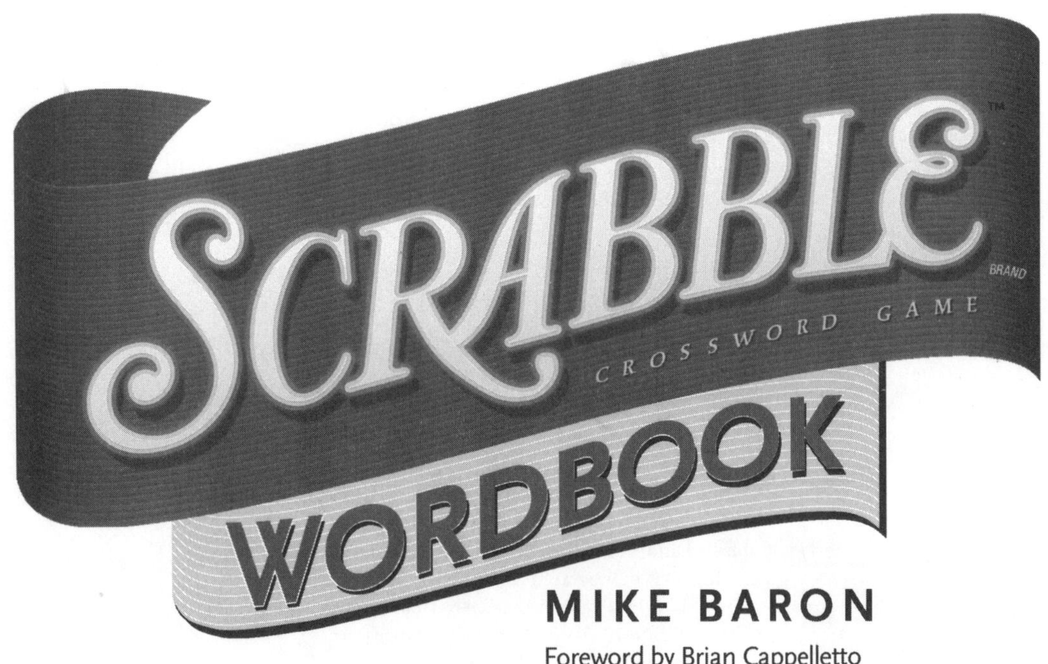

SCRABBLE Crossword Game WORDBOOK

MIKE BARON

Foreword by Brian Cappelletto

New York / London
www.sterlingpublishing.com

DEDICATED TO PAMINA AND MELINA

Formatting provided by Dr. Amit Chakrabarti

Word lists given in this book have been compiled from the vocabulary of the *Official SCRABBLE® Players Dictionary, Fourth Edition.*

Library of Congress Cataloging-in-Publication Data

Baron, Mike.
Scrabble wordbook / Mike Baron ; foreword by Brian Cappelletto.
p. cm.
"This book is a revised and expanded version of
The complete wordbook for game players,
published and © in 2004 by Sterling Publishing Co."
Includes bibliographical references and index.
ISBN-13: 978-1-4027-5086-1 (alk. paper)
ISBN-10: 1-4027-5086-2 (alk. paper)
1. Scrabble (Game)--Glossaries, vocabularies, etc.
I. Baron, Mike. Complete wordbook for game players. II. Title.

GV1507.S3B277 2007
793.734--dc22

2007030228

2 4 6 8 10 9 7 5 3 1

Published by Sterling Publishing Co., Inc.
387 Park Avenue South, New York, NY 10016

This book is a revised and expanded version of *The Complete Wordbook for Game Players*,
published and © in 2004 by Sterling Publishing Co., Inc.
Distributed in Canada by Sterling Publishing
c/o Canadian Manda Group, 165 Dufferin Street
Toronto, Ontario, Canada M6K 3H6
Distributed in the United Kingdom by GMC Distribution Services
Castle Place, 166 High Street, Lewes, East Sussex, England BN7 1XU
Distributed in Australia by Capricorn Link (Australia) Pty. Ltd.
P.O. Box 704, Windsor, NSW 2756, Australia

Manufactured in the United States of America

Sterling ISBN-13: 978-1-4027-5086-1
ISBN-10: 1-4027-5086-2

For information about custom editions, special sales, premium and
corporate purchases, please contact Sterling Special Sales
Department at 800-805-5489 or specialsales@sterlingpublishing.com.

CONTENTS

FOREWORD
by Brian Cappelletto, World SCRABBLE™ Champion

I first started playing SCRABBLE tournaments in 1985. I was a junior in high school when I ventured out to Albuquerque for my first event. Somewhere along the way, I went up against Mike Baron. The game was pretty close for a while, until I made the mistake of pluralizing HEP with my S. The problem with this was that HEP is an adjective, and Mike knew it, so he promptly challenged the play off and I never recovered.

I had heard of Mike Baron before venturing out there. He had a lot of articles published in the *SCRABBLE News* throughout the 1980s. Most of the articles centered around word lists and which ones were the most cost-effective ones to study. That may seem trivial at this point in time. Back in the mid '80s and before that, however, there was very little in the way of computer innovation when it came to compiling SCRABBLE word lists. Anybody who wanted to learn all the words had to compile lists and flashcards by hand, or go through the *Official SCRABBLE® Players Dictionary* (OSPD) and mark it up accordingly. These hand-compiled lists were subject to some human error, as we would later learn, sometimes the hard way, over the board. Compiling lists by hand was a lot of hard work, and was a very tedious exercise. As a result, most people were not very willing to share their hand-compiled lists with anybody. It was their work, and they were entitled to all the benefits of having gone through such a laborious endeavor. Many really did feel that way. I'll explain how I saw the revolution, and I arrived in its midst, as best I can, but I'm sure that whatever I say here will fall far short of capturing the true impact Mike's endeavors, all captured in this book, had on the competitive landscape of the game. It cannot be stressed enough that the contents of this book, originally published piecemeal, revolutionized the competitive game. The contents of this book were theretofore revealed for the masses to see with their own eyes, instead of wondering how much was really there.

Mike was the one who got many of the lists you'll find in this book published in the newsletter. The secrets were out there, in plain view, for everyone to see. He got the whole list of three letter words and their hooks ("3s-to-Make-4s") published, and then the "4s-to-Make-5s" soon thereafter. Those lists, along with the widely published "2s-to-Make-3s," are the building blocks of the game, really. The ever important "5s-to-Make-6s" would make their appearance later on, also.

Besides the lists of shorter words and their hooks, Mike did extensive research on how likely a given 7- or 8-letter word had the potential to be played in a game of SCRABBLE, as dictated by the letter distribution in the game. He zeroed in on what the most probable sevens and eights would be. Back in the early days of tournament SCRABBLE, subsets of sevens based on six-letter "stems" were reasonably well known. One of the best known stems consisted of the letters in SATIRE. Based on the distribution of letters in the game, this stem had a decent likelihood of showing up often enough to know what sevens could be made from it. Add an A to it and you got ARISTAE, ASTERIA, and ATRESIA. B made BAITERS, BARITES, REBAITS, and TERBIAS, and so on. This stem list, and a few others like it, were widely known. There are a lot more stems out there, however. A number of top players had compiled these stems, also, but many weren't too excited about letting everyone in on their discoveries. Mike was able to compile hundreds of stems and devise a ranking system for the stems, which took tile-drawing probability into account, which he'll explain in detail in the book. No one had tried to rank stems in such a way before. Learning new words and relearning them takes up a lot of time, and not everyone is willing to put in insane amounts of time to learn all the words. This ranking system was part of the cost-effective learning experience. After he had finished his research, he then had the top 100 stems published in an issue of the newsletter, along with the letters one could add to make sevens, which of course were also included. This was a big revelation to a lot of people. I had compiled many of these lists by hand myself, but after the top 10 stems or so, it's hard to know exactly how important the others were. I used to look at that published list a lot, until I felt I had it down. That list of the top 100 six-letter stems and all their sevens was printed on two sides of paper the size of a place mat. He called them Listmats at the time. That was a very important piece of paper, without a doubt. It was all right there in front of me. Mike would add the list of all the possible eight-letter words that could be made from those six-letter stems in a later issue. Those were very important lists as well. All sevens and eights derived from these stems were what he called "Type I" words. He eventually published the "Type II" words, which were sevens and eights that consisted exclusively of letters drawn from the subset of ADEGILNORSTU (duplication of letters included in the list), and did not appear on the Type I list. Actually, the Type II list was an offshoot of his earlier work called the "3%ers." (There might have been slight differences between the two lists.) Filling in the cracks, he added the Type III list, which consisted of words that he deemed as probable as the least likely Type I word.

Mike added a few other important lists to this bunch, and they're all in this book. These lists I mentioned are a rock-solid foundation upon which to build. Once I felt comfortable enough with these lists, I tackled the seven- and eight-letter alphagrams found in the back of this book, otherwise known as "the rest of the sevens and eights." There were a lot of words to learn there, and I doubt I'll get to see most of them played, or get to play them, myself. These are not very cost-effective words to learn compared to the ones that are found in Mike's other lists, the ones that form the solid foundation. I was crazy enough to want to try to learn all the words to get that extra edge. There is an extra edge to be had in learning those other words, but it's a lot of work for an unknown return on the investment of time spent. It took a lot longer to feel comfortable with such a massive set of words that had a lower likelihood of being played. Mike realized early on the importance of at least having a list of all the alphagrams of the sevens and eights. Only a few of us were crazy enough to want to learn them all, but it was a great reference tool to have for looking up what bingos (the term for playing all seven letters and getting the 50 point bonus in SCRABBLE) might have been played.

I'm here today to tell you that all these lists that Mike generated and made available to the public, at very little profit for himself, played a huge part in my successes in this game, and I'm sure many, many others' successes in this game. It's possible that I would have gotten there without reaping the benefits of his work, but I think it would have been much, much more difficult to get there doing every single list by hand. Today's players might not be aware of how important Mike's work in the '80s was. Today, one can find word study tools on the Internet, and there are other underground programs and lists that people have used since. *The Wordbook* is the original book of SCRABBLE word lists, though. This inspired other people to delve further into the question of what are the most probable bingos, and it inspired others to create other lists and to exchange ideas about how to study. Before Mike, there was nowhere near as much exchange of ideas and sharing of lists.

I also put Mike's cost-effective method to good use in studying words in the international word source for the World SCRABBLE Championship that occurs in odd-numbered years. I knew that if I learned all the twos through fives, plus their hooks, along with all the Type I sevens and eights, I could compete in that event. I talk about cost-effectiveness in regard to this event because of how infrequently it's played. Playing in North America, we only use the words contained in this book. For this special event, I need to get the most bang for my buck, so to speak. If I tried to master the international book, I fear that it would interfere with my regular game, because I could easily get confused as to which book a word appears in. The cost-effective method has enabled me to compete well at this event. I won it in 2001, and I came very close back in 1991.

It is an honor to write the foreword to this book, and it is something I'm more than happy to do. I know that I am one of the biggest beneficiaries ever of Mike's work, and I hope that you, the reader, find yourself benefiting from what is in this book. I cannot express enough my appreciation for what Mike has done for my game. I only hope that others benefit as much as I have from this book.

—Brian Cappelletto
Chicago, Illinois

INTRODUCTION

"We don't stop playing because we grow old; we grow old because we stop playing."
—George Bernard Shaw, 1856–1950

"Man is never so authentically himself as when at play."
—Friedrich Schiller, 1759–1805

Melina, my daughter, was five years old when she and I were on a self-guided tour of the Ice Caves and Bandera Volcano in western New Mexico in April of 2000. "Melina, look!" I pointed to the trailside sign. "It says this is 'aa,' a kind of lava. That's the first word in the SCRABBLE dictionary." Children store things away and then take them out to play with when we least expect it. Election Day rolls around, and Melina pipes up:

> Melina: "Why do crows always say hot lava?"
> Dad (clueless): "I don't know. Why?"
> Melina (poised): "Because they say 'AA! ... AA!'"

Meanwhile, she's storing away that notorious Election Day debacle. Then, in April of 2001, she becomes the six-year-old incarnation of Mort Sahl:

> Melina: "What's the opposite of a gargoyle?"
> (mispronouncing the first syllable so it sounds like "gorgoyle")
> Dad (still clueless): "I don't know. What's the opposite?"
> Melina: "A bushgoyle!"

I give my goyle a big hug as we delight in her wordplay. Our family's fascination with words and wordplay goes back many years. During my first six years, in Brooklyn in the 1950s before a move "to the country" all of thirty miles east on Long Island, our family often played Key Word, an early rival to SCRABBLE. It was not until the early '70s that, while home on a college break, I would first dabble in SCRABBLE, playing Dad and Mom on lazy summer evenings.

I had just laid down my tiles onto the board forming "T-W-O." Dad tilted his head, inspecting my play. "Twoe?" he mused to himself, seeing my three-letter play but mispronouncing it as though it rhymed with "woe." "Hmm. What the heck is 'twoe'?" I struggled to conceal my utter disbelief. This well-read man, my father, has misread my innocent little play! "You challenge 'twoe'?" I coyly inquired. "Yeah," he replied confidently. "I challenge 'twoe'!" I passed him our big unabridged dictionary; and he began to carefully turn over its many pages, searching for what he knew would not be there. Suddenly he stopped, his eyes fixed upon a short space of bold type. His jaw dropped. "Oh my God!" he exclaimed, and we both joined in laughter.

In a game with Mom about that time, I could just tell she had a rack of great tiles and would soon have a seven-letter bonus play. "Hmm, what if I play a phony word one column short of the triple word score?" I think. So, I not-so-innocently play REW, knowing it is not in the dictionary we use. Sure enough, Mom hooks an S onto it, forming REWS, and plays SQUIRES for what would otherwise net her 108 points. Otherwise, save for the fact that, with a smile on my face somewhere along the Jack Nicholson–Steve Martin continuum of facial deviltry, I challenge REWS. "How can you challenge REWS!? You just played REW!" Mom exclaims. "I don't think it takes an S," I say, but I can no longer keep a straight face, as Mom offers, "Against your own mother?" and I burst out in laughter, while she's smiling. After her lost turn, my sonly guilt overcomes me, so, on the next play, I set her up for an allowable S-hook to the triple word score. We came to define "REW" as, uh, "disenfranchising one's own mother," but I remember we used a word other than "disenfranchising."

The joys of playing SCRABBLE with Mom and Dad gave way to finding graduate school friends in New Mexico who shared my proclivity and passion for the game. After a half-dozen years of playing informally, fellow student and now psychologist Dr. Dan Matthews and I started New Mexico's first SCRABBLE club in 1980. I hand-generated "The Cheat Sheet" of all allowable short words for newcomers, and our club quickly grew from a handful to a few dozen to, over the years, hundreds attending one or more times. That "Cheat Sheet" became a staple of the SCRABBLE Players Association (later renamed the National SCRABBLE Association), and is sent to all new members.

That seminal summer of 1980, I received an invitation to attend the Western Regionals in San Francisco, where the top five finishers would earn berths to the 32-player National Championship. My invitation was likely based solely upon getting a wider geographic representation as I had not played in any tournament during the qualifying period. I was the bottom-seeded player, #64, about to play the #1 seed, the redoubtable Charles Goldstein, arguably the best player in the country at the time. Players extended to me their condolences before the game. Charles started with RHOMB. I knew RHOMBUS but not RHOMB. "Challenge." Acceptable. Gulp. Now he adds an I on, forming RHOMBI, another word I did not know, while perpendicularly playing XI. I sheepishly muster PIC parallel to XI, forming RHOMBIC, a word I did know, and XI. We're on our way. Charles later lays down KNUR. "Challenge." I lose another turn. While down about 70 points, I play off one tile, setting up a hook-spot for my seven-letter bonus play on my next turn. I'm confident I'll soon be right back in this game against one of the legends of SCRABBLE. Charles not only takes my hook-spot, but he does so by laying down his own bonus word, KELVINS, for 90 points and about a 160-point lead. "Hold!" I only knew Kelvin as a capitalized word. I can't win if I'm 160 behind. "Challenge!" Acceptable. Oy! I go on to lose by 199 points before shaking Charles's hand. But I learn I can play this game if only I can learn more words. Inspired by KNUR, on the flight back to Albuquerque, I take out my *Official SCRABBLE® Players Dictionary* (OSPD) and begin to encircle all short words containing K. A few pages into the process, I realize I need to similarly highlight short words with J, Q, X, and Z. So began my first list of words beyond three letters' length. I'm hooked on learning more, and then upon learning "hooks," letters that can be hooked upon words to extend them (for example, X can be added to REDO to form REDOX, U can be front-hooked to LAMA to form ULAMA). By the end of 1980, I hand-generated the "3s-to-Make-4s" word list, which became another handout for new SCRABBLE Association members. On summer afternoons at some of Long Island's beaches in 1982, I went about the task of deconstructing the OSPD once again, this time teasing out all the four-letter words, nearly four thousand of them, determining what their hook-letters were, and seeing what three-letter words were contained within the fours. A year later, while vying for one of the 32 spots at the 1983 National Championship in Chicago, that list was published by the Association for all players.

A few weeks before going to the Chicago event that summer, I wended my way from Albuquerque, across the beautiful high desert terrain of mountains and mesas, with striated reds, oranges, and browns running through them, en route to Durango, Colorado. I would be meeting with Bobbie Sageser, Colorado's senior version of Mae West, and her coterie of friends to talk about starting a tournament at the "lodge," which was managed by Bobbie's husband. (Little did I know then that the "lodge," which I had presumed was a mom-and-pop group of bungalows, proved to be the gorgeous Tamarron Lodge, where former president Gerald Ford, Johnny Carson, Rock Hudson, and other celebrities have stayed. My jaw dropped at the majestic mountainside sight of it.) One of Bobbie's friends generously presented me with a gift, "a little something I found at a garage sale," she said. The little cardboard box (about 3 × 4 inches) reads: "CROSS-O-GRAMS, The Crossword Card Game Sensation." On another side of the box: "Trade Mark Registered 1932-U.S. Patent Office," and elsewhere: "American Newspaper Promotion Corp. 537 South Dearborn Street, Chicago, ILL," the very city I would be flying to in a few weeks. Within the box are two side-by-side piles of very small cards (each about 1.5 × 2.5 inches). There are 54 cards (52 + 2 jokers), with a letter on each card and a value of either 10, 20, 30, 40, or 50, with each joker worth 100. The Q is actually a "Qu" card "... to render the card more playable," say the sage instructions. Some excerpts:

> There are two Joker cards in each deck which may be used by the holder for any letter he himself designates. During the same game, the joker continues to represent only the letter originally designated.... The dealer distributes one card at a time until each player holds twelve cards.... The player at the left of the dealer begins the game by placing on the table, in the center, a word of three or four letters.... If the player is unable to form a word, he must draw a card from the top of the pack in the center of the table, and must then await his next turn.
>
> The new word must include one or more letters of a word previously played on the table...." A sample layout was provided:

```
        B
D       A
U       T
CAB PASS
T ATOM
  CORE
  KEEN
```

> Proper names, abbreviations and foreign words are not allowed. Players may use the dictionary as a means of settling disputes. If a word is questioned and is not found in the dictionary, the player must take back the word and lose his next turn. If the questioned word is in the dictionary, the one who disputed it must lose his next turn.

Game variations are provided, including AN-O-GRAMS ("... a fascinating new variation of the old parlor game") which, coincidentally, includes in one of its examples the word SCRAMBLE. Hmm. Mind you, there's no game board and no premium squares, but ....

At that summer's Nationals in Chicago, I learned that SCRABBLE inventor Alfred Butts, then about 82 or 83 years old, had conceded that 1983 was *not* the 50th anniversary of his invention of the game (I believe it having been a year or so later), which the Chicago event was being used to promote for the media, along with Butts himself being present for the event. Butts had said something to the effect of: "But at my age, who am I to argue?" willingly accepting at that time the kudos bestowed for the game's (premature) 50th anniversary. All this is to say that Cross-O-Grams may have been out from one to three years before Butts's "Criss-Crossword Game."

Now, have you seen the movie, *Marathon Man*, with Lawrence Olivier playing a former Nazi and Dustin Hoffman a Nazi hunter? Memory fails me a bit here, but "Is it safe?" was a code phrase which, if uttered to Olivier, would imply the utterer knew his (Olivier's) true identity. At one point in the movie, Hoffman meets Olivier, Olivier not knowing Hoffman's agenda, until Hoffman whispers to him, "Is it safe?" In Chicago, having then met Butts for the first time, there was a part of me that wanted, while passing by him, to whisper, in Hoffmanesque fashion, "Cross-O-Grams?" I just didn't have the heart to do that, and he lived another ten years thereafter.

Knowing how many players not in Chicago could hold their own at such an event, and, moreover, recognizing that SCRABBLE at a competitive level stood a better chance of expanding if we had more ambassadors, I suggested to then Association head Jim Houle to have our Championship become an "open" event, albeit with some modest amount of prerequisite tourney play. The 1985 event in Boston, where I would again meet Butts, thus had over 300 players. Richard Selchow, owner of Selchow & Righter, which owned the SCRABBLE trademark in North America since Butts's "Criss-Crossword Game" was renamed "SCRABBLE" in 1948, met with a dozen or so players at the Boston event to discuss players' concerns. Selchow, Houle, and I met a few months later, at which time I noted the potential of SCRABBLE as an international "sport," as well an educational tool for students. At the first players' Advisory Board meeting in 1987, the last time I met Butts, he was thrilled at how far his game had come outside the millions of homes where SCRABBLE is sometimes saved just for rainy days. He was awed by the degree to which players were studying words and strategy, the hundreds attending the Nationals, and that we were now laying the groundwork for the first World Championship. Seeds planted in the 1980s blossomed in the 1990s with both the first World Championship and, in the United States, a School SCRABBLE program, which is reported to have already reached over two million students.

In July 1988, *The Wordbook*, a compilation of my various word lists, some of which were previously published piecemeal, was introduced at the National Championship in Reno, Nevada. Little did I realize then that a year later I would propose marriage on a SCRABBLE board to a woman I met at that Reno tournament. How grateful I was when Pamina chose not to "challenge" my move, presumably believing the "play" was "acceptable." (The word LURE, formed along column I, was a subliminal suggestion, no doubt!) SCRABBLE, in the words of Garrett Morris's baseball player character on television's *Saturday Night Live*, "has been berry berry good to me."

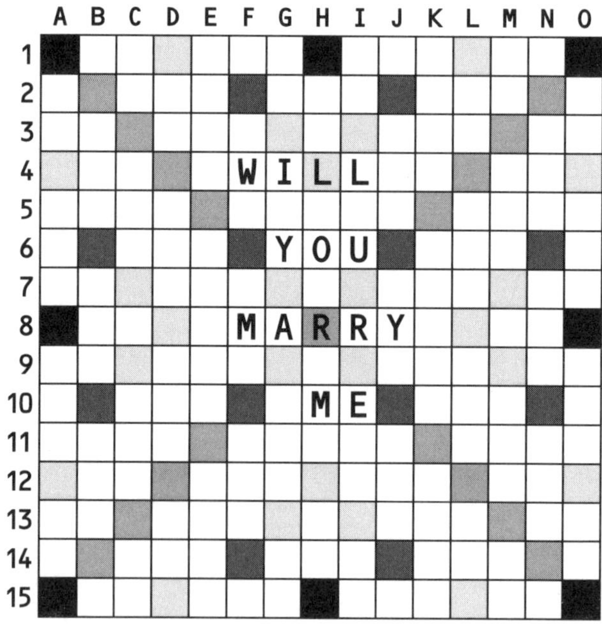

And for millions of other players as well. The game affords the opportunity to combine many skills, including vocabulary, anagramming, mathematics, visual-spatial perception, and psychological dexterity. This last term includes not only the ability to remain calm and focused, say, in a tournament situation when under time constraints, but "sizing up" your opponent and weighing the odds your opponent's play is a bluff or phony, as well as determining when *you* might attempt to play a word you are unsure of or that you know is as phony as a three-dollar bill.

SCRABBLE Wordbook attempts to organize words in such a way as to assist, maximally, players of SCRABBLE and other crossword games, as well as crossword puzzle aficionados. *The SCRABBLE Wordbook* is divided into three sections: (1) Specialty Word Lists, (2) The Hooks, and (3) The Alphagrams. Further instruction in the use of each can be found within each section.

If you are a casual player, you may wish to use *SCRABBLE Wordbook* while playing as a way of increasing your word power, assuming your opponent either won't mind or may use *SCRABBLE Wordbook*, too. If you are looking to increase your level of play, the single most effective page of words is "The Cheat Sheet," found on page 12. More than any other page of words, this "Cheat Sheet" has improved the playing strength of expert tournament-level players. Of course, at tournaments one cannot use any "Cheat Sheets," but most tourney players have gradually committed much, if not all, of its contents to memory. In informal play, you and your opponent may wish to limit use of *SCRABBLE Wordbook* just to this "Cheat Sheet," if access to the entire book seems too generous.

The serious player will likely want to learn "The Cheat Sheet" as well as a number of the other specialty word lists, as time permits. "The Hooks" is an unabridged list of all three- through eight-letter words, by length, and the "hook letters" they take. "The Alphagrams" is an unabridged list of all the three- through eight-letter combinations, by length, and the word or words they form when such letters are unscrambled. These two large sections are reference sections, though some of the very top players systematically study these lists.

Here is my unsolicited advice about SCRABBLE: Follow your passion, enjoy the game, and the people you meet through this wonderful, crazy enterprise. On average, you will have 13 turns per game. Consider each turn a riddle to solve or question to answer, where the question posed is along the lines of: "Given this rack, this board, my opponent's last play, the present score, and my present word knowledge, what is my best play?" On my 13 turns, I aspire to going 10-3 or better, in terms of best play selections. Realize, too, that there will be better plays possible that are not in your present word arsenal. Find joy in learning (and relearning) such words. When demonstrated, enjoy the beauty of your opponent's playmanship. Congratulate your opponent and yourself when either of you has come up with one of those special plays. Take pride in keeping your cool when the Tile Gods frown upon you. Be grateful that you have sufficient health and the opportunity to play this wonderful game and to befriend some fairly amazing people who share your passion for the game. The gratitude for connections to such special people may continue, even if or when one's health prohibits or limits one's playing or playmanship.

As I offered in *The Wordbook* (1988), regarding studying word lists, "If you opt instead to take a walk by a stream or in the mountains, or choose to chat with a friend or read a story to a child, you've no doubt made a much better choice and will be rewarded with JONQUIL on your opening play in your next game!" In *The Complete Wordbook* (1994) I added, "Or perhaps you will be blessed with the opportunity and be inspired to propose marriage." Now, in 2007, I recommend some major caution on this last suggestion if you are already married. Your spouse will much prefer you study these word lists. And since the '94 *Wordbook* when our daughter was born, I've read gobs of stories to her, and have *never* gotten JONQUIL on my opening rack. Go figure. Once asked by a TV news reporter, "What sort of person is attracted to SCRABBLE?" I immediately replied, "Obsessive-compulsive personalities deprived of summer camp experiences." He was initially stunned at my reply. "I was just kidding about the summer camp part."

SPECIALTY WORD LISTS

THE CHEAT SHEET

At the outset of a game, you have the tiles: DEGNORU. You immediately see GROUND, with the E left over. You search further, trying various prefixes (RE-, DE-, UN-) and suffixes (-ED, -ER). Then it comes to you: UNDERGO, a seven-letter bonus word! However, your opponent has the first turn. Will your word be playable after your opponent's move? Eagerly, you wait. Your opponent plays VOX in the center of the board. Your initial joy at finding UNDERGO is deflated when you find you can no longer play it. Instead of a 50-point bonus, you play GONER for 23 points as in the diagram below:

However, had you known that XU was an acceptable two-letter word (a monetary unit of Vietnam), you would have been able to play your 71-point bonus word as follows:

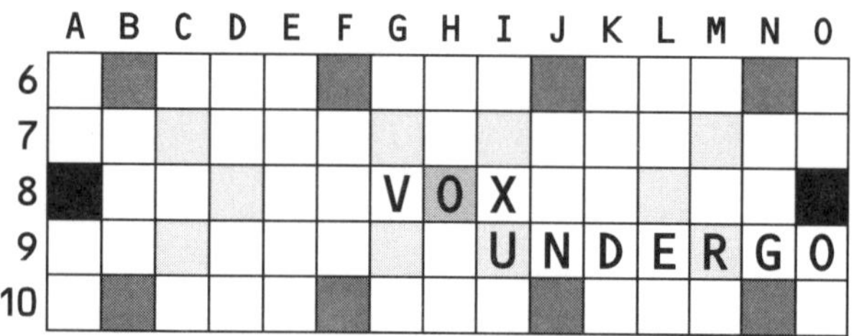

There are 101 acceptable two-letter words, half of which you probably know already. If you study no other list of words, attempt to learn all the twos. Encircle, highlight, or copy down just the ones you do not know. This brief list of the twos you do not know will require the least amount of study and provide the biggest payoff, as virtually every word played in a game affords the opportunity to build two-letter words parallel to it. Perhaps your opponent, not big on strategic placement but looking to impress you with a new word he learned, starts the game off with OXY, the X on the center square. You know by "hooking" your B in front, you could play:

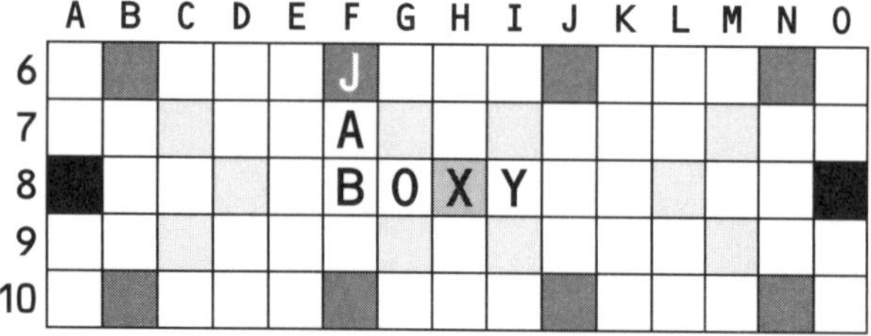

You would get a handsome 44 points for your play. But having just learned that JO is an acceptable two-letter word, you opt for 59 points by playing JAB while forming three two-letter words:

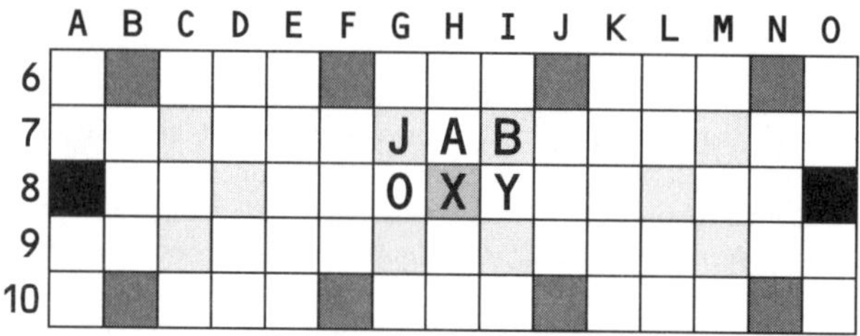

Your opponent's initial thrill over his OXY play is now a bit attenuated by your hard-hitting and high-scoring JAB. Let's assume your opponent now exchanges his tiles, and you have the JAB-atop-OXY board configuration as above and the following tiles: AEESSTY. If you learned some of the "2s-to-Make-3s" (i.e., the two-letter words that can be extended to three-letter words) and now knew that BY took an S, you might choose to score 47 points with YES:

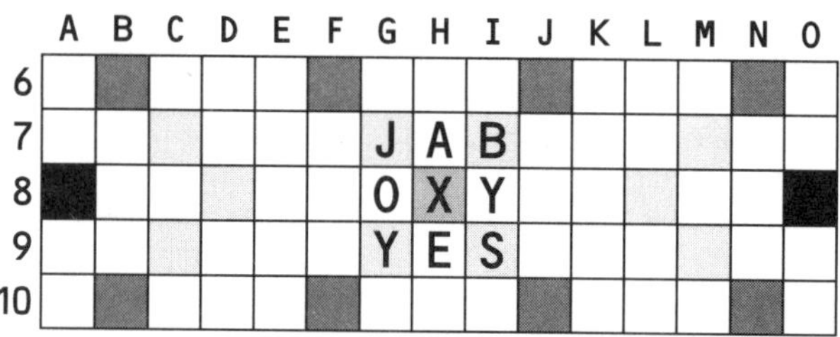

With the excellent letters AEST still in your possession, and a 106-26 lead, you are not as impressed with your opponent's first play of OXY as you are with your having learned JO and BYS. And you begin to wonder what other wondrous results can accrue from further study of "The Cheat Sheet."

There are 89 "vowel dumps" (the two- through five-letter "Words With 70+% Vowels" atop page 13). A vowel dump is a non-bonus word (fewer than 7 letters) with more than two-thirds of the letters vowels. What this really amounts to are the six words with all vowels (AA, AE, AI, OE, OI, EAU) plus the four- and five-letter words with only one consonant. These relatively few words can be real rack savers. Let's say you have AAAIIIL. Rather than passing your turn, you can play AALII, keeping AI, and likely enhancing your rack with the draw of five new letters. Or, suppose you have AEEIIUS and your opponent's first play was BRRR. (Often when one player's rack is vowel-heavy, the other's is consonant-heavy.) Through one of the R's you can play either AUREI or URAEI, with a very promising "rack leave" of EIS. Sometimes a vowel dump may lead to fairly high-scoring plays, as when AEEO is added to Z to form ZOEAE, say, on a triple word score for 42 points, or AAEU is wrapped around a Q to form AQUAE for a heap of points.

Here is a very unlikely rack and board scenario. You have AAEEIUU. The board configuration is as shown above right. By playing your duplicated letters, EAU, from (row/column) 8A to 8C, you would form four vowel dumps: EAUX (8A-8D), ZOEAE (A4-A8), AQUA (B8-B11), and EMEU (C5-C8), while scoring a whopping 94 points! And the AEIU leftover letters in your rack may be easily salvaged with just a few newly drawn consonants.

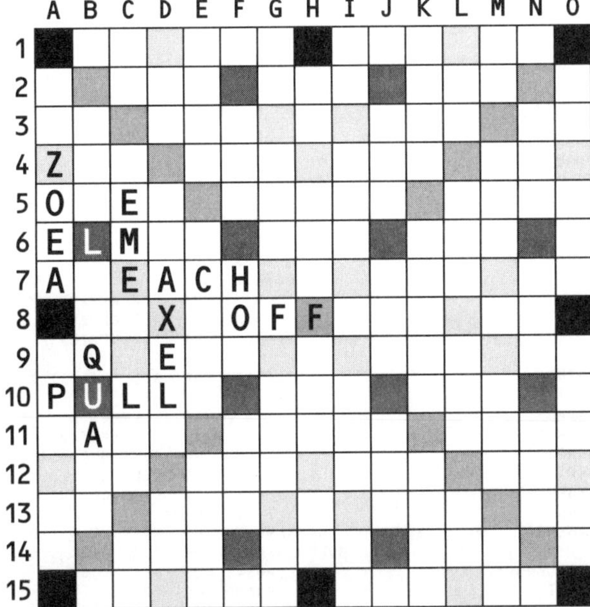

The conventional notation for indicating play locations, used in this book, indicates simply one letter and one number. In the example above, we would indicate our play as: EAUX (8A, 94), conveying that the word was formed along row 8, starting with column A, and was worth 94 points. If we also wished to indicate which letters were already on the board, we would underline them (EAUX). A vertical word would have the column letter indicated first, e.g., ZOEA (A4, 23).

The letters J, Q, X, and Z are the letters with the highest point value since there are fewer words that contain them. They are also, along with the letter K, the only unduplicated, or "frequency-1," tiles in the game. The general intent is to play these tiles quickly, usually for 25 to 35 points, in the hopes of not only scoring well, but of replacing them with low-point value letters, which are more conducive to "bingos." (A "bingo," or "bonus play," is a play made by using all seven tiles from one's rack, thereby netting 50 bonus points.) The most likely way to play off the J, Q, X, or Z will be in a short (two-, three-, or four-letter) word. And, if one of these letters can be placed on a double letter score (DLS) while also reaching a triple word score (TWS) with the other three letters, you will generate as many points as a seven-letter bingo. Plays like JOIN (H12, 57), QUIP (1L, 75), FLAX (A1, 66), and ZARF (A12, 78) should please the best of expert-level players, as well as yourself, assuming it is you and not your opponent who makes the play!

The final list on "The Cheat Sheet" includes all 1004 three-letter words. Master its contents, conquer "The Cheat Sheet," and you will prevail against all but the game's best experts, and you'll snatch a few victories from them as well. But how to digest nearly a thousand words?

Slowly. Here is the method I used: First, I wrote out the list of all the three-letter words I knew in alphabetical order. Sounds like a tall order, but here is how I went about it, thinking out loud:

"The first word will start with the letter A. The second letter is likely A. So, what letters could come after AA? Let's see: AAA? No, that's a car association. AAB? No. AAC? AAD? AAE? AAF? AAG? No. No. No. No. No. AAH? Yes! AAI? AAJ? AAK? No way. AAL? Sounds familiar. Okay, I'll put that one down." I continued this process, rejecting all but AAS (the plural of the two-letter lava word) on my way to AAZ. Then, I went on:

"Okay, that takes care of letters following AA. What letters come after AB? ABA? Yes. ABC? The alphabet? No. ABD? All but dissertation? No. ABE? Lincoln? No." In addition to ABA, the others are ABS and ABY, but I doubt I knew these at the start. I went on to words starting with AC, and I would hope I wrote down ACE and ACT. I continued this process, inserting the next letter of the alphabet as the second letter, then questioning which letters, A through Z, could "fill in the blank": AD + ? [answers: ADD, ADO, ADS, ADZ], AE + ? [answer: No three-letter words start with AE], AF + ? [AFF, AFT], and so on.

After trying AZ + ? [AZO], I then went on to BA + ? [BAD, BAG, BAH, BAL, BAM, BAN, BAP, BAR, BAS, BAT, BAY]. I could easily reject words starting with BB, BC, and BD, fast-forwarding to the next vowel, and testing myself on BE + ?. With three-letter words starting with consonants, the tendency is to simply insert a vowel as the second letter and determine what the final letters might be: BA + ?, BE + ?, BI + ?, BO + ?, BU + ?. But you would miss words like BRA, BRR, BYE, and BYS. I jumped from COZ to CUB, leaving out CRY.

You can see this will take a while. A few minutes each day may be best. When you are done (ZZZ is the last word), give yourself a pat on the back. Then the next step begins: "Which words did I omit?" Check your list against "The Cheat Sheet" and, in a different colored pen, write in the missing words. You can even "grade" yourself by counting the number of omissions and determining the percentage of words you successfully recalled. Of 1004 words, if you omitted 300, you would get a grade of 70% (which is a very high "pretest" score). You might also have included some bogus words. Put a big "×" through such ringers and (remember to) forget them!

The next task is to review all but your "forgivable omissions." A forgivable omission is a word you know you know, would never challenge if played by your opponent, would have little difficulty finding on your rack, and which was just an innocent omission; like my omission of CRY. If you are really committed to becoming an aspiring expert, having studied your omissions, you will then go on to the final step: the posttest. This involves generating the entire three-letter word list one more and final time. You will likely show considerable improvement over your pretest "grade." But even the best experts in the world will likely forget quite a few words. Pretest, study your omissions, posttest. The omissions on your posttest will be fewer in number, a manageable number to gradually review and commit to memory. Your family members may never want to play with you again. You're ready to challenge experts!

THE CHEAT SHEET

Two-Letter Words and Their Hooks

Here are all two-letter words, from AA to ZA. Next to each word are the letters that "hook" onto the word to make a three-letter word. For example, adding B to the front of AA makes BAA, and adding H, L, or S to the back of AA makes AAH, AAL, or AAS.

B	AA	HLS
CDFGJKLNSTW	AB	ASY
BCDFGHLMPRSTW	AD	DOSZ
GHKMNSTW	AE	
BDFGHJLMNRSTWYZ	AG	AEOS
ABDHNPRY	AH	AIS
R	AI	DLMNRST
ABDGPS	AL	ABELPST
BCDGHJLNPRTY	AM	AIPU
BCDFGMNPRTVW	AN	ADEITY
BCEFGJLMOPTVWY	AR	BCEFKMST
ABFGHKLMPRTVWZ	AS	HKPS
BCEFGHKLMOPQRSTVW	AT	ET
CDHJLMNPRSTVWY	AW	AELN
FLMPRSTWZ	AX	E
BCDFGHJKLMNPRSWY	AY	ES
AO	BA	ADGHLMNPRSTY
O	BE	DEGLNSTY
O	BI	BDGNOSTZ
	BO	ABDGOPSTWXY
A	BY	ES
O	DE	BEFLNVWXY
AU	DO	CEGLMNRSTW
BFGLMPRTWZ	ED	HS
DKR	EF	FST
FHPY	EH	
BCDEGMST	EL	DFKLMS
FGHMR	EM	ESU
BDFGHKMPSTWY	EN	DGS
FHPS	ER	AEGNRS
BFHOPRY	ES	S
BFGHJLMNPRSTVWY	ET	AH
DHKLRSV	EX	
	FA	BDGNRSTXY
	FE	DEHMNRSTUWYZ
AE	GO	ABDORSTX
ASW	HA	DEGHJMOPSTWY
ST	HE	HMNPRSTWXY
ACGKP	HI	CDEMNPST
O	HM	M
MORTW	HO	BDEGNPTWY
ABDFGHKLMRV	ID	S
DKR	IF	FS
ABDFGHJKLPRSTWYZ	IN	KNS
ABCDHKLMPQSTVWX	IS	M
ABDFGHKLNPSTWZ	IT	S
	JO	BEGTWY
OS	KA	BEFSTY
S	KI	DFNPRST
A	LA	BCDGMPRSTVWXY
	LI	BDENPST
	LO	BGOPTWX
A	MA	CDEGNPRSTWXY
E	ME	DGLMNTW
A	MI	BCDGLMRSX
HU	MM	
	MO	ABCDGLMNOPRSTW
AE	MU	DGMNST
	MY	C
A	NA	BEGHMNPWY
AO	NE	BEGTW
O	NO	BDGHMORSTW
G	NU	BNST
BCGHMNPRSTY	OD	ADES
DFHJRTVW	OE	S
	OF	FT
FNOP	OH	MOS
KP	OI	L
DMNRSTY	OM	S
CDEFHIMSTWY	ON	EOS
BCFHKLMPST	OP	EST
CDFGKMNT	OR	ABCEST
BCDGKMNSW	OS	E
BCDHJLMNPRSTVWY	OW	ELN
BCFGLPSV	OX	OY
BCFHJST	OY	
S	PA	CDHLMNPRSTWXY
AO	PE	ACDEGHNPRSTW
	PI	ACEGNPSTUX
	QI	S
AEIO	RE	BCDEFGIMPSTVX
A	SH	AEHY
P	SI	BCMNPRSTX
	SO	BDLMNPSTUWXY
EU	TA	BDEGJMNOPRSTUVWX
	TI	CELNPST
	TO	DEGMNOPRTWY
DH	UH	
BCGHLMRSVY	UM	MP
BDFGHJMNPRST	UN	S
CDHPSTY	UP	OS
BJMNP	US	E
BCGHJMNOPRT	UT	AES
AEO	WE	BDENT
T	WO	EKNOSTW
	XI	S
	XU	
PR	YA	GHKMPRWY
ABDEKLPRTW	YE	AHNPSTW
	YO	BDKMNUW
	ZA	GPSX

Three-Letter Words

AAH ALT AWE BIZ CAY DAH DOS ELS FER FUN GOR HIC IGG JUT LAM LUG MOA NEW OES OXO PIP RAG ROB SER SPY TEW UDO VIS WOO YUM
AAL AMA AWL BOA CEE DAK DOT EME FES FUR GOS HID ILK KAB LAP LUM MOB NIB OFF OXY PIS RAH ROC SET SRI THE UGH VOE WOS YUP
AAS AMI AWN BOB CEL DAL DOW EMS FET GAB GOT HIE ILL KAE LAR LUV MOC NIL OFT PAC PIT RAI ROD SEW STY THO UKE VOW WOT ZAG
ABA AMP AXE BOD CEP DAM DRY EMU FEU GAD GOX HIM IMP KAF LAS LUX MOD NIM OHM PAD PIU RAJ ROE SEX SUB THY ULU VOX WOW ZAP
ABS AMU AYE BOG CHI DAN DUB END FEW GAE GUL HIN INK KAS LAT LYE MOG NIP OHO PAH PIX RAM ROM SHA SUE TIC UMM VUG WRY ZAS
ABY ANA AYS BOO CIG DAP DUD ENG FEY GAG GUM HIP INN KAT LAV MAC MOL NIT OHS PAL PLY RAN ROT SHE SUK TIE UMP VUM WUD ZAX
ACE AND AZO BOP CIS DAW DUE ENS FEZ GAL GUN HIS INS KAY LAW MAD MOM NIX OIL PAM POD RAP ROW SHH SUM TIL UNS WAB WYE ZED
ACT ANE BAA BOS COB DAY DUG EON FIB GAM GUT HIT ION KEA LAX MAE MON NOB OKA PAN POH RAS RUB SHY SUN TIN UPO WAD WYN ZEE
ADD ANI BAD BOT COD DEB DUH ERA FID GAN GUV HMM IRE KEF LAY MAG MOO NOD OKE PAP POI RAT RUE SIB SUP TIP UPS WAE XIS ZEK
ADO ANT BAG BOW COG DEE DUI ERE FIE GAP GUY HOB IRK KEG LEA MAN MOP NOG OLD PAR POL RAW RUG SIC SUQ TIS URB WAG YAG ZEP
ADS ANY BAH BOX COL DEF DUN ERG FIG GAR GYM HOD ISM KEN LED MAP MOR NOH OLE PAS POP RAX RUM SIM SYN TIT URD WAN YAH ZIG
ADZ APE BAL BOY CON DEL DUO ERN FIL GAS GYP HOE ITS KEP LEE MAR MOS NOM OMS PAT POT RAY RUN SIN TAB TOD URN WAP YAK ZIN
AFF APO BAM BRA COO DEN DUP ERR FIN GAT HAD HOG IVY KEX LEG MAS MOT NOO ONE PAW POW REB RUT SIP TAD TOE URP WAR YAM ZIP
AFT APP BAN BRO COP DEV DYE ERS FIR GAY HAE HON JAB KEY LEI MAT MOW NOR ONO PAX POX REC RYA SIR TAE TOG USE WAS YAP ZIT
AGA APT BAP BRR COR DEW EAR ESS FIT GED HAG HOP JAG KHI LEK MAW MUD NOS ONS PAY PRO RED RYE SIS TAG TOM UTA WAT YAR ZOA
AGE ARB BAR BUB COS DEX EAT ETA FIX GEE HAH HOT JAM KID LET MAX MUG NOT OOH PEA PRY REE SAB SIT TAJ TON UTE WAW YAW ZOO
AGO ARC BAS BUD COT DEY EAU ETH FIZ GEL HAJ HOW JAR KIF LEU MAY MUM NOW OOT PEC PSI REF SAC SIX TAM TOO UTS WAX YAY ZUZ
AGS ARE BAT BUG COW DIB EBB EVE FLU GEM HAM HOY JAW KIN LEV MED MUN NTH OPE PED PST REG SAD SKA TAN TOP VAC WAY YEA ZZZ
AHA ARF BAY BUM COX DID ECU EWE FLY GEN HAO HUB JAY KIP LEX MEG MUS NUB OPS PEE PUB REI SAE SKI TAO TOR VAN WEB YEH
AHI ARK BED BUN COY DIE EDH EYE FOB GET HAP HUE JEE KIR LEY MEL MUT NUN OPT PEG PUD REM SAG SKY TAP TOT VAR WED YEN
AHS ARM BEE BUR COZ DIF EDS FAB FOE GEY HAS HUG JET KIS LIB MEM MYC NUS ORA PEH PUG REP SAL SLY TAR TOW VAS WEE YEP
AID ARS BEG BUS CRU DIG EEK FAD FOG GHI HAT HUH JEU KIT LID MEN NAB NUT ORB PEN PUL RES SAP SOB TAS TOY VAT WEN YES
AIL ART BEL BUT CRY DIM EEL FAG FOH GIB HAW HUM JIB KOA LIE MET NAE OAF ORC PEP PUN RET SAT SOD TAT TRY VAU WET YET
AIM ASH BEN BUY CUB DIN EFF FAN FON GID HAY HUN JIG KOB LIN MEW NAG OAK ORE PER PUP REV SAU SOL TAU TSK VAV WHA YEW
AIN ASK BES BYE CUD DIP EFS FAR FOP GIE HEH HUP JIN KOI LIP MHO NAH OAR ORS PES PUR REX SAW SOM TAV TUB VAW WHO YIN
AIR ASP BET BYS CUE DIS EFT FAS FOR GIG HEM HUT JOB KOP LIS MIB NAM OAT ORT PET PUS RHO SAX SON TAW TUG VEE WHY YIP
AIS ASS BEY CAB CUM DIT EGG FAT FOU GIN HEN HYP JOE KOR LIT MIC NAN OBA OSE PEW PUT RIA SAY SOP TAX TUI VEG WIG YOB
AIT ATE BIB CAD CUP DOC EGO FAX FOX GIP HEP ICE JOG KOS LOB MID NAP OBE OUD PHI PYA RIB SEA SOS TEA TUN VET WIN YOD
ALA ATT BID CAM CUR DOE EKE FAY FOY GIT HER ICH JOT KUE LOG MIG NAW OBI OUR PHT PYE RID SEC SOT TED TUP VEX WIS YOK
ALB AUK BIG CAN CUT DOG ELD FED FRO GNU HES ICK JOW KYE LOO MIL NAY OCA OUT PIA PYX RIF SEE SOU TEE TUT VIA WIT YOM
ALE AVA BIN CAP CWM DOL ELF FEE FRY GOA HET ICY JOY LAB LOP MIM NEB ODA OVA PIC QAT RIG SEG SOW TEG TUX VID WIZ YON
ALL AVE BIO CAR DAB DOM ELK FEH FUB GOB HEW IDS JUG LAC LOT MIR NEE ODD OWE PIE QIS RIM SEI SOX TEL TWA VIE WOE YOU
ALP AVO BIS CAT DAD DON ELL FEM FUD GOD HEX IFF JUN LAD LOW MIS NEG ODE OWL PIG QUA RIN SEL SOY TEN TWO VIG WOK YOW
ALS AWA BIT CAW DAG DOR ELM FEN FUG GOO HEY IFS JUS LAG LOX MIX NET ODS OWN PIN RAD RIP SEN SPA TET TYE VIM WON YUK

Two-, Three-, and Four-Letter Words With J, Q, X, and Z

J	JOE	HADJ	JATO	JEON	JINK	JOLT	JUKE	Q	QUID	COX	OXY	XIS	CRUX	FLEX	NIXE	TAXI	ZAP	AZAN	FUTZ	MOZO	TZAR	ZEST
JO	JOG	HAJI	JAUK	JERK	JINN	JOSH	JUKU	QI	QUIN	DEX	PAX	ZAX	DEXY	FLUX	NIXY	TEXT	ZAS	AZON	FUZE	NAZI	WHIZ	ZETA
HAJ	JOT	HAJJ	JAUP	JESS	JINS	JOSS	JUMP	QAT	QUIP	FAX	PIX	APEX	DOUX	FOXY	ONYX	VEXT	ZAX	BIZE	FUZZ	OOZE	YUTZ	ZIGS
JAB	JOW	JABS	JAVA	JEST	JINX	JOTA	JUNK	QIS	QUIT	FIX	POX	AXAL	DOXY	HOAX	ORYX	WAXY	ZED	BOZO	GAZE	OOZY	ZAGS	ZILL
JAG	JOY	JACK	JAWS	JETE	JIVE	JOTS	JUPE	QUA	QUIZ	FOX	PYX	AXED	EAUX	IBEX	OXEN	XYST	ZEE	BUZZ	GEEZ	ORZO	ZANY	ZINC
JAM	JUG	JADE	JAYS	JETS	JIVY	JOUK	JURA	SUQ	QUOD	GOX	RAX	AXEL	EXAM	ILEX	OXES		ZEK	CHEZ	HAZE	OUZO	ZAPS	ZINE
JAR	JUN	JAGG	JAZZ	JEUX	JOBS	JOWL	JURY	AQUA	SUQS	HEX	REX	AXES	EXEC	IXIA	OXID	Z	ZEP	COZY	HAZY	OYEZ	ZARF	ZING
JAW	JUS	JAGS	JEAN	JIAO	JOCK	JOWS	JUST	QADI		KEX	SAX	AXIL	EXED	JEUX	OXIM	ZA	ZIG	CZAR	IZAR	PHIZ	ZEAL	ZINS
JAY	JUT	JAIL	JEED	JIBB	JOES	JOYS	JUTE	QAID	X	LAX	SEX	AXIS	EXES	JINX	PIXY	ADZ	ZIN	DAZE	JAZZ	PREZ	ZEBU	ZIPS
JEE	RAJ	JAKE	JEEP	JIBE	JOEY	JUBA	JUTS	QATS	AX	LEX	SIX	AXLE	EXIT	LUXE	PLEX	AZO	ZIP	DITZ	JEEZ	PUTZ	ZEDS	ZITI
JET	TAJ	JAMB	JEER	JIBS	JOGS	JUBE	KOJI	QOPH	EX	LOX	SOX	AXON	EXON	LYNX	POXY	BIZ	ZIT	DOZE	LAZE	QUIZ	ZEES	ZITS
JEU	AJAR	JAMS	JEES	JIFF	JOHN	JUCO	MOJO	QUAD	OX	LUX	TAX	BOXY	EXPO	MAXI	PREX	COZ	ZOA	DOZY	LAZY	RAZE	ZEIN	ZOEA
JIB	AJEE	JANE	JEEZ	JIGS	JOIN	JUDO	PUJA	QUAG	XI	MAX	TUX	BRUX	FALX	MINX	ROUX	FEZ	ZOO	FAZE	LUTZ	RAZZ	ZEKS	ZOIC
JIG	DJIN	JAPE	JEFE	JILL	JOKE	JUGA	RAJA	QUAI	XU	MIX	VEX	CALX	FAUX	MIXT	SEXT	FIZ	ZUZ	FIZZ	MAZE	RITZ	ZEPS	ZONA
JIN	DOJO	JARL	JEHU	JILT	JOKY	JUGS	SOJA	QUAY	AXE	NIX	VOX	COAX	FIXT	MOXA	SEXY	WIZ	ZZZ	FOZY	MAZY	SIZE	ZERK	ZONE
JOB	FUJI	JARS	JELL	JIMP	JOLE	JUJU		QUEY	BOX	OXO	WAX	COXA	FLAX	NEXT	TAXA	ZAG	ADZE	FRIZ	MEZE	SIZY	ZERO	ZONK

ZOOM	
ZOON	
ZOOS	
ZORI	
ZOUK	
ZYME	

VOWEL-HEAVY WORDS

The following word lists contain all two- through eight-letter words that either consist of many vowels or can help rid oneself of multiple I's or U's. The other vowels (A, E, O) generally do not prove problematic as there are a far greater number of words containing duplicates of each of these letters. By way of contrast, while there are no three-letter words containing two I's and only one containing two U's (ULU), there are 12 with two A's, 22 with two E's, and 12 with two O's. Even combinations like GIIIINN may not be so bad if you can dump at least two of the four I's and one of the two N's, leaving GIIN. If an A, D, M, S, or T are available, INIA, NIDI, MINI, NISI, or INTI will do the trick.

Words With 70+% Vowels

AA	AGIO	AQUA	EAVE	IXIA	OHIA	UNAU	AREAE	OURIE	AEROBIA	AURORAE	NOUVEAU	ABOIDEAU
AE	AGUE	AREA	EIDE	JIAO	OLEA	UREA	AUDIO	QUEUE	ALIENEE	COUTEAU	OIDIOID	ABOITEAU
AI	AIDE	ARIA	EMEU	LIEU	OLEO	UVEA	AURAE	URAEI	AMOEBAE	EPINAOI	OOGONIA	AUREOLAE
OE	AJEE	ASEA	EPEE	LUAU	OLIO	ZOEA	AUREI	ZOEAE	ANAEMIA	EUCAINE	OUABAIN	EPOPOEIA
OI	AKEE	AURA	ETUI	MEOU	OOZE		COOEE		AQUARIA	EUGENIA	OUGUIYA	EULOGIAE
	ALAE	AUTO	EURO	MOUE	OUZO	AALII	EERIE	ABOULIA	AQUEOUS	EULOGIA	ROULEAU	
EAU	ALEE	AWEE	IDEA	NAOI	QUAI	ADIEU	LOOIE	ACEQUIA	AREOLAE	EUPNOEA	SEQUOIA	
	ALOE	BEAU	ILEA	OBIA	RAIA	AECIA	LOUIE	AECIDIA	AUDITEE	EVACUEE	TAENIAE	
AEON	AMIA	CIAO	ILIA	OBOE	ROUE	AERIE	MIAOU	AENEOUS	AUREATE	EXUVIAE	URAEMIA	
AERO	AMIE	EASE	INIA	ODEA	TOEA	AIOLI	OIDIA	AEOLIAN	AUREOLA	IPOMOEA	ZOOECIA	
AGEE	ANOA	EAUX	IOTA	OGEE	UNAI	AQUAE	OORIE	AEONIAN	AUREOLE	MIAOUED		

Multiple I- and U-Dumps

BIDI	PILI	CHILI	IDIOM	IODIN	LIPID	PIKIS	VILLI	JUJU	DURUM	QUIPU
HILI	TIKI	CILIA	IDIOT	IONIC	LIPIN	PILEI	VINIC	JUKU	FUCUS	RUBUS
IBIS	TIPI	CIRRI	ILIAC	IRIDS	LITAI	PILIS	VIRID	KUDU	FUGUE	SULUS
ILIA	TITI	CIVIC	ILIAD	IRING	LIVID	PIPIT	VISIT	KURU	FUGUS	SUNUP
IMID	ZITI	CIVIE	ILIAL	ISSEI	MEDII	PIXIE	VIVID	LUAU	GURUS	TUQUE
IMPI		CIVIL	ILIUM	IVIED	MIDIS	PRIMI	VIZIR	LULU	HUMUS	TUTUS
INIA	AALII	DIDIE	IMIDE	IVIES	MILIA	RADII	ZITIS	MUMU	JUGUM	UNAUS
INTI	ACINI	DIGIT	IMIDO	IXIAS	MIMIC	RICIN	ZIZIT	PUPU	JUJUS	UNCUS
IRID	AIOLI	DISCI	IMIDS	JINNI	MINIM	RIGID		SULU	JUKUS	UNCUT
IRIS	ALIBI	DIXIT	IMINE	KIBBI	MINIS	RISHI	BIKINI	TUTU	KUDUS	UNDUE
IWIS	AMICI	FICIN	IMINO	KIBEI	MIRIN	SIGIL	IMIDIC	ULUS	KUDZU	USQUE
IXIA	ANIMI	FILMI	IMMIX	KILIM	MITIS	TEIID	IRIDIC	UNAU	KURUS	USUAL
KIWI	BIALI	FINIS	IMPIS	KININ	NIHIL	TIBIA	IRITIC	URUS	LUAUS	USURP
LIRI	BIDIS	FIXIT	INDIE	KIWIS	NIMBI	TIKIS	IRITIS		LULUS	USURY
MIDI	BIFID	GENII	INDRI	LIBRI	NISEI	TIMID		AUGUR	LUPUS	UVULA
MINI	BIKIE	IAMBI	INFIX	LICHI	NITID	TIPIS	ULU	AURUM	LUSUS	WUSHU
MIRI	BINDI	ICIER	INION	LICIT	NIXIE	TITIS		BUBUS	MUCUS	
NIDI	BINIT	ICILY	INTIS	LIMBI	OIDIA	TORII	BUBU	BUTUT	MUMUS	MUUMUU
NISI	BLINI	ICING	IODIC	LIMIT	ORIBI	VIGIA	FUGU	CUTUP	PUPUS	
PIKI	CEILI	ICTIC	IODID	LININ	PIING	VIGIL	GURU	DUFUS	QUEUE	

Six-Letter Words With Four Vowels

AAAEgp AGAPAE
lz AZALEA
AAAIbs ABASIA
cc ACACIA
gp AGAPAI
tx ATAXIA
AAEEbm AMEBAE
gl GALEAE
lp PALEAE
rt AERATE
AAEIbl ABELIA
cd ACEDIA
cf FACIAE
cl AECIAL
lm LAMIAE
lr AERIAL
lr REALIA
lx ALEXIA
mn ANEMIA
nt TAENIA
tv AVIATE
AAEObm AMOEBA
cm CAEOMA
gr AGORAE
lr AREOLA
np APNOEA
rt AORTAE
AAEUbd AUBADE
bt BATEAU
ct ACUATE
fn FAUNAE
gt GATEAU
ll ALULAE
lr LAURAE
ns NAUSEA
rt AURATE
AAIIkz ZAIKAI
ls AALIIS
AAIOdg ADAGIO
dl ALODIA
gl LAOGAI
np ANOPIA
nt ATONIA
nx ANOXIA
pr APORIA
rz ZOARIA
AAIUbl ABULIA
cg GUAIAC
dl AUDIAL
gn IGUANA
kr UAKARI
lq QUALIA
ms AMUSIA
nr ANURIA
nr URANIA
ty YAUTIA
AAOUcj ACAJOU
dd AOUDAD
dm AMADOU
rr AURORA
AAUUbc AUCUBA
AEEIbl BAILEE
bn BEANIE
cp APIECE
dl AEDILE
dm MEDIAE
dn AEDINE
dr AERIED
dr DEARIE
dr REDIAE
dt IDEATE
fr FAERIE
fr FERIAE
lm MEALIE
mn MEANIE
nt TENIAE
pr PEREIA
rr AERIER
rs AERIES
rs EASIER
ss EASIES
AEEObr AEROBE
cr OCREAE
ct COATEE
dl ELODEA
dm OEDEMA
fv FOVEAE
gp APOGEE
gt GOATEE
lr AREOLE
lt OLEATE
AEEUbb BAUBEE
gl LEAGUE
hm HEAUME
kr EUREKA
lq QUELEA
lt ELUATE
np EUPNEA
ns AENEUS
ns UNEASE
nv AVENUE
qr QUAERE
qt EQUATE
rs RESEAU
rs UREASE
AEIIbl BAILIE
bt TIBIAE
ls LIAISE
rr AIRIER
AEIObl OBELIA
cd CODEIA
cn AEONIC
cz ZOECIA
dl EIDOLA
dr ROADIE
dt IODATE
fj FEIJOA
gh HOAGIE
gl GOALIE
kr OAKIER
ln EOLIAN
mn ANOMIE
nn EONIAN
pt OPIATE
pz EPIZOA
rs ARIOSE
AEIUcl ACULEI
cm AECIUM
cn UNCIAE
cq CAIQUE
cr CURIAE
dl AUDILE
dr UREDIA
ds ADIEUS
dt DAUTIE
dx ADIEUX
gn GUINEA
gt AUGITE
lv ELUVIA
mr UREMIA
nt AUNTIE
vx EXUVIA
AEOOdr ROADEO
AEOUct COTEAU
dt AUTOED
gr AERUGO
gt OUTAGE
pq OPAQUE
rs AROUSE
tt OUTATE
tt OUTEAT
vz ZOUAVE
AEUUbr BUREAU
lv UVULAE
rs AUREUS
rs URAEUS
rt AUTEUR
AIIOdk AIKIDO
dm DAIMIO
ls AIOLIS
mr MOIRAI
rs ARIOSI
AIOOcm OOMIAC
km OOMIAK
lr OORALI
rs ARIOSO
AIOUds AUDIOS
gr GIAOUR
gt AGOUTI
ms MIAOUS
nq QUINOA
pt UTOPIA
rr OURARI
rs SOUARI
AOUUbs AUSUBO
rs AUROUS
EEEEbb BEEBEE
pt TEEPEE
pv VEEPEE
pw PEEWEE
ww WEEWEE
EEEIlr EELIER
nw WEENIE
pr PEERIE
pw WEEPIE
rr EERIER
EEEOcn EOCENE
pp EPOPEE
EEEUkl EKUELE
mt EMEUTE
EEIIfr FEIRIE
hn HEINIE
mn MEINIE
nw WIENIE
EEIOdr OREIDE
ln OLEINE
lt ETOILE
ns EOSINE
rs SOIREE
EEIUdr UREIDE
nq EQUINE
EEOObt BOOTEE
cd COOEED
cs COOEES
dl DOOLEE
EEOUcl COULEE
dm MEOUED
pt TOUPEE
rv OEUVRE
st OUTSEE
EEUUdq QUEUED
qr QUEUER
qs QUEUES
EIIOdd IODIDE
dn IODINE
ds IODISE
dz IODIZE
lr OILIER
lt IOLITE
ns IONISE
nz IONIZE
EIIUlm MILIEU
pr EURIPI
EIOObd DOOBIE
bg BOOGIE
bk BOOKIE
bl BLOOIE
bt BOOTIE
ck COOKIE
cl COOLIE
ct COOTIE
df FOODIE
dg GOODIE
dh HOODIE
dl DOOLIE
dr OROIDE
dw WOODIE
dx EXODOI
dz DOOZIE
fl FLOOIE
fr ROOFIE
ft FOOTIE
gn GOONIE
gn NOOGIE
gr GOOIER
hl HOOLIE
kk KOOKIE
kr ROOKIE
ln LOONIE
lr ORIOLE
ls LOOIES
lt OOLITE
lw WOOLIE
mr ROOMIE
nn IONONE
nt TOONIE
rz OOZIER
rz ZOOIER
st OTIOSE
EIOUbg BOUGIE
br OUREBI
ls LOUIES
lt OUTLIE
tv OUTVIE
EIUUbq UBIQUE
nq UNIQUE
EOOOhp HOOPOE
EOUUsv UVEOUS
IIOOdp OPIOID
IIOUdm OIDIUM
mn IONIUM
IOOUds IODOUS
ds ODIOUS
kr KOUROI
OOOObb BOOBOO
bc BOOCOO
bh BOOHOO
bk BOOKOO
cc COOCOO
dd DOODOO
dh HOODOO
dk KOODOO
dv VOODOO
hp HOOPOO
OOUUbb BOUBOU
UUUUmm MUUMUU

Eight-Letter Words With Five Vowels

AAAAEbnn ANABAENA
AAAAIkmn KAMAAINA
mpr ARAPAIMA
rtx ATARAXIA
AAAEIcdm ACADEMIA
dmz MAZAEDIA
mns ANAEMIAS
AAAEOnpr PARANOEA
AAAEUcdq AQUACADE
cdt ACAUDATE
cgt AGUACATE
AAAIIdlr RADIALIA
mnp APIMANIA
npr APIARIAN
AAAIOnpr PARANOIA
AAAIUdlr ADULARIA
fnv AVIFAUNA
lqr AQUARIAL
mrs MAIASAUR
nqr AQUARIAN
AAAOUmtt AUTOMATA
AAAUUnqt AQUANAUT
AAEEEdrt DEAERATE
hrt HETAERAE
mrt AMEERATE
AAEEIcft FACETIAE
cmt EMACIATE
cnn ENCAENIA
crt ACIERATE
drt ERADIATE
gln ALIENAGE
gns AGENESIA
lnt ALIENATE
AAEEObmn AMOEBEAN
bnr ANAEROBE
dmt OEDEMATA
lrt AREOLATE
AAEEUcdt ECAUDATE
clt ACULEATE
crs CAESURAE
ctv EVACUATE
dqt ADEQUATE
kqs SEAQUAKE
lrt LAUREATE
ltv EVALUATE
nst NAUSEATE
AAEIIcdl AECIDIAL
cdm ACIDEMIA
cnt ACTINIAE
flr FILARIAE
hrt HETAIRAI
kns AKINESIA
nvz AVIANIZE
prs APIARIES
rsv AVIARIES
AAEIObnz ZABAIONE
clp ALOPECIA
cpr CAPOEIRA
ggt AGIOTAGE
gmn EGOMANIA
mnx ANOXEMIA
mtx TOXAEMIA
mtz AZOTEMIA
nrt AERATION
nrx ANOREXIA
AAEIUbrt AUBRETIA
brt AUBRIETA
ccl ACICULAE
cln ACAULINE
cqs ACEQUIAS
dps DIAPAUSE
fnn INFAUNAE
fnp EPIFAUNA
lll ALLELUIA
mrs URAEMIAS
qrt TAQUERIA
AAEOUcdt AUTOCADE
cls ACAULOSE
cnt OCEANAUT
crs ARACEOUS
gln ANALOGUE
lms MAUSOLEA
lrs AUREOLAS
mtt AUTOMATE
nqt AQUATONE
nrr AUROREAN
nrt AERONAUT
AAEUUbqs USQUABAE
dlq QUAALUDE
AAIIIlmr MILIARIA
AAIIOclm MAIOLICA
ntv AVIATION
AAIIUbhn BAUHINIA
cdr ACIDURIA
gnn IGUANIAN
llq QUILLAIA
lnx UNIAXIAL
AAIOOglp APOLOGIA
mnz ZOOMANIA
nps ANOOPSIA
AAIOUbls ABOULIAS
bns OUABAINS
cdt AUTACOID
cgl GUAIACOL
rtz AZOTURIA
AAIUUcgm GUAIACUM
clr AURICULA
mqr AQUARIUM
AAOUUcls ACAULOUS
AEEEEmrt EMEERATE
AEEEIcpr EARPIECE
cps SEAPIECE
dnt DETAINEE
lns ALIENEES
mnx EXAMINEE
mrt EMERITAE
rst EATERIES
AEEEUcsv EVACUEES
dgw AGUEWEED
lqs SEQUELAE
AEEIIcdp EPICEDIA
dfr AERIFIED
dls IDEALISE
dlz IDEALIZE
dtv IDEATIVE
frs AERIFIES
glw WEIGELIA
gst GAIETIES
nrt INERTIAE
AEEIOdll OEILLADE
dnp OEDIPEAN
lrt AEROLITE
ltt ETIOLATE
AEEIUbst BEAUTIES
cdd DECIDUAE
cdn AUDIENCE
clm LEUCEMIA
cns EUCAINES
cqr ACQUIREE
crs CAUSERIE
ddn UNIDEAED
dst AUDITEES
gkl AGUELIKE
gns EUGENIAS
gpq EQUIPAGE
klm LEUKEMIA
lqs EQUALISE
lqx EXEQUIAL
lqz EQUALIZE
ltv ELUVIATE
nrs UNEASIER
pps EUPEPSIA
qrs QUEASIER
qrz QUEAZIER
qst EQUISETA
stx EUTAXIES
tvx EXUVIATE
AEEOObkp PEEKABOO
cht OOTHECAE
flv FOVEOLAE
glz ZOOGLEAE
gmt OOGAMETE
hhp PAHOEHOE
kpp PEEKAPOO
AEEOUcqt COEQUATE
dlr AUREOLED
dmn EUDAEMON
hls ALEHOUSE
hst TEAHOUSE
lnr ALEURONE
lrs AUREOLES
nps EUPNOEAS
ntt OUTEATEN
rrs REAROUSE
AEEUUbqs USQUEBAE
lnr NEURULAE
rss URAEUSES
AEIIIntt INITIATE
rrt RETIARII
AEIIObgn IBOGAINE
dnt IDEATION
dnt IODINATE
hlm HEMIOLIA
AEIIUcdm AECIDIUM
cmt MAIEUTIC
cst ACUITIES
dnr UREDINIA
dtv AUDITIVE
gll AIGUILLE
lnq AQUILINE
lnq QUINIELA
lqs SILIQUAE
mnr URINEMIA
mnt MINUTIAE
ntt UINTAITE
AEIOObdm AMOEBOID
flr AEROFOIL
gms OOGAMIES
lmv MOVIEOLA
lrv OVARIOLE
mps IPOMOEAS
ptt PATOOTIE
AEIOUbmr AEROBIUM
cds EDACIOUS
cls EUSOCIAL
dgl DIALOGUE
dmn EUDAIMON
gls EULOGIAS
gst AGOUTIES
hpr EUPHORIA
hrt THIOUREA
jls JALOUSIE
mnx EXONUMIA
nqr AEQUORIN
nqt EQUATION
qss SEQUOIAS
rst OUTRAISE
rst SAUTOIRE
AEIUUflt FAUTEUIL
grs AUGURIES
ntt AUTUNITE
AEOOOglz ZOOGLOEA
AEOOUcls ACOELOUS
cps POACEOUS
glp APOLOGUE
mst AUTOSOME
AEOUUbcp BEAUCOUP
ctx COUTEAUX
grt OUTARGUE
lrs ROULEAUS
lrx ROULEAUX
ltv OUTVALUE
nss NAUSEOUS
rss ROUSSEAU
AIIIOcct OITICICA
AIIIUdqr DAIQUIRI
AIIOOdnt IODATION
AIIOUdnt AUDITION
glr OLIGURIA
gmn MIAOUING
AIOOOgln OOGONIAL
rrt ORATORIO
AIOOUcdt AUTOCOID
grt AUTOGIRO
AIOUUcgm GUAIOCUM
cst CAUTIOUS
gsy OUGUIYAS
AOOOUgms OOGAMOUS
AOOUUcmr COUMAROU
EEEEIcpy EYEPIECE
EEEEUgqs SQUEEGEE
EEEIOcpt TOEPIECE
EEEIUmnr MEUNIERE
ntx EUXENITE
qsx EXEQUIES
EEEOUfft ETOUFFEE
EEIIObrs BOISERIE
cds DIOECIES
dnz DEIONIZE
llp EOLIPILE
mst MOIETIES
ptz EPIZOITE
EEIIUbst UBIETIES
dpr PRIEDIEU
qst EQUITIES
EEIOOcgn COOEEING
gns OOGENIES
llp EOLOPILE
npt OPTIONEE
EEIOUchs ICEHOUSE
cnp EUPNOEIC
glp EPILOGUE
gls EULOGIES
gls EULOGISE
glz EULOGIZE
gps EPIGEOUS
kqv EQUIVOKE
krs EUROKIES
EEIUUdqt QUIETUDE
gnq QUEUEING
EIIIOcds IDIOCIES
EIIOUcds DIECIOUS
msx EXIMIOUS
nns UNIONISE
nnz UNIONIZE
EIIUUbnq BIUNIQUE
EIOOOgls OOLOGIES
EIOOUcmz ZOOECIUM
ctv OUTVOICE
dns IDONEOUS
gls ISOLOGUE
EIOUUbqt BOUTIQUE
dgt OUTGUIDE
glm EULOGIUM
gsx EXIGUOUS
mpr EUROPIUM
EOOOObdh BOOHOOED
ddh HOODOOED
ddv VOODOOED
EOOUUdgl DUOLOGUE
hst OUTHOUSE
krs EUROKOUS
qtt OUTQUOTE
IIIOUstt OUISTITI
IIOOUcds DIOICOUS
dnp DOUPIONI
IOOOUgmn OOGONIUM
IOOUUbks BOUSOUKI
bkz BOUZOUKI
rsx UXORIOUS
IOUUUrss USURIOUS

THE JQXZ NON-BINGO WORD LIST

As noted earlier, with the letters J, Q, X, and Z, the best strategy is to play off these high-value letters quickly, usually for 25–35 points, in the hopes of not only scoring well, but of replacing these high-point with low-point value letters, which are more conducive to bingos. Shorter words are generally more likely to be drawn and played than longer words. This is especially true of words containing J, Q, X, or Z. Moreover, with these letters, bingo-type scores are possible by playing four- or five-letter words. Plays like JIAO (A12, 57), JOINT (14J, 56), QAID (H12, 72), TRANQ (N2, 68), HAPAX (B2, 66), XYST (8L, 66), FRIZ (8A, 78), and ZILCH (1D, 87) surpass 50 points without using all seven tiles. If you feel you have amply reviewed the short JQXZ plays on "The Cheat Sheet," focus on the five- and six-letter words below.

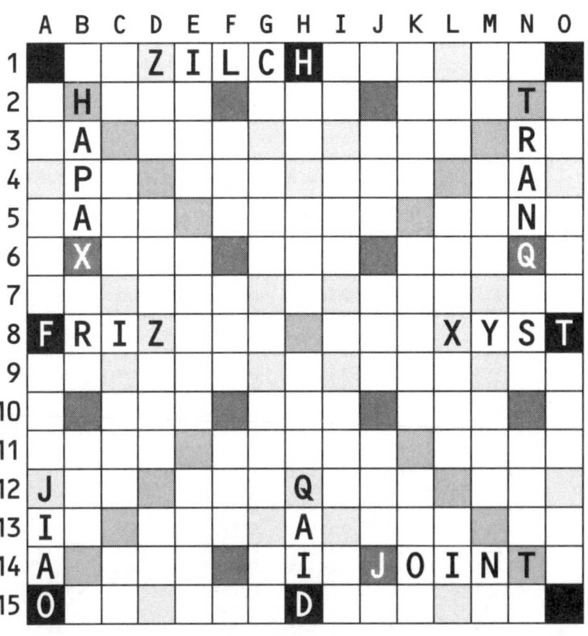

J
JO HAJ JAB JAG JAM JAR JAW JAY JEE JET JEU JIB JIG JIN JOB JOE JOG JOT JOW JOY JUG JUN JUS JUT RAJ TAJ AJAR AJEE DJIN DOJO FUJI HADJ HAJI HAJJ JABS JACK JADE JAGG JAGS JAIL JAKE JAMB JAMS JANE JAPE JARL JARS JATO JAUK JAUP JAVA JAWS JAYS JAZZ JEAN JEED JEEP JEER JEES JEEZ JEFE

JEHU JELL JEON JERK JESS JEST JETE JETS JEUX JIAO JIBB JIBE JIBS JIFF JIGS JILL JILT JIMP JINK JINN JINS JINX JIVE JIVY JOBS JOCK JOES JOEY JOGS JOHN JOIN JOKE JOKY JOLE JOLT JOSH JOSS JOTA JOTS JOUK JOWL JOWS JOYS JUBA JUBE JUCO JUDO JUGA JUGS JUJU JUKE JUKU JUMP JUNK JUPE JURA JURY JUST JUTE JUTS KOJI MOJO

PUJA RAJA SOJA AJIVA AJUGA BANJO BIJOU CAJON DJINN DJINS DOJOS EJECT ENJOY FJELD FJORD FUJIS GANJA HADJI HAJES HAJIS HAJJI HIJAB HIJRA JABOT JACAL JACKS JACKY JADED JADES JAGER JAGGS JAGGY JAGRA JAILS JAKES JALAP JALOP JAMBE JAMBS JAMMY JANES JANTY JAPAN JAPED JAPER JAPES JARLS JATOS JAUKS JAUNT JAUPS JAVAS JAWAN JAWED JAZZY JEANS JEBEL JEEPS JEERS JEFES JEHAD JEHUS

JELLO JELLS JELLY JEMMY JENNY JERID JERKS JERKY JERRY JESSE JESTS JETES JETON JETTY JEWEL JIBBS JIBED JIBER JIBES JIFFS JIFFY JIGGY JIHAD JILLS JILTS JIMMY JIMPY JINGO JINKS JINNI JINNS JIVED JIVER JIVES JIVEY JNANA JOCKO JOCKS JOEYS JOHNS JOINS JOINT JOIST JOKED JOKER JOKES JOKEY JOLES JOLLY JOLTS JOLTY JOMON JONES JORAM JORUM JOTAS JOTTY JOUAL JOUKS JOULE JOUST JOWAR

JOWED JOWLS JOWLY JOYED JUBAS JUBES JUCOS JUDAS JUDGE JUDOS JUGAL JUGUM JUICE JUICY JUJUS JUKED JUKES JUKUS JULEP JUMBO JUMPS JUMPY JUNCO JUNKS JUNKY JUNTA JUNTO JUPES JUPON JURAL JURAT JUREL JUROR JUSTS JUTES JUTTY KANJI KOJIS KOPJE MAJOR MOJOS MUJIK NINJA OBJET PUJAH PUJAS PUNJI RAJAH RAJAS RAJES REJIG RIOJA SAJOU SHOJI SLOJD SOJAS TAJES THUJA UNJAM ABJECT ABJURE ACAJOU

ADJOIN ADJURE ADJUST AJIVAS AJOWAN AJUGAS BANJAX BANJOS BIJOUS BIJOUX BOOJUM CAJOLE COJOIN CROJIK DEEJAY DEJECT DJEBEL DJINNI DJINNS DJINNY DONJON EJECTA EJECTS ENJOIN ENJOYS FAJITA FANJET FEIJOA FJELDS FJORDS FRIJOL GAIJIN GANJAH GANJAS GYTTJA HADJEE HADJES HADJIS HAJJES HAJJIS HEJIRA HIJABS HIJACK HIJRAH HIJRAS INJECT INJURE INJURY INKJET JABBED JABBER JABIRU JABOTS JACALS JACANA JACKAL JACKED JACKER JACKET JADING JADISH JAEGER

JAGERS JAGGED JAGGER JAGRAS JAGUAR JAILED JAILER JAILOR JALAPS JALOPS JALOPY JAMBED JAMBES JAMMED JAMMER JANGLE JANGLY JAPANS JAPERS JAPERY JAPING JARFUL JARGON JARINA JARRAH JARRED JARVEY JASMIN JASPER JASSID JAUKED JAUNCE JAUNTS JAUNTY JAUPED JAWANS JAWING JAYGEE JAYVEE JAZZBO JAZZED JAZZER JAZZES JEANED JEBELS JEEING JEEPED JEERED JEERER JEHADS JEJUNA JEJUNE JELLED JELLOS JENNET JERBOA JEREED JERIDS JERKED JERKER JERKIN JERRID

JERSEY JESSED JESSES JESTED JESTER JETLAG JETONS JETSAM JETSOM JETTED JETTON JETWAY JEWELS JEZAIL JIBBED JIBBER JIBERS JIBING JICAMA JIGGED JIGGER JIGGLE JIGGLY JIGSAW JIHADS JILTED JILTER JIMINY JIMMIE JIMPER JIMPLY JINGAL JINGKO JINGLE JINGLY JINKED JINKER JINNEE JINNIS JINXED JINXES JITNEY JITTER JIVERS JIVIER JIVING JNANAS JOBBED JOBBER JOCKEY JOCKOS JOCOSE JOCUND JOGGED JOGGER JOGGLE JOHNNY JOINED JOINER JOINTS JOISTS JOJOBA

JOKERS JOKIER JOKILY JOKING JOLTED JOLTER JORAMS JORDAN JORUMS JOSEPH JOSHED JOSHER JOSHES JOSSES JOSTLE JOTTED JOTTER JOUALS JOUKED JOULES JOUNCE JOUNCY JOURNO JOUSTS JOVIAL JOWARS JOWING JOWLED JOYFUL JOYING JOYOUS JOYPOP JUBBAH JUBHAH JUBILE JUDDER JUDGED JUDGER JUDGES JUDOKA JUGATE JUGFUL JUGGED JUGGLE JUGULA JUGUMS JUICED JUICER JUICES JUJUBE JUKING JULEPS JUMBAL JUMBLE JUMBOS JUMPED JUMPER JUNCOS JUNGLE JUNGLY JUNIOR JUNKED

JUNKER JUNKET JUNKIE JUNTAS JUNTOS JUPONS JURANT JURATS JURELS JURIED JURIES JURIST JURORS JUSTED JUSTER JUSTLE JUSTLY JUTTED KANJIS KOPJES LOGJAM MAJORS MASJID MOJOES MOUJIK MUJIKS MUSJID MUZJIK NINJAS OBJECT OBJETS OUTJUT PAJAMA PRAJNA PROJET PUJAHS PUNJIS PYJAMA RAJAHS RAMJET REJECT REJIGS REJOIN RIOJAS ROMAJI SAJOUS SANJAK SEJANT SHOJIS SLOJDS SVARAJ SWARAJ THUJAS TRIJET UNJAMS UNJUST VEEJAY

Q
QI QAT QIS

QUA SUQ AQUA QADI QAID QATS QOPH QUAD QUAG QUAI QUAY QUEY QUID QUIN QUIP QUIT QUIZ QUOD SUQS AQUAE AQUAS BURQA EQUAL EQUID EQUIP FAQIR FIQUE MAQUI PIQUE QADIS QAIDS QANAT QOPHS QUACK QUADS QUAFF QUAGS QUAIL QUAIS QUAKE QUAKY QUALE QUALM QUANT QUARE QUARK QUART QUASH QUASI QUASS QUATE QUAYS QUBIT QUEAN QUEEN QUEER QUELL QUERN QUERY QUEST QUEUE QUEYS

QUICK QUIDS QUIET QUIFF QUILL QUILT QUINS QUINT QUIPS QUIPU QUIRE QUIRK QUIRT QUITE QUITS QUODS QUOIN QUOIT QUOLL QUOTA QUOTE QUOTH QURSH ROQUE SQUAB SQUAD SQUAT SQUEG SQUIB SQUID TOQUE TRANQ TUQUE UMIAQ USQUE ACQUIT BARQUE BASQUE BISQUE BOSQUE BUQSHA BURQAS CAIQUE CALQUE CASQUE CHEQUE CINQUE CIRQUE CLAQUE CLIQUE CLIQUY CLOQUE COQUET DIQUAT EQUALS EQUATE EQUIDS EQUINE EQUIPS EQUITY EXEQUY FAQIRS

FAQUIR FIQUES LIQUID LIQUOR LOQUAT MANQUE MAQUIS MARQUE MASQUE MOSQUE OPAQUE PIQUED PIQUES PIQUET PLAQUE PULQUE QABALA QANATS QINDAR QINTAR QIVIUT QUACKS QUACKY QUAERE QUAFFS QUAGGA QUAGGY QUAHOG QUAICH QUAIGH QUAILS QUAINT QUAKED QUAKER QUAKES QUALIA QUALMS QUALMY QUANGO QUANTA QUANTS QUARKS QUARRY QUARTE QUARTO QUARTS QUARTZ QUASAR QUATRE QUAVER QUBITS QUBYTE QUEANS QUEASY QUEAZY QUEENS QUEERS QUELEA QUELLS QUENCH QUERNS QUESTS

QUEUED QUEUER QUEUES QUEZAL QUICHE QUICKS QUIETS QUIFFS QUILLS QUILTS QUINCE QUINIC QUININ QUINOA QUINOL QUINSY QUINTA QUINTE QUINTS QUIPPU QUIPPY QUIPUS QUIRED QUIRES QUIRKS QUIRKY QUIRTS QUITCH QUIVER QUOHOG QUOINS QUOITS QUOKKA QUOLLS QUORUM QUOTAS QUOTED QUOTER QUOTES QUOTHA QURUSH QWERTY REQUIN RISQUE ROQUES ROQUET SACQUE SEQUEL SEQUIN SHEQEL SQUABS SQUADS SQUALL SQUAMA SQUARE SQUARK SQUASH SQUATS SQUAWK SQUEAK SQUEAL SQUEGS

SQUIBS SQUIDS SQUILL SQUINT SQUIRE SQUIRM SQUIRT SQUISH SQUUSH TOQUES TOQUET TORQUE TRANQS TUQUES UBIQUE UMIAQS UNIQUE USQUES YANQUI

X
AX EX OX XI XU AXE BOX COX DEX FAX FIX FOX GOX HEX KEX LAX LEX LOX LUX MAX MIX NIX OXO OXY PAX PIX POX PYX RAX REX SAX SEX SIX SOX TAX TUX VEX VOX WAX XIS ZAX

APEX AXAL AXED AXEL AXES AXIL AXIS AXLE AXON BOXY BRUX CALX COAX COXA CRUX DEXY DOUX DOXY EAUX EXAM EXEC EXED EXES EXIT EXON EXPO FALX FAUX FIXT FLAX FLEX FLUX FOXY HOAX IBEX ILEX IXIA JEUX JINX LUXE LYNX MAXI MINX MIXT MOXA NEXT NIXE NIXY ONYX ORYX OXEN OXES OXID OXIM PIXY PLEX POXY PREX ROUX SEXT SEXY TAXA TAXI TEXT VEXT WAXY XYST ADDAX ADMIX AFFIX ANNEX ATAXY AUXIN AXELS AXIAL AXILE AXILS AXING AXIOM AXION AXITE AXLED AXLES AXMAN AXMEN AXONE AXONS BEAUX BEMIX BORAX BOXED BOXER

BOXES BRAXY BUXOM CALIX CALYX CAREX CIMEX CODEX COMIX COXAE COXAL COXED COXES CULEX CYLIX DEOXY DESEX DETOX DEWAX DEXES DEXIE DIXIT DOXIE EPOXY EXACT EXALT EXAMS EXCEL EXECS EXERT EXILE EXINE EXING EXIST EXITS EXONS EXPAT EXPEL EXPOS EXTOL EXTRA EXUDE EXULT EXURB FAXED FAXES FEDEX FIXED FIXER FIXES FIXIT FLAXY FOXED FOXES GALAX GOXES HAPAX HELIX HEXAD HEXED HEXER HEXES HEXYL HYRAX IMMIX INDEX INFIX IXIAS IXORA IXTLE KEXES KYLIX LATEX LAXER LAXES LAXLY LEXES LEXIS LOXED LOXES LUREX LUXES MAXED MAXES MAXIM MAXIS MIREX MIXED MIXER MIXES MIXUP MOXAS

MOXIE MUREX NEXUS NIXED NIXES NIXIE OXBOW OXEYE OXIDE OXIDS OXIME OXIMS OXLIP OXTER PAXES PHLOX PIXEL PIXES PIXIE POXED POXES PREXY PROXY PYREX PYXES PYXIE PYXIS RADIX RAXED RAXES REDOX REDUX REFIX RELAX REMEX REMIX RETAX REWAX REXES SAXES SEXED SEXES SEXTO SEXTS SILEX SIXES SIXMO SIXTE SIXTH SIXTY TAXED TAXER TAXES TAXIS TAXOL TAXON TAXUS TELEX TEXAS TEXTS TOXIC TOXIN TUXES TWIXT UNBOX UNFIX UNMIX UNSEX VARIX VEXED VEXER VEXES VEXIL VIXEN WAXED WAXEN WAXER WAXES XEBEC XENIA XENIC XENON XERIC XEROX XERUS XYLAN XYLEM XYLOL XYLYL XYSTI XYSTS ZAXES

ADIEUX ADMIXT ADNEXA AFFLUX ALEXIA ALEXIN ALKOXY ANNEXE ANOXIA ANOXIC APEXES ATAXIA ATAXIC AUSPEX AUXINS AXEMAN AXEMEN AXENIC AXILLA AXIOMS AXIONS AXISED AXISES AXITES AXLIKE AXONAL AXONES AXONIC AXSEED BANJAX BEMIXT BIAXAL BIFLEX BIJOUX BOLLIX BOLLOX BOMBAX BOMBYX BOXCAR BOXERS BOXFUL BOXIER BOXILY BOXING BRUXED BRUXES CALXES CAUDEX CERVIX CLAXON CLIMAX COAXAL COAXED COAXER COAXES COCCYX COMMIX CONVEX CORTEX COWPOX COXING CRUXES DEIXIS DELUXE DESOXY DEXIES DEXTER DEXTRO DIOXAN DIOXID DIOXIN DIPLEX DIXITS DOXIES DUPLEX EARWAX EFFLUX ELIXIR ETHOXY EUTAXY EXACTA EXACTS EXALTS EXAMEN EXARCH EXCEED EXCELS EXCEPT EXCESS EXCIDE EXCISE EXCITE

EXCUSE EXEDRA EXEMPT EXEQUY EXERTS EXEUNT EXHALE EXHORT EXHUME EXILED EXILER EXILES EXILIC EXINES EXISTS EXITED EXODOI EXODOS EXODUS EXOGEN EXONIC EXONYM EXOTIC EXPAND EXPATS EXPECT EXPELS EXPEND EXPERT EXPIRE EXPIRY EXPORT EXPOSE EXSECT EXSERT EXTANT EXTEND EXTENT EXTERN EXTOLL EXTOLS EXTORT EXTRAS EXUDED EXUDES EXULTS EXURBS EXUVIA FAXING FIXATE FIXERS FIXING FIXITY FIXURE FLAXEN FLAXES FLEXED FLEXES FLEXOR FLUXED FLUXES FORNIX FOXIER FOXILY FOXING GALAXY HALLUX HANDAX HATBOX HEXADE HEXADS HEXANE HEXERS HEXING HEXONE HEXOSE HEXYLS HOAXED HOAXER HOAXES HOTBOX IBEXES ICEBOX ILEXES INFLUX IXODID IXORAS IXTLES JINXED JINXES KLAXON LARYNX

LAXEST LAXITY LEXEME LEXICA LOXING LUMMOX LUXATE LUXURY LYNXES MASTIX MATRIX MAXIMA MAXIMS MAXING MAXIXE MENINX MINXES MIXERS MIXING MIXUPS MOXIES MUSKOX MYXOID MYXOMA NIXIES NIXING NONTAX ONYXES ORYXES OUTBOX OUTFOX OXALIC OXALIS OXBOWS OXCART OXEYES OXFORD OXIDES OXIDIC OXIMES OXLIKE OXLIPS OXTAIL OXTERS OXYGEN PAXWAX PEGBOX PEROXY PHENIX PICKAX PIXELS PIXIES PLEXAL PLEXES PLEXOR PLEXUS POLEAX POLLEX POXIER POXING PRAXES PRAXIS PREFIX PREMIX PRETAX PREXES PROLIX PYXIES RAXING REFLEX REFLUX REMIXT REXINE SAXONY SCOLEX SEXIER SEXILY SEXING SEXISM SEXIST SEXPOT SEXTAN SEXTET SEXTON SEXTOS SEXUAL SILVEX SIXMOS SIXTES SIXTHS SKYBOX SMILAX

SPADIX SPHINX SPHYNX STORAX STYRAX SUBFIX SUFFIX SURTAX SYNTAX SYRINX TAXEME TAXERS TAXIED TAXIES TAXING TAXITE TAXMAN TAXMEN TAXOLS TAXONS TEABOX THORAX TOXICS TOXINE TOXINS TOXOID TUXEDO UNAXED UNFIXT UNISEX UNMIXT UNSEXY UNVEXT URTEXT VERNIX VERTEX VEXERS VEXILS VEXING VIXENS VOLVOX VORTEX WAXERS WAXIER WAXILY WAXING XEBECS XENIAL XENIAS XENONS XYLANS XYLEMS XYLENE XYLOID XYLOLS XYLOSE XYLYLS XYSTER XYSTOI XYSTOS XYSTUS

Z

ZA ADZ AZO BIZ COZ FEZ FIZ WIZ ZAG ZAP ZAS ZAX ZED ZEE ZEK ZEP ZIG ZIN ZIP ZIT ZOA ZOO ZUZ ZZZ ADZE AZAN AZON BIZE BOZO

BUZZ CHEZ COZY CZAR DAZE DITZ DOZE DOZY FAZE FIZZ FOZY FRIZ FUTZ FUZE FUZZ GAZE GEEZ HAZE HAZY IZAR JAZZ JEEZ LAZE LAZY LUTZ MAZE MAZY MEZE MOZO NAZI OOZE OOZY ORZO OUZO OYEZ PHIZ PREZ PUTZ QUIZ RAZE RAZZ RITZ SIZE SIZY TZAR WHIZ YUTZ ZAGS ZANY ZAPS ZARF ZEAL ZEBU ZEDS ZEES ZEIN ZEKS ZEPS ZERK ZERO ZEST ZETA ZIGS ZILL ZINC ZINE ZING ZINS ZIPS ZITI ZITS ZOEA ZOIC ZONA ZONE ZONK ZOOM ZOON ZOOS ZORI ZOUK ZYME ABUZZ ADOZE ADZED ADZES AGAZE AMAZE AZANS AZIDE AZIDO AZINE

AZLON AZOIC AZOLE AZONS AZOTE AZOTH AZUKI AZURE BAIZA BAIZE BAZAR BAZOO BEZEL BEZIL BIZES BLAZE BLITZ BONZE BOOZE BOOZY BORTZ BOZOS BRAZA BRAZE CAPIZ CLOZE COLZA COZEN COZES COZEY COZIE CRAZE CRAZY CROZE CZARS DAZED DAZES DIAZO DITZY DIZEN DIZZY DOOZY DOZED DOZEN DOZER DOZES ENZYM FAZED FAZES FEAZE FEEZE FEZES FEZZY FIZZY FRITZ FRIZZ FROZE FURZE FURZY FUZED FUZEE FUZES FUZIL FUZZY GAUZE GAUZY GAZAR GAZED GAZER GAZES GHAZI GIZMO GLAZE GLAZY GLITZ GLOZE GONZO GRAZE GROSZ GYOZA HAFIZ HAMZA HAZAN HAZED HAZEL HAZER HAZES HEEZE HERTZ HUZZA IZARS JAZZY

KANZU KAZOO KLUTZ KUDZU LAZAR LAZED LAZES MAIZE MATZA MATZO MAZED MAZER MAZES MEZES MEZZO MIRZA MIZEN MOZOS MUZZY NAZIS NERTZ NIZAM NUDZH OOZED OOZES ORZOS OUZEL OUZOS OZONE PIZZA PLAZA PLOTZ PRIZE RAZED RAZEE RAZER RAZES RAZOR RITZY SCUZZ SEIZE SIZAR SIZED SIZER SIZES SMAZE SOYUZ SOZIN SPITZ TAZZA TAZZE TIZZY TOPAZ TROOZ TZARS UNZIP VIZIR VIZOR WALTZ WHIZZ WINZE WIZEN WIZES WOOZY ZAIRE ZAMIA ZANZA ZAPPY ZARFS ZAXES ZAYIN ZAZEN ZEALS ZEBEC ZEBRA ZEBUS ZEINS ZERKS ZEROS ZESTS ZESTY ZETAS ZIBET ZILCH ZILLS ZINCS ZINCY ZINEB ZINES ZINGS ZINGY ZINKY

ZIPPY ZIRAM ZITIS ZIZIT ZLOTE ZLOTY ZOEAE ZOEAL ZOEAS ZOMBI ZONAE ZONAL ZONED ZONER ZONES ZONKS ZOOEY ZOOID ZOOKS ZOOMS ZOONS ZOOTY ZORIL ZORIS ZOUKS ZOWIE ZUZIM ZYMES ABLAZE ADZING ADZUKI AGNIZE AMAZED AMAZES AMAZON ASSIZE AZALEA AZIDES AZINES AZLONS AZOLES AZONAL AZONIC AZOTED AZOTES AZOTHS AZOTIC AZUKIS AZURES AZYGOS BAIZAS BAIZES BANZAI BAZAAR BAZARS BAZOOS BEEZER BEGAZE BENZAL BENZIN BENZOL BENZYL BEZANT BEZAZZ BEZELS BEZILS BEZOAR BIZONE BIZZES BLAZED BLAZER BLAZES BLAZON BLINTZ BLOWZY BONZER BONZES BOOZED BOOZER BOOZES BORZOI BRAIZE BRAZAS BRAZED BRAZEN BRAZER BRAZES BRAZIL BREEZE BREEZY BRONZE BRONZY

BUZUKI BUZZED BUZZER BUZZES BYZANT CHAZAN CHINTZ CLOZES COLZAS CORYZA COZENS COZEYS COZIED COZIER COZIES COZILY COZZES CRAZED CRAZES CROZER CROZES DAZING DAZZLE DEFUZE DEZINC DIAZIN DITZES DIZENS DONZEL DOOZER DOOZIE DOZENS DOZERS DOZIER DOZILY DOZING ECZEMA ENZYME ENZYMS EPIZOA ERSATZ EVZONE FAZING FEAZED FEAZES FEEZED FEEZES FEZZED FEZZES FIZGIG FIZZED FIZZER FIZZES FIZZLE FLOOZY FOOZLE FOZIER FRAZIL FREEZE FRENZY FRIEZE FRIZED FRIZER FRIZES FRIZZY FROUZY FROWZY FROZEN FURZES FUTZED FUTZES FUZEES FUZILS FUZING FUZZED FUZZES GAUZES GAZABO GAZARS GAZEBO GAZERS GAZING GAZUMP GEEZER GHAZIS GIZMOS GLAZED GLAZER GLAZES GLITZY GLOZED GLOZES

GRAZED GRAZER GRAZES GROSZE GROSZY GUZZLE GYOZAS HALUTZ HAMZAH HAMZAS HAZANS HAZARD HAZELS HAZERS HAZIER HAZILY HAZING HAZMAT HAZZAN HEEZED HEEZES HUTZPA HUZZAH HUZZAS IODIZE IONIZE IZZARD JAZZBO JAZZED JAZZER JAZZES JEZAIL KANZUS KAZOOS KHAZEN KIBITZ KLUTZY KOLHOZ KOLKOZ KUDZUS KUVASZ KWANZA LAZARS LAZIED LAZIER LAZIES LAZILY LAZING LAZULI LIZARD LUTZES MAHZOR MAIZES MAMZER MATZAH MATZAS MATZOH MATZOS MATZOT MAZARD MAZERS MAZIER MAZILY MAZING MAZUMA MEZCAL MEZUZA MEZZOS MIRZAS MIZENS MIZUNA MIZZEN MIZZLE MIZZLY MOMZER MUZHIK MUZJIK MUZZLE NAZIFY NIZAMS NOZZLE NUZZLE OOZIER OOZILY OOZING OUZELS OYEZES OZALID OZONES OZONIC PANZER PATZER

PAZAZZ PHIZES PIAZZA PIAZZE PIZAZZ PIZZAS PIZZAZ PIZZLE PLAZAS PODZOL POTZER POZOLE PREZES PRIZED PRIZER PRIZES PUTZED PUTZES PUZZLE QUARTZ QUEAZY QUEZAL RAZEED RAZEES RAZERS RAZING RAZORS RAZZED RAZZES REBOZO RESIZE REZERO REZONE RITZES ROZZER SCHIZO SCHIZY SCHNOZ SCUZZY SEIZED SEIZER SEIZES SEIZIN SEIZOR SHAZAM SIZARS SIZERS SIZIER SIZING SIZZLE SLEAZE SLEAZO SLEAZY SMAZES SNAZZY SNEEZE SNEEZY SNOOZE SNOOZY SOZINE SOZINS SPELTZ SPRITZ STANZA SYZYGY TARZAN TAZZAS TEAZEL TEAZLE TOUZLE TWEEZE TZETZE TZURIS UNZIPS UPGAZE UPSIZE VIZARD VIZIER VIZIRS VIZORS VIZSLA WHEEZE WHEEZY WHIZZY WINZES WIZARD WIZENS WIZZEN WIZZES WURZEL YAKUZA YUTZES

ZADDIK ZAFFAR ZAFFER ZAFFIR ZAFFRE ZAFTIG ZAGGED ZAIKAI ZAIRES ZAMIAS ZANANA ZANDER ZANIER ZANIES ZANILY ZANZAS ZAPPED ZAPPER ZAREBA ZARIBA ZAYINS ZAZENS ZEALOT ZEATIN ZEBECK ZEBECS ZEBRAS ZECHIN ZENANA ZENITH ZEPHYR ZEROED ZEROES ZEROTH ZESTED ZESTER ZEUGMA ZIBETH ZIBETS ZIGGED ZIGZAG ZILLAH ZINCED ZINCIC ZINCKY ZINEBS ZINGED ZINGER ZINNIA ZIPPED ZIPPER ZIRAMS ZIRCON ZITHER ZIZITH ZIZZLE ZLOTYS ZOARIA ZOCALO ZODIAC ZOECIA ZOFTIG ZOMBIE ZOMBIS ZONARY ZONATE ZONERS ZONING ZONKED ZONULA ZONULE ZOOIDS ZOOIER ZOOMED ZOONAL ZOONED ZORILS ZOSTER ZOUAVE ZOUNDS ZOYSIA ZYDECO ZYGOID ZYGOMA ZYGOSE ZYGOTE ZYMASE

FOUR-LETTER WORDS

A bit of research I conducted of SCRABBLE games between experts revealed that 75% of all words formed in a game are short words—words of two, three, or four letters. Moreover, these words account for 50% of all points scored. With short words comprising only 5% of the dictionary, their contribution to the game is disproportionately great. It also suggests that word-studiers will get a much greater payoff by judiciously selecting the shorter words to study. Another part of the payoff is learning the root words to longer words, including bonus plays. DRAY can be extended into DRAYING, MAZY can become MAZIEST, while TINT is the root of TINTERS. Studying the 101 two-letter words and the 1004 three-letter words is no small accomplishment. So how does one approach 4002 four-letter words? Grab a highlighter and mark those words that you (a) do not know, (b) might consider challenging if played by your opponent, or (c) feel you may have difficulty seeing within a group of seven random letters. At your leisure, review only your highlighted words.

AAHS AALS ABAS ABBA ABBE ABED ABET ABLE ABLY ABRI ABUT ABYE ABYS ACED ACES ACHE ACHY ACID ACME ACNE ACRE ACTA ACTS ACYL ADDS ADIT ADOS ADZE AEON AERO AERY AFAR AGAR AGAS AGED AGEE AGER AGES AGHA AGIN AGIO AGLY AGMA AGOG AGON AGUE AHED AHEM AHIS AHOY AIDE AIDS AILS AIMS AINS AIRN AIRS AIRT AIRY AITS AJAR AJEE AKEE AKIN ALAE ALAN ALAR ALAS ALBA ALBS ALEC ALEE ALEF ALES ALFA ALGA ALIF ALIT ALKY ALLS ALLY

ALMA ALME ALMS ALOE ALOW ALPS ALSO ALTO ALTS ALUM AMAH AMAS AMBO AMEN AMIA AMID AMIE AMIN AMIR AMIS AMMO AMOK AMPS AMUS AMYL ANAL ANAS ANDS ANES ANEW ANGA ANIL ANIS ANKH ANNA ANOA ANON ANSA ANTA ANTE ANTI ANTS ANUS APED APER APES APEX APOD APOS APPS APSE AQUA ARAK ARBS ARCH ARCO ARCS AREA ARES ARFS ARIA ARID ARIL ARKS ARMS ARMY ARTS ARTY ARUM ARVO ARYL ASCI ASEA ASHY ASKS ASPS ATAP ATES ATMA ATOM ATOP

AUKS AULD AUNT AURA AUTO AVER AVES AVID AVOS AVOW AWAY AWED AWEE AWES AWLS AWNS AWNY AWOL AWRY AXAL AXED AXEL AXES AXIL AXIS AXLE AXON AYAH AYES AYIN AZAN AZON BAAL BAAS BABA BABE BABU BABY BACH BACK BADE BADS BAFF BAGS BAHT BAIL BAIT BAKE BALD BALE BALK BALL BALM BALS BAMS BAND BANE BANG BANI BANK BANS BAPS BARB BARD BARE BARF BARK BARM BARN BARS BASE BASH BASK BASS BAST BATE BATH BATS BATT BAUD BAWD

BAWL BAYS BEAD BEAK BEAM BEAN BEAR BEAT BEAU BECK BEDS BEDU BEEF BEEN BEEP BEER BEES BEET BEGS BELL BELS BELT BEMA BEND BENE BENS BENT BERG BERK BERM BEST BETA BETH BETS BEVY BEYS BHUT BIAS BIBB BIBS BICE BIDE BIDI BIDS BIER BIFF BIGS BIKE BILE BILK BILL BIMA BIND BINE BINS BINT BIOG BIOS BIRD BIRK BIRL BIRO BIRR BISE BISK BITE BITS BITT BIZE BLAB BLAE BLAH BLAM BLAT BLAW BLEB BLED BLET BLEW BLIN BLIP

BLOB BLOC BLOG BLOT BLOW BLUB BLUE BLUR BOAR BOAS BOAT BOBS BOCK BODE BODS BODY BOFF BOGS BOGY BOHO BOIL BOLA BOLD BOLE BOLL BOLO BOLT BOMB BOND BONE BONG BONK BONY BOOB BOOK BOOM BOON BOOR BOOS BOOT BOPS BORA BORE BORK BORN BORT BOSH BOSK BOSS BOTA BOTH BOTS BOTT BOUT BOWL BOWS BOXY BOYO BOYS BOZO BRAD BRAE BRAG BRAN BRAS BRAT BRAW BRAY BRED BREE BREN BREW BRIE BRIG BRIM BRIN BRIO BRIS BRIT BROO BROS

BROW BRRR BRUT BRUX BUBO BUBS BUBU BUCK BUDS BUFF BUGS BUHL BUHR BULB BULK BULL BUMF BUMP BUMS BUNA BUND BUNG BUNK BUNN BUNS BUNT BUOY BURA BURB BURD BURG BURL BURN BURP BURR BURS BURY BUSH BUSK BUSS BUST BUSY BUTE BUTS BUTT BUYS BUZZ BYES BYRE BYRL BYTE CABS CACA CADE CADI CADS CAFE CAFF CAGE CAGY CAID CAIN CAKE CAKY CALF CALK CALL CALM CALO CALX CAME CAMO CAMP CAMS CANE CANS CANT CAPE CAPH CAPO CAPS

CARB CARD CARE CARK CARL CARN CARP CARR CARS CART CASA CASE CASH CASK CAST CATE CATS CAUL CAVE CAVY CAWS CAYS CECA CEDE CEDI CEES CEIL CELL CELS CELT CENT CEPE CEPS CERE CERO CESS CETE CHAD CHAI CHAM CHAO CHAP CHAR CHAT CHAW CHAY CHEF CHEW CHEZ CHIA CHIC CHID CHIN CHIP CHIS CHIT CHON CHOP CHOW CHUB CHUG CHUM CIAO CIGS CINE CION CIRE CIST CITE CITY CLAD CLAG CLAM CLAN CLAP CLAW CLAY CLEF CLEW CLIP CLOD

CLOG CLON CLOP CLOT CLOY CLUB CLUE COAL COAT COAX COBB COBS COCA COCK COCO CODA CODE CODS COED COFF COFT COGS COHO COIF COIL COIN COIR COKE COKY COLA COLD COLE COLS COLT COLY COMA COMB COME COMP CONE CONI CONK CONN CONS CONY COOF COOK COOL COON COOP COOS COOT COPE COPS COPY CORD CORE CORF CORK CORM CORN CORS CORY COSH COSS COST COSY COTE COTS COUP COVE COWL COWS COWY COXA COYS COZY CRAB CRAG CRAM CRAP

CRAW CRED CREW CRIB CRIS CRIT CROC CROP CROW CRUD CRUS CRUX CUBE CUBS CUDS CUED CUES CUFF CUIF CUKE CULL CULM CULT CUPS CURB CURD CURE CURF CURL CURN CURR CURS CURT CUSK CUSP CUSS CUTE CUTS CWMS CYAN CYMA CYME CYST CZAR DABS DACE DADA DADO DADS DAFF DAFT DAGS DAHL DAHS DAIS DAKS DALE DALS DAME DAMN DAMP DAMS DANG DANK DANS DAPS DARB DARE DARK DARN DART DASH DATA DATE DATO DAUB DAUT DAVY DAWK DAWN DAWS

DAWT DAYS DAZE DEAD DEAF DEAL DEAN DEAR DEBS DEBT DECK DECO DEED DEEM DEEP DEER DEES DEET DEFI DEFT DEFY DEIL DEKE DELE DELF DELI DELL DELS DELT DEME DEMO DEMY DENE DENI DENS DENT DENY DERE DERM DESK DEVA DEVS DEWS DEWY DEXY DEYS DHAK DHAL DHOW DIAL DIBS DICE DICK DIDO DIDY DIED DIEL DIES DIET DIFF DIFS DIGS DIKE DILL DIME DIMS DINE DING DINK DINO DINS DINT DIOL DIPS DIPT DIRE DIRK DIRL DIRT DISC DISH

DISK DISS DITA DITE DITS DITZ DIVA DIVE DJIN DOAT DOBY DOCK DOCS DODO DOER DOES DOFF DOGE DOGS DOGY DOIT DOJO DOLE DOLL DOLS DOLT DOME DOMS DONA DONE DONG DONS DOOM DOOR DOPA DOPE DOPY DORE DORK DORM DORP DORR DORS DORY DOSE DOSS DOST DOTE DOTH DOTS DOTY DOUM DOUR DOUX DOVE DOWN DOWS DOXY DOZE DOZY DRAB DRAG DRAM DRAT DRAW DRAY DREE DREG DREK DREW DRIB DRIP DROP DRUB DRUG DRUM DRYS DUAD DUAL DUBS DUCE

DUCI DUCK DUCT DUDE DUDS DUEL DUES DUET DUFF DUGS DUIT DUKE DULL DULY DUMA DUMB DUMP DUNE DUNG DUNK DUNS DUNT DUOS DUPE DUPS DURA DURE DURN DURO DURR DUSK DUST DUTY DYAD DYED DYER DYES DYKE DYNE EACH EARL EARN EARS EASE EAST EASY EATH EATS EAUX EAVE EBBS EBON ECHE ECHO ECHT ECRU ECUS EDDO EDDY EDGE EDGY EDHS EDIT EELS EELY EERY EFFS EFTS EGAD EGAL EGER EGGS EGGY EGIS EGOS EIDE EKED EKES ELAN ELDS ELHI

ELKS ELLS ELMS ELMY ELSE EMES EMEU EMIC EMIR EMIT EMMY EMUS EMYD ENDS ENGS ENOL ENOW ENUF ENVY EONS EPEE EPHA EPIC EPOS ERAS ERGO ERGS ERNE ERNS EROS ERRS ERST ESES ESNE ESPY ETAS ETCH ETHS ETIC ETNA ETUI EURO EVEN EVER EVES EVIL EWER EWES EXAM EXEC EXED EXES EXIT EXON EXPO EYAS EYED EYEN EYER EYES EYNE EYRA EYRE EYRY FABS FACE FACT FADE FADO FADS FAGS FAIL FAIN FAIR FAKE FALL FALX FAME FANE FANG FANO

FANS FARD FARE FARL FARM FARO FASH FAST FATE FATS FAUN FAUX FAVA FAVE FAWN FAYS FAZE FEAL FEAR FEAT FECK FEDS FEEB FEED FEEL FEES FEET FEHS FELL FELT FEME FEMS FEND FENS FEOD FERE FERN FESS FEST FETA FETE FETS FEUD FEUS FIAR FIAT FIBS FICE FICO FIDO FIDS FIEF FIFE FIGS FILA FILE FILL FILM FILO FILS FIND FINE FINK FINO FINS FIRE FIRM FIRN FIRS FISC FISH FIST FITS FIVE FIXT FIZZ FLAB FLAG FLAK FLAM FLAN

FLAP FLAT FLAW FLAX FLAY FLEA FLED FLEE FLEW FLEX FLEY FLIC FLIP FLIR FLIT FLOC FLOE FLOG FLOP FLOW FLUB FLUE FLUS FLUX FOAL FOAM FOBS FOCI FOES FOGS FOGY FOHN FOIL FOIN FOLD FOLK FOND FONS FONT FOOD FOOL FOOT FOPS FORA FORB FORD FORE FORK FORM FORT FOSS FOUL FOUR FOWL FOXY FOYS FOZY FRAE FRAG FRAP FRAT FRAY FREE FRET FRIG FRIT FRIZ FROE FROG FROM FROW FRUG FUBS FUCI FUDS FUEL FUGS FUGU FUJI FULL FUME

FUMY
FUND
FUNK
FUNS
FURL
FURS
FURY
FUSE
FUSS
FUTZ
FUZE
FUZZ
FYCE
FYKE
GABS
GABY
GADI
GADS
GAED
GAEN
GAES
GAFF
GAGA
GAGE
GAGS
GAIN
GAIT
GALA
GALE
GALL
GALS
GAMA
GAMB
GAME
GAMP
GAMS
GAMY
GANE
GANG
GAOL
GAPE
GAPS
GAPY
GARB
GARS
GASH
GASP
GAST
GATE
GATS
GAUD
GAUM
GAUN
GAUR
GAVE
GAWK
GAWP
GAYS
GAZE
GEAR
GECK
GEDS
GEED
GEEK
GEES
GEEZ
GELD
GELS
GELT
GEMS
GENE
GENS
GENT
GENU
GERM
GEST
GETA
GETS
GEUM
GHAT
GHEE
GHIS
GIBE
GIBS
GIDS
GIED
GIEN
GIES
GIFT
GIGA
GIGS
GILD
GILL
GILT
GIMP
GINK

GINS
GIPS
GIRD
GIRL
GIRN
GIRO
GIRT
GIST
GITE
GITS
GIVE
GLAD
GLAM
GLED
GLEE
GLEG
GLEN
GLEY
GLIA
GLIB
GLIM
GLOB
GLOM
GLOP
GLOW
GLUE
GLUG
GLUM
GLUT
GNAR
GNAT
GNAW
GNUS
GOAD
GOAL
GOAS
GOAT
GOBO
GOBS
GOBY
GODS
GOER
GOES
GOGO
GOLD
GOLF
GONE
GONG
GOOD
GOOF
GOOK
GOON
GOOP
GOOS
GORE
GORM
GORP
GORY
GOSH
GOTH
GOUT
GOWD
GOWK
GOWN
GRAB
GRAD
GRAM
GRAN
GRAT
GRAY
GREE
GREW
GREY
GRID
GRIG
GRIM
GRIN
GRIP
GRIT
GROG
GROK
GROT
GROW
GRUB
GRUE
GRUM
GUAN
GUAR
GUCK
GUDE
GUFF
GUID
GULF
GULL
GULP
GULS

GUMS
GUNK
GUNS
GURU
GUSH
GUST
GUTS
GUVS
GUYS
GYBE
GYMS
GYPS
GYRE
GYRI
GYRO
GYVE
HAAF
HAAR
HABU
HACK
HADE
HADJ
HAED
HAEM
HAEN
HAES
HAET
HAFT
HAGS
HAHA
HAHS
HAIK
HAIL
HAIR
HAJI
HAJJ
HAKE
HAKU
HALE
HALF
HALL
HALM
HALO
HALT
HAME
HAMS
HAND
HANG
HANK
HANT
HAPS
HARD
HARE
HARK
HARL
HARM
HARP
HART
HASH
HASP
HAST
HATE
HATH
HATS
HAUL
HAUT
HAVE
HAWK
HAWS
HAYS
HAZE
HAZY
HEAD
HEAL
HEAP
HEAR
HEAT
HECK
HEED
HEEL
HEFT
HEHS
HEIL
HEIR
HELD
HELL
HELM
HELO
HELP
HEME
HEMP
HEMS
HENS
HENT
HERB
HERD

HERE
HERL
HERM
HERN
HERO
HERS
HEST
HETH
HETS
HEWN
HEWS
HICK
HIDE
HIED
HIES
HIGH
HIKE
HILA
HILI
HILL
HILT
HIMS
HIND
HINS
HINT
HIPS
HIRE
HISN
HISS
HIST
HITS
HIVE
HOAR
HOAX
HOBO
HOBS
HOCK
HODS
HOED
HOER
HOES
HOGG
HOGS
HOKE
HOLD
HOLE
HOLK
HOLM
HOLP
HOLS
HOLT
HOLY
HOME
HOMO
HOMY
HONE
HONG
HONK
HONS
HOOD
HOOF
HOOK
HOOP
HOOT
HOPE
HOPS
HORA
HORN
HOSE
HOST
HOTS
HOUR
HOVE
HOWE
HOWF
HOWK
HOWL
HOWS
HOYA
HOYS
HUBS
HUCK
HUED
HUES
HUFF
HUGE
HUGS
HUIC
HULA
HULK
HULL
HUMP
HUMS
HUNG
HUNH
HUNK

HUNS
HUNT
HURL
HURT
HUSH
HUSK
HUTS
HWAN
HYLA
HYMN
HYPE
HYPO
HYPS
HYTE
IAMB
IBEX
IBIS
ICED
ICES
ICHS
ICKY
ICON
IDEA
IDEM
IDES
IDLE
IDLY
IDOL
IDYL
IFFY
IGGS
IGLU
IKAT
IKON
ILEA
ILEX
ILIA
ILKA
ILKS
ILLS
ILLY
IMAM
IMID
IMMY
IMPI
IMPS
INBY
INCH
INFO
INIA
INKS
INKY
INLY
INNS
INRO
INTI
INTO
IONS
IOTA
IRED
IRES
IRID
IRIS
IRKS
IRON
ISBA
ISLE
ISMS
ITCH
ITEM
IWIS
IXIA
IZAR
JABS
JACK
JADE
JAGG
JAGS
JAIL
JAKE
JAMB
JAMS
JANE
JAPE
JARL
JARS
JATO
JAUK
JAUP
JAVA
JAWS
JAYS
JAZZ
JEAN
JEED
JEEP

JEER
JEES
JEEZ
JEFE
JEHU
JELL
JEON
JERK
JESS
JEST
JETE
JETS
JEUX
JIAO
JIBB
JIBE
JIBS
JIFF
JIGS
JILL
JILT
JIMP
JINK
JINN
JINS
JINX
JIVE
JIVY
JOBS
JOCK
JOES
JOEY
JOGS
JOHN
JOIN
JOKE
JOKY
JOLE
JOLT
JOSH
JOSS
JOTA
JOTS
JOUK
JOWL
JOWS
JOYS
JUBA
JUBE
JUCO
JUDO
JUGA
JUGS
JUJU
JUKE
JUKU
JUMP
JUNK
JUPE
JURA
JURY
JUST
JUTE
JUTS
KAAS
KABS
KADI
KAES
KAFS
KAGU
KAIF
KAIL
KAIN
KAKA
KAKI
KALE
KAME
KAMI
KANA
KANE
KAON
KAPA
KAPH
KARN
KART
KATA
KATS
KAVA
KAYO
KAYS
KBAR
KEAS
KECK
KEEF
KEEK
KEEL

KEEN
KEEP
KEET
KEFS
KEGS
KEIR
KELP
KELT
KEMP
KENO
KENS
KENT
KEPI
KEPS
KEPT
KERB
KERF
KERN
KETO
KEYS
KHAF
KHAN
KHAT
KHET
KHIS
KIBE
KICK
KIDS
KIEF
KIER
KIFS
KILL
KILN
KILO
KILT
KINA
KIND
KINE
KING
KINK
KINO
KINS
KIPS
KIRK
KIRN
KIRS
KISS
KIST
KITE
KITH
KITS
KIVA
KIWI
KLIK
KNAP
KNAR
KNEE
KNEW
KNIT
KNOB
KNOP
KNOT
KNOW
KNUR
KOAN
KOAS
KOBO
KOBS
KOEL
KOHL
KOIS
KOJI
KOLA
KOLO
KONK
KOOK
KOPH
KOPS
KORA
KORE
KORS
KOSS
KOTO
KRIS
KUDO
KUDU
KUES
KUFI
KUNA
KUNE
KURU
KVAS
KYAK
KYAR
KYAT
KYES

KYTE
LABS
LACE
LACK
LACS
LACY
LADE
LADS
LADY
LAGS
LAIC
LAID
LAIN
LAIR
LAKE
LAKH
LAKY
LALL
LAMA
LAMB
LAME
LAMP
LAMS
LAND
LANE
LANG
LANK
LAPS
LARD
LARI
LARK
LARS
LASE
LASH
LASS
LAST
LATE
LATH
LATI
LATS
LATU
LAUD
LAVA
LAVE
LAVS
LAWN
LAWS
LAYS
LAZE
LAZY
LEAD
LEAF
LEAK
LEAL
LEAN
LEAP
LEAR
LEAS
LECH
LEEK
LEER
LEES
LEET
LEFT
LEGS
LEHR
LEIS
LEKE
LEKS
LEKU
LEND
LENO
LENS
LENT
LEPT
LESS
LEST
LETS
LEUD
LEVA
LEVO
LEVY
LEWD
LEYS
LIAR
LIBS
LICE
LICH
LICK
LIDO
LIDS
LIED
LIEF
LIEN
LIER
LIES

LIEU
LIFE
LIFT
LIKE
LILO
LILT
LILY
LIMA
LIMB
LIME
LIMN
LIMO
LIMP
LIMY
LINE
LING
LINK
LINN
LINO
LINS
LINT
LINY
LION
LIPA
LIPE
LIPS
LIRA
LIRE
LIRI
LISP
LIST
LITE
LITS
LITU
LIVE
LOAD
LOAF
LOAM
LOAN
LOBE
LOBO
LOBS
LOCA
LOCH
LOCI
LOCK
LOCO
LODE
LOFT
LOGE
LOGO
LOGS
LOGY
LOID
LOIN
LOLL
LONE
LONG
LOOF
LOOK
LOOM
LOON
LOOP
LOOS
LOOT
LOPE
LOPS
LORD
LORE
LORN
LORY
LOSE
LOSS
LOST
LOTA
LOTH
LOTI
LOTS
LOUD
LOUP
LOUR
LOUT
LOVE
LOWE
LOWN
LOWS
LUAU
LUBE
LUCE
LUCK
LUDE
LUES
LUFF
LUGE
LUGS
LULL

LULU
LUMA
LUMP
LUMS
LUNA
LUNE
LUNG
LUNK
LUNT
LUNY
LURE
LURK
LUSH
LUST
LUTE
LUTZ
LUVS
LUXE
LWEI
LYCH
LYES
LYNX
LYRE
LYSE
MAAR
MABE
MACE
MACH
MACK
MACS
MADE
MADS
MAES
MAGE
MAGI
MAGS
MAID
MAIL
MAIM
MAIN
MAIR
MAKE
MAKO
MALE
MALL
MALM
MALT
MAMA
MANA
MANE
MANO
MANS
MANY
MAPS
MARA
MARC
MARE
MARK
MARL
MARS
MART
MASA
MASH
MASK
MASS
MAST
MATE
MATH
MATS
MATT
MAUD
MAUL
MAUN
MAUT
MAWN
MAWS
MAXI
MAYA
MAYO
MAYS
MAZE
MAZY
MEAD
MEAL
MEAN
MEAT
MEDS
MEED
MEEK
MEET
MEGA
MEGS
MELD
MELL
MELS
MELT

MEME
MEMO
MEMS
MEND
MENO
MENU
MEOU
MEOW
MERC
MERE
MERK
MERL
MESA
MESH
MESS
META
METE
METH
MEWL
MEWS
MEZE
MHOS
MIBS
MICA
MICE
MICS
MIDI
MIDS
MIEN
MIFF
MIGG
MIGS
MIKE
MILD
MILE
MILK
MILL
MILO
MILS
MILT
MIME
MINA
MIND
MINE
MINI
MINK
MINT
MINX
MIPS
MIRE
MIRI
MIRK
MIRS
MIRY
MISE
MISO
MISS
MIST
MITE
MITT
MITY
MIXT
MOAN
MOAS
MOAT
MOBS
MOCK
MOCS
MODE
MODI
MODS
MOGS
MOIL
MOJO
MOKE
MOLA
MOLD
MOLE
MOLL
MOLS
MOLT
MOLY
MOME
MOMI
MOMS
MONK
MONO
MONS
MONY
MOOD
MOOL
MOON
MOOR
MOOS
MOOT
MOPE

MOPS
MOPY
MORA
MORE
MORN
MORS
MORT
MOSH
MOSK
MOSS
MOST
MOTE
MOTH
MOTS
MOTT
MOUE
MOVE
MOWN
MOWS
MOXA
MOZO
MUCH
MUCK
MUDS
MUFF
MUGG
MUGS
MULE
MULL
MUMM
MUMP
MUMS
MUMU
MUNI
MUNS
MUON
MURA
MURE
MURK
MURR
MUSE
MUSH
MUSK
MUSS
MUST
MUTE
MUTS
MUTT
MYCS
MYNA
MYTH
NAAN
NABE
NABS
NADA
NAFF
NAGS
NAIF
NAIL
NALA
NAME
NANA
NANS
NAOI
NAOS
NAPA
NAPE
NAPS
NARC
NARD
NARK
NARY
NAVE
NAVY
NAYS
NAZI
NEAP
NEAR
NEAT
NEBS
NECK
NEED
NEEM
NEEP
NEGS
NEIF
NEMA
NENE
NEON
NERD
NESS
NEST
NETS
NETT
NEUK
NEUM

NEVE
NEVI
NEWS
NEWT
NEXT
NIBS
NICE
NICK
NIDE
NIDI
NIGH
NILL
NILS
NIMS
NINE
NIPA
NIPS
NISI
NITE
NITS
NIXE
NIXY
NOBS
NOCK
NODE
NODI
NODS
NOEL
NOES
NOGG
NOGS
NOIL
NOIR
NOLO
NOMA
NOME
NOMS
NONA
NONE
NOOK
NOON
NOPE
NORI
NORM
NOSE
NOSH
NOSY
NOTA
NOTE
NOUN
NOUS
NOVA
NOWS
NOWT
NUBS
NUDE
NUKE
NULL
NUMB
NUNS
NURD
NURL
NUTS
OAFS
OAKS
OAKY
OARS
OAST
OATH
OATS
OBAS
OBES
OBEY
OBIA
OBIS
OBIT
OBOE
OBOL
OCAS
ODAH
ODAS
ODDS
ODEA
ODES
ODIC
ODOR
ODYL
OFFS
OGAM
OGEE
OGLE
OGRE
OHED
OHIA
OHMS
OILS

OILY
OINK
OKAS
OKAY
OKEH
OKES
OKRA
OLDS
OLDY
OLEA
OLEO
OLES
OLIO
OLLA
OMEN
OMER
OMIT
ONCE
ONES
ONLY
ONOS
ONTO
ONUS
ONYX
OOHS
OOPS
OOTS
OOZE
OOZY
OPAH
OPAL
OPED
OPEN
OPES
OPTS
OPUS
ORAD
ORAL
ORBS
ORBY
ORCA
ORCS
ORDO
ORES
ORGY
ORLE
ORRA
ORTS
ORYX
ORZO
OSAR
OSES
OSSA
OTIC
OTTO
OUCH
OUDS
OUPH
OURS
OUST
OUTS
OUZO
OVAL
OVEN
OVER
OVUM
OWED
OWES
OWLS
OWNS
OWSE
OXEN
OXES
OXID
OXIM
OYER
OYES
OYEZ
PACA
PACE
PACK
PACS
PACT
PACY
PADI
PADS
PAGE
PAID
PAIK
PAIL
PAIN
PAIR
PALE
PALL
PALM
PALP

PALS
PALY
PAMS
PANE
PANG
PANS
PANT
PAPA
PAPS
PARA
PARD
PARE
PARK
PARR
PARS
PART
PASE
PASH
PASS
PAST
PATE
PATH
PATS
PATY
PAVE
PAWL
PAWN
PAWS
PAYS
PEAG
PEAK
PEAL
PEAN
PEAR
PEAS
PEAT
PECH
PECK
PECS
PEDS
PEEK
PEEL
PEEN
PEEP
PEER
PEES
PEGS
PEHS
PEIN
PEKE
PELE
PELF
PELT
PEND
PENS
PENT
PEON
PEPO
PEPS
PERE
PERI
PERK
PERM
PERP
PERT
PERV
PESO
PEST
PETS
PEWS
PFFT
PFUI
PHAT
PHEW
PHIS
PHIZ
PHON
PHOT
PHUT
PIAL
PIAN
PIAS
PICA
PICE
PICK
PICS
PIED
PIER
PIES
PIGS
PIKA
PIKE
PIKI
PILE
PILI
PILL

PILY PIMA PIMP PINA PINE PING PINK PINS PINT PINY PION PIPE PIPS PIPY PIRN PISH PISO PITA PITH PITS PITY PIXY PLAN PLAT PLAY PLEA PLEB PLED PLEW PLEX PLIE PLOD PLOP PLOT PLOW PLOY PLUG PLUM PLUS POCK POCO PODS POEM POET POGY POIS POKE POKY POLE POLL POLO POLS POLY POME POMO POMP POND PONE PONG PONS PONY POOD POOF POOH POOL POON POOP POOR POPE POPS PORE PORK PORN PORT POSE POSH POST POSY POTS POUF POUR POUT POWS POXY PRAM PRAO PRAT PRAU PRAY PREE

PREP PREX PREY PREZ PRIG PRIM PROA PROD PROF PROG PROM PROP PROS PROW PSIS PSST PTUI PUBS PUCE PUCK PUDS PUFF PUGH PUGS PUJA PUKE PULA PULE PULI PULL PULP PULS PUMA PUMP PUNA PUNG PUNK PUNS PUNT PUNY PUPA PUPS PUPU PURE PURI PURL PURR PURS PUSH PUSS PUTS PUTT PUTZ PYAS PYES PYIC PYIN PYRE PYRO QADI QAID QATS QOPH QUAD QUAG QUAI QUAY QUEY QUID QUIN QUIP QUIT QUIZ QUOD RACE RACK RACY RADS RAFF RAFT RAGA RAGE RAGG RAGI RAGS RAIA RAID RAIL RAIN RAIS

RAJA RAKE RAKI RAKU RALE RAMI RAMP RAMS RAND RANG RANI RANK RANT RAPE RAPS RAPT RARE RASE RASH RASP RATE RATH RATO RATS RAVE RAWS RAYA RAYS RAZE RAZZ READ REAL REAM REAP REAR REBS RECK RECS REDD REDE REDO REDS REED REEF REEK REEL REES REFS REFT REGS REIF REIN REIS RELY REMS REND RENT REPO REPP REPS RESH REST RETE RETS REVS RHEA RHOS RHUS RIAL RIAS RIBS RICE RICH RICK RIDE RIDS RIEL RIFE RIFF RIFS RIFT RIGS RILE RILL RIME RIMS RIMY RIND RING RINK

RINS RIOT RIPE RIPS RISE RISK RITE RITZ RIVE ROAD ROAM ROAN ROAR ROBE ROBS ROCK ROCS RODE RODS ROES ROIL ROLE ROLF ROLL ROMP ROMS ROOD ROOF ROOK ROOM ROOT ROPE ROPY ROSE ROSY ROTA ROTE ROTI ROTL ROTO ROTS ROUE ROUP ROUT ROUX ROVE ROWS RUBE RUBS RUBY RUCK RUDD RUDE RUED RUER RUES RUFF RUGA RUGS RUIN RULE RULY RUMP RUMS RUNE RUNG RUNS RUNT RUSE RUSH RUSK RUST RUTH RUTS RYAS RYES RYKE RYND RYOT SABE SABS SACK SACS SADE SADI SAFE SAGA SAGE SAGO SAGS

SAGY SAID SAIL SAIN SAKE SAKI SALE SALL SALP SALS SALT SAME SAMP SAND SANE SANG SANK SANS SAPS SARD SARI SARK SASH SASS SATE SATI SAUL SAVE SAWN SAWS SAYS SCAB SCAD SCAG SCAM SCAN SCAR SCAT SCOP SCOT SCOW SCRY SCUD SCUM SCUP SCUT SEAL SEAM SEAR SEAS SEAT SECS SECT SEED SEEK SEEL SEEM SEEN SEEP SEER SEES SEGO SEGS SEIF SEIS SELF SELL SELS SEME SEMI SEND SENE SENT SEPT SERA SERE SERF SERS SETA SETS SETT SEWN SEWS SEXT SEXY SHAD SHAG SHAH SHAM SHAW

SHAY SHEA SHED SHES SHEW SHIM SHIN SHIP SHIV SHMO SHOD SHOE SHOG SHOO SHOP SHOT SHOW SHRI SHUL SHUN SHUT SHWA SIAL SIBB SIBS SICE SICK SICS SIDE SIDH SIFT SIGH SIGN SIKA SIKE SILD SILK SILL SILO SILT SIMA SIMP SIMS SINE SING SINH SINK SINS SIPE SIPS SIRE SIRS SITE SITH SITS SIZE SIZY SKAG SKAS SKAT SKEE SKEG SKEP SKEW SKID SKIM SKIN SKIP SKIS SKIT SKUA SLAB SLAG SLAM SLAP SLAT SLAW SLAY SLED SLEW SLID SLIM SLIP SLIT SLOB SLOE SLOG SLOP SLOT SLOW

SLUB SLUE SLUG SLUM SLUR SLUT SMEW SMIT SMOG SMUG SMUT SNAG SNAP SNAW SNED SNIB SNIP SNIT SNOB SNOG SNOT SNOW SNUB SNUG SNYE SOAK SOAP SOAR SOBA SOBS SOCA SOCK SODA SODS SOFA SOFT SOIL SOJA SOKE SOLA SOLD SOLE SOLI SOLO SOLS SOMA SOME SOMS SONE SONG SONS SOOK SOON SOOT SOPH SOPS SORA SORB SORD SORE SORI SORN SORT SOTH SOTS SOUK SOUL SOUP SOUR SOUS SOWN SOWS SOYA SOYS SPAE SPAM SPAN SPAR SPAS SPAT SPAY SPEC SPED SPEW SPIN SPIT SPIV SPOT SPRY SPUD

SPUE SPUN SPUR SRIS STAB STAG STAR STAT STAW STAY STEM STEP STET STEW STEY STIR STOA STOB STOP STOT STOW STUB STUD STUM STUN STYE SUBA SUBS SUCH SUCK SUDD SUDS SUED SUER SUES SUET SUGH SUIT SUKS SULK SULU SUMO SUMP SUMS SUNG SUNK SUNN SUNS SUPE SUPS SUQS SURA SURD SURE SURF SUSS SWAB SWAG SWAM SWAN SWAP SWAT SWAY SWIG SWIM SWOB SWOP SWOT SWUM SYBO SYCE SYKE SYLI SYNC SYNE SYPH TABS TABU TACE TACH TACK TACO TACT TADS TAEL TAGS TAHR TAIL TAIN TAKA

TAKE TALA TALC TALE TALI TALK TALL TAME TAMP TAMS TANG TANK TANS TAOS TAPA TAPE TAPS TARE TARN TARO TARP TARS TART TASK TASS TATE TATS TAUS TAUT TAVS TAWS TAXA TAXI TEAK TEAL TEAM TEAR TEAS TEAT TECH TEDS TEED TEEL TEEM TEEN TEES TEFF TEGG TEGS TELA TELE TELL TELS TEMP TEND TENS TENT TEPA TERM TERN TEST TETH TETS TEWS TEXT THAE THAN THAT THAW THEE THEM THEN THEW THEY THIN THIO THIR THIS THOU THRO THRU THUD THUG THUS TICK TICS TIDE TIDY TIED TIER

TIES TIFF TIKE TIKI TILE TILL TILS TILT TIME TINE TING TINS TINT TINY TIPI TIPS TIRE TIRL TIRO TITI TITS TIVY TOAD TOBY TODS TODY TOEA TOED TOES TOFF TOFT TOFU TOGA TOGS TOIL TOIT TOKE TOLA TOLD TOLE TOLL TOLU TOMB TOME TOMS TONE TONG TONS TONY TOOK TOOL TOOM TOON TOOT TOPE TOPH TOPI TOPO TOPS TORA TORC TORE TORI TORN TORO TORR TORS TORT TORY TOSH TOSS TOST TOTE TOTS TOUR TOUT TOWN TOWS TOWY TOYO TOYS TRAD TRAM TRAP TRAY TREE TREF TREK TRES TRET

TREY TRIG TRIM TRIO TRIP TROD TROG TROP TROT TROW TROY TRUE TRUG TSAR TSKS TUBA TUBE TUBS TUCK TUFA TUFF TUFT TUGS TUIS TULE TUMP TUNA TUNE TUNG TUNS TUPS TURF TURK TURN TUSH TUSK TUTS TUTU TWAE TWAS TWEE TWIG TWIN TWIT TWOS TYEE TYER TYES TYIN TYKE TYNE TYPE TYPO TYPP TYPY TYRE TYRO TZAR UDON UDOS UGHS UGLY UKES ULAN ULNA ULUS ULVA UMBO UMPS UNAI UNAU UNBE UNCI UNCO UNDE UNDO UNDY UNIT UNTO UPAS UPBY UPDO UPON URBS URDS UREA URGE URIC URNS URPS

URSA URUS USED USER USES UTAS UTES UVEA VACS VAGI VAIL VAIN VAIR VALE VAMP VANE VANG VANS VARA VARS VARY VASA VASE VAST VATS VATU VAUS VAVS VAWS VEAL VEEP VEER VEES VEIL VEIN VELA VELD VENA VEND VENT VERA VERB VERT VERY VEST VETO VETS VEXT VIAL VIBE VICE VIDE VIDS VIED VIER VIES VIEW VIGA VIGS VILE VILL VIMS VINA VINE VINO VINY VIOL VIRL VISA VISE VITA VIVA VIVE VOES VOID VOLE VOLT VOTE VOWS VROW VUGG VUGH VUGS WABS WACK WADE WADI WADS WADY WAES

WAFF WAFT WAGE WAGS WAIF WAIL WAIN WAIR WAIT WAKE WALE WALK WALL WALY WAME WAND WANE WANS WANT WANY WAPS WARD WARE WARK WARM WARN WARP WARS WART WARY WASH WASP WAST WATS WATT WAUK WAUL WAUR WAVE WAVY WAWL WAWS WAXY WAYS WEAK WEAL WEAN WEAR WEBS WEDS WEED WEEK WEEL WEEN WEEP WEER WEES WEET WEFT WEIR WEKA WELD WELL WELT WEND WENS WENT WEPT WERE WERT WEST WETS WHAM WHAP WHAT WHEE WHEN WHET WHEW WHEY WHID WHIG WHIM WHIN WHIP WHIR WHIT WHIZ WHOA WHOM

WHOP WHUP WHYS WICH WICK WIDE WIFE WIGS WILD WILE WILL WILT WILY WIMP WIND WINE WING WINK WINO WINS WINY WIPE WIRE WIRY WISE WISH WISP WISS WIST WITE WITH WITS WIVE WOAD WOES WOKE WOKS WOLD WOLF WOMB WONK WONS WONT WOOD WOOF WOOL WOOS WORD WORE WORK WORM WORN WORT WOST WOTS WOVE WOWS WRAP WREN WRIT WUSS WYCH WYES WYLE WYND WYNN WYNS WYTE XYST YACK YAFF YAGI YAGS YAKS YALD YAMS YANG YANK YAPS YARD YARE YARN YAUD YAUP YAWL YAWN YAWP YAWS YAYS YEAH

YEAN YEAR YEAS YECH YEGG YELD YELK YELL YELP YENS YEPS YERK YETI YETT YEUK YEWS YILL YINS YIPE YIPS YIRD YIRR YLEM YOBS YOCK YODH YODS YOGA YOGH YOGI YOKE YOKS YOLK YOND YONI YORE YOUR YOUS YOWE YOWL YOWS YUAN YUCA YUCH YUCK YUGA YUKS YULE YUPS YURT YUTZ YWIS ZAGS ZANY ZAPS ZARF ZEAL ZEBU ZEDS ZEES ZEIN ZEKS ZEPS ZERK ZERO ZEST ZETA ZIGS ZILL ZINC ZINE ZING ZINS ZIPS ZITI ZITS ZOEA ZOIC ZONA ZONE ZONK ZOOM ZOON ZOOS ZORI ZOUK ZYME

SHORT WORDS THAT DO NOT TAKE S-ENDINGS

There I was, on my 36th birthday, a seasoned tourney player, paired against a 16-year-old in his first tournament. Tile tracking, which is not only permitted but encouraged at tournaments, led me to conclude which tiles he had remaining on his rack near game's end. Knowing he had an S, I added a P onto HE, forming HEP, and crossed my fingers. My opponent, who would have won with any acceptable play, made a high scoring play ending in S, and added the S onto HEP, forming HEPS. To his chagrin, I challenged his play off the board, played out, added the value of his tiles to my score, and eked out a 414-407 win. I was much impressed with this young man's playmanship, told him I'd be surprised if he hadn't won a couple of National Championships by the time he reached my age, and sent him some word lists. If anyone's birthday wish came true, it was his, as this teen, Brian Cappelletto, would become North America's top-ranked player just three years later at age 19, and has since gone on to win the National and World Championship titles.

It pays to know which words do not take an S that might otherwise appear to do so. They can be great defensive gems, or very HEP strategic lures, but don't press your luck more than once against the same player. As previously noted, the vast majority (75%) of words formed in an average expert-level game consist of two-, three-, and four-letter words. Most do take an added S-ending. Others clearly would not, for example, VOX, FIZ, CAGY, LOSS, ONLY. Herewith are short words that look as if they might take an S but actually do not.

AE	AFF	FOR	NAE	SAT	ABED	AVID	CURT	ERST	GLEG	IDEM	LANG	LOCA	NIDI	PIAL	SENE	SWAM	TROD	WEER
AM	AFT	FOU	NAH	SAU	ACTA	AWAY	DAFT	ETIC	GLIB	ILEA	LANK	LOCI	NISI	PICE	SENT	SWUM	TROP	WENT
AN	AGO	FRO	NAM	SEN	AERO	AWEE	DANK	EVER	GONE	ILIA	LATE	LONE	NODI	PIED	SERA	SYBO	TWEE	WEPT
AT	AHA	GAN	NAW	SHA	AGEE	AXAL	DATA	EYEN	GRAT	ILKA	LATI	LORN	NOPE	POCO	SEWN	SYNE	TYIN	WERE
AW	APT	GEY	NEE	SIS	AGIN	BACH	DEAF	EYNE	GREW	INBY	LATU	LOST	NOTA	POOR	SHAT	TALI	UNBE	WERT
EH	ATT	GOR	NOH	SYN	AGOG	BADE	DEFT	FAIN	GRIM	INIA	LEAL	LOTH	ODEA	PSST	SHMO	TAXA	UNCI	WHEE
ET	AVA	GOT	NOO	TAE	AHEM	BANI	DENI	FEAL	GRUM	INRO	LECH	LOTI	ODIC	PTUI	SHOD	TEED	UNDE	WHOA
HM	AWA	HAD	NOR	THE	AHOY	BEDU	DERE	FEET	GYRI	INTO	LEKE	LOUD	OHED	PUGH	SIDH	TELA	UNDO	WHOM
JO	AZO	HAO	NOT	THO	AJAR	BEEN	DIEL	FICO	HAED	IRED	LEKU	LOWN	OLEA	PULA	SITH	THAE	UNTO	WITH
LO	BAH	HEP	NTH	TOO	AJEE	BLAE	DIPT	FILA	HAEN	JEED	LENT	LYCH	ONCE	PURE	SLID	THAN	UPBY	WOKE
ME	BRR	HEY	OFT	UMM	AKIN	BLED	DIRE	FLAK	HALF	JEON	LEPT	MADE	ONTO	PYIC	SMIT	THAT	UPON	WORE
MM	CUM	HIC	OHO	UPO	ALAE	BLEW	DONE	FLED	HAST	JIAO	LEST	MAGI	ORAD	RAMI	SMUG	THEE	URIC	WORN
MY	DEF	HID	ORA	VEG	ALAR	BLIN	DORE	FOCI	HAUT	JIMP	LEVA	MAUN	ORRA	RANG	SOLA	THEM	URSA	WOST
NA	DID	HMM	OVA	VIA	ALEE	BORN	DOUR	FORA	HELD	JUGA	LEVO	MAWN	OSAR	RAPT	SOLD	THEY	VAGI	WOVE
NE	DUH	HUH	OXO	VUM	ALIT	BOTH	DREW	FRAE	HEWN	JURA	LEWD	MEEK	OSSA	RATH	SOLI	THIO	VAIN	WYCH
OF	DUI	HUP	PAH	WHA	ALOW	BRRR	DUCI	FROM	HIED	KAMI	LICE	MEGA	OTIC	REFT	SOME	THIR	VELA	YALD
OI	EAU	ICK	PER	WHO	ALSO	BUBO	EATH	FUCI	HILA	KENT	LICH	MENO	OVUM	RETE	SOON	THRO	VENA	YARE
OW	EEK	IFF	PHT	WUD	ANEW	CECA	ECHT	GAED	HISN	KEPT	LIED	META	OWSE	RIFE	SORI	THRU	VERA	YELD
TO	ELF	JEU	PIU	YAH	ANON	CHID	EDDO	GAEN	HOLP	KETO	LIEF	MICE	OXEN	RUDE	SOWN	TOLD	VETO	YOND
OY	ERE	JUN	POH	YAR	ANSA	CHON	EGAL	GAGA	HOVE	KNEW	LIFE	MIRI	PAID	RUGA	SPED	TOOK	VIDE	YUCH
UH	FAR	LED	PST	YEH	ARCO	CIAO	EIDE	GANE	HUED	KORE	LIPA	MODI	PENT	SALL	SPUN	TOOM	VILE	ZOIC
UM	FER	LEU	QUA	YET	ARID	COFT	ELHI	GAUN	HUGE	KRIS	LIPE	MOMI	PERT	SAME	STAW	TORI	VITA	ZONA
WE	FEW	LEV	RAH	YOM	ASCI	CONI	ELSE	GAVE	HUNG	KUNA	LIRE	MOWN	PFFT	SANG	STEY	TORN	VIVE	
XU	FEY	MEN	RAN	YON	ASEA	CORF	EMIC	GEED	HUNH	KUNE	LIRI	NAOI	PFUI	SANK	SUNG	TOST	WAUR	
YA	FIE	MET	SAD	YUM	ATOP	COXA	ENUF	GIED	HWAN	LAID	LITE	NEVI	PHAT	SAWN	SUNK	TRAD	WEAK	
YO	FOH	MIM	SAE	ZOA	AULD	CRIS	ERGO	GIEN	HYTE	LAIN	LITU	NICE	PHEW	SEEN	SURE	TREF	WEEL	

SHORTER WORDS THAT TAKE SURPRISE S-ENDINGS

While some words "should" take S-endings but do not, others defy expectation by accepting the S-ending. BAH, PAH, and RAH do not take an S-ending but AAH, DAH, and HAH do. DOST and TOST do not accept the S, but COST and HOST, of course, do. PALY and PILY do not take an S but POLY does. A word that we know does not take an S because its meaning precludes the addition of an S, prompts an "Oops!" from us when we learn there is an alternative meaning of the word, one permitting the S. Prepositions like BY and ON take the S because these words have alternative definitions as nouns. On the presumption that you know the S-ending and your opponent does not, such words may be effective setups for yourself when you possess the S. Another group of words that may initially appear not to take S-endings are those that already have an S-ending. For example, your opponent plays ABY. You confidently, and perhaps immodestly, lay down your bonus play, hooking your S to form ABYS. Your opponent then surprises you when she plays her bonus play, hooking her S to form ABYSS! It is easy to overlook even the most common single-to-double S-ending words. Here are some shorter words that take surprise S-endings.

AG	ADO	DUG	MED	TIL	AWOL	DUMB	HARD	NILL	THOU	ADIEU	CAMAS	FILMI	LEAST	TOXIC
AH	ALL	EDH	MIS	WHY	BIDI	ECHO	HENT	NONE	TOEA	AFRIT	CARES	FLYBY	LUNGI	TWEEN
AS	AND	ELK	MOS	WIS	BLAM	EGAD	HEST	NULL	TOFT	AFTER	CEILI	FOSSA	LYING	UNFIT
BE	ARE	FEH	MUS	WON	BOLD	EMMY	HIST	PECH	TORE	AGAPE	CHILI	FOVEA	MAYBE	VARIA
BY	ARF	GIT	NIL	YAY	BRIS	ENOW	HYPO	POLY	TORR	AGING	CHOSE	FRAIL	MICRO	WEIRD
ED	ATE	HAH	NOW	YEP	BRUT	EURO	IMPI	PROS	TRES	AHOLD	CIVIC	GIMME	MODAL	WITAN
ES	AVO	HAP	OFF	YOU	BUTE	EYAS	INTI	RIPE	UPDO	AIRER	CLACH	HAIKU	MOPED	WOMAN
GO	BAA	HEH	OLE	YUP	CALO	FICE	KIST	RODE	VAST	ALOHA	COLBY	HENRY	MORAS	WORSE
HE	BAD	HIM	OOH		CHIC	FLEW	KOBO	SAID	VIVA	AMUCK	CONCH	HEUCH	NAIRA	WORST
HO	BAS	HIS	PAS	ABLE	CUTE	FOND	KVAS	SANE	YEAH	ANIMI	CONIC	HOMEY	OGRES	YOUNG
IF	BIG	HOD	PIS	ABYS	DAFF	FULL	LOCH	SEXT	YECH	ASDIC	CRUDE	HYPER	PLATY	ZLOTY
OH	BOS	ICH	POW	AFAR	DAMP	GAST	MAUT	SICK	YORE	ASSES	CUBIC	INANE	PREST	
ON	BUS	KOI	PUS	AMEN	DEAD	GLAD	MILD	SNUG	ZORI	AWAKE	DATUM	INION	SAUCH	
OR	COR	KOS	RAW	AMID	DEAR	GLIA	MOOT	SOFT		BELOW	DREAR	IONIC	SAYED	
SO	COS	LAS	REI	AMIS	DECO	GLUM	MOST	TACH	AALII	BENDY	DURES	JINNI	SCANT	
WO	DAH	LEI	SEC	AMOK	DEEP	HAEM	MUST	TAKA	ABBES	BIALY	DYING	KAVAS	SHEER	
	DIS	LIT	SEI	ANTE	DRAB	HAET	NEAT	TALL	ABOVE	BOING	EAGER	KNOWN	STICH	
AAH	DOS	MAS	SHE	ANTI	DUAL	HAFT	NENE	TECH	ACUTE	BRACH	EAGRE	LAICH	TETRI	
ABY	DRY	MAY	TAS	ARVO	DUIT	HAHA	NIGH	THEN	ADEPT	BRAVO	FERAL	LAMED	TORIC	

THE HIGH FIVES

Let us say you have conquered "The Cheat Sheet," studied "The Vowel Dumps," familiarized yourself with The JQXZ Non-Bingos, and read over "The Fours." (By the way, try reading these lists, say, on a plane, subway, or bus or while waiting in line at a fast food restaurant, bank, or checkout line at the supermarket. Passersby can't help but notice the unusual layout of word lists upon these pages and will assume you are a brilliant encryptionologist working for the CIA.) So, with about five thousand short words behind you, what's next? Two routes to go, perhaps alternating your study paths: (1) The Best of the Bingos, the elixir of champions (see page 30), and (2) The Fives. Actually, I often recommend players begin studying at least those bingos that contain the top bingo "stems," TISANE, SATIRE, and RETINA, while also studying The Fours. But if you are done with The Fours, The Best of the Bingos should be tackled with gusto. The Fives, however, are also fruitful ground. But, with over eight thousand fives, that task may seem too daunting. So these considerably fewer "High Fives" may give you a taste and provide the best payoff with the least amount of study. These are the five-letter words that contain F, H, K, V, W, Y in the first and/or last position, and which neither start nor end with J, Q, X, or Z. Why these letters and these words? These letters are worth 4 or 5 points each, and, if you can place any one of these letters on a Triple Letter Score and simultaneously reach a Double Word Score with your five-letter word, you will garner 30-50 and possibly more points. WHACK played at, say, position B2, also forming KA nets 70 points! HEMPY at the same spot, also forming YA, nets 59 points. These High Fives, in addition to the JQXZ fives, may prove to be The Best of the Fives.

AARGH ABACK ABASH ABBEY ACIDY ACOCK AGLEY AGLOW AGONY AIRTH AITCH ALACK ALARY ALEPH ALLAY ALLEY ALLOW ALLOY ALMAH ALMEH ALOOF ALWAY AMBRY AMITY AMPLY AMUCK ANGRY ANNOY ANOMY ANTSY APEAK APEEK APERY APISH APPLY APTLY ARRAY ARROW ARTSY ASKEW ASSAY ATAXY ATOMY ATONY ATOPY AUNTY AWASH AZOTH BADDY BADLY BAFFY BAGGY BAITH BALDY BALKY BALLY BALMY BANDY BANTY BARKY BARMY BARNY BASSY BATCH BATIK BATTY BAULK BAWDY BAWTY BEACH BEADY BEAKY BEAMY

BEDEW BEECH BEEFY BEERY BEIGY BELAY BELCH BELLY BELOW BENCH BENDY BENNY BERRY BERTH BIALY BIDDY BIFFY BIGGY BIGLY BILBY BILGY BILLY BIMAH BIRCH BIRTH BITCH BITSY BITTY BLACK BLAFF BLANK BLEAK BLIMY BLINK BLOCK BLOWY BLUEY BLUFF BLUSH BOBBY BOGEY BOGGY BONEY BONNY BOOBY BOOGY BOOMY BOOTH BOOTY BOOZY BORTY BOSKY BOSSY BOTCH BOTHY BOUGH BOUSY BRACH BRAKY BRANK BRASH BRAXY BREAK BRICK BRIEF BRINK BRINY BRISK BRITH BROCK BROOK BROSY BROTH

BRUGH BRUSH BRUSK BUDDY BUFFY BUGGY BULGY BULKY BULLY BUMPH BUMPY BUNCH BUNNY BUPPY BURGH BURLY BURRY BUSBY BUSHY BUSTY BUTCH BUTTY BYLAW BYWAY CABBY CADDY CADGY CAGEY CAHOW CAKEY CALIF CAMPY CANDY CANNY CANTY CARNY CARRY CASKY CATCH CATTY CAULK CHAFF CHALK CHARK CHARY CHECK CHEEK CHETH CHEVY CHEWY CHICK CHIEF CHINK CHIRK CHIVY CHOCK CHOKY CHOOK CHUCK CHUFF CHUNK CINCH CISSY CIVVY CLACH CLACK CLANK CLARY CLASH CLEEK CLERK CLICK CLIFF

CLINK CLOAK CLOCK CLONK CLOTH CLUCK CLUNK COACH COALY COBBY COCKY COLBY COLLY COMFY COMMY CONCH CONEY CONKY COOCH COOEY COOKY COOLY COPAY CORBY CORKY CORNY COSEY COUCH COUGH COUTH COVEY COWRY COYLY COZEY CRACK CRANK CRASH CRAZY CREAK CREEK CREPY CRICK CROAK CROCK CRONY CROOK CRUCK CRUSH CRWTH CUBBY CUDDY CUISH CULCH CULLY CUPPY CURCH CURDY CURLY CURRY CURVY CUSHY CUTCH CUTEY CUTTY DADDY DAFFY DAILY DAIRY DAISY DALLY DANDY DASHY DAUBY

DEARY DEASH DEATH DECAF DECAY DECOY DECRY DEEDY DEIFY DEITY DELAY DELLY DEOXY DEPTH DERAY DERBY DERRY DIARY DICEY DICKY DICTY DILLY DIMLY DINGY DINKY DIPPY DIRTY DISHY DITCH DITSY DITTY DITZY DIVVY DIZZY DOBBY DODGY DOETH DOGEY DOGGY DOILY DOLLY DONSY DOODY DOOLY DOOMY DOOZY DOPEY DORKY DORMY DORTY DOTTY DOUGH DOWDY DOWNY DOWRY DOYLY DRAFF DRANK DRECK DRILY DRINK DROUK DRUNK DRYLY DUCHY DUCKY DUDDY DULLY DUMKY DUMMY DUMPY DUNCH DUNGY

DUSKY DUSTY DUTCH DWARF EARLY EARTH EBONY EBOOK EDIFY ELBOW ELEGY EMBAY EMBOW EMERY EMPTY ENDOW ENEMY ENJOY ENSKY ENTRY ENVOY EPHAH EPOCH EPOXY ESSAY EVERY FABLE FACED FACER FACES FACET FACIA FACTS FADDY FADED FADER FADES FADGE FADOS FAENA FAERY FAGIN FAGOT FAILS FAINT FAIRS FAIRY FAITH FAKED FAKER FAKES FAKEY FAKIR FALLS FALSE FAMED FAMES FANCY FANES FANGA FANGS FANNY FANON FANOS FANUM FAQIR FARAD FARCE FARCI FARCY FARDS FARED FARER

FARES FARLE FARLS FARMS FAROS FASTS FATAL FATED FATES FATLY FATTY FATWA FAUGH FAULD FAULT FAUNA FAUNS FAUVE FAVAS FAVES FAVOR FAVUS FAWNS FAWNY FAXED FAXES FAYED FAZED FAZES FEARS FEASE FEAST FEATS FEAZE FECAL FECES FECKS FEDEX FEEBS FEEDS FEELS FEEZE FEIGN FEINT FEIST FELID FELLA FELLS FELLY FELON FELTS FEMES FEMME FEMUR FENCE FENDS FENNY FEODS FEOFF FERAL FERES FERIA FERLY FERMI FERNS FERNY FERRY FESSE FESTS FETAL FETAS FETCH FETED

FETES FETID FETOR FETUS FEUAR FEUDS FEUED FEVER FEWER FEYER FEYLY FEZES FEZZY FIARS FIATS FIBER FIBRE FICES FICHE FICHU FICIN FICUS FIDGE FIDOS FIEFS FIELD FIEND FIERY FIFED FIFER FIFES FIFTH FIFTY FIGHT FILAR FILCH FILED FILER FILES FILET FILLE FILLO FILLS FILLY FILMI FILMS FILMY FILOS FILTH FILUM FINAL FINCA FINCH FINDS FINED FINER FINES FINIS FINKS FINNY FINOS FIORD FIQUE FIRED FIRER FIRES FIRMS FIRNS FIRRY FIRST FIRTH FISCS FISHY

FISTS FITCH FITLY FIVER FIVES FIXED FIXER FIXES FIXIT FIZZY FJELD FJORD FLABS FLACK FLAGS FLAIL FLAIR FLAKE FLAKY FLAME FLAMS FLAMY FLANK FLANS FLAPS FLARE FLASH FLASK FLATS FLAWS FLAWY FLAXY FLAYS FLEAM FLEAS FLECK FLEER FLEES FLEET FLESH FLEWS FLEYS FLICK FLICS FLIED FLIER FLIES FLING FLINT FLIPS FLIRS FLIRT FLITE FLITS FLOAT FLOCK FLOCS FLOES FLOGS FLONG FLOOD FLOOR FLOPS FLORA FLOSS FLOTA FLOUR FLOUT FLOWN FLOWS FLUBS FLUED FLUES

FLUFF FLUID FLUKE FLUKY FLUME FLUMP FLUNG FLUNK FLUOR FLUSH FLUTE FLUTY FLUYT FLYBY FLYER FLYTE FOALS FOAMS FOAMY FOCAL FOCUS FOEHN FOGEY FOGGY FOGIE FOHNS FOILS FOINS FOIST FOLDS FOLEY FOLIA FOLIC FOLIO FOLKS FOLKY FOLLY FONDS FONDU FONTS FOODS FOOLS FOOTS FOOTY FORAM FORAY FORBS FORBY FORCE FORDO FORDS FORES FORGE FORGO FORKS FORKY FORME FORMS FORTE FORTH FORTS FORTY FORUM FOSSA FOSSE FOULS FOUND FOUNT FOURS FOVEA FOWLS FOXED FOXES

FOYER FRAGS FRAIL FRAME FRANC FRANK FRAPS FRASS FRATS FRAUD FRAYS FREAK FREED FREER FREES FREMD FRENA FRERE FRESH FRETS FRIAR FRIED FRIER FRIES FRIGS FRILL FRISE FRISK FRITH FRITS FRITT FRITZ FRIZZ FROCK FROES FROGS FROND FRONS FRONT FRORE FROSH FROST FROTH FROWN FROWS FROZE FRUGS FRUIT FRUMP FRYER FUBSY FUCUS FUDDY FUDGE FUELS FUGAL FUGGY FUGIO FUGLE FUGUE FUGUS FUJIS FULLS FULLY FUMED FUMER FUMES FUMET FUNDI FUNDS FUNGI FUNGO FUNKS

FUNKY FUNNY FURAN FURLS FUROR FURRY FURZE FURZY FUSED FUSEE FUSEL FUSES FUSIL FUSSY FUSTY FUTON FUZED FUZEE FUZES FUZIL FUZZY FYCES FYKES FYTTE GABBY GAILY GALAH GALLY GAMAY GAMEY GAMMY GANEF GANEV GANOF GAPPY GARTH GASSY GAUDY GAUZY GAWKY GAWSY GAYLY GEEKY GEMMY GERAH GERMY GIDDY GILLY GIMPY GINNY GIPSY GIRLY GIRSH GIRTH GLADY GLARY GLAZY GLEEK GLIFF GLORY GLUEY GLYPH GNASH GODLY GOLLY GONEF GONIF GONOF GOODY GOOEY GOOFY GOOKY GOONY

GOOPY GOOSY GOPIK GORSY GOUTY GRAPH GRAPY GRAVY GREEK GRIEF GRIFF GRIMY GRIPY GRITH GRODY GRUFF GULCH GULFY GULLY GULPY GUMMY GUNKY GUNNY GUPPY GURRY GURSH GUSHY GUSSY GUSTY GUTSY GUTTY GYPSY HAAFS HAARS HABIT HABUS HACEK HACKS HADAL HADED HADES HADJI HADST HAEMS HAETS HAFIZ HAFTS HAHAS HAIKA HAIKS HAIKU HAILS HAINT HAIRS HAIRY HAJES HAJIS HAJJI HAKES HAKIM HAKUS HALAL HALED HALER HALES HALID HALLO HALLS HALMA HALMS HALON HALOS HALTS

HALVA HALVE HAMAL HAMES HAMMY HAMZA HANCE HANDS HANDY HANGS HANKS HANKY HANSA HANSE HANTS HAPAX HAPLY HAPPY HARDS HARDY HARED HAREM HARES HARKS HARLS HARMS HARPS HARPY HARRY HARSH HARTS HASPS HASTE HASTY HATCH HATED HATER HATES HAUGH HAULM HAULS HAUNT HAUTE HAVEN HAVER HAVES HAVOC HAWED HAWKS HAWSE HAYED HAYER HAYEY HAZAN HAZED HAZEL HAZER HAZES HEADS HEADY HEALS HEAPS HEAPY HEARD HEARS HEART HEATH HEATS HEAVE HEAVY HECKS HEDER HEDGE

HEDGY HEEDS HEELS HEEZE HEFTS HEFTY HEIGH HEILS HEIRS HEIST HELIO HELIX HELLO HELLS HELMS HELOS HELOT HELPS HELVE HEMAL HEMES HEMIC HEMIN HEMPS HEMPY HENCE HENGE HENNA HENRY HENTS HERBS HERBY HERDS HERES HERLS HERMA HERMS HERNS HERON HEROS HERRY HERTZ HESTS HETHS HEUCH HEUGH HEWED HEWER HEXAD HEXED HEXER HEXES HEXYL HICKS HIDED HIDER HIDES HIGHS HIGHT HIJAB HIJRA HIKED HIKER HIKES HILAR HILLO HILLS HILLY HILTS HILUM HILUS HINDS HINGE

HINKY HINNY HINTS HIPLY HIPPO HIPPY HIRED HIREE HIRER HIRES HISSY HISTS HITCH HIVED HIVES HOAGY HOARD HOARS HOARY HOBBY HOBOS HOCKS HOCUS HODAD HOERS HOGAN HOGGS HOICK HOISE HOIST HOKED HOKES HOKEY HOKKU HOKUM HOLDS HOLED HOLES HOLEY HOLKS HOLLA HOLLO HOLLY HOLMS HOLTS HOMED HOMER HOMES HOMEY HOMIE HOMOS HONAN HONDA HONED HONER HONES HONEY HONGI HONGS HONKS HONOR HOOCH HOODS HOODY HOOEY HOOFS HOOKA HOOKS HOOKY HOOLY HOOPS HOOTS HOOTY

HOPED HOPER HOPES HOPPY HORAH HORAL HORAS HORDE HORNS HORNY HORSE HORST HORSY HOSED HOSEL HOSEN HOSER HOSES HOSEY HOSTA HOSTS HOTCH HOTEL HOTLY HOUND HOURI HOURS HOUSE HOVEL HOVER HOWDY HOWES HOWFF HOWFS HOWKS HOWLS HOYAS HOYLE HUBBY HUCKS HUFFS HUFFY HUGER HULAS HULKS HULKY HULLO HULLS HUMAN HUMIC HUMID HUMOR HUMPH HUMPS HUMPY HUMUS HUNCH HUNKS HUNKY HUNTS HURDS HURLS HURLY HURRY HURST HURTS HUSKS HUSKY HUSSY HUTCH HUZZA HYDRA HYDRO

HYENA
HYING
HYLAS
HYMEN
HYMNS
HYOID
HYPED
HYPER
HYPES
HYPHA
HYPOS
HYRAX
HYSON
ICILY
IMPLY
INDOW
INLAY
IRONY
ITCHY
IVORY
JACKY
JAGGY
JAMMY
JANTY
JAZZY
JELLY
JEMMY
JENNY
JERKY
JERRY
JETTY
JIFFY
JIGGY
JIMMY
JIMPY
JIVEY
JOKEY
JOLLY
JOLTY
JOTTY
JOWLY
JUICY
JUMPY
JUNKY
JUTTY
KABAB
KABAR
KABOB
KADIS
KAFIR
KAGUS
KAIAK
KAIFS
KAILS
KAINS
KAKAS
KAKIS
KALAM
KALES
KALIF
KALPA
KAMES
KAMIK
KANAS
KANES
KANJI
KANZU
KAONS
KAPAS
KAPHS
KAPOK
KAPPA
KAPUT
KARAT
KARMA
KARNS
KAROO
KARST
KARTS
KASHA
KATAS
KAURI
KAURY
KAVAS
KAYAK
KAYOS
KAZOO
KBARS
KEBAB
KEBAR

KEBOB
KECKS
KEDGE
KEEFS
KEEKS
KEELS
KEENS
KEEPS
KEETS
KEEVE
KEFIR
KEIRS
KELEP
KELIM
KELLY
KELPS
KELPY
KELTS
KEMPS
KEMPT
KENAF
KENCH
KENDO
KENOS
KENTE
KEPIS
KERBS
KERFS
KERNE
KERNS
KERRY
KETCH
KETOL
KEVEL
KEVIL
KEXES
KEYED
KHADI
KHAFS
KHAKI
KHANS
KHAPH
KHATS
KHEDA
KHETH
KHETS
KHOUM
KIANG
KIBBE
KIBBI
KIBEI
KIBES
KIBLA
KICKS
KICKY
KIDDO
KIDDY
KIEFS
KIERS
KILIM
KILLS
KILNS
KILOS
KILTS
KILTY
KINAS
KINDS
KINES
KINGS
KININ
KINKS
KINKY
KINOS
KIOSK
KIRKS
KIRNS
KISSY
KISTS
KITED
KITER
KITES
KITHE
KITHS
KITTY
KIVAS
KIWIS
KLICK
KLIKS
KLONG
KLOOF

KLUGE
KLUTZ
KNACK
KNAPS
KNARS
KNAUR
KNAVE
KNAWE
KNEAD
KNEED
KNEEL
KNEES
KNELL
KNELT
KNIFE
KNISH
KNITS
KNOBS
KNOCK
KNOLL
KNOPS
KNOSP
KNOTS
KNOUT
KNOWN
KNOWS
KNURL
KNURS
KOALA
KOANS
KOBOS
KOELS
KOHLS
KOINE
KOJIS
KOLAS
KOLOS
KOMBU
KONKS
KOOKS
KOOKY
KOPEK
KOPHS
KOPJE
KOPPA
KORAI
KORAS
KORAT
KORMA
KORUN
KOTOS
KOTOW
KRAAL
KRAFT
KRAIT
KRAUT
KREEP
KREWE
KRILL
KRONA
KRONE
KROON
KRUBI
KUDOS
KUDUS
KUDZU
KUFIS
KUGEL
KUKRI
KULAK
KUMYS
KURTA
KURUS
KUSSO
KVASS
KVELL
KYACK
KYAKS
KYARS
KYATS
KYLIX
KYRIE
KYTES
KYTHE
LACEY
LAICH
LAIGH
LAITH
LAITY
LAMBY

LANKY
LARCH
LARDY
LARKY
LATCH
LATHY
LAUGH
LAWNY
LAXLY
LEACH
LEADY
LEAFY
LEAKY
LEARY
LEASH
LEAVY
LEDGY
LEECH
LEERY
LEFTY
LEGGY
LETCH
LIMBY
LIMEY
LINDY
LINEY
LINGY
LINKY
LINTY
LIPPY
LOACH
LOAMY
LOATH
LOBBY
LOFTY
LOGGY
LOLLY
LOOBY
LOOEY
LOONY
LOOPY
LOPPY
LORRY
LOSSY
LOTAH
LOUGH
LOURY
LOUSY
LOWLY
LUCKY
LUMPY
LUNCH
LURCH
LUSTY
LYMPH
LYNCH
MACAW
MADLY
MALMY
MALTY
MAMEY
MAMMY
MANGY
MANLY
MARCH
MARLY
MARRY
MARSH
MARVY
MASHY
MASSY
MATCH
MATEY
MEALY
MEANY
MEATY
MEINY
MELTY
MENSH
MERCH
MERCY
MERRY
MESHY
MESSY
MIAOW
MIDDY
MIFFY
MILCH
MILKY
MILTY

MINCY
MINGY
MINNY
MINTY
MIRKY
MIRTH
MISSY
MISTY
MOGGY
MOLDY
MOLLY
MOMMY
MONEY
MONTH
MOOCH
MOODY
MOONY
MOORY
MOPEY
MORAY
MORPH
MOSEY
MOSSY
MOTEY
MOTHY
MOTIF
MOUCH
MOUSY
MOUTH
MUCKY
MUDDY
MUGGY
MUHLY
MUJIK
MULCH
MULEY
MUMMY
MUNCH
MURKY
MURRY
MUSHY
MUSKY
MUSSY
MUSTH
MUSTY
MUTCH
MUZZY
MYNAH
MYOPY
MYRRH
MYTHY
NAGGY
NANNY
NAPPY
NARKY
NASTY
NATCH
NATTY
NAVVY
NEATH
NEDDY
NEEDY
NEIGH
NELLY
NERDY
NERVY
NETTY
NEWLY
NEWSY
NIFTY
NINNY
NINTH
NIPPY
NITTY
NOBBY
NOBLY
NODDY
NOHOW
NOILY
NOISY
NORTH
NOSEY
NOTCH
NOWAY
NUBBY
NUDZH
NUTSY
NUTTY
NYMPH
OBEAH

OCHRY
ODDLY
OLOGY
ONERY
ONLAY
OOMPH
ORACH
OUTBY
OVARY
OXBOW
PACEY
PADDY
PALLY
PALMY
PALSY
PANDY
PANSY
PANTY
PAPAW
PAPPY
PARCH
PARDY
PARRY
PARTY
PASTY
PATCH
PATLY
PATSY
PATTY
PAWKY
PEACH
PEAKY
PEATY
PEAVY
PECKY
PEERY
PENNY
PEONY
PEPPY
PERCH
PERDY
PERKY
PERRY
PESKY
PESTY
PETTY
PHONY
PICKY
PIETY
PIGGY
PIGMY
PILAF
PILAW
PINCH
PINEY
PINKY
PINNY
PITCH
PITHY
PLACK
PLANK
PLASH
PLATY
PLINK
PLONK
PLUCK
PLUMY
PLUNK
PLUSH
POACH
POBOY
POCKY
PODGY
POESY
POGEY
POKEY
POOCH
POPPY
POPSY
PORCH
PORGY
PORKY
PORNY
POTSY
POTTY
POUCH
POUFF
POUTY
PRANK
PREXY

PRICK
PRICY
PRINK
PRIVY
PROOF
PROSY
PROXY
PSHAW
PSYCH
PUDGY
PUFFY
PUGGY
PUJAH
PULIK
PULPY
PUNCH
PUNKY
PUNNY
PUNTY
PUPPY
PURSY
PURTY
PUSHY
PUSSY
PUTTY
PYGMY
QUACK
QUAFF
QUAKY
QUARK
QUASH
QUERY
QUICK
QUIFF
QUIRK
QUOTH
QURSH
RAGGY
RAINY
RAJAH
RALLY
RALPH
RAMMY
RANCH
RANDY
RANGY
RASPY
RATCH
RATTY
RAWLY
RAYAH
REACH
READY
REBUY
REDLY
REDRY
REEDY
REEFY
REEKY
REFLY
REFRY
REIFY
REINK
REKEY
RELAY
RENEW
REPAY
REPLY
RESAW
RESAY
RESEW
RESOW
RETCH
RETRY
RIBBY
RIDGY
RILEY
RINDY
RISKY
RITZY
ROACH
ROCKY
ROILY
ROOKY
ROOMY
ROOTY
ROPEY
ROTCH
ROUGH
ROUPY

ROUTH
ROWDY
ROWTH
RUBBY
RUDDY
RUGBY
RUMMY
RUNNY
RUNTY
RUSHY
RUSTY
RUTTY
SADLY
SAGGY
SAITH
SALLY
SALTY
SAMEK
SANDY
SANGH
SAPPY
SARKY
SASSY
SATAY
SAUCH
SAUCY
SAUGH
SAURY
SAVOY
SAVVY
SCALY
SCARF
SCARY
SCHAV
SCOFF
SCREW
SCUFF
SCULK
SCURF
SEAMY
SEDGY
SEEDY
SEELY
SEEPY
SELAH
SEPOY
SERIF
SEROW
SERRY
SHACK
SHADY
SHAKY
SHALY
SHANK
SHARK
SHEAF
SHEIK
SHELF
SHILY
SHINY
SHIRK
SHOCK
SHOOK
SHOWY
SHREW
SHTIK
SHUCK
SHUSH
SHYLY
SILKY
SILLY
SILTY
SINEW
SISSY
SIXTH
SIXTY
SKANK
SKIEY
SKIFF
SKINK
SKOSH
SKULK
SKUNK
SKYEY
SLACK
SLANK
SLASH
SLATY
SLEEK
SLICK

SLILY
SLIMY
SLINK
SLOSH
SLOTH
SLUFF
SLUNK
SLUSH
SLYLY
SMACK
SMASH
SMEEK
SMERK
SMIRK
SMITH
SMOCK
SMOKY
SMUSH
SNACK
SNAKY
SNARF
SNARK
SNASH
SNATH
SNEAK
SNECK
SNICK
SNIFF
SNOOK
SNOWY
SNUCK
SNUFF
SOAPY
SODDY
SOFTY
SOGGY
SONLY
SONNY
SONSY
SOOEY
SOOTH
SOOTY
SOPHY
SOPPY
SORRY
SOUGH
SOUPY
SOUTH
SPACY
SPANK
SPARK
SPEAK
SPECK
SPICY
SPIFF
SPIKY
SPINY
SPIRY
SPLAY
SPOOF
SPOOK
SPRAY
SPUMY
SPUNK
STACK
STAFF
STAGY
STALK
STANK
STAPH
STARK
STASH
STEAK
STEEK
STEWY
STICH
STICK
STIFF
STIMY
STINK
STIRK
STOCK
STOGY
STONY
STOOK
STORK
STORY
STRAW
STRAY
STREW

STROW
STROY
STUCK
STUDY
STUFF
STUNK
STYMY
SUBAH
SUCKY
SUDSY
SUETY
SULKY
SULLY
SUNNY
SURAH
SURFY
SURGY
SURLY
SWAMY
SWANK
SWARF
SWASH
SWATH
SWINK
SWISH
SWITH
SYLPH
SYNCH
SYNTH
TABBY
TACKY
TAFFY
TALKY
TALLY
TALUK
TAMMY
TANGY
TANSY
TARDY
TAROK
TARRY
TARTY
TASTY
TATTY
TAWNY
TEACH
TEARY
TECHY
TEDDY
TEENY
TEETH
TELLY
TENCH
TENTH
TENTY
TEPOY
TERRY
TESTY
TEUCH
TEUGH
THACK
THANK
THEWY
THICK
THIEF
THIGH
THINK
THRAW
THREW
THROW
THUNK
THYMY
TILAK
TILTH
TINNY
TIPPY
TIPSY
TITTY
TIZZY
TOADY
TODAY
TODDY
TOFFY
TOKAY
TOMMY
TONEY
TOOTH
TORAH
TORCH
TORSK

TOUCH
TOUGH
TOWNY
TRACK
TRAIK
TRANK
TRASH
TRICK
TROAK
TROCK
TROTH
TRUCK
TRULY
TRUNK
TRUTH
TUBBY
TUFTY
TUMMY
TUNNY
TUPIK
TURFY
TUSHY
TUTTY
TWEAK
TWINY
TYPEY
UMIAK
UNARY
UNCOY
UNIFY
UNITY
UNLAY
UNMEW
UNSAY
UNSEW
UPBOW
UPDRY
USURY
VACUA
VAGAL
VAGUE
VAGUS
VAILS
VAIRS
VAKIL
VALES
VALET
VALID
VALOR
VALSE
VALUE
VALVE
VAMPS
VAMPY
VANDA
VANED
VANES
VANGS
VAPID
VAPOR
VARAS
VARIA
VARIX
VARNA
VARUS
VARVE
VASAL
VASES
VASTS
VASTY
VATIC
VATUS
VAULT
VAUNT
VEALS
VEALY
VEENA
VEEPS
VEERS
VEERY
VEGAN
VEGES
VEGIE
VEILS
VEINS
VEINY
VELAR
VELDS
VELDT
VELUM

VENAE
VENAL
VENDS
VENGE
VENIN
VENOM
VENTS
VENUE
VENUS
VERBS
VERGE
VERSE
VERSO
VERST
VERTS
VERTU
VERVE
VESTA
VESTS
VETCH
VEXED
VEXER
VEXES
VEXIL
VIALS
VIAND
VIBES
VICAR
VICED
VICES
VICHY
VIDEO
VIERS
VIEWS
VIEWY
VIGAS
VIGIA
VIGIL
VIGOR
VILER
VILLA
VILLI
VILLS
VIMEN
VINAL
VINAS
VINCA
VINED
VINES
VINIC
VINOS
VINYL
VIOLA
VIOLS
VIPER
VIRAL
VIREO
VIRES
VIRGA
VIRID
VIRLS
VIRTU
VIRUS
VISAS
VISED
VISES
VISIT
VISOR
VISTA
VITAE
VITAL
VITTA
VIVAS
VIVID
VIXEN
VIZIR
VIZOR
VOCAB
VOCAL
VOCES
VODKA
VODOU
VODUN
VOGIE
VOGUE
VOICE
VOIDS
VOILA
VOILE
VOLAR

VOLED
VOLES
VOLTA
VOLTE
VOLTI
VOLTS
VOLVA
VOMER
VOMIT
VOTED
VOTER
VOTES
VOUCH
VOWED
VOWEL
VOWER
VROOM
VROUW
VROWS
VUGGS
VUGGY
VUGHS
VULGO
VULVA
VYING
WACKE
WACKO
WACKS
WACKY
WADDY
WADED
WADER
WADES
WADIS
WAFER
WAFFS
WAFTS
WAGED
WAGER
WAGES
WAGON
WAHOO
WAIFS
WAILS
WAINS
WAIRS
WAIST
WAITS
WAIVE
WAKED
WAKEN
WAKER
WAKES
WALED
WALER
WALES
WALKS
WALLA
WALLS
WALLY
WALTZ
WAMES
WAMUS
WANDS
WANED
WANES
WANEY
WANLY
WANTS
WARDS
WARED
WARES
WARKS
WARMS
WARNS
WARPS
WARTS
WARTY
WASHY
WASPS
WASPY
WASTE
WASTS
WATAP
WATCH
WATER
WATTS
WAUGH
WAUKS
WAULS

WAVED
WAVER
WAVES
WAVEY
WAWLS
WAXED
WAXEN
WAXER
WAXES
WEALD
WEALS
WEANS
WEARS
WEARY
WEAVE
WEBBY
WEBER
WECHT
WEDEL
WEDGE
WEDGY
WEEDS
WEEDY
WEEKS
WEENS
WEENY
WEEPS
WEEPY
WEEST
WEETS
WEFTS
WEIGH
WEIRD
WEIRS
WEKAS
WELCH
WELDS
WELLS
WELLY
WELSH
WELTS
WENCH
WENDS
WENNY
WESTS
WETLY
WHACK
WHALE
WHAMO
WHAMS
WHANG
WHAPS
WHARF
WHATS
WHAUP
WHEAL
WHEAT
WHEEL
WHEEN
WHEEP
WHELK
WHELM
WHELP
WHENS
WHERE
WHETS
WHEWS
WHEYS
WHICH
WHIDS
WHIFF
WHIGS
WHILE
WHIMS
WHINE
WHINS
WHINY
WHIPS
WHIPT
WHIRL
WHIRR
WHIRS
WHISH
WHISK
WHIST
WHITE
WHITS
WHITY
WHIZZ
WHOLE

WHOMP
WHOOF
WHOOP
WHOPS
WHORE
WHORL
WHORT
WHOSE
WHOSO
WHUMP
WHUPS
WICCA
WICKS
WIDDY
WIDEN
WIDER
WIDES
WIDOW
WIDTH
WIELD
WIFED
WIFES
WIFEY
WIFTY
WIGAN
WIGGY
WIGHT
WILCO
WILDS
WILED
WILES
WILLS
WILLY
WILTS
WIMPS
WIMPY
WINCE
WINCH
WINDS
WINDY
WINED
WINES
WINEY
WINGS
WINGY
WINKS
WINOS
WINZE
WIPED
WIPER
WIPES
WIRED
WIRER
WIRES
WIRRA
WISED
WISER
WISES
WISHA
WISPS
WISPY
WISTS
WITAN
WITCH
WITED
WITES
WITHE
WITHY
WITTY
WIVED
WIVER
WIVES
WIZEN
WIZES
WOADS
WOALD
WODGE
WOFUL
WOKEN
WOLDS
WOLFS
WOMAN
WOMBS
WOMBY
WOMEN
WOMYN
WONKS
WONKY
WONTS
WOODS

WOODY
WOOED
WOOER
WOOFS
WOOLS
WOOLY
WOOPS
WOOSH
WOOZY
WORDS
WORDY
WORKS
WORLD
WORMS
WORMY
WORRY
WORSE
WORST
WORTH
WORTS
WOULD
WOUND
WOVEN
WOWED
WRACK
WRANG
WRAPS
WRAPT
WRATH
WREAK
WRECK
WRENS
WREST
WRICK
WRIED
WRIER
WRIES
WRING
WRIST
WRITE
WRITS
WRONG
WROTE
WROTH
WRUNG
WRYER
WRYLY
WURST
WUSHU
WUSSY
WYLED
WYLES
WYNDS
WYNNS
WYTED
WYTES
YABBY
YACHT
YACKS
YAFFS
YAGER
YAGIS
YAHOO
YAIRD
YAMEN
YAMUN
YANGS
YANKS
YAPOK
YAPON
YARDS
YARER
YARNS
YAUDS
YAULD
YAUPS
YAWED
YAWEY
YAWLS
YAWNS
YAWPS
YCLAD
YEAHS
YEANS
YEARN
YEARS
YEAST
YECCH
YECHS
YECHY

YEGGS
YELKS
YELLS
YELPS
YENTA
YENTE
YERBA
YERKS
YESES
YETIS
YETTS
YEUKS
YEUKY
YIELD
YIKES
YILLS
YINCE
YIPES
YIRDS
YIRRS
YIRTH
YLEMS
YOBBO
YOCKS
YODEL
YODHS
YODLE
YOGAS
YOGEE
YOGHS
YOGIC
YOGIN
YOGIS
YOKED
YOKEL
YOKES
YOLKS
YOLKY
YOMIM
YONIC
YONIS
YORES
YOUNG
YOURN
YOURS
YOUSE
YOUTH
YOWED
YOWES
YOWIE
YOWLS
YUANS
YUCAS
YUCCA
YUCCH
YUCKS
YUCKY
YUGAS
YUKKY
YULAN
YULES
YUMMY
YUPON
YUPPY
YURTA
YURTS
ZAPPY
ZESTY
ZILCH
ZINCY
ZINGY
ZINKY
ZIPPY
ZLOTY
ZOOEY
ZOOTY

FRONT-HOOKS ONLY

The vast majority of end-hook letters include the frequent S, as well as D, R, and Y. When reading or writing, we do so from left to right, so the possible extension of a word with another letter leads a person, understandably, to look to the right side or the end of a word. We are less inclined to consider or see extending a word to the left. Moreover, there are far fewer front-extensions than rear-extensions to words. For the aspiring expert and word studier, particularly one who has mastered the 4s, and perhaps many of the 5s, the task of undertaking all the 6s, 7s, and 8s can be overwhelming. Within "The Hooks" section, the "5s-to-Make-6s" through the "8s-to-Make-9s" exceeds 100 pages. Here, however, are just a few pages of five- through eight-letter words and their less obvious front-hooks. Reviewing this section may increase your board awareness of opportunities you may find ... or wish to prevent. For example, seeing that LACKS can be extended to form BLACKS, CLACKS, FLACKS, PLACKS, and SLACKS, you are far better off, defensively, in playing CALKS instead. On the other hand, if you have CEEHKTV, you may confidently play VETCH, keeping EK, knowing you have the only K to form KVETCH on your next turn. If you wish to take just a small dose of these pages, confine your study to just those words taking front S-hooks. You'll savor moments, as I did, when I was able to place my common bingo word, ending in an S, onto GRAFFITI, forming SGRAFFITI.

5s-to-Make-6s

kABAKA kABAYA cABLED fABLED gABLED tABLED cABLER fABLER cABLES fABLES gABLES sABLES tABLES bABOON gABOON bACHED cACHED bACHES cACHES lACHES mACHES nACHES tACHES fACING lACING mACING pACING rACING hACKEE nACRED sACRED nACRES fACTOR gADDED mADDED pADDED rADDED wADDED bADDER gADDER lADDER mADDER pADDER sADDER wADDER dADDLE pADDLE rADDLE sADDLE wADDLE rADIOS bADMAN mADMAN bADMEN mADMEN pAEONS fAERIE dAFTER hAFTER rAFTER wAFTER cAGERS eAGERS gAGERS jAGERS lAGERS pAGERS wAGERS yAGERS bAGGER dAGGER gAGGER jAGGER lAGGER

nAGGER sAGGER tAGGER wAGGER bAGGIE vAGILE cAGING gAGING pAGING rAGING wAGING eAGLET mAGMAS wAGONS aAHING rAIDED rAIDER bAILED fAILED hAILED jAILED mAILED nAILED rAILED sAILED tAILED vAILED wAILED mAIMED mAIMER fAIRED hAIRED lAIRED pAIRED wAIRED fAIRER bAIRNS cAIRNS nAIVER wAIVER rAKEES sALARY mALATE pALATE bALDER cALIFS kALIFS mALIGN mALINE sALINE vALINE tALKIE cALLEE mALLEE gALLEY vALLEY bALLOT hALLOT cALLOW fALLOW hALLOW mALLOW sALLOW tALLOW wALLOW hALMAS hALOES kALONG fALTER hALTER pALTER sALTER cAMASS cAMBER

lAMBER gAMBIT gAMBLE rAMBLE wAMBLE mAMBOS sAMBOS yAMENS lAMENT lAMIAS zAMIAS mAMIES rAMIES fAMINE gAMINE gAMINS cAMPED dAMPED lAMPED rAMPED tAMPED vAMPED sAMPLE dAMPLY rANCHO fANGAS mANGAS pANGAS sANGAS mANGEL bANGER dANGER gANGER hANGER mANGER rANGER sANGER bANGLE dANGLE jANGLE mANGLE tANGLE wANGLE fANION wANION rANKLE cANNAS mANNAS tANNOY mANTAS cANTED hANTED pANTED rANTED wANTED mANTES cANTIC mANTIC mANTIS mANTRA tANTRA yANTRA cANYON cAPERS gAPERS jAPERS pAPERS rAPERS tAPERS jAPERY nAPERY pAPERY rAPHIS gAPING

jAPING rAPING tAPING rAPPEL dAPPLE lAPSES rAPTLY hARBOR fARCED gARGLE jARGON vARIAS cARLES fARLES pARLES fARMED hARMED wARMED fARMER hARMER wARMER bARROW fARROW hARROW mARROW nARROW yARROW cARSES mARSES pARSES pARSON hARTAL cARTEL lARUMS lARVAL pARVOS mASCOT bASHED cASHED dASHED fASHED gASHED hASHED lASHED mASHED pASHED sASHED wASHED bASHES cASHES dASHES fASHES gASHES hASHES lASHES mASHES pASHES rASHES sASHES wASHES bASKED cASKED mASKED tASKED mASKER gASPER jASPER rASPER bASSES gASSES lASSES mASSES pASSES sASSES tASSES bASSET

tASSET bASTER cASTER eASTER fASTER gASTER lASTER mASTER pASTER rASTER tASTER vASTER wASTER wATAPS bATMAN lATRIA cAUDAD gAUGER mAUGER sAUGER cAUGHT nAUGHT tAUGHT wAUGHT dAUNTS hAUNTS jAUNTS tAUNTS vAUNTS jAUNTY vAUNTY lAURAE lAURAS kAURIS sAVANT dAVENS hAVENS mAVENS rAVENS cAVERS hAVERS lAVERS pAVERS rAVERS sAVERS wAVERS vAWARD lAWFUL cAWING dAWING hAWING jAWING lAWING mAWING pAWING sAWING tAWING yAWING dAWNED fAWNED pAWNED yAWNED fAXING mAXING rAXING tAXING wAXING tAXITE tAXMAN tAXMEN tAXONS rAYAHS lAYINS zAYINS hAZANS aBASED

aBASER aBASES aBATED aBATES oBENTO iBICES aBIDED aBIDER aBIDES iBISES oBLAST aBLATE oBLATE aBLAZE aBLEST aBLOOM aBLUSH aBOARD aBODED aBODES oBOLES oBOLUS eBOOKS aBORAL aBORTS aBOUND aBROAD aBUSED aBUSES sCABBY sCALLS sCAMPI sCAMPS sCANTS sCANTY sCAPED sCAPES sCARED sCARER sCARES sCARPS sCARRY eCARTE sCARTS sCATTY oCELLI sCENTS eCHARD sCIONS yCLEPT sCOFFS sCOLDS iCONES sCONES iCONIC sCOOCH sCOOPS sCOOTS sCOPED sCOPES sCORED sCORER sCORES sCORIA aCORNS sCORNS sCOUTH sCOWED sCOWLS sCRAGS sCRAMS sCRAPE sCRAPS sCRAWL sCREAK sCREAM

sCREED sCREWS sCRIED sCRIES sCRIMP aCROSS sCUFFS sCULCH sCULLS sCURFS sCURRY sCURVY sCUTCH aCUTER aCUTES iDEALS aDEEMS aDRIFT aDROIT eDUCES eDUCTS mEAGER bEAGLE mEAGRE fEARED gEARED nEARED rEARED sEARED tEARED pEARLS dEARLY nEARLY pEARLY yEARLY lEARNS yEARNS dEARTH hEARTH cEASED fEASED lEASED tEASED tEASEL wEASEL cEASES fEASES lEASES pEASES tEASES bEASTS fEASTS lEASTS yEASTS bEATEN nEATEN bEATER fEATER hEATER nEATER sEATER dEAVED hEAVED lEAVED rEAVED wEAVED dEAVES hEAVES lEAVES rEAVES wEAVES wEBBED rEBOOK lECHED pECHED

tECHED lECHES oEDEMA hEDGED kEDGED wEDGED hEDGER lEDGER hEDGES kEDGES lEDGES sEDGES wEDGES aEDILE sEDILE dEDUCE rEDUCE sEDUCE dEDUCT pEERIE lEGERS bEGGAR sEGGAR bEGGED kEGGED lEGGED pEGGED vEGGED kEGGER rEGRET hEIGHT wEIGHT dEJECT rEJECT dEKING rELAND dELATE gELATE rELATE vELATE gELDER mELDER wELDER sELECT pELITE dELUDE dELVER dELVES hELVES pELVES sELVES rEMAIL mEMBER rEMEND dEMITS rEMITS hEMMER dEMOTE gEMOTE rEMOTE sENATE bENDED fENDED mENDED pENDED rENDED sENDED tENDED vENDED wENDED bENDER fENDER gENDER lENDER mENDER rENDER

sENDER tENDER vENDER vENDUE cENTER rENTER tENTER vENTER gENTRY sENTRY tENURE rENVOI tEPEES kERNES tERNES rEROSE tERROR pERSES vERSES aERUGO mESNES cESSES fESSES jESSES mESSES nESSES yESSES fESTER jESTER nESTER pESTER rESTER tESTER wESTER yESTER zESTER rETAPE aETHER nETHER tETHER wETHER mETHYL sEVENS rEVERT rEVERY dEVILS kEVILS rEVOKE hEWERS sEWERS rEXINE hEXING sEXING vEXING sEXIST kEYING aFIELD aFLAME aFLOAT aFRESH aFRITS aGAMAS aGAMIC aGAPES aGATES aGENES aGENTS eGESTS aGHAST aGISTS oGIVES aGLARE aGLEAM aGOUTY aGREED aGREES

sHACKS tHACKS wHACKS sHADED sHADES sHAFTS cHAIRS sHAKES sHALED wHALED tHALER wHALER sHALES wHALES sHAMES cHAMMY sHAMMY wHAMMY cHANCE sHANDY bHANGS cHANGS wHANGS sHANKS tHANKS cHANTS cHARDS sHARDS cHARED sHARED cHARES sHARES cHARKS sHARKS cHARMS tHARMS sHARPS sHARPY cHARRY gHARRY cHARTS cHASTE tHATCH sHAUGH sHAULS cHAUNT sHAVEN sHAVER sHAVES cHAWED sHAWED tHAWED cHAZAN sHEALS wHEALS cHEAPS sHEARS sHEATH cHEATS wHEATS sHEAVE tHEBES cHECKS cHEDER wHEELS wHEEZE tHEFTS tHEIRS tHEIST sHELLS wHELMS wHELPS sHELVE rHEMES tHEMES cHEMIC

tHENCE wHENCE sHERDS tHERES wHERES tHERMS cHERRY sHERRY wHERRY cHESTS cHETHS kHETHS sHEUCH sHEUGH cHEWED sHEWED cHEWER sHEWER cHICKS tHICKS cHIDED cHIDER cHIDES tHIGHS cHILLS sHILLS tHILLS cHILLY wHINGE cHINKY sHINNY wHINNY cHINTS cHIPPY wHIPPY sHIRES sHISTS wHISTS cHIVES sHIVES cHOCKS sHOCKS sHOERS cHOKED cHOKES cHOKEY aHOLDS tHOLED dHOLES tHOLES wHOLES cHOLLA wHOLLY pHONED pHONES pHONEY tHONGS pHOOEY wHOOFS cHOOKS sHOOKS dHOOLY wHOOPS bHOOTS sHOOTS cHOPPY cHORAL tHORNS tHORNY aHORSE cHOSEN cHOSES gHOSTS cHOUSE sHOVEL sHOVER

cHUBBY cHUCKS sHUCKS cHUFFS cHUFFY cHUMPS tHUMPS wHUMPS cHUNKS tHUNKS cHUNKY sHUNTS cHURLS tHURLS sHYING dICIER dICING rICING vICING bICKER dICKER kICKER lICKER nICKER pICKER sICKER tICKER wICKER rICTUS sIDLED sIDLER sIDLES dIGGED fIGGED gIGGED jIGGED pIGGED rIGGED wIGGED zIGGED eIKONS pILEUM pILEUS fILIAL cILIUM mILIUM bILLER fILLER gILLER hILLER kILLER mILLER sILLER tILLER wILLER lIMBED gIMPED lIMPED pIMPED wIMPED dIMPLY jIMPLY lIMPLY pIMPLY sIMPLY wINDOW dINGLE jINGLE mINGLE sINGLE tINGLE mINION pINION dINKED fINKED jINKED

kINKED lINKED oINKED pINKED wINKED jINKER lINKER pINKER sINKER tINKER wINKER tINKLE wINKLE bINNED dINNED fINNED gINNED pINNED sINNED tINNED wINNED dINNER gINNER pINNER sINNER tINNER wINNER hINTER lINTER mINTER sINTER tINTER wINTER bIONIC pIONIC bIOTAS tIRADE pIRATE aIRING fIRING hIRING mIRING sIRING tIRING wIRING dIRKED gIRONS aISLED mISLED aISLES lISLES tISSUE bITCHY fITCHY pITCHY wITCHY cITHER dITHER eITHER hITHER lITHER mITHER tITHER wITHER zITHER cIVIES sIZARS dJEBEL dJINNI dJINNS sKEENS sKEETS sKELPS sKERRY sKETCH sKIDDY

sKIERS sKILLS sKINKS sKITED sKITES pLACED pLACER gLACES pLACES bLACKS cLACKS fLACKS pLACKS sLACKS bLADED bLADER bLADES cLADES gLADES fLAIRS gLAIRS fLAKED sLAKED fLAKER sLAKER fLAKES sLAKES lLAMAS uLAMAS bLAMED fLAMED bLAMER fLAMER bLAMES fLAMES cLAMPS gLANCE aLANDS eLANDS gLANDS fLANES pLANES cLANKY eLAPSE bLARES fLARES gLARES aLARUM bLASTS cLASTS kLATCH sLATCH aLATED eLATED pLATED sLATED pLATEN eLATER pLATER sLATER sLAVED cLAVER sLAVER cLAVES sLAVES bLAWED cLAWED fLAWED fLAXES cLAYED fLAYED pLAYED sLAYED fLAYER pLAYER sLAYER

bLAZED
gLAZED
bLAZES
gLAZES
bLEACH
pLEACH
pLEADS
bLEAKS
cLEANS
gLEANS
bLEARS
cLEARS
bLEARY
pLEASE
cLEAVE
sLEAVE
fLEDGE
pLEDGE
sLEDGE
fLEDGY
fLEECH
cLEEKS
gLEEKS
sLEEKS
fLEERS
fLEETS
gLEETS
sLEETS
cLEFTS
eLEGIT
bLENDS
fLENSE
fLETCH
cLEVER
aLEVIN
cLEVIS
fLEXES
iLEXES
pLEXES
eLICIT
cLICKS
fLICKS
kLICKS
sLICKS
aLIENS
fLIERS
pLIERS
sLIEVE
cLIFTS
aLIGHT
bLIGHT
fLIGHT
pLIGHT
sLIGHT
cLIMBS
gLIMED
sLIMED
cLIMES
gLIMES
sLIMES
bLIMEY
bLIMPS
aLINED
aLINER
aLINES
cLINES
oLINGO
cLINGS
fLINGS
sLINGS
cLINGY
bLINKS
cLINKS
pLINKS
sLINKS
sLINKY
eLINTS
fLINTS
gLINTS
fLINTY
gLINTY
fLIPPY
sLIPPY
bLITHE
sLIVER

oLIVES
gLOAMS
gLOBBY
sLOBBY
gLOBED
gLOBES
bLOCKS
cLOCKS
fLOCKS
sLOGAN
cLOGGY
sLOIDS
aLOINS
eLOINS
cLONER
fLONGS
kLONGS
bLOOEY
fLOOEY
kLOOFS
bLOOIE
fLOOIE
bLOOMS
gLOOMS
bLOOPS
sLOOPS
cLOOTS
eLOPED
sLOPED
eLOPER
sLOPER
eLOPES
sLOPES
fLOPPY
gLOPPY
sLOPPY
fLORAL
cLOSER
cLOSES
fLOSSY
gLOSSY
fLOTAS
bLOTTO
cLOUGH
pLOUGH
sLOUGH
cLOURS
fLOURS
fLOURY
bLOUSE
bLOUSY
cLOUTS
fLOUTS
gLOUTS
gLOVED
cLOVER
gLOVER
pLOVER
cLOVES
gLOVES
bLOWED
fLOWED
gLOWED
pLOWED
sLOWED
bLOWER
fLOWER
gLOWER
pLOWER
sLOWER
sLOWLY
cLUCKS
pLUCKS
pLUCKY
eLUDES
bLUFFS
fLUFFS
sLUFFS
kLUGED
kLUGES
cLUMPS
fLUMPS
pLUMPS
sLUMPS
cLUMPY

gLUMPY
gLUNCH
bLUNGE
pLUNGE
cLUNKS
fLUNKS
pLUNKS
bLUNTS
eLUTED
fLUTED
eLUTES
fLUTES
gLUTES
fLUXES
fLYING
pLYING
sMACKS
iMAGES
eMAILS
sMALLS
sMALTS
sMARTS
aMAZED
aMAZES
sMAZES
sMELLS
sMELTS
aMENDS
eMENDS
oMENTA
eMERGE
sMERKS
sMIDGE
aMIDST
sMILER
sMILES
aMINES
iMINES
sMIRKS
sMIRKY
sMITER
sMITES
sMOCKS
sMOGGY
sMOKES
aMOLES
sMOLTS
sMOOCH
aMORAL
eMOTES
aMOUNT
aMUCKS
aMUSED
aMUSER
aMUSES
sMUTCH
sNAGGY
sNAILS
sNAKED
jNANAS
sNAPPY
sNARES
sNARKS
sNARKY
sNATCH
eNATES
gNATTY
kNAVES
sNEAPS
aNEARS
sNECKS
eNEMAS
iNERTS
sNICKS
kNIGHT
sNIPPY
uNITER
uNITES
kNOBBY
sNOBBY
kNOCKS
aNODAL
aNODES
gNOMES
sNOOKS

gNOSES
kNUBBY
sNUBBY
kNURLS
rOARED
sOARED
bOASTS
cOASTS
rOASTS
tOASTS
bOATER
cOATER
lOAVES
sOAVES
cOBIAS
gOBOES
hOBOES
tOCHER
cOCKER
dOCKER
hOCKER
lOCKER
mOCKER
rOCKER
lOCULI
cODDER
dODDER
fODDER
nODDER
pODIUM
sODIUM
bOFFED
dOFFED
cOFFER
dOFFER
gOFFER
sOFTEN
lOFTER
sOFTER
yOGEES
bOGLES
oOHING
bOILED
cOILED
dOILED
fOILED
mOILED
rOILED
sOILED
tOILED
bOILER
cOILER
mOILER
tOILER
bOINKS
tOKAYS
gOLDEN
hOLDEN
bOLDER
cOLDER
fOLDER
gOLDER
hOLDER
mOLDER
pOLDER
sOLDER
fOLIOS
pOLIOS
hOLLAS
oOLOGY
bOMBER
cOMBER
sOMBER
hOMBRE
sOMBRE
cOMERS
gOMERS
hOMERS
vOMERS
vOMITS
gONION
rONION
cONIUM
gONIUM
iONIUM

pOOHED
bOOZED
bOOZES
cOPALS
nOPALS
cOPENS
cOPING
dOPING
hOPING
lOPING
mOPING
rOPING
tOPING
bORALS
cORALS
gORALS
mORALS
bORATE
sORBED
bORDER
cORDER
mORGAN
dORMER
fORMER
wORMER
mORRIS
cOSIER
hOSIER
nOSIER
rOSIER
cOSMIC
bOTHER
mOTHER
nOTHER
pOTHER
tOTHER
cOTTAR
cOTTER
dOTTER
hOTTER
jOTTER
lOTTER
pOTTER
rOTTER
tOTTER
lOTTOS
mOTTOS
pOTTOS
bOUGHT
dOUGHT
fOUGHT
nOUGHT
sOUGHT
bOUNCE
jOUNCE
pOUNCE
hOUSEL
jOUSTS
rOUSTS
lOUTED
pOUTED
rOUTED
tOUTED
cOUTER
pOUTER
rOUTER
sOUTER
tOUTER
cOVARY
cOVENS
dOVENS
wOVENS
cOVERS
hOVERS
lOVERS
mOVERS
rOVERS
cOVERT
bOVINE
bOWING
cOWING
dOWING
jOWING
lOWING
mOWING

rOWING
sOWING
tOWING
vOWING
wOWING
yOWING
hOWLET
dOWNED
gOWNED
dOWNER
fOYERS
tOYERS
sPACED
sPACER
sPACES
sPACEY
ePACTS
sPAILS
sPALES
sPALLS
ePARCH
sPARED
sPARER
sPARES
sPARGE
sPARKS
sPARRY
sPARSE
uPASES
sPATES
sPAVIN
sPAWNS
sPAYED
sPEAKS
sPEANS
sPEARS
sPECKS
sPEELS
sPEERS
sPEISE
sPELTS
sPENCE
sPENDS
uPENDS
sPERMS
aPICAL
ePICAL
sPICAS
sPICKS
aPIECE
sPIERS
sPIKED
sPIKER
sPIKES
sPILED
sPILES
sPILLS
oPINED
sPINED
oPINES
sPINES
sPINNY
sPINTO
sPLASH
sPLATS
sPLAYS
uPLINK
sPOKED
sPOKES
sPOOFS
sPOOFY
sPOOLS
sPOONS
sPORED
sPORES
sPORTS
ePOSES
sPOTTY
sPOUTS
sPRANG
uPRATE
sPRATS
sPRAYS
sPREES
sPRIER

sPRIGS
sPRINT
uPRISE
uPROSE
sPRYER
sPUNKS
sPUNKY
sPURGE
oPUSES
sQUADS
sQUARE
sQUARK
sQUASH
eQUATE
eQUIDS
sQUIDS
sQUILL
sQUINT
eQUIPS
sQUIRE
sQUIRT
aRABIC
bRACED
gRACED
tRACED
bRACER
tRACER
bRACES
gRACES
tRACES
cRACKS
tRACKS
wRACKS
dRAFFS
cRAFTS
dRAFTS
gRAFTS
kRAFTS
dRAGEE
bRAGGY
cRAGGY
dRAGGY
bRAIDS
bRAILS
dRAILS
fRAILS
gRAILS
tRAILS
bRAINS
dRAINS
gRAINS
tRAINS
bRAINY
gRAINY
bRAISE
fRAISE
pRAISE
bRAKED
bRAKES
cRAKES
dRAKES
oRALLY
cRAMPS
gRAMPS
tRAMPS
pRANCE
tRANCE
bRANCH
cRANCH
bRANDS
gRANDS
bRANDY
gRANGE
oRANGE
oRANGY
bRANKS
cRANKS
fRANKS
pRANKS
tRANKS
bRANTS
gRANTS
cRAPED
dRAPED
dRAPER

cRAPES
dRAPES
gRAPES
tRAPES
uRARES
eRASED
eRASER
cRASES
eRASES
pRASES
uRASES
gRASPS
cRATCH
cRATED
gRATED
oRATED
pRATED
cRATER
fRATER
gRATER
iRATER
kRATER
pRATER
cRATES
gRATES
oRATES
pRATES
uRATES
bRATTY
bRAVED
cRAVED
gRAVED
gRAVEL
tRAVEL
cRAVEN
gRAVEN
bRAVER
cRAVER
gRAVER
bRAVES
cRAVES
gRAVES
tRAVES
bRAWER
dRAWER
bRAWLY
cRAWLY
dRAWLY
pRAXES
bRAYED
dRAYED
fRAYED
gRAYED
pRAYED
cRAYON
bRAZED
cRAZED
gRAZED
bRAZER
gRAZER
bRAZES
cRAZES
gRAZES
bREACH
pREACH
pREACT
bREADS
dREADS
oREADS
tREADS
bREADY
bREAMS
cREAMS
dREAMS
pREARM
dREARS
gREAVE
pREBID
pREBUY
dRECKS
wRECKS
pRECUT
bREDES
uREDIA
cREDOS

uREDOS
pREDRY
bREEDS
cREEDS
gREEDS
gREEDY
bREEKS
cREEKS
cREELS
fREEST
pREFER
pREFIX
bREGMA
pREMAN
pREMIX
tRENDS
bRENTS
pREPAY
pRESET
cRESTS
pRESTS
wRESTS
pRETAX
wRETCH
bREVET
tREVET
pREVUE
bREWED
cREWED
pREXES
tRIALS
uRIALS
bRIBES
tRIBES
pRICED
tRICED
pRICER
pRICES
tRICES
bRICKS
cRICKS
pRICKS
tRICKS
wRICKS
aRIDER
bRIDES
gRIDES
iRIDES
pRIDES
bRIDGE
fRIDGE
aRIELS
oRIELS
gRIFFS
tRIFLE
dRIFTS
gRIFTS
aRIGHT
bRIGHT
fRIGHT
wRIGHT
fRIGID
aRILED
gRILLE
bRILLS
dRILLS
fRILLS
gRILLS
kRILLS
pRILLS
tRILLS
gRIMED
pRIMED
pRIMER
tRIMER
cRIMES
gRIMES
pRIMES
gRINDS
bRINGS
wRINGS
bRINKS
dRINKS
pRINKS
gRIOTS

gRIPED
gRIPER
cRIPES
gRIPES
tRIPES
aRISEN
aRISES
bRISES
cRISES
fRISES
iRISES
kRISES
pRISES
bRISKS
fRISKS
fRISKY
fRITES
wRITES
dRIVEN
dRIVER
dRIVES
gRIVET
pRIVET
tRIVET
bROACH
bROADS
gROANS
pROBED
pROBES
bROCKS
cROCKS
fROCKS
tROCKS
eRODES
bROGUE
dROGUE
bROILS
pROLES
dROLLS
tROLLS
tROMPS
bROODS
pROOFS
bROOKS
cROOKS
bROOMS
gROOMS
vROOMS
bROOMY
gROPED
gROPER
pROPER
gROPES
tROPES
pROSED
bROSES
eROSES
pROSES
cROTCH
tROUGH
aROUND
gROUND
cROUPS
gROUPS
cROUPY
aROUSE
cROUSE
gROUSE
cROUTE
dROUTH
gROUTS
tROUTS
dROVED
gROVED
pROVED
pROVEN
dROVER
pROVER
tROVER
dROVES
gROVES
pROVES
tROVES
cROWDY
bROWED

cROWED
tROWED
tROWEL
cROWER
gROWER
pROWER
gROWTH
tROWTH
gRUBBY
cRUCKS
tRUCKS
cRUDDY
cRUDER
tRUFFE
gRUFFS
fRUGAL
tRUING
bRUINS
cRUMMY
cRUMPS
fRUMPS
gRUMPS
tRUMPS
pRUNES
bRUNTS
gRUNTS
cRURAL
cRUSES
dRUSES
uRUSES
bRUSHY
cRUSTS
tRUSTS
cRUSTY
tRUSTY
tRUTHS
uSABLE
tSADES
tSADIS
uSAGES
iSATIN
eSCAPE
eSCARP
eSCARS
aSCEND
aSCENT
aSCOTS
eSCOTS
eSCUDO
pSHAWS
aSHIER
aSHORE
aSIDES
aSLANT
aSLEEP
iSLING
aSLOPE
aSLOSH
tSORES
aSPICS
eSPIED
eSPIES
aSPIRE
eSPRIT
eSTATE
oSTEAL
aSTERN
aSTONY
eSTOPS
aSTRAY
eSTRAY
eSTRUM
uSURER
aSWARM
aSWIRL
aSWOON
sTABLE
sTACKS
sTAINS
sTAKES
sTALER
sTALES
sTALKS
sTALKY
sTALLS

eTALON
sTAMPS
sTANGS
sTANKS
eTAPES
sTAPES
sTARED
sTARES
sTARRY
sTARTS
sTATER
sTATES
sTEAKS
sTEALS
sTEAMS
sTEELS
sTELAE
sTELES
aTELIC
sTELIC
sTENCH
sTENTS
eTERNE
sTERNS
sTEWED
eTHANE
sTICKS
sTIFFS
sTILES
sTILLS
sTILTS
sTIMES
sTINGS
sTINTS
oTITIS
eTOILE
sTOKED
sTOKER
sTOKES
sTOLED
sTOLES
aTOLLS
aTONAL
aTONED
sTONED
aTONER
sTONER
aTONES
sTONES
sTONEY
aTONIC
sTOOLS
sTOPED
sTOPER
sTOPES
aTOPIC
sTORES
sTOURS
sTOUTS
sTOWED
sTRAIN
sTRAIT
sTRAPS
sTRASS
sTRAYS
sTRESS
sTREWS
aTRIAL
sTRICK
sTRIKE
sTRIPE
sTRIPS
sTRODE
sTROKE
sTROLL
sTROVE
sTROWS
sTROYS
sTRUCK
sTUBBY
sTUFFS
sTUMPS
aTWAIN
aTWEEN
sTYING

aTYPIC
bUDDER
jUDDER
mUDDER
rUDDER
yULANS
vULVAS
cUMBER
dUMBER
lUMBER
nUMBER
dUMBOS
gUMBOS
jUMBOS
bUMPED
dUMPED
hUMPED
jUMPED
lUMPED
mUMPED
pUMPED
tUMPED
nUNCLE
bUNCOS
jUNCOS
fUNDER
sUNDER
bUNION
dUNITE
gUNITE
rUNLET
sUNLIT
gUNMAN
sUNSET
aUNTIE
cUPPED
dUPPED
pUPPED
sUPPED
tUPPED
cUPPER
sUPPER
cURARE
cURARI
oURARI
aURATE
cURATE
rURBAN
tURBAN
gURGED
pURGED
sURGED
bURGER
pURGER
sURGER
gURGES
pURGES
sURGES
bURIAL
cURIAL
mURINE
pURINE
bURPED
bURSAE
mUSERS
bUSHER
gUSHER
lUSHER
mUSHER
pUSHER
rUSHER
bUSING
fUSING
mUSING
fUTILE
rUTILE
bUTTER
cUTTER
gUTTER
mUTTER
nUTTER
pUTTER
aVAILS
kVASES
aVAUNT

aVENGE
eVENTS
aVENUE
aVERSE
aVERTS
eVERTS
kVETCH
eVILER
oVINES
aVOIDS
oVOIDS
aVOUCH
aVOWED
aVOWER
sWAGED
sWAGER
sWAGES
sWAILS
sWAINS
tWAINS
aWAITS
aWAKED
aWAKEN
aWAKES
sWALES
sWANKS
aWARDS
sWARDS
sWARMS
sWARTY
sWATCH
sWEARS
aWEARY
tWEEDS
tWEEDY
tWEENS
sWEENY
tWEENY
sWEEPS
sWEEPY
sWEETS
tWEETS
aWEIGH
dWELLS
sWELLS
aWHILE
aWHIRL
tWIGGY
sWILLS
tWILLS
dWINED
tWINED
dWINES
tWINES
sWINGS
sWINGY
sWINKS
sWIPED
sWIPES
tWISTS
sWITCH
tWITCH
sWITHE
sWIVED
sWIVES
aWOKEN
sWOOPS
sWOOSH
sWORDS
sWOUND
aXENIC
kYACKS
cYESES
xYLEMS
aZINES
aZONAL
oZONES

6s-to-Make-7s

kABAKAS
kABAYAS
bABYING
bACHING
cACHING
hACKEES
tACNODE
fACTION
pACTION
tACTION
fACTORS
fACTUAL
tACTUAL
vACUITY
gADDERS
lADDERS
mADDERS
pADDERS
wADDERS
gADDING
mADDING
pADDING
rADDING
wADDING
dADDLED
pADDLED
rADDLED
sADDLED
wADDLED
dADDLES
pADDLES
rADDLES
sADDLES
wADDLES
fAERIES
hAFTERS
rAFTERS
wAFTERS
hAGGADA
bAGGERS
dAGGERS
gAGGERS
jAGGERS
lAGGERS
nAGGERS
sAGGERS
tAGGERS
wAGGERS
bAGGIES
jAGGIES
rAGGIES
pAGINGS
eAGLETS
mAGNATE
rAIDERS
rAIDING
bAILING
fAILING
hAILING
jAILING
mAILING
nAILING
rAILING
sAILING
tAILING
vAILING
wAILING
mAIMERS
mAIMING
fAIREST
hAIRIER
fAIRING
lAIRING
pAIRING
wAIRING
fAIRWAY
wAIVERS
mALATES
pALATES
vALGOID
mALIGNS
mALINES
sALINES
vALINES
tALIPED
tALKIES
cALLEES
mALLEES
gALLEYS
vALLEYS
dALLIED
gALLIED
rALLIED
sALLIED

tALLIED
bALLIES
dALLIES
gALLIES
rALLIES
sALLIES
tALLIES
wALLIES
gALLIUM
pALLIUM
bALLOTS
fALLOWS
gALLOWS
hALLOWS
mALLOWS
sALLOWS
tALLOWS
wALLOWS
fALTERS
hALTERS
pALTERS
sALTERS
cAMBERS
lAMBERS
gAMBITS
gAMBLED
rAMBLED
wAMBLED
gAMBLER
rAMBLER
gAMBLES
rAMBLES
wAMBLES
lAMENTS
fAMINES
gAMINES
cAMPING
dAMPING
lAMPING
rAMPING
tAMPING
vAMPING
sAMPLER
wAMUSES
bANALLY
rANCHOS
pANELED
mANGELS
bANGERS
dANGERS
gANGERS
hANGERS
mANGERS
rANGERS
sANGERS
dANGLED
jANGLED
mANGLED
tANGLED
wANGLED
dANGLER
jANGLER
mANGLER
tANGLER
wANGLER
bANGLES
dANGLES
jANGLES
mANGLES
tANGLES
wANGLES
fANIONS
wANIONS
rANKLED
rANKLES
tANNOYS
pANTHER
cANTING
hANTING
pANTING
rANTING
wANTING
tANTRUM
cANYONS
nAPHTHA
hAPLITE
rAPPELS
dAPPLES
pAPPOSE
pARABLE
hARBORS
hARBOUR
mARCHED
pARCHED

mARCHER
lARCHES
mARCHES
pARCHES
fARCING
mARGENT
gARGLED
gARGLES
jARGONS
pARISES
bARISTA
fARMERS
hARMERS
wARMERS
hARMFUL
fARMING
hARMING
wARMING
cAROUSE
bARRACK
cARRACK
wARRANT
bARROWS
fARROWS
hARROWS
mARROWS
nARROWS
yARROWS
mARROWY
pARSONS
cARTELS
pARTIER
tARTIER
wARTIER
tARTILY
nASCENT
mASCOTS
cASHIER
dASHIER
wASHIER
bASHING
cASHING
dASHING
fASHING
gASHING
hASHING
lASHING
mASHING
pASHING
sASHING
wASHING
mASKERS
bASKING
cASKING
gASKING
mASKING
tASKING
gASPERS
jASPERS
rASPERS
rASPISH
wASPISH
wASSAIL
bASSETS
tASSETS
bASSIST
eASTERN
pASTERN
bASTERS
cASTERS
eASTERS
gASTERS
lASTERS
mASTERS
pASTERS
rASTERS
tASTERS
wASTERS
gASTRAL
nATRIUM
fATTEST
wATTEST
lAUDING
gAUGERS
sAUGERS
nAUGHTS
wAUGHTS
vAUNTIE
gAUNTLY
hAUTEUR
vAWARDS
jAWLESS
lAWLESS
dAWNING
fAWNING
pAWNING

yAWNING
mAXILLA
tAXITES
wAXLIKE
aBASHED
aBASHES
aBASING
aBATING
oBENTOS
aBETTED
aBETTER
aBETTOR
aBIDERS
aBIDING
aBIOTIC
oBLASTS
aBODING
aBOUGHT
aBOUNDS
aBREAST
aBRIDGE
aBROACH
aBUBBLE
aBUSING
aBUTTED
aBUTTER
aBYSSAL
sCABBED
sCAMPED
sCAMPER
sCANNED
sCANNER
sCANTED
sCANTER
aCANTHI
sCARERS
oCARINA
sCARING
sCARPED
sCARPER
sCARTED
eCARTES
sCARVES
sCATTED
aCAUDAL
oCELLAR
aCERATE
aCEROUS
eCHARDS
aCHIRAL
yCLEPED
aCLINIC
sCOFFER
sCOLDER
sCOLLOP
sCOOPED
sCOOPER
sCOOTER
sCOPING
sCOPULA
sCORERS
sCORING
aCORNED
sCORNED
sCORNER
eCOTYPE
sCOUTER
sCOUTHS
sCOWING
sCOWLED
sCRAGGY
sCRAPED
sCRAPES
sCRAPPY
sCRATCH
sCRAWLS
sCRAWLY
sCREAKS
sCREAKY
sCREAMS
oCREATE
sCREEDS
sCREWED
sCRIMPS
sCRIMPY
sCRUNCH
sCRYING
sCUFFED
sCULLED
sCULLER
sCULTCH
sCUMMER
sCUNNER
sCUPPER
aCUTELY
aCUTEST

sCUTTER
sCUTTLE
aCYCLIC
aDEEMED
oDONATE
bEAGLES
fEARFUL
tEARFUL
bEARING
fEARING
gEARING
hEARING
nEARING
rEARING
sEARING
tEARING
wEARING
lEARNED
yEARNED
lEARNER
yEARNER
dEARTHS
hEARTHS
tEASELS
wEASELS
cEASING
fEASING
lEASING
tEASING
fEASTER
bEATERS
hEATERS
sEATERS
bEATING
hEATING
sEATING
wEBBING
rEBOOKS
lECHING
pECHING
nEDDIES
tEDDIES
oEDEMAS
hEDGERS
lEDGERS
hEDGIER
lEDGIER
sEDGIER
wEDGIER
hEDGING
kEDGING
wEDGING
aEDILES
dEDUCED
rEDUCED
sEDUCED
dEDUCES
rEDUCES
sEDUCES
dEDUCTS
bEERIER
lEERIER
lEERILY
bEGGARS
sEGGARS
kEGGERS
bEGGING
kEGGING
lEGGING
pEGGING
vEGGING
aEGISES
rEGRESS
rEGRETS
hEIGHTH
hEIGHTS
wEIGHTS
wEIGHTY
nEITHER
dEJECTA
dEJECTS
rEJECTS
rELANDS
rELAPSE
bELATED
dELATED
gELATED
rELATED
rELATER
dELATES
gELATES
rELATES
gELDERS
mELDERS
wELDERS
sELECTS

sELFISH
pELITES
vELITES
dELUDED
dELUDER
dELUDES
dELVERS
rEMAILS
mEMBERS
rEMENDS
dEMERGE
rEMERGE
nEMESES
nEMESIS
hEMMERS
dEMOTED
rEMOTER
dEMOTES
gEMOTES
rEMOTES
tENABLE
pENATES
sENATES
vENATIC
bENDERS
fENDERS
gENDERS
lENDERS
mENDERS
rENDERS
sENDERS
tENDERS
vENDERS
bENDING
fENDING
lENDING
mENDING
pENDING
rENDING
sENDING
tENDING
vENDING
wENDING
vENDUES
tENFOLD
kENOSIS
pENSILE
tENSILE
cENSURE
vENTAIL
cENTERS
rENTERS
tENTERS
vENTERS
tENURED
tENURES
rENVOIS
aEOLIAN
nEOLITH
aEONIAN
pEONISM
dEPOSES
rEPOSES
tERBIUM
xEROSES
cEROTIC
xEROTIC
hERRING
tERRORS
aERUGOS
gESTATE
rESTATE
tESTATE
fESTERS
jESTERS
nESTERS
pESTERS
rESTERS
tESTERS
wESTERS
zESTERS
vESTRAL
oESTRIN
oESTRUM
oESTRUS
rETAPES
fETCHED
lETCHED
rETCHED
tETCHED
fETCHER
fETCHES
kETCHES
lETCHES
rETCHES
vETCHES

mETHANE
aETHERS
tETHERS
wETHERS
mETHOXY
mETHYLS
rEVERTS
rEVILER
rEVOKED
rEVOKER
rEVOKES
dEVOLVE
rEVOLVE
rEXINES
sEXISTS
sEXTANT
aFEARED
aGAINST
aGAMETE
aGENTRY
aGINNER
aGROUND
sHACKED
tHACKED
wHACKED
wHACKER
sHACKLE
sHADING
sHAFTED
sHAGGED
cHAIRED
tHALERS
wHALERS
wHALING
cHALLAH
cHALLOT
sHALLOT
sHALLOW
cHALUTZ
sHAMMED
wHAMMED
sHAMMER
cHAMPER
cHANCES
cHANGED
wHANGED
cHANGER
sHANKED
tHANKED
tHANKER
cHANTED
cHAPPED
wHAPPED
cHARING
sHARING
cHARKED
sHARKED
cHARMED
cHARMER
sHARPED
sHARPER
cHASTEN
cHATTED
cHATTER
pHATTER
sHATTER
sHAUGHS
sHAULED
cHAUNTS
sHAVERS
sHAVING
cHAWING
sHAWING
tHAWING
cHAZANS
cHAZZAN
cHEAPER
sHEARER
cHEATED
cHEATER
tHEATER
sHEATHS
sHEAVED
sHEAVES
cHEDERS
wHEELED
wHEELER
wHEEZED
wHEEZES
tHEISTS
sHELLED
sHELLER
wHELMED
wHELPED
sHELVED
sHELVES

tHEREAT
wHEREAT
tHEREBY
wHEREBY
tHEREIN
wHEREIN
tHEREOF
wHEREOF
tHEREON
wHEREON
tHERETO
wHERETO
tHERMAE
tHERMIT
sHEUCHS
sHEUGHS
cHEWERS
sHEWERS
cHEWING
sHEWING
cHIDDEN
cHIDERS
cHIDING
cHILLED
sHILLED
cHILLER
wHINGED
wHINGER
wHINGES
cHIPPED
sHIPPED
wHIPPED
cHIPPER
sHIPPER
wHIPPER
cHIPPIE
wHISTED
tHITHER
wHITHER
cHITTER
wHITTER
cHOCKED
sHOCKED
sHOCKER
sHODDEN
sHOEING
sHOGGED
cHOKIER
cHOKING
tHOLING
wHOLISM
cHOLLAS
pHONEYS
pHONIED
pHONING
wHOOFED
wHOOPED
wHOOPER
wHOOPLA
sHOOTER
cHOPPED
sHOPPED
wHOPPED
cHOPPER
sHOPPER
wHOPPER
cHORDED
tHORNED
gHOSTED
gHOSTLY
sHOTTED
cHOUSED
cHOUSER
cHOUSES
sHOVELS
sHOVERS
cHUCKLE
cHUFFED
cHUGGED
cHUGGER
cHUMMED
cHUMPED
tHUMPED
wHUMPED
tHUMPER
sHUNTED
cHUNTER
sHUNTER
cHUPPAH
sHUSHED
sHUSHES
cHUTZPA
dICIEST
bICKERS
dICKERS
kICKERS

lICKERS
nICKERS
pICKERS
tICKERS
wICKERS
dICKIER
kICKIER
pICKIER
sIDLERS
sIDLING
mIFFIER
bIGGING
dIGGING
fIGGING
gIGGING
jIGGING
pIGGING
rIGGING
wIGGING
zIGGING
dIGNIFY
lIGNIFY
sIGNIFY
lIGNITE
sIGNORE
sILEXES
tILLITE
gIMMIES
jIMMIES
gIMPING
lIMPING
pIMPING
wIMPING
wIMPISH
dIMPLED
pIMPLED
rIMPLED
wIMPLED
cINCHED
pINCHED
wINCHED
pINCHER
wINCHER
cINCHES
fINCHES
pINCHES
wINCHES
zINCITE
lINDIES
wINDIGO
wINDOWS
pINFOLD
dINGLES
jINGLES
mINGLES
sINGLES
tINGLES
mINIONS
pINIONS
jINKERS
lINKERS
pINKERS
sINKERS
tINKERS
wINKERS
dINKIER
hINKIER
kINKIER
dINKING
fINKING
jINKING
kINKING
lINKING
oINKING
pINKING
sINKING
wINKING
tINKLES
wINKLES
pINNATE
dINNERS
gINNERS
pINNERS
sINNERS
tINNERS
wINNERS
bINNING
dINNING
fINNING
gINNING
pINNING
rINNING
sINNING
tINNING
wINNING
hINTERS

lINTERS
mINTERS
sINTERS
tINTERS
wINTERS
bIONICS
lIONISE
lIONIZE
tIRADES
dIREFUL
eIRENIC
dIRKING
tISSUED
tISSUES
bITCHED
dITCHED
hITCHED
pITCHED
wITCHED
aITCHES
bITCHES
dITCHES
fITCHES
hITCHES
pITCHES
wITCHES
gIZZARD
dJEBELS
sKELPED
sKELTER
sKIDDED
sKIDDER
sKILLED
sKINKED
sKIPPED
sKIPPER
sKITING
sKITTLE
pLACERS
gLACIER
pLACING
bLACKED
cLACKED
fLACKED
sLACKED
bLACKER
cLACKER
sLACKER
bLADDER
gLADDER
bLADERS
bLADING
cLAGGED
fLAGGED
sLAGGED
fLAGGER
gLAIRED
fLAKERS
sLAKERS
fLAKIER
fLAKING
sLAKING
cLAMBER
bLAMING
fLAMING
cLAMMED
fLAMMED
sLAMMED
cLAMPED
pLANATE
gLANCED
gLANCER
gLANCES
bLANDER
sLANDER
bLANKER
fLANKER
bLANKLY
pLANNER
cLAPPED
fLAPPED
sLAPPED
cLAPPER
fLAPPER
sLAPPER
eLAPSED
eLAPSES
aLARUMS
cLASHED
fLASHED
pLASHED
sLASHED
cLASHER
fLASHER
pLASHER
sLASHER

cLASHES
fLASHES
pLASHES
sLASHES
cLASSES
gLASSES
gLASSIE
cLASSIS
bLASTED
bLASTER
pLASTER
pLATENS
bLATHER
sLATHER
pLATINA
fLATTEN
bLATTER
cLATTER
fLATTER
pLATTER
cLAVERS
sLAVERS
sLAVING
sLAVISH
bLAWING
cLAWING
fLAWING
fLAYERS
pLAYERS
sLAYERS
cLAYING
fLAYING
pLAYING
sLAYING
pLAYOFF
gLAZIER
gLAZILY
bLAZING
gLAZING
pLEADED
pLEADER
bLEAKER
cLEANED
gLEANED
cLEANER
gLEANER
cLEANLY
pLEASED
pLEASER
pLEASES
cLEAVED
sLEAVED
cLEAVER
cLEAVES
sLEAVES
fLECHES
eLECTOR
pLEDGER
fLEDGES
pLEDGES
sLEDGES
fLEERED
eLEGIST
eLEGITS
bLENDER
sLENDER
fLENSED
fLENSES
bLESSER
pLESSOR
aLEVINS
pLIABLE
gLIBBER
cLICHES
cLICKED
fLICKED
sLICKED
cLICKER
fLICKER
sLICKER
aLIGHTS
bLIGHTS
fLIGHTS
pLIGHTS
sLIGHTS
cLIMBED
cLIMBER
sLIMIER
gLIMING
sLIMING
gLIMMER
sLIMMER
sLIMPSY
aLINERS
cLINGER
fLINGER

sLINGER
aLINING
bLINKED
cLINKED
pLINKED
sLINKED
bLINKER
cLINKER
pLINKER
fLINTED
gLINTED
bLIPPED
cLIPPED
fLIPPED
sLIPPED
cLIPPER
fLIPPER
sLIPPER
gLISTEN
bLISTER
gLISTER
kLISTER
bLITHER
sLITHER
fLITTER
gLITTER
sLITTER
cLIVERS
sLIVERS
gLOBATE
bLOBBED
cLOBBER
sLOBBER
gLOBULE
bLOCKED
cLOCKED
fLOCKED
bLOCKER
cLOCKER
sLOGANS
cLOGGED
fLOGGED
sLOGGED
bLOGGER
cLOGGER
fLOGGER
sLOGGER
cLONERS
bLOOMED
gLOOMED
bLOOPED
bLOOPER
eLOPERS
sLOPERS
eLOPING
sLOPING
cLOPPED
fLOPPED
gLOPPED
pLOPPED
sLOPPED
fLOPPER
gLORIES
cLOSERS
cLOSING
fLOSSES
gLOSSES
bLOTTED
cLOTTED
pLOTTED
sLOTTED
bLOTTER
pLOTTER
sLOTTER
cLOUGHS
pLOUGHS
sLOUGHS
cLOURED
fLOURED
bLOUSED
bLOUSES
cLOUTED
fLOUTED
gLOUTED
cLOVERS
gLOVERS
pLOVERS
gLOVING
pLOWBOY
bLOWERS
fLOWERS
gLOWERS
pLOWERS
fLOWERY
sLOWEST
bLOWING

fLOWING
gLOWING
pLOWING
sLOWING
sLOWISH
bLUBBER
cLUBBER
fLUBBER
sLUBBER
cLUCKED
pLUCKED
bLUFFED
fLUFFED
sLUFFED
gLUGGED
pLUGGED
sLUGGED
pLUGGER
sLUGGER
kLUGING
cLUMBER
pLUMBER
sLUMBER
aLUMINA
fLUMMOX
cLUMPED
fLUMPED
pLUMPED
sLUMPED
pLUMPEN
pLUMPER
bLUNGED
pLUNGED
bLUNGER
pLUNGER
bLUNGES
pLUNGES
cLUNKER
fLUNKER
pLUNKER
bLUNTED
bLUSHED
fLUSHED
sLUSHED
bLUSHER
fLUSHER
pLUSHER
bLUSHES
fLUSHES
pLUSHES
sLUSHES
pLUSHLY
bLUSTER
cLUSTER
fLUSTER
gLUTEAL
eLUTING
fLUTING
fLUTIST
kLUTZES
fLYINGS
eMAILED
sMARTED
sMARTEN
sMASHED
sMASHER
sMASHES
aMASSED
aMASSES
sMATTER
aMAZING
sMELLED
sMELTED
sMELTER
aMENDED
eMENDED
aMENDER
eMENDER
oMENTAL
oMENTUM
aMERCER
aMERCES
eMERGED
eMERGES
oMICRON
sMIDGES
oMIKRON

sMILERS
sMIRKER
sMITERS
sMITTEN
sMOCKED
sMOLDER
aMONGST
sMOTHER
aMOTION
eMOTION
eMOTIVE
aMOUNTS
sMUGGER
aMUSERS
sMUSHED
sMUSHES
aMUSING
sNAGGED
sNAILED
oNANISM
kNAPPED
sNAPPED
kNAPPER
sNAPPER
eNATION
aNEARED
uNEATEN
sNIBBED
sNICKED
sNICKER
sNIFFER
sNIGGER
sNIGGLE
kNIGHTS
sNIPPED
sNIPPER
uNITERS
kNOCKED
sNOGGED
aNOTHER
kNURLED
rOARING
sOARING
bOATERS
cOATERS
lOBELIA
tOCHERS
cOCKERS
dOCKERS
hOCKERS
lOCKERS
mOCKERS
rOCKERS
jOCULAR
lOCULAR
lOCULUS
pODIUMS
sODIUMS
cOFFERS
dOFFERS
gOFFERS
bOFFING
cOFFING
dOFFING
sOFTEST
bOILERS
cOILERS
mOILERS
tOILERS
rOILIER
bOILING
cOILING
fOILING
mOILING
rOILING
sOILING
tOILING
bOINKED
bOLDEST
cOLDEST
gOLDEST
cOLDISH
bOMBERS
cOMBERS
hOMBRES
lOMENTA
mOMENTA

tOMENTA
rONIONS
bONUSES
nONUSES
tONUSES
bOODLES
dOODLES
nOODLES
pOODLES
zOOGENY
pOOHING
zOOLOGY
wOORALI
bOOZIER
wOOZIER
bOOZILY
wOOZILY
bOOZING
cORACLE
mORALLY
bORATED
bORATES
sORBING
bORDERS
cORDERS
bORDURE
mORGANS
pORGIES
fORGONE
dORMERS
fORMERS
wORMERS
mORPHIC
hOSIERS
hOSTLER
jOSTLER
bOTHERS
mOTHERS
pOTHERS
cOTTARS
cOTTERS
dOTTERS
jOTTERS
lOTTERS
pOTTERS
rOTTERS
tOTTERS
cOUCHED
dOUCHED
mOUCHED
pOUCHED
tOUCHED
vOUCHED
cOUCHES
dOUCHES
mOUCHES
pOUCHES
rOUCHES
tOUCHES
vOUCHES
nOUGHTS
bOUNCES
jOUNCES
pOUNCES
hOUSELS
jOUSTED
rOUSTED
jOUSTER
rOUSTER
cOUTERS
pOUTERS
rOUTERS
sOUTERS
tOUTERS
lOUTING
pOUTING
rOUTING
tOUTING
cOVERED
hOVERED
lOVERLY
bOVINES
hOWLETS
dOWNERS
dOWNING
gOWNING
bOXLIKE

fOXLIKE
fOXTAIL
rOYSTER
sPACERS
sPACIER
oPACIFY
sPACING
sPALLED
sPANNED
sPANNER
sPARERS
sPARGED
sPARGES
sPARING
sPARKED
sPARKER
sPARRED
sPARSER
sPARTAN
sPATTED
sPATTER
sPAVINS
sPAWNED
sPAWNER
sPAYING
sPECKED
sPEELED
sPEERED
sPEISES
sPELTER
uPENDED
aPHASIC
aPHONIC
aPHOTIC
sPIKERS
sPIKING
sPILING
sPILLED
sPINIER
oPINING
oPINION
sPINNER
sPINTOS
sPITTED
sPLASHY
sPLAYED
aPLENTY
uPLIGHT
uPLINKS
sPOKING
sPONGED
sPOOLED
sPOOLER
sPORING
sPORTED
sPORTER
oPOSSUM
sPOTTED
sPOTTER
sPOUTED
sPOUTER
uPRAISE
sPRANGS
uPRATED
uPRATES
sPRAYED
sPRAYER
uPREACH
sPRIEST
sPRINTS
uPRISES
sPUNKIE
sPURGES
sPURRED
sPUTTER
sQUARKS
sQUILLS
sQUINTS
sQUIRED
sQUIRES
sQUIRTS
aQUIVER
dRABBET
bRABBLE
dRABBLE
gRABBLE
bRACERS

tRACERS
bRACHET
bRACING
gRACING
tRACING
cRACKED
tRACKED
wRACKED
cRACKER
tRACKER
bRACKET
cRACKLE
gRACKLE
bRADDED
cRAFTED
dRAFTED
gRAFTED
cRAFTER
dRAFTER
gRAFTER
dRAGEES
bRAGGED
cRAGGED
dRAGGED
fRAGGED
dRAGGLE
bRAIDED
bRAIDER
bRAILED
tRAILED
fRAILER
tRAILER
bRAINED
dRAINED
gRAINED
tRAINED
bRAISED
pRAISED
pRAISER
bRAISES
fRAISES
pRAISES
bRAKING
bRAMBLE
cRAMMED
dRAMMED
tRAMMED
cRAMMER
cRAMPED
tRAMPED
pRANCES
tRANCES
pRANGED
gRANGER
gRANGES
oRANGES
cRANKED
fRANKED
pRANKED
cRANKER
fRANKER
cRANKLE
cRANKLY
fRANKLY
tRANSOM
gRANTED
gRANTER
dRAPERS
gRAPIER
cRAPING
dRAPING
cRAPPED
fRAPPED
tRAPPED
wRAPPED
cRAPPER
tRAPPER
wRAPPER
eRASERS
bRASHER
cRASHER
tRASHER
bRASHES
cRASHES
tRASHES
bRASHLY
eRASING

gRASPED
gRASPER
wRASSLE
eRASURE
cRATERS
fRATERS
gRATERS
kRATERS
pRATERS
gRATIFY
gRATINE
cRATING
gRATING
oRATING
pRATING
oRATION
dRATTED
bRATTLE
pRATTLE
cRAUNCH
gRAVELS
tRAVELS
cRAVENS
bRAVERS
cRAVERS
gRAVERS
bRAVING
cRAVING
gRAVING
bRAWEST
bRAYING
dRAYING
fRAYING
gRAYING
pRAYING
cRAYONS
bRAZERS
gRAZERS
bRAZING
cRAZING
gRAZING
pREACTS
tREADER
aREALLY
bREAMED
cREAMED
dREAMED
cREAMER
dREAMER
pREARMS
tREASON
gREAVED
pREAVER
gREAVES
pREBIDS
pREBILL
pREBIND
pREBOIL
pREBOOK
pREBUYS
pRECAST
pRECEDE
pRECENT
pRECEPT
pRECESS
pRECIPE
wRECKED
pRECODE
pRECOOK
pRECOUP
eRECTOR
pRECUTS
pREDATE
tREDDLE
pREDIAL
uREDIAL
pREEDIT
cREELED
pREFACE
pREFECT
pREFERS
pREFILE
pREFIRE
pREFORM
pREFUND
pREHEAT
pRELATE

pRELOAD
pREMADE
cREMATE
pREMEET
pREMISE
pREMISS
pREMIXT
pREMOLD
tRENAIL
pRENAME
tRENDED
pREPACK
pREPAID
pREPAVE
pREPAYS
pREPLAN
pREPPED
pRESALE
pRESELL
pRESENT
pRESETS
fRESHES
pRESHIP
pRESHOW
pRESIDE
pRESIFT
pRESOAK
pRESOLD
pRESORT
cRESTED
wRESTED
pRESTER
wRESTER
pRESUME
pRETAPE
pRETELL
pRETEST
pRETOLD
pRETRIM
fRETTED
pRETYPE
pREVERB
bREVETS
tREVETS
pREVIEW
pREVISE
pREVUES
pREWARM
pREWASH
pREWIRE
pREWORK
pREWORN
pREWRAP
cRIBBED
dRIBBED
cRIBBER
dRIBLET
pRICERS
pRICING
tRICING
bRICKED
cRICKED
pRICKED
tRICKED
wRICKED
cRICKEY
gRIDDED
gRIDDER
gRIDDLE
tRIDENT
bRIDGED
bRIDGES
fRIDGES
gRIDING
pRIDING
gRIEVER
tRIFLED
tRIFLER
tRIFLES
dRIFTED
gRIFTED
fRIGGED
pRIGGED
tRIGGED
tRIGGER
bRIGHTS
fRIGHTS

wRIGHTS
dRILLED
fRILLED
gRILLED
pRILLED
tRILLED
gRILLES
pRIMERS
tRIMERS
gRIMIER
gRIMING
pRIMING
bRIMMED
pRIMMED
tRIMMED
bRIMMER
cRIMMER
gRIMMER
kRIMMER
pRIMMER
tRIMMER
cRIMPLE
bRINDED
gRINDED
cRINGED
fRINGED
wRINGED
bRINGER
cRINGER
wRINGER
gRIPING
dRIPPED
gRIPPED
tRIPPED
dRIPPER
gRIPPER
tRIPPER
cRIPPLE
gRIPPLE
aRISING
iRISING
pRISING
bRISKED
fRISKED
bRISKER
fRISKER
cRITTER
fRITTER
gRITTER
fRITZES
dRIVERS
gRIVETS
pRIVETS
tRIVETS
dRIVING
pROBAND
pROBING
cROCHET
cROCKED
fROCKED
tROCKED
bROCKET
cROCKET
pRODDED
eRODENT
bROGUES
dROGUES
bROILED
dROLLED
tROLLED
dROLLER
tROLLER
tROMPED
pROOFED
pROOFER
bROOKED
cROOKED
bROOKIE
bROOMED
gROOMED
vROOMED
gROOMER
gROPERS
pROPERS
gROPING
cROQUET
cROSIER

pROSIER
pROSILY
pROSING
tROTTED
tROTTER
oROTUND
tROUBLE
tROUGHS
gROUNDS
gROUPED
tROUPED
aROUSED
gROUSED
aROUSER
gROUSER
tROUSER
aROUSES
gROUSES
gROUTED
gROUTER
cROUTES
dROUTHS
dROVERS
pROVERS
tROVERS
dROVING
pROVING
tROWELS
cROWERS
gROWERS
cROWING
gROWING
tROWING
gROWTHS
tROWTHS
dRUBBED
gRUBBED
dRUBBER
gRUBBER
tRUCKED
tRUCKLE
cRUDELY
pRUDERY
cRUDEST
gRUFFED
tRUFFES
tRUFFLE
gRUFFLY
dRUGGED
fRUGGED
aRUGOLA
cRUMBLE
dRUMBLE
gRUMBLE
cRUMBLY
gRUMBLY
dRUMMER
gRUMMER
cRUMPLE
cRUMPLY
tRUNDLE
tRUNNEL
bRUSHED
cRUSHED
bRUSHER
cRUSHER
bRUSHES
cRUSHES
cRUSTED
tRUSTED
pSALTER
iSATINS
eSCAPED
eSCAPES
aSCARED
eSCARPS
aSCENDS
aSCENTS
aSCRIBE
aSEPSES
aSEPSIS
aSEPTIC
eSERINE
aSEXUAL
aSHAMED
pSHAWED
aSHIEST

aSOCIAL
iSOLATE
aSPIRED
aSPIRES
eSPOUSE
eSPRITS
eSPYING
aSQUINT
eSQUIRE
eSTATED
eSTATES
aSTATIC
aSTOUND
eSTRAYS
aSTRICT
aSTRIDE
eSTRUMS
aSTYLAR
aSUNDER
sTABBED
sTABLED
sTABLES
sTACKED
sTACKER
aTACTIC
sTAGGED
sTAGGER
sTAKING
sTALKED
sTALKER
eTALONS
sTAMPED
sTAMPER
sTANGED
sTANNIC
sTARING
sTARRED
sTARTED
sTARTER
sTATERS
aTAXIES
sTEAMED
sTEWING
eTHANES
aTHEISM
aTHEIST
aTHIRST
aTHWART
sTIBIAL
sTICKED
sTICKER
sTICKLE
sTIFFED
sTILLED
sTILLER
sTILTED
aTINGLE
sTINKER
sTINTED
sTINTER
sTIPPLE
eTOILES
sTOKERS
sTOKING
aTONERS
sTONERS
aTONICS
sTONIER
aTONING
sTONING
sTONISH
sTOOLED
sTOPERS
sTOPING
sTOPPED
sTOPPER
sTOPPLE
sTORIES
sTOTTED
sTOUTER
sTOWAGE
sTOWING
sTRAINS
sTRAITS
sTRICKS
sTRIKES
sTRIPES

sTROKED
sTROKES
sTROLLS
aTROPHY
aTROPIN
sTROWED
sTUBBED
sTUMBLE
sTUMPED
sTUNNED
dUBIETY
bUDDERS
jUDDERS
mUDDERS
rUDDERS
sULLAGE
cUMBERS
lUMBERS
nUMBERS
bUMBLES
fUMBLES
hUMBLES
jUMBLES
mUMBLES
nUMBLES
rUMBLES
tUMBLES
bUMPING
dUMPING
hUMPING
jUMPING
lUMPING
mUMPING
pUMPING
tUMPING
tUNABLE
sUNBELT
nUNCLES
fUNFAIR
bUNIONS
dUNITES
gUNITES
gUNLESS
rUNLESS
sUNLESS
nUNLIKE
sUNLIKE
gUNLOCK
sUNROOF
sUNSETS
gUNSHIP
aUNTIES
pUNTIES
sUNWISE
eUPHROE
cUPPERS
sUPPERS
cUPPING
dUPPING
pUPPING
sUPPING
tUPPING
pURANIC
cURARES
cURARIS
oURARIS
cURATES
tURGENT
bURGERS
pURGERS
sURGERS
gURGING
pURGING
sURGING
bURIALS
mURINES
pURINES
bURPING
mUSEFUL
bUSHERS
gUSHERS
mUSHERS
pUSHERS
rUSHERS
oUTMOST
bUTTERS
cUTTERS

gUTTERS
mUTTERS
nUTTERS
pUTTERS
aVAILED
eVANISH
oVARIES
aVENGED
aVENGES
aVENUES
oVERBID
oVERSET
aVIATIC
aVIATOR
eVICTOR
eVILEST
aVOIDED
aVOIDER
eVOLUTE
aVOWERS
aVOWING
sWADDLE
tWADDLE
sWAGERS
sWAGGED
sWAGGER
sWAGING
aWAITED
aWAITER
aWAKENS
aWAKING
sWALLOW
tWANGLE
sWANKED
sWANKER
sWANNED
sWAPPED
aWARDED
sWARDED
aWARDER
sWARMED
sWARMER
sWASHED
sWASHER
sWASHES
sWATTER
tWATTLE
sWEARER
sWEEPER
tWEETED
dWELLED
sWELLED
sWELTER
tWIDDLE
sWIGGED
tWIGGED
sWILLED
tWILLED
sWILLER
dWINDLE
sWINDLE
sWINGED
tWINGED
sWINGER
tWINIER
dWINING
tWINING
sWINISH
sWINKED
tWINKLE
tWINNED
sWIPING
sWISHED
sWISHER
sWISHES
sWISSES
tWISTED
tWITCHY
sWITHER
tWITTED
sWIVING
sWOTTED
sWOUNDS
oYESSES
tZADDIK
oZONATE

7s-to-Make-8s

lABILITY
lACERATE
mACERATE
tACNODES
tACONITE
fACTIONS
pACTIONS
tACTIONS
dADDLING
pADDLING
rADDLING
sADDLING
wADDLING
mADWOMAN
mADWOMEN
wAGELESS
hAGGADAH
hAGGADAS
hAGGADIC
hAGGADOT
vAGILITY
mAGNATES
bAILMENT
hAIRIEST
fAIRINGS
pAIRINGS
hAIRLESS
hAIRLIKE
hAIRLINE
fAIRWAYS
hALATION
kALEWIFE
mALIGNED
mALIGNER
pALIMONY
tALIPEDS
gALLIUMS
pALLIUMS
fALLOWED
hALLOWED
sALLOWED
tALLOWED
wALLOWED
dALLYING
gALLYING
rALLYING
sALLYING
tALLYING
fALTERED
hALTERED
pALTERED
fALTERER
pALTERER
cAMASSES
gAMBLERS
rAMBLERS
gAMBLING
rAMBLING
wAMBLING
hAMBONES
bANALITY
pANELING
dANGERED
dANGLERS
jANGLERS
mANGLERS
tANGLERS
wANGLERS
dANGLING
gANGLING
jANGLING
mANGLING
tANGLING
wANGLING
sANGUINE
lANGUISH
rANKLING
tANNATES
cANNULAR
pANTHERS
tANTRUMS
tAPELIKE
jAPERIES
nAPERIES
rAPHIDES
hAPLITES
cAPSIDAL
rAPTNESS
pARABLES
hARBORED
hARBOURS
mARCHERS
mARCHING
pARCHING
mARGENTS
gARGLING
bARISTAS
fARMINGS
hARMLESS
cAROUSAL
cAROUSED
cAROUSER
cAROUSES
bARRACKS
cARRACKS
fARROWED
hARROWED
mARROWED
nARROWED
pARTICLE
tARTIEST
wARTIEST
bARTISAN
pARTISAN
wARTLESS
hARUSPEX
dASHIEST
wASHIEST
cASHLESS
sASHLESS
gASKINGS
mASKINGS
wASSAILS
bASSISTS
yATAGHAN
nATRIUMS
lAUREATE
hAUTEURS
tAUTONYM
lAWFULLY
mAXILLAE
mAXILLAS
lAZURITE
aBASHING
aBEGGING
aBETTERS
aBETTING
aBETTORS
aBOUNDED
aBRACHIA
aBRIDGED
aBRIDGES
aBUTTALS
aBUTTERS
aBUTTING
sCABBING
sCAMPERS
sCAMPING
sCANDENT
sCANNERS
sCANNING
aCANTHUS
sCANTING
oCARINAS
sCARIOUS
sCARLESS
sCARPERS
sCARPING
sCARRIER
sCARTING
sCATTIER
sCATTING
aCAUDATE
eCAUDATE
aCAULINE
aCENTRIC
aCERATED
sCHILLER
aCHROMIC
sCOFFERS
sCOFFING
sCOLLOPS
iCONICAL
sCOOCHES
sCOOPERS
sCOOPING
sCOOTERS
sCOPULAE
sCOPULAS
sCORNERS
sCORNING
eCOTYPES
sCOUTERS
sCOUTHER
sCOWLING
sCRAGGED
sCRAMMED
sCRAPING
sCRAPPED
sCRAPPER
sCRAWLED
sCRAWLER
sCREAKED
sCREAMED
sCREAMER
sCREWING
sCRIMPED
sCRIMPER
sCRUNCHY
sCUFFING
sCULCHES
sCULLERS
sCULLING
sCULLION
sCUMMERS
sCUNNERS
sCUPPERS
sCURRIED
sCURRIES
sCURVIER
sCUTCHES
sCUTTERS
sCUTTLED
sCUTTLES
sCUTWORK
aDEEMING
eDENTATE
oDONATES
aDYNAMIC
mEAGERLY
wEANLING
yEANLING
tEARDROP
bEARINGS
gEARINGS
hEARINGS
fEARLESS
gEARLESS
tEARLESS
nEARLIER
pEARLIER
lEARNERS
yEARNERS
lEARNING
yEARNING
tEASELED
wEASELED
fEASTERS
fEASTING
yEASTING
bEATABLE
hEATABLE
bEATINGS
sEATINGS
oECOLOGY
pECTASES
oEDEMATA
hEDGIEST
lEDGIEST
sEDGIEST
wEDGIEST
sEDITION
dEDUCING
rEDUCING
sEDUCING
rEDUCTOR
bEERIEST
lEERIEST
hEIGHTHS
dEJECTED
rEJECTED
rEJECTOR
rELAPSED
rELAPSES
rELATERS
dELATING
gELATING
rELATING
dELATION
gELATION
rELATION
rELATIVE
sELECTED
sELECTEE
sELECTOR
dELUDERS
dELUDING
dELUSION
dELUSIVE
dELUSORY
rEMAILED
rEMENDED
dEMERGED
rEMERGED
dEMERGES
rEMERGES
mEMETICS
dEMITTED
rEMITTED
rEMITTER
dEMOTING
dEMOTION
rEMOTION
vENATION
pENCHANT
mENDINGS
bENDWAYS
bENDWISE
tENFOLDS
mENOLOGY
oENOLOGY
pENOLOGY
vENOLOGY
dENOUNCE
rENOUNCE
cENSURED
cENSURER
cENSURES
vENTAILS
cENTERED
tENTERED
gENTRIES
sENTRIES
tENURING
nEOLITHS
pEONISMS
lEPIDOTE
dEPILATE
rEQUITES
tERBIUMS
mERISTIC
vERISTIC
bESPOUSE
gESTATED
rESTATED
gESTATES
rESTATES
tESTATES
aESTHETE
aESTIVAL
fESTIVAL
oESTRINS
oESTRIOL
oESTRONE
oESTROUS
oESTRUMS
kETAMINE
fETCHERS
fETCHING
lETCHING
rETCHING
mETHANES
mETHANOL
aETHERIC
mETHOXYL
mETHYLIC
rEVERTED
rEVOKERS
rEVOKING
rEVOLUTE
dEVOLVED
rEVOLVED
rEVOLVER
dEVOLVES
rEVOLVES
rEVULSED
hEXAMINE
hEXARCHY
aFEBRILE
aFLUTTER
aGAMETES
aGENESES
aGENESIS
aGENETIC
aGINNERS
aGLIMMER
aGLITTER
aGNOSTIC
aGRAPHIC
aGREEING
wHACKERS
sHACKING
tHACKING
wHACKING
sHACKLED
sHACKLER
sHACKLES
cHADARIM
sHADDOCK
sHAFTING
sHAGGING
cHALLAHS
cHALLOTH
sHALLOWS
sHAMMERS
sHAMMING
wHAMMING
cHAMPERS
cHANDLER
cHANGERS
cHANGING
wHANGING
tHANKERS
sHANKING
tHANKING
cHANTING
cHAPPING
wHAPPING
cHARKING
sHARKING
cHARMERS
cHARMING
pHARMING
sHARPERS
sHARPIES
sHARPING
cHARRIER
gHARRIES
cHASTENS
tHATCHED
tHATCHER
tHATCHES
cHATTERS
sHATTERS
cHATTING
sHAULING
cHAUNTED
cHAUNTER
cHAZANIM
cHAZZANS
sHEALING
sHEARERS
sHEARING
cHEATERS
tHEATERS
sHEATHER
cHEATING
sHEAVING
wHEELERS
wHEELING
wHEEZING
sHELLERS
sHELLING
wHELMING
wHELPING
sHELVING
rHEMATIC
tHEMATIC
tHERMITS
wHERRIED
cHERRIES
sHERRIES
wHERRIES
cHEWABLE
tHICKISH
cHICKORY
cHILDING
cHILLERS
cHILLIER
cHILLING
sHILLING
wHINGERS
wHINGING
cHINKIER
sHINNIED
wHINNIED
sHINNIES
wHINNIES
sHIPLESS
wHIPLIKE
cHIPPIER
wHIPPIER
cHIPPIES
cHIPPING
sHIPPING
wHIPPING
wHISTING
sHITLESS
cHITTERS
wHITTERS
sHITTING
sHOCKERS
cHOCKING
sHOCKING
sHOGGING
cHOKIEST
wHOLISMS
pHONEYED
wHOOFING
wHOOPERS
wHOOPING
wHOOPLAS
sHOOTERS
sHOOTING
cHOPPERS
sHOPPERS
wHOPPERS
cHOPPIER
cHOPPING
sHOPPING
wHOPPING
cHORDING
tHORNIER
tHORNILY
tHORNING
gHOSTING
sHOTTING
cHOUSERS
cHOUSING
sHOVELED
cHUCKLES
cHUFFIER
cHUFFING
cHUGGERS
cHUGGING
cHUMMING
tHUMPERS
cHUMPING
tHUMPING
wHUMPING
cHUNKIER
cHUNTERS
sHUNTERS
sHUNTING
cHUPPAHS
dHURRIES
sHUSHING
sHUTTING
cHUTZPAH
cHUTZPAS
vICELESS
dICKIEST
kICKIEST
pICKIEST
rICTUSES
mIFFIEST
lIGNEOUS
lIGNITES
tILLITES
pINCHERS
wINCHERS
cINCHING
pINCHING
wINCHING
zINCITES
wINDIGOS
wINDOWED
pINFOLDS
dINKIEST
hINKIEST
kINKIEST
tINKLING
wINKLING
gINNINGS
wINNINGS
lIONISED
lIONISES
lIONIZED
lIONIZER
lIONIZES
fIRELESS
tIRELESS
wIRELESS
mISOGAMY
tISSUING
bITCHIER
pITCHIER
wITCHIER
bITCHILY
pITCHILY
bITCHING
dITCHING
hITCHING
pITCHING
wITCHING
lITERATE
gIZZARDS
dJELLABA
sKELPING
sKELTERS
sKERRIES
sKETCHES
sKIDDERS
sKIDDING
sKILLING
aKINETIC
sKINKING
sKINLESS
sKIPPERS
sKIPPING
sKITTLES
fLABELLA
gLABELLA
cLACKERS
sLACKERS
bLACKING
cLACKING
fLACKING
sLACKING
bLADDERS
bLADINGS
fLAGGERS
bLAGGING
cLAGGING
fLAGGING
sLAGGING
gLAIRING
fLAKIEST
cLAMBERS
cLAMMING
fLAMMING
sLAMMING
cLAMPERS
cLAMPING
gLANCERS
gLANCING
gLANDERS
sLANDERS
bLANKEST
cLANKIER
pLANNERS
cLAPPERS
fLAPPERS
sLAPPERS
cLAPPING
fLAPPING
sLAPPING
eLAPSING
cLASHERS
fLASHERS
pLASHERS
sLASHERS
cLASHING
fLASHING
pLASHING
sLASHING
gLASSIES
bLASTERS
pLASTERS
bLASTING
kLATCHES
sLATCHES
bLATHERS
sLATHERS
pLATINAS
fLATTENS
cLAWLESS
fLAWLESS
cLAWLIKE
pLAYOFFS
gLAZIEST
bLEACHED
pLEACHED
bLEACHER
bLEACHES
pLEACHES
pLEADERS
pLEADING
cLEANERS
gLEANERS
cLEANEST
cLEANING
gLEANING
bLEARIER
pLEASERS
pLEASING
pLEATHER
cLEAVERS
cLEAVING
sLEAVING
eLECTION
fLECTION
eLECTORS
pLEDGERS
fLEDGIER
fLEECHED
fLEECHES
fLEERING
eLEGISTS
bLENDERS
bLENDING
fLENSING
pLESSORS
fLETCHED
fLETCHES
eLEVATOR
cLICKERS
fLICKERS
sLICKERS
cLICKING
fLICKING
sLICKING
aLIGHTED
bLIGHTED
fLIGHTED
pLIGHTED
sLIGHTED
bLIGHTER
pLIGHTER
sLIGHTER
sLIGHTLY
cLIMBERS
cLIMBING
sLIMIEST
gLIMMERS
sLIMMERS
cLINGERS
fLINGERS
sLINGERS
cLINGIER
bLINKERS
cLINKERS
pLINKERS
bLINKING
cLINKING
pLINKING
sLINKING
fLINTIER
gLINTIER
fLINTING
gLINTING
sLIPLESS
cLIPPERS
fLIPPERS
sLIPPERS
sLIPPIER
bLIPPING
cLIPPING
fLIPPING
sLIPPING
gLISTENS
bLISTERS
gLISTERS
kLISTERS
bLITHELY
bLITHEST
cLITORAL
fLITTERS
gLITTERS
sLITTERS
gLITTERY
sLIVERED
gLOAMING
gLOBATED
cLOBBERS
sLOBBERS
bLOBBING
gLOBULAR
gLOBULES
bLOCKAGE
bLOCKERS
cLOCKERS
bLOCKING
cLOCKING
fLOCKING
bLOGGERS
cLOGGERS
fLOGGERS
sLOGGERS
cLOGGIER
bLOGGING
cLOGGING
fLOGGING
sLOGGING
aLOGICAL
bLOOMING
gLOOMING
bLOOPERS
bLOOPING
fLOPPERS
fLOPPIER
gLOPPIER
sLOPPIER
cLOPPING
fLOPPING
gLOPPING
pLOPPING
sLOPPING
cLOSABLE
cLOSINGS
bLOTTERS
pLOTTERS
sLOTTERS
bLOTTING
cLOTTING
pLOTTING
sLOTTING
cLOURING
fLOURING
bLOUSIER
bLOUSILY
bLOUSING
cLOUTING
fLOUTING
gLOUTING
bLOWBALL
pLOWBOYS
bLOWDOWN
sLOWDOWN
fLOWERED
gLOWERED
pLOWLAND
sLOWNESS
bLUBBERS
cLUBBERS
fLUBBERS
sLUBBERS
pLUCKIER
pLUCKILY
cLUCKING
pLUCKING
bLUFFING
fLUFFING
sLUFFING
pLUGGERS
sLUGGERS
gLUGGING
pLUGGING
sLUGGING
pLUMBAGO
cLUMBERS
pLUMBERS
sLUMBERS
pLUMPENS
pLUMPERS
cLUMPIER
gLUMPIER
gLUMPILY
cLUMPING
fLUMPING
pLUMPING
sLUMPING
cLUMPISH
pLUMPISH
gLUNCHED
gLUNCHES
bLUNGERS
pLUNGERS
bLUNGING
pLUNGING
cLUNKERS
fLUNKERS
pLUNKERS
bLUNTING
fLUSHEST
pLUSHEST
bLUSHING
fLUSHING
sLUSHING
bLUSTERS
cLUSTERS
fLUSTERS
fLUTINGS
fLUTISTS
pLYINGLY
eMAILING
sMARTENS
sMARTING
sMASHERS
sMASHING
aMASSING
sMATTERS
aMAZEDLY
sMELLING
sMELTERS
sMELTING
aMENDERS
eMENDERS
aMENDING
eMENDING
aMERCERS
eMERGING
oMICRONS
aMIDSHIP
eMIGRANT
eMIGRATE
oMIKRONS
sMIRKIER
sMIRKILY
eMISSION
oMISSION
eMISSIVE
oMISSIVE
sMITHERS
aMITOSES
aMITOSIS
aMITOTIC
sMOCKING
sMOLDERS
sMOOCHED
sMOOCHER
sMOOCHES
aMORALLY
aMORTISE
sMOTHERS
sMOTHERY
aMOTIONS
eMOTIONS
sMOULDER
aMOUNTED
sMUSHING
sMUTCHES
sNAGGIER
sNAGGING
sNAILING
oNANISMS
sNAPLESS
kNAPPERS
sNAPPERS
sNAPPIER
kNAPPING
sNAPPING
eNATIONS
gNATTIER
aNEARING
eNERVATE
sNIBBING
kNICKERS
sNICKERS
sNICKING
sNIFFERS
sNIGGERS
sNIGGLED
sNIGGLER
sNIGGLES
kNIGHTLY
sNIPPERS
sNIPPIER
sNIPPILY
sNIPPING
kNOBBIER
sNOBBIER
sNOBBILY
kNOCKING
aNODALLY
sNOGGING
kNUBBIER
sNUBBIER
kNURLING
bOARFISH
bOATLIKE
gOATLIKE
mOATLIKE
lOBELIAS
tOCHERED
cOCREATE
cOFFERED
gOFFERED
sOFTENER
rOILIEST
bOINKING
bOLDNESS
cOLDNESS
oOLOGIES
oOLOGIST
dOLOROSO
lOMENTUM
mOMENTUM
tOMENTUM
dONENESS
gONENESS
lONENESS
zONETIME
zOOLOGIC
zOOPHYTE
wOORALIS

zOOSPERM
zOOSPORE
bOOZIEST
wOOZIEST
cORACLES
mORALISM
mORALIST
mORALITY
bORATING
mORATORY
bORDERED
bORDERER
sORDINES
bORDURES
hOROLOGY
mORRISES
cOSMOSES
hOSTLERS
jOSTLERS
pOSTMARK
cOUCHING
dOUCHING
mOUCHING
pOUCHING
tOUCHING
vOUCHING
yOURSELF
jOUSTERS
rOUSTERS
jOUSTING
rOUSTING
cOVARIES
nOVATION
cOVERAGE
cOVERALL
hOVERFLY
cOVERING
hOVERING
cOVERLET
cOVERTLY
bOWLLIKE
fOXTAILS
rOYSTERS
sPACIEST
sPALLING
sPANNERS
sPANNING
sPARABLE
sPARGING
sPARKERS
sPARKING
sPARLING
sPARRIER
sPARRING
sPATTERS
sPATTING
sPAWNERS
sPAWNING
sPEAKING
sPECKING
sPECTATE
sPEELING
sPEERING
sPELTERS
sPENDING
uPENDING
aPHONICS
ePHORATE
sPILINGS
sPILLAGE
sPILLING
sPINIEST
oPINIONS
sPINNERS
sPINNIES
sPINNING
sPITTING
sPLASHED
sPLASHER
sPLASHES
aPLASTIC
sPLATTED
sPLATTER
sPLAYING
uPLIGHTS
uPLINKED
sPONGING
sPONTOON
sPOOLERS
sPOOLING
sPORTERS
sPORTING
oPOSSUMS
sPOTTERS
sPOTTIER
sPOTTING
sPOUTERS
sPOUTING
aPRACTIC
uPRAISED
uPRAISER
uPRAISES
uPRATING
sPRATTLE
sPRAYERS
sPRAYING
sPRIGGED
sPRINTED
sPRINTER
uPRISING
sPUDDING
sPUNKIER
sPUNKIES
sPURRING
sPUTTERS
aPYRETIC
sQUADDED
eQUALITY
sQUASHED
sQUASHER
sQUASHES
eQUIPPED
eQUIPPER
sQUIRING
sQUIRTED
dRABBETS
bRABBLED
dRABBLED
gRABBLED
bRABBLER
gRABBLER
bRABBLES
dRABBLES
gRABBLES
bRACHETS
bRACHIAL
bRACINGS
tRACINGS
cRACKERS
tRACKERS
bRACKETS
wRACKFUL
cRACKING
tRACKING
wRACKING
bRADDING
eRADIATE
dRAFFISH
cRAFTERS
dRAFTERS
gRAFTERS
cRAFTING
dRAFTING
gRAFTING
bRAGGING
dRAGGING
fRAGGING
dRAGGLES
bRAIDERS
bRAIDING
tRAILERS
bRAILING
tRAILING
bRAINIER
gRAINIER
bRAINILY
bRAINING
dRAINING
gRAINING
tRAINING
pRAISERS
bRAISING
pRAISING
bRAMBLED
bRAMBLES
cRAMMERS
cRAMMING
dRAMMING
tRAMMING
cRAMPING
tRAMPING
bRANCHED
cRANCHED
bRANCHES
cRANCHES
tRANCHES
bRANDIES
gRANGERS
oRANGIER
pRANGING
fRANKERS
cRANKEST
fRANKEST
cRANKING
fRANKING
pRANKING
cRANKISH
pRANKISH
cRANKLED
cRANKLES
tRANSOMS
gRANTERS
gRANTING
gRANULAR
cRAPPERS
tRAPPERS
wRAPPERS
cRAPPING
fRAPPING
tRAPPING
wRAPPING
cRASHERS
tRASHERS
bRASHEST
gRASPERS
gRASPING
wRASSLED
wRASSLES
eRASURES
cRATCHES
gRATINGS
oRATIONS
bRATTIER
dRATTING
bRATTISH
bRATTLED
pRATTLED
pRATTLER
bRATTLES
pRATTLES
gRAVELED
tRAVELED
tRAVELER
gRAVELLY
cRAVENED
cRAVINGS
bREACHED
pREACHED
bREACHER
pREACHER
bREACHES
pREACHES
pREACTED
pREADAPT
tREADERS
bREADING
dREADING
tREADING
pREADMIT
pREADOPT
pREALLOT
pREALTER
cREAMERS
dREAMERS
bREAMING
cREAMING
dREAMING
pREAPPLY
pREARMED
tREASONS
pREAVERS
pREBILLS
pREBINDS
pREBIRTH
pREBOARD
pREBOILS
pREBOOKS
pREBOUND
pREBUILD
pREBUILT
pRECASTS
pRECEDED
pRECEDES
pRECEPTS
pRECHECK
pRECHOSE
pRECIPES
pRECITED
wRECKING
pRECLEAN
pRECODED
pRECODES
pRECOOKS
eRECTORS
pREDATED
pREDATES
tREDDLED
tREDDLES
pREDRAFT
pREDRIED
pREDRIES
pREDRILL
gREEDIER
gREEDILY
bREEDING
pREEDITS
fREEDMAN
fREEDMEN
pREELECT
cREELING
pREENACT
pREERECT
pREFACED
pREFACES
pREFECTS
pREFIGHT
pREFILED
pREFILES
pREFIRED
pREFIRES
pREFIXED
pREFIXES
pREFOCUS
pREFORMS
pREFROZE
pREFUNDS
bREGMATA
pREGNANT
pREHEATS
pREJUDGE
pRELATES
pRELIVES
pRELOADS
cREMAINS
cREMATED
cREMATES
pREMISED
pREMISES
pREMIXED
pREMIXES
pREMOLDS
pREMORSE
tRENAILS
pRENAMES
tRENDING
pREORDER
pREPACKS
pREPAVED
pREPAVES
pREPLACE
pREPLANS
pREPLANT
pREPPING
pREPRESS
pREPRICE
pREPRINT
pRESALES
pRESCIND
pRESCORE
pRESELLS
pRESENTS
pRESERVE
pRESHAPE
pRESHIPS
pRESHOWN
pRESHOWS
pRESIDED
pRESIDER
pRESIDES
pRESIFTS
pRESOAKS
pRESOLVE
pRESORTS
pRESPLIT
pRESTAMP
pRESTERS
wRESTERS
cRESTING
wRESTING
pRESTORE
pRESUMED
pRESUMER
pRESUMES
pRETAPED
pRETAPES
pRETASTE
wRETCHED
wRETCHES
pRETELLS
pRETESTS
pRETRAIN
pRETREAT
pRETRIAL
pRETRIMS
fRETTING
pRETYPED
pRETYPES
pREUNION
pREUNITE
pREVALUE
pREVERBS
pREVIEWS
pREVISED
pREVISES
pREVISIT
pREVISOR
pREWARMS
pREWEIGH
pREWIRED
pREWIRES
pREWORKS
pREWRAPS
cRIBBERS
cRIBBING
dRIBBING
dRIBLETS
cRICKETS
pRICKETS
bRICKING
cRICKING
pRICKING
tRICKING
wRICKING
gRIDDERS
gRIDDLED
gRIDDLES
bRIDGING
gRIEVERS
tRIFLERS
tRIFLING
dRIFTING
gRIFTING
tRIGGERS
fRIGGING
pRIGGING
tRIGGING
fRIGHTED
bRIGHTER
bRIGHTLY
fRIGIDLY
dRILLING
fRILLING
gRILLING
pRILLING
tRILLING
gRIMIEST
bRIMLESS
bRIMMERS
cRIMMERS
kRIMMERS
tRIMMERS
bRIMMING
pRIMMING
tRIMMING
cRIMPLED
cRIMPLES
bRINGERS
cRINGERS
wRINGERS
bRINGING
cRINGING
fRINGING
wRINGING
gRINNING
dRIPPERS
gRIPPERS
tRIPPERS
dRIPPING
gRIPPING
tRIPPING
cRIPPLED
cRIPPLER
cRIPPLES
fRISKERS
fRISKIER
fRISKILY
bRISKING
fRISKING
cRITTERS
fRITTERS
gRITTERS
bROACHED
bROACHES
pROBANDS
cROCHETS
cROCKERY
bROCKETS
cROCKETS
cROCKING
fROCKING
tROCKING
pRODDING
bROGUERY
bROGUISH
bROILING
tROLLERS
dROLLING
tROLLING
tROMPING
pROOFERS
pROOFING
cROOKERY
bROOKIES
bROOKING
cROOKING
gROOMERS
bROOMIER
bROOMING
gROOMING
vROOMING
cROQUETS
pROSIEST
cROTCHES
tROTTERS
tROTTING
tROUBLES
cROUCHES
gROUCHES
gROUNDED
gROUNDER
cROUPIER
cROUPILY
gROUPING
tROUPING
aROUSERS
gROUSERS
tROUSERS
aROUSING
gROUSING
gROUTERS
gROUTING
gROWABLE
cROWDIES
tROWELED
dRUBBERS
gRUBBERS
dRUBBING
gRUBBING
tRUCKING
tRUCKLED
tRUCKLES
cRUDDIER
gRUFFING
tRUFFLED
tRUFFLES
dRUGGING
fRUGGING
aRUGOLAS
cRUMBLED
dRUMBLED
gRUMBLED
gRUMBLER
cRUMBLES
dRUMBLES
gRUMBLES
dRUMMERS
gRUMMEST
cRUMMIER
cRUMMIES
cRUMPLED
cRUMPLES
tRUNDLES
tRUNNELS
bRUSHERS
cRUSHERS
bRUSHIER
bRUSHING
cRUSHING
cRUSTIER
tRUSTIER
cRUSTILY
tRUSTILY
cRUSTING
tRUSTING
tRUTHFUL
pSALTERS
eSCALADE
eSCALLOP
eSCAPING
eSCARPED
aSCENDED
aSCRIBED
aSCRIBES
eSERINES
pSHAWING
iSLANDER
aSOCIALS
iSOLATED
iSOLATES
aSPARKLE
eSPECIAL
aSPHERIC
aSPIRANT
aSPIRING
eSPOUSAL
eSPOUSED
eSPOUSES
eSQUIRED
eSQUIRES
eSTATING
aSTERNAL
aSTEROID
aSTHENIA
aSTHENIC
oSTOMATE
aSTONISH
eSTOPPED
aSTOUNDS
eSTOVERS
eSTRANGE
eSTRAYED
sTABBING
sTABLING
sTACKERS
sTACKING
sTAGGERS
sTAGGING
sTAKEOUT
sTALKERS
sTALKIER
sTALKING
sTAMPERS
sTAMPING
sTANGING
sTARRIER
sTARRING
sTARTING
sTEAMING
aTECHNIC
sTENCHES
aTHEISMS
aTHEISTS
sTICKERS
sTICKING
sTICKLED
sTICKLER
sTICKLES
sTIFFING
sTILLING
sTILTING
sTINGING
sTINKERS
sTINTERS
sTINTING
sTIPPLED
sTIPPLER
sTIPPLES
sTOCCATA
aTONALLY
sTONIEST
sTOOLING
sTOPPERS
sTOPPING
sTOPPLED
sTOPPLES
sTOTTING
sTOWABLE
sTOWAGES
sTOWAWAY
sTRAINED
sTRAINER
sTRAPPED
sTRAPPER
sTRASSES
aTREMBLE
sTRESSED
sTRESSES
sTRICKLE
sTRIDENT
sTRIPPED
sTRIPPER
sTROKING
sTROLLED
sTROLLER
aTROPHIC
sTROPHIC
aTROPINE
aTROPINS
aTROPISM
sTROWING
sTRUMPET
sTUBBIER
sTUBBING
sTUMBLED
sTUMBLER
sTUMBLES
sTUMPING
sTUNNING
aTWITTER
aTYPICAL
sULLAGES
cUMBERED
lUMBERED
nUMBERED
sUNBAKED
sUNBELTS
sUNBLOCK
sUNBURNT
sUNCHOKE
fUNCTION
jUNCTION
sUNDRESS
fUNHOUSE
cUNIFORM
pUNITIVE
gUNLOCKS
sUNROOFS
rUNROUND
gUNSHIPS
eUPHROES
cUPPINGS
rURALITE
tURGENCY
fUSELESS
fUTILITY
bUTTERED
gUTTERED
mUTTERED
pUTTERED
mUTTERER
pUTTERER
aVAILING
eVALUATE
aVARICES
oVARIOLE
aVENGING
aVENTAIL
oVERBIDS
oVERSETS
aVERSION
eVERSION
kVETCHES
aVIATORS
eVICTORS
eVOCABLE
aVOIDERS
aVOIDING
eVOLUTES
aVOUCHED
aVOUCHER
aVOUCHES
sWADDLED
tWADDLED
tWADDLER
sWADDLES
tWADDLES
sWAGGERS
sWAGGING
aWAITERS
aWAITING
aWAKENED
aWAKENER
sWALLOWS
sWAMPISH
tWANGLED
tWANGLER
tWANGLES
sWANKING
sWANNING
sWAPPING
aWARDERS
aWARDING
sWARDING
sWARMERS
sWARMING
sWASHERS
sWASHING
sWATCHES
tWATTLED
tWATTLES
sWEARERS
sWEARING
aWEATHER
tWEEDIER
sWEENIES
tWEENIES
sWEEPERS
sWEEPIER
sWEEPING
sWEETING
tWEETING
dWELLING
sWELLING
sWELTERS
tWIDDLED
tWIDDLES
tWIGGIER
sWIGGING
tWIGGING
tWIGLESS
tWIGLIKE
sWILLERS
sWILLING
tWILLING
dWINDLED
sWINDLED
dWINDLES
sWINDLES
sWINGERS
sWINGIER
sWINGING
tWINGING
sWINGMAN
sWINGMEN
tWINIEST
sWINKING
tWINKLED
tWINKLES
tWINNING
sWISHERS
sWISHING
tWISTING
sWITCHED
tWITCHED
sWITCHES
tWITCHES
sWITHERS
tWITTING
sWOOSHED
sWOOSHES
sWOTTING
sWOUNDED
oZONATED
aZYGOSES

8s-to-Make-9s

lACERATED
mACERATED
tACONITES
mACRODONT
fACTUALLY
tACTUALLY
vACUITIES
hAGGADAHS
hAGGADOTH
bAILMENTS
hAIRBRUSH
hAIRINESS
hAIRLINES
hALATIONS
kALEWIVES
mALIGNERS
mALIGNING
dALLIANCE
fALLOWING
hALLOWING
sALLOWING
tALLOWING
wALLOWING
fALTERERS
pALTERERS
fALTERING
hALTERING
pALTERING
dANGERING
cANNULATE
gANTELOPE
nAPHTHOUS
hARBOROUS
hARBOURED
hARMONICA
cAROUSALS
cAROUSERS
cAROUSING
hARQUEBUS
fARROWING
hARROWING
mARROWING
nARROWING
pARTICLES
tARTINESS
bARTISANS
pARTISANS
wASHINESS
wASSAILED
wASSAILER
yATAGHANS
tAUTONYMS
nAVICULAR
nAVIGATOR
mAXILLARY
lAZURITES
aBASEMENT
aBIOGENIC
aBOUNDING
aBRIDGING
aBUILDING
sCANNINGS
sCATTIEST
aCELLULAR
aCEPHALIC
sCHILLERS
sCHILLING
aCHROMOUS
iCONICITY
sCOPULATE
sCORELESS
sCRAGGIER
sCRAGGILY
sCRAMMING
sCRAPPERS
sCRAPPIER
sCRAPPING
sCRATCHES
sCRAWLERS
sCRAWLIER
sCRAWLING
sCREAKING
sCREAMERS
sCREAMING
sCRIBBLED
sCRIMPERS
sCRIMPIER
sCRIMPING
aCRITICAL
sCRUNCHED
sCRUNCHES
sCULLIONS
sCULTCHES
sCURRYING
sCURVIEST
aCUTENESS
sCUTTLING
sCUTWORKS
wEANLINGS
yEANLINGS
tEARDROPS
nEARLIEST
pEARLIEST
lEARNINGS
yEARNINGS
bEASTINGS
sEDITIONS
dEDUCIBLE
rEDUCIBLE
sEDUCIBLE
dEDUCTION
rEDUCTION
sEDUCTION
dEDUCTIVE
rEDUCTIVE
sEDUCTIVE
rEDUCTORS
bEERINESS
lEERINESS
rEGRESSED
rEGRESSES
dEJECTING
rEJECTING
dEJECTION
rEJECTION
rEJECTIVE
rEJECTORS
rELAPSING
bELATEDLY
rELATEDLY
dELATIONS
gELATIONS
rELATIONS
rELATIVES
sELECTEES
sELECTING
sELECTION
sELECTIVE
sELECTORS
sELFISHLY
dELUSIONS
rEMAILING
rEMENDING
dEMERGING
rEMERGING
rEMIGRATE
dEMISSION
rEMISSION
rEMISSIVE
rEMITTERS
dEMITTING
rEMITTING
dEMOTIONS
rEMOTIONS
dEMULSIFY
vENATIONS
pENCHANTS
dENERVATE
oENOPHILE
xENOPHILE
kENOSISES
dENOUNCED
rENOUNCED
dENOUNCES
rENOUNCES
cENSURERS
cENSURING
pENTANGLE
cENTERING
tENTERING
nEOLITHIC
lEPIDOTES
dEPILATED
dEPILATES
dEPILATOR
rERADIATE
oESOPHAGI
bESPOUSED
bESPOUSES
hESSONITE
gESTATING
rESTATING
aESTHESIA
aESTHETES
aESTHETIC
aESTIVATE
oESTRIOLS
oESTROGEN
oESTRONES
oESTRUSES
kETAMINES
mETHANOLS
aETHEREAL
mETHYLATE
mETHYLENE
pETIOLATE
aETIOLOGY
dEVALUATE
rEVALUATE
nEVERMORE
rEVERSION
rEVERTING
rEVOCABLE
rEVOLVERS
dEVOLVING
rEVOLVING
rEVULSION
hEXAMINES
dEXTRORSE
aFOREHAND
aFORESAID
aFORETIME
sFORZANDI
sFORZANDO
aGENTRIES
aGNOSTICS
sGRAFFITI
sGRAFFITO
sHACKLERS
sHACKLING
sHADDOCKS
sHALLOWED
sHALLOWER
cHALUTZIM
cHANDLERS
cHARMLESS
cHASTENED
cHASTENER
tHATCHERS
tHATCHING
cHAUNTERS
cHAUNTING
cHAZZANIM
sHEARINGS
cHEATABLE
sHEATHERS
wHEATLESS
wHEELINGS
wHEELLESS
sHELLFIRE
wHELPLESS
tHEMATICS
cHEMOSTAT
tHEREINTO
wHEREINTO
tHEREUNTO
wHEREUNTO
tHEREUPON
wHEREUPON
tHEREWITH
wHEREWITH
wHERRYING
cHILLIEST
cHINKIEST
sHINNYING
wHINNYING
cHIPPIEST
wHIPPIEST
aHISTORIC
tHITHERTO
wHOLISTIC
pHONEYING
cHOPPIEST
sHOPPINGS
tHORNIEST
tHORNLESS
tHORNLIKE
sHOVELING
sHOVELLED
cHUFFIEST
cHUNKIEST
cHUTZPAHS
pICKINESS
mIFFINESS
dIGNIFIED
lIGNIFIED
sIGNIFIED
dIGNIFIES
lIGNIFIES
sIGNIFIES
lIMITABLE
vINDICATE
wINDOWING
pINFOLDED
kINKINESS
tINKLINGS
pINNATELY
pINSETTER
lIONISING
lIONIZERS
lIONIZING
dIREFULLY
eIRENICAL
bITCHIEST
pITCHIEST
wITCHIEST
wITCHINGS
lITERATES
eJACULATE
dJELLABAS
sKILLINGS
sKIPPERED
fLABELLUM
pLACELESS
aLACKADAY
bLAGGINGS
fLAGGINGS
gLANDLESS
sLANGUAGE
cLANKIEST
bLANKNESS
cLAPBOARD
fLASHINGS
sLASHINGS
bLASTINGS
eLATERITE
bLATHERED
sLATHERED
bLATHERER
pLATINIZE
pLATITUDE
sLAUGHTER
cLAVATION
sLAVISHLY
gLAZINESS
bLEACHERS
bLEACHING
pLEACHING
pLEADINGS
gLEANINGS
cLEANNESS
bLEARIEST
pLEATHERS
eLECTIONS
fLECTIONS
fLEDGIEST
fLEECHING
fLETCHING
eLEVATORS
aLIENABLE
bLIGHTERS
pLIGHTERS
sLIGHTERS
sLIGHTEST
aLIGHTING
bLIGHTING
fLIGHTING
pLIGHTING
sLIGHTING
aLIKENESS
sLIMINESS
sLIMPSIER
cLINGIEST
fLINTIEST
gLINTIEST
sLIPPERED
sLIPPIEST
cLIPPINGS
gLISTENED
aLITERACY
aLITERATE
fLITTERED
gLITTERED
aLIVENESS
sLIVERING
bLOCKABLE
bLOCKAGES
eLOCUTION
cLOGGIEST
bLOGGINGS
fLOGGINGS
aLONENESS
fLOPPIEST
gLOPPIEST
sLOPPIEST
bLOUSIEST
bLOWBALLS
bLOWDOWNS
sLOWDOWNS
fLOWERING
gLOWERING
pLOWLANDS
pLUCKIEST
pLUMBAGOS
sLUMBERED
sLUMBERER
aLUMINOUS
fLUMMOXES
cLUMPIEST
gLUMPIEST
gLUNCHING
fLUSHNESS
pLUSHNESS
bLUSTERED
cLUSTERED
fLUSTERED
sMATTERED
aMENDABLE
eMENDABLE
eMERGENCE
aMIDSHIPS
eMIGRANTS
eMIGRATED
eMIGRATES
sMIRKIEST
eMISSIONS
oMISSIONS
sMOLDERED
sMOOCHERS
sMOOCHING
aMORALISM
aMORALITY
aMORTISED
aMORTISES
sMOTHERED
eMOTIONAL
eMOTIVITY
sMOULDERS
aMOUNTING
aMUSINGLY
aMYOTONIA
sNAGGIEST
sNAPPIEST
gNATTIEST
pNEUMATIC
sNICKERED
sNIGGLERS
sNIGGLING
sNIPPIEST
kNOBBIEST
sNOBBIEST
kNUBBIEST
sNUBBIEST
eNUCLEATE
eNUMERATE
tOCHERING
jOCULARLY
iODOMETRY
pOENOLOGY
cOFFERING
gOFFERING
oOLOGISTS
lOMENTUMS
mOMENTUMS
zOOGAMETE
zOOGENIES
zOOLOGIES
zOOLOGIST
zOOPHYTES
zOOPHYTIC
zOOSPERMS
nOOSPHERE
zOOSPORES
zOOSPORIC
bOOZINESS
wOOZINESS
mORALISMS
mORALISTS
bORDERERS
bORDERING
pOSTMARKS
nOVATIONS
cOVERABLE
cOVERAGES
cOVERALLS
cOVERLETS
cOVERSLIP
cOVERTURE
rOYSTERED
oPACIFIED
oPACIFIER
oPACIFIES
sPARABLES
aPATHETIC
sPATTERED
sPECTATES
sPECULATE
aPERIODIC
aPETALOUS
aPHERESES
aPHERESIS
ePHORATES
ePICRITIC
sPILLAGES
sPINDLING
sPINELIKE
oPINIONED
sPLASHERS
sPLASHIER
sPLASHING
sPLATTERS
sPLATTING
uPLIGHTED
uPLINKING
sPONTOONS
sPOTTIEST
uPRAISERS
uPRAISING
sPRATTLED
sPRATTLES
uPREACHED
uPREACHES
sPRIGGING
sPRINTERS
sPRINTING
aPRIORITY
sPUNKIEST
sPUTTERED
sPUTTERER
sQUADDING
sQUASHERS
sQUASHING
eQUIPPERS
eQUIPPING
sQUIRTING
bRABBLERS
gRABBLERS
bRABBLING
dRABBLING
gRABBLING
bRACKETED
eRADIATED
eRADIATES
eRADICATE
cRAFTSMAN
dRAFTSMAN
cRAFTSMEN
dRAFTSMEN
tRAILHEAD
tRAINBAND
bRAINIEST
gRAINIEST
bRAINLESS
gRAINLESS
bRAINWASH
bRAMBLING
bRANCHING
cRANCHING
oRANGIEST
cRANKLING
fRANKNESS
bRASHNESS
wRASSLING
gRATIFIED
gRATIFIER
gRATIFIES
bRATTIEST
pRATTLERS
bRATTLING
pRATTLING
cRAUNCHES
tRAVELERS
gRAVELING
tRAVELING
gRAVELLED
tRAVELLED
tRAVELLER
cRAVENING
pREABSORB
pREACCUSE
bREACHERS
pREACHERS
bREACHING
pREACHING
pREACTING
pREADAPTS
pREADJUST
pREADMITS
pREADOPTS
pREALLOTS
pREALTERS
pREARMING
pREASSIGN
pREASSURE
pREBIDDEN
pREBILLED
pREBIRTHS
pREBOARDS
pREBOILED
pREBOOKED
pREBOUGHT
pREBUILDS
pREBUYING
pRECEDING
pRECENSOR
pRECEPTOR
pRECESSED
pRECESSES
pRECHARGE
pRECHECKS
pRECHOOSE
pRECHOSEN
pRECISION
pRECLEANS
pRECODING
pRECOOKED
pREDATING
tREDDLING
pREDEFINE
pREDIGEST
pREDRILLS
pREDRYING
gREEDIEST
bREEDINGS
pREEDITED
pREELECTS
pREENACTS
gREENGAGE
pREERECTS
pREEXPOSE
pREFACING
pREFERRED
pREFERRER
pREFIGURE
pREFILING
pREFILLED
pREFIRING
pREFIXING
pREFORMAT
pREFORMED
pREFREEZE
pREFROZEN
pREFUNDED
pREGNANCY
pREGROWTH
pREHANDLE
pREHARDEN
pREHEATED
pREHEATER
pREHIRING
pREIMPOSE
pREINFORM
pREINSERT
pREINVITE
pREJUDGED
pREJUDGES
pRELAUNCH
pRELOADED
pRELOCATE
pREMARKET
cREMATING
pREMISING
pREMIXING
pREMODIFY
pREMOLDED
cRENATURE
pRENOTIFY
pRENUMBER
pREOBTAIN
pREOCCUPY
pREORDAIN
pREORDERS
pREPACKED
pREPASTED
pREPAVING
pREPAYING
pREPLACED
pREPLACES
pREPRICED
pREPRICES
pREPRINTS
pRERECORD
pREREVIEW
pRESCHOOL
pRESCINDS
pRESCORED
pRESCORES
pRESCREEN
pRESCRIPT
pRESEASON
pRESELECT
pRESENTED
pRESERVED
pRESERVER
pRESERVES
pRESETTLE
pRESHAPED
pRESHAPES
pRESHOWED
pRESIDENT
pRESIDERS
pRESIDING
pRESIFTED
pRESOAKED
pRESOLVED
pRESOLVES
pRESORTED
pRESTAMPS
cRESTLESS
pRESTORED
pRESTORES
pRESTRESS
pRESTRIKE
pRESUMERS
pRESUMING
pRESURVEY
pRETAPING
pRETASTED
pRETASTES
pRETESTED
cRETINOID
pRETRAINS
pRETREATS
pRETRIALS
pRETYPING
pREUNIONS
pREUNITED
pREUNITES
pREVALUED
pREVALUES
bREVETTED
pREVIEWED
pREVIEWER
pREVISING
pREVISION
pREVISITS
pREVISORS
pREWARMED
pREWASHED
pREWASHES
pREWEIGHS
pREWIRING
pREWORKED
cRIBBINGS
gRIDDLING
tRIFLINGS
bRIGHTEST
fRIGHTFUL
fRIGHTING
fRIGIDITY
tRIMESTER
gRIMINESS
cRIMPLING
cRIPPLERS
cRIPPLING
fRISKIEST
bROACHING
bROADSIDE
cROCKETED
fROCKLESS
tROLLINGS
bROOMIEST
cROQUETED
cROQUETTE
pROSINESS
pROSTRATE
gROUNDERS
gROUNDING
cROUPIEST
tROUSSEAU
tROWELING
tROWELLED
dRUBBINGS
tRUCKLING
cRUDDIEST
cRUDENESS
pRUDERIES
gRUMBLERS
cRUMBLING
dRUMBLING
gRUMBLING
cRUMMIEST
cRUMPLIER
cRUMPLING
bRUSHIEST
tRUSTABLE
cRUSTIEST
tRUSTIEST
cRUSTLESS
tRUSTLESS
tRUTHLESS
eSCALADES
eSCALLOPS
eSCARPING
aSCENDING
aSCRIBING
aSEXUALLY
aSKEWNESS
iSLANDERS
iSOLATING
iSOLATION
aSPIRANTS
eSPOUSALS
eSPOUSING
eSQUIRING
eSTABLISH
aSTEROIDS
aSTHENIAS
aSTOMATAL
oSTOMATES
eSTOPPAGE
eSTOPPING
aSTOUNDED
aSTRADDLE
eSTRANGER
eSTRANGES
eSTRAYING
aSTRINGED
aSYLLABIC
aSYMMETRY
aSYNAPSES
aSYNAPSIS
aSYNDETIC
sTACKLESS
sTAKEOUTS
sTALKIEST
sTALKINGS
sTARRIEST
aTEMPORAL
aTHEISTIC
eTHIONINE
sTICKLERS
sTICKLING
sTICKSEED
sTIPPLERS
sTIPPLING
sTOCCATAS
aTONALITY
aTONICITY
sTOPPLING
sTOWAWAYS
sTRAINERS
sTRAINING
sTRAPPERS
sTRAPPING
sTRICKLED
sTRICKLES
sTRIPLING
sTRIPPERS
sTRIPPING
sTROLLERS
sTROLLING
aTROPHIED
aTROPHIES
aTROPINES
aTROPISMS
sTRUMPETS
sTUBBIEST
sTUMBLERS
sTUMBLING
dUBIETIES
cUMBERING
lUMBERING
nUMBERING
sUNBATHED
sUNBLOCKS
sUNBONNET
sUNBURNED
sUNCHOKES
rUNCINATE
fUNCTIONS
jUNCTIONS
gUNFOUGHT
pUNGENTLY
fUNHOUSES
cUNIFORMS
rUNROUNDS
sUNTANNED
cUPBEARER
rURALITES
bURSIFORM
pUSTULATE
mUTTERERS
pUTTERERS
bUTTERING
gUTTERING
mUTTERING
pUTTERING
eVAGINATE
eVALUABLE
eVALUATED
eVALUATES
eVALUATOR
eVANISHED
eVANISHES
oVARIOLES
aVASCULAR
aVENGEFUL
aVENTAILS
eVENTLESS
aVERSIONS
eVERSIONS
eVINCIBLE
aVIRULENT
aVOCATION
eVOCATION
eVOCATIVE
aVOIDABLE
aVOIDANCE
eVOLUTION
aVOUCHERS
aVOUCHING
tWADDLERS
sWADDLING
tWADDLING
aWAKENERS
aWAKENING
sWALLOWED
sWALLOWER
tWANGLERS
tWANGLING
tWATTLING
tWEEDIEST
sWEEPIEST
sWEEPINGS
sWELLHEAD
sWELTERED
tWIDDLING
tWIGGIEST
dWINDLING
sWINDLING
sWINGIEST
tWINKLING
tWINNINGS
tWITCHIER
sWITCHING
tWITCHING
sWITHERED
sWOOSHING
sWORDPLAY
sWOUNDING
tZADDIKIM
oZONATION

THE BEST OF THE BINGOS

While short words (those with two, three, or four letters) make a disproportionately high contribution to the number of words (75%) and total points scored (50%) in a typical game, my research showed that, more often than not, it is the long words (those with 7+ letters) that determine victory or defeat. On average, the winner plays two bingos to the loser's one, with virtually the entire margin of victory accounted for by points scored on long words. (Some long words are non-bingo plays, as when six letters are added to a seventh letter already on the board.) With such a compelling finding, the task then was to determine which of the over 50,000 bingos, of seven- and eight-letters' length, would be most cost-effective to study.

Al Weissman wrote a wonderful article on "Some SCRABBLE Game Mathematics" (*SCRABBLE Players Newspaper*[1], No. 29, February 1980) in which he addressed the issue of the probabilities of drawing individual tiles and various seven- and eight-letter combinations of tiles. He went on to list the most likely "natural occurring" (i.e., those without regard to blanks) bingos that could be drawn from a complete bag of 100 tiles. His thinking sensitized my own to the whole idea of probability in tile selection.

I considered how the most plentiful tiles were those worth only one or two points (i.e., ADEGILNORSTU). There are three or more of any one of these tiles in a full bag. In total, with blanks, they comprise 77% of the 100 tiles! These letters can spell out phrases like REGIONAL STUD, GOD IS NEUTRAL, D-REGULATIONS, OLD SIGNATURE, or, if you're doing too much word study, U DATE NO GIRLS. These are the "bingo prone" tiles, and the ones we generally hold on to (without duplications) in vying for a bingo. Taking probability into account, I devised the concept of a "3%er" bingo: A bingo composed solely of those letters that had a 3% chance or greater of being drawn from a full bag (ADEG, etc.). But the frequency with which any one of these letters could be repeated within the word would be as follows: A (3), D (1), E (4), G (1), I (3), L (1), N (2), O (2), R (2), S (2), T (2), U (1). These frequencies also represent the number of trios of each letter that can be formed from a full set of tiles. Since there are a total of nine A's, three trios of A's can be formed. Since there are only four D's, only one trio of D's can be formed. A 3%er bingo allows for the draw of one tile from any trio of letters. The exception is the almighty S. Since the S is the one tile we generally will hold on to because of its versatility, a second S might be drawn from the remaining trio of S's. Hence, two S's are allowed to appear in a 3%er. Such bonuses take both probability and usual rack management ploys into account. So, a list of about 50,000 was whittled down to about 4,000.

But how to learn all those 3%ers? I realized that a more efficient mode of learning bingos was through the study of "bingo stems." Bingo stems are generally combinations of six letters that can readily combine with a seventh letter to form a bingo. For example, if TISANE were your first six tiles drawn, of the remaining 94, all but the J, Q, and two Y's will combine to give you one of 67 different bingos. With 90 usable tiles out of 94, that's a 96% chance of getting a bingo! With SATIRE, there are 75 usable tiles to make 69 bingos. One could subsume many bingos under each family "name" (TISANE, SATIRE, etc.).

To determine which of the bingo stems were the best to study, I devised (are you ready for this?) the "Modified Modified Power Rating" or MMPR. I won't saddle you with the mathematical details of this, which you can learn in *SCRABBLE Players News*, No. 67, May 1986. Essentially, the stems are rank-ordered on the basis of the likelihood you will be able to obtain the six-letter stem and a usable seventh tile that will complete the stem to form one or more bingos. The Top 100 stems and the seven- and eight-letter bingos they generate are presented here. They are the "Type I" bingos. Almost one out of every seven words of seven- or eight-letters' length contains one of these 100 bingo stems.

So what happened to the 3%ers? Many contain a Top 100 bingo stem and could therefore be found on the Type I lists. ENTASIA and TAENIAS, for example, could be found under TISANE + A, while DELUSION, INSOULED, and UNSOILED were included under LESION + DU. However, there were a number of 3%ers that did not contain a Top 100 stem: words like ADAGIAL, STRIDOR, and SEGETAL. These "other" 3%ers became "Type II" bingos. Despite not having a Top 100 stem, given the kinds of letter combinations we might keep in our racks (ADIL, IST, AET, AEST, etc.) and the probability of drawing the remaining letters, Type II's became another source of useful and likely bingos.

Then there are words like EROTICA. It does not contain a Top 100 stem. In fact, in terms of seven-letter bingos, AEIORT can combine *only* with the letter C; not a versatile stem at all. And, as EROTICA contains that C, it could not qualify as a 3%er. Yet EROTICA is a very high probability bingo, especially with the blanks taken into account, higher in fact than many on the 3%er list. Obviously, EROTICA and other bingos like it had to be taken into consideration somewhere. They could not simply be ignored; due to their high-probability, they deserved to be recognized as valuable bingos to know. The solution was the establishment of the "Type III" list, the list of all bingos of high-probability that could not be included on the Type I list (due to the absence of a Top 100 stem) or the Type II list (due to the presence of a non-3%er tile). A frequency of 26.8793-per-million draws was selected as the cutoff point for "high probability." I figured that in order to qualify as a "high-probability" bingo, the word should be at least as likely as the least likely Top 100 bingo stem completed with a frequency-two tile (like H). TUNERS, as the Top 100 stem of lowest probability, when combined with H, made the bingo HUNTERS, which has a frequency of 26.8793-per-million draws from a full bag.

So, the Best of the Bingos are of three types:

Type I: Bingos containing a Top 100 stem (TISANE, etc.)
Type II: 3%ers not found in the Type I's (e.g., ADAGIAL)
Type III: High-probability bingos that are neither Type I's nor Type II's (e.g., EROTICA)

About one out of every four seven- and eight-letter words can be categorized as a Type I, II, or III. I would hazard a guess that they may account for two-thirds of all bingos played (or playable but overlooked) in a game between two experts.

As I see it, the best way to start learning the bingos is to review the TISANE, SATIRE, and RETINA lists of seven-letter words. Then, using a copy of the Master Study Sheet on page 39 (which may be photocopied for this purpose), fill in the words these stems form with each usable letter of the alphabet. Then, check your list against that given in the book, score yourself on the percentage you remember correctly, and study those you missed. You can retest yourself later and see how much your score improves. The number of correct answers can be quickly determined by using the Cross Index on page 31, where the number of "sevens" is listed for each stem.

Knowledge of the TISANE, SATIRE, and RETINA lists in combination with knowledge of the four-letter words will likely establish you as a full-fledged expert, presuming you have learned strategic skills along the way as well. Strategy is best learned from having "consultation" or "open rack" games with an expert player who can share her knowledge about the alternative plays available and the rationale for

---

[1] *SCRABBLE Players Newspaper* has since been renamed *SCRABBLE News* and is published eight times a year for members of the National SCRABBLE Association. For more information on becoming a member, and participating in local clubs and tournaments around North America and the world, contact: National SCRABBLE Association, Box 700, 401 Front Street, Greenport, NY 11944, or on the Web at www.scrabble-assoc.com, info@scrabble-assoc.com.

selecting one over another during each player's turn. A computer disk version of SCRABBLE, when set at the highest competitive level, may have the capacity to offer "suggestions" for your turn, a variety of rank-ordered selections that will equal or surpass those offered by most mere mortals, thereby indirectly "teaching" strategy.

The major difference between experts and non-experts is strategy. Two discriminators among experts are word knowledge and the ability to pluck such words from one's memory bank when needed. The experts study the five- and six-letter words and go beyond TISANE, SATIRE, and RETINA. The world's best know most of the 7000+ seven- and eight-letter bingos formed with the Top 100 stems and the 5000+ Type II's and III's. Some even attempt to learn the "Type IV" bingos, in other words, everything else! My own personal bias? Though the two are neither mutually inclusive nor exclusive, better that you should enjoy the game than become exceptionally proficient at it.

Top 100 Six-Letter Bingo Stems Based on MMPR

SN	STEM	MSP	UT	MMPR	SN	STEM	MSP	UT	MMPR	SN	STEM	MSP	UT	MMPR	SN	STEM	MSP	UT	MMPR
1	TISANE	1.500	90	135.000	26	SADTIE	1.000	55	55.000	51	SENATE	0.917	50	45.850	76	UNITER	0.667	57	38.019
2	SATIRE	1.500	75	112.500	27	ATONES	1.333	41	54.653	52	LEARNS	0.667	68	45.356	77	SOILED	0.593	64	37.952
3	RETAIN	1.500	68	102.000	28	SOLATE	0.889	60	53.340	53	SENITI	0.667	68	45.356	78	STEREO	0.815	46	37.490
4	ARSINE	1.500	61	91.500	29	ORALES	0.889	60	53.340	54	ORIENT	1.333	34	45.322	79	LINERS	0.667	56	37.352
5	SENIOR	1.333	68	90.644	30	ISATON	1.000	52	52.000	55	TRAINS	0.750	60	45.000	80	ALEROT	0.889	42	37.338
6	STERNA	1.000	86	86.000	31	SAINED	1.000	52	52.000	56	STRIDE	0.667	67	44.689	81	ENTOIL	0.889	42	37.338
7	TOESIN	1.333	62	82.646	32	DORIES	0.889	58	51.562	57	INTROS	0.667	67	44.689	82	GARNET	0.500	74	37.000
8	ORATES	1.333	61	81.313	33	GAINER	0.750	68	51.000	58	SANDER	0.667	66	44.022	83	EASING	0.750	49	36.750
9	REASON	1.333	57	75.981	34	LISTER	0.667	76	50.692	59	OATIES	2.000	22	44.000	84	OILSAT	0.667	55	36.685
10	INSERT	1.000	73	73.000	35	ENTERS	0.611	82	50.102	60	STORED	0.593	72	42.696	85	TINIER	0.667	55	36.685
11	TONERS	0.889	80	71.120	36	SALTER	0.667	75	50.025	61	TODIES	0.889	48	42.672	86	ATESOD	0.889	41	36.449
12	EASTER	0.917	77	70.609	37	TIRADE	1.000	50	50.000	62	OILERS	0.889	48	42.672	87	SNORED	0.593	61	36.173
13	AIDERS	1.000	70	70.000	38	SILENT	0.667	73	48.691	63	ANITOE	2.000	21	42.000	88	ELITES	0.611	59	36.049
14	RAINED	1.000	68	68.000	39	DIALER	0.667	72	48.024	64	STEROL	0.593	70	41.510	89	INMATE	0.500	72	36.000
15	LESION	0.889	75	66.675	40	LADIES	0.667	72	48.024	65	TENIAE	1.375	30	41.250	90	NEATER	0.917	39	35.763
16	TORIES	1.333	50	66.650	41	DATERS	0.667	72	48.024	66	TEARIE	1.375	30	41.250	91	LANOSE	0.889	40	35.560
17	TOILES	0.889	72	64.008	42	SNIDER	0.667	72	48.024	67	NEROLI	0.889	46	40.894	92	GREATS	0.500	71	35.500
18	SERIAL	1.000	64	64.000	43	ADORES	0.889	54	48.006	68	RANEES	0.917	44	40.348	93	ATTIRE	0.625	56	35.000
19	NAILER	1.000	59	59.000	44	SERINE	0.917	52	47.684	69	SOIGNE	0.667	60	40.020	94	TRONAS	0.667	52	34.684
20	ALIENS	1.000	59	59.000	45	SEENIT	0.917	52	47.684	70	ARIOSE	2.000	20	40.000	95	TUNERS	0.444	78	34.632
21	IONSEA	2.000	29	58.000	46	LATENS	0.667	71	47.357	71	DETAIN	1.000	40	40.000	96	PRAISE	0.500	68	34.000
22	SALTIE	1.000	57	57.000	47	STANED	0.667	71	47.357	72	SINGER	0.500	80	40.000	97	DOERAN	0.889	38	33.782
23	RETAIL	1.000	57	57.000	48	TENAIL	1.000	47	47.000	73	EASIER	1.375	29	39.875	98	SUITER	0.667	50	33.350
24	RETIES	0.917	60	55.020	49	TEINDS	0.667	70	46.690	74	EOLIAN	1.333	29	38.657	99	OALIES	1.333	25	33.325
25	ENTIRE	0.917	60	55.020	50	DESIRE	0.611	76	46.436	75	RESALE	0.611	63	38.493	100	ALDERS	0.444	75	33.300

SN: Stem Number, ranked according to MMPR value. (If two stems have identical MMPRs, one with higher MSP comes first. If equal MSPs, then listed aphabetically based on alphagram of stem.)

Stem: Here, a combination of six letters, arranged as a word, if one exists. Otherwise, stem may be comprised of shorter words. In three instances, OATIES (59), TEARIE (66), OALIES (99), a phony word is constructed.

MSP: Modified Stem Probability. Stem Probability was originally defined as the relative probability of obtaining a six-letter combination, where the Stem Probability of obtaining TISANE was set at 1. However, due to the frequent retention of the S in actual play, its attributed frequency was subsequently increased artificially by 50%. TISANE's Modified Stem Probability (MSP) thus became 1.500.

UT: Usable Tiles to complete stem, of the remaining 94 tiles.

MMPR: Modified Modified Power Rating = MSP × UT. A means of identifying the best bingo stems to study based on the likelihood of obtaining a six-letter stem (MSP) and the likelihood of completing the stem to form a bingo with a usable tile (UT).

Cross Index

STEM	SN	MNEMONIC	7s	8s	STEM	SN	MNEMONIC	7s	8s	STEM	SN	MNEMONIC	7s	8s	STEM	SN	MNEMONIC	7s	8s
ADEILR	39	DIALER	27	78	AEGNRT	82	GARNET	27	81	AELORT	80	ALE-ROT	18	86	EENRST	35	ENTERS	42	135
ADEILS	40	LADIES	30	105	AEGRST	92	GREATS	31	85	AELOST	28	SOLATE	22	100	EEORST	78	STEREO	17	105
ADEINR	14	RAINED	27	90	AEILNO	74	EOLIAN	8	36	AELRST	36	SALTER	58	187	EGINOS	69	SOIGNE	29	64
ADEINS	31	SAINED	25	99	AEILNR	19	NAILER	30	113	AENORS	9	REASON	25	104	EGINRS	72	SINGER	42	178
ADEINT	71	DETAIN	20	87	AEILNS	20	ALIENS	39	161	AENOST	27	ATONES	13	87	EIINRT	85	TINIER	23	69
ADEIRS	13	AIDERS	43	130	AEILNT	48	TENAIL	27	132	AENRST	6	STERNA	57	204	EIINST	53	SENITI	21	105
ADEIRT	37	TIRADE	30	103	AEILOS	99	OALIES*	7	73	AEORST	8	ORATES	30	171	EILNOR	67	NEROLI	8	44
ADEIST	26	SAD-TIE	28	104	AEILRS	18	SERIAL	35	167	AILOST	84	OIL-SAT	18	66	EILNOS	15	LESION	25	96
ADELRS	100	ALDERS	30	93	AEILRT	23	RETAIL	35	144	AINOST	30	I-SAT-ON	20	109	EILNOT	81	ENTOIL	15	52
ADENOR	97	DOE-RAN	15	75	AEILST	22	SALTIE	45	182	AINRST	55	TRAINS	30	152	EILNRS	79	LINERS	18	98
ADENRS	58	SANDER	31	97	AEIMNT	89	INMATE	24	82	ANORST	94	TRONAS	23	79	EILNST	38	SILENT	38	130
ADENST	47	STANED	24	71	AEINOS	21	I-ON-SEA	10	75	DEEIRS	50	DESIRE	40	149	EILORS	62	OILERS	19	90
ADEORS	43	ADORES	18	74	AEINOT	63	ANI-TOE	7	81	DEILOS	77	SOILED	19	66	EILOST	17	TOILES	24	100
ADEOST	86	ATE-SOD	11	52	AEINRS	4	ARSINE	41	213	DEINRS	42	SNIDER	37	104	EILRST	34	LISTER	44	154
ADERST	41	DATERS	42	115	AEINRT	3	RETAIN	55	201	DEINST	49	TEINDS	30	89	EINORS	5	SENIOR	36	150
AEEINT	65	TENIAE	10	64	AEINST	1	TISANE	69	247	DEIORS	32	DORIES	28	103	EINORT	54	ORIENT	17	109
AEEIRS	73	EASIER	12	78	AEIORS	70	ARIOSE	6	68	DEIOST	61	TODIES	26	81	EINOST	7	TOE-SIN	25	131
AEEIRT	66	TEARIE*	13	86	AEIOST	59	OATIES*	11	69	DEIRST	56	STRIDE	36	130	EINRST	10	INSERT	47	226
AEELRS	75	RESALE	36	127	AEIPRS	96	PRAISE	37	133	DENORS	87	SNORED	27	85	EINRTU	76	UNITER	24	79
AEENRS	68	RANEES	18	113	AEIRST	2	SATIRE	70	264	DEORST	60	STORED	32	91	EIORST	16	TORIES	38	166
AEENRT	90	NEATER	25	119	AEIRTT	93	ATTIRE	29	84	EEILST	88	ELITES	30	89	EIRSTU	98	SUITER	26	131
AEENST	51	SENATE	21	98	AELNOS	91	LANOSE	10	57	EEINRS	44	SERINE	32	164	ELORST	64	STEROL	35	106
AEERST	12	EASTER	50	207	AELNRS	52	LEARNS	25	113	EEINRT	25	ENTIRE	25	144	ENORST	11	TONERS	31	115
AEGINR	33	GAINER	48	175	AELNST	46	LATENS	36	93	EEINST	45	SEEN-IT	21	155	ENRSTU	95	TUNERS	31	100
AEGINS	83	EASING	34	145	AELORS	29	OR-ALES	27	117	EEIRST	24	RETIES	37	194	INORST	57	INTROS	24	87

Mnemonics for the Type I Sevens

Mnemonics are memory devices, techniques that can assist in recalling information. Mnemonics for learning bingos were published as early as 1982 (*SCRABBLE Players Newspaper*, No. 42, April 1982), at which time a psychologist with far too much time on his hands suggested a poem by which to learn all the two-letter combinations (of 3%er tiles) that could combine with GREAT to form forty-nine seven-letter bingos:

> My GREAT RELATION(S)
> (N)o-DENIALOR (O)r-DULTOR me,
> you could say I was an UN-ADATEREE!

GREAT could combine with the letters of RELATION + S as follows:

R(S) = GARRETS, GARTERS, GRATERS
E(S) = ERGATES, RESTAGE
L(S) = LARGEST
A(S) = TEARGAS, GASTREA
T(S) = TARGETS
I(S) = AIGRETS, GAITERS, SEAGIRT, STAGIER, TRIAGES
O(S) = GAROTES, ORGEATS, STORAGE
N(S) = ARGENTS, GARNETS, STRANGE

Similarly, GREAT could combine with the letters of DENIALOR + N, DULTOR + O, as well as with UN, AD, AT, ER, EE. The development, refinement, and publication of the best bingo stems occurred during the last half of the 1980s. In 1992, Charlie Carroll and Nick Ballard introduced "anamonics" to assist in remembering usable letters for bingo stems, and Ballard assembled the first 200 such anamonics in his wonderful but now defunct monthly, Medleys. Here's one example I devised: The seven-letter stem STINGER can combine with the following letters to form eight-letter bingos: ACDEILORSTW. The mnemonic should, at best, tie in with the stem. I imagined a person being afraid of a bee about to sting him. The mnemonic: COWARDLIEST. That's not a real word, but for mnemonic's sake, it provides me the information I need to know. Some stems do not spell real words and some of the letters they combine with lack vowels, making mnemonics a bit of a challenge. For example, the stem AEEIRT does not unscramble to an acceptable six-letter word, and the letters that combine with it, LMNPRST, hardly look promising for a mnemonic. But Dr. James Cherry rearranged the stem to spell TEARIE, and, by inserting vowels, got the mnemonic PERSONAL LAMENTATION. Dr. John Chew developed and maintains "The Canonical List of Anamonics" at http://www.math.toronto.edu/jjchew/scrabble/anamonics.html. The reader is referred to Chew's list for mnemonic authors (where known) as well as some alternatives to the ones I've selected below. He also invites the creation and submission of new mnemonics. On the list of stems below, some are hyphenated shorter words. Three asterisked stems (59-OATIES, 66-TEARIE, and 99-OALIES) are not acceptable words. A mnemonic preceded by an asterisk indicates that the stem takes *no* vowels, but have been inserted only for mnemonic purposes. With the exception of 65-TENIAE (+A = TAENIAE) and 74-EOLIAN (+A = AEOLIAN), all other stems with four vowels do not combine with a fifth vowel.

SN	Stem	Mnemonic
==	======	========
1	TISANE	TUCKSHOP WIZ FIXES MEDICINAL BEVERAGE
2	SATIRE	BAD SPEECH REVIEW--FLAMING WIT
3	RETAIN	SMUG WIFE KEEPS THE CHILDREN
4	ARSINE	POISON MIGHT KILL OFF THRIVING CHILD
5	SENIOR	OLD MVP JOGS WITH A CRUTCH
6	STERNA	MAN WORKING OUT DEVELOPS THICK BONE
7	TOE-SIN	IS TO MARCH WITH PLAIN BOOT WAX
8	ORATES	ADAMANT PREACHERS CALLED BRAGGARTS
9	REASON	BIG LECTURES TRIUMPH
10	INSERT	WOMEN SHOVED STUCK FLAGPOLE
11	TONERS	HARD PECKS OF BIG TOUGHMAN
12	EASTER	CHRIST BACK UP; GOD WILL FIX MAN
13	AIDERS	HELP FIX TRUCK BOMB? NEVER!
14	RAINED	DAMP RAINS BROUGHT HAVOC
15	LESION	TUMOR? PAGE SKILFUL DOCTOR
16	TORIES	BUNCH OF OLD GRUMPS
17	TOILES	PREZ GOT CAUGHT HAVING MONICA
18	SERIAL	A CHANGEABLE TV DRAMA (JAWS?)
19	NAILER	VEXES SPOCK MIGHTILY
20	ALIENS	SPOCK'S FOXY VW BUG HOLDS TO FORM
21	I-ON-SEA	*MIMIC ATOP GRAVEL
22	SALTIE	FIZZ BLOCKS DRIVING SHIP
23	RETAIL	CHUMP-Y LENDER TURNS BUCKS
24	RETIES	SHACKLED MAZE PREVENTS ESCAPE
25	ENTIRE	IN GREAT CHUNKS
26	SAD-TIE	CURES WOVEN GLUM
27	ATONES	TIP CUP--RID GUILT
28	SOLATE	FRIZZING VIBES HENPECKED ME
29	OR-ALES	AM: THE HANDSOME, PM: THE DOGFACED
30	I-SAT-ON	MEN ELECT A GREEK REBEL
31	SAINED	BRAVE FELT CRAMPED
32	DORIES	MEAN WAVES TOPPLE BOATS
33	GAINER	FAT PREZ WATCHED ELEVEN BALL GAMES
34	LISTER	CHIEF JOB: MAKING UP LISTS
35	ENTERS	CONVEX PORTALS GUIDE WAY
36	SALTER	MUCKED UP BEST OF PUDDING--VILE WHIFF
37	TIRADE	SHARP TALK BY AN ANGRY VAMP
38	SILENT	UNCLE SPEAKING NO WORD
39	DIALER	CALL UP YOUR BRAVEST G.I.
40	LADIES	DIMPLED VENUSES HURT BOYS
41	DATERS	NEWLY BETROTHED FEMME PICKED VEIL
42	SNIDER	WIMP KVETCHING ABOUT WIFE
43	ADORES	FIRM TRUST; VIVID GLOW
44	SEEN-IT	RIVAL HAD SIX DYNAMIC HANDS
45	SERINE	EXPERT CHEWS VEG, FEELS REDEEMED
46	LATENS	RUDE COP GAVE HIM A TICKET
47	STANED	PUT A LIGHT ROCK OVER ME
48	TENAIL	KEEPS MOVER GRUFF
49	TEINDS	GLUM TURK PAYS TEINDS
50	DESIRE	ZEALOUS FANS CRAVED TOP BALLGAME

SN	Stem	Mnemonic
==	======	========
51	SENATE	CHIMPS JIGGLING DIRT
52	LEARNS	GO, MIND, KEEP TRACK!
53	SENITI[1]	WE KEEP BANK OF TONGA VAULT LOCKED
54	ORIENT	JUST SNUG PUB CULT
55	TRAINS	GLOBAL CHOO-CHOO PUMPS AQUA STEAM
56	STRIDE	BRISK CHAP RUNS OVER HERE
57	INTROS	HUGGING PAL FACE TO FACE
58	SANDER	WHIZ-KID'S FLIGHT: SPRUCED LUMBER
59	OATIES*	*MONOPOLIZED MIKE
60	STORED	HE PUT AWAY ONE BOTTLE OF MILK
61	TODIES	MAJOR CHUTZPAH FOOD
62	OILERS	DUMP CRUD, GOBS, TONS
63	ANI-TOE	*SOME ANIS CLIMB
64	STEROL	COMPLETED FIVE WHIFF JOBS: AAH!
65	TENIAE	LABS AMASS LARVA
66	TEARIE*	*PERSONAL LAMENTATION
67	NEROLI	SEAPORT
68	RANEES	LOOK DOWN ON COMMON GROTTO
69	SOIGNE	A JEW BELCHED PROUDLY
70	ARIOSE	*PAN BAD VOICE
71	DETAIN	I'D VISIT FRUMP
72	SINGER[2]	WE LOVE THE CRAZY POP SOUND OF BOY GEORGE
73	EASIER	*LET MAID WIPE FLOOR
74	EOLIAN	STAR PARKA
75	RESALE	HOCKEY TICKET DID GET EXPENSIVE
76	UNITER	GRABBED MORE VOTES
77	SOILED	DRIBBLED MILK ON MY PARKA
78	STEREO	VANDALS MARK MAHARAJA'S TV
79	LINERS	KEPT ABOVE MIG
80	ALE-ROT	LURCH, GUV! PUFF BUDS
81	ENTOIL	A CHAP GUARDS A VW
82	GARNET	WONDROUSLY PUFFY MINERAL
83	EASING	BOOK ON COMFORT: GULP OUZO
84	OIL-SAT	NEXT BUG CRAMP
85	TINIER	MAN CHANGED A VW FLAT
86	ATE-SOD	RIN TIN TIN BIT CLIPPING
87	SNORED	CIVIL WHIMPER BURSTED
88	ELITES	POSH FOLKS GOVERNED COMPLEX
89	INMATE	RELAXING BY HIS CELL DOOR
90	NEATER	SLICK RV, RIGHT?
91	LANOSE	PITCHER
92	GREATS	HAVING PERSONALITY
93	ATTIRE	CAP, SCARF, AND BELT
94	TRONAS	MINUTE COPY
95	TUNERS	OLD PIANOS BECOME RIGHT
96	PRAISE	APPROVED MEN WATCH US
97	DOE-RAN	CLIMB UP GRID
98	SUITER	GROOM HOLDS OFF ON PVQ COMBO
99	OALIES*	*CON DEBATING
100	ALDERS	FIR'S THORNS PRICKLED TWO BUMS

[1]SENITI (#53) is a monetary unit of Tonga. This clever mnemonic was provided by Mic Barron (who, despite his name, looks nothing like me). Alternatively, especially when a stem takes many letters, one may devise a "negamonic," coined by Bob Lipton, a mnemonic using the letters with which the stem does *not* combine, here HIJMQRSXYZ. Thanks to Chris Cree's and Pat Barrett's suggestions, which led to this: Turn SENITI to TINIES (not a real word), then the negamonic would be: "SHRIM'Y, no biggies (JQXZ)." TINIES-SHRIMY works nicely for me.

[2]SINGER (#72) does not combine with IJKMQX. Think of a singer attempting a sound mix or voice-overs of a Jack, Queen, and King, or, more simply, a singer playing cards. The negamonic for SINGER is "MIX JQK."

Type I Sevens, by Bingo Stem, With Mnemonics

#	Stem	Mnemonic
1	TISANE	TUCKSHOP WIZ FIXES MEDICINAL BEVERAGE
2	SATIRE	BAD SPEECH REVIEW--FLAMING WIT
3	RETAIN	SMUG WIFE KEEPS THE CHILDREN
4	ARSINE	POISON MIGHT KILL OFF THRIVING CHILD
5	SENIOR	OLD MVP JOGS WITH A CRUTCH
6	STERNA	MAN WORKING OUT DEVELOPS THICK BONE
7	TOE-SIN	IS TO MARCH WITH PLAIN BOOT WAX
8	ORATES	ADAMANT PREACHERS CALLED BRAGGARTS
9	REASON	BIG LECTURES TRIUMPH
10	INSERT	WOMEN SHOVED STUCK FLAGPOLE
11	TONERS	HARD PECKS OF BIG TOUGHMAN
12	EASTER	CHRIST BACK UP; GOD WILL FIX MAN
13	AIDERS	HELP FIX TRUCK BOMB? NEVER!
14	RAINED	DAMP RAINS BROUGHT HAVOC
15	LESION	TUMOR? PAGE SKILFUL DOCTOR
16	TORIES	BUNCH OF OLD GRUMPS

1 TISANE

A ENTASIA
TAENIAS
B BANTIES
BASINET
C ACETINS
CINEAST
D DESTAIN
DETAINS
INSTEAD
NIDATES
SAINTED
STAINED
E ETESIAN
F FAINEST
G EASTING
EATINGS
INGATES
INGESTA
SEATING
TEASING
H SHEITAN
STHENIA
I ISATINE
K INTAKES
L ELASTIN
ENTAILS
NAILSET
SALIENT
SALTINE
SLAINTE
TENAILS
M ETAMINS
INMATES
TAMEINS
N INANEST
STANINE
O ATONIES
P PANTIES
PATINES
SAPIENT
SPINATE
R ANESTRI
ANTSIER
NASTIER
RATINES
RETAINS
RETINAS
RETSINA
STAINER
STEARIN
S ENTASIS
NASTIES
SEITANS
SESTINA
TANSIES
TISANES
T INSTATE
SATINET
U AUNTIES
SINUATE
V NAIVEST
NATIVES
VAINEST
W TAWNIES
WANIEST
X ANTISEX
SEXTAIN
Z ZANIEST
ZEATINS

2 SATIRE

A ARISTAE
ASTERIA
ATRESIA
B BAITERS
BARITES
REBAITS
TERBIAS
C ATRESIC
CRISTAE
RACIEST
STEARIC
D ARIDEST
ASTRIDE
DIASTER
DISRATE
STAIDER
TARDIES
TIRADES
E AERIEST
SERIATE
F FAIREST
G AIGRETS
GAITERS
SEAGIRT
STAGIER
TRIAGES
H HASTIER
I AIRIEST
L REALIST
RETAILS
SALTIER
SALTIRE
SLATIER
TAILERS
M IMARETS
MAESTRI
MISRATE
SMARTIE
N ANESTRI
ANTSIER
NASTIER
RATINES
RETAINS
RETINAS
RETSINA
STAINER
STEARIN
P PARTIES
PASTIER
PIASTER
PIASTRE
PIRATES
TRAIPSE
R ARTSIER
TARRIES
TARSIER
S SATIRES
T ARTIEST
ARTISTE
ATTIRES
IRATEST
RATITES
STRIATE
TASTIER
V VASTIER
VERITAS
W WAISTER
WAITERS
WARIEST
WASTRIE

3 RETAIN

C CERATIN
CERTAIN
CREATIN
TACRINE
D ANTIRED
DETRAIN
TRAINED
E ARENITE
RETINAE
TRAINEE
F FAINTER
G GRANITE
GRATINE
INGRATE
TANGIER
TEARING
H HAIRNET
INEARTH
THERIAN
I INERTIA
K KERATIN
L LATRINE
RATLINE
RELIANT
RETINAL
TRENAIL
M MINARET
RAIMENT
N ENTRAIN
P PAINTER
PERTAIN
REPAINT
R RETRAIN
TERRAIN
TRAINER
S ANESTRI
ANTSIER
NASTIER
RATINES
RETAINS
RETINAS
RETSINA
STAINER
STEARIN
T INTREAT
ITERANT
NATTIER
NITRATE
TERTIAN
U RUINATE
TAURINE
URANITE
URINATE
W TAWNIER
TINWARE

4 ARSINE

C ARCSINE
ARSENIC
CARNIES
D RANDIES
SANDIER
SARDINE
F INFARES
G EARINGS
ERASING
GAINERS
REAGINS
REGAINS
REGINAS
SEARING
SERINGA
H HERNIAS
I SENARII
K SNAKIER
L ALINERS
NAILERS
RENAILS
M MARINES
REMAINS
SEMINAR
N INSANER
INSNARE
O ERASION
P PANIERS
RAPINES
R SIERRAN
S ARSINES
T ANESTRI
ANTSIER
NASTIER
RATINES
RETAINS
RETINAS
RETSINA
STAINER
STEARIN
V RAVINES

5 SENIOR

A ERASION
C COINERS
CRONIES
ORCEINS
RECOINS
D DINEROS
INDORSE
ORDINES
ROSINED
SORDINE
G ERINGOS
IGNORES
REGIONS
SIGNORE
H HEROINS
INSHORE
I IRONIES
NOISIER
J JOINERS
REJOINS
L NEROLIS
M MERINOS
O EROSION
P ORPINES
R IRONERS
S SENIORS
SONSIER
T NORITES
OESTRIN
ORIENTS
STONIER
U URINOSE
V ENVIROS
RENVOIS
VERSION
W SNOWIER

6 STERNA

A SANTERA
B BANTERS
C CANTERS
CARNETS
NECTARS
RECANTS
SCANTER
TANRECS
TRANCES
D STANDER
E EARNEST
EASTERN
NEAREST
G ARGENTS
GARNETS
STRANGE
H ANTHERS
THENARS
I ANESTRI
ANTSIER
NASTIER
RATINES
RETAINS
RETINAS
RETSINA
STAINER
STEARIN
K RANKEST
TANKERS
L ANTLERS
RENTALS
SALTERN
STERNAL
M MARTENS
SARMENT
SMARTEN
N TANNERS
O ATONERS
SANTERO
SENATOR
TREASON
P ARPENTS
ENTRAPS
PARENTS
PASTERN
TREPANS
R ERRANTS
RANTERS
S SARSNET
T NATTERS
RATTENS
U NATURES
SAUNTER
V SERVANT
TAVERNS
VERSANT
W WANTERS

7 TOESIN

A ATONIES
B BONIEST
C NOTICES
SECTION
H ETHIONS
HISTONE
I INOSITE
L ENTOILS
M MESTINO
MOISTEN
SENTIMO
N INTONES
TENSION
O ISOTONE
TOONIES
P PINTOES
POINTES
R NORITES
OESTRIN
ORIENTS
STONIER
S NOSIEST
T TONIEST
W TOWNIES
X TOXINES

8 ORATES

A AEROSAT
B BOASTER
BOATERS
BORATES
REBATOS
SORBATE
C COASTER
COATERS
RECOATS
D ROASTED
TORSADE
E ROSEATE
G GAROTES
ORGEATS
STORAGE
H EARSHOT
L OLESTRA
M MAESTRO
N ATONERS
SANTERO
SENATOR
TREASON
P ESPARTO
PROTEAS
SEAPORT
R ROASTER
S OSETRAS
OSSETRA
T ROTATES
TOASTER

9 REASON

B BORANES
C CANOERS
COARSEN
CORNEAS
NARCOSE
E ARENOSE
G ONAGERS
ORANGES
H HOARSEN
SENHORA
I ERASION
L LOANERS
RELOANS
M ENAMORS
MOANERS
OARSMEN
P PERSONA
R SERRANO
S REASONS
SENORAS
T ATONERS
SANTERO
SENATOR
TREASON
U ARENOUS

10 INSERT

A ANESTRI
ANTSIER
NASTIER
RATINES
RETAINS
RETINAS
RETSINA
STAINER
STEARIN
C CISTERN
CRETINS
D TINDERS
E ENTIRES
ENTRIES
RETINES
TRIENES
F SNIFTER
G RESTING
STINGER
H HINTERS
K REKNITS
STINKER
TINKERS
L LINTERS
M MINSTER
MINTERS
REMINTS
N INTERNS
TINNERS
O NORITES
OESTRIN
ORIENTS
STONIER
P PTERINS
S ESTRINS
INSERTS
SINTERS
T RETINTS
STINTER
TINTERS
U NUTSIER
TRIUNES
UNITERS
V INVERTS
STRIVEN
W TWINERS
WINTERS

11 TONERS

A ATONERS
SANTERO
SENATOR
TREASON
B SORBENT
C CORNETS
D RODENTS
SNORTED
E ESTRONE
F FRONTES
G TONGERS
H HORNETS
SHORTEN
THRONES
I NORITES
OESTRIN
ORIENTS
STONIER
K REKNOTS
M MENTORS
MONSTER
N TONNERS
O ENROOTS
P POSTERN
R SNORTER
S NESTORS
STONERS
TENSORS
T STENTOR
U TENOURS
TONSURE

12 EASTER

A AERATES
B BEATERS
BERATES
REBATES
C CERATES
CREATES
ECARTES
D DEAREST
DERATES
REDATES
SEDATER
F AFREETS
FEASTER
G ERGATES
RESTAGE
H AETHERS
HEATERS
REHEATS
I AERIEST
SERIATE
K RETAKES
L ELATERS
REALEST
RELATES
RESLATE
STEALER
M REMATES
RETEAMS
STEAMER
N EARNEST
EASTERN
NEAREST
O ROSEATE
P REPEATS
RETAPES
R RETEARS
SERRATE
TEARERS
S EASTERS
RESEATS
SEAREST
SEATERS
TEASERS
TESSERA
T ESTREAT
RESTATE
RETASTE
U AUSTERE
W SWEATER
X RETAXES

13 AIDERS

B ABIDERS
BRAISED
DARBIES
SEABIRD
SIDEBAR
C RADICES
SIDECAR
E DEARIES
READIES
F FARSIDE
H AIRSHED
DASHIER
HARDIES
SHADIER
I DAIRIES
DIARIES
K DAIKERS
DARKIES
L DERAILS
DIALERS
REDIALS
M ADMIRES
MISREAD
SEDARIM
SIDEARM
N RANDIES
SANDIER
SARDINE
O ROADIES
P ASPIRED
DESPAIR
DIAPERS
PRAISED
R RAIDERS
T ARIDEST
ASTRIDE
DIASTER
DISRATE
STAIDER
TARDIES
TIRADES
U RESIDUA
V ADVISER
X RADIXES

14 RAINED

A ARANEID
B BRAINED
C CAIRNED
D DANDIER
DRAINED
G DERAIGN
GRADINE
GRAINED
READING
H HANDIER
I DENARII
M INARMED
N NARDINE
O ANEROID
P PARDINE
R DRAINER
RANDIER
S RANDIES
SANDIER
SARDINE
T ANTIRED
DETRAIN
TRAINED
U UNAIRED
URANIDE
V INVADER
RAVINED

15 LESION

A ANISOLE
C CINEOLS
INCLOSE
D INDOLES
E OLEINES
F OLEFINS
G ELOIGNS
LEGIONS
LINGOES
LONGIES
I ELISION
ISOLINE
LIONISE
K SONLIKE
L NIELLOS
M LOMEINS
O LOONIES
P EPSILON
PINOLES
R NEROLIS
S INSOLES
LESIONS
LIONESS
T ENTOILS
U ELUSION

16 TORIES

B ORBIEST
C EROTICS
D EDITORS
SORTIED
STEROID
STORIED
TRIODES
F FORTIES
G GOITERS
GOITRES
GORIEST
H HERIOTS
HOISTER
SHORTIE
L ESTRIOL
LOITERS
TOILERS
M EROTISM
MOISTER
MORTISE
TRISOME
N NORITES
OESTRIN
ORIENTS
STONIER
O SOOTIER
P PROSTIE
REPOSIT
RIPOSTE
ROPIEST
R RIOTERS
ROISTER
S ROSIEST
SORITES
SORTIES
STORIES
TRIOSES
U STOURIE

17 TOILES PREZ GOT CAUGHT HAVING MONICA
18 SERIAL A CHANGEABLE TV DRAMA (JAWS?)
19 NAILER VEXES SPOCK MIGHTILY
20 ALIENS SPOCK'S FOXY VW BUG HOLDS TO FORM
21 I-ON-SEA *MIMIC ATOP GRAVEL
22 SALTIE FIZZ BLOCKS DRIVING SHIP
23 RETAIL CHUMP-Y LENDER TURNS BUCKS
24 RETIES SHACKLED MAZE PREVENTS ESCAPE
25 ENTIRE IN GREAT CHUNKS
26 SAD-TIE CURES WOVEN GLUM
27 ATONES TIP CUP--RID GUILT
28 SOLATE FRIZZING VIBES HENPECKED ME
29 OR-ALES AM: THE HANDSOME, PM: THE DOGFACED
30 I-SAT-ON MEN ELECT A GREEK REBEL
31 SAINED BRAVE FELT CRAMPED
32 DORIES MEAN WAVES TOPPLE BOATS
33 GAINER FAT PREZ WATCHED ELEVEN BALL GAMES
34 LISTER CHIEF JOB: MAKING UP LISTS
35 ENTERS CONVEX PORTALS GUIDE WAY
36 SALTER MUCKED UP BEST OF PUDDING--VILE WHIFF

17 TOILES

A ISOLATE
C CITOLES
E ETOILES
G LOGIEST
H EOLITHS
HOLIEST
HOSTILE
I IOLITES
OILIEST
M MOTILES
N ENTOILS
O OOLITES
OSTIOLE
STOOLIE
P PIOLETS
PISTOLE
R ESTRIOL
LOITERS
TOILERS
T LITOTES
TOILETS
U OUTLIES
V VIOLETS
Z ZLOTIES

18 SERIAL

A AERIALS
B BAILERS
C CLARIES
ECLAIRS
SCALIER
D DERAILS
DIALERS
REDIALS
E REALISE
G GLAIRES
H HAILERS
SHALIER
J JAILERS
L RALLIES
SALLIER
M MAILERS
REALISM
REMAILS
N ALINERS
NAILERS
RENAILS
R RAILERS
S AIRLESS
RESAILS
SAILERS
SERAILS
SERIALS
T REALIST
RETAILS
SALTIER
SALTIRE
SLATIER
TAILERS
V REVISAL
W WAILERS

19 NAILER

C CARLINE
E ALIENER
G ALIGNER
ENGRAIL
NARGILE
REALIGN
REGINAL
H HERNIAL
INHALER
I AIRLINE
K LANKIER
L RALLINE
M MANLIER
MARLINE
MINERAL
O AILERON
ALIENOR
P PLAINER
PRALINE
S ALINERS
NAILERS
RENAILS
T LATRINE
RATLINE
RELIANT
RETINAL
TRENAIL
V RAVELIN
X RELAXIN
Y INLAYER

20 ALIENS

B LESBIAN
C INLACES
SANICLE
SCALENI
D DENIALS
SNAILED
F FINALES
G LEASING
LINAGES
SEALING
H INHALES
K ALKINES
L AINSELL
M MALINES
MENIALS
SEMINAL
O ANISOLE
P ALPINES
PINEALS
SPANIEL
SPLENIA
R ALINERS
NAILERS
RENAILS
S SALINES
SILANES
T ELASTIN
ENTAILS
NAILSET
SALIENT
SALTINE
SLAINTE
TENAILS
U INULASE
V ALEVINS
VALINES
W LAWINES
X ALEXINS
Y ELYSIAN

21 IONSEA

C ACINOSE
G AGONIES
AGONISE
L ANISOLE
M ANOMIES
P EPINAOS
SENOPIA
R ERASION
T ATONIES
V EVASION

22 SALTIE

B ABLEIST
ALBITES
ASTILBE
BASTILE
BESTIAL
BLASTIE
STABILE
C ELASTIC
LACIEST
LATICES
D DETAILS
DILATES
F FETIALS
SEALIFT
G AIGLETS
GELATIS
LIGATES
H HALITES
HELIAST
I LAITIES
K LAKIEST
TALKIES
L TAILLES
TALLIES
N ELASTIN
ENTAILS
NAILSET
SALIENT
SALTINE
SLAINTE
TENAILS
O ISOLATE
P APLITES
PALIEST
PLATIES
TALIPES
R REALIST
RETAILS
SALTIER
SALTIRE
SLATIER
TAILERS
S SALTIES
V ESTIVAL
Z LAZIEST

23 RETAIL

B LIBRATE
TRIABLE
C ARTICLE
RECITAL
D DILATER
REDTAIL
TRAILED
E ATELIER
H LATHIER
K RATLIKE
TALKIER
L LITERAL
TALLIER
M MALTIER
MARLITE
N LATRINE
RATLINE
RELIANT
RETINAL
TRENAIL
P PLAITER
PLATIER
R RETRIAL
TRAILER
S REALIST
RETAILS
SALTIER
SALTIRE
SLATIER
TAILERS
T TERTIAL
U URALITE
Y IRATELY
REALITY
TEARILY

24 RETIES

A AERIEST
SERIATE
C CERITES
RECITES
TIERCES
D DIESTER
DIETERS
REEDITS
RESITED
E EERIEST
H HEISTER
K KEISTER
KIESTER
L LEISTER
RETILES
STERILE
M MEISTER
METIERS
REEMITS
RETIMES
TRISEME
N ENTIRES
ENTRIES
RETINES
TRIENES
P PESTIER
RESPITE
R RETIRES
RETRIES
TERRIES
S RESITES
T TESTIER
V RESTIVE
SIEVERT
VERIEST
VERITES
Z ZESTIER

25 ENTIRE

A ARENITE
RETINAE
TRAINEE
C ENTERIC
ENTICER
E TEENIER
G INTEGER
TREEING
H NEITHER
THEREIN
I NITERIE
K KERNITE
N INTERNE
R REINTER
RENTIER
TERRINE
S ENTIRES
ENTRIES
RETINES
TRIENES
T NETTIER
TENTIER
U RETINUE
REUNITE
UTERINE

26 SADTIE

C DACITES
E IDEATES
G AGISTED
L DETAILS
DILATES
M DIASTEM
MISDATE
N DESTAIN
DETAINS
INSTEAD
NIDATES
SAINTED
STAINED
O IODATES
TOADIES
R ARIDEST
ASTRIDE
DIASTER
DISRATE
STAIDER
TARDIES
TIRADES
S DISSEAT
U DAUTIES
V DATIVES
VISTAED
W DAWTIES
WAISTED

27 ATONES

C OCTANES
D DONATES
G ONSTAGE
I ATONIES
L ETALONS
TOLANES
P TEOPANS
R ATONERS
SANTERO
SENATOR
TREASON
T NOTATES
U SOUTANE

28 SOLATE

B BOATELS
OBLATES
C LACTOSE
LOCATES
TALCOSE
D SOLATED
E OLEATES
F FOLATES
G GELATOS
LEGATOS
H LOATHES
I ISOLATE
K SKATOLE
M MALTOSE
N ETALONS
TOLANES
P APOSTLE
PELOTAS
R OLESTRA
S SOLATES
V SOLVATE
Z ZEALOTS

29 ORALES

A AREOLAS
C CLAROES
COALERS
ESCOLAR
ORACLES
RECOALS
SOLACER
D LOADERS
ORDEALS
RELOADS
E AREOLES
F LOAFERS
SAFROLE
G GALORES
GAOLERS
H SHOALER
M MORALES
N LOANERS
RELOANS
O AEROSOL
ROSEOLA
P PAROLES
REPOSAL
S LASSOER
OARLESS
SEROSAL
T OLESTRA

30 ISATON

A ATONIAS
B BASTION
BONITAS
OBTAINS
C ACTIONS
ATONICS
CATIONS
E ATONIES
G AGONIST
GITANOS
K KATIONS
L LATINOS
TALIONS
M MANITOS
N ANOINTS
NATIONS
ONANIST
R AROINTS
RATIONS
T STATION

31 SAINED

A NAIADES
B BANDIES
BASINED
C CANDIES
INCASED
D DANDIES
E ANISEED
F FADEINS
L DENIALS
SNAILED
M MAIDENS
MEDIANS
MEDINAS
SIDEMAN
P PANDIES
R RANDIES
SANDIER
SARDINE
T DESTAIN
DETAINS
INSTEAD
NIDATES
SAINTED
STAINED
V INVADES

32 DORIES

A ROADIES
B BORIDES
DISROBE
E OREIDES
OSIERED
L SOLDIER
SOLIDER
M MISDOER
N DINEROS
INDORSE
ORDINES
ROSINED
SORDINE
O OROIDES
P PERIODS
S DOSSIER
T EDITORS
SORTIED
STEROID
STORIED
TRIODES
V DEVISOR
DEVOIRS
VISORED
VOIDERS
W DOWRIES
ROWDIES
WEIRDOS

33 GAINER

A ANERGIA
B BEARING
C ANERGIC
D DERAIGN
GRADINE
GRAINED
READING
E REGINAE
F FEARING
G GEARING
NAGGIER
H HEARING
L ALIGNER
ENGRAIL
NARGILE
REALIGN
REGINAL
M GERMINA
MANGIER
REAMING
N AGINNER
EARNING
ENGRAIN
GRANNIE
NEARING
P REAPING
R ANGRIER
EARRING
GRAINER
RANGIER
REARING
S EARINGS
ERASING
GAINERS
REAGINS
REGAINS
REGINAS
SEARING
SERINGA
T GRANITE
GRATINE
INGRATE
TANGIER
TEARING
V REAVING
VINEGAR
W WEARING
Z ZINGARE

34 LISTER

A REALIST
RETAILS
SALTIER
SALTIRE
SLATIER
TAILERS
B BLISTER
BRISTLE
RIBLETS
C RELICTS
E LEISTER
RETILES
STERILE
F FILTERS
LIFTERS
STIFLER
TRIFLES
G GLISTER
GRISTLE
H SLITHER
I SILTIER
J JILTERS
K KILTERS
KIRTLES
KLISTER
L RILLETS
STILLER
TILLERS
TRELLIS
M MILTERS
N LINTERS
O ESTRIOL
LOITERS
TOILERS
P RESPLIT
TRIPLES
S LISTERS
RELISTS
T LITTERS
SLITTER
TILTERS
U LUSTIER
RULIEST
RUTILES

35 ENTERS

A EARNEST
EASTERN
NEAREST
C CENTERS
CENTRES
TENRECS
D TENDERS
E ENTREES
RETENES
TEENERS
G GERENTS
REGENTS
I ENTIRES
ENTRIES
RETINES
TRIENES
L NESTLER
RELENTS
N RENNETS
TENNERS
O ESTRONE
P PENSTER
PRESENT
REPENTS
SERPENT
R RENTERS
RERENTS
STERNER
S NESTERS
RENESTS
RESENTS
T NETTERS
TENTERS
U NEUTERS
RETUNES
TENURES
TUREENS
V VENTERS
W WESTERN
X EXTERNS
Y STYRENE
YESTERN

36 SALTER

B BLASTER
LABRETS
STABLER
C CARTELS
CLARETS
CRESTAL
SCARLET
D DARTLES
E ELATERS
REALEST
RELATES
RESLATE
STEALER
F FALTERS
G LARGEST
H HALTERS
HARSLET
LATHERS
SLATHER
THALERS
I REALIST
RETAILS
SALTIER
SALTIRE
SLATIER
TAILERS
K STALKER
TALKERS
L STELLAR
M ARMLETS
LAMSTER
TRAMELS
N ANTLERS
RENTALS
SALTERN
STERNAL
O OLESTRA
P PALTERS
PERSALT
PLASTER
PLATERS
PSALTER
STAPLER
S ARTLESS
LASTERS
SALTERS
SLATERS
T RATTLES
STARLET
STARTLE
U ESTRUAL
SALUTER
V TRAVELS
VARLETS
VESTRAL
W WARSTLE
WASTREL
WRASTLE

37	TIRADE	SHARP TALK BY AN ANGRY VAMP	48	TENAIL	KEEPS MOVER GRUFF
38	SILENT	UNCLE SPEAKING NO WORD	49	TEINDS	GLUM TURK PAYS TEINDS
39	DIALER	CALL UP YOUR BRAVEST G.I.	50	DESIRE	ZEALOUS FANS CRAVED TOP BALLGAME
40	LADIES	DIMPLED VENUSES HURT BOYS	51	SENATE	CHIMPS JIGGLING DIRT
41	DATERS	NEWLY BETROTHED FEMME PICKED VEIL	52	LEARNS	GO, MIND, KEEP TRACK!
42	SNIDER	WIMP KVETCHING ABOUT WIFE	53	SENITI	WE KEEP BANK OF TONGA VAULT LOCKED
43	ADORES	FIRM TRUST; VIVID GLOW	54	ORIENT	JUST SNUG PUB CULT
44	SERINE	EXPERT CHEWS VEG, FEELS REDEEMED	55	TRAINS	GLOBAL CHOO-CHOO PUMPS AQUA STEAM
45	SEEN-IT	RIVAL HAD SIX DYNAMIC HANDS	56	STRIDE	BRISK CHAP RUNS OVER HERE
46	LATENS	RUDE COP GAVE HIM A TICKET	57	INTROS	HUGGING PAL FACE TO FACE
47	STANED	PUT A LIGHT ROCK OVER ME	58	SANDER	WHIZ-KID'S FLIGHT: SPRUCED LUMBER

37 TIRADE

A AIRDATE
RADIATE
TIARAED
B REDBAIT
TRIBADE
G TRIAGED
H AIRTHED
K TRAIKED
L DILATER
REDTAIL
TRAILED
M READMIT
N ANTIRED
DETRAIN
TRAINED
P DIPTERA
PARTIED
PIRATED
R TARDIER
TARRIED
S ARIDEST
ASTRIDE
DIASTER
DISRATE
STAIDER
TARDIES
TIRADES
T ATTIRED
V TARDIVE
Y DIETARY

38 SILENT

A ELASTIN
ENTAILS
NAILSET
SALIENT
SALTINE
SLAINTE
TENAILS
C CLIENTS
LECTINS
STENCIL
D DENTILS
E LENITES
LISENTE
SETLINE
TENSILE
G GLISTEN
SINGLET
SNIGLET
TINGLES
I LINIEST
K LENTISK
TINKLES
L LENTILS
LINTELS
N LINNETS
O ENTOILS
P LEPTINS
PINTLES
PLENIST
R LINTERS
S ENLISTS
LISTENS
SILENTS
TINSELS
U LUNIEST
LUTEINS
UTENSIL
W WINTLES

39 DIALER

A RADIALE
B BEDRAIL
BRAILED
RIDABLE
C DECRIAL
RADICEL
RADICLE
E LEADIER
G GLADIER
GLAIRED
I DELIRIA
L DALLIER
DIALLER
RALLIED
O DARIOLE
P LIPREAD
PREDIAL
R LARDIER
S DERAILS
DIALERS
REDIALS
T DILATER
REDTAIL
TRAILED
U UREDIAL
V RIVALED
Y READILY

40 LADIES

B BALDIES
DISABLE
D LADDIES
E AEDILES
H HALIDES
I DAILIES
LIAISED
SEDILIA
L DALLIES
SALLIED
M MEDIALS
MISDEAL
MISLEAD
N DENIALS
SNAILED
O ISOLEAD
P ALIPEDS
ELAPIDS
LAPIDES
PALSIED
PLEIADS
R DERAILS
DIALERS
REDIALS
S AIDLESS
T DETAILS
DILATES
U AUDILES
V DEVISAL
Y DIALYSE

41 DATERS

B DABSTER
C REDACTS
SCARTED
D ADDREST
E DEAREST
DERATES
REDATES
SEDATER
F STRAFED
H DEARTHS
HARDEST
HARDSET
HATREDS
THREADS
TRASHED
I ARIDEST
ASTRIDE
DIASTER
DISRATE
STAIDER
TARDIES
TIRADES
K DARKEST
STRAKED
L DARTLES
M SMARTED
N STANDER
O ROASTED
TORSADE
P DEPARTS
PETARDS
R DARTERS
RETARDS
STARRED
TRADERS
T STARTED
TETRADS
V ADVERTS
STARVED
W STEWARD
STRAWED
Y STRAYED

42 SNIDER

A RANDIES
SANDIER
SARDINE
B BINDERS
INBREDS
REBINDS
C CINDERS
DISCERN
RESCIND
E DENIERS
NEREIDS
RESINED
F FINDERS
FRIENDS
REDFINS
REFINDS
G DINGERS
ENGIRDS
H HINDERS
NERDISH
SHRINED
I INSIDER
K REDSKIN
M MINDERS
REMINDS
N DINNERS
ENDRINS
O DINEROS
INDORSE
ORDINES
ROSINED
SORDINE
P PINDERS
T TINDERS
U INSURED
V VERDINS
W REWINDS
WINDERS

43 ADORES

D DEODARS
F FEDORAS
G DOGEARS
I ROADIES
L LOADERS
ORDEALS
RELOADS
M RADOMES
O ROADEOS
R ADORERS
DROSERA
S SARODES
T ROASTED
TORSADE
U AROUSED
V OVERSAD
SAVORED
W REDOWAS

44 SERINE

C SINCERE
D DENIERS
NEREIDS
RESINED
E ESERINE
F REFINES
G GREISEN
H HENRIES
INHERES
RESHINE
L LIERNES
RELINES
M ERMINES
P EREPSIN
REPINES
R RERISEN
S SEINERS
SEREINS
SERINES
T ENTIRES
ENTRIES
RETINES
TRIENES
V ENVIERS
INVERSE
VEINERS
VENIRES
VERSINE
W NEWSIER
WEINERS
WIENERS
X REXINES

45 SEENIT

A ETESIAN
C ENTICES
D DESTINE
ENDITES
H THEINES
I SIENITE
L LENITES
LISENTE
SETLINE
TENSILE
M EMETINS
N INTENSE
TENNIES
R ENTIRES
ENTRIES
RETINES
TRIENES
S SESTINE
V TENSIVE
X SIXTEEN
Y SYENITE

46 LATENS

A SEALANT
C CANTLES
CENTALS
LANCETS
D DENTALS
SLANTED
E LATEENS
LEANEST
G GELANTS
TANGLES
H HANTLES
I ELASTIN
ENTAILS
NAILSET
SALIENT
SALTINE
SLAINTE
TENAILS
K ANKLETS
LANKEST
M LAMENTS
MANTELS
MANTLES
O ETALONS
TOLANES
P PLANETS
PLATENS
R ANTLERS
RENTALS
SALTERN
STERNAL
T LATENTS
LATTENS
TALENTS
U ELUANTS
V LEVANTS

47 STANED

A ANSATED
C DECANTS
DESCANT
SCANTED
E STANDEE
G STANGED
H HANDSET
I DESTAIN
DETAINS
INSTEAD
NIDATES
SAINTED
STAINED
K DANKEST
L DENTALS
SLANTED
M TANDEMS
O DONATES
P PEDANTS
PENTADS
R STANDER
T ATTENDS
U UNSATED
V ADVENTS

48 TENAIL

E LINEATE
F INFLATE
G ATINGLE
ELATING
GELATIN
GENITAL
TAGLINE
K ANTLIKE
M AILMENT
ALIMENT
O ELATION
TOENAIL
P PANTILE
R LATRINE
RATLINE
RELIANT
RETINAL
TRENAIL
S ELASTIN
ENTAILS
NAILSET
SALIENT
SALTINE
SLAINTE
TENAILS
U ALUNITE
V VENTAIL

49 TEINDS

A DESTAIN
DETAINS
INSTEAD
NIDATES
SAINTED
STAINED
D DISTEND
E DESTINE
ENDITES
G NIDGETS
I INDITES
TINEIDS
K KINDEST
L DENTILS
M MINDSET
MISTEND
N DENTINS
INDENTS
INTENDS
P DIPNETS
STIPEND
R TINDERS
S DISSENT
SNIDEST
T DENTIST
DISTENT
STINTED
U DUNITES
Y DENSITY
DESTINY

50 DESIRE

A DEARIES
READIES
B DERBIES
C DECRIES
DEICERS
D DERIDES
DESIRED
RESIDED
E SEEDIER
F DEFIERS
SERIFED
G SEDGIER
L RESILED
M REMISED
N DENIERS
NEREIDS
RESINED
O OREIDES
OSIERED
P PRESIDE
SPEIRED
SPIERED
R DERRIES
DESIRER
REDRIES
RESIDER
SERRIED
S DESIRES
RESIDES
T DIESTER
DIETERS
REEDITS
RESITED
U RESIDUE
UREIDES
V DERIVES
DEVISER
DIVERSE
REVISED
Z RESIZED

51 SENATE

C CETANES
TENACES
D STANDEE
G NEGATES
H ETHANES
I ETESIAN
J SEJEANT
L LATEENS
LEANEST
M MEANEST
N NEATENS
P NEPETAS
PENATES
R EARNEST
EASTERN
NEAREST
S ENTASES
SATEENS
SENATES
SENSATE
T NEATEST

52 LEARNS

A ARSENAL
C LANCERS
D DARNELS
LANDERS
RELANDS
SLANDER
SNARLED
E LEANERS
G ANGLERS
I ALINERS
NAILERS
RENAILS
K RANKLES
M ALMNERS
N ENSNARL
LANNERS
O LOANERS
RELOANS
P PLANERS
REPLANS
R SNARLER
T ANTLERS
RENTALS
SALTERN
STERNAL

53 SENITI

A ISATINE
B STIBINE
C INCITES
D INDITES
TINEIDS
E SIENITE
F FINITES
NIFTIES
G IGNITES
K INKIEST
L LINIEST
N INTINES
O INOSITE
P PINIEST
PINITES
TIEPINS
T TINIEST
U UNITIES
V INVITES
VINIEST
W WINIEST

54 ORIENT

B BORNITE
C COINTER
NOTICER
G GENITOR
J JOINTER
L RETINOL
N INTONER
TERNION
P POINTER
PROTEIN
TROPINE
S NORITES
OESTRIN
ORIENTS
STONIER
T TRITONE
U ROUTINE

55 TRAINS

A ANTIARS
ARTISAN
TSARINA
B BRISANT
C NARCIST
E ANESTRI
ANTSIER
NASTIER
RATINES
RETAINS
RETINAS
RETSINA
STAINER
STEARIN
G GASTRIN
GRATINS
RATINGS
STARING
H TARNISH
L RATLINS
M MARTINS
O AROINTS
RATIONS
P SPIRANT
Q QINTARS
S INSTARS
SANTIRS
STRAINS
T TRANSIT
U NUTRIAS

56 STRIDE

A ARIDEST
ASTRIDE
DIASTER
DISRATE
STAIDER
TARDIES
TIRADES
B BESTRID
BISTRED
C CREDITS
DIRECTS
E DIESTER
DIETERS
REEDITS
RESITED
H DITHERS
I DIRTIES
DITSIER
TIDIERS
K SKIRTED
N TINDERS
O EDITORS
SORTIED
STEROID
STORIED
TRIODES
P SPIRTED
STRIPED
R STIRRED
STRIDER
S DISSERT
STRIDES
U DUSTIER
STUDIER
V DIVERTS
STRIVED

57 INTROS

A AROINTS
RATIONS
C CISTRON
CITRONS
CORTINS
E NORITES
OESTRIN
ORIENTS
STONIER
F FORINTS
G SORTING
STORING
TRIGONS
H HORNIST
I IRONIST
L NOSTRIL
N INTRONS
O NITROSO
TORSION
P TROPINS
T INTORTS
TRITONS
U NITROUS
TURIONS

58 SANDER

B BANDERS
C DANCERS
D DANDERS
E ENDEARS
F SNARFED
G DANGERS
GANDERS
GARDENS
H HANDERS
HARDENS
I RANDIES
SANDIER
SARDINE
K DARKENS
L DARNELS
LANDERS
RELANDS
SLANDER
SNARLED
M DAMNERS
REMANDS
P PANDERS
R DARNERS
ERRANDS
S SANDERS
T STANDER
U ASUNDER
DANSEUR
W WANDERS
WARDENS
Z ZANDERS

59	OATIES*	*MONOPOLIZED MIKE
60	STORED	HE PUT AWAY ONE BOTTLE OF MILK
61	TODIES	MAJOR CHUTZPAH FOOD
62	OILERS	DUMP CRUD, GOBS, TONS
63	ANI-TOE	*SOME ANIS CLIMB
64	STEROL	COMPLETED FIVE WHIFF JOBS: AAH!
65	TENIAE	LABS AMASS LARVA
66	TEARIE*	*PERSONAL LAMENTATION
67	NEROLI	SEAPORT
68	RANEES	LOOK DOWN ON COMMON GROTTO
69	SOIGNE	A JEW BELCHED PROUDLY
70	ARIOSE	*PAN BAD VOICE
71	DETAIN	I'D VISIT FRUMP
72	SINGER	WE LOVE THE CRAZY POP SOUND OF BOY GEORGE
73	EASIER	*LET MAID WIPE FLOOR
74	EOLIAN	STAR PARKA
75	RESALE	HOCKEY TICKET DID GET EXPENSIVE
76	UNITER	GRABBED MORE VOTES
77	SOILED	DRIBBLED MILK ON MY PARKA
78	STEREO	VANDALS MARK MAHARAJA'S TV
79	LINERS	KEPT ABOVE MIG
80	ALE-ROT	LURCH, GUV! PUFF BUDS
81	ENTOIL	A CHAP GUARDS A VW
82	GARNET	WONDROUSLY PUFFY MINERAL
83	EASING	BOOK ON COMFORT: GULP OUZO
84	OIL-SAT	NEXT BUG CRAMP
85	TINIER	MAN CHANGED A VW FLAT
86	ATE-SOD	RIN TIN TIN BIT CLIPPING
87	SNORED	CIVIL WHIMPER BURSTED

59 OATIES

D IODATES
TOADIES
K OAKIEST
L ISOLATE
M AMOSITE
ATOMIES
ATOMISE
N ATONIES
P ATOPIES
OPIATES
Z AZOTISE

60 STORED

A ROASTED
TORSADE
B DEBTORS
E OERSTED
TEREDOS
F DEFROST
FROSTED
H DEHORTS
SHORTED
I EDITORS
SORTIED
STEROID
STORIED
TRIODES
K STROKED
L OLDSTER
M STORMED
N RODENTS
SNORTED
O ROOSTED
P DEPORTS
REDTOPS
SPORTED
T DOTTERS
U DETOURS
DOUREST
REDOUTS
ROUSTED
W STROWED
WORSTED
Y DESTROY
STROYED

61 TODIES

A IODATES
TOADIES
C CESTOID
COEDITS
D TODDIES
F FOISTED
H HOISTED
J JOISTED
M DISTOME
MODISTE
O OSTEOID
P DEPOSIT
DOPIEST
PODITES
POSITED
SOPITED
TOPSIDE
R EDITORS
SORTIED
STEROID
STORIED
TRIODES
T DOTIEST
U OUTSIDE
TEDIOUS
Z DOZIEST

62 OILERS

B BOILERS
REBOILS
C COILERS
RECOILS
D SOLDIER
SOLIDER
G GLORIES
M MOILERS
N NEROLIS
O ORIOLES
P SPOILER
R LORRIES
S LORISES
RISSOLE
T ESTRIOL
LOITERS
TOILERS
U LOUSIER
SOILURE

63 ANITOE

B NIOBATE
C ACONITE
L ELATION
TOENAIL
M AMNIOTE
N ENATION
S ATONIES

64 STEROL

A OLESTRA
B BOLSTER
BOLTERS
LOBSTER
C COLTERS
CORSLET
COSTREL
LECTORS
D OLDSTER
E SOLERET
F FLORETS
LOFTERS
H HOLSTER
HOSTLER
I ESTRIOL
LOITERS
TOILERS
J JOLTERS
JOSTLER
L TOLLERS
M MERLOTS
MOLTERS
O LOOTERS
RETOOLS
ROOTLES
TOOLERS
P PETROLS
REPLOTS
S OSTLERS
STEROLS
T LOTTERS
SETTLOR
SLOTTER
V REVOLTS
W TROWELS

65 TENIAE

A TAENIAE
B BETAINE
L LINEATE
M ETAMINE
MATINEE
R ARENITE
RETINAE
TRAINEE
S ETESIAN
V NAIVETE

66 TEARIE

L ATELIER
M EMERITA
EMIRATE
MEATIER
N ARENITE
RETINAE
TRAINEE
P PEATIER
R TEARIER
S AERIEST
SERIATE
T ARIETTE
ITERATE

67 NEROLI

A AILERON
ALIENOR
E ELOINER
O LOONIER
P PROLINE
R LORINER
S NEROLIS
T RETINOL

68 RANEES

C CAREENS
CASERNE
RECANES
D ENDEARS
G ENRAGES
K SNEAKER
L LEANERS
M MEANERS
RENAMES
N ENSNARE
RENNASE
O ARENOSE
R EARNERS
REEARNS
T EARNEST
EASTERN
NEAREST
W WEANERS

69 SOIGNE

A AGONIES
AGONISE
B BINGOES
BIOGENS
C COGNISE
COIGNES
D DINGOES
E GENOISE
SOIGNEE
H HONGIES
SHOEING
J JINGOES
L ELOIGNS
LEGIONS
LINGOES
LONGIES
O GOONIES
ISOGONE
NOOGIES
P EPIGONS
PIGEONS
PINGOES
R ERINGOS
IGNORES
REGIONS
SIGNORE
U IGNEOUS
W WIGEONS
Y ISOGENY
Z GINZOES

70 ARIOSE

B ISOBARE
C SCORIAE
D ROADIES
N ERASION
P SOAPIER
V OVARIES

71 DETAIN

D NIDATED
F DEFIANT
I INEDITA
M MEDIANT
P DEPAINT
PAINTED
PATINED
R ANTIRED
DETRAIN
TRAINED
S DESTAIN
DETAINS
INSTEAD
NIDATES
SAINTED
STAINED
T TAINTED
U AUDIENT
V DEVIANT

72 SINGER

A EARINGS
ERASING
GAINERS
REAGINS
REGAINS
REGINAS
SEARING
SERINGA
B BINGERS
C CRINGES
D DINGERS
ENGIRDS
E GREISEN
F FINGERS
FRINGES
G GINGERS
NIGGERS
SERGING
SNIGGER
H HINGERS
L LINGERS
SLINGER
N GINNERS
O ERINGOS
IGNORES
REGIONS
SIGNORE
P PINGERS
SPRINGE
R RINGERS
S INGRESS
RESIGNS
SIGNERS
SINGERS
T RESTING
STINGER
U REUSING
V SERVING
VERSING
W SWINGER
WINGERS
Y SYRINGE
Z ZINGERS

73 EASIER

D DEARIES
READIES
F FAERIES
FREESIA
L REALISE
M SEAMIER
SERIEMA
P APERIES
R RERAISE
T AERIEST
SERIATE
W WEARIES

74 EOLIAN

A AEOLIAN
K KAOLINE
P OPALINE
R AILERON
ALIENOR
S ANISOLE
T ELATION
TOENAIL

75 RESALE

C CEREALS
RELACES
RESCALE
SCLERAE
D DEALERS
LEADERS
E RELEASE
G GALERES
REGALES
H HEALERS
I REALISE
K LEAKERS
N LEANERS
O AREOLES
P LEAPERS
PLEASER
PRESALE
RELAPSE
REPEALS
S EARLESS
LEASERS
RESALES
RESEALS
SEALERS
T ELATERS
REALEST
RELATES
RESLATE
STEALER
V LAVEERS
LEAVERS
REVEALS
SEVERAL
VEALERS
X RELAXES
Y SEALERY

76 UNITER

A RUINATE
TAURINE
URANITE
URINATE
B TRIBUNE
TURBINE
D INTRUDE
TURDINE
UNTIRED
UNTRIED
E RETINUE
REUNITE
UTERINE
G TRUEING
M MINUTER
UNMITER
UNMITRE
O ROUTINE
R RUNTIER
S NUTSIER
TRIUNES
UNITERS
T NUTTIER
V VENTURI

77 SOILED

A ISOLEAD
B BOLIDES
D DILDOES
E OILSEED
I DOILIES
IDOLISE
K KELOIDS
L DOLLIES
M MELOIDS
MIDSOLE
N INDOLES
O DOOLIES
P DESPOIL
DIPLOES
DIPOLES
SPOILED
R SOLDIER
SOLIDER
Y DOYLIES

78 STEREO

A ROSEATE
D OERSTED
TEREDOS
H HETEROS
J RESOJET
K RESTOKE
L SOLERET
M EMOTERS
METEORS
REMOTES
N ESTRONE
R RESTORE
S STEREOS
T ROSETTE
V OVERSET
REVOTES
VETOERS

79 LINERS

A ALINERS
NAILERS
RENAILS
B BERLINS
E LIERNES
RELINES
G LINGERS
SLINGER
I INLIERS
RESILIN
K LINKERS
RELINKS
M LIMNERS
MERLINS
O NEROLIS
P PILSNER
T LINTERS
V SILVERN

80 ALEROT

B BLOATER
C LOCATER
D DELATOR
LEOTARD
F FLOATER
REFLOAT
G GLOATER
LEGATOR
H LOATHER
RATHOLE
L REALLOT
P PROLATE
R REALTOR
RELATOR
S OLESTRA
T RETOTAL
U TORULAE
V LEVATOR

81 ENTOIL

A ELATION
TOENAIL
C LECTION
D LENTOID
G LENTIGO
H HOTLINE
NEOLITH
P POTLINE
TOPLINE
R RETINOL
S ENTOILS
U ELUTION
OUTLINE
V VIOLENT
W TOWLINE

82 GARNET

A TANAGER
D DRAGNET
GRANTED
E GRANTEE
GREATEN
NEGATER
REAGENT
F ENGRAFT
I GRANITE
GRATINE
INGRATE
TANGIER
TEARING
L TANGLER
M GARMENT
MARGENT
N REGNANT
O NEGATOR
P TREPANG
R GRANTER
REGRANT
S ARGENTS
GARNETS
STRANGE
U GAUNTER
W TWANGER
Y AGENTRY

83 EASING

B SABEING
C CEASING
INCAGES
F FEASING
G AGEINGS
SIGNAGE
K SINKAGE
L LEASING
LINAGES
SEALING
M ENIGMAS
GAMINES
SEAMING
N INNAGES
O AGONIES
AGONISE
P SPAEING
SPINAGE
R EARINGS
ERASING
GAINERS
REAGINS
REGAINS
REGINAS
SEARING
SERINGA
T EASTING
EATINGS
INGATES
INGESTA
SEATING
TEASING
U GUINEAS
Z AGNIZES

84 OILSAT

A SOLATIA
B OBLASTI
C CITOLAS
STOICAL
E ISOLATE
G GALIOTS
LATIGOS
M SOMITAL
N LATINOS
TALIONS
P APOSTIL
TOPSAIL
R ORALIST
RIALTOS
TAILORS
T ALTOIST
U OUTSAIL
X OXTAILS

85 TINIER

A INERTIA
C CITRINE
CRINITE
INCITER
NERITIC
D INDITER
NITRIDE
E NITERIE
F NIFTIER
G IGNITER
TIERING
H INHERIT
L LINTIER
NITRILE
M INTERIM
MINTIER
TERMINI
N TINNIER
T NITRITE
NITTIER
V INVITER
VITRINE
W TWINIER

86 ATESOD

B BOASTED
C COASTED
G DOTAGES
I IODATES
TOADIES
L SOLATED
N DONATES
P PODESTA
R ROASTED
TORSADE
T TOASTED

87 SNORED

B BONDERS
C SCORNED
D NODDERS
E ENDORSE
H DEHORNS
I DINEROS
INDORSE
ORDINES
ROSINED
SORDINE
L RONDELS
M MODERNS
RODSMEN
P PERNODS
PONDERS
RESPOND
R DRONERS
S SONDERS
T RODENTS
SNORTED
U ENDUROS
RESOUND
SOUNDER
UNDOERS
V VENDORS
W DOWNERS
WONDERS

88	ELITES	POSH FOLKS GOVERNED COMPLEX
89	INMATE	RELAXING BY HIS CELL DOOR
90	NEATER	SLICK RV, RIGHT?
91	LANOSE	PITCHER
92	GREATS	HAVING PERSONALITY
93	ATTIRE	CAP, SCARF, AND BELT
94	TRONAS	MINUTE COPY
95	TUNERS	OLD PIANOS BECOME RIGHT
96	PRAISE	APPROVED MEN WATCH US
97	DOE-RAN	CLIMB UP GRID
98	SUITER	GROOM HOLDS OFF ON PVQ COMBO
99	OALIES*	*CON DEBATING
100	ALDERS	FIR'S THORNS PRICKLED TWO BUMS

88 ELITES

C SECTILE
D ISLETED
E EELIEST
STEELIE
F FELSITE
LEFTIES
LIEFEST
G ELEGIST
ELEGITS
H SHELTIE
K SLEEKIT
L TELLIES
M ELMIEST
N LENITES
LISENTE
SETLINE
TENSILE
O ETOILES
P EPISTLE
PELITES
R LEISTER
RETILES
STERILE
S LISTEES
TELESIS
TIELESS
V EVILEST
LIEVEST
VELITES
X SEXTILE

89 INMATE

A AMENTIA
ANIMATE
B AMBIENT
C NEMATIC
D MEDIANT
E ETAMINE
MATINEE
G MINTAGE
TEAMING
TEGMINA
H HEMATIN
I INTIMAE
L AILMENT
ALIMENT
N MANNITE
O AMNIOTE
R MINARET
RAIMENT
S ETAMINS
INMATES
TAMEINS
X TAXIMEN
Y AMENITY
ANYTIME

90 NEATER

C CENTARE
CRENATE
REENACT
G GRANTEE
GREATEN
NEGATER
REAGENT
H EARTHEN
HEARTEN
I ARENITE
RETINAE
TRAINEE
K RETAKEN
L ENTERAL
ETERNAL
TELERAN
R TERRANE
S EARNEST
EASTERN
NEAREST
T ENTREAT
RATTEEN
TERNATE
V NERVATE
VETERAN

91 LANOSE

C SECONAL
E ENOLASE
H ENHALOS
I ANISOLE
P ESPANOL
NOPALES
R LOANERS
RELOANS
T ETALONS
TOLANES

92 GREATS

A GASTREA
TEARGAS
E ERGATES
RESTAGE
G GAGSTER
GARGETS
STAGGER
TAGGERS
H GATHERS
I AIGRETS
GAITERS
SEAGIRT
STAGIER
TRIAGES
L LARGEST
N ARGENTS
GARNETS
STRANGE
O GAROTES
ORGEATS
STORAGE
P PARGETS
R GARRETS
GARTERS
GRATERS
S GASTERS
STAGERS
T TARGETS
V GRAVEST
Y GRAYEST
GYRATES

93 ATTIRE

A ARIETTA
B BATTIER
BIRETTA
C ATRETIC
CATTIER
CITRATE
D ATTIRED
E ARIETTE
ITERATE
F FATTIER
L TERTIAL
N INTREAT
ITERANT
NATTIER
NITRATE
TERTIAN
P PARTITE
R RATTIER
TARTIER
S ARTIEST
ARTISTE
ATTIRES
IRATEST
RATITES
STRIATE
TASTIER
T ATTRITE
TATTIER
TITRATE

94 TRONAS

C CANTORS
CARTONS
CONTRAS
CRATONS
E ATONERS
SANTERO
SENATOR
TREASON
I AROINTS
RATIONS
M MATRONS
TRANSOM
N NATRONS
NONARTS
O RATOONS
SANTOOR
P PARTONS
PATRONS
TARPONS
T ATTORNS
RATTONS
U SANTOUR
Y AROYNTS

95 TUNERS

A NATURES
SAUNTER
B BRUNETS
BUNTERS
BURNETS
SUBRENT
C ENCRUST
D UNDREST
E NEUTERS
RETUNES
TENURES
TUREENS
G GURNETS
H HUNTERS
SHUNTER
I NUTSIER
TRIUNES
UNITERS
L RUNLETS
M MUNSTER
STERNUM
N STUNNER
O TENOURS
TONSURE
P PUNSTER
PUNTERS
R RETURNS
TURNERS
S UNRESTS
T ENTRUST
NUTTERS

96 PRAISE

A SPIRAEA
C SCRAPIE
SPACIER
D ASPIRED
DESPAIR
DIAPERS
PRAISED
E APERIES
H HARPIES
SHARPIE
M IMPRESA
N PANIERS
RAPINES
O SOAPIER
P APPRISE
SAPPIER
R ASPIRER
PARRIES
PRAISER
RAPIERS
RASPIER
REPAIRS
S ASPIRES
PARESIS
PARISES
PRAISES
SPIREAS
T PARTIES
PASTIER
PIASTER
PIASTRE
PIRATES
TRAIPSE
U UPRAISE
V PARVISE
PAVISER
W WASPIER

97 DOERAN

B BANDORE
BROADEN
C ACORNED
D ADORNED
G GROANED
I ANEROID
L LADRONE
M MADRONE
P APRONED
OPERAND
PADRONE
PANDORE
R ADORNER
READORN
U RONDEAU

98 SUITER

B BUSTIER
RUBIEST
C CURITES
ICTERUS
D DUSTIER
STUDIER
F FUSTIER
SURFEIT
G GUSTIER
GUTSIER
H HIRSUTE
L LUSTIER
RULIEST
RUTILES
M MUSTIER
N NUTSIER
TRIUNES
UNITERS
O STOURIE
P PERITUS
Q QUERIST
R RUSTIER
S SUITERS
V REVUIST
STUIVER
VIRTUES

99 OALIES

B OBELIAS
C CELOSIA
D ISOLEAD
G GOALIES
SOILAGE
N ANISOLE
T ISOLATE

100 ALDERS

B BLADERS
C CRADLES
RECLADS
D LADDERS
RADDLES
SADDLER
E DEALERS
LEADERS
F FARDELS
H HERALDS
I DERAILS
DIALERS
REDIALS
K DARKLES
L LADLERS
M MEDLARS
N DARNELS
LANDERS
RELANDS
SLANDER
SNARLED
O LOADERS
ORDEALS
RELOADS
P PEDLARS
R LARDERS
S RASSLED
T DARTLES
U LAUDERS
W WARSLED

Master Study Sheet

Stems: ____________ ____________ ____________

A			
B			
C			
D			
E			
F			
G			
H			
I			
J			
K			
L			
M			
N			
O			
P			
Q			
R			
S			
T			
U			
V			
W			
X			
Y			
Z			
	Total correct: / Total bingos: × 100 = ____ %	Total correct: / Total bingos: × 100 = ____ %	Total correct: / Total bingos: × 100 = ____ %

Type I Sevens, Alphabetized

ABIDERS
ABLEIST
ACETINS
ACINOSE
ACONITE
ACORNED
ACTIONS
ADDREST
ADMIRES
ADORERS
ADORNED
ADORNER
ADVENTS
ADVERTS
ADVISER
AEDILES
AEOLIAN
AERATES
AERIALS
AERIEST
AEROSAT
AEROSOL
AETHERS
AFREETS
AGEINGS
AGENTRY
AGINNER
AGISTED
AGNIZES
AGONIES
AGONISE
AGONIST
AIDLESS
AIGLETS
AIGRETS
AILERON
AILMENT
AINSELL
AIRDATE
AIRIEST
AIRLESS
AIRLINE
AIRSHED
AIRTHED
ALBITES
ALEVINS
ALEXINS
ALIENER
ALIENOR
ALIGNER
ALIMENT
ALINERS
ALIPEDS
ALKINES
ALMNERS
ALPINES
ALTOIST
ALUNITE
AMBIENT
AMENITY
AMENTIA
AMNIOTE
AMOSITE
ANERGIA
ANERGIC
ANEROID
ANESTRI
ANGLERS
ANGRIER
ANIMATE
ANISEED
ANISOLE
ANKLETS
ANOINTS
ANOMIES
ANSATED
ANTHERS
ANTIARS
ANTIRED
ANTISEX
ANTLERS
ANTLIKE
ANTSIER
ANYTIME
APERIES
APLITES
APOSTIL
APOSTLE
APPRISE
APRONED
ARANEID
ARCSINE
ARENITE
ARENOSE
ARENOUS
AREOLAS
AREOLES
ARGENTS
ARIDEST
ARIETTA
ARIETTE
ARISTAE
ARMLETS
AROINTS
AROUSED
AROYNTS
ARPENTS
ARSENAL
ARSENIC
ARSINES
ARTICLE
ARTIEST
ARTISAN
ARTISTE
ARTLESS
ARTSIER
ASPIRED
ASPIRER
ASPIRES
ASTERIA
ASTILBE
ASTRIDE
ASUNDER
ATELIER
ATINGLE
ATOMIES
ATOMISE
ATONERS
ATONIAS
ATONICS
ATONIES
ATOPIES
ATRESIA
ATRESIC
ATRETIC
ATTENDS
ATTIRED
ATTIRES
ATTORNS
ATTRITE
AUDIENT
AUDILES
AUNTIES
AUSTERE
AZOTISE
BAILERS
BAITERS
BALDIES
BANDERS
BANDIES
BANDORE
BANTERS
BANTIES
BARITES
BASINED
BASINET
BASTILE
BASTION
BATTIER
BEARING
BEATERS
BEDRAIL
BERATES
BERLINS
BESTIAL
BESTRID
BETAINE
BINDERS
BINGERS
BINGOES
BIOGENS
BIRETTA
BISTRED
BLADERS
BLASTER
BLASTIE
BLISTER
BLOATER
BOASTED
BOASTER
BOATELS
BOATERS
BOILERS
BOLIDES
BOLSTER
BOLTERS
BONDERS
BONIEST
BONITAS
BORANES
BORATES
BORIDES
BORNITE
BRAILED
BRAINED
BRAISED
BRISANT
BRISTLE
BROADEN
BRUNETS
BUNTERS
BURNETS
BUSTIER
CAIRNED
CANDIES
CANOERS
CANTERS
CANTLES
CANTORS
CAREENS
CARLINE
CARNETS
CARNIES
CARTELS
CARTONS
CASERNE
CATIONS
CATTIER
CEASING
CELOSIA
CENTALS
CENTARE
CENTERS
CENTRES
CERATES
CERATIN
CEREALS
CERITES
CERTAIN
CESTOID
CETANES
CINDERS
CINEAST
CINEOLS
CISTERN
CISTRON
CITOLAS
CITOLES
CITRATE
CITRINE
CITRONS
CLARETS
CLARIES
CLAROES
CLIENTS
COALERS
COARSEN
COASTED
COASTER
COATERS
COEDITS
COGNISE
COIGNES
COILERS
COINERS
COINTER
COLTERS
CONTRAS
CORNEAS
CORNETS
CORSLET
CORTINS
COSTREL
CRADLES
CRATONS
CREATES
CREATIN
CREDITS
CRENATE
CRESTAL
CRETINS
CRINGES
CRINITE
CRISTAE
CRONIES
CURITES
DABSTER
DACITES
DAIKERS
DAILIES
DAIRIES
DALLIER
DALLIES
DAMNERS
DANCERS
DANDERS
DANDIER
DANDIES
DANGERS
DANKEST
DANSEUR
DARBIES
DARIOLE
DARKENS
DARKEST
DARKLES
DARNELS
DARNERS
DARTERS
DARTLES
DASHIER
DATIVES
DAUTIES
DAWTIES
DEALERS
DEAREST
DEARIES
DEARTHS
DEBTORS
DECANTS
DECRIAL
DECRIES
DEFIANT
DEFIERS
DEFROST
DEHORNS
DEHORTS
DEICERS
DELATOR
DELIRIA
DENARII
DENIALS
DENIERS
DENSITY
DENTALS
DENTILS
DENTINS
DENTIST
DEODARS
DEPAINT
DEPARTS
DEPORTS
DEPOSIT
DERAIGN
DERAILS
DERATES
DERBIES
DERIDES
DERIVES
DERRIES
DESCANT
DESIRED
DESIRER
DESIRES
DESPAIR
DESPOIL
DESTAIN
DESTINE
DESTINY
DESTROY
DETAILS
DETAINS
DETOURS
DETRAIN
DEVIANT
DEVISAL
DEVISER
DEVISOR
DEVOIRS
DIALERS
DIALLER
DIALYSE
DIAPERS
DIARIES
DIASTEM
DIASTER
DIESTER
DIETARY
DIETERS
DILATER
DILATES
DILDOES
DINEROS
DINGERS
DINGOES
DINNERS
DIPLOES
DIPNETS
DIPOLES
DIPTERA
DIRECTS
DIRTIES
DISABLE
DISCERN
DISRATE
DISROBE
DISSEAT
DISSENT
DISSERT
DISTEND
DISTENT
DISTOME
DITHERS
DITSIER
DIVERSE
DIVERTS
DOGEARS
DOILIES
DOLLIES
DONATES
DOOLIES
DOPIEST
DOSSIER
DOTAGES
DOTIEST
DOTTERS
DOUREST
DOWNERS
DOWRIES
DOYLIES
DOZIEST
DRAGNET
DRAINED
DRAINER
DRONERS
DROSERA
DUNITES
DUSTIER
EARINGS
EARLESS
EARNERS
EARNEST
EARNING
EARRING
EARSHOT
EARTHEN
EASTERN
EASTERS
EASTING
EATINGS
ECARTES
ECLAIRS
EDITORS
EELIEST
EERIEST
ELAPIDS
ELASTIC
ELASTIN
ELATERS
ELATING
ELATION
ELEGIST
ELEGITS
ELISION
ELMIEST
ELOIGNS
ELOINER
ELUANTS
ELUSION
ELUTION
ELYSIAN
EMERITA
EMETINS
EMIRATE
EMOTERS
ENAMORS
ENATION
ENCRUST
ENDEARS
ENDITES
ENDORSE
ENDRINS
ENDUROS
ENGIRDS
ENGRAFT
ENGRAIL
ENGRAIN
ENHALOS
ENIGMAS
ENLISTS
ENOLASE
ENRAGES
ENROOTS
ENSNARE
ENSNARL
ENTAILS
ENTASES
ENTASIA
ENTASIS
ENTERAL
ENTERIC
ENTICER
ENTICES
ENTIRES
ENTOILS
ENTRAIN
ENTRAPS
ENTREAT
ENTREES
ENTRIES
ENTRUST
ENVIERS
ENVIROS
EOLITHS
EPIGONS
EPINAOS
EPISTLE
EPSILON
ERASING
ERASION
EREPSIN
ERGATES
ERINGOS
ERMINES
EROSION
EROTICS
EROTISM
ERRANDS
ERRANTS
ESCOLAR
ESERINE
ESPANOL
ESPARTO
ESTIVAL
ESTREAT
ESTRINS
ESTRIOL
ESTRONE
ESTRUAL
ETALONS
ETAMINE
ETAMINS
ETERNAL
ETESIAN
ETHANES
ETHIONS
ETOILES
EVASION
EVILEST
EXTERNS
FADEINS
FAERIES
FAINEST
FAINTED
FAINTER
FAIREST
FALTERS
FARDELS
FARSIDE
FATTIER
FEARING
FEASING
FEASTER
FEDORAS
FELSITE
FETIALS
FILTERS
FINALES
FINDERS
FINGERS
FINITES
FLOATER
FLORETS
FOISTED
FOLATES
FORINTS
FORTIES
FREESIA
FRIENDS
FRINGES
FRONTES
FROSTED
FUSTIER
GAGSTER
GAINERS
GAITERS
GALERES
GALIOTS
GALORES
GAMINES
GANDERS
GAOLERS
GARDENS
GARGETS
GARMENT
GARNETS
GAROTES
GARRETS
GARTERS
GASTERS
GASTREA
GASTRIN
GATHERS
GAUNTER
GEARING
GELANTS
GELATIN
GELATIS
GELATOS
GENITAL
GENITOR
GENOISE
GERENTS
GERMINA
GINGERS
GINNERS
GITANOS
GLADIER
GLAIRED
GLAIRES
GLISTEN
GLISTER
GLOATER
GLORIES
GOALIES
GOITERS
GOITRES
GOONIES
GORIEST
GRADINE
GRAINED
GRAINER
GRANITE
GRANNIE
GRANTED
GRANTEE
GRANTER
GRATERS
GRATINE
GRATINS
GRAVEST
GRAYEST
GREATEN
GREISEN
GRISTLE
GROANED
GUINEAS
GURNETS
GUSTIER
GUTSIER
GYRATES
HAILERS
HAIRNET
HALIDES
HALITES
HALTERS
HANDERS
HANDIER
HANDSET
HANTLES
HARDENS
HARDEST
HARDIES
HARDSET
HARPIES
HARSLET
HASTIER
HATREDS
HEALERS
HEARING
HEARTEN
HEATERS
HEISTER
HELIAST
HEMATIN
HENRIES
HERALDS
HERIOTS
HERNIAL
HERNIAS
HEROINS
HETEROS
HINDERS
HINGERS
HINTERS
HIRSUTE
HISTONE
HOARSEN
HOISTED
HOISTER
HOLIEST
HOLSTER
HONGIES
HORNETS
HORNIST
HOSTILE
HOSTLER
HOTLINE
HUNTERS
ICTERUS
IDEATES
IDOLISE
IGNEOUS
IGNITER
IGNITES
IGNORES
IMARETS
IMPRESA
INANEST
INARMED
INBREDS
INCAGES
INCASED
INCITER
INCITES
INCLOSE
INDENTS
INDITER
INDITES
INDOLES
INDORSE
INEARTH
INEDITA
INERTIA
INFARES
INFLATE
INGATES
INGESTA
INGRATE
INGRESS
INHALER
INHALES
INHERES
INHERIT
INKIEST
INLACES
INLAYER
INLIERS
INMATES
INNAGES
INOSITE
INSANER
INSERTS
INSHORE
INSIDER
INSNARE
INSOLES
INSTARS
INSTATE
INSTEAD
INSURED
INTAKES
INTEGER
INTENDS
INTENSE
INTERIM
INTERNE
INTERNS
INTIMAE
INTINES
INTONER
INTONES
INTORTS
INTREAT
INTRONS
INTRUDE
INULASE
INVADER
INVADES
INVERSE
INVERTS
INVITER
INVITES
IODATES
IOLITES
IRATELY
IRATEST
IRONERS
IRONIES
IRONIST
ISATINE
ISLETED
ISOBARE
ISOGENY
ISOGONE
ISOLATE
ISOLEAD
ISOLINE
ISOTONE
ITERANT
ITERATE
JAILERS
JILTERS
JINGOES
JOINERS
JOINTER
JOISTED
JOLTERS
JOSTLER
KAOLINE
KATIONS
KEISTER
KELOIDS
KERATIN
KERNITE
KIESTER
KILTERS
KINDEST
KIRTLES
KLISTER
LABRETS
LACIEST
LACTOSE
LADDERS
LADDIES
LADLERS
LADRONE
LAITIES
LAKIEST
LAMENTS
LAMSTER
LANCERS
LANCETS
LANDERS
LANKEST
LANKIER
LANNERS
LAPIDES
LARDERS
LARDIER
LARGEST
LASSOER
LASTERS
LATEENS
LATENTS
LATHERS
LATHIER
LATICES
LATIGOS
LATINOS
LATRINE
LATTENS
LAUDERS
LAVEERS
LAWINES
LAZIEST
LEADERS
LEADIER
LEAKERS
LEANERS
LEANEST
LEAPERS
LEASERS
LEASING
LEAVERS
LECTINS
LECTION
LECTORS
LEFTIES
LEGATOR
LEGATOS
LEGIONS
LEISTER
LENITES
LENTIGO
LENTILS
LENTISK
LENTOID
LEOTARD
LEPTINS
LESBIAN
LESIONS
LEVANTS
LEVATOR
LIAISED
LIBRATE
LIEFEST
LIERNES
LIEVEST
LIFTERS
LIGATES
LIMNERS
LINAGES
LINEATE
LINGERS
LINGOES
LINIEST
LINKERS
LINNETS
LINTELS
LINTERS
LINTIER
LIONESS
LIONISE
LIPREAD
LISENTE
LISTEES
LISTENS
LISTERS
LITERAL
LITOTES
LITTERS
LOADERS
LOAFERS
LOANERS
LOATHER
LOATHES
LOBSTER
LOCATER
LOCATES
LOFTERS
LOGIEST
LOITERS
LOMEINS
LONGIES
LOONIER
LOONIES
LOOTERS
LORINER
LORISES
LORRIES
LOTTERS
LOUSIER
LUNIEST
LUSTIER
LUTEINS
MADRONE
MAESTRI
MAESTRO
MAIDENS
MAILERS
MALINES
MALTIER
MALTOSE
MANGIER
MANITOS
MANLIER
MANNITE
MANTELS
MANTLES
MARGENT
MARINES
MARLINE
MARLITE
MARTENS
MARTINS
MATINEE
MATRONS
MEANERS
MEANEST
MEATIER
MEDIALS
MEDIANS
MEDIANT
MEDINAS
MEDLARS
MEISTER
MELOIDS
MENIALS
MENTORS
MERINOS
MERLINS
MERLOTS
MESTINO
METEORS
METIERS
MIDSOLE
MILTERS
MINARET
MINDERS
MINDSET
MINERAL
MINSTER
MINTAGE
MINTERS
MINTIER
MINUTER
MISDATE
MISDEAL
MISDOER
MISLEAD
MISRATE
MISREAD
MISTEND
MOANERS
MODERNS
MODISTE
MOILERS
MOISTEN
MOISTER
MOLTERS
MONSTER
MORALES
MORTISE
MOTILES
MUNSTER
MUSTIER
NAGGIER
NAIADES
NAILERS
NAILSET
NAIVEST
NAIVETE
NARCIST
NARCOSE
NARDINE
NARGILE
NASTIER
NASTIES
NATIONS
NATIVES
NATRONS
NATTERS
NATTIER
NATURES
NEAREST
NEARING
NEATENS
NEATEST
NECTARS
NEGATER
NEGATES
NEGATOR
NEITHER
NEMATIC
NEOLITH
NEPETAS
NERDISH
NEREIDS
NERITIC
NEROLIS
NERVATE
NESTERS
NESTLER
NESTORS
NETTERS
NETTIER
NEUTERS
NEWSIER
NIDATED
NIDATES
NIDGETS
NIELLOS
NIFTIER
NIFTIES
NIOBATE
NITERIE
NITRATE
NITRIDE
NITRILE
NITRITE
NITROSO
NITROUS
NITTIER
NODDERS
NOISIER
NONARTS
NOOGIES
NOPALES
NORITES
NOSIEST
NOSTRIL
NOTATES
NOTICER
NOTICES
NUTRIAS
NUTSIER
NUTTERS

NUTTIER
OAKIEST
OARLESS
OARSMEN
OBELIAS
OBLASTI
OBLATES
OBTAINS
OCTANES
OERSTED
OESTRIN
OILIEST
OILSEED
OLDSTER
OLEATES
OLEFINS
OLEINES
OLESTRA
ONAGERS
ONANIST
ONSTAGE
OOLITES
OPALINE
OPERAND
OPIATES
ORACLES
ORALIST
ORANGES
ORBIEST
ORCEINS
ORDEALS
ORDINES
OREIDES
ORGEATS
ORIENTS
ORIOLES
OROIDES
ORPINES
OSETRAS
OSIERED
OSSETRA
OSTEOID
OSTIOLE
OSTLERS
OUTLIES
OUTLINE
OUTSAIL
OUTSIDE
OVARIES
OVERSAD
OVERSET
OXTAILS
PADRONE
PAINTED
PAINTER
PALIEST
PALSIED
PALTERS
PANDERS
PANDIES
PANDORE
PANIERS
PANTIES
PANTILE
PARDINE
PARENTS
PARESIS
PARGETS
PARISES
PAROLES
PARRIES
PARTIED
PARTIES
PARTITE
PARTONS
PARVISE
PASTERN
PASTIER
PATINED
PATINES
PATRONS
PAVISER
PEATIER
PEDANTS
PEDLARS
PELITES
PELOTAS
PENATES
PENSTER
PENTADS
PERIODS
PERITUS
PERNODS
PERSALT
PERSONA
PERTAIN
PESTIER
PETARDS
PETROLS
PIASTER
PIASTRE
PIGEONS
PILSNER
PINDERS
PINEALS
PINGERS
PINGOES
PINIEST
PINITES
PINOLES
PINTLES
PINTOES
PIOLETS
PIRATED
PIRATES
PISTOLE
PLAINER
PLAITER
PLANERS
PLANETS
PLASTER
PLATENS
PLATERS
PLATIER
PLATIES
PLEASER
PLEIADS
PLENIST
PODESTA
PODITES
POINTER
POINTES
PONDERS
POSITED
POSTERN
POTLINE
PRAISED
PRAISER
PRAISES
PRALINE
PREDIAL
PRESALE
PRESENT
PRESIDE
PROLATE
PROLINE
PROSTIE
PROTEAS
PROTEIN
PSALTER
PTERINS
PUNSTER
PUNTERS
QINTARS
QUERIST
RACIEST
RADDLES
RADIALE
RADIATE
RADICEL
RADICES
RADICLE
RADIXES
RADOMES
RAIDERS
RAILERS
RAIMENT
RALLIED
RALLIES
RALLINE
RANDIER
RANDIES
RANGIER
RANKEST
RANKLES
RANTERS
RAPIERS
RAPINES
RASPIER
RASSLED
RATHOLE
RATINES
RATINGS
RATIONS
RATITES
RATLIKE
RATLINE
RATLINS
RATOONS
RATTEEN
RATTENS
RATTIER
RATTLES
RATTONS
RAVELIN
RAVINED
RAVINES
READIES
READILY
READING
READMIT
READORN
REAGENT
REAGINS
REALEST
REALIGN
REALISE
REALISM
REALIST
REALITY
REALLOT
REALTOR
REAMING
REAPING
REARING
REASONS
REAVING
REBAITS
REBATES
REBATOS
REBINDS
REBOILS
RECANES
RECANTS
RECITAL
RECITES
RECLADS
RECOALS
RECOATS
RECOILS
RECOINS
REDACTS
REDATES
REDBAIT
REDFINS
REDIALS
REDOUTS
REDOWAS
REDRIES
REDTAIL
REDTOPS
REEARNS
REEDITS
REEMITS
REENACT
REFINDS
REFINES
REFLOAT
REGAINS
REGALES
REGENTS
REGINAE
REGINAL
REGINAS
REGIONS
REGNANT
REGRANT
REHEATS
REINTER
REJOINS
REKNITS
REKNOTS
RELACES
RELANDS
RELAPSE
RELATES
RELATOR
RELAXES
RELAXIN
RELEASE
RELENTS
RELIANT
RELICTS
RELINES
RELINKS
RELISTS
RELOADS
RELOANS
REMAILS
REMAINS
REMANDS
REMATES
REMINDS
REMINTS
REMISED
REMOTES
RENAILS
RENAMES
RENESTS
RENNASE
RENNETS
RENTALS
RENTERS
RENTIER
RENVOIS
REPAINT
REPAIRS
REPEALS
REPEATS
REPENTS
REPINES
REPLANS
REPLOTS
REPOSAL
REPOSIT
RERAISE
RERENTS
RERISEN
RESAILS
RESALES
RESCALE
RESCIND
RESEALS
RESEATS
RESENTS
RESHINE
RESIDED
RESIDER
RESIDES
RESIDUA
RESIDUE
RESIGNS
RESILED
RESILIN
RESINED
RESITED
RESITES
RESIZED
RESLATE
RESOJET
RESOUND
RESPITE
RESPLIT
RESPOND
RESTAGE
RESTATE
RESTING
RESTIVE
RESTOKE
RESTORE
RETAILS
RETAINS
RETAKEN
RETAKES
RETAPES
RETARDS
RETASTE
RETAXES
RETEAMS
RETEARS
RETENES
RETILES
RETIMES
RETINAE
RETINAL
RETINAS
RETINES
RETINOL
RETINTS
RETINUE
RETIRES
RETOOLS
RETOTAL
RETRAIN
RETRIAL
RETRIES
RETSINA
RETUNES
RETURNS
REUNITE
REUSING
REVEALS
REVISAL
REVISED
REVOLTS
REVOTES
REVUIST
REWINDS
REXINES
RIALTOS
RIBLETS
RIDABLE
RILLETS
RINGERS
RIOTERS
RIPOSTE
RISSOLE
RIVALED
ROADEOS
ROADIES
ROASTED
ROASTER
RODENTS
RODSMEN
ROISTER
RONDEAU
RONDELS
ROOSTED
ROOTLES
ROPIEST
ROSEATE
ROSEOLA
ROSETTE
ROSIEST
ROSINED
ROTATES
ROUSTED
ROUTINE
ROWDIES
RUBIEST
RUINATE
RULIEST
RUNLETS
RUNTIER
RUSTIER
RUTILES
SABEING
SADDLER
SAFROLE
SAILERS
SAINTED
SALIENT
SALINES
SALLIED
SALLIER
SALTERN
SALTERS
SALTIER
SALTIES
SALTINE
SALTIRE
SALUTER
SANDERS
SANDIER
SANICLE
SANTERA
SANTERO
SANTIRS
SANTOOR
SANTOUR
SAPIENT
SAPPIER
SARDINE
SARMENT
SARODES
SARSNET
SATEENS
SATINET
SATIRES
SAUNTER
SAVORED
SCALENI
SCALIER
SCANTED
SCANTER
SCARLET
SCARTED
SCLERAE
SCORIAE
SCORNED
SCRAPIE
SEABIRD
SEAGIRT
SEALANT
SEALERS
SEALERY
SEALIFT
SEALING
SEAMIER
SEAMING
SEAPORT
SEAREST
SEARING
SEATERS
SEATING
SECONAL
SECTILE
SECTION
SEDARIM
SEDATER
SEDGIER
SEDILIA
SEEDIER
SEINERS
SEITANS
SEJEANT
SEMINAL
SEMINAR
SENARII
SENATES
SENATOR
SENHORA
SENIORS
SENOPIA
SENORAS
SENSATE
SENTIMO
SERAILS
SEREINS
SERGING
SERIALS
SERIATE
SERIEMA
SERIFED
SERINES
SERINGA
SEROSAL
SERPENT
SERRANO
SERRATE
SERRIED
SERVANT
SERVING
SESTINA
SESTINE
SETLINE
SETTLOR
SEVERAL
SEXTAIN
SEXTILE
SHADIER
SHALIER
SHARPIE
SHEITAN
SHELTIE
SHOALER
SHOEING
SHORTED
SHORTEN
SHORTIE
SHRINED
SHUNTER
SIDEARM
SIDEBAR
SIDECAR
SIDEMAN
SIENITE
SIERRAN
SIEVERT
SIGNAGE
SIGNERS
SIGNORE
SILANES
SILENTS
SILTIER
SILVERN
SINCERE
SINGERS
SINGLET
SINKAGE
SINTERS
SINUATE
SIXTEEN
SKATOLE
SKIRTED
SLAINTE
SLANDER
SLANTED
SLATERS
SLATHER
SLATIER
SLEEKIT
SLINGER
SLITHER
SLITTER
SLOTTER
SMARTED
SMARTEN
SMARTIE
SNAILED
SNAKIER
SNARFED
SNARLED
SNARLER
SNEAKER
SNIDEST
SNIFTER
SNIGGER
SNIGLET
SNORTED
SNORTER
SNOWIER
SOAPIER
SOIGNEE
SOILAGE
SOILURE
SOLACER
SOLATED
SOLATES
SOLATIA
SOLDIER
SOLERET
SOLIDER
SOLVATE
SOMITAL
SONDERS
SONLIKE
SONSIER
SOOTIER
SOPITED
SORBATE
SORBENT
SORDINE
SORITES
SORTIED
SORTIES
SORTING
SOUNDER
SOUTANE
SPACIER
SPAEING
SPANIEL
SPEIRED
SPIERED
SPINAGE
SPINATE
SPIRAEA
SPIRANT
SPIREAS
SPIRTED
SPLENIA
SPOILED
SPOILER
SPORTED
SPRINGE
STABILE
STABLER
STAGERS
STAGGER
STAGIER
STAIDER
STAINED
STAINER
STALKER
STANDEE
STANDER
STANGED
STANINE
STAPLER
STARING
STARLET
STARRED
STARTED
STARTLE
STARVED
STATION
STEALER
STEAMER
STEARIC
STEARIN
STEELIE
STELLAR
STENCIL
STENTOR
STEREOS
STERILE
STERNAL
STERNER
STERNUM
STEROID
STEROLS
STEWARD
STHENIA
STIBINE
STIFLER
STILLER
STINGER
STINKER
STINTED
STINTER
STIPEND
STIRRED
STOICAL
STONERS
STONIER
STOOLIE
STORAGE
STORIED
STORIES
STORING
STORMED
STOURIE
STRAFED
STRAINS
STRAKED
STRANGE
STRAWED
STRAYED
STRIATE
STRIDER
STRIDES
STRIPED
STRIVED
STRIVEN
STROKED
STROWED
STROYED
STUDIER
STUIVER
STUNNER
STYRENE
SUBRENT
SUITERS
SURFEIT
SWEATER
SWINGER
SYENITE
SYRINGE
TACRINE
TAENIAE
TAENIAS
TAGGERS
TAGLINE
TAILERS
TAILLES
TAILORS
TAINTED
TALCOSE
TALENTS
TALIONS
TALIPES
TALKERS
TALKIER
TALKIES
TALLIER
TALLIES
TAMEINS
TANAGER
TANDEMS
TANGIER
TANGLER
TANGLES
TANKERS
TANNERS
TANRECS
TANSIES
TARDIER
TARDIES
TARDIVE
TARGETS
TARNISH
TARPONS
TARRIED
TARRIES
TARSIER
TARTIER
TASTIER
TATTIER
TAURINE
TAVERNS
TAWNIER
TAWNIES
TAXIMEN
TEAMING
TEARERS
TEARGAS
TEARIER
TEARILY
TEARING
TEASERS
TEASING
TEDIOUS
TEENERS
TEENIER
TEGMINA
TELERAN
TELESIS
TELLIES
TENACES
TENAILS
TENDERS
TENNERS
TENNIES
TENOURS
TENRECS
TENSILE
TENSION
TENSIVE
TENSORS
TENTERS
TENTIER
TENURES
TEOPANS
TERBIAS
TEREDOS
TERMINI
TERNATE
TERNION
TERRAIN
TERRANE
TERRIES
TERRINE
TERTIAL
TERTIAN
TESSERA
TESTIER
TETRADS
THALERS
THEINES
THENARS
THEREIN
THERIAN
THREADS
THRONES
TIARAED
TIDIERS
TIELESS
TIEPINS
TIERCES
TIERING
TILLERS
TILTERS
TINDERS
TINEIDS
TINGLES
TINIEST
TINKERS
TINKLES
TINNERS
TINNIER
TINSELS
TINTERS
TINWARE
TIRADES
TISANES
TITRATE
TOADIES
TOASTED
TOASTER
TODDIES
TOENAIL
TOILERS
TOILETS
TOLANES
TOLLERS
TONGERS
TONIEST
TONNERS
TONSURE
TOOLERS
TOONIES
TOPLINE
TOPSAIL
TOPSIDE
TORSADE
TORSION
TORULAE
TOWLINE
TOWNIES
TOXINES
TRADERS
TRAIKED
TRAILED
TRAILER
TRAINED
TRAINEE
TRAINER
TRAIPSE
TRAMELS
TRANCES
TRANSIT
TRANSOM
TRASHED
TRAVELS
TREASON
TREEING
TRELLIS
TRENAIL
TREPANG
TREPANS
TRIABLE
TRIAGED
TRIAGES
TRIBADE
TRIBUNE
TRIENES
TRIFLES
TRIGONS
TRIODES
TRIOSES
TRIPLES
TRISEME
TRISOME
TRITONE
TRITONS
TRIUNES
TROPINE
TROPINS
TROWELS
TRUEING
TSARINA
TURBINE
TURDINE
TUREENS
TURIONS
TURNERS
TWANGER
TWINERS
TWINIER
UNAIRED
UNDOERS
UNDREST
UNITERS
UNITIES
UNMITER
UNMITRE
UNRESTS
UNSATED
UNTIRED
UNTRIED
UPRAISE
URALITE
URANIDE
URANITE
UREDIAL
UREIDES
URINATE
URINOSE
UTENSIL
UTERINE
VAINEST
VALINES
VARLETS
VASTIER
VEALERS
VEINERS
VELITES
VENDORS
VENIRES
VENTAIL
VENTERS
VENTURI
VERDINS
VERIEST
VERITAS
VERITES
VERSANT
VERSINE
VERSING
VERSION
VESTRAL
VETERAN
VETOERS
VINEGAR
VINIEST
VIOLENT
VIOLETS
VIRTUES
VISORED
VISTAED
VITRINE
VOIDERS
WAILERS
WAISTED
WAISTER
WAITERS
WANDERS
WANIEST
WANTERS
WARDENS
WARIEST
WARSLED
WARSTLE
WASPIER
WASTREL
WASTRIE
WEANERS
WEARIES
WEARING
WEINERS
WEIRDOS
WESTERN
WIENERS
WIGEONS
WINDERS
WINGERS
WINIEST
WINTERS
WINTLES
WONDERS
WORSTED
WRASTLE
YESTERN
ZANDERS
ZANIEST
ZEALOTS
ZEATINS
ZESTIER
ZINGARE
ZINGERS
ZLOTIES

Type I Eights, by Bingo Stem

1 TISANE

AC ESTANCIA
AF FANTASIE
AH ASTHENIA
AM AMENTIAS
ANIMATES
AR ANTISERA
RATANIES
SANTERIA
SEATRAIN
AS ENTASIAS
AT ASTATINE
SANITATE
AV SANATIVE
BC CABINETS
BE BETAINES
BG BEATINGS
BH ABSINTHE
BK BEATNIKS
SNAKEBIT
BL INSTABLE
BM AMBIENTS
BO BOTANIES
BOTANISE
NIOBATES
OBEISANT
BP BEPAINTS
BR BANISTER
BARNIEST
BS BASINETS
BASSINET
CD DISTANCE
CE CINEASTE
CF FANCIEST
CH ASTHENIC
CHANTIES
CI CANITIES
CL CANISTEL
CM AMNESTIC
SEMANTIC
CN ANCIENTS
CANNIEST
INSECTAN
INSTANCE
CO ACONITES
CANOEIST
SONICATE
CR CANISTER
CERATINS
CISTERNA
CREATINS
SCANTIER
TACRINES
CS CINEASTS
SCANTIES
CT ENTASTIC
NICTATES
TETANICS
CV VESICANT
CY CYANITES
CZ ZINCATES
DD DANDIEST
DE ANDESITE
DG SEDATING
STEADING
DH HANDIEST
DI ADENITIS
DAINTIES
DM MEDIANTS
DO ASTONIED
SEDATION
DP DEPAINTS
DR DETRAINS
RANDIEST
STRAINED
DS DESTAINS
SANDIEST
DT INSTATED
DU AUDIENTS
SINUATED
DV DEVIANTS
EM ETAMINES
MATINEES
MISEATEN
ER ARENITES
ARSENITE
RESINATE
STEARINE
TRAINEES
ES ETESIANS
TENIASES
ET ANISETTE
TETANIES
TETANISE
EV NAIVETES
FG FEASTING
FL INFLATES
FM MANIFEST
FN INFANTES
FR FAINTERS
FT FAINTEST
FW FAWNIEST
GG NAGGIEST
GH GAHNITES
GL GELATINS
GENITALS
STEALING
TAGLINES
GM MANGIEST
MINTAGES
MISAGENT
STEAMING
GN ANTIGENS
GENTIANS
GR ANGRIEST
ASTRINGE
GANISTER
GANTRIES
GRANITES
INGRATES
RANGIEST
GS EASTINGS
GIANTESS
SEATINGS
GT ESTATING
TANGIEST
GU SAUTEING
UNITAGES
GV VINTAGES
GW SWEATING
GY YEASTING
GZ TZIGANES
HH INSHEATH
HM HEMATINS
HP THESPIAN
HR HAIRNETS
INEARTHS
THERIANS
HS ANTHESIS
SHANTIES
SHEITANS
STHENIAS
HT HESITANT
HW INSWATHE
IK KAINITES
IL ALIENIST
LITANIES
IR INERTIAS
RAINIEST
IS ISATINES
SANITIES
SANITISE
TENIASIS
IV VANITIES
IZ SANITIZE
KL LANKIEST
KM MISTAKEN
KN NEATNIKS
KP SNAKEPIT
KR KERATINS
KS SNAKIEST
KU UNAKITES
KW TWANKIES
KY KYANITES
LM AILMENTS
ALIMENTS
MANLIEST
MELANIST
SMALTINE
LO ELATIONS
INSOLATE
TOENAILS
LP PANELIST
PANTILES
PLAINEST
LR ENTRAILS
LATRINES
RATLINES
RETINALS
TRENAILS
LS ELASTINS
NAILSETS
SALIENTS
SALTINES
LU ALUNITES
INSULATE
LV VENTAILS
MN MANNITES
MO AMNIOTES
MASONITE
MISATONE
MR MINARETS
RAIMENTS
MS MANTISES
MATINESS
NO ENATIONS
SONATINE
NR ENTRAINS
TRANNIES
NS INSANEST
STANINES
NT STANNITE
OP SAPONITE
OR NOTARIES
SENORITA
OS ASTONIES
PP NAPPIEST
PR PAINTERS
PANTRIES
PERTAINS
PINASTER
PRISTANE
REPAINTS
PS SAPIENTS
STEAPSIN
PT PATIENTS
PU PETUNIAS
SUPINATE
PY EPINASTY
QU ANTIQUES
RR RESTRAIN
RETRAINS
STRAINER
TERRAINS
TRAINERS
RS ARTINESS
RETSINAS
STAINERS
STEARINS
RT INTREATS
NITRATES
STRAITEN
TERTIANS
RU RUINATES
TAURINES
URANITES
URINATES
RW TINWARES
SS SESTINAS
ST ANTSIEST
INSTATES
NASTIEST
SATINETS
TITANESS
SU SINUATES
SX SEXTAINS
TT NATTIEST
TW TAWNIEST

2 SATIRE

AD AIRDATES
DATARIES
RADIATES
AH HETAIRAS
AM AMIRATES
AN ANTISERA
RATANIES
SANTERIA
SEATRAIN
AP ASPIRATE
PARASITE
SEPTARIA
AS ASTERIAS
ATRESIAS
AT ARIETTAS
ARISTATE
AV VARIATES
AW AWAITERS
BD REDBAITS
TRIBADES
BK BARKIEST
BRAKIEST
BL BLASTIER
LIBRATES
BM BARMIEST
BN BANISTER
BARNIEST
BR ARBITERS
RAREBITS
BT BIRETTAS
BV VIBRATES
BY BESTIARY
SYBARITE
CD ACRIDEST
CG AGRESTIC
CIGARETS
ERGASTIC
CH CHARIEST
THERIACS
CL ARTICLES
RECITALS
STERICAL
CM CERAMIST
MATRICES
MISTRACE
SCIMETAR
CN CANISTER
CERATINS
CISTERNA
CREATINS
SCANTIER
TACRINES
CP CRISPATE
PARETICS
PICRATES
PRACTISE
CR ERRATICS
CS SCARIEST
CT CITRATES
CRISTATE
SCATTIER
CU SURICATE
CZ CRAZIEST
DD DISRATED
DE READIEST
SERIATED
STEADIER
DH HARDIEST
DL DILATERS
LARDIEST
REDTAILS
DM MISRATED
READMITS
DN DETRAINS
RANDIEST
STRAINED
DO ASTEROID
DP RAPIDEST
TRAIPSED
DS DIASTERS
DISASTER
DISRATES
DT STRIATED
TARDIEST
DW TAWDRIES
EE EATERIES
EH HEARTIES
EL ATELIERS
EARLIEST
LEARIEST
REALTIES
EM EMERITAS
EMIRATES
STEAMIER
EN ARENITES
ARSENITE
RESINATE
STEARINE
TRAINEES
EP PARIETES
ER ARTERIES
ES SERIATES
ET ARIETTES
ITERATES
TEARIEST
TREATIES
TREATISE
EW SWEATIER
WASTERIE
WEARIEST
EY YEASTIER
FG FRIGATES
FI RATIFIES
FL FRAILEST
FN FAINTERS
GG STAGGIER
GL GLARIEST
GM MAGISTER
MIGRATES
RAGTIMES
STERIGMA
GN ANGRIEST
ASTRINGE
GANISTER
GANTRIES
GRANITES
INGRATES
RANGIEST
GP GRAPIEST
GV VIRGATES
HI HAIRIEST
HN HAIRNETS
INEARTHS
THERIANS
HO HOARIEST
HP TRIPHASE
HR TRASHIER
HU THESAURI
HW WATERISH
HY HYSTERIA
IL LISTERIA
IM AIRTIMES
SERIATIM
IN INERTIAS
RAINIEST
IP PARITIES
IR RARITIES
IS SATIRISE
IW WISTERIA
IX SEXTARII
IZ SATIRIZE
JO JAROSITE
KL LARKIEST
STALKIER
STARLIKE
KM MISTAKER
KN KERATINS
KS ASTERISK
SARKIEST
KW WATERSKI
LL LITERALS
TALLIERS
LM LAMISTER
MARLIEST
MARLITES
MISALTER
LN ENTRAILS
LATRINES
RATLINES
RETINALS
TRENAILS
LP PILASTER
PLAISTER
PLAITERS
LR RETRIALS
TRAILERS
LS REALISTS
SALTIERS
SALTIRES
LT TERTIALS
LU URALITES
MM MARMITES
RAMMIEST
MN MINARETS
RAIMENTS
MO AMORTISE
ATOMISER
MP PRIMATES
MS ASTERISM
MISRATES
SMARTIES
MT MISTREAT
TERATISM
MU MURIATES
MV VITAMERS
MW WARTIMES
MX MATRIXES
NN ENTRAINS
TRANNIES
NO NOTARIES
SENORITA
NP PAINTERS
PANTRIES
PERTAINS
PINASTER
PRISTANE
REPAINTS
NR RESTRAIN
RETRAINS
STRAINER
TERRAINS
TRAINERS
NS ARTINESS
RETSINAS
STAINERS
STEARINS
NT INTREATS
NITRATES
STRAITEN
TERTIANS
NU RUINATES
TAURINES
URANITES
URINATES
NW TINWARES
OR ROTARIES
OT TOASTIER
OU OUTRAISE
SAUTOIRE
OV TRAVOISE
VIATORES
VOTARIES
PP PERIAPTS
PR PARTIERS
PS PASTRIES
PIASTERS
PIASTRES
RASPIEST
TRAIPSES
PV PRIVATES
PW WIRETAPS
PY ASPERITY
RR STARRIER
TARRIERS
RS TARSIERS
RT STRAITER
TARRIEST
RW STRAWIER
SS ASSISTER
ST ARTISTES
ARTSIEST
STRIATES
SW WAISTERS
WAITRESS
WASTRIES
TT ATTRITES
RATTIEST
TARTIEST
TITRATES
TRISTATE
TW WARTIEST
TZ TRISTEZA
UZ AZURITES
VY VESTIARY

3 RETAIN

AB ATABRINE
AC CARINATE
CRANIATE
AG AERATING
AM ANIMATER
MARINATE
AO AERATION
AP ANTIRAPE
AS ANTISERA
RATANIES
SANTERIA
SEATRAIN
AT ATTAINER
REATTAIN
AW ANTIWEAR
AZ ATRAZINE
BC BACTERIN
BG BERATING
REBATING
TABERING
BO BARITONE
OBTAINER
REOBTAIN
TABORINE
BS BANISTER
BARNIEST
BU BRAUNITE
URBANITE
CC ACENTRIC
CD DICENTRA
CE CENTIARE
CREATINE
INCREATE
ITERANCE
CG ARGENTIC
CATERING
CREATING
REACTING
CL CLARINET
CO ACTIONER
ANORETIC
CREATION
REACTION
CS CANISTER
CERATINS
CISTERNA
CREATINS
SCANTIER
TACRINES
CT INTERACT
CU ANURETIC
CV NAVICERT
DE DETAINER
RETAINED
DG DERATING
GRADIENT
REDATING
TREADING
DH ANTHERID
DI DAINTIER
DO AROINTED
ORDINATE
RATIONED
DP DIPTERAN
DS DETRAINS
RANDIEST
STRAINED
DT NITRATED
DU INDURATE
RUINATED
URINATED
EG GRATINEE
INTERAGE
EH HERNIATE
EI INERTIAE
EK ANKERITE
EL ELATERIN
ENTAILER
TREENAIL
EM ANTIMERE
EP APERIENT
ER RETAINER
ES ARENITES
ARSENITE
RESINATE
STEARINE
TRAINEES
FL INFLATER
FS FAINTERS
GH EARTHING
HEARTING
INGATHER
GK RETAKING
GL ALERTING
ALTERING
INTEGRAL
RELATING
TANGLIER
TRIANGLE
GM EMIGRANT
REMATING
GP RETAPING
TAPERING
GS ANGRIEST
ASTRINGE
GANISTER
GANTRIES
GRANITES
INGRATES
RANGIEST
GT GNATTIER
TREATING
GV AVERTING
GRIEVANT
VINTAGER
GW TWANGIER
WATERING
GX RETAXING
HO ANTIHERO
HP PERIANTH
HS HAIRNETS
INEARTHS
THERIANS
IL INERTIAL
IN TRIENNIA
IP PAINTIER
IS INERTIAS
RAINIEST
IZ TRIAZINE
JU JAUNTIER
KS KERATINS
KW KNITWEAR
LM TERMINAL
TRAMLINE
LN INTERNAL
LO ORIENTAL
RELATION
LP INTERLAP
TRAPLINE
TRIPLANE
LS ENTRAILS
LATRINES
RATLINES
RETINALS
TRENAILS
LU AUNTLIER
RETINULA
TENURIAL
LV INTERVAL
LY INTERLAY
MN TRAINMEN
MS MINARETS
RAIMENTS
MT INTERMAT
MARTINET
MU RUMINATE
MY TYRAMINE
NO ANOINTER
REANOINT
NR INERRANT
NS ENTRAINS
TRANNIES
NT INTRANET
OP ATROPINE
OR ANTERIOR
OS NOTARIES
SENORITA
OT TENTORIA
OZ NOTARIZE
PR PRETRAIN
TERRAPIN
PS PAINTERS
PANTRIES
PERTAINS
PINASTER
PRISTANE
REPAINTS
PT TRIPTANE
QU ANTIQUER
QUAINTER
RS RESTRAIN
RETRAINS
STRAINER
TERRAINS
TRAINERS
RT RETIRANT
RV VERATRIN
RW INTERWAR
SS ARTINESS
RETSINAS
STAINERS
STEARINS
ST INTREATS
NITRATES
STRAITEN
TERTIANS
SU RUINATES
TAURINES
URANITES
URINATES
SW TINWARES

4 ARSINE

AC ACARINES
CANARIES
CESARIAN
SARCINAE
AD ARANEIDS
AG ANERGIAS
ANGARIES
ARGINASE
AT ANTISERA
RATANIES
SANTERIA
SEATRAIN
BC BRISANCE
CARBINES
BD BRANDIES
BG BEARINGS
SABERING
BH BANISHER
BI BINARIES
BK BEARSKIN
BL RINSABLE
BO BARONIES
SEAROBIN
BT BANISTER
BARNIEST
BU URBANISE
CE INCREASE
CF FANCIERS
CG CREASING
CH ARCHINES
INARCHES
CL CARLINES
LANCIERS
CM CARMINES
CREMAINS
CN CRANNIES
NARCEINS
CO SCENARIO
CS ARCSINES
ARSENICS
RACINESS
CT CANISTER
CERATINS
CISTERNA
CREATINS
SCANTIER
TACRINES
DD SARDINED
DE ARSENIDE
NEARSIDE
DG DERAIGNS
GRADINES
READINGS
DL ISLANDER
DN INSNARED
DO ANEROIDS
DP SPRAINED
DR DRAINERS
SERRANID
DS ARIDNESS
SARDINES
DT DETRAINS
RANDIEST
STRAINED
DU DENARIUS
UNRAISED
URANIDES
DV INVADERS
EG ANERGIES
GESNERIA
EK SNEAKIER
EL ALIENERS
EN ANSERINE
EP NAPERIES
ET ARENITES
ARSENITE
RESINATE
STEARINE
TRAINEES
EU UNEASIER
FO FARINOSE
FP FIREPANS
PANFRIES
FR REFRAINS
FS FAIRNESS
SANSERIF
FT FAINTERS
GG GEARINGS
GREASING
SNAGGIER
GH HEARINGS
HEARSING
SHEARING
GL ALIGNERS
ENGRAILS
NARGILES
REALIGNS
SIGNALER
SLANGIER
GM SMEARING
GN AGINNERS
EARNINGS
ENGRAINS
GRANNIES
GO ORGANISE
GP SPEARING
GR EARRINGS
GRAINERS
GS ASSIGNER
REASSIGN
SERINGAS
GT ANGRIEST
ASTRINGE
GANISTER
GANTRIES
GRANITES
INGRATES
RANGIEST
GV VINEGARS
GW RESAWING
SWEARING
GY RESAYING
SYNERGIA
HL INHALERS

HM HARMINES
HP HEPARINS
SERAPHIN
HT HAIRNETS
INEARTHS
THERIANS
HV ENRAVISH
VANISHER
IK KAISERIN
IL AIRLINES
IN SIRENIAN
IS AIRINESS
IT INERTIAS
RAINIEST
KK SKANKIER
KM RAMEKINS
KP RANPIKES
KR SNARKIER
KT KERATINS
KW SWANKIER
LM MARLINES
MINERALS
MISLEARN
LO AILERONS
ALIENORS
LP PRALINES
LR SNARLIER
LS RAINLESS
LT ENTRAILS
LATRINES
RATLINES
RETINALS
TRENAILS
LV RAVELINS
LX RELAXINS
LY INLAYERS
MN REINSMAN
MO MORAINES
ROMAINES
ROMANISE
MR MARINERS
MS SEMINARS
MT MINARETS
RAIMENTS
MU ANEURISM
MY SEMINARY
NO RAISONNE
NP PANNIERS
NR INSNARER
NS INSNARES
NT ENTRAINS
TRANNIES
NU ANEURINS
OS ERASIONS
SENSORIA
OT NOTARIES
SENORITA
OV AVERSION
PP SNAPPIER
PT PAINTERS
PANTRIES
PERTAINS
PINASTER
PRISTANE
REPAINTS
RT RESTRAIN
RETRAINS
STRAINER
TERRAINS
TRAINERS
ST ARTINESS
RETSINAS
STAINERS
STEARINS
SU ANURESIS
SENARIUS
SW WARINESS
TT INTREATS
NITRATES
STRAITEN
TERTIANS
TU RUINATES
TAURINES
URANITES
URINATES
TW TINWARES
UZ SUZERAIN
VV VERVAINS
ZZ SNAZZIER

5 SENIOR

AB BARONIES
SEAROBIN
AC SCENARIO
AD ANEROIDS
AF FARINOSE
AG ORGANISE
AL AILERONS
ALIENORS
AM MORAINES
ROMAINES
ROMANISE
AN RAISONNE
AS ERASIONS
SENSORIA
AT NOTARIES
SENORITA
AV AVERSION
BB SNOBBIER
BC BICORNES
BF BONFIRES
BG SOBERING
BI BRIONIES
BM BROMINES
BT BORNITES
BW BROWNIES
BY BRYONIES
CC CONCISER
CORNICES
CROCEINS
CD CONSIDER
CF COINFERS
CONIFERS
FORENSIC
FORNICES
CG COREIGNS
COSIGNER
CH CHORINES
CI RECISION
SORICINE
CL INCLOSER
LICENSOR
CM INCOMERS
SERMONIC
CP CONSPIRE
INCORPSE
CR RESORCIN
CS NECROSIS
CT COINTERS
CORNIEST
NOTICERS
CU COINSURE
DD INDORSED
DE INDORSEE
DG NEGROIDS
DH HORDEINS
DI DERISION
IRONSIDE
RESINOID
DJ JOINDERS
DP PRISONED
DR INDORSER
DS INDORSES
SORDINES
DU DOURINES
SOURDINE
EG ERINGOES
EH HEROINES
EK KEROSINE
EL ELOINERS
EM EMERSION
EP ISOPRENE
PEREIONS
PIONEERS
ET ONERIEST
SEROTINE
EV EVERSION
FK FORESKIN
FM ENSIFORM
FERMIONS
FN INFERNOS
GI SEIGNIOR
GL RESOLING
GN NEGRONIS
GP PERIGONS
REPOSING
SPONGIER
GR IGNORERS
GS GORINESS
GT GENITORS
GW RESOWING
GY SEIGNORY
HT HORNIEST
ORNITHES
IL LIONISER
IP RIPIENOS
IV REVISION
IZ IONIZERS
IRONIZES
JT JOINTERS
KM MONIKERS
KN EINKORNS
NONSKIER
KT INSTROKE
KV INVOKERS
LM MISENROL
LP PROLINES
LR LORINERS
LT RETINOLS
MM MISNOMER
MO IONOMERS
MOONRISE
MP PROMINES
MU MONSIEUR
MW WINSOMER
NS IRONNESS
NT INTONERS
TERNIONS
NU REUNIONS
NV ENVIRONS
OP POISONER
SNOOPIER
SPOONIER
OS EROSIONS
OT SNOOTIER
OW SWOONIER
OZ SNOOZIER
PP PROPINES
PR PRISONER
PS ROPINESS
PT POINTERS
PORNIEST
PROTEINS
TROPINES
PU PRUINOSE
PV OVERSPIN
RT INTRORSE
SS ROSINESS
ST OESTRINS
SU NEUROSIS
RESINOUS
SV VERSIONS
TT SNOTTIER
TENORIST
TRITONES
TU ROUTINES
SNOUTIER
TV INVESTOR
TY SEROTINY
TYROSINE
UV SOUVENIR

6 STERNA

AB ANTBEARS
RATSBANE
AC CATERANS
AE ARSENATE
SERENATA
AG TANAGERS
AI ANTISERA
RATANIES
SANTERIA
SEATRAIN
AL ASTERNAL
AM SARMENTA
AR NARRATES
AS SANTERAS
AV TAVERNAS
TSAREVNA
BD BARTENDS
BE ABSENTER
BI BANISTER
BARNIEST
BO BARONETS
BU URBANEST
CE CENTARES
REASCENT
REENACTS
SARCENET
CH CHANTERS
SNATCHER
STANCHER
TRANCHES
CI CANISTER
CERATINS
CISTERNA
CREATINS
SCANTIER
TACRINES
CK CRANKEST
CL CENTRALS
CO ANCESTOR
ENACTORS
CT TRANSECT
CU CENTAURS
RECUSANT
UNCRATES
CY ANCESTRY
DD DARNDEST
STRANDED
DG DRAGNETS
GRANDEST
DI DETRAINS
RANDIEST
STRAINED
DR STRANDER
DS STANDERS
DU DAUNTERS
TRANSUDE
UNTREADS
DX DEXTRANS
EE SERENATE
EF FASTENER
FENESTRA
REFASTEN
EG ESTRANGE
GRANTEES
GREATENS
NEGATERS
REAGENTS
SERGEANT
EH HASTENER
HEARTENS
EI ARENITES
ARSENITE
RESINATE
STEARINE
TRAINEES
EJ SERJEANT
EL ETERNALS
TELERANS
EO EARSTONE
RESONATE
ER TERRANES
ES ASSENTER
EARNESTS
SARSENET
ET ENTREATS
RATTEENS
EU SAUTERNE
EV VETERANS
FG ENGRAFTS
FI FAINTERS
FK FRANKEST
FM RAFTSMEN
FO SEAFRONT
FR TRANSFER
GG GANGSTER
GI ANGRIEST
ASTRINGE
GANISTER
GANTRIES
GRANITES
INGRATES
RANGIEST
GL STRANGLE
TANGLERS
GM GARMENTS
MARGENTS
GO ESTRAGON
NEGATORS
GP TREPANGS
GR GRANTERS
REGRANTS
STRANGER
GS STRANGES
GW TWANGERS
HI HAIRNETS
INEARTHS
THERIANS
HK THANKERS
HL ENTHRALS
HM TRASHMEN
HP PANTHERS
HU HAUNTERS
UNEARTHS
URETHANS
II INERTIAS
RAINIEST
IK KERATINS
IL ENTRAILS
LATRINES
RATLINES
RETINALS
TRENAILS
IM MINARETS
RAIMENTS
IN ENTRAINS
TRANNIES
IO NOTARIES
SENORITA
IP PAINTERS
PANTRIES
PERTAINS
PINASTER
PRISTANE
REPAINTS
IR RESTRAIN
RETRAINS
STRAINER
TERRAINS
TRAINERS
IS ARTINESS
RETSINAS
STAINERS
STEARINS
IT INTREATS
NITRATES
STRAITEN
TERTIANS
IU RUINATES
TAURINES
URANITES
URINATES
IW TINWARES
LN LANTERNS
LP PLANTERS
REPLANTS
LS SALTERNS
LT SLATTERN
LU NEUTRALS
LV VENTRALS
MN REMNANTS
MO MONSTERA
ONSTREAM
TONEARMS
MS SARMENTS
SMARTENS
MU MENSTRUA
MV VARMENTS
NO RESONANT
NT ENTRANTS
OP OPERANTS
PRONATES
PROTEANS
OR ANTRORSE
OS ASSENTOR
SANTEROS
SENATORS
STARNOSE
TREASONS
OU OUTEARNS
PR PARTNERS
PS PASTERNS
RAPTNESS
PT PATTERNS
TRANSEPT
TRAPNEST
SS SARSNETS
ST TARTNESS
SU ANESTRUS
SAUNTERS
SV SERVANTS
VERSANTS
TU TAUNTERS
UV VAUNTERS
WY STERNWAY

7 TOESIN

AB BOTANIES
BOTANISE
NIOBATES
OBEISANT
AC ACONITES
CANOEIST
SONICATE
AD ASTONIED
SEDATION
AL ELATIONS
INSOLATE
TOENAILS
AM AMNIOTES
MASONITE
MISATONE
AN ENATIONS
SONATINE
AP SAPONITE
AR NOTARIES
SENORITA
AS ASTONIES
BB NOBBIEST
BE BETONIES
EBONITES
BI NIOBITES
BK STEINBOK
BN BONNIEST
BO BONITOES
EOBIONTS
BR BORNITES
BU BOUNTIES
CC CONCEITS
CE SEICENTO
CG ESCOTING
CL LECTIONS
TELSONIC
CM CENTIMOS
CO COONTIES
CR COINTERS
CORNIEST
NOTICERS
CS SECTIONS
CT STENOTIC
TONETICS
CU COUNTIES
CX EXCITONS
CY CYTOSINE
DH HEDONIST
DI EDITIONS
SEDITION
DL LENTOIDS
DM DEMONIST
DW DOWNIEST
EG EGESTION
EM MONETISE
SEMITONE
ER ONERIEST
SEROTINE
ES ESSONITE
ET NOISETTE
TEOSINTE
FI NOTIFIES
FT FISTNOTE
GH HISTOGEN
GM MITOGENS
GO GOONIEST
GR GENITORS
HL HOLSTEIN
HOTLINES
NEOLITHS
HP PHONIEST
HR HORNIEST
ORNITHES
HS HISTONES
HU OUTSHINE
IS INOSITES
NOISIEST
JR JOINTERS
JT JETTISON
KM TOKENISM
KN INKSTONE
KR INSTROKE
KW WONKIEST
LN INSOLENT
LO LOONIEST
OILSTONE
LP POTLINES
TOPLINES
LR RETINOLS
LU ELUTIONS
OUTLINES
LV NOVELIST
LW TOWLINES
MN MENTIONS
MO EMOTIONS
MOONIEST
MP NEPOTISM
PIMENTOS
MS MESTINOS
MOISTENS
SENTIMOS
NR INTONERS
TERNIONS
NS TENSIONS
NT TINSTONE
TONTINES
OR SNOOTIER
OS ISOTONES
OW TWOONIES
PR POINTERS
PORNIEST
PROTEINS
TROPINES
PT NEPOTIST
PU POUTINES
QU QUESTION
RR INTRORSE
RS OESTRINS
RT SNOTTIER
TENORIST
TRITONES
RU ROUTINES
SNOUTIER
RV INVESTOR
RY SEROTINY
TYROSINE
SS SONSIEST
STENOSIS
ST STONIEST
SW SNOWIEST
VY VENOSITY

8 ORATES

AB AEROBATS
AR AERATORS
AS AEROSATS
AT AEROSTAT
BC CABESTRO
CABRESTO
BD BROADEST
BL BLOATERS
SORTABLE
STORABLE
BM BROMATES
BN BARONETS
BP PROBATES
BR ABORTERS
TABORERS
BS BOASTERS
SORBATES
BT ABETTORS
TABORETS
BU SABOTEUR
CC ECTOSARC
CD REDCOATS
CF FORECAST
CG ESCARGOT
CH THORACES
CL LOCATERS
SECTORAL
CN ANCESTOR
ENACTORS
CP POSTRACE
CR CREATORS
REACTORS
CS COARSEST
COASTERS
CU OUTRACES
CV OVERACTS
OVERCAST
CX EXACTORS
DI ASTEROID
DL DELATORS
LEOTARDS
LODESTAR
DP ADOPTERS
PASTORED
READOPTS
DR ROADSTER
DS ASSORTED
TORSADES
DU OUTDARES
OUTREADS
READOUTS
DX EXTRADOS
EK KERATOSE
EL OLEASTER
EN EARSTONE
RESONATE
EP OPERATES
PROTEASE
EV OVEREATS
FF AFFOREST
FG FAGOTERS
FL FLOATERS
FORESTAL
REFLOATS
FM FOREMAST
FORMATES
FN SEAFRONT
FP FOREPAST
FV OVERFAST
FW SOFTWARE
FY FORESTAY
GH SHORTAGE
GL GLOATERS
LEGATORS
GN ESTRAGON
NEGATORS
GO ROOTAGES
GP PORTAGES
GR GARROTES
GS STORAGES
GT GAROTTES
GU OUTRAGES
HI HOARIEST
HL LOATHERS
RATHOLES
HM TERAOHMS
HP PHORATES
HS EARSHOTS
HOARSEST
HT RHEOSTAT
HU OUTHEARS
HX OXHEARTS
THORAXES
IJ JAROSITE
IM AMORTISE
ATOMISER
IN NOTARIES
SENORITA
IR ROTARIES
IT TOASTIER
IU OUTRAISE
SAUTOIRE
IV TRAVOISE
VIATORES
VOTARIES
KV OVERTASK
KW SEATWORK
LL REALLOTS
ROSTELLA
LP PETROSAL
POLESTAR
LR REALTORS
RELATORS
RESTORAL
LS OLESTRAS
LT RETOTALS
LU ROSULATE
LV LEVATORS
OVERSALT
MM MARMOSET
MN MONSTERA
ONSTREAM
TONEARMS
MO TEAROOMS
MR REARMOST
MS MAESTROS
NN RESONANT
NP OPERANTS
PRONATES
PROTEANS
NR ANTRORSE
NS ASSENTOR
SANTEROS
SENATORS
STARNOSE
TREASONS
NU OUTEARNS
OR SORORATE
PP TRAPPOSE
PR PRAETORS
PRORATES
PS ESPARTOS
PROTASES
SEAPORTS
PT PROSTATE
PU APTEROUS
PV OVERPAST
QU EQUATORS
QUAESTOR
RR ARRESTOR
RS ASSERTOR
ASSORTER
ORATRESS
REASSORT
ROASTERS
RT ROSTRATE
SS OSSETRAS
ST TOASTERS
SU OSSATURE
SV VOTARESS
SX STORAXES
TT ATTESTOR
TESTATOR
TU OUTRATES
OUTSTARE
SEATROUT
UV OUTRAVES
UW OUTSWARE
OUTSWEAR
OUTWEARS
VY OVERSTAY

9 REASON

AM AMARONES
BB BASEBORN
BD BANDORES
BROADENS
BE SEABORNE
BG BEGROANS
BI BARONIES
SEAROBIN
BN BARONNES
BS BARONESS
BT BARONETS
BZ ZEBRANOS
CD ENDOSARC
CG ACROGENS
CI SCENARIO
CM ROMANCES
CS COARSENS
NARCOSES
CT ANCESTOR
ENACTORS
CU NACREOUS
DE REASONED
DH HARDNOSE
DI ANEROIDS
DL LADRONES
SOLANDER
DM MADRONES
RANSOMED
DP OPERANDS
PADRONES
PANDORES
DR ADORNERS
READORNS
EP PERSONAE
ER REASONER
ES RESEASON
SEASONER
ET EARSTONE
RESONATE
FI FARINOSE
FK FORSAKEN
FL FARNESOL
FM FORAMENS
FP PROFANES
FT SEAFRONT
FU FURANOSE
GI ORGANISE
GO OREGANOS
GR GROANERS
GT ESTRAGON
NEGATORS
GW WAGONERS
HM HORSEMAN
MENORAHS
RHAMNOSE
HS HOARSENS
SENHORAS
IL AILERONS
ALIENORS
IM MORAINES
ROMAINES
ROMANISE
IN RAISONNE
IS ERASIONS
SENSORIA
IT NOTARIES
SENORITA
IV AVERSION
LM ALMONERS
LP PERSONAL
PSORALEN
LU ALEURONS
NEUROSAL
MN MONERANS
SONARMEN
MP MANROPES
MR RANSOMER
MT MONSTERA
ONSTREAM
TONEARMS
MU ENAMOURS
NEUROMAS
MV OVERMANS
NT RESONANT
NU UNREASON
NY ANNOYERS
PP PROPANES
PS PERSONAS
RESPONSA
PT OPERANTS
PRONATES
PROTEANS
PY PYRANOSE
RS SERRANOS

RT ANTRORSE
ST ASSENTOR
SANTEROS
SENATORS
STARNOSE
TREASONS
SU ANSEROUS
ARSENOUS
TU OUTEARNS
UV RAVENOUS

10 INSERT

AA ANTISERA
RATANIES
SANTERIA
SEATRAIN
AB BANISTER
BARNIEST
AC CANISTER
CERATINS
CISTERNA
CREATINS
SCANTIER
TACRINES
AD DETRAINS
RANDIEST
STRAINED
AE ARENITES
ARSENITE
RESINATE
STEARINE
TRAINEES
AF FAINTERS
AG ANGRIEST
ASTRINGE
GANISTER
GANTRIES
GRANITES
INGRATES
RANGIEST
AH HAIRNETS
INEARTHS
THERIANS
AI INERTIAS
RAINIEST
AK KERATINS
AL ENTRAILS
LATRINES
RATLINES
RETINALS
TRENAILS
AM MINARETS
RAIMENTS
AN ENTRAINS
TRANNIES
AO NOTARIES
SENORITA
AP PAINTERS
PANTRIES
PERTAINS
PINASTER
PRISTANE
REPAINTS
AR RESTRAIN
RETRAINS
STRAINER
TERRAINS
TRAINERS
AS ARTINESS
RETSINAS
STAINERS
STEARINS
AT INTREATS
NITRATES
STRAITEN
TERTIANS
AU RUINATES
TAURINES
URANITES
URINATES
AW TINWARES
BI BRINIEST
BO BORNITES
BT BITTERNS
BU TRIBUNES
TURBINES
CE ENTERICS
ENTICERS
SECRETIN
CG CRESTING
CH CHRISTEN
CITHERNS
CITHRENS
SNITCHER
CI CITRINES
CRINITES
INCITERS
CK STRICKEN
CM CENTRISM
CO COINTERS
CORNIEST
NOTICERS
CS CISTERNS
CT CENTRIST
CITTERNS
DD STRIDDEN
DE INSERTED
NERDIEST
RESIDENT
SINTERED
TRENDIES
DG STRINGED
DI DISINTER
INDITERS
NITRIDES
DL TENDRILS
TRINDLES
DP SPRINTED
DT STRIDENT
TRIDENTS
DU INTRUDES
DX DEXTRINS
EE ETERNISE
TEENSIER
EF FERNIEST
INFESTER
EG GENTRIES
INTEGERS
REESTING
STEERING
EI NITERIES
EK KERNITES
EL ENLISTER
LISTENER
REENLIST
SILENTER
EM MISENTER
EN INTENSER
INTERNES
EO ONERIEST
SEROTINE
ER INSERTER
REINSERT
REINTERS
RENTIERS
TERRINES
ES SENTRIES
ET INSETTER
INTEREST
STERNITE
TRIENTES
EU ESURIENT
RETINUES
REUNITES
EV NERVIEST
REINVEST
SIRVENTE
EX INTERSEX
EY SERENITY
FN FERNINST
FS SNIFTERS
GI IGNITERS
RESITING
STINGIER
GL RINGLETS
STERLING
TINGLERS
GO GENITORS
GR RESTRING
STRINGER
GS STINGERS
TRIGNESS
GT GITTERNS
GW STREWING
WRESTING
HI INHERITS
HK RETHINKS
THINKERS
HN THINNERS
HO HORNIEST
ORNITHES
HZ ZITHERNS
IK STINKIER
IL NITRILES
IM INTERIMS
MINISTER
MISINTER
IP PRISTINE
IS INSISTER
SINISTER
IT NITRITES
IU NEURITIS
IV INVITERS
VITRINES
JO JOINTERS
KL TINKLERS
KO INSTROKE
KS STINKERS
KT KNITTERS
TRINKETS
LM MINSTREL
LO RETINOLS
LP SPLINTER
LU INSULTER
MS MINSTERS
TRIMNESS
MU TERMINUS
UNMITERS
UNMITRES
MY MISENTRY
NO INTONERS
TERNIONS
NU RUNNIEST
NV VINTNERS
OO SNOOTIER
OP POINTERS
PORNIEST
PROTEINS
TROPINES
OR INTRORSE
OS OESTRINS
OT SNOTTIER
TENORIST
TRITONES
OU ROUTINES
SNOUTIER
OV INVESTOR
OY SEROTINY
TYROSINE
PR PRINTERS
REPRINTS
SPRINTER
PS SPINSTER
PU UNRIPEST
QU SQUINTER
ST STINTERS
TU RUNTIEST
UV VENTURIS

11 TONERS

AB BARONETS
AC ANCESTOR
ENACTORS
AE EARSTONE
RESONATE
AF SEAFRONT
AG ESTRAGON
NEGATORS
AI NOTARIES
SENORITA
AM MONSTERA
ONSTREAM
TONEARMS
AN RESONANT
AP OPERANTS
PRONATES
PROTEANS
AR ANTRORSE
AS ASSENTOR
SANTEROS
SENATORS
STARNOSE
TREASONS
AU OUTEARNS
BH BETHORNS
BI BORNITES
BS SORBENTS
BU BURSTONE
BW BESTROWN
BROWNEST
CC CONCERTS
CH CHORTENS
NOTCHERS
CI COINTERS
CORNIEST
NOTICERS
CO CORONETS
CU CONSTRUE
COUNTERS
RECOUNTS
TROUNCES
CV CONVERTS
CW CROWNETS
DM MORDENTS
DP PORTENDS
PROTENDS
DU ROUNDEST
TONSURED
UNSORTED
DY DRYSTONE
EF RESOFTEN
SOFTENER
EG ESTROGEN
EH HONESTER
EI ONERIEST
SEROTINE
EL ENTRESOL
EN ENTERONS
TENONERS
EO OESTRONE
ES ESTRONES
EX EXTENSOR
FP FORSPENT
FR REFRONTS
FU FORTUNES
GI GENITORS
GN RONTGENS
GR STRONGER
GS SONGSTER
GU STURGEON
GW WRONGEST
HI HORNIEST
ORNITHES
HR NORTHERS
HS SHORTENS
HU SOUTHERN
IJ JOINTERS
IK INSTROKE
IL RETINOLS
IN INTONERS
TERNIONS
IO SNOOTIER
IP POINTERS
PORNIEST
PROTEINS
TROPINES
IR INTRORSE
IS OESTRINS
IT SNOTTIER
TENORIST
TRITONES
IU ROUTINES
SNOUTIER
IV INVESTOR
IY SEROTINY
TYROSINE
KT KNOTTERS
KW NETWORKS
LU TURNSOLE
MO MESOTRON
MONTEROS
MS MONSTERS
MT TORMENTS
MU MOUNTERS
REMOUNTS
NS STERNSON
NU NEUTRONS
OU OUTSNORE
PS POSTERNS
PT PORTENTS
RS SNORTERS
RT TORRENTS
ST STENTORS
SU TONSURES
UY TOURNEYS

12 EASTER

AF RATAFEES
AH HETAERAS
AM AMREETAS
AN ARSENATE
SERENATA
AP ASPERATE
SEPARATE
AT STEARATE
AW SEAWATER
TEAWARES
BC ACERBEST
BD BREASTED
DEBATERS
BG ABSTERGE
BH BREATHES
BL ARBELEST
BLEATERS
RESTABLE
RETABLES
BN ABSENTER
BR REBATERS
BT ABETTERS
BERETTAS
CC ACCRETES
CH CHEATERS
HECTARES
RECHEATS
TEACHERS
CL CLEAREST
TREACLES
CM CREMATES
CN CENTARES
REASCENT
REENACTS
SARCENET
CR CATERERS
RECRATES
RETRACES
TERRACES
CS CATERESS
CERASTES
CU SECATEUR
CX EXACTERS
DE RESEATED
DF DRAFTEES
DG RESTAGED
DH HEADREST
DI READIEST
SERIATED
STEADIER
DK STREAKED
DL DESALTER
RESLATED
TREADLES
DM MASTERED
STREAMED
DP PEDERAST
PREDATES
REPASTED
TRAPESED
DR ARRESTED
RETREADS
SERRATED
TREADERS
DS ASSERTED
DT RESTATED
RETASTED
DW DEWATERS
TARWEEDS
DY ESTRAYED
EG EAGEREST
ETAGERES
STEERAGE
EI EATERIES
EL TEASELER
EN SERENATE
ER ARRESTEE
ES ESTERASE
TESSERAE
FH FEATHERS
FL REFLATES
FN FASTENER
FENESTRA
REFASTEN
FR FERRATES
FS FEASTERS
FU FEATURES
GM GAMESTER
GN ESTRANGE
GRANTEES
GREATENS
NEGATERS
REAGENTS
SERGEANT
GR REGRATES
GS RESTAGES
GT GREATEST
HH HEATHERS
SHEATHER
HI HEARTIES
HK HEKTARES
HL HALTERES
LEATHERS
HN HASTENER
HEARTENS
HP PREHEATS
HT EARTHSET
THEATERS
THEATRES
HW WEATHERS
WREATHES
IL ATELIERS
EARLIEST
LEARIEST
REALTIES
IM EMERITAS
EMIRATES
STEAMIER
IN ARENITES
ARSENITE
RESINATE
STEARINE
TRAINEES
IP PARIETES
IR ARTERIES
IS SERIATES
IT ARIETTES
ITERATES
TEARIEST
TREATIES
TREATISE
IW SWEATIER
WASTERIE
WEARIEST
IY YEASTIER
JN SERJEANT
KM MEERKATS
KO KERATOSE
KR RETAKERS
STREAKER
LN ETERNALS
TELERANS
LO OLEASTER
LP PETRALES
PLEATERS
PRELATES
REPLATES
LR ALTERERS
REALTERS
RELATERS
LS RESLATES
STEALERS
TEARLESS
LT ALERTEST
LU RESALUTE
LX EXALTERS
LY EASTERLY
MM AMMETERS
METAMERS
MP TEMPERAS
MR REMASTER
STREAMER
MS MASSETER
SEAMSTER
STEAMERS
MT TEAMSTER
MW STEMWARE
NO EARSTONE
RESONATE
NR TERRANES
NS ASSENTER
EARNESTS
SARSENET
NT ENTREATS
RATTEENS
NU SAUTERNE
NV VETERANS
OP OPERATES
PROTEASE
OV OVEREATS
PP PREPASTE
PRETAPES
PR TAPERERS
PS TRAPESES
PT PEARTEST
PRETASTE
PZ TRAPEZES
RR ARRESTER
REARREST
RS ASSERTER
REASSERT
SERRATES
TERRASES
RT RETREATS
TREATERS
RU AUSTERER
TREASURE
RV AVERTERS
TRAVERSE
RW WATERERS
ST ESTREATS
RESTATES
RETASTES
SW SWEATERS
SZ ERSATZES
TT ATTESTER
WW WETWARES

13 AIDERS

AF FARADISE
SAFARIED
AH AIRHEADS
AL SALARIED
AM MADEIRAS
AN ARANEIDS
AP PARADISE
AT AIRDATES
DATARIES
RADIATES
BC ASCRIBED
CARBIDES
BG ABRIDGES
BRIGADES
BL BEDRAILS
DISABLER
BN BRANDIES
BR BRAIDERS
BS SEABIRDS
SIDEBARS
BT REDBAITS
TRIBADES
BU DAUBRIES
BW BAWDRIES
CE DECIARES
CG DISGRACE
CH RACHIDES
CL DECRIALS
RADICELS
RADICLES
CO IDOCRASE
CP PERACIDS
CS SIDECARS
CT ACRIDEST
DH DIEHARDS
DM DISARMED
DN SARDINED
DO ROADSIDE
DP DISPREAD
DT DISRATED
DW SIDEWARD
EG DISAGREE
EL REALISED
RESAILED
SIDEREAL
EN ARSENIDE
NEARSIDE
EP AIRSPEED
ER DREARIES
RERAISED
ET READIEST
SERIATED
STEADIER
FO FORESAID
FS FARSIDES
GH HAGRIDES
GM MISGRADE
GN DERAIGNS
GRADINES
READINGS
HM MISHEARD
SEMIHARD
HP RAPHIDES
HS AIRSHEDS
RADISHES
HT HARDIEST
HV RAVISHED
HW DISHWARE
RAWHIDES
HY HAYRIDES
IM SEMIARID
IP PRESIDIA
JM JEMIDARS
LL DALLIERS
DIALLERS
LM DISMALER
LN ISLANDER
LO DARIOLES
LP LIPREADS
PARSLIED
SPIRALED
LT DILATERS
LARDIEST
REDTAILS
LU RESIDUAL
LY DIALYSER
MM MERMAIDS
MR ADMIRERS
DISARMER
MARRIEDS
MS MISREADS
SIDEARMS
MT MISRATED
READMITS
MY MIDYEARS
NN INSNARED
NO ANEROIDS
NP SPRAINED
NR DRAINERS
SERRANID
NS ARIDNESS
SARDINES
NT DETRAINS
RANDIEST
STRAINED
NU DENARIUS
UNRAISED
URANIDES
NV INVADERS
OP DIASPORE
PARODIES
OT ASTEROID
OV AVODIRES
AVOIDERS
PP APPRISED
PS DESPAIRS
PT RAPIDEST
TRAIPSED
PU UPRAISED
PW RIPSAWED
QU QUERIDAS
ST DIASTERS
DISASTER
DISRATES
SU RADIUSES
SUDARIES
SV ADVISERS
TT STRIATED
TARDIEST
TW TAWDRIES

14 RAINED

AC RADIANCE
AG DRAINAGE
GARDENIA
AM MARINADE
AS ARANEIDS
BD BRANDIED
BG BEARDING
BREADING
BL BILANDER
BN ENDBRAIN
BO DEBONAIR
BS BRANDIES
CD CANDIDER
RIDDANCE
CH INARCHED
CI ACRIDINE
CN CRANNIED
CT DICENTRA
DG DREADING
READDING
DO ORDAINED
DS SARDINED
EG REGAINED
EL RENAILED
EM REMAINED
ES ARSENIDE
NEARSIDE
ET DETAINER
RETAINED
EV REINVADE
FP PANFRIED
FR INFRARED
GH ADHERING
GI DEAIRING
GL DANGLIER
DRAGLINE
GM DREAMING
MARGINED
MIDRANGE
GO ORGANDIE
GS DERAIGNS
GRADINES
READINGS
GT DERATING
GRADIENT
REDATING
TREADING
GY READYING
HL HARDLINE
HT ANTHERID
HU UNHAIRED
IM MERIDIAN
IT DAINTIER
IU UREDINIA
KP KIDNAPER
LN INLANDER
LS ISLANDER
MO RADIOMEN
MU MURAENID
MY DAIRYMEN
MZ ZEMINDAR
NS INSNARED
NZ RENDZINA
OR ORDAINER
REORDAIN
OS ANEROIDS
OT AROINTED
ORDINATE
RATIONED
PS SPRAINED
PT DIPTERAN
PU UNPAIRED
UNREPAID
RS DRAINERS
SERRANID
SS ARIDNESS
SARDINES
ST DETRAINS
RANDIEST
STRAINED
SU DENARIUS
UNRAISED
URANIDES
SV INVADERS
TT NITRATED
TU INDURATE
RUINATED
URINATED
UV UNVARIED
VY VINEYARD

15 LESION

AG GASOLINE
AK KAOLINES
AM LAMINOSE
SEMOLINA
AN SOLANINE
AP OPALINES
AR AILERONS
ALIENORS
AS ANISOLES
AT ELATIONS
INSOLATE
TOENAILS
AX SILOXANE
BC BINOCLES
BF LOBEFINS
BP BONSPIEL
BU NUBILOSE
BW BOWLINES
CD INCLOSED
CE CINEOLES
CH CHOLINES
HELICONS
CI ISOCLINE
SILICONE
CO COLONIES
COLONISE
ECLOSION
CP PINOCLES
CR INCLOSER
LICENSOR
CS INCLOSES
CT LECTIONS
TELSONIC
CX LEXICONS
DE LESIONED
DG SIDELONG
DI LIONISED
DO EIDOLONS
SOLENOID
DT LENTOIDS
DU DELUSION
INSOULED
UNSOILED
EF FELONIES
OLEFINES
EK NOSELIKE
ER ELOINERS
EV NOVELISE
FM FOILSMEN
FX FLEXIONS
GK SONGLIKE
GR RESOLING
GS LOGINESS
GU LIGNEOUS
GW LONGWISE
HK SINKHOLE
HL HELLIONS
HM LEMONISH

HP PINHOLES
HS HOLINESS
HT HOLSTEIN
HOTLINES
NEOLITHS
IR LIONISER
IS ELISIONS
ISOLINES
LIONISES
OILINESS
IV OLIVINES
IZ LIONIZES
KM MOLESKIN
KW SNOWLIKE
LM SEMILLON
MO OINOMELS
SIMOLEON
MR MISENROL
MU EMULSION
NT INSOLENT
NV NONLIVES
OT LOONIEST
OILSTONE
OV VIOLONES
PR PROLINES
PS EPSILONS
PT POTLINES
TOPLINES
RR LORINERS
RT RETINOLS
SU ELUSIONS
SW LEWISSON
TU ELUTIONS
OUTLINES
TV NOVELIST
TW TOWLINES
UV EVULSION
VV INVOLVES

16 TORIES

AD ASTEROID
AH HOARIEST
AJ JAROSITE
AM AMORTISE
ATOMISER
AN NOTARIES
SENORITA
AR ROTARIES
AT TOASTIER
AU OUTRAISE
SAUTOIRE
AV TRAVOISE
VIATORES
VOTARIES
BC BISECTOR
BD DEORBITS
BK REITBOKS
BL STROBILE
BN BORNITES
BR ORBITERS
BY SOBRIETY
CC CORTICES
CD CORDITES
CE COTERIES
ESOTERIC
CK CORKIEST
ROCKIEST
STOCKIER
CL CLOISTER
COISTREL
COSTLIER
CM MORTICES
CN COINTERS
CORNIEST
NOTICERS
CS CROSSTIE
CT COTTIERS
CU CITREOUS
OUTCRIES
CV EVICTORS
VORTICES
CW COWRITES
CX EXCITORS
EXORCIST
DG DIGESTOR
GRODIEST
STODGIER
DI DIORITES
DK DORKIEST
DL STOLIDER
DM MORTISED
DP DIOPTERS
DIOPTRES
PERIDOTS
PORTSIDE
PROTEIDS
RIPOSTED
TOPSIDER
DS STEROIDS
DU OUTRIDES
OUTSIDER
DW ROWDIEST
WORDIEST
EH ISOTHERE
THEORIES
THEORISE
EM TIRESOME
EN ONERIEST
SEROTINE
EP POETISER
POETRIES
EZ EROTIZES
FF FORFEITS
FK FORKIEST
FL TREFOILS
FM SETIFORM
FP FIREPOTS
PIEFORTS
POSTFIRE
FR FROSTIER
ROTIFERS
FU OUTFIRES
GH GHOSTIER
GM ERGOTISM
GN GENITORS
GS GORSIEST
STRIGOSE
GV VERTIGOS
HM ISOTHERM
HN HORNIEST
ORNITHES
HP TROPHIES
HR HERITORS
HS HOISTERS
HORSIEST
SHORTIES
HT THEORIST
THORITES
HW WORTHIES
IL ROILIEST
JN JOINTERS
KN INSTROKE
KO ROOKIEST
KP PORKIEST
LL TROLLIES
LN RETINOLS
LO OESTRIOL
LP POITRELS
LS ESTRIOLS
LT TRIOLETS
LU OUTLIERS
MO MOORIEST
MOTORISE
ROOMIEST
MP IMPOSTER
MR MORTISER
STORMIER
MS EROTISMS
MORTISES
TRISOMES
MT OMITTERS
MU MISROUTE
MOISTURE
MV VOMITERS
MW MISWROTE
WORMIEST
MY ISOMETRY
NN INTONERS
TERNIONS
NO SNOOTIER
NP POINTERS
PORNIEST
PROTEINS
TROPINES
NR INTRORSE
NS OESTRINS
NT SNOTTIER
TENORIST
TRITONES
NU ROUTINES
SNOUTIER
NV INVESTOR
NY SEROTINY
TYROSINE
OT ROOTIEST
TORTOISE
PR PIERROTS
SPORTIER
PS PROSIEST
PROSTIES
REPOSITS
RIPOSTES
TRIPOSES
PT SPOTTIER
PU ROUPIEST
PV OVERTIPS
SORPTIVE
SPORTIVE
RS RESISTOR
ROISTERS
SORRIEST
RV OVERSTIR
SERVITOR
SY SEROSITY
UV VIRTUOSE
VITREOUS

17 TOILES

AC COALIEST
SOCIETAL
AD DIASTOLE
ISOLATED
SODALITE
AF FOLIATES
AG LATIGOES
OTALGIES
AK KEITLOAS
AM LOAMIEST
AN ELATIONS
INSOLATE
TOENAILS
AP SPOLIATE
AS ISOLATES
AT TOTALISE
AV VIOLATES
BB BIBELOTS
BF BOTFLIES
BR STROBILE
BW BLOWIEST
CN LECTIONS
TELSONIC
CR CLOISTER
COISTREL
COSTLIER
CS SOLECIST
SOLSTICE
DD DELTOIDS
DG GODLIEST
DM MELODIST
MODELIST
MOLDIEST
DN LENTOIDS
DP PISTOLED
DR STOLIDER
DS SOLIDEST
DU SOLITUDE
TOLUIDES
EP PETIOLES
EZ ZEOLITES
FJ JETFOILS
FK FOLKIEST
FR TREFOILS
FT LOFTIEST
FU OUTFLIES
GG LOGGIEST
GU EULOGIST
HM HELOTISM
HN HOLSTEIN
HOTLINES
NEOLITHS
HP HELISTOP
HOPLITES
ISOPLETH
HS HOSTILES
IP PISOLITE
POLITIES
IR ROILIEST
JL JOLLIEST
JT JOLTIEST
JW JOWLIEST
KY YOLKIEST
LM MELILOTS
LR TROLLIES
LW LOWLIEST
MO TOILSOME
MP MILEPOST
POLEMIST
MT MOTLIEST
MU OUTSMILE
NN INSOLENT
NO LOONIEST
OILSTONE
NP POTLINES
TOPLINES
NR RETINOLS
NU ELUTIONS
OUTLINES
NV NOVELIST
NW TOWLINES
OP LOOPIEST
OR OESTRIOL
OS OSTIOLES
STOOLIES
OW WOOLIEST
OY OTIOSELY
PP LOPPIEST
PR POITRELS
PS PISTOLES
PT PLOTTIES
POLITEST
PX EXPLOITS
RS ESTRIOLS
RT TRIOLETS
RU OUTLIERS
SU LOUSIEST
TT STILETTO
UV OUTLIVES
UW OUTWILES

18 SERIAL

AB RAISABLE
AD SALARIED
AG GASALIER
AS ASSAILER
REASSAIL
SALARIES
AV REAVAILS
BC CALIBERS
CALIBRES
BD BEDRAILS
DISABLER
BF BARFLIES
BL BALLSIER
BRAILLES
LIBERALS
BN RINSABLE
BT BLASTIER
LIBRATES
BY BILAYERS
CD DECRIALS
RADICELS
RADICLES
CG GLACIERS
GRACILES
CH CHARLIES
CM CLAIMERS
MIRACLES
RECLAIMS
CN CARLINES
LANCIERS
CO CALORIES
CARIOLES
CP CALIPERS
REPLICAS
SPIRACLE
CS CLASSIER
CT ARTICLES
RECITALS
STERICAL
CU AURICLES
CV CAVILERS
CLAVIERS
VISCERAL
DE REALISED
RESAILED
SIDEREAL
DL DALLIERS
DIALLERS
DM DISMALER
DN ISLANDER
DO DARIOLES
DP LIPREADS
PARSLIED
SPIRALED
DT DILATERS
LARDIEST
REDTAILS
DU RESIDUAL
DY DIALYSER
EF FILAREES
EG GASELIER
EM MEASLIER
EN ALIENERS
EP ESPALIER
ER REALISER
ES REALISES
ET ATELIERS
EARLIEST
LEARIEST
REALTIES
EY YEARLIES
EZ REALIZES
SLEAZIER
FH FLASHIER
FO FORESAIL
FT FRAILEST
FU FAILURES
GG SLAGGIER
GM GREMIALS
GN ALIGNERS
ENGRAILS
NARGILES
REALIGNS
SIGNALER
SLANGIER
GO GASOLIER
GIRASOLE
SERAGLIO
GS GLASSIER
GT GLARIEST
GY GREASILY
GZ GLAZIERS
HK RASHLIKE
HN INHALERS
HO AIRHOLES
SHOALIER
HP EARLSHIP
HARELIPS
PLASHIER
HS HAIRLESS
HU HAULIERS
HV LAVISHER
SHRIEVAL
IM RAMILIES
IN AIRLINES
IT LISTERIA
IV VIRELAIS
KP SPARLIKE
KT LARKIEST
STALKIER
STARLIKE
LP PERILLAS
LR RALLIERS
LS SALLIERS
LT LITERALS
TALLIERS
LY SERIALLY
MN MARLINES
MINERALS
MISLEARN
MO MORALISE
MP IMPALERS
IMPEARLS
LEMPIRAS
MS REALISMS
MT LAMISTER
MARLIEST
MARLITES
MISALTER
MY MISLAYER
NO AILERONS
ALIENORS
NP PRALINES
NR SNARLIER
NS RAINLESS
NT ENTRAILS
LATRINES
RATLINES
RETINALS
TRENAILS
NV RAVELINS
NX RELAXINS
NY INLAYERS
OP PELORIAS
POLARISE
OS SOLARISE
OV VALORISE
VARIOLES
OZ SOLARIZE
PP APPLIERS
PR REPRISAL
PT PILASTER
PLAISTER
PLAITERS
PU SPIRULAE
PV PREVAILS
PW SLIPWARE
RT RETRIALS
TRAILERS
RU RURALISE
ST REALISTS
SALTIERS
SALTIRES
SV REVISALS
TT TERTIALS
TU URALITES
VV REVIVALS
VY VIRELAYS

19 NAILER

AB INARABLE
AG GERANIAL
AP AIRPLANE
AV VALERIAN
BD BILANDER
BG BLEARING
BH HIBERNAL
BI BILINEAR
BK BARNLIKE
BS RINSABLE
BU RUINABLE
CE RELIANCE
CG CLEARING
RELACING
CI IRENICAL
CK CLANKIER
CO ACROLEIN
COLINEAR
CS CARLINES
LANCIERS
CT CLARINET
DE RENAILED
DG DANGLIER
DRAGLINE
DH HARDLINE
DN INLANDER
DS ISLANDER
EF FLANERIE
EG ALGERINE
EP PERINEAL
ER NEARLIER
ES ALIENERS
ET ELATERIN
ENTAILER
TREENAIL
FG FINAGLER
FM INFLAMER
RIFLEMAN
FN INFERNAL
FT INFLATER
FU FRAULEIN
GG GANGLIER
LAGERING
REGALING
GH NARGHILE
NARGILEH
GI GAINLIER
GJ JANGLIER
GL ALLERGIN
GM GERMINAL
MALIGNER
MALINGER
GN LEARNING
GO GERANIOL
REGIONAL
GP GRAPLINE
PEARLING
GR GNARLIER
GS ALIGNERS
ENGRAILS
NARGILES
REALIGNS
SIGNALER
SLANGIER
GT ALERTING
ALTERING
INTEGRAL
RELATING
TANGLIER
TRIANGLE
GV RAVELING
GX RELAXING
GY LAYERING
RELAYING
YEARLING
HI HAIRLINE
HS INHALERS
HU INHAULER
IR AIRLINER
IS AIRLINES
IT INERTIAL
LY LINEARLY
MS MARLINES
MINERALS
MISLEARN
MT TERMINAL
TRAMLINE
NT INTERNAL
OP PELORIAN
OS AILERONS
ALIENORS
OT ORIENTAL
RELATION
OV OVERLAIN
PS PRALINES
PT INTERLAP
TRAPLINE
TRIPLANE
RS SNARLIER
SS RAINLESS
ST ENTRAILS
LATRINES
RATLINES
RETINALS
TRENAILS
SV RAVELINS
SX RELAXINS
SY INLAYERS
TU AUNTLIER
RETINULA
TENURIAL
TV INTERVAL
TY INTERLAY

20 ALIENS

AC CANALISE
AN ALANINES
AS NASALISE
AZ NASALIZE
BE BASELINE
BG SINGABLE
BK SINKABLE
BM BAILSMEN
BIMENSAL
BP BIPLANES
BR RINSABLE
BS LESBIANS
BT INSTABLE
CC CALCINES
SCENICAL
CE SALIENCE
CI SALICINE
CM MELANICS
MENISCAL
CP CAPELINS
PANICLES
PELICANS
CR CARLINES
LANCIERS
CS LACINESS
SANICLES
CT CANISTEL
CU LUNACIES
CY SALIENCY
DD ISLANDED
LANDSIDE
DE DELAINES
DG DEALINGS
LEADINGS
SIGNALED
DK SANDLIKE
DN ANNELIDS
LINDANES
DP SANDPILE
DR ISLANDER
EE ALIENEES
EG ENSILAGE
LINEAGES
EP PENALISE
SEPALINE
ER ALIENERS
EV VASELINE
EX ALEXINES
FG FINAGLES
FH SHINLEAF
FI FINALISE
FM FLAMINES
INFLAMES
FP LIFESPAN
FT INFLATES
FV FLAVINES
GH LEASHING
SHEALING
GK LINKAGES
SNAGLIKE
GL GALLEINS
NIGELLAS
GN EANLINGS
LEANINGS
GO GASOLINE
GP ELAPSING
PLEASING
GR ALIGNERS
ENGRAILS
NARGILES
REALIGNS
SIGNALER
SLANGIER
GS GAINLESS
GLASSINE
LEASINGS
GT GELATINS
GENITALS
STEALING
TAGLINES
GV LEAVINGS
SLEAVING
GY YEALINGS
HR INHALERS
HY HYALINES
IM ALIENISM
MILESIAN
IN ANILINES
IR AIRLINES
IT ALIENIST
LITANIES
IZ SALINIZE
JV JAVELINS
JW JAWLINES
KO KAOLINES
KP SKIPLANE
KS SEALSKIN
KT LANKIEST
KW SWANLIKE
KY SNEAKILY
LM MANILLES
LP SPLENIAL
LS AINSELLS
SENSILLA
MM MELANISM
MN LINESMAN
MELANINS
MO LAMINOSE
SEMOLINA
MP IMPANELS
MANIPLES
MR MARLINES
MINERALS
MISLEARN
MT AILMENTS
ALIMENTS
MANLIEST
MELANIST
SMALTINE
MU ALUMINES
NO SOLANINE
NY INSANELY
OP OPALINES
OR AILERONS
ALIENORS
OS ANISOLES
OT ELATIONS
INSOLATE
TOENAILS
OX SILOXANE
PR PRALINES
PS PAINLESS
SPANIELS
PT PANELIST
PANTILES
PLAINEST
PU SPINULAE
PW PINWALES
PX EXPLAINS
QU QUINELAS
RR SNARLIER
RS RAINLESS
RT ENTRAILS
LATRINES
RATLINES
RETINALS
TRENAILS
RV RAVELINS
RX RELAXINS
RY INLAYERS
ST ELASTINS
NAILSETS
SALIENTS
SALTINES
SU INULASES
SZ LAZINESS
TU ALUNITES
INSULATE
TV VENTAILS
UW LAUWINES
UY UNEASILY

21 IONSEA

BD BEDSONIA
BG BEGONIAS
BR BARONIES
SEAROBIN
BT BOTANIES
BOTANISE
NIOBATES
OBEISANT
CC COCAINES
CD CODEINAS
DIOCESAN
CG COINAGES
CN CANONISE
CP CANOPIES
CR SCENARIO
CT ACONITES
CANOEIST
SONICATE
DD ADENOIDS
DG AGONISED
DIAGNOSE
DH ADHESION
DM AMIDONES
DAIMONES
DOMAINES
DR ANEROIDS
DS ADENOSIS
ADONISES
DT ASTONIED
SEDATION
DX DIOXANES
DZ ANODIZES
FR FARINOSE
GG SEAGOING
GL GASOLINE
GN ANGINOSE
GR ORGANISE
GS AGONISES
GZ AGONIZES
KL KAOLINES
LM LAMINOSE
SEMOLINA
LN SOLANINE
LP OPALINES
LR AILERONS
ALIENORS
LS ANISOLES
LT ELATIONS
INSOLATE
TOENAILS
LX SILOXANE
MM SEMINOMA
MR MORAINES
ROMAINES
ROMANISE
MS ANEMOSIS
MT AMNIOTES
MASONITE
MISATONE
MW WOMANISE
NP SAPONINE
NR RAISONNE
NT ENATIONS
SONATINE
PS SENOPIAS
PT SAPONITE
RS ERASIONS
SENSORIA
RT NOTARIES
SENORITA
RV AVERSION
ST ASTONIES
SV EVASIONS
SX SAXONIES
XZ OXAZINES

22 SALTIE

AB LABIATES
SATIABLE
AP STAPELIA
AV AESTIVAL
SALIVATE
AX SAXATILE
BC BASILECT
BI SIBILATE

BK BALKIEST
BL BASTILLE
LISTABLE
BM BALMIEST
BIMETALS
LAMBIEST
TIMBALES
BN INSTABLE
BP EPIBLAST
BR BLASTIER
LIBRATES
BS ABLEISTS
ASTILBES
BASTILES
BLASTIES
STABILES
BU SUITABLE
CC CALCITES
CD CITADELS
DIALECTS
CG GESTICAL
CH ETHICALS
CI CILIATES
SILICATE
CM CLEMATIS
CLIMATES
METICALS
CN CANISTEL
CO COALIEST
SOCIETAL
CP SEPTICAL
TIECLASP
CR ARTICLES
RECITALS
STERICAL
CS ELASTICS
SCALIEST
CT LATTICES
CY CLAYIEST
DE LEADIEST
DG GLADIEST
DI IDEALIST
DM MEDALIST
MISDEALT
DO DIASTOLE
ISOLATED
SODALITE
DP TALIPEDS
DR DILATERS
LARDIEST
REDTAILS
DY STEADILY
EF FEALTIES
FETIALES
LEAFIEST
EG EGALITES
EK LEAKIEST
EL LEALTIES
EM MEALIEST
METALISE
EP EPILATES
ER ATELIERS
EARLIEST
LEARIEST
REALTIES
EV ELATIVES
LEAVIEST
VEALIEST
FI FETIALIS
FILIATES
FK FLAKIEST
FM FLAMIEST
FN INFLATES
FO FOLIATES
FP FLEAPITS
FR FRAILEST
FS SEALIFTS
FU FISTULAE
FV FESTIVAL
FW FLATWISE
FLAWIEST
FX FLAXIEST
GL LEGALIST
TILLAGES
GN GELATINS
GENITALS
STEALING
TAGLINES
GO LATIGOES
OTALGIES
GR GLARIEST
GZ GLAZIEST
HP HAPLITES
HS HELIASTS
SHALIEST
HT LATHIEST
HY HYALITES
IN ALIENIST
LITANIES
IR LISTERIA
IV VITALISE
IX LAXITIES
KL SALTLIKE
KM MASTLIKE
KN LANKIEST
KO KEITLOAS
KR LARKIEST
STALKIER
STARLIKE
KT TALKIEST
LP PALLIEST
PASTILLE
LR LITERALS
TALLIERS
LS TAILLESS
TALLISES
MM MALMIEST
MN AILMENTS
ALIMENTS
MANLIEST
MELANIST
SMALTINE
MO LOAMIEST
MP PALMIEST
MR LAMISTER
MARLIEST
MARLITES
MISALTER
MT MALTIEST
METALIST
SMALTITE
MU SIMULATE
MY STEAMILY
TALEYSIM
NO ELATIONS
INSOLATE
TOENAILS
NP PANELIST
PANTILES
PLAINEST
NR ENTRAILS
LATRINES
RATLINES
RETINALS
TRENAILS
NS ELASTINS
NAILSETS
SALIENTS
SALTINES
NU ALUNITES
INSULATE
NV VENTAILS
OP SPOLIATE
OS ISOLATES
OT TOTALISE
OV VIOLATES
PR PILASTER
PLAISTER
PLAITERS
PT PLATIEST
QU LIQUATES
TEQUILAS
RR RETRAILS
TRAILERS
RS REALISTS
SALTIERS
SALTIRES
RT TERTIALS
RU URALITES
ST SALTIEST
SLATIEST
VY VILAYETS
WY SWEATILY
YY YEASTILY

23 RETAIL

AC TAILRACE
AD LARIATED
AL ARILLATE
AM MATERIAL
AP PARIETAL
AR ARTERIAL
AV VARIETAL
BD LIBRATED
BE LIBERATE
BO LABORITE
BP PARTIBLE
BS BLASTIER
LIBRATES
BT TITRABLE
BW WRITABLE
CD ARTICLED
LACERTID
CM METRICAL
CN CLARINET
CO EROTICAL
LORICATE
CP PARTICLE
PRELATIC
CS ARTICLES
RECITALS
STERICAL
CT TRACTILE
CU RETICULA
CV VERTICAL
CY LITERACY
DE DETAILER
ELATERID
RETAILED
DO IDOLATER
TAILORED
DP DIPTERAL
TRIPEDAL
DS DILATERS
LARDIEST
REDTAILS
DT DETRITAL
EF FEATLIER
EL LAETRILE
EM MATERIEL
EN ELATERIN
ENTAILER
TREENAIL
EO AEROLITE
EP PEARLITE
ER RETAILER
ES ATELIERS
EARLIEST
LEARIEST
REALTIES
ET LATERITE
LITERATE
EV LEVIRATE
RELATIVE
EZ LATERIZE
FN INFLATER
FO FLOATIER
FS FRAILEST
FT FILTRATE
FU FAULTIER
FILATURE
GH LITHARGE
THIRLAGE
GN ALERTING
ALTERING
INTEGRAL
RELATING
TANGLIER
TRIANGLE
GS GLARIEST
GT AGLITTER
GU LIGATURE
GY REGALITY
HO AEROLITH
HY EARTHILY
HEARTILY
IN INERTIAL
IP REPTILIA
IS LISTERIA
IT LITERATI
KP TRAPLIKE
KS LARKIEST
STALKIER
STARLIKE
KW WARTLIKE
LS LITERALS
TALLIERS
LU TAILLEUR
MN TERMINAL
TRAMLINE
MO AMITROLE
ROLAMITE
MS LAMISTER
MARLIEST
MARLITES
MISALTER
MT REMITTAL
NN INTERNAL
NO ORIENTAL
RELATION
NP INTERLAP
TRAPLINE
TRIPLANE
NS ENTRAILS
LATRINES
RATLINES
RETINALS
TRENAILS
NU AUNTLIER
RETINULA
TENURIAL
NV INTERVAL
NY INTERLAY
OP EPILATOR
PETIOLAR
OR RETAILOR
OV VIOLATER
OZ TRIAZOLE
PR PALTRIER
PRETRIAL
PS PILASTER
PLAISTER
PLAITERS
PV LIVETRAP
QU QUARTILE
REQUITAL
RS RETRIALS
TRAILERS
RU RURALITE
RY LITERARY
SS REALISTS
SALTIERS
SALTIRES
ST TERTIALS
SU URALITES
TY ALTERITY
UV VAULTIER
UZ LAZURITE
VV TRIVALVE
WY WATERILY

24 RETIES

AD READIEST
SERIATED
STEADIER
AE EATERIES
AH HEARTIES
AL ATELIERS
EARLIEST
LEARIEST
REALTIES
AM EMERITAS
EMIRATES
STEAMIER
AN ARENITES
ARSENITE
RESINATE
STEARINE
TRAINEES
AP PARIETES
AR ARTERIES
AS SERIATES
AT ARIETTES
ITERATES
TEARIEST
TREATIES
TREATISE
AW SWEATIER
WASTERIE
WEARIEST
AY YEASTIER
BD BESTRIDE
BISTERED
BE BEERIEST
BF BRIEFEST
BH HERBIEST
BM BIMESTER
CD DESERTIC
DISCREET
DISCRETE
CF FIERCEST
CH CHESTIER
HERETICS
CL RETICLES
SCLERITE
TIERCELS
TRISCELE
CN ENTERICS
ENTICERS
SECRETIN
CO COTERIES
ESOTERIC
CP CREPIEST
RECEIPTS
CR RECITERS
CU CERUSITE
CUTESIER
EUCRITES
CV VERTICES
CX EXCITERS
DE REEDIEST
DF RESIFTED
DG DIGESTER
REDIGEST
DH DIETHERS
DI SIDERITE
DL RELISTED
DM DEMERITS
DEMISTER
DIMETERS
DN INSERTED
NERDIEST
RESIDENT
SINTERED
TRENDIES
DP PREEDITS
PRIESTED
RESPITED
DR DESTRIER
DS DIESTERS
EDITRESS
RESISTED
SISTERED
DT TIREDEST
DW WEIRDEST
EF REEFIEST
EK REEKIEST
EL LEERIEST
SLEETIER
STEELIER
EM EREMITES
EN ETERNISE
TEENSIER
ER RETIREES
FI FEISTIER
FERITIES
FIERIEST
FN FERNIEST
INFESTER
FR FERRITES
FT FRISETTE
FY ESTERIFY
GM GERMIEST
GN GENTRIES
INTEGERS
REESTING
STEERING
GP PRESTIGE
GR REGISTER
GT GRISETTE
TERGITES
HH ETHERISH
HM ERETHISM
HO ISOTHERE
THEORIES
THEORISE
HS HEISTERS
IN NITERIES
IV VERITIES
JK JERKIEST
KL TRISKELE
KN KERNITES
KP PERKIEST
KR RESTRIKE
KS KEISTERS
KIESTERS
KU KEIRETSU
LN ENLISTER
LISTENER
REENLIST
SILENTER
LP EPISTLER
PELTRIES
PERLITES
REPTILES
LS LEISTERS
TIRELESS
LT RETITLES
MM MERISTEM
STEMMIER
MN MISENTER
MO TIRESOME
MP EMPTIERS
MR MERRIEST
MITERERS
RIMESTER
TRIREMES
MS MEISTERS
MISSTEER
TRISEMES
MT EMITTERS
TERMITES
MU EMERITUS
NN INTENSER
INTERNES
NO ONERIEST
SEROTINE
NR INSERTER
REINSERT
REINTERS
RENTIERS
TERRINES
NS SENTRIES
NT INSETTER
INTEREST
STERNITE
TRIENTES
NU ESURIENT
RETINUES
REUNITES
NV NERVIEST
REINVEST
SIRVENTE
NX INTERSEX
NY SERENITY
OP POETISER
POETRIES
OZ EROTIZES
PS RESPITES
PT PRETTIES
PX PREEXIST
PY YPERITES
QU QUIETERS
REQUITES
RR RETIRERS
TERRIERS
RS RESISTER
TRESSIER
RV RESTRIVE
RIVETERS
RW REWRITES
SU SURETIES
SV SIEVERTS
VESTRIES
VV VETIVERS
VY SEVERITY

25 ENTIRE

AC CENTIARE
CREATINE
INCREATE
ITERANCE
AD DETAINER
RETAINED
AG GRATINEE
INTERAGE
AH HERNIATE
AI INERTIAE
AK ANKERITE
AL ELATERIN
ENTAILER
TREENAIL
AM ANTIMERE
AP APERIENT
AR RETAINER
AS ARENITES
ARSENITE
RESINATE
STEARINE
TRAINEES
BD INTERBED
CF FRENETIC
INFECTER
REINFECT
CG ERECTING
GENTRICE
CI REINCITE
CJ REINJECT
CN INCENTER
CO ERECTION
NEOTERIC
CP PRENTICE
TERPENIC
CS ENTERICS
ENTICERS
SECRETIN
CT RETICENT
CU CEINTURE
ENURETIC
DD DENDRITE
DK TINKERED
DM REMINTED
DN INDENTER
INTENDER
INTERNED
DO ORIENTED
DR INTERRED
TRENDIER
DS INSERTED
NERDIEST
RESIDENT
SINTERED
TRENDIES
DT RETINTED
DU RETINUED
REUNITED
DV INVERTED
DW WINTERED
DX DEXTRINE
EN INTERNEE
RETINENE
ES ETERNISE
TEENSIER
EZ ETERNIZE
FS FERNIEST
INFESTER
GG GREETING
GI REIGNITE
RETIEING
GL GREENLIT
GM METERING
REGIMENT
GN ENTERING
GP PETERING
GS GENTRIES
INTEGERS
REESTING
STEERING
GU GENITURE
GV EVERTING
GX EXERTING
HM THEREMIN
HN INHERENT
HO HEREINTO
HP NEPHRITE
TREPHINE
HT THIRTEEN
HW WHITENER
IS NITERIES
IT INTERTIE
RETINITE
IV REINVITE
JL JETLINER
KR TINKERER
KS KERNITES
LS ENLISTER
LISTENER
REENLIST
SILENTER
LT NETTLIER
LY ENTIRELY
LIENTERY
MS MISENTER
MU MUTINEER
NS INTENSER
INTERNES
NT RENITENT
NV INVENTER
REINVENT
OR ORIENTER
REORIENT
OS ONERIEST
SEROTINE
OT TENORITE
OX EXERTION
PU PREUNITE
PX INEXPERT
RS INSERTER
REINSERT
REINTERS
RENTIERS
TERRINES
RU REUNITER
UNRETIRE
RV INVERTER
RW WINTERER
RX INTERREX
SS SENTRIES
ST INSETTER
INTEREST
STERNITE
TRIENTES
SU ESURIENT
RETINUES
REUNITES
SV NERVIEST
REINVEST
SIRVENTE
SX INTERSEX
SY SERENITY
TY ENTIRETY
ETERNITY

26 SADTIE

AM ADAMSITE
DIASTEMA
AR AIRDATES
DATARIES
RADIATES
AS DIASTASE
AT SATIATED
BE BEADIEST
DIABETES
BP BAPTISED
BR REDBAITS
TRIBADES
BU DAUBIEST
BW BAWDIEST
CL CITADELS
DIALECTS
CM MISACTED
CN DISTANCE
CP SPICATED
CR ACRIDEST
CT DICTATES
DE STEADIED
DF FADDIEST
DM MISDATED
DN DANDIEST
DR DISRATED
EF SAFETIED
EH HEADIEST
EJ JADEITES
EL LEADIEST
EM MEDIATES
EN ANDESITE
ER READIEST
SERIATED
STEADIER
ES STEADIES
EU AUDITEES
EV DEVIATES
SEDATIVE
FF DAFFIEST
GL GLADIEST
GN SEDATING
STEADING
GO GODETIAS
GU GAUDIEST
HH SHITHEAD
HN HANDIEST
HP PITHEADS
HR HARDIEST
HS DASHIEST
SHADIEST
IL IDEALIST
IN ADENITIS
DAINTIES
LM MEDALIST
MISDEALT
LO DIASTOLE
ISOLATED
SODALITE
LP TALIPEDS
LR DILATERS
LARDIEST
REDTAILS
LY STEADILY
MM MISMATED
MN MEDIANTS
MO ATOMISED
MP IMPASTED
MR MISRATED
READMITS
MS DIASTEMS
MISDATES
MY DAYTIMES
NO ASTONIED
SEDATION
NP DEPAINTS
NR DETRAINS
RANDIEST
STRAINED
NS DESTAINS
SANDIEST
NT INSTATED
NU AUDIENTS
SINUATED
NV DEVIANTS
OP DIOPTASE
OR ASTEROID
OX OXIDATES
OZ AZOTISED
PR RAPIDEST
TRAIPSED
RS DIASTERS
DISASTER
DISRATES
RT STRIATED
TARDIEST
RW TAWDRIES
SS ASSISTED
DISSEATS
ST DISTASTE
STAIDEST
SV DISTAVES
TU SITUATED
UZ DEUTZIAS
WY TIDEWAYS

27 ATONES

BI BOTANIES
BOTANISE
NIOBATES
OBEISANT
BL NOTABLES
STONABLE
BM BOATSMEN
BR BARONETS
BY BAYONETS
CC COENACTS
COSECANT
CD ENDOCAST
TACNODES
CE ACETONES
NOTECASE
CG COAGENTS
COGNATES
CI ACONITES
CANOEIST
SONICATE
CJ JACONETS
CL LACTONES
CP CAPSTONE
OPENCAST
CR ANCESTOR
ENACTORS
CS CONTESSA
CV CENTAVOS
DE ENDOSTEA
DI ASTONIED
SEDATION
DO ODONATES
DP NOTEPADS
EN NEONATES
ER EARSTONE
RESONATE
FR SEAFRONT
GL TANGELOS
GM MAGNETOS
MEGATONS
MONTAGES
GN NEGATONS
TONNAGES
GR ESTRAGON
NEGATORS
HL ANETHOLS
ETHANOLS
HP PHAETONS
PHONATES
STANHOPE
IL ELATIONS
INSOLATE
TOENAILS
IM AMNIOTES
MASONITE
MISATONE
IN ENATIONS
SONATINE
IP SAPONITE
IR NOTARIES
SENORITA
IS ASTONIES
LP POLENTAS
LY ANOLYTES
MN MONTANES
MR MONSTERA
ONSTREAM
TONEARMS
MU SEAMOUNT
NP PENTOSAN
NR RESONANT
NU TONNEAUS
NX NONTAXES
OP TEASPOON
OZ OZONATES

PR OPERANTS
PRONATES
PROTEANS
PU AUTOPENS
RR ANTRORSE
RS ASSENTOR
SANTEROS
SENATORS
STARNOSE
TREASONS
RU OUTEARNS
SU SOUTANES

28 SOLATE

AC CATALOES
AM OATMEALS
AX OXALATES
BC OBSTACLE
BN NOTABLES
STONABLE
BP POTABLES
BR BLOATERS
SORTABLE
STORABLE
BU ABSOLUTE
BW BESTOWAL
STOWABLE
TEABOWLS
CH CHOLATES
ESCHALOT
CI COALIEST
SOCIETAL
CL COLLATES
CN LACTONES
CP POLECATS
CR LOCATERS
SECTORAL
CS COATLESS
LACTOSES
CT CALOTTES
CU LACTEOUS
LOCUSTAE
OSCULATE
CY ACOLYTES
DE DESOLATE
DI DIASTOLE
ISOLATED
SODALITE
DP TADPOLES
DR DELATORS
LEOTARDS
LODESTAR
DS TOADLESS
DU OUTLEADS
DV SOLVATED
ER OLEASTER
EV LOVESEAT
FG FLOTAGES
FI FOLIATES
FL FLOATELS
FR FLOATERS
FORESTAL
REFLOATS
FT FALSETTO
GI LATIGOES
OTALGIES
GL TOLLAGES
GN TANGELOS
GR GLOATERS
LEGATORS
GV VOLTAGES
HN ANETHOLS
ETHANOLS
HP TAPHOLES
HR LOATHERS
RATHOLES
HS SHOALEST
IK KEITLOAS
IM LOAMIEST
IN ELATIONS
INSOLATE
TOENAILS
IP SPOLIATE
IS ISOLATES
IT TOTALISE
IV VIOLATES
KS SKATOLES
LR REALLOTS
ROSTELLA
LY LOYALEST
MS MALTOSES
MT MATELOTS
MU SOULMATE
NP POLENTAS
NY ANOLYTES
PR PETROSAL
POLESTAR
PS APOSTLES
PT PALETOTS
PU OUTLEAPS
PETALOUS
RR REALTORS
RELATORS
RESTORAL
RS OLESTRAS
RT RETOTALS
RU ROSULATE
RV LEVATORS
OVERSALT
SV SOLVATES
TU TOLUATES
TW WASTELOT
UV OVULATES
UY AUTOLYSE

29 ORALES

AC ACEROLAS
AP PSORALEA
AU AUREOLAS
BB BELABORS
SORBABLE
BE EARLOBES
BR LABORERS
BT BLOATERS
SORTABLE
STORABLE
BU RUBEOLAS
BV ABSOLVER
CC CORACLES
CE ESCAROLE
CF ALFRESCO
CH CHOLERAS
CHORALES
CI CALORIES
CARIOLES
CJ CAJOLERS
CK EARLOCKS
CM SCLEROMA
CP PARCLOSE
CR CAROLERS
CS ESCOLARS
LACROSSE
SOLACERS
CT LOCATERS
SECTORAL
CU CAROUSEL
CY CALOYERS
COARSELY
DI DARIOLES
DM EARLDOMS
DN LADRONES
SOLANDER
DP LEOPARDS
PRELOADS
DS ROADLESS
DT DELATORS
LEOTARDS
LODESTAR
DU ROULADES
EG AEROGELS
EP PAROLEES
ET OLEASTER
EU AUREOLES
EV OVERSALE
FI FORESAIL
FN FARNESOL
FO SEAFLOOR
FS SAFROLES
FT FLOATERS
FORESTAL
REFLOATS
GI GASOLIER
GIRASOLE
SERAGLIO
GL ALLEGROS
GM GOMERALS
GP PERGOLAS
GT GLOATERS
LEGATORS
GV VORLAGES
HI AIRHOLES
SHOALIER
HM ARMHOLES
HT LOATHERS
RATHOLES
HY HOARSELY
IM MORALISE
IN AILERONS
ALIENORS
IP PELORIAS
POLARISE
IS SOLARISE
IV VALORISE
VARIOLES
IZ SOLARIZE
KM LARKSOME
LM SLALOMER
LT REALLOTS
ROSTELLA
LV ALLOVERS
OVERALLS
LW SALLOWER
MN ALMONERS
MO SALEROOM
MP RAMPOLES
MU RAMULOSE
MV REMOVALS
MY RAMOSELY
NP PERSONAL
PSORALEN
NU ALEURONS
NEUROSAL
OR ROSEOLAR
OS AEROSOLS
ROSEOLAS
PP PROLAPSE
SAPROPEL
PS REPOSALS
PT PETROSAL
POLESTAR
PV OVERLAPS
RT REALTORS
RELATORS
RESTORAL
SS LASSOERS
ST OLESTRAS
TT RETOTALS
TU ROSULATE
TV LEVATORS
OVERSALT
UU ROULEAUS
VY LAYOVERS
OVERLAYS

30 ISATON

AL ALATIONS
AN SONATINA
BD BANDITOS
BE BOTANIES
BOTANISE
NIOBATES
OBEISANT
BG BOASTING
BOATINGS
BJ BANJOIST
BN ANTISNOB
BO BONIATOS
BR TABORINS
BS ANTIBOSS
BASTIONS
BT BOTANIST
CE ACONITES
CANOEIST
SONICATE
CF FACTIONS
CG AGNOSTIC
COASTING
COATINGS
COTINGAS
CH CHITOSAN
CM MONASTIC
CN ACTINONS
CANONIST
CONTAINS
SANCTION
SONANTIC
CP CAPTIONS
PACTIONS
CR CAROTINS
CORTINAS
CT OSCITANT
TACTIONS
CU AUCTIONS
CAUTIONS
CW WAINSCOT
DE ASTONIED
SEDATION
DJ ADJOINTS
DM SAINTDOM
DP PINTADOS
SATINPOD
DR DIATRONS
INTRADOS
DU SUDATION
DX OXIDANTS
DY DYSTONIA
EL ELATIONS
INSOLATE
TOENAILS
EM AMNIOTES
MASONITE
MISATONE
EN ENATIONS
SONATINE
EP SAPONITE
ER NOTARIES
SENORITA
ES ASTONIES
FN FONTINAS
GG GIGATONS
GK GOATSKIN
GL ANTILOGS
SOLATING
GM ANTISMOG
GR ORGANIST
ROASTING
GS AGONISTS
GT TOASTING
GU OUTGAINS
HM MANIHOTS
HS ASTONISH
HZ HOATZINS
IT OSTINATI
JR JANITORS
KT STOTINKA
LL STALLION
LN ANTLIONS
LO SOLATION
LR TONSILAR
LY LANOSITY
MO AMOTIONS
MP MAINTOPS
PTOMAINS
TAMPIONS
MS STASIMON
MU MANITOUS
TINAMOUS
MW WOMANIST
NN SANTONIN
NP PINTANOS
NS ONANISTS
OR ORATIONS
OT OSTINATO
OV OVATIONS
PP APPOINTS
PR ATROPINS
PU OPUNTIAS
UTOPIANS
RS ARSONIST
RT STRONTIA
RU RAINOUTS
RW WAITRONS
ST STATIONS
TU TITANOUS

31 SAINED

AR ARANEIDS
AZ ZENAIDAS
BD SIDEBAND
BG BEADINGS
DEBASING
BH BANISHED
BK BANKSIDE
BO BEDSONIA
BR BRANDIES
BU UNBIASED
CF FACIENDS
CH ECHIDNAS
CI SCIAENID
CO CODEINAS
DIOCESAN
CS ACIDNESS
CT DISTANCE
CY CYANIDES
DL ISLANDED
LANDSIDE
DO ADENOIDS
DR SARDINED
DT DANDIEST
EL DELAINES
EN ADENINES
ER ARSENIDE
NEARSIDE
ES ANISEEDS
ET ANDESITE
GH DEASHING
HEADINGS
GL DEALINGS
LEADINGS
SIGNALED
GO AGONISED
DIAGNOSE
GR DERAIGNS
GRADINES
READINGS
GS ASSIGNED
GT SEDATING
STEADING
GW WINDAGES
HK SKINHEAD
HO ADHESION
HP DEANSHIP
HEADPINS
PINHEADS
HS DANISHES
SHANDIES
HT HANDIEST
HV VANISHED
IM AMIDINES
DIAMINES
IN SANIDINE
IT ADENITIS
DAINTIES
IZ DIAZINES
KL SANDLIKE
KY KYANISED
LN ANNELIDS
LINDANES
LP SANDPILE
LR ISLANDER
MM MISNAMED
MO AMIDONES
DAIMONES
DOMAINES
MT MEDIANTS
MU MAUNDIES
NR INSNARED
OR ANEROIDS
OS ADENOSIS
ADONISES
OT ASTONIED
SEDATION
OX DIOXANES
OZ ANODIZES
PR SPRAINED
PT DEPAINTS
PV SPAVINED
RR DRAINERS
SERRANID
RS ARIDNESS
SARDINES
RT DETRAINS
RANDIEST
STRAINED
RU DENARIUS
UNRAISED
URANIDES
RV INVADERS
ST DESTAINS
SANDIEST
SV AVIDNESS
TT INSTATED
TU AUDIENTS
SINUATED
TV DEVIANTS

32 DORIES

AC IDOCRASE
AD ROADSIDE
AF FORESAID
AL DARIOLES
AN ANEROIDS
AP DIASPORE
PARODIES
AT ASTEROID
AV AVODIRES
AVOIDERS
BD DISROBED
BE REBODIES
BM BROMIDES
BR BROIDERS
DISROBER
BS DISROBES
BT DEORBITS
BV OVERBIDS
CL SCLEROID
CN CONSIDER
CO CORODIES
CP PERCOIDS
CT CORDITES
CV CODRIVES
DISCOVER
DIVORCES
CW CROWDIES
DH SHODDIER
DM DERMOIDS
DN INDORSED
DP DROPSIED
DR DISORDER
EF FORESIDE
EM EMEROIDS
EN INDORSEE
EV OVERSIDE
EW DOWERIES
WEIRDOES
FG FIREDOGS
GG DISGORGE
GN NEGROIDS
GT DIGESTOR
GRODIEST
STODGIER
HM HEIRDOMS
HN HORDEINS
HP SPHEROID
HS HIDROSES
IL IDOLISER
IN DERISION
IRONSIDE
RESINOID
IP PRESIDIO
IT DIORITES
IX OXIDISER
IZ IODIZERS
JN JOINDERS
JY JOYRIDES
KS DROSKIES
KT DORKIEST
LP LEPORIDS
LS SOLDIERS
LT STOLIDER
LY SOLDIERY
MO MOIDORES
MP PROMISED
MR MISORDER
MS MISDOERS
MT MORTISED
MU DIMEROUS
MV MISDROVE
NP PRISONED
NR INDORSER
NS INDORSES
SORDINES
NU DOURINES
SOURDINE
OW WOODSIER
OZ ODORIZES
PS DISPOSER
DROPSIES
PT DIOPTERS
DIOPTRES
PERIDOTS
PORTSIDE
PROTEIDS
RIPOSTED
TOPSIDER
PV DISPROVE
PROVIDES
PX PEROXIDS
RS DROSSIER
RW DROWSIER
RY DERISORY
SS DOSSIERS
ST STEROIDS
SU DESIROUS
SV DEVISORS
TU OUTRIDES
OUTSIDER
TW ROWDIEST
WORDIEST
WW WIDOWERS

33 GAINER

AD DRAINAGE
GARDENIA
AL GERANIAL
AN ANEARING
AS ANERGIAS
ANGARIES
ARGINASE
AT AERATING
BD BEARDING
BREADING
BK BERAKING
BREAKING
BL BLEARING
BM BREAMING
BS BEARINGS
SABERING
BT BERATING
REBATING
TABERING
BW BEWARING
CF REFACING
CH REACHING
CI REAGINIC
CK CREAKING
CL CLEARING
RELACING
CM AMERCING
CREAMING
GERMANIC
CN RECANING
CP CAPERING
CS CREASING
CT ARGENTIC
CATERING
CREATING
REACTING
DD DREADING
READDING
DE REGAINED
DH ADHERING
DI DEAIRING
DL DANGLIER
DRAGLINE
DM DREAMING
MARGINED
MIDRANGE
DO ORGANDIE
DS DERAIGNS
GRADINES
READINGS
DT DERATING
GRADIENT
REDATING
TREADING
DY READYING
EG AGREEING
EL ALGERINE
EP PERIGEAN
ER REGAINER
ES ANERGIES
GESNERIA
ET GRATINEE
INTERAGE
EZ RAZEEING
FF FIREFANG
FH HANGFIRE
FK FREAKING
FL FINAGLER
FW WAFERING
GL GANGLIER
LAGERING
REGALING
GN ANGERING
ENRAGING
GS GEARINGS
GREASING
SNAGGIER
GW WAGERING
HL NARGHILE
NARGILEH
HS HEARINGS
HEARSING
SHEARING
HT EARTHING
HEARTING
INGATHER
HV HAVERING
IL GAINLIER
IM IMAGINER
MIGRAINE
IN ARGININE
IR GRAINIER
JL JANGLIER
KM REMAKING
KT RETAKING
KW REWAKING
WREAKING
LL ALLERGIN
LM GERMINAL
MALIGNER
MALINGER
LN LEARNING
LO GERANIOL
REGIONAL
LP GRAPLINE
PEARLING
LR GNARLIER
LS ALIGNERS
ENGRAILS
NARGILES
REALIGNS
SIGNALER
SLANGIER
LT ALERTING
ALTERING
INTEGRAL
RELATING
TANGLIER
TRIANGLE
LV RAVELING
LX RELAXING
LY LAYERING
RELAYING
YEARLING
MN RENAMING
MR REARMING
MS SMEARING
MT EMIGRANT
REMATING
MU GERANIUM
NS AGINNERS
EARNINGS
ENGRAINS
GRANNIES
NV RAVENING
NY YEARNING
OR ORANGIER
OS ORGANISE
OZ ORGANIZE
PP PAPERING
PS SPEARING
PT RETAPING
TAPERING
PV REPAVING
PY REPAYING
RS EARRINGS
GRAINERS
RV AVERRING
SS ASSIGNER
REASSIGN
SERINGAS
ST ANGRIEST
ASTRINGE
GANISTER
GANTRIES
GRANITES
INGRATES
RANGIEST
SV VINEGARS
SW RESAWING
SWEARING
SY RESAYING
SYNERGIA
TT GNATTIER
TREATING
TV AVERTING
GRIEVANT
VINTAGER
TW TWANGIER
WATERING
TX RETAXING
VW WAVERING
VY VINEGARY
WX REWAXING
WY WEARYING

34 LISTER

AB BLASTIER
LIBRATES
AC ARTICLES
RECITALS
STERICAL
AD DILATERS
LARDIEST
REDTAILS
AE ATELIERS
EARLIEST
LEARIEST
REALTIES
AF FRAILEST
AG GLARIEST
AI LISTERIA
AK LARKIEST
STALKIER
STARLIKE
AL LITERALS
TALLIERS
AM LAMISTER
MARLIEST
MARLITES
MISALTER
AN ENTRAILS
LATRINES
RATLINES
RETINALS
TRENAILS
AP PILASTER
PLAISTER
PLAITERS
AR RETRIALS
TRAILERS
AS REALISTS
SALTIERS
SALTIRES
AT TERTIALS
AU URALITES
BD BRISTLED
DRIBLETS
BF FILBERTS
BG GILBERTS
BH BLITHERS
BI TRILBIES
BM TIMBRELS
BO STROBILE
BS BLISTERS
BRISTLES
BT BRITTLES
BU BURLIEST
SUBTILER
BY BLISTERY
BZ BLITZERS
CC CIRCLETS
CE RETICLES
SCLERITE
TIERCELS
TRISCELE
CK STICKLER
STRICKLE
TICKLERS
TRICKLES
CO CLOISTER
COISTREL
COSTLIER
CU CURLIEST
UTRICLES
DD TIDDLERS
DE RELISTED
DN TENDRILS
TRINDLES
DO STOLIDER
DU DILUTERS
STUDLIER
EE LEERIEST
SLEETIER
STEELIER
EK TRISKELE
EN ENLISTER
LISTENER
REENLIST
SILENTER
EP EPISTLER
PELTRIES
PERLITES
REPTILES
ES LEISTERS
TIRELESS
ET RETITLES
FI FILISTER
FO TREFOILS
FR FLIRTERS
TRIFLERS
FS RIFTLESS
STIFLERS
FT FLITTERS
FW FEWTRILS
FY FLYTIERS
GH LIGHTERS
RELIGHTS
SLIGHTER
GI GIRLIEST
GN RINGLETS
STERLING
TINGLERS
GS GLISTERS
GRISTLES
GT GLITTERS
HP PHILTERS
PHILTRES
HS SLITHERS
HU LUTHIERS
HW WHISTLER
HY SLITHERY
IL STILLIER

IM LIMITERS
IN NITRILES
IO ROILIEST
IT SLITTIER
IU UTILISER
KN TINKLERS
KS KLISTERS
LO TROLLIES
LR TRILLERS
MN MINSTREL
NO RETINOLS
NP SPLINTER
NU INSULTER
OO OESTRIOL
OP POITRELS
OS ESTRIOLS
OT TRIOLETS
OU OUTLIERS
PP PRESPLIT
RIPPLETS
STIPPLER
TIPPLERS
PS RESPLITS
PT SPLITTER
TRIPLETS
PY PRIESTLY
QU QUILTERS
RU SULTRIER
RW TWIRLERS
ST SLITTERS
SU SURLIEST
SY SISTERLY
STYLISER
TU SLUTTIER
SURTITLE
TW WRISTLET
UV RIVULETS
YZ STYLIZER

35 ENTERS

AA ARSENATE
SERENATA
AB ABSENTER
AC CENTARES
REASCENT
REENACTS
SARCENET
AE SERENATE
AF FASTENER
FENESTRA
REFASTEN
AG ESTRANGE
GRANTEES
GREATENS
NEGATERS
REAGENTS
SERGEANT
AH HASTENER
HEARTENS
AI ARENITES
ARSENITE
RESINATE
STEARINE
TRAINEES
AJ SERJEANT
AL ETERNALS
TELERANS
AO EARSTONE
RESONATE
AR TERRANES
AS ASSENTER
EARNESTS
SARSENET
AT ENTREATS
RATTEENS
AU SAUTERNE
AV VETERANS
BP BESPRENT
BW BESTREWN
CC CRESCENT
CH TRENCHES
CI ENTERICS
ENTICERS
SECRETIN
CL LECTERNS
CN CENTNERS
CP PERCENTS
PRECENTS
DE RENESTED
RESENTED
DI INSERTED
NERDIEST
RESIDENT
SINTERED
TRENDIES
DP PRETENDS
DU DENTURES
SEDERUNT
UNDERSET
UNRESTED
EG GREENEST
EI ETERNISE
TEENSIER
EP PRETEENS
PRETENSE
TERPENES
ER ENTERERS
REENTERS
TERREENS
TERRENES
ES SERENEST
EW TWEENERS
EX EXTERNES
EY YESTREEN
FI FERNIEST
INFESTER
FM FERMENTS
FO RESOFTEN
SOFTENER
GH GREENTHS
GI GENTRIES
INTEGERS
REESTING
STEERING
GO ESTROGEN
HO HONESTER
II NITERIES
IK KERNITES
IL ENLISTER
LISTENER
REENLIST
SILENTER
IM MISENTER
IN INTENSER
INTERNES
IO ONERIEST
SEROTINE
IR INSERTER
REINSERT
REINTERS
RENTIERS
TERRINES
IS SENTRIES
IT INSETTER
INTEREST
STERNITE
TRIENTES
IU ESURIENT
RETINUES
REUNITES
IV NERVIEST
REINVEST
SIRVENTE
IX INTERSEX
IY SERENITY
LO ENTRESOL
LS NESTLERS
LT NETTLERS
MU MUENSTER
NO ENTERONS
TENONERS
OO OESTRONE
OS ESTRONES
OX EXTENSOR
PP PERPENTS
PS PENSTERS
PERTNESS
PRESENTS
SERPENTS
PV PREVENTS
ST STERNEST
SU TRUENESS
SW WESTERNS
SY STYRENES
UV VENTURES

36 SALTER

AB ARBALEST
RATABLES
AG AGRESTAL
AH TREHALAS
AL LATERALS
AN ASTERNAL
AP PALESTRA
AZ LAZARETS
BE ARBELEST
BLEATERS
RESTABLE
RETABLES
BH BLATHERS
HALBERTS
BI BLASTIER
LIBRATES
BM LAMBERTS
BO BLOATERS
SORTABLE
STORABLE
BS BLASTERS
STABLERS
BT BATTLERS
BLATTERS
BRATTLES
BU BALUSTER
RUSTABLE
CE CLEAREST
TREACLES
CH TRACHLES
CI ARTICLES
RECITALS
STERICAL
CK TACKLERS
CN CENTRALS
CO LOCATERS
SECTORAL
CP SCEPTRAL
SPECTRAL
CS SCARLETS
CT CLATTERS
DD STRADDLE
DE DESALTER
RESLATED
TREADLES
DI DILATERS
LARDIEST
REDTAILS
DO DELATORS
LEOTARDS
LODESTAR
DT STARTLED
DW WARSTLED
WRASTLED
EE TEASELER
EF REFLATES
EH HALTERES
LEATHERS
EI ATELIERS
EARLIEST
LEARIEST
REALTIES
EN ETERNALS
TELERANS
EO OLEASTER
EP PETRALES
PLEATERS
PRELATES
REPLATES
ER ALTERERS
REALTERS
RELATERS
ES RESLATES
STEALERS
TEARLESS
ET ALERTEST
EU RESALUTE
EX EXALTERS
EY EASTERLY
FI FRAILEST
FK FARTLEKS
FO FLOATERS
FORESTAL
REFLOATS
FT FLATTERS
FU REFUTALS
GG STRAGGLE
GI GLARIEST
GN STRANGLE
TANGLERS
GO GLOATERS
LEGATORS
GU GESTURAL
HM THERMALS
HN ENTHRALS
HO LOATHERS
RATHOLES
HS HARSLETS
SLATHERS
II LISTERIA
IK LARKIEST
STALKIER
STARLIKE
IL LITERALS
TALLIERS
IM LAMISTER
MARLIEST
MARLITES
MISALTER
IN ENTRAILS
LATRINES
RATLINES
RETINALS
TRENAILS
IP PILASTER
PLAISTER
PLAITERS
IR RETRIALS
TRAILERS
IS REALISTS
SALTIERS
SALTIRES
IT TERTIALS
IU URALITES
KP SPARKLET
KS STALKERS
LM TRAMELLS
LO REALLOTS
ROSTELLA
MM TRAMMELS
MP TEMPLARS
TRAMPLES
MS LAMSTERS
TRAMLESS
MT MALTSTER
MARTLETS
MU STAUMREL
MY MASTERLY
NN LANTERNS
NP PLANTERS
REPLANTS
NS SALTERNS
NT SLATTERN
NU NEUTRALS
NV VENTRALS
OP PETROSAL
POLESTAR
OR REALTORS
RELATORS
RESTORAL
OS OLESTRAS
OT RETOTALS
OU ROSULATE
OV LEVATORS
OVERSALT
PS PERSALTS
PLASTERS
PSALTERS
STAPLERS
PT PARTLETS
PLATTERS
PRATTLES
SPLATTER
SPRATTLE
PY PEYTRALS
PLASTERY
PSALTERY
RT RATTLERS
STARTLER
RW TRAWLERS
WARSTLER
SS STARLESS
ST STARLETS
STARTLES
SU SALUTERS
SW WARSTLES
WARTLESS
WASTRELS
WRASTLES
TT TARTLETS
TATTLERS
TU LUSTRATE
TUTELARS
UV VAULTERS
VESTURAL
WY TRAWLEYS
WZ WALTZERS

37 TIRADE

AC RADICATE
AD RADIATED
AE ERADIATE
AL LARIATED
AS AIRDATES
DATARIES
RADIATES
AV VARIATED
BB RABBITED
BE REBAITED
BI DIATRIBE
BL LIBRATED
BP BIPARTED
BS REDBAITS
TRIBADES
BV VIBRATED
CC ACCREDIT
CD READDICT
CH TRACHEID
CI RATICIDE
CL ARTICLED
LACERTID
CM TIMECARD
CN DICENTRA
CO CERATOID
CP PICRATED
CS ACRIDEST
CT CITRATED
TETRACID
TETRADIC
DS DISRATED
EL DETAILER
ELATERID
RETAILED
EM DIAMETER
EN DETAINER
RETAINED
ES READIEST
SERIATED
STEADIER
ET ITERATED
EV DERIVATE
EW WAITERED
FF TARIFFED
FG DRIFTAGE
FI RATIFIED
FR DRAFTIER
GI DIGERATI
GM MIGRATED
GN DERATING
GRADIENT
REDATING
TREADING
HN ANTHERID
HR TRIHEDRA
HS HARDIEST
IN DAINTIER
KM TIDEMARK
KO KERATOID
LO IDOLATER
TAILORED
LP DIPTERAL
TRIPEDAL
LS DILATERS
LARDIEST
REDTAILS
LT DETRITAL
MO MEDIATOR
MP IMPARTED
PREADMIT
MS MISRATED
READMITS
MT ADMITTER
MU MURIATED
NO AROINTED
ORDINATE
RATIONED
NP DIPTERAN
NS DETRAINS
RANDIEST
STRAINED
NT NITRATED
NU INDURATE
RUINATED
URINATED
OR ADROITER
OS ASTEROID
OT TERATOID
OV DEVIATOR
PS RAPIDEST
TRAIPSED
PU EUPATRID
PREAUDIT
RW TAWDRIER
SS DIASTERS
DISASTER
DISRATES
ST STRIATED
TARDIEST
SW TAWDRIES
TT ATTRITED
TITRATED
UV DURATIVE

38 SILENT

AB INSTABLE
AC CANISTEL
AF INFLATES
AG GELATINS
GENITALS
STEALING
TAGLINES
AI ALIENIST
LITANIES
AK LANKIEST
AM AILMENTS
ALIMENTS
MANLIEST
MELANIST
SMALTINE
AO ELATIONS
INSOLATE
TOENAILS
AP PANELIST
PANTILES
PLAINEST
AR ENTRAILS
LATRINES
RATLINES
RETINALS
TRENAILS
AS ELASTINS
NAILSETS
SALIENTS
SALTINES
AU ALUNITES
INSULATE
AV VENTAILS
BD BLINDEST
BE STILBENE
TENSIBLE
BG BELTINGS
BM NIMBLEST
BU BUSTLINE
BY TENSIBLY
BZ BLINTZES
CE CENTILES
CF INFLECTS
CO LECTIONS
TELSONIC
CS STENCILS
CU CUTLINES
LINECUTS
TUNICLES
DE ENLISTED
LISTENED
TINSELED
DO LENTOIDS
DP SPLINTED
DR TENDRILS
TRINDLES
DU DILUENTS
INSULTED
UNLISTED
EE ENLISTEE
SELENITE
EG GENTILES
SLEETING
STEELING
EH THEELINS
EI LENITIES
EK NESTLIKE
EN SENTINEL
EP PENLITES
PLENTIES
ER ENLISTER
LISTENER
REENLIST
SILENTER
ES LITENESS
SETLINES
ET ENTITLES
EV VEINLETS
FG FELTINGS
GH LIGHTENS
GI LIGNITES
LINGIEST
GK KINGLETS
GL GILLNETS
GM SMELTING
GN NESTLING
GP PESTLING
GR RINGLETS
STERLING
TINGLERS
GS GLISTENS
SINGLETS
SNIGLETS
GT SETTLING
GW WELTINGS
WINGLETS
HO HOLSTEIN
HOTLINES
NEOLITHS
HY ETHINYLS
IL NIELLIST
IR NITRILES
IT INTITLES
LINTIEST
IY SENILITY
KR TINKLERS
KS LENTISKS
KW TWINKLES
LM STILLMEN
LS LINTLESS
LY SILENTLY
TINSELLY
MR MINSTREL
NO INSOLENT
NU UNSILENT
OO LOONIEST
OILSTONE
OP POTLINES
TOPLINES
OR RETINOLS
OU ELUTIONS
OUTLINES
OV NOVELIST
OW TOWLINES
PR SPLINTER
PS PLENISTS
RU INSULTER
ST TINTLESS
SU UTENSILS
TU LUTENIST

39 DIALER

AB RADIABLE
AF FAIRLEAD
AH RAILHEAD
AP PRAEDIAL
AS SALARIED
AT LARIATED
BC CALIBRED
BE RIDEABLE
BL BRAILLED
BN BILANDER
BS BEDRAILS
DISABLER
BT LIBRATED
BV DRIVABLE
BY DIABLERY
CH HERALDIC
CS DECRIALS
RADICELS
RADICLES
CT ARTICLED
LACERTID
CU AURICLED
DE DEADLIER
DERAILED
REDIALED
DH DIHEDRAL
EM REMAILED
REMEDIAL
EN RENAILED
EP PEDALIER
ES REALISED
RESAILED
SIDEREAL
ET DETAILER
ELATERID
RETAILED
EZ REALIZED
FI AIRFIELD
GL GLADLIER
GRILLADE
GN DANGLIER
DRAGLINE
GO DIALOGER
HN HARDLINE
IP PERIDIAL
KL LARDLIKE
KR DARKLIER
LO ARILLODE
LP PILLARED
LS DALLIERS
DIALLERS
LV RIVALLED
MS DISMALER
MY DREAMILY
NN INLANDER
NS ISLANDER
OS DARIOLES
OT IDOLATER
TAILORED
OV OVERLAID
OX EXORDIAL
PS LIPREADS
PARSLIED
SPIRALED
PT DIPTERAL
TRIPEDAL
PU EPIDURAL
PV DEPRIVAL
RW DRAWLIER
RY DREARILY
ST DILATERS
LARDIEST
REDTAILS
SU RESIDUAL
SY DIALYSER
TT DETRITAL
VY VARIEDLY
YZ DIALYZER

40 LADIES

AC ALCAIDES
AD ALIDADES
AH HEADSAIL
AM MALADIES
AP PALISADE
AR SALARIED
AS ASSAILED
AV VEDALIAS
BD DISABLED
BE ABSEILED
BELADIES
BL SLIDABLE
BM SEMIBALD
BP PIEBALDS
BR BEDRAILS
DISABLER
BS DISABLES
BU AUDIBLES
BY BIASEDLY
CI LAICISED
CL CEDILLAS
CM CAMELIDS
DECIMALS
DECLAIMS
MEDICALS
CP DISPLACE
CR DECRIALS
RADICELS
RADICLES
CT CITADELS
DIALECTS
CY ECDYSIAL
DN ISLANDED
LANDSIDE
DY DIALYSED
EI IDEALISE
EK LAKESIDE
EM LIMEADES
EN DELAINES
EP PLEIADES
ER REALISED
RESAILED
SIDEREAL
ES IDEALESS
ET LEADIEST
FG GADFLIES
FH DEALFISH
FI SALIFIED
FY DAYFLIES
GN DEALINGS
LEADINGS
SIGNALED
GS GLISSADE
GT GLADIEST
HP HELIPADS
HV LAVISHED
IM IDEALISM
MILADIES
IT IDEALIST
KN SANDLIKE
KW SIDEWALK
LP SPADILLE
LR DALLIERS
DIALLERS
LW SIDEWALL
MM DILEMMAS
MO MELODIAS
MP IMPLEADS
MISPLEAD
MR DISMALER
MS MISDEALS
MISLEADS
MT MEDALIST
MISDEALT
NN ANNELIDS
LINDANES
NP SANDPILE
NR ISLANDER
OP SEPALOID
OR DARIOLES
OS ASSOILED
ISOLEADS
OT DIASTOLE
ISOLATED
SODALITE
OZ DIAZOLES
SLEAZOID
PR LIPREADS
PARSLIED
SPIRALED
PS DESPISAL
PT TALIPEDS
RT DILATERS
LARDIEST
REDTAILS
RU RESIDUAL
RY DIALYSER
SV DEVISALS
SY DIALYSES
TY STEADILY
UV DISVALUE
UZ DUALIZES
WY SLIDEWAY
XY DYSLEXIA
YZ DIALYZES

41 DATERS

AC CADASTER
CADASTRE
AG GRADATES
AI AIRDATES
DATARIES
RADIATES
AP ADAPTERS
READAPTS
AW EASTWARD
RADWASTE
BB DRABBEST
DRABBETS
BE BREASTED
DEBATERS
BH BREADTHS
BI REDBAITS
TRIBADES
BN BARTENDS
BO BROADEST
BS DABSTERS
BW BEDSTRAW
CH STARCHED
CI ACRIDEST
CO REDCOATS
CT DETRACTS
CU TRADUCES
DI DISRATED
DL STRADDLE
DN DARNDEST
STRANDED
EE RESEATED
EF DRAFTEES
EG RESTAGED
EH HEADREST
EI READIEST
SERIATED
STEADIER
EK STREAKED
EL DESALTER
RESLATED
TREADLES
EM MASTERED
STREAMED
EP PEDERAST
PREDATES
REPASTED
TRAPESED
ER ARRESTED
RETREADS
SERRATED
TREADERS
ES ASSERTED
ET RESTATED
RETASTED
EW DEWATERS
TARWEEDS
EY ESTRAYED

FR DRAFTERS
REDRAFTS
FW DWARFEST
GN DRAGNETS
GRANDEST
GR DRAGSTER
HH THRASHED
HI HARDIEST
HY HYDRATES
IL DILATERS
LARDIEST
REDTAILS
IM MISRATED
READMITS
IN DETRAINS
RANDIEST
STRAINED
IO ASTEROID
IP RAPIDEST
TRAIPSED
IS DIASTERS
DISASTER
DISRATES
IT STRIATED
TARDIEST
IW TAWDRIES
JU ADJUSTER
READJUST
LO DELATORS
LEOTARDS
LODESTAR
LT STARTLED
LW WARSTLED
WRASTLED
NR STRANDER
NS STANDERS
NU DAUNTERS
TRANSUDE
UNTREADS
NX DEXTRANS
OP ADOPTERS
PASTORED
READOPTS
OR ROADSTER
OS ASSORTED
TORSADES
OU OUTDARES
OUTREADS
READOUTS
OX EXTRADOS
PP STRAPPED
PU PASTURED
UPDATERS
UPSTARED
RT REDSTART
SW STEWARDS
UX SURTAXED
WW WESTWARD

42 SNIDER

AA ARANEIDS
AB BRANDIES
AD SARDINED
AE ARSENIDE
NEARSIDE
AG DERAIGNS
GRADINES
READINGS
AL ISLANDER
AN INSNARED
AO ANEROIDS
AP SPRAINED
AR DRAINERS
SERRANID
AS ARIDNESS
SARDINES
AT DETRAINS
RANDIEST
STRAINED
AU DENARIUS
UNRAISED
URANIDES
AV INVADERS
BE INBREEDS
BL BLINDERS
BRINDLES
BP PREBINDS
CO CONSIDER
CP PRESCIND
CS DISCERNS
RESCINDS
CU INDUCERS
DK KINDREDS
DO INDORSED
DT STRIDDEN
EE NEREIDES
REDENIES
EF DEFINERS
EG DESIGNER
ENERGIDS
REDESIGN
REEDINGS
RESIGNED
EH RESHINED
EK DEERSKIN
EL REDLINES
EO INDORSEE
EP SPENDIER
ES DIRENESS
ET INSERTED
NERDIEST
RESIDENT
SINTERED
TRENDIES
EV INVERSED
EW REWIDENS
WIDENERS
EX INDEXERS
FL FLINDERS
GI DESIRING
RESIDING
RINGSIDE
GO NEGROIDS
GP SPRINGED
GR GRINDERS
REGRINDS
GS DRESSING
GT STRINGED
GW REDWINGS
GY SYNERGID
SYRINGED
HO HORDEINS
IO DERISION
IRONSIDE
RESINOID
IP INSPIRED
IS INSIDERS
IT DISINTER
INDITERS
NITRIDES
IU URIDINES
IV DIVINERS
JO JOINDERS
KL KINDLERS
KR DRINKERS
KS REDSKINS
LP SPINDLER
LS RINDLESS
LT TENDRILS
TRINDLES
LW SWINDLER
NU UNRINSED
OP PRISONED
OR INDORSER
OS INDORSES
SORDINES
OU DOURINES
SOURDINE
PT SPRINTED
SU INSUREDS
SUNDRIES
TT STRIDENT
TRIDENTS
TU INTRUDES
TX DEXTRINS

43 ADORES

AB SEABOARD
AD DEODARAS
BB ABSORBED
BC BROCADES
BD ADSORBED
ROADBEDS
BN BANDORES
BROADENS
BR ADSORBER
BOARDERS
REBOARDS
BT BROADEST
BW SOWBREAD
CG CORDAGES
CI IDOCRASE
CM COMRADES
CN ENDOSARC
CP SCOREPAD
CR CORRADES
CT REDCOATS
CU CAROUSED
DI ROADSIDE
EH SOREHEAD
EK RESOAKED
EM SEADROME
EN REASONED
FI FORESAID
GM ORGASMED
GW DOWAGERS
WORDAGES
HN HARDNOSE
HP RHAPSODE
HR HOARDERS
HW SHADOWER
IL DARIOLES
IN ANEROIDS
IP DIASPORE
PARODIES
IT ASTEROID
IV AVODIRES
AVOIDERS
JP JEOPARDS
KM DARKSOME
LM EARLDOMS
LN LADRONES
SOLANDER
LP LEOPARDS
PRELOADS
LS ROADLESS
LT DELATORS
LEOTARDS
LODESTAR
LU ROULADES
MN MADRONES
RANSOMED
NP OPERANDS
PADRONES
PANDORES
NR ADORNERS
READORNS
PR EARDROPS
PT ADOPTERS
PASTORED
READOPTS
PU UPSOARED
RS DROSERAS
RT ROADSTER
ST ASSORTED
TORSADES
TU OUTDARES
OUTREADS
READOUTS
TX EXTRADOS
UV SAVOURED

44 SERINE

AC INCREASE
AD ARSENIDE
NEARSIDE
AG ANERGIES
GESNERIA
AK SNEAKIER
AL ALIENERS
AN ANSERINE
AP NAPERIES
AT ARENITES
ARSENITE
RESINATE
STEARINE
TRAINEES
AU UNEASIER
BD INBREEDS
BG REBEGINS
BL BERLINES
BZ ZEBRINES
CG GENERICS
CH ENRICHES
CK SICKENER
CL LICENSER
RECLINES
SILENCER
CR SINCERER
CT ENTERICS
ENTICERS
SECRETIN
CU INSECURE
SINECURE
DE NEREIDES
REDENIES
DF DEFINERS
DG DESIGNER
ENERGIDS
REDESIGN
REEDINGS
RESIGNED
DH RESHINED
DK DEERSKIN
DL REDLINES
DO INDORSEE
DP SPENDIER
DS DIRENESS
DT INSERTED
NERDIEST
RESIDENT
SINTERED
TRENDIES
DV INVERSED
DW REWIDENS
WIDENERS
DX INDEXERS
EG ENERGIES
ENERGISE
GREENIES
RESEEING
EH SHEENIER
ER SNEERIER
ES EERINESS
ESERINES
ET ETERNISE
TEENSIER
EV VENERIES
EW WEENSIER
EZ SNEEZIER
FG FEIGNERS
FI FINERIES
FR REFINERS
FS RIFENESS
FT FERNIEST
INFESTER
FU REINFUSE
FZ FRENZIES
GH GREENISH
REHINGES
SHEERING
GL REELINGS
GM REGIMENS
GN SNEERING
GO ERINGOES
GP SPEERING
GR RESIGNER
GS GREISENS
GT GENTRIES
INTEGERS
REESTING
STEERING
GU SEIGNEUR
GV SEVERING
GW RESEWING
SEWERING
HN ENSHRINE
HO HEROINES
HP INSPHERE
HR ERRHINES
HS RESHINES
IP PINERIES
IT NITERIES
IV VINERIES
IW WINERIES
KO KEROSINE
KT KERNITES
LO ELOINERS
LP PILSENER
LS REINLESS
LT ENLISTER
LISTENER
REENLIST
SILENTER
LV LIVENERS
SNIVELER
MM IMMENSER
MN REINSMEN
MO EMERSION
MP SPERMINE
MT MISENTER
NT INTENSER
INTERNES
NU NEURINES
NV INNERVES
NERVINES
OP ISOPRENE
PEREIONS
PIONEERS
OT ONERIEST
SEROTINE
OV EVERSION
PR PRERINSE
REPINERS
RIPENERS
PS EREPSINS
RIPENESS
PU PENURIES
RESUPINE
QU ENQUIRES
SQUIREEN
RT INSERTER
REINSERT
REINTERS
RENTIERS
TERRINES
RU REINSURE
RV VERNIERS
ST SENTRIES
SU ENURESIS
SV INVERSES
VERSINES
TT INSETTER
INTEREST
STERNITE
TRIENTES
TU ESURIENT
RETINUES
REUNITES
TV NERVIEST
REINVEST
SIRVENTE
TX INTERSEX
TY SERENITY
UV UNIVERSE
VX VERNIXES
WW NEWSWIRE

45 SEENIT

AB BETAINES
AC CINEASTE
AD ANDESITE
AM ETAMINES
MATINEES
MISEATEN
AR ARENITES
ARSENITE
RESINATE
STEARINE
TRAINEES
AS ETESIANS
TENIASES
AT ANISETTE
TETANIES
TETANISE
AV NAIVETES
BD BENDIEST
BF BENEFITS
BG BEIGNETS
BL STILBENE
TENSIBLE
BO BETONIES
EBONITES
CG GENETICS
CH SITHENCE
CI NICETIES
CK NECKTIES
CL CENTILES
CM CENTIMES
TENESMIC
CN NESCIENT
CO SEICENTO
CP PECTINES
CR ENTERICS
ENTICERS
SECRETIN
CS CENTESIS
CY CYSTEINE
DD DESTINED
DE NEEDIEST
DF INFESTED
DG INGESTED
SIGNETED
DL ENLISTED
LISTENED
TINSELED
DM SEDIMENT
DN DENTINES
DESINENT
DR INSERTED
NERDIEST
RESIDENT
SINTERED
TRENDIES
DS DESTINES
DT DINETTES
INSETTED
DU DETINUES
DV INVESTED
EL ENLISTEE
SELENITE
EM EMETINES
ER ETERNISE
TEENSIER
ET TEENIEST
EW TWEENIES
WEENIEST
FF FIFTEENS
FN FENNIEST
FR FERNIEST
INFESTER
GG EGESTING
GH SEETHING
SHEETING
GK STEEKING
GL GENTILES
SLEETING
STEELING
GM MEETINGS
GO EGESTION
GP STEEPING
GR GENTRIES
INTEGERS
REESTING
STEERING
GU EUGENIST
GV STEEVING
GW SWEETING
HL THEELINS
IL LENITIES
IM ENMITIES
IN EINSTEIN
NINETIES
IR NITERIES
IS SIENITES
IT ENTITIES
IV INVITEES
VEINIEST
KL NESTLIKE
KR KERNITES
LN SENTINEL
LP PENLITES
PLENTIES
LR ENLISTER
LISTENER
REENLIST
SILENTER
LS LITENESS
SETLINES
LT ENTITLES
LV VEINLETS
MO MONETISE
SEMITONE
MR MISENTER
MV MISEVENT
NR INTENSER
INTERNES
NS TENNISES
NT SENTIENT
NW ENTWINES
WENNIEST
NZ NETIZENS
OR ONERIEST
SEROTINE
OS ESSONITE
OT NOISETTE
TEOSINTE
QU QUIETENS
RR INSERTER
REINSERT
REINTERS
RENTIERS
TERRINES
RS SENTRIES
RT INSETTER
INTEREST
STERNITE
TRIENTES
RU ESURIENT
RETINUES
REUNITES
RV NERVIEST
REINVEST
SIRVENTE
RX INTERSEX
RY SERENITY
SS SESTINES
SW NEWSIEST
SX SIXTEENS
SY SYENITES
TT NETTIEST
TENTIEST
TW TWENTIES
TX EXISTENT

46 LATENS

AC ANALECTS
AK ALKANETS
AM TALESMAN
AP PLATANES
PLEASANT
AR ASTERNAL
AS SEALANTS
AT ATLANTES
AY ANALYTES
BD BLANDEST
BE NESTABLE
BI INSTABLE
BK BLANKEST
BLANKETS
BO NOTABLES
STONABLE
BU ABLUENTS
UNSTABLE
BY ABSENTLY
CE CLEANEST
CI CANISTEL
CO LACTONES
CR CENTRALS
CY SECANTLY
DH SHETLAND
DU UNSALTED
DW WETLANDS
EE SELENATE
EK KANTELES
EM TALESMEN
ER ETERNALS
TELERANS
ES LATENESS
FI INFLATES
FS FLATNESS
FT FLATTENS
GI GELATINS
GENITALS
STEALING
TAGLINES
GL GELLANTS
GO TANGELOS
GR STRANGLE
TANGLERS
GT GANTLETS
GU LANGUETS
GW TWANGLES
HO ANETHOLS
ETHANOLS
HR ENTHRALS
HS NATHLESS
II ALIENIST
LITANIES
IK LANKIEST
IM AILMENTS
ALIMENTS
MANLIEST
MELANIST
SMALTINE
IO ELATIONS
INSOLATE
TOENAILS
IP PANELIST
PANTILES
PLAINEST
IR ENTRAILS
LATRINES
RATLINES
RETINALS
TRENAILS
IS ELASTINS
NAILSETS
SALIENTS
SALTINES
IU ALUNITES
INSULATE
IV VENTAILS
KS TANKLESS
LS TALLNESS
MT MANTLETS
MY MESNALTY
NR LANTERNS
NU ANNULETS
OP POLENTAS
OY ANOLYTES
PR PLANTERS
REPLANTS
PX EXPLANTS
RS SALTERNS
RT SLATTERN
RU NEUTRALS
RV VENTRALS
SS SALTNESS

47 STANED

AM MANDATES
AN ANDANTES
AY ASYNDETA
AZ STANZAED
BD BEDSTAND
BE ABSENTED
BL BLANDEST
BR BARTENDS
BU UNBASTED
CH SNATCHED
STANCHED
CI DISTANCE
CN SCANDENT
CO ENDOCAST
TACNODES
CP PANDECTS
CS DESCANTS
DI DANDIEST
DM DAMNDEST
DR DARNDEST
STRANDED
EF FASTENED
EH HASTENED
EI ANDESITE
EK NAKEDEST
EM STAMENED
EO ENDOSTEA
ES ASSENTED
SENSATED
STANDEES
EU UNSEATED
EY ANDESYTE
FS DAFTNESS
GI SEDATING
STEADING
GR DRAGNETS
GRANDEST
HI HANDIEST
HL SHETLAND
HS HANDSETS
II ADENITIS
DAINTIES
IM MEDIANTS
IO ASTONIED
SEDATION
IP DEPAINTS
IR DETRAINS
RANDIEST
STRAINED
IS DESTAINS
SANDIEST
IT INSTATED
IU AUDIENTS
SINUATED
IV DEVIANTS
LU UNSALTED
LW WETLANDS
NP PENDANTS
OO ODONATES
OP NOTEPADS
RR STRANDER
RS STANDERS
RU DAUNTERS
TRANSUDE
UNTREADS
RX DEXTRANS
TU UNSTATED
UNTASTED
UW UNWASTED
UY UNSTAYED
UNSTEADY

48 TENAIL

AC ANALCITE
LAITANCE
AD DENTALIA
AE ALIENATE
AG AGENTIAL
ALGINATE
AH ANTHELIA
AK ANTILEAK
AL ALLANITE
AM ANTIMALE
LAMINATE
AP PALATINE
AV AVENTAIL
BD BIDENTAL
BG BLEATING
TANGIBLE
BL LIBELANT
BM BAILMENT
BO TAILBONE
BS INSTABLE
BV BIVALENT
BY BINATELY
CC CANTICLE
CG CLEATING
CH ETHNICAL
CL CLIENTAL
CR CLARINET
CS CANISTEL
DD TIDELAND
DE DATELINE
ENTAILED
LINEATED
DF INFLATED
DG DELATING
DN DENTINAL
DO DELATION
DP PANTILED
DV DIVALENT
EG GALENITE
GELATINE
LEGATINE
EL TENAILLE
EM MELANITE
EP PETALINE
TAPELINE
ER ELATERIN
ENTAILER
TREENAIL
FI ANTILIFE
FL FLATLINE
FM FILAMENT
FR INFLATER
FS INFLATES
FT ANTILEFT
GG GELATING
LEGATING
GH ATHELING
GK GNATLIKE
GM LIGAMENT
METALING
TEGMINAL
GN GANTLINE
LATENING
GO GELATION
LEGATION
GP PLEATING
GR ALERTING
ALTERING
INTEGRAL
RELATING
TANGLIER
TRIANGLE
GS GELATINS
GENITALS
STEALING
TAGLINES
GV VALETING
GX EXALTING
GZ TEAZLING
HX ANTHELIX
HZ ZENITHAL
IR INERTIAL
IS ALIENIST
LITANIES
IZ LATINIZE
KK TANKLIKE
KS LANKIEST
KU AUNTLIKE
MR TERMINAL
TRAMLINE
MS AILMENTS
ALIMENTS
MANLIEST
MELANIST
SMALTINE
NR INTERNAL
NY INNATELY
OP ANTIPOLE
OR ORIENTAL
RELATION
OS ELATIONS
INSOLATE
TOENAILS
PP PIEPLANT
PR INTERLAP
TRAPLINE
TRIPLANE
PS PANELIST
PANTILES
PLAINEST
PT TINPLATE
PY PENALITY
QU QUANTILE

RS ENTRAILS
LATRINES
RATLINES
RETINALS
TRENAILS
RU AUNTLIER
RETINULA
TENURIAL
RV INTERVAL
RY INTERLAY
SS ELASTINS
NAILSETS
SALIENTS
SALTINES
SU ALUNITES
INSULATE
SV VENTAILS
VY NATIVELY
VENALITY

49 TEINDS

AC DISTANCE
AD DANDIEST
AE ANDESITE
AG SEDATING
STEADING
AH HANDIEST
AI ADENITIS
DAINTIES
AM MEDIANTS
AO ASTONIED
SEDATION
AP DEPAINTS
AR DETRAINS
RANDIEST
STRAINED
AS DESTAINS
SANDIEST
AT INSTATED
AU AUDIENTS
SINUATED
AV DEVIANTS
BE BENDIEST
BL BLINDEST
CH SNITCHED
CY SYNDETIC
DE DESTINED
DR STRIDDEN
DS DISTENDS
EE NEEDIEST
EF INFESTED
EG INGESTED
SIGNETED
EL ENLISTED
LISTENED
TINSELED
EM SEDIMENT
EN DENTINES
DESINENT
ER INSERTED
NERDIEST
RESIDENT
SINTERED
TRENDIES
ES DESTINES
ET DINETTES
INSETTED
EU DETINUES
EV INVESTED
FU UNSIFTED
GI DINGIEST
GR STRINGED
GU DUNGIEST
HO HEDONIST
IK DINKIEST
IO EDITIONS
SEDITION
IR DISINTER
INDITERS
NITRIDES
IS INSISTED
TIDINESS
IU DISUNITE
NUDITIES
UNTIDIES
IV DIVINEST
IW WINDIEST
LO LENTOIDS
LP SPLINTED
LR TENDRILS
TRINDLES
LU DILUENTS
INSULTED
UNLISTED
MO DEMONIST
MS MINDSETS
MISTENDS
MU MISTUNED
NU DUNNITES
OW DOWNIEST
PR SPRINTED
PS STIPENDS
QU SQUINTED
RT STRIDENT
TRIDENTS
RU INTRUDES
RX DEXTRINS
SS DISSENTS
ST DENTISTS
UU UNSUITED

50 DESIRE

AC DECIARES
AG DISAGREE
AL REALISED
RESAILED
SIDEREAL
AN ARSENIDE
NEARSIDE
AP AIRSPEED
AR DREARIES
RERAISED
AT READIEST
SERIATED
STEADIER
BC DESCRIBE
BD BIRDSEED
DEBRIDES
BF DEBRIEFS
BN INBREEDS
BO REBODIES
BT BESTRIDE
BISTERED
BU DEBRUISE
BY BIRDSEYE
CD DECIDERS
DESCRIED
CL SCLEREID
CP PRECISED
CR DECRIERS
DESCRIER
CS DESCRIES
CT DESERTIC
DISCREET
DISCRETE
CU DECURIES
CV SCRIEVED
SERVICED
DL DREIDELS
DP PRESIDED
DR DERIDERS
EF REDEFIES
EM REMEDIES
EN NEREIDES
REDENIES
EP SPEEDIER
ES DIERESES
ET REEDIEST
EZ RESEIZED
FF SERIFFED
FI DEIFIERS
EDIFIERS
FIRESIDE
FL DEFILERS
FIELDERS
FN DEFINERS
FO FORESIDE
FT RESIFTED
GN DESIGNER
ENERGIDS
REDESIGN
REEDINGS
RESIGNED
GT DIGESTER
REDIGEST
GV DIVERGES
HK SHRIEKED
HL HIRSELED
RELISHED
SHIELDER
HN RESHINED
HP PERISHED
HT DIETHERS
HV SHIVERED
SHRIEVED
HW SHREWDIE
IS DIERESIS
IT SIDERITE
IV DERISIVE
IW WEIRDIES
KN DEERSKIN
LN REDLINES
LT RELISTED
LU LEISURED
LV DELIVERS
DESILVER
SILVERED
SLIVERED
LW WIELDERS
LY YIELDERS
MM IMMERSED
SIMMERED
MO EMEROIDS
MP DEMIREPS
EPIDERMS
IMPEDERS
PREMISED
SIMPERED
MS DERMISES
MT DEMERITS
DEMISTER
DIMETERS
NO INDORSEE
NP SPENDIER
NS DIRENESS
NT INSERTED
NERDIEST
RESIDENT
SINTERED
TRENDIES
NV INVERSED
NW REWIDENS
WIDENERS
NX INDEXERS
OV OVERSIDE
OW DOWERIES
WEIRDOES
PR PREDRIES
PRESIDER
REPRISED
RESPIRED
PS DESPISER
DISPERSE
PRESIDES
PT PREEDITS
PRIESTED
RESPITED
PU DUPERIES
PV DEPRIVES
PREVISED
QU ESQUIRED
RS DERRISES
DESIRERS
DRESSIER
RESIDERS
RT DESTRIER
RU RUDERIES
RV DERIVERS
REDRIVES
ST DIESTERS
EDITRESS
RESISTED
SISTERED
SU DIURESES
REISSUED
RESIDUES
SV DEVISERS
DISSERVE
DISSEVER
TT TIREDEST
TW WEIRDEST

51 SENATE

AM EMANATES
MANATEES
AR ARSENATE
SERENATA
AU NAUSEATE
BD ABSENTED
BE ABSENTEE
BI BETAINES
BL NESTABLE
BM BASEMENT
BR ABSENTER
BW NEWSBEAT
CC ACESCENT
CI CINEASTE
CL CLEANEST
CM CASEMENT
CN CANTEENS
CO ACETONES
NOTECASE
CR CENTARES
REASCENT
REENACTS
SARCENET
CX EXSECANT
DF FASTENED
DH HASTENED
DI ANDESITE
DK NAKEDEST
DM STAMENED
DO ENDOSTEA
DS ASSENTED
SENSATED
STANDEES
DU UNSEATED
DY ANDESYTE
EL SELENATE
EM EASEMENT
ER SERENATE
FR FASTENER
FENESTRA
REFASTEN
GH THENAGES
GR ESTRANGE
GRANTEES
GREATENS
NEGATERS
REAGENTS
SERGEANT
GT TENTAGES
GV VENTAGES
HH ENSHEATH
HEATHENS
HM METHANES
HP HAPTENES
HEPTANES
PHENATES
HR HASTENER
HEARTENS
HS ANTHESES
HW ENSWATHE
WHEATENS
IM ETAMINES
MATINEES
MISEATEN
IR ARENITES
ARSENITE
RESINATE
STEARINE
TRAINEES
IS ETESIANS
TENIASES
IT ANISETTE
TETANIES
TETANISE
IV NAIVETES
JR SERJEANT
KL KANTELES
LM TALESMEN
LR ETERNALS
TELERANS
LS LATENESS
MS TAMENESS
NO NEONATES
NP PENTANES
NS NEATNESS
NT SETENANT
OR EARSTONE
RESONATE
RR TERRANES
RS ASSENTER
EARNESTS
SARSENET
RT ENTREATS
RATTEENS
RU SAUTERNE
RV VETERANS
SS SENSATES
TV NAVETTES

52 LEARNS

AD ADRENALS
AS ARSENALS
AT ASTERNAL
AY ANALYSER
BE ENABLERS
BI RINSABLE
BY BLARNEYS
CD CANDLERS
CE CLEANERS
CLEANSER
RECLEANS
CG CLANGERS
GLANCERS
CH CHARNELS
CI CARLINES
LANCIERS
CK CRANKLES
CN SCRANNEL
CT CENTRALS
CU LUCARNES
DD DANDLERS
DG DANGLERS
GLANDERS
DH HANDLERS
DI ISLANDER
DL LANDLERS
DM MANDRELS
DO LADRONES
SOLANDER
DP SPANDREL
DS SLANDERS
DU LAUNDERS
LURDANES
EG ENLARGES
GENERALS
GLEANERS
EI ALIENERS
EP REPANELS
ER LEARNERS
RELEARNS
ES REALNESS
ET ETERNALS
TELERANS
EV ENSLAVER
EW RENEWALS
FG FLANGERS
FK FLANKERS
FO FARNESOL
FU FLANEURS
FUNERALS
GG GANGRELS
GI ALIGNERS
ENGRAILS
NARGILES
REALIGNS
SIGNALER
SLANGIER
GJ JANGLERS
GL LANGRELS
GM MANGLERS
GP GRAPNELS
GT STRANGLE
TANGLERS
GU GRANULES
GW WANGLERS
WRANGLES
GY LARYNGES
HI INHALERS
HP SHRAPNEL
HT ENTHRALS
II AIRLINES
IM MARLINES
MINERALS
MISLEARN
IO AILERONS
ALIENORS
IP PRALINES
IR SNARLIER
IS RAINLESS
IT ENTRAILS
LATRINES
RATLINES
RETINALS
TRENAILS
IV RAVELINS
IX RELAXINS
IY INLAYERS
KS RANKLESS
KV KLAVERNS
MO ALMONERS
MU MENSURAL
NUMERALS
NP PLANNERS
NS ENSNARLS
NT LANTERNS
NU UNLEARNS
OP PERSONAL
PSORALEN
OU ALEURONS
NEUROSAL
PP PREPLANS
PT PLANTERS
REPLANTS
PU PURSLANE
SUPERNAL
RS SNARLERS
ST SALTERNS
TT SLATTERN
TU NEUTRALS
TV VENTRALS
UU NEURULAS
UV UNRAVELS
XY LARYNXES

53 SENITI

AC CANITIES
AD ADENITIS
DAINTIES
AK KAINITES
AL ALIENIST
LITANIES
AR INERTIAS
RAINIEST
AS ISATINES
SANITIES
SANITISE
TENIASIS
AV VANITIES
AZ SANITIZE
BO NIOBITES
BR BRINIEST
BS STIBINES
BT STIBNITE
CE NICETIES
CH ICHNITES
NITCHIES
CK KINETICS
CM MINCIEST
CR CITRINES
CRINITES
INCITERS
CU CUTINISE
CY SYENITIC
CZ CITIZENS
ZINCITES
DG DINGIEST
DK DINKIEST
DO EDITIONS
SEDITION
DR DISINTER
INDITERS
NITRIDES
DS INSISTED
TIDINESS
DU DISUNITE
NUDITIES
UNTIDIES
DV DIVINEST
DW WINDIEST
EL LENITIES
EM ENMITIES
EN EINSTEIN
NINETIES
ER NITERIES
ES SIENITES
ET ENTITIES
EV INVITEES
VEINIEST
FM FEMINIST
FN FINNIEST
FO NOTIFIES
FT NIFTIEST
GH HEISTING
NIGHTIES
GL LIGNITES
LINGIEST
GM MINGIEST
GN GINNIEST
GR IGNITERS
RESITING
STINGIER
GW WINGIEST
GX EXISTING
GZ ZINGIEST
HK HINKIEST
HR INHERITS
HS SHINIEST
HW WHINIEST
KK KINKIEST
KN KINETINS
KR STINKIER
KW TWINKIES
LL NIELLIST
LR NITRILES
LT INTITLES
LINTIEST
LY SENILITY
MR INTERIMS
MINISTER
MISINTER
MT MINTIEST
MU MUTINIES
NS TININESS
NT TINNIEST
NW INTWINES
OS INOSITES
NOISIEST
PP NIPPIEST
PR PRISTINE
PS SPINIEST
PZ PINTSIZE
QU INQUIETS
RS INSISTER
SINISTER
RT NITRITES
RU NEURITIS
RV INVITERS
VITRINES
TT NITTIEST
TW TWINIEST
UZ UNITIZES

54 ORIENT

AA AERATION
AB BARITONE
OBTAINER
REOBTAIN
TABORINE
AC ACTIONER
ANORETIC
CREATION
REACTION
AD AROINTED
ORDINATE
RATIONED
AH ANTIHERO
AL ORIENTAL
RELATION
AN ANOINTER
REANOINT
AP ATROPINE
AR ANTERIOR
AS NOTARIES
SENORITA
AT TENTORIA
AZ NOTARIZE
BS BORNITES
CC CONCERTI
NECROTIC
CD CENTROID
DOCTRINE
CE ERECTION
NEOTERIC
CF INFECTOR
CG GERONTIC
CJ INJECTOR
CM INTERCOM
CP ENTROPIC
INCEPTOR
CR TRICORNE
CS COINTERS
CORNIEST
NOTICERS
CT CONTRITE
CU NEUROTIC
UNEROTIC
CV CONTRIVE
DD TRENDOID
DE ORIENTED
DI RETINOID
DM DORMIENT
DN INDENTOR
DP DIPTERON
DT INTORTED
EH HEREINTO
ER ORIENTER
REORIENT
ES ONERIEST
SEROTINE
ET TENORITE
EX EXERTION
FI NOTIFIER
FR FRONTIER
FY RENOTIFY
GN NITROGEN
GS GENITORS
GV REVOTING
GW TOWERING
HM THERMION
HN INTHRONE
HR THORNIER
HS HORNIEST
ORNITHES
HV OVERTHIN
IP POINTIER
IR INTERIOR
JS JOINTERS
JU JOINTURE
KS INSTROKE
KT KNOTTIER
LP TERPINOL
LS RETINOLS
LT TROTLINE
LU OUTLINER
MO MOTIONER
REMOTION
MP ORPIMENT
MW TIMEWORN
MY ENORMITY
NN NONINERT
NS INTONERS
TERNIONS
NU NEUTRINO
NV INVENTOR
OS SNOOTIER
PS POINTERS
PORNIEST
PROTEINS
TROPINES
PU ERUPTION
RS INTRORSE
RV INVERTOR
RW INTERROW
SS OESTRINS
ST SNOTTIER
TENORIST
TRITONES
SU ROUTINES
SNOUTIER
SV INVESTOR
SY SEROTINY
TYROSINE

55 TRAINS

AB BARTISAN
AD RADIANTS
AE ANTISERA
RATANIES
SANTERIA
SEATRAIN
AG GRANITAS
AI INTARSIA
AM MARTIANS
TAMARINS
AP ASPIRANT
PARTISAN
SPARTINA
AS ARTISANS
TSARINAS
AV VARIANTS
AY SANITARY
AZ TZARINAS
BE BANISTER
BARNIEST
BO TABORINS
BU URBANIST
BV VIBRANTS
CE CANISTER
CERATINS
CISTERNA
CREATINS
SCANTIER
TACRINES
CF INFARCTS
INFRACTS
CG SCARTING
TRACINGS
CO CAROTINS
CORTINAS
CP CANTRIPS
CS NARCISTS
CU CURTAINS
DE DETRAINS
RANDIEST
STRAINED
DF INDRAFTS
DI DISTRAIN
DK STINKARD
DO DIATRONS
INTRADOS
DU UNITARDS
EE ARENITES
ARSENITE
RESINATE
STEARINE
TRAINEES
EF FAINTERS
EG ANGRIEST
ASTRINGE
GANISTER
GANTRIES
GRANITES
INGRATES
RANGIEST
EH HAIRNETS
INEARTHS
THERIANS
EI INERTIAS
RAINIEST
EK KERATINS
EL ENTRAILS
LATRINES
RATLINES
RETINALS
TRENAILS
EM MINARETS
RAIMENTS
EN ENTRAINS
TRANNIES
EO NOTARIES
SENORITA
EP PAINTERS
PANTRIES
PERTAINS
PINASTER
PRISTANE
REPAINTS
ER RESTRAIN
RETRAINS
STRAINER
TERRAINS
TRAINERS
ES ARTINESS
RETSINAS
STAINERS
STEARINS
ET INTREATS
NITRATES
STRAITEN
TERTIANS
EU RUINATES
TAURINES
URANITES
URINATES
EW TINWARES
FG INGRAFTS
STRAFING
FK RATFINKS
FX TRANSFIX
GG GRATINGS
GH TRASHING
GK KARTINGS
GL STARLING
GM MIGRANTS
SMARTING
GO ORGANIST
ROASTING
GP PARTINGS
GR STARRING
GS GASTRINS
GT STARTING
GV STARVING
GW RINGTAWS
STRAWING
GY STINGRAY
STRAYING
HL INTHRALS
HP TRANSHIP
IM MARTINIS
MISTRAIN
IV VITRAINS
IZ TRIAZINS
JO JANITORS
LO TONSILAR
MT TANTRISM
TRANSMIT
MU NATRIUMS
NATURISM
MV VARMINTS
NT INTRANTS
NU INSURANT
OO ORATIONS
OP ATROPINS
OS ARSONIST
OT STRONTIA
OU RAINOUTS
OW WAITRONS
PS SPIRANTS
PT TRIPTANS
PU PURITANS
QU QUINTARS
ST TRANSITS
TT TITRANTS

TU ANTIRUST
NATURIST
TY TANISTRY

56 STRIDE

AA AIRDATES
DATARIES
RADIATES
AB REDBAITS
TRIBADES
AC ACRIDEST
AD DISRATED
AE READIEST
SERIATED
STEADIER
AH HARDIEST
AL DILATERS
LARDIEST
REDTAILS
AM MISRATED
READMITS
AN DETRAINS
RANDIEST
STRAINED
AO ASTEROID
AP RAPIDEST
TRAIPSED
AS DIASTERS
DISASTER
DISRATES
AT STRIATED
TARDIEST
AW TAWDRIES
BE BESTRIDE
BISTERED
BL BRISTLED
DRIBLETS
BO DEORBITS
CE DESERTIC
DISCREET
DISCRETE
CH DITCHERS
CO CORDITES
CP PREDICTS
SCRIPTED
CU CRUDITES
CURDIEST
CURTSIED
CV VERDICTS
DL TIDDLERS
DN STRIDDEN
DU RUDDIEST
STURDIED
EE REEDIEST
EF RESIFTED
EG DIGESTER
REDIGEST
EH DIETHERS
EI SIDERITE
EL RELISTED
EM DEMERITS
DEMISTER
DIMETERS
EN INSERTED
NERDIEST
RESIDENT
SINTERED
TRENDIES
EP PREEDITS
PRIESTED
RESPITED
ER DESTRIER
ES DIESTERS
EDITRESS
RESISTED
SISTERED
ET TIREDEST
EW WEIRDEST
FH REDSHIFT
FR DRIFTERS
GI RIDGIEST
GN STRINGED
GO DIGESTOR
GRODIEST
STODGIER
HI DISHERIT
HR REDSHIRT
HT THIRSTED
IN DISINTER
INDITERS
NITRIDES
IO DIORITES
IP RIPTIDES
SPIRITED
TIDERIPS
IT DIRTIEST
KO DORKIEST
LN TENDRILS
TRINDLES
LO STOLIDER
LU DILUTERS
STUDLIER
MM MIDTERMS
MO MORTISED
MU DIESTRUM
NP SPRINTED
NT STRIDENT
TRIDENTS
NU INTRUDES
NX DEXTRINS
OP DIOPTERS
DIOPTRES
PERIDOTS
PORTSIDE
PROTEIDS
RIPOSTED
TOPSIDER
OS STEROIDS
OU OUTRIDES
OUTSIDER
OW ROWDIEST
WORDIEST
PP STRIPPED
PU DISPUTER
STUPIDER
PZ SPRITZED
QU SQUIRTED
RS STRIDERS
RU STURDIER
SS DISSERTS
DISTRESS
SU DIESTRUS
STUDIERS
STURDIES
TU DETRITUS

57 INTROS

AB TABORINS
AC CAROTINS
CORTINAS
AD DIATRONS
INTRADOS
AE NOTARIES
SENORITA
AG ORGANIST
ROASTING
AJ JANITORS
AL TONSILAR
AO ORATIONS
AP ATROPINS
AS ARSONIST
AT STRONTIA
AU RAINOUTS
AW WAITRONS
BE BORNITES
BO BIOTRONS
CE COINTERS
CORNIEST
NOTICERS
CI CROSTINI
CO CROSTINO
CR TRICORNS
CS CISTRONS
CT STRONTIC
CU RUCTIONS
EE ONERIEST
SEROTINE
EG GENITORS
EH HORNIEST
ORNITHES
EJ JOINTERS
EK INSTROKE
EL RETINOLS
EN INTONERS
TERNIONS
EO SNOOTIER
EP POINTERS
PORNIEST
PROTEINS
TROPINES
ER INTRORSE
ES OESTRINS
ET SNOTTIER
TENORIST
TRITONES
EU ROUTINES
SNOUTIER
EV INVESTOR
EY SEROTINY
TYROSINE
FG FROSTING
FP FROSTNIP
GH SHORTING
GI IGNITORS
GK STROKING
GM STORMING
GN SNORTING
GO ROOSTING
GP SPORTING
GS RINGTOSS
GU OUTGRINS
OUTRINGS
ROUSTING
TOURINGS
GW STROWING
WORSTING
GY STORYING
STROYING
HN TINHORNS
HO HORNITOS
HS HORNISTS
IS IRONISTS
IT INTROITS
KW TINWORKS
LS NOSTRILS
LY NITROSYL
MO MONITORS
NO NOTORNIS
OP PORTIONS
POSITRON
SORPTION
OS TORSIONS
OT TORTONIS
OY SONORITY

58 SANDER

AC DRACENAS
AI ARANEIDS
AL ADRENALS
AV VERANDAS
BI BRANDIES
BO BANDORES
BROADENS
BR BRANDERS
BS DRABNESS
BT BARTENDS
CE ASCENDER
REASCEND
CL CANDLERS
CO ENDOSARC
CU DURANCES
DI SARDINED
DL DANDLERS
DT DARNDEST
STRANDED
DU DAUNDERS
EE SERENADE
EG DERANGES
GRANDEES
GRENADES
EI ARSENIDE
NEARSIDE
EK KNEADERS
EM AMENDERS
MEANDERS
EN ENSNARED
EO REASONED
ES DEARNESS
EU UNDERSEA
UNERASED
UNSEARED
EW ANSWERED
EY YEARENDS
GI DERAIGNS
GRADINES
READINGS
GL DANGLERS
GLANDERS
GT DRAGNETS
GRANDEST
HK REDSHANK
HL HANDLERS
HM HERDSMAN
HO HARDNOSE
HS HARDNESS
HU UNSHARED
HW SWANHERD
IL ISLANDER
IN INSNARED
IO ANEROIDS
IP SPRAINED
IR DRAINERS
SERRANID
IS ARIDNESS
SARDINES
IT DETRAINS
RANDIEST
STRAINED
IU DENARIUS
UNRAISED
URANIDES
IV INVADERS
KS DARKNESS
LL LANDLERS
LM MANDRELS
LO LADRONES
SOLANDER
LP SPANDREL
LS SLANDERS
LU LAUNDERS
LURDANES
MO MADRONES
RANSOMED
MU DURAMENS
MAUNDERS
SURNAMED
OP OPERANDS
PADRONES
PANDORES
OR ADORNERS
READORNS
PR PARDNERS
PU UNDRAPES
PW PREDAWNS
QU SQUANDER
RT STRANDER
RY REYNARDS
ST STANDERS
SU DANSEURS
TU DAUNTERS
TRANSUDE
UNTREADS
TX DEXTRANS

59 OATIES*

BC ICEBOATS
BN BOTANIES
BOTANISE
NIOBATES
OBEISANT
BV OBVIATES
CH ACHIOTES
CL COALIEST
SOCIETAL
CN ACONITES
CANOEIST
SONICATE
CP ECTOPIAS
DG GODETIAS
DL DIASTOLE
ISOLATED
SODALITE
DM ATOMISED
DN ASTONIED
SEDATION
DP DIOPTASE
DR ASTEROID
DX OXIDATES
DZ AZOTISED
FL FOLIATES
FM FOAMIEST
GL LATIGOES
OTALGIES
GU AGOUTIES
GX GEOTAXIS
HR HOARIEST
JR JAROSITE
KL KEITLOAS
KS STOKESIA
LM LOAMIEST
LN ELATIONS
INSOLATE
TOENAILS
LP SPOLIATE
LS ISOLATES
LT TOTALISE
LV VIOLATES
MN AMNIOTES
MASONITE
MISATONE
MR AMORTISE
ATOMISER
MS AMITOSES
AMOSITES
ATOMISES
MX TOXEMIAS
MZ ATOMIZES
NN ENATIONS
SONATINE
NP SAPONITE
NR NOTARIES
SENORITA
NS ASTONIES
PP APPOSITE
PS SOAPIEST
RR ROTARIES
RT TOASTIER
RU OUTRAISE
SAUTOIRE
RV TRAVOISE
VIATORES
VOTARIES
SZ AZOTISES
ZZ AZOTIZES

60 STORED

AB BROADEST
AC REDCOATS
AI ASTEROID
AL DELATORS
LEOTARDS
LODESTAR
AP ADOPTERS
PASTORED
READOPTS
AR ROADSTER
AS ASSORTED
TORSADES
AU OUTDARES
OUTREADS
READOUTS
AX EXTRADOS
BE BESTRODE
BI DEORBITS
BU DOUBTERS
OBTRUDES
REDOUBTS
CE CORSETED
ESCORTED
SECTORED
CI CORDITES
CU EDUCTORS
DL TODDLERS
EE STEREOED
EF DEFOREST
FORESTED
FOSTERED
EK RESTOKED
EM MODESTER
EP DOPESTER
ER RESORTED
RESTORED
ES DOSSERET
OERSTEDS
ET TETRODES
EX DEXTROSE
EY OYSTERED
STOREYED
FL TELFORDS
FS DEFROSTS
FROSTEDS
FW FROWSTED
GI DIGESTOR
GRODIEST
STODGIER
HP POTSHERD
II DIORITES
IK DORKIEST
IL STOLIDER
IM MORTISED
IP DIOPTERS
DIOPTRES
PERIDOTS
PORTSIDE
PROTEIDS
RIPOSTED
TOPSIDER
IS STEROIDS
IU OUTRIDES
OUTSIDER
IW ROWDIEST
WORDIEST
LL DROLLEST
STROLLED
LP DROPLETS
LS OLDSTERS
LT DOTTRELS
MN MORDENTS
MO DOOMSTER
NP PORTENDS
PROTENDS
NU ROUNDEST
TONSURED
UNSORTED
NY DRYSTONE
OP DOORSTEP
TORPEDOS
OR REDROOTS
OU OUTDOERS
PP STROPPED
PU POSTURED
PROUDEST
SPROUTED
SU OUTDRESS
SW WORSTEDS
SY DESTROYS
UX DEXTROUS

61 TODIES

AG GODETIAS
AL DIASTOLE
ISOLATED
SODALITE
AM ATOMISED
AN ASTONIED
SEDATION
AP DIOPTASE
AR ASTEROID
AX OXIDATES
AZ AZOTISED
BR DEORBITS
CK DIESTOCK
CM DEMOTICS
DOMESTIC
CP DESPOTIC
CR CORDITES
CS CESTOIDS
DG DODGIEST
DI ODDITIES
DL DELTOIDS
DW DOWDIEST
EP EPIDOTES
POETISED
GG DOGGIEST
GL GODLIEST
GP PODGIEST
GR DIGESTOR
GRODIEST
STODGIER
HM ETHMOIDS
HN HEDONIST
HO DHOOTIES
HOODIEST
HU HIDEOUTS
IN EDITIONS
SEDITION
IR DIORITES
IT OTITIDES
KR DORKIEST
LM MELODIST
MODELIST
MOLDIEST
LN LENTOIDS
LP PISTOLED
LR STOLIDER
LS SOLIDEST
LU SOLITUDE
TOLUIDES
MM IMMODEST
MN DEMONIST
MO DOOMIEST
MOODIEST
SODOMITE
MP IMPOSTED
MR MORTISED
MS DISTOMES
MODISTES
MT DEMOTIST
NW DOWNIEST
OS OSTEOIDS
OW WOODIEST
PR DIOPTERS
DIOPTRES
PERIDOTS
PORTSIDE
PROTEIDS
RIPOSTED
TOPSIDER
PS DEPOSITS
TOPSIDES
PV POSTDIVE
RS STEROIDS
RU OUTRIDES
OUTSIDER
RW ROWDIEST
WORDIEST
SU OUTSIDES
TT DOTTIEST
UW WIDEOUTS
UZ OUTSIZED

62 OILERS

AC CALORIES
CARIOLES
AD DARIOLES
AF FORESAIL
AG GASOLIER
GIRASOLE
SERAGLIO
AH AIRHOLES
SHOALIER
AM MORALISE
AN AILERONS
ALIENORS
AP PELORIAS
POLARISE
AS SOLARISE
AV VALORISE
VARIOLES
AZ SOLARIZE
BB SLOBBIER
BC BRICOLES
CORBEILS
BE EROSIBLE
BG OBLIGERS
BL BROLLIES
BM EMBROILS
BP PREBOILS
BR BROILERS
BT STROBILE
BU BLOUSIER
BW BLOWSIER
CD SCLEROID
CE CREOLISE
CH CEORLISH
CL COLLIERS
CN INCLOSER
LICENSOR
CP POLICERS
CT CLOISTER
COISTREL
COSTLIER
DI IDOLISER
DP LEPORIDS
DS SOLDIERS
DT STOLIDER
DY SOLDIERY
EK ROSELIKE
EN ELOINERS
EV OVERLIES
RELIEVOS
VOLERIES
FJ FRIJOLES
FK FOLKSIER
FP PROFILES
FS FLOSSIER
FT TREFOILS
GL GIROLLES
GM GOMERILS
GN RESOLING
GS GLOSSIER
HP POLISHER
REPOLISH
HS SLOSHIER
HU HOURLIES
IN LIONISER
IP LIRIOPES
IT ROILIEST
JL JOLLIERS
LT TROLLIES
LU ROUILLES
LZ ZORILLES
MN MISENROL
MP IMPLORES
MR LORIMERS
MY RIMOSELY
NP PROLINES
NR LORINERS
NT RETINOLS
OT OESTRIOL
PP SLOPPIER
PS SPOILERS
PT POITRELS
PU PERILOUS
PV OVERSLIP
SLIPOVER
SS RISSOLES
ST ESTRIOLS
SU SOILURES
TT TRIOLETS
TU OUTLIERS
UV RIVULOSE

63 ANITOE

AR AERATION
BD OBTAINED
BL TAILBONE
BR BARITONE
OBTAINER
REOBTAIN
TABORINE
BS BOTANIES
BOTANISE
NIOBATES
OBEISANT
BZ BOTANIZE
CC ACETONIC
CD CATENOID
CH INCHOATE
CM COINMATE
CR ACTIONER
ANORETIC
CREATION
REACTION
CS ACONITES
CANOEIST
SONICATE
CT TACONITE
CV CONATIVE
INVOCATE
CX EXACTION
DI IDEATION
IODINATE
DL DELATION
DM DOMINATE
DN ANOINTED
ANTINODE
DP ANTIPODE
DR AROINTED
ORDINATE
RATIONED
DS ASTONIED
SEDATION
DT ANTIDOTE
TETANOID
DV DONATIVE
FT FETATION
GL GELATION
LEGATION
GN NEGATION
HR ANTIHERO
HT THIONATE
LP ANTIPOLE
LR ORIENTAL
RELATION
LS ELATIONS
INSOLATE
TOENAILS
MM AMMONITE
MN ANTINOME
NOMINATE
MP PTOMAINE
MS AMNIOTES
MASONITE
MISATONE
MZ MONAZITE
NR ANOINTER
REANOINT
NS ENATIONS
SONATINE
NT INTONATE
NV INNOVATE
VENATION
PP ANTIPOPE
PR ATROPINE
PS SAPONITE
PZ TOPAZINE
QU EQUATION
RR ANTERIOR
RS NOTARIES
SENORITA
RT TENTORIA
RZ NOTARIZE
SS ASTONIES
VX VEXATION

64 STEROL

AB BLOATERS
SORTABLE
STORABLE
AC LOCATERS
SECTORAL
AD DELATORS
LEOTARDS
LODESTAR
AE OLEASTER
AF FLOATERS
FORESTAL
REFLOATS
AG GLOATERS
LEGATORS
AH LOATHERS
RATHOLES
AL REALLOTS
ROSTELLA
AP PETROSAL
POLESTAR
AR REALTORS
RELATORS
RESTORAL
AS OLESTRAS
AT RETOTALS
AU ROSULATE
AV LEVATORS
OVERSALT
BH BROTHELS
BI STROBILE
BM TEMBLORS
BS BOLSTERS
LOBSTERS
BT BLOTTERS
BOTTLERS
BU TROUBLES
CE CORSELET
ELECTORS
ELECTROS
SELECTOR
CH CHORTLES
CI CLOISTER
COISTREL
COSTLIER
CS CORSLETS
COSTRELS
CROSSLET
CU CLOTURES
CLOUTERS
COULTERS
DD TODDLERS
DF TELFORDS
DI STOLIDER
DL DROLLEST
STROLLED
DP DROPLETS
DS OLDSTERS
DT DOTTRELS
EH HOSTELER
EL SOLLERET
EM MOLESTER
EN ENTRESOL
ES SOLERETS
EU RESOLUTE
EV OVERLETS
FG FROGLETS
FI TREFOILS
FO FOOTLERS
FU FLOUTERS
FW FELWORTS
GG TOGGLERS
HS HOLSTERS
HOSTLERS
HT THROSTLE
HW WHORTLES
HY HOSTELRY
II ROILIEST
IL TROLLIES
IN RETINOLS
IO OESTRIOL
IP POITRELS
IS ESTRIOLS
IT TRIOLETS
IU OUTLIERS
JS JOSTLERS
LP POLLSTER
LR STROLLER
TROLLERS
LY TROLLEYS
MM TROMMELS
MO TREMOLOS
MT MOTTLERS
MU MOULTERS
NU TURNSOLE

OS ROOTLESS
OT ROOTLETS
TOOTLERS
PS PORTLESS
PT PLOTTERS
PU POULTERS
PY PROSTYLE
PROTYLES
ST SETTLORS
SLOTTERS
UY ELYTROUS
UROSTYLE

65 TENIAE

AL ALIENATE
BH THEBAINE
BS BETAINES
CG AGENETIC
CH ECHINATE
CP PATIENCE
CR CENTIARE
CREATINE
INCREATE
ITERANCE
CS CINEASTE
CV ENACTIVE
DD DETAINED
DE DETAINEE
DL DATELINE
ENTAILED
LINEATED
DM DEMENTIA
DR DETAINER
RETAINED
DS ANDESITE
DW ANTIWEED
GL GALENITE
GELATINE
LEGATINE
GM GEMINATE
GN ANTIGENE
GR GRATINEE
INTERAGE
GV AGENTIVE
NEGATIVE
HM HEMATEIN
HEMATINE
HR HERNIATE
IR INERTIAE
KM KETAMINE
KR ANKERITE
LL TENAILLE
LM MELANITE
LP PETALINE
TAPELINE
LR ELATERIN
ENTAILER
TREENAIL
MM MEANTIME
MR ANTIMERE
MS ETAMINES
MATINEES
MISEATEN
NV VENETIAN
PR APERIENT
RR RETAINER
RS ARENITES
ARSENITE
RESINATE
STEARINE
TRAINEES
SS ETESIANS
TENIASES
ST ANISETTE
TETANIES
TETANISE
SV NAIVETES
TZ TETANIZE

66 TEARIE*

AC ACIERATE
AD ERADIATE
BD REBAITED
BK TIEBREAK
BL LIBERATE
BT BATTERIE
CH AETHERIC
HETAERIC
CN CENTIARE
CREATINE
INCREATE
ITERANCE
CV CREATIVE
REACTIVE
DL DETAILER
ELATERID
RETAILED
DM DIAMETER
DN DETAINER
RETAINED
DS READIEST
SERIATED
STEADIER
DT ITERATED
DV DERIVATE
DW WAITERED
EM EMERITAE
ES EATERIES
FG FIGEATER
FL FEATLIER
FT FETERITA
GH HERITAGE
GM EMIGRATE
GN GRATINEE
INTERAGE
GT AIGRETTE
GV ERGATIVE
HH HEATHIER
HN HERNIATE
HR EARTHIER
HEARTIER
HS HEARTIES
IN INERTIAE
KN ANKERITE
KW TWEAKIER
LL LAETRILE
LM MATERIEL
LN ELATERIN
ENTAILER
TREENAIL
LO AEROLITE
LP PEARLITE
LR RETAILER
LS ATELIERS
EARLIEST
LEARIEST
REALTIES
LT LATERITE
LITERATE
LV LEVIRATE
RELATIVE
LZ LATERIZE
MN ANTIMERE
MS EMERITAS
EMIRATES
STEAMIER
NP APERIENT
NR RETAINER
NS ARENITES
ARSENITE
RESINATE
STEARINE
TRAINEES
PS PARIETES
RS ARTERIES
RW WATERIER
SS SERIATES
ST ARIETTES
ITERATES
TEARIEST
TREATIES
TREATISE
SW SWEATIER
WASTERIE
WEARIEST
SY YEASTIER

67 NEROLI

AC ACROLEIN
COLINEAR
AG GERANIOL
REGIONAL
AP PELORIAN
AS AILERONS
ALIENORS
AT ORIENTAL
RELATION
AV OVERLAIN
BM BROMELIN
CC CORNICLE
CH CHLORINE
CP REPLICON
CS INCLOSER
LICENSOR
DF INFOLDER
DH INHOLDER
EG ELOIGNER
EL LONELIER
EP LEPORINE
ES ELOINERS
FG FLORIGEN
FO ROOFLINE
FU FLUORINE
GI LIGROINE
RELIGION
REOILING
GS RESOLING
GW LOWERING
ROWELING
HK HORNLIKE
HU UNHOLIER
IK IRONLIKE
IS LIONISER
IZ LIONIZER
MS MISENROL
PS PROLINES
PT TERPINOL
RS LORINERS
ST RETINOLS
TT TROTLINE
TU OUTLINER
VV INVOLVER

68 RANEES

AC CESAREAN
AG SANGAREE
AT ARSENATE
SERENATA
BL ENABLERS
BO SEABORNE
BS BARENESS
BT ABSENTER
BV VERBENAS
CD ASCENDER
REASCEND
CH ENCHASER
CI INCREASE
CL CLEANERS
CLEANSER
RECLEANS
CM MENACERS
CS CASERNES
CT CENTARES
REASCENT
REENACTS
SARCENET
DE SERENADE
DG DERANGES
GRANDEES
GRENADES
DI ARSENIDE
NEARSIDE
DK KNEADERS
DM AMENDERS
MEANDERS
DN ENSNARED
DO REASONED
DS DEARNESS
DU UNDERSEA
UNERASED
UNSEARED
DW ANSWERED
DY YEARENDS
ET SERENATE
FM ENFRAMES
FT FASTENER
FENESTRA
REFASTEN
GG ENGAGERS
GH SHAGREEN
GI ANERGIES
GESNERIA
GL ENLARGES
GENERALS
GLEANERS
GT ESTRANGE
GRANTEES
GREATENS
NEGATERS
REAGENTS
SERGEANT
GV AVENGERS
ENGRAVES
HK HEARKENS
HT HASTENER
HEARTENS
HV RESHAVEN
IK SNEAKIER
IL ALIENERS
IN ANSERINE
IP NAPERIES
IT ARENITES
ARSENITE
RESINATE
STEARINE
TRAINEES
IU UNEASIER
JT SERJEANT
KS SNEAKERS
KW REWAKENS
WAKENERS
LP REPANELS
LR LEARNERS
RELEARNS
LS REALNESS
LT ETERNALS
TELERANS
LV ENSLAVER
LW RENEWALS
MP PRENAMES
SPEARMEN
MU USERNAME
MV VERSEMAN
MW MENSWEAR
NR ENSNARER
NS ENSNARES
NEARNESS
RENNASES
OP PERSONAE
OR REASONER
OS RESEASON
SEASONER
OT EARSTONE
RESONATE
RS RARENESS
RT TERRANES
RV RAVENERS
RW ANSWERER
RY YEARNERS
ST ASSENTER
EARNESTS
SARSENET
SU ANURESES
TT ENTREATS
RATTEENS
TU SAUTERNE
TV VETERANS

69 SOIGNE

AB BEGONIAS
AC COINAGES
AD AGONISED
DIAGNOSE
AG SEAGOING
AL GASOLINE
AN ANGINOSE
AR ORGANISE
AS AGONISES
AZ AGONIZES
BR SOBERING
CD CODESIGN
COGNISED
COSIGNED
CI ISOGENIC
CM GENOMICS
CR COREIGNS
COSIGNER
CS COGNISES
CT ESCOTING
CZ COGNIZES
DI INDIGOES
DL SIDELONG
DM MENDIGOS
SMIDGEON
DP DEPOSING
DR NEGROIDS
DW WENDIGOS
WIDGEONS
EO OOGENIES
EP EPIGONES
ER ERINGOES
ES GENOISES
ET EGESTION
GK GINGKOES
GINKGOES
HT HISTOGEN
HY HOSEYING
IR SEIGNIOR
JK JINGKOES
JN JONESING
KL SONGLIKE
LR RESOLING
LS LOGINESS
LU LIGNEOUS
LW LONGWISE
MT MITOGENS
MY MOSEYING
NO IONOGENS
NP OPENINGS
NR NEGRONIS
NU ENGINOUS
OS ISOGONES
OT GOONIEST
PR PERIGONS
REPOSING
SPONGIER
PU EPIGONUS
PX EXPOSING
RR IGNORERS
RS GORINESS
RT GENITORS
RW RESOWING
RY SEIGNORY

70 ARIOSE

BC AEROBICS
BM BIRAMOSE
BN BARONIES
SEAROBIN
BS ISOBARES
CD IDOCRASE
CL CALORIES
CARIOLES
CN SCENARIO
CS SCARIOSE
CV COVARIES
VARICOSE
DD ROADSIDE
DF FORESAID
DL DARIOLES
DN ANEROIDS
DP DIASPORE
PARODIES
DT ASTEROID
DV AVODIRES
AVOIDERS
FL FORESAIL
FN FARINOSE
GL GASOLIER
GIRASOLE
SERAGLIO
GN ORGANISE
GS ARGOSIES
GV VIRAGOES
HL AIRHOLES
SHOALIER
HP APHORISE
HT HOARIEST
JT JAROSITE
LM MORALISE
LN AILERONS
ALIENORS
LP PELORIAS
POLARISE
LS SOLARISE
LV VALORISE
VARIOLES
LZ SOLARIZE
MN MORAINES
ROMAINES
ROMANISE
MP MEROPIAS
MR ARMOIRES
ARMORIES
MT AMORTISE
ATOMISER
NN RAISONNE
NS ERASIONS
SENSORIA
NT NOTARIES
SENORITA
NV AVERSION
PV VAPORISE
RS ROSARIES
RT ROTARIES
RV SAVORIER
SV SAVORIES
TT TOASTIER
TU OUTRAISE
SAUTOIRE
TV TRAVOISE
VIATORES
VOTARIES

71 DETAIN

AG INDAGATE
AL DENTALIA
AM ANIMATED
DIAMANTE
AP PATINAED
AT ATTAINED
BG DEBATING
BL BIDENTAL
BO OBTAINED
CC ACCIDENT
CI ACTINIDE
CTENIDIA
INDICATE
CK ANTICKED
CM MEDICANT
CN INCANTED
CO CATENOID
CP PEDANTIC
CR DICENTRA
CS DISTANCE
CT NICTATED
CU INCUDATE
DE DETAINED
DL TIDELAND
DS DANDIEST
EE DETAINEE
EL DATELINE
ENTAILED
LINEATED
EM DEMENTIA
ER DETAINER
RETAINED
ES ANDESITE
EW ANTIWEED
FL INFLATED
GI IDEATING
GL DELATING
GR DERATING
GRADIENT
REDATING
TREADING
GS SEDATING
STEADING
HR ANTHERID
HS HANDIEST
IO IDEATION
IODINATE
IR DAINTIER
IS ADENITIS
DAINTIES
IV VANITIED
LN DENTINAL
LO DELATION
LP PANTILED
LV DIVALENT
MO DOMINATE
MS MEDIANTS
MY DYNAMITE
NO ANOINTED
ANTINODE
NP PINNATED
NU INUNDATE
OP ANTIPODE
OR AROINTED
ORDINATE
RATIONED
OS ASTONIED
SEDATION
OT ANTIDOTE
TETANOID
OV DONATIVE
PR DIPTERAN
PS DEPAINTS
QU ANTIQUED
RS DETRAINS
RANDIEST
STRAINED
RT NITRATED
RU INDURATE
RUINATED
URINATED
SS DESTAINS
SANDIEST
ST INSTATED
SU AUDIENTS
SINUATED
SV DEVIANTS

72 SINGER

AA ANERGIAS
ANGARIES
ARGINASE
AB BEARINGS
SABERING
AC CREASING
AD DERAIGNS
GRADINES
READINGS
AE ANERGIES
GESNERIA
AG GEARINGS
GREASING
SNAGGIER
AH HEARINGS
HEARSING
SHEARING
AL ALIGNERS
ENGRAILS
NARGILES
REALIGNS
SIGNALER
SLANGIER
AM SMEARING
AN AGINNERS
EARNINGS
ENGRAINS
GRANNIES
AO ORGANISE
AP SPEARING
AR EARRINGS
GRAINERS
AS ASSIGNER
REASSIGN
SERINGAS
AT ANGRIEST
ASTRINGE
GANISTER
GANTRIES
GRANITES
INGRATES
RANGIEST
AV VINEGARS
AW RESAWING
SWEARING
AY RESAYING
SYNERGIA
BE REBEGINS
BO SOBERING
BR BRINGERS
BW BREWINGS
CE GENERICS
CH GRINCHES
CL CLINGERS
CRINGLES
CO COREIGNS
COSIGNER
CR CRINGERS
CT CRESTING
CU RECUSING
RESCUING
SECURING
CW SCREWING
CY SYNERGIC
DE DESIGNER
ENERGIDS
REDESIGN
REEDINGS
RESIGNED
DI DESIRING
RESIDING
RINGSIDE
DO NEGROIDS
DP SPRINGED
DR GRINDERS
REGRINDS
DS DRESSING
DT STRINGED
DW REDWINGS
DY SYNERGID
SYRINGED
EE ENERGIES
ENERGISE
GREENIES
RESEEING
EF FEIGNERS
EH GREENISH
REHINGES
SHEERING
EL REELINGS
EM REGIMENS
EN SNEERING
EO ERINGOES
EP SPEERING
ER RESIGNER
ES GREISENS
ET GENTRIES
INTEGERS
REESTING
STEERING
EU SEIGNEUR
EV SEVERING
EW RESEWING
SEWERING
FH FRESHING
FL FLINGERS
FU GUNFIRES
REFUSING
GL NIGGLERS
SNIGGLER
GS SERGINGS
SNIGGERS
HK GHERKINS
HL SHINGLER
HP SPHERING
HR HERRINGS
HU USHERING
HW SHREWING
WHINGERS
IL RESILING
RIESLING
IM REMISING
IN RESINING
IO SEIGNIOR
IP SPEIRING
SPIERING
IR RERISING
IT IGNITERS
RESITING
STINGIER
IV REVISING
IW SWINGIER
IZ RESIZING
JL JINGLERS
KL ERLKINGS
KM SMERKING
LM GREMLINS
MINGLERS
LO RESOLING
LS SLINGERS
LT RINGLETS
STERLING
TINGLERS
LW NEWSGIRL
MP IMPREGNS
MS GRIMNESS
MU RESUMING
NO NEGRONIS
NR GRINNERS
NU ENSURING
NV NERVINGS
OP PERIGONS
REPOSING
SPONGIER
OR IGNORERS
OS GORINESS
OT GENITORS
OW RESOWING
OY SEIGNORY
PR RESPRING
SPRINGER
PS PRESSING
SPRINGES
PU PERUSING
SUPERING
RT RESTRING
STRINGER
RW WRINGERS
RY SERRYING
ST STINGERS
TRIGNESS
SV SERVINGS
SW SWINGERS
SY SYRINGES
TT GITTERNS
TW STREWING
WRESTING
VW SWERVING

73 EASIER

BF FIREBASE
BK BAKERIES
BM AMBERIES
CD DECIARES
CM CASIMERE
CN INCREASE
CR CREASIER
CU CAUSERIE
CW WISEACRE
DG DISAGREE
DL REALISED
RESAILED
SIDEREAL
DN ARSENIDE
NEARSIDE
DP AIRSPEED
DR DREARIES
RERAISED
DT READIEST
SERIATED
STEADIER
ET EATERIES
FI AERIFIES
FK FAKERIES
FL FILAREES
FR RAREFIES
FS FREESIAS
GL GASELIER
GM REIMAGES
GN ANERGIES
GESNERIA
GR GREASIER
HK SHIKAREE
HP PHARISEE
HT HEARTIES
HV SHIVAREE
JP JAPERIES
KN SNEAKIER
LM MEASLIER
LN ALIENERS
LP ESPALIER
LR REALISER
LS REALISES
LT ATELIERS
EARLIEST
LEARIEST
REALTIES
LY YEARLIES
LZ REALIZES
SLEAZIER
MR SMEARIER
MS SERIEMAS
MT EMERITAS
EMIRATES
STEAMIER
NN ANSERINE
NP NAPERIES
NT ARENITES
ARSENITE
RESINATE
STEARINE
TRAINEES
NU UNEASIER
PT PARIETES
QU QUEASIER
RS RERAISES
RT ARTERIES
ST SERIATES
TT ARIETTES
ITERATES
TEARIEST
TREATIES
TREATISE
TW SWEATIER
WASTERIE
WEARIEST
TY YEASTIER
VV AVERSIVE

74 EOLIAN

BC BIOCLEAN
COINABLE
BJ JOINABLE
BT TAILBONE
CR ACROLEIN
COLINEAR
DM MELANOID
DN NONIDEAL
DP PALINODE
DT DELATION
GR GERANIOL
REGIONAL
GS GASOLINE
GT GELATION
LEGATION
HP APHELION
PHELONIA
KS KAOLINES
KV NOVALIKE
LN LANOLINE
MS LAMINOSE
SEMOLINA
NS SOLANINE
PR PELORIAN
PS OPALINES
PT ANTIPOLE
RS AILERONS
ALIENORS
RT ORIENTAL
RELATION

RV OVERLAIN
SS ANISOLES
ST ELATIONS
INSOLATE
TOENAILS
SX SILOXANE

75 RESALE

AB ERASABLE
BL LABELERS
RELABELS
BN ENABLERS
BO EARLOBES
BT ARBELEST
BLEATERS
RESTABLE
RETABLES
BU REUSABLE
BV SERVABLE
BY BELAYERS
CD DECLARES
RESCALED
CH LEACHERS
CM RECLAMES
CN CLEANERS
CLEANSER
RECLEANS
CO ESCAROLE
CP PERCALES
REPLACES
CR CLEARERS
CS CARELESS
RESCALES
CT CLEAREST
TREACLES
CV CERVELAS
CLEAVERS
DD RESADDLE
DE RELEASED
RESEALED
DF FEDERALS
DH ASHLERED
DI REALISED
RESAILED
SIDEREAL
DM DEMERSAL
EMERALDS
DP PEDALERS
PLEADERS
RELAPSED
REPLEADS
DT DESALTER
RESLATED
TREADLES
DV SLAVERED
DW LEEWARDS
DY DELAYERS
ER RELEASER
ES RELEASES
ET TEASELER
FI FILAREES
FS FEARLESS
FT REFLATES
FW WELFARES
GI GASELIER
GL ALLEGERS
GM GLEAMERS
GN ENLARGES
GENERALS
GLEANERS
GO AEROGELS
GR REGALERS
GS EELGRASS
GEARLESS
LARGESSE
GU LEAGUERS
GZ REGLAZES
HT HALTERES
LEATHERS
HV HAVERELS
IM MEASLIER
IN ALIENERS
IP ESPALIER
IR REALISER
IS REALISES
IT ATELIERS
EARLIEST
LEARIEST
REALTIES
IY YEARLIES
IZ REALIZES
SLEAZIER
MP EMPALERS
RESAMPLE
NP REPANELS
NR LEARNERS
RELEARNS
NS REALNESS
NT ETERNALS
TELERANS
NV ENSLAVER
NW RENEWALS
OP PAROLEES
OT OLEASTER
OU AUREOLES
OV OVERSALE
PR PEARLERS
RELAPSER
PS PLEASERS
PRESALES
RELAPSES
PT PETRALES
PLEATERS
PRELATES
REPLATES
PU PLEASURE
PV VESPERAL
QU SQUEALER
RT ALTERERS
REALTERS
RELATERS
RV RAVELERS
REVERSAL
SLAVERER
RX RELAXERS
ST RESLATES
STEALERS
TEARLESS
SV SEVERALS
TT ALERTEST
TU RESALUTE
TX EXALTERS
TY EASTERLY
UV REVALUES
VY AVERSELY

76 UNITER

AB BRAUNITE
URBANITE
AC ANURETIC
AD INDURATE
RUINATED
URINATED
AJ JAUNTIER
AL AUNTLIER
RETINULA
TENURIAL
AM RUMINATE
AQ ANTIQUER
QUAINTER
AS RUINATES
TAURINES
URANITES
URINATES
BS TRIBUNES
TURBINES
BT UNBITTER
CC CINCTURE
CD REINDUCT
CE CEINTURE
ENURETIC
CG ERUCTING
CH RUTHENIC
CI NEURITIC
CO NEUROTIC
UNEROTIC
CT INTERCUT
TINCTURE
DD INTRUDED
DE RETINUED
REUNITED
DI UNTIDIER
DL UNDERLIT
DM RUDIMENT
UNMITRED
DN INTURNED
DR INTRUDER
DS INTRUDES
EG GENITURE
EM MUTINEER
EP PREUNITE
ER REUNITER
UNRETIRE
ES ESURIENT
RETINUES
REUNITES
FG REFUTING
GI INTRIGUE
GN RETUNING
TENURING
GP ERUPTING
REPUTING
GT UTTERING
IS NEURITIS
IZ UNITIZER
JO JOINTURE
KP TURNPIKE
LO OUTLINER
LS INSULTER
LV VIRULENT
MS TERMINUS
UNMITERS
UNMITRES
NO NEUTRINO
NS RUNNIEST
NT NUTRIENT
OP ERUPTION
OS ROUTINES
SNOUTIER
PR PRURIENT
PS UNRIPEST
PT INPUTTER
QS SQUINTER
QT QUITRENT
ST RUNTIEST
SV VENTURIS

77 SOILED

AM MELODIAS
AP SEPALOID
AR DARIOLES
AS ASSOILED
ISOLEADS
AT DIASTOLE
ISOLATED
SODALITE
AZ DIAZOLES
SLEAZOID
BE OBELISED
BO BLOODIES
BS BODILESS
BW DISBOWEL
CH CHELOIDS
CL COLLIDES
CN INCLOSED
CR SCLEROID
CS DISCLOSE
DG DISLODGE
DI IDOLISED
DP DISPLODE
LOPSIDED
DT DELTOIDS
EM MELODIES
MELODISE
EN LESIONED
ES OILSEEDS
GM MISLODGE
GN SIDELONG
GT GODLIEST
HM DEMOLISH
HO DHOOLIES
HP DEPOLISH
POLISHED
IN LIONISED
IP PLOIDIES
IR IDOLISER
IS IDOLISES
IZ IDOLIZES
MP IMPLODES
MS MIDSOLES
MT MELODIST
MODELIST
MOLDIEST
MU EMULSOID
NO EIDOLONS
SOLENOID
NT LENTOIDS
NU DELUSION
INSOULED
UNSOILED
OP POOLSIDE
PR LEPORIDS
PS DESPOILS
DIPLOSES
PT PISTOLED
PU EUPLOIDS
RS SOLDIERS
RT STOLIDER
RY SOLDIERY
ST SOLIDEST
SV DISSOLVE
TU SOLITUDE
TOLUIDES
VW OLDWIVES

78 STEREO

AK KERATOSE
AL OLEASTER
AN EARSTONE
RESONATE
AP OPERATES
PROTEASE
AV OVEREATS
BD BESTRODE
BS SOBEREST
BU TUBEROSE
BV OVERBETS
BW BESTOWER
CC COERECTS
CD CORSETED
ESCORTED
SECTORED
CG CORTEGES
CH TROCHEES
CI COTERIES
ESOTERIC
CJ EJECTORS
CL CORSELET
ELECTORS
ELECTROS
SELECTOR
CO CREOSOTE
CR ERECTORS
SECRETOR
CV COVETERS
CX COEXERTS
CORTEXES
DE STEREOED
DF DEFOREST
FORESTED
FOSTERED
DK RESTOKED
DM MODESTER
DP DOPESTER
DR RESORTED
RESTORED
DS DOSSERET
OERSTEDS
DT TETRODES
DX DEXTROSE
DY OYSTERED
STOREYED
EH SHOETREE
FM FRETSOME
FN RESOFTEN
SOFTENER
FR FORESTER
FOSTERER
REFOREST
GN ESTROGEN
GP PROTEGES
HI ISOTHERE
THEORIES
THEORISE
HL HOSTELER
HM THEOREMS
HN HONESTER
IM TIRESOME
IN ONERIEST
SEROTINE
IP POETISER
POETRIES
IZ EROTIZES
JK JOKESTER
JS RESOJETS
KS RESTOKES
LL SOLLERET
LM MOLESTER
LN ENTERSOL
LS SOLERETS
LU RESOLUTE
LV OVERLETS
MS SOMERSET
MT REMOTEST
NN ENTERONS
TENONERS
NO OESTRONE
NS ESTRONES
NX EXTENSOR
OP PROTEOSE
PR PRESTORE
PT PROETTES
TREETOPS
PV OVERSTEP
PY SEROTYPE
RR RESORTER
RESTORER
RETRORSE
RS RESTORES
RU REROUTES
RV EVERTORS
RESTROVE
RX EXTRORSE
RY OYSTERER
ST ROSETTES
SV ESTOVERS
OVERSETS
TU OUTSTEER
UV OUTSERVE
VW OVERWETS
VX VORTEXES

79 LINERS

AB RINSABLE
AC CARLINES
LANCIERS
AD ISLANDER
AE ALIENERS
AG ALIGNERS
ENGRAILS
NARGILES
REALIGNS
SIGNALER
SLANGIER
AH INHALERS
AI AIRLINES
AM MARLINES
MINERALS
MISLEARN
AO AILERONS
ALIENORS
AP PRALINES
AR SNARLIER
AS RAINLESS
AT ENTRAILS
LATRINES
RATLINES
RETINALS
TRENAILS
AV RAVELINS
AX RELAXINS
AY INLAYERS
BB NIBBLERS
BD BLINDERS
BRINDLES
BE BERLINES
BI RINSIBLE
BK BLINKERS
BY BYLINERS
CE LICENSER
RECLINES
SILENCER
CG CLINGERS
CRINGLES
CK CLINKERS
CRINKLES
CO INCLOSER
LICENSOR
DE REDLINES
DF FLINDERS
DK KINDLERS
DP SPINDLER
DS RINDLESS
DT TENDRILS
TRINDLES
DW SWINDLER
EG REELINGS
EO ELOINERS
EP PILSENER
ES REINLESS
ET ENLISTER
LISTENER
REENLIST
SILENTER
EV LIVENERS
SNIVELER
FF SNIFFLER
FG FLINGERS
GG NIGGLERS
SNIGGLER
GH SHINGLER
GI RESILING
RIESLING
GJ JINGLERS
GK ERLKINGS
GM GREMLINS
MINGLERS
GO RESOLING
GS SLINGERS
GT RINGLETS
STERLING
TINGLERS
GW NEWSGIRL
IK SLINKIER
IO LIONISER
IS RESILINS
IT NITRILES
KM KREMLINS
KP PLINKERS
SPRINKLE
KT TINKLERS
KW WRINKLES
MO MISENROL
MT MINSTREL
OP PROLINES
OR LORINERS
OT RETINOLS
PS PILSNERS
PT SPLINTER
PU PURLINES
TU INSULTER

80 ALEROT

AE AREOLATE
AY ALEATORY
BC BROCATEL
BI LABORITE
BL BALLOTER
BP PORTABLE
BS BLOATERS
SORTABLE
STORABLE
CC ACROLECT
CE CORELATE
RELOCATE
CH CHELATOR
CHLORATE
TROCHLEA
CI EROTICAL
LORICATE
CL COLLARET
CP PECTORAL
CS LOCATERS
SECTORAL
DF DEFLATOR
DI IDOLATER
TAILORED
DP PORTALED
DS DELATORS
LEOTARDS
LODESTAR
DW LEADWORT
EI AEROLITE
ES OLEASTER
ET TOLERATE
EV ELEVATOR
OVERLATE
FI FLOATIER
FL FELLATOR
FP TERAFLOP
FS FLOATERS
FORESTAL
REFLOATS
FW FLEAWORT
GS GLOATERS
LEGATORS
GU OUTGLARE
GV TRAVELOG
GW WATERLOG
HI AEROLITH
HP PLETHORA
HS LOATHERS
RATHOLES
IM AMITROLE
ROLAMITE
IN ORIENTAL
RELATION
IP EPILATOR
PETIOLAR
IR RETAILOR
IV VIOLATER
IZ TRIAZOLE
JV TOLARJEV
KP LAKEPORT
KV OVERTALK
LM MARTELLO
LP PREALLOT
LS REALLOTS
ROSTELLA
LT ALLOTTER
MP TEMPORAL
MU EMULATOR
MZ METRAZOL
NT TOLERANT
NU OUTLEARN
NY ORNATELY
OW WATERLOO
OZ ZOOLATER
PS PETROSAL
POLESTAR
RS REALTORS
RELATORS
RESTORAL
SS OLESTRAS
ST RETOTALS
SU ROSULATE
SV LEVATORS
OVERSALT
YZ ZEALOTRY

81 ENTOIL

AB TAILBONE
AD DELATION
AG GELATION
LEGATION
AP ANTIPOLE
AR ORIENTAL
RELATION
AS ELATIONS
INSOLATE
TOENAILS
CE ELECTION
CF FLECTION
CP LEPTONIC
CS LECTIONS
TELSONIC
DE DELETION
ENTOILED
DI TOLIDINE
DN INDOLENT
DS LENTOIDS
DU OUTLINED
EN NONELITE
GM LONGTIME
GW TOWELING
HP THOLEPIN
HS HOLSTEIN
HOTLINES
NEOLITHS
HX XENOLITH
IM LIMONITE
IN LENITION
KK KNOTLIKE
LP PLOTLINE
LU LUTEOLIN
MY MYLONITE
NS INSOLENT
NT NONTITLE
OS LOONIEST
OILSTONE
PR TERPINOL
PS POTLINES
TOPLINES
PU UNPOLITE
PY LINOTYPE
RS RETINOLS
RT TROTLINE
RU OUTLINER
SU ELUTIONS
OUTLINES
SV NOVELIST
SW TOWLINES
UV INVOLUTE

82 GARNET

AI AERATING
AL ARGENTAL
AS TANAGERS
AU RUNAGATE
BI BERATING
REBATING
TABERING
CI ARGENTIC
CATERING
CREATING
REACTING
DI DERATING
GRADIENT
REDATING
TREADING
DO DRAGONET
DS DRAGNETS
GRANDEST
EE GENERATE
TEENAGER
EI GRATINEE
INTERAGE
EL REGENTAL
ES ESTRANGE
GRANTEES
GREATENS
NEGATERS
REAGENTS
SERGEANT
FM FRAGMENT
FO FRONTAGE
FS ENGRAFTS
GS GANGSTER
HI EARTHING
HEARTING
INGATHER
IK RETAKING
IL ALERTING
ALTERING
INTEGRAL
RELATING
TANGLIER
TRIANGLE
IM EMIGRANT
REMATING
IP RETAPING
TAPERING
IS ANGRIEST
ASTRINGE
GANISTER
GANTRIES
GRANITES
INGRATES
RANGIEST
IT GNATTIER
TREATING
IV AVERTING
GRIEVANT
VINTAGER
IW TWANGIER
WATERING
IX RETAXING
LS STRANGLE
TANGLERS
LW TWANGLER
MS GARMENTS
MARGENTS
MU ARGENTUM
ARGUMENT
NO NEGATRON
NP PREGNANT
OS ESTRAGON
NEGATORS
OT TETRAGON
OU OUTRANGE
PS TREPANGS
RS GRANTERS
REGRANTS
STRANGER
SS STRANGES
SW TWANGERS

83 EASING

AE AGENESIA
AM MAGNESIA
AP PAGANISE
AR ANERGIAS
ANGARIES
ARGINASE
BD BEADINGS
DEBASING
BL SINGABLE
BM MISBEGAN
BO BEGONIAS
BR BEARINGS
SABERING
BT BEATINGS
CE AGENCIES
CM MAGNESIC
CN ENCASING
CO COINAGES
CP ESCAPING
CR CREASING
CS CAGINESS
DH DEASHING
HEADINGS
DL DEALINGS
LEADINGS
SIGNALED
DO AGONISED
DIAGNOSE
DR DERAIGNS
GRADINES
READINGS
DS ASSIGNED
DT SEDATING
STEADING
DW WINDAGES
EL ENSILAGE
LINEAGES
ER ANERGIES
GESNERIA
ES AGENESIS
ASSIGNEE
EU EUGENIAS
EV ENVISAGE
EZ AGENIZES
FH SHEAFING
FL FINAGLES
FT FEASTING
GO SEAGOING
GR GEARINGS
GREASING
SNAGGIER
GS SIGNAGES
GT NAGGIEST
HL LEASHING
SHEALING
HR HEARINGS
HEARSING
SHEARING
HT GAHNITES
HV SHEAVING
IM IMAGINES
KL LINKAGES
SNAGLIKE
KN SNEAKING
KP SPEAKING
KS SINKAGES
LL GALLEINS
NIGELLAS
LN EANLINGS
LEANINGS
LO GASOLINE
LP ELAPSING
PLEASING
LR ALIGNERS
ENGRAILS
NARGILES
REALIGNS
SIGNALER
SLANGIER
LS GAINLESS
GLASSINE
LEASINGS
LT GELATINS
GENITALS
STEALING
TAGLINES
LV LEAVINGS
SLEAVING
LY YEALINGS
MN MEANINGS
MR SMEARING
MS GAMINESS
MT MANGIEST
MINTAGES
MISAGENT
STEAMING
MV VEGANISM
NO ANGINOSE
NP SNEAPING
SPEANING
NR AGINNERS
EARNINGS
ENGRAINS
GRANNIES
NT ANTIGENS
GENTIANS
NU GUANINES
SANGUINE
OR ORGANISE
OS AGONISES
OZ AGONIZES
PP GENIPAPS
PR SPEARING
PS SPAEINGS
SPINAGES
PY GYPSEIAN
RR EARRINGS
GRAINERS
RS ASSIGNER
REASSIGN
SERINGAS

RT ANGRIEST
ASTRINGE
GANISTER
GANTRIES
GRANITES
INGRATES
RANGIEST
RV VINEGARS
RW RESAWING
SWEARING
RY RESAYING
SYNERGIA
ST EASTINGS
GIANTESS
SEATINGS
SY ESSAYING
TT ESTATING
TANGIEST
TU SAUTEING
UNITAGES
TV VINTAGES
TW SWEATING
TY YEASTING
TZ TZIGANES

84 OILSAT

AB SAILBOAT
AG OTALGIAS
AN ALATIONS
BB BOBTAILS
BD TABLOIDS
BR ORBITALS
STROBILA
BU BAILOUTS
TABOULIS
CE COALIEST
SOCIETAL
CL LOCALIST
CP CAPITOLS
COALPITS
CV VOCALIST
DE DIASTOLE
ISOLATED
SODALITE
DH SHITLOAD
DR DILATORS
DS SODALIST
DY SODALITY
EF FOLIATES
EG LATIGOES
OTALGIES
EK KEITLOAS
EM LOAMIEST
EN ELATIONS
INSOLATE
TOENAILS
EP SPOLIATE
ES ISOLATES
ET TOTALISE
EV VIOLATES
FK FLOKATIS
FX FOXTAILS
GH GOLIATHS
GL GALLIOTS
GN ANTILOGS
SOLATING
GP GALIPOTS
HP HOSPITAL
HZ THIAZOLS
LM MAILLOTS
MISALLOT
LN STALLION
LY LOYALIST
MR MORALIST
MT TOTALISM
MU SOLATIUM
MV VOLTAISM
NN ANTLIONS
NO SOLATION
NR TONSILAR
NY LANOSITY
OR ISOLATOR
OSTIOLAR
PS APOSTILS
TOPSAILS
PT TALIPOTS
QU ALIQUOTS
RS ORALISTS
RY ROYALIST
SOLITARY
ST ALTOISTS
SU OUTSAILS
TT TOTALIST

85 TINIER

AD DAINTIER
AE INERTIAE
AL INERTIAL
AN TRIENNIA
AP PAINTIER
AS INERTIAS
RAINIEST
AZ TRIAZINE
BS BRINIEST
CD INDICTER
INDIRECT
REINDICT
CE REINCITE
CG RECITING
CS CITRINES
CRINITES
INCITERS
CU NEURITIC
DD NITRIDED
DM DIRIMENT
DO RETINOID
DP INTREPID
DS DISINTER
INDITERS
NITRIDES
DU UNTIDIER
EG REIGNITE
RETIEING
ES NITERIES
ET INTERTIE
RETINITE
EV REINVITE
FL FLINTIER
FO NOTIFIER
FR FERRITIN
GL GLINTIER
RETILING
TINGLIER
GM MERITING
MITERING
RETIMING
GR RETIRING
GS IGNITERS
RESITING
STINGIER
GU INTRIGUE
GV RIVETING
HS INHERITS
KL TINKLIER
KS STINKIER
LS NITRILES
MS INTERIMS
MINISTER
MISINTER
MT INTERMIT
MX INTERMIX
NV INVERTIN
OP POINTIER
OR INTERIOR
PS PRISTINE
RW WINTRIER
SS INSISTER
SINISTER
ST NITRITES
SU NEURITIS
SV INVITERS
VITRINES
UZ UNITIZER
VY INVERITY

86 ATESOD

BR BROADEST
CC ACCOSTED
CH CATHODES
CK STOCKADE
CN ENDOCAST
TACNODES
CR REDCOATS
EL DESOLATE
EN ENDOSTEA
EP ADOPTEES
FH SOFTHEAD
FU FADEOUTS
GI GODETIAS
HH HOTHEADS
HK KATHODES
HM HEADMOST
HP POTHEADS
HW TOWHEADS
IL DIASTOLE
ISOLATED
SODALITE
IM ATOMISED
IN ASTONIED
SEDATION
IP DIOPTASE
IR ASTEROID
IX OXIDATES
IZ AZOTISED
KU OUTASKED
LP TADPOLES
LR DELATORS
LEOTARDS
LODESTAR
LS TOADLESS
LU OUTLEADS
LV SOLVATED
MO STOMODEA
NO ODONATES
NP NOTEPADS
PR ADOPTERS
PASTORED
READOPTS
PS PODESTAS
PT POSTDATE
RR ROADSTER
RS ASSORTED
TORSADES
RU OUTDARES
OUTREADS
READOUTS
RX EXTRADOS
TU OUTDATES

87 SNORED

AB BANDORES
BROADENS
AC ENDOSARC
AE REASONED
AH HARDNOSE
AI ANEROIDS
AL LADRONES
SOLANDER
AM MADRONES
RANSOMED
AP OPERANDS
PADRONES
PANDORES
AR ADORNERS
READORNS
BE DEBONERS
REDBONES
BU BOUNDERS
REBOUNDS
SUBORNED
CE CENSORED
ENCODERS
NECROSED
SECONDER
CI CONSIDER
CK DORNECKS
CO CONDORES
CU CRUNODES
CW DECROWNS
DE ENDORSED
DI INDORSED
DN DENDRONS
DU REDOUNDS
EE ENDORSEE
EI INDORSEE
EM MODERNES
ER ENDORSER
ES ENDORSES
EW ENDOWERS
REENDOWS
WORSENED
FF FORFENDS
FL FONDLERS
FO FRONDOSE
FU FOUNDERS
REFOUNDS
GI NEGROIDS
GU GUERDONS
HI HORDEINS
HU ENSHROUD
HOUNDERS
UNHORSED
II DERISION
IRONSIDE
RESINOID
IJ JOINDERS
IP PRISONED
IR INDORSER
IS INDORSES
SORDINES
IU DOURINES
SOURDINE
LP SPLENDOR
LU ROUNDELS
UNSOLDER
MT MORDENTS
MW SWORDMEN
MY SYNDROME
OR ENDORSOR
PP PROPENDS
PS RESPONDS
PT PORTENDS
PROTENDS
PU POUNDERS
RU RONDURES
ROUNDERS
RW DROWNERS
SU DOURNESS
RESOUNDS
SOUNDERS
TU ROUNDEST
TONSURED
UNSORTED
TY DRYSTONE
UU UNSOURED

88 ELITES

AD LEADIEST
AF FEALTIES
FETIALES
LEAFIEST
AG EGALITES
AK LEAKIEST
AL LEALTIES
AM MEALIEST
METALISE
AP EPILATES
AR ATELIERS
EARLIEST
LEARIEST
REALTIES
AV ELATIVES
LEAVIEST
VEALIEST
BN STILBENE
TENSIBLE
CN CENTILES
CR RETICLES
SCLERITE
TIERCELS
TRISCELE
CT TELESTIC
TESTICLE
CU LEUCITES
DD DELISTED
DG LEDGIEST
DN ENLISTED
LISTENED
TINSELED
DR RELISTED
DS TIDELESS
EN ENLISTEE
SELENITE
ER LEERIEST
SLEETIER
STEELIER
ES STEELIES
EV TELEVISE
FS FELSITES
FY EYELIFTS
GG LEGGIEST
GN GENTILES
SLEETING
STEELING
GS ELEGISTS
HN THEELINS
HS SHELTIES
IN LENITIES
IV LEVITIES
IW LEWISITE
KM STEMLIKE
KN NESTLIKE
KP SPIKELET
STEPLIKE
KR TRISKELE
KV VESTLIKE
LT STELLITE
LV EVILLEST
LW WELLSITE
MS TIMELESS
NN SENTINEL
NP PENLITES
PLENTIES
NR ENLISTER
LISTENER
REENLIST
SILENTER
NS LITENESS
SETLINES
NT ENTITLES
NV VEINLETS
OP PETIOLES
OZ ZEOLITES
PR EPISTLER
PELTRIES
PERLITES
REPTILES
PS EPISTLES
PY EPISTYLE
RS LEISTERS
TIRELESS
RT RETITLES
SX EXITLESS
SEXTILES
TX TEXTILES
UX ULEXITES

89 INMATE

AD ANIMATED
DIAMANTE
AG AGMINATE
ENIGMATA
AH ANTHEMIA
HAEMATIN
AL ANTIMALE
LAMINATE
AR ANIMATER
MARINATE
AS AMENTIAS
ANIMATES
AZ NIZAMATE
BL BAILMENT
BS AMBIENTS
CD MEDICANT
CG MAGNETIC
CH ANTHEMIC
CO COINMATE
CS AMNESTIC
SEMANTIC
CU NEUMATIC
DE DEMENTIA
DO DOMINATE
DS MEDIANTS
DY DYNAMITE
EG GEMINATE
EH HEMATEIN
HEMATINE
EK KETAMINE
EL MELANITE
EM MEANTIME
ER ANTIMERE
ES ETAMINES
MATINEES
MISEATEN
FL FILAMENT
FS MANIFEST
GL LIGAMENT
METALING
TEGMINAL
GR EMIGRANT
REMATING
GS MANGIEST
MINTAGES
MISAGENT
STEAMING
GU TEGUMINA
UMANGITE
HI THIAMINE
HS HEMATINS
IN ANTIMINE
IT INTIMATE
IU MINUTIAE
IV VITAMINE
KS MISTAKEN
LR TERMINAL
TRAMLINE
LS AILMENTS
ALIMENTS
MANLIEST
MELANIST
SMALTINE
MN IMMANENT
MO AMMONITE
NO ANTINOME
NOMINATE
NR TRAINMEN
NS MANNITES
OP PTOMAINE
OS AMNIOTES
MASONITE
MISATONE
OZ MONAZITE
RS MINARETS
RAIMENTS
RT INTERMAT
MARTINET
RU RUMINATE
RY TYRAMINE
SS MANTISES
MATINESS

90 NEATER

AS ARSENATE
SERENATA
AT ANTEATER
BC CABERNET
BD BANTERED
BE TENEBRAE
BL RENTABLE
BN BANNERET
BR BANTERER
BS ABSENTER
BT BATTENER
CC REACCENT
CD CANTERED
CRENATED
DECANTER
RECANTED
CI CENTIARE
CREATINE
INCREATE
ITERANCE
CN ENTRANCE
CO CAROTENE
CP PREENACT
CR RECANTER
RECREANT
CS CENTARES
REASCENT
REENACTS
SARCENET
CU UNCREATE
DH ADHERENT
NEATHERD
DI DETAINER
RETAINED
DL ANTLERED
DP PARENTED
DT ATTENDER
NATTERED
RATTENED
DU DENATURE
UNDERATE
UNDEREAT
EG GENERATE
TEENAGER
EL LATEENER
ES SERENATE
EV ENERVATE
VENERATE
FF AFFERENT
FS FASTENER
FENESTRA
REFASTEN
FT FATTENER
GI GRATINEE
INTERAGE
GL REGENTAL
GS ESTRANGE
GRANTEES
GREATENS
NEGATERS
REAGENTS
SERGEANT
HI HERNIATE
HL LEATHERN
HM EARTHMEN
HS HASTENER
HEARTENS
HT THREATEN
HU URETHANE
HW WATERHEN
WREATHEN
II INERTIAE
IK ANKERITE
IL ELATERIN
ENTAILER
TREENAIL
IM ANTIMERE
IP APERIENT
IR RETAINER
IS ARENITES
ARSENITE
RESINATE
STEARINE
TRAINEES
JS SERJEANT
LM LAMENTER
LN LANNERET
LR RELEARNT
LS ETERNALS
TELERANS
LV LEVANTER
RELEVANT
LW TREELAWN
LX EXTERNAL
MN REMANENT
MP PERMEANT
MU NUMERATE
MV AVERMENT
MW WATERMEN
NV REVENANT
OS EARSTONE
RESONATE
OV OVERNEAT
RENOVATE
PP PETNAPER
RS TERRANES
RT RATTENER
RU RENATURE
RV TAVERNER
SS ASSENTER
EARNESTS
SARSENET
ST ENTREATS
RATTEENS
SU SAUTERNE
SV VETERANS
TV ANTEVERT
TX EXTRANET
TY ENTREATY

91 LANOSE

AB ABALONES
AS SEASONAL
BT NOTABLES
STONABLE
BY BALONEYS
CC CONCEALS
CD CELADONS
CG CONGEALS
CH CHALONES
CN ALENCONS
CS SECONALS
CT LACTONES
CU LACUNOSE
CZ CALZONES
DR LADRONES
SOLANDER
EG GASOLENE
EH ENHALOES
ES ENOLASES
FR FARNESOL
FV FLAVONES
GH HALOGENS
GI GASOLINE
GL ALLONGES
GALLEONS
GT TANGELOS
GU ANGULOSE
HM MANHOLES
HT ANETHOLS
ETHANOLS
IK KAOLINES
IM LAMINOSE
SEMOLINA
IN SOLANINE
IP OPALINES
IR AILERONS
ALIENORS
IS ANISOLES
IT ELATIONS
INSOLATE
TOENAILS
IX SILOXANE
KY ANKYLOSE
LV NOVELLAS
MP NEOPLASM
PLEONASM
MR ALMONERS
MU MELANOUS
NU ANNULOSE
PR PERSONAL
PSORALEN
PT POLENTAS
PU APOLUNES
RU ALEURONS
NEUROSAL
SV OVALNESS
TY ANOLYTES

92 GREATS

AA GASTRAEA
AC CARTAGES
AD GRADATES
AL AGRESTAL
AM MEGASTAR
AN TANAGERS
AS GASTREAS
AT REGATTAS
AV STRAVAGE
AZ STARGAZE
BE ABSTERGE
BG BRAGGEST
BH BARGHEST
BU BARGUEST
CI AGRESTIC
CIGARETS
ERGASTIC
CO ESCARGOT
DE RESTAGED
DN DRAGNETS
GRANDEST
DR DRAGSTER
EE EAGEREST
ETAGERES
STEERAGE
EM GAMESTER
EN ESTRANGE
GRANTEES
GREATENS
NEGATERS
REAGENTS
SERGEANT
ER REGRATES
ES RESTAGES
ET GREATEST
FI FRIGATES
FN ENGRAFTS
FO FAGOTERS
FR GRAFTERS
REGRAFTS
GI STAGGIER
GL STRAGGLE
GN GANGSTER
GS GAGSTERS
STAGGERS
GY STAGGERY
HO SHORTAGE
IL GLARIEST
IM MAGISTER
MIGRATES
RAGTIMES
STERIGMA
IN ANGRIEST
ASTRINGE
GANISTER
GANTRIES
GRANITES
INGRATES
RANGIEST
IP GRAPIEST
IV VIRGATES
LN STRANGLE
TANGLERS
LO GLOATERS
LEGATORS
LU GESTURAL
MN GARMENTS
MARGENTS
NO ESTRAGON
NEGATORS
NP TREPANGS
NR GRANTERS
REGRANTS
STRANGER
NS STRANGES
NW TWANGERS
OO ROOTAGES
OP PORTAGES
OR GARROTES
OS STORAGES
OT GAROTTES
OU OUTRAGES
PU UPSTAGER
TY STRATEGY
UU AUGUSTER

93 ATTIRE

AH HATTERIA
AM AMARETTI
AN ATTAINER
REATTAIN
AP PATRIATE
AS ARIETTAS
ARISTATE
AZ ZARATITE
BC BRATTICE
BE BATTERIE
BL TITRABLE
BR BIRRETTA
BRATTIER
BS BIRETTAS
BY YTTERBIA
CD CITRATED
TETRACID
TETRADIC
CF TRIFECTA
CH CHATTIER
THEATRIC
CL TRACTILE
CN INTERACT
CS CITRATES
CRISTATE
SCATTIER
CU URTICATE
CV TRACTIVE
DE ITERATED
DL DETRITAL
DM ADMITTER
DN NITRATED
DO TERATOID
DS STRIATED
TARDIEST
DT ATTRITED
TITRATED
EF FETERITA
EG AIGRETTE
EL LATERITE
LITERATE
ES ARIETTES
ITERATES
TEARIEST
TREATIES
TREATISE
FL FILTRATE
GL AGLITTER
GN GNATTIER
TREATING
IL LITERATI
IR IRRITATE
LM REMITTAL
LS TERTIALS
LY ALTERITY
MN INTERMAT
MARTINET
MO AMORETTI
MS MISTREAT
TERATISM
NN INTRANET
NO TENTORIA
NP TRIPTANE
NR RETIRANT
NS INTREATS
NITRATES
STRAITEN
TERTIANS
OS TOASTIER
OV ROTATIVE
RS STRAITER
TARRIEST
RY TERTIARY
SS ARTISTES
ARTSIEST
STRIATES
ST ATTRITES
RATTIEST
TARTIEST
TITRATES
TRISTATE
SW WARTIEST
SZ TRISTEZA
TW ATWITTER

94 TRONAS

AT ARNATTOS
BE BARONETS
BI TABORINS
BL LASTBORN
BY BARYTONS

CE ANCESTOR
ENACTORS
CG CONGRATS
CH CHANTORS
CI CAROTINS
CORTINAS
CO CARTOONS
CORANTOS
OSTRACON
CT CONTRAST
CU COURANTS
DI DIATRONS
INTRADOS
DL TROLANDS
DM MORDANTS
DO DONATORS
ODORANTS
TANDOORS
TORNADOS
DU ROTUNDAS
DW SANDWORT
DY TARDYONS
EE EARSTONE
RESONATE
EF SEAFRONT
EG ESTRAGON
NEGATORS
EI NOTARIES
SENORITA
EM MONSTERA
ONSTREAM
TONEARMS
EN RESONANT
EP OPERANTS
PRONATES
PROTEANS
ER ANTRORSE
ES ASSENTOR
SANTEROS
SENATORS
STARNOSE
TREASONS
EU OUTEARNS
FF AFFRONTS
FL FRONTALS
FM FORMANTS
FW FANWORTS
GI ORGANIST
ROASTING
GM ANGSTROM
GR GRANTORS
HL ALTHORNS
IJ JANITORS
IL TONSILAR
IO ORATIONS
IP ATROPINS
IS ARSONIST
IT STRONTIA
IU RAINOUTS
IW WAITRONS
KO OSTRAKON
KU OUTRANKS
LO ORTOLANS
LP PLASTRON
MS TRANSOMS
MU ROMAUNTS
MY STRAMONY
NO SONORANT
OP PATROONS
OS SANTOORS
OT ARNOTTOS
RATTOONS
SU SANTOURS
VY SOVRANTY

95 TUNERS

AB URBANEST
AC CENTAURS
RECUSANT
UNCRATES
AD DAUNTERS
TRANSUDE
UNTREADS
AE SAUTERNE
AH HAUNTERS
UNEARTHS
URETHANS
AI RUINATES
TAURINES
URANITES
URINATES
AL NEUTRALS
AM MENSTRUA
AO OUTEARNS
AS ANESTRUS
SAUNTERS
AT TAUNTERS
AV VAUNTERS
BD SUBTREND
BH BURTHENS
BI TRIBUNES
TURBINES
BO BURSTONE
BS SUBRENTS
BY SUBENTRY
CH CHUNTERS
CK STRUCKEN
CM CENTRUMS
CO CONSTRUE
COUNTERS
RECOUNTS
TROUNCES
CR CURRENTS
CS CURTNESS
ENCRUSTS
DD DURNDEST
DE DENTURES
SEDERUNT
UNDERSET
UNRESTED
DG TRUDGENS
DH THUNDERS
DI INTRUDES
DK DRUNKEST
DL RUNDLETS
TRUNDLES
DO ROUNDEST
TONSURED
UNSORTED
DP UPTRENDS
DT STRUNTED
DU UNRUSTED
EI ESURIENT
RETINUES
REUNITES
EM MUENSTER
ES TRUENESS
EV VENTURES
FO FORTUNES
GL GRUNTLES
GO STURGEON
GR GRUNTERS
RESTRUNG
HL LUTHERNS
HO SOUTHERN
HS HUNTRESS
SHUNTERS
II NEURITIS
IL INSULTER
IM TERMINUS
UNMITERS
UNMITRES
IN RUNNIEST
IO ROUTINES
SNOUTIER
IP UNRIPEST
IQ SQUINTER
IT RUNTIEST
IV VENTURIS
KY TURNKEYS
LN TRUNNELS
LO TURNSOLE
MO MOUNTERS
REMOUNTS
MS MUNSTERS
STERNUMS
NO NEUTRONS
NS STUNNERS
OO OUTSNORE
OS TONSURES
OY TOURNEYS
PS PUNSTERS
RU NURTURES
SS UNSTRESS
ST ENTRUSTS
TU UNTRUEST

96 PRAISE

AC AIRSCAPE
AIRSPACE
AD PARADISE
AI APIARIES
AM SAPREMIA
AP APPRAISE
AR PAREIRAS
AS SPIRAEAS
AT ASPIRATE
PARASITE
SEPTARIA
BR SPARERIB
CC CAPRICES
CD PERACIDS
CH ASPHERIC
PARCHESI
SERAPHIC
CI PIRACIES
CL CALIPERS
REPLICAS
SPIRACLE
CM PARECISM
SAPREMIC
CP CRAPPIES
EPICARPS
CR PERISARC
CS SCRAPIES
CT CRISPATE
PARETICS
PICRATES
PRACTISE
DD DISPREAD
DE AIRSPEED
DH RAPHIDES
DI PRESIDIA
DL LIPREADS
PARSLIED
SPIRALED
DN SPRAINED
DO DIASPORE
PARODIES
DP APPRISED
DS DESPAIRS
DT RAPIDEST
TRAIPSED
DU UPRAISED
DW RIPSAWED
EH PHARISEE
EJ JAPERIES
EL ESPALIER
EN NAPERIES
ET PARIETES
FF PIAFFERS
FN FIREPANS
PANFRIES
GK GARPIKES
GM EPIGRAMS
PRIMAGES
GN SPEARING
GT GRAPIEST
HL EARLSHIP
HARELIPS
PLASHIER
HM SAMPHIRE
SERAPHIM
HN HEPARINS
SERAPHIN
HO APHORISE
HP SAPPHIRE
HS PARISHES
SHARPIES
HT TRIPHASE
IR PRAIRIES
IT PARITIES
KL SPARLIKE
KM RAMPIKES
KN RANPIKES
KR SPARKIER
LL PERILLAS
LM IMPALERS
IMPEARLS
LEMPIRAS
LN PRALINES
LO PELORIAS
POLARISE
LP APPLIERS
LR REPRISAL
LT PILASTER
PLAISTER
PLAITERS
LU SPIRULAE
LV PREVAILS
LW SLIPWARE
MO MEROPIAS
MS IMPRESAS
MISPARSE
MT PRIMATES
MV VAMPIRES
MW SWAMPIER
NN PANNIERS
NP SNAPPIER
NT PAINTERS
PANTRIES
PERTAINS
PINASTER
PRISTANE
REPAINTS
OV VAPORISE
PR APPRISER
PS APPRISES
PT PERIAPTS
PZ APPRIZES
RR PARRIERS
SPARRIER
RS ASPIRERS
PRAISERS
RT PARTIERS
RU UPRAISER
ST PASTRIES
PIASTERS
PIASTRES
RASPIEST
TRAIPSES
SU UPRAISES
SV PARVISES
PAVISERS
SX PRAXISES
TV PRIVATES
TW WIRETAPS
TY ASPERITY
VY VESPIARY
WW WARPWISE
XY PYREXIAS

97 DOERAN

BI DEBONAIR
BL BANDEROL
BM BOARDMEN
BS BANDORES
BROADENS
BW RAWBONED
BY BONEYARD
CH ANCHORED
CL COLANDER
CONELRAD
CM ROMANCED
CN ORDNANCE
CP ENDOCARP
CR RANCORED
CS ENDOSARC
CT CARTONED
NOTECARD
CY CRAYONED
DEACONRY
DI ORDAINED
DP PARDONED
EG RENEGADO
EL OLEANDER
RELOANED
EM DEMEANOR
ENAMORED
ES REASONED
EV ENDEAVOR
EY AERODYNE
FH FOREHAND
FL FORELAND
FP PROFANED
GI ORGANDIE
GJ JARGONED
GM DRAGOMEN
GN ANDROGEN
GP DOGNAPER
GT DRAGONET
HP ORPHANED
HS HARDNOSE
HV HANDOVER
OVERHAND
IM RADIOMEN
IR ORDAINER
REORDAIN
IS ANEROIDS
IT AROINTED
ORDINATE
RATIONED
LS LADRONES
SOLANDER
LU UNLOADER
LV OVERLAND
MN NORMANDE
MO MAROONED
MP POMANDER
MS MADRONES
RANSOMED
NT NONRATED
OT RATOONED
OW WANDEROO
PR PARDONER
PS OPERANDS
PADRONES
PANDORES
PT PRONATED
PX EXPANDOR
RS ADORNERS
READORNS
RW NARROWED
TT ATTORNED
TW DANEWORT
TEARDOWN
TY AROYNTED
UX RONDEAUX

98 SUITER

AC SURICATE
AH THESAURI
AL URALITES
AM MURIATES
AN RUINATES
TAURINES
URANITES
URINATES
AO OUTRAISE
SAUTOIRE
AZ AZURITES
BB STUBBIER
SUBTRIBE
BK BURKITES
BL BURLIEST
SUBTILER
BM IMBRUTES
RESUBMIT
TERBIUMS
BN TRIBUNES
TURBINES
BQ BRIQUETS
BR BRUITERS
BURRIEST
BS BUSTIERS
BT TRIBUTES
CD CRUDITES
CURDIEST
CURTSIED
CE CERUSITE
CUTESIER
EUCRITES
CL CURLIEST
UTRICLES
CO CITREOUS
OUTCRIES
CP CUPRITES
PICTURES
PIECRUST
CR CRUSTIER
RECRUITS
CS CITRUSES
CURTSIES
RICTUSES
CV CURVIEST
CY SECURITY
DD RUDDIEST
STURDIED
DL DILUTERS
STUDLIER
DM DIESTRUM
DN INTRUDES
DO OUTRIDES
OUTSIDER
DP DISPUTER
STUPIDER
DQ SQUIRTED
DR STURDIER
DS DIESTRUS
STUDIERS
STURDIES
DT DETRITUS
EK KEIRETSU
EM EMERITUS
EN ESURIENT
RETINUES
REUNITES
EQ QUIETERS
REQUITES
ES SURETIES
FF STUFFIER
FM FREMITUS
FO OUTFIRES
FR FRUITERS
FURRIEST
FS SURFEITS
SURFIEST
FT TURFIEST
FX FIXTURES
FZ FURZIEST
GT TURGITES
HL LUTHIERS
HP SUPERHIT
HS RUSHIEST
IL UTILISER
IN NEURITIS
IP PURITIES
JY JESUITRY
KM MURKIEST
LN INSULTER
LO OUTLIERS
LQ QUILTERS
LR SULTRIER
LS SURLIEST
LT SLUTTIER
SURTITLE
LV RIVULETS
MM RUMMIEST
MN TERMINUS
UNMITERS
UNMITRES
MO MISROUTE
MOISTURE
MP IMPUREST
IMPUTERS
STUMPIER
MT SMUTTIER
MX MIXTURES
NN RUNNIEST
NO ROUTINES
SNOUTIER
NP UNRIPEST
NQ SQUINTER
NT RUNTIEST
NV VENTURIS
OP ROUPIEST
OV VIRTUOSE
VITREOUS
PQ QUIPSTER
PS PURSIEST
PT PURTIEST
PUTTIERS
QR SQUIRTER
QS QUERISTS
QT QUITTERS
QU SEQUITUR
RT TRUSTIER
ST RUSTIEST
TRUSTIES
SV REVUISTS
STUIVERS
TT RUTTIEST

99 OALIES*

BC SOCIABLE
BK KILOBASE
BL ISOLABLE
LOBELIAS
CC CALICOES
CF FOCALISE
CL LOCALISE
CM CAMISOLE
CR CALORIES
CARIOLES
CS CELOSIAS
CT COALIEST
SOCIETAL
CU EUSOCIAL
CV VOCALISE
DM MELODIAS
DP SEPALOID
DR DARIOLES
DS ASSOILED
ISOLEADS
DT DIASTOLE
ISOLATED
SODALITE
DZ DIAZOLES
SLEAZOID
FG FOLIAGES
FR FORESAIL
FT FOLIATES
GN GASOLINE
GP SPOILAGE
GR GASOLIER
GIRASOLE
SERAGLIO
GS SOILAGES
GT LATIGOES
OTALGIES
GU EULOGIAS
HM HEMIOLAS
HR AIRHOLES
SHOALIER
JP JALOPIES
JU JALOUSIE
KN KAOLINES
KP SOAPLIKE
KT KEITLOAS
LS LOESSIAL
MN LAMINOSE
SEMOLINA
MP EPISOMAL
MR MORALISE
MT LOAMIEST
MV SEMIOVAL
MW WAILSOME
NN SOLANINE
NP OPALINES
NR AILERONS
ALIENORS
NS ANISOLES
NT ELATIONS
INSOLATE
TOENAILS
NX SILOXANE
PR PELORIAS
POLARISE
PT SPOLIATE
RS SOLARISE
RV VALORISE
VARIOLES
RZ SOLARIZE
ST ISOLATES
SX OXALISES
TT TOTALISE
TV VIOLATES

100 ALDERS

AC CALDERAS
AH ASHLARED
AI SALARIED
AN ADRENALS
BB DABBLERS
DRABBLES
BD BLADDERS
BH HALBERDS
BI BEDRAILS
DISABLER
BU DURABLES
CE DECLARES
RESCALED
CI DECRIALS
RADICELS
RADICLES
CN CANDLERS
CR CRADLERS
CW SCRAWLED
CY SACREDLY
DE RESADDLE
DN DANDLERS
DP PADDLERS
SPRADDLE
DS SADDLERS
DT STRADDLE
DW DAWDLERS
WADDLERS
DY SADDLERY
EE RELEASED
RESEALED
EF FEDERALS
EH ASHLERED
EI REALISED
RESAILED
SIDEREAL
EM DEMERSAL
EMERALDS
EP PEDALERS
PLEADERS
RELAPSED
REPLEADS
ET DESALTER
RESLATED
TREADLES
EV SLAVERED
EW LEEWARDS
EY DELAYERS
FP FELDSPAR
FW SELFWARD
GG DRAGGLES
GN DANGLERS
GLANDERS
HN HANDLERS
IL DALLIERS
DIALLERS
IM DISMALER
IN ISLANDER
IO DARIOLES
IP LIPREADS
PARSLIED
SPIRALED
IT DILATERS
LARDIEST
REDTAILS
IU RESIDUAL
IY DIALYSER
KP SPARKLED
LN LANDLERS
MN MANDRELS
MO EARLDOMS
NO LADRONES
SOLANDER
NP SPANDREL
NS SLANDERS
NU LAUNDERS
LURDANES
OP LEOPARDS
PRELOADS
OS ROADLESS
OT DELATORS
LEOTARDS
LODESTAR
OU ROULADES
PW SPRAWLED
RU RUDERALS
RW DRAWLERS
SW WARDLESS
WRASSLED
TT STARTLED
TW WARSTLED
WRASTLED
ZZ DAZZLERS

Type I Eights, Alphabetized

ABALONES ABETTERS ABETTORS ABLEISTS ABLUENTS ABORTERS ABRIDGES ABSEILED ABSENTED ABSENTEE ABSENTER ABSENTLY ABSINTHE ABSOLUTE ABSOLVER ABSORBED ABSTERGE ACARINES ACCIDENT ACCOSTED ACCREDIT ACCRETES ACENTRIC ACERBEST ACEROLAS ACESCENT ACETONES ACETONIC ACHIOTES ACIDNESS ACIERATE ACOLYTES ACONITES ACRIDEST ACRIDINE ACROGENS ACROLECT ACROLEIN ACTINIDE ACTINONS ACTIONER ADAMSITE ADAPTERS ADENINES ADENITIS ADENOIDS ADENOSIS ADHERENT ADHERING ADHESION ADJOINTS ADJUSTER ADMIRERS ADMITTER ADONISES ADOPTEES ADOPTERS ADORNERS ADRENALS ADROITER ADSORBED ADSORBER ADVISERS AERATING AERATION AERATORS AERIFIES AEROBATS AEROBICS AERODYNE AEROGELS AEROLITE AEROLITH AEROSATS AEROSOLS AEROSTAT AESTIVAL AETHERIC AFFERENT AFFOREST AFFRONTS AGENCIES AGENESIA AGENESIS AGENETIC AGENIZES AGENTIAL AGENTIVE AGINNERS AGLITTER AGMINATE AGNOSTIC AGONISED AGONISES

AGONISTS AGONIZES AGOUTIES AGREEING AGRESTAL AGRESTIC AIGRETTE AILERONS AILMENTS AINSELLS AIRDATES AIRFIELD AIRHEADS AIRHOLES AIRINESS AIRLINER AIRLINES AIRPLANE AIRSCAPE AIRSHEDS AIRSPACE AIRSPEED AIRTIMES ALANINES ALATIONS ALCAIDES ALEATORY ALENCONS ALERTEST ALERTING ALEURONS ALEXINES ALFRESCO ALGERINE ALGINATE ALIDADES ALIENATE ALIENEES ALIENERS ALIENISM ALIENIST ALIENORS ALIGNERS ALIMENTS ALIQUOTS ALKANETS ALLANITE ALLEGERS ALLEGROS ALLERGIN ALLONGES ALLOTTER ALLOVERS ALMONERS ALTERERS ALTERING ALTERITY ALTHORNS ALTOISTS ALUMINES ALUNITES AMARETTI AMARONES AMBERIES AMBIENTS AMENDERS AMENTIAS AMERCING AMIDINES AMIDONES AMIRATES AMITOSES AMITROLE AMMETERS AMMONITE AMNESTIC AMNIOTES AMORETTI AMORTISE AMOSITES AMOTIONS AMREETAS ANALCITE ANALECTS ANALYSER ANALYTES ANCESTOR ANCESTRY ANCHORED ANCIENTS ANDANTES ANDESITE ANDESYTE ANDROGEN

ANEARING ANEMOSIS ANERGIAS ANERGIES ANEROIDS ANESTRUS ANETHOLS ANEURINS ANEURISM ANGARIES ANGERING ANGINOSE ANGRIEST ANGSTROM ANGULOSE ANILINES ANIMATED ANIMATER ANIMATES ANISEEDS ANISETTE ANISOLES ANKERITE ANKYLOSE ANNELIDS ANNOYERS ANNULETS ANNULOSE ANODIZES ANOINTED ANOINTER ANOLYTES ANORETIC ANSERINE ANSEROUS ANSWERED ANSWERER ANTBEARS ANTEATER ANTERIOR ANTEVERT ANTHELIA ANTHELIX ANTHEMIA ANTHEMIC ANTHERID ANTHESES ANTHESIS ANTIBOSS ANTICKED ANTIDOTE ANTIGENE ANTIGENS ANTIHERO ANTILEAK ANTILEFT ANTILIFE ANTILOGS ANTIMALE ANTIMERE ANTIMINE ANTINODE ANTINOME ANTIPODE ANTIPOLE ANTIPOPE ANTIQUED ANTIQUER ANTIQUES ANTIRAPE ANTIRUST ANTISERA ANTISMOG ANTISNOB ANTIWEAR ANTIWEED ANTLERED ANTLIONS ANTRORSE ANTSIEST ANURESES ANURESIS ANURETIC APERIENT APHELION APHORISE APIARIES APOLUNES APOSTILS APOSTLES APPLIERS APPOINTS APPOSITE APPRAISE

APPRISED APPRISER APPRISES APPRIZES APTEROUS ARANEIDS ARBALEST ARBELEST ARBITERS ARCHINES ARCSINES ARENITES AREOLATE ARGENTAL ARGENTIC ARGENTUM ARGINASE ARGININE ARGOSIES ARGUMENT ARIDNESS ARIETTAS ARIETTES ARILLATE ARILLODE ARISTATE ARMHOLES ARMOIRES ARMORIES ARNATTOS ARNOTTOS AROINTED AROYNTED ARRESTED ARRESTEE ARRESTER ARRESTOR ARSENALS ARSENATE ARSENICS ARSENIDE ARSENITE ARSENOUS ARSONIST ARTERIAL ARTERIES ARTICLED ARTICLES ARTINESS ARTISANS ARTISTES ARTSIEST ASCENDER ASCRIBED ASHLARED ASHLERED ASPERATE ASPERITY ASPHERIC ASPIRANT ASPIRATE ASPIRERS ASSAILED ASSAILER ASSENTED ASSENTER ASSENTOR ASSERTED ASSERTER ASSERTOR ASSIGNED ASSIGNEE ASSIGNER ASSISTED ASSISTER ASSOILED ASSORTED ASSORTER ASTATINE ASTERIAS ASTERISK ASTERISM ASTERNAL ASTEROID ASTHENIA ASTHENIC ASTILBES ASTONIED ASTONIES ASTONISH ASTRINGE ASYNDETA ATABRINE ATELIERS

ATHELING ATLANTES ATOMISED ATOMISER ATOMISES ATOMIZES ATRAZINE ATRESIAS ATROPINE ATROPINS ATTAINED ATTAINER ATTENDER ATTESTER ATTESTOR ATTORNED ATTRITED ATTRITES ATWITTER AUCTIONS AUDIBLES AUDIENTS AUDITEES AUGUSTER AUNTLIER AUNTLIKE AUREOLAS AUREOLES AURICLED AURICLES AUSTERER AUTOLYSE AUTOPENS AVENGERS AVENTAIL AVERMENT AVERRING AVERSELY AVERSION AVERSIVE AVERTERS AVERTING AVIDNESS AVODIRES AVOIDERS AWAITERS AZOTISED AZOTISES AZOTIZES AZURITES BACTERIN BAILMENT BAILOUTS BAILSMEN BAKERIES BALKIEST BALLOTER BALMIEST BALONEYS BALUSTER BANDEROL BANDITOS BANDORES BANISHED BANISHER BANISTER BANJOIST BANKSIDE BANNERET BANTERED BANTERER BAPTISED BARENESS BARFLIES BARGHEST BARGUEST BARITONE BARKIEST BARMIEST BARNIEST BARNLIKE BARONESS BARONETS BARONIES BARONNES BARTENDS BARTISAN BARYTONS BASEBORN BASELINE BASEMENT BASILECT BASINETS BASSINET BASTILES BASTILLE

BASTIONS BATTENER BATTERIE BATTLERS BAWDIEST BAWDRIES BAYONETS BEADIEST BEADINGS BEARDING BEARINGS BEARSKIN BEATINGS BEATNIKS BEDRAILS BEDSONIA BEDSTAND BEDSTRAW BEERIEST BEGONIAS BEGROANS BEIGNETS BELABORS BELADIES BELAYERS BELTINGS BENDIEST BENEFITS BEPAINTS BERAKING BERATING BERETTAS BERLINES BESPRENT BESTIARY BESTOWAL BESTOWER BESTREWN BESTRIDE BESTRODE BESTROWN BETAINES BETHORNS BETONIES BEWARING BIASEDLY BIBELOTS BICORNES BIDENTAL BILANDER BILAYERS BILINEAR BIMENSAL BIMESTER BIMETALS BINARIES BINATELY BINOCLES BIOCLEAN BIOTRONS BIPARTED BIPLANES BIRAMOSE BIRDSEED BIRDSEYE BIRETTAS BIRRETTA BISECTOR BISTERED BITTERNS BIVALENT BLADDERS BLANDEST BLANKEST BLANKETS BLARNEYS BLASTERS BLASTIER BLASTIES BLATHERS BLATTERS BLEARING BLEATERS BLEATING BLINDERS BLINDEST BLINKERS BLINTZES BLISTERS BLISTERY BLITHERS BLITZERS BLOATERS BLOODIES BLOTTERS BLOUSIER

BLOWIEST BLOWSIER BOARDERS BOARDMEN BOASTERS BOASTING BOATINGS BOATSMEN BOBTAILS BODILESS BOLSTERS BONEYARD BONFIRES BONIATOS BONITOES BONNIEST BONSPIEL BORNITES BOTANIES BOTANISE BOTANIST BOTANIZE BOTFLIES BOTTLERS BOUNDERS BOUNTIES BOWLINES BRAGGEST BRAIDERS BRAILLED BRAILLES BRAKIEST BRANDERS BRANDIED BRANDIES BRATTICE BRATTIER BRATTLES BRAUNITE BREADING BREADTHS BREAKING BREAMING BREASTED BREATHES BREWINGS BRICOLES BRIEFEST BRIGADES BRINDLES BRINGERS BRINIEST BRIONIES BRIQUETS BRISANCE BRISTLED BRISTLES BRITTLES BROADENS BROADEST BROCADES BROCATEL BROIDERS BROILERS BROLLIES BROMATES BROMELIN BROMIDES BROMINES BROTHELS BROWNEST BROWNIES BRUITERS BRYONIES BURKITES BURLIEST BURRIEST BURSTONE BURTHENS BUSTIERS BUSTLINE BYLINERS CABERNET CABESTRO CABINETS CABRESTO CADASTER CADASTRE CAGINESS CAJOLERS CALCINES CALCITES CALDERAS CALIBERS CALIBRED CALIBRES

CALICOES CALIPERS CALORIES CALOTTES CALOYERS CALZONES CAMELIDS CAMISOLE CANALISE CANARIES CANDIDER CANDLERS CANISTEL CANISTER CANITIES CANNIEST CANOEIST CANONISE CANONIST CANOPIES CANTEENS CANTERED CANTICLE CANTRIPS CAPELINS CAPERING CAPITOLS CAPRICES CAPSTONE CAPTIONS CARBIDES CARBINES CARELESS CARINATE CARIOLES CARLINES CARMINES CAROLERS CAROTENE CAROTINS CAROUSED CAROUSEL CARTAGES CARTONED CARTOONS CASEMENT CASERNES CASIMERE CATALOES CATENOID CATERANS CATERERS CATERESS CATERING CATHODES CAUSERIE CAUTIONS CAVILERS CEDILLAS CEINTURE CELADONS CELOSIAS CENSORED CENTARES CENTAURS CENTAVOS CENTESIS CENTIARE CENTILES CENTIMES CENTIMOS CENTNERS CENTRALS CENTRISM CENTRIST CENTROID CENTRUMS CEORLISH CERAMIST CERASTES CERATINS CERATOID CERUSITE CERVELAS CESAREAN CESARIAN CESTOIDS CHALONES CHANTERS CHANTIES CHANTORS CHARIEST CHARLIES CHARNELS CHATTIER CHEATERS

CHELATOR CHELOIDS CHESTIER CHITOSAN CHLORATE CHLORINE CHOLATES CHOLERAS CHOLINES CHORALES CHORINES CHORTENS CHORTLES CHRISTEN CHUNTERS CIGARETS CILIATES CINCTURE CINEASTE CINEASTS CINEOLES CIRCLETS CISTERNA CISTERNS CISTRONS CITADELS CITHERNS CITHRENS CITIZENS CITRATED CITRATES CITREOUS CITRINES CITRUSES CITTERNS CLAIMERS CLANGERS CLANKIER CLARINET CLASSIER CLATTERS CLAVIERS CLAYIEST CLEANERS CLEANEST CLEANSER CLEARERS CLEAREST CLEARING CLEATING CLEAVERS CLEMATIS CLIENTAL CLIMATES CLINGERS CLINKERS CLOISTER CLOTURES CLOUTERS COAGENTS COALIEST COALPITS COARSELY COARSENS COARSEST COASTERS COASTING COATINGS COATLESS COCAINES CODEINAS CODESIGN CODRIVES COENACTS COERECTS COEXERTS COGNATES COGNISED COGNISES COGNIZES COINABLE COINAGES COINFERS COINMATE COINSURE COINTERS COISTREL COLANDER COLINEAR COLLARET COLLATES COLLIDES COLLIERS COLONIES COLONISE COMRADES

CONATIVE CONCEALS CONCEITS CONCERTI CONCERTS CONCISER CONDORES CONELRAD CONGEALS CONGRATS CONIFERS CONSIDER CONSPIRE CONSTRUE CONTAINS CONTESSA CONTRAST CONTRITE CONTRIVE CONVERTS COONTIES CORACLES CORANTOS CORBEILS CORDAGES CORDITES COREIGNS CORELATE CORKIEST CORNICES CORNICLE CORNIEST CORODIES CORONETS CORRADES CORSELET CORSETED CORSLETS CORTEGES CORTEXES CORTICES CORTINAS COSECANT COSIGNED COSIGNER COSTLIER COSTRELS COTERIES COTINGAS COTTIERS COULTERS COUNTERS COUNTIES COURANTS COVARIES COVETERS COWRITES CRADLERS CRANIATE CRANKEST CRANKLES CRANNIED CRANNIES CRAPPIES CRAYONED CRAZIEST CREAKING CREAMING CREASIER CREASING CREATINE CREATING CREATINS CREATION CREATIVE CREATORS CREMAINS CREMATES CRENATED CREOLISE CREOSOTE CREPIEST CRESCENT CRESTING CRINGERS CRINGLES CRINITES CRINKLES CRISPATE CRISTATE CROCEINS CROSSLET CROSSTIE CROSTINI CROSTINO CROWDIES

CROWNETS CRUDITES CRUNODES CRUSTIER CTENIDIA CUPRITES CURDIEST CURLIEST CURRENTS CURTAINS CURTNESS CURTSIED CURTSIES CURVIEST CUTESIER CUTINISE CUTLINES CYANIDES CYANITES CYSTEINE CYTOSINE DABBLERS DABSTERS DAFFIEST DAFTNESS DAIMONES DAINTIER DAINTIES DAIRYMEN DALLIERS DAMNDEST DANDIEST DANDLERS DANEWORT DANGLERS DANGLIER DANISHES DANSEURS DARIOLES DARKLIER DARKNESS DARKSOME DARNDEST DASHIEST DATARIES DATELINE DAUBIEST DAUBRIES DAUNDERS DAUNTERS DAWDLERS DAYFLIES DAYTIMES DAZZLERS DEACONRY DEADLIER DEAIRING DEALFISH DEALINGS DEANSHIP DEARNESS DEASHING DEBASING DEBATERS DEBATING DEBONAIR DEBONERS DEBRIDES DEBRIEFS DEBRUISE DECANTER DECIARES DECIDERS DECIMALS DECLAIMS DECLARES DECRIALS DECRIERS DECROWNS DECURIES DEERSKIN DEFILERS DEFINERS DEFLATOR DEFOREST DEFROSTS DEIFIERS DELAINES DELATING DELATION DELATORS DELAYERS DELETION DELISTED DELIVERS DELTOIDS

DELUSION DEMEANOR DEMENTIA DEMERITS DEMERSAL DEMIREPS DEMISTER DEMOLISH DEMONIST DEMOTICS DEMOTIST DENARIUS DENATURE DENDRITE DENDRONS DENTALIA DENTINAL DENTINES DENTISTS DENTURES DEODARAS DEORBITS DEPAINTS DEPOLISH DEPOSING DEPOSITS DEPRIVAL DEPRIVES DERAIGNS DERAILED DERANGES DERATING DERIDERS DERISION DERISIVE DERISORY DERIVATE DERIVERS DERMISES DERMOIDS DERRISES DESALTER DESCANTS DESCRIBE DESCRIED DESCRIER DESCRIES DESERTIC DESIGNER DESILVER DESINENT DESIRERS DESIRING DESIROUS DESOLATE DESPAIRS DESPISAL DESPISER DESPOILS DESPOTIC DESTAINS DESTINED DESTINES DESTRIER DESTROYS DETAILER DETAINED DETAINEE DETAINER DETINUES DETRACTS DETRAINS DETRITAL DETRITUS DEUTZIAS DEVIANTS DEVIATES DEVIATOR DEVISALS DEVISERS DEVISORS DEWATERS DEXTRANS DEXTRINE DEXTRINS DEXTROSE DEXTROUS DHOOLIES DHOOTIES DIABETES DIABLERY DIAGNOSE DIALECTS DIALLERS DIALOGER DIALYSED

DIALYSER
DIALYSES
DIALYZER
DIALYZES
DIAMANTE
DIAMETER
DIAMINES
DIASPORE
DIASTASE
DIASTEMA
DIASTEMS
DIASTERS
DIASTOLE
DIATRIBE
DIATRONS
DIAZINES
DIAZOLES
DICENTRA
DICTATES
DIEHARDS
DIERESES
DIERESIS
DIESTERS
DIESTOCK
DIESTRUM
DIESTRUS
DIETHERS
DIGERATI
DIGESTER
DIGESTOR
DIHEDRAL
DILATERS
DILATORS
DILEMMAS
DILUENTS
DILUTERS
DIMEROUS
DIMETERS
DINETTES
DINGIEST
DINKIEST
DIOCESAN
DIOPTASE
DIOPTERS
DIOPTRES
DIORITES
DIOXANES
DIPLOSES
DIPTERAL
DIPTERAN
DIPTERON
DIRENESS
DIRIMENT
DIRTIEST
DISABLED
DISABLER
DISABLES
DISAGREE
DISARMED
DISARMER
DISASTER
DISBOWEL
DISCERNS
DISCLOSE
DISCOVER
DISCREET
DISCRETE
DISGORGE
DISGRACE
DISHERIT
DISHWARE
DISINTER
DISLODGE
DISMALER
DISORDER
DISPERSE
DISPLACE
DISPLODE
DISPOSER
DISPREAD
DISPROVE
DISPUTER
DISRATED
DISRATES
DISROBED
DISROBER
DISROBES
DISSEATS
DISSENTS
DISSERTS
DISSERVE
DISSEVER
DISSOLVE
DISTANCE
DISTASTE
DISTAVES

DISTENDS
DISTOMES
DISTRAIN
DISTRESS
DISUNITE
DISVALUE
DITCHERS
DIURESES
DIVALENT
DIVERGES
DIVINERS
DIVINEST
DIVORCES
DOCTRINE
DODGIEST
DOGGIEST
DOGNAPER
DOMAINES
DOMESTIC
DOMINATE
DONATIVE
DONATORS
DOOMIEST
DOOMSTER
DOORSTEP
DOPESTER
DORKIEST
DORMIENT
DORNECKS
DOSSERET
DOSSIERS
DOTTIEST
DOTTRELS
DOUBTERS
DOURINES
DOURNESS
DOWAGERS
DOWDIEST
DOWERIES
DOWNIEST
DRABBEST
DRABBETS
DRABBLES
DRABNESS
DRACENAS
DRAFTEES
DRAFTERS
DRAFTIER
DRAGGLES
DRAGLINE
DRAGNETS
DRAGOMEN
DRAGONET
DRAGSTER
DRAINAGE
DRAINERS
DRAWLERS
DRAWLIER
DREADING
DREAMILY
DREAMING
DREARIES
DREARILY
DREIDELS
DRESSIER
DRESSING
DRIBLETS
DRIFTAGE
DRIFTERS
DRINKERS
DRIVABLE
DROLLEST
DROPLETS
DROPSIED
DROPSIES
DROSERAS
DROSKIES
DROSSIER
DROWNERS
DROWSIER
DRUNKEST
DRYSTONE
DUALIZES
DUNGIEST
DUNNITES
DUPERIES
DURABLES
DURAMENS
DURANCES
DURATIVE
DURNDEST
DWARFEST
DYNAMITE
DYSLEXIA
DYSTONIA
EAGEREST

EANLINGS
EARDROPS
EARLDOMS
EARLIEST
EARLOBES
EARLOCKS
EARLSHIP
EARNESTS
EARNINGS
EARRINGS
EARSHOTS
EARSTONE
EARTHIER
EARTHILY
EARTHING
EARTHMEN
EARTHSET
EASEMENT
EASTERLY
EASTINGS
EASTWARD
EATERIES
EBONITES
ECDYSIAL
ECHIDNAS
ECHINATE
ECLOSION
ECTOPIAS
ECTOSARC
EDIFIERS
EDITIONS
EDITRESS
EDUCTORS
EELGRASS
EERINESS
EGALITES
EGESTING
EGESTION
EIDOLONS
EINKORNS
EINSTEIN
EJECTORS
ELAPSING
ELASTICS
ELASTINS
ELATERID
ELATERIN
ELATIONS
ELATIVES
ELECTION
ELECTORS
ELECTROS
ELEGISTS
ELEVATOR
ELISIONS
ELOIGNER
ELOINERS
ELUSIONS
ELUTIONS
ELYTROUS
EMANATES
EMBROILS
EMERALDS
EMERITAE
EMERITAS
EMERITUS
EMEROIDS
EMERSION
EMETINES
EMIGRANT
EMIGRATE
EMIRATES
EMITTERS
EMOTIONS
EMPALERS
EMPTIERS
EMULATOR
EMULSION
EMULSOID
ENABLERS
ENACTIVE
ENACTORS
ENAMORED
ENAMOURS
ENATIONS
ENCASING
ENCHASER
ENCODERS
ENCRUSTS
ENDBRAIN
ENDEAVOR
ENDOCARP
ENDOCAST
ENDORSED
ENDORSEE
ENDORSER

ENDORSES
ENDORSOR
ENDOSARC
ENDOSTEA
ENDOWERS
ENERGIDS
ENERGIES
ENERGISE
ENERVATE
ENFRAMES
ENGAGERS
ENGINOUS
ENGRAFTS
ENGRAILS
ENGRAINS
ENGRAVES
ENHALOES
ENIGMATA
ENLARGES
ENLISTED
ENLISTEE
ENLISTER
ENMITIES
ENOLASES
ENORMITY
ENQUIRES
ENRAGING
ENRAVISH
ENRICHES
ENSHEATH
ENSHRINE
ENSHROUD
ENSIFORM
ENSILAGE
ENSLAVER
ENSNARED
ENSNARER
ENSNARES
ENSNARLS
ENSURING
ENSWATHE
ENTAILED
ENTAILER
ENTASIAS
ENTASTIC
ENTERERS
ENTERICS
ENTERING
ENTERONS
ENTHRALS
ENTICERS
ENTIRELY
ENTIRETY
ENTITIES
ENTITLES
ENTOILED
ENTRAILS
ENTRAINS
ENTRANCE
ENTRANTS
ENTREATS
ENTREATY
ENTRESOL
ENTROPIC
ENTRUSTS
ENTWINES
ENURESIS
ENURETIC
ENVIRONS
ENVISAGE
EOBIONTS
EPIBLAST
EPICARPS
EPIDERMS
EPIDOTES
EPIDURAL
EPIGONES
EPIGONUS
EPIGRAMS
EPILATES
EPILATOR
EPINASTY
EPISOMAL
EPISTLER
EPISTLES
EPISTYLE
EPSILONS
EQUATION
EQUATORS
ERADIATE
ERASABLE
ERASIONS
ERECTING
ERECTION
ERECTORS
EREMITES

EREPSINS
ERETHISM
ERGASTIC
ERGATIVE
ERGOTISM
ERINGOES
ERLKINGS
EROSIBLE
EROSIONS
EROTICAL
EROTISMS
EROTIZES
ERRATICS
ERRHINES
ERSATZES
ERUCTING
ERUPTING
ERUPTION
ESCAPING
ESCARGOT
ESCAROLE
ESCHALOT
ESCOLARS
ESCORTED
ESCOTING
ESERINES
ESOTERIC
ESPALIER
ESPARTOS
ESQUIRED
ESSAYING
ESSONITE
ESTANCIA
ESTATING
ESTERASE
ESTERIFY
ESTOVERS
ESTRAGON
ESTRANGE
ESTRAYED
ESTREATS
ESTRIOLS
ESTROGEN
ESTRONES
ESURIENT
ETAGERES
ETAMINES
ETERNALS
ETERNISE
ETERNITY
ETERNIZE
ETESIANS
ETHANOLS
ETHERISH
ETHICALS
ETHINYLS
ETHMOIDS
ETHNICAL
EUCRITES
EUGENIAS
EUGENIST
EULOGIAS
EULOGIST
EUPATRID
EUPLOIDS
EUSOCIAL
EVASIONS
EVERSION
EVERTING
EVERTORS
EVICTORS
EVILLEST
EVULSION
EXACTERS
EXACTION
EXACTORS
EXALTERS
EXALTING
EXCITERS
EXCITONS
EXCITORS
EXERTING
EXERTION
EXISTENT
EXISTING
EXITLESS
EXORCIST
EXORDIAL
EXPANDOR
EXPLAINS
EXPLANTS
EXPLOITS
EXPOSING
EXSECANT
EXTENSOR
EXTERNAL

EXTERNES
EXTRADOS
EXTRANET
EXTRORSE
EYELIFTS
FACIENDS
FACTIONS
FADDIEST
FADEOUTS
FAGOTERS
FAILURES
FAINTERS
FAINTEST
FAIRLEAD
FAIRNESS
FAKERIES
FALSETTO
FANCIERS
FANCIEST
FANTASIE
FANWORTS
FARADISE
FARINOSE
FARNESOL
FARSIDES
FARTLEKS
FASTENED
FASTENER
FATTENER
FAULTIER
FAWNIEST
FEALTIES
FEARLESS
FEASTERS
FEASTING
FEATHERS
FEATLIER
FEATURES
FEDERALS
FEIGNERS
FEISTIER
FELDSPAR
FELLATOR
FELONIES
FELSITES
FELTINGS
FELWORTS
FEMINIST
FENESTRA
FENNIEST
FERITIES
FERMENTS
FERMIONS
FERNIEST
FERNINST
FERRATES
FERRITES
FERRITIN
FESTIVAL
FETATION
FETERITA
FETIALES
FETIALIS
FEWTRILS
FIELDERS
FIERCEST
FIERIEST
FIFTEENS
FIGEATER
FILAMENT
FILAREES
FILATURE
FILBERTS
FILIATES
FILISTER
FILTRATE
FINAGLER
FINAGLES
FINALISE
FINERIES
FINNIEST
FIREBASE
FIREDOGS
FIREFANG
FIREPANS
FIREPOTS
FIRESIDE
FISTNOTE
FISTULAE
FIXTURES
FLAKIEST
FLAMIEST
FLAMINES
FLANERIE
FLANEURS
FLANGERS

FLANKERS
FLASHIER
FLATLINE
FLATNESS
FLATTENS
FLATTERS
FLATWISE
FLAVINES
FLAVONES
FLAWIEST
FLAXIEST
FLEAPITS
FLEAWORT
FLECTION
FLEXIONS
FLINDERS
FLINGERS
FLINTIER
FLIRTERS
FLITTERS
FLOATELS
FLOATERS
FLOATIER
FLOKATIS
FLORIGEN
FLOSSIER
FLOTAGES
FLOUTERS
FLUORINE
FLYTIERS
FOAMIEST
FOCALISE
FOILSMEN
FOLIAGES
FOLIATES
FOLKIEST
FOLKSIER
FONDLERS
FONTINAS
FOOTLERS
FORAMENS
FORECAST
FOREHAND
FORELAND
FOREMAST
FORENSIC
FOREPAST
FORESAID
FORESAIL
FORESIDE
FORESKIN
FORESTAL
FORESTAY
FORESTED
FORESTER
FORFEITS
FORFENDS
FORKIEST
FORMANTS
FORMATES
FORNICES
FORSAKEN
FORSPENT
FORTUNES
FOSTERED
FOSTERER
FOUNDERS
FOXTAILS
FRAGMENT
FRAILEST
FRANKEST
FRAULEIN
FREAKING
FREESIAS
FREMITUS
FRENETIC
FRENZIES
FRESHING
FRETSOME
FRIGATES
FRIJOLES
FRISETTE
FROGLETS
FRONDOSE
FRONTAGE
FRONTALS
FRONTIER
FROSTEDS
FROSTIER
FROSTING
FROSTNIP
FROWSTED
FRUITERS
FUNERALS
FURANOSE
FURRIEST

FURZIEST
GADFLIES
GAGSTERS
GAHNITES
GAINLESS
GAINLIER
GALENITE
GALIPOTS
GALLEINS
GALLEONS
GALLIOTS
GAMESTER
GAMINESS
GANGLIER
GANGRELS
GANGSTER
GANISTER
GANTLETS
GANTLINE
GANTRIES
GARDENIA
GARMENTS
GAROTTES
GARPIKES
GARROTES
GASALIER
GASELIER
GASOLENE
GASOLIER
GASOLINE
GASTRAEA
GASTREAS
GASTRINS
GAUDIEST
GEARINGS
GEARLESS
GELATINE
GELATING
GELATINS
GELATION
GELLANTS
GEMINATE
GENERALS
GENERATE
GENERICS
GENETICS
GENIPAPS
GENITALS
GENITORS
GENITURE
GENOISES
GENOMICS
GENTIANS
GENTILES
GENTRICE
GENTRIES
GEOTAXIS
GERANIAL
GERANIOL
GERANIUM
GERMANIC
GERMIEST
GERMINAL
GERONTIC
GESNERIA
GESTICAL
GESTURAL
GHERKINS
GHOSTIER
GIANTESS
GIGATONS
GILBERTS
GILLNETS
GINGKOES
GINKGOES
GINNIEST
GIRASOLE
GIRLIEST
GIROLLES
GITTERNS
GLACIERS
GLADIEST
GLADLIER
GLANCERS
GLANDERS
GLARIEST
GLASSIER
GLASSINE
GLAZIERS
GLAZIEST
GLEAMERS
GLEANERS
GLINTIER
GLISSADE
GLISTENS
GLISTERS

GLITTERS
GLOATERS
GLOSSIER
GNARLIER
GNATLIKE
GNATTIER
GOATSKIN
GODETIAS
GODLIEST
GOLIATHS
GOMERALS
GOMERILS
GOONIEST
GORINESS
GORSIEST
GRACILES
GRADATES
GRADIENT
GRADINES
GRAFTERS
GRAINERS
GRAINIER
GRANDEES
GRANDEST
GRANITAS
GRANITES
GRANNIES
GRANTEES
GRANTERS
GRANTORS
GRANULES
GRAPIEST
GRAPLINE
GRAPNELS
GRATINEE
GRATINGS
GREASIER
GREASILY
GREASING
GREATENS
GREATEST
GREENEST
GREENIES
GREENISH
GREENLIT
GREENTHS
GREETING
GREISENS
GREMIALS
GREMLINS
GRENADES
GRIEVANT
GRILLADE
GRIMNESS
GRINCHES
GRINDERS
GRINNERS
GRISETTE
GRISTLES
GROANERS
GRODIEST
GRUNTERS
GRUNTLES
GUANINES
GUERDONS
GUNFIRES
GYPSEIAN
HAEMATIN
HAGRIDES
HAIRIEST
HAIRLESS
HAIRLINE
HAIRNETS
HALBERDS
HALBERTS
HALOGENS
HALTERES
HANDIEST
HANDLERS
HANDOVER
HANDSETS
HANGFIRE
HAPLITES
HAPTENES
HARDIEST
HARDLINE
HARDNESS
HARDNOSE
HARELIPS
HARMINES
HARSLETS
HASTENED
HASTENER
HATTERIA
HAULIERS
HAUNTERS

HAVERELS
HAVERING
HAYRIDES
HEADIEST
HEADINGS
HEADMOST
HEADPINS
HEADREST
HEADSAIL
HEARINGS
HEARKENS
HEARSING
HEARTENS
HEARTIER
HEARTIES
HEARTILY
HEARTING
HEATHENS
HEATHERS
HEATHIER
HECTARES
HEDONIST
HEIRDOMS
HEISTERS
HEISTING
HEKTARES
HELIASTS
HELICONS
HELIPADS
HELISTOP
HELLIONS
HELOTISM
HEMATEIN
HEMATINE
HEMATINS
HEMIOLAS
HEPARINS
HEPTANES
HERALDIC
HERBIEST
HERDSMAN
HEREINTO
HERETICS
HERITAGE
HERITORS
HERNIATE
HEROINES
HERRINGS
HESITANT
HETAERAS
HETAERIC
HETAIRAS
HIBERNAL
HIDEOUTS
HIDROSES
HINKIEST
HIRSELED
HISTOGEN
HISTONES
HOARDERS
HOARIEST
HOARSELY
HOARSENS
HOARSEST
HOATZINS
HOISTERS
HOLINESS
HOLSTEIN
HOLSTERS
HONESTER
HOODIEST
HOPLITES
HORDEINS
HORNIEST
HORNISTS
HORNITOS
HORNLIKE
HORSEMAN
HORSIEST
HOSEYING
HOSPITAL
HOSTELER
HOSTELRY
HOSTILES
HOSTLERS
HOTHEADS
HOTLINES
HOUNDERS
HOURLIES
HUNTRESS
HYALINES
HYALITES
HYDRATES
HYSTERIA
ICEBOATS
ICHNITES

IDEALESS
IDEALISE
IDEALISM
IDEALIST
IDEATING
IDEATION
IDOCRASE
IDOLATER
IDOLISED
IDOLISER
IDOLISES
IDOLIZES
IGNITERS
IGNITORS
IGNORERS
IMAGINER
IMAGINES
IMBRUTES
IMMANENT
IMMENSER
IMMERSED
IMMODEST
IMPALERS
IMPANELS
IMPARTED
IMPASTED
IMPEARLS
IMPEDERS
IMPLEADS
IMPLODES
IMPLORES
IMPOSTED
IMPOSTER
IMPREGNS
IMPRESAS
IMPUREST
IMPUTERS
INARABLE
INARCHED
INARCHES
INBREEDS
INCANTED
INCENTER
INCEPTOR
INCHOATE
INCITERS
INCLOSED
INCLOSER
INCLOSES
INCOMERS
INCORPSE
INCREASE
INCREATE
INCUDATE
INDAGATE
INDENTER
INDENTOR
INDEXERS
INDICATE
INDICTER
INDIGOES
INDIRECT
INDITERS
INDOLENT
INDORSED
INDORSEE
INDORSER
INDORSES
INDRAFTS
INDUCERS
INDURATE
INEARTHS
INERRANT
INERTIAE
INERTIAL
INERTIAS
INEXPERT
INFANTES
INFARCTS
INFECTER
INFECTOR
INFERNAL
INFERNOS
INFESTED
INFESTER
INFLAMER
INFLAMES
INFLATED
INFLATER
INFLATES
INFLECTS
INFOLDER
INFRACTS
INFRARED
INGATHER
INGESTED

INGRAFTS
INGRATES
INHALERS
INHAULER
INHERENT
INHERITS
INHOLDER
INJECTOR
INKSTONE
INLANDER
INLAYERS
INNATELY
INNERVES
INNOVATE
INOSITES
INPUTTER
INQUIETS
INSANELY
INSANEST
INSECTAN
INSECURE
INSERTED
INSERTER
INSETTED
INSETTER
INSHEATH
INSIDERS
INSISTED
INSISTER
INSNARED
INSNARER
INSNARES
INSOLATE
INSOLENT
INSOULED
INSPHERE
INSPIRED
INSTABLE
INSTANCE
INSTATED
INSTATES
INSTROKE
INSULATE
INSULTED
INSULTER
INSURANT
INSUREDS
INSWATHE
INTARSIA
INTEGERS
INTEGRAL
INTENDER
INTENSER
INTERACT
INTERAGE
INTERBED
INTERCOM
INTERCUT
INTEREST
INTERIMS
INTERIOR
INTERLAP
INTERLAY
INTERMAT
INTERMIT
INTERMIX
INTERNAL
INTERNED
INTERNEE
INTERNES
INTERRED
INTERREX
INTERROW
INTERSEX
INTERTIE
INTERVAL
INTERWAR
INTHRALS
INTHRONE
INTIMATE
INTITLES
INTONATE
INTONERS
INTORTED
INTRADOS
INTRANET
INTRANTS
INTREATS
INTREPID
INTRIGUE
INTROITS
INTRORSE
INTRUDED
INTRUDER
INTRUDES
INTURNED

INTWINES
INULASES
INUNDATE
INVADERS
INVENTER
INVENTOR
INVERITY
INVERSED
INVERSES
INVERTED
INVERTER
INVERTIN
INVERTOR
INVESTED
INVESTOR
INVITEES
INVITERS
INVOCATE
INVOKERS
INVOLUTE
INVOLVER
INVOLVES
IODINATE
IODIZERS
IONIZERS
IONOGENS
IONOMERS
IRENICAL
IRONISTS
IRONIZES
IRONLIKE
IRONNESS
IRONSIDE
IRRITATE
ISATINES
ISLANDED
ISLANDER
ISOBARES
ISOCLINE
ISOGENIC
ISOGONES
ISOLABLE
ISOLATED
ISOLATES
ISOLATOR
ISOLEADS
ISOLINES
ISOMETRY
ISOPLETH
ISOPRENE
ISOTHERE
ISOTHERM
ISOTONES
ITERANCE
ITERATED
ITERATES
JACONETS
JADEITES
JALOPIES
JALOUSIE
JANGLERS
JANGLIER
JANITORS
JAPERIES
JARGONED
JAROSITE
JAUNTIER
JAVELINS
JAWLINES
JEMIDARS
JEOPARDS
JERKIEST
JETFOILS
JETLINER
JETTISON
JINGKOES
JINGLERS
JOINABLE
JOINDERS
JOINTERS
JOINTURE
JOKESTER
JOLLIERS
JOLLIEST
JOLTIEST
JONESING
JOSTLERS
JOWLIEST
JOYRIDES
KAINITES
KAISERIN
KANTELES
KAOLINES
KARTINGS
KATHODES
KEIRETSU
KEISTERS
KEITLOAS
KERATINS
KERATOID
KERATOSE
KERNITES
KEROSINE
KETAMINE
KIDNAPER
KIESTERS
KILOBASE
KINDLERS
KINDREDS
KINETICS
KINETINS
KINGLETS
KINKIEST
KLAVERNS
KLISTERS
KNEADERS
KNITTERS
KNITWEAR
KNOTLIKE
KNOTTERS
KNOTTIER
KREMLINS
KYANISED
KYANITES
LABELERS
LABIATES
LABORERS
LABORITE
LACERTID
LACINESS
LACROSSE
LACTEOUS
LACTONES
LACTOSES
LACUNOSE
LADRONES
LAETRILE
LAGERING
LAICISED
LAITANCE
LAKEPORT
LAKESIDE
LAMBERTS
LAMBIEST
LAMENTER
LAMINATE
LAMINOSE
LAMISTER
LAMSTERS
LANCIERS
LANDLERS
LANDSIDE
LANGRELS
LANGUETS
LANKIEST
LANNERET
LANOLINE
LANOSITY
LANTERNS
LARDIEST
LARDLIKE
LARGESSE
LARIATED
LARKIEST
LARKSOME
LARYNGES
LARYNXES
LASSOERS
LASTBORN
LATEENER
LATENESS
LATENING
LATERALS
LATERITE
LATERIZE
LATHIEST
LATIGOES
LATINIZE
LATRINES
LATTICES
LAUNDERS
LAUWINES
LAVISHED
LAVISHER
LAXITIES
LAYERING
LAYOVERS
LAZARETS
LAZINESS
LAZURITE
LEACHERS
LEADIEST
LEADINGS
LEADWORT
LEAFIEST
LEAGUERS
LEAKIEST
LEALTIES
LEANINGS
LEARIEST
LEARNERS
LEARNING
LEASHING
LEASINGS
LEATHERN
LEATHERS
LEAVIEST
LEAVINGS
LECTERNS
LECTIONS
LEDGIEST
LEERIEST
LEEWARDS
LEGALIST
LEGATINE
LEGATING
LEGATION
LEGATORS
LEGGIEST
LEISTERS
LEISURED
LEMONISH
LEMPIRAS
LENITIES
LENITION
LENTISKS
LENTOIDS
LEOPARDS
LEOTARDS
LEPORIDS
LEPORINE
LEPTONIC
LESBIANS
LESIONED
LEUCITES
LEVANTER
LEVATORS
LEVIRATE
LEVITIES
LEWISITE
LEWISSON
LEXICONS
LIBELANT
LIBERALS
LIBERATE
LIBRATED
LIBRATES
LICENSER
LICENSOR
LIENTERY
LIFESPAN
LIGAMENT
LIGATURE
LIGHTENS
LIGHTERS
LIGNEOUS
LIGNITES
LIGROINE
LIMEADES
LIMITERS
LIMONITE
LINDANES
LINEAGES
LINEARLY
LINEATED
LINECUTS
LINESMAN
LINGIEST
LINKAGES
LINOTYPE
LINTIEST
LINTLESS
LIONISED
LIONISER
LIONISES
LIONIZER
LIONIZES
LIPREADS
LIQUATES
LIRIOPES
LISTABLE
LISTENED
LISTENER
LISTERIA
LITANIES
LITENESS
LITERACY
LITERALS
LITERARY
LITERATE
LITERATI
LITHARGE
LIVENERS
LIVETRAP
LOAMIEST
LOATHERS
LOBEFINS
LOBELIAS
LOBSTERS
LOCALISE
LOCALIST
LOCATERS
LOCUSTAE
LODESTAR
LOESSIAL
LOFTIEST
LOGGIEST
LOGINESS
LONELIER
LONGTIME
LONGWISE
LOONIEST
LOOPIEST
LOPPIEST
LOPSIDED
LORICATE
LORIMERS
LORINERS
LOUSIEST
LOVESEAT
LOWERING
LOWLIEST
LOYALEST
LOYALIST
LUCARNES
LUNACIES
LURDANES
LUSTRATE
LUTENIST
LUTEOLIN
LUTHERNS
LUTHIERS
MADEIRAS
MADRONES
MAESTROS
MAGISTER
MAGNESIA
MAGNESIC
MAGNETIC
MAGNETOS
MAILLOTS
MAINTOPS
MALADIES
MALIGNER
MALINGER
MALMIEST
MALTIEST
MALTOSES
MALTSTER
MANATEES
MANDATES
MANDRELS
MANGIEST
MANGLERS
MANHOLES
MANIFEST
MANIHOTS
MANILLES
MANIPLES
MANITOUS
MANLIEST
MANNITES
MANROPES
MANTISES
MANTLETS
MARGENTS
MARGINED
MARINADE
MARINATE
MARINERS
MARLIEST
MARLINES
MARLITES
MARMITES
MARMOSET
MAROONED
MARRIEDS
MARTELLO
MARTIANS
MARTINET
MARTINIS
MARTLETS
MASONITE
MASSETER
MASTERED
MASTERLY
MASTLIKE
MATELOTS
MATERIAL
MATERIEL
MATINEES
MATINESS
MATRICES
MATRIXES
MAUNDERS
MAUNDIES
MEALIEST
MEANDERS
MEANINGS
MEANTIME
MEASLIER
MEDALIST
MEDIANTS
MEDIATES
MEDIATOR
MEDICALS
MEDICANT
MEERKATS
MEETINGS
MEGASTAR
MEGATONS
MEISTERS
MELANICS
MELANINS
MELANISM
MELANIST
MELANITE
MELANOID
MELANOUS
MELILOTS
MELODIAS
MELODIES
MELODISE
MELODIST
MENACERS
MENDIGOS
MENISCAL
MENORAHS
MENSTRUA
MENSURAL
MENSWEAR
MENTIONS
MERIDIAN
MERISTEM
MERITING
MERMAIDS
MEROPIAS
MERRIEST
MESNALTY
MESOTRON
MESTINOS
METALING
METALISE
METALIST
METAMERS
METERING
METHANES
METICALS
METRAZOL
METRICAL
MIDRANGE
MIDSOLES
MIDTERMS
MIDYEARS
MIGRAINE
MIGRANTS
MIGRATED
MIGRATES
MILADIES
MILEPOST
MILESIAN
MINARETS
MINCIEST
MINDSETS
MINERALS
MINGIEST
MINGLERS
MINISTER
MINSTERS
MINSTREL
MINTAGES
MINTIEST
MINUTIAE
MIRACLES
MISACTED
MISAGENT
MISALLOT
MISALTER
MISATONE
MISBEGAN
MISDATED
MISDATES
MISDEALS
MISDEALT
MISDOERS
MISDROVE
MISEATEN
MISENROL
MISENTER
MISENTRY
MISEVENT
MISGRADE
MISHEARD
MISINTER
MISLAYER
MISLEADS
MISLEARN
MISLODGE
MISMATED
MISNAMED
MISNOMER
MISORDER
MISPARSE
MISPLEAD
MISRATED
MISRATES
MISREADS
MISROUTE
MISSTEER
MISTAKEN
MISTAKER
MISTENDS
MISTRACE
MISTRAIN
MISTREAT
MISTUNED
MISWROTE
MITERERS
MITERING
MITOGENS
MIXTURES
MODELIST
MODERNES
MODESTER
MODISTES
MOIDORES
MOISTENS
MOISTURE
MOLDIEST
MOLESKIN
MOLESTER
MONASTIC
MONAZITE
MONERANS
MONETISE
MONIKERS
MONITORS
MONSIEUR
MONSTERA
MONSTERS
MONTAGES
MONTANES
MONTEROS
MOODIEST
MOONIEST
MOONRISE
MOORIEST
MORAINES
MORALISE
MORALIST
MORDANTS
MORDENTS
MORTICES
MORTISED
MORTISER
MORTISES
MOSEYING
MOTIONER
MOTLIEST
MOTORISE
MOTTLERS
MOULTERS
MOUNTERS
MUENSTER
MUNSTERS
MURAENID
MURIATED
MURIATES
MURKIEST
MUTINEER
MUTINIES
MYLONITE
NACREOUS
NAGGIEST
NAILSETS
NAIVETES
NAKEDEST
NAPERIES
NAPPIEST
NARCEINS
NARCISTS
NARCOSES
NARGHILE
NARGILEH
NARGILES
NARRATES
NARROWED
NASALISE
NASALIZE
NASTIEST
NATHLESS
NATIVELY
NATRIUMS
NATTERED
NATTIEST
NATURISM
NATURIST
NAUSEATE
NAVETTES
NAVICERT
NEARLIER
NEARNESS
NEARSIDE
NEATHERD
NEATNESS
NEATNIKS
NECKTIES
NECROSED
NECROSIS
NECROTIC
NEEDIEST
NEGATERS
NEGATION
NEGATIVE
NEGATONS
NEGATORS
NEGATRON
NEGROIDS
NEGRONIS
NEOLITHS
NEONATES
NEOPLASM
NEOTERIC
NEPHRITE
NEPOTISM
NEPOTIST
NERDIEST
NEREIDES
NERVIEST
NERVINES
NERVINGS
NESCIENT
NESTABLE
NESTLERS
NESTLIKE
NESTLING
NETIZENS
NETTIEST
NETTLERS
NETTLIER
NETWORKS
NEUMATIC
NEURINES
NEURITIC
NEURITIS
NEUROMAS
NEUROSAL
NEUROSIS
NEUROTIC
NEURULAS
NEUTRALS
NEUTRINO
NEUTRONS
NEWSBEAT
NEWSGIRL
NEWSIEST
NEWSWIRE
NIBBLERS
NICETIES
NICTATED
NICTATES
NIELLIST
NIFTIEST
NIGELLAS
NIGGLERS
NIGHTIES
NIMBLEST
NINETIES
NIOBATES
NIOBITES
NIPPIEST
NITERIES
NITRATED
NITRATES
NITRIDED
NITRIDES
NITRILES
NITRITES
NITROGEN
NITROSYL
NITTIEST
NIZAMATE
NOBBIEST
NOISETTE
NOISIEST
NOMINATE
NONELITE
NONIDEAL
NONINERT
NONLIVES
NONRATED
NONSKIER
NONTAXES
NONTITLE
NORMANDE
NORTHERS
NOSELIKE
NOSTRILS
NOTABLES
NOTARIES
NOTARIZE
NOTCHERS
NOTECARD
NOTECASE
NOTEPADS
NOTICERS
NOTIFIER
NOTIFIES
NOTORNIS
NOVALIKE
NOVELISE
NOVELIST
NOVELLAS
NUBILOSE
NUDITIES
NUMERALS
NUMERATE
NURTURES
NUTRIENT
OATMEALS
OBEISANT
OBELISED
OBLIGERS
OBSTACLE
OBTAINED
OBTAINER
OBTRUDES
OBVIATES
ODDITIES
ODONATES
ODORANTS
ODORIZES
OERSTEDS
OESTRINS
OESTRIOL
OESTRONE
OILINESS
OILSEEDS
OILSTONE
OINOMELS
OLDSTERS
OLDWIVES
OLEANDER
OLEASTER
OLEFINES
OLESTRAS
OLIVINES
OMITTERS
ONANISTS
ONERIEST
ONSTREAM
OOGENIES
OPALINES
OPENCAST
OPENINGS
OPERANDS
OPERANTS
OPERATES
OPUNTIAS
ORALISTS
ORANGIER
ORATIONS
ORATRESS
ORBITALS
ORBITERS
ORDAINED
ORDAINER
ORDINATE
ORDNANCE
OREGANOS
ORGANDIE
ORGANISE
ORGANIST
ORGANIZE
ORGASMED
ORIENTAL
ORIENTED
ORIENTER
ORNATELY
ORNITHES
ORPHANED
ORPIMENT
ORTOLANS
OSCITANT
OSCULATE
OSSATURE
OSSETRAS
OSTEOIDS
OSTINATI
OSTINATO
OSTIOLAR
OSTIOLES
OSTRACON
OSTRAKON
OTALGIAS
OTALGIES
OTIOSELY
OTITIDES
OUTASKED
OUTCRIES
OUTDARES
OUTDATES
OUTDOERS
OUTDRESS
OUTEARNS
OUTFIRES
OUTFLIES
OUTGAINS
OUTGLARE
OUTGRINS
OUTHEARS
OUTLEADS
OUTLEAPS
OUTLEARN
OUTLIERS
OUTLINED
OUTLINER
OUTLINES
OUTLIVES
OUTRACES
OUTRAGES
OUTRAISE
OUTRANGE
OUTRANKS
OUTRATES
OUTRAVES
OUTREADS
OUTRIDES
OUTRINGS
OUTSAILS
OUTSERVE
OUTSHINE
OUTSIDER
OUTSIDES
OUTSIZED
OUTSMILE
OUTSNORE
OUTSTARE
OUTSTEER
OUTSWARE
OUTSWEAR
OUTWEARS
OUTWILES
OVALNESS
OVATIONS
OVERACTS
OVERALLS
OVERBETS
OVERBIDS
OVERCAST
OVEREATS
OVERFAST
OVERHAND
OVERLAID
OVERLAIN
OVERLAND
OVERLAPS
OVERLATE
OVERLAYS
OVERLETS
OVERLIES
OVERMANS
OVERNEAT
OVERPAST
OVERSALE
OVERSALT
OVERSETS
OVERSIDE
OVERSLIP
OVERSPIN
OVERSTAY
OVERSTEP
OVERSTIR
OVERTALK
OVERTASK
OVERTHIN
OVERTIPS
OVERWETS
OVULATES
OXALATES
OXALISES
OXAZINES
OXHEARTS
OXIDANTS
OXIDATES
OXIDISER
OYSTERED
OYSTERER
OZONATES
PACTIONS
PADDLERS
PADRONES
PAGANISE
PAINLESS
PAINTERS
PAINTIER
PALATINE
PALESTRA
PALETOTS
PALINODE
PALISADE
PALLIEST
PALMIEST
PALTRIER
PANDECTS
PANDORES
PANELIST
PANFRIED
PANFRIES
PANICLES
PANNIERS
PANTHERS
PANTILED
PANTILES
PANTRIES
PAPERING
PARADISE
PARASITE
PARCHESI
PARCLOSE
PARDNERS
PARDONED
PARDONER
PARECISM
PAREIRAS
PARENTED
PARETICS
PARIETAL
PARIETES
PARISHES
PARITIES
PARODIES
PAROLEES
PARRIERS
PARSLIED
PARTIBLE
PARTICLE
PARTIERS
PARTINGS
PARTISAN
PARTLETS
PARTNERS
PARVISES
PASTERNS
PASTILLE
PASTORED
PASTRIES
PASTURED
PATIENCE
PATIENTS
PATINAED
PATRIATE
PATROONS
PATTERNS
PAVISERS
PEARLERS
PEARLING
PEARLITE
PEARTEST
PECTINES
PECTORAL
PEDALERS
PEDALIER
PEDANTIC
PEDERAST
PELICANS
PELORIAN
PELORIAS
PELTRIES
PENALISE
PENALITY
PENDANTS
PENLITES
PENSTERS
PENTANES
PENTOSAN
PENURIES
PERACIDS
PERCALES
PERCENTS
PERCOIDS
PEREIONS
PERGOLAS
PERIANTH
PERIAPTS
PERIDIAL
PERIDOTS
PERIGEAN
PERIGONS
PERILLAS
PERILOUS
PERINEAL
PERISARC
PERISHED
PERKIEST
PERLITES
PERMEANT
PEROXIDS
PERPENTS
PERSALTS
PERSONAE
PERSONAL
PERSONAS
PERTAINS
PERTNESS
PERUSING
PESTLING
PETALINE
PETALOUS
PETERING
PETIOLAR
PETIOLES
PETNAPER
PETRALES
PETROSAL
PETUNIAS
PEYTRALS
PHAETONS
PHARISEE
PHELONIA
PHENATES
PHILTERS
PHILTRES
PHONATES
PHONIEST
PHORATES
PIAFFERS
PIASTERS
PIASTRES
PICRATED
PICRATES
PICTURES
PIEBALDS
PIECRUST
PIEFORTS
PIEPLANT
PIERROTS
PILASTER
PILLARED
PILSENER
PILSNERS
PIMENTOS
PINASTER
PINERIES
PINHEADS
PINHOLES
PINNATED
PINOCLES
PINTADOS
PINTANOS
PINTSIZE
PINWALES
PIONEERS
PIRACIES
PISOLITE
PISTOLED
PISTOLES
PITHEADS
PLAINEST
PLAISTER
PLAITERS
PLANNERS
PLANTERS
PLASHIER
PLASTERS
PLASTERY
PLASTRON
PLATANES
PLATIEST
PLATTERS
PLEADERS
PLEASANT
PLEASERS
PLEASING
PLEASURE
PLEATERS
PLEATING
PLEIADES
PLENISTS
PLENTIES
PLEONASM
PLETHORA
PLINKERS
PLOIDIES
PLOTLINE
PLOTTERS
PLOTTIES
PODESTAS
PODGIEST
POETISED
POETISER
POETRIES
POINTERS
POINTIER
POISONER
POITRELS
POLARISE
POLECATS
POLEMIST
POLENTAS
POLESTAR
POLICERS
POLISHED
POLISHER
POLITEST
POLITIES
POLLSTER
POMANDER
POOLSIDE
PORKIEST
PORNIEST
PORTABLE
PORTAGES
PORTALED
PORTENDS
PORTENTS
PORTIONS
PORTLESS
PORTSIDE
POSITRON
POSTDATE
POSTDIVE
POSTERNS
POSTFIRE
POSTRACE
POSTURED
POTABLES
POTHEADS
POTLINES
POTSHERD
POULTERS
POUNDERS
POUTINES
PRACTISE
PRAEDIAL
PRAETORS
PRAIRIES
PRAISERS
PRALINES
PRATTLES
PRAXISES
PREADMIT
PREALLOT
PREAUDIT
PREBINDS
PREBOILS
PRECENTS
PRECISED
PREDATES
PREDAWNS
PREDICTS
PREDRIES

PREEDITS
PREENACT
PREEXIST
PREGNANT
PREHEATS
PRELATES
PRELATIC
PRELOADS
PREMISED
PRENAMES
PRENTICE
PREPASTE
PREPLANS
PRERINSE
PRESALES
PRESCIND
PRESENTS
PRESIDED
PRESIDER
PRESIDES
PRESIDIA
PRESIDIO
PRESPLIT
PRESSING
PRESTIGE
PRESTORE
PRETAPES
PRETASTE
PRETEENS
PRETENDS
PRETENSE
PRETRAIN
PRETRIAL
PRETTIES
PREUNITE
PREVAILS
PREVENTS
PREVISED
PRIESTED
PRIESTLY
PRIMAGES
PRIMATES
PRINTERS
PRISONED
PRISONER
PRISTANE
PRISTINE
PRIVATES
PROBATES
PROETTES
PROFANED
PROFANES
PROFILES
PROLAPSE
PROLINES
PROMINES
PROMISED
PRONATED
PRONATES
PROPANES
PROPENDS
PROPINES
PRORATES
PROSIEST
PROSTATE
PROSTIES
PROSTYLE
PROTASES
PROTEANS
PROTEASE
PROTEGES
PROTEIDS
PROTEINS
PROTENDS
PROTEOSE
PROTYLES
PROUDEST
PROVIDES
PRUINOSE
PRURIENT
PSALTERS
PSALTERY
PSORALEA
PSORALEN
PTOMAINE
PTOMAINS
PUNSTERS
PURITANS
PURITIES
PURLINES
PURSIEST
PURSLANE
PURTIEST
PUTTIERS
PYRANOSE
PYREXIAS
QUAESTOR
QUAINTER
QUANTILE
QUARTILE
QUEASIER
QUERIDAS
QUERISTS
QUESTION
QUIETENS
QUIETERS
QUILTERS
QUINELAS
QUINTARS
QUIPSTER
QUITRENT
QUITTERS
RABBITED
RACHIDES
RACINESS
RADIABLE
RADIANCE
RADIANTS
RADIATED
RADIATES
RADICATE
RADICELS
RADICLES
RADIOMEN
RADISHES
RADIUSES
RADWASTE
RAFTSMEN
RAGTIMES
RAILHEAD
RAIMENTS
RAINIEST
RAINLESS
RAINOUTS
RAISABLE
RAISONNE
RALLIERS
RAMEKINS
RAMILIES
RAMMIEST
RAMOSELY
RAMPIKES
RAMPOLES
RAMULOSE
RANCORED
RANDIEST
RANGIEST
RANKLESS
RANPIKES
RANSOMED
RANSOMER
RAPHIDES
RAPIDEST
RAPTNESS
RAREBITS
RAREFIES
RARENESS
RARITIES
RASHLIKE
RASPIEST
RATABLES
RATAFEES
RATANIES
RATFINKS
RATHOLES
RATICIDE
RATIFIED
RATIFIES
RATIONED
RATLINES
RATOONED
RATSBANE
RATTEENS
RATTENED
RATTENER
RATTIEST
RATTLERS
RATTOONS
RAVELERS
RAVELING
RAVELINS
RAVENERS
RAVENING
RAVENOUS
RAVISHED
RAWBONED
RAWHIDES
RAZEEING
REACCENT
REACHING
REACTING
REACTION
REACTIVE
REACTORS
READAPTS
READDICT
READDING
READIEST
READINGS
READJUST
READMITS
READOPTS
READORNS
READOUTS
READYING
REAGENTS
REAGINIC
REALIGNS
REALISED
REALISER
REALISES
REALISMS
REALISTS
REALIZED
REALIZES
REALLOTS
REALNESS
REALTERS
REALTIES
REALTORS
REANOINT
REARMING
REARMOST
REARREST
REASCEND
REASCENT
REASONED
REASONER
REASSAIL
REASSERT
REASSIGN
REASSORT
REATTAIN
REAVAILS
REBAITED
REBATERS
REBATING
REBEGINS
REBOARDS
REBODIES
REBOUNDS
RECANING
RECANTED
RECANTER
RECEIPTS
RECHEATS
RECISION
RECITALS
RECITERS
RECITING
RECLAIMS
RECLAMES
RECLEANS
RECLINES
RECOUNTS
RECRATES
RECREANT
RECRUITS
RECUSANT
RECUSING
REDATING
REDBAITS
REDBONES
REDCOATS
REDEFIES
REDENIES
REDESIGN
REDIALED
REDIGEST
REDLINES
REDOUBTS
REDOUNDS
REDRAFTS
REDRIVES
REDROOTS
REDSHANK
REDSHIFT
REDSHIRT
REDSTART
REDTAILS
REDWINGS
REEDIEST
REEDINGS
REEFIEST
REEKIEST
REELINGS
REENACTS
REENDOWS
REENLIST
REENTERS
REESTING
REFACING
REFASTEN
REFINERS
REFLATES
REFLOATS
REFOREST
REFOUNDS
REFRAINS
REFRONTS
REFUSING
REFUTALS
REFUTING
REGAINED
REGAINER
REGALERS
REGALING
REGALITY
REGATTAS
REGENTAL
REGIMENS
REGIMENT
REGIONAL
REGISTER
REGLAZES
REGRAFTS
REGRANTS
REGRATES
REGRINDS
REHINGES
REIGNITE
REIMAGES
REINCITE
REINDICT
REINDUCT
REINFECT
REINFUSE
REINJECT
REINLESS
REINSERT
REINSMAN
REINSMEN
REINSURE
REINTERS
REINVADE
REINVENT
REINVEST
REINVITE
REISSUED
REITBOKS
RELABELS
RELACING
RELAPSED
RELAPSER
RELAPSES
RELATERS
RELATING
RELATION
RELATIVE
RELATORS
RELAXERS
RELAXING
RELAXINS
RELAYING
RELEARNS
RELEARNT
RELEASED
RELEASER
RELEASES
RELEVANT
RELIANCE
RELIEVOS
RELIGHTS
RELIGION
RELISHED
RELISTED
RELOANED
RELOCATE
REMAILED
REMAINED
REMAKING
REMANENT
REMASTER
REMATING
REMEDIAL
REMEDIES
REMINTED
REMISING
REMITTAL
REMNANTS
REMOTEST
REMOTION
REMOUNTS
REMOVALS
RENAILED
RENAMING
RENATURE
RENDZINA
RENEGADO
RENESTED
RENEWALS
RENITENT
RENNASES
RENOTIFY
RENOVATE
RENTABLE
RENTIERS
REOBTAIN
REOILING
REORDAIN
REORIENT
REPAINTS
REPANELS
REPASTED
REPAVING
REPAYING
REPINERS
REPLACES
REPLANTS
REPLATES
REPLEADS
REPLICAS
REPLICON
REPOLISH
REPOSALS
REPOSING
REPOSITS
REPRINTS
REPRISAL
REPRISED
REPTILES
REPTILIA
REPUTING
REQUITAL
REQUITES
RERAISED
RERAISES
RERISING
REROUTES
RESADDLE
RESAILED
RESALUTE
RESAMPLE
RESAWING
RESAYING
RESCALED
RESCALES
RESCINDS
RESCUING
RESEALED
RESEASON
RESEATED
RESEEING
RESEIZED
RESENTED
RESEWING
RESHAVEN
RESHINED
RESHINES
RESIDENT
RESIDERS
RESIDING
RESIDUAL
RESIDUES
RESIFTED
RESIGNED
RESIGNER
RESILING
RESILINS
RESINATE
RESINING
RESINOID
RESINOUS
RESISTED
RESISTER
RESISTOR
RESITING
RESIZING
RESLATED
RESLATES
RESOAKED
RESOFTEN
RESOJETS
RESOLING
RESOLUTE
RESONANT
RESONATE
RESORCIN
RESORTED
RESORTER
RESOUNDS
RESOWING
RESPIRED
RESPITED
RESPITES
RESPLITS
RESPONDS
RESPONSA
RESPRING
RESTABLE
RESTAGED
RESTAGES
RESTATED
RESTATES
RESTOKED
RESTOKES
RESTORAL
RESTORED
RESTORER
RESTORES
RESTRAIN
RESTRIKE
RESTRING
RESTRIVE
RESTROVE
RESTRUNG
RESUBMIT
RESUMING
RESUPINE
RETABLES
RETAILED
RETAILER
RETAILOR
RETAINED
RETAINER
RETAKERS
RETAKING
RETAPING
RETASTED
RETASTES
RETAXING
RETHINKS
RETICENT
RETICLES
RETICULA
RETIEING
RETILING
RETIMING
RETINALS
RETINENE
RETINITE
RETINOID
RETINOLS
RETINTED
RETINUED
RETINUES
RETINULA
RETIRANT
RETIREES
RETIRERS
RETIRING
RETITLES
RETOTALS
RETRACES
RETRAINS
RETREADS
RETREATS
RETRIALS
RETRORSE
RETSINAS
RETUNING
REUNIONS
REUNITED
REUNITER
REUNITES
REUSABLE
REVALUES
REVENANT
REVERSAL
REVISALS
REVISING
REVISION
REVIVALS
REVOTING
REVUISTS
REWAKENS
REWAKING
REWAXING
REWIDENS
REWRITES
REYNARDS
RHAMNOSE
RHAPSODE
RHEOSTAT
RICTUSES
RIDDANCE
RIDEABLE
RIDGIEST
RIESLING
RIFENESS
RIFLEMAN
RIFTLESS
RIMESTER
RIMOSELY
RINDLESS
RINGLETS
RINGSIDE
RINGTAWS
RINGTOSS
RINSABLE
RINSIBLE
RIPENERS
RIPENESS
RIPIENOS
RIPOSTED
RIPOSTES
RIPPLETS
RIPSAWED
RIPTIDES
RISSOLES
RIVALLED
RIVETERS
RIVETING
RIVULETS
RIVULOSE
ROADBEDS
ROADLESS
ROADSIDE
ROADSTER
ROASTERS
ROASTING
ROCKIEST
ROILIEST
ROISTERS
ROLAMITE
ROMAINES
ROMANCED
ROMANCES
ROMANISE
ROMAUNTS
RONDEAUX
RONDURES
RONTGENS
ROOFLINE
ROOKIEST
ROOMIEST
ROOSTING
ROOTAGES
ROOTIEST
ROOTLESS
ROOTLETS
ROPINESS
ROSARIES
ROSELIKE
ROSEOLAR
ROSEOLAS
ROSETTES
ROSINESS
ROSTELLA
ROSTRATE
ROSULATE
ROTARIES
ROTATIVE
ROTIFERS
ROTUNDAS
ROUILLES
ROULADES
ROULEAUS
ROUNDELS
ROUNDERS
ROUNDEST
ROUPIEST
ROUSTING
ROUTINES
ROWDIEST
ROWELING
ROYALIST
RUBEOLAS
RUCTIONS
RUDDIEST
RUDERALS
RUDERIES
RUDIMENT
RUINABLE
RUINATED
RUINATES
RUMINATE
RUMMIEST
RUNAGATE
RUNDLETS
RUNNIEST
RUNTIEST
RURALISE
RURALITE
RUSHIEST
RUSTABLE
RUSTIEST
RUTHENIC
RUTTIEST
SABERING
SABOTEUR
SACREDLY
SADDLERS
SADDLERY
SAFARIED
SAFETIED
SAFROLES
SAILBOAT
SAINTDOM
SALARIED
SALARIES
SALEROOM
SALICINE
SALIENCE
SALIENCY
SALIENTS
SALIFIED
SALINIZE
SALIVATE
SALLIERS
SALLOWER
SALTERNS
SALTIERS
SALTIEST
SALTINES
SALTIRES
SALTLIKE
SALTNESS
SALUTERS
SAMPHIRE
SANATIVE
SANCTION
SANDIEST
SANDLIKE
SANDPILE
SANDWORT
SANGAREE
SANGUINE
SANICLES
SANIDINE
SANITARY
SANITATE
SANITIES
SANITISE
SANITIZE
SANSERIF
SANTERAS
SANTERIA
SANTEROS
SANTONIN
SANTOORS
SANTOURS
SAPIENTS
SAPONINE
SAPONITE
SAPPHIRE
SAPREMIA
SAPREMIC
SAPROPEL
SARCENET
SARCINAE
SARDINED
SARDINES
SARKIEST
SARMENTA
SARMENTS
SARSENET
SARSNETS
SATIABLE
SATIATED
SATINETS
SATINPOD
SATIRISE
SATIRIZE
SAUNTERS
SAUTEING
SAUTERNE
SAUTOIRE
SAVORIER
SAVORIES
SAVOURED
SAXATILE
SAXONIES
SCALIEST
SCANDENT
SCANTIER
SCANTIES
SCARIEST
SCARIOSE
SCARLETS
SCARTING
SCATTIER
SCENARIO
SCENICAL
SCEPTRAL
SCIAENID
SCIMETAR
SCLEREID
SCLERITE
SCLEROID
SCLEROMA
SCOREPAD
SCRANNEL
SCRAPIES
SCRAWLED
SCREWING
SCRIEVED
SCRIPTED
SEABIRDS
SEABOARD
SEABORNE
SEADROME
SEAFLOOR
SEAFRONT
SEAGOING
SEALANTS
SEALIFTS
SEALSKIN
SEAMOUNT
SEAMSTER
SEAPORTS
SEAROBIN
SEASONAL
SEASONER
SEATINGS
SEATRAIN
SEATROUT
SEATWORK
SEAWATER
SECANTLY
SECATEUR
SECONALS
SECONDER
SECRETIN
SECRETOR
SECTIONS
SECTORAL
SECTORED
SECURING
SECURITY
SEDATING
SEDATION
SEDATIVE
SEDERUNT
SEDIMENT
SEDITION
SEETHING
SEICENTO
SEIGNEUR
SEIGNIOR
SEIGNORY
SELECTOR
SELENATE
SELENITE
SELFWARD
SEMANTIC
SEMIARID
SEMIBALD
SEMIHARD
SEMILLON
SEMINARS
SEMINARY
SEMINOMA
SEMIOVAL
SEMITONE
SEMOLINA
SENARIUS
SENATORS
SENHORAS
SENILITY
SENOPIAS
SENORITA
SENSATED
SENSATES
SENSILLA
SENSORIA
SENTIENT
SENTIMOS
SENTINEL
SENTRIES
SEPALINE
SEPALOID
SEPARATE
SEPTARIA
SEPTICAL
SEQUITUR
SERAGLIO
SERAPHIC
SERAPHIM
SERAPHIN
SERENADE
SERENATA
SERENATE
SERENEST
SERENITY
SERGEANT
SERGINGS
SERIALLY
SERIATED
SERIATES
SERIATIM
SERIEMAS
SERIFFED
SERINGAS
SERJEANT
SERMONIC
SEROSITY
SEROTINE
SEROTINY
SEROTYPE
SERPENTS
SERRANID
SERRANOS
SERRATED
SERRATES
SERRYING
SERVABLE
SERVANTS
SERVICED
SERVINGS
SERVITOR
SESTINAS
SESTINES
SETENANT
SETIFORM
SETLINES
SETTLING
SETTLORS
SEVERALS
SEVERING
SEVERITY
SEWERING
SEXTAINS
SEXTARII
SEXTILES
SHADIEST
SHADOWER
SHAGREEN
SHALIEST
SHANDIES
SHANTIES
SHARPIES
SHEAFING
SHEALING
SHEARING
SHEATHER
SHEAVING
SHEENIER
SHEERING
SHEETING
SHEITANS
SHELTIES
SHETLAND
SHIELDER
SHIKAREE
SHINGLER
SHINIEST
SHINLEAF
SHIVAREE
SHIVERED
SHOALEST
SHOALIER
SHODDIER
SHOETREE
SHORTAGE
SHORTENS
SHORTIES
SHORTING
SHRAPNEL
SHREWDIE
SHREWING
SHRIEKED
SHRIEVAL
SHRIEVED
SHUNTERS
SIBILATE
SICKENER
SIDEARMS
SIDEBAND
SIDEBARS
SIDECARS
SIDELONG
SIDEREAL
SIDERITE
SIDEWALK
SIDEWALL
SIDEWARD
SIENITES
SIEVERTS
SIGNAGES
SIGNALED
SIGNALER
SIGNETED
SILENCER
SILENTER
SILENTLY
SILICATE
SILICONE
SILOXANE
SILVERED
SIMMERED
SIMOLEON
SIMPERED
SIMULATE
SINCERER
SINECURE
SINGABLE
SINGLETS
SINISTER
SINKABLE
SINKAGES
SINKHOLE
SINTERED
SINUATED
SINUATES
SIRENIAN
SIRVENTE
SISTERED
SISTERLY
SITHENCE
SITUATED
SIXTEENS
SKANKIER
SKATOLES
SKINHEAD
SKIPLANE
SLAGGIER
SLALOMER
SLANDERS
SLANGIER
SLATHERS
SLATIEST
SLATTERN
SLAVERED
SLAVERER
SLEAVING
SLEAZIER
SLEAZOID
SLEETIER
SLEETING
SLIDABLE
SLIDEWAY
SLIGHTER
SLINGERS
SLINKIER
SLIPOVER
SLIPWARE
SLITHERS
SLITHERY
SLITTERS
SLITTIER
SLIVERED
SLOBBIER
SLOPPIER
SLOSHIER
SLOTTERS
SLUTTIER
SMALTINE
SMALTITE
SMARTENS
SMARTIES
SMARTING
SMEARIER
SMEARING
SMELTING
SMERKING
SMIDGEON
SMUTTIER
SNAGGIER
SNAGLIKE
SNAKEBIT
SNAKEPIT
SNAKIEST
SNAPPIER
SNARKIER
SNARLERS
SNARLIER
SNATCHED
SNATCHER
SNAZZIER
SNEAKERS
SNEAKIER
SNEAKILY
SNEAKING
SNEAPING
SNEERIER
SNEERING
SNEEZIER
SNIFFLER
SNIFTERS
SNIGGERS
SNIGGLER
SNIGLETS
SNITCHED
SNITCHER
SNIVELER
SNOBBIER
SNOOPIER
SNOOTIER
SNOOZIER
SNORTERS
SNORTING
SNOTTIER
SNOUTIER
SNOWIEST
SNOWLIKE
SOAPIEST
SOAPLIKE
SOBEREST
SOBERING
SOBRIETY
SOCIABLE
SOCIETAL
SODALIST
SODALITE
SODALITY
SODOMITE
SOFTENER
SOFTHEAD
SOFTWARE
SOILAGES
SOILURES
SOLACERS
SOLANDER
SOLANINE
SOLARISE
SOLARIZE
SOLATING
SOLATION
SOLATIUM
SOLDIERS
SOLDIERY
SOLECIST
SOLENOID
SOLERETS
SOLIDEST
SOLITARY
SOLITUDE
SOLLERET
SOLSTICE
SOLVATED
SOLVATES
SOMERSET
SONANTIC
SONARMEN
SONATINA
SONATINE
SONGLIKE
SONGSTER
SONICATE
SONORANT
SONORITY
SONSIEST
SORBABLE
SORBATES
SORBENTS
SORDINES
SOREHEAD
SORICINE
SORORATE
SORPTION
SORPTIVE
SORRIEST
SORTABLE
SOULMATE
SOUNDERS
SOURDINE
SOUTANES
SOUTHERN
SOUVENIR
SOVRANTY
SOWBREAD

SPADILLE
SPAEINGS
SPANDREL
SPANIELS
SPARERIB
SPARKIER
SPARKLED
SPARKLET
SPARLIKE
SPARRIER
SPARTINA
SPAVINED
SPEAKING
SPEANING
SPEARING
SPEARMEN
SPECTRAL
SPEEDIER
SPEERING
SPEIRING
SPENDIER
SPERMINE
SPHERING
SPHEROID
SPICATED
SPIERING
SPIKELET
SPINAGES
SPINDLER
SPINIEST
SPINSTER
SPINULAE
SPIRACLE
SPIRAEAS
SPIRALED
SPIRANTS
SPIRITED
SPIRULAE
SPLATTER
SPLENDOR
SPLENIAL
SPLINTED
SPLINTER
SPLITTER
SPOILAGE
SPOILERS
SPOLIATE
SPONGIER
SPOONIER
SPORTIER
SPORTING
SPORTIVE
SPOTTIER
SPRADDLE
SPRAINED
SPRATTLE
SPRAWLED
SPRINGED
SPRINGER
SPRINGES
SPRINKLE
SPRINTED
SPRINTER
SPRITZED
SPROUTED
SQUANDER
SQUEALER
SQUINTED
SQUINTER
SQUIREEN
SQUIRTED
SQUIRTER
STABILES
STABLERS
STAGGERS
STAGGERY
STAGGIER
STAIDEST
STAINERS
STALKERS
STALKIER
STALLION
STAMENED
STANCHED
STANCHER
STANDEES
STANDERS
STANHOPE
STANINES
STANNITE
STANZAED
STAPELIA
STAPLERS
STARCHED
STARGAZE
STARLESS
STARLETS
STARLIKE
STARLING
STARNOSE
STARRIER
STARRING
STARTING
STARTLED
STARTLER
STARTLES
STARVING
STASIMON
STATIONS
STAUMREL
STEADIED
STEADIER
STEADIES
STEADILY
STEADING
STEALERS
STEALING
STEAMERS
STEAMIER
STEAMILY
STEAMING
STEAPSIN
STEARATE
STEARINE
STEARINS
STEEKING
STEELIER
STEELIES
STEELING
STEEPING
STEERAGE
STEERING
STEEVING
STEINBOK
STELLITE
STEMLIKE
STEMMIER
STEMWARE
STENCILS
STENOSIS
STENOTIC
STENTORS
STEPLIKE
STEREOED
STERICAL
STERIGMA
STERLING
STERNEST
STERNITE
STERNSON
STERNUMS
STERNWAY
STEROIDS
STEWARDS
STHENIAS
STIBINES
STIBNITE
STICKLER
STIFLERS
STILBENE
STILETTO
STILLIER
STILLMEN
STINGERS
STINGIER
STINGRAY
STINKARD
STINKERS
STINKIER
STINTERS
STIPENDS
STIPPLER
STOCKADE
STOCKIER
STODGIER
STOKESIA
STOLIDER
STOMODEA
STONABLE
STONIEST
STOOLIES
STORABLE
STORAGES
STORAXES
STOREYED
STORMIER
STORMING
STORYING
STOTINKA
STOWABLE
STRADDLE
STRAFING
STRAGGLE
STRAINED
STRAINER
STRAITEN
STRAITER
STRAMONY
STRANDED
STRANDER
STRANGER
STRANGES
STRANGLE
STRAPPED
STRATEGY
STRAVAGE
STRAWIER
STRAWING
STRAYING
STREAKED
STREAKER
STREAMED
STREAMER
STREWING
STRIATED
STRIATES
STRICKEN
STRICKLE
STRIDDEN
STRIDENT
STRIDERS
STRIGOSE
STRINGED
STRINGER
STRIPPED
STROBILA
STROBILE
STROKING
STROLLED
STROLLER
STRONGER
STRONTIA
STRONTIC
STROPPED
STROWING
STROYING
STRUCKEN
STRUNTED
STUBBIER
STUDIERS
STUDLIER
STUFFIER
STUIVERS
STUMPIER
STUNNERS
STUPIDER
STURDIED
STURDIER
STURDIES
STURGEON
STYLISER
STYLIZER
STYRENES
SUBENTRY
SUBORNED
SUBRENTS
SUBTILER
SUBTREND
SUBTRIBE
SUDARIES
SUDATION
SUITABLE
SULTRIER
SUNDRIES
SUPERHIT
SUPERING
SUPERNAL
SUPINATE
SURETIES
SURFEITS
SURFIEST
SURICATE
SURLIEST
SURNAMED
SURTAXED
SURTITLE
SUZERAIN
SWAMPIER
SWANHERD
SWANKIER
SWANLIKE
SWEARING
SWEATERS
SWEATIER
SWEATILY
SWEATING
SWEETING
SWERVING
SWINDLER
SWINGERS
SWINGIER
SWOONIER
SWORDMEN
SYBARITE
SYENITES
SYENITIC
SYNDETIC
SYNDROME
SYNERGIA
SYNERGIC
SYNERGID
SYRINGED
SYRINGES
TABERING
TABLOIDS
TABORERS
TABORETS
TABORINE
TABORINS
TABOULIS
TACKLERS
TACNODES
TACONITE
TACRINES
TACTIONS
TADPOLES
TAGLINES
TAILBONE
TAILLESS
TAILLEUR
TAILORED
TAILRACE
TALESMAN
TALESMEN
TALEYSIM
TALIPEDS
TALIPOTS
TALKIEST
TALLIERS
TALLISES
TALLNESS
TAMARINS
TAMENESS
TAMPIONS
TANAGERS
TANDOORS
TANGELOS
TANGIBLE
TANGIEST
TANGLERS
TANGLIER
TANISTRY
TANKLESS
TANKLIKE
TANTRISM
TAPELINE
TAPERERS
TAPERING
TAPHOLES
TARDIEST
TARDYONS
TARIFFED
TARRIERS
TARRIEST
TARSIERS
TARTIEST
TARTLETS
TARTNESS
TARWEEDS
TATTLERS
TAUNTERS
TAURINES
TAVERNAS
TAVERNER
TAWDRIER
TAWDRIES
TAWNIEST
TEABOWLS
TEACHERS
TEAMSTER
TEARDOWN
TEARIEST
TEARLESS
TEAROOMS
TEASELER
TEASPOON
TEAWARES
TEAZLING
TEENAGER
TEENIEST
TEENSIER
TEGMINAL
TEGUMINA
TELERANS
TELESTIC
TELEVISE
TELFORDS
TELSONIC
TEMBLORS
TEMPERAS
TEMPLARS
TEMPORAL
TENAILLE
TENDRILS
TENEBRAE
TENESMIC
TENIASES
TENIASIS
TENNISES
TENONERS
TENORIST
TENORITE
TENSIBLE
TENSIBLY
TENSIONS
TENTAGES
TENTIEST
TENTORIA
TENURIAL
TENURING
TEOSINTE
TEQUILAS
TERAFLOP
TERAOHMS
TERATISM
TERATOID
TERBIUMS
TERGITES
TERMINAL
TERMINUS
TERMITES
TERNIONS
TERPENES
TERPENIC
TERPINOL
TERRACES
TERRAINS
TERRANES
TERRAPIN
TERRASES
TERREENS
TERRENES
TERRIERS
TERRINES
TERTIALS
TERTIANS
TERTIARY
TESSERAE
TESTATOR
TESTICLE
TETANICS
TETANIES
TETANISE
TETANIZE
TETANOID
TETRACID
TETRADIC
TETRAGON
TETRODES
TEXTILES
THANKERS
THEATERS
THEATRES
THEATRIC
THEBAINE
THEELINS
THENAGES
THEOREMS
THEORIES
THEORISE
THEORIST
THEREMIN
THERIACS
THERIANS
THERMALS
THERMION
THESAURI
THESPIAN
THIAMINE
THIAZOLS
THINKERS
THINNERS
THIONATE
THIRLAGE
THIRSTED
THIRTEEN
THOLEPIN
THORACES
THORAXES
THORITES
THORNIER
THRASHED
THREATEN
THROSTLE
THUNDERS
TICKLERS
TIDDLERS
TIDELAND
TIDELESS
TIDEMARK
TIDERIPS
TIDEWAYS
TIDINESS
TIEBREAK
TIECLASP
TIERCELS
TILLAGES
TIMBALES
TIMBRELS
TIMECARD
TIMELESS
TIMEWORN
TINAMOUS
TINCTURE
TINGLERS
TINGLIER
TINHORNS
TININESS
TINKERED
TINKERER
TINKLERS
TINKLIER
TINNIEST
TINPLATE
TINSELED
TINSELLY
TINSTONE
TINTLESS
TINWARES
TINWORKS
TIPPLERS
TIREDEST
TIRELESS
TIRESOME
TITANESS
TITANOUS
TITRABLE
TITRANTS
TITRATED
TITRATES
TOADLESS
TOASTERS
TOASTIER
TOASTING
TODDLERS
TOENAILS
TOGGLERS
TOILSOME
TOKENISM
TOLARJEV
TOLERANT
TOLERATE
TOLIDINE
TOLLAGES
TOLUATES
TOLUIDES
TONEARMS
TONETICS
TONNAGES
TONNEAUS
TONSILAR
TONSURED
TONSURES
TONTINES
TOOTLERS
TOPAZINE
TOPLINES
TOPSAILS
TOPSIDER
TOPSIDES
TORMENTS
TORNADOS
TORPEDOS
TORRENTS
TORSADES
TORSIONS
TORTOISE
TORTONIS
TOTALISE
TOTALISM
TOTALIST
TOURINGS
TOURNEYS
TOWELING
TOWERING
TOWHEADS
TOWLINES
TOXEMIAS
TRACHEID
TRACHLES
TRACINGS
TRACTILE
TRACTIVE
TRADUCES
TRAILERS
TRAINEES
TRAINERS
TRAINMEN
TRAIPSED
TRAIPSES
TRAMELLS
TRAMLESS
TRAMLINE
TRAMMELS
TRAMPLES
TRANCHES
TRANNIES
TRANSECT
TRANSEPT
TRANSFER
TRANSFIX
TRANSHIP
TRANSITS
TRANSMIT
TRANSOMS
TRANSUDE
TRAPESED
TRAPESES
TRAPEZES
TRAPLIKE
TRAPLINE
TRAPNEST
TRAPPOSE
TRASHIER
TRASHING
TRASHMEN
TRAVELOG
TRAVERSE
TRAVOISE
TRAWLERS
TRAWLEYS
TREACLES
TREADERS
TREADING
TREADLES
TREASONS
TREASURE
TREATERS
TREATIES
TREATING
TREATISE
TREELAWN
TREENAIL
TREETOPS
TREFOILS
TREHALAS
TREMOLOS
TRENAILS
TRENCHES
TRENDIER
TRENDIES
TRENDOID
TREPANGS
TREPHINE
TRESSIER
TRIANGLE
TRIAZINE
TRIAZINS
TRIAZOLE
TRIBADES
TRIBUNES
TRIBUTES
TRICKLES
TRICORNE
TRICORNS
TRIDENTS
TRIENNIA
TRIENTES
TRIFECTA
TRIFLERS
TRIGNESS
TRIHEDRA
TRILBIES
TRILLERS
TRIMNESS
TRINDLES
TRINKETS
TRIOLETS
TRIPEDAL
TRIPHASE
TRIPLANE
TRIPLETS
TRIPOSES
TRIPTANE
TRIPTANS
TRIREMES
TRISCELE
TRISEMES
TRISKELE
TRISOMES
TRISTATE
TRISTEZA
TRITONES
TRIVALVE
TROCHEES
TROCHLEA
TROLANDS
TROLLERS
TROLLEYS
TROLLIES
TROMMELS
TROPHIES
TROPINES
TROTLINE
TROUBLES
TROUNCES
TRUDGENS
TRUENESS
TRUNDLES
TRUNNELS
TRUSTIER
TRUSTIES
TSAREVNA
TSARINAS
TUBEROSE
TUNICLES
TURBINES
TURFIEST
TURGITES
TURNKEYS
TURNPIKE
TURNSOLE
TUTELARS
TWANGERS
TWANGIER
TWANGLER
TWANGLES
TWANKIES
TWEAKIER
TWEENERS
TWEENIES
TWENTIES
TWINIEST
TWINKIES
TWINKLES
TWIRLERS
TWOONIES
TYRAMINE
TYROSINE
TZARINAS
TZIGANES
ULEXITES
UMANGITE
UNAKITES
UNBASTED
UNBIASED
UNBITTER
UNCRATES
UNCREATE
UNDERATE
UNDEREAT
UNDERLIT
UNDERSEA
UNDERSET
UNDRAPES
UNEARTHS
UNEASIER
UNEASILY
UNERASED
UNEROTIC
UNHAIRED
UNHOLIER
UNHORSED
UNITAGES
UNITARDS
UNITIZER
UNITIZES
UNIVERSE
UNLEARNS
UNLISTED
UNLOADER
UNMITERS
UNMITRED
UNMITRES
UNPAIRED
UNPOLITE
UNRAISED
UNRAVELS
UNREASON
UNREPAID
UNRESTED
UNRETIRE
UNRINSED
UNRIPEST
UNRUSTED
UNSALTED
UNSEARED
UNSEATED
UNSHARED
UNSIFTED
UNSILENT
UNSOILED
UNSOLDER
UNSORTED
UNSOURED
UNSTABLE
UNSTATED
UNSTAYED
UNSTEADY
UNSTRESS
UNSUITED
UNTASTED
UNTIDIER
UNTIDIES
UNTREADS
UNTRUEST
UNVARIED
UNWASTED
UPDATERS
UPRAISED
UPRAISER
UPRAISES
UPSOARED
UPSTAGER
UPSTARED
UPTRENDS
URALITES
URANIDES
URANITES
URBANEST
URBANISE
URBANIST
URBANITE
UREDINIA
URETHANE
URETHANS
URIDINES
URINATED
URINATES
UROSTYLE
URTICATE
USERNAME
USHERING
UTENSILS
UTILISER
UTOPIANS
UTRICLES
UTTERING
VALERIAN
VALETING
VALORISE
VAMPIRES
VANISHED
VANISHER
VANITIED
VANITIES
VAPORISE
VARIANTS
VARIATED
VARIATES
VARICOSE
VARIEDLY
VARIETAL
VARIOLES
VARMENTS
VARMINTS
VASELINE
VAULTERS
VAULTIER
VAUNTERS
VEALIEST
VEDALIAS
VEGANISM
VEINIEST
VEINLETS
VENALITY
VENATION
VENERATE
VENERIES
VENETIAN
VENOSITY
VENTAGES
VENTAILS
VENTRALS
VENTURES
VENTURIS
VERANDAS
VERATRIN
VERBENAS
VERDICTS
VERITIES
VERNIERS
VERNIXES
VERSANTS
VERSEMAN
VERSINES
VERSIONS
VERTICAL
VERTICES
VERTIGOS
VERVAINS
VESICANT
VESPERAL
VESPIARY
VESTIARY
VESTLIKE
VESTRIES
VESTURAL
VETERANS
VETIVERS
VEXATION
VIATORES
VIBRANTS
VIBRATED
VIBRATES
VILAYETS
VINEGARS
VINEGARY
VINERIES
VINEYARD
VINTAGER
VINTAGES
VINTNERS
VIOLATER
VIOLATES
VIOLONES
VIRAGOES
VIRELAIS
VIRELAYS
VIRGATES
VIRTUOSE
VIRULENT
VISCERAL
VITALISE
VITAMERS
VITAMINE
VITRAINS
VITREOUS
VITRINES
VOCALISE
VOCALIST
VOLERIES
VOLTAGES
VOLTAISM
VOMITERS
VORLAGES
VORTEXES
VORTICES
VOTARESS
VOTARIES
WADDLERS
WAFERING
WAGERING
WAGONERS
WAILSOME
WAINSCOT
WAISTERS
WAITERED
WAITRESS
WAITRONS
WAKENERS
WALTZERS
WANDEROO
WANGLERS
WARDLESS
WARINESS
WARPWISE
WARSTLED
WARSTLER
WARSTLES
WARTIEST
WARTIMES
WARTLESS
WARTLIKE
WASTELOT
WASTERIE
WASTRELS
WASTRIES
WATERERS
WATERHEN
WATERIER
WATERILY
WATERING
WATERISH
WATERLOG
WATERLOO
WATERMEN
WATERSKI
WAVERING
WEARIEST
WEARYING
WEATHERS
WEENIEST
WEENSIER
WEIRDEST
WEIRDIES
WEIRDOES
WELFARES
WELLSITE
WELTINGS
WENDIGOS
WENNIEST
WESTERNS
WESTWARD
WETLANDS
WETWARES
WHEATENS
WHINGERS
WHINIEST
WHISTLER
WHITENER
WHORTLES
WIDENERS
WIDEOUTS
WIDGEONS
WIDOWERS
WIELDERS
WINDAGES
WINDIEST
WINERIES
WINGIEST
WINGLETS
WINSOMER
WINTERED
WINTERER
WINTRIER
WIRETAPS
WISEACRE
WISTERIA
WOMANISE
WOMANIST
WONKIEST
WOODIEST
WOODSIER
WOOLIEST
WORDAGES
WORDIEST
WORMIEST
WORSENED
WORSTEDS
WORSTING
WORTHIES
WRANGLES
WRASSLED
WRASTLED
WRASTLES
WREAKING
WREATHEN
WREATHES
WRESTING
WRINGERS
WRINKLES
WRISTLET
WRITABLE
WRONGEST
XENOLITH
YEALINGS
YEARENDS
YEARLIES
YEARLING
YEARNERS
YEARNING
YEASTIER
YEASTILY
YEASTING
YESTREEN
YIELDERS
YOLKIEST
YPERITES
YTTERBIA
ZARATITE
ZEALOTRY
ZEBRANOS
ZEBRINES
ZEMINDAR
ZENAIDAS
ZENITHAL
ZEOLITES
ZINCATES
ZINCITES
ZINGIEST
ZITHERNS
ZOOLATER
ZORILLES

Type II Sevens, in Alphagram Order

AAADGIL ADAGIAL
AAADNRS SARDANA
AAAEGLT GALATEA
AAAENST ANATASE
AAAGILN ANALGIA
AAAGINR ANGARIA
AAAGISS ASSAGAI
AAAGLNS LASAGNA
AAAGLRS ARGALAS
AAAGNNS NAGANAS
AAAGNRU GUARANA
AAAILRT TALARIA
AAAISST ASTASIA
AAALNNT LANTANA
AAANRTT TANTARA
TARTANA
AAARSST SATARAS
AAARTTU TUATARA
AADEELT DEALATE
AADEENR ANEARED
AADEERT AERATED
AADEGLS GELADAS
AADEGNS AGENDAS
AADEGRT GRADATE
AADELNR ADRENAL
AADELNT LANATED
AADELRT LATERAD
AADELRU RADULAE
AADELTU ADULATE
AADENNT ANDANTE
AADENSU SAUNAED
AADERRS ARRASED
AADERTU AURATED
AADGIIR GIARDIA
AADGIOS ADAGIOS
AADGIOT AGATOID
AADGLNO GONADAL
AADGLNR GARLAND
AADGLRU GRADUAL
AADGNRT GARDANT
AADILNR LANIARD
NADIRAL
AADILRS RADIALS
AADILSS DALASIS
AADINRS RADIANS
AADINRT RADIANT
AADIRSU SUDARIA
AADISST STADIAS
AADLNSS SANDALS
AADLNSU LANDAUS
AADLRRU RADULAR
AADLRSU RADULAS
AADNNRS RANDANS
AADOSTT TOSTADA
AADRRSS SARDARS
AADRSTU DATURAS
AAEEGLT GALEATE
AAEELOR AREOLAE
AAEERTU AUREATE
AAEGILR REGALIA
AAEGISS ASSEGAI
AAEGITT AGITATE
AAEGLNN ANLAGEN
AAEGLNS ANLAGES
GALENAS
LASAGNE
AAEGLRR REALGAR
AAEGLRS ALEGARS
LAAGERS
AAEGNNT TANNAGE
AAEGNRR ARRANGE
AAEGNST AGNATES
AAEGNSU GUANASE
AAEGORS AGAROSE
AAEGRTT REGATTA
AAEGSSU ASSUAGE
SAUSAGE
AAEGSTU GATEAUS
AAEILNN ALANINE
AAEILSS ALIASES
AAEINNO AEONIAN
AAEISTT SATIATE
AAELNNS ANNEALS
AAELNSS ANLASES
AAELNTT TETANAL
AAELORR AREOLAR
AAELORU AUREOLA
AAELSST ATLASES
AAENNST ANNATES
AAENNTT TANNATE
AAENRRT NARRATE
AAENSSU NAUSEAS
AAEORRT AERATOR
AAEORRU AURORAE
AAERRSS ARRASES
AAERRST ERRATAS
AAERRTT TARTARE
AAERTTU TUATERA
AAGIINT IGNATIA
AAGILNN ANGINAL
AAGILNO LOGANIA
AAGILNS AGNAILS
AAGILOS LAOGAIS
AAGILOT OTALGIA
AAGILRS ARGALIS
AAGINNS ANGINAS
AAGINOS AGNOSIA
AAGINRR ARRAIGN
AAGINRS SANGRIA
AAGINRT GRANITA
AAGINRU GUARANI
AAGINST AGAINST
ANTISAG
AAGINSU IGUANAS
AAGIOTT AGITATO
AAGLNOR GRANOLA
AAGLNOS ANALOGS
AAGLNRS RAGLANS
AAGLNRU ANGULAR
AAGLNSU LAGUNAS
AAGLORU ARUGOLA
AAGLRST GASTRAL
AAGLSST STALAGS
AAGNNOS GOANNAS
AAGNORS ANGORAS
AAGNRSS SANGARS
AAGNSST SATANGS
AAGORSU SAGUARO
AAIINRT ANTIAIR
AAIINTT TITANIA
AAILNNS ALANINS
AAILNOT ALATION
AAILNSS SALINAS
AAILNST LATINAS
AAILORS SOLARIA
AAILRST LARIATS
LATRIAS
AAILRTT RATTAIL
AAINRSU ANURIAS
SAURIAN
URANIAS
AAINSTT ATTAINS
AAIORRS ROSARIA
AAIRSST ARISTAS
TARSIAS
AAIRSTT STRIATA
AALNNRU ANNULAR
AALNNSU ANNUALS
AALNRRU RANULAR
AALNRSU RANULAS
AALNRTU NATURAL
AALNSTT SALTANT
AALNSTU SULTANA
AALORRU AURORAL
AALORST ALASTOR
AALORSU AROUSAL
AALRSST ASTRALS
TARSALS
AALRSTT STRATAL
AALRSTU AUSTRAL
AALSSTU ASSAULT
AANNOTT ANNATTO
AANNRSU ANURANS
AANORTT ARNATTO
AANOSST SONATAS
AANOSTT ANATTOS
AANRSTT RATTANS
TANTRAS
TARTANS
AAORRSU AURORAS
AARRSTT TARTARS
AARSSTT STRATAS
ADEEELS EASELED
ADEEGLN ANGELED
GLEANED
ADEEGLR LAGERED
REGALED
ADEEGLT GELATED
LEGATED
ADEEGLU LEAGUED
ADEEGNR ANGERED
DERANGE
ENRAGED
GRANDEE
GRENADE
ADEEGNT AGENTED
NEGATED
ADEEGOT GOATEED
ADEEGRR REGRADE
ADEEGRS DRAGEES
GREASED
ADEEGSS DEGASES
ADEEILN ALIENED
DELAINE
ADEEINN ADENINE
ADEEIRR READIER
ADEEISS DISEASE
SEASIDE
ADEEITU AUDITEE
ADEELNR LEARNED
ADEELNS LEADENS
ADEELNT LATENED
ADEELOS ELODEAS
ADEELRT ALERTED
ALTERED
RELATED
TREADLE
ADEELST DELATES
ADEENNS ENNEADS
ADEENTT DENTATE
ADEERRS READERS
REDEARS
REREADS
ADEERRT RETREAD
TREADER
ADEERSS RESEDAS
ADEERTT TREATED
ADEESST SEDATES
ADEESTT ESTATED
ADEESTU SAUTEED
ADEGILN ALIGNED
DEALING
LEADING
ADEGILO GEOIDAL
ADEGILT LIGATED
ADEGINN DEANING
ADEGIOT GODETIA
ADEGIRU GAUDIER
ADEGISU GAUDIES
ADEGLNR DANGLER
GNARLED
ADEGLNS DANGLES
GLANDES
LAGENDS
SLANGED
ADEGLNT TANGLED
ADEGLOT GLOATED
ADEGLSS GLASSED
ADEGNNU DUNNAGE
ADEGNOT TANGOED
ADEGNRR GNARRED
GRANDER
ADEGNSU AUGENDS
ADEGNTU UNGATED
ADEGORT GAROTED
ADEGOSS DOSAGES
SEADOGS
ADEGOTT TOGATED
ADEGRRS GRADERS
REGARDS
ADEGRRU GUARDER
ADEGRSS GRASSED
ADEGRSU DESUGAR
SUGARED
ADEGSSU DEGAUSS
ADEIISS DAISIES
ADEILNN ANNELID
LINDANE
ADEILNU ALIUNDE
UNIDEAL
ADELNNU UNLADEN
ADELNOT TALONED
ADELNRU LAUNDER
LURDANE
ADELNSS SENDALS
ADELNSU UNLADES
UNLEADS
ADELNTU LUNATED
ADELORU ROULADE
ADELOSS ALDOSES
LASSOED
ADELOTT TOTALED
ADELOTU OUTLEAD
ADELRRU RUDERAL
ADELRTT RATTLED
ADELSST DESALTS
ADELSTT SLATTED
ADELSTU AULDEST
SALUTED
ADENNSU DUENNAS
ADENOOT ODONATE
ADENOTT NOTATED
ADENRTU DAUNTER
NATURED
UNRATED
UNTREAD
ADENSSU SUNDAES
ADENTTU ATTUNED
NUTATED
TAUNTED
ADEORTT ROTATED
ADEORTU OUTDARE
OUTREAD
READOUT
ADEOTTU OUTDATE
ADERSSU ASSURED
ADESTTU STATUED
ADGIILN DIALING
GLIADIN
ADGIILT DIGITAL
ADGIINO GONIDIA
ADGIINR RAIDING
ADGIINS SIGANID
ADGIINU IGUANID
ADGILNN LANDING
ADGILNO LOADING
ADGILNR DARLING
LARDING
ADGILNS LADINGS
LIGANDS
ADGILNU LANGUID
LAUDING
ADGILOR GOLIARD
ADGILOS DIALOGS
ADGINNR DARNING
ADGINNS SANDING
ADGINOR ADORING
ADGINOS GANOIDS
ADGINOT DOATING
ADGINRS DARINGS
GRADINS
ADGINRT DARTING
TRADING
ADGINSU AUDINGS
ADGINTU DAUTING
ADGIORT GORDITA
ADGIRSU GUISARD
ADGLNOO DONGOLA
GONDOLA
ADGLNOR GOLDARN
ADGNOOR DRAGOON
GADROON
ADGNORS DRAGONS
ADGNORU AGROUND
ADGNRRU GURNARD
ADGORTU OUTDRAG
ADGRSTU DUSTRAG
ADIILNO LIANOID
ADIILOS SIALOID
ADIILSS SIALIDS
ADIILST DIALIST
ADIINST DISTAIN
ADIINSU INDUSIA
ADIIRST DIARIST
ADILNNS INLANDS
ADILNOR ORDINAL
ADILNOS LADINOS
ADILNRS ALDRINS
ADILNRU DIURNAL
ADILNSS ISLANDS
ADILNSU SUNDIAL
ADILORT DILATOR
ADILOTU OUTLAID
ADILSTU DUALIST
TULADIS
ADINNOR ANDIRON
ADINNRS INNARDS
ADINORS INROADS
ORDAINS
SADIRON
ADINORT DIATRON
ADINRSU DURIANS
ADINRTU UNITARD
ADINSTT DISTANT
ADIORTU AUDITOR
ADIOSTU OUTSAID
ADIRRSS SIRDARS
ADIRRST RITARDS
ADIRSSU SARDIUS
ADLNNOR NORLAND
ADLNNSU SUNLAND
ADLNOOR LARDOON
ADLNOOS ONLOADS
ADLNORS LADRONS
LARDONS
ADLNORT TROLAND
ADLNORU NODULAR
ADLNOSS SOLANDS
SOLDANS
ADLNOST DALTONS
SANDLOT
ADLNOSU UNLOADS
ADLNOTU OUTLAND
ADLNRSU LURDANS
ADLNSSU SULDANS
ADLORSS DORSALS
ADLORSU SUDORAL
ADNNOSU ADNOUNS
ADNOORT DONATOR
ODORANT
TANDOOR
TORNADO
ADNORTU ROTUNDA
ADNOSSU SOUDANS
ADNOSTU ASTOUND
ADNRSST STRANDS
ADNRSTU TUNDRAS
ADOOSTT TOSTADO
ADORRSU ARDOURS
AEEEGLT LEGATEE
AEEEGNT TEENAGE
AEEEGRR EAGERER
AEEEGRT ETAGERE
AEEEILN ALIENEE
AEEGILN LINEAGE
AEEGILT EGALITE
AEEGINU EUGENIA
AEEGISS AEGISES
AEEGLNR ENLARGE
GENERAL
GLEANER
AEEGLNT ELEGANT
AEEGLNU EUGLENA
AEEGLOR AEROGEL
AEEGLRR REGALER
AEEGLRU LEAGUER
AEEGLSS AGELESS
AEEGLST EAGLETS
GELATES
LEGATES
SEGETAL
TELEGAS
AEEGLSU LEAGUES
AEEGLTT GALETTE
AEEGNRU UNEAGER
AEEGNSS SENEGAS
AEEGNTT TENTAGE
AEEGOST GOATEES
AEEGRRS GREASER
REGEARS
AEEGRRT GREATER
REGRATE
AEEGRRU REARGUE
AEEGRSS GREASES
AEEGSTT GESTATE
AEEILRR EARLIER
LEARIER
AEEISST EASIEST
AEELNRR LEARNER
RELEARN
AEELORU AUREOLE
AEELRRT ALERTER
ALTERER
REALTER
RELATER
AEELSST TEASELS
AEELSTU ELUATES
AEENNOT NEONATE
AEENNTU UNEATEN
AEENOSU AENEOUS
AEENSSU UNEASES
AEEORSS SEROSAE
AEERRSS ERASERS
AEERRSU ERASURE
AEERRTT RETREAT
TREATER
AEERSSU RESEAUS
UREASES
AEESSTT ESTATES
AEGILNN ANELING
EANLING
LEANING
AEGILNU LINGUAE
UNAGILE
AEGILOU EULOGIA
AEGILRR GLARIER
AEGILSS GLASSIE
LIGASES
SILAGES
AEGINNT ANTEING
ANTIGEN
GENTIAN
AEGINNU ANGUINE
GUANINE
AEGINTU UNITAGE
AEGIRSS GASSIER
AEGISST AGEISTS
SAGIEST
AEGISTU AUGITES
AEGLNOT TANGELO
AEGLNRU GRANULE
AEGLNSU ANGELUS
LAGUNES
LANGUES
AEGLNTT GANTLET
AEGLNTU LANGUET
AEGLOSS GLOSSAE
AEGLRRU REGULAR
AEGLRSS LARGESS
AEGLRTU TEGULAR
AEGLSTT GESTALT
AEGNNOS NONAGES
AEGNNOT NEGATON
TONNAGE
AEGNNST GANNETS
AEGNNTT TANGENT
AEGNNTU TUNNAGE
AEGNOOR OREGANO
AEGNORR GROANER
AEGNRRS GARNERS
RANGERS
AEGNRSS SANGERS
AEGOORT ROOTAGE
AEGORRT GARROTE
AEGORSU AERUGOS
AEGORTT GAROTTE
AEGORTU OUTRAGE
AEGOSSU GASEOUS
AEGOSTU OUTAGES
AEGRRSU ARGUERS
SUGARER
AEGRSSU ARGUSES
SAUGERS
AEIILNN ANILINE
AEIILSS LIAISES
SILESIA
AEIINNS ASININE
AEIINRR RAINIER
AEINNRU ANEURIN
AEINNSS SIENNAS
AEIRRSS ARRISES
RAISERS
SIERRAS
AEIRSSU SAURIES
AEISTTU SITUATE
AELNNRT LANTERN
AELNNRU UNLEARN
AELNNTU ANNULET
AELNORU ALEURON
AELNRTU NEUTRAL
AELNSSU SENSUAL
UNSEALS
AELOTTU TOLUATE
AELRRSU SURREAL
AELRRTT RATTLER
AELRSSU SAURELS
AELRTTU TUTELAR
AELSSTT LATESTS
SALTEST
STALEST
AELSSTU SALUTES
TALUSES
AENNOTU TONNEAU
AENNRTT ENTRANT
AENNSTT TANNEST
TENANTS
AENORTU OUTEARN
AENRRSS SNARERS
AENRTTU TAUNTER
AENSSTU UNSEATS
AENSTTU ATTUNES
NUTATES
TAUTENS
TETANUS
UNSTATE
AEORRSS SOARERS
AEORRSU AROUSER
AEORSSU AROUSES
AEORTTU OUTRATE
AEOSTTU OUTEATS
AERRSST ARRESTS
RASTERS
STARERS
AERRSSU ASSURER
RASURES
AERRSTT RATTERS
RESTART
STARTER

AERSSTT STARETS
STATERS
TASTERS
AERSTTU STATURE
AESSTTU STATUES
AGIILNN ALINING
NAILING
AGIILNR LAIRING
RAILING
AGIILNS NILGAIS
SAILING
AGIILNT INTAGLI
TAILING
AGIINNR INGRAIN
RAINING
AGIINNS SAINING
AGIINRS AIRINGS
ARISING
RAISING
AGIINRT AIRTING
AGILNNO LOANING
AGILNNS LIGNANS
LINSANG
AGILNOT ANTILOG
AGILNSS SIGNALS
AGILNST LASTING
SALTING
SLATING
STALING
AGILNSU NILGAUS
AGILORS GIRASOL
GLORIAS
AGINNOT ATONING
AGINNRS SNARING
AGINNRT RANTING
AGINNST ANTINGS
STANING
AGINNSU GUANINS
AGINNTU ANTIGUN
AGINORR ROARING
AGINORS ORIGANS
SIGNORA
SOARING
AGINORT ORATING
AGINOTU AUTOING
OUTGAIN
AGINRRT TARRING
AGINRTT RATTING
TARTING
AGINSTT STATING
TASTING
AGINTTU TAUTING
AGIORST ORGIAST
AGIORSU GIAOURS
AGIOSTU AGOUTIS
AGIRSTU GUITARS
AGLNNOS LONGANS
AGLNNSU LUNGANS
AGLNOOS LAGOONS
AGLNORU LANGUOR
AGLNOSS SLOGANS
AGLNOSU LANUGOS
AGLNRSU LANGURS
AGLOORS GOORALS
AGLOOST GALOOTS
AGLORSU RUGOLAS
AGNNOOR ORGANON
AGNNSSU UNSNAGS
AGNORRS GARRONS
AGNORRT GRANTOR
AGNORSS SARONGS
AGNORSU OURANGS
AGNORTU OUTRANG
AGNOSTU NOUGATS
OUTSANG
AGORSSU RUGOSAS
AGORSTU RAGOUTS
AGOSTTU TAUTOGS
AIIILNT INITIAL
AIILNNS ANILINS
AIILNOS LIAISON
AIILNTU NAUTILI
AIINRSS RAISINS
AIINSST ISATINS
AIINSTT TITIANS
AILNNOS SOLANIN
AILNNOT ANTLION
AILNNSU UNNAILS
AILNOTU OUTLAIN
AILNRSU INSULAR
URINALS
AILNSST INSTALS
AILNSTT LATTINS
AILOORS OORALIS
AILORSS SAILORS
AILRSTT STARLIT
AILRSTU RITUALS
AILRTTU TITULAR
AILSSTU TISSUAL
AINNOSS NASIONS
AINNRTT INTRANT
AINNSTT INSTANT
AINOORT ORATION
AINORTU RAINOUT
AINOSSU SANIOUS
SUASION
AINSSTT STATINS
TANISTS
AINSSTU ISSUANT
SUSTAIN
AIOORSS ARIOSOS
AIORRSU OURARIS
AIORRTT TRAITOR
AIORSST AORISTS
ARISTOS
SATORIS
AIORSSU SOUARIS
AIORSTU SAUTOIR
AIOSSTT TATSOIS
AIRRSST RISTRAS
AIRSSTT ARTISTS
STRAITS
TSARIST
AIRSSTU AURISTS
AIRSTTU TURISTA
AISSTTU AUTISTS
ALNNOOR NONORAL
ALNNRSU UNSNARL
ALNOORT ORTOLAN
ALNOOSS SALOONS
SOLANOS
ALNORSU SOLUNAR
ALNOSST SANTOLS
STANOLS
ALNSSTU SULTANS
ALOORRS SORORAL
ALORRST ROSTRAL
ALORSTU TORULAS
ALOSTTU OUTLAST
ANNOSST SONANTS
ANNSSTU SUNTANS
ANOORTT ARNOTTO
RATTOON
ANRSSTU SANTURS
ANRSTTU TRUANTS
AOORRST ORATORS
AOORRTT ROTATOR
AOORRTU OUTROAR
AOORSTU OUTSOAR
AORRSST SARTORS
AORRSSU ASSUROR
AORSSTT STATORS
ARSSTTU STRATUS
DEEEGLT GLEETED
DEEEGNR GREENED
RENEGED
DEEEGRS DEGREES
DEEEGRT DETERGE
GREETED
DEEEGST EGESTED
DEEEINR NEEDIER
DEEEIRR REEDIER
DEEELNR NEEDLER
DEEELNS NEEDLES
DEEELST DELETES
SLEETED
STEELED
DEEENRS NEEDERS
SNEERED
DEEENRT ENTERED
DEEENTT DETENTE
DEEERSS RESEEDS
SEEDERS
DEEERST REESTED
STEERED
DEEGILN DELEING
DEEGILR LEDGIER
DEEGINN ENGINED
NEEDING
DEEGINR DREEING
ENERGID
REEDING
REIGNED
DEEGINS SEEDING
DEEGIST EDGIEST
DEEGLNS LEGENDS
DEEGLNT GENTLED
DEEGLRS GELDERS
LEDGERS
REDLEGS
DEEGLRU GRUELED
REGLUED
DEEGLSS SLEDGES
DEEGLSU DELUGES
DEEGNNO ENDOGEN
DEEGNRS GENDERS
DEEGNSU DENGUES
DEEGORR ROGERED
DEEGOSS GESSOED
DEEGSSU GUESSED
DEEGSTU GUESTED
DEEIIST DEITIES
DEEILNO ELOINED
DEEILNR REDLINE
RELINED
DEEILNS ENISLED
ENSILED
LINSEED
DEEILNT LENITED
DEEILOR REOILED
DEEILRT RETILED
DEEILSS DIESELS
IDLESSE
SEIDELS
DEEINNS INDENES
DEEINNT DENTINE
DEEINRR DERNIER
NERDIER
DEEINTT DINETTE
DEEINTU DETINUE
DEEIRRT RETIRED
RETRIED
TIREDER
DEEIRTU ERUDITE
DEEISSU DISEUSE
DEELNRS LENDERS
RELENDS
SLENDER
DEELNSS ENDLESS
DEELNST NESTLED
DEELNTT NETTLED
DEELOOS DOOLEES
DEELORS RESOLED
DEELORU URODELE
DEELOSU DELOUSE
DEELRSS ELDRESS
DEELRSU DUELERS
ELUDERS
DEELSTT SETTLED
DEELSTU TELEDUS
DEENNOS DONNEES
DEENNOT ENDNOTE
TENONED
DEENORT ERODENT
DEENOST DENOTES
DEENRRS RENDERS
DEENRRU ENDURER
DEENRSS REDNESS
RESENDS
SENDERS
DEENRSU ENDURES
ENSURED
DEENRTU DENTURE
RETUNED
TENURED
DEENSST DENSEST
DEENSSU DUENESS
DEENSTT DETENTS
DEEORRS REREDOS
DEEORTT TETRODE
DEERRSS DRESSER
REDRESS
DEERSST DESERTS
DESSERT
TRESSED
DEERTTU UTTERED
DEESSTT DETESTS
DEGIILN ELIDING
DEGIINN INDIGEN
DEGIINR DINGIER
DEGIINS DINGIES
DEGIINT DIETING
EDITING
IGNITED
DEGIIRR RIDGIER
DEGILNN LENDING
DEGILNO GLENOID
DEGILNS DINGLES
ENGILDS
SINGLED
DEGILNT GLINTED
TINGLED
DEGILNU DUELING
ELUDING
INDULGE
DEGILOR GLORIED
GODLIER
DEGILRR GIRDLER
DEGILRS GILDERS
GIRDLES
GLIDERS
REGILDS
RIDGELS
DEGILRU GUILDER
DEGINNR GRINNED
RENDING
DEGINNS ENDINGS
SENDING
DEGINNT DENTING
TENDING
DEGINNU ENDUING
DEGINOR ERODING
GROINED
IGNORED
NEGROID
REDOING
DEGINOT INGOTED
DEGINRR GRINDER
REGRIND
DEGINRU DUNGIER
DEGINSS DESIGNS
DEGINSU SUEDING
DEGINTU DUETING
DEGIOOS GOODIES
DEGIORR GRODIER
DEGIRRS GIRDERS
DEGIRSS DIGRESS
DEGIRSU GUIDERS
DEGIRTT GRITTED
DEGISST DIGESTS
DEGISSU GUSSIED
DEGLNNO ENDLONG
DEGLNOS DONGLES
DEGLNOU LOUNGED
DEGLNSU GULDENS
DEGLORS LODGERS
DEGLOSS GLOSSED
GODLESS
DEGLOST GOLDEST
DEGLOTU GLOUTED
DEGLSSU SLUDGES
DEGLTTU GLUTTED
GUTTLED
DEGNNOU DUNGEON
DEGNOOS NOODGES
DEGNORU GUERDON
UNDERGO
DEGNOTU TONGUED
DEGNRSU GERUNDS
NUDGERS
DEGNRTU GRUNTED
TRUDGEN
DEGOOST STOOGED
DEGORSS GROSSED
DEGORSU DROGUES
GOURDES
GROUSED
DEGORTU GROUTED
DEGOSST STODGES
DEGRRTU TRUDGER
DEGRSTU TRUDGES
DEGSSTU DEGUSTS
DEIILNS LINDIES
DEIINOS IODINES
IONISED
DEIINOT EDITION
DEIINRU URIDINE
DEIINSS INSIDES
DEIIORT DIORITE
DEIIOSS IODISES
DEIIRRT DIRTIER
DEIISTT DITTIES
TIDIEST
DEILNNS LINDENS
DEILNNU UNLINED
DEILNOO EIDOLON
DEILNOU UNOILED
DEILNRT TENDRIL
TRINDLE
DEILNTU DILUENT
DEILOTU TOLUIDE
DEILRSS SIDLERS
SLIDERS
DEILRTU DILUTER
DEILSST DELISTS
DEILSTT SLITTED
STILTED
DEILSTU DILUTES
DUELIST
DEINNOT INTONED
DEINNRU INURNED
DEINNSU UNDINES
DEINNTU DUNNITE
DEINORU DOURINE
NEUROID
DEINRTT TRIDENT
DEINSSU NIDUSES
DEIOOSS ISODOSE
DEIORTT DOTTIER
DEIORTU OUTRIDE
DEIRRSU DURRIES
DEIRSSU DISEURS
SUDSIER
DEISSTU STUDIES
TISSUED
DELNOOS NOODLES
SNOOLED
DELNORU ROUNDEL
DELNOSS OLDNESS
DELNOSU LOUDENS
NODULES
DELNRSU RUNDLES
DELNRTU RUNDLET
TRUNDLE
DELNSSU DULNESS
DELOORT ROOTLED
DELOOST STOOLED
TOLEDOS
DELOOTT TOOTLED
DELORSS DORSELS
RODLESS
SOLDERS
DELORTT DOTTREL
DELOSTT DOTTELS
DOTTLES
SLOTTED
DELOSTU LOUDEST
TOUSLED
DELRRSU SLURRED
DELRSTU LUSTRED
RUSTLED
STRUDEL
DELRTTU TURTLED
DELSSTU TUSSLED
DENNORT DONNERT
DENNOST TENDONS
DENNOTU UNNOTED
DENNSSU DUNNESS
DENNSTU DUNNEST
STUNNED
DENOOST SNOOTED
DENOOTU DUOTONE
OUTDONE
DENORRU RONDURE
ROUNDER
DENOSTU SNOUTED
DENRSSU SUNDERS
UNDRESS
DENSTTU STUDENT
STUNTED
DEOORRT REDROOT
DEOORTU OUTDOER
OUTRODE
DEOOSTU OUTDOES
DEORRSS DORSERS
DEORRSU ORDURES
DEORSSU DOUSERS
DEORTTU TUTORED
DEOSTTU TESTUDO
DERSSTU DUSTERS
TRUSSED
DERSTTU TRUSTED
DGIILNO LOIDING
DGIILNR DIRLING
DGIILNS SIDLING
SLIDING
DGIILRS RIDGILS
DGIINNT DINTING
DGIINNU INDUING
DGIINOS INDIGOS
DGIINRS RIDINGS
DGIINSS DISSING
SIDINGS
DGIINST TIDINGS
DGILNOR LORDING
DGILOST DIGLOTS
DGINNOR DRONING
DGINNOU UNDOING
DGINNRU DURNING
DGINNTU DUNTING
DGINOSS DOSSING
DGINOSU DOUSING
GUIDONS
DGINOTT DOTTING
DGINRSU UNGIRDS
DGINSSU SUDSING
DGINSTU DUSTING
DGISSTU DISGUST
DGLNORU GOLDURN
DGLOOSU DUOLOGS
DGNNORU NONDRUG
DGNOORS DRONGOS
DGNOOSS GODSONS
DGNORSU GROUNDS
DGNOSSU SUNDOGS
DGOORTT DOGTROT
DIILNNU INDULIN
DIILNOT TOLIDIN
DIILRSU SILURID
DIILSST DISTILS
DIINORS SORDINI
DIINORT DINITRO
DIINRST NITRIDS
DILNNSU DUNLINS
DILNOOS OODLINS
DILNOSU UNSOLID
DILNSTU INDULTS
DILORTU DILUTOR
DILOSSU SOLIDUS
DILOSTU TOLUIDS
DINOORS INDOORS
SORDINO
DINORSU DIURONS
DURIONS
DINSSTU NUDISTS
DIOORST DISROOT
TOROIDS
DIOORTT RIDOTTO
DIORRST STRIDOR
DIORSTT DISTORT
DIOSSTU STUDIOS
DLOORSU DOLOURS
DLOOSTU OUTSOLD
DLOOTTU OUTTOLD
DNOORTU OROTUND
DNOSSTU STOUNDS
DOORRSS SORDORS
DORSSTU STROUDS
EEEGILS ELEGIES
ELEGISE
EEEGINR GREENIE
EEEGLNT GENTEEL
EEEGNNO NEOGENE
EEEGNRR GREENER
REGREEN
RENEGER
EEEGNRS RENEGES
EEEGNSS GENESES
EEEGNTT GENETTE
EEEGRRT GREETER
REGREET
EEEILRR LEERIER
EEEIRRT RETIREE
EEELNST STELENE
EEELRRS REELERS
EEELSST TELESES
EEELSTU EUSTELE
EEENNTT ENTENTE
EEENRRS SERENER
SNEERER
EEENRRT ENTERER
REENTER
TERREEN
TERRENE
EEENRSS SERENES
EEERRST STEERER
EEERSTT TEETERS
EEESSTT SETTEES
TESTEES
EEGILNR LEERING
REELING
EEGILNS SEELING
EEGILNT GENTILE
EEGINNS ENGINES
EEGINNU GENUINE
INGENUE
EEGINSS GENESIS
SEEINGS
SIGNEES
EEGIRTT TERGITE
EEGLNOR ERELONG
EEGLNOU EUGENOL
EEGLNRT GENTLER
EEGLNST GENTLES
EEGLNSU LUNGEES
EEGLOSS EGOLESS
EEGLRRU GRUELER
EEGLRST REGLETS
EEGLRSU REGLUES
EEGNSSU GENUSES
NEGUSES
EEGRRSS REGRESS
SERGERS
EEGRRST REGRETS
EEGRRSU RESURGE

EEGRSSU GUESSER
EEGRSTT GETTERS
EEGRSTU GESTURE
EEILNNO LEONINE
EEILNNT LENIENT
EEILNSS ENISLES
ENSILES
SENILES
EEILNTT ENTITLE
EEILRRS RELIERS
EEILRSS IRELESS
RESILES
EEILRSU LEISURE
EEILRTT RETITLE
EEILSSU ILEUSES
EEINNRU NEURINE
EEINORR ONERIER
EEINOSS EOSINES
EEIORSS SOIREES
EEIRRSS RERISES
SERRIES
SIRREES
EEIRSSU REISSUE
SEISURE
EELNOTU TOLUENE
EELNRSU UNREELS
EELNRTT NETTLER
EELNSST NESTLES
NETLESS
EELNSTT NETTLES
TELNETS
EELNSTU ELUENTS
UNSTEEL
EELNTTU LUNETTE
EELORSS RESOLES
EELOSST TOELESS
EELOSTT TELEOST
EELRSST STREELS
TRESSEL
EELRSTT LETTERS
SETTLER
STERLET
TRESTLE
EELSSTT SETTLES
EENNORT ENTERON
TENONER
EENNORU NEURONE
EENNOSS ONENESS
EENNSST SENNETS
EENORSS SENORES
EENOSTU OUTSEEN
EENRRSU ENSURER
EENRSSU ENSURES
EENSSTT TENSEST
EEORRTU REROUTE
EEOSSTU OUTSEES
EERRSST RESTERS
EERRSTT TERRETS
EERRSTU URETERS
EERRTTU REUTTER
UTTERER
EERSSTT RETESTS
SETTERS
STREETS
TERSEST
TESTERS
EERSTTU TRUSTEE
EESSTTU SUTTEES
EGIILNR LINGIER
EGIILNT LIGNITE
EGIILRR GIRLIER
EGIILRS GIRLIES
EGIINNR GINNIER
REINING
EGIINNS INSIGNE
SEINING
EGIINSS SEISING
EGILNNS LENSING
EGILNRT RINGLET
TINGLER
EGILNSS SINGLES
EGILNTT LETTING
EGILNTU ELUTING
EGILOOS OLOGIES
EGILRSS GRILSES
EGILRSU LIGURES
EGILRTT GLITTER
EGILSST LEGISTS
EGILSTU GLUIEST
UGLIEST
EGINNOO IONOGEN
EGINNOR NEGRONI
EGINNRR GRINNER
EGINNRT RENTING
RINGENT
EGINNRU ENURING
EGINNSS ENSIGNS
SENSING
EGINNST NESTING
TENSING
EGINNSU ENSUING
GUNNIES
EGINNTT NETTING
TENTING
EGINOOR GOONIER
EGINORR IGNORER
EGINRTT GITTERN
RETTING
EGINSST INGESTS
SIGNETS
EGINSTT SETTING
TESTING
EGINSTU GUNITES
EGIOORS GOOSIER
EGIOOST GOOIEST
EGIORRS GORSIER
EGIORTU GOUTIER
EGIOSST EGOISTS
STOGIES
EGIOSTT EGOTIST
EGIRRST GRISTER
EGIRRSU GURRIES
EGIRRTT GRITTER
EGIRSST TIGRESS
EGIRTTU GUTTIER
TURGITE
EGLNNSU GUNNELS
EGLNORS LONGERS
EGLNORU LOUNGER
EGLNOST LONGEST
EGLNOSU LOUNGES
EGLNRSU LUNGERS
EGLNRTU GRUNTLE
EGLNSSU GUNLESS
GUNSELS
EGLNSTU ENGLUTS
GLUTENS
EGLOORS REGOSOL
EGLORSS GLOSSER
REGLOSS
EGLRTTU GUTTLER
EGLSSTU GUTLESS
TUGLESS
EGLSTTU GUTTLES
EGNNOOS NONEGOS
EGNNORT RONTGEN
EGNNOSU GUENONS
EGNNRSU GUNNERS
EGNOORS ORGONES
EGNOOST GENTOOS
EGNOOTU OUTGONE
EGNORSS ENGROSS
EGNORSU SURGEON
EGNOSTU TONGUES
EGNRRTU GRUNTER
EGNRTTU GRUTTEN
TURGENT
EGOOSST STOOGES
EGOOSTU OUTGOES
EGORRSS GROSSER
EGORRSU GROUSER
EGORRTU GROUTER
EGORSSU GROUSES
EGOSSTU GUSTOES
EGRRSSU SURGERS
EGRSTTU GUTTERS
EIIILST ILEITIS
EIILNTT INTITLE
EIILNTU INUTILE
EIILORR ROILIER
EIILSTT ELITIST
EIILSTU UTILISE
EIINNOS INOSINE
EIINOSS IONISES
EILNNSS INNLESS
EILNSSU SILENUS
EILORTT TORTILE
TRIOLET
EILORTU OUTLIER
EILRRSU SURLIER
EINNOOS IONONES
EINNORU REUNION
EINNOSS SONNIES
EINNOTT TONTINE
EINNRRU RUNNIER
EINNRSS SINNERS
EINNRSU SUNNIER
UNRISEN
EINNSST SENNITS
EINNSTT INTENTS
TENNIST
EINNSTU TUNNIES
EINRRSS RINSERS
EINRRSU INSURER
RUINERS
EINRSSU INSURES
SUNRISE
EIOORRT ROOTIER
EIOOSTT TOOTSIE
EIORRSS ORRISES
EIORSSU SERIOUS
EIRRSTT RITTERS
TERRITS
EIRRTTU RUTTIER
EIRSSTT SITTERS
ELNNORS RONNELS
ELNNOSS NELSONS
ELNNRSU RUNNELS
ELNNRTU TRUNNEL
ELNNSTU TUNNELS
ELNOOSS LOOSENS
ELNOOSU UNLOOSE
ELNOSST TELSONS
ELNOSSU ENSOULS
ELNOSTT TONLETS
ELNRSSU RUNLESS
ELNSTTU NUTLETS
ELOORTT ROOTLET
TOOTLER
ELOOSST LOOSEST
LOTOSES
ELOOSTT TOOTLES
ELOOSTU OUTSOLE
ELORRSS SORRELS
ELOSSTU LOTUSES
SOLUTES
TOUSLES
ELOSTTU OUTLETS
ELRRSTU RUSTLER
ELRRTTU TURTLER
ELRSSTU LUSTERS
LUSTRES
RESULTS
RUSTLES
SUTLERS
ULSTERS
ELRSTTU TURTLES
ENNORSU NEURONS
NONUSER
ENNORTU NEUTRON
ENNOSST SONNETS
ENNOSSU NONUSES
ENNOSTU NEUSTON
ENNRRSU RUNNERS
ENOORSS NOOSERS
SOONERS
ENOORSU ONEROUS
ENOOSST SOONEST
ENOOSTT TESTOON
ENORRSS SNORERS
SORNERS
ENORRTT TORRENT
ENOSSTT STETSON
TESTONS
ENOSSTU TONUSES
ENOSTTU STOUTEN
TENUTOS
ENRRSSU NURSERS
EOORRSS ROOSERS
EOORRST ROOSTER
ROOTERS
TOREROS
EOORSTT TOOTERS
EOOSSTT TOOTSES
EORRSST RESORTS
ROSTERS
SORTERS
STORERS
EORRSSU ROUSERS
EORRSTT RETORTS
ROTTERS
STERTOR
EORRSTU ROUSTER
ROUTERS
TOURERS
TROUSER
EORRTTU TORTURE
EORSSTU ESTROUS
OESTRUS
OUSTERS
SOUREST
SOUTERS
STOURES
TUSSORE
EORSTTU OUTSERT
STOUTER
TOUTERS
EOSSTTU OUTSETS
SETOUTS
ERRSSTU TRUSSER
ERRSTTU TRUSTER
TURRETS
GIIINRS IRISING
GIILNNS LIGNINS
LININGS
GIILNNT LINTING
GIILNOR LIGROIN
ROILING
GIILNOS SILOING
SOILING
GIILNOT TOILING
GIILNRT TIRLING
GIILNST LISTING
SILTING
TILINGS
GIILNTT TILTING
TITLING
GIILRST STRIGIL
GIINNOR IRONING
GIINNOS NOISING
GIINNRS RINSING
GIINNRT TRINING
GIINNRU INURING
RUINING
GIINNTT TINTING
GIINNTU UNITING
GIINORS ORIGINS
SIGNIOR
SIGNORI
GIINORT IGNITOR
RIOTING
GIINOTT TOITING
GIINRSS RISINGS
GIINSSU ISSUING
GIINSTT SITTING
GIINSTU SUITING
GILNNOO GLONOIN
GILNNRU NURLING
GILNNSU UNSLING
GILNNTU LUNTING
GILNOOS LOGIONS
LOOSING
OLINGOS
SOLOING
GILNOOT LOOTING
TOOLING
GILNORU LOURING
GILNOSS LOSINGS
GILNOST TIGLONS
GILNOSU LOUSING
GILNOTT LOTTING
GILNOTU LOUTING
GILNRSU RULINGS
GILNSTU LUSTING
LUTINGS
GILOORS GIROSOL
GILOOSS ISOLOGS
GILOOST OLOGIST
GILOSTT GLOTTIS
GINNOOS NOOSING
GINNORS SNORING
SORNING
GINNORU GRUNION
GINNOSS NOSINGS
GINNOST STONING
GINNRSU NURSING
GINNRTU TURNING
GINNTTU NUTTING
GINOORS ROOSING
GINOORT ROOTING
GINOOSS ISOGONS
GINOOST SOOTING
GINOOTT TOOTING
GINORSS GRISONS
SIGNORS
SORINGS
GINORSU ROUSING
SOURING
GINORTT ROTTING
GINORTU OUTGRIN
OUTRING
ROUTING
TOURING
GINOSST STINGOS
TOSSING
GINOSSU SOUSING
GINOSTU OUSTING
OUTINGS
OUTSING
TOUSING
GINOTTU TOUTING
GINRSST STRINGS
GINRSTU RUSTING
GINRTTU RUTTING
GIORRSU RIGOURS
GIORSTU OUTRIGS
GLNNOOR LORGNON
GLNOTTU GLUTTON
GNOORST TROGONS
GOORSTT GROTTOS
GORRSTU TURGORS
GORSTTU ROTGUTS
IILNNOT NITINOL
IILNNSU INSULIN
INULINS
IILNORS SIRLOIN
IILNRST NITRILS
IILNSST INSTILS
IINORTT INTROIT
IINOTTU TUITION
IINSTTU INTUITS
ILNNORU LINURON
ILNOORS ROSINOL
ILNOOSS SOLIONS
ILNOOST LOTIONS
SOLITON
ILNOSST TONSILS
ILNOSSU INSOULS
ILNSSTU INSULTS
ILOOSST SOLOIST
ILORSTU TROILUS
ILSSTTU LUTISTS
INNOORS RONIONS
INNOOST NOTIONS
INNOSSU UNISONS
INNOSTU NONSUIT
INNRSTU INTURNS
INOORSS ORISONS
INOORTT TORTONI
INOSSTT STOTINS
INOSSTU OUTSINS
INRSTTU INTRUST
IOORSST TSOORIS
IOORSTT RISOTTO
IOORSTU RIOTOUS
IORSSTU SUITORS
TSOURIS
IORSTTU TOURIST
IOSSTTU OUTSITS
LNOOSST STOLONS
NNORSTU TURNONS
NOORSTU UNROOTS
NRSSTTU STRUNTS
ORRSTTU TRUSTOR

Type II Eights, in Alphagram Order

AAADGLNS SALADANG
AAADIILR RADIALIA
AAADILRU ADULARIA
AAADNRSS SARDANAS
AAAEGLST GALATEAS
AAAENSST ANATASES
AAAGILNS ANALGIAS
AAAGINRR AGRARIAN
AAAGINRS ANGARIAS
AAAGLNSS LASAGNAS
AAAGLRST ASTRAGAL
AAAGNRSU GUARANAS
AAAILRST SALARIAT
AAALNNST LANTANAS
AAALNRTT TARLATAN
AAANRSTT TANTARAS
TARANTAS
TARTANAS
AAARSTTU TUATARAS
AADEEERT DEAERATE
AADEEGLR LAAGERED
AADEEGLT GALEATED
AADEEGNR GADARENE
AADEELNN ANNEALED
AADEELST DEALATES
AADEENTT ANTEDATE
AADEGILT GLADIATE
AADEGIRR GERARDIA
AADEGITT AGITATED
AADEGLNS SELADANG
AADEGNRR ARRANGED
AADEGRTU GRADUATE
AADEGSSU ASSUAGED
AADEILTT DILATATE
AADELSTU ADULATES
AADENRRT NARRATED
AADGIINS GAINSAID
AADGIIRS GIARDIAS
AADGILNO DIAGONAL
GONADIAL
AADGINRU GUARDIAN
AADGLNOR LARGANDO
AADGLNRS GARLANDS
AADGLRSU GRADUALS
AADGNRTU GUARDANT
AADIILNS SIALIDAN
AADILNRS LANIARDS
AADILNTT DILATANT
AADILORR RAILROAD
AADILRST DIASTRAL
AADINNOT ADNATION
AADINORT ANTIDORA
AADIORRT RADIATOR
AADLORST LOADSTAR
AADLORTU ADULATOR
LAUDATOR
AADOSSTT TOSTADAS
AAEEGILN ALIENAGE
AAEEGLST STEALAGE
AAEELNNR ANNEALER
AAEELORU AUREOLAE
AAEELRTU LAUREATE
AAEELSST ELASTASE
AAEGILTT TAILGATE
AAEGISTT AGITATES
AAEGLNOU ANALOGUE
AAEGLNSS LASAGNES
AAEGLNTU ANGULATE
AAEGLRRS REALGARS
AAEGNNST TANNAGES
AAEGNRRS ARRANGES
AAEGNSSU GUANASES
AAEGNSTT STAGNATE
AAEGORRT ARROGATE
AAEGORSS AGAROSES
AAEGRSSU ASSUAGER
AAEISSTT SATIATES
AAELNNOT NEONATAL
AAELNNTU ANNULATE
AAELNRTT ALTERANT
TARLETAN
AAENNOTT ANNOTATE
AAENNSTT TANNATES
AAENNSTU NAUSEANT
AAENORRU AUROREAN
AAENORTU AERONAUT
AAERSTTU SATURATE
TUATERAS
AAGIILNS ALIASING
AAGIINNU IGUANIAN
AAGIINST IGNATIAS
AAGILNRR LARRIGAN
AAGILRTT ATTAGIRL
AAGILSTT SAGITTAL
AAGINNOT AGNATION
AAGINNSU SAUNAING
AAGINOSS AGNOSIAS
AAGINRRS ARRAIGNS
AAGINRSS SANGRIAS
AAGINRSU GUARANIS
AAGINSST ASSIGNAT
AAGIORTT AGITATOR
AAGLNORS GRANOLAS
AAGLNRRU GRANULAR
AAGLORSU ARUGOLAS
AAGLRSTU GASTRULA
AAGNNSTT STAGNANT
AAGNORRT ARROGANT
TARRAGON
AAGNORTU ARGONAUT
AAGORSSU SAGUAROS
AAGRSSTU SASTRUGA
AAIINNRT ANTIARIN
AAIINSTT TITANIAS
AAILNNOT NATIONAL
AAILNNRU LUNARIAN
AAILNNST ANNALIST
AAILNORS ORINASAL
AAILNORT NOTARIAL
RATIONAL
AAILORRS RASORIAL
AAILRSTT RATTAILS
AAINNOTT NATATION
AAINORRS ROSARIAN
AAINRSSU SAURIANS
AAINSSTT SATANIST
AALNNOST SONANTAL
AALNRSTU NATURALS
AALNSSTU SULTANAS
AALNSTTU TANTALUS
AALORSST ALASTORS
AALORSSU AROUSALS
AALRSSTU AUSTRALS
AANNOSST ASSONANT
AANNOSTT ANNATTOS
AANRSTTU SATURANT
ADEEEGLT DELEGATE
ADEEEGNR RENEGADE
ADEEEGNT TEENAGED
ADEEEGRR REGEARED
ADEEEGRS DEGREASE
ADEEELST TEASELED
ADEEENNT NEATENED
ADEEENRR REEARNED
ADEEENTT ATTENDEE
EDENTATE
ADEEGLNR ENLARGED
ADEEGLNT DANEGELT
ADEEGNNR ENDANGER
ADEEGNRR DERANGER
GARDENER
GARNERED
ADEEGNRU DUNGAREE
UNAGREED
UNDERAGE
ADEEGNSS AGEDNESS
ADEEGORT DEROGATE
ADEEGRRS REGRADES
ADEEGRRT GARRETED
GARTERED
REGRATED
ADEEGRRU REARGUED
REDARGUE
ADEEGRSS DEGASSER
DRESSAGE
ADEEGRTT TARGETED
ADEEGSTT GESTATED
ADEELNNU UNANELED
ADEELNSU UNLEASED
UNSEALED
ADEELNTT TALENTED
ADEELORR RELOADER
ADEELORU AUREOLED
ADEELRRT TREADLER
ADEELSST DATELESS
DETASSEL
TASSELED
ADEENNRU UNEARNED
ADEENNTT TENANTED
ADEENOSS ADENOSES
SEASONED
ADEENOTT DETONATE
ADEENSSU DANSEUSE
ADEENTTU TAUTENED
ADEESSTT SEDATEST
ADEGIILN GLIADINE
ADEGIITT DIGITATE
ADEGILNN LADENING
ADEGILOU DIALOGUE
ADEGLNSS GLADNESS
ADEGNNSU DUNNAGES
ADEGNRRU GRANDEUR
ADEGORRT GARROTED
ADEGORTT GAROTTED
ADEGORTU OUTRAGED
RAGOUTED
ADEGRRSU GUARDERS
ADEGRSSU DESUGARS
GRADUSES
ADEILNNU UNNAILED
ADEILTTU ALTITUDE
LATITUDE
ADELNNOT LENTANDO
ADELNRTU DENTURAL
ADELRRTU ULTRARED
ADENNOTU UNATONED
ADENNRRU UNDERRAN
ADENRTTU TRUANTED
ADEOORRT TOREADOR
ADEORTTU OUTRATED
OUTTRADE
ADGIILNO GONIDIAL
ADGIILNS DIALINGS
GLIADINS
ADGIILNT DILATING
ADGIILST DIGITALS
ADGIINNR DRAINING
ADGIINNT NIDATING
ADGIINNU GUANIDIN
ADGIINOR RADIOING
ADGIINOT IODATING
ADGIINSS SIGANIDS
ADGIINSU IGUANIDS
ADGIINTU AUDITING
ADGILNNS LANDINGS
SANDLING
ADGILNNU UNLADING
ADGILNOS LOADINGS
ADGILNRS DARLINGS
ADGILNRT DARTLING
ADGILOOS SOLIDAGO
ADGILORS GOLIARDS
ADGINNOR ADORNING
ADGINNOT DONATING
ADGINNRS DARNINGS
ADGINNRU UNDARING
ADGINNST STANDING
ADGINNTU DAUNTING
ADGINOOR RIGADOON
ADGINORU RIGAUDON
ADGINRRS GRANDSIR
ADGINRTT DRATTING
ADGINRTU ANTIDRUG
ADGIORST GORDITAS
ADGIRSSU GUISARDS
ADGLNOOS DONGOLAS
GONDOLAS
ADGLNORS GOLDARNS
ADGNNORS GRANDSON
ADGNOORS DRAGOONS
GADROONS
ADGNRRSU GURNARDS
ADGORSTU OUTDRAGS
ADGRSSTU DUSTRAGS
ADIILNOT DILATION
ADIILNSU INDUSIAL
ADIILSST DIALISTS
ADIINNOT NIDATION
ADIINOOT IODATION
ADIINOTU AUDITION
ADIINSST DISTAINS
ADIIRSST DIARISTS
ADIIRSTT DISTRAIT
ADILNNOT NONTIDAL
ADILNNSU DISANNUL
ADILNOOR DOORNAIL
ADILNORS ORDINALS
ADILNORT TRINODAL
ADILNRSU DIURNALS
ADILNSSU SUNDIALS
ADILOORT IDOLATOR
TOROIDAL
ADILSSTU DUALISTS
ADINNOOT DONATION
ADINNORS ANDIRONS
ADINOORT TANDOORI
ADINOOTT DOTATION
ADINORSS SADIRONS
ADINORSU DINOSAUR
ADINORTU DURATION
ADIORRTT TRADITOR
ADIORSST SARODIST
ADIORSTU AUDITORS
ADLNNORS NORLANDS
ADLNNOTU NONADULT
ADLNNSSU SUNLANDS
ADLNOORS LARDOONS
ADLNOSST SANDLOTS
ADLNOSTU OUTLANDS
ADNOSSTU ASTOUNDS
ADNOSTTU OUTSTAND
STANDOUT
ADOOSSTT TOSTADOS
ADRSSTTU STARDUST
AEEEGLRT EGLATERE
REGELATE
RELEGATE
AEEEGLST LEGATEES
AEEEGNSS AGENESES
AEEGIIST GAIETIES
AEEGILOU EULOGIAE
AEEGLNNT ENTANGLE
AEEGLNOT ELONGATE
AEEGLNRR ENLARGER
AEEGLNSU EUGLENAS
AEEGLRTU REGULATE
AEEGLSST GATELESS
AEEGLSTT GALETTES
AEEGLTTU TUTELAGE
AEEGRRSS GREASERS
AEEGRRSU REARGUES
AEEGRRTT RETARGET
AEEGSSTT GESTATES
AEEILOTT ETIOLATE
AEELNNSS LEANNESS
AEELNORU ALEURONE
AEELRRTU URETERAL
AEENOTTU OUTEATEN
AEEORRSU REAROUSE
AEERRSSU ERASURES
REASSURE
AEGIILNN ALIENING
AEGIILRR GLAIRIER
AEGIILTT LITIGATE
AEGIIRRT IRRIGATE
AEGILNNU UNGENIAL
AEGIRRSS GRASSIER
AEGIRRSU SUGARIER
AEGISSTT STAGIEST
AEGLNNOR NONGLARE
AEGLNNTU UNTANGLE
AEGLNTTU GAUNTLET
AEGLRRSU REGULARS
AEGLSSTT GESTALTS
AEGNNSTT TANGENTS
AEGNNSTU TUNNAGES
AEGNSTTU GAUNTEST
AEGORRTT GAROTTER
GARROTTE
AEGORTTU TUTORAGE
AEGRRSSU SUGARERS
AEIIINTT INITIATE
AEIIIRRT RETIARII
AEIINTTU UINTAITE
AEISSTTU SITUATES
AELNNORU NEURONAL
AELNNRTU UNLEARNT
AENNORTU UNORNATE
AENOORRT RATOONER
AENSSTTU TAUTNESS
UNSTATES
AEORRSSU AROUSERS
AERRSSTT RESTARTS
STARTERS
AERSSTTU STATURES
AGIIILNS LIAISING
AGIIINNS INSIGNIA
AGIILNNS SNAILING
AGIILNNU INGUINAL
AGIILNOR ORIGINAL
AGIILNOT INTAGLIO
LIGATION
AGIILNRS RAILINGS
AGIILNRT RINGTAIL
TRAILING
AGIILNSS SAILINGS
AGIILNST TAILINGS
AGIILNSU LINGUISA
AGIILNTT LITIGANT
AGIILORU OLIGURIA
AGIINNRS INGRAINS
AGIINNRT TRAINING
AGIINNST SAINTING
STAINING
AGIINNTT TAINTING
AGIINORT RIGATONI
AGIINRSS RAISINGS
AGIINRTT ATTIRING
AGILNNOS LOANINGS
AGILNNRS SNARLING
AGILNNSS LINSANGS
AGILNNST SLANTING
AGILNOOS ISOGONAL
AGILNORT TRIGONAL
AGILNOSS GLOSSINA
LASSOING
AGILNOTT TOTALING
AGILNRSS RASSLING
AGILNRSU SINGULAR
AGILNRTT RATTLING
AGILNSST LASTINGS
SALTINGS
SLATINGS
AGILNSTT SLATTING
AGILNSTU SALUTING
AGILORSS GIRASOLS
AGINNORT IGNORANT
AGINNOSU ANGINOUS
AGINNOTT NOTATING
AGINNTTU ATTUNING
NUTATING
TAUNTING
AGINOORT ROGATION
AGINORRS GARRISON
ROARINGS
AGINORSS ASSIGNOR
SIGNORAS
SOARINGS
AGINORSU AROUSING
AGINORTT ROTATING
AGINRSSU ASSURING
AGIOORTU AUTOGIRO
AGIORSST ORGIASTS
AGIRSSTU SASTRUGI
AGLNORSU LANGUORS
AGLNOSST GLASNOST
AGNNOORS ORGANONS
AGNNORSU NONSUGAR
AGNRSSTU NUTGRASS
AIIILNST INITIALS
AIILNOSS LIAISONS
AIILNRSU SILURIAN
AIINORTT ANTIRIOT
AIINRRTT IRRITANT
AIIORRST SARTORII
AIIRSSTT SATIRIST
SITARIST
AILNNOOT NOTIONAL
AILNNOSS SOLANINS
AILNNOSU UNISONAL
AILNNOTU LUNATION
AILNNSTU INSULANT
AILNRSSU INSULARS
AILNRTTU RUTILANT
AILNSSTU STUNSAIL
AILNSTTU LUTANIST
AILORTTU TUTORIAL
AILRRSTU RURALIST
AILRSSTU TISSULAR
AILRSTTU ALTRUIST
TITULARS
ULTRAIST
AINNOOTT NOTATION
AINNOTTU NUTATION
AINNSSTT INSTANTS
AINOORTT ROTATION
AINORRTT NITRATOR
AINORRTU URINATOR
AIORRSTT TRAITORS
AIORSSTU SAUTOIRS
AIORSTTU TOURISTA
AIRSSTTU TURISTAS
ALNNOORS NONSOLAR
ALNNORRU NONRURAL
ALNNRSSU UNSNARLS
ALOSSTTU OUTLASTS
ANNOSSTU STANNOUS
ANOORSSU ARSONOUS
AOORRSTT ROTATORS
AOORRSTU OUTROARS
AOORSSTU OUTSOARS
AORSSTTU STRATOUS
DEEEERTT TEETERED
DEEEGILS ELEGISED
DEEEGINS DESIGNEE
DEEEGIRR GREEDIER
DEEEGLSS EDGELESS
DEEEGNNR ENGENDER
DEEEGRRT DETERGER
DEEEGRSS EGRESSED
DEEEGRST DETERGES
DEEEGRTT GETTERED
DEEEILNS SELENIDE
DEEEINRR REINDEER
DEEEISST SEEDIEST
DEEELNRS NEEDLERS

DEEELNRT RELENTED
DEEELNRU UNREELED
DEEELNSS LESSENED
NEEDLESS
DEEELNTT TELNETED
DEEELRST STREELED
DEEELRTT LETTERED
DEEENRRT RERENTED
TENDERER
DEEENRTT TENTERED
DEEENRTU NEUTERED
DEEENSTT DETENTES
DEEERRST DESERTER
DEEERSTT DETESTER
RETESTED
DEEGIINN INDIGENE
DEEGILNN NEEDLING
DEEGILNO ELOIGNED
DEEGILNR ENGIRDLE
LINGERED
REEDLING
DEEGILNS SEEDLING
DEEGILNT DELETING
DEEGILNU EUGLENID
DEEGINRR DERINGER
DEEGINSS EDGINESS
DEEGISST SEDGIEST
DEEGLNOR GOLDENER
DEEGNNOS ENDOGENS
DEEGNSTU NUTSEDGE
DEEGRRSU RESURGED
DEEGRSTU GESTURED
DEEGRTTU GUTTERED
DEEGSSTU GUSSETED
DEEIILNS SIDELINE
DEEILNRR REDLINER
DEEILNRU UNDERLIE
DEEILNSS IDLENESS
LINSEEDS
DEEILNTT ENTITLED
DEEILORT DOLERITE
LOITERED
DEEILOTT TOILETED
DEEILRTT LITTERED
RETITLED
DEELNNTU TUNNELED
DEELNOOS LOOSENED
DEELNORT REDOLENT
RONDELET
DEELNOSS LESSONED
DEELNOSU ENSOULED
DEELNRTU UNDERLET
DEELNTTU UNLETTED
DEELOORT RETOOLED
DEELORRS RESOLDER
SOLDERER
DEELORSU DELOUSER
URODELES
DEELORTT DOTTEREL
DEELOSSU DELOUSES
DEELRSTU DELUSTER
LUSTERED
RESULTED
DEENNOSS DONENESS
DEENNOST ENDNOTES
SONNETED
DEENNRTU UNRENTED
DEENNSSU NUDENESS
DEENNTTU UNTENTED
DEENOORT ENROOTED
DEENORTU DEUTERON
DEENOSST STENOSED
DEENRRSU ENDURERS
SUNDERER
DEENRRTU RETURNED
DEENRSSU RUDENESS
DEENSTTU UNTESTED
DEEORRTT RETORTED
DEEORRTU REROUTED
DEERRTTU TURRETED
DEERSTTU TRUSTEED
DEGIILNS SIDELING
DEGIILNT DILIGENT
DEGIINNR NIDERING
DEGIINNS INDIGENS
DEGIINNT ENDITING
INDIGENT
DEGIISSU DISGUISE
DEGILNRU INDULGER
DEGILNSU INDULGES
DEGILOOR GOODLIER
DEGILRRS GIRDLERS
DEGILRSU GUILDERS
SLUDGIER
DEGINNOT DENOTING
DEGINNRT TRENDING
DEGINNRU ENDURING
DEGINNSU UNSIGNED
DEGINNTU UNTINGED
DEGINOOR RODEOING
DEGINORR ORDERING
DEGINORU GUERIDON
DEGINSSU DINGUSES
DEGINTTU DUETTING
DEGLNOOT GOLDTONE
DEGLNRTU GRUNTLED
DEGNNOSU DUNGEONS
DEGNOOSS GOODNESS
DEGNOOST STEGODON
DEGNORRU GROUNDER
REGROUND
DEGNORTU TRUDGEON
DEGOORTT GROTTOED
DEGRRSTU TRUDGERS
DEIILNNU INDULINE
DEIILNTT INTITLED
DEIILSTU UTILISED
DEIINTTU INTUITED
DEIIRSSU DIURESIS
DEIISSTT DITSIEST
DEILNTTU UNTILTED
UNTITLED
DEILOORR DROOLIER
DEILRRSU SLURRIED
DEILSSTU DUELISTS
DEINNOOT NOONTIDE
DEINNORU UNIRONED
DEINOOSU IDONEOUS
DEIORRTU OUTRIDER
DEISSTTU DUSTIEST
DELNOOSU NODULOSE
UNLOOSED
DELNORTU ROUNDLET
DELNOSSU LOUDNESS
DELNRRTU TRUNDLER
DELOORSS DOORLESS
LORDOSES
ODORLESS
DELRSSTU STRUDELS
DENNOSTU UNSTONED
DENOORTU UNROOTED
DENOOSTU DUOTONES
DENOSSTU SOUNDEST
DENSSTTU STUDENTS
DEORRTTU TORTURED
DEOSSTTU TESTUDOS
DGIIINNT INDITING
DGIIINOS IODISING
DGIILNTU DILUTING
DGIINNOR NONRIGID
DGIINORR GRIDIRON
DGIINOTT DITTOING
DGIINRST STRIDING
DGIINSSU DISUSING
DGILNNOO NOODLING
DGILNOOR DROOLING
DGILNORS LORDINGS
DGINNOOS SNOODING
DGINNORU INGROUND
ROUNDING
DGINNOSU SOUNDING
UNDOINGS
DGINOOTU OUTDOING
DGINSSTU DUSTINGS
DGLNORSU GOLDURNS
DGOORSTT DOGTROTS
DIILNNSU INDULINS
DIILNOST TOLIDINS
DIILNOTU DILUTION
TOLUIDIN
DIILORSU SILUROID
DIILORTU UTILIDOR
DIILRSSU SILURIDS
DIINNOSU DISUNION
DIINOSSU SINUSOID
DIIORSST SISTROID
DILNNOOS NONSOLID
DILOORSS LORDOSIS
DILORSTU DILUTORS
DINOORRS INDORSOR
DIOORSST DISROOTS
DIOORSTT RIDOTTOS
DIORRSST STRIDORS
DIORSSTT DISTORTS
DIRSSTTU DISTRUST
EEEGILRT GLEETIER
EEEGILSS ELEGISES
EEEGINNR ENGINEER
EEEGINRR GREENIER
EEEGLNRT GREENLET
EEEGNRRS REGREENS
RENEGERS
EEEGNSTT GENETTES
EEEGRRST GREETERS
REGREETS
EEELNRRU UNREELER
EEELRRTT LETTERER
RELETTER
EEELRSST TREELESS
EEELRSTT RESETTLE
EEELSSTU EUSTELES
EEENNSTT ENTENTES
EEENRRSS SNEERERS
EEENRRTU RETURNEE
EEENRSSU ENURESES
EEERRSST STEERERS
EEERRSTT RESETTER
EEGIILNR LINGERIE
EEGILNRR LINGERER
EEGILNRU REGULINE
EEGILOSU EULOGIES
EULOGISE
EEGINNSU INGENUES
UNSEEING
EEGINORR ERIGERON
EEGINSSU GENIUSES
EEGLNNTU UNGENTLE
EEGLNOSU EUGENOLS
EEGLNSTT GENTLEST
EEGLRRSU GRUELERS
EEGNNORT ROENTGEN
EEGNNOSS GONENESS
EEGNORSU GENEROUS
EEGRRSSU RESURGES
EEGRRSTU GESTURER
EEGRSSTU GESTURES
EEILORRT LOITERER
EEILRRTT LITTERER
EEILRSSU LEISURES
EEIORRSS ROSERIES
EEIRRSSU REISSUER
EELNNOSS LONENESS
EELNNRTU TUNNELER
EELNOORS LOOSENER
EELNOSST NOTELESS
TONELESS
EELNOSSU SELENOUS
EELNOSTU TOLUENES
EELNSSTT TENTLESS
EELNSSTU TUNELESS
UNSTEELS
EELNSTTU LUNETTES
UNSETTLE
EELORTTU ROULETTE
EELOSSTT TELEOSTS
EELOSSTU SETULOSE
EELRSSTT SETTLERS
STERLETS
TRESTLES
EELRSSTU STREUSEL
EENNOORT ROTENONE
EENNORSU NEURONES
EENORRTT ROTTENER
EENORSSU NEUROSES
EENRRSSU ENSURERS
EERRSSTU TRESSURE
EERRSTTU REUTTERS
UTTERERS
EERSSTTU TRUSTEES
EGIILNNO ELOINING
EGIILNNR RELINING
EGIILNNS ENISLING
ENSILING
EGIILNNT LENITING
EGIILNNU LINGUINE
EGIILRRS GRISLIER
EGIILRTU GUILTIER
EGIINNTU UNTIEING
EGIIRRTT GRITTIER
EGILNNTT NETTLING
EGILNNTU GLUTENIN
EGILNSSU GLUINESS
UGLINESS
EGILOOSU ISOLOGUE
EGINNRRU UNERRING
EGINNSTT NETTINGS
EGINSSTT SETTINGS
EGIOOSST GOOSIEST
EGIORRTT GROTTIER
EGIORRTU GROUTIER
EGIORSSU GRISEOUS
EGIOSSTT EGOTISTS
EGIOSTTU GOUTIEST
EGIRRSST GRISTERS
EGIRRSTT GRITTERS
EGISSTTU GUSTIEST
GUTSIEST
EGLNNOOR LONGERON
EGLNNOSS LONGNESS
EGLNORSU LOUNGERS
EGLNRSSU RUNGLESS
EGLOORSS REGOSOLS
EGLORSSU ROSESLUG
EGLRSTTU GUTTLERS
EGNNOSTU NONGUEST
EGNNOTTU UNGOTTEN
EGNNSTTU TUNGSTEN
EGNORSSU SURGEONS
EGOORSTT GROTTOES
EGORRSSU GROUSERS
EGORRSTU GROUTERS
EIIIRSST IRITISES
EIILNTTU INTITULE
EIILORTT TROILITE
EIILSSTT ELITISTS
SILTIEST
EIILSSTU UTILISES
EIINNOSS INOSINES
EIINNOSU UNIONISE
EIIOSSTT OSTEITIS
OTITISES
EILORRTU ULTERIOR
EILRRSSU SLURRIES
EILSSTTU LUSTIEST
EINNOSSU NONISSUE
UNSONSIE
EINNSSTT TENNISTS
EINNSSTU SUNNIEST
EINRRSSU INSURERS
EINSSTTU NUTSIEST
EIOOSSTT SOOTIEST
TOOTSIES
EIORRTTU TROUTIER
ELNNOOSU UNLOOSEN
ELNNORSS LORNNESS
ELNNOSSU NOUNLESS
ELNOOSST SOLONETS
ELNOOSSU UNLOOSES
ELOOSSTU OUTSOLES
ELRRSSTU RUSTLERS
ELRRSTTU TURTLERS
ENNORSSU NONUSERS
ENNOSSTU NEUSTONS
SUNSTONE
ENOOSSTT TESTOONS
ENOSSTTU STOUTENS
EOORRSST ROOSTERS
EOORSSTU OESTROUS
EORRSSTT STERTORS
EORRSSTU ROUSTERS
TRESSOUR
TROUSERS
EORRSTTU TORTURES
EORSSTTU OUTSERTS
TUTORESS
ERRSSTTU TRUSTERS
GIIILNNU LINGUINI
GIIINNOS IONISING
GIIINNOT IGNITION
GIIINORS SIGNIORI
GIILNORS LIGROINS
GIILNSST LISTINGS
GIILNSTT SLITTING
STILTING
GIILNSTU LINGUIST
GIILRSST STRIGILS
GIINNORS IRONINGS
NIGROSIN
ROSINING
GIINNORT IGNITRON
GIINNRSS RINSINGS
GIINNRSU INSURING
GIINNRTU UNTIRING
GIINNSTT STINTING
TINTINGS
GIINORSS SIGNIORS
GIINRRST STIRRING
GIINSSTT SITTINGS
GIINSSTU SUITINGS
TISSUING
GIIORRST RIGORIST
GILNNOOS GLONOINS
SNOOLING
GILNNOTU NONGUILT
GILNNRSU NURSLING
GILNNSSU UNSLINGS
GILNOORT ROOTLING
GILNOOST STOOLING
TOOLINGS
GILNOOTT TOOTLING
GILNOSTT SLOTTING
GILNOSTU TOUSLING
GILNRRSU SLURRING
GILNRSTU LUSTRING
RUSTLING
GILNRTTU TURTLING
GILNSSTU TUSSLING
GILOORSS GIROSOLS
GILOORSU GLORIOUS
GILOOSST OLOGISTS
GINNOOST SNOOTING
GINNORSU GRUNIONS
GINNOSTU SNOUTING
GINNRSSU NURSINGS
GINNRSTU TURNINGS
UNSTRING
GINNSTTU NUTTINGS
STUNTING
GINORTTU TUTORING
GINOSSTU OUTSINGS
GINRSSTU TRUSSING
GINRSTTU TRUSTING
GIOORRSU RIGOROUS
GIOORSTU GOITROUS
GLNNOORS LORGNONS
GLNOSTTU GLUTTONS
GOORSSTU OUTGROSS
IIIOSTTU OUISTITI
IILNNOST NITINOLS
IILNNSSU INSULINS
IILNOOST INOSITOL
IILNORSS SIRLOINS
IINNOSTU UNIONIST
IINNSTTU TINNITUS
IINOSTTU TUITIONS
ILNNORSU LINURONS
ILNOORSS ROSINOLS
ILNOOSST SOLITONS
ILNOOSTU SOLUTION
INNORTTU NOTTURNI
INNOSSTU NONSUITS
INOORSSU ROSINOUS
INRSSTTU INTRUSTS
IOORSSTT RISOTTOS
IOORSTTU TORTIOUS
IORSSTTU TOURISTS
NNOORTTU NOTTURNO
ORRSSTTU TRUSTORS

Type III Sevens and Eights, in Alphagram Order

One advantage of having familiarity with the Type III's is the gained confidence you will have in challenging your opponent. If, say, THURNEL were played, I might deduce, probability-wise, it should be equivalent to HUNTERS (both contain HUNTER, and both S and L are frequency-four tiles), which should then qualify THURNEL as a Type III seven-letter bingo, if it were good. If I couldn't recall it being on the list, I might then more readily challenge.

Let's say someone played DIABLOS against me. Let's assume I have no recollection of it being on the Type III listings. (I know that it is not a Type I since ADOILS is not a Top 100 stem, and I know that it is not a Type II because the B disqualifies it as a 3%er.) My only question to myself is: Is the probability of DIABLOS too low to qualify as a Type III? If its pobability is less than HUNTERS, I may be less willing to challenge. If its probability is equal to or greater than HUNTERS (and therefore should have been on the Type III list), I am more likely to challenge. How to determine its probability? Here's how:

1. Write out the two compared words with the letter frequency above each letter and cross off the letters in HUNTERS and DIABLOS that have identical letter frequencies:

2. Look at the remaining letters and frequencies: The NTER (6 × 6 × 12 × 6) of HUNTERS is just as likely as the IALO (9 × 9 × 4 × 8) of DIABLOS. Without completing the entire multiplication, we know (6 × 6) × (6 × 12) = (9 × 4) × (9 × 8), i.e., 36 × 72 = 36 × 72. We can conclude that the probabilities of DIABLOS and HUNTERS are identical.

3. Now, knowing that DIABLOS, were it good, would qualify as a Type III, and having no recollection of its appearance on the list, you may more confidently challenge.

Assigning frequency values to duplicated letters in a word is a bit trickier. Suffice it to say, a second E is assigned a value of 5.5, a second A or I is a 4, a second O equals 3.5, a second N, R, or T is 2.5, a second D, L, S. Or U rates a 1.5, and a second G gets a 1.

Is ERRHINE a Type III? First, compare with HUNTERS and cross off identical frequencies:

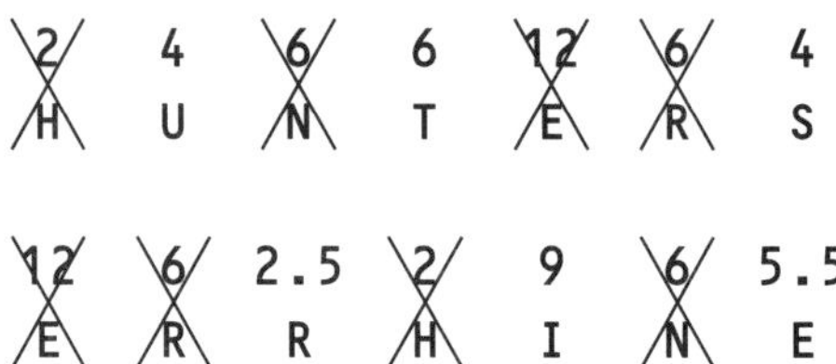

With HERN removed from both, we're left with UTS (4 × 6 × 4 = 96) of HUNTERS vs. RIE (2.5 × 9 × 5.5 = 123.75) of ERRHINE. Since 123.75 is greater than 96, we can conclude that ERRHINE is more likely than HUNTERS and therefore would qualify as a TYPE III word.

If one wishes to deduce the relative probability of an eight-letter word, it should be compared against NOTIFIED, which is tied for last among the least likely Type III eights. Remember that the second I is assigned a frequency of 4.

Type III Sevens, in Alphagram Order

AAAEIMN ANAEMIA
AABDEIS DIABASE
AABDELT ABLATED
DATABLE
AABDENU BANDEAU
AABDERS ABRADES
AABDINT TABANID
AABDNOR BANDORA
AABEELT EATABLE
AABEILN ABELIAN
AABEILS ABELIAS
AABEILT LABIATE
AABEIOR AEROBIA
AABELNO ABALONE
AABELRS ARABLES
AABELRT RATABLE
AABELST ABLATES
AABELTU TABLEAU
AABEMNO AMOEBAN
AABENRT ANTBEAR
AABEORT AEROBAT
AABERST ABATERS
ABREAST
AABERSU SUBAREA
AABILOU ABOULIA
AABINOU OUABAIN
AABINST ABSTAIN
AABIORS ABROSIA
AABIORT AIRBOAT
AABIRST BARISTA
AABLORT ABLATOR
AABNOST SABATON
AABORST ABATORS
RABATOS
AACDEII AECIDIA
AACDEIL ALCAIDE
AACDEIR CARDIAE
AACDEIS ACEDIAS
AACDELN CANALED
CANDELA
DECANAL
AACDELR CALDERA
CRAALED
AACDENR DRACENA
AACDERS ARCADES
ASCARED
AACDETU CAUDATE
AACDINT ANTACID
AACDIOR ACAROID
AACEEGR ACREAGE
AACEENT CATENAE
AACEERT ACERATE
AACEEST CASEATE
AACEGNR CARNAGE
AACEGRT CARTAGE
AACEHNO CHOANAE
AACEIMN ANAEMIC
AACEINR ACARINE
CARINAE
AACEIRV AVARICE
CAVIARE
AACELNS ANLACES
AACELNT LACTEAN
AACELNU CANULAE
LACUNAE
AACELOR ACEROLA
AACELRS SCALARE
AACELST ACETALS
LACTASE
AACENRT CATERAN
AACENST CATENAS
AACEOPT PEACOAT
AACEORS ROSACEA
AACERST CARATES
AACERSU CAESURA
AACERTU ARCUATE
AACIINT ACTINIA
AACILNR CARINAL
CRANIAL
AACILNT ACTINAL
AACILOS ASOCIAL
AACINOR OCARINA
AACINRS ACRASIN
ARNICAS
CARINAS
SARCINA
AACINRT ANTICAR
AACINST SATANIC
AACIRST CARITAS
AACNOST SACATON
AACORST OSTRACA
AADDEIL ALIDADE
AADDEOR DEODARA
AADEEFR AFEARED
AADEEMT EDEMATA
AADEERW AWARDEE
AADEHIR AIRHEAD
AADEILV AVAILED
VEDALIA
AADEIMR MADEIRA
AADEIMS AMIDASE
AADEINZ ZENAIDA
AADEITV AVIATED
AADEITW AWAITED
AADELMN LEADMAN
AADELMO ALAMODE
AADELMR ALARMED
AADELRY ALREADY
AADEMNO ADENOMA
AADEMNS ANADEMS
MAENADS
AADEMNT MANDATE
AADENRV VERANDA
AADENSW WEASAND
AADEPRS PARADES
AADEPRT ADAPTER
READAPT
AADERSW SEAWARD
AADERSY DARESAY
AADIMOR DIORAMA
AADINPT PINTADA
AADMNOR MADRONA
MONARDA
AADMORT MATADOR
AADNOPR PANDORA
AADOPRT ADAPTOR
AAEEFRT RATAFEE
AAEEGMT AGAMETE
AGEMATE
AAEEGRV AVERAGE
AAEEHRT HETAERA
AAEELMT MALEATE
AAEELPT PALEATE
AAEEMNT EMANATE
ENEMATA
MANATEE
AAEEMRT AMREETA
AAEERSW SEAWARE
AAEERTW TEAWARE
AAEFIRR AIRFARE
AAEGHNT THANAGE
AAEGINV VAGINAE
AAEGLOP APOGEAL
AAEGMNR MANAGER
AAEGMNT GATEMAN
MAGENTA
MAGNATE
NAMETAG
AAEGMRT REGMATA
AAEGNOP APOGEAN
AAEGNPT PAGEANT
AAEGNTV VANTAGE
AAEGNTW WANTAGE
AAEHIRT HETAIRA
AAEHLRT TREHALA
AAEHLST ALTHEAS
AAEILMN LAMINAE
AAEILMS MALAISE
AAEILRV REAVAIL
VELARIA
AAEIMNS AMNESIA
ANEMIAS
AAEIMRT AMIRATE
AAEIMRU URAEMIA
AAEIMTV AMATIVE
AAEINPS PAESANI
AAEINPT PATINAE
AAEIPRR PAREIRA
AAEIPRT APTERIA
AAEIPTT APATITE
AAEIRTV VARIATE
AAEIRTW AWAITER
AAEIRVW AIRWAVE
AAEISTV AVIATES
AAEISTX ATAXIES
AAELLRT LATERAL
AAELMNU ALUMNAE
AAELMOT OATMEAL
AAELMST MALATES
MALTASE
TAMALES
AAELNOP APNOEAL
AAELNPR PREANAL
AAELNPT PLANATE
PLATANE
AAELNSY ANALYSE
AAELNTY ANALYTE
AAELOTX OXALATE
AAELPRS EARLAPS
AAELPRT APTERAL
AAELPST PALATES
AAELPTU PLATEAU
AAELTUV VALUATE
AAEMNOR AMARONE
AAEMNRT RAMENTA
AAEMNTU MANTEAU
AAEMOTY ATEMOYA
AAEMRTU AMATEUR
AAENOPS APNOEAS
PAESANO
AAENPST ANAPEST
PEASANT
AAENRTV TAVERNA
AAENRUW UNAWARE
AAENSTW SEAWANT
AAFILNT FANTAIL
TAILFAN
AAFINRS FARINAS
AAGIMNO ANGIOMA
AAHINST SHAITAN
AAILMNR LAMINAR
AAILMNT MATINAL
AAILMRT MARITAL
MARTIAL
AAILNOV VALONIA
AAILNPT PLATINA
AAILNRY LANIARY
AAILNTV VALIANT
AAILNTY ANALITY
AAILORV OVARIAL
VARIOLA
AAILPRT PARTIAL
AAILRTV TRAVAIL
AAIMNOS ANOSMIA
AAIMNOT ANIMATO
AAIMNRS MARINAS
AAIMNRT MARTIAN
TAMARIN
AAIMNST STAMINA
AAIMRST AMRITAS
TAMARIS
AAIMRTU TIMARAU
AAINOPS ANOPIAS
ANOPSIA
PAISANO
AAINORV OVARIAN
AAINPRS PARIANS
PIRANAS
AAINPST PASTINA
PATINAS
PINATAS
TAIPANS
AAINRSV SAVARIN
AAINRTV VARIANT
AAINRTW ANTIWAR
AAIOPRS APORIAS
AAIORTV AVIATOR
AAMNORS OARSMAN
RAMONAS
AAMNOTU AUTOMAN
ABCDEIN CABINED
ABCDEIR CARBIDE
ABCDEOR BROCADE
ABCEILR CALIBER
CALIBRE
ABCEILT CITABLE
ABCEINR CARBINE
ABCEINT CABINET
ABCEIOR AEROBIC
ABCEIOT ICEBOAT
ABCEIRS ASCRIBE
CARIBES
ABCENOS BEACONS
ABCEORS BORACES
ABCINOR CORBINA
ABCINOT BOTANIC
ABDEEIR BEADIER
ABDEELN ENABLED
ABDEELR BLEARED
ABDEELT BELATED
BLEATED
ABDEERS BEADERS
DEBASER
SABERED
ABDEERT BERATED
DEBATER
REBATED
TABERED
ABDEEST BESTEAD
DEBATES
ABDEFOR FORBADE
ABDEGIN BEADING
ABDEGIR ABRIDGE
BRIGADE
ABDEGNO BONDAGE
DOGBANE
ABDEGOS BODEGAS
ABDEHIT HABITED
ABDEIIL ALIBIED
ABDEILU AUDIBLE
ABDEIMO AMEBOID
ABDEIRR BRAIDER
ABDEIRU DAUBIER
ABDEIRW BAWDIER
ABDEISU SUBIDEA
ABDELNR BLANDER
ABDELNU UNBALED
ABDELOR LABORED
ABDELOS ALBEDOS
ABDELOT BLOATED
LOBATED
ABDELRU DURABLE
ABDELST BALDEST
BLASTED
STABLED
ABDELTU ABLUTED
ABDEMNO ABDOMEN
ABDENRT BARTEND
ABDENSU SUBDEAN
UNBASED
ABDENTU UNBATED
ABDEOOT TABOOED
ABDEORR ARBORED
BOARDER
BROADER
REBOARD
ABDEORT ABORTED
BORATED
TABORED
ABDEORV BRAVOED
ABDERSU DAUBERS
EARBUDS
ABDGINO ABODING
ABDILOR LABROID
ABDILOT TABLOID
ABDINOR INBOARD
ABDINOT BANDITO
ABDINRS RIBANDS
ABDINRU UNBRAID
ABDINST BANDITS
ABDNORS ROBANDS
ABEEGLT GETABLE
ABEEGNR REBEGAN
ABEEGRS BAREGES
BARGEES
ABEEGRU AUBERGE
ABEEHNT BENEATH
ABEEHRT BREATHE
ABEEILS BAILEES
ABEEIMR BEAMIER
ABEEINS BEANIES
ABEEIST BEASTIE
ABEELNR ENABLER
ABEELNS BALEENS
ENABLES
ABEELNT TENABLE
ABEELNU NEBULAE
ABEELOR EARLOBE
ABEELRT BLEATER
RETABLE
ABEENRV VERBENA
ABEENRY BEANERY
ABEEORS AEROBES
ABEERRT REBATER
ABEERTT ABETTER
BERETTA
ABEFILN FINABLE
ABEFILR FRIABLE
ABEFIRT BAREFIT
ABEGINN BEANING
ABEGINO BEGONIA
ABEGINT BEATING
ABEGLOT GLOBATE
ABEGNOR BEGROAN
ABEGNOS NOSEBAG
ABEGNRS BANGERS
GRABENS
ABEGORS BORAGES
ABEHILR HIRABLE
ABEHINS BANSHIE
ABEHIRS BEARISH
ABEHITU HABITUE
ABEIILS ALIBIES
BAILIES
BIALIES
ABEIINN BIENNIA
ABEILLO LOBELIA
ABEILMN MINABLE
ABEILMR BALMIER
LAMBIER
ABEILMT BIMETAL
LIMBATE
TIMBALE
ABEILNP BIPLANE
ABEILRW BRAWLIE
WIRABLE
ABEILRY BILAYER
ABEIMRS AMBRIES
ABEINPT BEPAINT
ABEINRR BARNIER
ABEIOSS ABIOSES
ABEIOTV OBVIATE
ABEIPST BAPTISE
ABEIRRS BRASIER
ABEIRRT ARBITER
RAREBIT
ABEIRTV VIBRATE
ABEISTT BATISTE
BISTATE
ABEISTW BAWTIES
ABELNOT NOTABLE
ABELNOW OWNABLE
ABELNOY BALONEY
ABELNRU NEBULAR
ABELNSU NEBULAS
UNBALES
ABELNTU ABLUENT
TUNABLE
ABELOPR ROPABLE
ABELOPT POTABLE
ABELORR LABORER
ABELORU RUBEOLA
ABELORW ROWABLE
ABELOTT TOTABLE
ABELOTV VOTABLE
ABELOTW TEABOWL
TOWABLE
ABELSTU SUBLATE
ABEMNOS AMBONES
BEMOANS
ABEMNOT BOATMEN
ABEMORT BROMATE
ABEMOTU OUTBEAM
ABENNOR BARONNE
ABENORT BARONET
REBOANT
ABENOSY SOYBEAN
ABENOTY BAYONET
ABENRSU UNBEARS
ABENSTU BUTANES
ABEOOST SEABOOT
ABEOPRS SAPROBE
ABEOPRT PROBATE
ABEORRS ARBORES
ABEORRT ABORTER
TABORER
ABEORSV BRAVOES
ABEORSY ROSEBAY
ABEORTT ABETTOR
TABORET
ABERSTU ARBUTES
BURSATE
ABGILOR GARBOIL
ABGINOS BAGNIOS
GABIONS
ABGINOT BOATING
ABHIORT BOTHRIA
ABILNOS ALBINOS
ABILORS BAILORS
ABILORT ORBITAL
ABILOTU BAILOUT
TABOULI
ABILRST TRIBALS
ABINOOT BONIATO
ABINORT TABORIN
ABINORW RAINBOW
ABIORTV VIBRATO
ABLNOTU BUTANOL
ABLORST BORSTAL
ABORSTU ABORTUS
ROBUSTA
RUBATOS
TABOURS
ACDEEGN ENCAGED
ACDEEIR DECIARE
ACDEELN CLEANED
ENLACED
ACDEELR CLEARED
CREEDAL
DECLARE
RELACED
ACDEELT CLEATED
ACDEENR RECANED
ACDEENS DECANES
ENCASED
ACDEENT ENACTED
ACDEERS CREASED
DECARES
ACDEERT CATERED
CERATED
CREATED
REACTED
ACDEETU EDUCATE
ACDEFIN FACIEND
FANCIED
ACDEGIN INCAGED
ACDEGLO DECALOG
ACDEGNO CONGAED
DECAGON
ACDEGOR CORDAGE
ACDEHIN CHAINED
ECHIDNA
ACDEHIR CHAIRED
ACDEHOR ROACHED
ACDEHOT CATHODE
ACDEILN INLACED
ACDEILT CITADEL
DELTAIC
DIALECT
EDICTAL
ACDEINO CODEINA
ACDEINY CYANIDE
ACDEIOS CODEIAS
ACDEIPR PERACID
ACDEIRR ACRIDER
CARRIED
ACDEITT DICTATE
ACDEITY EDACITY
ACDELNO CELADON
ACDELNR CANDLER
ACDELNS CALENDS
CANDLES
ACDELNU UNLACED
ACDELOR CAROLED
ACDELOS COLEADS
SOLACED
ACDELOT LOCATED
ACDELST CASTLED
ACDEMOR CAROMED
COMRADE
ACDENOS ACNODES
DEACONS
ACDENOT TACNODE
ACDENRT TRANCED
ACDENRU DURANCE
ACDENSU UNCASED
ACDENTU UNACTED
ACDEOPT COAPTED
ACDEORR CORRADE
ACDEORT CORDATE
REDCOAT
ACDERSU CRUSADE
ACDERTU CURATED
TRADUCE
ACDGINO GONADIC
ACDIINO CONIDIA
ACDIIRT TRIACID
TRIADIC
ACDILNO NODICAL
ACDILOR CORDIAL
ACDILOT COTIDAL
ACDILRT TRICLAD
ACDINRU IRACUND
ACDINST DISCANT
ACDIORS SARCOID
ACDIORT CAROTID
ACDIOST DACOITS
ACDIRST DRASTIC
ACDIRTU DATURIC
ACDLNOR CALDRON
ACDNORS CANDORS
CARDONS
DACRONS
ACDNORU CANDOUR
ACDORST COSTARD
ACEEFIN FAIENCE
FIANCEE
ACEEGIL ELEGIAC
ACEEGNS ENCAGES
ACEEGOT ECOTAGE
ACEEHOR OCHREAE
ACEEHRT CHEATER
HECTARE
RECHEAT
RETEACH
TEACHER
ACEEILP CALIPEE
ACEEINU EUCAINE
ACEEISV VESICAE
ACEELNR CLEANER
RECLEAN
ACEELNS CLEANSE
ENLACES
SCALENE
ACEELRT TREACLE
ACEELST CELESTA
ACEEMNR MENACER
ACEEMNT CEMENTA
ACEEMRT CREMATE
ACEENNT CANTEEN
ACEENOT ACETONE
ACEENTU CUNEATE
ACEEORS ACEROSE
ACEEORT OCREATE
ACEEOST ACETOSE
COATEES
ACEERRT CATERER
RECRATE
RETRACE
TERRACE
ACEERSU CESURAE
ACEFINR FANCIER
ACEFINS FANCIES
FASCINE
FIANCES
ACEFINU UNIFACE
ACEFIRS FARCIES
FIACRES
ACEFOTU OUTFACE
ACEGILN ANGELIC
ANGLICE
GALENIC
ACEGILR GLACIER
GRACILE
ACEGINO COINAGE
ACEGIOP APOGEIC
ACEGIRT CIGARET
ACEGIST CAGIEST
ACEGLNO CONGEAL
ACEGLNR CLANGER
GLANCER
ACEGNOR ACROGEN
ACEGNOT COAGENT
COGNATE
ACEGORS CARGOES
CORSAGE
SOCAGER
ACEGORU COURAGE
ACEHILR CHARLIE
ACEHILT ETHICAL
ACEHINR ARCHINE
ACEHINS CHAINES
ACEHIOT ACHIOTE
ACEHIRS CAHIERS
CASHIER
ACEHIRT THERIAC
ACEHIST ACHIEST
AITCHES
ACEHLNO CHALONE
ACEHLOR CHOLERA
CHORALE
CHOREAL
ACEHLOT CHOLATE
ACEHNRT CHANTER
TRANCHE
ACEHORS CHOREAS
ORACHES
ROACHES
ACEIILS LAICISE
ACEIILT CILIATE
ACEILMN MELANIC
ACEILMR CLAIMER
MIRACLE
RECLAIM
ACEILMT CLIMATE
METICAL
ACEILNN ENCINAL
ACEILNP CAPELIN
PANICLE
PELICAN
ACEILNU CAULINE
ACEILOR CALORIE
CARIOLE
COALIER
LORICAE
ACEILOT ALOETIC
ACEILPR CALIPER
REPLICA
ACEILPT PLICATE
ACEILRU AURICLE
ACEILRV CAVILER
CLAVIER
VALERIC
ACEILRY CLAYIER

ACEILTT LATTICE
TACTILE
ACEIMNO ENCOMIA
ACEIMNR CARMINE
ACEIMNS AMNESIC
CINEMAS
ACEIMOR COREMIA
ACEIMRU URAEMIC
ACEIMST SEMATIC
ACEINNR CANNIER
NARCEIN
ACEINNS CANINES
ENCINAS
ACEINNT ANCIENT
ACEINOP APNOEIC
ACEINPR CAPRINE
ACEINPS INSCAPE
ACEINPT PICANTE
ACEINTT NICTATE
TETANIC
ACEINTU TUNICAE
ACEINTV VENATIC
ACEINTY CYANITE
ACEIOPT ECTOPIA
ACEIORT EROTICA
ACEIOTX EXOTICA
ACEIPRT PARETIC
PICRATE
ACEIPST ASEPTIC
PACIEST
SPICATE
ACEIRRS CARRIES
SCARIER
ACEIRRT CIRRATE
ERRATIC
ACEIRSU SAUCIER
ACEIRSV VARICES
VISCERA
ACEISTT CATTIES
STATICE
ACEISTV ACTIVES
ACELNNO ALENCON
ACELNOP NOPLACE
ACELNOR CORNEAL
ACELNOT LACTONE
ACELNRT CENTRAL
ACELNRU LUCARNE
NUCLEAR
UNCLEAR
ACELNSU CENSUAL
LACUNES
LAUNCES
UNLACES
ACELOPT POLECAT
ACELORR CAROLER
ACELORY CALOYER
ACELOTT CALOTTE
ACELOTY ACOLYTE
ACELRSU RECUSAL
SECULAR
ACELSTU SULCATE
ACEMNOR ROMANCE
ACEMORU MORCEAU
ACEMOST COMATES
ACENNOS ANCONES
SONANCE
ACENNOT CONNATE
ACENOOR CORONAE
ACENORT ENACTOR
ACENOTV CENTAVO
ACENRTU CENTAUR
UNCRATE
ACENRTY NECTARY
ACENSTU NUTCASE
ACEOPST CAPOTES
TOECAPS
ACEOPTU OUTPACE
ACEORRS COARSER
ACEORRT CREATOR
REACTOR
ACEORSU ACEROUS
CAROUSE
ACEORTU OUTRACE
ACEORTV OVERACT
ACEOSTT COSTATE
ACEOSTU ACETOUS
ACEOSTV AVOCETS
OCTAVES
ACERSTU CURATES
ACFINOT FACTION
ACGILNO COALING
ACGILOT OTALGIC
ACGINOR ORGANIC
ACGINOT COATING
COTINGA
ACGINRT CARTING
CRATING
TRACING
ACGIORT ARGOTIC
ACHIORT CHARIOT
HARICOT
ACIIRST SATIRIC
ACILNOR CLARION
ACILNOS ALNICOS
OILCANS
ACILNOU INOCULA
ACILNRS CARLINS
ACILNST CATLINS
TINCALS
ACILNTU LUNATIC
ACILRST CITRALS
ACILRTU CURTAIL
ACIMNOR MINORCA
ACINNOT ACTINON
CONTAIN
ACINOPT CAPTION
PACTION
ACINORR CARRION
ACINORT CAROTIN
CORTINA
ACINORV CORVINA
ACINOSU ACINOUS
ACINOTT TACTION
ACINOTU AUCTION
CAUTION
ACINRTT TANTRIC
ACINRTU CURTAIN
ACIOPRT APRICOT
APROTIC
PAROTIC
ACIORSU CARIOUS
CURIOSA
ACIORTT CITATOR
RICOTTA
ACLNORU CORNUAL
COURLAN
ACLORST SCROTAL
ACNOORT CARTOON
CORANTO
ACNORTU COURANT
ACNOSTU CONATUS
TOUCANS
ACORSTU CUATROS
SURCOAT
TURACOS
ADDEEIR DEAIRED
READIED
ADDEEIT IDEATED
ADDEELN LADENED
ADDEELT DELATED
ADDEENS DEADENS
ADDEERT DERATED
REDATED
TREADED
ADDEEST DEADEST
SEDATED
STEADED
ADDEIIS DAISIED
ADDEILT DILATED
ADDEINO ADENOID
ADDEINU UNAIDED
ADDEIOR RADIOED
ADDEIOT IODATED
TOADIED
ADDEIOV AVOIDED
ADDEITU AUDITED
ADDELNR DANDLER
ADDELRT DARTLED
ADDENOT DONATED
ADDENOU DUODENA
ADDENRU DAUNDER
ADDENTU DAUNTED
UNDATED
ADDINOR ANDROID
ADEEFLN ENDLEAF
ADEEFLR FEDERAL
ADEEFLT DEFLATE
ADEEFNS DEAFENS
ADEEFRT DRAFTEE
ADEEFST DEAFEST
DEFEATS
FEASTED
ADEEGMN ENDGAME
ADEEGNV AVENGED
ADEEGPR PREAGED
ADEEGRV GREAVED
ADEEGRW RAGWEED
WAGERED
ADEEHIR HEADIER
ADEEHNS DASHEEN
ADEEHRS ADHERES
HEADERS
HEARSED
SHEARED
ADEEHRT EARTHED
HEARTED
ADEEHST HEADSET
ADEEIJT JADEITE
ADEEILM EMAILED
LIMEADE
ADEEIMT MEDIATE
ADEEIRW WEARIED
ADEEISV ADVISEE
ADEEITV DEVIATE
ADEEKNR KNEADER
NAKEDER
ADEELMN LEADMEN
ADEELMR EMERALD
ADEELMT METALED
ADEELNP DEPLANE
PANELED
ADEELPR PEARLED
PEDALER
PLEADER
REPLEAD
ADEELPT PETALED
PLEATED
ADEELRV RAVELED
ADEELRW LEEWARD
ADEELRY DELAYER
LAYERED
RELAYED
ADEELTV VALETED
ADEEMNR AMENDER
MEANDER
REEDMAN
RENAMED
ADEEMNS DEMEANS
SEEDMAN
ADEEMOS OEDEMAS
ADEEMRS SMEARED
ADEEMRT REMATED
ADEEMST STEAMED
ADEENPS SNEAPED
SPEANED
ADEENRV RAVENED
ADEENRY DEANERY
YEAREND
YEARNED
ADEENSW DEEWANS
ADEEOPT ADOPTEE
ADEEPRS RESPADE
SPEARED
ADEEPRT ADEPTER
PREDATE
RETAPED
TAPERED
ADEERSV ADVERSE
EVADERS
ADEERSW DRAWEES
RESAWED
ADEERTV AVERTED
ADEERTW DEWATER
TARWEED
WATERED
ADEERTX RETAXED
ADEESTW SWEATED
ADEESTY YEASTED
ADEFGOR FORAGED
ADEFGOT FAGOTED
ADEFGRT GRAFTED
ADEFHIT FAITHED
ADEFLOR ALFREDO
ADEFLOT FLOATED
ADEFLRU DAREFUL
ADEFLTU DEFAULT
FAULTED
ADEFNSU SNAFUED
ADEFOOS SEAFOOD
ADEFORV FAVORED
ADEFORY FEODARY
FORAYED
ADEFOTU FADEOUT
ADEGHIN HEADING
ADEGHIR HAGRIDE
ADEGHOR HAGRODE
ADEGILV GLAIVED
ADEGIMS DEGAMIS
ADEGINV DEAVING
EVADING
ADEGINW WINDAGE
ADEGISV VISAGED
ADEGLOP GALOPED
ADEGNOV DOGVANE
ADEGNOW GOWANED
WAGONED
ADEGNPR PRANGED
ADEGNTW TWANGED
ADEGORW DOWAGER
WORDAGE
ADEGRTY GYRATED
TRAGEDY
ADEHILN INHALED
ADEHIMO HAEMOID
ADEHINP HEADPIN
PINHEAD
ADEHIPR RAPHIDE
ADEHIPT PITHEAD
ADEHIRR HARDIER
HARRIED
ADEHIRW RAWHIDE
ADEHIRY HAYRIDE
HYDRIAE
ADEHLNR HANDLER
ADEHLNS HANDLES
HANDSEL
ADEHLOS SHOALED
ADEHLOT LOATHED
ADEHLST DALETHS
ADEHNRU UNHEARD
ADEHNTU HAUNTED
ADEHOPT POTHEAD
ADEHORR HOARDER
ADEHOTW TOWHEAD
ADEIIMN AMIDINE
DIAMINE
ADEIINZ DIAZINE
ADEIIPR PERIDIA
ADEILLT TALLIED
ADEILMO MELODIA
ADEILMU MIAULED
ADEILNP PLAINED
ADEILNV ANVILED
ADEILOP OEDIPAL
ADEILOZ DIAZOLE
ADEILPT PLAITED
TALIPED
ADEIMNO AMIDONE
DOMAINE
ADEIMNU UNAIMED
ADEIMOU MIAOUED
ADEIMOW MIAOWED
ADEIMRR ADMIRER
MARRIED
ADEIMRY MIDYEAR
ADEIMTY DAYTIME
ADEINOV NAEVOID
ADEINOX DIOXANE
ADEINOZ ANODIZE
ADEIOPS ADIPOSE
ADEIOPT OPIATED
ADEIORV AVODIRE
AVOIDER
ADEIORX EXORDIA
ADEIOSX OXIDASE
ADEIOTX OXIDATE
ADEIPRR PARRIED
RAPIDER
ADEIQRU QUERIDA
ADEIRRV ARRIVED
ADEITUZ DEUTZIA
ADEITWY TIDEWAY
ADEKORT TROAKED
ADELLNR LANDLER
ADELMNR MANDREL
ADELMNT MANTLED
ADELMOR EARLDOM
ADELMOS DAMOSEL
ADELMRU MURALED
ADELMST MALTEDS
ADELNPT PLANTED
ADELNSY ADENYLS
ADELNTW WETLAND
ADELOPR LEOPARD
PAROLED
PRELOAD
ADELOPS DEPOSAL
PEDALOS
ADELOPT TADPOLE
ADELOSV SALVOED
ADELPST STAPLED
ADELRTW TRAWLED
ADELRTY LYRATED
ADELTUV VAULTED
ADEMNOS DAEMONS
MASONED
MONADES
ADEMNOW ADWOMEN
WOMANED
ADEMNRU DURAMEN
MANURED
MAUNDER
UNARMED
ADEMNSU MEDUSAN
ADEMNTU UNMATED
UNTAMED
ADEMORR ARMORED
ADEMRSU REMUDAS
ADEMRTU MATURED
ADENNOY ANNOYED
ANODYNE
ADENOPS DAPSONE
ADENOPT NOTEPAD
ADENOSY NOYADES
ADENOTZ ZONATED
ADENPRU UNDRAPE
ADENPTU UNADEPT
ADENRTV VERDANT
ADENRTX DEXTRAN
ADENRUY UNREADY
ADENSUV UNSAVED
ADENSUW UNSAWED
ADENTUV VAUNTED
ADEOPRR EARDROP
ADEOPRT ADOPTER
READOPT
ADEOPRV VAPORED
ADEORRW ARROWED
ADEPRTU UPDATER
UPRATED
ADEPSTU UPDATES
ADERSUY DASYURE
ADFINRT INDRAFT
ADFNOST FANTODS
ADHILOS HALOIDS
ADHINOT ANTHOID
ADHIORS HAIRDOS
ADHIOST TOADISH
ADHNORS HADRONS
ADHNOTU HANDOUT
ADIIMOS DAIMIOS
ADIIRTY ARIDITY
ADIJNOT ADJOINT
ADILMNR MANDRIL
RIMLAND
ADILMOS AMIDOLS
ADILMOU ALODIUM
ADILOPR DIPOLAR
ADILRTY TARDILY
ADIMNOS DAIMONS
DOMAINS
ADIMNST MANTIDS
ADIMOST DIATOMS
MASTOID
ADINOPR PADRONI
PONIARD
ADINOPT PINTADO
ADINOTX OXIDANT
ADINPST PANDITS
SANDPIT
ADINRSW INWARDS
ADIOOPR PARODOI
ADIOPRS SPAROID
ADIOPRT PAROTID
ADIOPSU ADIPOUS
ADIORSV ADVISOR
ADIPRST DISPART
ADIRSTY SATYRID
ADMNORS RANDOMS
RODSMAN
ADMNORT DORMANT
MORDANT
ADMORST STARDOM
TSARDOM
ADNOPRS PARDONS
ADNOPRU PANDOUR
ADNOPST DOPANTS
ADNORSW ONWARDS
ADNORTY TARDYON
ADORSTW TOWARDS
ADORTUW OUTDRAW
OUTWARD
AEEELTV ELEVATE
AEEFGLN FENAGLE
AEEFGRS SERFAGE
AEEFHRT FEATHER
TEREFAH
AEEFILR FILAREE
LEAFIER
AEEFILW ALEWIFE
AEEFLRT REFLATE
AEEFLRU FERULAE
AEEFMNR ENFRAME
FREEMAN
AEEFMRT FERMATE
AEEFOTV FOVEATE
AEEFRRT FERRATE
AEEFRTU FEATURE
AEEGHNT THENAGE
AEEGILL GALILEE
AEEGILM MILEAGE
AEEGILP EPIGEAL
AEEGILW WEIGELA
AEEGIMR REIMAGE
AEEGINP EPIGEAN
AEEGINZ AGENIZE
AEEGLMN GLEEMAN
MELANGE
AEEGLMR GLEAMER
AEEGLMT MELTAGE
AEEGLNV EVANGEL
AEEGLRY EAGERLY
AEEGLTV VEGETAL
AEEGMNR GERMANE
AEEGMNS MANEGES
MENAGES
AEEGMNT GATEMEN
AEEGMST GAMETES
METAGES
AEEGNOP PEONAGE
AEEGNRV AVENGER
ENGRAVE
AEEGNSV AVENGES
GENEVAS
AEEGNTV VENTAGE
AEEGOPS APOGEES
AEEGORV OVERAGE
AEEGPRS PRESAGE
AEEGPRU PUGAREE
AEEGPST SEPTAGE
AEEGRSV GREAVES
AEEHINR HERNIAE
AEEHIRV HEAVIER
AEEHISV HEAVIES
AEEHLNT LETHEAN
AEEHLRT HALTERE
LEATHER
AEEHMNT METHANE
AEEHMRT THERMAE
AEEHNPT HAPTENE
HEPTANE
PHENATE
AEEHNTW WHEATEN
AEEHPRT PREHEAT
AEEHRTT THEATER
THEATRE
THEREAT
AEEHRTW WEATHER
WHEREAT
WREATHE
AEEIKLR LEAKIER
AEEIKLT TEALIKE
AEEILMR MEALIER
AEEILMS MEALIES
AEEILNP ELAPINE
AEEILNX ALEXINE
AEEILPT EPILATE
PILEATE
AEEILRV LEAVIER
VEALIER
AEEILRZ REALIZE
AEEILTV ELATIVE
AEEIMNN ENAMINE
AEEIMNS MEANIES
AEEIMTT TEATIME
AEEINPR PERINEA
AEEINVW INWEAVE
AEEIPSV PEAVIES
AEEIRRW WEARIER
AEEKLNT KANTELE
AEELMNS ENAMELS
MELENAS
AEELMNT TELEMAN
AEELMTU EMULATE
AEELNPR REPANEL
AEELNPS SPELEAN
AEELNRW RENEWAL
AEELNSV ENSLAVE
LEAVENS
AEELOPR PAROLEE
AEELPRT PETRALE
PLEATER
PRELATE
REPLATE
AEELPRU PLEURAE
AEELPTU EPAULET
AEELRTX EXALTER
AEELRUV REVALUE
AEEMNNO ANEMONE
AEEMNPR PRENAME
AEEMOPT METOPAE
AEEMPRT TEMPERA
AEEMRSU MEASURE
AEENNOV NOVENAE
AEENNPT PENNATE
PENTANE
AEENOPU EUPNOEA
AEENPSU EUPNEAS
AEENRRV RAVENER
AEENRRY YEARNER
AEENSUV AVENUES
AEENTTV NAVETTE
AEEOPRT OPERATE
AEEORSV OVERSEA
AEEORTV OVERATE
OVEREAT
AEEORVW OVERAWE
AEEPRRT PEARTER
TAPERER
AEERRTV AVERTER
AEERRTW WATERER
AEFGILN FINAGLE
LEAFING
AEFGILO FOLIAGE
AEFGILR FRAGILE
AEFGIRT FRIGATE
AEFGIRU REFUGIA
AEFGITU FATIGUE
AEFGLNR FLANGER
AEFGLOT FLOTAGE
AEFGOOT FOOTAGE
AEFGORS FORAGES
AEFGORT FAGOTER
AEFIILT FILIATE
AEFIIRS FAIRIES
AEFILMN INFLAME
AEFILMR FLAMIER
AEFILNV FLAVINE
AEFILOT FOLIATE
AEFILPT FLEAPIT
AEFILRR FRAILER
AEFILRU FAILURE
AEFILRW FLAWIER
AEFIMNR FIREMAN
AEFIMNS FAMINES
AEFIMOR FOAMIER
AEFINNS FANNIES
AEFINNT INFANTE
AEFINPR FIREPAN
AEFINRR REFRAIN
AEFINRW FAWNIER
AEFINSW FANWISE
AEFISTT FATTIES
AEFLMOR FEMORAL
AEFLNOV FLAVONE
AEFLNRU FLANEUR
FRENULA
FUNERAL
AEFLRSU EARFULS
FERULAS
REFUSAL
AEFLRTU REFUTAL
TEARFUL
AEFLSTU SULFATE
AEFMNOR FORAMEN
FOREMAN
AEFMORS FOAMERS
AEFMORT FORMATE
AEFNOPR PROFANE
AEFNORR FORERAN
AEFNRSU FURANES
AEFORSW FORESAW
AEFORTV OVERFAT
AEGGIOS ISAGOGE
AEGHILN HEALING
AEGHINT GAHNITE
HEATING
AEGHIOS HOAGIES
AEGHIRS HEGARIS
HEGIRAS
AEGHLNO HALOGEN
AEGHLOS GALOSHE
AEGHNRS HANGERS
REHANGS
AEGHNST STENGAH
AEGHOST HOSTAGE
AEGIIMN IMAGINE
AEGILLN GALLEIN
NIGELLA
AEGILLT TILLAGE
AEGILMN GEMINAL
AEGILMR GREMIAL
AEGILMS MILAGES
AEGILNP LEAPING
PEALING
AEGILNV LEAVING
VEALING

AEGILNY YEALING
AEGILSV GLAIVES
AEGIMNN MEANING
AEGIMOS IMAGOES
AEGIMRR ARMIGER
AEGIMRS GISARME
IMAGERS
MIRAGES
AEGIMRT MIGRATE
RAGTIME
AEGIMST GAMIEST
SIGMATE
AEGINNW WEANING
AEGINNY YEANING
AEGINOZ AGONIZE
AEGINTV VINTAGE
AEGINTZ TZIGANE
AEGIPRR GRAPIER
AEGIRSV GRAVIES
RIVAGES
AEGIRSW EARWIGS
AEGIRTV VIRGATE
AEGISTY GASEITY
AEGLLNO ALLONGE
GALLEON
AEGLLOR ALLEGRO
AEGLLOT TOLLAGE
AEGLMNR MANGLER
AEGLMOR GLOMERA
GOMERAL
AEGLMOU MOULAGE
AEGLNPR GRAPNEL
AEGLNRW WANGLER
WRANGLE
AEGLNRY ANGERLY
AEGLNTW TWANGLE
AEGLOPR PERGOLA
AEGLORV VORLAGE
AEGLOSV LOVAGES
AEGLOTV VOLTAGE
AEGLRTY GREATLY
AEGMNOR MARENGO
MEGARON
AEGMNOS MANGOES
AEGMNOT MAGNETO
MEGATON
MONTAGE
AEGMNRS ENGRAMS
GERMANS
MANGERS
AEGMNST MAGNETS
AEGMNTU AUGMENT
MUTAGEN
AEGMOOR MOORAGE
AEGNORW WAGONER
AEGNORY ORANGEY
AEGNOSY NOSEGAY
AEGNRSW GNAWERS
AEGOPRT PORTAGE
AEGOPST GESTAPO
POSTAGE
POTAGES
AEGOSTW STOWAGE
TOWAGES
AEGOTUV OUTGAVE
AEHIIRR HAIRIER
AEHILMO HEMIOLA
AEHILNY HYALINE
AEHILOR AIRHOLE
AEHILPR HARELIP
AEHILPT HAPLITE
AEHILRU HAULIER
AEHILTY HYALITE
AEHIMNR HARMINE
AEHIMNS HAEMINS
AEHIMRS MISHEAR
AEHIMST ATHEISM
AEHINPR HEPARIN
AEHINPS INPHASE
AEHINSV EVANISH
VAHINES
AEHINSW WAHINES
AEHIORR HOARIER
AEHIRRS HARRIES
AEHIRSW WASHIER
WEARISH
AEHISTT ATHEIST
STAITHE
AEHLMNO MANHOLE
AEHLMOR ARMHOLE
AEHLNOT ANETHOL
ETHANOL
AEHLNRT ENTHRAL
AEHLNSU UNLEASH
AEHLOPR EPHORAL
AEHLOPT TAPHOLE

AEHLRSU HAULERS
AEHMNOR MENORAH
AEHMORT TERAOHM
AEHNOPT PHAETON
PHONATE
AEHNORT ANOTHER
AEHNPRT PANTHER
AEHNRTU HAUNTER
UNEARTH
URETHAN
AEHOPRT PHORATE
AEHOPST TEASHOP
AEHORRS HOARSER
AEHORTU OUTHEAR
AEIIKLR AIRLIKE
AEIIKNT KAINITE
AEIILMR RAMILIE
AEIILNX EXILIAN
AEIILRV VIRELAI
AEIIMPR IMPERIA
AEIIMRT AIRTIME
AEIIMRV VIREMIA
AEIIMST AMITIES
AEIIMTT IMITATE
AEIINOP EPINAOI
AEIIPRR PRAIRIE
AEIIRRV RIVIERA
AEIIRSW AIRWISE
AEIITTV VITIATE
AEIKLNU UNALIKE
AEIKLOR OARLIKE
AEIKLOT KEITLOA
OATLIKE
AEIKNNT NEATNIK
AEIKNTU UNAKITE
AEIKRSU KAURIES
AEILLOV ALVEOLI
AEILLRR RALLIER
AEILMNN LINEMAN
MELANIN
AEILMNP IMPANEL
MANIPLE
AEILMNU ALUMINE
AEILMOR LOAMIER
AEILMPR IMPALER
IMPEARL
LEMPIRA
PALMIER
AEILMRR MARLIER
AEILMTY MEATILY
AEILNNY INANELY
AEILNPW PINWALE
AEILNQU QUINELA
AEILNUW LAUWINE
AEILNVY NAIVELY
AEILOPR PELORIA
AEILORV VARIOLE
AEILOTV VIOLATE
AEILPRV PREVAIL
AEILQTU LIQUATE
TEQUILA
AEILRVY VIRELAY
AEILRWY WEARILY
AEILTVY VILAYET
AEIMNOR MORAINE
ROMAINE
AEIMNPR PERMIAN
AEIMNRR MARINER
AEIMNRV VERMIAN
AEIMNRW WIREMAN
AEIMNSW MANWISE
AEIMOOP IPOMOEA
AEIMOPR EMPORIA
MEROPIA
AEIMORR ARMOIRE
AEIMOTX TOXEMIA
AEIMOTZ ATOMIZE
AEIMPRT PRIMATE
AEIMPST IMPASTE
PASTIME
AEIMRRS MARRIES
AEIMRSU UREMIAS
AEIMRSV MISAVER
AEIMRSW SEMIRAW
AEIMRTU MURIATE
AEIMRTV VITAMER
AEIMRTW WARTIME
AEIMSTT ETATISM
MATIEST
AEINNPR PANNIER
AEINNPT PINNATE
AEINPSW WINESAP
AEINPTT PATIENT
AEINPTU PETUNIA
AEINQTU ANTIQUE
QUINATE

AEINSWY ANYWISE
AEINTUV VAUNTIE
AEINTVW VAWNTIE
AEINTVY NAIVETY
AEIOQSU SEQUOIA
AEIPRRT PARTIER
AEIPRTV PRIVATE
AEIPRTW WIRETAP
AEIPSTT PATTIES
AEIPSTV SPAVIET
AEIPSTW TAWPIES
AEIRRRT TARRIER
AEIRRSV ARRIVES
VARIERS
AEIRRTW WARTIER
AEIRRTY RETIARY
AEIRSVW WAIVERS
AEIRTUZ AZURITE
AEIRTVY VARIETY
AEISTTV STATIVE
AEISTTY SATIETY
AEISTVW WAVIEST
AELMNOR ALMONER
AELMNOT LOMENTA
OMENTAL
TELAMON
AELMNRU NUMERAL
AELMOPR RAMPOLE
AELMORU MORULAE
AELMORV REMOVAL
AELMOTT MATELOT
AELMRSU MAULERS
SERUMAL
AELMSTU AMULETS
MULETAS
AELNOPT POLENTA
AELNOPU APOLUNE
AELNOTV VOLANTE
AELNOTY ANOLYTE
AELNOUZ ZONULAE
AELNPRT PLANTER
REPLANT
AELNRTV VENTRAL
AELNRUU NEURULA
AELNRUV UNRAVEL
VENULAR
AELOPRR PERORAL
PREORAL
AELOPRV OVERLAP
AELOPTT PALETOT
AELOPTU OUTLEAP
AELORUU ROULEAU
AELORVY LAYOVER
OVERLAY
AELOTUV OVULATE
AELOTVY OVATELY
AELPRSU PERUSAL
PLEURAS
AELPSTU PULSATE
AELRSUV VALUERS
AELRTUV VAULTER
AEMNNOR MONERAN
AEMNNOS MANNOSE
AEMNNOT MONTANE
NONMEAT
AEMNNOU NOUMENA
AEMNNRT REMNANT
AEMNOPR MANROPE
AEMNORT TONEARM
AEMNORU ENAMOUR
NEUROMA
AEMNORV OVERMAN
AEMNORY ANYMORE
AEMNOTT TOMENTA
AEMNOTU AUTOMEN
AEMNRSU MANURES
SURNAME
AEMNRTV VARMENT
AEMOORT TEAROOM
AEMOOST OSTEOMA
AEMORRS REMORAS
ROAMERS
AEMORSW WOMERAS
AEMOSTT STOMATE
AEMOSTW TWASOME
AEMRSTU MATURES
STRUMAE
AENNORY ANNOYER
AENNOSV NOVENAS
AENNRTY TANNERY
AENOOTZ ENTOZOA
OZONATE
AENOPRT OPERANT
PRONATE
PROTEAN
AENOPSW WEAPONS

AENOPTU AUTOPEN
AENORRV OVERRAN
AENPRRT PARTNER
AENPRTT PATTERN
REPTANT
AENPSTU PEANUTS
AENRRTY TERNARY
AENRSUW UNSWEAR
AENRSUY SYNURAE
AENRTUV VAUNTER
AEOPRRT PRAETOR
PRORATE
AEOPRTV OVERAPT
AEOPSTT TEAPOTS
AEOPSTY TEAPOYS
AEOQRTU EQUATOR
AEORRSV SAVORER
SEROVAR
AEORSVW AVOWERS
OVERSAW
REAVOWS
AEORTUV OUTRAVE
AEORTUW OUTWEAR
AEPRSTU PASTURE
UPRATES
UPSTARE
UPTEARS
AERSTUU AUTEURS
AERSTUY ESTUARY
AFGILNO FOALING
LOAFING
AFGINOT ANTIFOG
AFGINRT INGRAFT
RAFTING
AFIILNT TAILFIN
AFIILOR AIRFOIL
AFIILRT AIRLIFT
AFILNTU ANTIFLU
AFINNOT FONTINA
AFINORS INSOFAR
AFINRTU ANTIFUR
AFINSTU FUSTIAN
AFIORTU FAITOUR
AFLNORT FRONTAL
AGHILNO HALOING
AGHILOT GOLIATH
AGHIOST GOATISH
AGIIMOR ORIGAMI
AGILMNO LOAMING
AGILOPT GALIPOT
AGILORW AIRGLOW
AGIMNOR ROAMING
AGIMNOT MOATING
AGIMNRT MARTING
MIGRANT
AGIMORS ISOGRAM
AGIMORU GOURAMI
AGINOPR PIGNORA
AGINOPS SOAPING
AGINPRT PARTING
PRATING
AGINRTW RINGTAW
AGIORSV VIRAGOS
AHIINST TAHINIS
AHILNRT INTHRAL
AHIMNOT MANIHOT
AHINRSU UNHAIRS
AHIORST AIRSHOT
SHORTIA
THORIAS
AHLNORT ALTHORN
AHLORST HARLOTS
AHORSTU AUTHORS
AIILMNT INTIMAL
AIILNPT PINTAIL
AIILNRY RAINILY
AIILNTV INVITAL
AIILNTY ANILITY
AIILORV RAVIOLI
AIILRTV TRIVIAL
AIIMNOR AMORINI
AIIMNRT MARTINI
AIIMNST ANIMIST
INTIMAS
SANTIMI
AIIMNTU MINUTIA
AIIMRST SIMITAR
AIINOPS SINOPIA
AIINPRS ASPIRIN
AIINPST PIANIST
AIINRSY RAISINY
AIINRTV VITRAIN
AIJNORT JANITOR
AIKORST TROIKAS
AILLORT LITORAL
AILMNOS MALISON

AILMNRS MARLINS
AILMNRU RUMINAL
AILMORS ORALISM
AILMRST MISTRAL
RAMTILS
AILNPST PLAINTS
AILNPTU NUPTIAL
UNPLAIT
AILNRTY RIANTLY
AILNSTY NASTILY
SAINTLY
AILOORW WOORALI
AILORTY ORALITY
AILRSTY TRYSAIL
AILRTUV VIRTUAL
AIMNNOR IRONMAN
AIMNOOR AMORINO
AIMNOOT AMOTION
AIMNOPR RAMPION
AIMNOPT MAINTOP
PTOMAIN
TAMPION
TIMPANO
AIMNOTU MANITOU
TINAMOU
AIMNRSU URANISM
AIMNRTU NATRIUM
AIMNSTU MANITUS
SANTIMU
TSUNAMI
AIMORST AMORIST
AIMORTT TRITOMA
AIMRSTU ATRIUMS
AINNOPT PINTANO
AINOOTV OVATION
AINOPRS SOPRANI
AINOPRT ATROPIN
AINOPTT ANTIPOT
AINOPTU OPUNTIA
UTOPIAN
AINORSW WARISON
AINORTW WAITRON
AINPRTT TRIPTAN
AINPRTU PURITAN
AINRRTY TRINARY
AINRTUY UNITARY
AIOPRRT AIRPORT
AIOPRST AIRPOST
AIOPRTT PATRIOT
AIOPRTY TOPIARY
AIOPSTU UTOPIAS
AIORSTV TRAVOIS
VIATORS
AIORSTY OSTIARY
AIORSUV SAVIOUR
VARIOUS
AIPRSTU UPSTAIR
ALMNORS NORMALS
ALMNORU UNMORAL
ALMORST MORTALS
STROMAL
ALMORTU TUMORAL
ALNOPRS PROLANS
ALNOPTU OUTPLAN
ALOPRST PATROLS
PORTALS
AMNORTU ROMAUNT
AMNOSTU AMOUNTS
OUTMANS
ANOOPRT PATROON
PRONOTA
ANOPSTU OUTSPAN
AORSTUW OUTWARS
BCEEIRT TEREBIC
BCEILNO BINOCLE
BCEILOR BRICOLE
CORBEIL
BCEINOR BICORNE
BCEINOS EBONICS
BCEIORS CORBIES
BDEEINR BENDIER
INBREED
BDEEIST BETIDES
BDEENOR DEBONER
ENROBED
REDBONE
BDEENOS DEBONES
BDEEORS BEDSORE
SOBERED
BDEGILO OBLIGED
BDEGIOT BIGOTED
BDEIIRS BIRDIES
BDEILNR BLINDER
BRINDLE
BDEILNS BINDLES
BDEILOR BROILED

BDEILRS BRIDLES
BDEILRT DRIBLET
BDEILRU BUILDER
REBUILD
BDEILST BILSTED
BDEIMOR BROMIDE
BDEINOU BEDOUIN
BDEINSU BEDUINS
BDEIOOS DOOBIES
BDEIORR BROIDER
BDEIORT DEORBIT
ORBITED
BDEIORV OVERBID
BDEIRSU BRUISED
BURDIES
BDEIRTU BRUITED
BDEISTU SUBEDIT
BDELNOR BLONDER
BDENORU BOUNDER
REBOUND
UNROBED
BDEORTU DOUBTER
OBTRUDE
OUTBRED
REDOUBT
BEEEILN BEELINE
BEEFINT BENEFIT
BEEGILO OBLIGEE
BEEGINR REBEGIN
BEEGINS BEIGNES
BEEGINT BEIGNET
BEEGINU BEGUINE
BEEILNR BERLINE
BEEILOS OBELISE
BEEILRS BELIERS
BEEINOS EBONIES
EBONISE
BEEINOT EBONITE
BEELNRT REBLENT
BEELOST BOLETES
BEENOOT BOTONEE
BEENORR ENROBER
BEENORS BOREENS
ENROBES
BEENOST BONESET
BEEOOST BOOTEES
BEFILNO LOBEFIN
BEFINOR BONFIRE
BEGILNO IGNOBLE
BEGILNT BELTING
BEGILOR OBLIGER
BEGILOS OBLIGES
BEGILRT GILBERT
BEGINST BESTING
BEGIOSU BOUGIES
BEGNORU BURGEON
BEHIOST BOTHIES
BEHNORT BETHORN
BEIILRS RISIBLE
BEIINOT NIOBITE
BEIINRS BRINIES
BEIIOTT BIOTITE
BEIIRST BITSIER
BEILMOR EMBROIL
BEILNOW BOWLINE
BEILNSU SUBLINE
BEILOOS LOOBIES
BEILOPR PREBOIL
BEILORR BROILER
BEILORW BLOWIER
BEILRTU REBUILT
BEILSTU SUBTILE
BEIMNOR BROMINE
BEINNOR BONNIER
BEINNOS BENISON
BEINOOS BOONIES
BEINOOT EOBIONT
BEINORW BROWNIE
BEINOSV BOVINES
BEINRSU BURNIES
SUBERIN
BEINRTT BITTERN
BEIOOST BOOTIES
BEIORRT ORBITER
BEIORSU OUREBIS
BEIORUV BOUVIER
BEIOSTY OBESITY
BELNOOR BORNEOL
BELNOST NOBLEST
BELNRTU BLUNTER
BELORTU TROUBLE
BENOOST OBENTOS
BENORSU BOURNES
UNROBES
UNSOBER
BENOSTU SUBTONE

BEOORST BOOSTER
REBOOTS
BEORSTU OBTUSER
BIINOST BIOTINS
BILNOTU BOTULIN
BILORST BRISTOL
STROBIL
BINOORT BIOTRON
BINORSU BOURSIN
CDEEIIT EIDETIC
CDEEILN DECLINE
CDEEINO CODEINE
CDEEINT ENTICED
CDEEIOS DIOCESE
CDEEIRT RECITED
TIERCED
CDEEIST DECEITS
CDEENOR ENCODER
ENCORED
CDEENOS ENCODES
SECONDE
CDEENRT CENTRED
CREDENT
CDEEORS RECODES
CDEEOST CESTODE
ESCOTED
CDEFINO CONFIDE
CDEGINO COIGNED
CDEGINR CRINGED
CDEGIOR ERGODIC
CDEHINO HEDONIC
CDEHIOR CHOIRED
CDEIILO EIDOLIC
CDEIINR DINERIC
CDEIINS INCISED
INDICES
CDEIINT IDENTIC
INCITED
CDEIIOR ERICOID
CDEIIRT DICTIER
CDEIIST DEISTIC
DICIEST
CDEILNU INCLUDE
NUCLIDE
CDEILOO OCELOID
CDEILRS CLERIDS
CDEILST DELICTS
CDEILTU DUCTILE
CDEIMNO DEMONIC
CDEIMOR DORMICE
CDEIMOT DEMOTIC
CDEINOS CODEINS
SECONDI
CDEINOT CTENOID
DEONTIC
NOTICED
CDEINRU INDUCER
CDEINSU INCUDES
INCUSED
INDUCES
CDEIOPR PERCOID
CDEIOPT PICOTED
CDEIORT CORDITE
CDEIORV CODRIVE
DIVORCE
CDEIORW CROWDIE
CDEIRSU CRUISED
CDENOOR CROONED
CDENORU CRUNODE
CDENOST DOCENTS
CDENOTU COUNTED
CDEORTU COURTED
EDUCTOR
CDIINOR CRINOID
CDIINOT DICTION
CDINOTU CONDUIT
NOCTUID
CEEGINR GENERIC
CEEGINT GENETIC
CEEGINU EUGENIC
CEEGORT CORTEGE
CEEHIOR CHEERIO
CEEHIRT ERETHIC
ETHERIC
HERETIC
TECHIER
CEEIINR EIRENIC
CEEILNO CINEOLE
CEEILNR RECLINE
CEEILNS LICENSE
SELENIC
SILENCE
CEEILNT CENTILE
LICENTE
CEEILNU LEUCINE
CEEILRS CEILERS

CEEILRT RETICLE
TIERCEL
CEEILTU LEUCITE
CEEIMNO MIOCENE
CEEIMNT CENTIME
CEEINOS SENECIO
CEEINRV CERVINE
CEEIOPT PICOTEE
CEEIORT COTERIE
CEEIORV REVOICE
CEEIOST COESITE
CEEIPRT RECEIPT
CEEIRRT RECITER
CEEIRTU EUCRITE
CEEISTU CUTESIE
CEELNOS ENCLOSE
CEELNRT LECTERN
CEELORS CREOLES
CEELORT ELECTOR
ELECTRO
CEENOOT ECOTONE
CEENORS ENCORES
NECROSE
CEENORU COENURE
CEENOST CENOTES
CEEORRT ERECTOR
CEFIIOR ORIFICE
CEFINOR COINFER
CONIFER
CEGILNR CLINGER
CRINGLE
CEGINOR COREIGN
CEGIORT ERGOTIC
CEGNORS CONGERS
CEGNOST CONGEST
CEHILNO CHOLINE
HELICON
CEHINOR CHORINE
CEHINRT CITHERN
CITHREN
CEHIORS COHEIRS
HEROICS
CEHIOTU COUTHIE
CEHNORT CHORTEN
NOTCHER
CEIILST ELICITS
CEIIMOT MEIOTIC
CEIINNO CONIINE
CEIINOR ONEIRIC
CEIINOS EOSINIC
NICOISE
CEIINOV INVOICE
CEIINRS IRENICS
SERICIN
CEIINSU CUISINE
CEIIRST ERISTIC
CEILMOT TELOMIC
CEILNOP PINOCLE
PLEONIC
CEILNSU LEUCINS
CEILNTU CUTLINE
LINECUT
TUNICLE
CEILOOS COOLIES
CEILOPR PELORIC
POLICER
CEILRTU UTRICLE
CEILSTU LUCITES
LUETICS
CEIMNOR INCOMER
CEIMNOS INCOMES
MESONIC
CEIMNOT CENTIMO
TONEMIC
CEIMORT MORTICE
CEINNOS CONINES
CEINOOT COONTIE
CEINOPR PORCINE
CEINOPT ENTOPIC
NEPOTIC
CEINORR CORNIER
CEINORU COENURI
CEINORV CORVINE
CEINOSV NOVICES
CEINOTT TONETIC
CEINOUV UNVOICE
CEINRTT CITTERN
CEINSTU NEUSTIC
CEIOOST COOTIES
CEIOPRS COPIERS
CEIOPST POETICS
CEIORRS CIRROSE
CORRIES
CROSIER
ORRICES
CEIORRU COURIER
CEIORSV VOICERS
CEIORSW COWRIES
CEIORTT COTTIER
CEIORTV EVICTOR
CEIORTW COWRITE
CEIOSTT SCOTTIE
CEIOSTV COSTIVE
CEIOSTW COWIEST
CEIOSTY SOCIETY
CELNOOR CORONEL
CELNORS CLONERS
CORNELS
CELNOTU NOCTULE
CELORTU CLOTURE
CLOUTER
COULTER
CENOORT CORONET
CENORTU CORNUTE
COUNTER
RECOUNT
TROUNCE
CENORTV CONVERT
CENORTW CROWNET
CENOSTU CONTUSE
CEOORST COOTERS
SCOOTER
CEOORTU ECOTOUR
CEORSTU COUTERS
CROUTES
SCOUTER
CIINORS INCISOR
CIINORT NORITIC
CIIORST SORITIC
CILNOTU LINOCUT
CILORST LICTORS
CINORTU RUCTION
CINOSTU SUCTION
CIORSTU CITROUS
DDEEILR DREIDEL
DDEEINS NEDDIES
DDEEINT ENDITED
DDEEIST TEDDIES
DDEENOT DENOTED
DDEENRT TRENDED
DDEGIOR DODGIER
DDEIINT INDITED
DDEIIOS IODIDES
IODISED
DDEIIRT DIRTIED
DDEILOT DELTOID
DDEILRT TIDDLER
DDEINOS NODDIES
DDEINOT DENTOID
DDEINRU UNDRIED
DDELORT TODDLER
DDENORT TRODDEN
DDENORU REDOUND
ROUNDED
UNDERDO
DEEEIRW WEEDIER
DEEEOTV DEVOTEE
DEEFGIN FEEDING
FEIGNED
DEEFIIR DEIFIER
EDIFIER
REIFIED
DEEFILR DEFILER
FIELDER
REFILED
DEEFILT FILETED
DEEFINR DEFINER
REFINED
DEEFINS DEFINES
DEEFINT FEINTED
DEEFLOT FEEDLOT
DEEGHIN HEEDING
NEIGHED
DEEGHIR HEDGIER
DEEGIMN DEEMING
DEEGINW WEEDING
DEEGIRV DIVERGE
GRIEVED
DEEGIRW WEDGIER
DEEHINR INHERED
DEEHIRT DIETHER
DEEHIST HEISTED
DEEHORS RESHOED
DEEIIRW WEIRDIE
DEEIKNR REINKED
DEEILNV LIVENED
DEEILNY NEEDILY
DEEILPR PERILED
REPLIED
DEEILRV DELIVER
LIVERED
RELIVED
REVILED
DEEILRW WIELDER
DEEILRY REEDILY
YIELDER
DEEIMNR ERMINED
DEEIMNS SIDEMEN
DEEIMOR EMEROID
DEEIMRT DEMERIT
DIMETER
MERITED
MITERED
RETIMED
DEEINPR REPINED
RIPENED
DEEINRW REWIDEN
WIDENER
DEEINRX INDEXER
REINDEX
DEEINSV DEVEINS
ENDIVES
DEEINSW ENDWISE
SINEWED
DEEINTV EVIDENT
DEEIOPS EPISODE
DEEIOPT EPIDOTE
DEEIPRT PREEDIT
DEEIPST DESPITE
DEEIRTV RIVETED
DEEISTW DEWIEST
DEELMOR MODELER
REMODEL
DEELOPR DEPLORE
DEELORW LOWERED
ROWELED
DEELORY YODELER
DEELOTW TOWELED
DEEMNOR MODERNE
DEEMNOT DEMETON
DEEMNOU EUDEMON
DEEMORS EMERODS
DEEMOST DEMOTES
DEENOPS DEPONES
SPONDEE
DEENOPT PENTODE
DEENORW ENDOWER
REENDOW
DEENPRT PRETEND
DEEOPRS DEPOSER
REPOSED
DEEORSW RESOWED
DEEORTV REVOTED
DEEORTW TOWERED
DEEORUV OVERDUE
DEEOSTV DEVOTES
DEFGINR FRINGED
DEFGIOR FIREDOG
DEFGIRT GRIFTED
DEFIILN INFIDEL
INFIELD
DEFIINU UNIFIED
DEFIIST FIDEIST
DEFILNR FLINDER
DEFILNT FLINTED
DEFILOO FOLIOED
DEFILRT FLIRTED
TRIFLED
DEFILRU DIREFUL
DEFILST STIFLED
DEFIMOR DEIFORM
DEFINRU UNFIRED
DEFINSU INFUSED
DEFIOOS FOODIES
DEFIRTU FRUITED
DEFISTU FEUDIST
DEFLNOR FONDLER
DEFLNOT TENFOLD
DEFLORT TELFORD
DEFNOOR FORDONE
DEFNORT FRONTED
DEFNORU FOUNDER
REFOUND
DEFNOST FONDEST
DEGHINO HONGIED
DEGHINR HERDING
DEGHIOT HOGTIED
DEGHIRT GIRTHED
RIGHTED
DEGHNOT THONGED
DEGIMNO DEMOING
MENDIGO
DEGINOW WENDIGO
WIDGEON
DEGINRW REDWING
WRINGED
DEGINTW TWINGED
DEGIOPR PODGIER
DEGNOPR PRONGED
DEGNORW WRONGED
DEHIIRS DISHIER
DEHILOT LITHOED
DEHILRS HIRSLED
DEHILRT THIRLED
DEHIMOR HEIRDOM
DEHIMOT ETHMOID
DEHINOP PHONIED
DEHINOR HORDEIN
DEHINOS HOIDENS
DEHINOY HYENOID
DEHINRU UNHIRED
DEHIOOR HOODIER
DEHIOOS HOODIES
DEHIOOT DHOOTIE
DEHIORT THEROID
DEHIOSU HIDEOUS
DEHIOTU HIDEOUT
DEHIRSU HURDIES
DEHNOOR HONORED
DEHNORT THORNED
THRONED
DEHNORU HOUNDER
DEHNRTU THUNDER
DEIILMN MIDLINE
DEIILMT DELIMIT
LIMITED
DEIIMNO DOMINIE
DEIIMRT TIMIDER
DEIIMST MISEDIT
STIMIED
DEIINOZ IONIZED
DEIINRV DIVINER
DEIINRW WINDIER
DEIINSV DIVINES
DEIINTV INVITED
DEIIORZ IODIZER
DEIIPRT RIPTIDE
TIDERIP
DEIISTV VISITED
DEIJNOR JOINDER
DEIJNOT JOINTED
DEIKLOR RODLIKE
DEIKNOS DOESKIN
DEILLRT TRILLED
DEILMNS MILDENS
DEILMOR MOLDIER
DEILMST MILDEST
DEILNPS SPINDLE
SPLINED
DEILNPU UNPILED
DEILNSW SWINDLE
WINDLES
DEILNSY SNIDELY
DEILNTW INDWELT
WINTLED
DEILNUV UNLIVED
DEILOPR LEPORID
DEILOPT PILOTED
DEILOPU EUPLOID
DEILPRT TRIPLED
DEILRSV DRIVELS
DEILRSW SWIRLED
WILDERS
DEILRSY RIDLEYS
DEILRTW TWIRLED
DEILRTY TIREDLY
DEILSTW WILDEST
DEIMNOP IMPONED
DEIMNOR MINORED
DEIMNOS DOMINES
EMODINS
MISDONE
DEIMNRU UNRIMED
DEIMNTU MINUTED
MUTINED
UNTIMED
DEIMOOR DOOMIER
MOIDORE
MOODIER
DEIMORR REMORID
DEIMOTT OMITTED
DEIMOTV MOTIVED
VOMITED
DEIMSTU TEDIUMS
DEINOPT POINTED
DEINOQU QUOINED
DEINORW DOWNIER
DEINPRT PRINTED
DEINRTX DEXTRIN
DEINRTY TINDERY
DEIOORW WOODIER
DEIOOSW WOODIES
DEIOPRT DIOPTER
DIOPTRE
PERIDOT
PROTEID
DEIOPRV PROVIDE
DEIOPTT TIPTOED
DEIOPTV PIVOTED
DEIOQTU QUOITED
DEIORRW ROWDIER
WORDIER
WORRIED
DEIOSUV DEVIOUS
DEIOTUV OUTVIED
DEIOTUW WIDEOUT
DEIPRSU SIRUPED
UPDRIES
DEIPSTU DISPUTE
DELLORT TROLLED
DELNOTW LETDOWN
DELNOTY NOTEDLY
DELOPRT DROPLET
PRETOLD
DEMNOOR DOORMEN
DEMNORT MORDENT
DEMNORU MOURNED
DEMNOST ENDMOST
DEMNOTU DEMOUNT
MOUNTED
DEMOORT MOTORED
DENOPRT PORTEND
PROTEND
DENOPRU POUNDER
UNROPED
DENORUW REWOUND
DENPRTU PRUDENT
UPTREND
DEOOPRT TORPEDO
TROOPED
DEOPRTU TROUPED
DEORTUW OUTDREW
DFILORT TRIFOLD
DFINOTU OUTFIND
DHINORS DRONISH
DIIMNOR MIDIRON
DILNOPT DIPLONT
DIMNORS DORMINS
NIMRODS
DINOTUW OUTWIND
DIOPRST DISPORT
TORPIDS
TRIPODS
EEEFORS FORESEE
EEEILRV RELIEVE
EEEIMNS ENEMIES
EEEIMNT EMETINE
EEEIMRS EMERIES
EEEIMRT EREMITE
EEEINRW WEENIER
EEEINSW WEENIES
EEEIPRS PEERIES
SEEPIER
EEEIPST EPEEIST
EEEIRSV VEERIES
EEEISTW SWEETIE
EEENPRT PRETEEN
TERPENE
EEENRTW TWEENER
EEEORSV OVERSEE
EEEORSY EYESORE
EEFGILN FEELING
FLEEING
EEFGINR FEIGNER
FREEING
REEFING
EEFGIST GIFTEES
EEFHIRT HEFTIER
EEFIIRS REIFIES
EEFILNO OLEFINE
EEFILNS FELINES
EEFILRS FERLIES
REFILES
REFLIES
RELIEFS
EEFILRT FERTILE
EEFIMNR FIREMEN
EEFINNR FENNIER
EEFINRR FERNIER
REFINER
EEFIRRT FERRITE
EEFLNOS ONESELF
EEFLOTU OUTFEEL
EEFNORT OFTENER
EEGHILN HEELING
EEGHINR REHINGE
EEGHNRT GREENTH
EEGILNP PEELING
EEGILRV VELIGER
EEGIMNR REGIMEN
EEGIMNS SEEMING
EEGIMNT MEETING
TEEMING
EEGIMRS EMIGRES
REGIMES
REMIGES
EEGINOP EPIGONE
EEGINPR PEERING
PREEING
EEGINPS SEEPING
EEGINRV REEVING
REGIVEN
VEERING
EEGINTW WEETING
EEGIRSV GRIEVES
REGIVES
EEGISTV VESTIGE
EEGOPRT PROTEGE
EEHIINS HEINIES
EEHILNT THEELIN
EEHINOR HEROINE
EEHINRR ERRHINE
EEHINRW WHEREIN
EEHIPRT PRITHEE
EEHIRTW THEWIER
EEHNOOR HONOREE
EEHNORS RESHONE
EEHNORT THEREON
EEHOOST TOESHOE
EEHORSU REHOUSE
EEHORTT THERETO
EEIIMNS MEINIES
EEIIMRT EMERITI
EEIIMST ITEMISE
EEIINRV VEINIER
EEIINSW EISWEIN
WIENIES
EEIINTV INVITEE
EEIIPST PIETIES
EEIKLNT NETLIKE
EEIKLOT TOELIKE
EEIKNOS EIKONES
EEILLNS NELLIES
EEILNPS PENSILE
EEILNPT PENLITE
EEILNRV LIVENER
EEILNSY YEELINS
EEILNTV VEINLET
EEILNUV VEINULE
EEILOPT PETIOLE
EEILORV OVERLIE
RELIEVO
EEILOTZ ZEOLITE
EEILPRS REPLIES
SPIELER
EEILPRT PERLITE
REPTILE
EEILPRU PUERILE
EEILRSV LEVIERS
RELIVES
REVILES
SERVILE
VEILERS
EEIMNNO NOMINEE
EEIMNNT EMINENT
EEIMNOT ONETIME
EEIMNRW WIREMEN
EEIMOPT EPITOME
EEIMOTV EMOTIVE
EEIMPRT EMPTIER
EEIMRRT MITERER
TRIREME
EEIMRTT EMITTER
TERMITE
EEINNRV INNERVE
NERVINE
EEINNRW WENNIER
EEINNTW ENTWINE
EEINOPR PEREION
PIONEER
EEINOPS PEONIES
EEINPRR REPINER
RIPENER
EEINQRU ENQUIRE
EEINQTU QUIETEN
EEINRRV NERVIER
VERNIER
EEIOPST POETISE
EEIORSV EROSIVE
EEIORTZ EROTIZE
EEIPRTT PETTIER
EEIPRTY YPERITE
EEIQRTU QUIETER
REQUITE
EEIRRTV RIVETER
EEIRRTW REWRITE
EELLNOR RELLENO
EELMNOO OENOMEL
EELMOST OMELETS
TELOMES
EELNOSV ELEVONS
EELOPRS ELOPERS
LEPROSE
EELOPTU EELPOUT
EELORSV RESOLVE
EELORSY EROSELY
EELORTV OVERLET
EELOTUV EVOLUTE
VELOUTE
EEMNOOS SOMEONE
EEMNORS MOREENS
EEMNOST TONEMES
EEMORRT REMOTER
EENNOTY NEOTENY
EENOPRS OPENERS
PEREONS
REOPENS
EENOPST OPENEST
PENTOSE
POSTEEN
POTEENS
EENOPTT POTTEEN
EENOSTW TOWNEES
EENRTUV VENTURE
EEOOPRS OPEROSE
EEOPRTT PROETTE
TREETOP
EEOPSTU TOUPEES
EEORRTV EVERTOR
EEORRTW REWROTE
EEORSUV OEUVRES
OVERUSE
EFGILNR FLINGER
EFGILNT FELTING
EFGINOR FOREIGN
EFGINRU GUNFIRE
EFGIOOR GOOFIER
EFGLORT FROGLET
EFGORST FORGETS
EFGORTU FOREGUT
EFIILRT FIRELIT
EFIINRU UNIFIER
EFIINSU UNIFIES
EFILMOT FILEMOT
EFILNNO NONLIFE
EFILOOS FLOOSIE
FOLIOSE
EFILOPR PROFILE
EFILORT LOFTIER
TREFOIL
EFILRTU FLUTIER
EFILSTU SULFITE
EFIMNOR FERMION
EFIMOST FOMITES
EFINNOR INFERNO
EFINRSU INFUSER
EFIOORS ROOFIES
EFIOORT FOOTIER
EFIOOST FOOTIES
FOOTSIE
EFIOPRT FIREPOT
PIEFORT
EFIORRT ROTIFER
EFIORTU OUTFIRE
EFIORTV OVERFIT
EFLNORU FLEURON
EFLNOST TEFLONS
EFLOORT FOOTLER
EFLORTU FLOUTER
EFNNORT FORNENT
EFNOOST EFTSOON
FESTOON
EFNORRT FRONTER
REFRONT
EFNORTU FORTUNE
EFNORTW FORWENT
EFOORST FOETORS
FOOTERS
EGHIINR HEIRING
EGHIINT NIGHTIE
EGHILNT LIGHTEN
EGHILOU GHOULIE
EGHILRT LIGHTER
RELIGHT
EGHINST NIGHEST
EGHIORS OGREISH
EGHIOST HOGTIES
EGHIOTU TOUGHIE

Alphagram	Word
EGHIRST	RESIGHT
	SIGHTER
EGHLNOR	LEGHORN
EGHNORS	GORHENS
EGHNORU	ROUGHEN
EGHNOTU	TOUGHEN
EGHORTU	TOUGHER
EGIIMNR	MINGIER
EGIIMNT	ITEMING
EGIINOP	EPIGONI
EGIINRV	REIVING
EGIINRW	WINGIER
EGIINTV	EVITING
EGIIOPR	PIEROGI
EGILLOR	GIROLLE
EGILMNR	GREMLIN
	MINGLER
EGILMNT	MELTING
EGILMOR	GOMERIL
EGILMOS	SEMILOG
EGILNOP	ELOPING
EGILNPT	PELTING
EGILNRY	RELYING
EGILNTW	WELTING
	WINGLET
EGILOPS	EPILOGS
EGIMNOT	EMOTING
	MITOGEN
EGIMNOU	MEOUING
EGIMNRT	METRING
	TERMING
EGIMORS	OGREISM
EGIMOST	EGOTISM
EGINOPR	PERIGON
	PIROGEN
EGINORV	OVERING
EGINORZ	ZEROING
EGINOTV	VETOING
EGINRTY	RETYING
EGINSTV	VESTING
EGINSTW	STEWING
	TWINGES
	WESTING
EGIOOPR	GOOPIER
EGIOPRS	PORGIES
	SERPIGO
EGIOPRU	GROUPIE
	PIROGUE
EGIORTV	VERTIGO
EGIOTUV	OUTGIVE
EGIRSTV	GRIVETS
EGLMNOR	MONGREL
EGMNORS	MONGERS
	MORGENS
EGMORTU	GOURMET
EGNOPRS	PRESONG
	SPONGER
EGNORSV	GOVERNS
EGNORSY	ERYNGOS
	GROYNES
EGNORUY	YOUNGER
EGORTUW	OUTGREW
EHIINRS	SHINIER
EHILNOP	PINHOLE
EHILOPT	HOPLITE
EHILRSU	HURLIES
EHILRTU	LUTHIER
EHIMNOS	HOMINES
EHIMORS	HEROISM
EHIMORT	MOTHIER
EHIMOST	HOMIEST
EHINNRT	THINNER
EHINOPR	PHONIER
EHINOPS	PHONIES
EHINORR	HORNIER
EHINOSU	HEINOUS
EHINRTV	THRIVEN
EHINRTW	WRITHEN
EHIOORT	HOOTIER
EHIOPRS	ROSEHIP
EHIOPST	OPHITES
EHIORRS	HORSIER
EHIORRT	HERITOR
EHIORSW	SHOWIER
EHIORSY	HOSIERY
EHIORTT	THORITE
EHIOSTT	HOTTIES
EHIOSTY	ISOHYET
EHLNRTU	LUTHERN
EHNOORS	ONSHORE
EHNORRT	HORRENT
	NORTHER
EHNORSU	UNHORSE
EHOORST	HOOTERS
	RESHOOT
	SHEROOT
	SHOOTER
	SOOTHER
EHORSTU	SHOUTER
	SOUTHER
EIILMRS	MILREIS
	SLIMIER
EIILMRT	LIMITER
	MILTIER
EIILMST	ELITISM
	LIMIEST
	LIMITES
EIILNOV	OLIVINE
EIILNOZ	LIONIZE
EIILNPS	SPLENII
EIILOPR	LIRIOPE
EIILORV	RILIEVO
EIILRSV	LIVIERS
EIILSTW	WILIEST
EIIMRST	MIRIEST
	MISTIER
	RIMIEST
EIINOPR	RIPIENO
EIINOPS	SINOPIE
EIINORZ	IONIZER
	IRONIZE
EIINOSZ	IONIZES
EIINPRS	INSPIRE
	SPINIER
EIINTUV	UNITIVE
EIIORSV	IVORIES
EIIOSTZ	ZOISITE
EIIPRST	PITIERS
	TIPSIER
EIIRSTV	REVISIT
	VISITER
EIIRSTW	WIRIEST
EIISTUV	UVEITIS
EIJLORT	JOLTIER
EIKLNRT	TINKLER
EILLORU	ROUILLE
EILMNOO	OINOMEL
EILMOPR	IMPLORE
EILMORR	LORIMER
EILMORT	MOTLIER
EILMRSU	MISRULE
EILNOOV	VIOLONE
EILNPRU	PURLINE
EILNPSU	LINEUPS
	LUPINES
	SPINULE
	UNPILES
EILNRTY	INERTLY
EILNSUV	UNLIVES
	UNVEILS
EILOOPR	LOOPIER
EILOORW	WOOLIER
EILOOSW	WOOLIES
EILOPRT	POITREL
	POLITER
EILOPSU	PILEOUS
EILORTV	OVERLIT
EILOTUV	OUTLIVE
EILOTUW	OUTWILE
EILPSTU	STIPULE
EILRSUV	SURVEIL
EILRTUV	RIVULET
EIMNNOR	IRONMEN
EIMNNOT	MENTION
EIMNOOR	IONOMER
	MOONIER
EIMNOOS	NOISOME
EIMNOOT	EMOTION
EIMNOPR	PROMINE
EIMNOPS	IMPONES
	PEONISM
EIMNOPT	PIMENTO
EIMNOSW	WINSOME
EIMNRSU	MUREINS
	MURINES
EIMNSTU	MINUETS
	MINUTES
	MISTUNE
	MUTINES
EIMOORR	MOORIER
	ROOMIER
EIMOORS	ROOMIES
EIMOPRS	IMPOSER
	PROMISE
	SEMIPRO
EIMOPST	MOPIEST
	OPTIMES
EIMORSU	MOUSIER
EIMORSV	VERISMO
EIMORTT	OMITTER
EIMORTV	VOMITER
EIMOSTU	TIMEOUS
EIMOSTV	MOTIVES
EIMOTTU	TIMEOUT
EINNOPS	PENSION
	PINONES
EINNOPT	PONTINE
EINNORV	ENVIRON
EINNOSV	VENISON
EINNRTV	VINTNER
EINOOTW	TWOONIE
EINOPRR	PORNIER
EINOPSW	WINESOP
EINOPTU	POUTINE
EINOSUV	ENVIOUS
	NIVEOUS
EINPRRT	PRINTER
	REPRINT
EINPRSU	PURINES
	UPRISEN
EINPSTU	PUNIEST
	PUNTIES
EINRSUW	UNWISER
EINRTTW	WRITTEN
EINRTWY	WINTERY
EIOOPST	ISOTOPE
EIOORTZ	ZOOTIER
EIOPRRS	PROSIER
EIOPRRT	PIERROT
	PRERIOT
EIOPRRU	ROUPIER
EIOPRSU	SOUPIER
EIOPRTT	POTTIER
EIOPRTU	POUTIER
EIOPRTV	OVERTIP
EIOPSTT	POTTIES
	TIPTOES
EIOPSTU	PITEOUS
EIOPSTY	ISOTYPE
EIOPTUW	WIPEOUT
EIORRSV	REVISOR
EIORRSW	WORRIES
EIOSTUV	OUTVIES
EIOSTUZ	OUTSIZE
ELLNORS	ENROLLS
ELLNOST	STOLLEN
ELMNOOT	MOONLET
ELMNORS	MERLONS
ELMNOST	LOMENTS
	MELTONS
ELMOORT	TREMOLO
ELMORTU	MOULTER
ELNOOPT	PELOTON
ELNOPRU	PLEURON
ELNOPST	LEPTONS
ELNOPTU	OPULENT
ELNORTY	ELYTRON
ELNOSTV	SOLVENT
ELNRSTY	STERNLY
ELOPRTU	POULTER
EMNOORS	MOONERS
EMNOORT	MONTERO
EMNOOST	MOONSET
EMNORTT	TORMENT
EMNORTU	MOUNTER
	REMOUNT
EMOORST	MOOTERS
EMORSTU	OESTRUM
ENOOPRS	OPERONS
	SNOOPER
ENOORSW	SWOONER
ENOPRTT	PORTENT
ENOPRTY	ENTROPY
ENORSUV	NERVOUS
ENORSUW	UNSWORE
ENORTUY	TOURNEY
ENOSTUU	TENUOUS
EOOPRST	POOREST
	STOOPER
EOORTUW	OUTWORE
EOPRSTU	PETROUS
	POSTURE
	POUTERS
	PROTEUS
	SPOUTER
	TROUPES
FIILNOT	TINFOIL
FILNORS	FLORINS
FILNORU	FLUORIN
FILORST	FLORIST
FILORTU	FLORUIT
GINOPRT	PORTING
GINORTW	TROWING
HIINORS	NOIRISH
HILORTU	UROLITH
HINOORT	HORNITO
HINORSU	NOURISH
IILNOPT	PINITOL
IILOPRT	TRIPOLI
IILORTV	VITRIOL
IINORSV	VIRIONS
IIORSTV	VISITOR
ILMORTU	TURMOIL
ILNOPRU	PURLOIN
ILNOPST	PONTILS
ILNOSTY	STONILY
	TYLOSIN
ILNOTUV	VOLUTIN
IMNOORT	MONITOR
IMORSTU	TOURISM
INOOPRT	PORTION
INOPRSU	INPOURS
INOPSTU	SPINOUT

Type III Eights, in Alphagram Order

Alphagram	Word
AABDEIOU	ABOIDEAU
AABDEORT	TEABOARD
AABEENOR	ANAEROBE
AABEIOTU	ABOITEAU
AABEIRTU	AUBRETIA
	AUBRIETA
AABELNOT	ATONABLE
AACDENOT	ANECDOTA
AACEIINT	ACTINIAE
AACENOTU	OCEANAUT
AACINORT	RAINCOAT
AADEOPRT	TAPADERO
AAEGIMNO	EGOMANIA
AAEHIIRT	HETAIRAI
AAEINORX	ANOREXIA
AAEMNORT	EMANATOR
AAIMNORT	ANIMATOR
ABCEIORT	BORACITE
ABDEEILN	DENIABLE
ABDEEILT	EDITABLE
ABDEORTU	OBDURATE
	TABOURED
ABEEISTU	BEAUTIES
ABEFIORT	BIFORATE
	FIREBOAT
ABEGIINO	IBOGAINE
ABEGILOT	OBLIGATE
ABEINORR	AIRBORNE
ABEIORTV	ABORTIVE
ACDEEILT	DELICATE
ACDEEINU	AUDIENCE
ACDEENOT	ANECDOTE
ACDEEORT	DECORATE
	RECOATED
ACDEIOSU	EDACIOUS
ACDENOTU	OUTDANCE
	UNCOATED
ACDEORTU	AERODUCT
	EDUCATOR
	OUTRACED
ACDINORT	TORNADIC
ACEEINSU	EUCAINES
ACEINOPR	APOCRINE
	CAPONIER
	PROCAINE
ACEINORV	VERONICA
ACEIOPRT	OPERATIC
ACENOORT	CORONATE
ACENORTU	COURANTE
	OUTRANCE
ACILNORT	CILANTRO
	CONTRAIL
ADEEFIIR	AERIFIED
ADEEFILN	ENFILADE
ADEEFORT	FOREDATE
ADEEHILN	HEADLINE
ADEEHNOT	HEADNOTE
ADEEIITV	IDEATIVE
ADEEILLO	OEILLADE
ADEEILMN	ENDEMIAL
ADEEILPT	DEPILATE
	EPILATED
	PILEATED
ADEEINOP	OEDIPEAN
ADEEMNOT	NEMATODE
ADEEMORT	MODERATE
ADEEOPRT	OPERATED
ADEFILOT	FOLIATED
ADEGIMNO	AMIDOGEN
ADEGIMOR	IDEOGRAM
ADEHORTU	AUTHORED
	OUTHEARD
ADEILOPT	PETALOID
ADEILOTV	DOVETAIL
	VIOLATED
ADEIMNOU	EUDAIMON
ADEMNOTU	AMOUNTED
ADEMORTU	OUTDREAM
ADENOTUY	AUTODYNE
ADEORTUV	OUTRAVED
AEEHLNOT	ANETHOLE
AEEILTUV	ELUVIATE
AEELNOPR	PERONEAL
AEELNOPT	ANTELOPE
AEFILOOR	AEROFOIL
AEFINOPR	PINAFORE
AEFIORTV	FAVORITE
AEGILOPT	PILOTAGE
AEGIORTV	RAVIGOTE
AEHIORTU	THIOUREA
AEIIMNRU	URINEMIA
AEILOORV	OVARIOLE
AEIMNORW	AIRWOMEN
AEINOQRU	AEQUORIN
AEINORRW	IRONWARE
AEIOPRRT	PRIORATE
AEMNOORT	ANTEROOM
AEMNORTU	ROUTEMAN
AFILNORT	FLATIRON
	INFLATOR
AHILNORT	HORNTAIL
BDEEINOT	OBEDIENT
BDEILORT	TRILOBED
BDEINOTU	BOUNTIED
BDEIORTU	TUBEROID
CDEEINOR	RECOINED
CDEINORU	DECURION
CDEINOTU	EDUCTION
CDEIORTU	OUTCRIED
CEEGINOR	EROGENIC
CEIILORT	ELICITOR
DEEIMNOR	DOMINEER
DEEINORW	IRONWEED
DEEINOTV	DENOTIVE
DEEIOPRT	PROTEIDE
DEEIORTV	OVEREDIT
DEFIINOT	NOTIFIED
DEFIORTU	OUTFIRED
DEIINOTY	IDONEITY
DEILORTY	ELYTROID
DEINOPRU	INPOURED
DEINOTUV	INDEVOUT
DEIORTUV	OUTDRIVE
EEHILORT	HOTELIER
EEINOOPT	OPTIONEE
EFILORTU	FLUORITE
EILORTUV	OUTLIVER

Top 100 Seven-Letter Bingo Stems Based on MMPR

In his bestseller *Word Freak* (Houghton Mifflin, 2001) Stefan Fatsis reported, "In the summer of 1986, in a centerfold pullout as sexy to SCRABBLE players as any Playboy Playmate, *SCRABBLE Players News* published Baron's 'Top 100' bonus word stems, about twenty-five hundred seven-letter bingos in all." Logo-titillationist me added the eight-letter bingos containing those 100 six-letter stems in the next issue. However, I had yet to apply the "MMPR" system of rank-ordering stems to determine which were the best *seven*-letter stems. It is far easier to learn when there is one degree of freedom (seven-letter stem plus singular tiles) than two degrees of freedom (six-letter stem plus two-tile combinations). In the months leading up to the 2000 National SCRABBLE Championship, I serialized such a list, along with mnemonics, to subscribers of "Crossword-Games-Pro," a worldwide listserv group of SCRABBLE tournament devotees. Those stems, bingos formed, and accompanying mnemonics are now provided.

SN	STEM	MSP	UT	MMPR
1	NASTIER	1.500	85	127.500
2	STONIER	1.333	72	95.976
3	AIRTONE	2.000	46	92.000
4	ENTRIES	0.917	82	75.194
5	ERASION	2.000	37	74.000
6	ATONERS	1.333	52	69.316
7	SARDINE	1.000	68	68.000
8	SERIATE	1.375	49	67.375
9	EASTERN	0.917	72	66.024
10	AIRTOES	2.000	33	66.000
11	NAILERS	1.000	65	65.000
12	RETAILS	1.000	65	65.000
13	ATONIES	2.000	32	64.000
14	SAINTED	1.000	63	63.000
15	TIRADES	1.000	62	62.000
16	TONEAID	1.333	44	58.652
17	ALERIOT	1.333	43	57.319
18	LATRINE	1.000	57	57.000
19	GAINERS	0.750	74	55.500
20	TRAINEE	1.375	39	53.625
21	RATIONS	1.000	53	53.000
22	DETRAIN	1.000	51	51.000
23	DINEROS	0.889	55	48.895
24	SALTINE	1.000	47	47.000
25	ROTSALE	0.889	52	46.228
26	SEERAIN	1.375	33	45.375
27	ISOLATE	1.333	34	45.322
28	REGIONS	0.667	67	44.689
29	NEROLIS	0.889	50	44.450
30	TOILERS	0.889	50	44.450
31	ATELIER	0.917	48	44.016
32	NOSEAID	1.333	33	43.989
33	TOADIER	1.333	33	43.989
34	OUTSEAR	0.889	49	43.561
35	ENDRIOT	0.889	49	43.561
36	NUTSIER	0.667	65	43.355
37	STEALER	0.611	69	42.159
38	DIETERS	0.611	69	42.159
39	REALIGN	0.500	84	42.000
40	ENTOILS	0.889	47	41.783
41	ANISOLE	1.333	31	41.323
42	ORALISE	1.333	31	41.323
43	TEARING	0.750	54	40.500
44	ARTIEST	0.625	64	40.000
45	SMARTIE	0.500	79	39.500
46	STEROID	0.889	44	39.116
47	DIALERS	0.667	58	38.686
48	RENTALS	0.667	58	38.686
49	SINRITE	0.667	58	38.686
50	ROADIES	1.333	29	38.657
51	ETESIAN	1.375	28	38.500
52	CINEAST	0.500	77	38.500
53	ESTRONE	0.815	47	38.305
54	TARRIES	0.625	61	38.125
55	DESTINE	0.611	62	37.882
56	TEASING	0.750	50	37.500
57	INSANER	0.625	60	37.500
58	NATURES	0.667	56	37.352
59	EARSNOD	0.889	41	36.449
60	DENIERS	0.611	59	36.049
61	LINTERS	0.667	54	36.018
62	IANURSE	1.000	36	36.000
63	ANEROID	1.333	27	35.991
64	TOADIES	1.333	27	35.991
65	IDEATES	0.917	39	35.763
66	ROASTER	0.556	63	35.028
67	INSTATE	0.625	56	35.000
68	REALISE	0.917	38	34.846
69	TENSILE	0.611	57	34.827
70	GREISEN	0.458	76	34.808
71	TINDERS	0.667	52	34.684
72	ONEDART	0.889	39	34.671
73	TENOURS	0.593	58	34.394
74	SEERONI	1.222	28	34.216
75	SEDATER	0.611	56	34.216
76	IREDATE	0.917	37	33.929
77	IRENTED	0.611	55	33.605
78	PARTIES	0.500	67	33.500
79	TEARAIN	1.000	33	33.000
80	INERTIA	1.000	33	33.000
81	GENITAL	0.500	65	32.500
82	ENDEARS	0.611	53	32.383
83	ETERNAL	0.611	53	32.383
84	LENTAID	0.667	48	32.016
85	LATINOS	0.667	48	32.016
86	AIRIEST	1.000	32	32.000
87	STRANGE	0.500	64	32.000
88	HASTIER	0.500	64	32.000
89	PAINTER	0.500	64	32.000
90	INMATES	0.500	63	31.500
91	STINGER	0.500	63	31.500
92	SANELIE	0.917	34	31.178
93	STOURIE	0.889	35	31.115
94	AGONIES	1.000	31	31.000
95	READING	0.500	62	31.000
96	SESTINA	0.375	82	30.750
97	DETAILS	0.667	46	30.682
98	TOENAIL	1.333	23	30.659
99	ONETIRE	1.222	25	30.550
100	ISONTEE	1.222	25	30.550

SN: Stem Number, ranked according to MMPR value. (If two stems have identical MMPRs, one with higher MSP comes first. If equal MSPs, then listed alphabetically based on alphagram of stem.)

Stem: Here, a combination of seven letters, arranged as a word, if one exists. Otherwise, stem may be comprised of shorter words. In three instances, TOADIER (33), OUTSEAR (34), ORALISE (42), a phony word is constructed.

MSP: Modified Stem Probability. The relative probability of obtaining a seven-letter combination, where the Modified Stem Probability of obtaining DETRAIN was set at 1, and, due to the retention of an S in actual game play, the first S in any stem was calculated as a frequency-6 tile.

UT: Usable Tiles to complete stem, of the remaining 93 tiles.

MMPR: Modified Modified Power Rating = MSP × UT. A means of identifying the best bingo stems to study based on the likelihood of obtaining a seven-letter stem (MSP) and the likelihood of completing the stem to form a bingo with a usable tile (UT).

Cross Index

STEM	SN	MNEMONIC	8s
AAEINRT	79	TEA-RAIN	16
ACEINST	52	CINEAST	32
ADEEIRT	76	I-REDATE	14
ADEEIST	65	IDEATES	16
ADEENRS	83	ENDEARS	19
ADEERST	75	SEDATER	29
ADEGINR	95	READING	23
ADEILNT	84	LENT-AID	12
ADEILRS	47	DIALERS	22
ADEILST	97	DETAILS	15
ADEINOR	63	ANEROID	10
ADEINOS	32	NOSE-AID	17
ADEINOT	16	TONE-AID	17
ADEINRS	7	SARDINE	23
ADEINRT	22	DETRAIN	20
ADEINST	14	SAINTED	21
ADEIORS	50	ROADIES	10
ADEIORT	33	TOADIER*	12
ADEIOST	64	TOADIES	11
ADEIRST	15	TIRADES	28
ADENORS	59	EARS-NOD	15
ADENORT	72	ONE-DART	13
AEEILNS	92	SANE-LIE	11
AEEILRS	68	REALISE	17
AEEILRT	31	ATELIER	22
AEEINRS	26	SEE-RAIN	15
AEEINRT	20	TRAINEE	22
AEEINST	51	ETESIAN	17
AEEIRST	8	SERIATE	29
AEELNRT	82	ETERNAL	17
AEELRST	37	STEALER	34
AEENRST	9	EASTERN	37
AEGILNR	39	REALIGN	42
AEGILNT	81	GELATIN	34
AEGINOS	94	AGONIES	10
AEGINRS	19	GAINERS	47
AEGINRT	43	TEARING	43
AEGINST	56	TEASING	34
AEGNRST	87	STRANGE	30
AEHIRST	88	HASTIER	15
AEIINRT	80	INERTIA	8
AEIIRST	86	AIRIEST	13
AEILNOS	41	ANISOLE	13
AEILNOT	98	TOENAIL	10
AEILNRS	11	NAILERS	29
AEILNRT	18	LATRINE	30
AEILNST	24	SALTINE	33
AEILORS	42	ORALISE*	18
AEILORT	17	ALE-RIOT	17
AEILOST	27	ISOLATE	17
AEILRST	12	RETAILS	39
AEIMNST	90	INMATES	29
AEIMRST	45	SMARTIE	38
AEINNRS	57	INSANER	17
AEINORS	5	ERASION	17
AEINORT	3	AIR-TONE	23
AEINOST	13	ATONIES	21
AEINPRT	89	PAINTER	20
AEINRST	1	NASTIER	69
AEINRSU	62	I-A-NURSE	14
AEINSST	96	SESTINA	44
AEINSTT	67	INSTATE	26
AEIORST	10	AIR-TOES	14
AEIPRST	78	PARTIES	33
AEIRRST	54	TARRIES	21
AEIRSTT	44	ARTIEST	33
AELNRST	48	RENTALS	19
AELORST	25	ROT-SALE	28
AENORST	6	ATONERS	24
AENRSTU	58	NATURES	22
AEORRST	66	ROASTER	23
AEORSTU	34	OUTSEAR*	22
AILNOST	85	LATINOS	11
AINORST	21	RATIONS	17
DEEINRS	60	DENIERS	26
DEEINRT	77	I-RENTED	23
DEEINST	55	DESTINE	23
DEEIRST	38	DIETERS	33
DEINORS	23	DINEROS	16
DEINORT	35	END-RIOT	12
DEINRST	71	TINDERS	20
DEIORST	46	STEROID	22
EEGINRS	70	GREISEN	32
EEILNST	69	TENSILE	25
EEINORS	74	SEE-RONI	12
EEINORT	99	ONE-TIRE	10
EEINOST	100	IS-ON-TEE	11
EEINRST	4	ENTRIES	50
EENORST	53	ESTRONE	14
EGINORS	28	REGIONS	17
EGINRST	91	STINGER	27
EIINRST	49	SIN-RITE	26
EILNORS	29	NEROLIS	11
EILNOST	40	ENTOILS	19
EILNRST	61	LINTERS	20
EILORST	30	TOILERS	14
EINORST	2	STONIER	31
EINRSTU	36	NUTSIER	22
EIORSTU	93	STOURIE	15
ENORSTU	73	TENOURS	21

Mnemonics for the Top 100 Seven-Letter Bingo Stems

As with the six-letter stems (page 31), asterisked stems are unacceptable words. Similarly, a mnemonic preceded by an asterisk indicates that the stem takes *no* vowels, but have been inserted only for mnemonic purposes. If the mnemonic is preceded by two asterisks (**), it means only the lower case vowel in the mnemonic can actually combine with the stem, while the others are inserted simply for mnemonic construction. I have sometimes included a "transition stem" in lower case letters under the mnemonic column, changing an acceptable word to a phrase, e.g., ATONIES to "into-sea," as the latter may then help access and remember the mnemonic (here, "SCRAMBLED POND") more effectively. Two words included in mnemonics, KNOX (#81) and COWARDLIEST (#91), are phonies and, so, are followed with asterisks. In devising some of these mnemonics ((#1, 4, 32, 42, 65, 75, 78, 92, 96), I personalized them, using my, my wife's, or a friend's name. What's most important is not that the mnemonic make sense, though many do, so much as that it can be effectively recalled. Precious time in a game can be saved knowing, as you look at your rack containing AEINRST, with a V between two triple word scores, that there is no eight-letter bingo there since the mnemonic for NASTIER contains no V. On the other hand, I once had AEIMNRT, and there was an E between two double word scores. I mentally "took out" the M and "replaced" it with the E on the board, making TRAINEE. Knowing that mnemonic for TRAINEE was "GIRL'S KID CHIMP," I knew it took the M, and spent the time to come up with ANTIMERE on the double-double for 90 points.

SN	Stem	Mnemonic
1	NASTIER	MICHAEL BARON'S WORD LIST FORGOT "PUKED"
2	STONIER	GO PROBE ROCKS: JUST HEAVENLY
3	AIR-TONE	BACH'S PLAN: DART CZAR
4	ENTRIES	ENTRY: CURVY FOX. MIKE'S GLAD.
5	ERASION	*BAFFLING SOME DETECTIVES
6	ATONERS	FRUMPS BEING NICE
7	SARDINE	PROVEN SALTED GRUB
8	SERIATE	HELPED MY NEW TERMS
9	EASTERN	BROUGHT JOVIAL FACES
10	AIR-TOES	**MJ HAD VENTuRED
11	NAILERS	PEGS HIT MY COVERED BOX
12	RETAILS	I GET CRUMPLED STUFF? BUNK!
13	ATONIES	*into-sea SCRAMBLED POND
14	SAINTED	GETS IMPROVED TOUCH
15	TIRADES	WOMAN-BLASTED SPEECHES
16	TONE-AID	**iMPROVES BENT MUSiCAL
17	ALE-RIOT	**FIVe-DOZeN-BeeR CHAMP
18	LATRINE	MOVING FUNNY SPICES
19	GAINERS	DANGER WAVY STOMACH PROBLEM
20	TRAINEE	GIRL'S KID CHIMP
21	RATIONS	BOTTLED BOWL JUG CUPS
22	DETRAIN	CHOOCHOO STOPS, I GET OUT
23	DINEROS	PAID RICH JUDGES
24	SALTINE	OBVIOUS COMBO FOR PORK GOMBO
25	ROT-SALE	VULTURES CHUGGED UP BEEF
26	SEE-RAIN	**PLuNKING CAT AND DOG
27	ISOLATE	*PACKING AND MOVING STUFF
28	REGIONS	WAY INCREDIBLE PARTS
29	NEROLIS	MAGIC CARPET
30	TOILERS	COULDN'T FLIP BUS
31	ATELIER	**lie-tear To FIVE DoZEN PRoBLEMS
32	NOSE-AID	*ZAX HAD BRIGHT MUCUS
33	TOADIER*	*SLICKER VARMINT
34	OUTSEAR*	BITCHING: TV WILL DIP IQS
35	END-RIOT	END PEACETIME
36	NUTSIER	BLAME IQ DIP ON TV
37	STEALER	STUPID BOXER "FRENCHY"
38	DIETERS	BLIMPS EATING CRAWFISH
39	REALIGN	SCRABBLING CHAMP FIXED JOVIALITY
40	ENTOILS	UNWRAP DA HAVOC
41	ANISOLE	*i-lose? na! EXPERT SMACKING
42	ORALISE*	*ZEV'S CHOMPING FOOD
43	TEARING	EX-VAMPS BELT-WHACKED
44	ARTIEST	AMAZES NOTABLE CROWD
45	SMARTIE	VALUES KNOWING, EXPECTS DUMB
46	STEROID	WIMP'S LUCK: BIG ABS
47	DIALERS	BELL COMPANY NUT
48	RENTALS	HAVING HUT SPACE
49	SIN-RITE	VAMP STABBED--HULK CAGED
50	ROADIES	*FLAT PAVED NICE
51	ETESIAN	*sane-tie DUMB CRAVATS
52	CINEAST	FANS OF THE DIRTY OLD MOVIE BIZ
53	ESTRONE	FLASHING FOX
54	TARRIES	BELCHER WON'T SPLIT
55	DESTINE	UNDERFED MAN: EAT VEGETABLES!
56	TEASING	FUZZY NURDS THUMB UGLY VW
57	INSANER	COMMITTED GROUPS
58	NATURES	THESE DO BECOME EVIL
59	EARS-NOD	PRIM BELCH
60	DENIERS	WHO GABS OF SEX TALK? PERVS!
61	LINTERS	GO AID MAKEUP
62	I-A-NURSE	**NUMBeD ZITS
63	ANEROID	*GOD'S BAROMETER
64	TOADIES	*PRIZING EX-ANIMALS
65	IDEATES	**MARVELOuS IDEA? JOHN FIBBED
66	ROASTER	ROASTING COLD BLIMPS
67	INSTATE	A FEW STRANGERS PREACHED
68	REALISE	*GAZED ON MY PROFITS
69	TENSILE	KEEPING STRETCHED VIBES
70	GREISEN	OLD STONE FACED BUMP HOWEVER
71	TINDERS	GUIDE LIT UP AX
72	ONE-DART	WINGY TOPIC
73	TENOURS	ten(h)ours COMBINING HALF-DAYS
74	SEE-RONI	*THE DOGLIKE VAMP
75	SEDATER	BIG MIKE FELT WHISPERY
76	I-REDATE	**TWO ENVIaBLE MaTES
77	I-RENTED	TOM BROKAW'S SUV AND AX
78	PARTIES	LIVELY PAMINA WAS CHARGED
79	TEA-RAIN	**BE TEAPoT'S MAGIC WIZ
80	INERTIA	**SPLeNDID Z'S
81	GELATIN	KNOX* VAMP'S GAZE BECHARMED
82	ETERNAL	EVER WISHING BED MIX
83	ENDEARS	SICKENS YOUNG WOMEN
84	LENT-AID	FOP GAVE BOND
85	LATINOS	ANGRY OLE (or, YEARLONG)
86	AIRIEST	*MAN WHO'LL FIX ZIPPERS
87	STRANGE	WEIRD FOG LAMPS
88	HASTIER	I POUNCED AND RODE AWAY
89	PAINTER	GATHERED OILS
90	INMATES	GANEFS OR BLOCKHEADS?
91	STINGER	COWARDLIEST*
92	SANE-LIE	CREE BEGGED "PREX?! VP?!"
93	STOURIE	NAVAL CAMP FAD
94	AGONIES	*SCRABBLING DAZE
95	READING	BED HABIT MOSTLY
96	SESTINA	sit-sane PAMINA DEUTSCH/MIKE BARON RELAXING
97	DETAILS	I MERGE COPY
98	TOENAIL	*GRIPS BED
99	ONE-TIRE	*EXHAUSTED CAR
100	IS-ON-TEE	*TIGER'S COMB

As with the six-letter stems, it is rare that a seven-letter stem with four vowels can take a fifth vowel to form an eight-letter word. Of the 1542 words generated by these seven-letter stems, there are but 12 with five vowels: AERATION, AEROLITE, AUDITEES, DETAINEE, EATERIES, ERADIATE, IDEATION-IODINATE, INERTIAE, OUTRAISE-SAUTOIRE, UNEASIER.

The Top 100 Seven-Letter Bingo Stems Based on MMPR and Bingos Formed, by Bingo Stem, With Mnemonics

#	Stem	Mnemonic	#	Stem	Mnemonic
1	NASTIER	MICHAEL BARON'S WORD LIST FORGOT "PUKED"	12	RETAILS	I GET CRUMPLED STUFF? BUNK!
2	STONIER	GO PROBE ROCKS: JUST HEAVENLY	13	ATONIES	*into-sea SCRAMBLED POND
3	AIR-TONE	BACH'S PLAN: DART CZAR	14	SAINTED	GETS iMPROVED TOUCH
4	ENTRIES	ENTRY: CURVY FOX. MIKE'S GLAD.	15	TIRADES	WOMAN-BLASTED SPEECHES
5	ERASION	*BAFFLING SOME DETECTIVES	16	TONE-AID	**iMPROVES BENT MUSiCAL
6	ATONERS	FRUMPS BEING NICE	17	ALE-RIOT	**FIVe-DOZeN-BeeR CHAMP
7	SARDINE	PROVEN SALTED GRUB	18	LATRINE	MOVING FUNNY SPICES
8	SERIATE	HELPED MY NEW TERMS	19	GAINERS	DANGER WAVY STOMACH PROBLEM
9	EASTERN	BROUGHT JOVIAL FACES	20	TRAINEE	GIRL'S KID CHIMP
10	AIR-TOES	**MJ HAD VENTuRED	21	RATIONS	BOTTLED BOWL JUG CUPS
11	NAILERS	PEGS HIT MY COVERED BOX			

1 NASTIER

A ANTISERA
RATANIES
SANTERIA
SEATRAIN
B BANISTER
BARNIEST
C CANISTER
CERATINS
CISTERNA
CREATINS
SCANTIER
TACRINES
D DETRAINS
RANDIEST
STRAINED
E ARENITES
ARSENITE
RESINATE
STEARINE
TRAINEES
F FAINTERS
G ANGRIEST
ASTRINGE
GANISTER
GANTRIES
GRANITES
INGRATES
RANGIEST
H HAIRNETS
INEARTHS
THERIANS
I INERTIAS
RAINIEST
K KERATINS
L ENTRAILS
LATRINES
RATLINES
RETINALS
TRENAILS
M MINARETS
RAIMENTS
N ENTRAINS
TRANNIES
O NOTARIES
SENORITA
P PAINTERS
PANTRIES
PERTAINS
PINASTER
PRISTANE
REPAINTS
R RESTRAIN
RETRAINS
STRAINER
TERRAINS
TRAINERS
S ARTINESS
RETSINAS
STAINERS
STEARINS
T INTREATS
NITRATES
STRAITEN
TERTIANS
U RUINATES
TAURINES
URANITES
URINATES
W TINWARES

2 STONIER

A NOTARIES
SENORITA
B BORNITES
C COINTERS
CORNIEST
NOTICERS
E ONERIEST
SEROTINE
G GENITORS
H HORNIEST
ORNITHES
J JOINTERS
K INSTROKE
L RETINOLS
N INTONERS
TERNIONS
O SNOOTIER
P POINTERS
PORNIEST
PROTEINS
TROPINES
R INTRORSE
S OESTRINS
T SNOTTIER
TENORIST
TRITONES
U ROUTINES
SNOUTIER
V INVESTOR
Y SEROTINY
TYROSINE

3 AIRTONE

A AERATION
B BARITONE
OBTAINER
REOBTAIN
TABORINE
C ACTIONER
ANORETIC
CREATION
REACTION
D AROINTED
ORDINATE
RATIONED
H ANTIHERO
L ORIENTAL
RELATION
N ANOINTER
REANOINT
P ATROPINE
R ANTERIOR
S NOTARIES
SENORITA
T TENTORIA
Z NOTARIZE

4 ENTRIES

A ARENITES
ARSENITE
RESINATE
STEARINE
TRAINEES
C ENTERICS
ENTICERS
SECRETIN
D INSERTED
NERDIEST
RESIDENT
SINTERED
TRENDIES
E ETERNISE
TEENSIER
F FERNIEST
INFESTER
G GENTRIES
INTEGERS
REESTING
STEERING
I NITERIES
K KERNITES
L ENLISTER
LISTENER
REENLIST
SILENTER
M MISENTER
N INTENSER
INTERNES
O ONERIEST
SEROTINE
R INSERTER
REINSERT
REINTERS
RENTIERS
TERRINES
S SENTRIES
T INSETTER
INTEREST
STERNITE
TRIENTES
U ESURIENT
RETINUES
REUNITES
V NERVIEST
REINVEST
SIRVENTE
X INTERSEX
Y SERENITY

5 ERASION

B BARONIES
SEAROBIN
C SCENARIO
D ANEROIDS
F FARINOSE
G ORGANISE
L AILERONS
ALIENORS
M MORAINES
ROMAINES
ROMANISE
N RAISONNE
S ERASIONS
SENSORIA
T NOTARIES
SENORITA
V AVERSION

6 ATONERS

B BARONETS
C ANCESTOR
ENACTORS
E EARSTONE
RESONATE
F SEAFRONT
G ESTRAGON
NEGATORS
I NOTARIES
SENORITA
M MONSTERA
ONSTREAM
TONEARMS
N RESONANT
P OPERANTS
PRONATES
PROTEANS
R ANTRORSE
S ASSENTOR
SANTEROS
SENATORS
STARNOSE
TREASONS
U OUTEARNS

7 SARDINE

A ARANEIDS
B BRANDIES
D SARDINED
E ARSENIDE
NEARSIDE
G DERAIGNS
GRADINES
READINGS
L ISLANDER
N INSNARED
O ANEROIDS
P SPRAINED
R DRAINERS
SERRANID
S ARIDNESS
SARDINES
T DETRAINS
RANDIEST
STRAINED
U DENARIUS
UNRAISED
URANIDES
V INVADERS

8 SERIATE

D READIEST
SERIATED
STEADIER
E EATERIES
H HEARTIES
L ATELIERS
EARLIEST
LEARIEST
REALTIES
M EMERITAS
EMIRATES
STEAMIER
N ARENITES
ARSENITE
RESINATE
STEARINE
TRAINEES
P PARIETES
R ARTERIES
S SERIATES
T ARIETTES
ITERATES
TEARIEST
TREATIES
TREATISE
W SWEATIER
WASTERIE
WEARIEST
Y YEASTIER

9 EASTERN

A ARSENATE
SERENATA
B ABSENTER
C CENTARES
REASCENT
REENACTS
SARCENET
E SERENATE
F FASTENER
FENESTRA
REFASTEN
G ESTRANGE
GRANTEES
GREATENS
NEGATERS
REAGENTS
SERGEANT
H HASTENER
HEARTENS
I ARENITES
ARSENITE
RESINATE
STEARINE
TRAINEES
J SERJEANT
L ETERNALS
TELERANS
O EARSTONE
RESONATE
R TERRANES
S ASSENTER
EARNESTS
SARSENET
T ENTREATS
RATTEENS
U SAUTERNE
V VETERANS

10 AIRTOES

D ASTEROID
H HOARIEST
J JAROSITE
M AMORTISE
ATOMISER
N NOTARIES
SENORITA
R ROTARIES
T TOASTIER
U OUTRAISE
SAUTOIRE
V TRAVOISE
VIATORES
VOTARIES

11 NAILERS

B RINSABLE
C CARLINES
LANCIERS
D ISLANDER
E ALIENERS
G ALIGNERS
ENGRAILS
NARGILES
REALIGNS
SIGNALER
SLANGIER
H INHALERS
I AIRLINES
M MARLINES
MINERALS
MISLEARN
O AILERONS
ALIENORS
P PRALINES
R SNARLIER
S RAINLESS
T ENTRAILS
LATRINES
RATLINES
RETINALS
TRENAILS
V RAVELINS
X RELAXINS
Y INLAYERS

12 RETAILS

B BLASTIER
LIBRATES
C ARTICLES
RECITALS
STERICAL
D DILATERS
LARDIEST
REDTAILS
E ATELIERS
EARLIEST
LEARIEST
REALTIES
F FRAILEST
G GLARIEST
I LISTERIA
K LARKIEST
STALKIER
STARLIKE
L LITERALS
TALLIERS
M LAMISTER
MARLIEST
MARLITES
MISALTER
N ENTRAILS
LATRINES
RATLINES
RETINALS
TRENAILS
P PILASTER
PLAISTER
PLAITERS
R RETRIALS
TRAILERS
S REALISTS
SALTIERS
SALTIRES
T TERTIALS
U URALITES

13 ATONIES

B BOTANIES
BOTANISE
NIOBATES
OBEISANT
C ACONITES
CANOEIST
SONICATE
D ASTONIED
SEDATION
L ELATIONS
INSOLATE
TOENAILS
M AMNIOTES
MASONITE
MISATONE
N ENATIONS
SONATINE
P SAPONITE
R NOTARIES
SENORITA
S ASTONIES

14 SAINTED

C DISTANCE
D DANDIEST
E ANDESITE
G SEDATING
STEADING
H HANDIEST
I ADENITIS
DAINTIES
M MEDIANTS
O ASTONIED
SEDATION
P DEPAINTS
R DETRAINS
RANDIEST
STRAINED
S DESTAINS
SANDIEST
T INSTATED
U AUDIENTS
SINUATED
V DEVIANTS

15 TIRADES

A AIRDATES
DATARIES
RADIATES
B REDBAITS
TRIBADES
C ACRIDEST
D DISRATED
E READIEST
SERIATED
STEADIER
H HARDIEST
L DILATERS
LARDIEST
REDTAILS
M MISRATED
READMITS
N DETRAINS
RANDIEST
STRAINED
O ASTEROID
P RAPIDEST
TRAIPSED
S DIASTERS
DISASTER
DISRATES
T STRIATED
TARDIEST
W TAWDRIES

16 TONEAID

B OBTAINED
C CATENOID
I IDEATION
IODINATE
L DELATION
M DOMINATE
N ANOINTED
ANTINODE
P ANTIPODE
R AROINTED
ORDINATE
RATIONED
S ASTONIED
SEDATION
T ANTIDOTE
TETANOID
V DONATIVE

17 ALERIOT

B LABORITE
C EROTICAL
LORICATE
D IDOLATER
TAILORED
E AEROLITE
F FLOATIER
H AEROLITH
M AMITROLE
ROLAMITE
N ORIENTAL
RELATION
P EPILATOR
PETIOLAR
R RETAILOR
V VIOLATER
Z TRIAZOLE

18 LATRINE

C CLARINET
E ELATERIN
ENTAILER
TREENAIL
F INFLATER
G ALERTING
ALTERING
INTEGRAL
RELATING
TANGLIER
TRIANGLE
I INERTIAL
M TERMINAL
TRAMLINE
N INTERNAL
O ORIENTAL
RELATION
P INTERLAP
TRAPLINE
TRIPLANE
S ENTRAILS
LATRINES
RATLINES
RETINALS
TRENAILS
U AUNTLIER
RETINULA
TENURIAL
V INTERVAL
Y INTERLAY

19 GAINERS

A ANERGIAS
ANGARIES
ARGINASE
B BEARINGS
SABERING
C CREASING
D DERAIGNS
GRADINES
READINGS
E ANERGIES
GESNERIA
G GEARINGS
GREASING
SNAGGIER
H HEARINGS
HEARSING
SHEARING
L ALIGNERS
ENGRAILS
NARGILES
REALIGNS
SIGNALER
SLANGIER
M SMEARING
N AGINNERS
EARNINGS
ENGRAINS
GRANNIES
O ORGANISE
P SPEARING
R EARRINGS
GRAINERS
S ASSIGNER
REASSIGN
SERINGAS
T ANGRIEST
ASTRINGE
GANISTER
GANTRIES
GRANITES
INGRATES
RANGIEST
V VINEGARS
W RESAWING
SWEARING
Y RESAYING
SYNERGIA

20 TRAINEE

C CENTIARE
CREATINE
INCREATE
ITERANCE
D DETAINER
RETAINED
G GRATINEE
INTERAGE
H HERNIATE
I INERTIAE
K ANKERITE
L ELATERIN
ENTAILER
TREENAIL
M ANTIMERE
P APERIENT
R RETAINER
S ARENITES
ARSENITE
RESINATE
STEARINE
TRAINEES

21 RATIONS

B TABORINS
C CAROTINS
CORTINAS
D DIATRONS
INTRADOS
E NOTARIES
SENORITA
G ORGANIST
ROASTING
J JANITORS
L TONSILAR
O ORATIONS
P ATROPINS
S ARSONIST
T STRONTIA
U RAINOUTS
W WAITRONS

22	DETRAIN	CHOOCHOO STOPS, I GET OUT
23	DINEROS	PAID RICH JUDGES
24	SALTINE	OBVIOUS COMBO FOR PORK GOMBO
25	ROT-SALE	VULTURES CHUGGED UP BEEF
26	SEE-RAIN	**PLuNKING CAT AND DOG
27	ISOLATE	*PACKING AND MOVING STUFF
28	REGIONS	WAY INCREDIBLE PARTS
29	NEROLIS	MAGIC CARPET
30	TOILERS	COULDN'T FLIP BUS
31	ATELIER	**lie-tear To FIVE DoZEN PRoBLEMS
32	NOSE-AID	*ZAX HAD BRIGHT MUCUS
33	TOADIER*	*SLICKER VARMINT
34	OUTSEAR*	BITCHING: TV WILL DIP IQS
35	END-RIOT	END PEACETIME
36	NUTSIER	BLAME IQ DIP ON TV
37	STEALER	STUPID BOXER "FRENCHY"
38	DIETERS	BLIMPS EATING CRAWFISH
39	REALIGN	SCRABBLING CHAMP FIXED JOVIALITY
40	ENTOILS	UNWRAP DA HAVOC
41	ANISOLE	*i-lose? na! EXPERT SMACKING
42	ORALISE*	*ZEV'S CHOMPING FOOD
43	TEARING	EX-VAMPS BELT-WHACKED
44	ARTIEST	AMAZES NOTABLE CROWD
45	SMARTIE	VALUES KNOWING, EXPECTS DUMB
46	STEROID	WIMP'S LUCK: BIG ABS
47	DIALERS	BELL COMPANY NUT

22 DETRAIN

C DICENTRA
E DETAINER
RETAINED
G DERATING
GRADIENT
REDATING
TREADING
H ANTHERID
I DAINTIER
O AROINTED
ORDINATE
RATIONED
P DIPTERAN
S DETRAINS
RANDIEST
STRAINED
T NITRATED
U INDURATE
RUINATED
URINATED

23 DINEROS

A ANEROIDS
C CONSIDER
D INDORSED
E INDORSEE
G NEGROIDS
H HORDEINS
I DERISION
IRONSIDE
RESINOID
J JOINDERS
P PRISONED
R INDORSER
S INDORSES
SORDINES
U DOURINES
SOURDINE

24 SALTINE

B INSTABLE
C CANISTEL
F INFLATES
G GELATINS
GENITALS
STEALING
TAGLINES
I ALIENIST
LITANIES
K LANKIEST
M AILMENTS
ALIMENTS
MANLIEST
MELANIST
SMALTINE
O ELATIONS
INSOLATE
TOENAILS
P PANELIST
PANTILES
PLAINEST
R ENTRAILS
LATRINES
RATLINES
RETINALS
TRENAILS
S ELASTINS
NAILSETS
SALIENTS
SALTINES
U ALUNITES
INSULATE
V VENTAILS

25 ROTSALE

B BLOATERS
SORTABLE
STORABLE
C LOCATERS
SECTORAL
D DELATORS
LEOTARDS
LODESTAR
E OLEASTER
F FLOATERS
FORESTAL
REFLOATS
G GLOATERS
LEGATORS
H LOATHERS
RATHOLES
L REALLOTS
ROSTELLA
P PETROSAL
POLESTAR
R REALTORS
RELATORS
RESTORAL
S OLESTRAS
T RETOTALS
U ROSULATE
V LEVATORS
OVERSALT

26 SEERAIN

C INCREASE
D ARSENIDE
NEARSIDE
G ANERGIES
GESNERIA
K SNEAKIER
L ALIENERS
N ANSERINE
P NAPERIES
T ARENITES
ARSENITE
RESINATE
STEARINE
TRAINEES
U UNEASIER

27 ISOLATE

C COALIEST
SOCIETAL
D DIASTOLE
ISOLATED
SODALITE
F FOLIATES
G LATIGOES
OTALGIES
K KEITLOAS
M LOAMIEST
N ELATIONS
INSOLATE
TOENAILS
P SPOLIATE
S ISOLATES
T TOTALISE
V VIOLATES

28 REGIONS

A ORGANISE
B SOBERING
C COREIGNS
COSIGNER
D NEGROIDS
E ERINGOES
I SEIGNIOR
L RESOLING
N NEGRONIS
P PERIGONS
REPOSING
SPONGIER
R IGNORERS
S GORINESS
T GENITORS
W RESOWING
Y SEIGNORY

29 NEROLIS

A AILERONS
ALIENORS
C INCLOSER
LICENSOR
E ELOINERS
G RESOLING
I LIONISER
M MISENROL
P PROLINES
R LORINERS
T RETINOLS

30 TOILERS

B STROBILE
C CLOISTER
COISTREL
COSTLIER
D STOLIDER
F TREFOILS
I ROILIEST
L TROLLIES
N RETINOLS
O OESTRIOL
P POITRELS
S ESTRIOLS
T TRIOLETS
U OUTLIERS

31 ATELIER

B LIBERATE
D DETAILER
ELATERID
RETAILED
F FEATLIER
L LAETRILE
M MATERIEL
N ELATERIN
ENTAILER
TREENAIL
O AEROLITE
P PEARLITE
R RETAILER
S ATELIERS
EARLIEST
LEARIEST
REALTIES
T LATERITE
LITERATE
V LEVIRATE
RELATIVE
Z LATERIZE

32 NOSEAID

B BEDSONIA
C CODEINAS
DIOCESAN
D ADENOIDS
G AGONISED
DIAGNOSE
H ADHESION
M AMIDONES
DAIMONES
DOMAINES
R ANEROIDS
S ADENOSIS
ADONISES
T ASTONIED
SEDATION
X DIOXANES
Z ANODIZES

33 TOADIER

C CERATOID
K KERATOID
L IDOLATER
TAILORED
M MEDIATOR
N AROINTED
ORDINATE
RATIONED
R ADROITER
S ASTEROID
T TERATOID
V DEVIATOR

34 OUTSEAR

B SABOTEUR
C OUTRACES
D OUTDARES
OUTREADS
READOUTS
G OUTRAGES
H OUTHEARS
I OUTRAISE
SAUTOIRE
L ROSULATE
N OUTEARNS
P APTEROUS
Q EQUATORS
QUAESTOR
S OSSATURE
T OUTRATES
OUTSTARE
SEATROUT
V OUTRAVES
W OUTSWARE
OUTSWEAR
OUTWEARS

35 ENDRIOT

A AROINTED
ORDINATE
RATIONED
C CENTROID
DOCTRINE
D TRENDOID
E ORIENTED
I RETINOID
M DORMIENT
N INDENTOR
P DIPTERON
T INTORTED

36 NUTSIER

A RUINATES
TAURINES
URANITES
URINATES
B TRIBUNES
TURBINES
D INTRUDES
E ESURIENT
RETINUES
REUNITES
I NEURITIS
L INSULTER
M TERMINUS
UNMITERS
UNMITRES
N RUNNIEST
O ROUTINES
SNOUTIER
P UNRIPEST
Q SQUINTER
T RUNTIEST
V VENTURIS

37 STEALER

B ARBELEST
BLEATERS
RESTABLE
RETABLES
C CLEAREST
TREACLES
D DESALTER
RESLATED
TREADLES
E TEASELER
F REFLATES
H HALTERES
LEATHERS
I ATELIERS
EARLIEST
LEARIEST
REALTIES
N ETERNALS
TELERANS
O OLEASTER
P PETRALES
PLEATERS
PRELATES
REPLATES
R ALTERERS
REALTERS
RELATERS
S RESLATES
STEALERS
TEARLESS
T ALERTEST
U RESALUTE
X EXALTERS
Y EASTERLY

38 DIETERS

A READIEST
SERIATED
STEADIER
B BESTRIDE
BISTERED
C DESERTIC
DISCREET
DISCRETE
E REEDIEST
F RESIFTED
G DIGESTER
REDIGEST
H DIETHERS
I SIDERITE
L RELISTED
M DEMERITS
DEMISTER
DIMETERS
N INSERTED
NERDIEST
RESIDENT
SINTERED
TRENDIES
P PREEDITS
PRIESTED
RESPITED
R DESTRIER
S DIESTERS
EDITRESS
RESISTED
SISTERED
T TIREDEST
W WEIRDEST

39 REALIGN

A GERANIAL
B BLEARING
C CLEARING
RELACING
D DANGLIER
DRAGLINE
E ALGERINE
F FINAGLER
G GANGLIER
LAGERING
REGALING
H NARGHILE
NARGILEH
I GAINLIER
J JANGLIER
L ALLERGIN
M GERMINAL
MALIGNER
MALINGER
N LEARNING
O GERANIOL
REGIONAL
P GRAPLINE
PEARLING
R GNARLIER
S ALIGNERS
ENGRAILS
NARGILES
REALIGNS
SIGNALER
SLANGIER
T ALERTING
ALTERING
INTEGRAL
RELATING
TANGLIER
TRIANGLE
V RAVELING
X RELAXING
Y LAYERING
RELAYING
YEARLING

40 ENTOILS

A ELATIONS
INSOLATE
TOENAILS
C LECTIONS
TELSONIC
D LENTOIDS
H HOLSTEIN
HOTLINES
NEOLITHS
N INSOLENT
O LOONIEST
OILSTONE
P POTLINES
TOPLINES
R RETINOLS
U ELUTIONS
OUTLINES
V NOVELIST
W TOWLINES

41 ANISOLE

G GASOLINE
K KAOLINES
M LAMINOSE
SEMOLINA
N SOLANINE
P OPALINES
R AILERONS
ALIENORS
S ANISOLES
T ELATIONS
INSOLATE
TOENAILS
X SILOXANE

42 ORALISE

C CALORIES
CARIOLES
D DARIOLES
F FORESAIL
G GASOLIER
GIRASOLE
SERAGLIO
H AIRHOLES
SHOALIER
M MORALISE
N AILERONS
ALIENORS
P PELORIAS
POLARISE
S SOLARISE
V VALORISE
VARIOLES
Z SOLARIZE

43 TEARING

A AERATING
B BERATING
REBATING
TABERING
C ARGENTIC
CATERING
CREATING
REACTING
D DERATING
GRADIENT
REDATING
TREADING
E GRATINEE
INTERAGE
H EARTHING
HEARTING
INGATHER
K RETAKING
L ALERTING
ALTERING
INTEGRAL
RELATING
TANGLIER
TRIANGLE
M EMIGRANT
REMATING
P RETAPING
TAPERING
S ANGRIEST
ASTRINGE
GANISTER
GANTRIES
GRANITES
INGRATES
RANGIEST
T GNATTIER
TREATING
V AVERTING
GRIEVANT
VINTAGER
W TWANGIER
WATERING
X RETAXING

44 ARTIEST

A ARIETTAS
ARISTATE
B BIRETTAS
C CITRATES
CRISTATE
SCATTIER
D STRIATED
TARDIEST
E ARIETTES
ITERATES
TEARIEST
TREATIES
TREATISE
L TERTIALS
M MISTREAT
TERATISM
N INTREATS
NITRATES
STRAITEN
TERTIANS
O TOASTIER
R STRAITER
TARRIEST
S ARTISTES
ARTSIEST
STRIATES
T ATTRITES
RATTIEST
TARTIEST
TITRATES
TRISTATE
W WARTIEST
Z TRISTEZA

45 SMARTIE

A AMIRATES
B BARMIEST
C CERAMIST
MATRICES
MISTRACE
SCIMETAR
D MISRATED
READMITS
E EMERITAS
EMIRATES
STEAMIER
G MAGISTER
MIGRATES
RAGTIMES
STERIGMA
I AIRTIMES
SERIATIM
K MISTAKER
L LAMISTER
MARLIEST
MARLITES
MISALTER
M MARMITES
RAMMIEST
N MINARETS
RAIMENTS
O AMORTISE
ATOMISER
P PRIMATES
S ASTERISM
MISRATES
SMARTIES
T MISTREAT
TERATISM
U MURIATES
V VITAMERS
W WARTIMES
X MATRIXES

46 STEROID

A ASTEROID
B DEORBITS
C CORDITES
G DIGESTOR
GRODIEST
STODGIER
I DIORITES
K DORKIEST
L STOLIDER
M MORTISED
P DIOPTERS
DIOPTRES
PERIDOTS
PORTSIDE
PROTEIDS
RIPOSTED
TOPSIDER
S STEROIDS
U OUTRIDES
OUTSIDER
W ROWDIEST
WORDIEST

47 DIALERS

A SALARIED
B BEDRAILS
DISABLER
C DECRIALS
RADICELS
RADICLES
E REALISED
RESAILED
SIDEREAL
L DALLIERS
DIALLERS
M DISMALER
N ISLANDER
O DARIOLES
P LIPREADS
PARSLIED
SPIRALED
T DILATERS
LARDIEST
REDTAILS
U RESIDUAL
Y DIALYSER

48 RENTALS HAVING HUT SPACE
49 SIN-RITE VAMP STABBED--HULK CAGED
50 ROADIES *FLAT PAVED NICE
51 ETESIAN *sane-tie DUMB CRAVATS
52 CINEAST FANS OF THE DIRTY OLD MOVIE BIZ
53 ESTRONE FLASHING FOX
54 TARRIES BELCHER WON'T SPLIT
55 DESTINE UNDERFED MAN: EAT VEGETABLES!
56 TEASING FUZZY NURDS THUMB UGLY VW
57 INSANER COMMITTED GROUPS
58 NATURES THESE DO BECOME EVIL
59 EARS-NOD PRIM BELCH
60 DENIERS WHO GABS OF SEX TALK? PERVS!
61 LINTERS GO AID MAKEUP
62 I-A-NURSE **NUMBeD ZITS
63 ANEROID *GOD'S BAROMETER
64 TOADIES *PRIZING EX-ANIMALS
65 IDEATES **MARVELOuS IDEA? JOHN FIBBED
66 ROASTER ROASTING COLD BLIMPS
67 INSTATE A FEW STRANGERS PREACHED
68 REALISE *GAZED ON MY PROFITS
69 TENSILE KEEPING STRETCHED VIBES
70 GREISEN OLD STONE FACED BUMP HOWEVER
71 TINDERS GUIDE LIT UP AX
72 ONE-DART WINGY TOPIC
73 TENOURS ten(h)ours COMBINING HALF-DAYS
74 SEE-RONI *THE DOGLIKE VAMP
75 SEDATER BIG MIKE FELT WHISPERY

48 RENTALS

A ASTERNAL
C CENTRALS
E ETERNALS
TELERANS
G STRANGLE
TANGLERS
H ENTHRALS
I ENTRAILS
LATRINES
RATLINES
RETINALS
TRENAILS
N LANTERNS
P PLANTERS
REPLANTS
S SALTERNS
T SLATTERN
U NEUTRALS
V VENTRALS

49 SINRITE

A INERTIAS
RAINIEST
B BRINIEST
C CITRINES
CRINITES
INCITERS
D DISINTER
INDITERS
NITRIDES
E NITERIES
G IGNITERS
RESITING
STINGIER
H INHERITS
K STINKIER
L NITRILES
M INTERIMS
MINISTER
MISINTER
P PRISTINE
S INSISTER
SINISTER
T NITRITES
U NEURITIS
V INVITERS
VITRINES

50 ROADIES

C IDOCRASE
D ROADSIDE
F FORESAID
L DARIOLES
N ANEROIDS
P DIASPORE
PARODIES
T ASTEROID
V AVODIRES
AVOIDERS

51 ETESIAN

B BETAINES
C CINEASTE
D ANDESITE
M ETAMINES
MATINEES
MISEATEN
R ARENITES
ARSENITE
RESINATE
STEARINE
TRAINEES
S ETESIANS
TENIASES
T ANISETTE
TETANIES
TETANISE
V NAIVETES

52 CINEAST

A ESTANCIA
B CABINETS
D DISTANCE
E CINEASTE
F FANCIEST
H ASTHENIC
CHANTIES
I CANITIES
L CANISTEL
M AMNESTIC
SEMANTIC
N ANCIENTS
CANNIEST
INSECTAN
INSTANCE
O ACONITES
CANOEIST
SONICATE
R CANISTER
CERATINS
CISTERNA
CREATINS
SCANTIER
TACRINES
S CINEASTS
SCANTIES
T ENTASTIC
NICTATES
TETANICS
V VESICANT
Y CYANITES
Z ZINCATES

53 ESTRONE

A EARSTONE
RESONATE
F RESOFTEN
SOFTENER
G ESTROGEN
H HONESTER
I ONERIEST
SEROTINE
L ENTRESOL
N ENTERONS
TENONERS
O OESTRONE
S ESTRONES
X EXTENSOR

54 TARRIES

B ARBITERS
RAREBITS
C ERRATICS
E ARTERIES
H TRASHIER
I RARITIES
L RETRIALS
TRAILERS
N RESTRAIN
RETRAINS
STRAINER
TERRAINS
TRAINERS
O ROTARIES
P PARTIERS
R STARRIER
TARRIERS
S TARSIERS
T STRAITER
TARRIEST
W STRAWIER

55 DESTINE

A ANDESITE
B BENDIEST
D DESTINED
E NEEDIEST
F INFESTED
G INGESTED
SIGNETED
L ENLISTED
LISTENED
TINSELED
M SEDIMENT
N DENTINES
DESINENT
R INSERTED
NERDIEST
RESIDENT
SINTERED
TRENDIES
S DESTINES
T DINETTES
INSETTED
U DETINUES
V INVESTED

56 TEASING

B BEATINGS
D SEDATING
STEADING
F FEASTING
G NAGGIEST
H GAHNITES
L GELATINS
GENITALS
STEALING
TAGLINES
M MANGIEST
MINTAGES
MISAGENT
STEAMING
N ANTIGENS
GENTIANS
R ANGRIEST
ASTRINGE
GANISTER
GANTRIES
GRANITES
INGRATES
RANGIEST
S EASTINGS
GIANTESS
SEATINGS
T ESTATING
TANGIEST
U SAUTEING
UNITAGES
V VINTAGES
W SWEATING
Y YEASTING
Z TZIGANES

57 INSANER

C CRANNIES
NARCEINS
D INSNARED
E ANSERINE
G AGINNERS
EARNINGS
ENGRAINS
GRANNIES
I SIRENIAN
M REINSMAN
O RAISONNE
P PANNIERS
R INSNARER
S INSNARES
T ENTRAINS
TRANNIES
U ANEURINS

58 NATURES

B URBANEST
C CENTAURS
RECUSANT
UNCRATES
D DAUNTERS
TRANSUDE
UNTREADS
E SAUTERNE
H HAUNTERS
UNEARTHS
URETHANS
I RUINATES
TAURINES
URANITES
URINATES
L NEUTRALS
M MENSTRUA
O OUTEARNS
S ANESTRUS
SAUNTERS
T TAUNTERS
V VAUNTERS

59 EARSNOD

B BANDORES
BROADENS
C ENDOSARC
E REASONED
H HARDNOSE
I ANEROIDS
L LADRONES
SOLANDER
M MADRONES
RANSOMED
P OPERANDS
PADRONES
PANDORES
R ADORNERS
READORNS

60 DENIERS

A ARSENIDE
NEARSIDE
B INBREEDS
E NEREIDES
REDENIES
F DEFINERS
G DESIGNER
ENERGIDS
REDESIGN
REEDINGS
RESIGNED
H RESHINED
K DEERSKIN
L REDLINES
O INDORSEE
P SPENDIER
S DIRENESS
T INSERTED
NERDIEST
RESIDENT
SINTERED
TRENDIES
V INVERSED
W REWIDENS
WIDENERS
X INDEXERS

61 LINTERS

A ENTRAILS
LATRINES
RATLINES
RETINALS
TRENAILS
D TENDRILS
TRINDLES
E ENLISTER
LISTENER
REENLIST
SILENTER
G RINGLETS
STERLING
TINGLERS
I NITRILES
K TINKLERS
M MINSTREL
O RETINOLS
P SPLINTER
U INSULTER

62 IANURSE

B URBANISE
D DENARIUS
UNRAISED
URANIDES
E UNEASIER
M ANEURISM
N ANEURINS
S ANURESIS
SENARIUS
T RUINATES
TAURINES
URANITES
URINATES
Z SUZERAIN

63 ANEROID

B DEBONAIR
D ORDAINED
G ORGANDIE
M RADIOMEN
R ORDAINER
REORDAIN
S ANEROIDS
T AROINTED
ORDINATE
RATIONED

64 TOADIES

G GODETIAS
L DIASTOLE
ISOLATED
SODALITE
M ATOMISED
N ASTONIED
SEDATION
P DIOPTASE
R ASTEROID
X OXIDATES
Z AZOTISED

65 IDEATES

B BEADIEST
DIABETES
D STEADIED
F SAFETIED
H HEADIEST
J JADEITES
L LEADIEST
M MEDIATES
N ANDESITE
R READIEST
SERIATED
STEADIER
S STEADIES
U AUDITEES
V DEVIATES
SEDATIVE

66 ROASTER

A AERATORS
B ABORTERS
TABORERS
C CREATORS
REACTORS
D ROADSTER
G GARROTES
I ROTARIES
L REALTORS
RELATORS
RESTORAL
M REARMOST
N ANTRORSE
O SORORATE
P PRAETORS
PRORATES
R ARRESTOR
S ASSERTOR
ASSORTER
ORATRESS
REASSORT
ROASTERS
T ROSTRATE

67 INSTATE

A ASTATINE
SANITATE
C ENTASTIC
NICTATES
TETANICS
D INSTATED
E ANISETTE
TETANIES
TETANISE
F FAINTEST
G ESTATING
TANGIEST
H HESITANT
N STANNITE
P PATIENTS
R INTREATS
NITRATES
STRAITEN
TERTIANS
S ANTSIEST
INSTATES
NASTIEST
SATINETS
TITANESS
T NATTIEST
W TAWNIEST

68 REALISE

D REALISED
RESAILED
SIDEREAL
F FILAREES
G GASELIER
M MEASLIER
N ALIENERS
P ESPALIER
R REALISER
S REALISES
T ATELIERS
EARLIEST
LEARIEST
REALTIES
Y YEARLIES
Z REALIZES
SLEAZIER

69 TENSILE

B STILBENE
TENSIBLE
C CENTILES
D ENLISTED
LISTENED
TINSELED
E ENLISTEE
SELENITE
G GENTILES
SLEETING
STEELING
H THEELINS
I LENITIES
K NESTLIKE
N SENTINEL
P PENLITES
PLENTIES
R ENLISTER
LISTENER
REENLIST
SILENTER
S LITENESS
SETLINES
T ENTITLES
V VEINLETS

70 GREISEN

A ANERGIES
GESNERIA
B REBEGINS
C GENERICS
D DESIGNER
ENERGIDS
REDESIGN
REEDINGS
RESIGNED
E ENERGIES
ENERGISE
GREENIES
RESEEING
F FEIGNERS
H GREENISH
REHINGES
SHEERING
L REELINGS
M REGIMENS
N SNEERING
O ERINGOES
P SPEERING
R RESIGNER
S GREISENS
T GENTRIES
INTEGERS
REESTING
STEERING
U SEIGNEUR
V SEVERING
W RESEWING
SEWERING

71 TINDERS

A DETRAINS
RANDIEST
STRAINED
D STRIDDEN
E INSERTED
NERDIEST
RESIDENT
SINTERED
TRENDIES
G STRINGED
I DISINTER
INDITERS
NITRIDES
L TENDRILS
TRINDLES
P SPRINTED
T STRIDENT
TRIDENTS
U INTRUDES
X DEXTRINS

72 ONEDART

C CARTONED
NOTECARD
G DRAGONET
I AROINTED
ORDINATE
RATIONED
N NONRATED
O RATOONED
P PRONATED
T ATTORNED
W DANEWORT
TEARDOWN
Y AROYNTED

73 TENOURS

A OUTEARNS
B BURSTONE
C CONSTRUE
COUNTERS
RECOUNTS
TROUNCES
D ROUNDEST
TONSURED
UNSORTED
F FORTUNES
G STURGEON
H SOUTHERN
I ROUTINES
SNOUTIER
L TURNSOLE
M MOUNTERS
REMOUNTS
N NEUTRONS
O OUTSNORE
S TONSURES
Y TOURNEYS

74 SEERONI

D INDORSEE
G ERINGOES
H HEROINES
K KEROSINE
L ELOINERS
M EMERSION
P ISOPRENE
PEREIONS
PIONEERS
T ONERIEST
SEROTINE
V EVERSION

75 SEDATER

B BREASTED
DEBATERS
E RESEATED
F DRAFTEES
G RESTAGED
H HEADREST
I READIEST
SERIATED
STEADIER
K STREAKED
L DESALTER
RESLATED
TREADLES
M MASTERED
STREAMED
P PEDERAST
PREDATES
REPASTED
TRAPESED
R ARRESTED
RETREADS
SERRATED
TREADERS
S ASSERTED
T RESTATED
RETASTED
W DEWATERS
TARWEEDS
Y ESTRAYED

No.	Stem	Mnemonic
76	I-REDATE	**TWO ENVIaBLE MaTES
77	I-RENTED	TOM BROKAW'S SUV AND AX
78	PARTIES	LIVELY PAMINA WAS CHARGED
79	TEA-RAIN	**BE TEAPoT'S MAGIC WIZ
80	INERTIA	**SPLeNDID Z'S
81	GELATIN	KNOX* VAMP'S GAZE BECHARMED
82	ETERNAL	EVER WISHING BED MIX
83	ENDEARS	SICKENS YOUNG WOMEN
84	LENT-AID	FOP GAVE BOND
85	LATINOS	ANGRY OLE (or, YEARLONG)
86	AIRIEST	*MAN WHO'LL FIX ZIPPERS
87	STRANGE	WEIRD FOG LAMPS
88	HASTIER	I POUNCED AND RODE AWAY
89	PAINTER	GATHERED OILS
90	INMATES	GANEFS OR BLOCKHEADS?
91	STINGER	COWARDLIEST*
92	SANE-LIE	CREE BEGGED "PREX?! VP?!"
93	STOURIE	NAVAL CAMP FAD
94	AGONIES	*SCRABBLING DAZE
95	READING	BED HABIT MOSTLY
96	SESTINA	sit-sane PAMINA DEUTSCH/MIKE BARON RELAXING
97	DETAILS	I MERGE COPY
98	TOENAIL	*GRIPS BED
99	ONE-TIRE	*EXHAUSTED CAR
100	IS-ON-TEE	*TIGER'S COMB

76 IREDATE

A ERADIATE
B REBAITED
L DETAILER
ELATERID
RETAILED
M DIAMETER
N DETAINER
RETAINED
S READIEST
SERIATED
STEADIER
T ITERATED
V DERIVATE
W WAITERED

77 IRENTED

A DETAINER
RETAINED
B INTERBED
D DENDRITE
K TINKERED
M REMINTED
N INDENTER
INTENDER
INTERNED
O ORIENTED
R INTERRED
TRENDIER
S INSERTED
NERDIEST
RESIDENT
SINTERED
TRENDIES
T RETINTED
U RETINUED
REUNITED
V INVERTED
W WINTERED
X DEXTRINE

78 PARTIES

A ASPIRATE
PARASITE
SEPTARIA
C CRISPATE
PARETICS
PICRATES
PRACTISE
D RAPIDEST
TRAIPSED
E PARIETES
G GRAPIEST
H TRIPHASE
I PARITIES
L PILASTER
PLAISTER
PLAITERS
M PRIMATES
N PAINTERS
PANTRIES
PERTAINS
PINASTER
PRISTANE
REPAINTS
P PERIAPTS
R PARTIERS
S PASTRIES
PIASTERS
PIASTRES
RASPIEST
TRAIPSES
V PRIVATES
W WIRETAPS
Y ASPERITY

79 TEARAIN

B ATABRINE
C CARINATE
CRANIATE
G AERATING
M ANIMATER
MARINATE
O AERATION
P ANTIRAPE
S ANTISERA
RATANIES
SANTERIA
SEATRAIN
T ATTAINER
REATTAIN
W ANTIWEAR
Z ATRAZINE

80 INERTIA

D DAINTIER
E INERTIAE
L INERTIAL
N TRIENNIA
P PAINTIER
S INERTIAS
RAINIEST
Z TRIAZINE

81 GELATIN

A AGENTIAL
ALGINATE
B BLEATING
TANGIBLE
C CLEATING
D DELATING
E GALENITE
GELATINE
LEGATINE
G GELATING
LEGATING
H ATHELING
K GNATLIKE
M LIGAMENT
METALING
TEGMINAL
N GANTLINE
LATENING
O GELATION
LEGATION
P PLEATING
R ALERTING
ALTERING
INTEGRAL
RELATING
TANGLIER
TRIANGLE
S GELATINS
GENITALS
STEALING
TAGLINES
V VALETING
X EXALTING
Z TEAZLING

82 ETERNAL

B RENTABLE
D ANTLERED
E LATEENER
G REGENTAL
H LEATHERN
I ELATERIN
ENTAILER
TREENAIL
M LAMENTER
N LANNERET
R RELEARNT
S ETERNALS
TELERANS
V LEVANTER
RELEVANT
W TREELAWN
X EXTERNAL

83 ENDEARS

C ASCENDER
REASCEND
E SERENADE
G DERANGES
GRANDEES
GRENADES
I ARSENIDE
NEARSIDE
K KNEADERS
M AMENDERS
MEANDERS
N ENSNARED
O REASONED
S DEARNESS
U UNDERSEA
UNERASED
UNSEARED
W ANSWERED
Y YEARENDS

84 LENTAID

A DENTALIA
B BIDENTAL
D TIDELAND
E DATELINE
ENTAILED
LINEATED
F INFLATED
G DELATING
N DENTINAL
O DELATION
P PANTILED
V DIVALENT

85 LATINOS

A ALATIONS
E ELATIONS
INSOLATE
TOENAILS
G ANTILOGS
SOLATING
L STALLION
N ANTLIONS
O SOLATION
R TONSILAR
Y LANOSITY

86 AIRIEST

F RATIFIES
H HAIRIEST
L LISTERIA
M AIRTIMES
SERIATIM
N INERTIAS
RAINIEST
P PARITIES
R RARITIES
S SATIRISE
W WISTERIA
X SEXTARII
Z SATIRIZE

87 STRANGE

A TANAGERS
D DRAGNETS
GRANDEST
E ESTRANGE
GRANTEES
GREATENS
NEGATERS
REAGENTS
SERGEANT
F ENGRAFTS
G GANGSTER
I ANGRIEST
ASTRINGE
GANISTER
GANTRIES
GRANITES
INGRATES
RANGIEST
L STRANGLE
TANGLERS
M GARMENTS
MARGENTS
O ESTRAGON
NEGATORS
P TREPANGS
R GRANTERS
REGRANTS
STRANGER
S STRANGES
W TWANGERS

88 HASTIER

A HETAIRAS
C CHARIEST
THERIACS
D HARDIEST
E HEARTIES
I HAIRIEST
N HAIRNETS
INEARTHS
THERIANS
O HOARIEST
P TRIPHASE
R TRASHIER
U THESAURI
W WATERISH
Y HYSTERIA

89 PAINTER

A ANTIRAPE
D DIPTERAN
E APERIENT
G RETAPING
TAPERING
H PERIANTH
I PAINTIER
L INTERLAP
TRAPLINE
TRIPLANE
O ATROPINE
R PRETRAIN
TERRAPIN
S PAINTERS
PANTRIES
PERTAINS
PINASTER
PRISTANE
REPAINTS
T TRIPTANE

90 INMATES

A AMENTIAS
ANIMATES
B AMBIENTS
C AMNESTIC
SEMANTIC
D MEDIANTS
E ETAMINES
MATINEES
MISEATEN
F MANIFEST
G MANGIEST
MINTAGES
MISAGENT
STEAMING
H HEMATINS
K MISTAKEN
L AILMENTS
ALIMENTS
MANLIEST
MELANIST
SMALTINE
N MANNITES
O AMNIOTES
MASONITE
MISATONE
R MINARETS
RAIMENTS
S MANTISES
MATINESS

91 STINGER

A ANGRIEST
ASTRINGE
GANISTER
GANTRIES
GRANITES
INGRATES
RANGIEST
C CRESTING
D STRINGED
E GENTRIES
INTEGERS
REESTING
STEERING
I IGNITERS
RESITING
STINGIER
L RINGLETS
STERLING
TINGLERS
O GENITORS
R RESTRING
STRINGER
S STINGERS
TRIGNESS
T GITTERNS
W STREWING
WRESTING

92 SANELIE

B BASELINE
C SALIENCE
D DELAINES
E ALIENEES
G ENSILAGE
LINEAGES
P PENALISE
SEPALINE
R ALIENERS
V VASELINE
X ALEXINES

93 STOURIE

A OUTRAISE
SAUTOIRE
C CITREOUS
OUTCRIES
D OUTRIDES
OUTSIDER
F OUTFIRES
L OUTLIERS
M MISROUTE
MOISTURE
N ROUTINES
SNOUTIER
P ROUPIEST
V VIRTUOSE
VITREOUS

94 AGONIES

B BEGONIAS
C COINAGES
D AGONISED
DIAGNOSE
G SEAGOING
L GASOLINE
N ANGINOSE
R ORGANISE
S AGONISES
Z AGONIZES

95 READING

A DRAINAGE
GARDENIA
B BEARDING
BREADING
D DREADING
READDING
E REGAINED
H ADHERING
I DEAIRING
L DANGLIER
DRAGLINE
M DREAMING
MARGINED
MIDRANGE
O ORGANDIE
S DERAIGNS
GRADINES
READINGS
T DERATING
GRADIENT
REDATING
TREADING
Y READYING

96 SESTINA

A ENTASIAS
B BASINETS
BASSINET
C CINEASTS
SCANTIES
D DESTAINS
SANDIEST
E ETESIANS
TENIASES
G EASTINGS
GIANTESS
SEATINGS
H ANTHESIS
SHANTIES
SHEITANS
STHENIAS
I ISATINES
SANITIES
SANITISE
TENIASIS
K SNAKIEST
L ELASTINS
NAILSETS
SALIENTS
SALTINES
M MANTISES
MATINESS
N INSANEST
STANINES
O ASTONIES
P SAPIENTS
STEAPSIN
R ARTINESS
RETSINAS
STAINERS
STEARINS
S SESTINAS
T ANTSIEST
INSTATES
NASTIEST
SATINETS
TITANESS
U SINUATES
X SEXTAINS

97 DETAILS

C CITADELS
DIALECTS
E LEADIEST
G GLADIEST
I IDEALIST
M MEDALIST
MISDEALT
O DIASTOLE
ISOLATED
SODALITE
P TALIPEDS
R DILATERS
LARDIEST
REDTAILS
Y STEADILY

98 TOENAIL

B TAILBONE
D DELATION
G GELATION
LEGATION
P ANTIPOLE
R ORIENTAL
RELATION
S ELATIONS
INSOLATE
TOENAILS

99 ONETIRE

C ERECTION
NEOTERIC
D ORIENTED
H HEREINTO
R ORIENTER
REORIENT
S ONERIEST
SEROTINE
T TENORITE
X EXERTION

100 ISONTEE

B BETONIES
EBONITES
C SEICENTO
G EGESTION
M MONETISE
SEMITONE
R ONERIEST
SEROTINE
S ESSONITE
T NOISETTE
TEOSINTE

The Top 100 Seven-Letter Bingo Stems Based on MMPR and Bingos Formed, Alphabetized

ABORTERS
ABSENTER
ACONITES
ACRIDEST
ACTIONER
ADENITIS
ADENOIDS
ADENOSIS
ADHERING
ADHESION
ADONISES
ADORNERS
ADROITER
AERATING
AERATION
AERATORS
AEROLITE
AEROLITH
AGENTIAL
AGINNERS
AGONISED
AGONISES
AGONIZES
AILERONS
AILMENTS
AIRDATES
AIRHOLES
AIRLINES
AIRTIMES
ALATIONS
ALERTEST
ALERTING
ALEXINES
ALGERINE
ALGINATE
ALIENEES
ALIENERS
ALIENIST
ALIENORS
ALIGNERS
ALIMENTS
ALLERGIN
ALTERERS
ALTERING
ALUNITES
AMBIENTS
AMENDERS
AMENTIAS
AMIDONES
AMIRATES
AMITROLE
AMNESTIC
AMNIOTES
AMORTISE
ANCESTOR
ANCIENTS
ANDESITE
ANERGIAS
ANERGIES
ANEROIDS
ANESTRUS
ANEURINS
ANEURISM
ANGARIES
ANGINOSE
ANGRIEST
ANIMATER
ANIMATES
ANISETTE
ANISOLES
ANKERITE
ANODIZES
ANOINTED
ANOINTER
ANORETIC
ANSERINE
ANSWERED
ANTERIOR
ANTHERID
ANTHESIS
ANTIDOTE
ANTIGENS
ANTIHERO
ANTILOGS
ANTIMERE
ANTINODE
ANTIPODE
ANTIPOLE
ANTIRAPE
ANTISERA
ANTIWEAR
ANTLERED
ANTLIONS
ANTRORSE
ANTSIEST
ANURESIS
APERIENT
APTEROUS
ARANEIDS
ARBELEST
ARBITERS
ARENITES
ARGENTIC
ARGINASE
ARIDNESS
ARIETTAS
ARIETTES
ARISTATE
AROINTED
AROYNTED
ARRESTED
ARRESTOR
ARSENATE
ARSENIDE
ARSENITE
ARSONIST
ARTERIES
ARTICLES
ARTINESS
ARTISTES
ARTSIEST
ASCENDER
ASPERITY
ASPIRATE
ASSENTER
ASSENTOR
ASSERTED
ASSERTOR
ASSIGNER
ASSORTER
ASTATINE
ASTERISM
ASTERNAL
ASTEROID
ASTHENIC
ASTONIED
ASTONIES
ASTRINGE
ATABRINE
ATELIERS
ATHELING
ATOMISED
ATOMISER
ATRAZINE
ATROPINE
ATROPINS
ATTAINER
ATTORNED
ATTRITES
AUDIENTS
AUDITEES
AUNTLIER
AVERSION
AVERTING
AVODIRES
AVOIDERS
AZOTISED
BANDORES
BANISTER
BARITONE
BARMIEST
BARNIEST
BARONETS
BARONIES
BASELINE
BASINETS
BASSINET
BEADIEST
BEARDING
BEARINGS
BEATINGS
BEDRAILS
BEDSONIA
BEGONIAS
BENDIEST
BERATING
BESTRIDE
BETAINES
BETONIES
BIDENTAL
BIRETTAS
BISTERED
BLASTIER
BLEARING
BLEATERS
BLEATING
BLOATERS
BORNITES
BOTANIES
BOTANISE
BRANDIES
BREADING
BREASTED
BRINIEST
BROADENS
BURSTONE
CABINETS
CALORIES
CANISTEL
CANISTER
CANITIES
CANNIEST
CANOEIST
CARINATE
CARIOLES
CARLINES
CAROTINS
CARTONED
CATENOID
CATERING
CENTARES
CENTAURS
CENTIARE
CENTILES
CENTRALS
CENTROID
CERAMIST
CERATINS
CERATOID
CHANTIES
CHARIEST
CINEASTE
CINEASTS
CISTERNA
CITADELS
CITRATES
CITREOUS
CITRINES
CLARINET
CLEAREST
CLEARING
CLEATING
CLOISTER
COALIEST
CODEINAS
COINAGES
COINTERS
COISTREL
CONSIDER
CONSTRUE
CORDITES
COREIGNS
CORNIEST
CORTINAS
COSIGNER
COSTLIER
COUNTERS
CRANIATE
CRANNIES
CREASING
CREATINE
CREATING
CREATINS
CREATION
CREATORS
CRESTING
CRINITES
CRISPATE
CRISTATE
CYANITES
DAIMONES
DAINTIER
DAINTIES
DALLIERS
DANDIEST
DANEWORT
DANGLIER
DARIOLES
DATARIES
DATELINE
DAUNTERS
DEAIRING
DEARNESS
DEBATERS
DEBONAIR
DECRIALS
DEERSKIN
DEFINERS
DELAINES
DELATING
DELATION
DELATORS
DEMERITS
DEMISTER
DENARIUS
DENDRITE
DENTALIA
DENTINAL
DENTINES
DEORBITS
DEPAINTS
DERAIGNS
DERANGES
DERATING
DERISION
DERIVATE
DESALTER
DESERTIC
DESIGNER
DESINENT
DESTAINS
DESTINED
DESTINES
DESTRIER
DETAILER
DETAINER
DETINUES
DETRAINS
DEVIANTS
DEVIATES
DEVIATOR
DEWATERS
DEXTRINE
DEXTRINS
DIABETES
DIAGNOSE
DIALECTS
DIALLERS
DIALYSER
DIAMETER
DIASPORE
DIASTERS
DIASTOLE
DIATRONS
DICENTRA
DIESTERS
DIETHERS
DIGESTER
DIGESTOR
DILATERS
DIMETERS
DINETTES
DIOCESAN
DIOPTASE
DIOPTERS
DIOPTRES
DIORITES
DIOXANES
DIPTERAN
DIPTERON
DIRENESS
DISABLER
DISASTER
DISCREET
DISCRETE
DISINTER
DISMALER
DISRATED
DISRATES
DISTANCE
DIVALENT
DOCTRINE
DOMAINES
DOMINATE
DONATIVE
DORKIEST
DORMIENT
DOURINES
DRAFTEES
DRAGLINE
DRAGNETS
DRAGONET
DRAINAGE
DRAINERS
DREADING
DREAMING
EARLIEST
EARNESTS
EARNINGS
EARRINGS
EARSTONE
EARTHING
EASTERLY
EASTINGS
EATERIES
EBONITES
EDITRESS
EGESTION
ELASTINS
ELATERID
ELATERIN
ELATIONS
ELOINERS
ELUTIONS
EMERITAS
EMERSION
EMIGRANT
EMIRATES
ENACTORS
ENATIONS
ENDOSARC
ENERGIDS
ENERGIES
ENERGISE
ENGRAFTS
ENGRAILS
ENGRAINS
ENLISTED
ENLISTEE
ENLISTER
ENSILAGE
ENSNARED
ENTAILED
ENTAILER
ENTASIAS
ENTASTIC
ENTERICS
ENTERONS
ENTHRALS
ENTICERS
ENTITLES
ENTRAILS
ENTRAINS
ENTREATS
ENTRESOL
EPILATOR
EQUATORS
ERADIATE
ERASIONS
ERECTION
ERINGOES
EROTICAL
ERRATICS
ESPALIER
ESSONITE
ESTANCIA
ESTATING
ESTRAGON
ESTRANGE
ESTRAYED
ESTRIOLS
ESTROGEN
ESTRONES
ESURIENT
ETAMINES
ETERNALS
ETERNISE
ETESIANS
EVERSION
EXALTERS
EXALTING
EXERTION
EXTENSOR
EXTERNAL
FAINTERS
FAINTEST
FANCIEST
FARINOSE
FASTENER
FEASTING
FEATLIER
FEIGNERS
FENESTRA
FERNIEST
FILAREES
FINAGLER
FLOATERS
FLOATIER
FOLIATES
FORESAID
FORESAIL
FORESTAL
FORTUNES
FRAILEST
GAHNITES
GAINLIER
GALENITE
GANGLIER
GANGSTER
GANISTER
GANTLINE
GANTRIES
GARDENIA
GARMENTS
GARROTES
GASELIER
GASOLIER
GASOLINE
GEARINGS
GELATINE
GELATING
GELATINS
GELATION
GENERICS
GENITALS
GENITORS
GENTIANS
GENTILES
GENTRIES
GERANIAL
GERANIOL
GERMINAL
GESNERIA
GIANTESS
GIRASOLE
GITTERNS
GLADIEST
GLARIEST
GLOATERS
GNARLIER
GNATLIKE
GNATTIER
GODETIAS
GORINESS
GRADIENT
GRADINES
GRAINERS
GRANDEES
GRANDEST
GRANITES
GRANNIES
GRANTEES
GRANTERS
GRAPIEST
GRAPLINE
GRATINEE
GREASING
GREATENS
GREENIES
GREENISH
GREISENS
GRENADES
GRIEVANT
GRODIEST
HAIRIEST
HAIRNETS
HALTERES
HANDIEST
HARDIEST
HARDNOSE
HASTENER
HAUNTERS
HEADIEST
HEADREST
HEARINGS
HEARSING
HEARTENS
HEARTIES
HEARTING
HEMATINS
HEREINTO
HERNIATE
HEROINES
HESITANT
HETAIRAS
HOARIEST
HOLSTEIN
HONESTER
HORDEINS
HORNIEST
HOTLINES
HYSTERIA
IDEALIST
IDEATION
IDOCRASE
IDOLATER
IGNITERS
IGNORERS
INBREEDS
INCITERS
INCLOSER
INCREASE
INCREATE
INDENTER
INDENTOR
INDEXERS
INDITERS
INDORSED
INDORSEE
INDORSER
INDORSES
INDURATE
INEARTHS
INERTIAE
INERTIAL
INERTIAS
INFESTED
INFESTER
INFLATED
INFLATER
INFLATES
INGATHER
INGESTED
INGRATES
INHALERS
INHERITS
INLAYERS
INSANEST
INSECTAN
INSERTED
INSERTER
INSETTED
INSETTER
INSISTER
INSNARED
INSNARER
INSNARES
INSOLATE
INSOLENT
INSTABLE
INSTANCE
INSTATED
INSTATES
INSTROKE
INSULATE
INSULTER
INTEGERS
INTEGRAL
INTENDER
INTENSER
INTERAGE
INTERBED
INTEREST
INTERIMS
INTERLAP
INTERLAY
INTERNAL
INTERNED
INTERNES
INTERRED
INTERSEX
INTERVAL
INTONERS
INTORTED
INTRADOS
INTREATS
INTRORSE
INTRUDES
INVADERS
INVERSED
INVERTED
INVESTED
INVESTOR
INVITERS
IODINATE
IRONSIDE
ISATINES
ISLANDER
ISOLATED
ISOLATES
ISOPRENE
ITERANCE
ITERATED
ITERATES
JADEITES
JANGLIER
JANITORS
JAROSITE
JOINDERS
JOINTERS
KAOLINES
KEITLOAS
KERATINS
KERATOID
KERNITES
KEROSINE
KNEADERS
LABORITE
LADRONES
LAETRILE
LAGERING
LAMENTER
LAMINOSE
LAMISTER
LANCIERS
LANKIEST
LANNERET
LANOSITY
LANTERNS
LARDIEST
LARKIEST
LATEENER
LATENING
LATERITE
LATERIZE
LATIGOES
LATRINES
LAYERING
LEADIEST
LEARIEST
LEARNING
LEATHERN
LEATHERS
LECTIONS
LEGATINE
LEGATING
LEGATION
LEGATORS
LENITIES
LENTOIDS
LEOTARDS
LEVANTER
LEVATORS
LEVIRATE
LIBERATE
LIBRATES
LICENSOR
LIGAMENT
LINEAGES
LINEATED
LIONISER
LIPREADS
LISTENED
LISTENER
LISTERIA
LITANIES
LITENESS
LITERALS
LITERATE
LOAMIEST
LOATHERS
LOCATERS
LODESTAR
LOONIEST
LORICATE
LORINERS
MADRONES
MAGISTER
MALIGNER
MALINGER
MANGIEST
MANIFEST
MANLIEST
MANNITES
MANTISES
MARGENTS
MARGINED
MARINATE
MARLIEST
MARLINES
MARLITES
MARMITES
MASONITE
MASTERED
MATERIEL
MATINEES
MATINESS
MATRICES
MATRIXES
MEANDERS
MEASLIER
MEDALIST
MEDIANTS
MEDIATES
MEDIATOR
MELANIST
MENSTRUA
METALING
MIDRANGE
MIGRATES
MINARETS
MINERALS
MINISTER
MINSTREL
MINTAGES
MISAGENT
MISALTER
MISATONE
MISDEALT
MISEATEN
MISENROL
MISENTER
MISINTER
MISLEARN
MISRATED
MISRATES
MISROUTE
MISTAKEN
MISTAKER
MISTRACE
MISTREAT
MOISTURE
MONETISE
MONSTERA
MORAINES
MORALISE
MORTISED
MOUNTERS
MURIATES
NAGGIEST
NAILSETS
NAIVETES
NAPERIES
NARCEINS
NARGHILE
NARGILEH
NARGILES
NASTIEST
NATTIEST
NEARSIDE
NEEDIEST
NEGATERS
NEGATORS
NEGROIDS
NEGRONIS
NEOLITHS
NEOTERIC
NERDIEST
NEREIDES
NERVIEST
NESTLIKE
NEURITIS
NEUTRALS
NEUTRONS
NICTATES
NIOBATES
NITERIES
NITRATED
NITRATES
NITRIDES
NITRILES
NITRITES
NOISETTE
NONRATED
NOTARIES
NOTARIZE
NOTECARD
NOTICERS
NOVELIST
OBEISANT
OBTAINED
OBTAINER
OESTRINS
OESTRIOL
OESTRONE
OILSTONE
OLEASTER
OLESTRAS

ONERIEST
ONSTREAM
OPALINES
OPERANDS
OPERANTS
ORATIONS
ORATRESS
ORDAINED
ORDAINER
ORDINATE
ORGANDIE
ORGANISE
ORGANIST
ORIENTAL
ORIENTED
ORIENTER
ORNITHES
OSSATURE
OTALGIES
OUTCRIES
OUTDARES
OUTEARNS
OUTFIRES
OUTHEARS
OUTLIERS
OUTLINES
OUTRACES
OUTRAGES
OUTRAISE
OUTRATES
OUTRAVES
OUTREADS
OUTRIDES
OUTSIDER
OUTSNORE
OUTSTARE
OUTSWARE
OUTSWEAR
OUTWEARS
OVERSALT
OXIDATES
PADRONES
PAINTERS
PAINTIER
PANDORES
PANELIST
PANNIERS
PANTILED
PANTILES
PANTRIES
PARASITE
PARETICS
PARIETES
PARITIES
PARODIES
PARSLIED
PARTIERS
PASTRIES
PATIENTS
PEARLING
PEARLITE
PEDERAST
PELORIAS
PENALISE
PENLITES
PEREIONS
PERIANTH
PERIAPTS
PERIDOTS
PERIGONS
PERTAINS
PETIOLAR
PETRALES
PETROSAL
PIASTERS
PIASTRES
PICRATES
PILASTER
PINASTER
PIONEERS

PLAINEST
PLAISTER
PLAITERS
PLANTERS
PLEATERS
PLEATING
PLENTIES
POINTERS
POITRELS
POLARISE
POLESTAR
PORNIEST
PORTSIDE
POTLINES
PRACTISE
PRAETORS
PRALINES
PREDATES
PREEDITS
PRELATES
PRETRAIN
PRIESTED
PRIMATES
PRISONED
PRISTANE
PRISTINE
PRIVATES
PROLINES
PRONATED
PRONATES
PRORATES
PROTEANS
PROTEIDS
PROTEINS
QUAESTOR
RADIATES
RADICELS
RADICLES
RADIOMEN
RAGTIMES
RAIMENTS
RAINIEST
RAINLESS
RAINOUTS
RAISONNE
RAMMIEST
RANDIEST
RANGIEST
RANSOMED
RAPIDEST
RAREBITS
RARITIES
RASPIEST
RATANIES
RATHOLES
RATIFIES
RATIONED
RATLINES
RATOONED
RATTEENS
RATTIEST
RAVELING
RAVELINS
REACTING
REACTION
REACTORS
READDING
READIEST
READINGS
READMITS
READORNS
READOUTS
READYING
REAGENTS
REALIGNS
REALISED
REALISER
REALISES
REALISTS
REALIZES

REALLOTS
REALTERS
REALTIES
REALTORS
REANOINT
REARMOST
REASCEND
REASCENT
REASONED
REASSIGN
REASSORT
REATTAIN
REBAITED
REBATING
REBEGINS
RECITALS
RECOUNTS
RECUSANT
REDATING
REDBAITS
REDENIES
REDESIGN
REDIGEST
REDLINES
REDTAILS
REEDIEST
REEDINGS
REELINGS
REENACTS
REENLIST
REESTING
REFASTEN
REFLATES
REFLOATS
REGAINED
REGALING
REGENTAL
REGIMENS
REGIONAL
REGRANTS
REHINGES
REINSERT
REINSMAN
REINTERS
REINVEST
RELACING
RELATERS
RELATING
RELATION
RELATIVE
RELATORS
RELAXING
RELAXINS
RELAYING
RELEARNT
RELEVANT
RELISTED
REMATING
REMINTED
REMOUNTS
RENTABLE
RENTIERS
REOBTAIN
REORDAIN
REORIENT
REPAINTS
REPASTED
REPLANTS
REPLATES
REPOSING
RESAILED
RESALUTE
RESAWING
RESAYING
RESEATED
RESEEING
RESEWING
RESHINED
RESIDENT
RESIDUAL

RESIFTED
RESIGNED
RESIGNER
RESINATE
RESINOID
RESISTED
RESITING
RESLATED
RESLATES
RESOFTEN
RESOLING
RESONANT
RESONATE
RESOWING
RESPITED
RESTABLE
RESTAGED
RESTATED
RESTORAL
RESTRAIN
RESTRING
RETABLES
RETAILED
RETAILER
RETAILOR
RETAINED
RETAINER
RETAKING
RETAPING
RETASTED
RETAXING
RETINALS
RETINOID
RETINOLS
RETINTED
RETINUED
RETINUES
RETINULA
RETOTALS
RETRAINS
RETREADS
RETRIALS
RETSINAS
REUNITED
REUNITES
REWIDENS
RINGLETS
RINSABLE
RIPOSTED
ROADSIDE
ROADSTER
ROASTERS
ROASTING
ROILIEST
ROLAMITE
ROMAINES
ROMANISE
ROSTELLA
ROSTRATE
ROSULATE
ROTARIES
ROUNDEST
ROUPIEST
ROUTINES
ROWDIEST
RUINATED
RUINATES
RUNNIEST
RUNTIEST
SABERING
SABOTEUR
SAFETIED
SALARIED
SALIENCE
SALIENTS
SALTERNS
SALTIERS
SALTINES
SALTIRES
SANDIEST

SANITATE
SANITIES
SANITISE
SANTERIA
SANTEROS
SAPIENTS
SAPONITE
SARCENET
SARDINED
SARDINES
SARSENET
SATINETS
SATIRISE
SATIRIZE
SAUNTERS
SAUTEING
SAUTERNE
SAUTOIRE
SCANTIER
SCANTIES
SCATTIER
SCENARIO
SCIMETAR
SEAFRONT
SEAGOING
SEAROBIN
SEATINGS
SEATRAIN
SEATROUT
SECRETIN
SECTORAL
SEDATING
SEDATION
SEDATIVE
SEDIMENT
SEICENTO
SEIGNEUR
SEIGNIOR
SEIGNORY
SELENITE
SEMANTIC
SEMITONE
SEMOLINA
SENARIUS
SENATORS
SENORITA
SENSORIA
SENTINEL
SENTRIES
SEPALINE
SEPTARIA
SERAGLIO
SERENADE
SERENATA
SERENATE
SERENITY
SERGEANT
SERIATED
SERIATES
SERIATIM
SERINGAS
SERJEANT
SEROTINE
SEROTINY
SERRANID
SERRATED
SESTINAS
SETLINES
SEVERING
SEWERING
SEXTAINS
SEXTARII
SHANTIES
SHEARING
SHEERING
SHEITANS
SHOALIER
SIDEREAL
SIDERITE
SIGNALER

SIGNETED
SILENTER
SILOXANE
SINISTER
SINTERED
SINUATED
SINUATES
SIRENIAN
SIRVENTE
SISTERED
SLANGIER
SLATTERN
SLEAZIER
SLEETING
SMALTINE
SMARTIES
SMEARING
SNAGGIER
SNAKIEST
SNARLIER
SNEAKIER
SNEERING
SNOOTIER
SNOTTIER
SNOUTIER
SOBERING
SOCIETAL
SODALITE
SOFTENER
SOLANDER
SOLANINE
SOLARISE
SOLARIZE
SOLATING
SOLATION
SONATINE
SONICATE
SORDINES
SORORATE
SORTABLE
SOURDINE
SOUTHERN
SPEARING
SPEERING
SPENDIER
SPIRALED
SPLINTER
SPOLIATE
SPONGIER
SPRAINED
SPRINTED
SQUINTER
STAINERS
STALKIER
STALLION
STANINES
STANNITE
STARLIKE
STARNOSE
STARRIER
STEADIED
STEADIER
STEADIES
STEADILY
STEADING
STEALERS
STEALING
STEAMIER
STEAMING
STEAPSIN
STEARINE
STEARINS
STEELING
STEERING
STERICAL
STERIGMA
STERLING
STERNITE
STEROIDS
STHENIAS

STILBENE
STINGERS
STINGIER
STINKIER
STODGIER
STOLIDER
STORABLE
STRAINED
STRAINER
STRAITEN
STRAITER
STRANGER
STRANGES
STRANGLE
STRAWIER
STREAKED
STREAMED
STREWING
STRIATED
STRIATES
STRIDDEN
STRIDENT
STRINGED
STRINGER
STROBILE
STRONTIA
STURGEON
SUZERAIN
SWEARING
SWEATIER
SWEATING
SYNERGIA
TABERING
TABORERS
TABORINE
TABORINS
TACRINES
TAGLINES
TAILBONE
TAILORED
TALIPEDS
TALLIERS
TANAGERS
TANGIBLE
TANGIEST
TANGLERS
TANGLIER
TAPERING
TARDIEST
TARRIERS
TARRIEST
TARSIERS
TARTIEST
TARWEEDS
TAUNTERS
TAURINES
TAWDRIES
TAWNIEST
TEARDOWN
TEARIEST
TEARLESS
TEASELER
TEAZLING
TEENSIER
TEGMINAL
TELERANS
TELSONIC
TENDRILS
TENIASES
TENIASIS
TENONERS
TENORIST
TENORITE
TENSIBLE
TENTORIA
TENURIAL
TEOSINTE
TERATISM
TERATOID
TERMINAL

TERMINUS
TERNIONS
TERRAINS
TERRANES
TERRAPIN
TERRINES
TERTIALS
TERTIANS
TETANICS
TETANIES
TETANISE
TETANOID
THEELINS
THERIACS
THERIANS
THESAURI
TIDELAND
TINGLERS
TINKERED
TINKLERS
TINSELED
TINWARES
TIREDEST
TITANESS
TITRATES
TOASTIER
TOENAILS
TONEARMS
TONSILAR
TONSURED
TONSURES
TOPLINES
TOPSIDER
TOTALISE
TOURNEYS
TOWLINES
TRAILERS
TRAINEES
TRAINERS
TRAIPSED
TRAIPSES
TRAMLINE
TRANNIES
TRANSUDE
TRAPESED
TRAPLINE
TRASHIER
TRAVOISE
TREACLES
TREADERS
TREADING
TREADLES
TREASONS
TREATIES
TREATING
TREATISE
TREELAWN
TREENAIL
TREFOILS
TRENAILS
TRENDIER
TRENDIES
TRENDOID
TREPANGS
TRIANGLE
TRIAZINE
TRIAZOLE
TRIBADES
TRIBUNES
TRIDENTS
TRIENNIA
TRIENTES
TRIGNESS
TRINDLES
TRIOLETS
TRIPHASE
TRIPLANE
TRIPTANE
TRISTATE
TRISTEZA

TRITONES
TROLLIES
TROPINES
TROUNCES
TURBINES
TURNSOLE
TWANGERS
TWANGIER
TYROSINE
TZIGANES
UNCRATES
UNDERSEA
UNEARTHS
UNEASIER
UNERASED
UNITAGES
UNMITERS
UNMITRES
UNRAISED
UNRIPEST
UNSEARED
UNSORTED
UNTREADS
URALITES
URANIDES
URANITES
URBANEST
URBANISE
URETHANS
URINATED
URINATES
VALETING
VALORISE
VARIOLES
VASELINE
VAUNTERS
VEINLETS
VENTAILS
VENTRALS
VENTURIS
VESICANT
VETERANS
VIATORES
VINEGARS
VINTAGER
VINTAGES
VIOLATER
VIOLATES
VIRTUOSE
VITAMERS
VITREOUS
VITRINES
VOTARIES
WAITERED
WAITRONS
WARTIEST
WARTIMES
WASTERIE
WATERING
WATERISH
WEARIEST
WEIRDEST
WIDENERS
WINTERED
WIRETAPS
WISTERIA
WORDIEST
WRESTING
YEARENDS
YEARLIES
YEARLING
YEASTIER
YEASTING
ZINCATES

WORDS ENDING WITH -ING(S), -LIKE, -ABLE, -IBLE

Words ending in -ING that can take an -S

==========

ACTING
AGEING
AGENTING
AGING
AIRING
ALIASING
ANGLING
ANTIKING
ANTING
ANYTHING
ARCADING
ARCHING
ARMING
ASKING
ATHELING
AUDING
AWNING
BABBLING
BACKING
BAGGING
BAKING
BANKING
BANTLING
BASHING
BASTING
BATTING
BEADING
BEARING
BEATING
BECOMING
BEDDING
BEESWING
BEING
BELLING
BELTING
BIDDING
BIGGING
BILLING
BINDING
BIRDING
BIRLING
BIRTHING
BITEWING
BITTING
BLACKING
BLADING
BLAGGING
BLASTING
BLEBBING
BLEEDING
BLESSING
BLOGGING
BLOODING
BLUEING
BLUING
BOARDING
BOATING
BODING
BOING
BOMBING
BONDING
BOOKING
BORING
BOTTLING
BOWING
BOWLING
BOXING
BRACING
BRAIDING
BRANDING
BREAKING
BREEDING
BREWING
BRIDGING
BRIEFING
BRING
BRISLING
BROKING
BRONZING
BUDDING
BUILDING
BULLRING
BUMBLING
BUNDLING
BUNGLING
BUNTING
BURNING
BUSHING
BUSING
BUSSING
CAGELING
CALKING
CALLING
CAMPING
CANNING
CAPPING
CARDING
CARLING
CARPING
CARVING
CASING
CASTING
CATLING
CAULKING
CAVING
CEILING
CENTRING
CHASING
CHITLING
CHROMING
CHURNING
CLADDING
CLEARING
CLING
CLIPPING
CLONING
CLOSING
CLOTHING
COAMING
COASTING
COATING
CODLING
COLORING
COMBING
COMING
COOKING
COPING
CORDING
COUCHING
COUPLING
COURSING
COVERING
COVING
COWLING
CRACKING
CRAVING
CRESTING
CRIBBING
CROSSING
CRUISING
CUNNING
CUPPING
CURBING
CURLING
CUTTING
CYCLING
CYMBLING
CYMLING
DABBLING
DAIRYING
DAMPING
DARING
DARKLING
DARLING
DARNING
DEALING
DECKING
DIALING
DIALLING
DIGGING
DING
DOING
DOPING
DRAFTING
DRAWING
DREDGING
DRESSING
DRILLING
DRINKING
DRIPPING
DRIVING
DROPPING
DRUBBING
DUBBING
DUCKLING
DUCTING
DUMPING
DUMPLING
DUSTING
DWELLING
DYEING
DYING
EANLING
EARING
EARNING
EARRING
EASTING
EATING
EDGING
ENDING
ERLKING
ETCHING
EVENING
FACING
FADING
FAGOTING
FAILING
FAIRING
FARMING
FARTHING
FASTING
FATLING
FEELING
FELTING
FENCING
FETTLING
FIGHTING
FILING
FILLING
FINDING
FINING
FIRING
FISHING
FITTING
FIXING
FLAGGING
FLASHING
FLATLING
FLESHING
FLING
FLOCKING
FLOGGING
FLOORING
FLUTING
FLYING
FLYTING
FONDLING
FOOTING
FOREWING
FORGING
FOULING
FOWLING
FOXING
FRAGGING
FRAMING
FRAYING
FRILLING
FROSTING
FURRING
GAMING
GASKING
GASSING
GATING
GEARING
GELDING
GHOSTING
GILDING
GINNING
GLAZING
GLEANING
GLEYING
GLOAMING
GLOOMING
GNAWING
GODLING
GOING
GOLFING
GOSLING
GRATING
GRAYLING
GRAZING
GREENING
GREETING
GROUPING
GRUELING
GUNNING
HANDLING
HANGING
HARPING
HATCHING
HAWKING
HAYING
HAZING
HEADING
HEARING
HEELING
HELPING
HERRING
HIDING
HILDING
HIRELING
HISSING
HOARDING
HOLDING
HOPPING
HORNING
HOUSING
HUNTING
HURLING
HUSKING
ICING
IMAGING
IMPING
INBEING
INCOMING
INDEXING
INKLING
INNING
IRONING
ITCHING
JESTING
JOGGING
JOINING
JOTTING
JUGGLING
KARTING
KAYAKING
KEEPING
KEGLING
KENNING
KILLING
KILTING
KINDLING
KING
KITLING
KNITTING
KNOTTING
KNOWING
LACEWING
LACING
LADING
LAGGING
LAKING
LANDING
LAPWING
LASHING
LASTING
LATHING
LAUGHING
LAWING
LAYERING
LEADING
LEANING
LEARNING
LEASING
LEAVING
LEGGING
LEMMING
LICKING
LIGHTING
LIKING
LING
LINING
LIPPING
LISTING
LIVING
LOADING
LOANING
LOATHING
LODGING
LOGGING
LONGING
LORDING
LORDLING
LOSING
LOWING
LUSTRING
LUTING
LYING
LYNCHING
MAILING
MAKING
MALLING
MANTLING
MAPPING
MARBLING
MARKING
MARLING
MASKING
MATING
MATTING
MAYING
MEANING
MEETING
MENDING
MIDDLING
MILLING
MINING
MISDOING
MODELING
MOLDING
MOORING
MORNING
MORPHING
MOSHING
MOTORING
MOULDING
MOUNTING
MOURNING
MOUSING
MOWING
MUGGING
MUNTING
MUSING
NAETHING
NECKING
NEEDLING
NERVING
NESTLING
NETTING
NIDERING
NIGGLING
NOGGING
NONBEING
NOONING
NORTHING
NOSING
NOTHING
NURSING
NURSLING
NUTTING
OFFERING
OFFING
ONCOMING
OPENING
OUTGOING
OUTING
OUTRING
OUTSING
OUTSWING
PACKING
PADDING
PADDLING
PAGING
PAINTING
PAIRING
PALING
PANELING
PARAWING
PARGING
PARING
PARKING
PARTING
PASSING
PAVING
PEELING
PETTING
PHARMING
PHRASING
PICKING
PIECING
PIERCING
PILING
PILOTING
PING
PINKING
PIPING
PITTING
PLAITING
PLANKING
PLANNING
PLANTING
PLATING
PLEADING
PLUMBING
POSTING
PRESSING
PRICKING
PRIMING
PRINTING
PUDDING
PUDDLING
PULING
PURFLING
PURGING
PURLING
QUILLING
QUILTING
QUISLING
RACING
RAILING
RAISING
RALLYING
RANKING
RASPING
RATING
RATTLING
RAVELING
RAVENING
RAVING
READING
REDWING
REEDING
REEDLING
REELING
RESPRING
RESTRING
RIBBING
RIDGLING
RIDING
RIESLING
RIFLING
RIGGING
RING
RINSING
RISING
ROARING
ROCKLING
ROLLING
ROOFING
ROVING
ROWING
RUBBING
RUCHING
RULING
RUMBLING
RUNNING
RUSHING
SACKING
SACRING
SAILING
SALTING
SAMPLING
SANDLING
SAPLING
SAVING
SAYING
SCANNING
SCOLDING
SCOURING
SCOUTING
SCRAPING
SEATING
SEEDLING
SEEING
SEEMING
SEISING
SEIZING
SERGING
SERVING
SETTING
SETTLING
SEWING
SHADING
SHAFTING
SHAVING
SHEALING
SHEARING
SHEETING
SHELVING
SHIELING
SHILLING
SHIPPING
SHIRRING
SHIRTING
SHOOTING
SHOPPING
SHORING
SHOWING
SHOWRING
SHUCKING
SIBLING
SIDING
SIFTING
SIGHTING
SING
SITTING
SIZING
SKATING
SKIING
SKILLING
SKIMMING
SKIORING
SKIRTING
SLAMMING
SLASHING
SLATING
SLATTING
SLEDDING
SLEEPING
SLING
SLUBBING
SMOCKING
SOARING
SORING
SOUNDING
SOUTHING
SPACING
SPAEING
SPANKING
SPARLING
SPEAKING
SPEEDING
SPEERING
SPELLING
SPILING
SPINNING
SPOOLING
SPOUTING
SPRING
STABLING
STAGING
STALKING
STANDING
STARLING
STEADING
STEALING
STEEVING
STERLING
STING
STIRRING
STOCKING
STRING
STRIPING
STUDDING
STUFFING
STYLING
SUBBING
SUBRING
SUCKLING
SUITING
SURFING
SWEEPING
SWEETING
SWELLING
SWIMMING
SWING
TACKLING
TAILING
TAKING
TALKING
TANNING
TAPPING
TATTING
TEACHING
TEETHING
THING
THINKING
TICKING
TIDING
TILING
TIMING
TING
TINKLING
TINTING
TITHING
TONGUING
TOOLING
TOPPING
TOURING
TOWELING
TRACING
TRACKING
TRAINING
TRAPPING
TRIFLING
TRIMMING
TRIPPING
TRITHING
TROLLING
TRUCKING
TRUSSING
TUBING
TUFTING
TUMBLING
TURNING
TURTLING
TWILLING
TWINNING
TWISTING
UNDOING
UNSLING
UNSTRING
UPFLING
UPPING
UPRISING
UPSPRING
UPSWING
VAPORING
VAULTING
VEILING
VEINING
VESTING
VIEWING
VIKING
VOGUEING
VOGUING
VOICING
WADDING
WAFFLING
WAISTING
WAITING
WAKENING
WALKING
WARNING
WASHING
WATERING
WAXING
WAXWING
WAYGOING
WEAKLING
WEANLING
WEBBING
WEDDING
WEEPING
WELTING
WESTING
WETTING
WHALING
WHEELING
WHIPPING
WHITING
WICKING
WIGGING
WILDING
WILDLING
WINDING
WINDLING
WING
WINNING
WIRING
WITCHING
WITLING
WITTING
WORDING
WORKING
WRAPPING
WRECKING
WRING
WRITING
YACHTING
YAWPING
YEALING
YEANLING
YEARLING
YEARNING
ZING

Words ending in -INGS that can't drop the -S

==========

ABLINGS
BEASTINGS
BEESTINGS
BIESTINGS
EMPTINGS
GAYWINGS
HUSTINGS

Words ending in -LIKE

==========

AGUELIKE
AIRLIKE
ALIKE
ANTLIKE
APELIKE
ARMLIKE
ASSLIKE
AUNTLIKE
AXLIKE
BAGLIKE
BALMLIKE
BARNLIKE
BATLIKE
BEADLIKE
BEAKLIKE
BEAMLIKE
BEANLIKE
BEARLIKE
BEDLIKE
BEELIKE
BELIKE
BIBLIKE
BIRDLIKE
BOATLIKE
BOLTLIKE
BOWLIKE
BOWLLIKE
BOXLIKE
BUDLIKE
BUSHLIKE
CAGELIKE
CALFLIKE
CATLIKE
CAVELIKE
CLAMLIKE
CLAWLIKE
CLAYLIKE
COCKLIKE
COKELIKE
COMBLIKE
CORDLIKE
CORKLIKE
CORMLIKE
CRABLIKE
CULTLIKE
CUPLIKE
DAWNLIKE
DEERLIKE
DISCLIKE
DISHLIKE
DISKLIKE
DISLIKE
DOGLIKE
DOMELIKE
DOVELIKE
DOWNLIKE
DRUMLIKE
DUNELIKE
DUSTLIKE
EELLIKE
ELFLIKE
EPICLIKE
EYELIKE
FADLIKE
FANGLIKE
FANLIKE
FATLIKE
FAUNLIKE
FAWNLIKE
FELTLIKE
FERNLIKE
FILMLIKE
FINLIKE
FISHLIKE
FOAMLIKE
FOLKLIKE
FOOTLIKE
FORKLIKE
FOXLIKE
FROGLIKE
FUMELIKE
FUSELIKE
GAMELIKE
GATELIKE
GEMLIKE
GERMLIKE
GLENLIKE
GLUELIKE
GNATLIKE
GOADLIKE
GOATLIKE
GODLIKE
GONGLIKE
GULFLIKE
GUMLIKE
GUTLIKE
HAIRLIKE
HALOLIKE
HANDLIKE
HARELIKE
HATLIKE
HAWKLIKE
HEMPLIKE
HENLIKE
HERBLIKE
HERDLIKE
HIPLIKE
HOBLIKE
HOELIKE
HOGLIKE
HOMELIKE
HOODLIKE
HOOFLIKE
HOOKLIKE
HOOPLIKE
HORNLIKE
HOSELIKE
HUSKLIKE
HUTLIKE
HYMNLIKE
ICELIKE
INKLIKE
IRONLIKE
IVYLIKE
JADELIKE
JAMLIKE
JAWLIKE
JAZZLIKE
JETLIKE
JIGLIKE
JUTELIKE
KIDLIKE
KILTLIKE
KINGLIKE
KITELIKE
KNOBLIKE
KNOTLIKE
LACELIKE
LADYLIKE
LAKELIKE
LAMBLIKE
LARDLIKE
LAVALIKE
LAWLIKE
LEAFLIKE
LEGLIKE
LIFELIKE
LIKE
LILYLIKE
LINELIKE
LIONLIKE
LIPLIKE
LOFTLIKE
LORDLIKE
MANLIKE
MAPLIKE
MASKLIKE
MASTLIKE
MAZELIKE
MISLIKE
MOATLIKE
MOONLIKE
MOSSLIKE
MOTHLIKE
NECKLIKE
NESTLIKE
NETLIKE
NIBLIKE
NOOKLIKE
NOSELIKE
NOVALIKE
NUNLIKE
NUTLIKE
OAKLIKE
OARLIKE
OATLIKE
OVENLIKE
OWLLIKE
OXLIKE
PALMLIKE
PARKLIKE
PEAKLIKE
PEALIKE
PEGLIKE
PIGLIKE
PINELIKE
PIPELIKE
PLAYLIKE
PLUMLIKE
PODLIKE
POETLIKE
POPELIKE
POTLIKE
PUMPLIKE
PUSLIKE
PUSSLIKE
QUAYLIKE
RASHLIKE
RATLIKE
RAYLIKE
REEDLIKE
RIBLIKE
RINGLIKE
ROCKLIKE
RODLIKE
ROOFLIKE
ROOTLIKE
ROPELIKE
ROSELIKE
RUBYLIKE
RUFFLIKE
RUGLIKE
RUNELIKE
RUSHLIKE
SACKLIKE
SACLIKE
SALTLIKE
SANDLIKE
SAWLIKE
SCABLIKE
SCUMLIKE
SEALLIKE
SEAMLIKE
SEEDLIKE
SERFLIKE
SHEDLIKE
SIGHLIKE
SILKLIKE
SKINLIKE
SKYLIKE
SLABLIKE
SLITLIKE
SNAGLIKE
SNOWLIKE
SOAPLIKE
SONGLIKE
SONLIKE
SOULLIKE
SOUPLIKE
SPARLIKE
STARLIKE
STEMLIKE
STEPLIKE
SUCHLIKE
SUITLIKE
SUNLIKE
SURFLIKE
SWANLIKE
TAGLIKE
TAILLIKE
TANKLIKE
TAPELIKE
TEALIKE
TENTLIKE
TIDELIKE
TILELIKE
TINLIKE
TOADLIKE
TOELIKE
TOMBLIKE
TOYLIKE
TRAPLIKE
TREELIKE
TUBELIKE
TUBLIKE
TURFLIKE
TUSKLIKE
TWIGLIKE
UNALIKE
UNLIKE
URNLIKE
VASELIKE
VEILLIKE
VEINLIKE
VESTLIKE
VISELIKE
WAIFLIKE
WARLIKE
WARTLIKE
WASPLIKE
WAVELIKE
WAXLIKE
WEBLIKE
WEEDLIKE
WHEYLIKE
WHIPLIKE
WIFELIKE
WIGLIKE
WINGLIKE
WIRELIKE
WISPLIKE
WOLFLIKE
WOOLLIKE
WORMLIKE

Words ending in -ABLE

==========

ABATABLE
ABLE
ABUSABLE
ACTABLE
ADDABLE
ADORABLE
AFFABLE
AGITABLE
ALLIABLE
AMENABLE
AMIABLE
AMICABLE
AMUSABLE
ARABLE
ARGUABLE
ATONABLE
AVOWABLE
BAILABLE
BANKABLE
BANNABLE
BARRABLE
BEARABLE
BEATABLE
BEDDABLE
BENDABLE
BIDDABLE
BILLABLE
BINDABLE
BITABLE
BITEABLE
BLAMABLE
BOATABLE
BOILABLE
BOMBABLE
BONDABLE
BOOKABLE
BOOTABLE
BRIBABLE
BUFFABLE
BURNABLE
BUYABLE
CABLE
CALLABLE
CAPABLE
CARTABLE
CASCABLE
CASHABLE
CASTABLE
CAUSABLE
CHEWABLE
CITABLE
CITEABLE
CLOSABLE
CLUBABLE
CODABLE
COINABLE
COOKABLE
COPYABLE
CULPABLE
CURABLE
CURBABLE
CUTTABLE
DAMNABLE
DATABLE
DATEABLE
DENIABLE
DIMMABLE
DIPPABLE
DISABLE
DOABLE
DOWABLE
DRAPABLE
DRAWABLE
DRIVABLE
DRYABLE
DUPABLE
DURABLE
DUTIABLE
DYABLE
DYEABLE
EATABLE
EDITABLE
EDUCABLE
EFFABLE
ENABLE
ENVIABLE
EQUABLE
ERASABLE
ERODABLE
ERRABLE
EVADABLE
EVITABLE
EVOCABLE
EXILABLE
EXORABLE
EXPIABLE
EYEABLE
FABLE
FACEABLE
FADABLE
FARMABLE
FEEDABLE
FELLABLE
FILEABLE
FILLABLE
FILMABLE
FINABLE
FINDABLE
FINEABLE
FIREABLE
FISHABLE
FITTABLE
FIXABLE
FLYABLE
FOAMABLE
FOILABLE
FOLDABLE
FORDABLE
FORMABLE
FRAMABLE
FRIABLE
FRYABLE
FURLABLE
GABLE
GAINABLE
GELABLE
GETABLE
GETTABLE
GIFTABLE
GIVEABLE
GNAWABLE
GRADABLE
GRAZABLE
GROWABLE
GUIDABLE
GULLABLE
GUSTABLE
HACKABLE
HANGABLE
HATABLE
HATEABLE
HEALABLE
HEARABLE
HEATABLE
HELPABLE
HEWABLE
HIDABLE
HIRABLE
HIREABLE
HITTABLE
HOLDABLE
HUGGABLE
HUMMABLE
HUNTABLE
IMITABLE
INARABLE
INSTABLE
INVIABLE
ISOLABLE
ISSUABLE
JAILABLE
JAMMABLE
JOINABLE
JUMPABLE
KEEPABLE
KICKABLE
KILLABLE
KISSABLE
KNOWABLE
LAPSABLE
LAUDABLE
LEASABLE
LENDABLE
LEVIABLE
LIABLE
LIENABLE
LIFTABLE
LIKABLE
LIKEABLE
LINABLE
LINEABLE
LINKABLE
LISTABLE
LIVABLE
LIVEABLE
LOANABLE
LOCKABLE
LOSABLE
LOVABLE
LOVEABLE
MAILABLE
MAKABLE
MAKEABLE
MAPPABLE
MASKABLE
MELTABLE
MENDABLE
MILLABLE
MINABLE
MINEABLE
MISSABLE
MIXABLE
MOCKABLE
MOLDABLE
MOVABLE
MOVEABLE
MUTABLE
NAMABLE
NAMEABLE
NESTABLE
NETTABLE
NOTABLE
OBEYABLE
OBVIABLE
OPENABLE
OPERABLE
OUTFABLE
OVERABLE
OWNABLE
OXIDABLE
PACKABLE
PALPABLE
PARABLE
PARSABLE
PASSABLE
PAWNABLE
PAYABLE
PECCABLE
PEELABLE
PETTABLE
PITIABLE
PLACABLE
PLAYABLE
PLIABLE
PLOWABLE
POKABLE
PORTABLE
POSABLE
POTABLE
POURABLE
PROBABLE
PROVABLE
PRUNABLE
QUOTABLE
RADIABLE
RAISABLE
RATABLE
RATEABLE
READABLE
REAPABLE
REEFABLE
REELABLE
RELIABLE
RENTABLE
RESTABLE
RETABLE
REUSABLE
RIDABLE
RIDEABLE
RINSABLE
RIPPABLE
ROCKABLE
ROPABLE
ROWABLE
RUINABLE
RULABLE
RUSTABLE
SABLE
SAILABLE
SALABLE
SALEABLE
SALVABLE
SANDABLE
SATIABLE
SAVABLE
SAVEABLE
SAYABLE
SCALABLE
SEALABLE
SEEABLE
SEISABLE
SEIZABLE
SELLABLE
SENDABLE
SERVABLE
SEWABLE
SHAKABLE
SHAMABLE
SHAPABLE
SHARABLE
SHAVABLE
SHEDABLE
SHOWABLE
SINGABLE
SINKABLE
SIZABLE
SIZEABLE
SKIABLE
SLAKABLE
SLAYABLE
SLIDABLE
SMOKABLE
SOCIABLE
SOLVABLE
SORBABLE
SORTABLE
SOWABLE
SPARABLE
STABLE
STATABLE
STEWABLE
STONABLE
STORABLE
STOWABLE
SUABLE
SUITABLE
SUMMABLE
SURFABLE
SWAYABLE
SYLLABLE
TABLE
TAKABLE
TAKEABLE
TALKABLE
TAMABLE
TAMEABLE
TANNABLE
TAPEABLE
TAPPABLE
TASTABLE
TAXABLE
TEARABLE
TEASABLE
TELLABLE
TENABLE
TESTABLE
TILLABLE
TILTABLE
TIPPABLE
TITHABLE
TITRABLE
TOTABLE
TOTEABLE
TOWABLE
TRADABLE
TRIABLE
TUBBABLE
TUNABLE
TUNEABLE
TURNABLE
TYPABLE
TYPEABLE
UNABLE
UNDOABLE
UNSTABLE
UNUSABLE
UNVIABLE
USABLE
USEABLE
VALUABLE
VARIABLE
VENDABLE
VIABLE
VIEWABLE
VIOLABLE
VITIABLE
VOCABLE
VOIDABLE
VOTABLE
VOTEABLE
WADABLE
WADEABLE
WALKABLE
WASHABLE
WASTABLE
WAXABLE
WEARABLE
WELDABLE
WETTABLE
WILLABLE
WINDABLE
WINNABLE
WIRABLE
WORKABLE
WRITABLE

Words ending in -IBLE

==========

ADDIBLE
ALIBLE
AUDIBLE
BIBLE
CREDIBLE
CRUCIBLE
EDIBLE
EDUCIBLE
ELIDIBLE
ELIGIBLE
ERODIBLE
EROSIBLE
EVADIBLE
EXIGIBLE
FALLIBLE
FEASIBLE
FENCIBLE
FLEXIBLE
FOIBLE
FORCIBLE
FUNGIBLE
FUSIBLE
GULLIBLE
HORRIBLE
INEDIBLE
LAPSIBLE
LEGIBLE
MANDIBLE
MISCIBLE
MIXIBLE
PARTIBLE
PASSIBLE
POSSIBLE
RENDIBLE
RINSIBLE
RISIBLE
SENSIBLE
TANGIBLE
TENSIBLE
TERRIBLE
THURIBLE
UNEDIBLE
VENDIBLE
VINCIBLE
VISIBLE

THE HOOKS

Before you approach the final game of the first annual World Open Championship (WOC), you've achieved a stellar 27–2 +3000 record (wins-losses, cumulative point-spread). Your opponent, however, is 28–1 +3372. You need not only to win but to win by 187 points to capture first place and the $100,000 prize money that accompanies it.

Your opponent starts off with CHAPEAU, with a less-than-best placement at 8H, for 80 points. You had to pass your VVWWUUU rack. Then, your opponent plops down OOLOGIES to run up a 148-0 advantage. Of course you couldn't keep your IEIEIEI rack, so you pass again. You don't want to accuse anyone of being awfully lucky, but after RATION[E]D is played through the O for a 214-0 lead, you're fuming. And, it gets worse.

Incredibly, you draw back your VVWWUUU rack! You have to continue passing. You angrily grab and vigorously shake the tile bag. Meanwhile, your opponent continues on his merry way, adding SENORITA, U[N]IVERSE, and FELTING to run the score up to a 578-0 lead.

You've got DCFJKOZ in your rack and the 15 unaccounted for tiles are ABEEGIILLNRSVXY. With divine inspiration, you pass all but DJZ. He, then, lays down BILLING at 13E for a 644-0 lead. You draw SEXY to join your DJZ combo and, with one tile in the bag, for the 22nd consecutive turn you pass your turn (this time without exchanging tiles).

Like the sadist you know he must be, your opponent's 23rd consecutive play is his 8th bingo, ECOFREAK (E4), for 118 points and a 762-0 lead. But, the fiend draws the final tile in the bag: the unplayable V. You are "Z SEXY DJ," but you're going to do what no sexy deejay ever did: win first place at WOC and $100K by saving your best for last. Here's how:

	A	B	C	D	E	F	G	H	I	J	K	L	M	N	O
1		M	U						A	N	I		A	R	
2	S	E	N	O	R	I	T	A			D	O	E		A
3	Q							P				O			W
4	U	N	I	V	E	R	S	E				L			E
5	I				C			R	A	T	I	O	N	E	D
6	R				O			Y				G			
7	E	T			F							I		O	E
8		O	W		R			C	H	A	P	E	A	U	
9		D			E							S		T	A
10					A										N
11					K										T
12															H
13					B	I	L	L	I	N	G			B	E
14											U			O	M
15								F	E	L	T	I	N	G	

Rack: ZSEXYDJ
Score: 0-762
Last Play: ECOFREAK (E4, 118)
Unseen: V

1. <u>ESQUIRE</u>D (A1) 198
2. <u>EXANTHEM</u>S (O7) 291 (489 total)
3. <u>JANIZARY</u> (1H) 452 (941 total)
+V from opponent × 2 = 8 (949 total)

You prevail upon your opponent 949-762, go 28–2 +3187, leaving your opponent a whisker behind at 28–2 +3185. Who says you need "tile turnover," blanks, and bingos to win?

But, in this scenario, you had to know your hooks. Hooks are letters that can be individually placed before or after a word to form a longer acceptable word. In our endgame above, E was a front-hook for MU to form EMU (1A), while D was a front-hook for OW to form DOW (8A), as ESQUIRED was concurrently played. Similarly, the J, Z, and Y were front-hooks for, respectively, APERY, OOLOGIES, and AWED to form JAPERY (H1), ZOOLOGIES (L1), and YAWED (O1), while also playing JANIZARY. At the other end, no pun intended, are the rear-hooks: X was a rear-hook for CHAPEAU to form CHAPEAUX while S was a rear-hook for FELTING to form FELTINGS, and thereby also creating XANTHEMS.

By learning all the two-letter words, you mastered the "1s-to-Make-2s," knowing which letters can individually go before or after an available letter. In the introduction to "The Cheat Sheet," knowing U could come "after" X to form XU allowed UNDERGO to go under VOX (see page 10).

The Hooks on the following pages include all the "3s-to-Make-4s" through the "8s-to-Make-9s." The "2s-to-Make-3s" are on "The Cheat Sheet" (page 12). Within a given list, the base word will be in capital letters, the front- and rear-hook letters, if any, in lowercase letters. Here is an example from the "4s-to-Make-5s" list:

```
bcd*RAVE dln
 gt       rs
bcd RAWS*
     RAYA*hs
bdf*RAYS*
gpt
```

RAVE can be extended by five different front-hook letters to form BRAVE, CRAVE, DRAVE, GRAVE, and TRAVE. As well, it can be extended by five different rear-hook letters to form RAVED, RAVEL, RAVEN, RAVER, and RAVES. In contrast, the next word, RAWS, can only take front-hook letters, and RAYA only rear-hook letters.

Also, you will see asterisks (*) before or after some base words, indicating that the base word contains a "parent" word, one letter shorter than the base word, which can be hooked or extended by the capitalized letter beside the asterisk. With our example above, the base word *RAVE contains the parent word AVE, which can be front-hooked or extended with the R, hence the asterisk calling attention to the R-hook of AVE. RAWS* and RAYA* contain the parent words RAW and RAY, and are extended by an S onto RAW and an A onto RAY. Finally, *RAYS* indicates RAY can add an S at the end and AYS can add an R at the front. In this example, you are simultaneously learning the four-letter words, the "3s-to-Make-4s," and the "4s-to-Make-5s." As you go from the shorter to longer word lists, the asterisks are giving you a "refresher course" on the list of parent words you just finished and the hook letters are giving you a "sneak preview" of the list of longer words next ahead of you.

The Hooks: 3s-to-Make-4s

*AAH*s
b*AAL*s
bk*AAS*
b*ABA*s
cdf ABS*
gjkl
nstw
bg*ABY*es
dfl ACE ds
mprt
fpt ACT as
ADD*s
df*ADO*s
bcd ADS*
fglm
prtw
ADZ*e
bcd AFF
gnr
wy
dhr AFT
w
grs AGA*rs
cgm AGE*der
prsw s
s*AGO*gn
bdf AGS*
ghjl
mnrs
twyz
h*AHA*
*AHI*s
adh AHS*
clm*AID*es
pqrs
bfh AIL*s
jkm
npr
stvw
m AIM*s
cfg*AIN*s
klm
prs
tvw
fhl AIR*nst
mpvw y
dr*AIS*
bgw*AIT*s
gnt*ALA*enr
s
ALB*as
bdg ALE*cef
hkm s
prs
tvw
bcf ALL*sy
ghlm
pstw
ps ALP*s
abd ALS*o
gps
hms ALT*os
glm*AMA*hs
kr*AMI*ade
nrs
cdg AMP*s
lrs
tv
*AMU*s
kmn*ANA*ls
bhl AND*s
rsw
bcf*ANE*sw
gjk
lmp
svw
br ANI*ls
chp ANT*aei
rw s
mwz ANY*
cgj*APE drs
nrt x
c APO ds
APP s
r APT
bcd ARB*s
g
mn ARC*hos
bcd*ARE*as
fhmp
rtwy
bz ARF*s
bcd ARK*s
hlm
npsw
bfh ARM*sy
w
bce ARS*
gjl
mop
tvw
cdh ART*sy
kmp
tw
bcd*ASH*y
fgh
lmp
rsw
bcm ASK*s
t
ghr ASP*s
w
blm ASS*
pst
bcd ATE*s
fgh
lmp
rst
bmw ATT*
jw AUK s
fjk AVA
l
cef AVE rs
ghln
prsw
AVO sw
AWA*y
*AWE*des
bpw AWL*s
y
dfl AWN*sy
mpsy
AXE*dls
*AYE*s
bcd AYS*
fgh
jkl
mnp
rswy
AZO n
*BAA*ls
*BAD*es
*BAG*s
*BAH*t
*BAL*dek
lms
*BAM*s
*BAN*deg
iks
BAP*s
k*BAR*bde
fkm
ns
ao*BAS*ehk
st
*BAT*ehs
t
*BAY*s
a*BED*su
BEE*fnp
rst
BEG*s
*BEL*lst
*BEN*des
t
o*BES*t
a*BET*ahs
o BEY*s
BIB*bs
*BID*eis
BIG*s
*BIN*des
t
BIO*gs
io*BIS*ek
o*BIT*est
BIZ*e
BOA*rst
BOB*s
*BOD*esy
BOG*sy
BOO*bkm
nrst
*BOP*s
*BOS*hks
BOT*ahs
t
*BOW*ls
*BOX*y
*BOY*os
BRA deg
nst
wy
BRO osw
BRR r
BUB osu
BUD s
BUG s
*BUM fps
*BUN adg
knst
BUR abd
gln
prsy
*BUS hks
ty
a*BUT est
BUY s
a*BYE*s
a BYS*
s*CAB s
s*CAD eis
s*CAM eop
s
s*CAN est
CAP eho
s
s*CAR bde
kln
prst
s*CAT es
*CAW s
*CAY s
CEE s
*CEL lst
CEP es
*CHI acd
npst
CIG s
*CIS t
COB bs
*COD aes
COG s
COL ade
sty
i*CON eik
nsy
COO fkl
npst
s*COP esy
*COR def
kmn
sy
*COS hst
y
s COT es
s*COW lsy
*COX a
*COY s
COZ y
e CRU dsx
s CRY
CUB es
s CUD s
CUE ds
s*CUM
s*CUP s
CUR bde
fln
rst
s*CUT es
CWM s
*DAB s
*DAD aos
*DAG s
o*DAH ls
DAK s
*DAL es
*DAM enp
s
*DAN gks
DAP s
*DAW kns
t
*DAY s
DEB*st
DEE*dmp
rst
*DEF*ity
*DEL*efi
lst
*DEN*eis
ty
DEV*as
DEW*sy
*DEX*y
DEY*s
DIB s
*DID oy
DIE dls
t
*DIF fs
DIG s
DIM es
*DIN egk
ost
DIP st
*DIS chk
s
ae*DIT aes
z
DOC*ks
*DOE*rs
DOG*esy
i DOL*els
t
*DOM*es
u*DON*aeg
s
o*DOR*ekm
prsy
au*DOS*est
DOT*ehs
y
*DOW*ns
DRY s
DUB s
DUD es
DUE lst
DUG s
*DUH
DUI t
*DUN egk
st
DUO s
*DUP es
*DYE drs
bdf*EAR lns
ghl
npr
stwy
bfh*EAT hs
mnp
st
b EAU x
EBB s
ECU s
EDH*s
bfg EDS*
mpr
twz
gkl EEK
mpr
sw
fhk*EEL sy
prs
tw
t EFF*s
kr EFS*
dhl EFT*s
rw
ty EGG sy
s*EGO s
dlp EKE ds
ghm ELD*s
vwy
dps ELF*
y ELK*s
bcd ELL*s
fhjm
stwy
h ELM*sy
bcd ELS*e
egm
st
dfh*EME*su
ms
fgh EMS*
mr
*EMU*s
bfl END*s
mpr
stvw
ENG*s
bdf ENS*
ghkl
ptwy
ajn*EON s
p
sv ERA*s
cdf*ERE*
hmp
sw
b ERG*os
fhk ERN*es
t
ERR*s
hs ERS*t
cfj ESS*
lmn
bfg*ETA*s
msz
bhm ETH*s
t
n EVE nrs
*EWE rs
*EYE dnr
s
*FAB*s
*FAD*eos
*FAG*s
*FAN*ego
a*FAR*del
mo
*FAS*ht
*FAT*es
FAX
*FAY*s
*FED*s
FEE*bdl
st
*FEH*s
*FEM*es
*FEN*ds
*FER*en
*FES*st
*FET*aes
FEU*ds
FEW*
FEY*
FEZ*
FIB s
*FID os
FIE f
FIG s
FIL ael
mos
*FIN dek
os
FIR emn
s
*FIT s
FIX t
FIZ z
FLU bes
x
FLY
FOB s
*FOE s
FOG sy
*FOH n
*FON dst
*FOP s
*FOR abd
ekmt
FOU lr
*FOX y
*FOY s
FRO egm
w
FRY
FUB s
FUD s
FUG su
*FUN dks
FUR lsy
*GAB sy
e*GAD is
*GAE dns
*GAG aes
e*GAL ael
s
o*GAM abe
psy
*GAN eg
GAP esy
a*GAR bs
a*GAS hpt
*GAT es
*GAY s
a*GED s
ao GEE dks
z
*GEL dst
*GEM s
*GEN est
u
*GET as
GEY
*GHI s
GIB es
*GID s
GIE dns
GIG as
a*GIN ks
GIP s
*GIT es
*GNU s
GOA*dls
t
GOB*osy
*GOD*s
GOO*dfk
nps
*GOR*emp
y
e*GOS*h
GOT*h
GOX
GUL flp
s
*GUM s
*GUN ks
*GUT s
GUV s
GUY s
GYM s
GYP s
cs*HAD*ej
t*HAE*dmn
st
s*HAG*s
s*HAH*as
HAJ*ij
csw*HAM*es
c HAO*
cw HAP*s
*HAS*hpt
cgk*HAT*ehs
ptw
cst*HAW*ks
cs*HAY*s
*HEH*s
at*HEM*eps
tw*HEN*st
HEP*
*HER*bde
lmn
os
s*HES*t
kw*HET*hs
cps HEW*ns
tw
HEX
tw HEY*
c HIC*k
cw*HID*e
HIE*ds
sw HIM*s
cst*HIN*dst
w
csw HIP*s
acg*HIS*nst
kpt
cw*HIT*s
HMM
HOB*os
s*HOD*s
s*HOE*drs
s HOG*gs
cp*HON*egk
s
csw*HOP*es
ps HOT*s
cds*HOW*efk
ls
a*HOY*as
c HUB s
HUE ds
ct HUG es
*HUH
c*HUM ps
s*HUN ghk
st
w*HUP
bps*HUT s
HYP eos
bdf ICE ds
lmn
prsv
lrw ICH s
dhk ICK y
lnp
rstw
ICY
abf IDS*
gkl
mrv
bdj IFF*y
mrt
dkr IFS*
m IGG s
bms ILK as
bdf ILL sy
ghjk
mnpr
stvw
yz
gjl IMP is
psw
dfg INK*sy
jkl
mop
rsw
jl INN*s
abd INS*
fgh
jkl
prs
twyz
clp*ION s
cdf*IRE ds
hlm
stw
bdk IRK s
m
ISM*s
abd ITS*
fgh
klnp
stwz
jt IVY
*JAB s
*JAG gs
*JAM bs
a*JAR ls
*JAW s
*JAY s
a JEE dpr
sz
*JET es
JEU x
JIB bes
JIG s
d*JIN kns
x
JOB*s
*JOE*sy
JOG*s
JOT*as
*JOW*ls
*JOY*s
JUG as
*JUN k
*JUS t
*JUT es
*KAB*s
*KAE*s
KAF*s
os*KAS*
is*KAT*as
o*KAY*os
KEA s
*KEF s
s KEG s
*KEN ost
s KEP ist
*KEX
KEY s
*KHI s
s*KID*s
*KIF*s
as*KIN*ade
gkos
s KIP*s
KIR*kns
s*KIS*st
s*KIT*ehs
KOA ns
KOB os
*KOI s
*KOP hs
*KOR aes
*KOS s
KUE s
*KYE s
bfs*LAB*s
LAC*eks
y
cg*LAD*esy
cfs*LAG*s
bcf*LAM*abe
gs ps
cfs LAP*s
a*LAR*dik
s
a*LAS*ehs
t
bfp*LAT*ehi
s su
LAV*aes
bcf*LAW*ns
s
f*LAX*
cfp*LAY*s
s
fio LEA dfk
p lnp
rs
bfg*LED
ps
afg LEE krs
t
g LEG s
LEI s
LEK esu
b*LET s
LEU d
LEV aoy
fip*LEX
fg LEY s
g LIB*s
s*LID*os
p LIE*dfn
rsu
b*LIN*egk
nos
ty
bcf LIP*aes
s
*LIS*pt
afs*LIT*esu
bgs LOB*eos
bcf LOG*eos
s y
LOO*fkm
npst
cfg*LOP*es
ps
bcp LOT*ahi
s s
abf*LOW*ens
gps
LOX
gps LUG es
agp*LUM aps
s
LUV s
f LUX e
*LYE s
MAC*ehk
s
*MAD*es
*MAE*s
*MAG*eis
*MAN*aeo
sy
MAP*s
*MAR*ace
klst
a*MAS*ahk
st
*MAT*ehs
t
*MAW*ns
*MAX*i
*MAY*aos
*MED*s
MEG*as
*MEL*dls
t
*MEM*eos
ao*MEN*dou
*MET*aeh
s MEW*ls
*MHO s
MIB*s

```
e MIC*aes
ai*MID*is
MIG*gs
MIL*dek
lost
MIM*e
ae MIR*eik
sy
a*MIS*eos
t
MIX*t
MOA*nst
MOB*s
MOC*ks
*MOD*eis
s MOG*s
MOL*ade
lsty
*MOM*eis
*MON*kos
y
MOO*dln
rst
*MOP*esy
*MOR*aen
st
*MOS*hks
t
MOT*ehs
t
*MOW*ns
MUD*s
s MUG*gs
*MUM*mps
u
*MUN*is
ae*MUS*ehk
st
s*MUT*est
MYC*s
*NAB*es
*NAE*
s*NAG*s
*NAH*
*NAM*e
*NAN*as
ks NAP*aes
gs*NAW*
*NAY*s
NEB*s
k NEE*dmp
NEG*s
*NET*st
ak NEW*st
s NIB s
a NIL ls
NIM s
s NIP as
ksu*NIT es
NIX ey
ks NOB*s
*NOD*eis
s NOG*gs
*NOH*
*NOM*aes
NOO*kn
*NOR*im
o*NOS*ehy
ks NOT*ae
eks*NOW*st
NTH
s NUB*s
*NUN*s
ago*NUS*
*NUT*s
l OAF s
s OAK sy

bhr*OAR s
s
bcd*OAT hs
gm
s*OBA s
lr*OBE sy
*OBI ast
cls OCA s
cs ODA*hs
ODD*s
bcl*ODE*as
mnr
bcg ODS*
hmnp
rsty
dfg*OES*
hjn
rtvw
bcd OFF*s
t
cls OFT*
t
*OHM*s
bc*OHO*
o OHS*
bcf OIL*sy
mnr
st
*OKA sy
chj OKE hs
mps
twy
bcf OLD sy
ghm
stw
bcd OLE aos
hjmp
rstv
dmn OMS*
rst
bcd*ONE*s
ghln
pstz
m*ONO*s
cde ONS*
fhim
pstw
p*OOH s
bcf OOT s
hlm
rst
cdh*OPE*dns
lmn
prt
bcf OPS*
hklm
opst
OPT*s
bfh ORA*dl
kmst
fs ORB*sy
t ORC*as
bcd*ORE*s
fgk
lmp
stwy
cdk ORS*
mt
bfm ORT*s
pstw
dhl OSE*s
npr
l OUD s
dfh OUR s
lps
ty

bgl*OUT s
prt
n OVA l
hly*OWE*ds
bcf OWL*s
hjy
dgl OWN*s
mst
OXO*
bdf OXY*
p
PAC*aek
sty
*PAD*is
o*PAH*
o*PAL*elm
psy
s*PAM*s
s*PAN*egs
t
PAP*as
s*PAR*ade
krst
su*PAS*ehs
t
s*PAT*ehs
y
*PAW*lns
*PAX*
s*PAY*s
PEA*gkl
nrst
s PEC*hks
aos*PED*s
e PEE*kln
prs
PEG*s
*PEH*s
o*PEN*dst
PEP*os
a*PER*eik
mptv
ao*PES*ot
*PET*s
s PEW*s
*PHI sz
PHT
PIA*lns
e PIC*aek
s
PIE*drs
PIG*s
s*PIN*aeg
ksty
PIP*esy
*PIS*ho
s*PIT*ahs
y
PIU*
PIX*y
PLY
a*POD s
*POH
*POI s
POL elo
sy
*POP es
s POT s
*POW s
*POX y
PRO adf
gmp
sw
s PRY
*PSI s
PST
PUB s

s PUD s
PUG hs
PUL aei
lps
s*PUN agk
sty
*PUP asu
s PUR eil
rs
o*PUS hs
*PUT stz
*PYA s
*PYE s
PYX
*QAT s
*QIS*
a QUA dgi
y
bgo*RAD s
t
bcd*RAG aeg
f is
*RAH
*RAI adl
ns
RAJ a
cdg*RAM ips
pt
bg*RAN dgi
kt
cft RAP est
w
be*RAS ehp
bdf*RAT eho
gp s
bcd*RAW s
*RAX
bdf*RAY as
gpt
REB*s
REC*ks
bci*RED*deo
s
bdf REE*dfk
gpt ls
t*REF*st
d REG*s
REI*fns
*REM*s
p REP*ops
aio*RES*ht
t
ft*RET*es
REV*s
p*REX*
*RHO s
a RIA ls
cd RIB s
agi*RID es
*RIF efs
t
bfg RIG s
pt
bgp RIM esy
t
bg*RIN dgk
s
dgt RIP es
ROB es
c ROC ks
pt*ROD es
f*ROE s
fp*ROM ps
gt ROT aei
los
bcf*ROW s
gptv

dg RUB esy
gt RUE drs
dft RUG as
adg*RUM ps
*RUN egs
t
b*RUT hs
*RYA s
*RYE s
*SAB es
SAC ks
*SAD ei
*SAE
*SAG aeo
sy
*SAL elp
st
SAP s
*SAT ei
SAU l
*SAW ns
*SAX
*SAY s
a SEA lmr
st
SEC st
SEE dkl
mnp
rs
SEG os
SEI fs
*SEL fls
*SEN det
u*SER aef
s
*SET ast
SEW ns
*SEX ty
*SHA*dgh
mwy
*SHE*ads
w
SHH*
a SHY*
SIB*bs
SIC*eks
SIM*aps
*SIN*egh
ks
SIP*es
SIR*es
p*SIS*
*SIT*ehs
SIX*
*SKA gst
*SKI dmn
pst
SKY
SLY
SOB*as
*SOD*as
SOL*ade
ios
*SOM*aes
*SON*egs
*SOP*hs
*SOS*
SOT*hs
SOU*klp
rs
*SOW*ns
*SOX*
*SOY*as
*SPA emn
rsty
e SPY
SRI s

STY e
SUB as
SUE drs
t
SUK s
*SUM ops
*SUN gkn
s
*SUP es
SUQ s
SYN ce
s*TAB*su
*TAD*s
*TAE*l
s*TAG*s
TAJ*
*TAM*eps
*TAN*gks
TAO*s
a TAP*aes
s*TAR*eno
pst
eu*TAS*ks
s*TAT*es
TAU*st
TAV*s
s*TAW*s
*TAX*ai
TEA klm
rst
*TED s
TEE dlm
ns
TEG gs
*TEL ael
s
*TEN dst
s*TET hs
s TEW s
*THE emn
wy
*THO u
THY
eo TIC*ks
TIE*drs
TIL*els
t
*TIN*egs
ty
TIP*is
*TIS*
*TIT*is
*TOD*sy
*TOE*ads
TOG*as
a*TOM*bes
*TON*egs
y
TOO*klm
nt
as*TOP*ehi
os
*TOR*ace
ino
rsty
s TOT*es
s*TOW*nsy
*TOY*os
TRY
TSK s
s TUB aes
TUG s
ep TUI s
s*TUN aeg
s
*TUP s
*TUT su

TUX
TWA es
*TWO s
s*TYE ers
jk*UDO ns
psv UGH s
cdj UKE s
np
ls ULU s
m*UMM*
bdh UMP*s
jlm
prst
bdf UNS*
ghmn
prst
UPO*n
cdp UPS*
sty
bc URB s
bcn URD s
s
bcd URN s
t
b URP s
fmr USE*drs
*UTA*s
bcj UTE*s
lm
bcg UTS*
hjmn
oprt
VAC s
*VAN egs
*VAR asy
k*VAS aet
*VAT su
VAU s
VAV s
*VAW s
VEE prs
VEG
*VET os
*VEX t
VIA l
a*VID es
VIE drs
w
VIG as
VIM s
*VIS ae
*VOE s
a*VOW s
*VOX
VUG ghs
o*VUM
s*WAB s
*WAD eis
y
t*WAE s
s*WAG es
hs*WAN des
ty
s WAP s
*WAR dek
mnp
sty
t*WAS hpt
s*WAT st
*WAW ls
*WAX y
as*WAY s
WEB*s
ao*WED*s
at WEE*dkl
npr
st

*WEN*dst
*WET*s
*WHA mpt
*WHO amp
WHY s
st WIG s
t*WIN deg
kosy
iy*WIS ehp
st
t*WIT ehs
WIZ
*WOE*s
WOK*es
*WON*kst
WOO*dfl
s
t*WOS*t
s WOT*s
*WOW*s
a WRY
WUD
*WYE s
WYN dns
a*XIS*
*YAG*is
a*YAH*
k YAK*s
*YAM*s
YAP*s
k*YAR*den
*YAW*lnp
s
*YAY*s
YEA*hnr
s
*YEH*
e*YEN*s
YEP*s
abd*YES*
eklo
prtw
*YET*it
YEW*s
apt*YIN s
YIP es
YOB*s
*YOD*hs
YOK*es
*YOM*
*YON*di
YOU*rs
*YOW*els
YUK s
*YUM
*YUP s
*ZAG*s
ZAP*s
*ZAS*
*ZAX*
*ZED s
ZEE s
ZEK s
ZEP s
ZIG s
*ZIN ceg
s
ZIP s
*ZIT is
ZOA
ZOO mns
ZUZ
ZZZ
```

The Hooks: 4s-to-Make-5s

AAHS
b*AALS*
b*ABAS*eh
ABBA s
ABBE sy
s*ABED
*ABET s
cfg ABLE drs
st
ABLY
ABRI s
*ABUT s
*ABYE*s
*ABYS*ms
flm ACED*
pr
dfl ACES*
mprt
cmt ACHE ds
ACHY
ACID sy
ACME s
ACNE ds
n ACRE ds
ACTA*
fpt ACTS*
ACYL s
ADDS*
*ADIT s
df*ADOS*
ADZE*ds
p*AEON s
AERO
f AERY
*AFAR s
*AGAR*s
rs*AGAS*
cgp*AGED*
rw
r*AGEE*
ceg AGER*s
jlp
swy
cgm AGES*
prsw
AGHA s
f*AGIN g
AGIO s
AGLY
m AGMA s
AGOG*
w AGON*esy
v AGUE s
a AHED
*AHEM
AHIS
*AHOY
AIDE*drs
cmq*AIDS*
rs
bfh AILS*
jkm
npr
stvw
m AIMS*
cgk*AINS*
mpr
stw
bc AIRN*s
fhl AIRS*
mpvw
AIRT*hs
dfh AIRY*
bgw*AITS*
*AJAR
*AJEE
r AKEE s
t*AKIN
ALAE*
ALAN*deg
st
mt*ALAR*my
bgn*ALAS*
t
ALBA*s
ALBS*
ALEC*s
ALEE
ALEF*s
bdg ALES*
hkm
prs
tvw
ALFA s
ALGA els
ck ALIF s
*ALIT
bt ALKY dl
bcf ALLS*
ghl
mptw
bdg ALLY*l
prs
tw
h ALMA hs
ALME hs
bch ALMS
mp
ALOE s
*ALOW
ps ALPS*
ALSO*
ALTO*s
hms ALTS*
*ALUM s
AMAH*s
cgl*AMAS*s
m
ms AMBO s
ry*AMEN dst
lz AMIA*s
*AMID*eos
mr AMIE*s
g AMIN*eos
*AMIR*s
t*AMIS*s
AMMO s
AMOK s
cdg AMPS*
lrs
tv
rw*AMUS*e
AMYL s
bc ANAL*
kmn ANAS*
bhl ANDS*
rsw
bcf ANES*
jklm
psvw
ANEW
fmp ANGA s
st
*ANIL*es
r ANIS*e
ANKH s
cm ANNA ls
ANOA s
cf ANON
h ANSA e
m ANTA*es
ANTE*ds
ANTI*cs
chp ANTS*y
rw
m*ANUS
cgj*APED*
rt
cgj*APER*sy
prt
cgj*APES*
nrt
APEX*
*APOD*s
c APOS*
APPS*
l APSE s
*AQUA es
ARAK s
bcd ARBS*
g
lmp ARCH*
n ARCO*
mn ARCS*
AREA*els
bcd*ARES*
fhl
mnp
rtw
bz ARFS*
mv*ARIA s
*ARID
ARIL s
bcd ARKS*
hlm
npsw
bfh ARMS*
w
b ARMY*
cdh ARTS*y
kmp
tw
ptw ARTY*
l*ARUM s
p ARVO s
ARYL s
ASCI
*ASEA
dmw*ASHY*
bcm ASKS*
t
ghr ASPS*
w
w*ATAP s
bcd ATES*
fgh
mnp
rst
ATMA ns
*ATOM sy
*ATOP y
jw AUKS*
cfy AULD
dgh AUNT sy
jtv
l AURA elr
s
AUTO s
chl AVER*st
prsw
cef AVES*
hlno
prsw
p*AVID
AVOS*
*AVOW*s
AWAY
cdh*AWED*
jlm
psty
AWEE
AWES*
bpw AWLS*
y
dfl AWNS*
py
flt AWNY*
AWOL s
*AWRY
AXAL
fmr AXED*
tw
AXEL*s
flm AXES*
prs
twz
AXIL es
mt*AXIS
AXLE ds
t AXON es
r*AYAH s
AYES
lz*AYIN s
h AZAN s
AZON*s
*BAAL*s
BAAS
*BABA s
BABE ls
BABU ls
*BABY
BACH
a BACK s
BADE*
BADS
*BAFF sy
BAGS
BAHT*s
*BAIL s
*BAIT hs
BAKE drs
BALD*sy
*BALE*drs
BALK*sy
*BALL*sy
BALM*sy
*BALS*a
BAMS*
*BAND*asy
*BANE*ds
BANG*s
BANI
BANK*s
BANS*
BAPS*
*BARB*es
BARD*es
*BARE*drs
*BARF*s
*BARK*sy
*BARM*sy
BARN*sy
k*BARS*
a BASE*drs
a*BASH*
*BASK*s
*BASS*ioy
BAST*es
a*BATE*ds
BATH*es
BATS*
*BATT*suy
BAUD s
BAWD sy
*BAWL s
BAYS
BEAD sy
BEAK sy
a BEAM sy
BEAN os
*BEAR ds
*BEAT s
*BEAU stx
BECK s
BEDS
BEDU*
BEEF*sy
BEEN*
BEEP*s
BEER*sy
BEES*
BEET*s
BEGS*
*BELL*esy
BELS
BELT*s
BEMA s
*BEND*sy
BENE*s
BENS
BENT*os
*BERG s
BERK s
BERM es
BEST*s
*BETA*s
*BETH*s
a BETS*
BEVY
o BEYS*
*BHUT s
o BIAS
BIBB*s
BIBS*
*BICE ps
a BIDE*drs
t
BIDI*s
BIDS
BIER s
*BIFF sy
BIGS*
BIKE drs
BILE s
*BILK s
*BILL sy
BIMA hs
BIND*is
BINE*rs
BINS
BINT*s
BIOG*s
BIOS*
BIRD s
*BIRK s
BIRL es
BIRO s
BIRR s
BISE*s
BISK*s
BITE*rs
o*BITS*y
BITT*sy
BIZE*s
*BLAB s
BLAE
BLAH s
*BLAM es
*BLAT es
*BLAW ns
BLEB s
a*BLED
*BLET s
BLEW
*BLIN dik
*BLIP s
*BLOB s
BLOC ks
*BLOG s
*BLOT s
*BLOW nsy
BLUB s
BLUE drs
ty
BLUR bst
*BOAR*dst
BOAS*t
*BOAT*s
BOBS*
BOCK s
a*BODE*ds
BODS
BODY*
*BOFF os
BOGS*
BOGY*
*BOHO s
a*BOIL s
BOLA rs
*BOLD s
o*BOLE s
BOLL s
BOLO s
BOLT s
BOMB es
BOND s
*BONE drs
y
BONG os
BONK s
e BONY
BOOB*sy
e BOOK*s
BOOM*sy
a BOON*s
BOOR*s
BOOS*t
*BOOT*hsy
BOPS
*BORA lsx
*BORE drs
BORK s
BORN e
a*BORT syz
BOSH*
BOSK*sy
BOSS*y
BOTA*s
BOTH*y
BOTS*
BOTT*s
a*BOUT s
*BOWL*s
BOWS*e
BOXY
BOYO*s
BOYS*
BOZO s
*BRAD*s
BRAE*s
*BRAG*s
*BRAN*dks
t
*BRAS*hs
*BRAT*s
*BRAW*lns
*BRAY*s
*BRED e
*BREE ds
BREN st
BREW s
BRIE frs
*BRIG s
*BRIM s
*BRIN egk
sy
BRIO s
a BRIS ks
BRIT hst
BROO*dkm
s
BROS*ey
*BROW*ns
BRRR*
*BRUT es
BRUX
BUBO*
BUBS*
BUBU*s
BUCK os
BUDS*
BUFF ios
y
BUGS*
BUHL s
BUHR s
BULB s
BULK sy
BULL asy
BUMF*s
*BUMP*hsy
BUMS*
BUNA*s
BUND*st
BUNG*s
BUNK*os
BUNN*sy
BUNS
BUNT*s
BUOY s
BURA*ns
*BURB*s
*BURD*s
BURG*hs
BURL*sy
*BURN*st
*BURP*s
BURR*osy
BURS*aet
BURY*
BUSH*y
BUSK*s
BUSS*
BUST*sy
BUSY*
*BUTE*os
a*BUTS*
BUTT*esy
BUYS*
a BUZZ
a*BYES*
BYRE s
BYRL s
BYTE s
s*CABS*
CACA os
CADE*st
CADI*s
s*CADS*
CAFE s
*CAFF s
*CAGE drs
y
CAGY
*CAID s
*CAIN s
CAKE dsy
CAKY
CALF s
CALK s
s*CALL as
CALM s
CALO s
CALX
CAME*los
CAMO*s
s*CAMP*ios
y
s CAMS*
*CANE*drs
s CANS*ot
s*CANT*osy
s*CAPE*drs
CAPH*s
*CAPO*ns
CAPS*
*CARB*os
CARD*s
s*CARE*drs
tx
*CARK*s
CARL*es
CARN*sy
s CARP*is
CARR*sy
s*CARS*e
s*CART*es
CASA s
CASE ds
*CASH
*CASK sy
CAST es
*CATE*rs
s CATS*
CAUL dks
*CAVE drs
CAVY
CAWS*
CAYS
CECA l
CEDE drs
CEDI s
CEES*
CEIL is
*CELL*aio
s
CELS
CELT*s
s CENT osu
CEPE*s
CEPS*
*CERE ds
CERO s
*CESS
CETE s
*CHAD s
CHAI nrs
*CHAM ps
*CHAO s
*CHAP est
CHAR dek
mrs
ty
*CHAT s
*CHAW s
*CHAY s
CHEF s
*CHEW sy
CHEZ
CHIA*os
*CHIC*ako
s
*CHID*e
*CHIN*aek
os
*CHIP*s
CHIS
*CHIT*s
*CHON
*CHOP s
*CHOW s
*CHUB s
*CHUG s
*CHUM ps
CIAO
CIGS*
CINE s
s*CION s
*CIRE s
CIST*s
CITE drs
CITY
y*CLAD es
*CLAG s
*CLAM ps
CLAN gks
*CLAP st
*CLAW s
*CLAY s
CLEF st
CLEW s
*CLIP st
CLOD s
*CLOG s
CLON eks
*CLOP s
*CLOT hs
CLOY s
CLUB s
CLUE ds
COAL asy
*COAT is
COAX
COBB*sy
COBS*
*COCA s
a COCK sy
COCO as
*CODA*s
*CODE*cdn
rsx
CODS
COED s
s*COFF s
*COFT
COGS*
*COHO gs
COIF s
*COIL s
COIN s
COIR s
*COKE ds
COKY
COLA*s
as*COLD*s
*COLE*ds
COLS*
COLT*s
COLY*
COMA els
COMB eos
COME rst
COMP ost
s*CONE*dsy
CONI*cn
CONK*sy
CONN*s
i*CONS*
CONY*
COOF*s
COOK*sy
COOL*sy
COON*s
s COOP*st
COOS*
s*COOT*s
s*COPE*dnr
s
s*COPS*e
COPY*
CORD*s
s*CORE*drs
CORF*
CORK*sy
CORM*s
as CORN*suy
*CORS*e
CORY*
COSH*
COSS*
COST*as
COSY*
COTE*ds
s COTS*
COUP es
COVE dnr
sty
s*COWL*s
s COWS*
COWY*
COXA*el
COYS*
COZY*
CRAB s
s*CRAG s
s*CRAM ps
s*CRAP es
*CRAW ls
a*CRED os
s CREW s
*CRIB s
CRIS p
CRIT s
*CROC iks
CROP s
*CROW dns
CRUD*es
e CRUS*eht
CRUX*
CUBE*bdr
s
CUBS*
s CUDS*
CUED*
CUES*
s CUFF s
CUIF s
*CUKE s
s CULL sy
CULM s
CULT is
s*CUPS*
*CURB*s
*CURD*sy
CURE*drs
t
s CURF*s
CURL*sy
*CURN*s
CURR*sy
CURS*et
CURT*

CUSK s
CUSP s
CUSS o
as*CUTE*rsy
s*CUTS*
CWMS*
CYAN os
CYMA ers
CYME s
CYST s
CZAR s
DABS
*DACE s
DADA*s
*DADO*s
DADS
*DAFF sy
*DAFT
DAGS
DAHL*s
o*DAHS*
*DAIS y
DAKS*
*DALE*s
DALS
DAME*s
DAMN*s
*DAMP*s
DAMS*
DANG*s
DANK*
DANS*
DAPS*
*DARB s
*DARE drs
*DARK s
DARN s
*DART s
*DASH iy
DATA
*DATE drs
DATO s
DAUB esy
DAUT s
DAVY
DAWK*s
*DAWN*s
DAWS*
DAWT*s
DAYS
DAZE ds
DEAD s
DEAF
i DEAL st
DEAN s
*DEAR sy
DEBS*
DEBT*s
DECK s
DECO rsy
DEED*sy
a DEEM*s
DEEP*s
DEER*s
DEES*
DEET*s
DEFI*s
DEFT
DEFY*
DEIL s
*DEKE ds
DELE*ds
*DELF*st
DELI*s
*DELL*sy
DELS
DELT*as
*DEME s
DEMO bns
DEMY
DENE*s
DENI*m
*DENS*e
DENT*s
DENY*
*DERE
DERM as
DESK s
DEVA*s
DEVS*
DEWS*
DEWY*
DEXY*
DEYS*
DHAK s
DHAL s

*DHOW s
DIAL s
DIBS*
*DICE drs
y
*DICK sy
DIDO*s
DIDY*
DIED*
DIEL*
DIES*
DIET*s
*DIFF*s
DIFS
DIGS*
DIKE drs
*DILL sy
DIME*rs
DIMS*
DINE*drs
DING*eos
y
*DINK*sy
DINO*s
DINS
DINT*s
DIOL s
DIPS*o
DIPT*
*DIRE r
*DIRK s
DIRL s
DIRT sy
DISC*ios
DISH*y
DISK*s
DISS*
DITA*s
DITE*s
ae*DITS*y
DITZ*y
DIVA ns
DIVE drs
*DJIN ns
*DOAT s
DOBY
DOCK*s
DOCS*
DODO s
DOER*s
*DOES*t
*DOFF s
DOGE*sy
DOGS*
DOGY*
DOIT s
DOJO s
*DOLE*ds
DOLL*sy
i DOLS*
DOLT*s
DOME*ds
DOMS
DONA*s
*DONE*e
DONG*as
u*DONS*y
DOOM sy
DOOR s
DOPA s
*DOPE drs
y
DOPY
a*DORE*
DORK*sy
DORM*sy
DORP*s
DORR*s
o*DORS*a
DORY*
*DOSE*drs
DOSS*
DOST*
DOTE*drs
DOTH*
DOTS*
DOTY*
DOUM as
o*DOUR a
DOUX
DOVE ns
a*DOWN*sy
DOWS*e
*DOXY
a DOZE dnr
s

DOZY
DRAB s
*DRAG s
*DRAM as
*DRAT s
*DRAW lns
*DRAY s
*DREE ds
*DREG s
DREK s
DREW
*DRIB s
*DRIP st
DROP st
*DRUB s
*DRUG s
*DRUM s
DRYS*
DUAD s
DUAL s
DUBS*
e DUCE s
DUCI
DUCK sy
e DUCT s
DUDE*ds
DUDS*
DUEL*s
DUES*
DUET*s
DUFF s
DUGS*
DUIT*s
*DUKE ds
DULL sy
DULY
DUMA s
DUMB os
*DUMP sy
DUNE*s
DUNG*sy
DUNK*s
DUNS
DUNT*s
DUOS*
DUPE*drs
DUPS
DURA ls
DURE ds
*DURN s
DURO cs
DURR as
DUSK sy
a DUST sy
DUTY
DYAD s
DYED*
DYER*s
DYES
DYKE ds
DYNE ls
blp EACH
rt
p EARL*sy
ly EARN*s
bdf*EARS*
ghl
npr
stwy
cfl EASE dls
pt
bfl EAST s
y
EASY
dhn EATH*
bfh EATS*
mnp
st
b EAUX*
dhl*EAVE ds
rw
EBBS*
EBON sy
ECHE ds
ECHO s
w ECHT
*ECRU s
ECUS*
EDDO
nt EDDY
hkl EDGE drs
sw
hls EDGY
w
EDHS*
*EDIT s

fhk*EELS*
prst
s EELY*
blp EERY
v
t EFFS*
hlw EFTS*
*EGAD s
lr*EGAL
l EGER s
ty EGGS*
l EGGY*
a EGIS
s*EGOS*
EIDE r
d EKED*
dp EKES*
ELAN ds
gmv ELDS*
w
ELHI
y ELKS*
bcd ELLS*
fhjm
stwy
h ELMS*
ELMY*
ELSE*
dfh EMES*
ms
EMEU*s
dh*EMIC
*EMIR s
dr EMIT s
gj EMMY s
EMUS
EMYD es
bfl ENDS*
mpr
stvw
ENGS*
ENOL s
*ENOW s
ENUF
ENVY
anp*EONS*
t*EPEE s
EPHA hs
s*EPIC s
pr EPOS
*ERAS*e
ERGO*t
b ERGS*
kt ERNE*s
fhk ERNS*
t
chz EROS e
ERRS*
v ERST*
by ESES
m ESNE s
*ESPY
bfg*ETAS*
z
fkl ETCH
rv
bhm ETHS*
t
*ETIC
ETNA s
*ETUI s
EURO s
s EVEN*st
fln EVER*ty
s
n EVES*
dk EVIL s
fhn EWER*s
s
EWES*
EXAM s
EXEC s
hsv EXED
dhk EXES
lrsv
EXIT s
EXON s
EXPO s
EYAS s
k EYED*
EYEN
f EYER*s
EYES
EYNE
EYRA s
EYRE s

EYRY
FABS
*FACE drs
t
*FACT s
FADE*drs
*FADO*s
FADS
FAGS
*FAIL s
*FAIN t
*FAIR sy
FAKE drs
y
*FALL s
FALX
FAME ds
*FANE*s
FANG*as
FANO*ns
FANS*
FARD*s
*FARE*drs
FARL*es
*FARM*s
FARO*s
FASH
FAST*s
*FATE*ds
FATS*
FAUN as
FAUX
*FAVA s
*FAVE s
*FAWN sy
FAYS
FAZE ds
FEAL
*FEAR s
*FEAT s
FECK s
FEDS
FEEB*s
FEED*s
*FEEL*s
FEES*
FEET*
FEHS*
*FELL asy
FELT s
*FEME*s
FEMS
*FEND*s
FENS
FEOD s
*FERE*s
*FERN*sy
*FESS*e
FEST*s
*FETA*ls
FETE*ds
FETS*
FEUD*s
FEUS*
FIAR s
FIAT s
FIBS*
*FICE s
FICO
FIDO*s
FIDS
FIEF*s
FIFE drs
FIGS*
FILA*r
FILE*drs
t
*FILL*eos
y
FILM*isy
FILO*s
FILS*
FIND*s
FINE*drs
*FINK*s
FINO*s
FINS
a*FIRE*drs
FIRM*s
FIRN*s
FIRS*t
FISC s
FISH y
FIST s
FITS
FIVE rs

FIXT*
FIZZ*y
*FLAB s
*FLAG s
FLAK ey
*FLAM esy
FLAN ks
*FLAP s
*FLAT s
*FLAW sy
*FLAX y
*FLAY s
*FLEA ms
*FLED
*FLEE rst
FLEW s
*FLEX
*FLEY s
FLIC ks
*FLIP s
FLIR st
*FLIT es
FLOC ks
FLOE s
*FLOG s
*FLOP s
*FLOW ns
FLUB*s
FLUE*ds
FLUS*h
FLUX
FOAL s
FOAM sy
FOBS*
FOCI
FOES
FOGS*
FOGY*
FOHN*s
*FOIL s
FOIN s
*FOLD s
FOLK sy
FOND*su
FONS
FONT*s
FOOD s
FOOL s
a*FOOT sy
FOPS
*FORA*my
*FORB*sy
FORD*os
a*FORE*s
FORK*sy
FORM*es
*FORT*ehs
y
FOSS ae
a FOUL*s
*FOUR*s
*FOWL s
FOXY
FOYS*
FOZY
FRAE
*FRAG s
*FRAP s
*FRAT s
*FRAY s
*FREE drs
*FRET s
*FRIG s
a FRIT hst
z
FRIZ z
*FROE*s
FROG*s
FROM
*FROW*ns
*FRUG s
FUBS*y
FUCI
FUDS*
FUEL s
FUGS*
FUGU*es
FUJI s
FULL sy
FUME drs
t
FUMY
FUND*is
FUNK*sy
FUNS
FURL*s

FURS*
FURY*
*FUSE del
s
FUSS y
FUTZ
FUZE des
FUZZ y
FYCE s
FYKE s
GABS
GABY
GADI*ds
e*GADS*
GAED*
GAEN*
GAES*
*GAFF es
GAGA
*GAGE*drs
GAGS
a*GAIN s
*GAIT s
*GALA*hsx
*GALE*as
*GALL*sy
GALS
a*GAMA*sy
GAMB*aes
GAME*drs
y
*GAMP*s
o GAMS*
GAMY*
*GANE*fv
GANG*s
GAOL s
a*GAPE*drs
GAPS*
GAPY*
*GARB*s
a*GARS*
GASH
*GASP*s
GAST*s
a*GATE*drs
GATS*
GAUD sy
GAUM s
GAUN t
GAUR s
a*GAVE l
GAWK sy
GAWP s
GAYS
a GAZE drs
*GEAR s
GECK os
GEDS
GEED*
*GEEK*sy
o GEES*et
GEEZ*
*GELD*s
GELS
GELT*s
GEMS
a GENE*st
GENS
a GENT*s
GENU*as
GERM sy
e GEST es
*GETA*s
GETS*
GEUM s
*GHAT s
GHEE s
GHIS
GIBE*drs
GIBS*
GIDS
GIED*
GIEN*
GIES*
GIFT s
GIGA*s
GIGS*
GILD s
*GILL sy
GILT s
*GIMP sy
*GINK*s
GINS
GIPS*y
GIRD s

GIRL sy
GIRN s
GIRO ns
GIRT hs
a GIST s
GITE*s
GITS
o GIVE nrs
*GLAD esy
*GLAM s
o*GLED es
a*GLEE dks
t
*GLEG
GLEN s
a*GLEY s
GLIA ls
*GLIB
GLIM es
*GLOB es
GLOM s
*GLOP s
a*GLOW s
GLUE drs
y
*GLUG s
*GLUM es
GLUT es
GNAR lrs
GNAT s
*GNAW ns
GNUS
GOAD*s
GOAL*s
GOAS*
*GOAT*s
GOBO*s
GOBS*
GOBY*
GODS
GOER s
*GOES
GOGO s
*GOLD s
GOLF s
a*GONE fr
GONG s
GOOD*sy
GOOF*sy
GOOK*sy
GOON*sy
GOOP*sy
GOOS*ey
*GORE*ds
GORM*s
GORP*s
GORY*
GOSH*
GOTH*s
*GOUT sy
GOWD s
GOWK s
*GOWN s
GRAB s
*GRAD es
*GRAM aps
*GRAN ads
t
*GRAT e
*GRAY s
a*GREE dkn
st
GREW
GREY s
*GRID es
*GRIG s
*GRIM ey
*GRIN ds
*GRIP est
y
GRIT hs
GROG s
GROK s
*GROT s
*GROW lns
*GRUB s
*GRUE ls
*GRUM ep
GUAN os
GUAR ds
GUCK s
GUDE s
GUFF s
GUID es
GULF*sy
GULL*sy

GULP*sy
GULS*
GUMS*
GUNK*sy
GUNS
GURU s
GUSH y
GUST osy
*GUTS*y
GUVS*
GUYS*
GYBE ds
GYMS*
GYPS*y
GYRE ds
GYRI
GYRO ns
GYVE ds
HAAF s
HAAR s
HABU s
stw HACK s
s HADE*ds
HADJ*i
HAED*
HAEM*s
HAEN*
HAES*
HAET*s
s*HAFT s
s*HAGS*
*HAHA*s
s*HAHS*
HAIK asu
*HAIL s
c*HAIR sy
HAJI*s
HAJJ*i
s HAKE s
HAKU s
sw*HALE drs
HALF
s*HALL os
HALM as
HALO ns
s*HALT s
s HAME*s
csw HAMS*
*HAND sy
bcw HANG s
st HANK sy
c*HANT s
cw HAPS*
cs HARD sy
cs*HARE dms
cs*HARK s
HARL s
ct*HARM s
s HARP sy
c*HART s
HASH
*HASP*s
g HAST*ey
*HATE*drs
HATH*
cgk HATS*
w
s HAUL ms
g HAUT e
s*HAVE nrs
HAWK*s
cst HAWS*e
cs*HAYS*
HAZE dlr
s
HAZY
a HEAD sy
sw HEAL s
c HEAP sy
s*HEAR dst
cw*HEAT hs
c HECK s
HEED s
w*HEEL s
t*HEFT sy
HEHS*
HEIL s
t HEIR s
*HELD
s*HELL os
w*HELM s
HELO st
w HELP s
rt*HEME*s
HEMP*sy
HEMS

tw*HENS*
s HENT*s
HERB*sy
s HERD*s
tw*HERE*s
HERL*s
t HERM*as
*HERN*s
HERO*ns
HERS
c HEST*s
ck*HETH*s
kw HETS*
s HEWN*
cst HEWS*
w
ct*HICK*s
c HIDE*drs
s HIED*
s HIES*
t HIGH st
HIKE drs
HILA r
c HILI
cst*HILL osy
HILT s
sw HIMS*
HIND*s
cst*HINS*
w
HINT*s
csw HIPS*
s*HIRE der
s
HISN*
HISS*y
sw HIST*s
cw*HITS*
cs HIVE ds
*HOAR dsy
HOAX
HOBO*s
HOBS*
cs HOCK s
HODS
s HOED*
s HOER*s
s*HOES*
HOGG*s
s HOGS*
c*HOKE dsy
a*HOLD s
dtw*HOLE dsy
HOLK s
HOLM s
HOLP
HOLS
HOLT s
HOLY
HOME drs
y
HOMO s
HOMY
ps*HONE*drs
y
t HONG*is
HONK*s
p*HONS*
HOOD sy
w HOOF s
cs HOOK asy
w HOOP s
bs*HOOT sy
*HOPE*drs
csw*HOPS*
*HORA hls
st HORN sy
ctw*HOSE dln
rsy
g HOST as
ps HOTS*
*HOUR is
s HOVE lr
*HOWE*s
HOWF*fs
HOWK*s
*HOWL*s
cds HOWS*
HOYA*s
HOYS*
c HUBS*
cs HUCK s
HUED*
HUES*
c HUFF sy
HUGE*r

ct HUGS*
HUIC
HULA s
HULK sy
a HULL os
ctw*HUMP*hsy
c HUMS*
HUNG*
HUNH*
ct HUNK*sy
s*HUNS*
s HUNT*s
ct HURL sy
HURT s
s HUSH
HUSK sy
bps*HUTS*
*HWAN
p HYLA s
HYMN s
HYPE*drs
HYPO*s
HYPS*
HYTE
IAMB is
IBEX
*IBIS
drv ICED*
bdf ICES*
rsv
ICHS*
dkp ICKY*
*ICON s
IDEA ls
IDEM
abh IDES
nrs
tw
s IDLE drs
IDLY
*IDOL s
IDYL ls
bjm IFFY*
m IGGS*
IGLU s
*IKAT s
e IKON s
p*ILEA cl
s*ILEX
cm ILIA cdl
ILKA*
bms ILKS*
bdf ILLS*
ghjk
mnpr
stvw
yz
bdf ILLY*
ghsw
IMAM s
t*IMID eos
j IMMY
IMPI*s
glp IMPS*
sw
INBY e
cfp INCH
w
INFO s
INIA
dfg INKS*
jkl
mop
rsw
dhk INKY*
lpz
INLY
jl INNS*
INRO
INTI s
p INTO
clp*IONS*
b IOTA s
afh*IRED*
mstw
cfh*IRES*
mst
vw
v*IRID s
IRIS
bdk IRKS*
m
g IRON esy
ISBA s
al ISLE dst
ISMS*

abd ITCH y
fhpw
ITEM s
k*IWIS
IXIA s
s IZAR s
JABS
JACK sy
JADE ds
JAGG*sy
JAGS
*JAIL s
JAKE s
JAMB*es
JAMS*
*JANE s
*JAPE drs
JARL*s
JARS
JATO s
*JAUK s
JAUP s
*JAVA s
JAWS*
JAYS
JAZZ y
JEAN s
JEED*
JEEP*s
JEER*s
JEES*
JEEZ*
JEFE s
JEHU s
*JELL osy
*JEON
JERK sy
*JESS e
JEST s
JETE*s
JETS*
JEUX*
JIAO
JIBB*s
JIBE*drs
JIBS*
*JIFF sy
JIGS*
*JILL s
JILT s
*JIMP y
*JINK*s
d*JINN*is
d*JINS*
JINX*
JIVE drs
y
*JIVY
JOBS*
JOCK os
JOES
JOEY*s
JOGS*
JOHN s
JOIN st
*JOKE drs
y
JOKY
*JOLE s
JOLT sy
JOSH
JOSS
JOTA*s
JOTS*
JOUK s
*JOWL*sy
JOWS*
JOYS*
JUBA s
JUBE s
JUCO s
*JUDO s
a JUGA*l
JUGS*
JUJU s
*JUKE ds
JUKU s
*JUMP sy
JUNK*sy
JUPE s
JURA lt
JURY
JUST*s
*JUTE*s
JUTS
*KAAS

KABS
KADI s
KAES*
KAFS*
KAGU s
KAIF s
*KAIL s
*KAIN s
KAKA s
KAKI s
*KALE s
KAME s
*KAMI k
*KANA s
*KANE s
KAON s
KAPA s
KAPH s
KARN s
*KART s
KATA*s
is KATS*
*KAVA s
KAYO*s
o*KAYS*
*KBAR s
KEAS*
KECK s
KEEF s
*KEEK s
*KEEL s
s KEEN s
KEEP s
s KEET s
KEFS
s KEGS*
KEIR s
s KELP sy
KELT s
KEMP st
KENO*s
KENS
KENT*e
KEPI*s
s KEPS*
KEPT*
KERB s
KERF s
*KERN es
KETO l
KEYS*
KHAF s
KHAN s
*KHAT s
*KHET hs
KHIS
KIBE is
*KICK sy
s*KIDS*
KIEF s
s KIER s
KIFS
s*KILL s
KILN s
KILO s
KILT sy
KINA*s
KIND*s
KINE*s
e KING*s
s*KINK*sy
KINO*s
s*KINS*
s KIPS*
*KIRK*s
KIRN*s
KIRS*
KISS*y
KIST*s
s KITE*drs
KITH*es
s*KITS*
KIVA s
KIWI s
KLIK s
*KNAP s
KNAR s
*KNEE dls
*KNEW
*KNIT s
*KNOB s
KNOP s
*KNOT s
*KNOW ns
KNUR ls
KOAN*s

KOAS*
KOBO*s
KOBS*
KOEL s
KOHL s
KOIS*
KOJI s
KOLA s
KOLO s
KONK s
KOOK sy
KOPH*s
KOPS
*KORA*ist
KORE
KORS
KOSS*
KOTO sw
KRIS
*KUDO s
KUDU s
KUES*
KUFI s
KUNA
KUNE
KURU s
*KVAS s
*KYAK s
*KYAR s
KYAT s
KYES
KYTE s
bfs*LABS*
gp*LACE*drs
y
abc LACK*s
fps
LACS*
LACY*
bcg LADE*dnr
s
cg*LADS*
g LADY*
cfs*LAGS*
LAIC hs
p*LAID
bep*LAIN
s
fg*LAIR ds
fs LAKE drs
LAKH s
f LAKY
*LALL s
lu*LAMA*s
LAMB*sy
bf LAME*drs
c*LAMP*s
bcf LAMS*
gs
abe*LAND s
g
ap*LANE s
acs LANG
bcf LANK y
ps
cfs LAPS*e
LARD*sy
LARI*s
*LARK*sy
LARS
b LASE*drs
cfp*LASH*
s
cg*LASS*io
bc LAST*s
abe*LATE*dnr
ps x
LATH*eis
y
LATI*
bfp LATS*
s
LATU*
LAUD s
*LAVA*s
cs*LAVE*drs
LAVS*
b*LAWN*sy
bcf LAWS*
s
cfp*LAYS*
s
bg LAZE ds
g LAZY
p LEAD*sy
LEAF*sy

b LEAK*sy
i LEAL*
cg LEAN*st
LEAP*st
bc*LEAR*nsy
fp LEAS*eht
LECH
cgs*LEEK*s
f LEER*sy
fg LEES*
fgs LEET*s
c*LEFT sy
LEGS*
LEHR s
LEIS*
LEKE
LEKS*
LEKU*
b*LEND s
LENO s
g*LENS e
b LENT o
cs LEPT a
b*LESS
b LEST
b LETS*
LEUD*s
LEVA*
LEVO*
LEVY*
LEWD
fg LEYS*
LIAR ds
LIBS*
s*LICE
*LICH it
cfk*LICK s
s
LIDO*s
LIDS
fp LIED*
LIEF*
a LIEN*s
fps LIER*s
fp LIES*
LIEU*s
LIFE r
c LIFT s
a LIKE dnr
s
LILO s
LILT s
s LILY
LIMA ns
c LIMB aio
sy
cgs LIME dns
y
LIMN s
LIMO s
b*LIMP as
bs LIMY
ac LINE*dnr
sy
cfs LING*aos
y
bcp*LINK*sy
s
*LINN*s
LINO*s
LINS
efg LINT*sy
LINY*
*LION s
LIPA*
s LIPE*
bcf LIPS*
s
LIRA s
*LIRE
LIRI
LISP*s
a LIST*s
bef LITE*r
fs*LITS*
LITU*
ao LIVE dnr
s
LOAD s
*LOAF s
g LOAM sy
LOAN s
g*LOBE*ds
LOBO*s
bgs LOBS*
*LOCA l

LOCH s
LOCI
bcf LOCK s
LOCO s
*LODE ns
a*LOFT sy
LOGE*s
LOGO*ins
bcf LOGS*
s
o LOGY*
s LOID s
ae LOIN s
LOLL sy
ac*LONE r
afk LONG es
ak LOOF*as
LOOK*s
bg LOOM*s
LOON*sy
bs LOOP*sy
LOOS*e
c*LOOT*s
es*LOPE*drs
cfg*LOPS*
ps
LORD s
*LORE s
LORN
g LORY
c*LOSE lrs
fg LOSS y
g LOST
f LOTA*hs
cs LOTH*
LOTI*c
bcp LOTS*
s
ac*LOUD
LOUP es
cf*LOUR sy
cfg*LOUT s
cg LOVE drs
*LOWE*drs
bcf*LOWN*
bfg LOWS*e
ps
LUAU s
LUBE ds
LUCE s
cp LUCK sy
e LUDE s
bcf LUES
gs
bfs LUFF as
k LUGE*drs
gps LUGS*
LULL s
*LULU s
LUMA*s
cfp*LUMP*sy
s
agp LUMS*
s
LUNA rs
LUNE st
cfs LUNG eis
cfp LUNK s
s
b LUNT s
LUNY
LURE drs
x
LURK s
bfp LUSH
s
LUST sy
efg*LUTE ads
k LUTZ
LUVS*
LUXE*s
LWEI s
LYCH
LYES
LYNX
LYRE s
LYSE ds
MAAR s
MABE s
*MACE*drs
MACH*eos
s MACK*s
MACS*
MADE*
MADS
MAES*

i*MAGE*s
MAGI*c
MAGS
*MAID s
e*MAIL els
*MAIM s
a*MAIN s
*MAIR s
MAKE rs
MAKO s
*MALE s
s*MALL s
MALM sy
s*MALT sy
*MAMA s
*MANA*st
*MANE*ds
MANO*rs
MANS*e
MANY
MAPS*
MARA*s
*MARC*hs
*MARE*s
*MARK*as
MARL*sy
*MARS*eh
s*MART*s
o MASA*s
s*MASH*y
*MASK*s
a*MASS*aey
MAST*s
*MATE*drs
y
MATH*s
MATS*
*MATT*es
MAUD s
MAUL s
MAUN d
MAUT s
MAWN
MAWS*
MAXI*ms
MAYA*ns
MAYO*rs
*MAYS*t
as MAZE drs
MAZY
MEAD s
MEAL sy
MEAN sty
*MEAT sy
MEDS
MEED s
s*MEEK
MEET s
o MEGA*
MEGS*
*MELD*s
s*MELL*s
MELS
s MELT*sy
*MEME*s
MEMO*s
MEMS
ae*MEND*s
MENO*
MENU*s
MEOU s
MEOW s
MERC hsy
*MERE rs
s MERK s
MERL es
MESA s
MESH y
*MESS y
*META*l
METE*drs
*METH*s
MEWL*s
s MEWS*
MEZE s
MHOS*
MIBS*
MICA*s
a*MICE*
MICS*
MIDI*s
ai*MIDS*t
MIEN s
*MIFF sy
*MIGG*s
MIGS*
MIKE ds
MILD*s
s MILE*rs
*MILK*sy
*MILL*es
MILO*s
MILS*
MILT*sy
MIME*dor
s
MINA es
MIND s
ai MINE drs
MINI ms
*MINK es
MINT sy
MINX
MIPS
*MIRE*dsx
MIRI*n
s*MIRK*sy
ae MIRS*
MIRY*
MISE*rs
MISO*s
a MISS*y
MIST*sy
s MITE rs
MITT s
a MITY
MIXT*
MOAN*s
MOAS*
*MOAT*s
MOBS*
s MOCK*s
MOCS*
*MODE*lms
MODI*
MODS
s MOGS*
*MOIL s
MOJO s
s*MOKE s
MOLA*lrs
*MOLD*sy
a*MOLE*s
MOLL*sy
MOLS*
s MOLT*os
MOLY*
MOME*s
MOMI*
MOMS
MONK*s
*MONO*s
MONS
MONY*
MOOD*sy
MOOL*as
MOON*sy
MOOR*sy
MOOS*e
*MOOT*s
*MOPE*drs
y
MOPS
MOPY*
*MORA*els
y
*MORE*ls
MORN*s
*MORS*e
a*MORT*s
MOSH*
MOSK*s
MOSS*oy
MOST*es
es MOTE*lst
y
MOTH*sy
MOTS*
MOTT*eos
MOUE s
MOVE drs
MOWN
MOWS*
MOXA s
MOZO s
MUCH o
a MUCK sy
MUDS*
MUFF s
MUGG*sy
MUGS*
MULE dsy
MULL as
*MUMM*sy
*MUMP*s
MUMS*
MUMU*s
MUNI*s
MUNS
MUON s
MURA ls
MURE dsx
MURK sy
MURR aes
y
a*MUSE*drs
s MUSH*y
MUSK*sy
MUSS*y
MUST*hsy
*MUTE*drs
s*MUTS*
MUTT*s
MYCS*
MYNA hs
MYTH sy
NAAN s
NABE*s
NABS
NADA s
*NAFF s
s*NAGS*
NAIF s
s*NAIL s
*NALA s
NAME*drs
j*NANA*s
NANS*
NAOI
NAOS
NAPA*s
*NAPE*s
ks NAPS*
*NARC os
NARD s
s*NARK sy
u NARY
k*NAVE ls
NAVY
NAYS
NAZI s
s NEAP s
a*NEAR s
*NEAT hs
NEBS*
s NECK s
k NEED*sy
NEEM*s
NEEP*s
NEGS*
NEIF s
e NEMA s
NENE s
*NEON s
NERD sy
*NESS
NEST s
NETS*
NETT*sy
NEUK s
NEUM es
*NEVE rs
NEVI
NEWS*y
NEWT*s
NEXT
s NIBS*
*NICE r
s*NICK s
s NIDE ds
NIDI
NIGH st
*NILL*s
a NILS*
NIMS*
NINE s
NIPA*s
s NIPS*
NISI
u NITE*rs
ksu*NITS*
NIXE*ds
NIXY*
ks NOBS*
k NOCK s
a*NODE*s
NODI*
NODS
NOEL s
*NOES
NOGG*s
s NOGS*
*NOIL sy
NOIR s
NOLO s
NOMA*ds
g NOME*ns
NOMS
NONA s
*NONE st
s NOOK*s
NOON*s
*NOPE
NORI*as
e NORM*s
*NOSE*dsy
NOSH*
NOSY*
NOTA*l
NOTE*drs
NOUN s
NOUS
*NOVA es
eks NOWS*
NOWT*s
s NUBS*
NUDE rs
*NUKE ds
NULL s
NUMB s
NUNS
*NURD s
k NURL s
*NUTS*y
l OAFS*
s OAKS*
OAKY*
bhr*OARS*
s
bcr OAST s
t
l OATH*s
bcd OATS*
gm
s*OBAS*
lr*OBES*e
*OBEY*s
c OBIA*s
OBIS
*OBIT*s
OBOE s
OBOL eis
cs OCAS*
*ODAH*s
cs ODAS*
ODDS*
ODEA*
bcl ODES*
mnr
is ODIC
*ODOR s
ODYL es
bcd OFFS*
t
*OGAM s
y*OGEE s
b OGLE drs
OGRE s
o OHED
OHIA s
OHMS*
bcf OILS*
mnr
st
dnr OILY*
*OINK s
OKAS
t*OKAY*s
OKEH*s
chj OKES*
mps
ty
OKRA s
bcf OLDS*
ghmw
m OLDY*
OLEA
OLEO*s
bcd OLES*
hjmp
rstv
fp OLIO s
h OLLA s
nw*OMEN s
cgh OMER s
v
v OMIT s
np ONCE t
bch ONES*
jnp
stz
s ONLY
m*ONOS*
c ONTO
bct*ONUS
ONYX
p*OOHS*
cgh*OOPS
lpw
bcf OOTS*
hlm
rst
b OOZE ds
bdw OOZY
*OPAH s
cn*OPAL s
cdh*OPED*
lmrt
c*OPEN*s
cdh*OPES*
lmp
rt
OPTS*
*OPUS
ORAD
bcg ORAL*s
hlm
fs ORBS*
cf ORBY*
ORCA*s
t ORCS*
f ORDO s
bcf*ORES*
glm
psty
p ORGY
ORLE s
ORRA
bfm ORTS*
pstw
ORYX
ORZO s
OSAR
cdh OSES*
lnpr
f OSSA
l*OTIC
lmp OTTO s
cmp OUCH
tv
OUDS*
OUPH es
fhl OURS*
psty
jr OUST s
bgl*OUTS*
prt
OUZO s
OVAL*s
cdr OVEN s
w
chl OVER st
mr
*OVUM
bcd*OWED*
jlm
rst
vwy
hly OWES*
bcf OWLS*
hjy
dgt OWNS*
bdl OWSE n
OXEN
bcf OXES
glp
OXID es
OXIM es
cft OYER s
*OYES
OYEZ
PACA*s
as*PACE*drs
y
PACK*s
PACS*
e*PACT*s
s PACY*
PADI*s
PADS
*PAGE drs
*PAID
PAIK s
s*PAIL s
*PAIN st
*PAIR s
s*PALE*adr
st
s*PALL*sy
PALM*sy
*PALP*is
o*PALS*y
PALY*
s PAMS*
*PANE*dls
s PANG*as
s PANS*y
*PANT*osy
PAPA*lsw
PAPS*
PARA*es
PARD*isy
s*PARE*dor
su
s*PARK*as
PARR*sy
s*PARS*e
a*PART*sy
PASE*os
*PASH*a
*PASS*e
PAST*aes
y
s*PATE*dnr
s
PATH*s
s PATS*y
PATY*
*PAVE drs
*PAWL*s
s*PAWN*s
PAWS*
s*PAYS*
PEAG*es
as PEAK*sy
PEAL*s
s PEAN*s
s*PEAR*lst
PEAS*e
*PEAT*sy
PECH*s
s PECK*sy
s PECS*
PEDS
a*PEEK*s
s*PEEL*s
PEEN*s
PEEP*s
s PEER*sy
e PEES*
PEGS*
PEHS*
PEIN s
*PEKE s
PELE s
*PELF s
s PELT s
su*PEND*s
o*PENS*
s PENT*
*PEON sy
PEPO*s
PEPS*
*PERE*as
PERI*ls
PERK*sy
s PERM*s
PERP*s
PERT*
PERV*s
PESO*s
PEST*osy
PETS*
s PEWS*
PFFT
PFUI
*PHAT
*PHEW
a*PHIS*
PHIZ*
*PHON eos
y
*PHOT os
*PHUT s
PIAL*
a PIAN*os
PIAS*
s PICA*ls
s*PICE*
*PICK*sy
e PICS*
s PIED*
s PIER*s
s PIES*
PIGS*
PIKA s
s PIKE drs
PIKI s
s PILE adi
s
PILI s
s*PILL s
PILY
PIMA s
*PIMP s
PINA*s
os PINE*dsy
ao PING*os
*PINK*osy
s*PINS*
PINT*aos
s PINY*
*PION s
PIPE*drs
t
PIPS*
PIPY*
PIRN s
a PISH*
PISO*s
PITA*s
PITH*sy
s*PITS*
PITY*
PIXY*
PLAN eks
t
s*PLAT esy
s*PLAY as
*PLEA dst
PLEB es
*PLED
PLEW s
*PLEX
*PLIE drs
PLOD s
*PLOP s
*PLOT sz
*PLOW s
PLOY s
*PLUG s
*PLUM bep
sy
PLUS h
POCK sy
POCO
a*PODS*
POEM s
POET s
POGY
POIS*e
s*POKE drs
y
POKY
*POLE*drs
POLL*s
POLO*s
POLS*
POLY*ps
POME s
POMO s
POMP s
POND s
*PONE s
PONG s
*PONS
PONY
POOD s
s POOF
*POOH s
s POOL s
s POON s
POOP s
s POOR i
*POPE*s
*POPS*y
s*PORE ds
PORK sy
PORN osy
as*PORT s
*POSE drs
POSH
POST s
POSY
s POTS*y
POUF fs
*POUR s
s*POUT sy
POWS*
e*POXY*
*PRAM s
PRAO s
s*PRAT es
PRAU s
s*PRAY s
s*PREE dns
*PREP s
*PREX y
PREY s
PREZ
s*PRIG s
*PRIM aei
ops
PROA*s
*PROD*s
PROF*s
PROG*s
*PROM*os
PROP*s
PROS*eos
ty
*PROW*ls
a*PSIS*
PSST
*PTUI
PUBS*
PUCE s
PUCK as
s PUDS*
PUFF sy
PUGH
PUGS*
PUJA hs
*PUKE ds
PULA*
PULE*drs
PULI*ks
PULL*s
PULP*sy
PULS*e
PUMA s
*PUMP s
PUNA*s
PUNG*s
s PUNK*asy
PUNS
PUNT*osy
PUNY*
PUPA*els
PUPS
PUPU*s
PURE*er
PURI*ns
PURL*s
PURR*s
s PURS*ey
PUSH*y
PUSS*y
PUTS
PUTT*ios
y
PUTZ*
PYAS*
PYES
PYIC
*PYIN s
PYRE sx
PYRO s
QADI s
*QAID s
QATS*
QOPH s
s QUAD*s
QUAG*s
QUAI*ls
QUAY*s
QUEY s
es QUID s
QUIN st
e QUIP su
QUIT es
QUIZ
QUOD s
bgt*RACE drs
ctw RACK s
RACY
bg*RADS*
d*RAFF s

cdg*RAFT s
k
*RAGA*s
*RAGE*des
RAGG*sy
t RAGI*s
bcd*RAGS*
f
RAIA*s
b*RAID*s
bdf*RAIL*s
gt
bdg*RAIN*sy
t
*RAIS*e
RAJA*hs
bcd RAKE der
s
RAKI s
RAKU s
*RALE s
*RAMI*e
cgt*RAMP*s
cdg RAMS*
pt
bg*RAND*sy
opw RANG*ey
*RANI*ds
bcd RANK*s
fpt
bg*RANT*s
cdg*RAPE*drs
cft RAPS*
w
tw*RAPT*
u*RARE drs
epu RASE*drs
bct*RASH*
g*RASP*sy
cgi*RATE*dlr
opu s
w RATH*e
RATO*s
bdf RATS*
p
bcd*RAVE dln
gt rs
bcd RAWS*
RAYA*hs
bdf*RAYS*
gpt
bcg RAZE der
s
RAZZ
bdo READ dsy
t
au REAL ms
bcd REAM s
REAP s
d*REAR ms
REBS*
dw RECK*s
RECS*
REDD*s
b REDE*ds
cu REDO*nsx
c*REDS*
bcd REED*sy
fgpt
REEF*sy
cg*REEK*sy
c*REEL*s
bdf REES*t
gpt
REFS
REFT
d REGS*
REIF*sy
REIN*ks
REIS*
RELY
REMS
t*REND s
b RENT es
REPO*st
REPP*s
p REPS*
f RESH*
cdp REST*s
w
a RETE*m
ft RETS*
REVS*
RHEA s
RHOS*
RHUS

tu RIAL*s
a RIAS*
cd RIBS*
pt*RICE drs
*RICH
bcp*RICK s
tw
bgp RIDE*rs
gi*RIDS*
ao RIEL s
RIFE*r
g*RIFF*s
RIFS
dg RIFT*s
bfg RIGS*
pt
RILE dsy
bdf*RILL es
gkpt
cgp RIME*drs
bpt RIMS*
g RIMY*
g RIND*sy
biw RING*s
bdp*RINK*s
bg*RINS*e
g RIOT s
cgt RIPE*dnr
s
dgt RIPS*
afp RISE nrs
bf RISK sy
tw RITE s
f RITZ y
d RIVE dnr
st
b ROAD s
ROAM s
g ROAN s
*ROAR s
p*ROBE*ds
ROBS*
bcf ROCK*sy
t
c ROCS*
et*RODE*os
p*RODS*
f*ROES*
b*ROIL sy
p*ROLE s
ROLF s
dt ROLL s
t ROMP*s
p*ROMS*
b ROOD s
p ROOF s
bc ROOK sy
bgv ROOM sy
*ROOT sy
gt*ROPE drs
y
ROPY
abe*ROSE dst
p
bp ROSY
ROTA*s
w ROTE*s
ROTI*s
ROTL*s
ROTO*rs
gt ROTS*
ROUE ns
cg ROUP sy
gt*ROUT ehs
ROUX
dgp ROVE dnr
t s
bcf ROWS*
gptv
RUBE*ls
dg RUBS*
RUBY*
ct RUCK s
RUDD sy
cp RUDE r
t RUED*
t RUER*s
gt RUES*
g RUFF es
RUGA*el
dft RUGS*
b RUIN gs
RULE drs
t RULY
cfg*RUMP*s
t

ad RUMS*
p RUNE*s
bw RUNG*s
RUNS
bg RUNT*sy
cd*RUSE s
bc RUSH y
b RUSK s
ct RUST sy
t RUTH*s
b*RUTS*
RYAS*
RYES
RYKE ds
RYND s
RYOT s
SABE*drs
SABS
SACK*s
SACS*
t SADE*s
t SADI*s
SAFE rs
*SAGA*s
u*SAGE*rs
*SAGO*s
SAGS
SAGY*
*SAID s
*SAIL s
*SAIN st
SAKE rs
SAKI s
*SALE*ps
*SALL*y
*SALP*as
*SALS*a
*SALT*sy
SAME k
*SAMP s
*SAND sy
*SANE drs
SANG ah
SANK
SANS
SAPS*
SARD s
SARI ns
*SARK sy
*SASH
*SASS y
*SATE*dms
SATI*ns
SAUL*st
*SAVE drs
SAWN
SAWS*
*SAYS*t
*SCAB s
*SCAD s
SCAG s
*SCAM ps
*SCAN st
e*SCAR efp
sty
*SCAT st
*SCOP es
ae*SCOT s
*SCOW ls
*SCRY
*SCUD ios
*SCUM s
*SCUP s
*SCUT aes
SEAL*s
SEAM*sy
*SEAR*s
SEAS*
*SEAT*s
SECS*
SECT*s
SEED*sy
*SEEK*s
*SEEL*sy
SEEM*s
SEEN*
SEEP*sy
SEER*s
SEES*
*SEGO*s
SEGS*
SEIF*s
SEIS*em
*SELF*s
*SELL*es
SELS

*SEME ns
SEMI s
*SEND*s
SENE*
SENT*ei
SEPT as
*SERA*cil
*SERE*drs
SERF*s
u*SERS*
*SETA*el
SETS*
SETT*s
SEWN*
SEWS*
SEXT*os
SEXY*
*SHAD*esy
*SHAG*s
*SHAH*s
*SHAM*es
p*SHAW*lmn
s
*SHAY*s
SHEA*flr
s
a SHED*s
a*SHES*
*SHEW*ns
*SHIM s
*SHIN esy
*SHIP s
SHIV aes
SHMO
*SHOD
*SHOE drs
*SHOG is
SHOO kln
st
*SHOP s
*SHOT est
*SHOW nsy
SHRI s
SHUL ns
*SHUN st
*SHUT es
SHWA s
SIAL s
SIBB*s
SIBS*
*SICE*s
*SICK*os
SICS*
a SIDE ds
SIDH e
SIFT s
SIGH st
SIGN as
SIKA s
SIKE rs
SILD s
*SILK sy
*SILL sy
SILO s
SILT sy
SIMA*rs
*SIMP*s
SIMS*
SINE*sw
u SING*es
SINH*s
*SINK*s
SINS
SIPE*ds
SIPS*
*SIRE*den
s
SIRS*
SITE*ds
SITH*
SITS
SIZE drs
SIZY
SKAG*s
SKAS
*SKAT*es
SKEE dns
t
*SKEG s
*SKEP s
a SKEW s
*SKID*s
SKIM*ps
*SKIN*kst
*SKIP*s
SKIS

*SKIT*es
SKUA s
*SLAB s
*SLAG s
*SLAM s
*SLAP s
*SLAT esy
*SLAW s
*SLAY s
i*SLED s
SLEW s
*SLID e
SLIM esy
*SLIP est
*SLIT s
*SLOB s
SLOE s
*SLOG s
*SLOP es
*SLOT hs
*SLOW s
SLUB s
SLUE ds
*SLUG s
*SLUM ps
SLUR bps
SLUT s
*SMEW s
SMIT eh
*SMOG s
*SMUG
*SMUT s
*SNAG s
*SNAP s
*SNAW s
SNED s
*SNIB s
*SNIP es
*SNIT s
*SNOB s
*SNOG s
*SNOT s
*SNOW sy
*SNUB s
SNUG s
SNYE s
*SOAK s
SOAP sy
*SOAR s
*SOBA*s
SOBS*
*SOCA s
SOCK os
*SODA*s
SODS
SOFA rs
*SOFT asy
*SOIL s
SOJA s
*SOKE s
SOLA*nr
*SOLD*io
*SOLE*dis
SOLI*d
SOLO*ns
SOLS*
SOMA*ns
SOME*
SOMS
*SONE*s
SONG*s
*SONS*y
SOOK s
SOON
*SOOT hsy
SOPH*sy
SOPS
*SORA s
*SORB s
SORD s
*SORE dlr
s
SORI
SORN s
*SORT as
SOTH*s
SOTS*
SOUK*s
SOUL*s
SOUP*sy
*SOUR*s
SOUS*e
SOWN
SOWS*
SOYA*s
SOYS*

SPAE*ds
*SPAM*s
*SPAN*gks
*SPAR*eks
*SPAS*m
*SPAT*es
*SPAY*s
*SPEC ks
*SPED
*SPEW s
*SPIN esy
*SPIT esz
SPIV s
*SPOT s
*SPRY
*SPUD s
SPUE ds
*SPUN k
*SPUR nst
SRIS*
*STAB s
*STAG esy
*STAR eks
t
*STAT es
*STAW
STAY s
STEM s
STEP s
*STET s
*STEW sy
STEY
a STIR kps
STOA eis
t
STOB s
e*STOP est
*STOT st
*STOW ps
*STUB s
STUD sy
STUM ps
*STUN gks
t
*STYE*ds
t SUBA*hs
SUBS*
SUCH
SUCK sy
SUDD s
SUDS y
SUED*e
SUER*s
SUES*
SUET*sy
*SUGH s
SUIT es
SUKS*
SULK sy
*SULU s
SUMO*s
*SUMP*s
SUMS*
SUNG*
SUNK*
SUNN*asy
SUNS
SUPE*rs
SUPS
SUQS*
SURA hls
*SURD s
SURE r
SURF sy
SUSS
*SWAB s
*SWAG es
SWAM ipy
*SWAN gks
*SWAP s
*SWAT hs
*SWAY s
*SWIG s
SWIM s
SWOB s
SWOP s
*SWOT s
SWUM
SYBO
SYCE es
SYKE s
SYLI s
SYNC*hs
SYNE*
SYPH s
s*TABS*

TABU*ns
*TACE st
TACH es
s TACK sy
TACO s
*TACT s
TADS
TAEL*s
s*TAGS*
TAHR s
*TAIL s
s*TAIN st
TAKA s
s TAKE nrs
*TALA rs
TALC s
s*TALE rs
TALI
s TALK sy
s*TALL sy
TAME*drs
s*TAMP*s
TAMS*
s TANG*aos
y
s TANK*as
TANS*y
TAOS*
TAPA*s
e*TAPE*drs
a TAPS*
s*TARE*ds
TARN*s
TARO*cks
t
TARP*s
s*TARS*i
s*TART*sy
*TASK*s
*TASS*e
s*TATE*rs
s TATS*
TAUS*
TAUT*s
TAVS*
TAWS*e
TAXA*
TAXI*s
s TEAK*s
s TEAL*s
s TEAM*s
*TEAR*sy
TEAS*e
*TEAT*s
TECH sy
TEDS
s TEED*
s*TEEL*s
TEEM*s
TEEN*sy
TEES*
*TEFF s
*TEGG*s
TEGS*
s TELA*e
s TELE*sx
*TELL*sy
TELS
TEMP ios
t
*TEND*su
*TENS*e
s TENT*hsy
TEPA ls
TERM s
s*TERN es
TEST asy
*TETH*s
s TETS*
s TEWS*
TEXT s
*THAE
THAN ek
*THAT
*THAW s
THEE*
*THEM*e
*THEN*s
*THEW*sy
THEY
*THIN egk
s
THIO l
THIR dl
*THIS
THOU*s

THRO bew
THRU m
THUD s
*THUG s
THUS
s*TICK*s
TICS*
TIDE ds
TIDY
s TIED*
TIER*s
s TIES*
s*TIFF s
TIKE s
TIKI s
su TILE*drs
s*TILL*s
TILS*
as TILT*hs
s TIME drs
TINE*ads
s TING*es
TINS
s TINT*s
TINY*
TIPI*s
TIPS*y
*TIRE ds
TIRL s
TIRO s
TITI*s
TITS
*TIVY
TOAD sy
TOBY
TODS
TODY*
TOEA*s
TOED*
TOES
*TOFF sy
*TOFT s
TOFU s
TOGA*es
TOGS*
*TOIL es
TOIT s
s*TOKE dnr
s
TOLA nrs
*TOLD
s*TOLE ds
a TOLL s
TOLU s
TOMB*s
TOME*s
a*TOMS*
as*TONE*drs
y
TONG*as
TONS
as TONY*
s TOOK*
s TOOL*s
TOOM*
TOON*s
*TOOT*hs
s*TOPE*der
s
TOPH*eis
TOPI*cs
TOPO*is
s*TOPS*
*TORA*hs
*TORC*hs
s*TORE*s
TORI*ci
TORN*
TORO*st
TORR*s
*TORS*eik
o
*TORT*aes
s TORY*
TOSH
s TOSS
TOST
TOTE*dmr
s
s TOTS*
s*TOUR s
s*TOUT s
*TOWN*sy
s TOWS*
TOWY*
TOYO*ns

TOYS*
*TRAD e
*TRAM ps
s*TRAP st
s*TRAY s
*TREE dns
*TREF
TREK s
*TRES s
*TRET s
TREY s
*TRIG os
*TRIM s
TRIO ls
as*TRIP es
*TROD e
TROG s
s TROP e
*TROT hs
s*TROW s
s TROY s
*TRUE drs
*TRUG s
TSAR s
TSKS*
TUBA*els
TUBE*drs
s TUBS*
s TUCK s
TUFA s
s TUFF s
TUFT sy
TUGS*
e TUIS*
TULE s
s*TUMP s
TUNA*s
TUNE*drs
s TUNG*s
s*TUNS*
TUPS
TURF sy
TURK s
*TURN s
TUSH y
TUSK s
TUTS
TUTU*s
*TWAE*s
TWAS
e*TWEE dnt
*TWIG s
*TWIN esy
*TWIT s
TWOS
TYEE*s
TYER*s
s*TYES*
*TYIN g
TYKE s
TYNE ds
TYPE dsy
TYPO s
TYPP s
TYPY
TYRE ds
TYRO s
TZAR s
*UDON*s
jk*UDOS*
sv UGHS*
UGLY
cdj UKES*
np
y ULAN s
ULNA der
s
ls ULUS*
v ULVA s
dgj UMBO s
bdh UMPS*
jlm
prst
UNAI s
UNAU s
UNBE
UNCI a
bj UNCO sy
UNDE er
UNDO
UNDY
*UNIT esy
jp UNTO
p*UPAS
UPBY e
UPDO s
jy UPON*
bc URBS*
bch URDS*
ns
UREA ls
gps URGE drs
a URIC
bcd URNS*
t
bt URPS*
b URSA e
gk URUS
bfm USED*
m*USER*s
bfm USES*
pr
UTAS
bcj UTES*
lm
UVEA ls
VACS*
VAGI
a*VAIL s
*VAIN
*VAIR s
*VALE st
*VAMP sy
*VANE*ds
VANG*s
VANS*
VARA*s
VARS
o VARY*
VASA*l
VASE*s
a VAST*sy
VATS*
VATU*s
VAUS*
VAVS*
VAWS*
u VEAL sy
VEEP*s
VEER*sy
VEES*
VEIL s
VEIN sy
VELA r
*VELD st
VENA el
*VEND s
e VENT s
*VERA
VERB s
aeo VERT su
e VERY
VEST as
VETO*
VETS*
VEXT*
VIAL*s
VIBE s
*VICE ds
VIDE*o
VIDS
i VIED*
VIER*s
i VIES*
VIEW*sy
VIGA*s
VIGS*
VILE r
*VILL ais
VIMS*
VINA ls
o VINE ds
VINO s
VINY l
VIOL as
VIRL s
VISA*s
VISE*ds
VITA el
VIVA s
VIVE
VOES
ao VOID s
*VOLE ds
VOLT aei
s
VOTE drs
a VOWS*
*VROW s
VUGG*sy
*VUGH*s
VUGS*
s*WABS*
WACK eos
y
WADE*drs
WADI*s
WADS
WADY*
t WAES*
*WAFF s
*WAFT s
s*WAGE*drs
s*WAGS*
WAIF s
s*WAIL s
st*WAIN s
*WAIR s
a*WAIT s
a WAKE dnr
s
s*WALE drs
WALK s
*WALL asy
WALY
WAME s
*WAND*s
*WANE*dsy
s WANS*
*WANT*s
WANY
s WAPS*
as WARD*s
as*WARE*ds
*WARK*s
s*WARM*s
WARN*s
WARP*s
WARS
s*WART*sy
WARY*
as*WASH*y
*WASP*sy
WAST*es
s WATS*
*WATT*s
*WAUK s
WAUL s
WAUR
*WAVE drs
y
WAVY
*WAWL*s
WAWS*
WAXY*
s*WAYS*
t WEAK
WEAL ds
WEAN s
s*WEAR sy
WEBS*
WEDS
t WEED*sy
*WEEK*s
WEEL
t WEEN*sy
s WEEP*sy
s WEER*
WEES*t
st WEET*s
*WEFT s
WEIR ds
WEKA s
*WELD s
ds*WELL sy
d WELT s
*WEND*s
WENS
WENT*
s WEPT
*WERE
WERT
WEST s
WETS*
*WHAM*os
*WHAP*s
*WHAT*s
WHEE lnp
*WHEN s
*WHET s
*WHEW s
*WHEY s
*WHID s
WHIG s
*WHIM s
*WHIN esy
*WHIP st
WHIR lrs
*WHIT esy
WHIZ z
WHOA*
WHOM*p
*WHOP*s
*WHUP s
WHYS*
*WICH
*WICK s
WIDE nrs
WIFE dsy
st WIGS*
WILD s
WILE ds
st*WILL sy
WILT s
WILY
*WIMP sy
WIND*sy
dgs WINE*dsy
t
aos WING*sy
s*WINK*s
WINO*s
t*WINS*
t WINY*
s WIPE drs
*WIRE drs
WIRY
WISE*drs
s WISH*a
WISP*sy
s WISS*
t WIST*s
WITE*ds
s WITH*ey
t*WITS*
s WIVE drs
WOAD s
WOES
a*WOKE*n
WOKS*
*WOLD s
WOLF s
WOMB sy
WONK*sy
WONS
WONT*s
WOOD*sy
WOOF*s
WOOL*sy
WOOS*h
s WORD sy
s*WORE
WORK s
WORM sy
s WORN
*WORT hs
WOST*
s WOTS*
WOVE n
WOWS*
*WRAP st
WREN s
WRIT es
WUSS y
WYCH
WYES
WYLE ds
WYND*s
WYNN*s
WYNS*
WYTE ds
XYST is
k YACK s
*YAFF s
YAGI*s
YAGS
k YAKS*
YALD
YAMS*
YANG s
YANK s
YAPS*
l YARD*s
*YARE*r
YARN*s
YAUD s
YAUP s
*YAWL*s
*YAWN*s
YAWP*s
YAWS*
YAYS
YEAH*s
YEAN*s
*YEAR*ns
YEAS*t
YECH sy
*YEGG s
*YELD
*YELK s
*YELL s
YELP s
YENS
YEPS*
YERK s
YETI*s
YETT*s
YEUK sy
YEWS*
*YILL s
ap*YINS*
YIPE*s
YIPS*
YIRD s
YIRR s
x YLEM s
YOBS*
YOCK s
YODH*s
YODS
YOGA s
YOGH s
YOGI cns
*YOKE*dls
YOKS*
YOLK sy
YOND*
YONI*cs
*YORE s
*YOUR*ns
YOUS*e
*YOWE*ds
*YOWL*s
YOWS*
YUAN s
YUCA s
YUCH
YUCK sy
YUGA s
YUKS*
YULE s
YUPS
YURT as
YUTZ
*YWIS
ZAGS
*ZANY
ZAPS*
*ZARF s
ZEAL s
ZEBU s
ZEDS
ZEES*
ZEIN s
ZEKS*
ZEPS*
ZERK s
ZERO s
ZEST sy
*ZETA s
ZIGS*
*ZILL s
ZINC*sy
a ZINE*bs
ZING*sy
ZINS
ZIPS*
ZITI*s
ZITS
ZOEA els
a ZOIC
ZONA el
o*ZONE drs
ZONK s
ZOOM*s
ZOON*s
ZOOS*
ZORI ls
ZOUK s
ZYME s

The Hooks: 5s-to-Make-6s

*AAHED
AALII s
AARGH
ABACA s
ABACI
*ABACK
ABAFT
k ABAKA s
ABAMP s
*ABASE*drs
ABASH
*ABATE drs
k ABAYA s
ABBAS*
ABBES*s
ABBEY*s
ABBOT s
*ABEAM
ABELE s
ABETS
ABHOR s
*ABIDE drs
cfg*ABLED*
t
cf ABLER*
cfg ABLES*t
st
ABMHO s
*ABODE ds
ABOHM s
*ABOIL
ABOMA s
bg*ABOON
*ABORT s
*ABOUT
ABOVE s
ABRIS
ABUSE drs
ABUTS
*ABUZZ
ABYES
ABYSM*s
ABYSS*
ACARI d
ACERB
ACETA l
bc ACHED*
bcl ACHES*
mnt
ACHOO
ACIDS*
ACIDY*
flm ACING
pr
ACINI c
h ACKEE s
ACMES*
ACMIC
ACNED*
ACNES*
*ACOCK
*ACOLD
*ACORN s
ns*ACRED*
n ACRES*
ACRID
ACTED
ACTIN gs
f ACTOR s
*ACUTE rs
ACYLS*
ADAGE s
ADAPT s
ADDAX
gmp ADDED
rw
bgl ADDER s
mpsw
dpr ADDLE ds
sw
*ADEEM s
ADEPT s
ADIEU sx
r ADIOS
ADITS
bm ADMAN
bm ADMEN
ADMIT s
ADMIX t
ADOBE s
ADOBO s
ADOPT s
*ADORE drs
ADORN s

*ADOWN
*ADOZE
ADULT s
ADUNC
*ADUST
ADYTA
ADZED*
ADZES*
AECIA l
AEDES
*AEGIS
p*AEONS*
f AERIE drs
AFARS*
AFFIX
*AFIRE
*AFOOT
*AFORE
*AFOUL
*AFRIT s
dhr AFTER s
w
*AGAIN
*AGAMA s
*AGAPE s
AGARS
*AGATE s
*AGAVE s
*AGAZE
*AGENE s
*AGENT s
ceg AGERS*
jlp
wy
bdg AGGER s
jln
stw
b AGGIE s
AGGRO s
AGHAS*t
v AGILE
cgp AGING*s
rw
AGIOS*
AGISM s
*AGIST s
AGITA s
*AGLEE
e AGLET s
*AGLEY
*AGLOW
m AGMAS*
*AGONE*s
w AGONS*
AGONY*
AGORA es
*AGREE ds
AGRIA s
AGUES*
*AHEAD
a AHING
*AHOLD s
*AHULL
r AIDED*
r AIDER*s
AIDES
bfh AILED
jmnr
stvw
m AIMED
m AIMER s
AIOLI s
fhl*AIRED
pw
f AIRER s
bc AIRNS*
AIRTH*s
AIRTS*
*AISLE ds
*AITCH
nw AIVER s
AJIVA s
*AJUGA s
r AKEES*
AKELA s
AKENE s
*ALACK
ALAMO s
*ALAND*s
ALANE
ALANG
ALANS*
ALANT*s
ALARM*s

s ALARY*
mp*ALATE ds
ALBAS*
ALBUM s
ALCID s
b ALDER s
ALDOL s
ALECS*
ALEFS*
ALEPH s
ALERT s
ALFAS*
ALGAE*
ALGAL*
ALGAS*
ALGID
ALGIN s
ALGOR s
ALGUM s
ALIAS
ALIBI s
*ALIEN s
ck ALIFS*
m ALIGN s
*ALIKE
msv*ALINE drs
*ALIST
*ALIVE
ALIYA hs
t ALKIE s
ALKYD*s
ALKYL*s
ALLAY s
cm ALLEE s
gv ALLEY s
ALLOD s
bh ALLOT s
cfh ALLOW s
mstw
ALLOY s
ALLYL*s
ALMAH*s
h ALMAS*
ALMEH*s
ALMES*
ALMUD es
ALMUG s
h ALOES*
*ALOFT
ALOHA s
*ALOIN s
*ALONE
k*ALONG
*ALOOF
*ALOUD
ALPHA s
ALTAR s
fhp ALTER s
s
ALTHO
ALTOS*
ALULA er
ALUMS
ALWAY s
AMAHS*
*AMAIN
c*AMASS*
*AMAZE ds
cl AMBER sy
g AMBIT s
grw AMBLE drs
ms AMBOS*
AMBRY
AMEBA ens
AMEER s
*AMEND*s
y AMENS*
l AMENT*s
lz AMIAS*
*AMICE s
AMICI
AMIDE*s
AMIDO*l
*AMIDS*t
mr AMIES*
AMIGA s
AMIGO s
fg*AMINE*s
AMINO*
g AMINS*
AMIRS
AMISS
*AMITY
AMMOS*

AMNIA
AMNIC
AMNIO ns
AMOKS*
*AMOLE s
AMONG
*AMORT
AMOUR s
cdl AMPED
rtv
s AMPLE r
d AMPLY
AMPUL es
*AMUCK s
*AMUSE*drs
AMYLS*
r ANCHO rs
ANCON e
ANDRO s
*ANEAR s
ANELE ds
ANENT
fmp ANGAS*
s
m ANGEL s
bdg ANGER s
hmrs
bdj ANGLE drs
mtw
ANGLO s
ANGRY
ANGST s
ANILE*
ANILS
ANIMA ls
ANIME s
ANIMI s
fw ANION s
ANISE*s
ANKHS*
r ANKLE dst
ANKUS h
ANLAS
ANNAL*s
cm ANNAS*
ANNEX e
t ANNOY s
ANNUL is
ANOAS*
*ANODE s
ANOLE s
ANOMY
ANSAE*
ANTAE*
m ANTAS*
chp ANTED*
rw
m ANTES*
cm ANTIC*ks
m ANTIS*
mty ANTRA l
ANTRE s
ANTSY*
ANVIL s
c ANYON es
AORTA els
*APACE
*APART
*APEAK
*APEEK
cgj APERS*
prt
jnp APERY*
APHID s
r*APHIS
*APIAN
gjr*APING
t
*APISH
APNEA ls
APODS
*APORT
APPAL ls
r APPEL s
d APPLE st
APPLY
APRES
APRON s
l APSES*
*APSIS
APTER
r APTLY
AQUAE*
AQUAS*
ARAKS*
ARAME s

h ARBOR s
f ARCED
ARCUS
ARDEB s
ARDOR s
AREAE*
AREAL
AREAS*
ARECA s
AREIC
ARENA s
ARENE s
AREPA s
*ARETE s
ARGAL ais
ARGIL s
g ARGLE ds
ARGOL s
j ARGON s
ARGOT s
ARGUE drs
ARGUS
ARHAT s
v*ARIAS*
*ARIEL s
ARILS*
*ARISE ns
cfp ARLES
fhw ARMED
fhw ARMER s
ARMET s
ARMOR sy
AROID s
AROMA s
*AROSE
ARPEN st
ARRAS
ARRAY s
ARRIS
bfh ARROW sy
mny
cmp ARSES
ARSIS
p ARSON s
h ARTAL
c ARTEL s
ARTSY*
l*ARUMS*
l ARVAL
p ARVOS*
ARYLS*
ASANA s
m*ASCOT s
ASCUS
ASDIC s
bcd*ASHED
fghl
mpsw
ASHEN
bcd*ASHES
fgh
lmp
rsw
*ASIDE s
bcm ASKED
t
m ASKER s
*ASKEW
ASKOI
ASKOS
ASPEN s
gjr ASPER s
ASPIC s
ASPIS h
ASSAI ls
ASSAY s
bgl ASSES s
mpst
bt ASSET s
bce ASTER ns
fgl
mpr
tvw
*ASTIR
ASYLA
w*ATAPS*
ATAXY
*ATILT
ATLAS
b ATMAN*s
ATMAS*
*ATOLL s
ATOMS
ATOMY*
*ATONE drs
*ATONY

ATOPY*
l ATRIA l
*ATRIP
ATTAR s
ATTIC s
c AUDAD s
AUDIO s
AUDIT s
gms AUGER s
cnt AUGHT s
w
AUGUR sy
AULIC
dhj AUNTS*
tv
jv AUNTY*
l AURAE*
AURAL*
AURAR*
l AURAS*
AUREI
AURES
*AURIC
k AURIS t
AURUM s
AUTOS*
AUXIN s
*AVAIL s
s AVANT
*AVAST
dhm AVENS
r
chl AVERS*e
prsw
*AVERT*s
AVGAS
AVIAN s
AVION s
AVISO s
*AVOID s
AVOWS
*AWAIT s
*AWAKE dns
v*AWARD s
*AWARE
*AWASH
l AWFUL
cdh*AWING
jlm
psty
dfp AWNED
y
*AWOKE n
AWOLS*
AXELS*
AXIAL
AXILE*
AXILS*
fmr AXING
tw
AXIOM s
AXION s
t AXITE s
AXLED*
AXLES*
t AXMAN
t AXMEN
AXONE*s
t AXONS*
r AYAHS*
lz*AYINS*
h AZANS*
AZIDE s
AZIDO
*AZINE s
AZLON s
*AZOIC
AZOLE s
AZONS*
AZOTE ds
AZOTH s
AZUKI s
AZURE s
BAAED
BAALS
BABAS
BABEL*s
BABES*
BABKA s
BABOO lns
BABUL*s
BABUS*
BACCA e
BACKS*
BACON s
BADDY

BADGE drs
BADLY
BAFFS*
BAFFY*
BAGEL s
BAGGY
BAHTS*
BAILS
*BAIRN s
BAITH*
BAITS
BAIZA s
BAIZE s
BAKED*
BAKER*sy
BAKES*
*BALAS
BALDS*
BALDY*
BALED*
BALER*s
BALES
BALKS*
BALKY
BALLS
BALLY
BALMS
BALMY*
BALSA*ms
*BANAL
BANCO s
BANDA*s
BANDS
BANDY*
BANED*
BANES
BANGS*
BANJO s
BANKS*
BANNS
BANTY
BARBE*dlr
st
BARBS
BARCA s
BARDE*ds
BARDS*
BARED*
BARER*
*BARES*t
BARFS
BARGE des
BARIC
BARKS
BARKY*
BARMS
BARMY
BARNS*
BARNY*
BARON gsy
BARRE dln
st
BARYE s
BASAL t
a BASED*
a BASER*
a BASES*t
BASIC s
BASIL s
BASIN gs
BASIS
BASKS
BASSI*
BASSO*s
BASSY*
BASTE*drs
BASTS*
BATCH
a BATED*
a*BATES*
BATHE*drs
BATHS*
BATIK s
BATON s
BATTS*
BATTU*e
BATTY*
BAUDS*
BAULK sy
BAWDS*
BAWDY*
BAWLS
BAWTY
BAYED
BAYOU s
BAZAR s

BAZOO s
*BEACH y
BEADS*
BEADY*
BEAKS*
BEAKY*
BEAMS*
BEAMY*
BEANO*s
BEANS*
BEARD*s
BEARS
*BEAST s
BEATS
BEAUS*
BEAUT*sy
BEAUX
BEBOP s
BECAP s
BECKS*
BEDEL ls
BEDEW s
BEDIM s
BEECH y
BEEDI
BEEFS*
BEEFY*
BEEPS*
BEERS*
BEERY
BEETS*
BEFIT s
BEFOG s
BEGAN
BEGAT
BEGET s
BEGIN s
BEGOT
BEGUM s
BEGUN
BEIGE s
BEIGY
BEING s
BELAY s
BELCH
BELGA s
BELIE dfr
s
BELLE*ds
BELLS
BELLY*
BELON gs
BELOW s
BELTS*
BEMAS*
BEMIX t
BENCH
BENDS
BENDY*s
BENES*
BENNE st
BENNI s
BENNY
o BENTO*s
BENTS*
BERET s
BERGS
BERKS*
BERME*ds
BERMS*
BERRY
BERTH as
BERYL s
*BESES
BESET s
BESOM s
BESOT s
BESTS*
BETAS
BETEL s
BETHS
BETON sy
BETTA s
BEVEL s
BEVOR s
BEWIG s
BEZEL s
BEZIL s
*BHANG s
*BHOOT s
BHUTS
BIALI s
BIALY s
BIBBS*
BIBLE s
BICEP*s

i*BICES*
BIDDY
a BIDED*
a BIDER*s
a*BIDES*
BIDET*s
BIDIS*
BIELD s
BIERS*
BIFFS*
BIFFY
BIFID
BIGGY
BIGHT s
BIGLY
BIGOS
BIGOT s
BIJOU sx
BIKED*
BIKER*s
BIKES*
BIKIE s
BILBO as
BILBY
BILES*
BILGE ds
BILGY
BILKS
BILLS
BILLY
BIMAH*s
BIMAS*
BIMBO s
BINAL
BINDI*s
BINDS*
BINER*s
BINES*
BINGE drs
BINGO s
BINIT s
BINTS*
BIOGS*
BIOME s
BIONT s
*BIOTA s
BIPED s
BIPOD s
BIRCH
BIRDS*
BIRKS
BIRLE*drs
BIRLS*
BIROS*
BIRRS*
BIRSE s
BIRTH s
i BISES*
BISKS*
BISON s
*BITCH y
BITER*s
BITES*
BITSY*
BITTS*
BITTY*
BIZES*
BLABS
*BLACK s
*BLADE drs
BLAFF s
BLAHS*
*BLAIN s
*BLAME*drs
BLAMS
*BLAND
*BLANK s
BLARE ds
*BLASE
o*BLAST sy
ao*BLATE*
BLATS
BLAWN
BLAWS
a*BLAZE drs
*BLEAK s
*BLEAR sy
BLEAT s
BLEBS*
BLEED s
BLEEP s
*BLEND es
*BLENT
*BLESS
a*BLEST
BLETS
*BLIMP s
*BLIMY
BLIND*s
BLINI*s
*BLINK*s
BLIPS
BLISS
*BLITE s
BLITZ
BLOAT s
BLOBS
*BLOCK*sy
BLOCS*
BLOGS
BLOKE s
BLOND es
BLOOD sy
a*BLOOM sy
*BLOOP s
BLOTS
BLOWN
*BLOWS*y
BLOWY*
BLUBS*
BLUED*
BLUER*
*BLUES*ty
BLUET*s
BLUEY*s
*BLUFF s
BLUME ds
*BLUNT s
BLURB*s
BLURS*
BLURT*s
a*BLUSH
BLYPE s
a BOARD*s
BOARS
BOART*s
*BOAST*s
BOATS
BOBBY
BOCCE s
BOCCI aes
BOCKS*
a BODED*
a*BODES*
BOFFO*s
BOFFS
BOGAN s
BOGEY s
BOGGY
BOGIE s
*BOGLE s
BOGUS
BOHEA s
BOHOS*
BOILS
BOING s
BOITE s
BOLAR*
BOLAS*
BOLDS
o*BOLES*
BOLLS*
BOLOS*
BOLTS*
o BOLUS
BOMBE*drs
BOMBS*
BONDS*
BONED*
BONER*s
BONES
BONEY*
BONGO*s
BONGS*
BONKS*
BONNE st
BONNY
*BONUS
BONZE rs
BOOBS*
BOOBY*
BOOED
BOOGY
e BOOKS*
BOOMS*
BOOMY*
BOONS*
BOORS*
BOOST*s
BOOTH*s
BOOTS
BOOTY*
*BOOZE drs
*BOOZY
a*BORAL*s
BORAS*
BORAX*
BORED*
BORER*s
BORES
BORIC
BORKS*
BORNE*
BORON s
a*BORTS*
BORTY*
BORTZ*
BOSKS*
BOSKY*
BOSOM sy
BOSON s
BOSSY*
BOSUN s
BOTAS*
BOTCH y
BOTEL s
BOTHY*
BOTTS*
BOUGH st
BOULE s
a BOUND s
BOURG s
BOURN es
BOUSE ds
BOUSY
BOUTS
BOVID s
*BOWED
BOWEL s
BOWER sy
BOWLS
*BOWSE*ds
BOXED
BOXER s
*BOXES
BOYAR ds
BOYLA s
BOYOS*
BOZOS*
*BRACE drs
BRACH s
BRACT s
BRADS
BRAES*
BRAGS
*BRAID s
*BRAIL s
*BRAIN sy
*BRAKE ds
BRAKY
*BRAND*sy
*BRANK*s
BRANS*
*BRANT*s
*BRASH*y
BRASS*y
BRATS
BRAVA s
*BRAVE drs
BRAVI
BRAVO s
BRAWL*sy
BRAWN*sy
BRAWS
BRAXY
BRAYS
BRAZA s
*BRAZE dnr
s
*BREAD sy
BREAK s
*BREAM s
*BREDE*s
*BREED*s
BREES
BRENS*
*BRENT*s
BREVE st
BREWS*
BRIAR dsy
BRIBE der
s
*BRICK sy
*BRIDE s
BRIEF*s
BRIER*sy
BRIES*
BRIGS
*BRILL os
BRIMS
BRINE*drs
*BRING*s
*BRINK*s
BRINS
BRINY*
BRIOS*
*BRISK*s
BRISS*
BRITH*s
BRITS*
BRITT*s
a*BROAD s
*BROCK s
*BROIL s
BROKE nr
BROME s
BROMO s
BRONC os
*BROOD*sy
*BROOK*s
*BROOM*sy
BROOS*
*BROSE*s
BROSY
BROTH sy
BROWN*sy
*BROWS*e
BRUGH s
*BRUIN s
BRUIT s
BRUME s
*BRUNG
*BRUNT s
*BRUSH y
*BRUSK
BRUTE*ds
BRUTS
BUBAL es
BUBUS*
BUCKO*s
BUCKS*
BUDDY
BUDGE drs
t
BUFFI*
BUFFO*s
BUFFS*
BUFFY*
BUGGY
BUGLE drs
BUHLS*
BUHRS*
BUILD s
BUILT
BULBS*
BULGE drs
BULGY
BULKS*
BULKY*
BULLA*e
BULLS*
BULLY*
BUMFS*
BUMPH*s
BUMPS
BUMPY*
BUNAS*
BUNCH y
*BUNCO s
BUNDS*
BUNDT*s
BUNGS*
BUNKO*s
BUNKS*
BUNNS*
BUNNY*
BUNTS*
BUNYA s
BUOYS*
BUPPY
BURAN*s
BURAS*
BURBS
BURDS
BURET s
BURGH*s
BURGS*
BURIN s
BURKA s
BURKE drs
BURLS*
BURLY*
BURNS
BURNT*
BURPS
BURQA s
BURRO*sw
BURRS*
BURRY*
*BURSA*elr
s
BURSE*s
BURST*s
BUSBY
a*BUSED
a*BUSES
BUSHY*
BUSKS*
BUSTS*
BUSTY*
BUTCH
BUTEO*s
BUTES
BUTLE drs
BUTTE*drs
BUTTS*
BUTTY*
BUTUT s
BUTYL s
BUXOM
BUYER s
BWANA s
BYLAW s
BYRES*
BYRLS*
BYSSI
BYTES*
BYWAY s
CABAL as
s CABBY
CABER s
CABIN s
*CABLE drs
t
CABOB s
CACAO*s
CACAS*
*CACHE dst
CACTI
CADDY
CADES*
CADET*s
CADGE drs
CADGY
CADIS*
CADRE s
CAECA l
CAFES*
CAFFS*
CAGED
*CAGER*s
CAGES
CAGEY*
CAHOW s
CAIDS
CAINS
CAIRD s
*CAIRN sy
CAJON
CAKED*
CAKES*
CAKEY*
CALFS*
*CALIF s
CALIX
CALKS*
CALLA*ns
s*CALLS*
CALMS
CALOS*
CALVE ds
CALYX
*CAMAS s
CAMEL*s
CAMEO*s
CAMES*
CAMOS*
s CAMPI*
CAMPO*s
s*CAMPS*
CAMPY*
*CANAL s
CANDY
CANED*
CANER*s
CANES
CANID s
*CANNA s
CANNY
CANOE drs
*CANON s
CANSO*s
CANST*
CANTO*nrs
s*CANTS*
s CANTY*
s*CAPED*
*CAPER*s
s*CAPES*
CAPHS*
CAPIZ
CAPON*s
CAPOS
CAPUT
CARAT es
CARBO*nsy
CARBS
CARDS*
s CARED*
s CARER*s
s*CARES*s
CARET*s
CAREX*
CARGO s
CARKS
CARLE*s
CARLS*
CARNS*
CARNY*
CAROB s
CAROL is
CAROM s
CARPI*
s CARPS*
CARRS*
s CARRY*
CARSE*s
e CARTE*dlr
s
s*CARTS*
CARVE dln
rs
CASAS*
CASED*
CASES*
CASKS
CASKY*
CASTE*rs
CASTS*
CASUS
CATCH y
CATER*s
CATES
s CATTY
*CAULD*s
CAULK*s
CAULS*
CAUSE drs
y
CAVED*
*CAVER*ns
CAVES
CAVIE s
CAVIL s
*CAWED
*CEASE ds
CEBID s
CECAL*
CECUM
CEDAR nsy
CEDED*
CEDER*s
CEDES*
CEDIS*
CEIBA s
CEILI*s
CEILS*
CELEB s
CELLA*er
o CELLI*
CELLO*s
CELLS
CELOM s
CELTS*
CENSE drs
CENTO*s
s CENTS*
CENTU*m
CEORL s
CEPES*
CERCI s
CERED*
CERES*
CERIA s
CERIC
CEROS
CESTA s
CESTI
CETES*
CHADS*
CHAFE drs
CHAFF sy
CHAIN*es
*CHAIR*s
*CHAIS*e
CHALK sy
CHAMP*sy
CHAMS
*CHANG es
*CHANT sy
CHAOS*
CHAPE*ls
CHAPS
CHAPT*
e*CHARD*s
*CHARE*ds
*CHARK*as
*CHARM*s
CHARR*osy
CHARS*
*CHART*s
CHARY*
CHASE drs
CHASM sy
CHATS
CHAWS
CHAYS
*CHEAP os
*CHEAT s
*CHECK s
CHEEK sy
CHEEP s
CHEER osy
CHEFS*
CHELA es
CHEMO s
CHERT sy
CHESS
*CHEST sy
*CHETH s
CHEVY
CHEWS
CHEWY*
CHIAO*
CHIAS*m
CHICA*s
*CHICK*s
CHICO*s
CHICS*
*CHIDE*drs
CHIEF s
CHIEL ds
CHILD e
CHILE s
*CHILI s
*CHILL isy
CHIMB s
CHIME drs
CHIMP s
CHINA*s
CHINE*ds
CHINK*sy
CHINO*s
CHINS
CHIPS
CHIRK s
CHIRM s
CHIRO s
CHIRP sy
CHIRR es
CHIRU s
CHITS
*CHIVE s
CHIVY
*CHOCK s
CHOIR s
*CHOKE drs
y
CHOKY
CHOLA s
CHOLO s
CHOMP s
*CHOOK s
CHOPS
CHORD s
CHORE ads
*CHOSE ns
CHOTT s
*CHOWS*e
CHUBS
*CHUCK sy
CHUFA s
*CHUFF sy
CHUGS
*CHUMP*s
CHUMS
*CHUNK sy
*CHURL s
CHURN s
CHURR os
CHUTE ds
CHYLE s
CHYME s
CIBOL s
CIDER s
CIGAR s
*CILIA
CIMEX
*CINCH
CINES*
s*CIONS*
CIRCA
CIRES
CIRRI
CISCO s
CISSY
CISTS*
CITED*
CITER*s
CITES*
CIVET s
CIVIC s
CIVIE s
CIVIL
CIVVY
CLACH s
*CLACK s
*CLADE*s
CLADS
CLAGS
CLAIM s
*CLAMP*s
CLAMS
*CLANG*s
*CLANK*sy
CLANS*
CLAPS
CLAPT*
CLARO s
CLARY
*CLASH
CLASP st
*CLASS y
*CLAST s
*CLAVE rs
CLAVI
CLAWS
CLAYS
*CLEAN s
*CLEAR s
CLEAT s
*CLEEK s
CLEFS*
*CLEFT*s
CLEPE ds
y*CLEPT
CLERK s
CLEWS*
*CLICK s
CLIFF sy
*CLIFT s
*CLIMB s
*CLIME s
*CLINE s
*CLING sy
*CLINK s
CLIPS
CLIPT*
CLOAK s
*CLOCK s
CLODS*
CLOGS
CLOMB
CLOMP s
*CLONE*drs
CLONK*s
CLONS*
*CLOOT s
CLOPS
*CLOSE drs
t
*CLOTH*es
CLOTS
*CLOUD sy
*CLOUR s
*CLOUT s
*CLOVE nrs
*CLOWN s

CLOYS*
CLOZE s
CLUBS*
*CLUCK s
CLUED*
CLUES
*CLUMP sy
*CLUNG
*CLUNK sy
CNIDA e
COACH
COACT s
COALA*s
COALS*
COALY*
COAPT s
*COAST s
COATI*s
COATS
COBBS*
COBBY*
*COBIA s
COBLE s
COBRA s
COCAS
COCCI cd
COCKS*
COCKY*
COCOA*s
COCOS*
CODAS
CODEC*s
CODED*
CODEN*s
CODER*s
CODES
CODEX*
CODON s
COEDS*
s*COFFS*
COGON s
COHOG*s
COHOS*ht
COIFS*
COIGN es
COILS
COINS*
COIRS*
COKED*
COKES
COLAS*
COLBY s
s*COLDS*
COLED*
COLES
COLIC s
COLIN s
COLLY
COLOG s
COLON eis y
COLOR s
COLTS*
COLZA s
COMAE*
COMAL*
COMAS*
COMBE*drs
COMBO*s
COMBS*
*COMER*s
COMES*
COMET*hs
COMFY
COMIC s
COMIX
COMMA s
COMMY
COMPO*s
COMPS*
COMPT*s
COMTE s
CONCH aos y
CONDO mrs
CONED*
is*CONES*
CONEY*s
CONGA s
CONGE ers
CONGO su
i CONIC*s
CONIN*egs
CONKS*
CONKY*
CONNS*
CONTE s
*CONTO s
*CONUS
s COOCH
COOED
COOEE ds
COOER s
COOEY s
COOFS*
COOKS*
COOKY*
COOLS*
COOLY*
COOMB es
COONS*
s*COOPS*
COOPT*s
s*COOTS*
*COPAL ms
COPAY s
s*COPED*
*COPEN*s
COPER*s
s*COPES*
COPRA hs
COPSE*s
*CORAL s
*CORBY
CORDS*
s CORED*
s CORER*s
s*CORES*
CORGI s
s CORIA
CORKS*
CORKY*
CORMS*
as CORNS*
CORNU*as
CORNY*
CORPS e
CORSE*st
COSEC s
*COSES
COSET s
COSEY s
COSIE drs
COSTA*elr
COSTS*
COTAN s
COTED*
COTES*
COTTA ers
*COUCH
COUDE
COUGH s
COULD
COUNT sy
COUPE*ds
COUPS*
COURT s
s COUTH s
COVED*
*COVEN*s
*COVER*st
COVES*
COVET*s
COVEY*s
COVIN gs
s*COWED
COWER s
s*COWLS*
COWRY
COXAE*
COXAL*
COXED
*COXES
COYED
*COYER
COYLY
COYPU s
COZEN s
COZES
COZEY s
COZIE drs
CRAAL s
CRABS*
*CRACK sy
*CRAFT sy
s*CRAGS*
*CRAKE s
*CRAMP*sy
s*CRAMS*
CRANE ds
*CRANK sy
s*CRAPE*ds
s*CRAPS*
*CRASH
CRASS
*CRATE drs
*CRAVE dnr s
s CRAWL*sy
CRAWS
*CRAZE ds
CRAZY
s CREAK sy
s*CREAM sy
*CREDO*s
CREDS
s*CREED s
*CREEK s
*CREEL s
CREEP sy
CREME s
CREPE dsy
CREPT
CREPY
CRESS y
*CREST s
s CREWS*
CRIBS
*CRICK s
s CRIED
CRIER s
s CRIES
*CRIME s
s CRIMP sy
*CRIPE s
CRISP*sy
CRITS*
CROAK sy
CROCI*
*CROCK*s
CROCS
CROFT s
CRONE s
CRONY
*CROOK s
CROON s
CROPS*
CRORE s
a CROSS e
*CROUP esy
CROWD*sy
CROWN*s
CROWS
CROZE rs
*CRUCK s
*CRUDE*rs
CRUDS*
CRUEL
CRUET s
CRUMB sy
*CRUMP s
CRUOR s
CRURA l
*CRUSE*st
CRUSH
*CRUST*sy
CRWTH s
CRYPT os
CUBBY
CUBEB*s
CUBED*
CUBER*s
CUBES*
CUBIC s
CUBIT is
CUDDY
s CUFFS*
CUIFS*
CUING
CUISH
CUKES
s CULCH
CULET s
CULEX
s CULLS*
CULLY*
CULMS*
CULPA e
CULTI*c
CULTS*
CUMIN s
CUPEL s
CUPID s
CUPPA s
CUPPY
CURBS
CURCH
CURDS
CURDY*
CURED*
CURER*s
CURES*
CURET*s
s CURFS*
CURIA el
CURIE s
CURIO s
CURLS*
CURLY*
CURNS
CURRS*
s CURRY*
CURSE*drs
CURST*
CURVE dst y
s CURVY
CUSEC s
CUSHY
CUSKS*
CUSPS*
CUSSO*s
s CUTCH
a CUTER*
as*CUTES*ty
CUTEY*s
CUTIE s
CUTIN s
CUTIS
CUTTY
CUTUP s
CUVEE s
CYANO*
CYANS*
CYBER
CYCAD s
CYCAS
CYCLE drs
CYCLO s
CYDER s
CYLIX
CYMAE*
CYMAR*s
CYMAS*
CYMES*
CYMOL s
CYNIC s
CYSTS*
CYTON s
CZARS*
DACES
DACHA s
DADAS*
DADDY
DADOS
DAFFS*
DAFFY*
DAGGA s
DAHLS*
DAILY
*DAIRY
DAISY*
DALES
*DALLY
DAMAN s
DAMAR s
DAMES*
DAMNS*
DAMPS
DANCE drs
DANDY
DANGS*
DANIO s
DARBS
DARED*
DARER*s
DARES
DARIC s
DARKS
DARNS*
DARTS
DASHI*s
DASHY
DATED*
DATER*s
DATES
DATOS*
DATTO s
DATUM s
DAUBE*drs
DAUBS*
DAUBY*
*DAUNT s
DAUTS*
DAVEN s
DAVIT s
*DAWED
DAWEN
DAWKS*
DAWNS
DAWTS*
DAZED*
DAZES*
DEADS*
DEAIR s
i DEALS*
DEALT*
DEANS*
DEARS
DEARY*
DEASH
*DEATH sy
*DEAVE ds
DEBAG s
DEBAR ks
DEBIT s
DEBTS*
DEBUG s
DEBUT s
DEBYE s
DECAF s
DECAL s
DECAY s
DECKS*
DECOR*s
DECOS*
DECOY*s
DECRY
DEDAL
DEEDS*
DEEDY*
a DEEMS*
DEEPS*
DEERS*
DEETS*
DEFAT s
DEFER s
DEFIS*
DEFOG s
DEGAS
DEGUM s
DEICE drs
DEIFY
DEIGN s
DEILS*
DEISM s
DEIST s
DEITY
DEKED
DEKES
DEKKO s
DELAY s
DELED*
DELES*
DELFS*
DELFT*s
DELIS*ht
DELLS
DELLY*
DELTA*s
DELTS*
DELVE drs
DEMES
*DEMIC
*DEMIT s
DEMOB*s
DEMON*s
DEMOS*
DEMUR es
DENAR isy
DENES*
DENIM*s
DENSE*r
DENTS*
DEOXY
DEPOT s
DEPTH s
DERAT es
DERAY s
DERBY
DERMA*ls
DERMS*
DERRY
DESEX
DESKS*
DETER s
DETOX
DEUCE ds
DEVAS*
DEVEL s
*DEVIL s
DEVON s
DEWAN s
DEWAR s
DEWAX
DEWED
*DEXES
DEXIE s
DHAKS*
DHALS*
DHOBI s
*DHOLE s
DHOTI s
DHOWS
DHUTI s
DIALS*
DIARY
DIAZO
DICED
DICER*s
DICES
DICEY*
DICKS*
DICKY
DICOT s
DICTA
DICTY
DIDIE s
DIDOS*
DIDST
DIENE s
DIETS*
DIFFS*
DIGHT s
DIGIT s
DIKED*
DIKER*s
DIKES*
DILDO es
DILLS
DILLY
DIMER*s
DIMES*
DIMLY
DINAR s
DINED*
DINER*os
DINES*
DINGE*drs y
DINGO*
DINGS*
DINGY*
DINKS
DINKY
DINOS*
DINTS*
DIODE s
DIOLS*
DIPPY
DIPSO*s
DIRAM s
DIRER*
DIRGE s
DIRKS
DIRLS*
DIRTS*
DIRTY*
DISCI*
DISCO*s
DISCS*
DISHY*
DISKS*
DISME s
DITAS*
*DITCH
DITES*
DITSY*
DITTO s
DITTY
DITZY*
DIVAN*s
DIVAS*
DIVED*
DIVER*st
DIVES*t
DIVOT s
DIVVY
DIWAN s
DIXIT s
DIZEN s
DIZZY
*DJINN*isy
DJINS
DOATS
DOBBY
DOBIE s
DOBLA s
DOBRA s
DOBRO s
DOCKS*
DODGE dmr s
DODGY
DODOS*
DOERS*
DOEST*
DOETH
DOFFS
DOGES*
DOGEY*s
DOGGO
DOGGY
DOGIE s
DOGMA s
*DOILY
DOING s
DOITS*
DOJOS*
DOLCE
DOLCI
DOLED*
DOLES
DOLLS*
DOLLY*
DOLMA ns
DOLOR s
DOLTS*
DOMAL
DOMED*
DOMES*
DOMIC
DONAS*
DONEE*s
DONGA*s
DONGS*
DONNA s
DONNE de
DONOR s
DONSY*
DONUT s
DOODY
DOOLY
DOOMS*
DOOMY*
DOORS*
*DOOZY
DOPAS*
DOPED
DOPER*s
DOPES
DOPEY*
DORKS*
DORKY*
DORMS*
DORMY*
DORPS*
DORRS*
DORSA*dl
DORTY
DOSED*
DOSER*s
DOSES
DOTAL
DOTED*
DOTER*s
DOTES*
DOTTY
DOUBT s
DOUCE
DOUGH sty
DOULA s
DOUMA*s
DOUMS*
DOURA*hs
DOUSE drs
*DOVEN*s
DOVES*
DOWDY
*DOWED
DOWEL s
DOWER sy
DOWIE
DOWNS
DOWNY*
DOWRY
*DOWSE*drs
DOXIE s
DOYEN s
DOYLY
DOZED*
DOZEN*s
DOZER*s
DOZES*
DRABS*
*DRAFF sy
*DRAFT sy
DRAGS
*DRAIL s
*DRAIN s
*DRAKE s
DRAMA*s
DRAMS
*DRANK
*DRAPE drs y
DRATS
*DRAVE
DRAWL*sy
DRAWN*
DRAWS
DRAYS
*DREAD s
*DREAM sty
*DREAR sy
*DRECK sy
DREED
DREES
DREGS
DREKS*
DRESS y
*DREST
DRIBS
DRIED
DRIER s
DRIES t
a*DRIFT sy
*DRILL s
DRILY
*DRINK s
DRIPS
DRIPT*
*DRIVE lnr s
DROID s
a DROIT s
*DROLL sy
DRONE drs
DROOL sy
DROOP sy
DROPS*y
DROPT*
DROSS y
DROUK s
*DROVE drs
DROWN ds
DRUBS
DRUGS
DRUID s
DRUMS
DRUNK s
DRUPE s
*DRUSE s
DRYAD s
DRYER s
DRYLY
DUADS*
DUALS*
DUCAL
DUCAT s
e DUCES*
DUCHY
DUCKS*
DUCKY*
e DUCTS*
DUDDY
DUDED*
DUDES*
DUELS*
DUETS*
DUFFS*
DUFUS
DUITS*
DUKED*
DUKES
DULIA s
DULLS*
DULLY*
DULSE s
DUMAS*
*DUMBO*s
DUMBS*
DUMKA
DUMKY
DUMMY
DUMPS
DUMPY*
DUNAM s

DUNCE s
DUNCH
DUNES*
DUNGS*
DUNGY*
DUNKS*
DUNTS*
DUOMI
DUOMO s
DUPED*
DUPER*sy
DUPES*
DUPLE x
DURAL*
DURAS*
DURED*
DURES*s
DURNS
DUROC*s
DUROS*
DURRA*s
DURRS*
DURST
DURUM s
DUSKS*
DUSKY*
DUSTS*
DUSTY*
DUTCH
DUVET s
DWARF s
DWEEB sy
*DWELL s
*DWELT
*DWINE ds
DYADS*
DYERS*
DYING s
DYKED*
DYKES*
DYNEL*s
DYNES*
m*EAGER s
b EAGLE dst
m EAGRE s
fgn EARED
rst
p EARLS*
dnp EARLY*
y
ly EARNS*
dh EARTH sy
cfl EASED*
t
tw EASEL*s
cfl EASES*
pt
bfl EASTS*
y
bn EATEN
bfh EATER sy
ns
dhl EAVED*
rw
dhl*EAVES*
rw
w EBBED
EBBET s
EBONS*
EBONY
r*EBOOK s
lpt ECHED*
l ECHES*
ECHOS*
ECLAT s
ECRUS
o EDEMA s
hkw EDGED*
hl EDGER*s
hkl EDGES*
sw
EDICT s
EDIFY
as EDILE s
EDITS
drs*EDUCE ds
d*EDUCT s
p EERIE r
EGADS
l EGERS*
*EGEST as
bs EGGAR s
bkl EGGED
pv
k EGGER s
r EGRET s

EIDER*s
EIDOS
hw EIGHT hsy
*EIKON s
dr EJECT as
d*EKING
*ELAIN s
r*ELAND*s
ELANS*
dgr*ELATE drs
v
ELBOW s
gmw ELDER s
s ELECT s
ELEGY
ELEMI s
ELFIN s
ELIDE ds
*ELINT s
p*ELITE s
*ELOIN s
*ELOPE drs
d*ELUDE drs
*ELUTE ds
d ELVER s
dhp ELVES
s
r*EMAIL s
EMBAR ks
EMBAY s
EMBED s
m EMBER s
EMBOW s
EMCEE ds
EMEER s
r*EMEND s
EMERY
EMEUS*
EMIRS
dr EMITS*
h EMMER s
EMMET s
EMMYS*
dgr*EMOTE drs
EMPTY
EMYDE*s
EMYDS*
ENACT s
s ENATE s
bfm ENDED
prs
tvw
bfg ENDER s
lmr
stv
ENDOW s
v ENDUE ds
*ENEMA s
ENEMY
ENJOY s
ENNUI s
ENOKI s
ENOLS*
*ENORM
ENOWS
ENROL ls
ENSKY
ENSUE ds
crt ENTER as
v
ENTIA
gs ENTRY
t ENURE ds
r ENVOI s
ENVOY s
ENZYM es
EOSIN es
*EPACT s
t*EPEES*
EPHAH*s
EPHAS*
EPHOD s
EPHOR is
EPICS
EPOCH s
EPODE s
*EPOXY
EQUAL s
*EQUID s
*EQUIP s
*ERASE*drs
ERECT s
ERGOT*s
ERICA s
kt ERNES*
*ERODE ds

r*EROSE*s
ERRED
t ERROR s
pv ERSES
ERUCT s
a ERUGO s
ERUPT s
ERVIL s
*ESCAR ps
*ESCOT s
ESKAR s
ESKER s
m ESNES*
ESSAY s
cfj ESSES
mny
fjn ESTER s
prt
wyz
*ESTOP s
r*ETAPE s
ant ETHER s
w
ETHIC s
ETHOS
m ETHYL s
ETNAS*
ETUDE s
ETUIS
*ETWEE s
ETYMA
EUROS*
EVADE drs
s EVENS*
*EVENT*s
r*EVERT*s
r*EVERY*
EVICT s
dk EVILS*
EVITE ds
r EVOKE drs
hs EWERS*
EXACT as
EXALT s
EXAMS*
EXCEL s
EXECS*
EXERT s
EXILE drs
r EXINE s
hsv EXING
s EXIST s
EXITS*
EXONS*
EXPAT s
EXPEL s
EXPOS*e
EXTOL ls
EXTRA s
EXUDE ds
EXULT s
EXURB s
EYASS*
EYERS*
k EYING
EYRAS*
EYRES*
EYRIE s
EYRIR
*FABLE drs
FACED
FACER*s
FACES
FACET*es
FACIA els
FACTS
FADDY
FADED*
FADER*s
FADES*
FADGE ds
FADOS
FAENA s
*FAERY
*FAGIN s
FAGOT s
FAILS
FAINT*s
FAIRS
FAIRY
FAITH s
FAKED*
FAKER*sy
FAKES*
FAKEY*
FAKIR s

FALLS
FALSE r
FAMED*
FAMES*
FANCY
FANES
*FANGA*s
FANGS*
FANNY
*FANON*s
FANOS*
FANUM s
FAQIR s
FARAD s
FARCE drs
FARCI e
FARCY
FARDS*
FARED*
FARER*s
FARES
FARLE*s
FARLS*
FARMS
FAROS*
FASTS*
FATAL
FATED*
FATES
FATLY
FATTY
FATWA s
FAUGH
*FAULD s
FAULT sy
FAUNA*els
FAUNS*
FAUVE s
FAVAS*
FAVES
FAVOR s
FAVUS
FAWNS
FAWNY
*FAXED
*FAXES
FAYED
FAZED*
FAZES*
FEARS
*FEASE ds
*FEAST s
FEATS
FEAZE ds
FECAL
FECES
FECKS*
FEDEX
FEEBS*
FEEDS*
FEELS
FEEZE ds
FEIGN s
FEINT s
FEIST sy
FELID s
FELLA*hs
FELLS
FELLY*
FELON sy
FELTS*
FEMES
FEMME s
FEMUR s
FENCE drs
FENDS
FENNY
FEODS*
FEOFF s
FERAL s
FERES*
FERIA els
FERLY
FERMI s
FERNS
FERNY*
FERRY
FESSE*ds
FESTS*
FETAL*
FETAS
*FETCH
FETED*
FETES*
FETID
FETOR s

FETUS
FEUAR s
FEUDS*
FEUED
*FEVER s
*FEWER
*FEYER
FEYLY
FEZES
FEZZY
FIARS*
FIATS*
FIBER s
FIBRE s
FICES
FICHE s
FICHU s
FICIN s
FICUS
FIDGE dst
FIDOS*
FIEFS*
a FIELD s
FIEND s
FIERY
FIFED*
FIFER*s
FIFES*
FIFTH s
FIFTY
FIGHT s
FILAR*
FILCH
FILED*
FILER*s
FILES*
FILET*s
FILLE*drs
t
FILLO*s
FILLS
FILLY
FILMI*cs
FILMS*
FILMY*
FILOS*e
FILTH sy
FILUM
FINAL es
FINCA s
*FINCH
FINDS*
FINED*
FINER*y
FINES*t
FINIS h
FINKS
FINNY
FINOS*
FIORD s
FIQUE s
FIRED
FIRER*s
FIRES
FIRMS*
FIRNS*
FIRRY
FIRST*s
FIRTH s
FISCS*
FISHY*
FISTS*
*FITCH y
FITLY
FIVER*s
FIVES*
FIXED
FIXER s
FIXES
FIXIT y
FIZZY*
FJELD s
FJORD s
FLABS
*FLACK s
FLAGS
FLAIL s
*FLAIR s
*FLAKE*drs
y
FLAKY
a*FLAME*dnr
s
FLAMS
FLAMY*
*FLANK*s

FLANS*
FLAPS
FLARE ds
*FLASH y
FLASK s
FLATS
FLAWS
FLAWY*
FLAXY*
FLAYS
FLEAM*s
FLEAS
FLECK sy
*FLEER*s
FLEES
*FLEET*s
FLESH y
FLEWS*
FLEYS
*FLICK*s
FLICS*
*FLIED
*FLIER s
*FLIES t
*FLING s
*FLINT sy
FLIPS
FLIRS*
FLIRT*sy
*FLITE*ds
FLITS
a FLOAT sy
*FLOCK*sy
FLOCS*
FLOES*
FLOGS
*FLONG s
FLOOD s
FLOOR s
FLOPS
FLORA els
*FLOSS y
*FLOTA s
*FLOUR sy
*FLOUT s
FLOWN
FLOWS
FLUBS*
FLUED*
FLUES
*FLUFF sy
FLUID s
FLUKE dsy
FLUKY
FLUME ds
*FLUMP s
*FLUNG
*FLUNK sy
FLUOR s
FLUSH
*FLUTE drs
y
FLUTY
FLUYT s
FLYBY s
FLYER s
FLYTE ds
FOALS*
FOAMS*
FOAMY*
FOCAL
FOCUS
FOEHN s
FOGEY s
FOGGY
FOGIE s
FOHNS*
FOILS
FOINS*
FOIST s
FOLDS
FOLEY s
FOLIA r
FOLIC
*FOLIO s
FOLKS*y
FOLKY*
FOLLY
FONDS*
FONDU*es
FONTS*
FOODS*
FOOLS*
*FOOTS*y
FOOTY*
FORAM*s

FORAY*s
FORBS
*FORBY*e
FORCE drs
FORDO
FORDS*
*FORES*t
FORGE drs
t
FORGO t
FORKS*
FORKY*
FORME*der
s
FORMS*
FORTE*s
FORTH*
FORTS
FORTY*
FORUM s
*FOSSA*es
FOSSE*s
FOULS*
FOUND s
FOUNT s
FOURS
FOVEA els
FOWLS
FOXED
*FOXES
*FOYER s
FRAGS
*FRAIL s
FRAME drs
FRANC s
*FRANK s
FRAPS
FRASS
FRATS
FRAUD s
FRAYS
FREAK sy
FREED
FREER*s
*FREES*t
FREMD
FRENA
FRERE s
a*FRESH
FRETS
FRIAR sy
FRIED
FRIER s
FRIES
FRIGS
*FRILL sy
*FRISE es
*FRISK sy
FRITH*s
a FRITS*
FRITT*s
FRITZ
FRIZZ*y
*FROCK s
FROES
FROGS*
FROND s
FRONS
FRONT s
FRORE
FROSH
FROST sy
FROTH sy
FROWN*s
*FROWS*ty
FROZE n
FRUGS
FRUIT sy
*FRUMP sy
FRYER s
FUBSY*
FUCUS
FUDDY
FUDGE ds
FUELS*
FUGAL
FUGGY
FUGIO s
FUGLE ds
FUGUE*ds
FUGUS*
FUJIS*
FULLS*
FULLY*
FUMED*
FUMER*s

FUMES*
FUMET*s
FUNDI*c
FUNDS*
FUNGI c
FUNGO
FUNKS*
FUNKY*
FUNNY
FURAN es
FURLS*
FUROR es
FURRY
FURZE s
FURZY
FUSED
FUSEE*s
FUSEL*s
FUSES
FUSIL es
FUSSY*
FUSTY
FUTON s
FUZED*
FUZEE*s
FUZES*
FUZIL s
FUZZY*
FYCES*
FYKES*
FYTTE s
GABBY
*GABLE ds
GADDI s
GADID*s
GADIS*
GAFFE*drs
GAFFS*
GAGED
*GAGER*s
GAGES
GAILY
*GAINS*t
GAITS
GALAH*s
GALAS
GALAX*y
GALEA*es
GALES
GALLS
GALLY
GALOP s
a*GAMAS*
GAMAY*s
GAMBA*s
GAMBE*s
GAMBS*
GAMED*
GAMER*s
GAMES*t
GAMEY*
a GAMIC
*GAMIN egs
GAMMA s
GAMMY
GAMPS
GAMUT s
GANEF*s
GANEV*s
GANGS*
GANJA hs
GANOF s
GAOLS*
GAPED
*GAPER*s
a*GAPES*
GAPPY
GARBS
GARDA i
GARNI
GARTH s
GASES
GASPS
GASSY
GASTS*
GATED*
GATER*s
a*GATES*
GATOR s
GAUDS*
GAUDY*
GAUGE drs
GAULT s
GAUMS*
GAUNT
GAURS*

GAUSS
GAUZE s
GAUZY
GAVEL*s
GAVOT s
GAWKS*
GAWKY*
GAWPS*
GAWSY
GAYAL s
GAYER
GAYLY
GAZAR s
GAZED*
GAZER*s
GAZES*
GEARS
GECKO*s
GECKS*
GEEKS*
GEEKY*
GEESE*
GEEST*s
GELDS
GELEE s
GELID
GELTS*
GEMMA e
*GEMMY
GEMOT es
a GENES*
GENET*s
GENIC
GENIE s
GENII
GENIP s
GENOA s
GENOM es
GENRE s
GENRO s
a GENTS*
GENUA*
GENUS*
GEODE s
GEOID s
GERAH s
GERMS*
GERMY*
GESSO
GESTE*s
e GESTS*
GETAS
GETUP s
GEUMS*
a*GHAST
GHATS
*GHAUT s
GHAZI s
GHEES*
*GHOST sy
GHOUL s
GHYLL s
GIANT s
GIBED*
GIBER*s
GIBES*
GIDDY
GIFTS*
GIGAS*
GIGHE
GIGOT s
GIGUE s
GILDS*
GILLS
GILLY
GILTS*
GIMEL s
GIMME s
GIMPS
GIMPY*
GINKS
GINNY
GIPON s
GIPSY*
GIRDS*
GIRLS*
GIRLY*
GIRNS*
*GIRON*s
GIROS*
GIRSH
GIRTH*s
GIRTS*
GISMO s
a GISTS*
GITES*

GIVEN*s
GIVER*s
o GIVES*
GIZMO s
*GLACE s
*GLADE*s
GLADS
GLADY
*GLAIR esy
GLAMS
*GLAND s
GLANS
a GLARE ds
GLARY
*GLASS y
*GLAZE drs
*GLAZY
a GLEAM sy
*GLEAN s
GLEBA e
GLEBE s
GLEDE*s
GLEDS*
GLEED*s
*GLEEK*s
GLEES
*GLEET*sy
GLENS
GLEYS
GLIAL*
GLIAS*
GLIDE drs
GLIFF s
*GLIME*ds
GLIMS*
*GLINT sy
GLITZ y
*GLOAM s
GLOAT s
*GLOBE*ds
GLOBS
GLOGG s
GLOMS*
*GLOOM sy
GLOPS
*GLORY
*GLOSS ay
*GLOST s
*GLOUT s
*GLOVE drs
GLOWS
GLOZE ds
GLUED*
GLUER*s
GLUES
GLUEY*
GLUGS
GLUME*s
GLUMS
GLUON s
*GLUTE*ins
GLUTS*
GLYPH s
GNARL*sy
GNARR*s
GNARS*
GNASH
GNATS*
GNAWN*
GNAWS*
*GNOME s
GOADS*
GOALS*
GOATS
GOBAN gs
GOBOS*
GODET s
GODLY
GOERS*
GOFER s
GOGOS*
GOING s
GOLDS
GOLEM s
GOLFS*
GOLLY
GOMBO s
*GOMER s
GONAD s
GONEF*s
GONER*s
GONGS*
GONIA
GONIF fs
GONOF s
GONZO

GOODS*
GOODY*
GOOEY
GOOFS*
GOOFY*
GOOKS*
GOOKY*
GOONS*
GOONY*
GOOPS
GOOPY*
GOOSE*dsy
GOOSY*
GOPIK
*GORAL s
GORED*
GORES
GORGE drs
t
GORMS*
GORPS*
GORSE s
GORSY
GOTHS*
GOUGE drs
GOURD es
GOUTS
a GOUTY*
GOWAN sy
GOWDS*
GOWKS*
GOWNS
*GOXES
GRAAL s
GRABS*
*GRACE ds
GRADE*drs
GRADS
*GRAFT s
*GRAIL s
*GRAIN sy
GRAMA*s
*GRAMP*as
GRAMS
GRANA*
*GRAND*s
GRANS*
*GRANT*s
*GRAPE sy
GRAPH s
GRAPY
*GRASP s
GRASS y
*GRATE*drs
*GRAVE dln
rs
GRAVY
GRAYS
*GRAZE drs
GREAT s
GREBE s
a*GREED*sy
GREEK
GREEN*sy
a*GREES*
GREET*s
GREGO s
GREYS*
*GRIDE*ds
GRIDS
GRIEF s
*GRIFF es
*GRIFT s
GRIGS
*GRILL es
*GRIME*ds
GRIMY
*GRIND*s
GRINS
*GRIOT s
*GRIPE*drs
y
GRIPS
GRIPT*
GRIPY*
GRIST s
GRITH*s
GRITS*
*GROAN s
GROAT s
GRODY
GROGS*
GROIN s
GROKS*
*GROOM s
*GROPE drs

GROSS
GROSZ ey
GROTS
*GROUP s
*GROUT sy
*GROVE dls
GROWL*sy
GROWN*
GROWS
GRUBS
GRUEL*s
GRUES
*GRUFF sy
GRUME*s
*GRUMP*sy
*GRUNT s
GUACO s
GUANO*s
GUANS*
GUARD*s
GUARS*
GUAVA s
GUCKS*
GUDES*
GUESS
GUEST s
GUFFS*
GUIDE*drs
GUIDS*
GUILD s
GUILE ds
GUILT sy
GUIRO s
GUISE ds
GULAG s
GULAR
GULCH
GULES
GULFS*
GULFY*
GULLS*
GULLY*
GULPS*
GULPY*
*GUMBO s
GUMMA s
GUMMY
GUNKS*
GUNKY*
GUNNY
GUPPY
*GURGE ds
GURRY
GURSH
GURUS
GUSHY*
GUSSY
GUSTO*
GUSTS*
GUSTY*
GUTSY*
GUTTA e
GUTTY
GUYED
GUYOT s
*GWINE
GYBED*
GYBES*
GYOZA s
GYPSY*
GYRAL
GYRED*
GYRES*
GYRON*s
GYROS*e
GYRUS
GYVED*
GYVES*
HAAFS*
HAARS*
HABIT s
HABUS*
HACEK s
stw HACKS*
HADAL
s HADED*
s HADES*
HADJI*s
HADST
HAEMS*
HAETS*
HAFIZ
s HAFTS*
HAHAS*
HAIKA*
HAIKS*

HAIKU*s
HAILS
HAINT s
c*HAIRS*
HAIRY
HAJES
HAJIS*
HAJJI*s
s HAKES*
HAKIM s
HAKUS*
HALAL as
sw HALED*
tw HALER*su
sw*HALES*t
HALID es
HALLO*aos
tw
HALLS
*HALMA*s
HALMS
HALON*s
HALOS*
HALTS
HALVA hs
HALVE ds
HAMAL s
s HAMES*
csw HAMMY
HAMZA hs
c HANCE s
HANDS
s HANDY*
bcw HANGS*
st HANKS*
HANKY*
*HANSA s
HANSE ls
c*HANTS*
HAPAX
HAPLY
HAPPY
cs HARDS*
HARDY*
cs HARED*
HAREM*s
cs*HARES*
cs*HARKS*
HARLS*
ct*HARMS*
s HARPS*
s HARPY*
cg HARRY
HARSH
c*HARTS*
HASPS
c HASTE*dns
HASTY*
t HATCH
HATED*
HATER*s
HATES
s HAUGH s
HAULM*sy
s HAULS*
c*HAUNT s
HAUTE*
s HAVEN*s
s*HAVER*s
s*HAVES*
HAVOC s
cst*HAWED
HAWKS*
HAWSE*rs
HAYED
HAYER s
HAYEY
c*HAZAN s
HAZED*
HAZEL*s
HAZER*s
HAZES*
HEADS*
HEADY*
sw HEALS*
c HEAPS*
HEAPY*
HEARD*
s*HEARS*e
HEART*hsy
s*HEATH*sy
cw*HEATS*
s*HEAVE dnr
s
HEAVY
c HECKS*

c HEDER s
*HEDGE drs
*HEDGY
HEEDS*
w*HEELS*
w HEEZE ds
t*HEFTS*
HEFTY*
HEIGH t
HEILS*
t HEIRS*
t HEIST s
HELIO s
HELIX
HELLO*s
s*HELLS*
w*HELMS*
HELOS*
HELOT*s
w HELPS*
s HELVE ds
HEMAL
rt*HEMES*
c*HEMIC
HEMIN s
HEMPS*
HEMPY*
tw HENCE
HENGE s
HENNA s
HENRY s
HENTS*
HERBS*
HERBY*
s HERDS*
tw HERES*y
HERLS*
HERMA*ei
t HERMS*
HERNS
HERON*s
HEROS
csw HERRY
HERTZ
c HESTS*
ck*HETHS*
s HEUCH s
s HEUGH s
cs HEWED
cs*HEWER s
HEXAD es
*HEXED
HEXER s
*HEXES
HEXYL s
ct HICKS*
c HIDED*
c HIDER*s
c*HIDES*
t HIGHS*
HIGHT*hs
HIJAB s
HIJRA hs
HIKED*
HIKER*s
HIKES*
HILAR*
HILLO*as
cst*HILLS*
c*HILLY*
HILTS*
HILUM
HILUS
HINDS*
w HINGE drs
c*HINKY
sw HINNY
c HINTS*
HIPLY
HIPPO s
cw HIPPY
HIRED
HIREE*s
HIRER*s
s*HIRES*
HISSY
sw HISTS*
*HITCH
HIVED*
cs HIVES*
HOAGY
HOARD*s
*HOARS*e
HOARY*
HOBBY
HOBOS*

cs HOCKS*
HOCUS
HODAD s
s HOERS*
HOGAN s
HOGGS*
HOICK s
HOISE ds
HOIST s
c HOKED*
c*HOKES*
c HOKEY*
HOKKU
HOKUM s
a*HOLDS*
t HOLED*
dtw*HOLES*
HOLEY*
HOLKS*
c*HOLLA s
HOLLO aos
w
w HOLLY
HOLMS*
HOLTS*
HOMED*
*HOMER*s
HOMES*
HOMEY*s
HOMIE rs
HOMOS*
HONAN s
HONDA s
p HONED*
HONER*s
p*HONES*t
p HONEY*s
HONGI*
t HONGS*
HONKS*
HONOR s
HOOCH
HOODS*
HOODY*
p HOOEY s
w HOOFS*
HOOKA*hs
cs HOOKS*
HOOKY*
d HOOLY
w*HOOPS*
bs*HOOTS*
HOOTY*
HOPED
HOPER*s
HOPES
c HOPPY
HORAH*s
c*HORAL*
HORAS*
HORDE ds
t HORNS*
t HORNY*
a HORSE dsy
HORST es
HORSY
HOSED*
HOSEL*s
c HOSEN*
HOSER*s
c*HOSES*
HOSEY*s
HOSTA*s
g HOSTS*
HOTCH
HOTEL s
HOTLY
HOUND s
HOURI*s
HOURS
c HOUSE dlr
s
s HOVEL*s
s*HOVER*s
HOWDY
HOWES
HOWFF*s
HOWFS*
HOWKS*
HOWLS
HOYAS*
HOYLE s
c HUBBY
cs HUCKS*
c HUFFS*
c HUFFY*

HUGER*
HULAS*
HULKS*
HULKY*
HULLO*aos
HULLS*
HUMAN es
HUMIC
HUMID
HUMOR s
HUMPH*s
ctw*HUMPS*
HUMPY*
HUMUS
HUNCH
ct HUNKS*
c HUNKY*
s HUNTS*
*HURDS
ct HURLS*
HURLY*
HURRY
HURST s
HURTS*
HUSKS*
HUSKY*
HUSSY
HUTCH
HUZZA hs
HYDRA es
HYDRO s
HYENA s
s HYING
HYLAS*
HYMEN s
HYMNS*
HYOID s
HYPED*
HYPER*s
HYPES*
HYPHA el
HYPOS*
HYRAX
HYSON s
IAMBI*c
IAMBS*
ICHOR s
d ICIER
ICILY
drv ICING s
bdk ICKER s
lnp
stw
ICONS
ICTIC
r ICTUS
*IDEAL*s
IDEAS*
IDIOM s
IDIOT s
s IDLED*
s IDLER*s
s IDLES*t
IDOLS
IDYLL*s
IDYLS*
dfg IGGED
jpr
wz
IGLOO s
IGLUS*
IHRAM s
IKATS
e IKONS*
ILEAC*
ILEAL
p ILEUM
p ILEUS
ILIAC*
ILIAD*s
f ILIAL*
cm ILIUM
bfg ILLER
hkm
stw
*IMAGE drs
IMAGO s
IMAMS*
IMAUM s
l IMBED s
IMBUE ds
IMIDE*s
IMIDO*
IMIDS
*IMINE s
IMINO

IMMIX
glp IMPED e
w
IMPEL s
IMPIS*h
djl IMPLY
ps
INANE rs
INAPT
INARM s
INBYE*
INCOG s
INCUR s
INCUS e
INDEX
INDIE s
INDOL es
w INDOW s
INDRI s
INDUE ds
INEPT
INERT s
INFER s
INFIX
INFOS*
INFRA
djm INGLE s
st
INGOT s
mp INION s
dfj INKED
klo
pw
jlp INKER s
stw
tw INKLE s
INLAY s
INLET s
bdf INNED
gps
tw
dgp INNER s
stw
INPUT s
INRUN s
INSET s
hlm INTER ns
stw
INTIS*
INTRO ns
INURE ds
INURN s
INVAR s
*IODIC
IODID es
IODIN es
bp IONIC s
b IOTAS*
t IRADE s
p*IRATE r
IRIDS
afh*IRING
mstw
d IRKED
IROKO s
IRONE*drs
g IRONS*
IRONY*
ISBAS*
am*ISLED*
al ISLES*
ISLET*s
ISSEI s
t ISSUE drs
ISTLE s
bfp ITCHY*
w
ITEMS*
cde ITHER
hlm
twz
*IVIED
c*IVIES
IVORY
IXIAS*
IXORA s
IXTLE s
s IZARS*
JABOT s
JACAL s
JACKS*
JACKY*
JADED*
JADES*
*JAGER s
JAGGS*
JAGGY*
JAGRA s
JAILS
JAKES*
JALAP s
JALOP sy
JAMBE*ds
JAMBS*
JAMMY
JANES
JANTY
JAPAN s
JAPED
*JAPER*sy
JAPES
JARLS*
JATOS*
JAUKS
*JAUNT sy
JAUPS*
JAVAS*
JAWAN s
*JAWED
JAZZY*
JEANS*
d JEBEL s
JEEPS*
JEERS*
JEFES*
JEHAD s
JEHUS*
JELLO*s
JELLS
JELLY*
*JEMMY
JENNY
JERID s
JERKS*
JERKY*
JERRY
JESSE*ds
JESTS*
JETES*
JETON s
JETTY
JEWEL s
JIBBS*
JIBED*
JIBER*s
JIBES*
JIFFS*
JIFFY
JIGGY
JIHAD s
JILLS
JILTS*
*JIMMY
JIMPY*
JINGO
JINKS
d JINNI*s
d*JINNS*
JIVED*
JIVER*s
JIVES*
JIVEY*
*JNANA s
JOCKO*s
JOCKS*
JOEYS*
JOHNS*
JOINS*
JOINT*s
JOIST s
JOKED*
JOKER*s
JOKES
JOKEY*
JOLES
JOLLY
JOLTS*
JOLTY*
JOMON
*JONES
JORAM s
JORUM s
JOTAS*
JOTTY
JOUAL s
JOUKS*
JOULE s
*JOUST s
JOWAR s
*JOWED
JOWLS
JOWLY*
JOYED
JUBAS*
JUBES*
JUCOS*
JUDAS
JUDGE drs
JUDOS
JUGAL*
JUGUM s
JUICE drs
JUICY
JUJUS*
JUKED*
JUKES
JUKUS*
JULEP s
*JUMBO s
JUMPS
JUMPY*
*JUNCO s
JUNKS*
JUNKY*
JUNTA s
*JUNTO s
JUPES*
*JUPON s
JURAL*
JURAT*s
JUREL s
JUROR s
JUSTS*
JUTES
JUTTY
KABAB s
KABAR s
KABOB s
KADIS*
KAFIR s
KAGUS*
KAIAK s
KAIFS*
KAILS
KAINS
KAKAS*
KAKIS*
KALAM s
KALES
*KALIF s
KALPA cks
KAMES*
KAMIK*s
KANAS
KANES
KANJI s
KANZU s
KAONS*
KAPAS*
KAPHS*
KAPOK s
KAPPA s
KAPUT t
KARAT es
KARMA s
KARNS*
KAROO s
KARST s
KARTS
KASHA s
KATAS*
KAURI s
KAURY
KAVAS*s
KAYAK s
KAYOS*
KAZOO s
KBARS
KEBAB s
KEBAR s
KEBOB s
KECKS*
*KEDGE ds
KEEFS*
KEEKS*
KEELS
s KEENS*
KEEPS*
s KEETS*
KEEVE s
KEFIR s
KEIRS*
KELEP s
KELIM s
KELLY
s KELPS*
KELPY*
KELTS*
KEMPS*
KEMPT*
KENAF s
KENCH
KENDO s
KENOS*
KENTE*s
KEPIS*
KERBS*
KERFS*
*KERNE*dls
KERNS
s KERRY
s*KETCH
KETOL*s
KEVEL s
*KEVIL s
*KEXES
*KEYED
KHADI s
KHAFS*
KHAKI s
KHANS*
KHAPH s
KHATS
KHEDA hs
*KHETH*s
KHETS
KHOUM s
KIANG s
KIBBE hs
KIBBI s
KIBEI*s
KIBES*
KIBLA hs
KICKS*
KICKY
KIDDO s
s KIDDY
KIEFS*
s KIERS*
KILIM s
s*KILLS*
KILNS*
KILOS*
KILTS*
KILTY*
KINAS*e
KINDS*
KINES*
KINGS*
KININ s
s*KINKS*
KINKY
KINOS*
KIOSK s
KIRKS
KIRNS*
KISSY*
KISTS*
s KITED*
KITER*s
s KITES*
KITHE*ds
KITHS*
KITTY
KIVAS*
KIWIS
*KLICK s
KLIKS*
*KLONG s
*KLOOF s
*KLUGE ds
*KLUTZ y
KNACK s
KNAPS
KNARS*
KNAUR s
*KNAVE s
KNAWE ls
KNEAD s
KNEED
KNEEL*s
KNEES*
KNELL s
KNELT
KNIFE drs
KNISH
KNITS
KNOBS
*KNOCK s
KNOLL sy
KNOPS*
KNOSP s
KNOTS*
KNOUT s
KNOWN*s
KNOWS
*KNURL*sy
KNURS*
KOALA s
KOANS*
KOBOS*
KOELS*
KOHLS*
KOINE s
KOJIS*
KOLAS*
KOLOS*
KOMBU s
KONKS*
KOOKS*
KOOKY*
KOPEK s
KOPHS*
KOPJE s
KOPPA s
KORAI*
KORAS*
KORAT*s
KORMA s
KORUN ay
KOTOS*
KOTOW*s
KRAAL s
*KRAFT s
KRAIT s
KRAUT s
KREEP s
KREWE s
*KRILL s
KRONA
KRONE nr
KROON is
KRUBI s
KUDOS
KUDUS*
KUDZU s
KUFIS*
KUGEL s
KUKRI s
KULAK is
KUMYS
KURTA s
KURUS
KUSSO s
KVASS*
KVELL s
*KYACK s
KYAKS
KYARS*
KYATS*
KYLIX
KYRIE s
KYTES*
KYTHE ds
LAARI
LABEL s
LABIA l
LABOR s
LABRA
p*LACED*
p LACER*s
gp*LACES*
LACEY*
bcf LACKS*
ps
b LADED*
LADEN*s
b LADER*s
bcg LADES*
LADLE drs
LAEVO
LAGAN s
*LAGER s
LAHAR s
LAICH*s
LAICS*
LAIGH s
LAIRD*s
fg*LAIRS*
LAITH
LAITY
fs LAKED*
fs LAKER*s
fs LAKES*
LAKHS*
LALLS
lu*LAMAS*
LAMBS*
LAMBY*
bf LAMED*hs
bf LAMER*
bf LAMES*t
*LAMIA es
c*LAMPS*
LANAI s
g LANCE drs
t
aeg*LANDS*
fp*LANES*
c LANKY*
LAPEL s
LAPIN s
LAPIS
e*LAPSE*drs
*LARCH
LARDS*
LARDY*
LAREE s
bfg*LARES
LARGE rs
LARGO s
LARIS*
LARKS
LARKY*
a*LARUM s
LARVA els
LASED*
LASER*s
LASES*
LASSI*es
LASSO*s
bc LASTS*
ks LATCH
aep LATED*
s
p LATEN*st
eps LATER*
LATEX*
LATHE*drs
LATHI*s
LATHS*
LATHY*
LATKE s
LATTE nrs
LAUAN s
LAUDS*
LAUGH s
*LAURA es
LAVAS*h
s LAVED*
cs*LAVER*s
cs*LAVES*
bcf*LAWED
LAWNS
LAWNY
LAXER
f*LAXES t
LAXLY
cfp LAYED
s
fps LAYER s
*LAYIN gs
LAYUP s
LAZAR s
bg LAZED*
bg LAZES*
bp*LEACH y
p LEADS*
LEADY*
LEAFS*
LEAFY*
b LEAKS*
LEAKY*
cg LEANS*
LEANT*
LEAPS*
LEAPT*
*LEARN*st
bc*LEARS*
b LEARY*
p*LEASE*drs
LEASH*
*LEAST*s
cs*LEAVE dnr
s
LEAVY
LEBEN s
fps*LEDGE rs
f*LEDGY
f LEECH
cgs LEEKS*
f LEERS*
LEERY
fgs LEETS*
c*LEFTS*
LEFTY*
*LEGAL s
*LEGER s
LEGES
*LEGGY
e LEGIT s
LEHRS*
LEHUA s
LEMAN s
LEMMA s
LEMON sy
LEMUR s
b*LENDS*
LENES
LENIS
LENOS*
f LENSE*ds
LENTO*s
LEONE s
LEPER s
LEPTA*
f*LETCH
LETHE s
LETUP s
LEUDS*
LEVEE ds
LEVEL s
c*LEVER s
a LEVIN s
c LEVIS
LEWIS
fip*LEXES
LEXIS
LIANA s
LIANE s
LIANG s
LIARD*s
LIARS*
LIBEL s
LIBER s
LIBRA es
LIBRI
LICHI*s
LICHT*s
e LICIT
cfk LICKS*
s
LIDAR s
LIDOS*
LIEGE s
a LIENS*
fp LIERS*
LIEUS*
s LIEVE r
LIFER*s
c LIFTS*
LIGAN ds
LIGER s
abf LIGHT s
ps
LIKED*
LIKEN*s
LIKER*s
LIKES*t
LILAC s
LILOS*
LILTS*
LIMAN*s
LIMAS*
LIMBA*s
LIMBI*c
LIMBO*s
c LIMBS*
LIMBY*
gs LIMED*
LIMEN*s
cgs LIMES*
b LIMEY*s
LIMIT s
LIMNS*
LIMOS*
LIMPA*s
b*LIMPS*y
LINAC s
LINDY
a LINED*
LINEN*sy
a LINER*s
ac LINES*
LINEY*
LINGA*ms
o LINGO*
cfs LINGS*
c LINGY*
LININ gs
bcp*LINKS*
s
s*LINKY*
LINNS
LINOS*
efg LINTS*
fg LINTY*
LINUM s
LIONS
LIPID es
LIPIN s
fs LIPPY
LIRAS*
LIROT h
*LISLE s
LISPS*
LISTS*
LITAI
LITAS
LITER*s
b LITHE r
LITHO s
LITRE s
LIVED*
LIVEN*s
s LIVER*sy
o LIVES*t
LIVID
LIVRE s
*LLAMA s
LLANO s
LOACH
LOADS*
LOAFS
g LOAMS*
LOAMY*
LOANS*
*LOATH e
LOBAR
gs LOBBY
g LOBED*
g*LOBES*
LOBOS*
LOCAL*es
LOCHS*
bcf LOCKS*
LOCOS*
LOCUM s
LOCUS t
LODEN*s
LODES
LODGE drs
LOESS
LOFTS*
LOFTY*
s LOGAN s
LOGES*
c LOGGY
LOGIA
LOGIC s
LOGIN s
LOGOI*
LOGON*s
LOGOS*
s LOIDS*
ae LOINS*
LOLLS*
LOLLY*
c LONER*s
LONGE*drs
fk LONGS*
LOOBY
LOOED
bf LOOEY s
LOOFA*hs
k LOOFS*
bf LOOIE s
LOOKS*
bg LOOMS*
LOONS*
LOONY*
bs*LOOPS*
LOOPY*
LOOSE*dnr
s
c*LOOTS*
es*LOPED*
es LOPER*s
es*LOPES*
fgs LOPPY
f*LORAL
LORAN s
LORDS*
LORES
LORIS
LORRY
LOSEL*s
c LOSER*s

c*LOSES*
fg LOSSY*
LOTAH*s
f LOTAS*
LOTIC
LOTOS
LOTTE drs
b*LOTTO s
LOTUS
cps LOUGH s
LOUIE s
LOUIS
LOUMA s
LOUPE*dns
LOUPS*
cf*LOURS*
f LOURY*
b LOUSE ds
b LOUSY
cfg*LOUTS*
LOVAT s
g LOVED*
cgp*LOVER*s
cg LOVES*
bfg*LOWED*
ps
bfg LOWER*sy
ps
*LOWES*t
s LOWLY
LOWSE
LOXED
*LOXES
LOYAL
LUAUS*
LUBED*
LUBES*
LUCES*
LUCID
cp LUCKS*
p LUCKY*
LUCRE s
e LUDES*
LUDIC
LUFFA*s
bfs LUFFS*
k LUGED*
LUGER*s
k LUGES*
LULLS*
LULUS
LUMAS*
LUMEN s
cfp*LUMPS*
s
cg LUMPY*
LUNAR*s
LUNAS*
g LUNCH
LUNES*
LUNET*s
bp LUNGE*der
s
LUNGI*s
LUNGS*
cfp LUNKS*
b LUNTS*
LUPIN es
LUPUS
LURCH
LURED*
LURER*s
LURES*
LUREX*
LURID
LURKS*
LUSTS*
LUSTY*
LUSUS
LUTEA*l
ef LUTED*
efg*LUTES*
f LUXES*
LWEIS*
*LYARD
LYART
LYASE s
LYCEA
LYCEE s
LYCRA s
fp LYING s
LYMPH s
LYNCH
LYRES*
LYRIC s
LYSED*
LYSES*
LYSIN egs
LYSIS
LYSSA s
LYTIC
LYTTA es
MAARS*
MABES*
MACAW s
MACED
MACER*s
MACES
*MACHE*s
MACHO*s
MACHS*
s MACKS*
MACLE ds
MACON s
MACRO ns
MADAM es
MADLY
MADRE s
MAFIA s
MAFIC
i*MAGES*
MAGIC*s
*MAGMA s
MAGOT s
MAGUS
MAHOE s
MAIDS
MAILE*drs
MAILL*s
e*MAILS*
MAIMS
MAINS
MAIRS
MAIST s
MAIZE s
MAJOR s
MAKAR s
MAKER*s
MAKES*
MAKOS*
*MALAR s
MALES
MALIC e
s*MALLS*
MALMS
MALMY*
s*MALTS*
MALTY*
MAMAS
MAMBA s
*MAMBO s
MAMEY s
*MAMIE s
MAMMA els
MAMMY
MANAS
MANAT*s
MANED*
MANES
*MANGA s
MANGE lrs
y
MANGO s
MANGY
MANIA cs
MANIC s
MANLY
*MANNA ns
MANOR*s
MANOS*
MANSE*s
*MANTA s
*MANUS
MAPLE s
MAQUI s
MARAS*
MARCH
MARCS
MARES
MARGE s
*MARIA
MARKA*s
MARKS
MARLS*
MARLY*
MARRY
MARSE*s
MARSH*y
s*MARTS*
MARVY
MASAS*
MASER s
MASHY
MASKS
MASON s
MASSA*s
MASSE*ds
MASSY*
MASTS*
MATCH
MATED*
MATER*s
MATES
MATEY*s
MATHS*
MATIN gs
MATTE*drs
MATTS*
MATZA hs
MATZO hst
MAUDS*
MAULS*
MAUND*sy
MAUTS*
MAUVE s
MAVEN s
MAVIE s
MAVIN s
MAVIS
*MAWED
*MAXED
*MAXES
MAXIM*as
MAXIS
MAYAN*
MAYAS*
MAYBE s
MAYED
MAYOR*s
MAYOS*
MAYST*
a MAZED*
MAZER*s
as MAZES*
MBIRA s
MEADS*
MEALS*
MEALY*
MEANS*
MEANT*
MEANY*
MEATS
MEATY*
MECCA s
MEDAL s
MEDIA del
ns
MEDIC kos
MEDII
MEEDS*
MEETS*
MEINY
MELDS
MELEE s
MELIC
s*MELLS*
MELON s
s MELTS*
MELTY*
MEMES
MEMOS*
MENAD s
ae*MENDS*
MENSA els
MENSE ds
MENSH
o MENTA l
MENUS*
MEOUS*
MEOWS*
MERCH*
MERCS*
MERCY*
MERER*
MERES*t
e MERGE der
s
MERIT s
s MERKS*
MERLE*s
MERLS*
MERRY
MESAS*
MESHY*
MESIC
*MESNE s
MESON s
MESSY*
METAL*s
METED*
METER*s
METES*
METHS
METIS
METOL s
METRE ds
METRO s
MEWED
MEWLS*
MEZES*
MEZZO s
MIAOU s
MIAOW s
MIASM as
MIAUL s
MICAS*
MICHE ds
MICRA
MICRO ns
MIDDY
s MIDGE st
MIDIS*
a MIDST*s
MIENS*
MIFFS*
MIFFY
MIGGS
MIGHT sy
MIKED*
MIKES*
MIKRA
MILCH
MILDS*
s MILER*s
s MILES*
*MILIA
MILKS
MILKY*
MILLE*drs
t
MILLS
MILOS*
MILPA s
MILTS*
MILTY*
MIMED*
MIMEO*s
MIMER*s
MIMES*
MIMIC s
MINAE*
MINAS*
MINCE drs
MINCY
MINDS*
MINED*
MINER*s
ai MINES*
MINGY
MINIM*as
MINIS*h
MINKE*s
MINKS
MINNY
MINOR s
MINTS*
MINTY*
MINUS
MIRED
MIRES
MIREX*
MIRIN*gs
s*MIRKS*
s MIRKY*
MIRTH s
MIRZA s
MISDO
MISER*sy
MISES*
MISOS*
MISSY*
MISTS*
MISTY*
s MITER*s
s MITES*
MITIS
MITRE ds
MITTS*
MIXED
MIXER s
MIXES
MIXUP s
MIZEN s
MOANS*
MOATS
MOCHA s
s MOCKS*
MODAL s
MODEL*s
MODEM*s
*MODES*t
MODUS
s MOGGY
MOGUL s
MOHEL s
MOHUR s
MOILS
MOIRA i
MOIRE s
MOIST
MOJOS*
s*MOKES*
MOLAL*
MOLAR*s
MOLAS*
MOLDS
MOLDY
a*MOLES*t
MOLLS*
MOLLY*
MOLTO*
s MOLTS*
MOMES*
MOMMA s
MOMMY
MOMUS
MONAD s
MONAS
MONDE s
MONDO s
MONEY s
MONGO els
MONIE ds
MONKS*
MONOS
MONTE s
MONTH s
s MOOCH
MOODS*
MOODY*
MOOED
MOOLA*hs
MOOLS*
MOONS*
MOONY*
MOORS*
MOORY*
MOOSE*
MOOTS
*MOPED*s
MOPER*sy
MOPES
MOPEY*
MORAE*
a*MORAL*es
MORAS*s
MORAY*s
MOREL*s
MORES
MORNS*
MORON s
MORPH os
MORRO sw
MORSE*l
MORTS
MOSEY s
MOSKS*
MOSSO*
MOSSY*
MOSTE*
MOSTS*
MOTEL*s
e MOTES*
MOTET*s
MOTEY*
MOTHS*
MOTHY*
MOTIF s
MOTOR s
MOTTE*s
*MOTTO*s
MOTTS*
*MOUCH
MOUES*
MOULD sy
MOULT s
MOUND s
a MOUNT s
MOURN s
MOUSE drs
y
MOUSY
MOUTH sy
MOVED*
*MOVER*s
MOVES*
MOVIE s
*MOWED
MOWER s
MOXAS*
MOXIE s
MOZOS*
MUCHO*
MUCID
MUCIN s
a MUCKS*
MUCKY*
MUCOR s
MUCRO
MUCUS
MUDDY
MUDRA s
MUFFS*
MUFTI s
MUGGS*
MUGGY*
MUHLY
MUJIK s
MULCH
MULCT s
MULED*
MULES*
MULEY*s
MULLA*hs
MULLS*
MUMMS*
MUMMY*
MUMPS
MUMUS*
MUNCH
MUNGO s
MUNIS*
MUONS*
MURAL*s
MURAS*
MURED*
MURES*
MUREX*
MURID s
MURKS*
MURKY*
MURRA*s
MURRE*sy
MURRS*
MURRY*
MUSCA et
a*MUSED*
a*MUSER*s
a*MUSES*
MUSHY*
MUSIC ks
MUSKS*
MUSKY*
MUSSY*
MUSTH*s
MUSTS*
MUSTY*
s MUTCH
MUTED*
MUTER*
*MUTES*t
MUTON s
MUTTS*
MUZZY
MYLAR s
MYNAH*s
MYNAS*
MYOID
MYOMA s
MYOPE s
MYOPY
MYRRH s
MYSID s
MYTHS*
MYTHY*
NAANS*
NABES*
NABIS
NABOB s
NACHO s
*NACRE ds
NADAS*
NADIR s
NAEVI
NAFFS*
s NAGGY
NAIAD s
NAIFS*
s*NAILS*
NAIRA s
NAIRU s
NAIVE rs
s NAKED
NAKFA s
NALAS
NALED s
NAMED*
NAMER*s
NAMES*
j*NANAS*
NANNY
NAPAS*
NAPES
NAPPA s
NAPPE drs
s NAPPY
*NARCO*s
NARCS
NARDS*
s*NARES
NARIC
NARIS
s*NARKS*
s NARKY*
NASAL s
NASTY
NATAL
s NATCH
e*NATES
g NATTY
NAVAL
NAVAR s
NAVEL*s
k*NAVES*
NAVVY
NAWAB s
NAZIS*
s NEAPS*
a*NEARS*
NEATH
NEATS
s NECKS*
*NEDDY
NEEDS*
NEEDY*
NEEMS*
NEEPS*
NEGUS
NEIFS*
NEIGH s
NEIST
NELLY
e NEMAS*
NENES*
NEONS
NERDS*
NERDY*
NEROL is
i NERTS
NERTZ
NERVE ds
NERVY
NESTS*
NETOP s
NETTS*
NETTY*
NEUKS*
NEUME*s
NEUMS*
NEVER
NEVES
NEVUS
NEWEL s
*NEWER
NEWIE s
NEWLY
NEWSY*
NEWTS*
NEXUS
NGWEE
NICAD s
NICER*
NICHE ds
s NICKS*
NICOL s
NIDAL
NIDED*
NIDES
NIDUS
NIECE s
NIEVE s
NIFTY
NIGHS*
k NIGHT*sy
NIHIL s
NILLS
NIMBI
NINES*
NINJA s
NINNY
NINON s
NINTH s
NIPAS*
s NIPPY
NISEI s
NISUS
u NITER*sy
u NITES*
NITID
NITON s
NITRE s
NITRO s
NITTY
NIVAL
NIXED*
NIXES*
NIXIE s
NIZAM s
ks NOBBY
NOBLE rs
NOBLY
k NOCKS*
a NODAL
NODDY
a*NODES*
NODUS
NOELS*
NOGGS*
NOHOW
NOILS
NOILY
NOIRS*
NOISE ds
NOISY
NOLOS*
NOMAD*s
NOMAS*
NOMEN
g NOMES*
NOMOI
NOMOS
NONAS*
*NONCE s
NONES
NONET*s
NONYL s
s NOOKS*
NOONS*
NOOSE drs
*NOPAL s
NORIA*s
NORIS*
NORMS*
NORTH s
NOSED*
g*NOSES*
NOSEY*
NOTAL*
NOTCH
NOTED*
NOTER*s
NOTES*
NOTUM
NOUNS*
NOVAE*
NOVAS*
NOVEL s
NOWAY s
NOWTS*
ks NUBBY
NUBIA s
NUCHA el
NUDER*
NUDES*t
NUDGE drs
NUDIE s
NUDZH
NUKED*
NUKES
NULLS*
NUMBS*
NUMEN
NURDS
k NURLS*
NURSE drs
NUTSY*
NUTTY

NYALA s
NYLON s
NYMPH aos
OAKEN
OAKUM s
rs OARED
OASES
OASIS
bcr OASTS*
t
OATEN
bc OATER s
OATHS*
ls*OAVES
OBEAH s
OBELI a
OBESE*
OBEYS
c*OBIAS*
OBITS
OBJET s
gh OBOES*
*OBOLE*s
OBOLI*
OBOLS*
OCCUR s
OCEAN s
t OCHER sy
OCHRE ads
OCHRY
cdh OCKER s
lmr
OCREA e
OCTAD s
OCTAL
OCTAN est
OCTET s
OCTYL s
l OCULI
ODAHS
cdf ODDER
n
ODDLY
ODEON s
ODEUM s
ODIST s
ps ODIUM s
ODORS
*ODOUR s
ODYLE*s
ODYLS*
OFFAL s
d OFFED
cdg OFFER s
s OFTEN
ls OFTER
OGAMS
y*OGEES*
OGHAM s
*OGIVE s
OGLED
OGLER*s
b OGLES*
OGRES*s
OHIAS*
o OHING
OHMIC
OIDIA
bcd OILED
fmr
st
bcm OILER s
t
OINKS
OKAPI s
t*OKAYS*
OKEHS*
OKRAS*
gh OLDEN
bcf OLDER
ghm
ps
OLDIE s
OLEIC
OLEIN es
OLEOS*
OLEUM s
fp OLIOS*
*OLIVE s
h OLLAS*
o*OLOGY
*OMASA
bcs OMBER s
hs OMBRE s
*OMEGA s
OMENS*

cgh OMERS*
v
v OMITS*
ONCET*
ONERY
gr ONION sy
cgi ONIUM
ONLAY s
ONSET s
ONTIC
p*OOHED
OOMPH s
OORIE
OOTID s
b OOZED*
b OOZES*
OPAHS*
cn*OPALS*
c*OPENS*
OPERA s
*OPINE ds
cdh*OPING
lmrt
OPIUM s
OPSIN s
OPTED
OPTIC s
ORACH e
bcg ORALS*
m
*ORANG esy
b*ORATE ds
s ORBED
ORBIT s
ORCAS*
ORCIN s
bc ORDER s
ORDOS*
*OREAD s
m ORGAN as
ORGIC
ORIBI s
*ORIEL s
ORLES*
ORLON s
ORLOP s
dfw ORMER s
ORNIS
ORPIN es
m ORRIS
ORTHO
ORZOS*
chn OSIER s
r
c OSMIC s
OSMOL es
OSSIA
OSTIA
bmn OTHER s
pt
c OTTAR s
cdh OTTER s
jlp
rt
lmp OTTOS*
bdf OUGHT s
ns
bjp OUNCE s
OUPHE*s
OUPHS*
OURIE
h OUSEL s
jr OUSTS*
OUTBY e
OUTDO
lpr OUTED
t
cpr OUTER s
st
OUTGO
OUTRE
OUZEL s
OUZOS*
OVALS*
c*OVARY
OVATE
cdw OVENS*
chl OVERS*
mr
c*OVERT*
b*OVINE s
*OVOID s
OVOLI
OVOLO s
OVULE s

bcd*OWING
jlm
rst
vwy
h OWLET s
dg OWNED
d OWNER s
OWSEN*
OXBOW s
OXEYE s
OXIDE*s
OXIDS*
OXIME*s
OXIMS*
OXLIP s
OXTER s
ft OYERS*
*OZONE s
PACAS*
s*PACED*
s PACER*s
s*PACES*
s PACEY*
PACHA s
PACKS*
e*PACTS*
PADDY
PADIS*
PADLE s
PADRE s
PADRI
PAEAN s
*PAEON s
PAGAN s
PAGED
*PAGER*s
PAGES
PAGOD as
PAIKS*
s*PAILS*
PAINS
PAINT*sy
PAIRS
PAISA ns
PAISE
PALEA*el
PALED*
PALER*
s*PALES*t
PALET*s
s*PALLS*
PALLY
PALMS
PALMY*
PALPI*
PALPS
PALSY*
PAMPA s
PANDA s
PANDY
PANED*
PANEL*s
PANES
*PANGA*s
PANGS*
PANIC s
PANNE drs
PANSY*
PANTO*s
PANTS
PANTY*
PAPAL*
PAPAS*
PAPAW*s
*PAPER sy
PAPPI
PAPPY
PARAE*
PARAS*
e*PARCH
PARDI*e
PARDS*
PARDY*
s PARED*
PAREO*s
s PARER*s
s*PARES*
PAREU*s
s PARGE dst
PARGO s
PARIS h
PARKA*s
s*PARKS*
PARLE dsy
PAROL es
PARRS*

s PARRY*
s PARSE*cdr
s
PARTS
PARTY
PARVE
*PARVO s
PASEO*s
u PASES*
PASHA*s
PASSE*del
rs
PASTA*s
PASTE*dlr
s
PASTS*
PASTY*
PATCH y
PATED*
PATEN*st
PATER*s
s*PATES*
PATHS*
PATIN aes
PATIO s
PATLY
PATSY*
PATTY
PAUSE drs
PAVAN es
PAVED*
*PAVER*s
PAVES
*PAVID
s PAVIN gs
PAVIS e
*PAWED
PAWER s
PAWKY
PAWLS
s*PAWNS*
*PAXES
s PAYED
PAYEE s
PAYER s
PAYOR s
PEACE ds
*PEACH y
PEAGE*s
PEAGS*
s PEAKS*
PEAKY*
PEALS*
s PEANS*
*PEARL*sy
s*PEARS*
PEART*
*PEASE*ns
PEATS
PEATY*
PEAVY
PECAN s
PECHS*
s PECKS*
PECKY*
PEDAL os
PEDES
PEDRO s
PEEKS*
s*PEELS*
PEENS*
PEEPS*
s PEERS*
PEERY
PEEVE ds
PEINS*
s PEISE ds
PEKAN s
PEKES
PEKIN s
PEKOE s
PELES*
PELFS*
PELON
s PELTS*
PENAL
s PENCE l
su*PENDS*
PENES
PENGO s
PENIS
PENNA e
PENNE dr
PENNI as
PENNY
PEONS

PEONY*
PEPLA
PEPOS
PEPPY
PERCH
PERDU es
PERDY
PEREA*
PERES*
PERIL*s
PERIS*h
PERKS*
PERKY*
s PERMS*
PERPS*
PERRY
PERSE s
PERVS*
PESKY
PESOS*
PESTO*s
PESTS*
PESTY*
PETAL s
PETER s
PETIT e
PETTI
PETTO
PETTY
PEWEE s
PEWIT s
PHAGE s
PHASE ds
PHIAL s
PHLOX
*PHONE*dsy
PHONO*ns
PHONS
PHONY*
PHOTO*gns
PHOTS
PHPHT
PHUTS
*PHYLA er
PHYLE
PIANO*s
PIANS*
PIBAL s
ae PICAL*
s PICAS*
PICKS*
PICKY
PICOT s
PICUL s
a PIECE drs
s PIERS*
PIETA s
PIETY
PIGGY
PIGMY
PIING
PIKAS*
s PIKED*
s PIKER*s
s PIKES*
PIKIS*
PILAF fs
PILAR
PILAU s
PILAW s
PILEA
s PILED*
PILEI*
s PILES*
PILIS*
s*PILLS*
PILOT s
PILUS
PIMAS*
PIMPS
PINAS*
*PINCH
os PINED*
os PINES*
PINEY*
PINGO*s
PINGS*
PINKO*s
PINKS
PINKY
PINNA els
s PINNY
PINON s
PINOT s
PINTA*s
s*PINTO*s

PINTS*
PINUP s
PIONS
PIOUS
PIPAL s
PIPED*
PIPER*s
PIPES*
PIPET*s
PIPIT s
PIQUE dst
PIRNS*
PIROG i
PISCO s
PISOS*
PISTE s
PITAS*
*PITCH y
PITHS*
PITHY*
PITON s
PITTA s
PIVOT s
PIXEL s
PIXES
PIXIE s
PIZZA sz
*PLACE drs
t
*PLACK s
PLAGE s
*PLAID s
*PLAIN st
PLAIT s
*PLANE*drs
t
*PLANK*s
PLANS*
PLANT*s
s*PLASH y
PLASM as
*PLATE*dnr
s
s*PLATS*
PLATY*s
PLAYA*s
s*PLAYS*
PLAZA s
*PLEAD*s
*PLEAS*e
PLEAT*s
PLEBE*s
PLEBS*
PLENA
PLEON s
PLEWS*
PLICA el
PLIED
*PLIER*s
PLIES
u*PLINK s
PLODS*
PLONK s
PLOPS
PLOTS
PLOTZ*
PLOWS
PLOYS*
*PLUCK sy
PLUGS
PLUMB*s
PLUME*ds
*PLUMP*s
PLUMS
PLUMY*
*PLUNK sy
*PLUSH*y
PLYER s
POACH y
POBOY s
POCKS*
POCKY*
PODGY
PODIA
POEMS*
POESY
POETS*
POGEY s
POILU s
POIND s
POINT esy
POISE*drs
s POKED*
POKER*s
s*POKES*
POKEY*s

POLAR s
POLED*
POLER*s
POLES
*POLIO s
POLIS h
POLKA s
POLLS*
POLOS*
POLYP*is
POLYS*
POMES*
POMOS*
POMPS*
*PONCE ds
PONDS*
PONES
PONGS*
POOCH
POODS*
POOHS
s POOLS*
s POONS*
POOPS
POORI*s
POPES
POPPA s
POPPY
POPSY*
PORCH
s PORED*
s*PORES*
*PORGY
PORKS*
PORKY*
PORNO*s
PORNS*
PORNY*
s*PORTS*
POSED*
POSER*s
e*POSES*
POSIT s
POSSE st
POSTS*
POTSY*
*POTTO s
s POTTY
*POUCH y
POUFF*esy
POUFS*
POULT s
POUND s
POURS
s*POUTS*
POUTY*
POWER s
POXED
*POXES
POYOU s
PRAAM s
PRAHU s
PRAMS
s*PRANG s
*PRANK s
PRAOS*
*PRASE s
u*PRATE*drs
s*PRATS*
PRAUS*
PRAWN s
s*PRAYS*
PREED
PREEN*s
s*PREES*
PREOP s
PREPS
PRESA
PRESE t
PRESS
*PREST os
PREXY*
PREYS*
*PRICE drs
y
*PRICK sy
PRICY
*PRIDE ds
PRIED
s PRIER s
PRIES t
s*PRIGS*
*PRILL s
PRIMA*ls
*PRIME*drs
PRIMI*

PRIMO*s
PRIMP*s
PRIMS
*PRINK s
s PRINT s
PRION s
PRIOR sy
u*PRISE ds
PRISM s
PRISS y
PRIVY
PRIZE drs
PROAS*
*PROBE drs
PRODS
PROEM s
PROFS*
PROGS*
*PROLE gs
PROMO*s
PROMS
PRONE
PRONG s
*PROOF s
PROPS*
u*PROSE*drs
PROSO*s
PROSS*
PROST*
PROSY
PROUD
*PROVE dnr
s
PROWL*s
PROWS
PROXY
*PRUDE s
*PRUNE drs
PRUTA h
s PRYER s
PSALM s
PSEUD os
*PSHAW s
PSOAE
PSOAI
PSOAS
PSYCH eos
PUBES
PUBIC
PUBIS
PUCES*
PUCKA*
PUCKS*
PUDGY
PUDIC
PUFFS*
PUFFY*
PUGGY
PUJAH*s
PUJAS*
PUKED*
PUKES
PUKKA
PULED*
PULER*s
PULES*
PULIK*
PULIS*
PULLS*
PULPS*
PULPY*
PULSE*drs
PUMAS*
PUMPS
PUNAS*
PUNCH y
PUNGS*
PUNJI s
PUNKA*hs
s PUNKS*
s PUNKY*
PUNNY
*PUNTO*s
PUNTS*
PUNTY*
PUPAE*
PUPAL*
PUPAS
PUPIL s
PUPPY
PUPUS*
PURDA hs
PUREE*ds
PURER*
s*PURGE drs
PURIN*es

PURIS*mt
PURLS*
PURRS*
PURSE*drs
PURSY*
PURTY
o*PUSES
PUSHY*
PUSSY*
PUTON s
PUTTI*e
PUTTO*
PUTTS*
PUTTY*
PYGMY
PYINS
PYLON s
PYOID
PYRAN s
PYRES*
PYREX*
PYRIC
PYROS*
PYXES
PYXIE s
PYXIS
QADIS*
QAIDS
QANAT s
QOPHS*
QUACK sy
s QUADS*
QUAFF s
QUAGS*
QUAIL*s
QUAIS*
QUAKE drs
QUAKY
QUALE
QUALM sy
QUANT as
s QUARE
s QUARK s
QUART eos
z
s QUASH
QUASI
QUASS
e QUATE
QUAYS*
QUBIT s
QUEAN s
QUEEN s
QUEER s
QUELL s
QUERN s
QUERY
QUEST s
QUEUE drs
QUEYS*
QUICK s
es QUIDS*
QUIET s
QUIFF s
s QUILL s
QUILT s
QUINS*y
s QUINT*aes
e QUIPS*
QUIPU*s
s QUIRE ds
QUIRK sy
s QUIRT s
QUITE*
QUITS*
QUODS*
QUOIN s
QUOIT s
QUOLL s
QUOTA s
QUOTE drs
QUOTH a
QURSH
RABAT os
RABBI nst
a RABIC
RABID
bgt*RACED*
bt RACER*s
bgt*RACES*
ctw RACKS*
RACON s
RADAR s
RADII
RADIO s
RADIX

RADON s
d RAFFS*
cdg RAFTS*
k
RAGAS
RAGED
d*RAGEE*s
RAGES
RAGGS*
bcd RAGGY*
RAGIS*
RAIAS*
b*RAIDS*
bdf*RAILS*
gt
bdg*RAINS*
t
bg RAINY*
bfp RAISE*drs
RAITA s
RAJAH*s
RAJAS*
RAJES
b RAKED*
*RAKEE*s
RAKER*s
bcd RAKES*
RAKIS*h
RAKUS*
RALES
o*RALLY e
RALPH s
RAMAL
RAMEE s
*RAMEN
RAMET s
*RAMIE*s
RAMMY
cgt*RAMPS*
*RAMUS
pt RANCE s
bc RANCH o
bg*RANDS*
b RANDY*
RANEE s
go RANGE*drs
o RANGY*
RANID*s
RANIS
bcf RANKS*
pt
bg*RANTS*
cd*RAPED*
d*RAPER*s
cdg*RAPES*
t
RAPHE s
RAPID s
RARED*
RARER*
u*RARES*t
e RASED*
e RASER*s
cep RASES*
u
g*RASPS*
RASPY*
RATAL s
RATAN sy
c RATCH
cgo RATED*
p
RATEL*s
cfg RATER*s
ikp
cgo*RATES*
pu
RATHE*r
RATIO ns
RATOS*
b RATTY
bcg RAVED*
gt RAVEL*s
cg RAVEN*s
bcg*RAVER*s
bcg*RAVES*
t
RAVIN egs
bd RAWER
RAWIN s
bcd RAWLY
*RAXED
p*RAXES
*RAYAH*s
RAYAS*

bdf RAYED
gp
c RAYON s
bcg RAZED*
RAZEE*ds
bg RAZER*s
bcg RAZES*
RAZOR s
bp*REACH
p REACT s
READD*s
bdo READS*
t
b READY*
REALM*s
REALS*
bcd REAMS*
REAPS*
p REARM*s
d*REARS*
REATA s
g*REAVE drs
REBAR s
REBBE s
REBEC ks
REBEL s
p REBID s
REBOP s
REBUS
REBUT s
p REBUY s
RECAP s
RECCE s
RECIT es
dw RECKS*
RECON s
RECTA l
RECTI
RECTO rs
RECUR s
p RECUT s
REDAN s
REDDS*
REDED*
b REDES*
u REDIA els
REDID
REDIP st
REDLY
REDON*es
cu REDOS*
REDOX*
p REDRY
REDUB s
REDUX
REDYE ds
bcg REEDS*
g REEDY*
REEFS*
REEFY*
bc REEKS*
REEKY*
c*REELS*
f REEST*s
REEVE ds
REFED
REFEL lst
p REFER s
REFIT s
p REFIX
REFLY
REFRY
*REGAL e
REGES
b REGMA
REGNA l
REHAB s
REHEM s
REIFS*
REIFY*
REIGN s
REINK*s
REINS*
REIVE drs
REJIG s
REKEY s
RELAX
RELAY s
RELET s
RELIC st
RELIT
p REMAN ds
REMAP s
REMET
REMEX
*REMIT s

p REMIX t
RENAL
t*RENDS*
RENEW s
RENIG s
RENIN s
RENTE*drs
b RENTS*
REOIL s
p REPAY s
REPEG s
REPEL s
REPIN es
REPLY
*REPOS*e
REPOT*s
REPPS*
REPRO s
RERAN
RERIG s
RERUN s
RESAT
RESAW ns
RESAY s
RESEE dkn
s
p RESET s
RESEW ns
RESID es
RESIN sy
RESIT es
RESOD s
RESOW ns
cpw RESTS*
RETAG s
p RETAX
w*RETCH
RETEM*s
RETIA l
RETIE ds
RETRO s
RETRY
REUSE ds
REVEL s
bt REVET s
p REVUE s
REWAN
REWAX
bc REWED s
REWET s
REWIN ds
REWON
p*REXES
RHEAS*
*RHEME s
RHEUM sy
RHINO s
RHOMB is
RHUMB as
RHYME drs
RHYTA
tu RIALS*
RIANT
RIATA s
RIBBY
bt RIBES
pt*RICED*
p RICER*s
pt*RICES*
RICIN gs
bcp RICKS*
tw
a RIDER*s
bgi*RIDES*
p
bf RIDGE dls
RIDGY
ao RIELS*
RIFER*
g RIFFS*
t RIFLE drs
dg RIFTS*
abf RIGHT osy
w
f RIGID
RIGOR s
a RILED*
RILES*
RILEY*
g RILLE*dst
bdf*RILLS*
gkpt
gp RIMED*
pt RIMER*s
cgp RIMES*
g RINDS*

RINDY*
bw RINGS*
bdp*RINKS*
RINSE*drs
RIOJA s
g RIOTS*
g RIPED*
RIPEN*s
g RIPER*
cgt RIPES*t
a RISEN*
RISER*s
abc RISES*
fikp
RISHI s
bf RISKS*
f RISKY*
RISUS
fw RITES*
RITZY*
RIVAL s
RIVED*
d RIVEN*
d RIVER*s
d RIVES*
gpt RIVET*s
RIYAL s
b ROACH
b ROADS*
ROAMS*
g ROANS*
ROARS
*ROAST s
p ROBED*
p*ROBES*
ROBIN gs
ROBLE s
ROBOT s
bcf ROCKS*
t
ROCKY*
RODEO*s
e*RODES*
ROGER s
bd ROGUE ds
b*ROILS*
ROILY
p*ROLES*
ROLFS*
dt ROLLS*
ROMAN os
ROMEO s
t ROMPS*
RONDO s
b ROODS*
p ROOFS*
bc ROOKS*
ROOKY*
bgv ROOMS*
b ROOMY*
ROOSE drs
ROOST s
ROOTS
ROOTY*
g*ROPED*
gp ROPER*sy
gt*ROPES*
ROPEY*
ROQUE st
p ROSED*
bep*ROSES*
ROSET*s
ROSHI s
ROSIN gsy
ROTAS*
c ROTCH e
ROTES*
ROTIS*
ROTLS*
ROTOR*s
ROTOS*
ROTTE dnr
s
ROUEN*s
ROUES*
ROUGE ds
t ROUGH sy
ag ROUND s
cg ROUPS*
c ROUPY*
acg ROUSE drs
*ROUST s
c ROUTE*drs
d ROUTH*s
gt*ROUTS*
dgp ROVED*

p*ROVEN*
dpt*ROVER*s
dgp ROVES*
t
ROWAN s
c ROWDY
bct*ROWED
t ROWEL s
ROWEN s
cgp ROWER s
gt ROWTH s
ROYAL s
RUANA s
g RUBBY
RUBEL*s
RUBES*
RUBLE s
RUBUS
RUCHE ds
ct RUCKS*
RUDDS*
c RUDDY*
c RUDER*y
RUERS*
t RUFFE*ds
g RUFFS*
RUGAE*
f RUGAL*
RUGBY
t RUING*
b RUINS*
RULED*
RULER*s
RULES*
RUMBA s
RUMEN s
c RUMMY
RUMOR s
cfg*RUMPS*
t
p RUNES*
RUNGS*
RUNIC
RUNNY
bg RUNTS*
RUNTY*
RUPEE s
c RURAL
cdu*RUSES*
b RUSHY*
RUSKS*
ct RUSTS*
ct RUSTY*
t RUTHS*
RUTIN s
RUTTY
RYKED*
RYKES*
RYNDS*
RYOTS*
SABAL s
SABED
SABER*s
SABES*
SABIN es
SABIR s
u*SABLE s
SABOT s
SABRA s
SABRE ds
SACKS*
SACRA l
t SADES*
SADHE s
SADHU s
t SADIS*mt
SADLY
SAFER*
SAFES*t
SAGAS
SAGER
u*SAGES*t
SAGGY
SAGOS*
SAGUM
SAHIB s
SAICE s
SAIDS
SAIGA s
SAILS
SAINS
SAINT*s
SAITH e
SAJOU s
SAKER*s
SAKES*

SAKIS*
SALAD s
SALAL s
SALEP*s
SALES
SALIC
SALLY
SALMI s
SALOL s
SALON s
SALPA*es
SALPS
SALSA*s
SALTS
SALTY*
SALVE drs
SALVO rs
SAMBA ls
*SAMBO s
SAMEK*hs
SAMPS
SANDS
SANDY*
SANED*
SANER*
*SANES*t
*SANGA*rs
SANGH*s
SANTO ls
SAPID
SAPOR s
SAPPY
SARAN s
SARDS*
SAREE s
SARGE s
SARGO s
SARIN*s
SARIS*
SARKS
SARKY*
SAROD es
SAROS
SASIN s
SASSY*
SATAY s
SATED*
SATEM*
SATES
i SATIN*gsy
SATIS*
SATYR s
SAUCE drs
SAUCH s
SAUCY
SAUGH sy
SAULS*
SAULT*s
SAUNA s
SAURY
SAUTE ds
SAVED*
*SAVER*s
SAVES
SAVIN egs
SAVOR sy
SAVOY s
SAVVY
*SAWED
SAWER s
*SAXES
SAYED s
SAYER s
SAYID s
SAYST*
SCABS
SCADS
SCAGS*
SCALD s
SCALE drs
*SCALL s
SCALP s
SCALY
*SCAMP*is
SCAMS
SCANS
*SCANT*sy
e*SCAPE ds
*SCARE*drs
y
SCARF*s
e*SCARP*hs
e*SCARS*
*SCART*s
SCARY*
SCATS

SCATT*sy
SCAUP s
SCAUR s
SCENA s
a SCEND s
SCENE s
a*SCENT s
SCHAV s
SCHMO es
SCHUL ns
SCHWA s
*SCION s
*SCOFF s
*SCOLD s
*SCONE s
*SCOOP s
*SCOOT s
*SCOPE*ds
SCOPS
*SCORE drs
*SCORN s
ae*SCOTS*
SCOUR s
SCOUT hs
*SCOWL*s
SCOWS
*SCRAG s
*SCRAM s
*SCRAP es
SCREE dns
*SCREW sy
SCRIM ps
SCRIP st
SCROD s
SCRUB s
SCRUM s
SCUBA s
SCUDI*
e SCUDO*
SCUDS
*SCUFF s
SCULK s
*SCULL s
SCULP st
SCUMS*
SCUPS
*SCURF sy
SCUTA*
*SCUTE*s
SCUTS
SCUZZ y
SEALS*
SEAMS*
SEAMY*
SEARS
SEATS
SEBUM s
SECCO s
SECTS*
SEDAN s
SEDER s
*SEDGE s
*SEDGY
SEDUM s
SEEDS*
SEEDY*
SEEKS*
SEELS
SEELY
SEEMS*
SEEPS*
SEEPY*
SEERS*
SEGNI
SEGNO s
SEGOS
SEGUE ds
SEIFS*
SEINE drs
SEISE*drs
SEISM*s
SEIZE drs
SELAH s
SELFS*
SELLE*rs
SELLS
SELVA s
SEMEN*s
SEMES
SEMIS*
SENDS
SENGI
SENNA s
SENOR as
SENSA
SENSE dis

SENTE*
SENTI*
SEPAL s
SEPIA s
*SEPIC
SEPOY s
SEPTA*l
SEPTS*
SERAC*s
SERAI*ls
SERAL*
SERED*
SERER*
SERES*t
SERFS*
SERGE drs
SERIF s
SERIN egs
SEROW s
SERRY
SERUM s
SERVE drs
SERVO s
SETAE*
SETAL*
SETON s
SETTS*
SETUP s
*SEVEN s
*SEVER es
SEWAN s
SEWAR s
SEWED
*SEWER s
*SEXED
*SEXES
SEXTO*ns
SEXTS*
*SHACK os
*SHADE*drs
SHADS*
SHADY*
*SHAFT s
SHAGS
SHAHS
*SHAKE nrs
SHAKO s
SHAKY
*SHALE dsy
*SHALL
*SHALT
SHALY
*SHAME*ds
SHAMS
*SHANK s
SHAPE dnr
s
*SHARD s
*SHARE drs
*SHARK s
SHARN sy
*SHARP sy
*SHAUL s
*SHAVE dnr
s
SHAWL*s
SHAWM*s
SHAWN*
p*SHAWS*
SHAYS
SHEAF*s
*SHEAL*s
*SHEAR*s
SHEAS*
SHEDS*
SHEEN sy
SHEEP
SHEER s
SHEET s
SHEIK hs
SHELF
*SHELL sy
SHEND s
*SHENT
SHEOL s
*SHERD s
SHEWN
SHEWS
*SHIED
SHIEL ds
a SHIER s
*SHIES t
SHIFT sy
*SHILL s
SHILY
SHIMS
SHINE*drs
SHINS
SHINY*
SHIPS
*SHIRE s
SHIRK s
SHIRR s
SHIRT sy
*SHIST s
SHIVA*hs
*SHIVE*rs
SHIVS*
SHLEP ps
SHLUB s
SHOAL sy
SHOAT s
*SHOCK s
SHOED
*SHOER*s
SHOES
SHOGI*s
SHOGS
SHOJI s
*SHONE
*SHOOK*s
SHOOL*s
SHOON*
SHOOS*
*SHOOT*s
SHOPS
a SHORE ds
SHORL s
*SHORN
SHORT sy
SHOTE*s
SHOTS
SHOTT*s
SHOUT s
*SHOVE dlr
s
SHOWN*
SHOWS
SHOWY*
SHOYU s
SHRED s
SHREW ds
SHRIS*
SHRUB s
SHRUG s
SHTIK s
*SHUCK s
SHULN*
SHULS*
SHUNS
*SHUNT*s
*SHUSH
SHUTE*ds
SHUTS
SHWAS*
SHYER s
SHYLY
SIALS*
SIBBS*
SIBYL s
SICES
SICKO*s
SICKS*
SIDED*
a*SIDES*
SIDHE*
*SIDLE drs
SIEGE ds
SIEUR s
SIEVE ds
SIFTS*
SIGHS*
SIGHT*s
SIGIL s
SIGLA
SIGMA s
SIGNA*l
SIGNS*
SIKAS*
SIKER*
SIKES*
SILDS*
*SILEX
SILKS
SILKY*
SILLS
SILLY
SILOS*
SILTS*
SILTY*
SILVA ens
SIMAR*s
SIMAS*
SIMPS
SINCE
SINES*
SINEW*sy
SINGE*drs
SINGS*
SINHS*
SINKS
SINUS
SIPED*
SIPES*
SIRED
SIREE*s
SIREN*s
SIRES
SIRRA hs
SIRUP sy
SISAL s
SISES
SISSY
SITAR s
SITED*
SITES*
SITUP s
SITUS
SIVER s
SIXES
SIXMO s
SIXTE s
SIXTH s
SIXTY
*SIZAR s
SIZED*
SIZER*s
SIZES*
SKAGS*
SKALD s
SKANK sy
SKATE*drs
SKATS
SKEAN es
SKEED*
*SKEEN*s
SKEES*
*SKEET*s
SKEGS
SKEIN s
SKELL s
SKELM s
*SKELP s
SKENE s
SKEPS
SKEWS*
SKIDS
SKIED
*SKIER s
SKIES
SKIEY
SKIFF s
*SKILL s
SKIMP*sy
SKIMS*
*SKINK*s
SKINS
SKINT*
SKIPS
SKIRL s
SKIRR s
SKIRT s
*SKITE*ds
SKITS
SKIVE drs
SKOAL s
SKORT s
SKOSH
SKUAS*
SKULK s
SKULL s
SKUNK sy
SKYED
SKYEY
SLABS
*SLACK s
SLAGS
*SLAIN
*SLAKE drs
SLAMS
*SLANG sy
*SLANK
a SLANT sy
SLAPS
*SLASH
*SLATE*drs
y
SLATS
SLATY*
*SLAVE drs
y
SLAWS
SLAYS
SLEDS*
*SLEEK sy
a SLEEP sy
*SLEET sy
*SLEPT
SLEWS*
*SLICE drs
*SLICK s
SLIDE*rs
*SLIER
*SLILY
*SLIME*ds
SLIMS*y
SLIMY
i*SLING s
*SLINK sy
*SLIPE*ds
SLIPS
SLIPT*
SLITS
SLOBS
SLOES*
SLOGS
*SLOID s
SLOJD s
*SLOOP s
a*SLOPE*drs
SLOPS
a SLOSH y
*SLOTH*s
SLOTS
SLOWS
SLOYD s
SLUBS*
SLUED*
SLUES
*SLUFF s
SLUGS
*SLUMP*s
SLUMS
*SLUNG
*SLUNK
SLURB*s
SLURP*s
SLURS*
*SLUSH y
SLUTS*
SLYER
SLYLY
SLYPE s
*SMACK s
*SMALL s
*SMALT ios
SMARM sy
*SMART sy
*SMASH
*SMAZE s
SMEAR sy
*SMEEK s
*SMELL sy
*SMELT s
*SMERK s
SMEWS
*SMILE drs
y
*SMIRK sy
*SMITE*rs
SMITH*sy
*SMOCK s
SMOGS
*SMOKE drs
y
SMOKY
*SMOLT s
*SMOTE
*SMUSH
SMUTS
SNACK s
SNAFU s
SNAGS
*SNAIL s
SNAKE dsy
SNAKY
SNAPS
SNARE drs
SNARF s
*SNARK sy
SNARL sy
SNASH
SNATH es
SNAWS*
SNEAK sy
*SNEAP s
*SNECK s
SNEDS*
SNEER sy
SNELL s
SNIBS
*SNICK s
*SNIDE r
SNIFF sy
SNIPE*drs
SNIPS
SNITS
SNOBS
SNOGS
SNOOD s
*SNOOK s
SNOOL s
SNOOP sy
SNOOT sy
SNORE drs
SNORT s
SNOTS*
SNOUT sy
SNOWS
SNOWY*
SNUBS
SNUCK
SNUFF sy
SNUGS*
SNYES*
SOAKS
SOAPS*
SOAPY*
SOARS
SOAVE s
SOBAS
SOBER s
SOCAS
SOCKO*
SOCKS*
SOCLE s
SODAS
SODDY
*SODIC
SODOM sy
SOFAR*s
SOFAS*
SOFTA*s
SOFTS*
SOFTY*
SOGGY
SOILS
SOJAS*
SOKES
SOKOL s
SOLAN*dos
SOLAR*
SOLDI*
SOLDO*
SOLED*
SOLEI*
SOLES
SOLID*is
SOLON*s
SOLOS*
SOLUM s
SOLUS
SOLVE drs
SOMAN*s
SOMAS*
SONAR s
SONDE rs
SONES
SONGS*
SONIC s
*SONLY
SONNY
SONSY*
SOOEY
SOOKS*
SOOTH*es
SOOTS
SOOTY*
SOPHS*
SOPHY*
SOPOR s
SOPPY
SORAS*
SORBS
SORDS*
SORED*
SOREL*sy
SORER*
t*SORES*t
SORGO s
SORNS*
SORRY
SORTA*
SORTS
SORUS
SOTHS*
SOTOL s
SOUGH st
SOUKS*
SOULS*
SOUND s
SOUPS*
SOUPY*
SOURS
SOUSE*ds
SOUTH s
SOWAR s
*SOWED
SOWER s
SOYAS*
SOYUZ
SOZIN es
*SPACE drs
y
*SPACY
SPADE drs
SPADO
SPAED*
SPAES*
SPAHI s
*SPAIL s
SPAIT s
SPAKE
*SPALE s
*SPALL s
SPAMS
SPANG
SPANK*s
SPANS
*SPARE*drs
*SPARK*sy
*SPARS*e
SPASM*s
*SPATE*s
SPATS
*SPAWN s
SPAYS
*SPEAK s
*SPEAN s
*SPEAR s
*SPECK*s
SPECS
SPEED osy
*SPEEL s
*SPEER s
SPEIL s
SPEIR s
SPELL s
*SPELT sz
*SPEND sy
*SPENT
*SPERM s
SPEWS
*SPICA es
*SPICE drs
y
SPICY
e*SPIED
SPIEL s
*SPIER s
e*SPIES
SPIFF sy
*SPIKE drs
y
SPIKY
*SPILE ds
*SPILL s
SPILT h
*SPINE*dls
t
SPINS
SPINY
a SPIRE adm
s
SPIRT s
SPIRY
SPITE*ds
SPITS
SPITZ*
SPIVS*
*SPLAT s
*SPLAY s
SPLIT s
SPODE s
SPOIL st
*SPOKE dns
*SPOOF sy
SPOOK sy
*SPOOL s
*SPOON sy
*SPOOR s
*SPORE ds
*SPORT sy
SPOTS
*SPOUT s
SPRAG s
*SPRAT s
*SPRAY s
*SPREE s
*SPRIG s
e SPRIT esz
SPRUE s
SPRUG s
SPUDS
SPUED*
SPUES*
SPUME ds
SPUMY
*SPUNK*sy
SPURN*s
SPURS
SPURT*s
SPUTA
SQUAB s
*SQUAD s
SQUAT s
SQUEG s
SQUIB s
*SQUID s
STABS
*STACK s
STADE s
STAFF s
STAGE*drs
y
STAGS
STAGY*
STAID
STAIG s
*STAIN s
STAIR s
*STAKE ds
*STALE drs
*STALK sy
*STALL s
*STAMP s
STAND s
STANE ds
*STANG s
*STANK s
STAPH s
*STARE*drs
STARK*
STARS
*START*s
STASH
e*STATE*drs
STATS
STAVE ds
STAYS*
STEAD sy
*STEAK s
o*STEAL s
*STEAM sy
*STEED s
STEEK s
*STEEL sy
STEEP s
STEER s
STEIN s
*STELA eir
*STELE s
STEMS*
STENO s
*STENT s
STEPS*
STERE os
a*STERN as
STETS
STEWS
STEWY*
STICH s
*STICK sy
*STIED
*STIES
*STIFF s
*STILE s
*STILL sy
*STILT s
*STIME s
STIMY
*STING osy
STINK osy
*STINT s
STIPE dls
STIRK*s
STIRP*s
STIRS*
STOAE*
STOAI*
STOAS*
STOAT*s
STOBS*
STOCK sy
STOGY
STOIC s
*STOKE drs
*STOLE dns
STOMA ls
STOMP s
*STONE drs
y
a*STONY
STOOD
*STOOK s
*STOOL s
STOOP s
*STOPE*drs
e*STOPS*
STOPT*
*STORE drs
y
STORK s
STORM sy
*STORY
*STOSS
STOTS
STOTT*s
STOUP s
*STOUR esy
*STOUT s
STOVE rs
STOWP*s
STOWS
*STRAP s
STRAW sy
ae*STRAY s
STREP s
STREW ns
STRIA e
*STRIP est
y
*STROP s
*STROW ns
*STROY s
e STRUM as
STRUT s
STUBS
*STUCK
STUDS*
STUDY*
*STUFF sy
STULL s
*STUMP*sy
STUMS*
STUNG
STUNK*
STUNS
STUNT*s
STUPA s
STUPE s
STURT s
STYED*
STYES
STYLE drs
t
STYLI
STYMY
SUAVE r
SUBAH*s
SUBAS*
SUBER s
SUCKS*
SUCKY*
SUCRE s
SUDDS*
SUDOR s
SUDSY*
SUEDE*ds
SUERS*
SUETS*
SUETY*
SUGAR sy
SUGHS
SUING
SUINT s
SUITE*drs
SUITS*

SULCI
SULFA s
SULFO
SULKS*
SULKY*
SULLY
SULUS
SUMAC hs
SUMMA es
SUMOS*
SUMPS
SUNNA*hs
SUNNS*
SUNNY*
SUNUP s
SUPER*bs
SUPES*
SUPRA
SURAH*s
SURAL*
SURAS*
SURDS
u SURER*
SURFS*
SURFY*
*SURGE drs
SURGY
SURLY
SURRA s
SUSHI s
SUTRA s
SUTTA s
SWABS
*SWAGE*drs
SWAGS
*SWAIL s
*SWAIN s
*SWALE s
SWAMI*s
SWAMP*sy
SWAMY*
SWANG*
SWANK*sy
SWANS
SWAPS
*SWARD s
*SWARE
SWARF s
a*SWARM s
*SWART hy
*SWASH
SWATH*es
SWATS
SWAYS
*SWEAR s
SWEAT sy
SWEDE s
*SWEEP sy
*SWEER
*SWEET s
*SWELL s
*SWEPT
SWIFT s
SWIGS
*SWILL s
SWIMS*
*SWINE
*SWING esy
*SWINK s
*SWIPE ds
a SWIRL sy
*SWISH y
*SWISS
*SWITH e
*SWIVE dls
t
SWOBS*
a SWOON sy
SWOOP sy
SWOPS*
*SWORD s
*SWORE
*SWORN
SWOTS
SWOUN ds
SWUNG
SYCEE*s
SYCES*
SYKES*
SYLIS*
SYLPH sy
SYLVA ens
SYNCH*s
SYNCS*
SYNOD s
SYNTH s

SYPHS*
SYREN s
SYRUP sy
SYSOP s
TABBY
TABER s
TABES
TABID
TABLA s
s*TABLE dst
TABOO s
TABOR s
TABUN*s
TABUS*
TACES
TACET*
*TACHE*s
TACHS*
TACIT
s TACKS*
TACKY*
TACOS*
TACTS
TAELS*
TAFFY
TAFIA s
TAHRS*
TAIGA s
TAILS
s*TAINS*
TAINT*s
TAJES
TAKAS*
TAKEN*
TAKER*s
s TAKES*
*TAKIN gs
*TALAR*s
TALAS
TALCS*
s TALER*s
s*TALES*
s TALKS*
s*TALKY*
s*TALLS*
TALLY
e TALON s
TALUK as
TALUS
TAMAL es
TAMED*
TAMER*s
TAMES*t
*TAMIS
TAMMY
s*TAMPS*
TANGA
TANGO*s
s TANGS*
TANGY*
TANKA*s
s TANKS*
TANSY*
TANTO
TAPAS*
TAPED
*TAPER*s
es*TAPES*
TAPIR s
TAPIS
TARDO
TARDY
s TARED*
s*TARES*
TARGE st
TARNS*
TAROC*s
TAROK*s
TAROS*
TAROT*s
TARPS*
TARRE ds
s TARRY
TARSI*a
s*TARTS*
TARTY
TASKS
TASSE*lst
TASTE drs
TASTY
TATAR s
s TATER*s
s*TATES*
TATTY
*TAUNT s
TAUON s

TAUPE s
TAUTS*
*TAWED
TAWER s
TAWIE
*TAWNY
TAWSE*ds
*TAXED
TAXER s
*TAXES
TAXIS
TAXOL s
*TAXON s
TAXUS
TAZZA s
TAZZE
*TEACH
s TEAKS*
s TEALS*
s TEAMS*
TEARS
TEARY*
*TEASE*dlr
s
TEATS
TECHS*
TECHY*
TECTA l
*TEDDY
s*TEELS*
TEEMS*
TEENS*y
TEENY*
TEETH e
TEFFS
TEGGS
TEGUA s
TEIID s
TEIND s
s TELAE*
TELCO s
s TELES*
TELEX*
TELIA l
as TELIC
TELLS
TELLY*s
TELOI
TELOS
TEMPI*
TEMPO*s
TEMPS*
TEMPT*s
s TENCH
TENDS
TENDU*s
TENET s
TENGE
TENIA es
TENON s
TENOR s
TENSE*drs
TENTH*s
s TENTS*
TENTY*
TEPAL*s
TEPAS*
*TEPEE s
TEPID
TEPOY s
TERAI s
TERCE lst
TERGA l
TERMS*
e*TERNE*s
s*TERNS*
TERRA es
TERRY
TERSE r
TESLA s
TESTA*e
TESTS*
TESTY*
TETHS
TETRA ds
TETRI s
TEUCH
TEUGH
s TEWED
TEXAS
TEXTS*
*THACK s
e THANE*s
*THANK*s
*THARM s
THAWS

THEBE s
THECA el
*THEFT s
THEGN s
THEIN es
*THEIR s
*THEME*ds
THENS
*THERE s
*THERM es
THESE s
THESP s
THETA s
THEWS
THEWY*
*THICK s
THIEF
*THIGH s
*THILL s
THINE*
THING*s
THINK*s
THINS
THIOL*s
THIRD*s
THIRL*s
*THOLE ds
*THONG s
*THORN sy
THORO n
THORP es
*THOSE
THOUS*
THRAW ns
THREE ps
THREW
THRIP s
THROB*s
THROE*s
THROW*ns
THRUM*s
THUDS*
THUGS
THUJA s
THUMB s
*THUMP s
*THUNK s
*THURL s
THUYA s
THYME sy
THYMI c
THYMY
TIARA s
TIBIA els
TICAL s
s TICKS*
TIDAL
TIDED*
TIDES
TIERS*
s TIFFS*
TIGER s
TIGHT s
TIGON s
TIKES*
TIKIS*
TIKKA s
TILAK s
TILDE s
TILED*
TILER*s
s TILES*
s*TILLS*
TILTH*s
s TILTS*
TIMED*
TIMER*s
s TIMES*
*TIMID
TINCT s
TINEA*ls
TINED*
TINES*
TINGE*ds
s TINGS*
TINNY
s TINTS*
TIPIS*
TIPPY
TIPSY*
TIRED
TIRES
TIRLS*
TIROS*
TITAN s
TITER s

TITHE drs
o TITIS*
TITLE ds
TITRE s
TITTY
TIZZY
TOADS*
TOADY*
*TOAST sy
TODAY s
TODDY
TOEAS*
TOFFS
TOFFY*
TOFTS*
TOFUS*
TOGAE*d
TOGAS*
TOGUE s
e TOILE*drs
t
TOILS
TOITS*
*TOKAY s
s TOKED*
TOKEN*s
s TOKER*s
s*TOKES*
TOLAN*es
TOLAR*s
TOLAS*
s TOLED*o
s*TOLES*
a TOLLS*
TOLUS*
TOLYL s
TOMAN s
TOMBS*
TOMES*
TOMMY
a TONAL
TONDI
TONDO s
as TONED*
as TONER*s
as*TONES*
s TONEY*
TONGA*s
TONGS*
a TONIC s
TONNE rs
*TONUS
s TOOLS*
TOONS*
TOOTH*sy
*TOOTS*y
TOPAZ
s*TOPED*
TOPEE*s
s TOPER*s
s*TOPES*
TOPHE*s
TOPHI*
TOPHS*
a TOPIC*s
TOPIS*
TOPOI*
TOPOS*
TOQUE st
TORAH*s
TORAS*
TORCH*y
TORCS
s*TORES*
TORIC*s
TORII*
TOROS*e
TOROT*h
TORRS*
TORSE*s
TORSI*
TORSK*s
TORSO*s
TORTA*s
TORTE*ns
TORTS
TORUS
TOTAL s
TOTED*
TOTEM*s
TOTER*s
TOTES*
*TOUCH ey
TOUGH sy
s*TOURS*
TOUSE ds

s*TOUTS*
s*TOWED
TOWEL s
TOWER sy
TOWIE s
TOWNS
TOWNY*
TOXIC s
TOXIN es
TOYED
*TOYER s
TOYON*s
TOYOS*
*TRACE drs
*TRACK s
TRACT s
TRADE*drs
*TRAGI c
TRAIK s
*TRAIL s
s*TRAIN s
s TRAIT s
*TRAMP*sy
TRAMS
*TRANK s
TRANQ s
TRANS
s*TRAPS*
TRAPT
*TRASH y
s TRASS
*TRAVE ls
TRAWL s
s*TRAYS*
*TREAD s
TREAT sy
TREED
TREEN*s
TREES
TREKS*
*TREND sy
s TRESS*y
TRETS
s TREWS
TREYS*
TRIAC s
TRIAD s
a*TRIAL s
TRIBE s
*TRICE dps
s*TRICK sy
TRIED
TRIER s
TRIES
TRIGO*ns
TRIGS
s TRIKE s
*TRILL s
TRIMS
TRINE ds
TRIOL*s
TRIOS*e
s*TRIPE*s
s*TRIPS*
*TRITE r
TROAK s
*TROCK s
s*TRODE*
TROGS*
TROIS
s TROKE ds
s*TROLL sy
*TROMP es
TRONA s
TRONE s
TROOP s
TROOZ
*TROPE*s
TROTH*s
TROTS
*TROUT sy
s*TROVE rs
s*TROWS*
s TROYS*
TRUCE ds
s*TRUCK s
TRUED
TRUER
*TRUES*t
TRUGS
TRULL s
*TRULY
*TRUMP s
TRUNK s
TRUSS
*TRUST sy

*TRUTH s
TRYMA
TRYST es
*TSADE s
*TSADI s
TSARS*
TSKED
*TSUBA
TUBAE*
TUBAL*
TUBAS*
s TUBBY
TUBED*
TUBER*s
TUBES*
TUCKS*
TUFAS*
s TUFFS*
TUFTS*
TUFTY*
TULES*
TULIP s
TULLE s
TUMID
TUMMY
TUMOR s
s*TUMPS*
TUNAS*
TUNED*
TUNER*s
TUNES*
TUNGS*
TUNIC as
TUNNY
TUPIK s
TUQUE s
TURBO st
TURFS*
TURFY*
TURKS*
TURNS
*TURPS
TUSHY*
TUSKS*
TUTEE s
TUTOR s
TUTTI s
TUTTY
TUTUS*
TUXES
TUYER es
TWAES
a*TWAIN s
TWANG sy
*TWEAK sy
*TWEED*sy
a*TWEEN*sy
*TWEET*s
TWERP s
TWICE
TWIER s
TWIGS
*TWILL s
*TWINE*drs
TWINS
TWINY
TWIRL sy
TWIRP s
*TWIST sy
TWITS
TWIXT
TWYER s
TYEES*
TYERS*
s TYING*
TYIYN
TYKES*
TYNED*
TYNES*
TYPAL
TYPED*
TYPES*
TYPEY*
a TYPIC
TYPOS*
TYPPS*
TYRED*
TYRES*
TYROS*
TYTHE ds
TZARS*
bjm UDDER s
r
UDONS
UHLAN s
UKASE s

*ULAMA s
y ULANS*
ULCER s
ULEMA s
ULNAD*
ULNAE*
ULNAR*
ULNAS*
ULPAN
ULTRA s
v ULVAS*
UMAMI s
UMBEL s
cdl UMBER s
n
dgj UMBOS*
UMBRA els
UMIAC ks
UMIAK s
UMIAQ s
bdh UMPED
jlm
pt
UNAIS*
UNAPT
UNARM s
*UNARY
UNAUS*
UNBAN s
UNBAR s
UNBID
UNBOX
UNCAP s
UNCIA*el
n UNCLE s
bj UNCOS*
UNCOY*
UNCUS
UNCUT e
UNDEE*
fs UNDER*
UNDID
UNDUE
UNFED
UNFIT s
UNFIX t
UNGOT
UNHAT s
UNHIP
UNIFY
b UNION s
dg*UNITE*drs
UNITS
UNITY*
UNJAM s
UNLAY s
UNLED
r UNLET
s UNLIT
g UNMAN s
UNMET
UNMEW s
UNMIX t
UNPEG s
UNPEN st
UNPIN s
UNRIG s
UNRIP es
UNSAY s
s UNSET s
UNSEW ns
UNSEX y
a UNTIE ds
UNTIL
UNWED
UNWET
UNWIT s
UNWON
UNZIP s
UPBOW s
UPBYE*
UPDOS*
UPDRY
*UPEND s
UPLIT
cdp UPPED
st
cs UPPER s
UPSET s
URAEI
c*URARE s
co URARI s
*URASE s
ac*URATE s
rt URBAN e
URBIA s

UREAL
UREAS*e
*UREDO s
UREIC
gps URGED*
bps URGER*s
gps URGES*
bc*URIAL s
mp URINE s
b URPED
b URSAE*
URSID s
*USAGE s
m*USERS*
bgl USHER s
mpr
bfm*USING
USNEA s
USQUE s
USUAL s
USURP s
USURY
UTERI
fr*UTILE
bcg UTTER s
mnp
UVEAL
UVEAS*
UVULA ers
VACUA
VAGAL
*VAGUE r
VAGUS
a*VAILS*
VAIRS
VAKIL s
VALES
VALET*s
VALID
VALOR s
VALSE s
VALUE drs
VALVE ds
VAMPS
VAMPY*
VANDA ls
VANED*
VANES
VANGS*
VAPID
VAPOR sy
VARAS*
*VARIA s
VARIX
VARNA s
VARUS
VARVE ds
VASAL*
k VASES*
VASTS*
VASTY*
VATIC
VATUS*
VAULT sy
a*VAUNT sy
VEALS*
VEALY*
VEENA s
VEEPS*
VEERS*
VEERY
VEGAN s
VEGES
VEGIE s
VEILS*
VEINS*
VEINY*
VELAR*s
VELDS
VELDT*s
VELUM
VENAE*
VENAL*
VENDS

a VENGE ds
VENIN es
VENOM s
e VENTS*
a VENUE s
VENUS
VERBS*
VERGE drs
a VERSE drs
t
VERSO s
*VERST es
ae VERTS*
VERTU*s
VERVE st
VESTA*ls
VESTS*
k*VETCH
*VEXED
VEXER s
*VEXES
VEXIL s
VIALS*
VIAND s
VIBES*
VICAR s
VICED
VICES
VICHY
VIDEO*s
VIERS*
VIEWS*
VIEWY*
VIGAS*
VIGIA s
VIGIL s
VIGOR s
e VILER*
VILLA*es
VILLI*
VILLS
VIMEN
VINAL*s
VINAS*
VINCA s
VINED*
o VINES*
VINIC
VINOS*
VINYL*s
VIOLA*s
VIOLS*
VIPER s
VIRAL
VIREO s
*VIRES
VIRGA s
*VIRID
VIRLS*
VIRTU es
VIRUS
VISAS*
VISED*
VISES*
VISIT s
VISOR s
VISTA s
VITAE*
VITAL*s
VITTA e
VIVAS*
VIVID
VIXEN s
VIZIR s
VIZOR s
VOCAB s
VOCAL s
VOCES
VODKA s
VODOU ns
VODUN s
VOGIE
VOGUE drs
VOICE drs

ao VOIDS*
VOILA
VOILE s
VOLAR
VOLED*
VOLES
VOLTA*
VOLTE*s
VOLTI*
VOLTS*
VOLVA s
*VOMER s
*VOMIT os
VOTED*
VOTER*s
VOTES*
a*VOUCH
a*VOWED
VOWEL s
a VOWER s
*VROOM s
VROUW s
VROWS
VUGGS*
VUGGY*
VUGHS
VULGO
*VULVA elr
s
VYING
WACKE*rs
WACKO*s
WACKS*
WACKY*
WADDY
WADED*
WADER*s
WADES*
WADIS*
WAFER sy
WAFFS*
WAFTS*
s*WAGED*
s*WAGER*s
s*WAGES*
*WAGON s
WAHOO s
WAIFS*
s*WAILS*
st*WAINS*
WAIRS
WAIST s
a*WAITS*
WAIVE drs
a WAKED*
a WAKEN*s
WAKER*s
a WAKES*
WALED*
WALER*s
s*WALES*
WALKS*
WALLA*hs
WALLS
WALLY
WALTZ
WAMES*
*WAMUS
WANDS
WANED*
WANES
WANEY*
WANLY
WANTS
as WARDS*
WARED*
WARES
WARKS
s*WARMS*
WARNS*
WARPS*
WARTS
s*WARTY*
WASHY

WASPS
WASPY*
WASTE*drs
WASTS*
*WATAP es
s WATCH
WATER sy
WATTS*
WAUGH t
WAUKS
WAULS*
WAVED*
*WAVER*sy
WAVES
WAVEY*s
WAWLS
*WAXED
WAXEN
WAXER s
*WAXES
WEALD*s
WEALS*
WEANS*
s*WEARS*
a WEARY*
*WEAVE drs
WEBBY
WEBER s
*WECHT s
WEDEL ns
*WEDGE ds
*WEDGY
t WEEDS*
t WEEDY*
WEEKS*
t WEENS*y
st WEENY*
s WEEPS*
s WEEPY*
WEEST*
st WEETS*
WEFTS
a WEIGH st
WEIRD*osy
WEIRS*
WEKAS*
WELCH
WELDS
ds*WELLS*
WELLY*
WELSH
WELTS*
WENCH
WENDS
WENNY
WESTS*
WETLY
*WHACK osy
*WHALE drs
WHAMO*
WHAMS
*WHANG s
WHAPS
WHARF s
WHATS
WHAUP s
*WHEAL s
*WHEAT s
*WHEEL*s
WHEEN*s
WHEEP*s
WHELK sy
*WHELM s
*WHELP s
WHENS
*WHERE s
WHETS
WHEWS
WHEYS*
WHICH
WHIDS*
WHIFF s
WHIGS*
a WHILE ds

*WHIMS*y
WHINE*drs
y
WHINS
WHINY*
WHIPS
WHIPT*
a WHIRL*sy
WHIRR*sy
WHIRS*
WHISH t
WHISK sy
*WHIST s
WHITE*dnr
sy
WHITS
WHITY*
WHIZZ*y
*WHOLE s
WHOMP*s
*WHOOF s
*WHOOP s
WHOPS
WHORE ds
WHORL s
WHORT s
*WHOSE
WHOSO
*WHUMP s
WHUPS*
WICCA ns
WICKS*
WIDDY
WIDEN*s
WIDER*
*WIDES*t
WIDOW s
WIDTH s
WIELD sy
WIFED*
WIFES*
WIFEY*s
WIFTY
WIGAN s
t WIGGY
WIGHT s
WILCO
WILDS*
WILED*
WILES*
st*WILLS*
WILLY
WILTS*
WIMPS
WIMPY*
WINCE drs
y
*WINCH
WINDS*
WINDY*
dt WINED*
dt WINES*
WINEY*
s WINGS*
s WINGY*
s*WINKS*
WINOS*
WINZE s
s WIPED*
WIPER*s
s WIPES*
WIRED
WIRER*s
WIRES
WIRRA
WISED*
WISER*
WISES*t
WISHA*
WISPS*
WISPY*
t WISTS*
WITAN s
st*WITCH y

WITED*
WITES*
s WITHE*drs
WITHY*
WITTY
s WIVED*
WIVER*ns
s WIVES*
WIZEN s
WIZES
WOADS*
WOALD s
WODGE s
WOFUL
a WOKEN*
WOLDS
WOLFS*
WOMAN s
WOMBS*
WOMBY*
*WOMEN
WOMYN
WONKS*
WONKY*
WONTS*
WOODS*y
WOODY*
WOOED
WOOER s
WOOFS*
WOOLS*
WOOLY*
s*WOOPS
s WOOSH*
*WOOZY
s WORDS*
WORDY*
WORKS*
WORLD s
WORMS*
WORMY*
WORRY
WORSE nrs
t
WORST s
WORTH*sy
WORTS
WOULD
s WOUND s
*WOVEN*s
*WOWED
*WRACK s
*WRANG s
WRAPS
WRAPT
*WRATH sy
WREAK s
*WRECK s
WRENS*
*WREST s
*WRICK s
WRIED
WRIER
WRIES t
*WRING s
WRIST sy
*WRITE*rs
WRITS*
WRONG s
*WROTE
WROTH
*WRUNG
WRYER
WRYLY
WURST s
WUSHU
WUSSY*
WYLED*
WYLES*
WYNDS*
WYNNS*
WYTED*
WYTES*
XEBEC s

XENIA ls
a XENIC
XENON s
XERIC
XEROX
XERUS
XYLAN s
*XYLEM s
XYLOL s
XYLYL s
XYSTI*
XYSTS*
YABBY
YACHT s
k YACKS*
YAFFS*
*YAGER s
YAGIS*
YAHOO s
YAIRD s
*YAMEN s
YAMUN s
YANGS*
YANKS*
YAPOK s
YAPON s
YARDS*
YARER*
YARNS*
YAUDS*
*YAULD
YAUPS*
*YAWED
YAWEY
YAWLS
YAWNS
YAWPS*
*YCLAD
YEAHS*
YEANS*
*YEARN*s
YEARS
*YEAST*sy
YECCH s
YECHS*
YECHY*
YEGGS
YELKS
YELLS
YELPS*
YENTA s
YENTE s
YERBA s
YERKS*
c*YESES
YETIS*
YETTS*
YEUKS*
YEUKY*
YIELD s
YIKES
YILLS
YINCE
YIPES*
YIRDS*
YIRRS*
YIRTH s
x YLEMS*
YOBBO s
YOCKS*
YODEL s
YODHS*
YODLE drs
YOGAS*
*YOGEE s
YOGHS*
YOGIC*
YOGIN*is
YOGIS*
YOKED*
YOKEL*s
YOKES
YOLKS*
YOLKY*

YOMIM
YONIC*
YONIS*
YORES
YOUNG s
YOURN*
YOURS
YOUSE*
YOUTH s
YOWED
YOWES
YOWIE s
YOWLS
YUANS*
YUCAS*
YUCCA s
YUCCH
YUCKS*
YUCKY*
YUGAS*
YUKKY
*YULAN s
YULES*
YUMMY
*YUPON s
YUPPY
YURTA*
YURTS*
ZAIRE s
*ZAMIA s
ZANZA s
ZAPPY
ZARFS
*ZAXES
*ZAYIN s
ZAZEN s
ZEALS*
ZEBEC ks
ZEBRA s
ZEBUS*
ZEINS*
ZERKS*
ZEROS
ZESTS*
ZESTY*
ZETAS
ZIBET hs
ZILCH
ZILLS
ZINCS*
ZINCY*
ZINEB*s
a ZINES*
ZINGS*
ZINGY*
*ZINKY
ZIPPY
ZIRAM s
ZITIS*
ZIZIT h
ZLOTE
ZLOTY s
ZOEAE*
ZOEAL*
ZOEAS*
ZOMBI es
ZONAE*
a ZONAL*
ZONED*
ZONER*s
o*ZONES*
ZONKS*
ZOOEY
ZOOID s
ZOOKS
ZOOMS*
ZOONS*
ZOOTY
ZORIL*s
ZORIS*
ZOUKS*
ZOWIE
ZUZIM
ZYMES*

The Hooks: 6s-to-Make-7s

*AAHING
AALIIS*
AARRGH h
ABACAS*
ABACUS
k ABAKAS*
ABAMPS*
ABASED
*ABASER*s
ABASES
ABASIA s
ABATED
ABATER*s
ABATES
ABATIS
ABATOR s
k ABAYAS*
ABBACY
ABBESS*
ABBEYS*
ABBOTS*
ABDUCE ds
ABDUCT s
ABELES*
ABELIA ns
ABHORS*
ABIDED
*ABIDER*s
ABIDES
ABJECT
ABJURE drs
*ABLATE ds
ABLAUT s
*ABLAZE
ABLEST
ABLINS
*ABLOOM
*ABLUSH
ABMHOS*
*ABOARD
ABODED
ABODES
ABOHMS*
ABOLLA e
ABOMAS*ai
*ABORAL
ABORTS
*ABOUND s
ABOVES*
ABRADE drs
*ABROAD
ABRUPT
ABSEIL s
ABSENT s
ABSORB s
ABSURD s
ABULIA s
ABULIC
ABUSED
ABUSER*s
ABUSES
ABVOLT s
ABWATT s
b ABYING
ABYSMS*
ACACIA s
ACAJOU s
ACARID*s
ACARUS
ACCEDE drs
ACCENT s
ACCEPT s
ACCESS
ACCORD s
ACCOST s
ACCRUE ds
ACCUSE drs
ACEDIA s
ACETAL*s
ACETIC
ACETIN s
ACETUM
ACETYL s
ACHENE s
ACHIER
bc ACHING
ACIDIC
ACIDLY
ACINAR
ACINIC*
ACINUS
h ACKEES*
t ACNODE s
ACORNS
ACQUIT s
*ACROSS
ACTING*s
ACTINS*
fpt ACTION s
ACTIVE s
f ACTORS*
ft ACTUAL
ACUATE
v ACUITY
ACULEI
ACUMEN s
ACUTER
*ACUTES*t
ADAGES*
ADAGIO s
ADAPTS*
ADDEND as
glm ADDERS*
pw
ADDICT s
gmp ADDING
rw
dpr ADDLED*
sw
dpr ADDLES*
sw
ADDUCE drs
ADDUCT s
ADEEMS
ADENYL s
ADEPTS*
ADHERE drs
ADIEUS*
ADIEUX*
ADIPIC
ADJOIN st
ADJURE drs
ADJUST s
ADMASS
ADMIRE drs
ADMITS*
ADMIXT*
ADNATE
ADNEXA l
ADNOUN s
ADOBES*
ADOBOS*
ADONIS
ADOPTS*
ADORED*
ADORER*s
ADORES*
ADORNS*
*ADRIFT
*ADROIT
ADSORB s
ADULTS*
ADVECT s
ADVENT s
ADVERB s
ADVERT s
ADVICE s
ADVISE der
s
ADYTUM
ADZING
ADZUKI s
AECIAL*
AECIUM
*AEDILE s
AEDINE
AENEUS
AEONIC
AERATE ds
AERIAL s
AERIED*
AERIER*
f AERIES*t
AERIFY
AERILY
AEROBE s
*AERUGO s
*AETHER s
AFEARD
AFFAIR es
AFFECT s
AFFINE ds
AFFIRM s
AFFLUX
AFFORD s
AFFRAY s
AFGHAN is
*AFIELD
*AFLAME
*AFLOAT
AFRAID
AFREET s
*AFRESH
AFRITS
hrw AFTERS*
AFTOSA s
AGAMAS
*AGAMIC
AGAMID s
AGAPAE
AGAPAI
AGAPES
AGARIC s
AGATES
AGAVES*
AGEDLY
AGEING s
AGEISM s
AGEIST s
AGENCY
AGENDA s
AGENES
AGENTS
h AGGADA hs
bdg AGGERS*
jln
stw
bjr AGGIES*
AGGROS*
AGHAST
p AGINGS*
AGISMS*
AGISTS
AGITAS*
*AGLARE
*AGLEAM
e AGLETS*
AGNAIL s
m AGNATE s
AGNIZE ds
AGONAL
AGONES*
AGONIC
AGORAE*
AGORAS*
AGOROT h
AGOUTI s
*AGOUTY
AGRAFE s
AGREED
AGREES
AGRIAS*
AGUISH
AHCHOO
AHIMSA s
AHOLDS
*AHORSE
r AIDERS*
AIDFUL
r AIDING
AIDMAN
AIDMEN
AIGLET s
AIGRET s
AIKIDO s
bfh AILING
jmnr
stvw
m AIMERS*
AIMFUL
m AIMING
AIOLIS*
AIRBAG s
AIRBUS
AIRERS*
f AIREST
h AIRIER
AIRILY
flp*AIRING s
w
AIRMAN
AIRMEN
AIRTED
AIRTHS*
f AIRWAY s
AISLED
AISLES
w AIVERS*
AJIVAS*
AJOWAN s
AJUGAS*
AKELAS*
AKENES*
AKIMBO
ALAMOS*
ALANDS
ALANIN es
ALANTS*
ALANYL s
ALARMS*
*ALARUM s
ALASKA s
ALATED
mp ALATES*
ALBATA s
ALBEDO s
ALBEIT
ALBINO s
ALBITE s
ALBUMS*
ALCADE s
ALCAIC s
ALCIDS*
ALCOVE ds
ALDERS*
ALDOLS*
ALDOSE s
ALDRIN s
ALEGAR s
ALEPHS*
ALERTS*
*ALEVIN s
ALEXIA s
ALEXIN es
ALFAKI s
ALGINS*
v ALGOID
ALGORS*
ALGUMS*
ALIBIS*
ALIBLE
ALIDAD es
ALIENS
*ALIGHT s
m ALIGNS*
ALINED
*ALINER*s
msv*ALINES*
t ALIPED s
ALIYAH*s
ALIYAS*
ALIYOS
ALIYOT
ALKALI cns
ALKANE st
ALKENE s
t ALKIES*
ALKINE s
ALKOXY
ALKYDS*
ALKYLS*
ALKYNE s
ALLAYS*
cm ALLEES*
ALLEGE drs
ALLELE s
gv ALLEYS*
dgr ALLIED
st
bdg ALLIES
rstw
gp ALLIUM s
ALLODS*
b ALLOTS*
fgh ALLOWS*
mstw
ALLOYS*
ALLUDE ds
ALLURE drs
ALLYLS*
ALMAHS*
ALMEHS*
ALMNER s
ALMOND sy
ALMOST
ALMUCE s
ALMUDE*s
ALMUDS*
ALMUGS*
ALNICO s
ALODIA l
ALOHAS*
ALOINS
ALPACA s
ALPHAS*
ALPHYL s
ALPINE s
ALSIKE s
ALTARS*
fhp ALTERS*
s
ALTHEA s
ALUDEL s
ALULAE*
ALULAR*
ALUMIN aes
ALUMNA e
ALUMNI
ALVINE
ALWAYS*
AMADOU s
AMARNA
AMATOL s
AMAZED
AMAZES
AMAZON s
AMBAGE s
AMBARI s
AMBARY
AMBEER s
cl AMBERS*
AMBERY*
g AMBITS*
grw AMBLED*
gr AMBLER*s
grw AMBLES*
AMBUSH
AMEBAE*
AMEBAN*
AMEBAS*
AMEBIC
AMEERS*
AMENDS
l AMENTS*
AMERCE drs
AMICES*
AMICUS
AMIDES*
AMIDIC
AMIDIN es
AMIDOL*s
AMIDST
AMIGAS*
AMIGOS*
fg*AMINES*
AMINIC
AMMINE s
AMMINO
AMMONO
AMNION*s
AMNIOS*
AMOEBA ens
AMOLES
*AMORAL
*AMOUNT s
AMOURS*
AMPERE s
cdl AMPING
rtv
s AMPLER*
AMPULE*s
AMPULS*
AMRITA s
AMTRAC ks
AMUCKS
AMULET s
AMUSED
*AMUSER*s
w*AMUSES*
AMUSIA s
AMYLIC
AMYLUM s
ANABAS
ANADEM s
b ANALLY
ANALOG sy
ANANKE s
ANARCH sy
ANATTO s
ANCHOR*s
r ANCHOS*
ANCONE*s
ANDROS*
ANEARS
p ANELED*
ANELES*
ANEMIA s
ANEMIC
ANENST
ANERGY
ANGARY
m ANGELS*
bdg ANGERS*
hmrs
ANGINA ls
djm ANGLED*
tw
djm ANGLER*s
tw
bdj ANGLES*
mtw
ANGLOS*
ANGORA s
ANGSTS*
ANILIN es
ANIMAL*s
ANIMAS*
ANIMES*
ANIMIS*mt
ANIMUS
fw ANIONS*
ANISES*
ANISIC
r ANKLED*
r ANKLES*
ANKLET*s
ANKUSH*
ANLACE s
ANLAGE ns
ANNALS*
ANNEAL s
ANNEXE*ds
ANNONA s
t ANNOYS*
ANNUAL s
ANNULI*
ANNULS*
*ANODAL
ANODES
ANODIC
ANOINT s
ANOLES*
ANOMIC
ANOMIE s
ANONYM s
ANOPIA s
ANORAK s
ANOXIA s
ANOXIC
ANSATE d
ANSWER s
ANTEED
ANTHEM s
p ANTHER s
ANTIAR s
ANTICK*s
ANTICS*
chp ANTING s
rw
ANTLER s
ANTRAL*
ANTRES*
t ANTRUM s
ANURAL
ANURAN s
ANURIA s
ANURIC
ANUSES
ANVILS*
ANYHOW
ANYONE*
c ANYONS*
ANYWAY s
AORIST s
AORTAE*
AORTAL*
AORTAS*
AORTIC
AOUDAD s
APACHE s
APATHY
APERCU s
APEXES
APHIDS*
n APHTHA e
APIARY
*APICAL s
APICES
*APIECE
h APLITE s
APLOMB s
APNEAL*
APNEAS*
APNEIC
APNOEA ls
APODAL
APOGEE s
APOLLO s
APOLOG sy
APORIA s
APPALL*s
APPALS*
APPEAL s
APPEAR s
r APPELS*
APPEND s
d APPLES*
APPLET*s
p APPOSE drs
APRONS*
APTEST
*ARABIC a
p ARABLE s
ARAMES*
ARAMID s
h ARBORS*
h ARBOUR s
ARBUTE s
ARCADE ds
ARCANA
ARCANE
mp ARCHED
m ARCHER sy
lmp ARCHES
ARCHIL s
ARCHLY
ARCHON s
f ARCING
ARCKED
ARCTIC s
ARDEBS*
ARDENT
ARDORS*
ARDOUR s
ARECAS*
ARENAS*
ARENES*
AREOLA ers
AREOLE s
AREPAS*
ARETES*
ARGALA*s
ARGALI*s
ARGALS*
m ARGENT s
ARGILS*
g ARGLED*
g ARGLES*
ARGOLS*
j ARGONS*
ARGOSY
ARGOTS*
ARGUED*
ARGUER*s
ARGUES*
ARGUFY
ARGYLE s
ARGYLL s
ARHATS*
ARIARY
*ARIDER
ARIDLY
ARIELS
*ARIGHT
*ARILED
ARIOSE
ARIOSI
ARIOSO s
ARISEN
p*ARISES*
b ARISTA es
ARISTO s
ARKOSE s
ARMADA s
fhw ARMERS*
ARMETS*
h ARMFUL s
ARMIES
fhw ARMING s
ARMLET s
ARMORS*
ARMORY*
ARMOUR sy
ARMPIT s
ARMURE s
ARNICA s
AROIDS*
AROINT s
AROMAS*
*AROUND
c*AROUSE drs
AROYNT s
ARPENS*
ARPENT*s
bc ARRACK s
w ARRANT

ARRAYS*
ARREAR s
ARREST s
ARRIBA
ARRIVE drs
ARROBA s
bfh ARROWS*
mny
m ARROWY*
ARROYO s
ARSENO
ARSHIN s
ARSINE s
ARSINO
p ARSONS*
c ARTELS*
ARTERY
ARTFUL
ptw ARTIER
t ARTILY
ARTIST es
ASANAS*
ASARUM s
*ASCEND s
n*ASCENT s
m*ASCOTS*
ASDICS*
ASHCAN s
cdw*ASHIER
bcd ASHING
fghl
mpsw
ASHLAR s
ASHLER s
ASHMAN
ASHMEN
*ASHORE
ASHRAM s
ASIDES
ASKANT
m ASKERS*
bcg ASKING s
mt
*ASLANT
*ASLEEP
*ASLOPE
*ASLOSH
ASPECT s
ASPENS*
gjr ASPERS*e
ASPICS*
*ASPIRE drs
rw ASPISH*
ASRAMA s
w ASSAIL*s
ASSAIS*
ASSAYS*
ASSENT s
ASSERT s
ASSESS*
bt ASSETS*
ASSIGN s
b ASSIST s
ASSIZE s
ASSOIL s
ASSORT s
ASSUME drs
ASSURE drs
ep*ASTERN*
bce ASTERS*
glm
prtw
ASTHMA s
*ASTONY
g ASTRAL s
*ASTRAY
ASTUTE
*ASWARM
*ASWIRL
*ASWOON
ASYLUM s
ATABAL s
ATAMAN s
ATAVIC
ATAXIA s
ATAXIC s
*ATELIC
ATLATL s
ATMANS*
ATOLLS
ATOMIC s
*ATONAL
ATONED
*ATONER*s
ATONES
ATONIA s

*ATONIC s
*ATOPIC
ATRIAL
n ATRIUM s
ATTACH e
ATTACK s
ATTAIN st
ATTARS*
ATTEND s
ATTENT
fw ATTEST s
ATTICS*
ATTIRE ds
ATTORN s
ATTRIT es
ATTUNE ds
*ATWAIN
*ATWEEN
*ATYPIC
AUBADE s
AUBURN s
AUCUBA s
AUDADS*
AUDIAL
AUDILE s
l AUDING s
AUDIOS*
AUDITS*
AUGEND s
gs AUGERS*
nw AUGHTS*
AUGITE s
AUGURS*
AUGURY*
AUGUST
AUKLET s
AULDER
v*AUNTIE s
g AUNTLY
*AURATE d
AUREUS
AURIST*s
AURORA els
AUROUS
AURUMS*
AUSPEX
AUSUBO s
h AUTEUR s
AUTHOR s
AUTISM s
AUTIST s
AUTOED
AUTUMN s
AUXINS*
AVAILS
AVATAR s
*AVAUNT
*AVENGE drs
*AVENUE s
AVERSE
AVERTS
AVIANS*
AVIARY
AVIATE ds
AVIDIN s
AVIDLY
AVIONS*
AVISOS*
AVOCET s
AVOIDS
AVOSET s
*AVOUCH
AVOWAL s
*AVOWED
*AVOWER s
AVULSE ds
AWAITS
AWAKED
*AWAKEN*s
AWAKES
v*AWARDS*
*AWEARY
*AWEIGH
AWEING
*AWHILE
*AWHIRL
jl AWLESS
AWMOUS
dfp AWNING s
y
AWOKEN
AXEMAN
AXEMEN
*AXENIC
m AXILLA ers
AXIOMS*

AXIONS*
AXISED
AXISES
t AXITES*
w AXLIKE
AXONAL
AXONES*
AXONIC
AXSEED s
AZALEA s
AZIDES*
AZINES
AZLONS*
AZOLES*
*AZONAL
AZONIC
AZOTED*
AZOTES*
AZOTHS*
AZOTIC
AZUKIS*
AZURES*
AZYGOS
BAAING
BAALIM
BAASES
BABBLE drs
BABELS*
BABIED
BABIER
BABIES t
BABKAS*
BABOOL*s
*BABOON*s
BABOOS*
BABULS*
BACCAE*
*BACHED
*BACHES
BACKED
BACKER s
BACKUP s
BACONS*
BACULA
*BADDER
BADDIE s
BADGED*
BADGER*s
BADGES*
*BADMAN
*BADMEN
BAFFED
BAFFLE drs
BAGASS e
BAGELS*
BAGFUL s
BAGGED
*BAGGER s
*BAGGIE rs
BAGMAN
BAGMEN
BAGNIO s
BAGUET s
BAGWIG s
*BAILED
BAILEE s
BAILER s
BAILEY s
BAILIE s
BAILOR s
BAIRNS
BAITED
BAITER s
BAIZAS*
BAIZES*
BAKERS*
BAKERY*
BAKING s
BALATA s
BALBOA s
BALDED
*BALDER
BALDLY
BALEEN s
BALERS*
BALING
BALKED
BALKER s
BALLAD es
BALLED
BALLER s
BALLET s
BALLON s
*BALLOT s
BALSAM*s
BALSAS*

BAMBOO s
BAMMED
BANANA s
BANCOS*
BANDAS*
BANDED
BANDER s
BANDIT os
BANDOG s
BANGED
*BANGER s
*BANGLE s
BANIAN s
BANING
BANISH
BANJAX
BANJOS*
BANKED
BANKER s
BANKIT s
BANNED
BANNER s
BANNET s
BANTAM s
BANTER s
BANYAN s
BANZAI s
BAOBAB s
BARBAL
BARBED*
BARBEL*ls
BARBER*s
BARBES*
BARBET*s
BARBIE s
BARBUT s
BARCAS*
BARDED*
BARDES*
BARDIC
BAREGE s
BARELY
BAREST*
BARFED
BARFLY
BARGED*
BARGEE*s
BARGES*
BARHOP s
BARING
BARITE s
BARIUM s
BARKED
BARKER s
BARLEY s
BARLOW s
BARMAN
BARMEN
BARMIE r
BARNED
BARNEY s
BARONG*s
BARONS*
BARONY*
BARQUE s
BARRED*
BARREL*s
BARREN*s
BARRES*
BARRET*s
BARRIO s
*BARROW s
BARTER s
BARYES*
BARYON s
BARYTA s
BARYTE s
BASALT*s
BASELY
BASEST*
BASHAW s
a*BASHED
BASHER s
a*BASHES
BASICS*
BASIFY
BASILS*
a BASING*
BASINS*
BASION s
*BASKED
BASKET s
BASQUE s
*BASSES
*BASSET st
BASSLY

BASSOS*
BASTED*
*BASTER*s
BASTES*
BATBOY s
BATEAU x
BATHED*
BATHER*s
BATHES*
BATHOS
BATIKS*
a BATING
*BATMAN
BATMEN
BATONS*
BATTED
BATTEN s
BATTER sy
BATTIK s
BATTLE drs
BATTUE*s
BAUBEE s
BAUBLE s
BAULKS*
BAULKY*
BAWBEE s
BAWDRY
BAWLED
BAWLER s
BAWTIE s
BAYAMO s
BAYARD s
BAYING
BAYMAN
BAYMEN
BAYOUS*
BAZAAR s
BAZARS*
BAZOOS*
BEACHY*
BEACON s
BEADED
BEADER s
BEADLE s
*BEAGLE s
BEAKED
BEAKER s
BEAMED
BEANED
BEANIE s
BEANOS*
BEARDS*
BEARER s
BEASTS
*BEATEN
*BEATER s
BEAUTS*
BEAUTY*
BEAVER s
BEBOPS*
BECALM s
BECAME
BECAPS*
BECKED
BECKET s
BECKON s
BECLOG s
BECOME s
BEDAMN s
BEDAUB s
BEDBUG s
BEDDED
BEDDER s
BEDECK s
BEDELL*s
BEDELS*
BEDEWS*
BEDIMS*
BEDLAM ps
BEDPAN s
BEDRID
BEDRUG s
BEDSIT s
BEDUIN s
BEDUMB s
BEEBEE s
BEECHY*
BEEFED
BEEPED
BEEPER s
BEETLE drs
BEEVES
BEEZER s
BEFALL s
BEFELL
BEFITS*

BEFLAG s
BEFLEA s
BEFOGS*
BEFOOL s
BEFORE
BEFOUL s
BEFRET s
BEGALL s
BEGAZE ds
BEGETS*
*BEGGAR sy
*BEGGED
BEGINS*
BEGIRD s
BEGIRT
BEGLAD s
BEGONE
BEGRIM es
BEGULF s
BEGUMS*
BEHALF
BEHAVE drs
BEHEAD s
BEHELD
BEHEST s
BEHIND s
BEHOLD s
BEHOOF
BEHOVE ds
BEHOWL s
BEIGES*
BEIGNE st
BEINGS*
BEKISS
BEKNOT s
BELADY
BELAUD s
BELAYS*
BELDAM es
BELEAP st
BELFRY
BELGAS*
BELIED*
BELIEF*s
BELIER*s
BELIES*
BELIKE
BELIVE
BELLED*
BELLES*
BELLOW s
BELONG*s
BELONS*
BELOWS*
BELTED
BELTER s
BELUGA s
BEMATA
BEMEAN s
BEMIRE ds
BEMIST s
BEMIXT*
BEMOAN s
BEMOCK s
BEMUSE ds
BENAME ds
BENDAY s
*BENDED
BENDEE s
*BENDER s
BENDYS*
BENIGN
BENNES*
BENNET*s
BENNIS*
o BENTOS*
BENUMB s
BENZAL
BENZIN es
BENZOL es
BENZYL s
BERAKE ds
BERATE ds
BEREFT
BERETS*
BERIME ds
BERLIN es
BERMED*
BERMES*
BERTHA*s
BERTHS*
BERYLS*
BESEEM s
BESETS*
BESIDE s
BESMUT s

BESNOW s
BESOMS*
BESOTS*
BESTED
BESTIR s
BESTOW s
BESTUD s
BETAKE ns
BETELS*
BETHEL s
BETIDE ds
BETIME s
BETISE s
BETONS*
BETONY*
BETOOK
BETRAY s
BETTAS*
a BETTED
a BETTER s
a BETTOR s
BEVELS*
BEVIES
BEVORS*
BEWAIL s
BEWARE ds
BEWEEP s
BEWEPT
BEWIGS*
BEWORM s
BEWRAP st
BEWRAY s
BEYLIC s
BEYLIK s
BEYOND s
BEZANT s
BEZAZZ
BEZELS*
BEZILS*
BEZOAR s
BHAKTA s
BHAKTI s
BHANGS
BHARAL s
BHOOTS
BIALIS*
BIALYS*
BIASED
BIASES
BIAXAL
BIBBED
BIBBER sy
BIBLES*s
BICARB s
BICEPS*
*BICKER s
BICORN es
BICRON s
BIDDEN
BIDDER s
a BIDERS*
BIDETS*
a BIDING
BIELDS*
BIFACE s
BIFFED
BIFFIN gs
BIFLEX
BIFOLD
BIFORM
BIGAMY
BIGEYE s
BIGGER
BIGGIE s
BIGGIN gs
BIGHTS*
BIGOTS*
BIGWIG s
BIJOUS*
BIJOUX*
BIKERS*
BIKIES*
BIKING
BIKINI s
BILBOA*s
BILBOS*
BILGED*
BILGES*
BILKED
BILKER s
BILLED
*BILLER s
BILLET s
BILLIE s
BILLON s
BILLOW sy

BIMAHS*
BIMBOS*
BINARY
BINATE
BINDER sy
BINDIS*
BINDLE s
BINERS*
BINGED*
BINGER*s
BINGES*
BINGOS*
BINITS*
*BINNED
BINOCS
BIOGAS
BIOGEN sy
BIOMES*
*BIONIC s
BIONTS*
BIOPIC s
BIOPSY
BIOTAS
a BIOTIC s
BIOTIN s
BIPACK s
BIPEDS*
BIPODS*
BIRDED
BIRDER s
BIRDIE ds
BIREME s
BIRKIE s
BIRLED*
BIRLER*s
BIRLES*
BIRRED
BIRSES*
BIRTHS*
BISECT s
BISHOP s
BISONS*
BISQUE s
BISTER s
BISTRE ds
BISTRO s
BITCHY
BITERS*
BITING
BITMAP s
BITTED
BITTEN
BITTER ns
BIZONE s
BIZZES
BLABBY
BLACKS
BLADED
*BLADER*s
BLADES
BLAFFS*
BLAINS*
BLAMED
*BLAMER*s
BLAMES
BLANCH
BLANKS*
BLARED*
BLARES
o*BLASTS*
BLASTY*
*BLAWED
BLAZED
BLAZER*s
BLAZES
BLAZON s
*BLEACH
BLEAKS
BLEARS
BLEARY
BLEATS*
BLEBBY
BLEEDS*
BLEEPS*
BLENCH
BLENDE*drs
BLENDS
BLENNY
*BLIGHT sy
*BLIMEY
BLIMPS
BLINDS*
BLINIS*
BLINKS
BLINTZ e
BLITES*
*BLITHE r
BLOATS*
BLOCKS
BLOCKY*
BLOKES*
BLONDE*rs
BLONDS*
BLOODS*
BLOODY*
*BLOOEY
*BLOOIE
BLOOMS
BLOOMY*
BLOOPS
BLOTCH y
*BLOTTO
BLOTTY
*BLOUSE ds
*BLOUSY
BLOWBY s
*BLOWED
*BLOWER s
BLOWSY*
BLOWUP s
BLOWZY
BLUDGE drs
BLUELY
BLUEST*
BLUESY*
BLUETS*
BLUEYS*
BLUFFS
BLUING s
BLUISH
BLUMED*
BLUMES*
*BLUNGE drs
BLUNTS
BLURBS*
BLURRY
BLURTS*
BLYPES*
BOARDS*
BOARTS*
BOASTS
BOATED
BOATEL s
*BOATER s
BOBBED
BOBBER sy
BOBBIN gs
BOBBLE ds
BOBCAT s
BOCCES*
BOCCIA*s
BOCCIE*s
BOCCIS*
BODEGA s
BODICE s
BODIED
BODIES
BODILY
a BODING s
BODKIN s
BOFFIN s
BOFFOS*
BOGANS*
BOGART s
BOGEYS*
BOGGED
BOGGLE drs
BOGIES*
BOGLES
BOHEAS*
BOHUNK s
*BOILED
*BOILER s
BOINGS*
BOITES*
*BOLDER
BOLDLY
BOLERO s
BOLETE s
BOLETI
BOLIDE s
BOLLED
BOLLIX
BOLLOX
BOLSHY
BOLSON s
BOLTED
BOLTER s
BOMBAX
BOMBED*
*BOMBER*s
BOMBES*
BOMBYX
BONACI s
BONBON s
BONDED
BONDER s
BONDUC s
BONERS*
BONGED
BONGOS*
BONIER
BONING
BONITA s
BONITO s
BONKED
BONNES*
BONNET*s
BONNIE r
BONOBO s
BONSAI
BONZER*
BONZES*
BOOBED
BOOBOO s
BOOCOO s
BOODLE drs
BOOGER s
BOOGEY s
BOOGIE ds
BOOHOO s
BOOING
BOOJUM s
BOOKED
BOOKER s
BOOKIE s
BOOKOO s
BOOMED
BOOMER s
BOOSTS*
BOOTED
BOOTEE s
BOOTHS*
BOOTIE s
BOOZED
BOOZER*s
BOOZES
BOPEEP s
BOPPED
BOPPER s
BORAGE s
BORALS
BORANE s
*BORATE ds
BORDEL s
*BORDER s
BOREAL
BOREAS
BOREEN s
BORERS*
BORIDE s
BORING s
BORKED
BORONS*
BORROW s
BORSCH t
BORSHT s
BORZOI s
BOSHES
BOSKER
BOSKET s
BOSOMS*
BOSOMY*
BOSONS*
BOSQUE st
BOSSED
BOSSES
BOSTON s
BOSUNS*
BOTANY
BOTCHY*
BOTELS*
BOTFLY
*BOTHER s
BOTTLE drs
BOTTOM s
BOUBOU s
BOUCLE s
BOUDIN s
BOUFFE s
BOUGHS*
a*BOUGHT*
BOUGIE s
BOULES*
BOULLE s
*BOUNCE drs
BOUNCY
a BOUNDS*
BOUNTY
BOURGS*
BOURNE*s
BOURNS*
BOURSE s
BOUSED*
BOUSES*
BOUTON s
BOVIDS*
*BOVINE s
BOWELS*
BOWERS*
BOWERY*
BOWFIN s
*BOWING s
BOWLED
BOWLEG s
BOWLER s
BOWMAN
BOWMEN
BOWPOT s
BOWSED*
BOWSES*
BOWWOW s
BOWYER s
BOXCAR s
BOXERS*
BOXFUL s
BOXIER
BOXILY
BOXING s
BOYARD*s
BOYARS*
BOYISH
BOYLAS*
BRACED
*BRACER*os
BRACES
BRACHS*
BRACTS*
*BRAGGY
BRAHMA s
BRAIDS
BRAILS
BRAINS
BRAINY
*BRAISE ds
BRAIZE s
BRAKED
BRAKES
*BRANCH y
BRANDS
BRANDY
BRANKS
BRANNY
BRANTS
BRASHY*
BRASIL s
BRASSY*
*BRATTY
BRAVAS*
BRAVED
*BRAVER*sy
*BRAVES*t
BRAVOS*
*BRAWER
BRAWLS*
BRAWLY
BRAWNS*
BRAWNY*
*BRAYED
BRAYER s
BRAZAS*
BRAZED
BRAZEN*s
*BRAZER*s
BRAZES
BRAZIL s
*BREACH
BREADS
BREADY
BREAKS*
BREAMS
a BREAST s
BREATH esy
BREDES
BREECH
BREEDS
*BREEKS
BREEZE ds
BREEZY
*BREGMA
BRENTS
BREVES*
*BREVET*s
*BREWED
BREWER sy
BREWIS
BRIARD*s
BRIARS*
BRIARY*
BRIBED*
BRIBEE*s
BRIBER*sy
BRIBES
BRICKS
BRICKY*
BRIDAL s
BRIDES
a*BRIDGE ds
BRIDLE drs
BRIEFS*
BRIERS*
BRIERY*
*BRIGHT s
BRILLO*s
BRILLS
BRINED*
BRINER*s
BRINES*
BRINGS
BRINKS
BRIONY
*BRISES
BRISKS
BRITHS*
BRITTS*
a*BROACH
BROADS
BROCHE
BROCKS
BROGAN s
*BROGUE s
BROILS
BROKEN*
BROKER*s
BROLLY
BROMAL s
BROMES*
BROMIC
BROMID es
BROMIN es
BROMOS*
BRONCO*s
BRONCS*
BRONZE drs
BRONZY
BROOCH
BROODS
BROODY*
BROOKS
BROOMS
BROOMY
BROSES
BROTHS*
BROTHY*
*BROWED
BROWNS*
BROWNY*
BROWSE*drs
BRUCIN es
BRUGHS*
BRUINS
BRUISE drs
BRUITS*
BRULOT s
BRUMAL
BRUMBY
BRUMES*
BRUNCH
BRUNET s
BRUNTS
BRUSHY
BRUTAL
BRUTED*
BRUTES*
BRUXED
BRUXES
BRYONY
BUBALE*s
BUBALS*
a BUBBLE drs
BUBBLY
BUBKES
BUBOED
BUBOES
BUCCAL
BUCKED
BUCKER s
BUCKET s
BUCKLE drs
BUCKOS*
BUDDED
*BUDDER s
BUDDHA s
BUDDLE s
BUDGED*
BUDGER*s
BUDGES*
BUDGET*s
BUDGIE s
BUFFED
BUFFER s
BUFFET s
BUFFOS*
BUGEYE s
BUGGED
BUGGER sy
BUGLED*
BUGLER*s
BUGLES*
BUGOUT s
BUGSHA s
BUILDS*
BULBAR
BULBED
BULBEL s
BULBIL s
BULBUL s
BULGED*
BULGER*s
BULGES*
BULGUR s
BULKED
BULLAE*
BULLED
BULLET s
BUMBLE drs
BUMKIN s
BUMMED
BUMMER s
*BUMPED
BUMPER s
BUMPHS*
BUNCHY*
BUNCOS
BUNDLE drs
BUNDTS*
BUNGED
BUNGEE s
BUNGLE drs
*BUNION s
BUNKED
BUNKER s
BUNKOS*
BUNKUM s
BUNTED
BUNTER s
BUNYAS*
BUOYED
BUPKES
BUPKUS
BUPPIE s
BUQSHA s
BURANS*
BURBLE drs
BURBLY
BURBOT s
BURDEN s
BURDIE s
BUREAU sx
BURETS*
BURGEE s
*BURGER s
BURGHS*
BURGLE ds
BURGOO s
*BURIAL s
BURIED
BURIER s
BURIES
BURINS*
BURKAS*
BURKED*
BURKER*s
BURKES*
BURLAP s
BURLED
BURLER s
BURLEY s
BURNED
BURNER s
BURNET s
BURNIE s
*BURPED
BURQAS*
BURRED
BURRER s
BURROS*
BURROW*s
BURSAE
BURSAL*
BURSAR*sy
BURSAS*
BURSES*
BURSTS*
BURTON s
BUSBAR s
BUSBOY s
BUSHED
BUSHEL s
*BUSHER s
BUSHES
BUSHWA hs
BUSIED
BUSIER
BUSIES t
BUSILY
a*BUSING s
BUSKED
BUSKER s
BUSKIN gs
BUSMAN
BUSMEN
BUSSED
BUSSES
BUSTED
BUSTER s
BUSTIC s
BUSTLE drs
BUTANE s
BUTENE s
BUTEOS*
BUTLED*
BUTLER*sy
BUTLES*
a BUTTED*
a*BUTTER*sy
BUTTES*
BUTTON sy
BUTUTS*
BUTYLS*
BUYERS*
BUYING
BUYOFF s
BUYOUT s
BUZUKI as
BUZZED
BUZZER s
BUZZES
BWANAS*
BYELAW s
BYGONE s
BYLAWS*
BYLINE drs
BYNAME s
BYPASS
BYPAST
BYPATH s
BYPLAY s
BYRLED
BYRNIE s
BYROAD s
a BYSSAL
BYSSUS
BYTALK s
BYWAYS*
BYWORD s
BYWORK s
BYZANT s
CABALA*s
CABALS*
CABANA s
s CABBED
CABBIE s
CABERS*
CABINS*
CABLED
*CABLER*s
CABLES
CABLET*s
CABMAN
CABMEN
CABOBS*
CACAOS*
CACHED
CACHES
CACHET*s
CACHOU s
CACKLE drs
CACTUS
CADDIE ds
CADDIS h
CADENT

CADETS*
CADGED*
CADGER*s
CADGES*
CADMIC
CADRES*
CAECAL*
CAECUM
CAEOMA s
CAESAR s
CAFTAN s
CAGERS
CAGIER
CAGILY
*CAGING
CAHIER s
CAHOOT s
CAHOWS*
CAIMAN s
CAIQUE s
CAIRDS*
CAIRNS
CAIRNY*
CAJOLE drs
CAKIER
CAKING
CALAMI
CALASH
CALCAR s
CALCES
CALCIC
CALESA s
CALICO s
CALIFS
CALIPH s
CALKED
CALKER s
CALKIN gs
CALLAN*st
CALLAS*
CALLED
*CALLEE s
CALLER s
CALLET s
*CALLOW
CALLUS
CALMED
CALMER
CALMLY
CALORY
CALPAC ks
CALQUE ds
CALVED*
CALVES*
CALXES
CAMAIL s
CAMASS
*CAMBER s
CAMBIA l
CAMELS*
CAMEOS*
CAMERA els
CAMION s
CAMISA s
CAMISE s
CAMLET s
CAMMIE s
s*CAMPED
s CAMPER s
CAMPOS*
CAMPUS
CANALS*
CANAPE s
CANARD s
CANARY
CANCAN s
CANCEL s
CANCER s
CANCHA s
CANDID as
CANDLE drs
CANDOR s
CANERS*
CANFUL s
CANGUE s
CANIDS*
CANINE s
CANING
CANKER s
CANNAS
s CANNED
CANNEL s
s CANNER sy
CANNIE r
CANNON s
CANNOT

CANOED*
CANOER*s
CANOES*
CANOLA s
CANONS*
CANOPY
CANSOS*
CANTAL as
s*CANTED
s CANTER s
a CANTHI
*CANTIC
CANTLE s
CANTON*s
CANTOR*s
CANTOS*
CANTUS
CANULA ers
CANVAS s
*CANYON s
CAPERS
CAPFUL s
CAPIAS
CAPITA l
CAPLET s
CAPLIN s
CAPONS*
CAPOTE s
CAPPED
CAPPER s
CAPRIC e
CAPRIS
CAPSID s
CAPTAN s
CAPTOR s
CARACK s
CARAFE s
CARATE*s
CARATS*
CARBON*s
CARBOS*
CARBOY*s
CARCEL s
CARDED
CARDER s
CARDIA ces
CARDIO
CARDON s
CAREEN s
CAREER s
s CARERS*
CARESS*
CARETS*
CARFUL s
CARGOS*
CARHOP s
CARIBE s
CARIED
CARIES
o CARINA els
s CARING
CARKED
*CARLES*s
CARLIN egs
CARMAN
CARMEN
CARNAL
CARNET s
CARNEY s
CARNIE s
CAROBS*
CAROCH e
CAROLI*
CAROLS*
CAROMS*
CARPAL es
s CARPED
CARPEL s
s CARPER s
CARPET s
CARPUS
CARREL ls
CARROM s
CARROT sy
CARSES
s CARTED*
*CARTEL*s
CARTER*s
e CARTES*
CARTON s
CARTOP
CARVED*
CARVEL*s
CARVEN*
CARVER*s
s CARVES*

CASABA s
CASAVA s
CASBAH s
CASEFY
CASEIC
CASEIN s
CASERN es
CASHAW s
*CASHED
*CASHES
CASHEW s
CASHOO s
CASING s
CASINI
CASINO s
CASITA s
*CASKED
CASKET s
CASQUE ds
CASSIA s
CASSIS
*CASTER*s
CASTES*
CASTLE ds
CASTOR s
CASUAL s
CATALO gs
CATCHY*
CATENA es
CATERS*
CATGUT s
CATION s
CATKIN s
CATLIN gs
CATNAP s
CATNIP s
CATSUP s
s CATTED
CATTIE rs
CATTLE
CAUCUS
*CAUDAD
a CAUDAL
CAUDEX
CAUDLE s
*CAUGHT
CAULDS*
CAULES
CAULIS
CAULKS*
CAUSAL s
CAUSED*
CAUSER*s
CAUSES*
CAUSEY*s
CAVEAT s
CAVERN*s
CAVERS
CAVIAR es
CAVIES*
CAVILS*
CAVING s
CAVITY
CAVORT s
*CAWING
CAYMAN s
CAYUSE s
CEASED
CEASES
CEBIDS*
CEBOID s
CECITY
CEDARN*
CEDARS*
CEDARY*
CEDERS*
CEDING
CEDULA s
CEIBAS*
CEILED
CEILER s
CEILIS*
CELEBS*
CELERY
CELIAC s
CELLAE*
o CELLAR*s
CELLED
CELLOS*
CELOMS*
CEMENT as
CENOTE s
CENSED*
CENSER*s
CENSES*
CENSOR s

CENSUS
CENTAI
CENTAL s
CENTAS
*CENTER s
CENTOS*
CENTRA l
CENTRE ds
CENTUM*s
CEORLS*
a CERATE ds
CERCAL
CERCIS*
CERCUS
CEREAL s
CEREUS
CERIAS*
CERING
CERIPH s
CERISE s
CERITE s
CERIUM s
CERMET s
a CEROUS
CERTES
CERUSE s
CERVID
CERVIX
CESIUM s
CESSED
*CESSES
CESTAS*
CESTOI d
CESTOS
CESTUS
CESURA es
CETANE s
CHABUK s
CHACMA s
CHADAR s
CHADOR s
CHADRI
CHAETA el
CHAFED*
CHAFER*s
CHAFES*
CHAFFS*
CHAFFY*
CHAINE*ds
CHAINS*
CHAIRS
CHAISE*s
CHAKRA s
CHALAH s
CHALEH s
CHALET s
CHALKS*
CHALKY*
CHALLA hs
CHALLY
CHALOT h
*CHAMMY
CHAMPS*
CHAMPY*
*CHANCE dlr
s
CHANCY
CHANGE*drs
CHANGS
CHANTS
CHANTY*
CHAPEL*s
CHAPES*
CHARAS
e*CHARDS*
CHARED
CHARES
CHARGE drs
CHARKA*s
CHARKS
CHARMS
CHARRO*s
CHARRS*
CHARRY
CHARTS
CHASED*
CHASER*s
CHASES*
CHASMS*
CHASMY*
CHASSE ds
*CHASTE nr
CHATTY
*CHAUNT s
*CHAWED
CHAWER s

*CHAZAN s
CHEAPO*s
CHEAPS
CHEATS
CHEBEC s
CHECKS
*CHEDER s
CHEEKS*
CHEEKY*
CHEEPS*
CHEERO*s
CHEERS*
CHEERY*
CHEESE ds
CHEESY
CHEFED
CHEGOE s
CHELAE*
CHELAS*
*CHEMIC s
CHEMOS*
CHEQUE rs
*CHERRY
CHERTS*
CHERTY*
CHERUB s
CHESTS
CHESTY*
CHETAH s
CHETHS
CHEVRE st
*CHEWED
*CHEWER s
CHIASM*ais
CHIAUS
CHICAS*
CHICER
CHICHI s
CHICKS
CHICLE s
CHICLY
CHICOS*
CHIDED
*CHIDER*s
CHIDES
CHIEFS*
CHIELD*s
CHIELS*
CHIGOE s
CHILDE*s
CHILES*
CHILIS*
CHILLI*s
CHILLS
CHILLY
CHIMAR s
CHIMBS*
CHIMED*
CHIMER*aes
CHIMES*
CHIMLA s
CHIMPS*
CHINAS*
CHINCH y
CHINED*
CHINES*
CHINKS*
CHINKY
CHINOS*
*CHINTS
CHINTZ y
*CHIPPY
a CHIRAL
CHIRKS*
CHIRMS*
CHIROS*
CHIRPS*
CHIRPY*
CHIRRE*dns
CHIRRS*
CHIRUS*
CHISEL s
CHITAL
CHITIN s
CHITON s
CHITTY
CHIVES
CHIVVY
CHOANA e
CHOCKS
CHOICE rs
CHOIRS*
CHOKED
CHOKER*s
CHOKES
CHOKEY

CHOLAS*
CHOLER as
*CHOLLA s
CHOLOS*
CHOMPS*
CHOOKS
CHOOSE rsy
CHOOSY
CHOPIN es
*CHOPPY
*CHORAL es
CHORDS*
CHOREA*ls
CHORED*
CHORES*
CHORIC
CHORUS
CHOSEN
CHOSES
CHOTTS*
CHOUGH s
*CHOUSE drs
CHOUSH
CHOWED
CHOWSE*ds
CHRISM as
CHROMA s
CHROME ds
CHROMO s
CHROMY l
*CHUBBY
CHUCKS
CHUCKY*
CHUFAS*
CHUFFS
CHUFFY
CHUKAR s
CHUKKA rs
CHUMMY
CHUMPS
CHUNKS
CHUNKY
CHUPPA hs
CHURCH y
CHURLS
CHURNS*
CHURRO*s
CHURRS*
CHUTED*
CHUTES*
CHYLES*
CHYMES*
CHYMIC s
CIBOLS*
CICADA es
CICALA s
CICALE
CICELY
CICERO s
CIDERS*
CIGARS*
CILICE s
*CILIUM
CINDER sy
CINEMA s
CINEOL es
CINQUE s
CIPHER s
CIRCLE drs
t
CIRCUS y
CIRQUE s
CIRRUS
CISCOS*
CISTED
CISTUS
CITERS*
*CITHER ns
CITIED
CITIES
CITIFY
CITING
CITOLA s
CITOLE s
CITRAL s
CITRIC
CITRIN es
CITRON s
CITRUS y
CIVETS*
CIVICS*
CIVIES
CIVISM s
CLACHS*
CLACKS
CLADES

CLAIMS*
CLAMMY
CLAMOR s
CLAMPS
CLANGS*
CLANKS*
CLANKY
CLAQUE rs
CLARET s
CLAROS*
CLASPS*
CLASPT*
CLASSY*
CLASTS
CLAUSE s
*CLAVER*s
CLAVES
CLAVUS
*CLAWED
CLAWER s
CLAXON s
*CLAYED
CLAYEY
*CLEANS*e
CLEARS
CLEATS*
*CLEAVE drs
CLEEKS
CLEFTS
CLENCH
CLEOME s
y CLEPED*
CLEPES*
CLERGY
CLERIC s
CLERID s
CLERKS*
*CLEVER
*CLEVIS
CLEWED
CLICHE ds
CLICKS
CLIENT s
CLIFFS*
CLIFFY*
CLIFTS
CLIMAX
CLIMBS
CLIMES
CLINAL
CLINCH
CLINES
CLINGS
CLINGY
a CLINIC s
CLINKS
CLIQUE dsy
CLIQUY
CLITIC s
CLIVIA s
CLOACA els
CLOAKS*
CLOCHE s
CLOCKS
CLODDY
*CLOGGY
CLOMPS*
CLONAL
CLONED*
*CLONER*s
CLONES*
CLONIC
CLONKS*
CLONUS
CLOOTS
CLOQUE s
CLOSED*
*CLOSER*s
*CLOSES*t
CLOSET*s
CLOTHE*ds
CLOTHS*
CLOTTY
CLOUDS*
CLOUDY*
*CLOUGH s
CLOURS
CLOUTS
CLOVEN*
*CLOVER*sy
CLOVES
CLOWNS*
CLOYED
CLOZES*
CLUBBY
CLUCKS

CLUING
CLUMPS
CLUMPY
CLUMSY
CLUNKS
CLUNKY*
CLUTCH y
CLYPEI
CNIDAE*
COACTS*
COALAS*
COALED
COALER s
COAPTS*
COARSE nr
COASTS
COATED
COATEE s
*COATER s
COATIS*
COAXAL
COAXED
COAXER s
COAXES
COBALT s
COBBER s
COBBLE drs
COBIAS
COBLES*
COBNUT s
COBRAS*
COBWEB s
COCAIN es
COCCAL
COCCIC*
COCCID*s
COCCUS
COCCYX
COCHIN s
COCKED
*COCKER s
COCKLE ds
COCKUP s
COCOAS*
COCOON s
CODDED
*CODDER s
CODDLE drs
CODECS*
CODEIA s
CODEIN aes
CODENS*
CODERS*
CODGER s
CODIFY
CODING
CODLIN gs
CODONS*
COEDIT s
COELOM es
COEMPT s
COERCE drs
COEVAL s
COFFEE s
s*COFFER s
COFFIN gs
COFFLE ds
COGENT
COGGED
COGITO s
COGNAC s
COGONS*
COGWAY s
COHEAD s
COHEIR s
COHERE drs
COHOGS*
COHORT s
COHOSH*
COHOST*s
COHUNE s
COIFED
COIFFE ds
COIGNE*ds
COIGNS*
*COILED
*COILER s
COINED
COINER s
COITAL
COITUS
COJOIN s
COKING
COLBYS*
s*COLDER
COLDLY
COLEAD s
COLEUS
COLICS*
COLIES
COLINS*
COLLAR ds
COLLET s
COLLIE drs
s COLLOP s
COLOBI
COLOGS*
COLONE*ls
COLONI*c
COLONS*
COLONY*
COLORS*
COLOUR s
COLTER s
COLUGO s
COLUMN s
COLURE s
COLZAS*
COMADE
COMAKE rs
COMATE s
COMBAT s
COMBED*
*COMBER*s
COMBES*
COMBOS*
COMEDO s
COMEDY
COMELY
COMERS
COMETH*
COMETS*
COMFIT s
COMICS*
COMING s
COMITY
COMMAS*
COMMIE s
COMMIT s
COMMIX t
COMMON s
COMOSE
COMOUS
COMPAS s
COMPED
COMPEL s
COMPLY
COMPOS*et
COMPTS*
COMTES*
CONCHA*els
CONCHO*s
CONCHS*
CONCHY*
CONCUR s
CONDOM*s
CONDOR*s
CONDOS*
CONEYS*
CONFAB s
CONFER s
CONFIT s
CONGAS*
CONGEE*ds
CONGER*s
CONGES*t
CONGII
CONGOS*
CONGOU*s
CONICS*
CONIES
CONINE*s
CONING*
CONINS*
*CONIUM s
CONKED
CONKER s
CONNED
CONNER s
CONOID s
CONSOL es
CONSUL st
CONTES*t
CONTOS*
CONTRA s
CONVEX
CONVEY s
CONVOY s
COOCOO
COOEED*
COOEES*
COOERS*
COOEYS*
COOING
COOKED
COOKER sy
COOKEY s
COOKIE s
COOLED
COOLER s
COOLIE s
COOLLY
COOLTH s
COOMBE*s
COOMBS*
s COOPED
s COOPER sy
COOPTS*
s COOTER s
COOTIE s
COPALM*s
COPALS
COPAYS*
COPECK s
COPENS
COPERS*
COPIED
COPIER s
COPIES
s*COPING s
COPLOT s
COPOUT s
COPPED
COPPER sy
COPPRA s
COPRAH*s
COPRAS*
COPSES*
COPTER s
s COPULA ers
COQUET s
CORALS
CORBAN s
CORBEL s
CORBIE s
CORDED
*CORDER s
CORDON s
s CORERS*
CORGIS*
s CORING
CORIUM
CORKED
CORKER s
CORMEL s
CORNEA ls
as CORNED
CORNEL s
s CORNER s
CORNET s
CORNUA*l
CORNUS*
CORODY
CORONA els
CORPSE*s
CORPUS
CORRAL s
CORRIE s
CORSAC s
CORSES*
CORSET*s
CORTEX
CORTIN as
CORVEE s
CORVES
CORVET s
CORVID s
CORYMB s
CORYZA ls
COSECS*
COSETS*
COSEYS*
COSHED
COSHER s
COSHES
COSIED*
COSIER
COSIES*t
COSIGN s
COSILY
COSINE s
*COSMIC
COSMID s
COSMOS
COSSET s
COSTAE*
COSTAL*
COSTAR*ds
COSTED
COSTER s
COSTLY
COTANS*
COTEAU x
COTING a
COTTAE*
*COTTAR*s
COTTAS*
*COTTER s
COTTON sy
e COTYPE s
COUGAR s
COUGHS*
COULEE s
COULIS
COUNTS*
COUNTY*
COUPED*
COUPES*
COUPLE drs
t
COUPON s
COURSE drs
COURTS*
COUSIN s
s*COUTER s
s COUTHS*
*COVARY
COVENS
COVERS
*COVERT*s
COVETS*
COVEYS*
COVING*s
COVINS*
COWAGE s
COWARD s
COWBOY s
COWERS*
COWIER
s*COWING
s COWLED
COWMAN
COWMEN
COWPAT s
COWPEA s
COWPIE s
COWPOX
COWRIE s
COXING
COYDOG s
COYEST
COYING
COYISH
COYOTE s
COYPOU s
COYPUS*
COZENS*
COZEYS*
COZIED*
COZIER*
COZIES*t
COZILY
COZZES
CRAALS*
CRABBY
CRACKS
CRACKY*
CRADLE drs
CRAFTS
CRAFTY*
s*CRAGGY
CRAKES
CRAMBE s
CRAMBO s
CRAMPS
CRAMPY*
*CRANCH
CRANED*
CRANES*
CRANIA l
CRANKS
CRANKY*
CRANNY
s*CRAPED*
s*CRAPES*
s CRAPPY
*CRASES
CRASIS
s*CRATCH
CRATED
*CRATER*s
CRATES
CRATON s
CRAVAT s
CRAVED
*CRAVEN*s
*CRAVER*s
CRAVES
s CRAWLS*
s*CRAWLY*
*CRAYON s
CRAZED
CRAZES
s CREAKS*
s CREAKY*
s*CREAMS*
CREAMY*
CREASE drs
CREASY
o CREATE ds
CRECHE s
CREDAL
CREDIT s
CREDOS
s*CREEDS*
CREEKS
CREELS
CREEPS*
CREEPY*
CREESE s
CREESH
CREMES*
CRENEL s
CREOLE s
CREPED*
CREPES*
CREPEY*
CREPON s
CRESOL s
CRESSY*
CRESTS
CRESYL s
CRETIC s
CRETIN s
s*CREWED
CREWEL s
CRICKS
CRIERS*
CRIKEY
CRIMES
s CRIMPS*
s CRIMPY*
CRINGE drs
CRINUM s
CRIPES
*CRISES
CRISIC
CRISIS
CRISPS*
CRISPY*
CRISSA l
CRISTA e
CRITIC s
CROAKS*
CROAKY*
CROCKS
CROCUS
CROFTS*
CROJIK s
CRONES*
CROOKS
CROONS*
CRORES*
CROSSE*drs
*CROTCH
CROTON s
CROUCH
CROUPE*s
CROUPS
CROUPY
*CROUSE
*CROUTE s
CROWDS*
CROWDY
*CROWED
*CROWER s
CROWNS*
CROZER*s
CROZES*
CRUCES
CRUCKS
*CRUDDY
CRUDER
CRUDES*t
CRUETS*
CRUISE drs
CRUMBS*
CRUMBY*
*CRUMMY
CRUMPS
s CRUNCH y
CRUORS*
CRURAL
CRUSES
CRUSET*s
CRUSTS
CRUSTY
CRUTCH
CRUXES
CRWTHS*
s CRYING
CRYPTO*s
CRYPTS*
CUATRO s
CUBAGE s
CUBEBS*
CUBERS*
CUBICS*
CUBING
CUBISM s
CUBIST s
CUBITI*
CUBITS*
CUBOID s
CUCKOO s
CUDDIE s
CUDDLE drs
CUDDLY
CUDGEL s
CUEING
CUESTA s
s CUFFED
CUISSE s
CULETS*
CULLAY s
s CULLED
s CULLER s
CULLET s
CULLIS
CULMED
CULPAE*
s CULTCH
CULTIC*
CULTUS
CULVER st
*CUMBER s
CUMBIA s
CUMINS*
s CUMMER s
CUMMIN s
CUMULI
CUNDUM s
CUNEAL
s CUNNER s
CUPELS*
CUPFUL s
CUPIDS*
CUPOLA s
CUPPAS*
*CUPPED
s*CUPPER s
CUPRIC
CUPRUM s
CUPULA er
CUPULE s
CURACY
CURAGH s
CURARA s
*CURARE s
*CURARI s
*CURATE ds
CURBED
CURBER s
CURDED
CURDLE drs
CURERS*
CURETS*
CURFEW s
CURIAE*
CURIAL
CURIES*
CURING
CURIOS*a
CURITE s
CURIUM s
CURLED
CURLER s
CURLEW s
CURRAN st
CURRED
CURRIE drs
CURSED*
CURSER*s
CURSES*
CURSOR sy
CURTAL s
CURTER
CURTLY
CURTSY
CURULE
CURVED*
CURVES*
CURVET*s
CURVEY*
CUSCUS
CUSECS*
CUSHAT s
CUSHAW s
CUSPAL
CUSPED
CUSPID s
CUSPIS
CUSSED
CUSSER s
CUSSES
CUSSOS*
CUSTOM s
CUSTOS
a CUTELY
a CUTEST*
CUTESY*
CUTEYS*
CUTIES*
CUTINS*
CUTLAS s
CUTLER sy
CUTLET s
CUTOFF s
CUTOUT s
s*CUTTER s
s CUTTLE ds
CUTUPS*
CUVEES*
CYANIC
CYANID es
CYANIN es
CYBORG s
CYCADS*
CYCLED*
CYCLER*sy
CYCLES*
a CYCLIC
CYCLIN gs
CYCLOS*
CYDERS*
*CYESES
CYESIS
CYGNET s
CYMARS*
CYMBAL s
CYMENE s
CYMLIN gs
CYMOID
CYMOLS*
CYMOSE
CYMOUS
CYNICS*
CYPHER s
CYPRES s
CYPRUS
CYSTIC
CYTONS*
DABBED
DABBER s
DABBLE drs
DACHAS*
DACITE s
DACKER s
DACOIT sy
DACRON s
DACTYL is
*DADDLE ds
DADGUM
DADOED
DADOES
DAEDAL
DAEMON s
DAFFED
*DAFTER
DAFTLY
DAGGAS*
*DAGGER s
DAGGLE ds
DAGOBA s
DAHLIA s
DAHOON s
DAIKER s
DAIKON s
DAIMEN
DAIMIO s
DAIMON s
DAIMYO s

DAINTY
DAISES
DAKOIT sy
DALASI s
DALEDH s
DALETH s
DALLES
DALTON s
DAMAGE drs
DAMANS*
DAMARS*
DAMASK s
DAMMAR s
DAMMED
DAMMER s
DAMMIT
DAMNED
DAMNER s
*DAMPED
DAMPEN s
DAMPER s
*DAMPLY
DAMSEL s
DAMSON s
DANCED*
DANCER*s
DANCES*
DANDER s
DANDLE drs
DANGED
*DANGER s
*DANGLE drs
DANGLY
DANIOS*
DANISH
DANKER
DANKLY
DAPHNE s
DAPPED
DAPPER
*DAPPLE ds
DARBAR s
DARERS*
DARICS*
DARING s
DARKED
DARKEN s
DARKER
DARKLE ds
DARKLY
DARNED
DARNEL s
DARNER s
DARTED
DARTER s
DARTLE ds
*DASHED
DASHER s
*DASHES
DASHIS*
DASSIE s
DATARY
DATCHA s
DATERS*
DATING
DATIVE s
DATTOS*
DATUMS*
DATURA s
DAUBED*
DAUBER*sy
DAUBES*
DAUBRY
DAUNTS
DAUTED
DAUTIE s
DAVENS
DAVIES
DAVITS*
DAWDLE drs
*DAWING
*DAWNED
DAWTED
DAWTIE s
DAYBED s
DAYFLY
DAYLIT
DAZING
DAZZLE drs
DEACON s
DEADEN s
DEADER
DEADLY
DEAFEN s
DEAFER
DEAFLY

DEAIRS*
DEALER s
DEANED
DEARER
DEARIE s
*DEARLY
*DEARTH s
DEASIL
DEATHS*
DEATHY*
DEAVED
DEAVES
DEBAGS*
DEBARK*s
DEBARS*
DEBASE drs
DEBATE drs
DEBEAK s
DEBITS*
DEBONE drs
DEBRIS
DEBTOR s
DEBUGS*
DEBUNK s
DEBUTS*
DEBYES*
DECADE s
DECAFS*
DECALS*
DECAMP s
DECANE s
DECANT s
DECARE s
DECAYS*
DECEIT s
DECENT
DECERN s
DECIDE drs
DECILE s
DECKED
DECKEL s
DECKER s
DECKLE s
DECLAW s
DECOCT s
DECODE drs
DECORS*
DECOYS*
DECREE drs
DECURY
DEDANS
*DEDUCE ds
*DEDUCT s
DEEDED
DEEJAY s
a DEEMED
DEEPEN s
DEEPER
DEEPLY
DEEWAN s
DEFACE drs
DEFAME drs
DEFANG s
DEFATS*
DEFEAT s
DEFECT s
DEFEND s
DEFERS*
DEFFER
DEFIED
DEFIER s
DEFIES
DEFILE drs
DEFINE drs
DEFLEA s
DEFOAM s
DEFOGS*
DEFORM s
DEFRAG s
DEFRAY s
DEFTER
DEFTLY
DEFUEL s
DEFUND s
DEFUSE drs
DEFUZE ds
DEGAGE
DEGAME s
DEGAMI s
DEGERM s
DEGREE ds
DEGUMS*
DEGUST s
DEHORN s
DEHORT s
DEICED*

DEICER*s
DEICES*
DEIFIC
DEIGNS*
DEISMS*
DEISTS*
DEIXIS
*DEJECT as
DEKARE s
*DEKING
DEKKOS*
*DELATE ds
DELAYS*
DELEAD s
DELETE ds
DELFTS*
DELICT s
DELIME ds
DELISH*
DELIST*s
DELTAS*
DELTIC
*DELUDE drs
DELUGE ds
DELUXE
DELVED*
*DELVER*s
DELVES
DEMAND s
DEMARK s
DEMAST s
DEMEAN s
DEMENT s
DEMIES
DEMISE ds
DEMITS
DEMOBS*
DEMODE d
DEMOED
DEMONS*
*DEMOTE ds
DEMURE*r
DEMURS*
DENARI*i
DENARS*
DENARY*
DENGUE s
DENIAL s
DENIED
DENIER s
DENIES
DENIMS*
DENNED
DENOTE ds
DENSER*
DENTAL s
DENTED
DENTIL s
DENTIN egs
DENUDE drs
DEODAR as
DEPART s
DEPEND s
DEPERM s
DEPICT s
DEPLOY s
DEPONE ds
DEPORT s
DEPOSE drs
DEPOTS*
DEPTHS*
DEPUTE ds
DEPUTY
DERAIL s
DERATE*ds
DERATS*
DERAYS*
DERIDE drs
DERIVE drs
DERMAL*
DERMAS*
DERMIC
DERMIS
DERRIS
DESALT s
DESAND s
DESCRY
DESERT s
DESIGN s
DESIRE drs
DESIST s
DESMAN s
DESMID s
DESORB s
DESOXY
DESPOT s

DETACH
DETAIL s
DETAIN s
DETECT s
DETENT es
DETERS*
DETEST s
DETICK s
DETOUR s
DEUCED*
DEUCES*
DEVEIN s
DEVELS*
DEVEST s
DEVICE s
DEVILS
DEVISE der
s
DEVOID
DEVOIR s
DEVONS*
DEVOTE des
DEVOUR s
DEVOUT
DEWANS*
DEWARS*
DEWIER
DEWILY
DEWING
DEWLAP s
DEWOOL s
DEWORM s
DEXIES*
DEXTER
DEXTRO
DEZINC s
DHARMA s
DHARNA s
DHOBIS*
DHOLES
*DHOOLY
DHOORA s
DHOOTI es
DHOTIS*
DHURNA s
DHUTIS*
DIACID s
DIADEM s
DIALED
DIALER s
DIALOG s
DIAMIN es
DIAPER s
DIAPIR s
DIATOM s
DIAZIN es
DIBBED
DIBBER s
DIBBLE drs
DIBBUK s
DICAST s
DICERS*
*DICIER
*DICING
*DICKER s
DICKEY s
DICKIE rs
DICOTS*
DICTUM s
DIDACT s
DIDDLE drs
y
DIDDLY
DIDIES*
DIDOES
DIEING
DIENES*
DIEOFF s
DIESEL s
DIESES
DIESIS
DIETED
DIETER s
DIFFER s
DIGAMY
DIGEST s
*DIGGED
DIGGER s
DIGHTS*
DIGITS*
DIGLOT s
DIKDIK s
DIKERS*
DIKING
DIKTAT s
DILATE drs

DILDOE*s
DILDOS*
DILLED
DILUTE drs
DIMERS*
DIMITY
DIMMED
DIMMER s
DIMOUT s
DIMPLE ds
*DIMPLY
DIMWIT s
DINARS*
DINDLE ds
DINERO*s
DINERS*
DINGED*
DINGER*s
DINGES*
DINGEY*s
DINGHY
*DINGLE s
DINGUS
DINING
*DINKED
DINKEY s
DINKLY
DINKUM s
*DINNED
*DINNER s
DINTED
DIOBOL s
DIODES*
DIOECY
DIOXAN es
DIOXID es
DIOXIN s
DIPLEX
DIPLOE s
DIPNET s
DIPODY
DIPOLE s
DIPPED
DIPPER s
DIPSAS
DIPSOS*
DIQUAT s
DIRAMS*
DIRDUM s
DIRECT s
DIRELY
DIREST
DIRGES*
DIRHAM s
*DIRKED
DIRLED
DIRNDL s
DISARM s
DISBAR s
DISBUD s
DISCED
DISCOS*
DISCUS s
DISEUR s
DISHED
DISHES
DISKED
DISMAL s
DISMAY s
DISMES*
DISOWN s
DISPEL s
DISSED
DISSES
DISTAL
DISTIL ls
DISUSE ds
*DITHER sy
DITTOS*
DITZES
DIURON s
DIVANS*
DIVERS*e
DIVERT*s
DIVEST*s
DIVIDE drs
DIVINE drs
DIVING
DIVOTS*
DIWANS*
DIXITS*
DIZENS*
*DJEBEL s
DJINNI
DJINNS
DJINNY*

DOABLE
DOATED
DOBBER s
DOBBIN s
DOBIES*
DOBLAS*
DOBLON s
DOBRAS*
DOBROS*
DOBSON s
DOCENT s
DOCILE
DOCKED
*DOCKER s
DOCKET s
DOCTOR s
*DODDER sy
DODGED*
DODGEM*s
DODGER*sy
DODGES*
DODOES
*DOFFED
*DOFFER s
DOGDOM s
DOGEAR s
DOGEYS*
DOGGED
DOGGER sy
DOGGIE rs
DOGIES*
DOGLEG s
DOGMAS*
DOGNAP s
*DOILED
DOINGS*
DOITED
DOLING
DOLLAR s
DOLLED
DOLLOP s
DOLMAN*s
DOLMAS*
DOLMEN s
DOLORS*
DOLOUR s
DOMAIN es
DOMINE s
DOMING
DOMINO s
o DONATE ds
DONEES*
DONGAS*
DONGLE s
DONJON s
DONKEY s
DONNAS*
DONNED*
DONNEE*s
DONORS*
DONSIE
DONUTS*
DONZEL s
DOOBIE s
DOODAD s
DOODLE drs
DOODOO s
DOOFUS
DOOLEE s
DOOLIE s
DOOMED
DOOWOP s
DOOZER s
DOOZIE s
DOPANT s
DOPERS*
DOPIER
DOPILY
*DOPING s
DORADO s
DORBUG s
DORIES
*DORMER s
DORMIE
DORMIN s
DORPER s
DORSAD*
DORSAL*s
DORSEL s
DORSER s
DORSUM
DOSAGE s
DOSERS*
DOSING
DOSSAL s
DOSSED

DOSSEL s
DOSSER s
DOSSES
DOSSIL s
DOTAGE s
DOTARD s
DOTERS*
DOTIER
DOTING
DOTTED
DOTTEL s
*DOTTER s
DOTTLE s
DOUBLE drs
t
DOUBLY
DOUBTS*
DOUCHE ds
DOUGHS*
*DOUGHT*y
DOUGHY*
DOULAS*
DOUMAS*
DOURAH*s
DOURAS*
DOURER
DOURLY
DOUSED*
DOUSER*s
DOUSES*
DOVENS
DOVISH
DOWELS*
DOWERS*
DOWERY*
*DOWING
*DOWNED
*DOWNER s
DOWSED*
DOWSER*s
DOWSES*
DOXIES*
DOYENS*
DOYLEY s
DOZENS*
DOZERS*
DOZIER
DOZILY
DOZING
DRABLY
DRACHM as
DRAFFS
DRAFFY*
DRAFTS
DRAFTY*
*DRAGEE s
*DRAGGY
DRAGON s
DRAILS
DRAINS
DRAKES
DRAMAS*
DRAPED
*DRAPER*sy
DRAPES
DRAPEY*
DRAWEE s
*DRAWER s
DRAWLS*
DRAWLY
*DRAYED
DREADS
DREAMS
DREAMT*
DREAMY*
DREARS
DREARY*
DRECKS
DRECKY*
DREDGE drs
DREGGY
DREICH
DREIDL s
DREIGH
DRENCH
DRESSY*
DRIEGH
DRIERS*
DRIEST*
DRIFTS
DRIFTY*
DRILLS
DRINKS
DRIPPY
DRIVEL*s
DRIVEN

*DRIVER*s
DRIVES
*DROGUE s
DROIDS*
DROITS*
DROLLS
DROLLY*
DROMON ds
DRONED*
DRONER*s
DRONES*
DRONGO s
DROOLS*
DROOLY*
DROOPS*
DROOPY*
DROPSY*
DROSKY
DROSSY*
DROUKS*
*DROUTH sy
DROVED
*DROVER*s
DROVES
DROWND*s
DROWNS*
DROWSE ds
DROWSY
DRUDGE drs
DRUGGY
DRUIDS*
DRUMLY
DRUNKS*
DRUPES*
DRUSES
DRYADS*
DRYERS*
DRYEST
DRYING
DRYISH
DRYLOT s
DUALLY
DUBBED
DUBBER s
DUBBIN gs
DUCATS*
DUCKED
DUCKER s
DUCKIE rs
DUCTAL
DUCTED
DUDDIE
DUDEEN s
DUDING
DUDISH
DUELED
DUELER s
DUELLI
DUELLO s
DUENDE s
DUENNA s
DUETED
DUFFEL s
DUFFER s
DUFFLE s
DUGONG s
DUGOUT s
DUIKER s
DUKING
DULCET s
DULIAS*
DULLED
DULLER
DULSES*
DUMBED
*DUMBER
DUMBLY
DUMBOS
DUMDUM s
*DUMPED
DUMPER s
DUNAMS*
DUNCES*
DUNGED
*DUNITE s
DUNKED
DUNKER s
DUNLIN s
DUNNED
DUNNER
DUNTED
DUOLOG s
DUOMOS*
DUPERS*
DUPERY*
DUPING
DUPLEX*
*DUPPED
DURBAR s
DURESS*
DURIAN s
DURING
DURION s
DURNED
DUROCS*
DURRAS*
DURRIE s
DURUMS*
DUSKED
DUSTED
DUSTER s
DUSTUP s
DUTIES
DUVETS*
DWARFS*
DWEEBS*
DWEEBY*
DWELLS
DWINED
DWINES
DYABLE
DYADIC s
DYBBUK s
DYEING s
DYINGS*
DYKING
DYNAMO s
DYNAST sy
DYNEIN s
DYNELS*
DYNODE s
DYVOUR s
EAGERS
EAGLED*
b EAGLES*
*EAGLET*s
EAGRES*
EARBUD s
ft EARFUL s
bfg EARING s
hnr
stw
EARLAP s
ly EARNED
ly EARNER s
dh EARTHS*
EARTHY*
EARWAX
EARWIG s
tw EASELS*
EASIER
EASIES t
EASILY
cfl EASING
t
f*EASTER ns
bhs EATERS*
EATERY*
bhs EATING s
EBBETS*
w EBBING
r*EBOOKS*
*ECARTE s
ECESIC
ECESIS
*ECHARD s
lp ECHING
ECHINI
ECHOED
ECHOER s
ECHOES
ECHOEY
ECHOIC
ECLAIR s
ECLATS*
ECTYPE s
ECZEMA s
EDDIED
nt EDDIES
EDDOES
o EDEMAS*
EDENIC
hl EDGERS*
hls EDGIER
w
EDGILY
hkw EDGING s
EDIBLE s
EDICTS*
a EDILES*
EDITED
EDITOR s
drs EDUCED*
drs*EDUCES*
d*EDUCTS*
EELIER
bl EERIER*
l EERILY
EFFACE drs
EFFECT s
EFFETE
EFFIGY
EFFLUX
EFFORT s
EFFUSE ds
EGESTA*
EGESTS
bs EGGARS*
EGGCUP s
k EGGERS*
bkl EGGING
pv
EGGNOG s
a EGISES
EGOISM s
EGOIST s
r EGRESS
r EGRETS*
EIDERS*
EIDOLA
h EIGHTH*s
hw EIGHTS*
w EIGHTY*
EIKONS
n*EITHER
d EJECTA*
dr EJECTS*
EKUELE
ELAINS*
r*ELANDS*
ELAPID s
r*ELAPSE ds
bdg*ELATED*
r
r*ELATER*s
dgr ELATES*
ELBOWS*
gmw ELDERS*
ELDEST
s ELECTS*
*ELEGIT s
ELEMIS*
ELEVEN s
ELEVON s
ELFINS*
s ELFISH
*ELICIT s
ELIDED*
ELIDES*
ELINTS
pv ELITES*
ELIXIR s
ELMIER
ELODEA s
ELOIGN s
ELOINS
ELOPED
*ELOPER*s
ELOPES
ELUANT s
ELUATE s
d ELUDED*
d ELUDER*s
d*ELUDES*
ELUENT s
ELUTED
ELUTES
ELUVIA l
d ELVERS*
ELVISH
ELYTRA
r*EMAILS*
EMBALM s
EMBANK s
EMBARK*s
EMBARS*
EMBAYS*
EMBEDS*
m EMBERS*
EMBLEM s
EMBODY
EMBOLI c
EMBOLY
EMBOSK s
EMBOSS
EMBOWS*
EMBRUE ds
EMBRYO ns
EMCEED*
EMCEES*
EMDASH
EMEERS*
r*EMENDS*
dr*EMERGE ds
EMEROD s
n EMESES
n EMESIS
EMETIC s
EMETIN es
EMEUTE s
EMIGRE s
h EMMERS*
EMMETS*
EMODIN s
d EMOTED*
r EMOTER*s
dgr*EMOTES*
EMPALE drs
EMPERY
EMPIRE s
EMPLOY es
EMYDES*
t ENABLE drs
ENACTS*
ENAMEL s
ENAMOR s
ps*ENATES*
v ENATIC
ENCAGE ds
ENCAMP s
ENCASE ds
ENCASH
ENCINA ls
ENCODE drs
ENCORE ds
ENCYST s
ENDASH
ENDEAR s
bfg ENDERS*
lmr
stv
bfl ENDING s
mpr
stvw
ENDITE ds
ENDIVE s
ENDOWS*
ENDRIN s
ENDUED*
v ENDUES*
ENDURE drs
ENDURO s
ENEMAS
ENERGY
ENFACE ds
t ENFOLD s
ENGAGE drs
ENGILD s
ENGINE ds
ENGIRD s
ENGIRT
ENGLUT s
ENGRAM s
ENGULF s
ENHALO s
ENIGMA s
ENISLE ds
ENJOIN s
ENJOYS*
ENLACE ds
ENLIST s
ENMESH
ENMITY
ENNEAD s
ENNUIS*
ENNUYE e
ENOKIS*
ENOLIC
k ENOSIS
ENOUGH s
ENRAGE ds
ENRAPT
ENRICH
ENROBE drs
ENROLL*s
ENROLS*
ENROOT s
ENSERF s
ENSIGN s
pt ENSILE ds
ENSOUL s
ENSUED*
ENSUES*
c ENSURE drs
v ENTAIL s
ENTERA*l
crt ENTERS*
v
ENTICE drs
ENTIRE s
ENTITY
ENTOIL s
ENTOMB s
ENTRAP s
ENTREE s
t ENURED*
t ENURES*
ENVIED
ENVIER s
ENVIES
ENVIRO ns
r ENVOIS*
ENVOYS*
ENWIND s
ENWOMB s
ENWRAP s
ENZYME*s
ENZYMS*
EOCENE
a EOLIAN
n EOLITH s
a EONIAN
p EONISM s
EOSINE*s
EOSINS*
EPACTS
*EPARCH sy
EPHAHS*
EPHEBE s
EPHEBI c
EPHODS*
EPHORI*
EPHORS*
*EPICAL
EPIGON eis
EPILOG s
EPIMER es
EPIZOA
EPOCHS*
EPODES*
EPONYM sy
EPOPEE s
dr*EPOSES
EQUALS*
*EQUATE ds
EQUIDS
EQUINE s
EQUIPS
EQUITY
ERASED
*ERASER*s
ERASES
t ERBIUM s
ERECTS*
ERENOW
ERGATE s
ERGOTS*
ERICAS*
ERINGO s
ERMINE ds
ERODED*
ERODES
x*EROSES*
cx EROTIC as
ERRAND s
ERRANT s
ERRATA s
h ERRING
t ERRORS*
ERSATZ
ERUCTS*
a ERUGOS*
ERUPTS*
ERVILS*
ERYNGO s
*ESCAPE der
s
*ESCARP*s
ESCARS
ESCHAR s
ESCHEW s
ESCORT s
ESCOTS
ESCROW s
*ESCUDO s
ESKARS*
ESKERS*
ESPIAL s
*ESPIED
*ESPIES
*ESPRIT s
ESSAYS*
ESSOIN s
grt*ESTATE ds
ESTEEM s
fjn ESTERS*
prt
wz
ESTOPS
v ESTRAL
*ESTRAY s
o ESTRIN s
o*ESTRUM s
o ESTRUS
*ETALON s
ETAMIN es
r*ETAPES*
flr ETCHED
t
f ETCHER s
fkl ETCHES
rv
*ETERNE
m*ETHANE s
ETHENE s
atw ETHERS*
ETHICS*
ETHION s
ETHNIC s
ETHNOS
m ETHOXY l
m ETHYLS*
ETHYNE s
*ETOILE s
ETUDES*
ETWEES*
ETYMON s
EUCHRE ds
EULOGY
EUNUCH s
EUPNEA s
EUREKA
EURIPI
EUROKY
EUTAXY
EVADED*
EVADER*s
EVADES*
EVENED
EVENER s
EVENLY
EVENTS
r*EVERTS*
EVICTS*
r*EVILER
EVILLY
EVINCE ds
EVITED*
EVITES*
r EVOKED*
r EVOKER*s
r EVOKES*
dr EVOLVE drs
EVULSE ds
EVZONE s
EXACTA*s
EXACTS*
EXALTS*
EXAMEN s
EXARCH sy
EXCEED s
EXCELS*
EXCEPT s
EXCESS
EXCIDE ds
EXCISE ds
EXCITE drs
EXCUSE drs
EXEDRA e
EXEMPT s
EXEQUY
EXERTS*
EXEUNT
EXHALE ds
EXHORT s
EXHUME drs
EXILED*
EXILER*s
EXILES*
EXILIC
r EXINES*
s EXISTS*
EXITED
EXODOI
EXODOS
EXODUS
EXOGEN s
EXONIC
EXONYM s
EXOTIC as
EXPAND s
EXPATS*
EXPECT s
EXPELS*
EXPEND s
EXPERT s
EXPIRE drs
EXPIRY
EXPORT s
EXPOSE*drs
EXSECT s
EXSERT s
s EXTANT
EXTEND s
EXTENT s
EXTERN es
EXTOLL*s
EXTOLS*
EXTORT s
EXTRAS*
EXUDED*
EXUDES*
EXULTS*
EXURBS*
EXUVIA el
EYASES
EYEBAR s
EYECUP s
EYEFUL s
EYEING
EYELET s
EYELID s
EYRIES*
FABBER
FABLED
*FABLER*s
FABLES
FABRIC s
FACADE s
FACERS*
FACETE*d
FACETS*
FACEUP
FACIAE*
FACIAL*s
FACIAS*
FACIES
FACILE
*FACING s
*FACTOR sy
FACULA er
FADEIN s
FADERS*
FADGED*
FADGES*
FADING s
FAECAL
FAECES
FAENAS*
*FAERIE s
FAGGED
FAGGOT s
FAGINS*
FAGOTS*
*FAILED
FAILLE s
FAINER
FAINTS*
*FAIRED
*FAIRER
FAIRLY
FAITHS*
FAJITA s
FAKEER s
FAKERS*
FAKERY*
FAKING
FAKIRS*
FALCES
FALCON s
FALLAL s
FALLEN
FALLER s
*FALLOW s
FALSER*
FALSIE s
*FALTER s
FAMILY
*FAMINE s
FAMING
FAMISH
FAMOUS

FAMULI
FANDOM s
FANEGA s
FANFIC s
FANGAS
FANGED
*FANION s
FANJET s
FANNED
FANNER s
FANONS*
FANTOD s
FANTOM s
FANUMS*
FAQIRS*
FAQUIR s
FARADS*
FARCED
FARCER*s
FARCES*
FARCIE*s
FARDED
FARDEL s
FARERS*
FARFAL s
FARFEL s
FARINA s
FARING
FARLES
*FARMED
*FARMER s
*FARROW s
FASCES
FASCIA els
*FASHED
*FASHES
FASTED
FASTEN s
*FASTER
FATHER s
FATHOM s
FATING
FATTED
FATTEN s
FATTER
FATWAS*
FAUCAL s
FAUCES
FAUCET s
FAULDS*
FAULTS*
FAULTY*
FAUNAE*
FAUNAL*
FAUNAS*
FAUVES*
FAVELA s
FAVISM s
FAVORS*
FAVOUR s
*FAWNED
FAWNER s
*FAXING
FAYING
FAZING
FEALTY
a*FEARED
FEARER s
FEASED
FEASES
FEASTS
*FEATER
FEATLY
FEAZED*
FEAZES*
FECIAL s
FECKLY
FECULA e
FECUND
FEDORA s
FEEBLE r
FEEBLY
FEEDER s
FEEING
FEELER s
FEEZED*
FEEZES*
FEIGNS*
FEIJOA s
FEINTS*
FEIRIE
FEISTS*
FEISTY*
FELIDS*
FELINE s
FELLAH*s
FELLAS*
FELLED
FELLER s
FELLOE s
FELLOW s
FELONS*
FELONY*
FELSIC
FELTED
FEMALE s
FEMMES*
FEMORA l
FEMURS*
FENCED*
FENCER*s
FENCES*
*FENDED
*FENDER s
FENNEC s
FENNEL s
FEOFFS*
FERALS*
FERBAM s
FERIAE*
FERIAL*
FERIAS*
FERINE
FERITY
FERLIE s
FERMIS*
FERREL s
FERRET sy
FERRIC
FERRUM s
FERULA es
FERULE ds
FERVID
FERVOR s
FESCUE s
FESSED*
FESSES
FESTAL
*FESTER s
FETIAL s
FETICH
FETING
FETISH
FETORS*
FETTED
FETTER s
FETTLE ds
FEUARS*
FEUDAL
FEUDED
FEUING
FEVERS*
FEWEST
FEYEST
FEZZED
FEZZES
FIACRE s
FIANCE es
FIASCO s
FIBBED
FIBBER s
FIBERS*
FIBRES*
FIBRIL s
FIBRIN s
FIBULA ers
FICHES*
FICHUS*
FICINS*
FICKLE r
FICKLY
FICOES
FIDDLE drs
FIDDLY
FIDGED*
FIDGES*
FIDGET*sy
FIELDS*
FIENDS*
FIERCE r
FIESTA s
FIFERS*
FIFING
FIFTHS*
*FIGGED
FIGHTS*
FIGURE drs
FILERS*
FILETS*
*FILIAL
FILING s
FILLED*
*FILLER*s
FILLES*
FILLET*s
FILLIP s
FILLOS*
FILMED
FILMER s
FILMIC*
FILMIS*
FILOSE*
FILTER s
FILTHS*
FILTHY*
FIMBLE s
FINALE*s
FINALS*
FINCAS*
FINDER s
FINELY
FINERY*
FINEST*
FINGER s
FINIAL s
FINING s
FINISH*
FINITE s
FINITO
*FINKED
*FINNED
FIORDS*
FIPPLE s
FIQUES*
FIRERS*
*FIRING s
FIRKIN s
FIRMAN s
FIRMED
FIRMER s
FIRMLY
FIRSTS*
FIRTHS*
FISCAL s
FISHED
FISHER sy
FISHES
FISTED
FISTIC
FITCHY
FITFUL
FITTED
FITTER s
FIVERS*
FIXATE ds
FIXERS*
FIXING s
FIXITY*
FIXURE s
FIZGIG s
FIZZED
FIZZER s
FIZZES
FIZZLE ds
FJELDS*
FJORDS*
FLABBY
FLACKS
FLACON s
FLAGGY
FLAGON s
FLAILS*
FLAIRS
FLAKED
*FLAKER*s
FLAKES
FLAKEY*
FLAMBE es
FLAMED
FLAMEN*s
*FLAMER*s
FLAMES
*FLANES
FLANGE drs
FLANKS*
FLAPPY
FLARED*
FLARES
FLASHY*
FLASKS*
FLATLY
FLATUS
FLAUNT sy
FLAUTA s
FLAVIN es
FLAVOR sy
*FLAWED
FLAXEN
*FLAXES
*FLAYED
*FLAYER s
FLEAMS*
FLECHE s
FLECKS*
FLECKY*
*FLEDGE ds
*FLEDGY
FLEECE drs
*FLEECH
FLEECY
FLEERS
FLEETS
FLENCH
*FLENSE drs
FLESHY*
*FLETCH
FLEURY
FLEXED
*FLEXES
FLEXOR s
FLEYED
FLICKS
FLIERS
FLIEST*
*FLIGHT sy
FLIMSY
FLINCH
FLINGS
FLINTS
FLINTY
*FLIPPY
FLIRTS*
FLIRTY*
FLITCH
FLITED*
FLITES*
FLOATS*
FLOATY*
FLOCCI
FLOCKS
FLOCKY*
FLONGS
FLOODS*
*FLOOEY
*FLOOIE
FLOORS*
FLOOSY
FLOOZY
*FLOPPY
FLORAE*
*FLORAL*s
FLORAS*
FLORET s
FLORID
FLORIN s
FLOSSY
FLOTAS
FLOURS
FLOURY
FLOUTS
*FLOWED
*FLOWER sy
FLUENT
FLUFFS
FLUFFY*
FLUIDS*
FLUISH
FLUKED*
FLUKES*
FLUKEY*
FLUMED*
FLUMES*
FLUMPS
FLUNKS
FLUNKY*
FLUORS*
FLURRY
FLUTED
FLUTER*s
FLUTES
FLUTEY*
FLUXED
*FLUXES
FLUYTS*
FLYBOY s
FLYBYS*
FLYERS*
*FLYING s
FLYMAN
FLYMEN
FLYOFF s
FLYSCH
FLYTED*
FLYTES*
FLYWAY s
FOALED
FOAMED
FOAMER s
FOBBED
*FODDER s
FODGEL
FOEHNS*
FOEMAN
FOEMEN
FOETAL
FOETID
FOETOR s
FOETUS
FOGBOW s
FOGDOG s
FOGEYS*
FOGGED
FOGGER s
FOGIES*
FOIBLE s
*FOILED
FOINED
FOISON s
FOISTS*
FOLATE s
FOLDED
*FOLDER s
FOLDUP s
FOLEYS*
FOLIAR*
*FOLIOS*e
FOLIUM s
FOLKIE rs
FOLKSY*
FOLLES
FOLLIS
FOLLOW s
FOMENT s
FOMITE s
FONDED
FONDER
FONDLE drs
FONDLY
FONDUE*ds
FONDUS*
FONTAL
FOODIE s
FOOLED
FOOTED
FOOTER s
FOOTIE rs
FOOTLE drs
FOOTSY*
FOOZLE drs
FOPPED
FORAGE drs
FORAMS*
FORAYS*
FORBAD e
FORBID s
FORBYE*
FORCED*
FORCER*s
FORCES*
FORDED
FORDID
FOREBY e
FOREDO
FOREGO
FOREST*s
FORGAT
FORGED*
FORGER*sy
FORGES*
FORGET*s
FORGOT*
FORINT s
FORKED
FORKER s
FORMAL s
FORMAT es
FORMED*
FORMEE*
*FORMER*s
FORMES*
FORMIC a
FORMOL s
FORMYL s
FORNIX
FORRIT
FORTES*
FORTIS
FORUMS*
FORWHY
FOSSAE*
FOSSAS*
FOSSES*
FOSSIL s
FOSTER s
*FOUGHT
FOULED
FOULER
FOULLY
FOUNDS*
FOUNTS*
FOURTH s
FOVEAE*
FOVEAL*
FOVEAS*
FOWLED
FOWLER s
FOXIER
FOXILY
FOXING s
FOYERS
FOZIER
FRACAS
FRACTI
FRAENA
FRAILS
*FRAISE s
FRAMED*
FRAMER*s
FRAMES*
FRANCS*
FRANKS
FRAPPE ds
*FRATER s
FRAUDS*
*FRAYED
FRAZIL s
FREAKS*
FREAKY*
FREELY
FREERS*
FREEST
FREEZE rs
FRENCH
FRENUM s
FRENZY
FRERES*
FRESCO s
FRETTY
FRIARS*
FRIARY*
*FRIDGE s
FRIEND s
FRIERS*
FRIEZE s
FRIGES
*FRIGHT s
*FRIGID
FRIJOL e
FRILLS
FRILLY*
FRINGE ds
FRINGY
FRISEE*s
FRISES
FRISKS
FRISKY
*FRITES
FRITHS*
FRITTS*
FRIVOL s
FRIZED
FRIZER s
FRIZES
FRIZZY*
FROCKS
FROGGY
FROLIC s
FRONDS*
FRONTS*
FROSTS*
FROSTY*
FROTHS*
FROTHY*
FROUZY
FROWNS*
FROWST*sy
FROWSY*
FROWZY
FROZEN*
*FRUGAL
FRUITS*
FRUITY*
FRUMPS
FRUMPY*
FRUSTA
FRYERS*
FRYING
FRYPAN s
FUBBED
FUCOID s
FUCOSE s
FUCOUS
FUDDLE ds
FUDGED*
FUDGES*
FUELED
FUELER s
FUGATO s
FUGGED
FUGIOS*
FUGLED*
FUGLES*
FUGUED*
FUGUES*
FUHRER s
FULCRA
FULFIL ls
FULGID
FULHAM s
FULLAM s
FULLED
FULLER sy
FULMAR s
FUMBLE drs
FUMERS*
FUMETS*
FUMIER
FUMING
FUMULI
FUNDED
*FUNDER s
FUNDIC*
FUNDUS
FUNEST
FUNGAL s
FUNGIC*
FUNGUS
FUNKED
FUNKER s
FUNKIA s
FUNNED
FUNNEL s
FUNNER
FURANE*s
FURANS*
FURFUR
FURIES
FURLED
FURLER s
FURORE*s
FURORS*
FURRED
FURROW sy
FURZES*
FUSAIN s
FUSEES*
FUSELS*
FUSILE*
FUSILS*
*FUSING
FUSION s
FUSSED
FUSSER s
FUSSES
FUSTIC s
FUSUMA
*FUTILE
FUTONS*
FUTURE s
FUTZED
FUTZES
FUZEES*
FUZILS*
FUZING
FUZZED
FUZZES
FYLFOT s
FYNBOS
FYTTES*
GABBED
GABBER s
GABBLE drs
GABBRO s
GABIES
GABION s
GABLED
GABLES
*GABOON s
*GADDED
*GADDER s
GADDIS*
GADFLY

GADGET sy
GADIDS*
GADOID s
GAEING
GAFFED*
GAFFER*s
GAFFES*
GAGAKU s
GAGERS
GAGGED
*GAGGER s
GAGGLE ds
*GAGING
GAGMAN
GAGMEN
GAIETY
GAIJIN
GAINED
GAINER s
GAINLY
a GAINST*
GAITED
GAITER s
GALAGO s
GALAHS*
GALAXY*
GALEAE*
GALEAS*
GALENA s
GALERE s
GALIOT s
GALLED
GALLET as
*GALLEY s
GALLIC a
GALLON s
GALLOP s
GALLUS
GALOOT s
GALOPS*
GALORE s
GALOSH e
GALYAC s
GALYAK s
GAMAYS*
GAMBAS*
GAMBES*
GAMBIA s
GAMBIR s
*GAMBIT s
*GAMBLE drs
GAMBOL s
GAMELY
GAMERS*
GAMEST*
a GAMETE s
GAMIER
GAMILY
*GAMINE*s
GAMING*s
GAMINS
GAMMAS*
GAMMED
GAMMER s
GAMMON s
GAMUTS*
GANDER s
GANEFS*
GANEVS*
GANGED
*GANGER s
GANGLY
GANGUE s
GANJAH*s
GANJAS*
GANNET s
GANOFS*
GANOID s
GANTRY
GAOLED
GAOLER s
GAPERS
*GAPING
GAPPED
GARAGE ds
GARBED
GARBLE drs
GARCON s
GARDAI*
GARDEN s
GARGET sy
*GARGLE drs
GARISH
GARLIC s
GARNER s
GARNET s
GAROTE ds
GARRED
GARRET s
GARRON s
GARTER s
GARTHS*
GARVEY s
GASBAG s
GASCON s
*GASHED
GASHER
*GASHES t
GASIFY
GASKET s
GASKIN gs
GASLIT
GASMAN
GASMEN
GASPED
*GASPER s
GASSED
GASSER s
*GASSES
GASTED
*GASTER s
GATEAU sx
GATERS*
GATHER s
GATING s
GATORS*
GAUCHE r
GAUCHO s
GAUGED*
*GAUGER*s
GAUGES*
GAULTS*
GAUMED
GAUZES*
GAVAGE s
GAVELS*
GAVIAL s
GAVOTS*
GAWKED
GAWKER s
GAWPED
GAWPER s
GAWSIE
GAYALS*
GAYDAR s
GAYEST
GAYETY
GAZABO s
GAZARS*
GAZEBO s
GAZERS*
GAZING
GAZUMP s
*GEARED
GECKED
GECKOS*
GEEGAW s
GEEING
GEEKED
GEESTS*
GEEZER s
GEISHA s
GELADA s
GELANT s
*GELATE ds
GELATI ns
GELATO s
GELCAP s
GELDED
*GELDER s
GELEES*
GELLED
GEMMAE*
GEMMED
*GEMOTE*s
GEMOTS*
*GENDER s
GENERA l
GENETS*
GENEVA s
GENIAL
GENIES*
GENIPS*
GENIUS
GENOAS*
GENOME*s
GENOMS*
GENRES*
GENROS*
GENTES
GENTIL e
GENTLE drs
GENTLY
GENTOO s
a*GENTRY
GEODES*y
GEODIC
GEOIDS*
GERAHS*
GERBIL s
GERENT s
GERMAN es
GERMEN s
GERUND s
GESTES*
GESTIC
GETTER s
GETUPS*
GEWGAW s
GEYSER s
GHARRI s
*GHARRY
GHAUTS*
GHAZIS*
GHERAO
GHETTO s
GHIBLI s
GHOSTS
GHOSTY*
GHOULS*
GHYLLS*
GIANTS*
GIAOUR s
GIBBED
GIBBER s
GIBBET s
GIBBON s
GIBERS*
GIBING
GIBLET s
GIBSON s
GIDDAP
GIEING
GIFTED
GIFTEE s
*GIGGED
GIGGLE drs
GIGGLY
GIGLET s
GIGLOT s
GIGOLO s
GIGOTS*
GIGUES*
GILDED
GILDER s
GILLED
*GILLER s
GILLIE ds
GIMBAL s
GIMELS*
GIMLET s
GIMMAL s
GIMMES*
GIMMIE s
*GIMPED
GINGAL ls
GINGER sy
GINGKO s
GINKGO s
*GINNED
a*GINNER s
GIPONS*
GIPPED
GIPPER s
GIRDED
GIRDER s
GIRDLE drs
GIRLIE rs
GIRNED
GIRONS
GIRTED
GIRTHS*
GISMOS*
GITANO s
GITTED
GITTIN g
GIVENS*
GIVERS*
GIVING
GIZMOS*
GLACES
GLACIS
GLADES
GLADLY
GLAIRE*ds
GLAIRS
GLAIRY*
GLAIVE ds
GLAMOR s
*GLANCE drs
GLANDS
GLARED*
GLARES
GLASSY*
GLAZED
GLAZER*s
GLAZES
GLEAMS*
GLEAMY*
GLEANS
GLEBAE*
GLEBES*
GLEDES*
GLEEDS*
GLEEKS
GLEETS
GLEETY*
GLEGLY
GLEYED
GLIBLY
GLIDED*
GLIDER*s
GLIDES*
GLIFFS*
GLIMED
GLIMES
GLINTS
GLINTY
GLIOMA s
GLITCH y
GLITZY*
GLOAMS
GLOATS*
GLOBAL
*GLOBBY
GLOBED
GLOBES
GLOBIN gs
GLOGGS*
GLOMUS
GLOOMS
GLOOMY*
*GLOPPY
GLORIA s
GLOSSA*els
GLOSSY
GLOSTS*
GLOUTS
GLOVED
*GLOVER*s
GLOVES
*GLOWED
*GLOWER s
GLOZED*
GLOZES*
GLUCAN s
GLUERS*
GLUIER
GLUILY
GLUING
GLUMES*
GLUMLY
*GLUMPY
*GLUNCH
GLUONS*
GLUTEI*
GLUTEN*s
GLUTES
GLYCAN s
GLYCIN es
GLYCOL s
GLYCYL s
GLYPHS*
GNARLS*
GNARLY*
GNARRS*
*GNATTY
GNAWED
GNAWER s
GNEISS
GNOMES
GNOMIC
GNOMON s
*GNOSES
GNOSIS
GOADED
GOALED
GOALIE s
GOANNA s
GOATEE ds
GOBANG*s
GOBANS*
GOBBED
GOBBET s
GOBBLE drs
GOBIES
GOBLET s
GOBLIN s
*GOBOES
GOBONY
GODDAM ns
GODDED
GODETS*
GODOWN s
GODSON s
GODWIT s
GOFERS*
*GOFFER s
GOGGLE drs
GOGGLY
GOGLET s
GOINGS*
GOITER s
GOITRE s
*GOLDEN
*GOLDER
GOLEMS*
GOLFED
GOLFER s
GOLOSH e
GOMBOS*
GOMERS
GOMUTI s
GONADS*
GONEFS*
GONERS*
GONGED
GONIFF*s
GONIFS*
*GONION
*GONIUM
GONOFS*
GONOPH s
GOOBER s
GOODBY es
GOODIE s
GOODLY
GOOFED
GOOGLY
GOOGOL s
GOOIER
GOONEY s
GOONIE rs
GOORAL s
GOOSED*
GOOSES*
GOOSEY*
GOPHER s
GORALS
GORGED*
GORGER*s
GORGES*
GORGET*s
GORGON s
GORHEN s
GORIER
GORILY
GORING
GORMED
GORSES*
GOSPEL s
GOSSAN s
GOSSIP sy
GOTCHA s
GOTHIC s
GOTTEN
GOUGED*
GOUGER*s
GOUGES*
GOURDE*s
GOURDS*
GOVERN s
GOWANS*
GOWANY*
*GOWNED
GRAALS*
GRABBY
GRABEN s
GRACED
GRACES
GRADED*
GRADER*s
GRADES*
GRADIN egs
GRADUS
GRAFTS
GRAHAM s
GRAILS
GRAINS
GRAINY
GRAMAS*
GRAMMA rs
GRAMME s
GRAMPA*s
GRAMPS
GRANDS
*GRANGE rs
GRANNY
GRANTS
GRANUM
GRAPES
GRAPEY*
GRAPHS*
GRAPPA s
GRASPS
GRASSY*
GRATED
*GRATER*s
GRATES
GRATIN egs
GRATIS
GRAVED
*GRAVEL*sy
GRAVEN
*GRAVER*s
*GRAVES*t
GRAVID a
*GRAYED
GRAYER
GRAYLY
GRAZED
*GRAZER*s
GRAZES
GREASE drs
GREASY
GREATS*
*GREAVE ds
GREBES*
GREEDS
GREEDY
GREENS*
GREENY*
GREETS*
GREGOS*
GREIGE s
GREMMY
GREYED
GREYER
GREYLY
GRIDED*
GRIDES
GRIEFS*
GRIEVE drs
GRIFFE*s
GRIFFS
GRIFTS
GRIGRI s
*GRILLE*drs
GRILLS
GRILSE s
GRIMED
GRIMES
GRIMLY
GRINCH
GRINDS
GRIOTS
GRIPED
*GRIPER*s
GRIPES
GRIPEY*
GRIPPE drs
GRIPPY
GRISLY
GRISON s
GRISTS*
GRITHS*
GRITTY
*GRIVET s
GROANS
GROATS*
GROCER sy
GROGGY
GROINS*
GROOMS
GROOVE drs
GROOVY
GROPED
*GROPER*s
GROPES
GROSZE*
GROSZY*
GROTTO s
GROTTY
GROUCH y
a*GROUND s
GROUPS
*GROUSE drs
GROUTS
GROUTY*
GROVED
GROVEL*s
GROVES
*GROWER s
GROWLS*
GROWLY*
*GROWTH sy
GROYNE s
*GRUBBY
GRUDGE drs
GRUELS*
GRUFFS
GRUFFY*
GRUGRU s
GRUMES*
GRUMPS
GRUMPY*
GRUNGE rs
GRUNGY
GRUNTS
GRUTCH
GUACOS*
GUAIAC s
GUANAY s
GUANIN es
GUANOS*
GUARDS*
GUAVAS*
GUENON s
GUESTS*
GUFFAW s
GUGGLE ds
GUGLET s
GUIDED*
GUIDER*s
GUIDES*
GUIDON s
GUILDS*
GUILED*
GUILES*
GUILTS*
GUILTY*
GUIMPE s
GUINEA s
GUIROS*
GUISED*
GUISES*
GUITAR s
GULAGS*
GULDEN s
GULFED
GULLED
GULLET s
GULLEY s
GULPED
GULPER s
GUMBOS
GUMMAS*
GUMMED
GUMMER s
GUNDOG s
*GUNITE s
*GUNMAN
GUNMEN
GUNNED
GUNNEL s
GUNNEN
GUNNER sy
GUNSEL s
GURGED
GURGES
GURGLE dst
GURNET s
GURNEY s
GUSHED
*GUSHER s
GUSHES
GUSSET s
GUSSIE ds
GUSTED
GUTTAE*
GUTTED
*GUTTER sy
GUTTLE drs
GUYING
GUYOTS*
GUZZLE drs
GWEDUC ks
GYBING
GYOZAS*
GYPPED
GYPPER s
GYPSUM s

GYRASE s
GYRATE ds
GYRENE s
GYRING
GYRONS*
GYROSE*
GYTTJA s
GYVING
HABILE
HABITS*
HABOOB s
HACEKS*
stw HACKED
*HACKEE s
w HACKER s
HACKIE s
s HACKLE drs
HACKLY
s HADING
HADITH s
HADJEE s
HADJES
HADJIS*
HADRON s
HAEING
HAEMAL
HAEMIC
HAEMIN s
HAERES
HAFFET s
HAFFIT s
s HAFTED
*HAFTER s
HAGBUT s
HAGDON s
s HAGGED
HAGGIS h
HAGGLE drs
HAIKUS*
*HAILED
HAILER s
HAINTS*
HAIRDO s
c*HAIRED
HAJJES
HAJJIS*
HAKEEM s
HAKIMS*
HALALA*hs
HALALS*
tw HALERS*
HALERU*
HALEST*
HALIDE*s
HALIDS*
w HALING
HALITE s
c HALLAH s
HALLAL
HALLEL s
HALLOA*s
HALLOO*s
HALLOS*
cs*HALLOT*h
s*HALLOW*s
HALLUX
HALMAS
HALOED
*HALOES
HALOID s
HALONS*
HALTED
*HALTER es
c HALUTZ
HALVAH*s
HALVAS*
HALVED*
HALVES*
HAMADA s
HAMALS*
HAMATE s
HAMAUL s
HAMLET s
HAMMAL s
HAMMAM s
sw HAMMED
s HAMMER s
c HAMPER s
HAMULI
HAMZAH*s
HAMZAS*
c HANCES*
HANDAX
HANDED
HANDER s
HANDLE drs
HANGAR s
cw HANGED
c*HANGER s
HANGUL
HANGUP s
HANIWA
st HANKED
t HANKER s
HANKIE s
HANSAS*
HANSEL*s
HANSES*
HANSOM s
c*HANTED
HANTLE s
cw HAPPED
HAPPEN s
HAPTEN es
HAPTIC
HARASS
*HARBOR s
HARDEN s
HARDER
HARDLY
HAREEM s
HAREMS*
cs HARING
cs HARKED
HARKEN s
HARLOT s
c*HARMED
c*HARMER s
HARMIN egs
s HARPED
s HARPER s
HARPIN gs
*HARROW s
*HARTAL s
*HASHED
*HASHES
HASLET s
HASPED
HASSEL s
HASSLE ds
HASTED*
c HASTEN*s
HASTES*
HATBOX
HATERS*
HATFUL s
HATING
HATPIN s
HATRED s
c HATTED
cps HATTER s
s HAUGHS*
s HAULED
HAULER s
HAULMS*
HAULMY*
HAUNCH
c*HAUNTS*
HAUSEN s
HAVENS
s*HAVERS*
s HAVING
HAVIOR s
HAVOCS*
HAWALA s
cst*HAWING
HAWKED
HAWKER s
HAWKEY s
HAWKIE s
HAWSER*s
HAWSES*
HAYERS*
HAYING s
HAYMOW s
c*HAZANS*
HAZARD s
HAZELS*
HAZERS*
HAZIER
HAZILY
HAZING s
HAZMAT s
c HAZZAN s
HEADED
HEADER s
HEALED
HEALER s
HEALTH sy
HEAPED
c HEAPER s
s HEARER s
HEARSE*ds
*HEARTH*s
HEARTS*
HEARTY*
c HEATED
ct*HEATER s
s HEATHS*
HEATHY*
HEAUME s
s*HEAVED*
HEAVEN*s
HEAVER*s
s*HEAVES*
HECKLE drs
HECTIC
HECTOR s
HEDDLE s
c HEDERS*
HEDGED
*HEDGER*s
HEDGES
HEEDED
HEEDER s
HEEHAW s
w HEELED
w HEELER s
w HEEZED*
w HEEZES*
HEFTED
HEFTER s
HEGARI s
HEGIRA s
HEIFER s
*HEIGHT*hs
HEILED
HEINIE s
HEIRED
HEISHI
t HEISTS*
HEJIRA s
HELIAC
HELIOS*
HELIUM s
s HELLED
s HELLER isy
HELLOS*
w HELMED
HELMET s
HELOTS*
w HELPED
HELPER s
s HELVED*
s*HELVES*
HEMINS*
HEMMED
*HEMMER s
HEMOID
HEMPEN
HEMPIE r
HENBIT s
HENGES*
HENLEY s
HENNAS*
HENRYS*
HENTED
HEPCAT s
HEPPER
HEPTAD s
HERALD s
HERBAL s
HERBED
HERDED
HERDER s
HERDIC s
tw HEREAT
tw HEREBY
tw HEREIN
tw HEREOF
tw HEREON
HERESY*
tw HERETO
HERIOT s
t HERMAE*
HERMAI*
t HERMIT s
HERNIA els
HEROES
HEROIC s
HEROIN es
HERONS*
HERPES
HETERO s
HETMAN s
s HEUCHS*
s HEUGHS*
cs*HEWERS*
cs HEWING
HEXADE*s
HEXADS*
HEXANE s
HEXERS*
*HEXING
HEXONE s
HEXOSE s
HEXYLS*
HEYDAY s
HEYDEY s
HIATAL
HIATUS
HICCUP s
HICKEY s
HICKIE s
c HIDDEN
c HIDERS*
c HIDING s
HIEING
HIEMAL
HIGGLE drs
HIGHER
HIGHLY
HIGHTH*s
HIGHTS*
HIJABS*
HIJACK s
HIJRAH*s
HIJRAS*
HIKERS*
HIKING
cs HILLED
c*HILLER s
HILLOA*s
HILLOS*
HILTED
HINDER s
w HINGED*
w HINGER*s
w HINGES*
HINTED
*HINTER s
csw HIPPED
csw HIPPER
c HIPPIE rs
HIPPOS*
HIREES*
HIRERS*
*HIRING
HIRPLE ds
HIRSEL s
HIRSLE ds
HISPID
HISSED
HISSER s
HISSES
w HISTED
tw*HITHER
HITMAN
HITMEN
cw HITTER s
HIVING
HOAGIE s
HOARDS*
HOARSE*nr
HOAXED
HOAXER s
HOAXES
HOBBED
HOBBER s
HOBBIT s
HOBBLE drs
HOBNOB s
HOBOED
*HOBOES
cs HOCKED
s*HOCKER s
HOCKEY s
HODADS*
s HODDEN s
HODDIN s
s HOEING
HOGANS*
s HOGGED
HOGGER s
HOGGET s
HOGNUT s
HOGTIE ds
HOICKS*
HOIDEN s
HOISED*
HOISES*
HOISTS*
c HOKIER
HOKILY
c HOKING
HOKUMS*
HOLARD s
*HOLDEN
*HOLDER s
HOLDUP s
HOLIER
HOLIES t
HOLILY
t HOLING
w HOLISM s
HOLIST s
HOLKED
c*HOLLAS*
HOLLER s
HOLLOA*s
HOLLOO*s
HOLLOS*
HOLLOW*s
HOLMIC
HOLPEN
HOMAGE drs
*HOMBRE s
HOMELY
HOMERS
HOMEYS*
HOMIER*
HOMIES*t
HOMILY
HOMING
HOMINY
HOMMOS
HONANS*
HONCHO s
HONDAS*
HONDLE ds
HONERS*
HONEST*y
p HONEYS*
p HONIED
p HONING
HONKED
HONKER s
HONORS*
HONOUR s
HOODED
HOODIE rs
HOODOO s
HOOEYS*
w HOOFED
HOOFER s
HOOKAH*s
HOOKAS*
HOOKED
HOOKER s
HOOKEY s
HOOKUP s
HOOLIE
w HOOPED
w HOOPER s
w HOOPLA s
HOOPOE s
HOOPOO s
HOORAH s
HOORAY s
HOOTCH
HOOTED
s HOOTER s
HOOVED
HOOVER s
HOOVES
HOPERS*
*HOPING
csw HOPPED
csw HOPPER s
HOPPLE ds
HORAHS*
HORARY
c HORDED*
HORDES*
t HORNED
HORNET s
HORRID
HORROR s
HORSED*
HORSES*
HORSEY*
HORSTE*s
HORSTS*
HOSELS*
HOSERS*
HOSEYS*
*HOSIER sy
HOSING
HOSTAS*
g HOSTED
HOSTEL s
g HOSTLY
HOTBED s
HOTBOX
HOTDOG s
HOTELS*
HOTROD s
s HOTTED
*HOTTER
HOTTIE s
HOUDAH s
HOUNDS*
HOURIS*
HOURLY
c HOUSED*
*HOUSEL*s
c HOUSER*s
c HOUSES*
s HOVELS*
s*HOVERS*
HOWDAH s
HOWDIE ds
HOWFFS*
HOWKED
HOWLED
HOWLER s
*HOWLET s
HOYDEN s
HOYLES*
HRYVNA s
HUBBLY
HUBBUB s
HUBCAP s
HUBRIS
c HUCKLE s
HUDDLE drs
c HUFFED
HUGELY
HUGEST
c HUGGED
c HUGGER s
HUIPIL s
HULKED
HULLED
HULLER s
HULLOA*s
HULLOO*s
HULLOS*
HUMANE*r
HUMANS*
HUMATE s
HUMBLE drs
HUMBLY
HUMBUG s
HUMERI
c HUMMED
HUMMER s
HUMMUS
HUMORS*
HUMOUR s
ctw*HUMPED
t HUMPER s
HUMPHS*
HUMVEE s
HUNGER s
HUNGRY
HUNKER s
s HUNTED
cs HUNTER s
c HUPPAH s
HURDLE drs
HURLED
HURLER s
HURLEY s
HURRAH s
HURRAY s
HURSTS*
HURTER s
HURTLE ds
s HUSHED
s HUSHES
HUSKED
HUSKER s
HUSSAR s
HUSTLE drs
HUTTED
c HUTZPA hs
HUZZAH*s
HUZZAS*
HYAENA s
HYALIN es
HYBRID s
HYBRIS
HYDRAE*
HYDRAS*e
HYDRIA e
HYDRIC
HYDRID es
HYDROS*
HYENAS*
HYENIC
HYETAL
HYMENS*
HYMNAL s
HYMNED
HYOIDS*
HYPERS*
HYPHAE*
HYPHAL*
HYPHEN s
HYPING
HYPNIC
HYPOED
HYSONS*
HYSSOP s
IAMBIC*s
IAMBUS
IATRIC
IBEXES
*IBICES
IBIDEM
*IBISES
ICEBOX
ICECAP s
ICEMAN
ICEMEN
ICHORS*
ICICLE ds
d ICIEST
ICINGS*
bdk ICKERS*
lnp
tw
dkp ICKIER
ICKILY
*ICONES
*ICONIC
IDEALS
IDEATE ds
IDIOCY
IDIOMS*
IDIOTS*
s IDLERS*
IDLEST*
s IDLING
IDYLLS*
m IFFIER
bdf IGGING
gjp
rwz
IGLOOS*
dls IGNIFY
l IGNITE drs
s IGNORE drs
IGUANA s
IHRAMS*
s*ILEXES
ILIADS*
ILLEST
t ILLITE s
ILLUDE ds
ILLUME ds
IMAGED*
IMAGER*sy
IMAGES
IMAGOS*
IMARET s
IMAUMS*
IMBALM s
IMBARK s
IMBEDS*
IMBIBE drs
IMBODY
IMBRUE ds
IMBUED*
IMBUES*
IMIDES*
IMIDIC
IMINES
IMMANE
IMMESH
gj IMMIES
IMMUNE s
IMMURE ds
IMPACT s
IMPAIR s
IMPALA s
IMPALE drs
IMPARK s
IMPART s
IMPAWN s
IMPEDE*drs

IMPELS*
IMPEND s
IMPHEE s
glp IMPING es
w
w IMPISH*
dpr IMPLED
w
IMPONE ds
IMPORT s
IMPOSE drs
IMPOST s
IMPROV es
IMPUGN s
IMPURE r
IMPUTE drs
INANER*
INANES*t
INARCH
INARMS*
INBORN
INBRED s
INCAGE ds
INCANT s
INCASE ds
INCENT s
INCEPT s
INCEST s
cpw INCHED
pw INCHER s
cfp INCHES
w
INCISE ds
z INCITE drs
INCLIP s
INCOGS*
INCOME rs
INCONY
INCUBI
INCULT
INCURS*
INCUSE*ds
INDABA s
INDEED
INDENE s
INDENT s
INDICT s
l INDIES*
INDIGN
w INDIGO s
INDITE drs
INDIUM s
INDOLE*s
INDOLS*
INDOOR s
w INDOWS*
INDRIS*
INDUCE drs
INDUCT s
INDUED*
INDUES*
INDULT s
INERTS
INFALL s
INFAMY
INFANT aes
INFARE s
INFECT s
INFERS*
INFEST s
INFILL
INFIRM s
INFLOW s
INFLUX
p INFOLD s
INFORM s
INFUSE drs
INGATE s
INGEST as
djm INGLES*
st
INGOTS*
INGULF s
INHALE drs
INHAUL s
INHERE ds
INHUME drs
mp INIONS*
INJECT s
INJURE drs
INJURY
jlp INKERS*
stw
dhk INKIER

dfj INKING
klo
psw
INKJET
tw INKLES*s
INKPOT s
INLACE ds
INLAID
INLAND s
INLAYS*
INLETS*
INLIER s
INMATE s
INMESH
INMOST
INNAGE s
p INNATE
dgp INNERS*
stw
bdf INNING s
gpr
stw
INPOUR s
INPUTS*
INROAD s
INRUNS*
INRUSH
INSANE r
INSEAM s
INSECT s
INSERT s
INSETS*
INSIDE rs
INSIST s
INSOLE s
INSOUL s
INSPAN s
INSTAL ls
INSTAR s
INSTEP s
INSTIL ls
INSULT s
INSURE drs
INTACT
INTAKE s
INTEND s
INTENT s
INTERN*es
hlm INTERS*
stw
INTIMA els
INTIME
INTINE s
INTOMB s
INTONE drs
INTORT s
INTOWN
INTRON*s
INTROS*
INTUIT s
INTURN s
INULIN s
INURED*
INURES*
INURNS*
INVADE drs
INVARS*
INVENT s
INVERT s
INVEST s
INVITE der
s
INVOKE drs
INWALL s
INWARD s
INWIND s
INWOVE n
INWRAP s
IODATE ds
IODIDE*s
IODIDS*
IODINE*s
IODINS*
IODISE ds
IODISM s
IODIZE drs
IODOUS
IOLITE s
b IONICS*
l IONISE ds
*IONIUM s
l IONIZE drs
IONONE s
IPECAC s
t IRADES*
IRATER

d IREFUL
e IRENIC s
*IRIDES
IRIDIC
IRISED
*IRISES
IRITIC
IRITIS
d IRKING
IROKOS*
IRONED*
IRONER*s
IRONES*
IRONIC
IRREAL
IRRUPT s
*ISATIN es
ISCHIA l
ISLAND s
ISLETS*
*ISLING
ISOBAR es
ISOGON esy
ISOHEL s
ISOLOG s
ISOMER s
ISOPOD s
ISSEIS*
t ISSUED*
ISSUER*s
t ISSUES*
ISTHMI c
ISTLES*
ITALIC s
bdh ITCHED
pw
abd ITCHES
fhpw
ITEMED
ITERUM
ITSELF
IXODID s
IXORAS*
IXTLES*
g IZZARD s
JABBED
JABBER s
JABIRU s
JABOTS*
JACALS*
JACANA s
JACKAL s
JACKED
JACKER s
JACKET s
JADING
JADISH
JAEGER s
JAGERS
JAGGED
*JAGGER sy
JAGRAS*
JAGUAR s
*JAILED
JAILER s
JAILOR s
JALAPS*
JALOPS*
JALOPY*
JAMBED*
JAMBES*
JAMMED
JAMMER s
*JANGLE drs
JANGLY
JAPANS*
JAPERS
JAPERY
*JAPING
JARFUL s
*JARGON sy
JARINA s
JARRAH s
JARRED
JARVEY s
JASMIN es
*JASPER sy
JASSID s
JAUKED
JAUNCE ds
JAUNTS
JAUNTY
JAUPED
JAWANS*
*JAWING
JAYGEE s

JAYVEE s
JAZZBO s
JAZZED
JAZZER s
JAZZES
JEANED
d JEBELS*
JEEING
JEEPED
JEERED
JEERER s
JEHADS*
JEJUNA l
JEJUNE
JELLED
JELLOS*
JENNET s
JERBOA s
JEREED s
JERIDS*
JERKED
JERKER s
JERKIN gs
JERRID s
JERSEY s
JESSED*
JESSES
JESTED
*JESTER s
JETLAG s
JETONS*
JETSAM s
JETSOM s
JETTED
JETTON s
JETWAY s
JEWELS*
JEZAIL s
JIBBED
JIBBER s
JIBERS*
JIBING
JICAMA s
*JIGGED
JIGGER s
JIGGLE ds
JIGGLY
JIGSAW ns
JIHADS*
JILTED
JILTER s
JIMINY
JIMMIE ds
JIMPER
*JIMPLY
JINGAL ls
JINGKO
*JINGLE drs
JINGLY
*JINKED
*JINKER s
JINNEE
JINNIS*
JINXED
JINXES
JITNEY s
JITTER sy
JIVERS*
JIVIER
JIVING
JNANAS
JOBBED
JOBBER sy
JOCKEY s
JOCKOS*
JOCOSE
JOCUND
JOGGED
JOGGER s
JOGGLE drs
JOHNNY
JOINED
JOINER sy
JOINTS*
JOISTS*
JOJOBA s
JOKERS*
JOKIER
JOKILY
JOKING
JOLTED
JOLTER s
JORAMS*
JORDAN s
JORUMS*
JOSEPH s

JOSHED
JOSHER s
JOSHES
JOSSES
JOSTLE drs
JOTTED
*JOTTER s
JOUALS*
JOUKED
JOULES*
*JOUNCE ds
JOUNCY
JOURNO s
JOUSTS
JOVIAL
JOWARS*
*JOWING
JOWLED
JOYFUL
JOYING
JOYOUS
JOYPOP s
JUBBAH s
JUBHAH s
JUBILE es
*JUDDER s
JUDGED*
JUDGER*s
JUDGES*
JUDOKA s
JUGATE
JUGFUL s
JUGGED
JUGGLE drs
JUGULA r
JUGUMS*
JUICED*
JUICER*s
JUICES*
JUJUBE s
JUKING
JULEPS*
JUMBAL s
JUMBLE drs
JUMBOS
*JUMPED
JUMPER s
JUNCOS
JUNGLE ds
JUNGLY
JUNIOR s
JUNKED
JUNKER s
JUNKET s
JUNKIE rs
JUNTAS*
JUNTOS*
JUPONS*
JURANT s
JURATS*
JURELS*
JURIED
JURIES
JURIST s
JURORS*
JUSTED
JUSTER s
JUSTLE ds
JUSTLY
JUTTED
KABABS*
*KABAKA s
KABALA s
KABARS*
*KABAYA s
KABIKI s
KABOBS*
KABUKI s
KAFFIR s
KAFIRS*
KAFTAN s
KAHUNA s
KAIAKS*
KAINIT es
KAISER s
KAKAPO s
KALAMS*
KALIAN s
KALIFS
KALIPH s
KALIUM s
KALMIA s
*KALONG s
KALPAC*s
KALPAK*s
KALPAS*

KAMALA s
KAMIKS*
KAMSIN s
KANBAN s
KANJIS*
KANTAR s
KANZUS*
KAOLIN es
KAONIC
KAPOKS*
KAPPAS*
KAPUTT*
KARATE*s
KARATS*
KARMAS*
KARMIC
KAROOS*
KAROSS
KARROO s
KARSTS*
KASBAH s
KASHAS*
KASHER s
KATION s
KAURIS
KAVASS*
KAYAKS*
KAYLES
KAYOED
KAYOES
KAZOOS*
KEBABS*
KEBARS*
KEBBIE s
KEBLAH s
KEBOBS*
KECKED
KECKLE ds
KEDDAH s
KEDGED
KEDGES
KEEKED
KEELED
KEENED
KEENER s
KEENLY
KEEPER s
KEEVES*
KEFIRS*
*KEGGED
*KEGGER s
KEGLER s
KELEPS*
KELIMS*
KELOID s
s KELPED
KELPIE s
KELSON s
s KELTER s
KELVIN s
KENAFS*
KENDOS*
KENNED
KENNEL s
KENTES*
KEPPED
KEPPEN
KERBED
KERFED
KERMES s
KERMIS
KERNED*
KERNEL*s
KERNES
KERRIA s
KERSEY s
KETENE s
KETOLS*
KETONE s
KETOSE s
KETTLE s
KEVELS*
KEVILS
KEWPIE s
*KEYING
KEYPAD s
KEYPAL s
KEYSET s
KEYWAY s
KHADIS*
KHAKIS*
KHALIF as
KHAPHS*
KHAZEN s
KHEDAH*s
KHEDAS*

KHETHS
KHOUMS*
KIANGS*
KIAUGH s
KIBBEH*s
KIBBES*
KIBBIS*
KIBBLE ds
KIBEIS*
KIBITZ
KIBLAH*s
KIBLAS*
KIBOSH
KICKED
*KICKER s
KICKUP s
s KIDDED
s KIDDER s
KIDDIE s
KIDDOS*
KIDNAP s
KIDNEY s
KIDVID s
KILIMS*
s KILLED
*KILLER s
KILLIE s
KILNED
KILTED
KILTER s
KILTIE s
KIMCHI s
KIMONO s
KINARA s
KINASE*s
KINDER
KINDLE drs
KINDLY
KINEMA s
KINGED
KINGLY
KININS*
s*KINKED
KIOSKS*
s KIPPED
KIPPEN
s KIPPER s
KIRNED
KIRSCH
KIRTLE ds
KISHKA s
KISHKE s
KISMAT s
KISMET s
KISSED
KISSER s
KISSES
KITBAG s
KITERS*
KITHED*
KITHES*
s KITING
KITSCH y
KITTED
KITTEL
KITTEN s
s KITTLE drs
*KLATCH
KLAXON s
KLEPHT s
KLEPTO s
KLICKS
KLONGS
KLOOFS
KLUDGE dsy
KLUDGY
KLUGED
KLUGES
KLUTZY*
KNACKS*
KNARRY
KNAURS*
KNAVES
KNAWEL*s
KNAWES*
KNEADS*
KNEELS*
KNELLS*
KNIFED*
KNIFER*s
KNIFES*
*KNIGHT s
KNIVES
*KNOBBY
KNOCKS
KNOLLS*

KNOLLY*
KNOSPS*
KNOTTY
KNOUTS*
KNOWER s
KNOWNS*
*KNUBBY
KNURLS
KNURLY*
KOALAS*
KOBOLD s
KOINES*
KOLHOZ y
KOLKOZ y
KOMBUS*
KONKED
KOODOO s
KOOKIE r
KOPECK s
KOPEKS*
KOPJES*
KOPPAS*
KOPPIE s
KORATS*
KORMAS*
KORUNA*s
KORUNY*
KOSHER s
KOTOWS*
KOUMIS s
KOUMYS s
KOUROI
KOUROS
KOUSSO s
KOWTOW s
KRAALS*
KRAFTS
KRAITS*
KRAKEN s
*KRATER s
KRAUTS*
KREEPS*
KREWES*
KRILLS
*KRISES
KRONEN*
KRONER*
KRONOR
KRONUR
KROONI*
KROONS*
KRUBIS*
KRUBUT s
KUCHEN s
KUDZUS*
KUGELS*
KUKRIS*
KULAKI*
KULAKS*
KULTUR s
KUMISS
KUMMEL s
KURGAN s
KURTAS*
KUSSOS*
KUVASZ
*KVASES
KVELLS*
*KVETCH y
KWACHA s
KWANZA s
KYACKS
KYBOSH
KYRIES*
KYTHED*
KYTHES*
LAAGER s
LABARA
LABELS*
LABIAL*s
LABILE
LABIUM
LABORS*
LABOUR s
LABRET s
LABRUM s
p LACERS*
*LACHES
g LACIER
LACILY
p*LACING s
bcf LACKED
s
bcs LACKER s
LACKEY s
LACTAM s

LACTIC
LACUNA elr
s
LACUNE s
bg*LADDER s
LADDIE s
LADENS*
b LADERS*
LADIES
b LADING s
LADINO s
LADLED*
LADLER*s
LADLES*
LADRON es
LAGANS*
LAGEND s
LAGERS
cfs LAGGED
f*LAGGER s
LAGOON s
LAGUNA s
LAGUNE s
LAHARS*
LAICAL
LAICHS*
LAIGHS*
LAIRDS*
g*LAIRED
fs LAKERS*
f LAKIER
fs LAKING s
LALLAN ds
LALLED
LAMBDA s
LAMBED
c*LAMBER st
LAMBIE rs
LAMEDH*s
LAMEDS*
LAMELY
*LAMENT s
LAMEST*
LAMIAE*
LAMIAS
LAMINA elr
s
bf LAMING
cfs LAMMED
LAMPAD s
LAMPAS
c*LAMPED
LANAIS*
p LANATE d
g LANCED*
g LANCER*s
g LANCES*
LANCET*s
LANDAU s
LANDED
bs LANDER s
LANELY
LANGUE st
LANGUR s
bf LANKER
b LANKLY
p LANNER s
LANOSE
LANUGO s
LAOGAI s
LAPDOG s
LAPELS*
LAPFUL s
LAPINS*
cfs LAPPED
cfs LAPPER s
LAPPET s
e LAPSED*
LAPSER*s
e*LAPSES*
LAPSUS
LAPTOP s
LARDED
LARDER s
LARDON s
LAREES*
LARGER*
LARGES*st
LARGOS*
LARIAT s
LARINE
LARKED
LARKER s
LARRUP s
a*LARUMS*
LARVAE*

LARVAL
LARVAS*
LARYNX
LASCAR s
LASERS*
cfp*LASHED
s
cfp LASHER s
s
cfp*LASHES
s
LASING
cg*LASSES
g LASSIE*s
c LASSIS*
LASSOS*
b LASTED
bp*LASTER s
LASTLY
LATEEN s
LATELY
p LATENS*
LATENT*s
LATEST s
LATHED*
bs LATHER*sy
LATHES*
LATHIS*
LATIGO s
p LATINA s
LATINO s
LATISH
LATKES*
*LATRIA s
f LATTEN*s
bcf LATTER*
p
LATTES*
LATTIN s
LAUANS*
LAUDED
LAUDER s
LAUGHS*
LAUNCE s
LAUNCH
LAURAE
LAURAS
LAUREL s
LAVABO s
LAVAGE s
LAVASH*
LAVEER s
cs*LAVERS*
s LAVING
s LAVISH
*LAWFUL
LAWINE s
bcf*LAWING s
LAWMAN
LAWMEN
LAWYER s
LAXEST*
LAXITY
fps LAYERS*
cfp LAYING*
s
LAYINS
LAYMAN
LAYMEN
p LAYOFF s
LAYOUT s
LAYUPS*
LAZARS*
LAZIED
g LAZIER
LAZIES t
g LAZILY
bg LAZING
LAZULI s
LEACHY*
p LEADED
LEADEN s
p LEADER s
LEAFED
LEAGUE drs
LEAKED
b LEAKER s
LEALLY
LEALTY
cg LEANED
cg LEANER s
c LEANLY
LEAPED
LEAPER s
LEARNS
LEARNT*

p*LEASED*
p LEASER*s
p*LEASES*
LEASTS
cs*LEAVED*
LEAVEN*s
c LEAVER*s
cs*LEAVES*
LEBENS*
*LECHED
LECHER sy
f*LECHES
LECHWE s
LECTIN s
e LECTOR s
p*LEDGER*s
fps*LEDGES*
f LEERED
LEEWAY s
LEFTER
LEGACY
LEGALS*
LEGATE des
LEGATO rs
LEGEND s
LEGERS
*LEGGED
LEGGIN gs
LEGION s
e LEGIST s
e LEGITS*
LEGMAN
LEGMEN
LEGONG s
LEGUME s
LEHUAS*
LEKKED
LEKVAR s
LEMANS*
LEMMAS*
LEMONS*
LEMONY*
LEMURS*
bs*LENDER s
LENGTH sy
LENITE ds
LENITY
f LENSED*
f LENSES*
LENTEN
LENTIC
LENTIL s
LENTOS*
LEONES*
LEPERS*
LEPTIN s
LEPTON s
LESION s
LESSEE s
LESSEN s
b LESSER
LESSON s
p LESSOR s
LETHAL s
LETHES*
LETTED
LETTER s
LETUPS*
LEUCIN es
LEUDES
LEUKON s
LEVANT s
LEVEED*
LEVEES*
LEVELS*
LEVERS*
LEVIED
LEVIER s
LEVIES
a LEVINS*
LEVITY
LEWDER
LEWDLY
LEXEME s
LEXICA l
p LIABLE
LIAISE ds
LIANAS*
LIANES*
LIANGS*
LIARDS*
LIBELS*
LIBERS*
LIBIDO s
LIBLAB s
LIBRAE*

LIBRAS*
LICHEE s
LICHEN s
c LICHES
LICHIS*
LICHTS*
cfs LICKED
cfs*LICKER s
LICTOR s
LIDARS*
LIDDED
LIEDER
LIEFER
LIEFLY
LIEGES*
LIENAL
LIERNE s
LIEVER*
LIFERS*
LIFTED
LIFTER s
LIGAND*s
LIGANS*
LIGASE s
LIGATE ds
LIGERS*
abf LIGHTS*
ps
LIGNAN s
LIGNIN s
LIGULA ers
LIGULE s
LIGURE s
LIKELY
LIKENS*
LIKERS*
LIKEST*
LIKING s
LIKUTA
LILACS*
LILIED
LILIES
LILTED
LIMANS*
LIMBAS*
c*LIMBED
c LIMBER s
LIMBIC*
LIMBOS*
LIMBUS
LIMENS*
LIMEYS*
s LIMIER
LIMINA l
gs LIMING
LIMITS*
gs LIMMER s
LIMNED
LIMNER s
LIMNIC
LIMPAS*
*LIMPED
LIMPER s
LIMPET s
LIMPID
*LIMPLY
s LIMPSY*
LIMULI
LINACS*
LINAGE s
LINDEN s
LINEAL
LINEAR
LINENS*
LINENY*
a LINERS*
LINEUP s
LINGAM*s
LINGAS*
cfs LINGER s
LINGUA el
LINIER
a LINING*s
LININS*
bcp*LINKED
s
bcp*LINKER s
LINKUP s
LINNET s
LINSEY s
fg LINTED
LINTEL s
*LINTER s
LINTOL s
LINUMS*
LIPASE s

LIPIDE*s
LIPIDS*
LIPINS*
LIPOID s
LIPOMA s
bcf LIPPED
s
LIPPEN s
cfs LIPPER s
LIQUID s
LIQUOR s
LIROTH*
LISLES
LISPED
LISPER s
LISSOM e
LISTED
LISTEE s
LISTEL s
g LISTEN s
bgk LISTER s
LITANY
LITCHI s
LITERS*
bs*LITHER*
LITHIA s
LITHIC
LITHOS*
LITMUS
LITRES*
LITTEN
fgs LITTER sy
LITTLE rs
LIVELY
LIVENS*
cs LIVERS*
LIVERY*
LIVEST*
LIVIER s
LIVING s
LIVRES*
LIVYER s
LIZARD s
LLAMAS
LLANOS*
LOADED
LOADER s
LOAFED
LOAFER s
LOAMED
LOANED
LOANER s
LOATHE*drs
*LOAVES
g LOBATE d
b LOBBED
cs LOBBER s
g LOBULE s
LOCALE*s
LOCALS*
LOCATE drs
LOCHAN s
LOCHIA l
bcf LOCKED
bc*LOCKER s
LOCKET s
LOCKUP s
LOCOED
LOCOES
LOCULE ds
*LOCULI
LOCUMS*
LOCUST*as
LODENS*
LODGED*
LODGER*s
LODGES*
LOFTED
*LOFTER s
s LOGANS*
cfs LOGGED
bcf LOGGER s
s
LOGGIA s
LOGGIE r
LOGICS*
LOGIER
LOGILY
LOGINS*
LOGION s
LOGJAM s
LOGONS*
LOGWAY s
LOIDED
LOITER s
LOLLED

LOLLER s
LOLLOP sy
LOMEIN s
LOMENT as
LONELY
c LONERS*
LONGAN s
LONGED*
LONGER*s
LONGES*t
LONGLY
LOOEYS*
LOOFAH*s
LOOFAS*
LOOIES*
LOOING
LOOKED
LOOKER s
LOOKUP s
bg LOOMED
LOONEY s
LOONIE rs
b LOOPED
b LOOPER s
LOOSED*
LOOSEN*s
LOOSER*
LOOSES*t
LOOTED
LOOTER s
es LOPERS*
es*LOPING
cfg LOPPED
ps
f LOPPER s
LOQUAT s
LORANS*
LORDED
LORDLY
LOREAL
LORICA e
g LORIES
LOSELS*
c LOSERS*
c LOSING s
fg LOSSES
LOTAHS*
LOTION s
bcp LOTTED*
s
bps*LOTTER*sy
LOTTES*
LOTTOS
LOUCHE
LOUDEN s
LOUDER
LOUDLY
cps LOUGHS*
LOUIES*
LOUMAS*
LOUNGE drs
LOUNGY
LOUPED*
LOUPEN*
LOUPES*
cf LOURED
b LOUSED*
b LOUSES*
cfg*LOUTED
LOUVER s
LOUVRE ds
LOVAGE s
LOVATS*
LOVELY
cgp*LOVERS*
g LOVING
p LOWBOY s
bfg LOWERS*
p
f LOWERY*
s LOWEST*
bfg*LOWING s
ps
s LOWISH
LOXING
bcf LUBBER s
s
LUBING
LUBRIC
LUCENT
LUCERN es
LUCITE s
cp LUCKED
LUCKIE rs
LUCRES*
LUETIC s

LUFFAS*
bfs LUFFED
LUGERS*
gps LUGGED
ps LUGGER s
LUGGIE s
k LUGING
LULLED
LULLER s
LUMBAR s
cps*LUMBER s
LUMENS*
a LUMINA l
f LUMMOX
cfp*LUMPED
s
p LUMPEN s
p LUMPER s
LUNACY
LUNARS*
LUNATE d
LUNETS*
LUNGAN s
bp LUNGED*
LUNGEE*s
bp LUNGER*s
bp LUNGES*
LUNGIS*
LUNGYI s
LUNIER
LUNIES t
cfp LUNKER s
b LUNTED
LUNULA er
LUNULE s
LUPINE*s
LUPINS*
LUPOUS
LURDAN es
LURERS*
LURING
LURKED
LURKER s
bfs LUSHED
bfp*LUSHER
bfp LUSHES t
s
p LUSHLY
LUSTED
bcf LUSTER s
LUSTRA l
LUSTRE ds
g LUTEAL*
LUTEIN s
LUTEUM
ef LUTING s
f LUTIST s
k LUTZES
LUXATE ds
LUXURY
LYASES*
LYCEES*
LYCEUM s
LYCHEE s
LYCHES
LYCRAS*
f LYINGS*
LYMPHS*
LYNXES
LYRATE d
LYRICS*
LYRISM s
LYRIST s
LYSATE s
LYSINE*s
LYSING*
LYSINS*
LYSSAS*
LYTTAE*
LYTTAS*
MACACO s
MACAWS*
MACERS*
MACHES
MACHOS*
*MACING
MACKLE ds
MACLED*
MACLES*
MACONS*
MACRON*s
MACROS*
MACULA ers
MACULE ds
MADAME*s
MADAMS*

MADCAP s
*MADDED
MADDEN s
*MADDER s
*MADMAN
*MADMEN
MADRAS a
MADRES*
MADTOM s
MADURO s
MAENAD s
MAFFIA s
MAFIAS*
MAFTIR s
MAGGOT sy
MAGIAN s
MAGICS*
MAGILP s
MAGLEV s
MAGMAS
MAGNET os
MAGNUM s
MAGOTS*
MAGPIE s
MAGUEY s
MAHOES*
MAHOUT s
MAHZOR s
MAIDEN s
MAIGRE
MAIHEM s
e*MAILED*
MAILER*s
MAILES*
MAILLS*
*MAIMED
*MAIMER s
MAINLY
MAISTS*
MAIZES*
MAJORS*
MAKARS*
MAKERS*
MAKEUP s
MAKING s
MAKUTA
MALADY
MALARS*
*MALATE s
MALFED
MALGRE
MALICE*s
*MALIGN s
*MALINE s
MALKIN s
MALLED
*MALLEE s
MALLEI
MALLET s
*MALLOW s
MALOTI
MALTED s
MALTHA s
MALTOL s
MAMBAS*
MAMBOS
MAMEYS*
MAMIES
MAMLUK s
MAMMAE*
MAMMAL*s
MAMMAS*
MAMMEE s
MAMMER s
MAMMET s
MAMMEY s
MAMMIE s
MAMMON s
MAMZER s
MANAGE drs
MANANA s
MANATS*
MANCHE st
MANEGE s
MANFUL
MANGAS
*MANGEL*s
*MANGER*s
MANGES*
MANGEY*
*MANGLE drs
MANGOS*
MANIAC*s
MANIAS*
MANICS*
MANILA s

MANIOC as
MANITO su
MANITU s
MANNAN*s
MANNAS
MANNED
MANNER s
MANORS*
MANQUE
MANSES*
MANTAS
MANTEL s
*MANTES
*MANTIC
MANTID s
*MANTIS
MANTLE dst
*MANTRA mps
MANTUA s
MANUAL s
MANURE drs
MAPLES*
MAPPED
MAPPER s
MAQUIS*
MARACA s
MARAUD s
MARBLE drs
MARBLY
MARCEL s
MARGAY s
MARGES*
MARGIN s
MARINA s
MARINE rs
MARISH
MARKAS*
MARKED
MARKER s
MARKET s
MARKKA as
MARKUP s
MARLED
MARLIN egs
MARMOT s
MAROON s
MARQUE es
MARRAM s
MARRED
MARRER s
MARRON s
*MARROW sy
MARSES
MARSHY*
s MARTED
s MARTEN s
MARTIN gis
MARTYR sy
MARVEL s
MASALA s
MASCON s
*MASCOT s
MASERS*
s*MASHED
s MASHER s
s*MASHES
MASHIE s
MASJID s
*MASKED
MASKEG s
*MASKER s
MASONS*
MASQUE rs
MASSAS*
a MASSED*
a*MASSES*
MASSIF s
MASTED
*MASTER sy
MASTIC s
MASTIX
MATERS*
MATEYS*
MATIER
MATING*s
MATINS*
MATRES
MATRIX
MATRON s
MATSAH s
MATTED*
s MATTER*sy
MATTES*
MATTIN gs
MATURE drs
MATZAH*s

MATZAS*
MATZOH*s
MATZOS*
MATZOT*h
*MAUGER
MAUGRE
MAULED
MAULER s
MAUMET s
MAUNDS*
MAUNDY*
MAUVES*
MAVENS
MAVIES*
MAVINS*
*MAWING
MAXIMA*l
MAXIMS*
*MAXING
MAXIXE s
MAYBES*
MAYDAY s
MAYEST
MAYFLY
MAYHAP
MAYHEM s
MAYING s
MAYORS*
MAYPOP s
MAYVIN s
MAZARD s
MAZERS*
MAZIER
MAZILY
a MAZING
MAZUMA s
MBIRAS*
MEADOW sy
*MEAGER
*MEAGRE
MEALIE rs
MEANER s
MEANIE s
MEANLY
MEASLE ds
MEASLY
MEATAL
MEATED
MEATUS
MECCAS*
MEDAKA s
MEDALS*
MEDDLE drs
MEDFLY
MEDIAD*
MEDIAE*
MEDIAL*s
MEDIAN*st
MEDIAS*
MEDICK*s
MEDICO*s
MEDICS*
MEDINA s
MEDIUM s
MEDIUS
MEDLAR s
MEDLEY s
MEDUSA eln
s
MEEKER
MEEKLY
MEETER s
MEETLY
MEGARA
MEGASS e
MEGILP hs
MEGOHM s
MEGRIM s
MEHNDI s
MEIKLE
MEINIE s
MELDED
*MELDER s
MELEES*
MELENA s
s MELLED
MELLOW s
MELODY
MELOID s
MELONS*
s MELTED
s MELTER s
MELTON s
*MEMBER s
MEMOIR s
MEMORY

MENACE drs
MENADS*
MENAGE s
ae*MENDED
ae*MENDER s
MENHIR s
MENIAL s
MENINX
MENSAE*
MENSAL*
MENSAS*
MENSCH y
MENSED*
MENSES*
o MENTAL*
MENTEE s
MENTOR s
o MENTUM
MENUDO s
MEOUED
MEOWED
a MERCER sy
a MERCES
MERELY
MEREST*
e MERGED*
MERGEE*s
MERGER*s
e MERGES*
MERINO s
MERITS*
MERLES*
MERLIN s
MERLON s
MERLOT s
MERMAN
MERMEN
MESCAL s
MESHED
MESHES
MESIAL
MESIAN
MESNES
MESONS*
MESSAN s
MESSED
*MESSES
MESTEE s
METAGE s
METALS*
METATE s
METEOR s
METEPA s
METERS*
METHOD s
*METHYL s
METIER s
METING
METOLS*
METOPE s
METRED*
METRES*
METRIC s
METROS*
METTLE ds
METUMP s
MEWING
MEWLED
MEWLER s
MEZCAL s
MEZUZA hs
MEZZOS*
MIAOUS*
MIAOWS*
MIASMA*ls
MIASMS*
MIAULS*
MICELL aes
MICHED*
MICHES*
MICKEY s
MICKLE rs
o MICRON*s
MICROS*
MIDAIR s
MIDCAP
MIDDAY s
MIDDEN s
MIDDLE drs
s MIDGES*
MIDGET*s
MIDGUT s
MIDLEG s
MIDRIB s
MIDSTS*
MIDWAY s

MIFFED
MIGGLE s
MIGHTS*
MIGHTY*
MIGNON s
MIHRAB s
MIKADO s
MIKING
o MIKRON s
MIKVAH s
MIKVEH s
MIKVOS
MIKVOT h
MILADI s
MILADY
MILAGE s
MILDED
MILDEN s
MILDER
MILDEW sy
MILDLY
s MILERS*
MILIEU sx
*MILIUM
MILKED
MILKER s
MILLED*
*MILLER*s
MILLES*
MILLET*s
MILNEB s
MILORD s
MILPAS*
MILTED
MILTER s
MIMBAR s
MIMEOS*
MIMERS*
MIMICS*
MIMING
MIMOSA s
MINCED*
MINCER*s
MINCES*
MINDED
MINDER s
MINERS*
*MINGLE drs
MINIFY
MINIMA*lx
MINIMS*
MINING s
*MINION s
MINISH*
MINIUM s
MINKES*
MINNOW s
MINORS*
MINTED
*MINTER s
MINUET s
MINUTE drs
MINXES
MINYAN s
MIOSES
MIOSIS
MIOTIC s
MIRAGE s
MIRIER
MIRING
MIRINS*
s MIRKER
MIRROR s
MIRTHS*
MIRZAS*
MISACT s
MISADD s
MISAIM s
MISATE
MISCUE ds
MISCUT s
MISDID
MISEAT s
MISERS*
MISERY*
MISFED
MISFIT s
MISHAP s
MISHIT s
MISKAL s
MISLAY s
*MISLED
MISLIE s
MISLIT
MISMET
MISPEN s

MISSAL s
MISSAY s
MISSED
MISSEL s
MISSES
MISSET s
MISSIS
MISSUS
MISTED
MISTER ms
MISUSE drs
s MITERS*
*MITHER s
MITIER
MITRAL
MITRED*
MITRES*
s MITTEN s
MIXERS*
MIXING
MIXUPS*
MIZENS*
MIZUNA s
MIZZEN s
MIZZLE ds
MIZZLY
MOANED
MOANER s
MOATED
MOBBED
MOBBER s
MOBCAP s
MOBILE s
MOBLED
MOCHAS*
s MOCKED
*MOCKER sy
MOCKUP s
MODALS*
MODELS*
MODEMS*
MODERN es
MODEST*y
MODICA
MODIFY
MODISH
MODULE s
MODULI
MODULO
MOGGED
MOGGIE s
MOGHUL s
MOGULS*
MOHAIR s
MOHAWK s
MOHELS*
MOHURS*
MOIETY
*MOILED
*MOILER s
MOIRAI*
MOIRES*
MOJOES
MOLARS*
MOLDED
s*MOLDER s
MOLEST*s
MOLIES
MOLINE
MOLLAH s
MOLLIE s
MOLOCH s
MOLTED
MOLTEN
MOLTER s
MOMENT aos
MOMISM s
MOMMAS*
MOMSER s
MOMZER s
MONADS*
MONDES*
MONDOS*
MONEYS*
MONGER s
MONGOE*s
MONGOL*s
MONGOS*
a MONGST
MONIED*
MONIES*
MONISH
MONISM s
MONIST s
MONKEY s
MONODY

MONTES*
MONTHS*
MOOING
MOOLAH*s
MOOLAS*
MOOLEY s
MOONED
MOONER s
MOORED
MOOTED
MOOTER s
MOPEDS*
MOPERS*
MOPERY*
MOPIER
*MOPING
MOPISH
MOPOKE s
MOPPED
MOPPER s
MOPPET s
MORALE*s
MORALS
MORASS*y
MORAYS*
MORBID
MOREEN s
MORELS*
*MORGAN s
MORGEN s
MORGUE s
MORION s
MORONS*
MOROSE
MORPHO*s
MORPHS*
*MORRIS
MORROS*
MORROW*s
MORSEL*s
MORTAL s
MORTAR sy
MORULA ers
MOSAIC s
MOSEYS*
MOSHAV
MOSHED
MOSHER s
MOSHES
MOSQUE s
MOSSED
MOSSER s
MOSSES
MOSTLY
MOTELS*
MOTETS*
s*MOTHER sy
MOTIFS*
MOTILE s
ae MOTION s
e MOTIVE ds
MOTLEY s
MOTMOT s
MOTORS*
MOTTES*
MOTTLE drs
MOTTOS
MOUJIK s
MOULDS*
MOULDY*
MOULIN s
MOULTS*
MOUNDS*
a MOUNTS*
MOURNS*
MOUSED*
MOUSER*s
MOUSES*
MOUSEY*
MOUSSE ds
MOUTHS*
MOUTHY*
MOUTON s
MOVERS
MOVIES*
MOVING
MOWERS*
*MOWING s
MOXIES*
MUCHES
MUCHLY
MUCINS*
MUCKED
MUCKER s
MUCKLE s
MUCLUC s

MUCOID s
MUCORS*
MUCOSA els
MUCOSE
MUCOUS
MUDBUG s
MUDCAP s
MUDCAT s
MUDDED
*MUDDER s
MUDDLE drs
MUDDLY
MUDHEN s
MUDRAS*
MUESLI s
MUFFED
MUFFIN gs
MUFFLE drs
MUFTIS*
MUGFUL s
MUGGAR s
MUGGED
MUGGEE s
s MUGGER s
MUGGUR s
MUGHAL s
MUJIKS*
MUKLUK s
MUKTUK s
MULCTS*
MULETA s
MULEYS*
MULING
MULISH
MULLAH*s
MULLAS*
MULLED
MULLEN s
MULLER s
MULLET s
MULLEY s
MUMBLE drs
MUMBLY
MUMMED
MUMMER sy
*MUMPED
MUMPER s
MUNGOS*
MUNTIN gs
MUONIC
MURALS*
MURDER s
MUREIN s
MURIDS*
*MURINE s
MURING
MURKER
MURKLY
MURMUR s
MURPHY
MURRAS*
MURRES*
MURREY*s
MURRHA s
MUSCAE*
MUSCAT*s
MUSCID s
MUSCLE ds
MUSCLY
a*MUSERS*
MUSEUM s
s MUSHED
*MUSHER s
s MUSHES
MUSICK*s
MUSICS*
a*MUSING s
MUSJID s
MUSKEG s
MUSKET s
MUSKIE rs
MUSKIT s
MUSKOX
MUSLIN s
MUSSED
MUSSEL s
MUSSES
MUSTED
MUSTEE s
MUSTER s
MUSTHS*
MUTANT s
MUTASE s
MUTATE ds
MUTELY
MUTEST*

MUTINE ds
MUTING
MUTINY
MUTISM s
MUTONS*
*MUTTER s
MUTTON sy
MUTUAL s
MUTUEL s
MUTULE s
MUUMUU s
MUZHIK s
MUZJIK s
MUZZLE drs
MYASES
MYASIS
MYCELE s
MYELIN es
MYLARS*
MYNAHS*
MYOMAS*
MYOPES*
MYOPIA s
MYOPIC
MYOSES
MYOSIN s
MYOSIS
MYOTIC s
MYRIAD s
MYRICA s
MYRRHS*
MYRTLE s
MYSELF
MYSIDS*
MYSOST s
MYSTIC s
MYTHIC
MYTHOI
MYTHOS
MYXOID
MYXOMA s
NABBED
NABBER s
NABOBS*
NACHAS
*NACHES
NACHOS*
NACRED
NACRES
NADIRS*
NAEVUS
NAFFED
NAGANA s
s NAGGED
*NAGGER s
NAIADS*
s*NAILED
NAILER s
NAIRAS*
NAIRUS*
NAIVER
NAIVES*t
NAKFAS*
NALEDS*
NAMELY
NAMERS*
NAMING
NANDIN as
o NANISM s
NANKIN s
NANNIE s
NAPALM s
*NAPERY
NAPKIN s
NAPPAS*
ks NAPPED*
ks NAPPER*s
NAPPES*
NAPPIE rs
NARCOS*e
NARIAL
NARINE
NARKED
*NARROW s
NARWAL s
NASALS*
NASIAL
NASION s
NASTIC
NATANT
e NATION s
NATIVE s
NATRON s
NATTER s
NATURE ds
*NAUGHT sy

NAUSEA s
NAUTCH
NAVAID s
NAVARS*
NAVELS*
NAVIES
NAWABS*
NAYSAY s
NAZIFY
NEARBY
a*NEARED
NEARER
*NEARLY
u*NEATEN s
*NEATER
NEATLY
NEBULA ers
NEBULE
NEBULY
NECKED
NECKER s
NECTAR sy
NEEDED
NEEDER s
NEEDLE drs
NEGATE drs
NEIGHS*
NEKTON s
NELLIE s
NELSON s
NEOCON s
NEONED
NEPETA s
NEPHEW s
NEREID s
NEREIS
NEROLI*s
NEROLS*
NERVED*
NERVES*
*NESSES
NESTED
*NESTER s
NESTLE drs
NESTOR s
*NETHER
NETOPS*
NETTED
NETTER s
NETTLE drs
NETTLY
NEUMES*
NEUMIC
NEURAL
NEURON es
NEUTER s
NEVOID
NEWBIE s
NEWELS*
NEWEST
NEWIES*
NEWISH
NEWSIE rs
NEWTON s
NIACIN s
s NIBBED
NIBBLE drs
NICADS*
NICELY
NICEST
NICETY
NICHED*
NICHES*
s NICKED
NICKEL s
s*NICKER s
NICKLE ds
NICOLS*
NIDATE ds
NIDGET s
NIDIFY
NIDING
NIECES*
NIELLI
NIELLO s
NIEVES*
s NIFFER s
s NIGGLE drs
NIGGLY
NIGHED
NIGHER
k NIGHTS*
NIGHTY*
NIHILS*
NILGAI s
NILGAU s

NILLED
NIMBLE r
NIMBLY
NIMBUS
NIMMED
NIMROD s
NINETY
NINJAS*
NINONS*
NINTHS*
NIOBIC
s NIPPED
s NIPPER s
NIPPLE ds
NISEIS*
u NITERS*
NITERY*
NITONS*
NITRES*
NITRIC
NITRID es
NITRIL es
NITROS*o
NITWIT s
NIXIES*
NIXING
NIZAMS*
NOBBLE drs
NOBLER*
NOBLES*t
NOBODY
NOCENT
k NOCKED
NODDED
*NODDER s
NODDLE ds
NODOSE
NODOUS
NODULE s
NOESIS
NOETIC
s NOGGED
NOGGIN gs
NOISED*
NOISES*
NOMADS*
NOMINA l
NOMISM s
NONAGE s
NONART s
NONCES*
NONCOM s
NONEGO s
NONETS*
NONFAN s
NONFAT
NONGAY s
NONMAN
NONMEN
NONPAR
NONTAX
NONUSE rs
NONWAR s
NONYLS*
NOODGE ds
NOODLE ds
NOOGIE s
NOOSED*
NOOSER*s
NOOSES*
NOPALS
NORDIC
NORIAS*
NORITE s
NORMAL s
NORMED
NORTHS*
NOSHED
NOSHER s
NOSHES
*NOSIER
NOSILY
NOSING s
NOSTOC s
NOTARY
NOTATE ds
NOTERS*
a*NOTHER
NOTICE drs
NOTIFY
NOTING
NOTION s
NOUGAT s
*NOUGHT s
NOUNAL
NOUSES

NOVELS*
NOVENA es
NOVICE s
NOWAYS*
NOWISE
NOYADE s
NOZZLE s
NUANCE ds
NUBBIN s
NUBBLE s
NUBBLY
NUBIAS*
NUBILE
NUBUCK s
NUCHAE*
NUCHAL*s
NUCLEI n
NUDELY
NUDEST*
NUDGED*
NUDGER*s
NUDGES*
NUDIES*
NUDISM s
NUDIST s
NUDITY
NUDNIK s
NUGGET sy
NUKING
NULLAH s
NULLED
NUMBAT s
NUMBED
*NUMBER s
NUMBLY
NUMINA
NUNCIO s
*NUNCLE s
k NURLED
NURSED*
NURSER*sy
NURSES*
NUTANT
NUTATE ds
NUTLET s
NUTMEG s
NUTRIA s
NUTTED
*NUTTER s
NUZZLE drs
NYALAS*
NYLONS*
NYMPHA*el
NYMPHO*s
NYMPHS*
OAFISH
OAKIER
OAKUMS*
rs OARING
bc OATERS*
OBEAHS*
l OBELIA*s
OBELUS
*OBENTO s
OBEYED
OBEYER s
OBIISM s
OBJECT s
OBJETS*
*OBLAST is
*OBLATE s
OBLIGE der
s
OBLONG s
OBOIST s
OBOLES
*OBOLUS
OBSESS
OBTAIN s
OBTECT
OBTEST s
OBTUND s
OBTUSE r
OBVERT s
OCCULT s
OCCUPY
OCCURS*
OCEANS*
*OCELLI
OCELOT s
t OCHERS*
OCHERY*
OCHONE
OCHREA*e
OCHRED*
OCHRES*

OCICAT s
cdh OCKERS*
lmr
OCREAE*
OCTADS*
OCTANE*s
OCTANS*
OCTANT*s
OCTAVE s
OCTAVO s
OCTETS*
OCTOPI
OCTROI s
OCTYLS*
jl OCULAR s
l OCULUS
ODDEST
ODDISH
ODDITY
ODEONS*
ODEUMS*
ODIOUS
ODISTS*
ps ODIUMS*
ODORED
ODOURS*
ODYLES*
*OEDEMA s
OEUVRE s
OFFALS*
OFFCUT s
OFFEND s
cdg OFFERS*
OFFICE rs
cd OFFING s
OFFISH
OFFKEY
OFFSET s
s OFTEST
OGDOAD s
OGHAMS*
OGIVAL
OGIVES
OGLERS*
OGLING
OGRESS*
OGRISH
OGRISM s
OHMAGE s
OIDIUM
OILCAN s
OILCUP s
bcm OILERS*
t
r OILIER
OILILY
bcf OILING
mrst
OILMAN
OILMEN
OILWAY s
*OINKED
OKAPIS*
OKAYED
bcg OLDEST
OLDIES*
c OLDISH
OLEATE s
OLEFIN es
OLEINE*s
OLEINS*
OLEUMS*
*OLINGO s
OLIVES
OMASUM
bc OMBERS*
h OMBRES*
OMEGAS*
OMELET s
OMENED
lmt*OMENTA l
ONAGER s
ONAGRI
r ONIONS*
ONIONY*
ONLAYS*
ONLINE
ONLOAD s
ONRUSH
ONSETS*
ONSIDE
bnt ONUSES
ONWARD s
ONYXES
OOCYST s
OOCYTE s

bdn OODLES
p
OOGAMY
z OOGENY
p*OOHING
OOLITE s
OOLITH s
z*OOLOGY
OOLONG s
OOMIAC ks
OOMIAK s
OOMPAH s
OOMPHS*
w OORALI s
OOTIDS*
bw OOZIER
bw OOZILY
b OOZING
OPAQUE drs
OPENED
OPENER s
OPENLY
OPERAS*
OPERON s
OPHITE s
OPIATE ds
OPINED
OPINES
OPIOID s
OPIUMS*
OPPOSE drs
OPPUGN s
OPSINS*
OPTICS*
OPTIMA l
OPTIME s
OPTING
OPTION s
*OPUSES
ORACHE*s
c ORACLE s
m*ORALLY
*ORANGE*sy
ORANGS*
ORANGY
b*ORATED*
b*ORATES*
ORATOR sy
ORBIER
s ORBING
ORBITS*
ORCEIN s
ORCHID s
ORCHIL s
ORCHIS
ORCINS*
ORDAIN s
ORDEAL s
bc ORDERS*
b ORDURE s
OREADS
OREIDE s
ORFRAY s
ORGANA*
m ORGANS*
ORGASM s
ORGEAT s
ORGIAC
p ORGIES
f ORGONE s
ORIBIS*
ORIELS
ORIENT s
ORIGAN s
ORIGIN s
ORIOLE s
ORISHA s
ORISON s
ORLONS*
ORLOPS*
dfw ORMERS*
ORMOLU s
ORNATE
ORNERY
OROIDE s
ORPHAN s
m ORPHIC
ORPINE*s
ORPINS*
ORRERY
ORRICE s
ORYXES
OSCINE s
OSCULA r
OSCULE s
OSETRA s
h OSIERS*
OSMICS*
OSMIUM s
OSMOLE*s
OSMOLS*
OSMOSE ds
OSMOUS
OSMUND as
OSPREY s
OSSEIN s
OSSIFY
*OSTEAL
OSTIUM
hj OSTLER s
OSTOMY
OTALGY
bmp OTHERS*
OTIOSE
OTITIC
*OTITIS
c OTTARS*
OTTAVA s
cdj OTTERS*
lprt
cdm OUCHED
ptv
cdm OUCHES
prtv
n OUGHTS*
bjp OUNCES*
OUPHES*
OURANG s
*OURARI s
OUREBI s
h OUSELS*
jr OUSTED
jr OUSTER s
OUTACT s
OUTADD s
OUTAGE s
OUTASK s
OUTATE
OUTBEG s
OUTBID s
OUTBOX
OUTBUY s
OUTBYE*
OUTCRY
OUTDID
OUTEAT s
cpr OUTERS*
st
OUTFIT s
OUTFLY
OUTFOX
OUTGAS
OUTGUN s
OUTHIT s
lpr OUTING s
t
OUTJUT s
OUTLAW s
OUTLAY s
OUTLED
OUTLET s
OUTLIE rs
OUTMAN s
OUTPUT s
OUTRAN gk
OUTRIG s
OUTROW s
OUTRUN gs
OUTSAT
OUTSAW
OUTSAY s
OUTSEE ns
OUTSET s
OUTSIN gs
OUTSIT s
OUTVIE ds
OUTWAR ds
OUTWIT hs
OUZELS*
OVALLY
OVERDO g
ch OVERED
l OVERLY
OVIBOS
b*OVINES*
OVISAC s
OVOIDS
OVOLOS*
OVONIC s
OVULAR y
OVULES*
h OWLETS*
OWLISH
d OWNERS*
dg OWNING
OXALIC
OXALIS
OXBOWS*
OXCART s
OXEYES*
OXFORD s
OXIDES*
OXIDIC
OXIMES*
bf OXLIKE
OXLIPS*
f OXTAIL s
OXTERS*
OXYGEN s
OYEZES
r OYSTER s
OZALID s
OZONES
OZONIC
PABLUM s
s PACERS*
PACHAS*
s PACIER
o PACIFY
s*PACING
PACKED
PACKER s
PACKET s
PACKLY
PADAUK s
*PADDED
*PADDER s
*PADDLE drs
PADLES*
PADNAG s
PADOUK s
PADRES*
PAEANS*
PAELLA s
PAEONS
PAESAN ios
PAGANS*
PAGERS
*PAGING s
PAGODA*s
PAGODS*
PAIKED
PAINCH
PAINED
PAINTS*
PAINTY*
*PAIRED
PAISAN*aos
PAISAS*
PAJAMA s
PAKEHA s
PAKORA s
PALACE ds
PALAIS
PALAPA s
*PALATE s
PALEAE*
PALEAL*
PALELY
PALEST*
PALETS*
PALIER
PALING s
PALISH
s PALLED
PALLET s
PALLIA l
PALLID
PALLOR s
PALMAR y
PALMED
PALMER s
PALPAL
PALPED
PALPUS
*PALTER s
PALTRY
PAMPAS*
PAMPER os
PANADA s
PANAMA s
PANDAS*
PANDER s
PANDIT s
PANELS*
PANFRY
PANFUL s
PANGAS
PANGED
PANGEN es
PANICS*
PANIER s
PANINI
PANINO
s PANNED*
s PANNER*s
PANNES*
*PANTED
PANTIE s
PANTOS*
PANTRY
PANZER s
PAPACY
PAPAIN s
PAPAWS*
PAPAYA ns
PAPERS
PAPERY
PAPPUS
PAPULA er
PAPULE s
PAPYRI
PARADE drs
PARAMO s
PARANG s
PARAPH s
PARCEL s
PARDAH s
PARDEE
PARDIE*
PARDON s
PARENT s
PAREOS*
s PARERS*
PAREUS*
PAREVE
s PARGED*
s PARGES*
PARGET*s
PARGOS*
PARIAH s
PARIAN s
PARIES
s PARING s
PARISH*
PARITY
PARKAS*
s PARKED
s PARKER s
PARLAY s
PARLED*
PARLES
PARLEY*s
PARLOR s
PARODY
PAROLE*des
PAROLS*
PAROUS
PARRAL s
s PARRED
PARREL s
PARROT sy
PARSEC*s
PARSED*
s PARSER*s
PARSES
*PARSON s
s PARTAN s
PARTED
PARTLY
PARTON s
PARURA s
PARURE s
PARVIS e
PARVOS
PASCAL s
PASEOS*
PASHAS*
*PASHED
*PASHES
PASSED*
PASSEE*
PASSEL*s
PASSER*s
PASSES
PASSIM
PASSUS
PASTAS*
PASTED*
PASTEL*s
*PASTER*ns
PASTES*
PASTIE rs
PASTIL s
PASTIS
PASTOR s
PASTRY
PATACA s
PATCHY*
PATENS*
PATENT*s
PATERS*
PATHOS
PATINA*es
PATINE*ds
PATINS*
PATIOS*
PATOIS
PATROL s
PATRON s
s PATTED
PATTEE
PATTEN s
s PATTER ns
PATTIE s
PATZER s
PAULIN s
PAUNCH y
PAUPER s
PAUSAL
PAUSED*
PAUSER*s
PAUSES*
PAVANE*s
PAVANS*
PAVEED
PAVERS
PAVING*s
s PAVINS*
PAVIOR s
PAVISE*rs
PAWERS*
*PAWING
s*PAWNED
PAWNEE s
s PAWNER s
PAWNOR s
PAWPAW s
PAXWAX
PAYDAY s
PAYEES*
PAYERS*
s PAYING
PAYNIM s
PAYOFF s
PAYOLA s
PAYORS*
PAYOUT s
PAZAZZ
PEACED*
PEACES*
PEACHY*
PEAGES*
PEAHEN s
PEAKED
PEALED
PEANUT s
PEARLS
PEARLY
PEASEN*
PEASES
PEAVEY s
PEBBLE ds
PEBBLY
PECANS*
PECHAN s
*PECHED
s PECKED
PECKER s
PECTEN s
PECTIC
PECTIN s
PEDALO*s
PEDALS*
PEDANT s
PEDATE
PEDDLE drs
PEDLAR sy
PEDLER sy
PEDROS*
PEEKED
s PEELED
PEELER s
PEENED
PEEPED
PEEPER s
PEEPUL s
s PEERED
*PEERIE s
PEEVED*
PEEVES*
PEEWEE s
PEEWIT s
PEGBOX
*PEGGED
PEINED
PEISED*
s PEISES*
PEKANS*
PEKINS*
PEKOES*
PELAGE s
*PELITE s
PELLET s
PELMET s
PELOTA s
PELTED
s PELTER s
PELTRY
*PELVES
PELVIC s
PELVIS
PENANG s
PENCEL*s
PENCIL s
u*PENDED
PENGOS*
PENIAL
PENILE
PENMAN
PENMEN
PENNAE*
PENNED*
PENNER*s
PENNIA*
PENNIS*
PENNON s
PENSEE s
PENSIL es
PENTAD s
PENTYL s
PENULT s
PENURY
PEONES
PEOPLE drs
PEPINO s
PEPLOS
PEPLUM s
PEPLUS
PEPPED
PEPPER sy
PEPSIN es
PEPTIC s
PEPTID es
PERDIE
PERDUE*s
PERDUS*
PEREIA
PEREON s
PERILS*
PERIOD s
PERISH*
PERITI
PERKED
PERMED
PERMIT s
PERNIO
PERNOD s
PEROXY
PERRON s
PERSES
PERSON as
PERTER
PERTLY
PERUKE ds
PERUSE drs
PESADE s
PESETA s
PESEWA s
*PESTER s
PESTLE ds
PESTOS*
PETALS*
PETARD s
PETERS*
PETITE*s
PETNAP s
PETREL s
PETROL s
PETSAI s
PETTED
PETTER s
PETTLE ds
PEWEES*
PEWITS*
PEWTER s
PEYOTE s
PEYOTL s
PHAGES*
PHALLI c
PHAROS
PHASED*
PHASES*
a PHASIC
PHASIS
PHATIC
PHENIX
PHENOL s
PHENOM s
PHENYL s
PHIALS*
PHIZES
PHLEGM sy
PHLOEM s
PHOBIA s
PHOBIC s
PHOEBE s
PHONAL
PHONED
PHONES
*PHONEY*s
a PHONIC s
PHONON*s
PHONOS*
*PHOOEY
a PHOTIC s
PHOTOG*s
PHOTON*s
PHOTOS*
PHRASE ds
PHREAK s
PHYLAE*
PHYLAR*
PHYLIC
PHYLLO s
PHYLON
PHYLUM
PHYSED s
PHYSES
PHYSIC s
PHYSIS
PHYTIN s
PHYTOL s
PHYTON s
PIAFFE drs
PIANIC
PIANOS*
PIAZZA s
PIAZZE
PIBALS*
PICARA s
PICARO s
PICKAX e
PICKED
*PICKER s
PICKET s
PICKLE ds
PICKUP s
PICNIC s
PICOTS*
PICRIC
PICULS*
PIDDLE drs
PIDDLY
PIDGIN s
PIECED*
PIECER*s
PIECES*
PIEING
PIERCE drs
PIETAS*
PIFFLE ds
PIGEON s
*PIGGED
PIGGIE rs
PIGGIN gs
PIGLET s
PIGNUS
PIGNUT s
PIGOUT s
PIGPEN s
PIGSTY
PIKAKE s
s PIKERS*
s PIKING
PILAFF*s
PILAFS*
PILAUS*
PILAWS*
*PILEUM
PILEUP s
*PILEUS

PILFER s
s PILING s
PILLAR s
s PILLED
PILLOW sy
PILOSE
PILOTS*
PILOUS
PILULE s
*PIMPED
PIMPLE ds
*PIMPLY
PINANG s
PINATA s
PINCER s
PINDER s
PINEAL s
PINENE s
PINERY
PINETA
PINGED
PINGER s
PINGOS*
s PINIER
o PINING
o*PINION s
PINITE s
*PINKED
PINKEN s
*PINKER s
PINKEY es
PINKIE s
PINKLY
PINKOS*
PINNAE*
PINNAL*
PINNAS*
*PINNED
s*PINNER s
PINOLE s
PINONS*
PINOTS*
PINTAS*
PINTLE s
s PINTOS*
PINUPS*
PINYIN
PINYON s
PIOLET s
*PIONIC
PIPAGE s
PIPALS*
PIPERS*
PIPETS*
PIPIER
PIPING s
PIPITS*
PIPKIN s
PIPPED
PIPPIN gs
PIQUED*
PIQUES*
PIQUET*s
PIRACY
PIRANA s
*PIRATE ds
PIRAYA s
PIROGI*
PISCOS*
PISHED
PISHER s
PISHES
PISTES*
PISTIL s
PISTOL es
PISTON s
PISTOU s
PITAYA s
PITCHY
PITHED
PITIED
PITIER s
PITIES
PITMAN s
PITMEN
PITONS*
PITSAW s
PITTAS*
s PITTED
PIVOTS*
PIXELS*
PIXIES*
PIZAZZ y
PIZZAS*
PIZZAZ*z
PIZZLE s

PLACED
*PLACER*s
PLACES
PLACET*s
PLACID
PLACKS
PLAGAL
PLAGES*
PLAGUE drs
y
PLAGUY
PLAICE s
PLAIDS*
PLAINS*
PLAINT*s
PLAITS*
PLANAR
PLANCH e
PLANED*
PLANER*s
PLANES
PLANET*s
PLANKS*
PLANTS*
PLAQUE s
s PLASHY*
PLASMA*s
PLASMS*
PLATAN es
PLATED
*PLATEN*s
*PLATER*s
PLATES*
PLATYS*
PLAYAS*
s*PLAYED
*PLAYER s
PLAZAS*
*PLEACH
PLEADS
*PLEASE*drs
PLEATS*
PLEBES*
*PLEDGE der
st
PLEIAD s
PLENCH
a PLENTY
PLENUM s
PLEONS*
PLEURA els
PLEXAL
*PLEXES
PLEXOR s
PLEXUS
PLIANT
PLICAE*
PLICAL*
PLIERS
u*PLIGHT s
u*PLINKS*
PLINTH s
PLISKY
PLISSE s
PLOIDY
PLONKS*
PLOTTY
*PLOUGH s
*PLOVER s
*PLOWED
*PLOWER s
PLOYED
PLUCKS
PLUCKY
PLUMBS*
PLUMED*
PLUMES*
PLUMMY
PLUMPS
*PLUNGE drs
PLUNKS
PLUNKY*
PLURAL s
PLUSES
PLUSHY*
PLUTEI
PLUTON s
PLYERS*
*PLYING
PNEUMA s
POACHY*
POBOYS*
POCKED
POCKET s
PODDED
PODITE s

*PODIUM s
PODSOL s
PODZOL s
POETIC s
POETRY
POGEYS*
POGIES
POGROM s
POILUS*
POINDS*
POINTE*drs
POINTS*
POINTY*
POISED*
POISER*s
POISES*
POISHA
POISON s
POKERS*
POKEYS*
POKIER
POKIES t
POKILY
s POKING
POLARS*
*POLDER s
POLEAX e
POLEIS
POLERS*
POLEYN s
POLICE drs
POLICY
POLIES
POLING
POLIOS
POLISH*
POLITE r
POLITY
POLKAS*
POLLED
POLLEE s
POLLEN s
POLLER s
POLLEX
POLYOL s
POLYPI*
POLYPS*
POMACE s
POMADE ds
POMELO s
POMMEE
POMMEL s
POMPOM s
POMPON s
PONCED*
PONCES*
PONCHO s
PONDED
PONDER s
PONENT
s PONGED
PONGEE s
PONGID s
PONIED
PONIES
PONTES
PONTIL s
PONTON s
POODLE s
*POOHED
s POOLED
s POOLER s
POOPED
POORER
POORIS*h
POORLY
POPGUN s
POPLAR s
POPLIN s
POPPAS*
POPPED
POPPER s
POPPET s
POPPLE ds
POPSIE s
s PORING
PORISM s
PORKED
PORKER s
PORNOS*
POROSE
POROUS
PORTAL s
s PORTED
s PORTER s
PORTLY

POSADA s
POSERS*
POSEUR s
POSHER
POSHLY
POSIES
POSING
POSITS*
POSOLE s
POSSES*s
POSSET*s
o POSSUM s
POSTAL s
POSTED
POSTER ns
POSTIE s
POSTIN gs
POSTOP s
POTAGE s
POTASH
POTATO
POTBOY s
POTEEN s
POTENT
POTFUL s
*POTHER bs
POTHOS
POTION s
POTMAN
POTMEN
POTPIE s
POTSIE s
s POTTED
s*POTTER sy
POTTLE s
POTTOS
POTZER s
POUCHY*
POUFED
POUFFE*ds
POUFFS*
POUFFY*
POULTS*
*POUNCE drs
POUNDS*
POURED
POURER s
s*POUTED
s*POUTER s
POWDER sy
POWERS*
POWTER s
POWWOW s
POXIER
POXING
POYOUS*
POZOLE s
PRAAMS*
PRAHUS*
u*PRAISE drs
PRAJNA s
*PRANCE drs
s PRANGS*
PRANKS
PRASES
u*PRATED*
*PRATER*s
u*PRATES*
PRAWNS*
*PRAXES
PRAXIS
s*PRAYED
s PRAYER s
u*PREACH y
*PREACT s
PREAMP s
*PREARM s
*PREBID s
*PREBUY s
PRECIS e
*PRECUT s
*PREDRY
PREENS*
PREFAB s
*PREFER s
*PREFIX
PRELAW
PRELIM s
*PREMAN
PREMED s
PREMEN
PREMIE rs
*PREMIX t
PREOPS*
*PREPAY s
PREPPY

*PRESET*s
PRESTO*s
PRESTS
*PRETAX
PRETOR s
PRETTY
*PREVUE ds
PREWAR mn
*PREXES
PREYED
PREYER s
PREZES
PRIAPI c
PRICED
*PRICER*s
PRICES
PRICEY*
PRICKS
PRICKY*
PRIDED*
PRIDES
PRIERS*
s PRIEST*s
PRILLS
PRIMAL*
PRIMAS*
PRIMED
*PRIMER*os
PRIMES
PRIMLY
PRIMOS*
PRIMPS*
PRIMUS
PRINCE s
PRINKS
s PRINTS*
PRIONS*
PRIORS*
PRIORY*
PRISED*
u*PRISES*
PRISMS*
PRISON s
PRISSY*
*PRIVET s
PRIZED*
PRIZER*s
PRIZES*
PROBED
PROBER*s
PROBES
PROBIT sy
PROEMS*
PROFIT s
PROGUN
PROJET s
PROLAN s
PROLEG*s
PROLES
PROLIX
PROLOG s
PROMOS*
PROMPT s
PRONGS*
PRONTO
PROOFS
PROPEL s
*PROPER s
PROPYL as
PROSED
PROSER*s
PROSES
PROSIT
PROSOS*
PROTEA ns
PROTEI dn
PROTON s
PROTYL es
PROVED
PROVEN
*PROVER*bs
PROVES
PROWAR
*PROWER
PROWLS*
PRUDES*
PRUNED*
PRUNER*s
PRUNES
PRUNUS
PRUTAH*
PRUTOT h
PRYERS*
PRYING
PSALMS*
PSEUDO*s

PSEUDS*
PSHAWS
PSOCID s
PSYCHE*ds
PSYCHO*s
PSYCHS*
PSYLLA s
PSYOPS
PSYWAR s
PTERIN s
PTISAN s
PTOOEY
PTOSES
PTOSIS
PTOTIC
PUBLIC s
PUCKER sy
PUDDLE drs
PUDDLY
PUEBLO s
PUFFED
PUFFER sy
PUFFIN gs
PUGGED
PUGGRY
PUGREE s
PUISNE s
PUJAHS*
PUKING
PULERS*
PULING s
PULLED
PULLER s
PULLET s
PULLEY s
PULLUP s
PULPAL
PULPED
PULPER s
PULPIT s
PULQUE s
PULSAR s
PULSED*
PULSER*s
PULSES*
PUMELO s
PUMICE drs
PUMMEL os
*PUMPED
PUMPER s
PUNCHY*
PUNDIT s
PUNGLE ds
PUNIER
PUNILY
PUNISH
PUNJIS*
PUNKAH*s
PUNKAS*
PUNKER s
PUNKEY s
s PUNKIE rs
PUNKIN s
PUNNED
PUNNER s
PUNNET s
PUNTED
PUNTER s
PUNTOS*
PUPATE ds
PUPILS*
*PUPPED
PUPPET s
PURANA s
PURDAH*s
PURDAS*
PUREED*
PUREES*
PURELY
PUREST
PURFLE drs
PURGED
*PURGER*s
s*PURGES*
PURIFY
*PURINE*s
PURINS*
PURISM*s
PURIST*s
PURITY
PURLED
PURLIN egs
PURPLE drs
PURPLY
s PURRED
PURSED*

PURSER*s
PURSES*
PURSUE drs
PURVEY s
PUSHED
*PUSHER s
PUSHES
PUSHUP s
PUSLEY s
PUSSES
PUSSLY
PUTLOG s
PUTOFF s
PUTONS*
PUTOUT s
PUTRID
PUTSCH
PUTTED
PUTTEE s
s*PUTTER s
PUTTIE*drs
PUTZED
PUTZES
PUZZLE drs
PYEMIA s
PYEMIC
PYJAMA s
PYKNIC s
PYLONS*
PYLORI c
PYOSES
PYOSIS
PYRANS*
PYRENE s
PYRITE s
PYROLA s
PYRONE s
PYROPE s
PYRROL es
PYTHON s
PYURIA s
PYXIES*
QABALA hs
QANATS*
QINDAR s
QINTAR s
QIVIUT s
QUACKS*
QUACKY*
QUAERE s
QUAFFS*
QUAGGA s
QUAGGY
QUAHOG s
QUAICH s
QUAIGH s
QUAILS*
QUAINT
QUAKED*
QUAKER*s
QUAKES*
QUALIA
QUALMS*
QUALMY*
QUANGO s
QUANTA*l
QUANTS*
s QUARKS*
QUARRY
QUARTE*rst
QUARTO*s
QUARTS*
QUARTZ*
QUASAR s
QUATRE s
QUAVER sy
QUBITS*
QUBYTE s
QUEANS*
QUEASY
QUEAZY
QUEENS*
QUEERS*
QUELEA s
QUELLS*
QUENCH
QUERNS*
QUESTS*
QUEUED*
QUEUER*s
QUEUES*
QUEZAL s
QUICHE s
QUICKS*
QUIETS*
QUIFFS*

s QUILLS*
QUILTS*
QUINCE s
QUINIC
QUININ aes
QUINOA s
QUINOL s
QUINSY*
QUINTA*lnr
s
QUINTE*st
s QUINTS*
QUIPPU s
QUIPPY
QUIPUS*
s QUIRED*
s QUIRES*
QUIRKS*
QUIRKY*
s QUIRTS*
QUITCH
a QUIVER sy
QUOHOG s
QUOINS*
QUOITS*
QUOKKA s
QUOLLS*
QUORUM s
QUOTAS*
QUOTED*
QUOTER*s
QUOTES*
QUOTHA*
QURUSH
QWERTY s
RABATO*s
RABATS*
d RABBET s
RABBIN*s
RABBIS*
RABBIT*sy
bdg RABBLE drs
RABIES
RACEME ds
bt RACERS*
b RACHET s
RACHIS
RACIAL
RACIER
RACILY
bgt*RACING s
RACISM s
RACIST s
ctw RACKED
ct RACKER s
b RACKET sy
cg RACKLE
RACONS*
RACOON s
RADARS*
b*RADDED
*RADDLE ds
RADIAL es
RADIAN st
RADIOS
RADISH
RADIUM s
RADIUS
RADOME s
RADONS*
RADULA ers
RAFFIA s
RAFFLE drs
cdg RAFTED
cdg*RAFTER s
RAGBAG s
d RAGEES*
bcd RAGGED y
f
RAGGEE s
d RAGGLE s
*RAGING
RAGLAN s
RAGMAN
RAGMEN
RAGOUT s
RAGTAG s
RAGTOP s
b*RAIDED
b*RAIDER s
bt*RAILED
ft RAILER s
bdg RAINED
t
bp RAISED*
p RAISER*s
bfp RAISES*
RAISIN gsy
RAITAS*
RAJAHS*
RAKEES
RAKERS*
b RAKING
RAKISH*
RALLYE*s
RALPHS*
RAMADA s
RAMATE
RAMBLA s
b*RAMBLE drs
RAMEES*
RAMETS*
RAMIES
RAMIFY
RAMJET s
cdt RAMMED
c RAMMER s
RAMONA s
RAMOSE
RAMOUS
ct*RAMPED
RAMROD s
RAMSON s
RAMTIL s
pt RANCES*
*RANCHO*s
RANCID
RANCOR s
RANDAN s
RANDOM s
RANEES*
p RANGED*
g*RANGER*s
go RANGES*
RANIDS*
cfp RANKED
cf RANKER s
c*RANKLE ds
cf RANKLY
t RANSOM s
g*RANTED
g RANTER s
RANULA rs
d*RAPERS*
RAPHAE
RAPHES*
RAPHIA s
*RAPHIS
RAPIDS*
g RAPIER s
RAPINE s
cd*RAPING
RAPINI
RAPIST s
cft RAPPED
w
RAPPEE s
*RAPPEL s
RAPPEN
tw RAPPER s
*RAPTLY
RAPTOR s
RAREFY
RARELY
RAREST*
RARIFY
RARING
RARITY
RASCAL s
e RASERS*
bct RASHER s
bct*RASHES t
b RASHLY
e RASING
g RASPED
g*RASPER s
w RASSLE ds
*RASTER s
e RASURE s
RATALS*
RATANS*
RATANY*
RATBAG s
RATELS*
cfg RATERS*
kp
RATHER*
g RATIFY
g RATINE s
cgo RATING s
p
o RATION*s
RATIOS*
RATITE s
RATLIN es
RATOON s
RATTAN s
d RATTED
RATTEN s
RATTER s
bp RATTLE drs
RATTLY
RATTON s
c RAUNCH y
RAVAGE drs
gt RAVELS*
c*RAVENS*
bcg*RAVERS*
RAVINE*ds
bcg RAVING*s
RAVINS*
RAVISH
b RAWEST
RAWINS*
RAWISH
*RAXING
RAYAHS
bdf RAYING
gp
c RAYONS*
RAZEED*
RAZEES*
bg RAZERS*
bcg RAZING
RAZORS*
RAZZED
RAZZES
p REACTS*
READDS*
t READER s
REAGIN s
REALER
REALES t
REALIA
a REALLY
REALMS*
REALTY
bcd REAMED
cd REAMER s
REAPED
REAPER s
*REARED
REARER s
p REARMS*
t REASON s
REATAS*
g*REAVED*
p REAVER*s
g*REAVES*
REAVOW s
REBAIT s
REBARS*
REBATE drs
REBATO s
REBBES*
REBECK*s
REBECS*
REBELS*
p REBIDS*
p REBILL s
p REBIND s
REBODY
p REBOIL s
p*REBOOK s
REBOOT s
REBOPS*
REBORE ds
REBORN
REBOZO s
REBRED
REBUFF s
REBUKE drs
REBURY
REBUTS*
p REBUYS*
RECALL s
RECANE ds
RECANT s
RECAPS*
p RECAST s
RECCES*
p RECEDE ds
p RECENT
p RECEPT s
p RECESS
RECHEW s
p RECIPE s
RECITE*drs
RECITS*
w RECKED
RECKON s
RECLAD s
RECOAL s
RECOAT s
RECOCK s
p RECODE ds
RECOIL s
RECOIN s
RECOMB s
RECONS*
p RECOOK s
RECOPY
RECORD s
RECORK s
p RECOUP es
RECTAL*
e RECTOR*sy
RECTOS*
RECTUM s
RECTUS
RECURS*
RECUSE ds
p RECUTS*
REDACT s
REDANS*
p REDATE ds
REDBAY s
REDBUD s
REDBUG s
REDCAP s
REDDED
REDDEN s
REDDER s
t REDDLE ds
REDEAR s
REDEEM s
REDEFY
REDENY
REDEYE s
REDFIN s
REDIAE*
pu REDIAL*s
REDIAS*
REDING
REDIPS*
REDIPT*
REDLEG s
REDOCK s
REDOES
REDONE*
REDONS*
REDOUT s
REDOWA s
REDRAW ns
REDREW
REDTOP s
REDUBS*
*REDUCE drs
REDYED*
REDYES*
REEARN s
REECHO
REECHY
REEDED
p REEDIT s
REEFED
REEFER s
REEKED
REEKER s
c REELED
REELER s
REEMIT s
REESTS*
REEVED*
REEVES*
p REFACE ds
REFALL s
p REFECT s
REFEED s
REFEEL s
REFELL*
REFELS*
REFELT*
p REFERS*
REFFED
p REFILE ds
REFILL s
REFILM s
REFIND s
REFINE drs
p REFIRE ds
REFITS*
REFLAG s
REFLET s
REFLEW
REFLEX
REFLOW ns
REFLUX
REFOLD s
p REFORM s
REFUEL s
REFUGE des
p REFUND s
REFUSE drs
REFUTE drs
REGAIN s
REGALE*drs
REGARD s
REGAVE
REGEAR s
REGENT s
REGGAE s
REGILD s
REGILT
REGIME ns
REGINA els
REGION s
REGIUS
REGIVE ns
REGLET s
REGLOW s
REGLUE ds
REGNAL*
REGNUM
*REGRET s
REGREW
REGROW ns
REGULI
REHABS*
REHANG s
REHASH
REHEAR ds
p REHEAT s
REHEEL s
REHEMS*
REHIRE ds
REHUNG
REIGNS*
REINED
REINKS*
REIVED*
REIVER*s
REIVES*
*REJECT s
REJIGS*
REJOIN s
REKEYS*
REKNIT s
REKNOT s
RELACE ds
RELAID
*RELAND s
p*RELATE drs
RELAYS*
RELEND s
RELENT s
RELETS*
RELEVE s
RELICS*
RELICT*s
RELIED
RELIEF s
RELIER s
RELIES
RELINE ds
RELINK s
RELISH
RELIST s
RELIVE ds
p RELOAD s
RELOAN s
RELOCK s
RELOOK s
RELUCT s
RELUME ds
p REMADE
*REMAIL s
REMAIN s
REMAKE rs
REMAND*s
REMANS*
REMAPS*
REMARK s
c REMATE ds
REMEDY
p REMEET s
REMELT s
*REMEND s
REMIND s
REMINT s
p REMISE ds
p REMISS
REMITS
p REMIXT*
p REMOLD s
REMORA s
*REMOTE rs
REMOVE drs
REMUDA s
t RENAIL s
p RENAME ds
t*RENDED
*RENDER s
RENEGE drs
RENEST s
RENEWS*
RENIGS*
RENINS*
RENNET s
RENNIN s
RENOWN s
RENTAL s
RENTED*
*RENTER*s
RENTES*
*RENVOI s
REOILS*
REOPEN s
p REPACK s
p REPAID
REPAIR s
REPAND
REPARK s
REPASS
REPAST s
p REPAVE ds
p REPAYS*
REPEAL s
REPEAT s
REPEGS*
REPELS*
REPENT s
REPERK s
REPINE*drs
REPINS*
p REPLAN st
REPLAY s
REPLED
REPLOT s
REPLOW s
REPOLL s
REPORT s
REPOSE*drs
REPOTS*
REPOUR s
p REPPED
REPROS*
REPUGN s
REPUMP s
REPUTE ds
REQUIN s
RERACK s
REREAD s
RERENT s
RERIGS*
RERISE ns
REROLL s
REROOF s
*REROSE
RERUNS*
RESAID
RESAIL s
p RESALE s
RESAWN*
RESAWS*
RESAYS*
RESCUE drs
RESEAL s
RESEAT s
RESEAU sx
RESECT s
RESEDA s
RESEED*s
RESEEK*s
RESEEN*
RESEES*
p RESELL s
RESEND s
p RESENT s
p RESETS*
RESEWN*
RESEWS*
f RESHES
p RESHIP s
RESHOD
RESHOE ds
RESHOT
p RESHOW ns
p RESIDE*drs
RESIDS*
p RESIFT s
RESIGN s
RESILE ds
RESINS*
RESINY*
RESIST s
RESITE*ds
RESITS*
RESIZE ds
p RESOAK s
RESODS*
p RESOLD
RESOLE ds
RESORB s
p RESORT s
RESOWN*
RESOWS*
RESPOT s
cw RESTED
pw*RESTER s
RESULT s
p RESUME drs
RETACK s
RETAGS*
RETAIL s
RETAIN s
RETAKE nrs
p*RETAPE ds
RETARD s
RETEAM s
RETEAR s
p RETELL s
RETEMS*
RETENE s
p RETEST s
RETIAL*
RETIED*
RETIES*
RETILE ds
RETIME ds
RETINA els
RETINE s
RETINT s
RETIRE der
s
p RETOLD
RETOOK
RETOOL s
RETORE
RETORN
RETORT s
RETRAL
p RETRIM s
RETROS*
f RETTED
RETUNE ds
RETURN s
RETUSE
p RETYPE ds
REUSED*
REUSES*
REVAMP s
REVEAL s
REVELS*
p REVERB s
REVERE drs
REVERS eo
*REVERT s
*REVERY
REVEST s
bt REVETS*
p REVIEW s
REVILE drs
p REVISE drs
REVIVE drs
*REVOKE drs
REVOLT s
REVOTE ds
p REVUES*
REVVED
REWAKE dns
REWARD s
p REWARM s
p REWASH
REWEAR s
REWEDS*
REWELD s
REWETS*
REWIND*s
REWINS*
p REWIRE ds
REWOKE n

REWORD s
REWORE
p REWORK s
p REWORN
REWOVE n
p REWRAP st
*REXINE s
REZERO s
REZONE ds
RHAPHE s
RHEBOK s
RHEMES
RHESUS
RHETOR s
RHEUMS*
RHEUMY*
RHINAL
RHINOS*
RHODIC
RHOMBI*c
RHOMBS*
RHOTIC
RHUMBA*s
RHUMBS*
RHUSES
RHYMED*
RHYMER*s
RHYMES*
RHYTHM s
RHYTON s
RIALTO s
RIATAS*
RIBALD s
RIBAND s
cd RIBBED
c RIBBER s
RIBBON sy
RIBIER s
d RIBLET s
RIBOSE s
p RICERS*
RICHEN s
RICHER
RICHES t
RICHLY
pt*RICING*
RICINS*
bcp RICKED
tw
c RICKEY s
RICRAC s
RICTAL
*RICTUS
g RIDDED
RIDDEN
g RIDDER s
g RIDDLE drs
t RIDENT
RIDERS*
b RIDGED*
RIDGEL*s
bf RIDGES*
RIDGIL s
gp RIDING s
RIDLEY s
g RIEVER s
RIFELY
RIFEST
RIFFED
RIFFLE drs
t RIFLED*
t RIFLER*sy
t RIFLES*
RIFLIP s
dg RIFTED
fpt*RIGGED
t RIGGER s
RIGHTO*
bfw RIGHTS*
RIGHTY*
RIGORS*
RIGOUR s
RILING
dfg RILLED*
pt
g RILLES*
RILLET*s
pt RIMERS*
g RIMIER
gp RIMING
bpt RIMMED
bcg RIMMER s
kpt
RIMOSE
RIMOUS
c RIMPLE ds
bg RINDED
cfw RINGED
bcw RINGER s
RINSED*
RINSER*s
RINSES*
RIOJAS*
RIOTED
RIOTER s
RIPELY
RIPENS*
RIPEST*
g RIPING
RIPOFF s
RIPOST es
dgt RIPPED
dgt RIPPER s
cg RIPPLE drs
t
RIPPLY
RIPRAP s
RIPSAW ns
RISERS*
RISHIS*
aip RISING s
bf RISKED
bf RISKER s
RISQUE
RISTRA s
RITARD s
cfg RITTER s
RITUAL s
f RITZES
RIVAGE s
RIVALS*
d RIVERS*
gpt RIVETS*
d RIVING
RIYALS*
ROADEO s
ROADIE s
ROAMED
ROAMER s
*ROARED
ROARER s
ROASTS
ROBALO s
p ROBAND s
ROBBED
ROBBER sy
ROBBIN gs
p ROBING*
ROBINS*
ROBLES*
ROBOTS*
ROBUST a
c ROCHET s
cft ROCKED
*ROCKER sy
bc ROCKET s
ROCOCO s
p RODDED
e RODENT s
RODEOS*
RODMAN
RODMEN
ROGERS*
ROGUED*
bd ROGUES*
b*ROILED
ROLFED
ROLFER s
dt ROLLED
dt ROLLER s
ROMAJI s
ROMANO*s
ROMANS*
ROMEOS*
t ROMPED
ROMPER s
RONDEL s
RONDOS*
*RONION s
RONNEL s
RONYON s
p ROOFED
p ROOFER s
ROOFIE s
bc ROOKED
b ROOKIE rs
bgv ROOMED
g ROOMER s
ROOMIE rs
ROOSED*
ROOSER*s
ROOSES*
ROOSTS*
ROOTED
ROOTER s
ROOTLE dst
gp ROPERS*
ROPERY*
ROPIER
ROPILY
g*ROPING
ROQUES*
c ROQUET*s
ROSARY
ROSCOE s
ROSERY
ROSETS*
ROSHIS*
cp*ROSIER
p ROSILY
p ROSING*
ROSINS*
ROSINY*
ROSTER s
ROSTRA l
ROTARY
ROTATE ds
ROTCHE*s
ROTGUT s
ROTORS*
t ROTTED*
ROTTEN*
t*ROTTER*s
ROTTES*
o ROTUND a
t ROUBLE s
ROUCHE s
ROUENS*
ROUGED*
ROUGES*
t ROUGHS*
ROUGHY*
g ROUNDS*
gt ROUPED
ROUPET
ag ROUSED*
agt ROUSER*s
ag ROUSES*
ROUSTS
g*ROUTED*
g*ROUTER*s
c ROUTES*
d ROUTHS*
dpt*ROVERS*
dp ROVING s
ROWANS*
t ROWELS*
ROWENS*
cg ROWERS*
cgt*ROWING s
gt ROWTHS*
ROYALS*
ROZZER s
RUANAS*
RUBACE s
RUBATI
RUBATO s
dg RUBBED
dg RUBBER sy
RUBBLE ds
RUBBLY
RUBELS*
RUBIED
RUBIER
RUBIES t
RUBIGO s
RUBLES*
RUBOFF s
RUBOUT s
RUBRIC s
RUCHED*
RUCHES*
t RUCKED
t RUCKLE ds
RUCKUS
*RUDDER s
RUDDLE ds
c RUDELY
p RUDERY*
c RUDEST
RUEFUL
g RUFFED*
t RUFFES*
t RUFFLE drs
g RUFFLY
RUFOUS
RUGATE
df RUGGED
RUGGER s
a RUGOLA s
RUGOSA s
RUGOSE
RUGOUS
RUINED
RUINER s
RULERS*
RULIER
RULING s
RUMAKI s
RUMBAS*
cdg RUMBLE drs
cg RUMBLY
RUMENS*
RUMINA l
dg RUMMER s
RUMORS*
RUMOUR s
c RUMPLE ds
c RUMPLY
RUMPUS
t RUNDLE st
RUNKLE ds
*RUNLET s
t RUNNEL s
RUNNER s
RUNOFF s
RUNOUT s
RUNWAY s
RUPEES*
RUPIAH s
*RURBAN
bc RUSHED
RUSHEE s
bc*RUSHER s
bc RUSHES
RUSINE
RUSSET sy
ct RUSTED
RUSTIC s
RUSTLE drs
*RUTILE s
RUTINS*
RUTTED
RYKING
RYOKAN s
SABALS*
SABBAT hs
SABBED
SABERS*
SABINE*s
SABINS*
SABIRS*
SABLES
SABOTS*
SABRAS*
SABRED*
SABRES*
SACBUT s
SACHEM s
SACHET s
SACKED
SACKER s
SACQUE s
SACRAL*s
*SACRED
SACRUM s
SADDEN s
*SADDER
SADDHU s
*SADDLE drs
SADHES*
SADHUS*
SADISM*s
SADIST*s
SAFARI s
SAFELY
SAFEST*
SAFETY
SAFROL es
SAGBUT s
SAGELY
SAGEST*
SAGGAR ds
SAGGED
*SAGGER s
SAGIER
SAHIBS*
SAICES*
SAIGAS*
*SAILED
SAILER s
SAILOR s
SAIMIN s
SAINED
SAINTS*
SAITHE*
SAIYID s
SAJOUS*
SAKERS*
SALAAM s
SALADS*
SALALS*
SALAMI s
*SALARY
SALEPS*
SALIFY
SALINA s
*SALINE s
SALIVA s
SALLET s
*SALLOW sy
SALMIS*
SALMON s
SALOLS*
SALONS*
SALOON s
SALOOP s
SALPAE*
SALPAS*
SALPID s
SALSAS*
SALTED
p*SALTER ns
SALTIE rs
SALUKI s
SALUTE drs
SALVED*
SALVER*s
SALVES*
SALVIA s
SALVOR*s
SALVOS*
SAMARA s
SAMBAL*s
SAMBAR*s
SAMBAS*
SAMBOS
SAMBUR s
SAMECH s
SAMEKH*s
SAMEKS*
SAMIEL s
SAMITE s
SAMLET s
SAMOSA s
SAMPAN s
*SAMPLE drs
SAMSHU s
SANCTA
SANDAL s
SANDED
SANDER s
SANDHI s
SANELY
SANEST*
SANGAR*s
SANGAS
*SANGER s
SANGHS*
SANIES
SANING
SANITY
SANJAK s
SANNOP s
SANNUP s
SANSAR s
SANSEI s
SANTIR s
SANTOL*s
SANTOS*
SANTUR s
SAPORS*
SAPOTA s
SAPOTE s
SAPOUR s
SAPPED
SAPPER s
SARANS*
SARAPE s
SARDAR s
SAREES*
SARGES*
SARGOS*
SARINS*
SARODE*s
SARODS*
SARONG s
SARSAR s
SARSEN s
SARTOR s
SASHAY s
*SASHED
*SASHES
SASINS*
SASSED
*SASSES
SATANG s
SATARA s
SATAYS*
SATEEN s
SATING*
i SATINS*
SATINY*
SATIRE s
SATORI s
SATRAP sy
SATYRS*
SAUCED*
SAUCER*s
SAUCES*
SAUCHS*
*SAUGER s
SAUGHS*
SAUGHY*
SAULTS*
SAUNAS*
SAUREL s
SAUTED*
SAUTES*
SAVAGE drs
*SAVANT s
SAVATE s
SAVERS
SAVINE*s
SAVING*s
SAVINS*
SAVIOR s
SAVORS*
SAVORY*
SAVOUR sy
SAVOYS*
SAWERS*
SAWFLY
*SAWING
SAWLOG s
SAWNEY s
SAWYER s
SAXONY
SAYEDS*
SAYERS*
SAYEST
SAYIDS*
SAYING s
SAYYID s
*SCABBY
SCALAR es
SCALDS*
SCALED*
SCALER*s
SCALES*
SCALLS
SCALPS*
SCAMPI
SCAMPS
SCANTS
SCANTY
e*SCAPED*
e*SCAPES*
SCARAB s
SCARCE r
a*SCARED*
*SCARER*s
SCARES
SCAREY*
SCARFS*
SCARPH*s
e*SCARPS*
*SCARRY
SCARTS
SCATHE ds
SCATTS*
SCATTY
SCAUPS*
SCAURS*
SCENAS*
a SCENDS*
SCENES*
SCENIC s
a*SCENTS*
SCHAVS*
SCHEMA s
SCHEME drs
SCHISM s
SCHIST s
SCHIZO s
SCHIZY
SCHLEP ps
SCHLUB s
SCHMOE*s
SCHMOS*
SCHNOZ z
SCHOOL s
SCHORL s
SCHRIK s
SCHROD s
SCHTIK s
SCHUIT s
SCHULN*
SCHULS*
SCHUSS
SCHWAS*
SCILLA s
SCIONS
SCLAFF s
SCLERA els
SCOFFS
SCOLDS
SCOLEX
SCONCE ds
SCONES
*SCOOCH
SCOOPS
SCOOTS
SCOPED
SCOPES
SCORCH
SCORED
*SCORER*s
SCORES
*SCORIA e
SCORNS
SCOTCH
SCOTER s
SCOTIA s
SCOURS*
SCOUSE s
*SCOUTH*s
SCOUTS*
*SCOWED
SCOWLS
SCRAGS
SCRAMS
*SCRAPE*drs
SCRAPS
*SCRAWL sy
*SCREAK sy
*SCREAM s
*SCREED*s
SCREEN*s
SCREES*
SCREWS
SCREWY*
a SCRIBE drs
*SCRIED
*SCRIES
*SCRIMP*sy
SCRIMS*
SCRIPS*
SCRIPT*s
SCRIVE ds
SCRODS*
SCROLL s
SCROOP s
SCROTA l
SCRUBS*
SCRUFF sy
SCRUMS*
SCUBAS*
SCUFFS
*SCULCH
SCULKS*
SCULLS
SCULPS*
SCULPT*s
SCUMMY
SCURFS
SCURFY*
*SCURRY
*SCURVY
*SCUTCH
SCUTES
SCUTUM
SCUZZY*
SCYPHI
SCYTHE ds
SEABAG s
SEABED s
SEADOG s
SEALED
SEALER sy
SEAMAN
SEAMED

SEAMEN
SEAMER s
SEANCE s
SEARCH
*SEARED
SEARER
SEASON s
SEATED
*SEATER s
SEAWAN st
SEAWAY s
SEBUMS*
SECANT s
SECCOS*
SECEDE drs
SECERN s
SECOND eio s
SECPAR s
SECRET es
SECTOR s
SECUND
SECURE drs
SEDANS*
SEDATE drs
SEDERS*
SEDGES
*SEDILE
*SEDUCE drs
SEDUMS*
SEEDED
SEEDER s
SEEING s
SEEKER s
SEELED
SEEMED
SEEMER s
SEEMLY
SEEPED
SEESAW s
SEETHE ds
*SEGGAR s
SEGNOS*
SEGUED*
SEGUES*
SEICHE s
SEIDEL s
SEINED*
SEINER*s
SEINES*
SEISED*
SEISER*s
SEISES*
SEISIN gs
SEISMS*
SEISOR s
SEITAN s
SEIZED*
SEIZER*s
SEIZES*
SEIZIN gs
SEIZOR s
SEJANT
SELAHS*
SELDOM
*SELECT s
SELFED
SELKIE s
SELLER*s
SELLES*
SELSYN s
SELVAS*
*SELVES
SEMEME s
SEMENS*
SEMINA lr
SEMPLE
SEMPRE
SENARY
*SENATE s
SENDAL s
*SENDED
*SENDER s
SENDUP s
SENECA s
SENEGA s
SENHOR as
SENILE s
SENIOR s
SENITI
SENNAS*
SENNET s
SENNIT s
SENORA*s
SENORS*
SENRYU

SENSED*
SENSEI*s
SENSES*
SENSOR sy
SENSUM
*SENTRY
SEPALS*
SEPIAS*
SEPOYS*
a SEPSES
a SEPSIS
SEPTAL*
SEPTET s
a SEPTIC s
SEPTUM s
SEQUEL as
SEQUIN s
SERACS*
SERAIL*s
SERAIS*
SERAPE s
SERAPH s
SERDAB s
SEREIN s
SERENE rs
SEREST*
SERGED*
SERGER*s
SERGES*
SERIAL s
SERIES
SERIFS*
e SERINE*s
SERING*a
SERINS*
SERMON s
SEROSA els
SEROUS
SEROWS*
SERUMS*
SERVAL s
SERVED*
SERVER*s
SERVES*
SERVOS*
SESAME s
SESTET s
SETOFF s
SETONS*
SETOSE
SETOUS
SETOUT s
SETTEE s
SETTER s
SETTLE drs
SETUPS*
SEVENS
SEVERE*dr
SEVERS*
SEWAGE s
SEWANS*
SEWARS*
SEWERS
SEWING s
SEXIER
SEXILY
*SEXING
SEXISM s
*SEXIST s
SEXPOT s
SEXTAN st
SEXTET s
SEXTON*s
SEXTOS*
a SEXUAL
SHABBY
SHACKO*s
SHACKS
SHADED
SHADER*s
SHADES
SHADOW sy
SHADUF s
SHAFTS
SHAGGY
SHAIRD s
SHAIRN s
SHAKEN*
SHAKER*s
SHAKES
SHAKOS*
SHALED
SHALES
SHALEY*
SHALOM s
SHAMAN s

SHAMAS
a SHAMED*
SHAMES
*SHAMMY
SHAMOS
SHAMOY s
SHAMUS
*SHANDY
SHANKS
SHANNY
SHANTI hs
SHANTY
SHAPED*
SHAPEN*
SHAPER*s
SHAPES*
SHARDS
SHARED
SHARER*s
SHARES
SHARIA hs
SHARIF s
SHARKS
SHARNS*
SHARNY*
SHARPS
SHARPY
*SHAUGH s
SHAULS
SHAVED*
SHAVEN
*SHAVER*s
SHAVES
SHAVIE s
p*SHAWED
SHAWLS*
SHAWMS*
SHAZAM
SHEAFS*
SHEALS
SHEARS
*SHEATH es
*SHEAVE ds
SHEENS*
SHEENY*
SHEERS*
SHEESH
SHEETS*
SHEEVE s
SHEIKH*s
SHEIKS*
SHEILA s
SHEKEL s
SHELLS
SHELLY*
SHELTA s
SHELTY
*SHELVE drs
SHELVY
SHENDS*
SHEOLS*
SHEQEL s
SHERDS
SHERIF fs
SHERPA s
*SHERRY
*SHEUCH s
*SHEUGH s
*SHEWED
*SHEWER s
SHIBAH s
SHIELD*s
SHIELS*
SHIERS*
a SHIEST*
SHIFTS*
SHIFTY*
SHIKAR is
SHILLS
SHIMMY
SHINDY s
SHINED*
SHINER*s
SHINES*
*SHINNY
SHIRES
SHIRKS*
SHIRRS*
SHIRTS*
SHIRTY*
SHISTS
SHIVAH*s
SHIVAS*
SHIVER*sy
SHIVES
SHLEPP*s

SHLEPS*
SHLOCK sy
SHLUBS*
SHLUMP sy
SHMEAR s
SHMOES
SHMUCK s
SHNAPS
SHNOOK s
SHOALS*
SHOALY*
SHOATS*
SHOCKS
SHODDY
SHOERS
SHOFAR s
SHOGIS*
SHOGUN s
SHOJIS*
SHOLOM s
SHOOED
SHOOKS
SHOOLS*
SHOOTS
SHOPPE drs
SHORAN s
SHORED*
SHORES*
SHORLS*
SHORTS*
SHORTY*
SHOTES*
SHOTTS*
SHOULD
SHOUTS*
SHOVED*
*SHOVEL*s
*SHOVER*s
SHOVES*
SHOWED
SHOWER sy
SHOYUS*
SHRANK
SHREDS*
SHREWD*
SHREWS*
SHRIEK sy
SHRIFT s
SHRIKE s
SHRILL sy
SHRIMP sy
SHRINE ds
SHRINK s
SHRIVE dln rs
SHROFF s
SHROUD s
SHROVE
SHRUBS*
SHRUGS*
SHRUNK
SHTETL s
SHTICK sy
SHTIKS*
SHUCKS
SHUNTS
SHUTED*
SHUTES*
SHYERS*
SHYEST
*SHYING
SIALIC
SIALID s
SIBYLS*
SICCAN
SICCED
SICKED
SICKEE s
SICKEN s
*SICKER
SICKIE s
SICKLE ds
SICKLY
SICKOS*
SIDDUR s
SIDING s
SIDLED
*SIDLER*s
SIDLES
SIEGED*
SIEGES*
SIENNA s
SIERRA ns
SIESTA s
SIEURS*
SIEVED*

SIEVES*
SIFAKA s
SIFTED
SIFTER s
SIGHED
SIGHER s
SIGHTS*
SIGILS*
SIGLOI
SIGLOS
SIGLUM
SIGMAS*
SIGNAL*s
SIGNED
SIGNEE s
SIGNER s
SIGNET s
SIGNOR aei sy
SILAGE s
SILANE s
SILENI
SILENT s
SILICA s
SILKED
SILKEN
SILKIE rs
*SILLER s
SILOED
SILTED
SILVAE*
SILVAN*s
SILVAS*
SILVER nsy
SILVEX
SIMARS*
SIMIAN s
SIMILE s
SIMLIN s
SIMMER s
SIMNEL s
SIMONY
SIMOOM s
SIMOON s
SIMPER s
SIMPLE rsx
*SIMPLY
SINEWS*
SINEWY*
SINFUL
SINGED*
SINGER*s
SINGES*
*SINGLE dst
SINGLY
*SINKER s
*SINNED
*SINNER s
*SINTER s
SIPHON s
SIPING
SIPPED
SIPPER s
SIPPET s
SIRDAR s
SIREES*
SIRENS*
*SIRING
SIRRAH*s
SIRRAS*
SIRREE s
SIRUPS*
SIRUPY*
SISALS*
SISKIN s
SISSES
SISTER s
SISTRA
SITARS*
SITCOM s
SITING
SITTEN
SITTER s
SITUPS*
SIVERS*
SIXMOS*
SIXTES*
SIXTHS*
SIZARS
SIZERS*
SIZIER
SIZING s
SIZZLE drs
SKALDS*
SKANKS*
SKANKY*

SKATED*
SKATER*s
SKATES*
SKATOL es
SKEANE*s
SKEANS*
SKEENS
SKEETS
SKEIGH
SKEINS*
SKELLS*
SKELMS*
SKELPS
SKENES*
*SKERRY
*SKETCH y
SKEWED
SKEWER s
SKIBOB s
*SKIDDY
SKIDOO s
SKIERS
SKIFFS*
SKIING s
SKILLS
SKIMPS*
SKIMPY*
SKINKS
SKINNY
SKIRLS*
SKIRRS*
SKIRTS*
SKITED
SKITES
SKIVED*
SKIVER*s
SKIVES*
SKIVVY
SKLENT s
SKOALS*
SKORTS*
SKULKS*
SKULLS*
SKUNKS*
SKUNKY*
SKYBOX
SKYCAP s
SKYING
SKYLIT
SKYMAN
SKYMEN
SKYWAY s
SLACKS
SLAGGY
SLAKED
*SLAKER*s
SLAKES
SLALOM s
SLANGS*
SLANGY*
SLANTS*
SLANTY*
*SLATCH
SLATED
*SLATER*s
SLATES*
SLATEY*
SLAVED
*SLAVER*sy
SLAVES
SLAVEY*s
*SLAYED
*SLAYER s
*SLEAVE ds
SLEAZE s
SLEAZO
SLEAZY
*SLEDGE ds
SLEEKS
SLEEKY*
SLEEPS*
SLEEPY*
SLEETS
SLEETY*
SLEEVE ds
SLEIGH st
SLEUTH s
SLEWED
SLICED*
SLICER*s
SLICES*
SLICKS
SLIDER*s
SLIDES*
SLIEST
*SLIEVE s

*SLIGHT s
SLIMED
SLIMES
SLIMLY
SLIMSY*
SLINGS
SLINKS
SLINKY
SLIPED*
SLIPES*
*SLIPPY
SLIPUP s
SLITTY
*SLIVER s
*SLOBBY
*SLOGAN s
SLOIDS
SLOJDS*
SLOOPS
SLOPED
*SLOPER*s
SLOPES
*SLOPPY
SLOSHY*
SLOTHS*
SLOUCH y
*SLOUGH sy
SLOVEN s
*SLOWED
*SLOWER
*SLOWLY
SLOYDS*
SLUDGE ds
SLUDGY
SLUFFS
SLUICE ds
SLUICY
SLUING
SLUMMY
SLUMPS
SLURBS*
SLURPS*
SLURRY
SLUSHY*
SLUTTY
SLYEST
SLYPES*
SMACKS
SMALLS
SMALTI*
SMALTO*s
SMALTS
SMARMS*
SMARMY*
SMARTS
SMARTY*
SMAZES
SMEARS*
SMEARY*
SMEEKS*
SMEGMA s
SMELLS
SMELLY*
SMELTS
SMERKS
*SMIDGE ns
SMILAX
SMILED*
*SMILER*s
SMILES
SMILEY*s
SMIRCH
SMIRKS
SMIRKY
*SMITER*s
SMITES
SMITHS*
SMITHY*
SMOCKS
*SMOGGY
SMOKED*
SMOKER*s
SMOKES
SMOKEY*
SMOLTS
*SMOOCH y
SMOOSH
SMOOTH sy
SMUDGE ds
SMUDGY
SMUGLY
*SMUTCH y
SMUTTY
SNACKS*
SNAFUS*
*SNAGGY

SNAILS
SNAKED
SNAKES*
SNAKEY*
*SNAPPY
SNARED*
SNARER*s
SNARES
SNARFS*
SNARKS
SNARKY
SNARLS*
SNARLY*
*SNATCH y
SNATHE*s
SNATHS*
SNAWED
SNAZZY
SNEAKS*
SNEAKY*
SNEAPS
SNECKS
SNEERS*
SNEERY*
SNEESH
SNEEZE drs
SNEEZY
SNELLS*
SNICKS
SNIDER*
SNIFFS*
SNIFFY*
SNIPED*
SNIPER*s
SNIPES*
*SNIPPY
SNITCH
SNIVEL s
*SNOBBY
SNOODS*
SNOOKS
SNOOLS*
SNOOPS*
SNOOPY*
SNOOTS*
SNOOTY*
SNOOZE drs
SNOOZY
SNORED*
SNORER*s
SNORES*
SNORTS*
SNOTTY
SNOUTS*
SNOUTY*
SNOWED
*SNUBBY
SNUFFS*
SNUFFY*
SNUGLY
SOAKED
SOAKER s
SOAPED
SOAPER s
*SOARED
SOARER s
SOAVES
SOBBED
SOBBER s
SOBEIT
SOBERS*
SOBFUL
SOCAGE rs
SOCCER s
a SOCIAL s
SOCKED
SOCKET s
SOCLES*
SOCMAN
SOCMEN
SODDED
SODDEN s
*SODIUM s
SODOMS*
SODOMY*
SOEVER
SOFARS*
SOFFIT s
SOFTAS*
*SOFTEN s
*SOFTER
SOFTIE s
SOFTLY
SOGGED
SOIGNE e
*SOILED

SOIREE s
SOKOLS*
SOLACE drs
SOLAND*s
SOLANO*s
SOLANS*
i SOLATE ds
SOLDAN s
*SOLDER s
SOLELY
SOLEMN
SOLEUS
SOLGEL
SOLIDI*
SOLIDS*
SOLING
SOLION s
SOLOED
SOLONS*
SOLUMS*
SOLUTE s
SOLVED*
SOLVER*s
SOLVES*
SOMANS*
SOMATA
*SOMBER
*SOMBRE
SOMITE s
SOMONI
SONANT s
SONARS*
SONATA s
SONDER*s
SONDES*
SONICS*
SONNET s
SONSIE r
SOONER s
SOOTED
SOOTHE*drs
SOOTHS*
SOPITE ds
SOPORS*
SOPPED
*SORBED
SORBET s
SORBIC
SORDID
SORDOR s
SORELS*
SORELY*
SOREST*
SORGHO s
SORGOS*
SORING s
SORNED
SORNER s
SORREL s
SORROW s
SORTED
SORTER s
SORTIE ds
SOTOLS*
SOTTED
SOUARI s
SOUCAR s
SOUDAN s
SOUGHS*
SOUGHT
SOULED
SOUNDS*
SOUPED
SOURCE ds
SOURED
SOURER
SOURLY
SOUSED*
SOUSES*
*SOUTER s
SOUTHS*
SOVIET s
SOVRAN s
SOWANS
SOWARS*
SOWCAR s
SOWENS
SOWERS*
*SOWING
SOZINE*s
SOZINS*
SPACED
*SPACER*s
SPACES
SPACEY
SPADED*

SPADER*s
SPADES*
SPADIX
SPAHEE s
SPAHIS*
SPAILS
SPAITS*
SPALES
SPALLS
SPANKS*
SPARED
*SPARER*s
*SPARES*t
*SPARGE drs
SPARID s
SPARKS
SPARKY*
*SPARRY
*SPARSE*r
SPASMS*
SPATES
SPATHE ds
SPAVIE st
*SPAVIN s
SPAWNS
*SPAYED
SPEAKS
SPEANS
SPEARS
SPECIE s
SPECKS
SPEECH
SPEEDO*s
SPEEDS*
SPEEDY*
SPEELS
SPEERS
SPEILS*
SPEIRS*
*SPEISE s
SPEISS
SPELLS*
SPELTS
SPELTZ*
*SPENCE rs
SPENDS
SPENDY*
SPENSE s
SPERMS
SPEWED
SPEWER s
SPHENE s
SPHERE ds
SPHERY
SPHINX
SPHYNX
SPICAE*
SPICAS
SPICED*
SPICER*sy
SPICES*
SPICEY*
SPIDER sy
SPIELS*
SPIERS
SPIFFS*
SPIFFY*
SPIGOT s
SPIKED
*SPIKER*s
SPIKES
SPIKEY*
SPILED
SPILES
SPILLS
SPILTH*s
SPINAL s
SPINED
SPINEL*s
SPINES
SPINET*s
*SPINNY
SPINOR s
*SPINTO s
SPIRAL s
SPIREA*s
a SPIRED*
SPIREM*es
a SPIRES*
SPIRIT s
SPIRTS*
SPITAL s
SPITED*
SPITES*
SPIVVY
SPLAKE s

*SPLASH y
SPLATS
SPLAYS
SPLEEN sy
SPLENT s
SPLICE drs
SPLIFF s
SPLINE ds
SPLINT s
SPLITS*
SPLORE s
SPLOSH
SPODES*
SPOILS*
SPOILT*
SPOKED
SPOKEN*
SPOKES
SPONGE drs
SPONGY
SPOOFS*
SPOOFY*
SPOOKS*
SPOOKY*
SPOOLS
SPOONS
SPOONY*
SPOORS*
SPORAL
SPORED
SPORES
SPORTS
SPORTY*
*SPOTTY
e SPOUSE ds
SPOUTS
SPRAGS*
SPRAIN s
*SPRANG s
SPRATS
SPRAWL sy
SPRAYS
SPREAD s
SPREES
SPRENT
*SPRIER
SPRIGS
SPRING esy
*SPRINT s
SPRITE*s
e SPRITS*
SPRITZ*
SPROUT s
SPRUCE drs
SPRUCY
SPRUES*
SPRUGS*
SPRUNG
*SPRYER
SPRYLY
SPUING
SPUMED*
SPUMES*
SPUNKS
SPUNKY
*SPURGE s
SPURNS*
SPURRY
SPURTS*
SPUTUM
e SPYING
SQUABS*
SQUADS
SQUALL sy
SQUAMA e
*SQUARE drs
*SQUARK s
*SQUASH y
SQUATS*
SQUAWK s
SQUEAK sy
SQUEAL s
SQUEGS*
SQUIBS*
SQUIDS
*SQUILL as
a*SQUINT sy
e*SQUIRE ds
SQUIRM sy
*SQUIRT s
SQUISH y
SQUUSH
SRADHA s
*STABLE drs
STABLY
STACKS

STACTE s
STADES*
STADIA s
STAFFS*
STAGED*
STAGER*s
STAGES*
STAGEY*
STAGGY
STAIGS*
STAINS
STAIRS*
STAKED*
STAKES
STALAG s
STALED*
STALER
*STALES*t
STALKS
STALKY
STALLS
STAMEN s
STAMPS
STANCE s
STANCH
STANDS*
STANED*
STANES*
STANGS
STANKS
STANOL s
STANZA s
*STAPES
STAPHS*
STAPLE drs
STARCH y
STARED
STARER*s
STARES
*STARRY
*STARTS*y
STARVE drs
STASES
STASIS
STATAL
e STATED*
*STATER*s
e*STATES*
a STATIC es
STATIN gs
STATOR s
STATUE ds
STATUS y
STAVED*
STAVES*
STAYED
STAYER s
STEADS*
STEADY*
STEAKS
STEALS
STEAMS
STEAMY*
STEEDS*
STEEKS*
STEELS
STEELY*
STEEPS*
STEERS*
STEEVE ds
STEINS*
STELAE
STELAI*
STELAR*
STELES
*STELIC
STELLA rs
STEMMA s
STEMMY
*STENCH y
STENOS*
STENTS
STEPPE drs
STEREO*s
STERES*
STERIC
STERNA*l
STERNS
STEROL s
*STEWED
STICHS*
STICKS
STICKY*
STIFFS
STIFLE drs
STIGMA ls

STILES
STILLS
STILLY*
STILTS
STIMES
STINGO*s
STINGS
STINGY*
STINKO*
STINKS*
STINKY*
STINTS
STIPED*
STIPEL*s
STIPES*
STIRKS*
STIRPS*
STITCH
STITHY
STIVER s
STOATS*
STOCKS*
STOCKY*
STODGE ds
STODGY
STOGEY s
STOGIE s
STOICS*
STOKED
*STOKER*s
STOKES
STOLED
STOLEN*
STOLES
STOLID
STOLON s
STOMAL*
STOMAS*
STOMPS*
STONED
*STONER*s
STONES
STONEY
STOOGE ds
STOOKS*
STOOLS
STOOPS*
STOPED
*STOPER*s
STOPES
STORAX
STORED*
STORER*s
STORES
STOREY*s
STORKS*
STORMS*
STORMY*
STOTIN s
STOTTS*
a STOUND s
STOUPS*
STOURE*s
STOURS
STOURY*
STOUTS
STOVER*s
STOVES*
*STOWED
STOWPS*
STRAFE drs
*STRAIN s
*STRAIT s
STRAKE ds
STRAND s
STRANG e
STRAPS
*STRASS
STRATA ls
STRATH s
STRATI
STRAWS*
STRAWY*
e*STRAYS*
STREAK sy
STREAM sy
STREEK s
STREEL s
STREET s
STREPS*
*STRESS
STREWN*
STREWS
STRIAE*
*STRICK s
a STRICT

a STRIDE rs
STRIFE s
*STRIKE rs
STRING sy
*STRIPE*drs
STRIPS
STRIPT*
STRIPY*
STRIVE dnr
s
STROBE s
*STRODE
*STROKE drs
*STROLL s
STROMA l
STRONG
STROOK
STROPS*
STROUD s
*STROVE
STROWN*
STROWS
STROYS
*STRUCK
STRUMA*es
e STRUMS*
STRUNG
STRUNT s
STRUTS*
*STUBBY
STUCCO s
STUDIO s
STUDLY
STUFFS
STUFFY*
STULLS*
STUMPS
STUMPY*
STUNTS*
STUPAS*
STUPES*
STUPID s
STUPOR s
STURDY
STURTS*
*STYING
a STYLAR
STYLED*
STYLER*s
STYLES*
STYLET*s
STYLUS
STYMIE ds
STYRAX
SUABLE
SUABLY
SUAVER*
SUBAHS*
SUBBED
SUBDEB s
SUBDUE drs
SUBERS*
SUBFIX
SUBGUM s
SUBITO
SUBLET s
SUBLOT s
SUBMIT s
SUBNET s
SUBORN s
SUBPAR t
SUBSEA
SUBSET s
SUBTLE r
SUBTLY
SUBURB s
SUBWAY s
SUCCAH s
SUCCOR sy
SUCKED
SUCKER s
SUCKLE drs
SUCRES*
SUDARY
SUDDEN s
SUDORS*
SUDSED
SUDSER s
SUDSES
SUEDED*
SUEDES*
SUFFER s
SUFFIX
SUGARS*
SUGARY*
SUGHED

SUINTS*
SUITED*
SUITER*s
SUITES*
SUITOR s
SUKKAH s
SUKKOT h
SULCAL
SULCUS
SULDAN s
SULFAS*
SULFID es
SULFUR sy
SULKED
SULKER s
SULLEN
SULPHA s
SULTAN as
SULTRY
SUMACH*s
SUMACS*
SUMMAE*
SUMMAS*
SUMMED
SUMMER sy
SUMMIT s
SUMMON s
SUNBOW s
SUNDAE s
a*SUNDER s
SUNDEW s
SUNDOG s
SUNDRY
SUNKEN
SUNKET s
*SUNLIT
SUNNAH*s
SUNNAS*
SUNNED
SUNRAY s
*SUNSET s
SUNTAN s
SUNUPS*
SUPERB*
SUPERS*
SUPINE s
*SUPPED
*SUPPER s
SUPPLE drs
SUPPLY
SURAHS*
SURELY
SUREST
SURETY
SURFED
SURFER s
SURGED
*SURGER*sy
SURGES
SURIMI s
SURRAS*
SURREY s
SURTAX
SURVEY s
SUSHIS*
SUSLIK s
SUSSED
SUSSES
SUTLER s
SUTRAS*
SUTTAS*
SUTTEE s
SUTURE ds
SVARAJ
SVELTE r
SWABBY
SWAGED
*SWAGER*s
SWAGES
SWAILS
SWAINS
SWALES
SWAMIS*
SWAMPS*
SWAMPY*
SWANKS*
SWANKY*
SWANNY
SWARAJ
SWARDS
SWARFS*
SWARMS
SWARTH*sy
SWARTY
*SWATCH
SWATHE*drs
SWATHS*
SWAYED
SWAYER s
SWEARS
SWEATS*
SWEATY*
SWEDES*
*SWEENY
SWEEPS
SWEEPY
SWEETS
SWELLS
SWERVE drs
SWEVEN s
SWIFTS*
SWILLS
SWIMMY
SWINGE*drs
SWINGS
SWINGY
SWINKS
SWIPED
SWIPES
SWIPLE s
SWIRLS*
SWIRLY*
SWISHY*
*SWITCH
*SWITHE*r
SWIVED
SWIVEL*s
SWIVES
SWIVET*s
SWOONS*
SWOONY*
SWOOPS
SWOOPY*
*SWOOSH
SWORDS
*SWOUND*s
SWOUNS*
SYBOES
SYCEES*
SYLPHS*
SYLPHY*
SYLVAE*
SYLVAN*s
SYLVAS*
SYLVIN es
SYMBOL s
SYNCED
SYNCHS*
SYNCOM s
SYNDET s
SYNDIC s
SYNGAS
SYNODS*
SYNTAX
SYNTHS*
SYNURA e
SYPHER s
SYPHON s
SYRENS*
SYRINX
SYRUPS*
SYRUPY*
SYSOPS*
SYSTEM s
SYZYGY
TABARD s
s TABBED
TABBIS
TABERS*
TABLAS*
s*TABLED*
s*TABLES*
TABLET*s
TABOOS*
TABORS*
TABOUR s
TABUED
TABULI s
TABUNS*
TACHES
s TACKED
s TACKER s
TACKET s
TACKEY
TACKLE drs
a TACTIC s
TAENIA es
TAFFIA s
TAFIAS*
s TAGGED
s*TAGGER s
TAGRAG s
TAHINI s
TAHSIL s
TAIGAS*
*TAILED
TAILER s
TAILLE s
TAILOR s
TAINTS*
TAIPAN s
TAKAHE s
TAKERS*
TAKEUP s
s TAKING*s
TAKINS*
TALARS*
TALCED
TALCKY
TALCUM s
TALENT s
TALERS*
TALION s
s TALKED
s TALKER s
*TALKIE rs
TALLER
TALLIS h
TALLIT hs
TALLOL s
*TALLOW sy
e TALONS*
TALUKA*s
TALUKS*
TAMALE*s
TAMALS*
TAMARI ns
TAMBAC s
TAMBAK s
TAMBUR as
TAMEIN s
TAMELY
TAMERS*
TAMEST*
TAMING
TAMMIE s
TAMPAN s
s*TAMPED
s TAMPER s
TAMPON s
TANDEM s
s TANGED
*TANGLE drs
TANGLY
TANGOS*
TANIST s
TANKAS*
TANKED
TANKER s
TANNED
TANNER sy
s TANNIC
TANNIN gs
*TANNOY s
TANREC s
*TANTRA s
TANUKI s
TAPALO s
TAPERS
TAPETA l
*TAPING
TAPIRS*
TAPPED
TAPPER s
TAPPET s
TARAMA s
TARGES*
TARGET*s
TARIFF s
s TARING
TARMAC s
TARNAL
TAROCS*
TAROKS*
TAROTS*
TARPAN s
TARPON s
s TARRED*
TARRES*
TARSAL s
TARSIA*s
TARSUS
TARTAN as
TARTAR es
s TARTED
s TARTER
TARTLY
TARZAN s
*TASKED
TASSEL*s
TASSES
*TASSET*s
TASSIE s
TASTED*
*TASTER*s
TASTES*
TATAMI s
TATARS*
s TATERS*
TATSOI s
TATTED
TATTER s
TATTIE rs
TATTLE drs
TATTOO s
*TAUGHT
TAUNTS
TAUONS*
TAUPES*
TAUTED
TAUTEN s
TAUTER
TAUTLY
TAUTOG s
TAVERN as
TAWDRY
TAWERS*
*TAWING
TAWNEY s
TAWPIE s
TAWSED*
TAWSES*
TAXEME s
TAXERS*
TAXIED
a TAXIES
*TAXING
*TAXITE s
*TAXMAN
*TAXMEN
TAXOLS*
TAXONS
TAZZAS*
TEABOX
TEACUP s
s TEAMED
TEAPOT s
TEAPOY s
*TEARED
TEARER s
TEASED
*TEASEL*s
TEASER*s
TEASES
TEATED
TEAZEL s
TEAZLE ds
*TECHED
TECHIE rs
TECHNO s
TECTAL*
TECTUM s
TEDDED
TEDDER s
TEDIUM s
TEEING
TEEMED
TEEMER s
TEENER s
TEENSY*
TEEPEE s
TEETER s
TEETHE*drs
TEFLON s
TEGMEN
TEGUAS*
TEIIDS*
TEINDS*
TEKKIE s
TELCOS*
TELEDU s
TELEGA s
TELFER s
TELIAL*
TELIUM
TELLER s
TELLYS*
TELNET s
TELOME s
TELSON s
TEMPED
TEMPEH s
TEMPER as
TEMPLE dst
TEMPOS*
TEMPTS*
TENACE s
TENAIL s
TENANT s
*TENDED
*TENDER s
TENDON s
TENDUS*
TENETS*
TENIAE*
TENIAS*
TENNER s
TENNIS t
TENONS*
TENORS*
TENOUR s
TENPIN s
TENREC s
TENSED*
TENSER*
TENSES*t
TENSOR s
TENTED
*TENTER s
TENTHS*
TENTIE r
TENUES
TENUIS
*TENURE ds
TENUTI
TENUTO s
TEOPAN s
TEPALS*
TEPEES
TEPEFY
TEPHRA s
TEPOYS*
TERAIS*
TERAPH
TERBIA s
TERBIC
TERCEL*s
TERCES*
TERCET*s
TEREDO s
TERETE
TERGAL*
TERGUM
TERMED
TERMER s
TERMLY
TERMOR s
TERNES
TERRAE*
TERRAS*
TERRET s
TERRIT s
*TERROR s
TERSER*
TESLAS*
TESTAE*
TESTED
TESTEE s
*TESTER s
TESTES
TESTIS
TESTON s
TETANY
TETCHY
*TETHER s
TETRAD*s
TETRAS*
TETRIS*
TETRYL s
TETTER s
s TEWING
THACKS
THAIRM s
*THALER s
THALLI c
e THANES*
THANKS
THARMS
*THATCH y
*THAWED
THAWER s
THEBES*
THECAE*
THECAL*
THEFTS
THEGNS*
THEINE*s
THEINS*
THEIRS
a THEISM s
a*THEIST s
THEMED*
THEMES
THENAL
THENAR s
*THENCE
THEORY
THERES
THERME*ls
THERMS
THESES*
THESIS
THESPS*
THETAS*
THETIC
THICKS
THIEVE ds
THIGHS
THILLS
THINGS*
THINKS*
THINLY
THIOLS*
THIRAM s
THIRDS*
THIRLS*
a THIRST sy
THIRTY
THOLED
THOLES
THOLOI
THOLOS
THONGS
THORAX
THORIA s
THORIC
THORNS
THORNY
THORON*s
THORPE*s
THORPS*
THOUED
THOUGH t
THRALL s
THRASH
THRAVE s
THRAWN*
THRAWS*
THREAD sy
THREAP s
THREAT s
THREEP*s
THREES*
THRESH
THRICE
THRIFT sy
THRILL s
THRIPS*
THRIVE dnr
s
THROAT sy
THROBS*
THROES*
THRONE ds
THRONG s
THROVE
THROWN*
THROWS*
THRUMS*
THRUSH
THRUST s
THUJAS*
THULIA s
THUMBS*
THUMPS
THUNKS
THURLS
THUSLY
THUYAS*
THWACK s
a THWART s
THYMES*
THYMEY*
THYMIC*
THYMOL s
THYMUS
THYRSE s
THYRSI
TIARAS*
TIBIAE*
s TIBIAL*
TIBIAS*
TICALS*
TICCED
s TICKED
s*TICKER s
TICKET s
s TICKLE drs
TICTAC s
TICTOC s
TIDBIT s
TIDDLY
TIDIED
TIDIER s
TIDIES t
TIDILY
TIDING s
TIEING
TIEPIN s
TIERCE dls
TIERED
s TIFFED
TIFFIN gs
TIGERS*
TIGHTS*
TIGLON s
TIGONS*
TIKKAS*
TILAKS*
TILDES*
TILERS*
TILING s
s TILLED
s*TILLER s
s TILTED
TILTER s
TILTHS*
TIMBAL es
TIMBER sy
TIMBRE ls
TIMELY
TIMERS*
TIMING s
TINCAL s
TINCTS*
TINDER sy
TINEAL*
TINEAS*
TINEID s
TINFUL s
TINGED*
TINGES*
a*TINGLE drs
TINGLY
TINIER
TINILY
TINING
s*TINKER s
*TINKLE drs
TINKLY
TINMAN
TINMEN
*TINNED
*TINNER s
TINPOT
TINSEL s
s TINTED
s*TINTER s
TIPCAT s
TIPOFF s
TIPPED
TIPPER s
TIPPET s
s TIPPLE drs
TIPTOE ds
TIPTOP s
*TIRADE s
*TIRING
TIRLED
TISANE s
*TISSUE dsy
TITANS*
TITBIT s
TITERS*
TITFER s
TITHED*
*TITHER*s
TITHES*
TITIAN s
TITLED*
TITLES*
TITMAN
TITMEN
TITRES*
TITTER s
TITTIE s
TITTLE s
TITTUP s
TMESES
TMESIS
TOASTS
TOASTY*

TOBIES
*TOCHER s
TOCSIN s
TODAYS*
TODDLE drs
TODIES
TOECAP s
TOEING
TOFFEE s
TOGAED*
TOGATE d
TOGGED
TOGGLE drs
TOGUES*
TOILED
*TOILER*s
e TOILES*
TOILET*s
TOITED
TOKAYS
TOKENS*
s TOKERS*
s TOKING
TOLANE*s
TOLANS*
TOLARS*
TOLEDO*s
TOLING
TOLLED
TOLLER s
TOLUIC
TOLUID es
TOLUOL es
TOLUYL s
TOLYLS*
TOMANS*
TOMATO
TOMBAC ks
TOMBAK s
TOMBAL
TOMBED
TOMBOY s
TOMCAT s
TOMCOD s
TOMTIT s
TONDOS*
TONEME s
as TONERS*
TONGAS*
TONGED
TONGER s
TONGUE ds
a TONICS*
s TONIER
as TONING
s TONISH
TONLET s
TONNER*s
TONNES*
TONSIL s
s TOOLED
TOOLER s
TOONIE s
TOOTED
TOOTER s
TOOTHS*
TOOTHY*
TOOTLE drs
TOOTSY*
TOPEES*
s TOPERS*
TOPFUL l
TOPHES*
TOPHUS
TOPICS*
s*TOPING
s TOPPED
s TOPPER s
s TOPPLE ds
TOQUES*
TOQUET*s
TORAHS*
TORCHY*
TORERO s
TORICS*
s TORIES
TOROID s
TOROSE*
TOROTH*
TOROUS
TORPID s
TORPOR s
TORQUE drs
TORRID
TORSES*
TORSKS*

TORSOS*
TORTAS*
TORTEN*
TORTES*
TORULA es
TOSHES
TOSSED
TOSSER s
TOSSES
TOSSUP s
TOTALS*
TOTEMS*
TOTERS*
*TOTHER
TOTING
s TOTTED
*TOTTER sy
TOUCAN s
TOUCHE*drs
TOUCHY*
TOUGHS*
TOUGHY*
TOUPEE s
TOURED
TOURER s
TOUSED*
TOUSES*
TOUSLE ds
*TOUTED
s*TOUTER s
TOUZLE ds
s TOWAGE s
TOWARD s
TOWELS*
TOWERS*
TOWERY*
TOWHEE s
TOWIES*
s*TOWING
TOWNEE s
TOWNIE s
TOXICS*
TOXINE*s
TOXINS*
TOXOID s
TOYERS
TOYING
TOYISH
TOYONS*
TRACED
*TRACER*sy
TRACES
TRACKS
TRACTS*
TRADED*
TRADER*s
TRADES*
TRAGIC*s
TRAGUS
TRAIKS*
TRAILS
s*TRAINS*
s TRAITS*
TRAMEL ls
TRAMPS
TRAMPY*
*TRANCE ds
TRANKS
TRANNY
TRANQS*
TRAPAN s
*TRAPES
TRASHY*
TRAUMA s
*TRAVEL*s
TRAVES
TRAWLS*
TREADS
TREATS*
TREATY*
TREBLE ds
TREBLY
TREENS*
TREFAH
TREMOR s
TRENCH
TRENDS
TRENDY*
TREPAN gs
TREPID
TRESSY*
*TREVET s
TRIACS*
TRIADS*
TRIAGE ds
TRIALS

TRIBAL s
TRIBES
TRICED
TRICEP*s
TRICES
s*TRICKS*y
TRICKY*
TRICOT s
TRIENE s
TRIENS
TRIERS*
TRIFID
*TRIFLE drs
TRIGLY
TRIGON*s
TRIGOS*
TRIJET s
s TRIKES*
TRILBY
TRILLS
*TRIMER s
TRIMLY
TRINAL
TRINED*
TRINES*
TRIODE s
TRIOLS*
TRIOSE*s
s*TRIPES*
TRIPLE dst
x
TRIPLY
TRIPOD sy
TRIPOS
TRIPPY
TRISTE
TRITER*
TRITON es
TRIUNE s
*TRIVET s
TRIVIA l
TROAKS*
TROCAR s
TROCHE es
TROCKS
TROGON s
TROIKA s
s TROKED*
s TROKES*
s*TROLLS*
TROLLY*
TROMPE*ds
TROMPS
TRONAS*
TRONES*
TROOPS*
TROPES
a TROPHY
TROPIC s
a TROPIN es
TROTHS*
TROTYL s
*TROUGH s
TROUPE drs
TROUTS
TROUTY*
*TROVER*s
TROVES
s*TROWED
*TROWEL s
*TROWTH s
TRUANT s
TRUCED*
TRUCES*
TRUCKS
TRUDGE dnr
s
TRUEST*
*TRUFFE s
*TRUING
TRUISM s
TRULLS*
TRUMPS
TRUNKS*
TRUSTS
TRUSTY
TRUTHS
TRYING
TRYOUT s
TRYSTE*drs
TRYSTS*
TSADES
TSADIS
TSETSE s
TSKING
TSKTSK s

*TSORES
TSORIS
TSURIS
TUBATE
s TUBBED
TUBBER s
TUBERS*
TUBFUL s
TUBING s
TUBIST s
TUBULE s
TUCHUN s
TUCKED
TUCKER s
TUCKET s
TUFFET s
TUFOLI
TUFTED
TUFTER s
TUGGED
TUGGER s
TUGRIK s
TUILLE s
TULADI s
TULIPS*
TULLES*
s TUMBLE drs
TUMEFY
TUMORS*
TUMOUR s
s*TUMPED
TUMULI
TUMULT s
TUNDRA s
TUNERS*
TUNEUP s
TUNICA*e
TUNICS*
TUNING
s TUNNED
TUNNEL s
TUPELO s
TUPIKS*
*TUPPED
TUQUES*
TURACO su
*TURBAN s
TURBID
TURBIT hs
TURBOS*
TURBOT*s
TUREEN s
TURFED
TURGID
TURGOR s
TURION s
TURKEY s
TURNED
TURNER sy
TURNIP s
TURNON s
TURNUP s
TURRET s
TURTLE drs
TURVES
TUSCHE s
TUSHED
TUSHES
TUSHIE s
TUSKED
TUSKER s
TUSSAH s
TUSSAL
TUSSAR s
TUSSEH s
TUSSER s
TUSSES
TUSSIS
TUSSLE ds
TUSSOR es
TUSSUR s
TUTEES*
TUTORS*
TUTTED
TUTTIS*
TUTUED
TUXEDO s
TUYERE*s
TUYERS*
TWAINS
TWANGS*
TWANGY*
TWANKY
TWEAKS*
TWEAKY*
TWEEDS

TWEEDY
TWEENS
TWEENY
TWEETS
TWEEZE drs
TWELVE s
TWENTY
TWERPS*
TWIBIL ls
TWIERS*
*TWIGGY
TWILIT
TWILLS
TWINED
TWINER*s
TWINES
TWINGE ds
TWIRLS*
TWIRLY*
TWIRPS*
TWISTS
TWISTY*
*TWITCH y
TWOFER s
TWYERS*
TYCOON s
TYMBAL s
TYMPAN aio
sy
TYNING
TYPHON s
TYPHUS
TYPIER
TYPIFY
TYPING
TYPIST s
TYRANT s
TYRING
TYTHED*
TYTHES*
TZETZE s
TZURIS
UAKARI s
d UBIETY
UBIQUE
bjm UDDERS*
r
UGLIER
UGLIES t
UGLIFY
UGLILY
UGSOME
UHLANS*
UKASES*
ULAMAS
ULCERS*
ULEMAS*
s ULLAGE ds
ULSTER s
ULTIMA s
ULTIMO
ULTRAS*
UMAMIS*
UMBELS*
cln UMBERS*
bfh UMBLES
jmn
rt
UMBRAE*
UMBRAL*
UMBRAS*
UMIACK*s
UMIACS*
UMIAKS*
UMIAQS*
UMLAUT s
bdh UMPING
jlm
pt
UMPIRE ds
t UNABLE
UNAGED
UNAKIN
UNARMS*
UNAWED
UNAXED
UNBALE ds
UNBANS*
UNBARS*
UNBEAR s
s UNBELT s
UNBEND s
UNBENT
UNBIND s
UNBOLT s
UNBORN

UNBRED
UNBUSY
UNCAGE ds
UNCAKE ds
UNCAPS*
UNCASE ds
UNCAST
UNCHIC
UNCIAE*
UNCIAL*s
UNCINI
UNCLAD
n UNCLES*
UNCLIP s
UNCLOG s
UNCOCK s
UNCOIL s
UNCOOL
UNCORK s
UNCUFF s
UNCURB s
UNCURL s
UNCUTE*
UNDEAD
UNDIES
UNDINE s
UNDOCK s
UNDOER s
UNDOES
UNDONE
UNDRAW ns
UNDREW
UNDULY
UNDYED
UNEASE s
UNEASY
UNEVEN
f UNFAIR
UNFELT
UNFITS*
UNFIXT*
UNFOLD s
UNFOND
UNFREE ds
UNFURL s
UNGIRD s
UNGIRT
UNGLUE ds
UNGUAL
UNGUES
UNGUIS
UNGULA er
UNHAIR s
UNHAND sy
UNHANG s
UNHATS*
UNHELM s
UNHEWN
UNHOLY
UNHOOD s
UNHOOK s
UNHUNG
UNHURT
UNHUSK s
UNIFIC
b UNIONS*
UNIPOD s
UNIQUE rs
UNISEX
UNISON s
UNITED*
*UNITER*s
dg*UNITES*
UNJAMS*
UNJUST
UNKEND
UNKENT
UNKEPT
UNKIND
UNKINK s
UNKNIT s
UNKNOT s
UNLACE ds
UNLADE dns
UNLAID
UNLASH
UNLAYS*
UNLEAD s
grs UNLESS
ns UNLIKE d
UNLINK s
UNLIVE ds
UNLOAD s
g UNLOCK s
UNMADE
UNMAKE rs

UNMANS*
UNMASK s
UNMEET
UNMESH
UNMEWS*
UNMIXT*
UNMOLD s
UNMOOR s
UNMOWN
UNNAIL s
UNOPEN
UNPACK s
UNPAID
UNPEGS*
UNPENS*
UNPENT*
UNPICK s
UNPILE ds
UNPINS*
UNPLUG s
UNPURE
UNREAD y
UNREAL
UNREEL s
UNRENT
UNREST s
UNRIGS*
UNRIPE*r
UNRIPS*
UNROBE ds
UNROLL s
s UNROOF s
UNROOT s
UNROVE n
UNRULY
UNSAFE
UNSAID
UNSAWN
UNSAYS*
UNSEAL s
UNSEAM s
UNSEAT s
UNSEEN
UNSELL s
UNSENT
s UNSETS*
UNSEWN*
UNSEWS*
UNSEXY*
UNSHED
g UNSHIP s
UNSHOD
UNSHUT
UNSNAG s
UNSNAP s
UNSOLD
UNSOWN
UNSPUN
UNSTEP s
UNSTOP s
UNSUNG
UNSUNK
UNSURE
UNTACK s
UNTAME d
UNTIDY
UNTIED*
ap UNTIES*
UNTOLD
UNTORN
UNTRIM s
UNTROD
UNTRUE r
UNTUCK s
UNTUNE ds
UNUSED
UNVEIL s
UNVEXT
UNWARY
UNWELL
UNWEPT
UNWIND s
s UNWISE r
UNWISH
UNWITS*
UNWORN
UNWOVE n
UNWRAP s
UNYOKE ds
UNZIPS*
*UPASES
UPBEAR s
UPBEAT s
UPBIND s
UPBOIL s
UPBORE

UPBOWS*
UPCAST s
UPCOIL s
UPCURL s
UPDART s
UPDATE drs
UPDIVE ds
UPDOVE
UPENDS
UPFLOW s
UPFOLD s
UPGAZE ds
UPGIRD s
UPGIRT
UPGREW
UPGROW ns
UPHEAP s
UPHELD
UPHILL s
UPHOLD s
UPHOVE
e UPHROE s
UPKEEP s
UPLAND s
UPLEAP st
UPLIFT s
*UPLINK s
UPLOAD s
UPMOST
cs UPPERS*
UPPILE ds
cdp UPPING s
st
UPPISH
UPPITY
UPPROP s
*UPRATE ds
UPREAR s
*UPRISE nrs
UPROAR s
UPROOT s
*UPROSE
UPRUSH
UPSEND s
UPSENT
UPSETS*
UPSHOT s
UPSIDE s
UPSIZE ds
UPSOAR s
UPSTEP s
UPSTIR s
UPTAKE s
UPTALK s
UPTEAR s
UPTICK s
UPTILT s
UPTIME s
UPTORE
UPTORN
UPTOSS
UPTOWN s
UPTURN s
UPWAFT s
UPWARD s
UPWELL s
UPWIND s
URACIL s
URAEUS
URANIA s
p URANIC
URANYL s
c*URARES*
co URARIS*
URASES
c*URATES*
URATIC
URBANE*r
URBIAS*
URCHIN s
UREASE*s
*UREDIA l
UREDOS
UREIDE s
UREMIA s
UREMIC
URETER s
URETIC
t URGENT
bps URGERS*
gps URGING
b*URIALS*
URINAL s
mp URINES*
UROPOD s
b URPING

URSIDS*
URSINE
URTEXT s
*URUSES
*USABLE
USABLY
USAGES
USANCE s
m USEFUL
bgm USHERS*
pr
USNEAS*
USQUES*
USUALS*
*USURER s
USURPS*
UTERUS
o UTMOST s
UTOPIA ns
bcg UTTERS*
mnp
UVEOUS
UVULAE*
UVULAR*s
UVULAS*
VACANT
VACATE ds
VACUUM s
VADOSE
VAGARY
*VAGILE
VAGINA els
VAGROM
VAGUER*
VAHINE s
a*VAILED
VAINER
VAINLY
VAKEEL s
VAKILS*
VALETS*
VALGUS
*VALINE s
VALISE s
VALKYR s
*VALLEY s
VALORS*
VALOUR s
VALSES*
VALUED*
VALUER*s
VALUES*
VALUTA s
VALVAL
VALVAR
VALVED*
VALVES*
VAMOSE ds
*VAMPED
VAMPER s
VANDAL*s
VANDAS*
e VANISH
VANITY
VANMAN
VANMEN
VANNED
VANNER s
VAPORS*
VAPORY*
VAPOUR sy
VARIAS
VARIED
VARIER s
o VARIES
VARLET s
VARNAS*
VAROOM s
VARVED*
VARVES*
VASSAL s
*VASTER
VASTLY
VATFUL s
VATTED
VAULTS*
VAULTY*
VAUNTS
VAUNTY
*VAWARD s
VEALED
VEALER s
VECTOR s
VEEJAY s
VEENAS*
VEEPEE s

VEERED
VEGANS*
VEGETE
*VEGGED
VEGGIE s
VEGIES*
VEILED
VEILER s
VEINAL
VEINED
VEINER s
VELARS*
*VELATE
VELCRO s
VELDTS*
VELLUM s
VELOCE
VELOUR s
VELURE ds
VELVET sy
*VENDED
VENDEE s
*VENDER s
VENDOR s
*VENDUE s
VENEER s
VENENE s
VENERY
a VENGED*
a VENGES*
VENIAL
VENINE*s
VENINS*
VENIRE s
VENOMS*
VENOSE
VENOUS
VENTED
*VENTER s
a VENUES*
VENULE s
VERBAL s
o VERBID s
VERDIN s
VERGED*
VERGER*s
VERGES*
VERIER
VERIFY
VERILY
VERISM os
VERIST s
VERITE s
VERITY
VERMES
VERMIN
VERMIS
VERNAL
VERNIX
VERSAL
VERSED*
VERSER*s
VERSES
o VERSET*s
VERSOS*
VERSTE*s
VERSTS*
VERSUS
VERTEX
VERTUS*
VERVES*
VERVET*s
VESICA el
VESPER s
VESPID s
VESSEL s
VESTAL*s
VESTAS*
VESTED
VESTEE s
VESTRY
VETOED
VETOER s
VETOES
VETTED
VETTER s
VEXERS*
VEXILS*
*VEXING
VIABLE
VIABLY
VIALED
VIANDS*
a VIATIC a
a VIATOR s
VIBIST s

VIBRIO ns
VICARS*
*VICING
VICTIM s
e VICTOR sy
VICUNA s
VIDEOS*
VIEWED
VIEWER s
VIGIAS*
VIGILS*
VIGORS*
VIGOUR s
VIKING s
VILELY
e VILEST
VILIFY
VILLAE*
VILLAS*
VILLUS
VIMINA l
VINALS*
VINCAS*
VINEAL
VINERY
VINIER
VINIFY
VINING
VINOUS
VINYLS*
VIOLAS*
VIOLET s
VIOLIN s
VIPERS*
VIRAGO s
VIREOS*
VIRGAS*
VIRGIN s
VIRILE
VIRION s
VIROID s
VIRTUE*s
VIRTUS*
VISAED
VISAGE ds
VISARD s
VISCID
VISCUS
VISEED
VISING
VISION s
VISITS*
VISIVE
VISORS*
VISTAS*
VISUAL s
VITALS*
VITRIC s
VITTAE*
VITTLE ds
VIVACE s
VIVARY
VIVERS
VIVIFY
VIXENS*
VIZARD s
VIZIER s
VIZIRS*
VIZORS*
VIZSLA s
VOCABS*
VOCALS*
VODKAS*
VODOUN*s
VODOUS*
VODUNS*
VOGUED*
VOGUER*s
VOGUES*
VOICED*
VOICER*s
VOICES*
a VOIDED
a VOIDER s
VOILES*
VOLANT e
VOLERY
VOLING
VOLLEY s
VOLOST s
VOLTES*
VOLUME ds
e VOLUTE ds
VOLVAS*
VOLVOX
VOMERS

VOMICA e
VOMITO*s
VOMITS
VOODOO s
VORTEX
VOTARY
VOTERS*
VOTING
VOTIVE s
VOUDON s
VOWELS*
a VOWERS*
a*VOWING
VOYAGE drs
VOYEUR s
VROOMS
VROUWS*
VULGAR s
VULGUS
VULVAE*
VULVAL*
VULVAR*
VULVAS
WABBLE drs
WABBLY
WACKER*
WACKES*t
WACKOS*
*WADDED
*WADDER s
WADDIE ds
st*WADDLE drs
WADDLY
WADERS*
WADIES
WADING
WADMAL s
WADMEL s
WADMOL ls
WADSET s
WAEFUL
WAFERS*
WAFERY*
WAFFED
WAFFIE s
WAFFLE drs
WAFFLY
WAFTED
*WAFTER s
s*WAGERS*
s WAGGED
s*WAGGER sy
WAGGLE ds
WAGGLY
WAGGON s
s*WAGING
WAGONS
WAHINE s
WAHOOS*
WAIFED
*WAILED
WAILER s
*WAIRED
WAISTS*
a WAITED
a WAITER s
WAIVED*
*WAIVER*s
WAIVES*
WAKAME s
a WAKENS*
WAKERS*
WAKIKI s
a WAKING
WALERS*
WALIES
WALING
WALKED
WALKER s
WALKUP s
WALLAH*s
WALLAS*
WALLED
WALLET s
WALLIE s
WALLOP s
s*WALLOW s
WALNUT s
WALRUS
*WAMBLE ds
WAMBLY
WAMMUS
WAMPUM s
WAMPUS
WANDER s
WANDLE

WANGAN s
t*WANGLE drs
WANGUN s
WANIER
WANING
*WANION s
s WANNED
WANNER
*WANTED
WANTER s
WANTON s
WAPITI s
s WAPPED
WARBLE drs
as WARDED
WARDEN s
a WARDER s
WARIER
WARILY
WARING
WARKED
s*WARMED
s*WARMER s
WARMLY
WARMTH s
WARMUP s
WARNED
WARNER s
WARPED
WARPER s
WARRED
WARREN s
WARSAW s
WARSLE drs
WARTED
WASABI s
s*WASHED
s WASHER s
s*WASHES
WASHUP s
WASTED*
*WASTER*sy
WASTES*
WASTRY
WATAPE*s
WATAPS
WATERS*
WATERY*
s WATTER
t WATTLE ds
WAUCHT s
*WAUGHT*s
WAUKED
WAULED
WAVERS
WAVERY*
WAVEYS*
WAVIER
WAVIES t
WAVILY
WAVING
WAWLED
WAXERS*
WAXIER
WAXILY
*WAXING s
WAYLAY s
WEAKEN s
WEAKER
WEAKLY
WEAKON s
WEALDS*
WEALTH sy
WEANED
WEANER s
WEAPON s
s WEARER s
*WEASEL sy
WEASON s
WEAVED
WEAVER*s
WEAVES
*WEBBED
WEBCAM s
WEBERS*
WEBFED
WEBLOG s
WECHTS*
WEDDED
WEDDER s
WEDELN*s
WEDELS*
WEDGED
WEDGES
WEDGIE rs
WEEDED

WEEDER s
WEEKLY
WEENED
WEENIE rs
WEENSY*
s WEEPER s
WEEPIE rs
t WEETED
WEEVER s
WEEVIL sy
WEEWEE ds
WEIGHS*
*WEIGHT*sy
WEINER s
WEIRDO*s
WEIRDS*
WEIRDY*
WELDED
*WELDER s
WELDOR s
WELKIN s
ds WELLED
WELLIE s
WELTED
s WELTER s
*WENDED
WESKIT s
*WESTER ns
*WETHER s
WETTED
WETTER s
WHACKO*s
WHACKS
WHACKY*
WHALED
*WHALER*s
WHALES
WHAMMO
*WHAMMY
WHANGS
WHARFS*
WHARVE s
WHAUPS*
WHEALS
WHEATS
WHEELS
WHEENS*
WHEEPS*
*WHEEZE drs
WHEEZY
WHELKS*
WHELKY*
WHELMS
WHELPS
WHENAS
*WHENCE
WHERES
*WHERRY
WHERVE s
WHEYEY
WHIDAH s
WHIFFS*
WHILED*
WHILES*
WHILOM
WHILST
WHIMSY*
WHINED*
WHINER*s
WHINES*
WHINEY*
*WHINGE drs
*WHINNY
*WHIPPY
WHIRLS*
WHIRLY*
WHIRRS*
WHIRRY*
WHISHT*s
WHISKS*
WHISKY*
WHISTS
WHITED*
WHITEN*s
WHITER*
WHITES*t
WHITEY*
WHIZZY*
WHOLES
*WHOLLY
WHOMPS*
WHOMSO
WHOOFS
WHOOPS
WHOOSH
WHORED*

WHORES*
WHORLS*
WHORTS*
WHOSIS
WHUMPS
WHYDAH s
WICCAN*s
WICCAS*
WICHES
WICKED
*WICKER s
WICKET s
WICOPY
WIDDER s
WIDDIE s
t WIDDLE ds
WIDELY
WIDENS*
WIDEST*
WIDGET s
WIDISH
WIDOWS*
WIDTHS*
WIELDS*
WIELDY*
WIENER s
WIENIE s
WIFELY
WIFEYS*
WIFING
WIGANS*
WIGEON s
st*WIGGED
WIGGLE drs
WIGGLY
WIGHTS*
WIGLET s
WIGWAG s
WIGWAM s
WIKIUP s
WILDED
WILDER s
WILDLY
WILFUL
WILIER
WILILY
WILING
st WILLED
s*WILLER s
WILLET s
WILLOW sy
WILTED
WIMBLE ds
WIMMIN
*WIMPED
WIMPLE ds
WINCED*
WINCER*s
WINCES*
WINCEY*s
WINDED
WINDER s
ds WINDLE ds
*WINDOW sy
WINDUP s
WINERY
st WINGED
s WINGER s
t WINIER
dt WINING
s WINISH
s*WINKED
*WINKER s
t*WINKLE ds
t*WINNED
*WINNER s
WINNOW s
WINOES
*WINTER sy
WINTLE ds
WINTRY
WINZES*
WIPERS*
s WIPING
WIRERS*
WIRIER
WIRILY
*WIRING s
WISDOM s
WISELY
WISENT s
WISEST*
s WISHED
s WISHER s
s WISHES
WISING
WISPED
WISSED
s WISSES
t WISTED
WITANS*
t*WITCHY*
WITHAL
WITHED*
s*WITHER*s
WITHES*
WITHIN gs
WITING
WITNEY s
t WITTED
WITTOL s
WIVERN*s
WIVERS*
s WIVING
WIZARD s
WIZENS*
WIZZEN s
WIZZES
WOADED
WOALDS*
WOBBLE drs
WOBBLY
WODGES*
WOEFUL
WOLFED
WOLFER s
WOLVER s
WOLVES
WOMANS*
WOMBAT s
WOMBED
WOMERA s
WONDER s
WONNED
WONNER s
WONTED
WONTON s
WOODED
WOODEN
WOODIE rs
WOODSY*
WOOERS*
WOOFED
WOOFER s
WOOING
WOOLED
WOOLEN s
WOOLER s
WOOLIE rs
WOOLLY
WORDED
WORKED
WORKER s
WORKUP s
WORLDS*
WORMED
*WORMER s
WORMIL s
WORRIT s
WORSEN*s
WORSER*
WORSES*
WORSET*s
WORSTS*
WORTHS*
WORTHY*
s WOTTED
s WOUNDS*
WOVENS
*WOWING
WOWSER s
WRACKS
WRAITH s
WRANGS*
WRASSE s
WRATHS*
WRATHY*
WREAKS*
WREATH esy
WRECKS
WRENCH
WRESTS
*WRETCH
WRICKS
WRIEST*
*WRIGHT s
WRINGS
WRISTS*
WRISTY*
WRITER*s
WRITES
WRITHE dnrs
WRONGS*
WRYEST
WRYING
WURSTS*
WURZEL s
WUSSES
WUTHER s
WYCHES
WYLING
WYTING
WYVERN s
XEBECS*
XENIAL*
XENIAS*
XENONS*
XYLANS*
XYLEMS
XYLENE s
XYLOID
XYLOLS*
XYLOSE s
XYLYLS*
XYSTER s
XYSTOI
XYSTOS
XYSTUS
YABBER s
YABBIE s
YACHTS*
YACKED
YAFFED
YAGERS
YAHOOS*
YAIRDS*
YAKKED
YAKKER s
YAKUZA
YAMENS
YAMMER s
YAMUNS*
YANKED
YANQUI s
*YANTRA s
YAPOCK s
YAPOKS*
YAPONS*
YAPPED
YAPPER s
YARDED
YARDER s
YARELY
YAREST
YARNED
YARNER s
*YARROW s
YASMAK s
YATTER s
YAUPED
YAUPER s
YAUPON s
YAUTIA s
*YAWING
YAWLED
*YAWNED
YAWNER s
YAWPED
YAWPER s
*YCLEPT
YEANED
*YEARLY
YEARNS
YEASTS
YEASTY*
YECCHS*
YEELIN s
YELLED
YELLER s
YELLOW sy
YELPED
YELPER s
YENNED
YENTAS*
YENTES*
YEOMAN
YEOMEN
YERBAS*
YERKED
YESSED
o*YESSES
*YESTER n
YEUKED
YIELDS*
YIPPED
YIPPEE
YIPPIE s
YIRRED
YIRTHS*
YOBBOS*
YOCKED
YODELS*
YODLED*
YODLER*s
YODLES*
YOGEES
YOGINI*s
YOGINS*
YOGURT s
YOICKS
YOKELS*
YOKING
YOLKED
YONDER
YONKER s
YOUNGS*
YOUPON s
YOUTHS*
YOWIES*
*YOWING
YOWLED
YOWLER s
YTTRIA s
YTTRIC
YUCCAS*
YUCKED
YUKKED
YULANS
YUPONS*
YUPPIE s
YUTZES
t ZADDIK
ZAFFAR s
ZAFFER s
ZAFFIR s
ZAFFRE s
ZAFTIG
ZAGGED
ZAIKAI s
ZAIRES*
ZAMIAS
ZANANA s
ZANDER s
ZANIER
ZANIES t
ZANILY
ZANZAS*
ZAPPED
ZAPPER s
ZAREBA s
ZARIBA s
ZAYINS
ZAZENS*
ZEALOT s
ZEATIN s
ZEBECK*s
ZEBECS*
ZEBRAS*s
ZECHIN s
ZENANA s
ZENITH s
ZEPHYR s
ZEROED
ZEROES
ZEROTH
ZESTED
*ZESTER s
ZEUGMA s
ZIBETH*s
ZIBETS*
*ZIGGED
ZIGZAG s
ZILLAH s
ZINCED
ZINCIC
ZINCKY
ZINEBS*
ZINGED
ZINGER s
ZINNIA s
ZIPPED
ZIPPER s
ZIRAMS*
ZIRCON s
*ZITHER ns
ZIZITH*
ZIZZLE ds
ZLOTYS*
ZOARIA l
ZOCALO s
ZODIAC s
ZOECIA
ZOFTIG
ZOMBIE*s
ZOMBIS*
ZONARY
o ZONATE d
ZONERS*
ZONING
ZONKED
ZONULA ers
ZONULE s
ZOOIDS*
ZOOIER
ZOOMED
ZOONAL
ZOONED
ZORILS*
ZOSTER s
ZOUAVE s
ZOUNDS
ZOYSIA s
ZYDECO s
ZYGOID
ZYGOMA s
ZYGOSE s
ZYGOTE s
ZYMASE s

The Hooks: 7s-to-Make-8s

AARRGHH*
ABALONE s
ABANDON s
ABASERS*
*ABASHED
*ABASHES
ABASIAS*
*ABASING
ABATERS*
*ABATING
ABATORS*
ABATTIS
ABAXIAL
ABAXILE
ABBOTCY
ABDOMEN s
ABDUCED*
ABDUCES*
ABDUCTS*
ABELIAN*
ABELIAS*
ABETTAL s
*ABETTED
*ABETTER s
*ABETTOR s
ABEYANT
ABFARAD s
ABHENRY s
ABIDERS
*ABIDING
ABIGAIL s
l ABILITY
ABIOSES
ABIOSIS
*ABIOTIC
ABJURED*
ABJURER*s
ABJURES*
ABLATED*
ABLATES*
ABLATOR s
ABLAUTS*
ABLEISM s
ABLEIST s
ABLINGS
ABLUENT s
ABLUTED
*ABODING
ABOLISH
ABOLLAE*
ABOMASA*l
ABOMASI*
ABORTED
ABORTER s
ABORTUS
*ABOUGHT
ABOULIA s
ABOULIC
ABOUNDS
ABRADED*
ABRADER*s
ABRADES*
ABREACT s
*ABREAST
*ABRIDGE drs
*ABROACH
ABROSIA s
ABSCESS
ABSCISE ds
ABSCOND s
ABSEILS*
ABSENCE s
ABSENTS*
ABSINTH es
ABSOLVE drs
ABSORBS*
ABSTAIN s
ABSURDS*
*ABUBBLE
ABULIAS*
ABUSERS*
*ABUSING
ABUSIVE
ABUTTAL s
*ABUTTED
*ABUTTER s
ABVOLTS*
ABWATTS*
ABYSMAL
*ABYSSAL
ABYSSES
ACACIAS*
ACADEME s
ACADEMY
ACAJOUS*
ACALEPH es
ACANTHA e
*ACANTHI
ACAPNIA s
ACARIDS*
ACARINE s
ACAROID
*ACAUDAL
ACCEDED*
ACCEDER*s
ACCEDES*
ACCENTS*
ACCEPTS*
ACCIDIA s
ACCIDIE s
ACCLAIM s
ACCORDS*
ACCOSTS*
ACCOUNT s
ACCRETE ds
ACCRUAL s
ACCRUED*
ACCRUES*
ACCURST
ACCUSAL s
ACCUSED*
ACCUSER*s
ACCUSES*
ACEDIAS*
ACEQUIA s
lm*ACERATE d
ACERBER
ACERBIC
ACEROLA s
ACEROSE
*ACEROUS
ACETALS*
ACETATE ds
ACETIFY
ACETINS*
ACETONE s
ACETOSE
ACETOUS
ACETYLS*
ACHENES*
ACHIEST
ACHIEVE drs
ACHIOTE s
*ACHIRAL
ACHOLIA s
ACICULA ers
ACIDIFY
ACIDITY
ACIFORM
ACINOSE
ACINOUS
*ACLINIC
ACMATIC
t ACNODES*
ACOLYTE s
t ACONITE s
*ACORNED
ACQUEST s
ACQUIRE der
s
ACQUITS*
ACRASIA s
ACRASIN s
ACREAGE s
ACRIDER
ACRIDLY
ACROBAT s
ACROGEN s
ACROMIA l
ACRONIC
ACRONYM s
ACROTIC
ACRYLIC s
ACTABLE
ACTINAL
ACTINGS*
ACTINIA ens
ACTINIC
ACTINON s
fpt ACTIONS*
ACTIVES*
ACTORLY
ACTRESS y
ACTUARY
ACTUATE ds
ACULEUS
ACUMENS*
*ACUTELY
ACUTEST
*ACYCLIC
ACYLATE ds
ACYLOIN s
ADAGIAL
ADAGIOS*
ADAMANT s
ADAPTED
ADAPTER s
ADAPTOR s
ADAXIAL
ADDABLE
ADDAXES
ADDEDLY
ADDENDA*
ADDENDS*
ADDIBLE
ADDICTS*
dpr ADDLING
sw
ADDRESS
ADDREST
ADDUCED*
ADDUCER*s
ADDUCES*
ADDUCTS*
*ADEEMED
ADENINE s
ADENOID s
ADENOMA s
ADENYLS*
ADEPTER
ADEPTLY
ADHERED*
ADHERER*s
ADHERES*
ADHIBIT s
ADIPOSE s
ADIPOUS
ADJOINS*
ADJOINT*s
ADJOURN s
ADJUDGE ds
ADJUNCT s
ADJURED*
ADJURER*s
ADJURES*
ADJUROR s
ADJUSTS*
ADMIRAL s
ADMIRED*
ADMIRER*s
ADMIRES*
ADMIXED
ADMIXES
ADNEXAL*
ADNOUNS*
ADOPTED
ADOPTEE s
ADOPTER s
ADORERS*
ADORING
ADORNED
ADORNER s
ADRENAL s
ADSORBS*
ADULATE ds
ADULTLY
ADVANCE drs
ADVECTS*
ADVENTS*
ADVERBS*
ADVERSE
ADVERTS*
ADVICES*
ADVISED*
ADVISEE*s
ADVISER*s
ADVISES*
ADVISOR sy
m ADWOMAN
m ADWOMEN
ADZUKIS*
AECIDIA l
AEDILES
*AEGISES
AENEOUS
*AEOLIAN
*AEONIAN
AERATED*
AERATES*
AERATOR s
AERIALS*
AERIEST*
AEROBAT s
AEROBES*
AEROBIA
AEROBIC s
AEROGEL s
AEROSAT s
AEROSOL s
AERUGOS
AETHERS
*AFEARED
AFFABLE
AFFABLY
AFFAIRE*s
AFFAIRS*
AFFECTS*
AFFIANT s
AFFICHE s
AFFINAL
AFFINED*
AFFINES*
AFFIRMS*
AFFIXAL
AFFIXED
AFFIXER s
AFFIXES
AFFLICT s
AFFORDS*
AFFRAYS*
AFFRONT s
AFGHANI*s
AFGHANS*
AFREETS*
AFTMOST
AFTOSAS*
*AGAINST
*AGAMETE s
AGAMIDS*
AGAMOUS
AGAPEIC
AGARICS*
AGAROSE s
AGATIZE ds
AGATOID
AGEINGS*
AGEISMS*
AGEISTS*
w AGELESS
AGELONG
AGEMATE s
AGENDAS*
AGENDUM s
AGENIZE ds
AGENTED
*AGENTRY
h AGGADAH*s
h AGGADAS*
h AGGADIC
h AGGADOT h
AGGRADE ds
AGGRESS
AGILELY
v AGILITY
*AGINNER s
AGISTED
AGITATE ds
AGITATO r
AGLYCON es
AGNAILS*
m AGNATES*
AGNATIC
AGNIZED*
AGNIZES*
AGNOMEN s
AGNOSIA s
AGONIES
AGONISE ds
AGONIST s
AGONIZE ds
AGOROTH*
AGOUTIS*
AGRAFES*
AGRAFFE s
AGRAPHA
AGRAVIC
*AGROUND
AHIMSAS*
AIBLINS
AIDLESS
AIGLETS*
AIGRETS*
AIKIDOS*
AILERON s
b AILMENT s
AIMLESS
AINSELL s
AIRBAGS*
AIRBOAT s
AIRCREW s
AIRDATE s
AIRDROP s
AIRFARE s
AIRFLOW s
AIRFOIL s
AIRGLOW s
AIRHEAD s
AIRHOLE s
h AIRIEST
fp AIRINGS*
h AIRLESS
AIRLIFT s
h AIRLIKE
h AIRLINE rs
AIRMAIL s
AIRPARK s
AIRPLAY s
AIRPORT s
AIRPOST s
AIRSHED s
AIRSHIP s
AIRSHOT s
AIRSHOW s
AIRSICK
AIRTHED
AIRTIME s
AIRTING
AIRWARD
AIRWAVE s
f AIRWAYS*
AIRWISE
*AITCHES
AJOWANS*
AKVAVIT s
ALAMEDA s
ALAMODE s
ALANINE*s
ALANINS*
ALANYLS*
ALARMED
ALARUMS
ALASKAS*
ALASTOR s
h ALATION s
ALBATAS*
ALBEDOS*
ALBINAL
ALBINIC
ALBINOS*
ALBITES*
ALBITIC
ALBIZIA s
ALBUMEN s
ALBUMIN s
ALCADES*
ALCAICS*
ALCAIDE s
ALCALDE s
ALCAYDE s
ALCAZAR s
ALCHEMY
ALCHYMY
ALCOHOL s
ALCOVED*
ALCOVES*
ALDOSES*
ALDRINS*
ALEGARS*
ALEMBIC s
ALENCON s
ALERTED
ALERTER
ALERTLY
ALEURON es
ALEVINS
k ALEWIFE
ALEXIAS*
ALEXINE*s
ALEXINS*
ALFAKIS*
ALFALFA s
ALFAQUI ns
ALFORJA s
ALFREDO
ALGEBRA s
ALIASES
ALIBIED
ALIBIES
ALIDADE*s
ALIDADS*
ALIENED
ALIENEE s
ALIENER s
ALIENLY
ALIENOR s
ALIFORM
ALIGHTS
m ALIGNED
m ALIGNER s
ALIMENT s
p ALIMONY
ALINERS
*ALINING
t ALIPEDS*
ALIQUOT s
ALIUNDE
ALIYAHS*
ALKALIC*
ALKALIN*e
ALKALIS*e
ALKANES*
ALKANET*s
ALKENES*
ALKINES*
ALKYLIC
ALKYNES*
ALLAYED
ALLAYER s
ALLEGED*
ALLEGER*s
ALLEGES*
ALLEGRO s
ALLELES*
ALLELIC
ALLERGY
ALLHEAL s
ALLICIN s
gp ALLIUMS*
ALLOBAR s
ALLODIA l
ALLONGE s
ALLONYM s
ALLOVER s
fhs ALLOWED
tw
ALLOXAN s
ALLOYED
ALLSEED s
ALLUDED*
ALLUDES*
ALLURED*
ALLURER*s
ALLURES*
ALLUVIA l
dgr ALLYING
st
ALLYLIC
ALMANAC ks
ALMEMAR s
ALMNERS*
ALMONDS*
ALMONDY*
ALMONER s
ALMONRY
ALMSMAN
ALMSMEN
ALMUCES*
ALMUDES*
ALNICOS*
ALODIAL*
ALODIUM
ALOETIC
ALOOFLY
ALPACAS*
ALPHORN s
ALPHYLS*
ALPINES*
ALREADY
ALRIGHT
ALSIKES*
fhp ALTERED
fp ALTERER s
ALTHAEA s
ALTHEAS*
ALTHORN s
ALTOIST s
ALUDELS*
*ALUMINA*s
ALUMINE*s
ALUMINS*
ALUMNAE*
ALUMNUS
ALUNITE s
ALVEOLI
ALYSSUM s
AMADOUS*
AMALGAM s
AMANITA s
AMARONE s
*AMASSED
AMASSER s
c*AMASSES
AMATEUR s
AMATIVE
AMATOLS*
AMATORY
*AMAZING
AMAZONS*
AMBAGES*
AMBARIS*
AMBEERS*
AMBIENT s
gr AMBLERS*
grw AMBLING
AMBOINA s
h AMBONES
AMBOYNA s
AMBRIES
AMBROID s
AMBSACE s
AMEBEAN
AMEBOID
*AMENDED
*AMENDER s
AMENITY
AMENTIA s
AMERCED*
*AMERCER*s
AMERCES
AMESACE s
AMIABLE
AMIABLY
AMIDASE s
AMIDINE*s
AMIDINS*
AMIDOLS*
AMIDONE s
AMINITY
AMIRATE s
AMITIES
AMMETER s
AMMINES*
AMMONAL s
AMMONIA cs
AMMONIC
AMNESIA cs
AMNESIC s
AMNESTY
AMNIONS*
AMNIOTE s
AMOEBAE*
AMOEBAN*
AMOEBAS*
AMOEBIC
*AMONGST
AMORINI
AMORINO
AMORIST s
AMOROSO
AMOROUS
AMOSITE s
*AMOTION s
AMOUNTS
AMPERES*
AMPHORA els
AMPLEST
AMPLIFY
AMPOULE s
AMPULES*
AMPULLA er
AMPUTEE s
AMREETA s
AMRITAS*
AMTRACK*s
AMTRACS*
AMULETS*
AMUSERS
AMUSIAS*
*AMUSING
AMUSIVE
AMYLASE s
AMYLENE s
AMYLOID s
AMYLOSE s
AMYLUMS*
ANADEMS*
ANAEMIA s
ANAEMIC
ANAGOGE s
ANAGOGY
ANAGRAM s
ANALGIA s
b ANALITY
ANALOGS*
ANALOGY*
ANALYSE drs

ANALYST s
ANALYTE s
ANALYZE drs
ANANKES*
ANAPEST s
ANAPHOR as
ANARCHS*
ANARCHY*
ANATASE s
ANATOMY
ANATTOS*
ANCHORS*
ANCHOVY
ANCHUSA s
ANCIENT s
ANCILLA es
ANCONAL
ANCONES*
ANCRESS
ANDANTE s
ANDIRON s
ANDROID s
*ANEARED
p ANELING
ANEMIAS*
ANEMONE s
ANERGIA s
ANERGIC
ANEROID s
ANESTRI
ANETHOL es
ANEURIN s
ANGAKOK s
ANGARIA s
ANGELED
ANGELIC a
ANGELUS
d ANGERED
ANGERLY
ANGINAL*
ANGINAS*
ANGIOMA s
djmtw ANGLERS*
ANGLICE
dgjmtw ANGLING s
ANGORAS*
ANGRIER
ANGRILY
s ANGUINE
l ANGUISH
ANGULAR
ANHINGA s
ANILINE*s
ANILINS*
ANILITY
ANIMACY
ANIMALS*
ANIMATE drs
ANIMATO r
ANIMISM*s
ANIMIST*s
ANIONIC
ANISEED s
ANISOLE s
ANKLETS*
r ANKLING
ANKUSES
ANLACES*
ANLAGEN*
ANLAGES*
ANLASES
t ANNATES
ANNATTO s
ANNEALS*
ANNELID s
ANNEXED*
ANNEXES*
ANNONAS*
ANNOYED
ANNOYER s
ANNUALS*
ANNUITY
c ANNULAR
ANNULET s
ANNULUS
ANODIZE ds
ANODYNE s
ANOINTS*
ANOLYTE s
ANOMALY
ANOMIES*
ANONYMS*
ANOPIAS*
ANOPSIA s

ANORAKS*
ANOREXY
ANOSMIA s
ANOSMIC
*ANOTHER
ANOXIAS*
ANSATED*
ANSWERS*
ANTACID s
ANTBEAR s
ANTEFIX a
ANTEING
ANTENNA els
ANTHEMS*
p ANTHERS*
ANTHILL s
ANTHOID
ANTHRAX
ANTIAIR
ANTIARS*
ANTIBUG
ANTICAR
ANTICKS*
ANTICLY
ANTIFAT
ANTIFLU
ANTIFOG
ANTIFUR
ANTIGAY
ANTIGEN es
ANTIGUN
ANTIJAM
ANTILOG sy
ANTIMAN
ANTINGS*
ANTIPOT
ANTIQUE drs
ANTIRED
ANTISAG
ANTISEX
ANTITAX
ANTIWAR
ANTLERS*
ANTLIKE
ANTLION s
ANTONYM sy
t ANTRUMS*
ANTSIER
ANURANS*
ANURIAS*
ANUROUS
ANVILED
ANXIETY
ANXIOUS
ANYBODY
ANYMORE
ANYTIME
ANYWAYS*
ANYWISE
AORISTS*
AOUDADS*
APACHES*
APAGOGE s
APANAGE s
APAREJO s
APATITE s
t APELIKE
APERCUS*
jn APERIES
APETALY
APHAGIA s
APHASIA cs
*APHASIC s
APHELIA n
APHESES
APHESIS
APHETIC
r APHIDES
APHONIA s
*APHONIC s
*APHOTIC
APHTHAE*
APHYLLY
APICALS*
APICULI
APISHLY
APLASIA s
*APLENTY
h APLITES*
APLITIC
APLOMBS*
APNOEAL*
APNOEAS*
APNOEIC
APOCARP sy
APOCOPE s

APODOUS
APOGAMY
APOGEAL
APOGEAN
APOGEES*
APOGEIC
APOLLOS*
APOLOGS*
APOLOGY*
APOLUNE s
APOMICT s
APORIAS*
APOSTIL s
APOSTLE s
APOTHEM s
APPALLS*
APPARAT s
APPAREL s
APPEALS*
APPEARS*
APPEASE drs
APPENDS*
APPLAUD s
APPLETS*
APPLIED
APPLIER s
APPLIES
APPOINT s
APPOSED*
APPOSER*s
APPOSES*
APPRISE drs
APPRIZE drs
APPROVE drs
APPULSE s
APRAXIA s
APRAXIC
APRICOT s
APRONED
APROPOS
APROTIC
c APSIDAL
APSIDES
APTERAL
APTERIA
APTERYX
r APTNESS
APYRASE s
AQUARIA ln
AQUATIC s
AQUAVIT s
AQUEOUS
AQUIFER s
*AQUIVER
ARABESK s
ARABICA*s
ARABIZE ds
p ARABLES*
ARAMIDS*
ARANEID s
ARAROBA s
ARBITER s
h ARBORED
ARBORES
h ARBOURS*
ARBUTES*
ARBUTUS
ARCADED*
ARCADES*
ARCADIA ns
ARCANUM s
ARCHAEA ln
ARCHAIC
ARCHEAN
m ARCHERS*
ARCHERY*
ARCHFOE s
ARCHILS*
ARCHINE s
mp ARCHING s
ARCHIVE ds
ARCHONS*
ARCHWAY s
ARCKING
ARCSINE s
ARCTICS*
ARCUATE d
ARCUSES
ARDENCY
ARDOURS*
ARDUOUS
*AREALLY
AREAWAY s
ARENITE s
ARENOSE
ARENOUS

AREOLAE*
AREOLAR*
AREOLAS*
AREOLES*
ARGALAS*
ARGALIS*
m ARGENTS*
g ARGLING
ARGOTIC
ARGUERS*
ARGUING
ARGUSES
ARGYLES*
ARGYLLS*
ARIDEST
ARIDITY
ARIETTA s
ARIETTE s
ARIOSOS*
*ARISING
ARISTAE*
b ARISTAS*
ARISTOS*
ARKOSES*
ARKOSIC
ARMADAS*
ARMBAND s
ARMFULS*
ARMHOLE s
ARMIGER os
ARMILLA es
f ARMINGS*
h ARMLESS
ARMLETS*
ARMLIKE
ARMLOAD s
ARMLOCK s
ARMOIRE s
ARMORED
ARMORER s
ARMOURS*
ARMOURY*
ARMPITS*
ARMREST s
ARMSFUL
ARMURES*
ARNATTO s
ARNICAS*
ARNOTTO s
AROINTS*
c AROUSAL s
c*AROUSED*
c*AROUSER*s
c*AROUSES*
AROYNTS*
ARPENTS*
bc ARRACKS*
ARRAIGN s
ARRANGE drs
ARRASED
ARRASES
ARRAYAL s
ARRAYED
ARRAYER s
ARREARS*
ARRESTS*
ARRISES
ARRIVAL s
ARRIVED*
ARRIVER*s
ARRIVES*
ARROBAS*
fhmn ARROWED
ARROYOS*
ARSENAL s
ARSENIC s
ARSHINS*
ARSINES*
p ARTICLE ds
tw ARTIEST
bp ARTISAN s
ARTISTE*s
ARTISTS*
w ARTLESS
ARTSIER
ARTWORK s
*ARUGOLA s
ARUGULA s
h ARUSPEX
ASARUMS*
*ASCARED
ASCARID s
ASCARIS
ASCENDS
ASCENTS

ASCESES
ASCESIS
ASCETIC s
ASCIDIA n
ASCITES
ASCITIC
*ASCRIBE ds
*ASEPSES
*ASEPSIS
*ASEPTIC
*ASEXUAL
*ASHAMED
ASHCAKE s
ASHCANS*
ASHFALL s
dw*ASHIEST
ASHLARS*
ASHLERS*
cs ASHLESS
ASHRAMS*
ASHTRAY s
ASININE
ASKANCE
ASKESES
ASKESIS
gm ASKINGS*
*ASOCIAL s
ASPECTS*
ASPERSE*drs
ASPHALT s
ASPHYXY
ASPIRED
ASPIRER*s
ASPIRES
ASPIRIN gs
ASPISES
*ASQUINT
ASRAMAS*
ASSAGAI s
w ASSAILS*
ASSAULT s
ASSAYED
ASSAYER s
ASSEGAI s
ASSENTS*
ASSERTS*
ASSIGNS*
b ASSISTS*
ASSIZES*
ASSLIKE
ASSOILS*
ASSORTS*
ASSUAGE drs
ASSUMED*
ASSUMER*s
ASSUMES*
ASSURED*s
ASSURER*s
ASSURES*
ASSUROR s
ASSWAGE ds
ASTASIA s
*ASTATIC
ASTERIA s
ASTHENY
ASTHMAS*
ASTILBE s
*ASTOUND s
ASTRALS*
*ASTRICT s
*ASTRIDE
*ASTYLAR
*ASUNDER
ASYLUMS*
ATABALS*
*ATACTIC
y ATAGHAN s
ATALAYA s
ATAMANS*
ATARAXY
ATAVISM s
ATAVIST s
ATAXIAS*
ATAXICS*
*ATAXIES
ATELIER s
ATEMOYA s
*ATHEISM s
*ATHEIST s
*ATHIRST
ATHLETE s
ATHODYD s
*ATHWART
*ATINGLE
ATLASES
ATLATLS*

ATOMICS*
ATOMIES
ATOMISE drs
ATOMISM s
ATOMIST s
ATOMIZE drs
ATONERS
ATONIAS*
ATONICS
ATONIES
*ATONING
ATOPIES
ATRESIA s
ATRESIC
ATRETIC
n ATRIUMS*
*ATROPHY
*ATROPIN es
ATTABOY
ATTACHE*drs
ATTACKS*
ATTAINS*
ATTAINT*s
ATTEMPT s
ATTENDS*
ATTESTS*
ATTIRED*
ATTIRES*
ATTORNS*
ATTRACT s
ATTRITE*ds
ATTRITS*
ATTUNED*
ATTUNES*
AUBADES*
AUBERGE s
AUBURNS*
AUCTION s
AUCUBAS*
AUDIBLE ds
AUDIBLY
AUDIENT s
AUDILES*
AUDINGS*
AUDITED
AUDITEE s
AUDITOR sy
AUGENDS*
AUGITES*
AUGITIC
AUGMENT s
AUGURAL
AUGURED
AUGURER s
AUKLETS*
AULDEST
AUNTIES
AURALLY
AURATED*
l AUREATE
AUREOLA es
AUREOLE ds
AURICLE ds
AURISTS*
AUROCHS
AURORAE*
AURORAL*
AURORAS*
AUSFORM s
AUSPICE s
AUSTERE r
AUSTRAL s
AUSUBOS*
AUTARCH sy
AUTARKY
h AUTEURS*
AUTHORS*
AUTISMS*
AUTISTS*
AUTOBUS
AUTOING
AUTOMAN
AUTOMAT aes
AUTOMEN
t AUTONYM s
AUTOPEN s
AUTOPSY
AUTUMNS*
AUXESES
AUXESIS
AUXETIC s
AUXINIC
*AVAILED
AVARICE s
AVATARS*
AVELLAN e

AVENGED
AVENGER*s
AVENGES
AVENSES
AVENUES
AVERAGE ds
AVERRED
AVERTED
AVERTER s
AVGASES
AVIATED*
AVIATES*
*AVIATIC
*AVIATOR s
AVIDINS*
AVIDITY
AVIONIC s
AVOCADO s
AVOCETS*
AVODIRE s
*AVOIDED
*AVOIDER s
AVOSETS*
AVOWALS*
AVOWERS
*AVOWING
AVULSED*
AVULSES*
*AWAITED
*AWAITER s
AWAKENS
*AWAKING
*AWARDED
AWARDEE s
*AWARDER s
AWELESS
AWESOME
l AWFULLY
AWKWARD
AWLWORT s
AWNINGS*
AWNLESS
AXIALLY
m AXILLAE*
AXILLAR*sy
m AXILLAS*
AXOLOTL s
AXONEME s
AXSEEDS*
AZALEAS*
AZIMUTH s
AZOTISE ds
AZOTIZE ds
AZULEJO s
l AZURITE s
AZYGOUS
BAALISM s
BAASKAP s
BABASSU s
BABBITT s
BABBLED*
BABBLER*s
BABBLES*
BABESIA s
BABICHE s
BABIEST*
BABOOLS*
BABOONS*
*BABYING
BABYISH
BABYSAT
BABYSIT s
BACALAO s
BACCARA st
BACCATE d
BACCHIC
BACCHII
*BACHING
BACILLI
BACKBIT e
BACKERS*
BACKFIT s
BACKHOE ds
BACKING s
BACKLIT
BACKLOG s
BACKOUT s
BACKSAW s
BACKSET s
BACKUPS*
BACULUM s
BADDEST
BADDIES*
BADGERS*
BADGING
BADLAND s

BADNESS
BAFFIES
BAFFING
BAFFLED*
BAFFLER*s
BAFFLES*
BAGASSE*s
BAGFULS*
BAGGAGE s
BAGGERS
BAGGIER*
*BAGGIES*t
BAGGILY
BAGGING s
BAGLIKE
BAGNIOS*
BAGPIPE drs
BAGSFUL
BAGUETS*
BAGWIGS*
BAGWORM s
BAHADUR s
BAILEES*
BAILERS*
BAILEYS*
BAILIES*
BAILIFF s
*BAILING
BAILORS*
BAILOUT s
BAIRNLY
BAITERS*
BAITING
BAKINGS*
BAKLAVA s
BAKLAWA s
BALANCE drs
BALASES
BALATAS*
BALBOAS*
BALCONY
BALDEST
BALDIES
BALDING
BALDISH
BALDRIC ks
BALEENS*
BALEFUL
BALKERS*
BALKIER
BALKILY
BALKING
BALLADE*s
BALLADS*
BALLAST s
BALLERS*
BALLETS*
*BALLIES
BALLING
BALLONS*
BALLOON s
BALLOTS
BALLUTE s
BALMIER
BALMILY
BALNEAL
BALONEY s
BALSAMS*
BAMBINI
BAMBINO s
BAMBOOS*
BAMMING
*BANALLY
BANANAS*
BANDAGE drs
BANDAID
BANDANA s
BANDBOX
BANDEAU sx
BANDERS*
BANDIED
BANDIES
BANDING
BANDITO*s
BANDITS*
BANDOGS*
BANDORA s
BANDORE s
BANDSAW s
BANEFUL
BANGERS
BANGING
BANGKOK s
BANGLES
BANIANS*
BANJOES

BANKERS*
BANKING s
BANKITS*
BANKSIA s
BANNERS*
BANNETS*
BANNING
BANNOCK s
BANQUET s
BANSHEE s
BANSHIE s
BANTAMS*
BANTENG s
BANTERS*
BANTIES
BANYANS*
BANZAIS*
BAOBABS*
BAPTISE ds
BAPTISM s
BAPTIST s
BAPTIZE drs
BARBATE
BARBELL*s
BARBELS*
BARBERS*
BARBETS*
BARBIES*
BARBING
BARBULE s
BARBUTS*
BARCHAN s
BARDING
BAREFIT
BAREGES*
BARFING
BARGAIN s
BARGEES*
BARGING
BARHOPS*
BARILLA s
*BARISTA s
BARITES*
BARIUMS*
BARKEEP s
BARKERS*
BARKIER
BARKING
BARLESS
BARLEYS*
BARLOWS*
BARMAID s
BARMIER*
BARNEYS*
BARNIER
BARNING
BARONET s
BARONGS*
BARONNE s
BAROQUE s
BARQUES*
*BARRACK s
BARRAGE ds
BARRELS*
BARRENS*
BARRETS*
BARRIER s
BARRING
BARRIOS*
BARROOM s
BARROWS
BARTEND s
BARTERS*
BARWARE s
BARYONS*
BARYTAS*
BARYTES*
BARYTIC
BARYTON es
BASALLY
BASALTS*
BASCULE s
BASEMAN
BASEMEN t
BASENJI s
BASHAWS*
BASHERS*
BASHFUL
a*BASHING s
BASHLYK s
BASIDIA l
BASILAR y
BASILIC a
BASINAL
BASINED
BASINET s

BASIONS*
BASKETS*
*BASKING
BASMATI s
BASQUES*
BASSETS
BASSETT*s
*BASSIST s
BASSOON s
BASTARD sy
BASTERS
BASTILE s
BASTING s
BASTION s
BATBOYS*
BATCHED
BATCHER s
BATCHES
BATEAUX*
BATFISH
BATFOWL s
BATGIRL s
BATHERS*
BATHING
BATHMAT s
BATHTUB s
BATHYAL
BATIKED
BATISTE s
BATLIKE
BATSMAN
BATSMEN
BATTEAU x
BATTENS*
BATTERS*
BATTERY*
BATTIER
BATTIKS*
BATTING s
BATTLED*
BATTLER*s
BATTLES*
BATTUES*
BATWING
BAUBEES*
BAUBLES*
BAULKED
BAUSOND
BAUXITE s
BAWBEES*
BAWCOCK s
BAWDIER
BAWDIES t
BAWDILY
BAWDRIC s
BAWLERS*
BAWLING
BAWSUNT
BAWTIES*
BAYAMOS*
BAYARDS*
BAYONET s
BAYWOOD s
BAZAARS*
BAZOOKA s
BEACHED
BEACHES
BEACONS*
BEADERS*
BEADIER
BEADILY
BEADING s
BEADLES*
BEADMAN
BEADMEN
BEAGLES
BEAKERS*
BEAKIER
BEAMIER
BEAMILY
BEAMING
BEAMISH
BEANBAG s
BEANERY
BEANIES*
BEANING
BEARCAT s
BEARDED
BEARERS*
BEARHUG s
*BEARING s
BEARISH
BEASTIE s
BEASTLY
BEATERS
BEATIFY

*BEATING s
BEATNIK s
BEAUISH
BEAVERS*
BEBEERU s
BEBLOOD s
BECALMS*
BECAUSE
BECHALK s
BECHARM s
BECKETS*
BECKING
BECKONS*
BECLASP s
BECLOAK s
BECLOGS*
BECLOUD s
BECLOWN s
BECOMES*
BECRAWL s
BECRIME ds
BECROWD s
BECRUST s
BECURSE ds
BECURST
BEDAMNS*
BEDAUBS*
BEDBUGS*
BEDDERS*
BEDDING s
BEDECKS*
BEDELLS*
BEDEMAN
BEDEMEN
BEDEVIL s
BEDEWED
BEDFAST
BEDGOWN s
BEDIGHT s
BEDIRTY
BEDIZEN s
BEDLAMP*s
BEDLAMS*
BEDLESS
BEDLIKE
BEDMATE s
BEDOUIN s
BEDPANS*
BEDPOST s
BEDRAIL s
BEDRAPE ds
BEDROCK s
BEDROLL s
BEDROOM s
BEDRUGS*
BEDSIDE s
BEDSITS*
BEDSORE s
BEDTICK s
BEDTIME s
BEDUINS*
BEDUMBS*
BEDUNCE ds
BEDWARD s
BEDWARF s
BEEBEES*
BEECHEN
BEECHES
BEEDIES
BEEFALO s
BEEFIER
BEEFILY
BEEFING
BEEHIVE s
BEELIKE
BEELINE ds
BEEPERS*
BEEPING
*BEERIER
BEESWAX
BEETLED*
BEETLER*s
BEETLES*
BEEYARD s
BEEZERS*
BEFALLS*
BEFLAGS*
BEFLEAS*
BEFLECK s
BEFOOLS*
BEFOULS*
BEFRETS*
BEGALLS*
BEGAZED*
BEGAZES*
BEGGARS

BEGGARY*
a*BEGGING
BEGIRDS*
BEGLADS*
BEGLOOM s
BEGONIA s
BEGORAH
BEGORRA h
BEGRIME*ds
BEGRIMS*
BEGROAN s
BEGUILE drs
BEGUINE s
BEGULFS*
BEHAVED*
BEHAVER*s
BEHAVES*
BEHEADS*
BEHESTS*
BEHINDS*
BEHOLDS*
BEHOOVE ds
BEHOVED*
BEHOVES*
BEHOWLS*
BEIGNES*
BEIGNET*s
BEJESUS
BEJEWEL s
BEKNOTS*
BELABOR s
BELACED
*BELATED
BELAUDS*
BELAYED
BELAYER s
BELCHED
BELCHER s
BELCHES
BELDAME*s
BELDAMS*
BELEAPS*
BELEAPT*
BELIEFS*
BELIERS*
BELIEVE drs
BELLBOY s
BELLEEK s
BELLHOP s
BELLIED
BELLIES
BELLING s
BELLMAN
BELLMEN
BELLOWS*
BELONGS*
BELOVED s
BELTERS*
BELTING s
BELTWAY s
BELUGAS*
BELYING
BEMADAM s
BEMEANS*
BEMIRED*
BEMIRES*
BEMISTS*
BEMIXED
BEMIXES
BEMOANS*
BEMOCKS*
BEMUSED*
BEMUSES*
BENAMED*
BENAMES*
BENCHED
BENCHER s
BENCHES
BENDAYS*
BENDEES*
BENDERS
BENDIER
*BENDING
BENEATH
BENEFIC e
BENEFIT s
BENEMPT
BENISON s
BENNETS*
BENNIES
BENOMYL s
BENTHAL
BENTHIC
BENTHON s
BENTHOS
BENUMBS*

BENZENE s
BENZINE*s
BENZINS*
BENZOIC
BENZOIN s
BENZOLE*s
BENZOLS*
BENZOYL s
BENZYLS*
BEPAINT s
BEQUEST s
BERAKED*
BERAKES*
BERATED*
BERATES*
BEREAVE drs
BERETTA s
BERGERE s
BERHYME ds
BERIMED*
BERIMES*
BERLINE*s
BERLINS*
BERMING
BEROBED
BERRIED
BERRIES
BERSEEM s
BERSERK s
BERTHAS*
BERTHED
BESCOUR s
BESEECH
BESEEMS*
BESHAME ds
BESHOUT s
BESHREW s
BESIDES*
BESIEGE drs
BESLIME ds
BESMEAR s
BESMILE ds
BESMOKE ds
BESMUTS*
BESNOWS*
BESPAKE
BESPEAK s
BESPOKE n
BESTEAD s
BESTIAL
BESTING
BESTIRS*
BESTOWS*
BESTREW ns
BESTRID e
BESTROW ns
BESTUDS*
BESWARM s
BETAINE s
BETAKEN*
BETAKES*
BETAXED
BETHANK s
BETHELS*
BETHINK s
BETHORN s
BETHUMP s
BETIDED*
BETIDES*
BETIMES*
BETISES*
BETOKEN s
BETRAYS*
BETROTH s
a BETTERS*
a BETTING
a BETTORS*
BETWEEN
BETWIXT
BEVELED
BEVELER s
BEVOMIT s
BEWAILS*
BEWARED*
BEWARES*
BEWEARY
BEWEEPS*
BEWITCH
BEWORMS*
BEWORRY
BEWRAPS*
BEWRAPT*
BEWRAYS*
BEYLICS*
BEYLIKS*
BEYONDS*

BEZANTS*
BEZIQUE s
BEZOARS*
BEZZANT s
BHAKTAS*
BHAKTIS*
BHANGRA s
BHARALS*
BHEESTY
BHISTIE s
BIALIES
BIASING
BIASSED
BIASSES
BIAXIAL
BIBASIC
BIBBERS*
BIBBERY*
BIBBING
BIBCOCK s
BIBELOT s
BIBLESS*
BIBLIKE
BIBLIST s
BICARBS*
BICKERS
BICOLOR s
BICORNE*s
BICORNS*
BICRONS*
BICYCLE drs
BIDARKA s
BIDDERS*
BIDDIES
BIDDING s
BIELDED
BIENNIA l
BIFACES*
BIFFIES
BIFFING*
BIFFINS*
BIFIDLY
BIFILAR
BIFOCAL s
BIGEYES*
BIGFEET
BIGFOOT s
BIGGEST
BIGGETY
BIGGIES*
*BIGGING*s
BIGGINS*
BIGGISH
BIGGITY
BIGHEAD s
BIGHORN s
BIGHTED
BIGNESS
BIGOSES
BIGOTED
BIGOTRY
BIGTIME
BIGWIGS*
BIKEWAY s
BIKINIS*
BILAYER s
BILBIES
BILBOAS*
BILBOES
BILEVEL s
BILGIER
BILGING
BILIARY
BILIOUS
BILKERS*
BILKING
BILLBUG s
BILLERS*
BILLETS*
BILLIES*
BILLING s
BILLION s
BILLONS*
BILLOWS*
BILLOWY*
BILOBED
BILSTED s
BILTONG s
BIMBOES
BIMETAL s
BIMODAL
BIMORPH s
BINDERS*
BINDERY*
BINDING s
BINDLES*

BINGERS*
BINGING
BINGOES
*BINNING
BINOCLE s
BIOCHIP s
BIOCIDE s
BIOFILM s
BIOFUEL s
BIOGENS*
BIOGENY*
BIOHERM s
BIOLOGY
BIOMASS
BIONICS
BIONOMY
BIONTIC
BIOPICS*
BIOPSIC
BIOPTIC
BIOTECH s
BIOTICS*
BIOTINS*
BIOTITE s
BIOTOPE s
BIOTRON s
BIOTYPE s
BIPACKS*
BIPARTY
BIPEDAL
BIPLANE s
BIPOLAR
BIRCHED
BIRCHEN
BIRCHES
BIRDDOG s
BIRDERS*
BIRDIED*
BIRDIES*
BIRDING s
BIRDMAN
BIRDMEN
BIREMES*
BIRETTA s
BIRIANI s
BIRKIES*
BIRLERS*
BIRLING s
BIRRING
BIRTHED
BIRYANI s
BISCUIT sy
BISECTS*
BISHOPS*
BISMUTH s
BISNAGA s
BISQUES*
BISTATE
BISTERS*
BISTORT s
BISTRED*
BISTRES*
BISTROS*
BITABLE
*BITCHED
BITCHEN
*BITCHES
BITMAPS*
BITSIER
BITTERN*s
BITTERS*
BITTIER
BITTING s
BITTOCK s
BITUMEN s
BIVALVE ds
BIVINYL s
BIVOUAC s
BIZARRE s
BIZARRO s
BIZNAGA s
BIZONAL
BIZONES*
BLABBED
BLABBER s
*BLACKED
BLACKEN s
*BLACKER
BLACKLY
*BLADDER sy
BLADERS
*BLADING s
BLAMERS*
*BLAMING
*BLANDER
BLANDLY
BLANKED
*BLANKER
BLANKET s
*BLANKLY
BLARING
BLARNEY s
*BLASTED
*BLASTER s
BLASTIE rs
BLATANT
*BLATHER s
BLATTED
*BLATTER s
BLAUBOK s
*BLAWING
BLAZERS*
*BLAZING
BLAZONS*
*BLEAKER
BLEAKLY
BLEARED
BLEATED
BLEATER s
BLEEDER s
BLEEPED
BLEEPER s
BLELLUM s
BLEMISH
BLENDED*
*BLENDER*s
BLENDES*
BLESBOK s
BLESSED
*BLESSER s
BLESSES
BLETHER s
BLIGHTS
BLIGHTY*
BLINDED
BLINDER s
BLINDLY
*BLINKED
*BLINKER s
BLINTZE*s
*BLIPPED
BLISSED
BLISSES
*BLISTER sy
*BLITHER*s
BLITZED
BLITZER s
BLITZES
BLOATED
BLOATER s
*BLOBBED
*BLOCKED
*BLOCKER s
*BLOGGER s
BLONDER*
BLONDES*t
BLOODED
*BLOOMED
BLOOMER sy
*BLOOPED
*BLOOPER s
BLOSSOM sy
BLOTCHY*
*BLOTTED
*BLOTTER s
BLOUSED
BLOUSES
BLOUSON s
BLOWBYS*
BLOWERS
BLOWFLY
BLOWGUN s
BLOWIER
*BLOWING
BLOWOFF s
BLOWOUT s
BLOWSED
BLOWUPS*
BLOWZED
BLUBBED
*BLUBBER sy
BLUCHER s
BLUDGED*
BLUDGER*s
BLUDGES*
BLUECAP s
BLUEFIN s
BLUEGUM s
BLUEING s
BLUEISH
BLUEJAY s
*BLUFFED
BLUFFER s
BLUFFLY
BLUINGS*
BLUMING
BLUNDER s
BLUNGED
*BLUNGER*s
BLUNGES
*BLUNTED
BLUNTER
BLUNTLY
BLURBED
BLURRED
BLURTED
BLURTER s
*BLUSHED
*BLUSHER s
*BLUSHES
*BLUSTER sy
BOARDED
BOARDER s
BOARISH
BOASTED
BOASTER s
BOATELS*
BOATERS
BOATFUL s
BOATING s
BOATMAN
BOATMEN
BOBBERS*
BOBBERY*
BOBBIES
BOBBING*
BOBBINS*
BOBBLED*
BOBBLES*
BOBCATS*
BOBECHE s
BOBSLED s
BOBSTAY s
BOBTAIL s
BOCCIAS*
BOCCIES*
BODEGAS*
BODHRAN s
BODICES*
BODINGS*
BODKINS*
BODYING
BOFFINS*
BOFFOLA s
BOGARTS*
BOGBEAN s
BOGEYED
BOGGIER
BOGGING
BOGGISH
BOGGLED*
BOGGLER*s
BOGGLES*
BOGUSLY
BOGWOOD s
BOGYISM s
BOGYMAN
BOGYMEN
BOHEMIA ns
BOHRIUM s
BOHUNKS*
BOILERS
*BOILING
BOILOFF s
BOLASES
*BOLDEST
BOLEROS*
BOLETES*
BOLETUS
BOLIDES*
BOLIVAR s
BOLIVIA s
BOLLARD s
BOLLING
BOLOGNA s
BOLONEY s
BOLSHIE s
BOLSONS*
BOLSTER s
BOLTERS*
BOLTING
BOLUSES
BOMBARD s
BOMBAST s
BOMBERS
BOMBING s
BOMBLET s
BONACIS*
BONANZA s
BONBONS*
BONDAGE s
BONDERS*
BONDING s
BONDMAN
BONDMEN
BONDUCS*
BONESET s
BONEYER
BONFIRE s
BONGING
BONGOES
BONIATO s
BONIEST
BONITAS*
BONITOS*
BONKERS
BONKING
BONNETS*
BONNIER*
BONNILY
BONNOCK s
BONOBOS*
*BONUSES
BOOBIES
BOOBING
BOOBIRD s
BOOBISH
BOOBOOS*
BOOCOOS*
BOODLED*
BOODLER*s
BOODLES
BOOGERS*
BOOGEYS*
BOOGIED*
BOOGIES*
BOOHOOS*
BOOJUMS*
BOOKEND s
BOOKERS*
BOOKFUL s
BOOKIES*
BOOKING s
BOOKISH
BOOKLET s
BOOKMAN
BOOKMEN
BOOKOOS*
BOOMBOX
BOOMERS*
BOOMIER
BOOMING
BOOMKIN s
BOOMLET s
BOONIES
BOORISH
BOOSTED
BOOSTER s
BOOTEES*
BOOTERY
BOOTIES*
BOOTING
BOOTLEG s
BOOZERS*
*BOOZIER
*BOOZILY
*BOOZING
BOPEEPS*
BOPPERS*
BOPPING
BORACES
BORACIC
BORAGES*
BORANES*
BORATED
BORATES
BORAXES
BORDELS*
BORDERS
*BORDURE s
BOREDOM s
BOREENS*
BORIDES*
BORINGS*
BORKING
BORNEOL s
BORNITE s
BORONIC
BOROUGH s
BORROWS*
BORSCHT*s
BORSHTS*
BORSTAL s
BORTZES
BORZOIS*
BOSCAGE s
BOSHBOK s
BOSKAGE s
BOSKETS*
BOSKIER
BOSOMED
BOSONIC
BOSQUES*
BOSQUET*s
BOSSDOM s
BOSSIER
BOSSIES t
BOSSILY
BOSSING
BOSSISM s
BOSTONS*
BOTANIC a
BOTCHED
BOTCHER sy
BOTCHES
BOTHERS
BOTHIES
BOTHRIA
BOTONEE
BOTTLED*
BOTTLER*s
BOTTLES*
BOTTOMS*
BOTULIN s
BOUBOUS*
BOUCHEE s
BOUCLES*
BOUDINS*
BOUDOIR s
BOUFFES*
BOUGHED
BOUGIES*
BOULDER sy
BOULLES*
BOUNCED*
BOUNCER*s
BOUNCES
a BOUNDED
BOUNDEN
BOUNDER s
BOUQUET s
BOURBON s
BOURDON s
BOURNES*
BOURREE s
BOURSES*
BOURSIN s
BOUSING
BOUTONS*
BOUVIER s
BOVINES
BOWELED
BOWERED
BOWFINS*
BOWHEAD s
BOWINGS*
BOWKNOT s
BOWLDER s
BOWLEGS*
BOWLERS*
BOWLESS
BOWLFUL s
BOWLIKE
BOWLINE s
BOWLING s
BOWPOTS*
BOWSHOT s
BOWSING
BOWWOWS*
BOWYERS*
BOXBALL s
BOXCARS*
BOXFISH
BOXFULS*
BOXHAUL s
BOXIEST
BOXINGS*
*BOXLIKE
BOXWOOD s
BOYARDS*
BOYCHIK s
BOYCOTT s
BOYHOOD s
*BRABBLE drs
BRACERO*s
BRACERS
BRACHES
*BRACHET s
a BRACHIA l
*BRACING s
BRACKEN s
*BRACKET s
BRACTED
BRADAWL s
*BRADDED
BRADOON s
*BRAGGED
BRAGGER s
BRAHMAS*
*BRAIDED
*BRAIDER s
*BRAILED
BRAILLE drs
*BRAINED
BRAISED
BRAISES
BRAIZES*
BRAKIER
*BRAKING
BRALESS
*BRAMBLE ds
BRAMBLY
BRANCHY*
BRANDED
BRANDER s
BRANNED
BRANNER s
*BRASHER
*BRASHES t
*BRASHLY
BRASIER s
BRASILS*
BRASSED
BRASSES
BRASSIE rs
*BRATTLE ds
BRAVADO s
BRAVELY
BRAVERS
BRAVERY*
BRAVEST*
*BRAVING
BRAVOED
BRAVOES
BRAVURA s
BRAVURE
*BRAWEST
BRAWLED
BRAWLER s
BRAWLIE r
BRAXIES
BRAYERS*
*BRAYING
BRAZENS*
BRAZERS
BRAZIER s
BRAZILS*
*BRAZING
BREADED
BREADTH s
BREAKER s
BREAKUP s
*BREAMED
BREASTS*
BREATHE*drs
BREATHS*
BREATHY*
BRECCIA ls
BRECHAM s
BRECHAN s
BREEDER s
BREEZED*
BREEZES*
BREVETS
BREVIER s
BREVITY
BREWAGE s
BREWERS*
BREWERY*
BREWING s
BREWPUB s
BREWSKI s
BRIARDS*
BRIBEES*
BRIBERS*
BRIBERY*
BRIBING
*BRICKED
BRICKLE s
BRICOLE s
BRIDALS*
a*BRIDGED*
a*BRIDGES*
BRIDLED*
BRIDLER*s
BRIDLES*
BRIDOON s
BRIEFED
BRIEFER s
BRIEFLY
BRIGADE ds
BRIGAND s
BRIGHTS
BRILLOS
BRIMFUL l
*BRIMMED
*BRIMMER s
*BRINDED
BRINDLE ds
BRINERS*
*BRINGER s
BRINIER
BRINIES t
BRINING
BRINISH
BRIOCHE s
BRIQUET s
BRISANT
*BRISKED
*BRISKER
BRISKET s
BRISKLY
BRISSES
BRISTLE ds
BRISTLY
BRISTOL s
BRITSKA s
BRITTLE drs
BRITTLY
BRITZKA s
BROADAX e
BROADEN s
BROADER
BROADLY
BROCADE ds
*BROCKET s
BROCOLI s
BROGANS*
BROGUES
BROIDER sy
*BROILED
BROILER s
BROKAGE s
BROKERS*
BROKING s
BROMALS*
BROMATE ds
BROMIDE*s
BROMIDS*
BROMINE*s
BROMINS*
BROMISM s
BROMIZE ds
BRONCHI a
BRONCHO s
BRONCOS*
BRONZED*
BRONZER*s
BRONZES*
BROODED
BROODER s
*BROOKED
*BROOKIE s
*BROOMED
BROTHEL s
BROTHER s
BROUGHT
BROWNED
BROWNER
BROWNIE rs
BROWSED*
BROWSER*s
BROWSES*
BRUCINE*s
BRUCINS*
BRUISED*
BRUISER*s
BRUISES*
BRUITED
BRUITER s
BRULOTS*
BRULYIE s
BRULZIE s
BRUMOUS
BRUNETS*
*BRUSHED
*BRUSHER s
*BRUSHES
BRUSHUP s
BRUSKER
BRUSQUE r
BRUTELY

BRUTIFY
BRUTING
BRUTISH
BRUTISM s
BRUXING
BRUXISM s
BUBALES*
BUBALIS
BUBBLED*
BUBBLER*s
BUBBLES*
BUBINGA s
BUBONIC
BUCKEEN s
BUCKERS*
BUCKETS*
BUCKEYE s
BUCKING
BUCKISH
BUCKLED*
BUCKLER*s
BUCKLES*
BUCKOES
BUCKRAM s
BUCKSAW s
BUCOLIC s
BUDDERS
BUDDHAS*
BUDDIED
BUDDIES
BUDDING s
BUDDLES*
BUDGERS*
BUDGETS*
BUDGIES*
BUDGING
BUDLESS
BUDLIKE
BUDWORM s
BUFFALO s
BUFFERS*
BUFFEST
BUFFETS*
BUFFIER
BUFFING
BUFFOON s
BUGABOO s
BUGBANE s
BUGBEAR s
BUGEYES*
BUGGERS*
BUGGERY*
BUGGIER
BUGGIES t
BUGGING
BUGLERS*
BUGLING
BUGLOSS
BUGOUTS*
BUGSEED s
BUGSHAS*
BUILDED
BUILDER s
BUILDUP s
BUIRDLY
BULBELS*
BULBILS*
BULBLET s
BULBOUS
BULBULS*
BULGERS*
BULGHUR s
BULGIER
BULGING
BULGURS*
BULIMIA cs
BULIMIC s
BULKAGE s
BULKIER
BULKILY
BULKING
BULLACE s
BULLATE
BULLBAT s
BULLDOG s
BULLETS*
BULLIED
BULLIER
BULLIES t
BULLING
BULLION s
BULLISH
BULLOCK sy
BULLOUS
BULLPEN s
BULRUSH

BULWARK s
BUMBLED*
BUMBLER*s
BUMBLES
BUMBOAT s
BUMELIA s
BUMKINS*
BUMMALO s
BUMMERS*
BUMMEST
BUMMING
BUMPERS*
BUMPIER
BUMPILY
*BUMPING
BUMPKIN s
BUNCHED
BUNCHES
BUNCOED
BUNDIST s
BUNDLED*
BUNDLER*s
BUNDLES*
BUNGEES*
BUNGING
BUNGLED*
BUNGLER*s
BUNGLES*
BUNIONS
BUNKERS*
BUNKING
BUNKOED
BUNKUMS*
BUNNIES
BUNRAKU s
BUNTERS*
BUNTING s
BUOYAGE s
BUOYANT
BUOYING
BUPPIES*
BUQSHAS*
BURBLED*
BURBLER*s
BURBLES*
BURBOTS*
BURDENS*
BURDIES*
BURDOCK s
BUREAUS*
BUREAUX*
BURETTE s
BURGAGE s
BURGEES*
BURGEON s
BURGERS
BURGESS
BURGHAL
BURGHER s
BURGLAR sy
BURGLED*
BURGLES*
BURGOOS*
BURGOUT s
BURIALS
BURIERS*
BURKERS*
BURKING
BURKITE s
BURLAPS*
BURLERS*
BURLESK s
BURLEYS*
BURLIER
BURLILY
BURLING
BURNERS*
BURNETS*
BURNIES*
BURNING s
BURNISH
BURNOUS
BURNOUT s
*BURPING
BURRERS*
BURRIER
BURRING
BURRITO s
BURROWS*
BURSARS*
BURSARY*
BURSATE
BURSEED s
BURSERA
BURSTED
BURSTER s

BURTHEN s
BURTONS*
BURWEED s
BURYING
BUSBARS*
BUSBIES
BUSBOYS*
BUSGIRL s
BUSHELS*
BUSHERS
BUSHIDO s
BUSHIER
BUSHILY
BUSHING s
BUSHMAN
BUSHMEN
BUSHPIG s
BUSHTIT s
BUSHWAH*s
BUSHWAS*
BUSIEST*
BUSINGS*
BUSKERS*
BUSKING*
BUSKINS*
BUSLOAD s
BUSSING s
BUSTARD s
BUSTERS*
BUSTICS*
BUSTIER s
BUSTING
BUSTLED*
BUSTLER*s
BUSTLES*
BUSYING
BUTANES*
BUTANOL s
BUTCHER sy
BUTCHES
BUTENES*
BUTLERS*
BUTLERY*
BUTLING
a BUTTALS
a*BUTTERS*
BUTTERY*
BUTTIES
a BUTTING
BUTTOCK s
BUTTONS*
BUTTONY*
BUTYRAL s
BUTYRIC
BUTYRIN s
BUTYRYL s
BUXOMER
BUXOMLY
BUYABLE
BUYBACK s
BUYOFFS*
BUYOUTS*
BUZUKIA*
BUZUKIS*
BUZZARD s
BUZZCUT s
BUZZERS*
BUZZING
BUZZWIG s
BYCATCH
BYELAWS*
BYGONES*
BYLINED*
BYLINER*s
BYLINES*
BYNAMES*
BYPATHS*
BYPLAYS*
BYRLING
BYRNIES*
BYROADS*
BYTALKS*
BYWORDS*
BYWORKS*
BYZANTS*
CABALAS*
CABANAS*
CABARET s
CABBAGE dsy
CABBAGY
CABBALA hs
CABBIES*
s CABBING
CABEZON es
CABILDO s
CABINED

CABINET s
CABLERS*
CABLETS*
CABLING
CABOMBA s
CABOOSE s
CACHETS*
CACHEXY
*CACHING
CACHOUS*
CACIQUE s
CACKLED*
CACKLER*s
CACKLES*
CACODYL s
CACONYM sy
CACTOID
CADAVER s
CADDICE s
CADDIED*
CADDIES*
CADDISH*
CADELLE s
CADENCE ds
CADENCY
CADENZA s
CADGERS*
CADGING
CADMIUM s
CADUCEI
CAEOMAS*
CAESARS*
CAESIUM s
CAESTUS
CAESURA els
CAFFEIN es
CAFTANS*
CAGEFUL s
CAGIEST
CAHIERS*
CAHOOTS*
CAIMANS*
CAIQUES*
CAIRNED
CAISSON s
CAITIFF s
CAJAPUT s
CAJEPUT s
CAJOLED*
CAJOLER*sy
CAJOLES*
CAJONES
CAJUPUT s
CAKIEST
CALAMAR isy
CALAMUS
CALANDO
CALATHI
CALCARS*
CALCIFY
CALCINE ds
CALCITE s
CALCIUM s
CALCULI
CALDERA s
CALDRON s
CALECHE s
CALENDS
CALESAS*
CALIBER s
CALIBRE ds
CALICES
CALICHE s
CALICLE s
CALICOS*
CALIPEE s
CALIPER s
CALIPHS*
CALKERS*
CALKING*s
CALKINS*
CALLANS*
CALLANT*s
CALLBOY s
CALLEES
CALLERS*
CALLETS*
CALLING s
CALLOSE s
CALLOUS
CALMEST
CALMING
CALOMEL s
CALORIC s
CALORIE s
CALOTTE s

CALOYER s
CALPACK*s
CALPACS*
CALPAIN s
CALQUED*
CALQUES*
CALTRAP s
CALTROP s
CALUMET s
CALUMNY
CALVARY
CALVING
CALYCES
CALYCLE s
CALYPSO s
CALYXES
CALZONE s
CAMAILS*
CAMASES
CAMBERS
CAMBIAL*
CAMBISM s
CAMBIST s
CAMBIUM s
CAMBRIC s
CAMELIA s
CAMELID s
CAMEOED
CAMERAE*
CAMERAL*
CAMERAS*
CAMIONS*
CAMISAS*
CAMISES*
CAMISIA s
CAMLETS*
CAMMIES*
CAMORRA s
s CAMPERS*
CAMPHOL s
CAMPHOR s
CAMPIER
CAMPILY
s*CAMPING s
CAMPION s
CAMPONG s
CAMPOUT s
CANAKIN s
CANALED
CANAPES*
CANARDS*
CANASTA s
CANCANS*
CANCELS*
CANCERS*
CANCHAS*
CANDELA s
s CANDENT
CANDIDA*ls
CANDIDS*
CANDIED
CANDIES
CANDLED*
CANDLER*s
CANDLES*
CANDORS*
CANDOUR s
CANELLA s
CANFULS*
CANGUES*
CANIKIN s
CANINES*
CANKERS*
CANNELS*
s CANNERS*
CANNERY*
CANNIER*
CANNILY
s CANNING s
CANNOLI s
CANNONS*
CANNULA ers
CANOERS*
CANOLAS*
CANONIC
CANONRY
CANOPIC
CANSFUL
CANTALA*s
CANTALS*
CANTATA s
CANTDOG s
CANTEEN s
CANTERS*
CANTHAL
a CANTHUS

CANTINA s
s*CANTING
CANTLES*
CANTONS*
CANTORS*
CANTRAP s
CANTRIP s
CANULAE*
CANULAR*
CANULAS*
CANVASS*
CANYONS
CANZONA s
CANZONE st
CANZONI
CAPABLE r
CAPABLY
CAPELAN s
CAPELET s
CAPELIN s
CAPERED
CAPERER s
CAPFULS*
CAPITAL*s
CAPITOL s
CAPIZES
CAPLESS
CAPLETS*
CAPLINS*
CAPORAL s
CAPOTES*
CAPOUCH
CAPPERS*
CAPPING s
CAPRICE*s
CAPRINE
CAPROCK s
CAPSIDS*
CAPSIZE ds
CAPSTAN s
CAPSULE ds
CAPTAIN s
CAPTANS*
CAPTION s
CAPTIVE s
CAPTORS*
CAPTURE drs
CAPUCHE ds
CARABAO s
CARABID s
CARABIN es
CARACAL s
CARACKS*
CARACOL es
CARACUL s
CARAFES*
CARAMBA
CARAMEL s
CARAPAX
CARATES*
CARAVAN s
CARAVEL s
CARAWAY s
CARBARN s
CARBIDE s
CARBINE s
CARBONS*
CARBORA s
CARBOYS*
CARCASE s
CARCASS
CARCELS*
CARDERS*
CARDIAC*s
CARDIAE*
CARDIAS*
CARDING s
CARDONS*
CARDOON s
CAREENS*
CAREERS*
CAREFUL
CARFARE s
CARFULS*
CARGOES
CARHOPS*
CARIBES*
CARIBOU s
CARICES
CARINAE*
CARINAL*
o CARINAS*
CARIOCA s
CARIOLE s
s CARIOUS
CARITAS

CARJACK s
CARKING
s CARLESS*
CARLINE*s
CARLING*s
CARLINS*
CARLISH
CARLOAD s
CARMINE s
CARNAGE s
CARNETS*
CARNEYS*
CARNIES*
CARNIFY
CAROACH
CAROCHE*s
CAROLED
CAROLER s
CAROLUS
CAROMED
CAROTID s
CAROTIN s
*CAROUSE dlr s
CARPALE*
CARPALS*
CARPELS*
s CARPERS*
CARPETS*
s CARPING s
CARPOOL s
CARPORT s
*CARRACK s
CARRELL*s
CARRELS*
CARRIED
s CARRIER s
CARRIES
CARRION s
CARROCH
CARROMS*
CARROTS*
CARROTY*
CARRYON s
CARSICK
CARTAGE s
CARTELS
CARTERS*
s CARTING
CARTONS*
CARTOON sy
CARVELS*
CARVERS*
CARVING s
CARWASH
CASABAS*
CASAVAS*
CASBAHS*
CASCADE ds
CASCARA s
CASEASE s
CASEATE ds
CASEINS*
CASEOSE s
CASEOUS
CASERNE*s
CASERNS*
CASETTE s
CASHAWS*
CASHBOX
CASHEWS*
*CASHIER s
*CASHING
CASHOOS*
CASINGS*
CASINOS*
CASITAS*
CASKETS*
*CASKING
CASQUED*
CASQUES*
CASSABA s
CASSATA s
CASSAVA s
CASSENA s
CASSENE s
CASSIAS*
CASSINA s
CASSINE s
CASSINO s
CASSOCK s
CASTERS
CASTING s
CASTLED*
CASTLES*
CASTOFF s

CASTORS*
CASUALS*
CASUIST s
CATALOG*s
CATALOS*
CATALPA s
CATARRH s
CATAWBA s
CATBIRD s
CATBOAT s
CATCALL s
CATCHER s
CATCHES
CATCHUP s
CATCLAW s
CATECHU s
CATENAE*
CATENAS*
CATERAN s
CATERED
CATERER s
CATFACE s
CATFALL s
CATFISH
CATGUTS*
CATHEAD s
CATHECT s
CATHODE s
CATIONS*
CATJANG s
CATKINS*
CATLIKE
CATLING*s
CATLINS*
CATMINT s
CATNAPS*
CATNIPS*
CATSPAW s
CATSUIT s
CATSUPS*
CATTAIL s
CATTALO s
CATTERY
s CATTIER*
CATTIES*t
CATTILY
s CATTING
CATTISH
CATWALK s
ae CAUDATE ds
CAUDLES*
a CAULINE
CAULKED
CAULKER s
CAUSALS*
CAUSERS*
CAUSEYS*
CAUSING
CAUSTIC s
CAUTERY
CAUTION s
CAVALLA s
CAVALLY
CAVALRY
CAVEATS*
CAVEMAN
CAVEMEN
CAVERNS*
CAVETTI
CAVETTO s
CAVIARE*s
CAVIARS*
CAVILED
CAVILER s
CAVINGS*
CAVORTS*
CAYENNE ds
CAYMANS*
CAYUSES*
CAZIQUE s
*CEASING
CEBOIDS*
CECALLY
CEDILLA s
CEDULAS*
CEILERS*
CEILIDH s
CEILING s
CELADON s
CELESTA s
CELESTE s
CELIACS*
CELLARS*
CELLING
CELLIST s
CELLULE s
CELOSIA s
CELOTEX
CEMBALI
CEMBALO s
CEMENTA*
CEMENTS*
CENACLE s
CENOTES*
CENSERS*
CENSING
CENSORS*
CENSUAL
*CENSURE drs
CENTALS*
CENTARE s
CENTAUR sy
CENTAVO s
CENTERS
CENTILE s
CENTIME s
CENTIMO s
CENTNER s
CENTRAL*s
CENTRED*
CENTRES*
a CENTRIC
CENTRUM s
CENTUMS*
CENTURY
CEPHEID s
CERAMAL s
CERAMIC s
a CERATED*
CERATES*
CERATIN s
CEREALS*
CEREBRA l
CERIPHS*
CERISES*
CERITES*
CERIUMS*
CERMETS*
*CEROTIC
CERTAIN
CERTIFY
CERUMEN s
CERUSES*
CERVEZA s
CERVINE
CESIUMS*
CESSING
CESSION s
CESSPIT s
CESTODE s
CESTOID*s
CESURAE*
CESURAS*
CETANES*
CEVICHE s
CHABLIS
CHABOUK s
CHABUKS*
CHACHKA s
CHACMAS*
CHADARS*
CHADORS*
CHAEBOL s
CHAETAE*
CHAETAL*
CHAFERS*
CHAFFED
CHAFFER s
CHAFING
CHAGRIN s
CHAINED*
CHAINES*
*CHAIRED
CHAISES*
CHAKRAS*
CHALAHS*
CHALAZA els
CHALCID s
CHALEHS*
CHALETS*
CHALICE ds
CHALKED
*CHALLAH*s
CHALLAS*
CHALLIE s
CHALLIS
*CHALLOT h
CHALONE s
CHALOTH*
CHALUPA s
*CHALUTZ
CHAMADE s
CHAMBER s
CHAMFER s
CHAMISA s
CHAMISE s
CHAMISO s
CHAMOIS
CHAMOIX
CHAMPAC as
CHAMPAK s
CHAMPED
*CHAMPER s
CHANCED*
CHANCEL*s
CHANCER*sy
CHANCES
CHANCRE s
CHANGED
*CHANGER*s
CHANGES*
CHANNEL s
CHANOYU s
CHANSON s
*CHANTED
CHANTER s
CHANTEY s
CHANTOR s
CHANTRY
CHAOSES
CHAOTIC
CHAPATI s
CHAPEAU sx
CHAPELS*
CHAPLET s
CHAPMAN
CHAPMEN
*CHAPPED
CHAPPIE s
CHAPTER s
CHARADE s
CHARGED*
CHARGER*s
CHARGES*
CHARIER
CHARILY
*CHARING
CHARIOT s
CHARISM as
CHARITY
CHARKAS*
*CHARKED
CHARKHA s
CHARLEY s
CHARLIE s
*CHARMED
*CHARMER s
CHARNEL s
CHARPAI s
CHARPOY s
CHARQUI ds
CHARRED
CHARROS*
CHARTED
CHARTER s
CHASERS*
CHASING s
CHASMAL
CHASMED
CHASMIC
CHASSED*
CHASSES*
CHASSIS
*CHASTEN*s
CHASTER*
CHATEAU sx
*CHATTED
CHATTEL s
*CHATTER sy
CHAUFER s
CHAUNTS
CHAWERS*
*CHAWING
CHAYOTE s
CHAZANS
*CHAZZAN s
CHAZZEN s
CHEAPEN s
*CHEAPER
CHEAPIE s
CHEAPLY
CHEAPOS*
*CHEATED
*CHEATER s
CHEBECS*
CHECKED
CHECKER s
CHECKUP s
CHEDDAR sy
CHEDERS
CHEDITE s
CHEEKED
CHEEPED
CHEEPER s
CHEERED
CHEERER s
CHEERIO s
CHEERLY
CHEEROS*
CHEESED*
CHEESES*
CHEETAH s
CHEFDOM s
CHEFFED
CHEFING
CHEGOES*
CHELATE ds
CHELOID s
CHEMICS*
CHEMISE s
CHEMISM s
CHEMIST s
CHEQUER*s
CHEQUES*
CHERISH
CHEROOT s
CHERUBS*
CHERVIL s
CHESSES
CHESTED
CHETAHS*
CHETRUM s
CHEVIED
CHEVIES
CHEVIOT s
CHEVRES*
CHEVRET*s
CHEVRON s
CHEWERS
CHEWIER
*CHEWING
CHEWINK s
CHIANTI s
CHIASMA*ls
CHIASMI*c
CHIASMS*
CHIBOUK s
CHICANE drs
CHICANO s
CHICEST
CHICHIS*
CHICKEE s
CHICKEN s
CHICLES*
CHICORY
*CHIDDEN
CHIDERS
*CHIDING
CHIEFER
CHIEFLY
CHIELDS*
CHIFFON s
CHIGGER s
CHIGNON s
CHIGOES*
CHILDES*
CHILDLY
CHILIAD s
CHILIES
*CHILLED
s*CHILLER s
CHILLIS*
CHILLUM s
CHIMARS*
CHIMBLY
CHIMERA*s
CHIMERE*s
CHIMERS*
CHIMING
CHIMLAS*
CHIMLEY s
CHIMNEY s
CHINCHY*
CHINING
CHINKED
CHINNED
CHINONE s
CHINOOK s
CHINTZY*
CHINWAG s
*CHIPPED
*CHIPPER s
*CHIPPIE rs
CHIRKED
CHIRKER
CHIRMED
CHIRPED
CHIRPER s
CHIRRED*
CHIRREN*
CHIRRES*
CHIRRUP sy
CHISELS*
CHITINS*
CHITLIN gs
CHITONS*
*CHITTER s
CHIVARI
CHIVIED
CHIVIES
CHLAMYS
CHLORAL s
CHLORIC
CHLORID es
CHLORIN es
CHOANAE*
*CHOCKED
CHOICER*
CHOICES*t
CHOIRED
CHOKERS*
*CHOKIER
*CHOKING
CHOLATE s
CHOLENT s
CHOLERA*s
CHOLERS*
CHOLINE s
CHOLLAS
CHOMPED
CHOMPER s
CHOOSER*s
CHOOSES*
CHOOSEY*
CHOPINE*s
CHOPINS*
*CHOPPED
*CHOPPER s
CHORAGI c
CHORALE*s
CHORALS*
CHORDAL
*CHORDED
CHOREAL*
CHOREAS*
CHOREGI
CHOREIC
CHORIAL
CHORINE s
CHORING
CHORION s
CHORIZO s
CHOROID s
CHORTEN s
CHORTLE drs
CHOUGHS*
CHOUSED
*CHOUSER*s
CHOUSES
CHOWDER s
CHOWING
CHOWSED*
CHOWSES*
CHRISMA*l
CHRISMS*
CHRISOM s
CHRISTY
CHROMAS*
CHROMED*
CHROMES*
a CHROMIC
CHROMOS*
CHROMYL*s
CHRONIC s
CHRONON s
CHUCKED
*CHUCKLE drs
CHUDDAH s
CHUDDAR s
CHUDDER s
*CHUFFED
CHUFFER
*CHUGGED
*CHUGGER s
CHUKARS*
CHUKKAR*s
CHUKKAS*
CHUKKER s
*CHUMMED
*CHUMPED
CHUNKED
CHUNNEL s
*CHUNTER s
*CHUPPAH*s
CHUPPAS*
CHURCHY*
CHURNED
CHURNER s
CHURRED
CHURROS*
CHUTING
CHUTIST s
CHUTNEE s
CHUTNEY s
*CHUTZPA hs
CHYLOUS
CHYMICS*
CHYMIST s
CHYMOUS
CHYTRID s
CIBORIA
CIBOULE s
CICADAE*
CICADAS*
CICALAS*
CICEROS*
CICHLID s
CICOREE s
CIGARET s
CILIARY
CILIATE ds
CILICES*
CIMICES
*CINCHED
*CINCHES
CINDERS*
CINDERY*
CINEAST es
CINEMAS*
CINEOLE*s
CINEOLS*
CINERIN s
CINGULA r
CINQUES*
CIPHERS*
CIPHONY
CIPOLIN s
CIRCLED*
CIRCLER*s
CIRCLES*
CIRCLET*s
CIRCUIT sy
CIRCUSY*
CIRQUES*
CIRRATE
CIRROSE
CIRROUS
CIRSOID
CISCOES
CISSIES
CISSOID s
CISTERN as
CISTRON s
CITABLE
CITADEL s
CITATOR sy
CITHARA s
CITHERN*s
CITHERS*
CITHREN s
CITIZEN s
CITOLAS*
CITOLES*
CITRALS*
CITRATE ds
CITRINE*s
CITRINS*
CITRONS*
CITROUS
CITRUSY*
CITTERN s
CIVILLY
CIVISMS*
CIVVIES
CLABBER s
CLACHAN s
*CLACKED
*CLACKER s
CLADDED
CLADISM s
CLADIST s
CLADODE s
*CLAGGED
CLAIMED
CLAIMER s
CLAMANT
*CLAMBER s
*CLAMMED
CLAMMER s
CLAMORS*
CLAMOUR s
*CLAMPED
CLAMPER s
CLANGED
CLANGER s
CLANGOR s
CLANKED
*CLAPPED
*CLAPPER s
CLAQUER*s
CLAQUES*
CLARETS*
CLARIES
CLARIFY
CLARION s
CLARITY
CLARKIA s
CLAROES
*CLASHED
*CLASHER s
*CLASHES
CLASPED
CLASPER s
CLASSED
CLASSER s
*CLASSES
CLASSIC os
*CLASSIS mt
CLASSON s
CLASTIC s
*CLATTER sy
CLAUCHT
CLAUGHT s
CLAUSAL
CLAUSES*
CLAVATE
CLAVERS
CLAVIER s
CLAWERS*
*CLAWING
CLAXONS*
CLAYIER
*CLAYING
CLAYISH
CLAYPAN s
*CLEANED
*CLEANER s
*CLEANLY
CLEANSE*drs
CLEANUP s
CLEARED
CLEARER s
CLEARLY
CLEATED
CLEAVED
*CLEAVER*s
CLEAVES
CLEEKED
CLEFTED
CLEMENT
CLEOMES*
CLEPING
CLERICS*
CLERIDS*
CLERISY
CLERKED
CLERKLY
CLEWING
CLICHED*
CLICHES
*CLICKED
*CLICKER s
CLIENTS*
CLIMATE s
*CLIMBED
*CLIMBER s
CLINGED
*CLINGER s
CLINICS*
*CLINKED
*CLINKER s
*CLIPPED
*CLIPPER s
CLIQUED*
CLIQUES*
CLIQUEY*
CLITICS*
*CLIVERS
CLIVIAS*
CLOACAE*
CLOACAL*
CLOACAS*

CLOAKED
*CLOBBER s
CLOCHES*
*CLOCKED
*CLOCKER s
*CLOGGED
*CLOGGER s
CLOMPED
CLONERS
CLONING s
CLONISM s
CLONKED
*CLOPPED
CLOQUES*
CLOSELY
CLOSERS
CLOSEST*
CLOSETS*
CLOSEUP s
*CLOSING s
CLOSURE ds
CLOTHED*
CLOTHES*
*CLOTTED
CLOTURE ds
CLOUDED
CLOUGHS
*CLOURED
*CLOUTED
CLOUTER s
CLOVERS
CLOVERY*
CLOWDER s
CLOWNED
CLOYING
CLUBBED
*CLUBBER s
CLUBMAN
CLUBMEN
*CLUCKED
CLUEING
*CLUMBER s
*CLUMPED
CLUNKED
*CLUNKER s
CLUPEID s
*CLUSTER sy
CLUTCHY*
CLUTTER sy
CLYPEAL
CLYPEUS
CLYSTER s
COACHED
COACHER s
COACHES
COACTED
COACTOR s
COADMIT s
COAEVAL s
COAGENT s
COAGULA
COALBIN s
COALBOX
COALERS*
COALIER
COALIFY
COALING
COALPIT s
COAMING s
COANNEX
COAPTED
COARSEN*s
COARSER*
COASTAL
COASTED
COASTER s
COATEES*
COATERS
COATING s
COAXERS*
COAXIAL
COAXING
COBALTS*
COBBERS*
COBBIER
COBBLED*
COBBLER*s
COBBLES*
COBNUTS*
COBWEBS*
COCAINE*s
COCAINS*
COCCIDS*
COCCOID s
COCCOUS
COCHAIR s
COCHINS*
COCHLEA ers
COCKADE ds
COCKERS
COCKEYE ds
COCKIER
COCKILY
COCKING
COCKISH
COCKLED*
COCKLES*
COCKNEY s
COCKPIT s
COCKSHY
COCKUPS*
COCOMAT s
COCONUT s
COCOONS*
COCOTTE s
COCOYAM s
CODABLE
CODDERS*
CODDING
CODDLED*
CODDLER*s
CODDLES*
CODEIAS*
CODEINA*s
CODEINE*s
CODEINS*
CODFISH
CODGERS*
CODICES
CODICIL s
CODLING*s
CODLINS*
CODRIVE nrs
CODROVE
COEDITS*
COELIAC
COELOME*s
COELOMS*
COEMPTS*
COENACT s
COENURE s
COENURI
COEQUAL s
COERCED*
COERCER*s
COERCES*
COERECT s
COESITE s
COEVALS*
COEXERT s
COEXIST s
COFFEES*
s*COFFERS*
s*COFFING*
COFFINS*
COFFLED*
COFFLES*
COFFRET s
COFOUND s
COGENCY
COGGING
COGITOS*
COGNACS*
COGNATE s
COGNISE ds
COGNIZE drs
COGWAYS*
COHABIT s
COHEADS*
COHEIRS*
COHERED*
COHERER*s
COHERES*
COHORTS*
COHOSTS*
COHUNES*
COIFFED*
COIFFES*
COIFING
COIGNED*
COIGNES*
COILERS
*COILING
COINAGE s
COINERS*
COINFER s
COINING
COINTER s
COITION s
COJOINS*
*COLDEST
*COLDISH
COLEADS*
COLICIN es
COLICKY
COLITIC
COLITIS
COLLAGE dns
COLLARD*s
COLLARS*
COLLATE ds
COLLECT s
COLLEEN s
COLLEGE rs
COLLETS*
COLLIDE drs
COLLIED*
COLLIER*sy
COLLIES*
COLLINS
COLLOID s
s COLLOPS*
COLLUDE drs
COLOBUS
COLOGNE ds
COLONEL*s
COLONES*
COLONIC*s
COLONUS
COLORED
COLORER s
COLOSSI
COLOURS*
COLTERS*
COLTISH
COLUGOS*
COLUMEL s
COLUMNS*
COLURES*
COMAKER*s
COMAKES*
COMATES*
COMATIC
COMATIK s
COMBATS*
COMBERS
COMBINE drs
COMBING s
COMBUST s
COMEDIC
COMEDOS*
COMETIC
COMFIER
COMFITS*
COMFORT s
COMFREY s
COMICAL
COMINGS*
COMITIA l
COMMAND os
COMMATA
COMMEND s
COMMENT s
COMMIES*
COMMITS*
COMMIXT*
COMMODE s
COMMONS*
COMMOVE ds
COMMUNE drs
COMMUTE drs
COMPACT s
COMPANY
COMPARE drs
COMPART s
COMPASS*
COMPEER s
COMPELS*
COMPEND s
COMPERE ds
COMPETE ds
COMPILE drs
COMPING
COMPLEX
COMPLIN es
COMPLOT s
COMPONE
COMPONY
COMPORT s
COMPOSE*drs
COMPOST*s
COMPOTE s
COMPTED
COMPUTE drs
COMRADE s
CONATUS
CONCAVE ds
CONCEAL s
CONCEDE drs
CONCEIT s
CONCENT s
CONCEPT is
CONCERN s
CONCERT ios
CONCHAE*
CONCHAL*
CONCHAS*
CONCHES
CONCHIE s
CONCHOS*
CONCISE r
CONCOCT s
CONCORD s
CONCURS*
CONCUSS
CONDEMN s
CONDIGN
CONDOES
CONDOLE drs
CONDOMS*
CONDONE drs
CONDORS*
CONDUCE drs
CONDUCT s
CONDUIT s
CONDYLE s
CONFABS*
CONFECT s
CONFERS*
CONFESS
CONFIDE drs
CONFINE drs
CONFIRM s
CONFITS*
CONFLUX
CONFORM s
CONFUSE ds
CONFUTE drs
CONGAED
CONGEAL s
CONGEED*
CONGEES*
CONGERS*
CONGEST*s
CONGIUS
CONGOES
CONGOUS*
i CONICAL
CONIDIA ln
CONIFER s
CONIINE s
CONINES*
CONIUMS*
CONJOIN st
CONJURE drs
CONKERS*
CONKING
CONNATE
CONNECT s
CONNERS*
CONNING
CONNIVE drs
CONNOTE ds
CONOIDS*
CONQUER s
CONSENT s
CONSIGN s
CONSIST s
CONSOLE*drs
CONSOLS*
CONSORT s
CONSULS*
CONSULT*s
CONSUME drs
CONTACT s
CONTAIN s
CONTEMN s
CONTEND s
CONTENT s
CONTEST*s
CONTEXT s
CONTORT s
CONTOUR s
CONTRAS*t
CONTROL s
CONTUSE ds
CONVECT s
CONVENE drs
CONVENT s
CONVERT s
CONVEYS*
CONVICT s
CONVOKE drs
CONVOYS*
s COOCHES
COOEYED
COOKERS*
COOKERY*
COOKEYS*
COOKIES*
COOKING s
COOKOFF s
COOKOUT s
COOKTOP s
COOLANT s
COOLERS*
COOLEST
COOLIES*
COOLING
COOLISH
COOLTHS*
COOMBES*
COONCAN s
COONTIE s
s COOPERS*
COOPERY*
s COOPING
COOPTED
s COOTERS*
COOTIES*
COPAIBA s
COPALMS*
COPECKS*
COPEPOD s
COPIERS*
COPIHUE s
COPILOT s
COPINGS*
COPIOUS
COPLOTS*
COPOUTS*
COPPERS*
COPPERY*
COPPICE ds
COPPING
COPPRAS*
COPRAHS*
COPTERS*
s COPULAE*
COPULAR*
s COPULAS*
COPYBOY s
COPYCAT s
COPYING
COPYIST s
COQUETS*
COQUINA s
COQUITO s
*CORACLE s
CORANTO s
CORBANS*
CORBEIL s
CORBELS*
CORBIES*
CORBINA s
CORDAGE s
CORDATE
CORDERS
CORDIAL s
CORDING s
CORDITE s
CORDOBA s
CORDONS*
COREIGN s
COREMIA
CORKAGE s
CORKERS*
CORKIER
CORKING
CORMELS*
CORMOID
CORMOUS
CORNCOB s
CORNEAL*
CORNEAS*
CORNELS*
s CORNERS*
CORNETS*
CORNFED
CORNICE ds
CORNIER
CORNIFY
CORNILY
s CORNING
CORNROW s
CORNUAL*
CORNUTE d
CORNUTO s
COROLLA s
CORONAE*
CORONAL*s
CORONAS*
CORONEL s
CORONER s
CORONET s
CORPORA l
CORPSES*
CORRADE ds
CORRALS*
CORRECT s
CORRIDA s
CORRIES*
CORRODE ds
CORRODY
CORRUPT s
CORSACS*
CORSAGE s
CORSAIR s
CORSETS*
CORSLET s
CORTEGE s
CORTINA*s
CORTINS*
CORULER s
CORVEES*
CORVETS*
CORVIDS*
CORVINA s
CORVINE
CORYMBS*
CORYZAL*
CORYZAS*
COSHERS*
COSHING
COSIEST*
COSIGNS*
COSINES*s
COSMIDS*
COSMISM s
COSMIST s
COSSACK s
COSSETS*
COSTARD*s
COSTARS*
COSTATE
COSTERS*
COSTING
COSTIVE
COSTREL s
COSTUME drs
y
COSYING
COTEAUX*
COTERIE s
COTHURN is
COTIDAL
COTINGA*s
COTTAGE rsy
COTTARS
COTTERS
COTTIER s
COTTONS*
COTTONY*
e COTYPES*
*COUCHED
COUCHER s
*COUCHES
COUGARS*
COUGHED
COUGHER s
COULDST
COULEES*
COULOIR s
COULOMB s
COULTER s
COUNCIL s
COUNSEL s
COUNTED
COUNTER s
COUNTRY
COUPING
COUPLED*
COUPLER*s
COUPLES*
COUPLET*s
COUPONS*
COURAGE s
COURANT eos
COURIER s
COURLAN s
COURSED*
COURSER*s
COURSES*
COURTED
COURTER s
COURTLY
COUSINS*
COUTEAU x
s*COUTERS*
s COUTHER
COUTHIE r
COUTURE s
COUVADE s
*COVERED
COVERER s
COVERTS*
COVERUP s
COVETED
COVETER s
COVINGS*
COWAGES*
COWARDS*
COWBANE s
COWBELL s
COWBIND s
COWBIRD s
COWBOYS*
COWEDLY
COWERED
COWFISH
COWFLAP s
COWFLOP s
COWGIRL s
COWHAGE s
COWHAND s
COWHERB s
COWHERD s
COWHIDE ds
COWIEST
COWLICK s
s COWLING s
COWPATS*
COWPEAS*
COWPIES*
COWPLOP s
COWPOKE s
COWRIES*
COWRITE rs
COWROTE
COWSHED s
COWSKIN s
COWSLIP s
COXALGY
COXCOMB s
COXITIS
COXLESS
COYDOGS*
COYNESS
COYOTES*
COYPOUS*
COZENED
COZENER s
COZIEST*
COZYING
CRAALED
CRABBED
CRABBER s
*CRACKED
*CRACKER s
*CRACKLE ds
CRACKLY
CRACKUP s
CRADLED*
CRADLER*s
CRADLES*
*CRAFTED
*CRAFTER s
s*CRAGGED
CRAMBES*
CRAMBOS*
s*CRAMMED
*CRAMMER s
*CRAMPED
CRAMPIT s
CRAMPON s
CRANIAL*
CRANING
CRANIUM s
*CRANKED
*CRANKER
*CRANKLE ds
*CRANKLY
CRANNOG es
s*CRAPING
CRAPOLA s
s*CRAPPED
CRAPPIE rs
CRASHED
*CRASHER s
*CRASHES
CRASSER
CRASSLY

CRATERS
*CRATING
CRATONS*
*CRAUNCH
CRAVATS*
CRAVENS
CRAVERS
*CRAVING s
CRAWDAD s
s CRAWLED
s CRAWLER s
CRAYONS
CRAZIER
CRAZIES t
CRAZILY
*CRAZING
s CREAKED
s*CREAMED
s*CREAMER sy
CREASED*
CREASER*s
CREASES*
CREATED*
CREATES*
CREATIN egs
CREATOR s
CRECHES*
CREDENT
CREDITS*
CREEDAL
*CREELED
CREEPED
CREEPER s
CREEPIE rs
CREESES*
*CREMATE ds
CREMINI s
CRENATE d
CRENELS*
CREOLES*
CREOSOL s
CREPIER
CREPING
CREPONS*
CRESOLS*
CRESSES
CRESSET s
CRESTAL
*CRESTED
CRESYLS*
CRETICS*
CRETINS*
CREVICE ds
CREWCUT s
CREWELS*
s CREWING
CREWMAN
CREWMEN
*CRIBBED
*CRIBBER s
*CRICKED
CRICKET s
*CRICKEY
CRICOID s
CRIMINE
CRIMINI s
CRIMINY
*CRIMMER s
s CRIMPED
s CRIMPER s
*CRIMPLE ds
CRIMSON s
CRINGED
*CRINGER*s
CRINGES*
CRINGLE s
CRINITE s
CRINKLE ds
CRINKLY
CRINOID s
CRINUMS*
CRIOLLO s
*CRIPPLE drs
CRISPED
CRISPEN s
CRISPER s
CRISPLY
CRISSAL*
CRISSUM
CRISTAE*
CRITICS*
*CRITTER s
CRITTUR s
CROAKED
CROAKER s
CROCEIN es
*CROCHET s
CROCINE
*CROCKED
*CROCKET s
CROFTER s
CROJIKS*
CRONIES
CRONISH
*CROOKED
CROOKER y
CROONED
CROONER s
CROPPED
CROPPER s
CROPPIE s
*CROQUET s
CROQUIS
*CROSIER s
CROSSED*
CROSSER*s
CROSSES*t
CROSSLY
CROTONS*
CROUPES*
CROUTES
CROUTON s
CROWBAR s
CROWDED
CROWDER s
CROWDIE s
CROWERS
*CROWING
CROWNED
CROWNER s
CROWNET s
CROZERS*
CROZIER s
CRUCIAL
CRUCIAN s
CRUCIFY
CRUDDED
*CRUDELY
CRUDEST
CRUDITY
CRUELER
CRUELLY
CRUELTY
CRUISED*
CRUISER*s
CRUISES*
CRULLER s
CRUMBED
CRUMBER s
*CRUMBLE ds
*CRUMBLY
CRUMBUM s
CRUMMIE rs
CRUMPED
CRUMPET s
*CRUMPLE ds
*CRUMPLY
s CRUNCHY*
CRUNODE s
CRUPPER s
CRUSADE drs
CRUSADO s
CRUSETS*
*CRUSHED
*CRUSHER s
*CRUSHES
CRUSILY
CRUSTAL
*CRUSTED
CRUZADO s
CRYBABY
CRYOGEN sy
CRYONIC s
CRYPTAL
CRYPTIC
CRYPTOS*
CRYSTAL s
CTENOID
CUATROS*
CUBAGES*
CUBBIES
CUBBISH
CUBICAL
CUBICLE s
CUBICLY
CUBISMS*
CUBISTS*
CUBITAL
CUBITUS
CUBOIDS*
CUCKOLD s
CUCKOOS*
CUDBEAR s
CUDDIES*
CUDDLED*
CUDDLER*s
CUDDLES*
CUDGELS*
CUDWEED s
CUESTAS*
s CUFFING
CUIRASS
CUISHES
CUISINE s
CUISSES*
CUITTLE ds
s CULCHES
CULEXES
CULICES
CULICID s
CULLAYS*
s CULLERS*
CULLETS*
CULLIED
CULLIES
s CULLING
s CULLION s
CULMING
CULOTTE s
CULPRIT s
CULTISH
CULTISM s
CULTIST s
CULTURE ds
CULVERS*
CULVERT*s
CUMARIN s
CUMBERS
CUMBIAS*
s CUMMERS*
CUMMINS*
CUMQUAT s
CUMSHAW s
CUMULUS
CUNDUMS*
CUNEATE d
s CUNNERS*
CUNNING s
CUPCAKE s
CUPELED
CUPELER s
CUPFULS*
CUPLIKE
CUPOLAS*
s*CUPPERS*
CUPPIER
*CUPPING s
CUPRITE s
CUPROUS
CUPRUMS*
CUPSFUL
CUPULAE*
CUPULAR*
CUPULES*
CURABLE
CURABLY
CURACAO s
CURACOA s
CURAGHS*
CURARAS*
CURARES
CURARIS
CURATED*
CURATES
CURATOR s
CURBERS*
CURBING s
CURCHES
CURCUMA s
CURDIER
CURDING
CURDLED*
CURDLER*s
CURDLES*
CURETTE ds
CURFEWS*
CURIOSA*
CURIOUS
CURITES*
CURIUMS*
CURLERS*
CURLEWS*
CURLIER
CURLILY
CURLING s
CURRACH s
CURRAGH s
CURRANS*
CURRANT*s
CURRENT s
s CURRIED*
CURRIER*sy
s CURRIES*
CURRING
CURRISH
CURSERS*
CURSING
CURSIVE s
CURSORS*
CURSORY*
CURTAIL s
CURTAIN s
CURTALS*
CURTATE
CURTEST
CURTESY
CURTSEY s
CURVETS*
s CURVIER
CURVING
CUSHATS*
CUSHAWS*
CUSHIER
CUSHILY
CUSHION sy
CUSPATE d
CUSPIDS*
CUSSERS*
CUSSING
CUSTARD sy
CUSTODY
CUSTOMS*
CUTAWAY s
CUTBACK s
CUTBANK s
s CUTCHES
CUTDOWN s
CUTESIE r
CUTICLE s
CUTISES
CUTLASS*
CUTLERS*
CUTLERY*
CUTLETS*
CUTLINE s
CUTOFFS*
CUTOUTS*
CUTOVER s
CUTTAGE s
s*CUTTERS*
CUTTIES
CUTTING s
s CUTTLED*
s CUTTLES*
s CUTWORK s
CUTWORM s
CUVETTE s
CYANATE s
CYANIDE*ds
CYANIDS*
CYANINE*s
CYANINS*
CYANITE s
CYBORGS*
CYCASES
CYCASIN s
CYCLASE s
CYCLERS*
CYCLERY*
CYCLING*s
CYCLINS*
CYCLIST s
CYCLIZE ds
CYCLOID s
CYCLONE s
CYCLOPS
CYGNETS*
CYLICES
CYMATIA
CYMBALS*
CYMENES*
CYMLING*s
CYMLINS*
CYNICAL
CYPHERS*
CYPRESS*
CYPRIAN s
CYPSELA e
CYSTEIN es
CYSTINE s
CYSTOID s
CYTOSOL s
CZARDAS
CZARDOM s
CZARINA s
CZARISM s
CZARIST s
DABBERS*
DABBING
DABBLED*
DABBLER*s
DABBLES*
DABSTER s
DACITES*
DACKERS*
DACOITS*
DACOITY*
DACRONS*
DACTYLI*c
DACTYLS*
DADAISM s
DADAIST s
DADDIES
DADDLED
DADDLES
DADOING
DAEMONS*
DAFFIER
DAFFILY
DAFFING
DAFTEST
DAGGERS
DAGGLED*
DAGGLES*
DAGLOCK s
DAGOBAS*
DAGWOOD s
DAHLIAS*
DAHOONS*
DAIKERS*
DAIKONS*
DAILIES
DAIMIOS*
DAIMONS*
DAIMYOS*
DAIRIES
DAISIED
DAISIES
DAKOITS*
DAKOITY*
DALAPON s
DALASIS*
DALEDHS*
DALETHS*
*DALLIED
DALLIER s
*DALLIES
DALTONS*
DAMAGED*
DAMAGER*s
DAMAGES*
DAMASKS*
DAMIANA s
DAMMARS*
DAMMERS*
DAMMING
DAMNERS*
DAMNIFY
DAMNING
DAMOSEL s
DAMOZEL s
DAMPENS*
DAMPERS*
DAMPEST
*DAMPING s
DAMPISH
DAMSELS*
DAMSONS*
DANAZOL s
DANCERS*
DANCING
DANDERS*
DANDIER
DANDIES t
DANDIFY
DANDILY
DANDLED*
DANDLER*s
DANDLES*
DANGERS
DANGING
DANGLED
*DANGLER*s
DANGLES
DANKEST
DANSEUR s
DAPHNES*
DAPHNIA s
DAPPING
DAPPLED*
DAPPLES
DAPSONE s
DARBARS*
DARBIES
DAREFUL
DARESAY
DARINGS*
DARIOLE s
DARKENS*
DARKEST
DARKING
DARKISH
DARKLED*
DARKLES*
DARLING s
DARNELS*
DARNERS*
DARNING s
DARSHAN s
DARTERS*
DARTING
DARTLED*
DARTLES*
DASHEEN s
DASHERS*
*DASHIER
DASHIKI s
*DASHING
DASHPOT s
DASSIES*
DASTARD s
DASYURE s
DATABLE
DATCHAS*
DATEDLY
DATIVAL
DATIVES*
DATURAS*
DATURIC
DAUBERS*
DAUBERY*
DAUBIER
DAUBING
DAUNDER s
DAUNTED
DAUNTER s
DAUPHIN es
DAUTIES*
DAUTING
DAVENED
DAWDLED*
DAWDLER*s
DAWDLES*
*DAWNING
DAWTIES*
DAWTING
DAYBEDS*
DAYBOOK s
DAYCARE s
DAYGLOW s
DAYLILY
DAYLONG
DAYMARE s
DAYROOM s
DAYSIDE s
DAYSMAN
DAYSMEN
DAYSTAR s
DAYTIME s
DAYWORK s
DAZEDLY
DAZZLED*
DAZZLER*s
DAZZLES*
DEACONS*
DEADENS*
DEADEST
DEADEYE s
DEADMAN
DEADMEN
DEADPAN s
DEAFENS*
DEAFEST
DEAFISH
DEAIRED
DEALATE ds
DEALERS*
DEALING s
DEANERY
DEANING
DEAREST
DEARIES*
DEARTHS
DEASHED
DEASHES
DEATHLY
DEAVING
DEBACLE s
DEBARKS*
DEBASED*
DEBASER*s
DEBASES*
DEBATED*
DEBATER*s
DEBATES*
DEBAUCH
DEBEAKS*
DEBEARD s
DEBITED
DEBONED*
DEBONER*s
DEBONES*
DEBOUCH e
DEBRIDE ds
DEBRIEF s
DEBTORS*
DEBUNKS*
DEBUTED
DECADAL
DECADES*
DECAGON s
DECALOG s
DECAMPS*
DECANAL
DECANES*
DECANTS*
DECAPOD s
DECARES*
DECAYED
DECAYER s
DECEASE ds
DECEITS*
DECEIVE drs
DECENCY
DECERNS*
DECIARE s
DECIBEL s
DECIDED*
DECIDER*s
DECIDES*
DECIDUA els
DECILES*
DECIMAL s
DECKELS*
DECKERS*
DECKING s
DECKLES*
DECLAIM s
DECLARE drs
DECLASS e
DECLAWS*
DECLINE drs
DECOCTS*
DECODED*
DECODER*s
DECODES*
DECOLOR s
DECORUM s
DECOYED
DECOYER s
DECREED*
DECREER*s
DECREES*
DECRIAL s
DECRIED
DECRIER s
DECRIES
DECROWN s
DECRYPT s
DECUMAN
DECUPLE ds
DECURVE ds
DEDUCED
DEDUCES
DEDUCTS
DEEDIER
DEEDING
DEEJAYS*
a DEEMING
DEEPENS*
DEEPEST
DEERFLY
DEEWANS*
DEFACED*
DEFACER*s
DEFACES*
DEFAMED*
DEFAMER*s
DEFAMES*
DEFANGS*
DEFAULT s
DEFEATS*

DEFECTS*
DEFENCE ds
DEFENDS*
DEFENSE ds
DEFFEST
DEFIANT
DEFICIT s
DEFIERS*
DEFILED*
DEFILER*s
DEFILES*
DEFINED*
DEFINER*s
DEFINES*
DEFLATE drs
DEFLEAS*
DEFLECT s
DEFOAMS*
DEFOCUS
DEFORCE drs
DEFORMS*
DEFRAGS*
DEFRAUD s
DEFRAYS*
DEFROCK s
DEFROST s
DEFTEST
DEFUELS*
DEFUNCT
DEFUNDS*
DEFUSED*
DEFUSER*s
DEFUSES*
DEFUZED*
DEFUZES*
DEFYING
DEGAMES*
DEGAMIS*
DEGASES
DEGAUSS
DEGERMS*
DEGLAZE ds
DEGRADE drs
DEGREED*
DEGREES*
DEGUSTS*
DEHISCE ds
DEHORNS*
DEHORTS*
DEICERS*
DEICIDE s
DEICING
DEICTIC s
DEIFIED
DEIFIER s
DEIFIES
DEIFORM
DEIGNED
DEISTIC
DEITIES
DEJECTA
DEJECTS
DEKARES*
DEKEING
DELAINE s
DELATED
DELATES
DELATOR s
DELAYED
DELAYER s
DELEADS*
DELEAVE ds
DELEING
DELETED*
DELETES*
DELICTS*
DELIGHT s
DELIMED*
DELIMES*
DELIMIT s
DELIRIA
DELISTS*
DELIVER sy
DELLIES
DELOUSE drs
DELPHIC
DELTAIC
DELTOID s
DELUDED
*DELUDER*s
DELUDES
DELUGED*
DELUGES*
DELVERS
DELVING
DEMAGOG sy

DEMANDS*
DEMARKS*
DEMASTS*
DEMEANS*
DEMENTS*
*DEMERGE drs
DEMERIT s
DEMESNE s
DEMETON s
DEMIGOD s
DEMIREP s
DEMISED*
DEMISES*
DEMODED*
DEMOING
DEMONIC
DEMOSES
DEMOTED
DEMOTES
DEMOTIC s
DEMOUNT s
DEMURER*
DENARII*
DENDRON s
DENGUES*
DENIALS*
DENIERS*
DENIMED
DENIZEN s
DENNING
DENOTED*
DENOTES*
DENSELY
DENSEST
DENSIFY
DENSITY
DENTALS*
e DENTATE d
DENTILS*
DENTINE*s
DENTING*
DENTINS*
DENTIST s
DENTOID
DENTURE s
DENUDED*
DENUDER*s
DENUDES*
DENYING
DEODAND s
DEODARA*s
DEODARS*
DEONTIC
DEORBIT s
DEPAINT s
DEPARTS*
DEPENDS*
DEPERMS*
DEPICTS*
DEPLANE ds
DEPLETE drs
DEPLORE drs
DEPLOYS*
DEPLUME ds
DEPONED*
DEPONES*
DEPORTS*
DEPOSAL s
DEPOSED*
DEPOSER*s
DEPOSES
DEPOSIT s
DEPRAVE drs
DEPRESS
DEPRIVE drs
DEPSIDE s
DEPUTED*
DEPUTES*
DERAIGN s
DERAILS*
DERANGE drs
DERATED*
DERATES*
DERBIES
DERIDED*
DERIDER*s
DERIDES*
DERIVED*
DERIVER*s
DERIVES*
DERMOID s
DERNIER
DERRICK s
DERRIES
DERVISH
DESALTS*

DESANDS*
DESCANT s
DESCEND s
DESCENT s
DESERTS*
DESERVE drs
DESEXED
DESEXES
DESIGNS*
DESIRED*
DESIRER*s
DESIRES*
DESISTS*
DESKMAN
DESKMEN
DESKTOP s
DESMANS*
DESMIDS*
DESMOID s
DESORBS*
DESPAIR s
DESPISE drs
DESPITE ds
DESPOIL s
DESPOND s
DESPOTS*
DESSERT s
DESTAIN s
DESTINE ds
DESTINY
DESTROY s
DESUGAR s
DETAILS*
DETAINS*
DETECTS*
DETENTE*s
DETENTS*
DETERGE drs
DETESTS*
DETICKS*
DETINUE s
DETOURS*
DETOXED
DETOXES
DETRACT s
DETRAIN s
DETRUDE ds
DEUCING
DEUTZIA s
DEVALUE ds
DEVEINS*
DEVELED
DEVELOP es
DEVESTS*
DEVIANT s
DEVIATE ds
DEVICES*
DEVILED
DEVILRY
DEVIOUS
DEVISAL s
DEVISED*
DEVISEE*s
DEVISER*s
DEVISES*
DEVISOR s
DEVOICE ds
DEVOIRS*
*DEVOLVE ds
DEVOTED*
DEVOTEE*s
DEVOTES*
DEVOURS*
DEWATER s
DEWAXED
DEWAXES
DEWCLAW s
DEWDROP s
DEWFALL s
DEWIEST
DEWLAPS*
DEWLESS
DEWOOLS*
DEWORMS*
DEXTRAL
DEXTRAN s
DEXTRIN es
DEZINCS*
DHARMAS*
DHARMIC
DHARNAS*
DHOORAS*
DHOOTIE*s
DHOOTIS*
DHOURRA s
DHURNAS*

DHURRIE s
DIABASE s
DIABOLO s
DIACIDS*
DIADEMS*
DIAGRAM s
DIALECT s
DIALERS*
DIALING s
DIALIST s
DIALLED
DIALLEL
DIALLER s
DIALOGS*
DIALYSE drs
DIALYZE drs
DIAMIDE s
DIAMINE*s
DIAMINS*
DIAMOND s
DIAPERS*
DIAPIRS*
DIAPSID s
DIARCHY
DIARIES
DIARIST s
DIASTEM as
DIASTER s
DIATOMS*
DIATRON s
DIAZINE*s
DIAZINS*
DIAZOLE s
DIBASIC
DIBBERS*
DIBBING
DIBBLED*
DIBBLER*s
DIBBLES*
DIBBUKS*
DICAMBA s
DICASTS*
*DICIEST
DICKENS
DICKERS
DICKEYS*
DICKIER
DICKIES*t
DICLINY
DICOTYL s
DICTATE ds
DICTIER
DICTION s
DICTUMS*
DICYCLY
DIDACTS*
DIDDLED*
DIDDLER*s
DIDDLES*
DIDDLEY*s
DIEBACK s
DIEHARD s
DIEOFFS*
DIESELS*
DIESTER s
DIETARY
DIETERS*
DIETHER s
DIETING
DIFFERS*
DIFFUSE drs
DIGAMMA s
DIGESTS*
DIGGERS*
*DIGGING s
DIGHTED
DIGITAL s
DIGLOTS*
*DIGNIFY
DIGNITY
DIGOXIN s
DIGRAPH s
DIGRESS
DIKDIKS*
DIKTATS*
DILATED*
DILATER*s
DILATES*
DILATOR sy
DILDOES*
DILEMMA s
DILLIES
DILUENT s
DILUTED*
DILUTER*s
DILUTES*

DILUTOR s
DILUVIA ln
DIMERIC
DIMETER s
DIMMERS*
DIMMEST
DIMMING
DIMNESS
DIMORPH s
DIMOUTS*
DIMPLED
DIMPLES*
DIMWITS*
DINDLED*
DINDLES*
DINERIC
DINEROS*
DINETTE s
DINGBAT s
DINGERS*
DINGEYS*
DINGIER
DINGIES t
DINGILY
DINGING
DINGLES
DINGOES
DINITRO
DINKEYS*
*DINKIER
DINKIES t
*DINKING
DINKUMS*
DINNERS
*DINNING
DINTING
DIOBOLS*
DIOCESE s
DIOPTER s
DIOPTRE s
DIORAMA s
DIORITE s
DIOXANE*s
DIOXANS*
DIOXIDE*s
DIOXIDS*
DIOXINS*
DIPHASE
DIPLOES*
DIPLOIC
DIPLOID sy
DIPLOMA st
DIPLONT s
DIPNETS*
DIPNOAN s
DIPODIC
DIPOLAR
DIPOLES*
DIPPERS*
DIPPIER
DIPPING
DIPTERA ln
DIPTYCA s
DIPTYCH s
DIQUATS*
DIRDUMS*
DIRECTS*
*DIREFUL
DIRHAMS*
*DIRKING
DIRLING
DIRNDLS*
DIRTBAG s
DIRTIED
DIRTIER
DIRTIES t
DIRTILY
DISABLE drs
DISARMS*
DISAVOW s
DISBAND s
DISBARS*
DISBUDS*
DISCANT s
DISCARD s
DISCASE ds
DISCEPT s
DISCERN s
DISCING
DISCOED
DISCOID s
DISCORD s
DISCUSS*
DISDAIN s
DISEASE ds
DISEURS*

DISEUSE s
DISGUST s
DISHELM s
DISHFUL s
DISHIER
DISHING
DISHPAN s
DISHRAG s
DISJECT s
DISJOIN st
DISKING
DISLIKE drs
DISLIMN s
DISMALS*
DISMAST s
DISMAYS*
DISMISS
DISOBEY s
DISOMIC
DISOWNS*
DISPART s
DISPELS*
DISPEND s
DISPLAY s
DISPORT s
DISPOSE drs
DISPUTE drs
DISRATE ds
DISROBE drs
DISROOT s
DISRUPT s
DISSAVE ds
DISSEAT s
DISSECT s
DISSENT s
DISSERT s
DISSING
DISTAFF s
DISTAIN s
DISTANT
DISTEND s
DISTENT
DISTICH s
DISTILL*s
DISTILS*
DISTOME s
DISTORT s
DISTURB s
DISUSED*
DISUSES*
DISYOKE ds
*DITCHED
DITCHER s
*DITCHES
DITHERS*
DITHERY*
DITHIOL
DITSIER
DITTANY
DITTIES
DITTOED
DITZIER
DIURNAL s
DIURONS*
DIVERGE ds
DIVERSE*
DIVERTS*
DIVESTS*
DIVIDED*
DIVIDER*s
DIVIDES*
DIVINED*
DIVINER*s
DIVINES*t
DIVISOR s
DIVORCE der
s
DIVULGE drs
DIVULSE ds
DIVVIED
DIVVIES
DIZENED
DIZZIED
DIZZIER
DIZZIES t
DIZZILY
DJEBELS
DOATING
DOBBERS*
DOBBIES
DOBBINS*
DOBLONS*
DOBSONS*
DOCENTS*
DOCETIC
DOCKAGE s

DOCKERS
DOCKETS*
DOCKING
DOCTORS*
DODDERS*
DODDERY*
DODGEMS*
DODGERS*
DODGERY*
DODGIER
DODGING
DODOISM s
DOESKIN s
DOFFERS
*DOFFING
DOGBANE s
DOGCART s
DOGDOMS*
DOGEARS*
DOGEDOM s
DOGFACE s
DOGFISH
DOGGERS*
DOGGERY*
DOGGIER*
DOGGIES*t
DOGGING
DOGGISH
DOGGONE drs
DOGGREL s
DOGLEGS*
DOGLIKE
DOGMATA
DOGNAPS*
DOGSLED s
DOGTROT s
DOGVANE s
DOGWOOD s
DOILIES
DOLEFUL
DOLLARS*
DOLLIED
DOLLIES
DOLLING
DOLLISH
DOLLOPS*
DOLMANS*
DOLMENS*
DOLOURS*
DOLPHIN s
DOLTISH
DOMAINE*s
DOMAINS*
DOMICAL
DOMICIL es
DOMINES*
DOMINIE s
DOMINOS*
DONATED*
o DONATES*
DONATOR s
DONGLES*
DONGOLA s
DONJONS*
DONKEYS*
DONNEES*
DONNERD
DONNERT
DONNING
DONNISH
DONZELS*
DOOBIES*
DOODADS*
DOODIES
DOODLED*
DOODLER*s
DOODLES
DOODOOS*
DOOLEES*
DOOLIES*
DOOMFUL
DOOMIER
DOOMILY
DOOMING
DOORMAN
DOORMAT s
DOORMEN
DOORWAY s
DOOWOPS*
DOOZERS*
DOOZIES*
DOPANTS*
DOPIEST
DOPINGS*
DORADOS*
DORBUGS*

DORHAWK s
DORKIER
DORMANT
DORMERS
DORMICE
DORMINS*
DORNECK s
DORNICK s
DORNOCK s
DORPERS*
DORSALS*
DORSELS*
DORSERS*
DOSAGES*
DOSSALS*
DOSSELS*
DOSSERS*
DOSSIER s
DOSSILS*
DOSSING
DOTAGES*
DOTARDS*
DOTIEST
DOTTELS*
DOTTERS
DOTTIER
DOTTILY
DOTTING
DOTTLES*
DOTTREL s
DOUBLED*
DOUBLER*s
DOUBLES*
DOUBLET*s
DOUBTED
DOUBTER s
DOUCELY
DOUCEUR s
DOUCHED
DOUCHES
DOUGHTY*
DOURAHS*
DOUREST
DOURINE s
DOUSERS*
DOUSING
DOVECOT es
DOVEKEY s
DOVEKIE s
DOVENED
DOWABLE
DOWAGER s
DOWDIER
DOWDIES t
DOWDILY
DOWELED
DOWERED
DOWNBOW s
DOWNERS
DOWNIER
*DOWNING
DOWRIES
DOWSERS*
DOWSING
DOYENNE s
DOYLEYS*
DOYLIES
DOZENED
DOZENTH s
DOZIEST
DRABBED
DRABBER
*DRABBET s
*DRABBLE ds
DRACENA s
DRACHMA*eis
DRACHMS*
*DRAFTED
DRAFTEE s
*DRAFTER s
DRAGEES
*DRAGGED
DRAGGER s
*DRAGGLE ds
DRAGNET s
DRAGONS*
DRAGOON s
*DRAINED
DRAINER s
DRAMADY
DRAMEDY
*DRAMMED
DRAPERS
DRAPERY*
*DRAPING
DRASTIC

*DRATTED
DRAUGHT sy
DRAWBAR s
DRAWEES*
DRAWERS*
DRAWING s
DRAWLED
DRAWLER s
DRAYAGE s
*DRAYING
DRAYMAN
DRAYMEN
DREADED
*DREAMED
*DREAMER s
DREDGED*
DREDGER*s
DREDGES*
DREEING
DREIDEL s
DREIDLS*
DRESSED
DRESSER s
DRESSES
*DRIBBED
DRIBBLE drs
t
DRIBBLY
*DRIBLET s
*DRIFTED
DRIFTER s
*DRILLED
DRILLER s
DRINKER s
*DRIPPED
*DRIPPER s
DRIVELS*
DRIVERS
*DRIVING s
DRIZZLE ds
DRIZZLY
DROGUES
*DROLLED
*DROLLER y
DROMOND*s
DROMONS*
DRONERS*
DRONGOS*
DRONING
DRONISH
DROOLED
DROOPED
DROPLET s
DROPOUT s
DROPPED
DROPPER s
DROSERA s
DROSHKY
DROSSES
DROUGHT sy
DROUKED
DROUTHS
DROUTHY*
DROVERS
*DROVING
DROWNDS*
DROWNED
DROWNER s
DROWSED*
DROWSES*
*DRUBBED
*DRUBBER s
DRUDGED*
DRUDGER*sy
DRUDGES*
*DRUGGED
DRUGGET s
DRUGGIE rs
DRUIDIC
*DRUMBLE ds
DRUMLIN s
DRUMMED
*DRUMMER s
DRUNKEN
DRUNKER
DRYABLE
DRYADES
DRYADIC
DRYLAND
DRYLOTS*
DRYNESS
DRYWALL s
DRYWELL s
DUALISM s
DUALIST s
DUALITY

DUALIZE ds
DUBBERS*
DUBBING*s
DUBBINS*
*DUBIETY
DUBIOUS
DUBNIUM s
DUCALLY
DUCHESS
DUCHIES
DUCKERS*
DUCKIER*
DUCKIES*t
DUCKING
DUCKPIN s
DUCTILE
DUCTING s
DUCTULE s
DUDEENS*
DUDGEON s
DUELERS*
DUELING
DUELIST s
DUELLED
DUELLER s
DUELLOS*
DUENDES*
DUENESS
DUENNAS*
DUETING
DUETTED
DUFFELS*
DUFFERS*
DUFFLES*
DUFUSES
DUGONGS*
DUGOUTS*
DUIKERS*
DUKEDOM s
DULCETS*
DULCIFY
DULLARD s
DULLEST
DULLING
DULLISH
DULNESS
DUMBEST
DUMBING
DUMDUMS*
DUMMIED
DUMMIES
DUMPERS*
DUMPIER
DUMPILY
*DUMPING s
DUMPISH
DUNCHES
DUNCISH
DUNGEON s
DUNGIER
DUNGING
DUNITES
DUNITIC
DUNKERS*
DUNKING
DUNLINS*
DUNNAGE s
DUNNESS
DUNNEST
DUNNING
DUNNITE s
DUNTING
DUODENA l
DUOLOGS*
DUOPOLY
DUOTONE s
DUPABLE
*DUPPING
DURABLE s
DURABLY
DURAMEN s
DURANCE s
DURBARS*
DURIANS*
DURIONS*
DURMAST s
DURNING
DURRIES*
DUSKIER
DUSKILY
DUSKING
DUSKISH
DUSTBIN s
DUSTERS*
DUSTIER
DUSTILY

DUSTING s
DUSTMAN
DUSTMEN
DUSTOFF s
DUSTPAN s
DUSTRAG s
DUSTUPS*
DUTEOUS
DUTIFUL
DUUMVIR is
DUVETYN es
DWARFED
DWARFER
DWARVES
*DWELLED
DWELLER s
*DWINDLE ds
*DWINING
DYADICS*
DYARCHY
DYBBUKS*
DYEABLE
DYEINGS*
DYEWEED s
DYEWOOD s
a DYNAMIC s
DYNAMOS*
DYNASTS*
DYNASTY*
DYNEINS*
DYNODES*
DYSPNEA ls
DYSURIA s
DYSURIC
DYVOURS*
EAGERER
m EAGERLY
EAGLETS
EAGLING
wy EANLING s
EARACHE s
EARBUDS*
t EARDROP s
EARDRUM s
EARFLAP s
EARFULS*
bgh EARINGS*
EARLAPS*
EARLDOM s
fgt EARLESS
np EARLIER
EARLOBE s
EARLOCK s
EARMARK s
EARMUFF s
ly EARNERS*
EARNEST s
ly EARNING s
EARPLUG s
EARRING s
EARSHOT s
EARTHED
EARTHEN
EARTHLY
EARWIGS*
EARWORM s
EASEFUL
tw EASELED
EASIEST*
EASTERN
f*EASTERS*
fy EASTING s
bh EATABLE s
bs EATINGS*
EBONICS
EBONIES
EBONISE ds
EBONITE s
EBONIZE ds
ECARTES
ECBOLIC s
ECCRINE
ECDYSES
ECDYSIS
ECDYSON es
ECHARDS
ECHELLE s
ECHELON s
ECHIDNA es
ECHINUS
ECHOERS*
ECHOING
ECHOISM s
ECLAIRS*
ECLIPSE drs
ECLOGUE s

ECOCIDE s
o ECOLOGY
ECONOMY
ECOTAGE s
ECOTONE s
ECOTOUR s
*ECOTYPE s
ECSTASY
p ECTASES
ECTASIS
ECTATIC
ECTHYMA
ECTOPIA s
ECTOPIC
ECTOZOA n
ECTYPAL
ECTYPES*
ECZEMAS*
EDACITY
EDAPHIC
EDDYING
o EDEMATA
hls EDGIEST
w
EDGINGS*
EDIBLES*
EDICTAL
EDIFICE s
EDIFIED
EDIFIER s
EDIFIES
EDITING
s EDITION s
EDITORS*
EDITRIX
EDUCATE ds
drs EDUCING
r EDUCTOR s
EELIEST
EELLIKE
EELPOUT s
EELWORM s
bl EERIEST
EFFABLE
EFFACED*
EFFACER*s
EFFACES*
EFFECTS*
EFFENDI s
EFFORTS*
EFFULGE ds
EFFUSED*
EFFUSES*
EFTSOON s
EGALITE s
EGESTED
EGGCUPS*
EGGHEAD s
EGGLESS
EGGNOGS*
EGOISMS*
EGOISTS*
EGOLESS
EGOTISM s
EGOTIST s
EIDETIC
EIDOLIC
EIDOLON s
h EIGHTHS*
EIGHTVO s
EIKONES
EINKORN s
*EIRENIC
EISWEIN s
dr EJECTED
r EJECTOR s
EKISTIC s
EKPWELE s
ELAPIDS*
ELAPINE
r*ELAPSED*
r*ELAPSES*
ELASTIC s
ELASTIN s
r ELATERS*
dgr ELATING
dgr ELATION s
r ELATIVE s
ELBOWED
ELDERLY
ELDRESS
ELDRICH
s ELECTED
s ELECTEE s
s*ELECTOR s
ELECTRO ns

ELEGANT
ELEGIAC s
ELEGIES
ELEGISE ds
*ELEGIST s
ELEGITS
ELEGIZE ds
ELEMENT s
ELENCHI c
ELEVATE ds
ELEVENS*
ELEVONS*
ELFLIKE
ELFLOCK s
ELICITS*
ELIDING
ELISION s
ELITISM s
ELITIST s
ELIXIRS*
ELLIPSE s
ELMIEST
ELODEAS*
ELOIGNS*
ELOINED
ELOINER s
ELOPERS
*ELOPING
ELUANTS*
ELUATES*
d ELUDERS*
d ELUDING
ELUENTS*
d ELUSION s
d ELUSIVE
d ELUSORY
*ELUTING
ELUTION s
ELUVIAL*
ELUVIUM s
ELYSIAN
ELYTRON
ELYTRUM
r*EMAILED
EMANANT
EMANATE ds
EMBALMS*
EMBANKS*
EMBARGO
EMBARKS*
EMBASSY
EMBAYED
EMBLAZE drs
EMBLEMS*
EMBOLIC*
EMBOLUS
EMBOSKS*
EMBOSOM s
EMBOWED
EMBOWEL s
EMBOWER s
EMBRACE drs
EMBROIL s
EMBROWN s
EMBRUED*
EMBRUES*
EMBRUTE ds
EMBRYON*s
EMBRYOS*
r*EMENDED
*EMENDER s
EMERALD s
dr*EMERGED*
dr*EMERGES*
EMERIES
EMERITA es
EMERITI
EMERODS*
EMEROID s
EMERSED
m EMETICS*
EMETINE*s
EMETINS*
EMEUTES*
EMIGRES*
EMINENT
EMIRATE s
dr EMITTED
r EMITTER s
EMODINS*
EMOTERS*
d EMOTING
dr*EMOTION s
*EMOTIVE
EMPALED*
EMPALER*s

EMPALES*
EMPANEL s
EMPATHY
EMPEROR s
EMPIRES*
EMPIRIC s
EMPLACE ds
EMPLANE ds
EMPLOYE*der
s
EMPLOYS*
EMPORIA
EMPOWER s
EMPRESS
EMPRISE s
EMPRIZE s
EMPTIED
EMPTIER s
EMPTIES t
EMPTILY
EMPTINS
EMPYEMA s
EMULATE ds
EMULOUS
ENABLED*
ENABLER*s
ENABLES*
ENACTED
ENACTOR sy
ENAMELS*
ENAMINE s
ENAMORS*
ENAMOUR s
v*ENATION s
ENCAGED*
ENCAGES*
ENCAMPS*
ENCASED*
ENCASES*
ENCHAIN s
p ENCHANT s
ENCHASE drs
ENCINAL*
ENCINAS*
ENCLASP s
ENCLAVE ds
ENCLOSE drs
ENCODED*
ENCODER*s
ENCODES*
ENCOMIA
ENCORED*
ENCORES*
ENCRUST s
ENCRYPT s
ENCYSTS*
ENDARCH y
ENDEARS*
ENDEMIC s
ENDGAME s
m ENDINGS*
ENDITED*
ENDITES*
ENDIVES*
ENDLEAF s
ENDLESS
ENDLONG
ENDMOST
ENDNOTE s
ENDOGEN sy
ENDOPOD s
ENDORSE der
s
ENDOWED
ENDOWER s
ENDPLAY s
ENDRINS*
ENDUING
ENDURED*
ENDURER*s
ENDURES*
ENDUROS*
b ENDWAYS
b ENDWISE
ENEMATA
ENEMIES
ENERGID s
ENFACED*
ENFACES*
ENFEOFF s
ENFEVER s
ENFLAME ds
t ENFOLDS*
ENFORCE drs
ENFRAME ds
ENGAGED*

ENGAGER*s
ENGAGES*
ENGILDS*
ENGINED*
ENGINES*
ENGIRDS*
ENGLISH
ENGLUTS*
ENGORGE ds
ENGRAFT s
ENGRAIL s
ENGRAIN s
ENGRAMS*
ENGRAVE drs
ENGROSS
ENGULFS*
ENHALOS*
ENHANCE drs
ENIGMAS*
ENISLED*
ENISLES*
ENJOINS*
ENJOYED
ENJOYER s
ENLACED*
ENLACES*
ENLARGE drs
ENLISTS*
ENLIVEN s
ENNEADS*
ENNOBLE drs
ENNUYEE*
ENOLASE s
mop ENOLOGY
v
ENOUGHS*
dr ENOUNCE ds
ENPLANE ds
ENQUIRE ds
ENQUIRY
ENRAGED*
ENRAGES*
ENROBED*
ENROBER*s
ENROBES*
ENROLLS*
ENROOTS*
ENSERFS*
ENSIGNS*
ENSILED*
ENSILES*
ENSKIED
ENSKIES
ENSKYED
ENSLAVE drs
ENSNARE drs
ENSNARL s
ENSOULS*
ENSUING
c ENSURED*
c ENSURER*s
c ENSURES*
v ENTAILS*
ENTASES
ENTASIA s
ENTASIS
ENTENTE s
ENTERAL*
ct ENTERED
ENTERER s
ENTERIC s
ENTERON s
ENTHRAL ls
ENTHUSE ds
ENTICED*
ENTICER*s
ENTICES*
ENTIRES*
ENTITLE ds
ENTOILS*
ENTOMBS*
ENTOPIC
ENTOZOA ln
ENTRAIN s
ENTRANT s
ENTRAPS*
ENTREAT sy
ENTREES*
gs ENTRIES
ENTROPY
ENTRUST s
ENTWINE ds
ENTWIST s
t ENURING
ENVELOP es
ENVENOM s

ENVIERS*
ENVIOUS
ENVIRON*s
ENVIROS*
ENVYING
ENWHEEL s
ENWINDS*
ENWOMBS*
ENWOUND
ENWRAPS*
ENZYMES*
ENZYMIC
EOBIONT s
n EOLITHS*
p EONISMS*
EOSINES*
EOSINIC
EPARCHS*
EPARCHY*
EPAULET s
EPAZOTE s
EPEEIST s
EPEIRIC
EPERGNE s
EPHEBES*
EPHEBIC*
EPHEBOI
EPHEBOS
EPHEBUS
EPHEDRA s
EPHORAL
EPIBOLY
EPICARP s
EPICENE s
EPICURE s
EPIDERM s
l EPIDOTE s
EPIGEAL
EPIGEAN
EPIGEIC
EPIGENE
EPIGONE*s
EPIGONI*c
EPIGONS*
EPIGRAM s
EPIGYNY
d EPILATE ds
EPILOGS*
EPIMERE*s
EPIMERS*
EPINAOI
EPINAOS
EPISCIA s
EPISODE s
EPISOME s
EPISTLE rs
EPITAPH s
EPITAXY
EPITHET s
EPITOME s
EPITOPE s
EPIZOIC
EPIZOON
EPOCHAL
EPONYMS*
EPONYMY*
EPOPEES*
EPOXIDE s
EPOXIED
EPOXIES
EPOXYED
EPSILON s
EQUABLE
EQUABLY
EQUALED
EQUALLY
EQUATED*
EQUATES*
EQUATOR s
EQUERRY
EQUINES*
EQUINOX
r EQUITES
ERASERS
*ERASING
ERASION s
*ERASURE s
t ERBIUMS*
ERECTED
ERECTER s
ERECTLY
*ERECTOR s
ERELONG
EREMITE s
EREMURI
EREPSIN s

ERETHIC
ERGATES*
ERGODIC
ERGOTIC
ERICOID
ERINGOS*
mv ERISTIC s
ERLKING s
ERMINED*
ERMINES*
*ERODENT
ERODING
EROSELY
EROSION s
EROSIVE
EROTICA*l
EROTICS*
EROTISM s
EROTIZE ds
ERRABLE
ERRANCY
ERRANDS*
ERRANTS*
ERRATAS*
ERRATIC s
ERRATUM
ERRHINE s
ERUCTED
ERUDITE
ERUPTED
ERYNGOS*
ESCALOP es
ESCAPED
ESCAPEE*s
ESCAPER*s
ESCAPES
ESCARPS
ESCHARS*
ESCHEAT s
ESCHEWS*
ESCOLAR s
ESCORTS*
ESCOTED
ESCROWS*
ESCUAGE s
ESCUDOS*
*ESERINE s
ESPANOL
ESPARTO s
ESPIALS*
b*ESPOUSE drs
ESPRITS
*ESPYING
*ESQUIRE ds
ESSAYED
ESSAYER s
ESSENCE s
ESSOINS*
gr*ESTATED*
grt*ESTATES*
ESTEEMS*
a ESTHETE s
af ESTIVAL
ESTRAYS
ESTREAT s
o ESTRINS*
o ESTRIOL s
o ESTRONE s
o ESTROUS
ESTRUAL
o*ESTRUMS*
ESTUARY
ETAGERE s
ETALONS
k ETAMINE*s
ETAMINS*
ETATISM s
ETATIST
ETCHANT s
f ETCHERS*
flr ETCHING s
ETERNAL s
ETESIAN s
m*ETHANES*
m ETHANOL s
ETHENES*
a ETHERIC
ETHICAL s
ETHINYL s
ETHIONS*
ETHMOID s
ETHNICS*
ETHOSES
m ETHOXYL*s
m ETHYLIC
ETHYNES*

ETHYNYL s
ETOILES
ETYMONS*
EUCAINE s
EUCHRED*
EUCHRES*
EUCLASE s
EUCRITE s
EUDEMON s
EUGENIA s
EUGENIC s
EUGENOL s
EUGLENA s
EULOGIA es
EUNUCHS*
EUPEPSY
EUPHONY
*EUPHROE s
EUPLOID sy
EUPNEAS*
EUPNEIC
EUPNOEA s
EURIPUS
EURYOKY
EUSTACY
EUSTASY
EUSTELE s
EVACUEE s
EVADERS*
EVADING
EVANGEL s
*EVANISH
EVASION s
EVASIVE
EVENERS*
EVENEST
EVENING s
r EVERTED
EVERTOR s
EVICTED
EVICTEE s
*EVICTOR s
EVIDENT
*EVILEST
EVILLER
EVINCED*
EVINCES*
EVITING
r EVOKERS*
r EVOKING
r*EVOLUTE s
dr EVOLVED*
r EVOLVER*s
dr EVOLVES*
r EVULSED*
EVULSES*
EVZONES*
EXABYTE s
EXACTAS*
EXACTED
EXACTER s
EXACTLY
EXACTOR s
EXALTED
EXALTER s
EXAMENS*
h EXAMINE der
s
EXAMPLE ds
EXAPTED
EXARCHS*
h EXARCHY*
EXCEEDS*
EXCEPTS*
EXCERPT s
EXCIDED*
EXCIDES*
EXCIMER s
EXCIPLE s
EXCISED*
EXCISES*
EXCITED*
EXCITER*s
EXCITES*
EXCITON s
EXCITOR s
EXCLAIM s
EXCLAVE s
EXCLUDE drs
EXCRETA l
EXCRETE drs
EXCUSED*
EXCUSER*s
EXCUSES*
EXECUTE drs
EXEDRAE*

EXEGETE s
EXEMPLA r
EXEMPTS*
EXERGUE s
EXERTED
EXHALED*
EXHALES*
EXHAUST s
EXHEDRA e
EXHIBIT s
EXHORTS*
EXHUMED*
EXHUMER*s
EXHUMES*
EXIGENT
EXILERS*
EXILIAN
EXILING
EXISTED
EXITING
EXOCARP s
EXODERM s
EXOGAMY
EXOGENS*
EXONYMS*
EXORDIA l
EXOSMIC
EXOTICA*
EXOTICS*
EXOTISM s
EXPANDS*
EXPANSE s
EXPECTS*
EXPENDS*
EXPENSE ds
EXPERTS*
EXPIATE ds
EXPIRED*
EXPIRER*s
EXPIRES*
EXPLAIN s
EXPLANT s
EXPLODE drs
EXPLOIT s
EXPLORE drs
EXPORTS*
EXPOSAL s
EXPOSED*
EXPOSER*s
EXPOSES*
EXPOSIT s
EXPOUND s
EXPRESS o
EXPULSE ds
EXPUNGE drs
EXSCIND s
EXSECTS*
EXSERTS*
EXTENDS*
EXTENTS*
EXTERNE*s
EXTERNS*
EXTINCT s
EXTOLLS*
EXTORTS*
EXTRACT s
EXTREMA
EXTREME rs
EXTRUDE drs
EXUDATE s
EXUDING
EXULTED
EXURBAN
EXURBIA s
EXUVIAE*
EXUVIAL*
EXUVIUM
EYASSES
EYEABLE
EYEBALL s
EYEBARS*
EYEBEAM s
EYEBOLT s
EYEBROW s
EYECUPS*
EYEFOLD s
EYEFULS*
EYEHOLE s
EYEHOOK s
EYELASH
EYELESS
EYELETS*
EYELIDS*
EYELIFT s
EYELIKE
EYESHOT s

EYESOME
EYESORE s
EYESPOT s
EYEWASH
EYEWEAR
EYEWINK s
FABBEST
FABLERS*
FABLIAU x
FABLING
FABRICS*
FABULAR
FACADES*
FACETED*
FACIALS*
FACIEND s
FACINGS*
FACTFUL
*FACTION s
FACTOID s
FACTORS
FACTORY*
*FACTUAL
FACTURE s
FACULAE*
FACULAR*
FACULTY
FADABLE
FADDIER
FADDISH
FADDISM s
FADDIST s
FADEDLY
FADEINS*
FADEOUT s
FADGING
FADINGS*
FADLIKE
FAERIES
FAGGING
FAGGOTS*
FAGOTED
FAGOTER s
FAIENCE s
*FAILING s
FAILLES*
FAILURE s
FAINEST
FAINTED
FAINTER s
FAINTLY
*FAIREST
FAIRIES
*FAIRING s
FAIRISH
*FAIRWAY s
FAITHED
FAITOUR s
FAJITAS*
FAKEERS*
FALAFEL s
FALBALA s
FALCATE d
FALCONS*
FALLACY
FALLALS*
FALLERS*
FALLING
FALLOFF s
FALLOUT s
FALLOWS
FALSELY
FALSEST
FALSIES*
FALSIFY
FALSITY
FALTERS
FAMINES
FAMULUS
FANATIC s
FANCIED
FANCIER s
FANCIES t
FANCIFY
FANCILY
FANDOMS*
FANEGAS*
FANFARE s
FANFICS*
FANFOLD s
FANIONS
FANJETS*
FANLIKE
FANNERS*
FANNIES
FANNING

FANTAIL s
FANTASM s
FANTAST s
FANTASY
FANTODS*
FANTOMS*
FANWISE
FANWORT s
FANZINE s
FAQUIRS*
FARADAY s
FARADIC
FARAWAY
FARCERS*
FARCEUR s
FARCIES*
*FARCING
FARDELS*
FARDING
FAREBOX
FARFALS*
FARFELS*
FARINAS*
FARINHA s
FARMERS
*FARMING s
FARNESS
FARRAGO
FARRIER sy
FARROWS
FARSIDE s
FARTHER
FARTLEK s
FASCIAE*
FASCIAL*
FASCIAS*
FASCINE s
FASCISM s
FASCIST s
*FASHING
FASHION s
FASTENS*
FASTEST
FASTING s
FATALLY
FATBACK s
FATBIRD s
FATEFUL
FATHEAD s
FATHERS*
FATHOMS*
FATIDIC
FATIGUE ds
FATLESS
FATLIKE
FATLING s
FATNESS
FATTENS*
*FATTEST
FATTIER
FATTIES t
FATTILY
FATTING
FATTISH
FATUITY
FATUOUS
FATWOOD s
FAUCALS*
FAUCETS*
FAUCIAL
FAULTED
FAUVISM s
FAUVIST s
FAVELAS*
FAVELLA s
FAVISMS*
FAVORED
FAVORER s
FAVOURS*
FAVUSES
FAWNERS*
FAWNIER
*FAWNING
FAZENDA s
FEARERS*
*FEARFUL
*FEARING
*FEASING
FEASTED
*FEASTER s
FEATEST
FEATHER sy
FEATURE ds
FEAZING
a FEBRILE
FECIALS*

FECULAE*
FEDAYEE n
FEDERAL s
FEDEXED
FEDEXES
FEDORAS*
FEEBLER*
FEEDBAG s
FEEDBOX
FEEDERS*
FEEDING
FEEDLOT s
FEELERS*
FEELESS
FEELING s
FEEZING
FEIGNED
FEIGNER s
FEIJOAS*
FEINTED
FELAFEL s
FELINES*
FELLAHS*
FELLATE ds
FELLERS*
FELLEST
FELLIES
FELLING
FELLOES*
FELLOWS*
FELONRY
FELSITE s
FELSPAR s
FELTING s
FELUCCA s
FELWORT s
FEMALES*
FEMINIE
FEMORAL*
FENAGLE ds
FENCERS*
FENCING s
FENDERS
*FENDING
FENLAND s
FENNECS*
FENNELS*
FENNIER
FENURON s
FEODARY
FEOFFED
FEOFFEE s
FEOFFER s
FEOFFOR s
FERBAMS*
FERLIES*
FERMATA s
FERMATE
FERMENT s
FERMION s
FERMIUM s
FERNERY
FERNIER
FERRATE s
FERRELS*
FERRETS*
FERRETY*
FERRIED
FERRIES
FERRITE s
FERROUS
FERRULE ds
FERRUMS*
FERTILE
FERULAE*
FERULAS*
FERULED*
FERULES*
FERVENT
FERVORS*
FERVOUR s
FESCUES*
FESSING
FESTERS
FESTIVE
FESTOON s
*FETCHED
*FETCHER s
*FETCHES
FETIALS*
FETIDLY
FETLOCK s
FETTERS*
FETTING
FETTLED*
FETTLES*

FETUSES
FEUDARY
FEUDING
FEUDIST s
FEVERED
FEWNESS
FEYNESS
FIACRES*
FIANCEE*s
FIANCES*
FIASCHI
FIASCOS*
FIBBERS*
FIBBING
FIBERED
FIBRILS*
FIBRINS*
FIBROID s
FIBROIN s
FIBROMA s
FIBROUS
FIBSTER s
FIBULAE*
FIBULAR*
FIBULAS*
FICKLER*
FICTILE
FICTION s
FICTIVE
FICUSES
FIDDLED*
FIDDLER*s
FIDDLES*
FIDEISM s
FIDEIST s
FIDGETS*
FIDGETY*
FIDGING
FIEFDOM s
FIELDED
FIELDER s
FIERCER*
FIERIER
FIERILY
FIESTAS*
FIFTEEN s
FIFTHLY
FIFTIES
*FIGGING
FIGHTER s
FIGMENT s
FIGURAL
FIGURED*
FIGURER*s
FIGURES*
FIGWORT s
FILAREE s
FILARIA eln
FILBERT s
FILCHED
FILCHER s
FILCHES
FILEMOT
FILETED
FILIATE ds
FILIBEG s
FILINGS*
FILLERS*
FILLETS*
FILLIES
FILLING s
FILLIPS*
FILMDOM s
FILMERS*
FILMIER
FILMILY
FILMING
FILMSET s
FILTERS*
FIMBLES*
FIMBRIA el
FINABLE
FINAGLE drs
FINALES*
FINALIS emt
FINALLY
FINANCE ds
FINBACK s
*FINCHES
FINDERS*
FINDING s
FINESSE ds
FINFISH
FINFOOT s
FINGERS*
FINIALS*

FINICAL
FINICKY
FINIKIN g
FININGS*
FINISES
FINITES*
*FINKING
FINLESS
FINLIKE
FINMARK s
FINNIER
*FINNING
FIPPLES*
FIREARM s
FIREBOX
FIREBUG s
FIREDOG s
FIREFLY
FIRELIT
FIREMAN
FIREMEN
FIREPAN s
FIREPOT s
FIRINGS*
FIRKINS*
FIRMANS*
FIRMERS*
FIRMEST
FIRMING
FIRRIER
FIRSTLY
FISCALS*
FISHERS*
FISHERY*
FISHEYE s
FISHGIG s
FISHIER
FISHILY
FISHING s
FISHNET s
FISHWAY s
FISSATE
FISSILE
FISSION s
FISSURE ds
FISTFUL s
FISTING
FISTULA ers
FITCHEE
*FITCHES
FITCHET s
FITCHEW s
FITMENT s
FITNESS
FITTERS*
FITTEST
FITTING s
FIXABLE
FIXATED*
FIXATES*
FIXATIF s
FIXEDLY
FIXINGS*
FIXTURE s
FIXURES*
FIZGIGS*
FIZZERS*
FIZZIER
FIZZING
FIZZLED*
FIZZLES*
FJORDIC
FLACCID
*FLACKED
FLACONS*
*FLAGGED
*FLAGGER s
FLAGMAN
FLAGMEN
FLAGONS*
FLAILED
FLAKERS
*FLAKIER
FLAKILY
*FLAKING
FLAMBEE*d
FLAMBES*
FLAMENS*
FLAMERS*
FLAMIER
*FLAMING o
*FLAMMED
FLANEUR s
FLANGED*
FLANGER*s
FLANGES*

FLANKED
FLANKEN
*FLANKER s
FLANNEL s
*FLAPPED
*FLAPPER s
FLAREUP s
FLARING
*FLASHED
*FLASHER s
*FLASHES
FLASKET s
FLATBED s
FLATCAP s
FLATCAR s
FLATLET s
FLATTED
*FLATTEN s
*FLATTER sy
FLATTOP s
FLAUNTS*
FLAUNTY*
FLAUTAS*
FLAVINE*s
FLAVINS*
FLAVONE s
FLAVORS*
FLAVORY*
FLAVOUR sy
FLAWIER
*FLAWING
FLAXIER
FLAYERS
*FLAYING
FLEABAG s
FLEAPIT s
FLECHES
FLECKED
FLEDGED*
FLEDGES
FLEECED*
FLEECER*s
FLEECES*
FLEEING
*FLEERED
FLEETED
FLEETER
FLEETLY
FLEHMEN s
FLEMISH
FLENSED
FLENSER*s
FLENSES
FLESHED
FLESHER s
FLESHES
FLESHLY
FLEURON s
FLEXILE
FLEXING
FLEXION s
FLEXORS*
FLEXURE s
FLEYING
*FLICKED
*FLICKER sy
FLIGHTS
FLIGHTY*
FLINDER s
*FLINGER s
*FLINTED
*FLIPPED
*FLIPPER s
FLIRTED
FLIRTER s
FLITING
FLITTED
*FLITTER s
FLIVVER s
FLOATED
FLOATEL s
FLOATER s
FLOCCED
FLOCCUS
*FLOCKED
*FLOGGED
*FLOGGER s
FLOKATI s
FLOODED
FLOODER s
FLOORED
FLOORER s
FLOOSIE s
FLOOZIE s
*FLOPPED
*FLOPPER s

FLORALS*
FLORETS*
FLORINS*
FLORIST s
FLORUIT s
FLOSSED
FLOSSER s
*FLOSSES
FLOSSIE rs
FLOTAGE s
FLOTSAM s
FLOUNCE ds
FLOUNCY
*FLOURED
*FLOUTED
FLOUTER s
FLOWAGE s
FLOWERS
FLOWERY
*FLOWING
FLUBBED
*FLUBBER s
FLUBDUB s
FLUENCY
FLUERIC s
*FLUFFED
FLUFFER s
FLUIDAL
FLUIDIC s
FLUIDLY
FLUKIER
FLUKILY
FLUKING
FLUMING
*FLUMMOX
*FLUMPED
FLUNKED
*FLUNKER s
FLUNKEY s
FLUNKIE s
FLUORIC
FLUORID es
FLUORIN es
*FLUSHED
*FLUSHER s
*FLUSHES t
*FLUSTER s
FLUTERS*
FLUTIER
*FLUTING s
*FLUTIST s
a FLUTTER sy
FLUVIAL
FLUXING
FLUXION s
FLYABLE
FLYAWAY s
FLYBELT s
FLYBLEW
FLYBLOW ns
FLYBOAT s
FLYBOYS*
FLYINGS
FLYLEAF
FLYLESS
FLYOFFS*
FLYOVER s
FLYPAST s
FLYTIER s
FLYTING s
FLYTRAP s
FLYWAYS*
FOALING
FOAMERS*
FOAMIER
FOAMILY
FOAMING
FOBBING
FOCALLY
FOCUSED
FOCUSER s
FOCUSES
FODDERS*
FOETORS*
FOGBOWS*
FOGDOGS*
FOGGAGE s
FOGGERS*
FOGGIER
FOGGILY
FOGGING
FOGHORN s
FOGLESS
FOGYISH
FOGYISM s
FOIBLES*

*FOILING
FOINING
FOISONS*
FOISTED
FOLACIN s
FOLATES*
FOLDERS*
FOLDING
FOLDOUT s
FOLDUPS*
FOLIAGE ds
FOLIATE ds
FOLIOED
FOLIOSE*
FOLIOUS
FOLIUMS*
FOLKIER*
FOLKIES*t
FOLKISH
FOLKMOT es
FOLKWAY s
FOLLIES
FOLLOWS*
FOMENTS*
FOMITES*
FONDANT s
FONDEST
FONDING
FONDLED*
FONDLER*s
FONDLES*
FONDUED*
FONDUES*
FONTINA s
FOODIES*
FOOLERY
FOOLING
FOOLISH
FOOTAGE s
FOOTBAG s
FOOTBOY s
FOOTERS*
FOOTIER*
FOOTIES*t
FOOTING s
FOOTLED*
FOOTLER*s
FOOTLES*s
FOOTMAN
FOOTMEN
FOOTPAD s
FOOTSIE s
FOOTWAY s
FOOZLED*
FOOZLER*s
FOOZLES*
FOPPERY
FOPPING
FOPPISH
FORAGED*
FORAGER*s
FORAGES*
FORAMEN s
FORAYED
FORAYER s
FORBADE*
FORBARE
FORBEAR s
FORBIDS*
FORBODE ds
FORBORE
FORCEPS
FORCERS*
FORCING
FORDING
FORDOES
FORDONE
FOREARM s
FOREBAY s
FOREBYE*
FOREDID
FOREGUT s
FOREIGN
FORELEG s
FOREMAN
FOREMEN
FOREPAW s
FORERAN k
FORERUN s
FORESAW
FORESEE nrs
FORESTS*
FORETOP s
FOREVER s
FORFEIT s
FORFEND s

FORGAVE
FORGERS*
FORGERY*
FORGETS*
FORGING s
FORGIVE nrs
FORGOER s
FORGOES
*FORGONE
FORINTS*
FORKERS*
FORKFUL s
FORKIER
FORKING
FORLORN
FORMALS*
FORMANT s
FORMATE*s
FORMATS*
FORMERS
FORMFUL
FORMICA*s
FORMING
FORMOLS*
FORMULA es
FORMYLS*
FORNENT
FORSAKE nrs
FORSOOK
FORTIES
FORTIFY
FORTUNE ds
FORWARD s
FORWENT
FORWORN
FOSSATE
FOSSICK s
FOSSILS*
FOSTERS*
FOUETTE s
FOULARD s
FOULEST
FOULING s
FOUNDED
FOUNDER s
FOUNDRY
FOURGON s
FOURTHS*
FOVEATE d
FOVEOLA ers
FOVEOLE st
FOWLERS*
FOWLING s
FOWLPOX
FOXFIRE s
FOXFISH
FOXHOLE s
FOXHUNT s
FOXIEST
FOXINGS*
*FOXLIKE
FOXSKIN s
*FOXTAIL s
FOXTROT s
FOZIEST
FRACTAL s
FRACTED
FRACTUR es
FRACTUS
FRAENUM s
*FRAGGED
FRAGILE
*FRAILER
FRAILLY
FRAILTY
FRAISES
FRAKTUR s
FRAMERS*
FRAMING s
*FRANKED
*FRANKER s
*FRANKLY
FRANTIC
FRAPPED
FRAPPES*
FRASSES
FRATERS
FRAUGHT s
*FRAYING s
FRAZILS*
FRAZZLE ds
FREAKED
FRECKLE ds
FRECKLY
FREEBEE s
FREEBIE s

FREEDOM s
FREEING
FREEMAN
FREEMEN
FREESIA s
FREEWAY s
FREEZER*s
FREEZES*
FREIGHT s
FRENULA r
FRENUMS*
FRESCOS*
FRESHED
FRESHEN s
FRESHER
*FRESHES t
FRESHET s
FRESHLY
FRESNEL s
FRETFUL
FRETSAW s
*FRETTED
FRETTER s
FRIABLE
FRIARLY
FRIBBLE drs
FRIDGES
FRIENDS*
FRIEZES*
FRIGATE s
*FRIGGED
FRIGHTS
FRIJOLE*s
*FRILLED
FRILLER s
FRINGED
FRINGES*
FRISBEE s
FRISEES*
FRISEUR s
*FRISKED
*FRISKER s
FRISKET s
FRISSON s
FRITTED
*FRITTER s
*FRITZES
FRIVOLS*
FRIZERS*
FRIZING
FRIZZED
FRIZZER s
FRIZZES
FRIZZLE drs
FRIZZLY
*FROCKED
FROGEYE ds
FROGGED
FROGLET s
FROGMAN
FROGMEN
FROLICS*
FROMAGE s
FRONDED
FRONTAL s
FRONTED
FRONTER
FRONTES
FRONTON s
FROSTED s
FROTHED
FROTHER s
FROUNCE ds
FROWARD
FROWNED
FROWNER s
FROWSTS*
FROWSTY*
*FRUGGED
FRUITED
FRUITER s
FRUSTUM s
FRYABLE
FRYPANS*
FUBBING
FUBSIER
FUCHSIA s
FUCHSIN es
FUCOIDS*
FUCOSES*
FUCUSES
FUDDIES
FUDDLED*
FUDDLES*
FUDGING
FUEHRER s

FUELERS*
FUELING
FUELLED
FUELLER s
FUGALLY
FUGATOS*
FUGGIER
FUGGILY
FUGGING
FUGLING
FUGUING
FUGUIST s
FUHRERS*
FULCRUM s
FULFILL*s
FULFILS*
FULGENT
FULHAMS*
FULLAMS*
FULLERS*
FULLERY*
FULLEST
FULLING
FULMARS*
FULMINE ds
FULNESS
FULSOME
FULVOUS
FUMARIC
FUMBLED*
FUMBLER*s
FUMBLES
FUMETTE s
FUMIEST
FUMULUS
FUNCTOR s
FUNDERS*
FUNDING
FUNERAL s
*FUNFAIR s
FUNFEST s
FUNGALS*
FUNGOES
FUNGOID s
FUNGOUS
FUNICLE s
FUNKERS*
FUNKIAS*
FUNKIER
FUNKILY
FUNKING
FUNNELS*
FUNNEST
FUNNIER
FUNNIES t
FUNNILY
FUNNING
FUNPLEX
FURANES*
FURBISH
FURCATE ds
FURCULA er
FURIOSO
FURIOUS
FURLERS*
FURLESS
FURLING
FURLONG s
FURMETY
FURMITY
FURNACE ds
FURNISH
FURORES*
FURRIER sy
FURRILY
FURRING s
FURROWS*
FURROWY*
FURTHER s
FURTIVE
FURZIER
FUSAINS*
FUSARIA
FUSCOUS
FUSIBLE
FUSIBLY
FUSILLI s
FUSIONS*
FUSSERS*
FUSSIER
FUSSILY
FUSSING
FUSSPOT s
FUSTIAN s
FUSTICS*
FUSTIER

FUSTILY
FUTHARC s
FUTHARK s
FUTHORC s
FUTHORK s
FUTTOCK s
FUTURAL
FUTURES*
FUTZING
FUZZIER
FUZZILY
FUZZING
FYLFOTS*
GABBARD s
GABBART s
GABBERS*
GABBIER
GABBING
GABBLED*
GABBLER*s
GABBLES*
GABBROS*
GABELLE ds
GABFEST s
GABIONS*
GABLING
GABOONS*
GADDERS
*GADDING
GADGETS*
GADGETY*
GADOIDS*
GADROON s
GADWALL s
GAFFERS*
GAFFING
GAGAKUS*
GAGGERS
GAGGING
GAGGLED*
GAGGLES*
GAGSTER s
GAHNITE s
GAINERS*
GAINFUL
GAINING
GAINSAY s
GAITERS*
GAITING
GALABIA s
GALAGOS*
GALANGA ls
GALATEA s
GALAXES
GALEATE d
GALENAS*
GALENIC
GALERES*
GALETTE s
GALILEE s
GALIOTS*
GALIPOT s
GALLANT s
GALLATE s
GALLEIN s
GALLEON s
GALLERY
GALLETA*s
GALLETS*
GALLEYS
GALLFLY
GALLICA*ns
*GALLIED
*GALLIES
GALLING
GALLIOT s
*GALLIUM s
GALLNUT s
GALLONS*
GALLOON s
GALLOOT s
GALLOPS*
GALLOUS
*GALLOWS
GALOOTS*
GALOPED
GALORES*
GALOSHE*ds
GALUMPH s
GALYACS*
GALYAKS*
GAMBADE s
GAMBADO s
GAMBIAS*
GAMBIER s
GAMBIRS*

GAMBITS
GAMBLED
*GAMBLER*s
GAMBLES
GAMBOGE s
GAMBOLS*
GAMBREL s
GAMELAN s
GAMETAL
a GAMETES*
GAMETIC
GAMIEST
*GAMINES*s
GAMINGS*
GAMMERS*
GAMMIER
GAMMING
GAMMONS*
GANACHE s
GANDERS*
GANGERS
GANGING
GANGLIA lr
GANGREL s
GANGSTA s
GANGUES*
GANGWAY s
GANJAHS*
GANNETS*
GANOIDS*
GANTLET s
GAOLERS*
GAOLING
GAPLESS
GAPOSIS
GAPPIER
GAPPING
GARAGED*
GARAGES*
GARBAGE sy
GARBAGY
GARBING
GARBLED*
GARBLER*s
GARBLES*s
GARBOIL s
GARCONS*
GARDANT
GARDENS*
GARFISH
GARGETS*
GARGETY*
GARGLED
GARGLER*s
GARGLES
GARIGUE s
GARLAND s
GARLICS*
GARMENT s
GARNERS*
GARNETS*
GARNISH
GAROTED*
GAROTES*
GAROTTE drs
GARPIKE s
GARRETS*
GARRING
GARRONS*
GARROTE drs
GARTERS*
GARVEYS*
GASBAGS*
GASCONS*
GASEITY
GASEOUS
GASHEST*
*GASHING
GASKETS*
*GASKING*s
GASKINS*
GASLESS
GASOHOL s
GASPERS
GASPING
GASSERS*
GASSIER
GASSILY
GASSING s
GASTERS
GASTING
*GASTRAL
GASTREA s
GASTRIC
GASTRIN s
GATEAUS*

GATEAUX*
GATEMAN
GATEMEN
GATEWAY s
GATHERS*
GATINGS*
GAUCHER*
GAUCHOS*
GAUDERY
GAUDIER
GAUDIES t
GAUDILY
GAUFFER s
GAUGERS
GAUGING
GAUMING
GAUNTER
*GAUNTLY
GAUNTRY
GAUSSES
GAUZIER
GAUZILY
GAVAGES*
GAVELED
GAVIALS*
GAVOTTE ds
GAWKERS*
GAWKIER
GAWKIES t
GAWKILY
GAWKING
GAWKISH
GAWPERS*
GAWPING
GAYDARS*
GAYNESS
GAZABOS*
GAZANIA s
GAZEBOS*
GAZELLE s
GAZETTE ds
GAZUMPS*
GEARBOX
*GEARING s
GECKING
GECKOES
GEEGAWS*
GEEKDOM s
GEEKIER
GEEZERS*
GEISHAS*
GELABLE
GELADAS*
GELANTS*
GELATED
GELATES
GELATIN*egs
GELATIS*
GELATOS*
GELCAPS*
GELDERS
GELDING s
GELIDLY
GELLANT s
GELLING
GEMINAL
GEMLIKE
GEMMATE ds
GEMMIER
GEMMILY
GEMMING
GEMMULE s
GEMOTES
GEMSBOK s
GENDERS
GENERAL*s
GENERIC s
a GENESES
a GENESIS
a GENETIC s
GENETTE s
GENEVAS*
GENIPAP s
GENITAL s
GENITOR s
GENOISE s
GENOMES*
GENOMIC s
GENSENG s
GENTEEL
GENTIAN s
GENTILE*s
GENTLED*
GENTLER*
GENTLES*t
GENTOOS*

GENUINE
GENUSES
GEODESY*
GEODUCK s
GEOIDAL
GEOLOGY
GEORGIC s
GERBERA s
GERBILS*
GERENTS*
GERENUK s
GERMANE*
GERMANS*
GERMENS*
GERMIER
GERMINA l
GERUNDS*
GESSOED
GESSOES
GESTALT s
GESTAPO s
*GESTATE ds
GESTURE drs
GETABLE
GETAWAY s
GETTERS*
GETTING
GEWGAWS*
GEYSERS*
GHARIAL s
GHARRIS*
GHASTLY
GHAZIES
GHERKIN s
GHETTOS*
GHIBLIS*
GHILLIE s
*GHOSTED
*GHOSTLY
GHOULIE s
GIAOURS*
GIARDIA s
GIBBERS*
GIBBETS*
GIBBING
GIBBONS*
GIBBOSE
GIBBOUS
GIBLETS*
GIBSONS*
GIDDIED
GIDDIER
GIDDIES t
GIDDILY
GIDDYAP
GIDDYUP
GIFTEES*
GIFTING
GIGABIT s
GIGATON s
*GIGGING
GIGGLED*
GIGGLER*s
GIGGLES*
GIGLETS*
GIGLOTS*
GIGOLOS*
GILBERT s
GILDERS*
GILDING s
GILLERS*
GILLIED*
GILLIES*
GILLING
GILLNET s
GIMBALS*
GIMLETS*
GIMMALS*
GIMMICK sy
GIMMIES
GIMPIER
*GIMPING
GINGALL*s
GINGALS*
GINGELI s
GINGELY
GINGERS*
GINGERY*
GINGHAM s
GINGILI s
GINGIVA el
GINGKOS*
GINKGOS*
a*GINNERS*
GINNIER
*GINNING s

GINSENG s
GIPPERS*
GIPPING
GIPSIED
GIPSIES
GIRAFFE s
GIRASOL es
GIRDERS*
GIRDING
GIRDLED*
GIRDLER*s
GIRDLES*
GIRLIER*
GIRLIES*t
GIRLISH
GIRNING
GIROLLE s
GIROSOL s
GIRSHES
GIRTHED
GIRTING
GISARME s
GITANOS*
GITTERN s
GITTING*
*GIZZARD s
GJETOST s
GLACEED
GLACIAL
*GLACIER s
GLADDED
GLADDEN s
*GLADDER
GLADIER
GLAIKET
GLAIKIT
GLAIRED
GLAIRES*
GLAIVED*
GLAIVES*
GLAMORS*
GLAMOUR s
GLANCED
*GLANCER*s
GLANCES
GLANDES
GLARIER
GLARING
GLASSED
*GLASSES
*GLASSIE rs
GLAZERS*
*GLAZIER sy
*GLAZILY
*GLAZING s
GLEAMED
GLEAMER s
*GLEANED
*GLEANER s
GLEEFUL
GLEEKED
GLEEMAN
GLEEMEN
GLEETED
GLENOID
GLEYING s
GLIADIN es
GLIBBER
GLIDERS*
GLIDING
*GLIMING
a*GLIMMER s
GLIMPSE drs
*GLINTED
GLIOMAS*
*GLISTEN s
*GLISTER s
GLITCHY*
a*GLITTER sy
GLITZED
GLITZES
GLOATED
GLOATER s
*GLOBATE d
GLOBING*
GLOBINS*
GLOBOID s
GLOBOSE
GLOBOUS
*GLOBULE s
GLOCHID s
GLOMERA
GLOMMED
GLONOIN s
*GLOOMED
*GLOPPED

GLORIAS*
GLORIED
*GLORIES
GLORIFY
GLOSSAE*
GLOSSAL*
GLOSSAS*
GLOSSED
GLOSSER s
*GLOSSES
GLOTTAL
GLOTTIC
GLOTTIS
*GLOUTED
GLOVERS
*GLOVING
GLOWERS
GLOWFLY
*GLOWING
GLOZING
GLUCANS*
GLUCOSE s
GLUEING
GLUEPOT s
*GLUGGED
GLUIEST
GLUMMER
*GLUTEAL
GLUTENS*
GLUTEUS
GLUTTED
GLUTTON sy
GLYCANS*
GLYCINE*s
GLYCINS*
GLYCOLS*
GLYCYLS*
GLYPHIC
GLYPTIC s
GNARLED
GNARRED
GNASHED
GNASHES
GNATHAL
GNATHIC
GNAWERS*
GNAWING s
GNOCCHI
GNOMISH
GNOMIST s
GNOMONS*
a GNOSTIC s
GOADING
GOALIES*
GOALING
GOANNAS*
GOATEED*
GOATEES*
GOATISH
GOBANGS*
GOBBETS*
GOBBING
GOBBLED*
GOBBLER*s
GOBBLES*
GOBIOID s
GOBLETS*
GOBLINS*
GOBONEE
GODDAMN*s
GODDAMS*
GODDESS
GODDING
GODETIA s
GODHEAD s
GODHOOD s
GODLESS
GODLIER
GODLIKE
GODLILY
GODLING s
GODOWNS*
GODROON s
GODSEND s
GODSHIP s
GODSONS*
GODWITS*
GOFFERS
GOGGLED*
GOGGLER*s
GOGGLES*
GOGLETS*
GOITERS*
GOITRES*
GOLDARN s
GOLDBUG s
*GOLDEST
GOLDEYE s
GOLDURN s
GOLFERS*
GOLFING s
GOLIARD s
GOLIATH s
GOLOSHE*s
GOMBEEN s
GOMERAL s
GOMEREL s
GOMERIL s
GOMUTIS*
GONADAL
GONADIC
GONDOLA s
GONGING
GONIDIA l
GONIDIC
GONIFFS*
GONOPHS*
GOOBERS*
GOODBYE*s
GOODBYS*
GOODIES*
GOODISH
GOODMAN
GOODMEN
GOOFIER
GOOFILY
GOOFING
GOOGOLS*
GOOIEST
GOOMBAH s
GOOMBAY s
GOONEYS*
GOONIER*
GOONIES*t
GOOPIER
GOORALS*
GOOSIER
GOOSING
GOPHERS*
GORCOCK s
GORDITA s
GORGERS*
GORGETS*
GORGING
GORGONS*
GORHENS*
GORIEST
GORILLA s
GORMAND s
GORMING
GORSIER
GOSHAWK s
GOSLING s
GOSPELS*
GOSPORT s
GOSSANS*
GOSSIPS*
GOSSIPY*
GOSSOON s
GOTCHAS*
GOTHICS*
GOTHITE s
GOUACHE s
GOUGERS*
GOUGING
GOULASH
GOURAMI s
GOURDES*
GOURMET s
GOUTIER
GOUTILY
GOVERNS*
GOWANED
*GOWNING
GRABBED
GRABBER s
*GRABBLE drs
GRABENS*
GRACILE s
*GRACING
*GRACKLE s
GRADATE ds
GRADERS*
GRADINE*s
GRADING*
GRADINS*
GRADUAL s
*GRAFTED
*GRAFTER s
GRAHAMS*
*GRAINED
GRAINER s
GRAMARY e
GRAMMAR*s
GRAMMAS*
GRAMMES*
GRAMPAS*
GRAMPUS
GRANARY
GRANDAD s
GRANDAM es
GRANDEE s
GRANDER
GRANDLY
GRANDMA s
GRANDPA s
*GRANGER*s
GRANGES
GRANITA s
GRANITE s
GRANNIE s
GRANOLA s
*GRANTED
GRANTEE s
*GRANTER s
GRANTOR s
GRANULE s
GRAPERY
GRAPHED
a GRAPHIC s
*GRAPIER
GRAPLIN es
GRAPNEL s
GRAPPAS*
GRAPPLE drs
*GRASPED
*GRASPER s
GRASSED
GRASSES
GRATERS
*GRATIFY
*GRATINE*e
*GRATING*s
GRATINS*
GRAUPEL s
GRAVELS
GRAVELY*
GRAVERS
GRAVEST*
GRAVIDA*es
GRAVIES
*GRAVING
GRAVITY
GRAVLAX
GRAVURE s
GRAYEST
*GRAYING
GRAYISH
GRAYLAG s
GRAYOUT s
GRAZERS
GRAZIER s
*GRAZING s
GREASED*
GREASER*s
GREASES*
GREATEN s
GREATER
GREATLY
GREAVED
GREAVES
GRECIZE ds
a GREEING
GREENED
GREENER y
GREENIE rs
GREENLY
GREENTH s
GREETED
GREETER s
GREIGES*
GREISEN s
GREMIAL s
GREMLIN s
GREMMIE s
GRENADE s
GREYEST
GREYHEN s
GREYING
GREYISH
GREYLAG s
GRIBBLE s
*GRIDDED
*GRIDDER s
*GRIDDLE ds
*GRIDING
GRIEVED*
*GRIEVER*s
GRIEVES*
GRIFFES*
GRIFFIN s
GRIFFON s
*GRIFTED
GRIFTER s
GRIGRIS*
GRILLED
GRILLER*sy
GRILLES
GRILSES*
GRIMACE drs
*GRIMIER
GRIMILY
*GRIMING
*GRIMMER
*GRINDED
GRINDER sy
GRINNED
GRINNER s
GRIPERS*
GRIPIER
*GRIPING
GRIPMAN
GRIPMEN
GRIPPED
*GRIPPER*s
GRIPPES*
*GRIPPLE
GRISKIN s
GRISONS*
GRISTER s
GRISTLE s
GRISTLY
GRITTED
*GRITTER s
GRIVETS
GRIZZLE drs
GRIZZLY
GROANED
GROANER s
GROCERS*
GROCERY*
GRODIER
GROGRAM s
GROINED
GROKKED
GROMMET s
*GROOMED
*GROOMER s
GROOVED*
GROOVER*s
GROOVES*
GROPERS
*GROPING
GROSSED
GROSSER s
GROSSES t
GROSSLY
GROTTOS*
GROUCHY*
GROUNDS
*GROUPED
GROUPER s
GROUPIE s
GROUSED
*GROUSER*s
GROUSES
*GROUTED
*GROUTER s
GROVELS*
GROWERS
*GROWING
GROWLED
GROWLER s
GROWNUP s
GROWTHS
GROWTHY*
GROYNES*
*GRUBBED
*GRUBBER s
GRUDGED*
GRUDGER*s
GRUDGES*
GRUELED
GRUELER s
*GRUFFED
GRUFFER
*GRUFFLY
GRUGRUS*
*GRUMBLE drs
*GRUMBLY
*GRUMMER
GRUMMET s
GRUMOSE
GRUMOUS
GRUMPED
GRUMPHY
GRUNGER*s
GRUNGES*
GRUNION s
GRUNTED
GRUNTER s
GRUNTLE ds
GRUSHIE
GRUTTEN
GRUYERE s
GRYPHON s
GUAIACS*
GUANACO s
GUANASE s
GUANAYS*
GUANINE*s
GUANINS*
GUARANA s
GUARANI s
GUARDED
GUARDER s
GUAYULE s
GUDGEON s
GUENONS*
GUERDON s
GUESSED
GUESSER s
GUESSES
GUESTED
GUFFAWS*
GUGGLED*
GUGGLES*
GUGLETS*
GUIDERS*
GUIDING
GUIDONS*
GUILDER s
GUILING
GUIMPES*
GUINEAS*
GUIPURE s
GUISARD s
GUISING
GUITARS*
GULCHES
GULDENS*
GULFIER
GULFING
GULLETS*
GULLEYS*
GULLIED
GULLIES
GULLING
GULPERS*
GULPIER
GULPING
GUMBALL s
GUMBOIL s
GUMBOOT s
GUMDROP s
GUMLESS
GUMLIKE
GUMLINE s
GUMMATA
GUMMERS*
GUMMIER
GUMMING
GUMMITE s
GUMMOSE s
GUMMOUS
GUMSHOE ds
GUMTREE s
GUMWEED s
GUMWOOD s
GUNBOAT s
GUNDOGS*
GUNFIRE s
GUNITES
GUNKIER
*GUNLESS
*GUNLOCK s
GUNNELS*
GUNNERS*
GUNNERY*
GUNNIES
GUNNING s
GUNPLAY s
GUNROOM s
GUNSELS*
*GUNSHIP s
GUNSHOT s
GUNWALE s
GUPPIES
*GURGING
GURGLED*
GURGLES*
GURGLET*s
GURNARD s
GURNETS*
GURNEYS*
GURRIES
GURSHES
GUSHERS
GUSHIER
GUSHILY
GUSHING
GUSSETS*
GUSSIED*
GUSSIES*
GUSTIER
GUSTILY
GUSTING
GUSTOES
GUTLESS
GUTLIKE
GUTSIER
GUTSILY
GUTTATE d
GUTTERS
GUTTERY*
GUTTIER
GUTTING
GUTTLED*
GUTTLER*s
GUTTLES*
GUYLINE s
GUZZLED*
GUZZLER*s
GUZZLES*
GWEDUCK*s
GWEDUCS*
GYMNAST s
GYNECIA
GYNECIC
GYPLURE s
GYPPERS*
GYPPING
GYPSIED
GYPSIES
GYPSTER s
GYPSUMS*
GYRALLY
GYRASES*
GYRATED*
GYRATES*
GYRATOR sy
GYRENES*
GYTTJAS*
HABITAN st
HABITAT s
HABITED
HABITUE s
HABITUS
HABOOBS*
HACHURE ds
HACKBUT s
HACKEES
w HACKERS*
HACKIES*
stw HACKING
s HACKLED*
s HACKLER*s
s HACKLES*
HACKMAN
HACKMEN
HACKNEY s
HACKSAW ns
c HADARIM
HADDEST
s HADDOCK s
HADITHS*
HADJEES*
HADRONS*
HAEMINS*
HAEMOID
HAFFETS*
HAFFITS*
HAFIZES
HAFNIUM s
HAFTARA hs
HAFTERS
s HAFTING
HAGADIC
HAGBORN
HAGBUSH
HAGBUTS*
HAGDONS*
HAGFISH
*HAGGADA hs
HAGGARD s
s HAGGING
HAGGISH*
HAGGLED*
HAGGLER*s
HAGGLES*
HAGRIDE rs
HAGRODE
HAHNIUM s
HAILERS*
*HAILING
HAIMISH
HAIRCAP s
HAIRCUT s
HAIRDOS*
*HAIRIER
HAIRNET s
HAIRPIN s
HAKEEMS*
HALACHA s
HALAKAH s
HALAKHA hs
HALAKIC
HALALAH*s
HALALAS*
HALAVAH s
HALBERD s
HALBERT s
HALCYON s
HALFWAY
HALIBUT s
HALIDES*
HALIDOM es
HALITES*
HALITUS
c HALLAHS*
HALLELS*
HALLOAS*
HALLOED
HALLOES
HALLOOS*
c HALLOTH*
s*HALLOWS*
HALLWAY s
HALOGEN s
HALOIDS*
HALOING
HALTERE*ds
HALTERS
HALTING
HALVAHS*
HALVERS
HALVING
HALYARD s
HAMADAS*
HAMATES*
HAMAULS*
HAMBONE ds
HAMBURG s
HAMLETS*
HAMMADA s
HAMMALS*
HAMMAMS*
s HAMMERS*
HAMMIER
HAMMILY
sw HAMMING
HAMMOCK s
c HAMPERS*
HAMSTER s
HAMULAR
HAMULUS
HAMZAHS*
HANAPER s
HANDBAG s
HANDCAR st
HANDERS*
HANDFUL s
HANDGUN s
HANDIER
HANDILY
HANDING
HANDLED*
c HANDLER*s
HANDLES*s
HANDOFF s
HANDOUT s
HANDSAW s
HANDSEL s
HANDSET s
HANGARS*
HANGDOG s
c*HANGERS*
cw HANGING s
HANGMAN
HANGMEN
HANGOUT s
HANGTAG s

HANGUPS*
t HANKERS*
HANKIES*
st HANKING
HANSELS*
HANSOMS*
c*HANTING
HANTLES*
HANUMAN s
HAPAXES
HAPKIDO s
HAPLESS
*HAPLITE s
HAPLOID sy
HAPLONT s
HAPPENS*
HAPPIER
HAPPILY
cw HAPPING
HAPTENE*s
HAPTENS*
HARBORS
*HARBOUR s
HARDENS*
HARDEST
HARDHAT s
HARDIER
HARDIES t
HARDILY
HARDPAN s
HARDSET
HARDTOP s
HAREEMS*
HARELIP s
HARIANA s
HARICOT s
HARIJAN s
HARISSA s
HARKENS*
cs HARKING
HARLOTS*
c*HARMERS*
*HARMFUL
HARMINE*s
cp*HARMING*
HARMINS*
HARMONY
HARNESS
s HARPERS*
s HARPIES
s HARPING*s
HARPINS*
HARPIST s
HARPOON s
HARRIED
c HARRIER s
g HARRIES
HARROWS
HARSHEN s
HARSHER
HARSHLY
HARSLET s
HARTALS*
HARUMPH s
HARVEST s
*HASHING
HASHISH
HASLETS*
HASPING
HASSELS*
HASSIUM s
HASSLED*
HASSLES*
HASSOCK s
HASTATE
c HASTENS*
HASTIER
HASTILY
HASTING
HATABLE
HATBAND s
t HATCHED
HATCHEL s
t HATCHER sy
t HATCHES
HATCHET s
HATEFUL
HATFULS*
HATLESS
HATLIKE
HATPINS*
HATRACK s
HATREDS*
HATSFUL
cs HATTERS*
c HATTING

HAUBERK s
HAUGHTY
HAULAGE s
HAULERS*
HAULIER s
s HAULING
c HAUNTED
c HAUNTER s
HAUSENS*
HAUTBOY s
*HAUTEUR s
HAVARTI s
HAVENED
HAVERED
HAVEREL s
HAVIORS*
HAVIOUR s
HAWALAS*
HAWKERS*
HAWKEYS*
HAWKIES*
HAWKING s
HAWKISH
HAWSERS*
HAYCOCK s
HAYFORK s
HAYINGS*
HAYLAGE s
HAYLOFT s
HAYMOWS*
HAYRACK s
HAYRICK s
HAYRIDE s
HAYSEED s
HAYWARD s
HAYWIRE s
c HAZANIM
HAZARDS*
HAZELLY
HAZIEST
HAZINGS*
HAZMATS*
c HAZZANS*
HEADEND s
HEADERS*
HEADFUL s
HEADIER
HEADILY
HEADING s
HEADMAN
HEADMEN
HEADPIN s
HEADSET s
HEADWAY s
HEALERS*
s HEALING
HEALTHS*
HEALTHY*
HEAPERS*
HEAPING
s HEARERS*
s*HEARING s
HEARKEN s
HEARSAY s
HEARSED*
HEARSES*
HEARTED
HEARTEN s
HEARTHS
ct*HEATERS*
HEATHEN s
s HEATHER sy
c*HEATING
HEAUMES*
HEAVENS*
HEAVERS*
HEAVIER
HEAVIES t
HEAVILY
s HEAVING
HEBETIC
HECKLED*
HECKLER*s
HECKLES*
HECTARE s
HECTORS*
HEDDLES*
HEDGERS
*HEDGIER
*HEDGING
HEDONIC s
HEEDERS*
HEEDFUL
HEEDING
HEEHAWS*
w HEELERS*

w HEELING s
HEELTAP s
w HEEZING
HEFTERS*
HEFTIER
HEFTILY
HEFTING
HEGARIS*
HEGEMON sy
HEGIRAS*
HEGUMEN esy
HEIFERS*
*HEIGHTH*s
HEIGHTS
HEILING
HEIMISH
HEINIES*
HEINOUS
HEIRDOM s
HEIRESS
HEIRING
HEISTED
HEISTER s
HEJIRAS*
HEKTARE s
HELIAST s
HELICAL
HELICES
HELICON s
HELIPAD s
HELIUMS*
HELIXES
HELLBOX
HELLCAT s
HELLERI*s
s HELLERS*
HELLERY*
s HELLING
HELLION s
HELLISH
HELLOED
HELLOES
HELLUVA
HELMETS*
w HELMING
HELOTRY
HELPERS*
HELPFUL
w HELPING s
s HELVING
HEMAGOG s
HEMATAL
rt HEMATIC s
HEMATIN es
HEMIOLA s
HEMLINE s
HEMLOCK s
HEMMERS
HEMMING
HEMPIER*
HENBANE s
HENBITS*
HENCOOP s
HENLEYS*
HENLIKE
HENNAED
HENNERY
HENNISH
HENPECK s
HENRIES
HENTING
HEPARIN s
HEPATIC as
HEPCATS*
HEPPEST
HEPTADS*
HEPTANE s
HEPTOSE s
HERALDS*
HERBAGE ds
HERBALS*
HERBIER
HERDERS*
HERDICS*
HERDING
HERDMAN
HERDMEN
HEREDES
HERETIC s
HERIOTS*
HERITOR s
t HERMITS*
HERNIAE*
HERNIAL*
HERNIAS*
HEROICS*

HEROINE*s
HEROINS*
HEROISM s
HEROIZE ds
HERONRY
w HERRIED
csw HERRIES
*HERRING s
HERSELF
HERTZES
HESSIAN s
HESSITE s
HETAERA es
HETAIRA is
HETEROS*
HETMANS*
c HEWABLE
HEXADES*
HEXADIC
HEXAGON s
HEXANES*
HEXAPLA rs
HEXAPOD sy
HEXEREI s
HEXONES*
HEXOSAN s
HEXOSES*
HEXYLIC
HEYDAYS*
HEYDEYS*
HIBACHI s
HICCUPS*
HICKEYS*
HICKIES*
t HICKISH
c HICKORY
HIDABLE
HIDALGO s
HIDEOUS
HIDEOUT s
HIDINGS*
HIGGLED*
HIGGLER*s
HIGGLES*
HIGHBOY s
HIGHEST
HIGHTED
HIGHTHS*
HIGHTOP s
HIGHWAY s
HIJACKS*
HIJINKS
HIJRAHS*
c HILDING s
c HILLERS*
c HILLIER
cs HILLING
HILLOAS*
HILLOCK sy
HILLOED
HILLOES
HILLTOP s
HILTING
HIMATIA
HIMSELF
HINDERS*
HINDGUT s
w HINGERS*
w HINGING
c*HINKIER
sw HINNIED
sw HINNIES
HINTERS
HINTING
HIPBONE s
s HIPLESS
w HIPLIKE
HIPLINE s
HIPNESS
HIPPEST
cw HIPPIER*
c HIPPIES*t
csw HIPPING
HIPPISH
HIPSHOT
HIPSTER s
HIRABLE
HIRCINE
HIRPLED*
HIRPLES*
HIRSELS*
HIRSLED*
HIRSLES*
HIRSUTE
HIRUDIN s
HISSELF

HISSERS*
HISSIER
HISSIES t
HISSING s
w HISTING
HISTOID
HISTONE s
HISTORY
*HITCHED
HITCHER s
*HITCHES
HITLESS
cw HITTERS*
HITTING
HOAGIES*
HOARDED
HOARDER s
HOARIER
HOARILY
HOARSEN*s
HOARSER*
HOATZIN s
HOAXERS*
HOAXING
HOBBERS*
HOBBIES
HOBBING
HOBBITS*
HOBBLED*
HOBBLER*s
HOBBLES*
HOBLIKE
HOBNAIL s
HOBNOBS*
HOBOING
HOBOISM s
s*HOCKERS*
HOCKEYS*
cs HOCKING
HOCUSED
HOCUSES
HODADDY
HODDENS*
HODDINS*
HOECAKE s
HOEDOWN s
HOELIKE
HOGBACK s
HOGFISH
HOGGERS*
HOGGETS*
s HOGGING
HOGGISH
HOGLIKE
HOGMANE s
HOGNOSE s
HOGNUTS*
HOGTIED*
HOGTIES*
HOGWASH
HOGWEED s
HOICKED
HOIDENS*
HOISING
HOISTED
HOISTER s
c HOKIEST
HOLARDS*
HOLDALL s
HOLDERS*
HOLDING s
HOLDOUT s
HOLDUPS*
HOLIBUT s
HOLIDAY s
HOLIEST*
w HOLISMS*
HOLISTS*
HOLKING
HOLLAED
HOLLAND s
HOLLERS*
HOLLIES
HOLLOAS*
HOLLOED
HOLLOES
HOLLOOS*
HOLLOWS*
HOLMIUM s
HOLSTER s
HOLYDAY s
HOMAGED*
HOMAGER*s
HOMAGES*
HOMBRES
HOMBURG s

HOMEBOY s
HOMERED
HOMERIC
HOMIEST*
HOMINES s
HOMINID s
HOMMOCK s
HOMOLOG sy
HOMONYM sy
HOMOSEX
HONCHOS*
HONDLED*
HONDLES*
HONESTY*
p HONEYED
HONGIED
HONGIES
HONKERS*
HONKING
HONORED
HONOREE s
HONORER s
HONOURS*
HOOCHES
HOOCHIE s
HOODIER*
HOODIES*t
HOODING
HOODLUM s
HOODOOS*
HOOFERS*
w HOOFING
HOOKAHS*
HOOKERS*
HOOKEYS*
HOOKIER
HOOKIES t
HOOKING
HOOKLET s
HOOKUPS*
w HOOPERS*
w HOOPING
w HOOPLAS*
HOOPOES*
HOOPOOS*
HOORAHS*
HOORAYS*
HOOSGOW s
s HOOTERS*
HOOTIER
s HOOTING
HOOVERS*
HOPEFUL s
HOPHEAD s
HOPLITE s
csw HOPPERS*
c HOPPIER
csw HOPPING s
HOPPLED*
HOPPLES*
HOPSACK s
HOPTOAD s
HORDEIN s
c HORDING
HORIZON s
HORMONE s
HORNETS*
t HORNIER
t HORNILY
t HORNING s
HORNIST s
HORNITO s
HORRENT
HORRIFY
HORRORS*
HORSIER
HORSILY
HORSING
HORSTES*
HOSANNA hs
HOSEYED
HOSIERS
HOSIERY*
HOSPICE s
HOSTAGE s
HOSTELS*
HOSTESS
HOSTILE s
g HOSTING
*HOSTLER s
HOTBEDS*
HOTCAKE s
HOTCHED
HOTCHES
HOTDOGS*
HOTFOOT s

HOTHEAD s
HOTLINE s
HOTLINK s
HOTNESS
HOTRODS*
HOTSHOT s
HOTSPOT s
HOTSPUR s
HOTTEST
HOTTIES*
s HOTTING
HOTTISH
HOUDAHS*
HOUNDED
HOUNDER s
HOUSELS
c HOUSERS*
c HOUSING s
s HOVELED
*HOVERED
HOVERER s
HOWBEIT
HOWDAHS*
HOWDIED*
HOWDIES*
HOWEVER
HOWKING
HOWLERS*
HOWLETS
HOWLING
HOYDENS*
HRYVNAS*
HRYVNIA s
HUBBIES
HUBBUBS*
HUBCAPS*
c HUCKLES*
HUDDLED*
HUDDLER*s
HUDDLES*
HUELESS
c HUFFIER
HUFFILY
c HUFFING
HUFFISH
HUGEOUS
c HUGGERS*
c HUGGING
HUIPILS*
HULKIER
HULKING
HULLERS*
HULLING
HULLOAS*
HULLOED
HULLOES
HULLOOS*
HUMANER*
HUMANLY
HUMATES*
HUMBLED*
HUMBLER*s
*HUMBLES*t
HUMBUGS*
HUMDRUM s
HUMERAL s
HUMERUS
HUMIDEX
HUMIDLY
HUMIDOR s
HUMMERS*
c HUMMING
HUMMOCK sy
HUMORAL
HUMORED
HUMOURS*
t HUMPERS*
HUMPHED
HUMPIER
ctw*HUMPING
HUMUSES
HUMVEES*
HUNCHED
HUNCHES
HUNDRED s
HUNGERS*
HUNKERS*
c HUNKIER
HUNNISH
cs HUNTERS*
s HUNTING s
c HUPPAHS*
HURDIES
HURDLED*
HURDLER*s
HURDLES*

HURLERS*
HURLEYS*
HURLIES
HURLING s
HURRAHS*
HURRAYS*
HURRIED
HURRIER s
d HURRIES
HURTERS*
HURTFUL
HURTING
HURTLED*
HURTLES*s
HUSBAND s
HUSHABY
HUSHFUL
s HUSHING
HUSKERS*
HUSKIER
HUSKIES t
HUSKILY
HUSKING s
HUSSARS*
HUSSIES
HUSTLED*
HUSTLER*s
HUSTLES*
HUSWIFE s
HUTCHED
HUTCHES
HUTLIKE
HUTMENT s
s HUTTING
c HUTZPAH*s
c HUTZPAS*
HUZZAED
HUZZAHS*
HYAENAS*
HYAENIC
HYALINE*s
HYALINS*
HYALITE s
HYALOID s
HYBRIDS*
HYDATID s
HYDRANT hs
HYDRASE*s
HYDRATE ds
HYDRIAE*
HYDRIDE*s
HYDRIDS*
HYDROID s
HYDROPS y
HYDROUS
HYDROXY l
HYENINE
HYENOID
HYGEIST s
HYGIENE s
HYMENAL
HYMENIA l
HYMNALS*
HYMNARY
HYMNING
HYMNIST s
HYMNODY
HYOIDAL
HYPERON s
HYPHENS*
HYPNOID
HYPOGEA ln
HYPOING
HYPONEA s
HYPONYM sy
HYPOXIA s
HYPOXIC
HYRACES
HYRAXES
HYSSOPS*
IAMBICS*
ICEBERG s
ICEBOAT s
ICECAPS*
ICEFALL s
v ICELESS
ICELIKE
ICHNITE s
ICICLED*
ICICLES*
ICINESS
dkp ICKIEST
ICTERIC s
ICTERUS
r ICTUSES
IDEALLY
IDEATED*
IDEATES*
IDENTIC
IDIOTIC
IDLESSE s
IDOLISE drs
IDOLISM s
IDOLIZE drs
IDYLIST s
IDYLLIC
m IFFIEST
IGNATIA s
l IGNEOUS
IGNITED*
IGNITER*s
l IGNITES*
IGNITOR s
IGNOBLE
IGNOBLY
IGNORED*
IGNORER*s
IGNORES*
IGUANAS*
IGUANID s
IKEBANA s
ILEITIS
ILEUSES
ILLEGAL s
ILLICIT
t ILLITES*
ILLITIC
ILLNESS
ILLOGIC s
ILLUDED*
ILLUDES*
ILLUMED*
ILLUMES*
ILLUVIA l
IMAGERS*
IMAGERY*
IMAGINE drs
IMAGING s
IMAGISM s
IMAGIST s
IMAGOES
IMAMATE s
IMARETS*
IMBALMS*
IMBARKS*
IMBIBED*
IMBIBER*s
IMBIBES*
IMBLAZE ds
IMBOSOM s
IMBOWER s
IMBROWN s
IMBRUED*
IMBRUES*
IMBRUTE ds
IMBUING
IMITATE ds
IMMENSE r
IMMERGE ds
IMMERSE ds
IMMIXED
IMMIXES
IMMORAL
IMMUNES*
IMMURED*
IMMURES*
IMPACTS*
IMPAINT s
IMPAIRS*
IMPALAS*
IMPALED*
IMPALER*s
IMPALES*
IMPANEL s
IMPARKS*
IMPARTS*
IMPASSE s
IMPASTE ds
IMPASTO s
IMPAVID
IMPAWNS*
IMPEACH
IMPEARL s
IMPEDED*
IMPEDER*s
IMPEDES*
IMPENDS*
IMPERIA l
IMPERIL s
IMPETUS
IMPHEES*
IMPIETY
IMPINGE*drs
IMPINGS*
IMPIOUS
IMPLANT s
IMPLEAD s
IMPLIED
IMPLIES
IMPLODE ds
IMPLORE drs
IMPONED*
IMPONES*
IMPORTS*
IMPOSED*
IMPOSER*s
IMPOSES*
IMPOSTS*
IMPOUND s
IMPOWER s
IMPREGN s
IMPRESA s
IMPRESE s
IMPRESS
IMPREST s
IMPRINT s
IMPROVE*drs
IMPROVS*
IMPUGNS*
IMPULSE ds
IMPURER*
IMPUTED*
IMPUTER*s
IMPUTES*
INANELY
INANEST*
INANITY
INAPTLY
INARMED
INBEING s
INBOARD s
INBOUND s
INBREDS*
INBREED s
INBUILT
INBURST s
INCAGED*
INCAGES*
INCANTS*
INCASED*
INCASES*
INCENSE ds
INCENTS*
INCEPTS*
INCESTS*
pw INCHERS*
cpw INCHING
INCIPIT s
INCISAL
INCISED*
INCISES*
INCISOR sy
INCITED*
INCITER*s
z INCITES*
INCIVIL
INCLASP s
INCLINE drs
INCLIPS*
INCLOSE drs
INCLUDE ds
INCOMER*s
INCOMES*
INCONNU s
INCROSS
INCRUST s
INCUBUS
INCUDAL
INCUDES
INCURVE ds
INCUSED*
INCUSES*
INDABAS*
INDAMIN es
INDENES*
INDENTS*
INDEXED
INDEXER s
INDEXES
INDICAN st
INDICES
INDICIA s
INDICTS*
INDIGEN est
w INDIGOS*
INDITED*
INDITER*s
INDITES*
INDIUMS*
INDOLES*
INDOORS*
INDORSE der
s
w INDOWED
INDOXYL s
INDRAFT s
INDRAWN
INDUCED*
INDUCER*s
INDUCES*
INDUCTS*
INDUING
INDULGE drs
INDULIN es
INDULTS*
INDUSIA l
INDWELL s
INDWELT
INEARTH s
INEDITA
INEPTLY
INERTIA els
INERTLY
INEXACT
INFALLS*
INFANCY
INFANTA*s
INFANTE*s
INFANTS*
INFARCT s
INFARES*
INFAUNA els
INFECTS*
INFEOFF s
INFERNO s
INFESTS*
INFIDEL s
INFIELD s
INFIGHT s
INFIRMS*
INFIXED
INFIXES
INFLAME drs
INFLATE drs
INFLECT s
INFLICT s
INFLOWS*
p INFOLDS*
INFORMS*
INFRACT s
INFUSED*
INFUSER*s
INFUSES*
INGATES*
INGENUE s
INGESTA*
INGESTS*
INGOING
INGOTED
INGRAFT s
INGRAIN s
INGRATE s
INGRESS
INGROUP s
INGROWN
INGULFS*
INHABIT s
INHALED*
INHALER*s
INHALES*
INHAULS*
INHERED*
INHERES*
INHERIT s
INHIBIN s
INHIBIT s
INHUMAN e
INHUMED*
INHUMER*s
INHUMES*
INITIAL s
INJECTS*
INJURED*
INJURER*s
INJURES*
INKBLOT s
INKHORN s
dhk INKIEST
INKLESS*
INKLIKE
tw INKLING s
INKPOTS*
INKWELL s
INKWOOD s
INLACED*
INLACES*
INLANDS*
INLAYER s
INLIERS*
INLYING
INMATES*
INNAGES*
INNARDS
INNERLY
INNERVE ds
gw INNINGS*
INNLESS
INOCULA
INOSINE s
INOSITE s
INPHASE
INPOURS*
INQUEST s
INQUIET s
INQUIRE drs
INQUIRY
INROADS*
INSANER*
INSCAPE s
INSCULP s
INSEAMS*
INSECTS*
INSERTS*
INSHORE
INSIDER*s
INSIDES*
INSIGHT s
INSIGNE
INSIPID
INSISTS*
INSNARE drs
INSOFAR
INSOLES*
INSOULS*
INSPANS*
INSPECT s
INSPIRE drs
INSTALL*s
INSTALS*
INSTANT s
INSTARS*
INSTATE ds
INSTEAD
INSTEPS*
INSTILL*s
INSTILS*
INSULAR s
INSULIN s
INSULTS*
INSURED*s
INSURER*s
INSURES*
INSWEPT
INTAGLI o
INTAKES*
INTEGER s
INTENDS*
INTENSE r
INTENTS*
INTERIM s
INTERNE*des
INTERNS*
INTHRAL ls
INTIMAE*
INTIMAL*
INTIMAS*
INTINES*
INTITLE ds
INTOMBS*
INTONED*
INTONER*s
INTONES*
INTORTS*
INTRANT s
INTREAT s
INTROFY
INTROIT s
INTRONS*
INTRUDE drs
INTRUST s
INTUITS*
INTURNS*
INTWINE ds
INTWIST s
INULASE s
INULINS*
INURING
INURNED
INUTILE
INVADED*
INVADER*s
INVADES*
INVALID s
INVEIGH s
INVENTS*
INVERSE ds
INVERTS*
INVESTS*
INVITAL
INVITED*
INVITEE*s
INVITER*s
INVITES*
INVOICE ds
INVOKED*
INVOKER*s
INVOKES*
INVOLVE drs
INWALLS*
INWARDS*
INWEAVE ds
INWINDS*
INWOUND
INWOVEN*
INWRAPS*
IODATED*
IODATES*
IODIDES*
IODINES*
IODISED*
IODISES*
IODISMS*
IODIZED*
IODIZER*s
IODIZES*
IOLITES*
l IONISED*
l IONISES*
IONIUMS*
l IONIZED*
l IONIZER*s
l IONIZES*
IONOGEN s
IONOMER s
IONONES*
IPECACS*
IPOMOEA s
IRACUND
IRATELY
IRATEST
ftw IRELESS
IRENICS*
IRIDIUM s
*IRISING
IRKSOME
IRONERS*
IRONIES
IRONING s
IRONIST s
IRONIZE ds
IRONMAN
IRONMEN
IRRUPTS*
ISAGOGE s
ISATINE*s
ISATINS
ISCHIAL*
ISCHIUM
ISLANDS*
ISLETED
ISOBARE*s
ISOBARS*
ISOBATH s
ISOCHOR es
ISODOSE
ISOFORM s
m ISOGAMY
ISOGENY
ISOGONE*s
ISOGONS*
ISOGONY*
ISOGRAM s
ISOGRIV s
ISOHELS*
ISOHYET s
*ISOLATE ds
ISOLEAD s
ISOLINE s
ISOLOGS*
ISOMERS*
ISONOMY
ISOPACH s
ISOPODS*
ISOSPIN s
ISOTACH s
ISOTONE s
ISOTOPE s
ISOTOPY
ISOTYPE s
ISOZYME s
ISSUANT
ISSUERS*
t ISSUING
ISTHMIC*
ISTHMUS
ITALICS*
bpw ITCHIER
bp ITCHILY
bdh ITCHING s
pw
ITEMING
ITEMISE ds
ITEMIZE drs
ITERANT
l ITERATE ds
IVORIES
IVYLIKE
IXODIDS*
g IZZARDS*
JABBERS*
JABBING
JABIRUS*
JACALES
JACAMAR s
JACANAS*
JACINTH es
JACKALS*
JACKASS
JACKDAW s
JACKERS*
JACKETS*
JACKIES
JACKING
JACKLEG s
JACKPOT s
JACOBIN s
JACOBUS
JACONET s
JACUZZI s
JADEDLY
JADEITE s
JADITIC
JAEGERS*
JAGGARY
JAGGERS
JAGGERY*
JAGGIER
*JAGGIES t
JAGGING
JAGLESS
JAGUARS*
JAILERS*
*JAILING
JAILORS*
JALAPIC
JALAPIN s
JALOPPY
JAMBEAU x
JAMBING
JAMLIKE
JAMMERS*
JAMMIER
JAMMIES t
JAMMING
JANGLED
*JANGLER*s
JANGLES
JANITOR s
JARFULS*
JARGONS
JARGONY*
JARGOON s
JARHEAD s
JARINAS*
JARLDOM s
JARRAHS*
JARRING
JARSFUL
JARVEYS*
JASMINE*s
JASMINS*
JASPERS
JASPERY*
JASSIDS*
JAUKING
JAUNCED*
JAUNCES*
JAUNTED
JAUPING
JAVELIN as
JAWBONE drs
*JAWLESS

JAWLIKE
JAWLINE s
JAYBIRD s
JAYGEES*
JAYVEES*
JAYWALK s
JAZZBOS*
JAZZERS*
JAZZIER
JAZZILY
JAZZING
JAZZMAN
JAZZMEN
JEALOUS y
JEEPERS
JEEPING
JEEPNEY s
JEERERS*
JEERING
JEJUNAL*
JEJUNUM
d JELLABA s
JELLIED
JELLIES
JELLIFY
JELLING
JEMADAR s
JEMIDAR s
JEMMIED
JEMMIES
JENNETS*
JENNIES
JEOPARD sy
JERBOAS*
JEREEDS*
JERKERS*
JERKIER
JERKIES t
JERKILY
JERKING*
JERKINS*
JERREED s
JERRIDS*
JERRIES
JERSEYS*
JESSANT
JESSING
JESTERS
JESTFUL
JESTING s
JETBEAD s
JETFOIL s
JETLAGS*
JETLIKE
JETPORT s
JETSAMS*
JETSOMS*
JETTIED
JETTIER
JETTIES t
JETTING
JETTONS*
JETWAYS*
JEWELED
JEWELER s
JEWELRY
JEWFISH
JEZAILS*
JEZEBEL s
JIBBERS*
JIBBING
JIBBOOM s
JICAMAS*
JIFFIES
JIGGERS*
JIGGIER
*JIGGING
JIGGISH
JIGGLED*
JIGGLES*
JIGLIKE
JIGSAWN*
JIGSAWS*
JILLION s
JILTERS*
JILTING
JIMJAMS
JIMMIED*
JIMMIES
JIMMINY
JIMPEST
JINGALL*s
JINGALS*
JINGLED*
JINGLER*s
JINGLES
JINGOES
JINKERS
*JINKING
JINXING
JITNEYS*
JITTERS*
JITTERY*
JIVEASS
JIVIEST
JOANNES
JOBBERS*
JOBBERY*
JOBBING
JOBLESS
JOBNAME s
JOCKEYS*
*JOCULAR
JODHPUR s
JOGGERS*
JOGGING s
JOGGLED*
JOGGLER*s
JOGGLES*
JOHNNIE s
JOINDER s
JOINERS*
JOINERY*
JOINING s
JOINTED
JOINTER s
JOINTLY
JOISTED
JOJOBAS*
JOKIEST
JOLLIED
JOLLIER s
JOLLIES t
JOLLIFY
JOLLILY
JOLLITY
JOLTERS*
JOLTIER
JOLTILY
JOLTING
JONESED
JONESES
JONQUIL s
JORDANS*
JOSEPHS*
JOSHERS*
JOSHING
JOSTLED*
*JOSTLER*s
JOSTLES*
JOTTERS
JOTTING s
JOUKING
JOUNCED*
JOUNCES
JOURNAL s
JOURNEY s
JOURNOS*
*JOUSTED
*JOUSTER s
JOWLIER
JOYANCE s
JOYLESS
JOYPOPS*
JOYRIDE rs
JOYRODE
JUBBAHS*
JUBHAHS*
JUBILEE*s
JUBILES*
JUDASES
JUDDERS
JUDGERS*
JUDGING
JUDOIST s
JUDOKAS*
JUGFULS*
JUGGING
JUGGLED*
JUGGLER*sy
JUGGLES*
JUGHEAD s
JUGSFUL
JUGULAR*s
JUGULUM
JUICERS*
JUICIER
JUICILY
JUICING
JUJITSU s
JUJUBES*
JUJUISM s
JUJUIST s
JUJUTSU s
JUKEBOX
JUMBALS*
JUMBLED*
JUMBLER*s
JUMBLES
JUMBUCK s
JUMPERS*
JUMPIER
JUMPILY
*JUMPING
JUMPOFF s
JUNCOES
JUNGLED*
JUNGLES*
JUNIORS*
JUNIPER s
JUNKERS*
JUNKETS*
JUNKIER*
JUNKIES*t
JUNKING
JUNKMAN
JUNKMEN
JURALLY
JURANTS*
JURIDIC
JURISTS*
JURYING
JURYMAN
JURYMEN
JUSSIVE s
JUSTERS*
JUSTEST
JUSTICE s
JUSTIFY
JUSTING
JUSTLED*
JUSTLES*
JUTTIED
JUTTIES
JUTTING
JUVENAL s
KABAKAS
KABALAS*
KABAYAS
KABBALA hs
KABIKIS*
KABUKIS*
KACHINA s
KADDISH
KAFFIRS*
KAFTANS*
KAHUNAS*
KAINITE*s
KAINITS*
KAISERS*
KAJEPUT s
KAKAPOS*
KALENDS
KALIANS*
KALIMBA s
KALIPHS*
KALIUMS*
KALMIAS*
KALONGS*
KALPACS*
KALPAKS*
KAMALAS*
KAMPONG s
KAMSEEN s
KAMSINS*
KANBANS*
KANTARS*
KANTELE s
KAOLINE*s
KAOLINS*
KARAKUL s
KARAOKE s
KARATES*
KARROOS*
KARSTIC
KARTING s
KASBAHS*
KASHERS*
KASHMIR s
KASHRUT hs
KATCINA s
KATHODE s
KATIONS*
KATSURA s
KATYDID s
KAURIES
KAYAKED
KAYAKER s
KAYOING
KEBBIES*
KEBBOCK s
KEBBUCK s
KEBLAHS*
KECKING
KECKLED*
KECKLES*
KEDDAHS*
*KEDGING
KEEKING
KEELAGE s
KEELING
KEELSON s
KEENERS*
KEENEST
KEENING
KEEPERS*
KEEPING s
KEESTER s
KEGELER s
KEGGERS
*KEGGING
KEGLERS*
KEGLING s
KEISTER s
KEITLOA s
KELLIES
KELOIDS*
KELPIES*
s KELPING
KELSONS*
s KELTERS*
KELVINS*
KENCHES
KENNELS*
KENNING s
*KENOSIS
KENOTIC
KEPPING
KERAMIC s
KERATIN s
KERBING
KERCHOO
KERFING
KERMESS*e
KERNELS*
KERNING
KERNITE s
KEROGEN s
KERRIAS*
s KERRIES
KERSEYS*
KERYGMA s
KESTREL s
s*KETCHES
KETCHUP s
KETENES*
KETONES*
KETONIC
KETOSES*
KETOSIS
KETOTIC
KETTLES*
KEWPIES*
KEYCARD s
KEYHOLE s
KEYLESS
KEYNOTE drs
KEYPADS*
KEYPALS*
KEYSETS*
KEYSTER s
KEYWAYS*
KEYWORD s
KHADDAR s
KHALIFA*s
KHALIFS*
KHAMSIN s
KHANATE s
KHAZENS*
KHEDAHS*
KHEDIVE s
KHIRKAH s
KIAUGHS*
KIBBEHS*
KIBBITZ
KIBBLED*
KIBBLES*
KIBBUTZ
KIBLAHS*
KICKBOX
KICKERS
*KICKIER
KICKING
KICKOFF s
KICKUPS*
s KIDDERS*
KIDDIES*
s KIDDING
KIDDISH
KIDDOES
KIDDUSH
KIDLIKE
KIDNAPS*
KIDNEYS*
KIDSKIN s
KIDVIDS*
KIESTER s
KILLDEE rs
KILLERS*
KILLICK s
KILLIES*
s KILLING s
KILLJOY s
KILLOCK s
KILNING
KILOBAR s
KILOBIT s
KILORAD s
KILOTON s
KILTERS*
KILTIES*
KILTING s
KIMCHEE s
KIMCHIS*
KIMONOS*
KINARAS*
KINASES*
KINDEST
KINDLED*
KINDLER*s
KINDLES*s
KINDRED s
KINEMAS*
KINESES
KINESIC s
KINESIS
a KINETIC s
KINETIN s
KINFOLK s
KINGCUP s
KINGDOM s
KINGING
KINGLET s
KINGPIN s
*KINKIER
KINKILY
s*KINKING
s KINLESS
KINSHIP s
KINSMAN
KINSMEN
s KIPPERS*
s KIPPING
KIPSKIN s
KIRKMAN
KIRKMEN
KIRMESS
KIRNING
KIRTLED*
KIRTLES*
KISHKAS*
KISHKES*
KISMATS*
KISMETS*
KISSERS*
KISSING
KISTFUL s
KITBAGS*
KITCHEN s
KITHARA s
KITHING
KITLING s
KITSCHY*
KITTENS*
KITTIES
KITTING
KITTLED*
KITTLER*
s KITTLES*t
KLATSCH
KLAVERN s
KLAXONS*
KLEAGLE s
KLEENEX
KLEPHTS*
KLEPTOS*
KLEZMER s
*KLISTER s
KLUDGED*
KLUDGES*
KLUDGEY*
*KLUGING
*KLUTZES
KNACKED
KNACKER sy
*KNAPPED
*KNAPPER s
KNARRED
KNAVERY
KNAVISH
KNAWELS*
KNEADED
KNEADER s
KNEECAP s
KNEEING
KNEELED
KNEELER s
KNEEPAD s
KNEEPAN s
KNELLED
KNESSET s
KNIFERS*
KNIFING
KNIGHTS
KNISHES
KNITTED
KNITTER s
KNOBBED
KNOBBLY
*KNOCKED
KNOCKER s
KNOLLED
KNOLLER s
KNOPPED
KNOTTED
KNOTTER s
KNOUTED
KNOWERS*
KNOWING s
KNUCKLE drs
KNUCKLY
*KNURLED
KOBOLDS*
KOKANEE s
KOLACKY
KOLBASI s
KOLHOZY*
KOLKHOS y
KOLKHOZ y
KOLKOZY*
KOMATIK s
KONKING
KOODOOS*
KOOKIER*
KOPECKS*
KOPIYKA s
KOPPIES*
KORUNAS*
KOSHERS*
KOTOWED
KOTOWER s
KOUMISS*
KOUMYSS*
KOUPREY s
KOUSSOS*
KOWTOWS*
KRAALED
KRAKENS*
KRATERS
KREMLIN s
KREUZER s
*KRIMMER s
KRUBUTS*
KRULLER s
KRYPTON s
KUCHENS*
KULTURS*
KUMMELS*
KUMQUAT s
KUMYSES
KUNZITE s
KURBASH
KURGANS*
KVASSES
KVELLED
KVETCHY*
KWACHAS*
KWANZAS*
KYANISE ds
KYANITE s
KYANIZE ds
KYLIKES
KYTHING
LAAGERS*
LABARUM s
LABELED
LABELER s
fg LABELLA
LABIALS*
LABIATE ds
LABORED
LABORER s
LABOURS*
LABRETS*
LABROID s
LABRUMS*
LACIEST
LACINGS*
cs LACKERS*
LACKEYS*
bcf LACKING
s
LACONIC
LACQUER s
LACQUEY s
LACTAMS*
LACTARY
LACTASE s
LACTATE ds
LACTEAL s
LACTEAN
LACTONE s
LACTOSE s
LACUNAE*
LACUNAL*
LACUNAR*sy
LACUNAS*
LACUNES*
LADANUM s
b*LADDERS*
LADDIES*
LADDISH
LADENED
LADHOOD s
b LADINGS*
LADINOS*
LADLERS*
LADLING
LADRONE*s
LADRONS*
LADYBUG s
LADYISH
LADYKIN s
LAGENDS*
LAGERED
LAGGARD s
f*LAGGERS*
bcf LAGGING s
s
LAGOONS*
LAGUNAS*
LAGUNES*
LAICISE ds
LAICISM s
LAICIZE ds
LAIRDLY
g*LAIRING
LAITHLY
LAITIES
LAKEBED s
f LAKIEST
LAKINGS*
LALIQUE s
LALLAND*s
LALLANS*
LALLING
LAMBADA s
LAMBAST es
LAMBDAS*
LAMBENT
c*LAMBERS*
LAMBERT*s
LAMBIER*
LAMBIES*t
LAMBING
LAMBKIN s
LAMEDHS*
LAMELLA ers
LAMENTS
LAMINAE*
LAMINAL*s
LAMINAR*y
LAMINAS*
LAMININ s
cfs LAMMING
LAMPADS*
c LAMPERS
c*LAMPING
LAMPION s
LAMPOON s
LAMPREY s
LAMSTER s

LANATED*
g LANCERS*
LANCETS*
g LANCING
LANDAUS*
gs LANDERS*
LANDING s
LANDLER s
LANDMAN
LANDMEN
LANEWAY s
LANGLEY s
LANGREL s
LANGUES*
LANGUET*s
LANGUID
LANGUOR s
LANGURS*
LANIARD s
LANIARY
LANITAL s
b LANKEST
c LANKIER
LANKILY
p LANNERS*
LANOLIN es
LANTANA s
LANTERN s
LANUGOS*
LANYARD s
LAOGAIS*
LAPDOGS*
LAPELED
LAPFULS*
LAPIDES
LAPILLI
LAPISES
cfs LAPPERS*
LAPPETS*
cfs LAPPING
LAPSERS*
e LAPSING
LAPTOPS*
LAPWING s
LARCENY
LARCHEN
*LARCHES
LARDERS*
LARDIER
LARDING
LARDONS*
LARDOON s
LARGELY
LARGESS*e
LARGEST*
LARGISH
LARIATS*
LARKERS*
LARKIER
LARKING
LARKISH
LARRUPS*
LASAGNA s
LASAGNE s
LASCARS*
cfp LASHERS* s
cfp*LASHING s s
LASHINS
LASHKAR s
g LASSIES*
LASSOED
LASSOER s
LASSOES
bp*LASTERS*
b LASTING s
LATAKIA s
LATCHED
ks LATCHES
LATCHET s
LATEENS*
LATENCY
LATENED
LATENTS*
LATERAD
LATERAL s
LATESTS*
LATEXES
bs LATHERS*
LATHERY*
LATHIER
LATHING s
LATICES
LATIGOS*
LATILLA s

p LATINAS*
LATINOS*
LATOSOL s
LATRIAS*
LATRINE s
f LATTENS*
LATTICE ds
LATTINS*
LAUDERS*
*LAUDING
LAUGHED
LAUGHER s
LAUNCES*
LAUNDER s
LAUNDRY
LAURELS*
LAUWINE s
LAVABOS*
LAVAGES*
LAVEERS*
LAVROCK s
LAWBOOK s
LAWINES*
LAWINGS*
cf*LAWLESS
c LAWLIKE
LAWSUIT s
LAWYERS*
LAXNESS
LAYAWAY s
LAYERED
LAYETTE s
p LAYOFFS*
LAYOUTS*
LAYOVER s
LAZARET s
g LAZIEST*
LAZULIS*
LAZYING
LAZYISH
bp LEACHED
b LEACHER s
bp LEACHES
LEADENS*
p LEADERS*
LEADIER
p LEADING s
LEADMAN
LEADMEN
LEADOFF s
LEAFAGE s
LEAFIER
LEAFING
LEAFLET s
LEAGUED*
LEAGUER*s
LEAGUES*
LEAKAGE s
LEAKERS*
LEAKIER
LEAKILY
LEAKING
cg LEANERS*
c LEANEST
cg LEANING s
LEAPERS*
LEAPING
b LEARIER
*LEARNED
*LEARNER s
p LEASERS*
LEASHED
LEASHES
p*LEASING s
p LEATHER nsy
LEAVENS*
c LEAVERS*
LEAVIER
cs LEAVING s
LECHERS*
LECHERY*
*LECHING
LECHWES*
LECTERN s
LECTINS*
ef LECTION s
e LECTORS*
LECTURE drs
LECYTHI s
p*LEDGERS*
f*LEDGIER
f LEECHED
f LEECHES
*LEERIER
*LEERILY
f LEERING

LEEWARD s
LEEWAYS*
LEFTEST
LEFTIES
LEFTISH
LEFTISM s
LEFTIST s
LEGALLY
LEGATED*
LEGATEE*s
LEGATES*
LEGATOR*s
LEGATOS*
LEGENDS*
LEGGIER o
*LEGGING*s
LEGGINS*
LEGHORN s
LEGIBLE
LEGIBLY
LEGIONS*
e LEGISTS*
LEGLESS
LEGLIKE
LEGONGS*
LEGROOM s
LEGUMES*
LEGUMIN s
LEGWORK s
LEHAYIM s
LEISTER s
LEISURE ds
LEKKING
LEKVARS*
LEKYTHI
LEMMATA
LEMMING s
LEMPIRA s
LEMURES
b*LENDERS*
b*LENDING
LENGTHS*
LENGTHY*
LENIENT
LENITED*
LENITES*
f LENSING
LENSMAN
LENSMEN
LENTIGO
LENTILS*
LENTISK s
LENTOID s
LEONINE
LEOPARD s
LEOTARD s
LEPORID s
LEPROSE
LEPROSY
LEPROUS
LEPTINS*
LEPTONS*
LESBIAN s
LESIONS*
LESSEES*
LESSENS*
LESSONS*
p LESSORS*
f*LETCHED
f*LETCHES
LETDOWN s
LETHALS*
LETHEAN
LETTERS*
LETTING
LETTUCE s
LEUCINE*s
LEUCINS*
LEUCITE s
LEUCOMA s
LEUKOMA s
LEUKONS*
LEVANTS*
e LEVATOR s
LEVELED
LEVELER s
LEVELLY
LEVERED
LEVERET s
LEVIERS*
LEVULIN s
LEVYING
LEWDEST
LEWISES
LEXEMES*
LEXEMIC

LEXICAL*
LEXICON s
LIAISED*
LIAISES*
LIAISON s
LIANOID
LIBELED
LIBELEE s
LIBELER s
LIBERAL s
LIBERTY
LIBIDOS*
LIBLABS*
LIBRARY
LIBRATE ds
LICENCE der s
LICENSE der s
LICENTE
LICHEES*
LICHENS*
LICHTED
LICHTLY
LICITLY
cfs*LICKERS*
cfs LICKING s
LICTORS*
LIDDING
LIDLESS
LIEFEST
LIERNES*
LIEVEST
LIFEFUL
LIFEWAY s
LIFTERS*
LIFTING
LIFTMAN
LIFTMEN
LIFTOFF s
LIGANDS*
LIGASES*
LIGATED*
LIGATES*
abf LIGHTED ps
LIGHTEN s
bps LIGHTER s
s LIGHTLY
LIGNANS*
*LIGNIFY
LIGNINS*
*LIGNITE s
LIGROIN es
LIGULAE*
LIGULAR*
LIGULAS*
LIGULES*
LIGURES*
LIKABLE
LIKENED
LIKINGS*
LILTING
LIMACON s
LIMBATE
LIMBECK s
c LIMBERS*
LIMBIER
c LIMBING
LIMEADE s
s LIMIEST
LIMINAL*
LIMITED s
LIMITER s
LIMITES
gs LIMMERS*
LIMNERS*
LIMNING
LIMPERS*
LIMPEST
LIMPETS*
*LIMPING
LIMPKIN s
LIMPSEY
LIMULUS
LINABLE
LINAGES*
LINALOL s
LINDANE s
LINDENS*
*LINDIES
LINEAGE s
LINEATE d
LINECUT s
LINEMAN
LINEMEN

LINEUPS*
LINGAMS*
LINGCOD s
cfs LINGERS*
c LINGIER
LINGOES
LINGUAE*
LINGUAL*s
LINGULA er
LINIEST
LININGS*
LINKAGE s
LINKBOY s
bcp*LINKERS*
bcp*LINKING s
LINKMAN
LINKMEN
LINKUPS*
LINNETS*
LINOCUT s
LINSANG s
LINSEED s
LINSEYS*
LINTELS*
LINTERS
fg LINTIER
fg LINTING
LINTOLS*
LINURON s
LIONESS
*LIONISE drs
*LIONIZE drs
LIPASES*
LIPIDES*
LIPIDIC
s LIPLESS
LIPLIKE
LIPOIDS*
LIPOMAS*
LIPPENS*
cfs LIPPERS*
s LIPPIER
bcf LIPPING s s
LIPREAD s
LIQUATE ds
LIQUEFY
LIQUEUR s
LIQUIDS*
LIQUIFY
LIQUORS*
LIRIOPE s
LISENTE
LISPERS*
LISPING
LISSOME*
LISTEES*
LISTELS*
g LISTENS*
bgk LISTERS*
LISTING s
LITCHIS*
LITERAL s
b LITHELY
b LITHEST
LITHIAS*
LITHIFY
LITHIUM s
LITHOED
LITHOID
LITHOPS
c LITORAL
LITOTES
LITOTIC
fgs LITTERS*
g LITTERY*
LITTLER*
LITTLES*t
LITURGY
LIVABLE
LIVENED
LIVENER s
s LIVERED
LIVIDLY
LIVIERS*
LIVINGS*
LIVYERS*
LIXIVIA l
LIZARDS*
LOACHES
LOADERS*
LOADING s
LOAFERS*
LOAFING
LOAMIER

g LOAMING
LOANERS*
LOANING s
LOATHED*
LOATHER*s
LOATHES*
LOATHLY
g LOBATED*
cs LOBBERS*
LOBBIED
LOBBIES
b LOBBING
LOBBYER s
LOBEFIN s
*LOBELIA s
LOBSTER s
g LOBULAR
g LOBULES*
LOBWORM s
LOCALES*
LOCALLY
LOCATED*
LOCATER*s
LOCATES*
LOCATOR s
LOCHANS*
LOCHIAL*
b LOCKAGE s
LOCKBOX
bc*LOCKERS*
LOCKETS*
bcf LOCKING
LOCKJAW s
LOCKNUT s
LOCKOUT s
LOCKRAM s
LOCKSET s
LOCKUPS*
LOCOING
LOCOISM s
*LOCULAR
LOCULED*
LOCULES*
*LOCULUS
LOCUSTA*el
LOCUSTS*
LODGERS*
LODGING s
LOESSAL
LOESSES
LOFTERS*
LOFTIER
LOFTILY
LOFTING
LOGANIA
LOGBOOK s
LOGGATS
bcf LOGGERS* s
LOGGETS
LOGGIAS*
c LOGGIER*
bcf LOGGING s s
LOGGISH
a LOGICAL
LOGIEST
LOGIONS*
LOGJAMS*
LOGROLL s
LOGWAYS*
LOGWOOD s
LOIDING
LOITERS*
LOLLERS*
LOLLIES
LOLLING
LOLLOPS*
LOLLOPY*
LOMEINS*
LOMENTA
LOMENTS*
LONGANS*
LONGBOW s
LONGERS*
LONGEST*
LONGIES
LONGING s
LONGISH
LOOBIES
LOOFAHS*
LOOKERS*
LOOKING
LOOKISM s
LOOKIST s
LOOKOUT s

LOOKUPS*
bg LOOMING
LOONEYS*
LOONIER*
LOONIES*t
LOONILY
b LOOPERS*
LOOPIER
LOOPILY
b LOOPING
LOOSELY
LOOSENS*
LOOSEST*
LOOSING
LOOTERS*
LOOTING
f LOPPERS*
fgs LOPPIER
cfg LOPPING ps
LOQUATS*
LORDING s
LORDOMA s
LORGNON s
LORICAE*
LORIMER s
LORINER s
LORISES
LORRIES
c LOSABLE
c LOSINGS*
LOTIONS*
LOTOSES
bps*LOTTERS*
LOTTERY*
bcp LOTTING s
LOTUSES
LOUDENS*
LOUDEST
LOUDISH
LOUNGED*
LOUNGER*s
LOUNGES*
LOUPING
cf LOURING
b LOUSIER
b LOUSILY
b LOUSING
cfg*LOUTING
LOUTISH
LOUVERS*
LOUVRED*
LOUVRES*
LOVABLE
LOVABLY
LOVAGES*
LOVEBUG s
*LOVERLY
b LOWBALL s
LOWBORN
p LOWBOYS*
LOWBRED
LOWBROW s
bs LOWDOWN s
fg LOWERED
LOWINGS*
p LOWLAND s
LOWLIER
LOWLIFE rs
LOWLILY
s LOWNESS
LOYALER
LOYALLY
LOYALTY
LOZENGE s
bcf LUBBERS* s
LUCARNE s
LUCENCE s
LUCENCY
LUCERNE*s
LUCERNS*
LUCIDLY
LUCIFER s
LUCITES*
p LUCKIER*
LUCKIES*t
p LUCKILY
cp LUCKING
LUETICS*
bfs LUFFING
LUGEING
LUGGAGE s
ps LUGGERS*
LUGGIES*

gps LUGGING
LUGSAIL s
LUGWORM s
LULLABY
LULLERS*
LULLING
p LUMBAGO s
LUMBARS*
cps*LUMBERS*
LUMENAL
LUMINAL*
p LUMPENS*
p LUMPERS*
cg LUMPIER
g LUMPILY
cfp*LUMPING
s
cp LUMPISH
LUNATED*
LUNATIC s
g LUNCHED
LUNCHER s
g LUNCHES
LUNETTE s
LUNGANS*
LUNGEES*
bp LUNGERS*
LUNGFUL s
bp LUNGING
LUNGYIS*
LUNIEST*
cfp LUNKERS*
b LUNTING
LUNULAE*
LUNULAR*
LUNULES*
LUPANAR s
LUPINES*
LUPULIN s
LUPUSES
LURCHED
LURCHER s
LURCHES
LURDANE*s
LURDANS*
LUREXES
LURIDLY
LURKERS*
LURKING
fp LUSHEST*
bfs LUSHING
bcf LUSTERS*
LUSTFUL
LUSTIER
LUSTILY
LUSTING
LUSTRAL*
LUSTRED*
LUSTRES*
LUSTRUM s
LUSUSES
LUTEINS*
LUTEOUS
LUTFISK s
LUTHERN s
LUTHIER s
f LUTINGS*
f LUTISTS*
LUXATED*
LUXATES*
LYCEUMS*
LYCHEES*
LYCHNIS
LYCOPOD s
LYDDITE s
p LYINGLY
LYNCEAN
LYNCHED
LYNCHER s
LYNCHES
LYRATED*
LYRICAL
LYRICON s
LYRISMS*
LYRISTS*
LYSATES*
LYSINES*
LYSOGEN sy
MACABER
MACABRE
MACACOS*
MACADAM s
MACAQUE s
MACCHIA
MACCHIE
MACHETE s
MACHINE ds
MACHREE s
MACHZOR s
MACKLED*
MACKLES*
MACRAME s
MACRONS*
MACULAE*
MACULAR*
MACULAS*
MACULED*
MACULES*
MACUMBA s
MADAMES*
MADCAPS*
MADDENS*
MADDERS
MADDEST
*MADDING
MADDISH
MADEIRA s
MADNESS
MADONNA s
MADRASA*hs
MADRONA s
MADRONE s
MADRONO s
MADTOMS*
MADUROS*
MADWORT s
MADZOON s
MAENADS*
MAESTRI
MAESTRO s
MAFFIAS*
MAFFICK s
MAFIOSI
MAFIOSO s
MAFTIRS*
MAGALOG s
MAGENTA s
MAGGOTS*
MAGGOTY*
MAGIANS*
MAGICAL
MAGILPS*
MAGLEVS*
MAGMATA
*MAGNATE s
MAGNETO*ns
MAGNETS*
MAGNIFY
MAGNUMS*
MAGPIES*
MAGUEYS*
MAHATMA s
MAHJONG gs
MAHONIA s
MAHOUTS*
MAHUANG s
MAHZORS*
MAIDENS*
MAIDISH
MAIHEMS*
MAILBAG s
MAILBOX
MAILERS*
e*MAILING s
MAILLOT s
MAILMAN
MAILMEN
MAIMERS
*MAIMING
MAINTOP s
MAJAGUA s
MAJESTY
MAJORED
MAJORLY
MAKABLE
MAKEUPS*
MAKINGS*
MALACCA s
MALAISE s
MALANGA s
MALARIA lns
MALARKY
MALATES
MALEATE s
MALEFIC
MALICES*
MALIGNS
MALINES
MALISON s
MALKINS*
MALLARD s
MALLEES
MALLETS*
MALLEUS
MALLING s
MALLOWS
MALMIER
MALMSEY s
MALODOR s
MALTASE s
MALTEDS*
MALTHAS*
MALTIER
MALTING
MALTOLS*
MALTOSE s
MAMBOED
MAMBOES
MAMEYES
MAMLUKS*
MAMMALS*
MAMMARY
MAMMATE
MAMMATI
MAMMEES*
MAMMERS*
MAMMETS*
MAMMEYS*
MAMMIES*
MAMMOCK s
MAMMONS*
MAMMOTH s
MAMZERS*
MANACLE ds
MANAGED*
MANAGER*s
MANAGES*
MANAKIN s
MANANAS*
MANATEE s
MANCHES*
MANCHET*s
MANDALA s
MANDATE ds
MANDOLA s
MANDREL s
MANDRIL ls
MANEGES*
MANGABY
MANGELS
MANGERS
MANGIER
MANGILY
MANGLED
*MANGLER*s
MANGLES
MANGOES
MANGOLD s
MANHOLE s
MANHOOD s
MANHUNT s
MANIACS*
MANIHOT s
MANIKIN s
MANILAS*
MANILLA s
MANILLE s
MANIOCA*s
MANIOCS*
MANIPLE s
MANITOS*
MANITOU*s
MANITUS*
MANKIND
MANLESS
MANLIER
MANLIKE
MANLILY
MANMADE
MANNANS*
MANNERS*
MANNING
MANNISH
MANNITE s
MANNOSE s
MANPACK
MANROPE s
MANSARD s
MANSION s
MANTEAU sx
MANTELS*
MANTIDS*
MANTLED*
MANTLES*
MANTLET*s
MANTRAM*s
MANTRAP*s
MANTRAS*
MANTRIC
MANTUAS*
MANUALS*
MANUARY
MANUMIT s
MANURED*
MANURER*s
MANURES*
MANWARD s
MANWISE
MAPLIKE
MAPPERS*
MAPPING s
MAQUILA s
MARABOU st
MARACAS*
MARANTA s
MARASCA s
MARAUDS*
MARBLED*
MARBLER*s
MARBLES*
MARCATO s
MARCELS*
*MARCHED
MARCHEN
*MARCHER s
*MARCHES aei
MAREMMA
MAREMME
MARENGO
MARGAYS*
*MARGENT s
MARGINS*
MARIMBA s
MARINAS*
MARINER*s
MARINES*
MARITAL
MARKERS*
MARKETS*
MARKHOR s
MARKING s
MARKKAA*
MARKKAS*
MARKUPS*
MARLIER
MARLINE*s
MARLING*s
MARLINS*
MARLITE s
MARMITE s
MARMOTS*
MAROONS*
MARPLOT s
MARQUEE*s
MARQUES*s
MARQUIS e
MARRAMS*
MARRANO s
MARRERS*
MARRIED s
MARRIER s
MARRIES
MARRING
MARRONS*
MARROWS
MARROWY
MARSALA s
MARSHAL ls
MARSHES
s MARTENS*
MARTIAL
MARTIAN s
s MARTING*
MARTINI*s
MARTINS*
MARTLET s
MARTYRS*
MARTYRY*
MARVELS*
MASALAS*
MASCARA s
MASCONS*
MASCOTS
s MASHERS*
MASHIES*
s*MASHING
MASJIDS*
MASKEGS*
MASKERS
*MASKING s
MASONED
MASONIC
MASONRY
MASQUER*s
MASQUES*
MASSAGE drs
MASSEUR s
MASSIER
MASSIFS*
a MASSING
MASSIVE
MASTABA hs
MASTERS
MASTERY*
MASTICS*
MASTIFF s
MASTING
MASTOID s
MATADOR s
MATCHED
MATCHER s
MATCHES
MATCHUP s
MATELOT es
MATIEST
MATILDA s
MATINAL
MATINEE s
MATINGS*
MATLESS
MATRASS
MATRONS*
MATSAHS*
s MATTERS*
MATTERY*
MATTING*s
MATTINS*
MATTOCK s
MATTOID s
MATURED*
MATURER*s
MATURES*t
MATZAHS*
MATZOHS*
MATZOON s
MATZOTH*
MAUDLIN
MAULERS*
MAULING
MAUMETS*
MAUNDER s
MAVISES
MAWKISH
*MAXILLA es
MAXIMAL*s
MAXIMIN s
MAXIMUM s
MAXIXES*
MAXWELL s
MAYBIRD s
MAYBUSH
MAYDAYS*
MAYHEMS*
MAYINGS*
MAYORAL
MAYPOLE s
MAYPOPS*
MAYVINS*
MAYWEED s
MAZARDS*
a MAZEDLY
MAZIEST
MAZUMAS*
MAZURKA s
MAZZARD s
MEADOWS*
MEADOWY*
MEALIER*
MEALIES*t
MEANDER s
MEANERS*
MEANEST
MEANIES*
MEANING s
MEASLED*
MEASLES*
MEASURE drs
MEATIER
MEATILY
MEATMAN
MEATMEN
MEDAKAS*
MEDALED
MEDDLED*
MEDDLER*s
MEDDLES*
MEDEVAC s
MEDIACY
MEDIALS*
MEDIANS*
MEDIANT*s
MEDIATE ds
MEDICAL s
MEDICKS*
MEDICOS*
MEDIGAP s
MEDINAS*
MEDIUMS*
MEDIVAC s
MEDLARS*
MEDLEYS*
MEDULLA ers
MEDUSAE*
MEDUSAL*
MEDUSAN*s
MEDUSAS*
MEEKEST
MEERKAT s
MEETERS*
MEETING s
MEGABAR s
MEGABIT s
MEGAHIT s
MEGAPOD es
MEGARON
MEGASSE*s
MEGATON s
MEGILLA hs
MEGILPH*s
MEGILPS*
MEGOHMS*
MEGRIMS*
MEHNDIS*
MEINIES*
MEIOSES
MEIOSIS
MEIOTIC
MEISTER s
MELAMED
MELANGE s
MELANIC s
MELANIN s
MELDERS
MELDING
MELENAS*
MELILOT s
MELISMA s
s MELLING
MELLOWS*
MELODIA s
MELODIC a
MELOIDS*
MELTAGE s
s MELTERS*
s MELTING
MELTONS*
MEMBERS
MEMENTO s
MEMOIRS*
MENACED*
MENACER*s
MENACES*
MENAGES*
MENAZON s
ae*MENDERS*
MENDIGO s
ae*MENDING s
MENFOLK s
MENHIRS*
MENIALS*
MENISCI
MENORAH s
MENSCHY*
MENSHEN
MENSHES
MENSING
MENTEES*
MENTHOL s
MENTION s
MENTORS*
MENUDOS*
MEOUING
MEOWING
a MERCERS*
MERCERY*
MERCHES
MERCIES
MERCURY
MERGEES*
MERGERS*
e MERGING
MERINOS*
MERISES
MERISIS
MERITED
MERLINS*
MERLONS*
MERLOTS*
MERMAID s
MEROPIA s
MEROPIC
MERRIER
MERRILY
MESALLY
MESARCH
MESCALS*
MESCLUN s
MESEEMS
MESHIER
MESHING
MESHUGA h
MESONIC
MESQUIT es
MESSAGE ds
MESSANS*
MESSIAH s
MESSIER
MESSILY
MESSING
MESSMAN
MESSMEN
MESTEES*
MESTESO s
MESTINO s
MESTIZA s
MESTIZO s
METAGES*
METALED
METAMER es
METATAG s
METATES*
METAZOA ln
METEORS*
METEPAS*
METERED
*METHANE s
METHODS*
*METHOXY l
METHYLS
METICAL s
METIERS*
METISSE s
METONYM sy
METOPAE
METOPES*
METOPIC
METOPON s
METRICS*
METRIFY
METRING
METRIST s
METTLED*
METTLES*
METUMPS*
MEWLERS*
MEWLING
MEZCALS*
MEZQUIT es
MEZUZAH*s
MEZUZAS*
MEZUZOT h
MIAOUED
MIAOWED
MIASMAL*
MIASMAS*
MIASMIC
MIAULED
MICELLA*er
MICELLE*s
MICELLS*
MICHING
MICKEYS*
MICKLER*
MICKLES*t
MICRIFY
MICROBE s
MICROHM s
o MICRONS*
MIDAIRS*
MIDCULT s
MIDDAYS*
MIDDENS*
MIDDIES
MIDDLED*
MIDDLER*s
MIDDLES*
MIDGETS*
MIDGUTS*
MIDIRON s
MIDLAND s
MIDLEGS*
MIDLIFE r

MIDLINE s
MIDLIST s
MIDMOST s
MIDNOON s
MIDRASH
MIDRIBS*
MIDRIFF s
a MIDSHIP s
MIDSIZE d
MIDSOLE s
MIDTERM s
MIDTOWN s
MIDWAYS*
MIDWEEK s
MIDWIFE ds
MIDYEAR s
*MIFFIER
MIFFING
MIGGLES*
MIGNONS*
e MIGRANT s
e MIGRATE ds
MIHRABS*
MIKADOS*
o MIKRONS*
MIKVAHS*
MIKVEHS*
MIKVOTH*
MILADIS*
MILAGES*
MILCHIG
MILDENS*
MILDEST
MILDEWS*
MILDEWY*
MILDING
MILEAGE s
MILFOIL s
MILIARY
MILIEUS*
MILIEUX*
MILITIA s
MILKERS*
MILKIER
MILKILY
MILKING
MILKMAN
MILKMEN
MILKSOP s
MILLAGE s
MILLDAM s
MILLERS*
MILLETS*
MILLIER s
MILLIME s
MILLINE rs
MILLING s
MILLION s
MILLRUN s
MILNEBS*
MILORDS*
MILREIS
MILTERS*
MILTIER
MILTING
MIMBARS*
MIMEOED
MIMESES
MIMESIS
MIMETIC
MIMICAL
MIMICRY
MIMOSAS*
MINABLE
MINARET s
MINCERS*
MINCIER
MINCING
MINDERS*
MINDFUL
MINDING
MINDSET s
MINERAL s
MINGIER
MINGLED*
MINGLER*s
MINGLES
MINIBAR s
MINIBUS
MINICAB s
MINICAM ps
MINICAR s
MINIKIN s
MINILAB s
MINIMAL*s
MINIMAX*
MINIMUM s
MININGS*
MINIONS
MINISKI s
MINIUMS*
MINIVAN s
MINIVER s
MINNIES
MINNOWS*
MINORCA s
MINORED
MINSTER s
MINTAGE s
MINTERS
MINTIER
MINTING
MINUEND s
MINUETS*
MINUSES
MINUTED*
MINUTER*
MINUTES*t
MINUTIA el
MINXISH
MINYANS*
MIOCENE
MIOTICS*
MIRACLE s
MIRADOR s
MIRAGES*
MIREXES
MIRIEST
MIRKEST
s MIRKIER
s MIRKILY
MIRRORS*
MISACTS*
MISADDS*
MISAIMS*
MISALLY
MISAVER s
MISBIAS
MISBILL s
MISBIND s
MISCALL s
MISCAST s
MISCITE ds
MISCODE ds
MISCOIN s
MISCOOK s
MISCOPY
MISCUED*
MISCUES*
MISCUTS*
MISDATE ds
MISDEAL st
MISDEED s
MISDEEM s
MISDIAL s
MISDOER s
MISDOES
MISDONE
MISDRAW ns
MISDREW
MISEASE s
MISEATS*
MISEDIT s
MISERLY
MISFEED s
MISFILE ds
MISFIRE ds
MISFITS*
MISFORM s
MISGAVE
MISGIVE ns
MISGREW
MISGROW ns
MISHAPS*
MISHEAR ds
MISHITS*
MISJOIN s
MISKALS*
MISKEEP s
MISKEPT
MISKICK s
MISKNEW
MISKNOW ns
MISLAID
MISLAIN
MISLAYS*
MISLEAD s
MISLIES*
MISLIKE drs
MISLIVE ds
MISMADE
MISMAKE s
MISMARK s
MISMATE ds
MISMEET s
MISMOVE ds
MISNAME ds
MISPAGE ds
MISPART s
MISPENS*
MISPLAN st
MISPLAY s
MISPLED
MISRATE ds
MISREAD s
MISRELY
MISRULE ds
MISSAID
MISSALS*
MISSAYS*
MISSEAT s
MISSELS*
MISSEND s
MISSENT
MISSETS*
MISSHOD
MISSIES
MISSILE s
MISSING
eo MISSION s
eo MISSIVE s
MISSORT s
MISSOUT s
MISSTEP s
MISSTOP s
MISSUIT s
MISTAKE nrs
MISTBOW s
MISTEND s
MISTERM*s
MISTERS*
MISTEUK
MISTIER
MISTILY
MISTIME ds
MISTING
MISTOOK
MISTRAL s
MISTUNE ds
MISTYPE ds
MISUSED*
MISUSER*s
MISUSES*
MISWORD s
MISWRIT e
MISYOKE ds
MITERED
MITERER s
s MITHERS*
MITIEST
MITISES
MITOGEN s
a MITOSES
a MITOSIS
a MITOTIC
MITRING
MITSVAH s
MITTENS*
MITZVAH s
MIXABLE
MIXEDLY
MIXIBLE
MIXTURE s
MIZUNAS*
MIZZENS*
MIZZLED*
MIZZLES*
MOANERS*
MOANFUL
MOANING
MOATING
MOBBERS*
MOBBING
MOBBISH
MOBBISM s
MOBCAPS*
MOBILES*
MOBSTER s
MOCHILA s
MOCKERS
MOCKERY*
s MOCKING
MOCKUPS*
MODALLY
MODELED
MODELER s
MODEMED
MODERNE*rs
MODERNS*
MODESTY*
MODICUM s
MODIOLI
MODISTE s
MODULAR s
MODULES*
MODULUS
MOFETTE s
MOGGIES*
MOGGING
MOGHULS*
MOGULED
MOHAIRS*
MOHALIM
MOHAWKS*
MOHELIM
MOIDORE s
MOILERS
*MOILING
MOISTEN s
MOISTER
MOISTLY
MOJARRA s
s MOLDERS*
MOLDIER
MOLDING s
MOLESTS*
MOLLAHS*
MOLLIES*
MOLLIFY
MOLLUSC as
MOLLUSK s
MOLOCHS*
MOLTERS*
MOLTING
MOMENTA
MOMENTO*s
MOMENTS*
MOMISMS*
MOMMIES
MOMSERS*
MOMUSES
MOMZERS*
MONACID s
MONADAL
MONADES
MONADIC
MONARCH sy
MONARDA s
MONAXON s
MONERAN s
MONEYED
MONEYER s
MONGERS*
MONGOES*
MONGOLS*
MONGREL s
MONIKER s
MONISMS*
MONISTS*
MONITOR sy
MONKERY
MONKEYS*
MONKISH
MONOCLE ds
MONOCOT s
MONODIC
MONOECY
MONOFIL s
MONOLOG sy
MONOMER s
MONOPOD esy
MONSOON s
MONSTER as
MONTAGE ds
MONTANE s
MONTERO s
MONTHLY
MONURON s
s MOOCHED
s MOOCHER s
s MOOCHES
MOODIER
MOODILY
MOOLAHS*
MOOLEYS*
MOONBOW s
MOONERS*
MOONEYE s
MOONIER
MOONILY
MOONING
MOONISH
MOONLET s
MOONLIT
MOONSET s
MOORAGE s
MOORHEN s
MOORIER
MOORING s
MOORISH
MOOTERS*
MOOTING
MOPIEST
MOPOKES*
MOPPERS*
MOPPETS*
MOPPING
MORAINE s
MORALES*
a*MORALLY
MORASSY*
MORCEAU x
MORDANT s
MORDENT s
MOREENS*
MORELLE s
MORELLO s
MORGANS
MORGENS*
MORGUES*
MORIONS*
MORNING s
MOROCCO s
MORONIC
MORPHED
MORPHIA s
*MORPHIC
MORPHIN egs
MORPHOS*
MORRION s
MORROWS*
MORSELS*
MORTALS*
MORTARS*
MORTARY*
MORTICE ds
MORTIFY
a MORTISE drs
MORULAE*
MORULAR*
MORULAS*
MOSAICS*
MOSEYED
MOSHERS*
MOSHING s
MOSQUES*
MOSSERS*
MOSSIER
MOSSING
MOSTEST s
s*MOTHERS*
s MOTHERY*
MOTHIER
MOTIFIC
MOTILES*
ae MOTIONS*
MOTIVED*
MOTIVES*
MOTIVIC
MOTLEYS*
MOTLIER
MOTMOTS*
MOTORED
MOTORIC
MOTTLED*
MOTTLER*s
MOTTLES*
MOTTOES
*MOUCHED
*MOUCHES
MOUFLON s
MOUILLE
MOUJIKS*
MOULAGE s
MOULDED
s MOULDER s
MOULINS*
MOULTED
MOULTER s
MOUNDED
a MOUNTED
MOUNTER s
MOURNED
MOURNER s
MOUSAKA s
MOUSERS*
MOUSIER
MOUSILY
MOUSING s
MOUSSED*
MOUSSES*
MOUTHED
MOUTHER s
MOUTONS*
MOVABLE s
MOVABLY
MOVIOLA s
MOWINGS*
MOZETTA s
MOZETTE
MUCKERS*
MUCKIER
MUCKILY
MUCKING
MUCKLES*
MUCLUCS*
MUCOIDS*
MUCOSAE*
MUCOSAL*
MUCOSAS*
MUCUSES
MUDBUGS*
MUDCAPS*
MUDCATS*
MUDDERS
MUDDIED
MUDDIER
MUDDIES t
MUDDILY
MUDDING
MUDDLED*
MUDDLER*s
MUDDLES*
MUDFISH
MUDFLAP s
MUDFLAT s
MUDFLOW s
MUDHENS*
MUDHOLE s
MUDLARK s
MUDPACK s
MUDROCK s
MUDROOM s
MUDSILL s
MUEDDIN s
MUESLIS*
MUEZZIN s
MUFFING*
MUFFINS*
MUFFLED*
MUFFLER*s
MUFFLES*
MUGFULS*
MUGGARS*
MUGGEES*
MUGGERS*
MUGGIER
MUGGILY
MUGGING s
MUGGINS
MUGGURS*
MUGHALS*
MUGWORT s
MUGWUMP s
MUHLIES
MUKLUKS*
MUKTUKS*
MULATTO s
MULCHED
MULCHES
MULCTED
MULETAS*
MULLAHS*
MULLEIN s
MULLENS*
MULLERS*
MULLETS*
MULLEYS*
MULLING
MULLION s
MULLITE s
MULLOCK sy
MULTURE s
MUMBLED*
MUMBLER*s
MUMBLES
MUMMERS*
MUMMERY*
MUMMIED
MUMMIES
MUMMIFY
MUMMING
MUMPERS*
*MUMPING
MUNCHED
MUNCHER s
MUNCHES
MUNDANE
MUNGOES
MUNNION s
MUNSTER s
MUNTING*s
MUNTINS*
MUNTJAC s
MUNTJAK s
MUONIUM s
MURALED
MURDERS*
MUREINS*
MUREXES
MURIATE ds
MURICES
MURINES
MURKEST
MURKIER
MURKILY
MURMURS*
MURRAIN s
MURREYS*
MURRHAS*
MURRIES
MURRINE
MURTHER s
MUSCATS*
MUSCIDS*
MUSCLED*
MUSCLES*
*MUSEFUL
MUSETTE s
MUSEUMS*
MUSHERS
MUSHIER
MUSHILY
s MUSHING
MUSICAL es
MUSICKS*
MUSINGS*
MUSJIDS*
MUSKEGS*
MUSKETS*
MUSKIER*
MUSKIES*t
MUSKILY
MUSKITS*
MUSKRAT s
MUSLINS*
MUSPIKE s
MUSSELS*
MUSSIER
MUSSILY
MUSSING
MUSTANG s
MUSTARD sy
MUSTEES*
MUSTERS*
MUSTIER
MUSTILY
MUSTING
MUTABLE
MUTABLY
MUTAGEN s
MUTANTS*
MUTASES*
MUTATED*
MUTATES*
s MUTCHES
MUTEDLY
MUTINED*
MUTINES*
MUTISMS*
MUTTERS
MUTTONS*
MUTTONY*
MUTUALS*
MUTUELS*
MUTULAR
MUTULES*
MUUMUUS*
MUZHIKS*
MUZJIKS*
MUZZIER
MUZZILY
MUZZLED*
MUZZLER*s
MUZZLES*
MYALGIA s
MYALGIC
MYCELES*
MYCELIA ln
MYCOSES
MYCOSIS
MYCOTIC

MYELINE*s
MYELINS*
MYELOID
MYELOMA s
MYIASES
MYIASIS
MYNHEER s
MYOLOGY
MYOMATA
MYOPIAS*
MYOPIES
MYOSINS*
MYOSOTE s
MYOTICS*
MYOTOME s
MYRIADS*
MYRICAS*
MYRRHIC
MYRTLES*
MYSOSTS*
MYSTERY
MYSTICS*
MYSTIFY
MYTHIER
MYXOMAS*
NABBERS*
NABBING
NACELLE s
NADIRAL
NAEVOID
NAFFING
NAGANAS*
NAGGERS
s NAGGIER
s NAGGING
NAIADES
NAILERS*
s*NAILING
NAILSET s
NAIVELY
NAIVEST*
NAIVETE s
NAIVETY
NAKEDER
NAKEDLY
NAMABLE
NAMETAG s
NANDINA*s
NANDINS*
o NANISMS*
NANKEEN s
NANKINS*
NANNIES*
NAPALMS*
*NAPHTHA s
NAPHTOL s
NAPKINS*
s NAPLESS
ks NAPPERS*
s NAPPIER*
NAPPIES*t
ks NAPPING
NARCEIN es
NARCISM s
NARCIST s
NARCOMA s
NARCOSE*s
NARDINE
NARGILE hs
NARKING
NARRATE drs
NARROWS
NARTHEX
NARWALS*
NARWHAL es
NASALLY
*NASCENT
NASIONS*
NASTIER
NASTIES t
NASTILY
e NATIONS*
NATIVES*
*NATRIUM s
NATRONS*
NATTERS*
g NATTIER
NATTILY
NATURAL s
NATURED*
NATURES*
NAUGHTS
NAUGHTY*
NAUPLII
NAUSEAS*
NAUTILI

NAVAIDS*
NAVALLY
NAVETTE s
NAVVIES
NAYSAID
NAYSAYS*
NEAREST
a*NEARING
NEATENS*
NEATEST
NEATNIK s
NEBBISH y
NEBULAE*
NEBULAR*
NEBULAS*
NECKERS*
NECKING s
NECKTIE s
NECROSE ds
NECTARS*
NECTARY*
*NEDDIES
NEEDERS*
NEEDFUL s
NEEDIER
NEEDILY
NEEDING
NEEDLED*
NEEDLER*s
NEEDLES*s
NEGATED*
NEGATER*s
NEGATES*
NEGATON s
NEGATOR s
NEGLECT s
NEGLIGE es
NEGROID s
NEGRONI s
NEGUSES
NEIGHED
*NEITHER
NEKTONS*
NELLIES*
NELSONS*
NELUMBO s
NEMATIC
*NEMESES
*NEMESIS
NEOCONS*
NEOGENE
*NEOLITH s
NEOLOGY
NEONATE s
NEOTENY
NEOTYPE s
NEPETAS*
NEPHEWS*
NEPHRIC
NEPHRON s
NEPOTIC
NERDIER
NERDISH
NEREIDS*
NERITIC
NEROLIS*
e NERVATE
NERVIER
NERVILY
NERVINE s
NERVING s
NERVOUS
NERVULE s
NERVURE s
NESTERS
NESTING
NESTLED*
NESTLER*s
NESTLES*
NESTORS*
NETIZEN s
NETLESS
NETLIKE
NETSUKE s
NETTERS*
NETTIER
NETTING s
NETTLED*
NETTLER*s
NETTLES*
NETWORK s
NEURINE s
NEUROID
NEUROMA s
NEURONE*s
NEURONS*

NEURULA ers
NEUSTIC
NEUSTON s
NEUTERS*
NEUTRAL s
NEUTRON s
NEWBIES*
NEWBORN s
NEWMOWN
NEWNESS
NEWSBOY s
NEWSIER*
NEWSIES*t
NEWSMAN
NEWSMEN
NEWTONS*
NEXUSES
NIACINS*
s NIBBING
NIBBLED*
NIBBLER*s
NIBBLES*
NIBLICK s
NIBLIKE
NICHING
NICKELS*
ks*NICKERS*
s NICKING
NICKLED*
NICKLES*
NICOISE
NICOTIN es
NICTATE ds
NIDATED*
NIDATES*
NIDGETS*
NIDUSES
NIELLOS*
s NIFFERS*
NIFTIER
NIFTIES t
NIFTILY
NIGELLA s
NIGGARD s
s NIGGLED*
s NIGGLER*s
s NIGGLES*
NIGHEST
NIGHING
NIGHTIE s
k NIGHTLY
NIGRIFY
NILGAIS*
NILGAUS*
NILGHAI s
NILGHAU s
NILLING
NIMBLER*
NIMIETY
NIMIOUS
NIMMING
NIMRODS*
NINEPIN s
NINNIES
NINTHLY
NIOBATE s
NIOBITE s
NIOBIUM s
NIOBOUS
s NIPPERS*
s NIPPIER
s NIPPILY
s NIPPING
NIPPLED*
NIPPLES*
NIRVANA s
NITERIE s
NITINOL s
NITPICK sy
NITRATE ds
NITRIDE*ds
NITRIDS*
NITRIFY
NITRILE*s
NITRILS*
NITRITE s
NITROSO*
NITROUS
NITTIER
NITWITS*
NIVEOUS
ks NOBBIER
s NOBBILY
NOBBLED*
NOBBLER*s
NOBBLES*

NOBLEST*
k NOCKING
NOCTUID s
NOCTULE s
NOCTURN es
NOCUOUS
a NODALLY
NODDERS*
NODDIES
NODDING
NODDLED*
NODDLES*
NODICAL
NODULAR
NODULES*
s NOGGING*s
NOGGINS*
NOIRISH
NOISIER
NOISILY
NOISING
NOISOME
NOMADIC
NOMARCH sy
NOMBLES
NOMBRIL s
NOMINAL*s
NOMINEE s
NOMISMS*
NONACID s
NONAGES*
NONAGON s
NONARTS*
NONBANK s
NONBODY
NONBOOK s
NONCASH
NONCOLA s
NONCOMS*
NONCORE
NONDRIP
NONDRUG
NONEGOS*
NONFACT s
NONFANS*
NONFARM
NONFOOD
NONFUEL
NONGAME
NONGAYS*
NONHEME
NONHERO
NONHOME
NONIRON
NONJURY
NONLIFE
NONMEAT
NONNEWS
NONOILY
NONORAL
NONPAID
NONPAST s
NONPEAK
NONPLAY s
NONPLUS
NONPOOR
NONPROS
NONSELF
NONSKED s
NONSKID
NONSLIP
NONSTOP s
NONSUCH
NONSUIT s
NONUPLE s
NONUSER*s
NONUSES
NONWAGE
NONWARS*
NONWOOL
NONWORD s
NONWORK
NONZERO
NOODGED*
NOODGES*
NOODLED*
NOODLES
NOOGIES*
NOONDAY s
NOONING s
NOOSERS*
NOOSING
NOPALES
NOPLACE
NORITES*
NORITIC

NORLAND s
NORMALS*
NORTHER ns
NOSEBAG s
NOSEGAY s
NOSHERS*
NOSHING
NOSIEST
NOSINGS*
NOSTOCS*
NOSTRIL s
NOSTRUM s
NOTABLE s
NOTABLY
NOTATED*
NOTATES*
NOTCHED
NOTCHER s
NOTCHES
NOTEDLY
NOTEPAD s
NOTHING s
NOTICED*
NOTICER*s
NOTICES*
NOTIONS*
NOUGATS*
NOUGHTS
NOUMENA l
NOURISH
NOUVEAU
NOVELLA s
NOVELLE
NOVELLY
NOVELTY
NOVENAE*
NOVENAS*
NOVICES*
NOWHERE s
NOWNESS
NOXIOUS
NOYADES*
NOZZLES*
NUANCED*
NUANCES*
ks NUBBIER
NUBBINS*
NUBBLES*
NUBUCKS*
NUCELLI
NUCHALS*
NUCLEAL
NUCLEAR
NUCLEIN*s
NUCLEON s
NUCLEUS
NUCLIDE s
NUDGERS*
NUDGING
NUDISMS*
NUDISTS*
NUDNICK s
NUDNIKS*
NUDZHED
NUDZHES
NUGGETS*
NUGGETY*
NULLAHS*
NULLIFY
NULLING
NULLITY
NUMBATS*
NUMBERS
NUMBEST
NUMBING
*NUMBLES
NUMERAL s
NUMERIC s
NUMMARY
NUNATAK s
NUNCIOS*
NUNCLES
*NUNLIKE
NUNNERY
NUNNISH
NUPTIAL s
k NURLING
NURSERS*
NURSERY*
NURSING s
NURTURE drs
NUTATED*
NUTATES*
NUTCASE s
NUTGALL s
NUTLETS*

NUTLIKE
NUTMEAT s
NUTMEGS*
NUTPICK s
NUTRIAS*
NUTSIER
NUTTERS
NUTTIER
NUTTILY
NUTTING s
NUTWOOD s
NUZZLED*
NUZZLER*s
NUZZLES*
NYLGHAI s
NYLGHAU s
NYMPHAE*
NYMPHAL*
NYMPHET s
NYMPHOS*
OAKIEST
OAKLIKE
OAKMOSS
b OARFISH
OARLESS
OARLIKE
OARLOCK s
OARSMAN
OARSMEN
OATCAKE s
bgm OATLIKE
OATMEAL s
OBCONIC
l OBELIAS*
OBELISE ds
OBELISK s
OBELISM s
OBELIZE ds
OBENTOS
OBESELY
OBESITY
OBEYERS*
OBEYING
OBIISMS*
OBJECTS*
OBLASTI*
OBLASTS
OBLATES*
OBLIGED*
OBLIGEE*s
OBLIGER*s
OBLIGES*
OBLIGOR s
OBLIQUE ds
OBLONGS*
OBLOQUY
OBOISTS*
OBOVATE
OBOVOID
OBSCENE r
OBSCURE drs
OBSEQUY
OBSERVE drs
OBTAINS*
OBTESTS*
OBTRUDE drs
OBTUNDS*
OBTUSER*
OBVERSE s
OBVERTS*
OBVIATE ds
OBVIOUS
*OCARINA s
OCCIPUT s
OCCLUDE ds
OCCULTS*
OCEANIC
*OCELLAR
OCELLUS
OCELOID
OCELOTS*
t OCHERED
OCHREAE*
OCHRING
OCHROID
OCHROUS
OCICATS*
c*OCREATE
OCTADIC
OCTAGON s
OCTANES*
OCTANOL s
OCTANTS*
OCTAVAL
OCTAVES*
OCTAVOS*

OCTETTE s
OCTOPOD s
OCTOPUS
OCTROIS*
OCTUPLE dst
x
OCTUPLY
OCULARS*
OCULIST s
ODALISK s
ODDBALL s
ODDMENT s
ODDNESS
*ODONATE s
ODORANT s
ODORFUL
ODORIZE ds
ODOROUS
ODYSSEY s
OEDEMAS
OEDIPAL
OENOMEL s
OERSTED s
*OESTRIN s
*OESTRUM s
*OESTRUS
OEUVRES*
OFFBEAT s
OFFCAST s
OFFCUTS*
OFFENCE s
OFFENDS*
OFFENSE s
cg OFFERED
OFFERER s
OFFEROR s
OFFHAND
OFFICER*s
OFFICES*
OFFINGS*
OFFLINE
OFFLOAD s
OFFRAMP s
OFFSETS*
OFFSIDE s
s OFTENER
OGDOADS*
OGHAMIC
OGREISH
OGREISM s
OGRISMS*
OHMAGES*
OIDIOID
OILBIRD s
OILCAMP s
OILCANS*
OILCUPS*
OILHOLE s
r OILIEST
OILSEED s
OILSKIN s
OILWAYS*
*OINKING
OINOMEL s
OKAYING
bc OLDNESS
OLDSTER s
OLDWIFE
OLEATES*
OLEFINE*s
OLEFINS*
OLEINES*
OLESTRA s
OLICOOK s
OLINGOS*
OLIVARY
OLIVINE s
o OLOGIES
o OLOGIST s
d OLOROSO s
OMELETS*
OMENING
OMENTAL
lmt*OMENTUM s
*OMICRON s
*OMIKRON s
OMINOUS
OMITTED
OMITTER s
OMNIBUS
OMNIFIC
OMPHALI
ONAGERS*
*ONANISM s
ONANIST s
ONBOARD

ONEFOLD
ONEIRIC
dgl ONENESS
ONERIER
ONEROUS
ONESELF
z ONETIME
ONGOING
ONLOADS*
ONSHORE
ONSTAGE
ONWARDS*
OOCYSTS*
OOCYTES*
OODLINS
OOGONIA l
OOLITES*
OOLITHS*
OOLITIC
z OOLOGIC
OOLONGS*
OOMIACK*s
OOMIACS*
OOMIAKS*
OOMPAHS*
z OOPHYTE s
w OORALIS*
z OOSPERM s
z OOSPORE s
OOTHECA el
bw OOZIEST
*OPACIFY
OPACITY
OPALINE s
OPAQUED*
OPAQUER*
OPAQUES*t
OPENERS*
OPENEST
OPENING s
OPERAND s
OPERANT s
OPERATE ds
OPERONS*
OPEROSE
OPHITES*
OPHITIC
OPIATED*
OPIATES*
*OPINING
*OPINION s
OPIOIDS*
*OPOSSUM s
OPPIDAN s
OPPOSED*
OPPOSER*s
OPPOSES*
OPPRESS
OPPUGNS*
OPSONIC
OPSONIN s
OPTICAL
OPTIMAL*
OPTIMES*
OPTIMUM s
OPTIONS*
OPULENT
OPUNTIA s
OQUASSA s
ORACHES*
c ORACLES*
m ORALISM s
m ORALIST s
m ORALITY
ORANGES
ORANGEY*
b*ORATING
*ORATION s
ORATORS*
m ORATORY*
ORATRIX
ORBIEST
ORBITAL s
ORBITED
ORBITER s
ORBLESS
ORCEINS*
ORCHARD s
ORCHIDS*
ORCHILS*
ORCINOL s
ORDAINS*
ORDEALS*
b ORDERED
b ORDERER s
ORDERLY
ORDINAL s
s ORDINES
b ORDURES*
ORECTIC
OREGANO s
OREIDES*
ORFRAYS*
ORGANDY
ORGANIC s
ORGANON s
ORGANUM s
ORGANZA s
ORGASMS*
ORGEATS*
ORGIAST s
ORGONES*
ORIENTS*
ORIFICE s
ORIGAMI s
ORIGANS*
ORIGINS*
ORIOLES*
ORISHAS*
ORISONS*
ORMOLUS*
OROGENY
OROIDES*
h OROLOGY
*OROTUND
ORPHANS*
ORPHISM s
ORPHREY s
ORPINES*
ORRICES*
m ORRISES
ORTOLAN s
OSCINES*
OSCULAR*
OSCULES*
OSCULUM
OSETRAS*
OSIERED
OSMATIC
OSMIOUS
OSMIUMS*
OSMOLAL
OSMOLAR
OSMOLES*
OSMOSED*
c OSMOSES*
OSMOSIS
OSMOTIC
OSMUNDA*s
OSMUNDS*
OSPREYS*
OSSEINS*
OSSEOUS
OSSETRA s
OSSICLE s
OSSIFIC
OSSUARY
OSTEOID s
OSTEOMA s
OSTIARY
OSTIOLE s
hj OSTLERS*
p OSTMARK s
OSTOSES
OSTOSIS
OSTRACA
OSTRAKA
OSTRICH
OTALGIA s
OTALGIC
OTOCYST s
OTOLITH s
OTOLOGY
OTTAVAS*
OTTOMAN s
OUABAIN s
cdm OUCHING
ptv
OUGHTED
OUGUIYA s
OURANGS*
OURARIS
OUREBIS*
y OURSELF
jr OUSTERS*
jr OUSTING
OUTACTS*
OUTADDS*
OUTAGES*
OUTASKS*
OUTBACK s
OUTBAKE ds
OUTBARK s
OUTBAWL s
OUTBEAM s
OUTBEGS*
OUTBIDS*
OUTBRAG s
OUTBRED
OUTBULK s
OUTBURN st
OUTBUYS*
OUTCALL s
OUTCAST es
OUTCHID e
OUTCITY
OUTCOME s
OUTCOOK s
OUTCROP s
OUTCROW ds
OUTDARE ds
OUTDATE ds
OUTDOER s
OUTDOES
OUTDONE
OUTDOOR s
OUTDRAG s
OUTDRAW ns
OUTDREW
OUTDROP s
OUTDUEL s
OUTEARN s
OUTEATS*
OUTECHO
OUTFACE ds
OUTFALL s
OUTFAST s
OUTFAWN s
OUTFEEL s
OUTFELT
OUTFIND s
OUTFIRE ds
OUTFISH
OUTFITS*
OUTFLEW
OUTFLOW ns
OUTFOOL s
OUTFOOT s
OUTGAIN s
OUTGAVE
OUTGAZE ds
OUTGIVE ns
OUTGLOW s
OUTGNAW ns
OUTGOES
OUTGONE
OUTGREW
OUTGRIN s
OUTGROW ns
OUTGUNS*
OUTGUSH
OUTHAUL s
OUTHEAR ds
OUTHITS*
OUTHOWL s
OUTHUNT s
OUTINGS*
OUTJINX
OUTJUMP s
OUTJUTS*
OUTKEEP s
OUTKEPT
OUTKICK s
OUTKILL s
OUTKISS
OUTLAID
OUTLAIN
OUTLAND s
OUTLAST s
OUTLAWS*
OUTLAYS*
OUTLEAD s
OUTLEAP st
OUTLETS*
OUTLIER*s
OUTLIES*
OUTLINE drs
OUTLIVE drs
OUTLOOK s
OUTLOVE ds
OUTMANS*
OUTMODE ds
*OUTMOST
OUTMOVE ds
OUTPACE ds
OUTPASS
OUTPITY
OUTPLAN s
OUTPLAY s
OUTPLOD s
OUTPLOT s
OUTPOLL s
OUTPORT s
OUTPOST s
OUTPOUR s
OUTPRAY s
OUTPULL s
OUTPUSH
OUTPUTS*
OUTRACE ds
OUTRAGE ds
OUTRANG*e
OUTRANK*s
OUTRATE ds
OUTRAVE ds
OUTREAD s
OUTRIDE rs
OUTRIGS*
OUTRING s
OUTROAR s
OUTROCK s
OUTRODE
OUTROLL s
OUTROOT s
OUTROWS*
OUTRUNG*
OUTRUNS*
OUTRUSH
OUTSAID
OUTSAIL s
OUTSANG
OUTSAYS*
OUTSEEN*
OUTSEES*
OUTSELL s
OUTSERT s
OUTSETS*
OUTSHOT
OUTSIDE rs
OUTSING*s
OUTSINS*
OUTSITS*
OUTSIZE ds
OUTSOAR s
OUTSOLD
OUTSOLE s
OUTSPAN s
OUTSPED
OUTSTAY s
OUTSULK s
OUTSUNG
OUTSWAM
OUTSWIM s
OUTSWUM
OUTTAKE s
OUTTALK s
OUTTASK s
OUTTELL s
OUTTOLD
OUTTROT s
OUTTURN s
OUTVIED*
OUTVIES*
OUTVOTE ds
OUTWAIT s
OUTWALK s
OUTWARD*s
OUTWARS*
OUTWASH
OUTWEAR sy
OUTWEEP s
OUTWENT
OUTWEPT
OUTWILE ds
OUTWILL s
OUTWIND s
OUTWISH
OUTWITH*
OUTWITS*
OUTWORE
OUTWORK s
OUTWORN
OUTWRIT e
OUTYELL s
OUTYELP s
OVALITY
OVARIAL
OVARIAN
c*OVARIES
OVATELY
n OVATION s
OVERACT s
c OVERAGE ds
c OVERALL s
OVERAPT
OVERARM s
OVERATE
OVERAWE ds
OVERBED
OVERBET s
*OVERBID s
OVERBIG
OVERBUY s
OVERCOY
OVERCUT s
OVERDID
OVERDOG*s
OVERDRY
OVERDUB s
OVERDUE
OVERDYE drs
OVEREAT s
OVERFAR
OVERFAT
OVERFED
OVERFIT
h OVERFLY
OVERHOT
ch OVERING
OVERJOY s
OVERLAP s
OVERLAX
OVERLAY s
c OVERLET s
OVERLIE s
OVERLIT
OVERMAN sy
OVERMEN
OVERMIX
OVERNEW
OVERPAY s
OVERPLY
OVERRAN k
OVERRUN s
OVERSAD
OVERSAW
OVERSEA s
OVERSEE dnr
s
*OVERSET s
OVERSEW ns
OVERSUP s
OVERTAX
OVERTIP s
c OVERTLY
OVERTOP s
OVERUSE ds
OVERWET s
OVICIDE s
OVIDUCT s
OVIFORM
OVIPARA
OVISACS*
OVOIDAL s
OVONICS*
OVULARY*
OVULATE ds
b OWLLIKE
OWNABLE
OXALATE ds
OXAZINE s
OXBLOOD s
OXCARTS*
OXFORDS*
OXHEART s
OXIDANT s
OXIDASE s
OXIDATE ds
OXIDISE drs
OXIDIZE drs
f OXTAILS*
OXYACID s
OXYGENS*
OXYMORA
OXYPHIL es
OXYSALT s
OXYSOME s
OXYTONE s
*OYESSES
r OYSTERS*
OZALIDS*
*OZONATE ds
OZONIDE s
OZONISE ds
OZONIZE drs
OZONOUS
PABLUMS*
PABULAR
PABULUM s
PACHISI s
PACHUCO s
s PACIEST
PACIFIC
PACKAGE drs
PACKERS*
PACKETS*
PACKING s
PACKMAN
PACKMEN
PACKWAX
*PACTION s
PADAUKS*
PADDERS
PADDIES
*PADDING s
PADDLED
PADDLER*s
PADDLES
PADDOCK s
PADLOCK s
PADNAGS*
PADOUKS*
PADRONE s
PADRONI
PADSHAH s
PAELLAS*
PAESANI*
PAESANO*s
PAESANS*
PAGEANT s
PAGEBOY s
PAGEFUL s
PAGINAL
PAGINGS
PAGODAS*
PAGURID s
PAHLAVI s
PAIKING
PAILFUL s
PAINFUL
PAINING
PAINTED
PAINTER s
*PAIRING s
PAISANA*s
PAISANO*s
PAISANS*
PAISLEY s
PAJAMAS*
PAKEHAS*
PAKORAS*
PALABRA s
PALACED*
PALACES*
PALADIN s
PALAPAS*
PALATAL s
PALATES
PALAVER s
PALAZZI
PALAZZO s
PALEATE
PALETOT s
PALETTE s
PALFREY s
PALIEST
PALIKAR s
PALINGS*
PALLETS*
PALLIAL*
PALLIER
s PALLING
*PALLIUM s
PALLORS*
PALMARY*
PALMATE d
PALMERS*
PALMFUL s
PALMIER
PALMING
PALMIST s
PALMTOP s
PALMYRA s
PALOOKA s
PALPATE ds
PALPING
PALSHIP s
PALSIED
PALSIES
PALTERS
PALUDAL
PAMPEAN s
PAMPERO*s
PAMPERS*
PANACEA ns
PANACHE s
PANADAS*
PANAMAS*
PANCAKE ds
PANCHAX
PANDANI
PANDECT s
PANDERS*
PANDIED
PANDIES
PANDITS*
PANDOOR s
PANDORA s
PANDORE s
PANDOUR s
PANDURA s
*PANELED
PANFISH
PANFULS*
PANGENE*s
PANGENS*
PANGING
PANGRAM s
PANICKY
PANICLE ds
PANICUM s
PANIERS*
s PANNERS*
PANNIER s
s PANNING
PANOCHA s
PANOCHE s
PANOPLY
PANPIPE s
PANSIES
*PANTHER s
PANTIES*
PANTILE ds
*PANTING
PANTOUM s
PANZERS*
PAPADAM s
PAPADOM s
PAPADUM s
PAPAINS*
PAPALLY
PAPAYAN*
PAPAYAS*
PAPERED
PAPERER s
PAPHIAN s
PAPILLA er
PAPOOSE s
PAPPIER
PAPPIES t
*PAPPOSE
PAPPOUS
PAPRICA s
PAPRIKA s
PAPULAE*
PAPULAR*
PAPULES*
PAPYRAL
PAPYRUS
s*PARABLE s
PARADED*
PARADER*s
PARADES*
PARADOR s
PARADOS
PARADOX
PARAGON s
PARAMOS*
PARANGS*
PARAPET s
PARAPHS*
PARASOL s
PARBAKE ds
PARBOIL s
PARCELS*
*PARCHED
*PARCHES i
PARDAHS*
PARDINE
PARDNER s
PARDONS*
PAREIRA s
PARENTS*
PARERGA
PARESES
PARESIS
PARETIC s
PARFAIT s
PARGETS*
s PARGING s
PARIAHS*
PARIANS*

PARINGS*
*PARISES
PARKADE s
s PARKERS*
s PARKING s
PARKWAY s
PARLAYS*
PARLEYS*
s PARLING
PARLORS*
PARLOUR s
PARLOUS
PARODIC
PARODOI
PARODOS
PAROLED*
PAROLEE*s
PAROLES*
PARONYM s
PAROTIC
PAROTID s
PARQUET s
PARRALS*
PARRELS*
PARRIED
s PARRIER s
PARRIES
s PARRING
PARROTS*
PARROTY*
PARSECS*
PARSERS*
PARSING
PARSLEY s
PARSNIP s
PARSONS
PARTAKE nrs
PARTANS*
PARTIAL s
PARTIED
*PARTIER s
PARTIES
PARTING s
PARTITA s
PARTITE
PARTLET s
PARTNER s
PARTONS*
PARTOOK
PARTWAY
PARTYER s
PARURAS*
PARURES*
PARVENU es
PARVISE*s
PASCALS*
PASCHAL s
*PASHING
PASQUIL s
PASSADE s
PASSADO s
PASSAGE ds
PASSANT
PASSELS*
PASSERS*
PASSING s
PASSION s
PASSIVE s
PASSKEY s
PASTELS*
*PASTERN*s
PASTERS
PASTEUP s
PASTIER*
PASTIES*t
PASTILS*
PASTIME s
PASTINA s
PASTING
PASTORS*
PASTURE drs
PATACAS*
PATAGIA l
PATAMAR s
PATCHED
PATCHER s
PATCHES
PATELLA ers
PATENCY
PATENTS*
PATHWAY s
PATIENT s
PATINAE*d
PATINAS*
PATINED*
PATINES*
PATNESS
PATRIOT s
PATROLS*
PATRONS*
PATROON s
PATSIES
PATTENS*
PATTERN*s
s PATTERS*
PATTIES*
s PATTING
PATZERS*
PAUCITY
PAUGHTY
PAULINS*
PAUNCHY*
PAUPERS*
PAUSERS*
PAUSING
PAVANES*
PAVINGS*
PAVIORS*
PAVIOUR s
PAVISER*s
PAVISES*
PAVISSE s
PAVLOVA s
PAWKIER
PAWKILY
PAWNAGE s
PAWNEES*
s PAWNERS*
s*PAWNING
PAWNORS*
PAWPAWS*
PAYABLE s
PAYABLY
PAYBACK s
PAYDAYS*
PAYLOAD s
PAYMENT s
PAYNIMS*
PAYOFFS*
PAYOLAS*
PAYOUTS*
PAYROLL s
PEACHED
PEACHER s
PEACHES
PEACING
PEACOAT s
PEACOCK sy
PEAFOWL s
PEAHENS*
PEAKIER
s PEAKING
PEAKISH
PEALIKE
PEALING
PEANUTS*
PEARLED
PEARLER s
PEARTER
PEARTLY
PEASANT s
PEASCOD s
PEATIER
PEAVEYS*
PEAVIES
PEBBLED*
PEBBLES*
PECCANT
PECCARY
PECCAVI s
PECHANS*
*PECHING
PECKERS*
PECKIER
s PECKING
PECKISH
PECTASE s
s PECTATE s
PECTENS*
PECTINS*
PECTIZE ds
PECULIA r
PEDAGOG sy
PEDALED
PEDALER s
PEDALOS*
PEDANTS*
PEDDLED*
PEDDLER*sy
PEDDLES*
PEDICAB s
PEDICEL s
PEDICLE ds
PEDLARS*
PEDLARY*
PEDLERS*
PEDLERY*
PEDOCAL s
PEEBEEN s
PEEKING
PEELERS*
s PEELING s
PEENING
PEEPERS*
PEEPING
PEEPULS*
PEERAGE s
PEERESS
PEERIES*
s PEERING
PEEVING
PEEVISH
PEEWEES*
PEEWITS*
*PEGGING
PEGLESS
PEGLIKE
PEINING
PEISING
PEKEPOO s
PELAGES*
PELAGIC s
PELICAN s
PELISSE s
PELITES
PELITIC
PELLETS*
PELMETS*
PELORIA ns
PELORIC
PELORUS
PELOTAS*
PELOTON s
PELTAST s
PELTATE
s PELTERS*
PELTING
PELVICS*
PEMBINA s
PEMICAN s
PEMPHIX
PENALLY
PENALTY
PENANCE ds
PENANGS*
*PENATES
PENCELS*
PENCILS*
PENDANT s
PENDENT s
su*PENDING
PENGUIN s
PENICIL s
PENISES
PENLITE s
PENNAME s
PENNANT s
PENNATE d
PENNERS*
PENNIES
PENNINE s
PENNING
PENNONS*
PENOCHE s
PENSEES*
PENSILE
PENSILS*
PENSION es
PENSIVE
PENSTER s
PENTADS*
PENTANE s
PENTENE s
PENTODE s
PENTOSE s
PENTYLS*
PENUCHE s
PENUCHI s
PENULTS*
PEONAGE s
PEONIES
*PEONISM s
PEOPLED*
PEOPLER*s
PEOPLES*
PEPINOS*
PEPLUMS*
PEPPERS*
PEPPERY*
PEPPIER
PEPPILY
PEPPING
PEPSINE*s
PEPSINS*
PEPTALK s
PEPTICS*
PEPTIDE*s
PEPTIDS*
PEPTIZE drs
PEPTONE s
PERACID s
PERCALE s
PERCENT s
PERCEPT s
PERCHED
PERCHER s
PERCHES
PERCOID s
PERCUSS
PERDUES*
PERDURE ds
PEREION s
PEREONS*
PERFECT aos
PERFIDY
PERFORM s
PERFUME drs
PERFUMY
PERFUSE ds
PERGOLA s
PERHAPS
PERIAPT s
PERIDIA l
PERIDOT s
PERIGEE s
PERIGON s
PERILED
PERILLA s
PERINEA l
PERIODS*
PERIQUE s
PERITUS
PERIWIG s
PERJURE drs
PERJURY
PERKIER
PERKILY
PERKING
PERKISH
PERLITE s
PERMIAN
PERMING
PERMITS*
PERMUTE ds
PERNODS*
PERORAL
PEROXID es
PERPEND s
PERPENT s
PERPLEX
PERRIES
PERRONS*
PERSALT s
PERSIST s
PERSONA*els
PERSONS*
PERSPEX
PERTAIN s
PERTEST
PERTURB s
PERUKED*
PERUKES*
PERUSAL s
PERUSED*
PERUSER*s
PERUSES*
PERVADE drs
PERVERT s
PESADES*
PESETAS*
PESEWAS*
PESKIER
PESKILY
PESSARY
PESTERS
PESTIER
PESTLED*
PESTLES*
PETALED
PETARDS*
PETASOS
PETASUS
PETCOCK s
PETERED
PETIOLE ds
PETITES*
PETNAPS*
PETRALE s
PETRELS*
PETRIFY
PETROLS*
PETROUS
PETSAIS*
PETTERS*
PETTIER
PETTILY
PETTING s
PETTISH
PETTLED*
PETTLES*
PETUNIA s
PEWTERS*
PEYOTES*
PEYOTLS*
PEYTRAL s
PEYTREL s
PFENNIG es
PHAETON s
PHALANX
PHALLIC*
PHALLUS
PHANTOM s
PHARAOH s
PHARYNX
PHASEAL
PHASING
PHASMID s
*PHATTER
PHELLEM s
PHENATE s
PHENOLS*
PHENOMS*
PHENOXY
PHENYLS*
PHILTER s
PHILTRA
PHILTRE ds
PHLEGMS*
PHLEGMY*
PHLOEMS*
PHLOXES
PHOBIAS*
PHOBICS*
PHOCINE
PHOEBES*
PHOEBUS
PHOENIX
PHONATE ds
PHONEME s
PHONEYS
a PHONICS*
*PHONIED
PHONIER
PHONIES t
PHONILY
*PHONING
PHONONS*
e PHORATE s
PHORESY
PHOTICS*
PHOTOED
PHOTOGS*
PHOTONS*
PHRASAL
PHRASED*
PHRASES*
PHRATRY
PHREAKS*
PHRENIC
PHRENSY
PHYLLOS*
PHYSEDS*
PHYSICS*
PHYTANE s
PHYTINS*
PHYTOID
PHYTOLS*
PHYTONS*
PIAFFED*
PIAFFER*s
PIAFFES*
PIANISM s
PIANIST s
PIASABA s
PIASAVA s
PIASTER s
PIASTRE s
PIAZZAS*
PIBROCH s
PICACHO s
PICADOR s
PICANTE
PICARAS*
PICAROS*
PICCATA
PICCOLO s
PICEOUS
PICKAXE*ds
PICKEER s
PICKERS
PICKETS*
*PICKIER
PICKING s
PICKLED*
PICKLES*
PICKOFF s
PICKUPS*
PICNICS*
PICOLIN es
PICOTED
PICOTEE s
PICQUET s
PICRATE ds
PICRITE s
PICTURE ds
PIDDLED*
PIDDLER*s
PIDDLES*
PIDDOCK s
PIDGINS*
PIEBALD s
PIECERS*
PIECING s
PIEFORT s
PIEHOLE s
PIERCED*
PIERCER*s
PIERCES*
PIEROGI
PIERROT s
PIETIES
PIETISM s
PIETIST s
PIFFLED*
PIFFLES*
PIGBOAT s
PIGEONS*
PIGFISH
PIGGERY
PIGGIER*
PIGGIES*t
PIGGING
PIGGINS*
PIGGISH
PIGLETS*
PIGLIKE
PIGMENT s
PIGMIES
PIGNOLI as
PIGNORA
PIGNUTS*
PIGOUTS*
PIGPENS*
PIGSKIN s
PIGSNEY s
PIGTAIL s
PIGWEED s
PIKAKES*
PIKEMAN
PIKEMEN
PILAFFS*
PILEATE d
PILEOUS
PILEUPS*
PILFERS*
PILGRIM s
s PILINGS*
s PILLAGE drs
PILLARS*
PILLBOX
s PILLING
PILLION s
PILLORY
PILLOWS*
PILLOWY*
PILOTED
PILSNER s
PILULAR
PILULES*
PIMENTO s
*PIMPING
PIMPLED
PIMPLES*
PINANGS*
PINATAS*
PINBALL s
PINBONE s
PINCERS*
*PINCHED
*PINCHER s
*PINCHES
PINDERS*
PINEALS*
PINENES*
PINESAP s
PINETUM
PINFISH
*PINFOLD s
PINGERS*
PINGING
PINGOES
PINGUID
PINHEAD s
PINHOLE s
s PINIEST
o*PINIONS*
PINITES*
PINITOL s
PINKENS*
PINKERS
PINKEST
PINKEYE*s
PINKEYS*
PINKIES*
*PINKING s
PINKISH
PINKOES
PINNACE s
*PINNATE d
s*PINNERS*
s PINNIES
s*PINNING
PINNULA er
PINNULE s
PINOCLE s
PINOLES*
PINONES
PINTADA s
PINTADO s
PINTAIL s
PINTANO s
PINTLES*
PINTOES
PINWALE s
PINWEED s
PINWORK s
PINWORM s
PINYONS*
PIOLETS*
PIONEER s
PIOSITY
PIOUSLY
PIPAGES*
PIPEAGE s
PIPEFUL s
PIPETTE ds
PIPIEST
PIPINGS*
PIPKINS*
PIPPING*
PIPPINS*
PIQUANT
PIQUETS*
PIQUING
PIRAGUA s
PIRANAS*
PIRANHA s
PIRATED*
PIRATES*
PIRATIC
PIRAYAS*
PIROGEN
PIROGHI
PIROGUE s
PIROJKI
PIROQUE s
PISCARY
PISCINA els
PISCINE
PISHERS*
PISHING
PISHOGE s
PISMIRE s
PISSOIR s
PISTILS*
PISTOLE*ds
PISTOLS*
PISTONS*
PISTOUS*
PITAPAT s
PITAYAS*
*PITCHED

PITCHER s
*PITCHES
PITEOUS
PITFALL s
PITHEAD s
PITHIER
PITHILY
PITHING
PITIERS*
PITIFUL
PITMANS*
PITSAWS*
s PITTING s
PITYING
PIVOTAL
PIVOTED
PIXYISH
PIZAZZY*
PIZZAZZ*y
PIZZLES*
PLACARD s
PLACATE drs
PLACEBO s
PLACERS
PLACETS*
*PLACING
PLACKET s
PLACOID s
PLAFOND s
PLAGUED*
PLAGUER*s
PLAGUES*
PLAGUEY*
PLAICES*
PLAIDED
PLAINED
PLAINER
PLAINLY
PLAINTS*
PLAITED
PLAITER s
*PLANATE
PLANCHE*st
PLANERS*
PLANETS*
PLANING
PLANISH
PLANKED
PLANNED
*PLANNER s
PLANTAR
PLANTED
PLANTER s
PLANULA er
PLAQUES*
s*PLASHED
s*PLASHER s
s*PLASHES
PLASMAS*
PLASMIC
PLASMID s
PLASMIN s
PLASMON s
*PLASTER sy
a PLASTIC s
PLASTID s
PLATANE*s
PLATANS*
PLATEAU sx
PLATENS
PLATERS*
PLATIER
PLATIES t
*PLATINA s
PLATING s
PLATOON s
s PLATTED
s*PLATTER s
PLATYPI
PLAUDIT s
PLAYACT s
PLAYBOY s
PLAYDAY s
PLAYERS
PLAYFUL
s*PLAYING
PLAYLET s
*PLAYOFF s
PLAYPEN s
*PLEADED
*PLEADER s
PLEASED
*PLEASER*s
PLEASES
PLEATED
PLEATER s

PLECTRA
PLEDGED*
PLEDGEE*s
*PLEDGER*s
PLEDGES
PLEDGET*s
PLEDGOR s
PLEIADS*
PLENARY
PLENISH
PLENISM s
PLENIST s
PLENUMS*
PLEONAL
PLEONIC
PLEOPOD s
*PLESSOR s
PLEURAE*
PLEURAL*
PLEURAS*
PLEURON
PLEXORS*
*PLIABLE
PLIABLY
PLIANCY
PLICATE d
u*PLIGHTS*
PLIMSOL els
u*PLINKED
*PLINKER s
PLINTHS*
PLISKIE s
PLISSES*
PLODDED
PLODDER s
PLONKED
*PLOPPED
PLOSION s
PLOSIVE s
*PLOTTED
*PLOTTER s
PLOTZED
PLOTZES
PLOUGHS
PLOVERS
*PLOWBOY s
PLOWERS
*PLOWING
PLOWMAN
PLOWMEN
PLOYING
*PLUCKED
PLUCKER s
*PLUGGED
*PLUGGER s
PLUGOLA s
PLUMAGE ds
PLUMATE
PLUMBED
*PLUMBER sy
PLUMBIC
PLUMBUM s
PLUMIER
PLUMING
PLUMMER
PLUMMET s
PLUMOSE
*PLUMPED
*PLUMPEN s
*PLUMPER s
PLUMPLY
PLUMULE s
PLUNDER s
PLUNGED
*PLUNGER*s
PLUNGES
PLUNKED
*PLUNKER s
PLURALS*
*PLUSHER
*PLUSHES t
*PLUSHLY
PLUSSES
PLUTEUS
PLUTONS*
PLUVIAL s
PLUVIAN
PLYWOOD s
PNEUMAS*
POACHED
POACHER s
POACHES
POBLANO s
POCHARD s
POCKETS*
POCKIER

POCKILY
POCKING
POCOSEN s
POCOSIN s
POCOSON s
PODAGRA ls
PODDING
PODESTA s
PODGIER
PODGILY
PODITES*
PODITIC
PODIUMS
PODLIKE
PODSOLS*
PODZOLS*
POESIES
POETESS
POETICS*
POETISE drs
POETIZE drs
POGONIA s
POGONIP s
POGROMS*
POINDED
POINTED*
POINTER*s
POINTES*
POISERS*
POISING
POISONS*
POITREL s
POKABLE
POKIEST*
POLARON s
POLDERS*
POLEAXE*ds
POLECAT s
POLEMIC s
POLENTA s
POLEYNS*
POLICED*
POLICER*s
POLICES*
POLITER*
POLITIC kos
POLKAED
POLLACK s
POLLARD s
POLLEES*
POLLENS*
POLLERS*
POLLING
POLLIST s
POLLOCK s
POLLUTE drs
POLOIST s
POLYCOT s
POLYENE s
POLYGON sy
POLYMER s
POLYNYA s
POLYNYI
POLYOLS*
POLYOMA s
POLYPED s
POLYPOD sy
POLYPUS
POMACES*
POMADED*
POMADES*
POMATUM s
POMELOS*
POMFRET s
POMMELS*
POMPANO s
POMPOMS*
POMPONS*
POMPOUS
PONCHOS*
PONCING
PONDERS*
PONDING
PONGEES*
PONGIDS*
s PONGING
PONIARD s
PONTIFF s
PONTILS*
PONTINE
PONTONS*
s PONTOON s
PONYING
POOCHED
POOCHES
POODLES

*POOHING
s POOLERS*
s POOLING
POOPING
POOREST
POORISH*
POPCORN s
POPEDOM s
POPEYED
POPGUNS*
POPLARS*
POPLINS*
POPOVER s
POPPERS*
POPPETS*
POPPIED
POPPIES
POPPING
POPPLED*
POPPLES*
POPSIES*
POPULAR
PORCHES
PORCINE
PORCINI s
PORCINO
*PORGIES
PORISMS*
PORKERS*
PORKIER
PORKIES t
PORKING
PORKPIE s
PORNIER
PORRECT
PORTAGE ds
PORTALS*
PORTEND s
PORTENT s
s PORTERS*
PORTICO s
s PORTING
PORTION s
PORTRAY s
POSABLE
POSADAS*
POSEURS*
POSHEST
POSITED
POSOLES*
POSSESS*
POSSETS*
o POSSUMS*
POSTAGE s
POSTALS*
POSTBAG s
POSTBOX
POSTBOY s
POSTDOC s
POSTEEN s
POSTERN*s
POSTERS*
POSTFIX
POSTIES*
POSTING*s
POSTINS*
POSTMAN
POSTMEN
POSTOPS*
POSTTAX
POSTURE drs
POSTWAR
POTABLE s
POTAGES*
POTAMIC
POTBOIL s
POTBOYS*
POTEENS*
POTENCE s
POTENCY
POTFULS*
POTHEAD s
POTHEEN s
POTHERB*s
POTHERS
POTHOLE ds
POTHOOK s
POTICHE s
POTIONS*
POTLACH e
POTLIKE
POTLINE s
POTLUCK s
POTPIES*
POTSHOT s
POTSIES*

POTTAGE s
POTTEEN s
s*POTTERS*
POTTERY*
s POTTIER
POTTIES t
s POTTING
POTTLES*
POTZERS*
*POUCHED
*POUCHES
POUFFED*
POUFFES*
POULARD es
POULTER s
POULTRY
POUNCED*
POUNCER*s
POUNCES
POUNDAL s
POUNDED
POUNDER s
POURERS*
POURING
POUSSIE s
s*POUTERS*
POUTFUL
POUTIER
POUTINE s
s*POUTING
POVERTY
POWDERS*
POWDERY*
POWERED
POWTERS*
POWWOWS*
POXIEST
POZOLES*
a PRACTIC e
PRAETOR s
PRAIRIE s
u*PRAISED*
u*PRAISER*s
u*PRAISES*
PRAJNAS*
PRALINE s
PRANCED*
PRANCER*s
PRANCES
*PRANGED
*PRANKED
PRATERS
u*PRATING
s*PRATTLE drs
PRAWNED
PRAWNER s
s PRAYERS*
s*PRAYING
PREACHY*
PREACTS
PREAGED
PREAMPS*
PREANAL
PREARMS
*PREAVER s
PREBADE
PREBAKE ds
PREBEND s
PREBIDS
*PREBILL s
*PREBIND s
*PREBOIL s
*PREBOOK s
PREBOOM
PREBUYS
*PRECAST s
PRECAVA el
*PRECEDE ds
*PRECENT s
*PRECEPT s
*PRECESS
*PRECIPE s
PRECISE*drs
*PRECODE ds
*PRECOOK s
PRECOOL s
*PRECOUP
PRECURE ds
PRECUTS
*PREDATE ds
PREDAWN s
*PREDIAL
PREDICT s
PREDIVE
PREDUSK s
*PREEDIT s

PREEING
PREEMIE s
PREEMPT s
PREENED
PREENER s
PREFABS*
*PREFACE drs
PREFADE ds
*PREFECT s
PREFERS
*PREFILE ds
*PREFIRE ds
*PREFORM s
*PREFUND s
PREGAME s
*PREHEAT s
PRELACY
*PRELATE s
PRELECT s
PRELIFE
PRELIMS*
*PRELOAD s
PRELUDE drs
*PREMADE
PREMEAL
PREMEDS*
*PREMEET
PREMIER*es
PREMIES*
*PREMISE ds
*PREMISS
PREMIUM s
PREMIXT
*PREMOLD s
PREMOLT
PREMUNE
*PRENAME s
PRENOON
PREORAL
*PREPACK s
*PREPAID
PREPARE drs
*PREPAVE ds
PREPAYS
PREPILL
*PREPLAN st
*PREPPED
PREPPIE rs
PREPREG s
PREPUCE s
PREPUPA els
PREQUEL s
PRERACE
PRERIOT
PREROCK
PRESAGE drs
*PRESALE s
*PRESELL s
*PRESENT s
PRESETS
*PRESHIP s
*PRESHOW ns
*PRESIDE drs
*PRESIFT s
*PRESOAK s
*PRESOLD
PRESONG
*PRESORT s
PRESSED
PRESSER s
PRESSES
PRESSOR s
*PRESTER s
PRESTOS*
*PRESUME drs
*PRETAPE ds
PRETEEN s
*PRETELL s
PRETEND s
PRETERM s
*PRETEST s
PRETEXT s
*PRETOLD
PRETORS*
*PRETRIM s
*PRETYPE ds
PRETZEL s
PREVAIL s
PREVENT s
*PREVERB s
*PREVIEW s
*PREVISE ds
PREVUED*
PREVUES
*PREWARM*s
PREWARN*s

*PREWASH
*PREWIRE ds
*PREWORK s
*PREWORN
*PREWRAP s
PREXIES
PREYERS*
PREYING
PRIAPIC*
PRIAPUS
PRICERS
PRICIER
PRICILY
*PRICING
*PRICKED
PRICKER s
PRICKET s
PRICKLE ds
PRICKLY
*PRIDING
PRIESTS*
s*PRIGGED
*PRILLED
PRIMACY
PRIMAGE s
PRIMARY
PRIMATE s
PRIMELY
PRIMERO*s
PRIMERS
PRIMINE s
*PRIMING s
*PRIMMED
*PRIMMER
PRIMPED
PRIMSIE
PRIMULA s
PRINCES*s
PRINCOX
PRINKED
PRINKER s
s PRINTED
s PRINTER sy
PRIORLY
PRISERE s
u*PRISING
PRISONS*
PRISSED
PRISSES
PRITHEE
PRIVACY
PRIVATE rs
PRIVETS
PRIVIER
PRIVIES t
PRIVILY
PRIVITY
PRIZERS*
PRIZING
*PROBAND s
PROBANG s
PROBATE ds
PROBERS*
*PROBING
PROBITS*
PROBITY*
PROBLEM s
PROCARP s
PROCEED s
PROCESS
PROCTOR s
PROCURE drs
*PRODDED
PRODDER s
PRODIGY
PRODRUG s
PRODUCE drs
PRODUCT s
PROETTE s
PROFANE drs
PROFESS
PROFFER s
PROFILE drs
PROFITS*
PROFUSE
PROGENY
PROGGED
PROGGER s
PROGRAM s
PROJECT s
PROJETS*
PROLANS*
PROLATE
PROLEGS*
PROLINE s
PROLOGS*

PROLONG es
PROMINE s
PROMISE der
s
PROMOED
PROMOTE drs
PROMPTS*
PRONATE ds
PRONELY
PRONGED
PRONOTA
PRONOUN s
*PROOFED
*PROOFER s
PROPANE s
PROPELS*
PROPEND s
PROPENE s
PROPERS
PROPHET s
PROPINE ds
PROPJET s
PROPMAN
PROPMEN
PROPONE ds
PROPOSE drs
PROPPED
PROPRIA
PROPYLA*
PROPYLS*
PRORATE ds
PROSAIC
PROSECT s
PROSERS*
*PROSIER
*PROSILY
*PROSING
PROSODY
PROSOMA ls
PROSPER s
PROSSES
PROSSIE s
PROSTIE s
PROTEAN*s
PROTEAS*e
PROTECT s
PROTEGE es
PROTEID*es
PROTEIN*s
PROTEND s
PROTEST s
PROTEUS
PROTIST s
PROTIUM s
PROTONS*
PROTYLE*s
PROTYLS*
PROUDER
PROUDLY
PROVERB*s
PROVERS
PROVIDE drs
*PROVING
PROVISO s
PROVOKE drs
PROVOST s
PROWESS
PROWEST
PROWLED
PROWLER s
PROXIES
PROXIMO
PRUDENT
*PRUDERY
PRUDISH
PRUNERS*
PRUNING
PRURIGO s
PRUSSIC
PRUTOTH*
PRYTHEE
PSALMED
PSALMIC
*PSALTER sy
PSALTRY
PSAMMON s
PSCHENT s
PSEUDOS*
*PSHAWED
PSOATIC
PSOCIDS*
PSYCHED*
PSYCHES*
PSYCHIC s
PSYCHOS*
PSYLLAS*
PSYLLID s
PSYWARS*
PTERINS*
PTERYLA e
PTISANS*
PTOMAIN es
PTYALIN s
PUBERAL
PUBERTY
PUBLICS*
PUBLISH
PUCCOON s
PUCKERS*
PUCKERY*
PUCKISH
s PUDDING s
PUDDLED*
PUDDLER*s
PUDDLES*
PUDENCY
PUDENDA l
PUDGIER
PUDGILY
PUEBLOS*
PUERILE
PUFFERS*
PUFFERY*
PUFFIER
PUFFILY
PUFFING*
PUFFINS*
PUGAREE s
PUGGIER
PUGGING
PUGGISH
PUGGREE s
PUGMARK s
PUGREES*
PUISNES*
PULINGS*
PULLERS*
PULLETS*
PULLEYS*
PULLING
PULLMAN s
PULLOUT s
PULLUPS*
PULPERS*
PULPIER
PULPILY
PULPING
PULPITS*
PULPOUS
PULQUES*
PULSANT
PULSARS*
PULSATE ds
PULSERS*
PULSING
PULSION s
PULVINI
PUMELOS*
PUMICED*
PUMICER*s
PUMICES*
PUMMELO*s
PUMMELS*
PUMPERS*
*PUMPING
PUMPKIN s
PUNCHED
PUNCHER s
PUNCHES
PUNDITS*
PUNGENT
PUNGLED*
PUNGLES*
PUNIEST
PUNKAHS*
PUNKERS*
PUNKEST
PUNKEYS*
s PUNKIER*
s PUNKIES*t
PUNKINS*
PUNKISH
PUNNERS*
PUNNETS*
PUNNIER
PUNNING
PUNSTER s
PUNTERS*
*PUNTIES
PUNTING
PUPARIA l
PUPATED*
PUPATES*
PUPFISH
PUPILAR y
PUPPETS*
PUPPIES
*PUPPING
PURANAS*
*PURANIC
PURDAHS*
PURFLED*
PURFLER*s
PURFLES*
PURGERS
*PURGING s
PURINES
PURISMS*
PURISTS*
PURITAN s
PURLIEU s
PURLINE*s
PURLING*s
PURLINS*
PURLOIN s
PURPLED*
PURPLER*
PURPLES*t
PURPORT s
PURPOSE ds
PURPURA s
PURPURE s
s PURRING
PURSERS*
PURSIER
PURSILY
PURSING
PURSUED*
PURSUER*s
PURSUES*
PURSUIT s
PURTIER
PURVEYS*
PURVIEW s
PUSHERS
PUSHFUL
PUSHIER
PUSHILY
PUSHING
PUSHPIN s
PUSHROD s
PUSHUPS*
PUSLEYS*
PUSLIKE
PUSSIER
PUSSIES t
PUSSLEY s
PUSTULE ds
PUTAMEN
PUTDOWN s
PUTLOGS*
PUTOFFS*
PUTOUTS*
PUTREFY
PUTTEES*
s*PUTTERS*
PUTTIED*
PUTTIER*s
PUTTIES*
PUTTING
PUTZING
PUZZLED*
PUZZLER*s
PUZZLES*
PYAEMIA s
PYAEMIC
PYEMIAS*
PYGIDIA l
PYGMEAN
PYGMIES
PYGMOID
PYJAMAS*
PYKNICS*
PYLORIC*
PYLORUS
PYRALID s
PYRAMID s
PYRENES*
a PYRETIC
PYREXES
PYREXIA ls
PYREXIC
PYRIDIC
PYRITES*
PYRITIC
PYROGEN s
PYROLAS*
PYRONES*
PYROPES*
PYROSIS
PYRRHIC s
PYRROLE*s
PYRROLS*
PYTHONS*
PYURIAS*
PYXIDES
PYXIDIA
QABALAH*s
QABALAS*
QINDARS*
QINTARS*
QIVIUTS*
QUACKED
s QUADDED
QUADRAT es
QUADRIC s
QUAERES*
QUAFFED
QUAFFER s
QUAGGAS*
QUAHAUG s
QUAHOGS*
QUAICHS*
QUAIGHS*
QUAILED
QUAKERS*
QUAKIER
QUAKILY
QUAKING
QUALIFY
e QUALITY
QUAMASH
QUANGOS*
QUANTAL*
QUANTED
QUANTIC s
QUANTUM
QUARREL s
QUARTAN s
QUARTER*ns
QUARTES*
QUARTET*s
QUARTIC s
QUARTOS*
QUASARS*
s QUASHED
s QUASHER s
s QUASHES
QUASSES
QUASSIA s
QUASSIN s
QUATRES*
QUAVERS*
QUAVERY*
QUAYAGE s
QUBYTES*
QUEENED
QUEENLY
QUEERED
QUEERER
QUEERLY
QUELEAS*
QUELLED
QUELLER s
QUERIDA s
QUERIED
QUERIER s
QUERIES
QUERIST s
QUESTED
QUESTER s
QUESTOR s
QUETZAL s
QUEUERS*
QUEUING
QUEZALS*
QUIBBLE drs
QUICHES*
QUICKEN s
QUICKER
QUICKIE s
QUICKLY
QUIETED
QUIETEN s
QUIETER s
QUIETLY
QUIETUS
QUILLAI as
QUILLED
QUILLET s
QUILTED
QUILTER s
QUINARY
QUINATE
QUINCES*
QUINELA s
QUININA*s
QUININE*s
QUININS*
QUINNAT s
QUINOAS*
QUINOID s
QUINOLS*
QUINONE s
QUINTAL*s
QUINTAN*s
QUINTAR*s
QUINTAS*
QUINTES*
QUINTET*s
QUINTIC s
QUINTIN s
e QUIPPED
e QUIPPER s
QUIPPUS*
s QUIRING
QUIRKED
s QUIRTED
QUITTED
QUITTER s
QUITTOR s
QUIVERS*
QUIVERY*
QUIXOTE s
QUIZZED
QUIZZER s
QUIZZES
QUOHOGS*
QUOINED
QUOITED
QUOKKAS*
QUOMODO s
QUONDAM
QUORUMS*
QUOTERS*
QUOTING
QURSHES
QWERTYS*
RABATOS*
d RABBETS*
RABBIES
RABBINS*
RABBITS*
RABBITY*
bdg RABBLED*
bg RABBLER*s
bdg RABBLES*
RABBONI s
RABIDLY
RACCOON s
RACEMED*
RACEMES*
RACEMIC
RACEWAY s
b RACHETS*
b RACHIAL
RACIEST
bt RACINGS*
RACISMS*
RACISTS*
ct RACKERS*
b RACKETS*
RACKETY*
w RACKFUL s
ctw RACKING
RACOONS*
RACQUET s
b*RADDING
RADDLED
RADDLES
RADIALE*
RADIALS*
RADIANS*
RADIANT*s
e RADIATE ds
RADICAL s
RADICEL s
RADICES
RADICLE s
RADIOED
RADIUMS*
RADIXES
RADOMES*
RADULAE*
RADULAR*
RADULAS*
RAFFIAS*
d RAFFISH
RAFFLED*
RAFFLER*s
RAFFLES*
cdg*RAFTERS*
cdg RAFTING
RAGBAGS*
RAGGEDY*
RAGGEES*
*RAGGIES
bdf RAGGING
d RAGGLES*
RAGLANS*
RAGOUTS*
RAGTAGS*
RAGTIME s
RAGTOPS*
RAGWEED s
RAGWORT s
b*RAIDERS*
b*RAIDING
RAILBUS
RAILCAR s
t RAILERS*
bt*RAILING s
RAILWAY s
RAIMENT s
RAINBOW s
bg RAINIER
b RAINILY
bdg RAINING
t
RAINOUT s
p RAISERS*
bp RAISING*s
RAISINS*
RAISINY*
RAKEOFF s
*RALLIED
RALLIER s
*RALLIES
RALLINE
RALLYES*
RALPHED
RAMADAS*
RAMBLAS*
b*RAMBLED*
*RAMBLER*s
b*RAMBLES*
RAMEKIN s
RAMENTA
RAMILIE s
RAMJETS*
c RAMMERS*
RAMMIER
cdt RAMMING
RAMMISH
RAMONAS*
RAMPAGE drs
RAMPANT
RAMPART s
RAMPIKE s
ct*RAMPING
RAMPION s
RAMPOLE s
RAMRODS*
RAMSONS*
RAMTILS*
bc RANCHED
RANCHER os
bct RANCHES
RANCHOS
RANCORS*
RANCOUR s
RANDANS*
RANDIER
b RANDIES t
RANDOMS*
g*RANGERS*
o RANGIER
p RANGING
f RANKERS*
cf RANKEST
cfp RANKING s
cp RANKISH
c*RANKLED*
c*RANKLES*s
RANPIKE s
RANSACK s
t RANSOMS*
g RANTERS*
g*RANTING
g RANULAR*
RANULAS*
RAPHIAS*
RAPHIDE s
RAPIDER
RAPIDLY
RAPIERS*
RAPINES*
RAPISTS*
RAPPEES*
RAPPELS
tw RAPPERS*
cft RAPPING
w
RAPPINI
RAPPORT s
RAPTORS*
RAPTURE ds
RAREBIT s
RASBORA s
RASCALS*
ct RASHERS*
b RASHEST*
g*RASPERS*
RASPIER
g RASPING s
*RASPISH
w RASSLED*
w RASSLES*
RASTERS
e RASURES*
RATABLE s
RATABLY
RATAFEE s
RATAFIA s
RATATAT s
RATBAGS*
c RATCHES
RATCHET s
RATFINK s
RATFISH
RATHOLE s
RATINES*
g RATINGS*
o RATIONS*
RATITES*
RATLIKE
RATLINE*s
RATLINS*
RATOONS*
RATTAIL s
RATTANS*
RATTEEN s
RATTENS*
RATTERS*
b RATTIER
d RATTING
b RATTISH
bp RATTLED*
p RATTLER*s
bp RATTLES*
RATTONS*
RATTOON s
RATTRAP s
RAUCITY
RAUCOUS
RAUNCHY*
RAVAGED*
RAVAGER*s
RAVAGES*
gt RAVELED
t RAVELER s
RAVELIN gs
g RAVELLY
c RAVENED
RAVENER s
RAVINED*
RAVINES*
c RAVINGS*
RAVIOLI s
RAWHIDE ds
RAWNESS
RAYLESS
RAYLIKE
RAZORED
RAZZING
bp REACHED
bp REACHER s
bp REACHES
p REACTED
REACTOR s
p READAPT s
READDED
t READERS*
READIED
READIER
READIES t
READILY
bdt READING s
p READMIT s
p READOPT s
READORN s
READOUT s

REAFFIX
REAGENT s
REAGINS*
REALEST*
REALGAR s
REALIGN s
REALISE drs
REALISM s
REALIST s
REALITY
REALIZE drs
p REALLOT s
p REALTER s
REALTOR s
cd REAMERS*
bcd REAMING
REANNEX
REAPERS*
REAPING
p REAPPLY
REARERS*
REARGUE ds
*REARING
p REARMED
t REASONS*
REAVAIL s
p REAVERS*
REAVING
REAVOWS*
REAWAKE dns
REAWOKE n
REBAITS*
REBATED*
REBATER*s
REBATES*
REBATOS*
REBECKS*
REBEGAN
REBEGIN s
REBEGUN
p REBILLS*
p REBINDS*
p REBIRTH s
REBLEND s
REBLENT
REBLOOM s
REBOANT
p REBOARD s
p REBOILS*
p*REBOOKS*
REBOOTS*
REBORED*
REBORES*
p REBOUND s
REBOZOS*
REBREED s
REBUFFS*
p REBUILD s
p REBUILT
REBUKED*
REBUKER*s
REBUKES*
REBUSES
RECALLS*
RECANED*
RECANES*
RECANTS*
RECARRY
p RECASTS*
p RECEDED*
p RECEDES*
RECEIPT s
RECEIVE drs
RECENCY
p RECEPTS*
RECHART s
RECHEAT s
p RECHECK s
RECHEWS*
p RECHOSE n
p RECIPES*
RECITAL s
p RECITED*
RECITER*s
RECITES*
w RECKING
RECKONS*
RECLADS*
RECLAIM s
RECLAME s
RECLASP s
p RECLEAN s
RECLINE drs
RECLUSE s
RECOALS*
RECOATS*
RECOCKS*
p RECODED*
p RECODES*
RECOILS*
RECOINS*
RECOLOR s
RECOMBS*
p RECOOKS*
RECORDS*
RECORKS*
RECOUNT s
RECOUPE*d
RECOUPS*
RECOVER sy
RECRATE ds
RECROSS
RECROWN s
RECRUIT s
RECTIFY
e RECTORS*
RECTORY*
RECTRIX
RECTUMS*
RECURVE ds
RECUSAL s
RECUSED*
RECUSES*
RECYCLE drs
REDACTS*
p REDATED*
p REDATES*
REDBAIT s
REDBAYS*
REDBIRD s
REDBONE s
REDBUDS*
REDBUGS*
REDCAPS*
REDCOAT s
REDDENS*
REDDERS*
REDDEST
REDDING
REDDISH
t REDDLED*
t REDDLES*
REDEARS*
REDEEMS*
REDEYES*
REDFINS*
REDFISH
REDHEAD s
REDIALS*
REDLEGS*
REDLINE drs
REDNESS
REDOCKS*
REDOING
REDOUBT s
REDOUND s
REDOUTS*
REDOWAS*
REDOXES
REDPOLL s
p REDRAFT s
REDRAWN*
REDRAWS*
REDREAM st
REDRESS
p REDRIED
p REDRIES
p REDRILL s
REDRIVE ns
REDROOT s
REDROVE
REDTAIL s
REDTOPS*
REDUCED
REDUCER*s
REDUCES
REDWARE s
REDWING s
REDWOOD s
REEARNS*
g REEDIER
REEDIFY
g REEDILY
b REEDING s
p REEDITS*
f REEDMAN
f REEDMEN
REEFERS*
REEFIER
REEFING
REEJECT s
REEKERS*
REEKIER
REEKING
p REELECT s
REELERS*
c REELING s
REEMITS*
p REENACT s
REENDOW s
REENJOY s
REENTER s
REENTRY
REEQUIP s
p REERECT s
REESTED
REEVING
REEVOKE ds
REEXPEL s
p REFACED*
p REFACES*
REFALLS*
p REFECTS*
REFEEDS*
REFEELS*
REFENCE ds
REFEREE ds
REFFING
p REFIGHT s
p REFILED*
p REFILES*
REFILLS*
REFILMS*
REFINDS*
REFINED*
REFINER*sy
REFINES*
p REFIRED*
p REFIRES*
p REFIXED
p REFIXES
REFLAGS*
REFLATE ds
REFLECT s
REFLETS*
REFLIES
REFLOAT s
REFLOOD s
REFLOWN*
REFLOWS*
p REFOCUS
REFOLDS*
REFORGE ds
p REFORMS*
REFOUND s
REFRACT s
REFRAIN s
REFRAME ds
REFRESH
REFRIED
REFRIES
REFRONT s
p REFROZE n
REFUELS*
REFUGED*
REFUGEE*s
REFUGES*
REFUGIA
p REFUNDS*
REFUSAL s
REFUSED*
REFUSER*s
REFUSES*
REFUTAL s
REFUTED*
REFUTER*s
REFUTES*
REGAINS*
REGALED*
REGALER*s
REGALES*
REGALIA
REGALLY
REGARDS*
REGATTA s
REGAUGE ds
REGEARS*
REGENCY
REGENTS*
REGGAES*
REGILDS*
REGIMEN*st
REGIMES*
REGINAE*
REGINAL*
REGINAS*
REGIONS*
REGIVEN*
REGIVES*
REGLAZE ds
REGLETS*
REGLOSS
REGLOWS*
REGLUED*
REGLUES*
b REGMATA
p REGNANT
REGORGE ds
REGOSOL s
REGRADE ds
REGRAFT s
REGRANT s
REGRATE ds
REGREEN s
REGREET s
*REGRESS
REGRETS
REGRIND s
REGROOM s
REGROUP s
REGROWN*
REGROWS*
REGULAR s
REGULUS
REHANGS*
REHEARD*
REHEARS*e
p REHEATS*
REHEELS*
REHINGE ds
REHIRED*
REHIRES*
REHOUSE ds
REIFIED
REIFIER s
REIFIES
REIGNED
REIMAGE ds
REINCUR s
REINDEX
REINING
REINKED
REINTER s
REISSUE drs
REITBOK s
REIVERS*
REIVING
REJECTS
REJOICE drs
REJOINS*
p REJUDGE ds
REKEYED
REKNITS*
REKNOTS*
RELABEL s
RELACED*
RELACES*
RELANDS
*RELAPSE drs
RELATED
*RELATER*s
p*RELATES*
RELATOR s
RELAXED
RELAXER s
RELAXES
RELAXIN gs
RELAYED
RELEARN st
RELEASE drs
RELENDS*
RELENTS*
RELEVES*
RELIANT
RELICTS*
RELIEFS*
RELIERS*
RELIEVE drs
RELIEVO s
RELIGHT s
RELINED*
RELINES*
RELINKS*
RELIQUE s
RELISTS*
RELIVED*
p RELIVES*
RELLENO s
p RELOADS*
RELOANS*
RELOCKS*
RELOOKS*
RELUCTS*
RELUMED*
RELUMES*
RELYING
REMAILS
c REMAINS*
REMAKER*s
REMAKES*
REMANDS*
REMARKS*
REMARRY
REMATCH
c REMATED*
c REMATES*
REMEETS*
REMELTS*
REMENDS
*REMERGE ds
REMIGES
REMINDS*
REMINTS*
p REMISED*
p REMISES*
p REMIXED
p REMIXES
REMNANT s
REMODEL s
p REMOLDS*
REMORAS*
REMORID
p REMORSE s
REMOTER
*REMOTES*t
REMOUNT s
REMOVAL s
REMOVED*
REMOVER*s
REMOVES*
REMUDAS*
t RENAILS*
RENAMED*
p RENAMES*
RENDERS
t*RENDING
RENEGED*
RENEGER*s
RENEGES*
RENESTS*
RENEWAL s
RENEWED
RENEWER s
RENNASE s
RENNETS*
RENNINS*
RENOWNS*
RENTALS*
RENTERS
RENTIER s
RENTING
RENVOIS
REOCCUR s
REOFFER s
REOILED
REOPENS*
p REORDER s
p REPACKS*
REPAINT s
REPAIRS*
REPANEL s
REPAPER s
REPARKS*
REPASTS*
REPATCH
p REPAVED*
p REPAVES*
REPEALS*
REPEATS*
REPENTS*
REPERKS*
REPINED*
REPINER*s
REPINES*
p REPLACE drs
p REPLANS*
p REPLANT*s
REPLATE ds
REPLAYS*
REPLEAD s
REPLETE s
REPLEVY
REPLICA s
REPLIED
REPLIER s
REPLIES
REPLOTS*
REPLOWS*
REPLUMB s
REPOLLS*
REPORTS*
REPOSAL s
REPOSED*
REPOSER*s
REPOSES
REPOSIT s
REPOURS*
REPOWER s
p REPPING
p REPRESS
p REPRICE ds
p REPRINT s
REPRISE ds
REPROBE ds
REPROOF s
REPROVE drs
REPTANT
REPTILE s
REPUGNS*
REPULSE drs
REPUMPS*
REPUTED*
REPUTES*
REQUEST s
REQUIEM s
REQUINS*
REQUIRE drs
REQUITE drs
RERACKS*
RERAISE ds
REREADS*
REREDOS
RERENTS*
RERISEN*
RERISES*
REROLLS*
REROOFS*
REROUTE ds
RESAILS*
p RESALES*
RESAWED
RESCALE ds
p RESCIND s
p RESCORE ds
RESCUED*
RESCUER*s
RESCUES*
RESEALS*
RESEATS*
RESEAUS*
RESEAUX*
RESECTS*
RESEDAS*
RESEEDS*
RESEEKS*
RESEIZE ds
p RESELLS*
RESENDS*
p RESENTS*
p RESERVE drs
RESEWED
p RESHAPE drs
RESHAVE dns
RESHINE ds
p RESHIPS*
RESHOED*
RESHOES*
RESHONE
RESHOOT s
p RESHOWN*
p RESHOWS*
p RESIDED*
p RESIDER*s
p RESIDES*
RESIDUA l
RESIDUE s
p RESIFTS*
RESIGHT s
RESIGNS*
RESILED*
RESILES*
RESILIN gs
RESINED
RESISTS*
RESITED*
RESITES*
RESIZED*
RESIZES*
RESLATE ds
RESMELT s
p RESOAKS*
RESOJET s
RESOLED*
RESOLES*
p RESOLVE drs
RESORBS*
p RESORTS*
RESOUND s
RESOWED
RESPACE ds
RESPADE ds
RESPEAK s
RESPECT s
RESPELL s
RESPELT
RESPIRE ds
RESPITE ds
p RESPLIT s
RESPOKE n
RESPOND s
RESPOOL s
RESPOTS*
RESPRAY s
RESTACK s
RESTAFF s
RESTAGE ds
p RESTAMP s
RESTART s
*RESTATE ds
pw*RESTERS*
RESTFUL
cw RESTING
RESTIVE
RESTOCK s
RESTOKE ds
p RESTORE drs
RESTUDY
RESTUFF s
RESTYLE ds
RESULTS*
p RESUMED*
p RESUMER*s
p RESUMES*
RESURGE ds
RETABLE s
RETACKS*
RETAILS*
RETAINS*
RETAKEN*
RETAKER*s
RETAKES*
RETALLY
p RETAPED*
p*RETAPES*
RETARDS*
p RETASTE ds
RETAXED
RETAXES
w*RETCHED
w*RETCHES
RETEACH
RETEAMS*
RETEARS*
p RETELLS*
RETENES*
p RETESTS*
RETHINK s
RETIARY
RETICLE s
RETILED*
RETILES*
RETIMED*
RETIMES*
RETINAE*
RETINAL*s
RETINAS*
RETINES*
RETINOL s
RETINTS*
RETINUE ds
RETIRED*
RETIREE*s
RETIRER*s
RETIRES*
RETITLE ds
RETOOLS*
RETORTS*
RETOTAL s
RETOUCH
RETRACE drs
RETRACK s
RETRACT s
p RETRAIN s
RETREAD s
p RETREAT s
p RETRIAL s
RETRIED
RETRIES
p RETRIMS*
RETSINA s
f RETTING
RETUNED*

RETUNES*
RETURNS*
RETWIST s
RETYING
p RETYPED*
p RETYPES*
REUNIFY
p REUNION s
p REUNITE drs
REUSING
REUTTER s
p REVALUE ds
REVAMPS*
REVEALS*
REVELED
REVELER s
REVELRY
REVENGE drs
REVENUE drs
p REVERBS*
REVERED*
REVERER*s
REVERES*
REVERIE s
REVERSE*drs
REVERSO*s
REVERTS
REVESTS*
p REVIEWS*
REVILED*
*REVILER*s
REVILES*
REVISAL s
p REVISED*
REVISER*s
p REVISES*
p REVISIT s
p REVISOR sy
REVIVAL s
REVIVED*
REVIVER*s
REVIVES*
REVOICE ds
REVOKED
*REVOKER*s
REVOKES
REVOLTS*
*REVOLVE drs
REVOTED*
REVOTES*
REVUIST s
REVVING
REWAKED*
REWAKEN*s
REWAKES*
REWARDS*
p REWARMS*
REWAXED
REWAXES
REWEARS*
REWEAVE ds
p REWEIGH s
REWELDS*
REWIDEN s
REWINDS*
p REWIRED*
p REWIRES*
REWOKEN*
REWORDS*
p REWORKS*
REWOUND
REWOVEN*
p REWRAPS*
REWRAPT*
REWRITE rs
REWROTE
REXINES
REYNARD s
REZEROS*
REZONED*
REZONES*
RHABDOM es
RHACHIS
RHAMNUS
RHAPHAE
RHAPHES*
RHATANY
RHEBOKS*
RHENIUM s
RHETORS*
RHEUMIC
RHIZOID s
RHIZOMA
RHIZOME s
RHIZOPI
RHODIUM s

RHODORA s
RHOMBIC*
RHOMBUS
RHONCHI
RHUBARB s
RHUMBAS*
RHYMERS*
RHYMING
RHYTHMS*
RHYTONS*
RIALTOS*
RIANTLY
RIBALDS*
RIBANDS*
RIBBAND s
c RIBBERS*
RIBBIER
cd RIBBING s
RIBBONS*
RIBBONY*
RIBIERS*
RIBLESS
d RIBLETS*
RIBLIKE
RIBOSES*
RIBWORT s
RICHENS*
RICHEST*
RICINUS
cp RICKETS
RICKETY
RICKEYS*
bcp RICKING
tw
RICKSHA sw
RICOTTA s
RICRACS*
RIDABLE
g RIDDERS*
RIDDING
g RIDDLED*
RIDDLER*s
g RIDDLES*
RIDGELS*
RIDGIER
RIDGILS*
b RIDGING
RIDINGS*
RIDLEYS*
RIDOTTO s
g RIEVERS*
RIFFING
RIFFLED*
RIFFLER*s
RIFFLES*
t RIFLERS*
RIFLERY*
t RIFLING s
RIFLIPS*
dg RIFTING
t RIGGERS*
fpt*RIGGING s
f RIGHTED
b RIGHTER s
b RIGHTLY
f RIGIDLY
RIGOURS*
RIKISHA s
RIKSHAW s
RILIEVI
RILIEVO
RILLETS*
dfg RILLING
pt
RIMFIRE s
g RIMIEST
RIMLAND s
b RIMLESS
bck RIMMERS*
t
bpt RIMMING
c*RIMPLED*
c RIMPLES*
RIMROCK s
RIMSHOT s
RINGENT
bcw RINGERS*
RINGGIT s
bcf RINGING
w
RINGLET s
RINGTAW s
g*RINNING
RINSERS*
RINSING s
RIOTERS*

RIOTING
RIOTOUS
RIPCORD s
RIPENED
RIPENER s
RIPIENI
RIPIENO s
RIPOFFS*
RIPOSTE*ds
RIPOSTS*
dgt RIPPERS*
dgt RIPPING
c RIPPLED*
c RIPPLER*s
c RIPPLES*
RIPPLET*s
RIPRAPS*
RIPSAWN*
RIPSAWS*
RIPSTOP s
RIPTIDE s
RISIBLE s
RISIBLY
RISINGS*
f RISKERS*
f RISKIER
f RISKILY
bf RISKING
RISOTTO s
RISSOLE s
RISTRAS*
RISUSES
RITARDS*
cfg RITTERS*
RITUALS*
RITZIER
RITZILY
RIVAGES*
RIVALED
RIVALRY
RIVETED
RIVETER s
RIVIERA s
RIVIERE s
RIVULET s
b ROACHED
b ROACHES
ROADBED s
ROADEOS*
ROADIES*
ROADWAY s
ROAMERS*
ROAMING
ROARERS*
*ROARING s
ROASTED
ROASTER s
ROBALOS*
p ROBANDS*
ROBBERS*
ROBBERY*
ROBBING*
ROBBINS*
ROBOTIC s
ROBOTRY
ROBUSTA*s
c ROCHETS*
ROCKABY e
ROCKERS
c ROCKERY*
bc ROCKETS*
ROCKIER
cft ROCKING
ROCKOON s
ROCOCOS*
p RODDING
RODENTS*
RODEOED
RODLESS
RODLIKE
RODSMAN
RODSMEN
ROEBUCK s
ROGERED
b ROGUERY
ROGUING
b ROGUISH
*ROILIER
b*ROILING
ROISTER s
ROLFERS*
ROLFING
t ROLLERS*
ROLLICK sy
dt ROLLING s
ROLLMOP s

ROLLOUT s
ROLLTOP
ROLLWAY s
ROMAINE s
ROMAJIS*
ROMANCE drs
ROMANOS*
ROMAUNT s
ROMPERS*
t ROMPING
ROMPISH
RONDEAU x
RONDELS*
RONDURE s
RONIONS
RONNELS*
RONTGEN s
RONYONS*
p ROOFERS*
ROOFIES*
p ROOFING s
ROOFTOP s
c ROOKERY
ROOKIER*
b ROOKIES*t
bc ROOKING
g ROOMERS*
ROOMFUL s
b ROOMIER*
ROOMIES*t
ROOMILY
bgv ROOMING
ROOSERS*
ROOSING
ROOSTED
ROOSTER s
ROOTAGE s
ROOTCAP s
ROOTERS*
ROOTIER
ROOTING
ROOTLED*
ROOTLES*s
ROOTLET*s
ROPABLE
ROPEWAY s
ROPIEST
c ROQUETS*
RORQUAL s
ROSACEA s
ROSARIA n
ROSCOES*
ROSEATE
ROSEBAY s
ROSEBUD s
ROSEHIP s
ROSELLE s
ROSEOLA rs
ROSETTE s
p ROSIEST
ROSINED
ROSINOL s
ROSOLIO s
ROSTERS*
ROSTRAL*
ROSTRUM s
ROTATED*
ROTATES*
ROTATOR sy
c ROTCHES*
ROTGUTS*
ROTIFER s
t*ROTTERS*
t ROTTING
ROTUNDA*s
t ROUBLES*
cg*ROUCHES*
ROUGHED
ROUGHEN s
ROUGHER s
ROUGHLY
ROUGING
ROUILLE s
ROULADE s
ROULEAU sx
g ROUNDED
ROUNDEL s
g ROUNDER s
ROUNDLY
ROUNDUP s
c ROUPIER
c ROUPILY
gt ROUPING
agt ROUSERS*
ag ROUSING
*ROUSTED

*ROUSTER s
g*ROUTERS*
ROUTINE s
g*ROUTING
ROVINGS*
g ROWABLE
ROWBOAT s
ROWDIER
c ROWDIES t
ROWDILY
t ROWELED
ROWINGS*
ROWLOCK s
ROYALLY
ROYALTY
*ROYSTER s
ROZZERS*
RUBABOO s
RUBACES*
RUBASSE s
RUBATOS*
dg RUBBERS*
RUBBERY*
RUBBIES
dg RUBBING s
RUBBISH y
RUBBLED*
RUBBLES*
RUBDOWN s
RUBELLA s
RUBEOLA rs
RUBIDIC
RUBIEST*
RUBIGOS*
RUBIOUS
RUBOFFS*
RUBOUTS*
RUBRICS*
RUBYING
RUCHING s
t RUCKING
t RUCKLED*
t RUCKLES*
RUCTION s
RUDDERS
c RUDDIER
RUDDILY
RUDDLED*
RUDDLES*
RUDDOCK s
RUDERAL s
RUDESBY
RUFFIAN s
g RUFFING
t RUFFLED*
RUFFLER*s
t RUFFLES*
RUFIYAA
RUGBIES
RUGGERS*
df RUGGING
RUGLIKE
a RUGOLAS*
RUGOSAS*
RUINATE ds
RUINERS*
RUINING
RUINOUS
RULABLE
RULIEST
RULINGS*
RUMAKIS*
RUMBAED
cdg RUMBLED*
g RUMBLER*s
cdg*RUMBLES*
RUMINAL*
RUMMAGE drs
d RUMMERS*
g RUMMEST
c RUMMIER
c RUMMIES t
RUMORED
RUMOURS*
c RUMPLED*
c RUMPLES*s
RUNAWAY s
RUNBACK s
t RUNDLES*
RUNDLET*s
RUNDOWN s
RUNKLED*
RUNKLES*
*RUNLESS
RUNLETS*
t RUNNELS*

RUNNERS*
RUNNIER
RUNNING s
RUNOFFS*
RUNOUTS*
RUNOVER s
RUNTIER
RUNTISH
RUNWAYS*
RUPIAHS*
RUPTURE ds
RURALLY
RUSHEES*
bc*RUSHERS*
b RUSHIER
bc RUSHING s
RUSSETS*
RUSSETY*
RUSSIFY
RUSTICS*
ct RUSTIER
ct RUSTILY
ct RUSTING
RUSTLED*
RUSTLER*s
RUSTLES*s
t RUTHFUL
RUTILES*
RUTTIER
RUTTILY
RUTTING
RUTTISH
RYOKANS*
SABATON s
SABAYON s
SABBATH*s
SABBATS*
SABBING
SABEING
SABERED
SABINES*
SABRING
SACATON s
SACBUTS*
SACCADE s
SACCATE
SACCULE s
SACCULI
SACHEMS*
SACHETS*
SACKBUT s
SACKERS*
SACKFUL s
SACKING s
SACLIKE
SACQUES*
SACRALS*
SACRING s
SACRIST sy
SACRUMS*
SADDENS*
SADDEST
SADDHUS*
SADDLED
SADDLER*sy
SADDLES
SADIRON s
SADISMS*
SADISTS*
SADNESS
SAFARIS*
SAFFRON s
SAFROLE*s
SAFROLS*
SAGAMAN
SAGAMEN
SAGBUTS*
SAGGARD*s
SAGGARS*
SAGGERS
SAGGIER
SAGGING
SAGIEST
SAGUARO s
SAHIWAL s
SAHUARO s
SAILERS*
*SAILING s
SAILORS*
SAIMINS*
SAINING
SAINTED
SAINTLY
SAIYIDS*
SALAAMS*
SALABLE

SALABLY
SALAMIS*
SALCHOW s
SALICIN es
SALIENT s
SALINAS*
SALINES
SALIVAS*
SALLETS*
*SALLIED
SALLIER s
*SALLIES
SALLOWS
SALLOWY*
SALMONS*
SALOONS*
SALOOPS*
SALPIAN s
SALPIDS*
SALPINX
SALSIFY
SALTANT
SALTBOX
SALTERN*s
p*SALTERS*
SALTEST
SALTIER*s
SALTIES*t
SALTILY
SALTINE s
SALTING s
SALTIRE s
SALTISH
SALTPAN s
SALUKIS*
SALUTED*
SALUTER*s
SALUTES*
SALVAGE der
s
SALVERS*
SALVIAS*
SALVING
SALVOED
SALVOES
SALVORS*
SAMADHI s
SAMARAS*
SAMBAED
SAMBALS*
SAMBARS*
SAMBHAR s
SAMBHUR s
SAMBUCA s
SAMBUKE s
SAMBURS*
SAMECHS*
SAMEKHS*
SAMIELS*
SAMISEN s
SAMITES*
SAMLETS*
SAMOSAS*
SAMOVAR s
SAMOYED s
SAMPANS*
SAMPLED*
*SAMPLER*s
SAMPLES*
SAMSARA s
SAMSHUS*
SAMURAI s
SANCTUM s
SANDALS*
SANDBAG s
SANDBAR s
SANDBOX
SANDBUR rs
SANDDAB s
SANDERS*
SANDFLY
SANDHIS*
SANDHOG s
SANDIER
SANDING
SANDLOT s
SANDMAN
SANDMEN
SANDPIT s
SANGARS*
SANGERS
SANGRIA s
SANICLE s
SANIOUS
SANJAKS*
SANNOPS*

SANNUPS*
SANSARS*
SANSEIS*
SANTERA s
SANTERO s
SANTIMI
SANTIMS
SANTIMU
SANTIRS*
SANTOLS*
SANTOOR s
SANTOUR s
SANTURS*
SAPAJOU s
SAPHEAD s
SAPHENA es
SAPIENS
SAPIENT s
SAPLESS
SAPLING s
SAPONIN es
SAPOTAS*
SAPOTES*
SAPOURS*
SAPPERS*
SAPPHIC s
SAPPIER
SAPPILY
SAPPING
SAPROBE s
SAPSAGO s
SAPWOOD s
SARAPES*
SARCASM s
SARCINA es
SARCOID s
SARCOMA s
SARCOUS
SARDANA s
SARDARS*
SARDINE ds
SARDIUS
SARKIER
SARMENT as
SARODES*
SARONGS*
SAROSES
SARSARS*
SARSENS*
SARSNET s
SARTORS*
SASHAYS*
SASHIMI s
*SASHING
SASSABY
SASSIER
SASSIES t
SASSILY
SASSING
SATANGS*
SATANIC
SATARAS*
SATCHEL s
SATEENS*
SATIATE ds
SATIETY
SATINET s
SATIRES*
SATIRIC
SATISFY
SATORIS*
SATRAPS*
SATRAPY*
SATSUMA s
SATYRIC
SATYRID s
SAUCERS*
SAUCIER s
SAUCILY
SAUCING
SAUGERS
SAUNAED
SAUNTER s
SAURELS*
SAURIAN s
SAURIES
SAUSAGE s
SAUTEED
SAUTOIR es
SAVABLE
SAVAGED*
SAVAGER*y
SAVAGES*t
SAVANNA hs
SAVANTS*
SAVARIN s
SAVATES*
SAVELOY s
SAVINES*
SAVINGS*
SAVIORS*
SAVIOUR s
SAVORED
SAVORER s
SAVOURS*
SAVOURY*
SAVVIED
SAVVIER
SAVVIES t
SAVVILY
SAWBILL s
SAWBUCK s
SAWDUST sy
SAWFISH
SAWLIKE
SAWLOGS*
SAWMILL s
SAWNEYS*
SAWYERS*
SAXHORN s
SAXTUBA s
SAYABLE
SAYINGS*
SAYYIDS*
*SCABBED
SCABBLE ds
SCABIES
e SCALADE s
SCALADO s
SCALAGE s
SCALARE*s
SCALARS*
SCALDED
SCALDIC
SCALENE
SCALENI
SCALERS*
SCALEUP s
SCALIER
SCALING
e SCALLOP s
SCALPED
SCALPEL s
SCALPER s
SCAMMED
SCAMMER s
*SCAMPED
*SCAMPER s
SCANDAL s
SCANDIA s
SCANDIC
*SCANNED
*SCANNER s
*SCANTED
*SCANTER
SCANTLY
e SCAPING
SCAPOSE
SCAPULA ers
SCARABS*
SCARCER*
SCARERS
SCARFED
SCARFER s
SCARIER
SCARIFY
SCARILY
*SCARING
SCARLET s
e*SCARPED
*SCARPER s
SCARPHS*
SCARRED
*SCARTED
*SCARVES
SCATHED*
SCATHES*
*SCATTED
SCATTER s
SCAUPER s
a SCENDED
SCENERY
SCENICS*
SCENTED
SCEPTER s
SCEPTIC s
SCEPTRE ds
SCHAPPE s
SCHEMAS*
SCHEMED*
SCHEMER*s
SCHEMES*
SCHERZI
SCHERZO s
SCHISMS*
SCHISTS*
SCHIZOS*
SCHIZZY
SCHLEPP*s
SCHLEPS*
SCHLOCK sy
SCHLUBS*
SCHLUMP sy
SCHMALZ y
SCHMEAR s
SCHMEER s
SCHMOES*
SCHMOOS e
SCHMUCK s
SCHNAPS
SCHNOOK s
SCHNOZZ*
SCHOLAR s
SCHOLIA
SCHOOLS*
SCHORLS*
SCHRIKS*
SCHRODS*
SCHTICK s
SCHTIKS*
SCHUITS*
SCIATIC as
SCIENCE s
SCILLAS*
SCIRRHI
SCISSOR s
SCIURID s
SCLAFFS*
SCLERAE*
SCLERAL*
SCLERAS*
SCOFFED
*SCOFFER s
SCOLDED
*SCOLDER s
*SCOLLOP s
SCONCED*
SCONCES*
*SCOOPED
*SCOOPER s
SCOOTCH
SCOOTED
*SCOOTER s
*SCOPING
*SCOPULA es
SCORERS
SCORIAE*
SCORIFY
*SCORING
*SCORNED
*SCORNER s
SCOTERS*
SCOTIAS*
SCOTOMA s
SCOTTIE s
SCOURED
SCOURER s
SCOURGE drs
SCOUSES*
SCOUTED
*SCOUTER s
SCOUTHS
SCOWDER s
*SCOWING
*SCOWLED
SCOWLER s
*SCRAGGY
SCRAICH s
SCRAIGH s
SCRAPED
SCRAPER*s
SCRAPES
SCRAPIE s
*SCRAPPY
*SCRATCH y
SCRAWLS
SCRAWLY
SCRAWNY
SCREAKS
SCREAKY
SCREAMS
SCREECH y
SCREEDS
SCREENS*
*SCREWED
SCREWER s
SCREWUP s
SCRIBAL
a SCRIBED*
SCRIBER*s
a SCRIBES*
SCRIEVE ds
SCRIMPS
SCRIMPY
SCRIPTS*
SCRIVED*
SCRIVES*
SCROGGY
SCROLLS*
SCROOCH
SCROOGE s
SCROOPS*
SCROTAL*
SCROTUM s
SCROUGE ds
SCRUBBY
SCRUFFS*
SCRUFFY*
*SCRUNCH y
SCRUPLE ds
*SCRYING
SCUBAED
SCUDDED
*SCUFFED
SCUFFER s
SCUFFLE drs
SCULKED
SCULKER s
*SCULLED
*SCULLER sy
SCULPED
SCULPIN gs
SCULPTS*
*SCULTCH
SCUMBAG s
SCUMBLE ds
SCUMMED
*SCUMMER s
*SCUNNER s
*SCUPPER s
SCURRIL e
SCUTAGE s
SCUTATE
*SCUTTER s
*SCUTTLE ds
SCUZZES
SCYPHUS
SCYTHED*
SCYTHES*
SEABAGS*
SEABEDS*
SEABIRD s
SEABOOT s
SEACOCK s
SEADOGS*
SEAFOOD s
SEAFOWL s
SEAGIRT
SEAGULL s
SEALANT s
SEALERS*
SEALERY*
SEALIFT s
SEALING
SEAMARK s
SEAMERS*
SEAMIER
SEAMING
SEANCES*
SEAPORT s
SEAREST
*SEARING
SEASICK
SEASIDE s
SEASONS*
SEATERS
*SEATING s
SEAWALL s
SEAWANS*
SEAWANT*s
SEAWARD s
SEAWARE s
SEAWAYS*
SEAWEED s
SEBACIC
SEBASIC
SECANTS*
SECEDED*
SECEDER*s
SECEDES*
SECERNS*
SECLUDE ds
SECONAL s
SECONDE*drs
SECONDI*
SECONDO*
SECONDS*
SECPARS*
SECRECY
SECRETE*drs
SECRETS*
SECTARY
SECTILE
SECTION s
SECTORS*
SECULAR s
SECURED*
SECURER*s
SECURES*t
SEDARIM
SEDATED*
SEDATER*
SEDATES*t
*SEDGIER
SEDILIA
SEDUCED
SEDUCER*s
SEDUCES
SEEABLE
SEEDBED s
SEEDERS*
SEEDIER
SEEDILY
SEEDING
SEEDMAN
SEEDMEN
SEEDPOD s
SEEINGS*
SEEKERS*
SEEKING
SEELING
SEEMERS*
SEEMING s
SEEPAGE s
SEEPIER
SEEPING
SEERESS
SEESAWS*
SEETHED*
SEETHES*
SEGETAL
SEGGARS
SEGMENT s
SEICHES*
SEIDELS*
SEINERS*
SEINING
SEISERS*
SEISING*s
SEISINS*
SEISMAL
SEISMIC
SEISORS*
SEISURE s
SEITANS*
SEIZERS*
SEIZING*s
SEIZINS*
SEIZORS*
SEIZURE s
SEJEANT
SELECTS
SELENIC
SELFDOM s
SELFING
*SELFISH
SELKIES*
SELLERS*
SELLING
SELLOFF s
SELLOUT s
SELSYNS*
SELTZER s
SELVAGE ds
SEMATIC
SEMEMES*
SEMEMIC
SEMIDRY
SEMIFIT
SEMILOG
SEMIMAT t
SEMINAL*
SEMINAR*sy
SEMIPRO s
SEMIRAW
SEMISES
SENARII
SENATES
SENATOR s
SENDALS*
SENDERS
*SENDING
SENDOFF s
SENDUPS*
SENECAS*
SENECIO s
SENEGAS*
SENHORA*s
SENHORS*
SENILES*
SENIORS*
SENNETS*
SENNITS*
SENOPIA s
SENORAS*
SENORES
SENSATE ds
SENSEIS*
SENSING
SENSORS*
SENSORY*
SENSUAL
SENTIMO s
SEPALED
SEPPUKU s
SEPTAGE s
SEPTATE
SEPTETS*
SEPTICS*
SEPTIME s
SEPTUMS*
SEQUELA*e
SEQUELS*
SEQUENT s
SEQUINS*
SEQUOIA s
SERAILS*
SERAPES*
SERAPHS*
SERDABS*
SEREINS*
SERENER*
SERENES*t
SERFAGE s
SERFDOM s
SERFISH
SERGERS*
SERGING s
SERIALS*
SERIATE ds
SERICIN s
SERIEMA s
SERIFED
e SERINES*
SERINGA*s
SERIOUS
SERMONS*
SEROSAE*
SEROSAL*
SEROSAS*
SEROVAR s
SERPENT s
SERPIGO s
SERRANO s
SERRATE ds
SERRIED
SERRIES
SERUMAL
SERVALS*
SERVANT s
SERVERS*
SERVICE drs
SERVILE
SERVING s
SESAMES*
SESSILE
SESSION s
SESTETS*
SESTINA s
SESTINE s
SETBACK s
SETLINE s
SETOFFS*
SETOUTS*
SETTEES*
SETTERS*
SETTING s
SETTLED*
SETTLER*s
SETTLES*
SETTLOR s
SEVENTH s
SEVENTY
SEVERAL s
SEVERED*
SEVERER*
SEVICHE s
SEVRUGA s
SEWABLE
SEWAGES*
SEWERED
SEWINGS*
SEXIEST
SEXISMS*
SEXISTS
SEXLESS
SEXPOTS*
SEXTAIN s
SEXTANS*
*SEXTANT*s
SEXTETS*
SEXTILE s
SEXTONS*
SFERICS
SFUMATO s
*SHACKED
*SHACKLE drs
SHACKOS*
SHADERS*
SHADFLY
SHADIER
SHADILY
*SHADING s
SHADOOF s
SHADOWS*
SHADOWY*
SHADUFS*
*SHAFTED
*SHAGGED
SHAHDOM s
SHAIRDS*
SHAIRNS*
SHAITAN s
SHAKERS*
SHAKEUP s
SHAKIER
SHAKILY
SHAKING
SHAKOES
SHALIER
SHALLOP s
*SHALLOT s
*SHALLOW s
SHALOMS*
SHAMANS*
SHAMBLE ds
SHAMING
SHAMMAS h
*SHAMMED
*SHAMMER s
SHAMMES
SHAMMOS
SHAMOIS
SHAMOYS*
SHAMPOO s
*SHANKED
SHANTEY s
SHANTIH*s
SHANTIS*
SHAPELY
SHAPERS*
SHAPEUP s
SHAPING
SHARERS*
SHARIAH*s
SHARIAS*
SHARIFS*
*SHARING
*SHARKED
SHARKER s
*SHARPED
SHARPEN s
*SHARPER s
SHARPIE s
SHARPLY
SHASLIK s
*SHATTER s
SHAUGHS
*SHAULED
SHAVERS
SHAVIES*
*SHAVING s
p*SHAWING
SHAWLED
SHEAFED
SHEARED
*SHEARER s
SHEATHE*drs
SHEATHS
SHEAVED
SHEAVES
SHEBANG s

SHEBEAN s
SHEBEEN s
SHEDDED
SHEDDER s
SHEENED
SHEERED
SHEERER
SHEERLY
SHEETED
SHEETER s
SHEEVES*
SHEIKHS*
SHEILAS*
SHEITAN s
SHEKELS*
SHELLAC ks
*SHELLED
*SHELLER s
SHELTAS*
SHELTER s
SHELTIE s
SHELVED
SHELVER*s
SHELVES
SHEQELS*
SHERBET s
SHEREEF s
SHERIFF*s
SHERIFS*
SHEROOT s
SHERPAS*
SHERRIS
SHEUCHS
SHEUGHS
SHEWERS
*SHEWING
SHIATSU s
SHIATZU s
SHIBAHS*
SHICKER s
SHIELDS*
SHIFTED
SHIFTER s
SHIKARI*s
SHIKARS*
SHIKKER s
*SHILLED
SHILPIT
SHIMMED
SHIMMER sy
SHINDIG s
SHINDYS*
SHINERS*
SHINGLE drs
SHINGLY
SHINIER
SHINILY
SHINING
SHINNED
SHINNEY s
SHIPLAP s
SHIPMAN
SHIPMEN t
*SHIPPED
SHIPPEN s
*SHIPPER s
SHIPPON s
SHIPWAY s
SHIRKED
SHIRKER s
SHIRRED
SHITAKE s
SHITTAH s
SHITTIM s
SHIVAHS*
SHIVERS*
SHIVERY*
SHIVITI s
SHLEPPS*
SHLOCKS*
SHLOCKY*
SHLUMPS*
SHLUMPY*
SHMALTZ y
SHMEARS*
SHMOOZE ds
SHMUCKS*
SHNAPPS
SHNOOKS*
SHOALED
SHOALER
*SHOCKED
*SHOCKER s
*SHODDEN
SHOEBOX
*SHOEING

SHOEPAC ks
SHOFARS*
*SHOGGED
SHOGUNS*
SHOLOMS*
SHOOFLY
SHOOING
SHOOLED
*SHOOTER s
SHOPBOY s
SHOPHAR s
SHOPMAN
SHOPMEN
SHOPPED
*SHOPPER*s
SHOPPES*
SHORANS*
SHORING s
SHORTED
SHORTEN s
SHORTER
SHORTIA s
SHORTIE s
SHORTLY
SHOTGUN s
*SHOTTED
SHOTTEN
SHOUTED
SHOUTER s
SHOVELS
SHOVERS
SHOVING
SHOWBIZ
SHOWERS*
SHOWERY*
SHOWIER
SHOWILY
SHOWING s
SHOWMAN
SHOWMEN
SHOWOFF s
SHREWED
SHRIEKS*
SHRIEKY*
SHRIEVE ds
SHRIFTS*
SHRIKES*
SHRILLS*
SHRILLY*
SHRIMPS*
SHRIMPY*
SHRINED*
SHRINES*
SHRINKS*
SHRIVED*
SHRIVEL*s
SHRIVEN*
SHRIVER*s
SHRIVES*
SHROFFS*
SHROUDS*
SHRUBBY
SHTETEL s
SHTETLS*
SHTICKS*
SHTICKY*
SHUCKED
SHUCKER s
SHUDDER sy
SHUFFLE drs
SHUNNED
SHUNNER s
*SHUNTED
*SHUNTER s
*SHUSHED
SHUSHER s
*SHUSHES
SHUTEYE s
SHUTING
SHUTOFF s
SHUTOUT s
SHUTTER s
SHUTTLE drs
SHYLOCK s
SHYNESS
SHYSTER s
SIALIDS*
SIALOID
SIAMANG s
SIAMESE s
SIBLING s
SIBYLIC
SICCING
SICKBAY s
SICKBED s
SICKEES*

SICKENS*
SICKEST
SICKIES*
SICKING
SICKISH
SICKLED*
SICKLES*
SICKOUT s
SIDDURS*
SIDEARM s
SIDEBAR s
SIDECAR s
SIDEMAN
SIDEMEN
SIDEWAY s
SIDINGS*
SIDLERS
*SIDLING
SIEGING
SIEMENS
SIENITE s
SIENNAS*
SIERRAN*
SIERRAS*
SIESTAS*
SIEVERT s
SIEVING
SIFAKAS*
SIFTERS*
SIFTING s
SIGANID s
SIGHERS*
SIGHING
SIGHTED
SIGHTER s
SIGHTLY
SIGMATE
SIGMOID s
SIGNAGE s
SIGNALS*
SIGNEES*
SIGNERS*
SIGNETS*
*SIGNIFY
SIGNING
SIGNIOR isy
SIGNORA*s
SIGNORE
SIGNORI*
SIGNORS*
SIGNORY*
SILAGES*
SILANES*
SILENCE drs
SILENTS*
SILENUS
SILESIA s
*SILEXES
SILICAS*
SILICIC
SILICLE s
SILICON es
SILIQUA e
SILIQUE s
SILKIER*
SILKIES*t
SILKILY
SILKING
SILLERS*
SILLIER
SILLIES t
SILLILY
SILOING
SILTIER
SILTING
SILURID s
SILVANS*
SILVERN*
SILVERS*
SILVERY*
SILVICS
SIMIANS*
SIMILAR
SIMILES*
SIMIOID
SIMIOUS
SIMITAR s
SIMLINS*
SIMMERS*
SIMNELS*
SIMOOMS*
SIMOONS*
SIMPERS*
SIMPLER*
SIMPLES*t
SIMPLEX*

SIMULAR s
SINCERE r
SINEWED
SINGERS*
SINGING
SINGLED*
SINGLES
SINGLET*s
SINKAGE s
SINKERS
*SINKING
SINLESS
SINNERS
*SINNING
SINOPIA s
SINOPIE
SINSYNE
SINTERS
SINUATE ds
SINUOUS
SINUSES
SIPHONS*
SIPPERS*
SIPPETS*
SIPPING
SIRDARS*
SIRLOIN s
SIROCCO s
SIRRAHS*
SIRREES*
SIRUPED
SISKINS*
SISSIER
SISSIES t
SISTERS*
SISTRUM s
SITCOMS*
SITHENS
SITTERS*
SITTING s
SITUATE ds
SITUSES
SIXFOLD
SIXTEEN s
SIXTHLY
SIXTIES
SIZABLE
SIZABLY
SIZIEST
SIZINGS*
SIZZLED*
SIZZLER*s
SIZZLES*
SJAMBOK s
SKALDIC
SKANKED
SKANKER s
SKATERS*
SKATING s
SKATOLE*s
SKATOLS*
SKEANES*
SKEEING
SKEETER s
SKEINED
SKELLUM s
*SKELPED
SKELPIT
*SKELTER s
SKEPSIS
SKEPTIC s
SKETCHY*
SKEWERS*
SKEWING
SKIABLE
SKIBOBS*
*SKIDDED
*SKIDDER s
SKIDDOO s
SKIDOOS*
SKIDWAY s
SKIFFLE ds
SKIINGS*
SKILFUL
*SKILLED
SKILLET s
SKIMMED
SKIMMER s
SKIMPED
SKINFUL s
*SKINKED
SKINKER s
SKINNED
SKINNER s
*SKIPPED
*SKIPPER s

SKIPPET s
SKIRLED
SKIRRED
SKIRRET s
SKIRTED
SKIRTER s
*SKITING
SKITTER sy
*SKITTLE s
SKIVERS*
SKIVING
SKIWEAR
SKLENTS*
SKOALED
SKOOKUM
SKOSHES
SKREEGH s
SKREIGH s
SKULKED
SKULKER s
SKULLED
SKUNKED
SKYCAPS*
SKYDIVE drs
SKYDOVE
SKYHOOK s
SKYJACK s
SKYLARK s
SKYLIKE
SKYLINE s
SKYPHOI
SKYPHOS
SKYSAIL s
SKYSURF s
SKYWALK s
SKYWARD s
SKYWAYS*
SLABBED
SLABBER sy
*SLACKED
SLACKEN s
*SLACKER s
SLACKLY
*SLAGGED
SLAINTE
SLAKERS
*SLAKING
SLALOMS*
*SLAMMED
SLAMMER s
i*SLANDER s
SLANGED
SLANTED
SLANTLY
*SLAPPED
*SLAPPER s
*SLASHED
*SLASHER s
*SLASHES
SLATERS*
*SLATHER s
SLATIER
SLATING s
SLATTED
SLAVERS
SLAVERY*
SLAVEYS*
*SLAVING
*SLAVISH
SLAYERS
*SLAYING
SLEAVED
SLEAVES
SLEAZES*
SLEDDED
SLEDDER s
SLEDGED*
SLEDGES
SLEEKED
SLEEKEN s
SLEEKER s
SLEEKIT
SLEEKLY
SLEEPER s
SLEETED
SLEEVED*
SLEEVES*
SLEIGHS*
SLEIGHT*s
*SLENDER
SLEUTHS*
SLEWING
SLICERS*
SLICING
*SLICKED
SLICKEN s

*SLICKER s
SLICKLY
SLIDDEN
SLIDERS*
SLIDING
SLIEVES*
SLIGHTS
*SLIMIER
SLIMILY
*SLIMING
SLIMMED
*SLIMMER s
*SLIMPSY
*SLINGER s
*SLINKED
SLIPING
SLIPOUT s
*SLIPPED
*SLIPPER sy
SLIPUPS*
SLIPWAY s
*SLITHER sy
SLITTED
*SLITTER s
SLIVERS
*SLOBBER sy
SLOGANS
*SLOGGED
*SLOGGER s
SLOPERS
*SLOPING
*SLOPPED
SLOSHED
SLOSHES
*SLOTTED
*SLOTTER s
SLOUCHY*
SLOUGHS
SLOUGHY*
SLOVENS*
*SLOWEST
*SLOWING
*SLOWISH
SLUBBED
*SLUBBER s
SLUDGED*
SLUDGES*
*SLUFFED
*SLUGGED
*SLUGGER s
SLUICED*
SLUICES*
*SLUMBER sy
SLUMGUM s
SLUMISM s
SLUMMED
SLUMMER s
*SLUMPED
SLURBAN
SLURPED
SLURRED
*SLUSHED
*SLUSHES
SLYNESS
SMACKED
SMACKER s
SMALLER
SMALTOS*
SMARAGD es
*SMARTED
*SMARTEN s
SMARTER
SMARTIE s
SMARTLY
*SMASHED
*SMASHER s
*SMASHES
SMASHUP s
*SMATTER s
SMEARED
SMEARER s
SMECTIC
SMEDDUM s
SMEEKED
SMEGMAS*
*SMELLED
SMELLER s
*SMELTED
*SMELTER sy
SMERKED
SMIDGEN*s
SMIDGES
SMIDGIN s
SMILERS
SMILEYS*
SMILING

SMIRKED
*SMIRKER s
SMITERS
SMITING
*SMITTEN
*SMOCKED
SMOKERS*
SMOKIER
SMOKILY
SMOKING
*SMOLDER s
SMOOCHY*
SMOOTHS*
SMOOTHY*
*SMOTHER sy
SMUDGED*
SMUDGES*
*SMUGGER
SMUGGLE drs
*SMUSHED
*SMUSHES
SMUTCHY*
SMUTTED
SNACKED
SNACKER s
SNAFFLE ds
SNAFUED
*SNAGGED
*SNAILED
SNAKIER
SNAKILY
SNAKING
*SNAPPED
*SNAPPER s
SNARERS*
SNARFED
SNARING
SNARLED
SNARLER s
SNASHES
SNATCHY*
SNATHES*
SNAWING
SNEAKED
SNEAKER s
SNEAPED
SNEDDED
SNEERED
SNEERER s
SNEEZED*
SNEEZER*s
SNEEZES*
SNELLED
SNELLER
*SNIBBED
*SNICKED
*SNICKER sy
SNIDELY
SNIDEST
SNIFFED
*SNIFFER s
SNIFFLE drs
SNIFFLY
SNIFTER s
SNIGGER s
*SNIGGLE drs
SNIGLET s
SNIPERS*
SNIPING
*SNIPPED
*SNIPPER s
SNIPPET sy
SNIVELS*
*SNOGGED
SNOODED
SNOOKED
SNOOKER s
SNOOLED
SNOOPED
SNOOPER s
SNOOTED
SNOOZED*
SNOOZER*s
SNOOZES*
SNOOZLE ds
SNORERS*
SNORING
SNORKEL s
SNORTED
SNORTER s
SNOUTED
SNOWCAP s
SNOWCAT s
SNOWIER
SNOWILY
SNOWING

SNOWMAN
SNOWMEN
SNUBBED
SNUBBER s
SNUFFED
SNUFFER s
SNUFFLE drs
SNUFFLY
SNUGGED
SNUGGER y
SNUGGLE ds
SOAKAGE s
SOAKERS*
SOAKING
SOAPBOX
SOAPERS*
SOAPIER
SOAPILY
SOAPING
SOARERS*
*SOARING s
SOBBERS*
SOBBING
SOBERED
SOBERER
SOBERLY
SOCAGER*s
SOCAGES*
SOCCAGE s
SOCCERS*
a SOCIALS*
SOCIETY
SOCKETS*
SOCKEYE s
SOCKING
SOCKMAN
SOCKMEN
SODDENS*
SODDIES
SODDING
SODIUMS
SOFABED s
SOFFITS*
SOFTENS*
*SOFTEST
SOFTIES*
SOFTISH
SOGGIER
SOGGILY
SOIGNEE*
SOILAGE s
*SOILING
SOILURE s
SOIREES*
SOJOURN s
SOKEMAN
SOKEMEN
SOLACED*
SOLACER*s
SOLACES*
SOLANDS*
SOLANIN es
SOLANOS*
SOLANUM s
SOLARIA
i SOLATED*
i SOLATES*
SOLATIA
SOLDANS*
SOLDERS*
SOLDIER sy
SOLERET s
SOLFEGE s
SOLICIT s
SOLIDER
SOLIDLY
SOLIDUS
SOLIONS*
SOLITON s
SOLOING
SOLOIST s
SOLUBLE s
SOLUBLY
SOLUNAR
SOLUTES*
SOLVATE ds
SOLVENT s
SOLVERS*
SOLVING
SOMATIC
SOMEDAY
SOMEHOW
SOMEONE s
SOMEWAY s
SOMITAL
SOMITES*

SOMITIC
SONANCE s
SONANTS*
SONATAS*
SONDERS*
SONGFUL
SONHOOD s
SONLESS
SONLIKE
SONNETS*
SONNIES
SONOVOX
SONSHIP s
SONSIER*
SOONERS*
SOONEST
SOOTHED*
SOOTHER*s
SOOTHES*t
SOOTHLY
SOOTIER
SOOTILY
SOOTING
SOPHIES
SOPHISM s
SOPHIST s
SOPITED*
SOPITES*
SOPPIER
SOPPING
SOPRANI
SOPRANO s
SORBATE s
SORBENT s
SORBETS*
*SORBING
SORBOSE s
SORCERY
SORDINE s
SORDINI
SORDINO
SORDORS*
SORGHOS*
SORGHUM s
SORINGS*
SORITES
SORITIC
SORNERS*
SORNING
SOROCHE s
SORORAL
SOROSES
SOROSIS
SORRELS*
SORRIER
SORRILY
SORROWS*
SORTERS*
SORTIED*
SORTIES*
SORTING
SOTTISH
SOUARIS*
SOUBISE s
SOUCARS*
SOUDANS*
SOUFFLE ds
SOUGHED
SOUKOUS
SOULFUL
SOUNDED
SOUNDER s
SOUNDLY
SOUPCON s
SOUPIER
SOUPING
SOURCED*
SOURCES*
SOUREST
SOURING
SOURISH
SOURSOP s
SOUSING
SOUSLIK s
SOUTANE s
SOUTERS
SOUTHED
SOUTHER ns
SOVIETS*
SOVKHOZ y
SOVRANS*
SOWABLE
SOWCARS*
SOYBEAN s
SOYMILK s
SOYUZES

SOZINES*
SOZZLED
SPACERS
SPACIAL
*SPACIER
*SPACING s
SPACKLE ds
SPADERS*
SPADING
SPAEING s
SPAHEES*
*SPALLED
SPALLER s
SPAMBOT s
SPAMMED
SPAMMER s
SPANCEL s
SPANDEX
SPANGLE ds
SPANGLY
SPANIEL s
SPANKED
SPANKER s
*SPANNED
*SPANNER s
SPARELY
SPARERS
SPAREST*
SPARGED
SPARGER*s
SPARGES
SPARIDS*
*SPARING
*SPARKED
*SPARKER s
a SPARKLE drs
t
SPARKLY
SPAROID s
*SPARRED
SPARROW s
SPARSER
*SPARTAN
SPASMED
SPASTIC s
SPATHAL
SPATHED*
SPATHES*
SPATHIC
SPATIAL
*SPATTED
*SPATTER s
SPATULA rs
SPATZLE s
SPAVIES*
SPAVIET*
SPAVINS
*SPAWNED
*SPAWNER s
*SPAYING
SPEAKER s
SPEANED
SPEARED
SPEARER s
SPECCED
e SPECIAL s
SPECIES*
SPECIFY
*SPECKED
SPECKLE ds
SPECTER s
SPECTRA l
SPECTRE s
SPECULA r
SPEEDED
SPEEDER s
SPEEDOS*
SPEEDUP s
*SPEELED
*SPEERED
SPEILED
SPEIRED
SPEISES
SPELEAN
SPELLED
SPELLER s
*SPELTER s
SPELUNK s
SPENCER*s
SPENCES*
SPENDER s
SPENSES*
SPERMIC
SPEWERS*
SPEWING
SPHENES*

SPHENIC
SPHERAL
SPHERED*
SPHERES*
a SPHERIC s
SPICATE d
SPICERS*
SPICERY*
SPICIER
SPICILY
SPICING
SPICULA er
SPICULE s
SPIDERS*
SPIDERY*
SPIEGEL s
SPIELED
SPIELER s
SPIERED
SPIFFED
SPIGOTS*
SPIKERS
SPIKIER
SPIKILY
*SPIKING
*SPILING s
*SPILLED
SPILLER s
SPILTHS*
SPINACH y
SPINAGE s
SPINALS*
SPINATE
SPINDLE drs
SPINDLY
SPINELS*
SPINETS*
*SPINIER
*SPINNER sy
SPINNEY s
SPINOFF s
SPINORS*
SPINOSE
SPINOUS
SPINOUT s
SPINTOS
SPINULA e
SPINULE s
SPIRAEA s
SPIRALS*
a SPIRANT s
SPIREAS*
SPIREME*s
SPIREMS*
SPIRIER
a SPIRING
SPIRITS*
SPIROID
SPIRTED
SPIRULA es
SPITALS*
SPITING
*SPITTED
SPITTER s
SPITTLE s
SPITZES
SPLAKES*
SPLASHY
*SPLAYED
SPLEENS*
SPLEENY*
SPLENIA l
SPLENIC
SPLENII
SPLENTS*
SPLICED*
SPLICER*s
SPLICES*
SPLIFFS*
SPLINED*
SPLINES*
SPLINTS*
SPLODGE ds
SPLORES*
SPLOTCH y
SPLURGE drs
SPLURGY
SPOILED
SPOILER s
*SPOKING
SPONDEE s
SPONGED
SPONGER*s
SPONGES*
SPONGIN gs
SPONSAL

SPONSON s
SPONSOR s
SPOOFED
SPOOFER sy
SPOOKED
*SPOOLED
*SPOOLER s
SPOONED
SPOONEY s
SPOORED
*SPORING
SPOROID
SPORRAN s
*SPORTED
*SPORTER s
SPORTIF
SPORULE s
SPOTLIT
*SPOTTED
*SPOTTER s
e SPOUSAL s
e SPOUSED*
e SPOUSES*
*SPOUTED
*SPOUTER s
SPRAINS*
SPRANGS
SPRAWLS*
SPRAWLY*
*SPRAYED
*SPRAYER s
SPREADS*
*SPRIEST
SPRIGGY
SPRIGHT s
SPRINGE*drs
SPRINGS*
SPRINGY*
SPRINTS
SPRITES*
SPROUTS*
SPRUCED*
SPRUCER*
SPRUCES*t
SPRYEST
SPUDDED
SPUDDER s
SPUMIER
SPUMING
SPUMONE s
SPUMONI s
SPUMOUS
SPUNKED
*SPUNKIE rs
SPURGES
SPURNED
SPURNER s
*SPURRED
SPURRER s
SPURREY s
SPURTED
SPURTER s
SPURTLE s
SPUTNIK s
*SPUTTER sy
SQUABBY
SQUALID
SQUALLS*
SQUALLY*
SQUALOR s
SQUAMAE*
SQUARED*
SQUARER*s
SQUARES*t
SQUARKS
SQUASHY*
SQUATLY
SQUATTY
SQUAWKS*
SQUEAKS*
SQUEAKY*
SQUEALS*
SQUEEZE drs
SQUELCH y
SQUIFFY
SQUILLA*es
SQUILLS
SQUINCH
SQUINNY
SQUINTS
SQUINTY*
e*SQUIRED*
e*SQUIRES*
SQUIRMS*
SQUIRMY*
SQUIRTS

SQUISHY*
SQUOOSH y
SRADDHA s
SRADHAS*
*STABBED
STABBER s
STABILE s
STABLED
STABLER*s
*STABLES*t
*STACKED
*STACKER s
STACKUP s
STACTES*
STADDLE s
STADIAS*
STADIUM s
STAFFED
STAFFER s
STAGERS*
*STAGGED
*STAGGER sy
STAGGIE rs
STAGIER
STAGILY
STAGING s
STAIDER
STAIDLY
STAINED
STAINER s
STAITHE s
*STAKING
STALAGS*
STALELY
STALEST*
STALING
*STALKED
*STALKER s
STALLED
STAMENS*
STAMINA ls
STAMMEL s
STAMMER s
*STAMPED e
*STAMPER s
STANCES*
STANDBY s
STANDEE s
STANDER s
STANDUP s
*STANGED
STANINE s
STANING
*STANNIC
STANNUM s
STANOLS*
STANZAS*
STAPLED*
STAPLER*s
STAPLES*
STARCHY*
STARDOM s
STARERS*
STARETS
*STARING
STARKER s
STARKLY
STARLET s
STARLIT
*STARRED
*STARTED
*STARTER s
STARTLE drs
STARTSY*
STARTUP s
STARVED*
STARVER*s
STARVES*
STASHED
STASHES
STASIMA
STATANT
STATELY
STATERS
STATICE*s
STATICS*
e STATING*
STATINS*
STATION s
STATISM s
STATIST s
STATIVE s
STATORS*
STATUED*
STATUES*
STATURE s

STATUSY*
STATUTE s
STAUNCH
STAVING
STAYERS*
STAYING
STEADED
STEALER s
STEALTH sy
*STEAMED
STEAMER s
STEARIC
STEARIN es
STEEKED
STEELED
STEELIE rs
STEEPED
STEEPEN s
STEEPER s
STEEPLE ds
STEEPLY
STEERED
STEERER s
STEEVED*
STEEVES*
STELENE
STELLAR*
STELLAS*
STEMMAS*
STEMMED
STEMMER sy
STEMSON s
STENCHY*
STENCIL s
STENGAH s
STENOKY
STENTOR s
STEPPED*
STEPPER*s
STEPPES*
STEPSON s
STEREOS*
STERILE
STERLET s
a STERNAL*
STERNER
STERNLY
STERNUM s
a STEROID s
STEROLS*
STERTOR s
STETSON s
STETTED
STEWARD s
STEWBUM s
*STEWING
STEWPAN s
a STHENIA s
a STHENIC
*STIBIAL
STIBINE s
STIBIUM s
STICHIC
*STICKED
*STICKER s
STICKIT
*STICKLE drs
STICKUM s
STICKUP s
*STIFFED
STIFFEN s
STIFFER
STIFFLY
STIFLED*
STIFLER*s
STIFLES*
STIGMAL*
STIGMAS*
*STILLED
*STILLER
*STILTED
STIMIED
STIMIES
STIMULI
STINGER s
STINGOS*
*STINKER s
*STINTED
*STINTER s
STIPELS*
STIPEND s
*STIPPLE drs
STIPULE ds
STIRPES
STIRRED
STIRRER s

STIRRUP s
STIVERS*
STOBBED
STOCKED
STOCKER s
STODGED*
STODGES*
STOGEYS*
STOGIES*
STOICAL
STOKERS
*STOKING
STOLLEN s
STOLONS*
STOMACH sy
STOMATA l
o STOMATE s
STOMPED
STOMPER s
STONERS
*STONIER
STONILY
*STONING
a*STONISH
STOOGED*
STOOGES*
STOOKED
STOOKER s
*STOOLED
STOOLIE s
STOOPED
STOOPER s
STOPERS
STOPGAP s
*STOPING
STOPOFF s
e*STOPPED
*STOPPER s
*STOPPLE ds
STORAGE s
STORERS*
STOREYS*
STORIED
*STORIES
STORING
STORMED
STOTINS*
*STOTTED
a STOUNDS*
STOURES*
STOURIE
STOUTEN s
*STOUTER
STOUTLY
e STOVERS*
*STOWAGE s
*STOWING
STRAFED*
STRAFER*s
STRAFES*
STRAINS
STRAITS
STRAKED*
STRAKES*
STRANDS*
e STRANGE*rs
STRAPPY
STRATAL*
STRATAS*
STRATHS*
STRATUM s
STRATUS
STRAWED
e STRAYED
STRAYER s
STREAKS*
STREAKY*
STREAMS*
STREAMY*
STREEKS*
STREELS*
STREETS*
STRETCH y
STRETTA s
STRETTE
STRETTI
STRETTO s
STREWED
STREWER s
STRIATA
STRIATE ds
STRICKS
STRIDER*s
STRIDES*
STRIDOR s
STRIFES*
STRIGIL s
STRIKER*s
STRIKES
STRINGS*
STRINGY*
STRIPED*
STRIPER*s
STRIPES
STRIVED*
STRIVEN*
STRIVER*s
STRIVES*
STROBES*
STROBIC
STROBIL aei
s
STROKED
STROKER*s
STROKES
STROLLS
STROMAL*
STROPHE s
STROPPY
STROUDS*
*STROWED
STROYED
STROYER s
STRUDEL s
STRUMAE*
STRUMAS*
STRUNTS*
*STUBBED
STUBBLE ds
STUBBLY
STUCCOS*
STUDDED
STUDDIE s
STUDENT s
STUDIED
STUDIER s
STUDIES
STUDIOS*
STUFFED
STUFFER s
STUIVER s
*STUMBLE drs
STUMMED
*STUMPED
STUMPER s
*STUNNED
STUNNER s
STUNTED
STUPEFY
STUPIDS*
STUPORS*
STUTTER s
STYGIAN
STYLATE
STYLERS*
STYLETS*
STYLING s
STYLISE drs
STYLISH
STYLIST s
STYLITE s
STYLIZE drs
STYLOID
STYMIED*
STYMIES*
STYPSIS
STYPTIC s
STYRENE s
SUASION s
SUASIVE
SUASORY
SUAVELY
SUAVEST
SUAVITY
SUBACID
SUBADAR s
SUBALAR
SUBAREA s
SUBARID
SUBATOM s
SUBBASE s
SUBBASS
SUBBING s
SUBCELL s
SUBCLAN s
SUBCODE s
SUBCOOL s
SUBCULT s
SUBDEAN s
SUBDEBS*
SUBDUAL s
SUBDUCE ds
SUBDUCT s
SUBDUED*
SUBDUER*s
SUBDUES*
SUBECHO
SUBEDIT s
SUBERIC
SUBERIN s
SUBFILE s
SUBFUSC s
SUBGOAL s
SUBGUMS*
SUBHEAD s
SUBIDEA s
SUBITEM s
SUBJECT s
SUBJOIN s
SUBLATE ds
SUBLETS*
SUBLIME drs
SUBLINE s
SUBLOTS*
SUBMENU s
SUBMISS
SUBMITS*
SUBNETS*
SUBORAL
SUBORNS*
SUBOVAL
SUBPART*s
SUBPENA s
SUBPLOT s
SUBRACE s
SUBRENT s
SUBRING s
SUBRULE s
SUBSALE s
SUBSECT s
SUBSERE s
SUBSETS*
SUBSIDE drs
SUBSIDY
SUBSIST s
SUBSITE s
SUBSOIL s
SUBSUME ds
SUBTASK s
SUBTAXA
SUBTEEN s
SUBTEND s
SUBTEST s
SUBTEXT s
SUBTILE r
SUBTLER*
SUBTONE s
SUBTYPE s
SUBUNIT s
SUBURBS*
SUBVENE ds
SUBVERT s
SUBWAYS*
SUBZERO
SUBZONE s
SUCCAHS*
SUCCEED s
SUCCESS
SUCCORS*
SUCCORY*
SUCCOTH
SUCCOUR s
SUCCUBA es
SUCCUBI
SUCCUMB s
SUCCUSS
SUCKERS*
SUCKIER
SUCKING
SUCKLED*
SUCKLER*s
SUCKLES*s
SUCRASE s
SUCROSE s
SUCTION s
SUDARIA
SUDDENS*
SUDORAL
SUDSERS*
SUDSIER
SUDSING
SUEDING
SUFFARI s
SUFFERS*
SUFFICE drs
SUFFUSE ds
SUGARED
SUGARER s
SUGGEST s
SUGHING
SUICIDE ds
SUITERS*
SUITING s
SUITORS*
SUKKAHS*
SUKKOTH*
SULCATE d
SULDANS*
SULFATE ds
SULFIDE*s
SULFIDS*
SULFITE s
SULFONE s
SULFURS*
SULFURY*l
SULKERS*
SULKIER
SULKIES t
SULKILY
SULKING
*SULLAGE s
SULLIED
SULLIES
SULPHAS*
SULPHID es
SULPHUR sy
SULTANA*s
SULTANS*
SUMACHS*
SUMLESS
SUMMAND s
SUMMARY
SUMMATE ds
SUMMERS*
SUMMERY*
SUMMING
SUMMITS*
SUMMONS*
SUMOIST s
SUMPTER s
SUNBACK
SUNBATH es
SUNBEAM sy
*SUNBELT s
SUNBIRD s
SUNBOWS*
SUNBURN st
SUNDAES*
SUNDECK s
SUNDERS*
SUNDEWS*
SUNDIAL s
SUNDOGS*
SUNDOWN s
SUNFAST
SUNFISH
SUNGLOW s
SUNKETS*
SUNLAMP s
SUNLAND s
*SUNLESS
*SUNLIKE
SUNNAHS*
SUNNIER
SUNNILY
SUNNING
SUNRAYS*
SUNRISE s
*SUNROOF s
SUNROOM s
SUNSETS
SUNSPOT s
SUNSUIT s
SUNTANS*
SUNWARD s
*SUNWISE
SUPERED
SUPINES*
SUPPERS
*SUPPING
SUPPLED*
SUPPLER*
SUPPLES*t
SUPPORT s
SUPPOSE drs
SUPREME rs
SUPREMO s
SURBASE ds
SURCOAT s
SURFACE drs
SURFEIT s
SURFERS*
SURFIER
SURFING s
SURFMAN
SURFMEN
SURGEON s
SURGERS
SURGERY*
*SURGING
SURIMIS*
SURLIER
SURLILY
SURMISE drs
SURNAME drs
SURPASS
SURPLUS
SURREAL
SURREYS*
SURTOUT s
SURVEIL s
SURVEYS*
SURVIVE drs
SUSLIKS*
SUSPECT s
SUSPEND s
SUSPIRE ds
SUSSING
SUSTAIN s
SUTLERS*
SUTTEES*
SUTURAL
SUTURED*
SUTURES*
SVELTER*
SWABBED
SWABBER s
SWABBIE s
SWACKED
*SWADDLE ds
SWAGERS
*SWAGGED
*SWAGGER s
SWAGGIE s
*SWAGING
SWAGMAN
SWAGMEN
*SWALLOW s
SWAMIES
SWAMPED
SWAMPER s
SWANKED
SWANKER
*SWANNED
SWANPAN s
*SWAPPED
SWAPPER s
*SWARDED
*SWARMED
*SWARMER s
SWARTHS*
SWARTHY*
*SWASHED
*SWASHER s
*SWASHES
SWATHED*
SWATHER*s
SWATHES*
SWATTED
*SWATTER s
SWAYERS*
SWAYFUL
SWAYING
*SWEARER s
SWEATED
SWEATER s
SWEENEY s
*SWEEPER s
SWEETEN s
SWEETER
SWEETIE s
SWEETLY
*SWELLED
SWELLER
*SWELTER s
SWELTRY
SWERVED*
SWERVER*s
SWERVES*
SWEVENS*
SWIDDEN s
SWIFTER s
SWIFTLY
*SWIGGED
SWIGGER s
*SWILLED
*SWILLER s
SWIMMER s
*SWINDLE drs
SWINGBY s
SWINGED
*SWINGER*s
SWINGES*
SWINGLE ds
*SWINISH
*SWINKED
SWINNEY s
*SWIPING
SWIPLES*
SWIPPLE s
SWIRLED
*SWISHED
*SWISHER s
*SWISHES
*SWISSES
*SWITHER*s
SWITHLY
SWIVELS*
SWIVETS*
*SWIVING
SWIZZLE drs
SWOBBED
SWOBBER s
SWOLLEN
SWOONED
SWOONER s
SWOOPED
SWOOPER s
SWOPPED
*SWOTTED
SWOTTER s
SWOUNDS
SWOUNED
SYCONIA
SYCOSES
SYCOSIS
SYENITE s
SYLLABI c
SYLPHIC
SYLPHID s
SYLVANS*
SYLVINE*s
SYLVINS*
SYLVITE s
SYMBION st
SYMBIOT es
SYMBOLS*
SYMPTOM s
SYNAGOG s
SYNANON s
SYNAPSE ds
SYNCARP sy
SYNCHED
SYNCHRO s
SYNCING
SYNCOMS*
SYNCOPE s
SYNDETS*
SYNDICS*
SYNERGY
SYNESIS
SYNFUEL s
SYNGAMY
SYNODAL
SYNODIC
SYNONYM esy
SYNOVIA ls
SYNTAGM as
SYNTONY
SYNURAE*
SYPHERS*
SYPHONS*
SYRETTE s
SYRINGA s
SYRINGE ds
SYRPHID s
SYRUPED
SYSTEMS*
SYSTOLE s
SYZYGAL
TABANID s
TABARDS*
TABARET s
TABBIED
TABBIES
s TABBING
TABERED
TABETIC s
TABLEAU sx
TABLETS*
s TABLING
TABLOID s
TABOOED
TABORED
TABORER s
TABORET s
TABORIN egs
TABOULI s
TABOURS*
TABUING
TABULAR
TABULIS*
TACHISM es
TACHIST es
TACHYON s
TACITLY
s TACKERS*
TACKETS*
TACKIER
TACKIFY
TACKILY
s TACKING
TACKLED*
TACKLER*s
TACKLES*s
*TACNODE s
TACRINE s
TACTFUL
TACTICS*
TACTILE
*TACTION s
*TACTUAL
TADPOLE s
TAENIAE*
TAENIAS*
TAFFETA s
TAFFIAS*
TAFFIES
TAGGANT s
s*TAGGERS*
s TAGGING
TAGLIKE
TAGLINE s
TAGMEME s
TAGRAGS*
TAHINIS*
TAHSILS*
TAILERS*
TAILFAN s
TAILFIN s
*TAILING s
TAILLES*s
TAILORS*
TAINTED
TAIPANS*
TAKABLE
TAKAHES*
TAKEOFF s
s TAKEOUT s
TAKEUPS*
TAKINGS*
TALARIA
TALCING
TALCKED
TALCOSE
TALCOUS
TALCUMS*
TALENTS*
TALIONS*
*TALIPED s
TALIPES
TALIPOT s
s TALKERS*
s TALKIER*
*TALKIES*t
s TALKING s
TALLAGE ds
TALLBOY s
TALLEST
*TALLIED
TALLIER s
*TALLIES
TALLISH*
TALLITH*s
TALLITS*
TALLOLS*
TALLOWS
TALLOWY*
TALLYHO s
TALONED
TALOOKA s
TALUKAS*
TALUSES
TAMABLE
TAMALES*
TAMANDU as
TAMARAO s
TAMARAU s
TAMARIN*ds
TAMARIS*k
TAMASHA s
TAMBACS*

TAMBAKS*
TAMBALA s
TAMBOUR as
TAMBURA*s
TAMBURS*
TAMEINS*
TAMISES
TAMMIES*
TAMPALA s
TAMPANS*
s TAMPERS*
s*TAMPING
TAMPION s
TAMPONS*
TANAGER s
TANBARK s
TANDEMS*
TANDOOR is
TANGELO s
TANGENT s
TANGIER
s TANGING
TANGLED
*TANGLER*s
TANGLES
TANGOED
TANGRAM s
TANISTS*
TANKAGE s
TANKARD s
TANKERS*
TANKFUL s
TANKING
TANKINI s
TANNAGE s
TANNATE s
TANNERS*
TANNERY*
TANNEST
TANNING*s
TANNINS*
TANNISH
TANNOYS
TANRECS*
TANSIES
TANTARA s
TANTIVY
TANTRAS*
TANTRIC
*TANTRUM s
TANUKIS*
TANYARD s
TAPALOS*
TAPERED
TAPERER s
TAPETAL*
TAPETUM
TAPHOLE s
TAPIOCA s
TAPISES
TAPPERS*
TAPPETS*
TAPPING s
TAPROOM s
TAPROOT s
TAPSTER s
TARAMAS*
TARBUSH
TARDIER
TARDIES t
TARDILY
TARDIVE
TARDYON s
TARGETS*
TARIFFS*
TARMACS*
TARNISH
TARPANS*
TARPONS*
TARRIED
s TARRIER s
TARRIES t
s TARRING
TARSALS*
TARSIAS*
TARSIER s
TARTANA*s
TARTANS*
TARTARE*
TARTARS*
TARTEST
*TARTIER
*TARTILY
s TARTING
TARTISH
TARTLET s

TARTUFE s
TARWEED s
TARZANS*
TASKBAR s
*TASKING
TASSELS*
TASSETS
TASSIES*
TASTERS
TASTIER
TASTILY
TASTING
TATAMIS*
TATOUAY s
TATSOIS*
TATTERS*
TATTIER*
TATTIES*t
TATTILY
TATTING s
TATTLED*
TATTLER*s
TATTLES*
TATTOOS*
TAUNTED
TAUNTER s
TAURINE s
TAUTAUG s
TAUTENS*
TAUTEST
TAUTING
TAUTOGS*
TAVERNA*s
TAVERNS*
TAWNEYS*
TAWNIER
TAWNIES t
TAWNILY
TAWPIES*
TAWSING
TAXABLE s
TAXABLY
TAXEMES*
TAXEMIC
TAXICAB s
TAXIING
TAXIMAN
TAXIMEN
TAXITES
TAXITIC
TAXIWAY s
TAXLESS
TAXPAID
TAXWISE
TAXYING
TEABOWL s
TEACAKE s
TEACART s
TEACHER s
TEACHES
TEACUPS*
TEALIKE
s TEAMING
TEAPOTS*
TEAPOYS*
TEARERS*
*TEARFUL
TEARGAS
TEARIER
TEARILY
*TEARING
TEAROOM s
TEASELS
TEASERS*
TEASHOP s
*TEASING
TEATIME s
TEAWARE s
TEAZELS*
TEAZLED*
TEAZLES*
TECHIER*
TECHIES*t
TECHILY
a TECHNIC s
TECHNOS*
TECTITE s
TECTRIX
TECTUMS*
TEDDERS*
*TEDDIES
TEDDING
TEDIOUS
TEDIUMS*
TEEMERS*
TEEMING

TEENAGE dr
TEENERS*
TEENFUL
TEENIER
TEENTSY
TEEPEES*
TEETERS*
TEETHED*
TEETHER*s
TEETHES*
TEFLONS*
TEGMINA l
TEGULAR
TEGUMEN t
TEKKIES*
TEKTITE s
TELAMON
TELECOM s
TELEDUS*
TELEFAX
TELEGAS*
TELEMAN
TELEMEN
TELEOST s
TELERAN s
TELESES
TELESIS
TELEXED
TELEXES
TELFERS*
TELFORD s
TELLERS*
TELLIES
TELLING
TELNETS*
TELOMES*
TELOMIC
TELPHER s
TELSONS*
TEMBLOR s
TEMPEHS*
TEMPERA*s
TEMPERS*
TEMPEST s
TEMPING
TEMPLAR s
TEMPLED*
TEMPLES*
TEMPLET*s
TEMPTED
TEMPTER s
TEMPURA s
*TENABLE
TENABLY
TENACES*
TENAILS*
TENANCY
TENANTS*
s TENCHES
TENDERS
*TENDING
TENDONS*
TENDRIL s
*TENFOLD s
TENNERS*
TENNIES
TENNIST*s
TENONED
TENONER s
TENOURS*
TENPINS*
TENRECS*
TENSELY
TENSEST*
*TENSILE
TENSING
TENSION s
TENSITY
TENSIVE
TENSORS*
TENTAGE s
TENTERS
TENTHLY
TENTIER*
TENTING
TENUITY
TENUOUS
TENURED
TENURES
TENUTOS*
TEOPANS*
TEPHRAS*
TEPIDLY
TEQUILA s
TERAOHM s
TERBIAS*

*TERBIUM s
TERCELS*
TERCETS*
TEREBIC
TEREDOS*
TEREFAH
TERGITE s
TERMERS*
TERMING
TERMINI
TERMITE s
TERMORS*
TERNARY
TERNATE
TERNION s
TERPENE s
TERRACE ds
TERRAIN s
TERRANE s
TERREEN s
TERRENE s
TERRETS*
TERRIER s
TERRIES
TERRIFY
TERRINE s
TERRITS*
TERRORS
TERSELY
TERSEST
TERTIAL s
TERTIAN s
TESSERA e
TESTACY
*TESTATE s
TESTEES*
TESTERS
TESTIER
TESTIFY
TESTILY
TESTING
TESTONS*
TESTOON s
TESTUDO s
TETANAL
TETANIC s
TETANUS
*TETCHED
TETHERS
TETOTUM s
TETRADS*
TETRODE s
TETRYLS*
TETTERS*
TEUGHLY
TEXASES
TEXTILE s
TEXTUAL
TEXTURE ds
*THACKED
THAIRMS*
THALAMI c
THALERS
THALLIC*
THALLUS
THALWEG s
THANAGE s
*THANKED
*THANKER s
THATCHY*
THAWERS*
*THAWING
*THEATER s
THEATRE s
THECATE
THEELIN s
THEELOL s
THEGNLY
THEINES*
a THEISMS*
a*THEISTS*
THEMING
THENAGE s
THENARS*
THEOLOG sy
THEORBO s
THEOREM s
THERAPY
*THEREAT
*THEREBY
*THEREIN
*THEREOF
*THEREON
*THERETO
THERIAC as
THERIAN s

*THERMAE
THERMAL s
THERMEL*s
THERMES*
THERMIC
*THERMIT es
THERMOS
THEROID
THEURGY
THEWIER
THIAMIN es
THIAZIN es
THIAZOL es
THICKEN s
THICKER
THICKET sy
THICKLY
THIEVED*
THIEVES*
THIGHED
THIMBLE s
THINKER s
THINNED
THINNER s
THIOLIC
THIONIC
THIONIN es
THIONYL s
THIRAMS*
THIRDLY
THIRLED
THIRSTS*
THIRSTY*
THISTLE s
THISTLY
*THITHER
*THOLING
THONGED
THORIAS*
THORITE s
THORIUM s
*THORNED
THORONS*
THORPES*
THOUGHT*s
THOUING
THRALLS*
THRAVES*
THRAWED
THREADS*
THREADY*
THREAPS*
THREATS*
THREEPS*
THRIFTS*
THRIFTY*
THRILLS*
THRIVED*
THRIVEN*
THRIVER*s
THRIVES*
THROATS*
THROATY*
THROMBI n
THRONED*
THRONES*
THRONGS*
THROUGH
THROWER s
THRUMMY
THRUPUT s
THRUSTS*
THRUWAY s
THUDDED
THUGGEE s
THULIAS*
THULIUM s
THUMBED
*THUMPED
*THUMPER s
THUNDER sy
THUNKED
THWACKS*
THWARTS*
THYMIER
THYMINE s
THYMOLS*
THYROID s
THYRSES*
THYRSUS
THYSELF
TIARAED
TICCING
s*TICKERS*
TICKETS*
s TICKING s

s TICKLED*
s TICKLER*s
s TICKLES*
TICTACS*
TICTOCS*
TIDALLY
TIDBITS*
TIDDLER s
TIDERIP s
TIDEWAY s
TIDIERS*
TIDIEST*
TIDINGS*
TIDYING
TIEBACK s
TIELESS
TIEPINS*
TIERCED*
TIERCEL*s
TIERCES*
TIERING
TIFFANY
s TIFFING*
TIFFINS*
TIGHTEN s
TIGHTER
TIGHTLY
TIGLONS*
TIGRESS
TIGRISH
TILAPIA s
TILBURY
TILINGS*
TILLAGE s
TILLERS*
s TILLING
*TILLITE s
TILTERS*
s TILTING
TIMARAU s
TIMBALE*s
TIMBALS*
TIMBERS*
TIMBERY*
TIMBRAL
TIMBREL*s
TIMBRES*
TIMEOUS
TIMEOUT s
TIMIDER
TIMIDLY
TIMINGS*
TIMOLOL s
TIMOTHY
TIMPANA
TIMPANI
TIMPANO
TINAMOU s
TINCALS*
TINCTED
TINDERS*
TINDERY*
TINEIDS*
TINFOIL s
TINFULS*
s TINGING
TINGLED*
TINGLER*s
TINGLES
TINHORN s
TINIEST
s*TINKERS*
TINKLED*
TINKLER*s
TINKLES
TINLIKE
TINNERS
TINNIER
TINNILY
*TINNING
TINSELS*
s*TINTERS*
s TINTING s
TINTYPE s
TINWARE s
TINWORK s
TIPCART s
TIPCATS*
TIPLESS
TIPOFFS*
TIPPERS*
TIPPETS*
TIPPIER
TIPPING
s TIPPLED*
s TIPPLER*s

s TIPPLES*
TIPSIER
TIPSILY
TIPSTER s
TIPTOED*
TIPTOES*
TIPTOPS*
TIRADES
TIREDER
TIREDLY
TIRLING
TISANES*
TISSUAL
TISSUED
TISSUES
TISSUEY*
TITANIA s
TITANIC
TITBITS*
TITFERS*
TITHERS*
TITHING s
TITIANS*
TITLARK s
TITLING
TITLIST s
TITMICE
TITRANT s
TITRATE ds
TITTERS*
TITTIES*
TITTLES*
TITTUPS*
TITULAR sy
TIZZIES
TOADIED
TOADIES
TOADISH
TOASTED
TOASTER s
TOBACCO s
s TOCCATA s
TOCCATE
TOCHERS
TOCSINS*
TODDIES
TODDLED*
TODDLER*s
TODDLES*
TOECAPS*
TOEHOLD s
TOELESS
TOELIKE
TOENAIL s
TOESHOE s
TOFFEES*
TOFFIES
TOFUTTI s
TOGATED*
TOGGERY
TOGGING
TOGGLED*
TOGGLER*s
TOGGLES*
TOILERS
TOILETS*
TOILFUL
*TOILING
TOITING
TOKAMAK s
TOKENED
TOKOMAK s
TOLANES*
TOLEDOS*
TOLIDIN es
TOLLAGE s
TOLLBAR s
TOLLERS*
TOLLING
TOLLMAN
TOLLMEN
TOLLWAY s
TOLUATE s
TOLUENE s
TOLUIDE*s
TOLUIDS*
TOLUOLE*s
TOLUOLS*
TOLUYLS*
TOMBACK*s
TOMBACS*
TOMBAKS*
TOMBING
TOMBOLA s
TOMBOLO s
TOMBOYS*

TOMCATS*
TOMCODS*
*TOMENTA
TOMFOOL s
TOMMIES
TOMPION s
TOMTITS*
a TONALLY
TONEARM s
TONEMES*
TONEMIC
TONETIC s
TONETTE s
TONGERS*
TONGING
TONGMAN
TONGMEN
TONGUED*
TONGUES*
s TONIEST
TONIGHT s
TONLETS*
TONNAGE s
TONNEAU sx
TONNERS*
TONNISH
TONSILS*
TONSURE ds
TONTINE s
*TONUSES
TOOLBAR s
TOOLBOX
TOOLERS*
s TOOLING s
TOONIES*
TOOTERS*
TOOTHED
TOOTING
TOOTLED*
TOOTLER*s
TOOTLES*
TOOTSES
TOOTSIE s
TOPAZES
TOPCOAT s
TOPFULL*
TOPIARY
TOPICAL
TOPKICK s
TOPKNOT s
TOPLESS
TOPLINE s
TOPMAST s
TOPMOST
TOPONYM sy
s TOPPERS*
s TOPPING s
s TOPPLED*
s TOPPLES*
TOPSAIL s
TOPSIDE rs
TOPSOIL s
TOPSPIN s
TOPWORK s
TOQUETS*
TORCHED
TORCHES
TORCHON s
TOREROS*
TORMENT s
TORNADO s
TOROIDS*
TORPEDO s
TORPIDS*
TORPORS*
TORQUED*
TORQUER*s
TORQUES*
TORREFY
TORRENT s
TORRIFY
TORSADE s
TORSION s
TORTILE
TORTONI s
TORTRIX
TORTURE drs
TORULAE*
TORULAS*
TOSSERS*
TOSSING
TOSSPOT s
TOSSUPS*
TOSTADA s
TOSTADO s
TOTABLE

TOTALED
TOTALLY
TOTEMIC
TOTTERS
TOTTERY*
s TOTTING
TOUCANS*
TOUCHED
TOUCHER*s
TOUCHES
TOUCHUP s
TOUGHED
TOUGHEN s
TOUGHER
TOUGHIE s
TOUGHLY
TOUPEES*
TOURACO s
TOURERS*
TOURING s
TOURISM s
TOURIST asy
TOURNEY s
TOUSING
TOUSLED*
TOUSLES*
TOUTERS
*TOUTING
TOUZLED*
TOUZLES*
s TOWABLE
s TOWAGES*
TOWARDS*
s TOWAWAY s
TOWBOAT s
TOWELED
TOWERED
TOWHEAD s
TOWHEES*
TOWLINE s
TOWMOND s
TOWMONT s
TOWNEES*
TOWNIES*
TOWNISH
TOWNLET s
TOWPATH s
TOWROPE s
TOWSACK s
TOXEMIA s
TOXEMIC
TOXICAL
TOXINES*
TOXOIDS*
TOYLESS
TOYLIKE
TOYSHOP s
TRACERS
TRACERY*
TRACHEA els
TRACHLE ds
*TRACING s
*TRACKED
*TRACKER s
TRACTOR s
TRADERS*
TRADING
TRADUCE drs
TRAFFIC s
TRAGEDY
TRAGICS*
TRAIKED
*TRAILED
*TRAILER s
s*TRAINED
TRAINEE s
s TRAINER s
TRAIPSE ds
TRAITOR s
TRAJECT s
TRAMCAR s
TRAMELL*s
TRAMELS*
*TRAMMED
TRAMMEL s
*TRAMPED
TRAMPER s
TRAMPLE drs
TRAMWAY s
TRANCED*
TRANCES
TRANCHE s
TRANGAM s
TRANSIT s
*TRANSOM s
TRAPANS*

TRAPEZE s
s*TRAPPED
s*TRAPPER s
TRASHED
*TRASHER s
*TRASHES
s TRASSES
TRAUMAS*
TRAVAIL s
TRAVELS
TRAVOIS e
TRAWLED
TRAWLER s
TRAWLEY s
TRAYFUL s
TREACLE s
TREACLY
TREADED
*TREADER s
TREADLE drs
*TREASON s
TREATED
TREATER s
TREBLED*
TREBLES*
*TREDDLE ds
TREEING
TREETOP s
TREFOIL s
TREHALA s
TREKKED
TREKKER s
TRELLIS
a TREMBLE drs
TREMBLY
TREMOLO s
TREMORS*
*TRENAIL s
*TRENDED
TREPANG*s
TREPANS*
s TRESSED
TRESSEL s
s TRESSES
TRESTLE s
TREVETS
TRIABLE
TRIACID s
TRIADIC s
TRIAGED*
TRIAGES*
TRIAZIN es
TRIBADE s
TRIBALS*
TRIBUNE s
TRIBUTE s
TRICEPS*
*TRICING
*TRICKED
TRICKER sy
TRICKIE r
s TRICKLE ds
TRICKLY
TRICKSY*
TRICLAD s
TRICORN es
TRICOTS*
s*TRIDENT s
TRIDUUM s
TRIENES*
TRIFLED
*TRIFLER*s
TRIFLES
TRIFOLD
TRIFORM
*TRIGGED
*TRIGGER s
TRIGONS*
TRIGRAM s
TRIJETS*
TRILITH s
*TRILLED
TRILLER s
TRILOGY
TRIMERS
*TRIMMED
*TRIMMER s
TRINARY
TRINDLE ds
TRINING
TRINITY
TRINKET s
TRIODES*
TRIOLET s
TRIOSES*
TRIOXID es

TRIPACK s
TRIPART
TRIPLED*
TRIPLES*
TRIPLET*s
TRIPLEX*
TRIPODS*
TRIPODY*
TRIPOLI s
s*TRIPPED
s*TRIPPER s
TRIPPET s
TRIPTAN es
TRIREME s
TRISECT s
TRISEME s
TRISHAW s
TRISMIC
TRISMUS
TRISOME s
TRISOMY
TRITELY
TRITEST
TRITIUM s
TRITOMA s
TRITONE*s
TRITONS*
TRIUMPH s
TRIUNES*
TRIVETS
TRIVIAL*
TRIVIUM
TROAKED
TROCARS*
TROCHAL
TROCHAR s
TROCHEE*s
TROCHES*
TROCHIL is
*TROCKED
TRODDEN
TROFFER s
TROGONS*
TROIKAS*
TROILUS
s TROKING
TROLAND s
s*TROLLED
s*TROLLER s
TROLLEY s
TROLLOP sy
TROMMEL s
TROMPED
TROMPES*
TROOPED
TROOPER s
as TROPHIC
TROPICS*
a TROPINE*s
a TROPINS*
a TROPISM s
TROTHED
*TROTTED
*TROTTER s
TROTYLS*
*TROUBLE drs
TROUGHS
TROUNCE drs
TROUPED
TROUPER*s
TROUPES*
*TROUSER s
TROVERS
TROWELS
s*TROWING
TROWTHS
TRUANCY
TRUANTS*
TRUCING
*TRUCKED
TRUCKER s
*TRUCKLE drs
TRUDGED*
TRUDGEN*s
TRUDGER*s
TRUDGES*
TRUEING
TRUFFES
*TRUFFLE ds
TRUISMS*
TRUMEAU x
TRUMPED
s TRUMPET s
*TRUNDLE drs
TRUNKED
*TRUNNEL s

TRUSSED
TRUSSER s
TRUSSES
*TRUSTED
TRUSTEE ds
TRUSTER s
TRUSTOR s
TRYMATA
TRYOUTS*
TRYPSIN s
TRYPTIC
TRYSAIL s
TRYSTED*
TRYSTER*s
TRYSTES*
TSADDIK
TSARDOM s
TSARINA s
TSARISM s
TSARIST s
TSATSKE s
TSETSES*
TSIMMES
TSKTSKS*
TSOORIS
TSOURIS
TSUNAMI cs
TUATARA s
TUATERA s
TUBAIST s
TUBBERS*
s TUBBIER
s TUBBING
TUBFULS*
TUBIFEX
TUBINGS*
TUBISTS*
TUBLIKE
TUBULAR
TUBULES*
TUBULIN s
TUCHUNS*
TUCKERS*
TUCKETS*
TUCKING
TUFFETS*
TUFTERS*
TUFTIER
TUFTILY
TUFTING s
TUGBOAT s
TUGGERS*
TUGGING
TUGHRIK s
TUGLESS
TUGRIKS*
TUILLES*
TUITION s
TULADIS*
s TUMBLED*
s TUMBLER*s
s*TUMBLES*
TUMBREL s
TUMBRIL s
TUMESCE ds
TUMIDLY
TUMMIES
TUMMLER s
TUMORAL
TUMOURS*
s*TUMPING
TUMULAR
TUMULTS*
TUMULUS
*TUNABLE
TUNABLY
TUNDISH
TUNDRAS*
TUNEFUL
TUNEUPS*
TUNICAE*
TUNICLE s
TUNNAGE s
TUNNELS*
TUNNIES
s TUNNING
TUPELOS*
*TUPPING
TURACOS*
TURACOU*s
TURBANS*
TURBARY
TURBETH s
TURBINE s
TURBITH*s
TURBITS*

TURBOTS*
TURDINE
TUREENS*
TURFIER
TURFING
TURFMAN
TURFMEN
TURFSKI s
*TURGENT
TURGITE s
TURGORS*
TURIONS*
TURISTA s
TURKEYS*
TURKOIS
TURMOIL s
TURNERS*
TURNERY*
TURNING s
TURNIPS*
TURNKEY s
TURNOFF s
TURNONS*
TURNOUT s
TURNUPS*
TURPETH s
TURRETS*
TURTLED*
TURTLER*s
TURTLES*
TUSCHES*
TUSHERY
TUSHIES*
TUSHING
TUSKERS*
TUSKING
TUSSAHS*
TUSSARS*
TUSSEHS*
TUSSERS*
TUSSIVE
TUSSLED*
TUSSLES*
TUSSOCK sy
TUSSORE*s
TUSSORS*
TUSSUCK s
TUSSURS*
TUTELAR sy
TUTORED
TUTOYED
TUTOYER s
TUTTIES
TUTTING
TUXEDOS*
TUYERES*
*TWADDLE drs
TWANGED
TWANGER s
*TWANGLE drs
TWASOME s
*TWATTLE ds
TWEAKED
TWEEDLE ds
TWEENER s
*TWEETED
TWEETER s
TWEEZED*
TWEEZER*s
TWEEZES*
TWELFTH s
TWELVES*
TWIBILL*s
TWIBILS*
*TWIDDLE drs
TWIDDLY
*TWIGGED
TWIGGEN
*TWILLED
TWINERS*
TWINGED
TWINGES*
*TWINIER
*TWINING
TWINJET s
TWINKIE s
*TWINKLE drs
TWINKLY
*TWINNED
TWINSET s
TWIRLED
TWIRLER s
*TWISTED
TWISTER s
TWITCHY
*TWITTED

a TWITTER sy
TWOFERS*
TWOFOLD s
TWOONIE s
TWOSOME s
TYCOONS*
TYLOSIN s
TYMBALS*
TYMPANA*l
TYMPANI*c
TYMPANO*
TYMPANS*
TYMPANY*
TYPABLE
TYPEBAR s
TYPESET s
TYPHOID s
TYPHONS*
TYPHOON s
TYPHOSE
TYPHOUS
a TYPICAL
TYPIEST
TYPISTS*
TYRANNY
TYRANTS*
TYRONIC
TYTHING
*TZADDIK
TZARDOM s
TZARINA s
TZARISM s
TZARIST s
TZETZES*
TZIGANE s
TZIMMES
TZITZIS
TZITZIT h
UAKARIS*
UFOLOGY
UGLIEST*
UKELELE s
UKULELE s
ULCERED
ULEXITE s
ULLAGED*
s ULLAGES*
ULPANIM
ULSTERS*
ULTIMAS*
ULULANT
ULULATE ds
UMBELED
cln UMBERED
UMBONAL
UMBONES
UMBONIC
UMBRAGE s
UMIACKS*
UMLAUTS*
UMPIRED*
UMPIRES*
UMPTEEN
UNACTED
UNADDED
UNADEPT
UNADULT
UNAGILE
UNAGING
UNAIDED
UNAIMED
UNAIRED
UNAKITE s
UNALIKE
UNAPTLY
UNARMED
UNASKED
UNAWAKE d
UNAWARE s
s UNBAKED
UNBALED*
UNBALES*
UNBASED
UNBATED
UNBEARS*
UNBEING
s UNBELTS*
UNBENDS*
UNBINDS*
UNBLEST
s UNBLOCK s
UNBOLTS*
UNBONED
UNBOSOM s
UNBOUND
UNBOWED

UNBOXED
UNBOXES
UNBRACE ds
UNBRAID s
UNBRAKE ds
UNBROKE n
UNBUILD s
UNBUILT
UNBULKY
s UNBURNT
UNCAGED*
UNCAGES*
UNCAKED*
UNCAKES*
UNCANNY
UNCASED*
UNCASES*
UNCEDED
UNCHAIN s
UNCHAIR s
UNCHARY
s UNCHOKE ds
UNCIALS*
UNCINAL
UNCINUS
UNCIVIL
UNCLAMP s
UNCLASP s
UNCLEAN
UNCLEAR
UNCLEFT
UNCLIPS*
UNCLOAK s
UNCLOGS*
UNCLOSE ds
UNCLOUD sy
UNCOCKS*
UNCODED
UNCOILS*
UNCOMIC
UNCORKS*
UNCOUTH
UNCOVER s
UNCRATE ds
UNCRAZY
UNCROSS
UNCROWN s
fj UNCTION s
UNCUFFS*
UNCURBS*
UNCURED
UNCURLS*
UNDATED
UNDERDO g
UNDERGO d
UNDINES*
UNDOCKS*
UNDOERS*
UNDOING s
UNDRAPE ds
UNDRAWN*
UNDRAWS*
s UNDRESS
UNDREST
UNDRIED
UNDRUNK
UNDULAR
UNDYING
UNEAGER
UNEARTH s
UNEASES*
*UNEATEN
UNENDED
UNEQUAL s
UNFADED
UNFAITH s
UNFAKED
UNFANCY
UNFAZED
UNFENCE ds
UNFIRED
UNFITLY
UNFIXED
UNFIXES
UNFOLDS*
UNFOUND
UNFREED*
UNFREES*
UNFROCK s
UNFROZE n
UNFUNNY
UNFURLS*
UNFUSED
UNFUSSY
UNGATED
UNGIRDS*
UNGLOVE ds
UNGLUED*
UNGLUES*
UNGODLY
UNGUARD s
UNGUENT as
UNGULAE*
UNGULAR*
UNHAIRS*
UNHANDS*
UNHANDY*
UNHANGS*
UNHAPPY
UNHASTY
UNHEARD
UNHELMS*
UNHINGE ds
UNHIRED
UNHITCH
UNHOODS*
UNHOOKS*
UNHOPED
UNHORSE ds
f UNHOUSE ds
UNHUMAN
UNHUSKS*
UNIBODY
UNICORN s
UNIDEAL
UNIFACE s
UNIFIED
UNIFIER s
UNIFIES
c UNIFORM s
UNIPODS*
UNIQUER*
UNIQUES*t
UNISIZE
UNISONS*
UNITAGE s
UNITARD s
UNITARY
UNITERS
UNITIES
UNITING
p UNITIVE
UNITIZE drs
UNJADED
UNJOINT s
UNKEMPT
UNKINKS*
UNKNITS*
UNKNOTS*
UNKNOWN s
UNLACED*
UNLACES*
UNLADED*
UNLADEN*
UNLADES*
UNLATCH
UNLEADS*
UNLEARN st
UNLEASH
UNLEVEL s
UNLIKED*
UNLINED
UNLINKS*
UNLIVED*
UNLIVES*
UNLOADS*
UNLOBED
g UNLOCKS*
UNLOOSE dns
UNLOVED
UNLUCKY
UNMACHO
UNMAKER*s
UNMAKES*
UNMANLY
UNMASKS*
UNMATED
UNMEANT
UNMERRY
UNMEWED
UNMINED
UNMITER s
UNMITRE ds
UNMIXED
UNMIXES
UNMOLDS*
UNMOORS*
UNMORAL
UNMOVED
UNNAILS*
UNNAMED
UNNERVE ds
UNNOISY
UNNOTED
UNOILED
UNOWNED
UNPACKS*
UNPAGED
UNPAVED
UNPICKS*
UNPILED*
UNPILES*
UNPLAIT s
UNPLUGS*
UNPOSED
UNQUIET s
UNQUOTE ds
UNRAKED
UNRATED
UNRAVEL s
UNRAZED
UNREADY*
UNREELS*
UNREEVE ds
UNRESTS*
UNRIMED
UNRIPER*
UNRISEN
UNROBED*
UNROBES*
UNROLLS*
s UNROOFS*
UNROOTS*
UNROPED
UNROUGH
r UNROUND s
UNROVEN*
UNRULED
UNSATED
UNSAVED
UNSAWED
UNSCREW s
UNSEALS*
UNSEAMS*
UNSEATS*
UNSELLS*
UNSEWED
UNSEXED
UNSEXES
UNSHARP
UNSHELL s
UNSHIFT s
g UNSHIPS*
UNSHORN
UNSHOWY
UNSIGHT s
UNSIZED
UNSLICK
UNSLING s
UNSLUNG
UNSMART
UNSNAGS*
UNSNAPS*
UNSNARL s
UNSOBER
UNSOLID
UNSONCY
UNSONSY
UNSOUND
UNSOWED
UNSPEAK s
UNSPENT
UNSPILT
UNSPLIT
UNSPOKE n
UNSPOOL s
UNSTACK s
UNSTATE ds
UNSTEEL s
UNSTEPS*
UNSTICK s
UNSTOPS*
UNSTRAP s
UNSTUCK
UNSTUNG
UNSWEAR s
UNSWEPT
UNSWORE
UNSWORN
UNTACKS*
UNTAKEN
UNTAMED*
UNTAXED
UNTEACH
UNTHINK s
UNTIMED
UNTIRED
UNTRACK s
UNTREAD s
UNTRIED
UNTRIMS*
UNTRUER*
UNTRULY
UNTRUSS
UNTRUTH s
UNTUCKS*
UNTUNED*
UNTUNES*
UNTWINE ds
UNTWIST s
UNTYING
UNURGED
UNUSUAL
UNVEILS*
UNVEXED
UNVOCAL
UNVOICE ds
UNWAXED
UNWEARY
UNWEAVE s
UNWHITE
UNWINDS*
UNWISER*
UNWOOED
UNWOUND
UNWOVEN*
UNWRAPS*
UNWRUNG
UNYOKED*
UNYOKES*
UNYOUNG
UNZONED
UPBEARS*
UPBEATS*
UPBINDS*
UPBOILS*
UPBORNE
UPBOUND
UPBRAID s
UPBUILD s
UPBUILT
UPCASTS*
UPCHUCK s
UPCLIMB s
UPCOAST
UPCOILS*
UPCOURT
UPCURLS*
UPCURVE ds
UPDARTS*
UPDATED*
UPDATER*s
UPDATES*
UPDIVED*
UPDIVES*
UPDRAFT s
UPDRIED
UPDRIES
*UPENDED
UPFIELD
UPFLING s
UPFLOWS*
UPFLUNG
UPFOLDS*
UPFRONT
UPGAZED*
UPGAZES*
UPGIRDS*
UPGOING
UPGRADE ds
UPGROWN*
UPGROWS*
UPHEAPS*
UPHEAVE drs
UPHILLS*
UPHOARD s
UPHOLDS*
e UPHROES*
UPKEEPS*
UPLANDS*
UPLEAPS*
UPLEAPT*
UPLIFTS*
*UPLIGHT s
UPLINKS
UPLOADS*
UPPILED*
UPPILES*
c UPPINGS*
UPPROPS*
*UPRAISE drs
UPRATED
UPRATES
*UPREACH
UPREARS*
UPRIGHT s
UPRISEN*
UPRISER*s
UPRISES
UPRIVER s
UPROARS*
UPROOTS*
UPROUSE ds
UPSCALE ds
UPSENDS*
UPSHIFT s
UPSHOOT s
UPSHOTS*
UPSIDES*
UPSILON s
UPSIZED*
UPSIZES*
UPSLOPE
UPSOARS*
UPSTAGE drs
UPSTAIR s
UPSTAND s
UPSTARE ds
UPSTART s
UPSTATE rs
UPSTEPS*
UPSTIRS*
UPSTOOD
UPSURGE ds
UPSWEEP s
UPSWELL s
UPSWEPT
UPSWING s
UPSWUNG
UPTAKES*
UPTALKS*
UPTEARS*
UPTEMPO s
UPTHREW
UPTHROW ns
UPTICKS*
UPTIGHT
UPTILTS*
UPTIMES*
UPTOWNS*
UPTREND s
UPTURNS*
UPWAFTS*
UPWARDS*
UPWELLS*
UPWINDS*
URACILS*
URAEMIA s
URAEMIC
r URALITE s
URANIAS*
URANIDE s
URANISM s
URANITE s
URANIUM s
URANOUS
URANYLS*
URBANER*
URCHINS*
UREASES*
UREDIAL
UREDIUM
UREIDES*
UREMIAS*
URETERS*
URETHAN es
URETHRA els
t URGENCY
URIDINE s
URINALS*
URINARY
URINATE ds
URINOSE
URINOUS
URNLIKE
URODELE s
UROLITH s
UROLOGY
UROPODS*
URTEXTS*
USANCES*
USAUNCE s
USEABLE
USEABLY
f USELESS
USHERED
USUALLY
USURERS*
USURIES
USURPED
USURPER s
UTENSIL s
UTERINE
UTILISE drs
f UTILITY
UTILIZE drs
UTMOSTS*
UTOPIAN*s
UTOPIAS*
UTOPISM s
UTOPIST s
UTRICLE s
bgm UTTERED
p
mp UTTERER s
UTTERLY
UVEITIC
UVEITIS
UVULARS*
UXORIAL
VACANCY
VACATED*
VACATES*
VACCINA ls
VACCINE es
*VACUITY
VACUOLE s
VACUOUS
VACUUMS*
VAGALLY
VAGINAE*
VAGINAL*
VAGINAS*
VAGRANT s
VAGUELY
VAGUEST
VAHINES*
a*VAILING
VAINEST
VAKEELS*
VALANCE ds
VALENCE s
VALENCY
VALERIC
VALETED
*VALGOID
VALIANT s
VALIDLY
VALINES
VALISES*
VALKYRS*
VALLATE
VALLEYS
VALONIA s
VALOURS*
e VALUATE ds
VALUERS*
VALUING
VALUTAS*
VALVATE
VALVING
VALVULA er
VALVULE s
VAMOOSE ds
VAMOSED*
VAMOSES*
VAMPERS*
VAMPIER
*VAMPING
VAMPIRE s
VAMPISH
VANADIC
VANDALS*
VANDYKE ds
VANILLA s
VANLOAD s
VANNERS*
VANNING
VANPOOL s
VANTAGE s
VANWARD
VAPIDLY
VAPORED
VAPORER s
VAPOURS*
VAPOURY*
VAQUERO s
VARIANT s
VARIATE ds
a VARICES
VARIERS*
VARIETY
VARIOLA rs
o VARIOLE s
VARIOUS
VARLETS*
VARMENT s
VARMINT s
VARNISH y
VAROOMS*
VARSITY
VARUSES
VARYING
VASCULA r
VASSALS*
VASTEST
VASTIER
VASTITY
VATFULS*
VATICAL
VATTING
VAULTED
VAULTER s
VAUNTED
VAUNTER s
*VAUNTIE
VAVASOR s
VAWARDS
VAWNTIE
VEALERS*
VEALIER
VEALING
VECTORS*
VEDALIA s
VEDETTE s
VEEJAYS*
VEEPEES*
VEERIES
VEERING
VEGETAL
VEGGIES*
*VEGGING
VEHICLE s
VEILERS*
VEILING s
VEINERS*
VEINIER
VEINING s
VEINLET s
VEINULE st
VELAMEN
VELARIA
VELCROS*
VELIGER s
*VELITES
VELLUMS*
VELOURS*
VELOUTE s
VELURED*
VELURES*
VELVETS*
VELVETY*
VENALLY
*VENATIC
VENDACE s
VENDEES*
VENDERS
*VENDING
VENDORS*
VENDUES
VENEERS*
VENENES*
a VENGING
VENINES*
VENIRES*
VENISON s
VENOMED
VENOMER s
VENTAGE s
a*VENTAIL s
VENTERS
VENTING
VENTRAL s
VENTURE drs
VENTURI s
VENULAR
VENULES*
VENUSES
VERANDA hs
VERBALS*
VERBENA s
o VERBIDS*
VERBIFY
VERBILE s
VERBOSE
VERDANT
VERDICT s
VERDINS*
VERDURE ds
VERGERS*
VERGING
VERGLAS

VERIDIC
VERIEST
VERISMO*s
VERISMS*
VERISTS*
VERITAS
VERITES*
VERMEIL s
VERMIAN
VERMUTH s
VERNIER s
VERRUCA es
VERSANT s
VERSERS*
o VERSETS*
VERSIFY
VERSINE s
VERSING
ae VERSION s
VERSTES*
VERTIGO s
VERVAIN s
VERVETS*
VESICAE*
VESICAL*
VESICLE s
VESPERS*
VESPIDS*
VESPINE
VESSELS*
VESTALS*
VESTEES*
VESTIGE s
VESTING s
*VESTRAL
VESTURE ds
k*VETCHES
VETERAN s
VETIVER st
VETOERS*
VETOING
VETTERS*
VETTING
VEXEDLY
VEXILLA r
VIADUCT s
VIALING
VIALLED
VIATICA*l
a VIATORS*
VIBISTS*
VIBRANT s
VIBRATE ds
VIBRATO rs
VIBRION*s
VIBRIOS*
VICARLY
VICEROY s
VICHIES
VICINAL
VICIOUS
VICOMTE s
VICTIMS*
e VICTORS*
VICTORY*
VICTUAL s
VICUGNA s
VICUNAS*
VIDETTE s
VIDICON s
VIDUITY
VIEWERS*
VIEWIER
VIEWING s
VIGOURS*
VIKINGS*
VILAYET s
VILLAGE rs
VILLAIN sy
VILLEIN s
VILLOSE
VILLOUS
VIMINAL*
VINASSE s
VINCULA
VINEGAR sy
VINIEST
VINTAGE rs
VINTNER s
VINYLIC
VIOLATE drs
VIOLENT
VIOLETS*
VIOLINS*
VIOLIST s
VIOLONE s

VIRAGOS*
VIRALLY
VIRELAI s
VIRELAY s
VIREMIA s
VIREMIC
VIRGATE s
VIRGINS*
VIRGULE s
VIRIONS*
VIROIDS*
VIROSES
VIROSIS
VIRTUAL
VIRTUES*
VIRUSES
VISAGED*
VISAGES*
VISAING
VISARDS*
VISCERA l
VISCOID
VISCOSE s
VISCOUS
VISEING
VISIBLE
VISIBLY
VISIONS*
VISITED
VISITER s
VISITOR s
VISORED
VISTAED
VISUALS*
VITALLY
VITAMER s
VITAMIN es
VITESSE s
VITIATE ds
VITRAIN s
VITRICS*
VITRIFY
VITRINE s
VITRIOL s
VITTATE
VITTLED*
VITTLES*
VIVACES*
VIVARIA
VIVIDER
VIVIDLY
VIVIFIC
VIXENLY
VIZARDS*
VIZIERS*
VIZORED
VIZSLAS*
e VOCABLE s
VOCABLY
VOCALIC s
VOCALLY
VOCODER s
VODOUNS*
VOGUERS*
VOGUING s
VOGUISH
VOICERS*
VOICING s
a VOIDERS*
a VOIDING
VOLANTE*
VOLCANO s
VOLLEYS*
VOLOSTS*
VOLTAGE s
VOLTAIC
VOLUBLE
VOLUBLY
VOLUMED*
VOLUMES*
VOLUTED*
e VOLUTES*
VOLUTIN s
VOLVATE
VOLVULI
VOMICAE*
VOMITED
VOMITER s
VOMITOS*
VOMITUS
VOODOOS*
VORLAGE s
VOTABLE
VOTIVES*
VOTRESS
a*VOUCHED

VOUCHEE s
a VOUCHER s
a*VOUCHES
VOUDONS*
VOUDOUN s
VOUVRAY s
VOWLESS
VOYAGED*
VOYAGER*s
VOYAGES*
VOYEURS*
*VROOMED
VUGGIER
VULGARS*
VULGATE s
VULPINE
VULTURE s
VULVATE
VYINGLY
WABBLED*
WABBLER*s
WABBLES*
WACKEST*
WACKIER
WACKILY
WADABLE
WADDERS
WADDIED*
WADDIES*
*WADDING s
st*WADDLED*
t WADDLER*s
st*WADDLES*
WADMAAL s
WADMALS*
WADMELS*
WADMOLL*s
WADMOLS*
WADSETS*
WAENESS
WAESUCK s
WAFERED
WAFFIES*
WAFFING
WAFFLED*
WAFFLER*s
WAFFLES*
WAFTAGE s
WAFTERS
WAFTING
WAFTURE s
WAGERED
WAGERER s
s*WAGGERS*
WAGGERY*
s WAGGING
WAGGISH
WAGGLED*
WAGGLES*
WAGGONS*
WAGONED
WAGONER s
WAGSOME
WAGTAIL s
WAHINES*
WAIFING
WAIFISH
WAILERS*
WAILFUL
*WAILING
*WAIRING
WAISTED
WAISTER s
a WAITERS*
a WAITING s
WAITRON s
WAIVERS
WAIVING
WAKAMES*
WAKANDA s
WAKEFUL
a WAKENED
a WAKENER s
WAKIKIS*
WALKERS*
WALKING s
WALKOUT s
WALKUPS*
WALKWAY s
WALLABY
WALLAHS*
WALLETS*
WALLEYE ds
WALLIES
WALLING
WALLOPS*

s*WALLOWS*
WALNUTS*
WALTZED
WALTZER s
WALTZES
WAMBLED
WAMBLES
WAMEFOU s
WAMEFUL s
s WAMPISH
WAMPUMS*
*WAMUSES
WANDERS*
WANGANS*
t*WANGLED*
t*WANGLER*s
t*WANGLES*
WANGUNS*
WANIEST
WANIGAN s
WANIONS
WANNABE es
WANNESS
WANNEST
s WANNING
WANTAGE s
WANTERS*
*WANTING
WANTONS*
WAPITIS*
s WAPPING
WARBLED*
WARBLER*s
WARBLES*
WARDENS*
a WARDERS*
as WARDING
WARFARE s
WARHEAD s
WARIEST
WARISON s
WARKING
WARLESS
WARLIKE
WARLOCK s
WARLORD s
s*WARMERS*
WARMEST
s*WARMING
WARMISH
WARMTHS*
WARMUPS*
WARNERS*
WARNING s
WARPAGE s
WARPATH s
WARPERS*
WARPING
*WARRANT sy
WARRENS*
WARRING
WARRIOR s
WARSAWS*
WARSHIP s
WARSLED*
WARSLER*s
WARSLES*
WARSTLE drs
WARTHOG s
*WARTIER
WARTIME s
WARWORK s
WARWORN
WASABIS*
WASHDAY s
s WASHERS*
*WASHIER
s*WASHING s
WASHOUT s
WASHRAG s
WASHTUB s
WASHUPS*
WASPIER
WASPILY
*WASPISH
*WASSAIL s
WASTAGE s
WASTERS
WASTERY*
WASTING
WASTREL s
WASTRIE s
WATAPES*
WATCHED
WATCHER s
s WATCHES

WATERED
WATERER s
WATTAGE s
WATTAPE s
*WATTEST
t WATTLED*
t WATTLES*s
WAUCHTS*
WAUGHTS
WAUKING
WAULING
WAVELET s
WAVEOFF s
WAVERED
WAVERER s
WAVICLE s
WAVIEST*
WAWLING
WAXABLE
WAXBILL s
WAXIEST
WAXINGS*
*WAXLIKE
WAXWEED s
WAXWING s
WAXWORK s
WAXWORM s
WAYBILL s
WAYLAID
WAYLAYS*
WAYLESS
WAYSIDE s
WAYWARD
WAYWORN
WEAKENS*
WEAKEST
WEAKISH
WEAKONS*
WEALTHS*
WEALTHY*
WEANERS*
WEANING
WEAPONS*
s WEARERS*
WEARIED
WEARIER
WEARIES t
WEARILY
s*WEARING
WEARISH
WEASAND s
WEASELS
WEASELY*
WEASONS*
a WEATHER s
WEAVERS*
WEAVING
WEAZAND s
WEBBIER
*WEBBING s
WEBCAMS*
WEBCAST s
WEBFEET
WEBFOOT
WEBLESS
WEBLIKE
WEBLOGS*
WEBPAGE s
WEBSITE s
WEBSTER s
WEBWORK s
WEBWORM s
WEDDERS*
WEDDING s
WEDELED
WEDELNS*
WEDGIER
WEDGIES*t
*WEDGING
WEDLOCK s
WEEDERS*
t WEEDIER
WEEDILY
WEEDING
WEEKDAY s
WEEKEND s
WEENIER*
st WEENIES*t
WEENING
s WEEPERS*
s WEEPIER*
WEEPIES*t
s WEEPING s
st WEETING
WEEVERS*
WEEVILS*

WEEVILY*
WEEWEED*
WEEWEES*
WEIGELA s
WEIGHED
WEIGHER s
WEIGHTS
WEIGHTY
WEINERS*
WEIRDED
WEIRDER
WEIRDIE s
WEIRDLY
WEIRDOS*
WELCHED
WELCHER s
WELCHES
WELCOME drs
WELDERS
WELDING
WELDORS*
WELFARE s
WELKINS*
WELLIES*
ds WELLING
WELSHED
WELSHER s
WELSHES
s WELTERS*
WELTING s
WENCHED
WENCHER s
WENCHES
WENDIGO s
*WENDING
WENNIER
WENNISH
WERGELD s
WERGELT s
WERGILD s
WERWOLF
WESKITS*
WESSAND s
WESTERN*s
WESTERS
WESTING s
WETHERS
WETLAND s
WETNESS
WETSUIT s
WETTERS*
WETTEST
WETTING s
WETTISH
WETWARE s
*WHACKED
*WHACKER s
WHACKOS*
WHALERS
*WHALING s
*WHAMMED
*WHANGED
WHANGEE s
*WHAPPED
WHAPPER s
WHARFED
WHARVES*
WHATNOT s
WHATSIS
WHATSIT s
WHEATEN s
WHEEDLE drs
*WHEELED
*WHEELER s
WHEELIE s
WHEEPED
WHEEPLE ds
WHEEZED
WHEEZER*s
WHEEZES
*WHELMED
*WHELPED
WHEREAS
*WHEREAT
*WHEREBY
*WHEREIN
*WHEREOF
*WHEREON
*WHERETO
WHERVES*
WHETHER
WHETTED
WHETTER s
WHEYISH
WHICKER s
WHIDAHS*

WHIDDED
WHIFFED
WHIFFER s
WHIFFET s
WHIFFLE drs
WHILING
WHIMPER s
WHIMSEY s
WHINERS*
WHINGED
*WHINGER*s
WHINGES
WHINIER
WHINING
*WHIPPED
*WHIPPER s
WHIPPET s
WHIPRAY s
WHIPSAW ns
WHIRLED
WHIRLER s
WHIRRED
WHISHED
WHISHES
WHISHTS*
WHISKED
WHISKER sy
WHISKEY s
WHISPER sy
*WHISTED
WHISTLE drs
WHITELY
WHITENS*
WHITEST*
*WHITHER
WHITIER
WHITING s
WHITISH
WHITLOW s
*WHITTER s
WHITTLE drs
WHIZZED
WHIZZER s
WHIZZES
WHOEVER
*WHOLISM s
WHOMPED
*WHOOFED
*WHOOPED
WHOOPEE s
*WHOOPER s
WHOOPIE s
*WHOOPLA s
WHOOSIS
*WHOPPED
*WHOPPER s
WHORING
WHORISH
WHORLED
WHORTLE s
*WHUMPED
WHUPPED
WHYDAHS*
WICCANS*
WICKAPE s
WICKERS
WICKETS*
WICKING s
WICKIUP s
WICKYUP s
WIDDERS*
WIDDIES*
t WIDDLED*
t WIDDLES*
WIDENED
WIDENER s
WIDEOUT s
WIDGEON s
WIDGETS*
WIDOWED
WIDOWER s
WIELDED
WIELDER s
WIENERS*
WIENIES*
WIFEDOM s
WIFTIER
WIGEONS*
WIGGERY
t WIGGIER
st*WIGGING s
WIGGLED*
WIGGLER*s
WIGGLES*
t WIGLESS
WIGLETS*

t WIGLIKE
WIGWAGS*
WIGWAMS*
WIKIUPS*
WILDCAT s
WILDERS*
WILDEST
WILDING s
WILDISH
WILIEST
s WILLERS*
WILLETS*
WILLFUL
WILLIED
WILLIES
st WILLING
WILLOWS*
WILLOWY*
WILTING
WIMBLED*
WIMBLES*
WIMPIER
*WIMPING
*WIMPISH
WIMPLED
WIMPLES*
WINCERS*
WINCEYS*
*WINCHED
*WINCHER s
*WINCHES
WINCING
WINDAGE s
WINDBAG s
WINDERS*
WINDIER
*WINDIGO s
WINDILY
WINDING s
ds WINDLED*
ds WINDLES*s
WINDOWS
WINDOWY*
WINDROW s
WINDUPS*
WINDWAY s
WINESAP s
WINESOP s
WINGBOW s
s WINGERS*
s WINGIER
st WINGING
WINGLET s
s WINGMAN
s WINGMEN
WINGTIP s
t WINIEST
WINKERS
s*WINKING
t WINKLED*
t*WINKLES*
WINLESS
WINNERS
t*WINNING s
WINNOCK s
WINNOWS*
WINSOME r
WINTERS
WINTERY*
WINTLED*
WINTLES*
WIPEOUT s
WIRABLE
WIREMAN
WIREMEN
WIRETAP s
WIREWAY s
WIRIEST
WIRINGS*
WISDOMS*
WISEASS
WISEGUY s
WISENTS*
s WISHERS*
WISHFUL
s WISHING
WISPIER
WISPILY
WISPING
WISPISH
WISSING
WISTFUL
t WISTING
st*WITCHED
st*WITCHES
s WITHERS*
WITHIER
WITHIES t
WITHING*
WITHINS*
WITHOUT s
WITLESS
WITLING s
WITLOOF s
WITNESS
WITNEYS*
WITTIER
WITTILY
t WITTING s
WITTOLS*
WIVERNS*
WIZARDS*
WIZENED
WIZZENS*
WOADWAX
WOBBLED*
WOBBLER*s
WOBBLES*
WOENESS
WOESOME
WOFULLY
WOLFERS*
WOLFING
WOLFISH
WOLFRAM s
WOLVERS*
WOMANED
WOMANLY
WOMBATS*
WOMBIER
WOMERAS*
WOMMERA s
WONDERS*
WONKIER
WONNERS*
WONNING
WONTING
WONTONS*
WOODBIN des
WOODBOX
WOODCUT s
WOODHEN s
WOODIER*
WOODIES*t
WOODING
WOODLOT s
WOODMAN
WOODMEN
WOODSIA s
WOODWAX
WOOFERS*
WOOFING
WOOLENS*
WOOLERS*
WOOLHAT s
WOOLIER*
WOOLIES*t
WOOLLED
WOOLLEN s
WOOLMAN
WOOLMEN
WOOMERA s
WOOPSED
WOOPSES
*WOORALI s
WOORARI s
s WOOSHED
s WOOSHES
*WOOZIER
*WOOZILY
WORDAGE s
WORDIER
WORDILY
WORDING s
WORKBAG s
WORKBOX
WORKDAY s
WORKERS*
WORKING s
WORKMAN
WORKMEN
WORKOUT s
WORKUPS*
WORLDLY
WORMERS
WORMIER
WORMILS*
WORMING
WORMISH
WORRIED
WORRIER s
WORRIES
WORRITS*
WORSENS*
WORSETS*
WORSHIP s
WORSTED s
WORTHED
s WOTTING
WOULDST
s WOUNDED
WOWSERS*
*WRACKED
WRAITHS*
WRANGLE drs
*WRAPPED
*WRAPPER s
WRASSES*
*WRASSLE ds
WRASTLE ds
WRATHED
WREAKED
WREAKER s
WREATHE*dnr
s
WREATHS*
WREATHY*
*WRECKED
WRECKER s
*WRESTED
*WRESTER s
WRESTLE drs
*WRICKED
WRIGGLE drs
WRIGGLY
WRIGHTS
*WRINGED
*WRINGER s
WRINKLE ds
WRINKLY
WRITERS*
WRITHED*
WRITHEN*
WRITHER*s
WRITHES*
WRITING s
WRITTEN
WRONGED
WRONGER s
WRONGLY
WROUGHT
WRYNECK s
WRYNESS
WURZELS*
WUSSIER
WUSSIES t
WUTHERS*
WYVERNS*
XANTHAN s
XANTHIC
XANTHIN es
XENOPUS
XERARCH
*XEROSES
XEROSIS
*XEROTIC
XEROXED
XEROXES
XERUSES
XIPHOID s
XYLENES*
XYLIDIN es
XYLITOL s
XYLOSES*
XYSTERS*
YABBERS*
YABBIES*
YACHTED
YACHTER s
YACKING
YAFFING
YAKKERS*
YAKKING
YAMALKA s
YAMMERS*
YAMULKA s
YANKING
YANQUIS*
YANTRAS*
YAPOCKS*
YAPPERS*
YAPPING
YARDAGE s
YARDARM s
YARDERS*
YARDING
YARDMAN
YARDMEN
YARNERS*
YARNING
YARROWS
YASHMAC s
YASHMAK s
YASMAKS*
YATAGAN s
YATTERS*
YAUPERS*
YAUPING
YAUPONS*
YAUTIAS*
YAWLING
YAWNERS*
*YAWNING
YAWPERS*
YAWPING s
*YCLEPED
YEALING s
YEANING
YEAREND s
*YEARNED
*YEARNER s
YEASTED
YEELINS*
YEGGMAN
YEGGMEN
YELLERS*
YELLING
YELLOWS*
YELLOWY*
YELPERS*
YELPING
YENNING
YERKING
YESHIVA hs
YESSING
YESTERN*
YEUKING
YIELDED
YIELDER s
YIPPIES*
YIPPING
YIRRING
YOBBOES
YOCKING
YODELED
YODELER s
YODLERS*
YODLING
YOGHURT s
YOGINIS*
YOGURTS*
YOHIMBE s
YOLKIER
YONKERS*
YOUNGER s
YOUNKER s
YOUPONS*
YOUTHEN s
YOWLERS*
YOWLING
YPERITE s
YTTRIAS*
YTTRIUM s
YUCKIER
YUCKING
YUKKIER
YUKKING
YUMMIER
YUMMIES t
YUPPIES*
YUPPIFY
ZACATON s
ZADDICK
ZAFFARS*
ZAFFERS*
ZAFFIRS*
ZAFFRES*
ZAGGING
ZAIKAIS*
ZAMARRA s
ZAMARRO s
ZANANAS*
ZANDERS*
ZANIEST*
ZANYISH
ZAPATEO s
ZAPPERS*
ZAPPIER
ZAPPING
ZAPTIAH s
ZAPTIEH s
ZAREBAS*
ZAREEBA s
ZARIBAS*
ZEALOTS*
ZEALOUS
ZEATINS*
ZEBECKS*
ZEBRAIC
ZEBRANO s
ZEBRASS*
ZEBRINE s
ZEBROID
ZECCHIN ios
ZECHINS*
ZEDOARY
ZELKOVA s
ZEMSTVA
ZEMSTVO s
ZENAIDA s
ZENANAS*
ZENITHS*
ZEOLITE s
ZEPHYRS*
ZEPPOLE s
ZEPPOLI
ZEROING
ZESTERS
ZESTFUL
ZESTIER
ZESTILY
ZESTING
ZEUGMAS*
ZIBETHS*
*ZIGGING
ZIGZAGS*
ZIKURAT s
ZILCHES
ZILLAHS*
ZILLION s
ZINCATE s
ZINCIFY
ZINCING
*ZINCITE s
ZINCKED
ZINCOID
ZINCOUS
ZINGANI
ZINGANO
ZINGARA
ZINGARE
ZINGARI
ZINGARO
ZINGERS*
ZINGIER
ZINGING
ZINKIFY
ZINNIAS*
ZIPLESS
ZIPLOCK
ZIPPERS*
ZIPPIER
ZIPPING
ZIRCONS*
ZITHERN*s
ZITHERS*
ZIZZLED*
ZIZZLES*
ZLOTIES
ZLOTYCH
ZOARIAL*
ZOARIUM
ZOCALOS*
ZODIACS*
ZOECIUM
ZOISITE s
ZOMBIES*
ZOMBIFY
ZONALLY
o ZONATED*
ZONKING
ZONULAE*
ZONULAR*
ZONULAS*
ZONULES*
ZOOECIA
*ZOOGENY
ZOOGLEA els
ZOOIDAL
ZOOIEST
*ZOOLOGY
ZOOMING
ZOONING
ZOOTIER
ZOOTOMY
ZORILLA s
ZORILLE s
ZORILLO s
ZOSTERS*
ZOUAVES*
ZOYSIAS*
ZYDECOS*
ZYGOMAS*
a ZYGOSES*
ZYGOSIS
ZYGOTES*
ZYGOTIC
ZYMASES*
ZYMOGEN es
ZYMOSAN s
ZYMOSES
ZYMOSIS
ZYMOTIC
ZYMURGY
ZYZZYVA s

The Hooks: 8s-to-Make-9s

AARDVARK s
AARDWOLF
AASVOGEL s
ABACUSES
ABALONES*
ABAMPERE s
ABANDONS*
ABAPICAL
ABASEDLY
*ABASHING
ABATABLE
ABATISES
ABATTOIR s
ABBACIES
ABBATIAL
ABBESSES
ABDICATE ds
ABDOMENS*
ABDOMINA l
ABDUCENS
ABDUCENT
ABDUCING
ABDUCTED
ABDUCTEE s
ABDUCTOR s
*ABEGGING
ABELMOSK s
ABERRANT s
ABETMENT s
ABETTALS*
ABETTERS
*ABETTING
ABETTORS
ABEYANCE s
ABEYANCY
ABFARADS*
ABHENRYS*
ABHORRED
ABHORRER s
ABIDANCE s
ABIGAILS*
ABJECTLY
ABJURERS*
ABJURING
ABLATING
ABLATION s
ABLATIVE s
ABLATORS*
ABLEGATE s
ABLEISMS*
ABLEISTS*
ABLUENTS*
ABLUTION s
ABNEGATE ds
ABNORMAL s
ABOIDEAU sx
ABOITEAU sx
ABOMASAL*
ABOMASUM
ABOMASUS
ABORALLY
ABORNING
ABORTERS*
ABORTING
ABORTION s
ABORTIVE
ABOULIAS*
*ABOUNDED
*ABRACHIA s
ABRADANT s
ABRADERS*
ABRADING
ABRASION s
ABRASIVE s
ABREACTS*
ABRIDGED
ABRIDGER*s
ABRIDGES
ABROGATE ds
ABROSIAS*
ABRUPTER
ABRUPTLY
ABSCISED*
ABSCISES*
ABSCISIN gs
ABSCISSA es
ABSCONDS*
ABSEILED
ABSENCES*
ABSENTED
ABSENTEE s
ABSENTER s
ABSENTLY
ABSINTHE*s

ABSINTHS*
ABSOLUTE rs
ABSOLVED*
ABSOLVER*s
ABSOLVES*
ABSONANT
ABSORBED
ABSORBER s
ABSTAINS*
ABSTERGE ds
ABSTRACT s
ABSTRICT s
ABSTRUSE r
ABSURDER
ABSURDLY
ABUNDANT
ABUSABLE
ABUTILON s
ABUTMENT s
ABUTTALS
ABUTTERS
*ABUTTING
ACADEMES*
ACADEMIA s
ACADEMIC s
ACALEPHE*s
ACALEPHS*
ACANTHAE*
*ACANTHUS
ACAPNIAS*
ACARBOSE s
ACARIDAN s
ACARINES*
ACARPOUS
*ACAUDATE
*ACAULINE
ACAULOSE
ACAULOUS
ACCEDERS*
ACCEDING
ACCENTED
ACCENTOR s
ACCEPTED
ACCEPTEE s
ACCEPTER s
ACCEPTOR s
ACCESSED
ACCESSES
ACCIDENT s
ACCIDIAS*
ACCIDIES*
ACCLAIMS*
ACCOLADE ds
ACCORDED
ACCORDER s
ACCOSTED
ACCOUNTS*
ACCOUTER s
ACCOUTRE ds
ACCREDIT s
ACCRETED*
ACCRETES*
ACCRUALS*
ACCRUING
ACCURACY
ACCURATE
ACCURSED
ACCUSALS*
ACCUSANT s
ACCUSERS*
ACCUSING
ACCUSTOM s
ACELDAMA s
*ACENTRIC
ACEQUIAS*
lm*ACERATED*
ACERBATE ds
ACERBEST
ACERBITY
ACEROLAS*
ACERVATE
ACERVULI
ACESCENT s
ACETAMID es
ACETATED*
ACETATES*
ACETONES*
ACETONIC
ACETOXYL s
ACETYLIC
ACHENIAL
ACHIEVED*
ACHIEVER*s
ACHIEVES*

ACHILLEA s
ACHINESS
ACHINGLY
ACHIOTES*
ACHOLIAS*
ACHROMAT s
*ACHROMIC
ACICULAE*
ACICULAR*
ACICULAS*
ACICULUM s
ACIDEMIA s
ACIDHEAD s
ACIDNESS
ACIDOSES
ACIDOSIS
ACIDOTIC
ACIDURIA s
ACIERATE ds
ACOELOUS
ACOLYTES*
t ACONITES*
ACONITIC
ACONITUM s
ACOUSTIC s
ACQUAINT s
ACQUESTS*
ACQUIRED*
ACQUIREE*s
ACQUIRER*s
ACQUIRES*
ACRASIAS*
ACRASINS*
ACREAGES*
ACRIDEST
ACRIDINE s
ACRIDITY
ACRIMONY
ACROBATS*
m ACRODONT s
ACROGENS*
ACROLECT s
ACROLEIN s
ACROLITH s
ACROMIAL*
ACROMION
ACRONYMS*
ACROSOME s
ACROSTIC s
ACROTISM s
ACRYLATE s
ACRYLICS*
ACTINIAE*
ACTINIAN*s
ACTINIAS*
ACTINIDE s
ACTINISM s
ACTINIUM s
ACTINOID s
ACTINONS*
ACTIONER s
ACTIVATE ds
ACTIVELY
ACTIVISM s
ACTIVIST s
ACTIVITY
ACTIVIZE ds
ACTORISH
ACTRESSY*
ft ACTUALLY
ACTUATED*
ACTUATES*
ACTUATOR s
v ACUITIES
ACULEATE d
ACUTANCE s
ACYLATED*
ACYLATES*
ACYLOINS*
ADAMANCE s
ADAMANCY
ADAMANTS*
ADAMSITE s
ADAPTERS*
ADAPTING
ADAPTION s
ADAPTIVE
ADAPTORS*
ADDENDUM s
ADDICTED
ADDITION s
ADDITIVE s
ADDITORY
ADDUCENT

ADDUCERS*
ADDUCING
ADDUCTED
ADDUCTOR s
*ADEEMING
ADENINES*
ADENITIS
ADENOIDS*
ADENOMAS*
ADENOSES
ADENOSIS
ADEPTEST
ADEQUACY
ADEQUATE
ADHEREND s
ADHERENT s
ADHERERS*
ADHERING
ADHESION s
ADHESIVE s
ADHIBITS*
ADIPOSES*
ADIPOSIS
ADJACENT
ADJOINED
ADJOINTS*
ADJOURNS*
ADJUDGED*
ADJUDGES*
ADJUNCTS*
ADJURERS*
ADJURING
ADJURORS*
ADJUSTED
ADJUSTER s
ADJUSTOR s
ADJUTANT s
ADJUVANT s
ADMASSES
ADMIRALS*
ADMIRERS*
ADMIRING
ADMITTED
ADMITTEE s
ADMITTER s
ADMIXING
ADMONISH
ADNATION s
ADONISES
ADOPTEES*
ADOPTERS*
ADOPTING
ADOPTION s
ADOPTIVE
ADORABLE
ADORABLY
ADORNERS*
ADORNING
ADRENALS*
ADROITER
ADROITLY
ADSCRIPT s
ADSORBED
ADSORBER s
ADULARIA s
ADULATED*
ADULATES*
ADULATOR sy
ADULTERY
ADUMBRAL
ADUNCATE
ADUNCOUS
ADVANCED*
ADVANCER*s
ADVANCES*
ADVECTED
ADVERTED
ADVISEES*
ADVISERS*
ADVISING
ADVISORS*
ADVISORY*
ADVOCACY
ADVOCATE ds
ADVOWSON s
ADYNAMIA s
*ADYNAMIC
AECIDIAL*
AECIDIUM
AEQUORIN s
AERATING
AERATION s
AERATORS*
AERIALLY
AERIFIED
AERIFIES

AERIFORM
AEROBATS*
AEROBICS*
AEROBIUM
AERODUCT s
AERODYNE s
AEROFOIL s
AEROGELS*
AEROGRAM s
AEROLITE s
AEROLITH s
AEROLOGY
AERONAUT s
AERONOMY
AEROSATS*
AEROSOLS*
AEROSTAT s
*AESTHETE s
*AESTIVAL
*AETHERIC
*AFEBRILE
AFFAIRES*
AFFECTED
AFFECTER s
AFFERENT s
AFFIANCE ds
AFFIANTS*
AFFICHES*
AFFINELY
AFFINITY
AFFIRMED
AFFIRMER s
AFFIXERS*
AFFIXIAL
AFFIXING
AFFLATUS
AFFLICTS*
AFFLUENT s
AFFLUXES
AFFORDED
AFFOREST s
AFFRAYED
AFFRAYER s
AFFRIGHT s
AFFRONTS*
AFFUSION s
AFGHANIS*
*AFLUTTER
AFTERTAX
AGALLOCH s
AGALWOOD s
AGAMETES
AGAROSES*
AGATIZED*
AGATIZES*
AGEDNESS
AGEMATES*
AGENCIES
AGENDUMS*
*AGENESES
AGENESIA s
*AGENESIS
*AGENETIC
AGENIZED*
AGENIZES*
AGENTIAL
AGENTING s
AGENTIVE s
AGERATUM s
h AGGADAHS*
h AGGADOTH*
AGGRADED*
AGGRADES*
AGGRIEVE ds
AGINNERS
AGIOTAGE s
AGISTING
AGITABLE
AGITATED*
AGITATES*
AGITATOR*s
AGITPROP s
*AGLIMMER
*AGLITTER
AGLYCONE*s
AGLYCONS*
AGMINATE
AGNATION s
AGNIZING
AGNOMENS*
AGNOMINA
AGNOSIAS*
*AGNOSTIC s
AGONISED*
AGONISES*
AGONISTS*

AGONIZED*
AGONIZES*
AGOUTIES
AGRAFFES*
AGRAPHIA s
*AGRAPHIC
AGRARIAN s
*AGREEING
AGRESTAL
AGRESTIC
AGRIMONY
AGROLOGY
AGRONOMY
AGRYPNIA s
AGUACATE s
AGUELIKE
AGUEWEED s
AGUISHLY
AIGRETTE s
AIGUILLE s
AILERONS*
b AILMENTS*
AIMFULLY
AINSELLS*
AIRBOATS*
AIRBORNE
AIRBOUND
h AIRBRUSH
AIRBURST s
AIRBUSES
AIRCHECK s
AIRCOACH
AIRCRAFT
AIRCREWS*
AIRDATES*
AIRDROME s
AIRDROPS*
AIRFARES*
AIRFIELD s
AIRFLOWS*
AIRFOILS*
AIRFRAME s
AIRGLOWS*
AIRHEADS*
AIRHOLES*
h AIRINESS
AIRLIFTS*
AIRLINER*s
h AIRLINES*
AIRMAILS*
AIRPARKS*
AIRPLANE s
AIRPLAYS*
AIRPORTS*
AIRPOSTS*
AIRPOWER s
AIRPROOF s
AIRSCAPE s
AIRSCREW s
AIRSHEDS*
AIRSHIPS*
AIRSHOTS*
AIRSHOWS*
AIRSPACE s
AIRSPEED s
AIRSTRIP s
AIRTHING
AIRTIGHT
AIRTIMES*
AIRWAVES*
AIRWOMAN
AIRWOMEN
AISLEWAY s
AKINESIA s
*AKINETIC
AKVAVITS*
ALACHLOR s
ALACRITY
ALAMEDAS*
ALAMODES*
ALANINES*
ALARMING
ALARMISM s
ALARMIST s
ALARUMED
ALASTORS*
h ALATIONS*
ALBACORE s
ALBEDOES
ALBICORE s
ALBINISM s
ALBIZIAS*
ALBIZZIA s
ALBUMENS*
ALBUMINS*
ALBUMOSE s

ALBURNUM s
ALCAHEST s
ALCAIDES*
ALCALDES*
ALCAYDES*
ALCAZARS*
ALCHEMIC
ALCIDINE
ALCOHOLS*
ALDEHYDE s
ALDERFLY
ALDERMAN
ALDERMEN
ALDICARB s
ALDOLASE s
ALEATORY
ALEHOUSE s
ALEMBICS*
ALENCONS*
ALERTEST
ALERTING
ALEURONE*s
ALEURONS*
k ALEWIVES
ALEXINES*
ALFALFAS*
ALFAQUIN*s
ALFAQUIS*
ALFORJAS*
ALFRESCO
ALGAROBA s
ALGEBRAS*
ALGERINE s
ALGICIDE s
ALGIDITY
ALGINATE s
ALGOLOGY
ALGORISM s
ALIASING s
ALIBIING
ALIDADES*
ALIENAGE s
ALIENATE ds
ALIENEES*
ALIENERS*
ALIENING
ALIENISM s
ALIENIST s
ALIENORS*
*ALIGHTED
m ALIGNERS*
m ALIGNING
ALIMENTS*
ALIQUANT
ALIQUOTS*
ALIZARIN es
ALKAHEST s
ALKALIES
ALKALIFY
ALKALINE*
ALKALISE*ds
ALKALIZE drs
ALKALOID s
ALKANETS*
ALKOXIDE s
ALKYLATE ds
ALLANITE s
ALLAYERS*
ALLAYING
ALLEGERS*
ALLEGING
ALLEGORY
ALLEGROS*
ALLELISM s
ALLELUIA s
ALLERGEN s
ALLERGIC
ALLERGIN s
ALLEYWAY s
ALLHEALS*
ALLIABLE
d ALLIANCE s
ALLICINS*
ALLOBARS*
ALLOCATE ds
ALLODIAL*
ALLODIUM
ALLOGAMY
ALLONGES*
ALLONYMS*
ALLOPATH sy
ALLOSAUR s
ALLOTTED
ALLOTTEE s
ALLOTTER s
ALLOTYPE s

ALLOTYPY
ALLOVERS*
fhs ALLOWING
tw
ALLOXANS*
ALLOYING
ALLSEEDS*
ALLSORTS
ALLSPICE s
ALLUDING
ALLURERS*
ALLURING
ALLUSION s
ALLUSIVE
ALLUVIAL*s
ALLUVION s
ALLUVIUM s
ALMAGEST s
ALMANACK*s
ALMANACS*
ALMEMARS*
ALMIGHTY
ALMONERS*
*ALOGICAL
ALOPECIA s
ALOPECIC
ALPHABET s
ALPHORNS*
ALPHOSIS
ALPINELY
ALPINISM s
ALPINIST s
ALTERANT s
fp ALTERERS*
fhp ALTERING
ALTERITY
ALTHAEAS*
ALTHORNS*
ALTHOUGH
ALTITUDE s
ALTOISTS*
ALTRUISM s
ALTRUIST s
ALUMINAS*
ALUMINES*
ALUMINIC
ALUMINUM s
ALUMROOT s
ALUNITES*
ALVEOLAR s
ALVEOLUS
ALYSSUMS*
AMADAVAT s
AMALGAMS*
AMANDINE
AMANITAS*
AMANITIN s
AMARANTH s
AMARELLE s
AMARETTI
AMARETTO s
AMARONES*
AMASSERS*
*AMASSING
AMATEURS*
*AMAZEDLY
AMBARIES
AMBERIES
AMBERINA s
AMBEROID s
AMBIANCE s
AMBIENCE s
AMBIENTS*
AMBITION s
AMBIVERT s
AMBOINAS*
AMBOYNAS*
AMBROIDS*
AMBROSIA lns
AMBSACES*
AMBULANT
AMBULATE ds
AMBUSHED
AMBUSHER s
AMBUSHES
AMEERATE s
AMELCORN s
AMENABLE
AMENABLY
AMENDERS
*AMENDING
AMENTIAS*
AMERCERS
AMERCING
AMESACES*
AMETHYST s
AMIANTUS
AMICABLE
AMICABLY
AMIDASES*
AMIDINES*
AMIDOGEN s
AMIDONES*
*AMIDSHIP s
AMIRATES*
*AMITOSES
*AMITOSIS
*AMITOTIC
AMITROLE s
AMMETERS*
AMMOCETE s
AMMONALS*
AMMONIAC*s
AMMONIAS*
AMMONIFY
AMMONITE s
AMMONIUM s
AMMONOID s
AMNESIAC*s
AMNESIAS*
AMNESICS*
AMNESTIC
AMNIONIC
AMNIOTES*
AMNIOTIC
AMOEBEAN
AMOEBOID
*AMORALLY
AMORETTI
AMORETTO s
AMORISTS*
*AMORTISE ds
AMORTIZE ds
AMOSITES*
AMOTIONS
*AMOUNTED
AMPERAGE s
AMPHIBIA n
AMPHIOXI
AMPHIPOD s
AMPHORAE*
AMPHORAL*
AMPHORAS*
AMPLEXUS
AMPOULES*
AMPULLAE*
AMPULLAR*y
AMPUTATE ds
AMPUTEES*
AMREETAS*
AMTRACKS*
AMUSABLE
AMUSEDLY
AMYGDALA e
AMYGDALE s
AMYGDULE s
AMYLASES*
AMYLENES*
AMYLOGEN s
AMYLOIDS*
AMYLOSES*
ANABAENA s
ANABASES
ANABASIS
ANABATIC
ANABLEPS
ANABOLIC
ANACONDA s
ANAEMIAS*
ANAEROBE s
ANAGLYPH s
ANAGOGES*
ANAGOGIC
ANAGRAMS*
ANALCIME s
ANALCITE s
ANALECTA
ANALECTS
ANALEMMA s
ANALGIAS*
ANALOGIC
ANALOGUE s
ANALYSED*
ANALYSER*s
ANALYSES*
ANALYSIS
ANALYSTS*
ANALYTES*
ANALYTIC s
ANALYZED*
ANALYZER*s
ANALYZES*
ANAPAEST s
ANAPESTS*
ANAPHASE s
ANAPHORA*ls
ANAPHORS*
ANARCHIC
ANASARCA s
ANATASES*
ANATHEMA s
ANATOMIC
ANATOXIN s
ANCESTOR s
ANCESTRY
ANCHORED
ANCHORET s
ANCHUSAS*
ANCHUSIN s
ANCIENTS*
ANCILLAE*
ANCILLAS*
ANCONEAL
ANCONOID
ANDANTES*
ANDESITE s
ANDESYTE s
ANDIRONS*
ANDROGEN s
ANDROIDS*
*ANEARING
ANECDOTA l
ANECDOTE s
ANECHOIC
ANEMONES*
ANEMOSES
ANEMOSIS
ANERGIAS*
ANERGIES
ANEROIDS*
ANESTRUS
ANETHOLE*s
ANETHOLS*
ANEURINS*
ANEURISM s
ANEURYSM s
ANGAKOKS*
ANGARIAS*
ANGARIES
ANGELICA*ls
ANGELING
d ANGERING
ANGINOSE
ANGINOUS
ANGIOMAS*
ANGLEPOD s
ANGLINGS*
ANGRIEST
ANGSTROM s
ANGULATE ds
ANGULOSE
ANGULOUS
ANHINGAS*
ANILINES*
ANIMALIC
ANIMALLY
ANIMATED*
ANIMATER*s
ANIMATES*
ANIMATOR*s
ANIMISMS*
ANIMISTS*
ANIMUSES
ANISEEDS*
ANISETTE s
ANISOLES*
ANKERITE s
ANKUSHES
ANKYLOSE ds
ANNALIST s
ANNATTOS*
ANNEALED
ANNEALER s
ANNELIDS*
ANNEXING
ANNOTATE ds
ANNOUNCE drs
ANNOYERS*
ANNOYING
ANNUALLY
c ANNULATE d
ANNULETS*
ANNULLED
ANNULOSE
*ANODALLY
ANODIZED*
ANODIZES*
ANODYNES*
ANODYNIC
ANOINTED
ANOINTER s
ANOLYTES*
ANOOPSIA s
ANOPSIAS*
ANORETIC s
ANOREXIA s
ANOREXIC s
ANORTHIC
ANOSMIAS*
ANOVULAR
ANOXEMIA s
ANOXEMIC
ANSERINE s
ANSEROUS
ANSWERED
ANSWERER s
ANTACIDS*
ANTALGIC s
ANTBEARS*
ANTEATER s
ANTECEDE ds
ANTEDATE ds
ANTEFIXA*el
g ANTELOPE s
ANTENNAE*
ANTENNAL*
ANTENNAS*
ANTEPAST s
ANTERIOR
ANTEROOM s
ANTETYPE s
ANTEVERT s
ANTHELIA
ANTHELIX
ANTHEMED
ANTHEMIA
ANTHEMIC
ANTHERAL
ANTHERID s
ANTHESES
ANTHESIS
ANTHILLS*
ANTHODIA
ANTIACNE
ANTIARIN s
ANTIATOM s
ANTIBIAS
ANTIBODY
ANTIBOSS
ANTICITY
ANTICKED
ANTICOLD
ANTICULT s
ANTIDORA
ANTIDOTE ds
ANTIDRUG
ANTIFOAM
ANTIGANG
ANTIGENE*s
ANTIGENS*
ANTIHERO
ANTIKING s
ANTILEAK
ANTILEFT
ANTILIFE r
ANTILOCK
ANTILOGS*
ANTILOGY*
ANTIMALE
ANTIMASK s
ANTIMERE s
ANTIMINE
ANTIMONY l
ANTINODE s
ANTINOME s
ANTINOMY
ANTINUKE rs
ANTIPHON sy
ANTIPILL
ANTIPODE s
ANTIPOLE s
ANTIPOPE s
ANTIPORN
ANTIPYIC s
ANTIQUED*
ANTIQUER*s
ANTIQUES*
ANTIRAPE
ANTIRIOT
ANTIROCK
ANTIROLL
ANTIRUST s
ANTISERA
ANTISHIP
ANTISKID
ANTISLIP
ANTISMOG
ANTISMUT
ANTISNOB s
ANTISPAM
ANTISTAT es
ANTITANK
ANTITYPE s
ANTIWEAR
ANTIWEED
ANTLERED
ANTLIONS*
ANTONYMS*
ANTONYMY*
ANTRORSE
ANTSIEST
ANURESES
ANURESIS
ANURETIC
ANVILING
ANVILLED
ANVILTOP s
ANYPLACE
ANYTHING s
ANYWHERE s
AORISTIC
APAGOGES*
APAGOGIC
APANAGES*
APAREJOS*
APATETIC
APATHIES
APATITES*
APERIENT s
APERITIF s
APERTURE ds
APHAGIAS*
APHANITE s
APHASIAC*s
APHASIAS*
APHASICS*
APHELIAN*
APHELION s
APHIDIAN s
APHOLATE s
APHONIAS*
APHONICS
APHORISE ds
APHORISM s
APHORIST s
APHORIZE drs
n APHTHOUS
APIARIAN s
APIARIES
APIARIST s
APICALLY
APICULUS
APIMANIA s
APIOLOGY
APLASIAS*
*APLASTIC
APOAPSES
APOAPSIS
APOCARPS*
APOCARPY*
APOCOPES*
APOCOPIC
APOCRINE
APODOSES
APODOSIS
APOGAMIC
APOLOGAL
APOLOGIA es
APOLOGUE s
APOLUNES*
APOMICTS*
APOMIXES
APOMIXIS
APOPHONY
APOPHYGE s
APOPLEXY
APOSPORY
APOSTACY
APOSTASY
APOSTATE s
APOSTILS*
APOSTLES*
APOTHECE s
APOTHEGM s
APOTHEMS*
APPALLED
APPANAGE s
APPARATS*
APPARELS*
APPARENT
APPEALED
APPEALER s
APPEARED
APPEASED*
APPEASER*s
APPEASES*
APPELLEE s
APPELLOR s
APPENDED
APPENDIX
APPESTAT s
APPETENT
APPETITE s
APPLAUDS*
APPLAUSE s
APPLIERS*
APPLIQUE ds
APPLYING
APPOINTS*
APPOSERS*
APPOSING
APPOSITE
APPRAISE der
s
APPRISED*
APPRISER*s
APPRISES*
APPRIZED*
APPRIZER*s
APPRIZES*
APPROACH
APPROVAL s
APPROVED*
APPROVER*s
APPROVES*
APPULSES*
*APRACTIC
APRAXIAS*
APRICOTS*
APRONING
APTERIUM
APTEROUS
APTITUDE s
APYRASES*
*APYRETIC
AQUACADE s
AQUAFARM s
AQUALUNG s
AQUANAUT s
AQUARIAL*
AQUARIAN*s
AQUARIST s
AQUARIUM s
AQUATICS*
AQUATINT s
AQUATONE s
AQUAVITS*
AQUEDUCT s
AQUIFERS*
AQUILINE
ARABESKS*
ARABICAS*
ARABIZED*
ARABIZES*
ARACEOUS
ARACHNID s
ARANEIDS*
ARAPAIMA s
ARAROBAS*
ARBALEST s
ARBALIST s
ARBELEST s
ARBITERS*
ARBITRAL
ARBOREAL
ARBORETA
ARBORIST s
ARBORIZE ds
h ARBOROUS
h ARBOURED
ARBUSCLE s
ARBUTEAN
ARCADIAN*s
ARCADIAS*
ARCADING s
ARCANUMS*
ARCATURE s
ARCHAEAL*
ARCHAEAN*s
ARCHAEON
ARCHAISE ds
ARCHAISM s
ARCHAIST s
ARCHAIZE drs
ARCHDUKE s
ARCHFOES*
ARCHINES*
ARCHINGS*
ARCHIVAL
ARCHIVED*
ARCHIVES*
ARCHNESS
ARCHWAYS*
ARCIFORM
ARCSINES*
ARCUATED*
ARDENTLY
AREAWAYS*
ARENITES*
AREOLATE d
AREOLOGY
ARETHUSA s
ARGENTAL
ARGENTIC
ARGENTUM s
ARGINASE s
ARGININE s
ARGONAUT s
ARGOSIES
ARGUABLE
ARGUABLY
ARGUFIED
ARGUFIER s
ARGUFIES
ARGUMENT as
ARIDNESS
ARIETTAS*
ARIETTES*
ARILLATE
ARILLODE s
ARILLOID
ARISTATE
ARMAGNAC s
ARMAMENT s
ARMATURE ds
ARMBANDS*
ARMCHAIR s
ARMHOLES*
ARMIGERO*s
ARMIGERS*
ARMILLAE*
ARMILLAS*
ARMLOADS*
ARMLOCKS*
ARMOIRES*
h ARMONICA s
ARMORERS*
ARMORIAL s
ARMORIES
ARMORING
ARMOURED
ARMOURER s
ARMRESTS*
ARMYWORM s
ARNATTOS*
ARNOTTOS*
AROINTED
AROMATIC s
c AROUSALS*
c*AROUSERS*
c*AROUSING
AROYNTED
ARPEGGIO s
h ARQUEBUS
ARRAIGNS*
ARRANGED*
ARRANGER*s
ARRANGES*
ARRANTLY
ARRAYALS*
ARRAYERS*
ARRAYING
ARRESTED
ARRESTEE s
ARRESTER s
ARRESTOR s
ARRHIZAL
ARRIVALS*
ARRIVERS*
ARRIVING
ARROGANT
ARROGATE ds
fhm ARROWING
n
ARSENALS*
ARSENATE s
ARSENICS*
ARSENIDE s
ARSENITE s
ARSENOUS
ARSONIST s
ARSONOUS

ARTEFACT s
ARTERIAL s
ARTERIES
ARTFULLY
ARTICLED*
p ARTICLES*
ARTIFACT s
ARTIFICE rs
t ARTINESS
bp ARTISANS*
ARTISTES*
ARTISTIC
ARTISTRY
ARTSIEST
ARTWORKS*
ARUGOLAS
ARUGULAS*
ARYTHMIA s
ARYTHMIC
ASBESTIC
ASBESTOS
ASBESTUS
ASCARIDS*
*ASCENDED
ASCENDER s
ASCETICS*
ASCIDIAN*s
ASCIDIUM
ASCOCARP s
ASCORBIC
ASCRIBED
ASCRIBES
ASHCAKES*
ASHFALLS*
w ASHINESS
ASHLARED
ASHLERED
ASHPLANT s
ASHTRAYS*
ASOCIALS
*ASPARKLE
ASPERATE ds
ASPERGES
ASPERITY
ASPERSED*
ASPERSER*s
ASPERSES*
ASPERSOR s
ASPHALTS*
*ASPHERIC
ASPHODEL s
ASPHYXIA ls
*ASPIRANT s
ASPIRATA e
ASPIRATE ds
ASPIRERS*
ASPIRING
ASPIRINS*
ASSAGAIS*
w ASSAILED
w ASSAILER s
ASSASSIN s
ASSAULTS*
ASSAYERS*
ASSAYING
ASSEGAIS*
ASSEMBLE drs
ASSEMBLY
ASSENTED
ASSENTER s
ASSENTOR s
ASSERTED
ASSERTER s
ASSERTOR s
ASSESSED
ASSESSES
ASSESSOR s
ASSIGNAT s
ASSIGNED
ASSIGNEE s
ASSIGNER s
ASSIGNOR s
ASSISTED
ASSISTER s
ASSISTOR s
ASSOILED
ASSONANT s
ASSORTED
ASSORTER s
ASSUAGED*
ASSUAGER*s
ASSUAGES*
ASSUMERS*
ASSUMING
ASSUREDS*
ASSURERS*
ASSURING
ASSURORS*
ASSWAGED*
ASSWAGES*
ASTASIAS*
ASTATINE s
ASTERIAS*
ASTERISK s
ASTERISM s
*ASTERNAL
*ASTEROID s
*ASTHENIA s
*ASTHENIC s
ASTIGMIA s
ASTILBES*
ASTOMOUS
ASTONIED
ASTONIES
*ASTONISH
ASTOUNDS
ASTRAGAL is
ASTRALLY
ASTRICTS*
ASTRINGE ds
ASTUTELY
ASYNDETA
ATABRINE s
y ATAGHANS*
ATALAYAS*
ATAMASCO s
ATARAXIA s
ATARAXIC s
ATAVISMS*
ATAVISTS*
*ATECHNIC
ATELIERS*
ATEMOYAS*
ATENOLOL s
ATHANASY
ATHEISMS
ATHEISTS
ATHELING s
ATHENEUM s
ATHEROMA s
ATHETOID
ATHLETES*
ATHLETIC s
ATHODYDS*
ATLANTES
ATOMICAL
ATOMISED*
ATOMISER*s
ATOMISES*
ATOMISMS*
ATOMISTS*
ATOMIZED*
ATOMIZER*s
ATOMIZES*
ATONABLE
*ATONALLY
ATRAZINE s
*ATREMBLE
ATRESIAS*
ATROCITY
ATROPHIA s
*ATROPHIC
*ATROPINE*s
ATROPINS
*ATROPISM s
ATTACHED*
ATTACHER*s
ATTACHES*
ATTACKED
ATTACKER s
ATTAGIRL
ATTAINED
ATTAINER s
ATTAINTS*
ATTEMPER s
ATTEMPTS*
ATTENDED
ATTENDEE s
ATTENDER s
ATTESTED
ATTESTER s
ATTESTOR s
ATTICISM s
ATTICIST s
ATTICIZE ds
ATTIRING
ATTITUDE s
ATTORNED
ATTORNEY s
ATTRACTS*
ATTRITED*
ATTRITES*
ATTUNING
*ATWITTER
*ATYPICAL
AUBERGES*
AUBRETIA s
AUBRIETA s
AUCTIONS*
AUDACITY
AUDIBLED*
AUDIBLES*
AUDIENCE s
AUDIENTS*
AUDITEES*
AUDITING
AUDITION s
AUDITIVE s
AUDITORS*
AUDITORY*
AUGMENTS*
AUGURERS*
AUGURIES
AUGURING
AUGUSTER
AUGUSTLY
AUNTHOOD s
AUNTLIER
AUNTLIKE
AURALITY
AUREOLAE*
AUREOLAS*
AUREOLED*
AUREOLES*
AURICLED*
AURICLES*
AURICULA ers
AURIFORM
AUROREAN
AUSFORMS*
AUSPICES*
AUSTERER*
AUSTRALS*
AUTACOID s
AUTARCHS*
AUTARCHY*
AUTARKIC
AUTECISM s
AUTHORED
AUTISTIC s
AUTOBAHN s
AUTOCADE s
AUTOCOID s
AUTOCRAT s
AUTODYNE s
AUTOGAMY
AUTOGENY
AUTOGIRO s
AUTOGYRO s
AUTOHARP s
AUTOLYSE ds
AUTOLYZE ds
AUTOMATA*
AUTOMATE*ds
AUTOMATS*
AUTONOMY
t AUTONYMS*
AUTOPENS*
AUTOPSIC
AUTOSOME s
AUTOTOMY
AUTOTYPE s
AUTOTYPY
AUTUMNAL
AUTUNITE s
AUXETICS*
AVADAVAT s
*AVAILING
AVARICES
AVELLANE*
AVENGERS*
*AVENGING
*AVENTAIL s
AVERAGED*
AVERAGES*
AVERMENT s
AVERRING
AVERSELY
*AVERSION s
AVERSIVE s
AVERTERS*
AVERTING
AVGASSES
AVIANIZE ds
AVIARIES
AVIARIST s
AVIATING
AVIATION s
AVIATORS
AVIATRIX
n AVICULAR
AVIDNESS
AVIFAUNA els
n AVIGATOR s
AVIONICS*
AVOCADOS*
AVODIRES*
AVOIDERS
*AVOIDING
*AVOUCHED
*AVOUCHER s
*AVOUCHES
AVOWABLE
AVOWABLY
AVOWEDLY
AVULSING
AVULSION s
AWAITERS
*AWAITING
*AWAKENED
*AWAKENER s
AWARDEES*
AWARDERS
*AWARDING
AWAYNESS
*AWEATHER
AWFULLER
AWLWORTS*
AWNINGED
AXIALITY
AXILLARS*
m AXILLARY*
AXIOLOGY
AXLETREE s
AXOLOTLS*
AXONEMAL
AXONEMES*
AXOPLASM s
AYURVEDA s
AZIMUTHS*
AZOTEMIA s
AZOTEMIC
AZOTISED*
AZOTISES*
AZOTIZED*
AZOTIZES*
AZOTURIA s
AZULEJOS*
l AZURITES*
*AZYGOSES
BAALISMS*
BAASKAAP s
BAASKAPS*
BAASSKAP s
BABASSUS*
BABBITRY
BABBITTS*
BABBLERS*
BABBLING s
BABESIAS*
BABICHES*
BABIRUSA s
BABUSHKA s
BABYDOLL s
BABYHOOD s
BABYSITS*
BACALAOS*
BACCARAS*
BACCARAT*s
BACCATED*
BACCHANT es
BACCHIUS
BACHELOR s
BACILLAR y
BACILLUS
BACKACHE s
BACKBEAT s
BACKBEND s
BACKBITE*rs
BACKBONE ds
BACKCAST s
BACKCHAT s
BACKDATE ds
BACKDOOR
BACKDROP st
BACKFILL s
BACKFIRE ds
BACKFITS*
BACKFLIP s
BACKFLOW s
BACKHAND s
BACKHAUL s
BACKHOED*
BACKHOES*
BACKINGS*
BACKLAND s
BACKLASH
BACKLESS
BACKLIST s
BACKLOAD s
BACKLOGS*
BACKMOST
BACKOUTS*
BACKPACK s
BACKREST s
BACKROOM s
BACKRUSH
BACKSAWS*
BACKSEAT s
BACKSETS*
BACKSIDE s
BACKSLAP s
BACKSLID e
BACKSPIN s
BACKSTAB s
BACKSTAY s
BACKSTOP s
BACKWARD s
BACKWASH
BACKWOOD s
BACKWRAP s
BACKYARD s
BACLOFEN s
BACTERIA ls
BACTERIN s
BACULINE
BACULUMS*
BADGERED
BADGERLY
BADINAGE ds
BADLANDS*
BADMOUTH s
BAFFLERS*
BAFFLING
BAGASSES*
BAGGAGES*
BAGGIEST*
BAGGINGS*
BAGHOUSE s
BAGPIPED*
BAGPIPER*s
BAGPIPES*
BAGUETTE s
BAGWORMS*
BAHADURS*
BAIDARKA s
BAILABLE
BAILIFFS*
*BAILMENT s
BAILOUTS*
BAILSMAN
BAILSMEN
BAIRNISH
BAITFISH
BAKELITE s
BAKEMEAT s
BAKERIES
BAKESHOP s
BAKEWARE s
BAKLAVAS*
BAKLAWAS*
BAKSHISH
BALANCED*
BALANCER*s
BALANCES*
BALDHEAD s
BALDNESS
BALDPATE ds
BALDRICK*s
BALDRICS*
BALEFIRE s
BALISAUR s
BALKIEST
BALKLINE s
BALLADES*
BALLADIC
BALLADRY
BALLASTS*
BALLETIC
BALLGAME s
BALLHAWK s
BALLISTA e
BALLONET s
BALLONNE s
BALLOONS*
BALLOTED
BALLOTER s
BALLPARK s
BALLROOM s
BALLUTES*
BALLYARD s
BALLYHOO s
BALLYRAG s
BALMIEST
BALMLIKE
BALMORAL s
BALONEYS*
BALSAMED
BALSAMIC
BALUSTER s
BAMBINOS*
*BANALITY
BANALIZE ds
BANAUSIC
BANDAGED*
BANDAGER*s
BANDAGES*
BANDANAS*
BANDANNA s
BANDEAUS*
BANDEAUX*
BANDEROL es
BANDITOS*
BANDITRY
BANDITTI
BANDMATE s
BANDORAS*
BANDORES*
BANDSAWS*
BANDSMAN
BANDSMEN
BANDYING
BANGKOKS*
BANGTAIL s
BANISHED
BANISHER s
BANISHES
BANISTER s
BANJAXED
BANJAXES
BANJOIST s
BANKABLE
BANKBOOK s
BANKCARD s
BANKERLY
BANKINGS*
BANKNOTE s
BANKROLL s
BANKRUPT s
BANKSIAS*
BANKSIDE s
BANNABLE
BANNERED
BANNERET s
BANNEROL s
BANNOCKS*
BANQUETS*
BANSHEES*
BANSHIES*
BANTENGS*
BANTERED
BANTERER s
BANTLING s
BAPTISED*
BAPTISES*
BAPTISIA s
BAPTISMS*
BAPTISTS*
BAPTIZED*
BAPTIZER*s
BAPTIZES*
BARATHEA s
BARBARIC
BARBASCO s
BARBECUE drs
BARBELLS*
BARBEQUE ds
BARBERED
BARBERRY
BARBETTE s
BARBICAN s
BARBICEL s
BARBITAL s
BARBLESS
BARBULES*
BARBWIRE s
BARCHANS*
BAREBACK
BAREBOAT s
BAREFOOT
BAREHAND s
BAREHEAD
BARENESS
BARESARK s
BARFLIES
BARGAINS*
BARGELLO s
BARGEMAN
BARGEMEN
BARGHEST s
BARGUEST s
BARILLAS*
BARISTAS
BARITONE s
BARKEEPS*
BARKIEST
BARKLESS
BARLEDUC s
BARMAIDS*
BARMIEST
BARNACLE ds
BARNIEST
BARNLIKE
BARNYARD s
BAROGRAM s
BARONAGE s
BARONESS
BARONETS*
BARONIAL
BARONIES
BARONNES*
BAROQUES*
BAROSAUR s
BAROUCHE s
BARRABLE
BARRACKS
BARRAGED*
BARRAGES*
BARRANCA s
BARRANCO s
BARRATER s
BARRATOR s
BARRATRY
BARRELED
BARRENER
BARRENLY
BARRETOR s
BARRETRY
BARRETTE s
BARRIERS*
BARROOMS*
BARSTOOL s
BARTENDS*
BARTERED
BARTERER s
*BARTISAN s
BARTIZAN s
BARWARES*
BARYONIC
BARYTONE*s
BARYTONS*
BASALTES
BASALTIC
BASCULES*
BASEBALL s
BASEBORN
BASELESS
BASELINE rs
a BASEMENT*s
BASENESS
BASENJIS*
BASHINGS*
BASHLYKS*
BASICITY
BASIDIAL*
BASIDIUM
BASIFIED
BASIFIER s
BASIFIES
BASILARY*
BASILECT s
BASILICA*eln
s
BASILISK s
BASINETS*
BASINFUL s
BASKETRY
BASMATIS*
BASOPHIL es
BASSETED
BASSETTS*
BASSINET s
BASSISTS
BASSNESS
BASSOONS*
BASSWOOD s
BASTARDS*
BASTARDY*
BASTILES*
BASTILLE s
BASTINGS*
BASTIONS*

BATCHERS*
BATCHING
BATFOWLS*
BATGIRLS*
BATHETIC
BATHLESS
BATHMATS*
BATHOSES
BATHROBE s
BATHROOM s
BATHTUBS*
BATIKING
BATISTES*
BATTALIA s
BATTEAUX*
BATTENED
BATTENER s
BATTERED
BATTERER s
BATTERIE s
BATTIEST
BATTINGS*
BATTLERS*
BATTLING
BAUDEKIN s
BAUDRONS
BAUHINIA s
BAULKIER
BAULKING
BAUXITES*
BAUXITIC
BAWCOCKS*
BAWDIEST*
BAWDRICS*
BAWDRIES
BAYADEER s
BAYADERE s
BAYBERRY
BAYONETS*
BAYWOODS*
BAZOOKAS*
BDELLIUM s
BEACHBOY s
BEACHIER
BEACHING
BEACONED
BEADIEST
BEADINGS*
BEADLIKE
BEADROLL s
BEADSMAN
BEADSMEN
BEADWORK s
BEAKIEST
BEAKLESS
BEAKLIKE
BEAMIEST
BEAMLESS
BEAMLIKE
BEANBAGS*
BEANBALL s
BEANLIKE
BEANPOLE s
BEARABLE
BEARABLY
BEARCATS*
BEARDING
BEARHUGS*
BEARINGS
BEARLIKE
BEARSKIN s
BEARWOOD s
BEASTIES*
*BEATABLE
BEATIFIC
BEATINGS
BEATLESS
BEATNIKS*
BEAUCOUP s
BEAUTIES
BEAUTIFY
BEAVERED
BEBEERUS*
BEBLOODS*
BEBOPPER s
BECALMED
BECAPPED
BECARPET s
BECHALKS*
BECHAMEL s
BECHANCE ds
BECHARMS*
BECKONED
BECKONER s
BECLAMOR s
BECLASPS*

BECLOAKS*
BECLOTHE ds
BECLOUDS*
BECLOWNS*
BECOMING s
BECOWARD s
BECRAWLS*
BECRIMED*
BECRIMES*
BECROWDS*
BECRUSTS*
BECUDGEL s
BECURSED*
BECURSES*
BEDABBLE ds
BEDAMNED
BEDARKEN s
BEDAUBED
BEDAZZLE ds
BEDBOARD s
BEDCHAIR s
BEDCOVER s
BEDDABLE
BEDDINGS*
BEDEAFEN s
BEDECKED
BEDESMAN
BEDESMEN
BEDEVILS*
BEDEWING
BEDFRAME s
BEDGOWNS*
BEDIAPER s
BEDIGHTS*
BEDIMMED
BEDIMPLE ds
BEDIZENS*
BEDLAMPS*
BEDMAKER s
BEDMATES*
BEDOTTED
BEDOUINS*
BEDPLATE s
BEDPOSTS*
BEDQUILT s
BEDRAILS*
BEDRAPED*
BEDRAPES*
BEDRENCH
BEDRIVEL s
BEDROCKS*
BEDROLLS*
BEDROOMS*
BEDSHEET s
BEDSIDES*
BEDSONIA s
BEDSORES*
BEDSTAND s
BEDSTEAD s
BEDSTRAW s
BEDTICKS*
BEDTIMES*
BEDUMBED
BEDUNCED*
BEDUNCES*
BEDWARDS*
BEDWARFS*
BEEBREAD s
BEECHIER
BEECHNUT s
BEEFALOS*
BEEFCAKE s
BEEFIEST
BEEFLESS
BEEFWOOD s
BEEHIVES*
BEELINED*
BEELINES*
*BEERIEST
BEESWING s
BEETLERS*
BEETLING
BEETROOT s
BEEYARDS*
BEFALLEN
BEFINGER s
BEFITTED
BEFLEAED
BEFLECKS*
BEFLOWER s
BEFOGGED
BEFOOLED
BEFOULED
BEFOULER s
BEFRIEND s
BEFRINGE ds

BEFUDDLE ds
BEGALLED
BEGAZING
BEGETTER s
BEGGARED
BEGGARLY
BEGINNER s
BEGIRDED
BEGIRDLE ds
BEGLAMOR s
BEGLOOMS*
BEGONIAS*
BEGORRAH*
BEGOTTEN
BEGRIMED*
BEGRIMES*
BEGROANS*
BEGRUDGE drs
BEGUILED*
BEGUILER*s
BEGUILES*
BEGUINES*
BEGULFED
BEHALVES
BEHAVERS*
BEHAVING
BEHAVIOR s
BEHEADAL s
BEHEADED
BEHEADER s
BEHEMOTH s
BEHOLDEN
BEHOLDER s
BEHOOVED*
BEHOOVES*
BEHOVING
BEHOWLED
BEIGNETS*
BEJABERS
BEJEEZUS
BEJEWELS*
BEJUMBLE ds
BEKISSED
BEKISSES
BEKNIGHT s
BELABORS*
BELABOUR s
BELADIED
BELADIES
BELAUDED
BELAYERS*
BELAYING
BELCHERS*
BELCHING
BELDAMES*
BELEAPED
BELFRIED
BELFRIES
BELIEVED*
BELIEVER*s
BELIEVES*
BELIQUOR s
BELITTLE drs
BELLBIRD s
BELLBOYS*
BELLEEKS*
BELLHOPS*
BELLINGS*
BELLOWED
BELLOWER s
BELLPULL s
BELLWORT s
BELLYFUL s
BELLYING
BELONGED
BELOVEDS*
BELTINGS*
BELTLESS
BELTLINE s
BELTWAYS*
BEMADAMS*
BEMADDEN s
BEMEANED
BEMINGLE ds
BEMIRING
BEMISTED
BEMIXING
BEMOANED
BEMOCKED
BEMUDDLE ds
BEMURMUR s
BEMUSING
BEMUZZLE ds
BENADRYL s
BENAMING
BENCHERS*

BENCHING
BENCHTOP
BENDABLE
BENDAYED
BENDIEST
*BENDWAYS
*BENDWISE
BENEDICK s
BENEDICT s
BENEFICE*ds
BENEFITS*
BENIGNLY
BENISONS*
BENJAMIN s
BENOMYLS*
BENTHONS*
BENTWOOD s
BENUMBED
BENZENES*
BENZIDIN es
BENZINES*
BENZOATE s
BENZOINS*
BENZOLES*
BENZOYLS*
BENZYLIC
BEPAINTS*
BEPIMPLE ds
BEQUEATH s
BEQUESTS*
BERAKING
BERASCAL s
BERATING
BERBERIN es
BERBERIS
BERCEUSE s
BERDACHE s
BEREAVED*
BEREAVER*s
BEREAVES*
BERETTAS*
BERGAMOT s
BERGERES*
BERHYMED*
BERHYMES*
BERIBERI s
BERIMBAU s
BERIMING
BERINGED
BERLINES*
BERMUDAS
BERNICLE s
BEROUGED
BERRETTA s
BERRYING
BERSEEMS*
BERSERKS*
BERTHING
BERYLINE
BESCORCH
BESCOURS*
BESCREEN s
BESEEMED
BESETTER s
BESHADOW s
BESHAMED*
BESHAMES*
BESHIVER s
BESHOUTS*
BESHREWS*
BESHROUD s
BESIEGED*
BESIEGER*s
BESIEGES*
BESLAVED
BESLIMED*
BESLIMES*
BESMEARS*
BESMILED*
BESMILES*
BESMIRCH
BESMOKED*
BESMOKES*
BESMOOTH s
BESMUDGE ds
BESNOWED
BESOOTHE ds
BESOTTED
BESOUGHT
BESPEAKS*
BESPOKEN*
*BESPOUSE ds
BESPREAD s
BESPRENT
BESTEADS*
BESTIARY

BESTOWAL s
BESTOWED
BESTOWER s
BESTREWN*
BESTREWS*
BESTRIDE*s
BESTRODE
BESTROWN*
BESTROWS*
BESWARMS*
BETAINES*
BETAKING
BETATRON s
BETATTER s
BETELNUT s
BETHANKS*
BETHESDA s
BETHINKS*
BETHORNS*
BETHUMPS*
BETIDING
BETOKENS*
BETONIES
BETRAYAL s
BETRAYED
BETRAYER s
BETROTHS*
BETTERED
BEUNCLED
BEVATRON s
BEVELERS*
BEVELING
BEVELLED
BEVELLER s
BEVERAGE s
BEVOMITS*
BEWAILED
BEWAILER s
BEWARING
BEWIGGED
BEWILDER s
BEWINGED
BEWORMED
BEWRAYED
BEWRAYER s
BEZAZZES
BEZIQUES*
BEZZANTS*
BHANGRAS*
BHEESTIE s
BHISTIES*
BIACETYL s
BIANNUAL
BIASEDLY
BIASNESS
BIASSING
BIATHLON s
BIBCOCKS*
BIBELOTS*
BIBLICAL
BIBLISTS*
BIBULOUS
BICAUDAL
BICEPSES
BICHROME
BICKERED
BICKERER s
BICOLORS*
BICOLOUR s
BICONVEX
BICORNES*
BICUSPID s
BICYCLED*
BICYCLER*s
BICYCLES*
BICYCLIC
BIDARKAS*
BIDARKEE s
BIDDABLE
BIDDABLY
BIDDINGS*
BIDENTAL
BIELDING
BIENNALE s
BIENNIAL*s
BIENNIUM s
BIFACIAL
BIFIDITY
BIFOCALS*
BIFORATE
BIFORKED
BIFORMED
BIGAMIES
BIGAMIST s
BIGAMOUS
BIGARADE s

BIGAROON s
BIGEMINY
BIGFOOTS*
BIGGINGS*
BIGHEADS*
BIGHORNS*
BIGHTING
BIGMOUTH s
BIGNONIA s
BIGSTICK
BIHOURLY
BIJUGATE
BIJUGOUS
BIKEWAYS*
BIKINIED
BILABIAL s
BILANDER s
BILAYERS*
BILBERRY
BILEVELS*
BILGIEST
BILINEAR
BILLABLE
BILLBUGS*
BILLETED
BILLETER s
BILLFISH
BILLFOLD s
BILLHEAD s
BILLHOOK s
BILLIARD s
BILLINGS*
BILLIONS*
BILLOWED
BILLYCAN s
BILOBATE d
BILSTEDS*
BILTONGS*
BIMANOUS
BIMANUAL
BIMBETTE s
BIMENSAL
BIMESTER s
BIMETALS*
BIMETHYL s
BIMORPHS*
BINARIES
BINARISM s
BINATELY
BINAURAL
BINDABLE
BINDINGS*
BINDWEED s
BINGEING
BINNACLE s
BINOCLES*
BINOMIAL s
BIOASSAY s
BIOCHIPS*
BIOCIDAL
BIOCIDES*
BIOCLEAN
BIOCYCLE s
BIOETHIC s
BIOFILMS*
BIOFUELS*
BIOGASES
a BIOGENIC
BIOHERMS*
BIOLOGIC s
BIOLYSES
BIOLYSIS
BIOLYTIC
BIOMETER s
BIOMETRY
BIOMORPH s
BIONOMIC s
BIOPLASM s
BIOPSIED
BIOPSIES
BIOSCOPE s
BIOSCOPY
BIOSOLID s
BIOTECHS*
BIOTICAL
BIOTITES*
BIOTITIC
BIOTOPES*
BIOTOXIN s
BIOTRONS*
BIOTYPES*
BIOTYPIC
BIOVULAR
BIPAROUS
BIPARTED
BIPHASIC

BIPHENYL s
BIPLANES*
BIRACIAL
BIRADIAL
BIRAMOSE
BIRAMOUS
BIRCHING
BIRDBATH s
BIRDCAGE s
BIRDCALL s
BIRDDOGS*
BIRDFARM s
BIRDFEED s
BIRDINGS*
BIRDLIFE
BIRDLIKE
BIRDLIME ds
BIRDSEED s
BIRDSEYE s
BIRDSHOT
BIRDSONG s
BIRETTAS*
BIRIANIS*
BIRLINGS*
BIRRETTA s
BIRROTCH
BIRTHDAY s
BIRTHING s
BIRYANIS*
BISCOTTI
BISCOTTO
BISCUITS*
BISCUITY*
BISECTED
BISECTOR s
BISEXUAL s
BISHOPED
BISMUTHS*
BISNAGAS*
BISTERED
BISTORTS*
BISTOURY
BISTROIC
BITCHERY
*BITCHIER
*BITCHILY
*BITCHING
BITEABLE
BITEWING s
BITINGLY
BITSIEST
BITSTOCK s
BITTERED
BITTERER
BITTERLY
BITTERNS*
BITTIEST
BITTINGS*
BITTOCKS*
BITUMENS*
BIUNIQUE
BIVALENT s
BIVALVED*
BIVALVES*
BIVINYLS*
BIVOUACS*
BIWEEKLY
BIYEARLY
BIZARRES*
BIZARROS*
BIZNAGAS*
BLABBERS*
BLABBING
BLACKBOY s
BLACKCAP s
BLACKENS*
BLACKEST
BLACKFIN s
BLACKFLY
BLACKGUM s
*BLACKING s
BLACKISH
BLACKLEG s
BLACKOUT s
BLACKTOP s
BLADDERS
BLADDERY*
BLADINGS
*BLAGGING s
BLAMABLE
BLAMABLY
BLAMEFUL
BLANCHED
BLANCHER s
BLANCHES
BLANDEST

BLANDISH
*BLANKEST
BLANKETS*
BLANKING
BLARNEYS*
BLASTEMA ls
BLASTERS
BLASTIER*
BLASTIES*t
*BLASTING s
BLASTOFF s
BLASTOMA s
BLASTULA ers
BLATANCY
BLATHERS
BLATTERS*
BLATTING
BLAUBOKS*
BLAZERED
BLAZONED
BLAZONER s
BLAZONRY
*BLEACHED
*BLEACHER s
*BLEACHES
BLEAKEST
BLEAKISH
*BLEARIER
BLEARILY
BLEARING
BLEATERS*
BLEATING
BLEBBING s
BLEEDERS*
BLEEDING s
BLEEPERS*
BLEEPING
BLELLUMS*
BLENCHED
BLENCHER s
BLENCHES
BLENDERS
*BLENDING
BLENNIES
BLESBOKS*
BLESBUCK s
BLESSERS*
BLESSING s
BLETHERS*
*BLIGHTED
*BLIGHTER s
BLIMPISH
BLINDAGE s
BLINDERS*
BLINDEST
BLINDGUT s
BLINDING
BLINKARD s
BLINKERS
*BLINKING
BLINTZES*
*BLIPPING
BLISSFUL
BLISSING
BLISTERS
BLISTERY*
*BLITHELY
BLITHERS*
*BLITHEST
BLITZERS*
BLITZING
BLIZZARD sy
BLOATERS*
BLOATING
*BLOBBING
BLOCKADE drs
*BLOCKAGE s
BLOCKERS
BLOCKIER
*BLOCKING
BLOCKISH
BLOGGERS
*BLOGGING s
BLONDEST*
BLONDINE ds
BLONDISH
BLOODFIN s
BLOODIED
BLOODIER
BLOODIES t
BLOODILY
BLOODING s
BLOODRED
BLOOMERS*
BLOOMERY*
BLOOMIER

*BLOOMING
BLOOPERS
*BLOOPING
BLOSSOMS*
BLOSSOMY*
BLOTCHED
BLOTCHES
BLOTLESS
BLOTTERS
BLOTTIER
*BLOTTING
*BLOUSIER
*BLOUSILY
*BLOUSING
BLOUSONS*
BLOVIATE ds
BLOWBACK s
*BLOWBALL s
*BLOWDOWN s
BLOWFISH
BLOWGUNS*
BLOWHARD s
BLOWHOLE s
BLOWIEST
BLOWOFFS*
BLOWOUTS*
BLOWPIPE s
BLOWSIER
BLOWSILY
BLOWTUBE s
BLOWZIER
BLOWZILY
BLUBBERS
BLUBBERY*
BLUBBING
BLUCHERS*
BLUDGEON s
BLUDGERS*
BLUDGING
BLUEBALL s
BLUEBEAT s
BLUEBELL s
BLUEBILL s
BLUEBIRD s
BLUEBOOK s
BLUECAPS*
BLUECOAT s
BLUEFINS*
BLUEFISH
BLUEGILL s
BLUEGUMS*
BLUEHEAD s
BLUEINGS*
BLUEJACK s
BLUEJAYS*
BLUELINE rs
BLUENESS
BLUENOSE ds
BLUESIER
BLUESMAN
BLUESMEN
BLUESTEM s
BLUETICK s
BLUEWEED s
BLUEWOOD s
BLUFFERS*
BLUFFEST
*BLUFFING
BLUNDERS*
BLUNGERS
*BLUNGING
BLUNTEST
*BLUNTING
BLURBING
BLURBIST s
BLURRIER
BLURRILY
BLURRING
BLURTERS*
BLURTING
BLUSHERS*
BLUSHFUL
*BLUSHING
BLUSTERS
BLUSTERY*
BOARDERS*
BOARDING s
BOARDMAN
BOARDMEN
*BOARFISH
BOASTERS*
BOASTFUL
BOASTING
BOATABLE
BOATBILL s
BOATFULS*

BOATHOOK s
BOATINGS*
BOATLIFT s
*BOATLIKE
BOATLOAD s
BOATNECK s
BOATSMAN
BOATSMEN
BOATYARD s
BOBBINET s
BOBBLING
BOBBYSOX
BOBECHES*
BOBOLINK s
BOBSLEDS*
BOBSTAYS*
BOBTAILS*
BOBWHITE s
BOCACCIO s
BODEMENT s
BODHRANS*
BODILESS
BODINGLY
BODYSUIT s
BODYSURF s
BODYWORK s
BOEHMITE s
BOFFOLAS*
BOGARTED
BOGBEANS*
BOGEYING
BOGEYMAN
BOGEYMEN
BOGGIEST
BOGGLERS*
BOGGLING
BOGWOODS*
BOGYISMS*
BOHEMIAN*s
BOHEMIAS*
BOHRIUMS*
BOILABLE
BOILOFFS*
BOILOVER s
BOISERIE s
BOLDFACE ds
*BOLDNESS
BOLIVARS*
BOLIVIAS*
BOLLARDS*
BOLLIXED
BOLLIXES
BOLLOCKS
BOLLOXED
BOLLOXES
BOLLWORM s
BOLOGNAS*
BOLONEYS*
BOLSHIES*
BOLSTERS*
BOLTHEAD s
BOLTHOLE s
BOLTLESS
BOLTLIKE
BOLTONIA s
BOLTROPE s
BOMBABLE
BOMBARDS*
BOMBASTS*
BOMBESIN s
BOMBINGS*
BOMBLETS*
BOMBLOAD s
BOMBYCID s
BOMBYXES
BONANZAS*
BONDABLE
BONDAGES*
BONDINGS*
BONDLESS
BONDMAID s
BONDSMAN
BONDSMEN
BONEFISH
BONEHEAD s
BONELESS
BONEMEAL s
BONESETS*
BONEYARD s
BONEYEST
BONFIRES*
BONGOIST s
BONHOMIE s
BONIATOS*
BONIFACE s
BONINESS

BONITOES
BONNETED
BONNIEST
BONNOCKS*
BONSPELL s
BONSPIEL s
BONTEBOK s
BOOBIRDS*
BOODLERS*
BOODLING
BOOGEYED
BOOGYING
BOOGYMAN
BOOGYMEN
BOOHOOED
BOOKABLE
BOOKCASE s
BOOKENDS*
BOOKFULS*
BOOKINGS*
BOOKLETS*
BOOKLICE
BOOKLORE s
BOOKMARK s
BOOKRACK s
BOOKREST s
BOOKSHOP s
BOOKWORM s
BOOMIEST
BOOMKINS*
BOOMLETS*
BOOMTOWN s
BOONDOCK s
BOONLESS
BOOSTERS*
BOOSTING
BOOTABLE
BOOTJACK s
BOOTLACE s
BOOTLEGS*
BOOTLESS
BOOTLICK s
*BOOZIEST
BORACITE s
*BORATING
BORDEAUX
BORDELLO s
*BORDERED
*BORDERER s
BORDURES
BOREASES
BORECOLE s
BOREDOMS*
BOREHOLE s
BORESOME
BORINGLY
BORNEOLS*
BORNITES*
BORNITIC
BOROUGHS*
BORRELIA s
BORROWED
BORROWER s
BORSCHES
BORSCHTS*
BORSTALS*
BOSCAGES*
BOSCHBOK s
BOSHBOKS*
BOSHVARK s
BOSKAGES*
BOSKIEST
BOSOMING
BOSQUETS*
BOSSDOMS*
BOSSIEST*
BOSSISMS*
BOTANICA*ls
BOTANIES
BOTANISE ds
BOTANIST s
BOTANIZE drs
BOTCHERS*
BOTCHERY*
BOTCHIER
BOTCHILY
BOTCHING
BOTFLIES
BOTHERED
BOTHRIUM s
BOTONNEE
BOTRYOID
BOTRYOSE
BOTRYTIS
BOTTLERS*
BOTTLING s

BOTTOMED
BOTTOMER s
BOTTOMRY
BOTULINS*
BOTULISM s
BOUCHEES*
BOUDOIRS*
BOUFFANT s
BOUGHPOT s
BOUGHTEN
BOUILLON s
BOULDERS*
BOULDERY*
BOUNCERS*
BOUNCIER
BOUNCILY
BOUNCING
BOUNDARY
BOUNDERS*
a BOUNDING
BOUNTIED
BOUNTIES
BOUQUETS*
BOURBONS*
BOURDONS*
BOURGEON s
BOURREES*
BOURRIDE s
BOURSINS*
BOURTREE s
BOUSOUKI as
BOUTIQUE sy
BOUVIERS*
BOUZOUKI as
BOVINELY
BOVINITY
BOWELING
BOWELLED
BOWERIES
BOWERING
BOWFRONT
BOWHEADS*
BOWINGLY
BOWKNOTS*
BOWLDERS*
BOWLFULS*
BOWLINES*
BOWLINGS*
*BOWLLIKE
BOWSHOTS*
BOWSPRIT s
BOWWOWED
BOXBALLS*
BOXBERRY
BOXBOARD s
BOXHAULS*
BOXINESS
BOXTHORN s
BOXWOODS*
BOYARISM s
BOYCHICK s
BOYCHIKS*
BOYCOTTS*
BOYHOODS*
BOYISHLY
BRABBLED
*BRABBLER*s
BRABBLES
BRACELET s
BRACEROS*
BRACHETS
*BRACHIAL*s
BRACHIUM
BRACINGS
BRACIOLA s
BRACIOLE s
BRACKENS*
BRACKETS
BRACKISH
BRACONID s
BRACTEAL
BRACTLET s
BRADAWLS*
*BRADDING
BRADOONS*
BRAGGART s
BRAGGERS*
BRAGGEST
BRAGGIER
*BRAGGING
BRAIDERS
*BRAIDING s
*BRAILING
BRAILLED*
BRAILLER*s
BRAILLES*

BRAINIAC s
*BRAINIER
*BRAINILY
*BRAINING
BRAINISH
BRAINPAN s
*BRAISING
BRAKEAGE s
BRAKEMAN
BRAKEMEN
BRAKIEST
BRAMBLED
BRAMBLES
*BRANCHED
*BRANCHES
BRANCHIA el
BRANDERS*
BRANDIED
*BRANDIES
BRANDING s
BRANDISH
BRANNERS*
BRANNIER
BRANNING
BRANTAIL s
BRASHEST
BRASHIER
BRASIERS*
BRASILIN s
BRASSAGE s
BRASSARD s
BRASSART s
BRASSICA s
BRASSIER*e
BRASSIES*t
BRASSILY
BRASSING
BRASSISH
BRATTICE ds
*BRATTIER
*BRATTISH
BRATTLED
BRATTLES
BRAUNITE s
BRAVADOS*
BRAVOING
BRAVURAS*
BRAWLERS*
BRAWLIER*
BRAWLING
BRAWNIER
BRAWNILY
BRAZENED
BRAZENLY
BRAZIERS*
BRAZILIN s
*BREACHED
*BREACHER s
*BREACHES
BREADBOX
*BREADING
BREADNUT s
BREADTHS*
BREAKAGE s
BREAKERS*
BREAKING s
BREAKOUT s
BREAKUPS*
*BREAMING
BREASTED
BREATHED*
BREATHER*s
BREATHES*
BRECCIAL*
BRECCIAS*
BRECHAMS*
BRECHANS*
BREECHED
BREECHES
BREEDERS*
*BREEDING s
BREEZIER
BREEZILY
BREEZING
*BREGMATA
BREGMATE
BRETHREN
BREVETCY
BREVETED
BREVIARY
BREVIERS*
BREWAGES*
BREWINGS*
BREWISES
BREWPUBS*
BREWSKIS*

BRIBABLE
BRICKBAT s
BRICKIER
*BRICKING
BRICKLES*
BRICOLES*
BRIDALLY
a*BRIDGING s
BRIDLERS*
BRIDLING
BRIDOONS*
BRIEFERS*
BRIEFEST
BRIEFING s
BRIGADED*
BRIGADES*
BRIGANDS*
BRIGHTEN s
*BRIGHTER
*BRIGHTLY
BRIMFULL*y
*BRIMLESS
BRIMMERS
*BRIMMING
BRINDLED*
BRINDLES*
BRINGERS
*BRINGING
BRINIEST*
BRIOCHES*
BRIONIES
BRIQUETS*
BRISANCE s
BRISKEST
BRISKETS*
*BRISKING
BRISLING s
BRISTLED*
BRISTLES*
BRISTOLS*
BRITCHES
BRITSKAS*
BRITTLED*
BRITTLER*
BRITTLES*t
BRITZKAS*
BRITZSKA s
*BROACHED
BROACHER s
*BROACHES
BROADAXE*s
BROADENS*
BROADEST
BROADISH
BROCADED*
BROCADES*
BROCATEL s
BROCCOLI s
BROCHURE s
BROCKAGE s
BROCKETS
BROCOLIS*
*BROGUERY
*BROGUISH
BROIDERS*
BROIDERY*
BROILERS*
*BROILING
BROKAGES*
BROKENLY
BROKERED
BROKINGS*
BROLLIES
BROMATED*
BROMATES*
BROMELIN s
BROMIDES*
BROMIDIC
BROMINES*
BROMISMS*
BROMIZED*
BROMIZES*
BRONCHIA*l
BRONCHOS*
BRONCHUS
BRONZERS*
BRONZIER
BRONZING s
BROOCHES
BROODERS*
BROODIER
BROODILY
BROODING
BROOKIES
*BROOKING
BROOKITE s

BROOKLET s
*BROOMIER
*BROOMING
BROTHELS*
BROTHERS*
BROUGHAM s
BROUHAHA s
BROWBAND s
BROWBEAT s
BROWLESS
BROWNEST
BROWNIER*
BROWNIES*t
BROWNING
BROWNISH
BROWNOUT s
BROWSERS*
BROWSING
BRUCELLA es
BRUCINES*
BRUISERS*
BRUISING
BRUITERS*
BRUITING
BRULYIES*
BRULZIES*
BRUMBIES
BRUNCHED
BRUNCHER s
BRUNCHES
BRUNETTE s
BRUNIZEM s
BRUSHERS
*BRUSHIER
*BRUSHING
BRUSHOFF s
BRUSHUPS*
BRUSKEST
BRUSQUER*
BRUTALLY
BRUTISMS*
BRUXISMS*
BRYOLOGY
BRYONIES
BRYOZOAN s
BUBALINE
BUBBLERS*
BUBBLIER
BUBBLIES t
BUBBLING
BUBINGAS*
BUCCALLY
BUCKAROO s
BUCKAYRO s
BUCKBEAN s
BUCKEENS*
BUCKEROO s
BUCKETED
BUCKEYES*
BUCKLERS*
BUCKLING
BUCKRAMS*
BUCKSAWS*
BUCKSHEE s
BUCKSHOT
BUCKSKIN s
BUCKTAIL s
BUCOLICS*
BUDDINGS*
BUDDLEIA s
BUDDYING
BUDGETED
BUDGETER s
BUDWORMS*
BUFFABLE
BUFFALOS*
BUFFERED
BUFFETED
BUFFETER s
BUFFIEST
BUFFOONS*
BUGABOOS*
BUGBANES*
BUGBEARS*
BUGGERED
BUGGIEST*
BUGHOUSE s
BUGSEEDS*
BUHLWORK s
BUILDERS*
a BUILDING s
BUILDUPS*
BULBLETS*
BULGHURS*
BULGIEST
BULIMIAC*

BULIMIAS*
BULIMICS*
BULKAGES*
BULKHEAD s
BULKIEST
BULLACES*
BULLBATS*
BULLDOGS*
BULLDOZE drs
BULLETED
BULLETIN gs
BULLFROG s
BULLHEAD s
BULLHORN s
BULLIEST*
BULLIONS*
BULLNECK s
BULLNOSE s
BULLOCKS*
BULLOCKY*
BULLPENS*
BULLPOUT s
BULLRING s
BULLRUSH
BULLSHOT s
BULLWEED s
BULLWHIP s
BULLYBOY s
BULLYING
BULLYRAG s
BULWARKS*
BUMBLERS*
BUMBLING s
BUMBOATS*
BUMELIAS*
BUMMALOS*
BUMPERED
BUMPIEST
BUMPKINS*
BUNCHIER
BUNCHILY
BUNCHING
BUNCOING
BUNCOMBE s
BUNDISTS*
BUNDLERS*
BUNDLING s
BUNGALOW s
BUNGHOLE s
BUNGLERS*
BUNGLING s
BUNKERED
BUNKMATE s
BUNKOING
BUNRAKUS*
BUNTINGS*
BUNTLINE s
BUOYAGES*
BUOYANCE s
BUOYANCY
BURBLERS*
BURBLIER
BURBLING
BURDENED
BURDENER s
BURDOCKS*
BURETTES*
BURGAGES*
BURGEONS*
BURGHERS*
BURGLARS*
BURGLARY*
BURGLING
BURGONET s
BURGOUTS*
BURGRAVE s
BURGUNDY
BURKITES*
BURLESKS*
BURLIEST
BURNABLE s
BURNINGS*
BURNOOSE ds
BURNOUTS*
BURRIEST
BURRITOS*
BURROWED
BURROWER s
BURSEEDS*
BURSITIS
BURSTERS*
BURSTING
BURSTONE s
BURTHENS*
BURWEEDS*
BUSGIRLS*

BUSHBUCK s
BUSHELED
BUSHELER s
BUSHFIRE s
BUSHGOAT s
BUSHIDOS*
BUSHIEST
BUSHINGS*
BUSHLAND s
BUSHLESS
BUSHLIKE
BUSHPIGS*
BUSHTITS*
BUSHVELD s
BUSHWAHS*
BUSINESS
BUSKINED
BUSLOADS*
BUSSINGS*
BUSTARDS*
BUSTIERS*
BUSTIEST
BUSTLERS*
BUSTLINE s
BUSTLING
BUSULFAN s
BUSYBODY
BUSYNESS
BUSYWORK s
BUTANOLS*
BUTANONE s
BUTCHERS*
BUTCHERY*
*BUTTERED
BUTTHEAD s
BUTTOCKS*
BUTTONED
BUTTONER s
BUTTRESS
BUTYLATE ds
BUTYLENE s
BUTYRALS*
BUTYRATE s
BUTYRINS*
BUTYROUS
BUTYRYLS*
BUXOMEST
BUYBACKS*
BUZZARDS*
BUZZCUTS*
BUZZWIGS*
BUZZWORD s
BYLINERS*
BYLINING
BYPASSED
BYPASSES
BYSSUSES
BYSTREET s
CABALISM s
CABALIST s
CABALLED
CABARETS*
CABBAGED*
CABBAGES*
CABBAGEY*
CABBALAH*s
CABBALAS*
CABERNET s
CABESTRO s
CABEZONE*s
CABEZONS*
CABILDOS*
CABINETS*
CABINING
CABLEWAY s
CABOCHED
CABOCHON s
CABOMBAS*
CABOODLE s
CABOOSES*
CABOSHED
CABOTAGE s
CABRESTA s
CABRESTO s
CABRETTA s
CABRILLA s
CABRIOLE st
CABSTAND s
CACHALOT s
CACHEPOT s
CACHETED
CACHEXIA s
CACHEXIC
CACHUCHA s
CACIQUES*
CACKLERS*

CACKLING
CACODYLS*
CACOMIXL es
CACONYMS*
CACONYMY*
CACTUSES
CADASTER s
CADASTRE s
CADAVERS*
CADDICES*
CADDISED
CADDISES
CADDYING
CADELLES*
CADENCED*
CADENCES*
CADENZAS*
CADMIUMS*
CADUCEAN
CADUCEUS
CADUCITY
CADUCOUS
CAECALLY
CAESIUMS*
CAESURAE*
CAESURAL*
CAESURAS*
CAESURIC
CAFFEINE*s
CAFFEINS*
CAFTANED
CAGEFULS*
CAGELIKE
CAGELING s
CAGINESS
CAISSONS*
CAITIFFS*
CAJAPUTS*
CAJEPUTS*
CAJOLERS*
CAJOLERY*
CAJOLING
CAJUPUTS*
CAKEWALK s
CAKINESS
CALABASH
CALABAZA s
CALADIUM s
CALAMARI*s
CALAMARS*
CALAMARY*
CALAMATA s
CALAMINE ds
CALAMINT s
CALAMITE s
CALAMITY
CALASHES
CALATHOS
CALATHUS
CALCANEA l
CALCANEI
CALCARIA
CALCEATE
CALCIFIC
CALCINED*
CALCINES*
CALCITES*
CALCITIC
CALCIUMS*
CALCSPAR s
CALCTUFA s
CALCTUFF s
CALCULUS
CALDARIA
CALDERAS*
CALDRONS*
CALECHES*
CALENDAL
CALENDAR s
CALENDER s
CALFLIKE
CALFSKIN s
CALIBERS*
CALIBRED*
CALIBRES*
CALICHES*
CALICLES*
CALICOES
CALIFATE s
CALIPASH
CALIPEES*
CALIPERS*
CALIPHAL
CALISAYA s
CALKINGS*
CALLABLE

CALLALOO s
CALLANTS*
CALLBACK s
CALLBOYS*
CALLINGS*
CALLIOPE s
CALLIPEE s
CALLIPER s
CALLOSES*
CALLOWER
CALLUSED
CALLUSES
CALMNESS
CALOMELS*
CALORICS*
CALORIES*
CALORIZE ds
CALOTTES*
CALOTYPE s
CALOYERS*
CALPACKS*
CALPAINS*
CALQUING
CALTHROP s
CALTRAPS*
CALTROPS*
CALUMETS*
CALUTRON s
CALVADOS
CALVARIA lns
CALYCATE
CALYCEAL
CALYCINE
CALYCLES*
CALYCULI
CALYPSOS*
CALYPTER s
CALYPTRA s
CALZONES*
CAMAILED
*CAMASSES
CAMBERED
CAMBISMS*
CAMBISTS*
CAMBIUMS*
CAMBOGIA s
CAMBRICS*
CAMELEER s
CAMELIAS*
CAMELIDS*
CAMELLIA s
CAMEOING
CAMISADE s
CAMISADO s
CAMISIAS*
CAMISOLE s
CAMOMILE s
CAMORRAS*
CAMPAGNA
CAMPAGNE
CAMPAIGN s
CAMPFIRE s
CAMPHENE s
CAMPHINE s
CAMPHIRE s
CAMPHOLS*
CAMPHORS*
CAMPIEST
CAMPINGS*
CAMPIONS*
CAMPONGS*
CAMPOREE s
CAMPOUTS*
CAMPSITE s
CAMPUSED
CAMPUSES
CAMSHAFT s
CANAILLE s
CANAKINS*
CANALING
CANALISE ds
CANALIZE ds
CANALLED
CANALLER s
CANARIES
CANASTAS*
CANCELED
CANCELER s
CANCERED
CANCROID s
CANDELAS*
CANDIDAL*
CANDIDAS*
CANDIDER
CANDIDLY
CANDLERS*

CANDLING
CANDOURS*
CANDYING
CANELLAS*
CANEPHOR s
CANEWARE s
CANFIELD s
CANIKINS*
CANINITY
CANISTEL s
CANISTER s
CANITIES
CANKERED
CANNABIC
CANNABIN s
CANNABIS
CANNELON s
CANNIBAL s
CANNIEST
CANNIKIN s
s CANNINGS*
CANNOLIS*
CANNONED
CANNONRY
CANNULAE*
CANNULAR
CANNULAS*
CANOEING
CANOEIST s
CANONESS
CANONISE ds
CANONIST s
CANONIZE drs
CANOODLE ds
CANOPIED
CANOPIES
CANOROUS
CANTALAS*
CANTATAS*
CANTDOGS*
CANTEENS*
CANTERED
CANTICLE s
CANTINAS*
CANTONAL
CANTONED
CANTRAIP s
CANTRAPS*
CANTRIPS*
CANULATE ds
CANVASED
CANVASER s
CANVASES
CANZONAS*
CANZONES*
CANZONET*s
CAPABLER*
CAPACITY
CAPELANS*
CAPELETS*
CAPELINS*
CAPERERS*
CAPERING
CAPESKIN s
CAPEWORK s
CAPIASES
CAPITALS*
CAPITATE d
CAPITOLS*
CAPITULA r
CAPMAKER s
CAPOEIRA s
CAPONATA s
CAPONIER s
CAPONIZE ds
CAPORALS*
CAPPINGS*
CAPRICCI o
CAPRICES*
CAPRIFIG s
CAPRIOLE ds
CAPROCKS*
CAPSICIN s
CAPSICUM s
*CAPSIDAL
CAPSIZED*
CAPSIZES*
CAPSOMER es
CAPSTANS*
CAPSTONE s
CAPSULAR
CAPSULED*
CAPSULES*
CAPTAINS*
CAPTIONS*
CAPTIOUS

CAPTIVES*
CAPTURED*
CAPTURER*s
CAPTURES*
CAPUCHED*
CAPUCHES*
CAPUCHIN s
CAPYBARA s
CARABAOS*
CARABIDS*
CARABINE*rs
CARABINS*
CARACALS*
CARACARA s
CARACOLE*drs
CARACOLS*
CARACULS*
CARAGANA s
CARAGEEN s
CARAMELS*
CARANGID s
CARAPACE ds
CARASSOW s
CARAVANS*
CARAVELS*
CARAWAYS*
CARBAMIC
CARBAMYL s
CARBARNS*
CARBARYL s
CARBIDES*
CARBINES*
CARBINOL s
CARBOLIC s
CARBONIC
CARBONYL s
CARBORAS*
CARBOXYL s
CARBOYED
CARBURET s
CARCAJOU s
CARCANET s
CARCASES*
CARCERAL
CARDAMOM s
CARDAMON s
CARDAMUM s
CARDCASE s
CARDIACS*
CARDIGAN s
CARDINAL s
CARDINGS*
CARDIOID s
CARDITIC
CARDITIS
CARDOONS*
CAREENED
CAREENER s
CAREERED
CAREERER s
CAREFREE
CARELESS
CARESSED
CARESSER s
CARESSES
CARETAKE nrs
CARETOOK
CAREWORN
CARFARES*
CARIBOUS*
CARILLON s
CARINATE d
CARIOCAS*
CARIOLES*
CARJACKS*
CARLINES*
CARLINGS*
CARLOADS*
CARMAKER s
CARMINES*
CARNAGES*
CARNALLY
CARNAUBA s
CARNIVAL s
CAROCHES*
CAROLERS*
CAROLING
CAROLLED
CAROLLER s
CAROMING
CAROTENE s
CAROTIDS*
CAROTINS*
*CAROUSAL s
CAROUSED
CAROUSEL*s

*CAROUSER*s
CAROUSES
CARPALIA
CARPETED
CARPINGS*
CARPOOLS*
CARPORTS*
CARRACKS
CARRELLS*
CARRIAGE s
CARRIERS*
CARRIOLE s
CARRIONS*
CARRITCH
CARROMED
CARROTIN s
CARRYALL s
CARRYING
CARRYONS*
CARRYOUT s
CARTABLE
CARTAGES*
CARTLOAD s
CARTONED
CARTOONS*
CARTOONY*
CARTOUCH e
CARUNCLE s
CARVINGS*
CARYATIC
CARYATID s
CARYOTIN s
CASCABEL s
CASCABLE s
CASCADED*
CASCADES*
CASCARAS*
CASEASES*
CASEATED*
CASEATES*
CASEBOOK s
CASEFIED
CASEFIES
CASELOAD s
CASEMATE ds
CASEMENT s
CASEOSES*
CASERNES*
CASETTES*
CASEWORK s
CASEWORM s
CASHABLE
CASHBOOK s
CASHIERS*
*CASHLESS
CASHMERE s
CASIMERE s
CASIMIRE s
CASKETED
CASSABAS*
CASSATAS*
CASSAVAS*
CASSENAS*
CASSENES*
CASSETTE s
CASSINAS*
CASSINES*
CASSINOS*
CASSISES
CASSOCKS*
CASTABLE
CASTANET s
CASTAWAY s
CASTEISM s
CASTINGS*
CASTLING
CASTOFFS*
CASTRATE drs
CASTRATI
CASTRATO rs
CASUALLY
CASUALTY
CASUISTS*
CATACOMB s
CATALASE s
CATALOES
CATALOGS*
CATALPAS*
CATALYST s
CATALYZE drs
CATAMITE s
CATAPULT s
CATARACT s
CATARRHS*
CATAWBAS*
CATBIRDS*
CATBOATS*
CATBRIER s
CATCALLS*
CATCHALL s
CATCHERS*
CATCHFLY
CATCHIER
CATCHING
CATCHUPS*
CATCLAWS*
CATECHIN s
CATECHOL s
CATECHUS*
CATEGORY
CATENARY
CATENATE ds
CATENOID s
CATERANS*
CATERERS*
CATERESS
CATERING
CATFACES*
CATFALLS*
CATFIGHT s
CATHEADS*
CATHECTS*
CATHEDRA els
CATHETER s
CATHEXES
CATHEXIS
CATHODAL
CATHODES*
CATHODIC
CATHOLIC s
CATHOUSE s
CATIONIC
CATJANGS*
CATLINGS*
CATMINTS*
CATNAPER s
CATSPAWS*
CATSUITS*
CATTAILS*
CATTALOS*
s CATTIEST*
CATTLEYA s
CATWALKS*
CAUCUSED
CAUCUSES
CAUDALLY
CAUDATED*
CAUDATES*
CAUDEXES
CAUDICES
CAUDILLO s
CAULDRON s
CAULICLE s
CAULKERS*
CAULKING s
CAUSABLE
CAUSALLY
CAUSERIE s
CAUSEWAY s
CAUSTICS*
CAUTIONS*
CAUTIOUS
CAVALERO s
CAVALIER s
CAVALLAS*
CAVATINA s
CAVATINE
CAVEATED
CAVEATOR s
CAVEFISH
CAVELIKE
CAVERNED
CAVETTOS*
CAVIARES*
CAVICORN
CAVILERS*
CAVILING
CAVILLED
CAVILLER s
CAVITARY
CAVITATE ds
CAVITIED
CAVITIES
CAVORTED
CAVORTER s
CAYENNED*
CAYENNES*
CAZIQUES*
CECITIES
CECROPIA s
CEDILLAS*
CEILIDHS*
CEILINGS*
CEINTURE s
CELADONS*
CELERIAC s
CELERIES
CELERITY
CELESTAS*
CELESTES*
CELIBACY
CELIBATE s
CELLARED
CELLARER s
CELLARET s
CELLISTS*
CELLMATE s
a CELLULAR s
CELLULES*
CELOMATA
CELOSIAS*
CEMBALOS*
CEMENTED
CEMENTER s
CEMENTUM s
CEMETERY
CENACLES*
CENOBITE s
CENOTAPH s
CENOZOIC
CENSORED
CENSURED
*CENSURER*s
CENSURES
CENSUSED
CENSUSES
CENTARES*
CENTAURS*
CENTAURY*
CENTAVOS*
*CENTERED
CENTESES
CENTESIS
CENTIARE s
CENTILES*
CENTIMES*
CENTIMOS*
CENTNERS*
CENTONES
CENTRALS*
CENTRING s
CENTRISM s
CENTRIST s
CENTROID s
CENTRUMS*
CENTUPLE ds
CEORLISH
CEPHALAD
a CEPHALIC
CEPHALIN s
CEPHEIDS*
CERAMALS*
CERAMICS*
CERAMIDE s
CERAMIST s
CERASTES
CERATINS*
CERATOID
CERCARIA eln
s
CERCISES
CEREBRAL*s
CEREBRIC
CEREBRUM s
CEREMENT s
CEREMONY
CEREUSES
CERNUOUS
CEROTYPE s
CERULEAN s
CERUMENS*
CERUSITE s
CERVELAS
CERVELAT s
CERVEZAS*
CERVICAL
CERVICES
CERVIXES
CESAREAN s
CESARIAN s
CESSIONS*
CESSPITS*
CESSPOOL s
CESTODES*
CESTOIDS*
CESTUSES
CETACEAN s
CETOLOGY
CEVICHES*
CHABOUKS*
CHACHKAS*
CHACONNE s
*CHADARIM
CHADLESS
CHAEBOLS*
CHAFFERS*
CHAFFIER
CHAFFING
CHAGRINS*
CHAINING
CHAINMAN
CHAINMEN
CHAINSAW s
CHAIRING
CHAIRMAN s
CHAIRMEN
CHALAZAE*
CHALAZAL*
CHALAZAS*
CHALAZIA
CHALCIDS*
CHALDRON s
CHALICED*
CHALICES*
CHALKIER
CHALKING
CHALLAHS
CHALLIES*
CHALLOTH
CHALONES*
CHALUPAS*
CHAMADES*
CHAMBERS*
CHAMBRAY s
CHAMFERS*
CHAMFRON s
CHAMISAS*
CHAMISES*
CHAMISOS*
CHAMMIED
CHAMMIES
CHAMPACA*s
CHAMPACS*
CHAMPAKS*
CHAMPERS
CHAMPING
CHAMPION s
CHANCELS*
CHANCERS*
CHANCERY*
CHANCIER
CHANCILY
CHANCING
CHANCRES*
*CHANDLER sy
CHANFRON s
CHANGERS
CHANGEUP s
*CHANGING
CHANNELS*
CHANOYUS*
CHANSONS*
CHANTAGE s
CHANTERS*
CHANTEYS*
CHANTIES
*CHANTING
CHANTORS*
CHAPATIS*
CHAPATTI s
CHAPBOOK s
CHAPEAUS*
CHAPEAUX*
CHAPERON es
CHAPITER s
CHAPLAIN s
CHAPLETS*
CHAPPATI s
CHAPPIES*
*CHAPPING
CHAPTERS*
CHAQUETA s
CHARACID s
CHARACIN s
CHARADES*
CHARASES
CHARCOAL sy
CHARGERS*
CHARGING
CHARIEST
CHARIOTS*
CHARISMA*s
CHARISMS*
CHARKHAS*
*CHARKING
CHARLADY
CHARLEYS*
CHARLIES*
CHARLOCK s
CHARMERS
*CHARMING
CHARNELS*
CHARPAIS*
CHARPOYS*
CHARQUID*
CHARQUIS*
*CHARRIER
CHARRING
CHARTERS*
CHARTING
CHARTIST s
CHASINGS*
CHASSEUR s
CHASTELY
CHASTENS
CHASTEST
CHASTISE drs
CHASTITY
CHASUBLE s
CHATCHKA s
CHATCHKE s
CHATEAUS*
CHATEAUX*
CHATROOM s
CHATTELS*
CHATTERS
CHATTERY*
CHATTIER
CHATTILY
*CHATTING
CHAUFERS*
CHAUFFER s
*CHAUNTED
*CHAUNTER s
CHAUSSES
CHAYOTES*
*CHAZANIM
CHAZZANS
CHAZZENS*
CHEAPENS*
CHEAPEST
CHEAPIES*
CHEAPISH
CHEATERS
*CHEATING
CHECHAKO s
CHECKERS*
CHECKING
CHECKOFF s
CHECKOUT s
CHECKROW s
CHECKSUM s
CHECKUPS*
CHEDDARS*
CHEDDARY*
CHEDDITE s
CHEDITES*
CHEEKFUL s
CHEEKIER
CHEEKILY
CHEEKING
CHEEPERS*
CHEEPING
CHEERERS*
CHEERFUL
CHEERIER
CHEERILY
CHEERING
CHEERIOS*
CHEERLED
CHEESIER
CHEESILY
CHEESING
CHEETAHS*
CHEFDOMS*
CHEFFING
CHELATED*
CHELATES*
CHELATOR s
CHELIPED s
CHELOIDS*
CHEMICAL s
CHEMISES*
CHEMISMS*
CHEMISTS*
CHEMURGY
CHENILLE s
CHENOPOD s
CHEQUERS*
CHEROOTS*
*CHERRIES
CHERTIER
CHERUBIC
CHERUBIM s
CHERVILS*
CHESHIRE s
CHESSMAN
CHESSMEN
CHESTFUL s
CHESTIER
CHESTILY
CHESTNUT s
CHETRUMS*
CHEVALET s
CHEVERON s
CHEVIOTS*
CHEVRETS*
CHEVRONS*
CHEVYING
*CHEWABLE
CHEWIEST
CHEWINKS*
CHIANTIS*
CHIASMAL*
CHIASMAS*
CHIASMIC*
CHIASMUS
CHIASTIC
CHIAUSES
CHIBOUKS*
CHICANED*
CHICANER*sy
CHICANES*
CHICANOS*
CHICCORY
CHICHIER
CHICKEES*
CHICKENS*
*CHICKORY
CHICKPEA s
CHICNESS
CHIEFDOM s
CHIEFEST
CHIFFONS*
CHIGETAI s
CHIGGERS*
CHIGNONS*
CHILDBED s
*CHILDING
CHILDISH
CHILDREN
CHILIADS*
CHILIASM s
CHILIAST s
CHILIDOG s
s*CHILLERS*
CHILLEST
*CHILLIER
CHILLIES t
CHILLILY
s*CHILLING
CHILLUMS*
CHILOPOD s
CHIMAERA s
CHIMBLEY s
CHIMERAS*
CHIMERES*
CHIMERIC
CHIMLEYS*
CHIMNEYS*
CHINBONE s
CHINCHES
*CHINKIER
CHINKING
CHINLESS
CHINNING
CHINONES*
CHINOOKS*
CHINTSES
CHINTZES
CHINWAGS*
CHIPMUCK s
CHIPMUNK s
CHIPOTLE s
CHIPPERS*
CHIPPIER
*CHIPPIES*t
*CHIPPING
CHIRKEST
CHIRKING
CHIRMING
CHIRPERS*
CHIRPIER
CHIRPILY
CHIRPING
CHIRRING
CHIRRUPS*
CHIRRUPY*
CHISELED
CHISELER s
CHITCHAT s
CHITLING*s
CHITLINS*
CHITOSAN s
CHITTERS
CHITTIES
CHIVALRY
CHIVAREE ds
CHIVVIED
CHIVVIES
CHIVYING
CHLOASMA s
CHLORALS*
CHLORATE s
CHLORDAN es
CHLORIDE*s
CHLORIDS*
CHLORINE*s
CHLORINS*
CHLORITE s
CHLOROUS
CHOCKFUL l
*CHOCKING
CHOICELY
CHOICEST*
CHOIRBOY s
CHOIRING
*CHOKIEST
CHOLATES*
CHOLENTS*
CHOLERAS*
CHOLERIC
CHOLINES*
CHOMPERS*
CHOMPING
CHOOSERS*
CHOOSIER
CHOOSING
CHOPINES*
CHOPPERS
*CHOPPIER
CHOPPILY
*CHOPPING
CHORAGIC*
CHORAGUS
CHORALES*
CHORALLY
CHORDATE s
*CHORDING
CHOREGUS
CHOREMAN
CHOREMEN
CHOREOID
CHORIAMB s
CHORINES*
CHORIOID s
CHORIONS*
CHORIZOS*
CHOROIDS*
CHORTENS*
CHORTLED*
CHORTLER*s
CHORTLES*
CHORUSED
CHORUSES
CHOUSERS
CHOUSHES
*CHOUSING
CHOWCHOW s
CHOWDERS*
CHOWSING
CHOWTIME s
CHRESARD s
CHRISMAL*
CHRISMON s
CHRISOMS*
CHRISTEN s
CHRISTIE s
CHROMATE s
CHROMIDE s
CHROMIER
CHROMING s
CHROMITE s
CHROMIUM s
CHROMIZE ds
a CHROMOUS
CHROMYLS*
CHRONAXY
CHRONICS*
CHRONONS*
CHTHONIC
CHUBASCO s

CHUBBIER
CHUBBILY
CHUCKIES
CHUCKING
CHUCKLED*
CHUCKLER*s
CHUCKLES
CHUDDAHS*
CHUDDARS*
CHUDDERS*
CHUFFEST
*CHUFFIER
*CHUFFING
CHUGALUG s
CHUGGERS
*CHUGGING
CHUKKARS*
CHUKKERS*
CHUMMIER
CHUMMILY
*CHUMMING
*CHUMPING
CHUMSHIP s
*CHUNKIER
CHUNKILY
CHUNKING
CHUNNELS*
CHUNTERS
CHUPPAHS
CHURCHED
CHURCHES
CHURCHLY
CHURLISH
CHURNERS*
CHURNING s
CHURRING
CHUTISTS*
CHUTNEES*
CHUTNEYS*
*CHUTZPAH*s
CHUTZPAS
CHYMISTS*
CHYMOSIN s
CHYTRIDS*
CIBORIUM
CIBOULES*
CICATRIX
CICELIES
CICERONE s
CICERONI
CICHLIDS*
CICISBEI
CICISBEO s
CICOREES*
CIGARETS*
CILANTRO s
CILIATED*
CILIATES*
CIMBALOM s
*CINCHING
CINCHONA s
CINCTURE ds
CINDERED
CINEASTE*s
CINEASTS*
CINEOLES*
CINERARY
CINERINS*
CINGULAR*
CINGULUM
CINNABAR s
CINNAMIC
CINNAMON sy
CINNAMYL s
CINQUAIN s
CIOPPINO s
CIPHERED
CIPHERER s
CIPOLINS*
CIRCLERS*
CIRCLETS*
CIRCLING
CIRCUITS*
CIRCUITY*
CIRCULAR s
CIRCUSES
CIRRIPED es
CISLUNAR
CISSOIDS*
CISTERNA*el
CISTERNS*
CISTRONS*
CISTUSES
CITADELS*
CITATION s
CITATORS*
CITATORY*
CITEABLE
CITHARAS*
CITHERNS*
CITHRENS*
CITIFIED
CITIFIES
CITIZENS*
CITRATED*
CITRATES*
CITREOUS
CITRINES*
CITRININ s
CITRUSES
CITTERNS*
CITYFIED
CITYWARD
CITYWIDE
CIVICISM s
CIVILIAN s
CIVILISE ds
CIVILITY
CIVILIZE drs
CLABBERS*
CLACHANS*
CLACKERS
*CLACKING
CLADDAGH s
CLADDING s
CLADISMS*
CLADISTS*
CLADODES*
CLAFOUTI s
*CLAGGING
CLAIMANT s
CLAIMERS*
CLAIMING
CLAMBAKE s
CLAMBERS
CLAMLIKE
CLAMMERS*
CLAMMIER
CLAMMILY
*CLAMMING
CLAMORED
CLAMORER s
CLAMOURS*
CLAMPERS
*CLAMPING
CLAMWORM s
CLANGERS*
CLANGING
CLANGORS*
CLANGOUR s
*CLANKIER
CLANKING
CLANNISH
CLANSMAN
CLANSMEN
CLAPPERS
*CLAPPING
CLAPTRAP s
CLAQUERS*
CLAQUEUR s
CLARENCE s
CLARINET s
CLARIONS*
CLARKIAS*
CLASHERS
*CLASHING
CLASPERS*
CLASPING
CLASSERS*
CLASSICO*
CLASSICS*
CLASSIER
CLASSIFY
CLASSILY
CLASSING
CLASSISM*s
CLASSIST*s
CLASSONS*
CLASTICS*
CLATTERS*
CLATTERY*
CLAUGHTS*
CLAUSTRA l
CLAVERED
CLAVICLE s
CLAVIERS*
CLAWBACK s
*CLAWLESS
*CLAWLIKE
CLAYBANK s
CLAYIEST
CLAYLIKE
CLAYMORE s
CLAYPANS*
CLAYWARE s
CLEANERS
*CLEANEST
*CLEANING
CLEANSED*
CLEANSER*s
CLEANSES*
CLEANUPS*
CLEARCUT s
CLEARERS*
CLEAREST
CLEARING s
CLEATING
CLEAVAGE s
CLEAVERS
*CLEAVING
CLEEKING
CLEFTING
CLEIDOIC
CLEMATIS
CLEMENCY
CLENCHED
CLENCHER s
CLENCHES
CLERGIES
CLERICAL s
CLERIHEW s
CLERKDOM s
CLERKING
CLERKISH
CLEVEITE s
CLEVERER
CLEVERLY
CLEVISES
CLICKERS
*CLICKING
CLIENTAL
CLIFFIER
CLIMATAL
CLIMATES*
CLIMATIC
CLIMAXED
CLIMAXES
CLIMBERS
*CLIMBING
CLINALLY
CLINCHED
CLINCHER s
CLINCHES
CLINGERS
*CLINGIER
CLINGING
CLINICAL
CLINKERS
*CLINKING
CLIPPERS
*CLIPPING s
CLIQUIER
CLIQUING
CLIQUISH
CLITELLA
*CLITORAL
CLITORIC
CLITORIS
CLOAKING
CLOBBERS
CLOCHARD s
CLOCKERS
*CLOCKING
CLODDIER
CLODDISH
CLODPATE s
CLODPOLE s
CLODPOLL s
CLOGGERS
*CLOGGIER
CLOGGILY
*CLOGGING
CLOISTER s
CLOMPING
CLONALLY
CLONINGS*
CLONISMS*
CLONKING
CLONUSES
*CLOPPING
*CLOSABLE
CLOSEOUT s
CLOSETED
CLOSEUPS*
CLOSINGS
CLOSURED*
CLOSURES*
CLOTHIER s
CLOTHING s
*CLOTTING
CLOTURED*
CLOTURES*
CLOUDIER
CLOUDILY
CLOUDING
CLOUDLET s
*CLOURING
CLOUTERS*
*CLOUTING
CLOVERED
CLOWDERS*
CLOWNERY
CLOWNING
CLOWNISH
CLUBABLE
CLUBBERS
CLUBBIER
CLUBBING
CLUBBISH
CLUBFACE s
CLUBFEET
CLUBFOOT
CLUBHAND s
CLUBHAUL s
CLUBHEAD s
CLUBROOM s
CLUBROOT s
*CLUCKING
CLUELESS
CLUMBERS
*CLUMPIER
*CLUMPING
*CLUMPISH
CLUMSIER
CLUMSILY
CLUNKERS
CLUNKIER
CLUNKING
CLUPEIDS*
CLUPEOID s
CLUSTERS
CLUSTERY*
CLUTCHED
CLUTCHES
CLUTTERS*
CLUTTERY*
CLYPEATE
CLYSTERS*
COACHERS*
COACHING
COACHMAN
COACHMEN
COACTING
COACTION s
COACTIVE
COACTORS*
COADMIRE ds
COADMITS*
COAEVALS*
COAGENCY
COAGENTS*
COAGULUM s
COALBINS*
COALESCE ds
COALFISH
COALHOLE s
COALIEST
COALLESS
COALPITS*
COALSACK s
COALSHED s
COALYARD s
COAMINGS*
COANCHOR s
COAPPEAR s
COAPTING
COARSELY
COARSENS*
COARSEST
COASSIST s
COASSUME ds
COASTERS*
COASTING s
COATINGS*
COATLESS
COATRACK s
COATROOM s
COATTAIL s
COATTEND s
COATTEST s
COAUTHOR s
COBALTIC
COBBIEST
COBBLERS*
COBBLING
COBWEBBY
COCAINES*
COCCIDIA
COCCOIDS*
COCCYGES
COCCYXES
COCHAIRS*
COCHLEAE*
COCHLEAR*
COCHLEAS*
COCINERA s
COCKADED*
COCKADES*
COCKAPOO s
COCKATOO s
COCKBILL s
COCKBOAT s
COCKCROW s
COCKERED
COCKEREL s
COCKEYED*
COCKEYES*
COCKIEST
COCKLIKE
COCKLING
COCKLOFT s
COCKNEYS*
COCKPITS*
COCKSHUT s
COCKSPUR s
COCKSURE
COCKTAIL s
COCOANUT s
COCOBOLA s
COCOBOLO s
COCOMATS*
COCONUTS*
COCOONED
COCOPLUM s
COCOTTES*
COCOYAMS*
*COCREATE ds
CODDLERS*
CODDLING
CODEBOOK s
CODEBTOR s
CODEINAS*
CODEINES*
CODELESS
CODERIVE ds
CODESIGN s
CODICILS*
CODIFIED
CODIFIER s
CODIFIES
CODIRECT s
CODLINGS*
CODPIECE s
CODRIVEN*
CODRIVER*s
CODRIVES*
COEDITED
COEDITOR s
COEFFECT s
COELOMES*
COELOMIC
COEMBODY
COEMPLOY s
COEMPTED
COENACTS*
COENAMOR s
COENDURE ds
COENURES*
COENURUS
COENZYME s
COEQUALS*
COEQUATE ds
COERCERS*
COERCING
COERCION s
COERCIVE
COERECTS*
COESITES*
COEVALLY
COEVOLVE ds
COEXERTS*
COEXISTS*
COEXTEND s
COFACTOR s
*COFFERED
COFFINED
COFFLING
COFFRETS*
COFOUNDS*
COGENTLY
COGITATE ds
COGNATES*
COGNISED*
COGNISES*
COGNIZED*
COGNIZER*s
COGNIZES*
COGNOMEN s
COGNOVIT s
COGWHEEL s
COHABITS*
COHEADED
COHERENT
COHERERS*
COHERING
COHESION s
COHESIVE
COHOBATE ds
COHOLDER s
COHOSHES
COHOSTED
COIFFEUR s
COIFFING
COIFFURE ds
COIGNING
COINABLE
COINAGES*
COINCIDE ds
COINFECT s
COINFERS*
COINHERE ds
COINMATE s
COINSURE drs
COINTERS*
COINVENT s
COISTREL s
COISTRIL s
COITALLY
COITIONS*
COITUSES
COJOINED
COKEHEAD s
COKELIKE
COLANDER s
COLDCOCK s
*COLDNESS
COLEADER s
COLESEED s
COLESLAW s
COLESSEE s
COLESSOR s
COLEUSES
COLEWORT s
COLICINE*s
COLICINS*
COLIFORM s
COLINEAR
COLISEUM s
COLISTIN s
COLLAGED*
COLLAGEN*s
COLLAGES*
COLLAPSE ds
COLLARDS*
COLLARED
COLLARET s
COLLATED*
COLLATES*
COLLATOR s
COLLECTS*
COLLEENS*
COLLEGER*s
COLLEGES*
COLLEGIA ln
COLLETED
COLLIDED*
COLLIDER*s
COLLIDES*
COLLIERS*
COLLIERY*
COLLOGUE ds
COLLOIDS*
COLLOQUY
COLLUDED*
COLLUDER*s
COLLUDES*
COLLUVIA l
COLLYING
COLLYRIA
COLOBOMA
COLOCATE ds
COLOGNED*
COLOGNES*
COLONELS*
COLONIAL s
COLONICS*
COLONIES
COLONISE ds
COLONIST s
COLONIZE drs
COLOPHON sy
COLORADO
COLORANT s
COLORERS*
COLORFUL
COLORING s
COLORISM s
COLORIST s
COLORIZE drs
COLORMAN
COLORMEN
COLORWAY s
COLOSSAL
COLOSSUS
COLOTOMY
COLOURED
COLOURER s
COLPITIS
COLUBRID s
COLUMBIC
COLUMELS*
COLUMNAL
COLUMNAR
COLUMNEA s
COLUMNED
COMAKERS*
COMAKING
COMANAGE drs
COMATIKS*
COMATOSE
COMATULA e
COMBATED
COMBATER s
COMBINED*s
COMBINER*s
COMBINES*
COMBINGS*
COMBLIKE
COMBUSTS*
COMEBACK s
COMEDIAN s
COMEDIES
COMEDOWN s
COMELIER
COMELILY
COMEMBER s
COMETARY
COMETHER s
COMFIEST
COMFORTS*
COMFREYS*
COMINGLE ds
COMITIAL*
COMITIES
COMMANDO*s
COMMANDS*
COMMENCE drs
COMMENDS*
COMMENTS*
COMMERCE ds
COMMIXED
COMMIXES
COMMODES*
COMMONER s
COMMONLY
COMMOVED*
COMMOVES*
COMMUNAL
COMMUNED*
COMMUNER*s
COMMUNES*
COMMUTED*
COMMUTER*s
COMMUTES*
COMORBID
COMPACTS*
COMPADRE s
COMPARED*
COMPARER*s
COMPARES*
COMPARTS*
COMPEERS*
COMPENDS*
COMPERED*
COMPERES*
COMPETED*
COMPETES*
COMPILED*
COMPILER*s
COMPILES*
COMPLAIN st
COMPLEAT

COMPLECT s
COMPLETE drs
COMPLICE s
COMPLIED
COMPLIER s
COMPLIES
COMPLINE*s
COMPLINS*
COMPLOTS*
COMPORTS*
COMPOSED*
COMPOSER*s
COMPOSES*
COMPOSTS*
COMPOTES*
COMPOUND s
COMPRESS
COMPRISE ds
COMPRIZE ds
COMPTING
COMPUTED*
COMPUTER*s
COMPUTES*
COMRADES*
CONATION s
CONATIVE
CONCAVED*
CONCAVES*
CONCEALS*
CONCEDED*
CONCEDER*s
CONCEDES*
CONCEITS*
CONCEIVE drs
CONCENTS*
CONCEPTI*
CONCEPTS*
CONCERNS*
CONCERTI*
CONCERTO*s
CONCERTS*
CONCHIES*
CONCHOID s
CONCISER*
CONCLAVE s
CONCLUDE drs
CONCOCTS*
CONCORDS*
CONCOURS e
CONCRETE ds
CONDEMNS*
CONDENSE drs
CONDOLED*
CONDOLER*s
CONDOLES*
CONDONED*
CONDONER*s
CONDONES*
CONDORES
CONDUCED*
CONDUCER*s
CONDUCES*
CONDUCTS*
CONDUITS*
CONDYLAR
CONDYLES*
CONELRAD s
CONENOSE s
CONEPATE s
CONEPATL s
CONFECTS*
CONFEREE s
CONFERVA els
CONFETTI
CONFETTO
CONFIDED*
CONFIDER*s
CONFIDES*
CONFINED*
CONFINER*s
CONFINES*
CONFIRMS*
CONFLATE ds
CONFLICT s
CONFOCAL
CONFORMS*
CONFOUND s
CONFRERE s
CONFRONT s
CONFUSED*
CONFUSES*
CONFUTED*
CONFUTER*s
CONFUTES*
CONGAING
CONGEALS*
CONGENER s
CONGESTS*
CONGLOBE ds
CONGRATS
CONGRESS
i CONICITY
CONIDIAL*
CONIDIAN*
CONIDIUM
CONIFERS*
CONIINES*
CONIOSES
CONIOSIS
CONJOINS*
CONJOINT*
CONJUGAL
CONJUNCT s
CONJUNTO s
CONJURED*
CONJURER*s
CONJURES*
CONJUROR s
CONNECTS*
CONNIVED*
CONNIVER*sy
CONNIVES*
CONNOTED*
CONNOTES*
CONODONT s
CONOIDAL
CONQUERS*
CONQUEST s
CONQUIAN s
CONSENTS*
CONSERVE drs
CONSIDER s
CONSIGNS*
CONSISTS*
CONSOLED*
CONSOLER*s
CONSOLES*
CONSOMME s
CONSORTS*
CONSPIRE drs
CONSTANT s
CONSTRUE drs
CONSULAR
CONSULTS*
CONSUMED*
CONSUMER*s
CONSUMES*
CONTACTS*
CONTAGIA
CONTAINS*
CONTEMNS*
CONTEMPO
CONTEMPT s
CONTENDS*
CONTENTS*
CONTESSA s
CONTESTS*
CONTEXTS*
CONTINUA l
CONTINUE drs
CONTINUO s
CONTORTS*
CONTOURS*
CONTRACT s
CONTRAIL s
CONTRARY
CONTRAST*sy
CONTRITE
CONTRIVE drs
CONTROLS*
CONTUSED*
CONTUSES*
CONVECTS*
CONVENED*
CONVENER*s
CONVENES*
CONVENOR s
CONVENTS*
CONVERGE ds
CONVERSE drs
CONVERSO s
CONVERTS*
CONVEXES
CONVEXLY
CONVEYED
CONVEYER s
CONVEYOR s
CONVICTS*
CONVINCE drs
CONVOKED*
CONVOKER*s
CONVOKES*
CONVOLVE ds
CONVOYED
CONVULSE ds
COOEEING
COOEYING
COOINGLY
COOKABLE
COOKBOOK s
COOKINGS*
COOKLESS
COOKOFFS*
COOKOUTS*
COOKSHOP s
COOKTOPS*
COOKWARE s
COOLANTS*
COOLDOWN s
COOLNESS
COONCANS*
COONSKIN s
COONTIES*
COOPERED
COOPTING
COOPTION s
COPAIBAS*
COPARENT s
COPASTOR s
COPATRON s
COPEMATE s
COPEPODS*
COPIHUES*
COPILOTS*
COPLANAR
COPPERAH s
COPPERAS
COPPERED
COPPICED*
COPPICES*
COPREMIA s
COPREMIC
COPRINCE s
s COPULATE ds
COPURIFY
COPYABLE
COPYBOOK s
COPYBOYS*
COPYCATS*
COPYDESK s
COPYEDIT s
COPYGIRL s
COPYHOLD s
COPYISTS*
COPYLEFT s
COPYREAD s
COQUETRY
COQUETTE ds
COQUILLE s
COQUINAS*
COQUITOS*
CORACLES
CORACOID s
CORANTOS*
CORBEILS*
CORBELED
CORBINAS*
CORDAGES*
CORDELLE ds
CORDIALS*
CORDINGS*
CORDITES*
CORDLESS
CORDLIKE
CORDOBAS*
CORDONED
CORDOVAN s
CORDUROY s
CORDWAIN s
CORDWOOD s
COREDEEM s
COREIGNS*
CORELATE ds
s CORELESS
COREMIUM
CORKAGES*
CORKIEST
CORKLIKE
CORKWOOD s
CORMLIKE
CORNBALL s
CORNCAKE s
CORNCOBS*
CORNCRIB s
CORNEOUS
CORNERED
CORNETCY
CORNHUSK s
CORNICED*
CORNICES*
CORNICHE s
CORNICLE s
CORNIEST
CORNMEAL s
CORNPONE s
CORNROWS*
CORNUSES
CORNUTED*
CORNUTOS*
CORODIES
COROLLAS*
CORONACH s
CORONALS*
CORONARY
CORONATE ds
CORONELS*
CORONERS*
CORONETS*
CORONOID
COROTATE ds
CORPORAL*s
CORPSMAN
CORPSMEN
CORPUSES
CORRADED*
CORRADES*
CORRECTS*
CORRIDAS*
CORRIDOR s
CORRIVAL s
CORRODED*
CORRODES*
CORRUPTS*
CORSAGES*
CORSAIRS*
CORSELET s
CORSETED
CORSETRY
CORSLETS*
CORTEGES*
CORTEXES
CORTICAL
CORTICES
CORTINAS*
CORTISOL s
CORULERS*
CORUNDUM s
CORVETTE s
CORVINAS*
CORYBANT s
CORYMBED
CORYPHEE s
COSCRIPT s
COSECANT s
COSHERED
COSIGNED
COSIGNER s
COSINESS*
COSMETIC s
COSMICAL
COSMISMS*
COSMISTS*
*COSMOSES
COSSACKS*
COSSETED
COSTALLY
COSTARDS*
COSTLESS
COSTLIER
COSTMARY
COSTRELS*
COSTUMED*
COSTUMER*sy
COSTUMES*
COSTUMEY*
COTENANT s
COTERIES*
COTHURNI*
COTHURNS*
COTILLON s
COTINGAS*
COTININE s
COTQUEAN s
COTTAGER*s
COTTAGES*
COTTAGEY*
COTTERED
COTTIERS*
COTTONED
COTURNIX
COTYLOID
COUCHANT
COUCHERS*
*COUCHING s
COUGHERS*
COUGHING
COULDEST
COULISSE s
COULOIRS*
COULOMBS*
COULTERS*
COUMARIC
COUMARIN s
COUMAROU s
COUNCILS*
COUNSELS*
COUNTERS*
COUNTESS
COUNTIAN s
COUNTIES
COUNTING
COUPLERS*
COUPLETS*
COUPLING s
COURAGES*
COURANTE*s
COURANTO*s
COURANTS*
COURIERS*
COURLANS*
COURSERS*
COURSING s
COURTERS*
COURTESY
COURTIER s
COURTING
COUSCOUS
COUSINLY
COUSINRY
COUTEAUX*
COUTHEST
COUTHIER*
COUTURES*
COUVADES*
COVALENT
COVARIED
*COVARIES
COVENANT s
*COVERAGE s
*COVERALL s
COVERERS*
*COVERING s
*COVERLET s
COVERLID s
*COVERTLY
COVERUPS*
COVETERS*
COVETING
COVETOUS
COWARDLY
COWBANES*
COWBELLS*
COWBERRY
COWBINDS*
COWBIRDS*
COWBOYED
COWERING
COWFLAPS*
COWFLOPS*
COWGIRLS*
COWHAGES*
COWHANDS*
COWHERBS*
COWHERDS*
COWHIDED*
COWHIDES*
COWINNER s
COWLICKS*
COWLINGS*
COWORKER s
COWPLOPS*
COWPOKES*
COWPOXES
COWRITER*s
COWRITES*
COWSHEDS*
COWSKINS*
COWSLIPS*
COXALGIA s
COXALGIC
COXCOMBS*
COXSWAIN s
COZENAGE s
COZENERS*
COZENING
COZINESS
CRAALING
CRABBERS*
CRABBIER
CRABBILY
CRABBING
CRABLIKE
CRABMEAT s
CRABWISE
CRACKERS
*CRACKING s
CRACKLED*
CRACKLES*
CRACKNEL s
CRACKPOT s
CRACKUPS*
CRADLERS*
CRADLING
CRAFTERS
CRAFTIER
CRAFTILY
*CRAFTING
s CRAGGIER
s CRAGGILY
CRAGSMAN
CRAGSMEN
CRAMBOES
CRAMMERS
s*CRAMMING
CRAMOISY
CRAMPIER
*CRAMPING
CRAMPITS*
CRAMPONS*
CRAMPOON s
*CRANCHED
*CRANCHES
CRANIATE s
CRANIUMS*
*CRANKEST
CRANKIER
CRANKILY
*CRANKING
*CRANKISH
CRANKLED
CRANKLES
CRANKOUS
CRANKPIN s
CRANNIED
CRANNIES
CRANNOGE*s
CRANNOGS*
CRAPOLAS*
s CRAPPIER*
CRAPPIES*t
s*CRAPPING
CRASHERS
CRASHING
CRASSEST
s*CRATCHES
CRATERED
CRATONIC
*CRAVENED
CRAVENLY
CRAVINGS
CRAWDADS*
CRAWFISH
s CRAWLERS*
s CRAWLIER
s CRAWLING
CRAWLWAY s
CRAYFISH
CRAYONED
CRAYONER s
CRAZIEST*
CREAKIER
CREAKILY
s CREAKING
s*CREAMERS*
CREAMERY*
CREAMIER
CREAMILY
s*CREAMING
CREASERS*
CREASIER
CREASING
CREATINE*s
CREATING*
CREATINS*
CREATION s
CREATIVE s
CREATORS*
CREATURE s
CREDENCE s
CREDENDA
CREDENZA s
CREDIBLE
CREDIBLY
CREDITED
CREDITOR s
*CREELING
CREEPAGE s
CREEPERS*
CREEPIER*
CREEPIES*t
CREEPILY
CREEPING
CREESHED
CREESHES
*CREMAINS
CREMATED
CREMATES
CREMATOR sy
CREMINIS*
CRENATED*
CRENELED
CRENELLE ds
CRENSHAW s
CREODONT s
CREOLISE ds
CREOLIZE ds
CREOSOLS*
CREOSOTE ds
CREPIEST
CRESCENT s
CRESCIVE
CRESSETS*
*CRESTING s
CRESYLIC
CRETONNE s
CREVALLE s
CREVASSE ds
CREVICED*
CREVICES*
CREWCUTS*
CREWLESS
CREWMATE s
CREWNECK s
CRIBBAGE s
CRIBBERS
*CRIBBING s
s CRIBBLED
CRIBROUS
CRIBWORK s
CRICETID s
CRICKETS
*CRICKING
CRICOIDS*
CRIMINAL s
CRIMINIS*
CRIMMERS
s CRIMPERS*
s CRIMPIER
s CRIMPING
CRIMPLED
CRIMPLES
CRIMSONS*
CRINGERS
*CRINGING
CRINGLES*
CRINITES*
CRINKLED*
CRINKLES*
CRINOIDS*
CRIOLLOS*
CRIPPLED
*CRIPPLER*s
CRIPPLES
CRISPATE d
CRISPENS*
CRISPERS*
CRISPEST
CRISPIER
CRISPILY
CRISPING
CRISTATE d
CRITERIA l
a CRITICAL
CRITIQUE ds
CRITTERS
CRITTURS*
CROAKERS*
CROAKIER
CROAKILY
CROAKING
CROCEINE*s
CROCEINS*
CROCHETS
*CROCKERY
CROCKETS
*CROCKING
CROCKPOT s
CROCOITE s
CROCUSES
CROFTERS*
CROMLECH s
CRONYISM s

CROOKERY
CROOKEST
*CROOKING
CROONERS*
CROONING
CROPLAND s
CROPLESS
CROPPERS*
CROPPIES*
CROPPING
CROQUETS
CROSIERS*
CROSSARM s
CROSSBAR s
CROSSBOW s
CROSSCUT s
CROSSERS*
CROSSEST*
CROSSING s
CROSSLET s
CROSSTIE ds
CROSSWAY s
CROSTINI
CROSTINO
CROTCHED
*CROTCHES
CROTCHET sy
CROUCHED
*CROUCHES
*CROUPIER s
*CROUPILY
CROUPOUS
CROUSELY
CROUTONS*
CROWBARS*
CROWDERS*
CROWDIES
CROWDING
CROWFEET
CROWFOOT s
CROWNERS*
CROWNETS*
CROWNING
CROWSTEP s
CROZIERS*
CRUCIANS*
CRUCIATE
CRUCIBLE s
CRUCIFER s
CRUCIFIX
*CRUDDIER
CRUDDING
CRUDITES
CRUELEST
CRUELLER
CRUISERS*
CRUISING s
CRULLERS*
CRUMBERS*
CRUMBIER
CRUMBING
CRUMBLED
CRUMBLES
CRUMBUMS*
CRUMHORN s
CRUMMIER
*CRUMMIES*t
CRUMPETS*
CRUMPING
CRUMPLED
CRUMPLES
s CRUNCHED
CRUNCHER s
s CRUNCHES
CRUNODAL
CRUNODES*
CRUPPERS*
CRUSADED*
CRUSADER*s
CRUSADES*
CRUSADOS*
CRUSHERS
*CRUSHING
*CRUSTIER
*CRUSTILY
*CRUSTING
CRUSTOSE
CRUTCHED
CRUTCHES
CRUZADOS*
CRUZEIRO s
CRYINGLY
CRYOBANK s
CRYOGENS*
CRYOGENY*
CRYOLITE s

CRYONICS*
CRYOSTAT s
CRYOTRON s
CRYSTALS*
CTENIDIA
CUBATURE s
CUBICITY
CUBICLES*
CUBICULA
CUBIFORM
CUBISTIC
CUBOIDAL
CUCKOLDS*
CUCKOOED
CUCUMBER s
CUCURBIT s
CUDBEARS*
CUDDLERS*
CUDDLIER
CUDDLING
CUDGELED
CUDGELER s
CUDWEEDS*
CUFFLESS
CUFFLINK s
CUISINES*
CUITTLED*
CUITTLES*
CULICIDS*
CULICINE s
CULINARY
s CULLIONS*
CULLISES
CULLYING
CULOTTES*
CULPABLE
CULPABLY
CULPRITS*
s CULTCHES
CULTIGEN s
CULTISMS*
CULTISTS*
CULTIVAR s
CULTLIKE
CULTRATE d
CULTURAL
CULTURED*
CULTURES*
CULTUSES
CULVERIN s
CULVERTS*
CUMARINS*
*CUMBERED
CUMBERER s
CUMBROUS
CUMQUATS*
CUMSHAWS*
CUMULATE ds
CUMULOUS
CUNEATED*
CUNEATIC
*CUNIFORM s
CUNNINGS*
CUPBOARD s
CUPCAKES*
CUPELERS*
CUPELING
CUPELLED
CUPELLER s
CUPIDITY
CUPOLAED
CUPPIEST
CUPPINGS
CUPREOUS
CUPRITES*
CUPULATE
CURACAOS*
CURACIES
CURACOAS*
CURARINE s
CURARIZE ds
CURASSOW s
CURATING
CURATIVE s
CURATORS*
CURBABLE
CURBINGS*
CURBSIDE s
CURCULIO s
CURCUMAS*
CURDIEST
CURDLERS*
CURDLING
CURELESS
CURETTED*
CURETTES*

CURLICUE ds
CURLIEST
CURLINGS*
CURLYCUE s
CURRACHS*
CURRAGHS*
CURRANTS*
CURRENCY
CURRENTS*
CURRICLE s
CURRIERS*
CURRIERY*
s CURRYING
CURSEDER
CURSEDLY
CURSIVES*
CURTAILS*
CURTAINS*
CURTALAX
CURTNESS
CURTSEYS*
CURTSIED
CURTSIES
CURVEDLY
CURVETED
s CURVIEST
CUSCUSES
CUSHIEST
CUSHIONS*
CUSHIONY*
CUSPATED*
CUSPIDAL
CUSPIDES
CUSPIDOR s
CUSSEDLY
CUSSWORD s
CUSTARDS*
CUSTARDY*
CUSTODES
CUSTOMER s
CUSTUMAL s
CUTAWAYS*
CUTBACKS*
CUTBANKS*
CUTCHERY
CUTDOWNS*
a CUTENESS
CUTESIER*
CUTGRASS
CUTICLES*
CUTICULA er
CUTINISE ds
CUTINIZE ds
CUTLASES
CUTLINES*
CUTOVERS*
CUTPURSE s
CUTTABLE
CUTTAGES*
CUTTINGS*
s CUTTLING
CUTWATER s
s CUTWORKS*
CUTWORMS*
CUVETTES*
CYANAMID es
CYANATES*
CYANIDED*
CYANIDES*
CYANINES*
CYANITES*
CYANITIC
CYANOGEN s
CYANOSED
CYANOSES
CYANOSIS
CYANOTIC
CYBERSEX
CYCASINS*
CYCLAMEN s
CYCLASES*
CYCLECAR s
CYCLEWAY s
CYCLICAL s
CYCLICLY
CYCLINGS*
CYCLISTS*
CYCLITOL s
CYCLIZED*
CYCLIZES*
CYCLOIDS*
CYCLONAL
CYCLONES*
CYCLONIC
CYCLOPES
CYCLOSES

CYCLOSIS
CYLINDER s
CYMATIUM
CYMBALER s
CYMBALOM s
CYMBIDIA
CYMBLING s
CYMLINGS*
CYMOGENE s
CYMOSELY
CYNICISM s
CYNOSURE s
CYPHERED
CYPRESES
CYPRIANS*
CYPRINID s
CYPRUSES
CYPSELAE*
CYSTEINE*s
CYSTEINS*
CYSTINES*
CYSTITIS
CYSTOIDS*
CYTASTER s
CYTIDINE s
CYTOGENY
CYTOKINE s
CYTOLOGY
CYTOSINE s
CYTOSOLS*
CZARDOMS*
CZAREVNA s
CZARINAS*
CZARISMS*
CZARISTS*
CZARITZA s
DABBLERS*
DABBLING s
DABCHICK s
DABSTERS*
DACKERED
DACTYLIC*s
DACTYLUS
DADAISMS*
DADAISTS*
*DADDLING
DAEMONES
DAEMONIC
DAFFIEST
DAFFODIL s
DAFTNESS
DAGGERED
DAGGLING
DAGLOCKS*
DAGWOODS*
DAHABEAH s
DAHABIAH s
DAHABIEH s
DAHABIYA s
DAIDZEIN s
DAIKERED
DAIMONES
DAIMONIC
DAINTIER
DAINTIES t
DAINTILY
DAIQUIRI s
DAIRYING s
DAIRYMAN
DAIRYMEN
DAISHIKI s
DAKERHEN s
DALAPONS*
DALESMAN
DALESMEN
DALLIERS*
*DALLYING
DALMATIC s
DALTONIC
DAMAGERS*
DAMAGING
DAMASKED
DAMEWORT s
DAMIANAS*
DAMNABLE
DAMNABLY
DAMNDEST s
DAMNEDER
DAMOSELS*
DAMOZELS*
DAMPENED
DAMPENER s
DAMPINGS*
DAMPNESS
DANAZOLS*
DANDERED

DANDIEST*
DANDLERS*
DANDLING
DANDRIFF s
DANDRUFF sy
DANDYISH
DANDYISM s
DANEGELD s
DANEGELT s
DANEWEED s
DANEWORT s
*DANGERED
DANGLERS
DANGLIER
*DANGLING
DANISHES
DANKNESS
DANSEURS*
DANSEUSE s
DAPHNIAS*
DAPPERER
DAPPERLY
DAPPLING
DAPSONES*
DARINGLY
DARIOLES*
DARKENED
DARKENER s
DARKLIER
DARKLING s
DARKNESS
DARKROOM s
DARKSOME
DARLINGS*
DARNDEST s
DARNEDER
DARNINGS*
DARSHANS*
DARTLING
DASHEENS*
*DASHIEST
DASHIKIS*
DASHPOTS*
DASTARDS*
DASYURES*
DATABANK s
DATABASE ds
DATARIES
DATEABLE
DATEBOOK s
DATELESS
DATELINE ds
DATIVELY
DAUBIEST
DAUBRIES
DAUGHTER s
DAUNDERS*
DAUNTERS*
DAUNTING
DAUPHINE*s
DAUPHINS*
DAVENING
DAWDLERS*
DAWDLING
DAWNLIKE
DAYBOOKS*
DAYBREAK s
DAYCARES*
DAYDREAM sty
DAYFLIES
DAYGLOWS*
DAYLIGHT s
DAYMARES*
DAYROOMS*
DAYSIDES*
DAYSTARS*
DAYTIMES*
DAYWORKS*
DAZZLERS*
DAZZLING
DEACONED
DEACONRY
DEADBEAT s
DEADBOLT s
DEADENED
DEADENER s
DEADEYES*
DEADFALL s
DEADHEAD s
DEADLIER
DEADLIFT s
DEADLINE ds
DEADLOCK s
DEADNESS
DEADPANS*
DEADWOOD s

DEAERATE ds
DEAFENED
DEAFNESS
DEAIRING
DEALATED*
DEALATES*
DEALFISH
DEALINGS*
DEANSHIP s
DEARNESS
DEASHING
DEATHBED s
DEATHCUP s
DEATHFUL
DEBACLES*
DEBAGGED
DEBARKED
DEBARKER s
DEBARRED
DEBASERS*
DEBASING
DEBATERS*
DEBATING
DEBEAKED
DEBEARDS*
DEBILITY
DEBITING
DEBONAIR e
DEBONERS*
DEBONING
DEBOUCHE*ds
DEBRIDED*
DEBRIDES*
DEBRIEFS*
DEBRUISE ds
DEBTLESS
DEBUGGED
DEBUGGER s
DEBUNKED
DEBUNKER s
DEBUTANT es
DEBUTING
DECADENT s
DECAGONS*
DECAGRAM s
DECALOGS*
DECAMPED
DECANTED
DECANTER s
DECAPODS*
DECAYERS*
DECAYING
DECEASED*
DECEASES*
DECEDENT s
DECEIVED*
DECEIVER*s
DECEIVES*
DECEMVIR is
DECENARY
DECENNIA l
DECENTER s
DECENTLY
DECENTRE ds
DECERNED
DECIARES*
DECIBELS*
DECIDERS*
DECIDING
DECIDUAE*
DECIDUAL*
DECIDUAS*
DECIGRAM s
DECIMALS*
DECIMATE ds
DECIPHER s
DECISION s
DECISIVE
DECKHAND s
DECKINGS*
DECLAIMS*
DECLARED*
DECLARER*s
DECLARES*
DECLASSE*ds
DECLAWED
DECLINED*
DECLINER*s
DECLINES*
DECOCTED
DECODERS*
DECODING
DECOLORS*
DECOLOUR s
DECORATE ds
DECOROUS

DECORUMS*
DECOUPLE drs
DECOYERS*
DECOYING
DECREASE ds
DECREERS*
DECREPIT
DECRETAL s
DECRIALS*
DECRIERS*
DECROWNS*
DECRYING
DECRYPTS*
DECUPLED*
DECUPLES*
DECURIES
DECURION s
DECURVED*
DECURVES*
DEDICATE des
*DEDUCING
DEDUCTED
DEEDIEST
DEEDLESS
DEEJAYED
DEEMSTER s
DEEPENED
DEEPENER s
DEEPNESS
DEERLIKE
DEERSKIN s
DEERWEED s
DEERYARD s
DEFACERS*
DEFACING
DEFAMERS*
DEFAMING
DEFANGED
DEFATTED
DEFAULTS*
DEFEATED
DEFEATER s
DEFECATE ds
DEFECTED
DEFECTOR s
DEFENCED*
DEFENCES*
DEFENDED
DEFENDER s
DEFENSED*
DEFENSES*
DEFERENT s
DEFERRAL s
DEFERRED
DEFERRER s
DEFIANCE s
DEFICITS*
DEFILADE ds
DEFILERS*
DEFILING
DEFINERS*
DEFINING
DEFINITE
DEFLATED*
DEFLATER*s
DEFLATES*
DEFLATOR s
DEFLEAED
DEFLECTS*
DEFLEXED
DEFLOWER s
DEFOAMED
DEFOAMER s
DEFOGGED
DEFOGGER s
DEFORCED*
DEFORCER*s
DEFORCES*
DEFOREST s
DEFORMED
DEFORMER s
DEFRAUDS*
DEFRAYAL s
DEFRAYED
DEFRAYER s
DEFROCKS*
DEFROSTS*
DEFTNESS
DEFUELED
DEFUNDED
DEFUSERS*
DEFUSING
DEFUZING
DEGASSED
DEGASSER s
DEGASSES

DEGENDER s
DEGERMED
DEGLAZED*
DEGLAZES*
DEGRADED*
DEGRADER*s
DEGRADES*
DEGREASE drs
DEGUMMED
DEGUSTED
DEHISCED*
DEHISCES*
DEHORNED
DEHORNER s
DEHORTED
DEICIDAL
DEICIDES*
DEICTICS*
DEIFICAL
DEIFIERS*
DEIFYING
DEIGNING
DEIONIZE drs
DEIXISES
*DEJECTED
DEJEUNER s
DEKAGRAM s
DELAINES*
*DELATING
*DELATION s
DELATORS*
DELAYERS*
DELAYING
DELEADED
DELEAVED*
DELEAVES*
DELEGACY
DELEGATE des
DELETING
DELETION s
DELICACY
DELICATE s
DELIGHTS*
DELIMING
DELIMITS*
DELIRIUM s
DELISTED
DELIVERS*
DELIVERY*
DELOUSED*
DELOUSER*s
DELOUSES*
DELTOIDS*
DELUDERS
*DELUDING
DELUGING
*DELUSION s
*DELUSIVE
*DELUSORY
DELUSTER s
DEMAGOGS*
DEMAGOGY*
DEMANDED
DEMANDER s
DEMARCHE s
DEMARKED
DEMASTED
DEMEANED
DEMEANOR s
DEMENTED
DEMENTIA ls
DEMERARA ns
DEMERGED
DEMERGER*s
DEMERGES
DEMERITS*
DEMERSAL
DEMESNES*
DEMETONS*
DEMIGODS*
DEMIJOHN s
DEMILUNE s
DEMIREPS*
DEMISING
DEMISTER s
*DEMITTED
DEMIURGE s
DEMIVOLT es
DEMOBBED
DEMOCRAT s
DEMOLISH
DEMONESS
DEMONIAC s
DEMONIAN
DEMONISE ds
DEMONISM s
DEMONIST s
DEMONIZE ds
DEMOTICS*
*DEMOTING
*DEMOTION s
DEMOTIST s
DEMOUNTS*
DEMPSTER s
DEMURELY
DEMUREST
DEMURRAL s
DEMURRED
DEMURRER s
DENARIUS
DENATURE ds
DENAZIFY
DENDRITE s
DENDROID
DENDRONS*
DENIABLE
DENIABLY
DENIZENS*
DENOTING
DENOTIVE
*DENOUNCE drs
DENTALIA
DENTALLY
DENTATED*
DENTICLE s
DENTILED
DENTINAL
DENTINES*
DENTISTS*
DENTURAL
DENTURES*
DENUDATE ds
DENUDERS*
DENUDING
DEODANDS*
DEODARAS*
DEORBITS*
DEPAINTS*
DEPARTED
DEPARTEE s
DEPENDED
DEPEOPLE ds
DEPERMED
DEPICTED
DEPICTER s
DEPICTOR s
*DEPILATE ds
DEPLANED*
DEPLANES*
DEPLETED*
DEPLETER*s
DEPLETES*
DEPLORED*
DEPLORER*s
DEPLORES*
DEPLOYED
DEPLOYER s
DEPLUMED*
DEPLUMES*
DEPOLISH
DEPONENT s
DEPONING
DEPORTED
DEPORTEE s
DEPORTER s
DEPOSALS*
DEPOSERS*
DEPOSING
DEPOSITS*
DEPRAVED*
DEPRAVER*s
DEPRAVES*
DEPRENYL s
DEPRIVAL s
DEPRIVED*
DEPRIVER*s
DEPRIVES*
DEPSIDES*
DEPURATE ds
DEPUTIES
DEPUTING
DEPUTIZE ds
DERAIGNS*
DERAILED
DERANGED*
DERANGER*s
DERANGES*
DERATING
DERATTED
DERELICT s
DERIDERS*
DERIDING
DERINGER s
DERISION s
DERISIVE
DERISORY
DERIVATE s
DERIVERS*
DERIVING
DERMISES
DERMOIDS*
DEROGATE ds
DERRICKS*
DERRIERE s
DERRISES
DESALTED
DESALTER s
DESANDED
DESCANTS*
DESCENDS*
DESCENTS*
DESCRIBE drs
DESCRIED
DESCRIER s
DESCRIES
DESELECT s
DESERTED
DESERTER s
DESERTIC
DESERVED*
DESERVER*s
DESERVES*
DESEXING
DESIGNED
DESIGNEE s
DESIGNER s
DESILVER s
DESINENT
DESIRERS*
DESIRING
DESIROUS
DESISTED
DESKTOPS*
DESMOIDS*
DESOLATE drs
DESORBED
DESPAIRS*
DESPATCH
DESPISAL s
DESPISED*
DESPISER*s
DESPISES*
DESPITED*
DESPITES*
DESPOILS*
DESPONDS*
DESPOTIC
DESSERTS*
DESTAINS*
DESTINED*
DESTINES*
DESTRIER s
DESTROYS*
DESTRUCT s
DESUGARS*
DESULFUR s
DETACHED
DETACHER s
DETACHES
DETAILED
DETAILER s
DETAINED
DETAINEE s
DETAINER s
DETASSEL s
DETECTED
DETECTER s
DETECTOR s
DETENTES*
DETERGED*
DETERGER*s
DETERGES*
DETERRED
DETERRER s
DETESTED
DETESTER s
DETHATCH
DETHRONE drs
DETICKED
DETICKER s
DETINUES*
DETONATE ds
DETOURED
DETOXIFY
DETOXING
DETRACTS*
DETRAINS*
DETRITAL
DETRITUS
DETRUDED*
DETRUDES*
DEUCEDLY
DEUTERIC
DEUTERON s
DEUTZIAS*
DEVALUED*
DEVALUES*
DEVEINED
DEVELING
DEVELOPE*drs
DEVELOPS*
DEVERBAL s
DEVESTED
DEVIANCE s
DEVIANCY
DEVIANTS*
DEVIATED*
DEVIATES*
DEVIATOR sy
DEVILING
DEVILISH
DEVILKIN s
DEVILLED
DEVILTRY
DEVISALS*
DEVISEES*
DEVISERS*
DEVISING
DEVISORS*
DEVOICED*
DEVOICES*
DEVOLVED
DEVOLVES
DEVONIAN
DEVOTEES*
DEVOTING
DEVOTION s
DEVOURED
DEVOURER s
DEVOUTER
DEVOUTLY
DEWATERS*
DEWAXING
DEWBERRY
DEWCLAWS*
DEWDROPS*
DEWFALLS*
DEWINESS
DEWOOLED
DEWORMED
DEWORMER s
DEXTRANS*
DEXTRINE*s
DEXTRINS*
DEXTROSE s
DEXTROUS
DEZINCED
DHOOLIES
DHOOTIES*
DHOURRAS*
DHURRIES
DIABASES*
DIABASIC
DIABETES
DIABETIC s
DIABLERY
DIABOLIC
DIABOLOS*
DIACETYL s
DIACIDIC
DIACONAL
DIADEMED
DIAGNOSE ds
DIAGONAL s
DIAGRAMS*
DIAGRAPH s
DIALECTS*
DIALINGS*
DIALISTS*
DIALLAGE s
DIALLERS*
DIALLING s
DIALLIST s
DIALOGED
DIALOGER s
DIALOGIC
DIALOGUE drs
DIALYSED*
DIALYSER*s
DIALYSES*
DIALYSIS
DIALYTIC
DIALYZED*
DIALYZER*s
DIALYZES*
DIAMANTE s
DIAMETER s
DIAMIDES*
DIAMINES*
DIAMONDS*
DIANTHUS
DIAPASON s
DIAPAUSE ds
DIAPERED
DIAPHONE s
DIAPHONY
DIAPIRIC
DIAPSIDS*
DIARCHIC
DIARISTS*
DIARRHEA ls
DIASPORA s
DIASPORE s
DIASTASE s
DIASTEMA*s
DIASTEMS*
DIASTERS*
DIASTOLE s
DIASTRAL
DIATOMIC
DIATONIC
DIATRIBE s
DIATRONS*
DIAZEPAM s
DIAZINES*
DIAZINON s
DIAZOLES*
DIBBLERS*
DIBBLING
DIBBUKIM
DICAMBAS*
DICASTIC
DICENTRA s
DICHASIA l
DICHOTIC
DICHROIC
DICKERED
DICKIEST
DICOTYLS*
DICROTAL
DICROTIC
DICTATED*
DICTATES*
DICTATOR s
DICTIEST
DICTIONS*
DICYCLIC
DIDACTIC s
DIDACTYL
DIDAPPER s
DIDDLERS*
DIDDLEYS*
DIDDLIES
DIDDLING
DIDYMIUM s
DIDYMOUS
DIDYNAMY
DIEBACKS*
DIECIOUS
DIEHARDS*
DIELDRIN s
DIEMAKER s
DIERESES
DIERESIS
DIERETIC
DIESELED
DIESTERS*
DIESTOCK s
DIESTRUM s
DIESTRUS
DIETETIC s
DIETHERS*
DIFFERED
DIFFRACT s
DIFFUSED*
DIFFUSER*s
DIFFUSES*
DIFFUSOR s
DIGAMIES
DIGAMIST s
DIGAMMAS*
DIGAMOUS
DIGERATI
DIGESTED
DIGESTER s
DIGESTIF s
DIGESTOR s
DIGGINGS*
DIGHTING
DIGITALS*
DIGITATE d
DIGITIZE drs
DIGOXINS*
DIGRAPHS*
DIHEDRAL s
DIHEDRON s
DIHYBRID s
DIHYDRIC
DILATANT s
DILATATE
DILATERS*
DILATING
DILATION s
DILATIVE
DILATORS*
DILATORY*
DILEMMAS*
DILEMMIC
DILIGENT
DILUENTS*
DILUTERS*
DILUTING
DILUTION s
DILUTIVE
DILUTORS*
DILUVIAL*
DILUVIAN*
DILUVION s
DILUVIUM s
DIMERISM s
DIMERIZE ds
DIMEROUS
DIMETERS*
DIMETHYL s
DIMETRIC
DIMINISH
DIMITIES
DIMMABLE
DIMORPHS*
DIMPLIER
DIMPLING
DINDLING
DINETTES*
DINGBATS*
DINGDONG s
DINGHIES
DINGIEST*
DINGUSES
DINKIEST
DINOSAUR s
DIOBOLON s
DIOCESAN s
DIOCESES*
DIOECIES
DIOECISM s
DIOICOUS
DIOLEFIN s
DIOPSIDE s
DIOPTASE s
DIOPTERS*
DIOPTRAL
DIOPTRES*
DIOPTRIC s
DIORAMAS*
DIORAMIC
DIORITES*
DIORITIC
DIOXANES*
DIOXIDES*
DIPHASIC
DIPHENYL s
DIPLEGIA s
DIPLEGIC
DIPLEXER s
DIPLOIDS*
DIPLOIDY*
DIPLOMAS*
DIPLOMAT*aes
DIPLONTS*
DIPLOPIA s
DIPLOPIC
DIPLOPOD s
DIPLOSES
DIPLOSIS
DIPNOANS*
DIPODIES
DIPPABLE
DIPPIEST
DIPROTIC
DIPSADES
DIPSTICK s
DIPTERAL*
DIPTERAN*s
DIPTERON
DIPTYCAS*
DIPTYCHS*
DIRECTED
DIRECTER
DIRECTLY
DIRECTOR sy
DIRENESS
DIRGEFUL
DIRIMENT
DIRTBAGS*
DIRTIEST*
DIRTYING
DISABLED*
DISABLER*s
DISABLES*
DISABUSE ds
DISAGREE ds
DISALLOW s
DISANNUL s
DISARMED
DISARMER s
DISARRAY s
DISASTER s
DISAVOWS*
DISBANDS*
DISBOSOM s
DISBOUND
DISBOWEL s
DISBURSE drs
DISCANTS*
DISCARDS*
DISCASED*
DISCASES*
DISCEPTS*
DISCERNS*
DISCIPLE ds
DISCLAIM s
DISCLIKE
DISCLOSE drs
DISCOIDS*
DISCOING
DISCOLOR s
DISCORDS*
DISCOUNT s
DISCOVER sty
DISCREET
DISCRETE
DISCROWN s
DISCUSES
DISDAINS*
DISEASED*
DISEASES*
DISENDOW s
DISEUSES*
DISFAVOR s
DISFROCK s
DISGORGE ds
DISGRACE drs
DISGUISE drs
DISGUSTS*
DISHELMS*
DISHERIT s
DISHEVEL s
DISHFULS*
DISHIEST
DISHLIKE
DISHONOR s
DISHPANS*
DISHRAGS*
DISHWARE s
DISINTER s
DISJECTS*
DISJOINS*
DISJOINT*s
DISJUNCT s
DISKETTE s
DISKLIKE
DISLIKED*
DISLIKER*s
DISLIKES*
DISLIMNS*
DISLODGE ds
DISLOYAL
DISMALER
DISMALLY
DISMASTS*
DISMAYED
DISMOUNT s
DISOBEYS*
DISORDER s
DISOWNED
DISPARTS*
DISPATCH
DISPENDS*
DISPENSE drs
DISPERSE drs
DISPIRIT s
DISPLACE drs

DISPLANT s
DISPLAYS*
DISPLODE ds
DISPLUME ds
DISPORTS*
DISPOSAL s
DISPOSED*
DISPOSER*s
DISPOSES*
DISPREAD s
DISPRIZE ds
DISPROOF s
DISPROVE dnr s
DISPUTED*
DISPUTER*s
DISPUTES*
DISQUIET s
DISRATED*
DISRATES*
DISROBED*
DISROBER*s
DISROBES*
DISROOTS*
DISRUPTS*
DISSAVED*
DISSAVES*
DISSEATS*
DISSECTS*
DISSEISE des
DISSEIZE des
DISSENTS*
DISSERTS*
DISSERVE ds
DISSEVER s
DISSOLVE drs
DISSUADE drs
DISTAFFS*
DISTAINS*
DISTALLY
DISTANCE ds
DISTASTE ds
DISTAVES
DISTENDS*
DISTICHS*
DISTILLS*
DISTINCT
DISTOMES*
DISTORTS*
DISTRACT s
DISTRAIN st
DISTRAIT e
DISTRESS
DISTRICT s
DISTRUST s
DISTURBS*
DISULFID es
DISUNION s
DISUNITE drs
DISUNITY
DISUSING
DISVALUE ds
DISYOKED*
DISYOKES*
DITCHERS*
*DITCHING
DITHEISM s
DITHEIST s
DITHERED
DITHERER s
DITSIEST
DITTOING
DITZIEST
DIURESES
DIURESIS
DIURETIC s
DIURNALS*
DIVAGATE ds
DIVALENT
DIVEBOMB s
DIVERGED*
DIVERGES*
DIVERTED
DIVERTER s
DIVESTED
DIVIDEND s
DIVIDERS*
DIVIDING
DIVIDUAL
DIVINELY
DIVINERS*
DIVINEST*
DIVINING
DIVINISE ds
DIVINITY
DIVINIZE ds

DIVISION s
DIVISIVE
DIVISORS*
DIVORCED*
DIVORCEE*s
DIVORCER*s
DIVORCES*
DIVULGED*
DIVULGER*s
DIVULGES*
DIVULSED*
DIVULSES*
DIVVYING
DIZENING
DIZYGOUS
DIZZIEST*
DIZZYING
*DJELLABA hs
DOBLONES
DOCILELY
DOCILITY
DOCKAGES*
DOCKETED
DOCKHAND s
DOCKLAND s
DOCKSIDE s
DOCKYARD s
DOCTORAL
DOCTORED
DOCTORLY
DOCTRINE s
DOCUMENT s
DODDERED
DODDERER s
DODGIEST
DODOISMS*
DOESKINS*
DOGBANES*
DOGBERRY
DOGCARTS*
DOGEARED
DOGEDOMS*
DOGESHIP s
DOGFACES*
DOGFIGHT s
DOGGEDLY
DOGGEREL s
DOGGIEST*
DOGGONED*
DOGGONER*
DOGGONES*t
DOGGRELS*
DOGHOUSE s
DOGMATIC s
DOGNAPED
DOGNAPER s
DOGSBODY
DOGSLEDS*
DOGTEETH
DOGTOOTH
DOGTROTS*
DOGVANES*
DOGWATCH
DOGWOODS*
DOLCETTO s
DOLDRUMS
DOLERITE s
DOLESOME
DOLLOPED
DOLLYING
DOLMADES
DOLMENIC
DOLOMITE s
*DOLOROSO
DOLOROUS
DOLPHINS*
DOMAINES*
DOMELIKE
DOMESDAY s
DOMESTIC s
DOMICILE*ds
DOMICILS*
DOMINANT s
DOMINATE ds
DOMINEER s
DOMINICK s
DOMINIES*
DOMINION s
DOMINIUM s
DOMINOES
DONATING
DONATION s
DONATIVE s
DONATORS*
*DONENESS
DONGOLAS*

DONNERED
DONNIKER s
DOODLERS*
DOODLING
DOOFUSES
DOOMIEST
DOOMSDAY s
DOOMSTER s
DOORBELL s
DOORJAMB s
DOORKNOB s
DOORLESS
DOORMATS*
DOORNAIL s
DOORPOST s
DOORSILL s
DOORSTEP s
DOORSTOP s
DOORWAYS*
DOORYARD s
DOPAMINE s
DOPEHEAD s
DOPESTER s
DOPINESS
DORHAWKS*
DORKIEST
DORMANCY
DORMERED
DORMIENT
DORMOUSE
DORNECKS*
DORNICKS*
DORNOCKS*
DORSALLY
DOSSERET s
DOSSIERS*
DOTARDLY
DOTATION s
DOTINGLY
DOTTEREL s
DOTTIEST
DOTTRELS*
DOUBLERS*
DOUBLETS*
DOUBLING
DOUBLOON s
DOUBLURE s
DOUBTERS*
DOUBTFUL
DOUBTING
DOUCEURS*
*DOUCHING
DOUGHBOY s
DOUGHIER
DOUGHNUT s
DOUPIONI s
DOURINES*
DOURNESS
DOUZEPER s
DOVECOTE*s
DOVECOTS*
DOVEKEYS*
DOVEKIES*
DOVELIKE
DOVENING
DOVETAIL s
DOWAGERS*
DOWDIEST*
DOWDYISH
DOWELING
DOWELLED
DOWERIES
DOWERING
DOWNBEAT s
DOWNBOWS*
DOWNCAST s
DOWNCOME s
DOWNFALL s
DOWNHAUL s
DOWNHILL s
DOWNIEST
DOWNLAND s
DOWNLESS
DOWNLIKE
DOWNLINK s
DOWNLOAD s
DOWNPIPE s
DOWNPLAY s
DOWNPOUR s
DOWNSIDE s
DOWNSIZE ds
DOWNSPIN s
DOWNTICK s
DOWNTIME s
DOWNTOWN s
DOWNTROD

DOWNTURN s
DOWNWARD s
DOWNWASH
DOWNWIND
DOWNZONE ds
DOWSABEL s
DOXOLOGY
DOYENNES*
DOZENING
DOZENTHS*
DOZINESS
DRABBEST
DRABBETS
DRABBING
DRABBLED
DRABBLES
DRABNESS
DRACAENA s
DRACENAS*
DRACHMAE*
DRACHMAI*
DRACHMAS*
DRACONIC
DRAFFIER
*DRAFFISH
DRAFTEES*
DRAFTERS
DRAFTIER
DRAFTILY
*DRAFTING s
DRAGGERS*
DRAGGIER
*DRAGGING
DRAGGLED*
DRAGGLES
DRAGLINE s
DRAGNETS*
DRAGOMAN s
DRAGOMEN
DRAGONET s
DRAGOONS*
DRAGROPE s
DRAGSTER s
DRAINAGE s
DRAINERS*
*DRAINING
DRAMATIC s
*DRAMMING
DRAMMOCK s
DRAMSHOP s
DRAPABLE
*DRATTING
DRAUGHTS*
DRAUGHTY*
DRAWABLE
DRAWBACK s
DRAWBARS*
DRAWBORE s
DRAWDOWN s
DRAWINGS*
DRAWLERS*
DRAWLIER
DRAWLING
DRAWTUBE s
DRAYAGES*
DREADFUL s
*DREADING
DREAMERS
DREAMFUL
DREAMIER
DREAMILY
*DREAMING
DREARIER
DREARIES t
DREARILY
DREDGERS*
DREDGING s
DREGGIER
DREGGISH
DREIDELS*
DRENCHED
DRENCHER s
DRENCHES
DRESSAGE s
DRESSERS*
DRESSIER
DRESSILY
DRESSING s
*DRIBBING
DRIBBLED*
DRIBBLER*s
DRIBBLES*
DRIBBLET*s
DRIBLETS
DRIFTAGE s
DRIFTERS*

DRIFTIER
*DRIFTING
DRIFTPIN s
DRILLERS*
*DRILLING s
DRINKERS*
DRINKING s
DRIPLESS
DRIPPERS
DRIPPIER
DRIPPILY
*DRIPPING s
DRIVABLE
DRIVELED
DRIVELER s
DRIVEWAY s
DRIVINGS*
DRIZZLED*
DRIZZLES*
DROLLERY*
DROLLEST
*DROLLING
DROMONDS*
DROOLIER
DROOLING
DROOPIER
DROOPILY
DROOPING
DROPHEAD s
DROPKICK s
DROPLETS*
DROPOUTS*
DROPPERS*
DROPPING s
DROPSHOT s
DROPSIED
DROPSIES
DROPWORT s
DROSERAS*
DROSKIES
DROSSIER
DROUGHTS*
DROUGHTY*
DROUKING
DROWNDED
DROWNERS*
DROWNING
DROWSIER
DROWSILY
DROWSING
DRUBBERS
*DRUBBING s
DRUDGERS*
DRUDGERY*
DRUDGING
DRUGGETS*
DRUGGIER*
DRUGGIES*t
*DRUGGING
DRUGGIST s
DRUIDESS
DRUIDISM s
DRUMBEAT s
DRUMBLED
DRUMBLES
DRUMFIRE s
DRUMFISH
DRUMHEAD s
DRUMLIER
DRUMLIKE
DRUMLINS*
DRUMMERS
DRUMMING
DRUMROLL s
DRUNKARD s
DRUNKEST
DRUPELET s
DRUTHERS
DRYPOINT s
DRYSTONE
DRYWALLS*
DRYWELLS*
DUALISMS*
DUALISTS*
DUALIZED*
DUALIZES*
DUBBINGS*
DUBNIUMS*
DUBONNET s
DUCKBILL s
DUCKIEST*
DUCKLING s
DUCKPINS*
DUCKTAIL s
DUCKWALK s
DUCKWEED s

DUCTINGS*
DUCTLESS
DUCTULES*
DUCTWORK s
DUDGEONS*
DUDISHLY
DUECENTO s
DUELISTS*
DUELLERS*
DUELLING
DUELLIST s
DUETTING
DUETTIST s
DUKEDOMS*
DULCETLY
DULCIANA s
DULCIMER s
DULCINEA s
DULLARDS*
DULLNESS
DUMBBELL s
DUMBCANE s
DUMBHEAD s
DUMBNESS
DUMFOUND s
DUMMKOPF s
DUMMYING
DUMPCART s
DUMPIEST
DUMPINGS*
DUMPLING s
DUMPSITE s
DUMPSTER s
DUNCICAL
DUNELAND s
DUNELIKE
DUNGAREE ds
DUNGEONS*
DUNGHILL s
DUNGIEST
DUNNAGES*
DUNNITES*
DUODENAL*
DUODENUM s
DUOLOGUE s
DUOPSONY
DUOTONES*
DUPERIES
DUPLEXED
DUPLEXER s
DUPLEXES
DURABLES*
DURAMENS*
DURANCES*
DURATION s
DURATIVE s
DURESSES
DURMASTS*
DURNDEST
DURNEDER
DUSKIEST
DUSTBINS*
DUSTHEAP s
DUSTIEST
DUSTINGS*
DUSTLESS
DUSTLIKE
DUSTOFFS*
DUSTPANS*
DUSTRAGS*
DUTCHMAN
DUTCHMEN
DUTIABLE
DUUMVIRI*
DUUMVIRS*
DUVETINE s
DUVETYNE*s
DUVETYNS*
DUXELLES
DWARFEST
DWARFING
DWARFISH
DWARFISM s
DWEEBIER
DWEEBISH
DWELLERS*
*DWELLING s
DWINDLED
DWINDLES
DYARCHIC
DYBBUKIM
DYESTUFF s
DYEWEEDS*
DYEWOODS*
DYNAMICS*
DYNAMISM s

DYNAMIST s
DYNAMITE drs
DYNASTIC
DYNATRON s
DYSGENIC s
DYSLEXIA s
DYSLEXIC s
DYSPEPSY
DYSPNEAL*
DYSPNEAS*
DYSPNEIC
DYSPNOEA s
DYSPNOIC
DYSTAXIA s
DYSTOCIA s
DYSTONIA s
DYSTONIC
DYSTOPIA ns
DYSURIAS*
EAGEREST
wy EANLINGS*
EARACHES*
t EARDROPS*
EARDRUMS*
EARFLAPS*
EARLDOMS*
np EARLIEST
EARLOBES*
EARLOCKS*
EARLSHIP s
EARMARKS*
EARMUFFS*
EARNESTS*
ly EARNINGS*
EARPHONE s
EARPIECE s
EARPLUGS*
EARRINGS*
EARSHOTS*
EARSTONE s
EARTHIER
EARTHILY
EARTHING
EARTHMAN
EARTHMEN
EARTHNUT s
EARTHPEA s
EARTHSET s
EARWAXES
EARWORMS*
EASEMENT s
EASINESS
EASTERLY
b EASTINGS*
EASTWARD s
EATABLES*
EATERIES
EBONISED*
EBONISES*
EBONITES*
EBONIZED*
EBONIZES*
*ECAUDATE
ECBOLICS*
ECCLESIA el
ECDYSIAL
ECDYSONE*s
ECDYSONS*
ECESISES
ECHELLES*
ECHELONS*
ECHIDNAE*
ECHIDNAS*
ECHINATE d
ECHINOID s
ECHOGRAM s
ECHOISMS*
ECHOLESS
ECLECTIC s
ECLIPSED*
ECLIPSER*s
ECLIPSES*
ECLIPSIS
ECLIPTIC s
ECLOGITE s
ECLOGUES*
ECLOSION s
ECOCIDAL
ECOCIDES*
ECOFREAK s
ECOLOGIC
ECONOBOX
ECONOMIC s
ECOTAGES*
ECOTONAL
ECOTONES*

ECOTOURS*
ECOTYPES
ECOTYPIC
ECRASEUR s
ECSTATIC s
ECTODERM s
ECTOMERE s
ECTOPIAS*
ECTOSARC s
ECTOZOAN*s
ECTOZOON
ECUMENIC s
EDACIOUS
*EDENTATE s
EDGELESS
EDGEWAYS
EDGEWISE
EDGINESS
EDIFICES*
EDIFIERS*
EDIFYING
EDITABLE
s EDITIONS*
EDITRESS
EDUCABLE s
EDUCATED*
EDUCATES*
EDUCATOR sy
drs EDUCIBLE
drs EDUCTION s
drs EDUCTIVE
r EDUCTORS*
EELGRASS
EELPOUTS*
EELWORMS*
bl EERINESS
EFFACERS*
EFFACING
EFFECTED
EFFECTER s
EFFECTOR s
EFFENDIS*
EFFERENT s
EFFETELY
EFFICACY
EFFIGIAL
EFFIGIES
EFFLUENT s
EFFLUVIA l
EFFLUXES
EFFULGED*
EFFULGES*
EFFUSING
EFFUSION s
EFFUSIVE
EFTSOONS*
EGALITES*
EGESTING
EGESTION s
EGESTIVE
EGGFRUIT s
EGGHEADS*
EGGPLANT s
EGGSHELL s
EGLATERE s
EGLOMISE
EGOISTIC
EGOMANIA cs
EGOTISMS*
EGOTISTS*
r EGRESSED
r EGRESSES
EGYPTIAN s
EIDOLONS*
EIGHTEEN s
EIGHTHLY
EIGHTIES
EIGHTVOS*
EINKORNS*
EINSTEIN s
EISWEINS*
dr EJECTING
dr EJECTION s
r EJECTIVE s
r EJECTORS*
EKISTICS*
EKPWELES*
EKTEXINE s
ELAPHINE
r*ELAPSING
ELASTASE s
ELASTICS*
ELASTINS*
br ELATEDLY
ELATERID s
ELATERIN s

dgr ELATIONS*
r ELATIVES*
ELBOWING
ELDRITCH
s ELECTEES*
s ELECTING
s*ELECTION s
s ELECTIVE s
s*ELECTORS*
ELECTRET s
ELECTRIC s
ELECTRON*s
ELECTROS*
ELECTRUM s
ELEGANCE s
ELEGANCY
ELEGIACS*
ELEGISED*
ELEGISES*
ELEGISTS
ELEGIZED*
ELEGIZES*
ELEMENTS*
ELENCHIC*
ELENCHUS
ELENCTIC
ELEPHANT s
ELEVATED*s
ELEVATES*
*ELEVATOR s
ELEVENTH s
s ELFISHLY
ELFLOCKS*
ELICITED
ELICITOR s
ELIDIBLE
ELIGIBLE s
ELIGIBLY
ELISIONS*
ELITISMS*
ELITISTS*
ELKHOUND s
ELLIPSES*
ELLIPSIS
ELLIPTIC
ELOIGNED
ELOIGNER s
ELOINERS*
ELOINING
ELONGATE ds
ELOQUENT
d ELUSIONS*
ELUTIONS*
ELUVIATE ds
ELUVIUMS*
ELVISHLY
ELYTROID
ELYTROUS
EMACIATE ds
r*EMAILING
EMANATED*
EMANATES*
EMANATOR s
EMBALMED
EMBALMER s
EMBANKED
EMBARKED
EMBARRED
EMBATTLE ds
EMBAYING
EMBEDDED
EMBEZZLE drs
EMBITTER s
EMBLAZED*
EMBLAZER*s
EMBLAZES*
EMBLAZON s
EMBLEMED
EMBODIED
EMBODIER s
EMBODIES
EMBOLDEN s
EMBOLIES
EMBOLISM s
EMBORDER s
EMBOSKED
EMBOSOMS*
EMBOSSED
EMBOSSER s
EMBOSSES
EMBOWELS*
EMBOWERS*
EMBOWING
EMBRACED*
EMBRACER*sy
EMBRACES*

EMBROILS*
EMBROWNS*
EMBRUING
EMBRUTED*
EMBRUTES*
EMBRYOID s
EMBRYONS*
EMCEEING
EMDASHES
EMEERATE s
EMENDATE ds
EMENDERS
r*EMENDING
EMERALDS*
EMERGENT s
dr*EMERGING
EMERITAE*
EMERITAS*
EMERITUS
EMEROIDS*
EMERSION s
EMETINES*
*EMIGRANT s
r*EMIGRATE ds
EMINENCE s
EMINENCY
EMIRATES*
EMISSARY
dr*EMISSION s
r*EMISSIVE
r EMITTERS*
dr EMITTING
EMOTICON s
dr*EMOTIONS*
EMPALERS*
EMPALING
EMPANADA s
EMPANELS*
EMPATHIC
EMPERIES
EMPERORS*
EMPHASES
EMPHASIS e
EMPHATIC
EMPIRICS*
EMPLACED*
EMPLACES*
EMPLANED*
EMPLANES*
EMPLOYED*
EMPLOYEE*s
EMPLOYER*s
EMPLOYES*
EMPOISON s
EMPORIUM s
EMPOWERS*
EMPRISES*
EMPRIZES*
EMPTIERS*
EMPTIEST*
EMPTINGS
EMPTYING
EMPURPLE ds
EMPYEMAS*
EMPYEMIC
EMPYREAL
EMPYREAN s
EMULATED*
EMULATES*
EMULATOR s
d EMULSIFY
EMULSION s
EMULSIVE
EMULSOID s
ENABLERS*
ENABLING
ENACTING
ENACTIVE
ENACTORS*
ENACTORY*
ENAMELED
ENAMELER s
ENAMINES*
ENAMORED
ENAMOURS*
v*ENATIONS*
ENCAENIA
ENCAGING
ENCAMPED
ENCASHED
ENCASHES
ENCASING
ENCEINTE s
ENCHAINS*
p ENCHANTS*
ENCHASED*

ENCHASER*s
ENCHASES*
ENCHORIC
ENCIPHER s
ENCIRCLE ds
ENCLASPS*
ENCLAVED*
ENCLAVES*
ENCLITIC s
ENCLOSED*
ENCLOSER*s
ENCLOSES*
ENCODERS*
ENCODING
ENCOMIUM s
ENCORING
ENCROACH
ENCRUSTS*
ENCRYPTS*
ENCUMBER s
ENCYCLIC s
ENCYSTED
ENDAMAGE ds
ENDAMEBA es
ENDANGER s
ENDARCHY*
ENDASHES
ENDBRAIN s
ENDEARED
ENDEAVOR s
ENDEMIAL
ENDEMICS*
ENDEMISM s
ENDERMIC
ENDEXINE s
ENDGAMES*
ENDITING
ENDLEAFS*
ENDNOTES*
ENDOCARP s
ENDOCAST s
ENDODERM s
ENDOGAMY
ENDOGENS*
ENDOGENY*
ENDOPODS*
ENDORSED*
ENDORSEE*s
ENDORSER*s
ENDORSES*
ENDORSOR s
ENDOSARC s
ENDOSMOS
ENDOSOME s
ENDOSTEA l
ENDOWERS*
ENDOWING
ENDOZOIC
ENDPAPER s
ENDPLATE s
ENDPLAYS*
ENDPOINT s
ENDURERS*
ENDURING
ENERGIDS*
ENERGIES
ENERGISE ds
ENERGIZE drs
d*ENERVATE ds
ENFACING
ENFEEBLE drs
ENFEOFFS*
ENFETTER s
ENFEVERS*
ENFILADE ds
ENFLAMED*
ENFLAMES*
ENFOLDED
ENFOLDER s
ENFORCED*
ENFORCER*s
ENFORCES*
ENFRAMED*
ENFRAMES*
ENGAGERS*
ENGAGING
ENGENDER s
ENGILDED
ENGINEER s
ENGINERY
ENGINING
ENGINOUS
ENGIRDED
ENGIRDLE ds
ENGORGED*
ENGORGES*

ENGRAFTS*
ENGRAILS*
ENGRAINS*
ENGRAMME s
ENGRAVED*
ENGRAVER*s
ENGRAVES*
ENGULFED
ENHALOED
ENHALOES
ENHANCED*
ENHANCER*s
ENHANCES*
ENIGMATA
ENISLING
ENJAMBED
ENJOINED
ENJOINER s
ENJOYERS*
ENJOYING
ENKINDLE drs
ENLACING
ENLARGED*
ENLARGER*s
ENLARGES*
ENLISTED
ENLISTEE s
ENLISTER s
ENLIVENS*
ENMESHED
ENMESHES
ENMITIES
ENNEADIC
ENNEAGON s
ENNOBLED*
ENNOBLER*s
ENNOBLES*
ENOLASES*
ox ENOPHILE s
ENORMITY
ENORMOUS
k ENOSISES
dr ENOUNCED*
dr ENOUNCES*
ENPLANED*
ENPLANES*
ENQUIRED*
ENQUIRES*
ENRAGING
ENRAVISH
ENRICHED
ENRICHER s
ENRICHES
ENROBERS*
ENROBING
ENROLLED
ENROLLEE s
ENROLLER s
ENROOTED
ENSAMPLE s
ENSCONCE ds
ENSCROLL s
ENSEMBLE s
ENSERFED
ENSHEATH es
ENSHRINE des
ENSHROUD s
ENSIFORM
ENSIGNCY
ENSILAGE ds
ENSILING
ENSKYING
ENSLAVED*
ENSLAVER*s
ENSLAVES*
ENSNARED*
ENSNARER*s
ENSNARES*
ENSNARLS*
ENSORCEL ls
ENSOULED
ENSPHERE ds
c ENSURERS*
c ENSURING
ENSWATHE ds
ENTAILED
ENTAILER s
ENTAMEBA es
p ENTANGLE drs
ENTASIAS*
ENTASTIC
ENTELLUS
ENTENTES*
ENTERERS*
ENTERICS*
ct ENTERING

ENTERONS*
ENTHALPY
ENTHETIC
ENTHRALL*s
ENTHRALS*
ENTHRONE ds
ENTHUSED*
ENTHUSES*
ENTICERS*
ENTICING
ENTIRELY
ENTIRETY
ENTITIES
ENTITLED*
ENTITLES*
ENTODERM s
ENTOILED
ENTOMBED
ENTOZOAL*
ENTOZOAN*s
ENTOZOIC
ENTOZOON
ENTRAILS
ENTRAINS*
ENTRANCE ds
ENTRANTS*
ENTREATS*
ENTREATY*
ENTRENCH
ENTREPOT s
ENTRESOL s
ENTROPIC
ENTRUSTS*
ENTRYWAY s
ENTWINED*
ENTWINES*
ENTWISTS*
ENURESES
ENURESIS
ENURETIC s
ENVELOPE*drs
ENVELOPS*
ENVENOMS*
ENVIABLE
ENVIABLY
ENVIRONS*
ENVISAGE ds
ENVISION s
ENWHEELS*
ENWOMBED
ENZOOTIC s
EOBIONTS*
EOHIPPUS
EOLIPILE s
n EOLITHIC
EOLOPILE s
EPAULETS*
EPAZOTES*
EPEEISTS*
EPENDYMA s
EPERGNES*
EPHEDRAS*
EPHEDRIN es
EPHEMERA els
*EPHORATE s
EPIBLAST s
EPIBOLIC
EPICALLY
EPICALYX
EPICARPS*
EPICEDIA
EPICENES*
EPICLIKE
EPICOTYL s
EPICURES*
EPICYCLE s
EPIDEMIC s
EPIDERMS*
l EPIDOTES*
EPIDOTIC
EPIDURAL s
EPIFAUNA els
EPIFOCAL
EPIGENIC
EPIGEOUS
EPIGONES*
EPIGONIC*
EPIGONUS
EPIGRAMS*
EPIGRAPH sy
d EPILATED*
d EPILATES*
d EPILATOR s
EPILEPSY
EPILOGUE ds
EPIMERES*

EPIMERIC
EPIMYSIA
EPINASTY
EPIPHANY
EPIPHYTE s
EPISCIAS*
EPISCOPE s
EPISODES*
EPISODIC
EPISOMAL
EPISOMES*
EPISTASY
EPISTLER*s
EPISTLES*
EPISTOME s
EPISTYLE s
EPITAPHS*
EPITASES
EPITASIS
EPITAXIC
EPITHETS*
EPITOMES*
EPITOMIC
EPITOPES*
EPIZOISM s
EPIZOITE s
EPIZOOTY
EPONYMIC
EPOPOEIA s
EPOXIDES*
EPOXYING
EPSILONS*
EQUALING
EQUALISE drs
*EQUALITY
EQUALIZE drs
EQUALLED
EQUATING
EQUATION s
EQUATORS*
EQUINELY
EQUINITY
EQUIPAGE s
*EQUIPPED
*EQUIPPER s
EQUISETA
EQUITANT
EQUITIES
EQUIVOKE s
r*ERADIATE ds
ERASABLE
ERASIONS*
ERASURES
ERECTERS*
ERECTILE
ERECTING
ERECTION s
ERECTIVE
ERECTORS
EREMITES*
EREMITIC
EREMURUS
EREPSINS*
ERETHISM s
EREWHILE s
ERGASTIC
ERGATIVE s
ERGOTISM s
ERIGERON s
ERINGOES
ERISTICS*
ERLKINGS*
ERODABLE
ERODIBLE
EROGENIC
EROSIBLE
EROSIONS*
EROTICAL*
EROTISMS*
EROTIZED*
EROTIZES*
ERRANTLY
ERRANTRY
ERRATICS*
ERRHINES*
ERRINGLY
ERSATZES
ERUCTATE ds
ERUCTING
ERUMPENT
ERUPTING
ERUPTION s
ERUPTIVE s
ERYNGOES
ERYTHEMA s
ERYTHRON s

*ESCALADE drs
ESCALATE ds
*ESCALLOP s
ESCALOPE*ds
ESCALOPS*
ESCAPADE s
ESCAPEES*
ESCAPERS*
*ESCAPING
ESCAPISM s
ESCAPIST s
ESCARGOT s
ESCAROLE s
*ESCARPED
ESCHALOT s
ESCHEATS*
ESCHEWAL s
ESCHEWED
ESCHEWER s
ESCOLARS*
ESCORTED
ESCOTING
ESCROWED
ESCUAGES*
ESCULENT s
ESERINES
o ESOPHAGI
ESOTERIC a
ESPALIER s
ESPARTOS*
*ESPECIAL
ESPIEGLE
*ESPOUSAL s
b*ESPOUSED*
ESPOUSER*s
b*ESPOUSES*
ESPRESSO s
ESQUIRED
ESQUIRES
ESSAYERS*
ESSAYING
ESSAYIST s
ESSENCES*
h ESSONITE s
ESTANCIA s
gr*ESTATING
ESTEEMED
ESTERASE s
ESTERIFY
ESTHESES
a ESTHESIA s
ESTHESIS
a ESTHETES*
a ESTHETIC s
ESTIMATE ds
a ESTIVATE ds
*ESTOPPED
ESTOPPEL s
*ESTOVERS
ESTRAGON s
*ESTRANGE drs
*ESTRAYED
ESTREATS*
o ESTRIOLS*
o ESTROGEN s
o ESTRONES*
o ESTRUSES
ESURIENT
ETAGERES*
k ETAMINES*
ETATISMS*
ETCETERA s
ETCHANTS*
ETCHINGS*
ETERNALS*
ETERNISE ds
ETERNITY
ETERNIZE ds
ETESIANS*
m ETHANOLS*
ETHEPHON s
a ETHEREAL
ETHERIFY
ETHERISH
ETHERIZE drs
ETHICALS*
ETHICIAN s
ETHICIST s
ETHICIZE ds
ETHINYLS*
ETHMOIDS*
ETHNARCH sy
ETHNICAL
ETHNONYM s
ETHNOSES
ETHOGRAM s
ETHOLOGY
ETHOXIES
ETHOXYLS*
m ETHYLATE ds
m ETHYLENE s
ETHYNYLS*
p ETIOLATE ds
a ETIOLOGY
ETOUFFEE s
EUCAINES*
EUCALYPT is
EUCHARIS
EUCHRING
EUCLASES*
EUCRITES*
EUCRITIC
EUDAEMON s
EUDAIMON s
EUDEMONS*
EUGENIAS*
EUGENICS*
EUGENIST s
EUGENOLS*
EUGLENAS*
EUGLENID s
EULACHAN s
EULACHON s
EULOGIAE*
EULOGIAS*
EULOGIES
EULOGISE ds
EULOGIST s
EULOGIUM s
EULOGIZE drs
EUONYMUS
EUPATRID s
EUPEPSIA s
EUPEPTIC
EUPHENIC s
EUPHONIC
EUPHORIA s
EUPHORIC
EUPHOTIC
EUPHRASY
EUPHROES
EUPHUISM s
EUPHUIST s
EUPLOIDS*
EUPLOIDY*
EUPNOEAS*
EUPNOEIC
EUROKIES
EUROKOUS
EUROPIUM s
EURYBATH s
EURYTHMY
EUSOCIAL
EUSTATIC
EUSTELES*
EUTAXIES
EUTECTIC s
EUTROPHY
EUXENITE s
EVACUANT s
EVACUATE ds
EVACUEES*
EVADABLE
EVADIBLE
dr*EVALUATE ds
EVANESCE ds
EVANGELS*
EVASIONS*
EVECTION s
EVENFALL s
EVENINGS*
EVENNESS
EVENSONG s
EVENTFUL
EVENTIDE s
EVENTUAL
n EVERMORE
r*EVERSION s
r EVERTING
EVERTORS*
EVERYDAY s
EVERYMAN
EVERYMEN
EVERYONE
EVERYWAY
EVICTEES*
EVICTING
EVICTION s
EVICTORS
EVIDENCE ds
EVILDOER s
EVILLEST
EVILNESS
EVINCING
EVINCIVE
EVITABLE
r*EVOCABLE
EVOCATOR s
EVOLUTES
r EVOLVERS*
dr EVOLVING
EVONYMUS
EVULSING
r EVULSION s
EXABYTES*
EXACTERS*
EXACTEST
EXACTING
EXACTION s
EXACTORS*
EXAHERTZ
EXALTERS*
EXALTING
EXAMINED*
EXAMINEE*s
EXAMINER*s
h EXAMINES*
EXAMPLED*
EXAMPLES*
EXANTHEM as
EXAPTIVE
EXARCHAL
EXCAVATE ds
EXCEEDED
EXCEEDER s
EXCELLED
EXCEPTED
EXCERPTS*
EXCESSED
EXCESSES
EXCHANGE drs
EXCIDING
EXCIMERS*
EXCIPLES*
EXCISING
EXCISION s
EXCITANT s
EXCITERS*
EXCITING
EXCITONS*
EXCITORS*
EXCLAIMS*
EXCLAVES*
EXCLUDED*
EXCLUDER*s
EXCLUDES*
EXCRETAL*
EXCRETED*
EXCRETER*s
EXCRETES*
EXCURSUS
EXCUSERS*
EXCUSING
EXECRATE ds
EXECUTED*
EXECUTER*s
EXECUTES*
EXECUTOR sy
EXEGESES
EXEGESIS
EXEGETES*
EXEGETIC s
EXEMPLAR*sy
EXEMPLUM
EXEMPTED
EXEQUIAL
EXEQUIES
EXERCISE drs
EXERGUAL
EXERGUES*
EXERTING
EXERTION s
EXERTIVE
EXHALANT s
EXHALENT s
EXHALING
EXHAUSTS*
EXHEDRAE*
EXHIBITS*
EXHORTED
EXHORTER s
EXHUMERS*
EXHUMING
EXIGENCE s
EXIGENCY
EXIGIBLE
EXIGUITY
EXIGUOUS
EXILABLE
EXIMIOUS
EXISTENT s
EXISTING
EXITLESS
EXOCARPS*
EXOCRINE s
EXOCYTIC
EXODERMS*
EXODUSES
EXOERGIC
EXOGAMIC
EXONUMIA
EXORABLE
EXORCISE drs
EXORCISM s
EXORCIST s
EXORCIZE ds
EXORDIAL*
EXORDIUM s
EXOSMOSE s
EXOSPORE s
EXOTERIC
EXOTISMS*
EXOTOXIC
EXOTOXIN s
EXPANDED
EXPANDER s
EXPANDOR s
EXPANSES*
EXPECTED
EXPECTER s
EXPEDITE drs
EXPELLED
EXPELLEE s
EXPELLER s
EXPENDED
EXPENDER s
EXPENSED*
EXPENSES*
EXPERTED
EXPERTLY
EXPIABLE
EXPIATED*
EXPIATES*
EXPIATOR sy
EXPIRERS*
EXPIRIES
EXPIRING
EXPLAINS*
EXPLANTS*
EXPLICIT s
EXPLODED*
EXPLODER*s
EXPLODES*
EXPLOITS*
EXPLORED*
EXPLORER*s
EXPLORES*
EXPONENT s
EXPORTED
EXPORTER s
EXPOSALS*
EXPOSERS*
EXPOSING
EXPOSITS*
EXPOSURE s
EXPOUNDS*
EXPRESSO*s
EXPULSED*
EXPULSES*
EXPUNGED*
EXPUNGER*s
EXPUNGES*
EXSCINDS*
EXSECANT s
EXSECTED
EXSERTED
EXTENDED
EXTENDER s
EXTENSOR s
EXTERIOR s
EXTERNAL s
EXTERNES*
EXTINCTS*
EXTOLLED
EXTOLLER s
EXTORTED
EXTORTER s
EXTRACTS*
EXTRADOS
EXTRANET s
EXTREMER*
EXTREMES*t
EXTREMUM
d EXTRORSE
EXTRUDED*
EXTRUDER*s
EXTRUDES*
EXTUBATE ds
EXUDATES*
EXULTANT
EXULTING
EXURBIAS*
EXUVIATE ds
EYEBALLS*
EYEBEAMS*
EYEBLACK s
EYEBLINK s
EYEBOLTS*
EYEBROWS*
EYEDNESS
EYEDROPS
EYEFOLDS*
EYEGLASS
EYEHOLES*
EYEHOOKS*
EYELIFTS*
EYELINER s
EYEPIECE s
EYEPOINT s
EYESHADE s
EYESHINE s
EYESHOTS*
EYESIGHT s
EYESORES*
EYESPOTS*
EYESTALK s
EYESTONE s
EYETEETH
EYETOOTH
EYEWATER s
EYEWINKS*
FABLIAUX*
FABULATE ds
FABULIST s
FABULOUS
FACEABLE
FACEDOWN s
FACELESS
FACELIFT s
FACEMASK s
FACETELY
FACETIAE
FACETING
FACETTED
FACIALLY
FACIENDS*
FACILELY
FACILITY
FACTIONS
FACTIOUS
FACTOIDS*
FACTORED
FACTOTUM s
FACTURES*
FADDIEST
FADDISMS*
FADDISTS*
FADEAWAY s
FADELESS
FADEOUTS*
FAGGOTED
FAGOTERS*
FAGOTING s
FAHLBAND s
FAIENCES*
FAILINGS*
FAILURES*
FAINEANT s
FAINTERS*
FAINTEST
FAINTING
FAINTISH
FAIRGOER s
FAIRINGS
FAIRLEAD s
FAIRNESS
FAIRWAYS
FAIRYISM s
FAITHFUL s
FAITHING
FAITOURS*
FAKERIES
FALAFELS*
FALBALAS*
FALCATED*
FALCHION s
FALCONER s
FALCONET s
FALCONRY
FALDERAL s
FALDEROL s
FALLAWAY s
FALLBACK s
FALLFISH
FALLIBLE
FALLIBLY
FALLOFFS*
FALLOUTS*
*FALLOWED
FALSETTO s
FALTBOAT s
*FALTERED
*FALTERER s
FAMELESS
FAMILIAL
FAMILIAR s
FAMILIES
FAMILISM s
FAMISHED
FAMISHES
FAMOUSLY
FANATICS*
FANCIERS*
FANCIEST*
FANCIFUL
FANCYING
FANDANGO s
FANEGADA s
FANFARES*
FANFARON s
FANFOLDS*
FANGLESS
FANGLIKE
FANLIGHT s
FANTAILS*
FANTASIA s
FANTASIE ds
FANTASMS*
FANTASTS*
FANWORTS*
FANZINES*
FARADAIC
FARADAYS*
FARADISE ds
FARADISM s
FARADIZE drs
FARCEURS*
FARCICAL
FAREWELL s
FARFALLE
FARINHAS*
FARINOSE
FARMABLE
FARMHAND s
FARMINGS
FARMLAND s
FARMWIFE
FARMWORK s
FARMYARD s
FARNESOL s
FAROLITO s
FAROUCHE
FARRIERS*
FARRIERY*
*FARROWED
FARSIDES*
FARTHEST
FARTHING s
FARTLEKS*
FASCIATE d
FASCICLE ds
FASCINES*
FASCISMS*
FASCISTS*
FASCITIS
FASHIONS*
FASHIOUS
FASTBACK s
FASTBALL s
FASTENED
FASTENER s
FASTINGS*
FASTNESS
FASTUOUS
FATALISM s
FATALIST s
FATALITY
FATBACKS*
FATBIRDS*
FATHEADS*
FATHERED
FATHERLY
FATHOMED
FATHOMER s
FATIGUED*
FATIGUES*
FATLINGS*
FATSTOCK s
FATTENED
FATTENER s
FATTIEST*
FATWOODS*
FAUBOURG s
FAULTIER
FAULTILY
FAULTING
FAUNALLY
FAUNLIKE
FAUTEUIL s
FAUVISMS*
FAUVISTS*
FAVELLAS*
FAVONIAN
FAVORERS*
FAVORING
FAVORITE s
FAVOURED
FAVOURER s
FAWNIEST
FAWNLIKE
FAYALITE s
FAZENDAS*
FEALTIES
*FEARLESS
FEARSOME
FEASANCE s
FEASIBLE
FEASIBLY
FEASTERS
FEASTFUL
*FEASTING
FEATHERS*
FEATHERY*
FEATLIER
FEATURED*
FEATURES*
FEBRIFIC
FECKLESS
FECULENT
FEDAYEEN*
FEDERACY
FEDERALS*
FEDERATE ds
FEDEXING
FEEBLEST
FEEBLISH
FEEDABLE
FEEDBACK s
FEEDBAGS*
FEEDHOLE s
FEEDLOTS*
FEEDYARD s
FEELINGS*
FEETLESS
FEIGNERS*
FEIGNING
FEINTING
FEISTIER
FEISTILY
FELAFELS*
FELDSHER s
FELDSPAR s
FELICITY
FELINELY
FELINITY
FELLABLE
FELLAHIN
FELLATED*
FELLATES*
FELLATIO ns
FELLATOR s
FELLNESS
FELLOWED
FELLOWLY
FELONIES
FELSITES*
FELSITIC
FELSPARS*
FELSTONE s
FELTINGS*
FELTLIKE
FELUCCAS*
FELWORTS*
FEMINACY
FEMININE s
FEMINISE ds
FEMINISM s
FEMINIST s
FEMINITY
FEMINIZE ds
FENAGLED*
FENAGLES*

FENCEROW s
FENCIBLE s
FENCINGS*
FENDERED
FENESTRA el
FENLANDS*
FENNIEST
FENTANYL s
FENTHION s
FENURONS*
FEOFFEES*
FEOFFERS*
FEOFFING
FEOFFORS*
FERACITY
FERETORY
FERITIES
FERMATAS*
FERMENTS*
FERMIONS*
FERMIUMS*
FERNIEST
FERNINST
FERNLESS
FERNLIKE
FEROCITY
FERRATES*
FERRELED
FERREOUS
FERRETED
FERRETER s
FERRIAGE s
FERRITES*
FERRITIC
FERRITIN s
FERRULED*
FERRULES*
FERRYING
FERRYMAN
FERRYMEN
FERULING
FERVENCY
FERVIDLY
FERVOURS*
FESSWISE
FESTALLY
FESTERED
*FESTIVAL s
FESTOONS*
FETATION s
FETCHERS
*FETCHING
FETERITA s
FETIALES
FETIALIS
FETICHES
FETICIDE s
FETIDITY
FETISHES
FETLOCKS*
FETOLOGY
FETTERED
FETTERER s
FETTLING s
FEUDALLY
FEUDISTS*
FEVERFEW s
FEVERING
FEVERISH
FEVEROUS
FEWTRILS
FIANCEES*
FIASCOES
FIBERIZE ds
FIBRANNE s
FIBRILLA er
FIBROIDS*
FIBROINS*
FIBROMAS*
FIBROSES
FIBROSIS
FIBROTIC
FIBSTERS*
FICKLEST
FICTIONS*
FIDDLERS*
FIDDLING
FIDEISMS*
FIDEISTS*
FIDELITY
FIDGETED
FIDGETER s
FIDUCIAL
FIEFDOMS*
FIELDERS*
FIELDING
FIENDISH
FIERCELY
FIERCEST
FIERIEST
FIFTEENS*
FIFTIETH s
FIFTYISH
FIGEATER s
FIGHTERS*
FIGHTING s
FIGMENTS*
FIGULINE s
FIGURANT s
FIGURATE
FIGURERS*
FIGURINE s
FIGURING
FIGWORTS*
FILAGREE ds
FILAMENT s
FILAREES*
FILARIAE*
FILARIAL*
FILARIAN*
FILARIID s
FILATURE s
FILBERTS*
FILCHERS*
FILCHING
FILEABLE
FILEFISH
FILENAME s
FILETING
FILIALLY
FILIATED*
FILIATES*
FILIBEGS*
FILICIDE s
FILIFORM
FILIGREE ds
FILISTER s
FILLABLE
FILLETED
FILLINGS*
FILLIPED
FILMABLE
FILMCARD s
FILMDOMS*
FILMGOER s
FILMIEST
FILMLAND s
FILMLESS
FILMLIKE
FILMSETS*
FILTERED
FILTERER s
FILTHIER
FILTHILY
FILTRATE ds
FIMBRIAE*
FIMBRIAL*
FINAGLED*
FINAGLER*s
FINAGLES*
FINALISE*ds
FINALISM*s
FINALIST*s
FINALITY
FINALIZE drs
FINANCED*
FINANCES*
FINBACKS*
FINDABLE
FINDINGS*
FINEABLE
FINENESS
FINERIES
FINESPUN
FINESSED*
FINESSES*
FINFOOTS*
FINGERED
FINGERER s
FINIALED
FINICKIN g
FINIKING*
FINISHED
FINISHER s
FINISHES
FINITELY
FINITUDE s
FINMARKS*
FINNICKY
FINNIEST
FINNMARK s
FINOCHIO s
FIREABLE
FIREARMS*
FIREBACK s
FIREBALL s
FIREBASE s
FIREBIRD s
FIREBOAT s
FIREBOMB s
FIREBRAT s
FIREBUGS*
FIRECLAY s
FIREDAMP s
FIREDOGS*
FIREFANG s
FIREHALL s
*FIRELESS
FIRELOCK s
FIREPANS*
FIREPINK s
FIREPLUG s
FIREPOTS*
FIREROOM s
FIRESHIP s
FIRESIDE s
FIRETRAP s
FIREWALL s
FIREWEED s
FIREWOOD s
FIREWORK s
FIREWORM s
FIRMNESS
FIRMWARE s
FIRRIEST
FISCALLY
FISHABLE
FISHBOLT s
FISHBONE s
FISHBOWL s
FISHEYES*
FISHGIGS*
FISHHOOK s
FISHIEST
FISHINGS*
FISHKILL s
FISHLESS
FISHLIKE
FISHLINE s
FISHMEAL s
FISHNETS*
FISHPOLE s
FISHPOND s
FISHTAIL s
FISHWAYS*
FISHWIFE
FISHWORM s
FISSIONS*
FISSIPED s
FISSURAL
FISSURED*
FISSURES*
FISTFULS*
FISTNOTE s
FISTULAE*
FISTULAR*
FISTULAS*
FITCHETS*
FITCHEWS*
FITFULLY
FITMENTS*
FITTABLE
FITTINGS*
FIVEFOLD
FIVEPINS
FIXATIFS*
FIXATING
FIXATION s
FIXATIVE s
FIXITIES
FIXTURES*
FIZZIEST
FIZZLING
FLABBIER
FLABBILY
*FLABELLA
FLACKERY
*FLACKING
FLAGELLA r
FLAGGERS
FLAGGIER
*FLAGGING s
FLAGLESS
FLAGPOLE s
FLAGRANT
FLAGSHIP s
FLAILING
*FLAKIEST
FLAMBEAU sx
FLAMBEED*
FLAMENCO s
FLAMEOUT s
FLAMIEST
FLAMINES
FLAMINGO*s
*FLAMMING
FLANCARD s
FLANERIE s
FLANEURS*
FLANGERS*
FLANGING
FLANKERS*
FLANKING
FLANNELS*
FLAPERON s
FLAPJACK s
FLAPLESS
FLAPPERS
FLAPPIER
*FLAPPING
FLAREUPS*
FLASHERS
FLASHGUN s
FLASHIER
FLASHILY
*FLASHING s
FLASKETS*
FLATBEDS*
FLATBOAT s
FLATCAPS*
FLATCARS*
FLATFEET
FLATFISH
FLATFOOT s
FLATHEAD s
FLATIRON s
FLATLAND s
FLATLETS*
FLATLINE drs
FLATLING s
FLATLONG
FLATMATE s
FLATNESS
FLATTENS
FLATTERS*
FLATTERY*
FLATTEST
FLATTING
FLATTISH
FLATTOPS*
FLATUSES
FLATWARE s
FLATWASH
FLATWAYS
FLATWISE
FLATWORK s
FLATWORM s
FLAUNTED
FLAUNTER s
FLAUTIST s
FLAVANOL s
FLAVINES*
FLAVONES*
FLAVONOL s
FLAVORED
FLAVORER s
FLAVOURS*
FLAVOURY*
FLAWIEST
*FLAWLESS
FLAXIEST
FLAXSEED s
FLEABAGS*
FLEABANE s
FLEABITE s
FLEAPITS*
FLEAWORT s
FLECKING
*FLECTION s
*FLEDGIER
FLEDGING
FLEECERS*
*FLEECHED
*FLEECHES
FLEECIER
FLEECILY
FLEECING
*FLEERING
FLEETEST
FLEETING
FLEHMENS*
FLEISHIG
FLENCHED
FLENCHES
FLENSERS*
*FLENSING
FLESHERS*
FLESHIER
FLESHILY
FLESHING s
FLESHPOT s
*FLETCHED
FLETCHER s
*FLETCHES
FLEURONS*
FLEXAGON s
FLEXIBLE
FLEXIBLY
FLEXIONS*
FLEXTIME rs
FLEXUOSE
FLEXUOUS
FLEXURAL
FLEXURES*
FLICHTER s
FLICKERS
FLICKERY*
*FLICKING
*FLIGHTED
FLIMFLAM s
FLIMSIER
FLIMSIES t
FLIMSILY
FLINCHED
FLINCHER s
FLINCHES
FLINDERS*
FLINGERS
FLINGING
FLINKITE s
*FLINTIER
FLINTILY
*FLINTING
FLIPBOOK s
FLIPFLOP s
FLIPPANT
FLIPPERS
FLIPPEST
*FLIPPING
FLIRTERS*
FLIRTIER
FLIRTING
FLITCHED
FLITCHES
FLITTERS
FLITTING
FLIVVERS*
FLOATAGE s
FLOATELS*
FLOATERS*
FLOATIER
FLOATING
FLOCCING
FLOCCOSE
FLOCCULE s
FLOCCULI
FLOCKIER
*FLOCKING s
FLOGGERS
*FLOGGING s
FLOKATIS*
FLOODERS*
FLOODING
FLOODLIT
FLOODWAY s
FLOORAGE s
FLOORERS*
FLOORING s
FLOOSIES*
FLOOZIES*
FLOPOVER s
FLOPPERS
*FLOPPIER
FLOPPIES t
FLOPPILY
*FLOPPING
FLORALLY
FLORENCE s
FLORIDLY
FLORIGEN s
FLORISTS*
FLORUITS*
FLOSSERS*
FLOSSIER*
FLOSSIES*t
FLOSSILY
FLOSSING
FLOTAGES*
FLOTILLA s
FLOTSAMS*
FLOUNCED*
FLOUNCES*
FLOUNDER s
*FLOURING
FLOURISH
FLOUTERS*
*FLOUTING
FLOWAGES*
*FLOWERED
FLOWERER s
FLOWERET s
FLUBBERS
FLUBBING
FLUBDUBS*
FLUENTLY
FLUERICS*
FLUFFERS*
FLUFFIER
FLUFFILY
*FLUFFING
FLUIDICS*
FLUIDISE ds
FLUIDITY
FLUIDIZE drs
FLUIDRAM s
FLUKIEST
FLUMMERY
*FLUMPING
FLUNKERS
FLUNKEYS*
FLUNKIES*
FLUNKING
FLUORENE s
FLUORIDE*s
FLUORIDS*
FLUORINE*s
FLUORINS*
FLUORITE s
FLURRIED
FLURRIES
FLUSHERS*
FLUSHEST
*FLUSHING
FLUSTERS
FLUTIEST
FLUTINGS
FLUTISTS
FLUTTERS*
FLUTTERY*
FLUXGATE s
FLUXIONS*
FLYAWAYS*
FLYBELTS*
FLYBLOWN*
FLYBLOWS*
FLYBOATS*
FLYOVERS*
FLYPAPER s
FLYPASTS*
FLYSCHES
FLYSHEET s
FLYSPECK s
FLYTIERS*
FLYTINGS*
FLYTRAPS*
FLYWHEEL s
FOAMABLE
FOAMIEST
FOAMLESS
FOAMLIKE
FOCACCIA s
FOCALISE ds
FOCALIZE ds
FOCUSERS*
FOCUSING
FOCUSSED
FOCUSSES
FODDERED
FOETUSES
FOGBOUND
FOGEYISH
FOGEYISM s
FOGFRUIT s
FOGGAGES*
FOGGIEST
FOGHORNS*
FOGYISMS*
FOILABLE
FOILSMAN
FOILSMEN
FOISTING
FOLACINS*
FOLDABLE
FOLDAWAY s
FOLDBOAT s
FOLDEROL s
FOLDOUTS*
FOLIAGED*
FOLIAGES*
FOLIATED*
FOLIATES*
FOLIOING
FOLKIEST*
FOLKLIFE
FOLKLIKE
FOLKLORE s
FOLKMOOT s
FOLKMOTE*s
FOLKMOTS*
FOLKSIER
FOLKSILY
FOLKSONG s
FOLKTALE s
FOLKWAYS*
FOLLICLE s
FOLLOWED
FOLLOWER s
FOLLOWUP s
FOMENTED
FOMENTER s
FONDANTS*
FONDLERS*
FONDLING s
FONDNESS
FONDUING
FONTANEL s
FONTINAS*
FOODLESS
FOODWAYS
FOOFARAW s
FOOLFISH
FOOLSCAP s
FOOSBALL s
FOOTAGES*
FOOTBAGS*
FOOTBALL s
FOOTBATH s
FOOTBOYS*
FOOTFALL s
FOOTGEAR s
FOOTHILL s
FOOTHOLD s
FOOTIEST*
FOOTINGS*
FOOTLERS*
FOOTLESS*
FOOTLIKE
FOOTLING
FOOTMARK s
FOOTNOTE ds
FOOTPACE s
FOOTPADS*
FOOTPATH s
FOOTRACE s
FOOTREST s
FOOTROPE s
FOOTSIES*
FOOTSLOG s
FOOTSORE
FOOTSTEP s
FOOTWALL s
FOOTWAYS*
FOOTWEAR
FOOTWORK s
FOOTWORN
FOOZLERS*
FOOZLING
FORAGERS*
FORAGING
FORAMENS*
FORAMINA l
FORAYERS*
FORAYING
FORBEARS*
FORBIDAL s
FORBODED*
FORBODES*
FORBORNE
FORCEDLY
FORCEFUL
FORCIBLE
FORCIBLY
FORCIPES
FORDABLE
FORDLESS
FORDOING
FOREARMS*
FOREBAYS*
FOREBEAR s
FOREBODE drs
FOREBODY
FOREBOOM s

FORECAST s
FOREDATE ds
FOREDECK s
FOREDOES
FOREDONE
FOREDOOM s
FOREFACE s
FOREFEEL s
FOREFEET
FOREFELT
FOREFEND s
FOREFOOT
FOREGOER s
FOREGOES
FOREGONE
FOREGUTS*
a FOREHAND s
FOREHEAD s
FOREHOOF s
FOREKNEW
FOREKNOW ns
FORELADY
FORELAND s
FORELEGS*
FORELIMB s
FORELOCK s
FOREMAST s
FOREMILK s
FOREMOST
FORENAME ds
FORENOON s
FORENSIC s
FOREPART s
FOREPAST
FOREPAWS*
FOREPEAK s
FOREPLAY s
FORERANK*s
FORERUNS*
a FORESAID
FORESAIL s
FORESEEN*
FORESEER*s
FORESEES*
FORESHOW ns
FORESIDE s
FORESKIN s
FORESTAL l
FORESTAY s
FORESTED
FORESTER s
FORESTRY
FORETELL s
a FORETIME s
FORETOLD
FORETOPS*
FOREVERS*
FOREWARN s
FOREWENT
FOREWING s
FOREWORD s
FOREWORN
FOREYARD s
FORFEITS*
FORFENDS*
FORGINGS*
FORGIVEN*
FORGIVER*s
FORGIVES*
FORGOERS*
FORGOING
FORJUDGE ds
FORKBALL s
FORKEDLY
FORKFULS*
FORKIEST
FORKLESS
FORKLIFT s
FORKLIKE
FORKSFUL
FORMABLE
FORMABLY
FORMALIN s
FORMALLY
FORMANTS*
FORMATES*
FORMERLY
FORMICAS*
FORMLESS
FORMULAE*
FORMULAS*
FORMWORK s
FORNICAL
FORNICES
FORRADER
FORSAKEN*
FORSAKER*s
FORSAKES*
FORSOOTH
FORSPENT
FORSWEAR s
FORSWORE
FORSWORN
FORTIETH s
FORTRESS
FORTUITY
FORTUNED*
FORTUNES*
FORTYISH
FORWARDS*
s FORZANDI
s FORZANDO s
FOSSETTE s
FOSSICKS*
FOSTERED
FOSTERER s
FOUETTES*
FOUGHTEN
FOULARDS*
FOULINGS*
FOULNESS
FOUNDERS*
FOUNDING
FOUNTAIN s
FOURCHEE
FOUREYED
FOURFOLD
FOURGONS*
FOURPLEX
FOURSOME s
FOURTEEN s
FOURTHLY
FOVEATED*
FOVEOLAE*
FOVEOLAR*
FOVEOLAS*
FOVEOLES*
FOVEOLET*s
FOWLINGS*
FOXFIRES*
FOXGLOVE s
FOXHOLES*
FOXHOUND s
FOXHUNTS*
FOXINESS
FOXSKINS*
FOXTAILS
FOXTROTS*
FOZINESS
FRABJOUS
FRACASES
FRACTALS*
FRACTION s
FRACTURE*drs
FRACTURS*
FRAENUMS*
*FRAGGING s
FRAGMENT s
FRAGRANT
FRAILEST
FRAKTURS*
FRAMABLE
FRAMINGS*
FRANCIUM s
FRANCIZE ds
FRANKERS
*FRANKEST
*FRANKING
FRANKLIN s
*FRAPPING
FRAUGHTS*
FRAULEIN s
FRAYINGS*
FRAZZLED*
FRAZZLES*
FREAKIER
FREAKILY
FREAKING
FREAKISH
FREAKOUT s
FRECKLED*
FRECKLES*
FREEBASE drs
FREEBEES*
FREEBIES*
FREEBOOT s
FREEBORN
*FREEDMAN
*FREEDMEN
FREEDOMS*
FREEFORM
FREEHAND
FREEHOLD s
FREELOAD s
FREENESS
FREESIAS*
FREEWARE s
FREEWAYS*
FREEWILL
FREEZERS*
FREEZING
FREIGHTS*
FREMITUS
FRENCHED
FRENCHES
FRENETIC s
FRENULAR*
FRENULUM s
FRENZIED
FRENZIES
FRENZILY
FREQUENT s
FRESCOED
FRESCOER s
FRESCOES
FRESHENS*
FRESHEST*
FRESHETS*
FRESHING
FRESHMAN
FRESHMEN
FRESNELS*
FRETLESS
FRETSAWS*
FRETSOME
FRETTERS*
FRETTIER
*FRETTING
FRETWORK s
FRIARIES
FRIBBLED*
FRIBBLER*s
FRIBBLES*
FRICANDO
FRICTION s
FRIENDED
FRIENDLY
FRIGATES*
*FRIGGING
*FRIGHTED
FRIGHTEN s
*FRIGIDLY
FRIJOLES*
FRILLERS*
FRILLIER
*FRILLING s
FRINGIER
*FRINGING
FRIPPERY
FRISBEES*
FRISETTE s
FRISEURS*
FRISKERS
FRISKETS*
*FRISKIER
*FRISKILY
*FRISKING
FRISSONS*
FRITTATA s
FRITTERS
FRITTING
FRIVOLED
FRIVOLER s
FRIZETTE s
FRIZZERS*
FRIZZIER
FRIZZIES t
FRIZZILY
FRIZZING
FRIZZLED*
FRIZZLER*s
FRIZZLES*
*FROCKING
FROGEYED*
FROGEYES*
FROGFISH
FROGGIER
FROGGING
FROGLETS*
FROGLIKE
FROLICKY
FROMAGES*
FROMENTY
FRONDEUR s
FRONDOSE
FRONTAGE s
FRONTALS*
FRONTIER s
FRONTING
FRONTLET s
FRONTMAN
FRONTMEN
FRONTONS*
FROSTBIT e
FROSTEDS*
FROSTIER
FROSTILY
FROSTING s
FROSTNIP s
FROTHERS*
FROTHIER
FROTHILY
FROTHING
FROTTAGE s
FROTTEUR s
FROUFROU s
FROUNCED*
FROUNCES*
FROUZIER
FROWNERS*
FROWNING
FROWSIER
FROWSTED
FROWZIER
FROWZILY
FROZENLY
FRUCTIFY
FRUCTOSE s
FRUGALLY
*FRUGGING
FRUITAGE s
FRUITERS*
FRUITFUL
FRUITIER
FRUITILY
FRUITING
FRUITION s
FRUITLET s
FRUMENTY
FRUMPIER
FRUMPILY
FRUMPISH
FRUSTULE s
FRUSTUMS*
FRYBREAD s
FUBSIEST
FUCHSIAS*
FUCHSINE*s
FUCHSINS*
FUCOIDAL
FUDDLING
FUEHRERS*
FUELLERS*
FUELLING
FUELWOOD s
FUGACITY
FUGGIEST
FUGITIVE s
FUGLEMAN
FUGLEMEN
FUGUISTS*
FULCRUMS*
FULFILLS*
FULLBACK s
FULLERED
FULLFACE s
FULLNESS
FULMINED*
FULMINES*
FULMINIC
FUMARASE s
FUMARATE s
FUMAROLE s
FUMATORY
FUMBLERS*
FUMBLING
FUMELESS
FUMELIKE
FUMETTES*
FUMIGANT s
FUMIGATE ds
FUMINGLY
FUMITORY
*FUNCTION s
FUNCTORS*
FUNERALS*
FUNERARY
FUNEREAL
FUNFAIRS*
FUNFESTS*
FUNGIBLE s
FUNGOIDS*
FUNGUSES
*FUNHOUSE s
FUNICLES*
FUNICULI
FUNKIEST
FUNNELED
FUNNIEST*
FUNNYMAN
FUNNYMEN
FURANOSE s
FURBELOW s
FURCATED*
FURCATES*
FURCRAEA s
FURCULAE*
FURCULAR*
FURCULUM
FURFURAL s
FURFURAN s
FURFURES
FURIBUND
FURLABLE
FURLONGS*
FURLOUGH s
FURMENTY
FURNACED*
FURNACES*
FURRIERS*
FURRIERY*
FURRIEST
FURRINER s
FURRINGS*
FURROWED
FURROWER s
FURTHERS*
FURTHEST
FURUNCLE s
FURZIEST
FUSARIUM
FUSELAGE s
*FUSELESS
FUSELIKE
FUSIFORM
FUSILEER s
FUSILIER s
FUSILLIS*
FUSIONAL
FUSSIEST
FUSSPOTS*
FUSTIANS*
FUSTIEST
FUTHARCS*
FUTHARKS*
FUTHORCS*
FUTHORKS*
FUTILELY
*FUTILITY
FUTTOCKS*
FUTURISM s
FUTURIST s
FUTURITY
FUZZIEST
FUZZTONE s
GABBARDS*
GABBARTS*
GABBIEST
GABBLERS*
GABBLING
GABBROIC
GABBROID
GABELLED*
GABELLES*
GABFESTS*
GADABOUT s
GADARENE
GADFLIES
GADGETRY
GADROONS*
GADWALLS*
GADZOOKS
GAGGLING
GAGSTERS*
GAHNITES*
GAIETIES
GAINABLE
GAINLESS
GAINLIER
GAINSAID
GAINSAYS*
GALABIAS*
GALABIEH s
GALABIYA hs
GALACTIC
GALANGAL*s
GALANGAS*
GALATEAS*
GALAVANT s
GALAXIES
GALBANUM s
GALEATED*
GALENITE s
GALETTES*
GALILEES*
GALIPOTS*
GALIVANT s
GALLANTS*
GALLATES*
GALLEASS
GALLEINS*
GALLEONS*
GALLERIA s
GALLETAS*
GALLETED
GALLIARD s
GALLIASS
GALLICAN*
GALLICAS*
GALLIOTS*
GALLIPOT s
GALLIUMS
GALLNUTS*
GALLOONS*
GALLOOTS*
GALLOPED
GALLOPER s
GALLUSED
GALLUSES
*GALLYING
GALOPADE s
GALOPING
GALOSHED*
GALOSHES*
GALUMPHS*
GALVANIC
GAMASHES
GAMBADES*
GAMBADOS*
GAMBESON s
GAMBIERS*
GAMBLERS
*GAMBLING
GAMBOGES*
GAMBOLED
GAMBRELS*
GAMBUSIA s
GAMECOCK s
GAMELANS*
GAMELIKE
GAMENESS
GAMESMAN
GAMESMEN
GAMESOME
GAMESTER s
GAMINESS*
GAMMADIA
GAMMIEST
GAMMONED
GAMMONER s
GAMODEME s
GANACHES*
GANDERED
GANGBANG s
GANGLAND s
GANGLIAL*
GANGLIAR*
GANGLIER
*GANGLING
GANGLION s
GANGPLOW s
GANGRELS*
GANGRENE ds
GANGSTAS*
GANGSTER s
GANGWAYS*
GANISTER s
GANTLETS*
GANTLINE s
GANTLOPE s
GANTRIES
GANYMEDE s
GAPESEED s
GAPEWORM s
GAPINGLY
GAPPIEST
GARAGING
GARBAGES*
GARBAGEY*
GARBANZO s
GARBLERS*
GARBLESS*
GARBLING
GARBOARD s
GARBOILS*
GARDENED
GARDENER s
GARDENIA s
GARDYLOO
GARGANEY s
GARGLERS*
*GARGLING
GARGOYLE ds
GARIGUES*
GARISHLY
GARLANDS*
GARLICKY
GARMENTS*
GARNERED
GAROTING
GAROTTED*
GAROTTER*s
GAROTTES*
GARPIKES*
GARRETED
GARRISON s
GARROTED*
GARROTER*s
GARROTES*
GARROTTE ds
GARTERED
GASALIER s
GASELIER s
GASHOUSE s
GASIFIED
GASIFIER s
GASIFIES
GASIFORM
GASKINGS
GASLIGHT s
GASOGENE s
GASOHOLS*
GASOLENE s
GASOLIER s
GASOLINE s
GASSIEST
GASSINGS*
GASTIGHT
GASTNESS
GASTRAEA s
GASTREAS*
GASTRINS*
GASTRULA ers
GASWORKS
GATEFOLD s
GATELESS
GATELIKE
GATEPOST s
GATEWAYS*
GATHERED
GATHERER s
GAUCHELY
GAUCHEST
GAUDIEST*
GAUFFERS*
GAUNTEST
GAUNTLET s
GAUZIEST
GAVELING
GAVELLED
GAVELOCK s
GAVOTTED*
GAVOTTES*
GAWKIEST*
GAYETIES
GAYWINGS
GAZABOES
GAZANIAS*
GAZEBOES
GAZELLES*
GAZETTED*
GAZETTES*
GAZOGENE s
GAZPACHO s
GAZUMPED
GAZUMPER s
GEARCASE s
GEARHEAD s
GEARINGS
*GEARLESS
GEEKDOMS*
GEEKIEST
GEEPOUND s
GELATINE*s
GELATING
GELATINS*
*GELATION s
GELDINGS*
GELIDITY
GELLANTS*
GELSEMIA
GEMATRIA s

GEMINATE ds
GEMMATED*
GEMMATES*
GEMMIEST
GEMMULES*
GEMOLOGY
GEMSBOKS*
GEMSBUCK s
GEMSTONE s
GENDARME s
GENDERED
GENERALS*
GENERATE ds
GENERICS*
GENEROUS
GENETICS*
GENETTES*
GENIALLY
GENIPAPS*
GENITALS*
GENITIVE s
GENITORS*
GENITURE s
GENIUSES
GENNAKER s
GENOCIDE s
GENOGRAM s
GENOISES*
GENOMICS*
GENOTYPE s
GENSENGS*
GENTIANS*
GENTILES*
GENTLEST*
GENTLING
GENTRICE s
a*GENTRIES
GENTRIFY
GEODESIC s
GEODETIC s
GEODUCKS*
GEOGNOSY
GEOLOGER s
GEOLOGIC
GEOMANCY
GEOMETER s
GEOMETRY
GEOPHAGY
GEOPHONE s
GEOPHYTE s
GEOPONIC s
GEOPROBE s
GEORGICS*
GEOTAXES
GEOTAXIS
GERANIAL s
GERANIOL s
GERANIUM s
GERARDIA s
GERBERAS*
GERBILLE s
GERENUKS*
GERMANIC
GERMFREE
GERMIEST
GERMINAL*
GERMLIKE
GERONTIC
GESNERIA d
GESTALTS*
GESTAPOS*
GESTATED
GESTATES
GESTICAL
GESTURAL
GESTURED*
GESTURER*s
GESTURES*
GETAWAYS*
GETTABLE
GETTERED
GEWGAWED
GHARIALS*
*GHARRIES
GHASTFUL
GHERAOED
GHERAOES
GHERKINS*
GHETTOED
GHETTOES
GHILLIES*
GHOSTIER
*GHOSTING s
GHOULIES*
GHOULISH
GIANTESS

GIANTISM s
GIARDIAS*
GIBBERED
GIBBETED
GIBBSITE s
GIBINGLY
GIDDIEST*
GIDDYING
GIFTABLE s
GIFTEDLY
GIFTLESS
GIFTWARE s
GIFTWRAP s
GIGABITS*
GIGABYTE s
GIGAFLOP s
GIGANTIC
GIGATONS*
GIGAWATT s
GIGGLERS*
GIGGLIER
GIGGLING
GILBERTS*
GILDHALL s
GILDINGS*
GILLNETS*
GILLYING
GILTHEAD s
GIMBALED
GIMCRACK s
GIMLETED
GIMMICKS*
GIMMICKY*
GIMPIEST
GINGALLS*
GINGELEY s
GINGELIS*
GINGELLI s
GINGELLY
GINGERED
GINGERLY
GINGHAMS*
GINGILIS*
GINGILLI s
GINGIVAE*
GINGIVAL*
GINGKOES
GINKGOES
GINNIEST
GINNINGS
GINSENGS*
GIPSYING
GIRAFFES*
GIRASOLE*s
GIRASOLS*
GIRDLERS*
GIRDLING
GIRLHOOD s
GIRLIEST*
GIROLLES*
GIROSOLS*
GIRTHING
GISARMES*
GITTERNS*
GIVEABLE
GIVEAWAY s
GIVEBACK s
GIZZARDS
GJETOSTS*
*GLABELLA er
GLABRATE
GLABROUS
GLACEING
GLACIATE ds
GLACIERS*
GLACISES
GLADDENS*
GLADDEST
GLADDING
GLADIATE
GLADIEST
GLADIOLA rs
GLADIOLI
GLADLIER
GLADNESS
GLADSOME r
GLAIRIER
*GLAIRING
GLAMOURS*
GLANCERS
*GLANCING
*GLANDERS
GLANDULE s
GLARIEST
GLASNOST s
GLASSFUL s

GLASSIER*
*GLASSIES*t
GLASSILY
GLASSINE s
GLASSING
GLASSMAN
GLASSMEN
GLAUCOMA s
GLAUCOUS
GLAZIERS*
GLAZIERY*
*GLAZIEST
GLAZINGS*
GLEAMERS*
GLEAMIER
GLEAMING
GLEANERS
*GLEANING s
GLEEKING
GLEESOME
GLEETIER
GLEETING
GLEGNESS
GLENLIKE
GLEYINGS*
GLIADINE*s
GLIADINS*
GLIBBEST
GLIBNESS
GLIMMERS
GLIMPSED*
GLIMPSER*s
GLIMPSES*
*GLINTIER
*GLINTING
GLIOMATA
GLISSADE drs
GLISTENS
GLISTERS
GLITCHES
GLITTERS
GLITTERY
GLITZIER
GLITZING
*GLOAMING s
GLOATERS*
GLOATING
GLOBALLY
GLOBATED
GLOBBIER
GLOBOIDS*
*GLOBULAR s
GLOBULES
GLOBULIN s
GLOCHIDS*
GLOMMING
GLONOINS*
GLOOMFUL
GLOOMIER
GLOOMILY
*GLOOMING s
*GLOPPIER
*GLOPPING
GLORIOLE s
GLORIOUS
GLORYING
GLOSSARY
GLOSSEME s
GLOSSERS*
GLOSSIER
GLOSSIES t
GLOSSILY
GLOSSINA s
GLOSSING
*GLOUTING
*GLOWERED
GLOWWORM s
GLOXINIA s
GLUCAGON s
GLUCINIC
GLUCINUM s
GLUCOSES*
GLUCOSIC
GLUELIKE
GLUEPOTS*
*GLUGGING
GLUHWEIN s
GLUINESS
GLUMMEST
GLUMNESS
*GLUMPIER
*GLUMPILY
*GLUNCHED
*GLUNCHES
GLUTELIN s
GLUTENIN s

GLUTTING
GLUTTONS*
GLUTTONY*
GLYCERIC
GLYCERIN es
GLYCEROL s
GLYCERYL s
GLYCINES*
GLYCOGEN s
GLYCOLIC
GLYCONIC s
GLYCOSYL s
GLYPTICS*
GNARLIER
GNARLING
GNARRING
GNASHING
GNATHION s
GNATHITE s
GNATLIKE
*GNATTIER
GNAWABLE
GNAWINGS*
GNEISSES
GNEISSIC
GNOMICAL
GNOMISTS*
GNOMONIC
a GNOSTICS*
GOADLIKE
GOALLESS
GOALPOST s
GOALWARD
GOATFISH
GOATHERD s
*GOATLIKE
GOATSKIN s
GOBBLERS*
GOBBLING
GOBIOIDS*
GOBSHITE s
GODCHILD
GODDAMNS*
GODETIAS*
GODHEADS*
GODHOODS*
GODLIEST
GODLINGS*
GODROONS*
GODSENDS*
GODSHIPS*
GOETHITE s
*GOFFERED
GOGGLERS*
GOGGLIER
GOGGLING
GOITROUS
GOLCONDA s
GOLDARNS*
GOLDBUGS*
GOLDENER
GOLDENLY
GOLDEYES*
GOLDFISH
GOLDTONE
GOLDURNS*
GOLFINGS*
GOLGOTHA s
GOLIARDS*
GOLIATHS*
GOLLIWOG gs
GOLLYWOG s
GOLOSHES*
GOMBEENS*
GOMBROON s
GOMERALS*
GOMERELS*
GOMERILS*
GONADIAL
GONDOLAS*
*GONENESS
GONFALON s
GONFANON s
GONGLIKE
GONIDIAL*
GONIDIUM
GONOCYTE s
GONOPORE s
GOODBYES*
GOODLIER
GOODNESS
GOODWIFE
GOODWILL s
GOOFBALL s
GOOFIEST
GOOGLIES

GOOMBAHS*
GOOMBAYS*
GOONIEST*
GOOPIEST
GOOSIEST
GORBELLY
GORBLIMY
GORCOCKS*
GORDITAS*
GORGEDLY
GORGEOUS
GORGERIN s
GORGETED
GORILLAS*
GORINESS
GORMANDS*
GORMLESS
GORSIEST
GOSHAWKS*
GOSLINGS*
GOSPELER s
GOSPELLY
GOSPORTS*
GOSSAMER sy
GOSSIPED
GOSSIPER s
GOSSIPRY
GOSSOONS*
GOSSYPOL s
GOTHITES*
GOUACHES*
GOURAMIS*
GOURMAND s
GOURMETS*
GOUTIEST
GOVERNED
GOVERNOR s
GOWNSMAN
GOWNSMEN
GRABBERS*
GRABBIER
GRABBING
GRABBLED
*GRABBLER*s
GRABBLES
GRACEFUL
GRACILES*
GRACILIS
GRACIOSO s
GRACIOUS
GRACKLES*
GRADABLE
GRADATED*
GRADATES*
GRADIENT s
GRADINES*
GRADUALS*
GRADUAND s
GRADUATE ds
GRADUSES
GRAECIZE ds
s GRAFFITI s
s GRAFFITO
GRAFTAGE s
GRAFTERS
*GRAFTING
GRAINERS*
*GRAINIER
*GRAINING
GRAMARYE*s
GRAMERCY
GRAMMARS*
GRANDADS*
GRANDAME*s
GRANDAMS*
GRANDDAD s
GRANDDAM s
GRANDEES*
GRANDEST
GRANDEUR s
GRANDKID s
GRANDMAS*
GRANDPAS*
GRANDSIR es
GRANDSON s
GRANGERS
GRANITAS*
GRANITES*
GRANITIC
GRANNIES*
GRANOLAS*
GRANTEES*
GRANTERS
*GRANTING
GRANTORS*
*GRANULAR

GRANULES*
GRAPHEME s
GRAPHICS*
GRAPHING
GRAPHITE s
GRAPIEST
GRAPLINE*s
GRAPLINS*
GRAPNELS*
GRAPPLED*
GRAPPLER*s
GRAPPLES*
GRASPERS
*GRASPING
GRASSIER
GRASSILY
GRASSING
GRATEFUL
GRATINEE*ds
GRATINGS
GRATUITY
GRAUPELS*
GRAVAMEN s
*GRAVELED
*GRAVELLY
GRAVIDAE*
GRAVIDAS*
GRAVIDLY
GRAVITAS
GRAVITON s
GRAVLAKS
GRAVURES*
GRAYBACK s
GRAYFISH
GRAYLAGS*
GRAYLING s
GRAYMAIL s
GRAYNESS
GRAYOUTS*
GRAZABLE
GRAZIERS*
GRAZINGS*
GRAZIOSO
GREASERS*
GREASIER
GREASILY
GREASING
GREATENS*
GREATEST
GRECIZED*
GRECIZES*
*GREEDIER
*GREEDILY
GREEGREE s
GREENBUG s
GREENERY*
GREENEST
GREENFLY
GREENIER*
GREENIES*t
GREENING s
GREENISH
GREENLET s
GREENLIT
GREENTHS*
GREENWAY s
GREETERS*
GREETING s
GREISENS*
GREMIALS*
GREMLINS*
GREMMIES*
GRENADES*
GREWSOME r
GREYHENS*
GREYLAGS*
GREYNESS
GRIBBLES*
GRIDDERS
GRIDDLED
GRIDDLES
GRIDIRON s
GRIDLOCK s
GRIEVANT s
GRIEVERS
GRIEVING
GRIEVOUS
GRIFFINS*
GRIFFONS*
GRIFTERS*
*GRIFTING
GRILLADE s
GRILLAGE s
GRILLERS*
GRILLERY*
*GRILLING

GRIMACED*
GRIMACER*s
GRIMACES*
*GRIMIEST
GRIMMEST
GRIMNESS
GRINCHES
GRINDERS*
GRINDERY*
GRINDING
GRINNERS*
*GRINNING
GRIPIEST
GRIPPERS
GRIPPIER
*GRIPPING
GRIPSACK s
GRISEOUS
GRISETTE s
GRISKINS*
GRISLIER
GRISTERS*
GRISTLES*
GRITTERS
GRITTIER
GRITTILY
GRITTING
GRIZZLED*
GRIZZLER*s
GRIZZLES*
GROANERS*
GROANING
GRODIEST
GROGGERY
GROGGIER
GROGGILY
GROGRAMS*
GROGSHOP s
GROINING
GROKKING
GROMMETS*
GROMWELL s
GROOMERS
*GROOMING
GROOVERS*
GROOVIER
GROOVING
GROSBEAK s
GROSCHEN
GROSSERS*
GROSSEST*
GROSSING
GROTTIER
GROTTOED
GROTTOES
GROUCHED
*GROUCHES
*GROUNDED
*GROUNDER s
GROUPERS*
GROUPIES*
*GROUPING s
GROUPOID s
GROUSERS
*GROUSING
GROUTERS
GROUTIER
*GROUTING
GROVELED
GROVELER s
*GROWABLE
GROWLERS*
GROWLIER
GROWLING
GROWNUPS*
GRUBBERS
GRUBBIER
GRUBBILY
*GRUBBING
GRUBWORM s
GRUDGERS*
GRUDGING
GRUELERS*
GRUELING s
GRUELLED
GRUELLER s
GRUESOME r
GRUFFEST
GRUFFIER
GRUFFILY
*GRUFFING
GRUFFISH
GRUIFORM
GRUMBLED
*GRUMBLER*s
GRUMBLES

*GRUMMEST
GRUMMETS*
GRUMPHIE s
GRUMPIER
GRUMPILY
GRUMPING
GRUMPISH
GRUNGERS*
GRUNGIER
GRUNIONS*
GRUNTERS*
GRUNTING
GRUNTLED*
GRUNTLES*
GRUTCHED
GRUTCHES
GRUYERES*
GRYPHONS*
GUACHARO s
GUAIACOL s
GUAIACUM s
GUAIOCUM s
GUANACOS*
GUANASES*
GUANIDIN es
GUANINES*
GUARANAS*
GUARANIS*
GUARANTY
GUARDANT s
GUARDDOG s
GUARDERS*
GUARDIAN s
GUARDING
GUAYULES*
GUDGEONS*
GUERDONS*
GUERIDON s
GUERILLA s
GUERNSEY s
GUESSERS*
GUESSING
GUESTING
GUFFAWED
GUGGLING
GUIDABLE
GUIDANCE s
GUIDEWAY s
GUILDERS*
GUILEFUL
GUILTIER
GUILTILY
GUIPURES*
GUISARDS*
GUITGUIT s
GULFIEST
GULFLIKE
GULFWEED s
GULLABLE
GULLABLY
GULLIBLE
GULLIBLY
GULLWING
GULLYING
GULOSITY
GULPIEST
GUMBALLS*
GUMBOILS*
GUMBOOTS*
GUMBOTIL s
GUMDROPS*
GUMLINES*
GUMMIEST
GUMMITES*
GUMMOSES*
GUMMOSIS
GUMPTION s
GUMSHOED*
GUMSHOES*
GUMTREES*
GUMWEEDS*
GUMWOODS*
GUNBOATS*
GUNFIGHT s
GUNFIRES*
GUNFLINT s
GUNKHOLE ds
GUNKIEST
GUNLOCKS
GUNMETAL s
GUNNINGS*
GUNNYBAG s
GUNPAPER s
GUNPLAYS*
GUNPOINT s
GUNROOMS*
GUNSHIPS
GUNSHOTS*
GUNSMITH s
GUNSTOCK s
GUNWALES*
GURGLETS*
GURGLING
GURNARDS*
GURUSHIP s
GUSHIEST
GUSSETED
GUSSYING
GUSTABLE s
GUSTIEST
GUSTLESS
GUTSIEST
GUTTATED*
*GUTTERED
GUTTIEST
GUTTLERS*
GUTTLING
GUTTURAL s
GUYLINES*
GUZZLERS*
GUZZLING
GWEDUCKS*
GYMKHANA s
GYMNASIA l
GYMNASTS*
GYNAECEA
GYNAECIA
GYNANDRY
GYNARCHY
GYNECIUM
GYNECOID
GYNIATRY
GYNOECIA
GYPLURES*
GYPSEIAN
GYPSEOUS
GYPSTERS*
GYPSYDOM s
GYPSYING
GYPSYISH
GYPSYISM s
GYRATING
GYRATION s
GYRATORS*
GYRATORY*
GYROIDAL
GYROSTAT s
HABANERA s
HABANERO s
HABDALAH s
HABITANS*
HABITANT*s
HABITATS*
HABITING
HABITUAL
HABITUDE s
HABITUES*
HACHURED*
HACHURES*
HACIENDA s
HACKABLE
HACKBUTS*
s HACKLERS*
HACKLIER
s HACKLING
HACKNEYS*
HACKSAWN*
HACKSAWS*
HACKWORK s
s HADDOCKS*
HADRONIC
HAEMATAL
HAEMATIC s
HAEMATIN s
HAEREDES
HAFNIUMS*
HAFTARAH*s
HAFTARAS*
HAFTAROT h
HAFTORAH s
HAFTOROS
HAFTOROT h
HAGADIST s
HAGBERRY
*HAGGADAH*s
HAGGADAS
*HAGGADIC
*HAGGADOT h
HAGGARDS*
HAGGISES
HAGGLERS*
HAGGLING
HAGRIDER*s
HAGRIDES*
HAHNIUMS*
HAIRBALL s
HAIRBAND s
HAIRCAPS*
HAIRCUTS*
*HAIRIEST
*HAIRLESS
*HAIRLIKE
*HAIRLINE s
HAIRLOCK s
HAIRNETS*
HAIRPINS*
HAIRWORK s
HAIRWORM s
HALACHAS*
HALACHIC
HALACHOT h
HALAKAHS*
HALAKHAH*s
HALAKHAS*
HALAKHIC
HALAKHOT h
HALAKIST s
HALAKOTH
HALALAHS*
*HALATION s
HALAVAHS*
HALAZONE s
HALBERDS*
HALBERTS*
HALCYONS*
HALENESS
HALFBACK s
HALFBEAK s
HALFLIFE
HALFNESS
HALFPIPE s
HALFTIME s
HALFTONE s
HALIBUTS*
HALIDOME*s
HALIDOMS*
HALLIARD s
HALLMARK s
HALLOAED
HALLOING
HALLOOED
s*HALLOWED
s HALLOWER s
HALLUCAL
HALLUCES
HALLWAYS*
HALOGENS*
HALOLIKE
HALTERED
HALTERES*
HALTLESS
c HALUTZIM
HALYARDS*
HAMARTIA s
HAMBONED*
HAMBONES
HAMBURGS*
HAMMADAS*
HAMMERED
HAMMERER s
HAMMIEST
HAMMOCKS*
HAMPERED
HAMPERER s
HAMSTERS*
HAMULATE
HAMULOSE
HAMULOUS
HANAPERS*
HANDAXES
HANDBAGS*
HANDBALL s
HANDBELL s
HANDBILL s
HANDBOOK s
HANDCARS*
HANDCART*s
HANDCLAP s
HANDCUFF s
HANDFAST s
HANDFULS*
HANDGRIP s
HANDGUNS*
HANDHELD s
HANDHOLD s
HANDICAP s
HANDIEST
c HANDLERS*
HANDLESS*
HANDLIKE
HANDLING s
HANDLIST s
HANDLOOM s
HANDMADE
HANDMAID s
HANDOFFS*
HANDOUTS*
HANDOVER s
HANDPICK s
HANDRAIL s
HANDSAWS*
HANDSELS*
HANDSETS*
HANDSEWN
HANDSFUL
HANDSOME r
HANDWORK s
HANDWRIT e
HANDYMAN
HANDYMEN
HANGABLE
HANGARED
HANGBIRD s
HANGDOGS*
HANGFIRE s
HANGINGS*
HANGNAIL s
HANGNEST s
HANGOUTS*
HANGOVER s
HANGTAGS*
HANKERED
HANKERER s
HANSELED
HANUMANS*
HAPHTARA hs
HAPKIDOS*
HAPLITES
HAPLOIDS*
HAPLOIDY*
HAPLONTS*
HAPLOPIA s
HAPLOSES
HAPLOSIS
HAPPENED
HAPPIEST
HAPTENES*
HAPTENIC
HAPTICAL
HARANGUE drs
HARASSED
HARASSER s
HARASSES
*HARBORED
HARBORER s
HARBOURS
HARDBACK s
HARDBALL s
HARDBOOT s
HARDCASE
HARDCORE s
HARDEDGE s
HARDENED
HARDENER s
HARDHACK s
HARDHATS*
HARDHEAD s
HARDIEST*
HARDLINE
HARDNESS
HARDNOSE s
HARDPACK s
HARDPANS*
HARDSHIP s
HARDTACK s
HARDTOPS*
HARDWARE s
HARDWIRE ds
HARDWOOD s
HAREBELL s
HARELIKE
HARELIPS*
HARIANAS*
HARICOTS*
HARIJANS*
HARISSAS*
HARKENED
HARKENER s
HARLOTRY
HARMINES*
c*HARMLESS
HARMONIC as
HARPINGS*
HARPISTS*
HARPOONS*
HARRIDAN s
HARRIERS*
*HARROWED
HARROWER s
HARRUMPH s
HARRYING
HARSHENS*
HARSHEST
HARSLETS*
HARUMPHS*
*HARUSPEX
HARVESTS*
HASHEESH
HASHHEAD s
HASSIUMS*
HASSLING
HASSOCKS*
HASTEFUL
c HASTENED
c HASTENER s
HASTIEST
HATBANDS*
HATBOXES
HATCHECK s
HATCHELS*
t HATCHERS*
HATCHERY*
HATCHETS*
t HATCHING s
HATCHWAY s
HATEABLE
HATMAKER s
HATRACKS*
HATTERIA s
HAUBERKS*
HAULAGES*
HAULIERS*
HAULMIER
HAULYARD s
HAUNCHED
HAUNCHES
c HAUNTERS*
c HAUNTING
HAUSFRAU s
HAUTBOIS
HAUTBOYS*
HAUTEURS
HAVARTIS*
HAVDALAH s
HAVELOCK s
HAVENING
HAVERELS*
HAVERING
HAVIOURS*
HAVOCKED
HAVOCKER s
HAWFINCH
HAWKBILL s
HAWKEYED
HAWKINGS*
HAWKLIKE
HAWKMOTH s
HAWKNOSE s
HAWKSHAW s
HAWKWEED s
HAWTHORN sy
HAYCOCKS*
HAYFIELD s
HAYFORKS*
HAYLAGES*
HAYLOFTS*
HAYMAKER s
HAYRACKS*
HAYRICKS*
HAYRIDES*
HAYSEEDS*
HAYSTACK s
HAYWARDS*
HAYWIRES*
HAZARDED
HAZARDER s
HAZELHEN s
HAZELNUT s
HAZINESS
c HAZZANIM
HEADACHE sy
HEADACHY
HEADBAND s
HEADENDS*
HEADFISH
HEADFULS*
HEADGATE s
HEADGEAR s
HEADHUNT s
HEADIEST
HEADINGS*
HEADLAMP s
HEADLAND s
HEADLESS
HEADLINE drs
HEADLOCK s
HEADLONG
HEADMOST
HEADNOTE s
HEADPINS*
HEADRACE s
HEADREST s
HEADROOM s
HEADSAIL s
HEADSETS*
HEADSHIP s
HEADSMAN
HEADSMEN
HEADSTAY s
HEADWAYS*
HEADWIND s
HEADWORD s
HEADWORK s
HEALABLE
HEARABLE
s*HEARINGS*
HEARKENS*
HEARSAYS*
HEARSING
HEARTENS*
HEARTIER
HEARTIES t
HEARTILY
HEARTING
c*HEATABLE
HEATEDLY
HEATHENS*
s HEATHERS*
HEATHERY*
HEATHIER
w HEATLESS
HEAVENLY
HEAVIEST*
HEAVYSET
HEBDOMAD s
HEBETATE ds
HEBETUDE s
HEBRAIZE ds
HECATOMB s
HECKLERS*
HECKLING
HECTARES*
HECTICAL
HECTICLY
HECTORED
HEDGEHOG s
HEDGEHOP s
HEDGEPIG s
HEDGEROW s
*HEDGIEST
HEDONICS*
HEDONISM s
HEDONIST s
HEEDLESS
HEEHAWED
HEELBALL s
w HEELINGS*
w HEELLESS
HEELPOST s
HEELTAPS*
HEFTIEST
HEGEMONS*
HEGEMONY*
HEGUMENE*s
HEGUMENS*
HEGUMENY*
HEIGHTEN s
HEIGHTHS
HEIRDOMS*
HEIRLESS
HEIRLOOM s
HEIRSHIP s
HEISTERS*
HEISTING
HEKTARES*
HELIACAL
HELIASTS*
HELICITY
HELICOID s
HELICONS*
HELICOPT s
HELILIFT s
HELIPADS*
HELIPORT s
HELISTOP s
HELLBENT
HELLCATS*
HELLERIS*
s HELLFIRE s
HELLHOLE s
HELLIONS*
HELLKITE s
HELLOING
HELMETED
HELMINTH s
HELMLESS
HELMSMAN
HELMSMEN
HELOTAGE s
HELOTISM s
HELPABLE
HELPINGS*
w HELPLESS
HELPMATE s
HELPMEET s
HEMAGOGS*
HEMATEIN s
t HEMATICS*
HEMATINE*s
HEMATINS*
HEMATITE s
HEMATOID
HEMATOMA s
HEMIOLAS*
HEMIOLIA s
HEMIPTER s
HEMLINES*
HEMLOCKS*
HEMOCOEL s
HEMOCYTE s
HEMOLYZE ds
c HEMOSTAT s
HEMPIEST
HEMPLIKE
HEMPSEED s
HEMPWEED s
HENBANES*
HENCHMAN
HENCHMEN
HENCOOPS*
HENEQUEN s
HENEQUIN s
HENHOUSE s
HENIQUEN s
HENNAING
HENPECKS*
HEPARINS*
HEPATICA*es
HEPATICS*
HEPATIZE ds
HEPATOMA s
HEPTAGON s
HEPTANES*
HEPTARCH sy
HEPTOSES*
HERALDED
HERALDIC
HERALDRY
HERBAGED*
HERBAGES*
HERBARIA l
HERBIEST
HERBLESS
HERBLIKE
HERCULES
HERDLIKE
HERDSMAN
HERDSMEN
HEREAWAY s
HEREDITY
tw HEREINTO
HERESIES
HERETICS*
HERETRIX
tw HEREUNTO
tw HEREUPON
tw HEREWITH
HERITAGE s
HERITORS*
HERITRIX
HERMAEAN
HERMETIC
HERMITIC
HERMITRY
HERNIATE ds
HEROICAL
HEROINES*
HEROISMS*
HEROIZED*
HEROIZES*
HERPETIC
HERRINGS*

w HERRYING
HERSTORY
HESITANT
HESITATE drs
HESSIANS*
HESSITES*
HETAERAE*
HETAERAS*
HETAERIC
HETAIRAI*
HETAIRAS*
HEXAGONS*
HEXAGRAM s
*HEXAMINE s
HEXAPLAR*
HEXAPLAS*
HEXAPODS*
HEXAPODY*
*HEXARCHY
HEXEREIS*
HEXOSANS*
HIATUSES
HIBACHIS*
HIBERNAL
HIBISCUS
HICCOUGH s
HICCUPED
HIDALGOS*
HIDDENLY
HIDEAWAY s
HIDELESS
HIDEOUTS*
HIDROSES
HIDROSIS
HIDROTIC s
HIERARCH sy
HIERATIC
HIERURGY
HIGGLERS*
HIGGLING
HIGHBALL s
HIGHBORN
HIGHBOYS*
HIGHBRED
HIGHBROW s
HIGHBUSH
HIGHJACK s
HIGHLAND s
HIGHLIFE s
HIGHNESS
HIGHRISE s
HIGHROAD s
HIGHSPOT s
HIGHTAIL s
HIGHTING
HIGHTOPS*
HIGHWAYS*
HIJACKED
HIJACKER s
HILARITY
HILDINGS*
c HILLIEST
HILLOAED
HILLOCKS*
HILLOCKY*
HILLOING
HILLSIDE s
HILLTOPS*
HILTLESS
HIMATION s
HINDERED
HINDERER s
HINDGUTS*
HINDMOST
c*HINKIEST
sw HINNYING
HIPBONES*
HIPLINES*
HIPPARCH s
cw HIPPIEST*
HIPSTERS*
HIRAGANA s
HIREABLE
HIRELING s
HIRPLING
HIRSELED
HIRSLING
HIRUDINS*
HISSIEST*
HISSINGS*
HISTAMIN es
HISTIDIN es
HISTOGEN s
HISTONES*
a HISTORIC
HITCHERS*

*HITCHING
t HITHERTO
HITTABLE
HIVELESS
HIZZONER s
HOACTZIN s
HOARDERS*
HOARDING s
HOARIEST
HOARSELY
HOARSENS*
HOARSEST
HOATZINS*
HOBBLERS*
HOBBLING
HOBBYIST s
HOBNAILS*
HOBOISMS*
HOCKSHOP s
HOCUSING
HOCUSSED
HOCUSSES
HOECAKES*
HOEDOWNS*
HOGBACKS*
HOGMANAY s
HOGMANES*
HOGMENAY s
HOGNOSES*
HOGSHEAD s
HOGTYING
HOGWEEDS*
HOICKING
HOIDENED
HOISTERS*
HOISTING
HOKINESS
HOKYPOKY
HOLDABLE
HOLDALLS*
HOLDBACK s
HOLDDOWN s
HOLDFAST s
HOLDINGS*
HOLDOUTS*
HOLDOVER s
HOLELESS
HOLIBUTS*
HOLIDAYS*
HOLINESS
w HOLISTIC
HOLLAING
HOLLANDS*
HOLLERED
HOLLOAED
HOLLOING
HOLLOOED
HOLLOWED
HOLLOWER
HOLLOWLY
HOLMIUMS*
HOLOCENE
HOLOGAMY
HOLOGRAM s
HOLOGYNY
HOLOTYPE s
HOLOZOIC
HOLSTEIN s
HOLSTERS*
HOLYDAYS*
HOLYTIDE s
HOMAGERS*
HOMAGING
HOMBURGS*
HOMEBODY
HOMEBOYS*
HOMEBRED s
HOMEBREW s
HOMEGIRL s
HOMELAND s
HOMELESS
HOMELIER
HOMELIKE
HOMEMADE
HOMEOBOX
HOMEOTIC
HOMEPAGE s
HOMEPORT s
HOMERING
HOMEROOM s
HOMESICK
HOMESITE s
HOMESPUN s
HOMESTAY s
HOMETOWN s
HOMEWARD s

HOMEWORK s
HOMICIDE s
HOMILIES
HOMILIST s
HOMINESS*
HOMINIAN s
HOMINIDS*
HOMINIES
HOMININE
HOMINIZE ds
HOMINOID s
HOMMOCKS*
HOMMOSES
HOMOGAMY
HOMOGENY
HOMOGONY
HOMOLOGS*
HOMOLOGY*
HOMONYMS*
HOMONYMY*
HONCHOED
HONDLING
HONESTER
HONESTLY
HONEWORT s
HONEYBEE s
HONEYBUN s
HONEYDEW s
HONEYFUL
p HONEYING
HONEYPOT s
HONGIING
HONORAND s
HONORARY
HONOREES*
HONORERS*
HONORING
HONOURED
HONOURER s
HOOCHIES*
HOODIEST*
HOODLESS
HOODLIKE
HOODLUMS*
HOODMOLD s
HOODOOED
HOODWINK s
HOOFBEAT s
HOOFLESS
HOOFLIKE
HOOKIEST*
HOOKLESS
HOOKLETS*
HOOKLIKE
HOOKNOSE ds
HOOKWORM s
HOOLIGAN s
HOOPLESS
HOOPLIKE
HOOPSTER s
HOORAHED
HOORAYED
HOOSEGOW s
HOOSGOWS*
HOOTCHES
HOOTIEST
HOOVERED
HOPEFULS*
HOPELESS
HOPHEADS*
HOPINGLY
HOPLITES*
HOPLITIC
c HOPPIEST
s HOPPINGS*
HOPPLING
HOPSACKS*
HOPTOADS*
HORDEINS*
HORDEOLA
HORIZONS*
HORMONAL
HORMONES*
HORMONIC
HORNBEAM s
HORNBILL s
HORNBOOK s
HORNFELS
t HORNIEST
HORNINGS*
HORNISTS*
HORNITOS*
t HORNLESS
t HORNLIKE
HORNPIPE s
HORNPOUT s

HORNTAIL s
HORNWORM s
HORNWORT s
HOROLOGE rs
*HOROLOGY
HORRIBLE s
HORRIBLY
HORRIDER
HORRIDLY
HORRIFIC
HORSECAR s
HORSEFLY
HORSEMAN
HORSEMEN
HORSEPOX
HORSIEST
HOSANNAH*s
HOSANNAS*
HOSELIKE
HOSEPIPE s
HOSEYING
HOSPICES*
HOSPITAL s
HOSPITIA
HOSPODAR s
HOSTAGES*
HOSTELED
HOSTELER s
HOSTELRY
HOSTILES*
HOSTLERS
HOTBLOOD s
HOTBOXES
HOTCAKES*
HOTCHING
HOTCHPOT s
HOTELDOM s
HOTELIER s
HOTELMAN
HOTELMEN
HOTFOOTS*
HOTHEADS*
HOTHOUSE ds
HOTLINES*
HOTLINKS*
HOTPRESS
HOTSHOTS*
HOTSPOTS*
HOTSPURS*
HOUNDERS*
HOUNDING
HOURLIES
HOURLONG
HOUSEBOY s
HOUSEFLY
HOUSEFUL s
HOUSELED
HOUSEMAN
HOUSEMEN
HOUSESAT
HOUSESIT s
HOUSETOP s
HOUSINGS*
s HOVELING
s HOVELLED
HOVERERS*
*HOVERFLY
*HOVERING
HOWDYING
HOWITZER s
HOYDENED
HRYVNIAS*
HUARACHE s
HUARACHO s
HUBRISES
HUCKSTER s
HUDDLERS*
HUDDLING
c HUFFIEST
HUGENESS
HUGGABLE
HUIPILES
HUISACHE s
HULKIEST
HULLOAED
HULLOING
HULLOOED
HUMANELY
HUMANEST
HUMANISE ds
HUMANISM s
HUMANIST s
HUMANITY
HUMANIZE drs
HUMANOID s
HUMBLERS*

HUMBLEST*
HUMBLING
HUMDRUMS*
HUMERALS*
HUMIDIFY
HUMIDITY
HUMIDORS*
HUMIFIED
HUMILITY
HUMITURE s
HUMMABLE
HUMMOCKS*
HUMMOCKY*
HUMMUSES
HUMORFUL
HUMORING
HUMORIST s
HUMOROUS
HUMOURED
HUMPBACK s
HUMPHING
HUMPIEST
HUMPLESS
HUNCHING
HUNDREDS*
HUNGERED
HUNGOVER
HUNGRIER
HUNGRILY
HUNKERED
c HUNKIEST
HUNTABLE
HUNTEDLY
HUNTINGS*
HUNTRESS
HUNTSMAN
HUNTSMEN
HURDLERS*
HURDLING
HURLINGS*
HURRAHED
HURRAYED
HURRIERS*
HURRYING
HURTLESS*
HURTLING
HUSBANDS*
HUSHEDLY
HUSKIEST*
HUSKINGS*
HUSKLIKE
HUSTINGS
HUSTLERS*
HUSTLING
HUSWIFES*
HUSWIVES
HUTCHING
HUTMENTS*
c HUTZPAHS*
HUZZAHED
HUZZAING
HYACINTH s
HYALINES*
HYALITES*
HYALOGEN s
HYALOIDS*
HYBRISES
HYDATIDS*
HYDRACID s
HYDRAGOG s
HYDRANTH*s
HYDRANTS*
HYDRASES*
HYDRATED*
HYDRATES*
HYDRATOR s
HYDRIDES*
HYDRILLA s
HYDROGEL s
HYDROGEN s
HYDROIDS*
HYDROMEL s
HYDRONIC
HYDROPIC
HYDROPSY*
HYDROSKI s
HYDROSOL s
HYDROXYL*s
HYGEISTS*
HYGIEIST s
HYGIENES*
HYGIENIC s
HYLOZOIC
HYMENEAL s
HYMENIAL*
HYMENIUM s

HYMNBOOK s
HYMNISTS*
HYMNLESS
HYMNLIKE
HYOIDEAN
HYOSCINE s
HYPERGOL s
HYPERONS*
HYPEROPE s
HYPHEMIA s
HYPHENED
HYPHENIC
HYPNOSES
HYPNOSIS
HYPNOTIC s
HYPOACID
HYPODERM as
HYPOGEAL*
HYPOGEAN*
HYPOGENE
HYPOGEUM
HYPOGYNY
HYPONEAS*
HYPONOIA s
HYPONYMS*
HYPONYMY*
HYPOPNEA s
HYPOPYON s
HYPOTHEC s
HYPOXIAS*
HYRACOID s
HYSTERIA s
HYSTERIC s
IAMBUSES
IATRICAL
IBOGAINE s
ICEBERGS*
ICEBLINK s
ICEBOATS*
ICEBOUND
ICEBOXES
ICEFALLS*
ICEHOUSE s
ICEKHANA s
ICEMAKER s
ICHNITES*
ICHOROUS
ICHTHYIC
p ICKINESS
*ICONICAL
ICTERICS*
IDEALESS
IDEALISE ds
IDEALISM s
IDEALIST s
IDEALITY
IDEALIZE drs
IDEALOGY
IDEATING
IDEATION s
IDEATIVE
IDENTIFY
IDENTITY
IDEOGRAM s
IDEOLOGY
IDIOCIES
IDIOLECT s
IDIOTISM s
IDIOTYPE s
IDLENESS
IDLESSES*
IDOCRASE s
IDOLATER s
IDOLATOR s
IDOLATRY
IDOLISED*
IDOLISER*s
IDOLISES*
IDOLISMS*
IDOLIZED*
IDOLIZER*s
IDOLIZES*
IDONEITY
IDONEOUS
IDYLISTS*
IDYLLIST s
m IFFINESS
IGNATIAS*
dls IGNIFIED
dls IGNIFIES
IGNITERS*
IGNITING
IGNITION s
IGNITORS*
IGNITRON s
IGNOMINY

IGNORAMI
IGNORANT
IGNORERS*
IGNORING
IGUANIAN s
IGUANIDS*
IKEBANAS*
ILLATION s
ILLATIVE s
ILLEGALS*
ILLINIUM s
ILLIQUID
ILLOGICS*
ILLUDING
ILLUMINE ds
ILLUMING
ILLUSION s
ILLUSIVE
ILLUSORY
ILLUVIAL*
ILLUVIUM s
ILMENITE s
IMAGINAL
IMAGINED*
IMAGINER*s
IMAGINES*
IMAGINGS*
IMAGISMS*
IMAGISTS*
IMAMATES*
IMBALMED
IMBALMER s
IMBARKED
IMBECILE s
IMBEDDED
IMBIBERS*
IMBIBING
IMBITTER s
IMBLAZED*
IMBLAZES*
IMBODIED
IMBODIES
IMBOLDEN s
IMBOSOMS*
IMBOWERS*
IMBROWNS*
IMBRUING
IMBRUTED*
IMBRUTES*
l IMITABLE
IMITATED*
IMITATES*
IMITATOR s
IMMANENT
IMMATURE s
IMMENSER*
IMMERGED*
IMMERGES*
IMMERSED*
IMMERSES*
IMMESHED
IMMESHES
IMMINENT
IMMINGLE ds
IMMIXING
IMMOBILE
IMMODEST y
IMMOLATE ds
IMMORTAL s
IMMOTILE
IMMUNISE ds
IMMUNITY
IMMUNIZE drs
IMMURING
IMPACTED
IMPACTER s
IMPACTOR s
IMPAINTS*
IMPAIRED
IMPAIRER s
IMPALERS*
IMPALING
IMPANELS*
IMPARITY
IMPARKED
IMPARTED
IMPARTER s
IMPASSES*
IMPASTED*
IMPASTES*
IMPASTOS*
IMPAWNED
IMPEARLS*
IMPEDERS*
IMPEDING
IMPELLED

IMPELLER s
IMPELLOR s
IMPENDED
IMPERIAL*s
IMPERILS*
IMPERIUM s
IMPETIGO s
IMPINGED*
IMPINGER*s
IMPINGES*
IMPISHLY
IMPLANTS*
IMPLEADS*
IMPLEDGE ds
IMPLICIT
IMPLODED*
IMPLODES*
IMPLORED*
IMPLORER*s
IMPLORES*
IMPLYING
IMPOLICY
IMPOLITE
IMPONING
IMPOROUS
IMPORTED
IMPORTER s
IMPOSERS*
IMPOSING
IMPOSTED
IMPOSTER s
IMPOSTOR s
IMPOTENT s
IMPOUNDS*
IMPOWERS*
IMPREGNS*
IMPRESAS*
IMPRESES*
IMPRESTS*
IMPRIMIS
IMPRINTS*
IMPRISON s
IMPROPER
IMPROVED*
IMPROVER*s
IMPROVES*
IMPUDENT
IMPUGNED
IMPUGNER s
IMPULSED*
IMPULSES*
IMPUNITY
IMPURELY
IMPUREST
IMPURITY
IMPUTERS*
IMPUTING
INACTION s
INACTIVE
INARABLE
INARCHED
INARCHES
INARMING
INBEINGS*
INBOARDS*
INBOUNDS*
INBREEDS*
INBURSTS*
INCAGING
INCANTED
INCASING
INCENSED*
INCENSES*
INCENTED
INCENTER s
INCEPTED
INCEPTOR s
INCHMEAL
INCHOATE
INCHWORM s
INCIDENT s
INCIPITS*
INCISING
INCISION s
INCISIVE
INCISORS*
INCISORY*
INCISURE s
INCITANT s
INCITERS*
INCITING
INCLASPS*
INCLINED*
INCLINER*s
INCLINES*
INCLOSED*
INCLOSER*s
INCLOSES*
INCLUDED*
INCLUDES*
INCOMERS*
INCOMING s
INCONNUS*
INCORPSE ds
INCREASE drs
INCREATE
INCRUSTS*
INCUBATE ds
INCUDATE
INCUMBER s
INCURRED
INCURVED*
INCURVES*
INCUSING
INDAGATE ds
INDAMINE*s
INDAMINS*
INDEBTED
INDECENT
INDENTED
INDENTER s
INDENTOR s
INDEVOUT
INDEXERS*
INDEXING s
INDICANS*
INDICANT*s
v INDICATE ds
INDICIAS*
INDICIUM s
INDICTED
INDICTEE s
INDICTER s
INDICTOR s
INDIGENE*s
INDIGENS*
INDIGENT*s
INDIGNLY
INDIGOES
INDIGOID s
INDIRECT
INDITERS*
INDITING
INDOCILE
INDOLENT
INDORSED*
INDORSEE*s
INDORSER*s
INDORSES*
INDORSOR s
w INDOWING
INDOXYLS*
INDRAFTS*
INDUCERS*
INDUCING
INDUCTED
INDUCTEE s
INDUCTOR s
INDULGED*
INDULGER*s
INDULGES*
INDULINE*s
INDULINS*
INDURATE ds
INDUSIAL*
INDUSIUM
INDUSTRY
INDWELLS*
INEARTHS*
INEDIBLE
INEDIBLY
INEDITED
INEQUITY
INERRANT
INERTIAE*
INERTIAL*
INERTIAS*
INEXPERT s
INFAMIES
INFAMOUS
INFANTAS*
INFANTES*
INFANTRY
INFARCTS*
INFAUNAE*
INFAUNAL*
INFAUNAS*
INFECTED
INFECTER s
INFECTOR s
INFECUND
INFEOFFS*
INFERIOR s
INFERNAL
INFERNOS*
INFERRED
INFERRER s
INFESTED
INFESTER s
INFIDELS*
INFIELDS*
INFIGHTS*
INFINITE s
INFINITY
INFIRMED
INFIRMLY
INFIXING
INFIXION s
INFLAMED*
INFLAMER*s
INFLAMES*
INFLATED*
INFLATER*s
INFLATES*
INFLATOR s
INFLECTS*
INFLEXED
INFLICTS*
INFLIGHT
INFLUENT s
INFLUXES
INFOBAHN s
p INFOLDED
INFOLDER s
INFORMAL
INFORMED
INFORMER s
INFOUGHT
INFRACTS*
INFRARED s
INFRINGE drs
INFRUGAL
INFUSERS*
INFUSING
INFUSION s
INFUSIVE
INGATHER s
INGENUES*
INGESTED
INGOTING
INGRAFTS*
INGRAINS*
INGRATES*
INGROUND
INGROUPS*
INGROWTH s
INGUINAL
INGULFED
INHABITS*
INHALANT s
INHALERS*
INHALING
INHAULER s
INHERENT
INHERING
INHERITS*
INHESION s
INHIBINS*
INHIBITS*
INHOLDER s
INHUMANE*
INHUMERS*
INHUMING
INIMICAL
INIQUITY
INITIALS*
INITIATE ds
INJECTED
INJECTOR s
INJURERS*
INJURIES
INJURING
INKBERRY
INKBLOTS*
INKHORNS*
k INKINESS
t INKLINGS*
INKSTAND s
INKSTONE s
INKWELLS*
INKWOODS*
INLACING
INLANDER s
INLAYERS*
INLAYING
INMESHED
INMESHES
p INNATELY
INNERVED*
INNERVES*
INNOCENT s
INNOVATE ds
INNUENDO s
INOCULUM s
INOSINES*
INOSITES*
INOSITOL s
INPOURED
INPUTTED
INPUTTER s
INQUESTS*
INQUIETS*
INQUIRED*
INQUIRER*s
INQUIRES*
INRUSHES
INSANELY
INSANEST
INSANITY
INSCAPES*
INSCRIBE drs
INSCROLL s
INSCULPS*
INSECTAN
INSECURE
INSERTED
INSERTER s
INSETTED
p INSETTER s
INSHEATH es
INSHRINE ds
INSIDERS*
INSIGHTS*
INSIGNIA s
INSISTED
INSISTER s
INSNARED*
INSNARER*s
INSNARES*
INSOLATE ds
INSOLENT s
INSOMNIA cs
INSOMUCH
INSOULED
INSPECTS*
INSPHERE ds
INSPIRED*
INSPIRER*s
INSPIRES*
INSPIRIT s
INSTABLE
INSTALLS*
INSTANCE ds
INSTANCY
INSTANTS*
INSTATED*
INSTATES*
INSTILLS*
INSTINCT s
INSTROKE s
INSTRUCT s
INSULANT s
INSULARS*
INSULATE ds
INSULINS*
INSULTED
INSULTER s
INSURANT s
INSUREDS*
INSURERS*
INSURING
INSWATHE ds
INTACTLY
INTAGLIO*s
INTARSIA s
INTEGERS*
INTEGRAL s
INTENDED s
INTENDER s
INTENSER*
INTENTLY
INTERACT s
INTERAGE
INTERBED s
INTERCOM s
INTERCUT s
INTEREST s
INTERIMS*
INTERIOR s
INTERLAP s
INTERLAY s
INTERMAT s
INTERMIT s
INTERMIX
INTERNAL s
INTERNED*
INTERNEE*s
INTERNES*
INTERRED
INTERREX
INTERROW
INTERSEX
INTERTIE s
INTERVAL es
INTERWAR
INTHRALL*s
INTHRALS*
INTHRONE ds
INTIFADA hs
INTIMACY
INTIMATE drs
INTIMIST s
INTITLED*
INTITLES*
INTITULE ds
INTOMBED
INTONATE ds
INTONERS*
INTONING
INTORTED
INTRADAY
INTRADOS
INTRANET s
INTRANTS*
INTREATS*
INTRENCH
INTREPID
INTRIGUE drs
INTROITS*
INTROMIT s
INTRORSE
INTRUDED*
INTRUDER*s
INTRUDES*
INTRUSTS*
INTUBATE ds
INTUITED
INTURNED
INTWINED*
INTWINES*
INTWISTS*
INULASES*
INUNDANT
INUNDATE ds
INURBANE
INURNING
INVADERS*
INVADING
INVALIDS*
INVASION s
INVASIVE
INVECTED
INVEIGHS*
INVEIGLE drs
INVENTED
INVENTER s
INVENTOR sy
INVERITY
INVERSED*
INVERSES*
INVERTED
INVERTER s
INVERTIN gs
INVERTOR s
INVESTED
INVESTOR s
INVIABLE
INVIABLY
INVIRILE
INVISCID
INVITEES*
INVITERS*
INVITING
INVOCATE ds
INVOICED*
INVOICES*
INVOKERS*
INVOKING
INVOLUTE ds
INVOLVED*
INVOLVER*s
INVOLVES*
INWALLED
INWARDLY
INWEAVED*
INWEAVES*
IODATING
IODATION s
IODINATE ds
IODISING
IODIZERS*
IODIZING
IODOFORM s
IODOPHOR s
IODOPSIN s
IONICITY
l IONISING
l IONIZERS*
l IONIZING
IONOGENS*
IONOMERS*
IOTACISM s
IPOMOEAS*
d IREFULLY
e IRENICAL
IRIDIUMS*
IRITISES
IRONBARK s
IRONCLAD s
IRONICAL
IRONINGS*
IRONISTS*
IRONIZED*
IRONIZES*
IRONLIKE
IRONNESS
IRONSIDE s
IRONWARE s
IRONWEED s
IRONWOOD s
IRONWORK s
IRRIGATE ds
IRRITANT s
IRRITATE ds
IRRUPTED
ISAGOGES*
ISAGOGIC s
ISARITHM s
ISATINES*
ISATINIC
ISCHEMIA s
ISCHEMIC
ISLANDED
*ISLANDER s
ISLELESS
ISOBARES*
ISOBARIC
ISOBATHS*
ISOBUTYL s
ISOCHEIM s
ISOCHIME s
ISOCHORE*s
ISOCHORS*
ISOCHRON es
ISOCLINE s
ISOCRACY
ISOFORMS*
ISOGENIC
ISOGLOSS
ISOGONAL s
ISOGONES*
ISOGONIC s
ISOGRAFT s
ISOGRAMS*
ISOGRAPH s
ISOGRIVS*
ISOHYETS*
ISOLABLE
ISOLATED
ISOLATES
ISOLATOR s
ISOLEADS*
ISOLINES*
ISOLOGUE s
ISOMERIC
ISOMETRY
ISOMORPH s
ISONOMIC
ISOPACHS*
ISOPHOTE s
ISOPLETH s
ISOPODAN s
ISOPRENE s
ISOSPINS*
ISOSPORY
ISOSTACY
ISOSTASY
ISOTACHS*
ISOTHERE s
ISOTHERM s
ISOTONES*
ISOTONIC
ISOTOPES*
ISOTOPIC
ISOTROPY
ISOTYPES*
ISOTYPIC
ISOZYMES*
ISOZYMIC
ISSUABLE
ISSUABLY
ISSUANCE s
ISTHMIAN s
ISTHMOID
bpw ITCHIEST
w ITCHINGS*
ITEMISED*
ITEMISES*
ITEMIZED*
ITEMIZER*s
ITEMIZES*
ITERANCE s
ITERATED*
l ITERATES*
JABBERED
JABBERER s
JACAMARS*
JACINTHE*s
JACINTHS*
JACKAROO s
JACKBOOT s
JACKDAWS*
JACKEROO s
JACKETED
JACKFISH
JACKLEGS*
JACKPOTS*
JACKROLL s
JACKSTAY s
JACOBINS*
JACONETS*
JACQUARD s
e JACULATE ds
JACUZZIS*
JADEITES*
JADELIKE
JADISHLY
JAGGEDER
JAGGEDLY
JAGGHERY
JAGGIEST*
JAILABLE
JAILBAIT
JAILBIRD s
JALAPENO s
JALAPINS*
JALOPIES
JALOUSIE ds
JAMBEAUX*
JAMBOREE s
JAMMABLE
JAMMIEST*
JANGLERS
JANGLIER
*JANGLING
JANIFORM
JANISARY
JANITORS*
JANIZARY
JAPANIZE ds
JAPANNED
JAPANNER s
*JAPERIES
JAPINGLY
JAPONICA s
JARGONED
JARGONEL s
JARGOONS*
JARHEADS*
JARLDOMS*
JAROSITE s
JAROVIZE ds
JASMINES*
JAUNCING
JAUNDICE ds
JAUNTIER
JAUNTILY
JAUNTING
JAVELINA*s
JAVELINS*
JAWBONED*
JAWBONER*s
JAWBONES*
JAWLINES*
JAYBIRDS*
JAYWALKS*
JAZZIEST
JAZZLIKE
JEALOUSY*
JEEPNEYS*
JEJUNELY
JEJUNITY

d JELLABAS*
JELLYING
JELUTONG s
JEMADARS*
JEMIDARS*
JEMMYING
JEOPARDS*
JEOPARDY*
JEREMIAD s
JERKIEST*
JEROBOAM s
JERREEDS*
JERRICAN s
JERRYCAN s
JERSEYED
JESTINGS*
JETBEADS*
JETFOILS*
JETLINER s
JETPORTS*
JETTIEST*
JETTISON s
JETTYING
JEWELERS*
JEWELING
JEWELLED
JEWELLER sy
JEZEBELS*
JIBBOOMS*
JIBINGLY
JIGGERED
JIGGIEST
JIGGLIER
JIGGLING
JIGSAWED
JILLIONS*
JIMMYING
JINGALLS*
JINGKOES
JINGLERS*
JINGLIER
JINGLING
JINGOISH
JINGOISM s
JINGOIST s
JIPIJAPA s
JITTERED
JIUJITSU s
JIUJUTSU s
JOBNAMES*
JOCKETTE s
JOCKEYED
JOCOSELY
JOCOSITY
JOCUNDLY
JODHPURS*
JOGGINGS*
JOGGLERS*
JOGGLING
JOHANNES
JOHNBOAT s
JOHNNIES*
JOINABLE
JOINDERS*
JOININGS*
JOINTERS*
JOINTING
JOINTURE ds
JOISTING
JOKESTER s
JOKINESS
JOKINGLY
JOLLIERS*
JOLLIEST*
JOLLYING
JOLTIEST
JONESING
JONGLEUR s
JONQUILS*
JOSTLERS
JOSTLING
JOTTINGS*
JOUNCIER
JOUNCING
JOURNALS*
JOURNEYS*
JOUSTERS
*JOUSTING
JOVIALLY
JOVIALTY
JOWLIEST
JOYANCES*
JOYFULLY
JOYOUSLY
JOYRIDER*s
JOYRIDES*
JOYSTICK s
JUBILANT
JUBILATE ds
JUBILEES*
JUDDERED
JUDGMENT s
JUDICIAL
JUDOISTS*
JUGGLERS*
JUGGLERY*
JUGGLING s
JUGHEADS*
JUGULARS*
JUGULATE ds
JUICIEST
JUJITSUS*
JUJUISMS*
JUJUISTS*
JUJUTSUS*
JULIENNE ds
JUMBLERS*
JUMBLING
JUMBUCKS*
JUMPABLE
JUMPIEST
JUMPOFFS*
JUMPSUIT s
*JUNCTION s
JUNCTURE s
JUNGLIER
JUNIPERS*
JUNKETED
JUNKETER s
JUNKIEST*
JUNKYARD s
JURASSIC
JURATORY
JURISTIC
JURYLESS
JUSSIVES*
JUSTICES*
JUSTLING
JUSTNESS
JUTELIKE
JUTTYING
JUVENALS*
JUVENILE s
KABALISM s
KABALIST s
KABBALAH*s
KABBALAS*
KABELJOU s
KACHINAS*
KAFFIYAH s
KAFFIYEH s
KAILYARD s
KAINITES*
KAISERIN s
KAJEPUTS*
KAKEMONO s
KAKIEMON s
KALAMATA s
*KALEWIFE
KALEYARD s
KALIFATE s
KALIMBAS*
KALLIDIN s
KALYPTRA s
KAMAAINA s
KAMACITE s
KAMIKAZE s
KAMPONGS*
KAMSEENS*
KANGAROO s
KANTELES*
KAOLIANG s
KAOLINES*
KAOLINIC
KARAKULS*
KARAOKES*
KAROSSES
KARTINGS*
KARYOTIN s
KASHERED
KASHMIRS*
KASHRUTH*s
KASHRUTS*
KATAKANA s
KATCHINA s
KATCINAS*
KATHODAL
KATHODES*
KATHODIC
KATSURAS*
KATYDIDS*
KAVAKAVA s
KAVASSES
KAYAKERS*
KAYAKING s
KAZACHKI
KAZACHOK
KAZATSKI
KAZATSKY
KEBBOCKS*
KEBBUCKS*
KECKLING
KEDGEREE s
KEELAGES*
KEELBOAT s
KEELHALE ds
KEELHAUL s
KEELLESS
KEELSONS*
KEENNESS
KEEPABLE
KEEPINGS*
KEEPSAKE s
KEESHOND s
KEESTERS*
KEFFIYAH s
KEFFIYEH s
KEGELERS*
KEGLINGS*
KEIRETSU s
KEISTERS*
KEITLOAS*
KELOIDAL
KENNELED
KENNINGS*
KENOTRON s
KEPHALIN s
KERAMICS*
KERATINS*
KERATOID
KERATOMA s
KERATOSE s
KERCHIEF s
KERMESSE*s
KERMISES
KERNELED
KERNELLY
KERNITES*
KEROGENS*
KEROSENE s
KEROSINE s
KERPLUNK s
KERYGMAS*
KESTRELS*
*KETAMINE s
KETCHUPS*
KEYBOARD s
KEYCARDS*
KEYHOLES*
KEYNOTED*
KEYNOTER*s
KEYNOTES*
KEYPUNCH
KEYSTERS*
KEYSTONE s
KEYWORDS*
KHADDARS*
KHALIFAS*
KHAMSEEN s
KHAMSINS*
KHANATES*
KHAZENIM
KHEDIVAL
KHEDIVES*
KHIRKAHS*
KIBBLING
KIBITZED
KIBITZER s
KIBITZES
KIBOSHED
KIBOSHES
KICKABLE
KICKBACK s
KICKBALL s
*KICKIEST
KICKOFFS*
KICKSHAW s
KIDNAPED
KIDNAPEE s
KIDNAPER s
KIDSKINS*
KIELBASA s
KIELBASI
KIELBASY
KIESTERS*
KILLABLE
KILLDEER*s
KILLDEES*
KILLICKS*
s KILLINGS*
KILLJOYS*
KILLOCKS*
KILOBARS*
KILOBASE s
KILOBAUD s
KILOBITS*
KILOBYTE s
KILOGRAM s
KILOMOLE s
KILORADS*
KILOTONS*
KILOVOLT s
KILOWATT s
KILTINGS*
KILTLIKE
KIMCHEES*
KIMONOED
KINDLERS*
KINDLESS*
KINDLIER
KINDLING s
KINDNESS
KINDREDS*
KINESICS*
KINETICS*
KINETINS*
KINFOLKS*
KINGBIRD s
KINGBOLT s
KINGCUPS*
KINGDOMS*
KINGFISH
KINGHOOD s
KINGLESS
KINGLETS*
KINGLIER
KINGLIKE
KINGPINS*
KINGPOST s
KINGSHIP s
KINGSIDE s
KINGWOOD s
KINKAJOU s
*KINKIEST
KINSFOLK
KINSHIPS*
s KIPPERED
KIPPERER s
KIPSKINS*
KIRIGAMI s
KIRSCHES
KISMETIC
KISSABLE
KISSABLY
KISTFULS*
KITCHENS*
KITELIKE
KITHARAS*
KITLINGS*
KITSCHES
KITTENED
KITTLEST*
KITTLING
*KLATCHES
KLAVERNS*
KLEAGLES*
KLEPHTIC
KLEZMERS*
KLISTERS
KLONDIKE s
KLUDGIER
KLUDGING
KLUTZIER
KLYSTRON s
KNACKERS*
KNACKERY*
KNACKING
KNAPPERS
*KNAPPING
KNAPSACK s
KNAPWEED s
KNEADERS*
KNEADING
KNEECAPS*
KNEEHOLE s
KNEELERS*
KNEELING
KNEEPADS*
KNEEPANS*
KNEESIES
KNEESOCK s
KNELLING
KNESSETS*
*KNICKERS
KNIGHTED
*KNIGHTLY
KNITTERS*
KNITTING s
KNITWEAR
*KNOBBIER
KNOBLIKE
KNOCKERS*
*KNOCKING
KNOCKOFF s
KNOCKOUT s
KNOLLERS*
KNOLLING
KNOTHOLE s
KNOTLESS
KNOTLIKE
KNOTTERS*
KNOTTIER
KNOTTILY
KNOTTING s
KNOTWEED s
KNOUTING
KNOWABLE
KNOWINGS*
*KNUBBIER
KNUCKLED*
KNUCKLER*s
KNUCKLES*
KNURLIER
*KNURLING
KOHLRABI
KOKANEES*
KOLBASIS*
KOLBASSI s
KOLHOZES
KOLINSKI
KOLINSKY
KOLKHOSY*
KOLKHOZY*
KOLKOZES
KOMATIKS*
KOMONDOR s
KOOKIEST
KOPIYKAS*
KOSHERED
KOTOWERS*
KOTOWING
KOUMISES
KOUMYSES
KOUPREYS*
KOWTOWED
KOWTOWER s
KRAALING
KREMLINS*
KREPLACH
KREPLECH
KREUTZER s
KREUZERS*
KRIMMERS
KRULLERS*
KRUMHORN s
KRUMKAKE s
KRYOLITE s
KRYOLITH s
KRYPTONS*
KUMISSES
KUMQUATS*
KUNZITES*
KURTOSES
KURTOSIS
KUVASZOK
KVELLING
KVETCHED
KVETCHER s
*KVETCHES
KYANISED*
KYANISES*
KYANITES*
KYANIZED*
KYANIZES*
KYBOSHED
KYBOSHES
KYMOGRAM s
KYPHOSES
KYPHOSIS
KYPHOTIC
LAAGERED
LABARUMS*
LABDANUM s
LABELERS*
LABELING
LABELLED
LABELLER s
f LABELLUM
LABIALLY
LABIATED*
LABIATES*
*LABILITY
LABORERS*
LABORING
LABORITE s
LABOURED
LABOURER s
LABRADOR s
LABROIDS*
LABRUSCA
LABURNUM s
p LACELESS
LACELIKE
*LACERATE ds
LACERTID s
LACEWING s
LACEWOOD s
LACEWORK s
LACINESS
a LACKADAY
LACKERED
LACKEYED
LACONISM s
LACQUERS*
LACQUEYS*
LACRIMAL s
LACROSSE s
LACTASES*
LACTATED*
LACTATES*
LACTEALS*
LACTEOUS
LACTONES*
LACTONIC
LACTOSES*
LACUNARS*
LACUNARY*
LACUNATE
LACUNOSE
LADANUMS*
LADDERED
LADENING
LADHOODS*
LADLEFUL s
LADRONES*
LADYBIRD s
LADYBUGS*
LADYFISH
LADYHOOD s
LADYKINS*
LADYLIKE
LADYLOVE s
LADYPALM s
LADYSHIP s
LAETRILE s
LAGERING
LAGGARDS*
bf LAGGINGS*
LAGNAPPE s
LAGOONAL
LAICALLY
LAICISED*
LAICISES*
LAICISMS*
LAICIZED*
LAICIZES*
LAITANCE s
LAKEBEDS*
LAKELIKE
LAKEPORT s
LAKESIDE s
LALIQUES*
LALLANDS*
LALLYGAG s
LAMASERY
LAMBADAS*
LAMBASTE*ds
LAMBASTS*
LAMBDOID
LAMBENCY
LAMBERTS*
LAMBIEST*
LAMBKILL s
LAMBKINS*
LAMBLIKE
LAMBSKIN s
LAMELLAE*
LAMELLAR*
LAMELLAS*
LAMENESS
LAMENTED
LAMENTER s
LAMINALS*
LAMINARY*
LAMINATE ds
LAMININS*
LAMINOSE
LAMINOUS
LAMISTER s
LAMPASES
LAMPIONS*
LAMPOONS*
LAMPPOST s
LAMPREYS*
LAMPYRID s
LAMSTERS*
LANCELET s
LANCETED
LANCIERS
LANDFALL s
LANDFILL s
LANDFORM s
LANDGRAB s
LANDINGS*
LANDLADY
LANDLERS*
g LANDLESS
LANDLINE s
LANDLORD s
LANDMARK s
LANDMASS
LANDSIDE s
LANDSKIP s
LANDSLID e
LANDSLIP s
LANDSMAN
LANDSMEN
LANDWARD s
LANEWAYS*
LANGLAUF s
LANGLEYS*
LANGRAGE s
LANGRELS*
LANGSHAN s
LANGSYNE s
s LANGUAGE s
LANGUETS*
*LANGUISH
LANGUORS*
LANIARDS*
LANITALS*
c LANKIEST
b LANKNESS
LANNERET s
LANOLINE*s
LANOLINS*
LANOSITY
LANTANAS*
LANTERNS*
LANTHORN s
LANYARDS*
c LAPBOARD s
LAPELLED
LAPIDARY
LAPIDATE ds
LAPIDIFY
LAPIDIST s
LAPILLUS
LAPPERED
LAPPETED
LAPSABLE
LAPSIBLE
LAPWINGS*
LARBOARD s
LARCENER s
LARDIEST
LARDLIKE
LARDOONS*
LARGANDO
LARGESSE*s
LARIATED
LARKIEST
LARKSOME
LARKSPUR s
LARRIGAN s
LARRIKIN s
LARRUPED
LARRUPER s
LARYNGAL s
LARYNGES
LARYNXES
LASAGNAS*
LASAGNES*
fs LASHINGS*
LASHKARS*
LASSOERS*
LASSOING
LASTBORN s
b LASTINGS*
LATAKIAS*
LATCHETS*
LATCHING

LATCHKEY s
LATEENER s
LATENESS
LATENING
LATENTLY
LATERALS*
e LATERITE s
LATERIZE ds
LATEWOOD s
bs LATHERED
b LATHERER s
LATHIEST
LATHINGS*
LATHWORK s
LATIGOES
LATILLAS*
LATINITY
p LATINIZE ds
p LATITUDE s
LATOSOLS*
LATRINES*
LATTERLY
LATTICED*
LATTICES*
LAUDABLE
LAUDABLY
LAUDANUM s
LAUDATOR sy
LAUGHERS*
LAUGHING s
s LAUGHTER s
LAUNCHED
LAUNCHER s
LAUNCHES
LAUNDERS*
*LAUREATE ds
LAURELED
LAUWINES*
LAVABOES
LAVALAVA s
LAVALIER es
LAVALIKE
LAVASHES
c LAVATION s
LAVATORY
LAVEERED
LAVENDER s
LAVEROCK s
LAVISHED
LAVISHER s
LAVISHES t
s LAVISHLY
LAVROCKS*
LAWBOOKS*
*LAWFULLY
LAWGIVER s
LAWMAKER s
LAWSUITS*
LAWYERED
LAWYERLY
LAXATION s
LAXATIVE s
LAXITIES
LAYABOUT s
LAYAWAYS*
LAYERAGE s
LAYERING s
LAYETTES*
LAYOVERS*
LAYWOMAN
LAYWOMEN
LAZARETS*
g LAZINESS
LAZULITE s
*LAZURITE s
LEACHATE s
b LEACHERS*
LEACHIER
bp LEACHING
LEADENED
LEADENLY
LEADIEST
p LEADINGS*
LEADLESS
LEADOFFS*
LEADSMAN
LEADSMEN
LEADWORK s
LEADWORT s
LEAFAGES*
LEAFIEST
LEAFLESS
LEAFLETS*
LEAFLIKE
LEAFWORM s
LEAGUERS*

LEAGUING
LEAKAGES*
LEAKIEST
LEAKLESS
LEALTIES
g LEANINGS*
c LEANNESS
LEAPFROG s
b LEARIEST
LEARNERS
*LEARNING s
LEASABLE
LEASHING
LEASINGS*
LEATHERN*
p LEATHERS*
LEATHERY*
LEAVENED
LEAVIEST
LEAVINGS*
LECHAYIM s
LECHERED
LECITHIN s
LECTERNS*
ef LECTIONS*
LECTURED*
LECTURER*s
LECTURES*
LECYTHIS*
LECYTHUS
f*LEDGIEST
LEEBOARD s
f LEECHING
*LEERIEST
LEEWARDS*
LEFTISMS*
LEFTISTS*
LEFTMOST s
LEFTOVER s
LEFTWARD s
LEFTWING
LEGACIES
LEGALESE s
LEGALISE ds
LEGALISM s
LEGALIST s
LEGALITY
LEGALIZE drs
LEGATEES*
LEGATINE
LEGATING
LEGATION s
LEGATORS*
LEGENDRY
LEGERITY
LEGGIERO*
LEGGIEST
LEGGINGS*
LEGHORNS*
LEGROOMS*
LEGUMINS*
LEGWORKS*
LEHAYIMS*
LEISTERS*
LEISURED*
LEISURES*
LEKYTHOI
LEKYTHOS
LEKYTHUS
LEMMINGS*
LEMNISCI
LEMONADE s
LEMONISH
LEMPIRAS*
LEMURINE
LEMUROID s
LENDABLE
LENGTHEN s
LENIENCE s
LENIENCY
LENITIES
LENITING
LENITION s
LENITIVE s
LENSLESS
LENTANDO
LENTICEL s
LENTISKS*
LENTOIDS*
LEOPARDS*
LEOTARDS*
*LEPIDOTE s
LEPORIDS*
LEPORINE
LEPROTIC
LEPTONIC

LESBIANS*
LESIONED
LESSENED
LESSONED
f*LETCHING
LETDOWNS*
LETHALLY
LETHARGY
LETTERED
LETTERER s
LETTUCES*
LEUCEMIA s
LEUCEMIC
LEUCINES*
LEUCITES*
LEUCITIC
LEUCOMAS*
LEUKEMIA s
LEUKEMIC s
LEUKOMAS*
LEUKOSES
LEUKOSIS
LEUKOTIC
LEVANTED
LEVANTER s
e LEVATORS*
LEVEEING
LEVELERS*
LEVELING
LEVELLED
LEVELLER s
LEVERAGE ds
LEVERETS*
LEVERING
LEVIABLE
LEVIGATE ds
LEVIRATE s
LEVITATE ds
LEVITIES
LEVODOPA s
LEVOGYRE
LEVULINS*
LEVULOSE s
LEWDNESS
LEWISITE s
LEWISSON s
LEXICONS*
LIAISING
LIAISONS*
LIBATION s
LIBECCIO s
LIBELANT s
LIBELEES*
LIBELERS*
LIBELING
LIBELIST s
LIBELLED
LIBELLEE s
LIBELLER s
LIBELOUS
LIBERALS*
LIBERATE ds
LIBRATED*
LIBRATES*
LIBRETTI
LIBRETTO s
LICENCED*
LICENCEE*s
LICENCER*s
LICENCES*
LICENSED*
LICENSEE*s
LICENSER*s
LICENSES*
LICENSOR s
LICHENED
LICHENIN gs
LICHTING
LICKINGS*
LICKSPIT s
LICORICE s
LIEGEMAN
LIEGEMEN
a LIENABLE
LIENTERY
LIFEBOAT s
LIFECARE s
LIFELESS
LIFELIKE
LIFELINE s
LIFELONG
LIFESPAN s
LIFETIME s
LIFEWAYS*
LIFEWORK s
LIFTABLE

LIFTGATE s
LIFTOFFS*
LIGAMENT s
LIGATING
LIGATION s
LIGATIVE
LIGATURE ds
LIGHTENS*
bps LIGHTERS*
s LIGHTEST
LIGHTFUL
abf LIGHTING s
ps
LIGHTISH
*LIGNEOUS
LIGNITES
LIGNITIC
LIGROINE*s
LIGROINS*
LIGULATE d
LIGULOID
LIKEABLE
LIKELIER
a LIKENESS
LIKENING
LIKEWISE
LILLIPUT s
LILYLIKE
LIMACINE
LIMACONS*
LIMBECKS*
LIMBERED
LIMBERER
LIMBERLY
LIMBIEST
LIMBLESS
LIMBUSES
LIMEADES*
LIMEKILN s
LIMELESS
LIMERICK s
s LIMINESS
LIMITARY
LIMITEDS*
LIMITERS*
LIMITING
LIMNETIC
LIMONENE s
LIMONITE s
LIMPIDLY
LIMPKINS*
LIMPNESS
s LIMPSIER
LIMULOID s
LINALOLS*
LINALOOL s
LINCHPIN s
LINDANES*
LINEABLE
LINEAGES*
LINEALLY
LINEARLY
LINEATED*
LINEBRED
LINECUTS*
LINELESS
LINELIKE
LINESMAN
LINESMEN
LINGCODS*
LINGERED
LINGERER s
LINGERIE s
c LINGIEST
LINGUALS*
LINGUICA s
LINGUINE s
LINGUINI s
LINGUISA s
LINGUIST s
LINGULAE*
LINGULAR*
LINIMENT s
LINKABLE
LINKAGES*
LINKBOYS*
LINKSMAN
LINKSMEN
LINKWORK s
LINOCUTS*
LINOLEUM s
LINOTYPE drs
LINSANGS*
LINSEEDS*
LINSTOCK s
fg LINTIEST

LINTLESS
LINURONS*
LIONFISH
LIONISED
LIONISER*s
LIONISES
LIONIZED
*LIONIZER*s
LIONIZES
LIONLIKE
LIPOCYTE s
LIPOIDAL
LIPOMATA
LIPOSOME s
LIPPENED
s LIPPERED
s LIPPIEST
c LIPPINGS*
LIPREADS*
LIPSTICK s
LIQUATED*
LIQUATES*
LIQUEURS*
LIQUIDLY
LIQUORED
LIRIOPES*
LIRIPIPE s
LISSOMLY
LISTABLE
g LISTENED
LISTENER s
LISTERIA s
LISTINGS*
LISTLESS
LITANIES
LITENESS
a LITERACY
LITERALS*
LITERARY
a*LITERATE s
LITERATI m
LITHARGE s
LITHEMIA s
LITHEMIC
LITHIUMS*
LITHOING
LITHOSOL s
LITIGANT s
LITIGATE ds
LITMUSES
fg LITTERED
LITTERER s
LITTLEST*
LITTLISH
LITTORAL s
LITURGIC s
LIVEABLE
LIVELIER
LIVELILY
LIVELONG
LIVENERS*
a LIVENESS
LIVENING
LIVERIED
LIVERIES
s LIVERING
LIVERISH
LIVETRAP s
LIVIDITY
LIVINGLY
LIXIVIAL*
LIXIVIUM s
LOADINGS*
LOADSTAR s
LOAMIEST
LOAMLESS
LOANABLE
LOANINGS*
LOANWORD s
LOATHERS*
LOATHFUL
LOATHING s
LOBATELY
LOBATION s
LOBBYERS*
LOBBYGOW s
LOBBYING
LOBBYISM s
LOBBYIST s
LOBEFINS*
LOBELIAS
LOBELINE s
LOBLOLLY
LOBOTOMY
LOBSTERS*
LOBSTICK s

LOBULATE d
LOBULOSE
LOBWORMS*
LOCALISE ds
LOCALISM s
LOCALIST s
LOCALITE s
LOCALITY
LOCALIZE drs
LOCATERS*
LOCATING
LOCATION s
LOCATIVE s
LOCATORS*
b LOCKABLE
b LOCKAGES*
LOCKDOWN s
LOCKJAWS*
LOCKNUTS*
LOCKOUTS*
LOCKRAMS*
LOCKSETS*
LOCKSTEP s
LOCOFOCO s
LOCOISMS*
LOCOMOTE ds
LOCOWEED s
LOCULATE d
LOCUSTAE*
LOCUSTAL*
e LOCUTION s
LOCUTORY
LODESTAR s
LODGINGS*
LODGMENT s
LODICULE s
LOESSIAL
LOFTIEST
LOFTLESS
LOFTLIKE
LOGBOOKS*
c LOGGIEST
bf LOGGINGS*
LOGICIAN s
LOGICISE ds
LOGICIZE ds
LOGINESS
LOGISTIC s
LOGOGRAM s
LOGOMACH sy
LOGOTYPE s
LOGOTYPY
LOGROLLS*
LOGWOODS*
LOITERED
LOITERER s
LOLLIPOP s
LOLLOPED
LOLLYGAG s
LOLLYPOP s
*LOMENTUM s
LONELIER
LONELILY
a*LONENESS
LONESOME s
LONGBOAT s
LONGBOWS*
LONGEING
LONGERON s
LONGHAIR s
LONGHAND s
LONGHEAD s
LONGHORN s
LONGINGS*
LONGJUMP s
LONGLEAF
LONGLINE s
LONGNECK s
LONGNESS
LONGSHIP s
LONGSOME
LONGSPUR s
LONGTIME
LONGUEUR s
LONGWAYS
LONGWISE
LOOKDOWN s
LOOKISMS*
LOOKISTS*
LOOKOUTS*
LOOKSISM s
LOONIEST*
LOOPHOLE ds
LOOPIEST
LOOSENED
LOOSENER s

LOPPERED
fgs LOPPIEST
LOPSIDED
LOPSTICK s
LORDINGS*
LORDLESS
LORDLIER
LORDLIKE
LORDLING s
LORDOMAS*
LORDOSES
LORDOSIS
LORDOTIC
LORDSHIP s
LORGNONS*
LORICATE ds
LORIKEET s
LORIMERS*
LORINERS*
LORNNESS
LOSINGLY
LOSSLESS
LOSTNESS
LOTHARIO s
LOTHSOME
LOUDENED
LOUDLIER
LOUDNESS
LOUNGERS*
LOUNGING
b LOUSIEST
LOUVERED
LOVEABLE
LOVEABLY
LOVEBIRD s
LOVEBUGS*
LOVEFEST s
LOVELESS
LOVELIER
LOVELIES t
LOVELILY
LOVELOCK s
LOVELORN
LOVESEAT s
LOVESICK
LOVESOME
LOVEVINE s
LOVINGLY
b LOWBALLS*
LOWBROWS*
bs LOWDOWNS*
fg LOWERING
p LOWLANDS*
LOWLIEST
LOWLIFER*s
LOWLIFES*
LOWLIGHT s
LOWLIVES
LOWRIDER s
LOYALEST
LOYALISM s
LOYALIST s
LOZENGES*
LUBBERLY
LUBRICAL
LUCARNES*
LUCENCES*
LUCENTLY
LUCERNES*
LUCIDITY
LUCIFERS*
p LUCKIEST*
LUCKLESS
LUCULENT
LUGGAGES*
LUGSAILS*
LUGWORMS*
LUKEWARM
p LUMBAGOS*
s*LUMBERED
s LUMBERER s
LUMBERLY
LUMINARY
LUMINISM s
LUMINIST s
a LUMINOUS
f LUMMOXES
LUMPFISH
cg LUMPIEST
LUNACIES
LUNARIAN s
LUNATELY
LUNATICS*
LUNATION s
LUNCHBOX
LUNCHEON s

LUNCHERS*
g LUNCHING
LUNETTES*
LUNGFISH
LUNGFULS*
LUNGWORM s
LUNGWORT s
LUNKHEAD s
LUNULATE d
LUPANARS*
LUPULINS*
LURCHERS*
LURCHING
LURDANES*
LURINGLY
LUSCIOUS
fp LUSHNESS
bcf LUSTERED
LUSTIEST
LUSTRATE ds
LUSTRING s
LUSTROUS
LUSTRUMS*
LUTANIST s
LUTECIUM s
LUTEFISK s
LUTENIST s
LUTEOLIN s
LUTETIUM s
LUTFISKS*
LUTHERNS*
LUTHIERS*
LUXATING
LUXATION s
LUXURIES
LYCOPENE s
LYCOPODS*
LYDDITES*
LYMPHOID
LYMPHOMA s
LYNCHERS*
LYNCHING s
LYNCHPIN s
LYOPHILE d
LYRATELY
LYREBIRD s
LYRICISE ds
LYRICISM s
LYRICIST s
LYRICIZE ds
LYRICONS*
LYRIFORM
LYSOGENS*
LYSOGENY*
LYSOSOME s
LYSOZYME s
MACADAMS*
MACAQUES*
MACARONI cs
MACAROON s
MACCABAW s
MACCABOY s
MACCOBOY s
*MACERATE drs
MACHETES*
MACHINED*
MACHINES*
MACHISMO s
MACHOISM s
MACHREES*
MACHZORS*
MACKEREL s
MACKINAW s
MACKLING
MACRAMES*
MACRURAL
MACRURAN s
MACULATE ds
MACULING
MACUMBAS*
MADDENED
MADEIRAS*
MADERIZE ds
MADHOUSE s
MADONNAS*
MADRASAH*s
MADRASAS*
MADRASES
MADRASSA hs
MADRIGAL s
MADRONAS*
MADRONES*
MADRONOS*
*MADWOMAN
*MADWOMEN
MADWORTS*

MADZOONS*
MAENADES
MAENADIC
MAESTOSO s
MAESTROS*
MAFFICKS*
MAFIOSOS*
MAGALOGS*
MAGAZINE s
MAGDALEN es
MAGENTAS*
MAGICIAN s
MAGICKED
MAGISTER s
MAGMATIC
MAGNATES
MAGNESIA ns
MAGNESIC
MAGNETIC s
MAGNETON*s
MAGNETOS*
MAGNIFIC o
MAGNOLIA s
MAHARAJA hs
MAHARANI s
MAHATMAS*
MAHIMAHI s
MAHJONGG*s
MAHJONGS*
MAHOGANY
MAHONIAS*
MAHUANGS*
MAHZORIM
MAIASAUR as
MAIDENLY
MAIDHOOD s
MAIEUTIC
MAILABLE
MAILBAGS*
MAILGRAM s
MAILINGS*
MAILLESS
MAILLOTS*
MAILROOM s
MAINLAND s
MAINLINE drs
MAINMAST s
MAINSAIL s
MAINSTAY s
MAINTAIN s
MAINTOPS*
MAIOLICA s
MAJAGUAS*
MAJESTIC
MAJOLICA s
MAJORING
MAJORITY
MAKEABLE
MAKEBATE s
MAKEFAST s
MAKEOVER s
MAKIMONO s
MALACCAS*
MALADIES
MALAISES*
MALAMUTE s
MALANGAS*
MALAPERT s
MALAPROP s
MALARIAL*
MALARIAN*
MALARIAS*
MALARKEY s
MALAROMA s
MALEATES*
MALEDICT s
MALEMIUT s
MALEMUTE s
MALENESS
*MALIGNED
*MALIGNER s
MALIGNLY
MALIHINI s
MALINGER s
MALISONS*
MALLARDS*
MALLEOLI
MALLINGS*
MALMIEST
MALMSEYS*
MALODORS*
MALPOSED
MALTASES*
MALTIEST
MALTOSES*
MALTREAT s

MALTSTER s
MALVASIA ns
MAMALIGA s
MAMBOING
MAMELUKE s
MAMMATUS
MAMMERED
MAMMILLA e
MAMMITIS
MAMMOCKS*
MAMMOTHS*
MANACLED*
MANACLES*
MANAGERS*
MANAGING
MANAKINS*
MANATEES*
MANATOID
MANCHETS*
MANCIPLE s
MANDALAS*
MANDALIC
MANDAMUS
MANDARIN s
MANDATED*
MANDATES*
MANDATOR sy
MANDIBLE s
MANDIOCA s
MANDOLAS*
MANDOLIN es
MANDRAKE s
MANDRELS*
MANDRILL*s
MANDRILS*
MANELESS
MANEUVER s
MANFULLY
MANGABEY s
MANGANIC
MANGANIN s
MANGIEST
MANGLERS
*MANGLING
MANGOLDS*
MANGONEL s
MANGROVE s
MANHOLES*
MANHOODS*
MANHUNTS*
MANIACAL
MANICURE ds
MANIFEST os
MANIFOLD s
MANIHOTS*
MANIKINS*
MANILLAS*
MANILLES*
MANIOCAS*
MANIPLES*
MANITOUS*
MANLIEST
MANNERED
MANNERLY
MANNIKIN s
MANNITES*
MANNITIC
MANNITOL s
MANNOSES*
MANORIAL
MANPOWER s
MANROPES*
MANSARDS*
MANSIONS*
MANTEAUS*
MANTEAUX*
MANTELET s
MANTILLA s
MANTISES
MANTISSA s
MANTLETS*
MANTLING s
MANTRAMS*
MANTRAPS*
MANUALLY
MANUBRIA l
MANUMITS*
MANURERS*
MANURIAL
MANURING
MANWARDS*
MANYFOLD
MAPMAKER s
MAPPABLE
MAPPINGS*
MAQUETTE s

MAQUILAS*
MARABOUS*
MARABOUT*s
MARANTAS*
MARASCAS*
MARASMIC
MARASMUS
MARATHON s
MARAUDED
MARAUDER s
MARAVEDI s
MARBLERS*
MARBLIER
MARBLING s
MARCATOS*
MARCHERS
MARCHESA*
MARCHESE*
MARCHESI*
*MARCHING
MARGARIC
MARGARIN es
MARGENTS
MARGINAL s
MARGINED
MARGRAVE s
MARIACHI s
MARIGOLD s
MARIMBAS*
MARINADE ds
MARINARA s
MARINATE ds
MARINERS*
MARIPOSA s
MARISHES
MARITIME
MARJORAM s
MARKDOWN s
MARKEDLY
MARKETED
MARKETER s
MARKHOOR s
MARKHORS*
MARKINGS*
MARKSMAN
MARKSMEN
MARLIEST
MARLINES*
MARLINGS*
MARLITES*
MARLITIC
MARMITES*
MARMOSET s
MAROCAIN s
MAROONED
MARPLOTS*
MARQUEES*
MARQUESS*
MARQUISE*s
MARRANOS*
MARRIAGE s
MARRIEDS*
MARRIERS*
*MARROWED
MARRYING
MARSALAS*
MARSHALL*s
MARSHALS*
MARSHIER
MARSUPIA l
MARTAGON s
MARTELLO s
MARTIANS*
MARTINET s
MARTINIS*
MARTLETS*
MARTYRED
MARTYRLY
MARVELED
MARYJANE s
MARZIPAN s
MASCARAS*
MASHGIAH
MASKABLE
MASKINGS
MASKLIKE
MASONING
MASONITE s
MASQUERS*
MASSACRE drs
MASSAGED*
MASSAGER*s
MASSAGES*
MASSCULT s
MASSEDLY
MASSETER s

MASSEURS*
MASSEUSE s
MASSICOT s
MASSIEST
MASSLESS
MASTABAH*s
MASTABAS*
MASTERED
MASTERLY
MASTHEAD s
MASTICHE s
MASTIFFS*
MASTITIC
MASTITIS
MASTIXES
MASTLESS
MASTLIKE
MASTODON st
MASTOIDS*
MASURIUM s
MATADORS*
MATCHBOX
MATCHERS*
MATCHING
MATCHUPS*
MATELESS
MATELOTE*s
MATELOTS*
MATERIAL s
MATERIEL s
MATERNAL
MATESHIP s
MATILDAS*
MATINEES*
MATINESS
MATRICES
MATRIXES
MATRONAL
MATRONLY
MATTEDLY
s MATTERED
MATTINGS*
MATTOCKS*
MATTOIDS*
MATTRASS
MATTRESS
MATURATE ds
MATURELY
MATURERS*
MATUREST*
MATURING
MATURITY
MATZOONS*
MAUMETRY
MAUNDERS*
MAUNDIES
MAUSOLEA n
MAVERICK s
MAXICOAT s
MAXILLAE
MAXILLAS
MAXIMALS*
MAXIMINS*
MAXIMISE ds
MAXIMITE s
MAXIMIZE drs
MAXIMUMS*
MAXWELLS*
MAYAPPLE s
MAYBIRDS*
MAYFLIES
MAYORESS
MAYPOLES*
MAYWEEDS*
MAZAEDIA
MAZELIKE
MAZELTOV
MAZINESS
MAZOURKA s
MAZURKAS*
MAZZARDS*
MBAQANGA s
*MEAGERLY
MEAGRELY
MEALIEST*
MEALLESS
MEALTIME s
MEALWORM s
MEALYBUG s
MEANDERS*
MEANINGS*
MEANNESS
MEANTIME s
MEASLIER
MEASURED*
MEASURER*s

MEASURES*
MEATBALL s
MEATHEAD s
MEATIEST
MEATLESS
MEATLOAF
MEATUSES
MECHANIC s
MECHITZA s
MECONIUM s
MEDALING
MEDALIST s
MEDALLED
MEDALLIC
MEDDLERS*
MEDDLING
MEDEVACS*
MEDFLIES
MEDIALLY
MEDIANLY
MEDIANTS*
MEDIATED*
MEDIATES*
MEDIATOR sy
MEDICAID s
MEDICALS*
MEDICANT s
MEDICARE s
MEDICATE ds
MEDICIDE s
MEDICINE ds
MEDIEVAL s
MEDIGAPS*
MEDIOCRE
MEDITATE ds
MEDIVACS*
MEDULLAE*
MEDULLAR*y
MEDULLAS*
MEDUSANS*
MEDUSOID s
MEEKNESS
MEERKATS*
MEETINGS*
MEETNESS
MEGABARS*
MEGABITS*
MEGABUCK s
MEGABYTE s
MEGACITY
MEGADEAL s
MEGADOSE s
MEGADYNE s
MEGAFLOP s
MEGAHITS*
MEGALITH s
MEGALOPS
MEGAPLEX
MEGAPODE*s
MEGAPODS*
MEGASSES*
MEGASTAR s
MEGATONS*
MEGAVOLT s
MEGAWATT s
MEGILLAH*s
MEGILLAS*
MEGILPHS*
MEISTERS*
MELAMDIM
MELAMINE s
MELANGES*
MELANIAN
MELANICS*
MELANINS*
MELANISM s
MELANIST s
MELANITE s
MELANIZE ds
MELANOID s
MELANOMA s
MELANOUS
MELILITE s
MELILOTS*
MELINITE s
MELISMAS*
MELLIFIC
MELLOWED
MELLOWER
MELLOWLY
MELODEON s
MELODIAS*
MELODICA*s
MELODIES
MELODISE ds
MELODIST s

MELODIZE drs
MELTABLE
MELTAGES*
MELTDOWN s
MEMBERED
MEMBRANE ds
MEMENTOS*
*MEMETICS
MEMORIAL s
MEMORIES
MEMORISE ds
MEMORIZE drs
MEMSAHIB s
MENACERS*
MENACING
MENARCHE s
MENAZONS*
ae MENDABLE
MENDIGOS*
MENDINGS
MENFOLKS*
MENHADEN s
MENIALLY
MENINGES
MENISCAL
MENISCUS
*MENOLOGY
MENORAHS*
MENSCHEN
MENSCHES
MENSEFUL
MENSTRUA l
MENSURAL
MENSWEAR
MENTALLY
MENTHENE s
MENTHOLS*
MENTIONS*
MENTORED
MEPHITIC
MEPHITIS
MERCAPTO
MERCHANT s
MERCIFUL
MERCURIC
MERENGUE s
e MERGENCE s
MERIDIAN s
MERINGUE s
MERISTEM s
*MERISTIC
MERITING
MERMAIDS*
MEROPIAS*
MERRIEST
MESCLUNS*
MESDAMES
MESEEMED
MESHIEST
MESHUGAH*
MESHUGGA h
MESHUGGE
MESHWORK s
MESIALLY
MESMERIC
MESNALTY
MESOCARP s
MESODERM s
MESOGLEA ls
MESOMERE s
MESOPHYL ls
MESOSOME s
MESOTRON s
MESOZOAN s
MESOZOIC
MESQUITE*s
MESQUITS*
MESSAGED*
MESSAGES*
MESSIAHS*
MESSIEST
MESSMATE s
MESSUAGE s
MESTESOS*
MESTINOS*
MESTIZAS*
MESTIZOS*
METALING
METALISE ds
METALIST s
METALIZE ds
METALLED
METALLIC s
METAMERE*s
METAMERS*
METAPHOR s

METATAGS*
METAZOAL*
METAZOAN*s
METAZOIC
METAZOON
METEORIC
METERAGE s
METERING
METHADON es
METHANES
*METHANOL s
METHINKS
METHODIC
METHOXYL
METHYLAL s
*METHYLIC
METICAIS
METICALS*
METISSES*
METONYMS*
METONYMY*
METOPONS*
METRAZOL s
METRICAL
METRISTS*
METRITIS
MEUNIERE
MEZEREON s
MEZEREUM s
MEZQUITE*s
MEZQUITS*
MEZUZAHS*
MEZUZOTH*
MIAOUING
MIAOWING
MIASMATA
MIAULING
MICAWBER s
MICELLAE*
MICELLAR*
MICELLES*
MICKLEST*
MICROBAR s
MICROBES*
MICROBIC
MICROBUS
MICROCAP
MICRODOT s
MICROHMS*
MICROLUX
MICROMHO s
MICRURGY
MIDBRAIN s
MIDCULTS*
MIDDLERS*
MIDDLING s
MIDFIELD s
MIDIRONS*
MIDLANDS*
MIDLIFER*s
MIDLINES*
MIDLISTS*
MIDLIVES
MIDMONTH s
MIDMOSTS*
MIDNIGHT s
MIDNOONS*
MIDPOINT s
MIDRANGE s
MIDRIFFS*
a MIDSHIPS*
MIDSIZED*
MIDSOLES*
MIDSPACE s
MIDSTORY
MIDTERMS*
MIDTOWNS*
MIDWATCH
MIDWEEKS*
MIDWIFED*
MIDWIFES*
MIDWIVED
MIDWIVES
MIDYEARS*
*MIFFIEST
MIGHTIER
MIGHTILY
MIGNONNE
MIGRAINE s
e MIGRANTS*
e MIGRATED*
e MIGRATES*
MIGRATOR sy
MIJNHEER s
MILADIES
MILDENED

MILDEWED
MILDNESS
MILEAGES*
MILEPOST s
MILESIAN
MILESIMO s
MILFOILS*
MILIARIA ls
MILITANT s
MILITARY
MILITATE ds
MILITIAS*
MILKFISH
MILKIEST
MILKLESS
MILKMAID s
MILKSHED s
MILKSOPS*
MILKWEED s
MILKWOOD s
MILKWORT s
MILLABLE
MILLAGES*
MILLCAKE s
MILLDAMS*
MILLEPED es
MILLIARD s
MILLIARE s
MILLIARY
MILLIBAR s
MILLIEME s
MILLIERS*
MILLIGAL s
MILLILUX
MILLIMES*
MILLIMHO s
MILLINER*sy
MILLINES*
MILLINGS*
MILLIOHM s
MILLIONS*
MILLIPED es
MILLIREM s
MILLPOND s
MILLRACE s
MILLRUNS*
MILLWORK s
MILTIEST
MIMEOING
MIMETITE s
MIMICKED
MIMICKER s
MINACITY
MINARETS*
MINATORY
MINCIEST
MINDLESS
MINDSETS*
MINEABLE
MINERALS*
MINGIEST
MINGLERS*
MINGLING
MINIBARS*
MINIBIKE rs
MINICABS*
MINICAMP*s
MINICAMS*
MINICARS*
MINIDISC s
MINIFIED
MINIFIES
MINIKINS*
MINILABS*
MINIMALS*
MINIMILL s
MINIMISE ds
MINIMIZE drs
MINIMUMS*
MINIPARK s
MINIPILL s
MINISHED
MINISHES
MINISKIS*
MINISTER s
MINISTRY
MINIVANS*
MINIVERS*
MINORCAS*
MINORING
MINORITY
MINSTERS*
MINSTREL s
MINTAGES*
MINTIEST
MINUENDS*

MINUTELY
MINUTEST*
MINUTIAE*
MINUTIAL*
MINUTING
MINYANIM
MIQUELET s
MIRACLES*
MIRADORS*
MIREPOIX
MIRINESS
s MIRKIEST
MIRLITON s
MIRRORED
MIRTHFUL
MISACTED
MISADAPT s
MISADDED
MISAGENT s
MISAIMED
MISALIGN s
MISALLOT s
MISALTER s
MISANDRY
MISAPPLY
MISASSAY s
MISATONE ds
MISAVERS*
MISAWARD s
MISBEGAN
MISBEGIN s
MISBEGOT
MISBEGUN
MISBILLS*
MISBINDS*
MISBOUND
MISBRAND s
MISBUILD s
MISBUILT
MISCALLS*
MISCARRY
MISCASTS*
MISCHIEF s
MISCHOSE n
MISCIBLE
MISCITED*
MISCITES*
MISCLAIM s
MISCLASS
MISCODED*
MISCODES*
MISCOINS*
MISCOLOR s
MISCOOKS*
MISCOUNT s
MISCUING
MISDATED*
MISDATES*
MISDEALS*
MISDEALT*
MISDEEDS*
MISDEEMS*
MISDIALS*
MISDOERS*
MISDOING s
MISDOUBT s
MISDRAWN*
MISDRAWS*
MISDRIVE ns
MISDROVE
MISEASES*
MISEATEN
MISEDITS*
MISENROL ls
MISENTER s
MISENTRY
MISERERE s
MISERIES
MISEVENT s
MISFAITH s
MISFEEDS*
MISFIELD s
MISFILED*
MISFILES*
MISFIRED*
MISFIRES*
MISFOCUS
MISFORMS*
MISFRAME ds
MISGAUGE ds
MISGIVEN*
MISGIVES*
MISGRADE ds
MISGRAFT s
MISGROWN*
MISGROWS*

MISGUESS
MISGUIDE drs
MISHEARD*
MISHEARS*
MISHMASH
MISHMOSH
MISINFER s
MISINTER s
MISJOINS*
MISJUDGE ds
MISKEEPS*
MISKICKS*
MISKNOWN*
MISKNOWS*
MISLABEL s
MISLABOR s
MISLAYER s
MISLEADS*
MISLEARN st
MISLIGHT s
MISLIKED*
MISLIKER*s
MISLIKES*
MISLIVED*
MISLIVES*
MISLODGE ds
MISLYING
MISMAKES*
MISMARKS*
MISMATCH
MISMATED*
MISMATES*
MISMEETS*
MISMOVED*
MISMOVES*
MISNAMED*
MISNAMES*
MISNOMER s
*MISOGAMY
MISOGYNY
MISOLOGY
MISORDER s
MISPAGED*
MISPAGES*
MISPAINT s
MISPARSE ds
MISPARTS*
MISPATCH
MISPLACE ds
MISPLANS*
MISPLANT*s
MISPLAYS*
MISPLEAD s
MISPOINT s
MISPOISE ds
MISPRICE ds
MISPRINT s
MISPRIZE drs
MISQUOTE drs
MISRAISE ds
MISRATED*
MISRATES*
MISREADS*
MISREFER s
MISROUTE ds
MISRULED*
MISRULES*
MISSABLE
MISSEATS*
MISSENDS*
MISSENSE s
MISSHAPE dnr
s
MISSILES*
MISSILRY
eo MISSIONS*
MISSISES
MISSIVES*
MISSORTS*
MISSOUND s
MISSOUTS*
MISSPACE ds
MISSPEAK s
MISSPELL s
MISSPELT
MISSPEND s
MISSPENT
MISSPOKE n
MISSTAMP s
MISSTART s
MISSTATE ds
MISSTEER s
MISSTEPS*
MISSTOPS*
MISSTYLE ds
MISSUITS*

MISSUSES
MISTAKEN*
MISTAKER*s
MISTAKES*
MISTBOWS*
MISTEACH
MISTENDS*
MISTERMS*
MISTHINK s
MISTHREW
MISTHROW ns
MISTIEST
MISTIMED*
MISTIMES*
MISTITLE ds
MISTOUCH
MISTRACE ds
MISTRAIN s
MISTRALS*
MISTREAT s
MISTRESS
MISTRIAL s
MISTRUST s
MISTRUTH s
MISTRYST s
MISTUNED*
MISTUNES*
MISTUTOR s
MISTYPED*
MISTYPES*
MISUNION s
MISUSAGE s
MISUSERS*
MISUSING
MISVALUE ds
MISWORDS*
MISWRITE*s
MISWROTE
MISYOKED*
MISYOKES*
MITERERS*
MITERING
MITICIDE s
MITIGATE ds
MITOGENS*
MITSVAHS*
MITSVOTH
MITTENED
MITTIMUS
MITZVAHS*
MITZVOTH
MIXOLOGY
MIXTURES*
MIZZLING
MNEMONIC s
*MOATLIKE
MOBBISMS*
MOBILISE ds
MOBILITY
MOBILIZE drs
MOBOCRAT s
MOBSTERS*
MOCCASIN s
MOCHILAS*
MOCKABLE
MOCKTAIL s
MODALITY
MODELERS*
MODELING s
MODELIST s
MODELLED
MODELLER s
MODEMING
MODERATE ds
MODERATO rs
MODERNER*
MODERNES*t
MODERNLY
MODESTER
MODESTLY
MODICUMS*
MODIFIED
MODIFIER s
MODIFIES
MODIOLUS
MODISHLY
MODISTES*
MODULARS*
MODULATE ds
MOFETTES*
MOFFETTE s
MOIDORES*
MOIETIES
MOISTENS*
MOISTEST
MOISTFUL

MOISTURE s
MOJARRAS*
MOLALITY
MOLARITY
MOLASSES
MOLDABLE
s MOLDERED
MOLDIEST
MOLDINGS*
MOLDWARP s
MOLECULE s
MOLEHILL s
MOLESKIN s
MOLESTED
MOLESTER s
MOLLUSCA*n
MOLLUSCS*
MOLLUSKS*
MOLTENLY
MOLYBDIC
MOMENTLY
MOMENTOS*
*MOMENTUM s
MONACHAL
MONACIDS*
MONADISM s
MONANDRY
MONARCHS*
MONARCHY*
MONARDAS*
MONASTIC s
MONAURAL
MONAXIAL
MONAXONS*
MONAZITE s
MONECIAN
MONELLIN s
MONERANS*
MONETARY
MONETISE ds
MONETIZE ds
MONEYBAG s
MONEYERS*
MONEYMAN
MONEYMEN
MONGEESE
MONGERED
MONGOOSE s
MONGRELS*
MONICKER s
MONIKERS*
MONISHED
MONISHES
MONISTIC
MONITION s
MONITIVE
MONITORS*
MONITORY*
MONKEYED
MONKFISH
MONKHOOD s
MONOACID s
MONOCARP s
MONOCLED*
MONOCLES*
MONOCOTS*
MONOCRAT s
MONOCYTE s
MONODIES
MONODIST s
MONOFILS*
MONOFUEL s
MONOGAMY
MONOGENY
MONOGERM
MONOGLOT s
MONOGRAM s
MONOGYNY
MONOHULL s
MONOKINE s
MONOLITH s
MONOLOGS*
MONOLOGY*
MONOMERS*
MONOMIAL s
MONOPODE*s
MONOPODS*
MONOPODY*
MONOPOLE s
MONOPOLY
MONORAIL s
MONOSOME s
MONOSOMY
MONOTINT s
MONOTONE s
MONOTONY

MONOTYPE s
MONOXIDE s
MONSIEUR
MONSOONS*
MONSTERA*s
MONSTERS*
MONTAGED*
MONTAGES*
MONTANES*
MONTEITH s
MONTEROS*
MONUMENT s
MONURONS*
s MOOCHERS*
s MOOCHING
MOODIEST
MOONBEAM s
MOONBOWS*
MOONCALF
MOONDUST s
MOONEYES*
MOONFISH
MOONIEST
MOONLESS
MOONLETS*
MOONLIKE
MOONPORT s
MOONRISE s
MOONROOF s
MOONSAIL s
MOONSEED s
MOONSETS*
MOONSHOT s
MOONWALK s
MOONWARD s
MOONWORT s
MOORAGES*
MOORCOCK s
MOORFOWL s
MOORHENS*
MOORIEST
MOORINGS*
MOORLAND s
MOORWORT s
MOOTNESS
MOPBOARD s
MOPERIES
MOPINESS
MOPINGLY
MOPISHLY
MOQUETTE s
MORAINAL
MORAINES*
MORAINIC
MORALISE ds
a*MORALISM s
*MORALIST s
a*MORALITY
MORALIZE drs
MORASSES
*MORATORY
MORBIDLY
MORBIFIC
MORBILLI
MORCEAUX*
MORDANCY
MORDANTS*
MORDENTS*
MORELLES*
MORELLOS*
MORENESS
MOREOVER
MORESQUE s
MORIBUND
MORNINGS*
MOROCCOS*
MORONISM s
MORONITY
MOROSELY
MOROSITY
MORPHEME s
MORPHIAS*
MORPHINE*s
MORPHING*s
MORPHINS*
MORRIONS*
*MORRISES
MORSELED
MORTALLY
MORTARED
MORTGAGE der
s
MORTICED*
MORTICES*
a MORTISED*
MORTISER*s

a MORTISES*
MORTMAIN s
MORTUARY
MOSASAUR s
MOSCHATE l
MOSEYING
MOSHAVIM
MOSHINGS*
MOSQUITO s
MOSSBACK s
MOSSIEST
MOSSLIKE
MOSTESTS*
MOTHBALL s
s MOTHERED
MOTHERLY
MOTHIEST
MOTHLIKE
MOTILITY
e MOTIONAL
MOTIONED
MOTIONER s
MOTIVATE ds
MOTIVING
e MOTIVITY
MOTLEYER
MOTLIEST
MOTORBUS
MOTORCAR s
MOTORDOM s
MOTORING s
MOTORISE ds
MOTORIST s
MOTORIZE ds
MOTORMAN
MOTORMEN
MOTORWAY s
MOTTLERS*
MOTTLING
*MOUCHING
MOUCHOIR s
MOUFFLON s
MOUFLONS*
MOULAGES*
s MOULDERS*
MOULDIER
MOULDING s
MOULTERS*
MOULTING
MOUNDING
MOUNTAIN sy
MOUNTERS*
a MOUNTING s
MOURNERS*
MOURNFUL
MOURNING s
MOUSAKAS*
MOUSEPAD s
MOUSIEST
MOUSINGS*
MOUSSAKA s
MOUSSING
MOUTHERS*
MOUTHFUL s
MOUTHIER
MOUTHILY
MOUTHING
MOVABLES*
MOVEABLE s
MOVEABLY
MOVELESS
MOVEMENT s
MOVIEDOM s
MOVIEOLA s
MOVINGLY
MOVIOLAS*
MOZETTAS*
MOZZETTA s
MOZZETTE
MRIDANGA ms
MUCHACHO s
MUCHNESS
MUCIDITY
MUCILAGE s
MUCINOID
MUCINOUS
MUCKIEST
MUCKLUCK s
MUCKRAKE drs
MUCKWORM s
MUCOIDAL
MUCOSITY
MUCRONES
MUDDIEST*
MUDDLERS*
MUDDLING
MUDDYING
MUDFLAPS*
MUDFLATS*
MUDFLOWS*
MUDGUARD s
MUDHOLES*
MUDLARKS*
MUDPACKS*
MUDPUPPY
MUDROCKS*
MUDROOMS*
MUDSILLS*
MUDSLIDE s
MUDSTONE s
MUEDDINS*
MUENSTER s
MUEZZINS*
MUFFLERS*
MUFFLING
MUGGIEST
MUGGINGS*
MUGWORTS*
MUGWUMPS*
MULATTOS*
MULBERRY
MULCHING
MULCTING
MULETEER s
MULISHLY
MULLEINS*
MULLIGAN s
MULLIONS*
MULLITES*
MULLOCKS*
MULLOCKY*
MULTIAGE
MULTICAR
MULTIDAY
MULTIFID
MULTIJET
MULTIPED es
MULTIPLE stx
MULTIPLY
MULTITON e
MULTIUSE r
MULTURES*
MUMBLERS*
MUMBLING
MUMMYING
MUNCHERS*
MUNCHIES
MUNCHING
MUNCHKIN s
MUNDUNGO s
MUNGOOSE s
MUNIMENT s
MUNITION s
MUNNIONS*
MUNSTERS*
MUNTINGS*
MUNTJACS*
MUNTJAKS*
MUONIUMS*
MURAENID s
MURALIST s
MURALLED
MURDERED
MURDEREE s
MURDERER s
MURIATED*
MURIATES*
MURICATE d
MURKIEST
MURMURED
MURMURER s
MURPHIES
MURRAINS*
MURRELET s
MURRHINE
MURTHERS*
MUSCADEL s
MUSCADET s
MUSCATEL s
MUSCLING
MUSCULAR
MUSETTES*
MUSHIEST
MUSHROOM s
MUSICALE*s
MUSICALS*
MUSICIAN s
MUSICKED
a MUSINGLY
MUSKETRY
MUSKIEST*
MUSKOXEN
MUSKRATS*
MUSKROOT s
MUSPIKES*
MUSQUASH
MUSSIEST
MUSTACHE ds
MUSTANGS*
MUSTARDS*
MUSTARDY*
MUSTELID s
MUSTERED
MUSTIEST
MUTAGENS*
MUTATING
MUTATION s
MUTATIVE
MUTCHKIN s
MUTENESS
MUTICOUS
MUTILATE ds
MUTINEER s
MUTINIED
MUTINIES
MUTINING
MUTINOUS
*MUTTERED
*MUTTERER s
MUTUALLY
MUZZIEST
MUZZLERS*
MUZZLING
MYALGIAS*
MYCELIAL*
MYCELIAN*
MYCELIUM
MYCELOID
MYCETOMA s
MYCOLOGY
MYELINES*
MYELINIC
MYELITIS
MYELOMAS*
MYLONITE s
MYNHEERS*
MYOBLAST s
MYOGENIC
MYOGRAPH s
MYOLOGIC
MYOPATHY
MYOSCOPE s
MYOSITIS
MYOSOTES*
MYOSOTIS
MYOTOMES*
a MYOTONIA s
MYOTONIC
MYRIAPOD s
MYRIOPOD s
MYRMIDON s
MYSTAGOG sy
MYSTICAL
MYSTICLY
MYSTIQUE s
MYTHICAL
MYTHIEST
MYXAMEBA es
MYXEDEMA s
MYXOCYTE s
MYXOMATA
NABOBERY
NABOBESS
NABOBISH
NABOBISM s
NACELLES*
NACREOUS
NAETHING s
s NAGGIEST
NAILFOLD s
NAILHEAD s
NAILSETS*
NAINSOOK s
NAIVETES*
NAKEDEST
NALOXONE s
NAMEABLE
NAMELESS
NAMESAKE s
NAMETAGS*
NANDINAS*
NANKEENS*
NANNYISH
NANOGRAM s
NANOTECH s
NANOTUBE s
NANOWATT s
NAPALMED
*NAPERIES
NAPHTHAS*
NAPHTHOL s
NAPHTHYL s
NAPHTOLS*
NAPIFORM
NAPOLEON s
s NAPPIEST*
NAPROXEN s
NARCEINE*s
NARCEINS*
NARCISMS*
NARCISSI
NARCISTS*
NARCOMAS*
NARCOSES*
NARCOSIS
NARCOTIC s
NARGHILE s
NARGILEH*s
NARGILES*
NARRATED*
NARRATER*s
NARRATES*
NARRATOR s
*NARROWED
NARROWER
NARROWLY
NARWHALE*s
NARWHALS*
NASALISE ds
NASALISM s
NASALITY
NASALIZE ds
NASCENCE s
NASCENCY
NASTIEST*
NATALITY
NATANTLY
NATATION s
NATATORY
NATHLESS
NATIONAL s
NATIVELY
NATIVISM s
NATIVIST s
NATIVITY
NATRIUMS
NATTERED
g NATTIEST
NATURALS*
NATURISM s
NATURIST s
NAUMACHY
NAUPLIAL
NAUPLIUS
NAUSEANT s
NAUSEATE ds
NAUSEOUS
NAUTCHES
NAUTICAL
NAUTILUS
NAVETTES*
NAVICERT s
NAVIGATE ds
NAYSAYER s
NAZIFIED
NAZIFIES
*NEARLIER
NEARNESS
NEARSIDE s
NEATENED
NEATHERD s
NEATNESS
NEATNIKS*
NEBBISHY*
NEBULISE ds
NEBULIZE drs
NEBULOSE
NEBULOUS
NECKBAND s
NECKINGS*
NECKLACE ds
NECKLESS
NECKLIKE
NECKLINE s
NECKTIES*
NECKWEAR
NECROPSY
NECROSED*
NECROSES*
NECROSIS
NECROTIC
NEEDFULS*
NEEDIEST
NEEDLERS*
NEEDLESS*
NEEDLING s
NEGATERS*
NEGATING
NEGATION s
NEGATIVE ds
NEGATONS*
NEGATORS*
NEGATRON s
NEGLECTS*
NEGLIGEE*s
NEGLIGES*
NEGROIDS*
NEGRONIS*
NEIGHBOR s
NEIGHING
NEKTONIC
NELUMBOS*
NEMATODE s
NEOLITHS
NEOLOGIC
NEOMORPH s
NEOMYCIN s
NEONATAL
NEONATES*
NEOPHYTE s
NEOPLASM s
NEOPRENE s
NEOTENIC
NEOTERIC s
NEOTYPES*
NEPENTHE s
NEPHRISM s
NEPHRITE s
NEPHRONS*
NEPOTISM s
NEPOTIST s
NERDIEST
NEREIDES
NERVIEST
NERVINES*s
NERVINGS*
NERVULES*
NERVURES*
NESCIENT s
NESTABLE
NESTLERS*
NESTLIKE
NESTLING s
NETIZENS*
NETSUKES*
NETTABLE
NETTIEST
NETTINGS*
NETTLERS*
NETTLIER
NETTLING
NETWORKS*
p NEUMATIC
NEURALLY
NEURAXON s
NEURINES*
NEURITIC s
NEURITIS
NEUROMAS*t
NEURONAL
NEURONES*
NEURONIC
NEUROSAL
NEUROSES
NEUROSIS
NEUROTIC s
NEURULAE*
NEURULAR*
NEURULAS*
NEUSTONS*
NEUTERED
NEUTRALS*
NEUTRINO s
NEUTRONS*
NEWBORNS*
NEWCOMER s
NEWFOUND
NEWLYWED s
NEWSBEAT s
NEWSBOYS*
NEWSCAST s
NEWSDESK s
NEWSGIRL s
NEWSHAWK s
NEWSIEST*
NEWSLESS
NEWSPEAK s
NEWSREEL s
NEWSROOM s
NEWSWIRE s
NEWWAVER s
NEXTDOOR
NGULTRUM s
NIBBLERS*
NIBBLING
NIBLICKS*
NICENESS
NICETIES
NICKELED
NICKELIC
s NICKERED
NICKLING
NICKNACK s
NICKNAME drs
NICOTINE*s
NICOTINS*
NICTATED*
NICTATES*
NIDATING
NIDATION s
NIDERING s
NIDIFIED
NIDIFIES
NIELLIST s
NIELLOED
NIFFERED
NIFTIEST*
NIGELLAS*
NIGGARDS*
s NIGGLERS*
NIGGLIER
s NIGGLING s
NIGHNESS
NIGHTCAP s
NIGHTIES*
NIGHTJAR s
NIGROSIN es
NIHILISM s
NIHILIST s
NIHILITY
NILGHAIS*
NILGHAUS*
NIMBLEST
NIMBUSED
NIMBUSES
NINEBARK s
NINEFOLD
NINEPINS*
NINETEEN s
NINETIES
NINNYISH
NIOBATES*
NIOBITES*
NIOBIUMS*
s NIPPIEST
NIRVANAS*
NIRVANIC
NITERIES*
NITINOLS*
NITPICKS*
NITPICKY*
NITRATED*
NITRATES*
NITRATOR s
NITRIDED*
NITRIDES*
NITRILES*
NITRITES*
NITROGEN s
NITROLIC
NITROSYL s
NITTIEST
NIZAMATE s
ks NOBBIEST
NOBBLERS*
NOBBLING
NOBELIUM s
NOBILITY
NOBLEMAN
NOBLEMEN
NOBLESSE s
NOBODIES
NOCTUIDS*
NOCTULES*
NOCTUOID
NOCTURNE*s
NOCTURNS*
NODALITY
NODDLING
NODOSITY
NODULOSE
NODULOUS
NOESISES
NOGGINGS*
NOISETTE s
NOISIEST
NOMADISM s
NOMARCHS*
NOMARCHY*
NOMBRILS*
NOMINALS*
NOMINATE ds
NOMINEES*
NOMISTIC
NOMOGRAM s
NOMOLOGY
NONACIDS*
NONACTOR s
NONADULT s
NONAGONS*
NONBANKS*
NONBASIC
NONBEING s
NONBLACK s
NONBOOKS*
NONBRAND
NONCLASS
NONCLING
NONCOLAS*
NONCOLOR s
NONCRIME s
NONDAIRY
NONDANCE rs
NONELECT
NONELITE
NONEMPTY
NONENTRY
NONEQUAL s
NONESUCH
NONEVENT s
NONFACTS*
NONFATAL
NONFATTY
NONFINAL
NONFLUID s
NONFOCAL
NONGLARE s
NONGREEN
NONGUEST s
NONGUILT s
NONHARDY
NONHUMAN s
NONIDEAL
NONIMAGE s
NONINERT
NONIONIC
NONISSUE s
NONJUROR s
NONLABOR
NONLEAFY
NONLEGAL
NONLEVEL
NONLIVES
NONLOCAL s
NONLOYAL
NONLYRIC
NONMAJOR s
NONMETAL s
NONMETRO
NONMODAL
NONMONEY
NONMORAL
NONMUSIC s
NONNASAL
NONNAVAL
NONNOBLE
NONNOVEL s
NONOBESE
NONOHMIC
NONOWNER s
NONPAGAN s
NONPAPAL
NONPARTY
NONPASTS*
NONPLAYS*
NONPOINT
NONPOLAR
NONPRINT
NONQUOTA
NONRATED
NONRIGID
NONRIVAL s
NONROYAL
NONRURAL
NONSENSE s
NONSKEDS*
NONSKIER s
NONSOLAR
NONSOLID s
NONSTICK y
NONSTOPS*
NONSTORY

NONSTYLE s
NONSUGAR s
NONSUITS*
NONTAXES
NONTIDAL
NONTITLE
NONTONAL
NONTONIC
NONTOXIC
NONTRUMP
NONTRUTH s
NONUNION s
NONUPLES*
NONURBAN
NONUSERS*
NONUSING
NONVALID
NONVIRAL
NONVITAL
NONVOCAL s
NONVOTER s
NONWHITE s
NONWOODY
NONWORDS*
NONWOVEN s
NOODGING
NOODLING
NOOKLIKE
NOONDAYS*
NOONINGS*
NOONTIDE s
NOONTIME s
NOPALITO s
NORLANDS*
NORMALCY
NORMALLY
NORMANDE
NORMLESS
NORTHERN*s
NORTHERS*
NORTHING s
NOSEBAGS*
NOSEBAND s
NOSEDIVE ds
NOSEDOVE
NOSEGAYS*
NOSELESS
NOSELIKE
NOSINESS
NOSOLOGY
NOSTRILS*
NOSTRUMS*
NOTABLES*
NOTARIAL
NOTARIES
NOTARIZE ds
NOTATING
NOTATION s
NOTCHERS*
NOTCHING
NOTEBOOK s
NOTECARD s
NOTECASE s
NOTELESS
NOTEPADS*
NOTHINGS*
NOTICERS*
NOTICING
NOTIFIED
NOTIFIER s
NOTIFIES
NOTIONAL
NOTORNIS
NOTTURNI
NOTTURNO
NOUMENAL*
NOUMENON
NOUNALLY
NOUNLESS
NOUVELLE s
NOVALIKE
*NOVATION s
NOVELISE ds
NOVELIST s
NOVELIZE drs
NOVELLAS*
NOVERCAL
NOWADAYS
NOWHERES*
ks NUBBIEST
NUBBLIER
NUBILITY
NUBILOSE
NUBILOUS
NUCELLAR
NUCELLUS
NUCLEASE s
e NUCLEATE ds
NUCLEINS*
NUCLEOID s
NUCLEOLE s
NUCLEOLI
NUCLEONS*
NUCLIDES*
NUCLIDIC
NUDENESS
NUDICAUL
NUDITIES
NUDNICKS*
NUDZHING
NUGATORY
NUISANCE s
*NUMBERED
NUMBERER s
NUMBFISH
NUMBNESS
NUMCHUCK s
NUMERACY
NUMERALS*
NUMERARY
e NUMERATE ds
NUMERICS*
NUMEROUS
NUMINOUS
NUMMULAR
NUMSKULL s
NUNATAKS*
NUNCHAKU s
NUPTIALS*
NURSINGS*
NURSLING s
NURTURAL
NURTURED*
NURTURER*s
NURTURES*
NUTATING
NUTATION s
NUTBROWN
NUTCASES*
NUTGALLS*
NUTGRASS
NUTHATCH
NUTHOUSE s
NUTMEATS*
NUTPICKS*
NUTRIENT s
NUTSEDGE s
NUTSHELL s
NUTSIEST
NUTTIEST
NUTTINGS*
NUTWOODS*
NUZZLERS*
NUZZLING
NYLGHAIS*
NYLGHAUS*
NYMPHEAN
NYMPHETS*
NYSTATIN s
OAFISHLY
OARLOCKS*
OATCAKES*
OATMEALS*
OBDURACY
OBDURATE
OBEAHISM s
OBEDIENT
OBEISANT
OBELISED*
OBELISES*
OBELISKS*
OBELISMS*
OBELIZED*
OBELIZES*
OBEYABLE
OBITUARY
OBJECTED
OBJECTOR s
OBLATELY
OBLATION s
OBLATORY
OBLIGATE ds
OBLIGATI
OBLIGATO rs
OBLIGEES*
OBLIGERS*
OBLIGING
OBLIGORS*
OBLIQUED*
OBLIQUES*
OBLIVION s
OBLONGLY
OBSCENER*
OBSCURED*
OBSCURER*
OBSCURES*t
OBSERVED*
OBSERVER*s
OBSERVES*
OBSESSED
OBSESSES
OBSESSOR s
OBSIDIAN s
OBSOLETE ds
OBSTACLE s
OBSTRUCT s
OBTAINED
OBTAINER s
OBTECTED
OBTESTED
OBTRUDED*
OBTRUDER*s
OBTRUDES*
OBTUNDED
OBTURATE ds
OBTUSELY
OBTUSEST
OBTUSITY
OBVERSES*
OBVERTED
OBVIABLE
OBVIATED*
OBVIATES*
OBVIATOR s
OBVOLUTE
OCARINAS
OCCASION s
OCCIDENT s
OCCIPITA l
OCCIPUTS*
OCCLUDED*
OCCLUDES*
OCCLUSAL
OCCULTED
OCCULTER s
OCCULTLY
OCCUPANT s
OCCUPIED
OCCUPIER s
OCCUPIES
OCCURRED
OCEANAUT s
OCELLATE d
t OCHERING
OCHEROUS
OCHREOUS
OCOTILLO s
OCTAGONS*
OCTANGLE s
OCTANOLS*
OCTANTAL
OCTARCHY
OCTETTES*
OCTONARY
OCTOPODS*
OCTOROON s
OCTUPLED*
OCTUPLES*
OCTUPLET*s
OCTUPLEX*
j OCULARLY
OCULISTS*
ODALISKS*
ODDBALLS*
ODDITIES
ODDMENTS*
ODIOUSLY
ODOGRAPH s
ODOMETER s
i ODOMETRY
ODONATES
ODONTOID s
ODORANTS*
ODORIZED*
ODORIZES*
ODORLESS
ODOURFUL
ODYSSEYS*
*OECOLOGY
*OEDEMATA
OEDIPEAN
OEILLADE s
p*OENOLOGY
OENOMELS*
OERSTEDS*
OESTRINS
*OESTRIOL s
*OESTRONE s
*OESTROUS
OESTRUMS
OFFBEATS*
OFFCASTS*
OFFENCES*
OFFENDED
OFFENDER s
OFFENSES*
OFFERERS*
cg OFFERING s
OFFERORS*
OFFICERS*
OFFICIAL s
OFFISHLY
OFFLOADS*
OFFPRINT s
OFFRAMPS*
OFFSHOOT s
OFFSHORE s
OFFSIDES*
OFFSTAGE s
OFFTRACK
OFTENEST
OFTTIMES
OGHAMIST s
OGREISMS*
OGRESSES
OGRISHLY
OHMMETER s
OILBIRDS*
OILCAMPS*
OILCLOTH s
OILHOLES*
OILINESS
OILPAPER s
OILPROOF
OILSEEDS*
OILSKINS*
OILSTONE s
OILTIGHT
OINOLOGY
OINOMELS*
OINTMENT s
OITICICA s
OKEYDOKE y
OLDSQUAW s
OLDSTERS*
OLDSTYLE s
OLDWIVES
OLEANDER s
OLEASTER s
OLEFINES*
OLEFINIC
OLESTRAS*
OLIBANUM s
OLICOOKS*
OLIGARCH sy
OLIGOMER s
OLIGURIA s
OLIVINES*
OLIVINIC
o OLOGISTS*
OLOROSOS*
OLYMPIAD s
OMELETTE s
lm OMENTUMS*
OMICRONS
OMIKRONS
*OMISSION s
*OMISSIVE
OMITTERS*
OMITTING
OMNIARCH s
OMNIFORM
OMNIMODE
OMNIVORA
OMNIVORE s
OMOPHAGY
OMPHALOS
ONANISMS
ONANISTS*
ONCIDIUM s
ONCOGENE s
ONCOLOGY
ONCOMING s
ONDOGRAM s
ONERIEST
ONLOADED
ONLOOKER s
ONRUSHES
ONSCREEN
ONSTREAM
ONTOGENY
ONTOLOGY
z OOGAMETE s
OOGAMIES
OOGAMOUS
z OOGENIES
OOGONIAL*
OOGONIUM s
OOLACHAN s
z*OOLOGIES
z*OOLOGIST s
OOMIACKS*
OOMPAHED
z OOPHYTES*
z OOPHYTIC
z OOSPERMS*
n OOSPHERE s
z OOSPORES*
z OOSPORIC
OOTHECAE*
OOTHECAL*
bw OOZINESS
OPALESCE ds
OPALINES*
OPAQUELY
OPAQUEST*
OPAQUING
OPENABLE
OPENCAST
OPENINGS*
OPENNESS
OPENWORK s
OPERABLE
OPERABLY
OPERANDS*
OPERANTS*
OPERATED*
OPERATES*
OPERATIC s
OPERATOR s
OPERCELE s
OPERCULA r
OPERCULE s
OPERETTA s
OPHIDIAN s
OPIATING
OPINIONS
OPIUMISM s
OPOSSUMS
OPPIDANS*
OPPILANT
OPPILATE ds
OPPONENT s
OPPOSERS*
OPPOSING
OPPOSITE s
OPPUGNED
OPPUGNER s
OPSONIFY
OPSONINS*
OPSONIZE ds
OPTATIVE s
OPTICIAN s
OPTICIST s
OPTIMISE ds
OPTIMISM s
OPTIMIST s
OPTIMIZE drs
OPTIMUMS*
OPTIONAL s
OPTIONED
OPTIONEE s
OPULENCE s
OPULENCY
OPUNTIAS*
OPUSCULA r
OPUSCULE s
OQUASSAS*
ORACULAR
m ORALISMS*
m ORALISTS*
ORANGERY
*ORANGIER
ORANGISH
ORATIONS
ORATORIO s
ORATRESS
ORBITALS*
ORBITERS*
ORBITING
ORCHARDS*
ORCHISES
ORCHITIC
ORCHITIS
ORCINOLS*
ORDAINED
ORDAINER s
b ORDERERS*
b ORDERING
ORDINALS*
ORDINAND s
ORDINARY
ORDINATE s
ORDNANCE s
ORDUROUS
ORECTIVE
OREGANOS*
OREODONT s
ORGANDIE s
ORGANICS*
ORGANISE drs
ORGANISM s
ORGANIST s
ORGANIZE drs
ORGANONS*
ORGANUMS*
ORGANZAS*
ORGASMED
ORGASMIC
ORGASTIC
ORGIASTS*
ORGULOUS
ORIBATID s
ORIENTAL s
ORIENTED
ORIENTER s
ORIFICES*
ORIGAMIS*
ORIGANUM s
ORIGINAL s
ORINASAL s
ORNAMENT s
ORNATELY
ORNERIER
ORNITHES
ORNITHIC
OROGENIC
OROMETER s
ORPHANED
ORPHICAL
ORPHISMS*
ORPHREYS*
ORPIMENT s
ORRERIES
ORTHICON s
ORTHODOX y
ORTHOEPY
ORTHOSES
ORTHOSIS
ORTHOTIC s
ORTOLANS*
OSCININE
OSCITANT
OSCULANT
OSCULATE ds
OSMOSING
OSMUNDAS*
OSNABURG s
OSSATURE s
OSSETRAS*
OSSICLES*
OSSIFIED
OSSIFIER s
OSSIFIES
OSTEITIC
OSTEITIS
OSTEOIDS*
OSTEOMAS*
OSTEOSES
OSTEOSIS
OSTINATI
OSTINATO s
OSTIOLAR
OSTIOLES*
p OSTMARKS*
*OSTOMATE s
OSTOMIES
OSTRACOD es
OSTRACON
OSTRAKON
OTALGIAS*
OTALGIES
OTIOSELY
OTIOSITY
OTITIDES
OTITISES
OTOCYSTS*
OTOLITHS*
OTOSCOPE s
OTOSCOPY
OTOTOXIC
OTTOMANS*
OUABAINS*
OUGHTING
OUGUIYAS*
OUISTITI s
OUTACTED
OUTADDED
OUTARGUE ds
OUTASKED
OUTBACKS*
OUTBAKED*
OUTBAKES*
OUTBARKS*
OUTBAWLS*
OUTBEAMS*
OUTBITCH
OUTBLAZE ds
OUTBLEAT s
OUTBLESS
OUTBLOOM s
OUTBLUFF s
OUTBLUSH
OUTBOARD s
OUTBOAST s
OUTBOUND
OUTBOXED
OUTBOXES
OUTBRAGS*
OUTBRAVE ds
OUTBRAWL s
OUTBREAK s
OUTBREED s
OUTBRIBE ds
OUTBUILD s
OUTBUILT
OUTBULGE ds
OUTBULKS*
OUTBULLY
OUTBURNS*
OUTBURNT*
OUTBURST s
OUTCALLS*
OUTCAPER s
OUTCASTE*s
OUTCASTS*
OUTCATCH
OUTCAVIL s
OUTCHARM s
OUTCHEAT s
OUTCHIDE*ds
OUTCLASS
OUTCLIMB s
OUTCLOMB
OUTCOACH
OUTCOMES*
OUTCOOKS*
OUTCOUNT s
OUTCRAWL s
OUTCRIED
OUTCRIES
OUTCROPS*
OUTCROSS
OUTCROWD*s
OUTCROWS*
OUTCURSE ds
OUTCURVE s
OUTDANCE ds
OUTDARED*
OUTDARES*
OUTDATED*
OUTDATES*
OUTDODGE ds
OUTDOERS*
OUTDOING
OUTDOORS*y
OUTDRAGS*
OUTDRANK
OUTDRAWN*
OUTDRAWS*
OUTDREAM st
OUTDRESS
OUTDRINK s
OUTDRIVE ns
OUTDROPS*
OUTDROVE
OUTDRUNK
OUTDUELS*
OUTEARNS*
OUTEATEN
OUTFABLE ds
OUTFACED*
OUTFACES*
OUTFALLS*
OUTFASTS*
OUTFAWNS*
OUTFEAST s
OUTFEELS*
OUTFENCE ds
OUTFIELD s
OUTFIGHT s
OUTFINDS*

OUTFIRED*
OUTFIRES*
OUTFLANK s
OUTFLIES
OUTFLOAT s
OUTFLOWN*
OUTFLOWS*
OUTFOOLS*
OUTFOOTS*
OUTFOUND
OUTFOXED
OUTFOXES
OUTFROWN s
OUTGAINS*
OUTGAZED*
OUTGAZES*
OUTGIVEN*
OUTGIVES*
OUTGLARE ds
OUTGLEAM s
OUTGLOWS*
OUTGNAWN*
OUTGNAWS*
OUTGOING s
OUTGRINS*
OUTGROSS
OUTGROUP s
OUTGROWN*
OUTGROWS*
OUTGUESS
OUTGUIDE ds
OUTHAULS*
OUTHEARD*
OUTHEARS*
OUTHOMER s
OUTHOUSE s
OUTHOWLS*
OUTHUMOR s
OUTHUNTS*
OUTJUMPS*
OUTKEEPS*
OUTKICKS*
OUTKILLS*
OUTLANDS*
OUTLASTS*
OUTLAUGH s
OUTLAWED
OUTLAWRY
OUTLEADS*
OUTLEAPS*
OUTLEAPT*
OUTLEARN st
OUTLIERS*
OUTLINED*
OUTLINER*s
OUTLINES*
OUTLIVED*
OUTLIVER*s
OUTLIVES*
OUTLOOKS*
OUTLOVED*
OUTLOVES*
OUTLYING
OUTMARCH
OUTMATCH
OUTMODED*
OUTMODES*
OUTMOVED*
OUTMOVES*
OUTPACED*
OUTPACES*
OUTPAINT s
OUTPITCH
OUTPLACE ds
OUTPLANS*
OUTPLAYS*
OUTPLODS*
OUTPLOTS*
OUTPOINT s
OUTPOLLS*
OUTPORTS*
OUTPOSTS*
OUTPOURS*
OUTPOWER s
OUTPRAYS*
OUTPREEN s
OUTPRESS
OUTPRICE ds
OUTPULLS*
OUTPUNCH
OUTPUPIL s
OUTQUOTE ds
OUTRACED*
OUTRACES*
OUTRAGED*
OUTRAGES*
OUTRAISE ds
OUTRANCE s
OUTRANGE*ds
OUTRANKS*
OUTRATED*
OUTRATES*
OUTRAVED*
OUTRAVES*
OUTREACH
OUTREADS*
OUTRIDER*s
OUTRIDES*
OUTRIGHT
OUTRINGS*
OUTRIVAL s
OUTROARS*
OUTROCKS*
OUTROLLS*
OUTROOTS*
OUTROWED
OUTSAILS*
OUTSAVOR s
OUTSCOLD s
OUTSCOOP s
OUTSCORE ds
OUTSCORN s
OUTSELLS*
OUTSERTS*
OUTSERVE ds
OUTSHAME ds
OUTSHINE ds
OUTSHONE
OUTSHOOT s
OUTSHOUT s
OUTSIDER*s
OUTSIDES*
OUTSIGHT s
OUTSINGS*
OUTSIZED*
OUTSIZES*
OUTSKATE ds
OUTSKIRT s
OUTSLEEP s
OUTSLEPT
OUTSLICK s
OUTSMART s
OUTSMELL s
OUTSMELT
OUTSMILE ds
OUTSMOKE ds
OUTSNORE ds
OUTSOARS*
OUTSOLES*
OUTSPANS*
OUTSPEAK s
OUTSPEED s
OUTSPELL s
OUTSPELT
OUTSPEND s
OUTSPENT
OUTSPOKE n
OUTSTAND s
OUTSTARE ds
OUTSTART s
OUTSTATE ds
OUTSTAYS*
OUTSTEER s
OUTSTOOD
OUTSTRIP s
OUTSTUDY
OUTSTUNT s
OUTSULKS*
OUTSWARE
OUTSWEAR s
OUTSWEEP s
OUTSWEPT
OUTSWIMS*
OUTSWING s
OUTSWORE
OUTSWORN
OUTSWUNG
OUTTAKES*
OUTTALKS*
OUTTASKS*
OUTTELLS*
OUTTHANK s
OUTTHINK s
OUTTHREW
OUTTHROB s
OUTTHROW ns
OUTTOWER s
OUTTRADE ds
OUTTRICK s
OUTTROTS*
OUTTRUMP s
OUTTURNS*
OUTVALUE ds
OUTVAUNT s
OUTVOICE ds
OUTVOTED*
OUTVOTES*
OUTVYING
OUTWAITS*
OUTWALKS*
OUTWARDS*
OUTWASTE ds
OUTWATCH
OUTWEARS*
OUTWEARY*
OUTWEEPS*
OUTWEIGH s
OUTWHIRL s
OUTWILED*
OUTWILES*
OUTWILLS*
OUTWINDS*
OUTWORKS*
OUTWRITE*s
OUTWROTE
OUTYELLS*
OUTYELPS*
OUTYIELD s
OVALNESS
*OVARIOLE s
OVARITIS
n OVATIONS*
OVENBIRD s
OVENLIKE
OVENWARE s
c OVERABLE
OVERACTS*
OVERAGED*
c OVERAGES*
c OVERALLS*
OVERARCH
OVERARMS*
OVERAWED*
OVERAWES*
OVERBAKE ds
OVERBEAR s
OVERBEAT s
OVERBETS*
OVERBIDS
OVERBILL s
OVERBITE s
OVERBLEW
OVERBLOW ns
OVERBOIL s
OVERBOLD
OVERBOOK s
OVERBORE
OVERBORN e
OVERBRED
OVERBURN st
OVERBUSY
OVERBUYS*
OVERCALL s
OVERCAME
OVERCAST s
OVERCOAT s
OVERCOLD
OVERCOME rs
OVERCOOK s
OVERCOOL s
OVERCRAM s
OVERCROP s
OVERCURE ds
OVERCUTS*
OVERDARE ds
OVERDEAR
OVERDECK s
OVERDOER s
OVERDOES
OVERDOGS*
OVERDONE
OVERDOSE ds
OVERDRAW ns
OVERDREW
OVERDUBS*
OVERDYED*
OVERDYER*s
OVERDYES*
OVEREASY
OVEREATS*
OVEREDIT s
OVERFAST
OVERFEAR s
OVERFEED s
OVERFILL s
OVERFISH
OVERFLEW
OVERFLOW ns
OVERFOND
OVERFOUL
OVERFREE
OVERFULL
OVERFUND s
OVERGILD s
OVERGILT
OVERGIRD s
OVERGIRT
OVERGLAD
OVERGOAD s
OVERGREW
OVERGROW ns
OVERHAND s
OVERHANG s
OVERHARD
OVERHATE ds
OVERHAUL s
OVERHEAD s
OVERHEAP s
OVERHEAR ds
OVERHEAT s
OVERHELD
OVERHIGH
OVERHOLD s
OVERHOLY
OVERHOPE ds
OVERHUNG
OVERHUNT s
OVERHYPE ds
OVERIDLE
OVERJOYS*
OVERJUST
OVERKEEN
OVERKILL s
OVERKIND
OVERLADE dns
OVERLAID
OVERLAIN
OVERLAND s
OVERLAPS*
OVERLATE
OVERLAYS*
OVERLEAF
OVERLEAP st
OVERLEND s
OVERLENT
c OVERLETS*
OVERLEWD
OVERLIES*
OVERLIVE ds
OVERLOAD s
OVERLONG
OVERLOOK s
OVERLORD s
OVERLOUD
OVERLOVE ds
OVERLUSH
OVERMANS*
OVERMANY*
OVERMEEK
OVERMELT s
OVERMILD
OVERMILK s
OVERMINE ds
OVERMUCH
OVERNEAR
OVERNEAT
OVERNICE
OVERPACK s
OVERPAID
OVERPASS
OVERPAST
OVERPAYS*
OVERPERT
OVERPLAN st
OVERPLAY s
OVERPLOT s
OVERPLUS
OVERPUMP s
OVERRANK*
OVERRASH
OVERRATE ds
OVERRICH
OVERRIDE s
OVERRIFE
OVERRIPE
OVERRODE
OVERRUDE
OVERRUFF s
OVERRULE ds
OVERRUNS*
OVERSALE s
OVERSALT s
OVERSAVE ds
OVERSEAS*
OVERSEED*s
OVERSEEN*
OVERSEER*s
OVERSEES*
OVERSELL s
OVERSETS
OVERSEWN*
OVERSEWS*
OVERSHOE s
OVERSHOT s
OVERSICK
OVERSIDE s
OVERSIZE ds
c OVERSLIP st
OVERSLOW
OVERSOAK s
OVERSOFT
OVERSOLD
OVERSOON
OVERSOUL s
OVERSPIN s
OVERSTAY s
OVERSTEP s
OVERSTIR s
OVERSUDS
OVERSUPS*
OVERSURE
OVERTAKE ns
OVERTALK s
OVERTAME
OVERTART
OVERTASK s
OVERTHIN k
OVERTIME ds
OVERTIPS*
OVERTIRE ds
OVERTOIL s
OVERTONE s
OVERTOOK
OVERTOPS*
OVERTRIM s
c OVERTURE ds
OVERTURN s
OVERURGE ds
OVERUSED*
OVERUSES*
OVERVIEW s
OVERVOTE ds
OVERWARM s
OVERWARY
OVERWEAK
OVERWEAR sy
OVERWEEN s
OVERWETS*
OVERWIDE
OVERWILY
OVERWIND s
OVERWISE
OVERWORD s
OVERWORE
OVERWORK s
OVERWORN
OVERZEAL s
OVICIDAL
OVICIDES*
OVIDUCAL
OVIDUCTS*
OVIPOSIT s
OVOIDALS*
OVULATED*
OVULATES*
OWLISHLY
OXALATED*
OXALATES*
OXALISES
OXAZEPAM s
OXAZINES*
OXBLOODS*
OXHEARTS*
OXIDABLE
OXIDANTS*
OXIDASES*
OXIDASIC
OXIDATED*
OXIDATES*
OXIDISED*
OXIDISER*s
OXIDISES*
OXIDIZED*
OXIDIZER*s
OXIDIZES*
OXIMETER s
OXIMETRY
OXPECKER s
OXTONGUE s
OXYACIDS*
OXYGENIC
OXYMORON s
OXYPHILE*s
OXYPHILS*
OXYSALTS*
OXYSOMES*
OXYTOCIC s
OXYTOCIN s
OXYTONES*
r OYSTERED
OYSTERER s
OZONATED
OZONATES*
OZONIDES*
OZONISED*
OZONISES*
OZONIZED*
OZONIZER*s
OZONIZES*
PABULUMS*
PACHADOM s
PACHALIC s
PACHINKO s
PACHISIS*
PACHOULI s
PACHUCOS*
o PACIFIED
o PACIFIER s
o PACIFIES
PACIFISM s
PACIFIST s
PACKABLE
PACKAGED*
PACKAGER*s
PACKAGES*
PACKETED
PACKINGS*
PACKNESS
PACKSACK s
PACTIONS
PADDINGS*
PADDLERS*
*PADDLING s
PADDOCKS*
PADISHAH s
PADLOCKS*
PADRONES*
PADSHAHS*
PADUASOY s
PAEANISM s
PAESANOS*
PAGANDOM s
PAGANISE ds
PAGANISH
PAGANISM s
PAGANIST s
PAGANIZE drs
PAGEANTS*
PAGEBOYS*
PAGEFULS*
PAGINATE ds
PAGURIAN s
PAGURIDS*
PAHLAVIS*
PAHOEHOE s
PAILFULS*
PAILLARD s
PAILSFUL
PAINCHES
PAINLESS
PAINTERS*
PAINTIER
PAINTING s
PAIRINGS
PAISANAS*
PAISANOS*
PAISLEYS*
PAJAMAED
PALABRAS*
PALADINS*
PALATALS*
PALATIAL
PALATINE s
PALAVERS*
PALAZZOS*
PALEFACE s
PALENESS
PALEOSOL s
PALESTRA els
PALETOTS*
PALETTES*
PALEWAYS
PALEWISE
PALFREYS*
PALIKARS*
*PALIMONY
PALINODE s
PALISADE ds
PALLADIA
PALLADIC
PALLETED
PALLETTE s
PALLIATE ds
PALLIDLY
PALLIEST
PALLIUMS
PALMATED*
PALMETTE s
PALMETTO s
PALMFULS*
PALMIEST
PALMISTS*
PALMITIN s
PALMLIKE
PALMTOPS*
PALMYRAS*
PALOMINO s
PALOOKAS*
PALPABLE
PALPABLY
PALPATED*
PALPATES*
PALPATOR sy
PALPEBRA els
PALSHIPS*
PALSYING
*PALTERED
*PALTERER s
PALTRIER
PALTRILY
PALUDISM s
PAMPEANS*
PAMPERED
PAMPERER s
PAMPEROS*
PAMPHLET s
PANACEAN*
PANACEAS*
PANACHES*
PANATELA s
PANBROIL s
PANCAKED*
PANCAKES*
PANCETTA s
PANCREAS
PANDANUS
PANDECTS*
PANDEMIC s
PANDERED
PANDERER s
PANDOORS*
PANDORAS*
PANDORES*
PANDOURS*
PANDOWDY
PANDURAS*
PANDYING
PANELESS
*PANELING s
PANELIST s
PANELLED
PANETELA s
PANFRIED
PANFRIES
PANGENES*
PANGOLIN s
PANGRAMS*
PANHUMAN
PANICKED
PANICLED*
PANICLES*
PANICUMS*
PANMIXES
PANMIXIA s
PANMIXIS
PANNIERS*
PANNIKIN s
PANOCHAS*
PANOCHES*
PANOPTIC
PANORAMA s
PANPIPES*
PANSOPHY
PANTALET s
PANTHEON s
PANTHERS
PANTILED*
PANTILES*
PANTOFLE s
PANTOUMS*
PANTRIES
PANTSUIT s

PAPACIES
PAPADAMS*
PAPADOMS*
PAPADUMS*
PAPERBOY s
PAPERERS*
PAPERING
PAPHIANS*
PAPILLAE*
PAPILLAR*y
PAPILLON s
PAPOOSES*
PAPPADAM s
PAPPIEST*
PAPPOOSE s
PAPRICAS*
PAPRIKAS*
PAPULOSE
PAPYRIAN
PAPYRINE
s*PARABLES*
PARABOLA s
PARACHOR s
PARADERS*
PARADIGM s
PARADING
PARADISE s
PARADORS*
PARADROP s
PARAFFIN es
PARAFOIL s
PARAFORM s
PARAGOGE s
PARAGONS*
PARAKEET s
PARAKITE s
PARALLAX
PARALLEL s
PARALYSE ds
PARALYZE drs
PARAMENT as
PARAMOUR s
PARANOEA s
PARANOIA cs
PARANOIC s
PARANOID s
PARAPETS*
PARAQUAT s
PARAQUET s
PARASAIL s
PARASANG s
PARASHAH s
PARASHOT h
PARASITE s
PARASOLS*
PARAVANE s
PARAWING s
PARAZOAN s
PARBAKED*
PARBAKES*
PARBOILS*
PARCELED
PARCENER s
PARCHESI*s
*PARCHING
PARCHISI s
PARCLOSE s
PARDNERS*
PARDONED
PARDONER s
PARECISM s
PAREIRAS*
PARENTAL
PARENTED
PARERGON
PARETICS*
PARFAITS*
PARFLESH
PARFOCAL
PARGETED
PARGINGS*
PARHELIA
PARHELIC
PARIETAL s
PARIETES
PARISHES
PARITIES
PARKADES*
PARKETTE s
PARKINGS*
PARKLAND s
PARKLIKE
PARKWAYS*
PARLANCE s
PARLANDO
PARLANTE
PARLAYED
PARLEYED
PARLEYER s
PARLOURS*
PARMESAN s
PARODIED
PARODIES
PARODIST s
PAROLEES*
PAROLING
PARONYMS*
PAROQUET s
PAROSMIA s
PAROTIDS*
PAROTOID s
PAROXYSM s
PARQUETS*
PARRIDGE s
PARRIERS*
PARRITCH
PARROKET s
PARROTED
PARROTER s
PARRYING
PARSABLE
PARSLEYS*
PARSLIED
PARSNIPS*
PARSONIC
PARTAKEN*
PARTAKER*s
PARTAKES*
PARTERRE s
PARTIALS*
PARTIBLE
*PARTICLE s
PARTIERS*
PARTINGS*
*PARTISAN s
PARTITAS*
PARTIZAN s
PARTLETS*
PARTNERS*
PARTYERS*
PARTYING
PARVENUE*s
PARVENUS*
PARVISES*
PARVOLIN es
PASCHALS*
PASHADOM s
PASHALIC s
PASHALIK s
PASHMINA s
PASQUILS*
PASSABLE
PASSABLY
PASSADES*
PASSADOS*
PASSAGED*
PASSAGES*
PASSBAND s
PASSBOOK s
PASSERBY
PASSIBLE
PASSINGS*
PASSIONS*
PASSIVES*
PASSKEYS*
PASSLESS
PASSOVER s
PASSPORT s
PASSUSES
PASSWORD s
PASTERNS*
PASTEUPS*
PASTICCI o
PASTICHE s
PASTIEST*
PASTILLE s
PASTIMES*
PASTINAS*
PASTISES
PASTITSO s
PASTLESS
PASTNESS
PASTORAL eis
PASTORED
PASTORLY
PASTRAMI s
PASTRIES
PASTROMI s
PASTURAL
PASTURED*
PASTURER*s
PASTURES*
PATAGIAL*
PATAGIUM
PATAMARS*
PATCHERS*
PATCHIER
PATCHILY
PATCHING
PATELLAE*
PATELLAR*
PATELLAS*
PATENTED
PATENTEE s
PATENTLY
PATENTOR s
PATERNAL
a PATHETIC
PATHLESS
PATHOGEN esy
PATHOSES
PATHWAYS*
PATIENCE s
PATIENTS*
PATINAED*
PATINATE ds
PATINING
PATINIZE ds
PATOOTIE s
PATRIATE ds
PATRIOTS*
PATRONAL
PATRONLY
PATROONS*
PATTAMAR s
PATTENED
s PATTERED
PATTERER s
PATTERNS*
PATTYPAN s
PATULENT
PATULOUS
PAULDRON s
PAUNCHED
PAUNCHES
PAUPERED
PAVEMENT s
PAVILION s
PAVILLON s
PAVIOURS*
PAVISERS*
PAVISSES*
PAVLOVAS*
PAVONINE
PAWKIEST
PAWNABLE
PAWNAGES*
PAWNSHOP s
PAXWAXES
PAYABLES*
PAYBACKS*
PAYCHECK s
PAYGRADE s
PAYLOADS*
PAYMENTS*
PAYROLLS*
PAZAZZES
PEACEFUL
PEACENIK s
PEACHERS*
PEACHIER
PEACHING
PEACOATS*
PEACOCKS*
PEACOCKY*
PEAFOWLS*
PEAKIEST
PEAKLESS
PEAKLIKE
PEARLASH
PEARLERS*
*PEARLIER
PEARLING
PEARLITE s
PEARMAIN s
PEARTEST
PEARWOOD s
PEASANTS*
PEASCODS*
PEASECOD s
PEATIEST
PEBBLIER
PEBBLING
PECCABLE
PECCANCY
PECCAVIS*
PECKIEST
PECORINI
PECORINO s
PECTASES
s PECTATES*
PECTINES
PECTIZED*
PECTIZES*
PECTORAL s
s PECULATE ds
PECULIAR*s
PECULIUM
PEDAGOGS*
PEDAGOGY*
PEDALERS*
PEDALFER s
PEDALIER s
PEDALING
PEDALLED
PEDALLER s
PEDANTIC
PEDANTRY
PEDATELY
PEDDLERS*
PEDDLERY*
PEDDLING
PEDERAST sy
PEDESTAL s
PEDICABS*
PEDICELS*
PEDICLED*
PEDICLES*
PEDICURE ds
PEDIFORM
PEDIGREE ds
PEDIMENT s
PEDIPALP s
PEDOCALS*
PEDOLOGY
PEDUNCLE ds
PEEBEENS*
PEEKABOO s
PEEKAPOO s
PEELABLE
PEELINGS*
PEEPHOLE s
PEEPSHOW s
PEERAGES*
PEERLESS
PEESWEEP s
PEETWEET s
PEGBOARD s
PEGBOXES
PEIGNOIR s
PEKEPOOS*
PELAGIAL
PELAGICS*
PELERINE s
PELICANS*
PELISSES*
PELLAGRA s
PELLETAL
PELLETED
PELLICLE s
PELLMELL s
PELLUCID
PELORIAN*
PELORIAS*
PELOTONS*
PELTASTS*
PELTERED
PELTLESS
PELTRIES
PELVISES
PEMBINAS*
PEMICANS*
PEMMICAN s
PEMOLINE s
PENALISE ds
PENALITY
PENALIZE ds
PENANCED*
PENANCES*
*PENCHANT s
PENCILED
PENCILER s
PENDANTS*
PENDENCY
PENDENTS*
PENDULAR
PENDULUM s
PENGUINS*
PENICILS*
PENITENT s
PENKNIFE
PENLIGHT s
PENLITES*
PENNAMES*
PENNANTS*
PENNATED*
PENNINES*
PENNONED
PENOCHES*
*PENOLOGY
PENONCEL s
PENPOINT s
PENSIONE*drs
PENSIONS*
PENSTERS*
PENSTOCK s
PENTACLE s
PENTAGON s
PENTANES*
PENTANOL s
PENTARCH sy
PENTENES*
PENTODES*
PENTOMIC
PENTOSAN s
PENTOSES*
PENUCHES*
PENUCHIS*
PENUCHLE s
PENUCKLE s
PENUMBRA els
PENURIES
PEONAGES*
PEONISMS
PEOPLERS*
PEOPLING
PEPERONI s
PEPLOSES
PEPLUMED
PEPLUSES
PEPONIDA s
PEPONIUM s
PEPPERED
PEPPERER s
PEPPIEST
PEPSINES*
PEPTALKS*
PEPTIDES*
PEPTIDIC
PEPTIZED*
PEPTIZER*s
PEPTIZES*
PEPTONES*
PEPTONIC
PERACIDS*
PERCALES*
PERCEIVE drs
PERCENTS*
PERCEPTS*
PERCHERS*
PERCHING
PERCOIDS*
PERDURED*
PERDURES*
PEREGRIN es
PEREIONS*
PEREOPOD s
PERFECTA*s
PERFECTO*s
PERFECTS*
PERFORCE
PERFORMS*
PERFUMED*
PERFUMER*sy
PERFUMES*
PERFUSED*
PERFUSES*
PERGOLAS*
PERIANTH s
PERIAPTS*
PERIBLEM s
PERICARP s
PERICOPE s
PERIDERM s
PERIDIAL*
PERIDIUM
PERIDOTS*
PERIGEAL
PERIGEAN
PERIGEES*
PERIGONS*
PERIGYNY
PERILING
PERILLAS*
PERILLED
PERILOUS
PERILUNE s
PERINEAL*
PERINEUM
a PERIODIC
PERIODID s
PERIOTIC
PERIPETY
PERIPTER s
PERIQUES*
PERISARC s
PERISHED
PERISHES
PERIWIGS*
PERJURED*
PERJURER*s
PERJURES*
PERKIEST
PERLITES*
PERLITIC
PERMEANT
PERMEASE s
PERMEATE ds
PERMUTED*
PERMUTES*
PERONEAL
PERORATE ds
PEROXIDE*ds
PEROXIDS*
PERPENDS*
PERPENTS*
PERSALTS*
PERSISTS*
PERSONAE*
PERSONAL*s
PERSONAS*
PERSPIRE ds
PERSPIRY
PERSUADE drs
PERTAINS*
PERTNESS
PERTURBS*
PERUSALS*
PERUSERS*
PERUSING
PERVADED*
PERVADER*s
PERVADES*
PERVERSE
PERVERTS*
PERVIOUS
PESKIEST
PESTERED
PESTERER s
PESTHOLE s
PESTIEST
PESTLING
PETABYTE s
PETALINE
PETALLED
PETALODY
PETALOID
a PETALOUS
PETCOCKS*
PETECHIA el
PETERING
PETIOLAR
PETIOLED*
PETIOLES*
PETITION s
PETNAPER s
PETRALES*
PETROLIC
PETRONEL s
PETROSAL
PETTABLE
PETTEDLY
PETTIEST
PETTIFOG s
PETTINGS*
PETTLING
PETULANT
PETUNIAS*
PETUNTSE s
PETUNTZE s
PEWTERER s
PEYTRALS*
PEYTRELS*
PFENNIGE*
PFENNIGS*
PHAETONS*
PHALANGE rs
PHALLISM s
PHALLIST s
PHANTASM as
PHANTAST s
PHANTASY
PHANTOMS*
PHARAOHS*
PHARISEE s
PHARMACY
*PHARMING s
PHAROSES
PHASEOUT s
PHASMIDS*
PHATTEST
PHEASANT s
PHELLEMS*
PHELONIA
PHENATES*
PHENAZIN es
PHENETIC s
PHENETOL es
PHENIXES
PHENOLIC s
PHENYLIC
a PHERESES
a PHERESIS
PHILABEG s
PHILIBEG s
PHILOMEL as
PHILTERS*
PHILTRED*
PHILTRES*
PHILTRUM
PHIMOSES
PHIMOSIS
PHIMOTIC
PHONATED*
PHONATES*
PHONEMES*
PHONEMIC s
PHONETIC s
*PHONEYED
PHONIEST*
PHONYING
e PHORATES*
PHORONID s
PHOSGENE s
PHOSPHID es
PHOSPHIN es
PHOSPHOR eis
PHOTOING
PHOTOMAP s
PHOTONIC s
PHOTOPIA s
PHOTOPIC
PHOTOSET s
PHRASING s
PHRATRAL
PHRATRIC
PHREAKED
PHREAKER s
PHREATIC
PHTHALIC
PHTHALIN s
PHTHISES
PHTHISIC s
PHTHISIS
PHYLAXIS
PHYLESES
PHYLESIS
PHYLETIC s
PHYLLARY
PHYLLITE s
PHYLLODE s
PHYLLOID s
PHYLLOME s
PHYSICAL s
PHYSIQUE ds
PHYTANES*
PHYTONIC
PIACULAR
PIAFFERS*
PIAFFING
PIANISMS*
PIANISTS*
PIASABAS*
PIASAVAS*
PIASSABA s
PIASSAVA s
PIASTERS*
PIASTRES*
PIBROCHS*
PICACHOS*
PICADORS*
PICAROON s
PICAYUNE s
PICCOLOS*
PICIFORM
PICKADIL s
PICKAXED*
PICKAXES*
PICKEERS*
PICKEREL s
PICKETED
PICKETER s

*PICKIEST
PICKINGS*
PICKLING
PICKLOCK s
PICKOFFS*
PICKWICK s
PICLORAM s
PICNICKY
PICOGRAM s
PICOLINE*s
PICOLINS*
PICOMOLE s
PICOTEES*
PICOTING
PICOWAVE ds
PICQUETS*
PICRATED*
PICRATES*
PICRITES*
e PICRITIC
PICTURED*
PICTURES*
PIDDLERS*
PIDDLING
PIDDOCKS*
PIEBALDS*
PIECINGS*
PIECRUST s
PIEDFORT s
PIEDMONT s
PIEFORTS*
PIEHOLES*
PIEPLANT s
PIERCERS*
PIERCING s
PIERROTS*
PIETISMS*
PIETISTS*
PIFFLING
PIGBOATS*
PIGGIEST*
PIGMENTS*
PIGNOLIA*s
PIGNOLIS*
PIGSKINS*
PIGSNEYS*
PIGSTICK s
PIGSTIES
PIGTAILS*
PIGWEEDS*
PILASTER s
PILCHARD s
PILEATED*
PILELESS
PILEWORT s
PILFERED
PILFERER s
PILGRIMS*
PILIFORM
PILLAGED*
PILLAGER*s
s PILLAGES*
PILLARED
PILLIONS*
PILLOWED
PILOSITY
PILOTAGE s
PILOTING s
PILSENER s
PILSNERS*
PIMENTOS*
PIMIENTO s
PIMPLIER
PINAFORE ds
PINASTER s
PINBALLS*
PINBONES*
PINCHBUG s
PINCHECK s
PINCHERS
*PINCHING
s PINDLING
PINECONE s
PINELAND s
s PINELIKE
PINERIES
PINESAPS*
PINEWOOD s
PINFOLDS
PINGRASS
PINHEADS*
PINHOLES*
o PINIONED
PINITOLS*
PINKENED
PINKEYES*

PINKINGS*
PINKNESS
PINKROOT s
PINNACES*
PINNACLE ds
PINNATED*
PINNIPED s
PINNULAE*
PINNULAR*
PINNULES*
PINOCHLE s
PINOCLES*
PINPOINT s
PINPRICK s
PINSCHER s
PINTADAS*
PINTADOS*
PINTAILS*
PINTANOS*
PINTSIZE d
PINWALES*
PINWEEDS*
PINWHEEL s
PINWORKS*
PINWORMS*
PIONEERS*
PIPEAGES*
PIPEFISH
PIPEFULS*
PIPELESS
PIPELIKE
PIPELINE ds
PIPERINE s
PIPESTEM s
PIPETTED*
PIPETTES*
PIPINESS
PIPINGLY
PIQUANCE s
PIQUANCY
PIRACIES
PIRAGUAS*
PIRANHAS*
PIRARUCU s
PIRATING
PIRIFORM
PIROGIES
PIROGUES*
PIROQUES*
PIROSHKI
PIROZHKI
PIROZHOK
PISCATOR sy
PISCINAE*
PISCINAL*
PISCINAS*
PISHOGES*
PISHOGUE s
PISIFORM s
PISMIRES*
PISOLITE s
PISOLITH s
PISSOIRS*
PISTACHE s
PISTOLED*
PISTOLES*
PITAHAYA s
PITAPATS*
PITCHERS*
*PITCHIER
*PITCHILY
*PITCHING
PITCHMAN
PITCHMEN
PITCHOUT s
PITFALLS*
PITHEADS*
PITHIEST
PITHLESS
PITIABLE
PITIABLY
PITILESS
PITTANCE s
PITTINGS*
PIVOTING
PIVOTMAN
PIVOTMEN
PIXIEISH
PIXINESS
PIZAZZES
PIZZAZES
PIZZAZZY*
PIZZELLE s
PIZZERIA s
PLACABLE
PLACABLY

PLACARDS*
PLACATED*
PLACATER*s
PLACATES*
PLACEBOS*
PLACEMAN
PLACEMEN t
PLACENTA els
PLACIDLY
PLACKETS*
PLACOIDS*
PLAFONDS*
PLAGIARY
PLAGUERS*
PLAGUILY
PLAGUING
PLAINEST
PLAINING
PLAISTER s
PLAITERS*
PLAITING s
PLANARIA ns
PLANCHES*
PLANCHET*s
PLANFORM s
PLANGENT
PLANKING s
PLANKTER s
PLANKTON s
PLANLESS
PLANNERS
PLANNING s
PLANOSOL s
PLANTAIN s
PLANTERS*
PLANTING s
PLANTLET s
PLANULAE*
PLANULAR*
s*PLASHERS*
s PLASHIER
s*PLASHING
PLASMIDS*
PLASMINS*
PLASMOID s
PLASMONS*
PLASTERS
PLASTERY*
PLASTICS*
PLASTIDS*
PLASTRAL
PLASTRON s
PLASTRUM s
PLATANES*
PLATEAUS*
PLATEAUX*
PLATEFUL s
PLATELET s
PLATFORM s
PLATIEST*
PLATINAS
PLATINGS*
PLATINIC
PLATINUM s
PLATONIC
PLATOONS*
s PLATTERS*
s PLATTING
PLATYPUS
PLAUDITS*
PLAUSIVE
PLAYABLE
PLAYACTS*
PLAYBACK s
PLAYBILL s
PLAYBOOK s
PLAYBOYS*
PLAYDATE s
PLAYDAYS*
PLAYDOWN s
PLAYGIRL s
PLAYGOER s
PLAYLAND s
PLAYLESS
PLAYLETS*
PLAYLIKE
PLAYLIST s
PLAYMATE s
PLAYOFFS
PLAYPENS*
PLAYROOM s
PLAYSUIT s
PLAYTIME s
PLAYWEAR
*PLEACHED
*PLEACHES

PLEADERS
*PLEADING s
PLEASANT
PLEASERS
*PLEASING
PLEASURE ds
PLEATERS*
*PLEATHER s
PLEATING
PLEBEIAN s
PLECTRON s
PLECTRUM s
PLEDGEES*
PLEDGEOR s
PLEDGERS
PLEDGETS*
PLEDGING
PLEDGORS*
PLEIADES
PLENCHES
PLENISMS*
PLENISTS*
PLENTIES
PLEONASM s
PLEOPODS*
PLESSORS
PLETHORA s
PLEURISY
PLEUSTON s
PLEXUSES
PLIANTLY
PLICATED*
u*PLIGHTED
*PLIGHTER s
PLIMSOLE*s
PLIMSOLL*s
PLIMSOLS*
PLINKERS
u*PLINKING
PLIOCENE
PLIOFILM s
PLIOTRON s
PLISKIES*
PLODDERS*
PLODDING
PLOIDIES
PLONKING
*PLOPPING
PLOSIONS*
PLOSIVES*
PLOTLESS
PLOTLINE s
PLOTTAGE s
PLOTTERS
PLOTTIER
PLOTTIES t
*PLOTTING
PLOTZING
PLOUGHED
PLOUGHER s
PLOWABLE
PLOWBACK s
PLOWBOYS
PLOWHEAD s
*PLOWLAND s
PLUCKERS*
*PLUCKIER
*PLUCKILY
*PLUCKING
PLUGGERS
*PLUGGING
PLUGLESS
PLUGOLAS*
PLUGUGLY
PLUMAGED*
PLUMAGES*
*PLUMBAGO s
PLUMBERS
PLUMBERY*
PLUMBING s
PLUMBISM s
PLUMBOUS
PLUMBUMS*
PLUMELET s
PLUMERIA s
PLUMIEST
PLUMIPED s
PLUMLIKE
PLUMMEST
PLUMMETS*
PLUMMIER
PLUMPENS
PLUMPERS
PLUMPEST
*PLUMPING
*PLUMPISH

PLUMULAR
PLUMULES*
PLUNDERS*
PLUNGERS
*PLUNGING
PLUNKERS
PLUNKIER
PLUNKING
PLURALLY
PLUSHEST
PLUSHIER
PLUSHILY
PLUSSAGE s
PLUTONIC
PLUVIALS*
PLUVIOSE
PLUVIOUS
*PLYINGLY
PLYWOODS*
POACEOUS
POACHERS*
POACHIER
POACHING
POBLANOS*
POCHARDS*
POCKETED
POCKETER s
POCKIEST
POCKMARK s
POCOSENS*
POCOSINS*
POCOSONS*
PODAGRAL*
PODAGRAS*
PODAGRIC
PODESTAS*
PODGIEST
PODIATRY
PODOCARP
PODOMERE s
PODSOLIC
PODZOLIC
POECHORE s
POETICAL
POETISED*
POETISER*s
POETISES*
POETIZED*
POETIZER*s
POETIZES*
POETLESS
POETLIKE
POETRIES
POGONIAS*
POGONIPS*
POGROMED
POIGNANT
POINDING
POINTERS*
POINTIER
POINTING
POINTMAN
POINTMEN
POISONED
POISONER s
POITRELS*
POKEROOT s
POKEWEED s
POKINESS
POLARISE ds
POLARITY
POLARIZE drs
POLARONS*
POLEAXED*
POLEAXES*
POLECATS*
POLELESS
POLEMICS*
POLEMIST s
POLEMIZE ds
POLENTAS*
POLESTAR s
POLEWARD
POLICERS*
POLICIES
POLICING
POLISHED
POLISHER s
POLISHES
POLITELY
POLITEST
POLITICK*s
POLITICO*s
POLITICS*
POLITIES
POLKAING

POLLACKS*
POLLARDS*
POLLENED
POLLICAL
POLLICES
POLLINIA
POLLINIC
POLLISTS*
POLLIWOG s
POLLOCKS*
POLLSTER s
POLLUTED*
POLLUTER*s
POLLUTES*
POLLYWOG s
POLOISTS*
POLONIUM s
POLTROON s
POLYBRID s
POLYCOTS*
POLYENES*
POLYENIC
POLYGALA s
POLYGAMY
POLYGENE s
POLYGLOT s
POLYGONS*
POLYGONY*
POLYGYNY
POLYMATH sy
POLYMERS*
POLYNYAS*
POLYOMAS*
POLYPARY
POLYPEDS*
POLYPIDE s
POLYPNEA s
POLYPODS*
POLYPODY*
POLYPOID
POLYPORE s
POLYPOUS
POLYSEMY
POLYSOME s
POLYTENE
POLYTENY
POLYTYPE s
POLYURIA s
POLYURIC
POLYZOAN s
POLYZOIC
POMADING
POMANDER s
POMATUMS*
POMFRETS*
POMMELED
POMOLOGY
POMPANOS*
PONCHOED
PONDERED
PONDERER s
PONDWEED s
PONIARDS*
PONTIFEX
PONTIFFS*
PONTIFIC
s PONTOONS*
PONYTAIL s
POOCHING
POOLHALL s
POOLROOM s
POOLSIDE s
POORNESS
POORTITH s
POPCORNS*
POPEDOMS*
POPELESS
POPELIKE
POPINJAY s
POPLITEI
POPLITIC
POPOVERS*
POPPADOM s
POPPADUM s
POPPLING
POPSICLE s
POPULACE s
POPULATE ds
POPULISM s
POPULIST s
POPULOUS
PORCINIS*
PORKIEST*
PORKPIES*
PORKWOOD s
PORNIEST

POROSITY
POROUSLY
PORPHYRY
PORPOISE ds
PORRIDGE s
PORRIDGY
PORTABLE s
PORTABLY
PORTAGED*
PORTAGES*
PORTALED
PORTANCE s
PORTAPAK s
PORTENDS*
PORTENTS*
PORTERED
PORTHOLE s
PORTICOS*
PORTIERE s
PORTIONS*
PORTLESS
PORTLIER
PORTRAIT s
PORTRAYS*
PORTRESS
PORTSIDE
POSHNESS
POSINGLY
POSITING
POSITION s
POSITIVE rs
POSITRON s
POSOLOGY
POSSIBLE r
POSSIBLY
POSTAGES*
POSTALLY
POSTANAL
POSTBAGS*
POSTBASE
POSTBOYS*
POSTBURN
POSTCARD s
POSTCAVA els
POSTCODE s
POSTCOUP
POSTDATE ds
POSTDIVE
POSTDOCS*
POSTDRUG
POSTEENS*
POSTERNS*
POSTFACE s
POSTFIRE
POSTFORM s
POSTGAME
POSTGRAD s
POSTHEAT s
POSTHOLE s
POSTICHE s
POSTINGS*
POSTIQUE s
POSTLUDE s
*POSTMARK s
POSTORAL
POSTPAID
POSTPONE drs
POSTPOSE ds
POSTPUNK
POSTRACE
POSTRIOT
POSTSHOW
POSTSYNC s
POSTTEEN s
POSTTEST s
POSTURAL
POSTURED*
POSTURER*s
POSTURES*
POTABLES*
POTASHES
POTASSIC
POTATION s
POTATOES
POTATORY
POTBELLY
POTBOILS*
POTBOUND
POTENCES*
POTENTLY
POTHEADS*
POTHEENS*
POTHERBS*
POTHERED
POTHOLED*
POTHOLES*

POTHOOKS*
POTHOUSE s
POTICHES*
POTLACHE*s
POTLATCH
POTLINES*
POTLUCKS*
POTSHARD s
POTSHERD s
POTSHOTS*
POTSTONE s
POTTAGES*
POTTEENS*
POTTERED
POTTERER s
s POTTIEST*
POUCHIER
*POUCHING
POULARDE*s
POULARDS*
POULTERS*
POULTICE ds
POUNCERS*
POUNCING
POUNDAGE s
POUNDALS*
POUNDERS*
POUNDING
POURABLE
POUSSIES*
POUTIEST
POUTINES*
POWDERED
POWDERER s
POWERFUL
POWERING
POWWOWED
POXVIRUS
POZZOLAN as
PRACTICE*drs
PRACTISE ds
PRAECIPE s
PRAEDIAL
PRAEFECT s
PRAELECT s
PRAETORS*
PRAIRIES*
u*PRAISERS*
u*PRAISING
PRALINES*
PRANCERS*
PRANCING
PRANDIAL
*PRANGING
*PRANKING
*PRANKISH
PRATFALL s
PRATIQUE s
s*PRATTLED*
*PRATTLER*s
s*PRATTLES*
PRAWNERS*
PRAWNING
PRAXISES
u*PREACHED
*PREACHER s
u*PREACHES
*PREACTED
*PREADAPT s
*PREADMIT s
*PREADOPT s
PREADULT s
*PREALLOT s
*PREALTER s
PREAMBLE ds
*PREAPPLY
*PREARMED
PREAUDIT s
PREAVERS
PREAXIAL
PREBAKED*
PREBAKES*
PREBASAL
PREBENDS*
PREBILLS
PREBINDS
*PREBIRTH s
PREBLESS
*PREBOARD s
PREBOILS
PREBOOKS
*PREBOUND
*PREBUILD s
*PREBUILT
PRECASTS
PRECAVAE*

PRECAVAL*
PRECEDED
PRECEDES
PRECENTS*
PRECEPTS
*PRECHECK s
PRECHILL s
*PRECHOSE n
PRECIEUX
PRECINCT s
PRECIOUS
PRECIPES
PRECISED*
PRECISER*
PRECISES*t
*PRECITED
*PRECLEAN s
PRECLEAR s
PRECLUDE ds
PRECODED
PRECODES
PRECOOKS
PRECOOLS*
PRECRASH
PRECURED*
PRECURES*
PREDATED
PREDATES
PREDATOR sy
PREDAWNS*
PREDEATH s
PREDELLA s
PREDICTS*
*PREDRAFT
*PREDRIED
*PREDRIES
*PREDRILL s
PREDUSKS*
PREEDITS
*PREELECT s
PREEMIES*
PREEMPTS*
*PREENACT s
PREENERS*
PREENING
*PREERECT s
PREEXIST s
PREFACED
PREFACER*s
PREFACES
PREFADED*
PREFADES*
PREFECTS
*PREFIGHT
PREFILED
PREFILES
PREFIRED
PREFIRES
PREFIXAL
*PREFIXED
*PREFIXES
PREFLAME
*PREFOCUS
PREFORMS
PREFRANK s
*PREFROZE n
PREFUNDS
PREGAMES*
PREGGERS
*PREGNANT
PREGUIDE ds
PREHEATS
PREHUMAN s
*PREJUDGE drs
PRELATES
PRELATIC
PRELECTS*
PRELEGAL
PRELIMIT s
*PRELIVES
PRELOADS
PRELUDED*
PRELUDER*s
PRELUDES*
PRELUNCH
PREMEDIC s
PREMIERE*ds
PREMIERS*
PREMISED
PREMISES
PREMIUMS*
*PREMIXED
*PREMIXES
PREMOLAR s
PREMOLDS
PREMORAL

*PREMORSE
PRENAMES
PRENATAL
PRENOMEN s
PRENTICE ds
*PREORDER s
PREOWNED
PREPACKS
PREPARED*
PREPARER*s
PREPARES*
PREPASTE ds
PREPAVED
PREPAVES
PREPENSE
*PREPLACE ds
PREPLANS
PREPLANT
PREPPIER*
PREPPIES*t
PREPPILY
*PREPPING
PREPREGS*
*PREPRESS
*PREPRICE ds
*PREPRINT s
PREPUBES
PREPUBIS
PREPUCES*
PREPUNCH
PREPUPAE*
PREPUPAL*
PREPUPAS*
PREQUELS*
PRERADIO
PRERENAL
PRERINSE ds
PRESAGED*
PRESAGER*s
PRESAGES*
PRESALES
*PRESCIND s
*PRESCORE ds
PRESELLS
PRESENCE s
PRESENTS
*PRESERVE drs
*PRESHAPE ds
PRESHIPS
PRESHOWN
PRESHOWS
PRESIDED
*PRESIDER*s
PRESIDES
PRESIDIA l
PRESIDIO s
PRESIFTS
PRESLEEP
PRESLICE ds
PRESOAKS
*PRESOLVE ds
PRESORTS
*PRESPLIT
PRESSERS*
PRESSING s
PRESSMAN
PRESSMEN
PRESSORS*
PRESSRUN s
PRESSURE ds
*PRESTAMP s
PRESTERS
PRESTIGE s
*PRESTORE ds
PRESUMED
*PRESUMER*s
PRESUMES
PRETAPED
PRETAPES
*PRETASTE ds
PRETEENS*
PRETELLS
PRETENCE s
PRETENDS*
PRETENSE s
PRETERIT es
PRETERMS*
PRETESTS
PRETEXTS*
*PRETRAIN s
*PRETREAT s
*PRETRIAL s
PRETRIMS
PRETTIED
PRETTIER
PRETTIES t

PRETTIFY
PRETTILY
PRETYPED
PRETYPES
PRETZELS*
*PREUNION s
*PREUNITE ds
PREVAILS*
*PREVALUE ds
PREVENTS*
PREVERBS
PREVIEWS
PREVIOUS
PREVISED
PREVISES
*PREVISIT s
*PREVISOR s
PREVUING
PREWARMS
PREWARNS*
*PREWEIGH s
PREWIRED
PREWIRES
PREWORKS
PREWRAPS
PRIAPEAN
PRIAPISM s
PRICIEST
PRICKERS*
PRICKETS
PRICKIER
*PRICKING s
PRICKLED*
PRICKLES*
PRIDEFUL
PRIEDIEU sx
PRIESTED
PRIESTLY
PRIGGERY
s*PRIGGING
PRIGGISH
PRIGGISM s
*PRILLING
PRIMAGES*
PRIMATAL s
PRIMATES*
PRIMEROS*
PRIMEVAL
PRIMINES*
PRIMINGS*
PRIMMEST
*PRIMMING
PRIMNESS
PRIMPING
PRIMROSE s
PRIMULAS*
PRIMUSES
PRINCELY
PRINCESS*e
PRINCIPE
PRINCIPI a
PRINCOCK s
PRINKERS*
PRINKING
s PRINTERS*
PRINTERY*
s PRINTING s
PRINTOUT s
PRIORATE s
PRIORESS
PRIORIES
a PRIORITY
PRISERES*
PRISMOID s
PRISONED
PRISONER s
PRISSIER
PRISSIES t
PRISSILY
PRISSING
PRISTANE s
PRISTINE
PRIVATER*
PRIVATES*t
PRIVIEST*
PROBABLE s
PROBABLY
PROBANDS
PROBANGS*
PROBATED*
PROBATES*
PROBLEMS*
PROCAINE s
PROCARPS*
PROCEEDS*
PROCHAIN

PROCHEIN
PROCLAIM s
PROCTORS*
PROCURAL s
PROCURED*
PROCURER*s
PROCURES*s
PRODDERS*
*PRODDING
PRODIGAL s
PRODROME s
PRODRUGS*
PRODUCED*
PRODUCER*s
PRODUCES*
PRODUCTS*
PROEMIAL
PROETTES*
PROFANED*
PROFANER*s
PROFANES*
PROFFERS*
PROFILED*
PROFILER*s
PROFILES*
PROFITED
PROFITER s
PROFORMA
PROFOUND s
PROGERIA s
PROGGERS*
PROGGING
PROGNOSE ds
PROGRADE
PROGRAMS*
PROGRESS
PROHIBIT s
PROJECTS*
PROLABOR
PROLAMIN es
PROLAPSE ds
PROLIFIC
PROLINES*
PROLIXLY
PROLOGED
PROLOGUE ds
PROLONGE*drs
PROLONGS*
PROMINES*
PROMISED*
PROMISEE*s
PROMISER*s
PROMISES*
PROMISOR s
PROMOING
PROMOTED*
PROMOTER*s
PROMOTES*
PROMPTED
PROMPTER s
PROMPTLY
PROMULGE ds
PRONATED*
PRONATES*
PRONATOR s
PRONGING
PRONOTUM
PRONOUNS*
PROOFERS
*PROOFING
PROPANES*
PROPENDS*
PROPENES*
PROPENOL s
PROPENSE
PROPENYL
PROPERER
PROPERLY
PROPERTY
PROPHAGE s
PROPHASE s
PROPHECY
PROPHESY
PROPHETS*
PROPINED*
PROPINES*
PROPJETS*
PROPOLIS
PROPONED*
PROPONES*
PROPOSAL s
PROPOSED*
PROPOSER*s
PROPOSES*
PROPOUND s
PROPPING

PROPRIUM
PROPYLIC
PROPYLON
PRORATED*
PRORATES*
PROROGUE ds
PROSAISM s
PROSAIST s
PROSECTS*
*PROSIEST
PROSODIC
PROSOMAL*
PROSOMAS*
PROSPECT s
PROSPERS*
PROSSIES*
PROSTATE s
PROSTIES*
PROSTYLE s
PROTAMIN es
PROTASES
PROTASIS
PROTATIC
PROTEANS*
PROTEASE*s
PROTECTS*
PROTEGEE*s
PROTEGES*
PROTEIDE*s
PROTEIDS*
PROTEINS*
PROTENDS*
PROTEOME s
PROTEOSE s
PROTESTS*
PROTISTS*
PROTIUMS*
PROTOCOL s
PROTONIC
PROTOPOD s
PROTOXID es
PROTOZOA ln
PROTRACT s
PROTRADE
PROTRUDE ds
PROTYLES*
PROUDEST
PROUDFUL
PROUNION
PROVABLE
PROVABLY
PROVENLY
PROVERBS*
PROVIDED*
PROVIDER*s
PROVIDES*
PROVINCE s
PROVIRAL
PROVIRUS
PROVISOS*
PROVOKED*
PROVOKER*s
PROVOKES*
PROVOSTS*
PROWLERS*
PROWLING
PROXEMIC s
PROXIMAL
PRUDENCE s
PRUINOSE
PRUNABLE
PRUNELLA s
PRUNELLE s
PRUNELLO s
PRUNUSES
PRURIENT
PRURIGOS*
PRURITIC
PRURITUS
PRYINGLY
PSALMING
PSALMIST s
PSALMODY
PSALTERS
PSALTERY*
PSAMMITE s
PSAMMONS*
PSCHENTS*
PSEPHITE s
*PSHAWING
PSILOCIN s
PSILOSES
PSILOSIS
PSILOTIC
PSORALEA s
PSORALEN s

PSYCHICS*
PSYCHING
PSYLLIDS*
PSYLLIUM s
PTEROPOD s
PTERYGIA l
PTERYLAE*
PTOMAINE*s
PTOMAINS*
PTYALINS*
PTYALISM s
PUBERTAL
PUBLICAN s
PUBLICLY
PUCCOONS*
PUCKERED
PUCKERER s
PUDDINGS*
PUDDLERS*
PUDDLIER
PUDDLING s
PUDENDAL*
PUDENDUM
PUDGIEST
PUDIBUND
PUERPERA el
PUFFBALL s
PUFFIEST
PUGAREES*
PUGGAREE s
PUGGIEST
PUGGREES*
PUGGRIES
PUGILISM s
PUGILIST s
PUGMARKS*
PUISSANT
PULICENE
PULICIDE s
PULINGLY
PULLBACK s
PULLMANS*
PULLOUTS*
PULLOVER s
PULMONIC
PULMOTOR s
PULPALLY
PULPIEST
PULPITAL
PULPLESS
PULPWOOD s
PULSATED*
PULSATES*
PULSATOR sy
PULSEJET s
PULSIONS*
PULSOJET s
PULVILLI
PULVINAR
PULVINUS
PUMICERS*
PUMICING
PUMICITE s
PUMMELED
PUMMELOS*
PUMPKINS*
PUMPLESS
PUMPLIKE
PUNCHEON s
PUNCHERS*
PUNCHIER
PUNCHILY
PUNCHING
PUNCTATE d
PUNCTUAL
PUNCTURE ds
PUNDITIC
PUNDITRY
PUNGENCY
PUNGLING
PUNINESS
PUNISHED
PUNISHER s
PUNISHES
PUNITION s
*PUNITIVE
PUNITORY
s PUNKIEST*
PUNNIEST
PUNSTERS*
PUPARIAL*
PUPARIUM
PUPATING
PUPATION s
PUPILAGE s
PUPILARY*

PUPPETRY
PUPPYDOM s
PUPPYISH
PURBLIND
PURCHASE drs
PUREBRED s
PUREEING
PURENESS
PURFLERS*
PURFLING s
PURGINGS*
PURIFIED
PURIFIER s
PURIFIES
PURISTIC
PURITANS*
PURITIES
PURLIEUS*
PURLINES*
PURLINGS*
PURLOINS*
PURPLEST*
PURPLING
PURPLISH
PURPORTS*
PURPOSED*
PURPOSES*
PURPURAS*
PURPURES*
PURPURIC
PURPURIN s
PURSIEST
PURSLANE s
PURSUANT
PURSUERS*
PURSUING
PURSUITS*
PURTIEST
PURULENT
PURVEYED
PURVEYOR s
PURVIEWS*
PUSHBALL s
PUSHCART s
PUSHDOWN s
PUSHIEST
PUSHOVER s
PUSHPINS*
PUSHRODS*
PUSSIEST*
PUSSLEYS*
PUSSLIES
PUSSLIKE
PUSSYCAT s
PUSTULAR
PUSTULED*
PUSTULES*
PUTAMINA
PUTATIVE
PUTDOWNS*
PUTRIDLY
PUTSCHES
s*PUTTERED
s*PUTTERER s
PUTTIERS*
PUTTYING
PUZZLERS*
PUZZLING
PYAEMIAS*
PYCNIDIA l
PYCNOSES
PYCNOSIS
PYCNOTIC
PYELITIC
PYELITIS
PYGIDIAL*
PYGIDIUM
PYGMAEAN
PYGMYISH
PYGMYISM s
PYKNOSES
PYKNOSIS
PYKNOTIC
PYODERMA s
PYOGENIC
PYORRHEA ls
PYRALIDS*
PYRAMIDS*
PYRANOID
PYRANOSE s
PYRENOID s
PYREXIAL*
PYREXIAS*
PYRIDINE s
PYRIFORM
PYRITOUS

PYROGENS*
PYROLIZE ds
PYROLOGY
PYROLYZE drs
PYRONINE s
PYROSTAT s
PYROXENE s
PYRRHICS*
PYRROLES*
PYRROLIC
PYRUVATE s
PYTHONIC
PYXIDIUM
QABALAHS*
QINDARKA
QUAALUDE s
QUACKERY
QUACKIER
QUACKING
QUACKISH
QUACKISM s
s QUADDING
QUADPLEX
QUADRANS
QUADRANT s
QUADRATE*ds
QUADRATS*
QUADRICS*
QUADRIGA e
QUADROON s
QUAESTOR s
QUAFFERS*
QUAFFING
QUAGGIER
QUAGMIRE s
QUAGMIRY
QUAHAUGS*
QUAICHES
QUAILING
QUAINTER
QUAINTLY
QUAKIEST
QUALMIER
QUALMISH
QUANDANG s
QUANDARY
QUANDONG s
QUANTICS*
QUANTIFY
QUANTILE s
QUANTING
QUANTITY
QUANTIZE drs
QUANTONG s
QUARRELS*
QUARRIED
QUARRIER s
QUARRIES
QUARTANS*
QUARTERN*s
QUARTERS*
QUARTETS*
QUARTICS*
QUARTIER s
QUARTILE s
QUARTZES
s QUASHERS*
s QUASHING
QUASSIAS*
QUASSINS*
QUATORZE s
QUATRAIN s
QUAVERED
QUAVERER s
QUAYAGES*
QUAYLIKE
QUAYSIDE s
QUEASIER
QUEASILY
QUEAZIER
QUEENDOM s
QUEENING
QUEEREST
QUEERING
QUEERISH
QUELLERS*
QUELLING
QUENCHED
QUENCHER s
QUENCHES
QUENELLE s
QUERCINE
QUERIDAS*
QUERIERS*
QUERISTS*
QUERYING

QUESTERS*
QUESTING
QUESTION s
QUESTORS*
QUETZALS*
QUEUEING
QUEZALES
QUIBBLED*
QUIBBLER*s
QUIBBLES*
QUICKENS*
QUICKEST
QUICKIES*
QUICKSET s
QUIDDITY
QUIDNUNC s
QUIETENS*
QUIETERS*
QUIETEST
QUIETING
QUIETISM s
QUIETIST s
QUIETUDE s
QUILLAIA*s
QUILLAIS*
QUILLAJA s
QUILLETS*
QUILLING s
QUILTERS*
QUILTING s
QUINCUNX
QUINELAS*
QUINELLA s
QUINIELA s
QUININAS*
QUININES*
QUINNATS*
QUINOIDS*
QUINOLIN es
QUINONES*
QUINSIED
QUINSIES
QUINTAIN s
QUINTALS*
QUINTANS*
QUINTARS*
QUINTETS*
QUINTICS*
QUINTILE s
QUINTINS*
e QUIPPERS*
QUIPPIER
e QUIPPING
QUIPPISH
QUIPSTER s
QUIRKIER
QUIRKILY
QUIRKING
QUIRKISH
s QUIRTING
QUISLING s
QUITCHES
QUITRENT s
QUITTERS*
QUITTING
QUITTORS*
QUIVERED
QUIVERER s
QUIXOTES*
QUIXOTIC
QUIXOTRY
QUIZZERS*
QUIZZING
QUOINING
QUOITING
QUOMODOS*
QUOTABLE
QUOTABLY
QUOTIENT s
QURUSHES
RABBETED
RABBINIC
RABBITED
RABBITER s
RABBITRY
bg RABBLERS*
bdg RABBLING
RABBONIS*
RABIDITY
RABIETIC
RACCOONS*
RACEMATE s
RACEMISM s
RACEMIZE ds
RACEMOID
RACEMOSE

RACEMOUS
RACEWALK s
RACEWAYS*
RACHETED
RACHIDES
RACHILLA e
RACHISES
RACHITIC
RACHITIS
RACIALLY
RACINESS
b RACKETED
RACKFULS*
RACKWORK s
RACLETTE s
RACQUETS*
*RADDLING
RADIABLE
RADIALIA
RADIALLY
RADIANCE s
RADIANCY
RADIANTS*
e RADIATED*
e RADIATES*
RADIATOR s
RADICALS*
RADICAND s
e RADICATE ds
RADICELS*
RADICLES*
RADIOING
RADIOMAN
RADIOMEN
RADISHES
RADIUSES
RADWASTE s
RAFFLERS*
RAFFLING
RAFTERED
cd RAFTSMAN
cd RAFTSMEN
RAGGEDER
RAGGEDLY
RAGINGLY
RAGOUTED
RAGTIMES*
RAGWEEDS*
RAGWORTS*
RAILBIRD s
RAILCARS*
t RAILHEAD s
RAILINGS*
RAILLERY
RAILROAD s
RAILWAYS*
RAIMENTS*
t RAINBAND s
RAINBIRD s
RAINBOWS*
RAINCOAT s
RAINDROP s
RAINFALL s
bg RAINIEST
bg RAINLESS
RAINOUTS*
b RAINWASH
RAINWEAR
RAISABLE
RAISINGS*
RAISONNE
RAKEHELL sy
RAKEOFFS*
RAKISHLY
RALLIERS*
*RALLYING s
RALLYIST s
RALPHING
RAMBLERS
b*RAMBLING
RAMBUTAN s
RAMEKINS*
RAMENTUM
RAMEQUIN s
RAMIFIED
RAMIFIES
RAMIFORM
RAMILIES*
RAMILLIE s
RAMMIEST
RAMOSELY
RAMOSITY
RAMPAGED*
RAMPAGER*s
RAMPAGES*
RAMPANCY

RAMPARTS*
RAMPIKES*
RAMPIONS*
RAMPOLES*
RAMSHORN s
RAMTILLA s
RAMULOSE
RAMULOUS
RANCHERO*s
RANCHERS*
bc RANCHING
RANCHMAN
RANCHMEN
RANCIDLY
RANCORED
RANCOURS*
RANDIEST*
RANDOMLY
o RANGIEST
RANKINGS*
RANKLESS*
c*RANKLING
f RANKNESS
RANPIKES*
RANSACKS*
RANSOMED
RANSOMER s
RAPACITY
RAPESEED s
RAPHIDES
RAPIDEST
RAPIDITY
RAPIERED
RAPPAREE s
RAPPELED
RAPPORTS*
*RAPTNESS
RAPTURED*
RAPTURES*
RAREBITS*
RAREFIED
RAREFIER s
RAREFIES
RARENESS
RARERIPE s
RARIFIED
RARIFIES
RARITIES
RASBORAS*
RASCALLY
RASHLIKE
b RASHNESS
RASORIAL
RASPIEST
RASPINGS*
w RASSLING
RATABLES*
RATAFEES*
RATAFIAS*
RATANIES
RATAPLAN s
RATATATS*
RATCHETS*
RATEABLE
RATEABLY
RATFINKS*
RATHOLES*
RATICIDE s
g RATIFIED
g RATIFIER s
g RATIFIES
RATIONAL es
RATIONED
RATLINES*
RATOONED
RATOONER s
RATSBANE s
RATTAILS*
RATTEENS*
RATTENED
RATTENER s
b RATTIEST
p RATTLERS*
bp RATTLING s
RATTOONS*
RATTRAPS*
c RAUNCHES
RAVAGERS*
RAVAGING
t RAVELERS*
gt RAVELING*s
RAVELINS*
gt RAVELLED
t RAVELLER s
RAVENERS*
c RAVENING s

RAVENOUS
RAVIGOTE s
RAVINGLY
RAVINING
RAVIOLIS*
RAVISHED
RAVISHER s
RAVISHES
RAWBONED
RAWHIDED*
RAWHIDES*
RAYGRASS
RAZEEING
RAZORING
p REABSORB s
REACCEDE ds
REACCENT s
REACCEPT s
p REACCUSE ds
bp REACHERS*
bp REACHING
REACTANT s
p REACTING
REACTION s
REACTIVE
REACTORS*
READABLE
READABLY
p READAPTS*
READDICT s
READDING
READERLY
READIEST*
READINGS*
p READJUST s
p READMITS*
p READOPTS*
READORNS*
READOUTS*
READYING
REAFFIRM s
REAGENTS*
REAGINIC
REALGARS*
REALIGNS*
REALISED*
REALISER*s
REALISES*
REALISMS*
REALISTS*
REALIZED*
REALIZER*s
REALIZES*
p REALLOTS*
REALNESS
p REALTERS*
REALTIES
REALTORS*
REANOINT s
REAPABLE
REAPHOOK s
REAPPEAR s
REARGUED*
REARGUES*
REARMICE
p REARMING
REARMOST
REAROUSE ds
REARREST s
REARWARD s
REASCEND s
REASCENT s
REASONED
REASONER s
REASSAIL s
REASSERT s
REASSESS
p REASSIGN s
REASSORT s
REASSUME ds
p REASSURE ds
REATTACH
REATTACK s
REATTAIN s
REAVAILS*
REAVOWED
REAWAKED*
REAWAKEN*s
REAWAKES*
REAWOKEN*
REBAITED
REBATERS*
REBATING
REBEGINS*
REBELDOM s
REBELLED

p REBIDDEN
p REBILLED
p REBIRTHS*
REBLENDS*
REBLOOMS*
p REBOARDS*
REBODIED
REBODIES
p REBOILED
p REBOOKED
REBOOTED
REBORING
REBOTTLE ds
p REBOUGHT
REBOUNDS*
REBRANCH
REBREEDS*
REBUFFED
p REBUILDS*
REBUKERS*
REBUKING
REBURIAL s
REBURIED
REBURIES
REBUTTAL s
REBUTTED
REBUTTER s
REBUTTON s
p REBUYING
RECALLED
RECALLER s
RECAMIER s
RECANING
RECANTED
RECANTER s
RECAPPED
RECARPET s
p RECEDING
RECEIPTS*
RECEIVED*
RECEIVER*s
RECEIVES*
RECEMENT s
p RECENSOR s
RECENTER
RECENTLY
p RECEPTOR s
p RECESSED
p RECESSES
RECHANGE ds
p RECHARGE drs
RECHARTS*
RECHEATS*
p RECHECKS*
RECHEWED
p RECHOOSE s
p RECHOSEN*
RECIRCLE ds
p RECISION s
RECITALS*
RECITERS*
RECITING
RECKLESS
RECKONED
RECKONER s
RECLAIMS*
RECLAMES*
RECLASPS*
p RECLEANS*
RECLINED*
RECLINER*s
RECLINES*
RECLOTHE ds
RECLUSES*
RECOALED
RECOATED
RECOCKED
RECODIFY
p RECODING
RECOILED
RECOILER s
RECOINED
RECOLORS*
RECOMBED
RECOMMIT s
RECONFER s
RECONNED
RECONVEY s
p RECOOKED
RECOPIED
RECOPIES
RECORDED
RECORDER s
RECORKED
RECOUNTS*
RECOUPED*

RECOUPLE ds
RECOURSE s
RECOVERS*
RECOVERY*
RECRATED*
RECRATES*
RECREANT s
RECREATE ds
RECROWNS*
RECRUITS*
RECTALLY
RECURRED
RECURVED*
RECURVES*
RECUSALS*
RECUSANT s
RECUSING
RECYCLED*
RECYCLER*s
RECYCLES*
REDACTED
REDACTOR s
REDAMAGE ds
REDARGUE ds
p REDATING
REDBAITS*
REDBIRDS*
REDBONES*
REDBRICK s
REDCOATS*
REDDENED
t REDDLING
REDECIDE ds
REDEEMED
REDEEMER s
REDEFEAT s
REDEFECT s
REDEFIED
REDEFIES
p REDEFINE ds
REDEMAND s
REDENIED
REDENIES
REDEPLOY s
REDESIGN s
REDHEADS*
REDHORSE s
REDIALED
p REDIGEST s
REDIPPED
REDIRECT s
REDIVIDE ds
REDLINED*
REDLINER*s
REDLINES*
REDOCKED
REDOLENT
REDONNED
REDOUBLE drs
REDOUBTS*
REDOUNDS*
REDPOLLS*
REDRAFTS*
REDRAWER s
REDREAMS*
REDREAMT*
p REDRILLS*
REDRIVEN*
REDRIVES*
REDROOTS*
p REDRYING
REDSHANK s
REDSHIFT s
REDSHIRT s
REDSTART s
REDTAILS*
REDUBBED
REDUCERS*
*REDUCING
*REDUCTOR s
REDUVIID s
REDWARES*
REDWINGS*
REDWOODS*
REDYEING
REEARNED
REECHIER
REECHOED
REECHOES
REEDBIRD s
REEDBUCK s
g REEDIEST
b REEDINGS*
p REEDITED
REEDLIKE
REEDLING s

REEFABLE
REEFIEST
REEJECTS*
REEKIEST
REELABLE
p REELECTS*
REELINGS*
REEMBARK s
REEMBODY
REEMERGE ds
REEMPLOY s
p REENACTS*
REENDOWS*
g REENGAGE ds
REENJOYS*
REENLIST s
REENROLL s
REENTERS*
REEQUIPS*
p REERECTS*
REESTING
REEVOKED*
REEVOKES*
REEXPELS*
REEXPORT s
p REEXPOSE ds
p REFACING
REFALLEN
REFASTEN s
REFECTED
REFELLED
REFENCED*
REFENCES*
REFEREED*
REFEREES*
REFERENT s
REFERRAL s
p REFERRED
p REFERRER s
REFIGHTS*
p REFIGURE ds
p REFILING
p REFILLED
REFILMED
REFILTER s
REFINERS*
REFINERY*
REFINING
REFINISH
p REFIRING
REFITTED
p REFIXING
REFLATED*
REFLATES*
REFLECTS*
REFLEXED
REFLEXES
REFLEXLY
REFLOATS*
REFLOODS*
REFLOWED
REFLOWER s
REFLUENT
REFLUXED
REFLUXES
REFLYING
REFOLDED
REFOREST s
REFORGED*
REFORGES*
p REFORMAT es
p REFORMED
REFORMER s
REFOUGHT
REFOUNDS*
REFRACTS*
REFRAINS*
REFRAMED*
REFRAMES*
p REFREEZE s
REFRONTS*
p REFROZEN*
REFRYING
REFUELED
REFUGEES*
REFUGING
REFUGIUM
p REFUNDED
REFUNDER s
REFUSALS*
REFUSERS*
REFUSING
REFUSNIK s
REFUTALS*
REFUTERS*
REFUTING

REGAINED
REGAINER s
REGALERS*
REGALING
REGALITY
REGARDED
REGATHER s
REGATTAS*
REGAUGED*
REGAUGES*
REGEARED
REGELATE ds
REGENTAL
REGICIDE s
REGILDED
REGIMENS*
REGIMENT*s
REGIONAL s
REGISTER s
REGISTRY
REGIVING
REGLAZED*
REGLAZES*
REGLOWED
REGLUING
p REGNANCY
REGOLITH s
REGORGED*
REGORGES*
REGOSOLS*
REGRADED*
REGRADES*
REGRAFTS*
REGRANTS*
REGRATED*
REGRATES*
REGREENS*
REGREETS*
REGRINDS*
REGROOMS*
REGROOVE ds
REGROUND
REGROUPS*
p REGROWTH s
REGULARS*
REGULATE ds
REGULINE
REHABBED
REHABBER s
REHAMMER s
p REHANDLE ds
REHANGED
p REHARDEN s
REHASHED
REHASHES
REHEARSE*drs
p REHEATED
p REHEATER s
REHEELED
REHEMMED
REHINGED*
REHINGES*
p REHIRING
REHOBOAM s
REHOUSED*
REHOUSES*
REIFIERS*
REIFYING
REIGNING
REIGNITE ds
REIMAGED*
REIMAGES*
REIMPORT s
p REIMPOSE ds
REINCITE ds
REINCURS*
REINDEER s
REINDICT s
REINDUCE ds
REINDUCT s
REINFECT s
p REINFORM s
REINFUSE ds
REINJECT s
REINJURE ds
REINJURY
REINKING
REINLESS
p REINSERT s
REINSMAN
REINSMEN
REINSURE drs
REINTERS*
REINVADE ds
REINVENT s
REINVEST s

p REINVITE ds
REINVOKE ds
REISSUED*
REISSUER*s
REISSUES*
REITBOKS*
REJACKET s
*REJECTED
REJECTEE s
REJECTER s
*REJECTOR s
REJIGGED
REJIGGER s
REJOICED*
REJOICER*s
REJOICES*
REJOINED
p REJUDGED*
p REJUDGES*
REJUGGLE ds
REKEYING
REKINDLE ds
RELABELS*
RELACING
RELANDED
RELAPSED
RELAPSER*s
RELAPSES
RELATERS
*RELATING
*RELATION s
*RELATIVE s
RELATORS*
p RELAUNCH
RELAXANT s
RELAXERS*
RELAXING*
RELAXINS*
RELAYING
RELEARNS*
RELEARNT*
RELEASED*
RELEASER*s
RELEASES*
RELEGATE ds
RELENTED
RELETTER s
RELEVANT
RELIABLE s
RELIABLY
RELIANCE s
RELIEVED*
RELIEVER*s
RELIEVES*
RELIEVOS*
RELIGHTS*
RELIGION s
RELINING
RELINKED
RELIQUES*
RELISHED
RELISHES
RELISTED
RELIVING
RELLENOS*
p RELOADED
RELOADER s
RELOANED
p RELOCATE des
RELOCKED
RELOOKED
RELUCENT
RELUCTED
RELUMINE ds
RELUMING
*REMAILED
REMAINED
REMAKERS*
REMAKING
REMANDED
REMANENT
REMANNED
REMAPPED
REMARKED
REMARKER s
p REMARKET s
REMARQUE s
REMASTER s
c REMATING
REMEDIAL
REMEDIED
REMEDIES
REMELTED
REMEMBER s
*REMENDED
REMERGED

REMERGES
REMIGIAL
REMINDED
REMINDER s
REMINTED
p REMISING
REMISSLY
REMITTAL s
*REMITTED
*REMITTER s
REMITTOR s
p REMIXING
REMNANTS*
REMODELS*
p REMODIFY
REMOLADE s
p REMOLDED
REMORSES*
REMOTELY
REMOTEST*
*REMOTION s
REMOUNTS*
REMOVALS*
REMOVERS*
REMOVING
RENAILED
RENAMING
c RENATURE ds
RENDERED
RENDERER s
RENDIBLE
RENDZINA s
RENEGADE ds
RENEGADO s
RENEGERS*
RENEGING
RENESTED
RENEWALS*
RENEWERS*
RENEWING
RENIFORM
RENIGGED
RENITENT
RENMINBI
RENNASES*
RENOGRAM s
p RENOTIFY
*RENOUNCE drs
RENOVATE ds
RENOWNED
RENTABLE
RENTIERS*
p RENUMBER s
REOBJECT s
p REOBTAIN s
p REOCCUPY
REOCCURS*
REOFFERS*
REOILING
REOPENED
REOPPOSE ds
p REORDAIN s
p REORDERS*
REORIENT s
REOUTFIT s
REOVIRUS
REPACIFY
p REPACKED
REPAINTS*
REPAIRED
REPAIRER s
REPANDLY
REPANELS*
REPAPERS*
REPARKED
REPARTEE s
REPASSED
REPASSES
p REPASTED
p REPAVING
p REPAYING
REPEALED
REPEALER s
REPEATED
REPEATER s
REPEGGED
REPELLED
REPELLER s
REPENTED
REPENTER s
REPEOPLE ds
REPERKED
REPETEND s
REPHRASE ds
REPINERS*
REPINING

REPINNED
p REPLACED*
REPLACER*s
p REPLACES*
REPLANTS*
REPLATED*
REPLATES*
REPLAYED
REPLEADS*
REPLEDGE ds
REPLETES*
REPLEVIN s
REPLICAS*e
REPLICON s
REPLIERS*
REPLOWED
REPLUMBS*
REPLUNGE ds
REPLYING
REPOLISH
REPOLLED
REPORTED
REPORTER s
REPOSALS*
REPOSERS*
REPOSING
REPOSITS*
REPOTTED
REPOURED
REPOUSSE s
REPOWERS*
p REPRICED*
p REPRICES*
REPRIEVE ds
p REPRINTS*
REPRISAL s
REPRISED*
REPRISES*
REPROACH
REPROBED*
REPROBES*
REPROOFS*
REPROVAL s
REPROVED*
REPROVER*s
REPROVES*
REPTILES*
REPTILIA n
REPUBLIC s
REPUGNED
REPULSED*
REPULSER*s
REPULSES*
REPUMPED
REPURIFY
REPURSUE ds
REPUTING
REQUESTS*
REQUIEMS*
REQUIRED*
REQUIRER*s
REQUIRES*
REQUITAL s
REQUITED*
REQUITER*s
REQUITES
RERACKED
RERAISED*
RERAISES*
p RERECORD s
REREMICE
REREMIND s
RERENTED
REREPEAT s
p REREVIEW s
REREWARD s
RERIGGED
RERISING
REROLLED
REROLLER s
REROOFED
REROUTED*
REROUTES*
RESADDLE ds
RESAILED
RESALUTE ds
RESAMPLE ds
RESAWING
RESAYING
RESCALED*
RESCALES*
p RESCHOOL s
p RESCINDS*
p RESCORED*
p RESCORES*
p RESCREEN s

p RESCRIPT s
RESCUERS*
RESCUING
RESCULPT s
RESEALED
RESEARCH
p RESEASON s
RESEATED
RESECTED
RESECURE ds
RESEEDED
RESEEING
RESEIZED*
RESEIZES*
p RESELECT s
RESELLER s
RESEMBLE drs
p RESENTED
p RESERVED*
p RESERVER*s
p RESERVES*
RESETTER s
p RESETTLE ds
RESEWING
p RESHAPED*
RESHAPER*s
p RESHAPES*
RESHAVED*
RESHAVEN*
RESHAVES*
RESHINED*
RESHINES*
RESHOOTS*
p RESHOWED
RESHOWER s
p RESIDENT s
p RESIDERS*
p RESIDING
RESIDUAL*s
RESIDUES*
RESIDUUM s
p RESIFTED
RESIGHTS*
RESIGNED
RESIGNER s
RESILING*
RESILINS*
RESILVER s
RESINATE ds
RESINIFY
RESINING
RESINOID s
RESINOUS
RESISTED
RESISTER s
RESISTOR s
RESITING
RESIZING
RESKETCH
RESLATED*
RESLATES*
RESMELTS*
RESMOOTH s
p RESOAKED
RESODDED
RESOFTEN s
RESOJETS*
RESOLDER s
RESOLING
RESOLUTE rs
p RESOLVED*
RESOLVER*s
p RESOLVES*
RESONANT s
RESONATE ds
RESORBED
RESORCIN s
p RESORTED
RESORTER s
RESOUGHT
RESOUNDS*
RESOURCE s
RESOWING
RESPACED*
RESPACES*
RESPADED*
RESPADES*
RESPEAKS*
RESPECTS*
RESPELLS*
RESPIRED*
RESPIRES*
RESPITED*
RESPITES*
RESPLICE ds
RESPLITS*

RESPOKEN*
RESPONDS*
RESPONSA
RESPONSE s
RESPOOLS*
RESPRANG
RESPRAYS*
RESPREAD s
RESPRING s
RESPROUT s
RESPRUNG
RESTABLE ds
RESTACKS*
RESTAFFS*
RESTAGED*
RESTAGES*
p RESTAMPS*
RESTARTS*
RESTATED
RESTATES
RESTITCH
c RESTLESS
RESTOCKS*
RESTOKED*
RESTOKES*
RESTORAL s
p RESTORED*
RESTORER*s
p RESTORES*
RESTRAIN st
p RESTRESS
RESTRICT s
p RESTRIKE s
RESTRING s
RESTRIVE ns
RESTROOM s
RESTROVE
RESTRUCK
RESTRUNG
RESTUFFS*
RESTYLED*
RESTYLES*
RESUBMIT s
RESULTED
p RESUMERS*
p RESUMING
RESUMMON s
RESUPINE
RESUPPLY
RESURGED*
RESURGES*
p RESURVEY s
RETABLES*
RETACKED
RETACKLE ds
RETAGGED
RETAILED
RETAILER s
RETAILOR s
RETAINED
RETAINER s
RETAKERS*
RETAKING
p RETAPING
RETARDED
RETARDER s
RETARGET s
p RETASTED*
p RETASTES*
RETAUGHT
RETAXING
*RETCHING
RETEAMED
RETEMPER s
p RETESTED
RETHINKS*
RETHREAD s
RETIARII
RETICENT
RETICLES*
RETICULA r
RETICULE s
RETIEING
RETIFORM
RETILING
RETIMING
RETINALS*
RETINENE s
RETINITE s
c RETINOID s
RETINOLS*
RETINTED
RETINUED*
RETINUES*
RETINULA ers
RETIRANT s
RETIREES*
RETIRERS*
RETIRING
RETITLED*
RETITLES*
RETOOLED
RETORTED
RETORTER s
RETOTALS*
RETRACED*
RETRACER*s
RETRACES*
RETRACKS*
RETRACTS*
p RETRAINS*
RETRALLY
RETREADS*
p RETREATS*
RETRENCH
p RETRIALS*
RETRIEVE drs
RETROACT s
RETROFIT s
RETRONYM s
RETRORSE
RETRYING
RETSINAS*
RETUNING
RETURNED
RETURNEE s
RETURNER s
RETWISTS*
p RETYPING
p REUNIONS*
p REUNITED*
REUNITER*s
p REUNITES*
REUPTAKE s
REUSABLE s
REUTTERS*
p REVALUED*
p REVALUES*
REVAMPED
REVAMPER s
REVANCHE s
REVEALED
REVEALER s
REVEHENT
REVEILLE s
REVELERS*
REVELING
REVELLED
REVELLER s
REVENANT s
REVENGED*
REVENGER*s
REVENGES*
REVENUAL
REVENUED*
REVENUER*s
REVENUES*
REVERBED
REVEREND s
REVERENT
REVERERS*
REVERIES*
REVERIFY
REVERING
REVERSAL s
REVERSED*
REVERSER*s
REVERSES*
REVERSOS*
*REVERTED
REVERTER s
REVESTED
b REVETTED
REVIEWAL s
p REVIEWED
p REVIEWER s
REVILERS*
REVILING
REVISALS*
REVISERS*
p REVISING
p REVISION s
p REVISITS*
p REVISORS*
REVISORY*
REVIVALS*
REVIVERS*
REVIVIFY
REVIVING
REVOICED*
REVOICES*
REVOKERS
*REVOKING
REVOLTED
REVOLTER s
*REVOLUTE
REVOLVED
*REVOLVER*s
REVOLVES
REVOTING
REVUISTS*
*REVULSED
REWAKENS*
REWAKING
REWARDED
REWARDER s
p REWARMED
p REWASHED
p REWASHES
REWAXING
REWEAVED*
REWEAVES*
REWEDDED
p REWEIGHS*
REWELDED
REWETTED
REWIDENS*
REWINDED
REWINDER s
p REWIRING
REWORDED
p REWORKED
REWRITER*s
REWRITES*
REYNARDS*
REZEROED
REZEROES
REZONING
RHABDOME*s
RHABDOMS*
RHAMNOSE s
RHAPSODE s
RHAPSODY
*RHEMATIC
RHENIUMS*
RHEOBASE s
RHEOLOGY
RHEOPHIL e
RHEOSTAT s
RHESUSES
RHETORIC s
RHEUMIER
RHINITIS
RHIZOBIA l
RHIZOIDS*
RHIZOMES*
RHIZOMIC
RHIZOPOD s
RHIZOPUS
RHODAMIN es
RHODIUMS*
RHODORAS*
RHOMBOID s
RHONCHAL
RHONCHUS
RHUBARBS*
RHUMBAED
RHYOLITE s
RHYTHMIC s
RIBALDLY
RIBALDRY
RIBBANDS*
RIBBIEST
c RIBBINGS*
RIBBONED
RIBGRASS
RIBOSOME s
RIBOZYME s
RIBWORTS*
RICEBIRD s
RICERCAR eis
RICHENED
RICHNESS
RICHWEED s
RICKRACK s
RICKSHAS*
RICKSHAW*s
RICOCHET s
RICOTTAS*
*RICTUSES
RIDDANCE s
RIDDLERS*
g RIDDLING
RIDEABLE
RIDGETOP s
RIDGIEST
RIDGLING s
RIDICULE drs
RIDOTTOS*
RIESLING s
RIFAMPIN s
RIFENESS
RIFFLERS*
RIFFLING
RIFFRAFF s
RIFLEMAN
RIFLEMEN
t RIFLINGS*
RIFTLESS
RIGADOON s
RIGATONI s
RIGAUDON s
RIGGINGS*
RIGHTERS*
b RIGHTEST
f RIGHTFUL
RIGHTIES
f RIGHTING
RIGHTISM s
RIGHTIST s
RIGIDIFY
f RIGIDITY
RIGORISM s
RIGORIST s
RIGOROUS
RIKISHAS*
RIKSHAWS*
t RIMESTER s
RIMFIRES*
g RIMINESS
RIMLANDS*
RIMOSELY
RIMOSITY
c RIMPLING
RIMROCKS*
RIMSHOTS*
RINDLESS
RINGBARK s
RINGBOLT s
RINGBONE s
RINGDOVE s
RINGGITS*
RINGHALS
RINGLETS*
RINGLIKE
RINGNECK s
RINGSIDE s
RINGTAIL s
RINGTAWS*
RINGTOSS
RINGWORM s
RINSABLE
RINSIBLE
RINSINGS*
RIPARIAN
RIPCORDS*
RIPENERS*
RIPENESS
RIPENING
RIPIENOS*
RIPOSTED*
RIPOSTES*
RIPPABLE
c RIPPLERS*
RIPPLETS*
RIPPLIER
c RIPPLING
RIPSAWED
RIPSTOPS*
RIPTIDES*
RISIBLES*
f RISKIEST
RISKLESS
RISOTTOS*
RISSOLES*
RITUALLY
RITZIEST
RIVALING
RIVALLED
RIVERBED s
RIVERINE
RIVETERS*
RIVETING
RIVETTED
RIVIERAS*
RIVIERES*
RIVULETS*
RIVULOSE
b ROACHING
ROADBEDS*
ROADKILL s
ROADLESS
ROADSHOW s
b ROADSIDE s
ROADSTER s
ROADWAYS*
ROADWORK s
ROARINGS*
ROASTERS*
ROASTING
ROBORANT s
ROBOTICS*
ROBOTISM s
ROBOTIZE ds
ROBUSTAS*
ROBUSTER
ROBUSTLY
ROCAILLE s
ROCKABLE
ROCKABYE*s
ROCKAWAY s
c ROCKETED
ROCKETER s
ROCKETRY
ROCKFALL s
ROCKFISH
ROCKIEST
f ROCKLESS
ROCKLIKE
ROCKLING s
ROCKOONS*
ROCKROSE s
ROCKWEED s
ROCKWORK s
RODEOING
ROEBUCKS*
ROENTGEN s
ROGATION s
ROGATORY
ROGERING
ROGUEING
*ROILIEST
ROISTERS*
ROLAMITE s
ROLLAWAY s
ROLLBACK s
ROLLICKS*
ROLLICKY*
t ROLLINGS*
ROLLMOPS*
ROLLOUTS*
ROLLOVER s
ROLLWAYS*
ROMAINES*
ROMANCED*
ROMANCER*s
ROMANCES*
ROMANISE ds
ROMANIZE ds
ROMANTIC s
ROMAUNTS*
RONDEAUX*
RONDELET s
RONDELLE s
RONDURES*
RONTGENS*
ROOFINGS*
ROOFLESS
ROOFLIKE
ROOFLINE s
ROOFTOPS*
ROOFTREE s
ROOKIEST*
ROOMETTE s
ROOMFULS*
b ROOMIEST*
ROOMMATE s
ROORBACH s
ROORBACK s
ROOSTERS*
ROOSTING
ROOTAGES*
ROOTCAPS*
ROOTHOLD s
ROOTIEST
ROOTLESS*
ROOTLETS*
ROOTLIKE
ROOTLING
ROOTWORM s
ROPELIKE
ROPERIES
ROPEWALK s
ROPEWAYS*
ROPINESS
c ROQUETED
c ROQUETTE s
RORQUALS*
ROSACEAS*
ROSARIAN*s
ROSARIES
ROSARIUM s
ROSEBAYS*
ROSEBUDS*
ROSEBUSH
ROSEFISH
ROSEHIPS*
ROSELIKE
ROSELLES*
ROSEMARY
ROSEOLAR*
ROSEOLAS*
ROSERIES
ROSEROOT s
ROSESLUG s
ROSETTES*
ROSEWOOD s
p ROSINESS
ROSINING
ROSINOLS*
ROSINOUS
ROSOLIOS*
ROSTELLA r
p ROSTRATE
ROSTRUMS*
ROSULATE
ROTARIES
ROTATING
ROTATION s
ROTATIVE
ROTATORS*
ROTATORY*
ROTENONE s
ROTIFERS*
ROTIFORM
ROTOTILL s
ROTTENER
ROTTENLY
ROTUNDAS*
ROTUNDLY
ROTURIER s
ROUGHAGE s
ROUGHDRY
ROUGHENS*
ROUGHERS*
ROUGHEST
ROUGHHEW ns
ROUGHIES
ROUGHING
ROUGHISH
ROUGHLEG s
ROUILLES*
ROULADES*
ROULEAUS*
ROULEAUX*
ROULETTE ds
ROUNDELS*
g ROUNDERS*
ROUNDEST
g ROUNDING
ROUNDISH
ROUNDLET s
ROUNDUPS*
c ROUPIEST
t ROUSSEAU s
ROUSTERS
*ROUSTING
ROUTEMAN
ROUTEMEN
ROUTEWAY s
ROUTINES*
ROVINGLY
ROWBOATS*
ROWDIEST*
ROWDYISH
ROWDYISM s
t ROWELING
t ROWELLED
ROWLOCKS*
ROYALISM s
ROYALIST s
ROYSTERS
RUBABOOS*
RUBAIYAT
RUBASSES*
RUBBABOO s
RUBBERED
d RUBBINGS*
RUBBISHY*
RUBBLIER
RUBBLING
RUBBOARD s
RUBDOWNS*
RUBELLAS*
RUBEOLAR*
RUBEOLAS*
RUBICUND
RUBIDIUM s
RUBRICAL
RUBYLIKE
RUCHINGS*
t RUCKLING
RUCKSACK s
RUCKUSES
RUCTIONS*
RUCTIOUS
c RUDDIEST
RUDDLING
RUDDOCKS*
c RUDENESS
RUDERALS*
p RUDERIES
RUDIMENT s
RUEFULLY
RUFFIANS*
RUFFLERS*
RUFFLIER
RUFFLIKE
RUFFLING
RUGALACH
RUGELACH
RUGGEDER
RUGGEDLY
RUGOSELY
RUGOSITY
RUGULOSE
RUINABLE
RUINATED*
RUINATES*
RULELESS
RUMBAING
g RUMBLERS*
cdg RUMBLING s
RUMINANT s
RUMINATE ds
RUMMAGED*
RUMMAGER*s
RUMMAGES*
c RUMMIEST*
RUMORING
RUMOURED
RUMPLESS*
c RUMPLIER
c RUMPLING
RUMPUSES
RUNABOUT s
RUNAGATE s
RUNAWAYS*
RUNBACKS*
RUNDLETS*
RUNDOWNS*
RUNELIKE
RUNGLESS
RUNKLING
RUNNIEST
RUNNINGS*
RUNOVERS*
*RUNROUND s
RUNTIEST
RUPTURED*
RUPTURES*
RURALISE ds
RURALISM s
RURALIST s
*RURALITE s
RURALITY
RURALIZE ds
b RUSHIEST
RUSHINGS*
RUSHLIKE
t RUSTABLE
RUSTICAL s
RUSTICLY
ct RUSTIEST
RUSTLERS*
ct RUSTLESS*
RUSTLING
RUTABAGA s
RUTHENIC
t RUTHLESS
RUTILANT
RUTTIEST
RYEGRASS
SABATONS*
SABAYONS*
SABBATHS*
SABBATIC s
SABERING
SABOTAGE ds
SABOTEUR s
SABULOSE
SABULOUS

SACATONS*
SACCADES*
SACCADIC
SACCULAR
SACCULES*
SACCULUS
SACHEMIC
SACHETED
SACKBUTS*
SACKFULS*
SACKINGS*
SACKLIKE
SACKSFUL
SACRARIA l
SACREDLY
SACRINGS*
SACRISTS*
SACRISTY*
SADDENED
SADDLERS*
SADDLERY*
*SADDLING
SADIRONS*
SADISTIC
SAFARIED
SAFENESS
SAFETIED
SAFETIES
SAFFRONS*
SAFRANIN es
SAFROLES*
SAGACITY
SAGAMORE s
SAGANASH
SAGENESS
SAGGARDS*
SAGGARED
SAGGERED
SAGGIEST
SAGITTAL
SAGUAROS*
SAHIWALS*
SAHUAROS*
SAILABLE
SAILBOAT s
SAILFISH
SAILINGS*
SAILLESS
SAILORLY
SAINFOIN s
SAINTDOM s
SAINTING
SALAAMED
SALACITY
SALADANG s
SALARIAT s
SALARIED
SALARIES
SALCHOWS*
SALEABLE
SALEABLY
SALEROOM s
SALESMAN
SALESMEN
SALICINE*s
SALICINS*
SALIENCE s
SALIENCY
SALIENTS*
SALIFIED
SALIFIES
SALINITY
SALINIZE ds
SALIVARY
SALIVATE ds
SALLIERS*
*SALLOWED
SALLOWER
SALLOWLY
*SALLYING
SALMONID s
SALPIANS*
SALSILLA s
SALTBUSH
SALTERNS*
SALTIERS*
SALTIEST*
SALTINES*s
SALTINGS*
SALTIRES*
SALTLESS
SALTLIKE
SALTNESS
SALTPANS*
SALTWORK s
SALTWORT s
SALUTARY
SALUTERS*
SALUTING
SALVABLE
SALVABLY
SALVAGED*
SALVAGEE*s
SALVAGER*s
SALVAGES*
SALVIFIC
SALVOING
SAMADHIS*
SAMARIUM s
SAMBAING
SAMBHARS*
SAMBHURS*
SAMBUCAS*
SAMBUKES*
SAMENESS
SAMISENS*
SAMIZDAT s
SAMOVARS*
SAMOYEDS*
SAMPHIRE s
SAMPLERS*
SAMPLING s
SAMSARAS*
SAMURAIS*
SANATIVE
SANCTIFY
SANCTION s
SANCTITY
SANCTUMS*
SANDABLE
SANDALED
SANDARAC s
SANDBAGS*
SANDBANK s
SANDBARS*
SANDBURR*s
SANDBURS*
SANDDABS*
SANDFISH
SANDHOGS*
SANDIEST
SANDLESS
SANDLIKE
SANDLING s
SANDLOTS*
SANDPEEP s
SANDPILE s
SANDPITS*
SANDSHOE s
SANDSOAP s
SANDSPUR s
SANDWICH
SANDWORM s
SANDWORT s
SANENESS
SANGAREE s
SANGRIAS*
*SANGUINE s
SANICLES*
SANIDINE s
SANITARY
SANITATE ds
SANITIES
SANITISE ds
SANITIZE drs
SANNYASI ns
SANSERIF s
SANTALIC
SANTALOL s
SANTERAS*
SANTERIA s
SANTEROS*
SANTONIN s
SANTOORS*
SANTOURS*
SAPAJOUS*
SAPHEADS*
SAPHENAE*
SAPHENAS*
SAPIDITY
SAPIENCE s
SAPIENCY
SAPIENTS*
SAPLINGS*
SAPONIFY
SAPONINE*s
SAPONINS*
SAPONITE s
SAPOROUS
SAPPHICS*
SAPPHIRE s
SAPPHISM s
SAPPHIST s
SAPPIEST
SAPREMIA s
SAPREMIC
SAPROBES*
SAPROBIC
SAPROPEL s
SAPSAGOS*
SAPWOODS*
SARABAND es
SARCASMS*
SARCENET s
SARCINAE*
SARCINAS*
SARCOIDS*
SARCOMAS*
SARDANAS*
SARDINED*
SARDINES*
SARDONIC
SARDONYX
SARGASSO s
SARKIEST
SARMENTA*
SARMENTS*
SARODIST s
SARSENET s
SARSNETS*
SARTORII
SASHAYED
SASHIMIS*
*SASHLESS
SASSIEST*
SASSWOOD s
SASTRUGA
SASTRUGI
SATANISM s
SATANIST s
SATCHELS*
SATIABLE
SATIABLY
SATIATED*
SATIATES*
SATINETS*
SATINPOD s
SATIRISE ds
SATIRIST s
SATIRIZE drs
SATSUMAS*
SATURANT s
SATURATE drs
SATYRIDS*
SAUCEBOX
SAUCEPAN s
SAUCEPOT s
SAUCIERS*
SAUCIEST
SAUNAING
SAUNTERS*
SAURIANS*
SAUROPOD s
SAUSAGES*
SAUTEING
SAUTERNE s
SAUTOIRE*s
SAUTOIRS*
SAVAGELY
SAVAGERY*
SAVAGEST*
SAVAGING
SAVAGISM s
SAVANNAH*s
SAVANNAS*
SAVARINS*
SAVEABLE
SAVELOYS*
SAVINGLY
SAVIOURS*
SAVORERS*
SAVORIER
SAVORIES t
SAVORILY
SAVORING
SAVOROUS
SAVOURED
SAVOURER s
SAVVIEST*
SAVVYING
SAWBILLS*
SAWBONES
SAWBUCKS*
SAWDUSTS*
SAWDUSTY*
SAWFLIES
SAWHORSE s
SAWMILLS*
SAWTEETH
SAWTOOTH
SAXATILE
SAXHORNS*
SAXONIES
SAXTUBAS*
SAYONARA s
SCABBARD s
SCABBIER
SCABBILY
*SCABBING
SCABBLED*
SCABBLES*
SCABIOSA s
SCABIOUS
SCABLAND s
SCABLIKE
SCABROUS
SCAFFOLD s
SCALABLE
SCALABLY
e SCALADES*
SCALADOS*
SCALAGES*
SCALARES*
SCALAWAG s
SCALDING
SCALENUS
SCALEPAN s
SCALEUPS*
SCALIEST
SCALLION s
e SCALLOPS*
SCALPELS*
SCALPERS*
SCALPING
SCAMMERS*
SCAMMING
SCAMMONY
SCAMPERS
SCAMPIES
*SCAMPING
SCAMPISH
SCAMSTER s
SCANDALS*
*SCANDENT
SCANDIAS*
SCANDIUM s
SCANNERS
*SCANNING s
SCANSION s
SCANTEST
SCANTIER
SCANTIES t
SCANTILY
*SCANTING
SCAPHOID s
SCAPULAE*
SCAPULAR*sy
SCAPULAS*
SCARCELY
SCARCEST
SCARCITY
SCAREDER
SCARFERS*
SCARFING
SCARFPIN s
SCARIEST
SCARIOSE
*SCARIOUS
*SCARLESS
SCARLETS*
SCARPERS
SCARPHED
e*SCARPING
*SCARRIER
SCARRING
*SCARTING
SCATBACK s
SCATHING
SCATTERS*
*SCATTIER
*SCATTING
SCAUPERS*
SCAVENGE drs
SCENARIO s
a SCENDING
SCENICAL
SCENTING
SCEPTERS*
SCEPTICS*
SCEPTRAL
SCEPTRED*
SCEPTRES*
SCHAPPES*
SCHEDULE drs
SCHEMATA
SCHEMERS*
SCHEMING
SCHERZOS*
*SCHILLER s
SCHIZIER
SCHIZOID s
SCHIZONT s
SCHLEPPS*
SCHLIERE n
SCHLOCKS*
SCHLOCKY*
SCHLUMPS*
SCHLUMPY*
SCHMALTZ y
SCHMALZY*
SCHMATTE s
SCHMEARS*
SCHMEERS*
SCHMELZE s
SCHMOOSE*ds
SCHMOOZE drs
SCHMOOZY
SCHMUCKS*
SCHNAPPS
SCHNECKE n
SCHNOOKS*
SCHNOZES
SCHOLARS*
SCHOLIUM s
SCHOOLED
SCHOONER s
SCHTICKS*
SCHUSSED
SCHUSSER s
SCHUSSES
SCIAENID s
SCIATICA*s
SCIATICS*
SCIENCES*
SCILICET
SCIMETAR s
SCIMITAR s
SCIMITER s
SCINCOID s
SCIOLISM s
SCIOLIST s
SCIROCCO s
SCIRRHUS
SCISSILE
SCISSION s
SCISSORS*
SCISSURE s
SCIURIDS*
SCIURINE s
SCIUROID
SCLAFFED
SCLAFFER s
SCLEREID s
SCLERITE s
SCLEROID
SCLEROMA s
SCLEROSE ds
SCLEROUS
SCOFFERS
*SCOFFING
SCOFFLAW s
SCOLDERS*
SCOLDING s
SCOLECES
SCOLICES
SCOLIOMA s
SCOLLOPS
SCOMBRID s
SCONCING
SCOOCHED
*SCOOCHES
SCOOPERS
SCOOPFUL s
*SCOOPING
SCOOTERS
SCOOTING
SCOPULAE
SCOPULAS
SCORCHED
SCORCHER s
SCORCHES
SCOREPAD s
SCORNERS
SCORNFUL
*SCORNING
SCORPION s
SCOTCHED
SCOTCHES
SCOTOMAS*
SCOTOPIA s
SCOTOPIC
SCOTTIES*
SCOURERS*
SCOURGED*
SCOURGER*s
SCOURGES*
SCOURING s
SCOUTERS
*SCOUTHER s
SCOUTING s
SCOWDERS*
SCOWLERS*
*SCOWLING
SCRABBLE drs
SCRABBLY
*SCRAGGED
SCRAGGLY
SCRAICHS*
SCRAIGHS*
SCRAMBLE drs
SCRAMJET s
*SCRAMMED
SCRANNEL s
SCRAPERS*
SCRAPIES*
*SCRAPING s
*SCRAPPED
SCRAPPER s
SCRAPPLE s
SCRATCHY*
*SCRAWLED
*SCRAWLER s
*SCREAKED
*SCREAMED
*SCREAMER s
SCREECHY*
SCREEDED
SCREENED
SCREENER s
SCREWERS*
SCREWIER
*SCREWING
SCREWUPS*
SCRIBBLE drs
SCRIBBLY
SCRIBERS*
a SCRIBING
SCRIEVED*
SCRIEVES*
*SCRIMPED
*SCRIMPER s
SCRIMPIT
SCRIPTED
SCRIPTER s
SCRIVING
SCROFULA s
SCROLLED
SCROOGES*
SCROOPED
SCROOTCH
SCROTUMS*
SCROUGED*
SCROUGES*
SCROUNGE drs
SCROUNGY
SCRUBBED
SCRUBBER s
SCRUMMED
SCRUNCHY
SCRUPLED*
SCRUPLES*
SCRUTINY
SCUBAING
SCUDDING
SCUFFERS*
*SCUFFING
SCUFFLED*
SCUFFLER*s
SCUFFLES*
*SCULCHES
SCULKERS*
SCULKING
SCULLERS
SCULLERY*
*SCULLING
*SCULLION s
SCULPING*
SCULPINS*
SCULPTED
SCULPTOR s
SCUMBAGS*
SCUMBLED*
SCUMBLES*
SCUMLESS
SCUMLIKE
SCUMMERS
SCUMMIER
SCUMMILY
SCUMMING
SCUNNERS
SCUPPAUG s
SCUPPERS
SCURFIER
*SCURRIED
*SCURRIES
SCURRILE*
*SCURVIER
SCURVIES t
SCURVILY
SCUTAGES*
SCUTCHED
SCUTCHER s
*SCUTCHES
SCUTELLA r
SCUTTERS
SCUTTLED
SCUTTLES
*SCUTWORK s
SCUZZIER
SCYPHATE
SCYTHING
SEABEACH
SEABIRDS*
SEABOARD s
SEABOOTS*
SEABORNE
SEACOAST s
SEACOCKS*
SEACRAFT s
SEADROME s
SEAFARER s
SEAFLOOR s
SEAFOODS*
SEAFOWLS*
SEAFRONT s
SEAGOING
SEAGULLS*
SEAHORSE s
SEALABLE
SEALANTS*
SEALIFTS*
SEALLIKE
SEALSKIN s
SEAMANLY
SEAMARKS*
SEAMIEST
SEAMLESS
SEAMLIKE
SEAMOUNT s
SEAMSTER s
SEAPIECE s
SEAPLANE s
SEAPORTS*
SEAQUAKE s
SEARCHED
SEARCHER s
SEARCHES
SEAROBIN s
SEASCAPE s
SEASCOUT s
SEASHELL s
SEASHORE s
SEASIDES*
SEASONAL s
SEASONED
SEASONER s
SEATBACK s
SEATBELT s
SEATINGS
SEATLESS
SEATMATE s
SEATRAIN s
SEATROUT s
SEATWORK s
SEAWALLS*
SEAWANTS*
SEAWARDS*
SEAWARES*
SEAWATER s
SEAWEEDS*
SECALOSE s
SECANTLY
SECATEUR s
SECEDERS*
SECEDING
SECERNED
SECLUDED*
SECLUDES*
SECONALS*
SECONDED*
SECONDER*s
SECONDES*

SECONDLY
SECRETED*
SECRETER*
SECRETES*t
SECRETIN gs
SECRETLY
SECRETOR sy
SECTIONS*
SECTORAL
SECTORED
SECULARS*
SECUNDLY
SECUNDUM
SECURELY
SECURERS*
SECUREST*
SECURING
SECURITY
SEDATELY
SEDATEST*
SEDATING
SEDATION s
SEDATIVE s
SEDERUNT s
*SEDGIEST
SEDILIUM
SEDIMENT s
*SEDITION s
SEDUCERS*
*SEDUCING
SEDUCIVE
SEDULITY
SEDULOUS
SEECATCH
SEEDBEDS*
SEEDCAKE s
SEEDCASE s
SEEDIEST
SEEDLESS
SEEDLIKE
SEEDLING s
SEEDPODS*
SEEDSMAN
SEEDSMEN
SEEDTIME s
SEEMINGS*
SEEMLIER
SEEPAGES*
SEEPIEST
SEESAWED
SEETHING
SEGMENTS*
SEGUEING
SEICENTO s
SEIGNEUR sy
SEIGNIOR sy
SEIGNORY
SEISABLE
SEISINGS*
SEISMISM s
SEISURES*
SEIZABLE
SEIZINGS*
SEIZURES*
SELADANG s
SELAMLIK s
SELCOUTH
SELDOMLY
*SELECTED
*SELECTEE s
SELECTLY
*SELECTOR s
SELENATE s
SELENIDE s
SELENITE s
SELENIUM s
SELENOUS
SELFDOMS*
SELFHEAL s
SELFHOOD s
SELFLESS
SELFNESS
SELFSAME
SELFWARD s
SELLABLE
SELLOFFS*
SELLOUTS*
SELTZERS*
SELVAGED*
SELVAGES*
SELVEDGE ds
SEMANTIC s
SEMESTER s
SEMIARID
SEMIBALD
SEMICOMA s
SEMIDEAF
SEMIDOME ds
SEMIGALA
SEMIHARD
SEMIHIGH
SEMIHOBO s
SEMILLON s
SEMIMATT*e
SEMIMILD
SEMIMUTE
SEMINARS*
SEMINARY*
SEMINOMA ds
SEMINUDE
SEMIOPEN
SEMIOSES
SEMIOSIS
SEMIOTIC s
SEMIOVAL
SEMIPROS*
SEMISOFT
SEMITIST s
SEMITONE s
SEMIWILD
SEMOLINA s
SEMPLICE
SENARIUS
SENATORS*
SENDABLE
SENDOFFS*
SENECIOS*
SENHORAS*
SENHORES
SENILELY
SENILITY
SENNIGHT s
SENOPIAS*
SENORITA s
SENSATED*
SENSATES*
SENSEFUL
SENSIBLE rs
SENSIBLY
SENSILLA e
SENSORIA l
SENSUOUS
SENTENCE drs
SENTIENT s
SENTIMOS*
SENTINEL s
*SENTRIES
SEPALINE
SEPALLED
SEPALOID
SEPALOUS
SEPARATE ds
SEPPUKUS*
SEPTAGES*
SEPTARIA n
SEPTETTE s
SEPTICAL
SEPTIMES*
SEPTUPLE dst
SEQUELAE*
SEQUENCE drs
SEQUENCY
SEQUENTS*
SEQUINED
SEQUITUR s
SEQUOIAS*
SERAGLIO s
SERAPHIC
SERAPHIM s
SERAPHIN
SERENADE drs
SERENATA s
SERENATE
SERENELY
SERENEST*
SERENITY
SERFAGES*
SERFDOMS*
SERFHOOD s
SERFLIKE
SERGEANT sy
SERGINGS*
SERIALLY
SERIATED*
SERIATES*
SERIATIM
SERICINS*
SERIEMAS*
SERIFFED
SERINGAS*
SERJEANT sy
SERMONIC
SEROLOGY
SEROSITY
SEROTINE s
SEROTINY
SEROTYPE ds
SEROVARS*
SERPENTS*
SERPIGOS*
SERRANID s
SERRANOS*
SERRATED*
SERRATES*
SERRYING
SERVABLE
SERVANTS*
SERVICED*
SERVICER*s
SERVICES*
SERVINGS*
SERVITOR s
SESAMOID s
SESSIONS*
SESSPOOL s
SESTERCE s
SESTINAS*
SESTINES*
SETBACKS*
SETENANT s
SETIFORM
SETLINES*
SETSCREW s
SETTINGS*
SETTLERS*
SETTLING s
SETTLORS*
SETULOSE
SETULOUS
SEVENTHS*
SEVERALS*
SEVERELY
SEVEREST
SEVERING
SEVERITY
SEVICHES*
SEVRUGAS*
SEWERAGE s
SEWERING
SEXINESS
SEXOLOGY
SEXTAINS*
SEXTANTS*
SEXTARII
SEXTETTE s
SEXTILES*
SEXTUPLE dst
SEXTUPLY
a SEXUALLY
SFORZATO s
SFUMATOS*
SHABBIER
SHABBILY
*SHACKING
SHACKLED
*SHACKLER*s
SHACKLES
SHACKOES
SHADBLOW s
SHADBUSH
SHADCHAN s
*SHADDOCK s
SHADIEST
SHADINGS*
SHADKHAN s
SHADOOFS*
SHADOWED
SHADOWER s
SHADRACH s
*SHAFTING s
SHAGBARK s
SHAGGIER
SHAGGILY
*SHAGGING
SHAGREEN s
SHAHDOMS*
SHAITANS*
SHAKABLE
SHAKEOUT s
SHAKEUPS*
SHAKIEST
SHALIEST
SHALLOON s
SHALLOPS*
SHALLOTS*
SHALLOWS
SHAMABLE
SHAMABLY
SHAMANIC
SHAMBLED*
SHAMBLES*
SHAMEFUL
SHAMISEN s
SHAMMASH*
SHAMMERS
SHAMMIED
SHAMMIES
*SHAMMING
SHAMOSIM
SHAMOYED
SHAMPOOS*
SHAMROCK s
SHAMUSES
SHANDIES
SHANGHAI s
*SHANKING
SHANNIES
SHANTEYS*
SHANTIES
SHANTIHS*
SHANTUNG s
SHAPABLE
SHAPEUPS*
SHARABLE
SHARIAHS*
SHARKERS*
*SHARKING
SHARPENS*
SHARPERS
SHARPEST
SHARPIES
*SHARPING
SHASHLIK s
SHASLIKS*
SHATTERS
*SHAULING
SHAVABLE
SHAVINGS*
SHAWLING
SHEAFING
*SHEALING s
SHEARERS
*SHEARING s
SHEATHED*
*SHEATHER*s
SHEATHES*
*SHEAVING
SHEBANGS*
SHEBEANS*
SHEBEENS*
SHEDABLE
SHEDDERS*
SHEDDING
SHEDLIKE
SHEENFUL
SHEENIER
SHEENING
SHEEPCOT es
SHEEPDOG s
SHEEPISH
SHEEPMAN
SHEEPMEN
SHEEREST
SHEERING
SHEETERS*
SHEETFED
SHEETING s
SHEIKDOM s
SHEITANS*
SHEKALIM
SHEKELIM
SHELDUCK s
SHELFFUL s
SHELLACK*s
SHELLACS*
SHELLERS
SHELLIER
*SHELLING
SHELTERS*
SHELTIES*
SHELVERS*
SHELVIER
*SHELVING s
SHENDING
SHEPHERD s
SHEQALIM
SHERBERT s
SHERBETS*
SHEREEFS*
SHERIFFS*
SHERLOCK s
SHEROOTS*
*SHERRIES
SHETLAND s
SHIATSUS*
SHIATZUS*
SHICKERS*
SHIELDED
SHIELDER s
SHIELING s
SHIFTERS*
SHIFTIER
SHIFTILY
SHIFTING
SHIGELLA es
SHIITAKE s
SHIKAREE s
SHIKARIS*
SHIKKERS*
SHILINGI
SHILLALA hs
*SHILLING s
SHIMMERS*
SHIMMERY*
SHIMMIED
SHIMMIES
SHIMMING
SHINBONE s
SHINDIES
SHINDIGS*
SHINGLED*
SHINGLER*s
SHINGLES*
SHINIEST
SHINLEAF s
SHINNERY
SHINNEYS*
*SHINNIED
*SHINNIES
SHINNING
SHIPLAPS*
*SHIPLESS
SHIPLOAD s
SHIPMATE s
SHIPMENT*s
SHIPPENS*
SHIPPERS*
*SHIPPING s
SHIPPONS*
SHIPSIDE s
SHIPWAYS*
SHIPWORM s
SHIPYARD s
SHIRKERS*
SHIRKING
SHIRRING s
SHIRTIER
SHIRTING s
SHITAKES*
SHITTAHS*
SHITTIMS*
SHIVAREE ds
SHIVERED
SHIVERER s
SHIVITIS*
SHLEMIEL s
SHLEPPED
SHLUMPED
SHMALTZY*
SHMOOZED*
SHMOOZES*
SHNORRER s
SHOALEST
SHOALIER
SHOALING
SHOCKERS
*SHOCKING
SHODDIER
SHODDIES t
SHODDILY
SHOEBILL s
SHOEHORN s
SHOELACE s
SHOELESS
SHOEPACK*s
SHOEPACS*
SHOETREE s
SHOFROTH
*SHOGGING
SHOGUNAL
SHOOLING
SHOOTERS
*SHOOTING s
SHOOTOUT s
SHOPBOYS*
SHOPGIRL s
SHOPHARS*
SHOPLIFT s
SHOPPERS
*SHOPPING s
SHOPTALK s
SHOPWORN
SHORINGS*
SHORTAGE s
SHORTCUT s
SHORTENS*
SHORTEST
SHORTIAS*
SHORTIES*
SHORTING
SHORTISH
SHOTGUNS*
SHOTHOLE s
*SHOTTING
SHOULDER s
SHOULDST
SHOUTERS*
SHOUTING
*SHOVELED
SHOVELER s
SHOWABLE
SHOWBOAT s
SHOWCASE ds
SHOWDOWN s
SHOWERED
SHOWERER s
SHOWGIRL s
SHOWIEST
SHOWINGS*
SHOWOFFS*
SHOWRING s
SHOWROOM s
SHOWTIME s
SHRAPNEL
SHREDDED
SHREDDER s
SHREWDER
SHREWDIE s
SHREWDLY
SHREWING
SHREWISH
SHRIEKED
SHRIEKER s
SHRIEVAL
SHRIEVED*
SHRIEVES*
SHRILLED
SHRILLER
SHRIMPED
SHRIMPER s
SHRINING
SHRINKER s
SHRIVELS*
SHRIVERS*
SHRIVING
SHROFFED
SHROUDED
SHRUGGED
SHRUNKEN
SHTETELS*
SHUCKERS*
SHUCKING s
SHUDDERS*
SHUDDERY*
SHUFFLED*
SHUFFLER*s
SHUFFLES*
SHUNNERS*
SHUNNING
SHUNPIKE drs
SHUNTERS
*SHUNTING
SHUSHERS*
*SHUSHING
SHUTDOWN s
SHUTEYES*
SHUTOFFS*
SHUTOUTS*
SHUTTERS*
*SHUTTING
SHUTTLED*
SHUTTLER*s
SHUTTLES*
SHWANPAN s
SHYLOCKS*
SHYSTERS*
SIALIDAN s
SIAMANGS*
SIAMESES*
SIBILANT s
SIBILATE ds
SIBLINGS*
SIBYLLIC
SICKBAYS*
SICKBEDS*
SICKENED
SICKENER s
SICKERLY
SICKLIED
SICKLIER
SICKLIES t
SICKLILY
SICKLING
SICKNESS
SICKOUTS*
SICKROOM s
SIDDURIM
SIDEARMS*
SIDEBAND s
SIDEBARS*
SIDECARS*
SIDEHILL s
SIDEKICK s
SIDELINE drs
SIDELING
SIDELONG
SIDEREAL
SIDERITE s
SIDESHOW s
SIDESLIP s
SIDESPIN s
SIDESTEP s
SIDEWALK s
SIDEWALL s
SIDEWARD s
SIDEWAYS*
SIDEWISE
SIENITES*
SIEROZEM s
SIEVERTS*
SIFFLEUR s
SIFTINGS*
SIGANIDS*
SIGHLESS
SIGHLIKE
SIGHTERS*
SIGHTING s
SIGHTSAW
SIGHTSEE nrs
SIGMOIDS*
SIGNAGES*
SIGNALED
SIGNALER s
SIGNALLY
SIGNETED
SIGNIORI*
SIGNIORS*
SIGNIORY*
SIGNORAS*
SIGNPOST s
SILENCED*
SILENCER*s
SILENCES*
SILENTER
SILENTLY
SILESIAS*
SILICATE s
SILICIDE s
SILICIFY
SILICIUM s
SILICLES*
SILICONE*s
SILICONS*
SILICULA e
SILIQUAE*
SILIQUES*
SILKIEST*
SILKLIKE
SILKWEED s
SILKWORM s
SILLABUB s
SILLIBUB s
SILLIEST*
SILOXANE s
SILTIEST
SILURIAN
SILURIDS*
SILUROID s
SILVERED
SILVERER s
SILVERLY
SILVEXES
SILVICAL
SIMARUBA s
SIMAZINE s
SIMITARS*
SIMMERED
SIMOLEON s
SIMONIAC s
SIMONIES
SIMONIST s
SIMONIZE ds

SIMPERED
SIMPERER s
SIMPLEST*
SIMPLIFY
SIMPLISM s
SIMPLIST s
SIMULANT s
SIMULARS*
SIMULATE ds
SINAPISM s
SINCERER*
SINCIPUT s
SINECURE s
SINEWING
SINFONIA s
SINFONIE
SINFULLY
SINGABLE
SINGEING
SINGLETS*
SINGLING
SINGSONG sy
SINGULAR s
SINICIZE ds
SINISTER
SINKABLE
SINKAGES*
SINKHOLE s
SINOLOGY
SINOPIAS*
SINTERED
SINUATED*
SINUATES*
SINUSOID s
SIPHONAL
SIPHONED
SIPHONIC
SIRENIAN s
SIRLOINS*
SIROCCOS*
SIRUPIER
SIRUPING
SIRVENTE s
SISSIEST*
SISSYISH
SISTERED
SISTERLY
SISTROID
SISTRUMS*
SITARIST s
SITHENCE
SITOLOGY
SITTINGS*
SITUATED*
SITUATES*
SITZMARK s
SIXPENCE s
SIXPENNY
SIXTEENS*
SIXTIETH s
SIXTYISH
SIZEABLE
SIZEABLY
SIZINESS
SIZZLERS*
SIZZLING
SJAMBOKS*
SKANKERS*
SKANKIER
SKANKING
SKATINGS*
SKATOLES*
SKEETERS*
SKEINING
SKELETAL
SKELETON s
SKELLUMS*
*SKELPING
SKELTERS
SKEPTICS*
*SKERRIES
SKETCHED
SKETCHER s
*SKETCHES
SKEWBACK s
SKEWBALD s
SKEWERED
a SKEWNESS
SKIAGRAM s
SKIDDERS
SKIDDIER
*SKIDDING
SKIDDOOS*
SKIDOOED
SKIDWAYS*
SKIFFLED*

SKIFFLES*s
SKIJORER s
SKILLESS
SKILLETS*
SKILLFUL
*SKILLING s
SKIMMERS*
SKIMMING s
SKIMPIER
SKIMPILY
SKIMPING
SKINFULS*
SKINHEAD s
SKINKERS*
*SKINKING
*SKINLESS
SKINLIKE
SKINNERS*
SKINNIER
SKINNING
SKIORING s
SKIPJACK s
SKIPLANE s
SKIPPERS
SKIPPETS*
*SKIPPING
SKIRLING
SKIRMISH
SKIRRETS*
SKIRRING
SKIRTERS*
SKIRTING s
SKITTERS*
SKITTERY*
SKITTISH
SKITTLES
SKIVVIED
SKIVVIES
SKLENTED
SKOALING
SKREEGHS*
SKREIGHS*
SKULKERS*
SKULKING
SKULLCAP s
SKULLING
SKUNKIER
SKUNKING
SKYBOARD s
SKYBORNE
SKYBOXES
SKYDIVED*
SKYDIVER*s
SKYDIVES*
SKYHOOKS*
SKYJACKS*
SKYLARKS*
SKYLIGHT s
SKYLINES*
SKYSAILS*
SKYSURFS*
SKYWALKS*
SKYWARDS*
SKYWRITE rs
SKYWROTE
SLABBERS*
SLABBERY*
SLABBING
SLABLIKE
SLACKENS*
SLACKERS
SLACKEST
*SLACKING
SLAGGIER
*SLAGGING
SLAKABLE
SLALOMED
SLALOMER s
SLAMMERS*
*SLAMMING s
i*SLANDERS*
SLANGIER
SLANGILY
SLANGING
SLANTING
SLAPDASH
SLAPJACK s
SLAPPERS
*SLAPPING
SLASHERS
*SLASHING s
*SLATCHES
SLATHERS
SLATIEST
SLATINGS*
SLATTERN s

SLATTING s
SLAVERED
SLAVERER s
SLAYABLE
*SLEAVING
SLEAZIER
SLEAZILY
SLEAZOID s
SLEDDERS*
SLEDDING s
SLEDGING
SLEEKENS*
SLEEKERS*
SLEEKEST
SLEEKIER
SLEEKING
SLEEPERS*
SLEEPIER
SLEEPILY
SLEEPING s
SLEETIER
SLEETING
SLEEVING
SLEIGHED
SLEIGHER s
SLEIGHTS*
SLEUTHED
SLICKENS*
SLICKERS
SLICKEST
*SLICKING
SLIDABLE
SLIDEWAY s
*SLIGHTED
*SLIGHTER s
*SLIGHTLY
*SLIMIEST
SLIMMERS
SLIMMEST
SLIMMING
SLIMNESS
SLIMSIER
SLINGERS
SLINGING
SLINKIER
SLINKILY
*SLINKING
SLIPCASE ds
SLIPFORM s
SLIPKNOT s
*SLIPLESS
SLIPOUTS*
SLIPOVER s
SLIPPAGE s
SLIPPERS
SLIPPERY*
*SLIPPIER
SLIPPILY
*SLIPPING
SLIPSHOD
SLIPSLOP s
SLIPSOLE s
SLIPWARE s
SLIPWAYS*
SLITHERS*
SLITHERY*
SLITLESS
SLITLIKE
SLITTERS
SLITTIER
SLITTING
*SLIVERED
SLIVERER s
SLIVOVIC
SLOBBERS
SLOBBERY*
SLOBBIER
SLOBBISH
SLOGGERS
*SLOGGING
*SLOPPIER
SLOPPILY
*SLOPPING
SLOPWORK s
SLOSHIER
SLOSHING
SLOTBACK s
SLOTHFUL
SLOTTERS
*SLOTTING
SLOUCHED
SLOUCHER s
SLOUCHES
SLOUGHED
SLOVENLY
*SLOWDOWN s

*SLOWNESS
SLOWPOKE s
SLOWWORM s
SLUBBERS
SLUBBING s
SLUDGIER
SLUDGING
*SLUFFING
SLUGABED s
SLUGFEST s
SLUGGARD s
SLUGGERS
*SLUGGING
SLUGGISH
SLUICING
SLUMBERS
SLUMBERY*
SLUMGUMS*
SLUMISMS*
SLUMLORD s
SLUMMERS*
SLUMMIER
SLUMMING
*SLUMPING
SLURPING
SLURRIED
SLURRIES
SLURRING
SLUSHIER
SLUSHILY
*SLUSHING
SLUTTIER
SLUTTISH
SLYBOOTS
SMACKERS*
SMACKING
SMALLAGE s
SMALLEST
SMALLISH
SMALLPOX
SMALTINE s
SMALTITE s
SMARAGDE*s
SMARAGDS*
SMARMIER
SMARMILY
SMARTASS
SMARTENS
SMARTEST
SMARTIES*
*SMARTING
SMASHERS
*SMASHING
SMASHUPS*
SMATTERS
SMEARERS*
SMEARIER
SMEARING
SMECTITE s
SMEDDUMS*
SMEEKING
SMELLERS*
SMELLIER
*SMELLING
SMELTERS
SMELTERY*
*SMELTING
SMERKING
SMIDGENS*
SMIDGEON s
SMIDGINS*
SMILAXES
SMIRCHED
SMIRCHES
SMIRKERS*
*SMIRKIER
*SMIRKILY
SMIRKING
SMITHERS
SMITHERY
SMITHIES
*SMOCKING s
SMOGGIER
SMOGLESS
SMOKABLE
SMOKEPOT s
SMOKIEST
SMOLDERS
*SMOOCHED
*SMOOCHER s
*SMOOCHES
SMOOSHED
SMOOSHES
SMOOTHED
SMOOTHEN s
SMOOTHER s

SMOOTHES t
SMOOTHIE s
SMOOTHLY
SMOTHERS
SMOTHERY
*SMOULDER s
SMUDGIER
SMUDGILY
SMUDGING
SMUGGEST
SMUGGLED*
SMUGGLER*s
SMUGGLES*
SMUGNESS
*SMUSHING
SMUTCHED
*SMUTCHES
SMUTTIER
SMUTTILY
SMUTTING
SNACKERS*
SNACKING
SNAFFLED*
SNAFFLES*
SNAFUING
*SNAGGIER
*SNAGGING
SNAGLIKE
*SNAILING
SNAKEBIT e
SNAKEPIT s
SNAKIEST
SNAPBACK s
*SNAPLESS
SNAPPERS
*SNAPPIER
SNAPPILY
*SNAPPING
SNAPPISH
SNAPSHOT s
SNAPWEED s
SNARFING
SNARKIER
SNARKILY
SNARLERS*
SNARLIER
SNARLING
SNATCHED
SNATCHER s
SNATCHES
SNAZZIER
SNEAKERS*
SNEAKIER
SNEAKILY
SNEAKING
SNEAPING
SNEDDING
SNEERERS*
SNEERFUL
SNEERIER
SNEERING
SNEESHES
SNEEZERS*
SNEEZIER
SNEEZING
SNELLEST
SNELLING
*SNIBBING
SNICKERS
SNICKERY*
*SNICKING
SNIFFERS
SNIFFIER
SNIFFILY
SNIFFING
SNIFFISH
SNIFFLED*
SNIFFLER*s
SNIFFLES*
SNIFTERS*
SNIGGERS*
SNIGGLED
*SNIGGLER*s
SNIGGLES
SNIGLETS*
SNIPPERS
SNIPPETS*
SNIPPETY*
*SNIPPIER
*SNIPPILY
*SNIPPING
SNITCHED
SNITCHER s
SNITCHES
SNIVELED
SNIVELER s

SNOBBERY
*SNOBBIER
*SNOBBILY
SNOBBISH
SNOBBISM s
*SNOGGING
SNOODING
SNOOKERS*
SNOOKING
SNOOLING
SNOOPERS*
SNOOPIER
SNOOPILY
SNOOPING
SNOOTIER
SNOOTILY
SNOOTING
SNOOZERS*
SNOOZIER
SNOOZING
SNOOZLED*
SNOOZLES*
SNORKELS*
SNORTERS*
SNORTING
SNOTTIER
SNOTTILY
SNOUTIER
SNOUTING
SNOUTISH
SNOWBALL s
SNOWBANK s
SNOWBELL s
SNOWBELT s
SNOWBIRD s
SNOWBUSH
SNOWCAPS*
SNOWCATS*
SNOWDROP s
SNOWFALL s
SNOWIEST
SNOWLAND s
SNOWLESS
SNOWLIKE
SNOWMELT s
SNOWMOLD s
SNOWPACK s
SNOWPLOW s
SNOWSHED s
SNOWSHOE drs
SNOWSUIT s
SNUBBERS*
*SNUBBIER
SNUBBING
SNUBNESS
SNUFFBOX
SNUFFERS*
SNUFFIER
SNUFFILY
SNUFFING
SNUFFLED*
SNUFFLER*s
SNUFFLES*
SNUGGERY*
SNUGGEST
SNUGGIES
SNUGGING
SNUGGLED*
SNUGGLES*
SNUGNESS
SOAKAGES*
SOAPBARK s
SOAPIEST
SOAPLESS
SOAPLIKE
SOAPSUDS y
SOAPWORT s
SOARINGS*
SOBEREST
SOBERING
SOBERIZE ds
SOBRIETY
SOCAGERS*
SOCCAGES*
SOCIABLE s
SOCIABLY
SOCIALLY
SOCIETAL
SOCKETED
SOCKEYES*
SOCKLESS
SODALESS
SODALIST s
SODALITE s
SODALITY
SODAMIDE s

SODDENED
SODDENLY
SODOMIES
SODOMIST s
SODOMITE s
SODOMIZE ds
SOFABEDS*
SOFTBACK s
SOFTBALL s
SOFTCORE
SOFTENED
*SOFTENER s
SOFTHEAD s
SOFTNESS
SOFTWARE s
SOFTWOOD s
SOGGIEST
SOILAGES*
SOILLESS
SOILURES*
SOJOURNS*
SOLACERS*
SOLACING
SOLANDER s
SOLANINE*s
SOLANINS*
SOLANUMS*
SOLARISE ds
SOLARISM s
SOLARIUM s
SOLARIZE ds
i SOLATING
i SOLATION s
SOLATIUM
SOLDERED
SOLDERER s
SOLDIERS*
SOLDIERY*
SOLECISE ds
SOLECISM s
SOLECIST s
SOLECIZE ds
SOLELESS
SOLEMNER
SOLEMNLY
SOLENESS
SOLENOID s
SOLERETS*
SOLEUSES
SOLFEGES*
SOLFEGGI o
SOLICITS*
SOLIDAGO s
SOLIDARY
SOLIDEST
SOLIDIFY
SOLIDITY
SOLIQUID s
SOLITARY
SOLITONS*
SOLITUDE s
SOLLERET s
SOLOISTS*
SOLONETS
SOLONETZ
SOLSTICE s
SOLUBLES*
SOLUTION s
SOLVABLE
SOLVATED*
SOLVATES*
SOLVENCY
SOLVENTS*
SOMBERLY
SOMBRELY
SOMBRERO s
SOMBROUS
SOMEBODY
SOMEDEAL
SOMEONES*
SOMERSET s
SOMETIME s
SOMEWAYS*
SOMEWHAT s
SOMEWHEN
SOMEWISE
SONANCES*
SONANTAL
SONANTIC
SONARMAN
SONARMEN
SONATINA s
SONATINE
SONGBIRD s
SONGBOOK s
SONGFEST s

SONGLESS
SONGLIKE
SONGSTER s
SONHOODS*
SONICATE ds
SONNETED
SONOBUOY s
SONOGRAM s
SONORANT s
SONORITY
SONOROUS
SONSHIPS*
SONSIEST
SOOCHONG s
SOOTHERS*
SOOTHEST*
SOOTHING
SOOTHSAY s
SOOTIEST
SOPHISMS*
SOPHISTS*
SOPITING
SOPPIEST
SOPRANOS*
SORBABLE
SORBATES*
SORBENTS*
SORBITOL s
SORBOSES*
SORCERER s
SORDIDLY
SORDINES
SOREHEAD s
SORENESS
SORGHUMS*
SORICINE
SOROCHES*
SORORATE s
SORORITY
SORPTION s
SORPTIVE
SORRIEST
SORROWED
SORROWER s
SORTABLE
SORTABLY
SOTTEDLY
SOUBISES*
SOUCHONG s
SOUFFLED*
SOUFFLES*
SOUGHING
SOULLESS
SOULLIKE
SOULMATE s
SOUNDBOX
SOUNDERS*
SOUNDEST
SOUNDING s
SOUNDMAN
SOUNDMEN
SOUPCONS*
SOUPIEST
SOUPLESS
SOUPLIKE
SOURBALL s
SOURCING
SOURDINE s
SOURNESS
SOURPUSS
SOURSOPS*
SOURWOOD s
SOUSLIKS*
SOUTACHE s
SOUTANES*
SOUTHERN*s
SOUTHERS*
SOUTHING s
SOUTHPAW s
SOUTHRON s
SOUVENIR s
SOUVLAKI as
SOVKHOZY*
SOVRANLY
SOVRANTY
SOWBELLY
SOWBREAD s
SOYBEANS*
SOYMILKS*
SPACEMAN
SPACEMEN
*SPACIEST
SPACINGS*
SPACIOUS
SPACKLED*
SPACKLES*
SPADEFUL s
SPADICES
SPADILLE s
SPADIXES
SPADONES
SPAEINGS*
SPAETZLE s
SPAGYRIC s
SPALDEEN s
SPALLERS*
*SPALLING
SPALPEEN s
SPAMBOTS*
SPAMMERS*
SPAMMING
SPANCELS*
SPANDREL s
SPANDRIL s
SPANGLED*
SPANGLES*
SPANIELS*
SPANKERS*
SPANKING s
SPANLESS
SPANNERS
*SPANNING
SPANSULE s
SPANWORM s
*SPARABLE s
SPARERIB s
SPARGERS*
*SPARGING
SPARKERS
SPARKIER
SPARKILY
*SPARKING
SPARKISH
SPARKLED*
SPARKLER*s
SPARKLES*
SPARKLET*s
SPARLIKE
*SPARLING s
SPAROIDS*
*SPARRIER
*SPARRING
SPARROWS*
SPARSELY
SPARSEST
SPARSITY
SPARTINA s
SPASMING
SPASTICS*
SPATHOSE
SPATTERS
*SPATTING
SPATULAR*
SPATULAS*
SPATZLES*
SPAVINED
SPAWNERS
*SPAWNING
SPEAKERS*
*SPEAKING s
SPEANING
SPEARERS*
SPEARGUN s
SPEARING
SPEARMAN
SPEARMEN
SPECCING
SPECIALS*
SPECIATE ds
SPECIFIC s
SPECIMEN s
SPECIOUS
*SPECKING
SPECKLED*
SPECKLES*
*SPECTATE ds
SPECTERS*
SPECTRAL*
SPECTRES*
SPECTRUM s
SPECULAR*
SPECULUM s
SPEECHES
SPEEDERS*
SPEEDIER
SPEEDILY
SPEEDING s
SPEEDUPS*
SPEEDWAY s
*SPEELING
*SPEERING s
SPEILING
SPEIRING
SPEISSES
SPELAEAN
SPELLERS*
SPELLING s
SPELTERS
SPELTZES
SPELUNKS*
SPENCERS*
SPENDERS*
SPENDIER
*SPENDING
SPERMARY
SPERMINE s
SPERMOUS
SPHAGNUM s
SPHENOID s
SPHERICS*
SPHERIER
SPHERING
SPHEROID s
SPHERULE s
SPHINGES
SPHINGID s
SPHINXES
SPHYGMIC
SPHYGMUS
SPHYNXES
SPICATED*
SPICCATO s
SPICIEST
SPICULAE*
SPICULAR*
SPICULES*
SPICULUM
SPIEGELS*
SPIELERS*
SPIELING
SPIERING
SPIFFIED
SPIFFIER
SPIFFIES t
SPIFFILY
SPIFFING
SPIKELET s
SPIKIEST
SPILIKIN s
SPILINGS
*SPILLAGE s
SPILLERS*
*SPILLING
SPILLWAY s
SPINACHY*
SPINAGES*
SPINALLY
SPINDLED*
SPINDLER*s
SPINDLES*
SPINELLE s
*SPINIEST
SPINIFEX
SPINLESS
SPINNERS
SPINNERY*
SPINNEYS*
*SPINNIES
*SPINNING s
SPINOFFS*
SPINOUTS*
SPINSTER s
SPINULAE*
SPINULES*
SPIRACLE s
SPIRAEAS*
SPIRALED
SPIRALLY
a SPIRANTS*
SPIREMES*
SPIRIEST
SPIRILLA
SPIRITED
SPIRTING
SPIRULAE*
SPIRULAS*
SPITBALL s
SPITEFUL
SPITFIRE s
SPITTERS*
*SPITTING
SPITTLES*
SPITTOON s
*SPLASHED
*SPLASHER s
*SPLASHES
*SPLATTED
*SPLATTER s
*SPLAYING
SPLENDID
SPLENDOR s
SPLENIAL*
SPLENIUM
SPLENIUS
SPLICERS*
SPLICING
SPLINING
SPLINTED
SPLINTER sy
SPLITTER s
SPLODGED*
SPLODGES*
SPLOSHED
SPLOSHES
SPLOTCHY*
SPLURGED*
SPLURGER*s
SPLURGES*
SPLUTTER sy
SPODOSOL s
SPOILAGE s
SPOILERS*
SPOILING
SPOLIATE ds
SPONDAIC s
SPONDEES*
SPONGERS*
SPONGIER
SPONGILY
SPONGING
SPONGINS*
SPONSION s
SPONSONS*
SPONSORS*
*SPONTOON s
SPOOFERS*
SPOOFERY*
SPOOFING
SPOOKERY
SPOOKIER
SPOOKILY
SPOOKING
SPOOKISH
SPOOLERS
*SPOOLING s
SPOONEYS*
SPOONFUL s
SPOONIER
SPOONIES t
SPOONILY
SPOONING
SPOORING
SPORADIC
SPOROZOA ln
SPORRANS*
SPORTERS
SPORTFUL
SPORTIER
SPORTILY
*SPORTING
SPORTIVE
SPORULAR
SPORULES*
SPOTLESS
SPOTTERS
*SPOTTIER
SPOTTILY
*SPOTTING
e SPOUSALS*
e SPOUSING
SPOUTERS
*SPOUTING s
SPRADDLE ds
SPRAINED
*SPRATTLE ds
SPRAWLED
SPRAWLER s
SPRAYERS
*SPRAYING
SPREADER s
*SPRIGGED
SPRIGGER s
SPRIGHTS*
SPRINGAL ds
SPRINGED*
SPRINGER*s
SPRINGES*
SPRINKLE drs
*SPRINTED
*SPRINTER s
SPRITZED
SPRITZER s
SPRITZES
SPROCKET s
SPROUTED
SPRUCELY
SPRUCEST*
SPRUCIER
SPRUCING
SPRYNESS
SPUDDERS*
*SPUDDING
SPUMIEST
SPUMONES*
SPUMONIS*
SPUNKIER
*SPUNKIES*t
SPUNKILY
SPUNKING
SPURGALL s
SPURIOUS
SPURNERS*
SPURNING
SPURRERS*
SPURREYS*
SPURRIER s
SPURRIES
*SPURRING
SPURTERS*
SPURTING
SPURTLES*
SPUTNIKS*
SPUTTERS
SPUTTERY*
SPYGLASS
SQUABBLE drs
*SQUADDED
SQUADRON s
SQUALENE s
SQUALLED
SQUALLER s
SQUALORS*
SQUAMATE s
SQUAMOSE
SQUAMOUS
SQUANDER s
SQUARELY
SQUARERS*
SQUAREST*
SQUARING
SQUARISH
*SQUASHED
*SQUASHER s
*SQUASHES
SQUATTED
SQUATTER s
SQUAWKED
SQUAWKER s
SQUEAKED
SQUEAKER s
SQUEALED
SQUEALER s
SQUEEGEE ds
SQUEEZED*
SQUEEZER*s
SQUEEZES*
SQUEGGED
SQUELCHY*
SQUIBBED
SQUIDDED
SQUIFFED
SQUIGGLE ds
SQUIGGLY
SQUILGEE ds
SQUILLAE*
SQUILLAS*
SQUINTED
SQUINTER s
SQUIREEN s
e*SQUIRING
SQUIRISH
SQUIRMED
SQUIRMER s
SQUIRREL sy
*SQUIRTED
SQUIRTER s
SQUISHED
SQUISHES
SQUOOSHY*
SQUUSHED
SQUUSHES
SRADDHAS*
STABBERS*
*STABBING
STABILES*
STABLERS*
STABLEST*
*STABLING s
e STABLISH
STACCATI
STACCATO s
STACKERS
*STACKING
STACKUPS*
STADDLES*
STADIUMS*
STAFFERS*
STAFFING
STAGEFUL s
STAGGARD s
STAGGART s
STAGGERS
STAGGERY*
STAGGIER*
STAGGIES*t
*STAGGING
STAGIEST
STAGINGS*
STAGNANT
STAGNATE ds
STAIDEST
STAINERS*
STAINING
STAIRWAY s
STAITHES*
*STAKEOUT s
STALKERS
*STALKIER
STALKILY
*STALKING s
STALLING
STALLION s
STALWART s
STAMENED
STAMINAL*
STAMINAS*
STAMMELS*
STAMMERS*
STAMPEDE*drs
STAMPERS
*STAMPING
STANCHED
STANCHER s
STANCHES t
STANCHLY
STANDARD s
STANDBYS*
STANDEES*
STANDERS*
STANDING s
STANDISH
STANDOFF s
STANDOUT s
STANDPAT
STANDUPS*
*STANGING
STANHOPE s
STANINES*
STANNARY
STANNITE s
STANNOUS
STANNUMS*
STANZAED
STANZAIC
STAPEDES
STAPELIA s
STAPLERS*
STAPLING
STARCHED
STARCHES
STARDOMS*
STARDUST s
STARFISH
STARGAZE drs
STARKERS*
STARKEST
STARLESS
STARLETS*
STARLIKE
STARLING s
STARNOSE s
*STARRIER
*STARRING
STARSHIP s
STARTERS*
*STARTING
STARTLED*
STARTLER*s
STARTLES*
STARTUPS*
STARVERS*
STARVING
STARWORT s
STASHING
STASIMON
STATABLE
STATEDLY
STATICAL
STATICES*
STATICKY
STATIONS*
STATISMS*
STATISTS*
STATIVES*
STATUARY
STATURES*
STATUSES
STATUTES*
STAUMREL s
STAYSAIL s
STEADIED
STEADIER s
STEADIES t
STEADILY
STEADING s
STEALAGE s
STEALERS*
STEALING s
STEALTHS*
STEALTHY*
STEAMERS*
STEAMIER
STEAMILY
*STEAMING
STEAPSIN s
STEARATE s
STEARINE*s
STEARINS*
STEATITE s
STEDFAST
STEEKING
STEELIER*
STEELIES*t
STEELING
STEENBOK s
STEEPENS*
STEEPERS*
STEEPEST
STEEPING
STEEPISH
STEEPLED*
STEEPLES*
STEERAGE s
STEERERS*
STEERING
STEEVING s
STEGODON s
STEINBOK s
STELLATE d
STELLIFY
STELLITE s
STEMLESS
STEMLIKE
STEMMATA
STEMMERS*
STEMMERY*
STEMMIER
STEMMING
STEMSONS*
STEMWARE s
*STENCHES
STENCILS*
STENGAHS*
STENOSED
STENOSES
STENOSIS
STENOTIC
STENTORS*
STEPDAME s
STEPLIKE
STEPPERS*
STEPPING
STEPSONS*
STEPWISE
STEREOED
STERICAL
STERIGMA s
STERLETS*
STERLING s
STERNEST
STERNITE s
STERNSON s
STERNUMS*
STERNWAY s
a STEROIDS*
STERTORS*
STETSONS*
STETTING
STEWABLE
STEWARDS*
STEWBUMS*
STEWPANS*

a STHENIAS*
STIBINES*
STIBIUMS*
STIBNITE s
STICKERS
STICKFUL s
STICKIER
STICKIES t
STICKILY
*STICKING
STICKLED
*STICKLER*s
STICKLES
STICKMAN
STICKMEN
STICKOUT s
STICKPIN s
STICKUMS*
STICKUPS*
STICTION s
STIFFENS*
STIFFEST
*STIFFING
STIFFISH
STIFLERS*
STIFLING
STIGMATA
STILBENE s
STILBITE s
STILETTO s
STILLEST
STILLIER
*STILLING
STILLMAN
STILLMEN
*STILTING
STIMULUS
STIMYING
STINGERS*
STINGIER
STINGILY
*STINGING
STINGRAY s
STINKARD s
STINKBUG s
STINKERS
STINKIER
STINKING
STINKPOT s
STINTERS
*STINTING
STIPENDS*
STIPITES
STIPPLED
*STIPPLER*s
STIPPLES
STIPULAR
STIPULED*
STIPULES*
STIRRERS*
STIRRING s
STIRRUPS*
STITCHED
STITCHER sy
STITCHES
STITHIED
STITHIES
STOBBING
STOCCADO s
*STOCCATA s
STOCKADE ds
STOCKAGE s
STOCKCAR s
STOCKERS*
STOCKIER
STOCKILY
STOCKING s
STOCKISH
STOCKIST s
STOCKMAN
STOCKMEN
STOCKPOT s
STODGIER
STODGILY
STODGING
STOICISM s
STOKESIA s
STOLIDER
STOLIDLY
STOLLENS*
STOLONIC
STOLPORT s
STOMACHS*
STOMACHY*
a STOMATAL*
o STOMATES*
STOMATIC
STOMODEA l
STOMPERS*
STOMPING
STONABLE
STONEFLY
*STONIEST
STOOGING
STOOKERS*
STOOKING
STOOLIES*
*STOOLING
STOOPERS*
STOOPING
STOPBANK s
STOPCOCK s
STOPGAPS*
STOPOFFS*
STOPOVER s
e STOPPAGE s
STOPPERS
e*STOPPING
STOPPLED
STOPPLES
STOPWORD s
STORABLE s
STORAGES*
STORAXES
STOREYED
STORMIER
STORMILY
STORMING
STORYING
STOTINKA
STOTINKI
STOTINOV
*STOTTING
a STOUNDED
STOUTENS*
STOUTEST
STOUTISH
*STOWABLE
STOWAGES
*STOWAWAY s
a STRADDLE drs
STRAFERS*
STRAFING
STRAGGLE drs
STRAGGLY
STRAIGHT s
*STRAINED
*STRAINER s
STRAITEN s
STRAITER
STRAITLY
STRAMASH
STRAMONY
STRANDED
STRANDER s
e STRANGER*s
e STRANGES*t
STRANGLE drs
*STRAPPED
*STRAPPER s
*STRASSES
STRATEGY
STRATIFY
STRATOUS
STRATUMS*
STRAVAGE ds
STRAVAIG s
STRAWHAT
STRAWIER
STRAWING
STRAYERS*
e STRAYING
STREAKED
STREAKER s
STREAMED
STREAMER s
STREEKED
STREEKER s
STREELED
STRENGTH s
*STRESSED
*STRESSES
STRESSOR s
STRETCHY*
STRETTAS*
STRETTOS*
STREUSEL s
STREWERS*
STREWING
STRIATED*
STRIATES*
STRIATUM
STRICKEN
*STRICKLE ds
STRICTER
STRICTLY
STRIDDEN
*STRIDENT
STRIDERS*
STRIDING
STRIDORS*
STRIGILS*
STRIGOSE
STRIKERS*
STRIKING
a STRINGED
STRINGER s
STRIPERS*
STRIPIER
STRIPING s
*STRIPPED
*STRIPPER s
STRIVERS*
STRIVING
STROBILA*er
STROBILE*s
STROBILI*
STROBILS*
STROKERS*
*STROKING
*STROLLED
*STROLLER s
STROMATA
STRONGER
STRONGLY
STRONGYL es
STRONTIA ns
STRONTIC
STROPHES*
*STROPHIC
STROPPED
STROPPER s
*STROWING
STROYERS*
STROYING
STRUCKEN
STRUDELS*
STRUGGLE drs
STRUMMED
STRUMMER s
STRUMOSE
STRUMOUS
*STRUMPET s
STRUNTED
STRUTTED
STRUTTER s
*STUBBIER
STUBBILY
*STUBBING
STUBBLED*
STUBBLES*
STUBBORN
STUCCOED
STUCCOER s
STUCCOES
STUDBOOK s
STUDDIES*
STUDDING s
STUDENTS*
STUDFISH
STUDIERS*
STUDIOUS
STUDLIER
STUDWORK s
STUDYING
STUFFERS*
STUFFIER
STUFFILY
STUFFING s
STUIVERS*
STULTIFY
STUMBLED
*STUMBLER*s
STUMBLES
STUMMING
STUMPAGE s
STUMPERS*
STUMPIER
*STUMPING
STUNNERS*
*STUNNING
STUNSAIL s
STUNTING
STUNTMAN
STUNTMEN
STUPIDER
STUPIDLY
STURDIED
STURDIER
STURDIES t
STURDILY
STURGEON s
STUTTERS*
STYLINGS*
STYLISED*
STYLISER*s
STYLISES*
STYLISTS*
STYLITES*
STYLITIC
STYLIZED*
STYLIZER*s
STYLIZES*
STYLUSES
STYMYING
STYPTICS*
STYRAXES
STYRENES*
SUASIONS*
SUBABBOT s
SUBACRID
SUBACUTE
SUBADARS*
SUBADULT s
SUBAGENT s
SUBAHDAR s
SUBAREAS*
SUBATOMS*
SUBAURAL
SUBAXIAL
SUBBASES*
SUBBASIN s
SUBBINGS*
SUBBLOCK s
SUBBREED s
SUBCASTE s
SUBCAUSE s
SUBCELLS*
SUBCHIEF s
SUBCLAIM s
SUBCLANS*
SUBCLASS
SUBCLERK s
SUBCODES*
SUBCOOLS*
SUBCULTS*
SUBCUTES
SUBCUTIS
SUBDEANS*
SUBDEPOT s
SUBDUALS*
SUBDUCED*
SUBDUCES*
SUBDUCTS*
SUBDUERS*
SUBDUING
SUBDURAL
SUBDWARF s
SUBEDITS*
SUBENTRY
SUBEPOCH s
SUBERECT
SUBERINS*
SUBERISE ds
SUBERIZE ds
SUBEROSE
SUBEROUS
SUBFIELD s
SUBFILES*
SUBFIXES
SUBFLOOR s
SUBFLUID
SUBFRAME s
SUBFUSCS*
SUBGENRE s
SUBGENUS
SUBGOALS*
SUBGRADE s
SUBGRAPH s
SUBGROUP s
SUBHEADS*
SUBHUMAN s
SUBHUMID
SUBIDEAS*
SUBINDEX
SUBITEMS*
SUBJECTS*
SUBJOINS*
SUBLATED*
SUBLATES*
SUBLEASE ds
SUBLEVEL s
SUBLIMED*
SUBLIMER*s
SUBLIMES*t
SUBLIMIT sy
SUBLINES*
SUBLUNAR y
SUBMENUS*
SUBMERGE ds
SUBMERSE ds
SUBNASAL
SUBNICHE s
SUBNODAL
SUBOCEAN
SUBOPTIC
SUBORDER s
SUBORNED
SUBORNER s
SUBOVATE
SUBOXIDE s
SUBPANEL s
SUBPARTS*
SUBPENAS*
SUBPHASE s
SUBPHYLA r
SUBPLOTS*
SUBPOENA s
SUBPOLAR
SUBPUBIC
SUBRACES*
SUBRENTS*
SUBRINGS*
SUBRULES*
SUBSALES*
SUBSCALE s
SUBSECTS*
SUBSENSE s
SUBSERES*
SUBSERVE ds
SUBSHAFT s
SUBSHELL s
SUBSHRUB s
SUBSIDED*
SUBSIDER*s
SUBSIDES*
SUBSISTS*
SUBSITES*
SUBSKILL s
SUBSOILS*
SUBSOLAR
SUBSONIC
SUBSPACE s
SUBSTAGE s
SUBSTATE s
SUBSUMED*
SUBSUMES*
SUBTASKS*
SUBTAXON s
SUBTEENS*
SUBTENDS*
SUBTESTS*
SUBTEXTS*
SUBTHEME s
SUBTILER*
SUBTILIN s
SUBTILTY
SUBTITLE ds
SUBTLEST
SUBTLETY
SUBTONES*
SUBTONIC s
SUBTOPIA s
SUBTOPIC s
SUBTOTAL s
SUBTRACT s
SUBTREND s
SUBTRIBE s
SUBTUNIC s
SUBTYPES*
SUBULATE
SUBUNITS*
SUBURBAN s
SUBURBED
SUBURBIA s
SUBVENED*
SUBVENES*
SUBVERTS*
SUBVICAR s
SUBVIRAL
SUBVIRUS
SUBVOCAL
SUBWAYED
SUBWORLD s
SUBZONES*
SUCCEEDS*
SUCCINCT
SUCCINIC
SUCCINYL s
SUCCORED
SUCCORER s
SUCCOURS*
SUCCUBAE*
SUCCUBAS*
SUCCUBUS
SUCCUMBS*
SUCHLIKE
SUCHNESS
SUCKERED
SUCKFISH
SUCKIEST
SUCKLERS*
SUCKLESS*
SUCKLING s
SUCRASES*
SUCROSES*
SUCTIONS*
SUDARIES
SUDARIUM
SUDATION s
SUDATORY
SUDDENLY
SUDSIEST
SUDSLESS
SUFFARIS*
SUFFERED
SUFFERER s
SUFFICED*
SUFFICER*s
SUFFICES*
SUFFIXAL
SUFFIXED
SUFFIXES
SUFFLATE ds
SUFFRAGE s
SUFFUSED*
SUFFUSES*
SUGARERS*
SUGARIER
SUGARING
SUGGESTS*
SUICIDAL
SUICIDED*
SUICIDES*
SUITABLE
SUITABLY
SUITCASE s
SUITINGS*
SUITLIKE
SUKIYAKI s
SULCATED*
SULFATED*
SULFATES*
SULFIDES*
SULFINYL s
SULFITES*
SULFITIC
SULFONES*
SULFONIC
SULFONYL s
SULFURED
SULFURET s
SULFURIC
SULFURYL*s
SULKIEST*
SULLAGES
SULLENER
SULLENLY
SULLYING
SULPHATE ds
SULPHIDE*s
SULPHIDS*
SULPHITE s
SULPHONE s
SULPHURS*
SULPHURY*
SULTANAS*
SULTANIC
SULTRIER
SULTRILY
SUMMABLE
SUMMANDS*
SUMMATED*
SUMMATES*
SUMMERED
SUMMERLY
SUMMITAL
SUMMITED
SUMMITRY
SUMMONED
SUMMONER s
SUMOISTS*
SUMPTERS*
SUMPWEED s
*SUNBAKED
SUNBATHE*drs
SUNBATHS*
SUNBEAMS*
SUNBEAMY*
SUNBELTS
SUNBIRDS*
*SUNBLOCK s
SUNBURNS*
SUNBURNT
SUNBURST s
*SUNCHOKE s
SUNDECKS*
SUNDERED
SUNDERER s
SUNDIALS*
SUNDOWNS*
*SUNDRESS
SUNDRIES
SUNDRILY
SUNDROPS
SUNGLASS
SUNGLOWS*
SUNLAMPS*
SUNLANDS*
SUNLIGHT s
SUNNIEST
SUNPORCH
SUNPROOF
SUNRISES*
SUNROOFS
SUNROOMS*
SUNSCALD s
SUNSHADE s
SUNSHINE s
SUNSHINY
SUNSPOTS*
SUNSTONE s
SUNSUITS*
SUNWARDS*
SUPERADD s
SUPERBAD
SUPERBER
SUPERBLY
SUPERBUG s
SUPERCAR s
SUPERCOP s
SUPEREGO s
SUPERFAN s
SUPERFIX
SUPERHIT s
SUPERHOT
SUPERING
SUPERIOR s
SUPERJET s
SUPERLAY
SUPERLIE s
SUPERMAN
SUPERMEN
SUPERMOM s
SUPERNAL
SUPERPRO s
SUPERSEX
SUPERSPY
SUPERTAX
SUPINATE ds
SUPINELY
SUPPLANT s
SUPPLELY
SUPPLEST*
SUPPLIED
SUPPLIER s
SUPPLIES
SUPPLING
SUPPORTS*
SUPPOSAL s
SUPPOSED*
SUPPOSER*s
SUPPOSES*
SUPPRESS
SUPREMER*
SUPREMES*t
SUPREMOS*
SURBASED*
SURBASES*
SURCEASE ds
SURCOATS*
SUREFIRE
SURENESS
SURETIES
SURFABLE
SURFACED*
SURFACER*s
SURFACES*
SURFBIRD s
SURFBOAT s
SURFEITS*
SURFFISH

SURFIEST
SURFINGS*
SURFLIKE
SURFSIDE
SURGEONS*
SURGICAL
SURICATE s
SURLIEST
SURMISED*
SURMISER*s
SURMISES*
SURMOUNT s
SURNAMED*
SURNAMER*s
SURNAMES*
SURPLICE ds
SURPRINT s
SURPRISE drs
SURPRIZE ds
SURROUND s
SURROYAL s
SURTAXED
SURTAXES
SURTITLE s
SURTOUTS*
SURVEILS*
SURVEYED
SURVEYOR s
SURVIVAL s
SURVIVED*
SURVIVER*s
SURVIVES*
SURVIVOR s
SUSPECTS*
SUSPENDS*
SUSPENSE rs
SUSPIRED*
SUSPIRES*
SUSTAINS*
SUSURRUS
SUTURING
SUZERAIN s
SVARAJES
SVEDBERG s
SVELTELY
SVELTEST
SWABBERS*
SWABBIES*
SWABBING
SWADDLED
SWADDLES
SWAGGERS
SWAGGIES*
*SWAGGING
SWAINISH
SWALLOWS
SWAMPERS*
SWAMPIER
SWAMPING
*SWAMPISH
SWANHERD s
SWANKEST
SWANKIER
SWANKILY
SWANKING
SWANLIKE
SWANNERY
*SWANNING
SWANPANS*
SWANSKIN s
SWAPPERS*
*SWAPPING
SWARAJES
*SWARDING
SWARMERS
*SWARMING
SWASHERS
*SWASHING
SWASTICA s
SWASTIKA s
*SWATCHES
SWATHERS*
SWATHING
SWATTERS*
SWATTING
SWAYABLE
SWAYBACK s
SWEARERS
*SWEARING
SWEATBOX
SWEATERS*
SWEATIER
SWEATILY
SWEATING
SWEENEYS*
*SWEENIES
SWEEPERS
*SWEEPIER
*SWEEPING s
SWEETENS*
SWEETEST
SWEETIES*
*SWEETING s
SWEETISH
SWEETSOP s
SWELLEST
*SWELLING s
SWELTERS
SWERVERS*
SWERVING
SWIDDENS*
SWIFTERS*
SWIFTEST
SWIFTLET s
SWIGGERS*
*SWIGGING
SWILLERS
*SWILLING
SWIMMERS*
SWIMMIER
SWIMMILY
SWIMMING s
SWIMSUIT s
SWIMWEAR
SWINDLED
SWINDLER*s
SWINDLES
SWINEPOX
SWINGBYS*
SWINGERS
*SWINGIER
*SWINGING s
SWINGLED*
SWINGLES*
*SWINGMAN
*SWINGMEN
*SWINKING
SWINNEYS*
SWIPPLES*
SWIRLIER
SWIRLING
SWISHERS
SWISHIER
*SWISHING
*SWITCHED
SWITCHER s
*SWITCHES
SWITHERS
SWIVELED
SWIZZLED*
SWIZZLER*s
SWIZZLES*
SWOBBERS*
SWOBBING
SWOONERS*
SWOONIER
SWOONING
SWOOPERS*
SWOOPIER
SWOOPING
*SWOOSHED
*SWOOSHES
SWOPPING
SWORDMAN
SWORDMEN
SWOTTERS*
*SWOTTING
*SWOUNDED
SWOUNING
SYBARITE s
SYCAMINE s
SYCAMORE s
SYCOMORE s
SYCONIUM
SYENITES*
SYENITIC
a SYLLABIC*s
SYLLABLE ds
SYLLABUB s
SYLLABUS
SYLPHIDS*
SYLPHISH
SYLVATIC
SYLVINES*
SYLVITES*
SYMBIONS*
SYMBIONT*s
SYMBIOTE*s
SYMBIOTS*
SYMBOLED
SYMBOLIC
a SYMMETRY
SYMPATHY
SYMPATRY
SYMPHONY
SYMPODIA l
SYMPOSIA c
SYMPTOMS*
SYNAGOGS*
SYNANONS*
SYNAPSED*
a SYNAPSES*
SYNAPSID s
a SYNAPSIS
SYNAPTIC
SYNCARPS*
SYNCARPY*
SYNCHING
SYNCHROS*
SYNCLINE s
SYNCOPAL
SYNCOPES*
SYNCOPIC
SYNCYTIA l
SYNDESES
SYNDESIS
a SYNDETIC
SYNDICAL
SYNDROME s
SYNECTIC
SYNERGIA s
SYNERGIC
SYNERGID s
SYNFUELS*
SYNGAMIC
SYNGASES
SYNGENIC
SYNKARYA
SYNONYME*s
SYNONYMS*
SYNONYMY*
SYNOPSES
SYNOPSIS
SYNOPTIC
SYNOVIAL*
SYNOVIAS*
SYNTAGMA*s
SYNTAGMS*
SYNTAXES
SYNTHPOP s
SYNTONIC
SYPHERED
SYPHILIS
SYPHONED
SYRETTES*
SYRINGAS*
SYRINGED*
SYRINGES*
SYRINXES
SYRPHIAN s
SYRPHIDS*
SYRUPIER
SYRUPING
SYSADMIN s
SYSTEMIC s
SYSTOLES*
SYSTOLIC
SYZYGIAL
SYZYGIES
TABANIDS*
TABARDED
TABARETS*
TABBISES
TABBYING
TABERING
TABETICS*
TABLEAUS*
TABLEAUX*
TABLEFUL s
TABLETED
TABLETOP s
TABLOIDS*
TABOOING
TABOOLEY s
TABORERS*
TABORETS*
TABORINE*s
TABORING*
TABORINS*
TABOULEH s
TABOULIS*
TABOURED
TABOURER s
TABOURET s
TABULATE ds
TACHINID s
TACHISME*s
TACHISMS*
TACHISTE*s
TACHISTS*
TACHYONS*
TACITURN
TACKIEST
TACKLERS*
s TACKLESS*
TACKLING s
TACNODES
*TACONITE s
TACRINES*
TACTICAL
TACTIONS
TACTLESS
TADPOLES*
TAFFAREL s
TAFFEREL s
TAFFETAS*
TAFFRAIL s
TAGALONG s
TAGBOARD s
TAGGANTS*
TAGLINES*
TAGMEMES*
TAGMEMIC s
TAIGLACH
TAILBACK s
TAILBONE s
TAILCOAT s
TAILFANS*
TAILFINS*
TAILGATE drs
TAILINGS*
TAILLAMP s
TAILLESS*
TAILLEUR s
TAILLIKE
TAILORED
TAILPIPE s
TAILRACE s
TAILSKID s
TAILSPIN s
TAILWIND s
TAINTING
TAKEABLE
TAKEAWAY s
TAKEDOWN s
TAKEOFFS*
s TAKEOUTS*
TAKEOVER s
TAKINGLY
TALAPOIN s
TALCKING
TALEGGIO s
TALENTED
TALESMAN
TALESMEN
TALEYSIM
TALIPEDS
TALIPOTS*
TALISMAN s
TALKABLE
TALKBACK s
s TALKIEST*
s TALKINGS*
TALLAGED*
TALLAGES*
TALLBOYS*
TALLIERS*
TALLISES
TALLISIM
TALLITHS*
TALLITIM
TALLNESS
*TALLOWED
TALLYHOS*
*TALLYING
TALLYMAN
TALLYMEN
TALMUDIC
TALOOKAS*
TAMANDUA*s
TAMANDUS*
TAMARACK s
TAMARAOS*
TAMARAUS*
TAMARIND*s
TAMARINS*
TAMARISK*s
TAMASHAS*
TAMBALAS*
TAMBOURA*s
TAMBOURS*
TAMBURAS*
TAMEABLE
TAMELESS
TAMENESS
TAMPALAS*
TAMPERED
TAMPERER s
TAMPIONS*
TAMPONED
TANAGERS*
TANBARKS*
TANDOORI*s
TANDOORS*
TANGELOS*
TANGENCE s
TANGENCY
TANGENTS*
TANGIBLE s
TANGIBLY
TANGIEST
TANGLERS
TANGLIER
*TANGLING
TANGOING
TANGRAMS*
TANISTRY
TANKAGES*
TANKARDS*
TANKFULS*
TANKINIS*
TANKLESS
TANKLIKE
TANKSHIP s
TANNABLE
TANNAGES*
TANNATES
TANNINGS*
TANTALIC
TANTALUM s
TANTALUS
TANTARAS*
TANTRISM s
TANTRUMS
TANYARDS*
TAPADERA s
TAPADERO s
TAPEABLE
TAPELESS
*TAPELIKE
TAPELINE s
TAPENADE s
TAPERERS*
TAPERING
TAPESTRY
TAPEWORM s
TAPHOLES*
TAPHOUSE s
TAPIOCAS*
TAPPABLE
TAPPINGS*
TAPROOMS*
TAPROOTS*
TAPSTERS*
TAQUERIA s
TARANTAS
TARBOOSH
TARDIEST*
TARDYONS*
TARGETED
TARIFFED
TARLATAN s
TARLETAN s
TARNALLY
TARPAPER s
TARRAGON s
TARRIERS*
s TARRIEST*
TARRYING
TARSIERS*
TARTANAS*
TARTARIC
*TARTIEST
TARTLETS*
TARTNESS
TARTRATE ds
TARTUFES*
TARTUFFE s
TARWEEDS*
TASKBARS*
TASKWORK s
TASSELED
TASTABLE
TASTEFUL
TASTIEST
TATOUAYS*
TATTERED
TATTIEST*
TATTINGS*
TATTLERS*
TATTLING
TATTOOED
TATTOOER s
TAUNTERS*
TAUNTING
TAURINES*
TAUTAUGS*
TAUTENED
TAUTNESS
TAUTOMER s
*TAUTONYM sy
TAVERNAS*
TAVERNER s
TAWDRIER
TAWDRIES t
TAWDRILY
TAWNIEST*
TAXABLES*
TAXATION s
TAXICABS*
TAXINGLY
TAXIWAYS*
TAXONOMY
TAXPAYER s
TEABERRY
TEABOARD s
TEABOWLS*
TEABOXES
TEACAKES*
TEACARTS*
TEACHERS*
TEACHING s
TEAHOUSE s
TEAKWOOD s
TEAMAKER s
TEAMMATE s
TEAMSTER s
TEAMWORK s
TEARABLE
TEARAWAY s
TEARDOWN s
*TEARDROP s
TEARIEST
*TEARLESS
TEAROOMS*
TEASABLE
*TEASELED
TEASELER s
TEASHOPS*
TEASPOON s
TEATIMES*
TEAWARES*
TEAZELED
TEAZLING
TECHIEST*
TECHNICS*
TECTITES*
TECTONIC s
TEDDERED
TEENAGED*
TEENAGER*s
TEENIEST
TEENSIER
TEENYBOP
TEETERED
TEETHERS*
TEETHING s
TEETOTAL s
TEETOTUM s
TEFILLIN
TEGMENTA l
TEGMINAL*
TEGUMENT*s
TEGUMINA
TEIGLACH
TEKTITES*
TEKTITIC
TELECAST s
TELECOMS*
TELEFILM s
TELEGONY
TELEGRAM s
TELEMARK s
TELEOSTS*
TELEPATH sy
TELEPLAY s
TELEPORT s
TELERANS*
TELESHOP s
TELESTIC hs
TELETEXT s
TELETHON s
TELETYPE ds
TELEVIEW s
TELEVISE ds
TELEXING
TELFERED
TELFORDS*
TELLABLE
TELLTALE s
TELLURIC
TELNETED
TELOMERE s
TELPHERS*
TELSONIC
TEMBLORS*
TEMERITY
TEMPERAS*
TEMPERED
TEMPERER s
TEMPESTS*
TEMPLARS*
TEMPLATE s
TEMPLETS*
a TEMPORAL s
TEMPTERS*
TEMPTING
TEMPURAS*
TENACITY
TENACULA
TENAILLE s
TENANTED
TENANTRY
TENDANCE s
TENDENCE s
TENDENCY
TENDERED
TENDERER s
TENDERLY
TENDRILS*
TENEBRAE
TENEMENT s
TENESMIC
TENESMUS
TENFOLDS
TENIASES
TENIASIS
TENNISES
TENNISTS*
TENONERS*
TENONING
TENORIST s
TENORITE s
TENOTOMY
TENPENCE s
TENPENNY
TENSIBLE
TENSIBLY
TENSIONS*
TENTACLE ds
TENTAGES*
*TENTERED
TENTIEST
TENTLESS
TENTLIKE
TENTORIA l
TENURIAL
*TENURING
TEOCALLI s
TEOSINTE s
TEPEFIED
TEPEFIES
TEPHRITE s
TEPIDITY
TEQUILAS*
TERABYTE s
TERAFLOP s
TERAOHMS*
TERAPHIM
TERATISM s
TERATOID
TERATOMA s
TERAWATT s
TERBIUMS
TERCELET s
TEREBENE s
TERGITES*
TERIYAKI s
TERMINAL s
TERMINUS
TERMITES*
TERMITIC
TERMLESS
TERMTIME s
TERNIONS*
TERPENES*
TERPENIC
TERPINOL s
TERRACED*
TERRACES*
TERRAINS*
TERRANES*

TERRAPIN s
TERRARIA
TERRASES
TERRAZZO s
TERREENS*
TERRELLA s
TERRENES*
TERRIBLE
TERRIBLY
TERRIERS*
TERRIFIC
TERRINES*
TERTIALS*
TERTIANS*
TERTIARY
TERYLENE s
TESSERAE*
TESTABLE
TESTATES
TESTATOR s
TESTICLE s
TESTIEST
TESTOONS*
TESTUDOS*
TETANICS*
TETANIES
TETANISE ds
TETANIZE ds
TETANOID
TETCHIER
TETCHILY
TETHERED
TETOTUMS*
TETRACID s
TETRADIC
TETRAGON s
TETRAMER s
TETRAPOD s
TETRARCH sy
TETRODES*
TETROXID es
TEVATRON s
TEXTBOOK s
TEXTILES*
TEXTLESS
TEXTUARY
TEXTURAL
TEXTURED*
TEXTURES*
*THACKING
THALAMIC*
THALAMUS
THALLIUM s
THALLOID
THALLOUS
THALWEGS*
THANAGES*
THANATOS
THANKERS
THANKFUL
*THANKING
THATAWAY
*THATCHED
*THATCHER s
*THATCHES
THAWLESS
THEARCHY
THEATERS
THEATRES*
THEATRIC s
THEBAINE s
THEELINS*
THEELOLS*
a THEISTIC
THELITIS
*THEMATIC s
THENAGES*
THEOCRAT s
THEODICY
THEOGONY
THEOLOGS*
THEOLOGY*
THEONOMY
THEORBOS*
THEOREMS*
THEORIES
THEORISE ds
THEORIST s
THEORIZE drs
THEREFOR e
THEREMIN s
THERIACA*ls
THERIACS*
THERIANS*
THERMALS*
THERMELS*

THERMION s
THERMITE*s
THERMITS
THEROPOD s
THESAURI
THESPIAN s
THETICAL
THEURGIC
THEWIEST
THEWLESS
THIAMINE*s
THIAMINS*
THIAZIDE s
THIAZINE*s
THIAZINS*
THIAZOLE*s
THIAZOLS*
THICKENS*
THICKEST
THICKETS*
THICKETY*
*THICKISH
THICKSET s
THIEVERY
THIEVING
THIEVISH
THIMBLES*
THINCLAD s
THINDOWN s
THINKERS*
THINKING s
THINNERS*
THINNESS
THINNEST
THINNING
THINNISH
THIONATE s
e THIONINE*s
THIONINS*
THIONYLS*
THIOPHEN es
THIOTEPA s
THIOUREA s
THIRLAGE s
THIRLING
THIRSTED
THIRSTER s
THIRTEEN s
THIRTIES
THISAWAY
THISTLES*
THOLEPIN s
THORACAL
THORACES
THORACIC
THORAXES
THORITES*
THORIUMS*
*THORNIER
*THORNILY
*THORNING
THOROUGH
THOUGHTS*
THOUSAND s
THOWLESS
THRALDOM s
THRALLED
THRASHED
THRASHER s
THRASHES
THRAWART
THRAWING
THRAWNLY
THREADED
THREADER s
THREAPED
THREAPER s
THREATED
THREATEN s
THREEPED
THRENODE s
THRENODY
THRESHED
THRESHER s
THRESHES
THRILLED
THRILLER s
THRIVERS*
THRIVING
THROATED
THROBBED
THROBBER s
THROMBIN*s
THROMBUS
THRONGED
THRONING

THROSTLE s
THROTTLE drs
THROWERS*
THROWING
THRUMMED
THRUMMER s
THRUPUTS*
THRUSHES
THRUSTED
THRUSTER s
THRUSTOR s
THRUWAYS*
THUDDING
THUGGEES*
THUGGERY
THUGGISH
THULIUMS*
THUMBING
THUMBKIN s
THUMBNUT s
THUMPERS
*THUMPING
THUNDERS*
THUNDERY*
THUNKING
THURIBLE s
THURIFER s
THWACKED
THWACKER s
THWARTED
THWARTER s
THWARTLY
THYMIEST
THYMINES*
THYMOSIN s
THYMUSES
THYREOID
THYROIDS*
THYROXIN es
THYRSOID
TICKETED
TICKINGS*
s TICKLERS*
s TICKLING
TICKLISH
s TICKSEED s
TICKTACK s
TICKTOCK s
TIDDLERS*
TIDELAND s
TIDELESS
TIDELIKE
TIDEMARK s
TIDERIPS*
TIDEWAYS*
TIDINESS
TIDYTIPS
TIEBACKS*
TIEBREAK s
TIECLASP s
TIERCELS*
TIFFINED
TIGEREYE s
TIGERISH
TIGHTENS*
TIGHTEST
TIGHTWAD s
TILAPIAS*
TILEFISH
TILELIKE
TILLABLE
TILLAGES*
TILLERED
TILLITES
TILTABLE
TILTYARD s
TIMARAUS*
TIMBALES*
TIMBERED
TIMBRELS*
TIMECARD s
TIMELESS
TIMELIER
TIMELINE s
TIMEOUTS*
TIMEWORK s
TIMEWORN
TIMIDEST
TIMIDITY
TIMOLOLS*
TIMOROUS
TIMPANUM s
TINAMOUS*
TINCTING
TINCTURE ds
TINFOILS*

TINGEING
TINGLERS*
TINGLIER
TINGLING
TINHORNS*
TININESS
TINKERED
TINKERER s
TINKLERS*
TINKLIER
*TINKLING s
TINNIEST
TINNITUS
TINPLATE s
TINSELED
TINSELLY
TINSMITH s
TINSNIPS
TINSTONE s
TINTINGS*
TINTLESS
TINTYPES*
TINWARES*
TINWORKS*
TIPCARTS*
TIPPABLE
TIPPIEST
s TIPPLERS*
s TIPPLING
TIPPYTOE ds
TIPSHEET s
TIPSIEST
TIPSTAFF s
TIPSTERS*
TIPSTOCK s
TIRAMISU s
TIREDEST
*TIRELESS
TIRESOME
TIRRIVEE s
*TISSUING
TISSULAR
TITANATE s
TITANESS
TITANIAS*
TITANISM s
TITANITE s
TITANIUM s
TITANOUS
TITHABLE
TITHINGS*
TITHONIA s
TITIVATE ds
TITLARKS*
TITLISTS*
TITMOUSE
TITRABLE
TITRANTS*
TITRATED*
TITRATES*
TITRATOR s
TITTERED
TITTERER s
TITTUPED
TITTUPPY
TITUBANT
TITULARS*
TITULARY*
TOADFISH
TOADFLAX
TOADLESS
TOADLIKE
TOADYING
TOADYISH
TOADYISM s
TOASTERS*
TOASTIER
TOASTING
TOBACCOS*
TOBOGGAN s
s TOCCATAS*
*TOCHERED
TOCOLOGY
TODDLERS*
TODDLING
TOEHOLDS*
TOENAILS*
TOEPIECE s
TOEPLATE s
TOESHOES*
TOFUTTIS*
TOGETHER
TOGGLERS*
TOGGLING
TOILETED
TOILETRY

TOILETTE s
TOILSOME
TOILWORN
TOKAMAKS*
TOKENING
TOKENISM s
TOKOLOGY
TOKOMAKS*
TOKONOMA s
TOLARJEV
TOLBOOTH s
TOLERANT
TOLERATE ds
TOLIDINE*s
TOLIDINS*
TOLLAGES*
TOLLBARS*
TOLLGATE s
TOLLWAYS*
TOLUATES*
TOLUENES*
TOLUIDES*
TOLUIDIN es
TOLUOLES*
TOMAHAWK s
TOMALLEY s
TOMATOES
TOMATOEY
TOMBACKS*
TOMBLESS
TOMBLIKE
TOMBOLAS*
TOMBOLOS*
*TOMENTUM
TOMFOOLS*
TOMMYROT s
TOMOGRAM s
TOMORROW s
TOMPIONS*
a TONALITY
TONEARMS*
TONELESS
TONETICS*
TONETTES*
TONGUING s
a TONICITY
TONIGHTS*
TONISHLY
TONNAGES*
TONNEAUS*
TONNEAUX*
TONSILAR
TONSURED*
TONSURES*
TONTINES*
TOOLBARS*
TOOLHEAD s
TOOLINGS*
TOOLLESS
TOOLROOM s
TOOLSHED s
TOOTHIER
TOOTHILY
TOOTHING
TOOTLERS*
TOOTLING
TOOTSIES*
TOPAZINE
TOPCOATS*
TOPCROSS
TOPKICKS*
TOPKNOTS*
TOPLINES*
TOPLOFTY
TOPMASTS*
TOPNOTCH
TOPOLOGY
TOPONYMS*
TOPONYMY*
TOPOTYPE s
TOPPINGS*
s TOPPLING
TOPSAILS*
TOPSIDER*s
TOPSIDES*
TOPSOILS*
TOPSPINS*
TOPSTONE s
TOPWORKS*
TORCHERE s
TORCHIER es
TORCHING
TORCHONS*
TOREADOR s
TOREUTIC s
TORMENTS*

TORNADIC
TORNADOS*
TORNILLO s
TOROIDAL
TOROSITY
TORPEDOS*
TORPIDLY
TORQUATE
TORQUERS*
TORQUING
TORRENTS*
TORRIDER
TORRIDLY
TORSADES*
TORSIONS*
TORTILLA s
TORTIOUS
TORTOISE s
TORTONIS*
TORTUOUS
TORTURED*
TORTURER*s
TORTURES*
TOSSPOTS*
TOSTADAS*
TOSTADOS*
TOTALING
TOTALISE ds
TOTALISM s
TOTALIST s
TOTALITY
TOTALIZE drs
TOTALLED
TOTEABLE
TOTEMISM s
TOTEMIST s
TOTEMITE s
TOTTERED
TOTTERER s
TOUCHERS*
TOUCHIER
TOUCHILY
*TOUCHING
TOUCHPAD s
TOUCHUPS*
TOUGHENS*
TOUGHEST
TOUGHIES*
TOUGHING
TOUGHISH
TOURACOS*
TOURINGS*
TOURISMS*
TOURISTA*s
TOURISTS*
TOURISTY*
TOURNEYS*
TOUSLING
TOUZLING
TOVARICH
TOVARISH
TOWARDLY
s TOWAWAYS*
TOWBOATS*
TOWELING s
TOWELLED
TOWERIER
TOWERING
TOWHEADS*
TOWLINES*
TOWMONDS*
TOWMONTS*
TOWNFOLK
TOWNHOME s
TOWNLESS
TOWNLETS*
TOWNSHIP s
TOWNSMAN
TOWNSMEN
TOWNWEAR
TOWPATHS*
TOWPLANE s
TOWROPES*
TOWSACKS*
TOXAEMIA s
TOXAEMIC
TOXEMIAS*
TOXICANT s
TOXICITY
TOYSHOPS*
TRABEATE d
TRACHEAE*
TRACHEAL*
TRACHEAS*
TRACHEID s
TRACHLED*

TRACHLES*
TRACHOMA s
TRACHYTE s
TRACINGS
TRACKAGE s
TRACKERS
*TRACKING s
TRACKMAN
TRACKMEN
TRACKPAD s
TRACKWAY s
TRACTATE s
TRACTILE
TRACTION s
TRACTIVE
TRACTORS*
TRADABLE
TRADEOFF s
TRADITOR
TRADUCED*
TRADUCER*s
TRADUCES*
TRAFFICS*
TRAGICAL
TRAGOPAN s
TRAIKING
TRAILERS
*TRAILING
TRAINEES*
s TRAINERS*
TRAINFUL s
s*TRAINING s
TRAINMAN
TRAINMEN
TRAINWAY s
TRAIPSED*
TRAIPSES*
TRAITORS*
TRAJECTS*
TRAMCARS*
TRAMELED
TRAMELLS*
TRAMLESS
TRAMLINE s
TRAMMELS*
*TRAMMING
TRAMPERS*
TRAMPIER
*TRAMPING
TRAMPISH
TRAMPLED*
TRAMPLER*s
TRAMPLES*
TRAMROAD s
TRAMWAYS*
TRANCHES
TRANCING
TRANGAMS*
TRANNIES
TRANQUIL
TRANSACT s
TRANSECT s
TRANSEPT s
TRANSFER s
TRANSFIX t
TRANSHIP s
TRANSITS*
TRANSMIT s
TRANSOMS
TRANSUDE ds
TRAPBALL s
TRAPDOOR s
TRAPESED
TRAPESES
TRAPEZES*
TRAPEZIA l
TRAPEZII
TRAPLIKE
TRAPLINE s
TRAPNEST s
TRAPPEAN
s*TRAPPERS*
s*TRAPPING s
TRAPPOSE
TRAPPOUS
TRAPROCK s
TRAPUNTO s
TRASHERS
TRASHIER
TRASHILY
TRASHING
TRASHMAN
TRASHMEN
TRAUCHLE ds
TRAUMATA
TRAVAILS*

*TRAVELED
*TRAVELER s
TRAVELOG s
TRAVERSE drs
TRAVESTY
TRAVOISE*s
TRAWLERS*
TRAWLEYS*
TRAWLING
TRAWLNET s
TRAYFULS*
TREACLES*
TREADERS
*TREADING
TREADLED*
TREADLER*s
TREADLES*s
TREASONS
TREASURE drs
TREASURY
TREATERS*
TREATIES
TREATING
TREATISE s
TREBLING
TRECENTO s
TREDDLED
TREDDLES
TREELAWN s
TREELESS
TREELIKE
TREENAIL s
TREETOPS*
TREFOILS*
TREHALAS*
TREKKERS*
TREKKING
TREMBLED*
TREMBLER*s
TREMBLES*
TREMOLOS*
TRENAILS
TRENCHED
TRENCHER s
TRENCHES
TRENDIER
TRENDIES t
TRENDILY
*TRENDING
TRENDOID s
TREPANGS*
TREPHINE ds
TRESPASS
TRESSELS*
TRESSIER
TRESSOUR s
TRESSURE s
TRESTLES*
TREVALLY s
TRIACIDS*
TRIADICS*
TRIADISM s
TRIAGING
TRIANGLE ds
TRIARCHY
TRIASSIC
TRIAXIAL
TRIAZINE*s
TRIAZINS*
TRIAZOLE s
TRIBADES*
TRIBADIC
TRIBALLY
TRIBASIC
TRIBRACH s
TRIBUNAL s
TRIBUNES*
TRIBUTES*
TRICHINA els
TRICHITE s
TRICHOID
TRICHOME s
TRICKERS*
TRICKERY*
TRICKIER*
TRICKILY
*TRICKING
TRICKISH
s TRICKLED*
s TRICKLES*
TRICLADS*
TRICOLOR s
TRICORNE*s
TRICORNS*
TRICTRAC s
TRICYCLE s

TRIDENTS*
TRIDUUMS*
TRIENNIA l
TRIENTES
TRIETHYL
TRIFECTA s
TRIFLERS
*TRIFLING s
TRIFOCAL s
TRIFORIA
TRIGGERS
TRIGGEST
*TRIGGING
TRIGLYPH s
TRIGNESS
TRIGONAL
TRIGRAMS*
TRIGRAPH s
TRIHEDRA l
TRILBIES
TRILITHS*
TRILLERS*
*TRILLING
TRILLION s
TRILLIUM s
TRILOBAL
TRILOBED
TRIMARAN s
TRIMERIC
TRIMETER s
TRIMMERS
TRIMMEST
*TRIMMING s
TRIMNESS
TRIMORPH s
TRIMOTOR s
TRINDLED*
TRINDLES*
TRINKETS*
TRINKUMS
TRINODAL
TRIOLETS*
TRIOXIDE*s
TRIOXIDS*
TRIPACKS*
TRIPEDAL
TRIPHASE
TRIPLANE s
TRIPLETS*
s TRIPLING
TRIPLITE s
TRIPLOID sy
TRIPODAL
TRIPODIC
TRIPOLIS*
TRIPOSES
s*TRIPPERS*
TRIPPETS*
TRIPPIER
s*TRIPPING s
TRIPTANE*s
TRIPTANS*
TRIPTYCA s
TRIPTYCH s
TRIPWIRE s
TRIREMES*
TRISCELE s
TRISECTS*
TRISEMES*
TRISEMIC
TRISHAWS*
TRISKELE s
TRISOMES*
TRISOMIC s
TRISTATE
TRISTEZA s
TRISTFUL
TRISTICH s
TRITHING s
TRITICUM s
TRITIUMS*
TRITOMAS*
TRITONES*
TRIUMPHS*
TRIUMVIR is
TRIUNITY
TRIVALVE s
TROAKING
TROCHAIC s
TROCHARS*
TROCHEES*
TROCHILI*
TROCHILS*
TROCHLEA ers
TROCHOID s
*TROCKING

TROFFERS*
TROILISM s
TROILITE s
TROLANDS*
s*TROLLERS*
TROLLEYS*
TROLLIED
TROLLIES
s*TROLLING s
TROLLOPS*
TROLLOPY*
TROMBONE s
TROMMELS*
*TROMPING
TROOPERS*
TROOPIAL s
TROOPING
a TROPHIED
a TROPHIES
TROPICAL s
a TROPINES*
a TROPISMS*
TROPONIN s
TROTHING
TROTLINE s
TROTTERS
*TROTTING
TROUBLED*
TROUBLER*s
TROUBLES
TROUNCED*
TROUNCER*s
TROUNCES*
TROUPERS*
TROUPIAL s
*TROUPING
TROUSERS
TROUTIER
TROUVERE s
TROUVEUR s
*TROWELED
TROWELER s
TROWSERS
TRUANTED
TRUANTLY
TRUANTRY
TRUCKAGE s
TRUCKERS*
TRUCKFUL s
*TRUCKING s
TRUCKLED
TRUCKLER*s
TRUCKLES
TRUCKMAN
TRUCKMEN
TRUDGENS*
TRUDGEON s
TRUDGERS*
TRUDGING
TRUEBLUE s
TRUEBORN
TRUEBRED
TRUELOVE s
TRUENESS
TRUFFLED
TRUFFLES
TRUISTIC
TRUMEAUX*
TRUMPERY
s TRUMPETS*
TRUMPING
TRUNCATE ds
TRUNDLED*
TRUNDLER*s
TRUNDLES
TRUNKFUL s
TRUNNELS
TRUNNION s
TRUSSERS*
TRUSSING s
TRUSTEED*
TRUSTEES*
TRUSTERS*
TRUSTFUL
*TRUSTIER
TRUSTIES t
*TRUSTILY
*TRUSTING
TRUSTORS*
*TRUTHFUL
TRYINGLY
TRYPSINS*
TRYSAILS*
TRYSTERS*
TRYSTING
TRYWORKS

TSARDOMS*
TSAREVNA s
TSARINAS*
TSARISMS*
TSARISTS*
TSARITZA s
TSATSKES*
TSKTSKED
TSORRISS
TSUNAMIC*
TSUNAMIS*
TUATARAS*
TUATERAS*
TUBAISTS*
TUBBABLE
s TUBBIEST
TUBELESS
TUBELIKE
TUBENOSE s
TUBERCLE s
TUBEROID
TUBEROSE s
TUBEROUS
TUBEWORK s
TUBEWORM s
TUBIFORM
TUBULATE ds
TUBULINS*
TUBULOSE
TUBULOUS
TUBULURE s
TUCKAHOE s
TUCKERED
TUCKSHOP s
TUFTIEST
TUFTINGS*
TUGBOATS*
TUGHRIKS*
TUITIONS*
TULLIBEE s
s TUMBLERS*
s TUMBLING s
TUMBRELS*
TUMBRILS*
TUMEFIED
TUMEFIES
TUMESCED*
TUMESCES*
TUMIDITY
TUMMLERS*
TUMOROUS
TUMPLINE s
TUMULOSE
TUMULOUS
TUNEABLE
TUNEABLY
TUNELESS
TUNGSTEN s
TUNGSTIC
TUNICATE ds
TUNICLES*
TUNNAGES*
TUNNELED
TUNNELER s
TUPPENCE s
TUPPENNY
TURACOUS*
TURBANED
TURBETHS*
TURBIDLY
TURBINAL s
TURBINES*
TURBITHS*
TURBOCAR s
TURBOFAN s
TURBOJET s
TURFIEST
TURFLESS
TURFLIKE
TURFSKIS*
*TURGENCY
TURGIDLY
TURGITES*
TURISTAS*
TURMERIC s
TURMOILS*
TURNABLE
TURNCOAT s
TURNDOWN s
TURNHALL s
TURNINGS*
TURNKEYS*
TURNOFFS*
TURNOUTS*
TURNOVER s
TURNPIKE s

TURNSOLE s
TURNSPIT s
TURPETHS*
TURQUOIS e
TURRETED
TURRICAL
TURTLERS*
TURTLING s
TUSKLESS
TUSKLIKE
TUSSISES
TUSSLING
TUSSOCKS*
TUSSOCKY*
TUSSORES*
TUSSUCKS*
TUTELAGE s
TUTELARS*
TUTELARY*
TUTORAGE s
TUTORESS
TUTORIAL s
TUTORING
TUTOYERS*
TUXEDOED
TUXEDOES
TWADDLED
*TWADDLER*s
TWADDLES
TWANGERS*
TWANGIER
TWANGING
TWANGLED
*TWANGLER*s
TWANGLES
TWANKIES
TWASOMES*
TWATTLED
TWATTLES
TWEAKIER
TWEAKING
*TWEEDIER
TWEEDLED*
TWEEDLES*
TWEENERS*
TWEENESS
*TWEENIES
TWEETERS*
*TWEETING
TWEEZERS*
TWEEZING
TWELFTHS*
TWELVEMO s
TWENTIES
TWIBILLS*
TWIDDLED
TWIDDLER*s
TWIDDLES
*TWIGGIER
*TWIGGING
*TWIGLESS
*TWIGLIKE
TWILIGHT s
*TWILLING s
TWINBORN
*TWINGING
*TWINIEST
TWINIGHT
TWINJETS*
TWINKIES*
TWINKLED
TWINKLER*s
TWINKLES
*TWINNING s
TWINSETS*
TWINSHIP s
TWIRLERS*
TWIRLIER
TWIRLING
TWISTERS*
TWISTIER
*TWISTING s
*TWITCHED
TWITCHER s
*TWITCHES
TWITTERS*
TWITTERY*
*TWITTING
TWOFOLDS*
TWOONIES*
TWOPENCE s
TWOPENNY
TWOSOMES*
TYLOSINS*
TYMPANAL*
TYMPANIC*

TYMPANUM s
TYPEABLE
TYPEBARS*
TYPECASE s
TYPECAST s
TYPEFACE s
TYPESETS*
TYPHOIDS*
TYPHONIC
TYPHOONS*
TYPHUSES
TYPIFIED
TYPIFIER s
TYPIFIES
TYPOLOGY
TYRAMINE s
TYRANNIC
TYROSINE s
TZARDOMS*
TZAREVNA s
TZARINAS*
TZARISMS*
TZARISTS*
TZARITZA s
TZIGANES*
TZITZITH*
d UBIETIES
UBIQUITY
UDOMETER s
UDOMETRY
UGLIFIED
UGLIFIER s
UGLIFIES
UGLINESS
UINTAITE s
UKELELES*
UKULELES*
ULCERATE ds
ULCERING
ULCEROUS
ULEXITES*
ULTERIOR
ULTIMACY
ULTIMATA
ULTIMATE ds
ULTRADRY
ULTRAHIP
ULTRAHOT
ULTRAISM s
ULTRAIST s
ULTRALOW
ULTRARED s
ULULATED*
ULULATES*
UMANGITE s
UMBELLAR
UMBELLED
UMBELLET s
cln UMBERING
UMBILICI
UMBONATE
UMBRAGES*
UMBRELLA s
UMBRETTE s
UMLAUTED
UMPIRAGE s
UMPIRING
UMTEENTH
UNABATED
UNABUSED
UNACIDIC
UNAFRAID
UNAGEING
UNAGREED
UNAKITES*
UNALLIED
UNAMAZED
UNAMUSED
UNANCHOR s
UNANELED
UNARCHED
UNARGUED
UNARMING
UNARTFUL
UNATONED
UNAVOWED
UNAWAKED*
UNAWARES*
UNBACKED
UNBALING
UNBANDED
UNBANNED
UNBARBED
UNBARRED
UNBASTED
s UNBATHED

UNBEARED
UNBEATEN
UNBELIEF s
UNBELTED
UNBENDED
UNBENIGN
UNBIASED
UNBIDDEN
UNBILLED
UNBITTED
UNBITTEN
UNBITTER
UNBLAMED
s UNBLOCKS*
UNBLOODY
UNBOBBED
UNBODIED
UNBOILED
UNBOLTED
UNBONDED
s UNBONNET s
UNBOOTED
UNBOSOMS*
UNBOTTLE ds
UNBOUGHT
UNBOUNCY
UNBOWING
UNBOXING
UNBRACED*
UNBRACES*
UNBRAIDS*
UNBRAKED*
UNBRAKES*
UNBREECH
UNBRIDLE ds
UNBRIGHT
UNBROKEN*
UNBUCKLE ds
UNBUILDS*
UNBUNDLE ds
UNBURDEN s
UNBURIED
s UNBURNED
UNBUSTED
UNBUTTON s
UNCAGING
UNCAKING
UNCALLED
UNCANDID
UNCANNED
UNCAPPED
UNCARDED
UNCARING
UNCARTED
UNCARVED
UNCASHED
UNCASING
UNCASKED
UNCATCHY
UNCAUGHT
UNCAUSED
UNCHAINS*
UNCHAIRS*
UNCHANCY
UNCHARGE ds
UNCHASTE r
UNCHEWED
UNCHICLY
UNCHOKED*
s UNCHOKES*
UNCHOSEN
UNCHURCH
UNCIALLY
UNCIFORM s
r UNCINATE
UNCLAMPS*
UNCLASPS*
UNCLASSY
UNCLAWED
UNCLENCH
UNCLINCH
UNCLOAKS*
UNCLOSED*
UNCLOSES*
UNCLOTHE ds
UNCLOUDS*
UNCLOUDY*
UNCLOYED
UNCOATED
UNCOCKED
UNCOFFIN s
UNCOILED
UNCOINED
UNCOMBED
UNCOMELY
UNCOMMON

UNCOOKED
UNCOOLED
UNCORKED
UNCOUPLE drs
UNCOVERS*
UNCRATED*
UNCRATES*
UNCREATE ds
UNCREWED
UNCROWNS*
fj UNCTIONS*
UNCTUOUS
UNCUFFED
UNCURBED
UNCURLED
UNCURSED
UNDAMPED
UNDARING
UNDECKED
UNDENIED
UNDENTED
UNDERACT s
UNDERAGE ds
UNDERARM s
UNDERATE
UNDERBID s
UNDERBUD s
UNDERBUY s
UNDERCUT s
UNDERDID
UNDERDOG*s
UNDEREAT s
UNDERFED
UNDERFUR s
UNDERGOD*s
UNDERJAW s
UNDERLAP s
UNDERLAY s
UNDERLET s
UNDERLIE s
UNDERLIP s
UNDERLIT
UNDERPAY s
UNDERPIN s
UNDERRAN
UNDERRUN s
UNDERSEA s
UNDERSET s
UNDERTAX
UNDERTOW s
UNDERUSE ds
UNDERWAY
UNDEVOUT
UNDIMMED
UNDOABLE
UNDOCILE
UNDOCKED
UNDOINGS*
UNDOTTED
UNDOUBLE ds
UNDRAPED*
UNDRAPES*
UNDREAMT
UNDUBBED
UNDULANT
UNDULATE ds
UNDULLED
UNEARNED
UNEARTHS*
UNEASIER
UNEASILY
UNEDIBLE
UNEDITED
UNENDING
UNENVIED
UNEQUALS*
UNERASED
UNEROTIC
UNERRING
UNEVADED
UNEVENER
UNEVENLY
UNEXOTIC
UNEXPERT
UNFADING
UNFAIRER
UNFAIRLY
UNFAITHS*
UNFALLEN
UNFAMOUS
UNFASTEN s
UNFEARED
UNFELTED
UNFENCED*
UNFENCES*
UNFETTER s
UNFILIAL
UNFILLED
UNFILMED
UNFISHED
UNFITTED
UNFIXING
UNFLASHY
UNFLAWED
UNFLEXED
UNFLUTED
UNFOILED
UNFOLDED
UNFOLDER s
UNFORCED
UNFORGED
UNFORGOT
UNFORKED
UNFORMED
g UNFOUGHT
UNFRAMED
UNFREEZE s
UNFROCKS*
UNFROZEN*
UNFUNDED
UNFURLED
UNGAINLY
UNGALLED
UNGARBED
UNGAZING
UNGELDED
UNGENIAL
UNGENTLE
p UNGENTLY
UNGIFTED
UNGIRDED
UNGIVING
UNGLAZED
UNGLOVED*
UNGLOVES*
UNGLUING
UNGOTTEN
UNGOWNED
UNGRACED
UNGRADED
UNGREEDY
UNGROUND
UNGUARDS*
UNGUENTA*
UNGUENTS*
UNGUIDED
UNGULATE s
UNHAILED
UNHAIRED
UNHAIRER s
UNHALLOW s
UNHALVED
UNHANDED
UNHANGED
UNHARMED
UNHATTED
UNHEALED
UNHEATED
UNHEDGED
UNHEEDED
UNHELMED
UNHELPED
UNHEROIC
UNHINGED*
UNHINGES*
UNHOLIER
UNHOLILY
UNHOODED
UNHOOKED
UNHORSED*
UNHORSES*
UNHOUSED*
f UNHOUSES*
UNHUSKED
UNIALGAL
UNIAXIAL
UNICOLOR
UNICORNS*
UNICYCLE ds
UNIDEAED
UNIFACES*
UNIFIERS*
UNIFILAR
c UNIFORMS*
UNIFYING
UNILOBED
UNIMBUED
UNIONISE ds
UNIONISM s
UNIONIST s
UNIONIZE drs
UNIPOLAR
UNIQUELY
UNIQUEST*
UNIRONED
UNIRONIC
UNISEXES
UNISONAL
UNISSUED
UNITAGES*
UNITARDS*
UNITEDLY
UNITIZED*
UNITIZER*s
UNITIZES*
UNITRUST s
UNIVALVE ds
UNIVERSE s
UNIVOCAL s
UNJAMMED
UNJOINED
UNJOINTS*
UNJOYFUL
UNJUDGED
UNJUSTLY
UNKEELED
UNKENNED
UNKENNEL s
UNKINDER
UNKINDLY
UNKINGLY
UNKINKED
UNKISSED
UNKNOWNS*
UNKOSHER
UNLACING
UNLADING
UNLASHED
UNLASHES
UNLAWFUL
UNLAYING
UNLEADED s
UNLEARNS*
UNLEARNT*
UNLEASED
UNLETHAL
UNLETTED
UNLEVELS*
UNLEVIED
UNLICKED
UNLIKELY
UNLIMBER s
UNLINKED
UNLISTED
UNLIVELY
UNLIVING
UNLOADED
UNLOADER s
UNLOCKED
UNLOOSED*
UNLOOSEN*s
UNLOOSES*
UNLOVELY
UNLOVING
UNMAILED
UNMAKERS*
UNMAKING
UNMANFUL
UNMANNED
UNMAPPED
UNMARKED
UNMARRED
UNMASKED
UNMASKER s
UNMATTED
UNMEETLY
UNMELLOW
UNMELTED
UNMENDED
UNMESHED
UNMESHES
UNMEWING
UNMILLED
UNMINGLE ds
UNMITERS*
UNMITRED*
UNMITRES*
UNMIXING
UNMODISH
UNMOLDED
UNMOLTEN
UNMOORED
UNMOVING
UNMUFFLE ds
UNMUZZLE ds
UNNAILED
UNNEEDED
UNNERVED*
UNNERVES*
UNOPENED
UNORNATE
UNPACKED
UNPACKER s
UNPADDED
UNPAIRED
UNPARTED
UNPAYING
UNPEELED
UNPEGGED
UNPENNED
UNPEOPLE ds
UNPERSON s
UNPICKED
UNPILING
UNPINNED
UNPITIED
UNPITTED
UNPLACED
UNPLAITS*
UNPLAYED
UNPLIANT
UNPLOWED
UNPOETIC
UNPOISED
UNPOLITE
UNPOLLED
UNPOSTED
UNPOTTED
UNPRETTY
UNPRICED
UNPRIMED
UNPRIZED
UNPROBED
UNPROVED
UNPROVEN
UNPRUNED
UNPUCKER s
UNPURELY
UNPURGED
UNPUZZLE ds
UNQUIETS*
UNQUOTED*
UNQUOTES*
UNRAISED
UNRANKED
UNRAVELS*
UNREALLY
UNREASON s
UNREELED
UNREELER s
UNREEVED*
UNREEVES*
UNRENTED
UNREPAID
UNREPAIR s
UNRESTED
UNRETIRE ds
UNRHYMED
UNRIBBED
UNRIDDLE drs
UNRIFLED
UNRIGGED
UNRINSED
UNRIPELY
UNRIPEST
UNRIPPED
UNROBING
UNROLLED
UNROOFED
UNROOTED
r UNROUNDS*
UNRULIER
UNRUSHED
UNRUSTED
UNSADDLE ds
UNSAFELY
UNSAFETY
UNSALTED
UNSAVORY
UNSAYING
UNSCALED
UNSCREWS*
UNSEALED
UNSEAMED
UNSEARED
UNSEATED
UNSEEDED
UNSEEING
UNSEEMLY
UNSEIZED
UNSERVED
UNSETTLE ds
UNSEWING
UNSEXING
UNSEXUAL
UNSHADED
UNSHAKEN
UNSHAMED
UNSHAPED
UNSHAPEN
UNSHARED
UNSHAVED
UNSHAVEN
UNSHELLS*
UNSHIFTS*
UNSHRUNK
UNSICKER
UNSIFTED
UNSIGHTS*
UNSIGNED
UNSILENT
UNSINFUL
UNSLAKED
UNSLICED
UNSLINGS*
UNSMOKED
UNSNARLS*
UNSOAKED
UNSOCIAL
UNSOILED
UNSOLDER s
UNSOLVED
UNSONSIE
UNSORTED
UNSOUGHT
UNSOURED
UNSPEAKS*
UNSPHERE ds
UNSPOILT
UNSPOKEN*
UNSPOOLS*
UNSPRUNG
UNSTABLE r
UNSTABLY
UNSTACKS*
UNSTATED*
UNSTATES*
UNSTAYED
UNSTEADY
UNSTEELS*
UNSTICKS*
UNSTITCH
UNSTONED
UNSTRAPS*
UNSTRESS
UNSTRING s
UNSTRUNG
UNSTUFFY
UNSUBTLE
UNSUBTLY
UNSUITED
UNSURELY
UNSWATHE ds
UNSWAYED
UNSWEARS*
UNTACKED
UNTAGGED
UNTANGLE ds
s UNTANNED
UNTAPPED
UNTASTED
UNTAUGHT
UNTENDED
UNTENTED
UNTESTED
UNTETHER s
UNTHAWED
UNTHINKS*
UNTHREAD s
UNTHRONE ds
UNTIDIED
UNTIDIER
UNTIDIES t
UNTIDILY
UNTIEING
UNTILLED
UNTILTED
UNTIMELY
UNTINGED
UNTIPPED
UNTIRING
UNTITLED
UNTOWARD
UNTRACED
UNTRACKS*
UNTREADS*
UNTRENDY
UNTRUEST
UNTRUSTY
UNTRUTHS*
UNTUCKED
UNTUFTED
UNTUNING
UNTURNED
UNTWINED*
UNTWINES*
UNTWISTS*
UNUNBIUM s
UNUNITED
UNUSABLE
UNVALUED
UNVARIED
UNVEILED
UNVEINED
UNVERSED
UNVESTED
UNVIABLE
UNVOICED*
UNVOICES*
UNWALLED
UNWANING
UNWANTED
UNWARIER
UNWARILY
UNWARMED
UNWARNED
UNWARPED
UNWASHED s
UNWASTED
UNWEANED
UNWEAVES*
UNWEDDED
UNWEEDED
UNWEIGHT s
UNWELDED
UNWETTED
UNWIELDY
UNWIFELY
UNWILLED
UNWINDER s
UNWISDOM s
UNWISELY
UNWISEST
UNWISHED
UNWISHES
UNWITTED
UNWONTED
UNWOODED
UNWORKED
UNWORTHY
UNYEANED
UNYOKING
UNZIPPED
c UPBEARER s
UPBOILED
UPBRAIDS*
UPBUILDS*
UPCHUCKS*
UPCLIMBS*
UPCOILED
UPCOMING
UPCURLED
UPCURVED*
UPCURVES*
UPDARTED
UPDATERS*
UPDATING
UPDIVING
UPDRAFTS*
UPDRYING
*UPENDING
UPFLINGS*
UPFLOWED
UPFOLDED
UPGATHER s
UPGAZING
UPGIRDED
UPGRADED*
UPGRADES*
UPGROWTH s
UPHEAPED
UPHEAVAL s
UPHEAVED*
UPHEAVER*s
UPHEAVES*
UPHOARDS*
UPHOLDER s
UPLANDER s
UPLEAPED
UPLIFTED
UPLIFTER s
UPLIGHTS
*UPLINKED
UPLOADED
UPMARKET
UPPERCUT s
UPPILING
UPPISHLY
UPRAISED
*UPRAISER*s
UPRAISES
*UPRATING
UPREARED
UPRIGHTS*
UPRISERS*
*UPRISING s
UPRIVERS*
UPROOTAL s
UPROOTED
UPROOTER s
UPROUSED*
UPROUSES*
UPRUSHED
UPRUSHES
UPSCALED*
UPSCALES*
UPSETTER s
UPSHIFTS*
UPSHOOTS*
UPSILONS*
UPSIZING
UPSOARED
UPSPRANG
UPSPRING s
UPSPRUNG
UPSTAGED*
UPSTAGER*s
UPSTAGES*
UPSTAIRS*
UPSTANDS*
UPSTARED*
UPSTARES*
UPSTARTS*
UPSTATER*s
UPSTATES*
UPSTREAM
UPSTROKE s
UPSURGED*
UPSURGES*
UPSWEEPS*
UPSWELLS*
UPSWINGS*
UPTALKED
UPTEMPOS*
UPTHROWN*
UPTHROWS*
UPTHRUST s
UPTILTED
UPTOSSED
UPTOSSES
UPTOWNER s
UPTRENDS*
UPTURNED
UPWAFTED
UPWARDLY
UPWELLED
URAEMIAS*
URAEUSES
r URALITES*
URALITIC
URANIDES*
URANISMS*
URANITES*
URANITIC
URANIUMS*
URANYLIC
URBANELY
URBANEST
URBANISE ds
URBANISM s
URBANIST s
URBANITE s
URBANITY
URBANIZE ds
UREDINIA l
URETERAL
URETERIC
URETHANE*s
URETHANS*
URETHRAE*
URETHRAL*
URETHRAS*
URGENTLY
URGINGLY
URIDINES*
URINATED*
URINATES*
URINATOR s
URINEMIA s
URINEMIC
UROCHORD s
URODELES*

UROLITHS*
UROLOGIC
UROPODAL
UROPYGIA l
UROSCOPY
UROSTYLE s
b URSIFORM
URTICANT s
URTICATE ds
URUSHIOL s
USAUNCES*
USEFULLY
USERNAME s
USHERING
USQUABAE s
USQUEBAE s
p USTULATE
USUFRUCT s
USURIOUS
USURPERS*
USURPING
UTENSILS*
UTERUSES
UTILIDOR s
UTILISED*
UTILISER*s
UTILISES*
UTILIZED*
UTILIZER*s
UTILIZES*
UTOPIANS*
UTOPISMS*
UTOPISTS*
UTRICLES*
UTRICULI
mp UTTERERS*
bgm UTTERING
p
UVULARLY
UVULITIS
UXORIOUS
VACANTLY
VACATING
VACATION s
VACCINAL*
VACCINAS*
VACCINEE*s
VACCINES*
VACCINIA ls
VACUOLAR
VACUOLES*
VACUUMED
VAGABOND s
VAGARIES
*VAGILITY
e VAGINATE d
VAGOTOMY
VAGRANCY
VAGRANTS*
VAINNESS
VALANCED*
VALANCES*
VALENCES*
VALENCIA s
VALERATE s
VALERIAN s
VALETING
VALGUSES
VALIANCE s
VALIANCY
VALIANTS*
VALIDATE ds
VALIDITY
VALKYRIE s
VALLEYED
VALONIAS*
VALORISE ds
VALORIZE ds
VALOROUS
e VALUABLE s
VALUABLY
e VALUATED*
e VALUATES*
e VALUATOR s
VALVELET s
VALVULAE*
VALVULAR*
VALVULES*
VAMBRACE ds
VAMOOSED*
VAMOOSES*
VAMOSING
VAMPIEST
VAMPIRES*
VAMPIRIC
VANADATE s
VANADIUM s
VANADOUS
VANDALIC
VANDYKED*
VANDYKES*
VANGUARD s
VANILLAS*
VANILLIC
VANILLIN s
e VANISHED
VANISHER s
e VANISHES
VANITIED
VANITIES
VANITORY
VANLOADS*
VANPOOLS*
VANQUISH
VANTAGES*
VAPIDITY
VAPORERS*
VAPORING s
VAPORISE ds
VAPORISH
VAPORIZE drs
VAPOROUS
VAPOURED
VAPOURER s
VAQUEROS*
VARACTOR s
VARIABLE s
VARIABLY
VARIANCE s
VARIANTS*
VARIATED*
VARIATES*
VARICOSE ds
VARIEDLY
VARIETAL s
VARIFORM
VARIOLAR*
VARIOLAS*
o VARIOLES*
VARIORUM s
VARISTOR s
VARLETRY
VARMENTS*
VARMINTS*
VARNISHY*
VAROOMED
a VASCULAR*
VASCULUM s
VASELIKE
VASELINE s
VASIFORM
VASOTOMY
VASTIEST
VASTNESS
VATICIDE s
VAULTERS*
VAULTIER
VAULTING s
VAUNTERS*
VAUNTFUL
VAUNTING
VAVASORS*
VAVASOUR s
VAVASSOR s
VEALIEST
VECTORED
VEDALIAS*
VEDETTES*
VEGANISM s
VEGETANT
VEGETATE ds
VEGETIST s
VEGETIVE
VEHEMENT
VEHICLES*
VEILEDLY
VEILINGS*
VEILLIKE
VEINIEST
VEININGS*
VEINLESS
VEINLETS*
VEINLIKE
VEINULES*
VEINULET*s
VELAMINA
VELARIUM
VELARIZE ds
VELIGERS*
VELLEITY
VELOCITY
VELOUTES*
VELURING
VELVERET s
VELVETED
VENALITY
*VENATION s
VENDABLE s
VENDACES*
VENDETTA s
VENDEUSE s
VENDIBLE s
VENDIBLY
VENEERED
VENEERER s
VENENATE ds
VENENOSE
VENERATE ds
VENEREAL
VENERIES
VENETIAN s
a VENGEFUL
VENIALLY
VENISONS*
VENOGRAM s
*VENOLOGY
VENOMERS*
VENOMING
VENOMOUS
VENOSITY
VENOUSLY
VENTAGES*
a*VENTAILS*
e VENTLESS
VENTRALS*
VENTURED*
VENTURER*s
VENTURES*
VENTURIS*
VENULOSE
VENULOUS
VERACITY
VERANDAH*s
VERANDAS*
VERATRIA s
VERATRIN es
VERATRUM s
VERBALLY
VERBATIM
VERBENAS*
VERBIAGE s
VERBILES*
VERBLESS
VERBOTEN
VERDANCY
VERDERER s
VERDEROR s
VERDICTS*
VERDITER s
VERDURED*
VERDURES*
VERECUND
VERGENCE s
VERIFIED
VERIFIER s
VERIFIES
VERISMOS*
*VERISTIC
VERITIES
VERJUICE s
VERMEILS*
VERMOULU
VERMOUTH s
VERMUTHS*
VERNACLE s
VERNALLY
VERNICLE s
VERNIERS*
VERNIXES
VERONICA s
VERRUCAE*
VERRUCAS*
VERSANTS*
VERSEMAN
VERSEMEN
VERSICLE s
VERSINES*
ae VERSIONS*
VERTEBRA els
VERTEXES
VERTICAL s
VERTICES
VERTICIL s
VERTIGOS*
VERVAINS*
VESICANT s
VESICATE ds
VESICLES*
VESICULA er
VESPERAL s
VESPIARY
VESSELED
VESTALLY
VESTIARY
VESTIGES*
VESTIGIA l
VESTINGS*
VESTLESS
VESTLIKE
VESTMENT s
VESTRIES
VESTURAL
VESTURED*
VESTURES*
VESUVIAN s
VETERANS*
VETIVERS*
VETIVERT*s
VEXATION s
VEXILLAR*y
VEXILLUM
VEXINGLY
VIADUCTS*
VIALLING
VIATICAL*s
VIATICUM s
VIATORES
VIBRANCE s
VIBRANCY
VIBRANTS*
VIBRATED*
VIBRATES*
VIBRATOR*sy
VIBRATOS*
VIBRIOID
VIBRIONS*
VIBRISSA el
VIBRONIC
VIBURNUM s
VICARAGE s
VICARATE s
VICARIAL
*VICELESS
VICENARY
VICEROYS*
VICINAGE s
VICINITY
VICOMTES*
VICTORIA s
VICTRESS
VICTUALS*
VICUGNAS*
VIDEOTEX t
VIDETTES*
VIDICONS*
VIEWABLE
VIEWDATA
VIEWIEST
VIEWINGS*
VIEWLESS
VIGILANT e
VIGNERON s
VIGNETTE drs
VIGORISH
VIGOROSO
VIGOROUS
VILAYETS*
VILENESS
VILIFIED
VILIFIER s
VILIFIES
VILIPEND s
VILLADOM s
VILLAGER*sy
VILLAGES*
VILLAINS*
VILLAINY*
VILLATIC
VILLEINS*
VINASSES*
e VINCIBLE
VINCIBLY
VINCULUM s
VINDALOO s
VINEGARS*
VINEGARY*
VINERIES
VINEYARD s
VINIFERA s
VINIFIED
VINIFIES
VINOSITY
VINOUSLY
VINTAGER*s
VINTAGES*
VINTNERS*
VIOLABLE
VIOLABLY
VIOLATED*
VIOLATER*s
VIOLATES*
VIOLATOR s
VIOLENCE s
VIOLISTS*
VIOLONES*
VIOMYCIN s
VIPERINE
VIPERISH
VIPEROUS
VIRAGOES
VIRELAIS*
VIRELAYS*
VIREMIAS*
VIRGATES*
VIRGINAL s
VIRGULES*
VIRICIDE s
VIRIDIAN s
VIRIDITY
VIRILELY
VIRILISM s
VIRILITY
VIRILIZE ds
VIROLOGY
VIRTUOSA s
VIRTUOSE
VIRTUOSI c
VIRTUOSO s
VIRTUOUS
VIRUCIDE s
a VIRULENT
VIRUSOID s
VISCACHA s
VISCERAL*
VISCIDLY
VISCOSES*
VISCOUNT sy
VISELIKE
VISIONAL
VISIONED
VISITANT s
VISITERS*
VISITING
VISITORS*
VISORING
VISUALLY
VITALISE ds
VITALISM s
VITALIST s
VITALITY
VITALIZE drs
VITAMERS*
VITAMINE*s
VITAMINS*
VITELLIN es
VITELLUS
VITESSES*
VITIABLE
VITIATED*
VITIATES*
VITIATOR s
VITILIGO s
VITRAINS*
VITREOUS
VITRINES*
VITRIOLS*
VITTLING
VITULINE
VIVACITY
VIVARIES
VIVARIUM s
VIVERRID s
VIVIDEST
VIVIFIED
VIVIFIER s
VIVIFIES
VIVIPARA
VIVISECT s
VIXENISH
VIZARDED
VIZCACHA s
VIZIRATE s
VIZIRIAL
VIZORING
VOCABLES*
VOCALESE s
VOCALICS*
VOCALISE ds
VOCALISM s
VOCALIST s
VOCALITY
VOCALIZE drs
ae VOCATION s
e VOCATIVE s
VOCODERS*
VOGUEING s
VOGUINGS*
VOICEFUL
VOICINGS*
a VOIDABLE
a VOIDANCE s
VOIDNESS
VOLATILE s
VOLCANIC s
VOLCANOS*
VOLERIES
VOLITANT
VOLITION s
VOLITIVE
VOLLEYED
VOLLEYER s
VOLPLANE ds
VOLTAGES*
VOLTAISM s
VOLUMING
VOLUTINS*
e VOLUTION s
VOLVOXES
VOLVULUS
VOMERINE
VOMITERS*
VOMITING
VOMITIVE s
VOMITORY
VOMITOUS
VOODOOED
VORACITY
VORLAGES*
VORTEXES
VORTICAL
VORTICES
VOTARESS
VOTARIES
VOTARIST s
VOTEABLE
VOTELESS
VOTIVELY
VOUCHEES*
a VOUCHERS*
a*VOUCHING
VOUDOUNS*
VOUSSOIR s
VOUVRAYS*
VOWELIZE ds
VOYAGERS*
VOYAGEUR s
VOYAGING
*VROOMING
VUGGIEST
VULCANIC
VULGARER
VULGARLY
VULGATES*
VULGUSES
VULTURES*
VULVITIS
WABBLERS*
WABBLIER
WABBLING
WACKIEST
WADDINGS*
t WADDLERS*
st*WADDLING
WADDYING
WADEABLE
WADMAALS*
WADMOLLS*
WAESUCKS*
WAFERING
WAFFLERS*
WAFFLIER
WAFFLING s
WAFTAGES*
WAFTURES*
*WAGELESS
WAGERERS*
WAGERING
WAGGLIER
WAGGLING
WAGGONED
WAGGONER s
WAGONAGE s
WAGONERS*
WAGONING
WAGTAILS*
WAHCONDA s
WAIFLIKE
WAILSOME
WAINSCOT s
WAISTERS*
WAISTING s
WAITERED
WAITINGS*
WAITLIST s
WAITRESS
WAITRONS*
WAKANDAS*
WAKELESS
a WAKENERS*
a WAKENING s
WAKERIFE
WALKABLE
WALKAWAY s
WALKINGS*
WALKOUTS*
WALKOVER s
WALKWAYS*
WALKYRIE s
WALLAROO s
WALLEYED*
WALLEYES*
WALLOPED
WALLOPER s
s*WALLOWED
s WALLOWER s
WALRUSES
WALTZERS*
WALTZING
WAMBLIER
*WAMBLING
WAMEFOUS*
WAMEFULS*
WAMMUSES
WAMPUSES
WANDERED
WANDERER s
WANDEROO s
t*WANGLERS*
t*WANGLING
WANIGANS*
WANNABEE*s
WANNABES*
WANNIGAN s
WANTAGES*
WANTONED
WANTONER s
WANTONLY
WARBLERS*
WARBLING
WARCRAFT s
WARDENRY
WARDLESS
WARDRESS
WARDROBE ds
WARDROOM s
WARDSHIP s
WAREROOM s
WARFARES*
WARFARIN s
WARHEADS*
WARHORSE s
WARINESS
WARISONS*
WARLOCKS*
WARLORDS*
WARMAKER s
WARMNESS
WARMOUTH s
WARNINGS*
WARPAGES*
WARPATHS*
WARPLANE s
WARPOWER s
WARPWISE
WARRAGAL s
WARRANTS*
WARRANTY*
WARRENER s
WARRIGAL s
WARRIORS*
WARSHIPS*
WARSLERS*
WARSLING
WARSTLED*
WARSTLER*s
WARSTLES*
WARTHOGS*
*WARTIEST
WARTIMES*
*WARTLESS
WARTLIKE
WARWORKS*

WASHABLE s
WASHBOWL s
WASHDAYS*
*WASHIEST
WASHINGS*
WASHOUTS*
WASHRAGS*
WASHROOM s
WASHTUBS*
WASPIEST
WASPLIKE
WASSAILS
WASTABLE
WASTAGES*
WASTEFUL
WASTELOT s
WASTERIE s
WASTEWAY s
WASTRELS*
WASTRIES*
WATCHCRY
WATCHDOG s
WATCHERS*
WATCHEYE s
WATCHFUL
WATCHING
WATCHMAN
WATCHMEN
WATCHOUT s
WATERAGE s
WATERBED s
WATERBUS
WATERDOG s
WATERERS*
WATERHEN s
WATERIER
WATERILY
WATERING s
WATERISH
WATERJET s
WATERLOG s
WATERLOO s
WATERMAN
WATERMEN
WATERSKI s
WATERWAY s
WATTAGES*
WATTAPES*
WATTHOUR s
WATTLESS*
t WATTLING
WAUCHTED
WAUGHTED
WAVEBAND s
WAVEFORM s
WAVELESS
WAVELETS*
WAVELIKE
WAVEOFFS*
WAVERERS*
WAVERING
WAVICLES*
WAVINESS
WAXBERRY
WAXBILLS*
WAXINESS
WAXPLANT s
WAXWEEDS*
WAXWINGS*
WAXWORKS*
WAXWORMS*
WAYBILLS*
WAYFARER s
WAYGOING s
WAYLAYER s
WAYPOINT s
WAYSIDES*
WEAKENED
WEAKENER s
WEAKFISH
WEAKLIER
WEAKLING s
WEAKNESS
WEAKSIDE s
*WEANLING s
WEAPONED
WEAPONRY
WEARABLE s
WEARIEST*
WEARIFUL
WEARYING
WEASANDS*
*WEASELED
WEASELLY
WEATHERS*
WEAZANDS*

WEBBIEST
WEBBINGS*
WEBCASTS*
WEBPAGES*
WEBSITES*
WEBSTERS*
WEBWORKS*
WEBWORMS*
WEDDINGS*
WEDELING
WEDGIEST
WEDLOCKS*
t WEEDIEST
WEEDLESS
WEEDLIKE
WEEKDAYS*
WEEKENDS*
WEEKLIES
WEEKLONG
WEENIEST*
WEENSIER
s WEEPIEST*
s WEEPINGS*
WEEVILED
WEEVILLY
WEFTWISE
WEIGELAS*
WEIGELIA s
WEIGHERS*
WEIGHING
WEIGHMAN
WEIGHMEN
WEIGHTED
WEIGHTER s
WEIRDEST
WEIRDIES*
WEIRDING
WEIRDOES
WELCHERS*
WELCHING
WELCOMED*
WELCOMER*s
WELCOMES*
WELDABLE
WELDLESS
WELDMENT s
WELFARES*
WELLADAY s
WELLAWAY s
WELLBORN
WELLCURB s
WELLDOER s
s WELLHEAD s
WELLHOLE s
WELLNESS
WELLSITE s
WELSHERS*
WELSHING
s WELTERED
WELTINGS*
WENCHERS*
WENCHING
WENDIGOS*
WENNIEST
WEREGILD s
WEREWOLF
WERGELDS*
WERGELTS*
WERGILDS*
WESSANDS*
WESTERED
WESTERLY
WESTERNS*
WESTINGS*
WESTMOST
WESTWARD s
WETLANDS*
WETPROOF
WETSUITS*
WETTABLE
WETTINGS*
WETWARES*
WHACKERS
WHACKIER
*WHACKING
WHALEMAN
WHALEMEN
WHALINGS*
WHAMMIES
*WHAMMING
WHANGEES*
*WHANGING
WHAPPERS*
*WHAPPING
WHARFAGE s
WHARFING

WHATEVER
WHATNESS
WHATNOTS*
WHATSITS*
WHEATEAR s
WHEATENS*
WHEEDLED*
WHEEDLER*s
WHEEDLES*
WHEELERS
WHEELIES*
*WHEELING s
WHEELMAN
WHEELMEN
WHEEPING
WHEEPLED*
WHEEPLES*
WHEEZERS*
WHEEZIER
WHEEZILY
*WHEEZING
WHELKIER
*WHELMING
*WHELPING
WHENEVER
WHEREVER
*WHERRIED
*WHERRIES
WHETTERS*
WHETTING
WHEYFACE ds
WHEYLIKE
WHICKERS*
WHIDDING
WHIFFERS*
WHIFFETS*
WHIFFING
WHIFFLED*
WHIFFLER*s
WHIFFLES*
WHIMBREL s
WHIMPERS*
WHIMSEYS*
WHIMSIED
WHIMSIES
WHINCHAT s
WHINGERS
*WHINGING
WHINIEST
*WHINNIED
WHINNIER
*WHINNIES t
WHIPCORD s
WHIPLASH
*WHIPLIKE
WHIPPERS*
WHIPPETS*
*WHIPPIER
*WHIPPING s
WHIPRAYS*
WHIPSAWN*
WHIPSAWS*
WHIPTAIL s
WHIPWORM s
WHIRLERS*
WHIRLIER
WHIRLIES t
WHIRLING
WHIRRIED
WHIRRIES
WHIRRING
WHISHING
WHISHTED
WHISKERS*
WHISKERY*
WHISKEYS*
WHISKIES
WHISKING
WHISPERS*
WHISPERY*
*WHISTING
WHISTLED*
WHISTLER*s
WHISTLES*
WHITECAP s
WHITEFLY
WHITENED
WHITENER s
WHITEOUT s
WHITIEST
WHITINGS*
WHITLOWS*
WHITRACK s
WHITTERS
WHITTLED*
WHITTLER*s

WHITTLES*
WHITTRET s
WHIZBANG s
WHIZZERS*
WHIZZIER
WHIZZING
WHODUNIT s
WHOLISMS
WHOMEVER
WHOMPING
*WHOOFING
WHOOPEES*
WHOOPERS
WHOOPIES*
*WHOOPING
WHOOPLAS
WHOOSHED
WHOOSHES
WHOPPERS
*WHOPPING
WHOREDOM s
WHORESON s
WHORTLES*
WHOSEVER
WHOSISES
*WHUMPING
WHUPPING
WICKAPES*
WICKEDER
WICKEDLY
WICKINGS*
WICKIUPS*
WICKLESS
WICKYUPS*
WICOPIES
t WIDDLING
WIDEBAND
WIDEBODY
WIDENERS*
WIDENESS
WIDENING
WIDEOUTS*
WIDGEONS*
WIDOWERS*
WIDOWING
WIDTHWAY s
WIELDERS*
WIELDIER
WIELDING
WIFEDOMS*
WIFEHOOD s
WIFELESS
WIFELIER
WIFELIKE
WIFTIEST
t WIGGIEST
WIGGINGS*
WIGGLERS*
WIGGLIER
WIGGLING
WIGMAKER s
WILDCARD s
WILDCATS*
WILDERED
WILDFIRE s
WILDFOWL s
WILDINGS*
WILDLAND s
WILDLIFE
WILDLING s
WILDNESS
WILDWOOD s
WILFULLY
WILINESS
WILLABLE
WILLIWAU s
WILLIWAW s
WILLOWED
WILLOWER s
WILLYARD
WILLYART
WILLYING
WILLYWAW s
WIMBLING
WIMPIEST
WIMPLING
WINCHERS
*WINCHING
WINDABLE
WINDAGES*
WINDBAGS*
WINDBELL s
WINDBURN st
WINDFALL s
WINDFLAW s
WINDGALL s

WINDIEST
WINDIGOS
WINDINGS*
WINDLASS
WINDLESS*
ds WINDLING s
WINDMILL s
*WINDOWED
WINDPIPE s
WINDROWS*
WINDSOCK s
WINDSURF s
WINDWARD s
WINDWAYS*
WINELESS
WINERIES
WINESAPS*
WINESHOP s
WINESKIN s
WINESOPS*
WINGBACK s
WINGBOWS*
WINGDING s
WINGEDLY
s WINGIEST
WINGLESS
WINGLETS*
WINGLIKE
WINGOVER s
WINGSPAN s
WINGTIPS*
t*WINKLING
WINNABLE
t*WINNINGS*
WINNOCKS*
WINNOWED
WINNOWER s
WINSOMER*
WINTERED
WINTERER s
WINTERLY
WINTLING
WINTRIER
WINTRILY
WIPEOUTS*
WIREDRAW ns
WIREDREW
WIREHAIR s
*WIRELESS
WIRELIKE
WIRETAPS*
WIREWAYS*
WIREWORK s
WIREWORM s
WIRINESS
WISEACRE s
WISEGUYS*
WISELIER
WISENESS
WISHBONE s
WISHLESS
WISPIEST
WISPLIKE
WISTARIA s
WISTERIA s
WITCHERY
t*WITCHIER
st*WITCHING s
WITHDRAW ns
WITHDREW
s WITHERED
WITHERER s
WITHEROD s
WITHHELD
WITHHOLD s
WITHIEST*
WITHOUTS*
WITLINGS*
WITLOOFS*
WITTIEST
WITTINGS*
WIZARDLY
WIZARDRY
WIZENING
WOBBLERS*
WOBBLIER
WOBBLIES t
WOBBLING
WOBEGONE
WOEFULLY
WOFULLER
WOLFFISH
WOLFLIKE
WOLFRAMS*
WOMANING
WOMANISE ds

WOMANISH
WOMANISM s
WOMANIST s
WOMANIZE
drs
WOMBIEST
WOMMERAS*
WONDERED
WONDERER s
WONDROUS
WONKIEST
WONTEDLY
WOODBIND*s
WOODBINE*s
WOODBINS*
WOODCHAT s
WOODCOCK s
WOODCUTS*
WOODENER
WOODENLY
WOODHENS*
WOODIEST*
WOODLAND s
WOODLARK s
WOODLESS
WOODLORE s
WOODLOTS*
WOODNOTE s
WOODPILE s
WOODRUFF s
WOODSHED s
WOODSIAS*
WOODSIER
WOODSMAN
WOODSMEN
WOODTONE s
WOODWIND s
WOODWORK s
WOODWORM s
WOOINGLY
WOOLFELL s
WOOLHATS*
WOOLIEST*
WOOLLENS*
WOOLLIER
WOOLLIES t
WOOLLIKE
WOOLLILY
WOOLPACK s
WOOLSACK s
WOOLSHED s
WOOLSKIN s
WOOLWORK s
WOOMERAS*
WOOPSING
WOORALIS
WOORARIS*
s WOOSHING
*WOOZIEST
WORDAGES*
WORDBOOK s
WORDIEST
WORDINGS*
WORDLESS
s WORDPLAY s
WORKABLE
WORKABLY
WORKADAY
WORKBAGS*
WORKBOAT s
WORKBOOK s
WORKDAYS*
WORKFARE s
WORKFLOW s
WORKFOLK s
WORKHOUR s
WORKINGS*
WORKLESS
WORKLOAD s
WORKMATE s
WORKOUTS*
WORKROOM s
WORKSHOP s
WORKWEEK s
WORMGEAR s
WORMHOLE s
WORMIEST
WORMLIKE
WORMROOT s
WORMSEED s
WORMWOOD s
WORNNESS
WORRIERS*
WORRITED
WORRYING
WORSENED

WORSHIPS*
WORSTEDS*
WORSTING
WORTHFUL
WORTHIER
WORTHIES t
WORTHILY
WORTHING
WOULDEST
s WOUNDING
*WRACKFUL
*WRACKING
WRANGLED*
WRANGLER*s
WRANGLES*
WRAPPERS
*WRAPPING s
WRASSLED
WRASSLES
WRASTLED*
WRASTLES*
WRATHFUL
WRATHIER
WRATHILY
WRATHING
WREAKERS*
WREAKING
WREATHED*
WREATHEN*
WREATHER*s
WREATHES*
WRECKAGE s
WRECKERS*
WRECKFUL
*WRECKING s
WRENCHED
WRENCHER s
WRENCHES
WRESTERS
*WRESTING
WRESTLED*
WRESTLER*s
WRESTLES*
*WRETCHED
*WRETCHES
*WRICKING
WRIGGLED*
WRIGGLER*s
WRIGGLES*
WRINGERS
*WRINGING
WRINKLED*
WRINKLES*
WRISTIER
WRISTLET s
WRITABLE
WRITERLY
WRITHERS*
WRITHING
WRITINGS*
WRONGERS*
WRONGEST
WRONGFUL
WRONGING
WROTHFUL
WRYNECKS*
WURTZITE s
WUSSIEST*
WUTHERED
XANTHANS*
XANTHATE s
XANTHEIN s
XANTHENE s
XANTHINE*s
XANTHINS*
XANTHOMA s
XANTHONE s
XANTHOUS
XENOGAMY
XENOGENY
XENOLITH s
XEROSERE s
XEROXING
XIPHOIDS*
XYLIDINE*s
XYLIDINS*
XYLITOLS*
XYLOCARP s
XYLOTOMY
YABBERED
YACHTERS*
YACHTING s
YACHTMAN
YACHTMEN
YAHOOISM s
YAHRZEIT s

YAKITORI s
YAMALKAS*
YAMMERED
YAMMERER s
YAMULKAS*
YARDAGES*
YARDARMS*
YARDBIRD s
YARDLAND s
YARDWAND s
YARDWORK s
YARMELKE s
YARMULKE s
YASHMACS*
YASHMAKS*
YATAGANS*
*YATAGHAN s
YATTERED
YAWMETER s
YAWPINGS*
YEALINGS*
*YEANLING s
YEARBOOK s
YEARENDS*
YEARLIES
YEARLING s
YEARLONG
YEARNERS
*YEARNING s
YEASAYER s
YEASTIER
YEASTILY
*YEASTING
YELLOWED
YELLOWER
YELLOWLY
YEOMANLY
YEOMANRY
YESHIVAH*s
YESHIVAS*
YESHIVOT h
YESTREEN s
YIELDERS*
YIELDING
YODELERS*
YODELING
YODELLED
YODELLER s
YOGHOURT s
YOGHURTS*
YOHIMBES*
YOKELESS
YOKELISH
YOKEMATE s
YOKOZUNA s
YOLKIEST
YOUNGERS*
YOUNGEST
YOUNGISH
YOUNKERS*
*YOURSELF
YOUTHENS*
YOUTHFUL
YPERITES*
YTTERBIA s
YTTERBIC
YTTRIUMS*
YUCKIEST
YUKKIEST
YULETIDE s
YUMMIEST*
ZABAIONE s
ZABAJONE s
ZACATONS*
t ZADDIKIM
ZAIBATSU
ZAMARRAS*
ZAMARROS*
ZAMINDAR is
ZANINESS
ZAPATEOS*
ZAPPIEST
ZAPTIAHS*
ZAPTIEHS*
ZARATITE s
ZAREEBAS*
ZARZUELA s
ZASTRUGA
ZASTRUGI
ZEALOTRY
ZEBRANOS*
ZEBRINES*
ZECCHINI*
ZECCHINO*s
ZECCHINS*
ZELKOVAS*
ZEMINDAR sy
ZEMSTVOS*
ZENAIDAS*
ZENITHAL
ZEOLITES*
ZEOLITIC
ZEPPELIN s
ZEPPOLES*
ZESTIEST
ZESTLESS
ZIBELINE s
ZIGGURAT s
ZIGZAGGY
ZIKKURAT s
ZIKURATS*
ZILLIONS*
ZINCATES*
ZINCITES
ZINCKING
ZINGIEST
ZIPPERED
ZIPPIEST
ZIRCALOY s
ZIRCONIA s
ZIRCONIC
ZITHERNS*
ZIZZLING
ZODIACAL
ZOISITES*
ZOMBIISM s
o ZONATION s
ZONELESS
*ZONETIME s
ZOOCHORE s
ZOOECIUM
ZOOGENIC
ZOOGLEAE*
ZOOGLEAL*
ZOOGLEAS*
ZOOGLOEA
els
ZOOLATER s
ZOOLATRY
*ZOOLOGIC
ZOOMANIA s
ZOOMETRY
ZOOMORPH s
ZOONOSES
ZOONOSIS
ZOONOTIC
ZOOPHILE s
ZOOPHILY
ZOOPHOBE s
*ZOOPHYTE s
*ZOOSPERM s
*ZOOSPORE s
ZOOTIEST
ZOOTOMIC
ZORILLAS*
ZORILLES*
ZORILLOS*
ZUCCHINI s
ZUGZWANG s
ZWIEBACK s
ZYGOMATA
ZYGOSITY
ZYGOTENE s
ZYMOGENE*s
ZYMOGENS*
ZYMOGRAM s
ZYMOLOGY
ZYMOSANS*
ZYZZYVAS*

THE ALPHAGRAMS

You're midway through a close game and on your rack are the tiles YDOIALH. You might, perhaps, find DAILY, leaving HO after your play. An "alphagram" is the alphabetical sequencing of letters contained within a word. Were you to have arranged your rack into its alphabetical sequence, ADHILOY, and looked it up on the list of "7-Letter Alphagrams," you would discover that such letters can form the words HOLIDAY, HYALOID, and HYOIDAL. ADHILOY is the alphagram shared by each of these three words. As such, they are anagrams of one another. In contrast, ADHILOS is the alphagram of HALOIDS and only HALOIDS. Therefore, HALOIDS has no anagram.

The shortest words (two and three letters) are easily anagrammable. However, as the words get longer, the possible sequence of letters within an acceptable word increases geometrically. With two letters, like A and T, there are only two possible sequences to consider: AT and TA, both acceptable. With three letters, like A, E, and T, there are six possible sequences: AET, ATE, EAT, ETA, TAE, and TEA, all but the first being acceptable words. With four letters, there are 24 possible sequences, often generating at least two or three words, with as many as eight in one instance (AEST). Some longer words have a dozen anagrams. With this in mind, if you are preparing to study words of four letters' length or greater, you may wish to use this alphagram section. By seeing all the anagrams of an alphagram, you will associate one word with one or more others, thereby increasing your playing arsenal. For example:

ORTY	RYOT TORY TROY TYRO

You may have known only TORY before studying this list. Now you have not only learned three more words, but have three other word associations when you think of TORY. In an actual game, while TORY might not fit or score well, one of the others might. Moreover, if all four are equally playable for the same offensive and defensive gains, you might choose the most unusual looking one, perhaps RYOT, in the hopes of securing a challenge from your opponent.

By far the most frequent use of The Alphagrams has been when players have wondered, "Did I have a playable bingo in my rack?" The player who had HOLIDAY, HYALOID, or HYOIDAL in his rack, even if he saw such alternatives, might not have been able to play any one of them. Perhaps, though, there might have been a P on the board. By "putting" the P "into" his rack, forming the new alphagram ADHILOPY, he would see in the "8-Letter Alphagrams" section, to his surprise, HAPLOIDY. Sometimes, "surprise" may not be the appropriate word. It has been my experience that after some highly competitive player has lost a game and looks up the alphagram, only to see the "obvious" bingo he could have played, I thereafter have heard more four-letter words than I care to repeat! Use The Alphagrams at your own risk ... and, hopefully, pleasure.

3-Letter Alphagrams

AAB ABA
BAA
AAG AGA
AAH AAH
AHA
AAL AAL
ALA
AAM AMA
AAN ANA
AAS AAS
AAV AVA
AAW AWA
ABC CAB
ABD BAD
DAB
ABF FAB
ABG BAG
GAB
ABH BAH
ABJ JAB
ABK KAB
ABL ALB
BAL
LAB
ABM BAM
ABN BAN
NAB
ABO BOA
OBA
ABP BAP
ABR ARB
BAR
BRA
ABS ABS
BAS
SAB
ABT BAT
TAB
ABW WAB
ABY ABY
BAY
ACD CAD
ACE ACE
ACL LAC
ACM CAM
MAC
ACN CAN
ACO OCA
ACP CAP
PAC
ACR ARC
CAR
ACS SAC
ACT ACT
CAT
ACV VAC
ACW CAW
ACY CAY
ADD ADD
DAD
ADF FAD
ADG DAG
GAD
ADH DAH
HAD
ADI AID
ADK DAK
ADL DAL
LAD
ADM DAM
MAD
ADN AND
DAN
ADO ADO
ODA
ADP DAP
PAD
ADR RAD
ADS ADS
SAD
ADT TAD
ADW DAW
WAD
ADY DAY
ADZ ADZ
AEG AGE
GAE
AEH HAE
AEK KAE
KEA
AEL ALE
LEA
AEM MAE
AEN ANE
NAE
AEP APE
PEA
AER ARE
EAR
ERA
AES SAE
SEA
AET ATE
EAT
ETA
TAE
TEA
AEU EAU
AEV AVE
AEW AWE
WAE
AEX AXE
AEY AYE
YEA
AFF AFF
AFG FAG
AFK KAF
AFN FAN
AFO OAF
AFR ARF
FAR
AFS FAS
AFT AFT
FAT
AFX FAX
AFY FAY
AGG GAG
AGH HAG
AGJ JAG
AGL GAL
LAG
AGM GAM
MAG
AGN GAN
NAG
AGO AGO
GOA
AGP GAP
AGR GAR
RAG
AGS AGS
GAS
SAG
AGT GAT
TAG
AGW WAG
AGY GAY
YAG
AGZ ZAG
AHH HAH
AHI AHI
AHJ HAJ
AHM HAM
AHN NAH
AHO HAO
AHP HAP
PAH
AHR RAH
AHS AHS
ASH
HAS
SHA
AHT HAT
AHW HAW
WHA
AHY HAY
YAH
AIL AIL
AIM AIM
AMI
AIN AIN
ANI
AIP PIA
AIR AIR
RAI
RIA
AIS AIS
AIT AIT
AIV VIA
AJM JAM
AJR JAR
RAJ
AJT TAJ
AJW JAW
AJY JAY
AKO KOA
OAK
OKA
AKR ARK
AKS ASK
KAS
SKA
AKT KAT
AKU AUK
AKY KAY
YAK
ALL ALL
ALM LAM
ALP ALP
LAP
PAL
ALR LAR
ALS ALS
LAS
SAL
ALT ALT
LAT
ALV LAV
ALW AWL
LAW
ALX LAX
ALY LAY
AMN MAN
NAM
AMO MOA
AMP AMP
MAP
PAM
AMR ARM
MAR
RAM
AMS MAS
AMT MAT
TAM
AMU AMU
AMW MAW
AMX MAX
AMY MAY
YAM
ANN NAN
ANP NAP
PAN
ANR RAN
ANT ANT
TAN
ANV VAN
ANW AWN
NAW
WAN
ANY ANY
NAY
AOP APO
AOR OAR
ORA
AOT OAT
TAO
AOV AVO
OVA
AOZ AZO
ZOA
APP APP
PAP
APR PAR
RAP
APS ASP
PAS
SAP
SPA
APT APT
PAT
TAP
APW PAW
WAP
APX PAX
APY PAY
PYA
YAP
APZ ZAP
AQT QAT
AQU QUA
ARS ARS
RAS
ART ART
RAT
TAR
ARV VAR
ARW RAW
WAR
ARX RAX
ARY RAY
RYA
YAR
ASS ASS
AST SAT
TAS
ASU SAU
ASV VAS
ASW SAW
WAS
ASX SAX
ASY AYS
SAY
ASZ ZAS
ATT ATT
TAT
ATU TAU
UTA
ATV TAV
VAT
ATW TAW
TWA
WAT
ATX TAX
AUV VAU
AVV VAV
AVW VAW
AWW WAW
AWX WAX
AWY WAY
YAW
AXZ ZAX
AYY YAY
BBE EBB
BBI BIB
BBO BOB
BBU BUB
BCO COB
BCU CUB
BDE BED
DEB
BDI BID
DIB
BDO BOD
BDU BUD
DUB
BEE BEE
BEG BEG
BEL BEL
BEN BEN
NEB
BEO OBE
BER REB
BES BES
BET BET
BEW WEB
BEY BEY
BYE
BFI FIB
BFO FOB
BFU FUB
BGI BIG
GIB
BGO BOG
GOB
BGU BUG
BHO HOB
BHU HUB
BIJ JIB
BIL LIB
BIM MIB
BIN BIN
NIB
BIO BIO
OBI
BIR RIB
BIS BIS
SIB
BIT BIT
BIZ BIZ
BJO JOB
BKO KOB
BLO LOB
BMO MOB
BMU BUM
BNO NOB
BNU BUN
NUB
BOO BOO
BOP BOP
BOR BRO
ORB
ROB
BOS BOS
SOB
BOT BOT
BOW BOW
BOX BOX
BOY BOY
YOB
BPU PUB
BRR BRR
BRU BUR
RUB
URB
BSU BUS
SUB
BSY BYS
BTU BUT
TUB
BUY BUY
CDO COD
DOC
CDU CUD
CEE CEE
CEI ICE
CEL CEL
CEP CEP
PEC
CER REC
CES SEC
CEU CUE
ECU
CGI CIG
CGO COG
CHI CHI
HIC
ICH
CIK ICK
CIM MIC
CIP PIC
CIS CIS
SIC
CIT TIC
CIY ICY
CLO COL
CMO MOC
CMU CUM
CMW CWM
CMY MYC
CNO CON
COO COO
COP COP
COR COR
ORC
ROC
COS COS
COT COT
COW COW
COX COX
COY COY
COZ COZ
CPU CUP
CRU CRU
CUR
CRY CRY
CTU CUT
DDI DID
DDO ODD
DDU DUD
DEE DEE
DEF DEF
FED
DEG GED
DEH EDH
DEI DIE
DEL DEL
ELD
LED
DEM MED
DEN DEN
END
DEO DOE
ODE
DEP PED
DER RED
DES EDS
DET TED
DEU DUE
DEV DEV
DEW DEW
WED
DEX DEX
DEY DEY
DYE
DEZ ZED
DFI DIF
FID
DFU FUD
DGI DIG
GID
DGO DOG
GOD
DGU DUG
DHI HID
DHO HOD
DHU DUH
DIK KID
DIL LID
DIM DIM
MID
DIN DIN
DIP DIP
DIR RID
DIS DIS
IDS
DIT DIT
DIU DUI
DIV VID
DLO DOL
OLD
DMO DOM
MOD
DMU MUD
DNO DON
NOD
DNU DUN
DOP POD
DOR DOR
ROD
DOS DOS
ODS
SOD
DOT DOT
TOD
DOU DUO
OUD
UDO
DOW DOW
DOY YOD
DPU DUP
PUD
DRU URD
DRY DRY
DUW WUD
EEF FEE
EEG GEE
EEJ JEE
EEK EEK
EKE
EEL EEL
LEE
EEM EME
EEN NEE
EEP PEE
EER ERE
REE
EES SEE
EET TEE
EEV EVE
VEE
EEW EWE
WEE
EEY EYE
EEZ ZEE
EFF EFF
EFH FEH
EFI FIE
EFK KEF
EFL ELF
EFM FEM
EFN FEN
EFO FOE
EFR FER
REF
EFS EFS
FES
EFT EFT
FET
EFU FEU
EFW FEW
EFY FEY
EFZ FEZ
EGG EGG
EGI GIE
EGK KEG
EGL GEL
LEG
EGM GEM
MEG
EGN ENG
GEN
NEG
EGO EGO
EGP PEG
EGR ERG
REG
EGS SEG
EGT GET
TEG
EGV VEG
EGY GEY
EHH HEH
EHI HIE
EHM HEM
EHN HEN
EHO HOE
EHP HEP
PEH
EHR HER
EHS HES
SHE
EHT ETH
HET
THE
EHU HUE
EHW HEW
EHX HEX
EHY HEY
YEH
EIL LEI
LIE
EIP PIE
EIR IRE
REI
EIS SEI
EIT TIE
EIV VIE
EJO JOE
EJT JET
EJU JEU
EKL ELK
LEK
EKN KEN
EKO OKE
EKP KEP
EKU KUE
UKE
EKX KEX
EKY KEY
KYE
EKZ ZEK
ELL ELL
ELM ELM
MEL
ELO OLE
ELS ELS
SEL
ELT LET
TEL
ELU LEU
ELV LEV
ELX LEX
ELY LEY
LYE
EMM MEM
EMN MEN
EMR REM
EMS EMS
EMT MET
EMU EMU
EMW MEW
ENO EON
ONE
ENP PEN
ENR ERN
ENS ENS
SEN
ENT NET
TEN
ENW NEW
WEN
ENY YEN
EOP OPE
EOR ORE
ROE
EOS OES
OSE
EOT TOE
EOV VOE
EOW OWE
WOE
EPP PEP
EPR PER
REP
EPS PES
EPT PET
EPW PEW
EPY PYE
YEP
EPZ ZEP
ERR ERR
ERS ERS
RES
SER
ERT RET
ERU RUE
ERV REV
ERX REX
ERY RYE
ESS ESS
EST SET
ESU SUE
USE
ESW SEW
ESX SEX
ESY YES
ETT TET
ETU UTE
ETV VET
ETW TEW
WET
ETY TYE
YET
EVX VEX
EWY WYE
YEW
FFI IFF
FFO OFF
FGI FIG
FGO FOG
FGU FUG
FHO FOH
FIK KIF
FIL FIL
FIN FIN
FIR FIR
RIF
FIS IFS
FIT FIT
FIX FIX
FIZ FIZ
FLU FLU
FLY FLY
FNO FON
FNU FUN
FOP FOP
FOR FOR
FRO
FOT OFT
FOU FOU
FOX FOX
FOY FOY
FRU FUR
FRY FRY
GGI GIG
IGG
GHI GHI
GHO HOG
GHU HUG
UGH
GIJ JIG
GIM MIG
GIN GIN
GIP GIP
PIG
GIR RIG
GIT GIT
GIV VIG
GIW WIG
GIZ ZIG
GJO JOG
GJU JUG
GLO LOG
GLU GUL
LUG
GMO MOG
GMU GUM
MUG
GMY GYM
GNO NOG
GNU GNU
GUN
GOO GOO
GOR GOR
GOS GOS
GOT GOT
TOG
GOX GOX
GPU PUG
GPY GYP
GRU RUG
GTU GUT
TUG
GUV GUV
VUG
GUY GUY
HHS SHH
HHU HUH
HIK KHI
HIM HIM
HIN HIN
HIP HIP
PHI
HIS HIS
HIT HIT
HMM HMM
HMO MHO
OHM
HMU HUM
HNO HON
NOH
HNT NTH
HNU HUN
HOO OHO
OOH
HOP HOP
POH
HOR RHO
HOS OHS
HOT HOT
THO
HOW HOW
WHO
HOY HOY
HPT PHT
HPU HUP
HPY HYP
HSY SHY
HTU HUT
HTY THY
HWY WHY
IJN JIN
IKL ILK
IKN INK
KIN
IKO KOI
IKP KIP
IKR IRK
KIR
IKS KIS
SKI
IKT KIT
ILL ILL
ILM MIL
ILN LIN
NIL
ILO OIL
ILP LIP
ILS LIS
ILT LIT
TIL
IMM MIM
IMN NIM
IMP IMP
IMR MIR
RIM
IMS ISM
MIS
SIM
IMV VIM
IMX MIX
INN INN
INO ION
INP NIP
PIN
INR RIN
INS INS
SIN
INT NIT
TIN
INW WIN
INX NIX
INY YIN
INZ ZIN
IOP POI
IPP PIP
IPR RIP
IPS PIS
PSI
SIP
IPT PIT
TIP
IPU PIU
IPX PIX
IPY YIP
IPZ ZIP
IQS QIS
IRS SIR
SRI
ISS SIS
IST ITS
SIT
TIS
ISV VIS
ISW WIS
ISX SIX
XIS
ITT TIT
ITU TUI
ITW WIT
ITZ ZIT
IVY IVY
IWZ WIZ
JNU JUN
JOT JOT
JOW JOW
JOY JOY
JSU JUS
JTU JUT
KOP KOP
KOR KOR
KOS KOS
KOW WOK
KOY YOK
KST TSK
KSU SUK
KSY SKY
KUY YUK
LMO MOL
LMU LUM
LOO LOO
LOP LOP
POL
LOS SOL
LOT LOT
LOW LOW
OWL
LOX LOX
LPU PUL
LPY PLY
LSY SLY
LUU ULU
LUV LUV
LUX LUX
MMO MOM
MMU MUM
UMM
MNO MON
NOM
MNU MUN
MOO MOO
MOP MOP
MOR MOR
ROM
MOS MOS
OMS
SOM
MOT MOT
TOM
MOW MOW
MOY YOM
MPU UMP
MRU RUM
MSU MUS
SUM
MTU MUT
MUV VUM
MUY YUM
NNU NUN
NOO NOO
ONO
NOR NOR
NOS NOS
ONS
SON
NOT NOT
TON
NOW NOW
OWN
WON
NOY YON
NPU PUN
NRU RUN
URN
NSU NUS
SUN
UNS
NSY SYN
NTU NUT
TUN
NWY WYN
OOT OOT
TOO
OOW WOO
OOX OXO
OOZ ZOO
OPP POP
OPR PRO
OPS OPS
SOP
OPT OPT
POT
TOP
OPU UPO
OPW POW
OPX POX
ORS ORS
ORT ORT
ROT
TOR
ORU OUR
ORW ROW
OSS SOS
OST SOT
OSU SOU
OSW SOW
WOS
OSX SOX
OSY SOY
OTT TOT
OTU OUT
OTW TOW
TWO
WOT
OTY TOY
OUY YOU
OVW VOW
OVX VOX
OWW WOW
OWY YOW
OXY OXY
PPU PUP
PRU PUR
URP
PRY PRY
PST PST
PSU PUS
SUP
UPS
PSY SPY
PTU PUT
TUP
PUY YUP
PXY PYX
QSU SUQ
RTU RUT
RTY TRY
RWY WRY
STU UTS
STY STY
TTU TUT
TUX TUX
UZZ ZUZ
ZZZ ZZZ

4-Letter Alphagrams

AABB ABBA
BABA
AABL ALBA
BAAL
AABS ABAS
BAAS
AACC CACA
AACP PACA
AACS CASA
AACT ACTA
AADD DADA
AADN NADA
AADT DATA
AAEL ALAE
AAER AREA
AAES ASEA
AAFH HAAF
AAFL ALFA
AAFR AFAR
AAFV FAVA
AAGG GAGA
AAGH AGHA
AAGL ALGA
GALA
AAGM AGMA
GAMA
AAGN ANGA
AAGR AGAR
RAGA
AAGS AGAS
SAGA
AAHH HAHA
AAHM AMAH
AAHR HAAR
AAHS AAHS
AAHY AYAH
AAIM AMIA
AAIR ARIA
RAIA
AAJR AJAR
RAJA
AAJV JAVA
AAKK KAKA
AAKN KANA
AAKP KAPA
AAKR ARAK
AAKS KAAS
AAKT KATA
TAKA
AAKV KAVA
AALM ALMA
LAMA
AALN ALAN
ANAL
NALA
AALR ALAR
AALS AALS
ALAS
AALT TALA
AALV LAVA
AALX AXAL
AAMM MAMA
AAMN MANA
AAMR MAAR
MARA
AAMS AMAS
MASA
AAMT ATMA
AAMY MAYA
AANN ANNA
NAAN
NANA
AANO ANOA
AANP NAPA
AANS ANAS
ANSA
AANT ANTA
AANZ AZAN
AAPP PAPA
AAPR PARA
AAPT ATAP
TAPA
AAQU AQUA
AARU AURA
AARV VARA
AARY RAYA
AASV VASA
AATX TAXA
AAWY AWAY
ABBE ABBE
BABE
ABBL BLAB
ABBR BARB
ABBU BABU
ABBY BABY
ABCH BACH
ABCK BACK
ABCR CARB
CRAB
ABCS CABS
SCAB
ABDE ABED
BADE
BEAD
ABDL BALD
ABDN BAND
ABDR BARD
BRAD
DARB
DRAB
ABDS BADS
DABS
ABDU BAUD
DAUB
ABDW BAWD
ABEK BAKE
BEAK
ABEL ABLE
BALE
BLAE
ABEM BEAM
BEMA
MABE
ABEN BANE
BEAN
NABE
ABER BARE
BEAR
BRAE
ABES BASE
SABE
ABET ABET
BATE
BEAT
BETA
ABEU BEAU
ABEY ABYE
ABFF BAFF
ABFL FLAB
ABFR BARF
ABFS FABS
ABGM GAMB
ABGN BANG
ABGR BRAG
GARB
GRAB
ABGS BAGS
GABS
ABGY GABY
ABHL BLAH
ABHS BASH
ABHT BAHT
BATH
ABHU HABU
ABIL BAIL
ABIM BIMA
IAMB
ABIN BANI
ABIO OBIA
ABIR ABRI
ABIS BIAS
ISBA
ABIT BAIT
ABJM JAMB
ABJS JABS
ABJU JUBA
ABKL BALK
ABKN BANK
ABKR BARK
KBAR
ABKS BASK
KABS
ABLL BALL
ABLM BALM
BLAM
LAMB
ABLO BOLA
ABLS ALBS
BALS
LABS
SLAB
ABLT BLAT
ABLW BAWL
BLAW
ABLY ABLY
ABMO AMBO
ABMR BARM
ABMS BAMS
ABNR BARN
BRAN
ABNS BANS
NABS
ABNU BUNA
ABOR BOAR
BORA
ABOS BOAS
OBAS
SOBA
ABOT BOAT
BOTA
ABPS BAPS
ABRS ARBS
BARS
BRAS
ABRT BRAT
ABRU BURA
ABRW BRAW
ABRY BRAY
ABSS BASS
SABS
ABST BAST
BATS
STAB
TABS
ABSU SUBA
ABSW SWAB
WABS
ABSY ABYS
BAYS
ABTT BATT
ABTU ABUT
TABU
TUBA
ACCE CECA
ACCO COCA
ACDE ACED
CADE
DACE
ACDH CHAD
ACDI ACID
CADI
CAID
ACDL CLAD
ACDO CODA
ACDR CARD
ACDS CADS
SCAD
ACEF CAFE
FACE
ACEG CAGE
ACEH ACHE
EACH
ACEK CAKE
ACEL ALEC
LACE
ACEM ACME
CAME
MACE
ACEN ACNE
CANE
ACEP CAPE
PACE
ACER ACRE
CARE
RACE
ACES ACES
CASE
ACET CATE
TACE
ACEV CAVE
ACFF CAFF
ACFL CALF
ACFT FACT
ACGL CLAG
ACGR CRAG
ACGS SCAG
ACGY CAGY
ACHI CHAI
CHIA
ACHK HACK
ACHM CHAM
MACH
ACHO CHAO
ACHP CAPH
CHAP
ACHR ARCH
CHAR
ACHS CASH
ACHT CHAT
TACH
ACHW CHAW
ACHY ACHY
CHAY
ACIL LAIC
ACIM MICA
ACIN CAIN
ACIO CIAO
ACIP PICA
ACIS ASCI
ACJK JACK
ACKL CALK
LACK
ACKM MACK
ACKP PACK
ACKR CARK
RACK
ACKS CASK
SACK
ACKT TACK
ACKW WACK
ACKY CAKY
YACK
ACLL CALL
ACLM CALM
CLAM
ACLN CLAN
ACLO CALO
COAL
COLA
LOCA
ACLP CLAP
ACLR CARL
ACLS LACS
ACLT TALC
ACLU CAUL
ACLW CLAW
ACLX CALX
ACLY ACYL
CLAY
LACY
ACMO CAMO
COMA
ACMP CAMP
ACMR CRAM
MARC
ACMS CAMS
MACS
SCAM
ACMY CYMA
ACNR CARN
NARC
ACNS CANS
SCAN
ACNT CANT
ACNY CYAN
ACOP CAPO
ACOR ARCO
ORCA
ACOS OCAS
SOCA
ACOT COAT
TACO
ACOX COAX
COXA
ACPR CARP
CRAP
ACPS CAPS
PACS
ACPT PACT
ACPY PACY
ACRR CARR
ACRS ARCS
CARS
SCAR
ACRT CART
ACRW CRAW
ACRY RACY
ACRZ CZAR
ACSS SACS
ACST ACTS
CAST
CATS
SCAT
ACSV VACS
ACSW CAWS
ACSY CAYS
ACTT TACT
ACUY YUCA
ACVY CAVY
ADDE DEAD
ADDO DADO
ADDS ADDS
DADS
ADDU DUAD
ADDY DYAD
ADEF DEAF
FADE
ADEG AGED
EGAD
GAED
ADEH AHED
HADE
HAED
HEAD
ADEI AIDE
IDEA
ADEJ JADE
ADEL DALE
DEAL
LADE
LEAD
ADEM DAME
MADE
MEAD
ADEN DEAN
ADEO ODEA
ADEP APED
ADER DARE
DEAR
READ
ADES SADE
ADET DATE
ADEV DEVA
ADEW AWED
WADE
ADEX AXED
ADEZ ADZE
DAZE
ADFF DAFF
ADFO FADO
ADFR FARD
ADFS FADS
ADFT DAFT
ADGI GADI
ADGL GLAD
ADGN DANG
ADGO GOAD
ADGR DRAG
GRAD
ADGS DAGS
GADS
ADGU GAUD
ADHJ HADJ
ADHK DHAK
ADHL DAHL
DHAL
ADHN HAND
ADHO ODAH
ADHR HARD
ADHS DAHS
DASH
SHAD
ADIK KADI
ADIL DIAL
LAID
ADIM AMID
MAID
ADIP PADI
PAID
ADIQ QADI
QAID
ADIR ARID
RAID
ADIS AIDS
DAIS
SADI
SAID
ADIT ADIT
DITA
ADIV AVID
DIVA
ADIW WADI
ADKN DANK
ADKR DARK
ADKS DAKS
ADKW DAWK
ADLN LAND
ADLO LOAD
ADLR LARD
ADLS DALS
LADS
ADLU AULD
DUAL
LAUD
ADLY LADY
YALD
ADMN DAMN
ADMP DAMP
ADMR DRAM
ADMS DAMS
MADS
ADMU DUMA
MAUD
ADNO DONA
ADNR DARN
NARD
RAND
ADNS ANDS
DANS
SAND
ADNW DAWN
WAND
ADOP APOD
DOPA
ADOR ORAD
ROAD
ADOS ADOS
ODAS
SODA
ADOT DATO
DOAT
TOAD
ADOW WOAD
ADPR PARD
ADPS DAPS
PADS
ADQU QUAD
ADRS RADS
SARD
ADRT DART
DRAT
TRAD
ADRU DURA
ADRW DRAW
WARD
ADRY DRAY
YARD
ADST TADS
ADSW DAWS
WADS
ADSY DAYS
ADTU DAUT
ADTW DAWT
ADUY YAUD
ADVY DAVY
ADWY WADY
AEEG AGEE
AEEJ AJEE
AEEK AKEE
AEEL ALEE
AEES EASE
AEEV EAVE
AEEW AWEE
AEFK FAKE
AEFL ALEF
FEAL
FLEA
LEAF
AEFM FAME
AEFN FANE
AEFR FARE
FEAR
FRAE
AEFS SAFE
AEFT FATE
FEAT
FETA
AEFV FAVE
AEFZ FAZE
AEGG GAGE
AEGL EGAL
GALE
AEGM GAME
MAGE
MEGA
AEGN GAEN
GANE
AEGP GAPE
PAGE
PEAG
AEGR AGER
GEAR
RAGE
AEGS AGES
GAES
SAGE
AEGT GATE
GETA
AEGU AGUE
AEGV GAVE
AEGW WAGE
AEGZ GAZE
AEHK HAKE
AEHL HALE
HEAL
AEHM AHEM
HAEM
HAME
AEHN HAEN
AEHP EPHA
HEAP
AEHR HARE
HEAR
RHEA
AEHS HAES
SHEA
AEHT EATH
HAET
HATE
HEAT
THAE
AEHV HAVE
AEHY YEAH
AEHZ HAZE
AEIL ILEA
AEIM AMIE
AEJK JAKE
AEJN JANE
JEAN
AEJP JAPE
AEKL KALE
LAKE
LEAK
AEKM KAME
MAKE
AEKN KANE
AEKP PEAK
AEKR RAKE
AEKS KAES
KEAS
SAKE
AEKT TAKE
TEAK
AEKW WAKE
WEAK
WEKA
AELL LEAL
AELM ALME
LAME
MALE
MEAL
AELN ELAN
LANE
LEAN
AELO ALOE
OLEA
AELP LEAP
PALE
PEAL
PLEA
AELR EARL
LEAR
RALE
REAL
AELS ALES
LASE
LEAS
SALE
SEAL
AELT LATE
TAEL
TALE
TEAL
TELA
AELV LAVE
LEVA
VALE
VEAL
VELA
AELW WALE
WEAL
AELX AXEL
AXLE
AELZ LAZE
ZEAL
AEMN AMEN
MANE
MEAN
NAME
NEMA
AEMR MARE
REAM
AEMS MAES
MESA
SAME
SEAM
AEMT MATE
MEAT
META
TAME
TEAM
AEMW WAME
AEMX EXAM
AEMZ MAZE
AENO AEON
AENP NAPE
NEAP
PANE
PEAN
AENR EARN
NEAR
AENS ANES
SANE
AENT ANTE
ETNA
NEAT
AENV NAVE
VANE
VENA
AENW ANEW
WANE
WEAN
AENY YEAN
AEOR AERO
AEOT TOEA
AEOZ ZOEA
AEPR APER
PARE
PEAR
RAPE
REAP
AEPS APES
APSE
PASE
PEAS
SPAE
AEPT PATE
PEAT
TAPE
TEPA
AEPV PAVE
AEPX APEX
AERR RARE
REAR
AERS ARES
EARS
ERAS
RASE
SEAR
SERA
AERT RATE
TARE
TEAR
AERU UREA
AERV AVER
RAVE
VERA
AERW WARE
WEAR
AERY AERY
EYRA
YARE
YEAR
AERZ RAZE
AESS SEAS
AEST ATES
EAST
EATS
ETAS
SATE
SEAT
SETA
TEAS
AESV AVES
SAVE
VASE
AESW AWES
WAES
AESX AXES
AESY AYES
EASY
EYAS
YEAS
AETT TATE
TEAT
AETW TWAE
AETZ ZETA
AEUV UVEA
AEUX EAUX
AEVW WAVE
AFFG GAFF
AFFN NAFF
AFFR RAFF
AFFW WAFF
AFFY YAFF
AFGL FLAG
AFGN FANG
AFGR FRAG
AFGS FAGS
AFHK KHAF
AFHL HALF
AFHS FASH
AFHT HAFT
AFIK KAIF
AFIL ALIF
FAIL
FILA
AFIN FAIN
NAIF
AFIR FAIR
FIAR
AFIT FIAT
AFIW WAIF
AFKL FLAK
AFKS KAFS
AFLL FALL
AFLM FLAM
AFLN FLAN
AFLO FOAL
LOAF
AFLP FLAP
AFLR FARL
AFLT FLAT
AFLW FLAW
AFLX FALX
FLAX
AFLY FLAY
AFMO FOAM
AFMR FARM
AFNO FANO
AFNS FANS
AFNU FAUN
AFNW FAWN
AFOR FARO
FORA
AFOS OAFS
SOFA
AFPR FRAP
AFRS ARFS
AFRT FRAT
RAFT
AFRY FRAY
AFRZ ZARF
AFST FAST
FATS
AFSY FAYS
AFTU TUFA
AFTW WAFT
AFUX FAUX
AGGI GIGA
AGGJ JAGG
AGGN GANG
AGGO AGOG
AGGR RAGG
AGGS GAGS
AGHN HANG
AGHS GASH
HAGS
SHAG
AGHT GHAT
AGIL GLIA
AGIM MAGI
AGIN AGIN
GAIN
AGIO AGIO
AGIR RAGI
AGIT GAIT
AGIV VAGI
VIGA
AGIY YAGI
AGJS JAGS
AGJU JUGA
AGKS SKAG
AGKU KAGU
AGKW GAWK
AGLL GALL
AGLM GLAM
AGLN LANG
AGLO GAOL
GOAL
AGLS GALS
LAGS
SLAG
AGLY AGLY
AGMO OGAM
AGMP GAMP
AGMR GRAM
AGMS GAMS
MAGS
AGMU GAUM
AGMY GAMY
AGNO AGON
AGNP PANG
AGNR GNAR
GRAN
RANG
AGNS NAGS
SANG
SNAG
AGNT GNAT
TANG
AGNU GAUN
GUAN
AGNV VANG
AGNW GNAW
AGNY YANG
AGOS GOAS
SAGO
AGOT GOAT
TOGA
AGOY YOGA
AGPS GAPS
GASP
AGPW GAWP
AGPY GAPY
AGQU QUAG
AGRS GARS
RAGS
AGRT GRAT
AGRU GAUR
GUAR
RUGA
AGRY GRAY
AGSS SAGS
AGST GAST
GATS
STAG
TAGS
AGSW SWAG
WAGS
AGSY GAYS
SAGY
YAGS
AGSZ ZAGS
AGUY YUGA
AHHS HAHS
HASH
SHAH
AHHT HATH
AHIJ HAJI
AHIK HAIK
AHIL HAIL
HILA
AHIO OHIA
AHIR HAIR
AHIS AHIS
AHJJ HAJJ
AHKL LAKH
AHKN ANKH
HANK
KHAN
AHKP KAPH
AHKR HARK
AHKT KHAT
AHKU HAKU
AHKW HAWK
AHLL HALL
AHLM HALM
AHLO HALO
AHLR HARL
AHLS LASH
AHLT HALT
LATH
AHLU HAUL
HULA
AHLY HYLA
AHMR HARM
AHMS HAMS
MASH
SHAM
AHMT MATH
AHMW WHAM
AHNT HANT
THAN
AHNW HWAN
AHOP OPAH
AHOR HOAR
HORA
AHOT OATH
AHOW WHOA
AHOX HOAX
AHOY AHOY
HOYA
AHPR HARP
AHPS HAPS
HASP
PASH
AHPT PATH
PHAT
AHPW WHAP
AHRS RASH
AHRT HART
RATH
TAHR
AHSS SASH
AHST HAST
HATS
AHSW HAWS
SHAW
SHWA
WASH
AHSY ASHY
HAYS
SHAY
AHTT THAT
AHTU HAUT
AHTW THAW
WHAT
AHYZ HAZY
AIIL ILIA
AIIN INIA
AIIX IXIA
AIJL JAIL
AIJO JIAO
AIKK KAKI
AIKL ILKA
KAIL
AIKM KAMI
AIKN AKIN
KAIN
KINA
AIKP PAIK
PIKA
AIKR RAKI
AIKS SAKI
SIKA
AIKT IKAT
AIKV KIVA
AILM LIMA
MAIL
AILN ANIL
LAIN
NAIL
AILP LIPA
PAIL
PIAL
AILR ARIL
LAIR
LARI
LIAR
LIRA
RAIL
RIAL
AILS AILS
SAIL
SIAL
AILT ALIT
LATI
TAIL
TALI
AILV VAIL
VIAL
AILW WAIL
AILX AXIL
AIMM IMAM
MAIM
AIMN AMIN
MAIN
MINA
AIMP PIMA
AIMR AMIR
MAIR
RAMI
AIMS AIMS
AMIS
SIMA
AIMX MAXI
AINO NAOI
AINP NIPA
PAIN
PIAN
PINA
AINR AIRN
RAIN
RANI
AINS AINS
ANIS
SAIN
AINT ANTI
TAIN
AINU UNAI
AINV VAIN
VINA
AINW WAIN
AINY AYIN
AINZ NAZI
AIOT IOTA

AIPR	PAIR
AIPS	PIAS
AIPT	PITA
AIQU	QUAI
AIRS	AIRS
	RAIS
	RIAS
	SARI
AIRT	AIRT
AIRV	VAIR
AIRW	WAIR
AIRY	AIRY
AIRZ	IZAR
AIST	AITS
	SATI
AISV	VISA
AISX	AXIS
AITV	VITA
AITW	WAIT
AITX	TAXI
AIVV	VIVA
AJKU	JAUK
AJLR	JARL
AJMS	JAMS
AJOS	SOJA
AJOT	JATO
	JOTA
AJPU	JAUP
	PUJA
AJRS	JARS
AJRU	JURA
AJSW	JAWS
AJSY	JAYS
AJZZ	JAZZ
AKKY	KYAK
AKLN	LANK
AKLO	KOLA
AKLR	LARK
AKLT	TALK
AKLW	WALK
AKLY	ALKY
	LAKY
AKMO	AMOK
	MAKO
AKMR	MARK
AKMS	MASK
AKNO	KAON
	KOAN
AKNP	KNAP
AKNR	KARN
	KNAR
	NARK
	RANK
AKNS	SANK
AKNT	TANK
AKNU	KUNA
AKNY	YANK
AKOR	KORA
	OKRA
AKOS	KOAS
	OAKS
	OKAS
	SOAK
AKOY	KAYO
	OAKY
	OKAY
AKPR	PARK
AKRS	ARKS
	SARK
AKRT	KART
AKRU	RAKU
AKRW	WARK
AKRY	KYAR
AKSS	ASKS
	SKAS
AKST	KATS
	SKAT
	TASK
AKSU	AUKS
	SKUA
AKSV	KVAS
AKSY	KAYS
	YAKS
AKTY	KYAT
AKUW	WAUK
ALLL	LALL
ALLM	MALL
ALLO	OLLA
ALLP	PALL
ALLS	ALLS
	SALL
ALLT	TALL
ALLW	WALL
ALLY	ALLY
ALMM	MALM
ALMO	LOAM
	MOLA
ALMP	LAMP
	PALM
ALMR	MARL
ALMS	ALMS
	LAMS
	SLAM
ALMT	MALT
ALMU	ALUM
	LUMA
	MAUL
ALMY	AMYL
ALNO	LOAN
ALNP	PLAN
ALNU	LUNA
	ULAN
	ULNA
ALNW	LAWN
ALOP	OPAL
ALOR	ORAL
ALOS	ALSO
	SOLA
ALOT	ALTO
	LOTA
	TOLA
ALOV	OVAL
ALOW	ALOW
	AWOL
ALPP	PALP
ALPS	ALPS
	LAPS
	PALS
	SALP
	SLAP
ALPT	PLAT
ALPU	PULA
ALPW	PAWL
ALPY	PALY
	PLAY
ALRS	LARS
ALRY	ARYL
ALSS	LASS
	SALS
ALST	ALTS
	LAST
	LATS
	SALT
	SLAT
ALSU	SAUL
ALSV	LAVS
ALSW	AWLS
	LAWS
	SLAW
ALSY	LAYS
	SLAY
ALTU	LATU
ALUU	LUAU
ALUV	ULVA
ALUW	WAUL
ALWW	WAWL
ALWY	WALY
	YAWL
ALYZ	LAZY
AMMO	AMMO
AMNO	MANO
	MOAN
	NOMA
AMNS	MANS
AMNU	MAUN
AMNW	MAWN
AMNY	MANY
	MYNA
AMOR	MORA
	ROAM
AMOS	MOAS
	SOMA
AMOT	ATOM
	MOAT
AMOX	MOXA
AMOY	MAYO
AMPR	PRAM
	RAMP
AMPS	AMPS
	MAPS
	PAMS
	SAMP
	SPAM
AMPT	TAMP
AMPU	PUMA
AMPV	VAMP
AMRS	ARMS
	MARS
	RAMS
AMRT	MART
	TRAM
AMRU	ARUM
	MURA
AMRW	WARM
AMRY	ARMY
AMSS	MASS
AMST	MAST
	MATS
	TAMS
AMSU	AMUS
AMSW	MAWS
	SWAM
AMSY	MAYS
	YAMS
AMTT	MATT
AMTU	MAUT
AMYZ	MAZY
ANNO	ANON
	NONA
ANNS	NANS
ANOR	ROAN
ANOS	NAOS
ANOT	NOTA
ANOV	NOVA
ANOX	AXON
ANOZ	AZON
	ZONA
ANPS	NAPS
	PANS
	SNAP
	SPAN
ANPT	PANT
ANPU	PUNA
ANPW	PAWN
ANRT	RANT
	TARN
ANRW	WARN
ANRY	NARY
	YARN
ANSS	SANS
ANST	ANTS
	TANS
ANSU	ANUS
ANSV	VANS
ANSW	AWNS
	SAWN
	SNAW
	SWAN
	WANS
ANSY	NAYS
ANTU	AUNT
	TUNA
ANTW	WANT
ANUU	UNAU
ANUY	YUAN
ANVY	NAVY
ANWY	AWNY
	WANY
	YAWN
ANYZ	ZANY
AOPR	PRAO
	PROA
AOPS	APOS
	SOAP
AOPT	ATOP
AORR	ORRA
	ROAR
AORS	OARS
	OSAR
	SOAR
	SORA
AORT	RATO
	ROTA
	TARO
	TORA
AORV	ARVO
AOSS	OSSA
AOST	OAST
	OATS
	STOA
	TAOS
AOSV	AVOS
AOSY	SOYA
AOTU	AUTO
AOVW	AVOW
APPS	APPS
	PAPS
APPU	PUPA
APRR	PARR
APRS	PARS
	RAPS
	RASP
	SPAR
APRT	PART
	PRAT
	RAPT
	TARP
	TRAP
APRU	PRAU
APRW	WARP
	WRAP
APRY	PRAY
APSS	ASPS
	PASS
	SAPS
	SPAS
APST	PAST
	PATS
	SPAT
	TAPS
APSU	UPAS
APSW	PAWS
	SWAP
	WAPS
	WASP
APSY	PAYS
	PYAS
	SPAY
	YAPS
APSZ	ZAPS
APTY	PATY
APUY	YAUP
APWY	YAWP
AQST	QATS
AQUY	QUAY
ARST	ARTS
	RATS
	STAR
	TARS
	TSAR
ARSU	SURA
	URSA
ARSV	VARS
ARSW	RAWS
	WARS
ARSY	RAYS
	RYAS
ARTT	TART
ARTW	WART
ARTY	ARTY
	TRAY
ARTZ	TZAR
ARUW	WAUR
ARVY	VARY
ARWY	AWRY
	WARY
ARZZ	RAZZ
ASSS	SASS
ASST	TASS
ASSW	SAWS
ASSY	SAYS
ASTT	STAT
	TATS
ASTU	TAUS
	UTAS
ASTV	TAVS
	VAST
	VATS
ASTW	STAW
	SWAT
	TAWS
	TWAS
	WAST
	WATS
ASTY	STAY
ASUV	VAUS
ASVV	VAVS
ASVW	VAWS
ASWW	WAWS
ASWY	SWAY
	WAYS
	YAWS
ASYY	YAYS
ATTU	TAUT
ATTW	WATT
ATUV	VATU
AVWY	WAVY
AWXY	WAXY
BBBI	BIBB
BBCO	COBB
BBEL	BLEB
BBES	EBBS
BBIJ	JIBB
BBIS	BIBS
	SIBB
BBLO	BLOB
BBLU	BLUB
	BULB
BBMO	BOMB
BBOO	BOOB
BBOS	BOBS
BBOU	BUBO
BBRU	BURB
BBSU	BUBS
BBUU	BUBU
BCEI	BICE
BCEK	BECK
BCEU	CUBE
BCHU	CHUB
BCIR	CRIB
BCKO	BOCK
BCKU	BUCK
BCLO	BLOC
BCLU	CLUB
BCMO	COMB
BCOS	COBS
BCRU	CURB
BCSU	CUBS
BDEI	BIDE
BDEL	BLED
BDEN	BEND
BDEO	BODE
BDER	BRED
BDES	BEDS
	DEBS
BDET	DEBT
BDEU	BEDU
BDII	BIDI
BDIN	BIND
BDIR	BIRD
	DRIB
BDIS	BIDS
	DIBS
BDLO	BOLD
BDMU	DUMB
BDNO	BOND
BDNU	BUND
BDOS	BODS
BDOY	BODY
	DOBY
BDRU	BURD
	DRUB
BDSU	BUDS
	DUBS
BEEF	BEEF
	FEEB
BEEN	BEEN
	BENE
BEEP	BEEP
BEER	BEER
	BREE
BEES	BEES
BEET	BEET
BEGI	GIBE
BEGR	BERG
BEGS	BEGS
BEGY	GYBE
BEHR	HERB
BEHT	BETH
BEIJ	JIBE
BEIK	BIKE
	KIBE
BEIL	BILE
BEIN	BINE
BEIR	BIER
	BRIE
BEIS	BISE
BEIT	BITE
BEIV	VIBE
BEIX	IBEX
BEIZ	BIZE
BEJU	JUBE
BEKR	BERK
	KERB
BELL	BELL
BELO	BOLE
	LOBE
BELP	PLEB
BELS	BELS
BELT	BELT
	BLET
BELU	BLUE
	LUBE
BELW	BLEW
BEMR	BERM
BENO	BONE
	EBON
BENR	BREN
BENS	BENS
	NEBS
BENT	BENT
BENU	UNBE
BEOO	OBOE
BEOR	BORE
	ROBE
BEOS	OBES
BEOY	OBEY
BERS	REBS
BERU	RUBE
BERV	VERB
BERW	BREW
BERY	BYRE
BEST	BEST
	BETS
BESW	WEBS
BESY	BEYS
	BYES
BETU	BUTE
	TUBE
BETY	BYTE
BEUZ	ZEBU
BEVY	BEVY
BFFI	BIFF
BFFO	BOFF
BFFU	BUFF
BFIS	FIBS
BFLU	FLUB
BFMU	BUMF
BFOR	FORB
BFOS	FOBS
BFSU	FUBS
BGIL	GLIB
BGIO	BIOG
BGIR	BRIG
BGIS	BIGS
	GIBS
BGLO	BLOG
	GLOB
BGNO	BONG
BGNU	BUNG
BGOO	GOBO
BGOS	BOGS
	GOBS
BGOY	BOGY
	GOBY
BGRU	BURG
	GRUB
BGSU	BUGS
BHLU	BUHL
BHOO	BOHO
	HOBO
BHOS	BOSH
	HOBS
BHOT	BOTH
BHRU	BUHR
BHSU	BUSH
	HUBS
BHTU	BHUT
BIIS	IBIS
BIJS	JIBS
BIKL	BILK
BIKR	BIRK
BIKS	BISK
BILL	BILL
BILM	LIMB
BILN	BLIN
BILO	BOIL
BILP	BLIP
BILR	BIRL
BILS	LIBS
BIMR	BRIM
BIMS	MIBS
BINR	BRIN
BINS	BINS
	NIBS
	SNIB
BINT	BINT
BINY	INBY
BIOR	BIRO
	BRIO
BIOS	BIOS
	OBIS
BIOT	OBIT
BIRR	BIRR
BIRS	BRIS
	RIBS
BIRT	BRIT
BISS	SIBS
BIST	BITS
BITT	BITT
BJOS	JOBS
BKLU	BULK
BKNO	BONK
	KNOB
BKNU	BUNK
BKOO	BOOK
	KOBO
BKOR	BORK
BKOS	BOSK
	KOBS
BKSU	BUSK
BLLO	BOLL
BLLU	BULL
BLOO	BOLO
	LOBO
	OBOL
BLOS	LOBS
	SLOB
BLOT	BLOT
	BOLT
BLOW	BLOW
	BOWL
BLRU	BLUR
	BURL
BLRY	BYRL
BLSU	SLUB
BMNU	NUMB
BMOO	BOOM
BMOS	MOBS
BMOT	TOMB
BMOU	UMBO
BMOW	WOMB
BMPU	BUMP
BMSU	BUMS
BNNU	BUNN
BNOO	BOON
BNOR	BORN
BNOS	NOBS
	SNOB
BNOY	BONY
BNRU	BURN
BNSU	BUNS
	NUBS
	SNUB
BNTU	BUNT
BOOR	BOOR
	BROO
BOOS	BOOS
BOOT	BOOT
BOOY	BOYO
BOOZ	BOZO
BOPS	BOPS
BORS	BROS
	ORBS
	ROBS
	SORB
BORT	BORT
BORW	BROW
BORY	ORBY
BOSS	BOSS
	SOBS
BOST	BOTS
	STOB
BOSW	BOWS
	SWOB
BOSY	BOYS
	SYBO
	YOBS
BOTT	BOTT
BOTU	BOUT
BOTY	TOBY
BOUY	BUOY
BOXY	BOXY
BPRU	BURP
BPSU	PUBS
BPUY	UPBY
BRRR	BRRR
BRRU	BURR
BRSU	BURS
	RUBS
	URBS
BRTU	BRUT
BRUX	BRUX
BRUY	BURY
	RUBY
BSSU	BUSS
	SUBS
BSTU	BUST
	BUTS
	STUB
	TUBS
BSUY	BUSY
	BUYS
BTTU	BUTT
BUZZ	BUZZ
CCHI	CHIC
CCKO	COCK
CCOO	COCO
CCOR	CROC
CDEE	CEDE
CDEI	CEDI
	DICE
	ICED
CDEK	DECK
CDEO	CODE
	COED
	DECO
CDER	CRED
CDEU	CUED
	DUCE
CDHI	CHID
CDIK	DICK
CDIO	ODIC
CDIS	DISC
CDIU	DUCI
CDKO	DOCK
CDKU	DUCK
CDLO	CLOD
	COLD
CDOR	CORD
CDOS	CODS
	DOCS
CDRU	CRUD
	CURD
CDSU	CUDS
	SCUD
CDTU	DUCT
CEEH	ECHE
CEEP	CEPE
CEER	CERE
CEES	CEES
CEET	CETE
CEEX	EXEC
CEFH	CHEF
CEFI	FICE
CEFK	FECK
CEFL	CLEF
CEFY	FYCE
CEGK	GECK
CEHK	HECK
CEHL	LECH
CEHO	ECHO
CEHP	PECH
CEHT	ECHT
	ETCH
	TECH
CEHW	CHEW
CEHY	YECH
CEHZ	CHEZ
CEIL	CEIL
	LICE
CEIM	EMIC
	MICE
CEIN	CINE
	NICE
CEIP	EPIC
	PICE
CEIR	CIRE
	RICE
CEIS	ICES
	SICE
CEIT	CITE
	ETIC
CEIV	VICE
CEKK	KECK
CEKN	NECK
CEKO	COKE
CEKP	PECK
CEKR	RECK
CEKU	CUKE
CELL	CELL
CELO	COLE
CELS	CELS
CELT	CELT
CELU	CLUE
	LUCE
CELW	CLEW
CEMO	COME
CEMR	MERC
CEMY	CYME
CENO	CONE
	ONCE
CENT	CENT
CEOP	COPE
CEOR	CERO
	CORE
CEOT	COTE
CEOV	COVE
CEPS	CEPS
	PECS
	SPEC
CEPU	PUCE
CERS	RECS
CERU	CURE
	ECRU
CERW	CREW
CESS	CESS
	SECS
CEST	SECT
CESU	CUES
	ECUS
CESY	SYCE
CETU	CUTE
CFFO	COFF
CFFU	CUFF
CFIL	FLIC
CFIO	COIF
	FICO
	FOCI
CFIS	FISC
CFIU	CUIF
	FUCI
CFLO	FLOC
CFOO	COOF
CFOR	CORF
CFOT	COFT
CFRU	CURF
CGHU	CHUG
CGIS	CIGS
CGKU	GUCK
CGLO	CLOG
CGOS	COGS
CHIK	HICK
CHIL	LICH
CHIN	CHIN
	INCH
CHIP	CHIP
CHIR	RICH
CHIS	CHIS
	ICHS
CHIT	CHIT
	ITCH
CHIU	HUIC
CHIW	WICH
CHKO	HOCK
CHKU	HUCK
CHLO	LOCH
CHLY	LYCH
CHMU	CHUM
	MUCH
CHNO	CHON
CHOO	COHO
CHOP	CHOP
CHOS	COSH
CHOU	OUCH
CHOW	CHOW
CHSU	SUCH
CHUY	YUCH
CHWY	WYCH
CIKK	KICK
CIKL	LICK
CIKN	NICK
CIKP	PICK
CIKR	RICK
CIKS	SICK
CIKT	TICK
CIKW	WICK
CIKY	ICKY
CILO	COIL
	LOCI
CILP	CLIP
CIMS	MICS
CINO	CION
	COIN
	CONI
	ICON
CINU	UNCI
CINZ	ZINC
CIOR	COIR
CIOT	OTIC
CIOZ	ZOIC
CIPS	PICS
CIPY	PYIC
CIRS	CRIS
CIRT	CRIT
CIRU	URIC
CISS	SICS
CIST	CIST
	TICS
CITY	CITY
CJKO	JOCK
CJOU	JUCO
CKLO	LOCK
CKLU	LUCK
CKMO	MOCK
CKMU	MUCK
CKNO	CONK
	NOCK
CKOO	COOK
CKOP	POCK
CKOR	CORK
	ROCK
CKOS	SOCK
CKOY	COKY
	YOCK
CKPU	PUCK
CKRU	RUCK
CKSU	CUSK
	SUCK
CKTU	TUCK
CKUY	YUCK
CLLU	CULL
CLMU	CULM
CLNO	CLON
CLOO	COOL
	LOCO
CLOP	CLOP
CLOS	COLS
CLOT	CLOT
	COLT
CLOW	COWL
CLOY	CLOY
	COLY
CLRU	CURL
CLTU	CULT
CMOP	COMP
CMOR	CORM
CMOS	MOCS
CMSU	SCUM
CMSW	CWMS
CMSY	MYCS
CNNO	CONN
CNOO	COON
CNOR	CORN
CNOS	CONS
CNOU	UNCO
CNOY	CONY
CNRU	CURN
CNSY	SYNC
COOP	COOP
	POCO
COOS	COOS
COOT	COOT
COPR	CROP
COPS	COPS
	SCOP
COPU	COUP
COPY	COPY
CORS	CORS
	ORCS
	ROCS
CORT	TORC
CORW	CROW
CORY	CORY
COSS	COSS
COST	COST
	COTS
	SCOT
COSW	COWS
	SCOW
COSY	COSY
	COYS
COWY	COWY
COYZ	COZY
CPSU	CUPS
	CUSP
	SCUP
CRRU	CURR
CRSU	CRUS
	CURS
CRSY	SCRY
CRTU	CURT
CRUX	CRUX
CSSU	CUSS
CSTU	CUTS
	SCUT
CSTY	CYST
DDEE	DEED
DDEI	DIED
DDEO	EDDO
DDER	REDD
DDEU	DUDE
DDEY	DYED
	EDDY
DDIO	DIDO
DDIY	DIDY
DDOO	DODO
DDOS	ODDS
DDRU	RUDD
DDSU	DUDS
	SUDD
DEEF	FEED
DEEG	EDGE
	GEED
DEEH	HEED
DEEI	EIDE
DEEJ	JEED
DEEK	DEKE
	EKED
DEEL	DELE
DEEM	DEEM
	DEME
	MEED
DEEN	DENE
	NEED
DEEP	DEEP
DEER	DEER
	DERE
	DREE
	REDE
	REED
DEES	DEES
	SEED
DEET	DEET
	TEED
DEEW	WEED
DEEX	EXED
DEEY	EYED
DEFI	DEFI
DEFL	DELF
	FLED
DEFN	FEND
DEFO	FEOD
DEFS	FEDS
DEFT	DEFT
DEFU	FEUD
DEFY	DEFY
DEGI	GIED
DEGL	GELD
	GLED
DEGO	DOGE
DEGR	DREG
DEGS	GEDS
DEGU	GUDE
DEGY	EDGY
DEHI	HIDE
	HIED
DEHL	HELD
DEHO	HOED
	OHED
DEHR	HERD
DEHS	EDHS
	SHED
DEHU	HUED
DEIK	DIKE
DEIL	DEIL
	DELI
	DIEL
	IDLE
	LIED
DEIM	DIME
	IDEM
DEIN	DENI
	DINE
	NIDE
DEIP	PIED
DEIR	DIRE
	IRED
	RIDE
DEIS	DIES
	IDES
	SIDE
DEIT	DIET
	DITE
	EDIT
	TIDE
	TIED
DEIV	DIVE
	VIDE
	VIED
DEIW	WIDE
DEKR	DREK
DEKS	DESK
DEKU	DUKE
DEKY	DYKE
DELL	DELL
DELM	MELD
DELN	LEND
DELO	DOLE
	LODE
DELP	PLED
DELS	DELS
	ELDS
	SLED
DELT	DELT
DELU	DUEL
	LEUD
	LUDE
DELV	VELD
DELW	LEWD
	WELD
DELY	YELD
DEMN	MEND
DEMO	DEMO
	DOME
	MODE
DEMR	DERM
DEMS	MEDS
DEMY	DEMY
	EMYD

DENO DONE NODE
DENP PEND
DENR NERD REND
DENS DENS ENDS SEND SNED
DENT DENT TEND
DENU DUNE NUDE UNDE
DENV VEND
DENW WEND
DENY DENY DYNE
DEOP DOPE OPED
DEOR DOER DORE REDO RODE
DEOS DOES DOSE ODES
DEOT DOTE TOED
DEOV DOVE
DEOW OWED
DEOZ DOZE
DEPS PEDS SPED
DEPU DUPE
DERS REDS
DERU DURE RUDE RUED
DERW DREW
DERY DYER
DEST TEDS
DESU DUES SUED USED
DESV DEVS
DESW DEWS WEDS
DESY DEYS DYES
DESZ ZEDS
DETU DUET
DEWY DEWY
DEXY DEXY
DFFI DIFF
DFFO DOFF
DFFU DUFF
DFIN FIND
DFIO FIDO
DFIS DIFS FIDS
DFLO FOLD
DFNO FOND
DFNU FUND
DFOO FOOD
DFOR FORD
DFSU FUDS
DGIL GILD
DGIN DING
DGIR GIRD GRID
DGIS DIGS GIDS
DGIU GUID
DGLO GOLD
DGNO DONG
DGNU DUNG
DGOO GOOD
DGOS DOGS GODS
DGOW GOWD
DGOY DOGY
DGRU DRUG
DGSU DUGS
DHIN HIND
DHIS DISH SIDH
DHIW WHID
DHLO HOLD
DHOO HOOD
DHOS HODS SHOD
DHOT DOTH
DHOW DHOW
DHOY YODH
DHTU THUD
DIIM IMID MIDI
DIIN NIDI
DIIR IRID
DIJN DJIN
DIKN DINK KIND
DIKR DIRK
DIKS DISK KIDS SKID
DILL DILL
DILM MILD
DILO DIOL IDOL LIDO LOID
DILR DIRL
DILS LIDS SILD SLID
DILW WILD
DILY IDLY IDYL
DIMN MIND
DIMO MODI
DIMS DIMS MIDS
DINO DINO NODI
DINR RIND
DINS DINS
DINT DINT
DINW WIND
DIOT DOIT
DIOV VOID
DIOX OXID
DIPR DRIP
DIPS DIPS
DIPT DIPT
DIQU QUID
DIRS RIDS
DIRT DIRT
DIRY YIRD
DISS DISS
DIST DITS
DISV VIDS
DITU DUIT
DITY TIDY
DITZ DITZ
DJOO DOJO
DJOU JUDO
DKNU DUNK
DKOR DORK
DKOU KUDO
DKSU DUSK
DKUU KUDU
DLLO DOLL
DLLU DULL
DLMO MOLD
DLOP PLOD
DLOR LORD
DLOS DOLS OLDS SOLD
DLOT DOLT TOLD
DLOU LOUD
DLOW WOLD
DLOY ODYL OLDY
DLUY DULY
DMOO DOOM MOOD
DMOR DORM
DMOS DOMS MODS
DMOU DOUM
DMPU DUMP
DMRU DRUM
DMSU MUDS
DNOP POND
DNOS DONS NODS
DNOU UDON UNDO
DNOW DOWN
DNOY YOND
DNRU DURN NURD
DNRY RYND
DNSU DUNS
DNTU DUNT
DNUY UNDY
DNWY WYND
DOOP POOD
DOOR DOOR ODOR ORDO ROOD
DOOW WOOD
DOPR DORP DROP PROD
DOPS PODS
DOPU UPDO
DOPY DOPY
DOQU QUOD
DORR DORR
DORS DORS RODS SORD
DORT TROD
DORU DOUR DURO
DORW WORD
DORY DORY
DOSS DOSS SODS
DOST DOST DOTS TODS
DOSU DUOS OUDS UDOS
DOSW DOWS
DOSY YODS
DOTY DOTY TODY
DOUX DOUX
DOXY DOXY
DOYZ DOZY
DPSU DUPS PUDS SPUD
DRRU DURR
DRSU SURD URDS
DRSY DRYS
DSSU SUDS
DSTU DUST STUD
DTUY DUTY
EEEP EPEE
EEFJ JEFE
EEFK KEEF
EEFL FEEL FLEE
EEFM FEME
EEFR FERE FREE REEF
EEFS FEES
EEFT FEET FETE
EEGH GHEE
EEGK GEEK
EEGL GLEE
EEGN GENE
EEGO OGEE
EEGR EGER GREE
EEGS GEES
EEGZ GEEZ
EEHL HEEL
EEHM HEME
EEHR HERE
EEHT THEE
EEHW WHEE
EEJP JEEP
EEJR JEER
EEJS JEES
EEJT JETE
EEJZ JEEZ
EEKK KEEK
EEKL KEEL LEEK LEKE
EEKM MEEK
EEKN KEEN KNEE
EEKP KEEP PEEK PEKE
EEKR REEK
EEKS EKES SEEK SKEE
EEKT KEET
EEKW WEEK
EELP PEEL PELE
EELR LEER REEL
EELS EELS ELSE LEES SEEL
EELT LEET TEEL TELE
EELW WEEL
EELY EELY
EEMM MEME
EEMN NEEM
EEMR MERE
EEMS EMES SEEM SEME
EEMT MEET METE TEEM
EEMU EMEU
EEMZ MEZE
EENN NENE
EENP NEEP PEEN
EENR ERNE
EENS ESNE SEEN SENE
EENT TEEN
EENV EVEN NEVE
EENW WEEN
EENY EYEN EYNE
EEPP PEEP
EEPR PEER PERE PREE
EEPS PEES SEEP
EEPV VEEP
EEPW WEEP
EERS REES SEER SERE
EERT RETE TREE
EERV EVER VEER
EERW EWER WERE
EERY EERY EYER EYRE
EESS ESES SEES
EEST TEES
EESV EVES
EESW EWES WEES
EESX EXES
EESY EYES
EESZ ZEES
EETW TWEE WEET
EETY TYEE
EFFI FIEF FIFE
EFFS EFFS
EFFT TEFF
EFHS FEHS
EFHT HEFT
EFIK KIEF
EFIL FILE LIEF LIFE
EFIN FINE NEIF
EFIR FIRE REIF RIFE
EFIS SEIF
EFIV FIVE
EFIW WIFE
EFKR KERF
EFKS KEFS
EFKY FYKE
EFLL FELL
EFLO FLOE
EFLP PELF
EFLS SELF
EFLT FELT LEFT
EFLU FLUE FUEL
EFLW FLEW
EFLX FLEX
EFLY FLEY
EFMS FEMS
EFMU FUME
EFNR FERN
EFNS FENS
EFNU ENUF
EFOR FORE FROE
EFOS FOES
EFRS REFS SERF
EFRT FRET REFT TREF
EFSS FESS
EFST EFTS FEST FETS
EFSU FEUS FUSE
EFTW WEFT
EFUZ FUZE
EGGL GLEG
EGGS EGGS
EGGT TEGG
EGGY EGGY YEGG
EGHU HUGE
EGIN GIEN
EGIS EGIS GIES
EGIT GITE
EGIV GIVE
EGKS KEGS SKEG
EGLN GLEN
EGLO LOGE OGLE
EGLS GELS LEGS
EGLT GELT
EGLU GLUE LUGE
EGLY GLEY
EGMR GERM
EGMS GEMS MEGS
EGMU GEUM
EGNO GONE
EGNS ENGS GENS NEGS
EGNT GENT
EGNU GENU
EGOR ERGO GOER GORE OGRE
EGOS EGOS GOES SEGO
EGPS PEGS
EGRS ERGS REGS
EGRU GRUE URGE
EGRW GREW
EGRY GREY GYRE
EGSS SEGS
EGST GEST GETS TEGS
EGVY GYVE
EHHS HEHS
EHHT HETH
EHIK HIKE
EHIL ELHI HEIL
EHIR HEIR HIRE
EHIS HIES
EHIV HIVE
EHJU JEHU
EHKO HOKE OKEH
EHKT KHET
EHLL HELL
EHLM HELM
EHLO HELO HOLE
EHLP HELP
EHLR HERL LEHR
EHMO HOME
EHMP HEMP
EHMR HERM
EHMS HEMS MESH
EHMT METH THEM
EHNO HONE
EHNR HERN
EHNS HENS
EHNT HENT THEN
EHNW HEWN WHEN
EHOP HOPE
EHOR HERO HOER
EHOS HOES HOSE SHOE
EHOV HOVE
EHOW HOWE
EHPS PEHS
EHPW PHEW
EHPY HYPE
EHRS HERS RESH
EHSS SHES
EHST ETHS HEST HETS
EHSU HUES
EHSW HEWS SHEW
EHTT TETH
EHTW THEW WHET
EHTY HYTE THEY
EHWW WHEW
EHWY WHEY
EIJV JIVE
EIKL LIKE
EIKM MIKE
EIKN KINE
EIKP KEPI PIKE
EIKR KEIR KIER
EIKS SIKE
EIKT KITE TIKE
EILM LIME MILE
EILN LIEN LINE
EILP LIPE PILE PLIE
EILR LIER LIRE RIEL RILE
EILS ISLE LEIS LIES
EILT LITE TILE
EILU LIEU
EILV EVIL LIVE VEIL VILE
EILW LWEI WILE
EILX ILEX
EIMM MIME
EIMN MIEN MINE
EIMR EMIR MIRE RIME
EIMS MISE SEMI
EIMT EMIT ITEM MITE TIME
EINN NINE
EINP PEIN PINE
EINR REIN
EINS SINE
EINT NITE TINE
EINV NEVI VEIN VINE
EINW WINE
EINX NIXE
EINZ ZEIN ZINE
EIPP PIPE
EIPR PERI PIER RIPE
EIPS PIES SIPE
EIPW WIPE
EIPY YIPE
EIRS IRES REIS RISE SIRE
EIRT RITE TIER TIRE
EIRV RIVE VIER
EIRW WEIR WIRE
EISS SEIS
EIST SITE TIES
EISV VIES VISE
EISW WISE
EISZ SIZE
EITU ETUI
EITW WITE
EITX EXIT
EITY YETI
EIVV VIVE
EIVW VIEW WIVE
EJKO JOKE
EJKR JERK
EJKU JUKE
EJLL JELL
EJLO JOLE
EJNO JEON
EJOS JOES
EJOY JOEY
EJPU JUPE
EJSS JESS
EJST JEST JETS
EJTU JUTE
EJUX JEUX
EKLO KOEL
EKLP KELP
EKLS ELKS LEKS
EKLT KELT
EKLU LEKU
EKLY YELK
EKMO MOKE
EKMP KEMP
EKMR MERK
EKNO KENO
EKNR KERN
EKNS KENS
EKNT KENT
EKNU KUNE NEUK NUKE
EKNW KNEW
EKOP POKE
EKOR KORE
EKOS OKES SOKE
EKOT KETO TOKE
EKOW WOKE
EKOY YOKE
EKPR PERK
EKPS KEPS SKEP
EKPT KEPT
EKPU PUKE
EKRT TREK
EKRY RYKE YERK
EKRZ ZERK
EKSU KUES UKES
EKSW SKEW
EKSY KEYS KYES SYKE
EKSZ ZEKS
EKTY KYTE TYKE
EKUY YEUK
ELLM MELL
ELLS ELLS SELL
ELLT TELL
ELLW WELL
ELLY YELL
ELMO MOLE
ELMR MERL
ELMS ELMS MELS
ELMT MELT
ELMU MULE
ELMW MEWL
ELMY ELMY YLEM
ELNO ENOL LENO LONE NOEL
ELNS LENS
ELNT LENT
ELNU LUNE
ELOO OLEO
ELOP LOPE POLE
ELOR LORE ORLE ROLE
ELOS LOSE OLES SLOE SOLE
ELOT TOLE
ELOV LEVO LOVE VOLE
ELOW LOWE
ELPT LEPT PELT
ELPU PULE
ELPW PLEW
ELPX PLEX
ELPY YELP
ELRU LURE RULE
ELRY LYRE RELY
ELSS LESS SELS
ELST LEST LETS TELS
ELSU LUES SLUE
ELSW SLEW
ELSY LEYS LYES LYSE
ELTU LUTE TULE
ELTW WELT
ELUX LUXE
ELUY YULE
ELVY LEVY
ELWY WYLE
EMMO MEMO MOME
EMMS MEMS
EMMY EMMY
EMNO MENO NOME OMEN
EMNU MENU NEUM
EMOP MOPE POEM POME
EMOR MORE OMER
EMOS SOME
EMOT MOTE TOME
EMOU MEOU MOUE
EMOV MOVE
EMOW MEOW
EMPR PERM
EMPT TEMP
EMRS REMS
EMRT TERM
EMRU MURE
EMSS MESS
EMST STEM
EMSU EMUS MUSE
EMSW MEWS SMEW
EMTU MUTE
EMYZ ZYME
ENNO NEON NONE
ENOP NOPE OPEN PEON PONE
ENOS EONS NOES NOSE ONES SONE
ENOT NOTE TONE
ENOV OVEN
ENOW ENOW
ENOX EXON OXEN
ENOZ ZONE
ENPS PENS
ENPT PENT
ENRS ERNS
ENRT RENT TERN
ENRU RUNE
ENRW WREN
ENSS NESS
ENST NEST NETS SENT TENS
ENSW NEWS SEWN WENS
ENSY SNYE SYNE YENS
ENTT NETT TENT
ENTU TUNE
ENTV VENT
ENTW NEWT WENT
ENTX NEXT
ENTY TYNE
ENVY ENVY
EOOZ OOZE
EOPP PEPO POPE
EOPR PORE REPO ROPE
EOPS EPOS OPES PESO POSE
EOPT POET TOPE
EOPX EXPO
EORS EROS ORES ROES ROSE SORE
EORT ROTE TORE
EORU EURO ROUE
EORV OVER ROVE
EORW WORE
EORY OYER YORE
EORZ ZERO
EOSS OSES
EOST TOES
EOSV VOES
EOSW OWES OWSE WOES
EOSX OXES
EOSY OYES
EOTT TOTE
EOTV VETO VOTE
EOVW WOVE
EOWY YOWE
EOYZ OYEZ
EPPR PERP PREP REPP
EPPS PEPS
EPRS REPS
EPRT PERT
EPRU PURE
EPRV PERV
EPRX PREX
EPRY PREY PYRE
EPRZ PREZ
EPST PEST PETS SEPT STEP
EPSU SPUE SUPE
EPSW PEWS SPEW
EPSY ESPY PYES YEPS
EPSZ ZEPS
EPTW WEPT
EPTY TYPE
EQUY QUEY
ERRS ERRS
ERRU RUER
ERSS SERS
ERST ERST REST RETS TRES
ERSU RUES RUSE SUER SURE USER
ERSV REVS
ERSY RYES
ERTT TRET
ERTU TRUE
ERTV VERT
ERTW WERT
ERTY TREY TYER TYRE
ERVY VERY
ERYY EYRY
ESST SETS
ESSU SUES USES
ESSW SEWS
ESTT SETT STET TEST TETS
ESTU SUET UTES
ESTV VEST VETS
ESTW STEW TEWS WEST WETS
ESTX SEXT
ESTY STEY STYE TYES
ESTZ ZEST
ESWY WYES YEWS
ESXY SEXY
ETTX TEXT
ETTY YETT
ETVX VEXT
ETWY WYTE
FFGU GUFF
FFHU HUFF
FFIJ JIFF
FFIM MIFF
FFIR RIFF
FFIT TIFF
FFIY IFFY
FFLU LUFF
FFMU MUFF
FFOS OFFS
FFOT TOFF
FFPT PFFT
FFPU PUFF
FFRU RUFF
FFTU TUFF
FGIR FRIG
FGIS FIGS
FGIT GIFT
FGLO FLOG GOLF
FGLU GULF
FGOO GOOF
FGOR FROG
FGOS FOGS
FGOY FOGY
FGRU FRUG
FGSU FUGS
FGUU FUGU
FHIS FISH
FHNO FOHN
FHOO HOOF
FHOW HOWF
FIJU FUJI
FIKN FINK
FIKS KIFS
FIKU KUFI
FILL FILL
FILM FILM
FILO FILO FOIL
FILP FLIP
FILR FLIR
FILS FILS
FILT FLIT LIFT
FIMR FIRM
FINO FINO FOIN INFO
FINR FIRN
FINS FINS
FIPU PFUI
FIRS FIRS RIFS
FIRT FRIT RIFT
FIRZ FRIZ
FIST FIST FITS SIFT
FITX FIXT
FIZZ FIZZ
FKLO FOLK
FKNU FUNK
FKOR FORK
FLLU FULL
FLOO FOOL LOOF
FLOP FLOP
FLOR ROLF
FLOT LOFT
FLOU FOUL
FLOW FLOW FOWL WOLF
FLRU FURL
FLSU FLUS
FLUX FLUX
FMOR FORM FROM
FMUY FUMY
FNOS FONS
FNOT FONT
FNSU FUNS
FOOP POOF
FOOR ROOF
FOOT FOOT
FOOW WOOF
FOPR PROF
FOPS FOPS
FOPU POUF
FORT FORT
FORU FOUR
FORW FROW
FOSS FOSS
FOST SOFT
FOSY FOYS
FOTT TOFT
FOTU TOFU
FOXY FOXY
FOYZ FOZY
FRSU FURS SURF
FRTU TURF
FRUY FURY
FSSU FUSS
FTTU TUFT
FTUZ FUTZ
FUZZ FUZZ
GGHO HOGG
GGIM MIGG
GGIR GRIG

GGIS GIGS
IGGS
GGLU GLUG
GGMU MUGG
GGNO GONG
NOGG
GGOO GOGO
GGOR GROG
GGUV VUGG
GHHI HIGH
GHIN NIGH
GHIS GHIS
SIGH
GHIW WHIG
GHNO HONG
GHNU HUNG
GHOS GOSH
HOGS
SHOG
GHOT GOTH
GHOY YOGH
GHPU PUGH
GHSU GUSH
HUGS
SUGH
UGHS
GHTU THUG
GHUV VUGH
GIJS JIGS
GIKN GINK
KING
GILL GILL
GILM GLIM
GILN LING
GILR GIRL
GILT GILT
GILU IGLU
GIMP GIMP
GIMR GRIM
GIMS MIGS
GINP PING
GINR GIRN
GRIN
RING
GINS GINS
SIGN
SING
GINT TING
GINW WING
GINZ ZING
GIOR GIRO
GIOY YOGI
GIPR GRIP
PRIG
GIPS GIPS
PIGS
GIRS RIGS
GIRT GIRT
GRIT
TRIG
GIRY GYRI
GIST GIST
GITS
GISV VIGS
GISW SWIG
WIGS
GISZ ZIGS
GITW TWIG
GJOS JOGS
GJSU JUGS
GKNU GUNK
GKOO GOOK
GKOR GROK
GKOW GOWK
GLLU GULL
GLMO GLOM
GLMU GLUM
GLNO LONG
GLNU LUNG
GLOO LOGO
GLOP GLOP
GLOS LOGS
SLOG
GLOW GLOW
GLOY LOGY
GLPU GULP
PLUG
GLSU GULS
LUGS
SLUG
GLTU GLUT
GLUY UGLY
GMOR GORM
GMOS MOGS
SMOG
GMRU GRUM
GMSU GUMS
MUGS
SMUG
GMSY GYMS
GNOO GOON
GNOP PONG
GNOS NOGS
SNOG
SONG
GNOT TONG
GNOW GOWN
GNPU PUNG
GNRU RUNG
GNSU GNUS
GUNS
SNUG
SUNG
GNTU TUNG
GOOP GOOP
GOOS GOOS
GOPR GORP
PROG
GOPY POGY
GORT GROT
TROG
GORW GROW
GORY GORY
GYRO
ORGY
GOST TOGS
GOTU GOUT
GPSU PUGS
GPSY GYPS
GRSU RUGS
GRTU TRUG
GRUU GURU
GSTU GUST
GUTS
TUGS
GSUV GUVS
VUGS
GSUY GUYS
HHNU HUNH
HHSU HUSH
HIIL HILI
HIKS KHIS
HIKT KITH
HILL HILL
HILT HILT
HIMS HIMS
SHIM
HIMW WHIM
HINS HINS
HISN
SHIN
SINH
HINT HINT
THIN
HINW WHIN
HIOT THIO
HIPS HIPS
PHIS
PISH
SHIP
HIPT PITH
HIPW WHIP
HIPZ PHIZ
HIRS SHRI
HIRT THIR
HIRW WHIR
HISS HISS
HIST HIST
HITS
SITH
THIS
HISV SHIV
HISW WISH
HITW WHIT
WITH
HIWZ WHIZ
HJNO JOHN
HJOS JOSH
HKLO HOLK
KOHL
HKLU HULK
HKNO HONK
HKNU HUNK
HKOO HOOK
HKOP KOPH
HKOW HOWK
HKSU HUSK
HLLU HULL
HLMO HOLM
HLOP HOLP
HLOS HOLS
HLOT HOLT
LOTH
HLOW HOWL
HLOY HOLY
HLRU HURL
HLSU LUSH
SHUL
HMNY HYMN
HMOO HOMO
HMOS MHOS
MOSH
OHMS
SHMO
HMOT MOTH
HMOW WHOM
HMOY HOMY
HMPU HUMP
HMSU HUMS
MUSH
HMTY MYTH
HNOP PHON
HNOR HORN
HNOS HONS
NOSH
HNSU HUNS
SHUN
HNTU HUNT
HOOP HOOP
POOH
HOOS OOHS
SHOO
HOOT HOOT
HOPQ QOPH
HOPS HOPS
POSH
SHOP
SOPH
HOPT PHOT
TOPH
HOPU OUPH
HOPW WHOP
HOPY HYPO
HORS RHOS
HORT THRO
HORU HOUR
HOST HOST
HOTS
SHOT
SOTH
TOSH
HOSW HOWS
SHOW
HOSY HOYS
HOTU THOU
HPSU PUSH
HPSY HYPS
SYPH
HPTU PHUT
HPUW WHUP
HRSU RHUS
RUSH
HRTU HURT
RUTH
THRU
HSTU HUTS
SHUT
THUS
TUSH
HSWY WHYS
IIKP PIKI
IIKT TIKI
IIKW KIWI
IILP PILI
IILR LIRI
IIMN MINI
IIMP IMPI
IIMR MIRI
IINS NISI
IINT INTI
IIPT TIPI
IIRS IRIS
IISW IWIS
IITT TITI
IITZ ZITI
IJKN JINK
IJKO KOJI
IJLL JILL
IJLT JILT
IJMP JIMP
IJNN JINN
IJNO JOIN
IJNS JINS
IJNX JINX
IJVY JIVY
IKKL KLIK
IKKN KINK
IKKR KIRK
IKLL KILL
IKLM MILK
IKLN KILN
LINK
IKLO KILO
IKLS ILKS
SILK
IKLT KILT
IKMN MINK
IKMR MIRK
IKMS SKIM
IKNO IKON
KINO
OINK
IKNP PINK
IKNR KIRN
RINK
IKNS INKS
KINS
SINK
SKIN
IKNT KNIT
IKNW WINK
IKNY INKY
IKOS KOIS
IKPS KIPS
SKIP
IKRS IRKS
KIRS
KRIS
RISK
IKSS KISS
SKIS
IKST KIST
KITS
SKIT
ILLM MILL
ILLN NILL
ILLO LILO
ILLP PILL
ILLR RILL
ILLS ILLS
SILL
ILLT LILT
TILL
ILLV VILL
ILLW WILL
ILLY ILLY
LILY
YILL
ILLZ ZILL
ILMN LIMN
ILMO LIMO
MILO
MOIL
ILMP LIMP
ILMS MILS
SLIM
ILMT MILT
ILMY LIMY
ILNN LINN
ILNO LINO
LION
LOIN
NOIL
ILNS LINS
NILS
ILNT LINT
ILNY INLY
LINY
ILOO OLIO
ILOR ROIL
ILOS OILS
SILO
SOIL
SOLI
ILOT LOTI
TOIL
ILOV VIOL
ILOY OILY
ILPS LIPS
LISP
SLIP
ILPU PULI
ILPY PILY
ILRT TIRL
ILRV VIRL
ILST LIST
LITS
SILT
SLIT
TILS
ILSY SYLI
ILTT TILT
ILTU LITU
ILTW WILT
ILWY WILY
IMMO MOMI
IMMY IMMY
IMNS NIMS
IMNT MINT
IMNU MUNI
IMNX MINX
IMOS MISO
IMOT OMIT
IMOX OXIM
IMPP PIMP
IMPR PRIM
IMPS IMPS
MIPS
SIMP
IMPW WIMP
IMRS MIRS
RIMS
IMRT TRIM
IMRY MIRY
RIMY
IMSS ISMS
MISS
SIMS
IMST MIST
SMIT
IMSV VIMS
IMSW SWIM
IMTT MITT
IMTX MIXT
IMTY MITY
INNS INNS
INOP PION
INOR INRO
IRON
NOIR
NORI
INOS IONS
INOT INTO
INOV VINO
INOW WINO
INOY YONI
INPR PIRN
INPS NIPS
PINS
SNIP
SPIN
INPT PINT
INPY PINY
PYIN
INQU QUIN
INRS RINS
INRU RUIN
INSS SINS
INST NITS
SNIT
TINS
INSW WINS
INSY YINS
INSZ ZINS
INTT TINT
INTU UNIT
INTW TWIN
INTY TINY
TYIN
INVY VINY
INWY WINY
INXY NIXY
IOPS PISO
POIS
IOPT TOPI
IORS SORI
IORT RIOT
ROTI
TIRO
TORI
TRIO
IORZ ZORI
IOTT TOIT
IPPS PIPS
IPPY PIPY
IPQU QUIP
IPRS RIPS
IPRT TRIP
IPRU PURI
IPSS PSIS
IPST PITS
SIPS
SPIT
TIPS
IPSV SPIV
IPSW WISP
IPSY YIPS
IPSZ ZIPS
IPTU PTUI
IPTY PITY
IPXY PIXY
IQTU QUIT
IQUZ QUIZ
IRRY YIRR
IRSS SIRS
SRIS
IRST STIR
IRTW WRIT
IRTZ RITZ
IRWY WIRY
ISST SITS
ISSW WISS
ISTT TITS
ISTU SUIT
TUIS
ISTW WIST
WITS
ISTZ ZITS
ISWY YWIS
ISYZ SIZY
ITTW TWIT
ITVY TIVY
JJUU JUJU
JKNU JUNK
JKOU JOUK
JKOY JOKY
JKUU JUKU
JLOT JOLT
JLOW JOWL
JMOO MOJO
JMPU JUMP
JOSS JOSS
JOST JOTS
JOSW JOWS
JOSY JOYS
JRUY JURY
JSTU JUST
JUTS
KKNO KONK
KKOO KOOK
KLNU LUNK
KLOO KOLO
LOOK
KLOY YOLK
KLRU LURK
KLSU SULK
KMNO MONK
KMOS MOSK
KMRU MURK
KMSU MUSK
KNOO NOOK
KNOP KNOP
KNOT KNOT
KNOW KNOW
WONK
KNOZ ZONK
KNPU PUNK
KNRU KNUR
KNSU SUNK
KOOR ROOK
KOOS SOOK
KOOT KOTO
TOOK
KOPR PORK
KOPS KOPS
KOPY POKY
KORS KORS
KORW WORK
KOSS KOSS
KOSU SOUK
KOSW WOKS
KOSY YOKS
KOUZ ZOUK
KRSU RUSK
KRTU TURK
KRUU KURU
KSST TSKS
KSSU SUKS
KSTU TUSK
KSUY YUKS
LLLO LOLL
LLLU LULL
LLMO MOLL
LLMU MULL
LLNU NULL
LLOP POLL
LLOR ROLL
LLOT TOLL
LLPU PULL
LLUU LULU
LMOO LOOM
MOOL
LMOS MOLS
LMOT MOLT
LMOY MOLY
LMPU LUMP
PLUM
LMSU LUMS
SLUM
LNOO LOON
NOLO
LNOR LORN
LNOW LOWN
LNOY ONLY
LNRU NURL
LNTU LUNT
LNUY LUNY
LNXY LYNX
LOOP LOOP
POLO
POOL
LOOS LOOS
SOLO
LOOT LOOT
TOOL
LOOW WOOL
LOPP PLOP
LOPS LOPS
POLS
SLOP
LOPT PLOT
LOPU LOUP
LOPW PLOW
LOPY PLOY
POLY
LORT ROTL
LORU LOUR
LORY LORY
LOSS LOSS
SOLS
LOST LOST
LOTS
SLOT
LOSU SOUL
LOSW LOWS
OWLS
SLOW
LOTU LOUT
TOLU
LOTV VOLT
LOWY YOWL
LPPU PULP
LPRU PURL
LPSU PLUS
PULS
LRSU SLUR
LRUY RULY
LSTU LUST
SLUT
LSUU SULU
ULUS
LSUV LUVS
LTUZ LUTZ
MMMU MUMM
MMOS MOMS
MMPU MUMP
MMSU MUMS
MMUU MUMU
MNOO MONO
MOON
MNOR MORN
NORM
MNOS MONS
NOMS
MNOU MUON
MNOW MOWN
MNOY MONY
MNSU MUNS
MOOP POMO
MOOR MOOR
ROOM
MOOS MOOS
MOOT MOOT
TOOM
MOOZ MOZO
ZOOM
MOPP POMP
MOPR PROM
ROMP
MOPS MOPS
MOPY MOPY
MORS MORS
ROMS
MORT MORT
MORW WORM
MOSS MOSS
SOMS
MOST MOST
MOTS
TOMS
MOSU SUMO
MOSW MOWS
MOTT MOTT
MOUV OVUM
MPPU PUMP
MPRU RUMP
MPSU SUMP
UMPS
MPTU TUMP
MRRU MURR
MRSU RUMS
MSSU MUSS
SUMS
MSTU MUST
MUTS
SMUT
STUM
MSUW SWUM
MTTU MUTT
NNOO NOON
NNOU NOUN
NNSU NUNS
SUNN
NNWY WYNN
NOOP POON
NOOS ONOS
SOON
NOOT ONTO
TOON
NOOZ ZOON
NOPR PORN
NOPS PONS
NOPU UPON
NOPY PONY
NORS SORN
NORT TORN
NORW WORN
NOSS SONS
NOST SNOT
TONS
NOSU NOUS
ONUS
NOSW NOWS
OWNS
SNOW
SOWN
WONS
NOSY NOSY
NOTU UNTO
NOTW NOWT
TOWN
WONT
NOTY TONY
NOXY ONYX
NPSU PUNS
SPUN
NPTU PUNT
NPUY PUNY
NRSU RUNS
URNS
NRTU RUNT
TURN
NSSU SUNS
NSTU NUTS
STUN
TUNS
NSWY WYNS
OOPP POOP
OOPR POOR
OOPS OOPS
OOPT TOPO
OORT ROOT
ROTO
TORO
OORZ ORZO
OOST OOTS
SOOT
OOSW WOOS
OOSZ ZOOS
OOTT OTTO
TOOT
OOTY TOYO
OOUZ OUZO
OOYZ OOZY
OPPR PROP
OPPS POPS
OPRS PROS
OPRT PORT
TROP
OPRU POUR
ROUP
OPRW PROW
OPRY PYRO
ROPY
OPSS SOPS
OPST OPTS
POST
POTS
SPOT
STOP
TOPS
OPSU OPUS
SOUP
OPSW POWS
SWOP
OPSY POSY
OPTU POUT
OPTY TYPO
OPXY POXY
ORRT TORR
ORST ORTS
ROTS
SORT
TORS
ORSU OURS
SOUR
ORSW ROWS
ORSY ROSY
ORTT TORT
TROT
ORTU ROUT
TOUR
ORTW TROW
WORT
ORTY RYOT
TORY
TROY
TYRO
ORUX ROUX
ORUY YOUR
ORVW VROW
ORXY ORYX
OSST SOTS
TOSS
OSSU SOUS
OSSW SOWS
OSSY SOYS
OSTT STOT
TOST
TOTS
OSTU OUST
OUTS
OSTW STOW
SWOT
TOWS
TWOS
WOST
WOTS
OSTY TOYS
OSUY YOUS
OSVW VOWS
OSWW WOWS
OSWY YOWS
OTTU TOUT
OTWY TOWY
PPSU PUPS
PPTY TYPP
PPUU PUPU
PRRU PURR
PRSU PURS
SPUR
URPS
PRSY SPRY
PSST PSST
PSSU PUSS
SUPS
PSTU PUTS
TUPS
PSUY YUPS
PTTU PUTT
PTUZ PUTZ
PTYY TYPY
QSSU SUQS
RSTU RUST
RUTS
RSUU URUS
RTUY YURT
SSSU SUSS
SSUW WUSS
STTU TUTS
STXY XYST
TTUU TUTU
TUYZ YUTZ

5-Letter Alphagrams

AAABC ABACA
AAABK ABAKA
AAABY ABAYA
AAAGM AGAMA
AAANS ASANA
AABBK BABKA
KABAB
AABBS ABBAS
BABAS
AABCC BACCA
AABCI ABACI
AABCK ABACK
AABCL CABAL
AABCR BARCA
AABDE BAAED
AABDN BANDA
AABEM ABEAM
AMEBA
AABES ABASE
AABET ABATE
AABFT ABAFT
AABGM GAMBA
AABHS ABASH
AABIL LABIA
AABIZ BAIZA
AABKR KABAR
AABLN BANAL
AABLR LABRA
AABLS ALBAS
BAALS
BALAS
BALSA
BASAL
SABAL
AABLT TABLA
AABMM MAMBA
AABMO ABOMA
AABMP ABAMP
AABMS SAMBA
AABNW BWANA
NAWAB
AABRS SABRA
AABRT RABAT
AABRV BRAVA
AABRZ BAZAR
BRAZA
AACCE CAECA
AACCO CACAO
AACCS CACAS
AACDH DACHA
AACEI AECIA
AACEP APACE
AACER ARECA
AACET ACETA
AACFI FACIA
AACHP PACHA
AACIR ACARI
AACJL JACAL
AACKL ALACK
AACLL CALLA
AACLN CANAL
AACLO COALA
AACLR CRAAL
AACMS CAMAS
AACMW MACAW
AACNN CANNA
AACPS PACAS
AACRS SACRA
AACRT CARAT
AACSS CASAS
AACUV VACUA
AADDS DADAS
AADDU AUDAD
AADDX ADDAX
AADEG ADAGE
AADEH AAHED
AHEAD
AADFR FARAD
AADGG DAGGA
AADGR GARDA
AADHL HADAL
AADIN NAIAD
AADLN ALAND
AADLS SALAD
AADMM MADAM
AADMN ADMAN
DAMAN
AADMR DAMAR
DRAMA
AADNP PANDA
AADNS NADAS
AADNV VANDA
AADPT ADAPT
AADRR RADAR
AADRW AWARD
AADTY ADYTA
AAEER AREAE
AAEFN FAENA
AAEGL ALGAE
GALEA
AAEGP AGAPE
AAEGT AGATE
AAEGV AGAVE
AAEGZ AGAZE
AAEKL AKELA
AAEKP APEAK
AAEKW AWAKE
AAELN ALANE
AAELP PALEA
AAELR AREAL
AAELT ALATE
AAEMR ARAME
AAEMZ AMAZE
AAENP APNEA
PAEAN
AAENR ANEAR
ARENA
AAENS ANSAE
AAENT ANTAE
AAEPR AREPA
PARAE
AAEQU AQUAE
AAERS AREAS
AAERT REATA
AAERU AURAE
AAERW AWARE
AAFGN FANGA
AAFHS HAAFS
AAFIM MAFIA
AAFIT TAFIA
AAFKN NAKFA
AAFLS ALFAS
AAFLT FATAL
AAFNU FAUNA
AAFRS AFARS
AAFSV FAVAS
AAFTW FATWA
AAGHL GALAH
AAGHR AARGH
AAGHS AGHAS
AAGIM AMIGA
AAGIN AGAIN
AAGIR AGRIA
AAGIS SAIGA
AAGIT AGITA
TAIGA
AAGJN GANJA
AAGJR JAGRA
AAGJU AJUGA
AAGLL ALGAL
AAGLN ALANG
LAGAN
AAGLR ARGAL
GRAAL
AAGLS ALGAS
GALAS
AAGLV VAGAL
AAGLX GALAX
AAGLY GAYAL
AAGMM GAMMA
MAGMA
AAGMN MANGA
AAGMR GRAMA
AAGMS AGMAS
GAMAS
AAGMY GAMAY
AAGNP PAGAN
PANGA
AAGNR GRANA
AAGNS ANGAS
SANGA
AAGNT TANGA
AAGOR AGORA
AAGRS AGARS
RAGAS
AAGRZ GAZAR
AAGSS SAGAS
AAGSV AVGAS
AAGUV GUAVA
AAHHS HAHAS
AAHIK HAIKA
AAHJR RAJAH
AAHKS KASHA
AAHLL HALAL
AAHLM ALMAH
HALMA
HAMAL
AAHLO ALOHA
AAHLP ALPHA
AAHLR LAHAR
AAHLV HALVA
AAHMS AMAHS
AAHMZ HAMZA
AAHNS HANSA
AAHNZ HAZAN
AAHPS PASHA
AAHPX HAPAX
AAHRS HAARS
AAHRT ARHAT
AAHRY RAYAH
AAHSW AWASH
AAHSY AYAHS
AAIIL AALII
AAIJV AJIVA
AAIKK KAIAK
AAILM LAMIA
AAILN LANAI
LIANA
AAILR LAARI
AAILS ALIAS
AAILV AVAIL
AAILX AXIAL
AAILY ALIYA
AAIMN AMAIN
AMNIA
ANIMA
MANIA
AAIMR MARIA
AAIMS AMIAS
AAIMZ ZAMIA
AAINP APIAN
AAINR NAIRA
AAINV AVIAN
AAIPS PAISA
AAIRS ARIAS
RAIAS
AAIRT ATRIA
RAITA
RIATA
TIARA
AAIRV VARIA
AAISS ASSAI
AAITW AWAIT
AAJLP JALAP
AAJNN JNANA
AAJNP JAPAN
AAJNW JAWAN
AAJRS RAJAS
AAJSV JAVAS
AAKKS KAKAS
AAKKY KAYAK
AAKLM KALAM
AAKLO KOALA
AAKLP KALPA
AAKLR KRAAL
AAKMR KARMA
MAKAR
MARKA
AAKNS KANAS
AAKNT TANKA
AAKPP KAPPA
AAKPR PARKA
AAKPS KAPAS
AAKRS ARAKS
AAKRT KARAT
AAKST KATAS
TAKAS
AAKSV KAVAS
AALLM LLAMA
AALLS SALAL
AALLU ALULA
AALLW WALLA
AALLY ALLAY
AALMO ALAMO
AALMR ALARM
MALAR
RAMAL
AALMS ALMAS
LAMAS
AALMT TAMAL
AALMU ULAMA
AALNN ANNAL
AALNS ALANS
ANLAS
NALAS
NASAL
AALNT ALANT
NATAL
AALNU LAUAN
AALNV NAVAL
AALNY NYALA
AALPP APPAL
PAPAL
AALPS SALPA
AALPY PLAYA
AALPZ PLAZA
AALRT ALTAR
ARTAL
RATAL
TALAR
AALRU AURAL
LAURA
AALRV ARVAL
LARVA
AALRY ALARY
AALRZ LAZAR
AALSS SALSA
AALST ATLAS
TALAS
AALSV LAVAS
VASAL
AALSY ASYLA
AALWY ALWAY
AAMMM MAMMA
AAMMS MAMAS
AAMNN MANNA
AAMNS MANAS
AAMNT ATMAN
MANAT
MANTA
AAMNX AXMAN
AAMNY MAYAN
AAMOR AROMA
AAMOS OMASA
AAMPP PAMPA
AAMPR PRAAM
AAMRS MAARS
MARAS
AAMSS AMASS
MASAS
MASSA
AAMST ATMAS
AAMSY MAYAS
AAMTZ MATZA
AANNS ANNAS
NAANS
NANAS
AANOS ANOAS
AANPP NAPPA
AANPS NAPAS
AANPV PAVAN
AANQT QANAT
AANRS SARAN
AANRT ANTRA
RATAN
AANRU RUANA
AANRV NAVAR
VARNA
AANST ANTAS
AANSU SAUNA
AANSZ AZANS
AANTV AVANT
AANZZ ZANZA
AAORT AORTA
AAPPS PAPAS
AAPPW PAPAW
AAPRS PARAS
AAPRT APART
AAPST ATAPS
PASTA
TAPAS
AAPTW WATAP
AAQSU AQUAS
AARRS ARRAS
AARRU AURAR
AARRY ARRAY
AARSU AURAS
AARSV VARAS
AARSY RAYAS
AARTT ATTAR
TATAR
AASSY ASSAY
AASTV AVAST
AASTY SATAY
AATXY ATAXY
AATZZ TAZZA
ABBCO CABOB
ABBCY CABBY
ABBEK KEBAB
ABBEL BABEL
ABBER BARBE
ABBES ABBES
BABES
ABBEY ABBEY
ABBGY GABBY
ABBIR RABBI
ABBKO KABOB
ABBLS BLABS
ABBLU BABUL
BUBAL
ABBNO NABOB
ABBOO BABOO
ABBOT ABBOT
ABBRS BARBS
ABBSU BABUS
ABBTY TABBY
ABBYY YABBY
ABCEH BEACH
ABCEI CEIBA
ABCEL CABLE
ABCEP BECAP
ABCER ACERB
BRACE
CABER
ABCHR BRACH
ABCHT BATCH
ABCIN CABIN
ABCIO COBIA
ABCIR BARIC
RABIC
ABCIS BASIC
ABCKL BLACK
ABCKS BACKS
ABCNO BACON
BANCO
ABCOR CARBO
CAROB
COBRA
ABCOV VOCAB
ABCRS CARBS
CRABS
ABCRT BRACT
ABCSS SCABS
ABCSU SCUBA
ABDDY BADDY
ABDEG BADGE
DEBAG
ABDEI ABIDE
ABDEK BAKED
ABDEL ABLED
BALED
BLADE
ABDEN BANED
ABDEO ABODE
ADOBE
ABDER ARDEB
BARDE
BARED
BEARD
BREAD
DEBAR
ABDES BASED
BEADS
SABED
ABDET BATED
ABDEU DAUBE
ABDEY BAYED
BEADY
ABDIR BRAID
RABID
ABDIT TABID
ABDLN BLAND
ABDLO DOBLA
ABDLS BALDS
ABDLY BADLY
BALDY
ABDNR BRAND
ABDNS BANDS
ABDNY BANDY
ABDOO ADOBO
ABDOR BOARD
BROAD
DOBRA
ABDRS BARDS
BRADS
DARBS
DRABS
ABDSU BAUDS
DAUBS
ABDSW BAWDS
ABDUY DAUBY
ABDWY BAWDY
ABEEL ABELE
ABEFL FABLE
ABEGL BAGEL
BELGA
GABLE
GLEBA
ABEGM GAMBE
ABEGN BEGAN
ABEGR BARGE
ABEGT BEGAT
ABEHO BOHEA
OBEAH
ABEHR REHAB
ABEHT BATHE
ABEIZ BAIZE
ABEJM JAMBE
ABEKL BLEAK
ABEKR BAKER
BRAKE
BREAK
KEBAR
ABEKS BAKES
BEAKS
ABEKY BEAKY
ABELL LABEL
ABELM AMBLE
BLAME
ABELR ABLER
BALER
BLARE
BLEAR
ABELS ABLES
BALES
BLASE
SABLE
ABELT BLATE
BLEAT
TABLE
ABELY BELAY
ABELZ BLAZE
ABEMR AMBER
BREAM
EMBAR
ABEMS BEAMS
BEMAS
MABES
ABEMY BEAMY
EMBAY
MAYBE
ABENO BEANO
ABENS BANES
BEANS
NABES
ABEOV ABOVE
ABERR BARER
BARRE
REBAR
ABERS BARES
BASER
BEARS
BRAES
SABER
SABRE
ABERT TABER
ABERV BRAVE
ABERY BARYE
YERBA
ABERZ BRAZE
ZEBRA
ABESS BASES
SABES
ABEST ABETS
BASTE
BATES
BEAST
BEATS
BETAS
TABES
ABESU ABUSE
BEAUS
ABESY ABYES
ABETT BETTA
ABETU BEAUT
TUBAE
ABEUX BEAUX
ABFFL BLAFF
ABFFS BAFFS
ABFFY BAFFY
ABFLS FLABS
ABFRS BARFS
ABGGY BAGGY
ABGHN BHANG
ABGMS GAMBS
ABGNO BOGAN
GOBAN
ABGNS BANGS
ABGRS BRAGS
GARBS
GRABS
ABHIJ HIJAB
ABHIM BIMAH
ABHIS SAHIB
ABHIT BAITH
HABIT
ABHLS BLAHS
ABHMO ABMHO
ABOHM
ABHOR ABHOR
ABHRS BRASH
ABHST BAHTS
BATHS
ABHSU HABUS
SUBAH
ABIIL ALIBI
BIALI
ABIIM IAMBI
ABIIT TIBIA
ABIKL KIBLA
ABIKT BATIK
ABILM LIMBA
ABILN BINAL
BLAIN
ABILO ABOIL
ABILP PIBAL
ABILR BRAIL
LIBRA
ABILS BAILS
BASIL
ABILY BIALY
ABIMR MBIRA
ABIMS BIMAS
IAMBS
ABIMT AMBIT
ABINR BAIRN
BRAIN
ABINS BASIN
NABIS
SABIN
ABINU NUBIA
ABIOS OBIAS
ABIOT BIOTA
ABIRR BRIAR
ABIRS ABRIS
SABIR
ABIRU URBIA
ABIRV BRAVI
ABISS BASIS
BASSI
ISBAS
ABIST BAITS
ABJMS JAMBS
ABJNO BANJO
ABJOT JABOT
ABJSU JUBAS
ABKLN BLANK
ABKLS BALKS
ABKLU BAULK
ABKLY BALKY
ABKNR BRANK
ABKNS BANKS
ABKRS BARKS
KBARS
ABKRU BURKA
ABKRY BARKY
BRAKY
ABKSS BASKS
ABLLS BALLS
ABLLU BULLA
ABLLY BALLY
ABLMS BALMS
BLAMS
LAMBS
ABLMU ALBUM
ABLMY BALMY
LAMBY
ABLNW BLAWN
ABLOR BOLAR
BORAL
LABOR
LOBAR
ABLOS BOLAS
ABLOT BLOAT
ABLOY BOYLA
ABLRW BRAWL
ABLSS SLABS
ABLST BLAST
BLATS
ABLSW BAWLS
BLAWS
ABLTU TUBAL
ABLWY BYLAW
ABMMO MAMBO
ABMOS AMBOS
SAMBO
ABMRS BARMS
ABMRU RUMBA
UMBRA
ABMRY AMBRY
BARMY
ABMSY ABYSM
ABNNS BANNS
ABNNU UNBAN
ABNOO ABOON
ABNOR BARON
ABNOT BATON
ABNRS BARNS
BRANS
ABNRT BRANT
ABNRU BURAN
UNBAR
URBAN
ABNRW BRAWN
ABNRY BARNY
ABNSU BUNAS
ABNTU TABUN
ABNTY BANTY
ABNUY BUNYA
ABOOT TABOO
ABOOZ BAZOO
ABORR ARBOR
ABORS BOARS
BORAS
ABORT ABORT
BOART
TABOR
ABORV BRAVO
ABORX BORAX
ABORY BOYAR
ABOSS BASSO
SOBAS
ABOST BOAST
BOATS
BOTAS
SABOT
ABOTU ABOUT
ABOUY BAYOU
ABQRU BURQA
ABQSU SQUAB
ABRSS BRASS
ABRST BRATS
ABRSU BURAS
BURSA
ABRSW BRAWS
ABRSY BRAYS
ABRXY BRAXY
ABSST BASTS
STABS
ABSSU SUBAS
ABSSW SWABS
ABSSY ABYSS
BASSY
ABSTT BATTS
ABSTU ABUTS
TABUS
TSUBA
TUBAS
ABTTU BATTU
ABTTY BATTY
ABTWY BAWTY
ABUZZ ABUZZ
ABWYY BYWAY
ACCDY CYCAD
ACCEH CACHE
ACCEL CECAL
ACCEM MECCA
ACCHI CHICA
ACCHL CLACH
ACCHO COACH
ACCHT CATCH
ACCIM ACMIC
ACCIR CIRCA
ACCIT CACTI
ACCIW WICCA
ACCKL CLACK
ACCKO ACOCK
ACCKR CRACK
ACCOO COCOA
ACCOS COCAS
ACCOT COACT
ACCSY CYCAS
ACCUY YUCCA
ACDDY CADDY
ACDEF DECAF
FACED
ACDEG CADGE
CAGED
ACDEH ACHED
ACDEK CAKED
ACDEL CLADE
DECAL
LACED
ACDEM MACED
ACDEN ACNED
CANED
DANCE
ACDEP CAPED
PACED
ACDER ACRED
ARCED
CADRE
CARED
CEDAR
RACED
ACDES CADES
CASED
DACES
ACDET ACTED
CADET
ACDEV CAVED
ACDEW CAWED
ACDEY DECAY
ACDGY CADGY
ACDHR CHARD
ACDHS CHADS
ACDIL ALCID
ACDIN CANID
CNIDA
NICAD
ACDIR ACRID
CAIRD
DARIC
ACDIS ACIDS
ASDIC
CADIS
CAIDS
ACDIT DICTA
ACDIY ACIDY
ACDLO ACOLD
ACDLS CLADS
SCALD
ACDLU CAULD
DUCAL
ACDLY YCLAD
ACDNU ADUNC
ACDNY CANDY
ACDOS CODAS
ACDOT OCTAD
ACDRS CARDS
ACDSS SCADS
ACDTU DUCAT
ACEEK ACKEE
ACEEP PEACE
ACEES CEASE
ACEFH CHAFE
ACEFL FECAL
ACEFR FACER
FARCE
ACEFS CAFES
FACES
ACEFT FACET
ACEGL GLACE
ACEGR CAGER
GRACE
ACEGS CAGES
ACEGY CAGEY
ACEHK HACEK
ACEHL CHELA
LEACH
ACEHM MACHE
ACEHN HANCE
ACEHP CHAPE
CHEAP
PEACH
ACEHR CHARE
REACH
ACEHS ACHES
CHASE
ACEHT CHEAT
TACHE
TEACH
THECA
ACEIL ILEAC
ACEIM AMICE
ACEIR AREIC
CERIA
ERICA
ACEIS SAICE
ACEIV CAVIE
ACEKR CRAKE
CREAK
ACEKS CAKES
ACEKW WACKE
ACEKY CAKEY
ACELL CELLA
ACELM CAMEL
MACLE
ACELN CLEAN
LANCE
ACELP PLACE
ACELR CARLE
CLEAR
LACER

ACELS ALECS
LACES
SCALE
ACELT CLEAT
ECLAT
ACELV CALVE
CLAVE
ACELY LACEY
LYCEA
ACEMO CAMEO
COMAE
ACEMR CREAM
MACER
ACEMS ACMES
CAMES
MACES
ACEMY CYMAE
ACENO CANOE
OCEAN
ACENP PECAN
ACENR CANER
CRANE
NACRE
RANCE
ACENS ACNES
CANES
SCENA
ACENT ENACT
ACEOR OCREA
ACEOX COXAE
ACEPR CAPER
CRAPE
PACER
RECAP
ACEPS CAPES
PACES
SCAPE
SPACE
ACEPT EPACT
ACEPY PACEY
ACERR CARER
RACER
ACERS ACRES
CARES
CARSE
ESCAR
RACES
SCARE
SERAC
ACERT CARET
CARTE
CATER
CRATE
REACT
RECTA
TRACE
ACERV CARVE
CAVER
CRAVE
ACERX CAREX
ACERZ CRAZE
ACESS CASES
ACEST CASTE
CATES
CESTA
TACES
ACESU CAUSE
SAUCE
ACESV CAVES
ACETT TACET
TECTA
ACETU ACUTE
ACETX EXACT
ACFFH CHAFF
ACFFS CAFFS
ACFHU CHUFA
ACFIL CALIF
ACFIM MAFIC
ACFIN FINCA
ACFIR FARCI
ACFKL FLACK
ACFLO FOCAL
ACFLS CALFS
ACFNR FRANC
ACFNY FANCY
ACFRS SCARF
ACFRT CRAFT
ACFRY FARCY
ACFST FACTS
ACGHN CHANG
ACGIM GAMIC
MAGIC
ACGIN ACING
ACGIR CIGAR
ACGLN CLANG
ACGLS CLAGS
ACGNO CONGA
ACGOR CARGO
ACGOU GUACO
ACGRS CRAGS
SCRAG
ACGSS SCAGS
ACHHT HATCH
ACHIL LAICH
ACHIN CHAIN
CHINA
ACHIO CHIAO
ACHIR CHAIR
ACHIS CHAIS
CHIAS
ACHIT AITCH
ACHKL CHALK
ACHKR CHARK
ACHKS HACKS
SHACK
ACHKT THACK
ACHKW WHACK
ACHLO CHOLA
LOACH
ACHLR LARCH
ACHLS CLASH
ACHLT LATCH
ACHMO MACHO
MOCHA
ACHMP CHAMP
ACHMR CHARM
MARCH
ACHMS CHAMS
CHASM
MACHS
ACHMT MATCH
ACHNO ANCHO
NACHO
ACHNR RANCH
ACHNT CHANT
NATCH
ACHNU NUCHA
ACHOO ACHOO
ACHOP POACH
ACHOR ORACH
ROACH
ACHOS CHAOS
ACHOV HAVOC
ACHOW CAHOW
ACHPR PARCH
ACHPS CAPHS
CHAPS
ACHPT CHAPT
PATCH
ACHRR CHARR
ACHRS CHARS
CRASH
ACHRT CHART
RATCH
ACHRY CHARY
ACHST CHATS
TACHS
ACHSU SAUCH
ACHSV SCHAV
ACHSW CHAWS
SCHWA
ACHSY CHAYS
ACHTW WATCH
ACHTY YACHT
ACIIL CILIA
ILIAC
ACIIM AMICI
ACIIN ACINI
ACILL LILAC
ACILM CLAIM
MALIC
ACILN LINAC
ACILP PICAL
PLICA
ACILS LAICS
SALIC
ACILT TICAL
ACILU AULIC
ACILV CAVIL
CLAVI
ACILX CALIX
ACIMN AMNIC
MANIC
ACIMP CAMPI
ACIMR MICRA
ACIMS MICAS
ACIMU UMIAC
ACINP PANIC
ACINR CAIRN
NARIC
ACINS CAINS
ACINT ACTIN
ANTIC
ACINU UNCIA
ACINV VINCA
ACIOR CORIA
ACIOT COATI
ACIOZ AZOIC
ACIPR CARPI
ACIPS ASPIC
PICAS
SPICA
ACIPZ CAPIZ
ACIRT TRIAC
ACIRU AURIC
CURIA
ACIRV VICAR
ACITT ATTIC
TACIT
ACITV VATIC
ACJKS JACKS
ACJKY JACKY
ACJNO CAJON
ACKKN KNACK
ACKKY KYACK
ACKLN CLANK
ACKLO CLOAK
ACKLP PLACK
ACKLS CALKS
LACKS
SLACK
ACKLU CAULK
ACKMS MACKS
SMACK
ACKMU AMUCK
ACKNR CRANK
ACKNS SNACK
ACKOR CROAK
ACKOW WACKO
ACKPS PACKS
ACKPU PUCKA
ACKQU QUACK
ACKRS CARKS
RACKS
ACKRT TRACK
ACKRW WRACK
ACKSS CASKS
SACKS
ACKST STACK
TACKS
ACKSW WACKS
ACKSY CASKY
YACKS
ACKTY TACKY
ACKWY WACKY
ACLLO LOCAL
ACLLS CALLS
SCALL
ACLMO COMAL
ACLMP CLAMP
ACLMS CALMS
CLAMS
ACLNS CLANS
ACLOP COPAL
ACLOR CAROL
CLARO
CORAL
ACLOS CALOS
COALS
COLAS
ACLOT OCTAL
ACLOV VOCAL
ACLOX COXAL
ACLOY COALY
ACLOZ COLZA
ACLPS CLAPS
CLASP
SCALP
ACLPT CLAPT
ACLPU CULPA
ACLRS CARLS
ACLRW CRAWL
ACLRY CLARY
LYCRA
ACLSS CLASS
ACLST CLAST
TALCS
ACLSU CAULS
ACLSW CLAWS
ACLSY ACYLS
CLAYS
SCALY
ACLXY CALYX
ACMMO COMMA
ACMNO MACON
ACMOP CAMPO
ACMOR CAROM
MACRO
ACMOS CAMOS
COMAS
ACMPR CRAMP
ACMPS CAMPS
SCAMP
ACMPY CAMPY
ACMRS CRAMS
MARCS
SCRAM
ACMRY CYMAR
ACMSS SCAMS
ACMSU MUSCA
SUMAC
ACMSY CYMAS
ACNNO ANCON
CANON
ACNNY CANNY
ACNOP CAPON
ACNOR ACORN
NARCO
RACON
ACNOS CANSO
ACNOT CANTO
COTAN
OCTAN
ACNOY CYANO
ACNPU UNCAP
ACNRS CARNS
NARCS
ACNRY CARNY
ACNSS SCANS
ACNST CANST
CANTS
SCANT
ACNSY CYANS
ACNTY CANTY
ACOPR COPRA
ACOPS CAPOS
ACOPT COAPT
ACOPY COPAY
ACORS ORCAS
ACORT ACTOR
TAROC
ACOSS SOCAS
ACOST ASCOT
COAST
COATS
COSTA
TACOS
ACOTT COTTA
ACPPU CUPPA
ACPRS CARPS
CRAPS
SCARP
SCRAP
ACPST PACTS
ACPSU SCAUP
ACPSY SPACY
ACPTU CAPUT
ACRRS CARRS
ACRRU CRURA
ACRRY CARRY
ACRSS CRASS
SCARS
ACRST CARTS
SCART
ACRSU ARCUS
SCAUR
ACRSW CRAWS
ACRSY SCARY
ACRSZ CZARS
ACRTT TRACT
ACRYZ CRAZY
ACSST CASTS
SCATS
ACSSU ASCUS
CASUS
ACSTT SCATT
TACTS
ACSTU SCUTA
ACSUY SAUCY
YUCAS
ACTTY CATTY
ADDDE ADDED
ADDDY DADDY
ADDEF FADED
ADDEH HADED
ADDEI AIDED
ADDEJ JADED
ADDEL ADDLE
DEDAL
LADED
ADDER ADDER
DARED
DREAD
READD
ADDES DEADS
ADDET DATED
ADDEW DAWED
WADED
ADDEZ ADZED
DAZED
ADDFY FADDY
ADDGI GADDI
GADID
ADDHO HODAD
ADDNY DANDY
ADDOS DADOS
ADDPY PADDY
ADDRY DRYAD
ADDSU DUADS
ADDSY DYADS
ADDWY WADDY
ADEEM ADEEM
EDEMA
ADEER EARED
ADEES AEDES
EASED
ADEEV DEAVE
EAVED
EVADE
ADEFG FADGE
ADEFK FAKED
ADEFM FAMED
ADEFR FADER
FARED
ADEFS FADES
ADEFT DEFAT
FATED
ADEFX FAXED
ADEFY FAYED
ADEFZ FAZED
ADEGG GAGED
ADEGL GLADE
ADEGM GAMED
ADEGP GAPED
PAGED
ADEGR GRADE
RAGED
ADEGS DEGAS
EGADS
ADEGT GATED
ADEGW WAGED
ADEGZ GAZED
ADEHJ JEHAD
ADEHK KHEDA
ADEHL HALED
ADEHR HARED
HEARD
ADEHS ASHED
DEASH
HADES
HEADS
SADHE
SHADE
ADEHT DEATH
HATED
ADEHW HAWED
ADEHX HEXAD
ADEHY HAYED
HEADY
ADEHZ HAZED
ADEIL AILED
IDEAL
ADEIM AIMED
AMIDE
MEDIA
ADEIR AIDER
AIRED
DEAIR
IRADE
REDIA
ADEIS AIDES
ASIDE
IDEAS
ADEIU ADIEU
ADEIZ AZIDE
ADEJP JAPED
ADEJS JADES
ADEJW JAWED
ADEKL LAKED
ADEKN KNEAD
NAKED
ADEKR DRAKE
RAKED
ADEKS ASKED
ADEKW WAKED
ADELL LADLE
ADELM LAMED
MEDAL
ADELN ELAND
LADEN
NALED
ADELP PADLE
PALED
PEDAL
PLEAD
ADELR ALDER
LADER
ADELS DALES
DEALS
LADES
LASED
LEADS
ADELT DEALT
DELTA
LATED
ADELV LAVED
ADELW LAWED
WALED
WEALD
ADELX AXLED
ADELY DELAY
LAYED
LEADY
ADELZ LAZED
ADEMN ADMEN
AMEND
MANED
MENAD
NAMED
ADEMP AMPED
ADEMR ARMED
DERMA
DREAM
MADRE
ADEMS DAMES
MEADS
ADEMT MATED
TAMED
ADEMW MAWED
ADEMX MAXED
ADEMY MAYED
ADEMZ MAZED
ADENO ANODE
ADENP PANED
ADENR DENAR
REDAN
ADENS DEANS
SANED
SEDAN
ADENT ANTED
ADENV DAVEN
VANED
ADENW AWNED
DAWEN
DEWAN
WANED
ADEOR ADORE
OARED
OREAD
ADEOZ ADOZE
ADEPR DRAPE
PADRE
PARED
RAPED
ADEPS SPADE
SPAED
ADEPT ADEPT
PATED
TAPED
ADEPV PAVED
ADEPW PAWED
ADEPY PAYED
ADERR DARER
DREAR
RARED
ADERS DARES
DEARS
RASED
READS
ADERT DATER
DERAT
RATED
TARED
TRADE
TREAD
ADERV DRAVE
RAVED
ADERW DEWAR
WADER
WARED
ADERX RAXED
ADERY DEARY
DERAY
RAYED
READY
ADERZ RAZED
ADESS SADES
ADEST DATES
SATED
STADE
STEAD
TSADE
ADESV DEVAS
SAVED
ADESW SAWED
WADES
ADESY SAYED
ADESZ ADZES
DAZES
ADETW TAWED
ADETX TAXED
ADEVW WAVED
ADEWX DEWAX
WAXED
ADEWY YAWED
ADFFR DRAFF
ADFFS DAFFS
ADFFY DAFFY
ADFLU FAULD
ADFOS FADOS
ADFRS FARDS
ADFRT DRAFT
ADFRU FRAUD
ADFRW DWARF
ADGIL ALGID
ADGIS GADIS
ADGLN GLAND
ADGLS GLADS
ADGLY GLADY
ADGMO DOGMA
ADGNO DONGA
GONAD
ADGNR GRAND
ADGNS DANGS
ADGOP PAGOD
ADGOS GOADS
ADGRS DRAGS
GRADS
ADGRU GUARD
ADGSU GAUDS
ADGUY GAUDY
ADHIJ HADJI
JIHAD
ADHIK KHADI
ADHIL HALID
ADHIP APHID
ADHIS DASHI
ADHKS DHAKS
ADHLO AHOLD
ADHLS DAHLS
DHALS
ADHNO HONDA
ADHNS HANDS
ADHNY HANDY
ADHOR HOARD
ADHOS ODAHS
ADHRS HARDS
SHARD
ADHRY HARDY
HYDRA
ADHSS SHADS
ADHST HADST
ADHSU SADHU
ADHSY DASHY
SHADY
ADIIL ILIAD
ADIIO OIDIA
ADIIR RADII
ADIKS KADIS
ADILN NIDAL
ADILP PLAID
ADILR DRAIL
LAIRD
LIARD
LIDAR
ADILS DIALS
ADILT TIDAL
ADILU DULIA
ADILV VALID
ADILY DAILY
ADIMO AMIDO
ADIMR DIRAM
ADIMS AMIDS
MAIDS
ADIMT ADMIT
ADIMX ADMIX
ADINO DANIO
ADINR DINAR
DRAIN
NADIR
RANID
ADINV DIVAN
VIAND
ADINW DIWAN
ADIOP PODIA
ADIOR AROID
RADIO
ADIOS ADIOS
ADIOU AUDIO
ADIOV AVOID
ADIOZ AZIDO
DIAZO
ADIPR PADRI
PARDI
RAPID
ADIPS PADIS
SAPID
ADIPV PAVID
VAPID
ADIQS QADIS
QAIDS
ADIRS RAIDS
ADIRT TRIAD
ADIRX RADIX
ADIRY DAIRY
DIARY
YAIRD
ADISS SADIS
SAIDS
ADIST ADITS
DITAS
STAID
TSADI
ADISV DIVAS
ADISW WADIS
ADISY DAISY
SAYID
ADITU AUDIT
ADITV DAVIT
ADJSU JUDAS
ADKLS SKALD
ADKLY ALKYD
ADKMU DUMKA
ADKNR DRANK
ADKOV VODKA
ADKRS DARKS
ADKSW DAWKS
ADLLO ALDOL
ALLOD
ADLLY DALLY
ADLMO DOLMA
DOMAL
MODAL
ADLMU ALMUD
ADLMY MADLY
ADLNO NODAL
ADLNS LANDS
ADLNU ULNAD
ADLOS LOADS
ADLOT DOTAL
ADLOU ALOUD
DOULA
ADLOW WOALD
ADLRS LARDS
ADLRU DURAL
ADLRW DRAWL
ADLRY LARDY
LYARD
ADLSU DUALS
LAUDS
ADLSY SADLY
ADLTU ADULT
ADLUY YAULD
ADMNO MONAD
NOMAD
ADMNS DAMNS
ADMNU DUNAM
MAUND
ADMOU DOUMA
ADMPS DAMPS
ADMRS DRAMS
ADMRU MUDRA
ADMSU DUMAS
MAUDS
ADMTU DATUM
ADNNO DONNA
ADNOR ADORN
ANDRO
RADON
ADNOS DONAS
ADNOW ADOWN
ADNPY PANDY
ADNRS DARNS
NARDS
RANDS
ADNRW DRAWN
ADNRY RANDY
ADNSS SANDS
ADNST STAND
ADNSW DAWNS
WANDS
ADNSY SANDY
ADNTU DAUNT
ADOPS APODS
DOPAS
SPADO
ADOPT ADOPT
ADORR ARDOR
ADORS DORSA
ROADS
SAROD
ADORT TARDO
ADORU DOURA
ADOSS SODAS
ADOST DATOS
DOATS
TOADS
ADOSW WOADS
ADOTT DATTO
ADOTY TOADY
TODAY
ADPRS PARDS
ADPRU PURDA
ADPRY PARDY
ADQSU QUADS
SQUAD
ADRRU DURRA
ADRSS SARDS
ADRST DARTS
DRATS
ADRSU DURAS
ADRSW DRAWS
SWARD
WARDS
ADRSY DRAYS
YARDS
ADRTY TARDY
ADSTU ADUST
DAUTS
ADSTW DAWTS
ADSUY YAUDS
AEEFS FEASE
AEEFZ FEAZE
AEEGL AGLEE
EAGLE
AEEGN AGENE
AEEGP PEAGE
AEEGR AGREE
EAGER
EAGRE
RAGEE
AEEHV HEAVE
AEEIR AERIE
AEEKN AKENE
AEEKP APEEK
AEEKR RAKEE
AEEKS AKEES
AEELL ALLEE
AEELN ANELE
AEELR LAREE
AEELS EASEL
LEASE
AEELT ELATE
TELAE
AEELV LEAVE
AEEMN ENEMA
AEEMR AMEER
RAMEE
AEENR ARENE
RANEE
AEENT EATEN
ENATE
AEENV VEENA
VENAE
AEEOZ ZOEAE
AEEPR PEREA
AEEPS PEASE
AEEPT ETAPE
AEEPY PAYEE
AEERS ERASE
SAREE
AEERT ARETE
EATER
AEERV REAVE
AEERZ RAZEE
AEESS EASES
AEEST SETAE
TEASE

AEESV EAVES
AEEVW WEAVE
AEFFG GAFFE
AEFGN GANEF
AEFHS SHEAF
AEFIR AFIRE
FERIA
AEFKL FLAKE
AEFKN KENAF
AEFKR FAKER
FREAK
AEFKS FAKES
AEFKY FAKEY
AEFLL FELLA
AEFLM FLAME
FLEAM
AEFLR FARLE
FERAL
FLARE
AEFLS ALEFS
FALSE
FLEAS
LEAFS
AEFLT FETAL
AEFLY LEAFY
AEFMR FRAME
AEFMS FAMES
AEFNR FRENA
AEFNS FANES
AEFOR AFORE
AEFOV FOVEA
AEFRR FARER
AEFRS FARES
FEARS
SAFER
AEFRT AFTER
AEFRU FEUAR
AEFRW WAFER
AEFRY FAERY
AEFSS SAFES
AEFST FATES
FEAST
FEATS
FETAS
AEFSV FAVES
AEFSX FAXES
AEFSZ FAZES
AEFUV FAUVE
AEGGI AGGIE
AEGGR AGGER
EGGAR
GAGER
AEGGS GAGES
AEGGU GAUGE
AEGHP PHAGE
AEGHR GERAH
AEGIL AGILE
AEGIM IMAGE
AEGIS AEGIS
AEGJR JAGER
AEGLL LEGAL
AEGLM GLEAM
AEGLN ANGEL
ANGLE
GLEAN
AEGLP PLAGE
AEGLR ARGLE
GLARE
LAGER
LARGE
REGAL
AEGLS GALES
AEGLT AGLET
AEGLV GAVEL
AEGLY AGLEY
AEGLZ GLAZE
AEGMM GEMMA
AEGMN MANGE
AEGMO OMEGA
AEGMR GAMER
MARGE
REGMA
AEGMS GAMES
MAGES
AEGMY GAMEY
AEGNO AGONE
GENOA
AEGNR ANGER
RANGE
REGNA
AEGNT AGENT
AEGNU GENUA
AEGNV GANEV
VEGAN
AEGOT TOGAE

AEGPR GAPER
GRAPE
PAGER
PARGE
AEGPS GAPES
PAGES
PEAGS
AEGRS AGERS
GEARS
RAGES
SAGER
SARGE
AEGRT GATER
GRATE
GREAT
RETAG
TARGE
TERGA
AEGRU ARGUE
AUGER
RUGAE
AEGRV GRAVE
AEGRW WAGER
AEGRY GAYER
YAGER
AEGRZ GAZER
GRAZE
AEGSS GASES
SAGES
AEGST GATES
GETAS
STAGE
AEGSU AGUES
USAGE
AEGSW SWAGE
WAGES
AEGSZ GAZES
AEGTU TEGUA
AEGUV VAGUE
AEGUZ GAUZE
AEHHP EPHAH
AEHHT HEATH
AEHJS HAJES
AEHKS HAKES
SHAKE
AEHLM ALMEH
HEMAL
AEHLP ALEPH
AEHLR HALER
AEHLS HALES
HEALS
LEASH
SELAH
SHALE
SHEAL
AEHLT LATHE
AEHLU LEHUA
AEHLV HALVE
AEHLW WHALE
WHEAL
AEHLZ HAZEL
AEHMO MAHOE
AEHMR HAREM
HERMA
AEHMS HAEMS
HAMES
SHAME
AEHNN HENNA
AEHNS ASHEN
HANSE
AEHNT NEATH
THANE
AEHNV HAVEN
AEHNY HYENA
AEHPR RAPHE
AEHPS EPHAS
HEAPS
PHASE
SHAPE
AEHPY HEAPY
AEHRS HARES
HEARS
RHEAS
SHARE
SHEAR
AEHRT EARTH
HATER
HEART
RATHE
AEHRV HAVER
AEHRY HAYER
AEHRZ HAZER
AEHSS ASHES
SHEAS

AEHST HAETS
HASTE
HATES
HEATS
AEHSV HAVES
SHAVE
AEHSW HAWSE
AEHSY YEAHS
AEHSZ HAZES
AEHTT THETA
AEHTU HAUTE
AEHTW WHEAT
AEHVY HEAVY
AEHYY HAYEY
AEIKL ALIKE
ALKIE
AEILL ILEAL
AEILM EMAIL
MAILE
AEILN ALIEN
ALINE
ANILE
ELAIN
LIANE
AEILP PILEA
AEILR ARIEL
AEILS AISLE
AEILT TELIA
AEILV ALIVE
AEILX AXILE
AEIMM MAMIE
AEIMN AMINE
ANIME
MINAE
AEIMR AIMER
RAMIE
AEIMS AMIES
AEIMV MAVIE
AEIMZ MAIZE
AEINN INANE
AEINS ANISE
AEINT ENTIA
TENIA
TINEA
AEINV NAEVI
NAIVE
AEINX XENIA
AEINZ AZINE
AEIPS PAISE
SEPIA
AEIPT PIETA
AEIRR AIRER
AEIRS ARISE
RAISE
SERAI
AEIRT IRATE
RETIA
TERAI
AEIRU AUREI
URAEI
AEIRV AIVER
AEIRZ ZAIRE
AEITV VITAE
AEITW TAWIE
AEITX AXITE
AEIVW WAIVE
AEJKS JAKES
AEJNS JANES
JEANS
AEJPR JAPER
AEJPS JAPES
AEJRS RAJES
AEJST TAJES
AEKLN ANKLE
AEKLR LAKER
AEKLS KALES
LAKES
LEAKS
SLAKE
AEKLT LATKE
AEKLY LEAKY
AEKMR MAKER
AEKMS KAMES
MAKES
SAMEK
AEKNO OAKEN
AEKNP PEKAN
AEKNS KANES
SKEAN
SNAKE
SNEAK
AEKNT TAKEN
AEKNV KNAVE
AEKNW KNAWE
WAKEN
AEKOW AWOKE

AEKPS PEAKS
SPAKE
SPEAK
AEKPY PEAKY
AEKQU QUAKE
AEKRR RAKER
AEKRS ASKER
ESKAR
RAKES
SAKER
AEKRT TAKER
AEKRW WAKER
WREAK
AEKSS SAKES
AEKST SKATE
STAKE
STEAK
TAKES
TEAKS
AEKSU UKASE
AEKSW ASKEW
WAKES
WEKAS
AEKTW TWEAK
AELLP LAPEL
AELLY ALLEY
AELMM LEMMA
AELMN LEMAN
AELMO AMOLE
AELMP AMPLE
MAPLE
AELMR LAMER
REALM
AELMS ALMES
LAMES
MALES
MEALS
AELMT METAL
AELMU ULEMA
AELMY MEALY
AELNO ALONE
ANOLE
AELNP PANEL
PENAL
PLANE
PLENA
AELNR LEARN
RENAL
AELNS ELANS
LANES
LEANS
AELNT LATEN
LEANT
AELNU ULNAE
AELNV NAVEL
VENAL
AELOS ALOES
AELOV LAEVO
AELOZ AZOLE
ZOEAL
AELPP APPEL
APPLE
PEPLA
AELPR PALER
PARLE
PEARL
AELPS LAPSE
LEAPS
PALES
PEALS
PLEAS
SALEP
SEPAL
SPALE
AELPT LEAPT
LEPTA
PALET
PETAL
PLATE
PLEAT
TEPAL
AELQU EQUAL
QUALE
AELRS ARLES
EARLS
LARES
LASER
LEARS
RALES
REALS
SERAL

AELRT ALERT
ALTER
ARTEL
LATER
RATEL
TALER
AELRU UREAL
AELRV LAVER
RAVEL
VELAR
AELRW WALER
AELRX LAXER
RELAX
AELRY EARLY
LAYER
LEARY
RELAY
AELSS LASES
SALES
SEALS
AELST LEAST
SETAL
SLATE
STALE
STEAL
STELA
TAELS
TALES
TEALS
TESLA
AELSV LAVES
SALVE
SELVA
SLAVE
VALES
VALSE
VEALS
AELSW SWALE
WALES
WEALS
AELSX AXELS
AXLES
LAXES
AELSY LYASE
AELSZ LAZES
ZEALS
AELTT LATTE
AELTU LUTEA
AELTV VALET
AELTX EXALT
LATEX
AELUV UVEAL
VALUE
AELVV VALVE
AELVY LEAVY
VEALY
AEMMY MAMEY
AEMNR NAMER
RAMEN
REMAN
AEMNS AMENS
MANES
MANSE
MEANS
MENSA
NAMES
NEMAS
AEMNT AMENT
MEANT
MENTA
AEMNV MAVEN
AEMNX AXMEN
AEMNY MEANY
YAMEN
AEMOR MORAE
AEMPR REMAP
AEMRR ARMER
REARM
AEMRS MARES
MARSE
MASER
REAMS
SMEAR
AEMRT ARMET
MATER
RAMET
TAMER
AEMRZ MAZER
AEMSS MASSE
MESAS
SEAMS

AEMST MATES
MEATS
SATEM
STEAM
TAMES
TEAMS
AEMSU AMUSE
AEMSW WAMES
AEMSX EXAMS
MAXES
AEMSY SEAMY
AEMSZ MAZES
SMAZE
AEMTT MATTE
AEMTY ETYMA
MATEY
MEATY
AEMUV MAUVE
AENNP PANNE
PENNA
AENNS SENNA
AENNT ANENT
AENNX ANNEX
AENOP PAEON
AENOS AEONS
AENOT ATONE
OATEN
AENOV NOVAE
AENOX AXONE
AENOZ ZONAE
AENPP NAPPE
AENPR ARPEN
AENPS ASPEN
NAPES
NEAPS
PANES
PEANS
SNEAP
SPEAN
AENPT PATEN
AENQU QUEAN
AENRR RERAN
AENRS EARNS
NARES
NEARS
SANER
SNARE
AENRT ANTRE
AENRV RAVEN
AENRW REWAN
AENRY YEARN
AENSS SANES
SENSA
AENST ANTES
ETNAS
NATES
NEATS
STANE
AENSU USNEA
AENSV AVENS
NAVES
VANES
AENSW SEWAN
WANES
WEANS
AENSY YEANS
AENTY YENTA
AENWX WAXEN
AENWY WANEY
AENZZ ZAZEN
AEOPR OPERA
PAREO
AEOPS PASEO
PSOAE
AEORS AROSE
AEORT OATER
ORATE
AEOSS OASES
AEOST STOAE
TOEAS
AEOSV OAVES
SOAVE
AEOSZ ZOEAS
AEOTV OVATE
AEOTZ AZOTE
AEPPR PAPER
AEPPU PUPAE
AEPRR PARER
RAPER

AEPRS APERS
APRES
ASPER
PARES
PARSE
PEARS
PRASE
PRESA
RAPES
REAPS
SPARE
SPEAR
AEPRT APTER
PATER
PEART
PRATE
TAPER
AEPRU PAREU
AEPRV PARVE
PAVER
AEPRW PAWER
AEPRY APERY
PAYER
REPAY
AEPSS APSES
PASES
PASSE
SPAES
AEPST PASTE
PATES
PEATS
SEPTA
SPATE
TAPES
TEPAS
AEPSU PAUSE
AEPSV PAVES
AEPSX PAXES
AEPTU TAUPE
AEPTX EXPAT
AEPTY PEATY
AEPVY PEAVY
AEQRU QUARE
AEQTU QUATE
AERRR RARER
AERRS RARES
RASER
REARS
AERRT RATER
TARRE
TERRA
AERRU URARE
AERRV RAVER
AERRW RAWER
AERRY YARER
AERRZ RAZER
AERSS ARSES
RASES
SEARS
AERST ASTER
RATES
RESAT
STARE
TARES
TEARS
AERSU AURES
URASE
UREAS
URSAE
AERSV AVERS
RAVES
SAVER
AERSW RESAW
SAWER
SEWAR
SWARE
SWEAR
WARES
WEARS
AERSX RAXES
AERSY EYRAS
RESAY
SAYER
YEARS
AERSZ RAZES
AERTT TATER
TETRA
TREAT
AERTU URATE
AERTV AVERT
TRAVE
AERTW TAWER
WATER
AERTX EXTRA
RETAX
TAXER

AERTY TEARY
AERUZ AZURE
AERVV VARVE
AERVW WAVER
AERWX REWAX
WAXER
AERWY WEARY
AESSS ASSES
AESST ASSET
EASTS
SATES
SEATS
TASSE
AESSV SAVES
VASES
AESSX SAXES
AESSY ESSAY
EYASS
AESTT STATE
TASTE
TATES
TEATS
TESTA
AESTU SAUTE
AESTV STAVE
VESTA
AESTW SWEAT
TAWSE
TWAES
WASTE
AESTX TAXES
TEXAS
AESTY YEAST
AESTZ ZETAS
AESUV SUAVE
UVEAS
AESVW WAVES
AESWX WAXES
AESXZ ZAXES
AETZZ TAZZE
AEVWY WAVEY
AEWYY YAWEY
AFFGS GAFFS
AFFIX AFFIX
AFFLO OFFAL
AFFLU LUFFA
AFFNS NAFFS
AFFQU QUAFF
AFFRS RAFFS
AFFST STAFF
AFFSW WAFFS
AFFSY YAFFS
AFFTY TAFFY
AFGHU FAUGH
AFGIN FAGIN
AFGLS FLAGS
AFGLU FUGAL
AFGNO GANOF
AFGNS FANGS
AFGOT FAGOT
AFGRS FRAGS
AFGRT GRAFT
AFHIT FAITH
AFHIZ HAFIZ
AFHKS KHAFS
AFHLS FLASH
AFHRW WHARF
AFHST HAFTS
SHAFT
AFIKL KALIF
AFIKR FAKIR
KAFIR
AFIKS KAIFS
AFILL FLAIL
AFILN FINAL
AFILO FOLIA
AFILP PILAF
AFILR FILAR
FLAIR
FRAIL
AFILS ALIFS
FAILS
AFINR INFRA
AFINS NAIFS
AFINT FAINT
AFIQR FAQIR
AFIRR FRIAR
AFIRS FAIRS
FIARS
AFIRT AFRIT
AFIRY FAIRY
AFIST FIATS
AFISW WAIFS
AFKLN FLANK
AFKLS FLASK
AFKLY FLAKY

AFKNR FRANK
AFKRT KRAFT
AFLLS FALLS
AFLMS FLAMS
AFLMY FLAMY
AFLNS FLANS
AFLOO ALOOF
LOOFA
AFLOR FLORA
AFLOS FOALS
LOAFS
AFLOT ALOFT
FLOAT
FLOTA
AFLOU AFOUL
AFLPS FLAPS
AFLRS FARLS
AFLST FLATS
AFLSU SULFA
AFLSW FLAWS
AFLSY FLAYS
AFLTU FAULT
AFLTY FATLY
AFLUW AWFUL
AFLWY FLAWY
AFLXY FLAXY
AFMNU FANUM
AFMOR FORAM
AFMOS FOAMS
AFMOY FOAMY
AFMRS FARMS
AFNNO FANON
AFNNY FANNY
AFNOS FANOS
AFNRS SNARF
AFNRU FURAN
AFNSU FAUNS
SNAFU
AFNSW FAWNS
AFNWY FAWNY
AFOOT AFOOT
AFORS FAROS
SOFAR
AFORV FAVOR
AFORY FORAY
AFOSS FOSSA
SOFAS
AFOST SOFTA
AFPRS FRAPS
AFRSS FRASS
AFRST FRATS
RAFTS
AFRSW SWARF
AFRSY FRAYS
AFRSZ ZARFS
AFSST FASTS
AFSTU TUFAS
AFSTW WAFTS
AFSUV FAVUS
AFTTY FATTY
AGGIN AGING
AGGIS GIGAS
AGGJS JAGGS
AGGJY JAGGY
AGGLU GULAG
AGGNS GANGS
AGGNY NAGGY
AGGOR AGGRO
AGGRS RAGGS
AGGRY RAGGY
AGGSY SAGGY
AGHHU HAUGH
AGHIL LAIGH
AGHIN AHING
AGHIZ GHAZI
AGHLU LAUGH
AGHMO OGHAM
AGHNO HOGAN
AGHNS GNASH
HANGS
SANGH
AGHNW WHANG
AGHOY HOAGY
AGHPR GRAPH
AGHRT GARTH
AGHSS SHAGS
AGHST GHAST
GHATS
AGHSU SAUGH
AGHTU AUGHT
GHAUT
AGHUW WAUGH
AGIIV VIGIA
AGIKN KIANG
AGILL GLIAL

AGILN ALGIN
ALIGN
LIANG
LIGAN
LINGA
AGILO LOGIA
AGILR ARGIL
GLAIR
GRAIL
AGILS GLIAS
SIGLA
AGILY GAILY
AGIMN GAMIN
AGIMO AMIGO
IMAGO
AGIMS AGISM
SIGMA
AGINO GONIA
AGINP APING
AGINR GARNI
GRAIN
AGINS GAINS
SIGNA
AGINT GIANT
AGINW AWING
WIGAN
AGINX AXING
AGIOS AGIOS
AGIRS RAGIS
AGIRT TRAGI
AGIRV VIRGA
AGIST AGIST
GAITS
STAIG
AGISV VIGAS
AGISY YAGIS
AGJLU JUGAL
AGKSS SKAGS
AGKSU KAGUS
AGKSW GAWKS
AGKWY GAWKY
AGLLS GALLS
AGLLY GALLY
AGLMO GLOAM
AGLMS GLAMS
AGLMU ALGUM
ALMUG
AGLNO ALONG
ANGLO
LOGAN
AGLNR GNARL
AGLNS GLANS
SLANG
AGLOP GALOP
AGLOR ALGOR
ARGOL
GORAL
LARGO
AGLOS GAOLS
GOALS
AGLOT GLOAT
AGLOW AGLOW
AGLRU GULAR
RUGAL
AGLRY GLARY
GYRAL
AGLSS GLASS
SLAGS
AGLTU GAULT
AGLYY GAYLY
AGLYZ GLAZY
AGMMU GUMMA
AGMMY GAMMY
AGMNO AMONG
MANGO
AGMNY MANGY
AGMOS OGAMS
AGMOT MAGOT
AGMPR GRAMP
AGMPS GAMPS
AGMRS GRAMS
AGMSU GAUMS
MAGUS
SAGUM
AGMTU GAMUT
AGNNW GNAWN
AGNOR ARGON
GROAN
ORANG
ORGAN
AGNOS AGONS
AGNOT TANGO
TONGA
AGNOU GUANO
AGNOW GOWAN
WAGON

AGNOY AGONY
AGNPR PRANG
AGNPS PANGS
SPANG
AGNRR GNARR
AGNRS GNARS
GRANS
AGNRT GRANT
AGNRW WRANG
AGNRY ANGRY
RANGY
AGNSS SNAGS
AGNST ANGST
GNATS
STANG
TANGS
AGNSU GUANS
AGNSV VANGS
AGNSW GNAWS
SWANG
AGNSY YANGS
AGNTU GAUNT
AGNTW TWANG
AGNTY TANGY
AGOPR PARGO
AGORS SARGO
AGORT ARGOT
GATOR
GROAT
AGOSS SAGOS
AGOST GOATS
TOGAS
AGOSY YOGAS
AGOTV GAVOT
AGOYZ GYOZA
AGPPY GAPPY
AGPRS GRASP
SPRAG
AGPRY GRAPY
AGPSS GASPS
AGPSW GAWPS
AGQSU QUAGS
AGRSS GRASS
AGRSU ARGUS
GAURS
GUARS
SUGAR
AGRSY GRAYS
AGRUU AUGUR
AGRVY GRAVY
AGSST GASTS
STAGS
AGSSU GAUSS
AGSSW SWAGS
AGSSY GASSY
AGSTY STAGY
AGSUV VAGUS
AGSUY YUGAS
AGSWY GAWSY
AGTTU GUTTA
AGUYZ GAUZY
AHHKP KHAPH
AHHOR HORAH
AHHPY HYPHA
AHHRS HARSH
AHHSS SHAHS
AHIJJ HAJJI
AHIJR HIJRA
AHIJS HAJIS
AHIKK KHAKI
AHIKM HAKIM
AHIKS HAIKS
AHIKU HAIKU
AHILP PHIAL
AHILR HILAR
AHILS HAILS
AHILT LAITH
LATHI
AHIMR IHRAM
AHINT HAINT
AHIOS OHIAS
AHIPS APHIS
APISH
SPAHI
AHIRS HAIRS
AHIRT AIRTH
AHIRY HAIRY
AHIST SAITH
AHISV SHIVA
AHISW WISHA
AHJPU PUJAH
AHJTU THUJA
AHKLS LAKHS

AHKNS ANKHS
HANKS
KHANS
SHANK
AHKNT THANK
AHKNY HANKY
AHKOO HOOKA
AHKOS SHAKO
AHKPS KAPHS
AHKRS HARKS
SHARK
AHKST KHATS
AHKSU HAKUS
AHKSW HAWKS
AHKSY SHAKY
AHLLO HALLO
HOLLA
AHLLS HALLS
SHALL
AHLLU AHULL
AHLMS HALMS
AHLMU HAULM
AHLNO HALON
AHLNU UHLAN
AHLOR HORAL
AHLOS HALOS
SHOAL
AHLOT ALTHO
LOATH
LOTAH
AHLPR RALPH
AHLPS PLASH
AHLPY HAPLY
PHYLA
AHLRS HARLS
AHLSS SLASH
AHLST HALTS
LATHS
SHALT
AHLSU HAULS
HULAS
SHAUL
AHLSW SHAWL
AHLSY HYLAS
SHALY
AHLTY LATHY
AHMMY HAMMY
AHMNU HUMAN
AHMNY MYNAH
AHMOW WHAMO
AHMRS HARMS
MARSH
AHMRT THARM
AHMSS SHAMS
SMASH
AHMST MATHS
AHMSW SHAWM
WHAMS
AHMSY MASHY
AHNNO HONAN
AHNRS SHARN
AHNSS SNASH
AHNST HANTS
SNATH
AHNSW SHAWN
AHNTU HAUNT
UNHAT
AHOOW WAHOO
AHOOY YAHOO
AHOPS OPAHS
AHORS HOARS
HORAS
AHORT TORAH
AHORY HOARY
AHOST HOSTA
OATHS
SHOAT
AHOSY HOYAS
AHOTZ AZOTH
AHPPY HAPPY
AHPRS HARPS
SHARP
AHPRU PRAHU
AHPRY HARPY
AHPSS HASPS
AHPST PATHS
STAPH
AHPSW PSHAW
WHAPS
AHPUW WHAUP
AHQSU QUASH
AHRRY HARRY
AHRST HARTS
TAHRS
TRASH
AHRSU SURAH

AHRTW THRAW
WRATH
AHRTY RHYTA
AHRXY HYRAX
AHSST STASH
AHSSW SHAWS
SHWAS
SWASH
AHSSY SHAYS
AHSTW SWATH
THAWS
WHATS
AHSTY HASTY
AHSWY WASHY
AHTUY THUYA
AHUZZ HUZZA
AIILL ILIAL
AIILM MILIA
AIILO AIOLI
AIILT LITAI
AIIMN ANIMI
AIISX IXIAS
AIJKN KANJI
AIJLS JAILS
AIJNN NINJA
AIJOR RIOJA
AIKKM KAMIK
AIKKS KAKIS
AIKKT TIKKA
AIKLS KAILS
AIKLT TILAK
AIKLV VAKIL
AIKMR MIKRA
AIKMU UMIAK
AIKNS KAINS
KINAS
AIKNT TAKIN
AIKOP OKAPI
AIKOR KORAI
AIKOS ASKOI
AIKPS PAIKS
PIKAS
AIKRS RAKIS
AIKRT KRAIT
TRAIK
AIKRU KAURI
AIKSS SAKIS
SIKAS
AIKST IKATS
AIKSV KIVAS
AIKUZ AZUKI
AILLM MAILL
AILLV VILLA
AILMN LIMAN
AILMP LIMPA
MILPA
AILMS LIMAS
MAILS
SALMI
AILMU MIAUL
AILNO ALOIN
AILNP LAPIN
PLAIN
AILNS ANILS
NAILS
SLAIN
SNAIL
AILNV ANVIL
NIVAL
VINAL
AILNY INLAY
LAYIN
AILOV VIOLA
VOILA
AILPP PALPI
PIPAL
AILPR PILAR
AILPS LAPIS
PAILS
SPAIL
AILPT PLAIT
AILPU PILAU
AILPW PILAW
AILQU QUAIL
AILRS ARILS
LAIRS
LARIS
LIARS
LIRAS
RAILS
RIALS
AILRT TRAIL
TRIAL
AILRU URIAL
AILRV RIVAL
VIRAL

AILRY RIYAL
AILSS LASSI
SAILS
SIALS
SISAL
AILST ALIST
LITAS
TAILS
AILSV SILVA
VAILS
VIALS
AILSW SWAIL
WAILS
AILSX AXILS
AILTT ATILT
AILTV VITAL
AILTY LAITY
AIMMS IMAMS
MAIMS
MIASM
AIMMU IMAUM
UMAMI
AIMMX MAXIM
AIMNO AMINO
AMNIO
AIMNR INARM
AIMNS AMINS
MAINS
MINAS
AIMNT MATIN
AIMNV MAVIN
AIMNZ NIZAM
AIMOR MOIRA
AIMOU MIAOU
AIMOW MIAOW
AIMOX AXIOM
AIMPR PRIMA
AIMPS PIMAS
AIMQU MAQUI
UMIAQ
AIMRS AMIRS
MAIRS
SIMAR
AIMRZ MIRZA
ZIRAM
AIMSS AMISS
SIMAS
AIMST MAIST
TAMIS
AIMSV MAVIS
AIMSW SWAMI
AIMSX MAXIS
AIMTY AMITY
AINNO ANION
AINNP PINNA
AINOP PIANO
AINOR NORIA
AINOV AVION
AINOX AXION
AINPS NIPAS
PAINS
PIANS
PINAS
AINPT INAPT
PAINT
PATIN
PINTA
AINPV PAVIN
AINRS AIRNS
NARIS
RAINS
RANIS
SARIN
AINRT RIANT
TRAIN
AINRU NAIRU
AINRV INVAR
RAVIN
AINRW RAWIN
AINRY RAINY
AINSS SAINS
SASIN
AINST ANTIS
SAINT
SATIN
STAIN
TAINS
AINSU UNAIS
AINSV SAVIN
VINAS
AINSW SWAIN
WAINS
AINSY AYINS
AINSZ NAZIS
AINTT TAINT
TITAN

AINTW TWAIN
WITAN
AINUX AUXIN
AINYZ ZAYIN
AIOPS PSOAI
AIOPT PATIO
AIORT RATIO
AIORX IXORA
AIOSS OASIS
OSSIA
AIOST IOTAS
OSTIA
STOAI
AIOSV AVISO
AIPPP PAPPI
AIPRS PAIRS
PARIS
AIPRT ATRIP
TAPIR
AIPSS APSIS
ASPIS
AIPST PITAS
SPAIT
TAPIS
AIPSV PAVIS
AIPTT PITTA
AIPZZ PIZZA
AIQSU QUAIS
QUASI
AIRRS ARRIS
SIRRA
AIRRU URARI
AIRRW WIRRA
AIRSS ARSIS
SARIS
AIRST AIRTS
ASTIR
SITAR
STAIR
STRIA
TARSI
AIRSU AURIS
AIRSV VAIRS
AIRSW WAIRS
AIRSZ IZARS
SIZAR
AIRTT TRAIT
AIRVX VARIX
AISST SATIS
AISSV VISAS
AISTV VISTA
AISTW WAIST
WAITS
AISTX TAXIS
AISVV VIVAS
AITTV VITTA
AJKSU JAUKS
AJLOP JALOP
AJLOU JOUAL
AJLRS JARLS
AJLRU JURAL
AJMMY JAMMY
AJMNU UNJAM
AJMOR JORAM
MAJOR
AJNTU JAUNT
JUNTA
AJNTY JANTY
AJORW JOWAR
AJOSS SOJAS
AJOST JATOS
JOTAS
AJOSU SAJOU
AJPSU JAUPS
PUJAS
AJRTU JURAT
AJYZZ JAZZY
AKKLU KULAK
AKKNS SKANK
AKKOP KAPOK
AKKPU PUKKA
AKKSY KYAKS
AKLLY ALKYL
AKLNP PLANK
AKLNS SLANK
AKLNY LANKY
AKLOP POLKA
AKLOS KOLAS
SKOAL
AKLRS LARKS
AKLRY LARKY
AKLST STALK
TALKS
AKLSW WALKS
AKLTU TALUK
AKLTY TALKY

AKMOR KORMA
AKMOS AMOKS
MAKOS
AKMOU OAKUM
AKMRS MARKS
AKMSS MASKS
AKNOR KRONA
AKNOS KAONS
KOANS
AKNPR PRANK
AKNPS KNAPS
SPANK
AKNPU PUNKA
AKNRS KARNS
KNARS
NARKS
RANKS
SNARK
AKNRT TRANK
AKNRU KNAUR
AKNRY NARKY
AKNST STANK
TANKS
AKNSU ANKUS
AKNSW SWANK
AKNSY SNAKY
YANKS
AKNUZ KANZU
AKOOR KAROO
AKOOZ KAZOO
AKOPP KOPPA
AKOPY YAPOK
AKORS KORAS
OKRAS
AKORT KORAT
TAROK
TROAK
AKOSS ASKOS
SOAKS
AKOSY KAYOS
OKAYS
AKOTY TOKAY
AKPRS PARKS
SPARK
AKPTU KAPUT
AKPWY PAWKY
AKQRU QUARK
AKQUY QUAKY
AKRSS SARKS
AKRST KARST
KARTS
STARK
AKRSU RAKUS
AKRSW WARKS
AKRSY KYARS
SARKY
AKRTU KRAUT
KURTA
AKRUY KAURY
AKSST SKATS
TASKS
AKSSU SKUAS
AKSSV KVASS
AKSTY KYATS
AKSUW WAUKS
ALLLS LALLS
ALLLY ALLYL
ALLMO MOLAL
ALLMS MALLS
SMALL
ALLMU MULLA
ALLNO LLANO
ALLOR LORAL
ALLOS OLLAS
SALOL
ALLOT ALLOT
ATOLL
ALLOW ALLOW
ALLOY ALLOY
LOYAL
ALLPS PALLS
SPALL
ALLPY PALLY
ALLRY RALLY
ALLST STALL
TALLS
ALLSW WALLS
ALLSY SALLY
ALLTY TALLY
ALLWY WALLY
ALLXY LAXLY
ALMMS MALMS
ALMMY MALMY
ALMNY MANLY
ALMOO MOOLA

ALMOR MOLAR
MORAL
ALMOS LOAMS
MOLAS
ALMOU LOUMA
ALMOY LOAMY
ALMPS LAMPS
PALMS
PLASM
PSALM
ALMPU AMPUL
ALMPY AMPLY
PALMY
ALMQU QUALM
ALMRS MARLS
ALMRU LARUM
MURAL
ALMRY MARLY
MYLAR
ALMSS SLAMS
ALMST MALTS
SMALT
ALMSU ALUMS
LUMAS
MAULS
ALMSY AMYLS
ALMTY MALTY
ALNNU ANNUL
ALNOP NOPAL
ALNOR LORAN
ALNOS LOANS
SALON
SOLAN
ALNOT NOTAL
TALON
TOLAN
TONAL
ALNOY ONLAY
ALNOZ AZLON
ZONAL
ALNPS PLANS
ALNPT PLANT
ALNPU ULPAN
ALNRS SNARL
ALNRU LUNAR
ULNAR
ALNST SLANT
ALNSU LUNAS
ULANS
ULNAS
ALNSW LAWNS
ALNUY UNLAY
YULAN
ALNWY LAWNY
WANLY
ALNXY XYLAN
ALOPR PAROL
POLAR
ALOPS OPALS
ALORS ORALS
SOLAR
ALORT TOLAR
ALORV VALOR
VOLAR
ALORY ROYAL
ALOSS LASSO
ALOST ALTOS
LOTAS
TOLAS
ALOSV OVALS
SALVO
ALOSW AWOLS
ALOTT TOTAL
ALOTV LOVAT
VOLTA
ALOTX TAXOL
ALOVV VOLVA
ALPPS PALPS
ALPPU PUPAL
ALPPY APPLY
ALPSS SALPS
SLAPS
ALPST PLATS
SPLAT
ALPSW PAWLS
ALPSY PALSY
PLAYS
SPLAY
ALPTY APTLY
PATLY
PLATY
TYPAL
ALPUY LAYUP
ALRRU RURAL
ALRSU SURAL
ALRSY ARYLS

ALRTU ULTRA
ALRTW TRAWL
ALRTY LYART
ALRWY RAWLY
ALSST LASTS
SALTS
SLATS
ALSSU SAULS
ALSSW SLAWS
ALSSY LYSSA
SLAYS
ALSTU SAULT
TALUS
ALSTY SALTY
SLATY
ALSUU LUAUS
USUAL
ALSUV ULVAS
ALSUW WAULS
ALSVY SYLVA
ALSWW WAWLS
ALSWY YAWLS
ALTTY LYTTA
ALTUV VAULT
ALTWZ WALTZ
ALUUV UVULA
ALUVV VULVA
AMMMO MOMMA
AMMMY MAMMY
AMMOS AMMOS
AMMOY MYOMA
AMMRS SMARM
AMMRY RAMMY
AMMSU SUMMA
AMMTY TAMMY
AMNNU UNMAN
AMNOR MANOR
ROMAN
AMNOS MANOS
MASON
MOANS
MONAS
NOMAS
SOMAN
AMNOT TOMAN
AMNOW WOMAN
AMNOY ANOMY
AMNRU UNARM
AMNSU MANUS
AMNSY MYNAS
AMNUY YAMUN
AMORR ARMOR
AMORS MORAS
ROAMS
AMORT AMORT
AMORU AMOUR
AMORY MAYOR
MORAY
AMOSS SOMAS
AMOST ATOMS
MOATS
STOMA
AMOSX MOXAS
AMOSY MAYOS
AMOTY ATOMY
AMOTZ MATZO
AMPRS PRAMS
RAMPS
AMPRT TRAMP
AMPSS SAMPS
SPAMS
SPASM
AMPST STAMP
TAMPS
AMPSU PUMAS
AMPSV VAMPS
AMPSW SWAMP
AMPVY VAMPY
AMRRU MURRA
AMRRY MARRY
AMRST MARTS
SMART
TRAMS
AMRSU ARUMS
MURAS
RAMUS
AMRSW SWARM
WARMS
AMRTY TRYMA
AMRUU AURUM
AMRVY MARVY
AMSST MASTS
AMSSY MASSY
AMSTT MATTS
AMSTU MAUTS
AMSTY MAYST

AMSUW WAMUS
AMSWY SWAMY
ANNNY NANNY
ANNOS NONAS
ANNOY ANNOY
ANYON
ANNSU SUNNA
ANOPR APRON
ANOPT PANTO
ANOPY YAPON
ANORS ARSON
ROANS
SONAR
ANORT TRONA
ANORW ROWAN
ANORY RAYON
ANOST SANTO
ANOSV NOVAS
ANOSX AXONS
ANOSZ AZONS
ANOTT TANTO
ANOTU TAUON
ANOTX TAXON
ANOTY ATONY
ANOWY NOWAY
ANPPY NAPPY
ANPRW PRAWN
ANPRY PYRAN
ANPSS SNAPS
SPANS
ANPST PANTS
ANPSU PUNAS
ANPSW PAWNS
SPAWN
ANPSY PANSY
ANPTU UNAPT
ANPTY PANTY
ANQRT TRANQ
ANQTU QUANT
ANRST RANTS
TARNS
TRANS
ANRSW WARNS
ANRSY YARNS
ANRUY UNARY
ANSSW SNAWS
SWANS
ANSTU AUNTS
TUNAS
ANSTW WANTS
ANSTY ANTSY
NASTY
TANSY
ANSUU UNAUS
ANSUY UNSAY
YUANS
ANSWY YAWNS
ANTTU TAUNT
ANTTY NATTY
ANTUV VAUNT
ANTUY AUNTY
ANTWY TAWNY
ANVVY NAVVY
AOPPP POPPA
AOPRS PRAOS
PROAS
SAPOR
AOPRT APORT
AOPRV PARVO
VAPOR
AOPRY PAYOR
AOPSS PSOAS
SOAPS
AOPSY SOAPY
AOPTY ATOPY
AOPTZ TOPAZ
AOQTU QUOTA
AORRS ROARS
AORRW ARROW
AORRZ RAZOR
AORSS SAROS
SOARS
SORAS
AORST RATOS
ROAST
ROTAS
SORTA
TAROS
TORAS
AORSV ARVOS
SAVOR
AORSW SOWAR
AORTT OTTAR
TAROT
TORTA
AORVY OVARY

AOSST OASTS
STOAS
AOSSY SOYAS
AOSTT STOAT
TOAST
AOSTU AUTOS
AOSVW AVOWS
AOSVY SAVOY
APPPY PAPPY
APPSU PUPAS
APPSY SAPPY
APPYZ ZAPPY
APRRS PARRS
APRRY PARRY
APRSS RASPS
SPARS
APRST PARTS
PRATS
SPRAT
STRAP
TARPS
TRAPS
APRSU PRAUS
SUPRA
APRSW WARPS
WRAPS
APRSY PRAYS
RASPY
SPRAY
APRTT TRAPT
APRTU PRUTA
APRTW WRAPT
APRTY PARTY
APSST PASTS
SPATS
APSSW SWAPS
WASPS
APSSY SPAYS
APSTU SPUTA
STUPA
APSTY PASTY
PATSY
APSUY YAUPS
APSWY WASPY
YAWPS
APTTY PATTY
AQRTU QUART
AQSSU QUASS
AQSTU SQUAT
AQSUY QUAYS
ARRSU SURRA
ARRTY TARRY
ARSST STARS
TRASS
TSARS
ARSSU SURAS
ARSTT START
TARTS
ARSTU SUTRA
ARSTW STRAW
SWART
WARTS
ARSTY ARTSY
SATYR
STRAY
TRAYS
ARSTZ TZARS
ARSUV VARUS
ARSUY SAURY
ARTTY RATTY
TARTY
ARTUY YURTA
ARTWY WARTY
ASSSY SASSY
ASSTT STATS
ASSTV VASTS
ASSTW SWATS
WASTS
ASSTY SAYST
STAYS
ASSWY SWAYS
ASTTU SUTTA
TAUTS
ASTTW WATTS
ASTTY TASTY
ASTUV VATUS
ASTUX TAXUS
ASTVY VASTY
ASVVY SAVVY
ATTTY TATTY
BBBIS BIBBS
BBBOY BOBBY
BBCEU CUBEB
BBCOS COBBS
BBCOY COBBY
BBCUY CUBBY

BBDEE EBBED
BBDOY DOBBY
BBEER REBBE
BBEET EBBET
BBEIK KIBBE
BBEIL BIBLE
BBEIR BRIBE
BBEKO KEBOB
BBELS BLEBS
BBEMO BOMBE
BBEOP BEBOP
BBEWY WEBBY
BBHOY HOBBY
BBHUY HUBBY
BBIIK KIBBI
BBIJS JIBBS
BBILO BILBO
BBILY BILBY
BBIMO BIMBO
BBIRY RIBBY
BBISS SIBBS
BBLOS BLOBS
BBLOY LOBBY
BBLRU BLURB
BBLSU BLUBS
BULBS
BBMOS BOMBS
BBNOY NOBBY
BBNUY NUBBY
BBOOS BOOBS
BBOOY BOOBY
YOBBO
BBRSU BURBS
BBRUY RUBBY
BBSUU BUBUS
BBSUY BUSBY
BBTUY TUBBY
BCCEO BOCCE
BCCIO BOCCI
BCCIU CUBIC
BCDEI CEBID
BCDEU CUBED
BCEEH BEECH
BCEEL CELEB
BCEER REBEC
BCEEX XEBEC
BCEEZ ZEBEC
BCEHL BELCH
BCEHN BENCH
BCEIP BICEP
BCEIS BICES
BCEKS BECKS
BCELO COBLE
BCEMO COMBE
BCERU CUBER
BCERY CYBER
BCESU CUBES
BCHIM CHIMB
BCHIR BIRCH
BCHIT BITCH
BCHNU BUNCH
BCHOT BOTCH
BCHSU CHUBS
BCHTU BUTCH
BCIKR BRICK
BCILM CLIMB
BCILO CIBOL
BCIOR BORIC
BCIPU PUBIC
BCIRS CRIBS
BCITU CUBIT
BCKLO BLOCK
BCKOR BROCK
BCKOS BOCKS
BCKOU BUCKO
BCKSU BUCKS
BCLMO CLOMB
BCLOS BLOCS
BCLOY COLBY
BCLSU CLUBS
BCMOO COMBO
COOMB
BCMOS COMBS
BCMRU CRUMB
BCNOR BRONC
BCNOU BUNCO
BCORY CORBY
BCRSU CURBS
SCRUB
BDDEI BIDED
BDDEO BODED
BDDIY BIDDY
BDDUY BUDDY
BDEEI BEEDI
BDEEL BEDEL
BLEED

BDEEM EMBED
BDEER BREDE
BREED
BDEEW BEDEW
DWEEB
BDEEY DEBYE
BDEGI GIBED
BDEGU BUDGE
DEBUG
BDEGY GYBED
BDEIJ JIBED
BDEIK BIKED
BDEIL BIELD
BDEIM BEDIM
IMBED
BDEIO DOBIE
BDEIP BIPED
BDEIR BIDER
BRIDE
REBID
BDEIS BIDES
BDEIT BIDET
DEBIT
BDELN BLEND
BDELO LOBED
BDELU BLUED
LUBED
BDEMO DEMOB
BDENO BONED
BDENS BENDS
BDENY BENDY
BDEOO BOOED
BDEOR BORED
ORBED
ROBED
BDEOS BODES
BDEOW BOWED
BDEOX BOXED
BDERU REDUB
BDERY DERBY
BDEST DEBTS
BDESU BUSED
BDETU DEBUT
TUBED
BDFII BIFID
BDHIO DHOBI
BDIIN BINDI
BDIIS BIDIS
BDILN BLIND
BDILU BUILD
BDINS BINDS
BDINU UNBID
BDIOP BIPOD
BDIOV BOVID
BDIRS BIRDS
DRIBS
BDLNO BLOND
BDLOO BLOOD
BDLOS BOLDS
BDMOU DUMBO
BDMSU DUMBS
BDNOS BONDS
BDNOU BOUND
BDNSU BUNDS
BDNTU BUNDT
BDOOR BROOD
DOBRO
BDOTU DOUBT
BDRSU BURDS
DRUBS
BEEFS BEEFS
FEEBS
BEEFY BEEFY
BEEGI BEIGE
BEEGL GLEBE
BEEGR GREBE
BEEGT BEGET
BEEHT THEBE
BEEIL BELIE
BEEJL JEBEL
BEELL BELLE
BEELN LEBEN
BEELP BLEEP
PLEBE
BEELR REBEL
BEELT BETEL
BEELV BEVEL
BEELZ BEZEL
BEEMR BERME
EMBER
BEENN BENNE
BEENS BENES
BEEOS OBESE
BEEPS BEEPS
BEERS BEERS
BREES

BEERT BERET
BEERV BREVE
BEERW WEBER
BEERY BEERY
BEESS BESES
BEEST BEETS
BESET
BEFGO BEFOG
BEFIR BRIEF
FIBER
FIBRE
BEFIT BEFIT
BEGIL BILGE
BEGIN BEGIN
BEING
BINGE
BEGIO BOGIE
BEGIR GIBER
BEGIS GIBES
BEGIW BEWIG
BEGIY BEIGY
BEGLO BOGLE
GLOBE
BEGLU BUGLE
BULGE
BEGMU BEGUM
BEGNU BEGUN
BEGOT BEGOT
BEGOY BOGEY
BEGRS BERGS
BEGSY GYBES
BEHRS HERBS
BEHRT BERTH
BEHRY HERBY
BEHST BETHS
BEIIK BIKIE
KIBEI
BEIJR JIBER
BEIJS JIBES
BEIKR BIKER
BEIKS BIKES
KIBES
BEILL LIBEL
BEILO OBELI
BEILR BIRLE
LIBER
BEILS BILES
BEILT BLITE
BEILZ BEZIL
BEIMO BIOME
BEIMU IMBUE
BEIMX BEMIX
BEINN BENNI
BEINR BINER
BRINE
BEINS BINES
BEINY INBYE
BEINZ ZINEB
BEIOT BOITE
BEIRR BRIER
BEIRS BIERS
BIRSE
BRIES
RIBES
BEIRT BITER
TRIBE
BEISS BISES
BEIST BITES
BEISV VIBES
BEISZ BIZES
BEITZ ZIBET
BEJOT OBJET
BEJSU JUBES
BEKLO BLOKE
BEKOO EBOOK
BEKOR BROKE
BEKRS BERKS
KERBS
BEKRU BURKE
BELLS BELLS
BELLY BELLY
BELMU BLUME
UMBEL
BELNO BELON
NOBLE
BELNT BLENT
BELOO OBOLE
BELOR ROBLE
BELOS BOLES
LOBES
BELOT BOTEL
BELOU BOULE
BELOW BELOW
BOWEL
ELBOW
BELPS PLEBS

BELPY BLYPE
BELRU BLUER
RUBEL
RUBLE
BELRY BERYL
BELSS BLESS
BELST BELTS
BLEST
BLETS
BELSU BLUES
LUBES
BELTU BLUET
BUTLE
BELUY BLUEY
BEMOR BROME
OMBER
OMBRE
BEMOS BESOM
BEMOW EMBOW
BEMRS BERMS
BEMRU BRUME
UMBER
BEMSU SEBUM
BENNO BONNE
BENNY BENNY
BENOR BONER
BORNE
BENOS BONES
EBONS
BENOT BENTO
BETON
BENOY BONEY
EBONY
BENOZ BONZE
BENRS BRENS
BENRT BRENT
BENST BENTS
BEOOS OBOES
BEOOZ BOOZE
BEOPR PROBE
REBOP
BEORR BORER
BEORS BORES
BROSE
ROBES
SOBER
BEORV BEVOR
BEORW BOWER
BEORX BOXER
BEOST BESOT
BEOSU BOUSE
BEOSW BOWSE
BEOSX BOXES
BEOSY OBEYS
BEOTU BUTEO
BEPSU PUBES
BEPUY UPBYE
BERRY BERRY
BERSU BURSE
REBUS
RUBES
SUBER
BERSV VERBS
BERSW BREWS
BERSY BYRES
BERTU BRUTE
BURET
REBUT
TUBER
BERUX EXURB
BERUY BUYER
REBUY
BESST BESTS
BESSU BUSES
BESTU BUTES
TUBES
BESTY BYTES
BESUZ ZEBUS
BETTU BUTTE
BFFIS BIFFS
BFFIU BUFFI
BFFIY BIFFY
BFFLU BLUFF
BFFOO BOFFO
BFFOS BOFFS
BFFOU BUFFO
BFFSU BUFFS
BFFUY BUFFY
BFLSU FLUBS
BFLYY FLYBY
BFMSU BUMFS
BFORS FORBS
BFORY FORBY
BFSUY FUBSY
BGGIY BIGGY
BGGOY BOGGY

BGGUY BUGGY
BGHIT BIGHT
BGHOU BOUGH
BGHRU BRUGH
BURGH
BGILY BIGLY
BILGY
BGINO BINGO
BOING
BGINR BRING
BGIOS BIGOS
BIOGS
BGIOT BIGOT
BGIRS BRIGS
BGLOS BLOGS
GLOBS
BGLUY BULGY
BGMOO GOMBO
BGMOU GUMBO
BGNOO BONGO
BGNOS BONGS
BGNRU BRUNG
BGNSU BUNGS
BGOOS GOBOS
BGOOY BOOGY
BGORU BOURG
BGOSU BOGUS
BGRSU BURGS
GRUBS
BGRUY RUGBY
BHIRT BIRTH
BRITH
BHLSU BLUSH
BUHLS
SHLUB
BHMOR RHOMB
BHMPU BUMPH
BHMRU RHUMB
BHMTU THUMB
BHOOS BOHOS
HOBOS
BHOOT BHOOT
BOOTH
BHORT BROTH
THROB
BHOTY BOTHY
BHRSU BRUSH
BUHRS
SHRUB
BHSTU BHUTS
BHSUY BUSHY
BIILM LIMBI
BIILN BLINI
BIILR LIBRI
BIIMN NIMBI
BIINT BINIT
BIIOR ORIBI
BIJOU BIJOU
BIKLN BLINK
BIKLS BILKS
BIKNR BRINK
BIKRS BIRKS
BRISK
BIKRU KRUBI
BIKSS BISKS
BILLR BRILL
BILLS BILLS
BILLY BILLY
BILMO LIMBO
BILMP BLIMP
BILMS LIMBS
BILMY BLIMY
LIMBY
BILOO OBOLI
BILOR BROIL
BILOS BOILS
BILPS BLIPS
BILRS BIRLS
BILSS BLISS
BILSY SIBYL
BILTU BUILT
BILTZ BLITZ
BIMOZ ZOMBI
BIMRS BRIMS
BINOR ROBIN
BINOS BISON
BINOT BIONT
BINRS BRINS
BINRU BRUIN
BURIN
BINRY BRINY
BINSS SNIBS
BINST BINTS
BIORS BIROS
BRIOS
BIORT ORBIT

BIOST OBITS
BIPSU PUBIS
BIQSU SQUIB
BIQTU QUBIT
BIRRS BIRRS
BIRSS BRISS
BIRST BRITS
BIRTT BRITT
BIRTU BRUIT
BISSY BYSSI
BISTT BITTS
BISTY BITSY
BITTY BITTY
BJMOU JUMBO
BKLSU BULKS
BKLUY BULKY
BKMOU KOMBU
BKNOS BONKS
KNOBS
BKNOU BUNKO
BKNSU BUNKS
BKOOR BROOK
BKOOS BOOKS
KOBOS
BKORS BORKS
BKOSS BOSKS
BKOSY BOSKY
BKRSU BRUSK
BKSSU BUSKS
BLLOS BOLLS
BLLSU BULLS
BLLUY BULLY
BLMOO BLOOM
BLMPU PLUMB
BLNOW BLOWN
BLNOY NOBLY
BLNTU BLUNT
BLOOP BLOOP
BLOOS BOLOS
LOBOS
OBOLS
BLOOY LOOBY
BLOSS SLOBS
BLOST BLOTS
BOLTS
BLOSU BOLUS
BLOSW BLOWS
BOWLS
BLOWY BLOWY
BLRSU BLURS
BURLS
SLURB
BLRSY BYRLS
BLRTU BLURT
BLRUY BURLY
BLSSU SLUBS
BLTUY BUTYL
BMNSU NUMBS
BMOOR BROMO
BROOM
BMOOS BOOMS
BOSOM
BMOOY BOOMY
BMOST TOMBS
BMOSU UMBOS
BMOSW WOMBS
BMOUX BUXOM
BMOWY WOMBY
BMPSU BUMPS
BMPUY BUMPY
BNNOY BONNY
BNNSU BUNNS
BNNUY BUNNY
BNOOR BORON
BNOOS BOONS
BOSON
BNORU BOURN
BNORW BROWN
BNOSS SNOBS
BNOSU BONUS
BOSUN
BNOUX UNBOX
BNRSU BURNS
BNRTU BRUNT
BURNT
BNSSU SNUBS
BNSTU BUNTS
BOOPY POBOY
BOORS BOORS
BROOS
BOORT ROBOT
BOOST BOOST
BOOTS
BOOSY BOYOS
BOOSZ BOZOS
BOOTY BOOTY

BOOWX OXBOW
BOOYZ BOOZY
BOPUW UPBOW
BORRU BURRO
BORSS SORBS
BORST BORTS
BORSW BROWS
BORSY BROSY
BORTU TURBO
BORTY BORTY
BORTZ BORTZ
BOSST STOBS
BOSSW SWOBS
BOSSY BOSSY
BOSTT BOTTS
BOSTU BOUTS
BOSUY BOUSY
BUOYS
BOTUY OUTBY
BPPUY BUPPY
BPRSU BURPS
BRRSU BURRS
BRRUY BURRY
BRSTU BRUTS
BURST
BRSUU RUBUS
BSSTU BUSTS
STUBS
BSTTU BUTTS
BSTUY BUSTY
BTTUU BUTUT
BTTUY BUTTY
CCCIO COCCI
CCDEO CODEC
CCEER RECCE
CCEHK CHECK
CCEHY YECCH
CCEIR CERCI
CERIC
CCELY CYCLE
CCEMU CECUM
CCEOS COSEC
SECCO
CCESU CUSEC
CCHIK CHICK
CCHIN CINCH
CCHIO CHICO
CCHIS CHICS
CCHKO CHOCK
CCHKU CHUCK
CCHLU CULCH
CCHNO CONCH
CCHOO COOCH
CCHOU COUCH
CCHRU CURCH
CCHTU CUTCH
CCHUY YUCCH
CCIIT ICTIC
CCIIV CIVIC
CCIKL CLICK
CCIKR CRICK
CCILO COLIC
CCIMO COMIC
CCINO CONIC
CCINY CYNIC
CCIOR CROCI
CCIOS CISCO
CCKLO CLOCK
CCKLU CLUCK
CCKOR CROCK
CCKOS COCKS
CCKOY COCKY
CCKRU CRUCK
CCLOY CYCLO
CCOOS COCOS
CCORS CROCS
CCORU OCCUR
CDDEE CEDED
CDDEI DICED
CDDEO CODED
CDDUY CUDDY
CDEEH ECHED
CDEEI DEICE
CDEER CEDER
CERED
CREED
CDEES CEDES
CDEEU DEUCE
EDUCE
CDEHI CHIDE
CDEIM DEMIC
MEDIC
CDEIR CIDER
CRIED
DICER
RICED

CDEIS CEDIS
DICES
CDEIT CITED
EDICT
CDEIV VICED
CDEIY DICEY
CDEKO COKED
CDEKR DRECK
CDEKS DECKS
CDELO COLED
DOLCE
CDELU CLUED
CDENO CODEN
CONED
CDENS SCEND
CDENU DUNCE
CDEOO COOED
CDEOP COPED
CDEOR CODER
CORED
CREDO
DECOR
CDEOS CODES
COEDS
DECOS
CDEOT COTED
CDEOU COUDE
DOUCE
CDEOV COVED
CDEOW COWED
CDEOX CODEX
COXED
CDEOY COYED
DECOY
CDERS CREDS
CDERU CRUDE
CURED
CDERY CYDER
DECRY
CDESU DUCES
CDETU EDUCT
CDHIL CHILD
CDHIT DITCH
CDHNU DUNCH
CDHOR CHORD
CDHTU DUTCH
CDHUY DUCHY
CDIIO IODIC
CDIIS DISCI
CDIKS DICKS
CDIKY DICKY
CDILO DOLCI
CDILU LUCID
LUDIC
CDIMO DOMIC
CDIMU MUCID
CDIOS DISCO
SODIC
CDIOT DICOT
CDIPU CUPID
PUDIC
CDISS DISCS
CDISU SCUDI
CDITY DICTY
CDKOS DOCKS
CDKSU DUCKS
CDKUY DUCKY
CDLOS CLODS
COLDS
SCOLD
CDLOU CLOUD
COULD
CDNOO CODON
CONDO
CDORS CORDS
SCROD
CDORU DUROC
CDORW CROWD
CDOSU SCUDO
CDRSU CRUDS
CURDS
CDRUY CURDY
CDSSU SCUDS
CDSTU DUCTS
CEEEM EMCEE
CEEFN FENCE
CEEFS FECES
CEEHK CHEEK
CEEHL LEECH
CEEHN HENCE
CEEHP CHEEP
CEEHR CHEER
CEEHS ECHES
CEEIN NIECE
CEEIP PIECE
CEEJT EJECT
CEEKL CLEEK
CEEKR CREEK
CEELP CLEPE
CEELR CREEL
CEELT ELECT
CEELX EXCEL
CEELY LYCEE
CEEMR CREME
CEENP PENCE
CEENS CENSE
SCENE
CEEOO COOEE
CEEPR CREEP
CREPE
CEEPS CEPES
CEERS CERES
SCREE
CEERT ERECT
TERCE
CEEST CETES
CEESX EXECS
CEESY SYCEE
CEEUV CUVEE
CEFHI CHIEF
FICHE
CEFHS CHEFS
CEFHT FETCH
CEFIS FICES
CEFKL FLECK
CEFKS FECKS
CEFLS CLEFS
CEFLT CLEFT
CEFOR FORCE
CEFSY FYCES
CEGIN GENIC
CEGKO GECKO
CEGKS GECKS
CEGNO CONGE
CEHHT CHETH
CEHHU HEUCH
CEHIL CHIEL
CHILE
CEHIM CHIME
HEMIC
MICHE
CEHIN CHINE
NICHE
CEHIT ETHIC
CEHIV CHIVE
CEHKN KENCH
CEHKO CHOKE
CEHKS HECKS
CEHKT KETCH
CEHLT LETCH
CEHLW WELCH
CEHLY CHYLE
CEHMO CHEMO
CEHMR MERCH
CEHMY CHYME
CEHNT TENCH
CEHNW WENCH
CEHOP EPOCH
CEHOR CHORE
OCHER
OCHRE
CEHOS CHOSE
ECHOS
CEHPR PERCH
CEHPS PECHS
CEHRT CHERT
RETCH
CEHRU RUCHE
CEHSS CHESS
CEHST CHEST
TECHS
CEHSW CHEWS
CEHSY YECHS
CEHTU CHUTE
TEUCH
CEHTV VETCH
CEHTW WECHT
CEHTY TECHY
CEHVY CHEVY
CEHWY CHEWY
CEHYY YECHY
CEIIL CEILI
CEIIR ICIER
CEIIV CIVIE
CEIJU JUICE
CEIKR ICKER
CEILL CELLI
CEILM CLIME
MELIC
CEILN CLINE
CEILO OLEIC
CEILR RELIC
CEILS CEILS
SLICE
CEILT TELIC
CEIMN MINCE
CEIMR CRIME
CEIMS MESIC
CEIMX CIMEX
CEINR NICER
CEINS CINES
SINCE
CEINW WINCE
CEINX XENIC
CEINY YINCE
CEIOS COSIE
CEIOV VOICE
CEIOZ COZIE
CEIPR CRIPE
PRICE
CEIPS EPICS
SEPIC
SPICE
CEIRR CRIER
RICER
CEIRS CIRES
CRIES
RICES
CEIRT CITER
RECIT
RECTI
TRICE
CEIRU CURIE
UREIC
CEIRX XERIC
CEISS SICES
CEIST CESTI
CITES
CEISV VICES
CEITU CUTIE
CEITV CIVET
EVICT
CEITW TWICE
CEKKS KECKS
CEKLR CLERK
CEKNS NECKS
SNECK
CEKOR OCKER
CEKOS COKES
CEKPS PECKS
SPECK
CEKPY PECKY
CEKRS RECKS
CEKRW WRECK
CEKSU CUKES
CELLO CELLO
CELLS CELLS
CELMO CELOM
CELNO CLONE
CELNU UNCLE
CELOR CEORL
CELOS CLOSE
COLES
SOCLE
CELOT TELCO
CELOV CLOVE
CELOZ CLOZE
CELPT CLEPT
CELPU CUPEL
CELRU CRUEL
LUCRE
ULCER
CELST CELTS
CELSU CLUES
LUCES
CELSW CLEWS
CELTU CULET
CELUX CULEX
CEMOR COMER
CEMOS COMES
CEMOT COMET
COMTE
CEMRS MERCS
CEMRY MERCY
CEMSY CYMES
CENNO NONCE
CENOP COPEN
PONCE
CENOR CRONE
RECON
CENOS CONES
SCONE
CENOT CENTO
CONTE
ONCET
CENOU OUNCE
CENOV COVEN
CENOY CONEY
CENOZ COZEN
CENST CENTS
SCENT
CENTU CENTU
CEOOR COOER
CEOOY COOEY
CEOPR COPER
CEOPS COPES
COPSE
SCOPE
CEOPU COUPE
CEORR CORER
CRORE
CEORS CEROS
CORES
CORSE
SCORE
CEORT RECTO
CEORV COVER
CEORW COWER
CEORY COYER
CEORZ CROZE
CEOSS COSES
CEOST COSET
COTES
ESCOT
CEOSV COVES
VOCES
CEOSX COXES
CEOSY COSEY
CEOSZ COZES
CEOTT OCTET
CEOTV COVET
CEOVY COVEY
CEOYZ COZEY
CEPRT CREPT
CEPRY CREPY
CEPSS SPECS
CEPSU PUCES
CERRU CURER
RECUR
CERSS CRESS
CERST CREST
CERSU CRUSE
CURES
CURSE
ECRUS
SUCRE
CERSW CREWS
SCREW
CERTU CRUET
CURET
CUTER
ERUCT
RECUT
TRUCE
CERUV CURVE
CESST SECTS
CESSY SYCES
CESTU CUTES
SCUTE
CETUY CUTEY
CFFHU CHUFF
CFFIL CLIFF
CFFOS COFFS
SCOFF
CFFSU CUFFS
SCUFF
CFHIL FILCH
CFHIN FINCH
CFHIT FITCH
CFHIU FICHU
CFIIN FICIN
CFIKL FLICK
CFILO FOLIC
CFILS FLICS
CFILT CLIFT
CFIOS COIFS
CFISS FISCS
CFISU CUIFS
FICUS
CFKLO FLOCK
CFKOR FROCK
CFLOS FLOCS
CFMOY COMFY
CFOOS COOFS
CFORT CROFT
CFOSU FOCUS
CFRSU CURFS
SCURF
CFSUU FUCUS
CGHLU GULCH
CGHOO COHOG
CGHOU COUGH
CGHSU CHUGS
CGIIN ICING
CGILN CLING
CGILO LOGIC
CGINO COIGN
INCOG
CGINU CUING
CGIOR CORGI
ORGIC
CGIOY YOGIC
CGKSU GUCKS
CGLNU CLUNG
CGLOO COLOG
CGLOS CLOGS
CGNOO COGON
CONGO
CHHIT HITCH
CHHIW WHICH
CHHNU HUNCH
CHHOO HOOCH
CHHOT HOTCH
CHHTU HUTCH
CHIIL CHILI
LICHI
CHIKN CHINK
CHIKO HOICK
CHIKR CHIRK
CHIKS HICKS
CHIKT THICK
CHILL CHILL
CHILM MILCH
CHILT LICHT
CHILZ ZILCH
CHIMO OHMIC
CHIMP CHIMP
CHIMR CHIRM
CHIMU HUMIC
CHINO CHINO
CHINP PINCH
CHINS CHINS
CHINW WINCH
CHIOR CHIRO
CHOIR
ICHOR
CHIPR CHIRP
CHIPS CHIPS
CHIPT PITCH
CHIRR CHIRR
CHIRU CHIRU
CHIST CHITS
STICH
CHISU CUISH
CHITW WITCH
CHITY ITCHY
CHIVY CHIVY
VICHY
CHKNU CHUNK
CHKOO CHOOK
CHKOS HOCKS
SHOCK
CHKOY CHOKY
CHKSU HUCKS
SHUCK
CHLMU MULCH
CHLNU LUNCH
CHLNY LYNCH
CHLOO CHOLO
CHLOS LOCHS
CHLOT CLOTH
CHLRU CHURL
LURCH
CHLSU SCHUL
CHMNU MUNCH
CHMOO MOOCH
CHMOP CHOMP
CHMOS SCHMO
CHMOU MOUCH
MUCHO
CHMPU CHUMP
CHMSU CHUMS
CHMTU MUTCH
CHNOT NOTCH
CHNPU PUNCH
CHNRU CHURN
CHNSY SYNCH
CHOOP POOCH
CHOOS COHOS
CHOPR PORCH
CHOPS CHOPS
CHOPU POUCH
CHORT ROTCH
TORCH
CHORY OCHRY
CHOSU HOCUS
CHOSW CHOWS
CHOTT CHOTT
CHOTU COUTH
TOUCH
CHOUV VOUCH
CHPSY PSYCH
CHRRU CHURR
CHRSU CRUSH
CHRTW CRWTH
CHSUY CUSHY
CIILT LICIT
CIILV CIVIL
CIILY ICILY
CIIMM MIMIC
CIINO IONIC
CIINR RICIN
CIINV VINIC
CIIRR CIRRI
CIJUY JUICY
CIKKL KLICK
CIKKS KICKS
CIKKY KICKY
CIKLN CLINK
CIKLS LICKS
SLICK
CIKNS NICKS
SNICK
CIKOS SICKO
CIKPR PRICK
CIKPS PICKS
CIKPY PICKY
CIKQU QUICK
CIKRS RICKS
CIKRT TRICK
CIKRW WRICK
CIKSS SICKS
CIKST STICK
TICKS
CIKSW WICKS
CILNO COLIN
NICOL
CILOS COILS
CILOT LOTIC
CILOU OCULI
CILOW WILCO
CILPS CLIPS
CILPT CLIPT
CILPU PICUL
CILRY LYRIC
CILSU SULCI
CILTU CULTI
CILTY LYTIC
CILXY CYLIX
CIMNU CUMIN
MUCIN
CIMNY MINCY
CIMOR MICRO
CIMOS OSMIC
CIMOX COMIX
CIMPR CRIMP
CIMRS SCRIM
CIMSU MUSIC
CINNO CONIN
CINOR ORCIN
CINOS CIONS
COINS
ICONS
SCION
SONIC
CINOT ONTIC
TONIC
CINOV COVIN
CINOY YONIC
CINRU INCUR
RUNIC
CINSU INCUS
CINSZ ZINCS
CINTT TINCT
CINTU CUTIN
TUNIC
CINYZ ZINCY
CIOPS PISCO
CIOPT OPTIC
PICOT
TOPIC
CIORS COIRS
CIORT TORIC
CIORU CURIO
CIOST STOIC
CIOTX TOXIC
CIPRS CRISP
SCRIP
CIPRY PRICY
PYRIC
CIPSY SPICY
CIPTY TYPIC
CIRST CRITS
CISST CISTS
CISSY CISSY
CISTU CUTIS
ICTUS
CIVVY CIVVY
CJKOO JOCKO
CJKOS JOCKS
CJNOU JUNCO
CJOSU JUCOS
CKKNO KNOCK
CKLNO CLONK
CKLNU CLUNK
CKLOS LOCKS
CKLPU PLUCK
CKLSU LUCKS
SCULK
CKLUY LUCKY
CKMOS MOCKS
SMOCK
CKMSU MUCKS
CKMUY MUCKY
CKNOS CONKS
NOCKS
CKNOY CONKY
CKNSU SNUCK
CKOOR CROOK
CKOOS COOKS
SOCKO
CKOOY COOKY
CKOPS POCKS
CKOPY POCKY
CKORS CORKS
ROCKS
CKORT TROCK
CKORY CORKY
ROCKY
CKOSS SOCKS
CKOST STOCK
CKOSY YOCKS
CKPSU PUCKS
CKRSU RUCKS
CKRTU TRUCK
CKSSU CUSKS
SUCKS
CKSTU STUCK
TUCKS
CKSUY SUCKY
YUCKS
CKUYY YUCKY
CLLOY COLLY
CLLSU CULLS
SCULL
CLLUY CULLY
CLMOP CLOMP
CLMOU LOCUM
CLMOY CYMOL
CLMPU CLUMP
CLMSU CULMS
CLMTU MULCT
CLNOO COLON
CLNOS CLONS
CLNOW CLOWN
CLOOR COLOR
CLOOS COOLS
LOCOS
CLOOT CLOOT
CLOOY COOLY
CLOPS CLOPS
CLORU CLOUR
CLOST CLOTS
COLTS
CLOSU LOCUS
CLOSW COWLS
SCOWL
CLOSY CLOYS
CLOTU CLOUT
CLOTY OCTYL
CLOYY COYLY
CLPSU SCULP
CLRSU CURLS
CLRUY CURLY
CLSTU CULTS
CMMOY COMMY
CMOOP COMPO
CMOPS COMPS
CMOPT COMPT
CMORS CORMS
CMORU MUCOR
MUCRO
CMPRU CRUMP
CMRSU SCRUM
CMSSU SCUMS
CMSUU MUCUS
CNNOS CONNS
CNOOR CROON
CNOOS COONS
CNOOT CONTO
CNORS CORNS
SCORN
CNORU CORNU
CNORW CROWN
CNORY CORNY
CRONY
CNOSU CONUS
UNCOS
CNOTU COUNT
CNOTY CYTON
CNOUY UNCOY
CNRSU CURNS
CNSSY SYNCS
CNSUU UNCUS
CNTUU UNCUT
COOPS COOPS
SCOOP
COOPT COOPT
COOST COOTS
SCOOT
COPRS CORPS
CROPS
COPRU CROUP
COPSS SCOPS
COPSU COUPS
COPUY COYPU
CORRU CRUOR
CORSS CROSS
CORST TORCS
CORSU SCOUR
CORSW CROWS
CORTU COURT
CORWY COWRY
COSST COSTS
SCOTS
COSSU CUSSO
COSSW SCOWS
COSTU SCOUT
CPPUY CUPPY
CPRTY CRYPT
CPSSU CUSPS
SCUPS
CPTUU CUTUP
CRRSU CURRS
CRRUY CURRY
CRSTU CRUST
CURST
CRUVY CURVY
CSSTU SCUTS
CSSTY CYSTS
CSUZZ SCUZZ
CTTUY CUTTY
DDDEU DUDED
DDDUY DUDDY
DDEEG EDGED
DDEEK DEKED
DDEEL DELED
DDEEN ENDED
DDEER DREED
REDED
DDEES DEEDS
DDEEW DEWED
DDEEY DEEDY
DDEGO DODGE
DDEHI HIDED
DDEII DIDIE
DDEIK DIKED
DDEIL IDLED
DDEIN DINED
NIDED
DDEIO DIODE
DDEIR DRIED
REDID
DDEIS SIDED
DDEIT TIDED
DDEIV DIVED
DDEKU DUKED
DDEKY DYKED
DDELO DOLED
DDEMO DOMED
DDENY NEDDY
DDEOP DOPED
DDEOR ODDER
DDEOS DOSED
DDEOT DOTED
DDEOW DOWED
DDEOZ DOZED
DDEPU DUPED
DDERS REDDS
DDERU DURED
UDDER
DDESU DUDES
DDETY TEDDY
DDFUY FUDDY
DDGIY GIDDY
DDGOY DODGY
DDIIO IODID
DDIKO KIDDO
DDIKY KIDDY
DDILO DILDO
DDIMY MIDDY
DDINU UNDID
DDIOR DROID
DDIOS DIDOS
DDIRU DRUID
DDIST DIDST
DDIWY WIDDY
DDLOY ODDLY
DDMUY MUDDY
DDNOY NODDY
DDOOS DODOS
DDOOY DOODY
DDOSY SODDY
DDOTY TODDY
DDOWY DOWDY
DDRSU RUDDS
DDRUY RUDDY
DDSSU SUDDS
DEEFR DEFER
FREED
REFED
DEEFS FEEDS
DEEFT FETED
DEEFU FEUED
DEEFX FEDEX
DEEGG EGGED
DEEGH HEDGE
DEEGK KEDGE
DEEGL GLEDE
GLEED
LEDGE
DEEGO GEODE
DEEGR EDGER
GREED
DEEGS EDGES
SEDGE
DEEGW WEDGE
DEEHR HEDER
DEEHS HEEDS
DEEHW HEWED
DEEHX HEXED
DEEIL EDILE
ELIDE
DEEIN DIENE
DEEIR EIDER
DEEIX DEXIE
DEEKN KNEED
DEEKS DEKES
SKEED
DEEKY KEYED
DEELR ELDER
DEELS DELES
DEELU ELUDE
DEELV DELVE
DEVEL
DEELW WEDEL
DEEMN EMEND
DEEMS DEEMS
DEMES
MEEDS
DEEMT METED
DEEMW MEWED
DEEMY EMYDE
DEENO DONEE
DEENR ENDER
DEENS DENES
DENSE
NEEDS
DEENU ENDUE
UNDEE
DEENY NEEDY
DEEOP EPODE
DEEOR ERODE
DEEPR PREED
DEEPS DEEPS
PEDES
SPEED
DEERR ERRED
DEERS DEERS
DREES
REDES
REEDS
SEDER
SERED
DEERT DETER
TREED
DEERW REWED
DEERY REDYE
REEDY
DEESS SEEDS
DEEST DEETS
STEED

DEESU SUEDE
DEESW SEWED
SWEDE
WEEDS
DEESX DESEX
DEXES
SEXED
DEESY SEEDY
DEETU ETUDE
DEETW TEWED
TWEED
DEEUX EXUDE
DEEVX VEXED
DEEWY WEEDY
DEFFI FIFED
DEFFO OFFED
DEFGI FIDGE
DEFGO DEFOG
DEFGU FUDGE
DEFIL FELID
FIELD
FILED
FLIED
DEFIN FIEND
FINED
DEFIR FIRED
FRIED
DEFIS DEFIS
DEFIT FETID
DEFIW WIFED
DEFIX FIXED
DEFIY DEIFY
EDIFY
DEFJL FJELD
DEFLS DELFS
DEFLT DELFT
DEFLU FLUED
DEFMR FREMD
DEFMU FUMED
DEFNS FENDS
DEFNU UNFED
DEFOS FEODS
DEFOX FOXED
DEFSU FEUDS
FUSED
DEFUZ FUZED
DEGGI IGGED
DEGHY HEDGY
DEGIL GELID
GLIDE
DEGIM MIDGE
DEGIN DEIGN
DINGE
DEGIO DOGIE
GEOID
DEGIR DIRGE
GRIDE
RIDGE
DEGIU GUIDE
DEGJU JUDGE
DEGLO LODGE
OGLED
DEGLS GELDS
GLEDS
DEGLU GLUED
LUGED
DEGLY LEDGY
DEGMU DEGUM
DEGNU NUDGE
DEGOR GORED
DEGOS DOGES
DEGOT GODET
DEGOW WODGE
DEGOY DOGEY
DEGRS DREGS
DEGRU URGED
DEGRY GYRED
DEGSU GUDES
DEGSY SEDGY
DEGUY GUYED
DEGVY GYVED
DEGWY WEDGY
DEHIK HIKED
DEHIR HIDER
HIRED
DEHIS HIDES
SHIED
SIDHE
DEHIV HIVED
DEHKO HOKED
DEHLO DHOLE
HOLED
DEHMO HOMED
DEHNO HONED
DEHNS SHEND
DEHOO OOHED

DEHOP EPHOD
HOPED
DEHOR HORDE
DEHOS HOSED
SHOED
DEHOT DOETH
DEHPT DEPTH
DEHPY HYPED
DEHRS HERDS
SHERD
SHRED
DEHSS SHEDS
DEIIM IMIDE
MEDII
DEIIN INDIE
DEIIT TEIID
DEIIV IVIED
DEIJR JERID
DEIJV JIVED
DEIKL LIKED
DEIKM MIKED
DEIKN INKED
DEIKP PIKED
DEIKR DIKER
IRKED
DEIKS DIKES
SKIED
DEIKT KITED
DEILM LIMED
DEILN LINED
DEILO OILED
OLDIE
DEILP PILED
PLIED
DEILR IDLER
RILED
DEILS DEILS
DELIS
IDLES
ISLED
SIDLE
SLIDE
DEILT TILDE
TILED
DEILV DEVIL
LIVED
DEILW WIELD
WILED
DEILY YIELD
DEIMM MIMED
DEIMN DENIM
MINED
DEIMP IMPED
DEIMR DIMER
MIRED
RIMED
DEIMS DEISM
DIMES
DISME
DEIMT DEMIT
TIMED
DEIMX MIXED
DEINN INNED
DEINP PINED
DEINR DINER
DEINS DINES
NIDES
SNIDE
DEINT TEIND
TINED
DEINU INDUE
NUDIE
DEINV VINED
DEINW DWINE
WIDEN
WINED
DEINX INDEX
NIXED
DEINZ DIZEN
DEIOS EIDOS
DEIOV VIDEO
DEIOW DOWIE
DEIOX DOXIE
OXIDE
DEIPP PIPED
DEIPR PRIDE
PRIED
REDIP
RIPED
DEIPS SIPED
SPIED
DEIPT TEPID
DEIPW WIPED
DEIQU EQUID

DEIRR DIRER
DRIER
RIDER
DEIRS DRIES
RESID
RIDES
SIRED
DEIRT TIRED
TRIED
DEIRV DIVER
DRIVE
RIVED
DEIRW WEIRD
WIDER
WIRED
WRIED
DEISS SIDES
DEIST DEIST
DIETS
DITES
EDITS
SITED
STIED
TIDES
DEISV DIVES
VISED
DEISW WIDES
WISED
DEISZ SIZED
DEITW WITED
DEITY DEITY
DEIVW WIVED
DEJKO JOKED
DEJKU JUKED
DEJOW JOWED
DEJOY JOYED
DEKKO DEKKO
DEKNO KENDO
DEKNU NUKED
DEKOP POKED
DEKOT TOKED
DEKOY YOKED
DEKPU PUKED
DEKRS DREKS
DEKRY RYKED
DEKSS DESKS
DEKST TSKED
DEKSU DUKES
DEKSY DYKES
SKYED
DELLS DELLS
DELLW DWELL
DELLY DELLY
DELMO MODEL
DELMS MELDS
DELMU MULED
DELNO LODEN
OLDEN
DELNS LENDS
DELNU UNLED
DELNY DYNEL
DELOO LOOED
DELOP LOPED
POLED
DELOR OLDER
DELOS DOLES
LODES
SOLED
DELOT TOLED
DELOV LOVED
VOLED
DELOW DOWEL
LOWED
DELOX LOXED
DELOY ODYLE
YODEL
YODLE
DELPU DUPLE
PULED
DELRU LURED
RULED
DELRY REDLY
DELSS SLEDS
DELST DELTS
DELSU DUELS
DULSE
LEUDS
LUDES
SLUED
DELSV VELDS
DELSW WELDS
DELSY LYSED
DELTU LUTED
DELTV VELDT
DELTW DWELT
DELWY WYLED

DEMMO MODEM
DEMNO DEMON
MONDE
DEMNS MENDS
DEMOO MOOED
DEMOP MOPED
DEMOS DEMOS
DOMES
MODES
DEMOU ODEUM
DEMOV MOVED
DEMOW MOWED
DEMPU UMPED
DEMRS DERMS
DEMRU DEMUR
MURED
DEMSU MUSED
SEDUM
DEMSY EMYDS
DEMTU MUTED
DENNO DONNE
DENOO ODEON
DENOR DRONE
REDON
DENOS NODES
NOSED
SONDE
DENOT NOTED
TONED
DENOV DEVON
DOVEN
DENOW ENDOW
OWNED
DENOY DOYEN
DENOZ DOZEN
ZONED
DENPS PENDS
SPEND
DENPU UPEND
DENRS NERDS
RENDS
DENRT TREND
DENRU NUDER
UNDER
DENRY NERDY
DENSS SENDS
SNEDS
DENST DENTS
TENDS
DENSU DUNES
NUDES
DENSV VENDS
DENSW WENDS
DENSY DYNES
DENTU TENDU
TUNED
DENTY TYNED
DENUU UNDUE
DENUW UNWED
DEOOR RODEO
DEOOW WOOED
DEOOZ OOZED
DEOPR DOPER
PEDRO
PORED
ROPED
DEOPS DOPES
POSED
SPODE
DEOPT DEPOT
OPTED
TOPED
DEOPX POXED
DEOPY DOPEY
DEORR ORDER
DEORS DOERS
DOSER
REDOS
RESOD
RODES
ROSED
SORED
DEORT DOTER
TRODE
DEORU UREDO
DEORV DROVE
ROVED
DEORW DOWER
ROWED
DEORX REDOX
DEORZ DOZER
DEOSS DOSES
DEOST DOEST
DOTES
DEOSU DOUSE
DEOSV DOVES

DEOSW DOWSE
SOWED
DEOSZ DOZES
DEOTT TOTED
DEOTU OUTED
DEOTV VOTED
DEOTW TOWED
DEOTX DETOX
DEOTY TOYED
DEOVW VOWED
DEOWW WOWED
DEOWY YOWED
DEOXY DEOXY
DEPPU UPPED
DEPRU DRUPE
DUPER
PERDU
PRUDE
URPED
DEPRY PERDY
DEPSU DUPES
PSEUD
SPUED
DEPTY TYPED
DERRU RUDER
DERRY DERRY
DRYER
REDRY
DERSS DRESS
DERST DREST
DERSU DRUSE
DURES
DERSY DYERS
DERTU TRUED
DERTY TYRED
DERUX REDUX
DESTU DUETS
DESTY STYED
DETUV DUVET
DETWY WYTED
DFFIS DIFFS
DFFOS DOFFS
DFFSU DUFFS
DFILU FLUID
DFINS FINDS
DFINU FUNDI
DFIOR FIORD
DFIOS FIDOS
DFIRT DRIFT
DFJOR FJORD
DFLOO FLOOD
DFLOS FOLDS
DFNOR FROND
DFNOS FONDS
DFNOU FONDU
FOUND
DFNSU FUNDS
DFOOR FORDO
DFOOS FOODS
DFORS FORDS
DFSUU DUFUS
DGGOO DOGGO
DGGOY DOGGY
DGHIT DIGHT
DGHOU DOUGH
DGIIR RIGID
DGIIT DIGIT
DGILS GILDS
DGILU GUILD
DGINO DINGO
DOING
DGINR GRIND
DGINS DINGS
DGINY DINGY
DYING
DGIRS GIRDS
GRIDS
DGIRY RIDGY
DGISU GUIDS
DGLOS GOLDS
DGLOY GODLY
DGNOS DONGS
DGNSU DUNGS
DGNUY DUNGY
DGOOS GOODS
DGOOY GOODY
DGOPY PODGY
DGORU GOURD
DGORY GRODY
DGOSW GOWDS
DGPUY PUDGY
DGRSU DRUGS
DHIMU HUMID
DHINS HINDS
DHIOT DHOTI
DHIOY HYOID

DHIRT THIRD
DHISW WHIDS
DHISY DISHY
DHITU DHUTI
DHITW WIDTH
DHLOS HOLDS
DHNOU HOUND
DHNUZ NUDZH
DHOOS HOODS
DHOOY HOODY
DHORY HYDRO
DHOSW DHOWS
DHOSY YODHS
DHOWY HOWDY
DHRSU HURDS
DHSTU THUDS
DIILP LIPID
DIILV LIVID
DIIMO IDIOM
IMIDO
DIIMS IMIDS
MIDIS
DIIMT TIMID
DIINO IODIN
DIINR INDRI
DIINT NITID
DIIOT IDIOT
DIIRS IRIDS
DIIRV VIRID
DIITX DIXIT
DIIVV VIVID
DIJNN DJINN
DIJNS DJINS
DIKNR DRINK
DIKNS DINKS
KINDS
DIKNY DINKY
DIKRS DIRKS
DIKSS DISKS
SKIDS
DILLR DRILL
DILLS DILLS
DILLY DILLY
IDYLL
DILMS MILDS
DILMY DIMLY
DILNO INDOL
DILNY LINDY
DILOS DIOLS
IDOLS
LIDOS
LOIDS
SLOID
SOLDI
SOLID
DILOY DOILY
DILRS DIRLS
DILRU LURID
DILRY DRILY
DILSS SILDS
DILSW WILDS
DILSY IDYLS
DIMNS MINDS
DIMOS MISDO
DIMOU DUOMI
ODIUM
DIMOY MYOID
DIMRU MURID
DIMST MIDST
DIMSY MYSID
DIMTU TUMID
DINOP POIND
DINOS DINOS
DINOT TONDI
DINOW INDOW
DINRS RINDS
DINRY RINDY
DINST DINTS
DINSU NIDUS
DINSW WINDS
DINWY WINDY
DIOOT OOTID
DIOOV OVOID
DIOOZ ZOOID
DIOPS DIPSO
DIOPY PYOID
DIORT DROIT
DIOST DOITS
ODIST
DIOSV VOIDS
DIOSX OXIDS
DIOTT DITTO
DIOTV DIVOT
DIOWW WIDOW
DIPPY DIPPY
DIPRS DRIPS

DIPRT DRIPT
DIQSU QUIDS
SQUID
DIRST DIRTS
DIRSU URSID
DIRSY YIRDS
DIRTY DIRTY
DISTU DUITS
DISTY DITSY
DITTY DITTY
DITYZ DITZY
DIVVY DIVVY
DIYZZ DIZZY
DJLOS SLOJD
DJOOS DOJOS
DJOSU JUDOS
DKMUY DUMKY
DKNRU DRUNK
DKNSU DUNKS
DKORS DORKS
DKORU DROUK
DKORY DORKY
DKOSU KUDOS
DKSSU DUSKS
DKSUU KUDUS
DKSUY DUSKY
DKUUZ KUDZU
DLLOR DROLL
DLLOS DOLLS
DLLOY DOLLY
DLLSU DULLS
DLLUY DULLY
DLMOS MOLDS
DLMOU MOULD
DLMOY MOLDY
DLOOR DOLOR
DROOL
DLOOS SOLDO
DLOOY DOOLY
DLOPS PLODS
DLORS LORDS
DLORW WORLD
DLOST DOLTS
DLOSW WOLDS
DLOSY ODYLS
SLOYD
DLOUW WOULD
DLOYY DOYLY
DLRYY DRYLY
DMMUY DUMMY
DMNOO MONDO
DMNOU MOUND
DMOOS DOOMS
MOODS
SODOM
DMOOU DUOMO
DMOOY DOOMY
MOODY
DMORS DORMS
DMORY DORMY
DMOSU DOUMS
MODUS
DMPSU DUMPS
DMPUY DUMPY
DMRSU DRUMS
DMRUU DURUM
DNOOR DONOR
RONDO
DNOOS SNOOD
DNOOT TONDO
DNOPS PONDS
DNOPU POUND
DNORU ROUND
DNORW DROWN
DNOSU NODUS
SOUND
UDONS
DNOSW DOWNS
DNOSY DONSY
SYNOD
DNOTU DONUT
DNOUV VODUN
DNOUW WOUND
DNOWY DOWNY
DNRSU DURNS
NURDS
DNRSY RYNDS
DNSTU DUNTS
DNSWY WYNDS
DOOPR DROOP
DOOPS POODS
DOORS DOORS
ODORS
ORDOS
ROODS
DOORU ODOUR

DOOST STOOD
DOOSW WOODS
DOOTU OUTDO
DOOUV VODOU
DOOWY WOODY
DOOYZ DOOZY
DOPRS DORPS
DROPS
PRODS
DOPRT DROPT
DOPRU PROUD
DOPSU UPDOS
DOQSU QUODS
DORRS DORRS
DORSS DROSS
SORDS
DORSU DUROS
SUDOR
DORSW SWORD
WORDS
DORTY DORTY
DORWY DOWRY
ROWDY
WORDY
DOTTY DOTTY
DPRUY UPDRY
DPSSU SPUDS
DRRSU DURRS
DRSSU SURDS
DRSTU DURST
DSSTU DUSTS
STUDS
DSSUY SUDSY
DSTUY DUSTY
STUDY
EEEFZ FEEZE
EEEGL GELEE
EEEGS GEESE
EEEHZ HEEZE
EEEIR EERIE
EEEKV KEEVE
EEELM MELEE
EEELV LEVEE
EEEMR EMEER
EEEPS EPEES
EEEPT TEPEE
EEEPV PEEVE
EEEPW PEWEE
EEERS RESEE
EEERV REEVE
EEETW ETWEE
EEFJS JEFES
EEFKS KEEFS
EEFLR FLEER
REFEL
EEFLS FEELS
FLEES
EEFLT FLEET
EEFMM FEMME
EEFMS FEMES
EEFRR FREER
FRERE
REFER
EEFRS FERES
FREES
REEFS
EEFRV FEVER
EEFRW FEWER
EEFRY FEYER
REEFY
EEFSS FESSE
EEFST FETES
EEFSU FUSEE
EEFSZ FEZES
EEFUZ FUZEE
EEGGR EGGER
EEGHN HENGE
EEGHS GHEES
EEGIL LIEGE
EEGIN GENIE
EEGIS SIEGE
EEGIV VEGIE
EEGKL GLEEK
EEGKR GREEK
EEGKS GEEKS
EEGKY GEEKY
EEGLR LEGER
EEGLS GLEES
LEGES
EEGLT GLEET
EEGLY ELEGY
EEGMR MERGE
EEGNR GENRE
GREEN
EEGNS GENES

EEGNT GENET
TENGE
EEGNV VENGE
EEGNW NGWEE
EEGOS OGEES
EEGOY YOGEE
EEGPR REPEG
EEGRS EGERS
GREES
REGES
SERGE
EEGRT EGRET
GREET
EEGRV VERGE
EEGST EGEST
GEEST
GESTE
EEGSU SEGUE
EEGSV VEGES
EEHIR HIREE
EEHLS HEELS
EEHLT LETHE
EEHLV HELVE
EEHLW WHEEL
EEHMR REHEM
RHEME
EEHMS HEMES
EEHMT THEME
EEHNS SHEEN
EEHNW WHEEN
EEHPS SHEEP
EEHPW WHEEP
EEHRS HERES
SHEER
EEHRT ETHER
THERE
THREE
EEHRW HEWER
WHERE
EEHRX HEXER
EEHST SHEET
THESE
EEHSX HEXES
EEHTT TEETH
EEILM ELEMI
EEILT ELITE
EEILV LIEVE
EEILX EXILE
EEINS SEINE
EEINV NIEVE
EEINW NEWIE
EEINX EXINE
EEIPS PEISE
EEIRS SIREE
EEIRT RETIE
EEIRV REIVE
EEIRY EYRIE
EEISS SEISE
EEISV SIEVE
EEISZ SEIZE
EEITV EVITE
EEJLW JEWEL
EEJPS JEEPS
EEJRS JEERS
EEJSS JESSE
EEJST JETES
EEKKS KEEKS
EEKLN KNEEL
EEKLP KELEP
EEKLS KEELS
LEEKS
SLEEK
EEKLV KEVEL
EEKMS SMEEK
EEKNR KERNE
EEKNS KEENS
KNEES
SKEEN
SKENE
EEKNT KENTE
EEKOP PEKOE
EEKOV EVOKE
EEKPR KREEP
EEKPS KEEPS
PEEKS
PEKES
EEKRS ESKER
REEKS
EEKRW KREWE
EEKRY REEKY
REKEY
EEKSS SEEKS
SKEES
EEKST KEETS
SKEET
STEEK

EEKSW WEEKS
EEKSX KEXES
EELLS SELLE
EELLV LEVEL
EELMR MERLE
EELNO LEONE
EELNS LENES
LENSE
EELNW NEWEL
EELOP ELOPE
EELPR LEPER
REPEL
EELPS PEELS
PELES
SLEEP
SPEEL
EELPX EXPEL
EELRS LEERS
REELS
EELRT RELET
EELRV ELVER
LEVER
REVEL
EELRY LEERY
EELSS SEELS
EELST LEETS
SLEET
STEEL
STELE
TEELS
TELES
EELSV ELVES
EELSX LEXES
EELSY SEELY
EELTU ELUTE
EELTX TELEX
EEMMR EMMER
EEMMS MEMES
EEMMT EMMET
EEMNS MENSE
MESNE
NEEMS
SEMEN
EEMNU NEUME
EEMNY ENEMY
EEMOT EMOTE
EEMRR MERER
EEMRS MERES
EEMRT METER
METRE
REMET
RETEM
EEMRX REMEX
EEMRY EMERY
EEMSS SEEMS
SEMES
EEMST MEETS
METES
TEEMS
EEMSU EMEUS
EEMSZ MEZES
EENNP PENNE
EENNS NENES
EENPR PREEN
EENPS NEEPS
PEENS
PENES
EENQU QUEEN
EENRS ERNES
SNEER
EENRT ENTER
RENTE
TERNE
TREEN
EENRU ENURE
EENRV NERVE
NEVER
EENRW NEWER
RENEW
EENSS ESNES
SENSE
EENST SENTE
TEENS
TENSE
EENSU ENSUE
EENSV EVENS
NEVES
SEVEN
EENSW WEENS
EENTT TENET
EENTV EVENT
EENTW TWEEN
EENTY TEENY
YENTE
EENUV VENUE
EENWY WEENY

EEOPT TOPEE
EEORS EROSE
EEOXY OXEYE
EEPPS PEEPS
EEPRS PEERS
PERES
PERSE
PREES
PRESE
SPEER
SPREE
EEPRT PETER
EEPRU PUREE
RUPEE
EEPRY PEERY
EEPSS SEEPS
EEPST STEEP
EEPSV VEEPS
EEPSW SWEEP
WEEPS
EEPSY SEEPY
EEPWY WEEPY
EEQRU QUEER
EEQUU QUEUE
EERRS SERER
EERSS ERSES
SEERS
SERES
EERST ESTER
REEST
RESET
STEER
STERE
TERSE
TREES
EERSU REUSE
EERSV SERVE
SEVER
VEERS
VERSE
EERSW EWERS
RESEW
SEWER
SWEER
EERSX REXES
EERSY EYERS
EYRES
EERTV EVERT
REVET
EERTW REWET
EERTX EXERT
EERUV REVUE
EERVV VERVE
EERVX VEXER
EERVY EVERY
VEERY
EESSS ESSES
EESSX SEXES
EESSY YESES
EESTW SWEET
WEEST
WEETS
EESTY TYEES
EESVX VEXES
EETTU TUTEE
EETTW TWEET
EFFFO FEOFF
EFFIR FIFER
EFFIS FIEFS
FIFES
EFFOR OFFER
EFFRU RUFFE
EFFST TEFFS
EFGIN FEIGN
EFGIO FOGIE
EFGIR GRIEF
EFGLU FUGLE
EFGNO GONEF
EFGOR FORGE
GOFER
EFGOY FOGEY
EFGUU FUGUE
EFHIT THIEF
EFHLS FLESH
SHELF
EFHNO FOEHN
EFHRS FRESH
EFHST HEFTS
EFHTT THEFT
EFHTY HEFTY
EFIKN KNIFE
EFIKR KEFIR
EFIKS KIEFS
EFILL FILLE
EFILN ELFIN

EFILR FILER
FLIER
LIFER
RIFLE
EFILS FILES
FLIES
EFILT FILET
FLITE
EFIMR FERMI
EFINR FINER
INFER
EFINS FINES
NEIFS
EFINT FEINT
EFIQU FIQUE
EFIRR FIRER
FRIER
RIFER
EFIRS FIRES
FRIES
FRISE
REIFS
SERIF
EFIRT REFIT
EFIRV FIVER
EFIRX FIXER
REFIX
EFIRY FIERY
REIFY
EFISS SEIFS
EFIST FEIST
EFISV FIVES
EFISW WIFES
EFISX FIXES
EFIWY WIFEY
EFKLU FLUKE
EFKRS KERFS
EFKSY FYKES
EFLLS FELLS
EFLLY FELLY
EFLMU FLUME
EFLNO FELON
EFLOS FLOES
EFLOY FOLEY
EFLPS PELFS
EFLRY FERLY
FLYER
REFLY
EFLSS SELFS
EFLST FELTS
LEFTS
EFLSU FLUES
FUELS
FUSEL
EFLSW FLEWS
EFLSY FLEYS
EFLTU FLUTE
EFLTY FLYTE
LEFTY
EFLYY FEYLY
EFMOR FORME
EFMRU FEMUR
FUMER
EFMSU FUMES
EFMTU FUMET
EFNNY FENNY
EFNOT OFTEN
EFNRS FERNS
EFNRY FERNY
EFORR FRORE
EFORS FORES
FROES
EFORT FETOR
FORTE
OFTER
EFORY FOYER
EFORZ FROZE
EFOSS FOSSE
EFOSX FOXES
EFRRY FERRY
FRYER
REFRY
EFRSS SERFS
EFRST FRETS
EFRUZ FURZE
EFSST FESTS
EFSSU FUSES
EFSTU FETUS
EFSTW WEFTS
EFSUZ FUZES
EFTTY FYTTE
EFYZZ FEZZY
EGGHI GIGHE
EGGIU GIGUE
EGGLY LEGGY

EGGOR GORGE
GREGO
EGGOU GOUGE
EGGRU GURGE
EGGST TEGGS
EGGSY YEGGS
EGHHI HEIGH
EGHHU HEUGH
EGHIN HINGE
NEIGH
EGHIT EIGHT
EGHIW WEIGH
EGHNT THEGN
EGHRU HUGER
EGHTU TEUGH
EGIIN GENII
EGIJR REJIG
EGIKN EKING
EGILM GIMEL
GLIME
EGILN INGLE
EGILR LIGER
EGILT LEGIT
EGILU GUILE
EGIMM GIMME
EGIMR GRIME
EGINP GENIP
EGINR REIGN
RENIG
EGINS SEGNI
SENGI
SINGE
EGINT TINGE
EGINV GIVEN
EGINW GWINE
EGINX EXING
EGINY EYING
EGIOV OGIVE
VOGIE
EGIPR GRIPE
EGIRR RERIG
EGIRT TIGER
EGIRV GIVER
EGIST GITES
EGISU GUISE
EGISV GIVES
EGKLU KLUGE
KUGEL
EGKSS SKEGS
EGLMO GOLEM
EGLMU GLUME
EGLNO LONGE
EGLNS GLENS
EGLNU LUNGE
EGLOR OGLER
EGLOS LOGES
OGLES
EGLOV GLOVE
EGLOZ GLOZE
EGLRU GLUER
GRUEL
LUGER
EGLST GELTS
EGLSU GLUES
GULES
LUGES
EGLSY GLEYS
EGLTU GLUTE
EGLUY GLUEY
EGMMY GEMMY
EGMNO GENOM
GNOME
EGMOR GOMER
EGMOT GEMOT
EGMRS GERMS
EGMRU GRUME
EGMRY GERMY
EGMSU GEUMS
EGNOP PENGO
EGNOR GENRO
GONER
EGNOS SEGNO
EGNPU UNPEG
EGNST GENTS
EGNSU GENUS
NEGUS
EGOOS GOOSE
EGOOY GOOEY
EGOPR GROPE
EGOPY POGEY
EGORR ROGER
EGORS GOERS
GORES
GORSE
OGRES
EGORT ERGOT

EGORU ERUGO
ROGUE
ROUGE
EGORV GROVE
EGOSS GESSO
SEGOS
EGOSX GOXES
EGOTU TOGUE
EGOUV VOGUE
EGPRU PURGE
EGPTU GETUP
EGQSU SQUEG
EGRRU URGER
EGRSU GRUES
SURGE
URGES
EGRSY GREYS
GYRES
EGSST GESTS
EGSSU GUESS
EGSTU GUEST
EGSVY GYVES
EHHKT KHETH
EHHST HETHS
EHIKR HIKER
EHIKS HIKES
SHEIK
EHIKT KITHE
EHILO HELIO
EHILS HEILS
SHIEL
EHILT LITHE
EHILW WHILE
EHILX HELIX
EHIMN HEMIN
EHIMO HOMIE
EHINS SHINE
EHINT THEIN
THINE
EHINW WHINE
EHIOS HOISE
EHIRR HIRER
EHIRS HEIRS
HIRES
SHIER
SHIRE
EHIRT ITHER
THEIR
EHISS SHIES
EHIST HEIST
EHISV HIVES
SHIVE
EHITT TITHE
EHITW WHITE
WITHE
EHJSU JEHUS
EHKLW WHELK
EHKOS HOKES
OKEHS
EHKOY HOKEY
EHKST KHETS
EHKTY KYTHE
EHLLO HELLO
EHLLS HELLS
SHELL
EHLMO MOHEL
EHLMS HELMS
EHLMW WHELM
EHLOS HELOS
HOLES
HOSEL
SHEOL
EHLOT HELOT
HOTEL
THOLE
EHLOV HOVEL
EHLOW WHOLE
EHLOY HOLEY
HOYLE
EHLPS HELPS
SHLEP
EHLPW WHELP
EHLPY PHYLE
EHLRS HERLS
LEHRS
EHLSW WELSH
EHLTY ETHYL
EHLXY HEXYL
EHMNS MENSH
EHMNY HYMEN
EHMOR HOMER
EHMOS HOMES
EHMOY HOMEY
EHMPS HEMPS
EHMPY HEMPY
EHMRS HERMS

EHMRT THERM
EHMRU RHEUM
EHMRY RHYME
EHMST METHS
EHMSY MESHY
EHMTY THYME
EHNOP PHONE
EHNOR HERON
HONER
EHNOS HONES
HOSEN
SHONE
EHNOY HONEY
EHNRS HERNS
EHNRY HENRY
EHNST HENTS
SHENT
THENS
EHNSW SHEWN
WHENS
EHNTT TENTH
EHOOY HOOEY
EHOPR EPHOR
HOPER
EHOPS HOPES
EHOPT TOPHE
EHOPU OUPHE
EHORS HEROS
HOERS
HORSE
HOSER
SHOER
SHORE
EHORT OTHER
THROE
EHORV HOVER
EHORW WHORE
EHOSS HOSES
SHOES
EHOST ETHOS
SHOTE
THOSE
EHOSU HOUSE
EHOSV SHOVE
EHOSW HOWES
WHOSE
EHOSY HOSEY
EHPRY HYPER
EHPST THESP
EHPSY HYPES
EHRRY HERRY
EHRSU USHER
EHRSW SHREW
EHRSY SHYER
EHRTW THREW
EHRTZ HERTZ
EHSST HESTS
EHSSW SHEWS
EHSTT TETHS
EHSTU SHUTE
EHSTW THEWS
WHETS
EHSWW WHEWS
EHSWY WHEYS
EHTTY TYTHE
EHTWY THEWY
EIILP PILEI
EIIMN IMINE
EIINS NISEI
EIINX NIXIE
EIIPX PIXIE
EIISS ISSEI
EIISV IVIES
EIJRV JIVER
EIJSV JIVES
EIJVY JIVEY
EIKLM KELIM
EIKLN INKLE
LIKEN
EIKLR LIKER
EIKLS LIKES
EIKLV KEVIL
EIKMN MINKE
EIKMS MIKES
EIKNO EIKON
ENOKI
KOINE
EIKNP PEKIN
EIKNR INKER
REINK
EIKNS KINES
SKEIN
EIKPR PIKER
EIKPS KEPIS
PIKES
SPIKE

EIKRS KEIRS
KIERS
SIKER
SKIER
EIKRT KITER
TRIKE
EIKRY KYRIE
EIKSS SIKES
SKIES
EIKST KITES
SKITE
TIKES
EIKSV SKIVE
EIKSY SKIEY
YIKES
EILLM MILLE
EILLR ILLER
RILLE
EILLS LISLE
EILMN LIMEN
EILMP IMPEL
EILMR MILER
EILMS LIMES
MILES
SLIME
SMILE
EILMU ILEUM
EILMY LIMEY
EILNN LINEN
EILNO ELOIN
OLEIN
EILNR LINER
EILNS LENIS
LIENS
LINES
EILNT ELINT
INLET
EILNV LEVIN
LIVEN
EILNY LINEY
EILOO LOOIE
EILOR OILER
ORIEL
REOIL
EILOS SOLEI
EILOT TELOI
TOILE
EILOU LOUIE
EILOV OLIVE
VOILE
EILPR PERIL
PLIER
EILPS PILES
PLIES
SLIPE
SPEIL
SPIEL
SPILE
EILPX PIXEL
EILRS LIERS
RIELS
RILES
SLIER
EILRT LITER
LITRE
RELIT
TILER
EILRV ERVIL
LIVER
LIVRE
VILER
EILRY RILEY
EILSS ISLES
EILST ISLET
ISTLE
STILE
TILES
EILSU ILEUS
LIEUS
EILSV EVILS
LEVIS
LIVES
VEILS
EILSW LEWIS
LWEIS
WILES
EILSX LEXIS
SILEX
EILTT TITLE
EILTU UTILE
EILTX IXTLE
EILVX VEXIL
EIMMO MIMEO
EIMMR MIMER
EIMMS MIMES
EIMNO MONIE

EIMNR MINER
EIMNS MIENS
MINES
EIMNV VIMEN
EIMNY MEINY
EIMNZ MIZEN
EIMOR MOIRE
EIMOV MOVIE
EIMOX MOXIE
OXIME
EIMPR PRIME
EIMPT TEMPI
EIMRR RIMER
EIMRS EMIRS
MIRES
MISER
RIMES
EIMRT MERIT
MITER
MITRE
REMIT
TIMER
EIMRX MIREX
MIXER
REMIX
EIMSS MISES
SEISM
SEMIS
EIMST EMITS
ITEMS
METIS
MITES
SMITE
STIME
TIMES
EIMSX MIXES
EINNP PENNI
EINNR INNER
RENIN
EINNS NINES
EINNU ENNUI
EINNV VENIN
EINOP OPINE
EINOR IRONE
EINOS EOSIN
NOISE
EINOV ENVOI
OVINE
EINPR REPIN
RIPEN
EINPS PEINS
PENIS
PINES
SNIPE
SPINE
EINPT INEPT
EINPY PINEY
EINRS REINS
RESIN
RINSE
RISEN
SERIN
SIREN
EINRT INERT
INTER
NITER
NITRE
TRINE
EINRU INURE
URINE
EINRV RIVEN
EINRW REWIN
EINSS SINES
EINST INSET
NEIST
NITES
SENTI
STEIN
TINES
EINSV VEINS
VINES
EINSW SINEW
SWINE
WINES
EINSX NIXES
EINSZ ZEINS
ZINES
EINTU UNITE
UNTIE
EINTW TWINE
EINVX VIXEN
EINVY VEINY
EINWY WINEY
EINWZ WINZE
WIZEN
EIOOR OORIE

EIOPS POISE
EIORS OSIER
EIORU OURIE
EIORV VIREO
EIOTW TOWIE
EIOWY YOWIE
EIOWZ ZOWIE
EIPPR PIPER
EIPPS PIPES
EIPPT PIPET
EIPQU EQUIP
PIQUE
EIPRR PRIER
RIPER
EIPRS PERIS
PIERS
PRIES
PRISE
RIPES
SPEIR
SPIER
SPIRE
EIPRT TRIPE
EIPRV VIPER
EIPRW WIPER
EIPRZ PRIZE
EIPSS SIPES
SPIES
EIPST PISTE
SPITE
STIPE
EIPSW SWIPE
WIPES
EIPSX PIXES
EIPSY YIPES
EIPTT PETIT
PETTI
EIPTW PEWIT
EIPTY PIETY
EIPXY PYXIE
EIQRU QUIRE
EIQTU QUIET
QUITE
EIRRS RISER
EIRRT TRIER
EIRRV RIVER
EIRRW WIRER
WRIER
EIRRY EYRIR
EIRSS RISES
SIRES
EIRST RESIT
RITES
TIERS
TIRES
TRIES
EIRSU SIEUR
EIRSV RIVES
SIVER
VIERS
VIRES
EIRSW WEIRS
WIRES
WISER
WRIES
EIRSZ SIZER
EIRTT TETRI
TITER
TITRE
TRITE
EIRTU UTERI
EIRTV RIVET
EIRTW TWIER
WRITE
EIRVW WIVER
EISSS SISES
EISST SITES
STIES
EISSU ISSUE
EISSV VISES
EISSW WISES
EISSX SIXES
EISSZ SIZES
EISTU ETUIS
SUITE
EISTW WITES
EISTX EXIST
EXITS
SIXTE
EISTY YETIS
EISVW SWIVE
VIEWS
WIVES
EISWZ WIZES
EIVWY VIEWY
EJKOP KOPJE

EJKOR JOKER
EJKOS JOKES
EJKOY JOKEY
EJKRS JERKS
EJKRY JERKY
EJKSU JUKES
EJLLO JELLO
EJLLS JELLS
EJLLY JELLY
EJLOS JOLES
EJLOU JOULE
EJLPU JULEP
EJLRU JUREL
EJMMY JEMMY
EJNNY JENNY
EJNOS JONES
EJNOT JETON
EJNOY ENJOY
EJOSY JOEYS
EJPSU JUPES
EJRRY JERRY
EJSST JESTS
EJSTU JUTES
EJTTY JETTY
EKKOP KOPEK
EKLLN KNELL
EKLLS SKELL
EKLLV KVELL
EKLLY KELLY
EKLMS SKELM
EKLNT KNELT
EKLOS KOELS
EKLOT KETOL
EKLOY YOKEL
EKLPS KELPS
SKELP
EKLPY KELPY
EKLST KELTS
EKLSY YELKS
EKMOS MOKES
SMOKE
EKMPS KEMPS
EKMPT KEMPT
EKMRS MERKS
SMERK
EKNOR KRONE
EKNOS KENOS
EKNOT TOKEN
EKNOW WOKEN
EKNRS KERNS
EKNSU NEUKS
NUKES
EKNSY ENSKY
EKOPR POKER
EKOPS POKES
SPOKE
EKOPY POKEY
EKORT TOKER
TROKE
EKOSS SOKES
EKOST STOKE
TOKES
EKOSY YOKES
EKPRS PERKS
EKPRY PERKY
EKPSS SKEPS
EKPSU PUKES
EKPSY PESKY
EKRRY KERRY
EKRST TREKS
EKRSY RYKES
YERKS
EKRSZ ZERKS
EKSSW SKEWS
EKSSY SYKES
EKSTY KYTES
TYKES
EKSUY YEUKS
EKSYY SKYEY
EKUYY YEUKY
ELLMS MELLS
SMELL
ELLNS SNELL
ELLNY NELLY
ELLOS LOSEL
ELLPS SPELL
ELLQU QUELL
ELLSS SELLS
ELLST TELLS
ELLSW SWELL
WELLS
ELLSY YELLS
ELLTU TULLE
ELLTY TELLY
ELLWY WELLY

ELMNO LEMON
MELON
ELMNU LUMEN
ELMOR MOREL
ELMOS MOLES
ELMOT METOL
MOTEL
ELMOU OLEUM
ELMPU PLUME
ELMRS MERLS
ELMRU LEMUR
ELMST MELTS
SMELT
ELMSU MULES
ELMSW MEWLS
ELMSY YLEMS
ELMTY MELTY
ELMUV VELUM
ELMUY MULEY
ELMXY XYLEM
ELNOP PELON
PLEON
ELNOR ENROL
LONER
NEROL
ELNOS ENOLS
LENOS
NOELS
ELNOT LENTO
ELNOV NOVEL
ELNSU LUNES
ELNTU LUNET
UNLET
ELNWY NEWLY
ELOOS LOOSE
OLEOS
ELOOY LOOEY
ELOPR LOPER
POLER
PROLE
ELOPS LOPES
POLES
SLOPE
ELOPU LOUPE
ELORS LORES
LOSER
ORLES
ROLES
SOREL
ELORV LOVER
ELORW LOWER
ROWEL
ELOSS LOESS
LOSES
SLOES
SOLES
ELOST STOLE
TELOS
TOLES
ELOSU LOUSE
OUSEL
ELOSV LOVES
SOLVE
VOLES
ELOSW LOWES
LOWSE
ELOSX LOXES
ELOTT LOTTE
ELOTV VOLTE
ELOTW OWLET
TOWEL
ELOTX EXTOL
ELOTZ ZLOTE
ELOUV OVULE
ELOUZ OUZEL
ELOVW VOWEL
ELPRU PULER
ELPRY PLYER
REPLY
ELPST PELTS
SLEPT
SPELT
ELPSU PULES
PULSE
ELPSW PLEWS
ELPSY SLYPE
YELPS
ELPTU LETUP
ELRRU LURER
RULER
ELRSU LURES
RULES
ELRSY LYRES
SLYER
ELRUX LUREX
ELSSU SLUES

ELSSW SLEWS
ELSSY LYSES
ELSTU LUTES
TULES
ELSTW WELTS
ELSTY STYLE
ELSUX LUXES
ELSUY YULES
ELSWY WYLES
ELTUX EXULT
ELTWY WETLY
EMMOS MEMOS
MOMES
EMMSY EMMYS
EMNNO NOMEN
EMNNU NUMEN
EMNOR ENORM
EMNOS MESON
NOMES
OMENS
EMNOT MONTE
EMNOV VENOM
EMNOW WOMEN
EMNOY MONEY
EMNRU RUMEN
EMNSU MENUS
NEUMS
EMNTU UNMET
EMNUW UNMEW
EMNYZ ENZYM
EMOOR ROMEO
EMOOS MOOSE
EMOPR MOPER
PROEM
EMOPS MOPES
POEMS
POMES
EMOPT TEMPO
EMOPY MOPEY
MYOPE
EMORR ORMER
EMORS MORES
MORSE
OMERS
EMORT METRO
EMORV MOVER
VOMER
EMORW MOWER
EMOST MOSTE
MOTES
SMOTE
TOMES
EMOSU MEOUS
MOUES
MOUSE
EMOSV MOVES
EMOSW MEOWS
EMOSY MOSEY
EMOTT MOTET
MOTTE
TOTEM
EMOTY MOTEY
EMOZZ MEZZO
EMPRS PERMS
SPERM
EMPST TEMPS
EMPSU SPUME
EMPTT TEMPT
EMPTY EMPTY
EMRRU MURRE
EMRRY MERRY
EMRST TERMS
EMRSU MURES
MUSER
SERUM
EMRTU MUTER
EMRUX MUREX
EMSST STEMS
EMSSU MUSES
EMSSW SMEWS
EMSSY MESSY
EMSTU MUTES
EMSYZ ZYMES
ENNOS NEONS
NONES
ENNOT NONET
TENON
TONNE
ENNOX XENON
ENNPU UNPEN
ENNPY PENNY
ENNWY WENNY
ENOOS NOOSE
ENOOZ OZONE
ENOPR PRONE

ENOPS OPENS
PEONS
PONES
ENOPT NETOP
ENOPY PEONY
ENORS SENOR
SNORE
ENORT NOTER
TENOR
TONER
TRONE
ENORU ROUEN
ENORV ROVEN
ENORW OWNER
REWON
ROWEN
ENORY ONERY
ENORZ ZONER
ENOSS NOSES
SONES
ENOST NOTES
ONSET
SETON
STENO
STONE
TONES
ENOSV OVENS
ENOSW ENOWS
OWSEN
ENOSX EXONS
ENOSY NOSEY
ENOSZ ZONES
ENOTY TONEY
ENOVW WOVEN
ENOVY ENVOY
ENPRU PRUNE
ENPST SPENT
ENQRU QUERN
ENRRU RERUN
ENRST NERTS
RENTS
STERN
TERNS
ENRSU NURSE
RUNES
ENRSW WRENS
ENRSY SYREN
ENRTU TUNER
ENRTY ENTRY
ENRTZ NERTZ
ENRVY NERVY
ENSST NESTS
ENSSY SNYES
ENSTT NETTS
STENT
TENTS
ENSTU TUNES
UNSET
ENSTV VENTS
ENSTW NEWTS
ENSTY TYNES
ENSUV NEVUS
VENUS
ENSUW UNSEW
ENSUX NEXUS
UNSEX
ENSWY NEWSY
ENTTY NETTY
TENTY
ENTUW UNWET
EOORS ROOSE
EOORW WOOER
EOOSY SOOEY
EOOSZ OOZES
EOOYZ ZOOEY
EOPPR PREOP
EOPPS PEPOS
POPES
EOPRR REPRO
ROPER
EOPRS PORES
POSER
PROSE
REPOS
ROPES
SPORE
EOPRT REPOT
TOPER
TROPE
EOPRV PROVE
EOPRW POWER
EOPRY ROPEY
EOPSS PESOS
POSES
POSSE

EOPST ESTOP
PESTO
POETS
STOPE
TOPES
EOPSX EXPOS
POXES
EOPSY POESY
SEPOY
EOPTT PETTO
EOPTY TEPOY
EOPXY EPOXY
EOQRU ROQUE
EOQTU QUOTE
TOQUE
EORRR ERROR
EORRS SORER
EORRT RETRO
EORRV ROVER
EORRW ROWER
EORSS ROSES
SORES
EORST ROSET
ROTES
STORE
TORES
TORSE
EORSU EUROS
ROUES
ROUSE
EORSV OVERS
ROVES
SERVO
VERSO
EORSW RESOW
SEROW
SOWER
SWORE
WORSE
EORSY OYERS
YORES
EORSZ ZEROS
EORTT OTTER
ROTTE
TORTE
TOTER
EORTU OUTER
OUTRE
ROUTE
EORTV OVERT
TROVE
VOTER
EORTW TOWER
WROTE
EORTX OXTER
EORTY TOYER
EORVW VOWER
EORXX XEROX
EOSSU SOUSE
EOSTT TOTES
EOSTU TOUSE
EOSTV STOVE
VOTES
EOSTX SEXTO
EOSUY YOUSE
EOSWY YOWES
EPPPY PEPPY
EPPRS PERPS
PREPS
REPPS
EPPRU UPPER
EPRRU PURER
EPRRY PERRY
PRYER
EPRSS PRESS
EPRST PREST
STREP
EPRSU PURSE
SPRUE
SUPER
EPRSV PERVS
EPRSY PREYS
PYRES
EPRTU ERUPT
EPRTW TWERP
EPRXY PREXY
PYREX
EPSST PESTS
SEPTS
STEPS
EPSSU PUSES
SPUES
SUPES
EPSSW SPEWS

EPSTU SETUP
STUPE
UPSET
EPSTW SWEPT
EPSTY PESTY
TYPES
EPSXY PYXES
EPTTY PETTY
EPTYY TYPEY
EQRUY QUERY
EQSTU QUEST
EQSUU USQUE
EQSUY QUEYS
EQTUU TUQUE
ERRSU RUERS
SURER
ERRSY SERRY
ERRTU TRUER
ERRTY RETRY
TERRY
ERRWY WRYER
ERSST RESTS
TRESS
ERSSU RUSES
SUERS
USERS
ERSTT TRETS
ERSTU TRUES
ERSTV VERST
VERTS
ERSTW STREW
TREWS
WREST
ERSTY TREYS
TYERS
TYRES
ERSUX XERUS
ERTTU UTTER
ERTUV VERTU
ERTUY TUYER
ERTWY TWYER
ESSTT SETTS
STETS
TESTS
ESSTU SUETS
ESSTV VESTS
ESSTW STEWS
WESTS
ESSTX SEXTS
ESSTY STYES
ESSTZ ZESTS
ESTTX TEXTS
ESTTY TESTY
YETTS
ESTUX TUXES
ESTUY SUETY
ESTWY STEWY
WYTES
ESTYZ ZESTY
FFFLU FLUFF
FFGIL GLIFF
FFGIR GRIFF
FFGRU GRUFF
FFGSU GUFFS
FFHIT FIFTH
FFHIW WHIFF
FFHOW HOWFF
FFHSU HUFFS
FFHUY HUFFY
FFIJS JIFFS
FFIJY JIFFY
FFIKS SKIFF
FFIMS MIFFS
FFIMY MIFFY
FFINS SNIFF
FFIPS SPIFF
FFIQU QUIFF
FFIRS RIFFS
FFIST STIFF
TIFFS
FFITY FIFTY
FFLSU LUFFS
FFMSU MUFFS
FFNSU SNUFF
FFOPU POUFF
FFOST TOFFS
FFOTY TOFFY
FFPSU PUFFS
FFPUY PUFFY
FFRSU RUFFS
FFSTU STUFF
TUFFS
FGGOY FOGGY
FGGUY FUGGY
FGHIT FIGHT

FGILN FLING
FGINO GONIF
FGINU FUNGI
FGIOU FUGIO
FGIRS FRIGS
FGIRT GRIFT
FGIST GIFTS
FGLNO FLONG
FGLNU FLUNG
FGLOS FLOGS
GOLFS
FGLSU GULFS
FGLUY GULFY
FGNOO GONOF
FGNOU FUNGO
FGOOR FORGO
FGOOS GOOFS
FGOOY GOOFY
FGORS FROGS
FGRSU FRUGS
FGSUU FUGUS
FHILT FILTH
FHIRT FIRTH
FRITH
FHIST SHIFT
FHISY FISHY
FHLSU FLUSH
FHNOS FOHNS
FHOOS HOOFS
FHOOW WHOOF
FHORS FROSH
FHORT FORTH
FROTH
FHOSW HOWFS
FIILM FILMI
FIINS FINIS
FIINX INFIX
FIITX FIXIT
FIJSU FUJIS
FIKNS FINKS
FIKRS FRISK
FIKSU KUFIS
FILLO FILLO
FILLR FRILL
FILLS FILLS
FILLY FILLY
FILMS FILMS
FILMU FILUM
FILMY FILMY
FILNT FLINT
FILOO FOLIO
FILOS FILOS
FOILS
FILPS FLIPS
FILRS FLIRS
FILRT FLIRT
FILST FLITS
LIFTS
FILSU FUSIL
FILTY FITLY
FILUZ FUZIL
FIMOT MOTIF
FIMRS FIRMS
FIMTU MUFTI
FINNY FINNY
FINOS FINOS
FOINS
INFOS
FINRS FIRNS
FINTU UNFIT
FINTY NIFTY
FINUX UNFIX
FINUY UNIFY
FIOST FOIST
FIRRY FIRRY
FIRST FIRST
FRITS
RIFTS
FIRTT FRITT
FIRTU FRUIT
FIRTZ FRITZ
FIRZZ FRIZZ
FISST FISTS
SIFTS
FISTW SWIFT
FITWY WIFTY
FIYZZ FIZZY
FKLNU FLUNK
FKLOO KLOOF
FKLOS FOLKS
FKLOY FOLKY
FKLUY FLUKY
FKNSU FUNKS
FKNUY FUNKY
FKORS FORKS
FKORY FORKY

FLLOY FOLLY
FLLSU FULLS
FLLUY FULLY
FLMPU FLUMP
FLNOW FLOWN
FLOOR FLOOR
FLOOS FOOLS
LOOFS
FLOPS FLOPS
FLORS ROLFS
FLORU FLOUR
FLUOR
FLOSS FLOSS
FLOST LOFTS
FLOSU FOULS
SULFO
FLOSW FLOWS
FOWLS
WOLFS
FLOTU FLOUT
FLOTY LOFTY
FLOUW WOFUL
FLRSU FURLS
FLTUY FLUTY
FLUYT
FMORS FORMS
FMORU FORUM
FMPRU FRUMP
FNNUY FUNNY
FNORS FRONS
FNORT FRONT
FNORW FROWN
FNOST FONTS
FNOTU FOUNT
FUTON
FOOPR PROOF
FOOPS SPOOF
FOORS ROOFS
FOOST FOOTS
FOOSW WOOFS
FOOTY FOOTY
FOPRS PROFS
FOPSU POUFS
FORRU FUROR
FORST FORTS
FROST
FORSU FOURS
FORSW FROWS
FORTY FORTY
FOSST SOFTS
FOSTT TOFTS
FOSTU TOFUS
FOSTY SOFTY
FRRUY FURRY
FRSSU SURFS
FRSTU TURFS
FRSUY SURFY
FRTUY TURFY
FRUYZ FURZY
FSSUY FUSSY
FSTTU TUFTS
FSTUY FUSTY
FTTUY TUFTY
FUYZZ FUZZY
GGGLO GLOGG
GGHOS HOGGS
GGIJY JIGGY
GGIMS MIGGS
GGINO GOING
GGIOT GIGOT
GGIPY PIGGY
GGIRS GRIGS
GGIWY WIGGY
GGLOY LOGGY
GGLSU GLUGS
GGMOY MOGGY
GGMSU MUGGS
GGMUY MUGGY
GGNOS GONGS
NOGGS
GGOOS GOGOS
GGORS GROGS
GGOSY SOGGY
GGPUY PUGGY
GGSUV VUGGS
GGUVY VUGGY
GHHIS HIGHS
GHHIT HIGHT
THIGH
GHILT LIGHT
GHIMT MIGHT
GHINO HONGI
OHING
GHINS NIGHS
GHINT NIGHT
THING

GHINY HYING
GHIOS SHOGI
GHIRS GIRSH
GHIRT GIRTH
GRITH
RIGHT
GHISS SIGHS
GHIST SIGHT
GHISW WHIGS
GHITT TIGHT
GHITW WIGHT
GHLLY GHYLL
GHLOU GHOUL
LOUGH
GHLPY GLYPH
GHNOS HONGS
GHNOT THONG
GHORU ROUGH
GHOSS SHOGS
GHOST GHOST
GOTHS
GHOSU SOUGH
GHOSY YOGHS
GHOTU OUGHT
TOUGH
GHRSU GURSH
SHRUG
GHSSU SUGHS
GHSTU THUGS
GHSUV VUGHS
GHSUY GUSHY
GIILS SIGIL
GIILV VIGIL
GIINP PIING
GIINR IRING
GIJNO JINGO
GIKNS GINKS
KINGS
GIKOP GOPIK
GILLR GRILL
GILLS GILLS
GILLY GILLY
GILMS GLIMS
GILNO LINGO
LOGIN
GILNS LINGS
SLING
GILNT GLINT
GILNU LUNGI
GILNY LINGY
LYING
GILOO IGLOO
LOGOI
GILRS GIRLS
GILRY GIRLY
GILST GILTS
GILSU IGLUS
GILTU GUILT
GILTZ GLITZ
GIMNY MINGY
GIMOS GISMO
GIMOZ GIZMO
GIMPS GIMPS
GIMPY GIMPY
PIGMY
GIMRY GRIMY
GINNY GINNY
GINOP GIPON
OPING
PINGO
GINOR GIRON
GROIN
GINOT INGOT
TIGON
GINOW OWING
GINOY YOGIN
GINPS PINGS
GINRS GIRNS
GRINS
RINGS
GINRU RUING
UNRIG
GINRW WRING
GINSS SIGNS
SINGS
GINST STING
TINGS
GINSU SUING
USING
GINSW SWING
WINGS
GINSZ ZINGS
GINTY TYING
GINVY VYING
GINWY WINGY
GINYZ ZINGY

GIOPR PIROG
GIORR RIGOR
GIORS GIROS
GIORT GRIOT
TRIGO
GIORU GUIRO
GIORV VIGOR
GIOSY YOGIS
GIPRS GRIPS
PRIGS
SPRIG
GIPRT GRIPT
GIPRY GRIPY
GIPSY GIPSY
GIRST GIRTS
GRIST
GRITS
TRIGS
GISST GISTS
GISSW SWIGS
GISTW TWIGS
GJMUU JUGUM
GKLNO KLONG
GKNSU GUNKS
GKNUY GUNKY
GKOOS GOOKS
GKOOY GOOKY
GKORS GROKS
GKOSW GOWKS
GLLOY GOLLY
GLLSU GULLS
GLLUY GULLY
GLMOO GLOOM
GLMOS GLOMS
GLMOU MOGUL
GLMSU GLUMS
GLNOO LOGON
GLNOS LONGS
GLNOU GLUON
GLNSU LUNGS
SLUNG
GLOOS LOGOS
GLOOY OLOGY
GLOPS GLOPS
GLORW GROWL
GLORY GLORY
GLOSS GLOSS
SLOGS
GLOST GLOST
GLOSW GLOWS
GLOTU GLOUT
GLOUV VULGO
GLPSU GULPS
PLUGS
GLPUY GULPY
GLSSU SLUGS
GLSTU GLUTS
GMMUY GUMMY
GMNOO MONGO
GMNOU MUNGO
GMOOR GROOM
GMORS GORMS
GMOSS SMOGS
GMPRU GRUMP
GMPYY PYGMY
GNNUY GUNNY
GNOOS GOONS
GNOOY GOONY
GNOOZ GONZO
GNOPR PRONG
GNOPS PONGS
GNORW GROWN
WRONG
GNORY GYRON
GNOSS SNOGS
SONGS
GNOST TONGS
GNOSW GOWNS
GNOTU UNGOT
GNOUY YOUNG
GNPSU PUNGS
GNRSU RUNGS
GNRTU GRUNT
GNRUW WRUNG
GNSSU SNUGS
GNSTU STUNG
TUNGS
GNSUW SWUNG
GOOPS GOOPS
GOOPY GOOPY
GOORS SORGO
GOOSY GOOSY
GOOTU OUTGO
GOPRS GORPS
PROGS

GOPRU GROUP
GOPRY PORGY
GORSS GROSS
GORST GROTS
TROGS
GORSW GROWS
GORSY GORSY
GYROS
GORSZ GROSZ
GORTU GROUT
GOSTU GOUTS
GUSTO
GOSTY STOGY
GOTUY GOUTY
GUYOT
GPPUY GUPPY
GPRSU SPRUG
GPSYY GYPSY
GRRUY GURRY
GRSTU TRUGS
GRSUU GURUS
GRSUY GYRUS
SURGY
GSSTU GUSTS
GSSUY GUSSY
GSTUY GUSTY
GUTSY
GTTUY GUTTY
HHISW WHISH
HHMPU HUMPH
HHPPT PHPHT
HHSSU SHUSH
HIILN NIHIL
HIIRS RISHI
HIJOS SHOJI
HIKNS KNISH
HIKNT THINK
HIKNY HINKY
HIKRS SHIRK
HIKST KITHS
SHTIK
HIKSW WHISK
HILLO HILLO
HILLS HILLS
SHILL
HILLT THILL
HILLY HILLY
HILMU HILUM
HILOT LITHO
THIOL
HILPY HIPLY
HILRT THIRL
HILRW WHIRL
HILST HILTS
HILSU HILUS
HILSY SHILY
HILTT TILTH
HIMRT MIRTH
HIMSS SHIMS
HIMST SMITH
HIMSW WHIMS
HIMTY THYMI
HINNT NINTH
HINNY HINNY
HINOR RHINO
HINPU UNHIP
HINSS SHINS
SINHS
HINST HINTS
THINS
HINSW WHINS
HINSY SHINY
HINWY WHINY
HIOPP HIPPO
HIOPT TOPHI
HIORS ROSHI
HIORU HOURI
HIOST HOIST
HIPPY HIPPY
HIPRT THRIP
HIPSS SHIPS
HIPST PITHS
HIPSW WHIPS
HIPTW WHIPT
HIPTY PITHY
HIRRS SHIRR
HIRRW WHIRR
HIRSS SHRIS
HIRST SHIRT
HIRSW WHIRS
HIRTY YIRTH
HISST HISTS
SHIST
HISSU SUSHI
HISSV SHIVS

HISSW SWISH
HISSY HISSY
HISTW SWITH
WHIST
WHITS
HISTX SIXTH
HITWY WHITY
WITHY
HIWZZ WHIZZ
HJNOS JOHNS
HKKOU HOKKU
HKLOS HOLKS
KOHLS
HKLSU HULKS
HKLUY HULKY
HKMOU HOKUM
KHOUM
HKNOS HONKS
HKNSU HUNKS
HKNTU THUNK
HKNUY HUNKY
HKOOS HOOKS
SHOOK
HKOOY HOOKY
HKOPS KOPHS
HKOSS SKOSH
HKOSW HOWKS
HKSSU HUSKS
HKSUY HUSKY
HLLOO HOLLO
HLLOU HULLO
HLLOY HOLLY
HLLSU HULLS
HLMOS HOLMS
HLMPY LYMPH
HLMUY MUHLY
HLNSU SHULN
HLOOS SHOOL
HLOOY HOOLY
HLOPX PHLOX
HLORS SHORL
HLORW WHORL
HLOSS SLOSH
HLOST HOLTS
SLOTH
HLOSW HOWLS
HLOTY HOTLY
HLPSU PLUSH
HLPSY SYLPH
HLRSU HURLS
HLRTU THURL
HLRUY HURLY
HLSSU SHULS
SLUSH
HLSYY SHYLY
HMNOT MONTH
HMNPY NYMPH
HMNSY HYMNS
HMOOP OOMPH
HMOOS HOMOS
HMOPR MORPH
HMOPW WHOMP
HMORU HUMOR
MOHUR
HMOST MOTHS
HMOTU MOUTH
HMOTY MOTHY
HMPSU HUMPS
HMPTU THUMP
HMPUW WHUMP
HMPUY HUMPY
HMRRY MYRRH
HMRTU THRUM
HMSSU SMUSH
HMSTU MUSTH
HMSTY MYTHS
HMSUU HUMUS
HMSUY MUSHY
HMTYY MYTHY
THYMY
HNOOP PHONO
HNOOR HONOR
HNOOS SHOON
HNOOW NOHOW
HNOPS PHONS
HNOPY PHONY
HNORS HORNS
SHORN
HNORT NORTH
THORN
HNORY HORNY
HNOSW SHOWN
HNOSY HYSON
HNSSU SHUNS

HNSTU HUNTS
SHUNT
HNSTY SYNTH
HOOPS HOOPS
POOHS
HOOPT PHOTO
HOOPW WHOOP
HOORT ORTHO
THORO
HOOSS SHOOS
HOOST HOOTS
SHOOT
SOOTH
HOOSW WHOSO
WOOSH
HOOTT TOOTH
HOOTY HOOTY
HOPPY HOPPY
HOPQS QOPHS
HOPRT THORP
HOPSS SHOPS
SOPHS
HOPST PHOTS
TOPHS
HOPSU OUPHS
HOPSW WHOPS
HOPSY HYPOS
SOPHY
HOQTU QUOTH
HORST HORST
SHORT
HORSU HOURS
HORSY HORSY
HORTT TROTH
HORTU ROUTH
HORTW ROWTH
THROW
WHORT
WORTH
WROTH
HOSST HOSTS
SHOTS
SOTHS
HOSSW SHOWS
HOSTT SHOTT
HOSTU SHOUT
SOUTH
THOUS
HOSUY SHOYU
HOSWY SHOWY
HOTUY YOUTH
HPSSY SYPHS
HPSTU PHUTS
HPSUW WHUPS
HPSUY PUSHY
HQRSU QURSH
HRRUY HURRY
HRSTU HURST
HURTS
RUTHS
HRSUY RUSHY
HRTTU TRUTH
HSSTU SHUTS
HSSUY HUSSY
HSTUY TUSHY
HSUUW WUSHU
IIJNN JINNI
IIKLM KILIM
IIKNN KININ
IIKPS PIKIS
IIKST TIKIS
IIKSW KIWIS
IILLV VILLI
IILMT LIMIT
IILMU ILIUM
IILNN LININ
IILNP LIPIN
IILPS PILIS
IIMMN MINIM
IIMMX IMMIX
IIMNO IMINO
IIMNR MIRIN
IIMNS MINIS
IIMPR PRIMI
IIMPS IMPIS
IIMST MITIS
IINNO INION
IINST INTIS
IIORT TORII
IIPPT PIPIT
IIPST TIPIS
IIRVZ VIZIR
IISTT TITIS
IISTV VISIT
IISTZ ZITIS

IITZZ ZIZIT
IJKMU MUJIK
IJKNS JINKS
IJKOS KOJIS
IJLLS JILLS
IJLST JILTS
IJMMY JIMMY
IJMPY JIMPY
IJNNS JINNS
IJNOS JOINS
IJNOT JOINT
IJNPU PUNJI
IJOST JOIST
IKKLS KLIKS
IKKNS KINKS
SKINK
IKKNY KINKY
IKKOS KIOSK
IKKRS KIRKS
IKKRU KUKRI
IKLLR KRILL
IKLLS KILLS
SKILL
IKLMS MILKS
IKLMY MILKY
IKLNP PLINK
IKLNS KILNS
LINKS
SLINK
IKLNY LINKY
IKLOS KILOS
IKLPU PULIK
IKLRS SKIRL
IKLSS SILKS
IKLST KILTS
IKLSY SILKY
IKLTY KILTY
IKLXY KYLIX
IKMNS MINKS
IKMPS SKIMP
IKMRS MIRKS
SMIRK
IKMRY MIRKY
IKMSS SKIMS
IKNOP PINKO
IKNOS IKONS
KINOS
OINKS
IKNPR PRINK
IKNPS PINKS
IKNPY PINKY
IKNRS KIRNS
RINKS
IKNSS SINKS
SKINS
IKNST KNITS
SKINT
STINK
IKNSW SWINK
WINKS
IKNYZ ZINKY
IKOOR IROKO
IKPSS SKIPS
IKPSY SPIKY
IKPTU TUPIK
IKQRU QUIRK
IKRRS SKIRR
IKRSS RISKS
IKRST SKIRT
STIRK
IKRSY RISKY
IKSST KISTS
SKITS
IKSSY KISSY
IKTTY KITTY
ILLMS MILLS
ILLNS NILLS
ILLOS LILOS
ILLPR PRILL
ILLPS PILLS
SPILL
ILLQU QUILL
ILLRS RILLS
ILLRT TRILL
ILLSS SILLS
ILLST LILTS
STILL
TILLS
ILLSV VILLS
ILLSW SWILL
WILLS
ILLSY SILLY
SLILY
YILLS
ILLSZ ZILLS

ILLTW TWILL
ILLWY WILLY
ILMNS LIMNS
ILMNU LINUM
ILMOS LIMOS
MILOS
MOILS
ILMPS LIMPS
ILMPY IMPLY
ILMSS SLIMS
ILMST MILTS
ILMSY SLIMY
ILMTY MILTY
ILNNS LINNS
ILNOS LINOS
LIONS
LOINS
NOILS
ILNOY NOILY
ILNPU LUPIN
ILNST LINTS
ILNSY LYSIN
ILNTU UNLIT
UNTIL
ILNTY LINTY
ILNVY VINYL
ILOOP POLIO
ILOOS OLIOS
ILOOV OVOLI
ILOPS POLIS
SPOIL
ILOPT PILOT
ILOPU POILU
ILOPX OXLIP
ILORS LORIS
ROILS
ILORT LIROT
TRIOL
ILORY ROILY
ILORZ ZORIL
ILOSS SILOS
SOILS
ILOST TOILS
ILOSU LOUIS
ILOSV VIOLS
ILOTV VOLTI
ILPPU PUPIL
ILPPY LIPPY
ILPSS LISPS
SLIPS
ILPST SLIPT
SPILT
SPLIT
ILPSU PILUS
PULIS
ILPTU TULIP
UPLIT
ILQTU QUILT
ILRST TIRLS
ILRSV VIRLS
ILRSW SWIRL
ILRTW TWIRL
ILSST LISTS
SILTS
SLITS
ILSSY LYSIS
SYLIS
ILSTT STILT
TILTS
ILSTW WILTS
ILSTY SILTY
STYLI
IMMOY YOMIM
IMNNY MINNY
IMNOO NOMOI
IMNOR MINOR
IMNOU ONIUM
IMNST MINTS
IMNSU MINUS
MUNIS
IMNTY MINTY
IMNUX UNMIX
IMOPR PRIMO
IMOPU OPIUM
IMOSS MISOS
IMOST MOIST
OMITS
IMOSX OXIMS
SIXMO
IMOTV VOMIT
IMPPR PRIMP
IMPPS PIMPS
IMPRS PRIMS
PRISM
IMPSS SIMPS

IMPSW WIMPS
IMPUX MIXUP
IMPWY WIMPY
IMRST TRIMS
IMSST MISTS
IMSSW SWIMS
IMSSY MISSY
IMSTT MITTS
IMSTY MISTY
IMUZZ ZUZIM
INNNO NINON
INNNY NINNY
INNOO ONION
INNOP PINON
INNOT NITON
INNOU UNION
INNPU UNPIN
INNPY PINNY
INNRU INRUN
INURN
INNTY TINNY
INOPR ORPIN
PRION
INOPS OPSIN
PIONS
INOPT PINOT
PINTO
PITON
POINT
INOQU QUOIN
INORS IRONS
NOIRS
NORIS
ORNIS
ROSIN
INORT INTRO
NITRO
INORY IRONY
INOSV VINOS
INOSW WINOS
INOSY NOISY
YONIS
INOSZ SOZIN
INOTX TOXIN
INPPU PINUP
INPPY NIPPY
INPRS PIRNS
INPRT PRINT
INPRU PURIN
UNRIP
INPSS SNIPS
SPINS
INPST PINTS
INPSY PYINS
SPINY
INPTU INPUT
INPUZ UNZIP
INQSU QUINS
INQTU QUINT
INRSU RUINS
INRTU RUTIN
INSST SNITS
INSSU NISUS
SINUS
INSTT STINT
TINTS
INSTU SUINT
UNITS
INSTW TWINS
INTTY NITTY
INTUW UNWIT
INTUY UNITY
INTWY TWINY
INTYY TYIYN
IOOPR POORI
IOOPT TOPOI
IOPRR PRIOR
IOPSS PISOS
IOPST POSIT
TOPIS
IOPSU PIOUS
IOPTV PIVOT
IOQTU QUOIT
IORRS ORRIS
IORST RIOTS
ROTIS
TIROS
TORSI
TRIOS
TROIS
IORSV VISOR
IORSZ ZORIS
IORVY IVORY
IORVZ VIZOR

IOSTT TOITS
IPPTY TIPPY
IPPYZ ZIPPY
IPQSU QUIPS
IPQUU QUIPU
IPRSS PRISS
IPRST SPIRT
SPRIT
STIRP
STRIP
TRIPS
IPRSU PURIS
SIRUP
IPRSY SPIRY
IPRTW TWIRP
IPRVY PRIVY
IPSST SPITS
IPSSV SPIVS
IPSSW WISPS
IPSTU SITUP
IPSTY TIPSY
IPSTZ SPITZ
IPSWY WISPY
IPSXY PYXIS
IPTTU PUTTI
IQRTU QUIRT
IQSTU QUITS
IRRSY YIRRS
IRSST STIRS
IRSSU RISUS
IRSTW WRIST
WRITS
IRSUV VIRUS
IRTUV VIRTU
IRTYZ RITZY
ISSSW SWISS
ISSSY SISSY
ISSTU SITUS
SUITS
ISSTW WISTS
ISTTW TWIST
TWITS
ISTXY SIXTY
XYSTI
ITTTU TUTTI
ITTTY TITTY
ITTWX TWIXT
ITTWY WITTY
ITYZZ TIZZY
JJSUU JUJUS
JKNSU JUNKS
JKNUY JUNKY
JKOSU JOUKS
JKSUU JUKUS
JLLOY JOLLY
JLOST JOLTS
JLOSW JOWLS
JLOTY JOLTY
JLOWY JOWLY
JMNOO JOMON
JMOOS MOJOS
JMORU JORUM
JMPSU JUMPS
JMPUY JUMPY
JNOPU JUPON
JNOTU JUNTO
JORRU JUROR
JOSTU JOUST
JOTTY JOTTY
JSSTU JUSTS
JTTUY JUTTY
KKLSU SKULK
KKNOS KONKS
KKNSU SKUNK
KKOOS KOOKS
KKOOY KOOKY
KKUYY YUKKY
KLLNO KNOLL
KLLSU SKULL
KLNOP PLONK
KLNPU PLUNK
KLNRU KNURL
KLNSU LUNKS
SLUNK
KLOOS KOLOS
LOOKS
KLOSY YOLKS
KLOYY YOLKY
KLRSU LURKS
KLSSU SULKS
KLSUY SULKY
KLTUZ KLUTZ
KMNOS MONKS
KMOSS MOSKS

KMOSY SMOKY
KMRSU MURKS
KMRUY MURKY
KMSSU MUSKS
KMSUY KUMYS
MUSKY
KNNOW KNOWN
KNOOR KROON
KNOOS NOOKS
SNOOK
KNOPS KNOPS
KNOSP
KNORU KORUN
KNOST KNOTS
KNOSW KNOWS
WONKS
KNOSZ ZONKS
KNOTU KNOUT
KNOWY WONKY
KNPSU PUNKS
SPUNK
KNPUY PUNKY
KNRSU KNURS
KNRTU TRUNK
KNSTU STUNK
KOOPS SPOOK
KOORS ROOKS
KOORY ROOKY
KOOSS SOOKS
KOOST KOTOS
STOOK
KOOSZ ZOOKS
KOOTW KOTOW
KOPRS PORKS
KOPRY PORKY
KORST SKORT
STORK
TORSK
KORSW WORKS
KOSSU KUSSO
SOUKS
KOSUZ ZOUKS
KRSSU RUSKS
KRSTU TURKS
KRSUU KURUS
KSSTU TUSKS
LLLOS LOLLS
LLLOY LOLLY
LLLSU LULLS
LLMOS MOLLS
LLMOY MOLLY
LLMSU MULLS
LLNSU NULLS
LLOPS POLLS
LLOQU QUOLL
LLORS ROLLS
LLORT TROLL
LLOST TOLLS
LLOTY TOLYL
LLOWY LOWLY
LLOXY XYLOL
LLPSU PULLS
LLRTU TRULL
LLSTU STULL
LLSUU LULUS
LLSUY SULLY
LLSYY SLYLY
LLXYY XYLYL
LMOOS LOOMS
MOOLS
OSMOL
LMOOT MOLTO
LMOST MOLTS
SMOLT
LMOSU SOLUM
LMOTU MOULT
LMPPU PLUMP
LMPSU LUMPS
PLUMS
SLUMP
LMPUY LUMPY
PLUMY
LMSSU SLUMS
LNNOY NONYL
NYLON
LNOOR ORLON
LNOOS LOONS
NOLOS
SNOOL
SOLON
LNOOY LOONY
LNOPY PYLON
LNOSY SONLY
LNRSU NURLS
LNSTU LUNTS

LOOOV OVOLO
LOOPR ORLOP
LOOPS LOOPS
POLOS
POOLS
SLOOP
SPOOL
LOOPY LOOPY
LOOSS SOLOS
LOOST LOOTS
LOTOS
SOTOL
STOOL
TOOLS
LOOSW WOOLS
LOOTT LOTTO
LOOWY WOOLY
LOPPS PLOPS
LOPPY LOPPY
POLYP
LOPRW PROWL
LOPSS SLOPS
LOPST PLOTS
LOPSU LOUPS
LOPSW PLOWS
LOPSY PLOYS
POLYS
LOPTU POULT
LOPTZ PLOTZ
LORRY LORRY
LORST ROTLS
LORSU LOURS
LORUY LOURY
LOSST SLOTS
LOSSU SOLUS
SOULS
LOSSW SLOWS
LOSSY LOSSY
LOSTU LOTUS
LOUTS
TOLUS
LOSTV VOLTS
LOSUY LOUSY
LOSWY YOWLS
LOTYZ ZLOTY
LPPSU PULPS
LPPUY PULPY
LPRSU PURLS
SLURP
LPSUU LUPUS
LRSSU SLURS
LRSUY SURLY
LRTUY TRULY
LRWYY WRYLY
LSSTU LUSTS
SLUTS
LSSUU LUSUS
SULUS
LSTUY LUSTY
MMMOY MOMMY
MMMSU MUMMS
MMMUY MUMMY
MMOSU MOMUS
MMOTY TOMMY
MMPSU MUMPS
MMRUY RUMMY
MMSUU MUMUS
MMTUY TUMMY
MMUYY YUMMY
MNOOR MORON
MNOOS MONOS
MOONS
NOMOS
MNOOY MOONY
MNORS MORNS
NORMS
MNORU MOURN
MNOSU MUONS
MNOTU MOUNT
MUTON
NOTUM
MNOWY WOMYN
MOOPR PROMO
MOOPS POMOS
MOORR MORRO
MOORS MOORS
ROOMS
MOORT MOTOR
MOORV VROOM
MOORY MOORY
ROOMY
MOOSS MOSSO
MOOST MOOTS
MOOSZ MOZOS
ZOOMS
MOOTT MOTTO
MOPPS POMPS
MOPRS PROMS
ROMPS
MOPRT TROMP
MOPST STOMP
MOPYY MYOPY
MORRU RUMOR
MORST MORTS
STORM
MORSW WORMS
MORTU TUMOR
MORWY WORMY
MOSST MOSTS
MOSSU SUMOS
MOSSY MOSSY
MOSTT MOTTS
MOSUY MOUSY
MPPSU PUMPS
MPRSU RUMPS
MPRTU TRUMP
MPSSU SUMPS
MPSTU STUMP
TUMPS
MPSUY SPUMY
MRRSU MURRS
MRRUY MURRY
MRSTU STRUM
MSSTU MUSTS
SMUTS
STUMS
MSSUY MUSSY
MSTTU MUTTS
MSTUY MUSTY
MSTYY STYMY
MUYZZ MUZZY
NNOOS NOONS
NNOSU NOUNS
NNOSY SONNY
NNOUW UNWON
NNPUY PUNNY
NNRUY RUNNY
NNSSU SUNNS
NNSUY SUNNY
NNSWY WYNNS
NNTUY TUNNY
NOOPR PORNO
NOOPS POONS
SNOOP
SPOON
NOOST SNOOT
TOONS
NOOSW SWOON
NOOSZ ZOONS
NOOTY TOYON
NOPRS PORNS
NOPRY PORNY
NOPTU PUNTO
PUTON
NOPUY YUPON
NORSS SORNS
NORST SNORT
NORSW SWORN
NORUY YOURN
NOSST SNOTS
NOSSW SNOWS
NOSSY SONSY
NOSTU SNOUT
TONUS
NOSTW NOWTS
TOWNS
WONTS
NOSTY STONY
NOSUW SWOUN
NOSWY SNOWY
NOTWY TOWNY
NPRSU SPURN
NPSTU PUNTS
NPSUU SUNUP
NPTUY PUNTY
NRSTU RUNTS
TURNS
NRTUY RUNTY
NSSTU STUNS
NSTTU STUNT
NSTUY NUTSY
NTTUY NUTTY
OOPPS POOPS
OOPRS PROSO
SOPOR
SPOOR
OOPRT TROOP
OOPST STOOP
TOPOS
OOPSW SWOOP
WOOPS
OOPTT POTTO
OOPUY POYOU
OORRT ROTOR
OORST ROOST
ROOTS
ROTOS
TOROS
TORSO
OORSZ ORZOS
OORTT TOROT
OORTY ROOTY
OORTZ TROOZ
OOSST SOOTS
OOSTT OTTOS
TOOTS
OOSTY SOOTY
TOYOS
OOSUZ OUZOS
OOTYZ ZOOTY
OOWYZ WOOZY
OPPPY POPPY
OPPRS PROPS
OPPSY POPSY
SOPPY
OPRSS PROSS
OPRST PORTS
PROST
SPORT
STROP
OPRSU POURS
ROUPS
OPRSW PROWS
OPRSY PROSY
PYROS
OPRUY ROUPY
OPRXY PROXY
OPSST POSTS
SPOTS
STOPS
OPSSU SOUPS
OPSSW SWOPS
OPSSY SYSOP
OPSTT STOPT
OPSTU POUTS
SPOUT
STOUP
OPSTW STOWP
OPSTY POTSY
TYPOS
OPSUY SOUPY
OPTTU PUTTO
OPTTY POTTY
OPTUY POUTY
ORRST TORRS
ORRSY SORRY
ORRWY WORRY
ORSST SORTS
ORSSU SORUS
SOURS
ORSTT TORTS
TROTS
ORSTU ROUST
ROUTS
STOUR
TORUS
TOURS
ORSTW STROW
TROWS
WORST
WORTS
ORSTY RYOTS
STORY
STROY
TROYS
TYROS
ORSUY YOURS
ORSVW VROWS
ORTTU TROUT
TUTOR
ORUVW VROUW
OSSST STOSS
OSSTU OUSTS
OSSTW STOWS
SWOTS
OSTTT STOTT
OSTTU STOUT
TOUTS
OSUYZ SOYUZ
PPPUY PUPPY
PPSTY TYPPS
PPSUU PUPUS
PPUYY YUPPY
PRRSU PURRS
PRSSU SPURS
PRSTU SPURT
TURPS
PRSUU USURP
PRSUY PURSY
SYRUP
PRTUY PURTY
PSSUY PUSSY
PSTTU PUTTS
PTTUY PUTTY
RSSTU RUSTS
TRUSS
RSTTU STRUT
STURT
TRUST
RSTTY TRYST
RSTUW WURST
RSTUY RUSTY
YURTS
RSUUY USURY
RTTUY RUTTY
SSTXY XYSTS
SSUWY WUSSY
STTUU TUTUS
TTTUY TUTTY

6-Letter Alphagrams

AAABCL CABALA
AAABCN CABANA
AAABCS ABACAS
CASABA
AAABIS ABASIA
AAABKK KABAKA
AAABKL KABALA
AAABKS ABAKAS
AAABKY KABAYA
AAABLQ QABALA
AAABLR LABARA
AAABLT ALBATA
ATABAL
BALATA
AAABNN BANANA
AAABNS ANABAS
AAABRZ BAZAAR
AAABSY ABAYAS
AAACCI ACACIA
AAACJN JACANA
AAACLP ALPACA
AAACMR MARACA
AAACNR ARCANA
AAACPT PATACA
AAACSV CASAVA
AAADGG AGGADA
AAADHM HAMADA
AAADMR ARMADA
RAMADA
AAADNP PANADA
AAAEGP AGAPAE
AAAELZ AZALEA
AAAGIP AGAPAI
AAAGLR ARGALA
AAAGMS AGAMAS
AAAGNN NAGANA
AAAHLL HALALA
AAAHLW HAWALA
AAAITX ATAXIA
AAAJMP PAJAMA
AAAKLM KAMALA
AAAKLS ALASKA
AAALMS MASALA
SALAAM
AAALPP PALAPA
AAAMNN MANANA
AAAMNP PANAMA
AAAMNR AMARNA
AAAMNT ATAMAN
AAAMRS ASRAMA
SAMARA
AAAMRT TARAMA
AAANNZ ZANANA
AAANSS ASANAS
AAAPPY PAPAYA
AAARST SATARA
AAARTV AVATAR
AABBBO BAOBAB
AABBCY ABBACY
AABBKS BABKAS
KABABS
AABBLO BALBOA
AABBLR BARBAL
AABBST SABBAT
AABCCE BACCAE
AABCHS CASBAH
AABCIM CAMBIA
AABCIR ARABIC
AABCLS CABALS
AABCLU BACULA
AABCMN CABMAN
AABCMT TAMBAC
AABCRS BARCAS
SCARAB
AABCSU ABACUS
AABCUU AUCUBA
AABDER ABRADE
AABDES ABASED
AABDET ABATED
AABDEU AUBADE
AABDGO DAGOBA
AABDIN INDABA
AABDLL BALLAD
AABDLM LAMBDA
AABDMN BADMAN
AABDNS BANDAS
AABDOR ABOARD
ABROAD
AABDRR DARBAR
AABDRT TABARD
AABDRY BAYARD
AABEEM AMEBAE
AABEGM AMBAGE
AABEGS SEABAG
AABEIL ABELIA
AABELR ARABLE
AABELT ABLATE
AABELZ ABLAZE
AABEMN AMEBAN
AABEMO AMOEBA
AABEMS AMEBAS
AABEMT BEMATA
AABERS ABASER
AABERT ABATER
AABERZ ZAREBA
AABESS ABASES
BAASES
AABEST ABATES
AABETU BATEAU
AABGGR RAGBAG
AABGGS GASBAG
AABGIM GAMBIA
AABGIN BAAING
AABGIR AIRBAG
AABGMN BAGMAN
AABGMS GAMBAS
AABGOZ GAZABO
AABGRT RATBAG
AABGSS BAGASS
AABHKS KASBAH
AABHKT BHAKTA
AABHLR BHARAL
AABHMR BRAHMA
AABHSW BASHAW
AABILL LABIAL
AABILM BAALIM
AABILU ABULIA
AABILX BIAXAL
AABIMR AMBARI
AABINN BANIAN
AABINZ BANZAI
AABIRR ARRIBA
AABIRZ ZARIBA
AABIST ABATIS
AABISW WASABI
AABISZ BAIZAS
AABJNX BANJAX
AABKMT TAMBAK
AABKNN KANBAN
AABKRS KABARS
AABLLO ABOLLA
AABLMR RAMBLA
AABLMS BALSAM
SAMBAL
AABLOR ABORAL
AABLOV LAVABO
AABLSS BALSAS
SABALS
AABLST BASALT
TABLAS
AABLTU ABLAUT
AABMMS MAMBAS
AABMNR BARMAN
AABMNT BANTAM
BATMAN
AABMNY BAYMAN
AABMOS ABOMAS
AABMOY BAYAMO
AABMPS ABAMPS
AABMRS SAMBAR
AABMRY AMBARY
AABMSS SAMBAS
AABNNY BANYAN
AABNSW BWANAS
NAWABS
AABORR ARROBA
AABORT ABATOR
RABATO
AABRSS SABRAS
AABRST RABATS
AABRSV BRAVAS
AABRSZ BAZARS
BRAZAS
AABRTY BARYTA
AABTTW ABWATT
AACCDI CICADA
AACCEL CAECAL
AACCHM CHACMA
AACCHN CANCHA
AACCIL ALCAIC
CICALA
AACCKR CARACK
AACCLO CLOACA
AACCLP CALPAC
AACCLR CALCAR
AACCMO MACACO
AACCNN CANCAN
AACCOS CACAOS
AACDDU CAUDAD
AACDEF FACADE
AACDEI ACEDIA
AACDEL ALCADE
AACDER ARCADE
AACDHR CHADAR
AACDHS DACHAS
AACDHT DATCHA
AACDIR ACARID
CARDIA
AACDLU CAUDAL
AACDMP MADCAP
AACDNR CANARD
AACEFI FACIAE
AACEFL FAECAL
AACEFR CARAFE
AACEHP APACHE
AACEHT CHAETA
AACEIL AECIAL
AACELN ANLACE
AACELP PALACE
AACELS CALESA
AACELT ACETAL
AACEMO CAEOMA
AACEMR CAMERA
AACENP CANAPE
AACENR ARCANE
AACENT CATENA
AACERS ARECAS
CAESAR
AACERT CARATE
AACETU ACUATE
AACETV CAVEAT
VACATE
AACETX EXACTA
AACFIL FACIAL
AACFIS FACIAS
FASCIA
AACFLU FACULA
FAUCAL
AACFNT CAFTAN
AACFRS FRACAS
AACGIM AGAMIC
AACGIR AGARIC
AACGIU GUAIAC
AACGLY GALYAC
AACHHL CHALAH
AACHKR CHAKRA
CHARKA
AACHKW KWACHA
AACHLL CHALLA
AACHLS CALASH
AACHNO CHOANA
AACHNR ANARCH
AACHNS ASHCAN
NACHAS
AACHNZ CHAZAN
AACHPS PACHAS
AACHRS CHARAS
AACHSW CASHAW
AACHTT ATTACH
AACIJM JICAMA
AACILL LAICAL
AACILM CALAMI
CAMAIL
AACILP APICAL
AACILR RACIAL
AACIMN CAIMAN
MANIAC
AACIMS CAMISA
AACINR ACINAR
ARNICA
CARINA
CRANIA
AACIPR PICARA
AACIPS CAPIAS
AACIPT CAPITA
AACIRV CAVIAR
AACISS CASSIA
AACIST CASITA
AACITV ATAVIC
AACITX ATAXIC
AACJKL JACKAL
AACJLS JACALS
AACJOU ACAJOU
AACKLP KALPAC
AACKRR ARRACK
AACKTT ATTACK
AACLLN CALLAN
AACLLS CALLAS
AACLMT LACTAM
AACLMU MACULA
AACLNO CANOLA
AACLNR CARNAL
AACLNS CANALS
AACLNT CANTAL
AACLNU CANULA
LACUNA
AACLOS COALAS
AACLOT CATALO
AACLOX COAXAL
AACLPR CARPAL
AACLPS PASCAL
AACLRS CRAALS
LASCAR
RASCAL
SACRAL
SCALAR
AACLSU CASUAL
CAUSAL
AACLTU ACTUAL
AACMNR CARMAN
AACMNY CAYMAN
AACMRT AMTRAC
TARMAC
AACMSS CAMASS
AACMSW MACAWS
AACNNS CANNAS
AACNPT CAPTAN
CATNAP
AACNRY CANARY
AACNST SANCTA
AACNSV CANVAS
AACNTV VACANT
AACPPY PAPACY
AACRRU CURARA
AACRST CARATS
AACRSU ACARUS
AACRTV CRAVAT
AADDEL DAEDAL
AADDIL ALIDAD
AADDOU AOUDAD
AADDSU AUDADS
AADEFR AFEARD
AADEGL GELADA
AADEGM DAMAGE
AADEGN AGENDA
AADEGS ADAGES
AADEKM MEDAKA
AADEKW AWAKED
AADELT ALATED
AADEMM MADAME
AADEMN ANADEM
MAENAD
AADEMZ AMAZED
AADENT ADNATE
AADENX ADNEXA
AADEPR PARADE
AADFIR AFRAID
AADFRS FARADS
AADGGS DAGGAS
AADGIM AGAMID
AADGIO ADAGIO
AADGIR GARDAI
AADGNP PADNAG
AADGOP PAGODA
AADGRY GAYDAR
AADHIL DAHLIA
AADHMR DHARMA
AADHNR DHARNA
AADHNX HANDAX
AADHPR PARDAH
AADHRS SRADHA
AADHRZ HAZARD
AADILO ALODIA
AADILR RADIAL
AADILS DALASI
AADILU AUDIAL
AADIMN AIDMAN
AADIMR ARAMID
AADINR RADIAN
AADINS NAIADS
AADINV NAVAID
AADIST STADIA
AADKMS DAMASK
AADKPU PADAUK
AADLMP LAMPAD
AADLMW WADMAL
AADLMY MALADY
AADLNO ANODAL
AADLNS ALANDS
SANDAL
AADLNU LANDAU
AADLNV VANDAL
AADLOP APODAL
AADLRU RADULA
AADLSS SALADS
AADMMN MADMAN
AADMMR DAMMAR
AADMMS MADAMS
AADMNS DAMANS
AADMOU AMADOU
AADMRS DAMARS
DRAMAS
MADRAS
AADMRU MARAUD
AADMRZ MAZARD
AADMSS ADMASS
AADMYY MAYDAY
AADNNR RANDAN
AADNPS PANDAS
AADNSV VANDAS
AADOPS POSADA
AADPST ADAPTS
AADPYY PAYDAY
AADRRS RADARS
SARDAR
AADRSW AWARDS
AADRTU DATURA
AADRTY DATARY
AADRVW VAWARD
AAEEGL GALEAE
AAEELP PALEAE
AAEERT AERATE
AAEFGN FANEGA
AAEFGR AGRAFE
AAEFLM AFLAME
AAEFLV FAVELA
AAEFNR FRAENA
AAEFNS FAENAS
AAEFNU FAUNAE
AAEGGR GARAGE
AAEGGV GAVAGE
AAEGLM AGLEAM
AAEGLN ANLAGE
GALENA
AAEGLR AGLARE
ALEGAR
LAAGER
AAEGLS GALEAS
AAEGLV LAVAGE
AAEGMN MANAGE
AAEGMR MEGARA
AAEGNT AGNATE
AAEGOR AGORAE
AAEGPS AGAPES
AAEGRV RAVAGE
AAEGST AGATES
AAEGSV AGAVES
SAVAGE
AAEGTU GATEAU
AAEHKP PAKEHA
AAEHKT TAKAHE
AAEHLM HAEMAL
AAEHLT ALTHEA
AAEHMT HAMATE
AAEHNY HYAENA
AAEHPR RAPHAE
AAEILM LAMIAE
AAEILR AERIAL
REALIA
AAEILX ALEXIA
AAEIMN ANEMIA
AAEINT TAENIA
AAEITV AVIATE
AAEKLN ALKANE
AAEKLS AKELAS
AAEKMW WAKAME
AAEKNN ANANKE
AAEKNW AWAKEN
AAEKRT KARATE
AAEKSW AWAKES
AAELLP PAELLA
PALEAL
AAELLU ALULAE
AAELMT MALATE
MEATAL
TAMALE
AAELNN ANNEAL
AAELNP APNEAL
AAELNT LANATE
AAELOR AREOLA
AAELPP APPEAL
AAELPR EARLAP
AAELPS SALPAE
AAELPT PALATE
AAELRU LAURAE
AAELRV LARVAE
AAELST ALATES
AAEMMM MAMMAE
AAEMNS SEAMAN
AAEMNX AXEMAN
AAEMRS ARAMES
AAEMRT RAMATE
AAEMSZ AMAZES
AAENNZ ZENANA
AAENOP APNOEA
AAENPS APNEAS
PAEANS
PAESAN
AAENPV PAVANE
AAENRS ANEARS
ARENAS
AAENST ANSATE
AAENSU NAUSEA
AAENSW SEAWAN
AAEORT AORTAE
AAEPPR APPEAR
AAEPRS AREPAS
SARAPE
AAEPTT TAPETA
AAEPTW WATAPE
AAERRR ARREAR
AAERRT ERRATA
AAERST REATAS
AAERTU AURATE
AAERWX EARWAX
AAERWY AWEARY
AAESTV SAVATE
AAESWY SEAWAY
AAFFIM MAFFIA
AAFFIR AFFAIR
RAFFIA
AAFFIT TAFFIA
AAFFLR FARFAL
AAFFRY AFFRAY
AAFFRZ ZAFFAR
AAFGHN AFGHAN
AAFGNS FANGAS
AAFIJT FAJITA
AAFIKL ALFAKI
AAFIKS SIFAKA
AAFIMS MAFIAS
AAFINR FARINA
AAFIRS SAFARI
AAFIST TAFIAS
AAFKNS NAKFAS
AAFKNT KAFTAN
AAFLLL FALLAL
AAFLNU FAUNAL
AAFLOT AFLOAT
AAFLTU FLAUTA
AAFNSU FAUNAS
AAFOST AFTOSA
AAFSTW FATWAS
AAGGKU GAGAKU
AAGGLO GALAGO
AAGGMN GAGMAN
AAGGQU QUAGGA
AAGGRS SAGGAR
AAGGRT RAGTAG
TAGRAG
AAGHIN AAHING
AAGHJN GANJAH
AAGHLS GALAHS
AAGHMR GRAHAM
AAGHNR HANGAR
AAGHRR AARRGH
AAGHST AGHAST
AAGILN AGNAIL
AAGILO LAOGAI
AAGILR ARGALI
AAGILV GAVIAL
AAGIMN MAGIAN
AAGIMS AMIGAS
AAGINN ANGINA
AAGINU IGUANA
AAGINV VAGINA
AAGIRS AGRIAS
AAGISS SAIGAS
AAGIST AGITAS
TAIGAS
AAGJNS GANJAS
AAGJRS JAGRAS
AAGJRU JAGUAR
AAGJSU AJUGAS
AAGKLY GALYAK
AAGLLP PLAGAL
AAGLNO AGONAL
ANALOG
AAGLNR RAGLAN
AAGLNS LAGANS
AAGLNU LAGUNA
AAGLRS ARGALS
GRAALS
AAGLST STALAG
AAGLSY GAYALS
AAGLXY GALAXY
AAGMMR GRAMMA
AAGMMS GAMMAS
MAGMAS
AAGMNR RAGMAN
AAGMNS GASMAN
MANGAS
AAGMPR GRAMPA
AAGMRS GRAMAS
AAGMRY MARGAY
AAGMSY GAMAYS
AAGNNO GOANNA
AAGNNW WANGAN
AAGNOR ANGORA
ORGANA
AAGNPR PARANG
AAGNPS PAGANS
PANGAS
AAGNRS SANGAR
AAGNRY ANGARY
AAGNSS SANGAS
AAGNST SATANG
AAGNUY GUANAY
AAGORS AGORAS
AAGPPR GRAPPA
AAGRSZ GAZARS
AAGRVY VAGARY
AAGSUV GUAVAS
AAHHLL HALLAH
AAHHLV HALVAH
AAHHMZ HAMZAH
AAHHPT APHTHA
AAHILT HIATAL
AAHILY ALIYAH
AAHIMS AHIMSA
AAHINW HANIWA
AAHIPR PARIAH
RAPHIA
AAHIRS SHARIA
AAHJRR JARRAH
AAHJRS RAJAHS
AAHKNU KAHUNA
AAHKSS KASHAS
AAHLLL HALLAL
AAHLLO HALLOA
AAHLLS HALALS
AAHLLW WALLAH
AAHLMM HAMMAL
AAHLMS ALMAHS
HALMAS
HAMALS
AAHLMT MALTHA
AAHLMU HAMAUL
AAHLOS ALOHAS
AAHLPS ALPHAS
AAHLRS ASHLAR
LAHARS
AAHLRT HARTAL
AAHLSV HALVAS
LAVASH
AAHMMM HAMMAM
AAHMNS ASHMAN
SHAMAN
AAHMPY MAYHAP
AAHMRS ASHRAM
AAHMSS SHAMAS
AAHMST ASTHMA
MATSAH
AAHMSZ HAMZAS
SHAZAM
AAHMTZ HAZMAT
MATZAH
AAHNSS HANSAS
AAHNSZ HAZANS
AAHNZZ HAZZAN
AAHPPR PARAPH
AAHPSS PASHAS
AAHPTY APATHY
AAHRSS HARASS
AAHRST ARHATS
AAHRSY RAYAHS
AAHSSY SASHAY
AAIIKZ ZAIKAI
AAIILS AALIIS
AAIJNR JARINA
AAIJSV AJIVAS
AAIKKS KAIAKS
AAIKLL ALKALI
AAIKLM KALMIA
AAIKLN KALIAN
AAIKNR KINARA
AAIKRU UAKARI
AAILLP PALLIA
AAILLX AXILLA
AAILMN ANIMAL
LAMINA
MANILA
AAILMP IMPALA
AAILMS LAMIAS
SALAMI
AAILNN ALANIN
AAILNR NARIAL
AAILNS LANAIS
LIANAS
NASIAL
SALINA
AAILNT LATINA
AAILPS PALAIS
AAILQU QUALIA
AAILRT ATRIAL
LARIAT
LATRIA
AAILSS ASSAIL
AAILSV AVAILS
SALIVA
SALVIA
AAILSY ALIYAS
AAIMMS MIASMA
AAIMMX MAXIMA
AAIMNR AIRMAN
MARINA
AAIMNS ANIMAS
MANIAS
AAIMRT AMRITA
TAMARI
AAIMSU AMUSIA
AAIMSZ ZAMIAS
AAIMTT TATAMI
AAINOP ANOPIA
AAINOT ATONIA
AAINOX ANOXIA
AAINPP PAPAIN
AAINPR PARIAN
PIRANA
AAINPS PAISAN
AAINPT PATINA
PINATA
TAIPAN
AAINRS NAIRAS
AAINRT ANTIAR
AAINRU ANURIA
URANIA
AAINSV AVIANS
AAINTT ATTAIN
AAINTW ATWAIN
AAIOPR APORIA
AAIORZ ZOARIA
AAIPRY APIARY
PIRAYA
AAIPSS PAISAS
AAIPTY PITAYA
AAIPZZ PIAZZA
AAIRRY ARIARY
AAIRST ARISTA
RAITAS
RIATAS
TARSIA
TIARAS
AAIRSV VARIAS
AAIRVY AVIARY
AAIRWY AIRWAY
AAISSS ASSAIS
AAISTW AWAITS
AAITUY YAUTIA
AAJKNS SANJAK
AAJLPS JALAPS
AAJMPY PYJAMA
AAJNNS JNANAS
AAJNOW AJOWAN
AAJNPR PRAJNA
AAJNPS JAPANS
AAJNSW JAWANS
AAJRSV SVARAJ
AAJRSW SWARAJ
AAKKLP KALPAK
AAKKMR MARKKA
AAKKOP KAKAPO
AAKKSY KAYAKS
AAKLMS KALAMS
AAKLOS KOALAS
AAKLPS KALPAS
AAKLRS KRAALS
AAKLTU TALUKA
AAKMRS KARMAS
MAKARS
MARKAS
AAKMSY YASMAK
AAKMTU MAKUTA
AAKNOR ANORAK
AAKNRT KANTAR
AAKNST ASKANT
TANKAS
AAKNWZ KWANZA
AAKOPR PAKORA
AAKPPS KAPPAS
AAKPRS PARKAS
AAKRST KARATS

AAKSSV KAVASS
AAKUYZ YAKUZA
AALLLN LALLAN
AALLMS LLAMAS
AALLNY ALANYL
ANALLY
AALLPP APPALL
PALPAL
AALLRU ALULAR
AALLRV LARVAL
AALLSS SALALS
AALLSW WALLAS
AALLSY ALLAYS
AALLTT ATLATL
AALLVV VALVAL
AALMMM MAMMAL
AALMNP NAPALM
AALMNU ALUMNA
MANUAL
AALMNW LAWMAN
AALMNY LAYMAN
AALMOR AMORAL
AALMOS ALAMOS
AALMOT AMATOL
AALMPR PALMAR
AALMPS LAMPAS
PLASMA
AALMRS ALARMS
MALARS
AALMRU ALARUM
AALMST TAMALS
AALMSU ULAMAS
AALNNS ANNALS
AALNNU ANNUAL
AALNOT ATONAL
AALNOX AXONAL
AALNOZ AZONAL
AALNPR PLANAR
AALNPT PLATAN
AALNRT ANTRAL
TARNAL
AALNRU ANURAL
RANULA
AALNRW NARWAL
AALNSS NASALS
AALNST ALANTS
ASLANT
AALNSU LAUANS
AALNSY NYALAS
AALOPT TAPALO
AALOPY PAYOLA
AALORT AORTAL
AALOVW AVOWAL
AALPPS APPALS
AALPPU PAPULA
AALPRR PARRAL
AALPRY PARLAY
AALPSS SALPAS
AALPSU PAUSAL
AALPSY PLAYAS
AALPSZ PLAZAS
AALRST ALTARS
ASTRAL
RATALS
TALARS
TARSAL
AALRSU LAURAS
AALRSV LARVAS
AALRSY SALARY
AALRSZ LAZARS
AALRVV VALVAR
AALSSS SALSAS
AALSSV VASSAL
AALSTT STATAL
AALSWY ALWAYS
AALTUV VALUTA
AALWYY WAYLAY
AAMMMS MAMMAS
AAMMRR MARRAM
AAMMUZ MAZUMA
AAMNNN MANNAN
AAMNNS MANNAS
AAMNNV VANMAN
AAMNOR RAMONA
AAMNOZ AMAZON
AAMNPS SAMPAN
AAMNPT TAMPAN
AAMNRT MANTRA
AAMNST ATMANS
MANATS
MANTAS
AAMNTU MANTUA
AAMNTX TAXMAN
AAMOPR PARAMO
AAMORS AROMAS
AAMOSS SAMOSA
AAMOST SOMATA
AAMPPS PAMPAS
AAMPRS PRAAMS
AAMQSU SQUAMA
AAMRSU ASARUM
AAMRSW ASWARM
AAMRTU TRAUMA
AAMSSS MASSAS
AAMSTZ MATZAS
AANNNO ANNONA
AANNRU ANURAN
AANNTT NATANT
AANOST SONATA
AANOTT ANATTO
AANPPS NAPPAS
AANPRT PARTAN
TARPAN
TRAPAN
AANPRU PURANA
AANPSV PAVANS
AANQST QANATS
AANQTU QUANTA
AANRRT ARRANT
AANRSS SANSAR
SARANS
AANRST RATANS
AANRSU RUANAS
AANRSV NAVARS
VARNAS
AANRTT RATTAN
TANTRA
TARTAN
AANRTY RATANY
YANTRA
AANRTZ TARZAN
AANSSU SAUNAS
AANSTV SAVANT
AANSTZ STANZA
AANSYY NAYSAY
AANSZZ ZANZAS
AANTUV AVAUNT
AANWYY ANYWAY
AAOPST SAPOTA
AAORRU AURORA
AAORST AORTAS
AAOTTV OTTAVA
AAPPSW PAPAWS
AAPPWW PAWPAW
AAPRRU PARURA
AAPRST SATRAP
AAPSST PASTAS
AAPSTW WATAPS
AAPWXX PAXWAX
AAPZZZ PAZAZZ
AAQRSU QUASAR
AARRSS SARSAR
AARRSY ARRAYS
AARRTT TARTAR
AARSTT ATTARS
STRATA
TATARS
AARSTY ASTRAY
AARSWW WARSAW
AASSSY ASSAYS
AASSTY SATAYS
AASTZZ TAZZAS
ABBBEL BABBLE
ABBBLY BLABBY
ABBCDE CABBED
ABBCEI CABBIE
ABBCIR BICARB
ABBCOS CABOBS
ABBCOT BOBCAT
ABBCRY CRABBY
ABBCSY SCABBY
ABBDDE DABBED
ABBDEG GABBED
ABBDEI BABIED
ABBDEJ JABBED
ABBDEL DABBLE
ABBDEN NABBED
ABBDER BARBED
DABBER
ABBDES SABBED
ABBDET TABBED
ABBDEU BEDAUB
ABBEEU BAUBEE
ABBEEW BAWBEE
ABBEFR FABBER
ABBEGL GABBLE
ABBEGR GABBER
ABBEIR BABIER
BARBIE
ABBEIS BABIES
ABBEIY YABBIE
ABBEJR JABBER
ABBEKS KEBABS
ABBELR BARBEL
RABBLE
ABBELS BABELS
ABBELU BAUBLE
BUBALE
ABBELW WABBLE
ABBENR NABBER
ABBERR BARBER
ABBERS BARBES
ABBERT BARBET
RABBET
ABBERY YABBER
ABBESS ABBESS
ABBESY ABBEYS
ABBFLY FLABBY
ABBGOR GABBRO
ABBGRY GRABBY
ABBHJU JUBBAH
ABBHOO HABOOB
ABBHSY SHABBY
ABBILL LIBLAB
ABBILO BILBOA
ABBINR RABBIN
ABBIRS RABBIS
ABBIRT RABBIT
ABBIST TABBIS
ABBKOS KABOBS
ABBLOO BABOOL
ABBLRU BULBAR
ABBLSU BABULS
BUBALS
ABBLWY WABBLY
ABBMOO BAMBOO
ABBMOX BOMBAX
ABBNOO BABOON
ABBNOS NABOBS
ABBOOS BABOOS
ABBORS ABSORB
ABBOST ABBOTS
ABBOTY BATBOY
ABBRSU BUSBAR
ABBRTU BARBUT
ABBSWY SWABBY
ABCCIO BOCCIA
ABCCLU BUCCAL
ABCDEH BACHED
ABCDEK BACKED
ABCDEL CABLED
ABCDER BRACED
ABCDEU ABDUCE
ABCDIR BARDIC
ABCDTU ABDUCT
ABCEEM BECAME
ABCEFI BIFACE
ABCEGU CUBAGE
ABCEHL BLEACH
ABCEHR BREACH
ABCEHS BACHES
ABCEHY BEACHY
ABCEIM AMEBIC
ABCEIR CARIBE
ABCEIS CEIBAS
ABCEJT ABJECT
ABCEKR BACKER
ABCELM BECALM
ABCELR CABLER
ABCELS CABLES
ABCELT CABLET
ABCEMN CABMEN
ABCEMR CAMBER
CRAMBE
ABCEMW WEBCAM
ABCENO BEACON
ABCEPS BECAPS
ABCERR BRACER
ABCERS BRACES
CABERS
ABCERU RUBACE
ABCFIR FABRIC
ABCFNO CONFAB
ABCHKU CHABUK
ABCHLN BLANCH
ABCHNR BRANCH
ABCHOR BROACH
ABCHPU HUBCAP
ABCHRS BRACHS
ABCIIM IAMBIC
ABCIKP BIPACK
ABCILU ABULIC
ABCIMU CUMBIA
ABCINO BONACI
ABCINS CABINS
ABCIOS COBIAS
ABCISS BASICS
ABCKLS BLACKS
ABCKPU BACKUP
ABCLMY CYMBAL
ABCLOT COBALT
ABCMOP MOBCAP
ABCMOR CRAMBO
ABCMOT COMBAT
TOMBAC
ABCNOR CARBON
CORBAN
ABCNOS BACONS
BANCOS
ABCORS CARBOS
CAROBS
COBRAS
ABCORX BOXCAR
ABCORY CARBOY
ABCOSV VOCABS
ABCRST BRACTS
ABCSSU SCUBAS
ABCSTU SACBUT
ABDDEE BEADED
ABDDEG BADGED
ABDDEI ABIDED
BADDIE
ABDDEL BALDED
BLADED
ABDDEN BANDED
ABDDEO ABODED
ABDDER BADDER
BARDED
ABDDEU DAUBED
ABDDEY DAYBED
ABDDHU BUDDHA
ABDEEH BEHEAD
ABDEEK BEAKED
DEBEAK
ABDEEL BEADLE
ABDEEM BEAMED
ABDEEN BEANED
ABDEER BEADER
ABDEES DEBASE
SEABED
ABDEET DEBATE
ABDEFF BAFFED
ABDEFL FABLED
ABDEFR BARFED
ABDEGG BAGGED
ABDEGL BEGLAD
GABLED
ABDEGN BANGED
ABDEGO BODEGA
ABDEGR BADGER
BARGED
GARBED
ABDEGS BADGES
DEBAGS
ABDEHS BASHED
ABDEHT BATHED
ABDEIL BAILED
ABDEIR ABIDER
ABDEIS ABIDES
BIASED
ABDEIT BAITED
ABDEJM JAMBED
ABDEKL BALKED
ABDEKN BANKED
ABDEKR BARKED
BRAKED
DEBARK
ABDEKS BASKED
ABDELL BALLED
ABDELM AMBLED
BEDLAM
BELDAM
BLAMED
LAMBED
ABDELO ALBEDO
DOABLE
ABDELR BALDER
BLADER
BLARED
ABDELS BLADES
ABDELT TABLED
ABDELU BELAUD
ABDELW BAWLED
BLAWED
ABDELY BELADY
DYABLE
ABDELZ BLAZED
ABDEMM BAMMED
ABDEMN BADMEN
BEDAMN
ABDENN BANNED
ABDENP BEDPAN
ABDENR BANDER
BARNED
ABDENY BENDAY
ABDEOS ABODES
ADOBES
ABDEOT BOATED
ABDERR BARRED
ABDERS ARDEBS
BARDES
BEARDS
BREADS
DEBARS
SABRED
SERDAB
ABDERU DAUBER
EARBUD
ABDERV ADVERB
BRAVED
ABDERY BRAYED
BREADY
REDBAY
ABDERZ BRAZED
ABDEST BASTED
ABDESU ABUSED
DAUBES
ABDETT BATTED
ABDETU TABUED
ABDFOR FORBAD
ABDGNO BANDOG
ABDILR BRIDAL
RIBALD
ABDINR RIBAND
ABDINT BANDIT
ABDIRR BRIARD
ABDIRS BRAIDS
DISBAR
ABDLLY BALDLY
ABDLOS DOBLAS
ABDLRY DRABLY
ABDNOR ROBAND
ABDNOU ABOUND
ABDNRS BRANDS
ABDNRY BRANDY
ABDOOS ADOBOS
ABDORS ADSORB
BOARDS
BROADS
DOBRAS
ABDORY BOYARD
BYROAD
ABDRRU DURBAR
ABDRSU ABSURD
ABDRUY DAUBRY
ABDRWY BAWDRY
ABEEFL BEFLEA
ABEEGL BEAGLE
GLEBAE
ABEEGR BAREGE
BARGEE
ABEEGZ BEGAZE
ABEEHV BEHAVE
ABEEIL BAILEE
ABEEIN BEANIE
ABEEKR BEAKER
BERAKE
ABEEKT BETAKE
ABEELN BALEEN
ENABLE
ABEELP BELEAP
ABEELS ABELES
ABEEMN BEMEAN
BENAME
ABEEMR AMBEER
ABEENT BEATEN
ABEEOR AEROBE
ABEERR BEARER
ABEERT BEATER
BERATE
REBATE
ABEERV BEAVER
ABEERW BEWARE
ABEERY EYEBAR
ABEFFL BAFFLE
ABEFGL BEFLAG
ABEFHL BEHALF
ABEFLL BEFALL
ABEFLM FLAMBE
ABEFLR FABLER
ABEFLS FABLES
ABEFMR FERBAM
ABEFPR PREFAB
ABEGGI BAGGIE
ABEGGR BAGGER
BEGGAR
ABEGIS GABIES
ABEGLL BEGALL
ABEGLM GAMBLE
ABEGLN BANGLE
ABEGLR GARBLE
ABEGLS BAGELS
BELGAS
GABLES
ABEGLU BELUGA
ABEGMN BAGMEN
ABEGMR BREGMA
ABEGMS GAMBES
ABEGNR BANGER
GRABEN
ABEGOR BORAGE
ABEGOZ GAZEBO
ABEGRS BARGES
ABEGTU BAGUET
ABEHIL HABILE
ABEHKL KEBLAH
ABEHLR HERBAL
ABEHOS BOHEAS
OBEAHS
ABEHRS BASHER
REHABS
ABEHRT BATHER
BERTHA
BREATH
ABEHSS BASHES
ABEHST BATHES
ABEIIL BAILIE
ABEIIT TIBIAE
ABEILL ALIBLE
LABILE
LIABLE
ABEILM LAMBIE
ABEILO OBELIA
ABEILR BAILER
LIBRAE
ABEILS ABSEIL
ABEILT ALBEIT
ALBITE
ABEILV VIABLE
ABEILW BEWAIL
ABEILY BAILEY
ABEIMR BARMIE
ABEINS SABINE
ABEINT BINATE
ABEIRS BRAISE
RABIES
ABEIRT BAITER
BARITE
REBAIT
TERBIA
ABEIRZ BRAIZE
ABEISS BIASES
ABEISZ BAIZES
ABEITW BAWTIE
ABEJMS JAMBES
ABEJOR JERBOA
ABEJRU ABJURE
ABEKLR BALKER
ABEKLS BLEAKS
ABEKMN EMBANK
ABEKMR EMBARK
ABEKNR BANKER
ABEKRR BARKER
ABEKRS BAKERS
BRAKES
BREAKS
KEBARS
ABEKRY BAKERY
ABEKST BASKET
ABELLR BALLER
ABELLS LABELS
ABELLT BALLET
ABELLU BULLAE
ABELMM EMBALM
ABELMR AMBLER
BLAMER
LAMBER
MARBLE
RAMBLE
ABELMS AMBLES
BLAMES
ABELMW WAMBLE
ABELNU NEBULA
UNABLE
UNBALE
ABELNZ BENZAL
ABELOR BOREAL
ABELOT BOATEL
LOBATE
OBLATE
ABELRR BARREL
ABELRS BALERS
BLARES
BLEARS
ABELRT LABRET
ABELRV VERBAL
ABELRW BAWLER
WARBLE
ABELRY BARELY
BARLEY
BLEARY
ABELRZ BLAZER
ABELSS SABLES
ABELST ABLEST
BLEATS
STABLE
TABLES
ABELSU SUABLE
USABLE
ABELSY BASELY
BELAYS
ABELSZ BLAZES
ABELTT BATTLE
TABLET
ABELWY BYELAW
ABEMNO BEMOAN
ABEMNR BARMEN
ABEMNT BATMEN
ABEMNY BAYMEN
BYNAME
ABEMRS AMBERS
BREAMS
EMBARS
ABEMRU UMBRAE
ABEMRY AMBERY
ABEMSY EMBAYS
MAYBES
ABENNR BANNER
ABENNT BANNET
ABENOR BORANE
ABENOS BEANOS
ABENRR BARREN
ABENRT BANTER
ABENRU UNBEAR
URBANE
ABENRY BARNEY
NEARBY
ABENRZ BRAZEN
ABENST ABSENT
ABENTT BATTEN
ABENTU BUTANE
ABENTZ BEZANT
ABEORS BOREAS
ABEORT BOATER
BORATE
REBATO
ABEORZ BEZOAR
ABEOSV ABOVES
ABEOTX TEABOX
ABEPRU UPBEAR
ABEPRW BEWRAP
ABEPTU UPBEAT
ABEQRU BARQUE
ABEQSU BASQUE
ABERRS BARRES
REBARS
ABERRT BARRET
BARTER
ABERRV BRAVER
ABERRW BRAWER
ABERRY BRAYER
ABERRZ BRAZER
ABERSS SABERS
SABRES
ABERST BAREST
BASTER
BREAST
TABERS
ABERSU ABUSER
BURSAE
ABERSV BRAVES
ABERSY BARYES
YERBAS
ABERSZ BRAZES
ZEBRAS
ABERTT BATTER
ABERTU ARBUTE
ABERTY BARYTE
BETRAY
ABERUU BUREAU
ABERWY BEWRAY
ABESSS BASSES
ABESST BASEST
BASSET
BASTES
BEASTS
ABESSU ABUSES
SUBSEA
ABESTT BETTAS
ABESTU BEAUTS
ABETTU BATTUE
TUBATE
ABETUY BEAUTY
ABEZZZ BEZAZZ
ABFFLS BLAFFS
ABFGLU BAGFUL
ABFILU FIBULA
ABFISY BASIFY
ABFLRY BARFLY
ABGGIW BAGWIG
ABGGNO GOBANG
ABGGRY BRAGGY
ABGHNS BHANGS
ABGHSU BUGSHA
ABGHTU HAGBUT
ABGIKN BAKING
ABGIKT KITBAG
ABGILM GIMBAL
ABGILN BALING
ABGIMR GAMBIR
ABGIMT GAMBIT
ABGIMY BIGAMY
ABGINN BANING
ABGINO BAGNIO
GABION
ABGINR BARING
ABGINS BASING
ABGINT BATING
ABGINY ABYING
BAYING
ABGIOS BIOGAS
ABGLLO GLOBAL
ABGLMO GAMBOL
ABGNOO GABOON
ABGNOR BARONG
BROGAN
ABGNOS BOGANS
GOBANS
ABGORT BOGART
ABGSTU SAGBUT
ABHHIS SHIBAH
ABHHJU JUBHAH
ABHIJS HIJABS
ABHIKL KIBLAH
ABHIKT BHAKTI
ABHIMR MIHRAB
ABHIMS BIMAHS
ABHINS BANISH
ABHIOP PHOBIA
ABHISS SAHIBS
ABHIST HABITS
ABHLSU ABLUSH
ABHMOS ABMHOS
ABOHMS
ABHMRU RHUMBA
ABHMSU AMBUSH
ABHOPR BARHOP
ABHORR HARBOR
ABHORS ABHORS
ABHOST BATHOS
ABHOTX HATBOX
ABHPTY BYPATH
ABHQSU BUQSHA
ABHRSY BRASHY
ABHSSU SUBAHS
ABHSUW BUSHWA
ABIIKK KABIKI
ABIILS ALIBIS
BIALIS
ABIILT TIBIAL
ABIIST TIBIAS
ABIJRU JABIRU
ABIKKU KABUKI
ABIKLS KIBLAS
ABIKMO AKIMBO
ABIKMR IMBARK
ABIKNT BANKIT
ABIKST BATIKS
ABIKTT BATTIK
ABILMM IMBALM
ABILMS LIMBAS
ABILMT TIMBAL
ABILMU LABIUM
ABILNO ALBINO
ABILNS ABLINS
BLAINS
ABILOR BAILOR
ABILPS PIBALS
ABILRS BRAILS
BRASIL
LIBRAS
ABILRT TRIBAL
ABILRU BURIAL
ABILRZ BRAZIL
ABILSS BASILS
ABILSY BIALYS
ABILTU TABULI
ABILVY VIABLY

ABIMMR MIMBAR
ABIMPT BITMAP
ABIMRS MBIRAS
ABIMRU BARIUM
ABIMST AMBITS
ABIMSU IAMBUS
ABINOS BASION
BONSAI
ABINOT BONITA
OBTAIN
ABINRS BAIRNS
BRAINS
ABINRY BINARY
BRAINY
ABINSS BASINS
SABINS
ABINSU NUBIAS
ABIORR BARRIO
ABIORS ISOBAR
ABIOST BIOTAS
ABIRRS BRIARS
ABIRRY BRIARY
ABIRSS SABIRS
ABIRSU AIRBUS
URBIAS
ABIRTU RUBATI
ABJJOO JOJOBA
ABJLMU JUMBAL
ABJNOS BANJOS
ABJOST JABOTS
ABJOZZ JAZZBO
ABKLNS BLANKS
ABKLSU BAULKS
ABKLTY BYTALK
ABKLUY BAULKY
ABKMOT TOMBAK
ABKNRS BRANKS
ABKRSU BURKAS
ABLLNO BALLON
ABLLOT BALLOT
ABLMOO ABLOOM
ABLMOP APLOMB
ABLMOR BROMAL
ABLMOT TOMBAL
ABLMPU PABLUM
ABLMRU BRUMAL
LABRUM
LUMBAR
UMBRAL
ABLMRY MARBLY
ABLMSU ALBUMS
ABLMTY TYMBAL
ABLMWY WAMBLY
ABLNOZ BLAZON
ABLOOR ROBALO
ABLORS BORALS
LABORS
ABLORU LABOUR
ABLORW BARLOW
ABLOST BLOATS
OBLAST
ABLOSY BOYLAS
ABLOTV ABVOLT
ABLPRU BURLAP
ABLPYY BYPLAY
ABLRSU BURSAL
ABLRSW BRAWLS
ABLRTU BRUTAL
ABLRWY BRAWLY
ABLSST BLASTS
ABLSSY BASSLY
BYSSAL
ABLSTY BLASTY
STABLY
ABLSUY SUABLY
USABLY
ABLSWY BYLAWS
ABMMOS MAMBOS
ABMNOW BOWMAN
ABMNSU BUSMAN
ABMNTU NUMBAT
ABMOSS SAMBOS
ABMOTW WOMBAT
ABMRSU RUMBAS
SAMBUR
UMBRAS
ABMRTU TAMBUR
ABMSSY ABYSMS
ABNNRY BRANNY
ABNNSU UNBANS
ABNORS BARONS
ABNORY BARONY
BARYON
ABNOST BATONS
ABNOTY BOTANY
ABNRRU RURBAN
ABNRST BRANTS
ABNRSU BURANS
UNBARS
ABNRSW BRAWNS
ABNRTU TURBAN
ABNRUU AUBURN
ABNRWY BRAWNY
ABNSTU TABUNS
ABNSUY BUNYAS
ABNTYZ BYZANT
ABOOST TABOOS
ABOOSZ BAZOOS
ABORRS ARBORS
ABORRU ARBOUR
ABORRW BARROW
ABORST ABORTS
BOARTS
TABORS
ABORSV BRAVOS
ABORSY BOYARS
ABORTU RUBATO
TABOUR
ABOSSS BASSOS
ABOSST BOASTS
SABOTS
ABOSUU AUSUBO
ABOSUY BAYOUS
ABPRSU SUBPAR
ABPRTU ABRUPT
ABPSSY BYPASS
ABPSTY BYPAST
ABQRSU BURQAS
ABQSSU SQUABS
ABRRSU BURSAR
ABRSSU BURSAS
ABRSSY BRASSY
ABRTTY BRATTY
ABSUWY SUBWAY
ABSWYY BYWAYS
ACCCIL CALCIC
ACCCLO COCCAL
ACCDEE ACCEDE
ACCDEH CACHED
ACCDII ACIDIC
ACCDIM CADMIC
ACCDOR ACCORD
ACCDSY CYCADS
ACCEHN CHANCE
ACCEHS CACHES
ACCEHT CACHET
ACCEIL CELIAC
CICALE
ACCEIP ICECAP
IPECAC
ACCEIS CASEIC
ACCEIT ACETIC
ACCEKL CACKLE
ACCELN CANCEL
ACCELR CARCEL
CERCAL
ACCELS CALCES
ACCEMS MECCAS
ACCEMU CAECUM
ACCENR CANCER
ACCENT ACCENT
ACCEPT ACCEPT
ACCERS SCARCE
ACCERU ACCRUE
ACCESS ACCESS
ACCESU ACCUSE
ACCGNO COGNAC
ACCHIS CHICAS
ACCHLS CLACHS
ACCHNO CONCHA
ACCHNR CRANCH
ACCHNY CHANCY
ACCHOR CAROCH
ACCHOU CACHOU
ACCHRT CRATCH
ACCHSU SUCCAH
ACCHTY CATCHY
ACCIIN ACINIC
ACCILO CALICO
ACCILT LACTIC
ACCINO COCAIN
ACCINS SICCAN
ACCINT CANTIC
ACCINW WICCAN
ACCINY CYANIC
ACCIOT OCICAT
ACCIPR CAPRIC
ACCIRR RICRAC
ACCIRT ARCTIC
ACCISW WICCAS
ACCITT TACTIC
TICTAC
ACCKLS CLACKS
ACCKRS CRACKS
ACCKRY CRACKY
ACCOOS COCOAS
ACCORS CORSAC
ACCOST ACCOST
COACTS
ACCRUY CURACY
ACCSTU CACTUS
ACCSUU CAUCUS
ACCSUY YUCCAS
ACDDEE DECADE
ACDDEG CADGED
ACDDEI CADDIE
ACDDEN DANCED
ACDDER CARDED
ACDDEU ADDUCE
ACDDII DIACID
ACDDIN CANDID
ACDDIS CADDIS
ACDDIT ADDICT
DIDACT
ACDDIY DYADIC
ACDDTU ADDUCT
ACDEEF DEFACE
ACDEEN DECANE
ACDEEP PEACED
ACDEER DECARE
ACDEES CEASED
ACDEFH CHAFED
ACDEFR FARCED
ACDEFS DECAFS
ACDEGR CADGER
GRACED
ACDEGS CADGES
ACDEHK HACKED
ACDEHO COHEAD
ACDEHR ARCHED
CHARED
ECHARD
ACDEHS CASHED
CHASED
ACDEHT DETACH
ACDEHW CHAWED
ACDEIN CNIDAE
ACDEIO CODEIA
ACDEIR CARIED
ACDEIT DACITE
ACDEIV ADVICE
ACDEJK JACKED
ACDEKL CALKED
LACKED
ACDEKP PACKED
ACDEKR ARCKED
CARKED
DACKER
RACKED
ACDEKS CASKED
SACKED
ACDEKT TACKED
ACDEKY YACKED
ACDELL CALLED
ACDELM CALMED
MACLED
ACDELN CANDLE
LANCED
ACDELO COALED
COLEAD
ACDELP PLACED
ACDELR CRADLE
CREDAL
RECLAD
ACDELS CLADES
DECALS
SCALED
ACDELT TALCED
ACDELU CAUDLE
CEDULA
ACDELV CALVED
ACDELW CLAWED
DECLAW
ACDELY CLAYED
ACDEMO COMADE
ACDEMP CAMPED
DECAMP
ACDENN CANNED
ACDENO ACNODE
CANOED
DEACON
ACDENR CEDARN
CRANED
DANCER
NACRED
ACDENS ASCEND
DANCES
ACDENT CADENT
CANTED
DECANT
ACDEOT COATED
ACDEOX COAXED
ACDEPP CAPPED
ACDEPR CARPED
CRAPED
REDCAP
ACDEPS SCAPED
SPACED
ACDERR CARDER
ACDERS CADRES
CEDARS
SACRED
SCARED
ACDERT CARTED
CRATED
REDACT
TRACED
ACDERV CARVED
CRAVED
ACDERY CEDARY
ACDERZ CRAZED
ACDEST CADETS
ACDESU CAUSED
SAUCED
ACDESY DECAYS
ACDETT CATTED
ACDETV ADVECT
ACDEUX CAUDEX
ACDHIR CHADRI
ACDHMR DRACHM
ACDHOR CHADOR
ACDHRS CHARDS
ACDIIM AMIDIC
ACDIIP ADIPIC
ACDILP PLACID
ACDILS ALCIDS
ACDILY ACIDLY
ACDIMO MODICA
ACDIMP MIDCAP
ACDINO ANODIC
ACDINR RANCID
ACDINS CANIDS
NICADS
ACDINY CYANID
ACDIOR CARDIO
ACDIOT DACOIT
ACDIOZ ZODIAC
ACDIPS CAPSID
ACDIRS CAIRDS
DARICS
ACDISS ASDICS
ACDIST DICAST
ACDLNU UNCLAD
ACDLSS SCALDS
ACDLSU CAULDS
ACDLTU DUCTAL
ACDLTY DACTYL
ACDMPU MUDCAP
ACDMTU MUDCAT
ACDNOR CANDOR
CARDON
DACRON
ACDORW COWARD
ACDOST OCTADS
ACDSTU DUCATS
ACEEFF EFFACE
ACEEFN ENFACE
ACEEFR REFACE
ACEEFS FAECES
ACEEFT FACETE
ACEEGN ENCAGE
ACEEHK HACKEE
ACEEHL CHELAE
ACEEHN ACHENE
ACEEHT THECAE
ACEEIP APIECE
ACEEJT EJECTA
ACEEKS ACKEES
ACEELL CALLEE
CELLAE
ACEELN ENLACE
ACEELR CEREAL
RELACE
ACEELV CLEAVE
ACEEMN MENACE
ACEEMR AMERCE
RACEME
ACEEMZ ECZEMA
ACEENR CAREEN
RECANE
ACEENS ENCASE
SEANCE
SENECA
ACEENT CETANE
TENACE
ACEEOR OCREAE
ACEEOT COATEE
ACEEPS ESCAPE
PEACES
ACEERR CAREER
ACEERS CREASE
ACEERT CERATE
CREATE
ECARTE
ACEESS CEASES
ACEFFT AFFECT
ACEFHR CHAFER
ACEFHS CHAFES
ACEFIL FACILE
FECIAL
ACEFIN FIANCE
ACEFIR FARCIE
FIACRE
ACEFIS FACIES
ACEFLS FALCES
ACEFLU FECULA
ACEFPU FACEUP
ACEFRR FARCER
ACEFRS FACERS
FARCES
ACEFSS FASCES
ACEFST FACETS
ACEFSU FAUCES
ACEFSY CASEFY
ACEFTU FAUCET
ACEGHN CHANGE
ACEGHR CHARGE
ACEGHU GAUCHE
ACEGIN INCAGE
ACEGIR CAGIER
ACEGLN GLANCE
ACEGLP GELCAP
ACEGLS GLACES
ACEGLY LEGACY
ACEGNU CANGUE
UNCAGE
ACEGNY AGENCY
ACEGOS SOCAGE
ACEGOW COWAGE
ACEGRS CAGERS
GRACES
ACEHHL CHALEH
ACEHHT CHETAH
ACEHIK HACKIE
ACEHIL HELIAC
ACEHIM HAEMIC
ACEHIN CHAINE
ACEHIR ACHIER
CAHIER
ACEHIS CHAISE
ACEHKL HACKLE
ACEHKR HACKER
ACEHKS HACEKS
ACEHLP CHAPEL
PLEACH
ACEHLS CHELAS
LACHES
ACEHLT CHALET
THECAL
ACEHLY LEACHY
ACEHMN MANCHE
ACEHMS MACHES
SACHEM
SAMECH
SCHEMA
ACEHNP PECHAN
ACEHNS ENCASH
HANCES
NACHES
ACEHNU NUCHAE
ACEHOP CHEAPO
ACEHOR CHOREA
OCHREA
ORACHE
ACEHPR EPARCH
PREACH
ACEHPS CHAPES
CHEAPS
ACEHPT HEPCAT
ACEHPY PEACHY
ACEHRR ARCHER
ACEHRS ARCHES
CHARES
CHASER
ESCHAR
SEARCH
ACEHRT RACHET
ACEHRW CHAWER
ACEHRX EXARCH
ACEHSS CASHES
CHASES
CHASSE
ACEHST CHASTE
CHEATS
SACHET
SCATHE
TACHES
ACEHSW CASHEW
ACEIKR CAKIER
ACEILM MALICE
ACEILN INLACE
ACEILP EPICAL
PLAICE
PLICAE
ACEILR ECLAIR
LACIER
ACEILT ATELIC
ACEILU ACULEI
ACEILX LEXICA
ACEIMM CAMMIE
ACEIMN ANEMIC
CINEMA
ICEMAN
ACEIMS AMICES
CAMISE
ACEIMU AECIUM
ACEINN CANINE
CANNIE
ENCINA
ACEINO AEONIC
ACEINP APNEIC
ACEINR CARNIE
ACEINS CASEIN
INCASE
ACEINT ACETIN
CENTAI
ENATIC
ACEINU UNCIAE
ACEINX AXENIC
ACEIOZ ZOECIA
ACEIPR PACIER
ACEIPS APICES
SPICAE
ACEIQU CAIQUE
ACEIRR RACIER
ACEIRS CARIES
CERIAS
ERICAS
ACEIRU CURIAE
ACEISS SAICES
ACEISV CAVIES
VESICA
ACEITT CATTIE
ACEITV ACTIVE
ACEIVV VIVACE
ACEJKR JACKER
ACEJKT JACKET
ACEJLO CAJOLE
ACEJNU JAUNCE
ACEKLM MACKLE
ACEKLR CALKER
LACKER
RACKLE
ACEKLT TACKLE
ACEKLY LACKEY
ACEKMO COMAKE
ACEKNR CANKER
ACEKNU UNCAKE
ACEKPR PACKER
REPACK
ACEKPT PACKET
ACEKRR RACKER
RERACK
ACEKRS CRAKES
CREAKS
SACKER
SCREAK
ACEKRT RACKET
RETACK
TACKER
ACEKRW WACKER
ACEKRY CREAKY
ACEKST CASKET
ACEKSW WACKES
ACEKTT TACKET
ACEKTY TACKEY
ACELLO LOCALE
ACELLR CALLER
CELLAR
RECALL
ACELLT CALLET
ACELMR CALMER
MARCEL
ACELMS CAMELS
MACLES
MESCAL
ACELMT CAMLET
ACELMU ALMUCE
MACULE
ACELMZ MEZCAL
ACELNN CANNEL
ACELNR LANCER
ACELNS CLEANS
LANCES
ACELNT CANTLE
CENTAL
LANCET
ACELNU CUNEAL
LACUNE
LAUNCE
UNLACE
ACELOR COALER
ORACLE
RECOAL
ACELOS SOLACE
ACELOT LOCATE
ACELOV ALCOVE
COEVAL
ACELPR CARPEL
PARCEL
PLACER
ACELPS PLACES
ACELPT CAPLET
PLACET
ACELPU CULPAE
ACELQU CALQUE
CLAQUE
ACELRR CARREL
ACELRS CARLES
CLEARS
LACERS
SCALER
SCLERA
ACELRT CARTEL
CLARET
RECTAL
ACELRV CARVEL
CLAVER
ACELRW CLAWER
ACELSS SCALES
ACELST CASTLE
CLEATS
ECLATS
ACELSU CAULES
CLAUSE
ACELSV CALVES
CLAVES
ACELSX CALXES
ACELTT CATTLE
TECTAL
ACELTY ACETYL
ACELYY CLAYEY
ACEMNP ENCAMP
ACEMNR CARMEN
ACEMNU ACUMEN
ACEMOP POMACE
ACEMOS CAMEOS
ACEMOT COMATE
ACEMPR CAMPER
ACEMRS CREAMS
MACERS
SCREAM
ACEMRY CREAMY
ACEMSU MUSCAE
ACEMTU ACETUM
ACENNO ANCONE
ACENNR CANNER
ACENNU NUANCE
ACENOR CANOER
CORNEA
ACENOS CANOES
OCEANS
ACENOT OCTANE
ACENPR PRANCE
ACENPS PECANS
ACENRS CANERS
CASERN
CRANES
NACRES
RANCES
ACENRT CANTER
CARNET
CENTRA
NECTAR
RECANT
TANREC
TRANCE
ACENRV CARVEN
CAVERN
CRAVEN
ACENRY CARNEY
ACENSS SCENAS
ACENST ASCENT
CENTAS
ENACTS
SECANT
STANCE
ACENSU UNCASE
USANCE
ACEOPT CAPOTE
TOECAP
ACEOPW COWPEA
ACEORS COARSE
ACEORT COATER
RECOAT
ACEORX COAXER
ACEOST COSTAE
ACEOSX COAXES
ACEOTT COTTAE
ACEOTU COTEAU
ACEOTV AVOCET
OCTAVE
ACEPPR CAPPER
ACEPRR CARPER
ACEPRS CAPERS
CRAPES
ESCARP
PACERS
PARSEC
RECAPS
SCRAPE
SECPAR
SPACER
ACEPRT CARPET
PREACT
ACEPRU APERCU
ACEPSS SCAPES
SPACES
ACEPST ASPECT
EPACTS
ACEPSY SPACEY
ACEPTU TEACUP
ACEQSU CASQUE
SACQUE
ACERRS CARERS
RACERS
SCARER
ACERRT CARTER
CRATER
TRACER
ACERRU CURARE
ACERRV CARVER
CRAVER
ACERSS CARESS
CARSES
CRASES
ESCARS
SCARES
SERACS
ACERST CARETS
CARTES
CASTER
CATERS
CRATES
REACTS
RECAST
TRACES
ACERSU CAUSER
CESURA
SAUCER
ACERSV CARVES
CAVERS
CRAVES
ACERSY CREASY
SCAREY
ACERSZ CRAZES
ACERTU ACUTER
CURATE
ACESST CASTES
CESTAS
ACESSU CAUSES
SAUCES
ACESTT STACTE
ACESTU ACUTES
CUESTA
ACESTX EXACTS
ACESUY CAUSEY
CAYUSE
ACFFHS CHAFFS
ACFFHY CHAFFY
ACFFIN FANFIC
ACFFLS SCLAFF
ACFGIN FACING

ACFHSU CHUFAS
ACFILS CALIFS
FISCAL
ACFINS FINCAS
ACFIOS FIASCO
ACFIPY PACIFY
ACFIRT FRACTI
ACFKLS FLACKS
ACFLNO FALCON
FLACON
ACFLNU CANFUL
ACFLPU CAPFUL
ACFLRU CARFUL
FULCRA
ACFNRS FRANCS
ACFORT FACTOR
ACFRSS SCARFS
ACFRST CRAFTS
ACFRTY CRAFTY
ACGGIN CAGING
ACGGRY CRAGGY
ACGHIN ACHING
ACGHNS CHANGS
ACGHOT GOTCHA
ACGHOU GAUCHO
ACGHRU CURAGH
ACGHTU CAUGHT
ACGIKN CAKING
ACGILL GALLIC
ACGILN LACING
ACGILR GARLIC
ACGILS GLACIS
ACGILY CAGILY
ACGIMN MACING
ACGIMS MAGICS
ACGINN CANING
ACGINO AGONIC
ACGINP PACING
ACGINR ARCING
CARING
RACING
ACGINS CASING
ACGINT ACTING
ACGINV CAVING
ACGINW CAWING
ACGIOR ORGIAC
ACGIRS CIGARS
ACGIRT TRAGIC
ACGLNS CLANGS
ACGLNU GLUCAN
ACGLNY GLYCAN
ACGNOR GARCON
ACGNOS CONGAS
GASCON
ACGORS CARGOS
ACGORU COUGAR
ACGOSU GUACOS
ACGOWY COGWAY
ACGRSS SCRAGS
ACGTTU CATGUT
ACHHNU HAUNCH
ACHHOO AHCHOO
ACHHTT THATCH
ACHIIS ISCHIA
ACHIJK HIJACK
ACHILM CHIMLA
ACHILO LOCHIA
ACHILP CALIPH
ACHILR ARCHIL
CHIRAL
ACHILS LAICHS
ACHILT CHITAL
ACHIMR CHIMAR
ACHIMS CHIASM
ACHINP PAINCH
ACHINR INARCH
ACHINS CHAINS
CHINAS
ACHINT CANTHI
ACHIPS PHASIC
ACHIPT HAPTIC
PHATIC
ACHIQU QUAICH
ACHIRS CHAIRS
RACHIS
ACHISU CHIAUS
ACHKKU CHUKKA
ACHKLS CHALKS
ACHKLT KLATCH
ACHKLY CHALKY
HACKLY
ACHKOS SHACKO
ACHKOW WHACKO
ACHKRS CHARKS
ACHKRU CHUKAR
ACHKSS SHACKS
ACHKST THACKS
ACHKSW WHACKS
ACHKTW THWACK
ACHKWY WHACKY
ACHLLO CHOLLA
ACHLLY CHALLY
ACHLNO LOCHAN
ACHLNP PLANCH
ACHLNU LAUNCH
NUCHAL
ACHLOR CHORAL
ACHLOS CHOLAS
ACHLOT CHALOT
ACHLRY ARCHLY
ACHLST SLATCH
ACHMMY CHAMMY
ACHMOR CHROMA
ACHMOS MACHOS
MOCHAS
ACHMPS CHAMPS
ACHMPY CHAMPY
ACHMRS CHARMS
ACHMSS CHASMS
ACHMSU SUMACH
ACHMSY CHASMY
ACHNOR ANCHOR
ARCHON
RANCHO
ACHNOS ANCHOS
NACHOS
ACHNPU PAUNCH
ACHNRU RAUNCH
ACHNST CHANTS
SNATCH
STANCH
ACHNTU CHAUNT
NAUTCH
ACHNTY CHANTY
ACHOOS CASHOO
ACHOOT CAHOOT
ACHOPR CARHOP
COPRAH
ACHOPY POACHY
ACHORR CHARRO
ACHOSV HAVOCS
ACHOSW CAHOWS
ACHOUV AVOUCH
ACHPPU CHUPPA
ACHPRS SCARPH
ACHPTY PATCHY
ACHRRS CHARRS
ACHRRY CHARRY
ACHRST CHARTS
STARCH
ACHSSU SAUCHS
ACHSSV SCHAVS
ACHSSW SCHWAS
ACHSTU CUSHAT
ACHSTW SWATCH
ACHSTY YACHTS
ACHSUW CUSHAW
ACHTTY CHATTY
ACHTUW WAUCHT
ACIILS SIALIC
SILICA
ACIILT ITALIC
ACIILV CLIVIA
ACIIMN AMINIC
ACIINN NIACIN
ACIINP PIANIC
ACIINS ANISIC
CASINI
ACIIRT IATRIC
ACIITV VIATIC
ACIKLN CALKIN
ACIKMR KARMIC
ACIKMU UMIACK
ACIKNO KAONIC
ACIKNT ANTICK
CATKIN
ACIKPX PICKAX
ACILLN CLINAL
ACILLP PLICAL
ACILLS LILACS
SCILLA
ACILLY LACILY
ACILMS CLAIMS
ACILMX CLIMAX
ACILMY AMYLIC
ACILNO ALNICO
OILCAN
ACILNP CAPLIN
ACILNR CARLIN
ACILNS LINACS
ACILNT CATLIN
TINCAL
ACILNU UNCIAL
ACILOR CAROLI
LORICA
ACILOS SOCIAL
ACILOT CITOLA
COITAL
ACILOX OXALIC
ACILRT CITRAL
RICTAL
ACILRU CURIAL
URACIL
ACILRY RACILY
ACILST TICALS
ACILSU CAULIS
ACILSV CAVILS
ACIMNO ANOMIC
CAMION
MANIOC
ACIMNS MANICS
ACIMNT MANTIC
ACIMOO OOMIAC
ACIMOS MOSAIC
ACIMOT ATOMIC
ACIMOV VOMICA
ACIMPS SCAMPI
ACIMPT IMPACT
ACIMRS RACISM
ACIMRY MYRICA
ACIMST MASTIC
MISACT
ACIMSU AMICUS
UMIACS
ACINNT INCANT
TANNIC
ACINNY CYANIN
ACINOS CASINO
ACINOT ACTION
ATONIC
CATION
ACINOX ANOXIC
AXONIC
ACINOZ AZONIC
ACINPS PANICS
ACINPT CATNIP
ACINRS CAIRNS
ACINRU ANURIC
URANIC
ACINRY CAIRNY
ACINST ACTINS
ANTICS
NASTIC
ACINSU ACINUS
ACINSV VINCAS
ACINTT INTACT
ACINTU TUNICA
ACINUV VICUNA
ACIOPR PICARO
ACIOPT ATOPIC
ACIORS SCORIA
ACIORT AORTIC
ACIOST COATIS
SCOTIA
ACIOSV OVISAC
ACIOTZ AZOTIC
ACIPRS CAPRIS
ACIPRY PIRACY
ACIPSS ASPICS
SPICAS
ACIPTT TIPCAT
ACIPTY ATYPIC
ACIQTU ACQUIT
ACIRRU CURARI
ACIRSS CRASIS
CRISSA
ACIRST CRISTA
RACIST
TRIACS
ACIRSV VICARS
ACIRTU URATIC
ACISSS CASSIS
ACISTT ATTICS
STATIC
ACITUY ACUITY
ACITVY CAVITY
ACKKNS KNACKS
ACKKSY KYACKS
ACKLNS CLANKS
ACKLNY CLANKY
ACKLOS CLOAKS
ACKLPS PLACKS
ACKLPY PACKLY
ACKLSS SLACKS
ACKLSU CAULKS
ACKLTY TALCKY
ACKMSS SMACKS
ACKMSU AMUCKS
ACKNPU UNPACK
ACKNRS CRANKS
ACKNRY CRANKY
ACKNSS SNACKS
ACKNTU UNTACK
ACKOPY YAPOCK
ACKORS CROAKS
ACKORY CROAKY
ACKOSW WACKOS
ACKPSY SKYCAP
ACKQSU QUACKS
ACKQUY QUACKY
ACKRST TRACKS
ACKRSW WRACKS
ACKSST STACKS
ACLLMY CALMLY
ACLLNO CLONAL
ACLLOR COLLAR
ACLLOS LOCALS
ACLLOW CALLOW
ACLLSS SCALLS
ACLLSU CALLUS
SULCAL
ACLLUY CULLAY
ACLMMY CLAMMY
ACLMOP COPALM
ACLMOR CLAMOR
ACLMPS CLAMPS
ACLMTU TALCUM
ACLNOX CLAXON
ACLNUY LUNACY
ACLOOZ ZOCALO
ACLOPS COPALS
ACLOPU COPULA
CUPOLA
ACLORR CORRAL
ACLORS CAROLS
CLAROS
CORALS
ACLORU OCULAR
ACLORY CALORY
ACLOST COSTAL
ACLOSU OSCULA
ACLOSV VOCALS
ACLOSZ COLZAS
ACLPSS CLASPS
SCALPS
ACLPST CLASPT
ACLPSU CUSPAL
ACLPUU CUPULA
ACLRRU CRURAL
ACLRSW CRAWLS
SCRAWL
ACLRSY LYCRAS
ACLRTU CURTAL
ACLRWY CRAWLY
ACLSST CLASTS
ACLSSY CLASSY
ACLSTU CUTLAS
ACLSUV CLAVUS
ACMMOS COMMAS
ACMNOR MACRON
ACMNOS MACONS
MASCON
SOCMAN
ACMNOW COWMAN
ACMOPS CAMPOS
COMPAS
ACMORR CARROM
ACMORS CAROMS
MACROS
ACMOST MASCOT
ACMOSU MUCOSA
ACMOTT TOMCAT
ACMPRS CRAMPS
ACMPRY CRAMPY
ACMPSS SCAMPS
ACMPSU CAMPUS
ACMRSS SCRAMS
ACMRSU SACRUM
ACMRSY CYMARS
ACMSSU SUMACS
ACMSTU MUSCAT
ACMUUV VACUUM
ACNNNO CANNON
ACNNOS CANONS
ACNNOT CANNOT
CANTON
ACNNOY CANYON
ACNNRY CRANNY
ACNOOR CORONA
RACOON
ACNOPS CAPONS
ACNOPY CANOPY
ACNORR RANCOR
ACNORS ACORNS
NARCOS
RACONS
ACNORT CANTOR
CARTON
CONTRA
CRATON
ACNORU CORNUA
ACNORY CRAYON
ACNOSS CANSOS
ACNOST CANTOS
COTANS
OCTANS
ACNOTT OCTANT
ACNOTU TOUCAN
ACNPSU UNCAPS
ACNRRU CURRAN
ACNSST SCANTS
ACNSTU CANTUS
UNCAST
ACNSTY SCANTY
ACOOTV OCTAVO
ACOPPR COPPRA
ACOPRS COPRAS
ACOPRT CAPTOR
CARTOP
ACOPST COAPTS
ACOPSY COPAYS
ACOPTW COWPAT
ACORRT CARROT
TROCAR
ACORSS ACROSS
ACORST ACTORS
CASTOR
COSTAR
SCROTA
TAROCS
ACORSU SOUCAR
ACORSW SOWCAR
ACORTT COTTAR
ACORTU CUATRO
TURACO
ACORTV CAVORT
ACORTX OXCART
ACORVY COVARY
ACORYZ CORYZA
ACOSST ASCOTS
COASTS
ACOSTT COTTAS
ACOTTU OUTACT
ACPPRY CRAPPY
ACPPSU CUPPAS
ACPRSS SCARPS
SCRAPS
ACPRSU CARPUS
ACPSSU SCAUPS
ACPSTU CATSUP
UPCAST
ACRRSY SCARRY
ACRSST SCARTS
ACRSSU SCAURS
ACRSTT TRACTS
ACSSTT SCATTS
ACSTTY SCATTY
ADDDEG GADDED
ADDDEL ADDLED
DADDLE
ADDDEM MADDED
ADDDEN ADDEND
ADDDEO DADOED
ADDDEP PADDED
ADDDER RADDED
ADDDEW WADDED
ADDDOO DOODAD
ADDEEH HEADED
ADDEEL DELEAD
LEADED
ADDEEN DEADEN
DEANED
ADDEER DEADER
ADDEEV DEAVED
EVADED
ADDEFF DAFFED
ADDEFG FADGED
ADDEFR FARDED
ADDEGN DANGED
ADDEGO GOADED
ADDEGR GADDER
GRADED
ADDEHK KEDDAH
ADDEHL DALEDH
ADDEHN HANDED
ADDEHS DASHED
SHADED
ADDEIL DIALED
LADDIE
ADDEIM DIADEM
MEDIAD
ADDEIR RAIDED
ADDEIW WADDIE
ADDEKR DARKED
ADDELL LADLED
ADDELN DANDLE
LANDED
ADDELO LOADED
ADDELP PADDLE
ADDELR LADDER
LARDED
RADDLE
ADDELS ADDLES
SADDLE
ADDELU LAUDED
ADDELW DAWDLE
WADDLE
ADDELY DEADLY
ADDEMM DAMMED
ADDEMN DAMNED
DEMAND
MADDEN
ADDEMP DAMPED
ADDEMR MADDER
ADDENR DANDER
DARNED
ADDENS DEDANS
DESAND
SADDEN
SANDED
ADDENU UNDEAD
ADDENW DAWNED
ADDEOR ADORED
DEODAR
ADDEOS DADOES
ADDEOT DOATED
ADDEOW WOADED
ADDEPP DAPPED
ADDEPR DRAPED
PADDER
ADDEPS SPADED
ADDERS ADDERS
DREADS
READDS
SADDER
ADDERT DARTED
TRADED
ADDERW WADDER
WARDED
ADDERY DRAYED
YARDED
ADDETU DAUTED
ADDETW DAWTED
ADDGIN ADDING
ADDGIO GADOID
ADDGIP GIDDAP
ADDGIS GADDIS
GADIDS
ADDGMO GODDAM
ADDGMU DADGUM
ADDGOO OGDOAD
ADDHOS HODADS
ADDHSU SADDHU
ADDIKZ ZADDIK
ADDIMS MISADD
ADDIMY MIDDAY
ADDLWY WADDLY
ADDOOR DORADO
ADDORS DORSAD
ADDORT DOTARD
ADDOTU OUTADD
ADDRSY DRYADS
ADEEFL DEFLEA
LEAFED
ADEEFM DEFAME
ADEEFN DEAFEN
ADEEFR DEAFER
FEARED
ADEEFS FEASED
ADEEFT DEFEAT
ADEEFZ FEAZED
ADEEGG DEGAGE
ADEEGL EAGLED
ADEEGM DEGAME
ADEEGR AGREED
DRAGEE
GEARED
ADEEHJ HADJEE
ADEEHL HEALED
ADEEHP HEAPED
ADEEHR ADHERE
HEADER
ADEEHT HEATED
ADEEHV HEAVED
ADEEHX HEXADE
ADEEIL AEDILE
ADEEIM MEDIAE
ADEEIN AEDINE
ADEEIR AERIED
DEARIE
REDIAE
ADEEIT IDEATE
ADEEJN JEANED
ADEEJY DEEJAY
ADEEKL LEAKED
ADEEKP PEAKED
ADEEKR DEKARE
ADEELN ANELED
LEADEN
LEANED
ADEELO ELODEA
ADEELP LEAPED
PEALED
ADEELR DEALER
LEADER
ADEELS LEASED
SEALED
ADEELT DELATE
ELATED
ADEELV LEAVED
VEALED
ADEEMN DEMEAN
ADEEMO OEDEMA
ADEEMR REAMED
REMADE
ADEEMS ADEEMS
EDEMAS
SEAMED
ADEEMT MEATED
TEAMED
ADEENN ENNEAD
ADEENR EARNED
ENDEAR
NEARED
ADEENT ANTEED
ADEENW DEEWAN
WEANED
ADEENY YEANED
ADEEPR PARDEE
REAPED
ADEEPS PESADE
ADEEPT PEDATE
ADEEPV PAVEED
ADEERR DEARER
READER
REARED
REDEAR
REREAD
ADEERS ERASED
RESEDA
SEARED
ADEERT DERATE
REDATE
TEARED
ADEERV EVADER
REAVED
ADEERW DRAWEE
ADEERX EXEDRA
ADEERZ RAZEED
ADEEST SEATED
SEDATE
TEASED
ADEESV DEAVES
EVADES
ADEESX AXSEED
ADEETT TEATED
ADEEVW WEAVED
ADEFFG GAFFED
ADEFFN NAFFED
ADEFFW WAFFED
ADEFFY YAFFED
ADEFGG FAGGED
ADEFGN DEFANG
FANGED
ADEFGR DEFRAG
ADEFGS FADGES
ADEFHS FASHED
ADEFHT HAFTED
ADEFIL AFIELD
FAILED
ADEFIN FADEIN
ADEFIR FAIRED
ADEFIW WAIFED
ADEFKL FLAKED
ADEFLM FLAMED
MALFED
ADEFLO FOALED
LOAFED
ADEFLR FARDEL
FLARED
ADEFLU FEUDAL
ADEFLW FLAWED
ADEFLY DEAFLY
FLAYED
ADEFMO DEFOAM
FOAMED
ADEFMR FARMED
FRAMED
ADEFNN FANNED
ADEFNW FAWNED
ADEFOR FEDORA
ADEFRS FADERS
ADEFRT DAFTER
RAFTED
ADEFRY DEFRAY
FRAYED
ADEFST DEFATS
FASTED
ADEFTT FATTED
ADEFTW WAFTED
ADEGGG GAGGED
ADEGGH HAGGED
ADEGGJ JAGGED
ADEGGL DAGGLE
LAGGED
ADEGGN GANGED
NAGGED
ADEGGR DAGGER
RAGGED
ADEGGS SAGGED
ADEGGT GADGET
TAGGED
ADEGGU GAUGED
ADEGGW WAGGED
ADEGGZ ZAGGED
ADEGHN HANGED
ADEGHS GASHED
ADEGIM DEGAMI
IMAGED
ADEGIN GAINED
ADEGIT GAITED
ADEGKW GAWKED
ADEGLL GALLED
ADEGLN ANGLED
DANGLE
LAGEND
ADEGLO GAOLED
GOALED
ADEGLR ARGLED
GLARED
ADEGLS GLADES
ADEGLY AGEDLY
ADEGLZ GLAZED
ADEGMM GAMMED
ADEGMU GAUMED
ADEGNP PANGED
ADEGNR DANGER
GANDER
GARDEN
RANGED
ADEGNT TANGED
ADEGNU AUGEND
UNAGED
ADEGNW GNAWED
ADEGOR DOGEAR
ADEGOS DOSAGE
SEADOG
ADEGOT DOTAGE
TOGAED
ADEGPP GAPPED
ADEGPR PARGED
ADEGPS GASPED
ADEGPW GAWPED
ADEGRR GARRED
GRADER
REGARD
ADEGRS GRADES
ADEGRT GRATED
ADEGRU ARGUED
ADEGRV GRAVED
ADEGRY GRAYED
ADEGRZ GRAZED
ADEGSS GASSED
ADEGST GASTED
STAGED
ADEGSW SWAGED
ADEHHK KHEDAH
ADEHHS HASHED
ADEHIL HAILED
HALIDE
ADEHIR HAIRED
ADEHJS HADJES
JEHADS
ADEHKN HANKED
ADEHKR HARKED
ADEHKS KHEDAS
ADEHKW HAWKED

ADEHLM LAMEDH
ADEHLN HANDLE
ADEHLO HALOED
ADEHLR HERALD
ADEHLS LASHED
SHALED
ADEHLT DALETH
HALTED
LATHED
ADEHLU HAULED
ADEHLV HALVED
ADEHLW WHALED
ADEHMM HAMMED
ADEHMR HARMED
ADEHMS EMDASH
MASHED
SHAMED
ADEHNP DAPHNE
ADEHNR HANDER
HARDEN
ADEHNS ENDASH
ADEHNT HANTED
ADEHOX HOAXED
ADEHPP HAPPED
ADEHPR HARPED
ADEHPS HASPED
PASHED
PHASED
SHAPED
ADEHPT HEPTAD
ADEHRR HARDER
ADEHRS DASHER
SHADER
SHARED
ADEHRT DEARTH
HATRED
THREAD
ADEHRY HYDRAE
ADEHSS DASHES
SADHES
SASHED
SHADES
ADEHST DEATHS
HASTED
ADEHSV SHAVED
ADEHSW SHAWED
WASHED
ADEHSX HEXADS
ADEHTT HATTED
ADEHTW THAWED
ADEHTY DEATHY
ADEHYY HEYDAY
ADEIJL JAILED
ADEIKP PAIKED
ADEIKR DAIKER
ADEILL ALLIED
ADEILM MAILED
MEDIAL
ADEILN ALINED
DENIAL
NAILED
ADEILO EIDOLA
ADEILP ALIPED
ELAPID
PLEIAD
ADEILR ARILED
DERAIL
DIALER
LAIRED
RAILED
REDIAL
RELAID
ADEILS AISLED
DEASIL
IDEALS
LADIES
SAILED
ADEILT DETAIL
DILATE
TAILED
ADEILU AUDILE
ADEILV VAILED
VIALED
ADEILW WAILED
ADEILZ LAZIED
ADEIMM MAIMED
ADEIMN AIDMEN
DAIMEN
MAIDEN
MEDIAN
MEDINA
ADEIMR ADMIRE
ADEIMS AMIDES
MEDIAS
ADEINP PAINED
ADEINR DENARI
RAINED
ADEINS SAINED
ADEINT DETAIN
NIDATE
ADEINV INVADE
ADEIOR ROADIE
ADEIOT IODATE
ADEIPR DIAPER
PAIRED
PARDIE
REPAID
ADEIRR ARIDER
RAIDER
ADEIRS AIDERS
DEAIRS
IRADES
RAISED
REDIAS
RESAID
ADEIRT AIRTED
TIRADE
ADEIRU UREDIA
ADEIRV VARIED
ADEIRW WAIRED
ADEISS ASIDES
DAISES
DASSIE
ADEISU ADIEUS
ADEISV ADVISE
DAVIES
VISAED
ADEISW WADIES
ADEISX AXISED
ADEISZ AZIDES
ADEITU DAUTIE
ADEITV DATIVE
ADEITW DAWTIE
WAITED
ADEITX TAXIED
ADEIUX ADIEUX
ADEIVW WAIVED
ADEJKU JAUKED
ADEJMM JAMMED
ADEJPU JAUPED
ADEJRR JARRED
ADEJRU ADJURE
ADEJZZ JAZZED
ADEKKY YAKKED
ADEKLN ANKLED
ADEKLR DARKLE
LARKED
ADEKLS SLAKED
ADEKLT TALKED
ADEKLW WALKED
ADEKMR DEMARK
MARKED
ADEKMS MASKED
ADEKNR DANKER
DARKEN
NARKED
RANKED
ADEKNS KNEADS
SNAKED
ADEKNT TANKED
ADEKNY YANKED
ADEKOS SOAKED
ADEKOY KAYOED
OKAYED
ADEKPR PARKED
ADEKPY KEYPAD
ADEKQU QUAKED
ADEKRR DARKER
ADEKRS DRAKES
ADEKRW WARKED
ADEKST SKATED
STAKED
TASKED
ADEKUW WAUKED
ADELLL LALLED
ADELLM MALLED
ADELLP PALLED
ADELLR LADLER
ADELLS DALLES
LADLES
ADELLU ALLUDE
ALUDEL
ADELLW WALLED
ADELMM LAMMED
ADELMO LOAMED
ADELMP LAMPED
PALMED
ADELMR DERMAL
MARLED
MEDLAR
ADELMS DAMSEL
LAMEDS
MEDALS
ADELMT MALTED
ADELMU ALMUDE
MAULED
ADELMW WADMEL
ADELNO LOANED
ADELNP PLANED
ADELNR DARNEL
LANDER
RELAND
ADELNS ELANDS
LADENS
NALEDS
SENDAL
ADELNT DENTAL
ADELNU UNLADE
UNLEAD
ADELNW WANDLE
ADELNY ADENYL
ADELOP PEDALO
ADELOR LOADER
ORDEAL
RELOAD
ADELOS ALDOSE
ADELPP DAPPLE
LAPPED
PALPED
ADELPR PARLED
PEDLAR
ADELPS LAPSED
PADLES
PEDALS
PLEADS
ADELPT PLATED
ADELPW DEWLAP
ADELPY PLAYED
ADELRR LARDER
ADELRS ALDERS
LADERS
ADELRT DARTLE
ADELRU AULDER
LAUDER
ADELRY DEARLY
ADELST DELTAS
DESALT
LASTED
SALTED
SLATED
STALED
ADELSV SALVED
SLAVED
ADELSW WEALDS
ADELSY DELAYS
SLAYED
ADELUV VALUED
ADELUW WAULED
ADELVV VALVED
ADELWW WAWLED
ADELWY YAWLED
ADELZZ DAZZLE
ADEMMN MADMEN
ADEMMR DAMMER
RAMMED
ADEMNN MANNED
ADEMNO DAEMON
MOANED
ADEMNP DAMPEN
ADEMNR DAMNER
REMAND
ADEMNS AMENDS
DESMAN
MENADS
ADEMNT TANDEM
ADEMNU UNMADE
ADEMOP POMADE
ADEMOR RADOME
ROAMED
ADEMOT MOATED
ADEMOW MEADOW
ADEMPP MAPPED
ADEMPR DAMPER
RAMPED
ADEMPT TAMPED
ADEMPV VAMPED
ADEMRR MARRED
ADEMRS DERMAS
DREAMS
MADRES
ADEMRT DREAMT
MARTED
ADEMRU REMUDA
ADEMRW WARMED
ADEMRY DREAMY
ADEMSS MASSED
ADEMST DEMAST
MASTED
ADEMSU AMUSED
MEDUSA
ADEMTT MATTED
ADENNP PANNED
ADENNT TANNED
ADENNU DUENNA
ADENNV VANNED
ADENNW WANNED
ADENOS ANODES
ADENOT ATONED
DONATE
ADENOY NOYADE
ADENPP APPEND
NAPPED
ADENPR PANDER
REPAND
ADENPT PANTED
PEDANT
PENTAD
ADENPW PAWNED
ADENPX EXPAND
ADENRR DARNER
ERRAND
ADENRS DENARS
REDANS
SANDER
SNARED
ADENRT ARDENT
RANTED
ADENRU UNREAD
ADENRW WANDER
WARDEN
WARNED
ADENRY DENARY
YARNED
ADENRZ ZANDER
ADENSS SEDANS
ADENST STANED
ADENSU SUNDAE
ADENSV DAVENS
ADENSW DEWANS
SNAWED
ADENTT ATTEND
ADENTV ADVENT
ADENTW WANTED
ADENUW UNAWED
ADENUX UNAXED
ADENWY YAWNED
ADEOOR ROADEO
ADEOPS SOAPED
ADEORR ADORER
ROARED
ADEORS ADORES
OREADS
SARODE
SOARED
ADEORT ORATED
ADEORW REDOWA
ADEOSV VADOSE
ADEOTU AUTOED
ADEOTZ AZOTED
ADEOVW AVOWED
ADEPPR DAPPER
RAPPED
ADEPPS SAPPED
ADEPPT TAPPED
ADEPPW WAPPED
ADEPPY YAPPED
ADEPPZ ZAPPED
ADEPRR DRAPER
PARRED
ADEPRS DRAPES
PADRES
PARSED
RASPED
SPADER
SPARED
SPREAD
ADEPRT DEPART
PARTED
PETARD
PRATED
ADEPRW WARPED
ADEPRY DRAPEY
PRAYED
ADEPSS PASSED
SPADES
ADEPST ADEPTS
PASTED
ADEPSU PAUSED
ADEPSY SPAYED
ADEPTT PATTED
ADEPTU UPDATE
ADEPUY YAUPED
ADEPWY YAWPED
ADERRS DARERS
DREARS
ADERRT DARTER
RETARD
TARRED
TRADER
ADERRW DRAWER
REDRAW
REWARD
WARDER
WARRED
ADERRY DREARY
YARDER
ADERST DATERS
DERATS
STARED
TRADES
TREADS
ADERSW DEWARS
WADERS
ADERSY DERAYS
ADERTT RATTED
TARTED
TETRAD
ADERTV ADVERT
ADERTW WARTED
ADERVV VARVED
ADERZZ RAZZED
ADESSS SASSED
ADESST STADES
STEADS
TSADES
ADESSY SAYEDS
ADESTT STATED
TASTED
ADESTU SAUTED
ADESTV STAVED
ADESTW TAWSED
WADSET
WASTED
ADESTY STAYED
STEADY
ADESWY SWAYED
ADETTT TATTED
ADETTU TAUTED
ADETTV VATTED
ADFFOR AFFORD
ADFFRS DRAFFS
ADFFRY DRAFFY
ADFGIN FADING
ADFGLY GADFLY
ADFHSU SHADUF
ADFILU AIDFUL
ADFIRT ADRIFT
ADFLSU FAULDS
ADFLTY DAFTLY
ADFLYY DAYFLY
ADFMNO FANDOM
ADFNOT FANTOD
ADFRST DRAFTS
ADFRSU FRAUDS
ADFRSW DWARFS
ADFRTY DRAFTY
ADGGRY DRAGGY
ADGHIN HADING
ADGHNO HAGDON
ADGIIN AIDING
ADGIJN JADING
ADGILN LADING
LIGAND
ADGILO ALGOID
DIALOG
ADGIMY DIGAMY
ADGINO GANOID
ADGINR DARING
GRADIN
ADGINT DATING
ADGINU AUDING
ADGINW DAWING
WADING
ADGINZ ADZING
DAZING
ADGIRV GRAVID
ADGLLY GLADLY
ADGLNS GLANDS
ADGLNY DANGLY
ADGLOP LAPDOG
ADGMOS DOGMAS
ADGNOP DOGNAP
ADGNOR DRAGON
ADGNOS DONGAS
GONADS
ADGNRS GRANDS
ADGOPS PAGODS
ADGRSU GRADUS
GUARDS
ADHHIT HADITH
ADHHIW WHIDAH
ADHHOU HOUDAH
ADHHOW HOWDAH
ADHHWY WHYDAH
ADHIJS HADJIS
JADISH
JIHADS
ADHIKS KHADIS
ADHILO HALOID
ADHILS HALIDS
ADHIMR DIRHAM
ADHINS DANISH
SANDHI
ADHIOR HAIRDO
ADHIPS APHIDS
ADHIRS RADISH
SHAIRD
ADHIRY HYDRIA
ADHISS DASHIS
ADHLOR HOLARD
ADHLOS AHOLDS
ADHLRY HARDLY
ADHNNU UNHAND
ADHNOO DAHOON
ADHNOR HADRON
ADHNOS HONDAS
ADHNRU DHURNA
ADHNSY SHANDY
ADHOOR DHOORA
ADHORS HOARDS
ADHORU DOURAH
ADHOSW SHADOW
ADHPRU PURDAH
ADHRSS SHARDS
ADHRSY HYDRAS
ADHSSU SADHUS
ADIIKO AIKIDO
ADIILM MILADI
ADIILN INLAID
ADIILS ILIADS
SIALID
ADIIMN AMIDIN
DIAMIN
ADIIMO DAIMIO
ADIIMR MIDAIR
ADIINV AVIDIN
ADIINZ DIAZIN
ADIIPR DIAPIR
ADIISY SAIYID
ADIJMS MASJID
ADIJNO ADJOIN
ADIJSS JASSID
ADIKMO MIKADO
ADIKNO DAIKON
ADIKNP KIDNAP
ADIKOT DAKOIT
ADIKTT DIKTAT
ADIKUZ ADZUKI
ADILLP PALLID
ADILMO AMIDOL
ADILMS DISMAL
ADILMY MILADY
ADILNN INLAND
ADILNO LADINO
ADILNR ALDRIN
ADILNS ISLAND
ADILNU UNLAID
ADILOZ OZALID
ADILPS PLAIDS
SALPID
ADILRS DRAILS
LAIRDS
LIARDS
LIDARS
ADILRY ARIDLY
ADILRZ LIZARD
ADILST DISTAL
ADILSU DULIAS
ADILTU TULADI
ADILTY DAYLIT
ADILVY AVIDLY
ADIMMT DAMMIT
ADIMNO DAIMON
DOMAIN
ADIMNT MANTID
ADIMOT DIATOM
ADIMOY DAIMYO
ADIMRS DIRAMS
DISARM
ADIMRU RADIUM
ADIMRY MYRIAD
ADIMSS SADISM
ADIMST ADMITS
AMIDST
ADIMSY DISMAY
ADIMTX ADMIXT
ADIMWY MIDWAY
ADINNN NANDIN
ADINOR INROAD
ORDAIN
ADINOS ADONIS
DANIOS
ADINOX DIOXAN
ADINPT PANDIT
ADINPU UNPAID
ADINQR QINDAR
ADINRS DINARS
DRAINS
NADIRS
RANIDS
ADINRU DURIAN
ADINRW INWARD
ADINSU UNSAID
ADINSV DIVANS
VIANDS
ADINSW DIWANS
ADINTY DAINTY
ADIORS AROIDS
RADIOS
ADIORT ADROIT
ADIOSU AUDIOS
ADIOSV AVOIDS
ADIPRS RAPIDS
SPARID
ADIPSS DIPSAS
ADIPSX SPADIX
ADIQTU DIQUAT
ADIRRS SIRDAR
ADIRRT RITARD
ADIRST TRIADS
ADIRSU RADIUS
ADIRSV VISARD
ADIRSY YAIRDS
ADIRVZ VIZARD
ADIRWZ WIZARD
ADIRZZ IZZARD
ADISST SADIST
TSADIS
ADISSY SAYIDS
ADISTU AUDITS
ADISTV DAVITS
ADISYY SAYYID
ADJKOU JUDOKA
ADJNOR JORDAN
ADJSTU ADJUST
ADKLNY DANKLY
ADKLRY DARKLY
ADKLSS SKALDS
ADKLSY ALKYDS
ADKOPU PADOUK
ADKOSV VODKAS
ADLLOR DOLLAR
ADLLOS ALDOLS
ALLODS
ADLLUY DUALLY
ADLMNO ALMOND
DOLMAN
ADLMOS DOLMAS
MODALS
ADLMOW WADMOL
ADLMPY DAMPLY
ADLMSU ALMUDS
ADLNOO ONLOAD
ADLNOR LADRON
LARDON
ADLNOS SOLAND
SOLDAN
ADLNOT DALTON
ADLNOU UNLOAD
ADLNPU UPLAND
ADLNRU LURDAN
ADLNSU SULDAN
ADLOPU UPLOAD
ADLORS DORSAL
ADLOSS DOSSAL
ADLOSU DOULAS
ADLOSW WOALDS
ADLRSW DRAWLS
ADLRWY DRAWLY
ADLSTU ADULTS
ADMMOT MADTOM
ADMNOR RANDOM
RODMAN
ADMNOS DAMSON
MONADS
NOMADS
ADMNOY DYNAMO
ADMNSU DUNAMS
MAUNDS
ADMNUY MAUNDY
ADMORR RAMROD
ADMORU MADURO
ADMOSU DOUMAS
ADMRSU MUDRAS
ADMSTU DATUMS
ADMTUY ADYTUM
ADNNOS DONNAS
ADNNOU ADNOUN
ADNOPR PARDON
ADNOPT DOPANT
ADNORS ADORNS
ANDROS
RADONS
ADNORU AROUND
ADNORW ONWARD
ADNOSU SOUDAN
ADNRST STRAND
ADNRTU TUNDRA
ADNRUW UNDRAW
ADNSST STANDS
ADNSTU DAUNTS
ADNSTY DYNAST
ADOPRY PARODY
ADOPST ADOPTS
ADORRS ARDORS
ADORRU ARDOUR
ADORSS SARODS
ADORSU DOURAS
ADORTW TOWARD
ADOSTT DATTOS
ADOSTY TODAYS
ADPRSU PURDAS
ADPRTU UPDART
ADPRUW UPWARD
ADQSSU SQUADS
ADRRSU DURRAS
ADRSSW SWARDS
ADRSUY SUDARY
ADRTWY TAWDRY
AEEFIR FAERIE
FERIAE
AEEFKR FAKEER
AEEFLM FEMALE
AEEFOV FOVEAE
AEEFRR FEARER
AEEFRT AFREET
FEATER
AEEFSS FEASES
AEEFSZ FEAZES
AEEGGN ENGAGE
AEEGGR RAGGEE
REGGAE
AEEGGW GEEGAW
AEEGJR JAEGER
AEEGJY JAYGEE
AEEGLL ALLEGE
AEEGLP PELAGE
AEEGLR GALERE
REGALE
AEEGLS EAGLES
AEEGLT EAGLET
GELATE
LEGATE
TELEGA
AEEGLU LEAGUE
AEEGMM GEMMAE
AEEGMN MANEGE
MENAGE
AEEGMR MEAGER
MEAGRE
AEEGMT GAMETE
METAGE
AEEGNR ENRAGE
GENERA
AEEGNS AGENES
SENEGA
AEEGNT NEGATE
AEEGNV AVENGE
GENEVA
AEEGOP APOGEE
AEEGOT GOATEE
AEEGPS PEAGES
AEEGRR REGEAR
AEEGRS AGREES
EAGERS
EAGRES
GREASE
RAGEES
AEEGRT ERGATE
AEEGRV GREAVE
REGAVE
AEEGST EGESTA
AEEGSW SEWAGE

AEEHHW HEEHAW
AEEHKM HAKEEM
AEEHLR HEALER
AEEHLX EXHALE
AEEHMR HAREEM
HERMAE
AEEHMU HEAUME
AEEHNP PEAHEN
AEEHNT ETHANE
AEEHNV HEAVEN
AEEHNX HEXANE
AEEHPR HEAPER
AEEHPS SPAHEE
AEEHRR HEARER
REHEAR
AEEHRS HAERES
HEARSE
AEEHRT AETHER
HEATER
HEREAT
REHEAT
AEEHRV HEAVER
AEEHSV HEAVES
SHEAVE
AEEILM MEALIE
AEEIMN MEANIE
AEEINT TENIAE
AEEIPR PEREIA
AEEIRR AERIER
AEEIRS AERIES
EASIER
AEEISS EASIES
AEEJVY JAYVEE
VEEJAY
AEEKLN ALKENE
AEEKLR LEAKER
AEEKLV VAKEEL
AEEKMR REMAKE
AEEKNS AKENES
SKEANE
AEEKNW WEAKEN
AEEKRS RAKEES
AEEKRT RETAKE
AEEKRU EUREKA
AEEKRW REWAKE
WEAKER
AEELLL ALLELE
AEELLM MALLEE
AEELLS ALLEES
AEELMN ENAMEL
MELENA
AEELMP EMPALE
AEELMS MEASLE
AEELNR LEANER
AEELNS ANELES
AEELNT LATEEN
AEELNV LEAVEN
AEELOR AREOLE
AEELOT OLEATE
AEELPR LEAPER
REPEAL
AEELPS ASLEEP
ELAPSE
PLEASE
AEELQU QUELEA
AEELRR REALER
AEELRS LAREES
LEASER
REALES
RESALE
RESEAL
SEALER
AEELRT ELATER
RELATE
AEELRV LAVEER
LEAVER
REVEAL
VEALER
AEELSS EASELS
LEASES
AEELST ELATES
STELAE
TEASEL
AEELSV LEAVES
SLEAVE
AEELSW WEASEL
AEELSZ SLEAZE
AEELTU ELUATE
AEELTV VELATE
AEELTZ TEAZEL
TEAZLE
AEELWY LEEWAY
AEEMMM MAMMEE
AEEMNR MEANER
RENAME

AEEMNS ENEMAS
MENSAE
SEAMEN
AEEMNX AXEMEN
EXAMEN
AEEMPR AMPERE
AEEMPT METEPA
AEEMRR REAMER
AEEMRS AMEERS
RAMEES
SEAMER
AEEMRT REMATE
RETEAM
AEEMSS SESAME
AEEMTT METATE
AEEMTX TAXEME
AEENNP PENNAE
AEENNT NEATEN
AEENNX ANNEXE
AEENPS PEASEN
AEENPT NEPETA
AEENPU EUPNEA
AEENPW PAWNEE
AEENRR EARNER
NEARER
REEARN
AEENRS ARENES
RANEES
AEENRT ENTERA
NEATER
AEENRW WEANER
AEENST ENATES
SATEEN
SENATE
AEENSU AENEUS
UNEASE
AEENSV VEENAS
AEENTW ATWEEN
AEENUV AVENUE
AEEPPR RAPPEE
AEEPRR REAPER
AEEPRS SERAPE
AEEPRT REPEAT
RETAPE
AEEPRV PAREVE
REPAVE
AEEPSS PASSEE
PEASES
AEEPST ETAPES
PESETA
AEEPSW PESEWA
AEEPSX APEXES
AEEPSY PAYEES
AEEPTT PATTEE
AEEPVY PEAVEY
AEEQRU QUAERE
AEEQTU EQUATE
AEERRR REARER
AEERRS ERASER
SEARER
AEERRT RETEAR
TEARER
TERRAE
AEERRV REAVER
AEERRW REWEAR
WEARER
AEERSS ERASES
SAREES
AEERST ARETES
EASTER
EATERS
RESEAT
SEATER
TEASER
AEERSU RESEAU
UREASE
AEERSV AVERSE
REAVES
AEERSZ RAZEES
AEERTY EATERY
AEERVW WEAVER
AEESST TEASES
AEESSW SEESAW
AEESSY EYASES
AEESTT ESTATE
TESTAE
AEESVW WEAVES
AEFFGR GAFFER
AEFFGS GAFFES
AEFFHT HAFFET
AEFFIN AFFINE
AEFFIP PIAFFE
AEFFIW WAFFIE
AEFFLR FARFEL
RAFFLE
AEFFLW WAFFLE

AEFFRZ ZAFFER
ZAFFRE
AEFGLN FLANGE
AEFGLR REFLAG
AEFGNS GANEFS
AEFGOR FORAGE
AEFHLL FELLAH
AEFHRS AFRESH
AEFHRT FATHER
HAFTER
TREFAH
AEFHSS FASHES
SHEAFS
AEFIJO FEIJOA
AEFILL FAILLE
AEFILN FINALE
AEFILR FERIAL
AEFILS FALSIE
AEFILT FETIAL
AEFIMN FAMINE
AEFINR FAINER
INFARE
AEFIRR FAIRER
AEFIRS FERIAS
FRAISE
AEFIRY AERIFY
AEFIST FIESTA
AEFITX FIXATE
AEFJNT FANJET
AEFKLR FLAKER
AEFKLS FLAKES
AEFKLY FLAKEY
AEFKNS KENAFS
AEFKRS FAKERS
FREAKS
AEFKRY FAKERY
FREAKY
AEFLLN FALLEN
AEFLLR FALLER
REFALL
AEFLLS FELLAS
AEFLMN FLAMEN
AEFLMR FLAMER
AEFLMS FLAMES
FLEAMS
AEFLNS FLANES
AEFLNX FLAXEN
AEFLOR FLORAE
LOAFER
AEFLOT FOETAL
FOLATE
AEFLOV FOVEAL
AEFLRS FALSER
FARLES
FERALS
FLARES
AEFLRT FALTER
AEFLRU EARFUL
FERULA
AEFLRY FLAYER
AEFLST FESTAL
AEFLSX FLAXES
AEFLSY SAFELY
AEFLTY FEALTY
FEATLY
AEFLUW WAEFUL
AEFMNO FOEMAN
AEFMOR FEMORA
FOAMER
AEFMRR FARMER
FRAMER
AEFMRS FRAMES
AEFNNR FANNER
AEFNRU FURANE
AEFNRW FAWNER
AEFNST FASTEN
AEFNSU UNSAFE
AEFNTT FATTEN
AEFOSS FOSSAE
AEFOSV FOVEAS
AEFPPR FRAPPE
AEFRRS FARERS
AEFRRT FRATER
RAFTER
AEFRRY RAREFY
AEFRST AFTERS
FASTER
STRAFE
AEFRSU FEUARS
AEFRSW WAFERS
AEFRTT FATTER
AEFRTW WAFTER
AEFRWY WAFERY
AEFSST FEASTS
SAFEST
AEFSTY SAFETY

AEFSUV FAUVES
AEGGGL GAGGLE
AEGGGR GAGGER
AEGGHL HAGGLE
AEGGIN AGEING
GAEING
AEGGIS AGGIES
AEGGJR JAGGER
AEGGLR GARGLE
LAGGER
RAGGLE
AEGGLW WAGGLE
AEGGMN GAGMEN
AEGGNR GANGER
GRANGE
NAGGER
AEGGNU GANGUE
AEGGRS AGGERS
EGGARS
GAGERS
SAGGER
SEGGAR
AEGGRT GARGET
TAGGER
AEGGRU GAUGER
AEGGRW WAGGER
AEGGSU GAUGES
AEGGWW GEWGAW
AEGHIN HAEING
AEGHIO HOAGIE
AEGHIR HEGARI
HEGIRA
AEGHIS GEISHA
AEGHIW AWEIGH
AEGHMO HOMAGE
OHMAGE
AEGHNR HANGER
REHANG
AEGHOR GHERAO
AEGHPS PHAGES
AEGHRS GASHER
GERAHS
AEGHRT GATHER
AEGHSS GASHES
AEGILM MILAGE
AEGILN GENIAL
LINAGE
AEGILO GOALIE
AEGILR GLAIRE
AEGILS LIGASE
SILAGE
AEGILT AIGLET
GELATI
LIGATE
AEGILV GLAIVE
VAGILE
AEGIMN ENIGMA
GAMINE
AEGIMP MAGPIE
AEGIMR GAMIER
IMAGER
MAIGRE
MIRAGE
AEGIMS AGEISM
IMAGES
AEGINN INNAGE
AEGINR EARING
GAINER
REAGIN
REGAIN
REGINA
AEGINS EASING
AEGINT EATING
INGATE
AEGINU GUINEA
AEGINW AWEING
AEGINZ AGNIZE
AEGIPP PIPAGE
AEGIRS SAGIER
AEGIRT AIGRET
GAITER
TRIAGE
AEGIRV RIVAGE
AEGIRW EARWIG
AEGIST AGEIST
AEGISV VISAGE
AEGISW GAWSIE
AEGITU AUGITE
AEGITY GAIETY
AEGJLN JANGLE
AEGJLT JETLAG
AEGJRS JAGERS
AEGJTU JUGATE
AEGKMS MASKEG
AEGKRW GAWKER
AEGKST GASKET

AEGLLS LEGALS
AEGLLT GALLET
AEGLLU ULLAGE
AEGLLY GALLEY
AEGLMN LEGMAN
MANGEL
MANGLE
AEGLMR MALGRE
AEGLMS GLEAMS
AEGLMV MAGLEV
AEGLMY GAMELY
GLEAMY
AEGLNR ANGLER
REGNAL
AEGLNS ANGELS
ANGLES
GLEANS
AEGLNT GELANT
TANGLE
AEGLNU LAGUNE
LANGUE
AEGLNW WANGLE
AEGLOR GALORE
GAOLER
AEGLOT GELATO
LEGATO
AEGLOV LOVAGE
AEGLPS PLAGES
AEGLPU PLAGUE
AEGLRR LARGER
AEGLRS ARGLES
GLARES
LAGERS
LARGES
AEGLRT TERGAL
AEGLRV GRAVEL
AEGLRY ARGYLE
AEGLRZ GLAZER
AEGLST AGLETS
AEGLSV GAVELS
AEGLSY SAGELY
AEGLSZ GLAZES
AEGMMR GAMMER
GRAMME
AEGMMS SMEGMA
AEGMNR ENGRAM
GERMAN
MANGER
RAGMEN
AEGMNS GASMEN
MANGES
AEGMNT MAGNET
AEGMNY MANGEY
AEGMOS OMEGAS
AEGMRS GAMERS
MARGES
AEGMRU MAUGER
MAUGRE
AEGMSS MEGASS
AEGMST GAMEST
AEGMUY MAGUEY
AEGMUZ ZEUGMA
AEGNNO NONAGE
AEGNNP PANGEN
PENANG
AEGNNT GANNET
AEGNOR ONAGER
ORANGE
AEGNOS AGONES
GENOAS
AEGNRR GARNER
RANGER
AEGNRS ANGERS
RANGES
SANGER
AEGNRT ARGENT
GARNET
AEGNRV GRAVEN
AEGNRW GNAWER
AEGNRY ANERGY
AEGNST AGENTS
AEGNSV GANEVS
VEGANS
AEGOPT POTAGE
AEGORT GAROTE
ORGEAT
AEGORU AERUGO
AEGOTT TOGATE
AEGOTU OUTAGE
AEGOTW TOWAGE
AEGOVY VOYAGE

AEGPRS GAPERS
GASPER
GRAPES
PAGERS
PARGES
SPARGE
AEGPRT PARGET
AEGPRW GAWPER
AEGPRY GRAPEY
AEGPUZ UPGAZE
AEGRRT GARRET
GARTER
GRATER
AEGRRU ARGUER
AEGRRV GRAVER
AEGRRY GRAYER
AEGRRZ GRAZER
AEGRSS GASSER
SARGES
AEGRST GASTER
GATERS
GRATES
GREATS
RETAGS
STAGER
TARGES
AEGRSU ARGUES
AUGERS
SAUGER
AEGRSV GRAVES
AEGRSW SWAGER
WAGERS
AEGRSY GREASY
GYRASE
YAGERS
AEGRSZ GAZERS
GRAZES
AEGRTT TARGET
AEGRTU RUGATE
AEGRTY GYRATE
AEGRUV VAGUER
AEGRVY GARVEY
AEGSSS GASSES
AEGSST SAGEST
STAGES
AEGSSU USAGES
AEGSSW SWAGES
AEGSTU TEGUAS
AEGSTY GAYEST
STAGEY
AEGSUZ GAUZES
AEGTTU GUTTAE
AEGTYY GAYETY
AEHHLT HEALTH
AEHHPR RHAPHE
AEHHPS EPHAHS
AEHHPY HYPHAE
AEHHRS REHASH
AEHHRT HEARTH
AEHHSS HASHES
AEHHST HEATHS
SHEATH
AEHHTY HEATHY
AEHIJR HEJIRA
AEHIKN HANKIE
AEHIKW HAWKIE
AEHILM HIEMAL
AEHILN INHALE
AEHILR HAILER
AEHILS SHEILA
AEHILT HALITE
AEHILW AWHILE
AEHIMM MAIHEM
AEHIMN HAEMIN
AEHIMR HERMAI
AEHIMS MASHIE
AEHINR HERNIA
AEHINV VAHINE
AEHINW WAHINE
AEHIRS ASHIER
AEHIRZ HAZIER
AEHIST SAITHE
AEHISV SHAVIE
AEHJJS HAJJES
AEHKMS SAMEKH
AEHKNR HANKER
HARKEN
AEHKNS SHAKEN
AEHKNZ KHAZEN
AEHKPR PHREAK
AEHKRS KASHER
SHAKER
AEHKRW HAWKER
AEHKSS SHAKES
AEHKWY HAWKEY
AEHLLL HALLEL

AEHLLT LETHAL
AEHLMS ALMEHS
AEHLMT HAMLET
AEHLNO ENHALO
AEHLNS HANSEL
AEHLNT HANTLE
THENAL
AEHLOS HALOES
AEHLOT LOATHE
AEHLPS ALEPHS
AEHLPY PHYLAE
AEHLRS ASHLER
HALERS
LASHER
AEHLRT HALTER
LATHER
THALER
AEHLRU HALERU
HAULER
AEHLRW WHALER
AEHLSS HASSEL
HASSLE
LASHES
SELAHS
SHALES
SHEALS
AEHLST HALEST
HASLET
LATHES
SHELTA
AEHLSU LEHUAS
AEHLSV HALVES
AEHLSW WHALES
WHEALS
AEHLSY SHALEY
AEHLSZ HAZELS
AEHLTW WEALTH
AEHLTY HYETAL
AEHMMR HAMMER
AEHMMY MAYHEM
AEHMNS ASHMEN
AEHMNT ANTHEM
HETMAN
AEHMNU HUMANE
AEHMOS MAHOES
AEHMPR HAMPER
AEHMRR HARMER
AEHMRS HAREMS
MASHER
SHMEAR
AEHMSS MASHES
SHAMES
AEHMTU HUMATE
AEHNNS HENNAS
AEHNPP HAPPEN
AEHNPS SHAPEN
AEHNPT HAPTEN
AEHNRT ANTHER
THENAR
AEHNSS HANSES
AEHNST HASTEN
SNATHE
THANES
AEHNSU HAUSEN
AEHNSV HAVENS
SHAVEN
AEHNSW WHENAS
AEHNSY HYENAS
AEHORS AHORSE
ASHORE
HOARSE
AEHORX HOAXER
AEHOSX HOAXES
AEHPPU UPHEAP
AEHPRR HARPER
AEHPRS PHRASE
RAPHES
SERAPH
SHAPER
SHERPA
AEHPRT TEPHRA
TERAPH
THREAP
AEHPSS PASHES
PHASES
SHAPES
AEHPST SPATHE
AEHRRS RASHER
SHARER
AEHRRT RATHER
AEHRSS RASHES
SHARES
SHEARS
AEHRST EARTHS
HATERS
HEARTS

AEHRSV HAVERS
SHAVER
AEHRSW HAWSER
REWASH
WASHER
AEHRSY HAYERS
AEHRSZ HAZERS
AEHRTT HATTER
THREAT
AEHRTV THRAVE
AEHRTW THAWER
WREATH
AEHRTY EARTHY
HEARTY
AEHRVW WHARVE
AEHSSS SASHES
AEHSST HASTES
AEHSSV SHAVES
AEHSSW HAWSES
WASHES
AEHSTT THETAS
AEHSTW SWATHE
WHEATS
AEIILS LIAISE
AEIIRR AIRIER
AEIJLR JAILER
AEIJLZ JEZAIL
AEIKKP PIKAKE
AEIKLN ALKINE
AEIKLR LAKIER
AEIKLS ALKIES
ALSIKE
AEIKLT TALKIE
AEIKLX AXLIKE
AEIKMN KINEMA
AEIKNS KINASE
AEIKNT INTAKE
AEIKOR OAKIER
AEIKRR KERRIA
AEIKRS KAISER
AEILLM MALLEI
AEILLN LIENAL
LINEAL
AEILLS ALLIES
AEILLT TAILLE
TELIAL
AEILLV VILLAE
AEILLW WALLIE
AEILMN MALINE
MENIAL
AEILMP IMPALE
AEILMR MAILER
REMAIL
AEILMS EMAILS
MAILES
MESIAL
SAMIEL
AEILNO EOLIAN
AEILNP ALPINE
PENIAL
PINEAL
AEILNR ALINER
LARINE
LINEAR
NAILER
RENAIL
AEILNS ALIENS
ALINES
ELAINS
LIANES
SALINE
SILANE
AEILNT ENTAIL
TENAIL
TINEAL
AEILNV ALEVIN
ALVINE
VALINE
VEINAL
VENIAL
VINEAL
AEILNW LAWINE
AEILNX ALEXIN
XENIAL
AEILPR PALIER
AEILPS ESPIAL
LIPASE
AEILPT APLITE
AEILRR IRREAL
RAILER
AEILRS ARIELS
RESAIL
SAILER
SERAIL
SERIAL

AEILRT RETAIL
RETIAL
TAILER
AEILRW WAILER
AEILRY AERILY
AEILRZ LAZIER
AEILSS AISLES
LASSIE
AEILST SALTIE
STELAI
AEILSV SILVAE
VALISE
AEILSW WALIES
AEILSY EASILY
AEILSZ LAZIES
AEILUV ELUVIA
AEIMMM MAMMIE
AEIMMN AMMINE
IMMANE
AEIMMR MAIMER
AEIMMS MAMIES
AEIMMT TAMMIE
AEIMNO ANOMIE
AEIMNR AIRMEN
MARINE
REMAIN
AEIMNS AMINES
ANIMES
INSEAM
MESIAN
SEMINA
AEIMNT ETAMIN
INMATE
TAMEIN
AEIMPY PYEMIA
AEIMRS AIMERS
ARMIES
RAMIES
AEIMRT IMARET
MATIER
AEIMRU UREMIA
AEIMRZ MAZIER
AEIMST MISATE
MISEAT
SAMITE
AEIMSV MAVIES
AEIMSZ MAIZES
AEIMXX MAXIXE
AEINNN NANNIE
AEINNO EONIAN
AEINNP PENNIA
PINNAE
AEINNR INANER
NARINE
AEINNS INANES
INSANE
SIENNA
AEINNT INNATE
AEINPP NAPPIE
AEINPR PANIER
RAPINE
AEINPT PANTIE
PATINE
PINETA
AEINRS ARISEN
ARSINE
AEINRT RATINE
RETAIN
RETINA
AEINRV NAIVER
RAVINE
VAINER
AEINRW WANIER
AEINRZ ZANIER
AEINSS ANISES
SANIES
SANSEI
AEINST SEITAN
TENIAS
TINEAS
TISANE
AEINSV NAIVES
NAVIES
SAVINE
AEINSX XENIAS
AEINSZ AZINES
ZANIES
AEINTU AUNTIE
AEINTV NATIVE
AEINTZ ZEATIN
AEIOPT OPIATE
AEIOPZ EPIZOA
AEIORS ARIOSE
AEIPRR RAPIER
REPAIR

AEIPRS ASPIRE
PARIES
PRAISE
SPIREA
AEIPRT PIRATE
AEIPSS SEPIAS
AEIPST PASTIE
PETSAI
PIETAS
AEIPSV PAVISE
SPAVIE
AEIPTT PATTIE
AEIPTW TAWPIE
AEIPZZ PIAZZE
AEIRRS AIRERS
RAISER
SIERRA
AEIRRT ARTIER
IRATER
AEIRRV ARRIVE
VARIER
AEIRRW WARIER
AEIRSS ARISES
RAISES
SERAIS
AEIRST AIREST
SATIRE
STRIAE
TERAIS
AEIRSV AIVERS
VARIES
AEIRSZ ZAIRES
AEIRTT ATTIRE
RATITE
AEIRTW WAITER
AEIRVW WAIVER
WAVIER
AEIRWX WAXIER
AEISST SIESTA
TASSIE
AEISSX AXISES
AEISSZ ASSIZE
AEISTX AXITES
TAXIES
AEISVW WAIVES
WAVIES
AEITTT TATTIE
AEITTV VITTAE
AEITTX TAXITE
AEIUVX EXUVIA
AEJJNU JEJUNA
AEJMMR JAMMER
AEJMRT RAMJET
AEJMST JETSAM
AEJNST SEJANT
AEJPRS JAPERS
JASPER
AEJPRY JAPERY
AEJRVY JARVEY
AEJRZZ JAZZER
AEJSZZ JAZZES
AEJTWY JETWAY
AEKKNR KRAKEN
AEKKRY YAKKER
AEKLNR LANKER
RANKLE
AEKLNS ANKLES
AEKLNT ANKLET
AEKLNW KNAWEL
AEKLNY ALKYNE
AEKLPS SPLAKE
AEKLPY KEYPAL
AEKLRR LARKER
AEKLRS LAKERS
SLAKER
AEKLRT TALKER
AEKLRV LEKVAR
AEKLRW WALKER
AEKLSS SLAKES
AEKLST LATKES
AEKLSY KAYLES
AEKLTU AUKLET
AEKLWY WEAKLY
AEKMNU UNMAKE
AEKMPU MAKEUP
AEKMRR MARKER
REMARK
AEKMRS MAKERS
MASKER
AEKMRT MARKET
AEKMSS SAMEKS
AEKNOW AWOKEN
WEAKON
AEKNPS PEKANS
AEKNRR RANKER
AEKNRT TANKER

AEKNSS SKEANS
SNAKES
SNEAKS
AEKNSV KNAVES
AEKNSW KNAWES
WAKENS
AEKNSY SNAKEY
SNEAKY
AEKORS ARKOSE
RESOAK
SOAKER
AEKOSY KAYOES
AEKPRR PARKER
REPARK
AEKPSS SPEAKS
AEKPTU TAKEUP
UPTAKE
AEKQRU QUAKER
AEKQSU QUAKES
SQUEAK
AEKRRS RAKERS
AEKRRT KRATER
AEKRSS ASKERS
ESKARS
SAKERS
AEKRST SKATER
STRAKE
STREAK
TAKERS
AEKRSW WAKERS
WREAKS
AEKSST SKATES
STAKES
STEAKS
AEKSSU UKASES
AEKSSV KVASES
AEKSTW TWEAKS
AEKTWY TWEAKY
AEKWYY KEYWAY
AELLLY LEALLY
AELLMT MALLET
AELLMY LAMELY
AELLNY LANELY
LEANLY
AELLOR LOREAL
AELLPS LAPELS
AELLPT PALLET
AELLPX PLEXAL
AELLPY PALELY
AELLRT TALLER
AELLRU ALLURE
LAUREL
AELLRY RALLYE
REALLY
AELLST SALLET
STELLA
AELLSY ALLEYS
AELLTU LUTEAL
AELLTW WALLET
AELLTY LATELY
LEALTY
AELLVY VALLEY
AELMMS LEMMAS
AELMNR ALMNER
AELMNS LEMANS
MENSAL
AELMNT LAMENT
MANTEL
MANTLE
MENTAL
AELMNW LAWMEN
AELMNY LAYMEN
MEANLY
NAMELY
AELMOR MORALE
AELMOS AMOLES
AELMPR AMPLER
PALMER
AELMPS MAPLES
SAMPLE
AELMPU AMPULE
AELMRS REALMS
AELMRT ARMLET
TRAMEL
AELMRU MAULER
AELMRV MARVEL
AELMST LAMEST
METALS
SAMLET
AELMSU ULEMAS
AELMSY MEASLY
AELMTU AMULET
MULETA
AELMTY TAMELY
AELNNR LANNER

AELNOR LOANER
RELOAN
AELNOS ANOLES
LANOSE
AELNOT ETALON
TOLANE
AELNPR PLANER
REPLAN
AELNPS PANELS
PLANES
AELNPT PLANET
PLATEN
AELNRS LEARNS
AELNRT ANTLER
LEARNT
RENTAL
AELNRU NEURAL
UNREAL
AELNRV VERNAL
AELNRY NEARLY
AELNST LATENS
AELNSU UNSEAL
AELNSV NAVELS
AELNSY SANELY
AELNTT LATENT
LATTEN
TALENT
AELNTU ELUANT
LUNATE
AELNTV LEVANT
AELNTY NEATLY
AELOPR PAROLE
AELOPS ASLOPE
AELOPT PELOTA
AELOPX POLEAX
AELOST OSTEAL
SOLATE
AELOSV LOAVES
AELOSZ AZOLES
SLEAZO
AELOTZ ZEALOT
AELPPR LAPPER
RAPPEL
AELPPS APPELS
APPLES
AELPPT APPLET
LAPPET
AELPPU PAPULE
UPLEAP
AELPQU PLAQUE
AELPRR PARREL
AELPRS LAPSER
PARLES
PEARLS
AELPRT PALTER
PLATER
AELPRU PLEURA
AELPRW PRELAW
AELPRY PARLEY
PEARLY
PLAYER
REPLAY
AELPSS LAPSES
PASSEL
SALEPS
SEPALS
SPALES
AELPST PALEST
PALETS
PASTEL
PETALS
PLATES
PLEATS
SEPTAL
STAPLE
TEPALS
AELQSU EQUALS
SQUEAL
AELQUZ QUEZAL
AELRRT RETRAL
AELRRY RARELY
AELRSS LASERS
RASSLE
AELRST ALERTS
ALTERS
ARTELS
ESTRAL
LASTER
RATELS
SALTER
SLATER
STALER
STELAR
TALERS
AELRSU SAUREL

AELRSV LAVERS
RAVELS
SALVER
SERVAL
SLAVER
VELARS
VERSAL
AELRSW WALERS
WARSLE
AELRSY LAYERS
RELAYS
SLAYER
AELRTT LATTER
RATTLE
AELRTV TRAVEL
VARLET
AELRTY ELYTRA
LYRATE
REALTY
AELRUV VALUER
AELRWY LAWYER
AELRYY YARELY
YEARLY
AELSSS LASSES
AELSST LEASTS
SLATES
STALES
STEALS
TASSEL
TESLAS
AELSSV SALVES
SELVAS
SLAVES
VALSES
AELSSW AWLESS
SWALES
AELSSY LYASES
AELSTT LATEST
LATTES
AELSTU SALUTE
AELSTV VALETS
VESTAL
AELSTX EXALTS
LAXEST
AELSTY LYSATE
SLATEY
AELSUV AVULSE
VALUES
AELSUX SEXUAL
AELSVV VALVES
AELSVY SLAVEY
SYLVAE
AELSYZ SLEAZY
AELTTT TATTLE
AELTTW WATTLE
AELTTY LYTTAE
AELTUX LUXATE
AELUUV UVULAE
AELUVV VULVAE
AEMMMR MAMMER
AEMMMT MAMMET
AEMMMY MAMMEY
AEMMNR MERMAN
AEMMRR RAMMER
AEMMRY YAMMER
AEMMRZ MAMZER
AEMMST STEMMA
AEMMSU SUMMAE
AEMMSY MAMEYS
AEMMTU MAUMET
AEMNNP PENMAN
AEMNNR MANNER
AEMNNV VANMEN
AEMNOR ENAMOR
MOANER
AEMNOT OMENTA
AEMNOY YEOMAN
AEMNPR PREMAN
AEMNPU PNEUMA
AEMNQU MANQUE
AEMNRS NAMERS
REMANS
AEMNRT MARTEN
AEMNRU MANURE
AEMNSS MANSES
MENSAS
MESSAN
AEMNST AMENTS
MANTES
STAMEN
AEMNSU UNSEAM
AEMNSV MAVENS
AEMNSY YAMENS
AEMNTU UNTAME
AEMNTX TAXMEN

AEMORR REMORA
ROAMER
AEMORS RAMOSE
AEMORW WOMERA
AEMOSV VAMOSE
AEMPPR MAPPER
PAMPER
PREAMP
AEMPRR PREARM
AEMPRS REMAPS
AEMPRT TAMPER
AEMPRV REVAMP
VAMPER
AEMQRU MARQUE
AEMQSU MASQUE
AEMRRR MARRER
AEMRRS ARMERS
REARMS
AEMRRU ARMURE
AEMRRW REWARM
WARMER
AEMRSS MARSES
MASERS
SMEARS
AEMRST ARMETS
MASTER
MATERS
MATRES
RAMETS
STREAM
TAMERS
AEMRSU AMUSER
AEMRSY SMEARY
AEMRSZ MAZERS
AEMRTT MATTER
AEMRTU MATURE
AEMSSS MASSES
AEMSST STEAMS
AEMSSU AMUSES
ASSUME
AEMSSY MYASES
AEMSSZ SMAZES
AEMSTT MATTES
TAMEST
AEMSTU MEATUS
MUTASE
AEMSTY MATEYS
MAYEST
STEAMY
AEMSUV MAUVES
AEMSYZ ZYMASE
AEMTTU MUTATE
AEMUZZ MEZUZA
AENNOV NOVENA
AENNOY ANYONE
AENNPR PANNER
AENNPS PANNES
AENNRT TANNER
AENNRV VANNER
AENNRW WANNER
AENNSS SENNAS
AENNST ANENST
AENNTT TENANT
AENOPS PAEONS
AENOPT TEOPAN
AENOPW WEAPON
AENORS ARSENO
REASON
SENORA
AENORT ATONER
ORNATE
AENOSS SEASON
AENOST ATONES
AENOSW WEASON
AENOSX AXONES
AENOTT NOTATE
AENOTZ ZONATE
AENPPR NAPPER
RAPPEN
AENPPS NAPPES
AENPPT PETNAP
AENPRS ARPENS
AENPRT ARPENT
ENRAPT
ENTRAP
PARENT
TREPAN
AENPRW ENWRAP
PAWNER
AENPRY NAPERY
AENPRZ PANZER
AENPSS ASPENS
SNEAPS
SPEANS
AENPST PATENS

AENPTT PATENT
PATTEN
AENPTU PEANUT
AENQSU QUEANS
AENRRS SNARER
AENRRT ERRANT
RANTER
AENRRW WARNER
WARREN
AENRRY YARNER
AENRSS SARSEN
SNARES
AENRST ANTRES
ASTERN
STERNA
AENRSV RAVENS
AENRSW ANSWER
RESAWN
AENRSY SENARY
YEARNS
AENRTT NATTER
RATTEN
AENRTU NATURE
AENRTV TAVERN
AENRTW WANTER
AENRWY YAWNER
AENSST ASSENT
SANEST
STANES
AENSSU ANUSES
USNEAS
AENSSW SEWANS
AENSTU UNSEAT
AENSTX SEXTAN
AENSTY YENTAS
AENSUV NAEVUS
AENSUY UNEASY
AENSWY SAWNEY
AENSZZ ZAZENS
AENTTT ATTENT
AENTTU ATTUNE
NUTATE
TAUTEN
AENTTX EXTANT
AENTTY TETANY
AENTWY TAWNEY
AEOPPS APPOSE
AEOPQU OPAQUE
AEOPRS OPERAS
PAREOS
SOAPER
AEOPRT PROTEA
AEOPSS PASEOS
AEOPST SAPOTE
AEOPTT TEAPOT
AEOPTY TEAPOY
AEORRR ROARER
AEORRS SOARER
AEORSS SEROSA
AEORST OATERS
ORATES
OSETRA
AEORSU AROUSE
AEORTT ROTATE
AEORVW AVOWER
REAVOW
AEOSSV SOAVES
AEOSTV AVOSET
AEOSTZ AZOTES
AEOTTU OUTATE
OUTEAT
AEOUVZ ZOUAVE
AEPPRR RAPPER
AEPPRS PAPERS
SAPPER
AEPPRT TAPPER
AEPPRU PAUPER
AEPPRY PAPERY
PREPAY
YAPPER
AEPPRZ ZAPPER
AEPPTT TAPPET
AEPPTU PUPATE
AEPRRS PARERS
PARSER
RAPERS
RASPER
SPARER
AEPRRT PRATER
AEPRRU PARURE
UPREAR
AEPRRW PREWAR
REWRAP
WARPER
AEPRRY PRAYER

AEPRSS ASPERS
PARSES
PASSER
PRASES
REPASS
SPARES
SPARSE
SPEARS
AEPRST PASTER
PATERS
PRATES
REPAST
TAPERS
TRAPES
AEPRSU PAREUS
PAUSER
AEPRSV PAVERS
AEPRSW PAWERS
AEPRSX PRAXES
AEPRSY PAYERS
REPAYS
AEPRTT PATTER
AEPRTU UPRATE
UPTEAR
AEPRTX PRETAX
AEPRTZ PATZER
AEPRUY YAUPER
AEPRWY YAWPER
AEPSSS PASSES
AEPSST PASTES
SPATES
STAPES
AEPSSU PAUSES
UPASES
AEPSTT APTEST
AEPSTU TAUPES
AEPSTX EXPATS
AEPSUX AUSPEX
AEQRSU SQUARE
AEQRTU QUARTE
QUATRE
AEQRUV QUAVER
AEQSUY QUEASY
AEQUYZ QUEAZY
AERRSS RASERS
AERRST ARREST
RAREST
RASTER
RATERS
STARER
TARRES
TERRAS
AERRSU RASURE
URARES
AERRSV RAVERS
AERRSZ RAZERS
AERRTT RATTER
TARTER
AERRTY ARTERY
AERSST ASSERT
ASTERS
STARES
AERSSU ASSURE
URASES
AERSSV SAVERS
AERSSW RESAWS
SAWERS
SEWARS
SWEARS
WRASSE
AERSSY RESAYS
SAYERS
AERSTT STATER
TASTER
TATERS
TETRAS
TREATS
AERSTU URATES
AERSTV AVERTS
STARVE
TRAVES
VASTER
AERSTW RAWEST
TAWERS
WASTER
WATERS
AERSTX EXTRAS
TAXERS
AERSTY ESTRAY
STAYER
YAREST
AERSTZ ERSATZ
AERSUU AUREUS
URAEUS
AERSUV SUAVER
AERSUZ AZURES

AERSVV VARVES
AERSVW WAVERS
AERSWX WAXERS
AERSWY SAWYER
SWAYER
AERSZZ RAZZES
AERTTT TATTER
AERTTU TAUTER
AERTTW WATTER
AERTTY TREATY
YATTER
AERTUU AUTEUR
AERTWY WATERY
AERVWY WAVERY
AESSSS ASSESS
SASSES
AESSST ASSETS
STASES
TASSES
AESSSY ESSAYS
AESSTT STATES
TASSET
TASTES
AESSTU SAUTES
AESSTV STAVES
VESTAS
AESSTW SWEATS
TAWSES
WASTES
AESSTY SAYEST
YEASTS
AESTTT ATTEST
AESTTU ASTUTE
STATUE
AESTWY SWEATY
AESTYY YEASTY
AESVWY WAVEYS
AETUXY EUTAXY
AFFGUW GUFFAW
AFFHIT HAFFIT
AFFIKR KAFFIR
AFFILP PILAFF
AFFIMR AFFIRM
AFFIRT TARIFF
AFFIRZ ZAFFIR
AFFLOS OFFALS
AFFLOY LAYOFF
AFFLSU LUFFAS
AFFLUX AFFLUX
AFFLWY WAFFLY
AFFOPY PAYOFF
AFFQSU QUAFFS
AFFSST STAFFS
AFGGLY FLAGGY
AFGGOT FAGGOT
AFGIKN FAKING
AFGIMN FAMING
AFGINR FARING
AFGINS FAGINS
AFGINT FATING
AFGINX FAXING
AFGINY FAYING
AFGINZ FAZING
AFGISY GASIFY
AFGITZ ZAFTIG
AFGLNO FLAGON
AFGLNU FUNGAL
AFGLRU FRUGAL
AFGNOS GANOFS
AFGORT FORGAT
AFGOST FAGOTS
AFGOTU FUGATO
AFGRST GRAFTS
AFGRUY ARGUFY
AFHIKL KHALIF
AFHIMS FAMISH
AFHIOS OAFISH
AFHIRS SHARIF
AFHIST FAITHS
AFHLMU FULHAM
AFHLOO LOOFAH
AFHLSY FLASHY
AFHLTU HATFUL
AFHMOT FATHOM
AFHORS SHOFAR
AFHRSW WHARFS
AFHSST SHAFTS
AFIILL FILIAL
AFIILN FINIAL
AFIKLS KALIFS
AFIKNU FUNKIA
AFIKRS FAKIRS
KAFIRS
AFILLN INFALL
AFILLS FLAILS
AFILMU AIMFUL
FAMULI
AFILMY FAMILY
AFILNS FINALS
AFILNV FLAVIN
AFILOR FOLIAR
AFILPS PILAFS
AFILRS FLAIRS
FRAILS
AFILRY FAIRLY
AFILRZ FRAZIL
AFILSY SALIFY
AFIMNR FIRMAN
AFIMNY INFAMY
AFIMRT MAFTIR
AFIMRY RAMIFY
AFIMSS MASSIF
AFIMSV FAVISM
AFINNO FANION
AFINNT INFANT
AFINRU UNFAIR
AFINST FAINTS
AFINSU FUSAIN
AFINYZ NAZIFY
AFIQRS FAQIRS
AFIQRU FAQUIR
AFIRRS FRIARS
AFIRRY FRIARY
RARIFY
AFIRST AFRITS
AFIRTY RATIFY
AFJLRU JARFUL
AFKLNS FLANKS
AFKLSS FLASKS
AFKNRS FRANKS
AFKRST KRAFTS
AFLLMU FULLAM
AFLLOR FLORAL
AFLLOW FALLOW
AFLLPU LAPFUL
AFLLTY FLATLY
AFLLUW LAWFUL
AFLMNU MANFUL
AFLMNY FLYMAN
AFLMOR FORMAL
AFLMRU ARMFUL
FULMAR
AFLMYY MAYFLY
AFLNOT FONTAL
AFLNPU PANFUL
AFLNTU FLAUNT
AFLOOS LOOFAS
AFLORS FLORAS
SAFROL
AFLORV FLAVOR
AFLOST FLOATS
FLOTAS
AFLOTY FLOATY
AFLPPY FLAPPY
AFLRTU ARTFUL
AFLSSU SULFAS
AFLSTU FAULTS
FLATUS
AFLSWY SAWFLY
AFLTUV VATFUL
AFLTUY FAULTY
AFLWYY FLYWAY
AFMNOT FANTOM
AFMNSU FANUMS
AFMORS FORAMS
AFMORT FORMAT
AFMOSU FAMOUS
AFMSUU FUSUMA
AFNNNO NONFAN
AFNNOS FANONS
AFNNOT NONFAT
AFNPRY FRYPAN
PANFRY
AFNRSS SNARFS
AFNRSU FURANS
AFNSSU SNAFUS
AFORRW FARROW
AFORRY ORFRAY
AFORSS SOFARS
AFORSV FAVORS
AFORSY FORAYS
AFORUV FAVOUR
AFOSSS FOSSAS
AFOSST SOFTAS
AFPTUW UPWAFT
AFRSSW SWARFS
AFRSTU FRUSTA
AGGGIN GAGING
AGGHIS HAGGIS
AGGHSY SHAGGY
AGGILN GINGAL
AGGILO LOGGIA
AGGIMN GAMING
AGGINP GAPING
PAGING
AGGINR RAGING
AGGINS AGINGS
AGGINT GATING
AGGINW WAGING
AGGINZ GAZING
AGGIWW WIGWAG
AGGIZZ ZIGZAG
AGGLNY GANGLY
AGGLSU GULAGS
AGGLSY SLAGGY
AGGLWY WAGGLY
AGGMOT MAGGOT
AGGMRU MUGGAR
AGGNOW WAGGON
AGGNSY SNAGGY
AGGORS AGGROS
AGGQUY QUAGGY
AGGSTY STAGGY
AGHHSU HAUGHS
SHAUGH
AGHIKU KIAUGH
AGHILN HALING
AGHILS LAIGHS
AGHILT ALIGHT
AGHINR HARING
AGHINS ASHING
AGHINT HATING
AGHINV HAVING
AGHINW HAWING
AGHINY HAYING
AGHINZ HAZING
AGHIQU QUAIGH
AGHIRR GHARRI
AGHIRS GARISH
AGHIRT ARIGHT
AGHISU AGUISH
AGHISZ GHAZIS
AGHLMU MUGHAL
AGHLNU HANGUL
AGHLOS GALOSH
AGHLSU LAUGHS
AGHMOS OGHAMS
AGHNNU UNHANG
AGHNOS HOGANS
AGHNPU HANGUP
AGHNSS SANGHS
AGHNSW WHANGS
AGHNTU NAUGHT
AGHOQU QUAHOG
AGHPRS GRAPHS
AGHRRY GHARRY
AGHRST GARTHS
AGHSSU SAUGHS
AGHSTU AUGHTS
GHAUTS
AGHSUY SAUGHY
AGHTTU TAUGHT
AGHTUW WAUGHT
AGIIJN GAIJIN
AGIILN AILING
NILGAI
AGIIMN AIMING
AGIINR AIRING
AGIISV VIGIAS
AGIJLN JINGAL
AGIJNP JAPING
AGIJNW JAWING
AGIJSW JIGSAW
AGIKLN LAKING
AGIKMN MAKING
AGIKNR RAKING
AGIKNS ASKING
GASKIN
KIANGS
AGIKNT TAKING
AGIKNW WAKING
AGILLU LIGULA
AGILMM GIMMAL
AGILMN LAMING
LINGAM
MALIGN
AGILMO GLIOMA
AGILMP MAGILP
AGILMY GAMILY
AGILNN LIGNAN
AGILNP PALING
AGILNS ALGINS
ALIGNS
LASING
LIANGS
LIGANS
LINGAS
SIGNAL
AGILNU LINGUA
NILGAU
AGILNV LAVING
AGILNW LAWING
WALING
AGILNY GAINLY
LAYING
AGILNZ LAZING
AGILOR GLORIA
AGILOT GALIOT
LATIGO
AGILOV OGIVAL
AGILRS ARGILS
GLAIRS
GRAILS
AGILRY GLAIRY
AGILST GASLIT
AGIMNN NAMING
AGIMNP AMPING
AGIMNR ARMING
MARGIN
AGIMNS GAMINS
AGIMNT MATING
TAMING
AGIMNW MAWING
AGIMNX MAXING
AGIMNY MAYING
AGIMNZ MAZING
AGIMOS AMIGOS
IMAGOS
AGIMSS AGISMS
SIGMAS
AGIMST STIGMA
AGIMWW WIGWAM
AGINNP PINANG
AGINNS SANING
AGINNT ANTING
AGINNU GUANIN
AGINNW AWNING
WANING
AGINOR OARING
ONAGRI
ORIGAN
AGINOT GITANO
AGINPR PARING
RAPING
AGINPT TAPING
AGINPV PAVING
AGINPW PAWING
AGINPY PAYING
AGINRR RARING
AGINRS GRAINS
RASING
AGINRT GRATIN
RATING
TARING
AGINRV RAVING
AGINRW WARING
AGINRX RAXING
AGINRY GRAINY
RAYING
AGINRZ RAZING
AGINSS ASSIGN
AGINST GAINST
GIANTS
SATING
AGINSV SAVING
AGINSW SAWING
WIGANS
AGINSY SAYING
AGINTW TAWING
AGINTX TAXING
AGINVW WAVING
AGINWX WAXING
AGINWY YAWING
AGIORU GIAOUR
AGIORV VIRAGO
AGIOTU AGOUTI
AGIRST GRATIS
AGIRSV VIRGAS
AGIRTU GUITAR
AGISST AGISTS
STAIGS
AGJLMO LOGJAM
AGJLNY JANGLY
AGJLUU JUGULA
AGJNOR JARGON
AGJTTY GYTTJA
AGKLNO KALONG
AGKNRU KURGAN
AGLLNO GALLON
AGLLOP GALLOP
AGLLRY ARGYLL
AGLLSU GALLUS
AGLMOR GLAMOR
AGLMOS GLOAMS
AGLMSU ALGUMS
ALMUGS
AGLNNO LONGAN
AGLNNU LUNGAN
AGLNOO LAGOON
AGLNOS ANGLOS
LOGANS
SLOGAN
AGLNOU LANUGO
AGLNRS GNARLS
AGLNRU LANGUR
AGLNRY GNARLY
AGLNSS SLANGS
AGLNSY SLANGY
AGLNTY TANGLY
AGLNUU UNGUAL
UNGULA
AGLOOP APOLOG
AGLOOR GOORAL
AGLOOT GALOOT
AGLOPS GALOPS
AGLORS ALGORS
ARGOLS
GORALS
LARGOS
AGLORU RUGOLA
AGLOSS GLOSSA
AGLOST GLOATS
AGLOSW SAWLOG
AGLOTY OTALGY
AGLOWY LOGWAY
AGLPUY PLAGUY
AGLRUV VULGAR
AGLRYY GRAYLY
AGLSSY GLASSY
AGLSTU GAULTS
AGLSUV VALGUS
AGMMNO GAMMON
AGMMNU MAGNUM
AGMMSU GUMMAS
AGMNNU GUNMAN
AGMNOR MORGAN
AGMNOS MANGOS
AGMNRU GRANUM
AGMOOY OOGAMY
AGMORS ORGASM
AGMORV VAGROM
AGMOST MAGOTS
AGMOYZ ZYGOMA
AGMPRS GRAMPS
AGMPUZ GAZUMP
AGMSTU GAMUTS
AGNNOY NONGAY
AGNNRY GRANNY
AGNNSU UNSNAG
AGNNUW WANGUN
AGNOQU QUANGO
AGNORR GARRON
AGNORS ARGONS
GROANS
ORANGS
ORGANS
SARONG
AGNORU OURANG
AGNORY ORANGY
AGNOSS GOSSAN
AGNOST TANGOS
TONGAS
AGNOSU GUANOS
AGNOSW GOWANS
WAGONS
AGNOTU NOUGAT
AGNOWY GOWANY
AGNPRS PRANGS
SPRANG
AGNRRS GNARRS
AGNRST GRANTS
STRANG
AGNRSW WRANGS
AGNRTY GANTRY
AGNSST ANGSTS
STANGS
AGNSSY SYNGAS
AGNSTW TWANGS
AGNTTY GNATTY
AGNTWY TWANGY
AGOORT AGOROT
AGOPRS PARGOS
AGOPRT RAGTOP
AGORSS SARGOS
AGORST ARGOTS
GATORS
GROATS
AGORSU RUGOSA
AGORSY ARGOSY
AGORTU RAGOUT
AGOSTU OUTGAS
AGOSTV GAVOTS
AGOSYZ AZYGOS
GYOZAS
AGOTTU TAUTOG
AGOTUY AGOUTY
AGPRSS GRASPS
SPRAGS
AGRSSU SUGARS
AGRSSY GRASSY
AGRSTU TRAGUS
AGRSUU AUGURS
AGRSUY SUGARY
AGRUUY AUGURY
AGSTUU AUGUST
AHHIJR HIJRAH
AHHISV SHIVAH
AHHKOO HOOKAH
AHHKPS KHAPHS
AHHLPY HYPHAL
AHHOOR HOORAH
AHHORS HORAHS
AHHPPU HUPPAH
AHHRRU HURRAH
AHHRST THRASH
AHHUZZ HUZZAH
AHIILT LITHIA
AHIINT TAHINI
AHIJJS HAJJIS
AHIJRS HIJRAS
AHIKKS KHAKIS
KISHKA
AHIKLP KALIPH
AHIKMS HAKIMS
AHIKMV MIKVAH
AHIKRS RAKISH
SHIKAR
AHIKSU HAIKUS
AHILLO HILLOA
AHILLP PHALLI
AHILLT THALLI
AHILLZ ZILLAH
AHILMU HAMULI
AHILNR RHINAL
AHILNU INHAUL
AHILNY HYALIN
AHILPS PALISH
PHIALS
AHILRW AWHIRL
AHILST LATHIS
LATISH
TAHSIL
AHILSV LAVISH
AHILTU THULIA
AHILTW WITHAL
AHILYZ HAZILY
AHIMNR HARMIN
AHIMNT HITMAN
AHIMOR MOHAIR
AHIMPS MISHAP
AHIMRS IHRAMS
MARISH
AHIMRT THAIRM
THIRAM
AHINPR HARPIN
AHINPT HATPIN
AHINRS ARSHIN
SHAIRN
AHINRU UNHAIR
AHINST HAINTS
SHANTI
AHINSV VANISH
AHIOPS POISHA
AHIORS ORISHA
AHIORT THORIA
AHIORV HAVIOR
AHIPRS PARISH
RAPHIS
AHIPRU RUPIAH
AHIPSS ASPISH
PHASIS
SPAHIS
AHIRRS SIRRAH
AHIRST AIRTHS
AHIRSV RAVISH
AHIRSW RAWISH
AHIRTW WRAITH
AHISSV SHIVAS
AHISTU HIATUS
AHJPSU PUJAHS
AHJSTU THUJAS
AHKKSU SUKKAH
AHKMOW MOHAWK
AHKNPU PUNKAH
AHKNRS SHRANK
AHKNSS SHANKS
AHKNST THANKS
AHKNSU ANKUSH
AHKOOS HOOKAS
AHKOSS SHAKOS
AHKRSS SHARKS
AHLLMO MOLLAH
AHLLMU MULLAH
AHLLNU NULLAH
AHLLOO HALLOO
HOLLOA
AHLLOS HALLOS
HOLLAS
AHLLOT HALLOT
AHLLOU HULLOA
AHLLOW HALLOW
AHLLPY ALPHYL
AHLLRT THRALL
AHLLUX HALLUX
AHLMNY HYMNAL
AHLMOO MOOLAH
AHLMOS SHALOM
AHLMSU HAULMS
AHLMUY HAULMY
AHLNOP PHONAL
AHLNOS HALONS
AHLNSU UHLANS
UNLASH
AHLOOP HOOPLA
AHLORT HARLOT
AHLOSS ASLOSH
SHOALS
AHLOST LOTAHS
AHLOSY SHOALY
AHLPRS RALPHS
AHLPRY PHYLAR
AHLPSS SPLASH
AHLPSU SULPHA
AHLPSY PLASHY
AHLRSY RASHLY
AHLSSU SHAULS
AHLSSW SHAWLS
AHLTUZ HALUTZ
AHMMOW WHAMMO
AHMMSY SHAMMY
AHMMWY WHAMMY
AHMNOS HANSOM
AHMNPY NYMPHA
AHMNSU HUMANS
AHMNSY MYNAHS
AHMOOP OOMPAH
AHMORZ MAHZOR
AHMOSS SHAMOS
AHMOSV MOSHAV
AHMOSY SHAMOY
AHMOTU MAHOUT
AHMOTZ MATZOH
AHMOWY HAYMOW
AHMRRU MURRHA
AHMRST THARMS
AHMRSY MARSHY
AHMRTW WARMTH
AHMSSU SAMSHU
SHAMUS
AHMSSW SHAWMS
AHNNOS HONANS
AHNNSU SUNNAH
AHNNSY SHANNY
AHNOPR ORPHAN
AHNORS SHORAN
AHNOWY ANYHOW
AHNPSS SHNAPS
AHNRSS SHARNS
AHNRSY SHARNY
AHNRTW THRAWN
AHNRVY HRYVNA
AHNSST SNATHS
AHNSTU HAUNTS
UNHATS
AHNSTY SHANTY
AHOORY HOORAY
AHOOSW WAHOOS
AHOOSY YAHOOS
AHOPRS PHAROS
AHOPST PATHOS
POTASH
AHOQTU QUOTHA
AHORRW HARROW
AHORRY HORARY
AHORST TORAHS
AHORTT THROAT
AHORTU AUTHOR
AHORTX THORAX
AHOSST HOSTAS
SHOATS
AHOSTZ AZOTHS
AHPRSS SHARPS
AHPRSU PRAHUS
AHPRSY SHARPY
AHPRTU PRUTAH
AHPSST STAPHS
AHPSSW PSHAWS
AHPSUW WASHUP
WHAUPS
AHPTUZ HUTZPA
AHQSSU SQUASH
AHRRUY HURRAY
AHRSSU HUSSAR
SURAHS
AHRSTT STRATH
AHRSTW SWARTH
THRAWS
WRATHS
AHRSTY TRASHY
AHRTTW THWART
AHRTWY WRATHY
AHSSTU TUSSAH
AHSSTW SWATHS
AHSTUY THUYAS
AHSUZZ HUZZAS
AIIKKW WAKIKI
AIIKNT KAINIT
AIILMN LIMINA
AIILNN ANILIN
AIILOS AIOLIS
AIILRY AIRILY
AIIMMN MINIMA
AIIMMS MISAIM
AIIMNS ANIMIS
SAIMIN
SIMIAN
AIIMNT INTIMA
AIIMNV VIMINA
AIIMOR MOIRAI
AIIMPR IMPAIR
AIINNP PANINI
AIINNZ ZINNIA
AIINPR RAPINI
AIINRS RAISIN
AIINST ISATIN
AIINTT TITIAN
AIIORS ARIOSI
AIIPPR PRIAPI
AIIPTW WAPITI
AIIRTV TRIVIA
AIJKNS KANJIS
AIJLOR JAILOR
AIJLOV JOVIAL
AIJMNS JASMIN
AIJMOR ROMAJI
AIJNNS NINJAS
AIJORS RIOJAS
AIKKLU KULAKI
AIKKMS KAMIKS
AIKKST TIKKAS
AIKLMN MALKIN
AIKLMS MISKAL
AIKLMU KALIUM
AIKLNO KAOLIN
AIKLST TILAKS
AIKLSU SALUKI
AIKLSV VAKILS
AIKLTU LIKUTA
AIKMNS KAMSIN
AIKMOO OOMIAK
AIKMPR IMPARK
AIKMRU RUMAKI
AIKMST KISMAT
AIKMSU UMIAKS
AIKNNN NANKIN
AIKNNP NAPKIN
AIKNNU UNAKIN
AIKNOT KATION
AIKNST TAKINS
AIKNTU TANUKI
AIKOPS OKAPIS
AIKORT TROIKA
AIKRST KRAITS
TRAIKS
AIKRSU KAURIS
AIKSUZ AZUKIS
AILLMS MAILLS
AILLMU ALLIUM
AILLNW INWALL
AILLPR PILLAR
AILLST TALLIS

AILLSV VILLAS
AILLTT TALLIT
AILLUZ LAZULI
AILLYZ LAZILY
AILMNO OILMAN
AILMNR MARLIN
AILMNS LIMANS
AILMNU ALUMIN
ALUMNI
LUMINA
AILMNY MAINLY
AILMOP LIPOMA
AILMOT MALOTI
AILMPR PRIMAL
AILMPS LIMPAS
MILPAS
AILMRT MITRAL
RAMTIL
AILMSS MISSAL
SALMIS
AILMST SMALTI
AILMSU MIAULS
AILMSX SMILAX
AILMSY MISLAY
AILMTU ULTIMA
AILMYZ MAZILY
AILNNP PINNAL
AILNNU ANNULI
UNNAIL
AILNOS ALOINS
AILNOT LATINO
TALION
AILNPS LAPINS
PLAINS
SPINAL
AILNPT PLAINT
PLIANT
AILNPU PAULIN
AILNRT RATLIN
TRINAL
AILNRU URINAL
AILNSS SNAILS
AILNST INSTAL
AILNSV ANVILS
SILVAN
VINALS
AILNSY INLAYS
LAYINS
AILNTT LATTIN
AILNTY LITANY
AILNVY VAINLY
AILNYZ ZANILY
AILOOR OORALI
AILORS SAILOR
AILORT RIALTO
TAILOR
AILOSS ASSOIL
AILOSV VIOLAS
AILOSX OXALIS
AILOSY ALIYOS
AILOTX OXTAIL
AILOTY ALIYOT
AILOWY OILWAY
AILPPS PIPALS
AILPRS SPIRAL
AILPSS SPAILS
AILPST PASTIL
PLAITS
SPITAL
AILPSU PILAUS
AILPSW PILAWS
AILQSU QUAILS
AILRST TRAILS
TRIALS
AILRSU URIALS
AILRSV RIVALS
AILRSW ASWIRL
AILRSY RIYALS
AILRTU RITUAL
AILRTY ARTILY
AILRWY WARILY
AILSSS LASSIS
SISALS
AILSSV SILVAS
AILSSW SWAILS
AILSTV VITALS
AILSUV VISUAL
AILSVZ VIZSLA
AILTXY LAXITY
AILVWY WAVILY
AILWXY WAXILY
AIMMNO AMMINO
AIMMOS MIMOSA
AIMMSS MIASMS
AIMMSU IMAUMS
UMAMIS
AIMMSX MAXIMS
AIMNNO AMNION
NOMINA
AIMNNS NANISM
AIMNNT TINMAN
AIMNNU NUMINA
AIMNNY MINYAN
AIMNOS AMNIOS
AIMNOT MANITO
AIMNPT PITMAN
AIMNPW IMPAWN
AIMNPY PAYNIM
AIMNRS INARMS
AIMNRT MARTIN
AIMNRU RUMINA
AIMNST MANTIS
MATINS
AIMNSU ANIMUS
AIMNSV MAVINS
AIMNSZ NIZAMS
AIMNTT MATTIN
TITMAN
AIMNTU MANITU
AIMNUZ MIZUNA
AIMNVY MAYVIN
AIMOPT OPTIMA
AIMOPY MYOPIA
AIMOSU MIAOUS
AIMOSW MIAOWS
AIMOSX AXIOMS
AIMPRS PRIMAS
AIMPRT ARMPIT
IMPART
AIMPSS PASSIM
AIMQSU MAQUIS
UMIAQS
AIMRSS SIMARS
AIMRSZ MIRZAS
ZIRAMS
AIMRTU ATRIUM
AIMRTX MATRIX
AIMSST MAISTS
AIMSSW SWAMIS
AIMSSY MISSAY
MYASIS
AIMSTU AUTISM
AIMSTX MASTIX
AINNNT TANNIN
AINNOP PANINO
AINNOS ANIONS
NASION
AINNOT ANOINT
NATION
AINNOW WANION
AINNPS INSPAN
PINNAS
AINOPS PIANOS
AINOQU QUINOA
AINORS ARSINO
NORIAS
AINORT AROINT
RATION
AINOSV AVIONS
AINOSX AXIONS
AINPRS SPRAIN
AINPRW INWRAP
AINPST PAINTS
PATINS
PINTAS
PTISAN
AINPSV PAVINS
SPAVIN
AINPTY PAINTY
AINQRT QINTAR
AINQTU QUAINT
QUINTA
AINQUY YANQUI
AINRSS SARINS
AINRST INSTAR
SANTIR
STRAIN
TRAINS
AINRSU NAIRUS
AINRSV INVARS
RAVINS
AINRSW RAWINS
AINRTU NUTRIA
AINSSS SASINS
AINSST SAINTS
SATINS
STAINS
AINSSV SAVINS
AINSSW SWAINS
AINSTT STATIN
TAINTS
TANIST
TITANS
AINSTW TWAINS
WITANS
AINSTY SANITY
SATINY
AINSUX AUXINS
AINSYZ ZAYINS
AINTVY VANITY
AIOORS ARIOSO
AIOPRV PAVIOR
AIOPST PATIOS
PATOIS
AIOPTU UTOPIA
AIORRU OURARI
AIORST AORIST
ARISTO
RATIOS
SATORI
AIORSU SOUARI
AIORSV SAVIOR
AIORSX IXORAS
AIORTV VIATOR
AIOSSV AVISOS
AIOSTT TATSOI
AIOSYZ ZOYSIA
AIPPRR RIPRAP
AIPPRY PAPYRI
AIPRST RAPIST
TAPIRS
AIPRSV PARVIS
AIPRSW RIPSAW
AIPRSX PRAXIS
AIPRTY PARITY
AIPRUY PYURIA
AIPSST PASTIS
SPAITS
AIPSTT PITTAS
AIPSTW PITSAW
AIPSZZ PIZZAS
AIPZZZ PIZAZZ
PIZZAZ
AIRRSS SIRRAS
AIRRST RISTRA
AIRRSU URARIS
AIRRTY RARITY
AIRSST SISTRA
SITARS
STAIRS
AIRSSZ SIZARS
AIRSTT ARTIST
STRAIT
STRATI
TRAITS
AIRSTU AURIST
AIRTTT ATTRIT
AIRTTY YTTRIA
AIRVVY VIVARY
AISSST ASSIST
STASIS
AISSTV VISTAS
AISSTW WAISTS
AISTTU AUTIST
AJLOPS JALOPS
AJLOPY JALOPY
AJLOSU JOUALS
AJMNSU UNJAMS
AJMORS JORAMS
MAJORS
AJNRTU JURANT
AJNSTU JAUNTS
JUNTAS
AJNTUY JAUNTY
AJORSW JOWARS
AJOSSU SAJOUS
AJRSTU JURATS
AKKLSU KULAKS
AKKNSS SKANKS
AKKNSY SKANKY
AKKOPS KAPOKS
AKKOQU QUOKKA
AKLLNY LANKLY
AKLLSY ALKYLS
AKLMMU MAMLUK
AKLNOX KLAXON
AKLNPS PLANKS
AKLNRY RANKLY
AKLOPS POLKAS
AKLOSS SKOALS
AKLOST SKATOL
AKLOXY ALKOXY
AKLPTU UPTALK
AKLPUW WALKUP
AKLRVY VALKYR
AKLSST STALKS
AKLSTU TALUKS
AKLSTY STALKY
AKMNSU UNMASK
AKMNSY SKYMAN
AKMORS KORMAS
AKMOSU OAKUMS
AKMPRU MARKUP
AKNORU KORUNA
AKNORY RYOKAN
AKNPRS PRANKS
AKNPSS SPANKS
AKNPSU PUNKAS
AKNRRY KNARRY
AKNRSS SNARKS
AKNRST TRANKS
AKNRSU KNAURS
AKNRSY SNARKY
AKNSST STANKS
AKNSSW SWANKS
AKNSUZ KANZUS
AKNSWY SWANKY
AKNTWY TWANKY
AKOORR KARROO
AKOORS KAROOS
AKOOSZ KAZOOS
AKOPPS KOPPAS
AKOPSY YAPOKS
AKORSS KAROSS
AKORST KORATS
TAROKS
TROAKS
AKOSTU OUTASK
AKOSTY TOKAYS
AKPRSS SPARKS
AKPRSY SPARKY
AKPTTU KAPUTT
AKQRSU QUARKS
SQUARK
AKQSUW SQUAWK
AKRSST KARSTS
AKRSTU KRAUTS
KURTAS
AKSUVZ KUVASZ
AKSWYY SKYWAY
ALLLOT TALLOL
ALLLSY ALLYLS
ALLMOS SLALOM
ALLMOT MALTOL
ALLMOW MALLOW
ALLMSS SMALLS
ALLMSU MULLAS
ALLNOS LLANOS
ALLNUU LUNULA
ALLOOP APOLLO
ALLOPR PALLOR
ALLOPW WALLOP
ALLORY ORALLY
ALLOSS SALOLS
ALLOST ALLOTS
ATOLLS
ALLOSW ALLOWS
SALLOW
ALLOSY ALLOYS
ALLOTW TALLOW
ALLOVY OVALLY
ALLOWW WALLOW
ALLPPU PULPAL
ALLPRU PLURAL
ALLPSS SPALLS
ALLPSY PSYLLA
ALLQSU SQUALL
ALLSST STALLS
ALLSTY LASTLY
ALLUVV VULVAL
ALMMUY AMYLUM
ALMNOR NORMAL
ALMNOS SALMON
ALMOOS MOOLAS
ALMORS MOLARS
MORALS
ALMORT MORTAL
ALMORU MORULA
ALMOST ALMOST
SMALTO
STOMAL
ALMOSU LOUMAS
ALMPSS PLASMS
PSALMS
ALMPSU AMPULS
ALMQSU QUALMS
ALMQUY QUALMY
ALMRSU LARUMS
MURALS
ALMRSY MYLARS
ALMRWY WARMLY
ALMSST SMALTS
ALMSUY ASYLUM
ALMTUU MUTUAL
UMLAUT
ALNNOU NOUNAL
ALNNSU ANNULS
ALNOOS SALOON
SOLANO
ALNOOZ ZOONAL
ALNOPR PROLAN
ALNOPS NOPALS
ALNORS LORANS
ALNOSS SALONS
SOLANS
ALNOST SANTOL
STANOL
TALONS
TOLANS
ALNOSY ONLAYS
ALNOSZ AZLONS
ALNOTV VOLANT
ALNOUZ ZONULA
ALNPST PLANTS
ALNRSS SNARLS
ALNRSU LUNARS
ALNRSY SNARLY
ALNRUY URANYL
ALNRXY LARYNX
ALNSST SLANTS
ALNSTU SULTAN
ALNSTY SLANTY
ALNSUY UNLAYS
YULANS
ALNSVY SYLVAN
ALNSXY XYLANS
ALNTUW WALNUT
ALNTUY AUNTLY
ALOOPS SALOOP
ALOPPR POPLAR
ALOPPT LAPTOP
ALOPRR PARLOR
ALOPRS PAROLS
POLARS
SPORAL
ALOPRT PATROL
PORTAL
ALOPRY PYROLA
ALOPST POSTAL
ALOQTU LOQUAT
ALORST TOLARS
ALORSV SALVOR
VALORS
ALORSY ROYALS
ALORTU TORULA
ALORUV OVULAR
VALOUR
ALOSSS LASSOS
ALOSSV SALVOS
ALOSTT TOTALS
ALOSTV LOVATS
ALOSTX TAXOLS
ALOSVV VOLVAS
ALOTUW OUTLAW
ALOTUY LAYOUT
OUTLAY
ALPPSU PALPUS
ALPRRU LARRUP
ALPRSU PULSAR
ALPRSW SPRAWL
ALPRTY PALTRY
PARTLY
RAPTLY
ALPSST SPLATS
ALPSSU LAPSUS
ALPSSY SPLAYS
ALPSTY PLATYS
ALPSUY LAYUPS
ALRSTU LUSTRA
ULTRAS
ALRSTW TRAWLS
ALRSTY STYLAR
ALRSUW WALRUS
ALRTTY RATTLY
TARTLY
ALRUUV UVULAR
ALRUVV VULVAR
ALSSSY LYSSAS
ALSSTU SAULTS
TUSSAL
ALSSUU USUALS
ALSSVY SYLVAS
ALSTTY LYTTAS
ALSTUV VAULTS
ALSTVY VASTLY
ALSUUV UVULAS
ALSUVV VULVAS
ALTTUY TAUTLY
ALTUVY VAULTY
AMMMNO MAMMON
AMMMOS MOMMAS
AMMNOO AMMONO
AMMORT MARMOT
AMMOSU OMASUM
AMMOSY MYOMAS
AMMOXY MYXOMA
AMMPUW WAMPUM
AMMRSS SMARMS
AMMRSY SMARMY
AMMSSU SUMMAS
AMMSUW WAMMUS
AMNNNO NONMAN
AMNNOY ANONYM
AMNNSU UNMANS
AMNOOR MAROON
ROMANO
AMNOPT POTMAN
TAMPON
AMNORR MARRON
AMNORS MANORS
RAMSON
RANSOM
ROMANS
AMNORT MATRON
AMNOSS MASONS
SOMANS
AMNOST TOMANS
AMNOSW WOMANS
AMNOTU AMOUNT
OUTMAN
AMNPTY TYMPAN
AMNRSU UNARMS
AMNRTU ANTRUM
AMNSUY YAMUNS
AMNTTU MUTANT
AMNTUU AUTUMN
AMOORV VAROOM
AMOOTT TOMATO
AMOPPY MAYPOP
AMORRS ARMORS
AMORRT MORTAR
AMORRU ARMOUR
AMORRW MARROW
AMORRY ARMORY
AMORSS MORASS
AMORST STROMA
AMORSU AMOURS
RAMOUS
AMORSY MAYORS
MORAYS
AMOSST STOMAS
AMOSTZ MATZOS
AMOSUW AWMOUS
AMOTTZ MATZOT
AMPRST TRAMPS
AMPRTY TRAMPY
AMPRUW WARMUP
AMPSSS SPASMS
AMPSST STAMPS
AMPSSW SWAMPS
AMPSUW WAMPUS
AMPSWY SWAMPY
AMRRSU MURRAS
AMRRTY MARTYR
AMRSST SMARTS
AMRSSW SWARMS
AMRSTU STRUMA
AMRSTY SMARTY
AMRSUU AURUMS
ANNOPR NONPAR
ANNOPS SANNOP
ANNORT NATRON
NONART
ANNORW NONWAR
ANNOST SONANT
ANNOSY ANNOYS
ANYONS
ANNOTW WANTON
ANNOTX NONTAX
ANNOTY TANNOY
ANNPSU SANNUP
UNSNAP
ANNRTY TRANNY
ANNSSU SUNNAS
ANNSTU SUNTAN
ANNSUW UNSAWN
ANNSWY SWANNY
ANNTTU NUTANT
ANOORT RATOON
ANOOSW ASWOON
ANOPRS APRONS
PARSON
ANOPRT PARTON
PATRON
TARPON
ANOPRW PAWNOR
ANOPST PANTOS
ANOPSY YAPONS
ANOPUY YAUPON
ANORRW NARROW
ANORSS ARSONS
SONARS
ANORST TRONAS
ANORSV SOVRAN
ANORSW ROWANS
ANORSY RAYONS
ANORTT ATTORN
RATTON
ANORTU OUTRAN
ANORTY AROYNT
NOTARY
ANORYZ ZONARY
ANOSST SANTOS
ANOSSW SOWANS
ANOSTU TAUONS
ANOSTX TAXONS
ANOSTY ASTONY
ANOSWY NOWAYS
ANOSXY SAXONY
ANPPSY SNAPPY
ANPRSW PRAWNS
ANPRSY PYRANS
ANPRTY PANTRY
ANPRUW UNWRAP
ANPSSW SPAWNS
ANQRST TRANQS
ANQSTU QUANTS
ANRSTU SANTUR
ANRSUY SUNRAY
SYNURA
ANRTTU TRUANT
ANRTTY TYRANT
ANRUWY RUNWAY
UNWARY
ANSSUY UNSAYS
ANSTTU TAUNTS
ANSTUV VAUNTS
ANSTXY SYNTAX
ANSYZZ SNAZZY
ANTUVY VAUNTY
AOOPTT POTATO
AOORRT ORATOR
AOORRY ARROYO
AOOTTT TATTOO
AOPPPS POPPAS
AOPRRT PARROT
RAPTOR
AOPRRU UPROAR
AOPRRW PROWAR
AOPRSS SAPORS
AOPRST PASTOR
AOPRSU PAROUS
SAPOUR
UPSOAR
AOPRSV PARVOS
VAPORS
AOPRSY PAYORS
AOPRUV VAPOUR
AOPRVY VAPORY
AOPTUY PAYOUT
AOQRTU QUARTO
AOQSTU QUOTAS
AORRST ROSTRA
SARTOR
AORRSW ARROWS
AORRSY ROSARY
AORRSZ RAZORS
AORRTY ROTARY
AORRWY ARROWY
YARROW
AORSST ASSORT
ROASTS
AORSSV SAVORS
AORSSW SOWARS
AORSTT OTTARS
STATOR
TAROTS
TORTAS
AORSTX STORAX
AORSUU AUROUS
AORSUV SAVOUR
AORSVY SAVORY
AORTUW OUTWAR
AORTVY VOTARY
AOSSTT STOATS
TOASTS
AOSSVY SAVOYS
AOSTTU OUTSAT
AOSTTY TOASTY
AOSTUW OUTSAW
AOSTUY OUTSAY
APPPSU PAPPUS
APRRSY SPARRY
APRSST SPRATS
STRAPS
APRSSY SPRAYS
APRSTY PASTRY
APRSWY PSYWAR
APSSSU PASSUS
APSSTU STUPAS
AQRRUY QUARRY
AQRSTU QUARTS
AQRTUZ QUARTZ
AQSSTU SQUATS
ARRSSU SURRAS
ARRSTY STARRY
ARSSST STRASS
ARSSTT STARTS
ARSSTU SUTRAS
TARSUS
TUSSAR
ARSSTW STRAWS
ARSSTY SATYRS
STRAYS
ARSTUX SURTAX
ARSTWY STRAWY
SWARTY
WASTRY
ARSTXY STYRAX
ASSTTU STATUS
SUTTAS
BBBDEI BIBBED
BBBDEO BOBBED
BBBEIR BIBBER
BBBELO BOBBLE
BBBELU BUBBLE
BBBELY BLEBBY
BBBEOR BOBBER
BBBHUU HUBBUB
BBBINO BOBBIN
BBBLUY BUBBLY
BBCELO COBBLE
BBCEOR COBBER
BBCEOW COBWEB
BBCESU CUBEBS
BBCHUY CHUBBY
BBCLUY CLUBBY
BBDDEI DIBBED
BBDDEU DUBBED
BBDEEW WEBBED
BBDEFI FIBBED
BBDEFO FOBBED
BBDEFU FUBBED
BBDEGI GIBBED
BBDEGO GOBBED
BBDEGU BEDBUG
BBDEHO HOBBED
BBDEIJ JIBBED
BBDEIL DIBBLE
BBDEIN NIBBED
BBDEIR BRIBED
DIBBER
RIBBED
BBDEJO JOBBED
BBDELO LOBBED
BBDELU BULBED
BBDEMO BOMBED
MOBBED
BBDEMU BEDUMB
BBDEOO BOOBED
BBDEOR DOBBER
ROBBED
BBDEOS SOBBED
BBDEOU BUBOED
BBDERU DUBBER
RUBBED
BBDESU SUBBED
SUBDEB
BBDETU TUBBED
BBDIKU DIBBUK
BBDINO DOBBIN
BBDINU DUBBIN
BBDKUY DYBBUK
BBEEEE BEEBEE
BBEEIK KEBBIE
BBEEIR BRIBEE
BBEELP PEBBLE
BBEERS REBBES
BBEEST EBBETS
BBEFIR FIBBER
BBEGIN EBBING
BBEGIR GIBBER
BBEGIT GIBBET
BBEGLO GOBBLE

BBEGOT GOBBET
BBEHIK KIBBEH
BBEHLO HOBBLE
BBEHOR HOBBER
BBEIIM IMBIBE
BBEIJR JIBBER
BBEIKL KIBBLE
BBEIKS KIBBES
BBEILN NIBBLE
BBEILS BIBLES
BBEIRR BRIBER
RIBBER
BBEIRS BRIBES
BBEJOR JOBBER
BBEKOS KEBOBS
BBEKSU BUBKES
BBELLU BULBEL
BBELMU BUMBLE
BBELNO NOBBLE
BBELNU NUBBLE
BBELOR LOBBER
BBELOW WOBBLE
BBELPY PEBBLY
BBELRU BURBLE
LUBBER
RUBBLE
BBEMNU BENUMB
BBEMOR BOMBER
MOBBER
BBEMOS BOMBES
BBEOPS BEBOPS
BBEORR ROBBER
BBEORS SOBBER
BBEOSU BUBOES
BBERRU RUBBER
BBERTU TUBBER
BBGINO GIBBON
BBGLOY GLOBBY
BBGRUY GRUBBY
BBHIOT HOBBIT
BBHLUY HUBBLY
BBHNOO HOBNOB
BBIIKS KIBBIS
BBIKOS SKIBOB
BBILLU BULBIL
BBILOS BILBOS
BBIMOS BIMBOS
BBINNU NUBBIN
BBINOR RIBBON
ROBBIN
BBKNOY KNOBBY
BBKNUY KNUBBY
BBLLUU BULBUL
BBLNUY NUBBLY
BBLOSY SLOBBY
BBLOWY BLOWBY
WOBBLY
BBLRSU BLURBS
BBLRUY BURBLY
RUBBLY
BBMOXY BOMBYX
BBMRUY BRUMBY
BBNNOO BONBON
BBNOOO BONOBO
BBNOSY SNOBBY
BBNSUY SNUBBY
BBOOOO BOOBOO
BBOOSY YOBBOS
BBOOUU BOUBOU
BBORTU BURBOT
BBOSUY BUSBOY
BBRSUU SUBURB
BBSTUY STUBBY
BCCEEH CHEBEC
BCCEIO BOCCIE
BCCEOS BOCCES
BCCIOS BOCCIS
BCCISU CUBICS
BCDEEK BECKED
BEDECK
BCDEIO BODICE
CEBOID
BCDEIS CEBIDS
BCDEKU BUCKED
BCDEMO COMBED
BCDERU CURBED
BCDIOU CUBOID
BCDNOU BONDUC
BCEEHR BREECH
BCEEHY BEECHY
BCEEKR REBECK
BCEEKT BECKET
BCEEKZ ZEBECK
BCEELS CELEBS
BCEEMO BECOME
BCEERS REBECS
BCEESX XEBECS
BCEESZ ZEBECS
BCEGLO BECLOG
BCEHLN BLENCH
BCEHOR BROCHE
BCEHRU CHERUB
BCEIIS IBICES
BCEIKR BICKER
BCEILY BEYLIC
BCEIOR CORBIE
BCEIOX ICEBOX
BCEIPS BICEPS
BCEIRS SCRIBE
BCEIRT TERBIC
BCEIST BISECT
BCEJOT OBJECT
BCEKLU BUCKLE
BCEKMO BEMOCK
BCEKNO BECKON
BCEKRU BUCKER
BCEKTU BUCKET
BCELOR CORBEL
BCELOS COBLES
BCELOU BOUCLE
BCEMOO COOMBE
BCEMOR COMBER
RECOMB
BCEMOS COMBES
BCEMRU CUMBER
BCENOU BOUNCE
BCEOTT OBTECT
BCERRU CURBER
BCERSU CUBERS
BCGINU CUBING
BCGORY CYBORG
BCHIMS CHIMBS
BCHIOP PHOBIC
BCHITY BITCHY
BCHLOT BLOTCH
BCHLSU SCHLUB
BCHNRU BRUNCH
BCHNUY BUNCHY
BCHOOR BROOCH
BCHORS BORSCH
BCHOTY BOTCHY
BCIILM LIMBIC
BCIINO BIONIC
NIOBIC
BCIINU INCUBI
BCIIOP BIOPIC
BCIIOT BIOTIC
BCIITU CUBITI
BCIKRS BRICKS
BCIKRY BRICKY
BCILMS CLIMBS
BCILOO COLOBI
BCILOS CIBOLS
BCILPU PUBLIC
BCILRU LUBRIC
BCIMOR BROMIC
BCIMSU CUBISM
BCINOR BICORN
BICRON
BCINOS BINOCS
BCINRU BRUCIN
BCIORS SORBIC
BCIRRU RUBRIC
BCISTU BUSTIC
CUBIST
CUBITS
BCKLOS BLOCKS
BCKLOY BLOCKY
BCKNUU NUBUCK
BCKORS BROCKS
BCKOSU BUCKOS
BCLOSY COLBYS
BCMOOS COMBOS
COOMBS
BCMORY CORYMB
BCMRSU CRUMBS
BCMRUY CRUMBY
BCNOOR BRONCO
BCNORS BRONCS
BCNOSU BUNCOS
BCNOTU COBNUT
BCNOUY BOUNCY
BCNRUU UNCURB
BCOOOO BOOCOO
BCOOWY COWBOY
BCRSSU SCRUBS
BDDDEE BEDDED
BDDDEU BUDDED
BDDEEN BENDED
BDDEER BEDDER
BDDEGU BUDGED
BDDEIN BIDDEN
BDDEIO BODIED
BDDEIR BEDRID
BIDDER
BIRDED
BDDELU BUDDLE
BDDEMU DUMBED
BDDENO DONDED
BDDERU BUDDER
REDBUD
BDDISU DISBUD
BDEEEF BEEFED
BDEEEN BENDEE
BDEEEP BEEPED
BDEEFW WEBFED
BDEEGG BEGGED
BDEEHL BEHELD
BDEEHR HERBED
BDEEIL BELIED
EDIBLE
BDEEIS BESIDE
BDEEIT BETIDE
BDEEJL DJEBEL
BDEEKR KERBED
BDEELL BEDELL
BELLED
BDEELN BLENDE
BDEELS BEDELS
BLEEDS
BDEELT BELTED
BDEEMR BERMED
BDEEMS EMBEDS
BDEENO DEBONE
BDEENR BENDER
BDEEOY OBEYED
BDEERR REBRED
BDEERS BREDES
BREEDS
BDEERW BREWED
BDEEST BESTED
BDEESW BEDEWS
DWEEBS
BDEESY DEBYES
BDEETT BETTED
BDEEWY DWEEBY
BDEFFI BIFFED
BDEFFU BUFFED
BDEGGO BOGGED
BDEGGU BUGGED
BDEGIL BILGED
BDEGIN BINGED
BDEGIR BEGIRD
BRIDGE
BDEGIU BUDGIE
BDEGLO GLOBED
BDEGLU BLUDGE
BUGLED
BULGED
BDEGNO BONGED
BDEGNU BUNGED
BDEGRU BEDRUG
BUDGER
REDBUG
BDEGSU BUDGES
DEBUGS
BDEGTU BUDGET
BDEHIN BEHIND
BDEHLO BEHOLD
BDEHOO HOBOED
BDEHOT HOTBED
BDEHSU BUSHED
BDEIIM IBIDEM
BDEIIR BIRDIE
BDEIKL BILKED
BDEILL BILLED
BDEILM LIMBED
BDEILN BINDLE
BDEILO BOILED
BOLIDE
BDEILR BIRLED
BRIDLE
BDEILS BIELDS
BDEIMS BEDIMS
IMBEDS
BDEIMU IMBUED
BDEINN BINNED
BDEINR BINDER
BRINED
INBRED
REBIND
BDEINU BEDUIN
BDEIOO DOOBIE
BDEIOR BORIDE
BDEIOS BODIES
DOBIES
BDEIPR PREBID
BDEIPS BIPEDS
BDEIRR BIRDER
BIRRED
BDEIRS BIDERS
BRIDES
DEBRIS
REBIDS
BDEIRU BURDIE
BURIED
RUBIED
BDEIRV VERBID
BDEIST BEDSIT
BIDETS
DEBITS
BDEISU BUSIED
BDEITT BITTED
BDEKLU BULKED
BDEKNO BONKED
BDEKNU BUNKED
DEBUNK
BDEKOO BOOKED
BDEKOR BORKED
BDEKRU BURKED
BDEKSU BUSKED
BDELLO BOLLED
BDELLU BULLED
BDELMO MOBLED
BDELMU BLUMED
BDELNO BLONDE
BDELNS BLENDS
BDELNU BUNDLE
BDELOO BOODLE
BDELOR BOLDER
BORDEL
BDELOT BOLTED
BDELOU DOUBLE
BDELOW BLOWED
BOWLED
BDELRU BURLED
BDELRY BYRLED
BDELTU BUTLED
BDEMMU BUMMED
BDEMNU NUMBED
BDEMOO BOOMED
BDEMOS DEMOBS
BDEMOT TOMBED
BDEMOW WOMBED
BDEMOY EMBODY
BDEMPU BUMPED
BDEMRU DUMBER
BDENNU UNBEND
BDENOR BONDER
BDENOY BEYOND
BDENRU BURDEN
BURNED
UNBRED
BDENSY BENDYS
BDENTU BUNTED
BDEOOT BOOTED
BDEOOZ BOOZED
BDEOPP BOPPED
BDEOPR PROBED
BDEORR BORDER
BDEORS DESORB
SORBED
BDEORT DEBTOR
BDEORW BROWED
BDEORY REBODY
BDEOSS BOSSED
BDEOSU BOUSED
BDEOSW BOWSED
BDEOUY BUOYED
BDEPRU BURPED
BDERRU BURRED
BDERSU REDUBS
BDERTU BRUTED
BDERUX BRUXED
BDESSU BUSSED
BDESTU BESTUD
BUSTED
DEBUTS
BDESUU SUBDUE
BDETTU BUTTED
BDEUZZ BUZZED
BDFILO BIFOLD
BDFIOR FORBID
BDGIIN BIDING
BDGINO BODING
BDGMUU MUDBUG
BDGOOY GOODBY
BDGORU DORBUG
BDHIOS DHOBIS
BDHIRY HYBRID
BDIILO LIBIDO
BDIIMR MIDRIB
BDIINS BINDIS
BDIITT TIDBIT
BDIKNO BODKIN
BDILNS BLINDS
BDILOO DIOBOL
BDILOY BODILY
BDILSU BUILDS
BDIMOR BROMID
MORBID
BDIMOY IMBODY
BDINNU UNBIND
BDINOU BOUDIN
BDINPU UPBIND
BDIOPS BIPODS
BDIOSV BOVIDS
BDIOTU OUTBID
BDIRTU TURBID
BDKLOO KOBOLD
BDLLOY BOLDLY
BDLMUY DUMBLY
BDLNOO DOBLON
BDLNOS BLONDS
BDLOOS BLOODS
BDLOOY BLOODY
BDLOUY DOUBLY
BDMOSU DUMBOS
BDNOOS DOBSON
BDNOOY NOBODY
BDNOSU BOUNDS
BDNOTU OBTUND
BDNSTU BUNDTS
BDOORS BROODS
DOBROS
BDOORY BROODY
BDORWY BYWORD
BDOSTU DOUBTS
BEEEFL FEEBLE
BEEEHP EPHEBE
BEEELT BEETLE
BEEEMS BESEEM
BEEEPR BEEPER
BEEEPW BEWEEP
BEEERZ BEEZER
BREEZE
BEEESV BEEVES
BEEFIL BELIEF
BEEFLL BEFELL
BEEFLY FEEBLY
BEEFOR BEFORE
BEEFRT BEFRET
BEREFT
BEEGIN BEIGNE
BEEGIS BEIGES
BEEGIY BIGEYE
BEEGLS GLEBES
BEEGNO BEGONE
BEEGNU BUNGEE
BEEGRS GREBES
BEEGRU BURGEE
BEEGST BEGETS
BEEGUY BUGEYE
BEEHIP EPHEBI
BEEHLT BETHEL
BEEHOP PHOEBE
BEEHOV BEHOVE
BEEHRY HEREBY
BEEHST BEHEST
THEBES
BEEIKL BELIKE
BEEILR BELIER
BEEILS BELIES
BEEILV BELIVE
BEEIMR BEMIRE
BERIME
BIREME
BEEIMT BETIME
BEEINW NEWBIE
BEEIST BETISE
BEEISV BEVIES
BEEISX IBEXES
BEEJLS JEBELS
BEEKRS BREEKS
BEEKRU REBUKE
BEELLS BELLES
BEELMM EMBLEM
BEELNS LEBENS
BEELNU NEBULE
BEELOT BOLETE
BEELPS BLEEPS
PLEBES
BEELRS REBELS
BEELRT BELTER
TREBLE
BEELST BETELS
BEELSV BEVELS
BEELSZ BEZELS
BEEMMR MEMBER
BEEMRS BERMES
EMBERS
BEEMRU EMBRUE
BEEMSU BEMUSE
BEENNS BENNES
BEENNT BENNET
BEENOR BOREEN
ENROBE
BEENTU BUTENE
BEEOOT BOOTEE
BEEOPP BOPEEP
BEEORR REBORE
BEEORY OBEYER
BEEPTW BEWEPT
BEERRV REVERB
BEERRW BREWER
BEERST BERETS
BEERSV BREVES
BEERSW WEBERS
BEERTT BETTER
BEERTV BREVET
BEERYZ BREEZY
BEESST BESETS
BEFFOU BOUFFE
BEFFRU BUFFER
REBUFF
BEFFTU BUFFET
BEFGLU BEGULF
BEFGOS BEFOGS
BEFHOO BEHOOF
BEFILM FIMBLE
BEFILO FOIBLE
BEFILX BIFLEX
BEFIRS BRIEFS
FIBERS
FIBRES
BEFIST BEFITS
BEFLMU FUMBLE
BEFLOO BEFOOL
BEFLOU BEFOUL
BEFLRY BELFRY
BEFORY FORBYE
FOREBY
BEGGII BIGGIE
BEGGIR BIGGER
BEGGLO BOGGLE
BEGGRU BUGGER
BEGILO OBLIGE
BEGILR GERBIL
BEGILS BILGES
BEGILT GIBLET
BEGIMR BEGRIM
BEGINN BENIGN
BEGINO BIOGEN
BEGINR BINGER
BEGINS BEGINS
BEINGS
BINGES
BEGIOO BOOGIE
BEGIOS BOGIES
GOBIES
BEGIOU BOUGIE
BEGIRS GIBERS
BEGIRT BEGIRT
BEGISW BEWIGS
BEGLNO BELONG
BEGLNU BLUNGE
BUNGLE
BEGLOS BOGLES
GLOBES
BEGLOT GOBLET
BEGLOW BOWLEG
WEBLOG
BEGLRU BUGLER
BULGER
BURGLE
BEGLSU BUGLES
BULGES
BEGMSU BEGUMS
BEGNOY BYGONE
BEGOOR BOOGER
GOOBER
BEGOOS GOBOES
BEGOOY BOOGEY
BEGOPX PEGBOX
BEGORU BROGUE
BEGOSY BOGEYS
BEGOTU OUTBEG
BEGRRU BURGER
BEHILT BLITHE
BEHINT HENBIT
BEHITZ ZIBETH
BEHKOR RHEBOK
BEHLMU HUMBLE
BEHLOW BEHOWL
BEHLSU BUSHEL
BEHMOR HOMBRE
BEHOOS HOBOES
BEHORT BOTHER
BEHOSS BOSHES
BEHRST BERTHS
BEHRSU BUSHER
BEHSSU BUSHES
BEIIKR BIRKIE
BEIIKS BIKIES
KIBEIS
BEIILL BILLIE
BEIIRR RIBIER
BEIISS IBISES
BEIJLU JUBILE
BEIJRS JIBERS
BEIKLR BILKER
BEIKLY BEYLIK
BEIKOO BOOKIE
BEIKRS BIKERS
BEIKSS BEKISS
BEILLR BILLER
REBILL
BEILLS LIBELS
BEILLT BILLET
BEILMN MILNEB
NIMBLE
BEILMO EMBOLI
MOBILE
BEILMR LIMBER
BEILMW WIMBLE
BEILMY BLIMEY
BEILNR BERLIN
BEILNU NUBILE
BEILNY BYLINE
BEILOO BLOOIE
BEILOR BOILER
REBOIL
BEILOT BOLETI
BEILRR BIRLER
BEILRS BIRLES
LIBERS
BEILRT RIBLET
BEILST BLITES
BEILSZ BEZILS
BEIMOS BIOMES
BEIMOZ ZOMBIE
BEIMRT TIMBER
TIMBRE
BEIMRU ERBIUM
IMBRUE
BEIMST BEMIST
BEIMSU IMBUES
BEIMTX BEMIXT
BEINNO BONNIE
BEINNS BENNIS
BEINNZ BENZIN
BEINOR BONIER
BEINOV BOVINE
BEINOZ BIZONE
BEINRR BRINER
BEINRS BINERS
BRINES
BEINRU BURNIE
BEINRY BYRNIE
BEINSZ ZINEBS
BEINTT BITTEN
BEIOOT BOOTIE
BEIORR ORBIER
BEIORS RIBOSE
BEIORU OUREBI
BEIORX BOXIER
BEIOST BOITES
SOBEIT
TOBIES
BEIPPU BUPPIE
BEIQSU BISQUE
BEIQUU UBIQUE
BEIRRS BRIERS
BEIRRU BURIER
RUBIER
BEIRRY BRIERY
BEIRSS BIRSES
BRISES
BEIRST BESTIR
BISTER
BISTRE
BITERS
TRIBES
BEIRSU BRUISE
BURIES
BUSIER
RUBIES
BEIRSW BREWIS
BEIRTT BITTER
BEISSU BUSIES
BEISTZ ZIBETS
BEISZZ BIZZES
BEITUY UBIETY
BEJJUU JUJUBE
BEJLMU JUMBLE
BEJOST OBJETS
BEKLOS BLOKES
BEKMOS EMBOSK
BEKNOR BROKEN
BEKNOT BEKNOT
BEKNRU BUNKER
BEKOOR BOOKER
REBOOK
BEKOOS EBOOKS
BEKOOT BETOOK
BEKORR BROKER
BEKORS BOSKER
BEKOST BOSKET
BEKPSU BUPKES
BEKRRU BURKER
BEKRSU BURKES
BUSKER
BELLOU BOULLE
LOBULE
BELLOW BELLOW
BELLTU BULLET
BELLUY BLUELY
BELMMU MUMBLE
BELMOY EMBOLY
BELMRU LUMBER
RUMBLE
BELMSU BLUMES
UMBELS
UMBLES
BELMTU TUMBLE
BELNNY BLENNY
BELNOR NOBLER
BELNOS BELONS
NOBLES
BELNOZ BENZOL
BELNTU UNBELT
BELNUY NEBULY
BELNYZ BENZYL
BELOOR BOLERO
BELOOS OBOLES
BELOOY BLOOEY
BELOPU PUEBLO
BELORS ROBLES
BELORT BOLTER
BELORU ROUBLE
BELORW BLOWER
BOWLER
BELOST BOTELS
BELOSU BLOUSE
BOULES
OBELUS
BELOSW BELOWS
BOWELS
ELBOWS
BELOTT BOTTLE
BELPSY BLYPES
BELRRU BURLER
BELRSU RUBELS
RUBLES
BELRSY BERYLS
BELRTU BUTLER
BELRTY TREBLY
BELRUY BURLEY
BELSTU BLUEST
BLUETS
BUSTLE
BUTLES
SUBLET
SUBTLE
BELSUY BLUESY
BLUEYS
BELTUU TUBULE
BEMMRU BUMMER
BEMNOT ENTOMB
BEMNOW BOWMEN
ENWOMB
BEMNRU NUMBER
BEMNSU BUSMEN
BEMOOR BOOMER
BEMORS BROMES
OMBERS
OMBRES
SOMBER
SOMBRE
BEMORW BEWORM
BEMORY EMBRYO
BEMOSS BESOMS
EMBOSS
BEMOSW EMBOWS
BEMPRU BUMPER
BEMRSU BRUMES
UMBERS

BEMSSU SEBUMS
BEMSTU BESMUT
BENNOS BONNES
BENNOT BONNET
BENNTU UNBENT
BENOOT OBENTO
BENORR REBORN
BENORS BONERS
BENORU BOURNE
UNROBE
BENORZ BONZER
BRONZE
BENOST BENTOS
BETONS
BENOSW BESNOW
BENOSZ BONZES
BENOTY BETONY
BENRRU BURNER
BENRST BRENTS
BENRTU BRUNET
BUNTER
BURNET
BENSTU SUBNET
BEOORT REBOOT
BEOORZ BOOZER
REBOZO
BEOOSZ BOOZES
BEOPPR BOPPER
BEOPRR PROBER
BEOPRS PROBES
REBOPS
BEOPRU UPBORE
BEOQSU BOSQUE
BEORRS BORERS
RESORB
BEORSS BROSES
SOBERS
BEORST SORBET
STROBE
BEORSU BOURSE
BEORSV BEVORS
BEORSW BOWERS
BROWSE
BEORSX BOXERS
BEORTT BETTOR
BEORTV OBVERT
BEORWY BOWERY
BOWYER
BEOSSS BOSSES
OBSESS
BEOSST BESOTS
BEOSSU BOUSES
BEOSSW BOWSES
BEOSSY SYBOES
BEOSTT OBTEST
BEOSTU BUTEOS
OBTUSE
BEOSTW BESTOW
BEOTUY OUTBYE
BEPRSU SUPERB
BEPRUY PREBUY
BEQTUY QUBYTE
BERRRU BURRER
BERRUY REBURY
BERSSU BURSES
SUBERS
BERSTU BRUTES
BURETS
BUSTER
REBUTS
TUBERS
BERSUX BRUXES
EXURBS
BERSUY BUYERS
REBUYS
BERTTU BUTTER
BERUZZ BUZZER
BESSSU BUSSES
BESSTU SUBSET
BESTTU BUTTES
BESUZZ BUZZES
BFFIIN BIFFIN
BFFINO BOFFIN
BFFLSU BLUFFS
BFFOOS BOFFOS
BFFORU RUBOFF
BFFOSU BUFFOS
BFFOUY BUYOFF
BFGOOW FOGBOW
BFIILR FIBRIL
BFIINR FIBRIN
BFIMOR BIFORM
BFINOW BOWFIN
BFISUX SUBFIX
BFLOSU SOBFUL
BFLOTY BOTFLY
BFLOUX BOXFUL
BFLOYY FLYBOY
BFLSYY FLYBYS
BFLTUU TUBFUL
BFNOSY FYNBOS
BGGIIN BIGGIN
GIBING
BGGIIW BIGWIG
BGGINY GYBING
BGHIIL GHIBLI
BGHILT BLIGHT
BGHIRT BRIGHT
BGHIST BIGHTS
BGHMUU HUMBUG
BGHOSU BOUGHS
BGHOTU BOUGHT
BGHRSU BRUGHS
BURGHS
BGIIJN JIBING
BGIIKN BIKING
BGIINT BITING
BGILLY GLIBLY
BGILNO GLOBIN
GOBLIN
BGILNU BLUING
LUBING
BGINNO BONING
BGINOO BOOING
BGINOR BORING
ORBING
ROBING
BGINOS BINGOS
BOINGS
GIBSON
BGINOW BOWING
BGINOX BOXING
BGINRS BRINGS
BGINSU BUSING
BGINTU TUBING
BGINUY BUYING
BGIORU RUBIGO
BGIOST BIGOTS
BGLNOO OBLONG
BGLRUU BULGUR
BGMOOS GOMBOS
BGMOSU GUMBOS
BGMSUU SUBGUM
BGNOOS BONGOS
BGNOOY GOBONY
BGOORU BURGOO
BGORSU BOURGS
BGOTUU BUGOUT
BHIKOS KIBOSH
BHILSU BLUISH
BHIMOR RHOMBI
BHIOPS BISHOP
BHIOSY BOYISH
BHIRST BIRTHS
BRITHS
BHIRSU HUBRIS
BHIRSY HYBRIS
BHKNOU BOHUNK
BHKOSY KYBOSH
BHLMUY HUMBLY
BHLOSY BOLSHY
BHLSSU SHLUBS
BHMORS RHOMBS
BHMPSU BUMPHS
BHMRSU RHUMBS
BHMSTU THUMBS
BHOOOO BOOHOO
BHOOST BHOOTS
BOOTHS
BHOOTX HOTBOX
BHORST BORSHT
BROTHS
THROBS
BHORTY BROTHY
BHRSSU SHRUBS
BHRSUY BRUSHY
BIIIKN BIKINI
BIIKTZ KIBITZ
BIILNS BLINIS
BIILTW TWIBIL
BIIMOS OBIISM
BIINOT BIOTIN
BIINST BINITS
BIIORS ORIBIS
BIIORV VIBRIO
BIISTV VIBIST
BIITTT TITBIT
BIJOSU BIJOUS
BIJOUX BIJOUX
BIKLNS BLINKS
BIKMNU BUMKIN
BIKNRS BRINKS
BIKNSU BUSKIN
BIKRSS BRISKS
BIKRSU KRUBIS
BIKUUZ BUZUKI
BILLNO BILLON
BILLOR BRILLO
BILLOW BILLOW
BILLOX BOLLIX
BILLRS BRILLS
BILMNY NIMBLY
BILMOS LIMBOS
BILMPS BLIMPS
BILMSU LIMBUS
BILNTZ BLINTZ
BILOPU UPBOIL
BILORS BROILS
BILOXY BOXILY
BILRTY TRILBY
BILSSY SIBYLS
BILSUY BUSILY
BIMNOR BROMIN
BIMNOT INTOMB
BIMNSU NIMBUS
BIMOSZ ZOMBIS
BIMSTU SUBMIT
BINNOR INBORN
BINNOU BUNION
BINOOT BONITO
BINORS ROBINS
BINORY BRIONY
BINOSS BISONS
BINOST BIONTS
BINRSU BRUINS
BURINS
BIOORZ BORZOI
BIOOST OBOIST
BIOOSV OVIBOS
BIOPRT PROBIT
BIOPSY BIOPSY
BIORST BISTRO
ORBITS
BIOSTU SUBITO
BIQSSU SQUIBS
BIQSTU QUBITS
BIRSTT BRITTS
BIRSTU BRUITS
BIRTTU TURBIT
BISTTU TUBIST
BJMOOU BOOJUM
BJMOSU JUMBOS
BKMNUU BUNKUM
BKMOSU KOMBUS
BKNOSU BUNKOS
BKOOOO BOOKOO
BKOORS BROOKS
BKORWY BYWORK
BKOSXY SKYBOX
BKPSUU BUPKUS
BKRTUU KRUBUT
BLLOOX BOLLOX
BLLORY BROLLY
BLMMUY MUMBLY
BLMNUY NUMBLY
BLMOOS BLOOMS
BLMOOY BLOOMY
BLMOSY SYMBOL
BLMPSU PLUMBS
BLMRUY RUMBLY
BLNOOS BOLSON
BLNOTU UNBOLT
BLNSTU BLUNTS
BLOOPS BLOOPS
BLOOSU OBOLUS
BLOOTT BLOTTO
BLOOWY LOWBOY
BLOPUW BLOWUP
BLORTU BRULOT
BLOSTU SUBLOT
BLOSUY BLOUSY
BLOSWY BLOWSY
BLOTTY BLOTTY
BLOWYZ BLOWZY
BLRRUY BLURRY
BLRSSU SLURBS
BLRSTU BLURTS
BLSTUY BUTYLS
SUBTLY
BMOORS BROMOS
BROOMS
BMOORY BROOMY
BMOOSS BOSOMS
BMOOSY BOSOMY
BMOOTT BOTTOM
BMOOTY TOMBOY
BNNORU UNBORN
BNOORS BORONS
BNOOSS BOSONS
BNOOST BOSTON
BNOOTU BOUTON
BNORSU BOURNS
SUBORN
BNORSW BROWNS
BNORTU BURTON
BNORWY BROWNY
BNORYY BRYONY
BNORYZ BRONZY
BNOSSU BOSUNS
BNOSUW SUNBOW
BNOTTU BUTTON
BNOTUY BOUNTY
BNRSTU BRUNTS
BNSUUY UNBUSY
BOOPSY POBOYS
BOOPTW BOWPOT
BOOPTY POTBOY
BOORRW BORROW
BOORST ROBOTS
BOOSST BOOSTS
BOOSWX OXBOWS
BOOTUX OUTBOX
BOOWWW BOWWOW
BOPSUW UPBOWS
BORRSU BURROS
BORRUW BURROW
BORSTU ROBUST
TURBOS
BORTTU TURBOT
BORTUU RUBOUT
BOTUUY BUYOUT
OUTBUY
BRSSTU BURSTS
BSSSUY BYSSUS
BSTTUU BUTUTS
CCCCIO COCCIC
CCCDIO COCCID
CCCILY CYCLIC
CCCOSU COCCUS
CCCOXY COCCYX
CCDEIS SICCED
CCDEIT TICCED
CCDEKO COCKED
CCDELY CYCLED
CCDEOS CODECS
CCDEOT DECOCT
CCEEHR CRECHE
CCEEIS ECESIC
CCEEOR COERCE
CCEERS RECCES
CCEHIL CHICLE
CLICHE
CCEHIM CHEMIC
CCEHIO CHOICE
ECHOIC
CCEHIR CHICER
CCEHIT HECTIC
CCEHKS CHECKS
CCEHLN CLENCH
CCEHLO CLOCHE
CCEHSY YECCHS
CCEIIL CILICE
ICICLE
CCEILR CIRCLE
CLERIC
CCEILY CICELY
CCEINS SCENIC
CCEIOR CICERO
CCEIPT PECTIC
CCEIRS CERCIS
CCEIRT CRETIC
CCEITY CECITY
CCEKLO COCKLE
CCEKOP COPECK
CCEKOR COCKER
RECOCK
CCELRY CYCLER
CCELSY CYCLES
CCENOS SCONCE
CCEORS SOCCER
CCEOSS COSECS
SECCOS
CCERSU CERCUS
CRUCES
CCESSU CUSECS
CCFILO FLOCCI
CCHHII CHICHI
CCHHIN CHINCH
CCHHRU CHURCH
CCHIKS CHICKS
CCHILN CLINCH
CCHILY CHICLY
CCHIMY CHYMIC
CCHINO COCHIN
CCHINU UNCHIC
CCHIOR CHORIC
CCHIOS CHICOS
CCHIPU HICCUP
CCHKOS CHOCKS
CCHKSU CHUCKS
CCHKUY CHUCKY
CCHLSU SCULCH
CCHLTU CLUTCH
CULTCH
CCHNOO CONCHO
CCHNOS CONCHS
CCHNOY CONCHY
CCHNRU CRUNCH
CCHOOS SCOOCH
CCHORS SCORCH
CCHORT CROTCH
CCHORU CROUCH
CCHOST SCOTCH
CCHRTU CRUTCH
CCHSTU SCUTCH
CCIILN CLINIC
CCIILT CLITIC
CCIINO ICONIC
CCIINP PICNIC
CCIINZ ZINCIC
CCIIPR PICRIC
CCIIRS CRISIC
CCIIRT CITRIC
CRITIC
CCIISV CIVICS
CCIKLS CLICKS
CCIKRS CRICKS
CCILNO CLONIC
CCILNY CYCLIN
CCILOS COLICS
CCILTU CULTIC
CCIMOS COMICS
COSMIC
CCINOS CONICS
CCINSY CYNICS
CCIOSS CISCOS
CCIOTT TICTOC
CCIPRU CUPRIC
CCIRSU CIRCUS
CCISTY CYSTIC
CCKLOS CLOCKS
CCKLSU CLUCKS
CCKNOU UNCOCK
CCKOOU CUCKOO
CCKOPU COCKUP
CCKORS CROCKS
CCKRSU CRUCKS
CCLMUU MUCLUC
CCLOSY CYCLOS
CCLOTU OCCULT
CCNOOO COCOON
CCNORU CONCUR
CCOOOO COOCOO
CCOOOR ROCOCO
CCOPUY OCCUPY
CCORSU CROCUS
OCCURS
SUCCOR
CCOSTU STUCCO
CCSSUU CUSCUS
CDDDEO CODDED
CDDEEI DECIDE
DEICED
CDDEEK DECKED
CDDEEO DECODE
CDDEEU DEDUCE
DEUCED
EDUCED
CDDEHI CHIDED
CDDEIS DISCED
CDDEIU CUDDIE
CDDEKO DOCKED
CDDEKU DUCKED
CDDELO CODDLE
CDDELU CUDDLE
CDDEOR CODDER
CORDED
CDDERU CURDED
CDDETU DEDUCT
DUCTED
CDDLOY CLODDY
CDDLUY CUDDLY
CDDRUY CRUDDY
CDEEEM EMCEED
CDEEER DECREE
RECEDE
CDEEES SECEDE
CDEEEX EXCEED
CDEEFH CHEFED
CDEEFN FENCED
CDEEFT DEFECT
CDEEGK GECKED
CDEEHL LECHED
CDEEHO ECHOED
CDEEHP PECHED
CDEEHR CHEDER
CDEEHT ETCHED
TECHED
CDEEHW CHEWED
CDEEIL CEILED
DECILE
CDEEIN EDENIC
CDEEIP PIECED
CDEEIR DEICER
CDEEIS DEICES
CDEEIT DECEIT
CDEEIV DEVICE
CDEEIX EXCIDE
CDEEJT DEJECT
CDEEKK KECKED
CDEEKL DECKEL
DECKLE
CDEEKN NECKED
CDEEKP PECKED
CDEEKR DECKER
RECKED
CDEELL CELLED
CDEELP CLEPED
CDEELW CLEWED
CDEENO ENCODE
CDEENR DECERN
CDEENS CENSED
CDEENT DECENT
CDEEOO COOEED
CDEEOR RECODE
CDEEPR CREPED
CDEERS CEDERS
CREEDS
SCREED
CDEERU REDUCE
CDEERW CREWED
CDEESS CESSED
CDEESU DEUCES
EDUCES
SEDUCE
CDEETT DETECT
CDEFFU CUFFED
CDEFII DEIFIC
CDEFIO COIFED
CDEFNU FECUND
CDEFOR FORCED
CDEGGO COGGED
CDEGIN CEDING
CDEGIO GEODIC
CDEGLU CUDGEL
CDEGOR CODGER
CDEGUW GWEDUC
CDEHIL CHIELD
CHILDE
CDEHIM CHIMED
MICHED
CDEHIN CHINED
INCHED
NICHED
CDEHIR CHIDER
DREICH
HERDIC
CDEHIS CHIDES
CDEHIT ITCHED
CDEHKO CHOKED
HOCKED
CDEHNR DRENCH
CDEHOR CHORED
OCHRED
CDEHOS COSHED
CDEHOU DOUCHE
OUCHED
CDEHOW CHOWED
CDEHRU RUCHED
CDEHTU CHUTED
CDEIIK DICKIE
CDEIIR DICIER
CDEIIT CITIED
CDEIJU JUICED
CDEIKK KICKED
CDEIKL LICKED
CDEIKM MEDICK
CDEIKN NICKED
CDEIKP PICKED
CDEIKR DICKER
RICKED
CDEIKS SICKED
CDEIKT DETICK
TICKED
CDEIKU DUCKIE
CDEIKW WICKED
CDEIKY DICKEY
CDEILO COILED
DOCILE
CDEILR CLERID
CDEILS SLICED
CDEILT DELICT
DELTIC
CDEIMN MINCED
CDEIMO MEDICO
CDEIMR DERMIC
CDEIMS MEDICS
CDEINO CODEIN
COINED
CDEINR CINDER
CDEINU INDUCE
CDEINW WINCED
CDEINZ DEZINC
ZINCED
CDEIOP COPIED
CDEIOS COSIED
CDEIOT COEDIT
CDEIOV VOICED
CDEIOY DIOECY
CDEIOZ COZIED
CDEIPR PRICED
CDEIPS SPICED
CDEIPT DEPICT
CDEIRS CIDERS
DICERS
SCRIED
CDEIRT CREDIT
DIRECT
TRICED
CDEIRV CERVID
CDEIST CISTED
EDICTS
CDEKLO LOCKED
CDEKLU LUCKED
CDEKMO MOCKED
CDEKMU MUCKED
CDEKNO CONKED
NOCKED
CDEKOO COOKED
CDEKOP POCKED
CDEKOR CORKED
DOCKER
REDOCK
ROCKED
CDEKOS SOCKED
CDEKOT DOCKET
CDEKOY YOCKED
CDEKRS DRECKS
CDEKRU DUCKER
RUCKED
CDEKRY DRECKY
CDEKSU SUCKED
CDEKTU TUCKED
CDEKUY YUCKED
CDELLU CULLED
CDELMU CULMED
CDELNO CLONED
CDELOO COOLED
LOCOED
CDELOR COLDER
CDELOS CLOSED
CDELOW COWLED
CDELOY CLOYED
CDELRU CURDLE
CURLED
CDELTU DULCET
CDEMOO COMEDO
CDEMOP COMPED
CDEMOY COMEDY
CDENNO CONNED
CDENOP PONCED
CDENOR CORNED
CDENOS CODENS
SECOND
CDENOT DOCENT
CDENSS SCENDS
CDENSU DUNCES
SECUND
CDENSY SYNCED
CDEOOP COOPED
CDEOPP COPPED
CDEOPS SCOPED
CDEOPU COUPED
CDEORR CORDER
RECORD
CDEORS CODERS
CREDOS
DECORS
SCORED
CDEORW CROWED
CDEOST COSTED
CDEOSU ESCUDO
CDEOSW SCOWED
CDEOSY DECOYS
CDEOYZ ZYDECO
CDEPPU CUPPED
CDEPSU CUSPED
CDERRU CRUDER
CURRED
CDERSU CRUDES
CURSED
CDERSY CYDERS
DESCRY
CDERTU TRUCED
CDERUV CURVED
CDERUY DECURY
CDESSU CUSSED
CDESTU EDUCTS
CDFINU FUNDIC
CDFIOU FUCOID
CDFIOY CODIFY
CDGIIN DICING
CDGINO CODING
CDGOOY COYDOG
CDHIOR ORCHID
RHODIC
CDHIRY HYDRIC
CDHORS CHORDS
SCHROD
CDIIIM IMIDIC
CDIIIR IRIDIC
CDIINT INDICT
CDIIOX OXIDIC
CDIIOY IDIOCY
CDIISV VISCID
CDILNO CODLIN
CDIMOS COSMID
CDIMOU MUCOID
CDIMOY CYMOID
CDIMSU MUSCID
CDIMTU DICTUM
CDINOO CONOID
CDINOR NORDIC
CDINSY SYNDIC
CDINTU INDUCT
CDIOPS PSOCID
CDIORV CORVID
CDIOSS DISCOS
CDIOST DICOTS
CDIPSU CUPIDS
CUSPID
CDISSU DISCUS
CDJNOU JOCUND
CDKNOU UNDOCK
CDLLOY COLDLY
CDLOSS SCOLDS
CDLOSU CLOUDS
CDLOUY CLOUDY
CDMNOO CONDOM
CDMNUU CUNDUM
CDMOOT TOMCOD
CDNOOR CONDOR
CORDON
CDNOOS CODONS
CONDOS
CDOORT DOCTOR
CDOORY CORODY
CDORSS SCRODS
CDORSU DUROCS
CDORSW CROWDS
CDORWY CROWDY
CEEEFL FLEECE
CEEEHS CHEESE
CEEEMS EMCEES
CEEENO EOCENE
CEEERS CREESE
CEEFFO COFFEE
CEEFFT EFFECT
CEEFHL FLECHE
FLEECH
CEEFIR FIERCE
CEEFLY FLEECY
CEEFNN FENNEC
CEEFNR FENCER
CEEFNS FENCES
CEEFRT REFECT
CEEFSU FESCUE
CEEGHO CHEGOE
CEEGNO CONGEE
CEEHIL LICHEE
CEEHIS SEICHE
CEEHIT TECHIE
CEEHKL HECKLE
CEEHKS CHEEKS
CEEHKY CHEEKY
CEEHLR LECHER
CEEHLS LECHES
CEEHLW LECHWE

CEEHLY LYCHEE
CEEHMS SCHEME
CEEHNT THENCE
CEEHNW WHENCE
CEEHOR CHEERO
COHERE
ECHOER
REECHO
CEEHOS ECHOES
CEEHOY ECHOEY
CEEHPS CHEEPS
SPEECH
CEEHQU CHEQUE
CEEHRS CHEERS
CREESH
CEEHRT ETCHER
CEEHRU EUCHRE
CEEHRV CHEVRE
CEEHRW CHEWER
RECHEW
CEEHRY CHEERY
REECHY
CEEHST ETCHES
CEEHSW ESCHEW
CEEHSY CHEESY
CEEIKS SICKEE
CEEILR CEILER
CEEIMN ICEMEN
CEEIMT EMETIC
CEEINS NIECES
CEEINT ENTICE
CEEINV EVINCE
CEEIPR PIECER
PIERCE
RECIPE
CEEIPS PIECES
SPECIE
CEEIRS CERISE
CEEIRT CERITE
RECITE
TIERCE
CEEISS ECESIS
CEEISX EXCISE
CEEITX EXCITE
CEEJRT REJECT
CEEJST EJECTS
CEEKKL KECKLE
CEEKLS CLEEKS
CEEKNR NECKER
CEEKPR PECKER
CEEKRS CREEKS
CEELMO CLEOME
CEELMY MYCELE
CEELNP PENCEL
CEELNR CRENEL
CEELOR CREOLE
CEELOU COULEE
CEELOV VELOCE
CEELPS CLEPES
CEELRS CREELS
CEELRT TERCEL
CEELRV CLEVER
CEELRW CREWEL
CEELRY CELERY
CEELST ELECTS
SELECT
CEELSX EXCELS
CEELSY LYCEES
CEEMNT CEMENT
CEEMNY CYMENE
CEEMRR MERCER
CEEMRS CREMES
MERCES
CEEMRT CERMET
CEENOR ENCORE
CEENOT CENOTE
CEENPS SPENCE
CEENPT PECTEN
CEENRS CENSER
SCREEN
SECERN
CEENRT CENTER
CENTRE
RECENT
TENREC
CEENSS CENSES
SCENES
CEEOOS COOEES
CEEORV CORVEE
CEEPRS CREEPS
CREPES
CEEPRT RECEPT
CEEPRY CREEPY
CREPEY
CEEPTX EXCEPT
EXPECT
CEEPTY ECTYPE
CEEPUY EYECUP
CEERSS RECESS
SCREES
CEERST CERTES
ERECTS
RESECT
SECRET
TERCES
CEERSU CEREUS
CERUSE
RECUSE
RESCUE
SECURE
CEERTT TERCET
CEESSS CESSES
CEESSX EXCESS
CEESSY CYESES
SYCEES
CEESTX EXSECT
CEESUV CUVEES
CEESUX EXCUSE
CEFFIO COIFFE
OFFICE
CEFFLO COFFLE
CEFFOR COFFER
CEFHIS CHIEFS
FICHES
CEFHIT FETICH
CEFHLN FLENCH
CEFHLT FLETCH
CEFHNR FRENCH
CEFIKL FICKLE
CEFILS FELSIC
CEFINT INFECT
CEFIOS FICOES
CEFIRR FERRIC
CEFKLS FLECKS
CEFKLY FECKLY
FLECKY
CEFLST CLEFTS
CEFNOR CONFER
CEFORR FORCER
CEFORS FORCES
FRESCO
CEFOSU FUCOSE
CEFRUW CURFEW
CEGGPU EGGCUP
CEGHIN ECHING
CEGHIO CHIGOE
CEGINO COIGNE
CEGINR CERING
CRINGE
CEGINU CUEING
CEGIST GESTIC
CEGKOS GECKOS
CEGLRY CLERGY
CEGNOR CONGER
CEGNOS CONGES
CEGNOT COGENT
CEGNTY CYGNET
CEGORR GROCER
CEHHST CHETHS
CEHHSU HEUCHS
SHEUCH
CEHIIK HICKIE
CEHIIN ECHINI
CEHIKY HICKEY
CEHILN LICHEN
CEHILS CHIELS
CHILES
CHISEL
LICHES
CEHIMR CHIMER
CEHIMS CHIMES
MICHES
CEHINR ENRICH
INCHER
RICHEN
CEHINS CHINES
INCHES
NICHES
CEHINT ETHNIC
CEHINY HYENIC
CEHINZ ZECHIN
CEHIOR COHEIR
HEROIC
CEHIPR CERIPH
CIPHER
CEHIQU QUICHE
CEHIRR CHIRRE
RICHER
CEHIRS RICHES
CEHIRT CITHER
THRICE
CEHIST ETHICS
ITCHES
CEHISV CHIVES
CEHISW WICHES
CEHITT THETIC
CEHKLU HUCKLE
CEHKNU KUCHEN
CEHKOR CHOKER
HOCKER
CEHKOS CHOKES
CEHKOY CHOKEY
HOCKEY
CEHKST SKETCH
CEHKTV KVETCH
CEHLNP PLENCH
CEHLOR CHOLER
CEHLOT CLOTHE
CEHLOU LOUCHE
CEHLPS SCHLEP
CEHLSY CHYLES
LYCHES
CEHMNS MENSCH
CEHMOR CHROME
CEHMOS CHEMOS
SCHMOE
CEHMOT COMETH
CEHMSU MUCHES
CEHMSY CHYMES
CEHNOO OCHONE
CEHNOS CHOSEN
CEHNOT TECHNO
CEHNOU COHUNE
CEHNQU QUENCH
CEHNRT TRENCH
CEHNRW WRENCH
CEHNST STENCH
CEHNUU EUNUCH
CEHOOS CHOOSE
CEHOPS EPOCHS
CEHORS CHORES
COSHER
OCHERS
OCHRES
CEHORT HECTOR
ROCHET
ROTCHE
TOCHER
TROCHE
CEHORU ROUCHE
CEHORY OCHERY
CEHOSS CHOSES
COSHES
CEHOSU CHOUSE
OUCHES
CEHOSW CHOWSE
CEHOTU TOUCHE
CEHPRY CYPHER
CEHPSY PSYCHE
CEHRRY CHERRY
CEHRST CHERTS
CEHRSU RUCHES
CEHRTW WRETCH
CEHRTY CHERTY
CEHSST CHESTS
CEHSTU CHUTES
TUSCHE
CEHSTW WECHTS
CEHSTY CHESTY
SCYTHE
CEHSWY WYCHES
CEHTTY TETCHY
CEIIKR ICKIER
CEIIKS SICKIE
CEIILS CEILIS
CEIILT ELICIT
CEIILX EXILIC
CEIINR IRENIC
CEIINS INCISE
CEIINT INCITE
CEIIST CITIES
ICIEST
CEIISV CIVIES
CEIJNT INJECT
CEIJRU JUICER
CEIJSU JUICES
CEIKKR KICKER
CEIKLM MICKLE
CEIKLN NICKEL
NICKLE
CEIKLP PICKLE
CEIKLR LICKER
CEIKLS SICKLE
CEIKLT TICKLE
CEIKLU LUCKIE
CEIKMY MICKEY
CEIKNR NICKER
CEIKNS SICKEN
CEIKOO COOKIE
CEIKPR PICKER
CEIKPT PICKET
CEIKRS ICKERS
SICKER
CEIKRT TICKER
CEIKRW WICKER
CEIKRY CRIKEY
RICKEY
CEIKTT TICKET
CEIKTW WICKET
CEILLM MICELL
CEILLO COLLIE
OCELLI
CEILMS CLIMES
CEILNO CINEOL
ENOLIC
CEILNP PENCIL
CEILNS CLINES
CEILNT CLIENT
LECTIN
LENTIC
CEILNU LEUCIN
NUCLEI
CEILNY NICELY
CEILOO COOLIE
CEILOP POLICE
CEILOR COILER
RECOIL
CEILOS COLIES
CEILOT CITOLE
CEILPS SPLICE
CEILPV PELVIC
CEILPY CLYPEI
CEILQU CLIQUE
CEILRS RELICS
SLICER
CEILRT RELICT
CEILSS SLICES
CEILST STELIC
CEILSU SLUICE
CEILSV CLEVIS
CEILTU LUCITE
LUETIC
CEIMMO COMMIE
CEIMNO INCOME
CEIMNR MINCER
CEIMNS MINCES
CEIMNU NEUMIC
CEIMPU PUMICE
CEIMPY PYEMIC
CEIMRS CRIMES
CEIMRT METRIC
CEIMRU CERIUM
UREMIC
CEIMSU CESIUM
MISCUE
CEINNO CONINE
CEINNT INCENT
CEINOR COINER
ORCEIN
RECOIN
CEINOS CONIES
COSINE
ICONES
OSCINE
CEINOT NOETIC
NOTICE
CEINOV NOVICE
CEINOX EXONIC
CEINPR PINCER
PRINCE
CEINPT INCEPT
PECTIN
CEINQU CINQUE
QUINCE
CEINRT CRETIN
CEINRW WINCER
CEINST INCEST
INSECT
NICEST
CEINSU INCUSE
CEINSW WINCES
CEINTY NICETY
CEINWY WINCEY
CEIOOT COOTIE
CEIOPR COPIER
CEIOPS COPIES
CEIOPT POETIC
CEIOPW COWPIE
CEIORR CORRIE
ORRICE
CEIORS COSIER
CEIORT EROTIC
CEIORV VOICER
CEIORW COWIER
COWRIE
CEIORZ COZIER
CEIOSS COSIES
CEIOST CESTOI
CEIOSV VOICES
CEIOSZ COZIES
CEIOTX EXOTIC
CEIPPT PEPTIC
CEIPRR PRICER
CEIPRS CRIPES
PRECIS
PRICES
SPICER
CEIPRT TRICEP
CEIPRY PRICEY
CEIPSS SPICES
CEIPST SEPTIC
CEIPSY SPICEY
CEIQRU CIRQUE
CEIRRS CRIERS
RICERS
CEIRRU CURRIE
CEIRSS CRISES
SCRIES
CEIRST CITERS
RECITS
STERIC
TRICES
CEIRSU CRUISE
CURIES
CEIRSV SCRIVE
CEIRTU CURITE
URETIC
CEIRVX CERVIX
CEISSU CUISSE
CEISSY CYESIS
CEISTU CUTIES
CEISTV CIVETS
EVICTS
CEJKOY JOCKEY
CEJNOU JOUNCE
CEJOOS JOCOSE
CEKKOP KOPECK
CEKLMU MUCKLE
CEKLOR LOCKER
RELOCK
CEKLOT LOCKET
CEKLRS CLERKS
CEKLRU RUCKLE
CEKLSU SUCKLE
CEKMOR MOCKER
CEKMRU MUCKER
CEKNOR CONKER
RECKON
CEKNSS SNECKS
CEKOOR COOKER
RECOOK
CEKOOY COOKEY
CEKOPT POCKET
CEKORR CORKER
RECORK
ROCKER
CEKORS OCKERS
CEKORT ROCKET
CEKOST SOCKET
CEKPRU PUCKER
CEKPSS SPECKS
CEKRSU SUCKER
CEKRSW WRECKS
CEKRTU TUCKER
CEKTTU TUCKET
CELLOS CELLOS
CELLOT COLLET
CELLOU LOCULE
CELLRU CULLER
CELLTU CULLET
CELMOO COELOM
CELMOP COMPEL
CELMOR CORMEL
CELMOS CELOMS
CELMOY COMELY
CELMSU MUSCLE
CELMUY LYCEUM
CELNNU NUNCLE
CELNOO COLONE
CELNOR CLONER
CORNEL
CELNOS CLONES
CELNOV CLOVEN
CELNRU LUCERN
CELNSU UNCLES
CELNTU LUCENT
CELOOR COOLER
CELOOS LOCOES
CELOOT OCELOT
CELOPU COUPLE
CELOQU CLOQUE
CELORS CEORLS
CLOSER
CRESOL
CELORT COLTER
LECTOR
CELORU COLURE
CELORV CLOVER
VELCRO
CELOSS CLOSES
SOCLES
CELOST CLOSET
TELCOS
CELOSU COLEUS
OSCULE
CELOSV CLOVES
CELOSX SCOLEX
CELOSZ CLOZES
CELPSU CUPELS
CELPTY YCLEPT
CELPUU CUPULE
CELRRU CURLER
CELRSU LUCRES
ULCERS
CELRSY CRESYL
CELRTU CUTLER
RELUCT
CELRUU CURULE
CELRUV CULVER
CELRUW CURLEW
CELSTU CULETS
CELTTU CUTLET
CUTTLE
CELTUY CUTELY
CEMMRU CUMMER
CEMNOS SOCMEN
CEMNOW COWMEN
CEMNTU CENTUM
CEMOOS COMOSE
CEMOPT COEMPT
CEMORS COMERS
CEMOST COMETS
COMTES
CEMOSU MUCOSE
CEMOSY CYMOSE
CEMRTU RECTUM
CEMTTU TECTUM
CENNOO NEOCON
CENNOR CONNER
CENNOS NONCES
CENNOT NOCENT
CENNRU CUNNER
CENOPR CREPON
CENOPS COPENS
PONCES
CENOPU POUNCE
CENORR CORNER
CENORS CENSOR
CRONES
RECONS
CENORT CORNET
CENOSS SCONES
CENOST CENTOS
CONTES
CENOSU OUNCES
CENOSV COVENS
CENOSY CONEYS
CENOSZ COZENS
CENOVX CONVEX
CENOVY CONVEY
CENSST SCENTS
CENSSU CENSUS
CENSTY ENCYST
CENTUU UNCUTE
CEOOPR COOPER
CEOORS COOERS
ROSCOE
CEOORT COOTER
CEOOSY COOEYS
CEOOTY COYOTE
OOCYTE
CEOPPR COPPER
CEOPRS COPERS
CORPSE
CEOPRT COPTER
CEOPRU CROUPE
RECOUP
CEOPRY RECOPY
CEOPSS COPSES
SCOPES
CEOPSU COUPES
CEOPTY COTYPE
CEOQTU COQUET
CEORRS CORERS
CRORES
SCORER
CEORRT RECTOR
CEORRW CROWER
CEORRZ CROZER
CEORSS CORSES
CROSSE
SCORES
CEORST CORSET
COSTER
ESCORT
RECTOS
SCOTER
SECTOR
CEORSU CEROUS
COURSE
CROUSE
SOURCE
CEORSV CORVES
COVERS
CEORSW COWERS
ESCROW
CEORSZ CROZES
CEORTT COTTER
CEORTU COUTER
CROUTE
CEORTV CORVET
COVERT
VECTOR
CEORTX CORTEX
CEOSST CESTOS
COSETS
COSSET
ESCOTS
CEOSSU SCOUSE
CEOSSY COSEYS
CEOSTT OCTETS
CEOSTV COVETS
CEOSTY COYEST
CEOSVY COVEYS
CEOSYZ COZEYS
CEOSZZ COZZES
CEPPRU CUPPER
CEPRSU SPRUCE
CEPRSY CYPRES
CEPRTU PRECUT
CERRSU CURERS
CURSER
RECURS
CERRTU CURTER
CERSST CRESTS
CERSSU CRUSES
CURSES
CUSSER
SUCRES
CERSSW SCREWS
CERSSY CRESSY
CERSTU CRUETS
CRUSET
CURETS
ERUCTS
RECTUS
RECUTS
TRUCES
CERSUV CURVES
CERSUX CRUXES
CERSWY SCREWY
CERTTU CUTTER
CERTUV CURVET
CERUVY CURVEY
CESSSU CUSSES
CESSTU CESTUS
SCUTES
CESTTU CUTEST
CESTUY CUTESY
CUTEYS
CFFHSU CHUFFS
CFFHUY CHUFFY
CFFILS CLIFFS
CFFILY CLIFFY
CFFINO COFFIN
CFFNUU UNCUFF
CFFOSS SCOFFS
CFFOTU CUTOFF
OFFCUT
CFFRSU SCRUFF
CFFSSU SCUFFS
CFGINU FUNGIC
CFHILN FLINCH
CFHILT FLITCH
CFHISU FICHUS
CFHITY FITCHY
CFHLSY FLYSCH
CFIILM FILMIC
CFIINS FICINS
CFIINU UNIFIC
CFIIST FISTIC
CFIITY CITIFY
CFIKLS FLICKS
CFIKLY FICKLY
CFILOR FROLIC
CFILST CLIFTS
CFIMOR FORMIC
CFIMOT COMFIT
CFINOT CONFIT
CFISTU FUSTIC
CFKLOS FLOCKS
CFKLOY FLOCKY
CFKORS FROCKS
CFLPUU CUPFUL
CFORST CROFTS
CFOSUU FUCOUS
CFRSSU SCURFS
CFRSUY SCURFY
CGGLOY CLOGGY
CGHHOU CHOUGH
CGHILT GLITCH
CGHINR GRINCH
CGHIOT GOTHIC
CGHLNU GLUNCH
CGHLOU CLOUGH
CGHOOS COHOGS
CGHORU GROUCH
CGHOSU COUGHS
CGHRTU GRUTCH
CGIINO CONGII
CGIINR RICING
CGIINS ICINGS
CGIINT CITING
CGIINV VICING
CGIKNO COKING
CGILNS CLINGS
CGILNU CLUING
CGILNY CLINGY
GLYCIN
CGILOS LOGICS
CGIMNO COMING
GNOMIC
CGINNO CONING
CGINOO COOING
CGINOP COPING
CGINOR CORING
CGINOS COIGNS
COSIGN
INCOGS
CGINOT COTING
CGINOV COVING
CGINOW COWING
CGINOX COXING
CGINOY COYING
CGINRU CURING
CGINRY CRYING
CGIOOT COGITO
CGIORS CORGIS
CGLLOY GLYCOL
CGLLYY GLYCYL
CGLNOU UNCLOG
CGLOOS COLOGS
CGLOOU COLUGO
CGNOOS COGONS
CONGOS
CGNOOU CONGOU
CHHNOO HONCHO
CHHOOS COHOSH
CHHOOT HOOTCH
CHHOSU CHOUSH
CHIIKM KIMCHI
CHIILL CHILLI
CHIILS CHILIS
LICHIS
CHIILT LITCHI
LITHIC
CHIINT CHITIN
CHIKNS CHINKS
CHIKNY CHINKY
CHIKOS HOICKS
CHIKRS CHIRKS
KIRSCH
SCHRIK
CHIKST KITSCH
SCHTIK
SHTICK
THICKS
CHILLS CHILLS
CHILLY CHILLY
CHILMO HOLMIC
CHILOR ORCHIL
CHILPY PHYLIC
CHILRY RICHLY
CHILST LICHTS
CHIMPS CHIMPS

CHIMRS CHIRMS
CHRISM
SMIRCH
CHIMSS SCHISM
CHIMTY MYTHIC
THYMIC
CHINOP CHOPIN
PHONIC
CHINOS CHINOS
CHINOT CHITON
CHINPY HYPNIC
CHINRU URCHIN
CHINST CHINTS
SNITCH
CHINTZ CHINTZ
CHIOPR ORPHIC
CHIOPT PHOTIC
CHIORS CHIROS
CHOIRS
ICHORS
ORCHIS
CHIORT RHOTIC
THORIC
CHIOSY COYISH
CHIOSZ SCHIZO
CHIPPY CHIPPY
CHIPRS CHIRPS
CHIPRY CHIRPY
CHIPSY PHYSIC
SCYPHI
CHIPTY PITCHY
CHIQTU QUITCH
CHIRRS CHIRRS
CHIRSU CHIRUS
CHISST SCHIST
STICHS
CHISTT STITCH
CHISTU SCHUIT
CHISTW SWITCH
CHISYZ SCHIZY
CHITTW TWITCH
CHITTY CHITTY
CHITWY WITCHY
CHIVVY CHIVVY
CHKLOS SHLOCK
CHKMSU SHMUCK
CHKNSU CHUNKS
CHKNUY CHUNKY
CHKOOS CHOOKS
CHKOSS SHOCKS
CHKSSU SHUCKS
CHLMOO MOLOCH
CHLMUY MUCHLY
CHLNSU SCHULN
CHLOOS CHOLOS
SCHOOL
CHLOOT COOLTH
CHLORS SCHORL
CHLOST CLOTHS
CHLOSU SLOUCH
CHLRSU CHURLS
CHLSSU SCHULS
CHMMUY CHUMMY
CHMOOR CHROMO
CHMOOS SMOOCH
CHMOPS CHOMPS
CHMORY CHROMY
CHMOSS SCHMOS
CHMPSU CHUMPS
CHMSTU SMUTCH
CHNOOP PONCHO
CHNOSZ SCHNOZ
CHNPUY PUNCHY
CHNRSU CHURNS
CHNSSY SYNCHS
CHNTUU TUCHUN
CHOORT COHORT
CHOOST COHOST
CHOOSY CHOOSY
CHOPPY CHOPPY
CHOPSY PSYCHO
CHOPUY POUCHY
CHORRU CHURRO
CHORSU CHORUS
CHORTY TORCHY
CHOSTT CHOTTS
CHOSTU COUTHS
SCOUTH
CHOTUY TOUCHY
CHPSSY PSYCHS
CHPSTU PUTSCH
CHRRSU CHURRS
CHRSTW CRWTHS
CHSSSU SCHUSS
CIIIRT IRITIC
CIIKLY ICKILY

CIILMN LIMNIC
CIILMU CILIUM
CIILNP INCLIP
CIIMMS MIMICS
CIIMOT MIOTIC
CIIMSV CIVISM
CIIMTV VICTIM
CIINNU UNCINI
CIINOP PIONIC
CIINOR IRONIC
CIINOS IONICS
CIINQU QUINIC
CIINRS RICINS
CIINRT CITRIN
NITRIC
CIIOTT OTITIC
CIIRSS CRISIS
CIIRTV VITRIC
CIJKOR CROJIK
CIJNOO COJOIN
CIKKLS KLICKS
CIKKPU KICKUP
CIKLNS CLINKS
CIKLSS SLICKS
CIKLSY SICKLY
CIKMSU MUSICK
CIKNPU UNPICK
CIKNPY PYKNIC
CIKNSS SNICKS
CIKNYZ ZINCKY
CIKOSS SICKOS
CIKOSY YOICKS
CIKPPU PICKUP
CIKPRS PRICKS
CIKPRY PRICKY
CIKPTU UPTICK
CIKQSU QUICKS
CIKRST STRICK
TRICKS
CIKRSW WRICKS
CIKRTY TRICKY
CIKSST STICKS
CIKSTY STICKY
CILLOU LOCULI
CILLSU CULLIS
CILMNY CYMLIN
CILMUU CUMULI
CILNOO COLONI
CILNOS COLINS
NICOLS
CILNOU UNCOIL
CILNPU UNCLIP
CILNTU INCULT
CILOPU OILCUP
UPCOIL
CILOPY POLICY
CILORT LICTOR
CILOSU COULIS
CILOSY COSILY
CILOTU TOLUIC
CILOYZ COZILY
CILPSU PICULS
CILQUY CLIQUY
CILRSY LYRICS
CILSUY SLUICY
CIMMNU CUMMIN
CIMMOT COMMIT
CIMMOX COMMIX
CIMNOR MICRON
CIMNOU CONIUM
MUONIC
CIMNRU CRINUM
CIMNSU CUMINS
MUCINS
CIMOPY MYOPIC
CIMORS MICROS
CIMORU CORIUM
CIMOSS OSMICS
CIMOST SITCOM
CIMOTY COMITY
MYOTIC
CIMPRS CRIMPS
SCRIMP
CIMPRY CRIMPY
CIMRSS SCRIMS
CIMRUU CURIUM
CIMSSU MUSICS
CIMSTU MISCUT
CIMSTY MYSTIC
CINNOS CONINS
CINNOU NUNCIO
CINNOY INCONY
CINOOV OVONIC
CINOOZ OZONIC
CINORS ORCINS

CINORT CITRON
CORTIN
CINORZ ZIRCON
CINOSS SCIONS
SONICS
CINOST TOCSIN
TONICS
CINOSU COUSIN
CINOSV COVINS
CINRSU INCURS
CINSTT TINCTS
CINSTU CUTINS
TUNICS
CIOOPT OCTOPI
CIOORT OCTROI
CIOPRT TROPIC
CIOPSS PISCOS
CIOPST OPTICS
PICOTS
TOPICS
CIOPTT PTOTIC
CIOPWY WICOPY
CIORST TORICS
CIORSU CURIOS
CIORTT TRICOT
CIORTV VICTOR
CIOSST STOICS
CIOSTU COITUS
CIOSTX TOXICS
CIPRSS CRISPS
SCRIPS
CIPRST SCRIPT
CIPRSY CRISPY
CIPSSU CUSPIS
CIRRSU CIRRUS
CIRSTT STRICT
CIRSTU CITRUS
RICTUS
RUSTIC
CIRTTY YTTRIC
CISSTU CISTUS
CISSUV VISCUS
CJKOOS JOCKOS
CJNOSU JUNCOS
CJNOUY JOUNCY
CKKNOS KNOCKS
CKLNOS CLONKS
CKLNOU UNLOCK
CKLNSU CLUNKS
CKLNUY CLUNKY
CKLOPU LOCKUP
CKLPSU PLUCKS
CKLPUY PLUCKY
CKLSSU SCULKS
CKMOPU MOCKUP
CKMOSS SMOCKS
CKNORU UNCORK
CKNTUU UNTUCK
CKOORS CROOKS
CKORST TROCKS
CKOSST STOCKS
CKOSTY STOCKY
CKRSTU STRUCK
TRUCKS
CKRSUU RUCKUS
CLLOOP COLLOP
CLLOOY COOLLY
CLLORS SCROLL
CLLSSU SCULLS
CLMNOU COLUMN
CLMOPS CLOMPS
CLMOPY COMPLY
CLMOSU LOCUMS
CLMOSY CYMOLS
CLMPSU CLUMPS
CLMPUY CLUMPY
CLMSTU MULCTS
CLMSUY CLUMSY
MUSCLY
CLNOOS COLONS
CONSOL
CLNOOU UNCOOL
CLNOOY COLONY
CLNOSU CLONUS
CONSUL
CLNOSW CLOWNS
CLNRUU UNCURL
CLOOPT COPLOT
CLOORS COLORS
CLOORU COLOUR
CLOOST CLOOTS
CLORSU CLOURS
CLOSSW SCOWLS
CLOSTU CLOUTS
LOCUST

CLOSTY COSTLY
OCTYLS
CLOSUU OCULUS
CLOTTY CLOTTY
CLPRUU UPCURL
CLPSSU SCULPS
CLPSTU SCULPT
CLRTUY CURTLY
CLSSUU SULCUS
CLSTUU CULTUS
CMMNOO COMMON
CMMRUY CRUMMY
CMMSUY SCUMMY
CMNNOO NONCOM
CMNOSY SYNCOM
CMOOPS COMPOS
CMOOSS COSMOS
CMOOSU COMOUS
CMOPST COMPTS
CMORSU MUCORS
CMOSTU CUSTOM
CMOSUU MUCOUS
CMOSUY CYMOUS
CMPRSU CRUMPS
CMPRUU CUPRUM
CMRSSU SCRUMS
CMSTUU SCUTUM
CNOOPU COUPON
CNOORS CROONS
CNOORT CROTON
CNOOST CONTOS
NOSTOC
CNOOTT COTTON
CNOOTY TYCOON
CNOOVY CONVOY
CNORSS SCORNS
CNORSU CORNUS
CNORSW CROWNS
CNOSTU COUNTS
CNOSTY CYTONS
CNOTUY COUNTY
COOPRS SCROOP
COOPSS SCOOPS
COOPST COOPTS
COOPTU COPOUT
COOPUY COYPOU
COOPWX COWPOX
COOSST SCOOTS
COOSTY OOCYST
COPRSU CORPUS
CROUPS
COPRTY CRYPTO
COPRUY CROUPY
COPSUY COYPUS
CORRSU CRUORS
CURSOR
CORSSU SCOURS
CORSTU COURTS
CORTUY OUTCRY
COSSSU CUSSOS
COSSTU CUSTOS
SCOUTS
COTTUU CUTOUT
CPRSTY CRYPTS
CPRSUY CYPRUS
SPRUCY
CPSTUU CUTUPS
CRRSUY SCURRY
CRSSTU CRUSTS
CRSTUY CRUSTY
CURTSY
CRSUVY SCURVY
CSUYZZ SCUZZY
DDDEEE DEEDED
DDDEEI EDDIED
DDDEER REDDED
DDDEET TEDDED
DDDEEW WEDDED
DDDEGO DODGED
GODDED
DDDEIK KIDDED
DDDEIL DIDDLE
LIDDED
DDDEIR RIDDED
DDDEIU DUDDIE
DDDEMU MUDDED
DDDENO NODDED
DDDEOP PODDED
DDDEOR DODDER
RODDED
DDDEOS SODDED
DDDILY DIDDLY
DDEEEH HEEDED
DDEEEM DEEMED
DDEEEN NEEDED
DDEEER REEDED

DDEEES SEEDED
DDEEEW WEEDED
DDEEFI DEFIED
DDEEFN DEFEND
FENDED
DDEEFU FEUDED
DDEEGH HEDGED
DDEEGK KEDGED
DDEEGL GELDED
DDEEGR DREDGE
DDEEGW WEDGED
DDEEHL HEDDLE
DDEEHR HERDED
DDEEIL ELIDED
DDEEIN DENIED
INDEED
DDEEIR DERIDE
DDEEIS EDDIES
DDEEIT DIETED
EDITED
DDEELM MEDDLE
MELDED
DDEELP PEDDLE
DDEELR REDDLE
DDEELU DELUDE
DUELED
ELUDED
DDEELV DELVED
DDEELW WELDED
DDEEMN MENDED
DDEEMO DEMODE
DEMOED
DDEENN DENNED
DDEENP DEPEND
PENDED
DDEENR REDDEN
RENDED
DDEENS SENDED
DDEENT DENTED
TENDED
DDEENU DENUDE
DUDEEN
DUENDE
ENDUED
DDEENV VENDED
DDEENW WENDED
DDEEOR ERODED
DDEEOS EDDOES
DDEERR REDDER
DDEERT TEDDER
DDEERW WEDDER
DDEERY REDYED
DDEESU SUEDED
DDEETU DUETED
DDEEUX EXUDED
DDEFFO DOFFED
DDEFGI FIDGED
DDEFGU FUDGED
DDEFIL FIDDLE
DDEFLO FOLDED
DDEFLU FUDDLE
DDEFNO FONDED
DDEFNU DEFUND
FUNDED
DDEFOR FODDER
FORDED
DDEGGI DIGGED
DDEGGO DOGGED
DDEGIL GILDED
GLIDED
DDEGIN DINGED
DDEGIR GIRDED
GRIDED
RIDGED
DDEGIU GUIDED
DDEGJU JUDGED
DDEGLO LODGED
DDEGMO DODGEM
DDEGNU DUNGED
NUDGED
DDEGOR DODGER
DDEGOS DODGES
DDEGRU DRUDGE
DDEHIN HIDDEN
DDEHIS DISHED
DDEHLU HUDDLE
DDEHNO HODDEN
DDEHOO HOODED
DDEHOR HORDED
DDEIIK KIDDIE
DDEIIO IODIDE
DDEIIS DIDIES
DDEIIT TIDIED
DDEIIV DIVIDE
DDEIIW WIDDIE
DDEIKN DINKED

DDEIKR DIRKED
KIDDER
DDEIKS DISKED
DDEILL DILLED
DDEILM MIDDLE
MILDED
DDEILN DINDLE
DDEILO DILDOE
DOILED
LOIDED
DDEILP PIDDLE
DDEILR DIRLED
DREIDL
RIDDLE
DDEILS SIDLED
DDEILW WIDDLE
WILDED
DDEIMM DIMMED
DDEIMN MIDDEN
MINDED
DDEIMS DESMID
DDEINN DINNED
DDEINR RIDDEN
RINDED
DDEINT DINTED
DDEINU INDUED
DDEINW DWINED
WINDED
DDEIOS DIDOES
DIODES
DDEIOT DOITED
DDEIOV DEVOID
VOIDED
DDEIPP DIPPED
DDEIPR PRIDED
DDEIRR RIDDER
DDEIRW WIDDER
DDEISS DISSED
DDEJRU JUDDER
DDEKNU DUNKED
DDEKSU DUSKED
DDELLO DOLLED
DDELLU DULLED
DDELMO MOLDED
DDELMU MUDDLE
DDELNO NODDLE
DDELOO DOODLE
DDELOR LORDED
DDELOT TODDLE
DDELOY YODLED
DDELPU PUDDLE
DDELRU RUDDLE
DDEMOO DOOMED
DDEMPU DUMPED
DDEMRU MUDDER
DDENNO DONNED
DDENNU DUNNED
DDENOP PONDED
DDENOR DRONED
NODDER
DDENOS SODDEN
DDENOW DOWNED
DDENOY DYNODE
DDENRU DURNED
DDENSU SUDDEN
DDENTU DUNTED
DDENUY UNDYED
DDEOOR ODORED
DDEOOS DODOES
DDEOOW WOODED
DDEORV DROVED
DDEORW WORDED
DDEOSS DOSSED
DDEOST ODDEST
DDEOSU DOUSED
DDEOSW DOWSED
DDEOTT DOTTED
DDEPPU DUPPED
DDERRU RUDDER
DDERSU UDDERS
DDESSU SUDSED
DDESTU DUSTED
DDFILY FIDDLY
DDFIOR FORDID
DDGINU DUDING
DDGMOO DOGDOM
DDHINO HODDIN
DDHIOS ODDISH
DDHIRY HYDRID
DDHISU DUDISH
DDHOSY SHODDY
DDIIKK DIKDIK
DDIIKV KIDVID
DDIIMS MISDID
DDIIOS IODIDS

DDIIOX DIOXID
IXODID
DDIKOS KIDDOS
DDIKSY SKIDDY
DDILNR DIRNDL
DDILOS DILDOS
DDILPY PIDDLY
DDILTY TIDDLY
DDIMRU DIRDUM
DDIOPY DIPODY
DDIORS DROIDS
SORDID
DDIOTU OUTDID
DDIOTY ODDITY
DDIRSU DRUIDS
SIDDUR
DDLMUY MUDDLY
DDLPUY PUDDLY
DDMMUU DUMDUM
DDNORW DROWND
DDOOOO DOODOO
DEEEFR FEEDER
REEFED
REFEED
DEEEFZ FEEZED
DEEEGK GEEKED
DEEEGR DEGREE
DEEEHL HEELED
DEEEHR HEEDER
DEEEHZ HEEZED
DEEEJP JEEPED
DEEEJR JEERED
JEREED
DEEEKK KEEKED
DEEEKL KEELED
DEEEKN KEENED
DEEEKP PEEKED
DEEEKR REEKED
DEEELN NEEDLE
DEEELP PEELED
DEEELR LEERED
REELED
DEEELS SEELED
DEEELT DELETE
DEEELV LEVEED
DEEEMR REDEEM
DEEEMS SEEMED
DEEEMT TEEMED
DEEENP DEEPEN
PEENED
DEEENR NEEDER
DEEENV EVENED
VENDEE
DEEENW WEENED
DEEEPP PEEPED
DEEEPR DEEPER
PEERED
DEEEPS SEEPED
DEEEPV PEEVED
DEEERS RESEED
SEEDER
DEEERV REEVED
VEERED
DEEERW WEEDER
DEEERY REDEYE
DEEETW WEETED
DEEFFR DEFFER
REFFED
DEEFGL FLEDGE
DEEFHT HEFTED
DEEFIL DEFILE
DEEFIN DEFINE
DEEFIR DEFIER
DEEFIS DEFIES
DEEFKR KERFED
DEEFLL FELLED
DEEFLS SELFED
DEEFLT FELTED
DEEFLU DEFUEL
FUELED
DEEFLX FLEXED
DEEFLY FLEYED
DEEFNR FENDER
DEEFRS DEFERS
DEEFRT DEFTER
DEEFRY REDEFY
DEEFSS FESSED
DEEFSU DEFUSE
DEEFTT FETTED
DEEFUZ DEFUZE
DEEFZZ FEZZED
DEEGGK KEGGED
DEEGGL LEGGED
DEEGGP PEGGED
DEEGGV VEGGED
DEEGHR HEDGER

DEEGHS HEDGES
DEEGIR EDGIER
DEEGIS SIEGED
DEEGIW WEDGIE
DEEGKS KEDGES
DEEGLL GELLED
DEEGLN LEGEND
DEEGLP PLEDGE
DEEGLR GELDER
LEDGER
REDLEG
DEEGLS GLEDES
GLEEDS
LEDGES
SLEDGE
DEEGLU DELUGE
DEEGLY GLEYED
DEEGMM GEMMED
DEEGMR DEGERM
MERGED
DEEGNR GENDER
DEEGNU DENGUE
DEEGNV VENGED
DEEGOS GEODES
DEEGRS EDGERS
GREEDS
SERGED
DEEGRV VERGED
DEEGRY GREEDY
GREYED
DEEGSS SEDGES
DEEGSU SEGUED
DEEGSW WEDGES
DEEHIL HEILED
DEEHIR HEIRED
DEEHLL HELLED
DEEHLM HELMED
DEEHLP HELPED
DEEHLV HELVED
DEEHMM HEMMED
DEEHMS MESHED
DEEHMT THEMED
DEEHNT HENTED
DEEHRR HERDER
DEEHRS HEDERS
DEEHSW SHEWED
DEEHYY HEYDEY
DEEILM DELIME
DEEILR LIEDER
RELIED
DEEILS DIESEL
EDILES
ELIDES
SEDILE
SEIDEL
DEEILV LEVIED
VEILED
DEEILX EXILED
DEEILY EYELID
DEEIMP IMPEDE
DEEIMS DEMIES
DEMISE
DEEIMT ITEMED
DEEINN INDENE
DEEINP PEINED
DEEINR DENIER
NEREID
REINED
DEEINS DENIES
DIENES
SEINED
DEEINT ENDITE
DEEINV DEVEIN
ENDIVE
ENVIED
VEINED
DEEIOR OREIDE
DEEIPR PERDIE
DEEIPS ESPIED
PEISED
DEEIRS DESIRE
EIDERS
RESIDE
DEEIRT DIETER
REEDIT
RETIED
TIERED
DEEIRU UREIDE
DEEIRV DERIVE
REIVED
DEEIRW DEWIER
DEEISS DIESES
SEISED
DEEISV DEVISE
SIEVED
VISEED

DEEISX DEXIES
DEEISZ SEIZED
DEEITV EVITED
DEEITX EXITED
DEEIVW VIEWED
DEEJKR JERKED
DEEJLL JELLED
DEEJSS JESSED
DEEJST JESTED
DEEJTT JETTED
DEEKKL LEKKED
DEEKLP KELPED
DEEKNN KENNED
DEEKNR KERNED
DEEKOV EVOKED
DEEKPP KEPPED
DEEKPR PERKED
DEEKRY YERKED
DEEKSW SKEWED
DEEKUY YEUKED
DEELLM MELLED
DEELLW WELLED
DEELLY YELLED
DEELMR MELDER
DEELMT MELTED
DEELMW MEWLED
DEELMY MEDLEY
DEELNR LENDER
RELEND
DEELNS LENSED
DEELNW WEDELN
DEELOO DOOLEE
DEELOP ELOPED
DEELPR PEDLER
REPLED
DEELPT PELTED
DEELPY DEEPLY
YELPED
DEELRS ELDERS
DEELRU DUELER
ELUDER
DEELRV DELVER
DEELRW LEWDER
REWELD
WELDER
DEELST ELDEST
DEELSU ELUDES
LEUDES
DEELSV DELVES
DEVELS
DEELSW SLEWED
WEDELS
DEELTT LETTED
DEELTU ELUTED
TELEDU
DEELTW WELTED
DEELUX DELUXE
DEEMNO OMENED
DEEMNR MENDER
REMEND
DEEMNS EMENDS
MENSED
DEEMNT DEMENT
DEEMOR EMEROD
DEEMOT DEMOTE
EMOTED
DEEMOU MEOUED
DEEMOW MEOWED
DEEMPR DEPERM
PERMED
PREMED
DEEMPT TEMPED
DEEMRT METRED
TERMED
DEEMRU DEMURE
DEEMRY REMEDY
DEEMSS MESSED
DEEMSY EMYDES
DEENNO DONNEE
NEONED
DEENNP PENNED
DEENNY YENNED
DEENOP DEPONE
OPENED
DEENOR REDONE
DEENOS DONEES
DEENOT DENOTE
DEENPX EXPEND
DEENRR RENDER
DEENRS DENSER
ENDERS
RESEND
SENDER
DEENRT RENTED
TENDER
DEENRU ENDURE
ENURED
DEENRV NERVED
VENDER
DEENRY REDENY
DEENSS SENSED
DEENST NESTED
TENSED
DEENSU ENDUES
ENSUED
DEENTT DETENT
NETTED
TENTED
DEENTV VENTED
DEENTX EXTEND
DEENUV VENDUE
DEEOPS DEPOSE
EPODES
SPEEDO
DEEORS ERODES
REDOES
DEEORT TEREDO
DEEORV OVERED
DEEORZ ZEROED
DEEOTV DEVOTE
VETOED
DEEPPP PEPPED
DEEPPR REPPED
DEEPRU PERDUE
PUREED
DEEPRY PREYED
DEEPSS SPEEDS
DEEPSW SPEWED
DEEPSY SPEEDY
DEEPTT PETTED
DEEPTU DEPUTE
DEEQUU QUEUED
DEERRW REDREW
DEERSS SEDERS
DEERST DESERT
DETERS
RESTED
DEERSU REUSED
DEERSV SERVED
VERSED
DEERSW REWEDS
DEERSY REDYES
DEERTT RETTED
DEERTX DEXTER
DEERVV REVVED
DEESST STEEDS
DEESSU SUEDES
DEESSW SWEDES
DEESSY YESSED
DEESTT DETEST
TESTED
DEESTU ETUDES
DEESTV DEVEST
VESTED
DEESTW STEWED
TWEEDS
DEESTZ ZESTED
DEESUX EXUDES
DEETTV VETTED
DEETTW WETTED
DEETWY TWEEDY
DEFFHU HUFFED
DEFFIM MIFFED
DEFFIO DIEOFF
DEFFIR DIFFER
RIFFED
DEFFIT TIFFED
DEFFLU DUFFEL
DUFFLE
LUFFED
DEFFMU MUFFED
DEFFNO OFFEND
DEFFOR DOFFER
DEFFPU PUFFED
DEFFRU DUFFER
RUFFED
DEFGGI FIGGED
DEFGGO FOGGED
DEFGGU FUGGED
DEFGIR FRIDGE
DEFGIS FIDGES
DEFGIT FIDGET
GIFTED
DEFGLO FODGEL
GOLFED
DEFGLU FUGLED
GULFED
DEFGLY FLEDGY
DEFGOO GOOFED
DEFGOR FORGED
DEFGOS DEFOGS
DEFGSU FUDGES
DEFGUU FUGUED
DEFHIS FISHED
DEFHOO HOOFED
DEFIKN FINKED
KNIFED
DEFILL FILLED
DEFILM FILMED
DEFILO FOILED
DEFILR RIFLED
DEFILS FELIDS
FIELDS
DEFILT FLITED
LIFTED
DEFIMR FIRMED
DEFIMS MISFED
DEFINN FINNED
DEFINO FOINED
DEFINR FINDER
FRIEND
REDFIN
REFIND
DEFINS FIENDS
DEFIOO FOODIE
DEFIOT FOETID
DEFIRT RIFTED
DEFIRV FERVID
DEFIRZ FRIZED
DEFIST FISTED
SIFTED
DEFITT FITTED
DEFIZZ FIZZED
DEFJLS FJELDS
DEFKLU FLUKED
DEFKNU FUNKED
DEFKOR FORKED
DEFLLU FULLED
DEFLMU FLUMED
DEFLMY MEDFLY
DEFLNO ENFOLD
FONDLE
DEFLOO FOOLED
DEFLOR FOLDER
REFOLD
ROLFED
DEFLOT LOFTED
DEFLOU FOULED
DEFLOW FLOWED
FOWLED
WOLFED
DEFLRU FURLED
DEFLST DELFTS
DEFLTU FLUTED
DEFLTY DEFTLY
FLYTED
DEFLUX FLUXED
DEFMOR DEFORM
FORMED
DEFNNU FUNNED
DEFNOR FONDER
DEFNOU FONDUE
DEFNRU FUNDER
REFUND
DEFOOR FOREDO
ROOFED
DEFOOT FOOTED
DEFOOW WOOFED
DEFOPP FOPPED
DEFOPU POUFED
DEFRRU FURRED
DEFRSU SURFED
DEFRTU TURFED
DEFSSU FUSSED
DEFTTU TUFTED
DEFTUZ FUTZED
DEFUZZ FUZZED
DEGGGI GIGGED
DEGGHO HOGGED
DEGGHU HUGGED
DEGGIJ JIGGED
DEGGIN EDGING
DEGGIO DOGGIE
DEGGIP PIGGED
DEGGIR DIGGER
RIGGED
DEGGIW WIGGED
DEGGIZ ZIGGED
DEGGJO JOGGED
DEGGJU JUGGED
DEGGLO DOGLEG
LOGGED
DEGGLU LUGGED
DEGGMO MOGGED
DEGGMU MUGGED
DEGGNO GONGED
NOGGED
DEGGOR DOGGER
GORGED
DEGGOS SOGGED
DEGGOT TOGGED
DEGGOU GOUGED
DEGGPU PUGGED
DEGGRU GRUDGE
GURGED
RUGGED
DEGGRY DREGGY
DEGGTU TUGGED
DEGHIN HINGED
NIGHED
DEGHIR DREIGH
DRIEGH
DEGHIS SIGHED
DEGHSU GUSHED
SUGHED
DEGIIN DIEING
DEGIKN DEKING
KINGED
DEGILL GILLED
DEGILM GLIMED
MIDLEG
DEGILN DINGLE
ENGILD
DEGILR GILDER
GIRDLE
GLIDER
REGILD
RIDGEL
DEGILS GLIDES
DEGILU GUILED
DEGILY EDGILY
DEGIMP GIMPED
DEGIMR GRIMED
DEGIMS MIDGES
SMIDGE
DEGIMT MIDGET
DEGINN ENDING
GINNED
DEGINP PINGED
DEGINR DINGER
ENGIRD
GIRNED
REDING
RINGED
DEGINS DEIGNS
DESIGN
DINGES
SIGNED
SINGED
DEGINT NIDGET
TINGED
DEGINW DEWING
WINGED
DEGINY DINGEY
DYEING
DEGINZ ZINGED
DEGIOO GOODIE
DEGIOS DOGIES
GEOIDS
DEGIPP GIPPED
DEGIPR GRIPED
DEGIRR GIRDER
DEGIRS DIRGES
GRIDES
RIDGES
DEGIRT GIRTED
DEGIRU GUIDER
DEGIST DIGEST
DEGISU GUIDES
GUISED
DEGITT GITTED
DEGITW WIDGET
DEGJRU JUDGER
DEGJSU JUDGES
DEGKLU KLUDGE
KLUGED
DEGLLU GULLED
DEGLNO DONGLE
GOLDEN
LONGED
DEGLNU GULDEN
LUNGED
DEGLOR GOLDER
LODGER
DEGLOS LODGES
DEGLOV GLOVED
DEGLOW GLOWED
DEGLOZ GLOZED
DEGLPU GULPED
DEGLSU SLUDGE
DEGMMU GUMMED
DEGMOR GORMED
DEGMSU DEGUMS
SMUDGE
DEGNNU GUNNED
DEGNOO NOODGE
DEGNOP PONGED
DEGNOT TONGED
DEGNOW GOWNED
DEGNRU GERUND
NUDGER
DEGNSU NUDGES
DEGOOS GOOSED
DEGOPR GROPED
DEGORU DROGUE
GOURDE
ROGUED
ROUGED
DEGORV GROVED
DEGOST GODETS
STODGE
DEGOSW WODGES
DEGOSY DOGEYS
DEGOUV VOGUED
DEGPPY GYPPED
DEGPRU PURGED
DEGRSU SURGED
DEGRTU TRUDGE
DEGSTU DEGUST
GUSTED
DEGTTU GUTTED
DEHHSU HUSHED
DEHIKT KITHED
DEHILL HILLED
DEHILS DELISH
SHIELD
DEHILT HILTED
DEHILW WHILED
DEHIMN MEHNDI
DEHIMO HEMOID
DEHINO HOIDEN
HONIED
DEHINR HINDER
DEHINS SHINED
DEHINT HINTED
DEHINW WHINED
DEHIOO HOODIE
DEHIOS HOISED
DEHIOW HOWDIE
DEHIPP HIPPED
DEHIPS PISHED
DEHIPT PITHED
DEHIRS HIDERS
DEHIRT DITHER
DEHISS DISHES
HISSED
DEHIST HISTED
DEHISW WISHED
DEHITT TITHED
DEHITW WHITED
WITHED
DEHJOS JOSHED
DEHKLO HOLKED
DEHKLU HULKED
DEHKNO HONKED
DEHKOO HOOKED
DEHKOW HOWKED
DEHKSU HUSKED
DEHKTY KYTHED
DEHLLU HULLED
DEHLNO HOLDEN
HONDLE
DEHLOR HOLDER
DEHLOS DHOLES
DEHLOT THOLED
DEHLOW HOWLED
DEHLPU UPHELD
DEHLRU HURDLE
HURLED
DEHLSU LUSHED
DEHMMU HUMMED
DEHMNU MUDHEN
DEHMNY HYMNED
DEHMOS MOSHED
DEHMOT METHOD
DEHMPU HUMPED
DEHMRY RHYMED
DEHMSU MUSHED
DEHNOP PHONED
DEHNOR DEHORN
HORNED
DEHNOS NOSHED
DEHNOY HOYDEN
DEHNSS SHENDS
DEHNSU UNSHED
DEHNTU HUNTED
DEHOOP HOOPED
POOHED
DEHOOS SHOOED
DEHOOT HOOTED
DEHOOV HOOVED
DEHOPP HOPPED
DEHOPS EPHODS
DEHOPY HYPOED
DEHORS HORDES
HORSED
RESHOD
SHORED
DEHORT DEHORT
DEHORW WHORED
DEHOST HOSTED
DEHOSU HOUSED
DEHOSV SHOVED
DEHOSW SHOWED
DEHOTT HOTTED
DEHOTU THOUED
DEHPST DEPTHS
DEHPSU PUSHED
DEHPSY PHYSED
DEHRSS SHERDS
SHREDS
DEHRSU RUSHED
DEHRSW SHREWD
DEHSTU SHUTED
TUSHED
DEHTTU HUTTED
DEHTTY TYTHED
DEIILL LILIED
DEIILP LIPIDE
DEIIMS IMIDES
DEIINO IODINE
DEIINS INDIES
INSIDE
DEIINT INDITE
TINEID
DEIINV DIVINE
DEIIOS IODISE
DEIIOZ IODIZE
DEIIPT PITIED
DEIIRS IRIDES
IRISED
DEIIRT TIDIER
DEIISS DIESIS
DEIIST TEIIDS
TIDIES
DEIISX DEIXIS
DEIJKN JINKED
DEIJLT JILTED
DEIJNO JOINED
DEIJNX JINXED
DEIJRR JERRID
DEIJRS JERIDS
DEIJRU JURIED
DEIKKN KINKED
DEIKLL KILLED
DEIKLM MILKED
DEIKLN KILNED
KINDLE
LINKED
DEIKLO KELOID
DEIKLS SILKED
DEIKLT KILTED
DEIKNO OINKED
DEIKNP PINKED
DEIKNR KINDER
KIRNED
DEIKNW WINKED
DEIKNY DINKEY
KIDNEY
DEIKPP KIPPED
DEIKPS SPIKED
DEIKRS DIKERS
RISKED
DEIKRU DUIKER
DEIKSS KISSED
DEIKST SKITED
DEIKSV SKIVED
DEIKTT KITTED
DEILLM MILLED
DEILLN NILLED
DEILLP PILLED
DEILLR RILLED
DEILLT LILTED
TILLED
DEILLU DUELLI
ILLUDE
DEILLW WILLED
DEILMN LIMNED
MILDEN
DEILMO MELOID
MOILED
DEILMP DIMPLE
IMPLED
LIMPED
DEILMR MILDER
DEILMS MISLED
SLIMED
SMILED
DEILMT MILTED
DEILMW MILDEW
DEILNN LINDEN
DEILNO INDOLE
DEILNT DENTIL
LINTED
DEILNW WINDLE
DEILOO DOOLIE
DEILOP DIPLOE
DIPOLE
DEILOR ROILED
DEILOS OLDIES
SILOED
SOILED
DEILOT TOILED
DEILPP LIPPED
DEILPS DISPEL
LISPED
SLIPED
SPILED
DEILPX DIPLEX
DEILRS IDLERS
SIDLER
SLIDER
DEILRT TIRLED
DEILRV DRIVEL
DEILRW WILDER
DEILRY DIRELY
RIDLEY
DEILSS SIDLES
SLIDES
DEILST DELIST
IDLEST
LISTED
SILTED
TILDES
DEILSV DEVILS
DEILSW WIELDS
DEILSY YIELDS
DEILTT TILTED
TITLED
DEILTU DILUTE
DEILTW WILTED
DEILWY DEWILY
WIDELY
WIELDY
DEIMMN NIMMED
DEIMMR DIMMER
RIMMED
DEIMMU MEDIUM
DEIMNO DOMINE
EMODIN
MONIED
DEIMNP IMPEND
DEIMNR MINDER
REMIND
DEIMNS DENIMS
DEIMNT MINTED
DEIMOR DORMIE
DEIMPP PIMPED
DEIMPR PRIMED
DEIMPW WIMPED
DEIMRS DERMIS
DIMERS
DEIMRT MITRED
DEIMSS DEISMS
DISMES
MISSED
DEIMST DEMITS
MISTED
DEIMSU MEDIUS
DEIMTU TEDIUM
DEINNP PINNED
DEINNR DINNER
ENDRIN
DEINNS SINNED
DEINNT DENTIN
INDENT
INTEND
TINNED
DEINNU UNDINE
DEINNW ENWIND
WINNED
DEINNY DYNEIN
DEINOP OPINED
PONIED
DEINOR DINERO
IRONED
DEINOS DONSIE
NOISED
ONSIDE
DEINOV NEVOID
DEINPP NIPPED
DEINPR PINDER
DEINPS SNIPED
SPINED
DEINPT DIPNET
DEINRS DINERS
RINSED
SNIDER
DEINRT RIDENT
TINDER
TRINED
DEINRU INURED
RUINED
DEINRV DRIVEN
VERDIN
DEINRW REWIND
WINDER
DEINST TEINDS
DEINSU INDUES
NUDIES
UNDIES
DEINSW DWINES
WIDENS
DEINSZ DIZENS
DEINTT TINTED
DEINTU DUNITE
UNITED
UNTIED
DEINTW TWINED
DEIOOR OROIDE
DEIOOW WOODIE
DEIOOX EXODOI
DEIOOZ DOOZIE
DEIOPR DOPIER
PERIOD
DEIOPS POISED
DEIOPT PODITE
DEIORS DORIES
DEIORT DOTIER
EDITOR
RIOTED
TRIODE
DEIORV DEVOIR
VOIDER
DEIORW WEIRDO
DEIORZ DOZIER
DEIOST TODIES
DEIOSV VIDEOS
DEIOSX DOXIES
OXIDES
DEIOTT TOITED
DEIPPP PIPPED
DEIPPR DIPPER
RIPPED
DEIPPS SIPPED
DEIPPT PEPTID
TIPPED
DEIPPY YIPPED
DEIPPZ ZIPPED
DEIPQU PIQUED
DEIPRS PRIDES
PRISED
REDIPS
SPIDER
SPIRED
DEIPRT REDIPT
TREPID
DEIPRZ PRIZED
DEIPST SPITED
STIPED
DEIPSU UPSIDE
DEIPSV VESPID
DEIPSW SWIPED
WISPED
DEIPTT PITTED
DEIPUV UPDIVE
DEIQRU QUIRED
DEIQSU EQUIDS
DEIRRS DERRIS
DRIERS
RIDERS
DEIRRU DURRIE
DEIRRV DRIVER
DEIRRY YIRRED
DEIRSS RESIDS
DEIRST DIREST
DRIEST
STRIDE
DEIRSU DISEUR
DEIRSV DIVERS
DRIVES
DEIRSW WEIRDS
DEIRTV DIVERT
DEIRWY WEIRDY
DEISSS DISSES

DEISST DEISTS
DESIST
DEISSU DISUSE
ISSUED
DEISSW WISSED
DEISTU DUTIES
SUITED
DEISTV DIVEST
DEISTW WIDEST
WISTED
DEISTZ DITZES
DEISVW SWIVED
DEITTW WITTED
DEJKNU JUNKED
DEJKOU JOUKED
DEJLOT JOLTED
DEJLOW JOWLED
DEJMPU JUMPED
DEJOTT JOTTED
DEJSTU JUSTED
DEJTTU JUTTED
DEKKNO KONKED
DEKKOS DEKKOS
DEKKUY YUKKED
DEKLOO LOOKED
DEKLOY YOLKED
DEKLRU LURKED
DEKLSU SULKED
DEKMOS SMOKED
DEKNNU UNKEND
DEKNOS KENDOS
DEKNOY DONKEY
DEKNOZ ZONKED
DEKNRU DUNKER
DEKOOR ROOKED
DEKOPR PORKED
DEKOPS SPOKED
DEKORT TROKED
DEKORW WORKED
DEKOST STOKED
DEKSTU TUSKED
DELLLO LOLLED
DELLLU LULLED
DELLMU MULLED
DELLNU NULLED
DELLOP POLLED
DELLOR ROLLED
DELLOT TOLLED
DELLOU DUELLO
DELLPU PULLED
DELLRU DULLER
DELLSW DWELLS
DELLWY LEWDLY
DELMNO DOLMEN
DELMOO LOOMED
DELMOR MOLDER
REMOLD
DELMOS MODELS
SELDOM
DELMOT MOLTED
DELMOU MODULE
DELMOY MELODY
DELMPU LUMPED
PLUMED
DELNOO NOODLE
DELNOR RONDEL
DELNOS LODENS
DELNOU LOUDEN
NODULE
DELNOZ DONZEL
DELNRU NURLED
RUNDLE
DELNSY DYNELS
DELNTU LUNTED
DELNUY NUDELY
DELOOP LOOPED
POODLE
POOLED
DELOOS LOOSED
OODLES
SOLOED
DELOOT LOOTED
TOLEDO
TOOLED
DELOOW DEWOOL
WOOLED
DELOPP LOPPED
DELOPR POLDER
DELOPS SLOPED
DELOPU LOUPED
DELOPW PLOWED
DELOPY DEPLOY
PLOYED
DELORS DORSEL
RESOLD
SOLDER

DELORT RETOLD
DELORU LOUDER
LOURED
DELORW WELDOR
DELORY YODLER
DELOSS DOSSEL
DELOST OLDEST
STOLED
DELOSU LOUSED
SOULED
DELOSV SOLVED
DELOSW DOWELS
SLOWED
DELOSY ODYLES
YODELS
YODLES
DELOTT DOTTEL
DOTTLE
LOTTED
DELOTU LOUTED
OUTLED
DELOWY YOWLED
DELOYY DOYLEY
DELPPU PULPED
DELPRU PURLED
DELPSU PULSED
DELPUX DUPLEX
DELRUY RUDELY
DELSSU DULSES
DELSTU LUSTED
DELSTV VELDTS
DELSTY STYLED
DEMMMU MUMMED
DEMMOS MODEMS
DEMMPU MUMPED
DEMMSU SUMMED
DEMNOO MOONED
DEMNOR MODERN
NORMED
DEMNOS DEMONS
MONDES
DEMNOU MENUDO
DEMOOR MOORED
ROOMED
DEMOOT MOOTED
DEMOOZ ZOOMED
DEMOPP MOPPED
DEMOPR ROMPED
DEMOPS MOPEDS
DEMORR DORMER
DEMORW DEWORM
WORMED
DEMOSS MOSSED
DEMOST MODEST
DEMOSU MOUSED
ODEUMS
DEMPPU PUMPED
DEMPRU DUMPER
DEMPSU SPUMED
DEMPTU TUMPED
DEMRRU MURDER
DEMRSU DEMURS
DEMSSU MUSSED
SEDUMS
DEMSTU MUSTED
DENNOT TENDON
DENNOU UNDONE
DENNOW WONNED
DENNPU PUNNED
DENNRU DUNNER
DENNSU SUNNED
DENNTU TUNNED
DENOOS NODOSE
NOOSED
ODEONS
DENOOW WOODEN
DENOOZ ZOONED
DENOPR PERNOD
PONDER
DENORR DRONER
DENORS DRONES
REDONS
SNORED
SONDER
SORNED
DENORT RODENT
DENORU ENDURO
UNDOER
DENORV VENDOR
DENORW DOWNER
WONDER
DENORY YONDER
DENOSS SONDES
DENOST STONED
DENOSU UNDOES

DENOSV DEVONS
DOVENS
DENOSW ENDOWS
SNOWED
DENOSY DOYENS
DENOSZ DOZENS
DENOTW WONTED
DENPRU PRUNED
DENPSS SPENDS
DENPSU SENDUP
UPENDS
UPSEND
DENPSY SPENDY
DENPTU PUNTED
DENRST TRENDS
DENRSU NURSED
SUNDER
DENRTU TURNED
DENRTY TRENDY
DENRUW UNDREW
DENSTU NUDEST
TENDUS
DENSTY SYNDET
DENSUU UNUSED
DENSUW SUNDEW
DENTTU NUTTED
DEOOPP POOPED
DEOORS RODEOS
ROOSED
DEOORT ROOTED
DEOORV OVERDO
DEOORZ DOOZER
DEOOST SOOTED
DEOOSX EXODOS
DEOOTT TOOTED
DEOPPP POPPED
DEOPPS SOPPED
DEOPPT TOPPED
DEOPRR DORPER
DEOPRS DOPERS
PEDROS
PROSED
SPORED
DEOPRT DEPORT
PORTED
REDTOP
DEOPRU POURED
ROUPED
DEOPRV PROVED
DEOPRW POWDER
DEOPSS SPODES
DEOPST DEPOTS
DESPOT
POSTED
STOPED
DEOPSU PSEUDO
SOUPED
DEOPTT POTTED
DEOPTU POUTED
DEOPUV UPDOVE
DEOQTU QUOTED
DEORRS DORSER
ORDERS
DEORRU DOURER
ORDURE
DEORRV DROVER
DEORRW REWORD
DEORSS DOSERS
DOSSER
RESODS
DEORST DOTERS
SORTED
STORED
STRODE
DEORSU DOUSER
ROUSED
SOURED
UREDOS
DEORSV DROVES
DEORSW DOWERS
DOWSER
DROWSE
DEORSZ DOZERS
DEORTT DOTTER
ROTTED
DEORTU DETOUR
REDOUT
ROUTED
TOURED
DEORTW TROWED
DEORTX DEXTRO
DEORUV DEVOUR
DEORWY DOWERY
DEOSSS DOSSES
DEOSST TOSSED

DEOSSU DOUSES
SOUSED
DEOSSW DOWSES
DEOSTT SOTTED
DEOSTU OUSTED
TOUSED
DEOSTW STOWED
DEOSUX EXODUS
DEOSXY DESOXY
DEOTTT TOTTED
DEOTTU TOUTED
DEOTTW WOTTED
DEOTUV DEVOUT
DEOTUX TUXEDO
DEPPPU PUPPED
DEPPSU SUPPED
DEPPTU TUPPED
DEPRRU PURRED
DEPRRY PREDRY
DEPRSU DRUPES
DUPERS
PERDUS
PRUDES
PURSED
DEPRUY DUPERY
DEPSSU PSEUDS
DEPTTU PUTTED
DEPTUY DEPUTY
DEPTUZ PUTZED
DERRSY DRYERS
DERRUY RUDERY
DERSSU DRUSES
DURESS
SUDSER
DERSSY DRESSY
DERSTU DUSTER
RUDEST
RUSTED
DERSTY DRYEST
DERTTU RUTTED
DESSSU SUDSES
SUSSED
DESTUV DUVETS
DETTTU TUTTED
DETTUU TUTUED
DFGGOO FOGDOG
DFGIIR FRIGID
DFGILU FULGID
DFIINY NIDIFY
DFIIRT TRIFID
DFILNO INFOLD
DFILOR FLORID
DFILSU FLUIDS
SULFID
DFIMOY MODIFY
DFIORS FIORDS
DFIRST DRIFTS
DFIRTY DRIFTY
DFJORS FJORDS
DFLNOU UNFOLD
DFLNOY FONDLY
DFLOOS FLOODS
DFLOPU FOLDUP
UPFOLD
DFNNOU UNFOND
DFNORS FRONDS
DFNOSU FONDUS
FOUNDS
DFNSUU FUNDUS
DFOORX OXFORD
DFOOSU DOOFUS
DGGNOU DUGONG
GUNDOG
DGGRUY DRUGGY
DGHIIN HIDING
DGHINY DINGHY
DGHIST DIGHTS
DGHOOT HOTDOG
DGHOSU DOUGHS
DGHOTU DOUGHT
DGHOUY DOUGHY
DGIIKN DIKING
DGIILN IDLING
DGIILR RIDGIL
DGIINN DINING
INDIGN
NIDING
DGIINO INDIGO
DGIINP PIDGIN
DGIINR RIDING
DGIINS SIDING
DGIINT TIDING
DGIINV DIVING
DGIIST DIGITS
DGIKNU DUKING
DGIKNY DYKING

DGILNO DOLING
DGILOT DIGLOT
DGILSU GUILDS
DGIMNO DOMING
DGIMTU MIDGUT
DGINOP DOPING
PONGID
DGINOS DOINGS
DOSING
DGINOT DOTING
DGINOU GUIDON
DGINOW DOWING
DGINOZ DOZING
DGINPU DUPING
DGINRS GRINDS
DGINRU DURING
UNGIRD
DGINRY DRYING
DGINSU DINGUS
DGINSY DYINGS
DGIOTW GODWIT
DGIOYZ ZYGOID
DGIPRU UPGIRD
DGIRTU TURGID
DGKLUY KLUDGY
DGLOOU DUOLOG
DGLOOY GOODLY
DGLSUY SLUDGY
DGMSUY SMUDGY
DGNOOR DRONGO
DGNOOS GODSON
DGNOOW GODOWN
DGNORU GROUND
DGNOSU SUNDOG
DGORSU GOURDS
DGOSTY STODGY
DGOTUU DUGOUT
DHIIPS HISPID
DHIISW WIDISH
DHILOS OLDISH
DHIMOS MODISH
DHINSY SHINDY
DHIOOT DHOOTI
DHIORR HORRID
DHIOST DHOTIS
DHIOSV DOVISH
DHIOSY HYOIDS
DHIRST THIRDS
DHIRSY DRYISH
DHISTU DHUTIS
DHISTW WIDTHS
DHLOOY DHOOLY
DHLOPU HOLDUP
UPHOLD
DHLOSU SHOULD
DHNOOU UNHOOD
DHNOSU HOUNDS
UNSHOD
DHOOOO HOODOO
DHOORT HOTROD
DHORSU SHROUD
DHORSY HYDROS
DHORTU DROUTH
DIIJNN DJINNI
DIILMP LIMPID
DIILOP LIPOID
DIILOS SOLIDI
DIILPS LIPIDS
DIILQU LIQUID
DIILST DISTIL
DIILTY TIDILY
DIIMNU INDIUM
DIIMOS IDIOMS
IODISM
DIIMOU OIDIUM
DIIMTW DIMWIT
DIIMTY DIMITY
DIINNW INWIND
DIINOS IODINS
DIINOX DIOXIN
DIINRS INDRIS
DIINRT NITRID
DIIOOP OPIOID
DIIORV VIROID
DIIOST IDIOTS
DIISTX DIXITS
DIJMSU MUSJID
DIJNNS DJINNS
DIJNNY DJINNY
DIKLNY DINKLY
KINDLY
DIKMNU DINKUM
DIKNNU NUDNIK
UNKIND
DIKNRS DRINKS
DIKOOS SKIDOO

DILLMY MILDLY
DILLRS DRILLS
DILLSY IDYLLS
DILLWY WILDLY
DILMOR MILORD
DILMOU MODULI
DILMPY DIMPLY
DILNNU DUNLIN
DILNOS INDOLS
DILNTU INDULT
DILOPY DOPILY
PLOIDY
DILOSS DOSSIL
SLOIDS
SOLIDS
DILOST STOLID
DILOTU TOLUID
DILOXY XYLOID
DILOYZ DOZILY
DIMNOO DOMINO
DIMNOR DORMIN
NIMROD
DIMNSU NUDISM
DIMOPU PODIUM
DIMOSU ODIUMS
SODIUM
DIMOSW WISDOM
DIMOTU DIMOUT
DIMOXY MYXOID
DIMRSU MURIDS
DIMSST MIDSTS
DIMSSY MYSIDS
DINNUW UNWIND
DINOOR INDOOR
DINOPS POINDS
DINOPU UNIPOD
DINORU DIURON
DURION
DINOSW DISOWN
INDOWS
DINOWW WINDOW
DINPTU PUNDIT
DINPUW UPWIND
WINDUP
DINSTU NUDIST
DINTUY NUDITY
UNTIDY
DIOOPS ISOPOD
DIOORT TOROID
DIOOST OOTIDS
DIOOSU IODOUS
ODIOUS
DIOOSV OVOIDS
DIOOSZ ZOOIDS
DIOOTX TOXOID
DIOPRT TORPID
TRIPOD
DIOPSS DIPSOS
DIORRT TORRID
DIORST DROITS
DIOSST ODISTS
DIOSTT DITTOS
DIOSTU STUDIO
DIOSTV DIVOTS
DIOSWW WIDOWS
DIPPRY DRIPPY
DIPRTU PUTRID
DIPSTU STUPID
DIQSSU SQUIDS
DIRSSU URSIDS
DJLOSS SLOJDS
DJNNOO DONJON
DKNRSU DRUNKS
DKOOOO KOODOO
DKORSU DROUKS
DKORSY DROSKY
DKSUUZ KUDZUS
DLLOOP DOLLOP
DLLORS DROLLS
DLLORY DROLLY
LORDLY
DLLOUY LOUDLY
DLMNOU UNMOLD
DLMOOU MODULO
DLMOSU MOULDS
DLMOUY MOULDY
DLMRUY DRUMLY
DLNOSU UNSOLD
DLNOTU UNTOLD
DLNUUY UNDULY
DLOOPS PODSOL
DLOOPZ PODZOL
DLOORS DOLORS
DROOLS
DLOORU DOLOUR
DLOORY DROOLY

DLORSW WORLDS
DLORTY DRYLOT
DLORUY DOURLY
DLOSSY SLOYDS
DLSTUY STUDLY
DMNOOR DROMON
DMNOOS MONDOS
DMNOOY MONODY
DMNOSU MOUNDS
OSMUND
DMOOSS SODOMS
DMOOSU DUOMOS
DMOOSY SODOMY
DMORSU DORSUM
DMRSUU DURUMS
DNOORS DONORS
RONDOS
DNOOSS SNOODS
DNOOST TONDOS
DNOOSU NODOUS
DNOOUV VODOUN
VOUDON
DNOPSU POUNDS
DNORSU ROUNDS
DNORSW DROWNS
DNORTU ROTUND
UNTROD
DNOSSU SOUNDS
DNOSSY SYNODS
DNOSTU DONUTS
STOUND
DNOSUV VODUNS
DNOSUW SWOUND
WOUNDS
DNOSUZ ZOUNDS
DNRSUY SUNDRY
DOOOOV VOODOO
DOOOPW DOOWOP
DOOPRS DROOPS
DOOPRU UROPOD
DOOPRY DROOPY
DOORRS SORDOR
DOORSU ODOURS
DOOSUV VODOUS
DOOSWY WOODSY
DOPRSY DROPSY
DORSSU SUDORS
DORSSW SWORDS
DORSSY DROSSY
DORSTU STROUD
DORSWY DROWSY
DORUVY DYVOUR
DPSTUU DUSTUP
DRSTUY STURDY
EEEEPT TEEPEE
EEEEPV VEEPEE
EEEEPW PEEWEE
EEEEWW WEEWEE
EEEFFT EFFETE
EEEFLR FEELER
REFEEL
EEEFRR REEFER
EEEFRZ FREEZE
EEEFSZ FEEZES
EEEGLS GELEES
EEEGMR EMERGE
MERGEE
EEEGNR RENEGE
EEEGRZ GEEZER
EEEGTV VEGETE
EEEHLR HEELER
REHEEL
EEEHNT ETHENE
EEEHST SEETHE
EEEHSV SHEEVE
EEEHSZ HEEZES
EEEHTT TEETHE
EEEHWZ WHEEZE
EEEILR EELIER
EEEINW WEENIE
EEEIPR PEERIE
EEEIPW WEEPIE
EEEIRR EERIER
EEEJRR JEERER
EEEKLU EKUELE
EEEKMR MEEKER
EEEKNR KEENER
EEEKNT KETENE
EEEKPR KEEPER
EEEKRR REEKER
EEEKRS RESEEK
SEEKER
EEEKSV KEEVES
EEELMS MELEES
EEELMX LEXEME
EEELNV ELEVEN

EEELPR PEELER
EEELRR REELER
EEELRV RELEVE
EEELSS LESSEE
EEELSV LEVEES
SLEEVE
EEELTY EYELET
EEEMMS SEMEME
EEEMNT MENTEE
EEEMRS EMEERS
SEEMER
EEEMRT MEETER
REMEET
TEEMER
EEEMSS EMESES
EEEMST ESTEEM
MESTEE
EEEMTU EMEUTE
EEENNV VENENE
EEENPS PENSEE
EEENRS RESEEN
SERENE
EEENRT ENTREE
ETERNE
RETENE
TEENER
EEENRV EVENER
VENEER
EEENSZ SNEEZE
EEEOPP EPOPEE
EEEPPR PEEPER
EEEPRW WEEPER
EEEPST TEPEES
EEEPSV PEEVES
EEEPSW PEWEES
EEERRV REVERE
EEERSS RESEES
EEERSV REEVES
SEVERE
EEERTT TEETER
TERETE
EEERVW WEEVER
EEESTT SETTEE
TESTEE
EEESTV STEEVE
VESTEE
EEESTW ETWEES
EEETWZ TWEEZE
EEFFOT TOFFEE
EEFFSU EFFUSE
EEFGIN FEEING
EEFGIT GIFTEE
EEFGRU REFUGE
EEFHIR HEIFER
EEFHOR HEREOF
EEFHRT HEFTER
EEFIIR FEIRIE
EEFILN FELINE
EEFILR FERLIE
LIEFER
REFILE
RELIEF
EEFINR FERINE
REFINE
EEFIRR REFIRE
EEFIRS FRISEE
EEFIRZ FRIEZE
EEFLLO FELLOE
EEFLLR FELLER
REFELL
EEFLNN FENNEL
EEFLNS FLENSE
EEFLRR FERREL
EEFLRS FLEERS
REFELS
EEFLRT LEFTER
REFELT
REFLET
TELFER
EEFLRU FERULE
FUELER
REFUEL
EEFLRW REFLEW
EEFLRX REFLEX
EEFLRY FREELY
EEFLST FLEETS
EEFLSX FLEXES
EEFLTT FETTLE
EEFLUY EYEFUL
EEFMMS FEMMES
EEFMNO FOEMEN
EEFMOR FORMEE
EEFNRS ENSERF
EEFNRU UNFREE
EEFPRR PREFER
EEFPTY TEPEFY

EEFRRS FREERS
FRERES
REFERS
EEFRRT FERRET
EEFRST FESTER
FREEST
EEFRSU REFUSE
EEFRSV FEVERS
EEFRTT FETTER
EEFRTU REFUTE
EEFSSS FESSES
EEFSSU FUSEES
EEFSTW FEWEST
EEFSTY FEYEST
EEFSUZ FUZEES
EEFSZZ FEZZES
EEGGIN GEEING
EEGGIR GREIGE
EEGGIV VEGGIE
EEGGKR KEGGER
EEGGMU MUGGEE
EEGGRS EGGERS
EEGHNS HENGES
EEGIJN JEEING
EEGILS LIEGES
EEGILT ELEGIT
EEGIMR EMIGRE
REGIME
EEGINN ENGINE
EEGINS GENIES
SEEING
SIGNEE
EEGINT TEEING
EEGINY EYEING
EEGIRV GRIEVE
REGIVE
EEGISS EGISES
SIEGES
EEGISV VEGIES
EEGKLR KEGLER
EEGKLS GLEEKS
EEGLMN LEGMEN
EEGLMU LEGUME
EEGLNT GENTLE
EEGLNU LUNGEE
EEGLRS LEGERS
EEGLRT REGLET
EEGLRU REGLUE
EEGLST GLEETS
EEGLTY GLEETY
EEGMNO GENOME
EEGMNR GERMEN
EEGMNT TEGMEN
EEGMOT GEMOTE
EEGMRR MERGER
EEGMRS MERGES
EEGNOP PONGEE
EEGNOX EXOGEN
EEGNRS GENRES
GREENS
EEGNRT GERENT
REGENT
EEGNRY ENERGY
GREENY
GYRENE
EEGNST GENETS
GENTES
EEGNSV VENGES
EEGOSY YOGEES
EEGPRS REPEGS
EEGPRU PUGREE
EEGRRS SERGER
EEGRRT REGRET
EEGRRV VERGER
EEGRRW REGREW
EEGRRY GREYER
EEGRSS EGRESS
SERGES
EEGRST EGRETS
GREETS
EEGRSV VERGES
EEGRSY GEYSER
EEGRTT GETTER
EEGSST EGESTS
GEESTS
GESTES
EEGSSU SEGUES
EEHHSS SHEESH
EEHIIN HEINIE
EEHIMP HEMPIE
IMPHEE
EEHINR HEREIN
INHERE
EEHINT THEINE
EEHIRR REHIRE
EEHIRS HIREES
EEHIRT EITHER
EEHITV THIEVE
EEHKLS SHEKEL
EEHLLR HELLER
EEHLMT HELMET
EEHLNY HENLEY
EEHLPR HELPER
EEHLQS SHEQEL
EEHLST LETHES
EEHLSV HELVES
SHELVE
EEHLSW WHEELS
EEHMMR HEMMER
EEHMNP HEMPEN
EEHMNS ENMESH
EEHMPT TEMPEH
EEHMRS REHEMS
RHEMES
EEHMRT THERME
EEHMSS MESHES
EEHMST THEMES
EEHMUV HUMVEE
EEHMUX EXHUME
EEHNOR HEREON
EEHNOX HEXONE
EEHNPS SPHENE
EEHNPW NEPHEW
EEHNRT NETHER
EEHNSS SHEENS
SNEESH
EEHNSW WHEENS
EEHNSY SHEENY
EEHNTY ETHYNE
EEHORS HEROES
RESHOE
EEHORT HERETO
HETERO
EEHOSX HEXOSE
EEHOTW TOWHEE
EEHPPR HEPPER
EEHPRS HERPES
SPHERE
EEHPRT THREEP
EEHPSW WHEEPS
EEHRSS RESHES
SHEERS
EEHRST ETHERS
THERES
THREES
EEHRSU RUSHEE
EEHRSW HEWERS
SHEWER
WHERES
EEHRSX HEXERS
EEHRSY HERESY
EEHRTT TETHER
EEHRTW WETHER
EEHRVW WHERVE
EEHSST SHEETS
THESES
EEHWYY WHEYEY
EEHWYZ WHEEZY
EEIIMN MEINIE
EEIINW WIENIE
EEIJNN JINNEE
EEIKKT TEKKIE
EEIKLM MEIKLE
EEIKLP KELPIE
EEIKLS SELKIE
EEIKPW KEWPIE
EEILLN NELLIE
EEILLW WELLIE
EEILMR ELMIER
EEILMS ELEMIS
EEILNO OLEINE
EEILNP PENILE
EEILNR LIERNE
RELINE
EEILNS ENISLE
ENSILE
SENILE
EEILNT LENITE
EEILNY YEELIN
EEILOT ETOILE
EEILPT PELITE
EEILRR RELIER
EEILRS RELIES
RESILE
EEILRT RETILE
EEILRV EVILER
LEVIER
LIEVER
RELIVE
REVILE
VEILER
EEILRX EXILER
EEILRY EERILY
EEILST ELITES
LISTEE
EEILSV LEVIES
SLIEVE
EEILSX EXILES
ILEXES
EEILVW WEEVIL
EEIMNR ERMINE
EEIMNT EMETIN
EEIMPR EMPIRE
EPIMER
PREMIE
EEIMRS REMISE
EEIMRT METIER
REEMIT
RETIME
EEIMSS EMESIS
EEINNP PINENE
EEINNV VENINE
EEINOS EOSINE
EEINPR REPINE
EEINQU EQUINE
EEINRS NEREIS
SEINER
SEREIN
SERINE
EEINRT ENTIRE
RETINE
TRIENE
EEINRV ENVIER
VEINER
VENIRE
EEINRW WEINER
WIENER
EEINRX REXINE
EEINSS SEINES
SENSEI
EEINSV ENVIES
NIEVES
EEINSW NEWIES
NEWSIE
EEINSX EXINES
EEINTT TENTIE
EEIORS SOIREE
EEIPPY YIPPEE
EEIPRX EXPIRE
EEIPSS ESPIES
PEISES
SPEISE
EEIPTT PETITE
EEIPTW PEEWIT
EEIRRS RERISE
SIRREE
EEIRRT RETIRE
EEIRRV REIVER
RIEVER
VERIER
EEIRRW REWIRE
EEIRSS SEISER
SERIES
SIREES
EEIRST RESITE
RETIES
EEIRSV REIVES
REVISE
EEIRSX SEXIER
EEIRSY EYRIES
EEIRSZ RESIZE
SEIZER
EEIRTV VERITE
EEIRVV REVIVE
EEIRVW REVIEW
VIEWER
EEISSS SEISES
EEISSV SIEVES
EEISSZ SEIZES
EEISTV EVITES
EEJJNU JEJUNE
EEJKRR JERKER
EEJLSW JEWELS
EEJNNT JENNET
EEJRST JESTER
EEJRSY JERSEY
EEJSSS JESSES
EEKLMY MEEKLY
EEKLNN KENNEL
EEKLNR KERNEL
EEKLNS KNEELS
EEKLNY KEENLY
EEKLPS KELEPS
EEKLRT KELTER
EEKLSS SLEEKS
EEKLSV KEVELS
EEKLSY SLEEKY
EEKLTT KETTLE
EEKLWY WEEKLY
EEKMRS KERMES
EEKMSS SMEEKS
EEKNOT KETONE
EEKNPP KEPPEN
EEKNRS KERNES
EEKNSS SKEENS
SKENES
EEKNST KENTES
EEKOPS PEKOES
EEKORV EVOKER
REVOKE
EEKORW REWOKE
EEKOST KETOSE
EEKOSV EVOKES
EEKPPU UPKEEP
EEKPRR REPERK
EEKPRS KREEPS
EEKPRU PERUKE
EEKRSS ESKERS
EEKRST STREEK
EEKRSW KREWES
SKEWER
EEKRSY KERSEY
REKEYS
EEKSST SKEETS
STEEKS
EEKSTY KEYSET
EELLOP POLLEE
EELLPT PELLET
EELLRS RESELL
SELLER
EELLRT RETELL
TELLER
EELLRY YELLER
EELLSS SELLES
EELLSV LEVELS
EELMOT OMELET
TELOME
EELMPS SEMPLE
EELMPT PELMET
TEMPLE
EELMRS MERLES
EELMRT MELTER
REMELT
EELMRU RELUME
EELMRW MEWLER
EELMRY MERELY
EELMSY SEEMLY
EELMTT METTLE
EELMTY MEETLY
EELNNT LENTEN
EELNOS LEONES
EELNOV ELEVON
EELNPS SPLEEN
EELNRT RELENT
EELNRU UNREEL
EELNSS LENSES
LESSEN
EELNST NESTLE
EELNSW NEWELS
EELNTT NETTLE
TELNET
EELNTU ELUENT
EELNUV VENULE
EELNVY EVENLY
EELNXY XYLENE
EELOPP PEOPLE
EELOPR ELOPER
EELOPS ELOPES
EELORS RESOLE
EELOVV EVOLVE
EELPPU PEEPUL
EELPRS LEPERS
REPELS
EELPRT PELTER
PETREL
EELPRY YELPER
EELPSS SLEEPS
SPEELS
EELPST PESTLE
EELPSV PELVES
EELPSX EXPELS
PLEXES
EELPSY SLEEPY
EELPTT PETTLE
EELQSU SEQUEL
EELRSS LESSER
EELRST RELETS
STREEL
EELRSV ELVERS
LEVERS
REVELS
EELRTT LETTER
EELRTW WELTER
EELRUV VELURE
EELSST SLEETS
STEELS
STELES
EELSSV SELVES
VESSEL
EELSTT SETTLE
EELSTU ELUTES
EELSTV SVELTE
EELSTY SLEETY
STEELY
EELSUV EVULSE
EELTVV VELVET
EELTVW TWELVE
EEMMNR MERMEN
EEMMOP POMMEE
EEMMRS EMMERS
EEMMST EMMETS
EEMNNP PENMEN
EEMNOR MOREEN
EEMNOT TONEME
EEMNOY YEOMEN
EEMNPR PREMEN
EEMNSS MENSES
MESNES
SEMENS
EEMNSU NEUMES
EEMNTU UNMEET
EEMNYZ ENZYME
EEMOPT METOPE
EEMORT EMOTER
METEOR
REMOTE
EEMORV REMOVE
EEMOST EMOTES
EEMPRS SEMPRE
EEMPRT TEMPER
EEMPRY EMPERY
EEMPTX EXEMPT
EEMRRT TERMER
EEMRST MEREST
METERS
METRES
RETEMS
EEMRSU RESUME
EEMRSV VERMES
EEMSSS MESSES
EEMSST TMESES
EEMSTU MUSTEE
EENNPR PENNER
EENNRT RENNET
TENNER
EENNST SENNET
EENNSU UNSEEN
EENNUV UNEVEN
EENNUY ENNUYE
EENOPR OPENER
PEREON
REOPEN
EENOPS PEONES
EENOPT POTEEN
EENORW ERENOW
EENORZ REZONE
EENOSV VENOSE
EENOTW TOWNEE
EENOVZ EVZONE
EENPRS PREENS
EENPRT REPENT
EENPRY PYRENE
EENPSS SPENSE
EENQSU QUEENS
EENRRT RENTER
RERENT
EENRSS SNEERS
EENRST ENTERS
NESTER
RENEST
RENTES
RESENT
TENSER
TERNES
TREENS
EENRSU ENSURE
ENURES
EENRSV NERVES
EENRSW RENEWS
RESEWN
EENRSY SNEERY
EENRTT NETTER
TENTER
EENRTU NEUTER
RETUNE
TENURE
TUREEN
EENRTV VENTER
EENRTX EXTERN
EENRVY VENERY
EENSSS NESSES
SENSES
EENSST TENSES
EENSSU ENSUES
EENSSV SEVENS
EENSTT TENETS
EENSTU TENUES
EENSTV EVENTS
EENSTW NEWEST
TWEENS
EENSTY TEENSY
YENTES
EENSUV VENUES
EENSVW SWEVEN
EENSWY SWEENY
WEENSY
EENSYZ SNEEZY
EENTTX EXTENT
EENTUX EXEUNT
EENTWY TWEENY
EEOPRS REPOSE
EEOPSS EPOSES
EEOPST TOPEES
EEOPSX EXPOSE
EEOPTU TOUPEE
EEOPTY PEYOTE
EEORRS REROSE
EEORRT RETORE
EEORRW REWORE
EEORRZ REZERO
EEORSS EROSES
EEORST STEREO
EEORSV SOEVER
EEORSZ ZEROES
EEORTV REVOTE
VETOER
EEORUV OEUVRE
EEORVW REWOVE
EEOSST SETOSE
EEOSTU OUTSEE
EEOSTV VETOES
EEOSXY OXEYES
EEOSYZ OYEZES
EEPPPR PEPPER
EEPPST STEPPE
EEPRRT PERTER
EEPRRY PREYER
EEPRSS PERSES
SPEERS
SPREES
EEPRST PESTER
PETERS
PRESET
EEPRSU PERUSE
PUREES
RUPEES
EEPRSV VESPER
EEPRSW SPEWER
EEPRSX PREXES
EEPRSZ PREZES
EEPRTT PETTER
EEPRTU REPUTE
EEPRTW PEWTER
EEPRTX EXPERT
EEPRTY RETYPE
EEPRUV PREVUE
EEPSSS SEPSES
EEPSST STEEPS
EEPSSW SWEEPS
EEPSTT SEPTET
EEPSWY SWEEPY
EEPTTU PUTTEE
EEQRSU QUEERS
EEQRUU QUEUER
EEQSUU QUEUES
EEQUXY EXEQUY
EERRST RESTER
TERSER
EERRSV REVERS
SERVER
VERSER
EERRTT TERRET
EERRTU URETER
EERRTV REVERT
EERRVY REVERY
EERSST ESTERS
REESTS
RESETS
SEREST
STEERS
STERES
EERSSU REUSES
EERSSV SERVES
SEVERS
VERSES
EERSSW RESEWS
SEWERS
EERSTT RETEST
SETTER
STREET
TESTER
EERSTU RETUSE
EERSTV EVERTS
REVEST
REVETS
VERSET
VERSTE
EERSTW REWETS
WESTER
EERSTX EXERTS
EXSERT
EERSTY YESTER
EERSTZ ZESTER
EERSUV REVUES
EERSVV VERVES
EERSVW SWERVE
EERSVX VEXERS
EERTTT TETTER
EERTTV TREVET
VETTER
EERTTW WETTER
EERTUY TUYERE
EERTVV VERVET
EERTVX VERTEX
EESSSY YESSES
EESSTT SESTET
TESTES
TSETSE
EESSTW SWEETS
EESTTU SUTTEE
TUTEES
EESTTW TWEETS
EESTTX SEXTET
EETTZZ TZETZE
EFFFOS FEOFFS
EFFGIR GRIFFE
EFFGIY EFFIGY
EFFGOR GOFFER
EFFIIR IFFIER
EFFILP PIFFLE
EFFILR RIFFLE
EFFINR NIFFER
EFFIRS FIFERS
EFFKOY OFFKEY
EFFLMU MUFFLE
EFFLRU RUFFLE
EFFLUX EFFLUX
EFFOPU POUFFE
EFFORS OFFERS
EFFORT EFFORT
EFFOST OFFSET
SETOFF
EFFPRU PUFFER
EFFRSU RUFFES
SUFFER
EFFRTU TRUFFE
EFFTTU TUFFET
EFGGOR FOGGER
EFGINR FINGER
FRINGE
EFGINS FEIGNS
EFGINT FETING
EFGINU FEUING
EFGIOS FOGIES
EFGIRS FRIGES
GRIEFS
EFGIRU FIGURE
EFGLNU ENGULF
EFGLOR GOLFER
EFGLSU FUGLES
EFGNOS GONEFS
EFGOOR FOREGO
EFGORR FORGER
EFGORS FORGES
GOFERS
EFGORT FORGET
EFGOSY FOGEYS
EFGSUU FUGUES
EFHILS ELFISH
EFHIRS FISHER
SHERIF
EFHISS FISHES
EFHIST FETISH
EFHLSY FLESHY
EFHNOS FOEHNS
EFHOOR HOOFER
EFHRRU FUHRER
EFHSTT THEFTS
EFIINT FINITE
EFIKLO FOLKIE
EFIKNR KNIFER
EFIKNS KNIFES
EFIKRS KEFIRS
EFILLR FILLER
REFILL
EFILLS FILLES
EFILLT FILLET
EFILLY LIEFLY
EFILMR FILMER
REFILM
EFILNO OLEFIN
EFILNS ELFINS
EFILNY FINELY
EFILOO FLOOIE
EFILOS FILOSE
EFILPP FIPPLE
EFILPR PILFER
EFILRR RIFLER
EFILRS FILERS
FLIERS
LIFERS
RIFLES
EFILRT FILTER
LIFTER
TRIFLE
EFILRU IREFUL
EFILRY RIFELY
EFILST FILETS
FLIEST
FLITES
ITSELF
STIFLE
EFILSU FUSILE
EFILTU FUTILE
EFILWY WIFELY
EFILZZ FIZZLE
EFIMOT FOMITE
EFIMRR FIRMER
EFIMRS FERMIS
EFIMRU FUMIER
EFINRS INFERS
EFINRY FINERY
EFINST FEINTS
FINEST
INFEST
EFINSU INFUSE
EFIOOR ROOFIE
EFIOOT FOOTIE
EFIORX FOXIER
EFIORZ FOZIER
EFIOST SOFTIE
EFIPRX PREFIX
EFIQSU FIQUES
EFIRRS FIRERS
FRIERS
EFIRRZ FRIZER
EFIRSS FRISES
SERIFS
EFIRST FRITES
REFITS
RESIFT
RIFEST
SIFTER
STRIFE
EFIRSU FURIES
EFIRSV FIVERS
EFIRSX FIXERS
EFIRSZ FRIZES
EFIRTT FITTER
TITFER
EFIRTY FERITY
EFIRUX FIXURE
EFIRVY VERIFY
EFIRZZ FIZZER
EFISST FEISTS
EFISTY FEISTY
EFISWY WIFEYS
EFISZZ FIZZES
EFKLSU FLUKES
EFKLUY FLUKEY
EFKNRU FUNKER
EFKORR FORKER
EFLLOS FOLLES
EFLLOW FELLOW
EFLLRU FULLER
EFLMNY FLYMEN
EFLMSU FLUMES
EFLMSY MYSELF
EFLNNU FUNNEL
EFLNOS FELONS
EFLNOT TEFLON
EFLNOY FELONY
EFLNTU FLUENT
UNFELT
EFLOOT FOOTLE
EFLOOY FLOOEY
EFLOOZ FOOZLE

EFLORR ROLFER
EFLORT FLORET
LOFTER
EFLORU FOULER
EFLORW FLOWER
FOWLER
REFLOW
WOLFER
EFLORX FLEXOR
EFLOSY FOLEYS
EFLOUW WOEFUL
EFLPRU PURFLE
EFLRRU FURLER
EFLRSY FLYERS
EFLRTU FLUTER
EFLRUU RUEFUL
EFLRUX REFLUX
EFLRUY FLEURY
EFLSSU FUSELS
EFLSTU FLUTES
EFLSTY FLYTES
EFLSUU USEFUL
EFLSUX FLUXES
EFLTUY FLUTEY
EFMNOT FOMENT
EFMNRU FRENUM
EFMORR FORMER
REFORM
EFMORS FORMES
EFMRRU FERRUM
EFMRSU FEMURS
FUMERS
EFMSTU FUMETS
EFMTUY TUMEFY
EFNNRU FUNNER
EFNORZ FROZEN
EFNOST SOFTEN
EFNRYZ FRENZY
EFNSTU FUNEST
EFOORR REROOF
ROOFER
EFOORT FOETOR
FOOTER
EFOORW WOOFER
EFORRU FURORE
EFORRV FERVOR
EFORST FETORS
FOREST
FORTES
FOSTER
SOFTER
EFORSY FOYERS
EFORTW TWOFER
EFOSSS FOSSES
EFOSTT OFTEST
EFOSTU FOETUS
EFRRSU SURFER
EFRRSY FRYERS
EFRSSU FUSSER
EFRSUZ FURZES
EFRTTU TUFTER
EFRTTY FRETTY
EFRTUU FUTURE
EFSSSU FUSSES
EFSTTY FYTTES
EFSTUZ FUTZES
EFSUZZ FUZZES
EGGGIL GIGGLE
EGGGIN EGGING
EGGGLO GOGGLE
EGGGLU GUGGLE
EGGGNO EGGNOG
EGGHIL HIGGLE
EGGHOR HOGGER
EGGHOT HOGGET
EGGHRU HUGGER
EGGIIN GIEING
EGGIIP PIGGIE
EGGIJL JIGGLE
EGGIJR JIGGER
EGGILM MIGGLE
EGGILN LEGGIN
NIGGLE
EGGILO LOGGIE
EGGILT GIGLET
EGGILU LUGGIE
EGGILW WIGGLE
EGGIMO MOGGIE
EGGINR GINGER
EGGIRR RIGGER
EGGISU GIGUES
EGGJLO JOGGLE
EGGJLU JUGGLE
EGGJOR JOGGER
EGGLLY GLEGLY
EGGLNO LEGONG

EGGLOR LOGGER
EGGLOT GOGLET
TOGGLE
EGGLRU GURGLE
LUGGER
EGGLTU GUGLET
EGGMRU MUGGER
EGGNRU GRUNGE
EGGNTU NUGGET
EGGORR GORGER
EGGORS GORGES
GREGOS
EGGORT GORGET
EGGORU GOUGER
EGGOSU GOUGES
EGGRRU RUGGER
EGGRSU GURGES
EGGRTU TUGGER
EGHHIR HIGHER
EGHHIT EIGHTH
HEIGHT
EGHHSU HEUGHS
SHEUGH
EGHIIN HIEING
EGHIKS SKEIGH
EGHILS SLEIGH
EGHINO HOEING
EGHINR HINGER
NIGHER
EGHINS HINGES
NEIGHS
EGHINW HEWING
WHINGE
EGHINX HEXING
EGHIOT HOGTIE
EGHIRS SIGHER
EGHIST EIGHTS
EGHISW WEIGHS
EGHITW WEIGHT
EGHITY EIGHTY
EGHLMP PHLEGM
EGHLNT LENGTH
EGHLUY HUGELY
EGHMMO MEGOHM
EGHNOR GORHEN
EGHNOU ENOUGH
EGHNRU HUNGER
REHUNG
EGHNST THEGNS
EGHOPR GOPHER
EGHOTT GHETTO
EGHRSU GUSHER
EGHSSU GUSHES
EGHSTU HUGEST
EGIILL GILLIE
EGIILR GIRLIE
EGIIMM GIMMIE
EGIINP PIEING
EGIINT IGNITE
TIEING
EGIJLN JINGLE
EGIJRS REJIGS
EGIKNY KEYING
EGILLR GILLER
GRILLE
EGILLU LIGULE
EGILMN MINGLE
EGILMP MEGILP
EGILMS GIMELS
GLIMES
EGILMT GIMLET
EGILNO ELOIGN
LEGION
EGILNR LINGER
EGILNS INGLES
SINGLE
EGILNT GENTIL
TINGLE
EGILOP EPILOG
EGILOR LOGIER
EGILPT PIGLET
EGILRS GRILSE
LIGERS
EGILRT REGILT
EGILRU GLUIER
LIGURE
REGULI
UGLIER
EGILST LEGIST
LEGITS
EGILSU GUILES
UGLIES
EGILTU GLUTEI
EGILTW WIGLET
EGIMMR MEGRIM
EGIMMS GIMMES

EGIMNT METING
EGIMNW MEWING
EGIMOS EGOISM
EGIMPU GUIMPE
EGIMRS GRIMES
EGINNR GINNER
EGINNS ENSIGN
EGINOO GOONIE
NOOGIE
EGINOP EPIGON
PIGEON
EGINOR ERINGO
IGNORE
REGION
EGINOS SOIGNE
EGINOT TOEING
EGINOW WIGEON
EGINPP PIGPEN
EGINPR PINGER
EGINPS GENIPS
EGINRR ERRING
RINGER
EGINRS REIGNS
RENIGS
RESIGN
SERING
SIGNER
SINGER
EGINRT ENGIRT
EGINRW WINGER
EGINRZ ZINGER
EGINSS GNEISS
SINGES
EGINST INGEST
SIGNET
TINGES
EGINSU GENIUS
EGINSV GIVENS
EGINSW SEWING
SWINGE
EGINSX SEXING
EGINTU GUNITE
EGINTW TEWING
TWINGE
EGINVX VEXING
EGIOOR GOOIER
EGIOPS POGIES
EGIORR GORIER
EGIORS ORGIES
EGIORT GOITER
GOITRE
EGIOST EGOIST
STOGIE
EGIOSV OGIVES
EGIPPR GIPPER
GRIPPE
EGIPRR GRIPER
EGIPRS GRIPES
EGIPRY GRIPEY
EGIRRS RERIGS
EGIRST TIGERS
EGIRSU REGIUS
EGIRSV GIVERS
EGIRTV GRIVET
EGISSU GUISES
GUSSIE
EGJLNU JUNGLE
EGKLSU KLUGES
KUGELS
EGKMSU MUSKEG
EGLLOS SOLGEL
EGLLTU GULLET
EGLLUY GULLEY
EGLMOS GOLEMS
EGLMSU GLUMES
EGLNNU GUNNEL
EGLNOR LONGER
EGLNOS LONGES
EGLNOU LOUNGE
EGLNPU PLUNGE
PUNGLE
EGLNRU LUNGER
EGLNSU GUNSEL
LUNGES
EGLNTU ENGLUT
GLUTEN
EGLNTY GENTLY
EGLNUU UNGLUE
EGLOPR PROLEG
EGLOPS GOSPEL
EGLORS OGLERS
EGLORV GLOVER
GROVEL
EGLORW GLOWER
REGLOW
EGLOSV GLOVES

EGLOSZ GLOZES
EGLOUY EULOGY
EGLPRU GULPER
EGLRSU GLUERS
GRUELS
LUGERS
EGLRYY GREYLY
EGLSTU GLUTES
EGLTTU GUTTLE
EGLUZZ GUZZLE
EGMMRU GUMMER
EGMMRY GREMMY
EGMNNU GUNMEN
EGMNOO MONGOE
EGMNOR MONGER
MORGEN
EGMNOS GENOMS
GNOMES
EGMNRU REGNUM
EGMNTU NUTMEG
EGMORS GOMERS
EGMORU MORGUE
EGMOST GEMOTS
EGMOSU UGSOME
EGMRSU GRUMES
EGMRTU TERGUM
EGNNNU GUNNEN
EGNNOO NONEGO
EGNNOU GUENON
EGNNRU GUNNER
EGNOOR ORGONE
EGNOOT GENTOO
EGNOOY GOONEY
OOGENY
EGNOPS PENGOS
SPONGE
EGNORS GENROS
GONERS
EGNORT TONGER
EGNORV GOVERN
EGNORY ERYNGO
GROYNE
EGNOSS GNOSES
SEGNOS
EGNOTT GOTTEN
EGNOTU TONGUE
EGNOXY OXYGEN
EGNPRU REPUGN
EGNPSU UNPEGS
EGNRTU GURNET
URGENT
EGNRTY GENTRY
EGNRUY GURNEY
EGNSUU UNGUES
EGOORV GROOVE
EGOOSS GOOSES
EGOOST STOOGE
EGOOSY GOOSEY
EGOPRR GROPER
EGOPRS GROPES
EGOPSY POGEYS
EGORRS ROGERS
EGORRW GROWER
REGROW
EGORSS GORSES
OGRESS
EGORST ERGOTS
EGORSU ERUGOS
GROUSE
ROGUES
ROUGES
RUGOSE
EGORSV GROVES
EGORSY GYROSE
EGORSZ GROSZE
EGORUV VOGUER
EGOSTU TOGUES
EGOSTY STOGEY
EGOSUV VOGUES
EGOSYZ ZYGOSE
EGOTYZ ZYGOTE
EGPPRY GYPPER
EGPRRU PURGER
EGPRSU PURGES
SPURGE
EGPRUW UPGREW
EGPSTU GETUPS
EGQSSU SQUEGS
EGRRSU SURGER
URGERS
EGRSSU SURGES
EGRTTU GUTTER
EGSSTU GUESTS
GUSSET
EHHIIS HEISHI
EHHIKS SHEIKH

EHHIRT HITHER
EHHKST KHETHS
EHHNPY HYPHEN
EHHRST THRESH
EHHSSU HUSHES
EHIIPP HIPPIE
EHIKKS KISHKE
EHIKMV MIKVEH
EHIKOR HOKIER
EHIKRS HIKERS
SHRIEK
SHRIKE
EHIKSS SHEIKS
EHIKST KITHES
EHILLR HILLER
EHILMU HELIUM
EHILOO HOOLIE
EHILOR HOLIER
EHILOS HELIOS
HOLIES
ISOHEL
EHILOT EOLITH
EHILPR HIRPLE
EHILRS HIRSEL
HIRSLE
RELISH
EHILRT LITHER
EHILSS SHIELS
EHILSV ELVISH
EHILSW WHILES
EHIMMS IMMESH
EHIMNR MENHIR
EHIMNS HEMINS
INMESH
EHIMNT HITMEN
EHIMNU INHUME
EHIMOR HOMIER
EHIMOS HOMIES
EHIMRT HERMIT
MITHER
EHIMRU HUMERI
EHIMST THEISM
EHINOR HEROIN
EHINOT ETHION
EHINPX PHENIX
EHINRS SHINER
SHRINE
EHINRT HINTER
EHINRW WHINER
EHINSS SHINES
EHINST THEINS
EHINSW NEWISH
WHINES
EHINTW WHITEN
EHINTZ ZENITH
EHINWY WHINEY
EHIOPR EPHORI
EHIOPT OPHITE
EHIORS HOSIER
EHIORT HERIOT
EHIOSS HOISES
EHIOTT HOTTIE
EHIPPR HIPPER
EHIPRS PERISH
PISHER
RESHIP
EHIPSS PISHES
EHIPSZ PHIZES
EHIRRS HIRERS
EHIRSS HISSER
SHIERS
SHIRES
EHIRST THEIRS
EHIRSV SHIVER
SHRIVE
EHIRSW WISHER
EHIRTT HITTER
TITHER
EHIRTV THRIVE
EHIRTW WHITER
WITHER
WRITHE
EHIRTZ ZITHER
EHISSS HISSES
EHISST HEISTS
SHIEST
THESIS
EHISSV SHIVES
EHISSW WISHES
EHISTT THEIST
TITHES
EHISTU TUSHIE
EHISTW SWITHE
WHITES
WITHES
EHITWY WHITEY

EHJOPS JOSEPH
EHJORS JOSHER
EHJOSS JOSHES
EHKLPT KLEPHT
EHKLSW WHELKS
EHKLWY WHELKY
EHKNOR HONKER
EHKNRU HUNKER
EHKOOR HOOKER
EHKOOY HOOKEY
EHKORS KOSHER
EHKRSU HUSKER
EHKSTY KYTHES
EHLLOR HOLLER
EHLLOS HELLOS
EHLLRU HULLER
EHLLSS SHELLS
EHLLSY SHELLY
EHLMNU UNHELM
EHLMOP PHLOEM
EHLMOS MOHELS
EHLMOY HOMELY
EHLMSW WHELMS
EHLMTY METHYL
EHLNOP HOLPEN
PHENOL
EHLNPY PHENYL
EHLOPP HOPPLE
EHLORW HOWLER
EHLOSS HOSELS
SHEOLS
EHLOST HELOTS
HOSTEL
HOTELS
THOLES
EHLOSU HOUSEL
EHLOSV HOVELS
SHOVEL
EHLOSW WHOLES
EHLOSY HOYLES
EHLOTW HOWLET
EHLPPS SHLEPP
EHLPSS SHLEPS
EHLPSW WHELPS
EHLRRU HURLER
EHLRSU LUSHER
EHLRTU HURTLE
EHLRUY HURLEY
EHLSSU LUSHES
EHLSTT SHTETL
EHLSTU HUSTLE
SLEUTH
EHLSTY ETHYLS
SHELTY
EHLSVY SHELVY
EHLSXY HEXYLS
EHMMRU HUMMER
EHMNOP PHENOM
EHMNSU UNMESH
EHMNSY HYMENS
EHMORS HOMERS
MOSHER
EHMORT MOTHER
EHMOSS MOSHES
SHMOES
EHMOSY HOMEYS
EHMPRU HUMPER
EHMRRY RHYMER
EHMRST THERMS
EHMRSU MUSHER
RHEUMS
EHMRSY RHYMES
EHMRUY RHEUMY
EHMSSU MUSHES
EHMSTY THYMES
EHMTYY THYMEY
EHNNUW UNHEWN
EHNOPS PHONES
EHNOPY PHONEY
EHNORS HERONS
HONERS
NOSHER
SENHOR
EHNORT HORNET
NOTHER
THRONE
EHNOSS NOSHES
EHNOST ETHNOS
HONEST
EHNOSY HONEYS
EHNRSY HENRYS
EHNRTU HUNTER
EHNSTT TENTHS
EHOOOP HOOPOE
EHOOPR HOOPER
EHOOPY PHOOEY

EHOORT HOOTER
EHOORV HOOVER
EHOOST SOOTHE
EHOOSV HOOVES
EHOOSY HOOEYS
EHOPPR HOPPER
EHOPPS SHOPPE
EHOPRS EPHORS
HOPERS
POSHER
EHOPRT POTHER
THORPE
EHOPRU UPHROE
EHOPST TOPHES
EHOPSU OUPHES
EHOPUV UPHOVE
EHORRT RHETOR
EHORSS HORSES
HOSERS
SHOERS
SHORES
EHORST HORSTE
OTHERS
RESHOT
THROES
EHORSU HOUSER
EHORSV HOVERS
SHOVER
SHROVE
EHORSW RESHOW
SHOWER
WHORES
EHORSY HORSEY
EHORTT HOTTER
TOTHER
EHORTV THROVE
EHORTX EXHORT
EHORTY THEORY
EHORTZ ZEROTH
EHOSST SHOTES
TOSHES
EHOSSU HOUSES
EHOSSV SHOVES
EHOSSY HOSEYS
EHOTXY ETHOXY
EHPRSU PUSHER
EHPRSY HYPERS
SPHERY
SYPHER
EHPRYZ ZEPHYR
EHPSST THESPS
EHPSSU PUSHES
EHPSSY PHYSES
EHRRSU RUSHER
EHRRSY SHERRY
EHRRTU HURTER
EHRRWY WHERRY
EHRSSU RHESUS
RHUSES
RUSHES
USHERS
EHRSSW SHREWS
EHRSSY SHYERS
EHRSTY THYRSE
EHRTUW WUTHER
EHSSTU SHUTES
TUSHES
TUSSEH
EHSSTY SHYEST
EHSTTY TYTHES
EIIJMM JIMMIE
EIIJRV JIVIER
EIIKLL KILLIE
EIIKLS SILKIE
EIIKLT KILTIE
EIIKNP PINKIE
EIIKNR INKIER
EIILLN NIELLI
EIILLS LILIES
EIILLT ILLITE
EIILMR LIMIER
EIILMS MISLIE
SIMILE
EIILMU MILIEU
EIILNR INLIER
LINIER
EIILNS SILENI
EIILOR OILIER
EIILOT IOLITE
EIILRV LIVIER
VIRILE
EIILRW WILIER
EIILRX ELIXIR
EIIMMS IMMIES
EIIMNS IMINES
EIIMNT INTIME

EIIMRR MIRIER
RIMIER
EIIMRT MITIER
EIINNT INTINE
EIINOS IONISE
EIINOZ IONIZE
EIINPR PINIER
EIINPT PINITE
TIEPIN
EIINRT TINIER
EIINRV VINIER
EIINRW WINIER
EIINSS NISEIS
SEISIN
EIINST SENITI
EIINSX NIXIES
EIINSZ SEIZIN
EIINTV INVITE
EIIPPR PIPIER
EIIPPY YIPPIE
EIIPRT PERITI
PITIER
EIIPRU EURIPI
EIIPST PITIES
EIIPSX PIXIES
EIIRRW WIRIER
EIIRSS IRISES
EIIRSZ SIZIER
EIIRVZ VIZIER
EIISSS ISSEIS
EIISVV VISIVE
EIITTT TITTIE
EIJKNR JERKIN
JINKER
EIJKNT INKJET
EIJKNU JUNKIE
EIJKOR JOKIER
EIJLRT JILTER
EIJMPR JIMPER
EIJNNO ENJOIN
EIJNOR JOINER
REJOIN
EIJNRU INJURE
EIJNSX JINXES
EIJNTY JITNEY
EIJRSU JURIES
EIJRSV JIVERS
EIJRTT JITTER
TRIJET
EIKKOO KOOKIE
EIKLLR KILLER
EIKLLY LIKELY
EIKLMR MILKER
EIKLMS KELIMS
EIKLNR LINKER
RELINK
EIKLNS INKLES
LIKENS
SILKEN
EIKLNT TINKLE
EIKLNU UNLIKE
EIKLNV KELVIN
EIKLNW WELKIN
WINKLE
EIKLOX OXLIKE
EIKLRS LIKERS
EIKLRT KILTER
KIRTLE
EIKLST LIKEST
EIKLSV KEVILS
EIKLTT KITTEL
KITTLE
EIKMNS MINKES
EIKMRR MIRKER
EIKMRS KERMIS
EIKMST KISMET
EIKMSU MUSKIE
EIKNNP PINKEN
EIKNOS EIKONS
ENOKIS
KOINES
EIKNOV INVOKE
EIKNPP KIPPEN
EIKNPR PINKER
EIKNPS PEKINS
EIKNPU PUNKIE
EIKNPY PINKEY
EIKNRS INKERS
REINKS
SINKER
EIKNRT REKNIT
TINKER
EIKNRW WINKER
EIKNSS SKEINS
EIKNSV KNIVES
EIKNTT KITTEN

EIKOOR ROOKIE
EIKOPP KOPPIE
EIKOPR POKIER
EIKOPS POKIES
EIKPPR KIPPER
EIKPRS PIKERS
SPIKER
EIKPSS SPIKES
EIKPSY SPIKEY
EIKRRS RISKER
EIKRSS KISSER
KRISES
SKIERS
EIKRST KITERS
STRIKE
TRIKES
EIKRSV SKIVER
EIKRSY KYRIES
EIKSSS KISSES
EIKSST SKITES
EIKSSV SKIVES
EIKSTW WESKIT
EILLMO MOLLIE
EILLMR MILLER
EILLMS MILLES
EILLMT MILLET
EILLMU ILLUME
EILLNO NIELLO
EILLNT LENTIL
LINTEL
EILLPU PILULE
EILLRS RILLES
SILLER
EILLRT RILLET
TILLER
EILLRW WILLER
EILLSS LISLES
EILLST ILLEST
LISTEL
EILLTT LITTLE
EILLTU TUILLE
EILLTW WILLET
EILLVY EVILLY
LIVELY
VILELY
EILMMR LIMMER
EILMNO LOMEIN
MOLINE
OILMEN
EILMNR LIMNER
MERLIN
EILMNS LIMENS
SIMNEL
EILMNY MYELIN
EILMOR MOILER
EILMOS MOLIES
EILMOT MOTILE
EILMPP PIMPLE
EILMPR LIMPER
PRELIM
RIMPLE
EILMPS IMPELS
SIMPLE
EILMPT LIMPET
EILMPU PILEUM
EILMPW WIMPLE
EILMRS MILERS
SMILER
EILMRT MILTER
EILMSS MISSEL
SLIMES
SMILES
EILMSU MUESLI
EILMSY LIMEYS
SMILEY
EILMTU TELIUM
EILMTY TIMELY
EILMZZ MIZZLE
EILNNO ONLINE
EILNNS LINENS
EILNNT LINNET
EILNNY LINENY
EILNOO LOONIE
EILNOP PINOLE
EILNOR NEROLI
EILNOS ELOINS
INSOLE
LESION
OLEINS
EILNOT ENTOIL
EILNPP LIPPEN
NIPPLE
EILNPS PENSIL
SPINEL
SPLINE
EILNPT LEPTIN
PINTLE
EILNPU LINEUP
LUPINE
UNPILE
EILNRS LINERS
EILNRT LINTER
EILNRU LUNIER
EILNST ELINTS
ENLIST
INLETS
LISTEN
SILENT
TINSEL
EILNSU LUNIES
EILNSV LEVINS
LIVENS
SNIVEL
EILNSY LINSEY
LYSINE
EILNTT LITTEN
EILNTU LUTEIN
EILNTW WINTLE
EILNTY LENITY
EILNUV UNLIVE
UNVEIL
EILOOR ORIOLE
EILOOS LOOIES
EILOOT OOLITE
EILOOW WOOLIE
EILOPS PILOSE
POLEIS
POLIES
EILOPT PIOLET
POLITE
EILORS LORIES
OILERS
ORIELS
REOILS
EILORT LOITER
TOILER
EILOST TOILES
EILOSU LOUIES
EILOSV OLIVES
VOILES
EILOTT TOILET
EILOTU OUTLIE
EILOTV VIOLET
EILPPR LIPPER
RIPPLE
EILPPT TIPPLE
EILPPU PILEUP
UPPILE
EILPRS LISPER
PERILS
PLIERS
EILPRT TRIPLE
EILPRY RIPELY
EILPSS PLISSE
SLIPES
SPEILS
SPIELS
SPILES
EILPST STIPEL
EILPSU PILEUS
EILPSV PELVIS
EILPSW SWIPLE
EILPSX PIXELS
EILPTU PLUTEI
EILPZZ PIZZLE
EILRRU RULIER
EILRST LISTER
LITERS
LITRES
RELIST
TILERS
EILRSV ERVILS
LIVERS
LIVRES
SILVER
SLIVER
EILRTT LITTER
TILTER
EILRTU RUTILE
EILRVY LIVERY
LIVYER
VERILY
EILSST ISLETS
ISTLES
SLIEST
STILES
EILSTT TITLES
EILSTV LIVEST
VILEST
EILSTX IXTLES
EILSVW SWIVEL
EILSVX SILVEX
VEXILS
EILSWY WISELY
EILSXY SEXILY
EILSZZ SIZZLE
EILTTT TITTLE
EILTTV VITTLE
EILTVY LEVITY
EILZZZ ZIZZLE
EIMMNU IMMUNE
EIMMOR MEMOIR
EIMMOS MIMEOS
EIMMRR RIMMER
EIMMRS MIMERS
SIMMER
EIMMRU IMMURE
EIMMST MISMET
EIMNNT TINMEN
EIMNNX MENINX
EIMNOP IMPONE
EIMNOR MERINO
EIMNOS EONISM
MONIES
EIMNPS MISPEN
EIMNPT PITMEN
EIMNRS MINERS
EIMNRT MINTER
REMINT
EIMNRU MUREIN
MURINE
EIMNRV VERMIN
EIMNSX MINXES
EIMNSZ MIZENS
EIMNTT MITTEN
TITMEN
EIMNTU MINUET
MINUTE
MUTINE
EIMNTY ENMITY
EIMNZZ MIZZEN
EIMOOR ROOMIE
EIMOPR MOPIER
EIMOPS IMPOSE
EIMOPT OPTIME
EIMORS ISOMER
MOIRES
RIMOSE
EIMOSS MIOSES
EIMOST SOMITE
EIMOSV MOVIES
EIMOSX MOXIES
OXIMES
EIMOTV MOTIVE
EIMOTY MOIETY
EIMPRR PRIMER
EIMPRS PRIMES
SIMPER
SPIREM
EIMPRT PERMIT
EIMPRU IMPURE
UMPIRE
EIMPRX PREMIX
EIMPTU IMPUTE
UPTIME
EIMRRS RIMERS
EIMRRT RETRIM
TRIMER
EIMRSS MISERS
REMISS
EIMRST MERITS
MISTER
MITERS
MITRES
REMITS
SMITER
TIMERS
EIMRSV VERISM
VERMIS
EIMRSX MIXERS
EIMRSY MISERY
EIMRTU ITERUM
EIMRTX REMIXT
EIMSSS MISSES
SEISMS
EIMSST MISSET
SMITES
STIMES
TMESIS
EIMSSU MISUSE
EIMSSX SEXISM
EIMSTY STYMIE
EINNNR RENNIN
EINNOO IONONE
EINNOT INTONE
EINNPR PINNER
EINNPS PENNIS
EINNPT TENPIN
EINNRS INNERS
RENINS
SINNER
EINNRT INTERN
TINNER
EINNRW WINNER
EINNST SENNIT
TENNIS
EINNSU ENNUIS
EINNSV VENINS
EINNTT INTENT
EINNTV INVENT
EINNTY NINETY
EINOOT TOONIE
EINOPP PEPINO
EINOPR ORPINE
PERNIO
EINOPS OPINES
PONIES
EINOPT POINTE
EINORR IRONER
EINORS IRONES
NOSIER
SENIOR
EINORT NORITE
ORIENT
TONIER
EINORV ENVIRO
RENVOI
EINOSS ENOSIS
EOSINS
ESSOIN
NOESIS
NOISES
OSSEIN
SONSIE
EINOSV ENVOIS
OVINES
EINOSW NOWISE
WINOES
EINOSZ SOZINE
EINOTW TOWNIE
EINOTX TOXINE
EINOVW INWOVE
EINPPR NIPPER
EINPPS PEPSIN
EINPRS REPINS
RIPENS
SNIPER
EINPRT PTERIN
EINPRU PUNIER
PURINE
UNRIPE
EINPRY PINERY
EINPSS SNIPES
SPINES
EINPST INSTEP
SPINET
EINPSU PUISNE
SUPINE
EINQRU REQUIN
EINQSU SEQUIN
EINQTU QUINTE
EINQUU UNIQUE
EINRRS RINSER
EINRRU RUINER
EINRSS RESINS
RINSES
SERINS
SIRENS
EINRST ESTRIN
INERTS
INSERT
INTERS
NITERS
NITRES
SINTER
TRIENS
TRINES
EINRSU INSURE
INURES
RUSINE
URINES
URSINE
EINRSW REWINS
EINRSY RESINY
EINRTT RETINT
TINTER
EINRTU TRIUNE
UNITER
EINRTV INVERT
EINRTW TWINER
WINTER
EINRTY NITERY
EINRVW WIVERN
EINRVX VERNIX
EINRVY VINERY
EINRWY WINERY
EINSST INSETS
STEINS
EINSSW SINEWS
EINSTT SITTEN
EINSTU TENUIS
UNITES
UNTIES
EINSTV INVEST
EINSTW TWINES
WISENT
EINSUW UNWISE
EINSUX UNISEX
EINSVX VIXENS
EINSWY SINEWY
EINSWZ WINZES
WIZENS
EINTTU TENUTI
EINTTY ENTITY
EINTWY WITNEY
EINWZZ WIZZEN
EIOORZ OOZIER
ZOOIER
EIOOST OTIOSE
EIOPPS POPSIE
EIOPPT POTPIE
EIOPRR ROPIER
EIOPRS POISER
EIOPRT PROTEI
EIOPRX POXIER
EIOPSS POISES
POSIES
EIOPST POSTIE
POTSIE
SOPITE
EIOPTT TIPTOE
EIORRS ROSIER
EIORRT RIOTER
EIORSS OSIERS
SEISOR
EIORST SORTIE
TORIES
TRIOSE
EIORSV VIREOS
EIORSZ SEIZOR
EIOSTV SOVIET
EIOSTW TOWIES
EIOSWY YOWIES
EIOTUV OUTVIE
EIOTVV VOTIVE
EIPPRR RIPPER
EIPPRS PIPERS
SIPPER
EIPPRT TIPPER
EIPPRZ ZIPPER
EIPPST PIPETS
SIPPET
EIPPTT TIPPET
EIPPUY YUPPIE
EIPQSU EQUIPS
PIQUES
EIPQTU PIQUET
EIPRRS PRIERS
SPRIER
EIPRRZ PRIZER
EIPRSS PRISES
SPEIRS
SPIERS
SPIRES
EIPRST ESPRIT
PRIEST
RIPEST
SPRITE
STRIPE
TRIPES
EIPRSU UPRISE
EIPRSV VIPERS
EIPRSW WIPERS
EIPRSZ PRIZES
EIPRTV PRIVET
EIPRTY PYRITE
TYPIER
EIPRXY EXPIRY
EIPSSS SEPSIS
SPEISS
EIPSST PISTES
SPITES
STIPES
EIPSSW SWIPES
EIPSTW PEWITS
EIPSUZ UPSIZE
EIPSXY PYXIES
EIPTTU PUTTIE
EIQRSU QUIRES
RISQUE
SQUIRE
EIQRUV QUIVER
EIQSTU QUIETS
EIQTUY EQUITY
EIRRSS RISERS
EIRRST TRIERS
EIRRSV RIVERS
EIRRSW WIRERS
EIRRTT RITTER
TERRIT
TRITER
EIRRTW WRITER
EIRSST RESIST
RESITS
SISTER
EIRSSU ISSUER
SIEURS
EIRSSV SIVERS
EIRSSZ SIZERS
EIRSTT SITTER
TETRIS
TITERS
TITRES
TRISTE
EIRSTU SUITER
EIRSTV RIVETS
STIVER
STRIVE
VERIST
EIRSTW TWIERS
WRIEST
WRITES
EIRSTZ RITZES
EIRSVV VIVERS
EIRSVW WIVERS
EIRTTT TITTER
EIRTTV TRIVET
EIRTUV VIRTUE
EIRTVY VERITY
EISSSS SISSES
EISSSU ISSUES
EISSSW WISSES
EISSTT TESTIS
EISSTU SUITES
TISSUE
EISSTW WISEST
EISSTX EXISTS
SEXIST
SIXTES
EISSVW SWIVES
EISTVW SWIVET
EISWZZ WIZZES
EJKNRU JUNKER
EJKNTU JUNKET
EJKOPS KOPJES
EJKORS JOKERS
EJLLOS JELLOS
EJLORT JOLTER
EJLOST JOSTLE
EJLOSU JOULES
EJLPSU JULEPS
EJLRSU JURELS
EJLSTU JUSTLE
EJMOOS MOJOES
EJMOST JETSOM
EJMPRU JUMPER
EJNOST JETONS
EJNOSY ENJOYS
EJNOTT JETTON
EJOPRT PROJET
EJORTT JOTTER
EJOSSS JOSSES
EJRSTU JUSTER
EKKOPS KOPEKS
EKLLNS KNELLS
EKLLSS SKELLS
EKLLSV KVELLS
EKLMMU KUMMEL
EKLMSS SKELMS
EKLNOS KELSON
EKLNOU LEUKON
EKLNRU LUNKER
RUNKLE
EKLNST SKLENT
EKLOOR LOOKER
RELOOK
EKLOPT KLEPTO
EKLOST KETOLS
EKLOSY YOKELS
EKLPSS SKELPS
EKLRRU LURKER
EKLRSU SULKER
EKMNOY MONKEY
EKMNSY SKYMEN
EKMOOP MOPOKE
EKMORS SMOKER
EKMOSS SMOKES
EKMOSY SMOKEY
EKMRRU MURKER
EKMRSS SMERKS
EKMSTU MUSKET
EKNNOR KRONEN
EKNNOT NEKTON
EKNNSU SUNKEN
EKNNTU UNKENT
EKNOPS SPOKEN
EKNORR KRONER
EKNORT REKNOT
EKNORW KNOWER
EKNORY YONKER
EKNOST TOKENS
EKNOUY UNYOKE
EKNPRU PUNKER
EKNPTU UNKEPT
EKNPUY PUNKEY
EKNSTU SUNKET
EKOORT RETOOK
EKOPRR PORKER
EKOPRS POKERS
EKOPSS SPOKES
EKOPSY POKEYS
EKORRW REWORK
WORKER
EKORST STOKER
STROKE
TOKERS
TROKES
EKORUY EUROKY
EKOSST STOKES
EKRRSY SKERRY
EKRSTU TUSKER
EKRTUY TURKEY
ELLLOR LOLLER
ELLLRU LULLER
ELLMNU MULLEN
ELLMOW MELLOW
ELLMRU MULLER
ELLMSS SMELLS
ELLMSY SMELLY
ELLMTU MULLET
ELLMUV VELLUM
ELLMUY MULLEY
ELLNOP POLLEN
ELLNOR ENROLL
ELLNOY LONELY
ELLNSS SNELLS
ELLNSU SULLEN
UNSELL
ELLNUU LUNULE
ELLNUW UNWELL
ELLOPR POLLER
REPOLL
ELLOPX POLLEX
ELLORR REROLL
ROLLER
ELLORT TOLLER
ELLOSS LOSELS
ELLOSY SOLELY
ELLOTX EXTOLL
ELLOVY LOVELY
VOLLEY
ELLOWY YELLOW
ELLPRU PULLER
ELLPSS SPELLS
ELLPTU PULLET
ELLPUW UPWELL
ELLPUY PULLEY
ELLQSU QUELLS
ELLSSW SWELLS
ELLSTU TULLES
ELLSTY TELLYS
ELMMOP POMMEL
ELMMPU PUMMEL
ELMNOR MERLON
ELMNOS LEMONS
MELONS
SOLEMN
ELMNOT LOMENT
MELTON
MOLTEN
ELMNOY LEMONY
ELMNPU LUMPEN
PLENUM
ELMNSU LUMENS
ELMOOP POMELO
ELMOOS OSMOLE
ELMOOY MOOLEY
ELMOPU PUMELO
ELMOPY EMPLOY
ELMORS MORELS
MORSEL
ELMORT MERLOT
MOLTER
ELMOST METOLS
MOLEST
MOTELS
ELMOSU OLEUMS
ELMOTT MOTTLE
ELMOTY MOTLEY
ELMOUV VOLUME
ELMPPU PEPLUM
ELMPRU LUMPER
RUMPLE
ELMPSU PLUMES
ELMRSU LEMURS
ELMRTY MYRTLE
TERMLY
ELMSST SMELTS
ELMSSU MUSSEL
ELMSUY MULEYS
ELMSXY XYLEMS
ELMTUU LUTEUM
MUTUEL
MUTULE
ELMTUY MUTELY
ELMUZZ MUZZLE
ELNNOR RONNEL
ELNNOS NELSON
ELNNRU RUNNEL
ELNNTU TUNNEL
ELNOOS LOOSEN
ELNOOW WOOLEN
ELNOOY LOONEY
ELNOPS PLEONS
ELNOPT LEPTON
ELNOPU LOUPEN
ELNOPY OPENLY
POLEYN
ELNORS ENROLS
LONERS
NEROLS
ELNOSS LESSON
ELNOST LENTOS
STOLEN
TELSON
ELNOSU ENSOUL
ELNOSV NOVELS
SLOVEN
ELNOTT TONLET
ELNOUZ ZONULE
ELNOZZ NOZZLE
ELNPST SPLENT
ELNPTU PENULT
ELNPTY PENTYL
PLENTY
ELNRTU RUNLET
ELNSSU UNLESS
ELNSSY SELSYN
ELNSTU LUNETS
ELNSXY LYNXES
ELNTTU NUTLET
ELNTTY NETTLY
ELNUZZ NUZZLE
ELOOPR LOOPER
POOLER
ELOOPS POSOLE
ELOOPZ POZOLE
ELOORS LOOSER
ELOORT LOOTER
RETOOL
ROOTLE
TOOLER
ELOORW WOOLER
ELOOSS LOOSES
ELOOSY LOOEYS
ELOOTT TOOTLE
ELOPPP POPPLE
ELOPPR LOPPER
PROPEL
ELOPPS PEPLOS
ELOPPT TOPPLE
ELOPRS LOPERS
POLERS
PROLES
SLOPER
SPLORE
ELOPRT PETROL
REPLOT
ELOPRV PLOVER
ELOPRW PLOWER
REPLOW
ELOPRX PLEXOR
ELOPSS SLOPES
ELOPSU LOUPES
ELOPTT POTTLE

ELOPTU TUPELO
ELOPTY PEYOTL
ELORRS SORREL
ELORSS LESSOR
LOSERS
SORELS
ELORST OSTLER
STEROL
ELORSV LOVERS
SOLVER
ELORSW LOWERS
ROWELS
SLOWER
ELORSY SORELY
ELORTT LOTTER
ELORTV REVOLT
ELORTW TROWEL
ELORUV LOUVER
LOUVRE
VELOUR
ELORVW WOLVER
ELORVY OVERLY
VOLERY
ELORWY LOWERY
YOWLER
ELOSSS LOSSES
ELOSST STOLES
ELOSSU LOUSES
OUSELS
SOLEUS
ELOSSV SOLVES
ELOSTT LOTTES
ELOSTU SOLUTE
TOUSLE
ELOSTV VOLTES
ELOSTW LOWEST
OWLETS
TOWELS
ELOSTX EXTOLS
ELOSUV OVULES
ELOSUZ OUZELS
ELOSVW VOWELS
WOLVES
ELOSXY XYLOSE
ELOTTU OUTLET
ELOTUV VOLUTE
ELOTUZ TOUZLE
ELPPRU PULPER
PURPLE
ELPPSU PEPLUS
SUPPLE
ELPQUU PULQUE
ELPRSU PULERS
PULSER
ELPRSY PLYERS
ELPRTY PELTRY
PERTLY
ELPRUY PURELY
ELPSST SPELTS
ELPSSU PLUSES
PULSES
ELPSSY SLYPES
ELPSTU LETUPS
ELPSTZ SPELTZ
ELPSUX PLEXUS
ELPSUY PUSLEY
ELPUZZ PUZZLE
ELRRSU LURERS
RULERS
ELRSTU LUSTER
LUSTRE
RESULT
RUSTLE
SUTLER
ULSTER
ELRSTY STYLER
ELRSUY SURELY
ELRTTU TURTLE
ELRTTY TETRYL
ELRUWZ WURZEL
ELSSTU TUSSLE
ELSSTY SLYEST
STYLES
ELSTTY STYLET
ELSTUX EXULTS
ELSTUZ LUTZES
EMMMRU MUMMER
EMMNOT MOMENT
EMMNTU MENTUM
EMMORS MOMSER
EMMORY MEMORY
EMMORZ MOMZER
EMMPRU MUMPER
EMMPTU METUMP
EMMRRU RUMMER
EMMRSU SUMMER

EMMSTY STEMMY
EMMSUU MUSEUM
EMNNNO NONMEN
EMNOOR MOONER
EMNOPT POTMEN
EMNOPY EPONYM
EMNORS SERMON
EMNORT MENTOR
EMNOSS MESONS
EMNOST MONTES
EMNOSV VENOMS
EMNOSY MONEYS
EMNOTY ETYMON
EMNOXY EXONYM
EMNRSU RUMENS
EMNSSU SENSUM
EMNSUW UNMEWS
EMNSYZ ENZYMS
EMOORR ROOMER
EMOORS MOROSE
ROMEOS
EMOORT MOOTER
EMOOSS OSMOSE
EMOPPR MOPPER
EMOPPT MOPPET
EMOPRR ROMPER
EMOPRS MOPERS
PROEMS
EMOPRT TROMPE
EMOPRY MOPERY
EMOPST TEMPOS
EMOPSY MYOPES
EMOQSU MOSQUE
EMORRS ORMERS
EMORRT TERMOR
TREMOR
EMORRW WORMER
EMORSS MOSSER
EMORST METROS
EMORSU MOUSER
EMORSV MOVERS
VOMERS
EMORSW MOWERS
EMOSSS MOSSES
EMOSSU MOUSES
MOUSSE
EMOSSY MOSEYS
MYOSES
EMOSTT MOTETS
MOTTES
TOTEMS
EMOSUY MOUSEY
EMOSZZ MEZZOS
EMPPRU PUMPER
REPUMP
EMPRSS SPERMS
EMPSSU SPUMES
EMPSTT TEMPTS
EMPSTU SEPTUM
EMRRSU MURRES
EMRRUY MURREY
EMRSSU MUSERS
SERUMS
EMRSTU ESTRUM
MUSTER
EMRTTU MUTTER
EMSSSU MUSSES
EMSSTY SYSTEM
EMSTTU MUTEST
ENNNOP PENNON
ENNOPT PONENT
ENNOPU UNOPEN
ENNORT TONNER
ENNORU NEURON
ENNORW RENOWN
WONNER
ENNOST NONETS
SONNET
TENONS
TONNES
ENNOSU NONUSE
ENNOSX XENONS
ENNOTW NEWTON
ENNPRU PUNNER
ENNPSU UNPENS
ENNPTU PUNNET
UNPENT
ENNRRU RUNNER
ENNRTU UNRENT
ENNSTU UNSENT
ENNSUW UNSEWN
ENNTUU UNTUNE
ENOOPR OPERON
ENOORS NOOSER
SOONER
ENOORT ENROOT

ENOOSS NOOSES
ENOOSZ OZONES
SNOOZE
ENOPRR PERRON
ENOPRS PERSON
ENOPRV PROVEN
ENOPRY PYRONE
ENOPST NETOPS
PONTES
ENOPTT POTENT
ENORRS SNORER
SORNER
ENORRT RETORN
ENORRW REWORN
ENORRY ORNERY
ENORSS SENORS
SENSOR
SNORES
ENORST NESTOR
NOTERS
STONER
TENORS
TENSOR
TONERS
TRONES
ENORSU ROUENS
ENORSW OWNERS
RESOWN
ROWENS
WORSEN
ENORSZ ZONERS
ENORTT ROTTEN
TORTEN
ENORTU TENOUR
ENORUV UNROVE
ENOSST ONSETS
SETONS
STENOS
STONES
ENOSSU NOUSES
ONUSES
ENOSSW SOWENS
ENOSTT TESTON
ENOSTX SEXTON
ENOSTY STONEY
ENOSUV VENOUS
ENOSVW WOVENS
ENOSVY ENVOYS
ENOSXY ONYXES
ENOTTU TENUTO
ENOUVW UNWOVE
ENPRRU PRUNER
ENPRST SPRENT
ENPRSU PRUNES
ENPRTU PUNTER
ENPRUU UNPURE
ENPRUY PENURY
ENPSTU UNSTEP
UPSENT
ENPTUU TUNEUP
ENPTUW UNWEPT
ENQRSU QUERNS
ENRRSU NURSER
RERUNS
ENRRTU RETURN
TURNER
ENRSST STERNS
ENRSSU NURSES
ENRSSY SYRENS
ENRSTU TUNERS
UNREST
ENRSTW STREWN
ENRSTY SENTRY
ENRSUU UNSURE
ENRSUY SENRYU
ENRTTU NUTTER
ENRTUU UNTRUE
ENRVWY WYVERN
ENSSTT STENTS
ENSSTU SUNSET
UNSETS
ENSSUW UNSEWS
ENSUXY UNSEXY
ENTTWY TWENTY
ENTUVX UNVEXT
EOOPPS OPPOSE
EOOPRR POORER
EOOPRS POROSE
EOOPTY PTOOEY
EOORRS ROOSER
EOORRT ROOTER
TORERO
EOORSS ROOSES
EOORST TOROSE
EOORSW WOOERS
EOORTT TOOTER

EOPPPR POPPER
EOPPPT POPPET
EOPPRR PROPER
EOPPRS PREOPS
EOPPRT TOPPER
EOPPRY PYROPE
EOPRRS PROSER
REPROS
ROPERS
EOPRRT PORTER
PRETOR
REPORT
EOPRRU POURER
REPOUR
EOPRRV PROVER
EOPRRW PROWER
EOPRRY ROPERY
EOPRSS POSERS
PROSES
SPORES
EOPRST POSTER
PRESTO
REPOTS
RESPOT
STOPER
TOPERS
TROPES
EOPRSU POSEUR
UPROSE
EOPRSV PROVES
EOPRSW POWERS
EOPRSY OSPREY
EOPRTT POTTER
EOPRTU POUTER
ROUPET
TROUPE
UPTORE
EOPRTW POWTER
EOPRTX EXPORT
EOPRTY POETRY
EOPRTZ POTZER
EOPRXY PEROXY
EOPSSS POSSES
EOPSST ESTOPS
PESTOS
POSSET
PTOSES
STOPES
EOPSSU OPUSES
SPOUSE
EOPSSY PYOSES
SEPOYS
EOPSTX SEXPOT
EOPSTY TEPOYS
EOQRSU ROQUES
EOQRTU QUOTER
ROQUET
TORQUE
EOQSTU QUOTES
TOQUES
EOQTTU TOQUET
EORRRS ERRORS
EORRRT TERROR
EORRRY ORRERY
EORRST RESORT
RETROS
ROSTER
SORTER
STORER
EORRSU ROUSER
SOURER
EORRSV ROVERS
EORRSW ROWERS
WORSER
EORRSY ROSERY
EORRTT RETORT
ROTTER
EORRTU ROUTER
TOURER
EORRTV TROVER
EORRZZ ROZZER
EORSST ROSETS
SOREST
STORES
TORSES
TOSSER
TSORES
EORSSU ROUSES
SEROUS
EORSSV SERVOS
VERSOS
EORSSW RESOWS
SEROWS
SOWERS
WORSES

EORSTT OTTERS
ROTTES
TORTES
TOTERS
EORSTU OUSTER
OUTERS
ROUTES
SOUTER
STOURE
EORSTV STOVER
STROVE
TROVES
VOTERS
EORSTW TOWERS
WORSET
EORSTX OXTERS
EORSTY OYSTER
STOREY
TOYERS
EORSTZ ZOSTER
EORSVW VOWERS
EORSWW WOWSER
EORSXY ORYXES
EORTTT TOTTER
EORTTU TOUTER
EORTTX EXTORT
EORTVX VORTEX
EORTWY TOWERY
EORUVY VOYEUR
EOSSST TOSSES
EOSSSU SOUSES
EOSSTU SETOUS
TOUSES
EOSSTV STOVES
EOSSTX SEXTOS
EOSTTU OUTSET
SETOUT
EOSUUV UVEOUS
EPPPRY PREPPY
EPPPTU PUPPET
EPPRSU SUPPER
UPPERS
EPPSTU UPSTEP
EPRRSU PURSER
EPRRSY PRYERS
SPRYER
EPRSST PRESTS
STREPS
EPRSSU PURSES
SPRUES
SUPERS
EPRSTU ERUPTS
PUREST
EPRSTW TWERPS
EPRSUU PURSUE
EPRTTU PUTTER
EPRTTY PRETTY
EPRUVY PURVEY
EPSSSU PUSSES
EPSSTU SETUPS
STUPES
UPSETS
EPSTUZ PUTZES
EQRTWY QWERTY
EQSSTU QUESTS
EQSSUU USQUES
EQSTUU TUQUES
ERRSUU USURER
ERRSUY SURREY
ERRTTU TURRET
ERSSST STRESS
ERSSTU ESTRUS
RUSSET
SUREST
TUSSER
ERSSTV VERSTS
ERSSTW STREWS
WRESTS
ERSSTY TRESSY
ERSSUU URUSES
ERSSUV VERSUS
ERSTTU TRUEST
UTTERS
ERSTTY TRYSTE
ERSTUU SUTURE
UTERUS
ERSTUV TURVES
VERTUS
ERSTUY SURETY
TUYERS
ERSTVY VESTRY
ERSTWY TWYERS
WRYEST
ERSTXY XYSTER
ERSUVY SURVEY
ERTTUX URTEXT

ESSSSU SUSSES
ESSSTU TUSSES
ESSSUW WUSSES
ESTUYZ YUTZES
FFFLOY FLYOFF
FFFLSU FLUFFS
FFFLUY FLUFFY
FFGIIN FIFING
FFGILS GLIFFS
FFGINO GONIFF
OFFING
FFGIRS GRIFFS
FFGRSU GRUFFS
FFGRUY GRUFFY
FFHIOS OFFISH
FFHIST FIFTHS
FFHISW WHIFFS
FFHORS SHROFF
FFHOSW HOWFFS
FFIINT TIFFIN
FFIKSS SKIFFS
FFILLU FULFIL
FFILPS SPLIFF
FFILTU FITFUL
FFIMNU MUFFIN
FFINPU PUFFIN
FFINSS SNIFFS
FFINSY SNIFFY
FFIOPR RIPOFF
FFIOPT TIPOFF
FFIOST SOFFIT
FFIPSS SPIFFS
FFIPSY SPIFFY
FFIQSU QUIFFS
FFISST STIFFS
FFISUX SUFFIX
FFLOTY FYLFOT
FFLRUY RUFFLY
FFLSSU SLUFFS
FFNORU RUNOFF
FFNSSU SNUFFS
FFNSUY SNUFFY
FFOPSU POUFFS
FFOPTU PUTOFF
FFOPUY POUFFY
FFRRUU FURFUR
FFSSTU STUFFS
FFSTUY STUFFY
FGGIIZ FIZGIG
FGGORY FROGGY
FGHILT FLIGHT
FGHIRT FRIGHT
FGHIST FIGHTS
FGHOTU FOUGHT
FGIILN FILING
FGIINN FINING
FGIINR FIRING
FGIINW WIFING
FGIINX FIXING
FGIINY IGNIFY
FGILNS FLINGS
FGILNU INGULF
FGILNY FLYING
FGILUY UGLIFY
FGIMNU FUMING
FGINOS GONIFS
FGINOX FOXING
FGINRY FRINGY
FRYING
FGINSU FUSING
FGINUZ FUZING
FGIOSU FUGIOS
FGIOTZ ZOFTIG
FGIRST GRIFTS
FGJLUU JUGFUL
FGLMUU MUGFUL
FGLNOS FLONGS
FGNOOS GONOFS
FGNSUU FUNGUS
FGOORT FORGOT
FHIINS FINISH
FHILST FILTHS
FHILSU FLUISH
FHILTY FILTHY
FHIRST FIRTHS
FRITHS
SHRIFT
FHIRTT THRIFT
FHISST SHIFTS
FHISTY SHIFTY
FHOOSW WHOOFS
FHORST FROTHS
FHORTU FOURTH
FHORTY FROTHY
FHORWY FORWHY
FIIKNR FIRKIN

FIILLN INFILL
FIILLP FILLIP
FIILMS FILMIS
FIILPR RIFLIP
FIILVY VILIFY
FIIMNR INFIRM
FIIMNY MINIFY
FIIMST MISFIT
FIINOT FINITO
FIINVY VINIFY
FIITXY FIXITY
FIIVVY VIVIFY
FIJLOR FRIJOL
FIKRSS FRISKS
FIKRSY FRISKY
FILLOS FILLOS
FOLLIS
FILLRS FRILLS
FILLRY FRILLY
FILLUW WILFUL
FILMOU FOLIUM
FILMRY FIRMLY
FILMSY FLIMSY
FILMUU FUMULI
FILNOR FLORIN
FILNOW INFLOW
FILNST FLINTS
FILNSU SINFUL
FILNTU TINFUL
FILNTY FLINTY
FILNUX INFLUX
FILOOS FOLIOS
FILORV FRIVOL
FILOSS FOSSIL
FILOTU TUFOLI
FILOXY FOXILY
FILPPY FLIPPY
FILPTU UPLIFT
FILRST FLIRTS
FILRTY FLIRTY
FILSSU FUSILS
FILSUZ FUZILS
FIMNOR INFORM
FIMOST MOTIFS
FIMSTU MUFTIS
FINOOS FOISON
FINORT FORINT
FINORX FORNIX
FINOSU FUSION
FINOTY NOTIFY
FINSTU UNFITS
FINTUX UNFIXT
FIOPRT PROFIT
FIORRT FORRIT
FIORST FORTIS
FIOSST FOISTS
FIOSSY OSSIFY
FIOTTU OUTFIT
FIPRUY PURIFY
FIPTYY TYPIFY
FIRSST FIRSTS
FIRSTT FRITTS
FIRSTU FRUITS
FIRTUY FRUITY
FIRYZZ FRIZZY
FISSTW SWIFTS
FJLOUY JOYFUL
FKLNSU FLUNKS
FKLNUY FLUNKY
FKLOOS KLOOFS
FKLOSY FOLKSY
FLLOOW FOLLOW
FLLOUY FOULLY
FLMOOR FORMOL
FLMORY FORMYL
FLMPSU FLUMPS
FLNRUU UNFURL
FLOORS FLOORS
FLOOSY FLOOSY
FLOOYZ FLOOZY
FLOPPY FLOPPY
FLOPTU POTFUL
TOPFUL
FLOPUW UPFLOW
FLORSU FLOURS
FLUORS
FLORUY FLOURY
FLOSSY FLOSSY
FLOSTU FLOUTS
FLOSTY SOFTLY
FLOTUY OUTFLY
FLRRUY FLURRY
FLRSUU SULFUR
FLSTUY FLUYTS
FMORSU FORUMS
FMPRSU FRUMPS

FMPRUY FRUMPY
FNOORU UNROOF
FNORST FRONTS
FNORSW FROWNS
FNOSTU FOUNTS
FUTONS
FOOPRS PROOFS
FOOPSS SPOOFS
FOOPSY SPOOFY
FOOSTY FOOTSY
FOOTUX OUTFOX
FORRSU FURORS
FORRUW FURROW
FORSST FROSTS
FORSTW FROWST
FORSTY FROSTY
FORSUU RUFOUS
FORSWY FROWSY
FORUYZ FROUZY
FORWYZ FROWZY
GGGIIN IGGING
GGGILY GIGGLY
GGGLOS GLOGGS
GGGLOY GOGGLY
GGGORY GROGGY
GGIINP PIGGIN
GGIINV GIVING
GGIIRR GRIGRI
GGIJLY JIGGLY
GGIKNO GINGKO
GINKGO
GGILNO OGLING
GGILNU GLUING
LUGING
GGILNY NIGGLY
GGILOO GIGOLO
GGILOT GIGLOT
GGILWY WIGGLY
GGINNO NOGGIN
GGINOR GORING
GGINOS GOINGS
GGINRU URGING
GGINRY GYRING
GGINUY GUYING
GGINVY GYVING
GGIOST GIGOTS
GGITWY TWIGGY
GGLOOO GOOGOL
GGLOOY GOOGLY
GGMOSY SMOGGY
GGMRUU MUGGUR
GGNOOR GORGON
GGNRUY GRUNGY
GGPRUY PUGGRY
GGRRUU GRUGRU
GHHHIT HIGHTH
GHHILY HIGHLY
GHHIST HIGHTS
THIGHS
GHHOTU THOUGH
GHIIKN HIKING
GHIINR HIRING
GHIINV HIVING
GHIKNO HOKING
GHIKNT KNIGHT
GHILNO HOLING
GHILPT PLIGHT
GHILST LIGHTS
SLIGHT
GHIMNO HOMING
GHIMST MIGHTS
GHIMTY MIGHTY
GHINNO HONING
GHINOO OOHING
GHINOP HOPING
GHINOS HOSING
GHINPY HYPING
GHINST NIGHTS
THINGS
GHINSY SHYING
GHINTY NIGHTY
GHIORS OGRISH
GHIORT RIGHTO
GHIOSS SHOGIS
GHIRST GIRTHS
GRITHS
RIGHTS
GHIRTW WRIGHT
GHIRTY RIGHTY
GHISST SIGHTS
GHISTT TIGHTS
GHISTW WIGHTS
GHLLSY GHYLLS
GHLMOU MOGHUL
GHLOOS GOLOSH
GHLOPU PLOUGH

GHLOSU GHOULS
LOUGHS
SLOUGH
GHLPSY GLYPHS
GHNNUU UNHUNG
GHNOOP GONOPH
GHNORT THRONG
GHNOST THONGS
GHNOSU SHOGUN
GHNOTU HOGNUT
NOUGHT
GHNRUY HUNGRY
GHOOPT PHOTOG
GHOOQU QUOHOG
GHOORS SORGHO
GHORSU ROUGHS
GHORTU TROUGH
GHORTW GROWTH
GHORUY ROUGHY
GHOSST GHOSTS
GHOSSU SOUGHS
GHOSTU OUGHTS
SOUGHT
TOUGHS
GHOSTY GHOSTY
GHOTUY TOUGHY
GHRSSU SHRUGS
GIIJNV JIVING
GIIKLN LIKING
GIIKMN MIKING
GIIKNN INKING
GIIKNP PIKING
GIIKNR IRKING
GIIKNS SKIING
GIIKNT KITING
GIIKNV VIKING
GIILMN LIMING
GIILNN LIGNIN
LINING
GIILNO OILING
GIILNP PILING
GIILNR RILING
GIILNS ISLING
GIILNT TILING
GIILNV LIVING
GIILNW WILING
GIILOS SIGLOI
GIILSS SIGILS
GIILSV VIGILS
GIIMMN MIMING
GIIMNN MINING
GIIMNP IMPING
GIIMNR MIRING
RIMING
GIIMNT TIMING
GIIMNX MIXING
GIINNN INNING
GIINNP PINING
GIINNT TINING
GIINNV VINING
GIINNW WINING
GIINNX NIXING
GIINOR ORIGIN
GIINOY YOGINI
GIINPP PIPING
GIINPR RIPING
GIINPS SIPING
GIINPW WIPING
GIINRS RISING
SIRING
GIINRT TIRING
GIINRV RIVING
VIRGIN
GIINRW WIRING
GIINST SITING
GIINSV VISING
GIINSW WISING
GIINSZ SIZING
GIINTT GITTIN
GIINTW WITING
GIINVW WIVING
GIIOPR PIROGI
GIJKNO JINGKO
JOKING
GIJKNU JUKING
GIJLNY JINGLY
GIJNOW JOWING
GIJNOY JOYING
GIKLNY KINGLY
GIKNNU NUKING
GIKNOP POKING
GIKNOT TOKING
GIKNOY YOKING
GIKNPU PUKING
GIKNRY RYKING
GIKNST TSKING

GIKNSY SKYING
GIKRTU TUGRIK
GILLOY LOGILY
GILLRS GRILLS
GILLUY GLUILY
UGLILY
GILMNU MULING
GILMRY GRIMLY
GILMSU SIGLUM
GILNOO LOGION
LOOING
OLINGO
GILNOP LOPING
POLING
GILNOS LOGINS
LOSING
SOLING
GILNOT TIGLON
TOLING
GILNOV LOVING
VOLING
GILNOW LOWING
GILNOX LOXING
GILNPU PULING
GILNPY PLYING
GILNRU LURING
RULING
GILNSS SLINGS
GILNST GLINTS
GILNSU LUNGIS
SLUING
GILNSY LYINGS
LYSING
SINGLY
GILNTU LUTING
GILNTY GLINTY
TINGLY
GILNUY LUNGYI
GILNWY WYLING
GILOOS IGLOOS
ISOLOG
GILORY GORILY
GILOSS SIGLOS
GILRSY GRISLY
GILRTY TRIGLY
GILSTU GUILTS
GILTUY GUILTY
GILTZY GLITZY
GIMNNO MIGNON
GIMNOO MOOING
GIMNOP MOPING
GIMNOU GONIUM
GIMNOV MOVING
GIMNOW MOWING
GIMNPU IMPUGN
UMPING
GIMNRU MURING
GIMNSU MUSING
GIMNTU MUTING
GIMORS OGRISM
GIMOSS GISMOS
GIMOSZ GIZMOS
GIMOTU GOMUTI
GINNOO GONION
GINNOS NOSING
GINNOT NOTING
TONING
GINNOW OWNING
GINNOZ ZONING
GINNTU TUNING
GINNTY TYNING
GINOOS ISOGON
GINOOW WOOING
GINOOZ OOZING
GINOPR PORING
ROPING
GINOPS GIPONS
PINGOS
POSING
GINOPT OPTING
TOPING
GINOPX POXING
GINORS GIRONS
GRISON
GROINS
ROSING
SIGNOR
SORING
GINORT TRIGON
GINORV ROVING
GINORW ROWING
GINOSS GNOSIS
GINOST INGOTS
STINGO
TIGONS
GINOSW SOWING

GINOSY YOGINS
GINOTT TOTING
GINOTU OUTING
GINOTV VOTING
GINOTW TOWING
GINOTY TOYING
GINOVW VOWING
GINOWW WOWING
GINOWY YOWING
GINPPU UPPING
GINPRS SPRING
GINPRU URPING
GINPRY PRYING
GINPSU PIGNUS
SPUING
GINPSY SPYING
GINPTU PIGNUT
GINPTY TYPING
GINRST STRING
GINRSU UNRIGS
GINRSW WRINGS
GINRTU TRUING
UNGIRT
GINRTY TRYING
TYRING
GINRWY WRYING
GINSST STINGS
GINSSW SWINGS
GINSTY STINGY
STYING
GINSUU UNGUIS
GINSWY SWINGY
GINTWY WYTING
GIOPSS GOSSIP
GIOPST SPIGOT
GIOPTU PIGOUT
GIORRS RIGORS
GIORRU RIGOUR
GIORST GRIOTS
TRIGOS
GIORSU GUIROS
GIORSV VIGORS
GIORTU OUTRIG
GIORUV VIGOUR
GIPPRY GRIPPY
GIPRSS SPRIGS
GIPRTU UPGIRT
GIPSTY PIGSTY
GIRSST GRISTS
GIRTTY GRITTY
GJLNUY JUNGLY
GJMSUU JUGUMS
GKLNOS KLONGS
GLLMUY GLUMLY
GLLNOY LONGLY
GLMNOO MONGOL
GLMOOS GLOOMS
GLMOOY GLOOMY
GLMOSU GLOMUS
MOGULS
GLMPUY GLUMPY
GLMSUY SMUGLY
GLNOOO OOLONG
GLNOOS LOGONS
GLNOSU GLUONS
GLNOUY LOUNGY
GLNPUU UNPLUG
GLNSUY SNUGLY
GLOOOY OOLOGY
GLOOPR PROLOG
GLOPPY GLOPPY
GLOPTU PUTLOG
GLORSW GROWLS
GLORWY GROWLY
GLOSST GLOSTS
GLOSSY GLOSSY
GLOSTU GLOUTS
GLSUUV VULGUS
GMNNOO GNOMON
GMNOOS MONGOS
GMNOST MONGST
GMNOSU MUNGOS
GMOOPR POGROM
GMOORS GROOMS
GMPRSU GRUMPS
GMPRUY GRUMPY
GMPSUY GYPSUM
GNNSUU UNSUNG
GNOORT TROGON
GNOPPU OPPUGN
POPGUN
GNOPRS PRONGS
GNOPRU PROGUN
GNOPSY SPONGY
GNORST STRONG
GNORSW WRONGS

GNORSY GYRONS
GNOSUY YOUNGS
GNOTUU OUTGUN
GNPRSU SPRUNG
GNRSTU GRUNTS
STRUNG
GOORSS SORGOS
GOORTT GROTTO
GOORVY GROOVY
GOPRSU GROUPS
GOPRUW UPGROW
GORRTU TURGOR
GORSTU GROUTS
GORSUU RUGOUS
GORSYZ GROSZY
GORTTU ROTGUT
GORTTY GROTTY
GORTUY GROUTY
YOGURT
GOSTUY GUYOTS
GPRSSU SPRUGS
GSYYYZ SYZYGY
HHISTW WHISHT
HHMPSU HUMPHS
HHMRTY RHYTHM
HHOOSW WHOOSH
HHRSTU THRUSH
HIILNS NIHILS
HIILPU HUIPIL
HIIMNS MINISH
HIIMPS IMPISH
HIIMST ISTHMI
MISHIT
HIINSW WINISH
HIINTW WITHIN
HIIRSS RISHIS
HIITZZ ZIZITH
HIJOSS SHOJIS
HIKLOY HOKILY
HIKMUZ MUZHIK
HIKNRS SHRINK
HIKNST THINKS
HIKRSS SHIRKS
HIKSST SHTIKS
HIKSSW WHISKS
HIKSWY WHISKY
HILLOS HILLOS
HILLOY HOLILY
HILLPU UPHILL
HILLRS SHRILL
HILLRT THRILL
HILLSS SHILLS
HILLST THILLS
HILMOS HOLISM
HILMOW WHILOM
HILMOY HOMILY
HILMSU MULISH
HILNPT PLINTH
HILNTY THINLY
HILOOT OOLITH
THOLOI
HILOPS POLISH
HILORT LIROTH
HILOST HOLIST
LITHOS
THIOLS
HILOSW LOWISH
OWLISH
HILPST SPILTH
HILRST THIRLS
HILRSW WHIRLS
HILRWY WHIRLY
HILSTT TILTHS
HILSTW WHILST
HIMMSY SHIMMY
HIMNOS MONISH
HIMNOY HOMINY
HIMOPS MOPISH
HIMOTY MYTHOI
HIMPRS SHRIMP
HIMRST MIRTHS
HIMSST SMITHS
HIMSTY SMITHY
HIMSWY WHIMSY
HINNST NINTHS
HINNSY SHINNY
HINNWY WHINNY
HINOPS SIPHON
HINORS RHINOS
HINOST TONISH
HINPSU PUNISH
UNSHIP
HINPSX SPHINX
HINPTY PHYTIN
HINRSU INRUSH
HINSUW UNWISH

HIOPPS HIPPOS
HIORSS ROSHIS
HIORSU HOURIS
HIOSST HOISTS
HIOSSW WHOSIS
HIOSTY TOYISH
HIOTTU OUTHIT
HIPPSU UPPISH
HIPPWY WHIPPY
HIPRST THRIPS
HIPSSY PHYSIS
HIQSSU SQUISH
HIRRSS SHIRRS
HIRRSW WHIRRS
HIRRWY WHIRRY
HIRSST SHIRTS
HIRSTT THIRST
HIRSTY SHIRTY
THYRSI
YIRTHS
HIRTTY THIRTY
HISSST SHISTS
HISSSU SUSHIS
HISSTW WHISTS
HISSTX SIXTHS
HISSWY SWISHY
HISTTY STITHY
HIWYZZ WHIZZY
HJNNOY JOHNNY
HKLOOZ KOLHOZ
HKMOSU HOKUMS
KHOUMS
HKNOOS SHNOOK
HKNOOU UNHOOK
HKNRSU SHRUNK
HKNSTU THUNKS
HKNSUU UNHUSK
HKOOPU HOOKUP
HKOOSS SHOOKS
HLLOOS HOLLOS
HLLOOU HULLOO
HLLOOW HOLLOW
HLLOPY PHYLLO
HLLOSU HULLOS
HLLOWY WHOLLY
HLLSUY LUSHLY
HLMOOS SHOLOM
HLMOTY THYMOL
HLMPSU SHLUMP
HLMPSY LYMPHS
HLMPUY PHYLUM
HLNOPY PHYLON
HLNOUY UNHOLY
HLOOSS SHOOLS
HLOOST THOLOS
HLOPSS SPLOSH
HLOPSY POSHLY
HLOPTY PHYTOL
HLORSS SHORLS
HLORSW WHORLS
HLORUY HOURLY
HLOSST SLOTHS
HLOSSY SLOSHY
HLOSTY HOSTLY
HLPSSY SYLPHS
HLPSUY PLUSHY
HLPSYY SYLPHY
HLRSTU THURLS
HLSSUY SLUSHY
HLSTUY THUSLY
HMMOOS HOMMOS
HMMSUU HUMMUS
HMNOPY NYMPHO
HMNOST MONTHS
HMNPSY NYMPHS
HMOOPR MORPHO
HMOOPS OOMPHS
HMOOSS SMOOSH
HMOOST SMOOTH
HMOOSW WHOMSO
HMOPRS MORPHS
HMOPSW WHOMPS
HMORSU HUMORS
MOHURS
HMORUU HUMOUR
HMOSTU MOUTHS
HMOSTY MYTHOS
HMOTUY MOUTHY
HMPRUY MURPHY
HMPSTU THUMPS
HMPSUW WHUMPS
HMRRSY MYRRHS
HMRSTU THRUMS
HMSSTU MUSTHS
HMSTUY THYMUS

HNNOOP PHONON
HNOOPS PHONOS
HNOOPT PHOTON
HNOORS HONORS
HNOORT THORON
HNOORU HONOUR
HNOPSY SYPHON
HNOPTY PHYTON
PYTHON
TYPHON
HNORST NORTHS
THORNS
HNORSU ONRUSH
HNORTW THROWN
HNORTY RHYTON
THORNY
HNOSSY HYSONS
HNPSXY SPHYNX
HNRTUU UNHURT
HNSSTU SHUNTS
HNSSTY SYNTHS
HNSTUU UNSHUT
HOOOOP HOOPOO
HOOPST PHOTOS
POTHOS
HOOPSW WHOOPS
HOORRR HORROR
HOORTT TOROTH
HOOSST SHOOTS
SOOTHS
HOOSSW SWOOSH
HOOSTT TOOTHS
HOOTTY TOOTHY
HOPRST THORPS
HOPRTY TROPHY
HOPSSY HYSSOP
HOPSTU TOPHUS
UPSHOT
HORSST HORSTS
SHORTS
HORSTT TROTHS
HORSTU ROUTHS
HORSTW ROWTHS
THROWS
WHORTS
WORTHS
HORSTY SHORTY
HORTTW TROWTH
HORTWY WORTHY
HOSSTT SHOTTS
HOSSTU SHOUTS
SOUTHS
HOSSUY SHOYUS
HOSTUY YOUTHS
HPPSUU PUSHUP
HPRSUU UPRUSH
HPSTUY TYPHUS
HQRSUU QURUSH
HQSSUU SQUUSH
HRSSTU HURSTS
HRSTTU THRUST
TRUTHS
IIIRST IRITIS
IIJMNY JIMINY
IIJNNS JINNIS
IIKLMS KILIMS
IIKNNS KININS
IIKNPP PIPKIN
IIKNSS SISKIN
IIKPUW WIKIUP
IILLMU LIMULI
IILLOY OILILY
IILLWY WILILY
IILMMU MILIUM
IILMNS SIMLIN
IILMST LIMITS
MISLIT
IILNNS LININS
IILNNU INULIN
IILNOV VIOLIN
IILNPS LIPINS
IILNRT NITRIL
IILNST INSTIL
IILNTY TINILY
IILPST PISTIL
IILRWY WIRILY
IILTTW TWILIT
IIMMNS MINIMS
IIMMNU MINIUM
IIMMNW WIMMIN
IIMNNO MINION
IIMNOU IONIUM
IIMNRS MIRINS
IIMOSS MIOSIS
IIMRSU SURIMI
IIMSSS MISSIS

IINNOP PINION
IINNOS INIONS
IINNPY PINYIN
IINNQU QUININ
IINORV VIRION
IINOSV VISION
IINPPP PIPPIN
IINSST INSIST
IINTTU INTUIT
IINTTW NITWIT
IIOSTT OTITIS
IIPPST PIPITS
IIPRST SPIRIT
IIQTUV QIVIUT
IIRSVZ VIZIRS
IISSTV VISITS
IJKLOY JOKILY
IJKMOU MOUJIK
IJKMSU MUJIKS
IJKMUZ MUZJIK
IJLMPY JIMPLY
IJNORU JUNIOR
IJNOST JOINTS
IJNPSU PUNJIS
IJNRUY INJURY
IJOSST JOISTS
IJRSTU JURIST
IKKNNU UNKINK
IKKNSS SKINKS
IKKOSS KIOSKS
IKKRSU KUKRIS
IKLLRS KRILLS
IKLLSS SKILLS
IKLNNU UNLINK
IKLNPS PLINKS
IKLNPU LINKUP
UPLINK
IKLNPY PINKLY
IKLNSS SLINKS
IKLNSY SLINKY
IKLNTY TINKLY
IKLOPY POKILY
IKLPSY PLISKY
IKLRSS SKIRLS
IKLSSU SUSLIK
IKLSTY SKYLIT
IKMNOO KIMONO
IKMNOR MIKRON
IKMOSU KOUMIS
IKMOSV MIKVOS
IKMOTV MIKVOT
IKMPSS SKIMPS
IKMPSY SKIMPY
IKMRSS SMIRKS
IKMRSY SMIRKY
IKMSSU KUMISS
IKMSTU MUSKIT
IKNNPU PUNKIN
IKNNSY SKINNY
IKNNTU UNKNIT
IKNOOR KROONI
IKNOPS PINKOS
IKNOPT INKPOT
IKNOST STINKO
IKNPRS PRINKS
IKNSST STINKS
IKNSSW SWINKS
IKNSTY STINKY
IKOORS IROKOS
IKOORU KOUROI
IKPSTU TUPIKS
IKQRSU QUIRKS
IKQRUY QUIRKY
IKRRSS SKIRRS
IKRSST SKIRTS
STIRKS
IKSVVY SKIVVY
ILLMPY LIMPLY
ILLMSY SLIMLY
ILLNOT LINTOL
ILLOPW PILLOW
ILLOWW WILLOW
ILLPRS PRILLS
ILLPSS SPILLS
ILLQSU QUILLS
SQUILL
ILLRST TRILLS
ILLSST STILLS
ILLSSW SWILLS
ILLSTW TWILLS
ILLSTY STILLY
ILLSUV VILLUS
ILMNOU MOULIN
ILMNSU LINUMS
MUSLIN
ILMORW WORMIL

ILMOSS LISSOM
ILMOTU ULTIMO
ILMPPY PIMPLY
ILMPRY PRIMLY
ILMPSY LIMPSY
SIMPLY
ILMRSY LYRISM
ILMRTY TRIMLY
ILMSSY SLIMSY
ILMSTU LITMUS
ILMTUU TUMULI
ILMYZZ MIZZLY
ILNOOS SOLION
ILNOOT LOTION
ILNOPP POPLIN
ILNOPT PONTIL
ILNOQU QUINOL
ILNOST TONSIL
ILNOSU INSOUL
ILNOSY NOSILY
ILNPRU PURLIN
ILNPST SPLINT
ILNPSU LUPINS
ILNPUY PUNILY
ILNSSY LYSINS
ILNSTU INSULT
SUNLIT
ILNSVY SYLVIN
VINYLS
ILOOPS POLIOS
ILOOYZ OOZILY
ILOPPY POLYPI
ILOPRX PROLIX
ILOPRY PYLORI
ROPILY
ILOPSS SPOILS
ILOPST PILOTS
PISTOL
SPOILT
ILOPSU PILOUS
POILUS
ILOPSX OXLIPS
ILOPTY POLITY
ILOQRU LIQUOR
ILORST TRIOLS
ILORSY ROSILY
ILORSZ ZORILS
ILOTTW WITTOL
ILPPRY RIPPLY
ILPPSU PUPILS
SLIPUP
ILPPSY SLIPPY
ILPPTU PULPIT
ILPRTY TRIPLY
ILPSST SPLITS
ILPSTU TULIPS
ILPTTU UPTILT
ILQSTU QUILTS
ILRSSW SWIRLS
ILRSTW TWIRLS
ILRSTY LYRIST
ILRSWY SWIRLY
ILRTWY TWIRLY
ILSSTT STILTS
ILSTTU LUTIST
ILSTTY SLITTY
IMMMOS MOMISM
IMMNOS MONISM
NOMISM
IMMOOS SIMOOM
IMMOSU OSMIUM
IMMSTU MUTISM
SUMMIT
IMMSWY SWIMMY
IMNNOW MINNOW
IMNNTU MUNTIN
IMNOOR MORION
IMNOOS SIMOON
SOMONI
IMNOOT MOTION
IMNORS MINORS
IMNOST INMOST
MONIST
IMNOSY MYOSIN
SIMONY
IMNRTU UNTRIM
IMNTUX UNMIXT
IMNTUY MUTINY
IMOOTV VOMITO
IMOPRS PORISM
PRIMOS
IMOPRT IMPORT
IMOPRV IMPROV
IMOPST IMPOST
IMOPSU OPIUMS
IMORRR MIRROR

IMORRS MORRIS
IMORSU RIMOUS
IMOSSX SIXMOS
IMOSSY MYOSIS
IMOSTU OSTIUM
IMOSTV VOMITS
IMOTTT TOMTIT
IMPPRS PRIMPS
IMPRSS PRISMS
IMPRSU PRIMUS
PURISM
IMPSUX MIXUPS
IMQRSU SQUIRM
IMRSTU TRUISM
IMSSSU MISSUS
INNNOS NINONS
INNOOR RONION
INNOOS ONIONS
INNOOT NOTION
INNOOY ONIONY
INNOPS PINONS
INNOPY PINYON
INNORT INTRON
INNOST NITONS
INNOSU UNIONS
UNISON
INNOTW INTOWN
INNOWW WINNOW
INNPSU UNPINS
INNPSY SPINNY
INNRSU INRUNS
INURNS
INNRTU INTURN
INOOPS POISON
INOOPT OPTION
POTION
INOORS ORISON
INOPRS ORPINS
PRIONS
PRISON
SPINOR
INOPRT TROPIN
INOPRU INPOUR
INOPSS OPSINS
INOPST PINOTS
PINTOS
PISTON
PITONS
POINTS
POSTIN
SPINTO
INOPTT TINPOT
INOPTY POINTY
INOQSU QUOINS

INORSS ROSINS
INORST INTROS
NITROS
INORSY ROSINY
INORTT INTORT
TRITON
INORTU TURION
INOSSZ SOZINS
INOSTT STOTIN
INOSTU OUTSIN
INOSTX TOXINS
INOSUV VINOUS
INPPSU PINUPS
INPPSY SNIPPY
INPRST PRINTS
SPRINT
INPRSU PURINS
UNRIPS
INPRTU TURNIP
INPSTU INPUTS
INPSUZ UNZIPS
INQSTU QUINTS
SQUINT
INQSUY QUINSY
INRSTU RUTINS
INRSXY SYRINX
INRTWY WINTRY
INSSTT STINTS
INSSTU SUINTS
INSTUW UNWITS
IOOPRS POORIS
IOPPTT TIPTOP
IOPRRS PRIORS
IOPRRY PRIORY
IOPRST PROSIT
RIPOST
TRIPOS
IOPSST POSITS
PTOSIS
IOPSSY PYOSIS
IOPSTU PISTOU
IOPSTV PIVOTS
IOQSTU QUOITS
IORRTW WORRIT
IORSST TSORIS
IORSSV VISORS
IORSTU SUITOR
IORSVZ VIZORS
IOSTTU OUTSIT
IOSTXY XYSTOI
IOTTUW OUTWIT
IPPQUU QUIPPU
IPPQUY QUIPPY
IPPRTY TRIPPY

IPPTUY UPPITY
IPQSUU QUIPUS
IPRRTU IRRUPT
IPRSST SPIRTS
SPRITS
STIRPS
STRIPS
IPRSSU SIRUPS
IPRSSY PRISSY
IPRSTT STRIPT
IPRSTU PURIST
UPSTIR
IPRSTW TWIRPS
IPRSTY STRIPY
IPRSTZ SPRITZ
IPRSUY SIRUPY
IPRTUY PURITY
IPSSTU SITUPS
IPSTTY TYPIST
IPSVVY SPIVVY
IPTTTU TITTUP
IQRSTU QUIRTS
SQUIRT
IRSSTU TSURIS
IRSSTW WRISTS
IRSTUV VIRTUS
IRSTUZ TZURIS
IRSTWY WRISTY
ISSSTU TUSSIS
ISSTTW TWISTS
ISTTTU TUTTIS
ISTTWY TWISTY
JLSTUY JUSTLY
JMORSU JORUMS
JNOORU JOURNO
JNOPSU JUPONS
JNOSTU JUNTOS
JNSTUU UNJUST
JOOPPY JOYPOP
JOOSUY JOYOUS
JORRSU JURORS
JOSSTU JOUSTS
JOTTUU OUTJUT
KKLMUU MUKLUK
KKLOOZ KOLKOZ
KKLSSU SKULKS
KKMTUU MUKTUK
KKNSSU SKUNKS
KKNSUY SKUNKY
KKOSTU SUKKOT
KKSSTT TSKTSK
KLLNOS KNOLLS
KLLNOY KNOLLY
KLLSSU SKULLS

KLMRUY MURKLY
KLNOPS PLONKS
KLNPSU PLUNKS
KLNPUY PLUNKY
KLNRSU KNURLS
KLNRUY KNURLY
KLOOPU LOOKUP
KLOOSS SOKOLS
KLRTUU KULTUR
KLTUYZ KLUTZY
KMOSUX MUSKOX
KMOSUY KOUMYS
KNNOSW KNOWNS
KNNOTU UNKNOT
KNNSUU UNSUNK
KNOORR KRONOR
KNOORS KROONS
KNOOSS SNOOKS
KNOPSS KNOSPS
KNORRU KRONUR
KNORUY KORUNY
KNOSTU KNOUTS
KNOTTY KNOTTY
KNPSSU SPUNKS
KNPSUY SPUNKY
KNRSTU TRUNKS
KOOPSS SPOOKS
KOOPSY SPOOKY
KOORST STROOK
KOORSU KOUROS
KOOSST STOOKS
KOOSSU KOUSSO
KOOSTW KOTOWS
KOOTWW KOWTOW
KOPRUW WORKUP
KORSST SKORTS
STORKS
TORSKS
KOSSSU KUSSOS
LLLOOP LOLLOP
LLNORU UNROLL
LLOOPY POLYOL
LLOOTU TOLUOL
LLOOWY WOOLLY
LLOQSU QUOLLS
LLORST STROLL
TROLLS
LLORTY TROLLY
LLOSTY TOLYLS
LLOSWY SLOWLY
LLOSXY XYLOLS
LLOTUY TOLUYL
LLPPUU PULLUP
LLRSTU TRULLS

LLSSTU STULLS
LLSXYY XYLYLS
LMMOUX LUMMOX
LMMPUY PLUMMY
LMMSUY SLUMMY
LMOORU ORMOLU
LMOOSS OSMOLS
LMOSST SMOLTS
LMOSSU SOLUMS
LMOSTU MOULTS
LMOSTY MOSTLY
LMPPSU PLUMPS
LMPRUY RUMPLY
LMPSSU SLUMPS
LMTTUU TUMULT
LNNOSY NONYLS
NYLONS
LNOORS ORLONS
LNOOSS SNOOLS
SOLONS
LNOOST STOLON
LNOPSY PYLONS
LNOPTU PLUTON
LNRUUY UNRULY
LOOOSV OVOLOS
LOOPRS ORLOPS
LOOPRY POORLY
LOOPSS SLOOPS
SPOOLS
LOOSST SOTOLS
STOOLS
LOOSTT LOTTOS
LOOSTV VOLOST
LOOVVX VOLVOX
LOPPRY PROPYL
LOPPSY POLYPS
SLOPPY
LOPRRY PYRROL
LOPRSW PROWLS
LOPRTY PORTLY
PROTYL
LOPSTU POULTS
LOPSUU LUPOUS
LOPTTY PLOTTY
LORSUY SOURLY
LORTTY TROTYL
LOSTYZ ZLOTYS
LPPRUY PURPLY
LPPSUY SUPPLY
LPRSSU SLURPS
LPRSYY SPRYLY
LPSSUY PUSSLY
LRRSUY SLURRY
LRSTUY SULTRY

LRUUXY LUXURY
LSSTUY STYLUS
LSTTUY SLUTTY
MMNOSU SUMMON
MMOOPP POMPOM
MMOOTT MOTMOT
MMRRUU MURMUR
MMUUUU MUUMUU
MNNOUW UNMOWN
MNOOPP POMPON
MNOORS MORONS
MNOORU UNMOOR
MNOOTU MOUTON
MNORSU MOURNS
MNOSTU MOUNTS
MUTONS
MNOTTU MUTTON
MOOPRS PROMOS
MOORRS MORROS
MOORRW MORROW
MOORST MOTORS
MOORSV VROOMS
MOOSSU OSMOUS
MOOSTT MOTTOS
MOOSTY OSTOMY
MOPPRT PROMPT
MOPRST TROMPS
MOPSST STOMPS
MOPSSU POSSUM
MOPSTU UPMOST
MOQRUU QUORUM
MORRSU RUMORS
MORRUU RUMOUR
MORSST STORMS
MORSTU TUMORS
MORSTY STORMY
MORTUU TUMOUR
MOSSTY MYSOST
MOSTTU UTMOST
MPRSTU TRUMPS
MPRSUU RUMPUS
MPSSTU STUMPS
MPSTUU SPUTUM
MPSTUY STUMPY
MRSSTU STRUMS
MSTTUY SMUTTY
NNOOPT PONTON
NNOORY RONYON
NNOOTW WONTON
NNORTU TURNON
UNTORN
NNORUW UNWORN
NNOSUW UNSOWN
NNPSUU UNSPUN

NOOPRS PORNOS
NOOPRT PRONTO
PROTON
NOOPSS SNOOPS
SPOONS
NOOPSY SNOOPY
SPOONY
NOOPUY YOUPON
NOORTU UNROOT
NOOSST SNOOTS
NOOSSW SWOONS
NOOSTY SNOOTY
TOYONS
NOOSWY SWOONY
NOOSYZ SNOOZY
NOPRTU UPTORN
NOPSTU PUNTOS
PUTONS
UNSTOP
NOPSUY YUPONS
NOPTUW UPTOWN
NORSST SNORTS
NORSTW STROWN
NORTUU OUTRUN
RUNOUT
NOSSTU SNOUTS
NOSSUW SWOUNS
NOSTTY SNOTTY
NOSTUY SNOUTY
NPRSSU SPURNS
NPRSUU PRUNUS
NPRTUU TURNUP
UPTURN
NPSSUU SUNUPS
NRSTTU STRUNT
NSSTTU STUNTS
OOPPST POSTOP
OOPRRT TORPOR
OOPRSS PROSOS
SOPORS
SPOORS
OOPRST TROOPS
OOPRSU POROUS
OOPRTU UPROOT
OOPSST STOOPS
OOPSSW SWOOPS
OOPSTT POTTOS
OOPSUY POYOUS
OOPSWY SWOOPY
OOPWWW POWWOW
OORRST ROTORS
OORRSW SORROW
OORSST ROOSTS
TORSOS

OORSTU TOROUS
OORTUW OUTROW
OOSTTY TOOTSY
OPPPRU UPPROP
OPPSSY PSYOPS
OPRSST SPORTS
STROPS
OPRSTU SPROUT
STUPOR
OPRSTY SPORTY
OPRTTU PRUTOT
OPSSSY SYSOPS
OPSSTU SPOUTS
STOUPS
TOSSUP
UPTOSS
OPSSTW STOWPS
OPSTTY SPOTTY
OPTTUU OUTPUT
PUTOUT
ORSSTU ROUSTS
STOURS
TUSSOR
ORSSTW STROWS
WORSTS
ORSSTY STROYS
ORSTTU TROUTS
TUTORS
ORSTUY STOURY
ORSUVW VROUWS
ORTTUY TROUTY
TRYOUT
OSSTTT STOTTS
OSSTTU STOUTS
OSSTXY XYSTOS
PRRSUY SPURRY
PRSSTU SPURTS
PRSSUU USURPS
PRSSUY SYRUPS
PRSUYY SYRUPY
RSSTTU STRUTS
STURTS
TRUSTS
RSSTTY TRYSTS
RSSTUU TUSSUR
RSSTUW WURSTS
RSTTUY TRUSTY
SSTUXY XYSTUS

7-Letter Alphagrams

AAAALTY ATALAYA
AAABBCL CABBALA
AAABBKL KABBALA
AAABCCR BACCARA
AAABCIR ARABICA
AAABCLO BACALAO
AAABCLS CABALAS
AAABCMR CARAMBA
AAABCNS CABANAS
AAABCOR CARABAO
AAABCSS CASABAS
CASSABA
AAABCTW CATAWBA
AAABDFR ABFARAD
AAABDLM LAMBADA
AAABDNN BANDANA
AAABFLL FALBALA
AAABGIL GALABIA
AAABHLQ QABALAH
AAABILX ABAXIAL
AAABIPS PIASABA
AAABISS ABASIAS
AAABKKS KABAKAS
AAABKLS KABALAS
AAABKLV BAKLAVA
AAABKLW BAKLAWA
AAABKPS BAASKAP
AAABKSY KABAYAS
AAABLMT TAMBALA
AAABLPR PALABRA
AAABLQS QABALAS
AAABLST ALBATAS
ATABALS
BALATAS
AAABMOS ABOMASA
AAABMST MASTABA
AAABNNS BANANAS
AAABORR ARAROBA
AAABRSZ BAZAARS
AAACCIS ACACIAS
AAACCLM MALACCA
AAACCLR CARACAL
AAACCRS CASCARA
AAACDIR ARCADIA
AAACDLU ACAUDAL
AAACDMM MACADAM
AAACEHR ARCHAEA
AAACENP PANACEA
AAACHHL HALACHA
AAACHLZ CHALAZA
AAACHNT ACANTHA
AAACINP ACAPNIA
AAACIRS ACRASIA
AAACJMR JACAMAR
AAACJNS JACANAS
AAACLLV CAVALLA
AAACLMN ALMANAC
AAACLMR CALAMAR
AAACLNT CANTALA
AAACLPS ALPACAS
AAACLPT CATALPA
AAACLRZ ALCAZAR
AAACMRS MARACAS
MARASCA
MASCARA
AAACNRV CARAVAN
AAACNST CANASTA
AAACNTT CANTATA
AAACPRX CARAPAX
AAACPST PATACAS
AAACRWY CARAWAY
AAACSST CASSATA
AAACSSV CASAVAS
CASSAVA
AAADELM ALAMEDA
AAADFRY FARADAY
AAADGGH AGGADAH
HAGGADA
AAADGGS AGGADAS
AAADGIL ADAGIAL
AAADHMM HAMMADA
AAADHMS HAMADAS
AAADILX ADAXIAL
AAADIMN DAMIANA
AAADKNW WAKANDA
AAADLMN MANDALA
AAADLMW WADMAAL
AAADMNT ADAMANT
AAADMPP PAPADAM
AAADMRS ARMADAS
MADRASA
RAMADAS
AAADNPS PANADAS
AAADNRS SARDANA
AAAEGLT GALATEA
AAAEGNP APANAGE
AAAEHLT ALTHAEA
AAAEIMN ANAEMIA
AAAELSZ AZALEAS
AAAENST ANATASE
AAAERWY AREAWAY
AAAFFLL ALFALFA
AAAFHRT HAFTARA
AAAFIRT RATAFIA
AAAFRWY FARAWAY
AAAGGLN GALANGA
AAAGHIP APHAGIA
AAAGHNT ATAGHAN
AAAGHPR AGRAPHA
AAAGILN ANALGIA
AAAGINR ANGARIA
AAAGINZ GAZANIA
AAAGIPT PATAGIA
AAAGISS ASSAGAI
AAAGJMU MAJAGUA
AAAGLMM AMALGAM
AAAGLMN MALANGA
AAAGLNS LASAGNA
AAAGLRS ARGALAS
AAAGMMT MAGMATA
AAAGMNR ANAGRAM
AAAGMNS SAGAMAN
AAAGNNS NAGANAS
AAAGNRU GUARANA
AAAGNTY YATAGAN
AAAHHKL HALAKAH
HALAKHA
AAAHHLL HALALAH
AAAHHLV HALAVAH
AAAHINR HARIANA
AAAHIPS APHASIA
AAAHLLS HALALAS
AAAHLSW HAWALAS
AAAHMMT MAHATMA
AAAHMST TAMASHA
AAAIKLT LATAKIA
AAAILMR MALARIA
AAAILPS APLASIA
AAAILRT TALARIA
AAAIMNT AMANITA
AAAINPS PAISANA
AAAIPRX APRAXIA
AAAIPSV PIASAVA
AAAIQRU AQUARIA
AAAISST ASTASIA
AAAISTX ATAXIAS
AAAJMPS PAJAMAS
AAAKKMR MARKKAA
AAAKLMS KAMALAS
AAAKLMY YAMALKA
AAAKLSS ALASKAS
AAALLPT PALATAL
AAALMPT TAMPALA
AAALMRS MARSALA
AAALMSS MASALAS
SALAAMS
AAALNNT LANTANA
AAALPPS PALAPAS
AAALRRY ARRAYAL
AAALWYY LAYAWAY
AAAMNNS MANANAS
AAAMNPS PANAMAS
AAAMNRT MARANTA
AAAMNST ATAMANS
AAAMORT TAMARAO
AAAMPRT PATAMAR
AAAMRRZ ZAMARRA
AAAMRSS ASRAMAS
SAMARAS
SAMSARA
AAAMRST TARAMAS
AAAMRTU TAMARAU
AAANNSV SAVANNA
AAANNSZ ZANANAS
AAANPPY PAPAYAN
AAANRTT TANTARA
TARTANA
AAAPPRT APPARAT
AAAPPSY PAPAYAS
AAARSST SATARAS
AAARSTV AVATARS
AAARTTT RATATAT
AAARTTU TUATARA
AAARTXY ATARAXY
AABBBOS BAOBABS
AABBCEG CABBAGE
AABBCGY CABBAGY
AABBCMO CABOMBA
AABBDGR GABBARD
AABBEGN BEANBAG
AABBEIS BABESIA
AABBERT BARBATE
AABBGRT GABBART
AABBHST SABBATH
AABBLOS BALBOAS
AABBSST SABBATS
AABBSSU BABASSU
AABBSTY BABYSAT
AABCCET BACCATE
AABCDIM DICAMBA
AABCDIR CARABID
AABCELN BALANCE
AABCELP CAPABLE
AABCELT ACTABLE
AABCEMR MACABER
MACABRE
AABCEMS AMBSACE
AABCERT ABREACT
BEARCAT
CABARET
AABCFKT FATBACK
AABCHIR BRACHIA
AABCHNR BARCHAN
AABCHOR ABROACH
AABCHSS CASBAHS
AABCILM CAMBIAL
AABCINR CARABIN
AABCIOP COPAIBA
AABCITX TAXICAB
AABCKPY PAYBACK
AABCKRR BARRACK
AABCKSW BACKSAW
AABCLPY CAPABLY
AABCMMU MACUMBA
AABCMST TAMBACS
AABCMSU SAMBUCA
AABCNRR CARBARN
AABCORR CARBORA
AABCORT ACROBAT
AABCOTT CATBOAT
AABCRSS SCARABS
AABCSUU AUCUBAS
AABDDEL ADDABLE
AABDDER ABRADED
AABDDIN BANDAID
AABDDLN BADLAND
AABDDNS SANDDAB
AABDEFL FADABLE
AABDEGM GAMBADE
AABDEGN BANDAGE
AABDEHS ABASHED
AABDEIS DIABASE
AABDELL BALLADE
AABDELT ABLATED
DATABLE
AABDELW WADABLE
AABDEMM BEMADAM
AABDEMN BEADMAN
AABDEMS SAMBAED
AABDENU BANDEAU
AABDERR ABRADER
AABDERS ABRADES
AABDESU AUBADES
AABDGHN HANDBAG
AABDGMO GAMBADO
AABDGNS SANDBAG
AABDGOS DAGOBAS
AABDHNT HATBAND
AABDHRU BAHADUR
AABDIIS BASIDIA
AABDIKR BIDARKA
AABDIMR BARMAID
AABDINS INDABAS
AABDINT TABANID
AABDLLS BALLADS
AABDLMS LAMBDAS
AABDLRW BRADAWL
AABDMNR ARMBAND
AABDNNO ABANDON
AABDNOR BANDORA
AABDNRS SANDBAR
AABDNSW BANDSAW
AABDORV BRAVADO
AABDORX BROADAX
AABDRRS DARBARS
AABDRRW DRAWBAR
AABDRST BASTARD
TABARDS
AABDRSU SUBADAR
AABDRSY BAYARDS
AABEELT EATABLE
AABEEMN AMEBEAN
AABEEMO AMOEBAE
AABEERZ ZAREEBA
AABEFFL AFFABLE
AABEFGL FLEABAG
AABEGGG BAGGAGE
AABEGGR GARBAGE
AABEGLR ALGEBRA
AABEGMR MEGABAR
AABEGMS AMBAGES
AABEGRR BARRAGE
AABEGSS BAGASSE
SEABAGS
AABEHLT HATABLE
AABEHSS ABASHES
AABEIKN IKEBANA
AABEILM AMIABLE
AABEILN ABELIAN
AABEILS ABELIAS
AABEILT LABIATE
AABEILX ABAXILE
AABEIOR AEROBIA
AABEIRZ ARABIZE
AABEJLL JELLABA
AABEJMU JAMBEAU
AABEKLM MAKABLE
AABEKLT TAKABLE
AABEKPR PARBAKE
AABEKRS ARABESK
AABELLL LABELLA
AABELLN BALNEAL
AABELLO ABOLLAE
AABELLS SALABLE
AABELMN NAMABLE
AABELMT TAMABLE
AABELNO ABALONE
AABELPR PARABLE
AABELPY PAYABLE
AABELRS ARABLES
AABELRT RATABLE
AABELSS BALASES
AABELST ABLATES
AABELSV SAVABLE
AABELSY SAYABLE
AABELTT ABETTAL
AABELTU TABLEAU
AABELTX TAXABLE
AABELWX WAXABLE
AABEMNO AMOEBAN
AABEMNS BASEMAN
AABEMOS AMOEBAS
AABENNW WANNABE
AABENRT ANTBEAR
AABENTY ABEYANT
AABEORT AEROBAT
AABERRW BARWARE
AABERSS ABASERS
AABERST ABATERS
ABREAST
AABERSU SUBAREA
AABERSZ ZAREBAS
AABERTT TABARET
AABETTU BATTEAU
AABETUX BATEAUX
AABFFLY AFFABLY
AABFILU FABLIAU
AABFLRU FABULAR
AABGGRS RAGBAGS
AABGGRY GARBAGY
AABGGSS GASBAGS
AABGHNR BHANGRA
AABGIIL ABIGAIL
AABGILM MAILBAG
AABGIMS GAMBIAS
AABGINR BARGAIN
AABGINS ABASING
BISNAGA
AABGINT ABATING
AABGINZ BIZNAGA
AABGIRS AIRBAGS
AABGMNY MANGABY
AABGOSZ GAZABOS
AABGRST RATBAGS
AABHINT HABITAN
AABHITT HABITAT
AABHKSS KASBAHS
AABHKST BHAKTAS
AABHLRS BHARALS
AABHLTY BATHYAL
AABHMRS BRAHMAS
SAMBHAR
AABHMTT BATHMAT
AABHSSW BASHAWS
AABIILX BIAXIAL
AABIILZ ALBIZIA
AABIKLM KALIMBA
AABIKNS BANKSIA
AABILLN ALBINAL
AABILLR BARILLA
AABILLS LABIALS
AABILMS BAALISM
AABILMY AMIABLY
AABILNS BASINAL
AABILOU ABOULIA
AABILRS BASILAR
AABILSU ABULIAS
AABIMMR MARIMBA
AABIMNO AMBOINA
AABIMOS ABOMASI
AABIMRS AMBARIS
AABIMST BASMATI
AABINNS BANIANS
AABINOU OUABAIN
AABINST ABSTAIN
AABINSZ BANZAIS
AABIORS ABROSIA
AABIORT AIRBOAT
AABIRST BARISTA
AABIRSZ ZARIBAS
AABISSW WASABIS
AABISTT ABATTIS
AABKMST TAMBAKS
AABKNNS KANBANS
AABKNRT TANBARK
AABKOOZ BAZOOKA
AABKRST TASKBAR
AABLLNY BANALLY
AABLLOR ALLOBAR
AABLLST BALLAST
AABLLSY BASALLY
SALABLY
AABLLWY WALLABY
AABLMRS RAMBLAS
AABLMRU LABARUM
AABLMSS BALSAMS
SAMBALS
AABLMST LAMBAST
AABLMSY ABYSMAL
AABLNTT BLATANT
AABLORT ABLATOR
AABLOSV LAVABOS
AABLPRU PABULAR
AABLPYY PAYABLY
AABLRSU SUBALAR
AABLRTU TABULAR
AABLRTY RATABLY
AABLSST BASALTS
AABLSSY ABYSSAL
AABLSTU ABLAUTS
AABLTTU ABUTTAL
AABLTXY TAXABLY
AABMNOT BOATMAN
AABMNOY AMBOYNA
AABMNST BANTAMS
BATSMAN
AABMORU MARABOU
AABMOSY BAYAMOS
AABMRSS SAMBARS
AABMRTU TAMBURA
AABNNOZ BONANZA
AABNNSY BANYANS
AABNOST SABATON
AABNOSY SABAYON
AABORRS ARROBAS
RASBORA
AABORST ABATORS
RABATOS
AABOTTY ATTABOY
AABRRUV BRAVURA
AABRSTY BARYTAS
AABSSSY SASSABY
AABSTTW ABWATTS
AABSTUX SAXTUBA
SUBTAXA
AACCDEI CICADAE
AACCDES CASCADE
SACCADE
AACCDII ACCIDIA
AACCDIR CARDIAC
AACCDIS CICADAS
AACCEFT CATFACE
AACCELO CLOACAE
AACCERS CARCASE
AACCEST SACCATE
AACCHHK CHACHKA
AACCHIM MACCHIA
AACCHIR ARCHAIC
AACCHLN CLACHAN
AACCHMP CHAMPAC
AACCHMS CHACMAS
AACCHNS CANCHAS
AACCHOR CAROACH
AACCILM ACCLAIM
AACCILS ALCAICS
CICALAS
AACCILU ACICULA
AACCIMT ACMATIC
AACCINV VACCINA
AACCIOR CARIOCA
AACCIPT PICCATA
AACCITT ATACTIC
AACCJKR CARJACK
AACCKLP CALPACK
AACCKRR CARRACK
AACCKRS CARACKS
AACCLLO CLOACAL
AACCLLT CATCALL
AACCLOR CARACOL
AACCLOS CLOACAS
AACCLPS CALPACS
AACCLRS CALCARS
AACCLRU ACCRUAL
CARACUL
AACCLSU ACCUSAL
AACCLTW CATCLAW
AACCMOS MACACOS
AACCNNS CANCANS
AACCNVY VACANCY
AACCORU CURACAO
CURACOA
AACCOTT TOCCATA
AACCRSS CARCASS
AACDDEL DECADAL
AACDDER ARCADED
AACDDIN CANDIDA
AACDDRW CRAWDAD
AACDEEM ACADEME
AACDEFS FACADES
AACDEHM CHAMADE
AACDEHR CHARADE
AACDEHT CATHEAD
AACDEII AECIDIA
AACDEIL ALCAIDE
AACDEIR CARDIAE
AACDEIS ACEDIAS
AACDELL ALCALDE
AACDELN CANALED
CANDELA
DECANAL
AACDELP PALACED
AACDELR CALDERA
CRAALED
AACDELS ALCADES
SCALADE
AACDELY ALCAYDE
AACDEMY ACADEMY
AACDENR DRACENA
AACDENV ADVANCE
AACDENZ CADENZA
AACDERS ARCADES
ASCARED
AACDERV CADAVER
AACDERY DAYCARE
AACDETU CAUDATE
AACDETV VACATED
AACDFIR FARADIC
AACDGGI AGGADIC
AACDGHI HAGADIC
AACDHMR DRACHMA
AACDHNR HANDCAR
AACDHRS CHADARS
AACDHST DATCHAS
AACDIIS ASCIDIA
AACDILR RADICAL
AACDINS SCANDIA
AACDINT ANTACID
AACDINV VANADIC
AACDIOR ACAROID
AACDIRS ACARIDS
ASCARID
CARDIAS
AACDJKW JACKDAW
AACDLNO CALANDO
AACDLNS SCANDAL
AACDLOR CARLOAD
AACDLOS SCALADO
AACDLPR PLACARD
AACDMPS MADCAPS
AACDNRS CANARDS
AACDOOV AVOCADO
AACDRSZ CZARDAS
AACEEGR ACREAGE
AACEEHR EARACHE
AACEEHT CHAETAE
AACEEKT TEACAKE
AACEEMR CAMERAE
AACEEMS AMESACE
AACEENT CATENAE
AACEERT ACERATE
AACEESS CASEASE
AACEEST CASEATE
AACEETT ACETATE
AACEFIS FASCIAE
AACEFLT FALCATE
AACEFLU FACULAE
AACEFRR CARFARE
AACEFRS CARAFES
AACEGHN GANACHE
AACEGIP AGAPEIC
AACEGKP PACKAGE
AACEGLS SCALAGE
AACEGNR CARNAGE
AACEGRT CARTAGE
AACEHKS ASHCAKE
AACEHLP ACALEPH
AACEHLT CHAETAL
AACEHNO CHOANAE
AACEHNP PANACHE
AACEHNR ARCHEAN
AACEHPS APACHES
AACEHPU CHAPEAU
AACEHRT TRACHEA
AACEHTT ATTACHE
AACEHTU CHATEAU
AACEILM CAMELIA
AACEIMN ANAEMIC
AACEINR ACARINE
CARINAE
AACEIQU ACEQUIA
AACEIRV AVARICE
CAVIARE
AACEJLS JACALES
AACEKNP PANCAKE
AACEKNS ASKANCE
AACEKOT OATCAKE
AACELLN CANELLA
AACELLT LACTEAL
AACELMN MANACLE
AACELMR CAMERAL
CARAMEL
CERAMAL
AACELMU MACULAE
AACELNP CAPELAN
AACELNS ANLACES
AACELNT LACTEAN
AACELNU CANULAE
LACUNAE
AACELNV VALANCE
AACELOR ACEROLA
AACELOV COAEVAL
AACELPR CARPALE
AACELPS PALACES
AACELPT PLACATE
AACELRS SCALARE
AACELRV CARAVEL
AACELSS CALESAS
AACELST ACETALS
LACTASE
AACELTT LACTATE
AACELTV CLAVATE
AACELTY ACYLATE
AACEMMR MACRAME
AACEMNV CAVEMAN
AACEMOS CAEOMAS
AACEMQU MACAQUE
AACEMRS CAMERAS
AACEMSS CAMASES
AACENPS CANAPES
AACENRT CATERAN
AACENSS CASSENA
AACENST CATENAS
AACENTY CYANATE
AACEOPT PEACOAT
AACEORS ROSACEA
AACEPRV PRECAVA
AACERSS CAESARS
AACERST CARATES
AACERSU CAESURA
AACERTT TEACART
AACERTU ACRUATE
AACERWY RACEWAY
AACESTV CAVEATS
VACATES
AACESTX EXACTAS
AACETTU ACTUATE
AACFILS FACIALS
FASCIAL
AACFILU FAUCIAL
AACFINT FANATIC
AACFISS FASCIAS
AACFLLT CATFALL
AACFLLY FALLACY
AACFLPT FLATCAP
AACFLRT FLATCAR
FRACTAL
AACFLRU FACULAR
AACFLSU FAUCALS

AACFLTU FACTUAL
AACFNST CAFTANS
AACGILL GALLICA
GLACIAL
AACGILM MAGICAL
AACGINT AGNATIC
AACGIRS AGARICS
AACGIRV AGRAVIC
AACGISU GUAIACS
AACGJNT CATJANG
AACGLOT CATALOG
AACGLOU COAGULA
AACGLSY GALYACS
AACGNOU GUANACO
AACHHKR CHARKHA
AACHHLL CHALLAH
AACHHLS CHALAHS
AACHIKL HALAKIC
AACHIKN KACHINA
AACHILO ACHOLIA
AACHILR ACHIRAL
RACHIAL
AACHILT CALATHI
AACHIMS CHAMISA
CHIASMA
AACHINT ACANTHI
AACHIPR CHARPAI
HAIRCAP
AACHIPS APHASIC
AACHIPT CHAPATI
AACHIRT CITHARA
AACHKMN HACKMAN
AACHKMP CHAMPAK
AACHKRS CHAKRAS
CHARKAS
AACHKRT HATRACK
AACHKRY HAYRACK
AACHKSW HACKSAW
KWACHAS
AACHLLS CHALLAS
AACHLMS CHASMAL
AACHLNT CANTHAL
AACHLPS PASCHAL
AACHLPU CHALUPA
AACHMNP CHAPMAN
AACHMSY YASHMAC
AACHNOP PANOCHA
AACHNPX PANCHAX
AACHNRS ANARCHS
AACHNRY ANARCHY
AACHNSS ASHCANS
AACHNSU ANCHUSA
AACHNSZ CHAZANS
AACHNZZ CHAZZAN
AACHRRT CATARRH
AACHRSW CARWASH
AACHRTU AUTARCH
AACHRWY ARCHWAY
AACHSSW CASHAWS
AACIIMS CAMISIA
AACIINT ACTINIA
AACIITV AVIATIC
VIATICA
AACIJLP JALAPIC
AACIJMS JICAMAS
AACIKLL ALKALIC
AACIKLR CLARKIA
AACIKNN CANAKIN
AACIKNT KATCINA
AACILLN ANCILLA
AACILMS CAMAILS
AACILNP CALPAIN
AACILNR CARINAL
CRANIAL
AACILNT ACTINAL
AACILOS ASOCIAL
AACILOX COAXIAL
AACILPS APICALS
SPACIAL
AACILPT CAPITAL
AACILRR RAILCAR
AACILTT CATTAIL
AACILTV VATICAL
AACIMNO MANIOCA
AACIMNS CAIMANS
MANIACS
AACIMNY ANIMACY
AACIMOR ACROMIA
AACIMSS CAMISAS
AACIMTY CYMATIA
AACINNT CANTINA
AACINOR OCARINA
AACINPT CAPTAIN
AACINRS ACRASIN
ARNICAS
CARINAS
SARCINA
AACINRT ANTICAR
AACINRZ CZARINA
AACINSS CASSINA
AACINST SATANIC
AACIOPT TAPIOCA
AACIPPR PAPRICA
AACIPRS PICARAS
AACIPRX APRAXIC
AACIQTU AQUATIC
AACIRSS ASCARIS
AACIRST CARITAS
AACIRSV CAVIARS
AACISSS CASSIAS
AACISST CASITAS
AACISTT ASTATIC
AACISTX ATAXICS
AACJKLS JACKALS
AACJKSS JACKASS
AACJOSU ACAJOUS
AACJPTU CAJAPUT
AACKLPS KALPACS
AACKLTW CATWALK
AACKMNP MANPACK
PACKMAN
AACKMRT AMTRACK
AACKNRS RANSACK
AACKPWX PACKWAX
AACKRRS ARRACKS
AACKSTT ATTACKS
AACLLNS CALLANS
AACLLNT CALLANT
AACLLNU LACUNAL
AACLLSU CLAUSAL
AACLLVY CAVALLY
AACLMNT CLAMANT
AACLMRU MACULAR
AACLMST LACTAMS
AACLMSU CALAMUS
MACULAS
AACLNNO ANCONAL
AACLNNU CANNULA
AACLNOS CANOLAS
AACLNPY CLAYPAN
AACLNRU CANULAR
LACUNAR
AACLNST CANTALS
AACLNSU CANULAS
LACUNAS
AACLOPR CAPORAL
CRAPOLA
AACLOST CATALOS
COASTAL
AACLOTT CATTALO
AACLOTV OCTAVAL
AACLPRS CARPALS
AACLPRT CALTRAP
AACLPSS PASCALS
AACLPSU SCAPULA
AACLPTY PLAYACT
AACLRSS LASCARS
RASCALS
SACRALS
SCALARS
AACLRTY LACTARY
AACLRVY CALVARY
CAVALRY
AACLSSU CASUALS
CAUSALS
AACLSUV VASCULA
AACLTTU TACTUAL
AACMMOT COMMATA
AACMNOR NARCOMA
AACMNRU ARCANUM
AACMNSY CAYMANS
AACMORR CAMORRA
AACMORS SARCOMA
AACMORT MARCATO
AACMRRT TRAMCAR
AACMRSS SARCASM
AACMRST AMTRACS
TARMACS
AACNNOZ CANZONA
AACNOST SACATON
AACNOTZ ZACATON
AACNPRT CANTRAP
AACNPST CAPSTAN
CAPTANS
CATNAPS
AACNSSV CANVASS
AACOPPR APOCARP
AACORST OSTRACA
AACPSTW CATSPAW
AACRRSU CURARAS
AACRSTV CRAVATS
AACRTTT ATTRACT
AACRTUY ACTUARY
AACTUWY CUTAWAY
AADDDEN ADDENDA
AADDEGM DAMAGED
AADDEIL ALIDADE
AADDEMN DEADMAN
AADDENP DEADPAN
AADDEOR DEODARA
AADDEPR PARADED
AADDEPT ADAPTED
AADDERW AWARDED
AADDESX ADDAXES
AADDGNR GRANDAD
AADDHKR KHADDAR
AADDHRS SRADDHA
AADDILS ALIDADS
AADDIMS DADAISM
AADDIST DADAIST
AADDMRY DRAMADY
AADDOSU AOUDADS
AADDRST DASTARD
AADEEFR AFEARED
AADEELT DEALATE
AADEEMT EDEMATA
AADEENR ANEARED
AADEERT AERATED
AADEERW AWARDEE
AADEFHT FATHEAD
AADEFNZ FAZENDA
AADEGGR AGGRADE
GARAGED
AADEGLS GELADAS
AADEGMN MANAGED
AADEGMR DAMAGER
AADEGMS DAMAGES
AADEGNS AGENDAS
AADEGRT GRADATE
AADEGRV RAVAGED
AADEGRY DRAYAGE
YARDAGE
AADEGSV SAVAGED
AADEHIR AIRHEAD
AADEHJR JARHEAD
AADEHMN HEADMAN
AADEHMS ASHAMED
AADEHPS SAPHEAD
AADEHRW WARHEAD
AADEHWY HEADWAY
AADEILR RADIALE
AADEILV AVAILED
VEDALIA
AADEIMR MADEIRA
AADEIMS AMIDASE
AADEINR ARANEID
AADEINS NAIADES
AADEINZ ZENAIDA
AADEIRT AIRDATE
RADIATE
TIARAED
AADEITV AVIATED
AADEITW AWAITED
AADEJMR JEMADAR
AADEKKY KAYAKED
AADEKLR KRAALED
AADEKMS MEDAKAS
AADEKPR PARKADE
AADELLY ALLAYED
AADELMN LEADMAN
AADELMO ALAMODE
AADELMR ALARMED
AADELNR ADRENAL
AADELNT LANATED
AADELNX ADNEXAL
AADELRT LATERAD
AADELRU RADULAE
AADELRY ALREADY
AADELTU ADULATE
AADEMMN MANMADE
AADEMMS MADAMES
AADEMNO ADENOMA
AADEMNS ANADEMS
MAENADS
AADEMNT MANDATE
AADEMRY DAYMARE
AADEMSS AMASSED
AADENNT ANDANTE
AADENRV VERANDA
AADENST ANSATED
AADENSU SAUNAED
AADENSW WEASAND
AADENWZ WEAZAND
AADEPRR PARADER
AADEPRS PARADES
AADEPRT ADAPTER
READAPT
AADEPSS PASSADE
AADERRS ARRASED
AADERRW AWARDER
AADERRY ARRAYED
AADERSW SEAWARD
AADERSY DARESAY
AADERTU AURATED
AADESSY ASSAYED
AADGGHR HAGGARD
AADGGLR LAGGARD
AADGGOT AGGADOT
AADGGRS SAGGARD
AADGIIR GIARDIA
AADGIMM DIGAMMA
AADGIMR DIAGRAM
AADGIMS AGAMIDS
AADGIOS ADAGIOS
AADGIOT AGATOID
AADGIRV GRAVIDA
AADGLLW GADWALL
AADGLNO GONADAL
AADGLNR GARLAND
AADGLRU GRADUAL
AADGMNR GRANDAM
GRANDMA
AADGMOT DOGMATA
AADGMRS SMARAGD
AADGNPR GRANDPA
AADGNPS PADNAGS
AADGNRT GARDANT
AADGOPR PODAGRA
AADGOPS PAGODAS
AADGRSY GAYDARS
AADHHPS PADSHAH
AADHHRT HARDHAT
AADHILS DAHLIAS
AADHIMR HADARIM
AADHIMS SAMADHI
AADHINP DAPHNIA
AADHLRY HALYARD
AADHMRS DHARMAS
AADHNPR HARDPAN
AADHNRS DARSHAN
DHARNAS
AADHNSW HANDSAW
AADHPRS PARDAHS
AADHRSS SRADHAS
AADHRSZ HAZARDS
AADHRWY HAYWARD
AADHSWY WASHDAY
AADILLO ALLODIA
ALODIAL
AADILMR ADMIRAL
AADILMT MATILDA
AADILNP PALADIN
AADILNR LANIARD
NADIRAL
AADILPS APSIDAL
AADILRS RADIALS
AADILSS DALASIS
AADILTV DATIVAL
AADILWY WAYLAID
AADIMOR DIORAMA
AADIMRS ARAMIDS
AADINNN NANDINA
AADINNP PANDANI
AADINPT PINTADA
AADINRS RADIANS
AADINRT RADIANT
AADINSV NAVAIDS
AADINSY NAYSAID
AADIPTX TAXPAID
AADIRRW AIRWARD
AADIRSU SUDARIA
AADISST STADIAS
AADKMSS DAMASKS
AADKNRT TANKARD
AADKPSU PADAUKS
AADKRWW AWKWARD
AADLLLN LALLAND
AADLLMR MALLARD
AADLLPU PALUDAL
AADLMNN LANDMAN
AADLMNO MANDOLA
MONADAL
AADLMNU LADANUM
AADLMOR ARMLOAD
AADLMPS LAMPADS
AADLMSW WADMALS
AADLNOP DALAPON
AADLNOV VANLOAD
AADLNOZ DANAZOL
AADLNRY LANYARD
AADLNSS SANDALS
AADLNSU LANDAUS
AADLNSV VANDALS
AADLOPY PAYLOAD
AADLPPU APPLAUD
AADLPYY PLAYDAY
AADLRRU RADULAR
AADLRSU RADULAS
AADMMRS DAMMARS
AADMNNO MADONNA
AADMNNS SANDMAN
AADMNOR MADRONA
MONARDA
AADMNOW ADWOMAN
AADMNRS MANSARD
AADMNRW MANWARD
AADMNRY DRAYMAN
YARDMAN
AADMNSY DAYSMAN
AADMNTU TAMANDU
AADMOPP PAPADOM
AADMORT MATADOR
AADMOSU AMADOUS
AADMPPU PAPADUM
AADMRRY YARDARM
AADMRSU MARAUDS
AADMRSZ MAZARDS
AADMRZZ MAZZARD
AADMSYY MAYDAYS
AADNNRS RANDANS
AADNOPR PANDORA
AADNPRU PANDURA
AADNRTY TANYARD
AADNRVW VANWARD
AADOPRR PARADOR
AADOPRS PARADOS
AADOPRT ADAPTOR
AADOPRX PARADOX
AADOPSS PASSADO
POSADAS
AADORWY ROADWAY
AADOSTT TOSTADA
AADOWWX WOADWAX
AADPSYY PAYDAYS
AADQRTU QUADRAT
AADRRSS SARDARS
AADRSTU DATURAS
AADRSTY DAYSTAR
AADRSVW VAWARDS
AADRWWY WAYWARD
AAEEFGL LEAFAGE
AAEEFRT RATAFEE
AAEEGKL LEAKAGE
AAEEGLT GALEATE
AAEEGMT AGAMETE
AGEMATE
AAEEGRV AVERAGE
AAEEHRT HETAERA
AAEEINT TAENIAE
AAEEKRW REAWAKE
AAEELMT MALEATE
AAEELOR AREOLAE
AAEELPT PALEATE
AAEEMNT EMANATE
ENEMATA
MANATEE
AAEEMRT AMREETA
AAEEPPS APPEASE
AAEERST AERATES
AAEERSW SEAWARE
AAEERTU AUREATE
AAEERTW TEAWARE
AAEFFGR AGRAFFE
AAEFFIR AFFAIRE
AAEFFLL FALAFEL
AAEFFNR FANFARE
AAEFFTT TAFFETA
AAEFGNS FANEGAS
AAEFGRS AGRAFES
AAEFGTW WAFTAGE
AAEFIRR AIRFARE
AAEFLLV FAVELLA
AAEFLPR EARFLAP
AAEFLSV FAVELAS
AAEFMRT FERMATA
AAEFRRW WARFARE
AAEGGNO ANAGOGE
AAEGGOP APAGOGE
AAEGGRS GARAGES
AAEGGSV GAVAGES
AAEGHLU HAULAGE
AAEGHLY HAYLAGE
AAEGHNT THANAGE
AAEGILR REGALIA
AAEGINR ANERGIA
AAEGINV VAGINAE
AAEGISS ASSEGAI
AAEGITT AGITATE
AAEGITZ AGATIZE
AAEGKNT TANKAGE
AAEGKOS SOAKAGE
AAEGLLT GALLATE
GALLETA
TALLAGE
AAEGLMN GAMELAN
AAEGLMT GAMETAL
AAEGLNN ANLAGEN
AAEGLNS ANLAGES
GALENAS
LASAGNE
AAEGLOP APOGEAL
AAEGLRR REALGAR
AAEGLRS ALEGARS
LAAGERS
AAEGLSV LAVAGES
SALVAGE
AAEGLSX GALAXES
AAEGMNR MANAGER
AAEGMNS MANAGES
SAGAMEN
AAEGMNT GATEMAN
MAGENTA
MAGNATE
NAMETAG
AAEGMPR RAMPAGE
AAEGMRT REGMATA
AAEGMSS MASSAGE
AAEGMTT METATAG
AAEGNNT TANNAGE
AAEGNOP APOGEAN
AAEGNPT PAGEANT
AAEGNPW PAWNAGE
AAEGNRR ARRANGE
AAEGNRT TANAGER
AAEGNST AGNATES
AAEGNSU GUANASE
AAEGNTV VANTAGE
AAEGNTW WANTAGE
AAEGORS AGAROSE
AAEGPRR PARERGA
AAEGPRW WARPAGE
AAEGPSS PASSAGE
AAEGQUY QUAYAGE
AAEGRRV RAVAGER
AAEGRST GASTREA
TEARGAS
AAEGRSV RAVAGES
SAVAGER
AAEGRTT REGATTA
AAEGSSU ASSUAGE
SAUSAGE
AAEGSSV AVGASES
SAVAGES
AAEGSSW ASSWAGE
AAEGSTU GATEAUS
AAEGSTW WASTAGE
AAEGTTW WATTAGE
AAEGTUX GATEAUX
AAEGTWY GATEWAY
GETAWAY
AAEHHPR RHAPHAE
AAEHHPT APHTHAE
AAEHILP APHELIA
AAEHIRT HETAIRA
AAEHKNT KHANATE
AAEHKPS PAKEHAS
AAEHKST TAKAHES
AAEHLLL ALLHEAL
AAEHLMT HEMATAL
AAEHLPS PHASEAL
AAEHLPX HEXAPLA
AAEHLRT TREHALA
AAEHLST ALTHEAS
AAEHMST HAMATES
AAEHNPR HANAPER
AAEHNPS SAPHENA
AAEHNSY HYAENAS
AAEHPSX HAPAXES
AAEHRSY HEARSAY
AAEHSTT HASTATE
AAEILLX AXILLAE
AAEILMN LAMINAE
AAEILMS MALAISE
AAEILNN ALANINE
AAEILNO AEOLIAN
AAEILRS AERIALS
AAEILRV REAVAIL
VELARIA
AAEILSS ALIASES
AAEILSX ALEXIAS
AAEIMMT IMAMATE
AAEIMNS AMNESIA
ANEMIAS
AAEIMNT AMENTIA
ANIMATE
AAEIMPY PYAEMIA
AAEIMRT AMIRATE
AAEIMRU URAEMIA
AAEIMTV AMATIVE
AAEINNO AEONIAN
AAEINPS PAESANI
AAEINPT PATINAE
AAEINST ENTASIA
TAENIAS
AAEIPRR PAREIRA
AAEIPRS SPIRAEA
AAEIPRT APTERIA
AAEIPTT APATITE
AAEIRST ARISTAE
ASTERIA
ATRESIA
AAEIRTT ARIETTA
AAEIRTV VARIATE
AAEIRTW AWAITER
AAEIRVW AIRWAVE
AAEISTT SATIATE
AAEISTV AVIATES
AAEISTX ATAXIES
AAEJOPR APAREJO
AAEKKOR KARAOKE
AAEKKRY KAYAKER
AAEKLNS ALKANES
AAEKLNT ALKANET
AAEKMRR EARMARK
AAEKMRS SEAMARK
AAEKMSW WAKAMES
AAEKNNS ANANKES
AAEKNSW AWAKENS
AAEKNUW UNAWAKE
AAEKPRT PARTAKE
AAEKRST KARATES
AAELLLM LAMELLA
AAELLNV AVELLAN
AAELLPS PAELLAS
AAELLPT PATELLA
AAELLRT LATERAL
AAELLRY ALLAYER
AREALLY
AAELLSW SEAWALL
AAELLTV VALLATE
AAELMMR ALMEMAR
AAELMMT LEMMATA
AAELMNU ALUMNAE
AAELMOT OATMEAL
AAELMPT PALMATE
AAELMST MALATES
MALTASE
TAMALES
AAELMSY AMYLASE
AAELNNS ANNEALS
AAELNOP APNOEAL
AAELNPR PREANAL
AAELNPT PLANATE
PLATANE
AAELNRS ARSENAL
AAELNSS ANLASES
AAELNST SEALANT
AAELNSY ANALYSE
AAELNTT TETANAL
AAELNTY ANALYTE
AAELNWY LANEWAY
AAELNYZ ANALYZE
AAELORR AREOLAR
AAELORS AREOLAS
AAELORU AUREOLA
AAELOTX OXALATE
AAELPPR APPAREL
AAELPPS APPEALS
AAELPPT PALPATE
AAELPPU PAPULAE
AAELPRS EARLAPS
AAELPRT APTERAL
AAELPRV PALAVER
AAELPST PALATES
AAELPTT TAPETAL
AAELPTU PLATEAU
AAELPTY APETALY
AAELRTZ LAZARET
AAELSST ATLASES
AAELSUX ASEXUAL
AAELTUV VALUATE
AAELTVV VALVATE
AAEMMMR MAREMMA
AAEMMMT MAMMATE
AAEMMNT MEATMAN
AAEMNNT EMANANT
AAEMNOR AMARONE
AAEMNPP PAMPEAN
AAEMNRT RAMENTA

AAEMNTU MANTEAU
AAEMOTY ATEMOYA
AAEMOTZ METAZOA
AAEMQSU SQUAMAE
AAEMRSS AMASSER
AAEMRTU AMATEUR
AAEMSSS AMASSES
AAENNNT ANTENNA
AAENNST ANNATES
AAENNSZ ZENANAS
AAENNTT TANNATE
AAENOPS APNOEAS
PAESANO
AAENPSS PAESANS
AAENPST ANAPEST
PEASANT
AAENPSV PAVANES
AAENRRT NARRATE
AAENRST SANTERA
AAENRTV TAVERNA
AAENRUW UNAWARE
AAENSSU NAUSEAS
AAENSSW SEAWANS
AAENSTW SEAWANT
AAEOPTZ ZAPATEO
AAEORRT AERATOR
AAEORRU AURORAE
AAEORST AEROSAT
AAEPPRS APPEARS
AAEPPRT PARAPET
AAEPRSS SARAPES
AAEPRSY APYRASE
AAEPSTW WATAPES
AAEPTTW WATTAPE
AAERRRS ARREARS
AAERRRY ARRAYER
AAERRSS ARRASES
AAERRST ERRATAS
AAERRTT TARTARE
AAERSSY ASSAYER
AAERTTU TUATERA
AAESSTV SAVATES
AAESSWY SEAWAYS
AAFFILN AFFINAL
AAFFILX AFFIXAL
AAFFIMS MAFFIAS
AAFFINT AFFIANT
AAFFIRS AFFAIRS
RAFFIAS
AAFFIST TAFFIAS
AAFFLRS FARFALS
AAFFRSY AFFRAYS
AAFFRSZ ZAFFARS
AAFGHIN AFGHANI
AAFGHNS AFGHANS
AAFGLMN FLAGMAN
AAFGORR FARRAGO
AAFHIKL KHALIFA
AAFHINR FARINHA
AAFHLLS ASHFALL
AAFHLWY HALFWAY
AAFIILR FILARIA
AAFIJST FAJITAS
AAFIKLS ALFAKIS
AAFIKSS SIFAKAS
AAFILNT FANTAIL
TAILFAN
AAFILQU ALFAQUI
AAFINNT INFANTA
AAFINNU INFAUNA
AAFINRS FARINAS
AAFINTT ANTIFAT
AAFIPRT PARFAIT
AAFIRSS SAFARIS
AAFIRSU FUSARIA
AAFIRUY RUFIYAA
AAFIRWY FAIRWAY
AAFJLOR ALFORJA
AAFKNST KAFTANS
AAFLLLS FALLALS
AAFLLTY FATALLY
AAFLSTU FLAUTAS
AAFLWYY FLYAWAY
AAFMNST FANTASM
AAFNSTT FANTAST
AAFNSTY FANTASY
AAFOSST AFTOSAS
AAGGHNT HANGTAG
AAGGILN GANGLIA
AAGGJRY JAGGARY
AAGGKSU GAGAKUS
AAGGLMO MAGALOG
AAGGLOS GALAGOS
AAGGLRY GRAYLAG
AAGGNOY ANAGOGY
AAGGNST GANGSTA
AAGGNTT TAGGANT
AAGGNWY GANGWAY
AAGGQSU QUAGGAS
AAGGRSS SAGGARS
AAGGRST RAGTAGS
TAGRAGS
AAGHHRR AARRGHH
AAGHILR GHARIAL
AAGHINN ANHINGA
AAGHJNS GANJAHS
AAGHLNT GNATHAL
AAGHMNN HANGMAN
AAGHMNU MAHUANG
AAGHMRS GRAHAMS
AAGHNRS HANGARS
AAGHQUU QUAHAUG
AAGHRSW WASHRAG
AAGIINT IGNATIA
AAGIKNW AWAKING
AAGILMY MYALGIA
AAGILNN ANGINAL
AAGILNO LOGANIA
AAGILNP PAGINAL
AAGILNS AGNAILS
AAGILNV VAGINAL
AAGILOS LAOGAIS
AAGILOT OTALGIA
AAGILRS ARGALIS
AAGILSV GAVIALS
AAGILTW WAGTAIL
AAGIMNO ANGIOMA
AAGIMNS MAGIANS
SIAMANG
AAGIMNZ AMAZING
AAGINNS ANGINAS
AAGINNW WANIGAN
AAGINOS AGNOSIA
AAGINRR ARRAIGN
AAGINRS SANGRIA
AAGINRT GRANITA
AAGINRU GUARANI
AAGINRZ ZINGARA
AAGINST AGAINST
ANTISAG
AAGINSU IGUANAS
AAGINSV VAGINAS
AAGINSY GAINSAY
AAGINTY ANTIGAY
AAGIOTT AGITATO
AAGIPRU PIRAGUA
AAGJRSU JAGUARS
AAGKKNO ANGAKOK
AAGKLSY GALYAKS
AAGLLNT GALLANT
AAGLLVY VAGALLY
AAGLNOR GRANOLA
AAGLNOS ANALOGS
AAGLNOY ANALOGY
AAGLNRS RAGLANS
AAGLNRU ANGULAR
AAGLNSU LAGUNAS
AAGLORU ARUGOLA
AAGLRST GASTRAL
AAGLRUU ARUGULA
AUGURAL
AAGLRVX GRAVLAX
AAGLSST STALAGS
AAGMMRR GRAMMAR
AAGMMRS GRAMMAS
AAGMMTU GUMMATA
AAGMNPR PANGRAM
AAGMNRT TANGRAM
TRANGAM
AAGMNSW SWAGMAN
AAGMOPY APOGAMY
AAGMOSU AGAMOUS
AAGMPRS GRAMPAS
AAGMRRY GRAMARY
AAGMRSY MARGAYS
AAGNNOS GOANNAS
AAGNNSW WANGANS
AAGNOPR PARAGON
AAGNORS ANGORAS
AAGNORZ ORGANZA
AAGNPRS PARANGS
AAGNRRY GRANARY
AAGNRSS SANGARS
AAGNRTV VAGRANT
AAGNSST SATANGS
AAGNSUY GUANAYS
AAGOPSS SAPSAGO
AAGORSU SAGUARO
AAGPPRS GRAPPAS
AAGTTUU TAUTAUG
AAHHIRS SHARIAH
AAHHLLS HALLAHS
AAHHLSV HALVAHS
AAHHMSZ HAMZAHS
AAHHNPT NAPHTHA
AAHHOPR PHARAOH
AAHIIMT HIMATIA
AAHIJNR HARIJAN
AAHIKRT KITHARA
AAHILMT THALAMI
AAHILPV PAHLAVI
AAHILSW SAHIWAL
AAHILSY ALIYAHS
AAHIMNO MAHONIA
AAHIMNZ HAZANIM
AAHIMSS AHIMSAS
AAHINOP APHONIA
AAHINPP PAPHIAN
AAHINPR PIRANHA
AAHINST SHAITAN
AAHIPRS PARIAHS
RAPHIAS
AAHIPTZ ZAPTIAH
AAHIRSS HARISSA
SHARIAS
AAHIRTV HAVARTI
AAHJRRS JARRAHS
AAHKLRS LASHKAR
AAHKMSY YASHMAK
AAHKNSU KAHUNAS
AAHLLOS HALLOAS
AAHLLSW WALLAHS
AAHLLWY HALLWAY
AAHLMMS HAMMALS
AAHLMRS MARSHAL
AAHLMRU HAMULAR
AAHLMST MALTHAS
AAHLMSU HAMAULS
AAHLNPX PHALANX
AAHLNRW NARWHAL
AAHLPRS PHRASAL
AAHLPST ASPHALT
SPATHAL
AAHLRSS ASHLARS
AAHLRST HARTALS
AAHMMMS HAMMAMS
AAHMMSS SHAMMAS
AAHMNNU HANUMAN
AAHMNSS SHAMANS
AAHMOPR AMPHORA
AAHMQSU QUAMASH
AAHMRSS ASHRAMS
AAHMSST ASTHMAS
MATSAHS
AAHMSTZ HAZMATS
MATZAHS
AAHNNOS HOSANNA
AAHNNTX XANTHAN
AAHNOPR ANAPHOR
AAHNRTX ANTHRAX
AAHNRTY RHATANY
AAHNSZZ HAZZANS
AAHORSU SAHUARO
AAHPPRS PARAPHS
AAHPRTW WARPATH
AAHPTWY PATHWAY
AAHRSTY ASHTRAY
AAHRTTW ATHWART
AAHSSSY SASHAYS
AAIIKSZ ZAIKAIS
AAIILMR AIRMAIL
AAIILPT TILAPIA
AAIINRT ANTIAIR
AAIINTT TITANIA
AAIIRVV VIVARIA
AAIJLNP JALAPIN
AAIJMNT ANTIJAM
AAIJNRS JARINAS
AAIKLLN ALKALIN
AAIKLLS ALKALIS
AAIKLMS KALMIAS
AAIKLNS KALIANS
AAIKLPR PALIKAR
AAIKMNN MANAKIN
AAIKNRS KINARAS
AAIKPPR PAPRIKA
AAIKPRR AIRPARK
AAIKRSU UAKARIS
AAIKTVV AKVAVIT
AAILLLP PALLIAL
AAILLLT LATILLA
AAILLMN LAMINAL
MANILLA
AAILLMR ARMILLA
AAILLMX MAXILLA
AAILLNT LANITAL
AAILLNV VANILLA
AAILLPP PAPILLA
AAILLRX AXILLAR
AAILLSX AXILLAS
AAILLUV ALLUVIA
AAILLXY AXIALLY
AAILMMN MAILMAN
AAILMMS MIASMAL
AAILMMX MAXIMAL
AAILMNR LAMINAR
AAILMNS ANIMALS
LAMINAS
MANILAS
AAILMNT MATINAL
AAILMNU ALUMINA
AAILMPS IMPALAS
AAILMQU MAQUILA
AAILMRT MARITAL
MARTIAL
AAILMSS SALAMIS
AAILNNS ALANINS
AAILNOT ALATION
AAILNOV VALONIA
AAILNPS SALPIAN
AAILNPT PLATINA
AAILNRY LANIARY
AAILNSS SALINAS
AAILNST LATINAS
AAILNTV VALIANT
AAILNTY ANALITY
AAILORS SOLARIA
AAILORV OVARIAL
VARIOLA
AAILORZ ZOARIAL
AAILOST SOLATIA
AAILPRT PARTIAL
AAILPRY AIRPLAY
AAILPST SPATIAL
AAILPZZ PALAZZI
AAILRRV ARRIVAL
AAILRST LARIATS
LATRIAS
AAILRTT RATTAIL
AAILRTV TRAVAIL
AAILRWY RAILWAY
AAILSSS ASSAILS
AAILSSV SALIVAS
SALVIAS
AAILSSW WASSAIL
AAIMMMT MAMMATI
AAIMMNO AMMONIA
AAIMMSS MIASMAS
AAIMNNT ANTIMAN
AAIMNOS ANOSMIA
AAIMNOT ANIMATO
AAIMNPT TIMPANA
AAIMNRS MARINAS
AAIMNRT MARTIAN
TAMARIN
AAIMNST STAMINA
AAIMNTX TAXIMAN
AAIMRST AMRITAS
TAMARIS
AAIMRSU SAMURAI
AAIMRTU TIMARAU
AAIMSST STASIMA
AAIMSSU AMUSIAS
AAIMSTT TATAMIS
AAIMSTV ATAVISM
AAINNRV NIRVANA
AAINOPS ANOPIAS
ANOPSIA
PAISANO
AAINORV OVARIAN
AAINOST ATONIAS
AAINOSX ANOXIAS
AAINPPS PAPAINS
AAINPRS PARIANS
PIRANAS
AAINPSS PAISANS
AAINPST PASTINA
PATINAS
PINATAS
TAIPANS
AAINRST ANTIARS
ARTISAN
TSARINA
AAINRSU ANURIAS
SAURIAN
URANIAS
AAINRSV SAVARIN
AAINRTV VARIANT
AAINRTW ANTIWAR
AAINRTZ TZARINA
AAINSTT ATTAINS
AAINTTT ATTAINT
AAINTTX ANTITAX
AAIOPRS APORIAS
AAIOPRV OVIPARA
AAIORRS ROSARIA
AAIORTV AVIATOR
AAIPPRU PUPARIA
AAIPPTT PITAPAT
AAIPRSY PIRAYAS
AAIPRTT PARTITA
AAIPSTY PITAYAS
AAIPSZZ PIAZZAS
AAIQSSU QUASSIA
AAIQTUV AQUAVIT
AAIRSST ARISTAS
TARSIAS
AAIRSTT STRIATA
AAIRSWY AIRWAYS
AAISTTV ATAVIST
AAISTUY YAUTIAS
AAITWXY TAXIWAY
AAJKLWY JAYWALK
AAJKNSS SANJAKS
AAJMNZZ JAZZMAN
AAJMORR MOJARRA
AAJMPSY PYJAMAS
AAJNOSW AJOWANS
AAJNPRS PRAJNAS
AAJOPSU SAPAJOU
AAKKLPS KALPAKS
AAKKLRU KARAKUL
AAKKMOT TOKAMAK
AAKKMRS MARKKAS
AAKKOPS KAKAPOS
AAKLMRY MALARKY
AAKLMUY YAMULKA
AAKLOOP PALOOKA
AAKLOOT TALOOKA
AAKLSTU TALUKAS
AAKLWWY WALKWAY
AAKMOSU MOUSAKA
AAKMRUZ MAZURKA
AAKMSSY YASMAKS
AAKNNTU NUNATAK
AAKNORS ANORAKS
AAKNRST KANTARS
AAKNSWZ KWANZAS
AAKOPRS PAKORAS
AAKORST OSTRAKA
AAKPRWY PARKWAY
AAKRSTU KATSURA
AAKRTUY AUTARKY
AALLLNS LALLANS
AALLMPU AMPULLA
AALLNOX ALLOXAN
AALLNPU PLANULA
AALLNSY ALANYLS
NASALLY
AALLNVY NAVALLY
AALLPPS APPALLS
AALLPPY PAPALLY
AALLRUY AURALLY
AALLSTT ATLATLS
AALLUVV VALVULA
AALMMMS MAMMALS
AALMMNO AMMONAL
AALMMNS ALMSMAN
AALMNOY ANOMALY
AALMNPS NAPALMS
AALMNSU MANUALS
AALMORY MAYORAL
AALMOST AMATOLS
AALMPRY PALMARY
PALMYRA
AALMPSS PLASMAS
AALMRSU ALARUMS
AALNNRU ANNULAR
AALNNSU ANNUALS
AALNPRT PLANTAR
AALNPRU LUPANAR
AALNPST PLATANS
SALTPAN
AALNQTU QUANTAL
AALNRRU RANULAR
AALNRSU RANULAS
AALNRSW NARWALS
AALNRTU NATURAL
AALNSTT SALTANT
AALNSTU SULTANA
AALNSTY ANALYST
AALOPRS PARASOL
AALOPST TAPALOS
AALOPSY PAYOLAS
AALOPVV PAVLOVA
AALOPZZ PALAZZO
AALORRU AURORAL
AALORST ALASTOR
AALORSU AROUSAL
AALOSVW AVOWALS
AALPPRU PAPULAR
AALPPRY PAPYRAL
AALPRRS PARRALS
AALPRSY PARLAYS
AALPSTU SPATULA
AALRSST ASTRALS
TARSALS
AALRSTT STRATAL
AALRSTU AUSTRAL
AALRSTY ASTYLAR
AALSSSV VASSALS
AALSSTU ASSAULT
AALSTUV VALUTAS
AALSWYY WAYLAYS
AAMMMRY MAMMARY
AAMMNRT MANTRAM
AAMMOTY MYOMATA
AAMMRRS MARRAMS
AAMMSUZ MAZUMAS
AAMNNNS MANNANS
AAMNORR MARRANO
AAMNORS OARSMAN
RAMONAS
AAMNOSZ AMAZONS
AAMNOTU AUTOMAN
AAMNOTY ANATOMY
AAMNPRT MANTRAP
RAMPANT
AAMNPSS SAMPANS
AAMNPST TAMPANS
AAMNPTY TYMPANA
AAMNRST MANTRAS
AAMNRUY MANUARY
AAMNSTU MANTUAS
AAMOPRS PARAMOS
AAMORRZ ZAMARRO
AAMORSV SAMOVAR
AAMORTY AMATORY
AAMOSSS SAMOSAS
AAMOSTT STOMATA
AAMOTTU AUTOMAT
AAMPRRT RAMPART
AAMRSST MATRASS
AAMRSSU ASARUMS
AAMRSTU TRAUMAS
AAMRTTY TRYMATA
AAMRTWY TRAMWAY
AAMSSTU SATSUMA
AANNNOS ANNONAS
AANNOTT ANNATTO
AANNPSW SWANPAN
AANNRSU ANURANS
AANORTT ARNATTO
AANOSST SONATAS
AANOSTT ANATTOS
AANPRST PARTANS
SPARTAN
TARPANS
TRAPANS
AANPRSU PURANAS
AANPSST PASSANT
AANQRTU QUARTAN
AANRRTW WARRANT
AANRSSS SANSARS
AANRSTT RATTANS
TANTRAS
TARTANS
AANRSTY YANTRAS
AANRSTZ TARZANS
AANRUWY RUNAWAY
AANSSTV SAVANTS
AANSSTZ STANZAS
AANSSYY NAYSAYS
AANSTTT STATANT
AANSWYY ANYWAYS
AAOPSST SAPOTAS
AAOQSSU OQUASSA
AAORRSU AURORAS
AAORSVV VAVASOR
AAOSTTV OTTAVAS
AAOTTUY TATOUAY
AAOTWWY TOWAWAY
AAPPSWW PAWPAWS
AAPRRSU PARURAS
AAPRRTT RATTRAP
AAPRSST SATRAPS
AAPRSTY SATRAPY
AAPRTWY PARTWAY
AAQRSSU QUASARS
AARRSSS SARSARS
AARRSTT TARTARS
AARSSTT STRATAS
AARSSWW WARSAWS
ABBBDEL BABBLED
BLABBED
ABBBELR BABBLER
BLABBER
BRABBLE
ABBBELS BABBLES
ABBBELU ABUBBLE
ABBBITT BABBITT
ABBCDER CRABBED
ABBCDES SCABBED
ABBCEHI BABICHE
ABBCEIS CABBIES
ABBCELR CLABBER
ABBCELS SCABBLE
ABBCERR CRABBER
ABBCGIN CABBING
ABBCIIS BIBASIC
ABBCIKT BACKBIT
ABBCIRS BICARBS
ABBCKUY BUYBACK
ABBCOST BOBCATS
ABBCOTY ABBOTCY
ABBCRYY CRYBABY
ABBDDEL DABBLED
ABBDDER DRABBED
ABBDEGL GABBLED
ABBDEGR GRABBED
ABBDEIT TABBIED
ABBDELR DABBLER
DRABBLE
RABBLED
ABBDELS DABBLES
SLABBED
ABBDELW WABBLED
ABBDERR DRABBER
ABBDERS DABBERS
ABBDERT DRABBET
ABBDEST STABBED
ABBDESU BEDAUBS
ABBDESW SWABBED
ABBDGIN DABBING
ABBDINR RIBBAND
ABBDMOR BOMBARD
ABBDNOX BANDBOX
ABBEESU BAUBEES
ABBEESW BAWBEES
ABBEFST FABBEST
ABBEGIR GABBIER
ABBEGLR GABBLER
GRABBLE
ABBEGLS GABBLES
ABBEGNO BOGBEAN
ABBEGNU BUGBANE
ABBEGRR GRABBER
ABBEGRS GABBERS
ABBEGRU BUGBEAR
ABBEILT BITABLE
ABBEIRS BARBIES
RABBIES
ABBEIST BABIEST
TABBIES
ABBEISW SWABBIE
ABBEISY YABBIES
ABBEJRS JABBERS
ABBELLR BARBELL
ABBELMR BRAMBLE
ABBELOR BELABOR
ABBELRR RABBLER
ABBELRS BARBELS
RABBLES
SLABBER
ABBELRU BARBULE
ABBELRW WABBLER
ABBELSU BAUBLES
BUBALES
ABBELSW WABBLES
ABBELUY BUYABLE
ABBENRS NABBERS
ABBERRS BARBERS
ABBERST BARBETS
RABBETS
STABBER
ABBERSW SWABBER
ABBERSY YABBERS
ABBESSU SUBBASE
ABBGGIN GABBING
ABBGIJN JABBING
ABBGINN NABBING
ABBGINR BARBING
ABBGINS SABBING
ABBGINT TABBING
ABBGINU BUBINGA
ABBGINY BABYING
ABBGOOU BUGABOO
ABBGORS GABBROS
ABBHISY BABYISH
ABBHJSU JUBBAHS
ABBHOOS HABOOBS

ABBHRRU RHUBARB
ABBHTTU BATHTUB
ABBIIMN BAMBINI
ABBILLS LIBLABS
ABBILOS BILBOAS
ABBILOT BOBTAIL
ABBILSU BUBALIS
ABBIMNO BAMBINO
ABBINOR RABBONI
ABBINRS RABBINS
ABBIRST RABBITS
ABBIRTY RABBITY
ABBISTY BABYSIT
ABBKLOU BLAUBOK
ABBLLOX BOXBALL
ABBLLTU BULLBAT
ABBLMRY BRAMBLY
ABBLOOS BABOOLS
ABBMOOS BAMBOOS
ABBMOST BOMBAST
ABBMOTU BUMBOAT
ABBNOOS BABOONS
ABBOORU RUBABOO
ABBORSS ABSORBS
ABBOSTY BATBOYS
BOBSTAY
ABBQSUY SQUABBY
ABBRSSU BUSBARS
ABBRSTU BARBUTS
ABBSSSU SUBBASS
ABCCCHI BACCHIC
ABCCEIR ACERBIC
BRECCIA
ABCCEIS SEBACIC
ABCCHII BACCHII
ABCCHTY BYCATCH
ABCCILU CUBICAL
ABCCIMR CAMBRIC
ABCCIOR BORACIC
ABCCIOS BOCCIAS
ABCCKOW BAWCOCK
ABCCKTU CUTBACK
ABCCOOT TOBACCO
ABCCSUU SUCCUBA
ABCDDEU ABDUCED
ABCDEEH BEACHED
ABCDEEL BELACED
DEBACLE
ABCDEHT BATCHED
ABCDEHU DEBAUCH
ABCDEIK DIEBACK
ABCDEIN CABINED
ABCDEIP PEDICAB
ABCDEIR CARBIDE
ABCDEKL BLACKED
ABCDELO CODABLE
ABCDEOR BROCADE
ABCDERT BRACTED
ABCDERU CUDBEAR
ABCDESU ABDUCES
SCUBAED
ABCDIIS DIBASIC
ABCDILO CABILDO
ABCDILR BALDRIC
ABCDIRT CATBIRD
ABCDIRW BAWDRIC
ABCDISU SUBACID
ABCDNOS ABSCOND
ABCDOOR CORDOBA
ABCDSTU ABDUCTS
ABCEEHS BEACHES
ABCEEMR EMBRACE
ABCEENS ABSENCE
ABCEERR ACERBER
CEREBRA
ABCEESU BECAUSE
ABCEFIS BIFACES
ABCEGOS BOSCAGE
ABCEGSU CUBAGES
ABCEHKL BECHALK
ABCEHKO BACKHOE
ABCEHLO CHAEBOL
ABCEHMR BECHARM
BRECHAM
CHAMBER
ABCEHNR BRECHAN
ABCEHRS BRACHES
ABCEHRT BATCHER
BRACHET
ABCEHST BATCHES
ABCEIKT TIEBACK
ABCEILM ALEMBIC
CEMBALI
ABCEILR CALIBER
CALIBRE
ABCEILT CITABLE

ABCEIMO AMOEBIC
ABCEINR CARBINE
ABCEINT CABINET
ABCEIOR AEROBIC
ABCEIOT ICEBOAT
ABCEIRS ASCRIBE
CARIBES
ABCEIRZ ZEBRAIC
ABCEISS ABSCISE
SCABIES
SEBASIC
ABCEITT TABETIC
ABCEKLN BLACKEN
ABCEKLO BECLOAK
ABCEKLR BLACKER
ABCEKNR BRACKEN
ABCEKRS BACKERS
ABCEKRT BRACKET
ABCEKST BACKSET
SETBACK
ABCELLU BULLACE
ABCELMO CEMBALO
ABCELMR CLAMBER
ABCELMS BECALMS
ABCELOP PLACEBO
ABCELOV VOCABLE
ABCELPS BECLASP
ABCELPU BLUECAP
ABCELRS CABLERS
ABCELRU CURABLE
ABCELRW BECRAWL
ABCELST CABLETS
ABCELSU BASCULE
ABCEMRS CAMBERS
CRAMBES
ABCEMSW WEBCAMS
ABCENOS BEACONS
ABCENOW COWBANE
ABCENOZ CABEZON
ABCENRU UNBRACE
ABCEOOS CABOOSE
ABCEORR BRACERO
ABCEORS BORACES
ABCERRS BRACERS
ABCERSU RUBACES
SUBRACE
ABCESSS ABSCESS
ABCESTW WEBCAST
ABCFIKN FINBACK
ABCFIKT BACKFIT
ABCFILO BIFOCAL
ABCFIRS FABRICS
ABCFNOS CONFABS
ABCGHIN BACHING
ABCGHKO HOGBACK
ABCGIKN BACKING
ABCGILN CABLING
ABCGINR BRACING
ABCGKLO BACKLOG
ABCGMSU SCUMBAG
ABCHHII HIBACHI
ABCHILS CHABLIS
ABCHIOT COHABIT
ABCHKOU CHABOUK
ABCHKSU CHABUKS
ABCHKTU HACKBUT
ABCHNRY BRANCHY
ABCHOSX CASHBOX
ABCHPSU HUBCAPS
ABCIILL BACILLI
ABCIILN ALBINIC
ABCIILS BASILIC
ABCIILT ALBITIC
ABCIIMN MINICAB
ABCIIMS IAMBICS
ABCIIOR CIBORIA
ABCIIOT ABIOTIC
ABCIJNO JACOBIN
ABCIKLT BACKLIT
ABCIKPS BIPACKS
ABCIKSY SICKBAY
ABCILNO COALBIN
ABCILOU ABOULIC
ABCILRS SCRIBAL
ABCILTU CUBITAL
ABCIMMS CAMBISM
ABCIMMU CAMBIUM
ABCIMST CAMBIST
ABCIMSU CUMBIAS
ABCINOR CORBINA
ABCINOS BONACIS
ABCINOT BOTANIC
ABCIORU CARIBOU
ABCIOUV BIVOUAC
ABCIRTY BARYTIC
ABCJOSU JACOBUS

ABCKLLY BLACKLY
ABCKMOT TOMBACK
ABCKMRU BUCKRAM
ABCKNNO BANNOCK
ABCKNRU RUNBACK
ABCKNSU SUNBACK
ABCKNTU CUTBANK
ABCKORY ROCKABY
ABCKOTU BACKOUT
OUTBACK
ABCKPSU BACKUPS
ABCKSTU SACKBUT
ABCKSUW BUCKSAW
SAWBUCK
ABCLLOY CALLBOY
ABCLMNU CLUBMAN
ABCLMSY CYMBALS
ABCLMUU BACULUM
ABCLNOY BALCONY
ABCLNSU SUBCLAN
ABCLOOX COALBOX
ABCLOST COBALTS
ABCLOVY VOCABLY
ABCLRUY CURABLY
ABCMOPS MOBCAPS
ABCMORS CRAMBOS
ABCMOST COMBATS
TOMBACS
ABCNORS CARBONS
CORBANS
ABCORRW CROWBAR
ABCORSX BOXCARS
ABCORSY CARBOYS
ABCSSTU SACBUTS
ABDDDER BRADDED
ABDDEER BEARDED
BREADED
DEBEARD
ABDDEES DEBASED
ABDDEET DEBATED
ABDDEIL ADDIBLE
ABDDEIN BANDIED
ABDDEIR BRAIDED
ABDDEIS BADDIES
ABDDELR BLADDER
ABDDENR BRANDED
ABDDEOR BOARDED
ROADBED
ABDDERW BEDWARD
ABDDEST BADDEST
ABDDESY DAYBEDS
ABDDHSU BUDDHAS
ABDDINS DISBAND
ABDDLLO ODDBALL
ABDEEFG FEEDBAG
ABDEEGZ BEGAZED
ABDEEHS BEHEADS
ABDEEHV BEHAVED
ABDEEIR BEADIER
ABDEEJT JETBEAD
ABDEEKL LAKEBED
ABDEEKR BERAKED
ABDEEKS DEBEAKS
ABDEELL LABELED
ABDEELM BELDAME
ABDEELN ENABLED
ABDEELR BLEARED
ABDEELS BEADLES
ABDEELT BELATED
BLEATED
ABDEELY BELAYED
DYEABLE
ABDEEMN BEADMEN
BEDEMAN
BENAMED
ABDEEMR BREAMED
ABDEEMT BEDMATE
ABDEEMY EMBAYED
ABDEEPR BEDRAPE
PREBADE
ABDEERS BEADERS
DEBASER
SABERED
ABDEERT BERATED
DEBATER
REBATED
TABERED
ABDEERW BEWARED
ABDEERY BEEYARD
ABDEESS DEBASES
SEABEDS
ABDEEST BESTEAD
DEBATES
ABDEETT ABETTED
ABDEETX BETAXED
ABDEFFL BAFFLED

ABDEFLT FLATBED
ABDEFOR FORBADE
ABDEFOS SOFABED
ABDEFRW BEDWARF
ABDEFST BEDFAST
ABDEGGR BRAGGED
ABDEGHI BIGHEAD
ABDEGIN BEADING
ABDEGIR ABRIDGE
BRIGADE
ABDEGLM GAMBLED
ABDEGLR GARBLED
ABDEGLS BEGLADS
ABDEGNO BONDAGE
DOGBANE
ABDEGOS BODEGAS
ABDEGRS BADGERS
ABDEHIL HIDABLE
ABDEHIT HABITED
ABDEHLR HALBERD
ABDEHOW BOWHEAD
ABDEHRT BREADTH
ABDEHSU SUBHEAD
ABDEIIL ALIBIED
ABDEIKT BATIKED
ABDEILP BIPEDAL
PIEBALD
ABDEILR BEDRAIL
BRAILED
RIDABLE
ABDEILS BALDIES
DISABLE
ABDEILU AUDIBLE
ABDEILY BEADILY
ABDEIMO AMEBOID
ABDEINR BRAINED
ABDEINS BANDIES
BASINED
ABDEIRR BRAIDER
ABDEIRS ABIDERS
BRAISED
DARBIES
SEABIRD
SIDEBAR
ABDEIRT REDBAIT
TRIBADE
ABDEIRU DAUBIER
ABDEIRW BAWDIER
ABDEISS BIASSED
ABDEISU SUBIDEA
ABDEISW BAWDIES
ABDEJRU ABJURED
ABDEKLN BLANKED
ABDEKLU BAULKED
ABDEKNU UNBAKED
ABDEKRS DEBARKS
ABDELMP BEDLAMP
ABDELMR MARBLED
RAMBLED
ABDELMS BEDLAMS
BELDAMS
ABDELMW WAMBLED
ABDELNR BLANDER
ABDELNU UNBALED
ABDELOR LABORED
ABDELOS ALBEDOS
ABDELOT BLOATED
LOBATED
ABDELOW DOWABLE
ABDELPU DUPABLE
ABDELRS BLADERS
ABDELRU DURABLE
ABDELRW BRAWLED
WARBLED
ABDELRY DRYABLE
ABDELST BALDEST
BLASTED
STABLED
ABDELSU BELAUDS
ABDELTT BATTLED
BLATTED
ABDELTU ABLUTED
ABDEMMO MAMBOED
ABDEMNO ABDOMEN
ABDEMNS BEDAMNS
ABDEMRU RUMBAED
ABDENNR BRANNED
ABDENOR BANDORE
BROADEN
ABDENPS BEDPANS
ABDENRR BRANDER
ABDENRS BANDERS
ABDENRT BARTEND
ABDENSS BADNESS
ABDENSU SUBDEAN
UNBASED

ABDENSY BENDAYS
ABDENTU UNBATED
ABDEOOT TABOOED
ABDEORR ARBORED
BOARDER
BROADER
REBOARD
ABDEORT ABORTED
BORATED
TABORED
ABDEORV BRAVOED
ABDEOST BOASTED
ABDERSS BRASSED
SERDABS
ABDERST DABSTER
ABDERSU DAUBERS
EARBUDS
ABDERSV ADVERBS
ABDERSY REDBAYS
ABDERUY DAUBERY
ABDETTU ABUTTED
ABDFIRT FATBIRD
ABDGGIN BADGING
ABDGIIN ABIDING
ABDGILN BALDING
BLADING
ABDGINN BANDING
ABDGINO ABODING
ABDGINR BARDING
BRIGAND
ABDGINT DINGBAT
ABDGINU DAUBING
ABDGINW WINDBAG
ABDGIRT DIRTBAG
ABDGLUY LADYBUG
ABDGNOS BANDOGS
ABDHIIT ADHIBIT
ABDHILS BALDISH
ABDHMOR RHABDOM
ABDHNOR BODHRAN
ABDHNSU HUSBAND
ABDIJRY JAYBIRD
ABDILMO BIMODAL
ABDILOO DIABOLO
ABDILOR LABROID
ABDILOT TABLOID
ABDILRS BRIDALS
RIBALDS
ABDILRY RABIDLY
ABDILUY AUDIBLY
ABDILWY BAWDILY
ABDIMNR BIRDMAN
ABDIMOR AMBROID
ABDIMRY MAYBIRD
ABDINOR INBOARD
ABDINOT BANDITO
ABDINRS RIBANDS
ABDINRU UNBRAID
ABDINST BANDITS
ABDIPRU UPBRAID
ABDIRRS BRIARDS
ABDIRSS DISBARS
ABDIRSU SUBARID
ABDKOOY DAYBOOK
ABDLLNY BLANDLY
ABDLLOR BOLLARD
ABDLORY BROADLY
ABDLOSU BUSLOAD
ABDLRUY DURABLY
ABDLSUU SUBDUAL
ABDMNNO BONDMAN
ABDNOOR BRADOON
ONBOARD
ABDNOPR PROBAND
ABDNORS ROBANDS
ABDNOSU ABOUNDS
BAUSOND
ABDNOSX SANDBOX
ABDNOYY ANYBODY
ABDNRSU SANDBUR
ABDNSTY STANDBY
ABDOOWY BAYWOOD
ABDORSS ADSORBS
ABDORSY BOYARDS
BYROADS
ABDRRSU DURBARS
ABDRSSU ABSURDS
ABDRSTU BUSTARD
ABDRUZZ BUZZARD
ABEEELS SEEABLE
ABEEELY EYEABLE
ABEEEMY EYEBEAM
ABEEERV BEREAVE
ABEEFFL EFFABLE
ABEEFLM FLAMBEE
ABEEFLO BEEFALO

ABEEFLS BEFLEAS
ABEEGHR HERBAGE
ABEEGLL GABELLE
GELABLE
ABEEGLS BEAGLES
ABEEGLT GETABLE
ABEEGNR REBEGAN
ABEEGPW WEBPAGE
ABEEGRR GERBERA
ABEEGRS BAREGES
BARGEES
ABEEGRU AUBERGE
ABEEGRW BREWAGE
ABEEGSZ BEGAZES
ABEEHLW HEWABLE
ABEEHMS BESHAME
ABEEHNN HENBANE
ABEEHNS BANSHEE
SHEBEAN
ABEEHNT BENEATH
ABEEHRT BREATHE
ABEEHRV BEHAVER
ABEEHSV BEHAVES
ABEEIKR BEAKIER
ABEEILS BAILEES
ABEEIMR BEAMIER
ABEEINS BEANIES
ABEEINT BETAINE
ABEEIST BEASTIE
ABEEKLR BLEAKER
ABEEKNT BETAKEN
ABEEKPR BARKEEP
PREBAKE
ABEEKPS BESPAKE
BESPEAK
ABEEKRR BREAKER
ABEEKRS BEAKERS
BERAKES
ABEEKST BETAKES
ABEELLR LABELER
RELABEL
ABEELLY EYEBALL
ABEELMZ EMBLAZE
ABEELNR ENABLER
ABEELNS BALEENS
ENABLES
ABEELNT TENABLE
ABEELNU NEBULAE
ABEELOR EARLOBE
ABEELPS BELEAPS
ABEELPT BELEAPT
ABEELQU EQUABLE
ABEELRR ERRABLE
ABEELRT BLEATER
RETABLE
ABEELRY BELAYER
ABEELSU USEABLE
ABEELSW SEWABLE
ABEEMNS BASEMEN
BEMEANS
BENAMES
ABEEMRS AMBEERS
BESMEAR
ABEENRV VERBENA
ABEENRY BEANERY
ABEEORS AEROBES
ABEERRS BEARERS
ABEERRT REBATER
ABEERST BEATERS
BERATES
REBATES
ABEERSV BEAVERS
ABEERSW BEWARES
ABEERSY EYEBARS
ABEERTT ABETTER
BERETTA
ABEERWY BEWEARY
ABEESWX BEESWAX
ABEETXY EXABYTE
ABEFFIS BAFFIES
ABEFFLR BAFFLER
ABEFFLS BAFFLES
ABEFFOT OFFBEAT
ABEFGLS BEFLAGS
ABEFGST GABFEST
ABEFILN FINABLE
ABEFILR FRIABLE
ABEFILU FIBULAE
ABEFILX FIXABLE
ABEFIRT BAREFIT
ABEFITY BEATIFY
ABEFLLS BEFALLS
ABEFLLU BALEFUL
ABEFLLY FLYABLE
ABEFLMS FLAMBES
ABEFLNU BANEFUL

ABEFLRS FABLERS
ABEFLRY FRYABLE
ABEFMRS FERBAMS
ABEFORR FORBARE
FORBEAR
ABEFORX FAREBOX
ABEFORY FOREBAY
ABEFPRS PREFABS
ABEGGIR BAGGIER
ABEGGIS BAGGIES
ABEGGMO GAMBOGE
ABEGGRR BRAGGER
ABEGGRS BAGGERS
BEGGARS
ABEGGRU BURGAGE
ABEGGRY BEGGARY
ABEGHNS SHEBANG
ABEGHOR BEGORAH
ABEGHRU BEARHUG
ABEGIKL BAGLIKE
ABEGIMN BEAMING
ABEGIMR GAMBIER
ABEGIMT MEGABIT
ABEGINN BEANING
ABEGINO BEGONIA
ABEGINR BEARING
ABEGINS SABEING
ABEGINT BEATING
ABEGIPP BAGPIPE
ABEGKLU BULKAGE
ABEGKOR BROKAGE
ABEGKOS BOSKAGE
ABEGLLS BEGALLS
ABEGLMR GAMBLER
GAMBREL
ABEGLMS GAMBLES
ABEGLNS BANGLES
ABEGLOT GLOBATE
ABEGLRR GARBLER
ABEGLRS GARBLES
ABEGLSU BELUGAS
ABEGMOR EMBARGO
ABEGMRU UMBRAGE
ABEGNNT BANTENG
ABEGNOR BEGROAN
ABEGNOS NOSEBAG
ABEGNRS BANGERS
GRABENS
ABEGOPY PAGEBOY
ABEGORR BEGORRA
ABEGORS BORAGES
ABEGORX GEARBOX
ABEGOSZ GAZEBOS
ABEGOUY BUOYAGE
ABEGSTU BAGUETS
ABEHILR HIRABLE
ABEHIMO BOHEMIA
ABEHIMS BEAMISH
ABEHINS BANSHIE
ABEHIRS BEARISH
ABEHISU BEAUISH
ABEHITU HABITUE
ABEHKLS KEBLAHS
ABEHKNT BETHANK
ABEHKRU HAUBERK
ABEHLMS SHAMBLE
ABEHLNT BENTHAL
ABEHLRS HERBALS
ABEHLRT BLATHER
HALBERT
ABEHMNO HAMBONE
ABEHNRY ABHENRY
ABEHRRS BRASHER
ABEHRSS BASHERS
BRASHES
ABEHRST BATHERS
BERTHAS
BREATHS
ABEHRTY BREATHY
ABEIILS ALIBIES
BAILIES
BIALIES
ABEIINN BIENNIA
ABEIJNS BASENJI
ABEIKLL LIKABLE
ABEIKLR BALKIER
ABEIKLS SKIABLE
ABEIKLT BATLIKE
ABEIKNT BEATNIK
ABEIKRR BARKIER
BRAKIER
ABEIKWY BIKEWAY
ABEILLN LINABLE
ABEILLO LOBELIA
ABEILLP PLIABLE

ABEILLR BRAILLE
LIBERAL
ABEILLS BALLIES
ABEILLV LIVABLE
ABEILMN MINABLE
ABEILMR BALMIER
LAMBIER
ABEILMS ABLEISM
LAMBIES
ABEILMT BIMETAL
LIMBATE
TIMBALE
ABEILMU BUMELIA
ABEILMX MIXABLE
ABEILMY BEAMILY
ABEILMZ IMBLAZE
ABEILNP BIPLANE
ABEILNS LESBIAN
ABEILOS OBELIAS
ABEILRS BAILERS
ABEILRT LIBRATE
TRIABLE
ABEILRW BRAWLIE
WIRABLE
ABEILRY BILAYER
ABEILSS ABSEILS
ABEILST ABLEIST
ALBITES
ASTILBE
BASTILE
BESTIAL
BLASTIE
STABILE
ABEILSW BEWAILS
ABEILSY BAILEYS
ABEILSZ SIZABLE
ABEILVV BIVALVE
ABEIMNP PEMBINA
ABEIMNT AMBIENT
ABEIMRR BARMIER
ABEIMRS AMBRIES
ABEINOT NIOBATE
ABEINPT BEPAINT
ABEINRR BARNIER
ABEINSS SABINES
ABEINST BANTIES
BASINET
ABEIORS ISOBARE
ABEIOSS ABIOSES
ABEIOTV OBVIATE
ABEIPST BAPTISE
ABEIPTZ BAPTIZE
ABEIRRR BARRIER
ABEIRRS BRASIER
ABEIRRT ARBITER
RAREBIT
ABEIRRZ BIZARRE
BRAZIER
ABEIRSS BRAISES
BRASSIE
ABEIRST BAITERS
BARITES
REBAITS
TERBIAS
ABEIRSX BRAXIES
ABEIRSZ BRAIZES
ABEIRTT BATTIER
BIRETTA
ABEIRTV VIBRATE
ABEIRUX EXURBIA
ABEISSS BIASSES
ABEISTT BATISTE
BISTATE
ABEISTW BAWTIES
ABEISUV ABUSIVE
ABEITUX BAUXITE
ABEJLUY BLUEJAY
ABEJMNO JOBNAME
ABEJNOS BANJOES
ABEJNOW JAWBONE
ABEJORS JERBOAS
ABEJRRU ABJURER
ABEJRSU ABJURES
ABEKLLY BLEAKLY
ABEKLNR BLANKER
ABEKLNT BLANKET
ABEKLOP POKABLE
ABEKLRS BALKERS
ABEKMNS EMBANKS
ABEKMRS EMBARKS
ABEKMSU SAMBUKE
ABEKNRS BANKERS
ABEKNRU UNBRAKE
ABEKOTU OUTBAKE
ABEKPRU BREAKUP
ABEKRRS BARKERS

ABEKSST BASKETS
ABELLMN BELLMAN
ABELLOS LOSABLE
ABELLOV LOVABLE
ABELLRS BALLERS
ABELLRU RUBELLA
RULABLE
ABELLST BALLETS
ABELLTU BALLUTE
BULLATE
ABELMMS EMBALMS
ABELMNT LAMBENT
ABELMNU ALBUMEN
ABELMOV MOVABLE
ABELMRR MARBLER
RAMBLER
ABELMRS AMBLERS
BLAMERS
LAMBERS
MARBLES
RAMBLES
ABELMRT LAMBERT
ABELMSW WAMBLES
ABELMTU MUTABLE
ABELNOT NOTABLE
ABELNOW OWNABLE
ABELNOY BALONEY
ABELNRU NEBULAR
ABELNRY BLARNEY
ABELNSU NEBULAS
UNBALES
ABELNTU ABLUENT
TUNABLE
ABELNTY TENABLY
ABELOPR ROPABLE
ABELOPS POSABLE
ABELOPT POTABLE
ABELORR LABORER
ABELORT BLOATER
ABELORU RUBEOLA
ABELORW ROWABLE
ABELOSS BOLASES
ABELOST BOATELS
OBLATES
ABELOSV ABSOLVE
ABELOSW SOWABLE
ABELOTT TOTABLE
ABELOTV VOTABLE
ABELOTW TEABOWL
TOWABLE
ABELPRU PUBERAL
ABELPTY TYPABLE
ABELQUY EQUABLY
ABELRRS BARRELS
ABELRRW BRAWLER
WARBLER
ABELRSS BARLESS
BRALESS
ABELRST BLASTER
LABRETS
STABLER
ABELRSV VERBALS
ABELRSW BAWLERS
WARBLES
ABELRSY BARLEYS
ABELRSZ BLAZERS
ABELRTT BATTLER
BLATTER
BRATTLE
ABELRVY BRAVELY
ABELSST STABLES
ABELSSU SUBSALE
ABELSTT BATTLES
TABLETS
ABELSTU SUBLATE
ABELSTY BEASTLY
ABELSUY USEABLY
ABELSWY BYELAWS
ABELTWY BELTWAY
ABEMMOS MAMBOES
ABEMNOS AMBONES
BEMOANS
ABEMNOT BOATMEN
ABEMNST BATSMEN
ABEMNSU SUNBEAM
ABEMNSY BYNAMES
ABEMORT BROMATE
ABEMOTU OUTBEAM
ABEMRSW BESWARM
ABEMSSY EMBASSY
ABENNOR BARONNE
ABENNRR BRANNER
ABENNRS BANNERS
ABENNST BANNETS
ABENORS BORANES

ABENORT BARONET
REBOANT
ABENORZ ZEBRANO
ABENOSY SOYBEAN
ABENOTY BAYONET
ABENPSU SUBPENA
ABENQTU BANQUET
ABENRRS BARRENS
ABENRRU URBANER
ABENRST BANTERS
ABENRSU UNBEARS
ABENRSY BARNEYS
ABENRSZ BRAZENS
ABENRUX EXURBAN
ABENSST ABSENTS
ABENSTT BATTENS
ABENSTU BUTANES
ABENSTZ BEZANTS
ABENTZZ BEZZANT
ABEOOST SEABOOT
ABEOOTV OBOVATE
ABEOPRS SAPROBE
ABEOPRT PROBATE
ABEOQRU BAROQUE
ABEORRS ARBORES
ABEORRT ABORTER
TABORER
ABEORST BOASTER
BOATERS
BORATES
REBATOS
SORBATE
ABEORSV BRAVOES
ABEORSX BORAXES
ABEORSY ROSEBAY
ABEORSZ BEZOARS
ABEORTT ABETTOR
TABORET
ABEPRSU UPBEARS
ABEPRSW BEWRAPS
ABEPRTW BEWRAPT
ABEPRTY TYPEBAR
ABEPSTU UPBEATS
ABEQRSU BARQUES
ABEQSSU BASQUES
ABERRST BARRETS
BARTERS
ABERRSU BURSERA
ABERRSV BRAVERS
ABERRSY BRAYERS
ABERRSZ BRAZERS
ABERRUV BRAVURE
ABERRVY BRAVERY
ABERSSS BRASSES
ABERSST BASTERS
BREASTS
ABERSSU ABUSERS
RUBASSE
SURBASE
ABERSSZ ZEBRASS
ABERSTT BATTERS
ABERSTU ARBUTES
BURSATE
ABERSTV BRAVEST
ABERSTW BRAWEST
ABERSTY BARYTES
BETRAYS
ABERSUU BUREAUS
ABERSWY BEWRAYS
ABERTTU ABUTTER
ABERTTY BATTERY
ABERUUX BUREAUX
ABESSST BASSETS
ABESSSY ABYSSES
ABESSTT BASSETT
ABESTTU BATTUES
ABFFGIN BAFFING
ABFFIIL BAILIFF
ABFFLOO BOFFOLA
ABFFLOU BUFFALO
ABFGILN FABLING
ABFGINR BARFING
ABFGLSU BAGFULS
BAGSFUL
ABFGOOT FOOTBAG
ABFHIST BATFISH
ABFHLSU BASHFUL
ABFIILR BIFILAR
ABFIIMR FIMBRIA
ABFILRU FIBULAR
ABFILSU FIBULAS
ABFIMOR FIBROMA
ABFLOTU BOATFUL
ABFLOTW BATFOWL
ABFLOTY FLYBOAT
ABGGGIN BAGGING

ABGGIIT GIGABIT
ABGGILN GABLING
ABGGILY BAGGILY
ABGGINN BANGING
ABGGINR BARGING
GARBING
ABGGISW BAGWIGS
ABGGNOS GOBANGS
ABGHHSU HAGBUSH
ABGHINS BASHING
ABGHINT BATHING
ABGHLRU BURGHAL
ABGHMOO GOOMBAH
ABGHMRU HAMBURG
ABGHNOR HAGBORN
ABGHOTU ABOUGHT
ABGHSSU BUGSHAS
ABGHSTU HAGBUTS
ABGIILN BAILING
ABGIINS BIASING
ABGIINT BAITING
ABGIJMN JAMBING
ABGIKLN BALKING
ABGIKNN BANKING
ABGIKNR BARKING
BRAKING
ABGIKNS BAKINGS
BASKING
ABGIKST KITBAGS
ABGILLN BALLING
ABGILMN AMBLING
BLAMING
LAMBING
ABGILMS GIMBALS
ABGILNR BLARING
ABGILNS ABLINGS
ABGILNT TABLING
ABGILNW BAWLING
BLAWING
ABGILNZ BLAZING
ABGILOR GARBOIL
ABGILRT BATGIRL
ABGIMMN BAMMING
ABGIMRS GAMBIRS
ABGIMST GAMBITS
ABGINNN BANNING
ABGINNR BARNING
ABGINOS BAGNIOS
GABIONS
ABGINOT BOATING
ABGINRR BARRING
ABGINRS SABRING
ABGINRV BRAVING
ABGINRY BRAYING
ABGINRZ BRAZING
ABGINST BASTING
ABGINSU ABUSING
ABGINTT BATTING
ABGINTU ANTIBUG
TABUING
ABGINTW BATWING
ABGIOPT PIGBOAT
ABGKKNO BANGKOK
ABGKORW WORKBAG
ABGLLMU GUMBALL
ABGLMOS GAMBOLS
ABGLMOU LUMBAGO
ABGLNOO BOLOGNA
ABGLOSU SUBGOAL
ABGLRRU BURGLAR
ABGMNOY BOGYMAN
ABGMOOY GOOMBAY
ABGMORW BAGWORM
ABGNOOS GABOONS
ABGNOPR PROBANG
ABGNORS BARONGS
BROGANS
ABGNOTU GUNBOAT
ABGOPST POSTBAG
ABGORST BOGARTS
ABGORTU OUTBRAG
ABGOTTU TUGBOAT
ABGSSTU SAGBUTS
ABHHISS SHIBAHS
ABHHJSU JUBHAHS
ABHHSUW BUSHWAH
ABHHSUY HUSHABY
ABHIINT INHABIT
ABHIKLS KIBLAHS
ABHIKST BHAKTIS
ABHILNO HOBNAIL
ABHILOS ABOLISH
ABHILTU HALIBUT
ABHIMRS MIHRABS
ABHINST ABSINTH
ABHIOPS PHOBIAS

ABHIORS BOARISH
ABHIORT BOTHRIA
ABHIOST ISOBATH
ABHISTU HABITUS
ABHKLSY BASHLYK
ABHKRSU KURBASH
ABHLOUX BOXHAUL
ABHLRSY BRASHLY
ABHMNSU BUSHMAN
ABHMRSU RHUMBAS
SAMBHUR
ABHMSUY MAYBUSH
ABHNSTU SUNBATH
ABHOPRS BARHOPS
ABHORRS HARBORS
ABHORRU HARBOUR
ABHOTUY HAUTBOY
ABHPSTY BYPATHS
ABHQSSU BUQSHAS
ABHRSTU TARBUSH
ABHSSUW BUSHWAS
ABHSTUW WASHTUB
ABIIINR BIRIANI
ABIIKKS KABIKIS
ABIILMN MINILAB
ABIILMU BULIMIA
ABIILNS AIBLINS
ABIILOV BOLIVIA
ABIILRY BILIARY
ABIILST STIBIAL
ABIILTY ABILITY
ABIIMNR MINIBAR
ABIIMSS MISBIAS
ABIINRY BIRYANI
ABIIOSS ABIOSIS
ABIJRSU JABIRUS
ABIKKSU KABUKIS
ABIKLLY BALKILY
ABIKLMN LAMBKIN
ABIKLOR KILOBAR
ABIKLOS KOLBASI
ABIKMRS IMBARKS
ABIKNST BANKITS
ABIKRST BRITSKA
ABIKRTZ BRITZKA
ABIKSTT BATTIKS
ABIKUUZ BUZUKIA
ABILLMY BALMILY
ABILLNP PINBALL
ABILLPY PLIABLY
ABILLSW SAWBILL
ABILLSY SYLLABI
ABILLWX WAXBILL
ABILLWY WAYBILL
ABILMMS IMBALMS
ABILMNU ALBUMIN
ABILMOX MAILBOX
ABILMRT TIMBRAL
ABILMST TIMBALS
ABILNOS ALBINOS
ABILNOZ BIZONAL
ABILNRY BAIRNLY
ABILOPR BIPOLAR
PARBOIL
ABILORS BAILORS
ABILORT ORBITAL
ABILORV BOLIVAR
ABILOST OBLASTI
ABILOTU BAILOUT
TABOULI
ABILRRY LIBRARY
ABILRSS BRASILS
ABILRST TRIBALS
ABILRSU BURIALS
RAILBUS
ABILRSZ BRAZILS
ABILSTU TABULIS
ABILSYZ SIZABLY
ABIMMRS MIMBARS
ABIMOSS BIOMASS
ABIMPST BAPTISM
BITMAPS
ABIMRSU BARIUMS
ABINOOT BONIATO
ABINORT TABORIN
ABINORW RAINBOW
ABINOSS BASIONS
ABINOST BASTION
BONITAS
OBTAINS
ABINRST BRISANT
ABINRTV VIBRANT
ABIORRS BARRIOS
ABIORRZ BIZARRO
ABIORSS ISOBARS
ABIORTV VIBRATO

ABIPRTY BIPARTY
ABIPSTT BAPTIST
ABISSST BASSIST
ABISTTU TUBAIST
ABJJOOS JOJOBAS
ABJKMOS SJAMBOK
ABJLMSU JUMBALS
ABJOSZZ JAZZBOS
ABKLLNY BLANKLY
ABKLOOW LAWBOOK
ABKLRUW BULWARK
ABKLSTY BYTALKS
ABKMNOO BOOKMAN
ABKMOST TOMBAKS
ABKNNNO NONBANK
ABKNRUU BUNRAKU
ABKORTU OUTBARK
ABKSSTU SUBTASK
ABLLLOW LOWBALL
ABLLLUY LULLABY
ABLLNOO BALLOON
ABLLNOS BALLONS
ABLLORT TOLLBAR
ABLLORU LOBULAR
ABLLOST BALLOTS
ABLLOTY TALLBOY
ABLLOVY LOVABLY
ABLMMOU BUMMALO
ABLMNOU UMBONAL
ABLMOOT TOMBOLA
ABLMOPS APLOMBS
ABLMORS BROMALS
ABLMOVY MOVABLY
ABLMPSU PABLUMS
ABLMPUU PABULUM
ABLMRSU LABRUMS
LUMBARS
ABLMSTY TYMBALS
ABLMTUY MUTABLY
ABLNOOP POBLANO
ABLNOSZ BLAZONS
ABLNOTU BUTANOL
ABLNOTY NOTABLY
ABLNRSU SLURBAN
ABLNTUY TUNABLY
ABLOORS ROBALOS
ABLOORT TOOLBAR
ABLOPYY PLAYBOY
ABLORST BORSTAL
ABLORSU LABOURS
SUBORAL
ABLORSW BARLOWS
ABLOSST OBLASTS
ABLOSTV ABVOLTS
ABLOSTX SALTBOX
ABLOSUV SUBOVAL
ABLOTUW OUTBAWL
ABLPRSU BURLAPS
ABLPSYY BYPLAYS
ABLRTUU TUBULAR
ABLRTUY BUTYRAL
ABLSTTU BUTTALS
ABMNSTU NUMBATS
ABMOORR BARROOM
ABMOPST SPAMBOT
ABMORTU TAMBOUR
ABMOSTU SUBATOM
ABMOSTW WOMBATS
ABMRSSU SAMBURS
ABMRSTU TAMBURS
ABNOOSS BASSOON
ABNORSY BARYONS
ABNORTY BARYTON
ABNOTUY BUOYANT
ABNRSTU TURBANS
ABNRSUU AUBURNS
ABNSTUW BAWSUNT
ABNSTYZ BYZANTS
ABOOPSX SOAPBOX
ABOORTW ROWBOAT
ABOOTTW TOWBOAT
ABORRSU ARBOURS
ABORRSW BARROWS
ABORSTU ABORTUS
ROBUSTA
RUBATOS
TABOURS
ABOSSUU AUSUBOS
ABOSTUU AUTOBUS
ABPRSTU SUBPART
ABRRSSU BURSARS
ABRRSUY BURSARY
ABRRTUY TURBARY
ABRSTUU ARBUTUS
ABSSUWY SUBWAYS
ACCCILY ACYCLIC

ACCDDEE ACCEDED
ACCDDEI CADDICE
ACCDEEN CADENCE
ACCDEER ACCEDER
ACCDEES ACCEDES
ACCDEHN CHANCED
ACCDEHO COACHED
ACCDEII ACCIDIE
ACCDEIU CADUCEI
ACCDEKL CACKLED
CLACKED
ACCDEKO COCKADE
ACCDEKR CRACKED
ACCDENY CADENCY
ACCDEOT COACTED
ACCDERU ACCRUED
ACCDESU ACCUSED
ACCDFIL FLACCID
ACCDHIL CHALCID
ACCDILS SCALDIC
ACCDINS SCANDIC
ACCDIOT CACTOID
OCTADIC
ACCDLOY CACODYL
ACCDORS ACCORDS
ACCEEHL CALECHE
ACCEELN CENACLE
ACCEERT ACCRETE
ACCEFLU FELUCCA
ACCEGOS SOCCAGE
ACCEHIL CALICHE
CHALICE
ACCEHIM MACCHIE
ACCEHIN CHICANE
ACCEHLN CHANCEL
ACCEHLO COCHLEA
ACCEHNO CONCHAE
ACCEHNR CHANCER
CHANCRE
ACCEHNS CHANCES
ACCEHOR CAROCHE
COACHER
ACCEHOS COACHES
ACCEHPU CAPUCHE
ACCEHRT CATCHER
ACCEHST CACHETS
CATCHES
ACCEHTT CATHECT
ACCEHTU CATECHU
ACCEHXY CACHEXY
ACCEILL CALICLE
ACCEILN CALCINE
ACCEILO COELIAC
ACCEILS CALICES
CELIACS
ACCEILT CALCITE
ACCEIMR CERAMIC
RACEMIC
ACCEINO COCAINE
OCEANIC
ACCEINV VACCINE
ACCEIPR CAPRICE
ACCEIPS ICECAPS
IPECACS
ACCEIPV PECCAVI
ACCEIQU CACIQUE
ACCEIRS CARICES
ACCEIST ASCETIC
ACCEITT ECTATIC
ACCEKLR CACKLER
CLACKER
CRACKLE
ACCEKLS CACKLES
ACCEKOP PEACOCK
ACCEKOS SEACOCK
ACCEKPU CUPCAKE
ACCEKRR CRACKER
ACCELLY CALYCLE
CECALLY
ACCELNO CONCEAL
ACCELNS CANCELS
ACCELOR CORACLE
ACCELRS CARCELS
ACCELSU SACCULE
ACCELSY CALYCES
CYCLASE
ACCENOT COENACT
ACCENOV CONCAVE
ACCENPT PECCANT
ACCENRS CANCERS
ACCENST ACCENTS
ACCEOTT TOCCATE
ACCEPRY PECCARY
ACCEPST ACCEPTS
ACCERRS SCARCER

ACCERSU ACCRUES
ACCUSER
ACCESSU ACCUSES
ACCESSY CYCASES
ACCFIIP PACIFIC
ACCFILY CALCIFY
ACCGHIN CACHING
ACCGNOS COGNACS
ACCHIMS CHASMIC
ACCHINO CHICANO
ACCHIOP PICACHO
ACCHIOR COCHAIR
ACCHIOT CHAOTIC
ACCHIRS SCRAICH
ACCHKOY HAYCOCK
ACCHLNO CONCHAL
ACCHLTU CLAUCHT
ACCHNOS CONCHAS
ACCHNRU CRAUNCH
ACCHOPU CAPOUCH
PACHUCO
ACCHORR CARROCH
ACCHOSU CACHOUS
ACCHPTU CATCHUP
ACCHRRU CURRACH
ACCHRST SCRATCH
ACCHSSU SUCCAHS
ACCIILN ACLINIC
ACCIINT ACTINIC
ACCIIST ASCITIC
SCIATIC
ACCIKRS CARSICK
ACCILLU CALCULI
ACCILMO COMICAL
ACCILMU CALCIUM
ACCILNO CONICAL
LACONIC
ACCILNY CYNICAL
ACCILOR CALORIC
ACCILOS CALICOS
ACCILOV VOCALIC
ACCILRU CRUCIAL
ACCILRY ACRYLIC
ACCILSS CLASSIC
ACCILST CLASTIC
ACCILSU SACCULI
ACCIMOT COMATIC
ACCINNO CANONIC
ACCINOP CANOPIC
ACCINOR ACRONIC
ACCINOS COCAINS
ACCINRU CRUCIAN
ACCINSW WICCANS
ACCINSY CYCASIN
ACCIORT ACROTIC
ACCIOST OCICATS
ACCIPRT PRACTIC
ACCIRRS RICRACS
ACCIRST ARCTICS
ACCISTT TACTICS
TICTACS
ACCISTU CAUSTIC
ACCKLRY CRACKLY
ACCKOPR CAPROCK
ACCKOSS CASSOCK
COSSACK
ACCKPRU CRACKUP
ACCMNOY CACONYM
ACCMOOT COCOMAT
ACCMOOY COCOYAM
ACCMOPT COMPACT
ACCMRUU CURCUMA
ACCNNOO COONCAN
ACCNOOR RACCOON
ACCNOTT CONTACT
ACCNOTU ACCOUNT
ACCOORT COACTOR
ACCOPTY COPYCAT
ACCORSS CORSACS
ACCOSST ACCOSTS
ACCRSTU ACCURST
ACDDDEI CADDIED
ACDDDEL CLADDED
ACDDDEU ADDUCED
ACDDEEF DEFACED
ACDDEES DECADES
ACDDEEY DECAYED
ACDDEHR CHEDDAR
ACDDEIN CANDIED
ACDDEIS CADDIES
ACDDEIU DECIDUA
ACDDELN CANDLED
ACDDELO CLADODE
ACDDELR CRADLED
ACDDELS SCALDED
ACDDEOP DECAPOD

ACDDERU ADDUCER
ACDDESU ADDUCES
ACDDHHU CHUDDAH
ACDDHIS CADDISH
ACDDHKO HADDOCK
ACDDHRU CHUDDAR
ACDDIIS DIACIDS
ACDDIKZ ZADDICK
ACDDINS CANDIDS
ACDDIRS DISCARD
ACDDIRY DRYADIC
ACDDIST ADDICTS
DIDACTS
ACDDISY DYADICS
ACDDKOP PADDOCK
ACDDSTU ADDUCTS
ACDEEES DECEASE
ACDEEFF EFFACED
ACDEEFN ENFACED
ACDEEFR DEFACER
REFACED
ACDEEFS DEFACES
ACDEEFT FACETED
ACDEEGL GLACEED
ACDEEGN ENCAGED
ACDEEHL LEACHED
ACDEEHP PEACHED
ACDEEHR REACHED
ACDEEHT CHEATED
ACDEEIR DECIARE
ACDEEJT DEJECTA
ACDEEKR CREAKED
ACDEELL CADELLE
ACDEELN CLEANED
ENLACED
ACDEELR CLEARED
CREEDAL
DECLARE
RELACED
ACDEELT CLEATED
ACDEELV CLEAVED
ACDEEMN MENACED
ACDEEMO CAMEOED
ACDEEMR AMERCED
CREAMED
RACEMED
ACDEEMV MEDEVAC
ACDEENR RECANED
ACDEENS DECANES
ENCASED
ACDEENT ENACTED
ACDEENV VENDACE
ACDEEPR CAPERED
ACDEEPS ESCAPED
ACDEERS CREASED
DECARES
ACDEERT CATERED
CERATED
CREATED
REACTED
ACDEERY DECAYER
ACDEETU EDUCATE
ACDEETX EXACTED
ACDEFFH CHAFFED
ACDEFGO DOGFACE
ACDEFIN FACIEND
FANCIED
ACDEFKL FLACKED
ACDEFRS SCARFED
ACDEFRT CRAFTED
FRACTED
ACDEGGL CLAGGED
ACDEGGR CRAGGED
ACDEGHN CHANGED
ACDEGHR CHARGED
ACDEGIN INCAGED
ACDEGKO DOCKAGE
ACDEGLN CLANGED
GLANCED
ACDEGLO DECALOG
ACDEGNO CONGAED
DECAGON
ACDEGNU UNCAGED
ACDEGOR CORDAGE
ACDEGRS CADGERS
ACDEHHT HATCHED
ACDEHIN CHAINED
ECHIDNA
ACDEHIP EDAPHIC
ACDEHIR CHAIRED
ACDEHIX HEXADIC
ACDEHKL CHALKED
HACKLED
ACDEHKR CHARKED
ACDEHKS SHACKED
ACDEHKT THACKED

ACDEHKW WHACKED
ACDEHLS CLASHED
ACDEHLT LATCHED
ACDEHMP CHAMPED
ACDEHMR CHARMED
MARCHED
ACDEHMS CHASMED
ACDEHMT MATCHED
ACDEHNR ENDARCH
RANCHED
ACDEHNT CHANTED
ACDEHOP POACHED
ACDEHOR ROACHED
ACDEHOS COHEADS
ACDEHOT CATHODE
ACDEHPP CHAPPED
ACDEHPR PARCHED
ACDEHPT PATCHED
ACDEHRR CHARRED
ACDEHRS CRASHED
ECHARDS
ACDEHRT CHARTED
ACDEHSS CHASSED
ACDEHST SCATHED
ACDEHTT CHATTED
ACDEHTW WATCHED
ACDEHTY YACHTED
ACDEILL CEDILLA
ACDEILM CAMELID
CLAIMED
DECIMAL
DECLAIM
MEDICAL
ACDEILN INLACED
ACDEILR DECRIAL
RADICEL
RADICLE
ACDEILT CITADEL
DELTAIC
DIALECT
EDICTAL
ACDEILV CAVILED
ACDEIMV MEDIVAC
ACDEIMY MEDIACY
ACDEINO CODEINA
ACDEINR CAIRNED
ACDEINS CANDIES
INCASED
ACDEINY CYANIDE
ACDEIOS CODEIAS
ACDEIPR PERACID
ACDEIRR ACRIDER
CARRIED
ACDEIRS RADICES
SIDECAR
ACDEISS DISCASE
ACDEIST DACITES
ACDEISV ADVICES
ACDEITT DICTATE
ACDEITY EDACITY
ACDEJLO CAJOLED
ACDEJNU JAUNCED
ACDEKKN KNACKED
ACDEKLM MACKLED
ACDEKLN CLANKED
ACDEKLO CLOAKED
ACDEKLS SLACKED
ACDEKLT TACKLED
TALCKED
ACDEKLU CAULKED
ACDEKMS SMACKED
ACDEKNR CRANKED
ACDEKNS SNACKED
ACDEKNU UNCAKED
ACDEKOR CROAKED
ACDEKQU QUACKED
ACDEKRS DACKERS
ACDEKRT TRACKED
ACDEKRW WRACKED
ACDEKRY KEYCARD
ACDEKST STACKED
ACDEKSW SWACKED
ACDELMM CLAMMED
ACDELMP CLAMPED
ACDELMU MACULED
ACDELNO CELADON
ACDELNR CANDLER
ACDELNS CALENDS
CANDLES
ACDELNU UNLACED
ACDELOP PEDOCAL
ACDELOR CAROLED
ACDELOS COLEADS
SOLACED
ACDELOT LOCATED
ACDELOV ALCOVED

ACDELPP CLAPPED
ACDELPS CLASPED
SCALPED
ACDELQU CALQUED
ACDELRR CRADLER
ACDELRS CRADLES
RECLADS
ACDELRW CRAWLED
ACDELSS CLASSED
DECLASS
ACDELST CASTLED
ACDELSU CAUDLES
CEDULAS
ACDELSW DECLAWS
ACDELWW DEWCLAW
ACDEMMR CRAMMED
ACDEMMS SCAMMED
ACDEMNU DECUMAN
ACDEMOR CAROMED
COMRADE
ACDEMPR CRAMPED
ACDEMPS DECAMPS
SCAMPED
ACDENNS SCANNED
ACDENNT CANDENT
ACDENNU NUANCED
ACDENOR ACORNED
ACDENOS ACNODES
DEACONS
ACDENOT TACNODE
ACDENPR PRANCED
ACDENPT PANDECT
ACDENRS DANCERS
ACDENRT TRANCED
ACDENRU DURANCE
ACDENRY ARDENCY
ACDENSS ASCENDS
ACDENST DECANTS
DESCANT
SCANTED
ACDENSU UNCASED
ACDENTU UNACTED
ACDEOPS PEASCOD
ACDEOPT COAPTED
ACDEORR CORRADE
ACDEORT CORDATE
REDCOAT
ACDEOST COASTED
ACDEOUV COUVADE
ACDEPPR CRAPPED
ACDEPRS REDCAPS
SCARPED
SCRAPED
ACDEQSU CASQUED
ACDERRS CARDERS
SCARRED
ACDERST REDACTS
SCARTED
ACDERSU CRUSADE
ACDERTT DETRACT
ACDERTU CURATED
TRADUCE
ACDESTT SCATTED
ACDESTV ADVECTS
ACDFIIT FATIDIC
ACDFIIY ACIDIFY
ACDFIOT FACTOID
ACDGGIN CADGING
ACDGINN DANCING
ACDGINO GONADIC
ACDGINR CARDING
ACDGKLO DAGLOCK
ACDGNOT CANTDOG
ACDGORT DOGCART
ACDHIIL CHILIAD
ACDHIMR DHARMIC
ACDHIRY DIARCHY
ACDHLOR CHORDAL
ACDHMRS DRACHMS
ACDHNOW COWHAND
ACDHOPR POCHARD
ACDHORR ORCHARD
ACDHORS CHADORS
ACDHRYY DYARCHY
ACDIIIN INDICIA
ACDIIJT JADITIC
ACDIINN INDICAN
ACDIINO CONIDIA
ACDIIRT TRIACID
TRIADIC
ACDIITY ACIDITY
ACDIKLS SKALDIC
ACDILMO DOMICAL
ACDILMS CLADISM
ACDILNO NODICAL
ACDILNU INCUDAL

ACDILOP PLACOID
ACDILOR CORDIAL
ACDILOT COTIDAL
ACDILRT TRICLAD
ACDILRY ACRIDLY
ACDILST CLADIST
ACDILTW WILDCAT
ACDILTY DACTYLI
ACDIMMU CADMIUM
ACDIMNO MONACID
MONADIC
NOMADIC
ACDIMNY DYNAMIC
ACDIMOT COADMIT
ACDINNO NONACID
ACDINRU IRACUND
ACDINST DISCANT
ACDINSY CYANIDS
ACDIOPR PARODIC
PICADOR
ACDIORR CORRIDA
ACDIORS SARCOID
ACDIORT CAROTID
ACDIOST DACOITS
ACDIOSZ ZODIACS
ACDIOTY DACOITY
ACDIOXY OXYACID
ACDIPSS CAPSIDS
ACDIPTY DIPTYCA
ACDIQRU QUADRIC
ACDIRST DRASTIC
ACDIRTU DATURIC
ACDISST DICASTS
ACDITUV VIADUCT
ACDJNTU ADJUNCT
ACDKLOP PADLOCK
ACDKMPU MUDPACK
ACDLLOR COLLARD
ACDLLUY DUCALLY
ACDLNOR CALDRON
ACDLSTY DACTYLS
ACDMMNO COMMAND
ACDMORZ CZARDOM
ACDMPSU MUDCAPS
ACDMSTU MUDCATS
ACDNOOR CARDOON
ACDNORS CANDORS
CARDONS
DACRONS
ACDNORU CANDOUR
ACDORST COSTARD
ACDORSU CRUSADO
ACDORSW COWARDS
ACDORUZ CRUZADO
ACDRSTU CUSTARD
ACEEEPS ESCAPEE
ACEEEUV EVACUEE
ACEEFFR EFFACER
ACEEFFS EFFACES
ACEEFIN FAIENCE
FIANCEE
ACEEFLU FECULAE
ACEEFNS ENFACES
ACEEFPR PREFACE
ACEEFRS REFACES
ACEEGIL ELEGIAC
ACEEGNS ENCAGES
ACEEGOT ECOTAGE
ACEEGSU ESCUAGE
ACEEHHT CHEETAH
ACEEHIP CHEAPIE
ACEEHIV ACHIEVE
ACEEHKO HOECAKE
ACEEHKS HACKEES
ACEEHLR LEACHER
ACEEHLS LEACHES
ACEEHLT CHELATE
ACEEHMR MACHREE
ACEEHMT MACHETE
ACEEHNN ENHANCE
ACEEHNP CHEAPEN
ACEEHNS ACHENES
ENCHASE
ACEEHOR OCHREAE
ACEEHPR CHEAPER
PEACHER
ACEEHPS PEACHES
ACEEHRR REACHER
ACEEHRS REACHES
ACEEHRT CHEATER
HECTARE
RECHEAT
RETEACH
TEACHER
ACEEHST ESCHEAT
TEACHES

ACEEHTT THECATE
ACEEILP CALIPEE
ACEEINU EUCAINE
ACEEISV VESICAE
ACEEKNP KNEECAP
ACEELLN NACELLE
ACEELLS CALLEES
ACEELMP EMPLACE
ACEELMR RECLAME
ACEELNR CLEANER
RECLEAN
ACEELNS CLEANSE
ENLACES
SCALENE
ACEELNV ENCLAVE
VALENCE
ACEELPR PERCALE
REPLACE
ACEELPT CAPELET
ACEELRR CLEARER
ACEELRS CEREALS
RELACES
RESCALE
SCLERAE
ACEELRT TREACLE
ACEELRV CLEAVER
ACEELST CELESTA
ACEELSU EUCLASE
ACEELSV CLEAVES
ACEELVX EXCLAVE
ACEEMNR MENACER
ACEEMNS MENACES
ACEEMNT CEMENTA
ACEEMNV CAVEMEN
ACEEMRR AMERCER
CREAMER
ACEEMRS AMERCES
RACEMES
ACEEMRT CREMATE
ACEEMSZ ECZEMAS
ACEENNP PENANCE
ACEENNT CANTEEN
ACEENNY CAYENNE
ACEENOT ACETONE
ACEENRS CAREENS
CASERNE
RECANES
ACEENRT CENTARE
CRENATE
REENACT
ACEENSS CASSENE
ENCASES
SEANCES
SENECAS
ACEENST CETANES
TENACES
ACEENTU CUNEATE
ACEEORS ACEROSE
ACEEORT OCREATE
ACEEOSS CASEOSE
ACEEOST ACETOSE
COATEES
ACEEPRR CAPERER
PRERACE
ACEEPRS ESCAPER
RESPACE
ACEEPSS ESCAPES
ACEEPST PECTASE
ACEEPTT PECTATE
ACEERRS CAREERS
CREASER
ACEERRT CATERER
RECRATE
RETRACE
TERRACE
ACEERSS CREASES
ACEERST CERATES
CREATES
ECARTES
ACEERSU CESURAE
ACEERTX EXACTER
EXCRETA
ACEERVZ CERVEZA
ACEESSS ASCESES
ACEESST ECTASES
ACEESTT CASETTE
ACEFFHI AFFICHE
ACEFFHR CHAFFER
ACEFFIN CAFFEIN
ACEFFST AFFECTS
ACEFGLU CAGEFUL
ACEFHMR CHAMFER
ACEFHOR ARCHFOE
ACEFHRS CHAFERS
ACEFHRU CHAUFER
ACEFILL ICEFALL

ACEFILM MALEFIC
ACEFILS FECIALS
ACEFINN FINANCE
ACEFINR FANCIER
ACEFINS FANCIES
FASCINE
FIANCES
ACEFINU UNIFACE
ACEFIRS FARCIES
FIACRES
ACEFITY ACETIFY
ACEFLRU CAREFUL
ACEFNRU FURNACE
ACEFOTU OUTFACE
ACEFRRS FARCERS
SCARFER
ACEFRRT CRAFTER
REFRACT
ACEFRRU FARCEUR
ACEFRSU SURFACE
ACEFRTU FACTURE
FURCATE
ACEFSTU FAUCETS
ACEGHNR CHANGER
ACEGHNS CHANGES
ACEGHOU GOUACHE
ACEGHOW COWHAGE
ACEGHRR CHARGER
ACEGHRS CHARGES
ACEGHRU GAUCHER
ACEGILN ANGELIC
ANGLICE
GALENIC
ACEGILP PELAGIC
ACEGILR GLACIER
GRACILE
ACEGIMR GRIMACE
ACEGIMT GAMETIC
ACEGINO COINAGE
ACEGINP PEACING
ACEGINR ANERGIC
ACEGINS CEASING
INCAGES
ACEGINY GYNECIA
ACEGIOP APOGEIC
ACEGIRT CIGARET
ACEGIST CAGIEST
ACEGJKL JACKLEG
ACEGKLO LOCKAGE
ACEGKLR GRACKLE
ACEGKOR CORKAGE
ACEGLLO COLLAGE
ACEGLNO CONGEAL
ACEGLNR CLANGER
GLANCER
ACEGLNS GLANCES
ACEGLPS GELCAPS
ACEGNOR ACROGEN
ACEGNOT COAGENT
COGNATE
ACEGNSU CANGUES
UNCAGES
ACEGORS CARGOES
CORSAGE
SOCAGER
ACEGORU COURAGE
ACEGOSS SOCAGES
ACEGOSW COWAGES
ACEGOTT COTTAGE
ACEGSTU SCUTAGE
ACEGTTU CUTTAGE
ACEHHLS CHALEHS
ACEHHLT HATCHEL
ACEHHRT HATCHER
ACEHHRU HACHURE
ACEHHST CHETAHS
HATCHES
ACEHHTT HATCHET
ACEHIKS HACKIES
ACEHILL CHALLIE
HELICAL
ACEHILR CHARLIE
ACEHILT ETHICAL
ACEHIMN MACHINE
ACEHIMP IMPEACH
ACEHIMR CHIMERA
ACEHIMS CHAMISE
ACEHIMT HEMATIC
ACEHINN ENCHAIN
ACEHINR ARCHINE
ACEHINS CHAINES
ACEHINY HYAENIC
ACEHIOT ACHIOTE
ACEHIPP CHAPPIE
ACEHIPT APHETIC
HEPATIC

ACEHIRR CHARIER
ACEHIRS CAHIERS
CASHIER
ACEHIRT THERIAC
ACEHIRV ARCHIVE
ACEHISS CHAISES
ACEHIST ACHIEST
AITCHES
ACEHKLR HACKLER
ACEHKLS HACKLES
SHACKLE
ACEHKMN HACKMEN
ACEHKNY HACKNEY
ACEHKOT HOTCAKE
ACEHKRS HACKERS
ACEHKRW WHACKER
ACEHLLS SHELLAC
ACEHLLT HELLCAT
ACEHLMY ALCHEMY
ACEHLNN CHANNEL
ACEHLNO CHALONE
ACEHLNP PLANCHE
ACEHLNR CHARNEL
LARCHEN
ACEHLOP EPOCHAL
ACEHLOR CHOLERA
CHORALE
CHOREAL
ACEHLOS LOACHES
ACEHLOT CHOLATE
ACEHLPS CHAPELS
ACEHLPT CHAPLET
ACEHLPY CHEAPLY
ACEHLRS CLASHER
LARCHES
ACEHLRT TRACHLE
ACEHLRY CHARLEY
ACEHLSS CLASHES
ACEHLST CHALETS
LATCHES
SATCHEL
ACEHLTT CHATTEL
LATCHET
ACEHMNP CHAPMEN
ACEHMNR MARCHEN
ACEHMNS MANCHES
ACEHMNT MANCHET
ACEHMPR CHAMPER
ACEHMRR CHARMER
MARCHER
ACEHMRS MARCHES
MESARCH
SCHMEAR
ACEHMRT MATCHER
REMATCH
ACEHMSS SACHEMS
SAMECHS
SCHEMAS
ACEHMST MATCHES
ACEHMTY ECTHYMA
ACEHNNT ENCHANT
ACEHNOP PANOCHE
ACEHNPS PECHANS
ACEHNRR RANCHER
ACEHNRS RANCHES
ACEHNRT CHANTER
TRANCHE
ACEHNST CHASTEN
ACEHNTT ETCHANT
ACEHNTU UNTEACH
ACEHNTY CHANTEY
ACEHNZZ CHAZZEN
ACEHOOT OOTHECA
ACEHOPR POACHER
ACEHOPS CHEAPOS
POACHES
SHOEPAC
ACEHORS CHOREAS
ORACHES
ROACHES
ACEHOSS CHAOSES
ACEHOTY CHAYOTE
ACEHPPS SCHAPPE
ACEHPRS EPARCHS
PARCHES
ACEHPRT CHAPTER
PATCHER
REPATCH
ACEHPRU UPREACH
ACEHPRY EPARCHY
PREACHY
ACEHPST HEPCATS
PATCHES
ACEHRRS ARCHERS
CRASHER

ACEHRRT CHARTER
RECHART
ACEHRRX XERARCH
ACEHRRY ARCHERY
ACEHRSS CHASERS
CRASHES
ESCHARS
ACEHRST CHASTER
RACHETS
RATCHES
ACEHRSW CHAWERS
ACEHRSX EXARCHS
ACEHRSY HYRACES
ACEHRTT CHATTER
RATCHET
ACEHRTW WATCHER
ACEHRTY YACHTER
ACEHRXY EXARCHY
ACEHSSS CHASSES
ACEHSST SACHETS
SCATHES
ACEHSSW CASHEWS
ACEHSTW WATCHES
ACEIILS LAICISE
ACEIILT CILIATE
ACEIILZ LAICIZE
ACEIIPS EPISCIA
ACEIJKS JACKIES
ACEIKLS SACLIKE
ACEIKLT CATLIKE
ACEIKMR KERAMIC
ACEIKPW WICKAPE
ACEIKPX PICKAXE
ACEIKRT TACKIER
ACEIKRW WACKIER
ACEIKSS SEASICK
ACEIKST CAKIEST
ACEILLL ALLELIC
ACEILLM MICELLA
ACEILLX LEXICAL
ACEILMN MELANIC
ACEILMR CLAIMER
MIRACLE
RECLAIM
ACEILMS MALICES
ACEILMT CLIMATE
METICAL
ACEILMX EXCLAIM
ACEILMY MYCELIA
ACEILNN ENCINAL
ACEILNP CAPELIN
PANICLE
PELICAN
ACEILNR CARLINE
ACEILNS INLACES
SANICLE
SCALENI
ACEILNU CAULINE
ACEILOR CALORIE
CARIOLE
COALIER
LORICAE
ACEILOS CELOSIA
ACEILOT ALOETIC
ACEILPR CALIPER
REPLICA
ACEILPS PLAICES
SPECIAL
ACEILPT PLICATE
ACEILPU PECULIA
ACEILRS CLARIES
ECLAIRS
SCALIER
ACEILRT ARTICLE
RECITAL
ACEILRU AURICLE
ACEILRV CAVILER
CLAVIER
VALERIC
ACEILRY CLAYIER
ACEILST ELASTIC
LACIEST
LATICES
ACEILSV VESICAL
ACEILTT LATTICE
TACTILE
ACEILVW WAVICLE
ACEIMMS CAMMIES
ACEIMNO ENCOMIA
ACEIMNP PEMICAN
ACEIMNR CARMINE
ACEIMNS AMNESIC
CINEMAS
ACEIMNT NEMATIC
ACEIMOR COREMIA
ACEIMOV VOMICAE

ACEIMPR CAMPIER
ACEIMPY PYAEMIC
ACEIMRU URAEMIC
ACEIMSS CAMISES
ACEIMST SEMATIC
ACEIMSU CAESIUM
ACEIMTX TAXEMIC
ACEINNP PINNACE
ACEINNR CANNIER
NARCEIN
ACEINNS CANINES
ENCINAS
ACEINNT ANCIENT
ACEINNY CYANINE
ACEINOP APNOEIC
ACEINOS ACINOSE
ACEINOT ACONITE
ACEINPR CAPRINE
ACEINPS INSCAPE
ACEINPT PICANTE
ACEINRS ARCSINE
ARSENIC
CARNIES
ACEINRT CERATIN
CERTAIN
CREATIN
TACRINE
ACEINSS CASEINS
CASSINE
INCASES
ACEINST ACETINS
CINEAST
ACEINTT NICTATE
TETANIC
ACEINTU TUNICAE
ACEINTV VENATIC
ACEINTX INEXACT
ACEINTY CYANITE
ACEINTZ ZINCATE
ACEIOOZ ZOOECIA
ACEIOPT ECTOPIA
ACEIORS SCORIAE
ACEIORT EROTICA
ACEIOTX EXOTICA
ACEIPPR CRAPPIE
EPICARP
ACEIPRS SCRAPIE
SPACIER
ACEIPRT PARETIC
PICRATE
ACEIPST ASEPTIC
PACIEST
SPICATE
ACEIPSU AUSPICE
ACEIPSZ CAPIZES
CAPSIZE
ACEIPTV CAPTIVE
ACEIQRU ACQUIRE
ACEIQSU CAIQUES
ACEIQUZ CAZIQUE
ACEIRRR CARRIER
ACEIRRS CARRIES
SCARIER
ACEIRRT CIRRATE
ERRATIC
ACEIRRW AIRCREW
ACEIRRZ CRAZIER
ACEIRST ATRESIC
CRISTAE
RACIEST
STEARIC
ACEIRSU SAUCIER
ACEIRSV VARICES
VISCERA
ACEIRSZ CRAZIES
ACEIRTT ATRETIC
CATTIER
CITRATE
ACEISSS ASCESIS
ACEISST ASCITES
ECTASIS
ACEISTT CATTIES
STATICE
ACEISTV ACTIVES
ACEISVV VIVACES
ACEITTV CAVETTI
ACEITUX AUXETIC
ACEJKRS JACKERS
ACEJKST JACKETS
ACEJLOR CAJOLER
ACEJLOS CAJOLES
ACEJNOS CAJONES
ACEJNOT JACONET
ACEJNOY JOYANCE
ACEJNSU JAUNCES
ACEJPTU CAJEPUT

ACEJRTT TRAJECT
ACEKKNR KNACKER
ACEKLMS MACKLES
ACEKLNR CRANKLE
ACEKLNS SLACKEN
ACEKLOR EARLOCK
ACEKLPS SPACKLE
ACEKLPT PLACKET
ACEKLRS CALKERS
LACKERS
SLACKER
ACEKLRT TACKLER
ACEKLRU CAULKER
ACEKLST TACKLES
ACEKLSY LACKEYS
ACEKMNP PACKMEN
ACEKMOR COMAKER
ACEKMOS COMAKES
ACEKMRS SMACKER
ACEKNRR CRANKER
ACEKNRS CANKERS
SNACKER
ACEKNSU UNCAKES
ACEKORR CROAKER
ACEKPPR PREPACK
ACEKPRS PACKERS
REPACKS
ACEKPST PACKETS
ACEKRRS RACKERS
RERACKS
ACEKRRT RETRACK
TRACKER
ACEKRSS SACKERS
SCREAKS
ACEKRST RACKETS
RESTACK
RETACKS
STACKER
TACKERS
ACEKRSY SCREAKY
ACEKRTY RACKETY
ACEKSST CASKETS
ACEKSTT TACKETS
ACEKSTW WACKEST
ACEKSUW WAESUCK
ACELLMO CALOMEL
ACELLNU NUCLEAL
ACELLNY CLEANLY
ACELLOR OCELLAR
ACELLOS CALLOSE
LOCALES
ACELLOT COLLATE
ACELLPS SCALPEL
ACELLPY CLYPEAL
ACELLRR CARRELL
ACELLRS CALLERS
CELLARS
RECALLS
SCLERAL
ACELLRY CLEARLY
ACELLST CALLETS
ACELMMR CLAMMER
ACELMOU LEUCOMA
ACELMPR CLAMPER
ACELMRS MARCELS
ACELMSS MESCALS
ACELMST CALMEST
CAMLETS
ACELMSU ALMUCES
MACULES
ACELMSZ MEZCALS
ACELMTU CALUMET
ACELNNO ALENCON
ACELNNS CANNELS
ACELNNU UNCLEAN
ACELNNY LYNCEAN
ACELNOP NOPLACE
ACELNOR CORNEAL
ACELNOS SECONAL
ACELNOT LACTONE
ACELNOZ CALZONE
ACELNPS ENCLASP
SPANCEL
ACELNPU CLEANUP
ACELNRS LANCERS
ACELNRT CENTRAL
ACELNRU LUCARNE
NUCLEAR
UNCLEAR
ACELNRY LARCENY
ACELNST CANTLES
CENTALS
LANCETS

ACELNSU CENSUAL
LACUNES
LAUNCES
UNLACES
ACELNTY LATENCY
ACELNVY VALENCY
ACELOPS ESCALOP
ACELOPT POLECAT
ACELOPU COPULAE
ACELOQU COEQUAL
ACELORR CAROLER
ACELORS CLAROES
COALERS
ESCOLAR
ORACLES
RECOALS
SOLACER
ACELORT LOCATER
ACELORY CALOYER
ACELOSS SOLACES
ACELOST LACTOSE
LOCATES
TALCOSE
ACELOSV ALCOVES
COEVALS
ACELOTT CALOTTE
ACELOTY ACOLYTE
ACELOUV VACUOLE
ACELPPR CLAPPER
ACELPRS CARPELS
CLASPER
PARCELS
PLACERS
RECLASP
SCALPER
ACELPRT PLECTRA
ACELPRY PRELACY
ACELPSS CAPLESS
ACELPST CAPLETS
PLACETS
ACELPSU CAPSULE
SCALEUP
SPECULA
UPSCALE
ACELPSY CYPSELA
ACELPTY ECTYPAL
ACELPUU CUPULAE
ACELQRU CLAQUER
LACQUER
ACELQSU CALQUES
CLAQUES
ACELQUY LACQUEY
ACELRRS CARRELS
ACELRRW CRAWLER
ACELRSS CARLESS
CLASSER
SCALERS
SCLERAS
ACELRST CARTELS
CLARETS
CRESTAL
SCARLET
ACELRSU RECUSAL
SECULAR
ACELRSV CARVELS
CLAVERS
ACELRSW CLAWERS
ACELRTT CLATTER
ACELRTY TREACLY
ACELSSS CLASSES
ACELSST CASTLES
ACELSSU CLAUSES
ACELSTU SULCATE
ACELSTY ACETYLS
ACELSUU ACULEUS
ACELSXY CALYXES
ACELTUY ACUTELY
ACELTXY EXACTLY
ACEMMRR CRAMMER
ACEMMRS SCAMMER
ACEMNOR ROMANCE
ACEMNPS ENCAMPS
ACEMNRW CREWMAN
ACEMNSU ACUMENS
ACEMOPR COMPARE
ACEMOPS POMACES
ACEMORU MORCEAU
ACEMOST COMATES
ACEMOSU MUCOSAE
ACEMPRS CAMPERS
SCAMPER
ACEMRSS SCREAMS
ACENNOS ANCONES
SONANCE
ACENNOT CONNATE
ACENNOX COANNEX

ACENNOZ CANZONE
ACENNRS CANNERS
SCANNER
ACENNRY CANNERY
ACENNST NASCENT
ACENNSU NUANCES
ACENNTY TENANCY
ACENOOR CORONAE
ACENORS CANOERS
COARSEN
CORNEAS
NARCOSE
ACENORT ENACTOR
ACENOST OCTANES
ACENOTV CENTAVO
ACENPRR PRANCER
ACENPRS PRANCES
ACENPTY PATENCY
ACENRRY ERRANCY
ACENRSS ANCRESS
CASERNS
ACENRST CANTERS
CARNETS
NECTARS
RECANTS
SCANTER
TANRECS
TRANCES
ACENRSV CAVERNS
CRAVENS
ACENRSY CARNEYS
ACENRTU CENTAUR
UNCRATE
ACENRTY NECTARY
ACENSST ASCENTS
SECANTS
STANCES
ACENSSU UNCASES
USANCES
ACENSTU NUTCASE
ACENSUU USAUNCE
ACEOOPP APOCOPE
ACEOOTZ ECTOZOA
ACEOPRX EXOCARP
ACEOPSS SCAPOSE
ACEOPST CAPOTES
TOECAPS
ACEOPSW COWPEAS
ACEOPTU OUTPACE
ACEORRS COARSER
ACEORRT CREATOR
REACTOR
ACEORST COASTER
COATERS
RECOATS
ACEORSU ACEROUS
CAROUSE
ACEORSX COAXERS
ACEORTU OUTRACE
ACEORTV OVERACT
ACEORTX EXACTOR
ACEOSSU CASEOUS
ACEOSTT COSTATE
ACEOSTU ACETOUS
ACEOSTV AVOCETS
OCTAVES
ACEOTTV CAVETTO
ACEOTUU COUTEAU
ACEOTUX COTEAUX
ACEPPRS CAPPERS
ACEPRRS CARPERS
SCARPER
SCRAPER
ACEPRSS ESCARPS
PARSECS
SCRAPES
SECPARS
SPACERS
ACEPRST CARPETS
PREACTS
PRECAST
SPECTRA
ACEPRSU APERCUS
SCAUPER
ACEPRTU CAPTURE
ACEPSST ASPECTS
ACEPSTU CUSPATE
TEACUPS
ACEQRTU RACQUET
ACEQSSU CASQUES
SACQUES
ACEQSTU ACQUEST
ACERRRY RECARRY
ACERRSS CRASSER
SCARERS

ACERRST CARTERS
CRATERS
TRACERS
ACERRSU CURARES
ACERRSV CARVERS
CRAVERS
ACERRTT RETRACT
ACERRTY TRACERY
ACERRUV VERRUCA
ACERSST ACTRESS
CASTERS
RECASTS
ACERSSU ARCUSES
CAUSERS
CESURAS
SAUCERS
SUCRASE
ACERSSV SCARVES
ACERSTT SCATTER
ACERSTU CURATES
ACERSTY SECTARY
ACERTTU CURTATE
ACERTTX EXTRACT
ACERTTY CATTERY
ACERTUY CAUTERY
ACESSTT STACTES
ACESSTU CAESTUS
CUESTAS
ACESSTY ECSTASY
ACESSUY CAUSEYS
CAYUSES
ACESTTU ACUTEST
SCUTATE
ACESTTY TESTACY
ACESTUY EUSTACY
ACFFIIT CAITIFF
ACFFIKM MAFFICK
ACFFILT AFFLICT
ACFFINS FANFICS
ACFFINY FANCIFY
ACFFIRT TRAFFIC
ACFFLSS SCLAFFS
ACFFLTU FACTFUL
ACFFOST CASTOFF
OFFCAST
ACFGHIN CHAFING
ACFGINR FARCING
ACFGINS FACINGS
ACFHIIS FIASCHI
ACFHIST CATFISH
ACFHISU FUCHSIA
ACFHRTU FUTHARC
ACFIILN FINICAL
ACFIKTY TACKIFY
ACFILNO FOLACIN
ACFILNY FANCILY
ACFILOY COALIFY
ACFILRY CLARIFY
ACFILSS FISCALS
ACFIMOR ACIFORM
FORMICA
ACFIMRU FUMARIC
ACFIMSS FASCISM
ACFINNY INFANCY
ACFINOT FACTION
ACFINRT FRANTIC
INFARCT
INFRACT
ACFINRY CARNIFY
ACFIOPY OPACIFY
ACFIOSS FIASCOS
ACFIRSY SCARIFY
ACFISST FASCIST
ACFKLRU RACKFUL
ACFKLSU SACKFUL
ACFLLOY FOCALLY
ACFLNOS FALCONS
FLACONS
ACFLNSU CANFULS
CANSFUL
ACFLOPW COWFLAP
ACFLPSU CAPFULS
ACFLRSU CARFULS
ACFLRUU FURCULA
ACFLTTU TACTFUL
ACFLTUY FACULTY
ACFNNOT NONFACT
ACFNNUY UNFANCY
ACFORST FACTORS
ACFORTY FACTORY
ACFRRTU FRACTUR
ACFRSTU FRACTUS
ACGGINR GRACING
ACGGRSY SCRAGGY
ACGHIKN HACKING
ACGHIMO OGHAMIC

ACGHINR ARCHING
CHAGRIN
CHARING
ACGHINS CASHING
CHASING
ACGHINT GNATHIC
ACGHINW CHAWING
CHINWAG
ACGHIOR CHORAGI
ACGHIPR GRAPHIC
ACGHIRS SCRAIGH
ACGHLTU CLAUGHT
ACGHOST GOTCHAS
ACGHOSU GAUCHOS
ACGHRRU CURRAGH
ACGHRSU CURAGHS
ACGIITU AUGITIC
ACGIJKN JACKING
ACGIKLN CALKING
LACKING
ACGIKNP PACKING
ACGIKNR ARCKING
CARKING
RACKING
ACGIKNS CASKING
SACKING
ACGIKNT TACKING
ACGIKNY YACKING
ACGILLN CALLING
ACGILLO LOGICAL
ACGILMN CALMING
ACGILMY MYALGIC
ACGILNN LANCING
ACGILNO COALING
ACGILNP PLACING
ACGILNR CARLING
ACGILNS LACINGS
SCALING
ACGILNT CATLING
TALCING
ACGILNU CINGULA
ACGILNV CALVING
ACGILNW CLAWING
ACGILNY CLAYING
ACGILOT OTALGIC
ACGILRS GARLICS
ACGIMNO COAMING
ACGIMNP CAMPING
ACGINNN CANNING
ACGINNR CRANING
ACGINNT CANTING
ACGINOR ORGANIC
ACGINOT COATING
COTINGA
ACGINOX COAXING
ACGINPP CAPPING
ACGINPR CARPING
CRAPING
ACGINPS SCAPING
SPACING
ACGINRS RACINGS
SACRING
SCARING
ACGINRT CARTING
CRATING
TRACING
ACGINRV CARVING
CRAVING
ACGINRZ CRAZING
ACGINSS CASINGS
ACGINST ACTINGS
CASTING
ACGINSU CAUSING
SAUCING
ACGINSV CAVINGS
ACGINTT CATTING
ACGINUV VICUGNA
ACGIORT ARGOTIC
ACGIRST GASTRIC
TRAGICS
ACGLNOR CLANGOR
ACGLNOY AGLYCON
ACGLNSU GLUCANS
ACGLNSY GLYCANS
ACGLOXY COXALGY
ACGMNOP CAMPONG
ACGNNOR CRANNOG
ACGNOOT OCTAGON
ACGNORS GARCONS
ACGNOSS GASCONS
ACGORSU COUGARS
ACGOSWY COGWAYS
ACGSTTU CATGUTS
ACHHIRS RHACHIS
ACHHLOT CHALOTH
ACHHPPU CHUPPAH
ACHHTTY THATCHY
ACHIILS ISCHIAL
ACHIIMS CHIASMI
ACHIINT CHIANTI
ACHIIPS PACHISI
ACHIIRV CHIVARI
ACHIJKS HIJACKS
ACHIJNT JACINTH
ACHIKRS RICKSHA
ACHIKRY HAYRICK
ACHILLO LOCHIAL
ACHILLP PHALLIC
ACHILLS CHALLIS
ACHILLT THALLIC
ACHILMO MOCHILA
ACHILMS CHIMLAS
ACHILOR CHORIAL
ACHILOS SCHOLIA
ACHILPS CALIPHS
ACHILRS ARCHILS
CARLISH
ACHILRY CHARILY
ACHILSY CLAYISH
ACHIMOS CHAMISO
CHAMOIS
ACHIMOX CHAMOIX
ACHIMRS CHARISM
CHIMARS
CHRISMA
ACHIMSS CHIASMS
ACHIMST TACHISM
ACHINNU UNCHAIN
ACHINOP APHONIC
ACHINPS SPINACH
ACHINRU UNCHAIR
ACHINTX XANTHIC
ACHIOPS ISOPACH
ACHIOPT APHOTIC
ACHIORT CHARIOT
HARICOT
ACHIOST ISOTACH
ACHIPPS SAPPHIC
ACHIPST SPATHIC
ACHIQRU CHARQUI
ACHIQSU QUAICHS
ACHIRTU HAIRCUT
ACHIRTY CHARITY
ACHISSS CHASSIS
ACHISTT CATTISH
TACHIST
ACHKKRU CHUKKAR
ACHKKSU CHUKKAS
ACHKLST KLATSCH
ACHKMMO HAMMOCK
ACHKOPS HOPSACK
ACHKOSS HASSOCK
SHACKOS
ACHKOSW WHACKOS
ACHKRSU CHUKARS
ACHKSTW THWACKS
ACHLLOO ALCOHOL
ACHLLOR CHLORAL
ACHLLOS CHOLLAS
ACHLLOT CHALLOT
ACHLMOP CAMPHOL
ACHLMSY CHLAMYS
ACHLMSZ SCHMALZ
ACHLMYY ALCHYMY
ACHLNOS LOCHANS
ACHLNOY HALCYON
ACHLNSU NUCHALS
ACHLNTU UNLATCH
ACHLOPT POTLACH
ACHLORS CHORALS
SCHOLAR
ACHLORT TROCHAL
ACHLOSW SALCHOW
ACHLTUZ CHALUTZ
ACHMNOR MONARCH
NOMARCH
ACHMNOU UNMACHO
ACHMOPR CAMPHOR
ACHMORS CHROMAS
ACHMORZ MACHZOR
ACHMOST STOMACH
ACHMPTU MATCHUP
ACHMSSU SUMACHS
ACHMSUW CUMSHAW
ACHNNOS CHANSON
NONCASH
ACHNORS ANCHORS
ARCHONS
RANCHOS
ACHNORT CHANTOR
ACHNOTY TACHYON
ACHNOUY CHANOYU
ACHNOVY ANCHOVY
ACHNPSS SCHNAPS
ACHNPUY PAUNCHY
ACHNRTY CHANTRY
ACHNRUY RAUNCHY
UNCHARY
ACHNSTU CANTHUS
CHAUNTS
STAUNCH
ACHNSTY SNATCHY
ACHOOSS CASHOOS
ACHOOST CAHOOTS
ACHOPRS CARHOPS
COPRAHS
ACHOPRY CHARPOY
ACHORRS CHARROS
ACHORRT TROCHAR
ACHORSU AUROCHS
ACHPPSU CHUPPAS
ACHPRSS SCARPHS
ACHPTUZ CHUTZPA
ACHRSTY STARCHY
ACHSSTU CUSHATS
ACHSSUW CUSHAWS
ACHSTUW WAUCHTS
ACIIKNN CANIKIN
ACIIKRS AIRSICK
ACIILLN ALLICIN
ACIILMM MIMICAL
ACIILMS LAICISM
ACIILNS INCISAL
SALICIN
ACIILNV VICINAL
ACIILPT APLITIC
ACIILPU APICULI
ACIILRY CILIARY
ACIILSS SILICAS
ACIILST ITALICS
ACIILSV CLIVIAS
ACIIMMN MINICAM
ACIIMMS MIASMIC
ACIIMNR MINICAR
ACIIMOT COMITIA
ACIINNO ANIONIC
ACIINNS NIACINS
ACIINOV AVIONIC
ACIINPS PISCINA
ACIINTT TITANIC
ACIINUX AUXINIC
ACIIPPR PRIAPIC
ACIIPRT PIRATIC
ACIIRST SATIRIC
ACIITTX TAXITIC
ACIJUZZ JACUZZI
ACIKLLY ALKYLIC
ACIKLNS CALKINS
ACIKLTY TACKILY
ACIKLWY WACKILY
ACIKMOO OOMIACK
ACIKMOT COMATIK
ACIKMSU UMIACKS
ACIKNPY PANICKY
ACIKNST ANTICKS
CATKINS
ACIKORS ARKOSIC
ACIKPRT TRIPACK
ACIKRST KARSTIC
ACILLLY ALLYLIC
ACILLMS MISCALL
ACILLRY LYRICAL
ACILLSS SCILLAS
ACILMNO LIMACON
ACILMOP OILCAMP
ACILMPS PLASMIC
PSALMIC
ACILMPY CAMPILY
ACILMSU MUSICAL
ACILNNO CANNOLI
ACILNNU UNCINAL
ACILNNY CANNILY
ACILNOR CLARION
ACILNOS ALNICOS
OILCANS
ACILNOU INOCULA
ACILNOY ACYLOIN
ACILNPS CAPLINS
INCLASP
ACILNPY PLIANCY
ACILNRS CARLINS
ACILNST CATLINS
TINCALS
ACILNSU UNCIALS
ACILNTU LUNATIC
ACILNTY ANTICLY
ACILNUV VINCULA
ACILOPT CAPITOL
COALPIT
OPTICAL
TOPICAL
ACILOSS SOCIALS
ACILOST CITOLAS
STOICAL
ACILOTV VOLTAIC
ACILOTX TOXICAL
ACILPST PLASTIC
ACILPSU SPICULA
ACILPTY TYPICAL
ACILRSS CRISSAL
ACILRST CITRALS
ACILRSU URACILS
ACILRSY SCARILY
ACILRTU CURTAIL
ACILRTY CLARITY
ACILRVY VICARLY
ACILRYZ CRAZILY
ACILSSS CLASSIS
ACILSUY SAUCILY
ACILTTY CATTILY
TACITLY
ACILTUV VICTUAL
ACIMMNO AMMONIC
ACIMNOP CAMPION
ACIMNOR MINORCA
ACIMNOS ANOSMIC
CAMIONS
MANIOCS
MASONIC
ACIMNPU PANICUM
ACIMNRS NARCISM
ACIMNRT MANTRIC
ACIMNRU CRANIUM
CUMARIN
ACIMNTT CATMINT
ACIMOOS OOMIACS
ACIMOPT APOMICT
POTAMIC
ACIMOSS MOSAICS
ACIMOST ATOMICS
OSMATIC
SOMATIC
ACIMPRT CRAMPIT
ACIMPRY PRIMACY
ACIMPST IMPACTS
ACIMRSS RACISMS
ACIMRSY MYRICAS
ACIMRSZ CZARISM
ACIMSST MASTICS
MISACTS
MISCAST
ACINNOT ACTINON
CONTAIN
ACINNOZ CANZONI
ACINNST INCANTS
STANNIC
ACINNSY CYANINS
ACINOPT CAPTION
PACTION
ACINOQU COQUINA
ACINORR CARRION
ACINORT CAROTIN
CORTINA
ACINORV CORVINA
ACINOSS CAISSON
CASINOS
CASSINO
ACINOST ACTIONS
ATONICS
CATIONS
ACINOSU ACINOUS
ACINOSY SYCONIA
ACINOTT TACTION
ACINOTU AUCTION
CAUTION
ACINPRT CANTRIP
ACINPRU PURANIC
ACINPRY CYPRIAN
ACINPST CATNIPS
ACINQTU QUANTIC
ACINRST NARCIST
ACINRTT TANTRIC
ACINRTU CURTAIN
ACINSUV VICUNAS
ACIOPRS PICAROS
PROSAIC
ACIOPRT APRICOT
APROTIC
PAROTIC
ACIOPST PSOATIC
ACIOPTY OPACITY
ACIORRS CORSAIR
ACIORSU CARIOUS
CURIOSA
ACIORTT CITATOR
RICOTTA
ACIOSST SCOTIAS
ACIOSSV OVISACS
ACIPRSY PISCARY
ACIPRTT TIPCART
ACIPRVY PRIVACY
ACIPSST SPASTIC
ACIPSTT TIPCATS
ACIPTUY PAUCITY
ACIQRTU QUARTIC
ACIQSTU ACQUITS
ACIRRSU CURARIS
ACIRSST RACISTS
SACRIST
ACIRSSU CUIRASS
ACIRSTT ASTRICT
ACIRSTY SATYRIC
ACIRSTZ CZARIST
ACIRTUY RAUCITY
ACISSTT STATICS
ACISSTU CASUIST
ACISTTU CATSUIT
ACITUVY VACUITY
ACJKKSY SKYJACK
ACJKLOW LOCKJAW
ACJKOPT JACKPOT
ACJLORU JOCULAR
ACJMNTU MUNTJAC
ACJPTUU CAJUPUT
ACKKLOY KOLACKY
ACKLLOP POLLACK
ACKLLSY SLACKLY
ACKLMOR ARMLOCK
LOCKRAM
ACKLNOU UNCLOAK
ACKLNRY CRANKLY
ACKLOOR OARLOCK
ACKLORV LAVROCK
ACKLORW WARLOCK
ACKMMMO MAMMOCK
ACKMNOS SOCKMAN
ACKMOTT MATTOCK
ACKNPSU UNPACKS
ACKNRTU UNTRACK
ACKNSTU UNSTACK
UNTACKS
ACKOPSY YAPOCKS
ACKOSTW TOWSACK
ACKPSSY SKYCAPS
ACKPSTU STACKUP
ACLLLOY LOCALLY
ACLLOOR COROLLA
ACLLOPS SCALLOP
ACLLORS COLLARS
ACLLORU LOCULAR
ACLLOSU CALLOUS
ACLLOTU OUTCALL
ACLLOVY VOCALLY
ACLLSUY CULLAYS
ACLMNPU UNCLAMP
ACLMNUY CALUMNY
ACLMOPS COPALMS
ACLMORS CLAMORS
ACLMORU CLAMOUR
ACLMOSU MUCOSAL
ACLMSTU TALCUMS
ACLNNOO NONCOLA
ACLNOOR CORONAL
ACLNOOT COOLANT
OCTANOL
ACLNOOV VOLCANO
ACLNORU CORNUAL
COURLAN
ACLNOSS CLASSON
ACLNOSX CLAXONS
ACLNOUV UNVOCAL
ACLNPSU UNCLASP
ACLNSTY SCANTLY
ACLOOPR CARPOOL
ACLOORT LOCATOR
ACLOOSZ ZOCALOS
ACLOPRT CALTROP
ACLOPRU COPULAR
ACLOPSU COPULAS
CUPOLAS
SCOPULA
ACLOPSY CALYPSO
ACLORRS CORRALS
ACLORST SCROTAL
ACLORSU CAROLUS
OCULARS
OSCULAR
ACLORTY ACTORLY
ACLORYZ CORYZAL
ACLOSTU LOCUSTA
TALCOUS
ACLPRTY CRYPTAL
ACLPRUU CUPULAR
ACLRSSW SCRAWLS
ACLRSSY CRASSLY
ACLRSTU CRUSTAL
CURTALS
ACLRSTY CRYSTAL
ACLRSWY SCRAWLY
ACLSSTU CUTLASS
ACMNOPR CRAMPON
ACMNOPY COMPANY
ACMNORS MACRONS
ACMNORY ACRONYM
ACMNOSS MASCONS
ACMNSTU SANCTUM
ACMOOST SCOTOMA
ACMOPRT COMPART
ACMOPSS COMPASS
ACMOPTU CAMPOUT
ACMORRS CARROMS
ACMOSST MASCOTS
ACMOSSU MUCOSAS
ACMOSTT TOMCATS
ACMQTUU CUMQUAT
ACMRSSU SACRUMS
ACMSSTU MUSCATS
ACMSUUV VACUUMS
ACNNNOS CANNONS
ACNNNUY UNCANNY
ACNNORY CANONRY
ACNNOST CANTONS
ACNNOSY CANYONS
ACNOORS CORONAS
RACOONS
ACNOORT CARTOON
CORANTO
ACNOPSW SNOWCAP
ACNORRS RANCORS
ACNORRU RANCOUR
ACNORRY CARRYON
ACNORST CANTORS
CARTONS
CONTRAS
CRATONS
ACNORSY CRAYONS
ACNORTU COURANT
ACNOSTT OCTANTS
ACNOSTU CONATUS
TOUCANS
ACNOSTW SNOWCAT
ACNPRSY SYNCARP
ACNRRSU CURRANS
ACNRRTU CURRANT
ACNRSWY SCRAWNY
ACNRTUY TRUANCY
ACNRUYZ UNCRAZY
ACOOPRR CORPORA
ACOOPRT ROOTCAP
ACOOPTT TOPCOAT
ACOORTU TOURACO
ACOOSTV OCTAVOS
ACOPPRR PROCARP
ACOPPRS COPPRAS
ACOPRRT CARPORT
ACOPRST CAPTORS
ACOPSTU UPCOAST
ACOPSTW COWPATS
ACORRST CARROTS
TROCARS
ACORRTT TRACTOR
ACORRTU CURATOR
ACORRTY CARROTY
ACORSST CASTORS
COSTARS
ACORSSU SARCOUS
SOUCARS
ACORSSW SOWCARS
ACORSTT COTTARS
ACORSTU CUATROS
SURCOAT
TURACOS
ACORSTV CAVORTS
ACORSTX OXCARTS
ACORSUU RAUCOUS
ACORSYZ CORYZAS
ACORTUU TURACOU
ACOSTTU OUTACTS
OUTCAST
ACOSUUV VACUOUS
ACPPRSY SCRAPPY
ACPSSTU CATSUPS
UPCASTS
ADDDDEL DADDLED
ADDDEER DREADED
READDED
ADDDEGL GLADDED
ADDDEIS DADDIES
ADDDEIW WADDIED
ADDDELN DANDLED
ADDDELP PADDLED
ADDDELR RADDLED
ADDDELS DADDLES
SADDLED
ADDDELW DAWDLED
WADDLED
ADDDELY ADDEDLY
ADDDENO DEODAND
ADDDENS ADDENDS
ADDDENU UNADDED
ADDDEQU QUADDED
ADDDHOY HODADDY
ADDDOOS DOODADS
ADDEEEM ADEEMED
ADDEEEY DEADEYE
ADDEEFM DEFAMED
ADDEEGR DEGRADE
ADDEEHN HEADEND
ADDEEHR ADHERED
REDHEAD
ADDEEHS DEASHED
ADDEEIR DEAIRED
READIED
ADDEEIT IDEATED
ADDEEKN KNEADED
ADDEELM MEDALED
ADDEELN LADENED
ADDEELP PEDALED
PLEADED
ADDEELS DELEADS
ADDEELT DELATED
ADDEELY DELAYED
ADDEEMN AMENDED
DEADMEN
ADDEEMR DREAMED
ADDEENS DEADENS
ADDEENV DAVENED
ADDEERT DERATED
REDATED
TREADED
ADDEEST DEADEST
SEDATED
STEADED
ADDEEWX DEWAXED
ADDEFIR FADDIER
ADDEFLY FADEDLY
ADDEFNU UNFADED
ADDEFRT DRAFTED
ADDEFRU DEFRAUD
ADDEFRW DWARFED
ADDEGGL DAGGLED
ADDEGGR DRAGGED
ADDEGHO GODHEAD
ADDEGJU ADJUDGE
ADDEGLN DANGLED
GLADDEN
ADDEGLR GLADDER
ADDEGRS GADDERS
ADDEGRU GUARDED
ADDEHIR DIEHARD
ADDEHKS KEDDAHS
ADDEHLN HANDLED
ADDEHLS DALEDHS
ADDEHOR HOARDED
ADDEHST HADDEST
ADDEIIM DIAMIDE
ADDEIIS DAISIED
ADDEILL DALLIED
DIALLED
ADDEILP PLAIDED
ADDEILS LADDIES
ADDEILT DILATED
ADDEIMR ADMIRED
ADDEIMS DIADEMS
ADDEIMX ADMIXED
ADDEINO ADENOID
ADDEINP PANDIED
ADDEINR DANDIER
DRAINED
ADDEINS DANDIES
ADDEINT NIDATED
ADDEINU UNAIDED
ADDEINV INVADED
ADDEIOR RADIOED
ADDEIOT IODATED
TOADIED
ADDEIOV AVOIDED
ADDEIPS PADDIES
ADDEISV ADVISED
ADDEISW WADDIES

ADDEISY DAYSIDE
ADDEITU AUDITED
ADDEJLY JADEDLY
ADDEJNU UNJADED
ADDEJRU ADJURED
ADDEKLR DARKLED
ADDELLU ALLUDED
ADDELNR DANDLER
ADDELNS DANDLES
ADDELNU UNLADED
ADDELPP DAPPLED
ADDELPR PADDLER
ADDELPS PADDLES
ADDELRS LADDERS
RADDLES
SADDLER
ADDELRT DARTLED
ADDELRW DAWDLER
DRAWLED
WADDLER
ADDELSS SADDLES
ADDELST STADDLE
ADDELSW DAWDLES
SWADDLE
WADDLES
ADDELTW TWADDLE
ADDELTY DATEDLY
ADDELYZ DAZEDLY
ADDELZZ DAZZLED
ADDEMMR DRAMMED
ADDEMNS DEMANDS
MADDENS
ADDEMOP POMADED
ADDEMRS MADDERS
ADDEMRY DRAMEDY
ADDEMST MADDEST
ADDENOR ADORNED
ADDENOT DONATED
ADDENOU DUODENA
ADDENPU PUDENDA
ADDENRS DANDERS
ADDENRU DAUNDER
ADDENSS DESANDS
SADDENS
ADDENTU DAUNTED
UNDATED
ADDEOPT ADOPTED
ADDEORS DEODARS
ADDEPRS PADDERS
ADDEPTU UPDATED
ADDERSS ADDRESS
ADDERST ADDREST
ADDERSW SWARDED
WADDERS
ADDERSY DRYADES
ADDERTT DRATTED
ADDESST SADDEST
ADDFHIS FADDISH
ADDFIMS FADDISM
ADDFINY DANDIFY
ADDFIST FADDIST
ADDGGIN GADDING
ADDGILN ADDLING
ADDGIMN MADDING
ADDGINO DADOING
ADDGINP PADDING
ADDGINR RADDING
ADDGINW WADDING
ADDGIOS GADOIDS
ADDGIPY GIDDYAP
ADDGMNO GODDAMN
ADDGMOS GODDAMS
ADDGOOS OGDOADS
ADDGOOW DAGWOOD
ADDHIKS KADDISH
ADDHILS LADDISH
ADDHIMS MADDISH
ADDHITY HYDATID
ADDHLOO LADHOOD
ADDHOTY ATHODYD
ADDHSSU SADDHUS
ADDIINS DISDAIN
ADDIIPS DIAPSID
ADDIKST TSADDIK
ADDIKTY KATYDID
ADDIKTZ TZADDIK
ADDILMN MIDLAND
ADDILNY DANDILY
ADDIMNO DIAMOND
ADDIMSS MISADDS
ADDIMSY MIDDAYS
ADDINOR ANDROID
ADDLLRU DULLARD
ADDLNRY DRYLAND
ADDOORS DORADOS
ADDORST DOTARDS
ADDOSTU OUTADDS
ADEEEFY FEDAYEE
ADEEELS EASELED
ADEEELV DELEAVE
ADEEERX EXEDRAE
ADEEESW SEAWEED
ADEEFHS SHEAFED
ADEEFKR FREAKED
ADEEFLN ENDLEAF
ADEEFLR FEDERAL
ADEEFLS DEFLEAS
ADEEFLT DEFLATE
ADEEFMR DEFAMER
ADEEFMS DEFAMES
ADEEFNS DEAFENS
ADEEFPR PREFADE
ADEEFRT DRAFTEE
ADEEFRW WAFERED
ADEEFST DEAFEST
DEFEATS
FEASTED
ADEEGGH EGGHEAD
ADEEGGN ENGAGED
ADEEGLL ALLEGED
ADEEGLM GLEAMED
ADEEGLN ANGELED
GLEANED
ADEEGLR LAGERED
REGALED
ADEEGLT GELATED
LEGATED
ADEEGLU LEAGUED
ADEEGLV GAVELED
ADEEGLZ DEGLAZE
ADEEGMN ENDGAME
ADEEGMS DEGAMES
ADEEGNR ANGERED
DERANGE
ENRAGED
GRANDEE
GRENADE
ADEEGNT AGENTED
NEGATED
ADEEGNV AVENGED
ADEEGOT GOATEED
ADEEGPR PREAGED
ADEEGRR REGRADE
ADEEGRS DRAGEES
GREASED
ADEEGRV GREAVED
ADEEGRW RAGWEED
WAGERED
ADEEGSS DEGASES
ADEEHIR HEADIER
ADEEHJS HADJEES
ADEEHLS LEASHED
ADEEHLX EXHALED
ADEEHMN HEADMEN
ADEEHNN HENNAED
ADEEHNS DASHEEN
ADEEHNV HAVENED
ADEEHPR EPHEDRA
ADEEHRR ADHERER
REHEARD
ADEEHRS ADHERES
HEADERS
HEARSED
SHEARED
ADEEHRT EARTHED
HEARTED
ADEEHRV HAVERED
ADEEHRX EXHEDRA
ADEEHSS DEASHES
ADEEHST HEADSET
ADEEHSV SHEAVED
ADEEHSX HEXADES
ADEEHSY HAYSEED
ADEEIJT JADEITE
ADEEILM EMAILED
LIMEADE
ADEEILN ALIENED
DELAINE
ADEEILR LEADIER
ADEEILS AEDILES
ADEEIMT MEDIATE
ADEEINN ADENINE
ADEEINS ANISEED
ADEEIRR READIER
ADEEIRS DEARIES
READIES
ADEEIRW WEARIED
ADEEISS DISEASE
SEASIDE
ADEEIST IDEATES
ADEEISV ADVISEE
ADEEITU AUDITEE
ADEEITV DEVIATE
ADEEJSY DEEJAYS
ADEEKNP KNEEPAD
ADEEKNR KNEADER
NAKEDER
ADEEKNS SNEAKED
ADEEKNW WAKENED
ADEEKRS DEKARES
ADEEKRW REWAKED
WREAKED
ADEEKTW TWEAKED
ADEEKWY WEEKDAY
ADEELLP LAPELED
ADEELLS ALLSEED
ADEELMM MELAMED
ADEELMN LEADMEN
ADEELMP EMPALED
ADEELMR EMERALD
ADEELMS MEASLED
ADEELMT METALED
ADEELNP DEPLANE
PANELED
ADEELNR LEARNED
ADEELNS LEADENS
ADEELNT LATENED
ADEELOS ELODEAS
ADEELPR PEARLED
PEDALER
PLEADER
REPLEAD
ADEELPS ELAPSED
PLEASED
SEPALED
ADEELPT PETALED
PLEATED
ADEELQU EQUALED
ADEELRS DEALERS
LEADERS
ADEELRT ALERTED
ALTERED
RELATED
TREADLE
ADEELRV RAVELED
ADEELRW LEEWARD
ADEELRX RELAXED
ADEELRY DELAYER
LAYERED
RELAYED
ADEELST DELATES
ADEELSV SLEAVED
ADEELTV VALETED
ADEELTX EXALTED
ADEELTZ TEAZLED
ADEELUV DEVALUE
ADEEMNR AMENDER
MEANDER
REEDMAN
RENAMED
ADEEMNS DEMEANS
SEEDMAN
ADEEMOS OEDEMAS
ADEEMPR PREMADE
ADEEMRR DREAMER
REARMED
REDREAM
ADEEMRS SMEARED
ADEEMRT REMATED
ADEEMST STEAMED
ADEEMSU MEDUSAE
ADEEMWY MAYWEED
ADEENNS ENNEADS
ADEENNX ANNEXED
ADEENPS SNEAPED
SPEANED
ADEENRS ENDEARS
ADEENRV RAVENED
ADEENRY DEANERY
YEAREND
YEARNED
ADEENST STANDEE
ADEENSW DEEWANS
ADEENTT DENTATE
ADEEOPT ADOPTEE
ADEEPPR PAPERED
ADEEPRS RESPADE
SPEARED
ADEEPRT ADEPTER
PREDATE
RETAPED
TAPERED
ADEEPRV DEPRAVE
PERVADE
REPAVED
ADEEPSS PESADES
ADEEPTX EXAPTED
ADEEQTU EQUATED
ADEERRS READERS
REDEARS
REREADS
ADEERRT RETREAD
TREADER
ADEERRV AVERRED
ADEERRW REDWARF
ADEERSS RESEDAS
ADEERST DEAREST
DERATES
REDATES
SEDATER
ADEERSV ADVERSE
EVADERS
ADEERSW DRAWEES
RESAWED
ADEERTT TREATED
ADEERTV AVERTED
ADEERTW DEWATER
TARWEED
WATERED
ADEERTX RETAXED
ADEERVW WAVERED
ADEERWX REWAXED
ADEESST SEDATES
ADEESSX AXSEEDS
ADEESSY ESSAYED
ADEESTT ESTATED
ADEESTU SAUTEED
ADEESTW SWEATED
ADEESTY YEASTED
ADEESWX DEWAXES
ADEETUX EXUDATE
ADEEWWX WAXWEED
ADEFFIN AFFINED
ADEFFIP PIAFFED
ADEFFIR DAFFIER
ADEFFIX AFFIXED
ADEFFLO LEADOFF
ADEFFLR RAFFLED
ADEFFLW WAFFLED
ADEFFQU QUAFFED
ADEFFST STAFFED
ADEFGGL FLAGGED
ADEFGGR FRAGGED
ADEFGLN FLANGED
ADEFGNS DEFANGS
ADEFGOR FORAGED
ADEFGOT FAGOTED
ADEFGRS DEFRAGS
ADEFGRT GRAFTED
ADEFHIS DEAFISH
ADEFHIT FAITHED
ADEFHLS FLASHED
ADEFHLU HEADFUL
ADEFHRW WHARFED
ADEFHST SHAFTED
ADEFIKL FADLIKE
ADEFILL FLAILED
ADEFINS FADEINS
ADEFINT DEFIANT
FAINTED
ADEFIRS FARSIDE
ADEFITX FIXATED
ADEFKLN FLANKED
ADEFKNR FRANKED
ADEFKNU UNFAKED
ADEFLLW DEWFALL
ADEFLMM FLAMMED
ADEFLNN FENLAND
ADEFLOR ALFREDO
ADEFLOT FLOATED
ADEFLPP FLAPPED
ADEFLRS FARDELS
ADEFLRU DAREFUL
ADEFLTT FLATTED
ADEFLTU DEFAULT
FAULTED
ADEFMOS DEFOAMS
ADEFNRS SNARFED
ADEFNSU SNAFUED
ADEFNUZ UNFAZED
ADEFOOS SEAFOOD
ADEFORS FEDORAS
ADEFORV FAVORED
ADEFORY FEODARY
FORAYED
ADEFOTU FADEOUT
ADEFPPR FRAPPED
ADEFRRT DRAFTER
REDRAFT
ADEFRRW DWARFER
ADEFRST STRAFED
ADEFRSY DEFRAYS
ADEFRUY FEUDARY
ADEFSTT DAFTEST
ADEGGGL GAGGLED
ADEGGHL HAGGLED
ADEGGHS SHAGGED
ADEGGLR DRAGGLE
GARGLED
ADEGGLS DAGGLES
SLAGGED
ADEGGLW WAGGLED
ADEGGMO DEMAGOG
ADEGGNS SNAGGED
ADEGGOP PEDAGOG
ADEGGRR DRAGGER
ADEGGRS DAGGERS
ADEGGRY RAGGEDY
ADEGGST GADGETS
STAGGED
ADEGGSW SWAGGED
ADEGGTY GADGETY
ADEGHIN HEADING
ADEGHIR HAGRIDE
ADEGHJU JUGHEAD
ADEGHLU LAUGHED
ADEGHMO HOMAGED
ADEGHNS GNASHED
ADEGHNW WHANGED
ADEGHOR HAGRODE
ADEGHPR GRAPHED
ADEGILL GALLIED
ADEGILN ALIGNED
DEALING
LEADING
ADEGILO GEOIDAL
ADEGILR GLADIER
GLAIRED
ADEGILT LIGATED
ADEGILV GLAIVED
ADEGIMP MEDIGAP
ADEGIMS DEGAMIS
ADEGINN DEANING
ADEGINR DERAIGN
GRADINE
GRAINED
READING
ADEGINV DEAVING
EVADING
ADEGINW WINDAGE
ADEGINZ AGNIZED
ADEGIOT GODETIA
ADEGIRT TRIAGED
ADEGIRU GAUDIER
ADEGIST AGISTED
ADEGISU GAUDIES
ADEGISV VISAGED
ADEGJLN JANGLED
ADEGLLU ULLAGED
ADEGLMN MANGLED
ADEGLNR DANGLER
GNARLED
ADEGLNS DANGLES
GLANDES
LAGENDS
SLANGED
ADEGLNT TANGLED
ADEGLNW WANGLED
ADEGLOP GALOPED
ADEGLOT GLOATED
ADEGLPU PLAGUED
ADEGLSS GLASSED
ADEGMNU AGENDUM
ADEGMOP MEGAPOD
ADEGNNU DUNNAGE
ADEGNOR GROANED
ADEGNOT TANGOED
ADEGNOV DOGVANE
ADEGNOW GOWANED
WAGONED
ADEGNPR PRANGED
ADEGNPU UNPAGED
ADEGNRR GNARRED
GRANDER
ADEGNRS DANGERS
GANDERS
GARDENS
ADEGNRT DRAGNET
GRANTED
ADEGNST STANGED
ADEGNSU AUGENDS
ADEGNTU UNGATED
ADEGNTW TWANGED
ADEGORS DOGEARS
ADEGORT GAROTED
ADEGORW DOWAGER
WORDAGE
ADEGOSS DOSAGES
SEADOGS
ADEGOST DOTAGES
ADEGOTT TOGATED
ADEGOVY VOYAGED
ADEGPRS GRASPED
SPARGED
ADEGPRU UPGRADE
ADEGPUZ UPGAZED
ADEGRRS GRADERS
REGARDS
ADEGRRU GUARDER
ADEGRSS GRASSED
ADEGRSU DESUGAR
SUGARED
ADEGRTY GYRATED
TRAGEDY
ADEGRUU AUGURED
ADEGRUY GAUDERY
ADEGSSU DEGAUSS
ADEHHKS KHEDAHS
ADEHHOP HOPHEAD
ADEHHOT HOTHEAD
ADEHILN INHALED
ADEHILP HELIPAD
ADEHILS HALIDES
ADEHILY HEADILY
ADEHIMO HAEMOID
ADEHINP HEADPIN
PINHEAD
ADEHINR HANDIER
ADEHIPR RAPHIDE
ADEHIPS APHIDES
DIPHASE
ADEHIPT PITHEAD
ADEHIRR HARDIER
HARRIED
ADEHIRS AIRSHED
DASHIER
HARDIES
SHADIER
ADEHIRT AIRTHED
ADEHIRW RAWHIDE
ADEHIRY HAYRIDE
HYDRIAE
ADEHKNS SHANKED
ADEHKNT THANKED
ADEHKOT KATHODE
ADEHKRS SHARKED
ADEHLLO HALLOED
HOLLAED
ADEHLMS LAMEDHS
ADEHLNR HANDLER
ADEHLNS HANDLES
HANDSEL
ADEHLOS SHOALED
ADEHLOT LOATHED
ADEHLPR RALPHED
ADEHLPS PLASHED
ADEHLRS HERALDS
ADEHLSS HASSLED
SLASHED
ADEHLST DALETHS
ADEHLSU SHAULED
ADEHLSW SHAWLED
ADEHLTY DEATHLY
ADEHMMS SHAMMED
ADEHMMW WHAMMED
ADEHMNR HERDMAN
ADEHMSS SMASHED
ADEHNPS DAPHNES
ADEHNRS HANDERS
HARDENS
ADEHNRU UNHEARD
ADEHNST HANDSET
ADEHNTU HAUNTED
ADEHOPT POTHEAD
ADEHOPX HEXAPOD
ADEHORR HOARDER
ADEHOTW TOWHEAD
ADEHPPW WHAPPED
ADEHPRS PHRASED
SHARPED
ADEHPST HEPTADS
SPATHED
ADEHPSW PSHAWED
ADEHQSU QUASHED
ADEHRSS DASHERS
SHADERS
ADEHRST DEARTHS
HARDEST
HARDSET
HATREDS
THREADS
TRASHED
ADEHRSY HYDRASE
ADEHRTW THRAWED
WRATHED
ADEHRTY HYDRATE
THREADY
ADEHSST STASHED
ADEHSSW SWASHED
ADEHSTW SWATHED
ADEHSYY HEYDAYS
ADEHUZZ HUZZAED
ADEIILR DELIRIA
ADEIILS DAILIES
LIAISED
SEDILIA
ADEIIMN AMIDINE
DIAMINE
ADEIINR DENARII
ADEIINT INEDITA
ADEIINZ DIAZINE
ADEIIPR PERIDIA
ADEIIRS DAIRIES
DIARIES
ADEIISS DAISIES
ADEIJMR JEMIDAR
ADEIKRS DAIKERS
ADEIKRT TRAIKED
ADEILLL DIALLEL
ADEILLR DALLIER
DIALLER
RALLIED
ADEILLS DALLIES
SALLIED
ADEILLT TALLIED
ADEILLV VIALLED
ADEILLY IDEALLY
ADEILMM DILEMMA
ADEILMO MELODIA
ADEILMP IMPALED
IMPLEAD
ADEILMS MEDIALS
MISDEAL
MISLEAD
ADEILMU MIAULED
ADEILNN ANNELID
LINDANE
ADEILNP PLAINED
ADEILNS DENIALS
SNAILED
ADEILNU ALIUNDE
UNIDEAL
ADEILNV ANVILED
ADEILOP OEDIPAL
ADEILOR DARIOLE
ADEILOS ISOLEAD
ADEILOZ DIAZOLE
ADEILPP APPLIED
ADEILPR LIPREAD
PREDIAL
ADEILPS ALIPEDS
ELAPIDS
LAPIDES
PALSIED
PLEIADS
ADEILPT PLAITED
TALIPED
ADEILQU QUAILED
ADEILRR LARDIER
ADEILRS DERAILS
DIALERS
REDIALS
ADEILRT DILATER
REDTAIL
TRAILED
ADEILRU UREDIAL
ADEILRV RIVALED
ADEILRY READILY
ADEILSS AIDLESS
ADEILST DETAILS
DILATES
ADEILSU AUDILES
ADEILSV DEVISAL
ADEILSY DIALYSE
ADEILUZ DUALIZE
ADEILYZ DIALYZE
ADEIMMR MERMAID
ADEIMMS MISMADE
ADEIMNO AMIDONE
DOMAINE
ADEIMNR INARMED
ADEIMNS MAIDENS
MEDIANS
MEDINAS
SIDEMAN
ADEIMNT MEDIANT
ADEIMNU UNAIMED
ADEIMOU MIAOUED
ADEIMOW MIAOWED
ADEIMRR ADMIRER
MARRIED

ADEIMRS ADMIRES
MISREAD
SEDARIM
SIDEARM
ADEIMRT READMIT
ADEIMRY MIDYEAR
ADEIMST DIASTEM
MISDATE
ADEIMSX ADMIXES
ADEIMTY DAYTIME
ADEINNR NARDINE
ADEINOR ANEROID
ADEINOV NAEVOID
ADEINOX DIOXANE
ADEINOZ ANODIZE
ADEINPR PARDINE
ADEINPS PANDIES
ADEINPT DEPAINT
PAINTED
PATINED
ADEINRR DRAINER
RANDIER
ADEINRS RANDIES
SANDIER
SARDINE
ADEINRT ANTIRED
DETRAIN
TRAINED
ADEINRU UNAIRED
URANIDE
ADEINRV INVADER
RAVINED
ADEINST DESTAIN
DETAINS
INSTEAD
NIDATES
SAINTED
STAINED
ADEINSV INVADES
ADEINTT TAINTED
ADEINTU AUDIENT
ADEINTV DEVIANT
ADEIOPS ADIPOSE
ADEIOPT OPIATED
ADEIORS ROADIES
ADEIORV AVODIRE
AVOIDER
ADEIORX EXORDIA
ADEIOST IODATES
TOADIES
ADEIOSX OXIDASE
ADEIOTX OXIDATE
ADEIPPR PREPAID
ADEIPRR PARRIED
RAPIDER
ADEIPRS ASPIRED
DESPAIR
DIAPERS
PRAISED
ADEIPRT DIPTERA
PARTIED
PIRATED
ADEIPSS APSIDES
ADEIQRU QUERIDA
ADEIRRS RAIDERS
ADEIRRT TARDIER
TARRIED
ADEIRRV ARRIVED
ADEIRST ARIDEST
ASTRIDE
DIASTER
DISRATE
STAIDER
TARDIES
TIRADES
ADEIRSU RESIDUA
ADEIRSV ADVISER
ADEIRSX RADIXES
ADEIRTT ATTIRED
ADEIRTV TARDIVE
ADEIRTY DIETARY
ADEISSS DASSIES
ADEISST DISSEAT
ADEISSV ADVISES
DISSAVE
ADEISTU DAUTIES
ADEISTV DATIVES
VISTAED
ADEISTW DAWTIES
WAISTED
ADEISVV SAVVIED
ADEISWY SIDEWAY
WAYSIDE
ADEITUZ DEUTZIA
ADEITWY TIDEWAY
ADEJMOR MAJORED

ADEJNTU JAUNTED
ADEJOPR JEOPARD
ADEJRRU ADJURER
ADEJRSU ADJURES
ADEJSSU JUDASES
ADEKKNS SKANKED
ADEKLNP PLANKED
ADEKLNR RANKLED
ADEKLNS KALENDS
ADEKLNY NAKEDLY
ADEKLOP POLKAED
ADEKLOS SKOALED
ADEKLRS DARKLES
ADEKLST STALKED
ADEKMNS DESKMAN
ADEKMRS DEMARKS
ADEKNPP KNAPPED
ADEKNPR PRANKED
ADEKNPS SPANKED
ADEKNRR KNARRED
ADEKNRS DARKENS
ADEKNRU UNRAKED
ADEKNST DANKEST
ADEKNSU UNASKED
ADEKNSW SWANKED
ADEKNVY VANDYKE
ADEKORT TROAKED
ADEKPRS SPARKED
ADEKPSY KEYPADS
ADEKRST DARKEST
STRAKED
ADELLMU MEDULLA
ADELLNR LANDLER
ADELLOW ALLOWED
ADELLOY ALLOYED
ADELLPS SPALLED
ADELLRS LADLERS
ADELLRU ALLURED
ADELLST STALLED
ADELLSU ALLUDES
ALUDELS
ADELMMS SLAMMED
ADELMNN LANDMEN
ADELMNR MANDREL
ADELMNT MANTLED
ADELMOR EARLDOM
ADELMOS DAMOSEL
ADELMOZ DAMOZEL
ADELMPS PSALMED
SAMPLED
ADELMRS MEDLARS
ADELMRU MURALED
ADELMSS DAMSELS
ADELMST MALTEDS
ADELMSU ALMUDES
MEDUSAL
ADELMSW WADMELS
ADELMYZ MAZEDLY
ADELNNP PLANNED
ADELNNU UNLADEN
ADELNOR LADRONE
ADELNOT TALONED
ADELNPT PLANTED
ADELNPY ENDPLAY
ADELNRS DARNELS
LANDERS
RELANDS
SLANDER
SNARLED
ADELNRU LAUNDER
LURDANE
ADELNSS SENDALS
ADELNST DENTALS
SLANTED
ADELNSU UNLADES
UNLEADS
ADELNSY ADENYLS
ADELNTU LUNATED
ADELNTW WETLAND
ADELOPR LEOPARD
PAROLED
PRELOAD
ADELOPS DEPOSAL
PEDALOS
ADELOPT TADPOLE
ADELORS LOADERS
ORDEALS
RELOADS
ADELORT DELATOR
LEOTARD
ADELORU ROULADE
ADELOSS ALDOSES
LASSOED
ADELOST SOLATED
ADELOSV SALVOED
ADELOTT TOTALED

ADELOTU OUTLEAD
ADELPPS DAPPLES
SLAPPED
ADELPRS PEDLARS
ADELPRY PEDLARY
ADELPST STAPLED
ADELPSW DEWLAPS
ADELPSY SPLAYED
ADELPTT PLATTED
ADELPTY ADEPTLY
ADELRRS LARDERS
ADELRRU RUDERAL
ADELRRW DRAWLER
ADELRSS RASSLED
ADELRST DARTLES
ADELRSU LAUDERS
ADELRSW WARSLED
ADELRTT RATTLED
ADELRTW TRAWLED
ADELRTX DEXTRAL
ADELRTY LYRATED
ADELRZZ DAZZLER
ADELSST DESALTS
ADELSTT SLATTED
ADELSTU AULDEST
SALUTED
ADELSUV AVULSED
ADELSZZ DAZZLES
ADELTTT TATTLED
ADELTTW WATTLED
ADELTUV VAULTED
ADELTUX LUXATED
ADELTWZ WALTZED
ADEMMPS SPAMMED
ADEMMRS DAMMERS
ADEMMRT TRAMMED
ADEMNNS SANDMEN
ADEMNNU MUNDANE
UNNAMED
ADEMNOR MADRONE
ADEMNOS DAEMONS
MASONED
MONADES
ADEMNOW ADWOMEN
WOMANED
ADEMNPS DAMPENS
ADEMNRS DAMNERS
REMANDS
ADEMNRU DURAMEN
MANURED
MAUNDER
UNARMED
ADEMNRY DRAYMEN
YARDMEN
ADEMNSS DESMANS
MADNESS
ADEMNST TANDEMS
ADEMNSU MEDUSAN
ADEMNSY DAYSMEN
ADEMNTU UNMATED
UNTAMED
ADEMOPS POMADES
ADEMORR ARMORED
ADEMORS RADOMES
ADEMOSV VAMOSED
ADEMOSW MEADOWS
ADEMOSY SAMOYED
SOMEDAY
ADEMOWY MEADOWY
ADEMPRS DAMPERS
ADEMPRT TRAMPED
ADEMPSS SPASMED
ADEMPST DAMPEST
STAMPED
ADEMPSW SWAMPED
ADEMRRU EARDRUM
ADEMRST SMARTED
ADEMRSU REMUDAS
ADEMRSW SWARMED
ADEMRTU MATURED
ADEMSST DEMASTS
ADEMSSU ASSUMED
MEDUSAS
ADEMTTU MUTATED
ADENNOY ANNOYED
ANODYNE
ADENNPS SPANNED
ADENNPT PENDANT
ADENNSU DUENNAS
ADENNSW SWANNED
ADENOOT ODONATE
ADENOPR APRONED
OPERAND
PADRONE
PANDORE
ADENOPS DAPSONE

ADENOPT NOTEPAD
ADENORR ADORNER
READORN
ADENORU RONDEAU
ADENOST DONATES
ADENOSY NOYADES
ADENOTT NOTATED
ADENOTZ ZONATED
ADENPPS APPENDS
SNAPPED
ADENPRR PARDNER
ADENPRS PANDERS
ADENPRU UNDRAPE
ADENPRW PRAWNED
PREDAWN
ADENPST PEDANTS
PENTADS
ADENPSW SPAWNED
ADENPSX EXPANDS
SPANDEX
ADENPSY DYSPNEA
ADENPTU UNADEPT
ADENPUV UNPAVED
ADENQTU QUANTED
ADENRRS DARNERS
ERRANDS
ADENRRW REDRAWN
ADENRRY REYNARD
ADENRSS SANDERS
ADENRST STANDER
ADENRSU ASUNDER
DANSEUR
ADENRSW WANDERS
WARDENS
ADENRSZ ZANDERS
ADENRTU DAUNTER
NATURED
UNRATED
UNTREAD
ADENRTV VERDANT
ADENRTX DEXTRAN
ADENRUY UNREADY
ADENRUZ UNRAZED
ADENSSS SADNESS
ADENSSU SUNDAES
ADENSSW WESSAND
ADENSTT ATTENDS
ADENSTU UNSATED
ADENSTV ADVENTS
ADENSUV UNSAVED
ADENSUW UNSAWED
ADENSWY ENDWAYS
ADENTTU ATTUNED
NUTATED
TAUNTED
ADENTUV VAUNTED
ADENTUX UNTAXED
ADENUWX UNWAXED
ADEOORS ROADEOS
ADEOPPS APPOSED
ADEOPQU OPAQUED
ADEOPRR EARDROP
ADEOPRT ADOPTER
READOPT
ADEOPRV VAPORED
ADEOPST PODESTA
ADEORRS ADORERS
DROSERA
ADEORRW ARROWED
ADEORRZ RAZORED
ADEORSS SARODES
ADEORST ROASTED
TORSADE
ADEORSU AROUSED
ADEORSV OVERSAD
SAVORED
ADEORSW REDOWAS
ADEORTT ROTATED
ADEORTU OUTDARE
OUTREAD
READOUT
ADEORYZ ZEDOARY
ADEOSTT TOASTED
ADEOTTU OUTDATE
ADEPPRT TRAPPED
ADEPPRW WRAPPED
ADEPPSW SWAPPED
ADEPPTU PUPATED
ADEPRRS DRAPERS
SPARRED
ADEPRRY DRAPERY
ADEPRSS SPADERS
SPREADS
ADEPRST DEPARTS
PETARDS
ADEPRSY SPRAYED

ADEPRTU UPDATER
UPRATED
ADEPSTT SPATTED
ADEPSTU UPDATES
ADEQRSU SQUARED
ADERRST DARTERS
RETARDS
STARRED
TRADERS
ADERRSW DRAWERS
REDRAWS
REWARDS
WARDERS
ADERRSY YARDERS
ADERSSU ASSURED
ADERSTT STARTED
TETRADS
ADERSTV ADVERTS
STARVED
ADERSTW STEWARD
STRAWED
ADERSTY STRAYED
ADERSUY DASYURE
ADERSVW DWARVES
ADESSTW WADSETS
ADESTTU STATUED
ADESTTW SWATTED
ADFFGIN DAFFING
ADFFHNO HANDOFF
OFFHAND
ADFFILY DAFFILY
ADFFIST DISTAFF
ADFFLNO FANFOLD
ADFFLOO OFFLOAD
ADFFORS AFFORDS
ADFGGIN FADGING
ADFGINR FARDING
ADFGINS FADINGS
ADFHLNU HANDFUL
ADFHLSY SHADFLY
ADFHOOS SHADOOF
ADFHSSU SHADUFS
ADFILLU FLUIDAL
ADFIMNY DAMNIFY
ADFINRT INDRAFT
ADFLMPU MUDFLAP
ADFLMTU MUDFLAT
ADFLNOP PLAFOND
ADFLNSY SANDFLY
ADFLORU FOULARD
ADFMNOS FANDOMS
ADFNNOT FONDANT
ADFNOST FANTODS
ADFOOPT FOOTPAD
ADFOOTW FATWOOD
ADFORRW FORWARD
FROWARD
ADFPRTU UPDRAFT
ADGGHNO HANGDOG
ADGGINN DANGING
ADGGINO GOADING
ADGGINR GRADING
NIGGARD
ADGHILO HIDALGO
ADGHINN HANDING
ADGHINS DASHING
SHADING
ADGHIPR DIGRAPH
ADGHIRS DISHRAG
ADGHNNU HANDGUN
ADGHNOS HAGDONS
SANDHOG
ADGHRTU DRAUGHT
ADGIILN DIALING
GLIADIN
ADGIILT DIGITAL
ADGIINO GONIDIA
ADGIINR RAIDING
ADGIINS SIGANID
ADGIINU IGUANID
ADGIIPY PYGIDIA
ADGIKNR DARKING
ADGILLN LADLING
ADGILNN LANDING
ADGILNO LOADING
ADGILNR DARLING
LARDING
ADGILNS LADINGS
LIGANDS
ADGILNU LANGUID
LAUDING
ADGILOR GOLIARD
ADGILOS DIALOGS
ADGILOV VALGOID
ADGILUY GAUDILY
ADGIMMN DAMMING

ADGIMNN DAMNING
ADGIMNP DAMPING
ADGINNR DARNING
ADGINNS SANDING
ADGINNW DAWNING
ADGINOR ADORING
ADGINOS GANOIDS
ADGINOT DOATING
ADGINPP DAPPING
ADGINPR DRAPING
ADGINPS SPADING
ADGINRS DARINGS
GRADINS
ADGINRT DARTING
TRADING
ADGINRW DRAWING
WARDING
ADGINRY DRAYING
YARDING
ADGINSU AUDINGS
ADGINTU DAUTING
ADGINTW DAWTING
ADGIORT GORDITA
ADGIPRU PAGURID
ADGIRSU GUISARD
ADGIRZZ GIZZARD
ADGLMNO MANGOLD
ADGLNOO DONGOLA
GONDOLA
ADGLNOR GOLDARN
ADGLNOY DAYLONG
ADGLNRY GRANDLY
ADGLOPS LAPDOGS
ADGLOWY DAYGLOW
ADGMNOO GOODMAN
ADGMNOR GORMAND
ADGNOOR DRAGOON
GADROON
ADGNOPS DOGNAPS
ADGNORS DRAGONS
ADGNORU AGROUND
ADGNORY ORGANDY
ADGNRRU GURNARD
ADGNRUU UNGUARD
ADGORTU OUTDRAG
ADGRSTU DUSTRAG
ADHHIST HADITHS
ADHHISW WHIDAHS
ADHHMOS SHAHDOM
ADHHOSU HOUDAHS
ADHHOSW HOWDAHS
ADHHSWY WHYDAHS
ADHIIKS DASHIKI
ADHIIMS MAIDISH
ADHIKOP HAPKIDO
ADHIKRS DARKISH
ADHILMO HALIDOM
ADHILNY HANDILY
ADHILOP HAPLOID
ADHILOS HALOIDS
ADHILOY HOLIDAY
HYALOID
HYOIDAL
ADHILRY HARDILY
ADHILSY LADYISH
SHADILY
ADHIMPS DAMPISH
PHASMID
ADHIMRS DIRHAMS
MIDRASH
ADHINOT ANTHOID
ADHINPS DISHPAN
ADHINPU DAUPHIN
ADHINSS SANDHIS
ADHIORS HAIRDOS
ADHIOST TOADISH
ADHIRSS SHAIRDS
ADHKORW DORHAWK
ADHLLLO HOLDALL
ADHLLNO HOLLAND
ADHLORS HOLARDS
ADHLOYY HOLYDAY
ADHMNOO MANHOOD
ADHNNSU UNHANDS
ADHNNUY UNHANDY
ADHNOOS DAHOONS
ADHNORS HADRONS
ADHNOTU HANDOUT
ADHNRSU DHURNAS
ADHNRTY HYDRANT
ADHOOPT HOPTOAD
ADHOORR RHODORA
ADHOORS DHOORAS
ADHOPRT HARDTOP
ADHOPRU UPHOARD
ADHOPST DASHPOT

ADHORRU DHOURRA
ADHORSU DOURAHS
ADHOSSW SHADOWS
ADHOSWY SHADOWY
ADHPRSU PURDAHS
ADIIKOS AIKIDOS
ADIILMS MILADIS
MISDIAL
MISLAID
ADIILNO LIANOID
ADIILNV INVALID
ADIILOS SIALOID
ADIILSS SIALIDS
ADIILST DIALIST
ADIILUV DILUVIA
ADIIMNN INDAMIN
ADIIMNS AMIDINS
DIAMINS
ADIIMOS DAIMIOS
ADIIMPV IMPAVID
ADIIMRS MIDAIRS
ADIIMSS MISSAID
ADIINST DISTAIN
ADIINSU INDUSIA
ADIINSV AVIDINS
ADIINSZ DIAZINS
ADIIPRS DIAPIRS
ADIIPXY PYXIDIA
ADIIRST DIARIST
ADIIRTY ARIDITY
ADIISSY SAIYIDS
ADIITVY AVIDITY
ADIJMSS MASJIDS
ADIJNOS ADJOINS
ADIJNOT ADJOINT
ADIJSSS JASSIDS
ADIKLNY LADYKIN
ADIKLOR KILORAD
ADIKLOS ODALISK
ADIKMNN MANKIND
ADIKMOS MIKADOS
ADIKNOS DAIKONS
ADIKNPS KIDNAPS
ADIKOST DAKOITS
ADIKOTY DAKOITY
ADIKSTT DIKTATS
ADIKSUZ ADZUKIS
ADIKSWY SKIDWAY
ADILLMM MILLDAM
ADILLRY LAIRDLY
ADILLTY TIDALLY
ADILLVY VALIDLY
ADILLYY DAYLILY
ADILMNR MANDRIL
RIMLAND
ADILMNU MAUDLIN
ADILMOP DIPLOMA
ADILMOS AMIDOLS
ADILMOU ALODIUM
ADILMOY AMYLOID
ADILMPS PLASMID
ADILMSS DISMALS
ADILMSU DUALISM
ADILNNS INLANDS
ADILNOR ORDINAL
ADILNOS LADINOS
ADILNRS ALDRINS
ADILNRU DIURNAL
ADILNSS ISLANDS
ADILNSU SUNDIAL
ADILOOV OVOIDAL
ADILOOZ ZOOIDAL
ADILOPR DIPOLAR
ADILORT DILATOR
ADILOSZ OZALIDS
ADILOTU OUTLAID
ADILPRY PYRALID
RAPIDLY
ADILPSS SALPIDS
ADILPST PLASTID
ADILPSY DISPLAY
ADILPTU PLAUDIT
ADILPVY VAPIDLY
ADILQSU SQUALID
ADILRSZ LIZARDS
ADILRTY TARDILY
ADILSTU DUALIST
TULADIS
ADILSTY STAIDLY
ADILTUY DUALITY
ADIMNOS DAIMONS
DOMAINS
ADIMNST MANTIDS
ADIMORR MIRADOR
ADIMOST DIATOMS
MASTOID

ADIMOSY DAIMYOS
ADIMOTT MATTOID
ADIMPRY PYRAMID
ADIMRSS DISARMS
ADIMRSU RADIUMS
ADIMRSW MISDRAW
ADIMRSY MYRIADS
ADIMSSS SADISMS
ADIMSST DISMAST
ADIMSSY DISMAYS
ADIMSTU STADIUM
ADIMSWY MIDWAYS
ADINNNS NANDINS
ADINNOP DIPNOAN
NONPAID
ADINNOR ANDIRON
ADINNRS INNARDS
ADINNRW INDRAWN
ADINOPP OPPIDAN
ADINOPR PADRONI
PONIARD
ADINOPT PINTADO
ADINORS INROADS
ORDAINS
SADIRON
ADINORT DIATRON
ADINOSX DIOXANS
ADINOTX OXIDANT
ADINPST PANDITS
SANDPIT
ADINQRS QINDARS
ADINRSU DURIANS
ADINRSW INWARDS
ADINRTU UNITARD
ADINSTT DISTANT
ADINTTY DITTANY
ADINWWY WINDWAY
ADIOOPR PARODOI
ADIOOSW WOODSIA
ADIOPRR AIRDROP
ADIOPRS SPAROID
ADIOPRT PAROTID
ADIOPSU ADIPOUS
ADIORSV ADVISOR
ADIORTU AUDITOR
ADIOSTU OUTSAID
ADIOSVW DISAVOW
ADIPRSS SPARIDS
ADIPRST DISPART
ADIQSTU DIQUATS
ADIRRSS SIRDARS
ADIRRST RITARDS
ADIRSSU SARDIUS
ADIRSSV VISARDS
ADIRSTY SATYRID
ADIRSUY DYSURIA
ADIRSVZ VIZARDS
ADIRSWZ WIZARDS
ADIRSZZ IZZARDS
ADISSST SADISTS
ADISSYY SAYYIDS
ADJKOSU JUDOKAS
ADJLMOR JARLDOM
ADJNORS JORDANS
ADJNORU ADJOURN
ADJORRU ADJUROR
ADJSSTU ADJUSTS
ADKLMRU MUDLARK
ADKOPSU PADOUKS
ADKORWY DAYWORK
WORKDAY
ADKRSWY SKYWARD
ADLLMOW WADMOLL
ADLLMOY MODALLY
ADLLNOW LOWLAND
ADLLNOY NODALLY
ADLLOPR POLLARD
ADLLORS DOLLARS
ADLLRWY DRYWALL
ADLLTUY ADULTLY
ADLMNOS ALMONDS
DOLMANS
ADLMNOY ALMONDY
ADLMOOR LORDOMA
MALODOR
ADLMORU MODULAR
ADLMOSW WADMOLS
ADLNNOR NORLAND
ADLNNSU SUNLAND
ADLNOOR LARDOON
ADLNOOS ONLOADS
ADLNOPU POUNDAL
ADLNORS LADRONS
LARDONS
ADLNORT TROLAND
ADLNORU NODULAR
ADLNOSS SOLANDS
SOLDANS
ADLNOST DALTONS
SANDLOT
ADLNOSU UNLOADS
ADLNOSY SYNODAL
ADLNOTU OUTLAND
ADLNPSU UPLANDS
ADLNRSU LURDANS
ADLNRUU UNDULAR
ADLNRUY LAUNDRY
ADLNSSU SULDANS
ADLNTUU UNADULT
ADLOPRU POULARD
ADLOPSU UPLOADS
ADLORRW WARLORD
ADLORSS DORSALS
ADLORSU SUDORAL
ADLOSSS DOSSALS
ADMMNSU SUMMAND
ADMMOST MADTOMS
ADMNOOR DOORMAN
MADRONO
ADMNOOW WOODMAN
ADMNOOZ MADZOON
ADMNOQU QUONDAM
ADMNORS RANDOMS
RODSMAN
ADMNORT DORMANT
MORDANT
ADMNOSS DAMSONS
ADMNOSU OSMUNDA
ADMNOSY DYNAMOS
ADMNSTU DUSTMAN
ADMOORT DOORMAT
ADMOORY DAYROOM
ADMORRS RAMRODS
ADMORST STARDOM
TSARDOM
ADMORSU MADUROS
ADMORTW MADWORT
ADMORTZ TZARDOM
ADMRSTU DURMAST
MUSTARD
ADNNOOY NOONDAY
ADNNOSU ADNOUNS
ADNNRUW UNDRAWN
ADNOOPR PANDOOR
ADNOORT DONATOR
ODORANT
TANDOOR
TORNADO
ADNOPRS PARDONS
ADNOPRU PANDOUR
ADNOPST DOPANTS
ADNORSW ONWARDS
ADNORTU ROTUNDA
ADNORTY TARDYON
ADNOSSU SOUDANS
ADNOSTU ASTOUND
ADNPSTU DUSTPAN
STANDUP
UPSTAND
ADNRSST STRANDS
ADNRSTU TUNDRAS
ADNRSUW SUNWARD
UNDRAWS
ADNSSTY DYNASTS
ADNSTYY DYNASTY
ADOOPRS PARODOS
ADOOPSU APODOUS
ADOOPSW SAPWOOD
ADOORWY DOORWAY
ADOOSTT TOSTADO
ADOOWWX WOODWAX
ADORRSU ARDOURS
ADORSTW TOWARDS
ADORSUU ARDUOUS
ADORTUW OUTDRAW
OUTWARD
ADPRSTU UPDARTS
ADPRSUW UPWARDS
ADSSTUW SAWDUST
AEEEGKL KEELAGE
AEEEGLT LEGATEE
AEEEGNT TEENAGE
AEEEGPR PEERAGE
AEEEGPS SEEPAGE
AEEEGRR EAGERER
AEEEGRT ETAGERE
AEEEILN ALIENEE
AEEELRS RELEASE
AEEELTV ELEVATE
AEEERVW REWEAVE
AEEERWY EYEWEAR
AEEFFLL FELAFEL
AEEFGLN FENAGLE
AEEFGRS SERFAGE
AEEFHRT FEATHER
TEREFAH
AEEFILR FILAREE
LEAFIER
AEEFILW ALEWIFE
AEEFIRS FAERIES
FREESIA
AEEFKRS FAKEERS
AEEFLLT FELLATE
LEAFLET
AEEFLMN ENFLAME
AEEFLMS FEMALES
AEEFLRT REFLATE
AEEFLRU FERULAE
AEEFLRW WELFARE
AEEFLSU EASEFUL
AEEFLTX TELEFAX
AEEFMNR ENFRAME
FREEMAN
AEEFMRR REFRAME
AEEFMRT FERMATE
AEEFOTV FOVEATE
AEEFRRS FEARERS
AEEFRRT FERRATE
AEEFRST AFREETS
FEASTER
AEEFRTU FEATURE
AEEFRWY FREEWAY
AEEFSTT FEATEST
AEEGGNR ENGAGER
AEEGGNS ENGAGES
AEEGGRS RAGGEES
REGGAES
AEEGGRU REGAUGE
AEEGGSW GEEGAWS
AEEGHNT THENAGE
AEEGHNW WHANGEE
AEEGILL GALILEE
AEEGILM MILEAGE
AEEGILN LINEAGE
AEEGILP EPIGEAL
AEEGILT EGALITE
AEEGILW WEIGELA
AEEGIMR REIMAGE
AEEGINP EPIGEAN
AEEGINR REGINAE
AEEGINU EUGENIA
AEEGINZ AGENIZE
AEEGIPP PIPEAGE
AEEGISS AEGISES
AEEGJRS JAEGERS
AEEGJSY JAYGEES
AEEGKLL KLEAGLE
AEEGLLR ALLEGER
AEEGLLS ALLEGES
AEEGLLZ GAZELLE
AEEGLMN GLEEMAN
MELANGE
AEEGLMR GLEAMER
AEEGLMT MELTAGE
AEEGLNR ENLARGE
GENERAL
GLEANER
AEEGLNT ELEGANT
AEEGLNU EUGLENA
AEEGLNV EVANGEL
AEEGLOR AEROGEL
AEEGLPS PELAGES
AEEGLRR REGALER
AEEGLRS GALERES
REGALES
AEEGLRU LEAGUER
AEEGLRY EAGERLY
AEEGLRZ REGLAZE
AEEGLSS AGELESS
AEEGLST EAGLETS
GELATES
LEGATES
SEGETAL
TELEGAS
AEEGLSU LEAGUES
AEEGLSV SELVAGE
AEEGLTT GALETTE
AEEGLTV VEGETAL
AEEGMMT GEMMATE
TAGMEME
AEEGMNR GERMANE
AEEGMNS MANEGES
MENAGES
AEEGMNT GATEMEN
AEEGMPR PREGAME
AEEGMSS MEGASSE
MESSAGE
AEEGMST GAMETES
METAGES
AEEGNNP PANGENE
AEEGNOP PEONAGE
AEEGNRS ENRAGES
AEEGNRT GRANTEE
GREATEN
NEGATER
REAGENT
AEEGNRU UNEAGER
AEEGNRV AVENGER
ENGRAVE
AEEGNSS SENEGAS
AEEGNST NEGATES
AEEGNSV AVENGES
GENEVAS
AEEGNTT TENTAGE
AEEGNTV VENTAGE
AEEGOPS APOGEES
AEEGORV OVERAGE
AEEGOST GOATEES
AEEGPRS PRESAGE
AEEGPRU PUGAREE
AEEGPST SEPTAGE
AEEGRRS GREASER
REGEARS
AEEGRRT GREATER
REGRATE
AEEGRRU REARGUE
AEEGRRW WAGERER
AEEGRSS GREASES
AEEGRST ERGATES
RESTAGE
AEEGRSV GREAVES
AEEGSSW SEWAGES
AEEGSTT GESTATE
AEEGTTZ GAZETTE
AEEHHNT HEATHEN
AEEHHRT HEATHER
AEEHHST SHEATHE
AEEHHSW HEEHAWS
AEEHINR HERNIAE
AEEHIRV HEAVIER
AEEHISV HEAVIES
AEEHKMS HAKEEMS
AEEHKNR HEARKEN
AEEHKRT HEKTARE
AEEHLNT LETHEAN
AEEHLPT HEELTAP
AEEHLRS HEALERS
AEEHLRT HALTERE
LEATHER
AEEHLRV HAVEREL
AEEHLSS LEASHES
AEEHLSX EXHALES
AEEHLSY EYELASH
AEEHLTT ATHLETE
AEEHMNT METHANE
AEEHMRS HAREEMS
AEEHMRT THERMAE
AEEHMSU HEAUMES
AEEHNPS PEAHENS
AEEHNPT HAPTENE
HEPTANE
PHENATE
AEEHNRT EARTHEN
HEARTEN
AEEHNST ETHANES
AEEHNSV HEAVENS
AEEHNSX HEXANES
AEEHNTW WHEATEN
AEEHPRS HEAPERS
RESHAPE
AEEHPRT PREHEAT
AEEHPSS APHESES
SPAHEES
AEEHPUV UPHEAVE
AEEHRRS HEARERS
REHEARS
SHEARER
AEEHRSS HEARSES
AEEHRST AETHERS
HEATERS
REHEATS
AEEHRSV HEAVERS
RESHAVE
AEEHRSW WHEREAS
AEEHRTT THEATER
THEATRE
THEREAT
AEEHRTW WEATHER
WHEREAT
WREATHE
AEEHSSV SHEAVES
AEEHSWY EYEWASH
AEEIKLP APELIKE
PEALIKE
AEEIKLR LEAKIER
AEEIKLT TEALIKE
AEEIKPR PEAKIER
AEEILMR MEALIER
AEEILMS MEALIES
AEEILNP ELAPINE
AEEILNR ALIENER
AEEILNT LINEATE
AEEILNX ALEXINE
AEEILPT EPILATE
PILEATE
AEEILRR EARLIER
LEARIER
AEEILRS REALISE
AEEILRT ATELIER
AEEILRV LEAVIER
VEALIER
AEEILRZ REALIZE
AEEILTV ELATIVE
AEEIMNN ENAMINE
AEEIMNS MEANIES
AEEIMNT ETAMINE
MATINEE
AEEIMNX EXAMINE
AEEIMRS SEAMIER
SERIEMA
AEEIMRT EMERITA
EMIRATE
MEATIER
AEEIMSS MISEASE
SIAMESE
AEEIMTT TEATIME
AEEINPR PERINEA
AEEINRT ARENITE
RETINAE
TRAINEE
AEEINST ETESIAN
AEEINTV NAIVETE
AEEINVW INWEAVE
AEEIPRS APERIES
AEEIPRT PEATIER
AEEIPSV PEAVIES
AEEIPTX EXPIATE
AEEIRRS RERAISE
AEEIRRT TEARIER
AEEIRRW WEARIER
AEEIRST AERIEST
SERIATE
AEEIRSW WEARIES
AEEIRTT ARIETTE
ITERATE
AEEISST EASIEST
AEEISVV EVASIVE
AEEIUVX EXUVIAE
AEEJNST SEJEANT
AEEJSVY JAYVEES
VEEJAYS
AEEKKNO KOKANEE
AEEKLNS ALKENES
AEEKLNT KANTELE
AEEKLRS LEAKERS
AEEKLSV VAKEELS
AEEKMNS KAMSEEN
AEEKMRR REMAKER
AEEKMRS REMAKES
AEEKMRT MEERKAT
AEEKNNN NANKEEN
AEEKNNP KNEEPAN
AEEKNRS SNEAKER
AEEKNRT RETAKEN
AEEKNRW REWAKEN
WAKENER
AEEKNSS SKEANES
AEEKNSW WEAKENS
AEEKORW REAWOKE
AEEKPRS RESPEAK
SPEAKER
AEEKRRT RETAKER
AEEKRRW WREAKER
AEEKRST RETAKES
AEEKRSW REWAKES
AEEKSSS ASKESES
AEEKSTW WEAKEST
AEELLLS ALLELES
AEELLMS MALLEES
AEELLWY WALLEYE
AEELMNP EMPANEL
EMPLANE
AEELMNS ENAMELS
MELENAS
AEELMNT TELEMAN
AEELMNV VELAMEN
AEELMNY AMYLENE
AEELMPR EMPALER
PREMEAL
AEELMPS EMPALES
AEELMPX EXAMPLE
EXEMPLA
AEELMSS MEASLES
AEELMTU EMULATE
AEELNNP ENPLANE
AEELNOS ENOLASE
AEELNPR REPANEL
AEELNPS SPELEAN
AEELNRR LEARNER
RELEARN
AEELNRS LEANERS
AEELNRT ENTERAL
ETERNAL
TELERAN
AEELNRW RENEWAL
AEELNST LATEENS
LEANEST
AEELNSV ENSLAVE
LEAVENS
AEELOPR PAROLEE
AEELOPX POLEAXE
AEELORS AREOLES
AEELORU AUREOLE
AEELOST OLEATES
AEELPRR PEARLER
AEELPRS LEAPERS
PLEASER
PRESALE
RELAPSE
REPEALS
AEELPRT PETRALE
PLEATER
PRELATE
REPLATE
AEELPRU PLEURAE
AEELPSS ELAPSES
PLEASES
AEELPTT PALETTE
PELTATE
AEELPTU EPAULET
AEELQSU QUELEAS
SEQUELA
AEELRRT ALERTER
ALTERER
REALTER
RELATER
AEELRRV RAVELER
AEELRRX RELAXER
AEELRSS EARLESS
LEASERS
RESALES
RESEALS
SEALERS
AEELRST ELATERS
REALEST
RELATES
RESLATE
STEALER
AEELRSV LAVEERS
LEAVERS
REVEALS
SEVERAL
VEALERS
AEELRSX RELAXES
AEELRSY SEALERY
AEELRTX EXALTER
AEELRUV REVALUE
AEELSST TEASELS
AEELSSV SLEAVES
AEELSSW AWELESS
WEASELS
AEELSSZ SLEAZES
AEELSTU ELUATES
AEELSTX LATEXES
AEELSTZ TEAZELS
TEAZLES
AEELSWY LEEWAYS
WEASELY
AEELTTY LAYETTE
AEELTVW WAVELET
AEEMMMR MAREMME
AEEMMMS MAMMEES
AEEMMNT MEATMEN
AEEMMPY EMPYEMA
AEEMMRT AMMETER
METAMER
AEEMMSY MAMEYES
AEEMNNO ANEMONE
AEEMNNP PENNAME
AEEMNOX AXONEME
AEEMNPR PRENAME
AEEMNRS MEANERS
RENAMES
AEEMNST MEANEST
AEEMNSX EXAMENS
AEEMOPT METOPAE
AEEMOSW AWESOME
AEEMPRS AMPERES
AEEMPRT TEMPERA
AEEMPST METEPAS
AEEMPTU AMPUTEE
AEEMQRU MARQUEE
AEEMRRS REAMERS
SMEARER
AEEMRSS SEAMERS
AEEMRST REMATES
RETEAMS
STEAMER
AEEMRSU MEASURE
AEEMRTX EXTREMA
AEEMSSS SESAMES
AEEMSTT METATES
AEEMSTX TAXEMES
AEENNOT NEONATE
AEENNOV NOVENAE
AEENNPT PENNATE
PENTANE
AEENNRS ENSNARE
RENNASE
AEENNRX REANNEX
AEENNST NEATENS
AEENNSX ANNEXES
AEENNTU UNEATEN
AEENOPU EUPNOEA
AEENORS ARENOSE
AEENOSU AENEOUS
AEENPST NEPETAS
PENATES
AEENPSU EUPNEAS
AEENPSW PAWNEES
AEENPSX EXPANSE
AEENRRS EARNERS
REEARNS
AEENRRT TERRANE
AEENRRV RAVENER
AEENRRY YEARNER
AEENRST EARNEST
EASTERN
NEAREST
AEENRSW WEANERS
AEENRTT ENTREAT
RATTEEN
TERNATE
AEENRTV NERVATE
VETERAN
AEENSST ENTASES
SATEENS
SENATES
SENSATE
AEENSSU UNEASES
AEENSSV AVENSES
AEENSSW WAENESS
AEENSTT NEATEST
AEENSUV AVENUES
AEENTTV NAVETTE
AEENUVW UNWEAVE
AEEOPRT OPERATE
AEEOPTZ EPAZOTE
AEEORSS SEROSAE
AEEORST ROSEATE
AEEORSV OVERSEA
AEEORTV OVERATE
OVEREAT
AEEORVW OVERAWE
AEEPPRR PAPERER
PREPARE
REPAPER
AEEPPRS RAPPEES
AEEPPRT PRETAPE
AEEPPRV PREPAVE
AEEPRRS REAPERS
SPEARER
AEEPRRT PEARTER
TAPERER
AEEPRRV PREAVER
AEEPRSS ASPERSE
PARESES
SERAPES
AEEPRST REPEATS
RETAPES
AEEPRSV REPAVES
AEEPRTZ TRAPEZE
AEEPSSS ASEPSES
AEEPSST PESETAS
AEEPSSW PESEWAS
AEEPSTT SEPTATE
AEEPSVY PEAVEYS
AEEQRSU QUAERES
AEEQSTU EQUATES

AEERRRS REARERS
AEERRSS ERASERS
AEERRST RETEARS
SERRATE
TEARERS
AEERRSU ERASURE
AEERRSV REAVERS
AEERRSW REWEARS
SWEARER
WEARERS
AEERRTT RETREAT
TREATER
AEERRTV AVERTER
AEERRTW WATERER
AEERRVW WAVERER
AEERSST EASTERS
RESEATS
SEAREST
SEATERS
TEASERS
TESSERA
AEERSSU RESEAUS
UREASES
AEERSSY ESSAYER
AEERSTT ESTREAT
RESTATE
RETASTE
AEERSTU AUSTERE
AEERSTW SWEATER
AEERSTX RETAXES
AEERSUX RESEAUX
AEERSVW WEAVERS
AEERSWX REWAXES
AEERTWW WETWARE
AEESSSW SEESAWS
AEESSSY EYASSES
AEESSTT ESTATES
AEESSTX TEXASES
AEESSUX AUXESES
AEESTTT TESTATE
AEFFGIR GIRAFFE
AEFFGRS GAFFERS
AEFFGRU GAUFFER
AEFFHST HAFFETS
AEFFINS AFFINES
AEFFIPR PIAFFER
AEFFIPS PIAFFES
AEFFIRX AFFIXER
REAFFIX
AEFFIST TAFFIES
AEFFISW WAFFIES
AEFFISX AFFIXES
AEFFKOR RAKEOFF
AEFFKOT TAKEOFF
AEFFLLY FLYLEAF
AEFFLNS SNAFFLE
AEFFLRR RAFFLER
AEFFLRS FARFELS
RAFFLES
AEFFLRU FEARFUL
AEFFLRW WAFFLER
AEFFLSW WAFFLES
AEFFLTU FATEFUL
AEFFMRU EARMUFF
AEFFOVW WAVEOFF
AEFFQRU QUAFFER
AEFFRST RESTAFF
STAFFER
AEFFRSZ ZAFFERS
ZAFFRES
AEFGGGO FOGGAGE
AEFGGLR FLAGGER
AEFGILN FINAGLE
LEAFING
AEFGILO FOLIAGE
AEFGILR FRAGILE
AEFGINR FEARING
AEFGINS FEASING
AEFGINZ FEAZING
AEFGIRT FRIGATE
AEFGIRU REFUGIA
AEFGITU FATIGUE
AEFGLMN FLAGMEN
AEFGLNR FLANGER
AEFGLNS FLANGES
AEFGLOT FLOTAGE
AEFGLOW FLOWAGE
AEFGLPU PAGEFUL
AEFGLRS REFLAGS
AEFGMOR FROMAGE
AEFGNRT ENGRAFT
AEFGOOT FOOTAGE
AEFGORR FORAGER
AEFGORS FORAGES
AEFGORT FAGOTER
AEFGORV FORGAVE
AEFGRRT GRAFTER
REGRAFT
AEFHISZ HAFIZES
AEFHLLS FELLAHS
AEFHLRS FLASHER
AEFHLSS FLASHES
AEFHLTU HATEFUL
AEFHRRT FARTHER
AEFHRST FATHERS
HAFTERS
AEFIILT FILIATE
AEFIIRS FAIRIES
AEFIJOS FEIJOAS
AEFIKLN FANLIKE
AEFIKLR FLAKIER
AEFIKLT FATLIKE
AEFILLS FAILLES
AEFILMN INFLAME
AEFILMR FLAMIER
AEFILNS FINALES
AEFILNT INFLATE
AEFILNV FLAVINE
AEFILOT FOLIATE
AEFILPT FLEAPIT
AEFILRR FRAILER
AEFILRU FAILURE
AEFILRW FLAWIER
AEFILRX FLAXIER
AEFILSS FALSIES
AEFILST FETIALS
SEALIFT
AEFILWY LIFEWAY
AEFIMNR FIREMAN
AEFIMNS FAMINES
AEFIMOR FOAMIER
AEFIMRR FIREARM
AEFINNS FANNIES
AEFINNT INFANTE
AEFINNZ FANZINE
AEFINPR FIREPAN
AEFINRR REFRAIN
AEFINRS INFARES
AEFINRT FAINTER
AEFINRW FAWNIER
AEFINST FAINEST
AEFINSW FANWISE
AEFINTX ANTEFIX
AEFIQRU AQUIFER
AEFIRRR FARRIER
AEFIRSS FRAISES
AEFIRST FAIREST
AEFIRTT FATTIER
AEFISST FIESTAS
FISSATE
AEFISTT FATTIES
AEFISTX FIXATES
AEFJNST FANJETS
AEFKLNN FLANKEN
AEFKLNR FLANKER
AEFKLRS FLAKERS
AEFKLRT FARTLEK
AEFKLST FLASKET
AEFKLUW WAKEFUL
AEFKNRR FRANKER
AEFKORS FORSAKE
AEFLLNN FLANNEL
AEFLLOT FLOATEL
AEFLLRS FALLERS
REFALLS
AEFLLSY FALSELY
AEFLLTT FLATLET
AEFLMNS FLAMENS
AEFLMOR FEMORAL
AEFLMRS FLAMERS
AEFLMUW WAMEFUL
AEFLNOV FLAVONE
AEFLNRU FLANEUR
FRENULA
FUNERAL
AEFLNTT FLATTEN
AEFLOOV FOVEOLA
AEFLOPW PEAFOWL
AEFLORS LOAFERS
SAFROLE
AEFLORT FLOATER
REFLOAT
AEFLOST FOLATES
AEFLOSW SEAFOWL
AEFLPPR FLAPPER
AEFLPRS FELSPAR
AEFLPRU FLAREUP
AEFLPRY PALFREY
AEFLRST FALTERS
AEFLRSU EARFULS
FERULAS
REFUSAL
AEFLRSY FLAYERS
AEFLRTT FLATTER
AEFLRTU REFUTAL
TEARFUL
AEFLRZZ FRAZZLE
AEFLSST FALSEST
FATLESS
AEFLSTU SULFATE
AEFMNOR FORAMEN
FOREMAN
AEFMNRU FRAENUM
AEFMORR FOREARM
AEFMORS FOAMERS
AEFMORT FORMATE
AEFMOUW WAMEFOU
AEFMRRS FARMERS
FRAMERS
AEFNNRS FANNERS
AEFNOPR PROFANE
AEFNORR FORERAN
AEFNRSS FARNESS
AEFNRSU FURANES
AEFNRSW FAWNERS
AEFNSST FASTENS
FATNESS
AEFNSTT FATTENS
AEFOPRW FOREPAW
AEFORRV FAVORER
OVERFAR
AEFORRY FORAYER
AEFORSW FORESAW
AEFORTV OVERFAT
AEFOSST FOSSATE
AEFPPRS FRAPPES
AEFRRST FRATERS
RAFTERS
STRAFER
AEFRSSS FRASSES
AEFRSST STRAFES
AEFRSTW FRETSAW
WAFTERS
AEFRTTU TARTUFE
AEFRTUW WAFTURE
AEFSSTT FASTEST
AEFSSUV FAVUSES
AEFSTTT FATTEST
AEGGGLS GAGGLES
AEGGGLU LUGGAGE
AEGGGRS GAGGERS
AEGGHLR HAGGLER
AEGGHLS HAGGLES
AEGGHMO HEMAGOG
AEGGIJR JAGGIER
AEGGIJS JAGGIES
AEGGILN EAGLING
AEGGINR GEARING
NAGGIER
AEGGINS AGEINGS
SIGNAGE
AEGGIOS ISAGOGE
AEGGIRS RAGGIES
SAGGIER
AEGGIRU GARIGUE
AEGGIST STAGGIE
AEGGISW SWAGGIE
AEGGJRS JAGGERS
AEGGJRY JAGGERY
AEGGLNO AGELONG
AEGGLNR GANGREL
AEGGLRR GARGLER
AEGGLRS GARGLES
LAGGERS
RAGGLES
AEGGLRY GREYLAG
AEGGLSW WAGGLES
AEGGMNY YEGGMAN
AEGGNRR GRANGER
AEGGNRS GANGERS
GRANGES
NAGGERS
AEGGNSU GANGUES
AEGGRSS AGGRESS
SAGGERS
SEGGARS
AEGGRST GAGSTER
GARGETS
STAGGER
TAGGERS
AEGGRSU GAUGERS
AEGGRSW SWAGGER
WAGGERS
AEGGRTY GARGETY
AEGGRWY WAGGERY
AEGGSWW GEWGAWS
AEGHILN HEALING
AEGHIMT MEGAHIT
AEGHINP HEAPING
AEGHINR HEARING
AEGHINT GAHNITE
HEATING
AEGHINV HEAVING
AEGHIOS HOAGIES
AEGHIRS HEGARIS
HEGIRAS
AEGHISS GEISHAS
AEGHISZ GHAZIES
AEGHLNO HALOGEN
AEGHLOS GALOSHE
AEGHLRU LAUGHER
AEGHLTW THALWEG
AEGHMNN HANGMEN
AEGHMNO HOGMANE
AEGHMOR HOMAGER
AEGHMOS HOMAGES
OHMAGES
AEGHMSU MESHUGA
AEGHNOX HEXAGON
AEGHNRS HANGERS
REHANGS
AEGHNSS GNASHES
AEGHNST STENGAH
AEGHOPY HYPOGEA
AEGHOST HOSTAGE
AEGHRST GATHERS
AEGHSST GASHEST
AEGIIMN IMAGINE
AEGIKLN LEAKING
LINKAGE
AEGIKLT GLAIKET
TAGLIKE
AEGIKNP PEAKING
AEGIKNS SINKAGE
AEGIKPR GARPIKE
AEGIKRW GAWKIER
AEGIKSW GAWKIES
AEGILLL ILLEGAL
AEGILLM MEGILLA
MILLAGE
AEGILLN GALLEIN
NIGELLA
AEGILLP PILLAGE
AEGILLS GALLIES
AEGILLT TILLAGE
AEGILLU LIGULAE
AEGILLV VILLAGE
AEGILLY AGILELY
AEGILMN GEMINAL
AEGILMR GREMIAL
AEGILMS MILAGES
AEGILNN ANELING
EANLING
LEANING
AEGILNP LEAPING
PEALING
AEGILNR ALIGNER
ENGRAIL
NARGILE
REALIGN
REGINAL
AEGILNS LEASING
LINAGES
SEALING
AEGILNT ATINGLE
ELATING
GELATIN
GENITAL
TAGLINE
AEGILNU LINGUAE
UNAGILE
AEGILNV LEAVING
VEALING
AEGILNY YEALING
AEGILOS GOALIES
SOILAGE
AEGILOU EULOGIA
AEGILRR GLARIER
AEGILRS GLAIRES
AEGILRZ GLAZIER
AEGILSS GLASSIE
LIGASES
SILAGES
AEGILST AIGLETS
GELATIS
LIGATES
AEGILSV GLAIVES
AEGIMMR GAMMIER
AEGIMNN MEANING
AEGIMNR GERMINA
MANGIER
REAMING
AEGIMNS ENIGMAS
GAMINES
SEAMING
AEGIMNT MINTAGE
TEAMING
TEGMINA
AEGIMOS IMAGOES
AEGIMPR EPIGRAM
PRIMAGE
AEGIMPS MAGPIES
MISPAGE
AEGIMRR ARMIGER
AEGIMRS GISARME
IMAGERS
MIRAGES
AEGIMRT MIGRATE
RAGTIME
AEGIMRY IMAGERY
AEGIMSS AGEISMS
AEGIMST GAMIEST
SIGMATE
AEGIMSV MISGAVE
AEGINNR AGINNER
EARNING
ENGRAIN
GRANNIE
NEARING
AEGINNS INNAGES
AEGINNT ANTEING
ANTIGEN
GENTIAN
AEGINNU ANGUINE
GUANINE
AEGINNW WEANING
AEGINNY YEANING
AEGINOS AGONIES
AGONISE
AEGINOZ AGONIZE
AEGINPP GENIPAP
AEGINPR REAPING
AEGINPS SPAEING
SPINAGE
AEGINRR ANGRIER
EARRING
GRAINER
RANGIER
REARING
AEGINRS EARINGS
ERASING
GAINERS
REAGINS
REGAINS
REGINAS
SEARING
SERINGA
AEGINRT GRANITE
GRATINE
INGRATE
TANGIER
TEARING
AEGINRV REAVING
VINEGAR
AEGINRW WEARING
AEGINRZ ZINGARE
AEGINST EASTING
EATINGS
INGATES
INGESTA
SEATING
TEASING
AEGINSU GUINEAS
AEGINSZ AGNIZES
AEGINTU UNITAGE
AEGINTV VINTAGE
AEGINTZ TZIGANE
AEGINVW WEAVING
AEGIPPR GAPPIER
AEGIPPS PIPAGES
AEGIPRR GRAPIER
AEGIRRZ GRAZIER
AEGIRSS GASSIER
AEGIRST AIGRETS
GAITERS
SEAGIRT
STAGIER
TRIAGES
AEGIRSV GRAVIES
RIVAGES
AEGIRSW EARWIGS
AEGIRTV VIRGATE
AEGIRUZ GAUZIER
AEGISST AGEISTS
SAGIEST
AEGISSV VISAGES
AEGISTU AUGITES
AEGISTY GASEITY
AEGJLNR JANGLER
AEGJLNS JANGLES
AEGJLSS JAGLESS
AEGJLST JETLAGS
AEGKMRY KERYGMA
AEGKMSS MASKEGS
AEGKRSW GAWKERS
AEGKSST GASKETS
AEGLLLY LEGALLY
AEGLLNO ALLONGE
GALLEON
AEGLLNR LANGREL
AEGLLNT GELLANT
AEGLLNY LANGLEY
AEGLLOR ALLEGRO
AEGLLOT TOLLAGE
AEGLLRY ALLERGY
GALLERY
LARGELY
REGALLY
AEGLLST GALLETS
AEGLLSU SEAGULL
SULLAGE
ULLAGES
AEGLLSY GALLEYS
AEGLLTU GLUTEAL
AEGLMNR MANGLER
AEGLMNS MANGELS
MANGLES
AEGLMOR GLOMERA
GOMERAL
AEGLMOU MOULAGE
AEGLMPU PLUMAGE
AEGLMSV MAGLEVS
AEGLNOT TANGELO
AEGLNPR GRAPNEL
AEGLNPS SPANGLE
AEGLNRS ANGLERS
AEGLNRT TANGLER
AEGLNRU GRANULE
AEGLNRW WANGLER
WRANGLE
AEGLNRY ANGERLY
AEGLNST GELANTS
TANGLES
AEGLNSU ANGELUS
LAGUNES
LANGUES
AEGLNSW WANGLES
AEGLNTT GANTLET
AEGLNTU LANGUET
AEGLNTW TWANGLE
AEGLNUU UNGULAE
AEGLNUW GUNWALE
AEGLOOZ ZOOGLEA
AEGLOPR PERGOLA
AEGLORS GALORES
GAOLERS
AEGLORT GLOATER
LEGATOR
AEGLORV VORLAGE
AEGLOSS GLOSSAE
AEGLOST GELATOS
LEGATOS
AEGLOSV LOVAGES
AEGLOTV VOLTAGE
AEGLPPR GRAPPLE
AEGLPRU EARPLUG
GRAUPEL
PLAGUER
AEGLPSS GAPLESS
AEGLPSU PLAGUES
AEGLPUY PLAGUEY
AEGLRRU REGULAR
AEGLRSS LARGESS
AEGLRST LARGEST
AEGLRSV GRAVELS
VERGLAS
AEGLRSY ARGYLES
AEGLRSZ GLAZERS
AEGLRTU TEGULAR
AEGLRTY GREATLY
AEGLRVY GRAVELY
AEGLSSS GASLESS
GLASSES
AEGLSTT GESTALT
AEGLTUV VULGATE
AEGLUUY GUAYULE
AEGLUVY VAGUELY
AEGMMRS GAMMERS
GRAMMES
AEGMMRU RUMMAGE
AEGMMSS SMEGMAS
AEGMNNO AGNOMEN
NONGAME
AEGMNOR MARENGO
MEGARON
AEGMNOS MANGOES
AEGMNOT MAGNETO
MEGATON
MONTAGE
AEGMNPY PYGMEAN
AEGMNRS ENGRAMS
GERMANS
MANGERS
AEGMNRT GARMENT
MARGENT
AEGMNST MAGNETS
AEGMNSW SWAGMEN
AEGMNTU AUGMENT
MUTAGEN
AEGMOOR MOORAGE
AEGMOSW WAGSOME
AEGMOXY EXOGAMY
AEGMSUY MAGUEYS
AEGMSUZ ZEUGMAS
AEGNNOS NONAGES
AEGNNOT NEGATON
TONNAGE
AEGNNOW NONWAGE
AEGNNPS PANGENS
PENANGS
AEGNNRT REGNANT
AEGNNST GANNETS
AEGNNTT TANGENT
AEGNNTU TUNNAGE
AEGNOOR OREGANO
AEGNORR GROANER
AEGNORS ONAGERS
ORANGES
AEGNORT NEGATOR
AEGNORW WAGONER
AEGNORY ORANGEY
AEGNOST ONSTAGE
AEGNOSY NOSEGAY
AEGNPRT TREPANG
AEGNRRS GARNERS
RANGERS
AEGNRRT GRANTER
REGRANT
AEGNRSS SANGERS
AEGNRST ARGENTS
GARNETS
STRANGE
AEGNRSW GNAWERS
AEGNRTU GAUNTER
AEGNRTW TWANGER
AEGNRTY AGENTRY
AEGNSSY GAYNESS
AEGOORT ROOTAGE
AEGOPRT PORTAGE
AEGOPST GESTAPO
POSTAGE
POTAGES
AEGOPTT POTTAGE
AEGORRT GARROTE
AEGORST GAROTES
ORGEATS
STORAGE
AEGORSU AERUGOS
AEGORTT GAROTTE
AEGORTU OUTRAGE
AEGORVY VOYAGER
AEGOSSU GASEOUS
AEGOSTU OUTAGES
AEGOSTW STOWAGE
TOWAGES
AEGOSVY VOYAGES
AEGOTTV GAVOTTE
AEGOTUV OUTGAVE
AEGOTUZ OUTGAZE
AEGPRRS GRASPER
SPARGER
AEGPRRY GRAPERY
AEGPRSS GASPERS
SPARGES
AEGPRST PARGETS
AEGPRSW GAWPERS
AEGPSTU UPSTAGE
AEGPSUZ UPGAZES
AEGRRST GARRETS
GARTERS
GRATERS
AEGRRSU ARGUERS
SUGARER
AEGRRSV GRAVERS
AEGRRSZ GRAZERS
AEGRRUU AUGURER
AEGRRUV GRAVURE
AEGRSSS GASSERS
GRASSES

AEGRSST GASTERS
STAGERS
AEGRSSU ARGUSES
SAUGERS
AEGRSSW SWAGERS
AEGRSSY GYRASES
AEGRSTT TARGETS
AEGRSTV GRAVEST
AEGRSTY GRAYEST
GYRATES
AEGRSUV SEVRUGA
AEGRSVY GARVEYS
AEGSSSU GAUSSES
AEGSTUV VAGUEST
AEGTTTU GUTTATE
AEHHLST HEALTHS
AEHHLTY HEALTHY
AEHHNRS HARSHEN
AEHHPRS RHAPHES
AEHHRRS HARSHER
AEHHRST HEARTHS
AEHHSST SHEATHS
AEHIIRR HAIRIER
AEHIJRS HEJIRAS
AEHIKLT HATLIKE
AEHIKNS HANKIES
AEHIKPS PEAKISH
AEHIKRS SHAKIER
AEHIKST SHITAKE
AEHIKSW HAWKIES
WEAKISH
AEHILMO HEMIOLA
AEHILMY LEHAYIM
AEHILNR HERNIAL
INHALER
AEHILNS INHALES
AEHILNY HYALINE
AEHILOR AIRHOLE
AEHILPR HARELIP
AEHILPT HAPLITE
AEHILRS HAILERS
SHALIER
AEHILRT LATHIER
AEHILRU HAULIER
AEHILSS SHEILAS
AEHILST HALITES
HELIAST
AEHILTY HYALITE
AEHILVY HEAVILY
AEHIMMR HAMMIER
AEHIMMS MAIHEMS
AEHIMNR HARMINE
AEHIMNS HAEMINS
AEHIMNT HEMATIN
AEHIMNY HYMENIA
AEHIMRS MISHEAR
AEHIMSS MASHIES
MESSIAH
AEHIMST ATHEISM
AEHINPR HEPARIN
AEHINPS INPHASE
AEHINRS HERNIAS
AEHINRT HAIRNET
INEARTH
THERIAN
AEHINSS HESSIAN
AEHINST SHEITAN
STHENIA
AEHINSV EVANISH
VAHINES
AEHINSW WAHINES
AEHIORR HOARIER
AEHIPPR HAPPIER
AEHIPPT EPITAPH
AEHIPRS HARPIES
SHARPIE
AEHIPSS APHESIS
AEHIPTZ ZAPTIEH
AEHIRRR HARRIER
AEHIRRS HARRIES
AEHIRST HASTIER
AEHIRSW WASHIER
WEARISH
AEHIRWY HAYWIRE
AEHISST ASHIEST
AEHISSV SHAVIES
AEHISTT ATHEIST
STAITHE
AEHISTZ HAZIEST
AEHISVY YESHIVA
AEHKMSS SAMEKHS
AEHKNRS HANKERS
HARKENS
AEHKNRT THANKER
AEHKNSZ KHAZENS
AEHKOSS SHAKOES
AEHKPRS PHREAKS
AEHKPSU SHAKEUP
AEHKRRS SHARKER
AEHKRSS KASHERS
SHAKERS
AEHKRSW HAWKERS
AEHKSWY HAWKEYS
AEHLLLS HALLELS
AEHLLOS HALLOES
AEHLLST LETHALS
AEHLLUV HELLUVA
AEHLLYZ HAZELLY
AEHLMNO MANHOLE
AEHLMNY HYMENAL
AEHLMOR ARMHOLE
AEHLMRT THERMAL
AEHLMRU HUMERAL
AEHLMST HAMLETS
AEHLNOS ENHALOS
AEHLNOT ANETHOL
ETHANOL
AEHLNRT ENTHRAL
AEHLNSS HANSELS
AEHLNST HANTLES
AEHLNSU UNLEASH
AEHLOPR EPHORAL
AEHLOPT TAPHOLE
AEHLORS SHOALER
AEHLORT LOATHER
RATHOLE
AEHLOST LOATHES
AEHLPRS PLASHER
SPHERAL
AEHLPSS HAPLESS
PLASHES
AEHLPSY SHAPELY
AEHLRSS ASHLERS
LASHERS
SLASHER
AEHLRST HALTERS
HARSLET
LATHERS
SLATHER
THALERS
AEHLRSU HAULERS
AEHLRSV HALVERS
AEHLRSW WHALERS
AEHLRTY EARTHLY
LATHERY
AEHLSSS ASHLESS
HASSELS
HASSLES
SLASHES
AEHLSST HASLETS
HATLESS
SHELTAS
AEHLSTT STEALTH
AEHLSTW WEALTHS
AEHLTWY WEALTHY
AEHMMRS HAMMERS
SHAMMER
AEHMMSS SHAMMES
AEHMMSY MAYHEMS
AEHMNOR MENORAH
AEHMNPY NYMPHAE
AEHMNRU HUMANER
AEHMNST ANTHEMS
HETMANS
AEHMOPT APOTHEM
AEHMORT TERAOHM
AEHMPRS HAMPERS
AEHMPTY EMPATHY
AEHMRRS HARMERS
AEHMRSS MARSHES
MASHERS
SHMEARS
SMASHER
AEHMRST HAMSTER
AEHMSSS SMASHES
AEHMSTU HUMATES
AEHMUZZ MEZUZAH
AEHNOPT PHAETON
PHONATE
AEHNOPY HYPONEA
AEHNORS HOARSEN
SENHORA
AEHNORT ANOTHER
AEHNOSX HEXOSAN
AEHNPPS HAPPENS
AEHNPRS SHARPEN
AEHNPRT PANTHER
AEHNPST HAPTENS
AEHNPTY PHYTANE
AEHNRSS HARNESS
AEHNRST ANTHERS
THENARS
AEHNRTU HAUNTER
UNEARTH
URETHAN
AEHNRTX NARTHEX
AEHNSSS SNASHES
AEHNSST HASTENS
SNATHES
AEHNSSU HAUSENS
AEHNSTY ASTHENY
SHANTEY
AEHOPRT PHORATE
AEHOPST TEASHOP
AEHORRS HOARSER
AEHORST EARSHOT
AEHORSX HOAXERS
AEHORTU OUTHEAR
AEHORTX OXHEART
AEHPPRS PERHAPS
AEHPPRW WHAPPER
AEHPPSU SHAPEUP
UPHEAPS
AEHPRRS HARPERS
SHARPER
AEHPRSS PHRASES
SERAPHS
SHAPERS
SHERPAS
AEHPRST TEPHRAS
THREAPS
AEHPRSW PREWASH
AEHPRTT PHATTER
AEHPRTY THERAPY
AEHPSST SPATHES
AEHQRSU QUASHER
AEHQSSU QUASHES
AEHRRSS RASHERS
SHARERS
AEHRRST TRASHER
AEHRRTU URETHRA
AEHRSST RASHEST
TRASHES
AEHRSSV SHAVERS
AEHRSSW HAWSERS
SWASHER
WASHERS
AEHRSTT HATTERS
SHATTER
THREATS
AEHRSTV HARVEST
THRAVES
AEHRSTW SWATHER
THAWERS
WREATHS
AEHRSVW WHARVES
AEHRSXY HYRAXES
AEHRTUU HAUTEUR
AEHRTWY WREATHY
AEHSSST STASHES
AEHSSSW SWASHES
AEHSSTW SWATHES
AEHSTUX EXHAUST
AEIIKLR AIRLIKE
AEIIKNT KAINITE
AEIILMR RAMILIE
AEIILNN ANILINE
AEIILNR AIRLINE
AEIILNX EXILIAN
AEIILRV VIRELAI
AEIILSS LIAISES
SILESIA
AEIILST LAITIES
AEIIMNT INTIMAE
AEIIMPR IMPERIA
AEIIMRT AIRTIME
AEIIMRV VIREMIA
AEIIMST AMITIES
AEIIMTT IMITATE
AEIINNS ASININE
AEIINOP EPINAOI
AEIINRR RAINIER
AEIINRS SENARII
AEIINRT INERTIA
AEIINST ISATINE
AEIIPRR PRAIRIE
AEIIRRV RIVIERA
AEIIRST AIRIEST
AEIIRSW AIRWISE
AEIITTV VITIATE
AEIJKLM JAMLIKE
AEIJKLW JAWLIKE
AEIJLNV JAVELIN
AEIJLNW JAWLINE
AEIJLRS JAILERS
AEIJLSZ JEZAILS
AEIJMMR JAMMIER
AEIJMMS JAMMIES
AEIJMNS JASMINE
AEIJRZZ JAZZIER
AEIJSSV JIVEASS
AEIKKLO OAKLIKE
AEIKKPS PIKAKES
AEIKLLW LAWLIKE
AEIKLLY LEAKILY
AEIKLMN MANLIKE
AEIKLMP MAPLIKE
AEIKLMR ARMLIKE
AEIKLNO KAOLINE
AEIKLNR LANKIER
AEIKLNS ALKINES
AEIKLNT ANTLIKE
AEIKLNU UNALIKE
AEIKLOR OARLIKE
AEIKLOT KEITLOA
OATLIKE
AEIKLRR LARKIER
AEIKLRT RATLIKE
TALKIER
AEIKLRW WARLIKE
AEIKLRY RAYLIKE
AEIKLSS ALSIKES
ASSLIKE
AEIKLST LAKIEST
TALKIES
AEIKLSW SAWLIKE
AEIKLWX WAXLIKE
AEIKMMS MISMAKE
AEIKMNP PIKEMAN
AEIKMNR RAMEKIN
AEIKMNS KINEMAS
AEIKMPR RAMPIKE
AEIKMST MISTAKE
AEIKNNT NEATNIK
AEIKNPR RANPIKE
AEIKNRS SNAKIER
AEIKNRT KERATIN
AEIKNSS KINASES
AEIKNST INTAKES
AEIKNSY KYANISE
AEIKNTU UNAKITE
AEIKNTY KYANITE
AEIKNYZ KYANIZE
AEIKOST OAKIEST
AEIKPRW PAWKIER
AEIKQRU QUAKIER
AEIKRRS KERRIAS
SARKIER
AEIKRSS KAISERS
AEIKRSU KAURIES
AEIKRSW SKIWEAR
AEIKSSS ASKESIS
AEILLMN MANILLE
AEILLNR RALLINE
AEILLNS AINSELL
AEILLNY ALIENLY
AEILLOV ALVEOLI
AEILLPR PALLIER
PERILLA
AEILLQU LALIQUE
AEILLRR RALLIER
AEILLRS RALLIES
SALLIER
AEILLRT LITERAL
TALLIER
AEILLSS SALLIES
AEILLST TAILLES
TALLIES
AEILLSW WALLIES
AEILLUV ELUVIAL
AEILLVX VEXILLA
AEILMMN MAILMEN
AEILMMR MALMIER
AEILMMS MELISMA
AEILMNN LINEMAN
MELANIN
AEILMNP IMPANEL
MANIPLE
AEILMNR MANLIER
MARLINE
MINERAL
AEILMNS MALINES
MENIALS
SEMINAL
AEILMNT AILMENT
ALIMENT
AEILMNU ALUMINE
AEILMOR LOAMIER
AEILMPR IMPALER
IMPEARL
LEMPIRA
PALMIER
AEILMPS IMPALES
AEILMRR MARLIER
AEILMRS MAILERS
REALISM
REMAILS
AEILMRT MALTIER
MARLITE
AEILMSS AIMLESS
SAMIELS
SEISMAL
AEILMTY MEATILY
AEILNNY INANELY
AEILNOP OPALINE
AEILNOR AILERON
ALIENOR
AEILNOS ANISOLE
AEILNOT ELATION
TOENAIL
AEILNPR PLAINER
PRALINE
AEILNPS ALPINES
PINEALS
SPANIEL
SPLENIA
AEILNPT PANTILE
AEILNPW PINWALE
AEILNPX EXPLAIN
AEILNQU QUINELA
AEILNRS ALINERS
NAILERS
RENAILS
AEILNRT LATRINE
RATLINE
RELIANT
RETINAL
TRENAIL
AEILNRV RAVELIN
AEILNRX RELAXIN
AEILNRY INLAYER
AEILNSS SALINES
SILANES
AEILNST ELASTIN
ENTAILS
NAILSET
SALIENT
SALTINE
SLAINTE
TENAILS
AEILNSU INULASE
AEILNSV ALEVINS
VALINES
AEILNSW LAWINES
AEILNSX ALEXINS
AEILNSY ELYSIAN
AEILNTU ALUNITE
AEILNTV VENTAIL
AEILNUW LAUWINE
AEILNVY NAIVELY
AEILOPR PELORIA
AEILORV VARIOLE
AEILOST ISOLATE
AEILOTV VIOLATE
AEILPPR APPLIER
AEILPPS APPLIES
AEILPRT PLAITER
PLATIER
AEILPRV PREVAIL
AEILPSS ESPIALS
LAPISES
LIPASES
PALSIES
AEILPST APLITES
PALIEST
PLATIES
TALIPES
AEILPSY PAISLEY
AEILQTU LIQUATE
TEQUILA
AEILRRS RAILERS
AEILRRT RETRIAL
TRAILER
AEILRSS AIRLESS
RESAILS
SAILERS
SERAILS
SERIALS
AEILRST REALIST
RETAILS
SALTIER
SALTIRE
SLATIER
TAILERS
AEILRSV REVISAL
AEILRSW WAILERS
AEILRTT TERTIAL
AEILRTU URALITE
AEILRTY IRATELY
REALITY
TEARILY
AEILRVV REVIVAL
AEILRVY VIRELAY
AEILRWY WEARILY
AEILSSS LASSIES
AEILSST SALTIES
AEILSSV VALISES
AEILSTV ESTIVAL
AEILSTZ LAZIEST
AEILTVY VILAYET
AEILUVX EXUVIAL
AEIMMMS MAMMIES
AEIMMNS AMMINES
MISNAME
AEIMMRR RAMMIER
AEIMMRS MAIMERS
AEIMMRT MARMITE
AEIMMST MISMATE
SEMIMAT
TAMMIES
AEIMNNT MANNITE
AEIMNOR MORAINE
ROMAINE
AEIMNOS ANOMIES
AEIMNOT AMNIOTE
AEIMNPR PERMIAN
AEIMNRR MARINER
AEIMNRS MARINES
REMAINS
SEMINAR
AEIMNRT MINARET
RAIMENT
AEIMNRV VERMIAN
AEIMNRW WIREMAN
AEIMNSS INSEAMS
SAMISEN
AEIMNST ETAMINS
INMATES
TAMEINS
AEIMNSW MANWISE
AEIMNTX TAXIMEN
AEIMNTY AMENITY
ANYTIME
AEIMOOP IPOMOEA
AEIMOPR EMPORIA
MEROPIA
AEIMORR ARMOIRE
AEIMOST AMOSITE
ATOMIES
ATOMISE
AEIMOTX TOXEMIA
AEIMOTZ ATOMIZE
AEIMPRS IMPRESA
AEIMPRT PRIMATE
AEIMPRV VAMPIER
VAMPIRE
AEIMPSS IMPASSE
AEIMPST IMPASTE
PASTIME
AEIMPSY PYEMIAS
AEIMRRR MARRIER
AEIMRRS MARRIES
AEIMRSS MASSIER
AEIMRST IMARETS
MAESTRI
MISRATE
SMARTIE
AEIMRSU UREMIAS
AEIMRSV MISAVER
AEIMRSW SEMIRAW
AEIMRTU MURIATE
AEIMRTV VITAMER
AEIMRTW WARTIME
AEIMSST MISEATS
MISSEAT
SAMITES
TAMISES
AEIMSSV MASSIVE
MAVISES
AEIMSSW SWAMIES
AEIMSSY MYIASES
AEIMSTT ETATISM
MATIEST
AEIMSTZ MAZIEST
MESTIZA
AEIMSUV AMUSIVE
AEIMSXX MAXIXES
AEINNNS NANNIES
AEINNOT ENATION
AEINNPR PANNIER
AEINNPT PINNATE
AEINNRS INSANER
INSNARE
AEINNRT ENTRAIN
AEINNRU ANEURIN
AEINNSS SIENNAS
AEINNST INANEST
STANINE
AEINOPS EPINAOS
SENOPIA
AEINORS ERASION
AEINOST ATONIES
AEINOSV EVASION
AEINOXZ OXAZINE
AEINPPP PANPIPE
AEINPPR NAPPIER
AEINPPS NAPPIES
PINESAP
AEINPRS PANIERS
RAPINES
AEINPRT PAINTER
PERTAIN
REPAINT
AEINPSS PANSIES
SAPIENS
AEINPST PANTIES
PATINES
SAPIENT
SPINATE
AEINPSW WINESAP
AEINPTT PATIENT
AEINPTU PETUNIA
AEINQTU ANTIQUE
QUINATE
AEINRRS SIERRAN
AEINRRT RETRAIN
TERRAIN
TRAINER
AEINRSS ARSINES
AEINRST ANESTRI
ANTSIER
NASTIER
RATINES
RETAINS
RETINAS
RETSINA
STAINER
STEARIN
AEINRSV RAVINES
AEINRTT INTREAT
ITERANT
NATTIER
NITRATE
TERTIAN
AEINRTU RUINATE
TAURINE
URANITE
URINATE
AEINRTW TAWNIER
TINWARE
AEINRVV VERVAIN
AEINSSS SANSEIS
AEINSST ENTASIS
NASTIES
SEITANS
SESTINA
TANSIES
TISANES
AEINSSV SAVINES
VINASSE
AEINSTT INSTATE
SATINET
AEINSTU AUNTIES
SINUATE
AEINSTV NAIVEST
NATIVES
VAINEST
AEINSTW TAWNIES
WANIEST
AEINSTX ANTISEX
SEXTAIN
AEINSTZ ZANIEST
ZEATINS
AEINSVV NAVVIES
AEINSWY ANYWISE
AEINTUV VAUNTIE
AEINTVW VAWNTIE
AEINTVY NAIVETY
AEINTXY ANXIETY
AEIOPRS SOAPIER
AEIOPST ATOPIES
OPIATES
AEIOQSU SEQUOIA
AEIORSV OVARIES
AEIOSTZ AZOTISE
AEIOTZZ AZOTIZE
AEIPPPR PAPPIER
AEIPPPS PAPPIES
AEIPPRS APPRISE
SAPPIER

AEIPPRT PERIAPT
AEIPPRZ APPRIZE
ZAPPIER
AEIPRRR PARRIER
AEIPRRS ASPIRER
PARRIES
PRAISER
RAPIERS
RASPIER
REPAIRS
AEIPRRT PARTIER
AEIPRSS ASPIRES
PARESIS
PARISES
PRAISES
SPIREAS
AEIPRST PARTIES
PASTIER
PIASTER
PIASTRE
PIRATES
TRAIPSE
AEIPRSU UPRAISE
AEIPRSV PARVISE
PAVISER
AEIPRSW WASPIER
AEIPRTT PARTITE
AEIPRTV PRIVATE
AEIPRTW WIRETAP
AEIPRXY PYREXIA
AEIPSSS ASEPSIS
ASPISES
AEIPSST PASTIES
PATSIES
PETSAIS
TAPISES
AEIPSSV PASSIVE
PAVISES
PAVISSE
SPAVIES
AEIPSTT PATTIES
AEIPSTV SPAVIET
AEIPSTW TAWPIES
AEIPTXY EPITAXY
AEIQRUV AQUIVER
AEIRRRT TARRIER
AEIRRRV ARRIVER
AEIRRSS ARRISES
RAISERS
SIERRAS
AEIRRST ARTSIER
TARRIES
TARSIER
AEIRRSV ARRIVES
VARIERS
AEIRRTT RATTIER
TARTIER
AEIRRTW WARTIER
AEIRRTY RETIARY
AEIRSSS SASSIER
AEIRSST SATIRES
AEIRSSU SAURIES
AEIRSTT ARTIEST
ARTISTE
ATTIRES
IRATEST
RATITES
STRIATE
TASTIER
AEIRSTV VASTIER
VERITAS
AEIRSTW WAISTER
WAITERS
WARIEST
WASTRIE
AEIRSVV SAVVIER
AEIRSVW WAIVERS
AEIRTTT ATTRITE
TATTIER
TITRATE
AEIRTUZ AZURITE
AEIRTVY VARIETY
AEIRWWY WIREWAY
AEISSSS SASSIES
AEISSST SIESTAS
TASSIES
AEISSSW WISEASS
AEISSSZ ASSIZES
AEISSUV SUASIVE
AEISSUX AUXESIS
AEISSVV SAVVIES
AEISTTT ETATIST
TATTIES
AEISTTU SITUATE
AEISTTV STATIVE
AEISTTX TAXITES
AEISTTY SATIETY
AEISTVW WAVIEST
AEISTWX TAXWISE
WAXIEST
AEITTTV VITTATE
AEJJLNU JEJUNAL
AEJKPTU KAJEPUT
AEJLNUV JUVENAL
AEJLOSU JEALOUS
AEJLOUZ AZULEJO
AEJLSSW JAWLESS
AEJMMRS JAMMERS
AEJMNZZ JAZZMEN
AEJMRST RAMJETS
AEJMSST JETSAMS
AEJMSTY MAJESTY
AEJNNOS JOANNES
AEJNSST JESSANT
AEJPRSS JASPERS
AEJPRSY JASPERY
AEJRSVY JARVEYS
AEJRSZZ JAZZERS
AEJSTWY JETWAYS
AEKKNRS KRAKENS
SKANKER
AEKKRSY YAKKERS
AEKLMOU LEUKOMA
AEKLNRS RANKLES
AEKLNRV KLAVERN
AEKLNST ANKLETS
LANKEST
AEKLNSW KNAWELS
AEKLNSY ALKYNES
AEKLOST SKATOLE
AEKLOVZ ZELKOVA
AEKLPPT PEPTALK
AEKLPRS SPARKLE
AEKLPSS SPLAKES
AEKLPSY KEYPALS
AEKLRRS LARKERS
AEKLRSS SLAKERS
AEKLRST STALKER
TALKERS
AEKLRSV LEKVARS
AEKLRSW WALKERS
AEKLSTU AUKLETS
AEKMNOS SOKEMAN
AEKMNRU UNMAKER
AEKMNSU UNMAKES
AEKMPSU MAKEUPS
AEKMRRS MARKERS
REMARKS
AEKMRSS MASKERS
AEKMRST MARKETS
AEKNNOP NONPEAK
AEKNNTU UNTAKEN
AEKNOSW WEAKONS
AEKNPPR KNAPPER
AEKNPRS SPANKER
AEKNPSU UNSPEAK
AEKNRRS RANKERS
AEKNRST RANKEST
TANKERS
AEKNRSW SWANKER
AEKNRVY KNAVERY
AEKNSSU ANKUSES
AEKOPRS PRESOAK
AEKORSS ARKOSES
RESOAKS
SOAKERS
AEKOTTU OUTTAKE
TAKEOUT
AEKPRRS PARKERS
REPARKS
SPARKER
AEKPSSY PASSKEY
AEKPSTU TAKEUPS
UPTAKES
AEKQRSU QUAKERS
AEKQSSU SQUEAKS
AEKQSUY SQUEAKY
AEKRRST KRATERS
STARKER
AEKRSST SKATERS
STRAKES
STREAKS
AEKRSTY STREAKY
AEKSSSV KVASSES
AEKSSTT TSATSKE
AEKSWYY KEYWAYS
AELLMNU LUMENAL
AELLMRS SMALLER
AELLMRT TRAMELL
AELLMST MALLETS
AELLMSU MALLEUS
AELLMSY MESALLY
AELLMWX MAXWELL
AELLNOP PLEONAL
AELLNOV NOVELLA
AELLNPY PENALLY
AELLNUU LUNULAE
AELLNVY VENALLY
AELLORT REALLOT
AELLORV ALLOVER
OVERALL
AELLORY LOYALER
AELLOSS LOESSAL
AELLPRS SPALLER
AELLPRU PLEURAL
AELLPST PALLETS
AELLPTY PLAYLET
AELLQUY EQUALLY
AELLRRU ALLURER
AELLRST STELLAR
AELLRSU ALLURES
LAURELS
AELLRSY RALLYES
AELLRTY ALERTLY
RETALLY
AELLRVY RAVELLY
AELLSST SALLETS
STELLAS
AELLSSW LAWLESS
AELLSTT TALLEST
AELLSTW WALLETS
AELLSTY STALELY
AELLSVY VALLEYS
AELLTUU ULULATE
AELLUVV VALVULE
AELMMNS ALMSMEN
AELMMOY MYELOMA
AELMMRS SLAMMER
AELMMRT TRAMMEL
AELMMST STAMMEL
AELMMSY MALMSEY
AELMNNS LENSMAN
AELMNOR ALMONER
AELMNOT LOMENTA
OMENTAL
TELAMON
AELMNRS ALMNERS
AELMNRU NUMERAL
AELMNSS MANLESS
AELMNST LAMENTS
MANTELS
MANTLES
AELMNTT MANTLET
AELMOPR RAMPOLE
AELMOPU AMPOULE
AELMOPY MAYPOLE
AELMORS MORALES
AELMORU MORULAE
AELMORV REMOVAL
AELMOST MALTOSE
AELMOSY AMYLOSE
AELMOTT MATELOT
AELMPRS LAMPERS
PALMERS
SAMPLER
AELMPRT TEMPLAR
TRAMPLE
AELMPRY LAMPREY
AELMPSS SAMPLES
AELMPST AMPLEST
AELMPSU AMPULES
AELMPTU PLUMATE
AELMRSS ARMLESS
AELMRST ARMLETS
LAMSTER
TRAMELS
AELMRSU MAULERS
SERUMAL
AELMRSV MARVELS
AELMRTT MARTLET
AELMSST MATLESS
SAMLETS
AELMSTU AMULETS
MULETAS
AELNNPR PLANNER
AELNNRS ENSNARL
LANNERS
AELNNRT LANTERN
AELNNRU UNLEARN
AELNNTU ANNULET
AELNOPS ESPANOL
NOPALES
AELNOPT POLENTA
AELNOPU APOLUNE
AELNORS LOANERS
RELOANS
AELNORU ALEURON
AELNOST ETALONS
TOLANES
AELNOTV VOLANTE
AELNOTY ANOLYTE
AELNOUZ ZONULAE
AELNPPR PREPLAN
AELNPPY PLAYPEN
AELNPRS PLANERS
REPLANS
AELNPRT PLANTER
REPLANT
AELNPRY PLENARY
AELNPSS NAPLESS
AELNPST PLANETS
PLATENS
AELNPTX EXPLANT
AELNPTY APLENTY
PENALTY
AELNQUU UNEQUAL
AELNRRS SNARLER
AELNRST ANTLERS
RENTALS
SALTERN
STERNAL
AELNRTU NEUTRAL
AELNRTV VENTRAL
AELNRUU NEURULA
AELNRUV UNRAVEL
VENULAR
AELNSSU SENSUAL
UNSEALS
AELNSSW AWNLESS
AELNSSX LAXNESS
AELNSTT LATENTS
LATTENS
TALENTS
AELNSTU ELUANTS
AELNSTV LEVANTS
AELOORS AEROSOL
ROSEOLA
AELOPRR PERORAL
PREORAL
AELOPRS PAROLES
REPOSAL
AELOPRT PROLATE
AELOPRV OVERLAP
AELOPST APOSTLE
PELOTAS
AELOPSX EXPOSAL
AELOPTT PALETOT
AELOPTU OUTLEAP
AELORRT REALTOR
RELATOR
AELORSS LASSOER
OARLESS
SEROSAL
AELORST OLESTRA
AELORTT RETOTAL
AELORTU TORULAE
AELORTV LEVATOR
AELORUU ROULEAU
AELORVX OVERLAX
AELORVY LAYOVER
OVERLAY
AELOSSS LASSOES
AELOSST SOLATES
AELOSSV SALVOES
AELOSTV SOLVATE
AELOSTZ ZEALOTS
AELOSUZ ZEALOUS
AELOSVY SAVELOY
AELOTTU TOLUATE
AELOTUV OVULATE
AELOTVV VOLVATE
AELOTVY OVATELY
AELPPRS LAPPERS
RAPPELS
SLAPPER
AELPPRY REAPPLY
AELPPST APPLETS
LAPPETS
AELPPSU APPULSE
PAPULES
UPLEAPS
AELPPTU UPLEAPT
AELPQSU PLAQUES
AELPRRS PARRELS
AELPRSS LAPSERS
AELPRST PALTERS
PERSALT
PLASTER
PLATERS
PSALTER
STAPLER
AELPRSU PERUSAL
PLEURAS
AELPRSY PARLEYS
PARSLEY
PLAYERS
REPLAYS
SPARELY
AELPRTT PARTLET
PLATTER
PRATTLE
AELPRTY PEARTLY
PEYTRAL
PTERYLA
AELPSSS PASSELS
SAPLESS
AELPSST PASTELS
STAPLES
AELPSTT PELTAST
AELPSTU PULSATE
AELPSTZ SPATZLE
AELQRRU QUARREL
AELQSSU SQUEALS
AELQSUZ QUEZALS
AELQTUZ QUETZAL
AELRRSU SURREAL
AELRRSW WARSLER
AELRRTT RATTLER
AELRRTW TRAWLER
AELRSSS RASSLES
AELRSST ARTLESS
LASTERS
SALTERS
SLATERS
AELRSSU SAURELS
AELRSSV SALVERS
SERVALS
SLAVERS
AELRSSW WARLESS
WARSLES
WRASSLE
AELRSSY RAYLESS
SLAYERS
AELRSTT RATTLES
STARLET
STARTLE
AELRSTU ESTRUAL
SALUTER
AELRSTV TRAVELS
VARLETS
VESTRAL
AELRSTW WARSTLE
WASTREL
WRASTLE
AELRSUV VALUERS
AELRSVY SLAVERY
AELRSWY LAWYERS
AELRTTT TARTLET
TATTLER
AELRTTU TUTELAR
AELRTUV VAULTER
AELRTWY TRAWLEY
AELRTWZ WALTZER
AELSSST TASSELS
AELSSTT LATESTS
SALTEST
STALEST
AELSSTU SALUTES
TALUSES
AELSSTV VESTALS
AELSSTX TAXLESS
AELSSTY LYSATES
AELSSUV AVULSES
AELSSVY SLAVEYS
AELSSWY WAYLESS
AELSTTT TATTLES
AELSTTW WATTLES
AELSTTY STATELY
STYLATE
AELSTUX LUXATES
AELSTWZ WALTZES
AELSUVY SUAVELY
AELTTTW TWATTLE
AELTTUX TEXTUAL
AELTUVV VULVATE
AEMMMRS MAMMERS
AEMMMST MAMMETS
AEMMMSY MAMMEYS
AEMMNOT MOMENTA
AEMMNSS MESSMAN
AEMMORW WOMMERA
AEMMPRS SPAMMER
AEMMRRS RAMMERS
AEMMRST STAMMER
AEMMRSY YAMMERS
AEMMRSZ MAMZERS
AEMMSST STEMMAS
AEMMSTU MAUMETS
SUMMATE
AEMNNOR MONERAN
AEMNNOS MANNOSE
AEMNNOT MONTANE
NONMEAT
AEMNNOU NOUMENA
AEMNNOZ MENAZON
AEMNNRS MANNERS
AEMNNRT REMNANT
AEMNNSW NEWSMAN
AEMNNTU UNMEANT
AEMNOPR MANROPE
AEMNORS ENAMORS
MOANERS
OARSMEN
AEMNORT TONEARM
AEMNORU ENAMOUR
NEUROMA
AEMNORV OVERMAN
AEMNORY ANYMORE
AEMNOTT TOMENTA
AEMNOTU AUTOMEN
AEMNPSU PNEUMAS
AEMNPTU PUTAMEN
AEMNPTY PAYMENT
AEMNRRU MANURER
AEMNRST MARTENS
SARMENT
SMARTEN
AEMNRSU MANURES
SURNAME
AEMNRTV VARMENT
AEMNSSS MESSANS
AEMNSST STAMENS
AEMNSSU UNSEAMS
AEMNSTY AMNESTY
AEMNTTU NUTMEAT
AEMOORT TEAROOM
AEMOORW WOOMERA
AEMOOST OSTEOMA
AEMOOSV VAMOOSE
AEMOPPR PAMPERO
AEMORRR ARMORER
AEMORRS REMORAS
ROAMERS
AEMORRV OVERARM
AEMORRW EARWORM
AEMORST MAESTRO
AEMORSW WOMERAS
AEMOSSV VAMOSES
AEMOSTT STOMATE
AEMOSTW TWASOME
AEMOSWY SOMEWAY
AEMOTTZ MOZETTA
AEMPPRS MAPPERS
PAMPERS
PREAMPS
AEMPRRS PREARMS
AEMPRRT TRAMPER
AEMPRRW PREWARM
AEMPRST RESTAMP
STAMPER
TAMPERS
AEMPRSV REVAMPS
VAMPERS
AEMPRSW SWAMPER
AEMPRTU TEMPURA
AEMPTTT ATTEMPT
AEMPTTU TAPETUM
AEMQRSU MARQUES
MASQUER
AEMQSSU MASQUES
AEMRRRS MARRERS
AEMRRRY REMARRY
AEMRRST ARMREST
SMARTER
AEMRRSU ARMURES
AEMRRSW REWARMS
SWARMER
WARMERS
AEMRRTU ERRATUM
MATURER
AEMRSST MASTERS
STREAMS
AEMRSSU AMUSERS
ASSUMER
MASSEUR
AEMRSTT MATTERS
SMATTER
AEMRSTU MATURES
STRUMAE
AEMRSTW WARMEST
AEMRSTY MASTERY
STREAMY
AEMRTTY MATTERY
AEMRTUU TRUMEAU
AEMSSSU ASSUMES
AEMSSTU MUTASES
AEMSSUW WAMUSES
AEMSSYZ ZYMASES
AEMSTTU MUTATES
AEMSTVZ ZEMSTVA
AEMSUZZ MEZUZAS
AENNNPT PENNANT
AENNORY ANNOYER
AENNOSV NOVENAS
AENNOTU TONNEAU
AENNPRS PANNERS
SPANNER
AENNRST TANNERS
AENNRSV VANNERS
AENNRTT ENTRANT
AENNRTY TANNERY
AENNSSW WANNESS
AENNSTT TANNEST
TENANTS
AENNSTW WANNEST
AENOOTZ ENTOZOA
OZONATE
AENOPPR PROPANE
AENOPRS PERSONA
AENOPRT OPERANT
PRONATE
PROTEAN
AENOPST TEOPANS
AENOPSW WEAPONS
AENOPTU AUTOPEN
AENORRS SERRANO
AENORRV OVERRAN
AENORSS REASONS
SENORAS
AENORST ATONERS
SANTERO
SENATOR
TREASON
AENORSU ARENOUS
AENORTU OUTEARN
AENORXY ANOREXY
AENOSSS SEASONS
AENOSSW WEASONS
AENOSTT NOTATES
AENOSTU SOUTANE
AENOUUV NOUVEAU
AENPPRS NAPPERS
SNAPPER
AENPPST PETNAPS
AENPRRT PARTNER
AENPRRW PRAWNER
PREWARN
AENPRST ARPENTS
ENTRAPS
PARENTS
PASTERN
TREPANS
AENPRSW ENWRAPS
PAWNERS
SPAWNER
AENPRSZ PANZERS
AENPRTT PATTERN
REPTANT
AENPRUV PARVENU
AENPSST APTNESS
PATNESS
AENPSSY SYNAPSE
AENPSTT PATENTS
PATTENS
AENPSTU PEANUTS
AENPSTW STEWPAN
AENRRSS SNARERS
AENRRST ERRANTS
RANTERS
AENRRSW WARNERS
WARRENS
AENRRSY YARNERS
AENRRTY TERNARY
AENRSSS SARSENS
AENRSST SARSNET
AENRSSW ANSWERS
RAWNESS
AENRSTT NATTERS
RATTENS
AENRSTU NATURES
SAUNTER
AENRSTV SERVANT
TAVERNS
VERSANT
AENRSTW WANTERS
AENRSUW UNSWEAR
AENRSUY SYNURAE
AENRSWY YAWNERS
AENRTTU TAUNTER
AENRTUV VAUNTER
AENRUWY UNWEARY

AENSSST ASSENTS
AENSSTU UNSEATS
AENSSTX SEXTANS
AENSSWY SAWNEYS
AENSTTU ATTUNES
NUTATES
TAUTENS
TETANUS
UNSTATE
AENSTTX SEXTANT
AENSTWY TAWNEYS
AEOOPPS PAPOOSE
AEOPPPS PAPPOSE
AEOPPRS APPOSER
AEOPPRV APPROVE
AEOPPSS APPOSES
AEOPQRU OPAQUER
AEOPQSU OPAQUES
AEOPRRT PRAETOR
PRORATE
AEOPRRV VAPORER
AEOPRSS SOAPERS
AEOPRST ESPARTO
PROTEAS
SEAPORT
AEOPRTV OVERAPT
AEOPRVY OVERPAY
AEOPRWY ROPEWAY
AEOPSST PETASOS
SAPOTES
AEOPSTT TEAPOTS
AEOPSTY TEAPOYS
AEOPSTZ TOPAZES
AEOQRTU EQUATOR
AEOQRUV VAQUERO
AEOQSUU AQUEOUS
AEORRRS ROARERS
AEORRSS SOARERS
AEORRST ROASTER
AEORRSU AROUSER
AEORRSV SAVORER
SEROVAR
AEORSSS SAROSES
SEROSAS
AEORSST OSETRAS
OSSETRA
AEORSSU AROUSES
AEORSTT ROTATES
TOASTER
AEORSVW AVOWERS
OVERSAW
REAVOWS
AEORTTU OUTRATE
AEORTUV OUTRAVE
AEORTUW OUTWEAR
AEORTVX OVERTAX
AEOSSTV AVOSETS
AEOSTTU OUTEATS
AEOSUVZ ZOUAVES
AEPPPRU PREPUPA
AEPPRRS RAPPERS
AEPPRRT TRAPPER
AEPPRRW PREWRAP
WRAPPER
AEPPRSS SAPPERS
AEPPRST TAPPERS
AEPPRSU PAUPERS
AEPPRSW SWAPPER
AEPPRSY PREPAYS
YAPPERS
AEPPRSZ ZAPPERS
AEPPSTT TAPPETS
AEPPSTU PASTEUP
PUPATES
AEPQRTU PARQUET
AEPRRSS PARSERS
RASPERS
SPARERS
SPARSER
AEPRRST PRATERS
AEPRRSU PARURES
UPREARS
AEPRRSW REWRAPS
WARPERS
AEPRRSY PRAYERS
RESPRAY
SPRAYER
AEPRRTU RAPTURE
AEPRRTW REWRAPT
AEPRRTY PARTYER
AEPRSSS PASSERS
AEPRSST PASTERS
REPASTS
SPAREST
AEPRSSU PAUSERS
AEPRSSY PESSARY

AEPRSTT PATTERS
SPATTER
TAPSTER
AEPRSTU PASTURE
UPRATES
UPSTARE
UPTEARS
AEPRSTZ PATZERS
AEPRSUX ARUSPEX
AEPRSUY YAUPERS
AEPRSWY YAWPERS
AEPRTXY APTERYX
AEPSSTU PETASUS
AEPSTTU UPSTATE
AEQRRSU SQUARER
AEQRRTU QUARTER
AEQRSSU SQUARES
AEQRSTU QUARTES
QUATRES
AEQRSUV QUAVERS
AEQRTTU QUARTET
AEQRUVY QUAVERY
AEQSSSU QUASSES
AERRSST ARRESTS
RASTERS
STARERS
AERRSSU ASSURER
RASURES
AERRSTT RATTERS
RESTART
STARTER
AERRSTV STARVER
AERRSTY STRAYER
AERSSST ASSERTS
TRASSES
AERSSSU ASSURES
AERSSSW WRASSES
AERSSTT STARETS
STATERS
TASTERS
AERSSTV STARVES
AERSSTW WASTERS
AERSSTY ESTRAYS
STAYERS
AERSSUV VARUSES
AERSSWY SAWYERS
SWAYERS
AERSTTT STRETTA
TARTEST
TATTERS
AERSTTU STATURE
AERSTTW SWATTER
AERSTTY YATTERS
AERSTUU AUTEURS
AERSTUY ESTUARY
AERSTWY WASTERY
AESSSTT TASSETS
AESSTTT ATTESTS
AESSTTU STATUES
AESSTTV VASTEST
AESSTUV SUAVEST
AESSTUY EUSTASY
AESTTTU STATUTE
TAUTEST
AESTTTW WATTEST
AFFFLLO FALLOFF
AFFGGIN GAFFING
AFFGINN NAFFING
AFFGINW WAFFING
AFFGINY YAFFING
AFFGSUW GUFFAWS
AFFHIRS RAFFISH
AFFHIST HAFFITS
AFFIITX FIXATIF
AFFIKRS KAFFIRS
AFFILPS PILAFFS
AFFILSY FALSIFY
AFFIMRS AFFIRMS
AFFIMST MASTIFF
AFFINRU FUNFAIR
RUFFIAN
AFFINTY TIFFANY
AFFIRST TARIFFS
AFFIRSU SUFFARI
AFFIRSZ ZAFFIRS
AFFLOPY PLAYOFF
AFFLOSY LAYOFFS
AFFMOPR OFFRAMP
AFFNORS SAFFRON
AFFNORT AFFRONT
AFFOPSY PAYOFFS
AFGGGIN FAGGING
AFGGOST FAGGOTS
AFGHHIS HAGFISH
AFGHINS FASHING
AFGHINT HAFTING

AFGHIRS GARFISH
AFGHRTU FRAUGHT
AFGIILN FAILING
AFGIINR FAIRING
AFGIINW WAIFING
AFGIKLN FLAKING
AFGILLN FALLING
AFGILMN FLAMING
AFGILNO FOALING
LOAFING
AFGILNR FLARING
AFGILNT FATLING
AFGILNU GAINFUL
AFGILNW FLAWING
AFGILNY FLAYING
AFGILRU FIGURAL
AFGIMNO FOAMING
AFGIMNR FARMING
FRAMING
AFGIMNY MAGNIFY
AFGINNN FANNING
AFGINNW FAWNING
AFGINOT ANTIFOG
AFGINRT INGRAFT
RAFTING
AFGINRY FRAYING
AFGINST FASTING
AFGINTT FATTING
AFGINTW WAFTING
AFGIRTY GRATIFY
AFGLLLY GALLFLY
AFGLLUY FUGALLY
AFGLNOS FLAGONS
AFGLNSU FUNGALS
AFGMNOR FROGMAN
AFGOSTU FUGATOS
AFHIIRS FAIRISH
AFHIISW WAIFISH
AFHIKLS KHALIFS
AFHIMNU HAFNIUM
AFHINOS FASHION
AFHINPS PANFISH
AFHINTU UNFAITH
AFHIORS OARFISH
AFHIRSS SHARIFS
AFHIRST RATFISH
AFHISSW SAWFISH
AFHISTT FATTISH
AFHISWY FISHWAY
AFHKORY HAYFORK
AFHKRTU FUTHARK
AFHLMRU HARMFUL
AFHLMSU FULHAMS
AFHLOOS LOOFAHS
AFHLOTY HAYLOFT
AFHLSTU HATFULS
HATSFUL
AFHMOST FATHOMS
AFHORSS SHOFARS
AFIILNS FINALIS
FINIALS
AFIILNT TAILFIN
AFIILOR AIRFOIL
AFIILRT AIRLIFT
AFIIMOS MAFIOSI
AFIKLLY FLAKILY
AFIKLOT FLOKATI
AFIKMNR FINMARK
AFIKNRT RATFINK
AFIKNSU FUNKIAS
AFILLNS INFALLS
AFILLNY FINALLY
AFILLPT PITFALL
AFILLPU PAILFUL
AFILLRY FRAILLY
AFILLUV FLUVIAL
AFILLUW WAILFUL
AFILMNT LIFTMAN
AFILMOR ALIFORM
AFILMOY FOAMILY
AFILMPY AMPLIFY
AFILNPU PAINFUL
AFILNSV FLAVINS
AFILNTU ANTIFLU
AFILNTY FAINTLY
AFILORW AIRFLOW
AFILOTX FOXTAIL
AFILQUY QUALIFY
AFILRRY FRIARLY
AFILRSZ FRAZILS
AFILRTY FRAILTY
AFILSSY SALSIFY
AFILSTU FISTULA
AFILSTY FALSITY
AFILTTY FATTILY
AFIMNRS FIRMANS

AFIMOOS MAFIOSO
AFIMRST MAFTIRS
AFIMSSS MASSIFS
AFIMSSV FAVISMS
AFIMSUV FAUVISM
AFINNOS FANIONS
AFINNOT FONTINA
AFINNST INFANTS
AFINORS INSOFAR
AFINRTU ANTIFUR
AFINSSU FUSAINS
AFINSTU FUSTIAN
AFIORTU FAITOUR
AFIQRSU FAQUIRS
AFISSTY SATISFY
AFISTUV FAUVIST
AFITTUY FATUITY
AFJLRSU JARFULS
JARSFUL
AFKLNRY FRANKLY
AFKLNTU TANKFUL
AFKLOWY FOLKWAY
AFKRRTU FRAKTUR
AFLLMPU PALMFUL
AFLLMSU FULLAMS
AFLLOOY ALOOFLY
AFLLORS FLORALS
AFLLOSW FALLOWS
AFLLOTU FALLOUT
OUTFALL
AFLLPSU LAPFULS
AFLLPUY PLAYFUL
AFLLUWY AWFULLY
AFLMNOU MOANFUL
AFLMORS FORMALS
AFLMORU FORMULA
AFLMORW WOLFRAM
AFLMOST FLOTSAM
AFLMRSU ARMFULS
ARMSFUL
FULMARS
AFLMSUU FAMULUS
AFLNORT FRONTAL
AFLNPSU PANFULS
AFLNSTU FLAUNTS
AFLNTUY FLAUNTY
AFLOPTT FLATTOP
AFLORSS SAFROLS
AFLORSV FLAVORS
AFLORUV FLAVOUR
AFLORVY FLAVORY
AFLPRTY FLYTRAP
AFLPSTY FLYPAST
AFLRTUU FUTURAL
AFLRTUY TRAYFUL
AFLSTUV VATFULS
AFLSUWY SWAYFUL
AFLSWYY FLYWAYS
AFMNNOR NONFARM
AFMNOOT FOOTMAN
AFMNORT FORMANT
AFMNOST FANTOMS
AFMNRSU SURFMAN
AFMNRTU TURFMAN
AFMORST FORMATS
AFMORSU AUSFORM
AFMOSTT AFTMOST
AFMOSTU SFUMATO
AFNNNOS NONFANS
AFNORTW FANWORT
AFNOTUW OUTFAWN
AFNPRSY FRYPANS
AFNSSTU SUNFAST
AFOOTWY FOOTWAY
AFORRSW FARROWS
AFORRSY ORFRAYS
AFORSUV FAVOURS
AFOSTTU OUTFAST
AFOSTUU FATUOUS
AFPSTUW UPWAFTS
AGGGGIN GAGGING
AGGGHIN HAGGING
AGGGIJN JAGGING
AGGGILN LAGGING
AGGGINN GANGING
NAGGING
AGGGINR RAGGING
AGGGINS SAGGING
AGGGINT TAGGING
AGGGINU GAUGING
AGGGINW WAGGING
AGGGINZ ZAGGING
AGGHHIS HAGGISH
AGGHIMN GINGHAM
AGGHINN HANGING
AGGHINS GASHING

AGGHISW WAGGISH
AGGIIMN IMAGING
AGGIINN GAINING
AGGIINT GAITING
AGGIINV GINGIVA
AGGIKNS GASKING
AGGIKNW GAWKING
AGGILLN GALLING
GINGALL
AGGILNN ANGLING
AGGILNO GAOLING
GOALING
AGGILNR ARGLING
GLARING
AGGILNS GINGALS
AGGILNZ GLAZING
AGGILOS LOGGIAS
AGGIMMN GAMMING
AGGIMNS GAMINGS
AGGIMNU GAUMING
AGGINNP PANGING
AGGINNR RANGING
AGGINNT TANGING
AGGINNU UNAGING
AGGINNW GNAWING
AGGINOT GIGATON
AGGINPP GAPPING
AGGINPR PARGING
AGGINPS GASPING
PAGINGS
AGGINPW GAWPING
AGGINRR GARRING
AGGINRT GRATING
AGGINRU ARGUING
AGGINRV GRAVING
AGGINRY GRAYING
AGGINRZ GRAZING
AGGINSS GASSING
AGGINST GASTING
GATINGS
STAGING
AGGINSW SWAGING
AGGISWW WIGWAGS
AGGISZZ ZIGZAGS
AGGLOST LOGGATS
AGGMORR GROGRAM
AGGMOST MAGGOTS
AGGMOTY MAGGOTY
AGGMRSU MUGGARS
AGGNOSW WAGGONS
AGGNOSY SYNAGOG
AGHHINS HASHING
AGHHIWY HIGHWAY
AGHHOSW HOGWASH
AGHHSSU SHAUGHS
AGHHTUY HAUGHTY
AGHIILN HAILING
NILGHAI
AGHIKNN HANKING
AGHIKNR HARKING
AGHIKNS SHAKING
AGHIKNW HAWKING
AGHIKSU KIAUGHS
AGHIKSW GAWKISH
AGHILNO HALOING
AGHILNS LASHING
AGHILNT HALTING
LATHING
AGHILNU HAULING
NILGHAU
AGHILNV HALVING
AGHILNW WHALING
AGHILNY NYLGHAI
AGHILOT GOLIATH
AGHILRS LARGISH
AGHILRT ALRIGHT
AGHILST ALIGHTS
AGHIMMN HAMMING
AGHIMNR HARMING
AGHIMNS MASHING
SHAMING
AGHINNT HANTING
AGHINOX HOAXING
AGHINPP HAPPING
AGHINPR HARPING
AGHINPS HASPING
PASHING
PHASING
SHAPING
AGHINRS GARNISH
SHARING
AGHINSS SASHING
AGHINST HASTING
AGHINSU ANGUISH
AGHINSV SHAVING

AGHINSW SHAWING
WASHING
AGHINSY HAYINGS
AGHINSZ HAZINGS
AGHINTT HATTING
AGHINTW THAWING
AGHIOST GOATISH
AGHIQSU QUAIGHS
AGHIRRS GHARRIS
AGHIRSY GRAYISH
AGHJMNO MAHJONG
AGHKOSW GOSHAWK
AGHLMPU GALUMPH
AGHLMSU MUGHALS
AGHLNUY NYLGHAU
AGHLOOS GASOHOL
AGHLOSU GOULASH
AGHLSTY GHASTLY
AGHNNSU UNHANGS
AGHNOTU HANGOUT
AGHNPSU HANGUPS
AGHNSTU NAUGHTS
AGHNTUY NAUGHTY
AGHOORT AGOROTH
AGHOQSU QUAHOGS
AGHORTW WARTHOG
AGHPTUY PAUGHTY
AGHSTUW WAUGHTS
AGIIJLN JAILING
AGIIKLT GLAIKIT
AGIIKNP PAIKING
AGIILMN MAILING
AGIILNN ALINING
NAILING
AGIILNR LAIRING
RAILING
AGIILNS NILGAIS
SAILING
AGIILNT INTAGLI
TAILING
AGIILNV VAILING
VIALING
AGIILNW WAILING
AGIILPT PIGTAIL
AGIILTY AGILITY
AGIIMMN MAIMING
AGIIMMS IMAGISM
AGIIMOR ORIGAMI
AGIIMST IMAGIST
AGIINNP PAINING
AGIINNR INGRAIN
RAINING
AGIINNS SAINING
AGIINNZ ZINGANI
AGIINPR PAIRING
AGIINRS AIRINGS
ARISING
RAISING
AGIINRT AIRTING
AGIINRW WAIRING
AGIINRZ ZINGARI
AGIINSV VISAING
AGIINTW WAITING
AGIINTX TAXIING
AGIINVW WAIVING
AGIJKNU JAUKING
AGIJLLN JINGALL
AGIJLNS JINGALS
AGIJMMN JAMMING
AGIJNPU JAUPING
AGIJNRR JARRING
AGIJNSW JIGSAWN
AGIJNZZ JAZZING
AGIJSSW JIGSAWS
AGIKKNY YAKKING
AGIKLNN ANKLING
AGIKLNR LARKING
AGIKLNS LAKINGS
SLAKING
AGIKLNT TALKING
AGIKLNW WALKING
AGIKLWY GAWKILY
AGIKMNR MARKING
AGIKMNS MAKINGS
MASKING
AGIKNNR NARKING
RANKING
AGIKNNS SNAKING
AGIKNNT TANKING
AGIKNNY YANKING
AGIKNOS SOAKING
AGIKNOY KAYOING
OKAYING
AGIKNPR PARKING
AGIKNQU QUAKING
AGIKNRT KARTING

AGIKNRW WARKING
AGIKNSS ASKINGS
GASKINS
AGIKNST SKATING
STAKING
TAKINGS
TASKING
AGIKNUW WAUKING
AGILLLN LALLING
AGILLMN MALLING
AGILLMU GALLIUM
AGILLNP PALLING
AGILLNU LINGUAL
LINGULA
AGILLNW WALLING
AGILLNY ALLYING
AGILLOR GORILLA
AGILLOT GALLIOT
AGILLRU LIGULAR
AGILLSU LIGULAS
LUGSAIL
AGILLYZ GLAZILY
AGILMMN LAMMING
AGILMMS GIMMALS
AGILMNO LOAMING
AGILMNP LAMPING
PALMING
AGILMNR MARLING
AGILMNS LINGAMS
MALIGNS
AGILMNT MALTING
AGILMNU MAULING
AGILMNY MANGILY
AGILMOS GLIOMAS
AGILMPS MAGILPS
AGILMST STIGMAL
AGILNNO LOANING
AGILNNP PLANING
AGILNNS LIGNANS
LINSANG
AGILNOT ANTILOG
AGILNPP LAPPING
PALPING
AGILNPR GRAPLIN
PARLING
AGILNPS LAPSING
PALINGS
SAPLING
AGILNPT PLATING
AGILNPW LAPWING
AGILNPY PLAYING
AGILNRY ANGRILY
AGILNSS SIGNALS
AGILNST LASTING
SALTING
SLATING
STALING
AGILNSU NILGAUS
AGILNSV SALVING
SLAVING
AGILNSW LAWINGS
AGILNSY SLAYING
AGILNUV VALUING
AGILNUW WAULING
AGILNVV VALVING
AGILNWW WAWLING
AGILNWY YAWLING
AGILNYZ LAZYING
AGILOPT GALIPOT
AGILORS GIRASOL
GLORIAS
AGILORW AIRGLOW
AGILOST GALIOTS
LATIGOS
AGILSSY GASSILY
AGILSTY STAGILY
AGILUYZ GAUZILY
AGIMMNR RAMMING
AGIMNNN MANNING
AGIMNNO MOANING
AGIMNNW WINGMAN
AGIMNOR ROAMING
AGIMNOT MOATING
AGIMNPP MAPPING
AGIMNPR GRIPMAN
RAMPING
AGIMNPT TAMPING
AGIMNPV VAMPING
AGIMNRR MARRING
AGIMNRS ARMINGS
MARGINS
AGIMNRT MARTING
MIGRANT
AGIMNRW WARMING
AGIMNSS MASSING

AGIMNST MASTING
MATINGS
AGIMNSU AMUSING
AGIMNSY MAYINGS
AGIMNTT MATTING
AGIMORS ISOGRAM
AGIMORU GOURAMI
AGIMOSY ISOGAMY
AGIMRRT TRIGRAM
AGIMSST STIGMAS
AGIMSWW WIGWAMS
AGINNNP PANNING
AGINNNT TANNING
AGINNNV VANNING
AGINNNW WANNING
AGINNOT ATONING
AGINNOZ ZINGANO
AGINNPP NAPPING
AGINNPS PINANGS
AGINNPT PANTING
AGINNPW PAWNING
AGINNRS SNARING
AGINNRT RANTING
AGINNRW WARNING
AGINNRY YARNING
AGINNST ANTINGS
STANING
AGINNSU GUANINS
AGINNSW AWNINGS
SNAWING
AGINNTU ANTIGUN
AGINNTW WANTING
AGINNWY YAWNING
AGINOOO OOGONIA
AGINOOP POGONIA
AGINOPR PIGNORA
AGINOPS SOAPING
AGINORR ROARING
AGINORS ORIGANS
SIGNORA
SOARING
AGINORT ORATING
AGINORZ ZINGARO
AGINOST AGONIST
GITANOS
AGINOTU AUTOING
OUTGAIN
AGINOVW AVOWING
AGINPPR RAPPING
AGINPPS SAPPING
AGINPPT TAPPING
AGINPPW WAPPING
AGINPPY YAPPING
AGINPPZ ZAPPING
AGINPRR PARRING
AGINPRS PARINGS
PARSING
RASPING
SPARING
AGINPRT PARTING
PRATING
AGINPRW WARPING
AGINPRY PRAYING
AGINPSS PASSING
AGINPST PASTING
AGINPSU PAUSING
AGINPSV PAVINGS
AGINPSY SPAYING
AGINPTT PATTING
AGINPUY YAUPING
AGINPWY YAWPING
AGINRRT TARRING
AGINRRW WARRING
AGINRST GASTRIN
GRATINS
RATINGS
STARING
AGINRSV RAVINGS
AGINRSY SYRINGA
AGINRTT RATTING
TARTING
AGINRTW RINGTAW
AGINRVY VARYING
AGINRZZ RAZZING
AGINSSS ASSIGNS
SASSING
AGINSSV SAVINGS
AGINSSY SAYINGS
AGINSTT STATING
TASTING
AGINSTV STAVING
AGINSTW TAWSING
WASTING
AGINSTY STAYING
STYGIAN
AGINSWX WAXINGS

AGINSWY SWAYING
AGINTTT TATTING
AGINTTU TAUTING
AGINTTV VATTING
AGINTXY TAXYING
AGINWWX WAXWING
AGIOPSS GAPOSIS
AGIORST ORGIAST
AGIORSU GIAOURS
AGIORSV VIRAGOS
AGIOSTU AGOUTIS
AGIOUUY OUGUIYA
AGIRSTU GUITARS
AGIRTVY GRAVITY
AGJLMOS LOGJAMS
AGJLRUU JUGULAR
AGJNOOR JARGOON
AGJNORS JARGONS
AGJNORY JARGONY
AGJSTTY GYTTJAS
AGKLNOS KALONGS
AGKMNOP KAMPONG
AGKMPRU PUGMARK
AGKNRSU KURGANS
AGLLNOO GALLOON
AGLLNOS GALLONS
AGLLNTU GALLNUT
NUTGALL
AGLLOOT GALLOOT
AGLLOPS GALLOPS
AGLLOPU PLUGOLA
AGLLOSS GLOSSAL
AGLLOSU GALLOUS
AGLLOSW GALLOWS
AGLLOTT GLOTTAL
AGLLRSY ARGYLLS
AGLLRYY GYRALLY
AGLMORS GLAMORS
AGLMORU GLAMOUR
AGLNNOS LONGANS
AGLNNSU LUNGANS
AGLNOOS LAGOONS
AGLNORU LANGUOR
AGLNOSS SLOGANS
AGLNOSU LANUGOS
AGLNPSY SPANGLY
AGLNPUY GUNPLAY
AGLNRSU LANGURS
AGLNRUU UNGULAR
AGLNTUY GAUNTLY
AGLOOPS APOLOGS
AGLOOPY APOLOGY
AGLOORS GOORALS
AGLOOST GALOOTS
AGLORSU RUGOLAS
AGLOSSS GLOSSAS
AGLOSSW SAWLOGS
AGLOSWY LOGWAYS
AGLRSUV VULGARS
AGLSYYZ SYZYGAL
AGMMNOS GAMMONS
AGMMNSU MAGNUMS
AGMNNOT TONGMAN
AGMNORS MORGANS
AGMNORU ORGANUM
AGMNOST AMONGST
AGMNSTU MUSTANG
AGMNSTY GYMNAST
SYNTAGM
AGMNSYY SYNGAMY
AGMOPRR PROGRAM
AGMORSS ORGASMS
AGMOSYZ ZYGOMAS
AGMPRSU GRAMPUS
AGMPSUZ GAZUMPS
AGNNNOO NONAGON
AGNNOOR ORGANON
AGNNOSY NONGAYS
AGNNSSU UNSNAGS
AGNNSUW WANGUNS
AGNOQSU QUANGOS
AGNORRS GARRONS
AGNORRT GRANTOR
AGNORSS SARONGS
AGNORSU OURANGS
AGNORTU OUTRANG
AGNOSSS GOSSANS
AGNOSTU NOUGATS
OUTSANG
AGNOTUW OUTGNAW
AGNPRSS SPRANGS
AGNRTUY GAUNTRY
AGOPPST STOPGAP
AGOPRST RAGTOPS
AGORRTW RAGWORT
AGORRTY GYRATOR

AGORSSU RUGOSAS
AGORSTU RAGOUTS
AGORTUY GRAYOUT
AGOSTTU TAUTOGS
AGOSUYZ AZYGOUS
AHHHISS HASHISH
AHHIIMS HAIMISH
AHHIJRS HIJRAHS
AHHIKKR KHIRKAH
AHHIKSW HAWKISH
AHHIMNU HAHNIUM
AHHINST SHANTIH
AHHISSV SHIVAHS
AHHISTT SHITTAH
AHHKOOS HOOKAHS
AHHLLOT HALLOTH
AHHLRSY HARSHLY
AHHMPRU HARUMPH
AHHOORS HOORAHS
AHHOPRS SHOPHAR
AHHPPSU HUPPAHS
AHHPTUZ HUTZPAH
AHHRRSU HURRAHS
AHHSUZZ HUZZAHS
AHIIKRS RIKISHA
SHIKARI
AHIILST LITHIAS
AHIIMNT THIAMIN
AHIIMSS SASHIMI
AHIINPR HAIRPIN
AHIINST TAHINIS
AHIINTZ THIAZIN
AHIIPRS AIRSHIP
AHIKKSS KISHKAS
AHIKLPS KALIPHS
AHIKLRS LARKISH
AHIKLSS SHASLIK
AHIKLSY SHAKILY
AHIKMNS KHAMSIN
AHIKMRS KASHMIR
AHIKMSV MIKVAHS
AHIKMSW MAWKISH
AHIKNRS RANKISH
AHIKNSV KNAVISH
AHIKRSS SHIKARS
AHIKRSW RIKSHAW
AHILLNT ANTHILL
AHILLOS HILLOAS
AHILLST TALLISH
AHILLSZ ZILLAHS
AHILLTT TALLITH
AHILLTY LAITHLY
AHILMMO MOHALIM
AHILMMY HAMMILY
AHILMOP OMPHALI
AHILNPS PLANISH
AHILNRT INTHRAL
AHILNSS LASHINS
AHILNSU INHAULS
AHILNSY HYALINS
AHILORY HOARILY
AHILOTZ THIAZOL
AHILPPS PALSHIP
SHIPLAP
AHILPPY HAPPILY
AHILPRT PHILTRA
AHILPSY APISHLY
AHILSST SALTISH
TAHSILS
AHILSSV SLAVISH
AHILSTU HALITUS
THULIAS
AHILSTY HASTILY
AHILSYZ LAZYISH
AHIMMRS RAMMISH
AHIMNNS MANNISH
AHIMNNU INHUMAN
AHIMNOT MANIHOT
AHIMNPS SHIPMAN
AHIMNRS HARMINS
AHIMOPR MORPHIA
AHIMORS MOHAIRS
AHIMORZ RHIZOMA
AHIMOSS SHAMOIS
AHIMPSS MISHAPS
AHIMPSV VAMPISH
AHIMPSW WAMPISH
AHIMRST THAIRMS
THIRAMS
AHIMRSW WARMISH
AHIMSSU HASSIUM
AHIMSTV MITSVAH
AHIMTUZ AZIMUTH
AHIMTVZ MITZVAH
AHINNST TANNISH
AHINNTX XANTHIN

AHINOTZ HOATZIN
AHINPRS HARPINS
AHINPST HATPINS
AHINRSS ARSHINS
SHAIRNS
AHINRST TARNISH
AHINRSU UNHAIRS
AHINRSV VARNISH
AHINRVY HRYVNIA
AHINSST SHANTIS
AHINSYZ ZANYISH
AHIOPXY HYPOXIA
AHIORSS ORISHAS
AHIORST AIRSHOT
SHORTIA
THORIAS
AHIORSV HAVIORS
AHIORSW AIRSHOW
AHIORUV HAVIOUR
AHIPRSS RASPISH
AHIPRST HARPIST
AHIPRSU RUPIAHS
AHIPRSW WARSHIP
AHIPRWY WHIPRAY
AHIPSSW WASPISH
AHIPSWW WHIPSAW
AHIPSWY SHIPWAY
AHIRRSS SIRRAHS
AHIRSTT ATHIRST
RATTISH
TARTISH
AHIRSTW TRISHAW
WRAITHS
AHISSTU SHIATSU
AHISSTW WHATSIS
AHISTTW WHATSIT
AHISTUZ SHIATZU
AHKKSSU SUKKAHS
AHKMORR MARKHOR
AHKMOSW MOHAWKS
AHKNPSU PUNKAHS
AHKRSTU KASHRUT
AHLLMOS MOLLAHS
AHLLMSU MULLAHS
AHLLNSU NULLAHS
AHLLOOS HALLOOS
HOLLOAS
AHLLOPS SHALLOP
AHLLOST SHALLOT
AHLLOSU HULLOAS
AHLLOSW HALLOWS
SHALLOW
AHLLOTY LOATHLY
TALLYHO
AHLLPSU PHALLUS
AHLLPSY ALPHYLS
AHLLPYY APHYLLY
AHLLRST THRALLS
AHLLSTU THALLUS
AHLMNPY NYMPHAL
AHLMNSY HYMNALS
AHLMNUY HUMANLY
AHLMOOS MOOLAHS
AHLMORU HUMORAL
AHLMOSS SHALOMS
AHLMSTZ SHMALTZ
AHLMSUU HAMULUS
AHLNOPR ALPHORN
AHLNOPT HAPLONT
NAPHTOL
AHLNORT ALTHORN
AHLOOPS HOOPLAS
AHLOOPW WHOOPLA
AHLOOTW WOOLHAT
AHLORST HARLOTS
AHLOTUU OUTHAUL
AHLPRSY SHARPLY
AHLPSSU SULPHAS
AHLPSSY SPLASHY
AHMMMOT MAMMOTH
AHMMOSS SHAMMOS
AHMNNTU MANHUNT
AHMNNUU UNHUMAN
AHMNOPS SHOPMAN
AHMNOPT PHANTOM
AHMNORY HARMONY
AHMNOSS HANSOMS
AHMNOSW SHOWMAN
AHMNRSU RHAMNUS
AHMNRYY HYMNARY
AHMOOPS OOMPAHS
SHAMPOO
AHMORSZ MAHZORS
AHMOSSY SHAMOYS
AHMOSTU MAHOUTS
AHMOSTZ MATZOHS

AHMOSWY HAYMOWS
AHMOTTZ MATZOTH
AHMPSSU SMASHUP
AHMRRSU MURRHAS
AHMRSTW WARMTHS
AHMSSSU SAMSHUS
AHNNSSU SUNNAHS
AHNOOPR HARPOON
AHNOPRS ORPHANS
AHNORSS SHORANS
AHNORSX SAXHORN
AHNOTTW WHATNOT
AHNPPSS SHNAPPS
AHNPPUY UNHAPPY
AHNPRSU UNSHARP
AHNPRXY PHARYNX
AHNRSVY HRYVNAS
AHNSTUY UNHASTY
AHOORSY HOORAYS
AHOPRTY ATROPHY
AHOPTTW TOWPATH
AHORRSW HARROWS
AHORSTT THROATS
AHORSTU AUTHORS
AHORTTY THROATY
AHOSTUW OUTWASH
WASHOUT
AHPRRTY PHRATRY
AHPSSUW WASHUPS
AHPSTUZ HUTZPAS
AHPSXYY ASPHYXY
AHQSSUY SQUASHY
AHRRSUY HURRAYS
AHRSSSU HUSSARS
AHRSSTT STRATHS
AHRSSTW SWARTHS
AHRSTTW THWARTS
AHRSTWY SWARTHY
AHRTUWY THRUWAY
AHSSSTU TUSSAHS
AIIILMT MILITIA
AIIILNT INITIAL
AIIILVX LIXIVIA
AIIKKSW WAKIKIS
AIIKMNN MANIKIN
AIIKNNT TANKINI
AIIKNST KAINITS
AIILLLP LAPILLI
AIILLMN LIMINAL
AIILLNV VILLAIN
AIILLQU QUILLAI
AIILLUV ILLUVIA
AIILMMN MINIMAL
AIILMNN LAMININ
AIILMNS MISLAIN
AIILMNT INTIMAL
AIILMNV VIMINAL
AIILMRS SIMILAR
AIILMRY MILIARY
AIILNNS ANILINS
AIILNOS LIAISON
AIILNPT PINTAIL
AIILNPU NAUPLII
AIILNRY RAINILY
AIILNTU NAUTILI
AIILNTV INVITAL
AIILNTY ANILITY
AIILORV RAVIOLI
AIILQSU SILIQUA
AIILRTV TRIVIAL
AIIMMNS ANIMISM
AIIMMNX MAXIMIN
MINIMAX
AIIMMSS MISAIMS
AIIMNNV MINIVAN
AIIMNOR AMORINI
AIIMNPS PIANISM
AIIMNPT IMPAINT
TIMPANI
AIIMNRT MARTINI
AIIMNSS SAIMINS
SIMIANS
AIIMNST ANIMIST
INTIMAS
SANTIMI
AIIMNTU MINUTIA
AIIMNTV VITAMIN
AIIMNTY AMINITY
AIIMPRS IMPAIRS
AIIMRST SIMITAR
AIIMSSY MYIASIS
AIINNQU QUININA
AIINNSZ ZINNIAS
AIINNTY INANITY
AIINOPS SINOPIA
AIINPPR RAPPINI

AIINPRS ASPIRIN
AIINPST PIANIST
AIINRSS RAISINS
AIINRSY RAISINY
AIINRTV VITRAIN
AIINRTZ TRIAZIN
AIINSST ISATINS
AIINSTT TITIANS
AIIPSTW WAPITIS
AIJJMMS JIMJAMS
AIJLORS JAILORS
AIJLYZZ JAZZILY
AIJMNSS JASMINS
AIJMORS ROMAJIS
AIJNORT JANITOR
AIKKMNR KIRKMAN
AIKKMOT KOMATIK
AIKKOPY KOPIYKA
AIKLLNY LANKILY
AIKLMMN MILKMAN
AIKLMNN LINKMAN
AIKLMNS MALKINS
AIKLMSS MISKALS
AIKLMSU KALIUMS
AIKLNOS KAOLINS
AIKLNSY SNAKILY
AIKLPWY PAWKILY
AIKLQUY QUAKILY
AIKLRTT TITLARK
AIKLSSU SALUKIS
AIKLSSY SKYSAIL
AIKMMRS MISMARK
AIKMNNS KINSMAN
AIKMNSS KAMSINS
AIKMOOS OOMIAKS
AIKMPRS IMPARKS
AIKMRSU RUMAKIS
AIKMSST KISMATS
AIKNNNS NANKINS
AIKNNPS NAPKINS
AIKNOST KATIONS
AIKNSTU TANUKIS
AIKORST TROIKAS
AIKRTUZ ZIKURAT
AILLLNO LINALOL
AILLMNU LUMINAL
AILLMNY MANLILY
AILLMOT MAILLOT
AILLMPU PALLIUM
AILLMSU ALLIUMS
AILLMSW SAWMILL
AILLMSY MISALLY
AILLNNO LANOLIN
AILLNPY PLAINLY
AILLNST INSTALL
AILLNSW INWALLS
AILLORT LITORAL
AILLORZ ZORILLA
AILLPRS PILLARS
AILLPRU PILULAR
AILLPUV PLUVIAL
AILLQSU SQUILLA
AILLRVY VIRALLY
AILLSTT TALLITS
AILLSTY SALTILY
AILLSUZ LAZULIS
AILLTVY VITALLY
AILMMOR IMMORAL
AILMNNO NOMINAL
AILMNOP LAMPION
AILMNOS MALISON
AILMNOY ALIMONY
AILMNPS MISPLAN
PLASMIN
AILMNPT IMPLANT
AILMNPU ULPANIM
AILMNRS MARLINS
AILMNRU RUMINAL
AILMNSU ALUMINS
AILMOOV MOVIOLA
AILMOPS LIPOMAS
AILMOPT OPTIMAL
AILMORS ORALISM
AILMOST SOMITAL
AILMPRU PRIMULA
AILMPST PALMIST
AILMPSY MISPLAY
AILMRST MISTRAL
RAMTILS
AILMRSU SIMULAR
AILMSSS MISSALS
AILMSSY MISLAYS
AILMSTU ULTIMAS
AILNNOS SOLANIN
AILNNOT ANTLION
AILNNPU PINNULA

AILNNSU UNNAILS
AILNOST LATINOS
TALIONS
AILNOTU OUTLAIN
AILNPSS SPINALS
AILNPST PLAINTS
AILNPSU PAULINS
SPINULA
AILNPSX SALPINX
AILNPTU NUPTIAL
UNPLAIT
AILNPTY INAPTLY
PTYALIN
AILNPUV PLUVIAN
AILNQTU QUINTAL
AILNRST RATLINS
AILNRSU INSULAR
URINALS
AILNRTY RIANTLY
AILNSST INSTALS
AILNSSV SILVANS
AILNSTT LATTINS
AILNSTY NASTILY
SAINTLY
AILNTTY NATTILY
AILNTWY TAWNILY
AILOORS OORALIS
AILOORW WOORALI
AILOPST APOSTIL
TOPSAIL
AILOPSY SOAPILY
AILOPTT TALIPOT
AILOPTV PIVOTAL
AILOQTU ALIQUOT
AILORSS SAILORS
AILORST ORALIST
RIALTOS
TAILORS
AILORTY ORALITY
AILORUX UXORIAL
AILORVY OLIVARY
AILOSSS ASSOILS
AILOSTT ALTOIST
AILOSTU OUTSAIL
AILOSTX OXTAILS
AILOSWY OILWAYS
AILOTVY OVALITY
AILPPRU PUPILAR
AILPPSY SAPPILY
AILPPTY PLATYPI
AILPQSU PASQUIL
AILPRSS SPIRALS
AILPRSU SPIRULA
AILPSST PASTILS
SPITALS
AILPSWY SLIPWAY
WASPILY
AILQTUY QUALITY
AILRRVY RIVALRY
AILRSTT STARLIT
AILRSTU RITUALS
AILRSTY TRYSAIL
AILRTTU TITULAR
AILRTTY TARTILY
AILRTUV VIRTUAL
AILSSSY SASSILY
AILSSTU TISSUAL
AILSSUV VISUALS
AILSSVZ VIZSLAS
AILSTTY TASTILY
AILSTUW LAWSUIT
AILSVVY SAVVILY
AILTTTY TATTILY
AIMMMUX MAXIMUM
AIMMNTU MANUMIT
AIMMOSS MIMOSAS
AIMMOST ATOMISM
AIMNNOR IRONMAN
AIMNNOS AMNIONS
MANSION
ONANISM
AIMNNSS NANISMS
AIMNNSY MINYANS
AIMNOOR AMORINO
AIMNOOT AMOTION
AIMNOPR RAMPION
AIMNOPT MAINTOP
PTOMAIN
TAMPION
TIMPANO
AIMNOST MANITOS
AIMNOTU MANITOU
TINAMOU
AIMNPST PITMANS
AIMNPSW IMPAWNS
AIMNPSY PAYNIMS

AIMNPTY TYMPANI
AIMNRRU MURRAIN
AIMNRST MARTINS
AIMNRSU URANISM
AIMNRTU NATRIUM
AIMNRTV VARMINT
AIMNRUU URANIUM
AIMNSST SANTIMS
AIMNSTT MATTINS
AIMNSTU MANITUS
SANTIMU
TSUNAMI
AIMNSUZ MIZUNAS
AIMNSVY MAYVINS
AIMOPST IMPASTO
AIMOPSY MYOPIAS
AIMORST AMORIST
AIMORTT TRITOMA
AIMORUZ ZOARIUM
AIMOSTT ATOMIST
AIMPRRY PRIMARY
AIMPRST ARMPITS
IMPARTS
MISPART
AIMQRSU MARQUIS
AIMRSST TSARISM
AIMRSTU ATRIUMS
AIMRSTZ TZARISM
AIMSSSY MISSAYS
AIMSSTT STATISM
AIMSSTU AUTISMS
AINNNST TANNINS
AINNOPS SAPONIN
AINNOPT PINTANO
AINNOSS NASIONS
AINNOST ANOINTS
NATIONS
ONANIST
AINNOSW WANIONS
AINNPSS INSPANS
AINNQTU QUINNAT
QUINTAN
AINNRTT INTRANT
AINNSTT INSTANT
AINNTUY ANNUITY
AINOORT ORATION
AINOOTV OVATION
AINOPPT APPOINT
AINOPRS SOPRANI
AINOPRT ATROPIN
AINOPSS PASSION
AINOPTT ANTIPOT
AINOPTU OPUNTIA
UTOPIAN
AINOQSU QUINOAS
AINORST AROINTS
RATIONS
AINORSW WARISON
AINORTU RAINOUT
AINORTW WAITRON
AINOSSU SANIOUS
SUASION
AINOSTT STATION
AINOSUX ANXIOUS
AINOSVY SYNOVIA
AINPPRS PARSNIP
AINPQTU PIQUANT
AINPRSS SPRAINS
AINPRST SPIRANT
AINPRSW INWRAPS
RIPSAWN
AINPRTT TRIPTAN
AINPRTU PURITAN
AINPSST PTISANS
AINPSSV SPAVINS
AINQRST QINTARS
AINQRTU QUINTAR
AINQRUY QUINARY
AINQSSU QUASSIN
AINQSTU ASQUINT
QUINTAS
AINQSUY YANQUIS
AINRRTY TRINARY
AINRRUY URINARY
AINRSST INSTARS
SANTIRS
STRAINS
AINRSTT TRANSIT
AINRSTU NUTRIAS
AINRTTT TITRANT
AINRTUY UNITARY
AINSSTT STATINS
TANISTS
AINSSTU ISSUANT
SUSTAIN
AINTTVY TANTIVY
AIOORRW WOORARI
AIOORSS ARIOSOS
AIOPPRR PROPRIA
AIOPPRT AIRPORT
AIOPRST AIRPOST
AIOPRSV PAVIORS
AIOPRTT PATRIOT
AIOPRTY TOPIARY
AIOPRUV PAVIOUR
AIOPSTU UTOPIAS
AIORRRW WARRIOR
AIORRSU OURARIS
AIORRTT TRAITOR
AIORRTX ORATRIX
AIORSST AORISTS
ARISTOS
SATORIS
AIORSSU SOUARIS
AIORSSV SAVIORS
AIORSTU SAUTOIR
AIORSTV TRAVOIS
VIATORS
AIORSTY OSTIARY
AIORSUV SAVIOUR
VARIOUS
AIOSSTT TATSOIS
AIOSSYZ ZOYSIAS
AIOTTUW OUTWAIT
AIPPRRS RIPRAPS
AIPPRSU PRIAPUS
AIPRRTT TRIPART
AIPRSST RAPISTS
AIPRSSW RIPSAWS
AIPRSTU UPSTAIR
AIPRSUY PYURIAS
AIPSSTW PITSAWS
AIPYZZZ PIZAZZY
AIPZZZZ PIZZAZZ
AIRRSST RISTRAS
AIRSSTT ARTISTS
STRAITS
TSARIST
AIRSSTU AURISTS
AIRSTTT ATTRITS
AIRSTTU TURISTA
AIRSTTY YTTRIAS
AIRSTTZ TZARIST
AIRSTVY VARSITY
AISSSST ASSISTS
AISSTTT STATIST
AISSTTU AUTISTS
AISTTVY VASTITY
AISTUVY SUAVITY
AJKMNNU JUNKMAN
AJKMNTU MUNTJAK
AJLLRUY JURALLY
AJLMORY MAJORLY
AJLNORU JOURNAL
AJLOPPY JALOPPY
AJMNRUY JURYMAN
AJNRSTU JURANTS
AKKLRSY SKYLARK
AKKLSWY SKYWALK
AKKMOOT TOKOMAK
AKKOQSU QUOKKAS
AKLMMSU MAMLUKS
AKLNOSX KLAXONS
AKLOSST SKATOLS
AKLOTTU OUTTALK
AKLOTUW OUTWALK
WALKOUT
AKLPRSY SPARKLY
AKLPSTU UPTALKS
AKLPSUW WALKUPS
AKLRSTY STARKLY
AKLRSVY VALKYRS
AKMNORW WORKMAN
AKMNSSU UNMASKS
AKMOOSS OAKMOSS
AKMORST OSTMARK
AKMPRSU MARKUPS
AKMQTUU KUMQUAT
AKMRSTU MUSKRAT
AKNORSU KORUNAS
AKNORSY RYOKANS
AKNORTU OUTRANK
AKOOPRT PARTOOK
AKOORRS KARROOS
AKORRTW ARTWORK
AKORRWW WARWORK
AKORWWX WAXWORK
AKOSSTU OUTASKS
AKOSTTU OUTTASK
AKQRSSU SQUARKS
AKQSSUW SQUAWKS
AKSSWYY SKYWAYS
ALLLOST TALLOLS
ALLLOYY LOYALLY
ALLMNOT TOLLMAN
ALLMNOY ALLONYM
ALLMNPU PULLMAN
ALLMOOS OSMOLAL
ALLMORY MORALLY
ALLMOSS SLALOMS
ALLMOST MALTOLS
ALLMOSW MALLOWS
ALLNOTY TONALLY
ALLNOYZ ZONALLY
ALLNRUU LUNULAR
ALLNSTY SLANTLY
ALLNTUU ULULANT
ALLOOPS APOLLOS
ALLOOST LATOSOL
ALLOOTX AXOLOTL
ALLOPRS PALLORS
ALLOPRY PAYROLL
ALLOPSW WALLOPS
ALLORWY ROLLWAY
ALLORYY ROYALLY
ALLOSSW SALLOWS
ALLOSTW TALLOWS
ALLOSWW SWALLOW
WALLOWS
ALLOSWY SALLOWY
ALLOTTY TOTALLY
ALLOTWY TALLOWY
TOLLWAY
ALLOTYY LOYALTY
ALLPRSU PLURALS
ALLPSSY PSYLLAS
ALLQSSU SQUALLS
ALLQSUY SQUALLY
ALLRRUY RURALLY
ALLRSTU LUSTRAL
ALLSUUY USUALLY
ALMMSUY AMYLUMS
ALMNNUY UNMANLY
ALMNOOP LAMPOON
ALMNOOW WOOLMAN
ALMNOPS PLASMON
ALMNOPW PLOWMAN
ALMNORS NORMALS
ALMNORU UNMORAL
ALMNORY ALMONRY
ALMNOSS SALMONS
ALMNOSU SOLANUM
ALMNOWY WOMANLY
ALMNPSU SUNLAMP
ALMNSUU ALUMNUS
ALMOOPY POLYOMA
ALMOORS OSMOLAR
ALMOPPT PALMTOP
ALMOPRT MARPLOT
ALMORRU MORULAR
ALMORST MORTALS
STROMAL
ALMORSU MORULAS
ALMORTU TUMORAL
ALMOSST SMALTOS
ALMOTTU MULATTO
ALMRSTY SMARTLY
ALMRTUU MUTULAR
TUMULAR
ALMSSUY ALYSSUM
ASYLUMS
ALMSTUU MUTUALS
UMLAUTS
ALNNOOR NONORAL
ALNNOPY NONPLAY
ALNNRSU UNSNARL
ALNNSUU ANNULUS
ALNOOPR POLARON
ALNOOPT PLATOON
ALNOOPV VANPOOL
ALNOORT ORTOLAN
ALNOOSS SALOONS
SOLANOS
ALNOPPY PANOPLY
ALNOPRS PROLANS
ALNOPSS SPONSAL
ALNOPTU OUTPLAN
ALNOPYY POLYNYA
ALNORSU SOLUNAR
ALNORUZ ZONULAR
ALNOSST SANTOLS
STANOLS
ALNOSUZ ZONULAS
ALNPSTU PULSANT
ALNPTUY UNAPTLY
ALNRSUY URANYLS
ALNSSTU SULTANS
ALNSSVY SYLVANS
ALNSTUW WALNUTS
ALNSUUU UNUSUAL
ALOOPSS SALOOPS
ALOORRS SORORAL
ALOPPRS POPLARS
ALOPPRU POPULAR
ALOPPRY PROPYLA
ALOPPST LAPTOPS
ALOPRRS PARLORS
ALOPRRU PARLOUR
ALOPRST PATROLS
PORTALS
ALOPRSU PARLOUS
ALOPRSY PYROLAS
ALOPSST POSTALS
ALOPSSU SPOUSAL
ALOPTUY OUTPLAY
ALOQRRU RORQUAL
ALOQRSU SQUALOR
ALOQSTU LOQUATS
ALORRST ROSTRAL
ALORSSV SALVORS
ALORSTU TORULAS
ALORSUV VALOURS
ALORTWW AWLWORT
ALORTYY ROYALTY
ALORUVY OVULARY
ALOSTTU OUTLAST
ALOSTUW OUTLAWS
ALOSTUY LAYOUTS
OUTLAYS
ALOSTXY OXYSALT
ALPRRSU LARRUPS
ALPRSSU PULSARS
ALPRSSW SPRAWLS
ALPRSTY PSALTRY
ALPRSWY SPRAWLY
ALQSTUY SQUATLY
ALRSTUU SUTURAL
ALRSUUV UVULARS
AMMMNOS MAMMONS
AMMNOPS PSAMMON
AMMNRUY NUMMARY
AMMOPTU POMATUM
AMMORST MARMOTS
AMMOSXY MYXOMAS
AMMPSUW WAMPUMS
AMMRSUY SUMMARY
AMNNOOX MONAXON
AMNNOSW SNOWMAN
AMNNOSY ANONYMS
AMNNOTY ANTONYM
AMNNSTU STANNUM
AMNOOPP POMPANO
AMNOORS MAROONS
ROMANOS
AMNOOTT OTTOMAN
AMNOOTZ MATZOON
AMNOPPR PROPMAN
AMNOPRY PARONYM
AMNOPST POSTMAN
TAMPONS
AMNOPTU PANTOUM
AMNOPTY TYMPANO
AMNORRS MARRONS
AMNORSS RAMSONS
RANSOMS
AMNORST MATRONS
TRANSOM
AMNORSY MASONRY
AMNORTU ROMAUNT
AMNOSTU AMOUNTS
OUTMANS
AMNOSYZ ZYMOSAN
AMNOTUY AUTONYM
AMNPSTY TYMPANS
AMNPTYY TYMPANY
AMNQTUU QUANTUM
AMNRSTU ANTRUMS
UNSMART
AMNRTTU TANTRUM
AMNSTTU MUTANTS
AMNSTUU AUTUMNS
AMOOORS AMOROSO
AMOOPRS PROSOMA
AMOOPRT TAPROOM
AMOORSU AMOROUS
AMOORSV VAROOMS
AMOORXY OXYMORA
AMOPPSY MAYPOPS
AMOPSTT TOPMAST
AMORRST MORTARS
AMORRSU ARMOURS
AMORRSW MARROWS
AMORRTY MORTARY
AMORRUY ARMOURY
AMORRWY MARROWY
AMORSSY MORASSY
AMORWWX WAXWORM
AMOSTUW OUTSWAM
AMPRSUW WARMUPS
AMRRSTY MARTYRS
AMRRTYY MARTYRY
AMRSSTU STRUMAS
AMRSTTU STRATUM
ANNNOSY SYNANON
ANNOPSS SANNOPS
ANNOPST NONPAST
ANNORST NATRONS
NONARTS
ANNORSW NONWARS
ANNOSST SONANTS
ANNOSTW WANTONS
ANNOSTY TANNOYS
ANNPSSU SANNUPS
UNSNAPS
ANNRTYY TYRANNY
ANNSSTU SUNTANS
ANOOPRS SOPRANO
ANOOPRT PATROON
PRONOTA
ANOORST RATOONS
SANTOOR
ANOORTT ARNOTTO
RATTOON
ANOPRRS SPORRAN
ANOPRSS PARSONS
ANOPRST PARTONS
PATRONS
TARPONS
ANOPRSW PAWNORS
ANOPSTU OUTSPAN
ANOPSUY YAUPONS
ANORRSW NARROWS
ANORRWW WARWORN
ANORSSV SOVRANS
ANORSTT ATTORNS
RATTONS
ANORSTU SANTOUR
ANORSTY AROYNTS
ANORSUU ANUROUS
URANOUS
ANORWWY WAYWORN
ANPRSTU UNSTRAP
ANPRSUW UNWRAPS
ANRSSTU SANTURS
ANRSSUY SUNRAYS
ANRSTTU TRUANTS
ANRSTTY TYRANTS
ANRSUWY RUNWAYS
AOOPPRS APROPOS
AOOPRTT TAPROOT
AOORRST ORATORS
AOORRSY ARROYOS
AOORRTT ROTATOR
AOORRTU OUTROAR
AOORRTY ORATORY
AOORSTU OUTSOAR
AOOSTTT TATTOOS
AOPPPSU PAPPOUS
AOPPRRT RAPPORT
AOPRRST PARROTS
RAPTORS
AOPRRSU UPROARS
AOPRRSW SPARROW
AOPRRTY PARROTY
PORTRAY
AOPRSST PASTORS
AOPRSSU SAPOURS
UPSOARS
AOPRSTW POSTWAR
AOPRSUV VAPOURS
AOPRTUY OUTPRAY
AOPRUVY VAPOURY
AOPSSTU OUTPASS
AOPSTTX POSTTAX
AOPSTUY AUTOPSY
PAYOUTS
AOQRSTU QUARTOS
AORRSST SARTORS
AORRSSU ASSUROR
AORRSWY YARROWS
AORSSST ASSORTS
AORSSTT STATORS
AORSSUV SAVOURS
AORSSUY OSSUARY
SUASORY
AORSTUW OUTWARS
AORSUVY SAVOURY
AORUVVY VOUVRAY
AOSSTUY OUTSAYS
AOSTTUY OUTSTAY
APPRRUU PURPURA
APPRSTY STRAPPY
APPRSUY PAPYRUS
APRSSSU SURPASS
APRSSWY PSYWARS
APRSTTU STARTUP
UPSTART
AQSTTUY SQUATTY
ARSSSTU TUSSARS
ARSSTTU STRATUS
ARSSTTY STARTSY
ASSTTUY STATUSY
AVYYZZZ ZYZZYVA
BBBDELO BLOBBED
BOBBLED
BBBDELU BLUBBED
BUBBLED
BBBEIOS BOBBIES
BBBEIRS BIBBERS
BBBEIRY BIBBERY
BBBELOS BOBBLES
BBBELRU BLUBBER
BUBBLER
BBBELSU BUBBLES
BBBEORS BOBBERS
BBBEORY BOBBERY
BBBGIIN BIBBING
BBBGINO BOBBING
BBBHSUU HUBBUBS
BBBINOS BOBBINS
BBCCIKO BIBCOCK
BBCDEIR CRIBBED
BBCDELO COBBLED
BBCDELU CLUBBED
BBCEEHO BOBECHE
BBCEIOR COBBIER
BBCEIRR CRIBBER
BBCEISU CUBBIES
BBCEKKO KEBBOCK
BBCEKKU KEBBUCK
BBCELOR CLOBBER
COBBLER
BBCELOS COBBLES
BBCELRU CLUBBER
BBCEORS COBBERS
BBCEOSW COBWEBS
BBCHISU CUBBISH
BBCINOU BUBONIC
BBCRSUY SCRUBBY
BBDDEIL DIBBLED
BBDDEIR DRIBBED
BBDDERU DRUBBED
BBDEELP PEBBLED
BBDEEOR BEROBED
BBDEFLU FLUBBED
BBDEGLO GOBBLED
BBDEGRU GRUBBED
BBDEGSU BEDBUGS
BBDEHLO HOBBLED
BBDEIIM IMBIBED
BBDEIKL KIBBLED
BBDEILN NIBBLED
BBDEILO BILOBED
LOBBIED
BBDEILR DIBBLER
DRIBBLE
BBDEILS DIBBLES
BBDEINS SNIBBED
BBDEIOS DOBBIES
BBDEIRS DIBBERS
BBDEKNO KNOBBED
BBDELMU BUMBLED
BBDELNO NOBBLED
BBDELOO BEBLOOD
BBDELOS BOBSLED
BBDELOW WOBBLED
BBDELRU BLURBED
BURBLED
RUBBLED
BBDELSU SLUBBED
BBDEMSU BEDUMBS
BBDENSU SNUBBED
BBDEORS DOBBERS
BBDEOST STOBBED
BBDEOSW SWOBBED
BBDERRU DRUBBER
BBDERSU DUBBERS
BBDESSU SUBDEBS
BBDESTU STUBBED
BBDFLUU FLUBDUB
BBDGIIN DIBBING
BBDGINU DUBBING
BBDIKSU DIBBUKS
BBDILRY DRIBBLY
BBDINOS DOBBINS
BBDINSU DUBBINS
BBDIOOR BOOBIRD
BBDKSUY DYBBUKS
BBEEEES BEEBEES
BBEEERU BEBEERU
BBEEIKS KEBBIES
BBEEIRS BRIBEES
BBEEIRW WEBBIER
BBEELPS PEBBLES
BBEFILR FRIBBLE
BBEFIRS FIBBERS
BBEFLRU FLUBBER
BBEGILR GLIBBER
GRIBBLE
BBEGINW WEBBING
BBEGIOS GIBBOSE
BBEGIRS GIBBERS
BBEGIST GIBBETS
BBEGLOR GOBBLER
BBEGLOS GOBBLES
BBEGOST GOBBETS
BBEGRRU GRUBBER
BBEHIKS KIBBEHS
BBEHINS NEBBISH
BBEHIOS HOBBIES
BBEHISU HUBBIES
BBEHLOR HOBBLER
BBEHLOS HOBBLES
BBEHORS HOBBERS
BBEIIKL BIBLIKE
BBEIILS BILBIES
BBEIIMR IMBIBER
BBEIIMS IMBIBES
BBEIIRR RIBBIER
BBEIJRS JIBBERS
BBEIKLS KIBBLES
BBEILNR NIBBLER
BBEILNS NIBBLES
BBEILOS BILBOES
LOBBIES
BBEILOT BIBELOT
BBEILQU QUIBBLE
BBEILSS BIBLESS
BBEIMOS BIMBOES
BBEINOR NOBBIER
BBEINRU NUBBIER
BBEIOOS BOOBIES
BBEIRRS BRIBERS
RIBBERS
BBEIRRY BRIBERY
BBEIRSU RUBBIES
BBEIRTU TUBBIER
BBEISSU BUSBIES
BBEJORS JOBBERS
BBEJORY JOBBERY
BBEKLOS BLESBOK
BBELLOY BELLBOY
BBELLSU BULBELS
BBELLTU BULBLET
BBELMOT BOMBLET
BBELMRU BUMBLER
BBELMSU BUMBLES
BBELNOR NOBBLER
BBELNOS NOBBLES
BBELNSU NUBBLES
BBELORS LOBBERS
SLOBBER
BBELORW WOBBLER
BBELORY LOBBYER
BBELOSW WOBBLES
BBELRRU BURBLER
BBELRSU BURBLES
LUBBERS
RUBBLES
SLUBBER
BBELSTU STUBBLE
BBEMNSU BENUMBS
BBEMORS BOMBERS
MOBBERS
BBENRSU SNUBBER
BBEOOSY YOBBOES
BBEORRS ROBBERS
BBEORRY ROBBERY
BBEORSS SOBBERS
BBEORSW SWOBBER
BBEPRUW BREWPUB
BBERRSU RUBBERS
BBERRUY RUBBERY
BBERSTU TUBBERS
BBFGIIN FIBBING
BBFGINO FOBBING
BBFGINU FUBBING
BBGGIIN GIBBING
BBGGINO GOBBING
BBGHINO HOBBING
BBGIIJN JIBBING
BBGIINN NIBBING

BBGIINR BRIBING
RIBBING
BBGIJNO JOBBING
BBGILLU BILLBUG
BBGILNO LOBBING
BBGIMNO BOMBING
MOBBING
BBGINOO BOOBING
BBGINOR ROBBING
BBGINOS GIBBONS
SOBBING
BBGINRU RUBBING
BBGINSU SUBBING
BBGINTU TUBBING
BBGIOSU GIBBOUS
BBHIMOS MOBBISH
BBHIOOS BOOBISH
BBHIOST HOBBITS
BBHIRSU RUBBISH
BBHKOOS BOSHBOK
BBHNOOS HOBNOBS
BBHRSUY SHRUBBY
BBIIKTZ KIBBITZ
BBIILST BIBLIST
BBIJMOO JIBBOOM
BBIKOSS SKIBOBS
BBIKTUZ KIBBUTZ
BBILLSU BULBILS
BBILNOY NOBBILY
BBIMMOS MOBBISM
BBINNSU NUBBINS
BBINORS RIBBONS
ROBBINS
BBINORY RIBBONY
BBKLNOY KNOBBLY
BBLLSUU BULBULS
BBLOSUU BULBOUS
BBLOSWY BLOWBYS
BBLSTUY STUBBLY
BBMOOOX BOOMBOX
BBNNOOS BONBONS
BBNOOOS BONOBOS
BBNOORU BOURBON
BBOOOOS BOOBOOS
BBOOSUU BOUBOUS
BBORSTU BURBOTS
BBOSSUY BUSBOYS
BBRSSUU SUBURBS
BCCEEHS CHEBECS
BCCEILO ECBOLIC
BCCEILU CUBICLE
BCCEILY BICYCLE
BCCEIOS BOCCIES
BCCILOU BUCOLIC
BCCILUY CUBICLY
BCCINOO OBCONIC
BCCISUU SUCCUBI
BCCMOOX COXCOMB
BCCMSUU SUCCUMB
BCCNOOR CORNCOB
BCDEEHL BELCHED
BCDEEHN BENCHED
BCDEEIL DECIBEL
BCDEEKS BEDECKS
BCDEENU BEDUNCE
BCDEHIR BIRCHED
BCDEHIT BITCHED
BCDEHNU BUNCHED
BCDEHOT BOTCHED
BCDEHOU DEBOUCH
BCDEIIO BIOCIDE
BCDEIKR BRICKED
BCDEIKS SICKBED
BCDEIKT BEDTICK
BCDEILM CLIMBED
BCDEIOS BODICES
CEBOIDS
BCDEIRS SCRIBED
BCDEKLO BLOCKED
BCDEKLU BUCKLED
BCDEKOR BEDROCK
BCDELOU BECLOUD
BCDEMRU CRUMBED
BCDENOU BOUNCED
BUNCOED
BCDEORW BECROWD
BCDEOSU SUBCODE
BCDESUU SUBDUCE
BCDIIRU RUBIDIC
BCDINOW COWBIND
BCDIORW COWBIRD
BCDIOSU CUBOIDS
BCDKORU BURDOCK
BCDNOSU BONDUCS
BCDSTUU SUBDUCT
BCEEEHN BEECHEN

BCEEEHS BEECHES
BESEECH
BCEEFIN BENEFIC
BCEEFKL BEFLECK
BCEEGIR ICEBERG
BCEEHIP EPHEBIC
BCEEHIT HEBETIC
BCEEHLR BELCHER
BCEEHLS BELCHES
BCEEHNR BENCHER
BCEEHNS BENCHES
BCEEHOU BOUCHEE
BCEEIMR BECRIME
BCEEIRT TEREBIC
BCEEKNU BUCKEEN
BCEEKRS REBECKS
BCEEKST BECKETS
BCEEKSZ ZEBECKS
BCEEKUY BUCKEYE
BCEEMOS BECOMES
BCEENOS OBSCENE
BCEERSU BECURSE
BCEGIKN BECKING
BCEGLOS BECLOGS
BCEHINR BIRCHEN
BCEHINT BENTHIC
BITCHEN
BCEHIOR BRIOCHE
BCEHIOT BIOTECH
BCEHIRS BIRCHES
BCEHIST BITCHES
BCEHITW BEWITCH
BCEHLRU BLUCHER
BCEHNSU BUNCHES
BCEHORT BOTCHER
BCEHORW COWHERB
BCEHOST BOTCHES
BCEHOSU SUBECHO
BCEHRSU CHERUBS
BCEHRTU BUTCHER
BCEHSTU BUTCHES
BCEIKLM LIMBECK
BCEIKLR BRICKLE
BCEIKRS BICKERS
BCEILMO EMBOLIC
BCEILMR CLIMBER
BCEILNO BINOCLE
BCEILOR BRICOLE
CORBEIL
BCEILOU CIBOULE
BCEILSY BEYLICS
BCEIMNO COMBINE
BCEIMOR MICROBE
BCEINOR BICORNE
BCEINOS EBONICS
BCEINOZ BENZOIC
BCEINRU BRUCINE
BCEIORS CORBIES
BCEIRRS SCRIBER
BCEIRSS SCRIBES
BCEIRSU SUBERIC
BCEISST BISECTS
BCEJOST OBJECTS
BCEJSTU SUBJECT
BCEKLOR BLOCKER
BCEKLRU BUCKLER
BCEKLSU BUCKLES
BCEKMOS BEMOCKS
BCEKNOS BECKONS
BCEKORT BROCKET
BCEKORU ROEBUCK
BCEKOSU BUCKOES
BCEKRSU BUCKERS
BCEKSTU BUCKETS
BCELLOW COWBELL
BCELLSU SUBCELL
BCELMNU CLUBMEN
BCELMRU CLUMBER
CRUMBLE
BCELMSU SCUMBLE
BCELNOW BECLOWN
BCELORS CORBELS
BCELOSU BOUCLES
BCEMOOS COOMBES
BCEMORS COMBERS
RECOMBS
BCEMRRU CRUMBER
BCEMRSU CUMBERS
BCENORU BOUNCER
BCENOSU BOUNCES
BCEORSU BESCOUR
OBSCURE
BCERRSU CURBERS
BCERSTU BECRUST
BECURST
BCESSTU SUBSECT

BCFSSUU SUBFUSC
BCGIKNU BUCKING
BCGIMNO COMBING
BCGINRU CURBING
BCGORSY CYBORGS
BCHIIOP BIOCHIP
BCHIKOU CHIBOUK
BCHIKOY BOYCHIK
BCHIKSU BUCKISH
BCHILMY CHIMBLY
BCHIMOR RHOMBIC
BCHINOR BRONCHI
BCHIOPR PIBROCH
BCHIOPS PHOBICS
BCHLOTY BLOTCHY
BCHLSSU SCHLUBS
BCHNOOR BRONCHO
BCHORST BORSCHT
BCIIKLN NIBLICK
BCIILMU BULIMIC
BCIILSY SIBYLIC
BCIINOS BIONICS
BCIINOT BIONTIC
BCIIOPS BIOPICS
BIOPSIC
BCIIOPT BIOPTIC
BCIIOST BIOTICS
BCIISTU BISCUIT
BCIKKOX KICKBOX
BCIKOTT BITTOCK
BCILMPU PLUMBIC
UPCLIMB
BCILOOR BICOLOR
BROCOLI
BCILPSU PUBLICS
BCIMNOU UMBONIC
BCIMSSU CUBISMS
BCINOOR BORONIC
BCINOOS BOSONIC
BCINORS BICORNS
BICRONS
BCINRSU BRUCINS
BCINSUU INCUBUS
BCIOORT ROBOTIC
BCIORST STROBIC
BCIRRSU RUBRICS
BCIRTUY BUTYRIC
BCISSTU BUSTICS
CUBISTS
BCISTUU CUBITUS
BCJKMUU JUMBUCK
BCKLLOU BULLOCK
BCKLNOU UNBLOCK
BCKLOOX LOCKBOX
BCKNNOO BONNOCK
BCKNSUU NUBUCKS
BCKOTTU BUTTOCK
BCLMOOU COULOMB
BCLMRUY CRUMBLY
BCLOOSU COLOBUS
SUBCOOL
BCLSTUU SUBCULT
BCMMRUU CRUMBUM
BCMORSY CORYMBS
BCMOSTU COMBUST
BCNOORS BRONCOS
BCNOSTU COBNUTS
BCNRSUU UNCURBS
BCOOOOS BOOCOOS
BCOOPYY COPYBOY
BCOOSWY COWBOYS
BCOOTTY BOYCOTT
BCTUUZZ BUZZCUT
BDDDEIU BUDDIED
BDDEEES SEEDBED
BDDEEEW BEDEWED
BDDEEIL BIELDED
BDDEEIR DEBRIDE
BDDEEIS BEDSIDE
BDDEEIT BETIDED
DEBITED
BDDEELN BLENDED
BDDEENO DEBONED
BDDEERS BEDDERS
BDDEETU DEBUTED
BDDEGIN BEDDING
BDDEGIR BRIDGED
BDDEGLU BLUDGED
BDDEIIR BIRDIED
BDDEIIS BIDDIES
BDDEILN BLINDED
BDDEILR BRIDLED
BDDEILU BUILDED
BDDEINR BRINDED
BDDEIRR REDBIRD
BDDEIRS BIDDERS

BDDEISU BUDDIES
BDDELNU BUNDLED
BDDELOO BLOODED
BOODLED
BDDELOU DOUBLED
BDDELSU BUDDLES
BDDENOU BOUNDED
BDDEOOR BROODED
BDDEOTU DOUBTED
BDDERSU BUDDERS
REDBUDS
BDDESUU SUBDUED
BDDGIIN BIDDING
BDDGINU BUDDING
BDDGIOR BIRDDOG
BDDISSU DISBUDS
BDEEEIS BEEDIES
BDEEELP BLEEPED
BDEEELR BLEEDER
BDEEELT BEETLED
BDEEELV BEVELED
BDEEEMN BEDEMEN
BDEEENS BENDEES
BDEEERR BREEDER
REBREED
BDEEERZ BREEZED
BDEEFIR BRIEFED
DEBRIEF
FIBERED
BDEEFOX FEEDBOX
BDEEGOY BOGEYED
BDEEGSU BUGSEED
BDEEHOV BEHOVED
BDEEHRT BERTHED
BDEEIKL BEDLIKE
BDEEILL BELLIED
LIBELED
BDEEILS EDIBLES
BDEEILV BEDEVIL
BDEEIMR BEMIRED
BERIMED
BDEEIMT BEDTIME
BDEEIMX BEMIXED
BDEEINR BENDIER
INBREED
BDEEINZ BEDIZEN
BDEEIRR BERRIED
BDEEIRS DERBIES
BDEEISS BESIDES
BDEEIST BETIDES
BDEEJLS DJEBELS
BDEEKRU REBUKED
BDEELLS BEDELLS
BDEELMU UMBELED
BDEELNR BLENDER
REBLEND
BDEELNS BLENDES
BDEELOV BELOVED
BDEELOW BOWELED
ELBOWED
BDEELRT TREBLED
BDEELSS BEDLESS
BLESSED
BDEEMOW EMBOWED
BDEEMRU EMBRUED
UMBERED
BDEEMSU BEMUSED
BDEENOR DEBONER
ENROBED
REDBONE
BDEENOS DEBONES
BDEENPR PREBEND
BDEENRS BENDERS
BDEEORR REBORED
BDEEORS BEDSORE
SOBERED
BDEEORV OVERBED
BDEEORW BOWERED
BDEERSU BURSEED
BDEERUW BURWEED
BDEFFLU BLUFFED
BDEFLMU FUMBLED
BDEFOOR FORBODE
BDEGGLO BOGGLED
BDEGHIT BEDIGHT
BIGHTED
BDEGHOU BOUGHED
BDEGILO OBLIGED
BDEGINN BENDING
BDEGIOO BOOGIED
BDEGIOT BIGOTED
BDEGIRS BEGIRDS
BRIDGES
BDEGISU BUDGIES
BDEGLNU BLUNGED
BUNGLED

BDEGLRU BLUDGER
BURGLED
BDEGLSU BLUDGES
BDEGNOW BEDGOWN
BDEGOOY GOODBYE
BDEGRSU BEDRUGS
BUDGERS
REDBUGS
BDEGSTU BUDGETS
BDEHINS BEHINDS
BDEHIRT BIRTHED
BDEHLMU HUMBLED
BDEHLOS BEHOLDS
BDEHLSU BLUSHED
BDEHMTU THUMBED
BDEHOST HOTBEDS
BDEHRSU BRUSHED
BDEIIRS BIRDIES
BDEIKLN BLINKED
BDEIKLU BUDLIKE
BDEIKRS BRISKED
BDEILLU BULLIED
BDEILMW WIMBLED
BDEILNR BLINDER
BRINDLE
BDEILNS BINDLES
BDEILNY BYLINED
BDEILOR BROILED
BDEILOS BOLIDES
BDEILPP BLIPPED
BDEILRR BRIDLER
BDEILRS BRIDLES
BDEILRT DRIBLET
BDEILRU BUILDER
REBUILD
BDEILSS BLISSED
BDEILST BILSTED
BDEILTZ BLITZED
BDEIMMR BRIMMED
BDEIMNR BIRDMEN
BDEIMOR BROMIDE
BDEIMRU IMBRUED
BDEINOU BEDOUIN
BDEINPR PREBIND
BDEINRS BINDERS
INBREDS
REBINDS
BDEINRY BINDERY
BDEINSU BEDUINS
BDEIOOS BOODIES
BDEIORR BROIDER
BDEIORS BORIDES
DISROBE
BDEIORT DEORBIT
ORBITED
BDEIORV OVERBID
BDEIORZ ZEBROID
BDEIOSY DISOBEY
BDEIPRS PREBIDS
BDEIRRS BIRDERS
BDEIRST BESTRID
BISTRED
BDEIRSU BRUISED
BURDIES
BDEIRSV VERBIDS
BDEIRTU BRUITED
BDEIRTY BEDIRTY
BDEISST BEDSITS
BDEISSU SUBSIDE
BDEISTU SUBEDIT
BDEITUY DUBIETY
BDEJLMU JUMBLED
BDEKNOO BOOKEND
BDEKNOU BUNKOED
BDEKNSU DEBUNKS
BDEKOOR BROOKED
BDELLOR BEDROLL
BDELMMU MUMBLED
BDELMOO BLOOMED
BDELMPU PLUMBED
BDELMRU DRUMBLE
RUMBLED
BDELMTU TUMBLED
BDELNOR BLONDER
BDELNOS BLONDES
BDELNOU UNLOBED
BDELNRU BLUNDER
BUNDLER
BDELNSU BUNDLES
BDELNTU BLUNTED
BDELOOP BLOOPED
BDELOOR BOODLER
BDELOOS BOODLES
BDELORS BORDELS
BDELORU BOULDER
DOUBLER

BDELORW BOWLDER
LOWBRED
BDELOST BOLDEST
BDELOSU BLOUSED
DOUBLES
BDELOSW BLOWSED
BDELOTT BLOTTED
BOTTLED
BDELOTU DOUBLET
BDELOWZ BLOWZED
BDELRRU BLURRED
BDELRTU BLURTED
BDELSSU BUDLESS
BDELSTU BUSTLED
BDEMNNO BONDMEN
BDEMOOR BEDROOM
BOREDOM
BROOMED
BDEMOOS BOSOMED
BDEMSTU DUMBEST
BDENNOU BOUNDEN
UNBONED
BDENNSU UNBENDS
BDENORS BONDERS
BDENORU BOUNDER
REBOUND
UNROBED
BDENORW BROWNED
BDENORZ BRONZED
BDENOSY BEYONDS
BDENOUW UNBOWED
BDENOUX UNBOXED
BDENRSU BURDENS
BDENSTU SUBTEND
BDEOORR BROODER
BDEOOST BOOSTED
BDEOPST BEDPOST
BDEORRS BORDERS
BDEORRU BORDURE
BDEORSS DESORBS
BDEORST DEBTORS
BDEORSU ROSEBUD
BDEORSW BROWSED
BDEORTU DOUBTER
OBTRUDE
OUTBRED
REDOUBT
BDEORUV OVERDUB
BDERSTU BURSTED
BDERSUU SUBDUER
BDERSUY RUDESBY
BDESSTU BESTUDS
BDESSUU SUBDUES
BDFIILY BIFIDLY
BDFIIOR FIBROID
BDFIORS FORBIDS
BDGGINU BUDGING
BDGGLOU GOLDBUG
BDGIINN BINDING
BDGIINR BIRDING
BDGIIOO GOBIOID
BDGILOO GLOBOID
BDGIMNU DUMBING
BDGINNO BONDING
BDGINOS BODINGS
BDGINOY BODYING
BDGLLOU BULLDOG
BDGMSUU MUDBUGS
BDGOOOW BOGWOOD
BDGOOSY GOODBYS
BDGORSU DORBUGS
BDHIOSU BUSHIDO
BDHIRSY HYBRIDS
BDHOOOY BOYHOOD
BDIILOR OILBIRD
BDIILOS LIBIDOS
BDIIMNS MISBIND
BDIIMRS MIDRIBS
BDIISTT TIDBITS
BDIKNOS BODKINS
BDILLNY BLINDLY
BDILNUU UNBUILD
BDILOOS DIOBOLS
BDILPUU BUILDUP
UPBUILD
BDILRUY BUIRDLY
BDIMNUU DUBNIUM
BDIMORS BROMIDS
BDINNOU INBOUND
BDINNSU UNBINDS
BDINOOR BRIDOON
BDINOOW WOODBIN
BDINOSU BOUDINS
BDINOUY UNIBODY
BDINPSU UPBINDS
BDINRSU SUNBIRD

BDINSTU BUNDIST
DUSTBIN
BDIOOOV OBOVOID
BDIOORU BOUDOIR
BDIOSTU OUTBIDS
BDIOSUU DUBIOUS
BDIRSTU DISTURB
BDISSUY SUBSIDY
BDKLOOS KOBOLDS
BDLNOOS DOBLONS
BDLOOOX OXBLOOD
BDMOOSS BOSSDOM
BDMORUW BUDWORM
BDNNOOY NONBODY
BDNNOUU UNBOUND
BDNOORU BOURDON
BDNOOSS DOBSONS
BDNOOWW DOWNBOW
BDNOPUU UPBOUND
BDNORUW RUBDOWN
BDNOSTU OBTUNDS
BDOOOWX BOXWOOD
WOODBOX
BDORSWY BYWORDS
BEEEEFR FREEBEE
BEEEENP PEEBEEN
BEEEFIR BEEFIER
FREEBIE
BEEEFLR FEEBLER
BEEEFTW WEBFEET
BEEEGIS BESIEGE
BEEEGRR BERGERE
BEEEHIV BEEHIVE
BEEEHNS SHEBEEN
BEEEHPS EPHEBES
BEEEIKL BEELIKE
BEEEILL LIBELEE
BEEEILN BEELINE
BEEEILV BELIEVE
BEEEIRR BEERIER
BEEEJLW BEJEWEL
BEEEJLZ JEZEBEL
BEEEKLL BELLEEK
BEEELPR BLEEPER
BEEELRT BEETLER
BEEELRV BEVELER
BEEELST BEETLES
BEEEMRS BERSEEM
BEEEMSS BESEEMS
BEEENNZ BENZENE
BEEENTW BETWEEN
BEEEPRS BEEPERS
BEEEPSW BEWEEPS
BEEERSZ BEEZERS
BREEZES
BEEFGIN BEEFING
BEEFGIT BIGFEET
BEEFILR FEBRILE
BEEFILS BELIEFS
BEEFILY BEEFILY
BEEFINT BENEFIT
BEEFIRR BRIEFER
BEEFIRS FRISBEE
BEEFORY FOREBYE
BEEFRST BEFRETS
BEEGILL LEGIBLE
BEEGILO OBLIGEE
BEEGILU BEGUILE
BEEGIMR BEGRIME
BEEGINP BEEPING
BEEGINR REBEGIN
BEEGINS BEIGNES
BEEGINT BEIGNET
BEEGINU BEGUINE
BEEGISY BIGEYES
BEEGMNO GOMBEEN
BEEGNOO GOBONEE
BEEGNRU REBEGUN
BEEGNSU BUNGEES
BEEGRSU BURGEES
BEEGSUY BUGEYES
BEEHIOP EPHEBOI
BEEHIRR HERBIER
BEEHLRT BLETHER
BEEHLST BETHELS
BEEHMRY BERHYME
BEEHOOV BEHOOVE
BEEHOPS EPHEBOS
PHOEBES
BEEHOSV BEHOVES
BEEHPSU EPHEBUS
BEEHRST SHERBET
BEEHRSW BESHREW
BEEHRTY THEREBY
BEEHRWY WHEREBY
BEEHSST BEHESTS

BEEHSTY BHEESTY
BEEIJLU JUBILEE
BEEIKLW WEBLIKE
BEEILLR LIBELER
BEEILLS BELLIES
BEEILLV BILEVEL
BEEILMS BESLIME
BESMILE
BEEILNR BERLINE
BEEILOS OBELISE
BEEILOZ OBELIZE
BEEILRS BELIERS
BEEILRV VERBILE
BEEIMRS BEMIRES
BERIMES
BIREMES
BEEIMST BETIMES
BEEIMSX BEMIXES
BEEINNS BENNIES
BEEINNZ BENZINE
BEEINOS EBONIES
EBONISE
BEEINOT EBONITE
BEEINOZ EBONIZE
BEEINRZ ZEBRINE
BEEINSW NEWBIES
BEEIQUZ BEZIQUE
BEEIRRS BERRIES
BEEIRRV BREVIER
BEEISST BETISES
BEEISTW WEBSITE
BEEJSSU BEJESUS
BEEKMOS BESMOKE
BEEKNOT BETOKEN
BEEKOPS BESPOKE
BEEKRRS BERSERK
BEEKRRU REBUKER
BEEKRSU REBUKES
BEELLMN BELLMEN
BEELMMS EMBLEMS
BEELMOW EMBOWEL
BEELMRT TREMBLE
BEELNNO ENNOBLE
BEELNOZ BENZOLE
BEELNRT REBLENT
BEELOST BOLETES
BEELOSY OBESELY
BEELOTY EYEBOLT
BEELRSS BLESSER
BEELRST BELTERS
TREBLES
BEELSSS BLESSES
BEELSSW WEBLESS
BEEMMRS MEMBERS
BEEMNPT BENEMPT
BEEMORW EMBOWER
BEEMRSU EMBRUES
BEEMRTU EMBRUTE
BEEMSSU BEMUSES
BEENNST BENNETS
BEENOOT BOTONEE
BEENORR ENROBER
BEENORS BOREENS
ENROBES
BEENORY BONEYER
BEENOST BONESET
BEENSTU BUTENES
SUBTEEN
BEENSUV SUBVENE
BEEOOST BOOTEES
BEEOPPS BOPEEPS
BEEOPRR REPROBE
BEEORRS REBORES
SOBERER
BEEORRU BOURREE
BEEORSV OBSERVE
OBVERSE
VERBOSE
BEEORSY OBEYERS
BEEORTV OVERBET
BEEORWY EYEBROW
BEEPRRV PREVERB
BEEQSTU BEQUEST
BEERRSV REVERBS
BEERRSW BREWERS
BEERRWY BREWERY
BEERSSU REBUSES
SUBSERE
BEERSTT BETTERS
BEERSTV BREVETS
BEERSTW BESTREW
WEBSTER
BEERTTU BURETTE
BEFFIIS BIFFIES
BEFFIRU BUFFIER
BEFFLRU BLUFFER
BEFFOSU BOUFFES
BEFFRSU BUFFERS
REBUFFS
BEFFSTU BUFFEST
BUFFETS
BEFGIIL FILIBEG
BEFGIRU FIREBUG
BEFGLSU BEGULFS
BEFILMS FIMBLES
BEFILNO LOBEFIN
BEFILNU BLUEFIN
BEFILOS FOIBLES
BEFILOU BIOFUEL
BEFILRT FILBERT
BEFILRY BRIEFLY
BEFILSU FUSIBLE
SUBFILE
BEFINOR BONFIRE
BEFIORX FIREBOX
BEFIRST FIBSTER
BEFIRSU FUBSIER
BEFIRVY VERBIFY
BEFITUX TUBIFEX
BEFLLTY FLYBELT
BEFLLWY FLYBLEW
BEFLMRU FUMBLER
BEFLMSU FUMBLES
BEFLOOS BEFOOLS
BEFLOSU BEFOULS
BEFOORR FORBORE
BEFOOTW WEBFOOT
BEGGGIN BEGGING
BEGGIIS BIGGIES
BEGGIOR BOGGIER
BEGGIRU BUGGIER
BEGGIST BIGGEST
BEGGISU BUGGIES
BEGGITY BIGGETY
BEGGLOR BLOGGER
BOGGLER
BEGGLOS BOGGLES
BEGGRSU BUGGERS
BEGGRUY BUGGERY
BEGHRRU BURGHER
BEGIILR BILGIER
BEGIIMT BIGTIME
BEGIINN INBEING
BEGIKNR KERBING
BEGILLN BELLING
BEGILLY LEGIBLY
BEGILNO IGNOBLE
BEGILNT BELTING
BEGILNU BLUEING
BEGILNY BELYING
BEGILOR OBLIGER
BEGILOS OBLIGES
BEGILRS GERBILS
BEGILRT GILBERT
BEGILRU BULGIER
BEGILST GIBLETS
BEGIMNR BERMING
BEGIMRS BEGRIMS
BEGINNU UNBEING
BEGINOS BINGOES
BIOGENS
BEGINOY BIOGENY
OBEYING
BEGINRR BRINGER
BEGINRS BINGERS
BEGINRW BREWING
BEGINSS BIGNESS
BEGINST BESTING
BEGINTT BETTING
BEGIOOS BOOGIES
BEGIORV OVERBIG
BEGIOSS BIGOSES
BEGIOSU BOUGIES
BEGIRSU RUGBIES
BEGKMOS GEMSBOK
BEGLLOU GLOBULE
BEGLMOO BEGLOOM
BEGLMRU GRUMBLE
BEGLMUU BLUEGUM
BEGLNOS BELONGS
BEGLNRU BLUNGER
BUNGLER
BEGLNSU BLUNGES
BUNGLES
BEGLOOS GLOBOSE
BEGLOOT BOOTLEG
BEGLOST GOBLETS
BEGLOSW BOWLEGS
WEBLOGS
BEGLOUV LOVEBUG
BEGLRSU BUGLERS
BULGERS
BURGLES
BEGMNOY BOGYMEN
BEGNOOS BONGOES
BEGNORU BURGEON
BEGNOSY BYGONES
BEGOORS BOOGERS
GOOBERS
BEGOOSY BOOGEYS
BEGORSU BROGUES
BEGOSTU OUTBEGS
BEGRRSU BURGERS
BEGRSSU BURGESS
BEHIIST BHISTIE
BEHIITX EXHIBIT
BEHIKLO HOBLIKE
BEHIKNT BETHINK
BEHILMS BLEMISH
BEHILMT THIMBLE
BEHILOS BOLSHIE
BEHILRT BLITHER
BEHILSU BLUEISH
BEHIMOR BIOHERM
BEHIMOY YOHIMBE
BEHINOP HIPBONE
BEHINST HENBITS
BEHIOST BOTHIES
BEHIOTW HOWBEIT
BEHIRRT REBIRTH
BEHIRSU BUSHIER
BEHISTZ ZIBETHS
BEHKORS RHEBOKS
BEHLLOP BELLHOP
BEHLLOX HELLBOX
BEHLMRU HUMBLER
BEHLMSU HUMBLES
BEHLORT BROTHEL
BEHLOSW BEHOWLS
BEHLRSU BLUSHER
BEHLSSU BLUSHES
BUSHELS
BEHMNSU BUSHMEN
BEHMOOY HOMEBOY
BEHMORS HOMBRES
BEHMPTU BETHUMP
BEHNNOT BENTHON
BEHNORT BETHORN
BEHNOST BENTHOS
BEHNRTU BURTHEN
BEHOORT THEORBO
BEHOOSX SHOEBOX
BEHOPRT POTHERB
BEHOPSU PHOEBUS
BEHORRT BROTHER
BEHORST BOTHERS
BEHORTT BETROTH
BEHOSTU BESHOUT
BEHRRSU BRUSHER
BEHRSSU BRUSHES
BUSHERS
BEHRTTU TURBETH
BEIIKLN NIBLIKE
BEIIKLR RIBLIKE
BEIIKRS BIRKIES
BEIILLS BILLIES
BEIILMR LIMBIER
BEIILMX MIXIBLE
BEIILRS RISIBLE
BEIILSV VISIBLE
BEIINOT NIOBITE
BEIINRR BRINIER
BEIINRS BRINIES
BEIINST STIBINE
BEIIOTT BIOTITE
BEIIRRS RIBIERS
BEIIRST BITSIER
BEIIRTT BITTIER
BEIJLSU JUBILES
BEIKLNR BLINKER
BEIKLOS OBELISK
BEIKLOW BOWLIKE
BEIKLOX BOXLIKE
BEIKLRS BILKERS
BEIKLRU BULKIER
BEIKLSY BEYLIKS
BEIKLTU TUBLIKE
BEIKOOR BROOKIE
BEIKOOS BOOKIES
BEIKORS BOSKIER
BEIKORT REITBOK
BEIKRRS BRISKER
BEIKRST BRISKET
BEIKRSW BREWSKI
BEIKRTU BURKITE
BEILLPR PREBILL
BEILLRS BILLERS
REBILLS
BEILLRU BULLIER
BEILLST BILLETS
BEILLSU BULLIES
BEILMNR NIMBLER
BEILMNS MILNEBS
BEILMOR EMBROIL
BEILMOS MOBILES
OBELISM
BEILMRS LIMBERS
BEILMRT TIMBREL
BEILMSU SUBLIME
BEILMSW WIMBLES
BEILNOW BOWLINE
BEILNRS BERLINS
BEILNRY BYLINER
BEILNSU SUBLINE
BEILNSY BYLINES
BEILNTZ BLINTZE
BEILOOS LOOBIES
BEILOPR PREBOIL
BEILOPY EPIBOLY
BEILOQU OBLIQUE
BEILORR BROILER
BEILORS BOILERS
REBOILS
BEILORW BLOWIER
BEILRRS BIRLERS
BEILRRU BURLIER
BEILRSS RIBLESS
BEILRST BLISTER
BRISTLE
RIBLETS
BEILRTT BRITTLE
BEILRTU REBUILT
BEILRTY LIBERTY
BEILRTZ BLITZER
BEILRUY BRULYIE
BEILRUZ BRULZIE
BEILSSS BLISSES
BEILSTU SUBTILE
BEILSTZ BLITZES
BEIMMRR BRIMMER
BEIMNOR BROMINE
BEIMNTU BITUMEN
BEIMOOR BOOMIER
BEIMORW IMBOWER
WOMBIER
BEIMORZ BROMIZE
BEIMOSZ ZOMBIES
BEIMOTV BEVOMIT
BEIMPRU BUMPIER
BEIMRST TIMBERS
TIMBRES
BEIMRSU ERBIUMS
IMBRUES
BEIMRTU IMBRUTE
TERBIUM
BEIMRTY TIMBERY
BEIMSST BEMISTS
BEIMSTU SUBITEM
BEINNOP PINBONE
BEINNOR BONNIER
BEINNOS BENISON
BEINNOZ BENZOIN
BEINNSU BUNNIES
BEINNSZ BENZINS
BEINOOS BOONIES
BEINOOT EOBIONT
BEINORT BORNITE
BEINORW BROWNIE
BEINOST BONIEST
BEINOSV BOVINES
BEINOSZ BIZONES
BEINRRS BRINERS
BEINRSU BURNIES
SUBERIN
BEINRSY BYRNIES
BEINRTT BITTERN
BEINRTU TRIBUNE
TURBINE
BEIOOPT BIOTOPE
BEIOORZ BOOZIER
BEIOOST BOOTIES
BEIOPTY BIOTYPE
BEIORRT ORBITER
BEIORSS BOSSIER
RIBOSES
BEIORST ORBIEST
BEIORSU OUREBIS
BEIORUV BOUVIER
BEIOSSS BOSSIES
BEIOSSU SOUBISE
BEIOSTX BOXIEST
BEIOSTY OBESITY
BEIPPSU BUPPIES
BEIQRTU BRIQUET
BEIQSSU BISQUES
BEIRRRU BURRIER
BEIRRSU BRUISER
BURIERS
BEIRRTU BRUITER
BEIRSSS BRISSES
BEIRSST BESTIRS
BISTERS
BISTRES
BEIRSSU BRUISES
BEIRSTT BITTERS
BEIRSTU BUSTIER
RUBIEST
BEIRTTU TRIBUTE
BEIRTVY BREVITY
BEISSTU BUSIEST
SUBSITE
BEISTTU BUTTIES
BEITTWX BETWIXT
BEJJSUU JUJUBES
BEJKOUX JUKEBOX
BEJLMRU JUMBLER
BEJLMSU JUMBLES
BEJLOSS JOBLESS
BEKLOOT BOOKLET
BEKLRSU BURLESK
BEKMNOO BOOKMEN
BEKMOSS EMBOSKS
BEKNORS BONKERS
BEKNORU UNBROKE
BEKNOST BEKNOTS
BEKNRSU BUNKERS
BEKOOPR PREBOOK
BEKOORS BOOKERS
REBOOKS
BEKORRS BROKERS
BEKORWW WEBWORK
BEKOSST BOSKETS
BEKRRSU BRUSKER
BURKERS
BEKRSSU BUSKERS
BELLLMU BLELLUM
BELLNPU BULLPEN
BELLOSU BOULLES
LOBULES
SOLUBLE
BELLOSW BELLOWS
BELLOUV VOLUBLE
BELLSTU BULLETS
BELMMRU MUMBLER
BELMMSU MUMBLES
BELMNOS NOMBLES
BELMNOU NELUMBO
BELMNOY BENOMYL
BELMNSU NUMBLES
BELMOOR BLOOMER
REBLOOM
BELMOOT BOOMLET
BELMOPR PROBLEM
BELMORT TEMBLOR
BELMOSU EMBOLUS
BELMPRU PLUMBER
REPLUMB
BELMRRU RUMBLER
BELMRSU LUMBERS
RUMBLES
SLUMBER
BELMRTU TUMBLER
TUMBREL
BELMRTY TREMBLY
BELMSTU STUMBLE
TUMBLES
BELNOOR BORNEOL
BELNOOY BOLONEY
BELNOST NOBLEST
BELNOSZ BENZOLS
BELNOYZ BENZOYL
BELNRTU BLUNTER
BELNSTU SUNBELT
UNBELTS
UNBLEST
BELNSYZ BENZYLS
BELOOPR BLOOPER
BELOORS BOLEROS
BELOPSU PUEBLOS
BELORSS ORBLESS
BELORST BOLSTER
BOLTERS
LOBSTER
BELORSU ROUBLES
BELORSW BLOWERS
BOWLERS
BELORSY SOBERLY
BELORTT BLOTTER
BOTTLER
BELORTU TROUBLE
BELOSSU BLOUSES
BOLUSES
BELOSSW BOWLESS
BELOSTT BOTTLES
BELOSTU BOLETUS
BELRRSU BURLERS
BELRRTU BLURTER
BELRSTU BLUSTER
BUSTLER
BUTLERS
SUBTLER
BELRSUU SUBRULE
BELRSUY BURLEYS
BELRTUY BRUTELY
BUTLERY
BELSSTU BUSTLES
SUBLETS
BELSTUU TUBULES
BEMMOOS EMBOSOM
BEMMRSU BUMMERS
BEMMSTU BUMMEST
BEMNORW EMBROWN
BEMNORY EMBRYON
BEMNOST ENTOMBS
BEMNOSU UMBONES
BEMNOSW ENWOMBS
BEMNRSU NUMBERS
BEMNSTU NUMBEST
BEMNSUU SUBMENU
BEMOOPR PREBOOM
BEMOORS BOOMERS
BEMORST MOBSTER
BEMORSW BEWORMS
BEMORSY EMBRYOS
BEMORUX BUXOMER
BEMORWW WEBWORM
BEMPRSU BUMPERS
BEMSSTU BESMUTS
BEMSSUU SUBSUME
BEMSTUW STEWBUM
BENNORW NEWBORN
BENNOST BONNETS
BENOOST OBENTOS
BENOPRU UPBORNE
BENORRW BROWNER
BENORRZ BRONZER
BENORST SORBENT
BENORSU BOURNES
UNROBES
UNSOBER
BENORSZ BRONZES
BENOSSU BONUSES
BENOSSW BESNOWS
BENOSTU SUBTONE
BENOSUX UNBOXES
BENOSUZ SUBZONE
BENOSWY NEWSBOY
BENRRSU BURNERS
BENRSTU BRUNETS
BUNTERS
BURNETS
SUBRENT
BENSSTU SUBNETS
BEOORSS SORBOSE
BEOORST BOOSTER
REBOOTS
BEOORSZ BOOZERS
REBOZOS
BEOORTY BOOTERY
BEOPPRS BOPPERS
BEOPRRS PROBERS
BEOPRRV PROVERB
BEOQSSU BOSQUES
BEOQSTU BOSQUET
BEOQSUY OBSEQUY
BEOQTUU BOUQUET
BEORRSS RESORBS
BEORRSW BROWSER
BEORRWY BEWORRY
BEORSST SORBETS
STROBES
BEORSSU BOURSES
BEORSSW BROWSES
BEORSTT BETTORS
BEORSTU OBTUSER
BEORSTV OBVERTS
BEORSTW BESTROW
BEORSTZ BORTZES
BEORSUZ SUBZERO
BEORSWY BOWYERS
BEORUVY OVERBUY
BEOSSTT OBTESTS
BEOSSTW BESTOWS
BEPRRTU PERTURB
BEPRSUY PREBUYS
BEPRTUY PUBERTY
BEPSTUY SUBTYPE
BEQRSUU BRUSQUE
BEQSTUY QUBYTES
BERRRSU BURRERS
BERRSTU BURSTER
BERSSTU BUSTERS
BERSTTU BUTTERS
BERSTUV SUBVERT
BERSUZZ BUZZERS
BERTTUY BUTTERY
BESSSTU SUBSETS
BESSTTU SUBTEST
BESTTUX SUBTEXT
BFFGIIN BIFFING
BFFGINU BUFFING
BFFIINS BIFFINS
BFFILOO BOILOFF
BFFINOS BOFFINS
BFFLLUY BLUFFLY
BFFLOOW BLOWOFF
BFFNOOU BUFFOON
BFFORSU RUBOFFS
BFFOSUY BUYOFFS
BFGIOOT BIGFOOT
BFGOOSW FOGBOWS
BFHIOSX BOXFISH
BFHIRSU FURBISH
BFIILMO BIOFILM
BFIILRS FIBRILS
BFIINOR FIBROIN
BFIINRS FIBRINS
BFILMRU BRIMFUL
BFILSUY FUSIBLY
BFIMOYZ ZOMBIFY
BFINOSW BOWFINS
BFIORSU FIBROUS
BFIRTUY BRUTIFY
BFKLOOU BOOKFUL
BFLLOUW BOWLFUL
BFLLOWY BLOWFLY
FLYBLOW
BFLOSUX BOXFULS
BFLOSYY FLYBOYS
BFLSTUU TUBFULS
BFOOOTY FOOTBOY
BGGGIIN BIGGING
BGGGINO BOGGING
BGGGINU BUGGING
BGGHIIS BIGGISH
BGGHIOS BOGGISH
BGGIILN BILGING
BGGIINN BINGING
BGGIINS BIGGINS
BGGIISW BIGWIGS
BGGIITY BIGGITY
BGGILNO GLOBING
BGGILNU BUGLING
BULGING
BGGINNO BONGING
BGGINNU BUNGING
BGHHIOY HIGHBOY
BGHIILS GHIBLIS
BGHILST BLIGHTS
BGHILTY BLIGHTY
BGHINOO HOBOING
BGHINOR BIGHORN
BGHINSU BUSHING
BGHIPSU BUSHPIG
BGHIRST BRIGHTS
BGHLRUU BULGHUR
BGHMORU HOMBURG
BGHMSUU HUMBUGS
BGHOORU BOROUGH
BGHORTU BROUGHT
BGIIKLN BILKING
BGIILLN BILLING
BGIILMN LIMBING
BGIILNO BOILING
BGIILNR BIRLING
BGIILNS SIBLING
BGIIMNU IMBUING
BGIINNN BINNING
BGIINNR BRINING
BGIINRR BIRRING
BGIINTT BITTING
BGIKLNU BULKING
BGIKNNO BONKING
BGIKNNU BUNKING
BGIKNOO BOOKING
BGIKNOR BORKING
BROKING
BGIKNRU BURKING
BGIKNSU BUSKING

BGILLNO BOLLING
BGILLNU BULLING
BGILMNU BLUMING
BGILMOU GUMBOIL
BGILNOS GLOBINS
GOBLINS
BGILNOT BILTONG
BOLTING
BGILNOW BLOWING
BOWLING
BGILNOY IGNOBLY
BGILNRU BURLING
BGILNRY BYRLING
BGILNSU BLUINGS
BGILNTU BUTLING
BGILOOR OBLIGOR
BGILOOY BIOLOGY
BGILRSU BUSGIRL
BGIMMNU BUMMING
BGIMNNU NUMBING
BGIMNOO BOOMING
BGIMNOT TOMBING
BGIMNPU BUMPING
BGIMOSY BOGYISM
BGINNRU BURNING
BGINNTU BUNTING
BGINOOT BOOTING
BGINOOZ BOOZING
BGINOPP BOPPING
BGINOPR PROBING
BGINORS BORINGS
SORBING
BGINOSS BOSSING
GIBSONS
BGINOSU BOUSING
BGINOSW BOWINGS
BOWSING
BGINOSX BOXINGS
BGINOUY BUOYING
BGINOWW WINGBOW
BGINPRU BURPING
BGINRRU BURRING
BGINRSU SUBRING
BGINRTU BRUTING
BGINRUX BRUXING
BGINRUY BURYING
RUBYING
BGINSSU BUSINGS
BUSSING
BGINSTU BUSTING
TUBINGS
BGINSUY BUSYING
BGINSWY SWINGBY
BGINTTU BUTTING
BGINUZZ BUZZING
BGIORSU RUBIGOS
BGIORTY BIGOTRY
BGIUWZZ BUZZWIG
BGKLOOO LOGBOOK
BGLMRUY GRUMBLY
BGLNOOS OBLONGS
BGLNOOW LONGBOW
BGLNOUW BLOWGUN
BGLOOSU GLOBOUS
BGLOSSU BUGLOSS
BGLOSUY BOGUSLY
BGLRSUU BULGURS
BGMOOTU GUMBOOT
BGMSSUU SUBGUMS
BGOORSU BURGOOS
BGORTUU BURGOUT
BGOSTUU BUGOUTS
BHIIINN INHIBIN
BHIIINT INHIBIT
BHIINRS BRINISH
BHIKOOS BOOKISH
BHILLSU BULLISH
BHILOTU HOLIBUT
BHILPSU PUBLISH
BHILSUY BUSHILY
BHIMOOS HOBOISM
BHIMOPR BIMORPH
BHIMORT THROMBI
BHIMORU BOHRIUM
BHIMSTU BISMUTH
BHINRSU BURNISH
BHIOORS BOORISH
BHIOPSS BISHOPS
BHIOSWZ SHOWBIZ
BHIRSTU BRUTISH
BHIRTTU TURBITH
BHISTTU BUSHTIT
BHKNOSU BOHUNKS
BHLRSUU BULRUSH
BHMORSU RHOMBUS
BHOOOOS BOOHOOS
BHOOPSY SHOPBOY
BHOOSTW BOWSHOT
BHORSST BORSHTS
BHPRSUU BRUSHUP
BIIIKNS BIKINIS
BIIKLOT KILOBIT
BIILLMS MISBILL
BIILLNO BILLION
BIILLTW TWIBILL
BIILNTU INBUILT
BIILNVY BIVINYL
BIILOSU BILIOUS
BIILRSY RISIBLY
BIILSTW TWIBILS
BIILSVY VISIBLY
BIIMNOU NIOBIUM
BIIMNSU MINIBUS
BIIMOSS OBIISMS
BIIMSTU STIBIUM
BIINORV VIBRION
BIINOST BIOTINS
BIIORSV VIBRIOS
BIISSTV VIBISTS
BIISTTT TITBITS
BIJNOSU SUBJOIN
BIKLLUY BULKILY
BIKLNOT INKBLOT
BIKLNOY LINKBOY
BIKLRSY BRISKLY
BIKMNOO BOOMKIN
BIKMNPU BUMPKIN
BIKMNSU BUMKINS
BIKNSSU BUSKINS
BIKSUUZ BUZUKIS
BILLNOS BILLONS
BILLNOU BULLION
BILLOPX PILLBOX
BILLORS BRILLOS
BILLOSW BILLOWS
BILLOWY BILLOWY
BILLRUY BURLILY
BILMNOR NOMBRIL
BILMPUY BUMPILY
BILMRTU TUMBRIL
BILNNOY BONNILY
BILNOTU BOTULIN
BILNTUU TUBULIN
UNBUILT
BILOOPT POTBOIL
BILOOYZ BOOZILY
BILOPSU UPBOILS
BILORST BRISTOL
STROBIL
BILOSSU SUBSOIL
BILOSSY BOSSILY
BILPTUU UPBUILT
BILRSTY BRISTLY
BILRTTY BRITTLY
BILRTUY TILBURY
BIMMOOS IMBOSOM
BIMMORS BROMISM
BIMNOOY BIONOMY
BIMNORS BROMINS
BIMNORW IMBROWN
BIMNOST INTOMBS
BIMNOSU OMNIBUS
BIMNOSY SYMBION
BIMOSSS BOSSISM
BIMOSTW MISTBOW
BIMOSTY SYMBIOT
BIMRSTU BRUTISM
BIMRSUX BRUXISM
BIMSSSU SUBMISS
BIMSSTU SUBMITS
BINNOSU BUNIONS
BINOORT BIOTRON
BINOOST BONITOS
BINOOSU NIOBOUS
BINORSU BOURSIN
BINRSTU INBURST
BINRTUY BUTYRIN
BINSTUU SUBUNIT
BIOORSZ BORZOIS
BIOOSST OBOISTS
BIOOSUV OBVIOUS
BIOPRST PROBITS
BIOPRTY PROBITY
BIORRTU BURRITO
BIORRTW RIBWORT
BIORSST BISTROS
BIORSTT BISTORT
BIORSUU RUBIOUS
BIRSTTU TURBITS
BISSSTU SUBSIST
BISSTTU TUBISTS
BJMOOSU BOOJUMS
BKLNUUY UNBULKY
BKLOTUU OUTBULK
BKMNSUU BUNKUMS
BKNNOOO NONBOOK
BKNOOTW BOWKNOT
BKOOOOS BOOKOOS
BKOORWX WORKBOX
BKORSWY BYWORKS
BKRSTUU KRUBUTS
BLLNTUY BLUNTLY
BLLOSUU BULLOUS
BLLOSUY SOLUBLY
BLLOUVY VOLUBLY
BLMMPUU PLUMBUM
BLMOOOT TOMBOLO
BLMOORW LOBWORM
BLMOOSS BLOSSOM
BLMOSSY SYMBOLS
BLMOUXY BUXOMLY
BLNOORW LOWBORN
BLNOOSS BOLSONS
BLNOOSU BLOUSON
BLNOSTU UNBOLTS
BLOOOTX TOOLBOX
BLOOPWY PLOWBOY
BLOOQUY OBLOQUY
BLOORWW LOWBROW
BLOOSWY LOWBOYS
BLOOTUW BLOWOUT
BLOPSTU SUBPLOT
BLOPSUW BLOWUPS
BLORSTU BRULOTS
BLOSSTU SUBLOTS
BLRTUYY BUTYRYL
BMNOOOW MOONBOW
BMNOOSU UNBOSOM
BMOOSTT BOTTOMS
BMOOSTY TOMBOYS
BMORSUU BRUMOUS
BNNRSUU SUNBURN
BNNRTUU UNBURNT
BNOOSST BOSTONS
BNOOSTU BOUTONS
BNORSSU SUBORNS
BNORSTU BURTONS
BNORSUU BURNOUS
BNORTUU BURNOUT
OUTBURN
BNOSSUW SUNBOWS
BNOSTTU BUTTONS
BNOTTUY BUTTONY
BOOPSTW BOWPOTS
BOOPSTX POSTBOX
BOOPSTY POSTBOY
POTBOYS
BOORRSW BORROWS
BOORRTY ROBOTRY
BOOSWWW BOWWOWS
BORRSUW BURROWS
BORSTTU TURBOTS
BORSTUU RUBOUTS
BOSTUUY BUYOUTS
OUTBUYS
CCCDIOO COCCOID
CCCDIOS COCCIDS
CCCNOOT CONCOCT
CCCOOSU COCCOUS
CCDEEHK CHECKED
CCDEEIO ECOCIDE
CCDEENO CONCEDE
CCDEENY DECENCY
CCDEEOR COERCED
CCDEEPS SPECCED
CCDEESU SUCCEED
CCDEFLO FLOCCED
CCDEHIL CLICHED
CCDEHIN CINCHED
CCDEHKO CHOCKED
CCDEHKU CHUCKED
CCDEHOU COUCHED
CCDEIIL ICICLED
CCDEIIT DEICTIC
CCDEIKL CLICKED
CCDEIKR CRICKED
CCDEILR CIRCLED
CCDEIMO COMEDIC
CCDEIOS CODICES
CCDEIOT DOCETIC
CCDEKLO CLOCKED
COCKLED
CCDEKLU CLUCKED
CCDEKOR CROCKED
CCDELOU OCCLUDE
CCDENOS SCONCED
CCDENOU CONDUCE
CCDEOST DECOCTS
CCDHIIL CICHLID
CCDIILO CODICIL
CCDIILU CULICID
CCDIIOR CRICOID
CCDILOY CYCLOID
CCDILYY DICYCLY
CCDKLOU CUCKOLD
CCDNOOR CONCORD
CCDNOTU CONDUCT
CCEEHIK CHICKEE
CCEEHIV CEVICHE
CCEEHKR CHECKER
RECHECK
CCEEHRS CRECHES
SCREECH
CCEEILN LICENCE
CCEEINR ECCRINE
CCEEINS SCIENCE
CCEEIOR CICOREE
CCEEIRV CREVICE
CCEEKOY COCKEYE
CCEELNU LUCENCE
CCEELRY RECYCLE
CCEENRY RECENCY
CCEEORR COERCER
CCEEORS COERCES
CCEEORT COERECT
CCEERSY SECRECY
CCEFNOT CONFECT
CCEGINY GYNECIC
CCEGNOY COGENCY
CCEHIKN CHICKEN
CCEHILS CHICLES
CLICHES
CCEHIMS CHEMICS
CCEHINO CONCHIE
CCEHINS CINCHES
CCEHINT TECHNIC
CCEHINZ ZECCHIN
CCEHIOR CHOICER
CHOREIC
CCEHIOS CHOICES
CCEHIST CHICEST
CCEHKLU CHUCKLE
CCEHKPU CHECKUP
CCEHLOS CLOCHES
CCEHLSU CULCHES
CCEHNOS CONCHES
CCEHOOS COOCHES
CCEHORT CROCHET
CCEHORU COUCHER
CCEHOSU COUCHES
CCEHRSU CURCHES
CCEHSTU CUTCHES
CCEIILS CILICES
ICICLES
CCEIIMS CIMICES
CCEIIRT ICTERIC
CCEIKLR CLICKER
CCEIKOR COCKIER
CCEIKRT CRICKET
CCEIKRY CRICKEY
CCEILRR CIRCLER
CCEILRS CIRCLES
CLERICS
CCEILRT CIRCLET
CCEILSU CULICES
CCEILSY CYLICES
CCEILTU CUTICLE
CCEILYZ CYCLIZE
CCEIMOT COMETIC
CCEIMST SMECTIC
CCEINOR CORNICE
CROCEIN
CROCINE
CCEINOS CONCISE
CCEINOT CONCEIT
CCEINRT CENTRIC
CCEINSS SCENICS
CCEIOPP COPPICE
CCEIOPT ECTOPIC
CCEIORS CICEROS
CCEIORT CEROTIC
ORECTIC
CCEIOSS CISCOES
CCEIPST SCEPTIC
CCEIRST CRETICS
CCEKLOR CLOCKER
CCEKLOS COCKLES
CCEKNOY COCKNEY
CCEKOPS COPECKS
CCEKOPT PETCOCK
CCEKORS COCKERS
RECOCKS
CCEKORT CROCKET
CCELLOT COLLECT
CCELNOY CYCLONE
CCELNUY LUCENCY
CCELRSY CYCLERS
CCELRYY CYCLERY
CCENNOR CONCERN
CCENNOT CONCENT
CONNECT
CCENOPT CONCEPT
CCENORT CONCERT
CCENOSS SCONCES
CCENOTV CONVECT
CCEOOTT COCOTTE
CCEORRT CORRECT
CCEORRU REOCCUR
CCEORSS SOCCERS
CCERTUW CREWCUT
CCESSSU SUCCESS
CCFIRUY CRUCIFY
CCFLOSU FLOCCUS
CCGHINO GNOCCHI
CCGIINS SICCING
CCGIINT TICCING
CCGIKNO COCKING
CCGILNY CYCLING
CCGKOOR GORCOCK
CCHHIIS CHICHIS
CCHHINY CHINCHY
CCHHRUY CHURCHY
CCHIIST STICHIC
CCHIKOS COCKISH
CCHIKST SCHTICK
CCHILOR CHLORIC
CCHIMOR CHROMIC
CCHIMSY CHYMICS
CCHINOR CHRONIC
CCHINOS COCHINS
CCHIORY CHICORY
CCHIPSU HICCUPS
CCHIPSY PSYCHIC
CCHKLOS SCHLOCK
CCHKMSU SCHMUCK
CCHKOSY COCKSHY
CCHKPUU UPCHUCK
CCHLSTU SCULTCH
CCHLTUY CLUTCHY
CCHNOOS CONCHOS
CCHNRSU SCRUNCH
CCHNRUY CRUNCHY
CCHOORS SCROOCH
CCHOOST SCOOTCH
CCHOSTU SUCCOTH
CCIIILS SILICIC
CCIILNO COLICIN
CCIILNS CLINICS
CCIILOT COLITIC
CCIILST CLITICS
CCIINPS PICNICS
CCIIRST CRITICS
CCIIRTU CIRCUIT
CCIKLOW COWLICK
CCIKLOY COCKILY
COLICKY
CCIKOPT COCKPIT
CCILNOO COLONIC
CCILNOU COUNCIL
CCILNSY CYCLINS
CCILOOP PICCOLO
CCILSTY CYCLIST
CCIMNOU UNCOMIC
CCIMOTY MYCOTIC
CCINORY CRYONIC
CCINOTV CONVICT
CCIOORS SIROCCO
CCIOPTU OCCIPUT
CCIOSTT TICTOCS
CCIPRTY CRYPTIC
CCIRSUY CIRCUSY
CCKNOSU UNCOCKS
CCKOOSU CUCKOOS
CCKOPSU COCKUPS
CCLMSUU MUCLUCS
CCLOPSY CYCLOPS
CCLOSTU OCCULTS
CCMOOOR MOROCCO
CCNOOOS COCOONS
CCNOOPU PUCCOON
CCNOOTU COCONUT
CCNORSU CONCURS
CCNOSSU CONCUSS
CCOOORS ROCOCOS
CCORSSU SUCCORS
CCORSUU SUCCOUR
CCORSUY SUCCORY
CCOSSTU STUCCOS
CCSSSUU SUCCUSS
CDDDEEI DECIDED
CDDDEEO DECODED
CDDDEEU DEDUCED
CDDDELO CODDLED
CDDDELU CUDDLED
CDDDERU CRUDDED
CDDDESU SCUDDED
CDDEEER DECREED
RECEDED
CDDEEES SECEDED
CDDEEII DEICIDE
CDDEEIR DECIDER
DECRIED
CDDEEIS DECIDES
CDDEEIX EXCIDED
CDDEENO ENCODED
CDDEENS DESCEND
SCENDED
CDDEENU UNCEDED
CDDEEOR DECODER
RECODED
CDDEEOS DECODES
CDDEEOY DECOYED
CDDEERU REDUCED
CDDEESU DEDUCES
SEDUCED
CDDEEUW CUDWEED
CDDEHIN CHIDDEN
CDDEHIT DITCHED
CDDEHOR CHORDED
CDDEHOU DOUCHED
CDDEHRU CHUDDER
CDDEINU INDUCED
CDDEIOS DISCOED
CDDEISU CUDDIES
CDDELOR CODDLER
CDDELOS CODDLES
SCOLDED
CDDELOU CLOUDED
CDDELRU CUDDLER
CURDLED
CDDELSU CUDDLES
CDDENOU UNCODED
CDDEORS CODDERS
CDDEORW CROWDED
CDDESTU DEDUCTS
CDDGINO CODDING
CDDIIOP DIPODIC
CDDIIOS DISCOID
CDDIIRU DRUIDIC
CDDIKOP PIDDOCK
CDDIORS DISCORD
CDDKORU RUDDOCK
CDEEEFL FLEECED
CDEEEFN DEFENCE
CDEEEHK CHEEKED
CDEEEHL LEECHED
CDEEEHP CHEEPED
CDEEEHR CHEERED
CDEEEHS CHEESED
CDEEEIV DECEIVE
CDEEEJT EJECTED
CDEEEKL CLEEKED
CDEEELR CREELED
CDEEELT ELECTED
CDEEEPR CREEPED
PRECEDE
CDEEERR DECREER
CDEEERS DECREES
RECEDES
SECEDER
CDEEERT ERECTED
CDEEESS SECEDES
CDEEESX EXCEEDS
CDEEFFH CHEFFED
CDEEFHT FETCHED
CDEEFII EDIFICE
CDEEFKL FLECKED
CDEEFLT CLEFTED
DEFLECT
CDEEFOR DEFORCE
CDEEFST DEFECTS
CDEEGNO CONGEED
CDEEHIP CEPHEID
CDEEHIS DEHISCE
CDEEHIT CHEDITE
CDEEHIV CHEVIED
CDEEHKL HECKLED
CDEEHLT LETCHED
CDEEHLW WELCHED
CDEEHMS SCHEMED
CDEEHNW WENCHED
CDEEHOR COHERED
OCHERED
CDEEHPR PERCHED
CDEEHRS CHEDERS
CDEEHRT RETCHED
CDEEHRU EUCHRED
CDEEHST CHESTED
CDEEHTT TETCHED
CDEEIIT EIDETIC
CDEEILN DECLINE
CDEEILP PEDICEL
PEDICLE
CDEEILS DECILES
CDEEIMN ENDEMIC
CDEEINO CODEINE
CDEEINT ENTICED
CDEEINV EVINCED
CDEEIOS DIOCESE
CDEEIOV DEVOICE
CDEEIPR PIERCED
CDEEIRR DECRIER
CDEEIRS DECRIES
DEICERS
CDEEIRT RECITED
TIERCED
CDEEIST DECEITS
CDEEISV DEVICES
CDEEISX EXCIDES
EXCISED
CDEEITV EVICTED
CDEEITX EXCITED
CDEEJST DEJECTS
CDEEKKL KECKLED
CDEEKLR CLERKED
CDEEKLS DECKELS
DECKLES
CDEEKPS SPECKED
CDEEKRS DECKERS
CDEEKRW WRECKED
CDEELPU CUPELED
DECUPLE
CDEELPY YCLEPED
CDEELRU ULCERED
CDEELSU SECLUDE
CDEELUX EXCLUDE
CDEENOR ENCODER
ENCORED
CDEENOS ENCODES
SECONDE
CDEENOZ COZENED
CDEENRS DECERNS
CDEENRT CENTRED
CREDENT
CDEENST DESCENT
SCENTED
CDEEOOY COOEYED
CDEEOPR PRECODE
PROCEED
CDEEORS RECODES
CDEEORV COVERED
CDEEORW COWERED
CDEEORY DECOYER
CDEEOST CESTODE
ESCOTED
CDEEOTV COVETED
CDEERRU REDUCER
CDEERSS SCREEDS
CDEERST CRESTED
CDEERSU RECUSED
REDUCES
RESCUED
SECURED
SEDUCER
CDEERSW SCREWED
CDEERTU ERUCTED
CDEERUV DECURVE
CDEESSU SEDUCES
CDEESSY ECDYSES
CDEESTT DETECTS
CDEESUX EXCUSED
CDEFFHU CHUFFED
CDEFFIO COIFFED
CDEFFLO COFFLED
CDEFFOS SCOFFED
CDEFFSU SCUFFED
CDEFHIL FILCHED
CDEFHMO CHEFDOM
CDEFIIT DEFICIT
CDEFIKL FLICKED
CDEFINO CONFIDE
CDEFKLO FLOCKED
CDEFKOR DEFROCK
FROCKED
CDEFNOR CORNFED
CDEFNTU DEFUNCT
CDEFOSU DEFOCUS
FOCUSED
CDEGGHU CHUGGED
CDEGGLO CLOGGED
CDEGHOU COUGHED
CDEGIIN DEICING

CDEGIKN DECKING
CDEGILN CLINGED
CDEGINO COIGNED
CDEGINR CRINGED
CDEGINU DEUCING
EDUCING
CDEGIOR ERGODIC
CDEGKOU GEODUCK
CDEGKUW GWEDUCK
CDEGLSU CUDGELS
CDEGORS CODGERS
CDEGSUW GWEDUCS
CDEHHIT HITCHED
CDEHHNU HUNCHED
CDEHHOT HOTCHED
CDEHHTU HUTCHED
CDEHIIL CEILIDH
CDEHIIV CHIVIED
CDEHIKN CHINKED
CDEHIKO HOICKED
CDEHIKR CHIRKED
CDEHILL CHILLED
CDEHILO CHELOID
CDEHILP DELPHIC
CDEHILR ELDRICH
CDEHILS CHIELDS
CHILDES
CDEHILT LICHTED
CDEHIMR CHIRMED
CDEHINN CHINNED
CDEHINO HEDONIC
CDEHINP PINCHED
CDEHINW WINCHED
CDEHIOR CHOIRED
CDEHIOW COWHIDE
CDEHIPP CHIPPED
CDEHIPR CHIRPED
CDEHIPT PITCHED
CDEHIRR CHIRRED
CDEHIRS CHIDERS
HERDICS
CDEHIRT DITCHER
CDEHIST DITCHES
CDEHISU DUCHIES
CDEHITW WITCHED
CDEHKNU CHUNKED
CDEHKOS SHOCKED
CDEHKSU SHUCKED
CDEHLMU MULCHED
CDEHLNU LUNCHED
CDEHLNY LYNCHED
CDEHLOT CLOTHED
CDEHLRU LURCHED
CDEHMMU CHUMMED
CDEHMNU MUNCHED
CDEHMOO MOOCHED
CDEHMOP CHOMPED
CDEHMOR CHROMED
CDEHMOU MOUCHED
CDEHMPU CHUMPED
CDEHNOT NOTCHED
CDEHNPU PUNCHED
CDEHNRU CHURNED
CDEHNSU DUNCHES
CDEHNSY SYNCHED
CDEHOOP POOCHED
CDEHOPP CHOPPED
CDEHOPU POUCHED
CDEHORT TORCHED
CDEHORW CHOWDER
COWHERD
CDEHOSU CHOUSED
DOUCHES
HOCUSED
CDEHOSW CHOWSED
COWSHED
CDEHOTU TOUCHED
CDEHOUV VOUCHED
CDEHPSY PSYCHED
CDEHRRU CHURRED
CDEHRSU CRUSHED
CDEHSSU DUCHESS
CDEHSTY SCYTHED
CDEIIKR DICKIER
CDEIIKS DICKIES
CDEIILO EIDOLIC
CDEIIMR DIMERIC
CDEIINR DINERIC
CDEIINS INCISED
INDICES
CDEIINT IDENTIC
INCITED
CDEIIOR ERICOID
CDEIIOV OVICIDE
CDEIIRT DICTIER
CDEIIRV VERIDIC
CDEIIST DEISTIC
DICIEST
CDEIISU SUICIDE
CDEIJST DISJECT
CDEIKLN CLINKED
NICKLED
CDEIKLP PICKLED
CDEIKLS SICKLED
SLICKED
CDEIKLT TICKLED
CDEIKMS MEDICKS
CDEIKNS DICKENS
SNICKED
CDEIKNZ ZINCKED
CDEIKPR PRICKED
CDEIKRR DERRICK
CDEIKRS DICKERS
CDEIKRT TRICKED
CDEIKRU DUCKIER
CDEIKRW WRICKED
CDEIKST DETICKS
STICKED
CDEIKSU DUCKIES
CDEIKSY DICKEYS
CDEILLO COLLIDE
COLLIED
CDEILLU CULLIED
CDEILMO MELODIC
CDEILNU INCLUDE
NUCLIDE
CDEILOO OCELOID
CDEILOP POLICED
CDEILPP CLIPPED
CDEILPS SPLICED
CDEILPU CLUPEID
CDEILQU CLIQUED
CDEILRS CLERIDS
CDEILST DELICTS
CDEILSU SLUICED
CDEILTU DUCTILE
CDEIMNO DEMONIC
CDEIMOR DORMICE
CDEIMOS MEDICOS
MISCODE
CDEIMOT DEMOTIC
CDEIMPR CRIMPED
CDEIMPU PUMICED
CDEIMSU MISCUED
CDEINOS CODEINS
SECONDI
CDEINOT CTENOID
DEONTIC
NOTICED
CDEINRS CINDERS
DISCERN
RESCIND
CDEINRU INDUCER
CDEINRY CINDERY
CDEINSU INCUDES
INCUSED
INDUCES
CDEINSX EXSCIND
CDEINSZ DEZINCS
CDEINTT TINCTED
CDEIOPR PERCOID
CDEIOPT PICOTED
CDEIORT CORDITE
CDEIORV CODRIVE
DIVORCE
CDEIORW CROWDIE
CDEIOST CESTOID
COEDITS
CDEIPRS CRISPED
CDEIPRT PREDICT
CDEIPST DEPICTS
DISCEPT
CDEIRRU CURDIER
CURRIED
CDEIRST CREDITS
DIRECTS
CDEIRSU CRUISED
CDEIRSV SCRIVED
CDEIRTV VERDICT
CDEISST DISSECT
CDEISSY ECDYSIS
CDEJNOU JOUNCED
CDEKKNO KNOCKED
CDEKLNO CLONKED
CDEKLNU CLUNKED
CDEKLOW WEDLOCK
CDEKLPU PLUCKED
CDEKLRU RUCKLED
CDEKLSU SCULKED
SUCKLED
CDEKMOS SMOCKED
CDEKNOR DORNECK
CDEKNSU SUNDECK
CDEKOOR CROOKED
CDEKORS DOCKERS
REDOCKS
CDEKORT TROCKED
CDEKOST DOCKETS
STOCKED
CDEKRSU DUCKERS
CDEKRTU TRUCKED
CDELLOU COLLUDE
LOCULED
CDELLSU SCULLED
CDELMOP CLOMPED
CDELMPU CLUMPED
CDELMSU MUSCLED
CDELMTU MULCTED
CDELNOO CONDOLE
CDELNOW CLOWNED
CDELNOY CONDYLE
CDELOOR COLORED
DECOLOR
CDELOPP CLOPPED
CDELOPU COUPLED
CDELORS SCOLDER
CDELORU CLOURED
CDELORW CLOWDER
CDELOST COLDEST
CDELOSW SCOWLED
CDELOTT CLOTTED
CDELOTU CLOUTED
CDELOUY DOUCELY
CDELOWY COWEDLY
CDELPSU SCULPED
CDELRRU CURDLER
CDELRSU CURDLES
CDELRUY CRUDELY
CDELSTU DULCETS
CDELTTU CUTTLED
CDELTUU DUCTULE
CDEMMNO COMMEND
CDEMMOO COMMODE
CDEMMSU SCUMMED
CDEMNNO CONDEMN
CDEMNOP COMPEND
CDEMOOS COMEDOS
CDEMOPT COMPTED
CDEMORU DECORUM
CDEMPRU CRUMPED
CDENNOO CONDONE
CDENNOT CONTEND
CDENOOR CROONED
CDENOOS CONDOES
SECONDO
CDENOPU POUNCED
CDENORS SCORNED
CDENORU CRUNODE
CDENORW CROWNED
DECROWN
CDENOSS SECONDS
CDENOST DOCENTS
CDENOSY ECDYSON
CDENOTU COUNTED
CDENPUY PUDENCY
CDENRUU UNCURED
CDEOOPP COPEPOD
CDEOOPS SCOOPED
CDEOOPT COOPTED
CDEOORR CORRODE
CDEOORV CODROVE
VOCODER
CDEOOST SCOOTED
CDEOOTV DOVECOT
CDEOPPR CROPPED
CDEOPRU PRODUCE
CDEORRS CORDERS
RECORDS
CDEORRW CROWDER
CDEORSS CROSSED
CDEORSU COURSED
SCOURED
SOURCED
CDEORSW SCOWDER
CDEORTU COURTED
EDUCTOR
CDEORUU DOUCEUR
CDEOSSU ESCUDOS
CDEOSTU SCOUTED
CDEOSYZ ZYDECOS
CDEPRSU SPRUCED
CDEPRTY DECRYPT
CDERSTU CRUDEST
CRUSTED
CDFHIOS CODFISH
CDFIILU FLUIDIC
CDFIJOR FJORDIC
CDFILUY DULCIFY
CDFIOSU FUCOIDS
CDFNOOU COFOUND
CDGHIIN CHIDING
CDGHILO GLOCHID
CDGIINO GONIDIC
CDGIINS DISCING
CDGIKNO DOCKING
CDGIKNU DUCKING
CDGILNO CODLING
LINGCOD
CDGINNO CONDIGN
CDGINOR CORDING
CDGINRU CURDING
CDGINTU DUCTING
CDGOOSY COYDOGS
CDHIIST DISTICH
CDHILLY CHILDLY
CDHILOR CHLORID
CDHILOS COLDISH
CDHINSU DUNCISH
CDHIOOR CHOROID
OCHROID
CDHIORS ORCHIDS
CDHIOTU OUTCHID
CDHIPTY DIPTYCH
CDHIRTY CHYTRID
CDHORSS SCHRODS
CDIIILP LIPIDIC
CDIIIOT IDIOTIC
CDIIJRU JURIDIC
CDIILLY IDYLLIC
CDIILMO DOMICIL
CDIILNY DICLINY
CDIILOP DIPLOIC
CDIIMOS DISOMIC
CDIINOR CRINOID
CDIINOT DICTION
CDIINOV VIDICON
CDIINOZ ZINCOID
CDIINST INDICTS
CDIINTU DUNITIC
CDIIOPT PODITIC
CDIIORS CIRSOID
CDIIOSS CISSOID
CDIIOSV VISCOID
CDIIPRY PYRIDIC
CDIIRSU SCIURID
CDIKNNU NUDNICK
CDIKNOR DORNICK
CDIKNPU DUCKPIN
CDILLOO COLLOID
CDILLUY LUCIDLY
CDILMTU MIDCULT
CDILNOS CODLINS
CDILOTY DICOTYL
CDIMMOU MODICUM
CDIMNOO MONODIC
CDIMOOR CORMOID
CDIMOSS COSMIDS
CDIMOSU MUCOIDS
CDIMSSU MUSCIDS
CDIMSTU DICTUMS
CDINOOS CONOIDS
CDINOSY SYNODIC
CDINOTU CONDUIT
NOCTUID
CDINSSY SYNDICS
CDINSTU INDUCTS
CDIOPRR RIPCORD
CDIOPSS PSOCIDS
CDIORSV CORVIDS
CDIOSTY CYSTOID
CDIOTUV OVIDUCT
CDIPSSU CUSPIDS
CDIRSUY DYSURIC
CDIRTUY CRUDITY
CDISSSU DISCUSS
CDKMORU MUDROCK
CDKNOOR DORNOCK
CDKNOSU UNDOCKS
CDLNOUU UNCLOUD
CDLOOPY LYCOPOD
CDLOSTU COULDST
CDMNOOS CONDOMS
CDMNSUU CUNDUMS
CDMOOST TOMCODS
CDNOORS CONDORS
CORDONS
CDNOTUW CUTDOWN
CDOOOPT OCTOPOD
CDOOPST POSTDOC
CDOORRY CORRODY
CDOORST DOCTORS
CDOOTUW WOODCUT
CDOPRTU PRODUCT
CDOSTUY CUSTODY
CEEEELT ELECTEE
CEEEFLR FLEECER
CEEEFLS FLEECES
CEEEFNR REFENCE
CEEEHLL ECHELLE
CEEEHLS LEECHES
CEEEHPR CHEEPER
CEEEHRR CHEERER
CEEEHSS CHEESES
CEEEINP EPICENE
CEEEIPR CREEPIE
CEEEIRV RECEIVE
CEEEITV EVICTEE
CEEEJRT REEJECT
CEEELRT REELECT
CEEELST CELESTE
CEEENSS ESSENCE
CEEEPRR CREEPER
CEEERRT ERECTER
REERECT
CEEERSS CREESES
CEEERST SECRETE
CEEERTX EXCRETE
CEEETUX EXECUTE
CEEFFNO OFFENCE
CEEFFOS COFFEES
CEEFFST EFFECTS
CEEFHIR CHIEFER
CEEFHIT FITCHEE
CEEFHLS FLECHES
CEEFHRT FETCHER
CEEFHST FETCHES
CEEFIRR FIERCER
CEEFKLR FRECKLE
CEEFLRT REFLECT
CEEFNNS FENNECS
CEEFNNU UNFENCE
CEEFNOR ENFORCE
CEEFNRS FENCERS
CEEFPRT PERFECT
PREFECT
CEEFRST REFECTS
CEEFSSU FESCUES
CEEGHOS CHEGOES
CEEGIIP EPIGEIC
CEEGINR GENERIC
CEEGINT GENETIC
CEEGINU EUGENIC
CEEGIRZ GRECIZE
CEEGKOS GECKOES
CEEGLLO COLLEGE
CEEGLNT NEGLECT
CEEGLOU ECLOGUE
CEEGNOS CONGEES
CEEGNRY REGENCY
CEEGORT CORTEGE
CEEHIKM KIMCHEE
CEEHILN ELENCHI
CEEHILS HELICES
LICHEES
CEEHILV VEHICLE
CEEHIMR CHIMERE
CEEHIMS CHEMISE
CEEHIOR CHEERIO
CEEHIRT ERETHIC
ETHERIC
HERETIC
TECHIER
CEEHIRW CHEWIER
CEEHISS SEICHES
CEEHIST TECHIES
CEEHISV CHEVIES
SEVICHE
CEEHKLR HECKLER
CEEHKLS HECKLES
CEEHKNP HENPECK
CEEHKNS KENCHES
CEEHKST KETCHES
CEEHLNO ECHELON
CEEHLRS LECHERS
CEEHLRW WELCHER
CEEHLRY CHEERLY
LECHERY
CEEHLST LETCHES
CEEHLSW LECHWES
WELCHES
CEEHLSY LYCHEES
CEEHMRS MERCHES
SCHEMER
SCHMEER
CEEHMSS SCHEMES
CEEHNOP PENOCHE
CEEHNPU PENUCHE
CEEHNRW WENCHER
CEEHNST TENCHES
CEEHNSW WENCHES
CEEHNTU CHUTNEE
CEEHORR COHERER
CEEHORS CHEEROS
COHERES
ECHOERS
RECHOSE
CEEHORT TROCHEE
CEEHOUV VOUCHEE
CEEHPRR PERCHER
CEEHPRS PERCHES
CEEHQRU CHEQUER
CEEHQSU CHEQUES
CEEHRST ETCHERS
RETCHES
CEEHRSU EUCHRES
CEEHRSV CHEVRES
CEEHRSW CHEWERS
RECHEWS
CEEHRTV CHEVRET
CEEHSSS CHESSES
CEEHSSW ESCHEWS
CEEHSTV VETCHES
CEEIIKL ICELIKE
CEEIINR EIRENIC
CEEIIPR EPEIRIC
CEEIJOR REJOICE
CEEIKNT NECKTIE
CEEIKPR PECKIER
PICKEER
CEEIKSS SICKEES
CEEILLM MICELLE
CEEILMX LEXEMIC
CEEILNO CINEOLE
CEEILNR RECLINE
CEEILNS LICENSE
SELENIC
SILENCE
CEEILNT CENTILE
LICENTE
CEEILNU LEUCINE
CEEILPS ECLIPSE
CEEILPX EXCIPLE
CEEILRS CEILERS
CEEILRT RETICLE
TIERCEL
CEEILSS ICELESS
CEEILST SECTILE
CEEILSV VESICLE
CEEILTU LEUCITE
CEEIMMS SEMEMIC
CEEIMNO MIOCENE
CEEIMNT CENTIME
CEEIMRS MERCIES
CEEIMRX EXCIMER
CEEIMST EMETICS
CEEINNS INCENSE
CEEINOS SENECIO
CEEINPU EUPNEIC
CEEINRS SINCERE
CEEINRT ENTERIC
ENTICER
CEEINRV CERVINE
CEEINST ENTICES
CEEINSV EVINCES
CEEIOPT PICOTEE
CEEIORT COTERIE
CEEIORV REVOICE
CEEIOST COESITE
CEEIPPR PRECIPE
CEEIPRR CREPIER
PIERCER
REPRICE
CEEIPRS PIECERS
PIERCES
PRECISE
RECIPES
CEEIPRT RECEIPT
CEEIPRU EPICURE
CEEIPSS SPECIES
CEEIPTZ PECTIZE
CEEIRRT RECITER
CEEIRSS CERISES
CEEIRST CERITES
RECITES
TIERCES
CEEIRSV SCRIEVE
SERVICE
CEEIRTU EUCRITE
CEEIRTX EXCITER
CEEISSX EXCISES
CEEISTU CUTESIE
CEEISTX EXCITES
CEEITTT TECTITE
CEEJORT EJECTOR
CEEJRST REJECTS
CEEKKLS KECKLES
CEEKLPS SPECKLE
CEEKNRS NECKERS
CEEKOSY SOCKEYE
CEEKPRS PECKERS
CEEKRRW WRECKER
CEELLLU CELLULE
CEELLNO COLLEEN
CEELMNT CLEMENT
CEELMOO COELOME
CEELMOS CLEOMES
CEELMOT TELECOM
CEELMOW WELCOME
CEELMSY MYCELES
CEELNOS ENCLOSE
CEELNPS PENCELS
CEELNRS CRENELS
CEELNRT LECTERN
CEELNRU LUCERNE
CEELORS CREOLES
CEELORT ELECTOR
ELECTRO
CEELOSU COULEES
CEELOTX CELOTEX
CEELPRT PRELECT
CEELPRU CUPELER
CEELRRU CRUELER
CEELRST TERCELS
CEELRSU RECLUSE
CEELRSW CREWELS
CEELRTU LECTURE
CEELRTY ERECTLY
CEELSST SELECTS
CEELSUX CULEXES
CEELTTU LETTUCE
CEEMNRU CERUMEN
CEEMNRW CREWMEN
CEEMNST CEMENTS
CEEMNSY CYMENES
CEEMOPR COMPEER
COMPERE
CEEMOPT COMPETE
CEEMRRS MERCERS
CEEMRRY MERCERY
CEEMRST CERMETS
CEEMSTU TUMESCE
CEENNOU ENOUNCE
CEENNOV CONVENE
CEENNRT CENTNER
CEENOOT ECOTONE
CEENOPT POTENCE
CEENORS ENCORES
NECROSE
CEENORU COENURE
CEENORZ COZENER
CEENOST CENOTES
CEENPRS SPENCER
CEENPRT PERCENT
PRECENT
CEENPSS SPENCES
CEENPST PECTENS
CEENRSS CENSERS
SCREENS
SECERNS
CEENRST CENTERS
CENTRES
TENRECS
CEENRSU CENSURE
CEENRSY SCENERY
CEEOPRU RECOUPE
CEEOPTY ECOTYPE
CEEORRS RESCORE
CEEORRT ERECTOR
CEEORRV COVERER
RECOVER
CEEORSV CORVEES
CEEORTV COVETER
CEEORTX COEXERT
CEEOTTT OCTETTE
CEEPPRT PERCEPT
PRECEPT
CEEPPRU PREPUCE
CEEPRRU PRECURE
CEEPRSS PRECESS
CEEPRST RECEPTS
RESPECT
SCEPTER
SCEPTRE
SPECTER
SPECTRE
CEEPRTX EXCERPT
CEEPSTX EXCEPTS
EXPECTS
CEEPSTY ECTYPES
CEEPSUY EYECUPS
CEERRSU RESCUER
SECURER

CEERRSW SCREWER
CEERRUV RECURVE
CEERSSS CRESSES
CEERSST CRESSET
RESECTS
SECRETS
CEERSSU CERUSES
RECUSES
RESCUES
SECURES
CEERSTT TERCETS
CEERSUX EXCUSER
CEERTTU CURETTE
CEESSTX EXSECTS
CEESSUX EXCUSES
CEETTUV CUVETTE
CEFFHRU CHUFFER
CEFFIOR OFFICER
CEFFIOS COIFFES
OFFICES
CEFFISU SUFFICE
CEFFLOS COFFLES
CEFFLSU SCUFFLE
CEFFORS COFFERS
SCOFFER
CEFFORT COFFRET
CEFFRSU SCUFFER
CEFGHIN CHEFING
CEFGINN FENCING
CEFHILR FILCHER
CEFHILS FILCHES
CEFHILY CHIEFLY
CEFHINS FINCHES
CEFHIST FITCHES
CEFHITT FITCHET
CEFHITW FITCHEW
CEFIILT FICTILE
CEFIIOR ORIFICE
CEFIITV FICTIVE
CEFIKLR FICKLER
FLICKER
CEFILNT INFLECT
CEFILNU FUNICLE
CEFILRU FLUERIC
LUCIFER
CEFIMOR COMFIER
CEFINNO CONFINE
CEFINOR COINFER
CONIFER
CEFINST INFECTS
CEFIPSY SPECIFY
CEFIRSS SFERICS
CEFIRTY CERTIFY
RECTIFY
CEFISSU FICUSES
CEFKLLO ELFLOCK
CEFKLOT FETLOCK
CEFKLRY FRECKLY
CEFLNOU FLOUNCE
CEFLNTU UNCLEFT
CEFLNUY FLUENCY
CEFMORY COMFREY
CEFNORS CONFERS
CEFNORU FROUNCE
CEFNOSS CONFESS
CEFNOSU CONFUSE
CEFNOTU CONFUTE
CEFOPRS FORCEPS
CEFORRS FORCERS
CEFORRT CROFTER
CEFORSS FRESCOS
CEFORSU FOCUSER
REFOCUS
CEFOSSU FOCUSES
FUCOSES
CEFRSUW CURFEWS
CEFSSUU FUCUSES
CEGGHIR CHIGGER
CEGGHRU CHUGGER
CEGGIKN GECKING
CEGGIOR GEORGIC
CEGGLOR CLOGGER
CEGGPSU EGGCUPS
CEGHILN LECHING
CEGHINO ECHOING
CEGHINP PECHING
CEGHINT ETCHING
CEGHINW CHEWING
CEGHIOR CHOREGI
CEGHIOS CHIGOES
CEGHLSU GULCHES
CEGHORU COUGHER
CEGIILN CEILING
CEGIINP PIECING
CEGIKKN KECKING
CEGIKNN NECKING
CEGIKNP PECKING
CEGIKNR RECKING
CEGILLN CELLING
CEGILNP CLEPING
CEGILNR CLINGER
CRINGLE
CEGILNU CLUEING
CEGILNW CLEWING
CEGILNY GLYCINE
CEGIMNO GENOMIC
CEGINNS CENSING
CEGINOR COREIGN
CEGINOS COGNISE
COIGNES
CEGINOZ COGNIZE
CEGINPR CREPING
CEGINRR CRINGER
CEGINRS CRINGES
CEGINRW CREWING
CEGINSS CESSING
CEGIORT ERGOTIC
CEGLNOO COLOGNE
CEGLOOY ECOLOGY
CEGLOSU GLUCOSE
CEGNOOS CONGOES
CEGNORS CONGERS
CEGNORY CRYOGEN
CEGNOST CONGEST
CEGNRUY URGENCY
CEGNSTY CYGNETS
CEGOORS SCROOGE
CEGORRS GROCERS
CEGORRY GROCERY
CEGORSU SCOURGE
SCROUGE
CEHHIOO HOOCHIE
CEHHIRS CHERISH
CEHHIRT HITCHER
CEHHIST HITCHES
CEHHNSU HUNCHES
CEHHOOS HOOCHES
CEHHOST HOTCHES
CEHHSSU SHEUCHS
CEHHSTU HUTCHES
CEHIIKS HICKIES
CEHIILS CHILIES
CEHIINR HIRCINE
CEHIINT ICHNITE
CEHIIPP CHIPPIE
CEHIIRT ITCHIER
CEHIISV CHIVIES
VICHIES
CEHIKNT KITCHEN
THICKEN
CEHIKNW CHEWINK
CEHIKOR CHOKIER
CEHIKPS PECKISH
CEHIKRR CHIRKER
CEHIKRS SHICKER
CEHIKRT THICKER
CEHIKRW WHICKER
CEHIKSY HICKEYS
CEHIKTT THICKET
CEHILLR CHILLER
CEHILMY CHIMLEY
CEHILNO CHOLINE
HELICON
CEHILNS LICHENS
CEHILRV CHERVIL
CEHILSS CHISELS
CEHILSZ ZILCHES
CEHILTY ETHYLIC
LECYTHI
TECHILY
CEHILXY HEXYLIC
CEHIMMS CHEMISM
CEHIMNY CHIMNEY
CEHIMOR HOMERIC
CEHIMOS ECHOISM
CEHIMRS CHIMERS
CEHIMRT THERMIC
CEHIMRU RHEUMIC
CEHIMST CHEMIST
CEHINNO CHINONE
CEHINOP CHOPINE
PHOCINE
CEHINOR CHORINE
CEHINPR NEPHRIC
PHRENIC
PINCHER
CEHINPS PINCHES
SPHENIC
CEHINPU PENUCHI
CEHINRR CHIRREN
CEHINRS INCHERS
RICHENS
CEHINRT CITHERN
CITHREN
CEHINRW WINCHER
CEHINST ETHNICS
STHENIC
CEHINSU ECHINUS
CEHINSW WINCHES
CEHINSZ ZECHINS
CEHIOPS HOSPICE
CEHIOPT POTICHE
CEHIOPU COPIHUE
CEHIORS COHEIRS
HEROICS
CEHIOTU COUTHIE
CEHIOTV CHEVIOT
CEHIPPR CHIPPER
CEHIPRR CHIRPER
CEHIPRS CERIPHS
CIPHERS
SPHERIC
CEHIPRT PITCHER
CEHIPST PITCHES
CEHIQSU QUICHES
CEHIRRS CHIRRES
CEHIRST CITHERS
RICHEST
CEHIRSU CUSHIER
CEHIRSZ SCHERZI
CEHIRTT CHITTER
CEHISSU CUISHES
CEHISTW WITCHES
CEHKKRU CHUKKER
CEHKLMO HEMLOCK
CEHKLSU HUCKLES
CEHKNOU UNCHOKE
CEHKNSU KUCHENS
CEHKOOR KERCHOO
CEHKORS CHOKERS
HOCKERS
SHOCKER
CEHKOSY HOCKEYS
CEHKPTU KETCHUP
CEHKRSU SHUCKER
CEHKSTY SKETCHY
CEHKTVY KVETCHY
CEHLMSU MULCHES
CEHLNNU CHUNNEL
CEHLNOT CHOLENT
CEHLNRU LUNCHER
CEHLNRY LYNCHER
CEHLNSU LUNCHES
CEHLNSY LYNCHES
CEHLORS CHOLERS
CEHLORT CHORTLE
CEHLOST CLOTHES
CEHLPPS SCHLEPP
CEHLPSS SCHLEPS
CEHLQSU SQUELCH
CEHLRRU LURCHER
CEHLRSU LURCHES
CEHMNRU MUNCHER
CEHMNSU MUNCHES
CEHMNSY MENSCHY
CEHMOOR MOOCHER
CEHMOOS MOOCHES
CEHMOPR CHOMPER
CEHMORS CHROMES
CEHMOSS SCHMOES
CEHMOSU MOUCHES
CEHMRTU CHETRUM
CEHMSTU MUTCHES
CEHNOOP HENCOOP
CEHNORT CHORTEN
NOTCHER
CEHNORV CHEVRON
CEHNOST NOTCHES
TECHNOS
CEHNOSU COHUNES
CEHNPRU PUNCHER
CEHNPST PSCHENT
CEHNPSU PUNCHES
CEHNRRU CHURNER
CEHNRTU CHUNTER
CEHNSTY STENCHY
CEHNSUU EUNUCHS
CEHNTUY CHUTNEY
CEHOOPS POOCHES
CEHOORS CHOOSER
SOROCHE
CEHOORT CHEROOT
CEHOOSS CHOOSES
CEHOOSY CHOOSEY
CEHOOTU OUTECHO
CEHOPPR CHOPPER
CEHOPRS PORCHES
CEHOPSU POUCHES
CEHORSS COSHERS
CEHORST HECTORS
ROCHETS
ROTCHES
TOCHERS
TORCHES
TROCHES
CEHORSU CHOUSER
ROUCHES
CEHORSZ SCHERZO
CEHORTU COUTHER
RETOUCH
TOUCHER
CEHORUV VOUCHER
CEHOSSU CHOUSES
HOCUSES
CEHOSSW CHOWSES
CEHOSTU TOUCHES
CEHOSUV VOUCHES
CEHPRSY CYPHERS
CEHPSSY PSYCHES
CEHRRSU CRUSHER
CEHRSSU CRUSHES
CEHRSTT STRETCH
CEHSSTU TUSCHES
CEHSSTY SCYTHES
CEIIJRU JUICIER
CEIIKKR KICKIER
CEIIKNS KINESIC
CEIIKNT KINETIC
CEIIKPR PICKIER
CEIIKQU QUICKIE
CEIIKRT TRICKIE
CEIIKSS SICKIES
CEIIKST EKISTIC
ICKIEST
CEIILLS SILICLE
CEIILNN INCLINE
CEIILNP PENICIL
CEIILPT PELITIC
CEIILST ELICITS
CEIIMMT MIMETIC
CEIIMNR CREMINI
CRIMINE
MINCIER
CEIIMNS MENISCI
CEIIMOT MEIOTIC
CEIIMPR EMPIRIC
CEIIMRV VIREMIC
CEIIMSS SEISMIC
CEIIMST MISCITE
CEIIMTT TITMICE
CEIINNO CONIINE
CEIINNR CINERIN
CEIINOR ONEIRIC
CEIINOS EOSINIC
NICOISE
CEIINOV INVOICE
CEIINPS PISCINE
CEIINRS IRENICS
SERICIN
CEIINRT CITRINE
CRINITE
INCITER
NERITIC
CEIINSS ICINESS
INCISES
CEIINST INCITES
CEIINSU CUISINE
CEIINTZ CITIZEN
ZINCITE
CEIIOPZ EPIZOIC
CEIIPRR PRICIER
CEIIPRS SPICIER
CEIIPRT PICRITE
CEIIRST ERISTIC
CEIISSS CISSIES
CEIISVV CIVVIES
CEIITUV UVEITIC
CEIJNST INJECTS
CEIJRSU JUICERS
CEIJSTU JUSTICE
CEIKKRS KICKERS
CEIKLMR MICKLER
CEIKLMS MICKLES
CEIKLNR CLINKER
CRINKLE
CEIKLNS NICKELS
NICKLES
SLICKEN
CEIKLPR PRICKLE
CEIKLPS PICKLES
CEIKLPU CUPLIKE
CEIKLRS LICKERS
SLICKER
CEIKLRT TICKLER
TRICKLE
CEIKLRU LUCKIER
CEIKLSS SICKLES
CEIKLST STICKLE
TICKLES
CEIKLSU LUCKIES
CEIKMRU MUCKIER
CEIKMSY MICKEYS
CEIKNOT KENOTIC
KETONIC
CEIKNQU QUICKEN
CEIKNRS NICKERS
SNICKER
CEIKNSS SICKENS
CEIKOOS COOKIES
CEIKOPR POCKIER
CEIKORR CORKIER
ROCKIER
CEIKOTT KETOTIC
CEIKPRR PRICKER
CEIKPRS PICKERS
CEIKPRT PRICKET
CEIKPST PICKETS
SKEPTIC
CEIKQRU QUICKER
CEIKRRT TRICKER
CEIKRST RICKETS
STICKER
TICKERS
CEIKRSU SUCKIER
CEIKRSW WICKERS
CEIKRSY RICKEYS
CEIKRTY RICKETY
CEIKRUY YUCKIER
CEIKSST SICKEST
CEIKSTT TICKETS
CEIKSTW WICKETS
CEILLMS MICELLS
CEILLNU NUCELLI
CEILLOR COLLIER
CEILLOS COLLIES
CEILLST CELLIST
CEILLSU CULLIES
CEILMOP COMPILE
POLEMIC
CEILMOT TELOMIC
CEILMPR CRIMPLE
CEILNNU NUCLEIN
CEILNOP PINOCLE
PLEONIC
CEILNOS CINEOLS
INCLOSE
CEILNOT LECTION
CEILNOX LEXICON
CEILNPS PENCILS
SPLENIC
CEILNST CLIENTS
LECTINS
STENCIL
CEILNSU LEUCINS
CEILNTU CUTLINE
LINECUT
TUNICLE
CEILOOS COOLIES
CEILOPR PELORIC
POLICER
CEILOPS POLICES
CEILORS COILERS
RECOILS
CEILOSS OSSICLE
CEILOST CITOLES
CEILPPR CLIPPER
CRIPPLE
CEILPRS SPLICER
CEILPSS SPLICES
CEILPSU SPICULE
CEILPSV PELVICS
CEILQSU CLIQUES
CEILQUY CLIQUEY
CEILRRU CURLIER
CEILRSS SLICERS
CEILRST RELICTS
CEILRSV CLIVERS
CEILRSY CLERISY
CEILRTU UTRICLE
CEILSSU SLUICES
CEILSTU LUCITES
LUETICS
CEILTTU CUITTLE
CEIMMOS COMMIES
CEIMMRR CRIMMER
CEIMMRU CRUMMIE
CEIMNOR INCOMER
CEIMNOS INCOMES
MESONIC
CEIMNOT CENTIMO
TONEMIC
CEIMNRS MINCERS
CEIMNRU NUMERIC
CEIMNYZ ENZYMIC
CEIMOPR MEROPIC
CEIMOPT METOPIC
CEIMORT MORTICE
CEIMOSX EXOSMIC
CEIMOTT TOTEMIC
CEIMOTV VICOMTE
CEIMOTX TOXEMIC
CEIMOUZ ZOECIUM
CEIMPRR CRIMPER
CEIMPRS SPERMIC
CEIMPRU PUMICER
CEIMPSU PUMICES
CEIMRST METRICS
CEIMRSU CERIUMS
MURICES
CEIMSSU CESIUMS
MISCUES
CEINNOS CONINES
CEINNOV CONNIVE
CEINNST INCENTS
CEINOOT COONTIE
CEINOPR PORCINE
CEINOPT ENTOPIC
NEPOTIC
CEINORR CORNIER
CEINORS COINERS
CRONIES
ORCEINS
RECOINS
CEINORT COINTER
NOTICER
CEINORU COENURI
CEINORV CORVINE
CEINOSS CESSION
COSINES
OSCINES
CEINOST NOTICES
SECTION
CEINOSV NOVICES
CEINOTT TONETIC
CEINOTX EXCITON
CEINOUV UNVOICE
CEINPRS CRISPEN
PINCERS
PRINCES
CEINPST INCEPTS
INSPECT
PECTINS
CEINQSU CINQUES
QUINCES
CEINRRU REINCUR
CEINRST CISTERN
CRETINS
CEINRSW WINCERS
CEINRTT CITTERN
CEINRUV INCURVE
CEINSST INCESTS
INSECTS
CEINSSU INCUSES
CEINSTU NEUSTIC
CEINSTY CYSTEIN
CYSTINE
CEINSWY WINCEYS
CEINTTX EXTINCT
CEIOOST COOTIES
CEIOPPR CROPPIE
CEIOPRS COPIERS
CEIOPST POETICS
CEIOPSU PICEOUS
CEIOPSW COWPIES
CEIORRS CIRROSE
CORRIES
CROSIER
ORRICES
CEIORRU COURIER
CEIORRZ CROZIER
CEIORST EROTICS
CEIORSV VOICERS
CEIORSW COWRIES
CEIORTT COTTIER
CEIORTV EVICTOR
CEIORTW COWRITE
CEIORTX EXCITOR
XEROTIC
CEIORVY VICEROY
CEIOSST COSIEST
CEIOSSV VISCOSE
CEIOSTT SCOTTIE
CEIOSTV COSTIVE
CEIOSTW COWIEST
CEIOSTX COEXIST
EXOTICS
CEIOSTY SOCIETY
CEIOSTZ COZIEST
CEIPPRU CUPPIER
CEIPPST PEPTICS
CEIPQTU PICQUET
CEIPRRS CRISPER
PRICERS
CEIPRSS SPICERS
CEIPRST TRICEPS
CEIPRSY SPICERY
CEIPRTU CUPRITE
PICTURE
CEIPRTY PYRETIC
CEIPRXY PYREXIC
CEIPSST CESSPIT
SEPTICS
CEIQRSU CIRQUES
CEIRRRU CURRIER
CEIRRSU CRUISER
CURRIES
CEIRRTT CRITTER
CEIRRTU RECRUIT
CEIRRTX RECTRIX
CEIRRUV CURVIER
CEIRSSU CRUISES
CEIRSSV SCRIVES
CEIRSTT TRISECT
CEIRSTU CURITES
ICTERUS
CEIRSUV CURSIVE
CEIRTTX TECTRIX
CEISSSU CUISSES
CEISSTU CUTISES
ICTUSES
CEISTTU CUTTIES
CEJKOSY JOCKEYS
CEJNORU CONJURE
CEJNOSU JOUNCES
JUNCOES
CEJOPRT PROJECT
CEKKLNU KNUCKLE
CEKKNOR KNOCKER
CEKKOPS KOPECKS
CEKLLRY CLERKLY
CEKLMSU MUCKLES
CEKLNRU CLUNKER
CEKLORS LOCKERS
RELOCKS
CEKLOST LOCKETS
LOCKSET
CEKLPRU PLUCKER
CEKLRSU RUCKLES
SCULKER
SUCKLER
CEKLRTU TRUCKLE
CEKLSSU SUCKLES
CEKMNOS SOCKMEN
CEKMORS MOCKERS
CEKMORY MOCKERY
CEKMRSU MUCKERS
CEKNOOV CONVOKE
CEKNORS CONKERS
RECKONS
CEKNRWY WRYNECK
CEKOOPR PRECOOK
CEKOOPW COWPOKE
CEKOORR CROOKER
CEKOORS COOKERS
RECOOKS
CEKOORY COOKERY
CEKOOSY COOKEYS
CEKOPRR PREROCK
CEKOPST POCKETS
CEKORRS CORKERS
RECORKS
ROCKERS
CEKORRY ROCKERY
CEKORST RESTOCK
ROCKETS
STOCKER
CEKOSST SOCKETS
CEKPRSU PUCKERS
CEKPRUY PUCKERY
CEKRRTU TRUCKER
CEKRSSU SUCKERS
CEKRSTU TUCKERS
CEKSTTU TUCKETS
CELLMOU COLUMEL
CELLNOO COLONEL
CELLOST COLLETS
CELLOSU LOCULES
OCELLUS
CELLOSY CLOSELY
CELLRRU CRULLER

CELLRSU CULLERS
SCULLER
CELLRUY CRUELLY
CELLSTU CULLETS
CELMNOO MONOCLE
CELMNSU MESCLUN
CELMOOS COELOMS
CELMOPS COMPELS
CELMOPX COMPLEX
CELMORS CORMELS
CELMPRU CRUMPLE
CELMSSU MUSCLES
CELMSUY LYCEUMS
CELNNOU NUCLEON
CELNNSU NUNCLES
CELNOOR CORONEL
CELNOOS COLONES
CONSOLE
CELNORS CLONERS
CORNELS
CELNOSU COUNSEL
UNCLOSE
CELNOTU NOCTULE
CELNRSU LUCERNS
CELNSUU NUCLEUS
CELOOPR PRECOOL
CELOORR COLORER
RECOLOR
CELOORS COOLERS
CREOSOL
CELOOST COOLEST
OCELOTS
CELOPRU COUPLER
CELOPSU CLOSEUP
COUPLES
CELOPTU COUPLET
OCTUPLE
CELOQSU CLOQUES
CELORRU CORULER
CELORSS CLOSERS
CRESOLS
CELORST COLTERS
CORSLET
COSTREL
LECTORS
CELORSU CLOSURE
COLURES
CELORSV CLOVERS
VELCROS
CELORSW SCOWLER
CELORTU CLOTURE
CLOUTER
COULTER
CELORVY CLOVERY
CELOSST CLOSEST
CLOSETS
CELOSSU OSCULES
CELOSSX COXLESS
CELOTTU CULOTTE
CELPRSU SCRUPLE
CELPSUU CUPULES
CELPSUY CLYPEUS
CELRRSU CURLERS
CELRSSY CRESYLS
CELRSTU CLUSTER
CUTLERS
RELUCTS
CELRSTY CLYSTER
CELRSUV CULVERS
CELRSUW CURLEWS
CELRTTU CLUTTER
CELRTUU CULTURE
CELRTUV CULVERT
CELRTUY CRUELTY
CUTLERY
CELSTTU CUTLETS
CUTTLES
SCUTTLE
CEMMNOT COMMENT
CEMMNOU COMMUNE
CEMMOOV COMMOVE
CEMMOTU COMMUTE
CEMMRSU CUMMERS
SCUMMER
CEMNNOT CONTEMN
CEMNOOP COMPONE
CEMNOOY ECONOMY
MONOECY
CEMNOSU CONSUME
CEMNRTU CENTRUM
CEMNSTU CENTUMS
CEMOOPS COMPOSE
CEMOOPT COMPOTE
CEMOOTU OUTCOME
CEMOPST COEMPTS
CEMOPTU COMPUTE

CEMOSSY MYCOSES
CEMOSTU COSTUME
CEMPRTU CRUMPET
CEMRRUY MERCURY
CEMRSTU RECTUMS
CEMSSUU MUCUSES
CEMSTTU TECTUMS
CENNOOR NONCORE
CENNOOS NEOCONS
CENNOOT CONNOTE
CENNORS CONNERS
CENNOST CONSENT
CENNOTT CONTENT
CENNOTV CONVENT
CENNRSU CUNNERS
SCUNNER
CENOOPS POCOSEN
CENOORR CORONER
CROONER
CENOORT CORONET
CENOPRS CREPONS
CENOPRU POUNCER
CENOPSU POUNCES
CENOPSY SYNCOPE
CENOPTY POTENCY
CENOQRU CONQUER
CENORRS CORNERS
SCORNER
CENORRW CROWNER
RECROWN
CENORSS CENSORS
CENORST CORNETS
CENORTU CORNUTE
COUNTER
RECOUNT
TROUNCE
CENORTV CONVERT
CENORTW CROWNET
CENORUV UNCOVER
CENOSSY COYNESS
CENOSTT CONTEST
CENOSTU CONTUSE
CENOSVY CONVEYS
CENOTTX CONTEXT
CENPRTY ENCRYPT
CENRRTU CURRENT
CENRSTU ENCRUST
CENRSUW UNSCREW
CENRTUY CENTURY
CENSSTY ENCYSTS
CEOOPRS COOPERS
SCOOPER
CEOOPRY COOPERY
CEOORSS ROSCOES
CEOORST COOTERS
SCOOTER
CEOORTU ECOTOUR
CEOORTW COWROTE
CEOORVY OVERCOY
CEOOSTY COYOTES
OOCYTES
CEOPPRR CROPPER
CEOPPRS COPPERS
CEOPPRU PRECOUP
CEOPPRY COPPERY
CEOPRRT PORRECT
CEOPRRU PROCURE
CEOPRSS CORPSES
PROCESS
CEOPRST COPTERS
PROSECT
CEOPRSU CROUPES
RECOUPS
CEOPRTT PROTECT
CEOPRUV COVERUP
CEOPSTY COTYPES
CEOQRTU CROQUET
CEOQSTU COQUETS
CEORRSS CROSSER
RECROSS
SCORERS
CEORRST RECTORS
CEORRSU COURSER
SCOURER
CEORRSW CROWERS
CEORRSY SORCERY
CEORRSZ CROZERS
CEORRTU COURTER
CEORRTY RECTORY
CEORSSS CROSSES
CEORSST CORSETS
COSTERS
ESCORTS
SCOTERS
SECTORS

CEORSSU COURSES
SOURCES
SUCROSE
CEORSSW ESCROWS
CEORSTT COTTERS
CEORSTU COUTERS
CROUTES
SCOUTER
CEORSTV CORVETS
COVERTS
VECTORS
CEORTUU COUTURE
CEORTUV CUTOVER
OVERCUT
CEOSSST COSSETS
CEOSSSU SCOUSES
CEOSSSY SYCOSES
CEPPRRU CRUPPER
CEPPRSU CUPPERS
SCUPPER
CEPRRSU SPRUCER
CEPRSSU PERCUSS
SPRUCES
CEPRSSY CYPRESS
CEPRSTU PRECUTS
CEPRSUW SCREWUP
CEPRUUV UPCURVE
CEPSSTU SUSPECT
CERRSSU CURSERS
CERSSSU CUSSERS
CERSSTU CRUSETS
CERSTTU CURTEST
CUTTERS
SCUTTER
CERSTUV CURVETS
CERSTUY CURTESY
CURTSEY
CESSUZZ SCUZZES
CFFGINO COFFING
CFFGINU CUFFING
CFFHINO CHIFFON
CFFIKKO KICKOFF
CFFIKOP PICKOFF
CFFINOS COFFINS
CFFKOOO COOKOFF
CFFNSUU UNCUFFS
CFFOSTU CUTOFFS
OFFCUTS
CFFRSSU SCRUFFS
CFFRSUY SCRUFFY
CFGIINO COIFING
CFGINOR FORCING
CFHINSU FUCHSIN
CFHIOSW COWFISH
CFHORTU FUTHORC
CFIIIVV VIVIFIC
CFIIKNY FINICKY
CFIILNT INFLICT
CFIIMNO OMNIFIC
CFIIMOT MOTIFIC
CFIIMRY MICRIFY
CFIINOT FICTION
CFIINYZ ZINCIFY
CFIIOSS OSSIFIC
CFIKOSS FOSSICK
CFILORS FROLICS
CFILORU FLUORIC
CFIMNOR CONFIRM
CFIMOST COMFITS
CFINORY CORNIFY
CFINOST CONFITS
CFIORSY SCORIFY
CFISSTU FUSTICS
CFKNORU UNFROCK
CFKOTTU FUTTOCK
CFLMRUU FULCRUM
CFLNOUX CONFLUX
CFLNOUY FLOUNCY
CFLOOPW COWFLOP
CFLPSUU CUPFULS
CUPSFUL
CFMNOOR CONFORM
CFMOORT COMFORT
CFNORTU FUNCTOR
CFOSSUU FUSCOUS
CGGGINO COGGING
CGGORSY SCROGGY
CGHHOSU CHOUGHS
CGHIILM MILCHIG
CGHIIMN CHIMING
MICHING
CGHIINN CHINING
INCHING
NICHING
CGHIINT ITCHING

CGHIKNO CHOKING
HOCKING
CGHILPY GLYPHIC
CGHILTY GLITCHY
CGHINNO CHIGNON
CGHINOR CHORING
OCHRING
CGHINOS COSHING
CGHINOU OUCHING
CGHINOW CHOWING
CGHINRU RUCHING
CGHINTU CHUTING
CGHIOST GOTHICS
CGHLOSU CLOUGHS
CGHORUY GROUCHY
CGIIJNU JUICING
CGIIKKN KICKING
CGIIKLN LICKING
CGIIKMM GIMMICK
CGIIKNN NICKING
CGIIKNP PICKING
CGIIKNR RICKING
CGIIKNS SICKING
CGIIKNT TICKING
CGIIKNW WICKING
CGIILLO ILLOGIC
CGIILNO COILING
CGIILNS SLICING
CGIIMNN MINCING
CGIINNO COINING
CGIINNW WINCING
CGIINNZ ZINCING
CGIINOV VOICING
CGIINPR PRICING
CGIINPS SPICING
CGIINRT TRICING
CGIKLNO LOCKING
CGIKLNU LUCKING
CGIKMNO MOCKING
CGIKMNU MUCKING
CGIKNNO CONKING
NOCKING
CGIKNOO COOKING
CGIKNOP POCKING
CGIKNOR CORKING
ROCKING
CGIKNOS SOCKING
CGIKNOY YOCKING
CGIKNPU KINGCUP
CGIKNRU RUCKING
CGIKNSU SUCKING
CGIKNTU TUCKING
CGIKNUY YUCKING
CGILLNU CULLING
CGILMNU CULMING
CGILMNY CYMLING
CGILNNO CLONING
CGILNOO COOLING
LOCOING
CGILNOS CLOSING
CGILNOW COWLING
CGILNOY CLOYING
CGILNRU CURLING
CGILNSY GLYCINS
CGILOOO OOLOGIC
CGILORW COWGIRL
CGILOTT GLOTTIC
CGILPTY GLYPTIC
CGIMNOP COMPING
CGIMNOS COMINGS
CGINNNO CONNING
CGINNNU CUNNING
CGINNOP PONCING
CGINNOR CORNING
CGINNOS CONSIGN
CGINNSY SYNCING
CGINOOP COOPING
CGINOPP COPPING
CGINOPS COPINGS
SCOPING
CGINOPU COUPING
CGINOPY COPYING
CGINORS SCORING
CGINORW CROWING
CGINOSS COSIGNS
CGINOST COSTING
GNOSTIC
CGINOSU CONGIUS
CGINOSV COVINGS
CGINOSW SCOWING
CGINOSY COSYING
CGINOYZ COZYING
CGINPPU CUPPING
CGINRRU CURRING
CGINRSU CURSING
CGINRSY SCRYING

CGINRTU TRUCING
CGINRUV CURVING
CGINSSU CUSSING
CGINTTU CUTTING
CGIOOST COGITOS
CGIOTYZ ZYGOTIC
CGKLNOU GUNLOCK
CGLLOSY GLYCOLS
CGLLSYY GLYCYLS
CGLNOSU UNCLOGS
CGLOOSU COLUGOS
CGNOOSU CONGOUS
CHHIIKS HICKISH
CHHINOR RHONCHI
CHHINTU UNHITCH
CHHNOOS HONCHOS
CHIIKMS KIMCHIS
CHIIKSS SICKISH
CHIILLS CHILLIS
CHIILNT CHITLIN
CHIILOT THIOLIC
CHIILST LITCHIS
CHIILTY ITCHILY
CHIIMST ISTHMIC
CHIIMSU ISCHIUM
CHIINOT THIONIC
CHIINST CHITINS
CHIIOPT OPHITIC
CHIIRRS SCIRRHI
CHIKLLO HILLOCK
CHIKLTY THICKLY
CHIKNOO CHINOOK
CHIKORY HICKORY
CHIKPSU PUCKISH
CHIKRSS SCHRIKS
CHIKSST SCHTIKS
SHTICKS
CHIKSTY KITSCHY
SHTICKY
CHILLMU CHILLUM
CHILLTY LICHTLY
CHILNOR CHLORIN
CHILNSY LYCHNIS
CHILOOS COOLISH
CHILORS ORCHILS
CHILORT TROCHIL
CHILOST COLTISH
CHILPSY SYLPHIC
CHILSTU CULTISH
CHILSUY CUSHILY
CHIMMOR MICROHM
CHIMOPR MORPHIC
CHIMORS CHRISOM
CHIMRRY MYRRHIC
CHIMRSS CHRISMS
CHIMSSS SCHISMS
CHIMSTY CHYMIST
CHINOOR CHORION
CHINOPS CHOPINS
PHONICS
CHINOPY CIPHONY
CHINORS CRONISH
CHINOST CHITONS
CHINOSU CUSHION
CHINQSU SQUINCH
CHINRSU URCHINS
CHINTYZ CHINTZY
CHIOORS ISOCHOR
CHIOORZ CHORIZO
CHIOPRT TROPHIC
CHIOPST PHOTICS
CHIOPXY HYPOXIC
CHIORST OSTRICH
CHIOSSZ SCHIZOS
CHIPRRU CHIRRUP
CHIPRRY PYRRHIC
CHIPSSY PHYSICS
CHIRRSU CURRISH
CHIRSTY CHRISTY
CHISSST SCHISTS
CHISSTU SCHUITS
CHISTTU CHUTIST
CHISYZZ SCHIZZY
CHITTWY TWITCHY
CHKLOSS SHLOCKS
CHKLOSY SHLOCKY
SHYLOCK
CHKMMOO HOMMOCK
CHKMMOU HUMMOCK
CHKMSSU SHMUCKS
CHKNOOS SCHNOOK
CHLMOOS MOLOCHS
CHLMORY CHROMYL
CHLMPSU SCHLUMP
CHLOOSS SCHOOLS
CHLOOST COOLTHS

CHLOPST SPLOTCH
CHLORSS SCHORLS
CHLOSUY CHYLOUS
SLOUCHY
CHLOTYZ ZLOTYCH
CHMOORS CHROMOS
CHMOOSS SCHMOOS
CHMOOSY SMOOCHY
CHMOSUY CHYMOUS
CHMSTUY SMUTCHY
CHNNOOR CHRONON
CHNNOSU NONSUCH
CHNOOPS PONCHOS
CHNOORT TORCHON
CHNORSY SYNCHRO
CHNORTU COTHURN
CHNOSZZ SCHNOZZ
CHNOTUU UNCOUTH
CHNSTUU TUCHUNS
CHOORST COHORTS
CHOORSU OCHROUS
CHOOSST COHOSTS
CHOPSSY PSYCHOS
CHOPTUU TOUCHUP
CHORRSU CHURROS
CHOSSTU SCOUTHS
CHPSSUY SCYPHUS
CIIILLT ILLICIT
ILLITIC
CIIILNV INCIVIL
CIIIMNR CRIMINI
CIIINPT INCIPIT
CIIJLUY JUICILY
CIIKKLL KILLICK
CIIKKMS MISKICK
CIIKNPT NITPICK
CIIKPUW WICKIUP
CIIKSTT STICKIT
CIILLTY LICITLY
CIILLVY CIVILLY
CIILNOP CIPOLIN
PICOLIN
CIILNOS SILICON
CIILNPS INCLIPS
CIILNUV UNCIVIL
CIILNVY VINYLIC
CIILOOT OOLITIC
CIILOPT POLITIC
CIILOST COLITIS
SOLICIT
CIILOTT LITOTIC
CIILPRY PRICILY
CIILPSY SPICILY
CIILSSV SILVICS
CIIMMRY MIMICRY
CIIMNOS MISCOIN
CIIMNRY CRIMINY
CIIMOST MIOTICS
SOMITIC
CIIMOTT MITOTIC
CIIMOTV MOTIVIC
CIIMRST TRISMIC
CIIMSSV CIVISMS
CIIMSTV VICTIMS
CIINNOT NICOTIN
CIINOOT COITION
CIINOPR PORCINI
CIINORS INCISOR
CIINORT NORITIC
CIINQTU QUINTIC
CIINRST CITRINS
CIINRSU RICINUS
CIIORST SORITIC
CIIOSTX COXITIS
CIIOSUV VICIOUS
CIIPRTY PYRITIC
CIIRSTV VITRICS
CIJKORS CROJIKS
CIJNNOO CONJOIN
CIJNOOS COJOINS
CIKKLLO KILLOCK
CIKKOPT TOPKICK
CIKKOTU OUTKICK
CIKKPSU KICKUPS
CIKLLOR ROLLICK
CIKLLSY SLICKLY
CIKLLUY LUCKILY
CIKLMUY MUCKILY
CIKLNRY CRINKLY
CIKLNSU UNSLICK
CIKLOOO OLICOOK
CIKLOPY POCKILY
CIKLOPZ ZIPLOCK
CIKLPRY PRICKLY
CIKLQUY QUICKLY
CIKLRTY TRICKLY

CIKMOOS MISCOOK
CIKMORR RIMROCK
CIKMSSU MUSICKS
CIKMSTU STICKUM
CIKNNOW WINNOCK
CIKNOSW COWSKIN
CIKNPSU UNPICKS
CIKNPSY PYKNICS
CIKNPTU NUTPICK
CIKNSTU UNSTICK
CIKOSTU SICKOUT
CIKPPSU PICKUPS
CIKPSTU STICKUP
UPTICKS
CIKPUWY WICKYUP
CIKRSST STRICKS
CIKRSTY TRICKSY
CILLNOS COLLINS
CILLNOU CULLION
CILLOOR CRIOLLO
CILLRUY CURLILY
CILMNOP COMPLIN
CILMNOS CLONISM
CILMNSY CYMLINS
CILMOOS LOCOISM
CILMSTU CULTISM
CILNOOR ORCINOL
CILNORY CORNILY
LYRICON
CILNOSU UNCOILS
CILNOTU LINOCUT
CILNPSU INSCULP
SCULPIN
UNCLIPS
CILOOPT COPILOT
CILOORU COULOIR
CILOOSS COLOSSI
CILOPRY PYLORIC
CILOPSU OILCUPS
UPCOILS
CILOPSW COWSLIP
CILORST LICTORS
CILOSTU OCULIST
CILPRSY CRISPLY
CILPRTU CULPRIT
CILRRSU SCURRIL
CILRSUY CRUSILY
CILSTTU CULTIST
CIMMNSU CUMMINS
CIMMOSS COSMISM
CIMMOST COMMITS
CIMMOTX COMMIXT
CIMNOOR MORONIC
OMICRON
CIMNORS CRIMSON
MICRONS
CIMNOSU CONIUMS
CIMNRSU CRINUMS
CIMOORT MOTORIC
CIMOOST OSMOTIC
CIMOPSY MISCOPY
CIMOSST COSMIST
SITCOMS
CIMOSSY MYCOSIS
CIMOSTY MYOTICS
CIMOTYZ ZYMOTIC
CIMPRSS SCRIMPS
CIMPRSY SCRIMPY
CIMRSSU CRISSUM
CIMRSUU CURIUMS
CIMSSTU MISCUTS
CIMSSTY MYSTICS
CINNNOU INCONNU
CINNORU UNICORN
CINNOSU NUNCIOS
CINNOTU UNCTION
CINNSUU UNCINUS
CINOOPR PORCINO
CINOOPS OPSONIC
POCOSIN
CINOOSV OVONICS
CINOPRX PRINCOX
CINORRT TRICORN
CINORSS INCROSS
CINORST CISTRON
CITRONS
CORTINS
CINORSZ ZIRCONS
CINORTU RUCTION
CINORTY TYRONIC
CINOSST CONSIST
TOCSINS
CINOSSU COUSINS
CINOSTU SUCTION
CINOSUZ ZINCOUS
CINRSTU INCRUST

CIOOPRT PORTICO
CIOOPSU COPIOUS
CIOOQTU COQUITO
CIOORST OCTROIS
CIOPRST TROPICS
CIOPSTY COPYIST
CIOQRSU CROQUIS
CIORRSU CIRROUS
CIORSSS SCISSOR
CIORSTT TRICOTS
CIORSTU CITROUS
CIORSTV VICTORS
CIORSUU CURIOUS
CIORTVY VICTORY
CIOSSSY SYCOSIS
CIOSSUV VISCOUS
CIOTTUY OUTCITY
CIPRSST SCRIPTS
CIPRSSU PRUSSIC
CIPRTTY TRYPTIC
CIPSTTY STYPTIC
CIRRTTU CRITTUR
CIRSSTU RUSTICS
CIRSTUY CITRUSY
CKKLNUY KNUCKLY
CKLLMOU MULLOCK
CKLLOOP POLLOCK
CKLNOSU UNLOCKS
CKLNOTU LOCKNUT
CKLNUUY UNLUCKY
CKLOORW ROWLOCK
CKLOOTU LOCKOUT
CKLOPSU LOCKUPS
CKLOPTU POTLUCK
CKMOPSU MOCKUPS
CKNOOOR ROCKOON
CKNORSU UNCORKS
CKNSTUU UNSTUCK
        UNTUCKS
CKOOOPT COOKTOP
CKOOOTU COOKOUT
        OUTCOOK
CKOORTU OUTROCK
CKORTUW CUTWORK
CKOSSTU TUSSOCK
CKSSTUU TUSSUCK
CLLMOSU MOLLUSC
CLLOOPS COLLOPS
        SCOLLOP
CLLORSS SCROLLS
CLLOSUU LOCULUS
CLMNOSU COLUMNS
CLMOOPT COMPLOT
CLMOSUU OSCULUM
CLMPRUY CRUMPLY
CLMSUUU CUMULUS
CLNOORT CONTROL
CLNOOSS CONSOLS
CLNOOSU COLONUS
CLNOSSU CONSULS
CLNOSTU CONSULT
CLNRSUU UNCURLS
CLOOPPW COWPLOP
CLOOPST COPLOTS
CLOOPTY POLYCOT
CLOORSU COLOURS
CLOOSTY CYTOSOL
CLOPTUY OCTUPLY
CLORSSY CROSSLY
CLORTUY COURTLY
CLOSSTU LOCUSTS
CLPRSUU UPCURLS
CLPSSTU SCULPTS
CMMNOOS COMMONS
CMNNOOS NONCOMS
CMNOOOT MONOCOT
CMNOOPY COMPONY
CMNOSSY SYNCOMS
CMOOPRT COMPORT
CMOOPST COMPOST
CMOORSU CORMOUS
CMORSTU SCROTUM
CMORTUW CUTWORM
CMOSSTU CUSTOMS
CMPRSUU CUPRUMS
CNNORTU NOCTURN
CNNORUW UNCROWN
CNNOSUY UNSONCY
CNOOOPS POCOSON
CNOOPPR POPCORN
CNOOPSU COUPONS
        SOUPCON
CNOORRW CORNROW
CNOORST CONSORT
        CROTONS
CNOORTT CONTORT
CNOORTU CONTOUR
        CORNUTO
        CROUTON
CNOOSST NOSTOCS
CNOOSTT COTTONS
CNOOSTY TYCOONS
CNOOSUU NOCUOUS
CNOOSVY CONVOYS
CNOOTTY COTTONY
CNORSSU UNCROSS
CNORTUY COUNTRY
COOPRRT PROCTOR
COOPRSS SCROOPS
COOPRTU OUTCROP
COOPSTU COPOUTS
        OCTOPUS
COOPSUY COYPOUS
COORTUW OUTCROW
COOSSTY OOCYSTS
COOSTTY OTOCYST
COPRRTU CORRUPT
COPRSTY CRYPTOS
COPRSUU CUPROUS
COPRTUU UPCOURT
CORRSSU CURSORS
CORRSUY CURSORY
COSTTUU CUTOUTS
DDDDEIL DIDDLED
DDDEEGR DREDGED
DDDEEHS SHEDDED
DDDEEIR DERIDED
DDDEELM MEDDLED
DDDEELP PEDDLED
DDDEELR REDDLED
DDDEELS SLEDDED
DDDEELU DELUDED
DDDEEMO DEMODED
DDDEENS SNEDDED
DDDEENU DENUDED
DDDEFIL FIDDLED
DDDEFLU FUDDLED
DDDEGII GIDDIED
DDDEGIR GRIDDED
DDDEGRU DRUDGED
DDDEHIW WHIDDED
DDDEHLU HUDDLED
DDDEHTU THUDDED
DDDEIIV DIVIDED
DDDEIKS SKIDDED
DDDEILM MIDDLED
DDDEILN DINDLED
DDDEILP PIDDLED
DDDEILR DIDDLER
        RIDDLED
DDDEILS DIDDLES
DDDEILW WIDDLED
DDDEILY DIDDLEY
DDDEIMU MUDDIED
DDDELMU MUDDLED
DDDELNO NODDLED
DDDELOO DOODLED
DDDELOP PLODDED
DDDELOT TODDLED
DDDELPU PUDDLED
DDDELRU RUDDLED
DDDEOPR PRODDED
DDDEORS DODDERS
DDDEORY DODDERY
DDDEPSU SPUDDED
DDDESTU STUDDED
DDEEEFX FEDEXED
DDEEEGR DEGREED
DDEEEIR DEEDIER
DDEEELN NEEDLED
DDEEELT DELETED
DDEEELV DEVELED
DDEEELW WEDELED
DDEEEMN EMENDED
DDEEEPS SPEEDED
DDEEESX DESEXED
DDEEEWY DYEWEED
DDEEFGL FLEDGED
DDEEFII DEIFIED
        EDIFIED
DDEEFIL DEFILED
        FIELDED
DDEEFIN DEFINED
DDEEFNS DEFENDS
DDEEFSU DEFUSED
DDEEFUZ DEFUZED
DDEEGIN DEEDING
        DEIGNED
DDEEGLP PLEDGED
DDEEGLS SLEDGED
DDEEGLU DELUGED
DDEEGRR DREDGER
DDEEGRS DREDGES
DDEEHLS HEDDLES
DDEEHRS SHEDDER
DDEEILM DELIMED
DDEEILR DREIDEL
DDEEILV DEVILED
DDEEILW WIELDED
DDEEILY YIELDED
DDEEIMN DENIMED
DDEEIMP IMPEDED
DDEEIMS DEMISED
        MISDEED
DDEEINS NEDDIES
DDEEINT ENDITED
DDEEINW WIDENED
DDEEINX INDEXED
DDEEINZ DIZENED
DDEEIPS DEPSIDE
DDEEIRR DERIDER
        REDRIED
DDEEIRS DERIDES
        DESIRED
        RESIDED
DDEEIRV DERIVED
DDEEIRW WEIRDED
DDEEIST TEDDIES
DDEEISV DEVISED
DDEELLU DUELLED
DDEELLW DWELLED
DDEELMO MODELED
DDEELMR MEDDLER
DDEELMS MEDDLES
DDEELOW DOWELED
DDEELOY YODELED
DDEELPR PEDDLER
DDEELPS PEDDLES
DDEELRS REDDLES
        SLEDDER
DDEELRT TREDDLE
DDEELRU DELUDER
DDEELSU DELUDES
DDEEMMO MODEMED
DDEEMOT DEMOTED
DDEENNU UNENDED
DDEENOP DEPONED
DDEENOT DENOTED
DDEENOV DOVENED
DDEENOW ENDOWED
DDEENOZ DOZENED
DDEENPS DEPENDS
DDEENPU UPENDED
DDEENRS REDDENS
DDEENRT TRENDED
DDEENRU DENUDER
        ENDURED
DDEENSU DENUDES
        DUDEENS
        DUENDES
DDEEOOR RODEOED
DDEEOPS DEPOSED
        SEEDPOD
DDEEORR ORDERED
DDEEORW DOWERED
DDEEOTV DEVOTED
DDEEOTX DETOXED
DDEEPTU DEPUTED
DDEERRS REDDERS
DDEERSS DRESSED
DDEERST REDDEST
        TEDDERS
DDEERSW WEDDERS
DDEERTU DETRUDE
DDEETTU DUETTED
DDEFILR FIDDLER
DDEFILS FIDDLES
DDEFIOR FOREDID
DDEFIRT DRIFTED
DDEFISU FUDDIES
DDEFLNO FONDLED
DDEFLOO FLOODED
DDEFLSU FUDDLES
DDEFNOR FRONDED
DDEFNOU FONDUED
        FOUNDED
DDEFNSU DEFUNDS
DDEFORS FODDERS
DDEGGRU DRUGGED
        GRUDGED
DDEGHIT DIGHTED
DDEGIIR GIDDIER
DDEGIIS GIDDIES
DDEGILR GIRDLED
        GRIDDLE
DDEGIMO DEMIGOD
DDEGINR GRINDED
        REDDING
DDEGINT TEDDING
DDEGINW WEDDING
DDEGINY EDDYING
DDEGIOR DODGIER
DDEGIRR GRIDDER
DDEGKLU KLUDGED
DDEGLOS DOGSLED
DDEGLSU SLUDGED
DDEGMOO DOGEDOM
DDEGMOS DODGEMS
DDEGMSU SMUDGED
DDEGNOO NOODGED
DDEGNOS GODSEND
DDEGNOU DUDGEON
DDEGORS DODGERS
DDEGORY DODGERY
DDEGOSS GODDESS
DDEGOST STODGED
DDEGRRU DRUDGER
DDEGRSU DRUDGES
DDEGRTU TRUDGED
DDEHIOW HOWDIED
DDEHIRS REDDISH
DDEHIRY HYDRIDE
DDEHLNO HONDLED
DDEHLRU HUDDLER
        HURDLED
DDEHLSU HUDDLES
DDEHNOS HODDENS
        SHODDEN
DDEHNOU HOUNDED
DDEHNRU HUNDRED
DDEHNUZ NUDZHED
DDEHRSU SHUDDER
DDEIIKS KIDDIES
DDEIIMS MIDDIES
DDEIINT INDITED
DDEIINV DIVINED
DDEIIOS IODIDES
        IODISED
DDEIIOX DIOXIDE
DDEIIOZ IODIZED
DDEIIRT DIRTIED
DDEIIRV DIVIDER
DDEIISV DIVIDES
DDEIISW WIDDIES
DDEIIVV DIVVIED
DDEIIZZ DIZZIED
DDEIKLN KINDLED
DDEIKNR KINDRED
DDEIKOS KIDDOES
DDEIKRS KIDDERS
        SKIDDER
DDEILLO DOLLIED
DDEILLR DRILLED
DDEILLU ILLUDED
DDEILMP DIMPLED
DDEILMR MIDDLER
DDEILMS MIDDLES
DDEILNS DINDLES
        SLIDDEN
DDEILNW DWINDLE
        WINDLED
DDEILOS DILDOES
DDEILOT DELTOID
DDEILPR PIDDLER
DDEILPS PIDDLES
DDEILRR RIDDLER
DDEILRS DREIDLS
        RIDDLES
DDEILRT TIDDLER
DDEILSW WIDDLES
DDEILTU DILUTED
DDEILTW TWIDDLE
DDEILTY LYDDITE
DDEIMMU DUMMIED
DDEIMNS MIDDENS
DDEIMNU MUEDDIN
DDEIMOR DERMOID
DDEIMOS DESMOID
DDEIMRU MUDDIER
DDEIMSS DESMIDS
DDEIMSU MUDDIES
DDEINOP POINDED
DDEINOS NODDIES
DDEINOT DENTOID
DDEINOW INDOWED
DDEINPS DISPEND
DDEINRU UNDRIED
DDEINST DISTEND
DDEINSW SWIDDEN
DDEIOOS DOODIES
DDEIORV OVERDID
DDEIORW DOWDIER
DDEIOSS SODDIES
DDEIOST TODDIES
DDEIOSW DOWDIES
DDEIOTT DITTOED
DDEIOWW WIDOWED
DDEIPPR DRIPPED
DDEIPRU UPDRIED
DDEIPUV UPDIVED
DDEIRRS RIDDERS
DDEIRRU RUDDIER
DDEIRSW WIDDERS
DDEISSU DISUSED
DDEISTU STUDDIE
        STUDIED
DDEJRSU JUDDERS
DDEKMOU DUKEDOM
DDEKORU DROUKED
DDELLOR DROLLED
DDELMOU MOULDED
DDELMRU MUDDLER
DDELMSU MUDDLES
DDELNOO NOODLED
DDELNOS NODDLES
DDELOOR DOODLER
        DROOLED
DDELOOS DOODLES
DDELOPR PLODDER
DDELORT TODDLER
DDELOST TODDLES
DDELPRU PUDDLER
DDELPSU PUDDLES
DDELRSU RUDDLES
DDEMMRU DRUMMED
DDEMMSU SMEDDUM
DDEMNOT ODDMENT
DDEMNOU MOUNDED
DDEMRSU MUDDERS
DDENNOR DENDRON
        DONNERD
DDENOOP ENDOPOD
DDENOOS SNOODED
DDENOPS DESPOND
DDENOPU POUNDED
DDENORS NODDERS
DDENORT TRODDEN
DDENORU REDOUND
        ROUNDED
        UNDERDO
DDENORW DROWNED
DDENOSS ODDNESS
        SODDENS
DDENOSU SOUNDED
DDENOSY DYNODES
DDENOUW WOUNDED
DDENSSU SUDDENS
DDEOOPR DROOPED
DDEOORW REDWOOD
DDEOOWY DYEWOOD
DDEOPPR DROPPED
DDEOPRR PRODDER
DDEOPRW DEWDROP
DDEORSW DROWSED
DDEPRSU SPUDDER
DDERRSU RUDDERS
DDGGINO DODGING
        GODDING
DDGHOOO GODHOOD
DDGIIKN KIDDING
DDGIILN LIDDING
DDGIILY GIDDILY
DDGIINR RIDDING
DDGIMNU MUDDING
DDGINNO NODDING
DDGINOP PODDING
DDGINOR RODDING
DDGINOS SODDING
DDGINPU PUDDING
DDGIPUY GIDDYUP
DDGMOOS DOGDOMS
DDGOOOW DOGWOOD
DDHIIKS KIDDISH
DDHIKSU KIDDUSH
DDHINOS HODDINS
DDHIORY HYDROID
DDHIRSY HYDRIDS
DDIIIOO OIDIOID
DDIIKKS DIKDIKS
DDIIKSV KIDVIDS
DDIILOP DIPLOID
DDIIOSX DIOXIDS
        IXODIDS
DDIKOOS SKIDDOO
DDILMUY MUDDILY
DDILNRS DIRNDLS
DDILOWY DOWDILY
DDILRUY RUDDILY
DDILTWY TWIDDLY
DDIMOOS DODOISM
DDIMRSU DIRDUMS
DDIRSSU SIDDURS
DDMMSUU DUMDUMS
DDMNOOR DROMOND
DDNORSW DROWNDS
DDOOOOS DOODOOS
DEEEEWW WEEWEED
DEEEFLR FLEERED
DEEEFLT FLEETED
DEEEFNS DEFENSE
DEEEFRS FEEDERS
        REFEEDS
DEEEFRV FEVERED
DEEEFSX FEDEXES
DEEEGKL GLEEKED
DEEEGLP PLEDGEE
DEEEGLT GLEETED
DEEEGMR DEMERGE
        EMERGED
DEEEGNR GREENED
        RENEGED
DEEEGRS DEGREES
DEEEGRT DETERGE
        GREETED
DEEEGST EGESTED
DEEEHLW WHEEDLE
        WHEELED
DEEEHNS SHEENED
DEEEHPW WHEEPED
DEEEHRS HEEDERS
        HEREDES
        SHEERED
DEEEHST SEETHED
        SHEETED
DEEEHTT TEETHED
DEEEHWZ WHEEZED
DEEEINR NEEDIER
DEEEIRR REEDIER
DEEEIRS SEEDIER
DEEEIRW WEEDIER
DEEEISV DEVISEE
DEEEJLW JEWELED
DEEEJRR JERREED
DEEEJRS JEREEDS
DEEEKLN KNEELED
DEEEKLS SLEEKED
DEEEKMS SMEEKED
DEEEKNW WEEKEND
DEEEKRY REKEYED
DEEEKST STEEKED
DEEELLV LEVELED
DEEELNR NEEDLER
DEEELNS NEEDLES
DEEELPS SPEELED
DEEELPT DEPLETE
DEEELRV LEVERED
        REVELED
DEEELST DELETES
        SLEETED
        STEELED
DEEELSV SLEEVED
DEEELTW TWEEDLE
DEEELTX TELEXED
DEEEMNR EMENDER
        REEDMEN
DEEEMNS DEMESNE
        SEEDMEN
DEEEMRS EMERSED
        REDEEMS
DEEEMRT METERED
DEEENPR PREENED
DEEENPS DEEPENS
DEEENQU QUEENED
DEEENRS NEEDERS
        SNEERED
DEEENRT ENTERED
DEEENRW RENEWED
DEEENSV VENDEES
DEEENSZ SNEEZED
DEEENTT DETENTE
DEEEOTV DEVOTEE
DEEEPRS SPEEDER
        SPEERED
DEEEPRT PETERED
DEEEPST DEEPEST
        STEEPED
DEEEQRU QUEERED
DEEERRV REVERED
DEEERSS RESEEDS
        SEEDERS
DEEERST REESTED
        STEERED
DEEERSV DESERVE
        SEVERED
DEEERSW RESEWED
        SEWERED
        WEEDERS
DEEERSY REDEYES
DEEERTV EVERTED
DEEERTX EXERTED
DEEESSX DESEXES
DEEESTV STEEVED
DEEETTV VEDETTE
DEEETTW TWEETED
DEEETWZ TWEEZED
DEEFFFO FEOFFED
DEEFFIN EFFENDI
DEEFFOR OFFERED
DEEFFST DEFFEST
DEEFFSU EFFUSED
DEEFGIN FEEDING
        FEIGNED
DEEFGLS FLEDGES
DEEFGRU REFUGED
DEEFHLS FLESHED
DEEFHLU HEEDFUL
DEEFHRS FRESHED
DEEFIIR DEIFIER
        EDIFIER
        REIFIED
DEEFIIS DEIFIES
        EDIFIES
DEEFILR DEFILER
        FIELDER
        REFILED
DEEFILS DEFILES
DEEFILT FILETED
DEEFIMS MISFEED
DEEFINR DEFINER
        REFINED
DEEFINS DEFINES
DEEFINT FEINTED
DEEFIRR FERRIED
        REFIRED
        REFRIED
DEEFIRS DEFIERS
        SERIFED
DEEFIRX REFIXED
DEEFIRY REEDIFY
DEEFLLU FUELLED
DEEFLNS FLENSED
DEEFLNU NEEDFUL
DEEFLOT FEEDLOT
DEEFLOY EYEFOLD
DEEFLRU FERULED
DEEFLRY DEERFLY
DEEFLSU DEFUELS
DEEFLTT FETTLED
DEEFMOR FREEDOM
DEEFNRS FENDERS
DEEFNRU UNFREED
DEEFORV OVERFED
DEEFRSU DEFUSER
        REFUSED
DEEFRTT FRETTED
DEEFRTU REFUTED
DEEFSSU DEFUSES
DEEFSTT DEFTEST
DEEFSUZ DEFUZES
DEEGHIN HEEDING
        NEIGHED
DEEGHIR HEDGIER
DEEGHIW WEIGHED
DEEGHOW HOGWEED
DEEGHRS HEDGERS
DEEGIKN DEKEING
DEEGILN DELEING
DEEGILR LEDGIER
DEEGIMN DEEMING
DEEGINN ENGINED
        NEEDING
DEEGINR DREEING
        ENERGID
        REEDING
        REIGNED
DEEGINS SEEDING
DEEGINW WEEDING
DEEGIPW PIGWEED
DEEGIRS SEDGIER
DEEGIRV DIVERGE
        GRIEVED
DEEGIRW WEDGIER
DEEGIST EDGIEST
DEEGISW WEDGIES
DEEGJRU REJUDGE
DEEGKMO GEEKDOM
DEEGLNS LEGENDS
DEEGLNT GENTLED
DEEGLOY GOLDEYE
DEEGLPR PLEDGER

DEEGLPS PLEDGES
DEEGLPT PLEDGET
DEEGLRS GELDERS
LEDGERS
REDLEGS
DEEGLRU GRUELED
REGLUED
DEEGLRW WERGELD
DEEGLSS SLEDGES
DEEGLSU DELUGES
DEEGMRS DEGERMS
DEEGMUW GUMWEED
DEEGNNO ENDOGEN
DEEGNRS GENDERS
DEEGNSU DENGUES
DEEGORR ROGERED
DEEGOSS GESSOED
DEEGOSY GEODESY
DEEGSSU GUESSED
DEEGSTU GUESTED
DEEHIKV KHEDIVE
DEEHINR INHERED
DEEHIRR HERRIED
REHIRED
DEEHIRT DIETHER
DEEHIST HEISTED
DEEHITV THIEVED
DEEHLLO HELLOED
DEEHLLS SHELLED
DEEHLMW WHELMED
DEEHLOV HOVELED
DEEHLPW WHELPED
DEEHLSV SHELVED
DEEHLSW WELSHED
DEEHMNR HERDMEN
DEEHMOR HOMERED
DEEHMUX EXHUMED
DEEHNOY HONEYED
DEEHORS RESHOED
DEEHORV HOVERED
DEEHOSY HOSEYED
DEEHPRS SPHERED
DEEHRRS HERDERS
DEEHRSU USHERED
DEEHRSW SHREWED
DEEHSYY HEYDEYS
DEEHTTW WHETTED
DEEIIRW WEIRDIE
DEEIIST DEITIES
DEEIJLL JELLIED
DEEIJMM JEMMIED
DEEIJTT JETTIED
DEEIKLL KILLDEE
DEEIKLN LIKENED
DEEIKMW MIDWEEK
DEEIKNR REINKED
DEEIKNS ENSKIED
SKEINED
DEEIKOV DOVEKIE
DEEILLS DELLIES
DEEILMS DELIMES
DEEILNO ELOINED
DEEILNR REDLINE
RELINED
DEEILNS ENISLED
ENSILED
LINSEED
DEEILNT LENITED
DEEILNV LIVENED
DEEILNY NEEDILY
DEEILOR REOILED
DEEILOS OILSEED
DEEILPR PERILED
REPLIED
DEEILPS SPEILED
SPIELED
DEEILRS RESILED
DEEILRT RETILED
DEEILRV DELIVER
LIVERED
RELIVED
REVILED
DEEILRW WIELDER
DEEILRY REEDILY
YIELDER
DEEILSS DIESELS
IDLESSE
SEIDELS
DEEILST ISLETED
DEEILSY EYELIDS
SEEDILY
DEEILWY WEEDILY
DEEIMMO MIMEOED
DEEIMMS MISDEEM
DEEIMNR ERMINED
DEEIMNS SIDEMEN

DEEIMOR EMEROID
DEEIMPR DEMIREP
EPIDERM
IMPEDER
DEEIMPS IMPEDES
DEEIMPT EMPTIED
DEEIMRS REMISED
DEEIMRT DEMERIT
DIMETER
MERITED
MITERED
RETIMED
DEEIMRX REMIXED
DEEIMSS DEMISES
DEEIMTT EMITTED
DEEINNS INDENES
DEEINNT DENTINE
DEEINNZ DENIZEN
DEEINPR REPINED
RIPENED
DEEINPW PINWEED
DEEINRR DERNIER
NERDIER
DEEINRS DENIERS
NEREIDS
RESINED
DEEINRW REWIDEN
WIDENER
DEEINRX INDEXER
REINDEX
DEEINST DESTINE
ENDITES
DEEINSV DEVEINS
ENDIVES
DEEINSW ENDWISE
SINEWED
DEEINSX INDEXES
DEEINTT DINETTE
DEEINTU DETINUE
DEEINTV EVIDENT
DEEINWZ WIZENED
DEEIOPS EPISODE
DEEIOPT EPIDOTE
DEEIOPX EPOXIDE
EPOXIED
DEEIORS OREIDES
OSIERED
DEEIPPT PEPTIDE
DEEIPRS PRESIDE
SPEIRED
SPIERED
DEEIPRT PREEDIT
DEEIPRV DEPRIVE
PREDIVE
DEEIPRX EXPIRED
DEEIPSS DESPISE
DEEIPST DESPITE
DEEIQRU QUERIED
DEEIQTU QUIETED
DEEIRRS DERRIES
DESIRER
REDRIES
RESIDER
SERRIED
DEEIRRT RETIRED
RETRIED
TIREDER
DEEIRRV DERIVER
REDRIVE
DEEIRRW REWIRED
WEIRDER
DEEIRSS DESIRES
RESIDES
DEEIRST DIESTER
DIETERS
REEDITS
RESITED
DEEIRSU RESIDUE
UREIDES
DEEIRSV DERIVES
DEVISER
DIVERSE
REVISED
DEEIRSZ RESIZED
DEEIRTU ERUDITE
DEEIRTV RIVETED
DEEIRVV REVIVED
DEEISSU DISEUSE
DEEISSV DEVISES
DEEISTW DEWIEST
DEEISTX EXISTED
DEEITTV VIDETTE
DEEJNOS JONESED
DEEJNOY ENJOYED
DEEKKRT TREKKED
DEEKLLN KNELLED

DEEKLLV KVELLED
DEEKLPS SKELPED
DEEKMNS DESKMEN
DEEKMRS SMERKED
DEEKNOT TOKENED
DEEKNSY ENSKYED
DEEKORV REVOKED
DEEKOVY DOVEKEY
DEEKPRU PERUKED
DEELLMS SMELLED
DEELLNS SNELLED
DEELLPS SPELLED
DEELLQU QUELLED
DEELLRU DUELLER
DEELLRW DWELLER
DEELLRY ELDERLY
DEELLSW SWELLED
DEELMOR MODELER
REMODEL
DEELMPT TEMPLED
DEELMPU DEPLUME
DEELMRS MELDERS
DEELMRU RELUMED
DEELMST SMELTED
DEELMSY MEDLEYS
DEELMTT METTLED
DEELNRS LENDERS
RELENDS
SLENDER
DEELNSS ENDLESS
DEELNST NESTLED
DEELNSW WEDELNS
DEELNSY DENSELY
DEELNTT NETTLED
DEELOOS DOOLEES
DEELOPP PEOPLED
DEELOPR DEPLORE
DEELOPV DEVELOP
DEELOPX EXPLODE
DEELORS RESOLED
DEELORU URODELE
DEELORW LOWERED
ROWELED
DEELORY YODELER
DEELOSU DELOUSE
DEELOTW TOWELED
DEELOVV DEVOLVE
EVOLVED
DEELPRS PEDLERS
DEELPRU PRELUDE
DEELPRY PEDLERY
DEELPST PESTLED
DEELPTT PETTLED
DEELRSS ELDRESS
DEELRSU DUELERS
ELUDERS
DEELRSV DELVERS
DEELRSW REWELDS
WELDERS
DEELRUV VELURED
DEELSSW DEWLESS
DEELSTT SETTLED
DEELSTU TELEDUS
DEELSTW LEWDEST
DEELSUV EVULSED
DEELTUX EXULTED
DEELVXY VEXEDLY
DEEMMST STEMMED
DEEMNOR MODERNE
DEEMNOT DEMETON
DEEMNOU EUDEMON
DEEMNOV VENOMED
DEEMNOY MONEYED
DEEMNRS MENDERS
REMENDS
DEEMNST DEMENTS
DEEMNUW UNMEWED
DEEMORS EMERODS
DEEMORV REMOVED
DEEMORX EXODERM
DEEMOSS DEMOSES
DEEMOST DEMOTES
DEEMOSY MOSEYED
DEEMPRS DEPERMS
PREMEDS
DEEMPTT TEMPTED
DEEMRRU DEMURER
DEEMRSU RESUMED
DEENNOS DONNEES
DEENNOT ENDNOTE
TENONED
DEENNOY DOYENNE
DEENNPT PENDENT
DEENOPS DEPONES
SPONDEE
DEENOPT PENTODE

DEENORS ENDORSE
DEENORT ERODENT
DEENORW ENDOWER
REENDOW
DEENORZ REZONED
DEENOST DENOTES
DEENPPR PERPEND
DEENPRS SPENDER
DEENPRT PRETEND
DEENPSX EXPENDS
DEENRRS RENDERS
DEENRRU ENDURER
DEENRSS REDNESS
RESENDS
SENDERS
DEENRST TENDERS
DEENRSU ENDURES
ENSURED
DEENRSV VENDERS
DEENRTU DENTURE
RETUNED
TENURED
DEENSST DENSEST
DEENSSU DUENESS
DEENSTT DETENTS
DEENSTX EXTENDS
DEENSUV VENDUES
DEENSUW UNSEWED
DEENSUX UNSEXED
DEENUVX UNVEXED
DEEOPPY POPEYED
DEEOPRS DEPOSER
REPOSED
DEEOPRW POWERED
DEEOPSS DEPOSES
SPEEDOS
DEEOPSX EXPOSED
DEEOPXY EPOXYED
DEEORRR ORDERER
REORDER
DEEORRS REREDOS
DEEORRV REDROVE
DEEORST OERSTED
TEREDOS
DEEORSW RESOWED
DEEORSX REDOXES
DEEORTT TETRODE
DEEORTV REVOTED
DEEORTW TOWERED
DEEORUV OVERDUE
DEEORVY OVERDYE
DEEORXX XEROXED
DEEOSTV DEVOTES
DEEOSTX DETOXES
DEEPPPR PREPPED
DEEPPST STEPPED
DEEPPSU SPEEDUP
DEEPRRU PERDURE
DEEPRSS DEPRESS
PRESSED
DEEPRSU PERDUES
PERUSED
SUPERED
DEEPRTU ERUPTED
REPUTED
DEEPRTY RETYPED
DEEPRUV PREVUED
DEEPSTU DEPUTES
DEEQSTU QUESTED
DEERRSS DRESSER
REDRESS
DEERRUV VERDURE
DEERSSS DRESSES
DEERSST DESERTS
DESSERT
TRESSED
DEERSTW STREWED
WRESTED
DEERSVW SWERVED
DEERTTU UTTERED
DEERTUX EXTRUDE
DEESSTT DETESTS
DEESSTV DEVESTS
DEESTTT STETTED
DEFFFLU FLUFFED
DEFFGRU GRUFFED
DEFFHIW WHIFFED
DEFFILP PIFFLED
DEFFILR RIFFLED
DEFFIMO FIEFDOM
DEFFINS SNIFFED
DEFFIOS DIEOFFS
OFFSIDE
DEFFIPS SPIFFED
DEFFIRS DIFFERS
DEFFIST STIFFED

DEFFISU DIFFUSE
DEFFLMU MUFFLED
DEFFLRU RUFFLED
DEFFLSU DUFFELS
DUFFLES
SLUFFED
DEFFNOR FORFEND
DEFFNOS OFFENDS
SENDOFF
DEFFNSU SNUFFED
DEFFOPU POUFFED
DEFFORS DOFFERS
DEFFRSU DUFFERS
DEFFSTU STUFFED
DEFGGIR FRIGGED
DEFGGLO FLOGGED
DEFGGOR FROGGED
DEFGGRU FRUGGED
DEFGINN FENDING
DEFGINR FRINGED
DEFGINU FEUDING
DEFGINY DEFYING
DEFGIOR FIREDOG
DEFGIRS FRIDGES
DEFGIRT GRIFTED
DEFGIRU FIGURED
DEFGIST FIDGETS
DEFGITY FIDGETY
DEFHIRS REDFISH
DEFHIST SHIFTED
DEFHLSU FLUSHED
DEFHOOW WHOOFED
DEFHORT FROTHED
DEFIILM MIDLIFE
DEFIILN INFIDEL
INFIELD
DEFIIMS FIDEISM
DEFIIMW MIDWIFE
DEFIINU UNIFIED
DEFIINX INFIXED
DEFIIST FIDEIST
DEFIKRS FRISKED
DEFILLR FRILLED
DEFILNR FLINDER
DEFILNT FLINTED
DEFILOO FOLIOED
DEFILOW OLDWIFE
DEFILPP FLIPPED
DEFILPU UPFIELD
DEFILRT FLIRTED
TRIFLED
DEFILRU DIREFUL
DEFILST STIFLED
DEFILSU SULFIDE
DEFILTT FLITTED
DEFILTY FETIDLY
DEFILXY FIXEDLY
DEFILZZ FIZZLED
DEFIMOR DEIFORM
DEFIMOW WIFEDOM
DEFINRS FINDERS
FRIENDS
REDFINS
REFINDS
DEFINRU UNFIRED
DEFINSU INFUSED
DEFINSY DENSIFY
DEFINUX UNFIXED
DEFIOOS FOODIES
DEFIOST FOISTED
DEFIPRY PERFIDY
DEFIRRT DRIFTER
DEFIRTT FRITTED
DEFIRTU FRUITED
DEFIRZZ FRIZZED
DEFISTU FEUDIST
DEFKLNU FLUNKED
DEFLLOU DOLEFUL
DEFLMOS SELFDOM
DEFLMPU FLUMPED
DEFLNOO ONEFOLD
DEFLNOR FONDLER
DEFLNOS ENFOLDS
FONDLES
DEFLNOT TENFOLD
DEFLOOR FLOODER
FLOORED
REFLOOD
DEFLOOT FOOTLED
DEFLOOZ FOOZLED
DEFLOPP FLOPPED
DEFLORS FOLDERS
REFOLDS
DEFLORT TELFORD
DEFLORU FLOURED
DEFLOSS FLOSSED

DEFLOTU FLOUTED
DEFLPRU PURFLED
DEFMORS DEFORMS
SERFDOM
DEFNOOR FORDONE
DEFNORT FRONTED
DEFNORU FOUNDER
REFOUND
DEFNORW FROWNED
DEFNOST FONDEST
DEFNOSU FONDUES
DEFNPRU PREFUND
DEFNRSU FUNDERS
REFUNDS
DEFNSUU UNFUSED
DEFOOPR PROOFED
DEFOOPS SPOOFED
DEFOORS FORDOES
DEFORST DEFROST
FROSTED
DEFSSUU DUFUSES
DEGGGIL GIGGLED
DEGGGLO GOGGLED
DEGGGLU GLUGGED
GUGGLED
DEGGHIL HIGGLED
DEGGHIN HEDGING
DEGGHOS SHOGGED
DEGGIJL JIGGLED
DEGGIKN KEDGING
DEGGILN GELDING
NIGGLED
DEGGILW WIGGLED
DEGGINS EDGINGS
DEGGINW WEDGING
DEGGIOR DOGGIER
DEGGIOS DOGGIES
DEGGIPR PRIGGED
DEGGIRS DIGGERS
DEGGIRT TRIGGED
DEGGIRU DRUGGIE
DEGGISW SWIGGED
DEGGITW TWIGGED
DEGGJLO JOGGLED
DEGGJLU JUGGLED
DEGGLOR DOGGREL
DEGGLOS DOGLEGS
SLOGGED
DEGGLOT TOGGLED
DEGGLPU PLUGGED
DEGGLRU GURGLED
DEGGLSU SLUGGED
DEGGNOO DOGGONE
DEGGNOS SNOGGED
DEGGNOU GUDGEON
DEGGNSU SNUGGED
DEGGOPR PROGGED
DEGGORS DOGGERS
DEGGORY DOGGERY
DEGGRRU GRUDGER
DEGGRSU GRUDGES
DEGGRTU DRUGGET
DEGHHIT HIGHTED
THIGHED
DEGHILT DELIGHT
LIGHTED
DEGHINO HONGIED
DEGHINR HERDING
DEGHINW WHINGED
DEGHIOT HOGTIED
DEGHIRT GIRTHED
RIGHTED
DEGHIST SIGHTED
DEGHNOT THONGED
DEGHORU ROUGHED
DEGHOST GHOSTED
DEGHOSU SOUGHED
DEGHOTU OUGHTED
TOUGHED
DEGIILL GILLIED
DEGIILN ELIDING
DEGIINN INDIGEN
DEGIINR DINGIER
DEGIINS DINGIES
DEGIINT DIETING
EDITING
IGNITED
DEGIIPS GIPSIED
DEGIIRR RIDGIER
DEGIJLN JINGLED
DEGIKLO DOGLIKE
GODLIKE
DEGILLR GRILLED
DEGILLU GULLIED
DEGILLY GELIDLY

DEGILMN MELDING
MINGLED
DEGILMS MIDLEGS
DEGILNN LENDING
DEGILNO GLENOID
DEGILNS DINGLES
ENGILDS
SINGLED
DEGILNT GLINTED
TINGLED
DEGILNU DUELING
ELUDING
INDULGE
DEGILNV DELVING
DEGILNW WELDING
DEGILOR GLORIED
GODLIER
DEGILRR GIRDLER
DEGILRS GILDERS
GIRDLES
GLIDERS
REGILDS
RIDGELS
DEGILRU GUILDER
DEGILRW WERGILD
DEGILTZ GLITZED
DEGILUV DIVULGE
DEGIMNN MENDING
DEGIMNO DEMOING
MENDIGO
DEGIMNS SMIDGEN
DEGIMSS SMIDGES
DEGIMST MIDGETS
DEGINNN DENNING
DEGINNP PENDING
DEGINNR GRINNED
RENDING
DEGINNS ENDINGS
SENDING
DEGINNT DENTING
TENDING
DEGINNU ENDUING
DEGINNV VENDING
DEGINNW WENDING
DEGINNY DENYING
DEGINOR ERODING
GROINED
IGNORED
NEGROID
REDOING
DEGINOS DINGOES
DEGINOT INGOTED
DEGINOW WENDIGO
WIDGEON
DEGINRR GRINDER
REGRIND
DEGINRS DINGERS
ENGIRDS
DEGINRU DUNGIER
DEGINRW REDWING
WRINGED
DEGINSS DESIGNS
DEGINST NIDGETS
DEGINSU SUEDING
DEGINSW SWINGED
DEGINSY DINGEYS
DYEINGS
DEGINTU DUETING
DEGINTW TWINGED
DEGINUX EXUDING
DEGIOOS GOODIES
DEGIOPR PODGIER
DEGIORR GRODIER
DEGIPPR GRIPPED
DEGIPRU PUDGIER
DEGIPSY GYPSIED
DEGIRRS GIRDERS
DEGIRSS DIGRESS
DEGIRSU GUIDERS
DEGIRTT GRITTED
DEGISST DIGESTS
DEGISSU GUSSIED
DEGISTW WIDGETS
DEGJLNU JUNGLED
DEGJRSU JUDGERS
DEGKKOR GROKKED
DEGKLSU KLUDGES
DEGKLUY KLUDGEY
DEGLMMO GLOMMED
DEGLMOO GLOOMED
DEGLMOU MOGULED
DEGLNNO ENDLONG
DEGLNOS DONGLES
DEGLNOU LOUNGED
DEGLNPU PLUNGED
PUNGLED

DEGLNSU GULDENS
DEGLNUU UNGLUED
DEGLOPP GLOPPED
DEGLOPR PLEDGOR
DEGLOPS SPLODGE
DEGLORS LODGERS
DEGLORW GROWLED
DEGLOSS GLOSSED
GODLESS
DEGLOST GOLDEST
DEGLOTU GLOUTED
DEGLSSU SLUDGES
DEGLTTU GLUTTED
GUTTLED
DEGLUZZ GUZZLED
DEGMNOO GOODMEN
DEGMOOR GROOMED
DEGMPRU GRUMPED
DEGMSSU SMUDGES
DEGNNOU DUNGEON
DEGNOOS NOODGES
DEGNOPR PRONGED
DEGNOPS SPONGED
DEGNORU GUERDON
UNDERGO
DEGNORW WRONGED
DEGNOTU TONGUED
DEGNRSU GERUNDS
NUDGERS
DEGNRTU GRUNTED
TRUDGEN
DEGNRUU UNURGED
DEGOORV GROOVED
OVERDOG
DEGOOST STOOGED
DEGOPRU GROUPED
DEGORSS GROSSED
DEGORSU DROGUES
GOURDES
GROUSED
DEGORTU GROUTED
DEGOSST STODGES
DEGRRTU TRUDGER
DEGRSTU TRUDGES
DEGSSTU DEGUSTS
DEHHISW WHISHED
DEHHMPU HUMPHED
DEHHSSU SHUSHED
DEHIINN HINNIED
DEHIIRS DISHIER
DEHIKRS SHIRKED
DEHIKSW WHISKED
DEHILLO HILLOED
DEHILLS SHILLED
DEHILMS DISHELM
DEHILOT LITHOED
DEHILPR HIRPLED
DEHILRS HIRSLED
DEHILRT THIRLED
DEHILRW WHIRLED
DEHILSS SHIELDS
DEHIMMS SHIMMED
DEHIMNS MEHNDIS
DEHIMNU INHUMED
DEHIMOR HEIRDOM
DEHIMOT ETHMOID
DEHIMUX HUMIDEX
DEHINNS SHINNED
DEHINNT THINNED
DEHINOP PHONIED
DEHINOR HORDEIN
DEHINOS HOIDENS
DEHINOY HYENOID
DEHINRS HINDERS
NERDISH
SHRINED
DEHINRU UNHIRED
DEHIOOR HOODIER
DEHIOOS HOODIES
DEHIOOT DHOOTIE
DEHIORT THEROID
DEHIOST HOISTED
DEHIOSU HIDEOUS
DEHIOSW HOWDIES
DEHIOTU HIDEOUT
DEHIPPS SHIPPED
DEHIPPW WHIPPED
DEHIRRS SHIRRED
DEHIRRU DHURRIE
HURRIED
DEHIRRW WHIRRED
DEHIRST DITHERS
DEHIRSU HURDIES
DEHIRSV DERVISH
SHRIVED
DEHIRTV THRIVED
DEHIRTW WRITHED
DEHIRTY DITHERY
DEHISSW SWISHED
DEHISTW WHISTED
DEHIWZZ WHIZZED
DEHKNTU THUNKED
DEHLLOO HOLLOED
DEHLLOU HULLOED
DEHLMOU MUDHOLE
DEHLNOS HONDLES
DEHLOOS SHOOLED
DEHLOOT TOEHOLD
DEHLOPP HOPPLED
DEHLORS HOLDERS
DEHLORW WHORLED
DEHLOSS SLOSHED
DEHLRRU HURDLER
DEHLRSU HURDLES
DEHLRTU HURTLED
DEHLSSU SLUSHED
DEHLSTU HUSTLED
DEHMNSU MUDHENS
DEHMOPR MORPHED
DEHMOPW WHOMPED
DEHMORU HUMORED
DEHMOST METHODS
DEHMOTU MOUTHED
DEHMPTU THUMPED
DEHMPUW WHUMPED
DEHMSSU SMUSHED
DEHNNSU SHUNNED
DEHNOOR HONORED
DEHNOOW HOEDOWN
WOODHEN
DEHNOPU UNHOPED
DEHNORS DEHORNS
DEHNORT THORNED
THRONED
DEHNORU HOUNDER
DEHNOSY HOYDENS
DEHNOTZ DOZENTH
DEHNRTU THUNDER
DEHNSTU SHUNTED
DEHNSUZ NUDZHES
DEHOOPT PHOTOED
DEHOOPW WHOOPED
DEHOOST SOOTHED
DEHOOSW WOOSHED
DEHOOTT TOOTHED
DEHOPPS SHOPPED
DEHOPPW WHOPPED
DEHORST DEHORTS
SHORTED
DEHORTT TROTHED
DEHORTW WORTHED
DEHOSTT SHOTTED
DEHOSTU SHOUTED
SOUTHED
DEHPPUW WHUPPED
DEHPSSY PHYSEDS
DEIIJMM JIMMIED
DEIIKKL KIDLIKE
DEIIKLS DISLIKE
DEIIKNR DINKIER
DEIIKNS DINKIES
DEIILLS DILLIES
DEIILLW WILLIED
DEIILMN MIDLINE
DEIILMP IMPLIED
DEIILMT DELIMIT
LIMITED
DEIILNS LINDIES
DEIILOS DOILIES
IDOLISE
DEIILOZ IDOLIZE
DEIILPS LIPIDES
DEIIMMX IMMIXED
DEIIMNO DOMINIE
DEIIMRT TIMIDER
DEIIMST MISEDIT
STIMIED
DEIIMSZ MIDSIZE
DEIINOS IODINES
IONISED
DEIINOT EDITION
DEIINOZ IONIZED
DEIINRS INSIDER
DEIINRT INDITER
NITRIDE
DEIINRU URIDINE
DEIINRV DIVINER
DEIINRW WINDIER
DEIINSS INSIDES
DEIINST INDITES
TINEIDS
DEIINSV DIVINES
DEIINTV INVITED
DEIIORT DIORITE
DEIIORZ IODIZER
DEIIOSS IODISES
DEIIOSX OXIDISE
DEIIOSZ IODIZES
DEIIOXZ OXIDIZE
DEIIPPR DIPPIER
DEIIPRT RIPTIDE
TIDERIP
DEIIRRT DIRTIER
DEIIRST DIRTIES
DITSIER
TIDIERS
DEIIRTX EDITRIX
DEIIRTZ DITZIER
DEIIRVV VIVIDER
DEIIRZZ DIZZIER
DEIISTT DITTIES
TIDIEST
DEIISTV VISITED
DEIISVV DIVVIES
DEIISZZ DIZZIES
DEIJLLO JOLLIED
DEIJNOR JOINDER
DEIJNOT JOINTED
DEIJNRU INJURED
DEIJORY JOYRIDE
DEIJOST JOISTED
DEIJRRS JERRIDS
DEIJTTU JUTTIED
DEIKKNS SKINKED
DEIKLLS SKILLED
DEIKLNP PLINKED
DEIKLNR KINDLER
DEIKLNS KINDLES
SLINKED
DEIKLNT TINKLED
DEIKLNU UNLIKED
DEIKLNW WINKLED
DEIKLOP PODLIKE
DEIKLOR RODLIKE
DEIKLOS KELOIDS
DEIKLRS SKIRLED
DEIKLRT KIRTLED
DEIKLTT KITTLED
DEIKMMS SKIMMED
DEIKMPS SKIMPED
DEIKMRS SMIRKED
DEIKNNS SKINNED
DEIKNOS DOESKIN
DEIKNOV INVOKED
DEIKNPR PRINKED
DEIKNRR DRINKER
DEIKNST KINDEST
DEIKNSW SWINKED
DEIKNSY DINKEYS
KIDNEYS
DEIKNTT KNITTED
DEIKORR DORKIER
DEIKOSY DISYOKE
DEIKPPS SKIPPED
DEIKQRU QUIRKED
DEIKRRS SKIRRED
DEIKRST SKIRTED
DEIKRSU DUIKERS
DUSKIER
DEIKSVY SKYDIVE
DEILLMU ILLUMED
DEILLNW INDWELL
DEILLOS DOLLIES
DEILLPR PRILLED
DEILLPS SPILLED
DEILLQU QUILLED
DEILLRR DRILLER
REDRILL
DEILLRT TRILLED
DEILLSS LIDLESS
DEILLST STILLED
DEILLSU ILLUDES
SULLIED
DEILLSW SWILLED
DEILLTW TWILLED
DEILMMS SLIMMED
DEILMNS MILDENS
DEILMOP IMPLODE
DEILMOR MOLDIER
DEILMOS MELOIDS
MIDSOLE
DEILMOY MYELOID
DEILMPP PIMPLED
DEILMPR RIMPLED
DEILMPS DIMPLES
MISPLED
DEILMPW WIMPLED
DEILMST MILDEST
DEILMSW MILDEWS
DEILMWY MILDEWY
DEILMXY MIXEDLY
DEILMZZ MIZZLED
DEILNNS LINDENS
DEILNNU UNLINED
DEILNOO EIDOLON
DEILNOS INDOLES
DEILNOT LENTOID
DEILNOU UNOILED
DEILNPP NIPPLED
DEILNPS SPINDLE
SPLINED
DEILNPU UNPILED
DEILNRT TENDRIL
TRINDLE
DEILNST DENTILS
DEILNSW SWINDLE
WINDLES
DEILNSY SNIDELY
DEILNTU DILUENT
DEILNTW INDWELT
WINTLED
DEILNUV UNLIVED
DEILOOS DOOLIES
DEILOPR LEPORID
DEILOPS DESPOIL
DIPLOES
DIPOLES
SPOILED
DEILOPT PILOTED
DEILOPU EUPLOID
DEILORS SOLDIER
SOLIDER
DEILOSY DOYLIES
DEILOTU TOLUIDE
DEILPPR RIPPLED
DEILPPS SLIPPED
DEILPPT TIPPLED
DEILPPU UPPILED
DEILPRT TRIPLED
DEILPSS DISPELS
DEILPTY TEPIDLY
DEILQTU QUILTED
DEILRSS SIDLERS
SLIDERS
DEILRSV DRIVELS
DEILRSW SWIRLED
WILDERS
DEILRSY RIDLEYS
DEILRTU DILUTER
DEILRTW TWIRLED
DEILRTY TIREDLY
DEILRVY DEVILRY
DEILRWY WEIRDLY
DEILRZZ DRIZZLE
DEILSST DELISTS
DEILSTT SLITTED
STILTED
DEILSTU DILUTES
DUELIST
DEILSTW WILDEST
DEILSUV DIVULSE
DEILSZZ SIZZLED
DEILTTV VITTLED
DEILZZZ ZIZZLED
DEIMMMU MUMMIED
DEIMMPR PRIMMED
DEIMMRS DIMMERS
DEIMMRT MIDTERM
TRIMMED
DEIMMRU IMMURED
DEIMMST DIMMEST
DEIMMSU DUMMIES
MEDIUMS
DEIMNNU MINUEND
UNMINED
DEIMNOP IMPONED
DEIMNOR MINORED
DEIMNOS DOMINES
EMODINS
MISDONE
DEIMNPS IMPENDS
DEIMNRS MINDERS
REMINDS
DEIMNRU UNRIMED
DEIMNSS DIMNESS
MISSEND
DEIMNST MINDSET
MISTEND
DEIMNTU MINUTED
MUTINED
UNTIMED
DEIMNUX UNMIXED
DEIMOOR DOOMIER
MOIDORE
MOODIER
DEIMOPS IMPOSED
DEIMORR REMORID
DEIMORS MISDOER
DEIMOSS MISDOES
DEIMOST DISTOME
MODISTE
DEIMOTT OMITTED
DEIMOTV MOTIVED
VOMITED
DEIMPPR PRIMPED
DEIMPRU DUMPIER
UMPIRED
DEIMPTU IMPUTED
DEIMRSW MISDREW
DEIMRSY SEMIDRY
DEIMRUU UREDIUM
DEIMSSU MISUSED
DEIMSTU TEDIUMS
DEIMSTY STYMIED
DEINNOT INTONED
DEINNRS DINNERS
ENDRINS
DEINNRU INURNED
DEINNST DENTINS
INDENTS
INTENDS
DEINNSU UNDINES
DEINNSW ENWINDS
DEINNSY DYNEINS
DEINNTU DUNNITE
DEINNTW TWINNED
DEINOOZ OZONIDE
DEINOPT POINTED
DEINOQU QUOINED
DEINORS DINEROS
INDORSE
ORDINES
ROSINED
SORDINE
DEINORU DOURINE
NEUROID
DEINORW DOWNIER
DEINPPS SNIPPED
DEINPRS PINDERS
DEINPRT PRINTED
DEINPST DIPNETS
STIPEND
DEINRST TINDERS
DEINRSU INSURED
DEINRSV VERDINS
DEINRSW REWINDS
WINDERS
DEINRTT TRIDENT
DEINRTU INTRUDE
TURDINE
UNTIRED
UNTRIED
DEINRTX DEXTRIN
DEINRTY TINDERY
DEINSST DISSENT
SNIDEST
DEINSSU NIDUSES
DEINSTT DENTIST
DISTENT
STINTED
DEINSTU DUNITES
DEINSTY DENSITY
DESTINY
DEINSUZ UNSIZED
DEIOORS OROIDES
DEIOORW WOODIER
DEIOORZ ODORIZE
DEIOOSS ISODOSE
DEIOOST OSTEOID
DEIOOSW WOODIES
DEIOOSZ DOOZIES
DEIOPPP POPPIED
DEIOPRS PERIODS
DEIOPRT DIOPTER
DIOPTRE
PERIDOT
PROTEID
DEIOPRV PROVIDE
DEIOPRX PEROXID
DEIOPSS DISPOSE
DEIOPST DEPOSIT
DOPIEST
PODITES
POSITED
SOPITED
TOPSIDE
DEIOPTT TIPTOED
DEIOPTV PIVOTED
DEIOQTU QUOITED
DEIORRW ROWDIER
WORDIER
WORRIED
DEIORSS DOSSIER
DEIORST EDITORS
SORTIED
STEROID
STORIED
TRIODES
DEIORSV DEVISOR
DEVOIRS
VISORED
VOIDERS
DEIORSW DOWRIES
ROWDIES
WEIRDOS
DEIORTT DOTTIER
DEIORTU OUTRIDE
DEIORVZ VIZORED
DEIORWW WIDOWER
DEIOSTT DOTIEST
DEIOSTU OUTSIDE
TEDIOUS
DEIOSTZ DOZIEST
DEIOSUV DEVIOUS
DEIOTUV OUTVIED
DEIOTUW WIDEOUT
DEIPPQU QUIPPED
DEIPPRR DRIPPER
DEIPPRS DIPPERS
DEIPPRT TRIPPED
DEIPPST PEPTIDS
DEIPRSS PRISSED
SPIDERS
DEIPRST SPIRTED
STRIPED
DEIPRSU SIRUPED
UPDRIES
DEIPRSY SPIDERY
DEIPSSU UPSIDES
DEIPSSV VESPIDS
DEIPSTT SPITTED
DEIPSTU DISPUTE
DEIPSUV UPDIVES
DEIPSUZ UPSIZED
DEIPSXY PYXIDES
DEIPTTU PUTTIED
DEIQRSU SQUIRED
DEIQRTU QUIRTED
DEIQTTU QUITTED
DEIQUZZ QUIZZED
DEIRRST STIRRED
STRIDER
DEIRRSU DURRIES
DEIRRSV DRIVERS
DEIRSST DISSERT
STRIDES
DEIRSSU DISEURS
SUDSIER
DEIRSTU DUSTIER
STUDIER
DEIRSTV DIVERTS
STRIVED
DEISSST DESISTS
DEISSSU DISUSES
DEISSTU STUDIES
TISSUED
DEISSTV DIVESTS
DEISTTW TWISTED
DEITTTW TWITTED
DEJLOST JOSTLED
DEJLSTU JUSTLED
DEJOORY JOYRODE
DEJOSTU JOUSTED
DEKKLSU SKULKED
DEKKNSU SKUNKED
DEKLLNO KNOLLED
DEKLLSU SKULLED
DEKLNOP PLONKED
DEKLNPU PLUNKED
DEKLNRU KNURLED
RUNKLED
DEKNNOS NONSKED
DEKNNRU DRUNKEN
DEKNOOS SNOOKED
DEKNOPP KNOPPED
DEKNOSY DONKEYS
DEKNOTT KNOTTED
DEKNOTU KNOUTED
DEKNOUY UNYOKED
DEKNPSU SPUNKED
DEKNRRU DRUNKER
DEKNRSU DUNKERS
DEKNRTU TRUNKED
DEKOOPS SPOOKED
DEKOOST STOOKED
DEKOOTW KOTOWED
DEKOPST DESKTOP
DEKORST STROKED
DEKORWY KEYWORD
DEKOSVY SKYDOVE
DEKPRSU PREDUSK
DELLOOW WOOLLED
DELLOPR REDPOLL
DELLORR DROLLER
DELLORT TROLLED
DELLOSU DUELLOS
DELLRWY DRYWELL
DELLSTU DULLEST
DELMMSU SLUMMED
DELMNOS DOLMENS
DELMOPR PREMOLD
DELMORS MOLDERS
REMOLDS
SMOLDER
DELMORU MOULDER
DELMOSU MODULES
DELMOTT MOTTLED
DELMOTU MOULTED
DELMOUV VOLUMED
DELMPPU PLUMPED
DELMPRU RUMPLED
DELMPSU SLUMPED
DELMTUY MUTEDLY
DELMUZZ MUZZLED
DELNOOS NOODLES
SNOOLED
DELNORS RONDELS
DELNORU ROUNDEL
DELNOSS OLDNESS
DELNOSU LOUDENS
NODULES
DELNOSZ DONZELS
DELNOTW LETDOWN
DELNOTY NOTEDLY
DELNOUV UNLOVED
DELNPRU PLUNDER
DELNRSU RUNDLES
DELNRTU RUNDLET
TRUNDLE
DELNRUU UNRULED
DELNSSU DULNESS
DELNUZZ NUZZLED
DELOOPP PLEOPOD
DELOOPS POODLES
SPOOLED
DELOORT ROOTLED
DELOOST STOOLED
TOLEDOS
DELOOSW DEWOOLS
DELOOTT TOOTLED
DELOPPP PLOPPED
POPPLED
DELOPPS SLOPPED
DELOPPT TOPPLED
DELOPPY POLYPED
DELOPRS POLDERS
PRESOLD
DELOPRT DROPLET
PRETOLD
DELOPRW PROWLED
DELOPSY DEPLOYS
DELOPTT PLOTTED
DELOPTZ PLOTZED
DELORRY ORDERLY
DELORSS DORSELS
RODLESS
SOLDERS
DELORST OLDSTER
DELORSW WELDORS
DELORSY YODLERS
DELORTT DOTTREL
DELORUV LOUVRED
DELOSSS DOSSELS
DELOSTT DOTTELS
DOTTLES
SLOTTED
DELOSTU LOUDEST
TOUSLED
DELOSYY DOYLEYS
DELOSZZ SOZZLED
DELOTUU OUTDUEL
DELOTUV VOLUTED
DELOTUZ TOUZLED
DELPPRU PURPLED
DELPPSU SUPPLED
DELPRSU SLURPED
DELPUZZ PUZZLED
DELRRSU SLURRED

DELRSTU LUSTRED
RUSTLED
STRUDEL
DELRTTU TURTLED
DELSSTU TUSSLED
DEMMRRU DRUMMER
DEMMSTU STUMMED
DEMNOOR DOORMEN
DEMNOOW WOODMEN
DEMNORS MODERNS
RODSMEN
DEMNORT MORDENT
DEMNORU MOURNED
DEMNOST ENDMOST
DEMNOSU MENUDOS
DEMNOTU DEMOUNT
MOUNTED
DEMNOUV UNMOVED
DEMNSTU DUSTMEN
DEMOOPP POPEDOM
DEMOOPR PROMOED
DEMOORT MOTORED
DEMOORV VROOMED
DEMOOSS OSMOSED
DEMOOTU OUTMODE
DEMOPRT TROMPED
DEMOPST STOMPED
DEMORRS DORMERS
DEMORRU RUMORED
DEMORST STORMED
DEMORSW DEWORMS
DEMOSSU MOUSSED
DEMOSTY MODESTY
DEMPRSU DUMPERS
DEMPRTU TRUMPED
DEMPSTU STUMPED
DEMRRSU MURDERS
DEMSTTU SMUTTED
DENNORT DONNERT
DENNOST TENDONS
DENNOTU UNNOTED
DENNOUW ENWOUND
UNOWNED
DENNOUZ UNZONED
DENNSSU DUNNESS
DENNSTU DUNNEST
STUNNED
DENNTUU UNTUNED
DENOOPS SNOOPED
SPOONED
DENOOST SNOOTED
DENOOSW SWOONED
DENOOSZ SNOOZED
DENOOTU DUOTONE
OUTDONE
DENOOUW UNWOOED
DENOPPR PROPEND
DENOPRS PERNODS
PONDERS
RESPOND
DENOPRT PORTEND
PROTEND
DENOPRU POUNDER
UNROPED
DENOPSU UNPOSED
DENOPUX EXPOUND
DENORRS DRONERS
DENORRU RONDURE
ROUNDER
DENORRW DROWNER
DENORSS SONDERS
DENORST RODENTS
SNORTED
DENORSU ENDUROS
RESOUND
SOUNDER
UNDOERS
DENORSV VENDORS
DENORSW DOWNERS
WONDERS
DENORUW REWOUND
DENOSTU SNOUTED
DENOSUW SWOUNED
UNSOWED
DENPRSU SPURNED
DENPRTU PRUDENT
UPTREND
DENPSSU SENDUPS
SUSPEND
UPSENDS
DENRSSU SUNDERS
UNDRESS
DENRSSY DRYNESS
DENRSTU UNDREST
DENSSTY SYNDETS
DENSSUW SUNDEWS
DENSTTU STUDENT
STUNTED
DENTUVY DUVETYN
DEOOPPS OPPOSED
DEOOPRS SPOORED
DEOOPRT TORPEDO
TROOPED
DEOOPST STOOPED
DEOOPSW SWOOPED
WOOPSED
DEOORRT REDROOT
DEOORST ROOSTED
DEOORSZ DOOZERS
DEOORTU OUTDOER
OUTRODE
DEOOSTU OUTDOES
DEOPPPR PROPPED
DEOPPRR DROPPER
DEOPPST STOPPED
DEOPPSW SWOPPED
DEOPRRS DORPERS
DEOPRRU PROUDER
DEOPRST DEPORTS
REDTOPS
SPORTED
DEOPRSW POWDERS
DEOPRTU TROUPED
DEOPRWY POWDERY
DEOPSST DESPOTS
DEOPSSU PSEUDOS
SPOUSED
DEOPSTT SPOTTED
DEOPSTU OUTSPED
SPOUTED
DEOQRTU TORQUED
DEORRSS DORSERS
DEORRSU ORDURES
DEORRSV DROVERS
DEORRSW REWORDS
DEORRVY OVERDRY
DEORSSS DOSSERS
DROSSES
DEORSSU DOUSERS
DEORSSW DOWSERS
DROWSES
DEORSTT DOTTERS
DEORSTU DETOURS
DOUREST
REDOUTS
ROUSTED
DEORSTW STROWED
WORSTED
DEORSTY DESTROY
STROYED
DEORSUV DEVOURS
DEORTTT TROTTED
DEORTTU TUTORED
DEORTUW OUTDREW
DEOSSYY ODYSSEY
DEOSTTT STOTTED
DEOSTTU TESTUDO
DEOSTTW SWOTTED
DEOSTUU DUTEOUS
DEOSTUX TUXEDOS
DEOTTUY TUTOYED
DEPRRSU SPURRED
DEPRRUY PRUDERY
DEPRSTU SPURTED
DEPRSUU PURSUED
USURPED
DEPRSUY SYRUPED
DERSSSU SUDSERS
DERSSTU DUSTERS
TRUSSED
DERSTTU TRUSTED
DERSTTY TRYSTED
DERSTUU SUTURED
DERSTUY RESTUDY
DFFGINO DOFFING
DFFIIMR MIDRIFF
DFFOSTU DUSTOFF
DFGGIIN FIDGING
DFGGINU FUDGING
DFGGOOS FOGDOGS
DFGHIOS DOGFISH
DFGIINN FINDING
DFGIINY DIGNIFY
DFGILNO FOLDING
DFGINNO FONDING
DFGINNU FUNDING
DFGINOR FORDING
DFGINOU FUNGOID
DFHILSU DISHFUL
DFHIMSU MUDFISH
DFILLUY FLUIDLY
DFILMMO FILMDOM
DFILMNU MINDFUL
DFILNOP PINFOLD
DFILNOS INFOLDS
DFILORT TRIFOLD
DFILORU FLUORID
DFILOSX SIXFOLD
DFILSSU SULFIDS
DFILTUU DUTIFUL
DFINOTU OUTFIND
DFLMOOU DOOMFUL
DFLMOUW MUDFLOW
DFLNOSU UNFOLDS
DFLOORU ODORFUL
DFLOOTU FOLDOUT
DFLOOTW TWOFOLD
DFLOPSU FOLDUPS
UPFOLDS
DFNNOOO NONFOOD
DFNNOUU UNFOUND
DFNORUY FOUNDRY
DFOORSX OXFORDS
DGGGIIN DIGGING
DGGGINO DOGGING
DGGHIOS DOGGISH
DGGIILN GILDING
GLIDING
DGGIINN DINGING
DGGIINR GIRDING
GRIDING
RIDGING
DGGIINU GUIDING
DGGIJNU JUDGING
DGGILNO GODLING
LODGING
DGGINNU DUNGING
NUDGING
DGGNOSU DUGONGS
GUNDOGS
DGHIILN HILDING
DGHIINS DISHING
HIDINGS
SHINDIG
DGHILNO HOLDING
DGHINOO HOODING
DGHINOR HORDING
DGHINTU HINDGUT
DGHIOOS GOODISH
DGHIOPS GODSHIP
DGHOOST HOTDOGS
DGHORTU DROUGHT
DGHOTUY DOUGHTY
DGIIKNN DINKING
DGIIKNR DIRKING
DGIIKNS DISKING
DGIILMN MILDING
DGIILNO LOIDING
DGIILNR DIRLING
DGIILNS SIDLING
SLIDING
DGIILNW WILDING
DGIILNY DINGILY
DGIILRS RIDGILS
DGIILRY RIGIDLY
DGIIMMN DIMMING
DGIIMNN MINDING
DGIIMNS SMIDGIN
DGIIMOS SIGMOID
DGIINNN DINNING
DGIINNT DINTING
DGIINNU INDUING
DGIINNW DWINING
WINDING
DGIINOS INDIGOS
DGIINOV VOIDING
DGIINOW WINDIGO
DGIINOX DIGOXIN
DGIINPP DIPPING
DGIINPR PRIDING
DGIINPS PIDGINS
DGIINPU PINGUID
DGIINRS RIDINGS
DGIINRV DRIVING
DGIINSS DISSING
SIDINGS
DGIINST TIDINGS
DGIINTY DIGNITY
TIDYING
DGIKMNO KINGDOM
DGIKNNU DUNKING
DGIKNSU DUSKING
DGILLNO DOLLING
DGILLNU DULLING
DGILLOY GODLILY
DGILMNO MOLDING
DGILNOR LORDING
DGILNOY YODLING
DGILOPY PODGILY
DGILOST DIGLOTS
DGILPUY PUDGILY
DGIMNOO DOOMING
DGIMNPU DUMPING
DGIMOPY PYGMOID
DGIMSTU MIDGUTS
DGINNNO DONNING
DGINNNU DUNNING
DGINNOP PONDING
DGINNOR DRONING
DGINNOU UNDOING
DGINNOW DOWNING
DGINNRU DURNING
DGINNTU DUNTING
DGINNUY UNDYING
DGINOOW WOODING
DGINOPS DOPINGS
PONGIDS
DGINORV DROVING
DGINORW WORDING
DGINOSS DOSSING
DGINOSU DOUSING
GUIDONS
DGINOSW DOWSING
DGINOTT DOTTING
DGINPPU DUPPING
DGINRSU UNGIRDS
DGINSSU SUDSING
DGINSTU DUSTING
DGIOPRY PRODIGY
DGIOSTW GODWITS
DGIPRSU UPGIRDS
DGISSTU DISGUST
DGLNORU GOLDURN
DGLNOUY UNGODLY
DGLOOOW LOGWOOD
DGLOOSU DUOLOGS
DGMOOUW GUMWOOD
DGMOPRU GUMDROP
DGNNORU NONDRUG
DGNOOOR GODROON
DGNOORS DRONGOS
DGNOOSS GODSONS
DGNOOSW GODOWNS
DGNORSU GROUNDS
DGNOSSU SUNDOGS
DGOORTT DOGTROT
DGOPRRU PRODRUG
DGOSTUU DUGOUTS
DHIILOT DITHIOL
LITHOID
DHIILSW WILDISH
DHIIMNO HOMINID
DHIIMPS MIDSHIP
DHIINRU HIRUDIN
DHIIOPX XIPHOID
DHIIORZ RHIZOID
DHIIOST HISTOID
DHIKSSU DUSKISH
DHILLOS DOLLISH
DHILLSU DULLISH
DHILMUY HUMIDLY
DHILNOP DOLPHIN
DHILOST DOLTISH
DHILOSU LOUDISH
DHILPSU SULPHID
DHILPSY SYLPHID
DHILRTY THIRDLY
DHIMOPR DIMORPH
DHIMORU HUMIDOR
RHODIUM
DHIMOSS MISSHOD
DHIMPSU DUMPISH
DHINNOS DONNISH
DHINOPY HYPNOID
DHINORS DRONISH
DHINSSY SHINDYS
DHINSTU TUNDISH
DHIOOST DHOOTIS
DHIOPTY PHYTOID
TYPHOID
DHIORTY THYROID
DHIPRSU PRUDISH
DHIPRSY SYRPHID
DHJOPRU JODHPUR
DHKORSY DROSHKY
DHLMOOU HOODLUM
DHLOOTU HOLDOUT
DHLOPSU HOLDUPS
UPHOLDS
DHMMRUU HUMDRUM
DHMNOYY HYMNODY
DHNOOOS SONHOOD
DHNOOSU UNHOODS
DHOOOOS HOODOOS
DHOORST HOTRODS
DHOPRSU PUSHROD
DHOPRSY HYDROPS
DHORSSU SHROUDS
DHORSTU DROUTHS
DHORSUY HYDROUS
DHORTUY DROUTHY
DHORXYY HYDROXY
DIIIMOS SIMIOID
DIIIMRU IRIDIUM
DIIINPS INSIPID
DIIJNOS DISJOIN
DIIKKNS KIDSKIN
DIILLST DISTILL
DIILLVY LIVIDLY
DIILMNS DISLIMN
DIILMOO MODIOLI
DIILMOS IDOLISM
DIILMST MIDLIST
DIILMTY TIMIDLY
DIILNNU INDULIN
DIILNOT TOLIDIN
DIILNWY WINDILY
DIILNXY XYLIDIN
DIILOPS LIPOIDS
DIILQSU LIQUIDS
DIILRSU SILURID
DIILRTY DIRTILY
DIILSST DISTILS
DIILSTY IDYLIST
DIILVVY VIVIDLY
DIILYZZ DIZZILY
DIIMNOR MIDIRON
DIIMNSU INDIUMS
DIIMOSS IODISMS
DIIMSSS DISMISS
DIIMSTW DIMWITS
DIINNSW INWINDS
DIINOQU QUINOID
DIINORS SORDINI
DIINORT DINITRO
DIINOSX DIOXINS
DIINRST NITRIDS
DIIOOPS OPIOIDS
DIIOPRS SPIROID
DIIORSV DIVISOR
VIROIDS
DIIORTX TRIOXID
DIITUVY VIDUITY
DIJMSSU MUSJIDS
DIJOSTU JUDOIST
DIKLSUY DUSKILY
DIKMNSU DINKUMS
DIKNNOS NONSKID
DIKNNSU NUDNIKS
DIKNOOW INKWOOD
DIKOOSS SKIDOOS
DILLMSU MUDSILL
DILLOSY SOLIDLY
DILLPSY PSYLLID
DILLRUY LURIDLY
DILMNRU DRUMLIN
DILMOOY DOOMILY
MOODILY
DILMORS MILORDS
DILMPUY DUMPILY
DILMTUY TUMIDLY
DILNNSU DUNLINS
DILNOOS OODLINS
DILNOPT DIPLONT
DILNOSU UNSOLID
DILNOXY INDOXYL
DILNPSY SPINDLY
DILNSTU INDULTS
DILORTU DILUTOR
DILORWY ROWDILY
WORDILY
DILOSSS DOSSILS
DILOSSU SOLIDUS
DILOSTU TOLUIDS
DILOSTY STYLOID
DILOTTY DOTTILY
DILRYZZ DRIZZLY
DILSTUY DUSTILY
DIMMOST MIDMOST
DIMNNOO MIDNOON
DIMNOOS DOMINOS
DIMNOPU IMPOUND
DIMNORS DORMINS
NIMRODS
DIMNOTW MIDTOWN
DIMNSSU NUDISMS
DIMOPSU PODIUMS
DIMORSW MISWORD
DIMOSSU SODIUMS
DIMOSSW WISDOMS
DIMOSTU DIMOUTS
DIMRTUU TRIDUUM
DIMRUUV DUUMVIR
DINNOPR NONDRIP
DINNOUW INWOUND
DINNSUW UNWINDS
DINOORS INDOORS
SORDINO
DINOPSU UNIPODS
DINORSU DIURONS
DURIONS
DINORWW WINDROW
DINOSSW DISOWNS
DINOSWW WINDOWS
DINOTUW OUTWIND
DINOWWY WINDOWY
DINPSTU PUNDITS
DINPSUW UPWINDS
WINDUPS
DINSSTU NUDISTS
DIOOPRS SPOROID
DIOOPSS ISOPODS
DIOORST DISROOT
TOROIDS
DIOORTT RIDOTTO
DIOOSTX TOXOIDS
DIOPRST DISPORT
TORPIDS
TRIPODS
DIOPRTY TRIPODY
DIORRST STRIDOR
DIORSTT DISTORT
DIOSSTU STUDIOS
DIPRSTU DISRUPT
DIPSSTU STUPIDS
DJNNOOS DONJONS
DKNNRUU UNDRUNK
DKOOOOS KOODOOS
DLLOOPS DOLLOPS
DLLORWY WORLDLY
DLMNOSU UNMOLDS
DLMOSUU MODULUS
DLNOOWW LOWDOWN
DLNORUY ROUNDLY
DLNOSUY SOUNDLY
DLOOOTW WOODLOT
DLOOPPY POLYPOD
DLOOPSS PODSOLS
DLOOPSZ PODZOLS
DLOOPTU OUTPLOD
DLOOPUY DUOPOLY
DLOOPWY PLYWOOD
DLOORSU DOLOURS
DLOOSTU OUTSOLD
DLOOTTU OUTTOLD
DLOPRUY PROUDLY
DLORSTY DRYLOTS
DLOSTUW WOULDST
DMMOORU MUDROOM
DMNOOOP MONOPOD
DMNOORS DROMONS
DMNOOTW TOWMOND
DMNOSSU OSMUNDS
DMOOOQU QUOMODO
DNNOORW NONWORD
DNNORUU UNROUND
DNNORUW RUNDOWN
DNNOSUU UNSOUND
DNNOSUW SUNDOWN
DNNOUUW UNWOUND
DNOORTU OROTUND
DNOOSUV VODOUNS
VOUDONS
DNOOTUW NUTWOOD
DNOOUUV VOUDOUN
DNOPRUU ROUNDUP
DNOPTUW PUTDOWN
DNOSSTU STOUNDS
DNOSSUW SWOUNDS
DOOOOSV VOODOOS
DOOOPSW DOOWOPS
DOOORSU ODOROUS
DOOORTU OUTDOOR
DOOPRSU UROPODS
DOOPRSY PROSODY
DOOPRTU DROPOUT
OUTDROP
DOOPSTU UPSTOOD
DOORRSS SORDORS
DORSSTU STROUDS
DORSUVY DYVOURS
DPSSTUU DUSTUPS
EEEEFRR REFEREE
EEEEGTX EXEGETE
EEEEPST TEEPEES
EEEEPSV VEEPEES
EEEEPSW PEEWEES
EEEESWW WEEWEES
EEEFFFO FEOFFEE
EEEFGRU REFUGEE
EEEFHRS SHEREEF
EEEFIRR REEFIER
EEEFLRS FEELERS
REFEELS
EEEFLRT FLEETER
EEEFLSS FEELESS
EEEFMNR FREEMEN
EEEFNRV ENFEVER
EEEFORS FORESEE
EEEFRRS REEFERS
EEEFRRZ FREEZER
EEEFRSZ FREEZES
EEEGIKR GEEKIER
EEEGILS ELEGIES
ELEGISE
EEEGILZ ELEGIZE
EEEGINP EPIGENE
EEEGINR GREENIE
EEEGIPR PERIGEE
EEEGKLR KEGELER
EEEGLMN GLEEMEN
EEEGLNT GENTEEL
EEEGMRR REMERGE
EEEGMRS EMERGES
MERGEES
EEEGNNO NEOGENE
EEEGNPR EPERGNE
EEEGNRR GREENER
REGREEN
RENEGER
EEEGNRS RENEGES
EEEGNRV REVENGE
EEEGNSS GENESES
EEEGNTT GENETTE
EEEGRRT GREETER
REGREET
EEEGRSZ GEEZERS
EEEGRUX EXERGUE
EEEHILW WHEELIE
EEEHIRX HEXEREI
EEEHLNW ENWHEEL
EEEHLOY EYEHOLE
EEEHLPW WHEEPLE
EEEHLRS HEELERS
REHEELS
EEEHLRW WHEELER
EEEHNST ETHENES
EEEHRRS SHEERER
EEEHRST SHEETER
EEEHRTT TEETHER
EEEHRWZ WHEEZER
EEEHSST SEETHES
EEEHSSV SHEEVES
EEEHSTT ESTHETE
TEETHES
EEEHSWZ WHEEZES
EEEIKLL EELLIKE
EEEIKLY EYELIKE
EEEIKRR REEKIER
EEEILRR LEERIER
EEEILRV RELIEVE
EEEILST EELIEST
STEELIE
EEEIMNS ENEMIES
EEEIMNT EMETINE
EEEIMPR EPIMERE
PREEMIE
EEEIMRS EMERIES
EEEIMRT EREMITE
EEEINRS ESERINE
EEEINRT TEENIER
EEEINRW WEENIER
EEEINSW WEENIES
EEEIPRS PEERIES
SEEPIER
EEEIPRW WEEPIER
EEEIPST EPEEIST
EEEIPSW WEEPIES
EEEIRRT RETIREE
EEEIRRV REVERIE
EEEIRST EERIEST
EEEIRSV VEERIES
EEEIRSZ RESEIZE
EEEISTW SWEETIE
EEEJLRW JEWELER
EEEJNPY JEEPNEY
EEEJPRS JEEPERS
EEEJRRS JEERERS
EEEKLLU UKELELE
EEEKLNR KNEELER
EEEKLNS SLEEKEN
EEEKLNX KLEENEX

EEEKLPW EKPWELE
EEEKLRS SLEEKER
EEEKMST MEEKEST
EEEKNRS KEENERS
EEEKNST KEENEST
KETENES
EEEKORV REEVOKE
EEEKPRS KEEPERS
EEEKRRS REEKERS
EEEKRSS RESEEKS
SEEKERS
EEEKRST KEESTER
SKEETER
EEELLRV LEVELER
EEELMNT ELEMENT
TELEMEN
EEELMSX LEXEMES
EEELNST STELENE
EEELNSV ELEVENS
EEELPRS PEELERS
SLEEPER
EEELPRT REPLETE
EEELPRX REEXPEL
EEELPST STEEPLE
EEELRRS REELERS
EEELRRV REVELER
EEELRSV RELEVES
EEELRTV LEVERET
EEELSSS LESSEES
EEELSST TELESES
EEELSSV SLEEVES
EEELSSY EYELESS
EEELSTU EUSTELE
EEELSTX TELEXES
EEELSTY EYELETS
EEEMMSS MESEEMS
SEMEMES
EEEMNSS NEMESES
EEEMNST MENTEES
EEEMOSY EYESOME
EEEMPRT PREMEET
EEEMRSS SEEMERS
EEEMRST MEETERS
REMEETS
TEEMERS
EEEMRTX EXTREME
EEEMSST ESTEEMS
MESTEES
EEEMSTU EMEUTES
EEENNPT PENTENE
EEENNSV VENENES
EEENNTT ENTENTE
EEENNUY ENNUYEE
EEENPRR PREENER
EEENPRT PRETEEN
TERPENE
EEENPSS PENSEES
EEENPST STEEPEN
EEENPSX EXPENSE
EEENRRS SERENER
SNEERER
EEENRRT ENTERER
REENTER
TERREEN
TERRENE
EEENRRW RENEWER
EEENRSS SERENES
EEENRST ENTREES
RETENES
TEENERS
EEENRSV EVENERS
VENEERS
EEENRSZ SNEEZER
EEENRTW TWEENER
EEENRTX EXTERNE
EEENRUV REVENUE
UNREEVE
EEENSSZ SNEEZES
EEENSTV EVENEST
EEENSTW SWEETEN
EEENSWY SWEENEY
EEEOPPS EPOPEES
EEEORSV OVERSEE
EEEORSY EYESORE
EEEPPRS PEEPERS
EEEPRSS PEERESS
EEEPRST STEEPER
EEEPRSW SWEEPER
WEEPERS
EEEQRRU QUEERER
EEEQSUZ SQUEEZE
EEERRRV REVERER
EEERRST STEERER
EEERRSV RESERVE
REVERES
REVERSE
SEVERER
EEERSSS SEERESS
EEERSTT TEETERS
EEERSTW SWEETER
EEERSVW WEEVERS
EEERTTW TWEETER
EEERTWZ TWEEZER
EEESSTT SETTEES
TESTEES
EEESSTV STEEVES
VESTEES
EEESTWZ TWEEZES
EEFFFNO ENFEOFF
EEFFFOR FEOFFER
EEFFGLU EFFULGE
EEFFINT FIFTEEN
EEFFNOS OFFENSE
EEFFORR OFFERER
REOFFER
EEFFOST TOFFEES
EEFFSSU EFFUSES
EEFGILN FEELING
FLEEING
EEFGINR FEIGNER
FREEING
REEFING
EEFGINZ FEEZING
EEFGIST GIFTEES
EEFGLLU GLEEFUL
EEFGLOR FORELEG
EEFGLOS SOLFEGE
EEFGORR REFORGE
EEFGORY FROGEYE
EEFGRSU REFUGES
EEFHIRS HEIFERS
EEFHIRT HEFTIER
EEFHISY FISHEYE
EEFHLMN FLEHMEN
EEFHLRS FLESHER
HERSELF
EEFHLSS FLESHES
EEFHNRS FRESHEN
EEFHORT THEREOF
EEFHORW WHEREOF
EEFHRRS FRESHER
REFRESH
EEFHRRU FUEHRER
EEFHRSS FRESHES
EEFHRST FRESHET
HEFTERS
EEFIIMN FEMINIE
EEFIIRR FIERIER
REIFIER
EEFIIRS REIFIES
EEFIKLL ELFLIKE
EEFILLS FELLIES
EEFILLX FLEXILE
EEFILNO OLEFINE
EEFILNS FELINES
EEFILPR PREFILE
PRELIFE
EEFILRS FERLIES
REFILES
REFLIES
RELIEFS
EEFILRT FERTILE
EEFILST FELSITE
LEFTIES
LIEFEST
EEFILTY EYELIFT
EEFIMNR FIREMEN
EEFINNR FENNIER
EEFINRR FERNIER
REFINER
EEFINRS REFINES
EEFINSS FINESSE
EEFIPRR PREFIRE
EEFIRRS FERRIES
REFIRES
REFRIES
EEFIRRT FERRITE
EEFIRSS FRISEES
EEFIRSX REFIXES
EEFIRSZ FRIEZES
EEFISTV FESTIVE
EEFLLOS FELLOES
EEFLLRS FELLERS
EEFLLRU FUELLER
EEFLLST FELLEST
EEFLLTY FLEETLY
EEFLNNS FENNELS
EEFLNOS ONESELF
EEFLNRS FLENSER
FRESNEL
EEFLNSS FLENSES
EEFLNTU TEENFUL
EEFLOOV FOVEOLE
EEFLOTU OUTFEEL
EEFLRRS FERRELS
EEFLRRU FERRULE
EEFLRST REFLETS
TELFERS
EEFLRSU FERULES
FUELERS
REFUELS
EEFLRUX FLEXURE
EEFLSTT FETTLES
LEFTEST
EEFLSUY EYEFULS
EEFMNOR FOREMEN
EEFMNRT FERMENT
EEFMOTT MOFETTE
EEFMPRU PERFUME
EEFMTTU FUMETTE
EEFNORT OFTENER
EEFNRRY FERNERY
EEFNRSS ENSERFS
EEFNRSU UNFREES
EEFNRTV FERVENT
EEFNSSW FEWNESS
EEFNSSY FEYNESS
EEFORRV FOREVER
EEFORRZ REFROZE
EEFOTTU FOUETTE
EEFPRRS PREFERS
EEFPRSU PERFUSE
EEFRRST FERRETS
EEFRRSU REFUSER
EEFRRTT FRETTER
EEFRRTU REFUTER
EEFRRTY FERRETY
EEFRSST FESTERS
EEFRSSU REFUSES
EEFRSTT FETTERS
EEFRSTU REFUTES
EEFSSTU FETUSES
EEGGHTU THUGGEE
EEGGILN NEGLIGE
EEGGILR LEGGIER
EEGGINR GREEING
EEGGIRS GREIGES
EEGGISV VEGGIES
EEGGKRS KEGGERS
EEGGLSS EGGLESS
EEGGMNY YEGGMEN
EEGGMSU MUGGEES
EEGGNNS GENSENG
EEGGNOR ENGORGE
EEGGORR REGORGE
EEGGPRU PUGGREE
EEGHILN HEELING
EEGHINR REHINGE
EEGHINY HYGIENE
EEGHINZ HEEZING
EEGHIRW REWEIGH
WEIGHER
EEGHKRS SKREEGH
EEGHMNO HEGEMON
EEGHMNU HEGUMEN
EEGHNRT GREENTH
EEGHNRY GREYHEN
EEGIJNP JEEPING
EEGIJNR JEERING
EEGIKKN KEEKING
EEGIKLL LEGLIKE
EEGIKLM GEMLIKE
EEGIKLN KEELING
EEGIKLP PEGLIKE
EEGIKNN KEENING
KNEEING
EEGIKNP KEEPING
PEEKING
EEGIKNR REEKING
EEGIKNS SEEKING
SKEEING
EEGILNP PEELING
EEGILNR LEERING
REELING
EEGILNS SEELING
EEGILNT GENTILE
EEGILPS SPIEGEL
EEGILRV VELIGER
EEGILST ELEGIST
ELEGITS
EEGIMMR GEMMIER
GREMMIE
IMMERGE
EEGIMNR REGIMEN
EEGIMNS SEEMING
EEGIMNT MEETING
TEEMING
EEGIMRR GERMIER
EEGIMRS EMIGRES
REGIMES
REMIGES
EEGINNP PEENING
EEGINNS ENGINES
EEGINNU GENUINE
INGENUE
EEGINNV EVENING
EEGINNW WEENING
EEGINOP EPIGONE
EEGINOS GENOISE
SOIGNEE
EEGINPP PEEPING
EEGINPR PEERING
PREEING
EEGINPS SEEPING
EEGINPV PEEVING
EEGINPW WEEPING
EEGINRS GREISEN
EEGINRT INTEGER
TREEING
EEGINRV REEVING
REGIVEN
VEERING
EEGINSS GENESIS
SEEINGS
SIGNEES
EEGINTW WEETING
EEGINTX EXIGENT
EEGIRRV GRIEVER
EEGIRSV GRIEVES
REGIVES
EEGIRTT TERGITE
EEGISTV VESTIGE
EEGKLRS KEGLERS
EEGKNOR KEROGEN
EEGKNRU GERENUK
EEGLLSS LEGLESS
EEGLMMU GEMMULE
EEGLMOR GOMEREL
EEGLMSU LEGUMES
EEGLNOR ERELONG
EEGLNOU EUGENOL
EEGLNOZ LOZENGE
EEGLNRT GENTLER
EEGLNRY GREENLY
EEGLNST GENTLES
EEGLNSU LUNGEES
EEGLOSS EGOLESS
EEGLPSS PEGLESS
EEGLRRU GRUELER
EEGLRST REGLETS
EEGLRSU REGLUES
EEGLRTW WERGELT
EEGMNOS GENOMES
EEGMNRS GERMENS
EEGMNST SEGMENT
EEGMNTU TEGUMEN
EEGMOST GEMOTES
EEGMRRS MERGERS
EEGMRTU GUMTREE
EEGNOPS PONGEES
EEGNOSX EXOGENS
EEGNPUX EXPUNGE
EEGNRST GERENTS
REGENTS
EEGNRSY GYRENES
EEGNSSU GENUSES
NEGUSES
EEGOPRT PROTEGE
EEGOSSS GESSOES
EEGPPRR PREPREG
EEGPRSU PUGREES
EEGRRSS REGRESS
SERGERS
EEGRRST REGRETS
EEGRRSU RESURGE
EEGRRSV VERGERS
EEGRRUY GRUYERE
EEGRSSU GUESSER
EEGRSSY GEYSERS
EEGRSTT GETTERS
EEGRSTU GESTURE
EEGRSTY GREYEST
EEGSSSU GUESSES
EEHHRTW WHETHER
EEHIINS HEINIES
EEHIKLN HENLIKE
EEHIKLO HOELIKE
EEHILLR HELLERI
EEHILMN HEMLINE
EEHILNT THEELIN
EEHILOP PIEHOLE
EEHILST SHELTIE
EEHILSX HELIXES
EEHIMPR HEMPIER
EEHIMPS IMPHEES
EEHIMRS MESHIER
EEHINNY HYENINE
EEHINOR HEROINE
EEHINRR ERRHINE
EEHINRS HENRIES
INHERES
RESHINE
EEHINRT NEITHER
THEREIN
EEHINRW WHEREIN
EEHINST THEINES
EEHIORZ HEROIZE
EEHIPRT PRITHEE
EEHIPSV PEEVISH
EEHIPTT EPITHET
EEHIRRS HERRIES
REHIRES
EEHIRSS HEIRESS
EEHIRST HEISTER
EEHIRSV SHRIEVE
EEHIRTW THEWIER
EEHISST HESSITE
EEHISTV THIEVES
EEHKLOY KEYHOLE
EEHKLSS SHEKELS
EEHKOOY EYEHOOK
EEHLLMP PHELLEM
EEHLLOS HELLOES
EEHLLOT THEELOL
EEHLLRS HELLERS
SHELLER
EEHLLRY HELLERY
EEHLMRT THERMEL
EEHLMST HELMETS
EEHLNSY HENLEYS
EEHLPRS HELPERS
EEHLPRT TELPHER
EEHLQSS SHEQELS
EEHLRST SHELTER
EEHLRSV SHELVER
EEHLRSW WELSHER
EEHLRSY SHEERLY
EEHLSSU HUELESS
EEHLSSV SHELVES
EEHLSSW WELSHES
EEHLSTT SHTETEL
EEHMMRS HEMMERS
EEHMNNO NONHEME
EEHMNNS MENSHEN
EEHMNOP PHONEME
EEHMNRY MYNHEER
EEHMNSS MENSHES
EEHMORT THEOREM
EEHMPST TEMPEHS
EEHMRST THERMES
EEHMRUX EXHUMER
EEHMSUV HUMVEES
EEHMSUX EXHUMES
EEHNNRY HENNERY
EEHNOOR HONOREE
EEHNOPT POTHEEN
EEHNORS RESHONE
EEHNORT THEREON
EEHNORW NOWHERE
WHEREON
EEHNOSX HEXONES
EEHNPSS SPHENES
EEHNPSW NEPHEWS
EEHNSTU ENTHUSE
EEHNSTV SEVENTH
EEHNSTY ETHYNES
EEHOOPW WHOOPEE
EEHOOST TOESHOE
EEHOPRU EUPHROE
EEHOPST HEPTOSE
EEHORRV HOVERER
EEHORSS RESHOES
EEHORST HETEROS
EEHORSU REHOUSE
EEHORTT THERETO
EEHORTW WHERETO
EEHORVW HOWEVER
WHOEVER
EEHOSST ETHOSES
EEHOSSX HEXOSES
EEHOSTW TOWHEES
EEHOSTY EYESHOT
EEHPPST HEPPEST
EEHPRSS SPHERES
EEHPRST THREEPS
EEHPRTY PRYTHEE
EEHRSSU RUSHEES
EEHRSSW SHEWERS
EEHRSTT TETHERS
EEHRSTW WETHERS
EEHRSTZ HERTZES
EEHRSVW WHERVES
EEHRTTW WHETTER
EEHSTUY SHUTEYE
EEIIMNS MEINIES
EEIIMRT EMERITI
EEIIMST ITEMISE
EEIIMTZ ITEMIZE
EEIINRT NITERIE
EEIINRV VEINIER
EEIINST SIENITE
EEIINSW EISWEIN
WIENIES
EEIINTV INVITEE
EEIIPST PIETIES
EEIIRRV RIVIERE
EEIIRVW VIEWIER
EEIJKLT JETLIKE
EEIJKRR JERKIER
EEIJKRS JERKIES
EEIJLLS JELLIES
EEIJMMS JEMMIES
EEIJNNS JENNIES
EEIJRRS JERRIES
EEIJRTT JETTIER
EEIJSTT JETTIES
EEIKKST TEKKIES
EEIKLLS KELLIES
EEIKLNT NETLIKE
EEIKLOT TOELIKE
EEIKLPS KELPIES
EEIKLSS SELKIES
EEIKLST SLEEKIT
EEIKMNP PIKEMEN
EEIKMPS MISKEEP
EEIKNOS EIKONES
EEIKNPY PINKEYE
EEIKNRT KERNITE
EEIKNSS ENSKIES
KINESES
EEIKNWY EYEWINK
EEIKPRR PERKIER
EEIKPRS PESKIER
EEIKPSW KEWPIES
EEIKRRS KERRIES
EEIKRST KEISTER
KIESTER
EEIKTTT TEKTITE
EEILLNS NELLIES
EEILLPS ELLIPSE
EEILLRV EVILLER
EEILLRY LEERILY
EEILLST TELLIES
EEILLSW WELLIES
EEILMNN LINEMEN
EEILMNY MYELINE
EEILMRV VERMEIL
EEILMST ELMIEST
EEILNNO LEONINE
EEILNNT LENIENT
EEILNNV ENLIVEN
EEILNOR ELOINER
EEILNOS OLEINES
EEILNPS PENSILE
EEILNPT PENLITE
EEILNRS LIERNES
RELINES
EEILNRV LIVENER
EEILNSS ENISLES
ENSILES
SENILES
EEILNST LENITES
LISENTE
SETLINE
TENSILE
EEILNSY YEELINS
EEILNTT ENTITLE
EEILNTV VEINLET
EEILNUV VEINULE
EEILOPT PETIOLE
EEILORV OVERLIE
RELIEVO
EEILOST ETOILES
EEILOTZ ZEOLITE
EEILPRR REPLIER
EEILPRS REPLIES
SPIELER
EEILPRT PERLITE
REPTILE
EEILPRU PUERILE
EEILPSS PELISSE
EEILPST EPISTLE
PELITES
EEILQRU RELIQUE
EEILRRS RELIERS
EEILRRV REVILER
EEILRSS IRELESS
RESILES
EEILRST LEISTER
RETILES
STERILE
EEILRSU LEISURE
EEILRSV LEVIERS
RELIVES
REVILES
SERVILE
VEILERS
EEILRSX EXILERS
EEILRTT RETITLE
EEILSSS SESSILE
EEILSST LISTEES
TELESIS
TIELESS
EEILSSU ILEUSES
EEILSSV SLIEVES
EEILSSW LEWISES
EEILSSX SILEXES
EEILSTV EVILEST
LIEVEST
VELITES
EEILSTX SEXTILE
EEILSUV ELUSIVE
EEILSVW WEEVILS
EEILTTX TEXTILE
EEILTUX ULEXITE
EEILVWY WEEVILY
EEIMMNS IMMENSE
EEIMMRS IMMERSE
EEIMMSS MIMESES
EEIMMST MISMEET
EEIMNNO NOMINEE
EEIMNNT EMINENT
EEIMNOT ONETIME
EEIMNRS ERMINES
EEIMNRW WIREMEN
EEIMNSS NEMESIS
SIEMENS
EEIMNST EMETINS
EEIMOPS EPISOME
EEIMOPT EPITOME
EEIMOSS MEIOSES
EEIMOTV EMOTIVE
EEIMPRR PREMIER
EEIMPRS EMPIRES
EMPRISE
EPIMERS
IMPRESE
PREMIES
PREMISE
SPIREME
EEIMPRT EMPTIER
EEIMPRZ EMPRIZE
EEIMPST EMPTIES
SEPTIME
EEIMQRU REQUIEM
EEIMRRR MERRIER
EEIMRRT MITERER
TRIREME
EEIMRRU EREMURI
EEIMRSS MERISES
MESSIER
REMISES
EEIMRST MEISTER
METIERS
REEMITS
RETIMES
TRISEME
EEIMRSX MIREXES
REMIXES
EEIMRTT EMITTER
TERMITE
EEIMSSS SEMISES
EEIMSST METISSE
EEINNNP PENNINE
EEINNPS PENNIES
PINENES
EEINNRT INTERNE
EEINNRU NEURINE
EEINNRV INNERVE
NERVINE
EEINNRW WENNIER
EEINNST INTENSE
TENNIES
EEINNSV VENINES
EEINNTW ENTWINE
EEINNTZ NETIZEN

EEINOPR PEREION
PIONEER
EEINOPS PEONIES
EEINORR ONERIER
EEINOSS EOSINES
EEINPPS PEPSINE
EEINPRR REPINER
RIPENER
EEINPRS EREPSIN
REPINES
EEINPSS PENISES
EEINPSV PENSIVE
VESPINE
EEINQRU ENQUIRE
EEINQSU EQUINES
EEINQTU QUIETEN
EEINRRS RERISEN
EEINRRT REINTER
RENTIER
TERRINE
EEINRRV NERVIER
VERNIER
EEINRSS SEINERS
SEREINS
SERINES
EEINRST ENTIRES
ENTRIES
RETINES
TRIENES
EEINRSV ENVIERS
INVERSE
VEINERS
VENIRES
VERSINE
EEINRSW NEWSIER
WEINERS
WIENERS
EEINRSX REXINES
EEINRTT NETTIER
TENTIER
EEINRTU RETINUE
REUNITE
UTERINE
EEINSSS SENSEIS
EEINSST SESTINE
EEINSSW NEWSIES
EEINSTV TENSIVE
EEINSTX SIXTEEN
EEINSTY SYENITE
EEIOPPT EPITOPE
EEIOPSS POESIES
EEIOPST POETISE
EEIOPSX EPOXIES
EEIOPTZ POETIZE
EEIORSS SOIREES
EEIORSV EROSIVE
EEIORTZ EROTIZE
EEIPPPR PEPPIER
PREPPIE
EEIPPTT PIPETTE
EEIPPTZ PEPTIZE
EEIPQRU PERIQUE
REEQUIP
EEIPRRS PERRIES
PRISERE
REPRISE
RESPIRE
EEIPRRW PREWIRE
EEIPRRX EXPIRER
EEIPRST PESTIER
RESPITE
EEIPRSV PREVISE
EEIPRSX EXPIRES
PREXIES
EEIPRTT PETTIER
EEIPRTY YPERITE
EEIPRVW PREVIEW
EEIPSSS SPEISES
EEIPSTT PETITES
EEIPSTW PEEWITS
EEIQRRU QUERIER
REQUIRE
EEIQRSU ESQUIRE
QUERIES
EEIQRTU QUIETER
REQUITE
EEIQSTU EQUITES
EEIRRRT RETIRER
TERRIER
EEIRRSS RERISES
SERRIES
SIRREES
EEIRRST RETIRES
RETRIES
TERRIES
EEIRRSV REIVERS
REVISER
RIEVERS
EEIRRSW REWIRES
EEIRRTV RIVETER
EEIRRTW REWRITE
EEIRRVV REVIVER
EEIRSSS SEISERS
EEIRSST RESITES
EEIRSSU REISSUE
SEISURE
EEIRSSV REVISES
EEIRSSZ RESIZES
SEIZERS
EEIRSTT TESTIER
EEIRSTV RESTIVE
SIEVERT
VERIEST
VERITES
EEIRSTZ ZESTIER
EEIRSUZ SEIZURE
EEIRSVV REVIVES
EEIRSVW REVIEWS
VIEWERS
EEIRTVV VETIVER
EEISSTV VITESSE
EEISSTX SEXIEST
EEJKRRS JERKERS
EEJLRWY JEWELRY
EEJNNST JENNETS
EEJNORY ENJOYER
REENJOY
EEJNOSS JONESES
EEJORST RESOJET
EEJPRRU PERJURE
EEJRSST JESTERS
EEJRSSY JERSEYS
EEKKRRT TREKKER
EEKLLSY SLEEKLY
EEKLLUU UKULELE
EEKLMRZ KLEZMER
EEKLNNS KENNELS
EEKLNOS KEELSON
EEKLNRS KERNELS
EEKLRST KELTERS
KESTREL
SKELTER
EEKLSSY KEYLESS
EEKLSTT KETTLES
EEKMNOS SOKEMEN
EEKMRSS KERMESS
EEKNORW REWOKEN
EEKNOST KETONES
EEKNOTY KEYNOTE
EEKNSST KNESSET
EEKNSTU NETSUKE
EEKOOPP PEKEPOO
EEKOPRS RESPOKE
EEKOPTU OUTKEEP
EEKORRV REVOKER
EEKORST RESTOKE
EEKORSV EVOKERS
REVOKES
EEKOSST KETOSES
EEKPPSU UPKEEPS
EEKPRRS REPERKS
EEKPRSU PERUKES
EEKRRUZ KREUZER
EEKRSST STREEKS
EEKRSSW SKEWERS
EEKRSSY KERSEYS
EEKRSTY KEYSTER
EEKSSTY KEYSETS
EELLLVY LEVELLY
EELLMOR MORELLE
EELLMRS SMELLER
EELLNOR RELLENO
EELLNOV NOVELLE
EELLNRS SNELLER
EELLNUV UNLEVEL
EELLOPS POLLEES
EELLORS ROSELLE
EELLPRS PRESELL
RESPELL
SPELLER
EELLPRT PRETELL
EELLPST PELLETS
EELLQRU QUELLER
EELLRSS RESELLS
SELLERS
EELLRST RETELLS
TELLERS
EELLRSW SWELLER
EELLRSY YELLERS
EELMNNS LENSMEN
EELMNOO OENOMEL
EELMOPY EMPLOYE
EELMORW EELWORM
EELMOST OMELETS
TELOMES
EELMPST PELMETS
TEMPLES
EELMPTT TEMPLET
EELMRST MELTERS
REMELTS
RESMELT
SMELTER
EELMRSU LEMURES
RELUMES
EELMRSW MEWLERS
EELMSTT METTLES
EELNOPV ENVELOP
EELNOPY POLYENE
EELNOSV ELEVONS
EELNOTU TOLUENE
EELNPSS SPLEENS
EELNPSY SPLEENY
EELNQUY QUEENLY
EELNRST NESTLER
RELENTS
EELNRSU UNREELS
EELNRTT NETTLER
EELNRUV NERVULE
EELNSSS LESSENS
EELNSST NESTLES
NETLESS
EELNSTT NETTLES
TELNETS
EELNSTU ELUENTS
UNSTEEL
EELNSTY TENSELY
EELNSUV VENULES
EELNSXY XYLENES
EELNTTU LUNETTE
EELOPPR PEOPLER
EELOPPS PEOPLES
EELOPPZ ZEPPOLE
EELOPRS ELOPERS
LEPROSE
EELOPRX EXPLORE
EELOPTU EELPOUT
EELORSS RESOLES
EELORST SOLERET
EELORSV RESOLVE
EELORSY EROSELY
EELORTV OVERLET
EELORVV EVOLVER
REVOLVE
EELOSSS LOESSES
EELOSST TOELESS
EELOSTT TELEOST
EELOSVV EVOLVES
EELOTUV EVOLUTE
VELOUTE
EELPPRX PERPLEX
EELPPSU PEEPULS
EELPQRU PREQUEL
EELPRST PELTERS
PETRELS
RESPELT
SPELTER
EELPRSU REPULSE
EELPRSY YELPERS
EELPRTY PEYTREL
EELPRTZ PRETZEL
EELPRVY REPLEVY
EELPSST PESTLES
EELPSTT PETTLES
EELPSTY STEEPLY
EELPSUX EXPULSE
EELQRUY QUEERLY
EELQSSU SEQUELS
EELRRVY REVELRY
EELRSST STREELS
TRESSEL
EELRSTT LETTERS
SETTLER
STERLET
TRESTLE
EELRSTV SVELTER
EELRSTW SWELTER
WELTERS
WRESTLE
EELRSTY RESTYLE
TERSELY
EELRSTZ SELTZER
EELRSUV VELURES
EELRSUX LUREXES
EELSSSU USELESS
EELSSSV VESSELS
EELSSSX SEXLESS
EELSSTT SETTLES
EELSSUV EVULSES
EELSTVV VELVETS
EELSTVW TWELVES
EELSTWY SWEETLY
EELTVVY VELVETY
EEMMNOT MEMENTO
EEMMNSS MESSMEN
EEMMRST STEMMER
EEMNNOV ENVENOM
EEMNNSW NEWSMEN
EEMNOOS SOMEONE
EEMNOOY MOONEYE
EEMNORS MOREENS
EEMNORV OVERMEN
VENOMER
EEMNORY MONEYER
EEMNOST TONEMES
EEMNPRU PREMUNE
EEMNPTU UMPTEEN
EEMNSYZ ENZYMES
EEMOOSW WOESOME
EEMOPRR EMPEROR
EEMOPRW EMPOWER
EEMOPST METOPES
EEMORRS REMORSE
EEMORRT REMOTER
EEMORRV REMOVER
EEMORST EMOTERS
METEORS
REMOTES
EEMORSV REMOVES
EEMOSST MESTESO
EEMOTTZ MOZETTE
EEMPPRT PREEMPT
EEMPRRT PRETERM
EEMPRSS EMPRESS
EEMPRST TEMPERS
EEMPRSU PRESUME
SUPREME
EEMPRTT TEMPTER
EEMPRTU PERMUTE
EEMPSTT TEMPEST
EEMPSTX EXEMPTS
EEMRRST TERMERS
EEMRRSU RESUMER
EEMRSSU RESUMES
EEMRSUX MUREXES
EEMSSTU MUSTEES
EEMSTTU MUSETTE
EENNORT ENTERON
TENONER
EENNORU NEURONE
EENNOSS ONENESS
EENNOTY NEOTENY
EENNPRS PENNERS
EENNRST RENNETS
TENNERS
EENNRUV UNNERVE
EENNSST SENNETS
EENNSSW NEWNESS
EENOPPR PROPENE
EENOPPT PEPTONE
EENOPRS OPENERS
PEREONS
REOPENS
EENOPST OPENEST
PENTOSE
POSTEEN
POTEENS
EENOPTT POTTEEN
EENOPTY NEOTYPE
EENORSS SENORES
EENORST ESTRONE
EENORSZ REZONES
EENORVW OVERNEW
REWOVEN
EENOSSW WOENESS
EENOSTU OUTSEEN
EENOSTW TOWNEES
EENOSVZ EVZONES
EENOTTT TONETTE
EENPPRT PERPENT
EENPRST PENSTER
PRESENT
REPENTS
SERPENT
EENPRSY PYRENES
EENPRTV PREVENT
EENPSSS SPENSES
EENQSTU SEQUENT
EENRRST RENTERS
RERENTS
STERNER
EENRRSU ENSURER
EENRRTY REENTRY
EENRRUV NERVURE
EENRSST NESTERS
RENESTS
RESENTS
EENRSSU ENSURES
EENRSTT NETTERS
TENTERS
EENRSTU NEUTERS
RETUNES
TENURES
TUREENS
EENRSTV VENTERS
EENRSTW WESTERN
EENRSTX EXTERNS
EENRSTY STYRENE
YESTERN
EENRTUV VENTURE
EENSSTT TENSEST
EENSSTW WETNESS
EENSSUV VENUSES
EENSSUX NEXUSES
UNSEXES
EENSSVW SWEVENS
EENSTTX EXTENTS
EENSTTY TEENTSY
EENSTVY SEVENTY
EEOOPRS OPEROSE
EEOPRRS REPOSER
EEOPRRV REPROVE
EEOPRRW REPOWER
EEOPRSS REPOSES
EEOPRSX EXPOSER
EEOPRTT PROETTE
TREETOP
EEOPSST POETESS
EEOPSSU ESPOUSE
EEOPSSX EXPOSES
EEOPSTU TOUPEES
EEOPSTY EYESPOT
PEYOTES
EEOPTUW OUTWEEP
EEORRST RESTORE
EEORRSV REVERSO
EEORRSZ REZEROS
EEORRTU REROUTE
EEORRTV EVERTOR
EEORRTW REWROTE
EEORSST STEREOS
EEORSSX XEROSES
EEORSTT ROSETTE
EEORSTV OVERSET
REVOTES
VETOERS
EEORSUV OEUVRES
OVERUSE
EEORSVW OVERSEW
EEORSXX XEROXES
EEORTVW OVERWET
EEOSSSY OYESSES
EEOSSTU OUTSEES
EEPPPRS PEPPERS
EEPPPRY PEPPERY
EEPPRST STEPPER
EEPPRSX PERSPEX
EEPPRTY PRETYPE
EEPPSST STEPPES
EEPPSUW UPSWEEP
EEPPSUY EUPEPSY
EEPRRSS PRESSER
REPRESS
EEPRRST PRESTER
EEPRRSU PERUSER
EEPRRSY PREYERS
EEPRRTV PERVERT
EEPRSSS PRESSES
EEPRSST PESTERS
PRESETS
EEPRSSU PERUSES
EEPRSSV VESPERS
EEPRSSW SPEWERS
EEPRSSX EXPRESS
EEPRSTT PERTEST
PETTERS
PRETEST
EEPRSTU REPUTES
EEPRSTW PEWTERS
EEPRSTX EXPERTS
EEPRSTY RETYPES
EEPRSUV PREVUES
EEPRSXY PYREXES
EEPRTTX PRETEXT
EEPSSTT SEPTETS
EEPSTTU PUTTEES
EEPSTTY TYPESET
EEQRRUY EQUERRY
EEQRSTU QUESTER
REQUEST
EEQRSUU QUEUERS
EERRSST RESTERS
EERRSSV SERVERS
VERSERS
EERRSTT TERRETS
EERRSTU URETERS
EERRSTV REVERTS
EERRSTW STREWER
WRESTER
EERRSVW SWERVER
EERRTTU REUTTER
UTTERER
EERSSST TRESSES
EERSSTT RETESTS
SETTERS
STREETS
TERSEST
TESTERS
EERSSTV REVESTS
VERSETS
VERSTES
EERSSTW WESTERS
EERSSTX EXSERTS
EERSSTZ ZESTERS
EERSSUX XERUSES
EERSSVW SWERVES
EERSTTT STRETTE
TETTERS
EERSTTU TRUSTEE
EERSTTV TREVETS
VETTERS
EERSTTW WETTERS
EERSTTY SYRETTE
EERSTUV VESTURE
EERSTUY TUYERES
EERSTVV VERVETS
EERTTUX TEXTURE
EESSSTT SESTETS
TSETSES
EESSTTU SUTTEES
EESSTTX SEXTETS
EESTTTW WETTEST
EESTTZZ TZETZES
EFFFINO INFEOFF
EFFFLRU FLUFFER
EFFFOOR FEOFFOR
EFFGINR REFFING
EFFGIRS GRIFFES
EFFGORS GOFFERS
EFFGRRU GRUFFER
EFFHILW WHIFFLE
EFFHIRS SHERIFF
EFFHIRU HUFFIER
EFFHIRW WHIFFER
EFFHITW WHIFFET
EFFHLSU SHUFFLE
EFFIIJS JIFFIES
EFFIIMR MIFFIER
EFFIIST FIFTIES
IFFIEST
EFFIKLS SKIFFLE
EFFILLU LIFEFUL
EFFILNO OFFLINE
EFFILNS SNIFFLE
EFFILPS PIFFLES
EFFILRR RIFFLER
EFFILRS RIFFLES
EFFILRY FIREFLY
EFFINRS NIFFERS
SNIFFER
EFFINST STIFFEN
EFFIORT FORFEIT
EFFIORX FOXFIRE
EFFIOST TOFFIES
EFFIPRU PUFFIER
EFFIRST STIFFER
EFFLLOS SELLOFF
EFFLMRU MUFFLER
EFFLMSU MUFFLES
EFFLNSU SNUFFLE
EFFLOSU SOUFFLE
EFFLRRU RUFFLER
EFFLRSU RUFFLES
EFFLRTU FRETFUL
TRUFFLE
EFFNRSU SNUFFER
EFFNSTU FUNFEST
EFFOORR OFFEROR
EFFOPRR PROFFER
EFFOPSU POUFFES
EFFORRT TROFFER
EFFORST EFFORTS
EFFOSST OFFSETS
SETOFFS
EFFPRSU PUFFERS
EFFPRUY PUFFERY
EFFRSSU SUFFERS
EFFRSTU RESTUFF
STUFFER
TRUFFES
EFFSSUU SUFFUSE
EFFSTTU TUFFETS
EFGGIOR FOGGIER
EFGGIRU FUGGIER
EFGGLOR FLOGGER
EFGGORS FOGGERS
EFGHINT HEFTING
EFGHIRT FIGHTER
FREIGHT
REFIGHT
EFGIKNR KERFING
EFGILLN FELLING
EFGILNR FLINGER
EFGILNS SELFING
EFGILNT FELTING
EFGILNU FUELING
EFGILNX FLEXING
EFGILNY FLEYING
EFGILRU GULFIER
EFGIMNT FIGMENT
EFGINNP PFENNIG
EFGINOR FOREIGN
EFGINRS FINGERS
FRINGES
EFGINRU GUNFIRE
EFGINSS FESSING
EFGINTT FETTING
EFGIOOR GOOFIER
EFGIORV FORGIVE
EFGIRRT GRIFTER
EFGIRRU FIGURER
EFGIRSU FIGURES
EFGLNSU ENGULFS
EFGLNTU FULGENT
EFGLORS GOLFERS
EFGLORT FROGLET
EFGLOSS FOGLESS
EFGMNOR FROGMEN
EFGNOOR FORGONE
EFGNOSU FUNGOES
EFGOORR FORGOER
EFGOORS FORGOES
EFGORRS FORGERS
EFGORRY FORGERY
EFGORST FORGETS
EFGORTU FOREGUT
EFHIIRS FISHIER
EFHIJSW JEWFISH
EFHILMS FLEMISH
HIMSELF
EFHILSS HISSELF
SELFISH
EFHILST LEFTISH
EFHILTY HEFTILY
EFHINST FISHNET
EFHIRSS FISHERS
SERFISH
SHERIFS
EFHIRST SHIFTER
EFHIRSY FISHERY
EFHISUW HUSWIFE
EFHLLPU HELPFUL
EFHLLSY FLESHLY
EFHLOOX FOXHOLE
EFHLOPU HOPEFUL
EFHLRSU FLUSHER
EFHLRSY FRESHLY
EFHLSSU FLUSHES
EFHLSTY THYSELF
EFHLTTW TWELFTH
EFHOORS HOOFERS
EFHORRT FROTHER
EFHRRSU FUHRERS
EFHRRTU FURTHER
EFIIKLN FINLIKE
EFIILLS FILLIES
EFIILMR FILMIER
EFIILMS MISFILE
EFIILRT FIRELIT
EFIILRY FIERILY
EFIILSS FISSILE
EFIIMRR RIMFIRE
EFIIMRS MISFIRE
EFIIMST SEMIFIT
EFIINNR FINNIER
EFIINRT NIFTIER
EFIINRU UNIFIER
EFIINSS FINISES
EFIINST FINITES
NIFTIES
EFIINSU UNIFIES
EFIINSX INFIXES

EFIIRRR FIRRIER
EFIIRTW WIFTIER
EFIIRZZ FIZZIER
EFIJLLY JELLIFY
EFIJLOR FRIJOLE
EFIJLOT JETFOIL
EFIKLNU FLUNKIE
EFIKLOR FOLKIER
EFIKLOS FOLKIES
EFIKLOX FOXLIKE
EFIKLRU FLUKIER
EFIKNRS KNIFERS
EFIKNRU FUNKIER
EFIKORR FORKIER
EFIKRRS FRISKER
EFIKRST FRISKET
EFILLOS FOLLIES
EFILLOW LOWLIFE
EFILLRR FRILLER
EFILLRS FILLERS
REFILLS
EFILLST FILLETS
EFILMNT LIFTMEN
EFILMNU FULMINE
EFILMOT FILEMOT
EFILMRS FILMERS
REFILMS
EFILMST FILMSET
LEFTISM
EFILNNO NONLIFE
EFILNOS OLEFINS
EFILNOX FLEXION
EFILNSS FINLESS
EFILOOS FLOOSIE
FOLIOSE
EFILOOZ FLOOZIE
EFILOPR PROFILE
EFILORT LOFTIER
TREFOIL
EFILOSS FLOSSIE
EFILPPR FLIPPER
EFILPPS FIPPLES
EFILPPU PIPEFUL
EFILPRS PILFERS
EFILQUY LIQUEFY
EFILRRS RIFLERS
EFILRRT FLIRTER
TRIFLER
EFILRRY RIFLERY
EFILRST FILTERS
LIFTERS
STIFLER
TRIFLES
EFILRTT FLITTER
EFILRTU FLUTIER
EFILRTY FLYTIER
EFILRVV FLIVVER
EFILRZZ FRIZZLE
EFILSST STIFLES
EFILSTT LEFTIST
EFILSTU SULFITE
EFILSZZ FIZZLES
EFIMMRU FERMIUM
EFIMNOR FERMION
EFIMNTT FITMENT
EFIMOST FOMITES
EFIMRRS FIRMERS
EFIMRST FIRMEST
EFIMRTY METRIFY
EFIMSTU FUMIEST
EFINNOR INFERNO
EFINNRU FUNNIER
EFINNSU FUNNIES
EFINRST SNIFTER
EFINRSU INFUSER
EFINRUY REUNIFY
EFINSST FITNESS
INFESTS
EFINSSU INFUSES
EFINSUX UNFIXES
EFIOORS ROOFIES
EFIOORT FOOTIER
EFIOOST FOOTIES
FOOTSIE
EFIOPRT FIREPOT
PIEFORT
EFIORRT ROTIFER
EFIORST FORTIES
EFIORTU OUTFIRE
EFIORTV OVERFIT
EFIOSST SOFTIES
EFIOSTX FOXIEST
EFIOSTZ FOZIEST
EFIPRST PRESIFT
EFIPRTY PETRIFY
EFIRRRU FURRIER
EFIRRSU FRISEUR
SURFIER
EFIRRSZ FRIZERS
EFIRRTT FRITTER
EFIRRTU FRUITER
TURFIER
EFIRRTY TERRIFY
EFIRRUZ FURZIER
EFIRRZZ FRIZZER
EFIRSST RESIFTS
SIFTERS
STRIFES
EFIRSSU FISSURE
FUSSIER
EFIRSTT FITTERS
TITFERS
EFIRSTU FUSTIER
SURFEIT
EFIRSTW SWIFTER
EFIRSTZ FRITZES
EFIRSUX FIXURES
EFIRSVY VERSIFY
EFIRSZZ FIZZERS
FRIZZES
EFIRTTU TUFTIER
EFIRTUV FURTIVE
EFIRTUX FIXTURE
EFIRUZZ FUZZIER
EFISTTT FITTEST
EFISTTY TESTIFY
EFJLSTU JESTFUL
EFKLMNO MENFOLK
EFKLNRU FLUNKER
EFKLNUY FLUNKEY
EFKNRSU FUNKERS
EFKORRS FORKERS
EFLLOSW FELLOWS
EFLLRSU FULLERS
EFLLRUY FULLERY
EFLLSSY FLYLESS
EFLLSTU FULLEST
EFLMOSU FULSOME
EFLMSUU MUSEFUL
EFLNNOS NONSELF
EFLNNOU NONFUEL
EFLNNSU FUNNELS
EFLNORU FLEURON
EFLNORW REFLOWN
EFLNORY FELONRY
EFLNOST TEFLONS
EFLNOSU SULFONE
EFLNPUX FUNPLEX
EFLNSSU FULNESS
EFLNSUY SYNFUEL
EFLNTUU TUNEFUL
EFLOORR FLOORER
EFLOORT FOOTLER
EFLOORY FOOLERY
EFLOORZ FOOZLER
EFLOOST FOOTLES
EFLOOSZ FOOZLES
EFLOPPR FLOPPER
EFLORRS ROLFERS
EFLORSS FLOSSER
EFLORST FLORETS
LOFTERS
EFLORSU OURSELF
EFLORSW FLOWERS
FOWLERS
REFLOWS
EFLORSX FLEXORS
EFLORTU FLOUTER
EFLORTW FELWORT
EFLORVY FLYOVER
OVERFLY
EFLORWW WERWOLF
EFLORWY FLOWERY
EFLOSSS FLOSSES
EFLOSTU FOULEST
EFLOTTU OUTFELT
EFLOTUW OUTFLEW
EFLPRRU PURFLER
EFLPRSU PURFLES
EFLRRSU FURLERS
EFLRSSU FURLESS
EFLRSTU FLUSTER
FLUTERS
RESTFUL
EFLRTTU FLUTTER
EFLSTUZ ZESTFUL
EFMNOOT FOOTMEN
EFMNOST FOMENTS
EFMNRSU FRENUMS
SURFMEN
EFMNRTU TURFMEN
EFMOPRR PERFORM
PREFORM
EFMOPRT POMFRET
EFMORRS FORMERS
REFORMS
EFMPRUY PERFUMY
EFMRRSU FERRUMS
EFMRTUY FURMETY
EFNNORT FORNENT
EFNNORU FENURON
EFNNSTU FUNNEST
EFNOOST EFTSOON
FESTOON
EFNORRT FRONTER
REFRONT
EFNORRU FORERUN
EFNORRW FROWNER
EFNORST FRONTES
EFNORTU FORTUNE
EFNORTW FORWENT
EFNORUZ UNFROZE
EFNOSST SOFTENS
EFOOPRR PROOFER
REPROOF
EFOOPRS SPOOFER
EFOOPRT FORETOP
EFOORRS REROOFS
ROOFERS
EFOORST FOETORS
FOOTERS
EFOORSW WOOFERS
EFOPPRY FOPPERY
EFOPRSS PROFESS
EFOPRSU PROFUSE
EFORRSU FERROUS
FURORES
EFORRSV FERVORS
EFORRTY TORREFY
EFORRUV FERVOUR
EFORSST FORESTS
FOSTERS
EFORSTW TWOFERS
EFOSSTT SOFTEST
EFPRTUY PUTREFY
EFPSTUY STUPEFY
EFRRSSU SURFERS
EFRSSSU FUSSERS
EFRSTTU TUFTERS
EFRSTUU FUTURES
EGGGIKN KEGGING
EGGGILN LEGGING
EGGGILR GIGGLER
EGGGILS GIGGLES
EGGGINP PEGGING
EGGGINV VEGGING
EGGGLOR GOGGLER
EGGGLOS GOGGLES
EGGGLSU GUGGLES
EGGGNOS EGGNOGS
EGGHILR HIGGLER
EGGHILS HIGGLES
EGGHORS HOGGERS
EGGHOST HOGGETS
EGGHRSU HUGGERS
EGGIIJR JIGGIER
EGGIILN GINGELI
EGGIINS SIEGING
EGGIIPR PIGGIER
EGGIIPS PIGGIES
EGGIIRW WIGGIER
EGGIJLS JIGGLES
EGGIJRS JIGGERS
EGGIKLN KEGLING
EGGILLN GELLING
EGGILMS MIGGLES
EGGILNR NIGGLER
EGGILNS LEGGINS
NIGGLES
SNIGGLE
EGGILNU GLUEING
LUGEING
EGGILNY GINGELY
GLEYING
EGGILOR LOGGIER
EGGILRW WIGGLER
WRIGGLE
EGGILST GIGLETS
EGGILSU LUGGIES
EGGILSW WIGGLES
EGGIMMN GEMMING
EGGIMNR MERGING
EGGIMOS MOGGIES
EGGIMRU MUGGIER
EGGINNS GINSENG
EGGINNV VENGING
EGGINRS GINGERS
SERGING
SNIGGER
EGGINRV VERGING
EGGINRY GINGERY
GREYING
EGGINTT GETTING
EGGINTW TWIGGEN
EGGIORS SOGGIER
EGGIPRU PUGGIER
EGGIPRY PIGGERY
EGGIRRS RIGGERS
EGGIRRT TRIGGER
EGGIRSW SWIGGER
EGGIRUV VUGGIER
EGGIRWY WIGGERY
EGGJLOR JOGGLER
EGGJLOS JOGGLES
EGGJLRU JUGGLER
EGGJLSU JUGGLES
EGGJORS JOGGERS
EGGLMSU SMUGGLE
EGGLNOS LEGONGS
EGGLNSU SNUGGLE
EGGLOOY GEOLOGY
EGGLORS LOGGERS
SLOGGER
EGGLORT TOGGLER
EGGLOST GOGLETS
LOGGETS
TOGGLES
EGGLPRU PLUGGER
EGGLRSU GURGLES
LUGGERS
SLUGGER
EGGLRTU GURGLET
EGGLSTU GUGLETS
EGGMRSU MUGGERS
SMUGGER
EGGNRRU GRUNGER
EGGNRSU GRUNGES
SNUGGER
EGGNSTU NUGGETS
EGGNTUY NUGGETY
EGGOPRR PROGGER
EGGORRS GORGERS
EGGORST GORGETS
EGGORSU GOUGERS
EGGORTY TOGGERY
EGGRRSU RUGGERS
EGGRSTU TUGGERS
EGGSSTU SUGGEST
EGHHHIT HEIGHTH
EGHHIST EIGHTHS
HEIGHTS
HIGHEST
EGHHSSU SHEUGHS
EGHIILL GHILLIE
EGHIILN HEILING
EGHIINR HEIRING
EGHIINT NIGHTIE
EGHIINV INVEIGH
EGHIKLO HOGLIKE
EGHIKNR GHERKIN
EGHIKRS SKREIGH
EGHILLN HELLING
EGHILMN HELMING
EGHILMP MEGILPH
EGHILNP HELPING
EGHILNS ENGLISH
SHINGLE
EGHILNT LIGHTEN
EGHILNV HELVING
EGHILOU GHOULIE
EGHILRT LIGHTER
RELIGHT
EGHILSS SLEIGHS
EGHILST SLEIGHT
EGHIMMN HEMMING
EGHIMNS MESHING
EGHIMNT THEMING
EGHINNT HENTING
EGHINNU UNHINGE
EGHINOS HONGIES
SHOEING
EGHINRR HERRING
EGHINRS HINGERS
EGHINRW WHINGER
EGHINST NIGHEST
EGHINSW SHEWING
WHINGES
EGHINTT TIGHTEN
EGHIOPS PISHOGE
EGHIORS OGREISH
EGHIOST HOGTIES
EGHIOTT GOTHITE
EGHIOTU TOUGHIE
EGHIOTV EIGHTVO
EGHIRRT RIGHTER
EGHIRSS GIRSHES
SIGHERS
EGHIRST RESIGHT
SIGHTER
EGHIRSU GRUSHIE
GUSHIER
EGHIRSY GREYISH
EGHIRTT TIGHTER
EGHISTW WEIGHTS
EGHISTY HYGEIST
EGHITWY WEIGHTY
EGHLMPS PHLEGMS
EGHLMPY PHLEGMY
EGHLNOR LEGHORN
EGHLNST LENGTHS
EGHLNTY LENGTHY
THEGNLY
EGHLOOS GOLOSHE
EGHLOOT THEOLOG
EGHLTUY TEUGHLY
EGHMMOS MEGOHMS
EGHMOSU GUMSHOE
EGHNOOS HOGNOSE
EGHNORS GORHENS
EGHNORU ROUGHEN
EGHNOSU ENOUGHS
EGHNOTU TOUGHEN
EGHNRSU HUNGERS
EGHOPRS GOPHERS
EGHORRU ROUGHER
EGHORTU TOUGHER
EGHOSTT GHETTOS
EGHOSUU HUGEOUS
EGHRSSU GURSHES
GUSHERS
EGHRTUY THEURGY
EGIIJKL JIGLIKE
EGIIKLP PIGLIKE
EGIIKLW WIGLIKE
EGIILLS GILLIES
EGIILNR LINGIER
EGIILNT LIGNITE
EGIILNV VEILING
EGIILNX EXILING
EGIILRR GIRLIER
EGIILRS GIRLIES
EGIIMMS GIMMIES
EGIIMNP IMPINGE
EGIIMNR MINGIER
EGIIMNT ITEMING
EGIIMPR GIMPIER
EGIIMPS PIGMIES
EGIIMRR GRIMIER
EGIIMSV MISGIVE
EGIINNP PEINING
EGIINNR GINNIER
REINING
EGIINNS INSIGNE
SEINING
EGIINNV VEINING
EGIINOP EPIGONI
EGIINPS PEISING
EGIINRT IGNITER
TIERING
EGIINRV REIVING
EGIINRW WINGIER
EGIINRZ ZINGIER
EGIINSS SEISING
EGIINST IGNITES
EGIINSV SIEVING
VISEING
EGIINSZ SEIZING
EGIINTV EVITING
EGIINTX EXITING
EGIINVW VIEWING
EGIIOPR PIEROGI
EGIIPRR GRIPIER
EGIIPRW PERIWIG
EGIIPSS GIPSIES
EGIJKNR JERKING
EGIJLLN JELLING
EGIJLNR JINGLER
EGIJLNS JINGLES
EGIJNOS JINGOES
EGIJNSS JESSING
EGIJNST JESTING
EGIJNTT JETTING
EGIKKLN LEKKING
EGIKLMU GUMLIKE
EGIKLNP KELPING
EGIKLNR ERLKING
EGIKLNT KINGLET
EGIKLRU RUGLIKE
EGIKLTU GUTLIKE
EGIKNNN KENNING
EGIKNNR KERNING
EGIKNOV EVOKING
EGIKNPP KEPPING
EGIKNPR PERKING
EGIKNRU GUNKIER
EGIKNRY YERKING
EGIKNSW SKEWING
EGIKNUY YEUKING
EGILLMN MELLING
EGILLNS SELLING
EGILLNT GILLNET
TELLING
EGILLNW WELLING
EGILLNY YELLING
EGILLOR GIROLLE
EGILLRR GRILLER
EGILLRS GILLERS
GRILLES
EGILLSU GULLIES
LIGULES
EGILMMN LEMMING
EGILMMR GLIMMER
EGILMMY GEMMILY
EGILMNR GREMLIN
MINGLER
EGILMNS MINGLES
EGILMNT MELTING
EGILMNU GUMLINE
LEGUMIN
EGILMNW MEWLING
EGILMOR GOMERIL
EGILMOS SEMILOG
EGILMPS GLIMPSE
MEGILPS
EGILMST GIMLETS
EGILNNS LENSING
EGILNOP ELOPING
EGILNOS ELOIGNS
LEGIONS
LINGOES
LONGIES
EGILNOT LENTIGO
EGILNPT PELTING
EGILNPY YELPING
EGILNRS LINGERS
SLINGER
EGILNRT RINGLET
TINGLER
EGILNRY RELYING
EGILNSS SINGLES
EGILNST GLISTEN
SINGLET
SNIGLET
TINGLES
EGILNSW SLEWING
SWINGLE
EGILNTT LETTING
EGILNTU ELUTING
EGILNTW WELTING
WINGLET
EGILNUY GUYLINE
EGILNVY LEVYING
EGILOOS OLOGIES
EGILOPS EPILOGS
EGILORS GLORIES
EGILOST LOGIEST
EGILPPR GRIPPLE
EGILPRU GULPIER
EGILPST PIGLETS
EGILRSS GRILSES
EGILRST GLISTER
GRISTLE
EGILRSU LIGURES
EGILRTT GLITTER
EGILRUV VIRGULE
EGILRZZ GRIZZLE
EGILSST LEGISTS
EGILSSW WIGLESS
EGILSTU GLUIEST
UGLIEST
EGILSTW WIGLETS
EGILSTZ GLITZES
EGIMMRR GRIMMER
EGIMMRS MEGRIMS
EGIMMRU GUMMIER
EGIMMTU GUMMITE
EGIMNNO OMENING
EGIMNNS MENSING
EGIMNNW WINGMEN
EGIMNOT EMOTING
MITOGEN
EGIMNOU MEOUING
EGIMNOW MEOWING
EGIMNPR GRIPMEN
IMPREGN
PERMING
EGIMNPT PIGMENT
TEMPING
EGIMNRT METRING
TERMING
EGIMNSS MESSING
EGIMORS OGREISM
EGIMOSS EGOISMS
EGIMOST EGOTISM
EGIMPSU GUIMPES
EGIMPSY PYGMIES
EGIMRSW MISGREW
EGINNNP PENNING
EGINNNY YENNING
EGINNOO IONOGEN
EGINNOP OPENING
EGINNOR NEGRONI
EGINNPU PENGUIN
EGINNRR GRINNER
EGINNRS GINNERS
EGINNRT RENTING
RINGENT
EGINNRU ENURING
EGINNRV NERVING
EGINNSS ENSIGNS
SENSING
EGINNST NESTING
TENSING
EGINNSU ENSUING
GUNNIES
EGINNTT NETTING
TENTING
EGINNTV VENTING
EGINNVY ENVYING
EGINOOR GOONIER
EGINOOS GOONIES
ISOGONE
NOOGIES
EGINOPR PERIGON
PIROGEN
EGINOPS EPIGONS
PIGEONS
PINGOES
EGINORR IGNORER
EGINORS ERINGOS
IGNORES
REGIONS
SIGNORE
EGINORT GENITOR
EGINORV OVERING
EGINORZ ZEROING
EGINOSU IGNEOUS
EGINOSW WIGEONS
EGINOSY ISOGENY
EGINOTV VETOING
EGINPPP PEPPING
EGINPPR REPPING
EGINPPS PIGPENS
EGINPRS PINGERS
SPRINGE
EGINPRY PREYING
EGINPSW SPEWING
EGINPSY ESPYING
PIGSNEY
EGINPTT PETTING
EGINPYY EPIGYNY
EGINQUU QUEUING
EGINRRS RINGERS
EGINRRW WRINGER
EGINRSS INGRESS
RESIGNS
SIGNERS
SINGERS
EGINRST RESTING
STINGER
EGINRSU REUSING
EGINRSV SERVING
VERSING
EGINRSW SWINGER
WINGERS
EGINRSY SYRINGE
EGINRSZ ZINGERS
EGINRTT GITTERN
RETTING
EGINRTU TRUEING
EGINRTY RETYING
EGINRVV REVVING
EGINSST INGESTS
SIGNETS
EGINSSW SEWINGS
SWINGES
EGINSSY YESSING
EGINSTT SETTING
TESTING

EGINSTU GUNITES
EGINSTV VESTING
EGINSTW STEWING
TWINGES
WESTING
EGINSTZ ZESTING
EGINTTV VETTING
EGINTTW WETTING
EGIOOPR GOOPIER
EGIOORS GOOSIER
EGIOOST GOOIEST
EGIOPRS PORGIES
SERPIGO
EGIOPRU GROUPIE
PIROGUE
EGIORRS GORSIER
EGIORST GOITERS
GOITRES
GORIEST
EGIORTU GOUTIER
EGIORTV VERTIGO
EGIOSST EGOISTS
STOGIES
EGIOSTT EGOTIST
EGIOTUV OUTGIVE
EGIPPRR GRIPPER
EGIPPRS GIPPERS
GRIPPES
EGIPPSU GUPPIES
EGIPRRS GRIPERS
EGIPRUU GUIPURE
EGIPSSY GYPSIES
EGIRRST GRISTER
EGIRRSU GURRIES
EGIRRTT GRITTER
EGIRSST TIGRESS
EGIRSTU GUSTIER
GUTSIER
EGIRSTV GRIVETS
EGIRTTU GUTTIER
TURGITE
EGISSSU GUSSIES
EGISUWY WISEGUY
EGJLNSU JUNGLES
EGJOSTT GJETOST
EGKLORW LEGWORK
EGKMSSU MUSKEGS
EGLLSTU GULLETS
EGLLSUY GULLEYS
EGLMMRU GLUMMER
EGLMNOR MONGREL
EGLMOOR LEGROOM
EGLMSSU GUMLESS
EGLNNSU GUNNELS
EGLNOOY ENOLOGY
NEOLOGY
EGLNORS LONGERS
EGLNORU LOUNGER
EGLNOST LONGEST
EGLNOSU LOUNGES
EGLNOSY LYSOGEN
EGLNOUV UNGLOVE
EGLNPRU PLUNGER
EGLNPSU PLUNGES
PUNGLES
EGLNRSU LUNGERS
EGLNRTU GRUNTLE
EGLNSSU GUNLESS
GUNSELS
EGLNSTU ENGLUTS
GLUTENS
EGLNSUU UNGLUES
EGLOORS REGOSOL
EGLOPRS PROLEGS
EGLOPSS GOSPELS
EGLOPTU GLUEPOT
EGLORRW GROWLER
EGLORSS GLOSSER
REGLOSS
EGLORSV GLOVERS
GROVELS
EGLORSW GLOWERS
REGLOWS
EGLOSSS GLOSSES
EGLPRSU GULPERS
SPLURGE
EGLPRUY GYPLURE
EGLRSUU REGULUS
EGLRTTU GUTTLER
EGLRUZZ GUZZLER
EGLSSTU GUTLESS
TUGLESS
EGLSTTU GUTTLES
EGLSTUU GLUTEUS
EGLSUZZ GUZZLES
EGMMORT GROMMET
EGMMOSU GUMMOSE
EGMMRRU GRUMMER
EGMMRSU GUMMERS
EGMMRTU GRUMMET
EGMNNOT TONGMEN
EGMNOOS MONGOES
EGMNORS MONGERS
MORGENS
EGMNOSU MUNGOES
EGMNOYZ ZYMOGEN
EGMNSTU NUTMEGS
EGMOORR GROOMER
REGROOM
EGMORSU GRUMOSE
MORGUES
EGMORTU GOURMET
EGNNOOS NONEGOS
EGNNORT RONTGEN
EGNNOSU GUENONS
EGNNPTU PUNGENT
EGNNRSU GUNNERS
EGNNRUY GUNNERY
EGNNTUU UNGUENT
EGNOORS ORGONES
EGNOORY OROGENY
EGNOOST GENTOOS
EGNOOSY GOONEYS
EGNOOTU OUTGONE
EGNOOYZ ZOOGENY
EGNOPRS PRESONG
SPONGER
EGNOPRY PROGENY
PYROGEN
EGNOPSS SPONGES
EGNORRW REGROWN
WRONGER
EGNORSS ENGROSS
EGNORST TONGERS
EGNORSU SURGEON
EGNORSV GOVERNS
EGNORSY ERYNGOS
GROYNES
EGNORUY YOUNGER
EGNOSTU TONGUES
EGNOSXY OXYGENS
EGNPRSU REPUGNS
EGNRRTU GRUNTER
EGNRSTU GURNETS
EGNRSUY GURNEYS
EGNRSYY SYNERGY
EGNRTTU GRUTTEN
TURGENT
EGOORRV GROOVER
EGOORSV GROOVES
EGOOSST STOOGES
EGOOSTU OUTGOES
EGOPRRS GROPERS
EGOPRRU GROUPER
REGROUP
EGORRSS GROSSER
EGORRSU GROUSER
EGORRSW GROWERS
REGROWS
EGORRTU GROUTER
EGORRUY ROGUERY
EGORSSS GROSSES
EGORSSU GROUSES
EGORSUV VOGUERS
EGORTUW OUTGREW
EGOSSTU GUSTOES
EGOSSTY STOGEYS
EGOSSYZ ZYGOSES
EGOSTYZ ZYGOTES
EGPPRSY GYPPERS
EGPRRSU PURGERS
EGPRSSU SPURGES
EGPRSTY GYPSTER
EGPRSUU UPSURGE
EGRRSSU SURGERS
EGRRSUY SURGERY
EGRSTTU GUTTERS
EGRTTUY GUTTERY
EGSSSTU GUSSETS
EHHIIMS HEIMISH
EHHIKSS SHEIKHS
EHHILLS HELLISH
EHHINNS HENNISH
EHHIRTT THITHER
EHHIRTW WHITHER
EHHISSW WHISHES
EHHISWY WHEYISH
EHHNPSY HYPHENS
EHHRSSU SHUSHER
EHHSSSU SHUSHES
EHIIKLP HIPLIKE
EHIIKNR HINKIER
EHIILLR HILLIER
EHIILNP HIPLINE
EHIINNS HINNIES
EHIINRS SHINIER
EHIINRT INHERIT
EHIINRW WHINIER
EHIIPPR HIPPIER
EHIIPPS HIPPIES
EHIIPRT PITHIER
EHIIRSS HISSIER
EHIIRTW WHITIER
WITHIER
EHIISSS HISSIES
EHIISTW WITHIES
EHIJNNO JOHNNIE
EHIKKRS SHIKKER
EHIKKSS KISHKES
EHIKLRU HULKIER
EHIKLTU HUTLIKE
EHIKLTY LEKYTHI
EHIKMSV MIKVEHS
EHIKNRT RETHINK
THINKER
EHIKNRU HUNKIER
EHIKNSS KNISHES
EHIKOOR HOOKIER
EHIKOOS HOOKIES
EHIKOST HOKIEST
EHIKPRS PERKISH
EHIKRRS SHIRKER
EHIKRSS SHRIEKS
SHRIKES
EHIKRSU HUSKIER
EHIKRSW WHISKER
EHIKRSY SHRIEKY
EHIKSSU HUSKIES
EHIKSWY WHISKEY
EHILLNO HELLION
EHILLOO OILHOLE
EHILLOS HILLOES
HOLLIES
EHILLRS HILLERS
EHILLTY LITHELY
EHILMMO MOHELIM
EHILMSU HELIUMS
MUHLIES
EHILNOP PINHOLE
EHILNOT HOTLINE
NEOLITH
EHILNPS PLENISH
EHILNTY ETHINYL
EHILOPT HOPLITE
EHILOSS ISOHELS
EHILOST EOLITHS
HOLIEST
HOSTILE
EHILPRS HIRPLES
EHILPRT PHILTER
PHILTRE
EHILPSS HIPLESS
EHILRRW WHIRLER
EHILRSS HIRSELS
HIRSLES
EHILRST SLITHER
EHILRSU HURLIES
EHILRSV SHRIVEL
EHILRTU LUTHIER
EHILSST HITLESS
EHILSTT LITHEST
THISTLE
EHILSTW WHISTLE
EHILTTW WHITTLE
EHILTWY WHITELY
EHIMMRS SHIMMER
EHIMNOS HOMINES
EHIMNPS SHIPMEN
EHIMNRS MENHIRS
EHIMNRU INHUMER
RHENIUM
EHIMNSU INHUMES
EHIMNTY THYMINE
EHIMORS HEROISM
EHIMORT MOTHIER
EHIMORZ RHIZOME
EHIMOST HOMIEST
EHIMPPX PEMPHIX
EHIMPRU HUMPIER
EHIMPRW WHIMPER
EHIMRST HERMITS
MITHERS
EHIMRSU MUSHIER
EHIMRTT THERMIT
EHIMRTY MYTHIER
THYMIER
EHIMSST THEISMS
EHIMSWY WHIMSEY
EHINNRT THINNER
EHINNSW WENNISH
EHINNSY SHINNEY
EHINOPR PHONIER
EHINOPS PHONIES
EHINOPX PHOENIX
EHINORR HORNIER
EHINORS HEROINS
INSHORE
EHINOST ETHIONS
HISTONE
EHINOSU HEINOUS
EHINPPS SHIPPEN
EHINPSS HIPNESS
EHINRSS SHINERS
SHRINES
EHINRST HINTERS
EHINRSV SHRIVEN
EHINRSW WHINERS
EHINRTV THRIVEN
EHINRTW WRITHEN
EHINRTZ ZITHERN
EHINSST SITHENS
EHINSTW WHITENS
EHINSTZ ZENITHS
EHINTUW UNWHITE
EHIOOPW WHOOPIE
EHIOORT HOOTIER
EHIOPPR HOPPIER
EHIOPRS ROSEHIP
EHIOPSS SOPHIES
EHIOPST OPHITES
EHIORRS HORSIER
EHIORRT HERITOR
EHIORSS HOSIERS
EHIORST HERIOTS
HOISTER
SHORTIE
EHIORSW SHOWIER
EHIORSY HOSIERY
EHIORTT THORITE
EHIOSTT HOTTIES
EHIOSTY ISOHYET
EHIPPRS PRESHIP
SHIPPER
EHIPPRW WHIPPER
EHIPPST HIPPEST
EHIPPTW WHIPPET
EHIPRSS PISHERS
RESHIPS
EHIPRST HIPSTER
EHIPRSU PUSHIER
EHIPRSW WHISPER
EHIPSTT PETTISH
EHIRRRU HURRIER
EHIRRSS SHERRIS
EHIRRSU HURRIES
RUSHIER
EHIRRSV SHRIVER
EHIRRTV THRIVER
EHIRRTW WRITHER
EHIRSSS HISSERS
EHIRSSV SHIVERS
SHRIVES
EHIRSSW SWISHER
WISHERS
EHIRSTT HITTERS
TITHERS
EHIRSTU HIRSUTE
EHIRSTV THRIVES
EHIRSTW SWITHER
WITHERS
WRITHES
EHIRSTZ ZITHERS
EHIRSVY SHIVERY
EHIRTTW WHITTER
EHIRWZZ WHIZZER
EHISSSU HUSSIES
EHISSSW SWISHES
EHISSTT THEISTS
EHISSTU TUSHIES
EHISTTW WETTISH
WHITEST
EHISWZZ WHIZZES
EHJOPSS JOSEPHS
EHJORSS JOSHERS
EHKLOOT HOOKLET
EHKLPST KLEPHTS
EHKNORS HONKERS
EHKNRSU HUNKERS
EHKOORS HOOKERS
EHKOOSY HOOKEYS
EHKORSS KOSHERS
EHKOSSS SKOSHES
EHKRSSU HUSKERS
EHLLNSU UNSHELL
EHLLOOS HOLLOES
EHLLORS HOLLERS
EHLLOSU HULLOES
EHLLRSU HULLERS
EHLMNOT MENTHOL
EHLMNSU UNHELMS
EHLMOPS PHLOEMS
EHLMSTY METHYLS
EHLNOPS PHENOLS
EHLNPSY PHENYLS
EHLNRTU LUTHERN
EHLNTTY TENTHLY
EHLNTYY ETHYNYL
EHLOOPT POTHOLE
EHLOPPS HOPPLES
EHLOPSX PHLOXES
EHLORST HOLSTER
HOSTLER
EHLORSW HOWLERS
EHLORTW WHORTLE
EHLORTY HELOTRY
EHLOSSS SLOSHES
EHLOSST HOSTELS
EHLOSSU HOUSELS
EHLOSSV SHOVELS
EHLOSTW HOWLETS
EHLOTXY ETHOXYL
EHLPPSS SHLEPPS
EHLPRSU PLUSHER
EHLPSSU PLUSHES
EHLRRSU HURLERS
EHLRSTU HURTLES
HUSTLER
EHLRSUY HURLEYS
EHLSSSU SLUSHES
EHLSSTT SHTETLS
EHLSSTU HUSTLES
LUSHEST
SLEUTHS
EHLSTTU SHUTTLE
EHMMRSU HUMMERS
EHMNNOO NONHOME
EHMNOOR HORMONE
MOORHEN
EHMNOPS PHENOMS
SHOPMEN
EHMNOSW SHOWMEN
EHMNPTY NYMPHET
EHMNTTU HUTMENT
EHMOOSW SOMEHOW
EHMOOSX HOMOSEX
EHMOOSZ SHMOOZE
EHMORSS MOSHERS
EHMORST MOTHERS
SMOTHER
THERMOS
EHMORTU MOUTHER
EHMORTY MOTHERY
EHMOTXY METHOXY
EHMPRSU HUMPERS
EHMPRTU THUMPER
EHMRRSY RHYMERS
EHMRRTU MURTHER
EHMRSSU MUSHERS
EHMRSUU HUMERUS
EHMRTUV VERMUTH
EHMSSSU SMUSHES
EHMSSUU HUMUSES
EHNNOOR NONHERO
EHNNOPR NEPHRON
EHNNRSU SHUNNER
EHNOORR HONORER
EHNOORS ONSHORE
EHNOPRY HYPERON
EHNOPSY PHONEYS
EHNOPUY EUPHONY
EHNOPXY PHENOXY
EHNORRT HORRENT
NORTHER
EHNORRY HERONRY
EHNORSS NOSHERS
SENHORS
EHNORST HORNETS
SHORTEN
THRONES
EHNORSU UNHORSE
EHNORSW RESHOWN
EHNOSST HOTNESS
EHNOSTT SHOTTEN
EHNOSTY HONESTY
EHNOSUU UNHOUSE
EHNOTUY YOUTHEN
EHNPRSY PHRENSY
EHNRSTU HUNTERS
SHUNTER
EHNSSSY SHYNESS
EHOOOPS HOOPOES
EHOOPRS HOOPERS
EHOOPRW WHOOPER
EHOOPTY OOPHYTE
EHOORST HOOTERS
RESHOOT
SHEROOT
SHOOTER
SOOTHER
EHOORSV HOOVERS
EHOORTV OVERHOT
EHOOSST SOOTHES
EHOOSSW WOOSHES
EHOPPRS HOPPERS
SHOPPER
EHOPPRT PROPHET
EHOPPRW WHOPPER
EHOPPSS SHOPPES
EHOPRRY ORPHREY
EHOPRST POTHERS
STROPHE
THORPES
EHOPRSU UPHROES
EHOPRSW PRESHOW
EHOPRSY PHORESY
EHOPSST POSHEST
EHOPSTY TYPHOSE
EHORRST RHETORS
SHORTER
EHORRTW THROWER
EHORSST HORSTES
EHORSSU HOUSERS
EHORSSV SHOVERS
EHORSSW RESHOWS
SHOWERS
EHORSTU SHOUTER
SOUTHER
EHORSTX EXHORTS
EHORSWY SHOWERY
EHOSSST HOSTESS
EHOSTTT HOTTEST
EHPRSSU PUSHERS
EHPRSSY SYPHERS
EHPRSYZ ZEPHYRS
EHPRTTU TURPETH
EHPRTUW UPTHREW
EHQRSSU QURSHES
EHRRSSU RUSHERS
EHRRSTU HURTERS
EHRSSTY SHYSTER
THYRSES
EHRSTTU SHUTTER
EHRSTUW WUTHERS
EHRSTUY TUSHERY
EHSSSTU TUSSEHS
EIIILRV RILIEVI
EIIILST ILEITIS
EIIINPR RIPIENI
EIIJMMS JIMMIES
EIIJSTV JIVIEST
EIIKKLN INKLIKE
EIIKKNR KINKIER
EIIKLLP LIPLIKE
EIIKLLS KILLIES
EIIKLMR MILKIER
EIIKLMS MISLIKE
EIIKLNT TINLIKE
EIIKLPS PLISKIE
EIIKLRS SILKIER
EIIKLSS SILKIES
EIIKLST KILTIES
EIIKLVY IVYLIKE
EIIKMRR MIRKIER
EIIKNNT KINETIN
EIIKNPS PINKIES
EIIKNSS KINESIS
EIIKNST INKIEST
EIIKNTW TWINKIE
EIIKPRS SPIKIER
EIIKRRS RISKIER
EIIKSTT KITTIES
EIILLMM MILLIME
EIILLMN MILLINE
EIILLMR MILLIER
EIILLNV VILLEIN
EIILLRS SILLIER
EIILLSS SILLIES
EIILLST ILLITES
EIILLSW WILLIES
EIILLTT TILLITE
EIILMPR IMPERIL
EIILMPS IMPLIES
EIILMRS MILREIS
SLIMIER
EIILMRT LIMITER
MILTIER
EIILMSS MISLIES
MISSILE
SIMILES
EIILMST ELITISM
LIMIEST
LIMITES
EIILMSU MILIEUS
EIILMSV MISLIVE
EIILMUX MILIEUX
EIILNOS ELISION
ISOLINE
LIONISE
EIILNOV OLIVINE
EIILNOZ LIONIZE
EIILNPS SPLENII
EIILNRS INLIERS
RESILIN
EIILNRT LINTIER
NITRILE
EIILNST LINIEST
EIILNTT INTITLE
EIILNTU INUTILE
EIILOPR LIRIOPE
EIILORR ROILIER
EIILORV RILIEVO
EIILOST IOLITES
OILIEST
EIILPPR LIPPIER
EIILQSU SILIQUE
EIILRST SILTIER
EIILRSV LIVIERS
EIILRSX ELIXIRS
EIILSTT ELITIST
EIILSTU UTILISE
EIILSTW WILIEST
EIILTUZ UTILIZE
EIIMMSS MIMESIS
EIIMMST MISTIME
EIIMMSX IMMIXES
EIIMNNS MINNIES
EIIMNPR PRIMINE
EIIMNRT INTERIM
MINTIER
TERMINI
EIIMNRV MINIVER
EIIMNTY NIMIETY
EIIMOSS MEIOSIS
EIIMPRS PISMIRE
PRIMSIE
EIIMPRW WIMPIER
EIIMPST PIETISM
EIIMPTY IMPIETY
EIIMRSS MERISIS
EIIMRST MIRIEST
MISTIER
RIMIEST
EIIMSSS MISSIES
EIIMSST MITISES
STIMIES
EIIMSSV MISSIVE
EIIMSTT MITIEST
EIINNNP NINEPIN
EIINNNS NINNIES
EIINNOS INOSINE
EIINNPS PINNIES
EIINNQU QUININE
EIINNRT TINNIER
EIINNST INTINES
EIINNTW INTWINE
EIINOPR RIPIENO
EIINOPS SINOPIE
EIINORS IRONIES
NOISIER
EIINORZ IONIZER
IRONIZE
EIINOSS IONISES
EIINOST INOSITE
EIINOSZ IONIZES
EIINPPR NIPPIER
EIINPRS INSPIRE
SPINIER
EIINPST PINIEST
PINITES
TIEPINS
EIINQRU INQUIRE
EIINQTU INQUIET
EIINRTT NITRITE
NITTIER
EIINRTV INVITER
VITRINE
EIINRTW TWINIER
EIINSSS SEISINS
EIINSSZ SEIZINS
EIINSTT TINIEST
EIINSTU UNITIES

EIINSTV INVITES
VINIEST
EIINSTW WINIEST
EIINSUZ UNISIZE
EIINTUV UNITIVE
EIINTUZ UNITIZE
EIIORSV IVORIES
EIIOSTZ ZOISITE
EIIPPRT TIPPIER
EIIPPRZ ZIPPIER
EIIPPST PIPIEST
EIIPPSY YIPPIES
EIIPRRS SPIRIER
EIIPRRV PRIVIER
EIIPRST PITIERS
TIPSIER
EIIPRSV PRIVIES
EIIPRSW WISPIER
EIIPSTT PIETIST
EIIRRTZ RITZIER
EIIRSSS SISSIER
EIIRSTV REVISIT
VISITER
EIIRSTW WIRIEST
EIIRSVZ VIZIERS
EIIRTTW WITTIER
EIISSSS SISSIES
EIISSTX SIXTIES
EIISSTZ SIZIEST
EIISTTT TITTIES
EIISTUV UVEITIS
EIISTZZ TIZZIES
EIJKLRY JERKILY
EIJKNRS JERKINS
JINKERS
EIJKNRU JUNKIER
EIJKNSU JUNKIES
EIJKOST JOKIEST
EIJLLOR JOLLIER
EIJLLOS JOLLIES
EIJLORT JOLTIER
EIJLORW JOWLIER
EIJLRST JILTERS
EIJMPRU JUMPIER
EIJMPST JIMPEST
EIJNNOS ENJOINS
EIJNORS JOINERS
REJOINS
EIJNORT JOINTER
EIJNORY JOINERY
EIJNPRU JUNIPER
EIJNRRU INJURER
EIJNRSU INJURES
EIJNSTY JITNEYS
EIJNTTW TWINJET
EIJRSTT JITTERS
TRIJETS
EIJRTTY JITTERY
EIJSSUV JUSSIVE
EIJSTTU JUTTIES
EIKKLSY KYLIKES
SKYLIKE
EIKKMNR KIRKMEN
EIKKNRS SKINKER
EIKKOOR KOOKIER
EIKKRUY YUKKIER
EIKLLNW INKWELL
EIKLLOW OWLLIKE
EIKLLRS KILLERS
EIKLLST SKILLET
EIKLMMN MILKMEN
EIKLMNN LINKMEN
EIKLMNR KREMLIN
EIKLMRS MILKERS
EIKLNNU NUNLIKE
EIKLNOS SONLIKE
EIKLNPR PLINKER
EIKLNRS LINKERS
RELINKS
EIKLNRT TINKLER
EIKLNRU URNLIKE
EIKLNRW WRINKLE
EIKLNSS INKLESS
KINLESS
EIKLNST LENTISK
TINKLES
EIKLNSU SUNLIKE
EIKLNSV KELVINS
EIKLNSW WELKINS
WINKLES
EIKLNSY SKYLINE
EIKLNTU NUTLIKE
EIKLNTW TWINKLE
EIKLOPT POTLIKE
EIKLORY YOLKIER
EIKLOTY TOYLIKE
EIKLPRY PERKILY
EIKLPST SKELPIT
EIKLPSU PUSLIKE
EIKLPSY PESKILY
EIKLRST KILTERS
KIRTLES
KLISTER
EIKLRSU SULKIER
EIKLRTT KITTLER
EIKLSSU SULKIES
EIKLSTT KITTLES
SKITTLE
EIKMMRR KRIMMER
EIKMMRS SKIMMER
EIKMNNS KINSMEN
EIKMNOR MONIKER
EIKMNSW MISKNEW
EIKMORS IRKSOME
SMOKIER
EIKMOSY MISYOKE
EIKMPST MISKEPT
EIKMPSU MUSPIKE
EIKMRRS SMIRKER
EIKMRRU MURKIER
EIKMRSS KIRMESS
EIKMRST MIRKEST
EIKMRSU MUSKIER
EIKMSST KISMETS
EIKMSSU MUSKIES
EIKMSTU MISTEUK
EIKNNOR EINKORN
EIKNNPS PINKENS
EIKNNRS SKINNER
EIKNOPS PINKOES
EIKNORV INVOKER
EIKNORW WONKIER
EIKNOSS KENOSIS
EIKNOSV INVOKES
EIKNPRR PRINKER
EIKNPRS PINKERS
EIKNPRU PUNKIER
EIKNPST PINKEST
EIKNPSU PUNKIES
SPUNKIE
EIKNPSY PINKEYS
EIKNRSS SINKERS
EIKNRST REKNITS
STINKER
TINKERS
EIKNRSW WINKERS
EIKNRTT KNITTER
TRINKET
EIKNSTT KITTENS
EIKNTUZ KUNZITE
EIKOORR ROOKIER
EIKOORS ROOKIES
EIKOPPR PORKPIE
EIKOPPS KOPPIES
EIKOPRR PORKIER
EIKOPRS PORKIES
EIKOPST POKIEST
EIKOSST KETOSIS
EIKPPRS KIPPERS
SKIPPER
EIKPPST SKIPPET
EIKPRSS SPIKERS
EIKPSSS SKEPSIS
EIKRRSS RISKERS
EIKRRST SKIRRET
SKIRTER
STRIKER
EIKRSSS KISSERS
EIKRSST STRIKES
EIKRSSV SKIVERS
EIKRSTT SKITTER
EIKSSTW WESKITS
EILLLOS LOLLIES
EILLMNU MULLEIN
EILLMOS MOLLIES
EILLMOT MELILOT
EILLMOU MOUILLE
EILLMRS MILLERS
EILLMST MILLETS
EILLMSU ILLUMES
EILLMTU MULLITE
EILLNOS NIELLOS
EILLNSS ILLNESS
EILLNST LENTILS
LINTELS
EILLNUV LEVULIN
EILLORU ROUILLE
EILLORW LOWLIER
EILLORZ ZORILLE
EILLOSV VILLOSE
EILLPPR PREPILL
EILLPRS SPILLER
EILLPSS LIPLESS
EILLPSU PILULES
EILLQTU QUILLET
EILLRRT TRILLER
EILLRSS SILLERS
EILLRST RILLETS
STILLER
TILLERS
TRELLIS
EILLRSW SWILLER
WILLERS
EILLRTT LITTLER
EILLSST LISTELS
EILLSSU SULLIES
EILLSTT LITTLES
EILLSTU TUILLES
EILLSTW WILLETS
EILMMRS LIMMERS
SLIMMER
EILMNOO OINOMEL
EILMNOS LOMEINS
EILMNPS PLENISM
EILMNRS LIMNERS
MERLINS
EILMNSS SIMNELS
EILMNSY MYELINS
EILMOPR IMPLORE
EILMORR LORIMER
EILMORS MOILERS
EILMORT MOTLIER
EILMOSS LISSOME
EILMOST MOTILES
EILMPPS PIMPLES
EILMPRS LIMPERS
PRELIMS
RIMPLES
SIMPLER
EILMPRU LUMPIER
PLUMIER
EILMPRY PRIMELY
EILMPSS SIMPLES
EILMPST LIMPEST
LIMPETS
EILMPSU IMPULSE
EILMPSW WIMPLES
EILMPSX SIMPLEX
EILMPSY LIMPSEY
EILMPTY EMPTILY
EILMRRY MERRILY
EILMRSS RIMLESS
SMILERS
EILMRST MILTERS
EILMRSU MISRULE
EILMRSY MISERLY
MISRELY
EILMSSS MISSELS
EILMSSU MUESLIS
EILMSSY MESSILY
SMILEYS
EILMSZZ MIZZLES
EILMUUV ELUVIUM
EILNNPU PINNULE
EILNNRY INNERLY
EILNNSS INNLESS
EILNNST LINNETS
EILNOOR LOONIER
EILNOOS LOONIES
EILNOOV VIOLONE
EILNOPR PROLINE
EILNOPS EPSILON
PINOLES
EILNOPT POTLINE
TOPLINE
EILNORR LORINER
EILNORS NEROLIS
EILNORT RETINOL
EILNOSS INSOLES
LESIONS
LIONESS
EILNOST ENTOILS
EILNOSU ELUSION
EILNOTU ELUTION
OUTLINE
EILNOTV VIOLENT
EILNOTW TOWLINE
EILNOVV INVOLVE
EILNPPS LIPPENS
NIPPLES
EILNPRS PILSNER
EILNPRU PURLINE
EILNPSS PENSILS
SPINELS
SPLINES
EILNPST LEPTINS
PINTLES
PLENIST
EILNPSU LINEUPS
LUPINES
SPINULE
UNPILES
EILNPTY INEPTLY
EILNPUV VULPINE
EILNRST LINTERS
EILNRSV SILVERN
EILNRTY INERTLY
EILNRVY NERVILY
EILNSSS SINLESS
EILNSST ENLISTS
LISTENS
SILENTS
TINSELS
EILNSSU SILENUS
EILNSSV SNIVELS
EILNSSW WINLESS
EILNSSY LINSEYS
LYSINES
EILNSTU LUNIEST
LUTEINS
UTENSIL
EILNSTW WINTLES
EILNSUV UNLIVES
UNVEILS
EILNSVY SYLVINE
EILNVXY VIXENLY
EILOOPR LOOPIER
EILOORS ORIOLES
EILOORW WOOLIER
EILOOST OOLITES
OSTIOLE
STOOLIE
EILOOSW WOOLIES
EILOPPR LOPPIER
EILOPPZ ZEPPOLI
EILOPRS SPOILER
EILOPRT POITREL
POLITER
EILOPST PIOLETS
PISTOLE
EILOPSU PILEOUS
EILOPSV PLOSIVE
EILOPTX EXPLOIT
EILORRS LORRIES
EILORSS LORISES
RISSOLE
EILORST ESTRIOL
LOITERS
TOILERS
EILORSU LOUSIER
SOILURE
EILORTT TORTILE
TRIOLET
EILORTU OUTLIER
EILORTV OVERLIT
EILOSTT LITOTES
TOILETS
EILOSTU OUTLIES
EILOSTV VIOLETS
EILOSTZ ZLOTIES
EILOTUV OUTLIVE
EILOTUW OUTWILE
EILPPPY PEPPILY
EILPPRR RIPPLER
EILPPRS LIPPERS
RIPPLES
SLIPPER
EILPPRT RIPPLET
TIPPLER
EILPPRU PULPIER
EILPPST STIPPLE
TIPPLES
EILPPSU PILEUPS
UPPILES
EILPPSW SWIPPLE
EILPRSS LISPERS
EILPRST RESPLIT
TRIPLES
EILPRTT TRIPLET
EILPRTX TRIPLEX
EILPRUU PURLIEU
EILPSSS PLISSES
EILPSST STIPELS
TIPLESS
EILPSSW SWIPLES
EILPSSZ ZIPLESS
EILPSTT SPITTLE
EILPSTU STIPULE
EILPSZZ PIZZLES
EILPTTY PETTILY
EILQRTU QUILTER
EILQRUU LIQUEUR
EILQTUY QUIETLY
EILRRSU SURLIER
EILRRTW TWIRLER
EILRSST LISTERS
RELISTS
EILRSSV SILVERS
SLIVERS
EILRSTT LITTERS
SLITTER
TILTERS
EILRSTU LUSTIER
RULIEST
RUTILES
EILRSUV SURVEIL
EILRSVY LIVYERS
SILVERY
EILRSZZ SIZZLER
EILRTTY LITTERY
TRITELY
EILRTUV RIVULET
EILSSTW WITLESS
EILSSTY STYLISE
EILSSVW SWIVELS
EILSSZZ SIZZLES
EILSTTT TITTLES
EILSTTV VITTLES
EILSTTY STYLITE
TESTILY
EILSTVY SYLVITE
EILSTYZ STYLIZE
ZESTILY
EILSWZZ SWIZZLE
EILSZZZ ZIZZLES
EIMMMOS MOMMIES
EIMMMSU MUMMIES
EIMMNSU IMMUNES
EIMMORS MEMOIRS
EIMMOST TOMMIES
EIMMOSV MISMOVE
EIMMPRR PRIMMER
EIMMPRU PREMIUM
EIMMRRS RIMMERS
EIMMRRT TRIMMER
EIMMRRU RUMMIER
EIMMRSS SIMMERS
EIMMRST MISTERM
EIMMRSU IMMURES
RUMMIES
EIMMRSW SWIMMER
EIMMRUY YUMMIER
EIMMSST TSIMMES
EIMMSTU TUMMIES
EIMMSTZ TZIMMES
EIMMSUY YUMMIES
EIMNNOR IRONMEN
EIMNNOT MENTION
EIMNOOR IONOMER
MOONIER
EIMNOOS NOISOME
EIMNOOT EMOTION
EIMNOPR PROMINE
EIMNOPS IMPONES
PEONISM
EIMNOPT PIMENTO
EIMNORS MERINOS
EIMNOSS EONISMS
EIMNOST MESTINO
MOISTEN
SENTIMO
EIMNOSW WINSOME
EIMNPSS MISPENS
EIMNPST EMPTINS
EIMNPTU PINETUM
EIMNRRU MURRINE
EIMNRST MINSTER
MINTERS
REMINTS
EIMNRSU MUREINS
MURINES
EIMNRTU MINUTER
UNMITER
UNMITRE
EIMNSST MISSENT
EIMNSSU MINUSES
EIMNSTT MITTENS
SMITTEN
EIMNSTU MINUETS
MINUTES
MISTUNE
MUTINES
EIMNSUX UNMIXES
EIMNSZZ MIZZENS
EIMNUZZ MUEZZIN
EIMOORR MOORIER
ROOMIER
EIMOORS ROOMIES
EIMOPRR PRIMERO
EIMOPRS IMPOSER
PROMISE
SEMIPRO
EIMOPRV IMPROVE
EIMOPRW IMPOWER
EIMOPSS IMPOSES
EIMOPST MOPIEST
OPTIMES
EIMOPSY MYOPIES
EIMORRW WORMIER
EIMORSS ISOMERS
MOSSIER
EIMORST EROTISM
MOISTER
MORTISE
TRISOME
EIMORSU MOUSIER
EIMORSV VERISMO
EIMORTT OMITTER
EIMORTV VOMITER
EIMORVX OVERMIX
EIMOSST MITOSES
SOMITES
EIMOSTU TIMEOUS
EIMOSTV MOTIVES
EIMOSTX EXOTISM
EIMOSTZ MESTIZO
EIMOSYZ ISOZYME
EIMOTTU TIMEOUT
EIMPRRS PRIMERS
EIMPRRT PRETRIM
EIMPRRU IMPURER
EIMPRSS IMPRESS
PREMISS
SIMPERS
SPIREMS
EIMPRST IMPREST
PERMITS
EIMPRSU SPUMIER
UMPIRES
EIMPRTU IMPUTER
EIMPRTX PREMIXT
EIMPSST MISSTEP
EIMPSTU IMPETUS
IMPUTES
UPTIMES
EIMPSTY MISTYPE
EIMQSTU MESQUIT
EIMQTUZ MEZQUIT
EIMRRST RETRIMS
TRIMERS
EIMRRSU MURRIES
EIMRSST MISTERS
SMITERS
EIMRSSU MISUSER
MUSSIER
SURMISE
EIMRSSV VERISMS
EIMRSTT METRIST
EIMRSTU MUSTIER
EIMRTUX MIXTURE
EIMRUZZ MUZZIER
EIMSSST MISSETS
EIMSSSU MISUSES
EIMSSSX SEXISMS
EIMSSTY STYMIES
EIMUUVX EXUVIUM
EINNNRS RENNINS
EINNOOS IONONES
EINNOPS PENSION
PINONES
EINNOPT PONTINE
EINNOQU QUINONE
EINNORT INTONER
TERNION
EINNORU REUNION
EINNORV ENVIRON
EINNOSS SONNIES
EINNOST INTONES
TENSION
EINNOSV VENISON
EINNOTT TONTINE
EINNOVW INWOVEN
EINNPRS PINNERS
SPINNER
EINNPRU PUNNIER
EINNPST TENPINS
EINNPSY SPINNEY
EINNRRU RUNNIER
EINNRSS SINNERS
EINNRST INTERNS
TINNERS
EINNRSU SUNNIER
UNRISEN
EINNRSW WINNERS
EINNRTV VINTNER
EINNSST SENNITS
EINNSSY SINSYNE
EINNSTT INTENTS
TENNIST
EINNSTU TUNNIES
EINNSTV INVENTS
EINNSWY SWINNEY
EINNTUW UNTWINE
EINOOPZ EPIZOON
EINOORS EROSION
EINOOST ISOTONE
TOONIES
EINOOSZ OZONISE
EINOOTW TWOONIE
EINOOZZ OZONIZE
EINOPPR PROPINE
EINOPPS PEPINOS
EINOPRR PORNIER
EINOPRS ORPINES
EINOPRT POINTER
PROTEIN
TROPINE
EINOPSS SPINOSE
EINOPST PINTOES
POINTES
EINOPSW WINESOP
EINOPTU POUTINE
EINOQUX EQUINOX
EINORRS IRONERS
EINORSS SENIORS
SONSIER
EINORST NORITES
OESTRIN
ORIENTS
STONIER
EINORSU URINOSE
EINORSV ENVIROS
RENVOIS
VERSION
EINORSW SNOWIER
EINORTT TRITONE
EINORTU ROUTINE
EINOSSS ESSOINS
OSSEINS
SESSION
EINOSST NOSIEST
EINOSSZ SOZINES
EINOSTT TONIEST
EINOSTW TOWNIES
EINOSTX TOXINES
EINOSUV ENVIOUS
NIVEOUS
EINPPRS NIPPERS
SNIPPER
EINPPSS PEPSINS
EINPPST SNIPPET
EINPRRT PRINTER
REPRINT
EINPRRU UNRIPER
EINPRSS SNIPERS
EINPRST PTERINS
EINPRSU PURINES
UPRISEN
EINPSST INSTEPS
SPINETS
EINPSSU PUISNES
SUPINES
EINPSTU PUNIEST
PUNTIES
EINPSTW INSWEPT
EINPTTY TINTYPE
EINQRSU REQUINS
EINQRUU UNIQUER
EINQRUY ENQUIRY
EINQSSU SEQUINS
EINQSTU INQUEST
QUINTES
EINQSUU UNIQUES
EINQTTU QUINTET
EINQTUU UNQUIET
EINRRSS RINSERS
EINRRSU INSURER
RUINERS
EINRRTU RUNTIER
EINRSST ESTRINS
INSERTS
SINTERS
EINRSSU INSURES
SUNRISE
EINRSTT RETINTS
STINTER
TINTERS
EINRSTU NUTSIER
TRIUNES
UNITERS

EINRSTV INVERTS
STRIVEN
EINRSTW TWINERS
WINTERS
EINRSUW UNWISER
EINRSVW WIVERNS
EINRTTU NUTTIER
EINRTTW WRITTEN
EINRTUV VENTURI
EINRTWY WINTERY
EINSSSU SINUSES
EINSSSY SYNESIS
EINSSTV INVESTS
EINSSTW WISENTS
WITNESS
EINSSUW SUNWISE
EINSTTW ENTWIST
TWINSET
EINSTTY TENSITY
EINSTWY WITNEYS
EINSWZZ WIZZENS
EINTTUY TENUITY
EIOOPST ISOTOPE
EIOORRT ROOTIER
EIOORST SOOTIER
EIOORTZ ZOOTIER
EIOORWZ WOOZIER
EIOOSTT TOOTSIE
EIOOSTZ OOZIEST
ZOOIEST
EIOPPPS POPPIES
EIOPPRS SOPPIER
EIOPPSS POPSIES
EIOPPST POTPIES
EIOPQRU PIROQUE
EIOPRRS PROSIER
EIOPRRT PIERROT
PRERIOT
EIOPRRU ROUPIER
EIOPRSS POISERS
PROSSIE
EIOPRST PROSTIE
REPOSIT
RIPOSTE
ROPIEST
EIOPRSU SOUPIER
EIOPRSX PROXIES
EIOPRTT POTTIER
EIOPRTU POUTIER
EIOPRTV OVERTIP
EIOPSST POSTIES
POTSIES
SOPITES
EIOPSSU POUSSIE
EIOPSTT POTTIES
TIPTOES
EIOPSTU PITEOUS
EIOPSTX EXPOSIT
POXIEST
EIOPSTY ISOTYPE
EIOPTUW WIPEOUT
EIOQTUX QUIXOTE
EIORRRS SORRIER
EIORRRW WORRIER
EIORRSS ORRISES
EIORRST RIOTERS
ROISTER
EIORRSV REVISOR
EIORRSW WORRIES
EIORSSS SEISORS
EIORSST ROSIEST
SORITES
SORTIES
STORIES
TRIOSES
EIORSSU SERIOUS
EIORSSV VIROSES
EIORSSX XEROSIS
EIORSSZ SEIZORS
EIORSTU STOURIE
EIOSSTV SOVIETS
EIOSTUV OUTVIES
EIOSTUZ OUTSIZE
EIOSTVV VOTIVES
EIPPPSU PUPPIES
EIPPQRU QUIPPER
EIPPRRS RIPPERS
EIPPRRT TRIPPER
EIPPRSS SIPPERS
EIPPRST TIPPERS
EIPPRSZ ZIPPERS
EIPPRTT TRIPPET
EIPPSST SIPPETS
EIPPSTT TIPPETS
EIPPSUY YUPPIES
EIPQSTU PIQUETS

EIPRRST STRIPER
EIPRRSU PURSIER
UPRISER
EIPRRSZ PRIZERS
EIPRRTU PURTIER
EIPRRUV UPRIVER
EIPRSSS PRISSES
EIPRSST ESPRITS
PERSIST
PRIESTS
SPRIEST
SPRITES
STIRPES
STRIPES
EIPRSSU PUSSIER
SUSPIRE
UPRISES
EIPRSTT SPITTER
TIPSTER
EIPRSTU PERITUS
EIPRSTV PRIVETS
EIPRSTY PYRITES
EIPRSUU EURIPUS
EIPRTTU PUTTIER
EIPRUVW PURVIEW
EIPSSSU PUSSIES
EIPSSTZ SPITZES
EIPSSUZ UPSIZES
EIPSTTU PUTTIES
EIPSTTY TYPIEST
EIQRSSU SQUIRES
EIQRSTU QUERIST
EIQRSUV QUIVERS
EIQRTTU QUITTER
EIQRUVY QUIVERY
EIQRUZZ QUIZZER
EIQSTUU QUIETUS
EIQSUZZ QUIZZES
EIRRRST STIRRER
EIRRSTT RITTERS
TERRITS
EIRRSTU RUSTIER
EIRRSTV STRIVER
EIRRSTW WRITERS
EIRRTTU RUTTIER
EIRSSST RESISTS
SISTERS
EIRSSSU ISSUERS
RISUSES
EIRSSTT SITTERS
EIRSSTU SUITERS
EIRSSTV STIVERS
STRIVES
VERISTS
EIRSSUU USURIES
EIRSSUV VIRUSES
EIRSSUW WUSSIER
EIRSTTT STRETTI
TITTERS
TRITEST
EIRSTTV TRIVETS
EIRSTTW RETWIST
TWISTER
EIRSTUV REVUIST
STUIVER
VIRTUES
EIRSUVV SURVIVE
EIRTTTW TWITTER
EISSSSW SWISSES
EISSSTU SITUSES
TISSUES
EISSSTX SEXISTS
EISSSUW WUSSIES
EISSTUV TUSSIVE
EISSTUY TISSUEY
EISSTVW SWIVETS
EISTTTU TUTTIES
EISTTUW WETSUIT
EJJMNUU JEJUNUM
EJKMNNU JUNKMEN
EJKNRSU JUNKERS
EJKNSTU JUNKETS
EJLORST JOLTERS
JOSTLER
EJLOSST JOSTLES
EJLOSSY JOYLESS
EJLSSTU JUSTLES
EJMNRUY JURYMEN
EJMOSST JETSOMS
EJMPRSU JUMPERS
EJNORUY JOURNEY
EJNOSTT JETTONS
EJOORVY OVERJOY
EJOPPRT PROPJET
EJOPRST PROJETS
EJOPRTT JETPORT

EJORSTT JOTTERS
EJORSTU JOUSTER
EJPRRUY PERJURY
EJRSSTU JUSTERS
EJSSTTU JUSTEST
EKKLRSU SKULKER
EKLLMSU SKELLUM
EKLLNOR KNOLLER
EKLLRRU KRULLER
EKLMMSU KUMMELS
EKLNORS SNORKEL
EKLNOSS KELSONS
EKLNOSU LEUKONS
EKLNPRU PLUNKER
EKLNPSU SPELUNK
EKLNRSU LUNKERS
RUNKLES
EKLNSST SKLENTS
EKLOORS LOOKERS
RELOOKS
EKLOPST KLEPTOS
EKLRRSU LURKERS
EKLRSSU SULKERS
EKLSTUZ KLUTZES
EKMNORW WORKMEN
EKMNORY MONKERY
EKMNOSY MONKEYS
EKMNPTU UNKEMPT
EKMOOPS MOPOKES
EKMORSS SMOKERS
EKMRSTU MURKEST
EKMSSTU MUSKETS
EKMSSUY KUMYSES
EKNNOST NEKTONS
EKNOORS SNOOKER
EKNOPSU UNSPOKE
EKNORST REKNOTS
EKNORSW KNOWERS
EKNORSY YONKERS
EKNORTT KNOTTER
EKNORTW NETWORK
EKNORUY YOUNKER
EKNOSTY STENOKY
EKNOSUY UNYOKES
EKNPRSU PUNKERS
EKNPSTU PUNKEST
EKNPSUY PUNKEYS
EKNRTUY TURNKEY
EKNSSTU SUNKETS
EKOOPRV PROVOKE
EKOORRY ROOKERY
EKOORST STOOKER
EKOORTW KOTOWER
EKOPRRS PORKERS
EKOPRRW PREWORK
EKOPRUY KOUPREY
EKOPTTU OUTKEPT
EKORRST STROKER
EKORRSW REWORKS
WORKERS
EKORSST STOKERS
STROKES
EKORUYY EURYOKY
EKPPSUU SEPPUKU
EKRSSTU TUSKERS
EKRSTUY TURKEYS
ELLLORS LOLLERS
ELLLRSU LULLERS
ELLMNOT TOLLMEN
ELLMNSU MULLENS
ELLMOOR MORELLO
ELLMOSW MELLOWS
ELLMPUU PLUMULE
ELLMRSU MULLERS
ELLMSTU MULLETS
ELLMSUV VELLUMS
ELLMSUY MULLEYS
ELLNOOW WOOLLEN
ELLNOPS POLLENS
ELLNORS ENROLLS
ELLNOST STOLLEN
ELLNOSW SWOLLEN
ELLNOVY NOVELLY
ELLNSSU UNSELLS
ELLNSUU LUNULES
ELLOOSY LOOSELY
ELLOOTU TOLUOLE
ELLOPRS POLLERS
REPOLLS
ELLOPTU POLLUTE
ELLORRS REROLLS
ROLLERS
ELLORRT TROLLER
ELLORST TOLLERS
ELLORTY TROLLEY
ELLORVY LOVERLY

ELLOSTU OUTSELL
SELLOUT
ELLOSTX EXTOLLS
ELLOSVY VOLLEYS
ELLOSWY YELLOWS
ELLOTTU OUTTELL
ELLOTUY OUTYELL
ELLOWYY YELLOWY
ELLPRSU PULLERS
ELLPSTU PULLETS
ELLPSUW UPSWELL
UPWELLS
ELLPSUY PULLEYS
ELMMOPS POMMELS
ELMMOPU PUMMELO
ELMMORT TROMMEL
ELMMPRU PLUMMER
ELMMPSU PUMMELS
ELMMPTU PLUMMET
ELMMRSU SLUMMER
ELMMRTU TUMMLER
ELMNOOT MOONLET
ELMNOOW WOOLMEN
ELMNOPW PLOWMEN
ELMNORS MERLONS
ELMNOST LOMENTS
MELTONS
ELMNPPU PLUMPEN
ELMNPSU LUMPENS
PLENUMS
ELMOOPS POMELOS
ELMOORT TREMOLO
ELMOOSS OSMOLES
ELMOOSY MOOLEYS
ELMOPRT PREMOLT
ELMOPRY POLYMER
ELMOPSU PLUMOSE
PUMELOS
ELMOPSY EMPLOYS
ELMORSS MORSELS
ELMORST MERLOTS
MOLTERS
ELMORTT MOTTLER
ELMORTU MOULTER
ELMOSST MOLESTS
ELMOSTT MOTTLES
ELMOSTY MOTLEYS
ELMOSUU EMULOUS
ELMOSUV VOLUMES
ELMPPRU PLUMPER
ELMPPSU PEPLUMS
ELMPRSU LUMPERS
RUMPLES
ELMRSTY MYRTLES
ELMRTUU MULTURE
ELMRTUY ELYTRUM
ELMRUZZ MUZZLER
ELMSSSU MUSSELS
SUMLESS
ELMSTUU MUTUELS
MUTULES
ELMSUZZ MUZZLES
ELNNOPU NONUPLE
ELNNORS RONNELS
ELNNOSS NELSONS
ELNNRSU RUNNELS
ELNNRTU TRUNNEL
ELNNSTU TUNNELS
ELNOOPT PELOTON
ELNOOSS LOOSENS
ELNOOSU UNLOOSE
ELNOOSW WOOLENS
ELNOOSY LOONEYS
ELNOOSZ SNOOZLE
ELNOPRU PLEURON
ELNOPRY PRONELY
ELNOPST LEPTONS
ELNOPSY POLEYNS
ELNOPTU OPULENT
ELNORTY ELYTRON
ELNOSSS LESSONS
SONLESS
ELNOSST TELSONS
ELNOSSU ENSOULS
ELNOSSV SLOVENS
ELNOSSW LOWNESS
ELNOSTT TONLETS
ELNOSTV SOLVENT
ELNOSUZ ZONULES
ELNOSZZ NOZZLES
ELNOTTW TOWNLET
ELNOTVY NOVELTY
ELNPSST SPLENTS
ELNPSTU PENULTS
ELNPSTY PENTYLS
ELNRSSU RUNLESS

ELNRSTU RUNLETS
ELNRSTY STERNLY
ELNRUZZ NUZZLER
ELNSSSU SUNLESS
ELNSSSY SELSYNS
SLYNESS
ELNSTTU NUTLETS
ELNSUZZ NUZZLES
ELOOPRS LOOPERS
POOLERS
RESPOOL
SPOOLER
ELOOPSS POSOLES
ELOOPSZ POZOLES
ELOORST LOOTERS
RETOOLS
ROOTLES
TOOLERS
ELOORSW WOOLERS
ELOORTT ROOTLET
TOOTLER
ELOOSST LOOSEST
LOTOSES
ELOOSTT TOOTLES
ELOOSTU OUTSOLE
ELOOTUV OUTLOVE
ELOPPPS POPPLES
ELOPPRS LOPPERS
PROPELS
ELOPPST STOPPLE
TOPPLES
ELOPPSU UPSLOPE
ELOPRRW PROWLER
ELOPRRY PYRROLE
ELOPRSS PLESSOR
SLOPERS
SPLORES
ELOPRST PETROLS
REPLOTS
ELOPRSU LEPROUS
PELORUS
SPORULE
ELOPRSV PLOVERS
ELOPRSW PLOWERS
REPLOWS
ELOPRSX PLEXORS
ELOPRSY LEPROSY
ELOPRTT PLOTTER
ELOPRTU POULTER
ELOPRTY PROTYLE
ELOPRVY OVERPLY
ELOPSST TOPLESS
ELOPSTT POTTLES
ELOPSTU TUPELOS
ELOPSTY PEYOTLS
ELOPSTZ PLOTZES
ELOPTUY OUTYELP
ELORRSS SORRELS
ELORSSS LESSORS
ELORSST OSTLERS
STEROLS
ELORSSV SOLVERS
ELORSTT LOTTERS
SETTLOR
SLOTTER
ELORSTV REVOLTS
ELORSTW TROWELS
ELORSUV LOUVERS
LOUVRES
VELOURS
ELORSUY ELUSORY
ELORSVW WOLVERS
ELORSWY YOWLERS
ELORTTY LOTTERY
ELORTVY OVERTLY
ELOSSTU LOTUSES
SOLUTES
TOUSLES
ELOSSTW SLOWEST
ELOSSTY SYSTOLE
TOYLESS
ELOSSVW VOWLESS
ELOSSXY XYLOSES
ELOSTTU OUTLETS
ELOSTUU LUTEOUS
ELOSTUV VOLUTES
ELOSTUZ TOUZLES
ELPPRRU PURPLER
ELPPRSU PULPERS
PURPLES
SUPPLER
ELPPSSU SUPPLES
ELPQSUU PULQUES
ELPRSSU PULSERS
ELPRSTU SPURTLE
ELPRUZZ PUZZLER

ELPSSSU PLUSSES
ELPSSUU LUPUSES
ELPSSUY PUSLEYS
PUSSLEY
ELPSTUU PLUTEUS
PUSTULE
ELPSUZZ PUZZLES
ELRRSTU RUSTLER
ELRRTTU TURTLER
ELRSSTU LUSTERS
LUSTRES
RESULTS
RUSTLES
SUTLERS
ULSTERS
ELRSSTY STYLERS
ELRSTTU TURTLES
ELRSTTY TETRYLS
ELRSTWY SWELTRY
ELRSUWZ WURZELS
ELRTTUY UTTERLY
ELRTUUV VULTURE
ELSSSTU TUSSLES
ELSSSUU LUSUSES
ELSSTTY STYLETS
EMMMRSU MUMMERS
EMMMRUY MUMMERY
EMMNOOR MONOMER
EMMNOST MOMENTS
EMMNOTU OMENTUM
EMMNOTY METONYM
EMMOOTY MYOTOME
EMMORSS MOMSERS
EMMORSZ MOMZERS
EMMOSSU MOMUSES
EMMPRSU MUMPERS
EMMPSTU METUMPS
EMMRRSU RUMMERS
EMMRSSU SUMMERS
EMMRSTU RUMMEST
EMMRSUY SUMMERY
EMMSSUU MUSEUMS
EMNNOSW SNOWMEN
EMNNOWW NEWMOWN
EMNOOPT METOPON
EMNOORS MOONERS
EMNOORT MONTERO
EMNOOST MOONSET
EMNOPPR PROPMEN
EMNOPST POSTMEN
EMNOPSU SPUMONE
EMNOPSY EPONYMS
EMNOPYY EPONYMY
EMNORRU MOURNER
EMNORSS SERMONS
EMNORST MENTORS
MONSTER
EMNORTT TORMENT
EMNORTU MOUNTER
REMOUNT
EMNOSST STEMSON
EMNOSTY ETYMONS
EMNOSXY EXONYMS
EMNRRUY UNMERRY
EMNRSTU MUNSTER
STERNUM
EMOOPRS OOSPERM
EMOOPRT PROMOTE
EMOORRS ROOMERS
EMOORST MOOTERS
EMOOSSS OSMOSES
EMOOSTT MOTTOES
EMOOSTW TWOSOME
EMOOSTY MYOSOTE
EMOOSXY OXYSOME
EMOOTUV OUTMOVE
EMOPPRS MOPPERS
EMOPPST MOPPETS
EMOPPTU UPTEMPO
EMOPRRS ROMPERS
EMOPRST STOMPER
TROMPES
EMOPRSU SUPREMO
EMOQSSU MOSQUES
EMORRST TERMORS
TREMORS
EMORRSW WORMERS
EMORSSS MOSSERS
EMORSSU MOUSERS
EMORSTU OESTRUM
EMOSSSU MOUSSES
EMOSSTT MOSTEST
EMOSSYZ ZYMOSES
EMOSTVZ ZEMSTVO
EMOTTTU TETOTUM

EMOTUZZ MEZUZOT
EMPPRSU PUMPERS
REPUMPS
EMPRSTU STUMPER
SUMPTER
EMPRTTU TRUMPET
EMPSSTU SEPTUMS
EMRRSUY MURREYS
EMRSSTU ESTRUMS
MUSTERS
EMRSTTU MUTTERS
EMRSTYY MYSTERY
EMSSSTY SYSTEMS
ENNNOPS PENNONS
ENNNOSW NONNEWS
ENNNRUY NUNNERY
ENNOOPR PRENOON
ENNOORZ NONZERO
ENNORST TONNERS
ENNORSU NEURONS
NONUSER
ENNORSW RENOWNS
WONNERS
ENNORTU NEUTRON
ENNORUV UNROVEN
ENNOSST SONNETS
ENNOSSU NONUSES
ENNOSSW NOWNESS
ENNOSTU NEUSTON
ENNOSTW NEWTONS
ENNOUVW UNWOVEN
ENNPRSU PUNNERS
ENNPSTU PUNNETS
UNSPENT
ENNRRSU RUNNERS
ENNRSTU STUNNER
ENNSTUU UNTUNES
ENOOPPR PROPONE
ENOOPRS OPERONS
SNOOPER
ENOOPSY SPOONEY
ENOORSS NOOSERS
SOONERS
ENOORST ENROOTS
ENOORSU ONEROUS
ENOORSW SWOONER
ENOORSZ SNOOZER
ENOOSST SOONEST
ENOOSSZ SNOOZES
ENOOSTT TESTOON
ENOOTXY OXYTONE
ENOPRRS PERRONS
ENOPRRW PREWORN
ENOPRSS PERSONS
ENOPRST POSTERN
ENOPRSY PYRONES
ENOPRTT PORTENT
ENOPRTY ENTROPY
ENOPSST STEPSON
ENOPSUX XENOPUS
ENOQTUU UNQUOTE
ENORRSS SNORERS
SORNERS
ENORRST SNORTER
ENORRTT TORRENT
ENORRUV OVERRUN
RUNOVER
ENORSSS SENSORS
ENORSST NESTORS
STONERS
TENSORS
ENORSSW WORSENS
ENORSSY SENSORY
ENORSTT STENTOR
ENORSTU TENOURS
TONSURE
ENORSUV NERVOUS
ENORSUW UNSWORE
ENORTUY TOURNEY
ENOSSTT STETSON
TESTONS
ENOSSTU TONUSES
ENOSSTX SEXTONS
ENOSTTU STOUTEN
TENUTOS
ENOSTUU TENUOUS
ENOTTUW OUTWENT
ENPRRSU PRUNERS
SPURNER
ENPRSTU PUNSTER
PUNTERS
ENPSSTU UNSTEPS
ENPSTUU TUNEUPS
ENPSTUW UNSWEPT
ENRRSSU NURSERS

ENRRSTU RETURNS
TURNERS
ENRRSUY NURSERY
ENRRTUU NURTURE
UNTRUER
ENRRTUY TURNERY
ENRSSTU UNRESTS
ENRSSWY WRYNESS
ENRSTTU ENTRUST
NUTTERS
ENRSVWY WYVERNS
ENSSSTU SUNSETS
EOOOPRS OOSPORE
EOOPPRS OPPOSER
PROPOSE
EOOPPRV POPOVER
EOOPPSS OPPOSES
EOOPRRT TROOPER
EOOPRST POOREST
STOOPER
EOOPRSW SWOOPER
EOOPRTV OVERTOP
EOOPRTW TOWROPE
EOOPSSW WOOPSES
EOORRSS ROOSERS
EOORRST ROOSTER
ROOTERS
TOREROS
EOORSSS SOROSES
EOORSTT TOOTERS
EOORTUW OUTWORE
EOOSSST OSTOSES
EOOSSSU OSSEOUS
EOOSSTT TOOTSES
EOOTTUV OUTVOTE
EOPPPRS POPPERS
EOPPPST POPPETS
EOPPRRS PROPERS
PROSPER
EOPPRSS OPPRESS
EOPPRST STOPPER
TOPPERS
EOPPRSU PURPOSE
EOPPRSY PYROPES
EOPPSSU SUPPOSE
EOPRRSS PRESSOR
PROSERS
EOPRRST PORTERS
PRESORT
PRETORS
REPORTS
SPORTER
EOPRRSU POURERS
REPOURS
EOPRRSV PROVERS
EOPRRTU TROUPER
EOPRSSS PROSSES
EOPRSST POSTERS
PRESTOS
RESPOTS
STOPERS
EOPRSSU POSEURS
EOPRSSW PROWESS
EOPRSSY OSPREYS
EOPRSTT POTTERS
PROTEST
SPOTTER
EOPRSTU PETROUS
POSTURE
POUTERS
PROTEUS
SPOUTER
TROUPES
EOPRSTW POWTERS
PROWEST
EOPRSTX EXPORTS
EOPRSTZ POTZERS
EOPRSUU UPROUSE
EOPRSUV OVERSUP
EOPRTTY POTTERY
EOPRTVY POVERTY
EOPSSSS POSSESS
EOPSSST POSSETS
EOPSSSU SPOUSES
EOPSSTX SEXPOTS
EOPTTUW OUTWEPT
EOQRRTU TORQUER
EOQRSTU QUESTOR
QUOTERS
ROQUETS
TORQUES
EOQSTTU TOQUETS
EORRRST TERRORS

EORRSST RESORTS
ROSTERS
SORTERS
STORERS
EORRSSU ROUSERS
EORRSTT RETORTS
ROTTERS
STERTOR
EORRSTU ROUSTER
ROUTERS
TOURERS
TROUSER
EORRSTV TROVERS
EORRSTY ROYSTER
STROYER
EORRSZZ ROZZERS
EORRTTT TROTTER
EORRTTU TORTURE
EORSSTT TOSSERS
EORSSTU ESTROUS
OESTRUS
OUSTERS
SOUREST
SOUTERS
STOURES
TUSSORE
EORSSTV STOVERS
VOTRESS
EORSSTW WORSETS
EORSSTY OYSTERS
STOREYS
EORSSTZ ZOSTERS
EORSSWW WOWSERS
EORSTTT STRETTO
TOTTERS
EORSTTU OUTSERT
STOUTER
TOUTERS
EORSTTW SWOTTER
EORSTTX EXTORTS
EORSUVY VOYEURS
EORTTTY TOTTERY
EORTTUY TUTOYER
EOSSTTU OUTSETS
SETOUTS
EOSSUYZ SOYUZES
EPPPSTU PUPPETS
EPPRRUU PURPURE
EPPRSSU SUPPERS
EPPSSTU UPSTEPS
EPPSTUW UPSWEPT
EPRRRSU SPURRER
EPRRSSU PURSERS
EPRRSTU SPURTER
EPRRSUU PURSUER
USURPER
EPRRSUY SPURREY
EPRRTUU RUPTURE
EPRSSTY SPRYEST
EPRSSUU PURSUES
EPRSTTU PUTTERS
SPUTTER
EPRSUVY PURVEYS
EQRSTWY QWERTYS
ERRSSTU TRUSSER
ERRSSUU USURERS
ERRSSUY SURREYS
ERRSTTU TRUSTER
TURRETS
ERRSTTY TRYSTER
ERSSSTU RUSSETS
TRUSSES
TUSSERS
ERSSTTY TRYSTES
ERSSTUU SUTURES
ERSSTUY RUSSETY
ERSSTXY XYSTERS
ERSSUVY SURVEYS
ERSTTTU STUTTER
ERSTTUX URTEXTS
FFFILOT LIFTOFF
FFFLOSY FLYOFFS
FFGHINU HUFFING
FFGIIMN MIFFING
FFGIINR GRIFFIN
RIFFING
FFGIINT TIFFING
FFGILNU LUFFING
FFGIMNU MUFFING
FFGINOR GRIFFON
FFGINOS GONIFFS
OFFINGS
FFGINPU PUFFING
FFGINRU RUFFING
FFGLRUY GRUFFLY
FFHHISU HUFFISH

FFHIINS FINFISH
FFHILTY FIFTHLY
FFHILUY HUFFILY
FFHIOSX FOXFISH
FFHOOSW SHOWOFF
FFHORSS SHROFFS
FFHOSTU SHUTOFF
FFIINST TIFFINS
FFILLLU FULFILL
FFILLSU FULFILS
FFILNSY SNIFFLY
FFILPSS SPLIFFS
FFILPUY PUFFILY
FFILSTU FISTFUL
FFILSTY STIFFLY
FFIMNSU MUFFINS
FFINOOT FINFOOT
FFINOPS SPINOFF
FFINOPT PONTIFF
FFINPSU PUFFINS
FFIOPRS RIPOFFS
FFIOPST TIPOFFS
FFIORTY FORTIFY
FFIOSST SOFFITS
FFIQSUY SQUIFFY
FFJMOPU JUMPOFF
FFKLORU FORKFUL
FFLMORU FORMFUL
FFLNSUY SNUFFLY
FFLOSTY FYLFOTS
FFNORSU RUNOFFS
FFNORTU TURNOFF
FFOOPST STOPOFF
FFOPSTU PUTOFFS
FGGGIIN FIGGING
FGGGINO FOGGING
FGGGINU FUGGING
FGGHIIS FISHGIG
FGGIINT GIFTING
FGGIISZ FIZGIGS
FGGILNO GOLFING
FGGILNU FUGLING
GULFING
FGGILOY FOGGILY
FGGILUY FUGGILY
FGGINOO GOOFING
FGGINOR FORGING
FGGINUU FUGUING
FGHHIOS HOGFISH
FGHIINS FISHING
FGHIINT INFIGHT
FGHIIPS PIGFISH
FGHILST FLIGHTS
FGHILTY FLIGHTY
FGHINOO HOOFING
FGHIOSY FOGYISH
FGHIRST FRIGHTS
FGHNOOR FOGHORN
FGIIKNN FINKING
KNIFING
FGIILLN FILLING
FGIILMN FILMING
FGIILNO FOILING
FGIILNR RIFLING
FGIILNS FILINGS
FGIILNT FLITING
LIFTING
FGIILNY LIGNIFY
FGIIMNR FIRMING
FGIINNN FINNING
FGIINNO FOINING
FGIINNS FININGS
FGIINRS FIRINGS
FGIINRT RIFTING
FGIINRY NIGRIFY
FGIINRZ FRIZING
FGIINST FISTING
SIFTING
FGIINSX FIXINGS
FGIINSY SIGNIFY
FGIINTT FITTING
FGIINZZ FIZZING
FGIKLNU FLUKING
FGIKNNU FUNKING
FGIKNOR FORKING
FGILLNU FULLING
FGILMNU FLUMING
FGILNOO FOOLING
FGILNOR ROLFING
FGILNOT LOFTING
FGILNOU FOULING
FGILNOW FLOWING
FOWLING
WOLFING
FGILNPU UPFLING
FGILNRU FURLING

FGILNSU INGULFS
FGILNSY FLYINGS
FGILNTU FLUTING
FGILNTY FLYTING
FGILNUX FLUXING
FGILOOY GOOFILY
FGILORY GLORIFY
FGIMNOR FORMING
FGIMOSY FOGYISM
FGINNNU FUNNING
FGINOOR ROOFING
FGINOOT FOOTING
FGINOOW WOOFING
FGINOPP FOPPING
FGINOSX FOXINGS
FGINRRU FURRING
FGINRSU SURFING
FGINRTU TURFING
FGINSSU FUSSING
FGINTTU TUFTING
FGINTUZ FUTZING
FGINUZZ FUZZING
FGIORTW FIGWORT
FGISTUU FUGUIST
FGJLSUU JUGFULS
JUGSFUL
FGLLNUU LUNGFUL
FGLLOWY GLOWFLY
FGLMSUU MUGFULS
FGLNORU FURLONG
FGLNOSU SONGFUL
FGLNPUU UPFLUNG
FGLOOUY UFOLOGY
FGNOORU FOURGON
FGNOSUU FUNGOUS
FHHLSUU HUSHFUL
FHIILSY FISHILY
FHIILTY LITHIFY
FHIINPS PINFISH
FHIKLOS FOLKISH
FHILOOS FOOLISH
FHILOSW WOLFISH
FHILSUW WISHFUL
FHINRSU FURNISH
FHINSSU SUNFISH
FHINSTU UNSHIFT
FHIOPPS FOPPISH
FHIORRY HORRIFY
FHIOSST SOFTISH
FHIOSTU OUTFISH
FHIPPSU PUPFISH
FHIPSTU UPSHIFT
FHIRSST SHRIFTS
FHIRSTT THRIFTS
FHIRTTY THRIFTY
FHKORTU FUTHORK
FHLOOSY SHOOFLY
FHLPSUU PUSHFUL
FHLRTUU HURTFUL
RUTHFUL
FHNOTUX FOXHUNT
FHOOOTT HOTFOOT
FHORSTU FOURTHS
FIIIKNN FINIKIN
FIIKNRS FIRKINS
FIIKNYZ ZINKIFY
FIILLMO MILFOIL
FIILLMY FILMILY
FIILLPS FILLIPS
FIILLSU FUSILLI
FIILNOT TINFOIL
FIILNTY NIFTILY
FIILPRS RIFLIPS
FIILPTU PITIFUL
FIILQUY LIQUIFY
FIIMNRS INFIRMS
FIIMSST MISFITS
FIINOSS FISSION
FIINRTY NITRIFY
FIIRTVY VITRIFY
FIJLLOY JOLLIFY
FIJSTUY JUSTIFY
FIKKLNO KINFOLK
FIKLLSU SKILFUL
FIKLLUY FLUKILY
FIKLNSU SKINFUL
FIKLNUY FUNKILY
FIKLSTU KISTFUL
LUTFISK
FIKNOSX FOXSKIN
FIKRSTU TURFSKI
FILLLUW WILLFUL
FILLMOY MOLLIFY
FILLNUY NULLIFY
FILLOTU TOILFUL
FILLOTY LOFTILY

FILMNOO MONOFIL
FILMOSU FOLIUMS
FILNNUY FUNNILY
FILNORS FLORINS
FILNORU FLUORIN
FILNOSW INFLOWS
FILNOUX FLUXION
FILNSTU TINFULS
FILNTUY UNFITLY
FILOOSU FOLIOUS
FILOOTW WITLOOF
FILORST FLORIST
FILORSV FRIVOLS
FILORTU FLORUIT
FILOSSS FOSSILS
FILPSTU UPLIFTS
FILRRUY FURRILY
FILRSTY FIRSTLY
FILRYZZ FRIZZLY
FILSSUY FUSSILY
FILSTTU FLUTIST
FILSTUW WISTFUL
FILSTUY FUSTILY
FILSTWY SWIFTLY
FILTTUY TUFTILY
FILUYZZ FUZZILY
FIMMMUY MUMMIFY
FIMMORS MISFORM
FIMNORS INFORMS
FIMNORU UNIFORM
FIMOORS ISOFORM
FIMOORV OVIFORM
FIMORRT TRIFORM
FIMORTY MORTIFY
FIMRTUY FURMITY
FIMSTYY MYSTIFY
FINOOSS FOISONS
FINORSS FRISSON
FINORST FORINTS
FINORTY INTROFY
FINOSSU FUSIONS
FIOORSU FURIOSO
FIOPRST PROFITS
SPORTIF
FIOPSTX POSTFIX
FIORRTY TORRIFY
FIORSUU FURIOUS
FIOSTTU OUTFITS
FIOTTTU TOFUTTI
FIPPUYY YUPPIFY
FIRSSUY RUSSIFY
FKLMOOT FOLKMOT
FKOOORS FORSOOK
FKRSSUY SKYSURF
FLLOOSW FOLLOWS
FLLOPTU TOPFULL
FLLOSUU SOULFUL
FLLOUWY WOFULLY
FLLSTUU LUSTFUL
FLMMOUX FLUMMOX
FLMNOOU MOUFLON
FLMOOOT TOMFOOL
FLMOORS FORMOLS
FLMOORU ROOMFUL
FLMORSY FORMYLS
FLMSUUU FUMULUS
FLNOORR FORLORN
FLNRSUU UNFURLS
FLOOOTU OUTFOOL
FLOOPWX FOWLPOX
FLOOTUW OUTFLOW
FLOPSTU POTFULS
FLOPSUW UPFLOWS
FLOPTUU POUTFUL
FLOSUUV FULVOUS
FLRSSUU SULFURS
FLRSUUY SULFURY
FMRSTUU FRUSTUM
FNNNUUY UNFUNNY
FNNOORT FRONTON
FNOORRW FORWORN
FNOORSU SUNROOF
UNROOFS
FNOPRTU UPFRONT
FNSSUUY UNFUSSY
FOOOPRT ROOFTOP
FOOOTTU OUTFOOT
FOORTTX FOXTROT
FOPSSTU FUSSPOT
FORRSUW FURROWS
FORRUWY FURROWY
FORSSTW FROWSTS
FORSTWY FROWSTY
GGGGIIN GIGGING
GGGHINO HOGGING
GGGHINU HUGGING

GGGIIJN JIGGING
GGGIINP PIGGING
GGGIINR RIGGING
GGGIINW WIGGING
GGGIINZ ZIGGING
GGGIJNO JOGGING
GGGIJNU JUGGING
GGGILNO LOGGING
GGGILNU LUGGING
GGGIMNO MOGGING
GGGIMNU MUGGING
GGGINNO GONGING
NOGGING
GGGINOR GORGING
GGGINOT TOGGING
GGGINOU GOUGING
GGGINPU PUGGING
GGGINRU GURGING
RUGGING
GGGINTU TUGGING
GGHHIOS HOGGISH
GGHIIJS JIGGISH
GGHIINN HINGING
NIGHING
GGHIINS SIGHING
GGHIIPS PIGGISH
GGHILOS LOGGISH
GGHINSU GUSHING
SUGHING
GGHIPSU PUGGISH
GGIIILN GINGILI
GGIIKNN KINGING
GGIILLN GILLING
GGIILMN GLIMING
GGIILNU GUILING
GGIIMNP GIMPING
GGIIMNR GRIMING
GGIINNN GINNING
GGIINNO INGOING
GGIINNP PINGING
GGIINNR GIRNING
RINGING
GGIINNS SIGNING
SINGING
GGIINNT TINGING
GGIINNW WINGING
GGIINNZ ZINGING
GGIINPP GIPPING
GGIINPR GRIPING
GGIINPS PIGGINS
GGIINRT GIRTING
RINGGIT
GGIINSU GUISING
GGIINTT GITTING
GGIIRRS GRIGRIS
GGIKLNU KLUGING
GGIKNOS GINGKOS
GINKGOS
GGILLNU GULLING
GGILMUY MUGGILY
GGILNNO LONGING
GGILNNU LUNGING
GGILNOS GOSLING
GGILNOV GLOVING
GGILNOW GLOWING
GGILNOZ GLOZING
GGILNPU GULPING
GGILOOS GIGOLOS
GGILOST GIGLOTS
GGILOSY SOGGILY
GGILRWY WRIGGLY
GGIMMNU GUMMING
GGIMNOR GORMING
GGIMNSU MUGGINS
GGINNNU GUNNING
GGINNOO ONGOING
GGINNOP PONGING
GGINNOS NOGGINS
GGINNOT TONGING
GGINNOW GOWNING
GGINOOS GOOSING
GGINOPR GROPING
GGINOPU UPGOING
GGINORU ROGUING
ROUGING
GGINORW GROWING
GGINOUV VOGUING
GGINPPY GYPPING
GGINPRU PURGING
GGINRSU SURGING
GGINSTU GUSTING
GGINTTU GUTTING
GGIPRSY SPRIGGY
GGLOOOS GOOGOLS
GGMRSUU MUGGURS
GGNOORS GORGONS

GGRRSUU GRUGRUS
GHHHIST HIGHTHS
GHHINSU HUSHING
GHHIOPT HIGHTOP
GHHORTU THROUGH
GHHOTTU THOUGHT
GHIIKNT KITHING
GHIILLN HILLING
GHIILNT HILTING
GHIILNW WHILING
GHIILRS GIRLISH
GHIINNS SHINING
GHIINNT HINTING
GHIINNW WHINING
GHIINOS HOISING
GHIINPP HIPPING
GHIINPS PISHING
GHIINPT PITHING
GHIINSS HISSING
GHIINST HISTING
INSIGHT
GHIINSW WISHING
GHIINTT HITTING
TITHING
GHIINTW WHITING
WITHING
GHIIOPR PIROGHI
GHIIRST TIGRISH
GHIJNOS JOSHING
GHIKLNO HOLKING
GHIKLNU HULKING
GHIKNNO HONKING
GHIKNOO HOOKING
GHIKNOW HOWKING
GHIKNST KNIGHTS
GHIKNSU HUSKING
GHIKNTY KYTHING
GHIKRTU TUGHRIK
GHILLNU HULLING
GHILLTY LIGHTLY
GHILNOS LONGISH
GHILNOT THOLING
GHILNOW HOWLING
GHILNRU HURLING
GHILNSU LUSHING
GHILNSY SHINGLY
GHILNTY NIGHTLY
GHILPST PLIGHTS
GHILPTU UPLIGHT
GHILRTY RIGHTLY
GHILSST SLIGHTS
GHILSTY SIGHTLY
GHILSUY GUSHILY
GHILTTY TIGHTLY
GHIMMNU HUMMING
GHIMNNY HYMNING
GHIMNOS GNOMISH
MOSHING
GHIMNPU HUMPING
GHIMNRY RHYMING
GHIMNSU MUSHING
GHINNOP PHONING
GHINNOR HORNING
GHINNOS NOSHING
GHINNOT NOTHING
GHINNTU HUNTING
GHINOOP HOOPING
POOHING
GHINOOS SHOOING
GHINOOT HOOTING
GHINOPP HOPPING
GHINOPY HYPOING
GHINORS HORSING
SHORING
GHINORW WHORING
GHINOST HOSTING
GHINOSU HOUSING
GHINOSV SHOVING
GHINOSW SHOWING
GHINOTT HOTTING
TONIGHT
GHINOTU THOUING
GHINPSU GUNSHIP
PUSHING
GHINRSU RUSHING
GHINRTU HURTING
GHINSTU SHUTING
TUSHING
UNSIGHT
GHINTTU HUTTING
GHINTTY TYTHING
GHIORSU ROGUISH
GHIOSUV VOGUISH
GHIPRST SPRIGHT
GHIPRTU UPRIGHT
GHIPTTU UPTIGHT

GHIRSTW WRIGHTS
GHLMOOO HOMOLOG
GHLMOSU MOGHULS
GHLOPSU PLOUGHS
GHLORUY ROUGHLY
GHLOSSU SLOUGHS
GHLOSTY GHOSTLY
GHLOSUY SLOUGHY
GHLOTUY TOUGHLY
GHMORSU SORGHUM
GHMPRUY GRUMPHY
GHNOOPS GONOPHS
GHNOPRY GRYPHON
GHNORST THRONGS
GHNORUU UNROUGH
GHNOSSU SHOGUNS
GHNOSTU GUNSHOT
HOGNUTS
NOUGHTS
SHOTGUN
GHOOOSW HOOSGOW
GHOOPST PHOTOGS
GHOOQSU QUOHOGS
GHOORSS SORGHOS
GHORSTU TROUGHS
GHORSTW GROWTHS
GHORTUW WROUGHT
GHORTUY YOGHURT
GHORTWY GROWTHY
GHOSTUU OUTGUSH
GIIINRS IRISING
GIIJKNN JINKING
GIIJLNT JILTING
GIIJNNO JOINING
GIIJNNX JINXING
GIIKKNN KINKING
GIIKLLN KILLING
GIIKLMN MILKING
GIIKLNN INKLING
KILNING
LINKING
GIIKLNS LIKINGS
SILKING
GIIKLNT KILTING
KITLING
GIIKNNO OINKING
GIIKNNP KINGPIN
PINKING
GIIKNNR KIRNING
GIIKNNS SINKING
GIIKNNW WINKING
GIIKNPP KIPPING
GIIKNPS PIGSKIN
SPIKING
GIIKNRS GRISKIN
RISKING
GIIKNSS KISSING
SKIINGS
GIIKNST SKITING
GIIKNSV SKIVING
VIKINGS
GIIKNTT KITTING
GIILLMN MILLING
GIILLNN NILLING
GIILLNP PILLING
GIILLNR RILLING
GIILLNT LILTING
TILLING
GIILLNW WILLING
GIILMNN LIMNING
GIILMNO MOILING
GIILMNP LIMPING
GIILMNS SLIMING
SMILING
GIILMNT MILTING
GIILMPR PILGRIM
GIILMRY GRIMILY
GIILNNS LIGNINS
LININGS
GIILNNT LINTING
GIILNNY INLYING
GIILNOP PIGNOLI
GIILNOR LIGROIN
ROILING
GIILNOS SILOING
SOILING
GIILNOT TOILING
GIILNPP LIPPING
GIILNPS LISPING
PILINGS
SLIPING
SPILING
GIILNRT TIRLING
GIILNST LISTING
SILTING
TILINGS

GIILNSV LIVINGS
GIILNTT TILTING
TITLING
GIILNTW WILTING
WITLING
GIILRST STRIGIL
GIIMMNN NIMMING
GIIMMNR RIMMING
GIIMNNS MININGS
GIIMNNT MINTING
GIIMNPP PIMPING
GIIMNPR PRIMING
GIIMNPS IMPINGS
GIIMNPW WIMPING
GIIMNRT MITRING
GIIMNSS MISSING
GIIMNST MISTING
SMITING
TIMINGS
GIINNNP PINNING
GIINNNR RINNING
GIINNNS INNINGS
SINNING
GIINNNT TINNING
GIINNNW WINNING
GIINNOP OPINING
GIINNOR IRONING
GIINNOS NOISING
GIINNPP NIPPING
GIINNPS SNIPING
GIINNRS RINSING
GIINNRT TRINING
GIINNRU INURING
RUINING
GIINNTT TINTING
GIINNTU UNITING
GIINNTW TWINING
GIINOPS POISING
GIINORS ORIGINS
SIGNIOR
SIGNORI
GIINORT IGNITOR
RIOTING
GIINOSY YOGINIS
GIINOTT TOITING
GIINPPP PIPPING
GIINPPR RIPPING
GIINPPS PIPINGS
SIPPING
GIINPPT TIPPING
GIINPPY YIPPING
GIINPPZ ZIPPING
GIINPQU PIQUING
GIINPRS PRISING
SPIRING
GIINPRZ PRIZING
GIINPST SPITING
GIINPSW SWIPING
WISPING
GIINPTT PITTING
GIINPTW WINGTIP
GIINPTY PITYING
GIINQRU QUIRING
GIINRRY YIRRING
GIINRSS RISINGS
GIINRSV VIRGINS
GIINRSW WIRINGS
GIINRTW WRITING
GIINSSU ISSUING
GIINSSW WISSING
GIINSSZ SIZINGS
GIINSTT SITTING
GIINSTU SUITING
GIINSTW WISTING
GIINSVW SWIVING
GIINTTW WITTING
GIIORSV ISOGRIV
GIJKNNU JUNKING
GIJKNOU JOUKING
GIJLNOT JOLTING
GIJMNPU JUMPING
GIJNOTT JOTTING
GIJNRUY JURYING
GIJNSTU JUSTING
GIJNTTU JUTTING
GIKKNNO KONKING
GIKKNUY YUKKING
GIKLNOO LOOKING
GIKLNRU LURKING
GIKLNSU SULKING
GIKMNOS SMOKING
GIKNNOW KNOWING
GIKNNOZ ZONKING
GIKNOOR ROOKING
GIKNOPR PORKING
GIKNOPS SPOKING

GIKNORT TROKING
GIKNORW WORKING
GIKNOST STOKING
GIKNSTU TUSKING
GIKRSTU TUGRIKS
GILLLNO LOLLING
GILLLNU LULLING
GILLMNU MULLING
GILLNNU NULLING
GILLNOP POLLING
GILLNOR ROLLING
GILLNOT TOLLING
GILLNPU PULLING
GILLNYY LYINGLY
GILMNOO LOOMING
GILMNOT MOLTING
GILMNPU LUMPING
PLUMING
GILNNOO GLONOIN
GILNNRU NURLING
GILNNSU UNSLING
GILNNTU LUNTING
GILNOOP LOOPING
POOLING
GILNOOS LOGIONS
LOOSING
OLINGOS
SOLOING
GILNOOT LOOTING
TOOLING
GILNOPP LOPPING
GILNOPS SLOPING
GILNOPU LOUPING
GILNOPW PLOWING
GILNOPY PLOYING
GILNORU LOURING
GILNOSS LOSINGS
GILNOST TIGLONS
GILNOSU LOUSING
GILNOSV SOLVING
GILNOSW LOWINGS
SLOWING
GILNOTT LOTTING
GILNOTU LOUTING
GILNOWY YOWLING
GILNPPU PULPING
GILNPRU PURLING
GILNPSU PULINGS
PULSING
GILNRSU RULINGS
GILNSTU LUSTING
LUTINGS
GILNSTY STYLING
GILNSUY LUNGYIS
GILNVYY VYINGLY
GILOORS GIROSOL
GILOOSS ISOLOGS
GILOOST OLOGIST
GILORTY TRILOGY
GILOSTT GLOTTIS
GILOTUY GOUTILY
GILRSTY GRISTLY
GILRTUY LITURGY
GILRYZZ GRIZZLY
GILSTUY GUSTILY
GUTSILY
GIMMMNU MUMMING
GIMMNPU MUMPING
GIMMNSU SUMMING
GIMNNOO MOONING
GIMNNOR MORNING
GIMNNOS MIGNONS
GIMNNTU MUNTING
GIMNOOR MOORING
ROOMING
GIMNOOT MOOTING
GIMNOOZ ZOOMING
GIMNOPP MOPPING
GIMNOPR ROMPING
GIMNORW WORMING
GIMNOSS MOSSING
GIMNOST GNOMIST
GIMNOSU MOUSING
GIMNOSW MOWINGS
GIMNPPU PUMPING
GIMNPSU IMPUGNS
SPUMING
GIMNPTU TUMPING
GIMNSSU MUSINGS
MUSSING
GIMNSTU MUSTING
GIMORSS OGRISMS
GIMORSW MISGROW
GIMOSTU GOMUTIS
GINNNOO NOONING
GINNNOW WONNING

GINNNPU PUNNING
GINNNRU RUNNING
GINNNSU SUNNING
GINNNTU TUNNING
GINNOOS NOOSING
GINNOOZ ZOONING
GINNOPS SPONGIN
GINNOPY PONYING
GINNORS SNORING
SORNING
GINNORU GRUNION
GINNORW INGROWN
GINNOSS NOSINGS
GINNOST STONING
GINNOSW SNOWING
GINNOTW WONTING
GINNPRU PRUNING
GINNPTU PUNTING
GINNRSU NURSING
GINNRTU TURNING
GINNTTU NUTTING
GINNTUY UNTYING
GINOOPP POGONIP
POOPING
GINOORS ROOSING
GINOORT ROOTING
GINOOSS ISOGONS
GINOOST SOOTING
GINOOSY ISOGONY
GINOOTT TOOTING
GINOPPP POPPING
GINOPPS SOPPING
GINOPPT TOPPING
GINOPRS PROSING
SPORING
GINOPRT PORTING
GINOPRU INGROUP
POURING
ROUPING
GINOPRV PROVING
GINOPST POSTING
STOPING
GINOPSU SOUPING
GINOPTT POTTING
GINOPTU POUTING
GINOQTU QUOTING
GINORSS GRISONS
SIGNORS
SORINGS
GINORST SORTING
STORING
TRIGONS
GINORSU ROUSING
SOURING
GINORSV ROVINGS
GINORSW ROWINGS
GINORSY SIGNORY
GINORTT ROTTING
GINORTU OUTGRIN
OUTRING
ROUTING
TOURING
GINORTW TROWING
GINOSST STINGOS
TOSSING
GINOSSU SOUSING
GINOSTU OUSTING
OUTINGS
OUTSING
TOUSING
GINOSTW STOWING
GINOTTT TOTTING
GINOTTU TOUTING
GINOTTW WOTTING
GINPPPU PUPPING
GINPPSU SUPPING
UPPINGS
GINPPTU TUPPING
GINPRRU PURRING
GINPRSS SPRINGS
GINPRSU PURSING
GINPRSY SPRINGY
GINPSTU PIGNUTS
GINPSUW UPSWING
GINPTTU PUTTING
GINPTUZ PUTZING
GINRSST STRINGS
GINRSTU RUSTING
GINRSTY STRINGY
GINRTTU RUTTING
GINSSSU SUSSING
GINTTTU TUTTING
GIOPRRU PRURIGO
GIOPSSS GOSSIPS
GIOPSST SPIGOTS
GIOPSSY GOSSIPY

GIOPSTU PIGOUTS
GIORRSU RIGOURS
GIORSTU OUTRIGS
GIORSUV VIGOURS
GIOSSYZ ZYGOSIS
GJLMUUU JUGULUM
GLLLOOR LOGROLL
GLMMSUU SLUMGUM
GLMNOOO MONOLOG
GLMNOOS MONGOLS
GLMOOYY MYOLOGY
GLMORUW LUGWORM
GLNNOOR LORGNON
GLNNSUU UNSLUNG
GLNOOOS OOLONGS
GLNOOPR PROLONG
GLNOOPY POLYGON
GLNORWY WRONGLY
GLNOSUW SUNGLOW
GLNOTTU GLUTTON
GLNPSUU UNPLUGS
GLOOORY OROLOGY
GLOOOTY OTOLOGY
GLOOOYZ ZOOLOGY
GLOOPRS PROLOGS
GLOORUY UROLOGY
GLOOTUW OUTGLOW
GLOPSTU PUTLOGS
GLORSSY GROSSLY
GLPRSUY SPLURGY
GMMOSUU GUMMOUS
GMMPUUW MUGWUMP
GMNNOOS GNOMONS
GMNOORU GUNROOM
GMOOPRS POGROMS
GMORSUU GRUMOUS
GMORTUW MUGWORT
GMPSSUY GYPSUMS
GMRUYYZ ZYMURGY
GNNOUUY UNYOUNG
GNNRUUW UNWRUNG
GNNSTUU UNSTUNG
GNOOOSS GOSSOON
GNOORST TROGONS
GNOPPSU OPPUGNS
POPGUNS
GNOPRUW GROWNUP
UPGROWN
GNORTUU OUTRUNG
GNOSTUU OUTGUNS
OUTSUNG
GNPSUUW UPSWUNG
GOOPRST GOSPORT
GOORSTT GROTTOS
GOORTUW OUTGROW
GOPRSUW UPGROWS
GORRSTU TURGORS
GORSTTU ROTGUTS
GORSTUY YOGURTS
HHIIPPS HIPPISH
HHIISTW WHITISH
HHINNSU HUNNISH
HHIOPST HIPSHOT
HHIORSW WHORISH
HHIOSTT HOTTISH
HHISSTW WHISHTS
HHMRSTY RHYTHMS
HHOOSTT HOTSHOT
HIIISTV SHIVITI
HIIJKNS HIJINKS
HIIKNPS KINSHIP
PINKISH
HIILMTU LITHIUM
HIILNSY SHINILY
HIILPST SHILPIT
HIILPSU HUIPILS
HIILPTY PITHILY
HIILRTT TRILITH
HIIMNSX MINXISH
HIIMPSW WIMPISH
HIIMSST MISHITS
HIIMSTT SHITTIM
HIINNOT THIONIN
HIINORS NOIRISH
HIINSSW SWINISH
HIINSTW WITHINS
HIIOPRZ RHIZOPI
HIIPSSW WISPISH
HIIPSXY PIXYISH
HIKLNOT HOTLINK
HIKLSUY HUSKILY
HIKMNOS MONKISH
HIKMOTV MIKVOTH
HIKMSUZ MUZHIKS
HIKNNOR INKHORN
HIKNNTU UNTHINK

HIKNPSU PUNKISH
HIKNRSS SHRINKS
HIKOPSY SKYPHOI
HILLOPT HILLTOP
HILLPSU UPHILLS
HILLRSS SHRILLS
HILLRST THRILLS
HILLRSY SHRILLY
HILMMOU HOLMIUM
HILMOSS HOLISMS
HILMOSW WHOLISM
HILMPSU LUMPISH
HILMSUY MUSHILY
HILMTUU THULIUM
HILNNTY NINTHLY
HILNOPY PHONILY
HILNORY HORNILY
HILNOTY THIONYL
HILNPST PLINTHS
HILOOST OOLITHS
HILOOTT OTOLITH
HILOPST LITHOPS
HILOPXY OXYPHIL
HILORSY HORSILY
HILORTU UROLITH
HILOSST HOLISTS
HILOSSW SLOWISH
HILOSTU LOUTISH
HILOSWY SHOWILY
HILOTWW WHITLOW
HILPSST SPILTHS
HILPSUY PUSHILY
HILSSTY STYLISH
HILSTTY THISTLY
HILSTWY SWITHLY
HILSTXY SIXTHLY
HIMNOOS MOONISH
HIMNOPR MORPHIN
HIMNSTY HYMNIST
HIMOORS MOORISH
HIMOPRS ORPHISM
ROMPISH
HIMOPSS SOPHISM
HIMORST RIMSHOT
HIMORSW WORMISH
HIMORTU THORIUM
HIMOTTY TIMOTHY
HIMPRSS SHRIMPS
HIMPRSY SHRIMPY
HIMPRTU TRIUMPH
HIMSSTU ISTHMUS
HINNNSU NUNNISH
HINNORT TINHORN
HINNOST TONNISH
HINOORT HORNITO
HINOORZ HORIZON
HINOPPS SHIPPON
HINOPSS SIPHONS
SONSHIP
HINORST HORNIST
HINORSU NOURISH
HINOSST STONISH
HINOSTW TOWNISH
HINPPSU PUSHPIN
HINPSSU UNSHIPS
HINPSTY PHYTINS
HINRSTU RUNTISH
HIOOPRS POORISH
HIOOSSW WHOOSIS
HIOPRSW WORSHIP
HIOPSST SOPHIST
HIORSSU SOURISH
HIORSTY HISTORY
HIOSSTT SOTTISH
HIOSTTU OUTHITS
HIOSTUW OUTWISH
HIOTTUW OUTWITH
WITHOUT
HIQSSUY SQUISHY
HIRSSTT THIRSTS
HIRSTTU RUTTISH
HIRSTTY THIRSTY
HKKLOOS KOLKHOS
HKKLOOZ KOLKHOZ
HKKOOSY SKYHOOK
HKKOSTU SUKKOTH
HKLOOYZ KOLHOZY
HKNOOSS SHNOOKS
HKNOOSU UNHOOKS
HKNSSUU UNHUSKS
HKOOOPT POTHOOK
HKOOPSU HOOKUPS
HKOOSVZ SOVKHOZ
HKOPSSY SKYPHOS
HLLOOOS HOLLOOS
HLLOOSU HULLOOS

HLLOOSW HOLLOWS
HLLOPSY PHYLLOS
HLLPSUY PLUSHLY
HLMNOTY MONTHLY
HLMOOSS SHOLOMS
HLMOSTY THYMOLS
HLMPSSU SHLUMPS
HLMPSUY SHLUMPY
HLOOSTY SOOTHLY
HLOOTUW OUTHOWL
HLOPSTY PHYTOLS
HLORSTY SHORTLY
HLPRSUU SULPHUR
HMMNOOY HOMONYM
HMMRTUY THRUMMY
HMNOPSY NYMPHOS
HMNOPYY HYPONYM
HMOOPRS MORPHOS
HMOOSST SMOOTHS
HMOOSTY SMOOTHY
HMORSUU HUMOURS
HNNOOPS PHONONS
HNNORSU UNSHORN
HNOOPST PHOTONS
HNOOPTY TYPHOON
HNOORST THORONS
HNOORSU HONOURS
HNOPSSY SYPHONS
HNOPSTY PHYTONS
PYTHONS
TYPHONS
HNORSTY RHYTONS
HNOSUWY UNSHOWY
HNOTTUU OUTHUNT
HNRTTUU UNTRUTH
HOOOOPS HOOPOOS
HOOPSTT HOTSPOT
POTSHOT
HOOPSTU UPSHOOT
HOOPSTY TOYSHOP
HOOQSSU SQUOOSH
HOORRRS HORRORS
HOOSTTU OUTSHOT
HOPRSTU HOTSPUR
HOPRTTU PRUTOTH
HOPRTUW UPTHROW
HOPSSSY HYSSOPS
HOPSSTU UPSHOTS
HOPSTUU OUTPUSH
HOPSTUY TYPHOUS
HORSTTW TROWTHS
HORSTUU OUTRUSH
HOSTTUU SHUTOUT
HPPSSUU PUSHUPS
HPRTTUU THRUPUT
HRSSTTU THRUSTS
HRSSTUY THYRSUS
IIIKMNN MINIKIN
IIIKMNS MINISKI
IIJKOPR PIROJKI
IIJLLNO JILLION
IIJMMNY JIMMINY
IIJMNOS MISJOIN
IIKKLNY KINKILY
IIKKNPS KIPSKIN
IIKLLMY MILKILY
IIKLLSY SILKILY
IIKLMNP LIMPKIN
IIKLMRY MIRKILY
IIKLNOS OILSKIN
IIKLPSY SPIKILY
IIKLRSY RISKILY
IIKNPPS PIPKINS
IIKNSSS SISKINS
IIKPSUW WIKIUPS
IILLLSY SILLILY
IILLMNO MILLION
IILLMSY SLIMILY
IILLNOP PILLION
IILLNOZ ZILLION
IILLNST INSTILL
IILMNSS SIMLINS
IILMSTU STIMULI
IILMSTY MISTILY
IILNNOT NITINOL
IILNNSU INSULIN
INULINS
IILNNTY TINNILY
IILNOPT PINITOL
IILNORS SIRLOIN
IILNOSV VIOLINS
IILNOSY NOISILY
IILNPPY NIPPILY
IILNPUV PULVINI
IILNRST NITRILS
IILNSST INSTILS

IILOPRT TRIPOLI
IILORTV VITRIOL
IILOSTV VIOLIST
IILPRVY PRIVILY
IILPSST PISTILS
IILPSTY TIPSILY
IILPSWY WISPILY
IILRTYZ RITZILY
IILSTTT TITLIST
IILTTUY UTILITY
IILTTWY WITTILY
IIMMMNU MINIMUM
IIMMNSU MINIUMS
IIMNNOS MINIONS
IIMNOSS MISSION
IIMNOSU IONIUMS
NIMIOUS
IIMNPRT IMPRINT
IIMOPSU IMPIOUS
IIMOSST MITOSIS
IIMOSSU SIMIOUS
IIMRSSU SURIMIS
IIMRSTW MISWRIT
IIMRTTU TRITIUM
IIMRTUV TRIVIUM
IIMSSTU MISSUIT
IINNOOP OPINION
IINNOPS PINIONS
IINNQSU QUININS
IINNQTU QUINTIN
IINOPSS ISOSPIN
IINORST IRONIST
IINORSV VIRIONS
IINORTT INTROIT
IINOSSV VISIONS
IINOTTU TUITION
IINPPPS PIPPINS
IINQRUY INQUIRY
IINRTTY TRINITY
IINSSST INSISTS
IINSTTU INTUITS
IINSTTW INTWIST
NITWITS
IIOPRSS PISSOIR
IIOPSTY PIOSITY
IIORSSV VIROSIS
IIORSTV VISITOR
IIPRSST SPIRITS
IIPRTVY PRIVITY
IIQSTUV QIVIUTS
IISTTZZ TZITZIS
IITTTZZ TZITZIT
IJJMSUU JUJUISM
IJJSTUU JUJITSU
JUJUIST
IJKLLOY KILLJOY
IJKMOSU MOUJIKS
IJKMSUZ MUZJIKS
IJLLLOY JOLLILY
IJLLOTY JOLLITY
JOLTILY
IJLMPUY JUMPILY
IJLNOQU JONQUIL
IJLNOTY JOINTLY
IJNNOTU UNJOINT
IJNORSU JUNIORS
IJNOTUX OUTJINX
IJRSSTU JURISTS
IKKNNSU UNKINKS
IKLLOTU OUTKILL
IKLLSUY SULKILY
IKLMOOS LOOKISM
IKLMOPS MILKSOP
IKLMOSY SMOKILY
SOYMILK
IKLMRUY MURKILY
IKLMSUY MUSKILY
IKLNNSU UNLINKS
IKLNOOT KILOTON
IKLNPSU LINKUPS
UPLINKS
IKLNRWY WRINKLY
IKLNTWY TWINKLY
IKLOOST LOOKIST
IKLOSSU SOUSLIK
IKLSSSU SUSLIKS
IKMNOOR OMIKRON
IKMNOOS KIMONOS
IKMNORS MIKRONS
IKMNOSW MISKNOW
IKMNPPU PUMPKIN
IKMOOST MISTOOK
IKMOSSU KOUMISS
IKMSSTU MUSKITS
IKNNPSU PUNKINS
IKNNSTU UNKNITS
IKNOPRW PINWORK
IKNOPST INKPOTS
IKNORTW TINWORK
IKNPSTU SPUTNIK
IKORSTU TURKOIS
IKOSSTU OUTKISS
ILLLOWY LOWLILY
ILLMNOU MULLION
ILLMNRU MILLRUN
ILLMOOT TIMOLOL
ILLMOPS PLIMSOL
ILLMPUY LUMPILY
ILLMSUU LIMULUS
ILLNOOY LOONILY
ILLNOST LINTOLS
ILLNPUU LUPULIN
ILLNTUY NULLITY
ILLOOPY LOOPILY
ILLOORZ ZORILLO
ILLOPRY PILLORY
ILLOPST POLLIST
ILLOPSW PILLOWS
ILLOPWY PILLOWY
ILLOSUV VILLOUS
ILLOSUY LOUSILY
ILLOSWW WILLOWS
ILLOTUW OUTWILL
ILLOTXY XYLITOL
ILLOUVV VOLVULI
ILLOWWY WILLOWY
ILLPPUY PULPILY
ILLQSSU SQUILLS
ILLRSUY SURLILY
ILLSTUY LUSTILY
ILMMSSU SLUMISM
ILMNOOT MOONLIT
ILMNOOY MOONILY
ILMNOSU MOULINS
ILMNSSU MUSLINS
ILMOORY ROOMILY
ILMORSW WORMILS
ILMORTU TURMOIL
ILMOSTY MOISTLY
ILMOSUY MOUSILY
ILMPSSY SLIMPSY
ILMRSSY LYRISMS
ILMSSUY MUSSILY
ILMSTUY MUSTILY
ILMUYZZ MUZZILY
ILNNOOY NONOILY
ILNNOPS NONSLIP
ILNNORU LINURON
ILNNSUY SUNNILY
ILNOOPS PLOSION
ILNOORS ROSINOL
ILNOOSS SOLIONS
ILNOOST LOTIONS
SOLITON
ILNOPPS POPLINS
ILNOPRU PURLOIN
ILNOPST PONTILS
ILNOPSU PULSION
UPSILON
ILNOPYY POLYNYI
ILNOQSU QUINOLS
ILNORST NOSTRIL
ILNOSST TONSILS
ILNOSSU INSOULS
ILNOSTY STONILY
TYLOSIN
ILNOSWY SNOWILY
ILNOTUV VOLUTIN
ILNPRSU PURLINS
ILNPSST SPLINTS
ILNPSTU UNSPILT
UNSPLIT
ILNSSTU INSULTS
ILNSSVY SYLVINS
ILNTTUY NUTTILY
ILOOORS ROSOLIO
ILOOPST POLOIST
TOPSOIL
ILOOSST SOLOIST
ILOOSTY SOOTILY
ILOOWYZ WOOZILY
ILOPRRY PRIORLY
ILOPRSY PROSILY
ILOPRUY ROUPILY
ILOPSST PISTOLS
ILOPSTT SPOTLIT
ILOPSTU SLIPOUT
ILOPSUY PIOUSLY
ILOQRSU LIQUORS
ILORRSY SORRILY
ILORSTU TROILUS
ILOSTTW WITTOLS
ILPPSSU SLIPUPS
ILPPSTU PULPITS
ILPRSUY PURSILY
ILPSTTU UPTILTS
ILRSSTY LYRISTS
ILRSTUY RUSTILY
ILRTTUY RUTTILY
ILSSTTU LUTISTS
ILSSTTY STYLIST
IMMMOSS MOMISMS
IMMNOSS MONISMS
NOMISMS
IMMNOUU MUONIUM
IMMOOSS SIMOOMS
IMMOPTU OPTIMUM
IMMOSSU OSMIUMS
IMMSSTU MUTISMS
SUMMITS
IMNNNOU MUNNION
IMNNOSW MINNOWS
IMNNSTU MUNTINS
IMNOOPT TOMPION
IMNOORR MORRION
IMNOORS MORIONS
IMNOORT MONITOR
IMNOOSS SIMOONS
IMNOOST MOTIONS
IMNOOSU OMINOUS
IMNOOSY ISONOMY
IMNOPRW PINWORM
IMNOPSU SPUMONI
IMNOSST MONISTS
IMNOSSY MYOSINS
IMNRSTU UNTRIMS
IMOOPRX PROXIMO
IMOOSSS OSMOSIS
IMOOSSU OSMIOUS
IMOOSTV VOMITOS
IMOPRSS PORISMS
IMOPRST IMPORTS
TROPISM
IMOPRSV IMPROVS
IMOPRTU PROTIUM
IMOPSST IMPOSTS
MISSTOP
IMOPSTU UTOPISM
IMORRRS MIRRORS
IMORSST MISSORT
IMORSTU TOURISM
IMORSTY TRISOMY
IMOSSTU MISSOUT
SUMOIST
IMOSSYZ ZYMOSIS
IMOSTTT TOMTITS
IMOSTUV VOMITUS
IMOSTUW OUTSWIM
IMPRSSU PURISMS
IMQRSSU SQUIRMS
IMQRSUY SQUIRMY
IMRSSTU SISTRUM
TRISMUS
TRUISMS
IMRTTUY YTTRIUM
INNNOOR NONIRON
INNOOPS OPSONIN
INNOORS RONIONS
INNOOST NOTIONS
INNOPSY PINYONS
INNORST INTRONS
INNOSSU UNISONS
INNOSTU NONSUIT
INNOSUY UNNOISY
INNOSWW WINNOWS
INNQSUY SQUINNY
INNRSTU INTURNS
INOOPRT PORTION
INOOPSS POISONS
INOOPST OPTIONS
POTIONS
INOORSS ORISONS
INOORST NITROSO
TORSION
INOORTT TORTONI
INOOSUX NOXIOUS
INOPPST TOPSPIN
INOPRSS PRISONS
SPINORS
INOPRST TROPINS
INOPRSU INPOURS
INOPSST PISTONS
POSTINS
SPINTOS
INOPSSU SPINOUS
INOPSTU SPINOUT
INORSTT INTORTS
TRITONS
INORSTU NITROUS
TURIONS
INORSUU RUINOUS
URINOUS
INOSSTT STOTINS
INOSSTU OUTSINS
INOSSUU SINUOUS
INPRSST SPRINTS
INPRSTU TURNIPS
INPRSTY TRYPSIN
INQSSTU SQUINTS
INQSTUY SQUINTY
INRSTTU INTRUST
INSSTUU SUNSUIT
INSTTUW UNTWIST
IOOPRSV PROVISO
IOOPSTY ISOTOPY
IOORSSS SOROSIS
IOORSST TSOORIS
IOORSTT RISOTTO
IOORSTU RIOTOUS
IOOSSST OSTOSIS
IOPPRST RIPSTOP
IOPPSTT TIPTOPS
IOPRSST RIPOSTS
IOPRSSY PYROSIS
IOPRSTT PROTIST
IOPSSTU PISTOUS
IOPSTTU UTOPIST
IOPTTUY OUTPITY
IOQRTTU QUITTOR
IORRSTW WORRITS
IORRTTX TORTRIX
IORSSTU SUITORS
TSOURIS
IORSTTU TOURIST
IORTTUW OUTWRIT
IOSSTTU OUTSITS
IOSTTUW OUTWITS
IPPQSUU QUIPPUS
IPRRSTU IRRUPTS
STIRRUP
IPRSSTU PURISTS
UPSTIRS
IPRSTUU PURSUIT
IPSSSTY STYPSIS
IPSSTTY TYPISTS
IPSTTTU TITTUPS
IQRSSTU SQUIRTS
JJSTUUU JUJUTSU
JMOPTUU OUTJUMP
JNNORUY NONJURY
JNOORSU JOURNOS
SOJOURN
JOOPPSY JOYPOPS
JOSTTUU OUTJUTS
KKLMSUU MUKLUKS
KKLOOYZ KOLKOZY
KKMOOSU SKOOKUM
KKMSTUU MUKTUKS
KKSSSTT TSKTSKS
KLLMOSU MOLLUSK
KLOOOTU LOOKOUT
OUTLOOK
KLOOPSU LOOKUPS
KLOSTUU OUTSULK
KLRSTUU KULTURS
KMOSSUY KOUMYSS
KNNNOUW UNKNOWN
KNNOORW NONWORK
KNNOSTU UNKNOTS
KNOOPTT TOPKNOT
KNOPRTY KRYPTON
KOOPRTW TOPWORK
KOORTUW OUTWORK
WORKOUT
KOOSSSU KOUSSOS
KOOSSUU SOUKOUS
KOOSTWW KOWTOWS
KOPRSUW WORKUPS
LLLOOPS LOLLOPS
LLLOOPY LOLLOPY
LLMOOPR ROLLMOP
LLMPPUY PLUMPLY
LLNORSU UNROLLS
LLOOPRT ROLLTOP
TROLLOP
LLOOPSY POLYOLS
LLOOPTU OUTPOLL
LLOORTU OUTROLL
ROLLOUT
LLOOSTU TOLUOLS
LLOPTUU OUTPULL
PULLOUT
LLORSST STROLLS
LLOSTUY TOLUYLS
LLPPSUU PULLUPS
LMOORSU ORMOLUS
LMRSTUU LUSTRUM
LMSTTUU TUMULTS
LMSTUUU TUMULUS
LNNOOOW NONWOOL
LNNOPSU NONPLUS
LNOOPSU UNSPOOL
LNOOSST STOLONS
LNOPSTU PLUTONS
LNRTUUY UNTRULY
LOOOORS OLOROSO
LOOPTTU OUTPLOT
LOOSSTV VOLOSTS
LOPPRSY PROPYLS
LOPPSUU PULPOUS
LOPPSUY POLYPUS
LOPRRSY PYRROLS
LOPRSTY PROTYLS
LOPRSUY PYLORUS
LOPRTUY POULTRY
LORSTTY TROTYLS
LOSTTUY STOUTLY
LPRSSUU SURPLUS
MMNOSSU SUMMONS
MMOOPPS POMPOMS
MMOOSTT MOTMOTS
MMOPSTY SYMPTOM
MMRRSUU MURMURS
MMSUUUU MUUMUUS
MNNOOOS MONSOON
MNNOORU MONURON
MNNOSYY SYNONYM
MNOOPPS POMPONS
MNOOPTY TOPONYM
MNOORSU SUNROOM
UNMOORS
MNOOSTU MOUTONS
MNOOTTW TOWMONT
MNORSTU NOSTRUM
MNOSTTU MUTTONS
MNOTTUY MUTTONY
MOOOTYZ ZOOTOMY
MOOPPSU POMPOUS
MOOPSSU OPOSSUM
MOOPSTT TOPMOST
MOORRSW MORROWS
MOOSTTU OUTMOST
MOPPRST PROMPTS
MOPSSSU POSSUMS
MOPSSUU SPUMOUS
MOQRSUU QUORUMS
MORRSTU ROSTRUM
MORRSUU RUMOURS
MORSTUU TUMOURS
MOSSSTY MYSOSTS
MOSSTTU UTMOSTS
MOSTUUW OUTSWUM
NNOOOPR NONPOOR
NNOOOPT PONTOON
NNOOPRS NONPROS
NNOOPRU PRONOUN
NNOOPSS SPONSON
NNOOPST NONSTOP
PONTONS
NNOORSY RONYONS
NNOOSTW WONTONS
NNORSTU TURNONS
NNORSUW UNSWORN
NNOSSUY UNSONSY
NNOSTYY SYNTONY
NOOOSUZ OZONOUS
NOOOSVX SONOVOX
NOOPRSS SPONSOR
NOOPRST PROTONS
NOOPSUY YOUPONS
NOORSTU UNROOTS
NOORTUW OUTWORN
NOPSSTU SUNSPOT
UNSTOPS
NOPSTUW UPTOWNS
NORSTUU OUTRUNS
RUNOUTS
NORTTUU OUTTURN
TURNOUT
NPRSTUU TURNUPS
UPTURNS
NRSSTTU STRUNTS
NRSSTUU UNTRUSS
OOORTTU OUTROOT
OOPPSST POSTOPS
OOPRRST TORPORS
OOPRSSU SOURSOP
OOPRSTU UPROOTS
OOPRSTV PROVOST
OOPRTTU OUTPORT
OOPRTUU OUTPOUR
OOPSSTT TOSSPOT
OOPSTTU OUTPOST
OOPSWWW POWWOWS
OORRSSW SORROWS
OORSTUW OUTROWS
OORTTTU OUTTROT
OPPPRSU UPPROPS
OPPRRTU PURPORT
OPPRSTU SUPPORT
OPPRSTY STROPPY
OPRSSTU SPROUTS
STUPORS
OPSSSTU TOSSUPS
OPSTTUU OUTPUTS
PUTOUTS
ORRSTTU TRUSTOR
ORSSSTU TUSSORS
ORSTTUU SURTOUT
ORSTTUY TRYOUTS
RSSSTUU TUSSURS

8-Letter Alphagrams

AAAABCLZ CALABAZA
AAAABENN ANABAENA
AAAABKPS BAASKAAP
AAAACCRR CARACARA
AAAACGNR CARAGANA
AAAACLMT CALAMATA
AAAACNRS ANASARCA
AAAADMTV AMADAVAT
AAAADTVV AVADAVAT
AAAAHJMR MAHARAJA
AAAAIKMN KAMAAINA
AAAAIMPR ARAPAIMA
AAAAIRTX ATARAXIA
AAAAKKNT KATAKANA
AAAAKKVV KAVAKAVA
AAAAKLMT KALAMATA
AAAALLVV LAVALAVA
AAAALSTY ATALAYAS
AAABBCHL CABBALAH
AAABBCLS CABBALAS
AAABBELT ABATABLE
AAABBHKL KABBALAH
AAABBILT ABBATIAL
AAABBKLS KABBALAS
AAABCCMW MACCABAW
AAABCCRS BACCARAS
AAABCCRT BACCARAT
AAABCHIR ABRACHIA
AAABCHLS CALABASH
AAABCILP ABAPICAL
AAABCINT ANABATIC
AAABCIRS ARABICAS
AAABCLOS BACALAOS
AAABCNRR BARRANCA
AAABCNRU CARNAUBA
AAABCORS CARABAOS
AAABCPRY CAPYBARA
AAABCSSS CASSABAS
AAABCSTW CATAWBAS
AAABDEHH DAHABEAH
AAABDEST DATABASE
AAABDFRS ABFARADS
AAABDHHI DAHABIAH
AAABDHHL HABDALAH
AAABDHIY DAHABIYA
AAABDIKR BAIDARKA
AAABDKNT DATABANK
AAABDLMS LAMBADAS
AAABDNNN BANDANNA
AAABDNNS BANDANAS
AAABDNRS SARABAND
AAABDNRT ABRADANT
AAABEHNR HABANERA
AAABEHRT BARATHEA
AAABENSS ANABASES
AAABFLLS FALBALAS
AAABGILS GALABIAS
AAABGILY GALABIYA
AAABGLOR ALGAROBA
AAABGMNQ MBAQANGA
AAABGRTU RUTABAGA
AAABHLQS QABALAHS
AAABHMST MASTABAH
AAABILTT BATTALIA
AAABINSS ANABASIS
AAABIPSS PIASABAS
PIASSABA
AAABKLSV BAKLAVAS
AAABKLSW BAKLAWAS
AAABKPSS BAASKAPS
BAASSKAP
AAABLMOS ABOMASAL
AAABLMST TAMBALAS
AAABLOPR PARABOLA
AAABLPRS PALABRAS
AAABMSST MASTABAS
AAABORRS ARAROBAS
AAACCELN CALCANEA
AAACCEPR CARAPACE
AAACCHMP CHAMPACA
AAACCILR CALCARIA
AAACCLMS MALACCAS
AAACCLRS CARACALS
AAACCRSS CASCARAS
AAACCRTT CATARACT
AAACDEIM ACADEMIA
AAACDELM ACELDAMA
AAACDEMN ADAMANCE
AAACDENR DRACAENA
AAACDEQU AQUACADE
AAACDETU ACAUDATE
AAACDFIR FARADAIC
AAACDILR CALDARIA
AAACDINR ACARIDAN
ARCADIAN
AAACDIRS ARCADIAS
AAACDKLY LACKADAY
AAACDMMS MACADAMS
AAACDMNY ADAMANCY
AAACDNNO ANACONDA
AAACDNRS SANDARAC
AAACEGTU AGUACATE
AAACEHLR ARCHAEAL
AAACEHLZ CHALAZAE
AAACEHNR ARCHAEAN
AAACEHNT ACANTHAE
AAACELNT ANALECTA
AAACELST CATALASE
AAACENNP PANACEAN
AAACENPS PANACEAS
AAACGLSW SCALAWAG
AAACGMNP CAMPAGNA
AAACGMNR ARMAGNAC
AAACHHLS HALACHAS
AAACHILZ CHALAZIA
AAACHIPS APHASIAC
AAACHLLZ CHALAZAL
AAACHLSZ CHALAZAS
AAACILMN MANIACAL
AAACILMR CALAMARI
AAACILPR CARPALIA
AAACILRV CALVARIA
AAACILSY CALISAYA
AAACINPS ACAPNIAS
AAACINTV CAVATINA
AAACIRRS SACRARIA
AAACIRSS ACRASIAS
AAACIRTX ATARAXIC
AAACJMRS JACAMARS
AAACKLMN ALMANACK
AAACKMRT TAMARACK
AAACLLSV CAVALLAS
AAACLMNS ALMANACS
AAACLMRS CALAMARS
AAACLMRY CALAMARY
AAACLNST CANTALAS
AAACLPST CATALPAS
AAACLRSZ ALCAZARS
AAACMOST ATAMASCO
AAACMRSS MARASCAS
MASCARAS
AAACNOPT CAPONATA
AAACNRSV CARAVANS
AAACNSST CANASTAS
AAACNSTT CANTATAS
AAACRSWY CARAWAYS
AAACSSST CASSATAS
AAACSSSV CASSAVAS
AAACSTWY CASTAWAY
AAADEFGN FANEGADA
AAADEFWY FADEAWAY
AAADEIMZ MAZAEDIA
AAADEJMP PAJAMAED
AAADELMS ALAMEDAS
SALAAMED
AAADEMNP EMPANADA
AAADENTV VANADATE
AAADEPRT TAPADERA
AAADFRSY FARADAYS
AAADGGHH HAGGADAH
AAADGGHS AGGADAHS
HAGGADAS
AAADGIMM GAMMADIA
AAADGLMY AMYGDALA
AAADGLNS SALADANG
AAADHHLV HAVDALAH
AAADHMMS HAMMADAS
AAADHMRS MADRASAH
AAADIILR RADIALIA
AAADILLP PALLADIA
AAADILRU ADULARIA
AAADIMNS DAMIANAS
AAADIMNY ADYNAMIA
AAADKNSW WAKANDAS
AAADKRRV AARDVARK
AAADLMNS MANDALAS
AAADLMSW WADMAALS
AAADMNST ADAMANTS
AAADMNTU TAMANDUA
AAADMPPP PAPPADAM
AAADMPPS PAPADAMS
AAADMRSS MADRASAS
MADRASSA
AAADNRSS SARDANAS
AAAEGLST GALATEAS
AAAEGNPP APPANAGE
AAAEGNPS APANAGES
AAAEGRST GASTRAEA
AAAEHLMT HAEMATAL
AAAEHLST ALTHAEAS
AAAEHMNT ANATHEMA
AAAEHNPS ANAPHASE
AAAEIMNS ANAEMIAS
AAAEKTWY TAKEAWAY
AAAELMMN ANALEMMA
AAAELNPT PANATELA
AAAENOPR PARANOEA
AAAENPRV PARAVANE
AAAENPST ANAPAEST
AAAENSST ANATASES
AAAERSWY AREAWAYS
AAAERTWY TEARAWAY
AAAFFLLS ALFALFAS
AAAFHHRT HAFTARAH
AAAFHRST HAFTARAS
AAAFINST FANTASIA
AAAFINUV AVIFAUNA
AAAFIRST RATAFIAS
AAAFLLWY FALLAWAY
AAAFMQRU AQUAFARM
AAAGGLLN GALANGAL
AAAGGLNS GALANGAS
AAAGHINR HIRAGANA
AAAGHIPR AGRAPHIA
AAAGHIPS APHAGIAS
AAAGHNSS SAGANASH
AAAGHNST ATAGHANS
AAAGHNTY YATAGHAN
AAAGILMM MAMALIGA
AAAGILNS ANALGIAS
AAAGILPT PATAGIAL
AAAGINRR AGRARIAN
AAAGINRS ANGARIAS
AAAGINSZ GAZANIAS
AAAGISSS ASSAGAIS
AAAGJMSU MAJAGUAS
AAAGLMMS AMALGAMS
AAAGLMNS MALANGAS
AAAGLNSS LASAGNAS
AAAGLNTV GALAVANT
AAAGLRRW WARRAGAL
AAAGLRST ASTRAGAL
AAAGMNRS ANAGRAMS
AAAGNPRS PARASANG
AAAGNRSU GUARANAS
AAAGNSTY YATAGANS
AAAHHHKL HALAKHAH
AAAHHKLS HALAKAHS
HALAKHAS
AAAHHLLS HALALAHS
AAAHHLSV HALAVAHS
AAAHHPRS PARASHAH
AAAHHPRT HAPHTARA
AAAHIMNR MAHARANI
AAAHIMRT HAMARTIA
AAAHINRS HARIANAS
AAAHIPSS APHASIAS
AAAHIPTY PITAHAYA
AAAHMMST MAHATMAS
AAAHMNRT AMARANTH
AAAHMSST TAMASHAS
AAAHNNSV SAVANNAH
AAAHNOPR ANAPHORA
AAAHNSTY ATHANASY
AAAHTTWY THATAWAY
AAAIIMNP APIMANIA
AAAIINPR APIARIAN
AAAIKLST LATAKIAS
AAAILLMR MALARIAL
AAAILLPT PALATIAL
AAAILMNR MALARIAN
AAAILMRS MALARIAS
AAAILMSV MALVASIA
AAAILNPR PLANARIA
AAAILPRS PARASAIL
AAAILPSS APLASIAS
AAAILQRU AQUARIAL
AAAILRST SALARIAT
AAAIMMST MIASMATA
AAAIMNRR MARINARA
AAAIMNST AMANITAS
AAAIMRSU MAIASAUR
AAAINOPR PARANOIA
AAAINPSS PAISANAS
AAAINQRU AQUARIAN
AAAIPRST ASPIRATA
AAAIPRSX APRAXIAS
AAAIPSSV PIASAVAS
PIASSAVA
AAAISSST ASTASIAS
AAAKLMSY YAMALKAS
AAAKLWWY WALKAWAY
AAALLPRX PARALLAX
AAALLPST PALATALS
AAALMMOR MALAROMA
AAALMPST TAMPALAS
AAALMRSS MARSALAS
AAALNNST LANTANAS
AAALNPRT RATAPLAN
AAALNRTT TARLATAN
AAALRRSY ARRAYALS
AAALSWYY LAYAWAYS
AAAMNOPR PANORAMA
AAAMNRST MARANTAS
AAAMORST TAMARAOS
AAAMOTTU AUTOMATA
AAAMPRST PATAMARS
AAAMPRTT PATTAMAR
AAAMRRSZ ZAMARRAS
AAAMRSSS SAMSARAS
AAAMRSTU TAMARAUS
AAAMRTTU TRAUMATA
AAANNSSV SAVANNAS
AAANOPRZ PARAZOAN
AAANORSY SAYONARA
AAANQTUU AQUANAUT
AAANRSTT TANTARAS
TARANTAS
TARTANAS
AAAPPRST APPARATS
AAAPQRTU PARAQUAT
AAARSTTT RATATATS
AAARSTTU TUATARAS
AABBCDEG CABBAGED
AABBCDRS SCABBARD
AABBCEGS CABBAGES
AABBCEGY CABBAGEY
AABBCEIS ABBACIES
AABBCEKR BAREBACK
AABBCEKT BACKBEAT
AABBCINR BARBICAN
AABBCIRR BARBARIC
AABBCIST SABBATIC
AABBCKST BACKSTAB
AABBCMOS CABOMBAS
AABBCORS BARBASCO
AABBDGRS GABBARDS
AABBEELR BEARABLE
AABBEELT BEATABLE
AABBEGNS BEANBAGS
AABBEILL BAILABLE
AABBEISS BABESIAS
AABBEKLN BANKABLE
AABBELLM BLAMABLE
AABBELLN BEANBALL
AABBELLS BASEBALL
AABBELNN BANNABLE
AABBELOT BOATABLE
AABBELRR BARRABLE
AABBELRY BEARABLY
AABBELSU ABUSABLE
AABBEORT BAREBOAT
AABBGRST GABBARTS
AABBHKSU BABUSHKA
AABBHSST SABBATHS
AABBIILL BILABIAL
AABBILRT BARBITAL
AABBIRSU BABIRUSA
AABBLLMY BLAMABLY
AABBSSSU BABASSUS
AABCCDET BACCATED
AABCCEHK BACKACHE
AABCCELS CASCABEL
CASCABLE
AABCCHKT BACKCHAT
AABCCHNT BACCHANT
AABCCIMR CARBAMIC
AABCCINN CANNABIC
AABCCKKP BACKPACK
AABCCKLL CALLBACK
AABCCKLP BLACKCAP
AABCCKLW CLAWBACK
AABCCKST BACKCAST
SCATBACK
AABCCMOT CATACOMB
AABCCMOY MACCABOY
AABCDEIN ABIDANCE
AABCDEIT ABDICATE
AABCDEKT BACKDATE
AABCDELL CABALLED
AABCDELN BALANCED
AABCDHKN BACKHAND
AABCDHKR HARDBACK
AABCDIIS DIABASIC
AABCDILL BALLADIC
AABCDILR ALDICARB
AABCDILU BICAUDAL
AABCDIMS DICAMBAS
AABCDIRS CARABIDS
AABCDKLN BACKLAND
AABCDKLO BACKLOAD
AABCDKNR BANKCARD
AABCDKRW BACKWARD
DRAWBACK
AABCDKRY BACKYARD
AABCDLNS SCABLAND
AABCDNST CABSTAND
AABCEEFL FACEABLE
AABCEEHS SEABEACH
AABCEENY ABEYANCE
AABCEERT ACERBATE
AABCEGOT CABOTAGE
AABCEHKL HACKABLE
AABCEHLS CASHABLE
AABCEILM AMICABLE
AABCEIMN AMBIANCE
AABCEINR CARABINE
AABCEIRT BACTERIA
AABCEKLM CLAMBAKE
AABCEKLP PACKABLE
AABCEKST BACKSEAT
SEATBACK
AABCELLL CALLABLE
AABCELLP PLACABLE
AABCELLS SCALABLE
AABCELNR BALANCER
BARNACLE
AABCELNS BALANCES
AABCELOR ALBACORE
AABCELPR CAPABLER
AABCELRS BERASCAL
AABCELRT BRACTEAL
CARTABLE
AABCELST CASTABLE
AABCELSU CAUSABLE
AABCELWY CABLEWAY
AABCEMRT CRABMEAT
AABCEMRV VAMBRACE
AABCEMSS AMBSACES
AABCENYY ABEYANCY
AABCEORS ACARBOSE
AABCERST ABREACTS
BEARCATS
CABARETS
CABRESTA
AABCERTT CABRETTA
AABCESSU ABACUSES
AABCFHKL HALFBACK
AABCFIIL BIFACIAL
AABCFKLL FALLBACK
AABCFKST FASTBACK
FATBACKS
AABCGIMO CAMBOGIA
AABCGKRY GRAYBACK
AABCHILR BRACHIAL
AABCHINR BRANCHIA
AABCHKLS BACKLASH
AABCHKLU BACKHAUL
AABCHKSW BACKWASH
AABCHMRY CHAMBRAY
AABCHNRS BARCHANS
AABCIILR BIRACIAL
AABCIILS BASILICA
AABCIINR BRAINIAC
AABCIKLT TAILBACK
AABCILLR BACILLAR
CABRILLA
AABCILMS BALSAMIC
CABALISM
AABCILMY AMICABLY
AABCILNN CANNIBAL
AABCILNO ANABOLIC
AABCILOR BRACIOLA
AABCILST BASALTIC
CABALIST
AABCINNN CANNABIN
AABCINNR CINNABAR
AABCINNS CANNABIS
AABCINOT BOTANICA
AABCINRS CARABINS
AABCINSU BANAUSIC
AABCIOPS COPAIBAS
AABCIOSS SCABIOSA
AABCIRSS BRASSICA
AABCISSS ABSCISSA
AABCISTX TAXICABS
AABCKKLT TALKBACK
AABCKLNY CLAYBANK
AABCKLPS BACKSLAP
AABCKLPY PLAYBACK
AABCKNPS SNAPBACK
AABCKPRW BACKWRAP
AABCKPSY PAYBACKS
AABCKRRS BARRACKS
AABCKSSW BACKSAWS
AABCKSTY BACKSTAY
AABCKSWY SWAYBACK
AABCLLPY PLACABLY
AABCLLSY SCALABLY
AABCLMRY CARBAMYL
AABCLNTY BLATANCY
AABCLRRY CARBARYL
AABCLRSU LABRUSCA
AABCMMSU MACUMBAS
AABCMSSU SAMBUCAS
AABCNORR BARRANCO
AABCNRRS CARBARNS
AABCORRS CARBORAS
AABCORST ACROBATS
AABCOSTT CATBOATS
AABCRSTT ABSTRACT
AABDDEET DEADBEAT
AABDDEGN BANDAGED
AABDDEHL BALDHEAD
AABDDEHN HEADBAND
AABDDERT TABARDED
AABDDLNS BADLANDS
AABDDNSS SANDDABS
AABDEEHL BEHEADAL
AABDEEHR BAREHEAD
AABDEELR READABLE
AABDEELT DATEABLE
AABDEELV EVADABLE
AABDEELW WADEABLE
AABDEEMN ENDAMEBA
AABDEERY BAYADEER
BAYADERE
AABDEGIN BADINAGE
AABDEGIR BIGARADE
AABDEGLR GRADABLE
AABDEGMS GAMBADES
AABDEGNR BANDAGER
AABDEGNS BANDAGES
AABDEGRR BARRAGED
AABDEHHI DAHABIEH
AABDEHNR BAREHAND
AABDEILR RADIABLE
AABDEILT LABIATED
AABDEIOU ABOIDEAU
AABDEIRZ ARABIZED
AABDEISS DIABASES
AABDEJLL DJELLABA
AABDEJNX BANJAXED
AABDEKPR PARBAKED
AABDEKRY DAYBREAK
AABDELLS BALLADES
AABDELLU LAUDABLE
AABDELMN DAMNABLE
AABDELMS BALSAMED
AABDELNS SANDABLE
AABDELOR ADORABLE
AABDELPR DRAPABLE
AABDELPT BALDPATE
AABDELRT TRADABLE
AABDELRW DRAWABLE
AABDELRY READABLY
AABDELSY ABASEDLY
AABDEMMS BEMADAMS
AABDEMNS BEADSMAN
AABDEMNT BANDMATE
AABDENSU BANDEAUS
AABDENTU UNABATED
AABDENUX BANDEAUX
AABDENVW WAVEBAND
AABDEORS SEABOARD
AABDEORT TEABOARD
AABDEORX BROADAXE
AABDERRS ABRADERS
AABDFHLN FAHLBAND
AABDGHNS HANDBAGS
AABDGINR ABRADING
AABDGLNR LANDGRAB
AABDGMOS GAMBADOS
AABDGNOV VAGABOND
AABDGNSS SANDBAGS
AABDGORR GARBOARD
AABDGORT TAGBOARD
AABDGOTU GADABOUT
AABDHINR HAIRBAND
AABDHLLN HANDBALL
AABDHLLR HARDBALL
AABDHNST HATBANDS
AABDHRSU BAHADURS
SUBAHDAR
AABDIILR BIRADIAL
AABDIILS BASIDIAL
AABDIKRS BIDARKAS
AABDIMNO ABDOMINA
AABDIMRS BARMAIDS
AABDINNR RAINBAND
AABDINST TABANIDS

AABDKNNS SANDBANK
AABDLLRY BALLADRY
BALLYARD
AABDLLUY LAUDABLY
AABDLMNU LABDANUM
AABDLMNY DAMNABLY
AABDLMRU ADUMBRAL
AABDLOOT BOATLOAD
AABDLOPR LAPBOARD
AABDLORR LABRADOR
LARBOARD
AABDLORY ADORABLY
AABDLRSW BRADAWLS
AABDMNNS BANDSMAN
AABDMNOR BOARDMAN
AABDMNRS ARMBANDS
AABDNNOS ABANDONS
AABDNNTU ABUNDANT
AABDNORS BANDORAS
AABDNPSS PASSBAND
AABDNRRY BARNYARD
AABDNRSS SANDBARS
AABDNSSW BANDSAWS
AABDORSV BRAVADOS
AABDORTY BOATYARD
AABDRRSS BRASSARD
AABDRRSW DRAWBARS
AABDRSST BASTARDS
AABDRSSU SUBADARS
AABDRSTY BASTARDY
AABEEFLN FLEABANE
AABEEGKR BRAKEAGE
BREAKAGE
AABEEGLT ABLEGATE
AABEEGNT ABNEGATE
AABEEHLL HEALABLE
AABEEHLR HEARABLE
AABEEHLT HATEABLE
HEATABLE
AABEEKLM MAKEABLE
AABEEKLT TAKEABLE
AABEEKMT BAKEMEAT
MAKEBATE
AABEEKRW BAKEWARE
AABEELLS LEASABLE
SALEABLE
SEALABLE
AABEELMN AMENABLE
NAMEABLE
AABEELMT TAMEABLE
AABEELPR REAPABLE
AABEELPT TAPEABLE
AABEELRS ERASABLE
AABEELRT RATEABLE
TEARABLE
AABEELRW WEARABLE
AABEELST EATABLES
TEASABLE
AABEELSV SAVEABLE
AABEEMNO AMOEBEAN
AABEEMNT ENTAMEBA
AABEEMPR ABAMPERE
AABEENNW WANNABEE
AABEENOR ANAEROBE
AABEERSZ ZAREEBAS
AABEERTT TRABEATE
AABEFGLS FLEABAGS
AABEFHKL HALFBEAK
AABEFLLL FLABELLA
AABEFLMO FOAMABLE
AABEFLMR FARMABLE
FRAMABLE
AABEFLMU FLAMBEAU
AABEFLTU FABULATE
AABEGGGS BAGGAGES
AABEGGRS GARBAGES
AABEGGRY GARBAGEY
AABEGHIL GALABIEH
AABEGHLN HANGABLE
AABEGILN GAINABLE
AABEGILT AGITABLE
AABEGLLL GLABELLA
AABEGLLM BALLGAME
AABEGLNW GNAWABLE
AABEGLRS ALGEBRAS
AABEGLRT GLABRATE
AABEGLRU ARGUABLE
AABEGLRZ GRAZABLE
AABEGMNR BARGEMAN
AABEGMNY MANGABEY
AABEGMRS MEGABARS
AABEGMRT BREGMATA
AABEGNOR BARONAGE
AABEGORT ABROGATE
AABEGOST SABOTAGE
AABEGOSZ GAZABOES
AABEGRRS BARRAGES
AABEGRSS BRASSAGE
AABEGSSS BAGASSES
AABEHIRR HERBARIA
AABEHKLS SHAKABLE
AABEHLMS SHAMABLE
AABEHLPS SHAPABLE
AABEHLPT ALPHABET
AABEHLRS SHARABLE
AABEHLSV SHAVABLE
AABEHLSW WASHABLE
AABEHNOR HABANERO
AABEIJLL JAILABLE
AABEIKLS KIELBASA
AABEIKNS IKEBANAS
AABEILLL ALLIABLE
AABEILLM MAILABLE
AABEILLS SAILABLE
AABEILNR INARABLE
AABEILNZ BANALIZE
AABEILRS RAISABLE
AABEILRV VARIABLE
AABEILST LABIATES
SATIABLE
AABEILTV ABLATIVE
AABEIMNR AMBERINA
AABEIMRS AMBARIES
AABEINOZ ZABAIONE
AABEINRT ATABRINE
AABEIOTU ABOITEAU
AABEIRSV ABRASIVE
AABEIRSZ ARABIZES
AABEIRTU AUBRETIA
AUBRIETA
AABEISST ABATISES
AABEJLLS JELLABAS
AABEJLMM JAMMABLE
AABEJMUX JAMBEAUX
AABEJNOZ ZABAJONE
AABEJNSX BANJAXES
AABEKLLS SLAKABLE
AABEKLLT TALKABLE
AABEKLLW WALKABLE
AABEKLMS MASKABLE
AABEKMNR BRAKEMAN
AABEKPRS PARBAKES
AABEKRRS BARESARK
AABEKRSS ARABESKS
AABELLMT MEATBALL
AABELLNO LOANABLE
AABELLPP PALPABLE
AABELLPS LAPSABLE
AABELLPY PLAYABLE
AABELLSV SALVABLE
AABELLSY SALEABLY
SLAYABLE
AABELLUV VALUABLE
AABELMNY AMENABLY
AABELMPP MAPPABLE
AABELMST BLASTEMA
LAMBASTE
AABELMSU AMUSABLE
AABELMTU AMBULATE
AABELNNT TANNABLE
AABELNOS ABALONES
AABELNOT ATONABLE
AABELNPS ANABLEPS
AABELNPW PAWNABLE
AABELORR ARBOREAL
AABELOSV LAVABOES
AABELOVW AVOWABLE
AABELPPR PALPEBRA
AABELPPT TAPPABLE
AABELPRS PARABLES
PARSABLE
PREBASAL
SPARABLE
AABELPSS PASSABLE
AABELPSY PAYABLES
AABELRST ARBALEST
RATABLES
AABELRTY BETRAYAL
RATEABLY
AABELSST BASALTES
AABELSTT ABETTALS
STATABLE
TASTABLE
AABELSTU TABLEAUS
AABELSTW WASTABLE
AABELSTX TAXABLES
AABELSWY SWAYABLE
AABELTTU TABULATE
AABELTUX TABLEAUX
AABEMMXY MYXAMEBA
AABENNSW WANNABES
AABENRRT ABERRANT
AABENRST ANTBEARS
RATSBANE
AABENRTU ARBUTEAN
AABEORRT ARBORETA
AABEORST AEROBATS
AABEQSUU USQUABAE
AABERRRT BARRATER
AABERRSW BARWARES
AABERSSU SUBAREAS
AABERSTT TABARETS
AABETTUX BATTEAUX
AABFILUX FABLIAUX
AABFLLST FASTBALL
AABFLOTT FALTBOAT
FLATBOAT
AABGGGNN GANGBANG
AABGGRRT BRAGGART
AABGHINS ABASHING
AABGHKRS SHAGBARK
AABGHNRS BHANGRAS
AABGIILS ABIGAILS
AABGILMS MAILBAGS
AABGILNT ABLATING
BANGTAIL
AABGIMNS SAMBAING
AABGIMSU GAMBUSIA
AABGINRS BARGAINS
AABGINSS BISNAGAS
AABGINSZ BIZNAGAS
AABGLLRY BALLYRAG
AABGLMNU GALBANUM
AABGLRUY ARGUABLY
AABGMORR BAROGRAM
AABGNORZ GARBANZO
AABHHORU BROUHAHA
AABHIIMP AMPHIBIA
AABHIINU BAUHINIA
AABHILLR HAIRBALL
AABHILTU HABITUAL
AABHINST HABITANS
AABHINTT HABITANT
AABHISTT HABITATS
AABHKLLW BALLHAWK
AABHLMSY SHAMABLY
AABHMRSS SAMBHARS
AABHMSTT BATHMATS
AABHNOTU AUTOBAHN
AABIIJLT JAILBAIT
AABIILSZ ALBIZIAS
AABIILZZ ALBIZZIA
AABIINST ANTIBIAS
AABIIPST BAPTISIA
AABIKLMS KABALISM
KALIMBAS
AABIKLST KABALIST
AABIKNSS BANKSIAS
AABILLLY LABIALLY
AABILLRS BARILLAS
AABILLST BALLISTA
AABILMNS BAILSMAN
AABILMNU BIMANUAL
AABILMSS BAALISMS
AABILNNU BIANNUAL
AABILNOR BARONIAL
AABILNOT ABLATION
AABILNRT BRANTAIL
AABILNRU BINAURAL
AABILNTY BANALITY
AABILOST SAILBOAT
AABILOSU ABOULIAS
AABILRRT ARBITRAL
AABILRST ARBALIST
AABILRSU BALISAUR
AABILRSY BASILARY
AABILRVY VARIABLY
AABILSTY SATIABLY
AABILSUX SUBAXIAL
AABIMMRS MARIMBAS
AABIMNOS AMBOINAS
AABIMNRU MANUBRIA
AABIMORS AMBROSIA
AABIMRSU SIMARUBA
AABIMSST BASMATIS
AABINNPR BRAINPAN
AABINORS ABRASION
AABINOSU OUABAINS
AABINRST BARTISAN
AABINRTZ BARTIZAN
AABINSST ABSTAINS
AABIORSS ABROSIAS
AABIORST AIRBOATS
AABIORTT ABATTOIR
AABIOSSY BIOASSAY
AABIRSST BARISTAS
AABIRTUY RUBAIYAT
AABISTUZ ZAIBATSU
AABKLLPR BALLPARK
AABKNRST TANBARKS
AABKOOSZ BAZOOKAS
AABKOPRS SOAPBARK
AABKRSST TASKBARS
AABLLMOR BALMORAL
AABLLORS ALLOBARS
AABLLORY ABORALLY
AABLLPPY PALPABLY
AABLLPRT TRAPBALL
AABLLSST BALLASTS
AABLLSTU BLASTULA
AABLLSVY SALVABLY
AABLLUVY VALUABLY
AABLMNOR ABNORMAL
AABLMNTU AMBULANT
AABLMOST BLASTOMA
AABLMRSU LABARUMS
AABLMSST LAMBASTS
AABLNSSU SUBNASAL
AABLORST ABLATORS
AABLOTUY LAYABOUT
AABLOVWY AVOWABLY
AABLPSSY PASSABLY
AABLRSUU SUBAURAL
AABLSTTU ABUTTALS
AABMMOSU ABOMASUM
AABMNOST BOATSMAN
AABMNOSY AMBOYNAS
AABMNRTU RAMBUTAN
AABMORSU MARABOUS
AABMORTU MARABOUT
TAMBOURA
AABMOSSU ABOMASUS
AABMRSTU TAMBURAS
AABNNOST ABSONANT
AABNNOSZ BONANZAS
AABNOSST SABATONS
AABNOSSY SABAYONS
AABORRRT BARRATOR
AABORRSS RASBORAS
AABORRSU BAROSAUR
AABRRRTY BARRATRY
AABRRSST BRASSART
AABRRSUV BRAVURAS
AABSSTUX SAXTUBAS
AACCCDIS SACCADIC
AACCCFIO FOCACCIA
AACCCHHU CACHUCHA
AACCCRUY ACCURACY
AACCDDES CASCADED
AACCDEIM ACADEMIC
AACCDELO ACCOLADE
AACCDENU CADUCEAN
AACCDERS CARDCASE
AACCDESS CASCADES
SACCADES
AACCDHIR CHARACID
AACCDIIS ACCIDIAS
AACCDIRS CARDIACS
AACCDOVY ADVOCACY
AACCEELT CALCEATE
AACCEENT CETACEAN
AACCEFST CATFACES
AACCEHIX CACHEXIA
AACCEILN CALCANEI
AACCEILU ACICULAE
AACCEIRR CERCARIA
AACCELLY CAECALLY
CALYCEAL
AACCELOR CARACOLE
AACCELRR CARCERAL
AACCELTY CALYCATE
AACCENRT CARCANET
AACCENTU ACUTANCE
AACCERSS CARCASES
AACCERTU ACCURATE
AACCFILR FARCICAL
AACCFLTU CALCTUFA
AACCGILT GALACTIC
AACCHHIL HALACHIC
AACCHHKS CHACHKAS
AACCHHKT CHATCHKA
AACCHILP PACHALIC
AACCHINR ANARCHIC
CHARACIN
AACCHIOR AIRCOACH
AACCHISV VISCACHA
AACCHIVZ VIZCACHA
AACCHLLT CATCHALL
AACCHLNS CLACHANS
AACCHLOR CHARCOAL
AACCHLOT CACHALOT
AACCHMNO COACHMAN
AACCHMPS CHAMPACS
AACCIINV VACCINIA
AACCIIST SCIATICA
AACCILMS ACCLAIMS
AACCILNV VACCINAL
AACCILRU ACICULAR
AACCILSU ACICULAS
AACCILTT TACTICAL
AACCINSV VACCINAS
AACCIORS CARIOCAS
AACCIPRT APRACTIC
AACCIPTY CAPACITY
AACCIRTY CARYATIC
AACCISTT STACCATI
AACCJKRS CARJACKS
AACCJORU CARCAJOU
AACCKKPS PACKSACK
AACCKLOS COALSACK
AACCKLPS CALPACKS
AACCKORT COATRACK
AACCKRRS CARRACKS
AACCLLST CATCALLS
AACCLORS CARACOLS
AACCLPRS CALCSPAR
AACCLRSU ACCRUALS
CARACULS
SACCULAR
AACCLSSU ACCUSALS
AACCLSTW CATCLAWS
AACCNSTU ACCUSANT
AACCOPRS ASCOCARP
AACCORSU CURACAOS
CURACOAS
AACCOSTT STACCATO
STOCCATA
TOCCATAS
AACDDEHI ACIDHEAD
AACDDENV ADVANCED
AACDDETU CAUDATED
AACDDGHL CLADDAGH
AACDDILN CANDIDAL
AACDDINR RADICAND
AACDDINS CANDIDAS
AACDDRSW CRAWDADS
AACDEEHH HEADACHE
AACDEEHR HEADRACE
AACDEELS ESCALADE
AACDEEMS ACADEMES
AACDEEPS ESCAPADE
AACDEERT ACERATED
AACDEEST CASEATED
AACDEETT ACETATED
AACDEETU ECAUDATE
AACDEETV CAVEATED
AACDEFLT FALCATED
AACDEFNT CAFTANED
AACDEGKP PACKAGED
AACDEGMR DECAGRAM
AACDEHHY HEADACHY
AACDEHIN HACIENDA
AACDEHLP CEPHALAD
AACDEHMR DRACHMAE
AACDEHMS CHAMADES
AACDEHRS CHARADES
HARDCASE
AACDEHRT CATHEDRA
AACDEHST CATHEADS
AACDEHTT ATTACHED
AACDEIIL AECIDIAL
AACDEIIM ACIDEMIA
AACDEILM CAMAILED
AACDEILS ALCAIDES
AACDEIMN MAENADIC
AACDEIMS CAMISADE
AACDEIMT ACETAMID
AACDEINR RADIANCE
AACDEIRT RADICATE
AACDEJNT ADJACENT
AACDEKNP PANCAKED
AACDEKTT ATTACKED
AACDELLN CALENDAL
CANALLED
AACDELLS ALCALDES
AACDELMN MANACLED
AACDELNR CALENDAR
AACDELNS CANDELAS
AACDELNV VALANCED
AACDELOS CASELOAD
AACDELPT PLACATED
AACDELRS CALDERAS
AACDELSS SCALADES
AACDELSY ALCAYDES
AACDELTT LACTATED
AACDELTY ACYLATED
AACDENOT ANECDOTA
AACDENRS DRACENAS
AACDENRV ADVANCER
AACDENSV ADVANCES
CANVASED
AACDENSZ CADENZAS
AACDENTU ADUNCATE
AACDEOTU AUTOCADE
AACDEOTV ADVOCATE
AACDEQUY ADEQUACY
AACDERST CADASTER
CADASTRE
AACDERSV CADAVERS
AACDERSY DAYCARES
AACDERTU ARCUATED
AACDESTU CAUDATES
AACDETTU ACTUATED
AACDFLNR FLANCARD
AACDGGHI HAGGADIC
AACDGINR ARCADING
CARANGID
CARDIGAN
AACDHHKR HARDHACK
AACDHHNS SHADCHAN
AACDHHRS SHADRACH
AACDHIIS DICHASIA
AACDHIMR CHADARIM
DRACHMAI
AACDHINP HANDICAP
AACDHINR ARACHNID
AACDHKPR HARDPACK
AACDHKRT HARDTACK
AACDHLNP HANDCLAP
AACDHLOT CATHODAL
AACDHLRY CHARLADY
AACDHMOP PACHADOM
AACDHMRS DRACHMAS
AACDHNOW WAHCONDA
AACDHNRS HANDCARS
AACDHNRT HANDCART
AACDIINS ASCIDIAN
AACDIIRU ACIDURIA
AACDILLP PALLADIC
AACDILMN MANDALIC
AACDILMT DALMATIC
AACDILMU CALADIUM
AACDILNO DIACONAL
AACDILNR CARDINAL
AACDILNU DULCIANA
AACDILNV VANDALIC
AACDILOZ ZODIACAL
AACDILPS CAPSIDAL
AACDILRS RADICALS
AACDIMNO MANDIOCA
AACDIMNY ADYNAMIC
CYANAMID
AACDIMOS CAMISADO
AACDIMRT DRAMATIC
AACDINRY RADIANCY
AACDINSS SCANDIAS
AACDINST ANTACIDS
AACDIOTU AUTACOID
AACDIRSS ASCARIDS
AACDIRTY CARYATID
AACDITUY AUDACITY
AACDJKSW JACKDAWS
AACDJQRU JACQUARD
AACDKPRT TRACKPAD
AACDLLUY CAUDALLY
AACDLNSS SCANDALS
AACDLORS CARLOADS
AACDLORT CARTLOAD
AACDLORY COALYARD
AACDLOSS SCALADOS
AACDLOSV CALVADOS
AACDLPRS PLACARDS
AACDMMOR CARDAMOM
AACDMMRU CARDAMUM
AACDMNOR CARDAMON
AACDOOSV AVOCADOS
AACEEFIT FACETIAE
AACEEFLP PALEFACE
AACEEFNS FEASANCE
AACEEGLV CLEAVAGE
AACEEGNR CARAGEEN
AACEEGNY GYNAECEA
AACEEGRS ACREAGES
GEARCASE
AACEEHLP ACALEPHE
AACEEHLT LEACHATE
AACEEHRS EARACHES
AACEEHRT TRACHEAE
AACEEIMT EMACIATE
AACEEINN ENCAENIA
AACEEIRT ACIERATE
AACEEKRT CARETAKE
AACEEKST TEACAKES
AACEELRT LACERATE
AACEELST ESCALATE

AACEELTU ACULEATE
AACEEMRT MACERATE
RACEMATE
AACEEMSS AMESACES
AACEEMST CASEMATE
AACEENRS CESAREAN
AACEENRW CANEWARE
AACEENTT CATENATE
AACEEPRV PRECAVAE
AACEEPSS SEASCAPE
AACEERSU CAESURAE
AACEERTV ACERVATE
AACEESSS CASEASES
AACEESST CASEATES
AACEESTT ACETATES
AACEETUV EVACUATE
AACEETVX EXCAVATE
AACEFFIN AFFIANCE
AACEFILT CALIFATE
AACEFIST FASCIATE
AACEFKMS FACEMASK
AACEFRRS CARFARES
AACEFRRU FURCRAEA
AACEFRSS FRACASES
AACEFRST SEACRAFT
AACEFRTT ARTEFACT
AACEGHNS GANACHES
AACEGHNT CHANTAGE
AACEGILN ANGELICA
AACEGILT GLACIATE
AACEGINY GYNAECIA
AACEGIRR CARRIAGE
AACEGIRV VICARAGE
AACEGKPR PACKAGER
AACEGKPS PACKAGES
AACEGKRT TRACKAGE
AACEGLSS SCALAGES
AACEGMNO COMANAGE
AACEGMNP CAMPAGNE
AACEGNRS CARNAGES
AACEGRST CARTAGES
AACEHHRU HUARACHE
AACEHIKN ICEKHANA
AACEHILL ACHILLEA
HELIACAL
AACEHILN ACHENIAL
AACEHIMR CHIMAERA
AACEHIMT HAEMATIC
AACEHIPT HEPATICA
AACEHIRS ARCHAISE
AACEHIRT THERIACA
AACEHIRZ ARCHAIZE
AACEHKSS ASHCAKES
AACEHLNU EULACHAN
AACEHLPS ACALEPHS
AACEHLRT TRACHEAL
AACEHLRX EXARCHAL
AACEHLSS CALASHES
AACEHLST ALCAHEST
AACEHMRS MARCHESA
AACEHMST SCHEMATA
AACEHNOR ARCHAEON
AACEHNPS PANACHES
AACEHPSU CHAPEAUS
AACEHPUX CHAPEAUX
AACEHQTU CHAQUETA
AACEHRSS CHARASES
AACEHRST TRACHEAS
AACEHRTT ATTACHER
REATTACH
AACEHSTT ATTACHES
AACEHSTU CHATEAUS
AACEHTUX CHATEAUX
AACEIINT ACTINIAE
AACEIKMT KAMACITE
AACEILLM CAMELLIA
AACEILLN ALLIANCE
ANCILLAE
CANAILLE
AACEILMN ANALCIME
CALAMINE
AACEILMS CAMELIAS
AACEILMT CALAMITE
AACEILNS CANALISE
AACEILNT ANALCITE
LAITANCE
AACEILNU ACAULINE
AACEILNV VALENCIA
VALIANCE
AACEILNZ CANALIZE
AACEILOP ALOPECIA
AACEILRT TAILRACE
AACEILRV CAVALIER
AACEIMNS AMNESIAC
AACEIMTT CATAMITE
AACEINNT ANTIACNE

AACEINRS ACARINES
CANARIES
CESARIAN
SARCINAE
AACEINRT CARINATE
CRANIATE
AACEINRV VARIANCE
AACEINST ESTANCIA
AACEINTV CAVATINE
AACEIOPR CAPOEIRA
AACEIPPS PAPACIES
AACEIPRS AIRSCAPE
AIRSPACE
AACEIPSS CAPIASES
AACEIPTT APATETIC
CAPITATE
AACEIQSU ACEQUIAS
AACEIRSV AVARICES
CAVIARES
AACEIRTV VICARATE
AACEITTV ACTIVATE
CAVITATE
AACEJLTU JACULATE
AACEKKLW CAKEWALK
AACEKLRW RACEWALK
AACEKMPR CAPMAKER
AACEKMRR CARMAKER
AACEKNPS PANCAKES
AACEKOST OATCAKES
AACEKRTT ATTACKER
REATTACK
AACELLNR CANALLER
AACELLNS CANELLAS
AACELLOT ALLOCATE
AACELLST LACTEALS
AACELMNP PLACEMAN
AACELMNS MANACLES
AACELMOT CELOMATA
AACELMRS CARAMELS
CERAMALS
AACELMTU MACULATE
AACELNNO ANCONEAL
AACELNNU CANNULAE
AACELNPR PARLANCE
AACELNPS CAPELANS
SCALEPAN
AACELNPT PLACENTA
AACELNPY ANYPLACE
AACELNST ANALECTS
AACELNSV VALANCES
AACELNTU CANULATE
LACUNATE
TENACULA
AACELORS ACEROLAS
AACELORV CAVALERO
AACELOST CATALOES
AACELOSU ACAULOSE
AACELOSV COAEVALS
AACELPRT PLACATER
AACELPRV PRECAVAL
AACELPST PLACATES
AACELPSU SCAPULAE
AACELRSS SCALARES
AACELRSU CAESURAL
AACELRSV CARAVELS
AACELRTY ACRYLATE
AACELRWY CLAYWARE
AACELSST LACTASES
AACELSTT LACTATES
AACELSTY ACYLATES
AACELTTY CATTLEYA
AACELTYZ CATALYZE
AACEMMRS MACRAMES
AACEMNPS SPACEMAN
AACEMQSU MACAQUES
AACEMRSS MASSACRE
AACEMSSS CAMASSES
AACENOTU OCEANAUT
AACENPRS PANCREAS
AACENPRT CATNAPER
AACENPSU SAUCEPAN
AACENPTT PANCETTA
AACENRST CATERANS
AACENRSV CANVASER
AACENRTT REACTANT
AACENRTY CATENARY
AACENRVZ CZAREVNA
AACENSSS CASSENAS
AACENSSV CANVASES
AACENSTT CASTANET
AACENSTY CYANATES
AACENTUV EVACUANT
AACEOPPR COAPPEAR
AACEOPST PEACOATS
AACEORSS ROSACEAS
AACEORSU ARACEOUS

AACEORTV CAVEATOR
AACEOSST SEACOAST
AACERRTU ARCATURE
AACERSSU CAESURAS
AACERSTT CASTRATE
TEACARTS
AACERSWY RACEWAYS
AACERTTT TRACTATE
AACESTTU ACTUATES
AACESUWY CAUSEWAY
AACFHMST CAMSHAFT
AACFILLY FACIALLY
AACFINST FANATICS
AACFIRRT AIRCRAFT
AACFIRTT ARTIFACT
AACFJKLP FLAPJACK
AACFLLST CATFALLS
AACFLOPR PARFOCAL
AACFLPST FLATCAPS
AACFLRST FLATCARS
FRACTALS
AACFRRTW WARCRAFT
AACGGINO ANAGOGIC
AACGGIOP APAGOGIC
AACGHILT TAIGLACH
AACGHIPR AGRAPHIC
AACGHLLO AGALLOCH
AACGHLRU RUGALACH
AACGHOPZ GAZPACHO
AACGHORU GUACHARO
AACGIIMN MAGICIAN
AACGILLN GALLICAN
AACGILLO ALOGICAL
AACGILLS GALLICAS
AACGILNN CANALING
AACGILNO ANALOGIC
AACGILNR CRAALING
AACGILNT ANTALGIC
AACGILNV GALVANIC
AACGILOU GUAIACOL
AACGILOX COXALGIA
AACGILRT TRAGICAL
AACGIMMT MAGMATIC
AACGIMNN MANGANIC
AACGIMNP CAMPAIGN
AACGIMOP APOGAMIC
AACGIMRR MARGARIC
AACGIMUU GUAIACUM
AACGINOT CONTAGIA
AACGINTV VACATING
AACGISTY SAGACITY
AACGJNST CATJANGS
AACGLMOU GLAUCOMA
AACGLOST CATALOGS
AACGMNRS CRAGSMAN
AACGNOSU GUANACOS
AACGNRVY VAGRANCY
AACHHIKL HALAKHIC
AACHHKRS CHARKHAS
AACHHLLS CHALLAHS
AACHHLOT HALACHOT
AACHHORU HUARACHO
AACHHTWY HATCHWAY
AACHIIMR MARIACHI
AACHIKKZ KAZACHKI
AACHIKNS KACHINAS
AACHIKNT KATCHINA
AACHILLP CALIPHAL
AACHILLR RACHILLA
AACHILMS CHIASMAL
AACHILMT THALAMIC
AACHILNP CHAPLAIN
AACHILOS ACHOLIAS
AACHILPS CALIPASH
PASHALIC
AACHILPT HAPTICAL
AACHILRV ARCHIVAL
AACHIMNN CHAINMAN
AACHIMNR CHAIRMAN
AACHIMNS SHAMANIC
AACHIMNZ CHAZANIM
AACHIMRR ARMCHAIR
AACHIMRS ARCHAISM
CHARISMA
AACHIMSS CHAMISAS
CHIASMAS
AACHINSW CHAINSAW
AACHIPPT CHAPPATI
AACHIPRS CHARPAIS
HAIRCAPS
AACHIPSS APHASICS
AACHIPST CHAPATIS
AACHIPTT CHAPATTI
AACHIRST ARCHAIST
CITHARAS
AACHKKOZ KAZACHOK

AACHKMPS CHAMPAKS
AACHKNSW HACKSAWN
AACHKRST HATRACKS
AACHKRSY HAYRACKS
AACHKSSW HACKSAWS
AACHKSTY HAYSTACK
AACHLLLU HALLUCAL
AACHLLOR ALACHLOR
AACHLMNO MONACHAL
AACHLMOS CHLOASMA
AACHLNOO OOLACHAN
AACHLORT THORACAL
AACHLOST CALATHOS
AACHLPSS PASCHALS
AACHLPSU CHALUPAS
AACHLSTU CALATHUS
AACHMNNR RANCHMAN
AACHMNTW WATCHMAN
AACHMNTY YACHTMAN
AACHMNUY NAUMACHY
AACHMORT ACHROMAT
TRACHOMA
AACHMPRY PHARMACY
AACHMSSY YASHMACS
AACHNOPS PANOCHAS
AACHNSSU ANCHUSAS
AACHNSTU ACANTHUS
AACHNSZZ CHAZZANS
AACHOPPR APPROACH
AACHOPRR PARACHOR
AACHRRST CATARRHS
AACHRSTU AUTARCHS
AACHRSWY ARCHWAYS
AACHRTUY AUTARCHY
AACIILMN ANIMALIC
AACIILMO MAIOLICA
AACIILRT IATRICAL
AACIILRV VICARIAL
AACIILTV VIATICAL
AACIIMSS CAMISIAS
AACIINNT ACTINIAN
AACIINST ACTINIAS
AACIJLMO MAJOLICA
AACIJNOP JAPONICA
AACIKLRS CLARKIAS
AACIKMNW MACKINAW
AACIKNNS CANAKINS
AACIKNST KATCINAS
AACIKRTU AUTARKIC
AACILLLY LAICALLY
AACILLMR LACRIMAL
AACILLMT CLIMATAL
AACILLNS ANCILLAS
AACILLPY APICALLY
AACILLRY RACIALLY
AACILMNT CALAMINT
CLAIMANT
AACILMOR ACROMIAL
AACILMOT ATOMICAL
AACILMTY CALAMITY
AACILNPS CALPAINS
AACILNRV CARNIVAL
AACILNST SANTALIC
AACILNTT TANTALIC
AACILNTU NAUTICAL
AACILNTY ANALYTIC
AACILNVY VALIANCY
AACILOSS ASOCIALS
AACILOTT COATTAIL
TAILCOAT
AACILPRU PIACULAR
AACILPST APLASTIC
CAPITALS
AACILPTU CAPITULA
AACILPTY ATYPICAL
AACILRRS RAILCARS
AACILRTY ALACRITY
AACILRUU AURICULA
AACILRUV AVICULAR
AACILSTT CATTAILS
STATICAL
AACILSTY SALACITY
AACIMMNO AMMONIAC
AACIMMRS MARASMIC
AACIMNOR ARMONICA
MACARONI
MAROCAIN
AACIMNOS MANIOCAS
AACIMNOT ANATOMIC
AACIMORT AROMATIC
AACIMOTX MAXICOAT
AACINNST CANTINAS
AACINOPR PARANOIC
AACINORS OCARINAS
AACINORT RAINCOAT
AACINOTV VACATION

AACINPRT CANTRAIP
AACINPST CAPTAINS
AACINQTU ACQUAINT
AACINRSS ACRASINS
SARCINAS
AACINRSZ CZARINAS
AACINSSS CASSINAS
AACINSTZ STANZAIC
AACIOPST TAPIOCAS
AACIPPRS PAPRICAS
AACIPRTY RAPACITY
AACIQSTU AQUATICS
AACIRRTT TARTARIC
AACIRSTT CASTRATI
AACIRTVY CAVITARY
AACIRTZZ CZARITZA
AACISSTW SWASTICA
AACJKLPS SLAPJACK
AACJKOOR JACKAROO
AACJKSTY JACKSTAY
AACJPSTU CAJAPUTS
AACKKNPS KNAPSACK
AACKLSTW CATWALKS
AACKMNRT TRACKMAN
AACKMRST AMTRACKS
AACKNRSS RANSACKS
AACKORWY ROCKAWAY
AACKRTWY TRACKWAY
AACLLLOO CALLALOO
AACLLNRY CARNALLY
AACLLNST CALLANTS
AACLLRRY CARRYALL
AACLLRSY RASCALLY
AACLLSUY CASUALLY
CAUSALLY
AACLLTUY ACTUALLY
AACLMNNS CLANSMAN
AACLMOTU COMATULA
AACLMRRU MACRURAL
AACLNNOT CANTONAL
AACLNNRU CANNULAR
AACLNNSU CANNULAS
AACLNOPR COPLANAR
AACLNOTT OCTANTAL
AACLNPSY CLAYPANS
AACLNRSU LACUNARS
AACLNRUY LACUNARY
AACLNTVY VACANTLY
AACLOPRS CAPORALS
CRAPOLAS
AACLORRU ORACULAR
AACLORSU CAROUSAL
AACLORUV VACUOLAR
AACLOSTT CATTALOS
AACLOSUU ACAULOUS
AACLPPRT CLAPTRAP
AACLPRST CALTRAPS
AACLPRSU CAPSULAR
SCAPULAR
AACLPRTY CALYPTRA
AACLPSSU SCAPULAS
AACLPSTY PLAYACTS
AACLPTTU CATAPULT
AACLRSTU CLAUSTRA
AACLRSUV VASCULAR
AACLRTUX CURTALAX
AACLRWWY CRAWLWAY
AACLSTTY CATALYST
AACLSTUY CASUALTY
AACMNOOR MACAROON
AACMNORS NARCOMAS
AACMNPRY RAMPANCY
AACMNRRU MACRURAN
AACMNRSU ARCANUMS
AACMORRS CAMORRAS
AACMORSS SARCOMAS
AACMORST MARCATOS
AACMRRST TRAMCARS
AACMRSSS SARCASMS
AACNNOSZ CANZONAS
AACNOSST SACATONS
AACNOSTZ ZACATONS
AACNPRST CANTRAPS
AACNPSST CAPSTANS
AACNRSTT TRANSACT
AACOPPRS APOCARPS
AACOPPRY APOCARPY
AACOPRSU ACARPOUS
AACOPSTV POSTCAVA
AACOPSTY APOSTACY
AACORRTV VARACTOR
AACORSSW CARASSOW
AACORSTT CASTRATO
AACORTTU ACTUATOR
AUTOCRAT
AACPSSTW CATSPAWS

AACRSTTT ATTRACTS
AACSTUWY CUTAWAYS
AADDDEEH DEADHEAD
AADDDGNR GRANDDAD
AADDEELT DEALATED
AADDEFLL DEADFALL
AADDEGGR AGGRADED
AADDEGRT GRADATED
AADDEHHR HARDHEAD
AADDEHLN HEADLAND
AADDEHMN HANDMADE
AADDEHRZ HAZARDED
AADDEILS ALIDADES
AADDEIRT RADIATED
AADDEKMS DAMASKED
AADDELNS SANDALED
AADDELTU ADULATED
AADDEMNT MANDATED
AADDEMRU MARAUDED
AADDEMRY DAYDREAM
AADDENPS DEADPANS
AADDEORS DEODARAS
AADDGMNR GRANDDAM
AADDGNRS GRANDADS
AADDGNRU GRADUAND
AADDHIMN HANDMAID
AADDHKRS KHADDARS
AADDHRSS SRADDHAS
AADDIMSS DADAISMS
AADDISST DADAISTS
AADDLLNY LANDLADY
AADDLNRW LANDWARD
AADDLNRY YARDLAND
AADDNRST STANDARD
AADDNRWY YARDWAND
AADDRSST DASTARDS
AADEEERT DEAERATE
AADEEGHR GEARHEAD
HEADGEAR
AADEEGHT HEADGATE
AADEEGLM MEGADEAL
AADEEGLR LAAGERED
AADEEGLT GALEATED
AADEEGMN ENDAMAGE
AADEEGMR REDAMAGE
AADEEGNR GADARENE
AADEEGRV AVERAGED
AADEEHMT MEATHEAD
AADEEIRT ERADIATE
AADEEKNW AWAKENED
AADEEKRW REAWAKED
AADEELNN ANNEALED
AADEELPP APPEALED
AADEELST DEALATES
AADEEMNS MAENADES
AADEEMNT EMANATED
AADEEMOT OEDEMATA
AADEEMRR DEMERARA
AADEENPT TAPENADE
AADEENTT ANTEDATE
AADEEPPR APPEARED
AADEEPPS APPEASED
AADEEQTU ADEQUATE
AADEERSW AWARDEES
AADEFFRY AFFRAYED
AADEFHLT FLATHEAD
AADEFHST FATHEADS
AADEFILR FAIRLEAD
AADEFIRS FARADISE
SAFARIED
AADEFIRZ FARADIZE
AADEFLLR FALDERAL
AADEFLRY DEFRAYAL
AADEFNSZ FAZENDAS
AADEGGRS AGGRADES
SAGGARED
AADEGHNR HANGARED
AADEGILL DIALLAGE
AADEGILT GLADIATE
AADEGINR DRAINAGE
GARDENIA
AADEGINT INDAGATE
AADEGIRR GERARDIA
AADEGIRV GRAVIDAE
AADEGITT AGITATED
AADEGITV DIVAGATE
AADEGITZ AGATIZED
AADEGKMR DEKAGRAM
AADEGLLT TALLAGED
AADEGLMN MAGDALEN
AADEGLMY AMYGDALE
AADEGLNS SELADANG
AADEGLOP GALOPADE
AADEGLSV SALVAGED
AADEGMNR GRANDAME
AADEGMPR RAMPAGED

AADEGMRS DAMAGERS
SMARAGDE
AADEGMSS MASSAGED
AADEGNRR ARRANGED
AADEGPRY PAYGRADE
AADEGPSS PASSAGED
AADEGRST GRADATES
AADEGRSY DRAYAGES
YARDAGES
AADEGRTU GRADUATE
AADEGSSU ASSUAGED
AADEGSSW ASSWAGED
AADEHHHS HASHHEAD
AADEHILN NAILHEAD
AADEHILR RAILHEAD
AADEHILS HEADSAIL
AADEHIRR DIARRHEA
AADEHIRS AIRHEADS
AADEHIWY HIDEAWAY
AADEHJRS JARHEADS
AADEHLLO HALLOAED
AADEHLMP HEADLAMP
AADEHLRS ASHLARED
AADEHMNS HEADSMAN
AADEHMST MASTHEAD
AADEHNRV VERANDAH
AADEHNSX HANDAXES
AADEHPSS SAPHEADS
AADEHRRW HARDWARE
AADEHRRZ HAZARDER
AADEHRSS HARASSED
AADEHRSW WARHEADS
AADEHSSY SASHAYED
AADEHSTY HEADSTAY
AADEHSWY HEADWAYS
AADEILMS MALADIES
AADEILNT DENTALIA
AADEILPR PRAEDIAL
AADEILPS PALISADE
AADEILPT LAPIDATE
AADEILRS SALARIED
AADEILRT LARIATED
AADEILSS ASSAILED
AADEILSV VEDALIAS
AADEILTT DILATATE
AADEILTV VALIDATE
AADEIMNN AMANDINE
AADEIMNR MARINADE
AADEIMNT ANIMATED
DIAMANTE
AADEIMPZ DIAZEPAM
AADEIMRS MADEIRAS
AADEIMRV MARAVEDI
AADEIMSS AMIDASES
AADEIMST ADAMSITE
DIASTEMA
AADEINPT PATINAED
AADEINRS ARANEIDS
AADEINSZ ZENAIDAS
AADEINTT ATTAINED
AADEIPRS PARADISE
AADEIPSU DIAPAUSE
AADEIPTV ADAPTIVE
AADEIRST AIRDATES
DATARIES
RADIATES
AADEIRTV VARIATED
AADEISST DIASTASE
AADEISTT SATIATED
AADEITVW VIEWDATA
AADEJMRS JEMADARS
AADEJNNP JAPANNED
AADEKLRY KALEYARD
AADEKMNR MANDRAKE
AADEKNUW UNAWAKED
AADEKPRS PARKADES
AADELLOS ALDOLASE
AADELLPP APPALLED
AADELLWY WELLADAY
AADELMNP NAPALMED
AADELMNR ALDERMAN
AADELMNS DALESMAN
LEADSMAN
AADELMOS ALAMODES
AADELMPT PALMATED
AADELMRU ALARUMED
AADELMYZ AMAZEDLY
AADELNRS ADRENALS
AADELNSY ANALYSED
AADELNYZ ANALYZED
AADELOTX OXALATED
AADELPPT PALPATED
AADELPRY PARLAYED
AADELPTY PLAYDATE
AADELQUU QUAALUDE
AADELSTU ADULATES
AADELTUV VALUATED
AADEMNOS ADENOMAS
AADEMNST MANDATES
AADEMNUZ UNAMAZED
AADEMRRU MARAUDER
AADEMRSS MADRASES
AADEMRSY DAYMARES
AADEMSSS ADMASSES
AADENNST ANDANTES
AADENRRT NARRATED
AADENRSV VERANDAS
AADENSSW WEASANDS
AADENSTY ASYNDETA
AADENSTZ STANZAED
AADENSWZ WEAZANDS
AADEOPRT TAPADERO
AADEPPRT PREADAPT
AADEPRRS PARADERS
AADEPRST ADAPTERS
READAPTS
AADEPSSS PASSADES
AADEQRTU QUADRATE
AADERRRW REARWARD
AADERRSW AWARDERS
AADERSSW SEAWARDS
AADERSTW EASTWARD
RADWASTE
AADERUVY AYURVEDA
AADFGNNO FANDANGO
AADFHMNR FARMHAND
AADFHNST HANDFAST
AADFIINT INTIFADA
AADFIMRS FARADISM
AADFINRU UNAFRAID
AADFLLLN LANDFALL
AADFLLNT FLATLAND
AADFLMNR FARMLAND
AADFLORW AARDWOLF
AADFLOTX TOADFLAX
AADFLOWY FOLDAWAY
AADFMRRY FARMYARD
AADGGHOT AGGADOTH
HAGGADOT
AADGGHRS HAGGARDS
AADGGIMN DAMAGING
AADGGLNN GANGLAND
AADGGLRS LAGGARDS
AADGGRSS SAGGARDS
AADGGRST STAGGARD
AADGHIPR DIAGRAPH
AADGHIST HAGADIST
AADGIINS GAINSAID
AADGIIRS GIARDIAS
AADGILLO GLADIOLA
AADGILLR GALLIARD
AADGILMR MADRIGAL
AADGILNO DIAGONAL
GONADIAL
AADGIMMS DIGAMMAS
AADGIMNR MRIDANGA
AADGIMPR PARADIGM
AADGIMRS DIAGRAMS
AADGINPR PARADING
AADGINPT ADAPTING
AADGINRU GUARDIAN
AADGINRW AWARDING
AADGIQRU QUADRIGA
AADGIRSV GRAVIDAS
AADGLLSW GADWALLS
AADGLNOR LARGANDO
AADGLNRS GARLANDS
AADGLOOW AGALWOOD
AADGLOPR PODAGRAL
AADGLORW GOALWARD
AADGLRSU GRADUALS
AADGMNOP PAGANDOM
AADGMNOR DRAGOMAN
AADGMNRS GRANDAMS
GRANDMAS
AADGMRSS SMARAGDS
AADGNNQU QUANDANG
AADGNPRS GRANDPAS
AADGNRTU GUARDANT
AADGNRUV VANGUARD
AADGOPRS PODAGRAS
AADHHIPS PADISHAH
AADHHKNS SHADKHAN
AADHHPSS PADSHAHS
AADHHRST HARDHATS
AADHIINP APHIDIAN
AADHILLR HALLIARD
AADHILNR HANDRAIL
AADHIMSS SAMADHIS
AADHINOT ANTHODIA
AADHINPS DAPHNIAS
AADHINRR HARRIDAN
AADHKLOT KATHODAL
AADHLPSS SLAPDASH
AADHLRSY HALYARDS
AADHLRUY HAULYARD
AADHMNNY HANDYMAN
AADHMOPS PASHADOM
AADHNPRS HARDPANS
AADHNRSS DARSHANS
AADHNSSW HANDSAWS
AADHRSWY HAYWARDS
AADHSSWY WASHDAYS
AADIILNS SIALIDAN
AADIKLLO ALKALOID
AADIKLRY KAILYARD
AADIKNQR QINDARKA
AADILLLO ALLODIAL
AADILLPR PAILLARD
AADILLRY RADIALLY
AADILMNN MAINLAND
AADILMRS ADMIRALS
AADILMST MATILDAS
AADILNPR PRANDIAL
AADILNPS PALADINS
AADILNRS LANIARDS
AADILNTT DILATANT
AADILORR RAILROAD
AADILPRY LAPIDARY
AADILRST DIASTRAL
AADIMNNR MANDARIN
AADIMNOR RADIOMAN
AADIMNOT MANATOID
AADIMNRT TAMARIND
AADIMNRY DAIRYMAN
AADIMNRZ ZAMINDAR
AADIMNUV VANADIUM
AADIMORS DIORAMAS
AADIMPST MISADAPT
AADIMRSW MISAWARD
AADIMSTZ SAMIZDAT
AADINNNS NANDINAS
AADINNOT ADNATION
AADINOPR PARANOID
AADINOPS DIAPASON
AADINOPT ADAPTION
AADINORT ANTIDORA
AADINPST PINTADAS
AADINRST RADIANTS
AADINRTY INTRADAY
AADIOPRS DIASPORA
AADIORRT RADIATOR
AADIRRSY DISARRAY
AADISTXY DYSTAXIA
AADJNTTU ADJUTANT
AADJNTUV ADJUVANT
AADKLMNR LANDMARK
AADKLNPR PARKLAND
AADKNRST TANKARDS
AADKORWY WORKADAY
AADLLLNS LALLANDS
AADLLMPY LADYPALM
AADLLMRS MALLARDS
AADLLNOY ANODALLY
AADLLNPY PLAYLAND
AADLMNNS LANDSMAN
AADLMNOS MANDOLAS
AADLMNSS LANDMASS
AADLMNSU LADANUMS
AADLMNUU LAUDANUM
AADLMORS ARMLOADS
AADLNOPR PARLANDO
AADLNOPS DALAPONS
AADLNOSV VANLOADS
AADLNOSZ DANAZOLS
AADLNRSY LANYARDS
AADLOPSY PAYLOADS
AADLORST LOADSTAR
AADLORTU ADULATOR
LAUDATOR
AADLPPSU APPLAUDS
AADLPSYY PLAYDAYS
AADMMNOW MADWOMAN
AADMMNSU MANDAMUS
AADMNNOS MADONNAS
AADMNORS MADRONAS
MONARDAS
AADMNORT MANDATOR
AADMNRSS MANSARDS
AADMNRSW MANWARDS
AADMNSTU TAMANDUS
AADMOPPS PAPADOMS
AADMORRT TRAMROAD
AADMORST MATADORS
AADMPPSU PAPADUMS
AADMRRSY YARDARMS
AADMRSZZ MAZZARDS
AADNNPSU PANDANUS
AADNOPRS PANDORAS
AADNOPSS SANDSOAP
AADNOSUV VANADOUS
AADNOSWY NOWADAYS
AADNPRSU PANDURAS
AADNPSTT STANDPAT
AADNQRSU QUADRANS
AADNQRTU QUADRANT
AADNQRUY QUANDARY
AADNRSTY TANYARDS
AADOPPRR PARADROP
AADOPRRS PARADORS
AADOPRST ADAPTORS
AADOPSSS PASSADOS
AADOPSUY PADUASOY
AADORSWY ROADWAYS
AADOSSTT TOSTADAS
AADQRSTU QUADRATS
AADRSSTY DAYSTARS
AAEEEHRT HETAERAE
AAEEEMRT AMEERATE
AAEEFGLS LEAFAGES
AAEEFRRS SEAFARER
AAEEFRST RATAFEES
AAEEGILN ALIENAGE
AAEEGINS AGENESIA
AAEEGKLS LEAKAGES
AAEEGLRY LAYERAGE
AAEEGLST STEALAGE
AAEEGLSV SALVAGEE
AAEEGMPR AMPERAGE
AAEEGMST AGAMETES
AGEMATES
AAEEGNRS SANGAREE
AAEEGRSV AVERAGES
AAEEGRTW WATERAGE
AAEEHMNR HERMAEAN
AAEEHNPS SAPHENAE
AAEEHPRT EARTHPEA
AAEEHRST HETAERAS
AAEEHRTW AWEATHER
WHEATEAR
AAEEHRWY HEREAWAY
AAEEILNT ALIENATE
AAEEKMNS NAMESAKE
AAEEKMRT TEAMAKER
AAEEKNRW AWAKENER
REAWAKEN
AAEEKPRT PARAKEET
AAEEKQSU SEAQUAKE
AAEEKRSW REAWAKES
AAEELLLM LAMELLAE
AAEELLMR AMARELLE
AAEELLNV AVELLANE
AAEELLPT PATELLAE
AAEELMST MALEATES
AAEELNNR ANNEALER
AAEELNPS SEAPLANE
SPELAEAN
AAEELNPT PANETELA
AAEELORT AREOLATE
AAEELORU AUREOLAE
AAEELPPR APPEALER
AAEELRTU LAUREATE
AAEELRTV VALERATE
AAEELSST ELASTASE
AAEELTUV EVALUATE
AAEEMMTT TEAMMATE
AAEEMNST EMANATES
MANATEES
AAEEMRST AMREETAS
AAEEMSTT SEATMATE
AAEENNNT ANTENNAE
AAEENRST ARSENATE
SERENATA
AAEENRTT ANTEATER
AAEENSTU NAUSEATE
AAEEPPRR RAPPAREE
REAPPEAR
AAEEPPRS APPEASER
AAEEPPSS APPEASES
AAEEPRST ASPERATE
SEPARATE
AAEERSSW SEAWARES
AAEERSTT STEARATE
AAEERSTW SEAWATER
TEAWARES
AAEERSWX EARWAXES
AAEERSYY YEASAYER
AAEFFGRS AGRAFFES
AAEFFIRS AFFAIRES
AAEFFLLR FARFALLE
AAEFFLLS FALAFELS
AAEFFLRT TAFFAREL
AAEFFNRS FANFARES
AAEFFRRY AFFRAYER
AAEFFSTT TAFFETAS
AAEFGGRT GRAFTAGE
AAEFGHRW WHARFAGE
AAEFGLLL FLAGELLA
AAEFGLOT FLOATAGE
AAEFGSTW WAFTAGES
AAEFIILR FILARIAE
AAEFIKLT KALIFATE
AAEFILTY FAYALITE
AAEFIMRR AIRFRAME
AAEFINNT FAINEANT
AAEFINNU INFAUNAE
AAEFINPU EPIFAUNA
AAEFINST FANTASIE
AAEFINTX ANTEFIXA
AAEFIRRS AIRFARES
AAEFKMST MAKEFAST
AAEFLLSV FAVELLAS
AAEFLMOT MEATLOAF
AAEFLMTT FLATMATE
AAEFLPRS EARFLAPS
AAEFLRTW FLATWARE
AAEFMRST FERMATAS
AAEFMRSU FUMARASE
AAEFMRTU FUMARATE
AAEFRRSW WARFARES
AAEFRRWY WAYFARER
AAEFRTTX AFTERTAX
AAEGGIOT AGIOTAGE
AAEGGLNR LANGRAGE
AAEGGLNU LANGUAGE
AAEGGNOS ANAGOGES
AAEGGNOW WAGONAGE
AAEGGNRY GARGANEY
AAEGGOPR PARAGOGE
AAEGGOPS APAGOGES
AAEGHLNP PHALANGE
AAEGHLSU HAULAGES
AAEGHLSY HAYLAGES
AAEGHMRX HEXAGRAM
AAEGHMSS GAMASHES
AAEGHNRU HARANGUE
AAEGHNST THANAGES
AAEGILLP PELAGIAL
AAEGILLR GALLERIA
AAEGILMS SEMIGALA
AAEGILNR GERANIAL
AAEGILNT AGENTIAL
ALGINATE
AAEGILRS GASALIER
AAEGILSX GALAXIES
AAEGILTT TAILGATE
AAEGIMNO EGOMANIA
AAEGIMNS MAGNESIA
AAEGIMNT AGMINATE
ENIGMATA
AAEGIMNZ MAGAZINE
AAEGIMRR MARRIAGE
AAEGIMRT GEMATRIA
AAEGINNR ANEARING
AAEGINPS PAGANISE
AAEGINPT PAGINATE
AAEGINPZ PAGANIZE
AAEGINRS ANERGIAS
ANGARIES
ARGINASE
AAEGINRT AERATING
AAEGINTV NAVIGATE
VAGINATE
AAEGIRSV VAGARIES
AAEGISSS ASSEGAIS
AAEGISTT AGITATES
AAEGISTZ AGATIZES
AAEGIVWY GIVEAWAY
AAEGKNST TANKAGES
AAEGKOSS SOAKAGES
AAEGLLMS SMALLAGE
AAEGLLPR PELLAGRA
AAEGLLSS GALLEASS
AAEGLLST GALLATES
GALLETAS
TALLAGES
AAEGLMNS GAMELANS
AAEGLMST ALMAGEST
AAEGLNOU ANALOGUE
AAEGLNPP LAGNAPPE
AAEGLNRT ARGENTAL
AAEGLNSS LASAGNES
AAEGLNTU ANGULATE
AAEGLOSV AASVOGEL
AAEGLRRS REALGARS
AAEGLRST AGRESTAL
AAEGLRSV SALVAGER
AAEGLSSV SALVAGES
AAEGLSVY SAVAGELY
AAEGMMNS GAMESMAN
AAEGMNPY PYGMAEAN
AAEGMNRS MANAGERS
AAEGMNRV GRAVAMEN
AAEGMNST MAGENTAS
MAGNATES
NAMETAGS
AAEGMORR AEROGRAM
AAEGMORS SAGAMORE
AAEGMPRR RAMPAGER
AAEGMPRS RAMPAGES
AAEGMRRV MARGRAVE
AAEGMRRY GRAMARYE
AAEGMRSS MASSAGER
AAEGMRST MEGASTAR
AAEGMRTU AGERATUM
AAEGMSSS MASSAGES
AAEGMSTT METATAGS
AAEGMTTW MEGAWATT
AAEGNNST TANNAGES
AAEGNPST PAGEANTS
AAEGNPSW PAWNAGES
AAEGNRRR ARRANGER
AAEGNRRS ARRANGES
AAEGNRST TANAGERS
AAEGNRTU RUNAGATE
AAEGNSSU GUANASES
AAEGNSTT STAGNATE
AAEGNSTV VANTAGES
AAEGNSTW WANTAGES
AAEGORRT ARROGATE
AAEGORSS AGAROSES
AAEGPRSW WARPAGES
AAEGPSSS PASSAGES
AAEGQSUY QUAYAGES
AAEGRRSV RAVAGERS
AAEGRSST GASTREAS
AAEGRSSU ASSUAGER
AAEGRSTT REGATTAS
AAEGRSTV STRAVAGE
AAEGRSTZ STARGAZE
AAEGRSVY SAVAGERY
AAEGSSSU ASSUAGES
SAUSAGES
AAEGSSSV AVGASSES
AAEGSSSW ASSWAGES
AAEGSSTV SAVAGEST
AAEGSSTW WASTAGES
AAEGSTTW WATTAGES
AAEGSTWY GATEWAYS
GETAWAYS
AAEHIIRT HETAIRAI
AAEHILNP APHELIAN
AAEHILNT ANTHELIA
AAEHILPR PARHELIA
AAEHIMNT ANTHEMIA
HAEMATIN
AAEHINPT APHANITE
AAEHINST ASTHENIA
AAEHIPST APATHIES
AAEHIRST HETAIRAS
AAEHIRTT HATTERIA
AAEHKLST ALKAHEST
AAEHKMRT HATMAKER
AAEHKMRY HAYMAKER
AAEHKNST KHANATES
AAEHLLLS ALLHEALS
AAEHLMNW WHALEMAN
AAEHLMTU HAMULATE
AAEHLNOZ HALAZONE
AAEHLNRT ANTHERAL
AAEHLNRW NARWHALE
AAEHLNTX EXHALANT
AAEHLOPT APHOLATE
AAEHLPRS PEARLASH
AAEHLPRX HEXAPLAR
AAEHLPSX HEXAPLAS
AAEHLPUV UPHEAVAL
AAEHLRST TREHALAS
AAEHLSSV LAVASHES
AAEHMMOT HEMATOMA
AAEHMNRT EARTHMAN
AAEHMOPR AMPHORAE
AAEHMOPT HEPATOMA
AAEHMORT ATHEROMA
AAEHNPRS HANAPERS
AAEHNPSS SAPHENAS
AAEHNPST PHEASANT
AAEHNTTX XANTHATE
AAEHRRSS HARASSER
AAEHRSSS HARASSES
AAEHRSSY HEARSAYS
AAEHRSTU ARETHUSA
AAEIIKNS AKINESIA
AAEIINVZ AVIANIZE
AAEIIPRS APIARIES
AAEIIRSV AVIARIES

AAEIJLNV JAVELINA
AAEIJNPZ JAPANIZE
AAEIKKMZ KAMIKAZE
AAEIKLLN ALKALINE
AAEIKLLS ALKALIES
ALKALISE
AAEIKLLV LAVALIKE
AAEIKLLZ ALKALIZE
AAEIKLNT ANTILEAK
AAEIKPRT PARAKITE
AAEILLLU ALLELUIA
AAEILLMR ARMILLAE
AAEILLMX MAXILLAE
AAEILLNT ALLANITE
AAEILLPP PAPILLAE
AAEILLPT PALLIATE
AAEILLRT ARILLATE
AAEILLRV LAVALIER
AAEILLRY AERIALLY
AAEILMNN MELANIAN
AAEILMNT ANTIMALE
LAMINATE
AAEILMNV VELAMINA
AAEILMRT MATERIAL
AAEILMSS MALAISES
AAEILNNS ALANINES
AAEILNPR AIRPLANE
AAEILNPT PALATINE
AAEILNRV VALERIAN
AAEILNSS NASALISE
AAEILNSZ NASALIZE
AAEILNTV AVENTAIL
AAEILPRT PARIETAL
AAEILPRX PREAXIAL
AAEILPST STAPELIA
AAEILRRT ARTERIAL
AAEILRSS ASSAILER
REASSAIL
SALARIES
AAEILRSV REAVAILS
AAEILRTV VARIETAL
AAEILSTV AESTIVAL
SALIVATE
AAEILSTX SAXATILE
AAEILSWY AISLEWAY
AAEILTVX LAXATIVE
AAEIMMST IMAMATES
AAEIMNOX ANOXEMIA
AAEIMNPR PEARMAIN
AAEIMNPS PAEANISM
AAEIMNRT ANIMATER
MARINATE
AAEIMNSS AMNESIAS
AAEIMNST AMENTIAS
ANIMATES
AAEIMNTZ NIZAMATE
AAEIMOTX TOXAEMIA
AAEIMOTZ AZOTEMIA
AAEIMPRS SAPREMIA
AAEIMPSY PYAEMIAS
AAEIMRST AMIRATES
AAEIMRSU URAEMIAS
AAEIMRTT AMARETTI
AAEINORT AERATION
AAEINORX ANOREXIA
AAEINPPR PRIAPEAN
AAEINPRT ANTIRAPE
AAEINPTT PATINATE
AAEINRRW RAINWEAR
AAEINRST ANTISERA
RATANIES
SANTERIA
SEATRAIN
AAEINRTT ATTAINER
REATTAIN
AAEINRTW ANTIWEAR
AAEINRTZ ATRAZINE
AAEINSST ENTASIAS
AAEINSTT ASTATINE
SANITATE
AAEINSTV SANATIVE
AAEINTTT TITANATE
AAEIPPRS APPRAISE
AAEIPRRS PAREIRAS
AAEIPRSS SPIRAEAS
AAEIPRST ASPIRATE
PARASITE
SEPTARIA
AAEIPRTT PATRIATE
AAEIPRTZ TRAPEZIA
AAEIPSTT APATITES
AAEIQRTU TAQUERIA
AAEIRRRT TERRARIA
AAEIRRTV VERATRIA
AAEIRSST ASTERIAS
ATRESIAS
AAEIRSTT ARIETTAS
ARISTATE
AAEIRSTV VARIATES
AAEIRSTW AWAITERS
AAEIRSVW AIRWAVES
AAEIRTTZ ZARATITE
AAEISSTT SATIATES
AAEJLNOP JALAPENO
AAEJMNRY MARYJANE
AAEJNNPR JAPANNER
AAEJOPRS APAREJOS
AAEJRSSV SVARAJES
AAEJRSSW SWARAJES
AAEKKORS KARAOKES
AAEKKRSY KAYAKERS
AAEKLLTY ALKYLATE
AAEKLMRW LAWMAKER
AAEKLMRY MALARKEY
AAEKLNST ALKANETS
AAEKLPRS ASPARKLE
AAEKMMPR MAPMAKER
AAEKMORT KERATOMA
AAEKMRRS EARMARKS
AAEKMRRW WARMAKER
AAEKMRSS SEAMARKS
AAEKNPRT PARTAKEN
AAEKPRRT PARTAKER
AAEKPRST PARTAKES
AAEKSSSV KAVASSES
AAELLLMR LAMELLAR
AAELLLMS LAMELLAS
AAELLLPR PARALLEL
AAELLMPU AMPULLAE
AAELLNPU PLANULAE
AAELLORV ALVEOLAR
AAELLPRT PATELLAR
AAELLPST PATELLAS
AAELLRST LATERALS
AAELLRSY ALLAYERS
AAELLSSW SEAWALLS
AAELLUVV VALVULAE
AAELLWWY WELLAWAY
AAELLWYY ALLEYWAY
AAELMMNO MELANOMA
AAELMMRS ALMEMARS
AAELMMTU MALAMUTE
AAELMNOX AXONEMAL
AAELMNRT MATERNAL
AAELMNSS SALESMAN
AAELMNST TALESMAN
AAELMNSY SEAMANLY
AAELMOST OATMEALS
AAELMOSU MAUSOLEA
AAELMOTZ METAZOAL
AAELMPPY MAYAPPLE
AAELMPRT MALAPERT
AAELMPSS LAMPASES
AAELMPTY PLAYMATE
AAELMRSY LAMASERY
AAELMRTT MALTREAT
AAELMSST MALTASES
AAELMSSY AMYLASES
AAELNNNT ANTENNAL
AAELNNOT NEONATAL
AAELNNTU ANNULATE
AAELNOSS SEASONAL
AAELNPRT PARENTAL
PARLANTE
PATERNAL
PRENATAL
AAELNPRW WARPLANE
AAELNPST PLATANES
PLEASANT
AAELNPTT PANTALET
AAELNRSS ARSENALS
AAELNRST ASTERNAL
AAELNRSY ANALYSER
AAELNRTT ALTERANT
TARLETAN
AAELNRTX RELAXANT
AAELNRYZ ANALYZER
AAELNSST SEALANTS
AAELNSSY ANALYSES
AAELNSTT ATLANTES
AAELNSTY ANALYTES
AAELNSWY LANEWAYS
AAELNSYZ ANALYZES
AAELOPRS PSORALEA
AAELORSU AUREOLAS
AAELORTY ALEATORY
AAELOSTX OXALATES
AAELPPRS APPARELS
AAELPPST PALPATES
AAELPPSU APPLAUSE
AAELPRST PALESTRA
AAELPRSV PALAVERS
AAELPRSY PARALYSE
AAELPRWY PLAYWEAR
AAELPRYZ PARALYZE
AAELPSTU PLATEAUS
AAELPSWY PALEWAYS
AAELPTUX PLATEAUX
AAELRSTZ LAZARETS
AAELRUZZ ZARZUELA
AAELRWYY WAYLAYER
AAELSTUV VALUATES
AAEMMNRT ARMAMENT
AAEMMSTT STEMMATA
AAEMNORS AMARONES
AAEMNORT EMANATOR
AAEMNOTZ METAZOAN
AAEMNPPS PAMPEANS
AAEMNPRS PARMESAN
SPEARMAN
AAEMNPRT PARAMENT
AAEMNRST SARMENTA
AAEMNRTW WATERMAN
AAEMNSTU MANTEAUS
AAEMNTUX MANTEAUX
AAEMOPXZ OXAZEPAM
AAEMORTT AMARETTO
TERATOMA
AAEMOSTY ATEMOYAS
AAEMOTTU AUTOMATE
AAEMPTTU AMPUTATE
AAEMQSTU SQUAMATE
AAEMRRTU ARMATURE
AAEMRSSS AMASSERS
AAEMRSTU AMATEURS
AAEMRTTU MATURATE
AAENNNST ANTENNAS
AAENNOTT ANNOTATE
AAENNSTT TANNATES
AAENNSTU NAUSEANT
AAENOPSS PAESANOS
AAENOQTU AQUATONE
AAENORRU AUROREAN
AAENORTU AERONAUT
AAENPPRT APPARENT
TRAPPEAN
AAENPSST ANAPESTS
PEASANTS
AAENPSTT ANTEPAST
AAENRRRT NARRATER
AAENRRST NARRATES
AAENRSST SANTERAS
AAENRSTV TAVERNAS
TSAREVNA
AAENRSUW UNAWARES
AAENRSYY NAYSAYER
AAENRTVZ TZAREVNA
AAENSSTW SEAWANTS
AAENSSWY AWAYNESS
AAEOPPSS APOAPSES
AAEOPSTT APOSTATE
AAEOPSTZ ZAPATEOS
AAEORRST AERATORS
AAEORSST AEROSATS
AAEORSTT AEROSTAT
AAEPPRRT TARPAPER
AAEPPRST PARAPETS
AAEPPSTT APPESTAT
AAEPQRTU PARAQUET
AAEPRSSY APYRASES
AAEPRTXY TAXPAYER
AAEPSTTW WATTAPES
AAEPSWXX PAXWAXES
AAEPSZZZ PAZAZZES
AAERRRSY ARRAYERS
AAERRTTT TARTRATE
AAERSSSY ASSAYERS
AAERSTTU SATURATE
TUATERAS
AAERTTTW TERAWATT
AAERTWWY WATERWAY
AAESTWWY WASTEWAY
AAFFHIKY KAFFIYAH
AAFFIILX AFFIXIAL
AAFFILRT TAFFRAIL
AAFFINPR PARAFFIN
AAFFINST AFFIANTS
AAFFLSTU AFFLATUS
AAFFNNOR FANFARON
AAFFOORW FOOFARAW
AAFGHINS AFGHANIS
AAFGLLNU LANGLAUF
AAFGLNRT FLAGRANT
AAFGNRRT FRAGRANT
AAFHHORT HAFTORAH
AAFHIKLS KHALIFAS
AAFHINRS FARINHAS
AAFHLLSS ASHFALLS
AAFHLSTW FLATWASH
AAFHORTT HAFTAROT
AAFHRSUU HAUSFRAU
AAFIILLM FAMILIAL
AAFIILLR FILARIAL
AAFIILMR FAMILIAR
AAFIILNR FILARIAN
AAFIKLLY ALKALIFY
AAFILLNR RAINFALL
AAFILMST FATALISM
AAFILNNU INFAUNAL
AAFILNQU ALFAQUIN
AAFILNST FANTAILS
TAILFANS
AAFILOPR PARAFOIL
AAFILQSU ALFAQUIS
AAFILSTT FATALIST
AAFILTTY FATALITY
AAFIMNOR FORAMINA
AAFIMNOT ANTIFOAM
AAFINNOV FAVONIAN
AAFINNRS SAFRANIN
AAFINNST INFANTAS
AAFINNSU INFAUNAS
AAFINRRW WARFARIN
AAFIPRST PARFAITS
AAFIRSWY FAIRWAYS
AAFIRTTT FRITTATA
AAFJLORS ALFORJAS
AAFLLNOV FLAVANOL
AAFLLNUY FAUNALLY
AAFLLPRT PRATFALL
AAFLNNOT NONFATAL
AAFLSTWY FLATWAYS
AAFLSWYY FLYAWAYS
AAFMNRST RAFTSMAN
AAFMNSST FANTASMS
AAFMOPRR PARAFORM
AAFNSSTT FANTASTS
AAGGGINR GARAGING
AAGGHNST HANGTAGS
AAGGILLN GANGLIAL
AAGGILNR GANGLIAR
AAGGIMNN MANAGING
AAGGINNT ANTIGANG
AAGGINRV RAVAGING
AAGGINSV SAVAGING
AAGGITTW GIGAWATT
AAGGLLLY LALLYGAG
AAGGLMOS MAGALOGS
AAGGLNOT TAGALONG
AAGGLRSY GRAYLAGS
AAGGNSST GANGSTAS
AAGGNSTT TAGGANTS
AAGGNSWY GANGWAYS
AAGGRSTT STAGGART
AAGHHIMS MASHGIAH
AAGHHINS SHANGHAI
AAGHILNN HANGNAIL
AAGHILRS GHARIALS
AAGHINNS ANHINGAS
AAGHINPS PAGANISH
AAGHKMNY GYMKHANA
AAGHLNNS LANGSHAN
AAGHLNPY ANAGLYPH
AAGHMNOY HOGMANAY
MAHOGANY
AAGHMNSU MAHUANGS
AAGHQSUU QUAHAUGS
AAGHRSSW WASHRAGS
AAGIILMN IMAGINAL
AAGIILNS ALIASING
AAGIILNV AVAILING
AAGIIMST ASTIGMIA
AAGIINNU IGUANIAN
AAGIINST IGNATIAS
AAGIINTV AVIATING
AAGIINTW AWAITING
AAGIKKNY KAYAKING
AAGIKLNO KAOLIANG
AAGIKLNR KRAALING
AAGIKMRS SKIAGRAM
AAGILLNU UNIALGAL
AAGILLNY ALLAYING
AAGILLSS GALLIASS
AAGILMMR MAILGRAM
AAGILMNO MAGNOLIA
AAGILMNR ALARMING
MARGINAL
AAGILMOT GLIOMATA
AAGILMRY GRAYMAIL
AAGILMSY MYALGIAS
AAGILNRR LARRIGAN
AAGILNTV GALIVANT
AAGILOOP APOLOGIA
AAGILOST OTALGIAS
AAGILPRY PLAGIARY
AAGILRRW WARRIGAL
AAGILRTT ATTAGIRL
AAGILSTT SAGITTAL
AAGILSTW WAGTAILS
AAGIMNNN MANGANIN
AAGIMNNO AGNOMINA
AAGIMNOS ANGIOMAS
AAGIMNPS PAGANISM
AAGIMNRR MARGARIN
AAGIMNSS AMASSING
SIAMANGS
AAGIMNSY GYMNASIA
AAGIMPTU PATAGIUM
AAGIMSSV SAVAGISM
AAGIMSTT STIGMATA
AAGINNNW WANNIGAN
AAGINNOT AGNATION
AAGINNSU SAUNAING
AAGINNSW WANIGANS
AAGINOSS AGNOSIAS
AAGINPRU PAGURIAN
AAGINPRW PARAWING
AAGINPRY AGRYPNIA
AAGINPST PAGANIST
AAGINRRS ARRAIGNS
AAGINRRY ARRAYING
AAGINRSS SANGRIAS
AAGINRST GRANITAS
AAGINRSU GUARANIS
AAGINSST ASSIGNAT
AAGINSSY ASSAYING
GAINSAYS
AAGIORTT AGITATOR
AAGIORTV AVIGATOR
AAGIPRSU PIRAGUAS
AAGIRSTV GRAVITAS
STRAVAIG
AAGKKNOS ANGAKOKS
AAGKLRSV GRAVLAKS
AAGKNOOR KANGAROO
AAGLLMOY ALLOGAMY
AAGLLNOO LAGOONAL
AAGLLNRY LARYNGAL
AAGLLNST GALLANTS
AAGLLOOP APOLOGAL
AAGLLOPY POLYGALA
AAGLMNSS GLASSMAN
AAGLNORS GRANOLAS
AAGLNQUU AQUALUNG
AAGLNRRU GRANULAR
AAGLORSU ARUGOLAS
AAGLRSTU GASTRULA
AAGLRSUU ARUGULAS
AAGMMRRS GRAMMARS
AAGMNNOR NANOGRAM
AAGMNORT MARTAGON
AAGMNPRS PANGRAMS
AAGMNRST TANGRAMS
TRANGAMS
AAGMNSTY SYNTAGMA
AAGMOTUY AUTOGAMY
AAGMOTYZ ZYGOMATA
AAGNNNOP NONPAGAN
AAGNNSTT STAGNANT
AAGNOPRS PARAGONS
AAGNOPRT TRAGOPAN
AAGNORRT ARROGANT
TARRAGON
AAGNORSZ ORGANZAS
AAGNORTU ARGONAUT
AAGNRSTV VAGRANTS
AAGNRTUY GUARANTY
AAGOPSSS SAPSAGOS
AAGORSSS SARGASSO
AAGORSSU SAGUAROS
AAGRRSSY RAYGRASS
AAGRSSTU SASTRUGA
AAGRSTUZ ZASTRUGA
AAGSTTUU TAUTAUGS
AAHHIIMM MAHIMAHI
AAHHIRSS SHARIAHS
AAHHKLOT HALAKHOT
HALAKOTH
AAHHKSWW HAWKSHAW
AAHHMMSS SHAMMASH
AAHHNNOS HOSANNAH
AAHHNPST NAPHTHAS
AAHHOPRS PHARAOHS
AAHIJNRS HARIJANS
AAHIKLPS PASHALIK
AAHIKLST HALAKIST
AAHIKRST KITHARAS
AAHILLLS SHILLALA
AAHILNNT INHALANT
AAHILNOT HALATION
AAHILOPP HAPLOPIA
AAHILPSV PAHLAVIS
AAHILRRZ ARRHIZAL
AAHILSSW SAHIWALS
AAHIMNOS MAHONIAS
AAHIMNPS PASHMINA
AAHIMNZZ HAZZANIM
AAHIMRTY ARYTHMIA
AAHINOPS APHONIAS
AAHINPPS PAPHIANS
AAHINPRS PIRANHAS
AAHINRSW RAINWASH
AAHINSST SHAITANS
AAHIOPRT ATROPHIA
AAHIPSTZ ZAPTIAHS
AAHIPSXY ASPHYXIA
AAHIRSSS HARISSAS
AAHIRSTV HAVARTIS
AAHISTWY THISAWAY
AAHKLLMR HALLMARK
AAHKLRSS LASHKARS
AAHKMOTW TOMAHAWK
AAHKMSSY YASHMAKS
AAHLLMRS MARSHALL
AAHLLOPT ALLOPATH
AAHLLSWY HALLWAYS
AAHLMOPR AMPHORAL
AAHLMRSS MARSHALS
AAHLMSTU THALAMUS
AAHLNPST ASHPLANT
AAHLNRSW NARWHALS
AAHLPRRT PHRATRAL
AAHLPSST ASPHALTS
AAHMNNPU PANHUMAN
AAHMNNSU HANUMANS
AAHMNORT MARATHON
AAHMNOTX XANTHOMA
AAHMNPST PHANTASM
AAHMNRST TRASHMAN
AAHMOPRS AMPHORAS
AAHMRSST STRAMASH
AAHNNOSS HOSANNAS
AAHNNPSW SHWANPAN
AAHNNSTX XANTHANS
AAHNOPRS ANAPHORS
AAHNOSTT THANATOS
AAHNPSTT PHANTAST
AAHNPSTY PHANTASY
AAHOPRST PARASHOT
AAHOPRTU AUTOHARP
AAHORSSU SAHUAROS
AAHPRSTW WARPATHS
AAHPSTWY PATHWAYS
AAHRRTTW THRAWART
AAHRSSTY ASHTRAYS
AAHRSTTW STRAWHAT
AAIIILMR MILIARIA
AAIIJJPP JIPIJAPA
AAIILLQU QUILLAIA
AAIILMNS MAINSAIL
AAIILMRS AIRMAILS
AAIILNRZ ALIZARIN
AAIILNUX UNIAXIAL
AAIILPST TILAPIAS
AAIILRTX TRIAXIAL
AAIILTXY AXIALITY
AAIIMNNT AMANITIN
MAINTAIN
AAIIMNPX PANMIXIA
AAIINNRT ANTIARIN
AAIINOTV AVIATION
AAIINPRR RIPARIAN
AAIINRST INTARSIA
AAIINSTT TITANIAS
AAIIPRST APIARIST
AAIIPRVV VIVIPARA
AAIIRSTV AVIARIST
AAIIRSTW WISTARIA
AAIIRTVX AVIATRIX
AAIJLLQU QUILLAJA
AAIJLNPS JALAPINS
AAIJNRSY JANISARY
AAIJNRYZ JANIZARY
AAIKKSTZ KAZATSKI
AAIKLPRS PALIKARS
AAIKMNNS MANAKINS
AAIKMNST ANTIMASK
AAIKMRST TAMARISK
AAIKNNTT ANTITANK
AAIKPPRS PAPRIKAS
AAIKPRRS AIRPARKS
AAIKSSTW SWASTIKA
AAIKSTVV AKVAVITS
AAILLLSS SALSILLA
AAILLLST LATILLAS
AAILLLUV ALLUVIAL

AAILLMMM MAMMILLA
AAILLMNS LAMINALS
MANILLAS
AAILLMNT MANTILLA
AAILLMNY ANIMALLY
AAILLMPT TAILLAMP
AAILLMRS ARMILLAS
AAILLMRT RAMTILLA
AAILLMSX MAXILLAS
AAILLNPU NAUPLIAL
AAILLNST LANITALS
AAILLNSV VANILLAS
AAILLPPR PAPILLAR
AAILLRSX AXILLARS
AAILLRXY AXILLARY
AAILMMRS ALARMISM
AAILMMSX MAXIMALS
AAILMNOR MANORIAL
MORAINAL
AAILMNOX MONAXIAL
AAILMNRU MANURIAL
AAILMNRY LAMINARY
AAILMNSS NASALISM
AAILMNST STAMINAL
TALISMAN
AAILMNSU ALUMINAS
AAILMOPT LIPOMATA
AAILMORR ARMORIAL
AAILMPRT PRIMATAL
AAILMQSU MAQUILAS
AAILMRST ALARMIST
AAILMTTU ULTIMATA
AAILNNOT NATIONAL
AAILNNPT PLANTAIN
AAILNNRU LUNARIAN
AAILNNST ANNALIST
AAILNOPT TALAPOIN
AAILNORS ORINASAL
AAILNORT NOTARIAL
RATIONAL
AAILNOST ALATIONS
AAILNOSV VALONIAS
AAILNOTV LAVATION
AAILNOTX LAXATION
AAILNPSS SALPIANS
AAILNPST PLATINAS
AAILNQTU ALIQUANT
AAILNSSY ANALYSIS
AAILNSTV VALIANTS
AAILNSTY NASALITY
AAILNTTY NATALITY
AAILORRS RASORIAL
AAILORRV VARIOLAR
AAILORSV VARIOLAS
AAILPPRU PUPARIAL
AAILPRST PARTIALS
AAILPRSY AIRPLAYS
AAILRRSV ARRIVALS
AAILRSTT RATTAILS
AAILRSTV TRAVAILS
AAILRSVY SALIVARY
AAILRSWY RAILWAYS
AAILRTUY AURALITY
AAILSSSW WASSAILS
AAILSSTY STAYSAIL
AAIMMNOS AMMONIAS
AAIMMNST MAINMAST
AAIMMRSU SAMARIUM
AAIMNNRT TRAINMAN
AAIMNOOZ ZOOMANIA
AAIMNORT ANIMATOR
AAIMNORW AIRWOMAN
AAIMNOSS ANOSMIAS
AAIMNOTT ANTIATOM
AAIMNPRZ MARZIPAN
AAIMNPST ANTISPAM
AAIMNPTU PUTAMINA
AAIMNRRT TRIMARAN
AAIMNRST MARTIANS
TAMARINS
AAIMNSST MANTISSA
SATANISM
STAMINAS
AAIMNSTU AMIANTUS
AAIMNSTY MAINSTAY
AAIMOPRS MARIPOSA
PAROSMIA
AAIMPRST PASTRAMI
AAIMPRSU MARSUPIA
AAIMQRUU AQUARIUM
AAIMRSSU SAMURAIS
AAIMRSTU TIMARAUS
AAIMSSSY MISASSAY
AAIMSSTV ATAVISMS
AAINNOST SONATINA
AAINNOTT NATATION
AAINNOTX ANATOXIN
AAINNRSV NIRVANAS
AAINNSSY SANNYASI
AAINOOPS ANOOPSIA
AAINOPSS ANOPSIAS
PAISANOS
AAINORRS ROSARIAN
AAINOTTX TAXATION
AAINPPRY PAPYRIAN
AAINPRST ASPIRANT
PARTISAN
SPARTINA
AAINPRTZ PARTIZAN
AAINPSST PASTINAS
AAINQRTU QUATRAIN
AAINQTTU AQUATINT
AAINRSST ARTISANS
TSARINAS
AAINRSSU SAURIANS
AAINRSSV SAVARINS
AAINRSTV VARIANTS
AAINRSTY SANITARY
AAINRSTZ TZARINAS
AAINRTWY TRAINWAY
AAINSSSS ASSASSIN
AAINSSTT SATANIST
AAINSTTT ANTISTAT
ATTAINTS
AAIOPPSS APOAPSIS
AAIORSTV AVIATORS
AAIORTUZ AZOTURIA
AAIPPSTT PITAPATS
AAIPRSTT PARTITAS
AAIQRSTU AQUARIST
AAIQSSSU QUASSIAS
AAIQSTUV AQUAVITS
AAIRSTTZ TSARITZA
AAIRSTWY STAIRWAY
AAIRTTZZ TZARITZA
AAISSTTV ATAVISTS
AAISTWXY TAXIWAYS
AAJKLSWY JAYWALKS
AAJMMORR MARJORAM
AAJMORRS MOJARRAS
AAJOPSSU SAPAJOUS
AAKKLRSU KARAKULS
AAKKMOST TOKAMAKS
AAKKSTYZ KAZATSKY
AAKLMSUY YAMULKAS
AAKLOOPS PALOOKAS
AAKLOOST TALOOKAS
AAKLPRTY KALYPTRA
AAKLSWWY WALKWAYS
AAKMMNRS MARKSMAN
AAKMORUZ MAZOURKA
AAKMOSSU MOUSAKAS
MOUSSAKA
AAKMRSUZ MAZURKAS
AAKNNSTU NUNATAKS
AAKNRSYY SYNKARYA
AAKOPPRT PORTAPAK
AAKPRSWY PARKWAYS
AAKRSSTU KATSURAS
AALLMNTY TALLYMAN
AALLMNUY MANUALLY
AALLMORY AMORALLY
AALLMPRU AMPULLAR
AALLNNUY ANNUALLY
AALLNOST SANTALOL
AALLNOSX ALLOXANS
AALLNOTY ATONALLY
AALLNPRU PLANULAR
AALLNRTY TARNALLY
AALLOORW WALLAROO
AALLORSU ALLOSAUR
AALLORWY ROLLAWAY
AALLPRST PLASTRAL
AALLRSTY ASTRALLY
AALLRUVV VALVULAR
AALMMNOS AMMONALS
AALMNORT MATRONAL
AALMNORU MONAURAL
AALMNOWY LAYWOMAN
AALMNPTY TYMPANAL
AALMNTTU TANTALUM
AALMNTUU AUTUMNAL
AALMOPPR MALAPROP
AALMOPSX AXOPLASM
AALMOSTT STOMATAL
AALMPRSY PALMYRAS
AALNNNOS NONNASAL
AALNNNOV NONNAVAL
AALNNOPP NONPAPAL
AALNNOST SONANTAL
AALNNTTY NATANTLY
AALNOPRT PATRONAL
AALNOPST POSTANAL
AALNORUV ANOVULAR
AALNPRSU LUPANARS
AALNPSST SALTPANS
AALNPTWX WAXPLANT
AALNRRTY ARRANTLY
AALNRSTU NATURALS
AALNSSTU SULTANAS
AALNSSTY ANALYSTS
AALNSTTU TANTALUS
AALOPPRT PALPATOR
AALOPPRV APPROVAL
AALOPRSS PARASOLS
AALOPRST PASTORAL
AALOPSVV PAVLOVAS
AALOPSZZ PALAZZOS
AALORSST ALASTORS
AALORSSU AROUSALS
AALORTUV VALUATOR
AALORTVY LAVATORY
AALPRSTU PASTURAL
SPATULAR
AALPSSTU SPATULAS
AALRSSTU AUSTRALS
AALRSTTW STALWART
AALRSTUY SALUTARY
AALSSSTU ASSAULTS
AAMMMSTU MAMMATUS
AAMMNRST MANTRAMS
AAMMOTXY MYXOMATA
AAMMRSSU MARASMUS
AAMNNORS SONARMAN
AAMNORRS MARRANOS
AAMNPRST MANTRAPS
AAMOPRRU PARAMOUR
AAMORRSZ ZAMARROS
AAMORSSU MOSASAUR
AAMORSSV SAMOVARS
AAMORSTT STROMATA
AAMOSTTU AUTOMATS
AAMPPRST RAMPARTS
AAMRSSST SMARTASS
AAMRSSTT MATTRASS
AAMRSTWY TRAMWAYS
AAMSSSTU SATSUMAS
AANNOSST ASSONANT
AANNOSTT ANNATTOS
AANNOTTW NANOWATT
AANNPSSW SWANPANS
AANNRSTY STANNARY
AANORRRT NARRATOR
AANORSTT ARNATTOS
AANORTTY NATATORY
AANPPTTY PATTYPAN
AANQRSTU QUARTANS
AANRRSTW WARRANTS
AANRRTWY WARRANTY
AANRSTTU SATURANT
AANRSUWY RUNAWAYS
AAOPSSTY APOSTASY
AAOQSSSU OQUASSAS
AAORSSVV VAVASORS
VAVASSOR
AAORSUVV VAVASOUR
AAOSTTUY TATOUAYS
AAOSTWWY STOWAWAY
TOWAWAYS
AAPRRSTT RATTRAPS
AARSTTUY STATUARY
ABBBDEEL BEDABBLE
ABBBDELR BRABBLED
ABBBEILR BRIBABLE
ABBBELMO BOMBABLE
ABBBELRR BRABBLER
ABBBELRS BABBLERS
BLABBERS
BRABBLES
ABBBELTU TUBBABLE
ABBBGILN BABBLING
BLABBING
ABBBIRTY BABBITRY
ABBBISTT BABBITTS
ABBBOORU RUBBABOO
ABBBOSTU SUBABBOT
ABBCDEKN BACKBEND
ABBCDELS SCABBLED
ABBCEERU BARBECUE
ABBCEGIR CRIBBAGE
ABBCEHIS BABICHES
ABBCEHOY BEACHBOY
ABBCEIKT BACKBITE
ABBCEILR BARBICEL
ABBCEIRR CRABBIER
ABBCEIRS SCABBIER
ABBCEKNO BACKBONE
ABBCEKNU BUCKBEAN
ABBCELLU CLUBABLE
ABBCELRS CLABBERS
SCRABBLE
ABBCELRU CURBABLE
ABBCELSS SCABBLES
ABBCERRS CRABBERS
ABBCGINR CRABBING
ABBCGINS SCABBING
ABBCGIOR GABBROIC
ABBCIILL BIBLICAL
ABBCIINR RABBINIC
ABBCIKRT BRICKBAT
ABBCILRY CRABBILY
ABBCILSY SCABBILY
ABBCKLOW BLOWBACK
ABBCKLOY BLACKBOY
ABBCKSUY BUYBACKS
ABBCLRSY SCRABBLY
ABBDDEEL BEDDABLE
ABBDDEEU BEDAUBED
ABBDDEIL BIDDABLE
ABBDDELR DRABBLED
ABBDDEOR BEDBOARD
ABBDDILY BIDDABLY
ABBDEEER BEEBREAD
ABBDEEHR REHABBED
ABBDEEJR JABBERED
ABBDEELN BENDABLE
ABBDEERR BARBERED
ABBDEERT RABBETED
ABBDEERY YABBERED
ABBDEGLR GRABBLED
ABBDEILN BINDABLE
ABBDEIRT RABBITED
ABBDELMR BRAMBLED
ABBDELNO BONDABLE
ABBDELRS DABBLERS
DRABBLES
ABBDENRU UNBARBED
ABBDEORS ABSORBED
ABBDEORX BREADBOX
ABBDERST DRABBEST
DRABBETS
ABBDGILN DABBLING
ABBDGINR DRABBING
ABBDGIOR GABBROID
ABBDHIRT BIRDBATH
ABBDHOOY BABYHOOD
ABBDINRS RIBBANDS
ABBDLLOY BABYDOLL
ABBDLMOO BOMBLOAD
ABBDMORS BOMBARDS
ABBDNORW BROWBAND
ABBDOORX BOXBOARD
ABBDORRU RUBBOARD
ABBEEHRR REHABBER
ABBEEILT BITEABLE
ABBEEJRR JABBERER
ABBEEJRS BEJABERS
ABBEELOY OBEYABLE
ABBEELTU BLUEBEAT
ABBEEQRU BARBEQUE
ABBEERTT BARBETTE
ABBEESSS ABBESSES
ABBEFFLU BUFFABLE
ABBEFILR FLABBIER
ABBEGIRR GRABBIER
ABBEGIST GABBIEST
ABBEGLRR GRABBLER
ABBEGLRS GABBLERS
GRABBLES
ABBEGNOS BOGBEANS
ABBEGNSU BUGBANES
ABBEGRRS GRABBERS
ABBEGRSU BUGBEARS
ABBEHIRS SHABBIER
ABBEHORT BATHROBE
ABBEILLL BILLABLE
ABBEILLO BOILABLE
ABBEILNU BUBALINE
ABBEILOT BILOBATE
ABBEILOV OBVIABLE
ABBEILRW WABBLIER
ABBEIMRU BERIMBAU
ABBEIRRT RABBITER
ABBEIRRW BARBWIRE
ABBEISST TABBISES
ABBEISSW SWABBIES
ABBEKLOO BOOKABLE
ABBELLLU BLUEBALL
ABBELLRS BARBELLS
ABBELMRS BRAMBLES
ABBELNRU BURNABLE
ABBELOOT BOOTABLE
ABBELOPR PROBABLE
ABBELORS BELABORS
SORBABLE
ABBELORU BELABOUR
ABBELQSU SQUABBLE
ABBELRRS RABBLERS
ABBELRSS BARBLESS
SLABBERS
ABBELRSU BARBULES
ABBELRSW WABBLERS
ABBELRSY SLABBERY
ABBENORS BASEBORN
ABBENORY NABOBERY
ABBENOSS NABOBESS
ABBEORRS ABSORBER
REABSORB
ABBEORTW BROWBEAT
ABBERRRY BARBERRY
ABBERRYY BAYBERRY
ABBERSST STABBERS
ABBERSSW SWABBERS
ABBESSSU SUBBASES
ABBFILLY FLABBILY
ABBGGILN GABBLING
ABBGGINR GRABBING
ABBGILNR RABBLING
ABBGILNS SLABBING
ABBGILNW WABBLING
ABBGINST STABBING
ABBGINSU BUBINGAS
ABBGINSW SWABBING
ABBGINTY TABBYING
ABBGOOSU BUGABOOS
ABBHILSY SHABBILY
ABBHINOS NABOBISH
ABBHRRSU RHUBARBS
ABBHSTTU BATHTUBS
ABBILLOT BOATBILL
ABBILLSU SILLABUB
ABBILOST BOBTAILS
ABBIMNOS BAMBINOS
NABOBISM
ABBINORS RABBONIS
ABBINSSU SUBBASIN
ABBIRRTY RABBITRY
ABBIRSUU SUBURBIA
ABBISSTY BABYSITS
ABBKKNOO BANKBOOK
ABBKLOSU BLAUBOKS
ABBLLLOW BLOWBALL
ABBLLOSX BOXBALLS
ABBLLSTU BULLBATS
ABBLLSUY SYLLABUB
ABBLOPRY PROBABLY
ABBMOSST BOMBASTS
ABBMOSTU BUMBOATS
ABBNRSUU SUBURBAN
ABBOORSU RUBABOOS
ABBOSSTY BOBSTAYS
ABCCCIOO BOCACCIO
ABCCDEHO CABOCHED
ABCCDHIK DABCHICK
ABCCEEHN BECHANCE
ABCCEELP PECCABLE
ABCCEFLU CLUBFACE
ABCCEILR BRECCIAL
ABCCEILY CELIBACY
ABCCEIRS BRECCIAS
ABCCEKMO COMEBACK
ABCCESUU SUCCUBAE
ABCCHISU BACCHIUS
ABCCHNOO CABOCHON
ABCCHOSU CHUBASCO
ABCCIKKK KICKBACK
ABCCILOR CARBOLIC
ABCCILOT COBALTIC
ABCCILUU CUBICULA
ABCCIMRS CAMBRICS
ABCCINOR CARBONIC
ABCCIORS ASCORBIC
ABCCKOOT COCKBOAT
ABCCKOSW BAWCOCKS
ABCCKSTU CUTBACKS
ABCCLLUY BUCCALLY
ABCCLOOO COCOBOLA
ABCCMOOY MACCOBOY
ABCCOOST TOBACCOS
ABCCSSUU SUCCUBAS
ABCDDEOR BROCADED
ABCDDETU ABDUCTED
ABCDEEFK FEEDBACK
ABCDEEHL BLEACHED
ABCDEEHR BERDACHE
BREACHED
ABCDEELM BECALMED
ABCDEELS DEBACLES
ABCDEELU EDUCABLE
ABCDEEMR CAMBERED
EMBRACED
ABCDEENO BEACONED
ABCDEEPP BECAPPED
ABCDEETU ABDUCTEE
ABCDEFLO BOLDFACE
ABCDEGIR BIRDCAGE
ABCDEHIR BEDCHAIR
ABCDEHKO BACKHOED
ABCDEHLN BLANCHED
ABCDEHLU CLUBHEAD
ABCDEHNR BRANCHED
ABCDEHOR BROACHED
ABCDEHOS CABOSHED
ABCDEIIT DIABETIC
ABCDEIKS BACKSIDE
DIEBACKS
ABCDEILR CALIBRED
ABCDEIPS PEDICABS
ABCDEIRS ASCRIBED
CARBIDES
ABCDEISS ABSCISED
ABCDEKLO BLOCKADE
ABCDEKNN NECKBAND
ABCDEKNU UNBACKED
ABCDELOO CABOODLE
ABCDELRU BARLEDUC
ABCDEMNU DUMBCANE
ABCDEMOT COMBATED
ABCDENRU UNBRACED
ABCDENSU ABDUCENS
ABCDENTU ABDUCENT
ABCDEORS BROCADES
ABCDEORW BECOWARD
ABCDEORY CARBOYED
ABCDERSU CUDBEARS
ABCDGINU ABDUCING
ABCDHKLO HOLDBACK
ABCDHLNU CLUBHAND
ABCDIILO BIOCIDAL
DIABOLIC
ABCDIIMY CYMBIDIA
ABCDIIRT TRIBADIC
ABCDIKLR BALDRICK
ABCDIKLS BACKSLID
ABCDILLR BIRDCALL
ABCDILOS CABILDOS
ABCDILOU CUBOIDAL
ABCDILRS BALDRICS
ABCDINOR BRACONID
ABCDIRST CATBIRDS
ABCDIRSU SUBACRID
ABCDIRSW BAWDRICS
ABCDKOOR BACKDOOR
ABCDKOOW BACKWOOD
ABCDKOPR BACKDROP
ABCDNOSS ABSCONDS
ABCDOORS CORDOBAS
ABCDOPRU CUPBOARD
ABCDORTU ABDUCTOR
ABCDORUY OBDURACY
ABCEEEFK BEEFCAKE
ABCEEHIR BEACHIER
ABCEEHLM BECHAMEL
ABCEEHLR BLEACHER
ABCEEHLS BLEACHES
ABCEEHLW CHEWABLE
ABCEEHRR BREACHER
ABCEEHRS BREACHES
ABCEEILT CELIBATE
CITEABLE
ABCEEIMN AMBIENCE
ABCEEKLY EYEBLACK
ABCEELOV EVOCABLE
ABCEELRR CEREBRAL
ABCEELRT BRACELET
ABCEEMRR EMBRACER
ABCEEMRS EMBRACES
ABCEENOZ CABEZONE
ABCEENRT CABERNET
ABCEENSS ABSENCES
ABCEEPRT BECARPET
ABCEERST ACERBEST
ABCEFIIT BEATIFIC
ABCEFIKR BACKFIRE
FIREBACK
ABCEFINO BONIFACE
ABCEFLNO BACLOFEN
ABCEGHIN BEACHING
ABCEGIKV GIVEBACK
ABCEGKLL BLACKLEG
ABCEGKLO BLOCKAGE
ABCEGKMU MEGABUCK
ABCEGKOR BROCKAGE
ABCEGOSS BOSCAGES
ABCEHITT BATHETIC

ABCEHKLS BECHALKS
ABCEHKOS BACKHOES
ABCEHLNR BLANCHER
ABCEHLNS BLANCHES
ABCEHLOR BACHELOR
ABCEHLOS CHAEBOLS
ABCEHLSU CHASUBLE
ABCEHMOT HECATOMB
ABCEHMRS BECHARMS
BRECHAMS
CHAMBERS
ABCEHNRR REBRANCH
ABCEHNRS BRANCHES
BRECHANS
ABCEHOOT COHOBATE
ABCEHORR BROACHER
ABCEHORS BROACHES
ABCEHORU BAROUCHE
ABCEHRST BATCHERS
BRACHETS
ABCEIIRT RABIETIC
ABCEIKKL KICKABLE
ABCEIKLR CRABLIKE
ABCEIKLS SCABLIKE
ABCEIKST TIEBACKS
ABCEIKWZ ZWIEBACK
ABCEILLT BALLETIC
ABCEILMS ALEMBICS
ABCEILNN BINNACLE
ABCEILNO BIOCLEAN
COINABLE
ABCEILNU BACULINE
ABCEILOR ALBICORE
BRACIOLE
CABRIOLE
ABCEILOS SOCIABLE
ABCEILRS CALIBERS
CALIBRES
ABCEILST BASILECT
ABCEILTY BIACETYL
ABCEIMRW MICAWBER
ABCEINRS BRISANCE
CARBINES
ABCEINRT BACTERIN
ABCEINRV VIBRANCE
ABCEINST CABINETS
ABCEINTU INCUBATE
ABCEIORS AEROBICS
ABCEIORT BORACITE
ABCEIOST ICEBOATS
ABCEIRRT CATBRIER
ABCEIRSS ASCRIBES
ABCEIRSW CRABWISE
ABCEIRTT BRATTICE
ABCEIRTY ACERBITY
ABCEISSS ABSCISES
ABCEISST ASBESTIC
ABCEISTT TABETICS
ABCEJKLU BLUEJACK
ABCEJLTY ABJECTLY
ABCEKKSW SKEWBACK
ABCEKLLO LOCKABLE
ABCEKLMO MOCKABLE
ABCEKLNS BLACKENS
ABCEKLOO COOKABLE
ABCEKLOR ROCKABLE
ABCEKLOS BECLOAKS
ABCEKLSS BACKLESS
ABCEKLST BLACKEST
ABCEKNOT BOATNECK
ABCEKNRS BRACKENS
ABCEKOOS BOOKCASE
CASEBOOK
ABCEKORY ROCKABYE
ABCEKRST BACKREST
BRACKETS
ABCEKSST BACKSETS
SETBACKS
ABCELLOS CLOSABLE
ABCELLPU CULPABLE
ABCELLRU BRUCELLA
ABCELLSU BULLACES
ABCELMNY LAMBENCY
ABCELMOR BECLAMOR
ABCELMOS CEMBALOS
ABCELMRS CLAMBERS
SCRAMBLE
ABCELMRY CYMBALER
ABCELOOT BOOTLACE
ABCELOPS PLACEBOS
ABCELOPY COPYABLE
ABCELORT BROCATEL
ABCELOST OBSTACLE
ABCELOSV VOCABLES
ABCELOTU BLUECOAT
ABCELPSS BECLASPS
ABCELPSU BLUECAPS
ABCELRSU ARBUSCLE
ABCELRSW BECRAWLS
ABCELRTT BRACTLET
ABCELSSU BASCULES
SUBSCALE
ABCELTTU CUTTABLE
ABCEMORS CRAMBOES
ABCEMORT COMBATER
ABCENOSU SUBOCEAN
ABCENOSW COWBANES
ABCENOSZ CABEZONS
ABCENOUY BUOYANCE
ABCENRSU UNBRACES
ABCEOOSS CABOOSES
ABCEOPUU BEAUCOUP
ABCEORRS BRACEROS
ABCEORST CABESTRO
CABRESTO
ABCEOSUX SAUCEBOX
ABCEPSSU SUBSPACE
ABCERRTU CARBURET
ABCERSSU SUBRACES
ABCERTUU CUBATURE
ABCESSTU SUBCASTE
ABCESSTW WEBCASTS
ABCESSUU SUBCAUSE
ABCESTUU SUBACUTE
ABCFIKLL BACKFILL
ABCFIKLN BLACKFIN
ABCFIKLP BACKFLIP
ABCFIKNS FINBACKS
ABCFIKST BACKFITS
ABCFILOS BIFOCALS
ABCFKLLU FULLBACK
ABCFKLLY BLACKFLY
ABCFKLOW BACKFLOW
ABCFKOST SOFTBACK
ABCGHINT BATCHING
ABCGHKOS HOGBACKS
ABCGIINN CABINING
ABCGIKLN BLACKING
ABCGIKNS BACKINGS
ABCGIKNW WINGBACK
ABCGINRS BRACINGS
ABCGINSU SCUBAING
ABCGKLMU BLACKGUM
ABCGKLOS BACKLOGS
ABCGMSSU SCUMBAGS
ABCHHIIS HIBACHIS
ABCHIIPS BIPHASIC
ABCHIKLS BLACKISH
ABCHIKRS BRACKISH
ABCHIMOR CHORIAMB
ABCHIMRU BRACHIUM
ABCHINOR BRONCHIA
ABCHIOST COHABITS
ABCHIRRT TRIBRACH
ABCHKMPU HUMPBACK
ABCHKOOP CHAPBOOK
ABCHKOOS CASHBOOK
ABCHKOSU CHABOUKS
ABCHKRSU BACKRUSH
ABCHKSTU HACKBUTS
ABCHLLUU CLUBHAUL
ABCHMOTX MATCHBOX
ABCHOORR ROORBACH
ABCIILMU BULIMIAC
ABCIILOT BIOTICAL
ABCIIMNS MINICABS
ABCIINSS ABSCISIN
ABCIIORS ISOBARIC
ABCIIRST TRIBASIC
ABCIISTY BASICITY
ABCIITUX BAUXITIC
ABCIJNOS JACOBINS
ABCIKKLL KICKBALL
ABCIKLST BACKLIST
ABCIKLTU BUCKTAIL
ABCIKNPS BACKSPIN
ABCIKSSY SICKBAYS
ABCILLNY BILLYCAN
ABCILLRU LUBRICAL
ABCILLSU BACILLUS
ABCILLSY SYLLABIC
ABCILMMO CIMBALOM
ABCILMSU SUBCLAIM
ABCILNOR CARBINOL
ABCILNOS COALBINS
ABCILNPU PUBLICAN
ABCILOSY SOCIABLY
ABCILRRU RUBRICAL
ABCIMMSS CAMBISMS
ABCIMMSU CAMBIUMS
ABCIMORR MICROBAR
ABCIMSST CAMBISTS
ABCINNOS NONBASIC
ABCINORS CORBINAS
ABCINORY BARYONIC
ABCINRVY VIBRANCY
ABCIOPRS SAPROBIC
ABCIORSU CARIBOUS
ABCIOSSU SCABIOUS
ABCIOSUV BIVOUACS
ABCIRSTT ABSTRICT
ABCIRSUV SUBVICAR
ABCJKOOT BOOTJACK
JACKBOOT
ABCKKOOR BOOKRACK
ABCKLLOR ROLLBACK
ABCKLLPU PULLBACK
ABCKLNNO NONBLACK
ABCKLOPT BLACKTOP
ABCKLOPW PLOWBACK
ABCKLOST SLOTBACK
ABCKLOTU BLACKOUT
ABCKMOOR BACKROOM
ABCKMOSS MOSSBACK
ABCKMOST BACKMOST
TOMBACKS
ABCKMRSU BUCKRAMS
ABCKNNOS BANNOCKS
ABCKNORY CRYOBANK
ABCKNRSU RUNBACKS
ABCKNSTU CUTBANKS
ABCKOORR ROORBACK
ABCKOORU BUCKAROO
ABCKOPST BACKSTOP
ABCKORUY BUCKAYRO
ABCKOSTU BACKOUTS
OUTBACKS
ABCKSSTU SACKBUTS
ABCKSSUW BUCKSAWS
SAWBUCKS
ABCLLNOR CORNBALL
ABCLLOSY CALLBOYS
ABCLLPUY CULPABLY
ABCLMMOY CYMBALOM
ABCLMOOO COLOBOMA
ABCLMSUU BACULUMS
ABCLNORY CARBONYL
ABCLNSSU SUBCLANS
ABCLORXY CARBOXYL
ABCLOSUV SUBVOCAL
ABCLSSSU SUBCLASS
ABCMOORT MOBOCRAT
ABCNORTY CORYBANT
ABCNOUYY BUOYANCY
ABCORRSS CROSSBAR
ABCORRSW CROWBARS
ABCORRTU TURBOCAR
ABCORSSU SCABROUS
ABCRSTTU SUBTRACT
ABDDEEEH BEHEADED
ABDDEEEK DEBEAKED
ABDDEEGG DEBAGGED
ABDDEEGR BADGERED
ABDDEEHT DEATHBED
ABDDEEIL BELADIED
ABDDEEKR DEBARKED
ABDDEELU BELAUDED
ABDDEEMN BEDAMNED
BEMADDEN
ABDDEENY BENDAYED
ABDDEEPR BEDRAPED
ABDDEERR DEBARRED
ABDDEERS DEBEARDS
ABDDEEST BEDSTEAD
ABDDEGIR ABRIDGED
BRIGADED
ABDDEHMO HEBDOMAD
ABDDEHMU DUMBHEAD
ABDDEILS DISABLED
ABDDEILU AUDIBLED
BUDDLEIA
ABDDEINR BRANDIED
ABDDEINS SIDEBAND
ABDDEINW WIDEBAND
ABDDELOT DEADBOLT
ABDDELRS BLADDERS
ABDDELRY BLADDERY
ABDDENNU UNBANDED
ABDDENOU ABOUNDED
ABDDENST BEDSTAND
ABDDEORS ADSORBED
ROADBEDS
ABDDERSW BEDWARDS
ABDDGINR BRADDING
ABDDILMO LAMBDOID
ABDDILRY LADYBIRD
ABDDIMNO BONDMAID
ABDDINSS DISBANDS
ABDDIRRY YARDBIRD
ABDDLLOS ODDBALLS
ABDEEEFL BEFLEAED
FEEDABLE
ABDEEEFN BEDEAFEN
ABDEEEHR BEHEADER
ABDEEELP BELEAPED
ABDEEEMN BEMEANED
ABDEEERV BEAVERED
BEREAVED
ABDEEFGS FEEDBAGS
ABDEEFLM FLAMBEED
ABDEEFMR BEDFRAME
ABDEEGGR BEGGARED
ABDEEGHR HERBAGED
ABDEEGLL BEGALLED
GABELLED
ABDEEHLS SHEDABLE
ABDEEHLU BLUEHEAD
ABDEEHMS BESHAMED
ABDEEHNO BONEHEAD
ABDEEHRT BREATHED
ABDEEHST BETHESDA
ABDEEIKL BEADLIKE
ABDEEIKR BIDARKEE
ABDEEILN DENIABLE
ABDEEILR RIDEABLE
ABDEEILS ABSEILED
BELADIES
ABDEEILT EDITABLE
ABDEEILV EVADIBLE
ABDEEILW BEWAILED
ABDEEIPR BEDIAPER
ABDEEIRT REBAITED
ABDEEIST BEADIEST
DIABETES
ABDEEJMN ENJAMBED
ABDEEJST JETBEADS
ABDEEKLS LAKEBEDS
ABDEEKMN EMBANKED
ABDEEKMR BEDMAKER
EMBARKED
ABDEEKNR BEDARKEN
ABDEEKPR PREBAKED
ABDEEKRR DEBARKER
ABDEELLL LABELLED
ABDEELLN LENDABLE
ABDEELLW WELDABLE
ABDEELMM EMBALMED
ABDEELMN MENDABLE
ABDEELMS BELDAMES
ABDEELMZ EMBLAZED
ABDEELNS SENDABLE
ABDEELNV VENDABLE
ABDEELOR ERODABLE
LEEBOARD
ABDEELOS ALBEDOES
ABDEELPT BEDPLATE
ABDEELRR BARRELED
ABDEELRV DEVERBAL
ABDEELRZ BLAZERED
ABDEELSV BESLAVED
ABDEELTT TABLETED
ABDEELZZ BEDAZZLE
ABDEEMNO BEMOANED
ABDEEMNS BEADSMEN
BEDESMAN
ABDEEMRR EMBARRED
ABDEEMST BEDMATES
ABDEENNR BANNERED
ABDEENRT BANTERED
ABDEENRU UNBEARED
ABDEENRZ BRAZENED
ABDEENST ABSENTED
ABDEENTT BATTENED
ABDEEPRS BEDRAPES
BESPREAD
ABDEERRT BARTERED
ABDEERSS DEBASERS
ABDEERST BREASTED
DEBATERS
ABDEERSY BEEYARDS
ABDEERTT BATTERED
ABDEERTW WATERBED
ABDEERTY BETRAYED
ABDEERWY BEWRAYED
ABDEESST BASSETED
BESTEADS
ABDEFIIS BASIFIED
ABDEFILN FINDABLE
ABDEFLLO FOLDABLE
ABDEFLOR FORDABLE
ABDEFLST FLATBEDS
ABDEFOSS SOFABEDS
ABDEFRRY FRYBREAD
ABDEFRSW BEDWARFS
ABDEGHIS BIGHEADS
ABDEGILM GIMBALED
ABDEGILN BLINDAGE
ABDEGILU GUIDABLE
ABDEGINR BEARDING
BREADING
ABDEGINS BEADINGS
DEBASING
ABDEGINT DEBATING
ABDEGIPP BAGPIPED
ABDEGIRR ABRIDGER
ABDEGIRS ABRIDGES
BRIGADES
ABDEGLMO GAMBOLED
ABDEGLOT GLOBATED
ABDEGLRY BADGERLY
ABDEGLSU SLUGABED
ABDEGNOS BONDAGES
DOGBANES
ABDEGNRU UNGARBED
ABDEGOPR PEGBOARD
ABDEGORT BOGARTED
ABDEGRSU SUBGRADE
ABDEHILL BILLHEAD
ABDEHINS BANISHED
ABDEHITU HABITUDE
ABDEHKLU BULKHEAD
ABDEHLLN HANDBELL
ABDEHLLO HOLDABLE
ABDEHLLU BULLHEAD
ABDEHLMS SHAMBLED
ABDEHLOT BOLTHEAD
ABDEHLRS HALBERDS
ABDEHMNO HAMBONED
ABDEHMOR RHABDOME
ABDEHMRU RHUMBAED
ABDEHMSU AMBUSHED
ABDEHNTU UNBATHED
ABDEHORR ABHORRED
HARBORED
ABDEHOSW BESHADOW
BOWHEADS
ABDEHRST BREADTHS
ABDEHSSU SUBHEADS
ABDEHTTU BUTTHEAD
ABDEIIRT DIATRIBE
ABDEIKMR IMBARKED
ABDEIKNS BANKSIDE
ABDEIKNU BAUDEKIN
ABDEILLR BRAILLED
ABDEILLS SLIDABLE
ABDEILMM DIMMABLE
IMBALMED
ABDEILMN MANDIBLE
ABDEILMS SEMIBALD
ABDEILMZ IMBLAZED
ABDEILNR BILANDER
ABDEILNT BIDENTAL
ABDEILNW WINDABLE
ABDEILNY DENIABLY
ABDEILOV VOIDABLE
ABDEILOX OXIDABLE
ABDEILPP DIPPABLE
ABDEILPS PIEBALDS
ABDEILRS BEDRAILS
DISABLER
ABDEILRT LIBRATED
ABDEILRV DRIVABLE
ABDEILRY DIABLERY
ABDEILSS DISABLES
ABDEILSU AUDIBLES
ABDEILSY BIASEDLY
ABDEILTU DUTIABLE
ABDEILVV BIVALVED
ABDEIMOO AMOEBOID
ABDEIMOR AMBEROID
ABDEINNR ENDBRAIN
ABDEINOR DEBONAIR
ABDEINOS BEDSONIA
ABDEINOT OBTAINED
ABDEINRS BRANDIES
ABDEINSU UNBIASED
ABDEIOTV OBVIATED
ABDEIPRT BIPARTED
ABDEIPST BAPTISED
ABDEIPTZ BAPTIZED
ABDEIRRS BRAIDERS
ABDEIRSS SEABIRDS
SIDEBARS
ABDEIRST REDBAITS
TRIBADES
ABDEIRSU DAUBRIES
ABDEIRSW BAWDRIES
ABDEIRTV VIBRATED
ABDEISSU DISABUSE
SUBIDEAS
ABDEISTU DAUBIEST
ABDEISTW BAWDIEST
ABDEJNOW JAWBONED
ABDEKLSW SKEWBALD
ABDEKNRU UNBRAKED
ABDEKNSU SUNBAKED
ABDEKOOT DATEBOOK
ABDEKORW BEADWORK
ABDEKORY KEYBOARD
ABDEKOTU OUTBAKED
ABDELLMO MOLDABLE
ABDELLOR BEADROLL
ABDELLOT BALLOTED
ABDELMNU UNBLAMED
ABDELMPS BEDLAMPS
ABDELNOR BANDEROL
ABDELNOU UNDOABLE
ABDELNOZ BLAZONED
ABDELNRY BENADRYL
ABDELNSS BALDNESS
ABDELNST BLANDEST
ABDELORU LABOURED
ABDELOSV ABSOLVED
ABDELOSW DOWSABEL
ABDELRSU DURABLES
ABDELRTT BRATTLED
ABDELSTU SUBLATED
ABDEMNNS BANDSMEN
ABDEMNOR BOARDMEN
ABDEMNOS ABDOMENS
ABDEMORT BROMATED
ABDEMRSU BERMUDAS
ABDEMRTU DRUMBEAT
ABDENNNU UNBANNED
ABDENNOS NOSEBAND
ABDENORS BANDORES
BROADENS
ABDENORW RAWBONED
ABDENORY BONEYARD
ABDENOTW DOWNBEAT
ABDENRRS BRANDERS
ABDENRRU UNBARRED
ABDENRSS DRABNESS
ABDENRST BARTENDS
ABDENRTU BREADNUT
TURBANED
ABDENSSU SUBDEANS
ABDENSTU UNBASTED
ABDENSUU UNABUSED
ABDENSWY BENDWAYS
ABDENTTU DEBUTANT
ABDEOORW BEARWOOD
ABDEOPRR PREBOARD
ABDEOPRT PROBATED
ABDEORRS ADSORBER
BOARDERS
REBOARDS
ABDEORRU ARBOURED
ABDEORRW DRAWBORE
WARDROBE
ABDEORST BROADEST
ABDEORSW SOWBREAD
ABDEORTU OBDURATE
TABOURED
ABDEORUX BORDEAUX
ABDEPRSU SUPERBAD
ABDEPSSY BYPASSED
ABDERRSU ABSURDER
ABDERSST DABSTERS
ABDERSSU SURBASED
ABDERSTW BEDSTRAW
ABDERTUW DRAWTUBE
ABDESUWY SUBWAYED
ABDFILOR FORBIDAL
ABDFIMRR BIRDFARM
ABDFIRST FATBIRDS
ABDFLOOT FOLDBOAT
ABDFRSUW SUBDWARF
ABDGHINR HANGBIRD
ABDGIINR BRAIDING
ABDGILNS BLADINGS
ABDGINNR BRANDING
ABDGINNY BANDYING
ABDGINOR BOARDING
ABDGINRS BRIGANDS
ABDGINST DINGBATS
ABDGINSW WINDBAGS
ABDGIRST DIRTBAGS
ABDGLSUY LADYBUGS
ABDHHSSU SHADBUSH
ABDHIIST ADHIBITS
ABDHILLN HANDBILL
ABDHILNS BLANDISH
ABDHINRS BRANDISH
ABDHIORS BROADISH
ABDHIRTY BIRTHDAY

ABDHKNOO HANDBOOK
ABDHLNSU BUSHLAND
ABDHLORW BLOWHARD
ABDHLOSW SHADBLOW
ABDHMORS RHABDOMS
ABDHMOTU BADMOUTH
ABDHNORS BODHRANS
ABDHNSSU HUSBANDS
ABDHOORT HARDBOOT
ABDIIJLR JAILBIRD
ABDIILLR BILLIARD
ABDIILRR RAILBIRD
ABDIIMNR MIDBRAIN
ABDIIMSU BASIDIUM
ABDIINOS OBSIDIAN
ABDIINRR RAINBIRD
ABDIINTT BANDITTI
ABDIIORT ORIBATID
ABDIIRTY RABIDITY
ABDIJRSY JAYBIRDS
ABDIKLNR BLINKARD
ABDIKLOU KILOBAUD
ABDILLRY BRIDALLY
RIBALDLY
ABDILOOS DIABOLOS
ABDILORS LABROIDS
ABDILOST TABLOIDS
ABDILRRY RIBALDRY
ABDILRZZ BLIZZARD
ABDIMNRS MISBRAND
ABDIMORS AMBROIDS
ABDIMRSY MAYBIRDS
ABDINORS INBOARDS
ABDINORU AIRBOUND
ABDINOST BANDITOS
ABDINOTY ANTIBODY
ABDINRSU UNBRAIDS
ABDINRTY BANDITRY
ABDIPRSU UPBRAIDS
ABDJMOOR DOORJAMB
ABDKOOSY DAYBOOKS
ABDKORSY SKYBOARD
ABDLLORS BOLLARDS
ABDLNOSU SUBNODAL
ABDLOSSU BUSLOADS
ABDLRSUU SUBDURAL
ABDLRSUY ABSURDLY
ABDLSSUU SUBDUALS
ABDLSTUU SUBADULT
ABDMNNOS BONDSMAN
ABDMOOPR MOPBOARD
ABDNNNOR NONBRAND
ABDNOORS BRADOONS
ABDNOPRS PROBANDS
ABDNORSU BAUDRONS
ABDNORUY BOUNDARY
ABDNRRSU SANDBURR
ABDNRSSU SANDBURS
ABDNSSTY STANDBYS
ABDOORTU OUTBOARD
ABDOOSSW BASSWOOD
ABDOOSWY BAYWOODS
ABDRSSTU BUSTARDS
ABDRSUZZ BUZZARDS
ABEEEFLR REEFABLE
ABEEEFRS FREEBASE
ABEEEGRV BEVERAGE
ABEEEHTT HEBETATE
ABEEEKLP KEEPABLE
ABEEELLP PEELABLE
ABEEELLR REELABLE
ABEEEMSY EYEBEAMS
ABEEENRT TENEBRAE
ABEEENST ABSENTEE
ABEEERRV BEREAVER
ABEEERSV BEREAVES
ABEEFILL FILEABLE
ABEEFILN FINEABLE
ABEEFILR AFEBRILE
BALEFIRE
FIREABLE
ABEEFILS FEASIBLE
ABEEFILT FLEABITE
ABEEFIRS FIREBASE
ABEEFLLL FELLABLE
ABEEFLLN BEFALLEN
ABEEFLOS BEEFALOS
ABEEFORR FOREBEAR
ABEEGHRS HERBAGES
ABEEGILV GIVEABLE
ABEEGIRV VERBIAGE
ABEEGLLS GABELLES
ABEEGLTT GETTABLE
ABEEGMNR BARGEMEN
ABEEGMRT BREGMATE
ABEEGMTY MEGABYTE
ABEEGOSZ GAZEBOES
ABEEGPSW WEBPAGES
ABEEGRRS GERBERAS
ABEEGRST ABSTERGE
ABEEGRSU AUBERGES
ABEEGRSW BREWAGES
ABEEGTTU BAGUETTE
ABEEHILR HIREABLE
ABEEHINT THEBAINE
ABEEHIRZ HEBRAIZE
ABEEHLLL HEELBALL
ABEEHLLP HELPABLE
ABEEHLLR HAREBELL
ABEEHLSV BEHALVES
ABEEHMSS BESHAMES
ABEEHNNS HENBANES
ABEEHNSS BANSHEES
SHEBEANS
ABEEHORS RHEOBASE
ABEEHQTU BEQUEATH
ABEEHRRT BREATHER
ABEEHRST BREATHES
ABEEHRSV BEHAVERS
ABEEIKKL BEAKLIKE
ABEEIKLL LIKEABLE
ABEEIKLM BEAMLIKE
ABEEIKLN BEANLIKE
ABEEIKLR BEARLIKE
ABEEIKLT BAKELITE
ABEEIKRS BAKERIES
ABEEIKRT TIEBREAK
ABEEIKST BEAKIEST
ABEEILLN LIENABLE
LINEABLE
ABEEILLR RELIABLE
ABEEILLV LEVIABLE
LIVEABLE
ABEEILLX EXILABLE
ABEEILMN MINEABLE
ABEEILNN BIENNALE
ABEEILNP PLEBEIAN
ABEEILNS BASELINE
ABEEILNV ENVIABLE
ABEEILPX EXPIABLE
ABEEILRR BLEARIER
ABEEILRT LIBERATE
ABEEILRW BEWAILER
ABEEILSS SEISABLE
ABEEILSZ SEIZABLE
SIZEABLE
ABEEILTV EVITABLE
ABEEILVW VIEWABLE
ABEEIMRS AMBERIES
ABEEIMST BEAMIEST
ABEEINST BETAINES
ABEEIRTT BATTERIE
ABEEISST BEASTIES
ABEEISTU BEAUTIES
ABEEJMOR JAMBOREE
ABEEKLOT KEELBOAT
ABEEKLSS BEAKLESS
ABEEKLST BLEAKEST
ABEEKMNR BRAKEMEN
ABEEKMRR REEMBARK
ABEEKOOP PEEKABOO
ABEEKORV OVERBAKE
ABEEKPRS BARKEEPS
PREBAKES
ABEEKPSS BESPEAKS
ABEEKRRS BREAKERS
ABEELLLR LABELLER
ABEELLLS SELLABLE
ABEELLLT TELLABLE
ABEELLMT MELTABLE
ABEELLOV LOVEABLE
ABEELLRS LABELERS
RELABELS
ABEELLSY EYEBALLS
ABEELMMR EMBALMER
ABEELMNO BONEMEAL
ABEELMOV MOVEABLE
ABEELMPR PREAMBLE
ABEELMRT ATREMBLE
ABEELMRZ EMBLAZER
ABEELMSS ASSEMBLE
BEAMLESS
ABEELMSZ EMBLAZES
ABEELMTT EMBATTLE
ABEELNOP BEANPOLE
OPENABLE
ABEELNRS ENABLERS
ABEELNRT RENTABLE
ABEELNST NESTABLE
ABEELNTT NETTABLE
ABEELNTU TUNEABLE
ABEELOPR OPERABLE
ABEELORS EARLOBES
ABEELORV OVERABLE
ABEELORX EXORABLE
ABEELOTT TOTEABLE
ABEELOTV VOTEABLE
ABEELPTT PETTABLE
ABEELPTY TYPEABLE
ABEELRST ARBELEST
BLEATERS
RESTABLE
RETABLES
ABEELRSU REUSABLE
ABEELRSV SERVABLE
ABEELRSY BELAYERS
ABEELSSS BASELESS
ABEELSST BEATLESS
ABEELSSU SUBLEASE
ABEELSTT SEATBELT
TESTABLE
ABEELSTW STEWABLE
ABEELTTW WETTABLE
ABEEMMNR MEMBRANE
ABEEMNST BASEMENT
ABEEMNTT ABETMENT
ABEEMRSS BESMEARS
ABEENNRT BANNERET
ABEENNTU UNBEATEN
ABEENORS SEABORNE
ABEENOTZ BENZOATE
ABEENRRR BARRENER
ABEENRRT BANTERER
ABEENRSS BARENESS
ABEENRST ABSENTER
ABEENRSV VERBENAS
ABEENRTT BATTENER
ABEENSSS BASENESS
ABEENSTW NEWSBEAT
ABEEORRV OVERBEAR
ABEEORSS BOREASES
ABEEORTV OVERBEAT
ABEEOSTX TEABOXES
ABEEPRRU UPBEARER
ABEEPTTY PETABYTE
ABEEQSUU USQUEBAE
ABEERRRT BARTERER
ABEERRST REBATERS
ABEERRTT BARRETTE
BATTERER
BERRETTA
ABEERRTV VERTEBRA
ABEERRTY BETRAYER
TEABERRY
ABEERRWY BEWRAYER
ABEERSTT ABETTERS
BERETTAS
ABEERTTT BETATTER
ABEERTTY TERABYTE
ABEESTXY EXABYTES
ABEESZZZ BEZAZZES
ABEETTUX EXTUBATE
ABEFFLRS BAFFLERS
ABEFFOST OFFBEATS
ABEFGILT GIFTABLE
ABEFGSST GABFESTS
ABEFHILS FISHABLE
ABEFHOOT HOOFBEAT
ABEFIIMR FIMBRIAE
ABEFIIRS BASIFIER
ABEFIISS BASIFIES
ABEFILLL FALLIBLE
FILLABLE
ABEFILLM FILMABLE
ABEFILLO FOILABLE
ABEFILLR FIREBALL
ABEFILLT LIFTABLE
ABEFILOT LIFEBOAT
ABEFILRS BARFLIES
ABEFILSY FEASIBLY
ABEFILTT FITTABLE
ABEFINNR FIBRANNE
ABEFIORT BIFORATE
FIREBOAT
ABEFIRRT FIREBRAT
ABEFITUY BEAUTIFY
ABEFLLMU BLAMEFUL
ABEFLLRU FURLABLE
ABEFLLTU TABLEFUL
ABEFLMOR FORMABLE
ABEFLOTU OUTFABLE
ABEFLRSU SURFABLE
ABEFMRSU SUBFRAME
ABEFOORT BAREFOOT
ABEFORRS FORBEARS
ABEFORSY FOREBAYS
ABEGGGIN ABEGGING
ABEGGHLU HUGGABLE
ABEGGINZ BEGAZING
ABEGGIRR BRAGGIER
ABEGGIST BAGGIEST
ABEGGITY GIGABYTE
ABEGGLRY BEGGARLY
ABEGGMOS GAMBOGES
ABEGGRRS BRAGGERS
ABEGGRST BRAGGEST
ABEGGRSU BURGAGES
ABEGHILP PHILABEG
ABEGHINV BEHAVING
ABEGHNSS SHEBANGS
ABEGHORR BEGORRAH
ABEGHOSU BAGHOUSE
ABEGHRRY HAGBERRY
ABEGHRST BARGHEST
ABEGHRSU BEARHUGS
ABEGIIMS BIGAMIES
ABEGIINO IBOGAINE
ABEGIJTU BIJUGATE
ABEGIKNR BERAKING
BREAKING
ABEGIKNT BETAKING
ABEGILLN LABELING
ABEGILNN ENABLING
ABEGILNR BLEARING
ABEGILNS SINGABLE
ABEGILNT BLEATING
TANGIBLE
ABEGILNY BELAYING
ABEGILOT OBLIGATE
ABEGIMNN BENAMING
ABEGIMNR BREAMING
ABEGIMNS MISBEGAN
ABEGIMNY EMBAYING
ABEGIMRS GAMBIERS
ABEGIMST MEGABITS
ABEGINOS BEGONIAS
ABEGINRS BEARINGS
SABERING
ABEGINRT BERATING
REBATING
TABERING
ABEGINRW BEWARING
ABEGINST BEATINGS
ABEGINTT ABETTING
ABEGIOSS BIOGASES
ABEGIPPR BAGPIPER
ABEGIPPS BAGPIPES
ABEGKLSU BULKAGES
ABEGKORS BROKAGES
GROSBEAK
ABEGKOSS BOSKAGES
ABEGLLLU GULLABLE
ABEGLLOR BARGELLO
ABEGLMOR BEGLAMOR
ABEGLMRS GAMBLERS
GAMBRELS
ABEGLMUY MEALYBUG
ABEGLORW GROWABLE
ABEGLRRS GARBLERS
ABEGLRSS GARBLESS
ABEGLSTU GUSTABLE
ABEGMNOS GAMBESON
ABEGMNOY BOGEYMAN
MONEYBAG
ABEGMORT BERGAMOT
ABEGMRSU UMBRAGES
ABEGNNST BANTENGS
ABEGNORS BEGROANS
ABEGNOSS NOSEBAGS
ABEGNSTU SUBAGENT
ABEGOPSY PAGEBOYS
ABEGOSUY BUOYAGES
ABEGRRUV BURGRAVE
ABEGRSTU BARGUEST
ABEGSSTU SUBSTAGE
ABEHIKLS BLEAKISH
ABEHILNR HIBERNAL
ABEHILTT HITTABLE
TITHABLE
ABEHIMMS MEMSAHIB
ABEHIMNO BOHEMIAN
ABEHIMOS BOHEMIAS
OBEAHISM
ABEHINRS BANISHER
ABEHINSS BANISHES
BANSHIES
ABEHINST ABSINTHE
ABEHIORV BEHAVIOR
ABEHIRRS BRASHIER
ABEHISTU HABITUES
ABEHKNST BETHANKS
ABEHKOPS BAKESHOP
ABEHKRSU HAUBERKS
ABEHLMMU HUMMABLE
ABEHLMSS SHAMBLES
ABEHLNTU HUNTABLE
ABEHLOSW SHOWABLE
ABEHLOTU TABOULEH
ABEHLRST BLATHERS
HALBERTS
ABEHLSST BATHLESS
ABEHMNOR HORNBEAM
ABEHMNOS HAMBONES
ABEHMOOR REHOBOAM
ABEHMRSU AMBUSHER
ABEHMSSU AMBUSHES
ABEHNRSY ABHENRYS
ABEHNSTU SUNBATHE
ABEHORRR ABHORRER
HARBORER
ABEHOSST BATHOSES
ABEHOSTX HATBOXES
ABEHPSSU SUBPHASE
ABEHRSST BRASHEST
ABEHRTUY EURYBATH
ABEIIKLS KIELBASI
ABEIILMT IMITABLE
ABEIILNN BIENNIAL
ABEIILNR BILINEAR
ABEIILNV INVIABLE
ABEIILPT PITIABLE
ABEIILST SIBILATE
ABEIILTV VITIABLE
ABEIINRR BRAINIER
ABEIINRS BINARIES
ABEIJLNO JOINABLE
ABEIJLTU JUBILATE
ABEIJMNN BENJAMIN
ABEIJNSS BASENJIS
ABEIKLLL KILLABLE
ABEIKLLM BALMLIKE
LAMBLIKE
ABEIKLLN BALKLINE
LINKABLE
ABEIKLLS SLABLIKE
ABEIKLNR BARNLIKE
ABEIKLNS SINKABLE
ABEIKLOS KILOBASE
ABEIKLOT BOATLIKE
ABEIKLRU BAULKIER
ABEIKLSS KISSABLE
ABEIKLST BALKIEST
ABEIKLSY KIELBASY
ABEIKNNR NINEBARK
ABEIKNRS BEARSKIN
ABEIKNST BEATNIKS
SNAKEBIT
ABEIKRST BARKIEST
BRAKIEST
ABEIKSWY BIKEWAYS
ABEILLLM MILLABLE
ABEILLLT TILLABLE
ABEILLLW WILLABLE
ABEILLMS MISLABEL
ABEILLNT LIBELANT
ABEILLOS ISOLABLE
LOBELIAS
ABEILLOV VIOLABLE
ABEILLPS LAPSIBLE
ABEILLRR BRAILLER
ABEILLRS BRAILLES
LIBERALS
ABEILLRY BLEARILY
RELIABLY
ABEILLST BASTILLE
LISTABLE
ABEILLTT TILTABLE
ABEILMMR IMBALMER
ABEILMNS BAILSMEN
BIMENSAL
ABEILMNT BAILMENT
ABEILMRR MARBLIER
ABEILMRW WAMBLIER
ABEILMSS ABLEISMS
MISSABLE
ABEILMST BALMIEST
BIMETALS
LAMBIEST
TIMBALES
ABEILMSU BUMELIAS
ABEILMSZ IMBLAZES
ABEILNNW WINNABLE
ABEILNOT TAILBONE
ABEILNPS BIPLANES
ABEILNRS RINSABLE
ABEILNRU RUINABLE
ABEILNSS LESBIANS
ABEILNST INSTABLE
ABEILNTV BIVALENT
ABEILNTY BINATELY
ABEILNUV UNVIABLE
ABEILNVY ENVIABLY
ABEILORR BORRELIA
ABEILORT LABORITE
ABEILOTV BLOVIATE
ABEILPPR RIPPABLE
ABEILPPT TIPPABLE
ABEILPRT PARTIBLE
ABEILPSS PASSIBLE
ABEILPST EPIBLAST
ABEILRRU REBURIAL
ABEILRRW BRAWLIER
ABEILRST BLASTIER
LIBRATES
ABEILRSY BILAYERS
ABEILRTT TITRABLE
ABEILRTW WRITABLE
ABEILRYY BIYEARLY
ABEILSST ABLEISTS
ASTILBES
BASTILES
BLASTIES
STABILES
ABEILSSU ISSUABLE
ABEILSTU SUITABLE
ABEILSUX BISEXUAL
ABEILSVV BIVALVES
ABEILSYZ SIZEABLY
ABEIMNPS PEMBINAS
ABEIMNST AMBIENTS
ABEIMORS BIRAMOSE
ABEIMORU AEROBIUM
ABEIMRST BARMIEST
ABEIMRTV AMBIVERT
VERBATIM
ABEIMSSU IAMBUSES
ABEINNRR BRANNIER
ABEINNRU INURBANE
ABEINORR AIRBORNE
ABEINORS BARONIES
SEAROBIN
ABEINORT BARITONE
OBTAINER
REOBTAIN
TABORINE
ABEINOST BOTANIES
BOTANISE
NIOBATES
OBEISANT
ABEINOTZ BOTANIZE
ABEINPST BEPAINTS
ABEINRRW BRAWNIER
ABEINRST BANISTER
BARNIEST
ABEINRSU URBANISE
ABEINRTU BRAUNITE
URBANITE
ABEINRUZ URBANIZE
ABEINSSS BIASNESS
ABEINSST BASINETS
BASSINET
ABEINTTU INTUBATE
ABEIORRZ ARBORIZE
ABEIORSS ISOBARES
ABEIORTV ABORTIVE
ABEIOSTV OBVIATES
ABEIPRRS SPARERIB
ABEIPRTZ BAPTIZER
ABEIPSST BAPTISES
ABEIPSTZ BAPTIZES
ABEIRRRS BARRIERS
ABEIRRSS BRASIERS
BRASSIER
ABEIRRST ARBITERS
RAREBITS
ABEIRRSZ BIZARRES
BRAZIERS
ABEIRRTT BIRRETTA
BRATTIER
ABEIRRVY BREVIARY
ABEIRSSS BRASSIES
ABEIRSSU AIRBUSES
ABEIRSTT BIRETTAS
ABEIRSTV VIBRATES
ABEIRSTY BESTIARY
SYBARITE
ABEIRSUX EXURBIAS
ABEIRTTY YTTERBIA
ABEISSTT BATISTES
ABEISTTT BATTIEST
ABEISTUX BAUXITES
ABEJKLOU KABELJOU
ABEJLMPU JUMPABLE
ABEJLSUY BLUEJAYS
ABEJMNOS JOBNAMES
ABEJMOOR JEROBOAM

ABEJNORW JAWBONER
ABEJNOSW JAWBONES
ABEJRRSU ABJURERS
ABEKLMOS ABELMOSK
SMOKABLE
ABEKLNOW KNOWABLE
ABEKLNRY BANKERLY
ABEKLNST BLANKEST
BLANKETS
ABEKLORW WORKABLE
ABEKLRSS BARKLESS
ABEKMNTU BUNKMATE
ABEKMSSU SAMBUKES
ABEKNNOT BANKNOTE
ABEKNRSU UNBRAKES
ABEKOORY YEARBOOK
ABEKORTU BREAKOUT
OUTBREAK
ABEKOSTU OUTBAKES
ABEKPRSU BREAKUPS
ABEKRSTY BASKETRY
ABELLLMU LABELLUM
ABELLLSY SYLLABLE
ABELLMRU UMBELLAR
UMBRELLA
ABELLNNO BALLONNE
ABELLNOT BALLONET
ABELLOPW PLOWABLE
ABELLORT BALLOTER
ABELLOSV SOLVABLE
ABELLOTU LOBULATE
ABELLOTY LOBATELY
OBLATELY
ABELLOVY LOVEABLY
ABELLRSU RUBELLAS
ABELLRVY VERBALLY
ABELLSTU BALLUTES
ABELMMSU SUMMABLE
ABELMNNO NOBLEMAN
ABELMNOZ EMBLAZON
ABELMNSU ALBUMENS
BLUESMAN
ABELMOSU ALBUMOSE
ABELMOSV MOVABLES
ABELMOVY MOVEABLY
ABELMRRS MARBLERS
RAMBLERS
ABELMRST LAMBERTS
ABELMSSY ASSEMBLY
ABELNNOR BANNEROL
ABELNORZ BLAZONER
ABELNOST NOTABLES
STONABLE
ABELNOSY BALONEYS
ABELNPRU PRUNABLE
ABELNPSU SUBPANEL
ABELNRRY BARRENLY
ABELNRSY BLARNEYS
ABELNRTU TURNABLE
ABELNRUY URBANELY
ABELNRYZ BRAZENLY
ABELNSTU ABLUENTS
UNSTABLE
ABELNSTY ABSENTLY
ABELNSUU UNUSABLE
ABELNTUY TUNEABLY
ABELOOTY TABOOLEY
ABELOPRT PORTABLE
ABELOPRU POURABLE
ABELOPRV PROVABLE
ABELOPRY OPERABLY
ABELOPST POTABLES
ABELOPTT TABLETOP
ABELOQTU QUOTABLE
ABELORRS LABORERS
ABELORRU LABOURER
RUBEOLAR
ABELORST BLOATERS
SORTABLE
STORABLE
ABELORSU RUBEOLAS
ABELORSV ABSOLVER
ABELOSSU SABULOSE
ABELOSSV ABSOLVES
ABELOSTU ABSOLUTE
ABELOSTW BESTOWAL
STOWABLE
TEABOWLS
ABELOTTU OUTBLEAT
ABELOTUZ OUTBLAZE
ABELPRTU PUBERTAL
ABELRRSW BRAWLERS
WARBLERS
ABELRSST BLASTERS
STABLERS
ABELRSTT BATTLERS
BLATTERS
BRATTLES
ABELRSTU BALUSTER
RUSTABLE
ABELRTTU REBUTTAL
ABELSSSU SUBSALES
ABELSSTT STABLEST
ABELSSTU SUBLATES
ABELSTUU SUBULATE
ABELSTWY BELTWAYS
ABELTTUU TUBULATE
ABELTTUY BUTYLATE
ABEMMNOO MOONBEAM
ABEMNOST BOATSMEN
ABEMNOTU UMBONATE
ABEMNPRU PENUMBRA
ABEMNSSU SUNBEAMS
ABEMNSUY SUNBEAMY
ABEMNTTU ABUTMENT
ABEMORST BROMATES
ABEMOSTU OUTBEAMS
ABEMRSSW BESWARMS
ABENNORS BARONNES
ABENNOTU BUTANONE
NANOTUBE
ABENNRRS BRANNERS
ABENOPSU SUBPOENA
ABENORSS BARONESS
ABENORST BARONETS
ABENORSZ ZEBRANOS
ABENORTT BETATRON
ABENORTV BEVATRON
ABENORTY BARYTONE
ABENOSSW SAWBONES
ABENOSSY SOYBEANS
ABENOSTY BAYONETS
ABENPSSU SUBPENAS
ABENQSTU BANQUETS
ABENRSTU URBANEST
ABENSSSS BASSNESS
ABENSTZZ BEZZANTS
ABEOOSST SEABOOTS
ABEOPPRY PAPERBOY
ABEOPRSS SAPROBES
ABEOPRST PROBATES
ABEOPSST POSTBASE
ABEOQRSU BAROQUES
ABEORRRT BARRETOR
ABEORRST ABORTERS
TABORERS
ABEORRTU TABOURER
ABEORSST BOASTERS
SORBATES
ABEORSSY ROSEBAYS
ABEORSTT ABETTORS
TABORETS
ABEORSTU SABOTEUR
ABEORTTU OBTURATE
TABOURET
ABEORTUV OUTBRAVE
ABEOSSST ASBESTOS
ABEOSTUV SUBOVATE
ABEOSTWX SWEATBOX
ABEPRRTU ABRUPTER
ABEPRSSY PASSERBY
ABEPRSTY TYPEBARS
ABEPSSSY BYPASSES
ABEQRSUU ARQUEBUS
ABERRRTY BARRETRY
ABERRWXY WAXBERRY
ABERSSSU RUBASSES
SURBASES
ABERSSTU ABSTRUSE
ABERSTTU ABUTTERS
ABERSTUW WATERBUS
ABERTTUY BUTYRATE
ABESSSTT BASSETTS
ABESSSTU ASBESTUS
ABESSTTU SUBSTATE
ABFFGILN BAFFLING
ABFFIILS BAILIFFS
ABFFLLPU PUFFBALL
ABFFLOOS BOFFOLAS
ABFFLOST BLASTOFF
ABFFLOSU BUFFALOS
ABFFNOTU BOUFFANT
ABFGLLOO GOOFBALL
ABFGOOST FOOTBAGS
ABFGORUU FAUBOURG
ABFHIIST BAITFISH
ABFHINNO INFOBAHN
ABFHIORS BOARFISH
ABFHOOTT FOOTBATH
ABFHSSTU SUBSHAFT
ABFIILLR FIBRILLA
ABFIILMR FIMBRIAL
ABFILLLY FALLIBLY
ABFILNSU BASINFUL
ABFILOTT BOATLIFT
ABFILSTU FABULIST
ABFIMORS FIBROMAS
ABFJORSU FRABJOUS
ABFKLLOR FORKBALL
ABFLLOOS FOOSBALL
ABFLLOOT FOOTBALL
ABFLLOST SOFTBALL
ABFLMORY FORMABLY
ABFLNSUU BUSULFAN
ABFLOSTU BOASTFUL
BOATFULS
ABFLOSTW BATFOWLS
ABFLOSTY FLYBOATS
ABFLOSUU FABULOUS
ABFNORTU TURBOFAN
ABFORSTU SURFBOAT
ABGGGILN BLAGGING
ABGGGINR BRAGGING
ABGGGINS BAGGINGS
ABGGIIST GIGABITS
ABGGILMN GAMBLING
ABGGILNR GARBLING
ABGGNNUY GUNNYBAG
ABGGNOOT TOBOGGAN
ABGHHILL HIGHBALL
ABGHIINT HABITING
ABGHINSS BASHINGS
ABGHINWZ WHIZBANG
ABGHMOOS GOOMBAHS
ABGHMORU BROUGHAM
ABGHMRSU HAMBURGS
ABGHOSTU BUSHGOAT
ABGHPRSU SUBGRAPH
ABGIIILN ALIBIING
ABGIIKNT BATIKING
ABGIILNR BRAILING
ABGIILOT OBLIGATI
ABGIIMST BIGAMIST
ABGIINNO BIGNONIA
ABGIINNR BRAINING
ABGIINRS BRAISING
ABGIINSS BIASSING
ABGIJNRU ABJURING
ABGIKLNN BLANKING
ABGIKLNU BAULKING
ABGIKNNS BANKINGS
ABGIKNRR RINGBARK
ABGILMNR MARBLING
RAMBLING
ABGILMNW WAMBLING
ABGILNNT BANTLING
ABGILNNU UNBALING
ABGILNOR LABORING
ABGILNOT BLOATING
ABGILNRW BRAWLING
WARBLING
ABGILNST BLASTING
STABLING
ABGILNTT BATTLING
BLATTING
ABGILNTY TANGIBLY
ABGILOOT OBLIGATO
ABGILORS GARBOILS
ABGILRST BATGIRLS
ABGIMMNO MAMBOING
ABGIMNRU RUMBAING
ABGIMOSU BIGAMOUS
ABGINNNR BRANNING
ABGINNOR ABORNING
ABGINOOR BIGAROON
ABGINOOT TABOOING
ABGINORT ABORTING
BORATING
TABORING
ABGINORV BRAVOING
ABGINOST BOASTING
BOATINGS
ABGINRSS BRASSING
ABGINSST BASTINGS
ABGINSTT BATTINGS
ABGINTTU ABUTTING
ABGIOPST PIGBOATS
ABGIRRSS RIBGRASS
ABGKKNOS BANGKOKS
ABGKORSW WORKBAGS
ABGLLLOY GLOBALLY
ABGLLLUY GULLABLY
ABGLLMSU GUMBALLS
ABGLLORU GLOBULAR
ABGLLRUY BULLYRAG
ABGLMOPU PLUMBAGO
ABGLMOSU LUMBAGOS
ABGLNOOS BOLOGNAS
ABGLNOOT LONGBOAT
ABGLNOUW BUNGALOW
ABGLORSU GLABROUS
ABGLOSSU SUBGOALS
ABGLRRSU BURGLARS
ABGLRRUY BURGLARY
ABGMNOOY BOOGYMAN
ABGMOOSY GOOMBAYS
ABGMORSW BAGWORMS
ABGNOPRS PROBANGS
ABGNORSU OSNABURG
ABGNOSTU GUNBOATS
ABGOPSST POSTBAGS
ABGORSTU OUTBRAGS
ABGOSTTU TUGBOATS
ABHHIKSS BAKSHISH
ABHHSSUW BUSHWAHS
ABHIINRS BAIRNISH
BRAINISH
ABHIINST INHABITS
ABHIIORZ RHIZOBIA
ABHIKLLW HAWKBILL
ABHIKLOR KOHLRABI
ABHILNOS HOBNAILS
ABHILNOT BIATHLON
ABHILOPS BASOPHIL
ABHILSST STABLISH
ABHILSTU HALIBUTS
ABHINSST ABSINTHS
ABHIOSST ISOBATHS
ABHIOSTU HAUTBOIS
ABHIRRSU AIRBRUSH
ABHIRSSS BRASSISH
ABHIRSTT BRATTISH
ABHJNOOT JOHNBOAT
ABHKLSSY BASHLYKS
ABHKOOOT BOATHOOK
ABHKORSV BOSHVARK
ABHLLMOT MOTHBALL
ABHLLOOY BALLYHOO
ABHLLPSU PUSHBALL
ABHLOSUX BOXHAULS
ABHLOSWW WASHBOWL
ABHLPSUY SUBPHYLA
ABHLSSTU SALTBUSH
ABHMNSUU SUBHUMAN
ABHMOORT BATHROOM
ABHMRSSU SAMBHURS
ABHNSSTU SUNBATHS
ABHOORST TARBOOSH
ABHOOSTW SHOWBOAT
ABHORRSU HARBOURS
ABHOSTUY HAUTBOYS
ABHSSTUW WASHTUBS
ABIIINRS BIRIANIS
ABIIKLSS BASILISK
ABIILLMR MILLIBAR
ABIILLTY LABILITY
ABIILMNO BINOMIAL
ABIILMNS ALBINISM
MINILABS
ABIILMSU BULIMIAS
ABIILNOT LIBATION
ABIILNRS BRASILIN
ABIILNRY BRAINILY
ABIILNRZ BRAZILIN
ABIILNST SIBILANT
ABIILNVY INVIABLY
ABIILOSV BOLIVIAS
ABIILPTY PITIABLY
ABIIMNOT AMBITION
ABIIMNRS BINARISM
MINIBARS
ABIINRSY BIRYANIS
ABIIRSSV VIBRISSA
ABIJLNTU JUBILANT
ABIJNOST BANJOIST
ABIKLLLM LAMBKILL
ABIKLMNS LAMBKINS
LAMBSKIN
ABIKLORS KILOBARS
ABIKLOSS KOLBASIS
KOLBASSI
ABIKLSSY KISSABLY
ABIKNORR IRONBARK
ABIKRSST BRITSKAS
ABIKRSTZ BRITZKAS
BRITZSKA
ABILLLPY PLAYBILL
ABILLNPS PINBALLS
ABILLORT TRILOBAL
ABILLOVY VIOLABLY
ABILLPST SPITBALL
ABILLRTY TRIBALLY
ABILLSSW SAWBILLS
ABILLSWX WAXBILLS
ABILLSWY WAYBILLS
ABILMNOU OLIBANUM
ABILMNSU ALBUMINS
ABILMOPS BIOPLASM
ABILMORS MISLABOR
ABILNOOT BOLTONIA
LOBATION
OBLATION
ABILNOPR PANBROIL
ABILNOTU ABLUTION
ABUTILON
ABILNRTU TRIBUNAL
TURBINAL
ABILNRWY BRAWNILY
ABILOPRS PARBOILS
ABILORST ORBITALS
STROBILA
ABILORSV BOLIVARS
ABILORUV BIOVULAR
ABILOSTU BAILOUTS
TABOULIS
ABILRSSY BRASSILY
ABILRSUV SUBVIRAL
ABILSSUY ISSUABLY
ABILSTUY SUITABLY
ABIMNOSU BIMANOUS
ABIMNRSU URBANISM
ABIMORSU BIRAMOUS
ABIMORSY BOYARISM
ABIMPSST BAPTISMS
ABINNOST ANTISNOB
ABINOORT ABORTION
ABINOOST BONIATOS
ABINORST TABORINS
ABINORSW RAINBOWS
ABINOSST ANTIBOSS
BASTIONS
ABINOSTT BOTANIST
ABINRSTU URBANIST
ABINRSTV VIBRANTS
ABINRTUY URBANITY
ABINTTTU TITUBANT
ABIOORTV OBVIATOR
ABIOPRSU BIPAROUS
ABIOPSTU SUBTOPIA
ABIORRST ARBORIST
ABIORRSZ BIZARROS
ABIORRTV VIBRATOR
ABIORSTV VIBRATOS
ABIORTUY OBITUARY
ABIPSSTT BAPTISTS
ABIRRSTU AIRBURST
ABISSSST BASSISTS
ABISSTTU TUBAISTS
ABJKMOSS SJAMBOKS
ABKKMOOR BOOKMARK
ABKLLNOR BANKROLL
ABKLOOPY PLAYBOOK
ABKLOOSW LAWBOOKS
ABKLORWY WORKABLY
ABKLRSUW BULWARKS
ABKNNNOS NONBANKS
ABKNNOSW SNOWBANK
ABKNOPST STOPBANK
ABKNPRTU BANKRUPT
ABKNRSUU BUNRAKUS
ABKOOPSS PASSBOOK
ABKOORTW WORKBOAT
ABKORSTU OUTBARKS
ABKSSSTU SUBTASKS
ABLLLOSW LOWBALLS
ABLLMOOR BALLROOM
ABLLNOOS BALLOONS
ABLLNOSW SNOWBALL
ABLLORST TOLLBARS
ABLLORSU SOURBALL
ABLLOSTY TALLBOYS
ABLLRTUY BRUTALLY
ABLLSSUY SYLLABUS
ABLMMOSU BUMMALOS
ABLMNRUU ALBURNUM
LABURNUM
ABLMOOST TOMBOLAS
ABLMOSTY MYOBLAST
ABLMPSUU PABULUMS
ABLNNOOR NONLABOR
ABLNOOPS POBLANOS
ABLNORST LASTBORN
ABLNORYZ BLAZONRY
ABLNOSTU BUTANOLS
ABLNRSUU SUBLUNAR
ABLNSTUY UNSTABLY
ABLOOPRR PROLABOR
ABLOORST BARSTOOL
TOOLBARS
ABLOORTY OBLATORY
ABLOPRSU SUBPOLAR
ABLOPRTY PORTABLY
ABLOPRVY PROVABLY
ABLOPSYY PLAYBOYS
ABLOQTUY QUOTABLY
ABLORSST BORSTALS
ABLORSSU SUBSOLAR
ABLORSTY SORTABLY
ABLORTUW OUTBRAWL
ABLOSSUU SABULOUS
ABLOSTTU SUBTOTAL
ABLOSTUW OUTBAWLS
ABLPRTUY ABRUPTLY
ABLRSTUY BUTYRALS
ABMOORRS BARROOMS
ABMOPSST SPAMBOTS
ABMORSTU TAMBOURS
ABMOSSTU SUBATOMS
ABNNNORU NONURBAN
ABNOORRT ROBORANT
ABNOORYZ BRYOZOAN
ABNOOSSS BASSOONS
ABNORSTY BARYTONS
ABNORTUU RUNABOUT
ABNOSTUX SUBTAXON
ABOORRSU ARBOROUS
ABOORSTW ROWBOATS
ABOOSTTU OUTBOAST
ABOOSTTW TOWBOATS
ABORSSTU ROBUSTAS
ABPRSSTU SUBPARTS
ACCCDIIO COCCIDIA
ACCCEHIX CACHEXIC
ACCCELRY CYCLECAR
ACCCENPY PECCANCY
ACCCFIIL CALCIFIC
ACCCIILT CALCITIC
ACCCIIPR CAPRICCI
ACCCILLY CYCLICAL
ACCDDEEN CADENCED
ACCDDEIS CADDICES
ACCDDEKO COCKADED
ACCDDEOR ACCORDED
ACCDDIII DIACIDIC
ACCDDIIT DIDACTIC
ACCDEEER REACCEDE
ACCDEEHT CACHETED
ACCDEELN CANCELED
ACCDEENR CANCERED
ACCDEENS CADENCES
ACCDEENT ACCENTED
ACCDEEPT ACCEPTED
ACCDEERS ACCEDERS
ACCDEERT ACCRETED
ACCDEESS ACCESSED
ACCDEGIN ACCEDING
ACCDEHIL CHALICED
ACCDEHIN CHICANED
ACCDEHNR CRANCHED
ACCDEHPU CAPUCHED
ACCDEIIS ACCIDIES
ACCDEILN CALCINED
ACCDEILO ECOCIDAL
ACCDEILY DELICACY
ACCDEINT ACCIDENT
ACCDEIRT ACCREDIT
ACCDEISU CAUDICES
ACCDEKLR CRACKLED
ACCDEKOS COCKADES
ACCDENOV CONCAVED
ACCDEORR ACCORDER
ACCDEOST ACCOSTED
ACCDERSU ACCURSED
ACCDESUU CADUCEUS
CAUCUSED
ACCDHIIR DIARCHIC
ACCDHILS CHALCIDS
ACCDHIOT CATHODIC
ACCDHIRY DYARCHIC
ACCDHLOR CLOCHARD
ACCDIINU UNACIDIC
ACCDIIOT ACIDOTIC
ACCDIIRT CARDITIC
ACCDIIST DICASTIC
ACCDILNU DUNCICAL
ACCDILTY DACTYLIC
ACCDINOR CANCROID
DRACONIC
ACCDIOOR CORACOID
ACCDITUY CADUCITY
ACCDLOSY CACODYLS
ACCDOOST STOCCADO
ACCDOSUU CADUCOUS
ACCEEEPT ACCEPTEE
ACCEEHLO COCHLEAE

ACCEEHLS CALECHES
ACCEEHST SEECATCH
ACCEEILR CELERIAC
ACCEEILS ECCLESIA
ACCEEINV VACCINEE
ACCEEKLN NECKLACE
ACCEELNR CANCELER
CLARENCE
ACCEELNS CENACLES
ACCEELOS COALESCE
ACCEENNS NASCENCE
ACCEENRT REACCENT
ACCEENST ACESCENT
ACCEEORT COCREATE
ACCEEPRT ACCEPTER
REACCEPT
ACCEERST ACCRETES
ACCEERSU REACCUSE
ACCEESSS ACCESSES
ACCEFFIY EFFICACY
ACCEFILS FASCICLE
ACCEFLSU FELUCCAS
ACCEGKMO GAMECOCK
ACCEGNOY COAGENCY
ACCEGOSS SOCCAGES
ACCEHHKO CHECHAKO
ACCEHHKT CHATCHKE
HATCHECK
ACCEHIKP CHICKPEA
ACCEHIKR AIRCHECK
ACCEHILM ALCHEMIC
CHEMICAL
ACCEHILP CEPHALIC
ACCEHILS CALICHES
CHALICES
ACCEHILT HECTICAL
ACCEHIMN MECHANIC
ACCEHIMS SACHEMIC
ACCEHINO ANECHOIC
ACCEHINR CHANCIER
CHICANER
ACCEHINS CHICANES
ACCEHINT ATECHNIC
CATECHIN
ACCEHIRT CATCHIER
ACCEHKPY PAYCHECK
ACCEHLNS CHANCELS
ACCEHLOR COCHLEAR
ACCEHLOS COCHLEAS
ACCEHLOT CATECHOL
ACCEHMNO COACHMEN
ACCEHNNO CHACONNE
ACCEHNOR ENCROACH
ACCEHNRS CHANCERS
CHANCRES
CRANCHES
ACCEHNRY CHANCERY
ACCEHOPT CACHEPOT
ACCEHORS CAROCHES
COACHERS
ACCEHPSU CAPUCHES
ACCEHRST CATCHERS
CRATCHES
ACCEHSTT CATHECTS
ACCEHSTU CATECHUS
ACCEILLR CLERICAL
ACCEILLS CALICLES
ACCEILLU CAULICLE
ACCEILLV CLAVICLE
ACCEILNS CALCINES
SCENICAL
ACCEILNT CANTICLE
ACCEILNY CALYCINE
ACCEILOP ALOPECIC
ACCEILOS CALICOES
ACCEILRV CERVICAL
ACCEILST CALCITES
ACCEILTY ACETYLIC
ACCEIMRS CERAMICS
ACCEINOR COCINERA
ACCEINOS COCAINES
ACCEINOT ACETONIC
ACCEINRT ACENTRIC
ACCEINSV VACCINES
ACCEINTU CUNEATIC
ACCEIOPR CECROPIA
ACCEIOTV COACTIVE
ACCEIPRS CAPRICES
ACCEIPRT PRACTICE
ACCEIPSV PECCAVIS
ACCEIQSU CACIQUES
ACCEIRRR RICERCAR
ACCEIRSU CAESURIC
CURACIES
ACCEIRTU CRUCIATE
ACCEISST ASCETICS
ACCEISTT ECSTATIC
ACCEKLNR CRACKNEL
ACCEKLRS CACKLERS
CLACKERS
CRACKLES
ACCEKNOR CORNCAKE
ACCEKOPS PEACOCKS
ACCEKOPY PEACOCKY
ACCEKOSS SEACOCKS
ACCEKPSU CUPCAKES
ACCEKRRS CRACKERS
ACCELLSY CALYCLES
ACCELMNY CYCLAMEN
ACCELNOS CONCEALS
ACCELNOV CONCLAVE
ACCELNRU CARUNCLE
ACCELOOT COLOCATE
ACCELORS CORACLES
ACCELORT ACROLECT
ACCELRSY SCARCELY
ACCELRTU CLEARCUT
ACCELSSU SACCULES
ACCELSSY CYCLASES
ACCELWYY CYCLEWAY
ACCENNSY NASCENCY
ACCENORT ACCENTOR
ACCENOST COENACTS
COSECANT
ACCENOSV CONCAVES
ACCEOPRT ACCEPTOR
ACCEORST ECTOSARC
ACCEORTU ACCOUTER
ACCOUTRE
ACCERSST SCARCEST
ACCERSSU ACCUSERS
ACCESSTU CACTUSES
ACCESSUU CAUCUSES
ACCFFLTU CALCTUFF
ACCFHLTY CATCHFLY
ACCFLNOO CONFOCAL
ACCFOORT COFACTOR
ACCGHINN CHANCING
ACCGHINO COACHING
ACCGHINT CATCHING
ACCGHIOR CHORAGIC
ACCGIKLN CACKLING
CLACKING
ACCGIKMR GIMCRACK
ACCGIKNR CRACKING
ACCGILOX COXALGIC
ACCGINOT COACTING
ACCGINRU ACCRUING
ACCGINSU ACCUSING
ACCHHITT CHITCHAT
ACCHHMOU MUCHACHO
ACCHIIMS CHIASMIC
ACCHIIRT RACHITIC
ACCHIIST CHIASTIC
ACCHILNY CHANCILY
ACCHILOT CATHOLIC
ACCHIMOR ACHROMIC
ACCHINNO CINCHONA
ACCHINOS CHICANOS
ACCHINPU CAPUCHIN
ACCHIOPS PICACHOS
ACCHIORS COCHAIRS
ACCHIORT THORACIC
TROCHAIC
ACCHIRRT CARRITCH
ACCHIRSS SCRAICHS
ACCHKLOR CHARLOCK
ACCHKOSY HAYCOCKS
ACCHNNUY UNCHANCY
ACCHNOOR COANCHOR
CORONACH
ACCHNOTU COUCHANT
ACCHNTUY UNCATCHY
ACCHOOTU OUTCOACH
ACCHOPSU PACHUCOS
ACCHORTU CARTOUCH
ACCHORTY OCTARCHY
ACCHOTTU OUTCATCH
ACCHPSTU CATCHUPS
ACCHRRSU CURRACHS
ACCHRSTY SCRATCHY
ACCHRTWY WATCHCRY
ACCIIIOT OITICICA
ACCIILLN CLINICAL
ACCIILMT CLIMATIC
ACCIILNO ICONICAL
ACCIILRT CRITICAL
ACCIIMNN CINNAMIC
ACCIINOT ACONITIC
CATIONIC
ACCIINPS CAPSICIN
ACCIINTY CYANITIC
ACCIIOPT OCCIPITA
ACCIIPST PASTICCI
ACCIIRTX CICATRIX
ACCIISST SCIATICS
ACCIKKNN NICKNACK
ACCIKKRR RICKRACK
ACCIKKTT TICKTACK
ACCIKLOT COCKTAIL
ACCILLUY CALYCULI
ACCILMOS COSMICAL
ACCILMOX CACOMIXL
ACCILMSU CALCIUMS
ACCILMUU ACICULUM
ACCILNOT LACTONIC
ACCILNOV VOLCANIC
ACCILNUV VULCANIC
ACCILORS CALORICS
ACCILORT CORTICAL
ACCILOSS CLASSICO
ACCILOSV VOCALICS
ACCILRRU CIRCULAR
ACCILRSY ACRYLICS
ACCILSSS CLASSICS
ACCILSST CLASTICS
ACCILTUU CUTICULA
ACCIMNOS MOCCASIN
ACCIMOPR MICROCAP
ACCIMORU COUMARIC
ACCIMPSU CAPSICUM
ACCINOOS OCCASION
ACCINOOT COACTION
ACCINORT CRATONIC
NARCOTIC
ACCINORV CAVICORN
ACCINOTY CYANOTIC
ACCINRSU CRUCIANS
ACCINSSY CYCASINS
ACCIOOPP APOCOPIC
ACCIOPST SPICCATO
ACCIORST ACROSTIC
ACCIORSY ISOCRACY
ACCIOSTU ACOUSTIC
ACCIRRTT TRICTRAC
ACCIRSTY SCARCITY
ACCISSTU CAUSTICS
ACCKKRSU RUCKSACK
ACCKOOOP COCKAPOO
ACCKOOOT COCKATOO
ACCKOPRS CAPROCKS
ACCKOPRT CRACKPOT
ACCKORST STOCKCAR
ACCKOSSS CASSOCKS
COSSACKS
ACCKPRSU CRACKUPS
ACCLLNOY CYCLONAL
ACCLLOSU OCCLUSAL
ACCLLSUU CALCULUS
ACCLSSUU SACCULUS
ACCMNOSY CACONYMS
ACCMNOYY CACONYMY
ACCMOOST COCOMATS
ACCMOOSY COCOYAMS
ACCMOPST COMPACTS
ACCMOSTU ACCUSTOM
ACCMRSUU CURCUMAS
ACCNNOOS COONCANS
ACCNOORS RACCOONS
ACCNOOTU COCOANUT
ACCNOPTU OCCUPANT
ACCNORTT CONTRACT
ACCNOSTT CONTACTS
ACCNOSTU ACCOUNTS
ACCOORST COACTORS
ACCOPSTY COPYCATS
ACDDDEIS CADDISED
ACDDDEIT ADDICTED
ACDDDETU ADDUCTED
ACDDEEES DECEASED
ACDDEEHO COHEADED
ACDDEEHT DETACHED
ACDDEEIT DEDICATE
ACDDEEIU DECIDUAE
ACDDEEKR DACKERED
ACDDEELR DECLARED
ACDDEELW DECLAWED
ACDDEEMP DECAMPED
ACDDEENO DEACONED
ACDDEENR CREDENDA
ACDDEENS ASCENDED
ACDDEENT DECADENT
DECANTED
ACDDEERT REDACTED
ACDDEETU EDUCATED
ACDDEETV ADVECTED
ACDDEHKN DECKHAND
ACDDEHRS CHEDDARS
ACDDEHRY CHEDDARY
ACDDEIIL DEICIDAL
ACDDEIIM MEDICAID
ACDDEILU DECIDUAL
ACDDEINR CANDIDER
RIDDANCE
ACDDEINY CYANIDED
ACDDEIRT READDICT
ACDDEISS CADDISES
DISCASED
ACDDEISU DECIDUAS
ACDDEITT DICTATED
ACDDEKLO DEADLOCK
ACDDELOS CLADODES
ACDDENRU UNCARDED
ACDDENTU ADDUCENT
ACDDEOPS DECAPODS
ACDDEORR CORRADED
ACDDERSU ADDUCERS
CRUSADED
ACDDERTU TRADUCED
ACDDGILN CLADDING
ACDDGINU ADDUCING
ACDDGINY CADDYING
ACDDHHSU CHUDDAHS
ACDDHIRY HYDRACID
ACDDHKNO DOCKHAND
ACDDHKOS HADDOCKS
SHADDOCK
ACDDHRSU CHUDDARS
ACDDIIOR CARDIOID
ACDDILNY CANDIDLY
ACDDILRW WILDCARD
ACDDILTY DIDACTYL
ACDDINNU UNCANDID
ACDDIRSS DISCARDS
ACDDKLNO DOCKLAND
ACDDKOPS PADDOCKS
ACDDKORY DOCKYARD
ACDDORTU ADDUCTOR
ACDEEEFT DEFECATE
ACDEEEKS SEEDCAKE
ACDEEENR CAREENED
ACDEEENT ANTECEDE
ACDEEERR CAREERED
ACDEEERS DECREASE
ACDEEESS DECEASES
SEEDCASE
ACDEEFFT AFFECTED
ACDEEFIN DEFIANCE
ACDEEFIS CASEFIED
ACDEEFPR PREFACED
ACDEEFRS DEFACERS
ACDEEFRY FEDERACY
ACDEEFTT FACETTED
ACDEEGLY DELEGACY
ACDEEHIN ECHIDNAE
ACDEEHIV ACHIEVED
ACDEEHKO COKEHEAD
ACDEEHLP PLEACHED
ACDEEHLT CHELATED
ACDEEHMR DEMARCHE
ACDEEHNN ENHANCED
ACDEEHNS ENCASHED
ENCHASED
ACDEEHPR PREACHED
ACDEEHRS SEARCHED
ACDEEHRT DETACHER
RACHETED
ACDEEHST DETACHES
SACHETED
ACDEEIIP EPICEDIA
ACDEEILT DELICATE
ACDEEIMR CERAMIDE
MEDICARE
ACDEEIMT DECIMATE
MEDICATE
ACDEEINN DECENNIA
ENNEADIC
ACDEEINU AUDIENCE
ACDEEINV DEVIANCE
ACDEEIRS DECIARES
ACDEEJKT JACKETED
ACDEEKLR LACKERED
ACDEEKLY LACKEYED
ACDEEKNR CANKERED
ACDEEKPR REPACKED
ACDEEKPT PACKETED
ACDEEKRR RERACKED
ACDEEKRS SCREAKED
ACDEEKRT RACKETED
RETACKED
ACDEEKST CASKETED
ACDEELLR CELLARED
RECALLED
ACDEELLS CADELLES
ACDEELMP EMPLACED
ACDEELNR CALENDER
ACDEELNS CLEANSED
ACDEELNT LANCETED
ACDEELNV ENCLAVED
ACDEELOR COLEADER
RECOALED
ACDEELPR PARCELED
REPLACED
ACDEELRR DECLARER
ACDEELRS DECLARES
RESCALED
ACDEELRT DECRETAL
ACDEELRV CLAVERED
ACDEELSS DECLASSE
ACDEEMNP ENCAMPED
ACDEEMRS SCREAMED
ACDEEMRT CREMATED
ACDEEMSV MEDEVACS
ACDEENNP PENANCED
ACDEENNT TENDANCE
ACDEENNY CAYENNED
ACDEENOT ANECDOTE
ACDEENRS ASCENDER
REASCEND
ACDEENRT CANTERED
CRENATED
DECANTER
RECANTED
ACDEENRV CAVERNED
CRAVENED
ACDEENRY DECENARY
ACDEENRZ CREDENZA
ACDEENSV VENDACES
ACDEENTU CUNEATED
ACDEEOPS PEASECOD
ACDEEORT DECORATE
RECOATED
ACDEEPPR RECAPPED
ACDEEPRS ESCARPED
RESPACED
ACDEEPRT CARPETED
PREACTED
ACDEERRS SCAREDER
ACDEERRT CRATERED
RECRATED
RETRACED
TERRACED
ACDEERSS CARESSED
ACDEERSY DECAYERS
ACDEESTU EDUCATES
ACDEESUX CAUDEXES
ACDEFFLS SCLAFFED
ACDEFGIN DEFACING
ACDEFGOS DOGFACES
ACDEFIIL DEIFICAL
ACDEFIIP PACIFIED
ACDEFILN CANFIELD
ACDEFINN FINANCED
ACDEFINS FACIENDS
ACDEFNOW FACEDOWN
ACDEFNRU FURNACED
ACDEFORT FACTORED
ACDEFOTU OUTFACED
ACDEFRSU SURFACED
ACDEFRTU FURCATED
ACDEGGRS SCRAGGED
ACDEGIIL ALGICIDE
ACDEGIKM MAGICKED
ACDEGIMR DECIGRAM
GRIMACED
ACDEGINU GUIDANCE
ACDEGINY DECAYING
ACDEGIRS DISGRACE
ACDEGKOS DOCKAGES
ACDEGLLO COLLAGED
ACDEGLOS DECALOGS
ACDEGNOS DECAGONS
ACDEGNRU UNGRACED
ACDEGORS CORDAGES
ACDEHHNU HAUNCHED
ACDEHHRU HACHURED
ACDEHHTT DETHATCH
THATCHED
ACDEHIJK HIJACKED
ACDEHILR HERALDIC
ACDEHIMM CHAMMIED
ACDEHIMN MACHINED
ACDEHINR INARCHED
ACDEHINS ECHIDNAS
ACDEHIRS RACHIDES
ACDEHIRT TRACHEID
ACDEHIRV ARCHIVED
ACDEHKLO HEADLOCK
ACDEHKLS SHACKLED
ACDEHKOV HAVOCKED
ACDEHKRU ARCHDUKE
ACDEHKTW THWACKED
ACDEHLNR CHANDLER
ACDEHLNU LAUNCHED
ACDEHLOS COALSHED
ACDEHLRT TRACHLED
ACDEHLSS CHADLESS
ACDEHNOR ANCHORED
ACDEHNPU PAUNCHED
ACDEHNRU UNARCHED
ACDEHNRY ENDARCHY
ACDEHNST SNATCHED
STANCHED
ACDEHNSU UNCASHED
ACDEHNTU CHAUNTED
ACDEHORR HARDCORE
ACDEHORT CHORDATE
ACDEHOST CATHODES
ACDEHOUV AVOUCHED
ACDEHPRS SCARPHED
ACDEHPST DESPATCH
ACDEHPTU DEATHCUP
ACDEHRRS CHRESARD
ACDEHRST STARCHED
ACDEHTUW WAUCHTED
ACDEIILN ALCIDINE
ACDEIILS LAICISED
ACDEIILT CILIATED
ACDEIILZ LAICIZED
ACDEIIMU AECIDIUM
ACDEIINR ACRIDINE
ACDEIINS SCIAENID
ACDEIINT ACTINIDE
CTENIDIA
INDICATE
ACDEIIRT RATICIDE
ACDEIITV CAVITIED
VATICIDE
ACDEIJNU JAUNDICE
ACDEIKNP PANICKED
ACDEIKNT ANTICKED
ACDEIKPX PICKAXED
ACDEILLM MEDALLIC
ACDEILLS CEDILLAS
ACDEILLV CAVILLED
ACDEILMO MELODICA
ACDEILMS CAMELIDS
DECIMALS
DECLAIMS
MEDICALS
ACDEILMT MALEDICT
ACDEILMX CLIMAXED
ACDEILNP PANICLED
ACDEILNU DULCINEA
ACDEILPS DISPLACE
ACDEILPT PLICATED
ACDEILRS DECRIALS
RADICELS
RADICLES
ACDEILRT ARTICLED
LACERTID
ACDEILRU AURICLED
ACDEILST CITADELS
DIALECTS
ACDEILSY ECDYSIAL
ACDEILTT LATTICED
ACDEILTY DIACETYL
ACDEIMNO COMEDIAN
DAEMONIC
DEMONIAC
ACDEIMNP PANDEMIC
ACDEIMNT MEDICANT
ACDEIMOR COADMIRE
RACEMOID
ACDEIMPS MIDSPACE
ACDEIMPT IMPACTED
ACDEIMRT TIMECARD
ACDEIMST MISACTED
ACDEIMSV MEDIVACS
ACDEINNR CRANNIED
ACDEINNT INCANTED
ACDEINOP CANOPIED
ACDEINOS CODEINAS
DIOCESAN
ACDEINOT CATENOID
ACDEINOV VOIDANCE
ACDEINPT PEDANTIC
ACDEINRT DICENTRA
ACDEINSS ACIDNESS
ACDEINST DISTANCE
ACDEINSY CYANIDES
ACDEINTT NICTATED
ACDEINTU INCUDATE
ACDEINVY DEVIANCY
ACDEIORS IDOCRASE
ACDEIORT CERATOID

ACDEIORV COVARIED
ACDEIOSS ACIDOSES
ACDEIOSU EDACIOUS
ACDEIPRS PERACIDS
ACDEIPRT PICRATED
ACDEIPSS SPADICES
ACDEIPST SPICATED
ACDEIPSZ CAPSIZED
ACDEIQRU ACQUIRED
ACDEIRSS SIDECARS
ACDEIRST ACRIDEST
ACDEIRTT CITRATED
TETRACID
TETRADIC
ACDEISSS DISCASES
ACDEISTT DICTATES
ACDEKLNR CRANKLED
ACDEKLPS SPACKLED
ACDEKNPU UNPACKED
ACDEKNSU UNCASKED
ACDEKNTU UNTACKED
ACDEKOST STOCKADE
ACDEKRSY KEYCARDS
ACDELLNU UNCALLED
ACDELLOR CAROLLED
COLLARED
ACDELLOT COLLATED
ACDELLSU CALLUSED
ACDELMOR CLAMORED
ACDELMSU MUSCADEL
ACDELNOO CANOODLE
ACDELNOR COLANDER
CONELRAD
ACDELNOS CELADONS
ACDELNPU UNPLACED
ACDELNRS CANDLERS
ACDELNSU UNSCALED
ACDELNUW UNCLAWED
ACDELOOW LACEWOOD
ACDELOPS PEDOCALS
ACDELOPT CLODPATE
ACDELOPU CUPOLAED
ACDELPSU CAPSULED
UPSCALED
ACDELRRS CRADLERS
ACDELRSW SCRAWLED
ACDELRSY SACREDLY
ACDELSTU SULCATED
ACDELSWW DEWCLAWS
ACDEMMRS SCRAMMED
ACDEMNOR ROMANCED
ACDEMOPR COMPADRE
COMPARED
ACDEMORR CARROMED
ACDEMORS COMRADES
ACDEMORT DEMOCRAT
ACDEMPSU CAMPUSED
ACDEMSTU MUSCADET
ACDEMUUV VACUUMED
ACDENNNO CANNONED
NONDANCE
ACDENNNU UNCANNED
ACDENNOR ORDNANCE
ACDENNOT CANTONED
ACDENNST SCANDENT
ACDENOPR ENDOCARP
ACDENORR RANCORED
ACDENORS ENDOSARC
ACDENORT CARTONED
NOTECARD
ACDENORY CRAYONED
DEACONRY
ACDENOST ENDOCAST
TACNODES
ACDENOSY CYANOSED
ACDENOTT COATTEND
ACDENOTU OUTDANCE
UNCOATED
ACDENPPU UNCAPPED
ACDENPST PANDECTS
ACDENRSU DURANCES
ACDENRTU UNCARTED
UNCRATED
UNDERACT
UNTRACED
ACDENRUV UNCARVED
ACDENRVY VERDANCY
ACDENSST DESCANTS
ACDENSUU UNCAUSED
ACDEOPRS SCOREPAD
ACDEOPRY COPYREAD
ACDEOPSS PEASCODS
ACDEOPTU OUTPACED
ACDEORRS CORRADES
ACDEORRT REDACTOR
ACDEORST REDCOATS
ACDEORSU CAROUSED
ACDEORTU AERODUCT
EDUCATOR
OUTRACED
ACDEORTV CAVORTED
ACDEOSUV COUVADES
ACDEOTTU OUTACTED
ACDEPPRS SCRAPPED
ACDEPRTU CAPTURED
ACDEPSTU CUSPATED
ACDEQTUU AQUEDUCT
ACDERRSU CRUSADER
ACDERRTU TRADUCER
ACDERSSU CRUSADES
ACDERSTT DETRACTS
ACDERSTU TRADUCES
ACDFFHNU HANDCUFF
ACDFFIRT DIFFRACT
ACDFFLOS SCAFFOLD
ACDFIILU FIDUCIAL
ACDFILMR FILMCARD
ACDFILOU FUCOIDAL
ACDFINOR FRICANDO
ACDFIOST FACTOIDS
ACDGHOTW DOGWATCH
WATCHDOG
ACDGIILO DIALOGIC
ACDGILNN CANDLING
ACDGILNR CRADLING
ACDGILNS SCALDING
ACDGIMOT DOGMATIC
ACDGINNY CANDYING
ACDGINRS CARDINGS
ACDGIOPR PODAGRIC
ACDGKLOS DAGLOCKS
ACDGLNOO GOLCONDA
ACDGNOST CANTDOGS
ACDGORST DOGCARTS
ACDHIILS CHILIADS
ACDHIINT TACHINID
ACDHIIPS DIPHASIC
ACDHIKNP HANDPICK
ACDHIKOT KATHODIC
ACDHILNT THINCLAD
ACDHILPR PILCHARD
ACDHIMTW MIDWATCH
ACDHINOR HADRONIC
ACDHINSW SANDWICH
ACDHIOPS SCAPHOID
ACDHIOPY HYPOACID
ACDHIORY HYRACOID
ACDHIPST DISPATCH
ACDHIQRU CHARQUID
ACDHLNOR CHALDRON
CHLORDAN
ACDHMNTU DUTCHMAN
ACDHNOSW COWHANDS
ACDHOOTW WOODCHAT
ACDHOPRS POCHARDS
ACDHOPTU TOUCHPAD
ACDHORRS ORCHARDS
ACDIIINS INDICIAS
ACDIIIPR DIAPIRIC
ACDIIJLU JUDICIAL
ACDIIKLP PICKADIL
ACDIILMS DISCLAIM
ACDIILNO CONIDIAL
ACDIILOV OVICIDAL
ACDIILSU SUICIDAL
ACDIILTY DIALYTIC
ACDIIMNO DAIMONIC
ACDIIMOR DIORAMIC
ACDIIMOT DIATOMIC
ACDIIMSU ASCIDIUM
ACDIINNO CONIDIAN
ACDIINNS INDICANS
ACDIINNT INDICANT
ACDIINOT ACTINOID
DIATONIC
ACDIINPY PYCNIDIA
ACDIIOSS ACIDOSIS
ACDIIOSX OXIDASIC
ACDIIRST CARDITIS
TRIACIDS
TRIADICS
ACDIIRTY ACRIDITY
ACDIISST SADISTIC
ACDIKLTU DUCKTAIL
ACDILLOU CAUDILLO
ACDILLPY PLACIDLY
ACDILMOU MUCOIDAL
ACDILMSS CLADISMS
ACDILMTU TALMUDIC
ACDILNOO CONOIDAL
ACDILNOR IRONCLAD
ACDILNOT ANTICOLD
DALTONIC
ACDILNRY RANCIDLY
ACDILNSY SYNDICAL
ACDILNUU NUDICAUL
ACDILOPS PLACOIDS
ACDILORS CORDIALS
ACDILORT DICROTAL
ACDILOUV OVIDUCAL
ACDILPSU CUSPIDAL
ACDILRST TRICLADS
ACDILSST CLADISTS
ACDILSTW WILDCATS
ACDIMMSU CADMIUMS
ACDIMNOO MONOACID
ACDIMNOS MONACIDS
ACDIMNSU SCANDIUM
ACDIMNSY DYNAMICS
ACDIMOST COADMITS
ACDINNOO ANCONOID
ACDINNOS NONACIDS
ACDINNOY ANODYNIC
ACDINOPS SPONDAIC
ACDINORS SARDONIC
ACDINORT TORNADIC
ACDINORW CORDWAIN
ACDINSST DISCANTS
ACDINSTY DYNASTIC
ACDIOOTU AUTOCOID
ACDIOPRS PICADORS
SPORADIC
ACDIORRS CORRIDAS
ACDIORSS SARCOIDS
ACDIORST CAROTIDS
ACDIORTT DICTATOR
ACDIOSTY DYSTOCIA
ACDIOSXY OXYACIDS
ACDIPRST ADSCRIPT
ACDIPSTY DIPTYCAS
ACDIQRSU QUADRICS
ACDIRSTT DISTRACT
ACDIRTWY CITYWARD
ACDISTUV VIADUCTS
ACDJNSTU ADJUNCTS
ACDKKLUW DUCKWALK
ACDKLOPS PADLOCKS
ACDKMMOR DRAMMOCK
ACDKMPSU MUDPACKS
ACDLLORS COLLARDS
ACDLNOPR CROPLAND
ACDLNORS CALDRONS
ACDLNORU CAULDRON
CRUNODAL
ACDLNORY CONDYLAR
ACDLNSSU SUNSCALD
ACDLOOOR COLORADO
ACDLOORT DOCTORAL
ACDLORWY COWARDLY
ACDLSTUY DACTYLUS
ACDMMNOO COMMANDO
ACDMMNOS COMMANDS
ACDMNORY DORMANCY
MORDANCY
ACDMORSZ CZARDOMS
ACDMPRTU DUMPCART
ACDNOORS CARDOONS
ACDNOORT ACRODONT
ACDNOORV CORDOVAN
ACDNORSU CANDOURS
ACDNOSTW DOWNCAST
ACDNOSUU ADUNCOUS
ACDOOPPR PODOCARP
ACDOORST OSTRACOD
ACDOPRST POSTCARD
ACDORSST COSTARDS
ACDORSSU CRUSADOS
ACDORSUZ CRUZADOS
ACDRSSTU CUSTARDS
ACDRSTUY CUSTARDY
ACEEEFRR CAREFREE
ACEEEGLN ELEGANCE
ACEEEGPR CREEPAGE
ACEEEIPR EARPIECE
ACEEEIPS SEAPIECE
ACEEELMR CAMELEER
ACEEENRR CAREENER
ACEEENSV EVANESCE
ACEEEPSS ESCAPEES
ACEEERRR CAREERER
ACEEERRT RECREATE
ACEEERTT ETCETERA
ACEEERTX EXECRATE
ACEEESUV EVACUEES
ACEEFFIN CAFFEINE
ACEEFFOR FOREFACE
ACEEFFRS EFFACERS
ACEEFFRT AFFECTER
ACEEFHWY WHEYFACE
ACEEFILR LIFECARE
ACEEFINS FAIENCES
FIANCEES
ACEEFISS CASEFIES
ACEEFKOR ECOFREAK
ACEEFLPU PEACEFUL
ACEEFLSS FACELESS
ACEEFLTY FACETELY
ACEEFPRR PREFACER
ACEEFPRS PREFACES
ACEEFPRT PERFECTA
PRAEFECT
ACEEFPTY TYPEFACE
ACEEGHNR RECHANGE
ACEEGHNX EXCHANGE
ACEEGHRR RECHARGE
ACEEGIKL CAGELIKE
ACEEGILS ELEGIACS
LEGACIES
ACEEGINS AGENCIES
ACEEGINT AGENETIC
ACEEGIRZ GRAECIZE
ACEEGKRW WRECKAGE
ACEEGLNY ELEGANCY
ACEEGNNT TANGENCE
ACEEGNOZ COZENAGE
ACEEGNSV SCAVENGE
ACEEGORV COVERAGE
ACEEGOST ECOTAGES
ACEEGSSU ESCUAGES
ACEEHHST CHEETAHS
ACEEHILR LEACHIER
ACEEHINT ECHINATE
ACEEHIPR PEACHIER
ACEEHIPS CHEAPIES
ACEEHIPT PETECHIA
ACEEHIRT AETHERIC
HETAERIC
ACEEHIRV ACHIEVER
CHIVAREE
ACEEHISV ACHIEVES
ACEEHKOS HOECAKES
ACEEHLOS SHOELACE
ACEEHLPS PLEACHES
ACEEHLRS LEACHERS
ACEEHLST CHELATES
ACEEHLSW ESCHEWAL
ACEEHLTV CHEVALET
ACEEHMNP CAMPHENE
ACEEHMNR MENARCHE
ACEEHMRS CASHMERE
MACHREES
MARCHESE
ACEEHMST MACHETES
ACEEHNNR ENHANCER
ACEEHNNS ENHANCES
ACEEHNPS CHEAPENS
ACEEHNRS ENCHASER
ACEEHNRV REVANCHE
ACEEHNSS ENCASHES
ENCHASES
ACEEHOOT OOTHECAE
ACEEHOPT APOTHECE
ACEEHPRR PREACHER
ACEEHPRS PEACHERS
PREACHES
ACEEHPST CHEAPEST
ACEEHRRS REACHERS
RESEARCH
SEARCHER
ACEEHRSS SEARCHES
ACEEHRST CHEATERS
HECTARES
RECHEATS
TEACHERS
ACEEHRTT CATHETER
ACEEHSST ESCHEATS
ACEEHSTX CATHEXES
ACEEHTWY WATCHEYE
ACEEIKLL LACELIKE
ACEEIKLV CAVELIKE
ACEEIKMR ICEMAKER
ACEEIKNP PEACENIK
ACEEIKRR CREAKIER
ACEEILLM MICELLAE
ACEEILLP CALLIPEE
ACEEILMU LEUCEMIA
ACEEILNR RELIANCE
ACEEILNS SALIENCE
ACEEILPS CALIPEES
ESPECIAL
ACEEIMRR CREAMIER
REARMICE
RECAMIER
ACEEIMRS CASIMERE
ACEEIMRZ RACEMIZE
ACEEINNR NARCEINE
ACEEINPS SAPIENCE
ACEEINPT PATIENCE
ACEEINRS INCREASE
ACEEINRT CENTIARE
CREATINE
INCREATE
ITERANCE
ACEEINST CINEASTE
ACEEINSU EUCAINES
ACEEINTV ENACTIVE
ACEEIPPR PRAECIPE
ACEEIPST SPECIATE
ACEEIQRU ACQUIREE
ACEEIRRS CREASIER
ACEEIRSU CAUSERIE
ACEEIRSW WISEACRE
ACEEIRTV CREATIVE
REACTIVE
ACEEISTV VESICATE
ACEEJKRT REJACKET
ACEEKLMR MACKEREL
ACEEKLRT RETACKLE
ACEEKNPS KNEECAPS
ACEEKNRW NECKWEAR
ACEELLMT CELLMATE
ACEELLNS NACELLES
ACEELLNT LANCELET
ACEELLOT OCELLATE
ACEELLRR CELLARER
RECALLER
ACEELLRT CELLARET
ACEELLRV CREVALLE
ACEELLSS LACELESS
ACEELMNP PLACEMEN
ACEELMPS EMPLACES
ACEELMRS RECLAMES
ACEELNPR PRECLEAN
ACEELNPT PENTACLE
ACEELNRR LARCENER
ACEELNRS CLEANERS
CLEANSER
RECLEANS
ACEELNRU CERULEAN
ACEELNRV VERNACLE
ACEELNSS CLEANSES
ACEELNST CLEANEST
ACEELNSU NUCLEASE
ACEELNSV ENCLAVES
VALENCES
ACEELNTT TENTACLE
ACEELNTU NUCLEATE
ACEELOPS ESCALOPE
OPALESCE
ACEELORS ESCAROLE
ACEELORT CORELATE
RELOCATE
ACEELOSS SECALOSE
ACEELOSV VOCALESE
ACEELPPR PREPLACE
ACEELPRR PRECLEAR
REPLACER
ACEELPRS PERCALES
REPLACES
ACEELPRT PRAELECT
ACEELPST CAPELETS
ACEELPSY CYPSELAE
ACEELPTU PECULATE
ACEELPTY CLYPEATE
ACEELRRS CLEARERS
ACEELRSS CARELESS
RESCALES
ACEELRST CLEAREST
TREACLES
ACEELRSV CERVELAS
CLEAVERS
ACEELRTT RACLETTE
ACEELRTU ULCERATE
ACEELRTV CERVELAT
ACEELRTX EXCRETAL
ACEELSST CELESTAS
ACEELSSU EUCLASES
ACEELSTT TELECAST
ACEELSVX EXCLAVES
ACEEMMOT AMMOCETE
ACEEMNPS SPACEMEN
ACEEMNRS MENACERS
ACEEMNST CASEMENT
ACEEMOPR CAMPOREE
ACEEMOPT COPEMATE
ACEEMORS RACEMOSE
ACEEMORV OVERCAME
ACEEMRRS AMERCERS
CREAMERS
SCREAMER
ACEEMRRY CREAMERY
ACEEMRST CREMATES
ACEEMRTW CREWMATE
ACEENNPS PENANCES
ACEENNRT ENTRANCE
ACEENNST CANTEENS
ACEENNSY CAYENNES
ACEENOPT CONEPATE
ACEENORT CAROTENE
ACEENOST ACETONES
NOTECASE
ACEENPRR PARCENER
ACEENPRT PREENACT
ACEENRRT RECANTER
RECREANT
ACEENRSS CASERNES
ACEENRST CENTARES
REASCENT
REENACTS
SARCENET
ACEENRTU UNCREATE
ACEENSSS CASSENES
ACEENSTX EXSECANT
ACEEOQTU COEQUATE
ACEEOSSS CASEOSES
ACEEPRRS CAPERERS
ACEEPRRT RECARPET
ACEEPRSS ESCAPERS
RESPACES
ACEEPSST PECTASES
ACEEPSTT PECTATES
SPECTATE
ACEEPSTY TYPECASE
ACEERRRT RETRACER
ACEERRSS CARESSER
CREASERS
ACEERRST CATERERS
RECRATES
RETRACES
TERRACES
ACEERRSU ECRASEUR
ACEERRTU CREATURE
ACEERRUV VERRUCAE
ACEERSSS CARESSES
ACEERSST CATERESS
CERASTES
ACEERSSU SURCEASE
ACEERSSV CREVASSE
ACEERSTU SECATEUR
ACEERSTX EXACTERS
ACEERSVZ CERVEZAS
ACEERTTU ERUCTATE
ACEESSTT CASETTES
CASSETTE
ACEESTTX EXACTEST
ACEFFGIN EFFACING
ACEFFHIR CHAFFIER
ACEFFHIS AFFICHES
ACEFFHRS CHAFFERS
ACEFFHRU CHAUFFER
ACEFFILT FACELIFT
ACEFFINS CAFFEINS
ACEFFLLU FULLFACE
ACEFFLRS SCLAFFER
ACEFGINN ENFACING
ACEFGINR REFACING
ACEFGINT FACETING
ACEFGLRU GRACEFUL
ACEFGLSU CAGEFULS
ACEFHISV CAVEFISH
ACEFHMRS CHAMFERS
ACEFHORS ARCHFOES
ACEFHORU FAROUCHE
ACEFHRSU CHAUFERS
ACEFIIPR PACIFIER
ACEFIIPS PACIFIES
ACEFIIRT ARTIFICE
ACEFIKLL CALFLIKE
ACEFILLS ICEFALLS
ACEFILLY FACILELY
ACEFILOP EPIFOCAL
ACEFILOS FOCALISE
ACEFILOZ FOCALIZE
ACEFILRY FIRECLAY
ACEFIMNY FEMINACY
ACEFIMPR CAMPFIRE
ACEFINNS FINANCES
ACEFINRS FANCIERS
ACEFINRZ FRANCIZE
ACEFINSS FASCINES
ACEFINST FANCIEST
ACEFINSU UNIFACES
ACEFIOSS FIASCOES

ACEFIPRY REPACIFY
ACEFIRRT CRAFTIER
ACEFIRTT TRIFECTA
ACEFIRTY FERACITY
ACEFKLRY FLACKERY
ACEFLMNO FLAMENCO
ACEFLNOR FALCONER
ACEFLNOT CONFLATE
FALCONET
ACEFLORS ALFRESCO
ACEFLRUU FURCULAE
ACEFNORV CONFERVA
ACEFNRSU FURNACES
ACEFOOPT FOOTPACE
ACEFOORT FOOTRACE
ACEFOPST POSTFACE
ACEFORST FORECAST
ACEFOSTU OUTFACES
ACEFRRSS SCARFERS
ACEFRRST CRAFTERS
REFRACTS
ACEFRRSU FARCEURS
SURFACER
ACEFRRTU FRACTURE
ACEFRSSU SURFACES
ACEFRSTU FACTURES
FURCATES
ACEGGILN CAGELING
GLACEING
ACEGGINN ENCAGING
ACEGGIRR CRAGGIER
ACEGHIIT CHIGETAI
ACEGHILN LEACHING
ACEGHILT TEIGLACH
ACEGHINP PEACHING
ACEGHINR REACHING
ACEGHINT CHEATING
TEACHING
ACEGHLRU RUGELACH
ACEGHLUY GAUCHELY
ACEGHMOR ECHOGRAM
ACEGHNPU CHANGEUP
ACEGHNRS CHANGERS
ACEGHNRU UNCHARGE
ACEGHOSU GOUACHES
ACEGHOSW COWHAGES
ACEGHRRS CHARGERS
ACEGHSTU GAUCHEST
ACEGIINR REAGINIC
ACEGIINV VICINAGE
ACEGIKNR CREAKING
ACEGILLO COLLEGIA
ACEGILLR ALLERGIC
ACEGILMU MUCILAGE
ACEGILNN CLEANING
ENLACING
ACEGILNR CLEARING
RELACING
ACEGILNT CLEATING
ACEGILNV CLEAVING
ACEGILNW LACEWING
ACEGILPS PELAGICS
ACEGILRS GLACIERS
GRACILES
ACEGILSS GLACISES
ACEGILST GESTICAL
ACEGIMMT TAGMEMIC
ACEGIMNN MENACING
ACEGIMNO CAMEOING
ACEGIMNR AMERCING
CREAMING
GERMANIC
ACEGIMNS MAGNESIC
ACEGIMNT MAGNETIC
ACEGIMOX EXOGAMIC
ACEGIMRR GRIMACER
ACEGIMRS GRIMACES
ACEGIMTY MEGACITY
ACEGINNO CANOEING
ACEGINNR RECANING
ACEGINNS ENCASING
ACEGINNT ENACTING
ACEGINOS COINAGES
ACEGINOY GYNOECIA
ACEGINPR CAPERING
ACEGINPS ESCAPING
ACEGINRS CREASING
ACEGINRT ARGENTIC
CATERING
CREATING
REACTING
ACEGINSS CAGINESS
ACEGINTX EXACTING
ACEGIOTT COGITATE

ACEGIRST AGRESTIC
CIGARETS
ERGASTIC
ACEGJKLS JACKLEGS
ACEGKLOS LOCKAGES
ACEGKLOV GAVELOCK
ACEGKLRS GRACKLES
ACEGKORS CORKAGES
ACEGKOST STOCKAGE
ACEGKRTU TRUCKAGE
ACEGLLNO COLLAGEN
ACEGLLOS COLLAGES
ACEGLNOS CONGEALS
ACEGLNOT OCTANGLE
ACEGLNOY AGLYCONE
ACEGLNRS CLANGERS
GLANCERS
ACEGMNOY GEOMANCY
ACEGMNRS CRAGSMEN
ACEGMRRY GRAMERCY
ACEGNNOR CRANNOGE
ACEGNNOY CYANOGEN
ACEGNNRY REGNANCY
ACEGNNTY TANGENCY
ACEGNORS ACROGENS
ACEGNOST COAGENTS
COGNATES
ACEGORSS CORSAGES
SOCAGERS
ACEGORST ESCARGOT
ACEGORSU COURAGES
ACEGORTT COTTAGER
ACEGORTY CATEGORY
ACEGOSTT COTTAGES
ACEGOTTY COTTAGEY
ACEGSSTU SCUTAGES
ACEGSTTU CUTTAGES
ACEHHIPS CHEAPISH
ACEHHIRR HIERARCH
ACEHHISU HUISACHE
ACEHHLST HATCHELS
ACEHHMNN HENCHMAN
ACEHHNRT ETHNARCH
ACEHHNSU HAUNCHES
ACEHHPRT HEPTARCH
ACEHHRST HATCHERS
ACEHHRSU HACHURES
ACEHHRTT THATCHER
ACEHHRTY HATCHERY
THEARCHY
ACEHHRXY HEXARCHY
ACEHHSTT HATCHETS
THATCHES
ACEHIIMS ISCHEMIA
ACEHIINT ETHICIAN
ACEHIIRT HIERATIC
ACEHIJKR HIJACKER
ACEHIJNT JACINTHE
ACEHIKLR CHALKIER
HACKLIER
ACEHIKRW WHACKIER
ACEHILLS CHALLIES
ACEHILMN INCHMEAL
ACEHILMY LECHAYIM
ACEHILNP CEPHALIN
ACEHILNT ETHNICAL
ACEHILOR HEROICAL
ACEHILPR PARHELIC
ACEHILRS CHARLIES
ACEHILST ETHICALS
ACEHILTT ATHLETIC
THETICAL
ACEHIMMS CHAMMIES
ACEHIMNN CHAINMEN
ACEHIMNP CAMPHINE
ACEHIMNR CHAIRMEN
ACEHIMNS MACHINES
ACEHIMNT ANTHEMIC
ACEHIMPR CAMPHIRE
ACEHIMPT EMPATHIC
EMPHATIC
ACEHIMRS CHIMERAS
MARCHESI
ACEHIMRT RHEMATIC
ACEHIMSS CHAMISES
ACEHIMST HEMATICS
MASTICHE
MISTEACH
TACHISME
ACEHIMTT THEMATIC
ACEHIMTZ MECHITZA
ACEHINNS ENCHAINS
ACEHINOT INCHOATE
ACEHINPS PAINCHES
ACEHINPT HAPTENIC

ACEHINRS ARCHINES
INARCHES
ACEHINSS ACHINESS
ACEHINST ASTHENIC
CHANTIES
ACEHIOPR POACHIER
ACEHIOST ACHIOTES
ACEHIPPS CHAPPIES
ACEHIPRS ASPHERIC
PARCHESI
SERAPHIC
ACEHIPRT CHAPITER
PATCHIER
PHREATIC
ACEHIPST HEPATICS
PASTICHE
PISTACHE
ACEHIPTT PATHETIC
ACEHIPTW WHITECAP
ACEHIQSU QUAICHES
ACEHIRRR CHARRIER
ACEHIRSS CASHIERS
RACHISES
ACEHIRST CHARIEST
THERIACS
ACEHIRSU EUCHARIS
ACEHIRSV ARCHIVES
ACEHIRTT CHATTIER
THEATRIC
ACEHISST CHASTISE
ACEHISSU CHIAUSES
ACEHISTT TACHISTE
ACEHISTX CATHEXIS
ACEHKLLS SHELLACK
ACEHKLOV HAVELOCK
ACEHKLPR KREPLACH
ACEHKLRS HACKLERS
SHACKLER
ACEHKLSS SHACKLES
ACEHKLST KLATCHES
ACEHKLTY LATCHKEY
ACEHKNSY HACKNEYS
ACEHKOPS SHOEPACK
ACEHKORV HAVOCKER
ACEHKOSS SHACKOES
ACEHKOST HOTCAKES
ACEHKOTU TUCKAHOE
ACEHKRSW WHACKERS
ACEHKRTW THWACKER
ACEHLLOO COALHOLE
ACEHLLSS SHELLACS
ACEHLLST HELLCATS
ACEHLLSU HALLUCES
ACEHLNNS CHANNELS
ACEHLNOS CHALONES
ACEHLNOU EULACHON
ACEHLNPS PLANCHES
ACEHLNPT PLANCHET
ACEHLNRS CHARNELS
ACEHLNRU LAUNCHER
RELAUNCH
ACEHLNSU LAUNCHES
ACEHLOOT OOTHECAL
ACEHLOPT POTLACHE
ACEHLORS CHOLERAS
CHORALES
ACEHLORT CHELATOR
CHLORATE
TROCHLEA
ACEHLOST CHOLATES
ESCHALOT
ACEHLPST CHAPLETS
ACEHLRSS CLASHERS
ACEHLRST TRACHLES
ACEHLRSY CHARLEYS
ACEHLRTU TRAUCHLE
ACEHLSSS CASHLESS
ACEHLSST SATCHELS
SLATCHES
ACEHLSTT CHATTELS
LATCHETS
ACEHLSTY CHASTELY
ACEHMNNR RANCHMEN
ACEHMNOR CHOREMAN
ACEHMNRT MERCHANT
ACEHMNSS CHESSMAN
ACEHMNST MANCHETS
ACEHMNTW WATCHMEN
ACEHMNTY YACHTMEN
ACEHMORT CHROMATE
ACEHMOST MOSCHATE
ACEHMPRS CHAMPERS
ACEHMRRS CHARMERS
MARCHERS
ACEHMRSS SCHMEARS
ACEHMRST MATCHERS

ACEHMSTT SCHMATTE
ACEHMSTU MUSTACHE
ACEHNNOT NANOTECH
ACEHNNPT PENCHANT
ACEHNNST ENCHANTS
ACEHNOPR CANEPHOR
CHAPERON
ACEHNOPS PANOCHES
ACEHNOPT CENOTAPH
ACEHNORR RANCHERO
ACEHNORT ANCHORET
ACEHNPRT PENTARCH
ACEHNPSU PAUNCHES
ACEHNRRS RANCHERS
ACEHNRSS ARCHNESS
ACEHNRST CHANTERS
SNATCHER
STANCHER
TRANCHES
ACEHNRSU RAUNCHES
ACEHNRSW CRENSHAW
ACEHNRTU CHAUNTER
ACEHNSST CHASTENS
SNATCHES
STANCHES
ACEHNSTT ETCHANTS
ACEHNSTU NAUTCHES
UNCHASTE
ACEHNSTY CHANTEYS
ACEHNSZZ CHAZZENS
ACEHOPPR COPPERAH
ACEHOPRR REPROACH
ACEHOPRS POACHERS
ACEHOPSS SHOEPACS
ACEHORRS HORSECAR
ACEHORRV OVERARCH
ACEHORST THORACES
ACEHORTT THEOCRAT
ACEHORTU OUTREACH
ACEHORUV AVOUCHER
ACEHOSSW SHOWCASE
ACEHOSTU CATHOUSE
SOUTACHE
ACEHOSTY CHAYOTES
ACEHOSUV AVOUCHES
ACEHOTTU OUTCHEAT
ACEHPPSS SCHAPPES
ACEHPRRS PRECRASH
ACEHPRST CHAPTERS
PATCHERS
ACEHPRSU PURCHASE
ACEHPSTY SCYPHATE
ACEHRRSS CRASHERS
ACEHRRST CHARTERS
RECHARTS
ACEHRRTT TETRARCH
ACEHRSST STARCHES
ACEHRSSU CHASSEUR
ACEHRSTT CHATTERS
RATCHETS
ACEHRSTW WATCHERS
ACEHRSTY YACHTERS
ACEHRTTY CHATTERY
TRACHYTE
ACEHSSSU CHAUSSES
ACEHSSTT CHASTEST
ACEHSSTW SWATCHES
ACEIIKNT AKINETIC
ACEIILMN LIMACINE
ACEIILNR IRENICAL
ACEIILNS SALICINE
ACEIILSS LAICISES
ACEIILST CILIATES
SILICATE
ACEIILSZ LAICIZES
ACEIIMRS CASIMIRE
ACEIIMST METICAIS
ACEIIMTU MAIEUTIC
ACEIINPS PISCINAE
ACEIINST CANITIES
ACEIINTV INACTIVE
ACEIIPRS PIRACIES
ACEIIPSS EPISCIAS
ACEIIPTX EPITAXIC
ACEIIRRT CRITERIA
ACEIISTU ACUITIES
ACEIISTV CAVITIES
ACEIITTZ ATTICIZE
ACEIITVZ ACTIVIZE
ACEIJMST MAJESTIC
ACEIJNRR JERRICAN
ACEIKKLS SACKLIKE
ACEIKLLM CLAMLIKE
MILLCAKE
ACEIKLLW CLAWLIKE
ACEIKLLY CLAYLIKE

ACEIKLNR CLANKIER
ACEIKLRY CREAKILY
ACEIKMNN NICKNAME
ACEIKMRS KERAMICS
ACEIKMRV MAVERICK
ACEIKNPS CAPESKIN
ACEIKNRR CRANKIER
ACEIKNSS CAKINESS
ACEIKORR CROAKIER
ACEIKPSW WICKAPES
ACEIKPSX PICKAXES
ACEIKQRU QUACKIER
ACEIKSTT TACKIEST
ACEIKSTW WACKIEST
ACEILLLT CLITELLA
ACEILLMR MICELLAR
MILLRACE
ACEILLMT METALLIC
ACEILLMY MYCELIAL
ACEILLNT CLIENTAL
ACEILLOP CALLIOPE
ACEILLOR ROCAILLE
ACEILLOS LOCALISE
ACEILLOT LOCALITE
TEOCALLI
ACEILLOZ LOCALIZE
ACEILLPR CALLIPER
ACEILLPS ALLSPICE
ACEILLPY EPICALLY
ACEILLRV CAVILLER
ACEILMMO CAMOMILE
ACEILMMR CLAMMIER
ACEILMNP MANCIPLE
ACEILMNS MELANICS
MENISCAL
ACEILMNY MYCELIAN
ACEILMOS CAMISOLE
ACEILMPS MISPLACE
ACEILMRS CLAIMERS
MIRACLES
RECLAIMS
ACEILMRT METRICAL
ACEILMRY CREAMILY
ACEILMST CLEMATIS
CLIMATES
METICALS
ACEILMSU MUSICALE
ACEILMSX CLIMAXES
EXCLAIMS
ACEILNNP PINNACLE
ACEILNOR ACROLEIN
COLINEAR
ACEILNPS CAPELINS
PANICLES
PELICANS
ACEILNRS CARLINES
LANCIERS
ACEILNRT CLARINET
ACEILNSS LACINESS
SANICLES
ACEILNST CANISTEL
ACEILNSU LUNACIES
ACEILNSY SALIENCY
ACEILOPR CAPRIOLE
ACEILOPT POETICAL
ACEILORR CARRIOLE
ACEILORS CALORIES
CARIOLES
ACEILORT EROTICAL
LORICATE
ACEILORZ CALORIZE
ACEILOSS CELOSIAS
ACEILOST COALIEST
SOCIETAL
ACEILOSU EUSOCIAL
ACEILOSV VOCALISE
ACEILOTV LOCATIVE
ACEILOVZ VOCALIZE
ACEILPRS CALIPERS
REPLICAS
SPIRACLE
ACEILPRT PARTICLE
PRELATIC
ACEILPRU PECULIAR
ACEILPSS SLIPCASE
SPECIALS
ACEILPST SEPTICAL
TIECLASP
ACEILPSU SPICULAE
ACEILPXY EPICALYX
ACEILRRW CRAWLIER
ACEILRSS CLASSIER
ACEILRST ARTICLES
RECITALS
STERICAL
ACEILRSU AURICLES

ACEILRSV CAVILERS
CLAVIERS
VISCERAL
ACEILRTT TRACTILE
ACEILRTU RETICULA
ACEILRTV VERTICAL
ACEILRTY LITERACY
ACEILRUV ACERVULI
ACEILSST ELASTICS
SCALIEST
ACEILSTT LATTICES
ACEILSTY CLAYIEST
ACEILSUV VESICULA
ACEILSVW WAVICLES
ACEILTVY ACTIVELY
ACEIMMNP PEMMICAN
ACEIMMOS SEMICOMA
ACEIMMRS RACEMISM
ACEIMNNO MONECIAN
ACEIMNOT COINMATE
ACEIMNOX ANOXEMIC
ACEIMNPS PEMICANS
ACEIMNRS CARMINES
CREMAINS
ACEIMNRU MANICURE
ACEIMNSS AMNESICS
ACEIMNST AMNESTIC
SEMANTIC
ACEIMNSY SYCAMINE
ACEIMNTU NEUMATIC
ACEIMOPR COPREMIA
ACEIMOTX TOXAEMIC
ACEIMOTZ AZOTEMIC
METAZOIC
ACEIMPRR CRAMPIER
ACEIMPRS PARECISM
SAPREMIC
ACEIMPRT IMPACTER
ACEIMPSS ESCAPISM
MISSPACE
SCAMPIES
ACEIMPST CAMPIEST
CAMPSITE
ACEIMRST CERAMIST
MATRICES
MISTRACE
SCIMETAR
ACEIMRTU MURICATE
ACEIMSST CASTEISM
ACEIMSSU CAESIUMS
ACEIMSTU AUTECISM
ACEINNOS CANONISE
ACEINNOZ CANONIZE
ACEINNPS PINNACES
ACEINNRS CRANNIES
NARCEINS
ACEINNST ANCIENTS
CANNIEST
INSECTAN
INSTANCE
ACEINNSU NUISANCE
ACEINNSY CYANINES
ACEINNTU UNCINATE
ACEINOPR APOCRINE
CAPONIER
PROCAINE
ACEINOPS CANOPIES
ACEINOPZ CAPONIZE
ACEINORS SCENARIO
ACEINORT ACTIONER
ANORETIC
CREATION
REACTION
ACEINORV VERONICA
ACEINORX ANOREXIC
ACEINOST ACONITES
CANOEIST
SONICATE
ACEINOTT TACONITE
ACEINOTV CONATIVE
INVOCATE
ACEINOTX EXACTION
ACEINPQU PIQUANCE
ACEINPSS INSCAPES
ACEINPSY SAPIENCY
ACEINPTT PITTANCE
ACEINPUY PICAYUNE
ACEINRRU CURARINE
ACEINRRY CINERARY
ACEINRSS ARCSINES
ARSENICS
RACINESS

ACEINRST CANISTER
CERATINS
CISTERNA
CREATINS
SCANTIER
TACRINES
ACEINRTT INTERACT
ACEINRTU ANURETIC
ACEINRTV NAVICERT
ACEINRVY VICENARY
ACEINSSS CASSINES
ACEINSST CINEASTS
SCANTIES
ACEINSSU ISSUANCE
ACEINSTT ENTASTIC
NICTATES
TETANICS
ACEINSTV VESICANT
ACEINSTY CYANITES
ACEINSTZ ZINCATES
ACEINTTU TUNICATE
ACEINTTX EXCITANT
ACEINTTY TENACITY
ACEIOPRT OPERATIC
ACEIOPST ECTOPIAS
ACEIOPVW PICOWAVE
ACEIORSS SCARIOSE
ACEIORSV COVARIES
VARICOSE
ACEIOTVV VOCATIVE
ACEIPPRR CRAPPIER
PERICARP
ACEIPPRS CRAPPIES
EPICARPS
ACEIPRRS PERISARC
ACEIPRSS SCRAPIES
ACEIPRST CRISPATE
PARETICS
PICRATES
PRACTISE
ACEIPRTY APYRETIC
ACEIPSST ESCAPIST
SPACIEST
ACEIPSSU AUSPICES
ACEIPSSZ CAPSIZES
ACEIPSTV CAPTIVES
ACEIQRRU ACQUIRER
ACEIQRSU ACQUIRES
ACEIQSUZ CAZIQUES
ACEIRRRS CARRIERS
SCARRIER
ACEIRRST ERRATICS
ACEIRRSW AIRCREWS
AIRSCREW
ACEIRRUZ CURARIZE
ACEIRSST SCARIEST
ACEIRSSU SAUCIERS
ACEIRSTT CITRATES
CRISTATE
SCATTIER
ACEIRSTU SURICATE
ACEIRSTZ CRAZIEST
ACEIRTTU URTICATE
ACEIRTTV TRACTIVE
ACEIRTUV CURATIVE
ACEIRTVY VERACITY
ACEISSSS CASSISES
ACEISSTT STATICES
ACEISSTU SAUCIEST
SUITCASE
ACEISTTT CATTIEST
ACEISTTU EUSTATIC
ACEISTUX AUXETICS
ACEJKOOR JACKEROO
ACEJLORS CAJOLERS
ACEJLORY CAJOLERY
ACEJMRST SCRAMJET
ACEJNOST JACONETS
ACEJNOSY JOYANCES
ACEJNRRY JERRYCAN
ACEJPSTU CAJEPUTS
ACEJRSTT TRAJECTS
ACEKKMRU MUCKRAKE
ACEKKNRS KNACKERS
ACEKKNRY KNACKERY
ACEKLNRS CRANKLES
ACEKLNSS SLACKENS
ACEKLORS EARLOCKS
ACEKLORV LAVEROCK
ACEKLORW LACEWORK
ACEKLPSS SPACKLES
ACEKLPST PLACKETS
ACEKLRSS SLACKERS
ACEKLRST TACKLERS
ACEKLRSU CAULKERS
ACEKLSST SLACKEST
TACKLESS
ACEKMNRT TRACKMEN
ACEKMORS COMAKERS
ACEKMRSS SMACKERS
ACEKNPRU UNPACKER
ACEKNPSS PACKNESS
ACEKNRSS SNACKERS
ACEKNRST CRANKEST
ACEKOORT CARETOOK
ACEKOORW COOKWARE
ACEKOPRV OVERPACK
ACEKOPRW CAPEWORK
ACEKORRS CROAKERS
ACEKORSW CASEWORK
ACEKPPRS PREPACKS
ACEKQRUY QUACKERY
ACEKRRST RETRACKS
TRACKERS
ACEKRSST RESTACKS
STACKERS
ACEKSSUW WAESUCKS
ACELLLRU CELLULAR
ACELLMOS CALOMELS
ACELLNRU NUCELLAR
ACELLOPS COLLAPSE
ESCALLOP
ACELLORR CAROLLER
ACELLORT COLLARET
ACELLORV COVERALL
OVERCALL
ACELLORW CALLOWER
ACELLOSS CALLOSES
COALLESS
ACELLOST COLLATES
ACELLOSW COLESLAW
ACELLOTU LOCULATE
ACELLOVY COEVALLY
ACELLPSS SCALPELS
ACELLRRS CARRELLS
ACELLRTY RECTALLY
ACELLSSU CALLUSES
ACELLSSW CLAWLESS
ACELLSTU SCUTELLA
ACELMMRS CLAMMERS
ACELMNNS CLANSMEN
ACELMNOR AMELCORN
CORNMEAL
ACELMNOU COLUMNEA
ACELMNSS CALMNESS
ACELMOPT COMPLEAT
ACELMORR CLAMORER
ACELMORS SCLEROMA
ACELMORY CLAYMORE
ACELMOSU LEUCOMAS
ACELMPRS CLAMPERS
ACELMSTU CALUMETS
MUSCATEL
ACELMTUU CUMULATE
ACELNNNO CANNELON
ACELNNOS ALENCONS
ACELNNRS SCRANNEL
ACELNOOT ECOTONAL
ACELNOPT CONEPATL
ACELNORV NOVERCAL
ACELNOSS SECONALS
ACELNOST LACTONES
ACELNOSU LACUNOSE
ACELNOSZ CALZONES
ACELNOTV COVALENT
ACELNPSS ENCLASPS
SPANCELS
ACELNPSU CLEANUPS
ACELNRST CENTRALS
ACELNRSU LUCARNES
ACELNRVY CRAVENLY
ACELNSSU SCALENUS
ACELNSTY SECANTLY
ACELOOSU ACOELOUS
ACELOPPU POPULACE
ACELOPRS PARCLOSE
ACELOPRT PECTORAL
ACELOPRU OPERCULA
ACELOPSS ESCALOPS
ACELOPST POLECATS
ACELOPSU SCOPULAE
ACELOPTU COPULATE
OUTPLACE
ACELOPTY CALOTYPE
ACELOQSU COEQUALS
ACELORRS CAROLERS
ACELORSS ESCOLARS
LACROSSE
SOLACERS
ACELORST LOCATERS
SECTORAL
ACELORSU CAROUSEL
ACELORSY CALOYERS
COARSELY
ACELOSST COATLESS
LACTOSES
ACELOSTT CALOTTES
ACELOSTU LACTEOUS
LOCUSTAE
OSCULATE
ACELOSTY ACOLYTES
ACELOSUV VACUOLES
ACELOTXY ACETOXYL
ACELPPRS CLAPPERS
SCRAPPLE
ACELPRSS CLASPERS
RECLASPS
SCALPERS
ACELPRST SCEPTRAL
SPECTRAL
ACELPRSU SPECULAR
ACELPRTY CALYPTER
ACELPSSU CAPSULES
SCALEUPS
UPSCALES
ACELPTUU CUPULATE
ACELPTUY EUCALYPT
ACELQRSU CLAQUERS
LACQUERS
ACELQRUU CLAQUEUR
ACELQSUY LACQUEYS
ACELRRSW CRAWLERS
SCRAWLER
ACELRSSS CLASSERS
SCARLESS
ACELRSST SCARLETS
ACELRSSU RECUSALS
SECULARS
ACELRSTT CLATTERS
ACELRTTU CULTRATE
ACELRTTY CLATTERY
ACELSSTT TACTLESS
ACELSSTU CUTLASES
ACEMMOTY MYCETOMA
ACEMMRRS CRAMMERS
ACEMMRSS SCAMMERS
ACEMNOOR COENAMOR
ACEMNORR ROMANCER
ACEMNORS ROMANCES
ACEMNRUY NUMERACY
ACEMOORS ACROSOME
ACEMOOST COMATOSE
ACEMOPRR COMPARER
ACEMOPRS CAPSOMER
COMPARES
MESOCARP
ACEMOPRT MERCAPTO
ACEMORRT CREMATOR
ACEMORRV OVERCRAM
ACEMORSU RACEMOUS
ACEMORSW CASEWORM
ACEMORSY SYCAMORE
ACEMORTY COMETARY
ACEMORUX MORCEAUX
ACEMOSSU COASSUME
ACEMPRSS SCAMPERS
ACEMPSSU CAMPUSES
ACEMRSST SCAMSTER
ACENNNOU ANNOUNCE
ACENNOSS CANONESS
SONANCES
ACENNOSZ CANZONES
ACENNOTT COTENANT
ACENNOTV COVENANT
ACENNOTZ CANZONET
ACENNRSS SCANNERS
ACENOORT CORONATE
ACENOOTZ ECTOZOAN
ACENOPRT COPARENT
PORTANCE
ACENOPST CAPSTONE
OPENCAST
ACENOQTU COTQUEAN
ACENORRW CAREWORN
ACENORRY CRAYONER
ACENORSS COARSENS
NARCOSES
ACENORST ANCESTOR
ENACTORS
ACENORSU NACREOUS
ACENORTU COURANTE
OUTRANCE
ACENORTY ENACTORY
ACENOSST CONTESSA
ACENOSSY CYANOSES
ACENOSTV CENTAVOS
ACENPRRS PRANCERS
ACENPTTU PUNCTATE
ACENRSTT TRANSECT
ACENRSTU CENTAURS
RECUSANT
UNCRATES
ACENRSTY ANCESTRY
ACENRTTU TRUNCATE
ACENRTUY CENTAURY
ACENSSTT SCANTEST
ACENSSTU NUTCASES
ACENSSTW NEWSCAST
ACENSSUU USAUNCES
ACEOOPPS APOCOPES
ACEOOPSU POACEOUS
ACEOORTT COROTATE
ACEOORTV EVOCATOR
OVERCOAT
ACEOPPRS COPPERAS
ACEOPRST POSTRACE
ACEOPRSX EXOCARPS
ACEOPRTU OUTCAPER
ACEOPSTU OUTPACES
SAUCEPOT
ACEORRST CREATORS
REACTORS
ACEORRSU CAROUSER
ACEORRTT RETROACT
ACEORRTV CAVORTER
ACEORSST COARSEST
COASTERS
ACEORSSU CAROUSES
ACEORSTU OUTRACES
ACEORSTV OVERACTS
OVERCAST
ACEORSTX EXACTORS
ACEOSSTU SEASCOUT
ACEOSTTT COATTEST
ACEOSTTU OUTCASTE
ACEOSTTV CAVETTOS
ACEOTUUX COUTEAUX
ACEPPRRS SCRAPPER
ACEPRRSS SCARPERS
SCRAPERS
ACEPRRSU SUPERCAR
ACEPRRTU CAPTURER
ACEPRSST PRECASTS
ACEPRSSU SCAUPERS
ACEPRSTU CAPTURES
ACEPSTTY TYPECAST
ACEQRSTU RACQUETS
ACEQSSTU ACQUESTS
ACERRSTT RETRACTS
ACERRSUV VERRUCAS
ACERSSST CRASSEST
ACERSSSU SUCRASES
ACERSSTT SCATTERS
ACERSSTY ACTRESSY
ACERSTTX EXTRACTS
ACERSTTY CYTASTER
ACERTTUW CUTWATER
ACFFGHIN CHAFFING
ACFFIILO OFFICIAL
ACFFIIST CAITIFFS
ACFFIKMS MAFFICKS
ACFFILNU FANCIFUL
ACFFILST AFFLICTS
ACFFIRST TRAFFICS
ACFFKORT OFFTRACK
ACFFLOSW SCOFFLAW
ACFFOSST CASTOFFS
OFFCASTS
ACFGHITT CATFIGHT
ACFGIIMN MAGNIFIC
ACFGIIPR CAPRIFIG
ACFGIKLN FLACKING
ACFGINNY FANCYING
ACFGINRS SCARFING
ACFGINRT CRAFTING
ACFGITUY FUGACITY
ACFHHINW HAWFINCH
ACFHIJKS JACKFISH
ACFHILNO FALCHION
ACFHILOS COALFISH
ACFHIRSW CRAWFISH
ACFHIRSY CRAYFISH
ACFHISSU FUCHSIAS
ACFHLTUW WATCHFUL
ACFHMNOR CHAMFRON
ACFHNNOR CHANFRON
ACFHRSTU FUTHARCS
ACFIILSV SALVIFIC
ACFIILTY FACILITY
ACFIIMPS PACIFISM
ACFIIPST PACIFIST
ACFIISST FASCITIS
ACFIKLNS CALFSKIN
ACFILLSY FISCALLY
ACFILNOR FORNICAL
ACFILNOS FOLACINS
ACFILORT TRIFOCAL
ACFILOTU CLAFOUTI
ACFILRTY CRAFTILY
ACFILSSY CLASSIFY
ACFIMNRU FRANCIUM
ACFIMORR ARCIFORM
ACFIMORS FORMICAS
ACFIMSSS FASCISMS
ACFINORT FRACTION
ACFINOST FACTIONS
ACFINPRS SCARFPIN
ACFINRST INFARCTS
INFRACTS
ACFINSTY SANCTIFY
ACFIOSTU FACTIOUS
ACFISSST FASCISTS
ACFKLLOR ROCKFALL
ACFKLRSU RACKFULS
ACFKLRUW WRACKFUL
ACFKLSSU SACKFULS
SACKSFUL
ACFKOSTT FATSTOCK
ACFLMNOO MOONCALF
ACFLNNOO NONFOCAL
ACFLNORY FALCONRY
ACFLOOPS FOOLSCAP
ACFLOPSW COWFLAPS
ACFLORSU SCROFULA
ACFLRRUU FURCULAR
ACFMOTTU FACTOTUM
ACFNNOST NONFACTS
ACFRRSTU FRACTURS
ACGGGILN CLAGGING
ACGGHINN CHANGING
ACGGHINR CHARGING
ACGGHLUU CHUGALUG
ACGGIINN INCAGING
ACGGIINT GIGANTIC
ACGGIIOS ISAGOGIC
ACGGILNN CLANGING
GLANCING
ACGGILRY CRAGGILY
ACGGINNO CONGAING
ACGGINNU UNCAGING
ACGGLNOU GLUCAGON
ACGGLRSY SCRAGGLY
ACGHHIJK HIGHJACK
ACGHHINT HATCHING
ACGHIINN CHAINING
ACGHIINR CHAIRING
ACGHIKLN CHALKING
HACKLING
ACGHIKNR CHARKING
ACGHIKNS SHACKING
ACGHIKNT THACKING
ACGHIKNW WHACKING
ACGHILNS CLASHING
ACGHILNT LATCHING
ACGHILNY ACHINGLY
ACGHILOR OLIGARCH
ACGHIMNP CHAMPING
ACGHIMNR CHARMING
MARCHING
ACGHIMNT MATCHING
ACGHINNR RANCHING
ACGHINNT CHANTING
ACGHINOP POACHING
ACGHINOR ROACHING
ACGHINPP CHAPPING
ACGHINPR PARCHING
ACGHINPT NIGHTCAP
PATCHING
ACGHINRR CHARRING
ACGHINRS ARCHINGS
CHAGRINS
CRASHING
ACGHINRT CHARTING
ACGHINSS CHASINGS
ACGHINST SCATHING
ACGHINSW CHINWAGS
ACGHINTT CHATTING
ACGHINTW WATCHING
ACGHINTY YACHTING
ACGHIPRS GRAPHICS
ACGHIRSS SCRAIGHS
ACGHLMOO LOGOMACH
ACGHLSTU CLAUGHTS
ACGHNRYY GYNARCHY
ACGHNTUU UNCAUGHT
ACGHORSU CHORAGUS
ACGHRRSU CURRAGHS
ACGIILMN CLAIMING
ACGIILNN INLACING
ACGIILNO LOGICIAN
ACGIILNU LINGUICA
ACGIILNV CAVILING
ACGIILRS GRACILIS
ACGIINNS INCASING
ACGIINRT GRANITIC
ACGIJLNO CAJOLING
ACGIJNNU JAUNCING
ACGIKKNN KNACKING
ACGIKLMN MACKLING
ACGIKLNN CLANKING
ACGIKLNO CLOAKING
ACGIKLNS CALKINGS
SLACKING
ACGIKLNT TACKLING
TALCKING
ACGIKLNU CAULKING
ACGIKLRY GARLICKY
ACGIKMNO COMAKING
ACGIKMNS SMACKING
ACGIKNNR CRANKING
ACGIKNNS SNACKING
ACGIKNNU UNCAKING
ACGIKNOR CROAKING
ACGIKNPS PACKINGS
ACGIKNQU QUACKING
ACGIKNRT TRACKING
ACGIKNRW WRACKING
ACGIKNSS SACKINGS
ACGIKNST STACKING
ACGIKPRS GRIPSACK
ACGILLNS CALLINGS
ACGILMMN CLAMMING
ACGILMNO GNOMICAL
ACGILMNP CLAMPING
ACGILMNU MACULING
ACGILNNU UNLACING
ACGILNOR CAROLING
ACGILNOS SOLACING
ACGILNOT LOCATING
ACGILNPP CLAPPING
ACGILNPS CLASPING
SCALPING
ACGILNQU CALQUING
ACGILNRS CARLINGS
ACGILNRU CINGULAR
ACGILNRW CRAWLING
ACGILNSS CLASSING
ACGILNST CASTLING
CATLINGS
ACGILRSU SURGICAL
ACGIMMNR CRAMMING
ACGIMMNS SCAMMING
ACGIMNOR CAROMING
ACGIMNOS COAMINGS
ACGIMNPR CRAMPING
ACGIMNPS CAMPINGS
SCAMPING
ACGIMNSY SYNGAMIC
ACGIMOPR PICOGRAM
ACGIMORS ORGASMIC
ACGIMOUU GUAIOCUM
ACGINNNS CANNINGS
SCANNING
ACGINNPR PRANCING
ACGINNRT TRANCING
ACGINNRU UNCARING
ACGINNST SCANTING
ACGINNSU UNCASING
ACGINOPT COAPTING
ACGINORS ORGANICS
ACGINOST AGNOSTIC
COASTING
COATINGS
COTINGAS
ACGINPPR CRAPPING
ACGINPPS CAPPINGS
ACGINPRS CARPINGS
SCARPING
SCRAPING
ACGINPSS SPACINGS
ACGINRRS SCARRING
ACGINRRY CARRYING
ACGINRSS SACRINGS
ACGINRST SCARTING
TRACINGS
ACGINRSV CARVINGS
CRAVINGS
ACGINRTU CURATING
ACGINSST CASTINGS
ACGINSTT SCATTING
ACGINSUV VICUGNAS
ACGIOORS GRACIOSO
ACGIORST ORGASTIC
ACGIORSU GRACIOUS
ACGIPRSY SPAGYRIC

ACGJLNOU CONJUGAL
ACGLMOUU COAGULUM
ACGLNORS CLANGORS
ACGLNORU CLANGOUR
ACGLNOSY AGLYCONS
ACGLOSUU GLAUCOUS
ACGMNOPS CAMPONGS
ACGNNORS CRANNOGS
ACGNOOST OCTAGONS
ACGNORST CONGRATS
ACGPPSUU SCUPPAUG
ACGRSSTU CUTGRASS
ACHHILPT PHTHALIC
ACHHINTW WHINCHAT
ACHHINTY HYACINTH
ACHHIPPR HIPPARCH
ACHHLLOT CHALLOTH
ACHHLNOR RHONCHAL
ACHHNTTU NUTHATCH
ACHHPPSU CHUPPAHS
ACHHPTUZ CHUTZPAH
ACHIILMS CHILIASM
ACHIILST CHILIAST
ACHIINRT TRICHINA
ACHIINST CHIANTIS
ACHIIPRS PARCHISI
ACHIIPSS PACHISIS
ACHIIRST RACHITIS
ACHIJNST JACINTHS
ACHIKKSW KICKSHAW
ACHIKLOR HAIRLOCK
ACHIKNOP PACHINKO
ACHIKNRS CRANKISH
ACHIKQSU QUACKISH
ACHIKRSS RICKSHAS
ACHIKRSW RICKSHAW
ACHIKRSY HAYRICKS
ACHIKRTW WHITRACK
ACHILMOS MOCHILAS
ACHILMRS CHRISMAL
ACHILMTY MYTHICAL
ACHILNNS CLANNISH
ACHILOPR ORPHICAL
ACHILOPU PACHOULI
ACHILORT ACROLITH
ACHILPSY PHYSICAL
ACHILPTY PATCHILY
ACHILRVY CHIVALRY
ACHILTTY CHATTILY
ACHIMMOS MACHISMO
MACHOISM
ACHIMMST MISMATCH
ACHIMNOP CHAMPION
ACHIMNOR HARMONIC
OMNIARCH
ACHIMNPT PITCHMAN
ACHIMOSS CHAMISOS
ACHIMPSS SCAMPISH
ACHIMPST MISPATCH
ACHIMRSS CHARISMS
ACHIMRTY ARYTHMIC
ACHIMSST TACHISMS
ACHIMSSU CHIASMUS
ACHINNSU ANCHUSIN
UNCHAINS
ACHINOPR PROCHAIN
ACHINOPS APHONICS
ACHINORT ANORTHIC
ACHINOST CHITOSAN
ACHINOTZ HOACTZIN
ACHINPSY SPINACHY
ACHINRSU UNCHAIRS
ACHIOPRT ATROPHIC
ACHIOPSS ISOPACHS
ACHIORST ACTORISH
CHARIOTS
HARICOTS
ACHIORTV TOVARICH
ACHIOSST ISOTACHS
ACHIPPSS SAPPHICS
ACHIPRRT PARRITCH
PHRATRIC
ACHIQRSU CHARQUIS
ACHIRRTY TRIARCHY
ACHIRSTT CHARTIST
ACHIRSTU HAIRCUTS
ACHISSTT TACHISTS
ACHISTTY CHASTITY
ACHKKORW HACKWORK
ACHKKRSU CHUKKARS
ACHKMMOS HAMMOCKS
ACHKMORS SHAMROCK
ACHKNNUU NUNCHAKU
ACHKOPSS HOPSACKS
ACHKOSSS HASSOCKS
ACHLLOOS ALCOHOLS
ACHLLORS CHLORALS
ACHLLORY CHORALLY
ACHLMOPS CAMPHOLS
ACHLMSTZ SCHMALTZ
ACHLMSYZ SCHMALZY
ACHLNOSY HALCYONS
ACHLNSTY STANCHLY
ACHLOPRT CALTHROP
ACHLOPTT POTLATCH
ACHLORSS SCHOLARS
ACHLOSSW SALCHOWS
ACHMNORS MONARCHS
NOMARCHS
ACHMNORY MONARCHY
NOMARCHY
ACHMOORT CHATROOM
ACHMOPRS CAMPHORS
ACHMORSZ MACHZORS
ACHMORTU OUTCHARM
OUTMARCH
ACHMOSST STOMACHS
ACHMOSTY STOMACHY
ACHMOTTU OUTMATCH
ACHMPSTU MATCHUPS
ACHMSSUW CUMSHAWS
ACHNNORU UNANCHOR
ACHNNOSS CHANSONS
ACHNORST CHANTORS
ACHNORXY CHRONAXY
ACHNOSTY TACHYONS
ACHNOSUY CHANOYUS
ACHNPPSS SCHNAPPS
ACHOORTU COAUTHOR
ACHOPRSY CHARPOYS
ACHORRST TROCHARS
ACHOTTUW OUTWATCH
WATCHOUT
ACHPRSTU PUSHCART
ACHPSTUZ CHUTZPAS
ACIIILMN INIMICAL
ACIIILNV CIVILIAN
ACIIINST ISATINIC
ACIIKLNO KAOLINIC
ACIIKNNN CANNIKIN
ACIIKNNS CANIKINS
ACIILLNS ALLICINS
ACIILLNV VANILLIC
ACIILLSU SILICULA
ACIILLSV SILVICAL
ACIILLTV VILLATIC
ACIILMMS MISCLAIM
ACIILMNR CRIMINAL
ACIILMNU ALUMINIC
ACIILMOT COMITIAL
ACIILMRT MARLITIC
ACIILMSS LAICISMS
ACIILNOR IRONICAL
ACIILNPS PISCINAL
ACIILNPT PLATINIC
ACIILNSS SALICINS
ACIILRTU URALITIC
ACIIMMNP MINICAMP
ACIIMMNS MINICAMS
ACIIMNNO AMNIONIC
ACIIMNNT MANNITIC
ACIIMNOR MORAINIC
ACIIMNOS SIMONIAC
ACIIMNOT AMNIOTIC
ACIIMNRS MINICARS
ACIIMNST ACTINISM
ACIIMNSU MUSICIAN
ACIIMNTU ACTINIUM
ACIIMNTY INTIMACY
MINACITY
ACIIMOST IOTACISM
ACIIMOTT AMITOTIC
ACIIMPRV VAMPIRIC
ACIIMRST SCIMITAR
ACIIMSTT ATTICISM
MASTITIC
ACIIMSTV ACTIVISM
ACIIMTUV VIATICUM
ACIINNOT INACTION
ACIINNQU CINQUAIN
ACIINNRV NIRVANIC
ACIINNTT INCITANT
ACIINNTY CANINITY
ACIINOPT OPTICIAN
ACIINORZ ZIRCONIA
ACIINOSV AVIONICS
ACIINOTT CITATION
ACIINPSS PISCINAS
ACIINPTY ANTIPYIC
ACIINRSS NARCISSI
ACIINRTU URANITIC
ACIINTTY ANTICITY
ACIIORST AORISTIC
ACIIORTV VICTORIA
ACIIRSST TRIASSIC
ACIIRSTT ARTISTIC
ACIISTTT ATTICIST
ACIISTTU AUTISTIC
ACIISTTV ACTIVIST
ACIITTVY ACTIVITY
ACIITVVY VIVACITY
ACIJKKPS SKIPJACK
ACIJRSSU JURASSIC
ACIJSUZZ JACUZZIS
ACIKLMOT MOCKTAIL
ACIKLNOT ANTILOCK
ACIKLNRY CRANKILY
ACIKLORY CROAKILY
ACIKMNST STICKMAN
ACIKMOOS OOMIACKS
ACIKMOST COMATIKS
ACIKMQSU QUACKISM
ACIKNNPR CRANKPIN
ACIKNORT ANTIROCK
ACIKPRST TRIPACKS
ACIKSTTY STATICKY
ACILLLNY CLINALLY
ACILLLOP POLLICAL
ACILLMMY CLAMMILY
ACILLMOS LOCALISM
ACILLMSS MISCALLS
ACILLNOO COLONIAL
ACILLNOR CARILLON
ACILLNOS SCALLION
ACILLNUY UNCIALLY
ACILLORT CLITORAL
ACILLORY COLLYRIA
ACILLOST LOCALIST
ACILLOSY SOCIALLY
ACILLOTY COITALLY
LOCALITY
ACILLOUV COLLUVIA
ACILLSSY CLASSILY
ACILMNNY CINNAMYL
ACILMNOP COMPLAIN
ACILMNOS LACONISM
LIMACONS
ACILMOOS SCOLIOMA
ACILMOPR PICLORAM
PROCLAIM
ACILMOPS OILCAMPS
ACILMOSV VOCALISM
ACILMRTU MULTICAR
ACILMSSS CLASSISM
MISCLASS
ACILMSSU MUSICALS
ACILMSTY MYSTICAL
ACILMTUY ULTIMACY
ACILNNOS CANNOLIS
ACILNOOT LOCATION
ACILNOPT PLATONIC
ACILNORS CLARIONS
ACILNORT CILANTRO
CONTRAIL
ACILNOSU UNSOCIAL
ACILNOSY ACYLOINS
ACILNOUV UNIVOCAL
ACILNPSS INCLASPS
ACILNRSU CISLUNAR
ACILNRUY CULINARY
URANYLIC
ACILNSTU LUNATICS
SULTANIC
ACILNSTY SCANTILY
ACILNTTU ANTICULT
ACILNTTY INTACTLY
ACILOPRT TROPICAL
ACILOPST CAPITOLS
COALPITS
ACILORRV CORRIVAL
ACILORTV VORTICAL
ACILORYZ ZIRCALOY
ACILOSTV VOCALIST
ACILOTUV OUTCAVIL
ACILOTVY VOCALITY
ACILPRSU SPICULAR
ACILPSST PLASTICS
ACILPSUU APICULUS
ACILRRTU TURRICAL
ACILRSTU CURTAILS
RUSTICAL
ACILRTUV CULTIVAR
ACILSSST CLASSIST
ACILSTUV VICTUALS
ACILSTVY SYLVATIC
ACIMMTUY CYMATIUM
ACIMNNNO CINNAMON
ACIMNOOR ACROMION
ACIMNOPS CAMPIONS
ACIMNORS MINORCAS
ACIMNORT ROMANTIC
ACIMNORU COUMARIN
ACIMNORY ACRIMONY
ACIMNOST MONASTIC
ACIMNOTU ACONITUM
ACIMNPSU PANICUMS
ACIMNPTY TYMPANIC
ACIMNRSS NARCISMS
ACIMNRSU CRANIUMS
CUMARINS
ACIMNSTT CATMINTS
ACIMNSTU TSUNAMIC
ACIMOPRT IMPACTOR
ACIMOPST APOMICTS
ACIMORST ACROTISM
ACIMORSY CRAMOISY
ACIMOSST MASSICOT
ACIMOSTT STOMATIC
ACIMPRST CRAMPITS
ACIMRRSY MISCARRY
ACIMRSSZ CZARISMS
ACIMSSST MISCASTS
ACINNOOT CONATION
ACINNOQU CONQUIAN
ACINNOSS SCANSION
ACINNOST ACTINONS
CANONIST
CONTAINS
SANCTION
SONANTIC
ACINNOTU CONTINUA
COUNTIAN
ACINNRTY TYRANNIC
ACINNSTY INSTANCY
ACINOOPR PICAROON
ACINOOTV VOCATION
ACINOPPT PANOPTIC
ACINOPRS PARSONIC
ACINOPST CAPTIONS
PACTIONS
ACINOQSU COQUINAS
ACINORRS CARRIONS
ACINORRT CARROTIN
ACINORSS NARCOSIS
ACINORST CAROTINS
CORTINAS
ACINORSV CORVINAS
ACINORTT TRACTION
ACINORTY CARYOTIN
ACINOSSS CAISSONS
CASSINOS
ACINOSSY CYANOSIS
ACINOSTT OSCITANT
TACTIONS
ACINOSTU AUCTIONS
CAUTIONS
ACINOSTW WAINSCOT
ACINOSWX COXSWAIN
ACINOTTX TOXICANT
ACINPQUY PIQUANCY
ACINPRST CANTRIPS
ACINPRSY CYPRIANS
ACINPSTY SYNAPTIC
ACINQSTU QUANTICS
ACINRSST NARCISTS
ACINRSTU CURTAINS
ACINRTTU TACITURN
URTICANT
ACINSTTY SANCTITY
ACINSTYY SYNCYTIA
ACIOOPST SCOTOPIA
ACIOPRST APRICOTS
PISCATOR
ACIOPRTT PROTATIC
ACIOPSST POTASSIC
ACIOPSSU SPACIOUS
ACIOPSTU AUTOPSIC
CAPTIOUS
ACIORRSS CORSAIRS
ACIORSSU SCARIOUS
ACIORSTT CITATORS
RICOTTAS
ACIORTTY ATROCITY
CITATORY
ACIORTVY VORACITY
ACIOSSST COASSIST
ACIOSSTY ISOSTACY
ACIOSTUU CAUTIOUS
ACIPRRUU PIRARUCU
ACIPRSTT TIPCARTS
ACIPRTTY TRIPTYCA
ACIPSSST SPASTICS
ACIQRSTU QUARTICS
ACIRSSST SACRISTS
ACIRSSTT ASTRICTS
ACIRSSTY SACRISTY
ACIRSSTZ CZARISTS
ACISSSTU CASUISTS
ACISSTTU CATSUITS
ACJKKSSY SKYJACKS
ACJKLLOR JACKROLL
ACJKLOSW LOCKJAWS
ACJKOPST JACKPOTS
ACJMNSTU MUNTJACS
ACJPSTUU CAJUPUTS
ACKKMOPR POCKMARK
ACKKORRW RACKWORK
ACKLLOPS POLLACKS
ACKLLPSU SKULLCAP
ACKLMORS ARMLOCKS
LOCKRAMS
ACKLNOSU UNCLOAKS
ACKLOOPW WOOLPACK
ACKLOORS OARLOCKS
ACKLOOSW WOOLSACK
ACKLORSV LAVROCKS
ACKLORSW WARLOCKS
ACKMMMOS MAMMOCKS
ACKMNOST STOCKMAN
ACKMNRTU TRUCKMAN
ACKMOSTT MATTOCKS
ACKNOPSW SNOWPACK
ACKNORSU CRANKOUS
ACKNRSTU UNTRACKS
ACKNSSTU UNSTACKS
ACKOPRRT TRAPROCK
ACKOSSTW TOWSACKS
ACKPSSTU STACKUPS
ACLLLNOY CLONALLY
ACLLMNOU COLUMNAL
ACLLMOSU MOLLUSCA
ACLLNNOO NONLOCAL
ACLLOORS COROLLAS
ACLLOORT COLLATOR
ACLLOOSS COLOSSAL
ACLLOPSS SCALLOPS
ACLLORUY OCULARLY
ACLLOSTU LOCUSTAL
OUTCALLS
ACLLOSTY COSTALLY
ACLLRTUU CULTURAL
ACLMMNOU COMMUNAL
ACLMMORW CLAMWORM
ACLMNOOR COLORMAN
ACLMNORU COLUMNAR
ACLMNORY NORMALCY
ACLMNPSU UNCLAMPS
ACLMORSU CLAMOURS
ACLMRSUU MUSCULAR
ACLMSSTU MASSCULT
ACLMSTUU CUSTUMAL
ACLMSUUV VASCULUM
ACLNNOOS NONCOLAS
ACLNNOOV NONVOCAL
ACLNNOSS NONCLASS
ACLNOORS CORONALS
ACLNOORT COLORANT
ACLNOOST COOLANTS
OCTANOLS
ACLNOOSV VOLCANOS
ACLNOPSY SYNCOPAL
ACLNORSU CONSULAR
COURLANS
ACLNORTU CALUTRON
ACLNOSSS CLASSONS
ACLNOSTU OSCULANT
ACLNPSSU UNCLASPS
ACLNPTUU PUNCTUAL
ACLNSSUY UNCLASSY
ACLOOPRR CORPORAL
ACLOOPRS CARPOOLS
ACLOORST LOCATORS
ACLOORWY COLORWAY
ACLOPRRU PROCURAL
ACLOPRST CALTROPS
ACLOPRXY XYLOCARP
ACLOPSSU SCOPULAS
ACLOPSSY CALYPSOS
ACLOPSUU OPUSCULA
ACLORTUW OUTCRAWL
ACLOSSTU OUTCLASS
ACLRSSTY CRYSTALS
ACMMNOSY SCAMMONY
ACMNOOPR CRAMPOON
MONOCARP
ACMNOORT MONOCRAT
ACMNOPRS CORPSMAN
CRAMPONS
ACMNORSY ACRONYMS
ACMNSSTU SANCTUMS
ACMOOORT COATROOM
ACMOORRT MOTORCAR
ACMOORUU COUMAROU
ACMOOSST SCOTOMAS
ACMOPRST COMPARTS
ACMOPSTU CAMPOUTS
ACMORRSS CROSSARM
ACMORSTY COSTMARY
ACMQSTUU CUMQUATS
ACNNNORY CANNONRY
ACNNOORT NONACTOR
ACNNOSTT CONSTANT
ACNOOPRT COPATRON
ACNOORRY CORONARY
ACNOORST CARTOONS
CORANTOS
OSTRACON
ACNOORSU CANOROUS
ACNOORTU COURANTO
ACNOORTY CARTOONY
OCTONARY
ACNOPSSW SNOWCAPS
ACNORRSU RANCOURS
ACNORRSY CARRYONS
ACNORRTY CONTRARY
ACNORSTT CONTRAST
ACNORSTU COURANTS
ACNORTTU TURNCOAT
ACNOSSTW SNOWCATS
ACNPRSSY SYNCARPS
ACNPRSYY SYNCARPY
ACNRRSTU CURRANTS
ACOOPRST COPASTOR
ROOTCAPS
ACOOPSTT TOPCOATS
ACOORSTU TOURACOS
ACOPPRRS PROCARPS
ACOPRRST CARPORTS
ACOPRRTT PROTRACT
ACORRSTT TRACTORS
ACORRSTU CURATORS
ACORRTUY CARRYOUT
ACORSSTU SURCOATS
ACORSSUW CURASSOW
ACORSSWY CROSSWAY
ACORSTTY CRYOSTAT
ACORSTUU TURACOUS
ACOSSTTU OUTCASTS
ACPSSTUY PUSSYCAT
ADDDEEEL DELEADED
ADDDEEEN DEADENED
ADDDEEGR DEGRADED
ADDDEEIM DIADEMED
ADDDEELR LADDERED
ADDDEEMN DEMANDED
MADDENED
ADDDEENR DANDERED
ADDDEENS DESANDED
SADDENED
ADDDEGJU ADJUDGED
ADDDEIMS MISADDED
ADDDELSW SWADDLED
ADDDELTW TWADDLED
ADDDEMNU ADDENDUM
ADDDENOS DEODANDS
ADDDENPU UNPADDED
ADDDEOOW DEADWOOD
ADDDEOTU OUTADDED
ADDDEQSU SQUADDED
ADDDGILN DADDLING
ADDEEEFL DEFLEAED
ADDEEEFN DEAFENED
ADDEEEFT DEFEATED
ADDEEEJY DEEJAYED
ADDEEELN LEADENED
ADDEEELV DELEAVED
ADDEEEMN DEMEANED
ADDEEENR DEADENER
ENDEARED
ADDEEENW DANEWEED
ADDEEESY DEADEYES
ADDEEFGN DEFANGED
ADDEEFIL DEFILADE
ADDEEFLT DEFLATED
ADDEEFMO DEFOAMED
ADDEEFPR PREFADED
ADDEEFRY DEFRAYED
FEEDYARD
ADDEEFTT DEFATTED
ADDEEGGR DAGGERED
ADDEEGHR HARDEDGE
ADDEEGLN DANEGELD
ADDEEGLZ DEGLAZED

ADDEEGNR DANGERED
DERANGED
GANDERED
GARDENED
ADDEEGOR DOGEARED
ADDEEGRR DEGRADER
REGARDED
REGRADED
ADDEEGRS DEGRADES
ADDEEGSS DEGASSED
ADDEEHLR HERALDED
ADDEEHLY ALDEHYDE
ADDEEHNR ADHEREND
HARDENED
ADDEEHNS HEADENDS
ADDEEHOP DOPEHEAD
ADDEEHRS REDHEADS
ADDEEHRT THREADED
ADDEEIKR DAIKERED
ADDEEILN DEADLINE
ADDEEILR DEADLIER
DERAILED
REDIALED
ADDEEILT DETAILED
ADDEEIMT MEDIATED
ADDEEINT DETAINED
ADDEEINU UNIDEAED
ADDEEIPR DIAPERED
ADDEEISS DISEASED
ADDEEIST STEADIED
ADDEEITV DEVIATED
ADDEEKMR DEMARKED
ADDEEKNR DARKENED
ADDEELLM MEDALLED
ADDEELLP PEDALLED
ADDEELNP DEPLANED
ADDEELNR RELANDED
ADDEELNU UNLEADED
ADDEELOR RELOADED
ADDEELRS RESADDLE
ADDEELRT TREADLED
ADDEELST DESALTED
ADDEELUV DEVALUED
ADDEEMNP DAMPENED
ADDEEMNR DAMNEDER
DEMANDER
REDEMAND
REMANDED
ADDEEMST DEMASTED
ADDEENPP APPENDED
ADDEENPR PANDERED
ADDEENPX EXPANDED
ADDEENRR DARNEDER
ADDEENRW WANDERED
ADDEENSS DEADNESS
ADDEENTT ATTENDED
DENTATED
ADDEENTU DENUDATE
ADDEENUV UNEVADED
ADDEEPRS RESPADED
ADDEEPRT DEPARTED
PREDATED
ADDEEPRV DEPRAVED
PERVADED
ADDEERRT RETARDED
ADDEERRW REWARDED
ADDEERRY DEERYARD
ADDEERTT DERATTED
ADDEERTV ADVERTED
ADDEFFOR AFFORDED
ADDEFILT DEADLIFT
ADDEFIST FADDIEST
ADDEFLRU DREADFUL
ADDEFRSU DEFRAUDS
ADDEGGLR DRAGGLED
ADDEGHOS GODHEADS
ADDEGILO DIALOGED
ADDEGINR DREADING
READDING
ADDEGJSU ADJUDGES
ADDEGLNS GLADDENS
ADDEGLST GLADDEST
ADDEGNOP DOGNAPED
ADDEGNRU UNGRADED
ADDEGPRU UPGRADED
ADDEHHLN HANDHELD
ADDEHILR DIHEDRAL
ADDEHINW HEADWIND
ADDEHIRS DIEHARDS
ADDEHIRW RAWHIDED
ADDEHMRU DRUMHEAD
ADDEHNNU UNHANDED
ADDEHNSU UNSHADED
ADDEHOPR DROPHEAD
ADDEHORW HEADWORD
ADDEHOSW SHADOWED
ADDEHRTY HYDRATED
ADDEIIMS DIAMIDES
ADDEIINZ DAIDZEIN
ADDEIITV ADDITIVE
ADDEIJNO ADJOINED
ADDEIKNP KIDNAPED
ADDEILNS ISLANDED
LANDSIDE
ADDEILNT TIDELAND
ADDEILSY DIALYSED
ADDEILUZ DUALIZED
ADDEILYZ DIALYZED
ADDEIMOS SODAMIDE
ADDEIMRS DISARMED
ADDEIMST MISDATED
ADDEIMSY DISMAYED
ADDEIMTT ADMITTED
ADDEINOR ORDAINED
ADDEINOS ADENOIDS
ADDEINOZ ANODIZED
ADDEINRS SARDINED
ADDEINST DANDIEST
ADDEIOPR PARODIED
ADDEIORS ROADSIDE
ADDEIOTX OXIDATED
ADDEIPPR DIDAPPER
ADDEIPRS DISPREAD
ADDEIPSS DIPSADES
ADDEIRST DISRATED
ADDEIRSW SIDEWARD
ADDEIRVZ VIZARDED
ADDEISSU DISSUADE
ADDEISSV DISSAVED
ADDEISSY DAYSIDES
ADDEJSTU ADJUSTED
ADDEKNVY VANDYKED
ADDELMOS DOLMADES
ADDELNNU DUNELAND
ADDELNOO ONLOADED
ADDELNOU DUODENAL
UNLOADED
ADDELNPU PUDENDAL
ADDELNRS DANDLERS
ADDELNSU UNSADDLE
ADDELOPU UPLOADED
ADDELPRS PADDLERS
SPRADDLE
ADDELRSS SADDLERS
ADDELRST STRADDLE
ADDELRSW DAWDLERS
WADDLERS
ADDELRSY SADDLERY
ADDELRTW TWADDLER
ADDELSST STADDLES
ADDELSSW SWADDLES
ADDELSTW TWADDLES
ADDEMNPU UNDAMPED
ADDEMNST DAMNDEST
ADDEMOSY DOMESDAY
ADDENOPR PARDONED
ADDENPRU UNDRAPED
ADDENRST DARNDEST
STRANDED
ADDENRSU DAUNDERS
ADDEORTU OUTDARED
ADDEOTTU OUTDATED
ADDEPRSU SUPERADD
ADDEPRTU UPDARTED
ADDFFILO DAFFODIL
ADDFFINR DANDRIFF
ADDFFNRU DANDRUFF
ADDFIMSS FADDISMS
ADDFISST FADDISTS
ADDGGILN GLADDING
ADDGGORU GUARDDOG
ADDGIKNR GRANDKID
ADDGILNN DANDLING
ADDGILNP PADDLING
ADDGILNR RADDLING
ADDGILNS SADDLING
ADDGILNW DAWDLING
WADDLING
ADDGINPS PADDINGS
ADDGINQU QUADDING
ADDGINSW WADDINGS
ADDGINWY WADDYING
ADDGMNOS GODDAMNS
ADDGMRUU MUDGUARD
ADDGOOSW DAGWOODS
ADDHHLNO HANDHOLD
ADDHIMOO MAIDHOOD
ADDHINSY DANDYISH
ADDHISTY HYDATIDS
ADDHLOOS LADHOODS
ADDHLOOY LADYHOOD
ADDHOORW HARDWOOD
ADDHOSTY ATHODYDS
ADDIIKMZ ZADDIKIM
ADDIILUV DIVIDUAL
ADDIINOT ADDITION
ADDIINSS DISDAINS
ADDIIPSS DIAPSIDS
ADDIKSTY KATYDIDS
ADDILLNS LANDSLID
ADDILLNW WILDLAND
ADDILMNS MIDLANDS
ADDIMNOS DIAMONDS
ADDIMNSY DANDYISM
ADDIMNYY DIDYNAMY
ADDINNOR ORDINAND
ADDINORS ANDROIDS
ADDINRWW WINDWARD
ADDIORTY ADDITORY
ADDKNRRU DRUNKARD
ADDLLNOR LANDLORD
ADDLLRSU DULLARDS
ADDLNNOW DOWNLAND
ADDLNOOW DOWNLOAD
WOODLAND
ADDLORTY DOTARDLY
ADDMOOSY DOOMSDAY
ADDNOPWY PANDOWDY
ADDNORWW DOWNWARD
DRAWDOWN
ADDOORRY DOORYARD
ADEEEFNY FEDAYEEN
ADEEEFRT DEFEATER
FEDERATE
REDEFEAT
ADEEEGLT DELEGATE
ADEEEGNR RENEGADE
ADEEEGNT TEENAGED
ADEEEGPS GAPESEED
ADEEEGRR REGEARED
ADEEEGRS DEGREASE
ADEEEGUW AGUEWEED
ADEEEHHW HEEHAWED
ADEEEHRS HAEREDES
ADEEEHRT REHEATED
ADEEEHRX EXHEDRAE
ADEEEHSY EYESHADE
ADEEEINT DETAINEE
ADEEEKNW WEAKENED
ADEEELMN ENAMELED
ADEEELNV LEAVENED
ADEEELPR REPEALED
ADEEELRS RELEASED
RESEALED
ADEEELRV LAVEERED
REVEALED
ADEEELST TEASELED
ADEEELSV DELEAVES
ADEEELSW WEASELED
ADEEELTV ELEVATED
ADEEELTZ TEAZELED
ADEEEMNT EMENDATE
ADEEEMRT RETEAMED
ADEEENNT NEATENED
ADEEENRR REEARNED
ADEEENRS SERENADE
ADEEENTT ATTENDEE
EDENTATE
ADEEEPRS RAPESEED
ADEEEPRT DEPARTEE
REPEATED
ADEEERST RESEATED
ADEEERVW REWEAVED
ADEEESSW SEAWEEDS
SEESAWED
ADEEFGLN FENAGLED
ADEEFHNR FREEHAND
ADEEFHOR FOREHEAD
ADEEFHRT FATHERED
ADEEFIIR AERIFIED
ADEEFILN ENFILADE
ADEEFIMS SEMIDEAF
ADEEFIRR RAREFIED
ADEEFIST SAFETIED
ADEEFLLT FELLATED
ADEEFLMN ENFLAMED
ADEEFLNS ENDLEAFS
ADEEFLOR FREELOAD
ADEEFLPR PEDALFER
ADEEFLRR DEFERRAL
ADEEFLRS FEDERALS
ADEEFLRT DEFLATER
FALTERED
REFLATED
ADEEFLSS FADELESS
ADEEFLST DEFLATES
ADEEFLSX FLAXSEED
ADEEFMNR ENFRAMED
FREEDMAN
ADEEFMOR DEFOAMER
ADEEFMRR REFRAMED
ADEEFMRS DEFAMERS
ADEEFNRU UNFEARED
ADEEFNSS DEAFNESS
ADEEFNST FASTENED
ADEEFNTT FATTENED
ADEEFORT FOREDATE
ADEEFOTV FOVEATED
ADEEFPRS PREFADES
ADEEFRRT RAFTERED
ADEEFRRY DEFRAYER
ADEEFRST DRAFTEES
ADEEFRTU FEATURED
ADEEGGHS EGGHEADS
ADEEGGJR JAGGEDER
ADEEGGRR RAGGEDER
ADEEGGRS SAGGERED
ADEEGGRT RETAGGED
ADEEGGRU REGAUGED
ADEEGGWW GEWGAWED
ADEEGHNR REHANGED
ADEEGHOR GHERAOED
ADEEGHRT GATHERED
ADEEGIMN ADEEMING
ADEEGIMR REIMAGED
ADEEGINR REGAINED
ADEEGINZ AGENIZED
ADEEGIRS DISAGREE
ADEEGLLT GALLETED
ADEEGLLV GAVELLED
ADEEGLNR ENLARGED
ADEEGLNT DANEGELT
ADEEGLRV GRAVELED
ADEEGLRZ REGLAZED
ADEEGLSV SELVAGED
ADEEGLSZ DEGLAZES
ADEEGMMO GAMODEME
ADEEGMMT GEMMATED
ADEEGMNR GENDARME
ADEEGMNS ENDGAMES
ADEEGMNY GANYMEDE
MEGADYNE
ADEEGMOP MEGAPODE
ADEEGMOS MEGADOSE
ADEEGMSS MESSAGED
ADEEGNNR ENDANGER
ADEEGNOR RENEGADO
ADEEGNRR DERANGER
GARDENER
GARNERED
ADEEGNRS DERANGES
GRANDEES
GRENADES
ADEEGNRU DUNGAREE
UNAGREED
UNDERAGE
ADEEGNRV ENGRAVED
ADEEGNSS AGEDNESS
ADEEGORT DEROGATE
ADEEGORV OVERAGED
ADEEGPRS PRESAGED
ADEEGPRT PARGETED
ADEEGRRS REGRADES
ADEEGRRT GARRETED
GARTERED
REGRATED
ADEEGRRU REARGUED
REDARGUE
ADEEGRSS DEGASSER
DRESSAGE
ADEEGRST RESTAGED
ADEEGRSW RAGWEEDS
ADEEGRTT TARGETED
ADEEGSSS DEGASSES
ADEEGSTT GESTATED
ADEEGSWY EDGEWAYS
ADEEGTTZ GAZETTED
ADEEHHRS REHASHED
ADEEHHST SHEATHED
ADEEHILN HEADLINE
ADEEHIST HEADIEST
ADEEHISV ADHESIVE
ADEEHKNR DAKERHEN
HANKERED
HARKENED
ADEEHKPR PHREAKED
ADEEHKRS KASHERED
ADEEHKWW HAWKWEED
ADEEHKWY HAWKEYED
ADEEHLLW WELLHEAD
ADEEHLNO ENHALOED
ADEEHLNR REHANDLE
ADEEHLNS HANSELED
ADEEHLNU UNHEALED
ADEEHLRS ASHLERED
ADEEHLRT HALTERED
LATHERED
ADEEHLSS HEADLESS
ADEEHLTY HEATEDLY
ADEEHMMO HOMEMADE
ADEEHMMR HAMMERED
ADEEHMNN MENHADEN
ADEEHMNS HEADSMEN
ADEEHMNT ANTHEMED
ADEEHMPR HAMPERED
ADEEHMSS EMDASHES
ADEEHNOT HEADNOTE
ADEEHNPP HAPPENED
ADEEHNRR HARDENER
REHARDEN
ADEEHNRT ADHERENT
NEATHERD
ADEEHNSS DASHEENS
ENDASHES
ADEEHNST HASTENED
ADEEHNTU UNHEATED
ADEEHORS SOREHEAD
ADEEHORV OVERHEAD
ADEEHPPU UPHEAPED
ADEEHPRS EPHEDRAS
RESHAPED
ADEEHPRT PREDEATH
THREAPED
ADEEHPUV UPHEAVED
ADEEHRRS ADHERERS
ADEEHRRT RETHREAD
THREADER
ADEEHRST HEADREST
ADEEHRSV RESHAVED
ADEEHRSW REWASHED
ADEEHRTT THREATED
ADEEHRTW WREATHED
ADEEHSST HEADSETS
ADEEHSSY HAYSEEDS
ADEEIILS IDEALISE
ADEEIILZ IDEALIZE
ADEEIITV IDEATIVE
ADEEIJKL JADELIKE
ADEEIJMR JEREMIAD
ADEEIJST JADEITES
ADEEIKLS LAKESIDE
ADEEIKMR DIEMAKER
ADEEIKNP KIDNAPEE
ADEEIKSW WEAKSIDE
ADEEILLO OEILLADE
ADEEILMN ENDEMIAL
ADEEILMR REMAILED
REMEDIAL
ADEEILMS LIMEADES
ADEEILMV MEDIEVAL
ADEEILNR RENAILED
ADEEILNS DELAINES
ADEEILNT DATELINE
ENTAILED
LINEATED
ADEEILPR PEDALIER
ADEEILPS PLEIADES
ADEEILPT DEPILATE
EPILATED
PILEATED
ADEEILRS REALISED
RESAILED
SIDEREAL
ADEEILRT DETAILER
ELATERID
RETAILED
ADEEILRZ REALIZED
ADEEILSS IDEALESS
ADEEILST LEADIEST
ADEEIMNR REMAINED
ADEEIMNT DEMENTIA
ADEEIMNX EXAMINED
ADEEIMRR DREAMIER
ADEEIMRT DIAMETER
ADEEIMRZ MADERIZE
ADEEIMST MEDIATES
ADEEIMTT ADMITTEE
MEDITATE
ADEEINNS ADENINES
ADEEINOP OEDIPEAN
ADEEINRS ARSENIDE
NEARSIDE
ADEEINRT DETAINER
RETAINED
ADEEINRV REINVADE
ADEEINSS ANISEEDS
ADEEINST ANDESITE
ADEEINTW ANTIWEED
ADEEINVW INWEAVED
ADEEIPRR RAPIERED
REPAIRED
ADEEIPRS AIRSPEED
ADEEIPTX EXPIATED
ADEEIRRR DREARIER
ADEEIRRS DREARIES
RERAISED
ADEEIRST READIEST
SERIATED
STEADIER
ADEEIRTT ITERATED
ADEEIRTV DERIVATE
ADEEIRTW WAITERED
ADEEISSS DISEASES
SEASIDES
ADEEISST STEADIES
ADEEISSV ADVISEES
ADEEISTU AUDITEES
ADEEISTV DEVIATES
SEDATIVE
ADEEKMRR REMARKED
ADEEKMRT MARKETED
ADEEKNPS KNEEPADS
ADEEKNPW KNAPWEED
ADEEKNRR DARKENER
ADEEKNRS KNEADERS
ADEEKNST NAKEDEST
ADEEKORS RESOAKED
ADEEKPRR REPARKED
ADEEKQSU SQUEAKED
ADEEKRST STREAKED
ADEEKSWY WEEKDAYS
ADEELLLP LAPELLED
ADEELLMT METALLED
ADEELLMU MEDULLAE
ADEELLNP PANELLED
ADEELLNY LEADENLY
ADEELLPR PEDALLER
PREDELLA
ADEELLPS SEPALLED
ADEELLPT PALLETED
PETALLED
ADEELLQU EQUALLED
ADEELLRU LAURELED
ADEELLRV RAVELLED
ADEELLSS ALLSEEDS
LEADLESS
ADEELLTY ELATEDLY
ADEELLVY VALLEYED
ADEELLWY WALLEYED
ADEELMNO LEMONADE
ADEELMNP EMPLANED
ADEELMNR ALDERMEN
ADEELMNS DALESMEN
LEADSMEN
ADEELMNT LAMENTED
ADEELMOR REMOLADE
ADEELMOS SOMEDEAL
ADEELMPX EXAMPLED
ADEELMRS DEMERSAL
EMERALDS
ADEELMRT TRAMELED
ADEELMRV MARVELED
ADEELMTU EMULATED
ADEELNNP ENPLANED
ADEELNNU UNANELED
ADEELNOR OLEANDER
RELOANED
ADEELNPS DEPLANES
SPALDEEN
ADEELNPT ENDPLATE
ADEELNRT ANTLERED
ADEELNRV LAVENDER
ADEELNSU UNLEASED
UNSEALED
ADEELNSV ENSLAVED
ADEELNTT TALENTED
ADEELNTV LEVANTED
ADEELOPX POLEAXED
ADEELORR RELOADER
ADEELORU AUREOLED
ADEELORV OVERLADE
ADEELOST DESOLATE
ADEELPPR LAPPERED
RAPPELED
ADEELPPT LAPPETED
ADEELPPU UPLEAPED
ADEELPRS PEDALERS
PLEADERS
RELAPSED
REPLEADS
ADEELPRT PALTERED
REPLATED
ADEELPRY PARLEYED
REPLAYED
ADEELPST PEDESTAL

ADEELPTY PEDATELY
ADEELQSU SQUEALED
ADEELRRT TREADLER
ADEELRRY READERLY
ADEELRST DESALTER
RESLATED
TREADLES
ADEELRSV SLAVERED
ADEELRSW LEEWARDS
ADEELRSY DELAYERS
ADEELRTV TRAVELED
ADEELRUV REVALUED
ADEELRWY LAWYERED
ADEELSST DATELESS
DETASSEL
TASSELED
ADEELSTY SEDATELY
ADEELSUV DEVALUES
ADEEMMMR MAMMERED
ADEEMMRY YAMMERED
ADEEMMSS MESDAMES
ADEEMMXY MYXEDEMA
ADEEMNNR MANNERED
REMANNED
ADEEMNOR DEMEANOR
ENAMORED
ADEEMNOS DAEMONES
ADEEMNOT NEMATODE
ADEEMNOU EUDAEMON
ADEEMNPR DAMPENER
ADEEMNPY EPENDYMA
ADEEMNRS AMENDERS
MEANDERS
ADEEMNSS SEEDSMAN
ADEEMNST STAMENED
ADEEMNSU UNSEAMED
ADEEMORS SEADROME
ADEEMORT MODERATE
ADEEMPPR PAMPERED
REMAPPED
ADEEMPRR PREARMED
ADEEMPRT TAMPERED
ADEEMPRV REVAMPED
ADEEMPST STAMPEDE
STEPDAME
ADEEMRRS DREAMERS
REDREAMS
ADEEMRRT REDREAMT
ADEEMRRW REWARMED
ADEEMRST MASTERED
STREAMED
ADEEMRSU MEASURED
ADEEMRTT MATTERED
ADEEMSWY MAYWEEDS
ADEENNPT PENNATED
ADEENNRS ENSNARED
ADEENNRU UNEARNED
ADEENNTT TENANTED
ADEENNUW UNWEANED
ADEENNUY UNYEANED
ADEENOPW WEAPONED
ADEENORS REASONED
ADEENORV ENDEAVOR
ADEENORY AERODYNE
ADEENOSS ADENOSES
SEASONED
ADEENOST ENDOSTEA
ADEENOTT DETONATE
ADEENPPR ENDPAPER
ADEENPPS SANDPEEP
ADEENPRR PANDERER
ADEENPRT PARENTED
ADEENPRX EXPANDER
ADEENPSW SNAPWEED
ADEENPTT PATENTED
PATTENED
ADEENRRW WANDERER
ADEENRSS DEARNESS
ADEENRSU UNDERSEA
UNERASED
UNSEARED
ADEENRSW ANSWERED
ADEENRSY YEARENDS
ADEENRTT ATTENDER
NATTERED
RATTENED
ADEENRTU DENATURE
UNDERATE
UNDEREAT
ADEENSST ASSENTED
SENSATED
STANDEES
ADEENSSU DANSEUSE
ADEENSTU UNSEATED
ADEENSTY ANDESYTE
ADEENTTU TAUTENED
ADEENTTV VENDETTA
ADEEOPRT OPERATED
ADEEOPST ADOPTEES
ADEEORRV OVERDARE
OVERDEAR
ADEEORVW OVERAWED
REAVOWED
ADEEPPRR DAPPERER
PREPARED
ADEEPPRT PRETAPED
ADEEPPRU PAUPERED
ADEEPPRV PREPAVED
ADEEPRRS RESPREAD
SPREADER
ADEEPRRU UPREARED
ADEEPRRV DEPRAVER
PERVADER
ADEEPRSS ASPERSED
REPASSED
RESPADES
ADEEPRST PEDERAST
PREDATES
REPASTED
TRAPESED
ADEEPRSU PERSUADE
ADEEPRSV DEPRAVES
PERVADES
ADEEPRTT PATTERED
ADEEPRTU DEPURATE
ADEEPSST STAPEDES
ADEEPSTT ADEPTEST
ADEEPSWY SPEEDWAY
ADEEQRUV QUAVERED
ADEERRRT RETARDER
ADEERRRW REDRAWER
REREWARD
REWARDER
ADEERRST ARRESTED
RETREADS
SERRATED
TREADERS
ADEERRSW REDWARES
ADEERSST ASSERTED
ADEERSTT RESTATED
RETASTED
ADEERSTW DEWATERS
TARWEEDS
ADEERSTY ESTRAYED
ADEERTTT TATTERED
ADEERTTY YATTERED
ADEERVYY EVERYDAY
ADEESSSS ASSESSED
ADEESSTT SEDATEST
ADEESTTT ATTESTED
ADEESTUX EXUDATES
ADEESWWX WAXWEEDS
ADEFFGUW GUFFAWED
ADEFFIMR AFFIRMED
ADEFFIRR DRAFFIER
ADEFFIRT TARIFFED
ADEFFIST DAFFIEST
ADEFFLNS SNAFFLED
ADEFFLOS LEADOFFS
ADEFFORT TRADEOFF
ADEFGGOT FAGGOTED
ADEFGIIS GASIFIED
ADEFGILN FINAGLED
ADEFGILO FOLIAGED
ADEFGILS GADFLIES
ADEFGIMN DEFAMING
ADEFGIRT DRIFTAGE
ADEFGIRU ARGUFIED
ADEFGITU FATIGUED
ADEFGLOT GATEFOLD
ADEFHHIS HEADFISH
ADEFHILS DEALFISH
ADEFHILY HAYFIELD
ADEFHIMS FAMISHED
ADEFHLSU HEADFULS
ADEFHLTU DEATHFUL
ADEFHMOT FATHOMED
ADEFHNOR FOREHAND
ADEFHOST SOFTHEAD
ADEFIILN FINIALED
ADEFIILR AIRFIELD
ADEFIILS SALIFIED
ADEFIILT FILIATED
ADEFIIMR RAMIFIED
ADEFIINZ NAZIFIED
ADEFIIRR RARIFIED
ADEFIIRT RATIFIED
ADEFILMN INFLAMED
ADEFILNT INFLATED
ADEFILOT FOLIATED
ADEFILSY DAYFLIES
ADEFIMPR FIREDAMP
ADEFINPR PANFRIED
ADEFINRR INFRARED
ADEFINYZ DENAZIFY
ADEFIORS FORESAID
ADEFIRRT DRAFTIER
ADEFIRSS FARSIDES
ADEFLLLU LADLEFUL
ADEFLLOR FALDEROL
ADEFLLOW FALLOWED
ADEFLLRY ALDERFLY
ADEFLLSW DEWFALLS
ADEFLLUY FEUDALLY
ADEFLMRU DREAMFUL
ADEFLNNS FENLANDS
ADEFLNOR FORELAND
ADEFLNTU FLAUNTED
ADEFLNUW UNFLAWED
ADEFLORT DEFLATOR
ADEFLORV FLAVORED
ADEFLORY FORELADY
ADEFLPRS FELDSPAR
ADEFLPSU SPADEFUL
ADEFLRSW SELFWARD
ADEFLRTW LEFTWARD
ADEFLRZZ FRAZZLED
ADEFLSTU DEFAULTS
SULFATED
ADEFMNRU UNFRAMED
ADEFNOPR PROFANED
ADEFNSST DAFTNESS
ADEFOOSS SEAFOODS
ADEFORRR FORRADER
ADEFORRW FARROWED
ADEFORRY FOREYARD
ADEFORUV FAVOURED
ADEFOSTU FADEOUTS
ADEFPRRT PREDRAFT
ADEFPTUW UPWAFTED
ADEFRRST DRAFTERS
REDRAFTS
ADEFRSTW DWARFEST
ADEFSSTT STEDFAST
ADEGGIRR DRAGGIER
ADEGGJLY JAGGEDLY
ADEGGLRS DRAGGLES
ADEGGLRY RAGGEDLY
ADEGGMOS DEMAGOGS
ADEGGMOY DEMAGOGY
ADEGGNOW WAGGONED
ADEGGNTU UNTAGGED
ADEGGOPS PEDAGOGS
ADEGGOPY PEDAGOGY
ADEGGRRS DRAGGERS
ADEGGRTY GADGETRY
ADEGHHOS HOGSHEAD
ADEGHILT ALIGHTED
GILTHEAD
ADEGHINR ADHERING
ADEGHINS DEASHING
HEADINGS
ADEGHIRR HAGRIDER
ADEGHIRS HAGRIDES
ADEGHJSU JUGHEADS
ADEGHLNO HEADLONG
LONGHEAD
ADEGHLOS GALOSHED
ADEGHNNU UNHANGED
ADEGHORT GOATHERD
ADEGHRTU DAUGHTER
ADEGHTUW WAUGHTED
ADEGIILN GLIADINE
ADEGIILP DIPLEGIA
ADEGIIMN IMAGINED
ADEGIIMS DIGAMIES
ADEGIINR DEAIRING
ADEGIINT IDEATING
ADEGIIRT DIGERATI
ADEGIITT DIGITATE
ADEGIJSW JIGSAWED
ADEGIKLO GOADLIKE
ADEGIKNN KNEADING
ADEGILLP PILLAGED
ADEGILLR GLADLIER
GRILLADE
ADEGILMN MALIGNED
MEDALING
ADEGILNN LADENING
ADEGILNP PEDALING
PLEADING
ADEGILNR DANGLIER
DRAGLINE
ADEGILNS DEALINGS
LEADINGS
SIGNALED
ADEGILNT DELATING
ADEGILNY DELAYING
ADEGILOR DIALOGER
ADEGILOU DIALOGUE
ADEGILOY IDEALOGY
ADEGILSS GLISSADE
ADEGILST GLADIEST
ADEGIMNN AMENDING
ADEGIMNO AMIDOGEN
ADEGIMNR DREAMING
MARGINED
MIDRANGE
ADEGIMOR IDEOGRAM
ADEGIMPS MEDIGAPS
MISPAGED
ADEGIMRS MISGRADE
ADEGIMRT MIGRATED
ADEGINNV DAVENING
ADEGINNW AWNINGED
ADEGINOR ORGANDIE
ADEGINOS AGONISED
DIAGNOSE
ADEGINOZ AGONIZED
ADEGINRS DERAIGNS
GRADINES
READINGS
ADEGINRT DERATING
GRADIENT
REDATING
TREADING
ADEGINRY READYING
ADEGINSS ASSIGNED
ADEGINST SEDATING
STEADING
ADEGINSW WINDAGES
ADEGINWX DEWAXING
ADEGIOST GODETIAS
ADEGIPRR PARRIDGE
ADEGISTU GAUDIEST
ADEGIUWY GUIDEWAY
ADEGJNOR JARGONED
ADEGLLNU GLANDULE
UNGALLED
ADEGLLOP GALLOPED
ADEGLLSU GALLUSED
ADEGLMOS GLADSOME
ADEGLMPU PLUMAGED
ADEGLMUY AMYGDULE
ADEGLNOP ANGLEPOD
ADEGLNPS SPANGLED
ADEGLNRS DANGLERS
GLANDERS
ADEGLNRW WRANGLED
ADEGLNSS GLADNESS
ADEGLNTW TWANGLED
ADEGLNUZ UNGLAZED
ADEGLORV OVERGLAD
ADEGLPPR GRAPPLED
ADEGMMNO GAMMONED
ADEGMMRU RUMMAGED
ADEGMNOR DRAGOMEN
ADEGMNOT MONTAGED
ADEGMNOY ENDOGAMY
ADEGMNSU AGENDUMS
ADEGMOPS MEGAPODS
ADEGMORS ORGASMED
ADEGMPUZ GAZUMPED
ADEGNNOR ANDROGEN
ADEGNNSU DUNNAGES
ADEGNOPR DOGNAPER
ADEGNOPU POUNDAGE
ADEGNORT DRAGONET
ADEGNOSV DOGVANES
ADEGNRRU GRANDEUR
ADEGNRST DRAGNETS
GRANDEST
ADEGNRUU UNARGUED
ADEGOORV OVERGOAD
ADEGOPRR DRAGROPE
PROGRADE
ADEGOPRT PORTAGED
ADEGORRT GARROTED
ADEGORSW DOWAGERS
WORDAGES
ADEGORTT GAROTTED
ADEGORTU OUTRAGED
RAGOUTED
ADEGORTW WATERDOG
ADEGOTTV GAVOTTED
ADEGOTUZ OUTGAZED
ADEGPRSU UPGRADES
ADEGPSTU UPSTAGED
ADEGRRST DRAGSTER
ADEGRRSU GUARDERS
ADEGRSSU DESUGARS
GRADUSES
ADEGTTTU GUTTATED
ADEHHIPS HEADSHIP
ADEHHNTU HEADHUNT
ADEHHOOR HOORAHED
ADEHHOPS HOPHEADS
ADEHHOST HOTHEADS
ADEHHRRU HURRAHED
ADEHHRST THRASHED
ADEHHUZZ HUZZAHED
ADEHIITZ THIAZIDE
ADEHIKLN HANDLIKE
ADEHIKLV KHEDIVAL
ADEHIKNS SKINHEAD
ADEHILLO HILLOAED
ADEHILMO HALIDOME
ADEHILNR HARDLINE
ADEHILNU UNHAILED
ADEHILPS HELIPADS
ADEHILSV LAVISHED
ADEHIMMS SHAMMIED
ADEHIMOT HEMATOID
ADEHIMRS MISHEARD
SEMIHARD
ADEHINOP DIAPHONE
ADEHINOS ADHESION
ADEHINOY HYOIDEAN
ADEHINPS DEANSHIP
HEADPINS
PINHEADS
ADEHINPU DAUPHINE
ADEHINRT ANTHERID
ADEHINRU UNHAIRED
ADEHINSS DANISHES
SHANDIES
ADEHINST HANDIEST
ADEHINSV VANISHED
ADEHIOTT ATHETOID
ADEHIPRS RAPHIDES
ADEHIPST PITHEADS
ADEHIRRT TRIHEDRA
ADEHIRRW HARDWIRE
ADEHIRSS AIRSHEDS
RADISHES
ADEHIRST HARDIEST
ADEHIRSV RAVISHED
ADEHIRSW DISHWARE
RAWHIDES
ADEHIRSY HAYRIDES
ADEHISST DASHIEST
SHADIEST
ADEHKLNU LUNKHEAD
ADEHKNRS REDSHANK
ADEHKORW HEADWORK
ADEHKOST KATHODES
ADEHLLOO HALLOOED
HOLLOAED
ADEHLLOU HULLOAED
ADEHLLOW HALLOWED
ADEHLLRT THRALLED
ADEHLMNO HOMELAND
ADEHLNRS HANDLERS
ADEHLNSS HANDLESS
HANDSELS
ADEHLNST SHETLAND
ADEHLNSU UNLASHED
ADEHLNUV UNHALVED
ADEHLOOR HORDEOLA
ADEHLOOT TOOLHEAD
ADEHLOPS ASPHODEL
ADEHLOPW PLOWHEAD
ADEHLPSS SPLASHED
ADEHLRRY HERALDRY
ADEHMNNY HANDYMEN
ADEHMNOS HANDSOME
ADEHMNOT METHADON
ADEHMNRS HERDSMAN
ADEHMNRU UNHARMED
ADEHMNSU UNSHAMED
ADEHMOOP OOMPAHED
ADEHMOOR HEADROOM
ADEHMORW HOMEWARD
ADEHMOST HEADMOST
ADEHMOSU MADHOUSE
ADEHMOSY SHAMOYED
ADEHNNSW HANDSEWN
ADEHNOPR ORPHANED
ADEHNOPT PHONATED
ADEHNORS HARDNOSE
ADEHNORV HANDOVER
OVERHAND
ADEHNOSS SANDSHOE
ADEHNPSU UNSHAPED
ADEHNRSS HARDNESS
ADEHNRSU UNSHARED
ADEHNRSW SWANHERD
ADEHNRTU UNTHREAD
ADEHNSST HANDSETS
ADEHNSSU SUNSHADE
ADEHNSUV UNSHAVED
ADEHNSUW UNWASHED
ADEHNTTU UNHATTED
ADEHNTUW UNTHAWED
ADEHOORY HOORAYED
ADEHOPRS RHAPSODE
ADEHOPST POTHEADS
ADEHOPSX HEXAPODS
ADEHOPXY HEXAPODY
ADEHORRS HOARDERS
ADEHORRV OVERHARD
ADEHORRW HARROWED
ADEHORSW SHADOWER
ADEHORTT THROATED
ADEHORTU AUTHORED
OUTHEARD
ADEHOSTW TOWHEADS
ADEHPSTU DUSTHEAP
ADEHQSSU SQUASHED
ADEHRRUY HURRAYED
ADEHRSSY HYDRASES
ADEHRSTY HYDRATES
ADEHRTTW THWARTED
ADEIILMS IDEALISM
MILADIES
ADEIILPR PERIDIAL
ADEIILST IDEALIST
ADEIILTV DILATIVE
ADEIILTY IDEALITY
ADEIIMMS MISAIMED
ADEIIMNN INDAMINE
ADEIIMNR MERIDIAN
ADEIIMNS AMIDINES
DIAMINES
ADEIIMPR IMPAIRED
ADEIIMRS SEMIARID
ADEIIMTT IMITATED
ADEIINNS SANIDINE
ADEIINOT IDEATION
IODINATE
ADEIINRT DAINTIER
ADEIINRU UREDINIA
ADEIINST ADENITIS
DAINTIES
ADEIINSZ DIAZINES
ADEIINTV VANITIED
ADEIIPRS PRESIDIA
ADEIITTV VITIATED
ADEIITUV AUDITIVE
ADEIJMRS JEMIDARS
ADEIKLLO KELOIDAL
ADEIKLLR LARDLIKE
ADEIKLLY LADYLIKE
ADEIKLNS SANDLIKE
ADEIKLNW DAWNLIKE
ADEIKLOT TOADLIKE
ADEIKLOX ALKOXIDE
ADEIKLRR DARKLIER
ADEIKLSW SIDEWALK
ADEIKMPR IMPARKED
ADEIKMRT TIDEMARK
ADEIKNPR KIDNAPER
ADEIKNSY KYANISED
ADEIKNYZ KYANIZED
ADEIKORT KERATOID
ADEILLMY MEDIALLY
ADEILLNN LANDLINE
ADEILLNU UNALLIED
ADEILLNV ANVILLED
ADEILLNW INWALLED
ADEILLOR ARILLODE
ADEILLPR PILLARED
ADEILLPS SPADILLE
ADEILLRS DALLIERS
DIALLERS
ADEILLRV RIVALLED
ADEILLSW SIDEWALL
ADEILMMM MELAMDIM
ADEILMMS DILEMMAS
ADEILMNO MELANOID
ADEILMNU UNMAILED
ADEILMNY MAIDENLY
MEDIANLY
ADEILMOS MELODIAS
ADEILMPS IMPLEADS
MISPLEAD
ADEILMRS DISMALER
ADEILMRY DREAMILY
ADEILMSS MISDEALS
MISLEADS
ADEILMST MEDALIST
MISDEALT
ADEILNNO NONIDEAL
ADEILNNP PINELAND
ADEILNNR INLANDER

ADEILNNS ANNELIDS
LINDANES
ADEILNNT DENTINAL
ADEILNNU UNNAILED
ADEILNOP PALINODE
ADEILNOT DELATION
ADEILNPS SANDPILE
ADEILNPT PANTILED
ADEILNRS ISLANDER
ADEILNTV DIVALENT
ADEILOPS SEPALOID
ADEILOPT PETALOID
ADEILORS DARIOLES
ADEILORT IDOLATER
TAILORED
ADEILORV OVERLAID
ADEILORX EXORDIAL
ADEILOSS ASSOILED
ISOLEADS
ADEILOST DIASTOLE
ISOLATED
SODALITE
ADEILOSZ DIAZOLES
SLEAZOID
ADEILOTV DOVETAIL
VIOLATED
ADEILPPP PEDIPALP
ADEILPRS LIPREADS
PARSLIED
SPIRALED
ADEILPRT DIPTERAL
TRIPEDAL
ADEILPRU EPIDURAL
ADEILPRV DEPRIVAL
ADEILPSS DESPISAL
ADEILPST TALIPEDS
ADEILQTU LIQUATED
ADEILRRW DRAWLIER
ADEILRRY DREARILY
ADEILRST DILATERS
LARDIEST
REDTAILS
ADEILRSU RESIDUAL
ADEILRSY DIALYSER
ADEILRTT DETRITAL
ADEILRVY VARIEDLY
ADEILRYZ DIALYZER
ADEILSSV DEVISALS
ADEILSSY DIALYSES
ADEILSTY STEADILY
ADEILSUV DISVALUE
ADEILSUZ DUALIZES
ADEILSWY SLIDEWAY
ADEILSXY DYSLEXIA
ADEILSYZ DIALYZES
ADEILTTU ALTITUDE
LATITUDE
ADEILTVY DATIVELY
ADEIMMNS MISNAMED
ADEIMMRS MERMAIDS
ADEIMMST MISMATED
ADEIMNNO DEMONIAN
ADEIMNOP DOPAMINE
ADEIMNOR RADIOMEN
ADEIMNOS AMIDONES
DAIMONES
DOMAINES
ADEIMNOT DOMINATE
ADEIMNOU EUDAIMON
ADEIMNPW IMPAWNED
ADEIMNRU MURAENID
ADEIMNRY DAIRYMEN
ADEIMNRZ ZEMINDAR
ADEIMNST MEDIANTS
ADEIMNSU MAUNDIES
ADEIMNTY DYNAMITE
ADEIMORR AIRDROME
ADEIMORT MEDIATOR
ADEIMOSS SESAMOID
ADEIMOST ATOMISED
ADEIMOTZ ATOMIZED
ADEIMPRT IMPARTED
PREADMIT
ADEIMPST IMPASTED
ADEIMRRS ADMIRERS
DISARMER
MARRIEDS
ADEIMRSS MISREADS
SIDEARMS
ADEIMRST MISRATED
READMITS
ADEIMRSY MIDYEARS
ADEIMRTT ADMITTER
ADEIMRTU MURIATED
ADEIMSST DIASTEMS
MISDATES
ADEIMSTY DAYTIMES
ADEINNOT ANOINTED
ANTINODE
ADEINNOV DEVONIAN
ADEINNPT PINNATED
ADEINNRS INSNARED
ADEINNRZ RENDZINA
ADEINNTU INUNDATE
ADEINOPP PEPONIDA
ADEINOPT ANTIPODE
ADEINORR ORDAINER
REORDAIN
ADEINORS ANEROIDS
ADEINORT AROINTED
ORDINATE
RATIONED
ADEINOSS ADENOSIS
ADONISES
ADEINOST ASTONIED
SEDATION
ADEINOSX DIOXANES
ADEINOSZ ANODIZES
ADEINOTT ANTIDOTE
TETANOID
ADEINOTV DONATIVE
ADEINPPX APPENDIX
ADEINPRS SPRAINED
ADEINPRT DIPTERAN
ADEINPRU UNPAIRED
UNREPAID
ADEINPST DEPAINTS
ADEINPSV SPAVINED
ADEINQTU ANTIQUED
ADEINRRS DRAINERS
SERRANID
ADEINRSS ARIDNESS
SARDINES
ADEINRST DETRAINS
RANDIEST
STRAINED
ADEINRSU DENARIUS
UNRAISED
URANIDES
ADEINRSV INVADERS
ADEINRTT NITRATED
ADEINRTU INDURATE
RUINATED
URINATED
ADEINRUV UNVARIED
ADEINRVY VINEYARD
ADEINSST DESTAINS
SANDIEST
ADEINSSV AVIDNESS
ADEINSTT INSTATED
ADEINSTU AUDIENTS
SINUATED
ADEINSTV DEVIANTS
ADEIOPRR PRERADIO
ADEIOPRS DIASPORE
PARODIES
ADEIOPRV OVERPAID
ADEIOPSS ADIPOSES
ADEIOPST DIOPTASE
ADEIOPTV ADOPTIVE
ADEIORRT ADROITER
ADEIORST ASTEROID
ADEIORSV AVODIRES
AVOIDERS
ADEIORTT TERATOID
ADEIORTV DEVIATOR
ADEIOSSX OXIDASES
ADEIOSTX OXIDATES
ADEIOSTZ AZOTISED
ADEIOTZZ AZOTIZED
ADEIPPRS APPRISED
ADEIPPRZ APPRIZED
ADEIPRSS DESPAIRS
ADEIPRST RAPIDEST
TRAIPSED
ADEIPRSU UPRAISED
ADEIPRSW RIPSAWED
ADEIPRTU EUPATRID
PREAUDIT
ADEIPSSX SPADIXES
ADEIPTTU APTITUDE
ADEIQRRU QUARRIED
ADEIQRSU QUERIDAS
ADEIQSUY QUAYSIDE
ADEIRRTW TAWDRIER
ADEIRRWW WIREDRAW
ADEIRSST DIASTERS
DISASTER
DISRATES
ADEIRSSU RADIUSES
SUDARIES
ADEIRSSV ADVISERS
ADEIRSTT STRIATED
TARDIEST
ADEIRSTW TAWDRIES
ADEIRTTT ATTRITED
TITRATED
ADEIRTUV DURATIVE
ADEIRVWY DRIVEWAY
ADEISSST ASSISTED
DISSEATS
ADEISSSV DISSAVES
ADEISSTT DISTASTE
STAIDEST
ADEISSTV DISTAVES
ADEISSWY SIDEWAYS
WAYSIDES
ADEISTTU SITUATED
ADEISTUZ DEUTZIAS
ADEISTWY TIDEWAYS
ADEITTTU ATTITUDE
ADEJMMNU UNJAMMED
ADEJNRUW UNDERJAW
ADEJOPRS JEOPARDS
ADEJOPRY JEOPARDY
ADEJRRSU ADJURERS
ADEJRSTU ADJUSTER
READJUST
ADEKLMRY MARKEDLY
ADEKLNSU UNSLAKED
ADEKLORW LEADWORK
ADEKLPRS SPARKLED
ADEKLPTU UPTALKED
ADEKMNRU UNMARKED
ADEKMNSU UNMASKED
ADEKMORS DARKSOME
ADEKNNRU UNRANKED
ADEKNNSS DANKNESS
ADEKNOSU UNSOAKED
ADEKNOTW TAKEDOWN
ADEKNRSS DARKNESS
ADEKNSVY VANDYKES
ADEKOOTW TEAKWOOD
ADEKOSTU OUTASKED
ADEKQSUW SQUAWKED
ADELLMOS SLALOMED
ADELLMRU MEDULLAR
MURALLED
ADELLMSU MEDULLAS
ADELLNNU ANNULLED
ADELLNRS LANDLERS
ADELLNSS LANDLESS
ADELLNTY DENTALLY
ADELLNUW UNWALLED
ADELLOPW WALLOPED
ADELLOSW SALLOWED
ADELLOTT ALLOTTED
TOTALLED
ADELLOTW TALLOWED
ADELLOVY LADYLOVE
ADELLOWW WALLOWED
ADELLQSU SQUALLED
ADELLTUU ULULATED
ADELMNNS LANDSMEN
ADELMNRS MANDRELS
ADELMOPS MALPOSED
ADELMORS EARLDOMS
ADELMOSS DAMOSELS
ADELMOSZ DAMOZELS
ADELMOTU MODULATE
ADELMPRT TRAMPLED
ADELMRRU DEMURRAL
ADELMSSY MASSEDLY
ADELMSUY AMUSEDLY
ADELMTTY MATTEDLY
ADELMTUU UMLAUTED
ADELNNOT LENTANDO
ADELNORS LADRONES
SOLANDER
ADELNORU UNLOADER
ADELNORV OVERLAND
ADELNPRS SPANDREL
ADELNPRU PENDULAR
UNDERLAP
UPLANDER
ADELNPRY REPANDLY
ADELNPSY DYSPNEAL
ENDPLAYS
ADELNPUY UNPLAYED
ADELNRSS SLANDERS
ADELNRSU LAUNDERS
LURDANES
ADELNRTU DENTURAL
ADELNRTY ARDENTLY
ADELNRUY UNDERLAY
ADELNSSS SANDLESS
ADELNSTU UNSALTED
ADELNSTW WETLANDS
ADELNTUU UNDULATE
ADELNUUV UNVALUED
ADELOOPV LEVODOPA
ADELOORV OVERLOAD
ADELOOTW LATEWOOD
ADELOPRS LEOPARDS
PRELOADS
ADELOPRT PORTALED
ADELOPRU POULARDE
ADELOPRW POLEWARD
ADELOPSS DEPOSALS
ADELOPST TADPOLES
ADELOPTY PETALODY
ADELORSS ROADLESS
ADELORST DELATORS
LEOTARDS
LODESTAR
ADELORSU ROULADES
ADELORTW LEADWORT
ADELOSSS SODALESS
ADELOSST TOADLESS
ADELOSTU OUTLEADS
ADELOSTV SOLVATED
ADELOTUV OVULATED
ADELOTUW OUTLAWED
ADELOVWY AVOWEDLY
ADELPPRY DAPPERLY
ADELPQUX QUADPLEX
ADELPRRU LARRUPED
ADELPRSW SPRAWLED
ADELPRTT PRATTLED
ADELPRTU PREADULT
ADELPSTT SPLATTED
ADELPSTU PULSATED
ADELRRSU RUDERALS
ADELRRSW DRAWLERS
ADELRRTU ULTRARED
ADELRSSW WARDLESS
WRASSLED
ADELRSTT STARTLED
ADELRSTW WARSTLED
WRASTLED
ADELRSZZ DAZZLERS
ADELRTUY ADULTERY
ADELSTTY STATEDLY
ADELTTTW TWATTLED
ADEMMNOW MADWOMEN
ADEMMSTU SUMMATED
ADEMNNNU UNMANNED
ADEMNNOR NORMANDE
ADEMNOOR MAROONED
ADEMNOPR POMANDER
ADEMNOPT TAMPONED
ADEMNORS MADRONES
RANSOMED
ADEMNOTU AMOUNTED
ADEMNPPU UNMAPPED
ADEMNPSS DAMPNESS
ADEMNRRU UNDERARM
UNMARRED
ADEMNRSU DURAMENS
MAUNDERS
SURNAMED
ADEMNRTU UNDREAMT
ADEMNRUW UNWARMED
ADEMNSSU MEDUSANS
ADEMNSUU UNAMUSED
ADEMNTTU UNMATTED
ADEMOORT MODERATO
ADEMOORV VAROOMED
ADEMOOST STOMODEA
ADEMOOSV VAMOOSED
ADEMOPRY PYODERMA
ADEMOPSU MOUSEPAD
ADEMORRT MORTARED
ADEMORRU ARMOURED
ADEMORRW MARROWED
ADEMORTU OUTDREAM
ADEMORTW DAMEWORT
ADEMOSSY SAMOYEDS
ADEMRRSU EARDRUMS
ADEMRRTY MARTYRED
ADENNNTU UNTANNED
ADENNORT NONRATED
ADENNOSY ANODYNES
ADENNOTU UNATONED
ADENNOTW WANTONED
ADENNPST PENDANTS
ADENNRRU UNDERRAN
ADENNRUW UNWARNED
ADENNTUW UNWANTED
ADENOORT RATOONED
ADENOORW WANDEROO
ADENOOST ODONATES
ADENOOTZ OZONATED
ADENOPRR PARDONER
ADENOPRS OPERANDS
PADRONES
PANDORES
ADENOPRT PRONATED
ADENOPRX EXPANDOR
ADENOPSS DAPSONES
SPADONES
ADENOPST NOTEPADS
ADENOPSY DYSPNOEA
ADENORRS ADORNERS
READORNS
ADENORRW NARROWED
ADENORTT ATTORNED
ADENORTW DANEWORT
TEARDOWN
ADENORTY AROYNTED
ADENORUX RONDEAUX
ADENOTUY AUTODYNE
ADENOUVW UNAVOWED
ADENPPTU UNTAPPED
ADENPRRS PARDNERS
ADENPRSU UNDRAPES
ADENPRSW PREDAWNS
ADENPRTU UNPARTED
ADENPRTY PEDANTRY
ADENPRUW UNWARPED
ADENPRUY UNDERPAY
ADENPSSY DYSPNEAS
SYNAPSED
ADENQRSU SQUANDER
ADENRRST STRANDER
ADENRRSY REYNARDS
ADENRRWY WARDENRY
ADENRSST STANDERS
ADENRSSU DANSEURS
ADENRSTU DAUNTERS
TRANSUDE
UNTREADS
ADENRSTX DEXTRANS
ADENRTTU TRUANTED
ADENRTUX UNDERTAX
ADENRUWY UNDERWAY
ADENSSSW WESSANDS
ADENSTTU UNSTATED
UNTASTED
ADENSTUW UNWASTED
ADENSTUY UNSTAYED
UNSTEADY
ADENSUWY UNSWAYED
ADEOOPRW PEARWOOD
ADEOOPSS APODOSES
ADEOORRT TOREADOR
ADEOOTTT TATTOOED
ADEOPPRT PREADOPT
ADEOPPRV APPROVED
ADEOPRRS EARDROPS
ADEOPRRT PARROTED
PREDATOR
PRORATED
PROTRADE
TEARDROP
ADEOPRST ADOPTERS
PASTORED
READOPTS
ADEOPRSU UPSOARED
ADEOPRTT TETRAPOD
ADEOPRUV VAPOURED
ADEOPSST PODESTAS
ADEOPSTT POSTDATE
ADEORRSS DROSERAS
ADEORRST ROADSTER
ADEORRVW OVERDRAW
ADEORSST ASSORTED
TORSADES
ADEORSTU OUTDARES
OUTREADS
READOUTS
ADEORSTX EXTRADOS
ADEORSUV SAVOURED
ADEORTTU OUTRATED
OUTTRADE
ADEORTUV OUTRAVED
ADEOSTTU OUTDATES
ADEPPRST STRAPPED
ADEPRRTU RAPTURED
ADEPRSTU PASTURED
UPDATERS
UPSTARED
ADEQSTTU SQUATTED
ADERRSSW WARDRESS
ADERRSTT REDSTART
ADERSSSU ASSUREDS
ADERSSTW STEWARDS
ADERSSUY DASYURES
ADERSTUX SURTAXED
ADERSTWW WESTWARD
ADFFHIRS DRAFFISH
ADFFHNOS HANDOFFS
ADFFISST DISTAFFS
ADFFLNOS FANFOLDS
ADFFLOOS OFFLOADS
ADFFNOST STANDOFF
ADFGINNU UNFADING
ADFGINRT DRAFTING
ADFGINRW DWARFING
ADFHILSY LADYFISH
ADFHINSS SANDFISH
ADFHIOST TOADFISH
ADFHIRSW DWARFISH
ADFHLNSU HANDFULS
HANDSFUL
ADFHLOST HOLDFAST
ADFHOOSS SHADOOFS
ADFIIILR FILARIID
ADFIILPY LAPIDIFY
ADFILLLN LANDFILL
ADFILLMN FILMLAND
ADFILLNO NAILFOLD
ADFILLNW WINDFALL
ADFILMNO MANIFOLD
ADFILMRU FLUIDRAM
ADFILNWW WINDFLAW
ADFILRTY DRAFTILY
ADFIMRSW DWARFISM
ADFINORZ FORZANDI
ADFINRST INDRAFTS
ADFIORSV DISFAVOR
ADFLLNOW DOWNFALL
ADFLMNOR LANDFORM
ADFLMNOY MANYFOLD
ADFLMPSU MUDFLAPS
ADFLMSTU MUDFLATS
ADFLNOPS PLAFONDS
ADFLOOWY FLOODWAY
ADFLORSU FOULARDS
ADFNNOST FONDANTS
ADFNOORZ FORZANDO
ADFOOPST FOOTPADS
ADFOOSTW FATWOODS
ADFOOSWY FOODWAYS
ADFORRSW FORWARDS
ADFPRSTU UPDRAFTS
ADGGGILN DAGGLING
ADGGGINR DRAGGING
ADGGHNOS HANGDOGS
ADGGHORY HYDRAGOG
ADGGILNN DANGLING
ADGGINRS NIGGARDS
ADGGINRU GUARDING
ADGGLRSU SLUGGARD
ADGHHILN HIGHLAND
ADGHHIOR HIGHROAD
ADGHILLL GILDHALL
ADGHILNN HANDLING
ADGHILOS HIDALGOS
ADGHILTY DAYLIGHT
ADGHINOR HOARDING
ADGHINPR HANDGRIP
ADGHINSS SHADINGS
ADGHIPRS DIGRAPHS
ADGHIRSS DISHRAGS
ADGHITTW TIGHTWAD
ADGHLNNO LONGHAND
ADGHNNSU HANDGUNS
ADGHNOSS SANDHOGS
ADGHOOPR ODOGRAPH
ADGHRSTU DRAUGHTS
ADGHRTUY DRAUGHTY
ADGIILLN DIALLING
ADGIILLO GLADIOLI
ADGIILNO GONIDIAL
ADGIILNS DIALINGS
GLIADINS
ADGIILNT DILATING
ADGIILPY PYGIDIAL
ADGIILST DIGITALS
ADGIILTY ALGIDITY
ADGIIMNR ADMIRING
ADGIIMNX ADMIXING
ADGIIMST DIGAMIST
ADGIINNR DRAINING
ADGIINNT NIDATING
ADGIINNU GUANIDIN
ADGIINNV INVADING
ADGIINOR RADIOING
ADGIINOT IODATING
ADGIINOV AVOIDING
ADGIINRY DAIRYING
ADGIINSS SIGANIDS
ADGIINSU IGUANIDS
ADGIINSV ADVISING
ADGIINTU AUDITING

ADGIJNRU ADJURING
ADGIKLNR DARKLING
ADGILLNU ALLUDING
ADGILLNW WINDGALL
ADGILLNY DALLYING
ADGILMOR MARIGOLD
ADGILNNS LANDINGS
SANDLING
ADGILNNU UNLADING
ADGILNOS LOADINGS
ADGILNPP DAPPLING
ADGILNRS DARLINGS
ADGILNRT DARTLING
ADGILNRW DRAWLING
ADGILNRY DARINGLY
ADGILNZZ DAZZLING
ADGILOOS SOLIDAGO
ADGILOPR PRODIGAL
ADGILORS GOLIARDS
ADGILORY GYROIDAL
ADGILRVY GRAVIDLY
ADGIMMNR DRAMMING
ADGIMNOP POMADING
ADGIMNPS DAMPINGS
ADGIMOSU DIGAMOUS
ADGINNOR ADORNING
ADGINNOT DONATING
ADGINNPY PANDYING
ADGINNRS DARNINGS
ADGINNRU UNDARING
ADGINNST STANDING
ADGINNTU DAUNTING
ADGINOOR RIGADOON
ADGINOPT ADOPTING
ADGINORU RIGAUDON
ADGINOTY TOADYING
ADGINPTU UPDATING
ADGINRRS GRANDSIR
ADGINRSW DRAWINGS
SWARDING
ADGINRTT DRATTING
ADGINRTU ANTIDRUG
ADGIORST GORDITAS
ADGIPRSU PAGURIDS
ADGIRSSU GUISARDS
ADGIRSZZ GIZZARDS
ADGKOOSZ GADZOOKS
ADGLMNOS MANGOLDS
ADGLNOOS DONGOLAS
GONDOLAS
ADGLNORS GOLDARNS
ADGLOORY GARDYLOO
ADGLOSWY DAYGLOWS
ADGMNOOR ONDOGRAM
ADGMNORS GORMANDS
ADGMNORU GOURMAND
ADGNNOQU QUANDONG
ADGNNORS GRANDSON
ADGNNRYY GYNANDRY
ADGNOORS DRAGOONS
GADROONS
ADGNRRSU GURNARDS
ADGNRSUU UNGUARDS
ADGOPRST POSTGRAD
ADGORSTU OUTDRAGS
ADGRSSTU DUSTRAGS
ADHHIPRS HARDSHIP
ADHHMOSS SHAHDOMS
ADHHNRTY HYDRANTH
ADHIIIKS DAISHIKI
ADHIIKSS DASHIKIS
ADHIIMPS AMIDSHIP
ADHIINOP OPHIDIAN
ADHIJLSY JADISHLY
ADHIKOPS HAPKIDOS
ADHILLOT THALLOID
ADHILLRY HYDRILLA
ADHILMOS HALIDOMS
ADHILNST HANDLIST
ADHILOPS HAPLOIDS
SHIPLOAD
ADHILOPY HAPLOIDY
ADHILOSY HOLIDAYS
HYALOIDS
ADHILPSY LADYSHIP
ADHIMNOR RHODAMIN
ADHIMNOS ADMONISH
ADHIMNOU HUMANOID
ADHIMOPP AMPHIPOD
ADHIMPSS PHASMIDS
ADHINOPY DIAPHONY
ADHINPSS DISHPANS
ADHINPSU DAUPHINS
ADHINRTW HANDWRIT
ADHINSST STANDISH
ADHINSTU DIANTHUS
ADHIOSTY TOADYISH
ADHIPRSW WARDSHIP
ADHIPRSY SHIPYARD
ADHIRTWW WITHDRAW
ADHITWWY WIDTHWAY
ADHKNORW HANDWORK
ADHKORSW DORHAWKS
ADHLLLOS HOLDALLS
ADHLLNOS HOLLANDS
ADHLMNOO HANDLOOM
ADHLMORT THRALDOM
ADHLNOUW DOWNHAUL
ADHLOSYY HOLYDAYS
ADHMNOOS MANHOODS
ADHMOPRS DRAMSHOP
ADHNNOOR HONORAND
ADHNNORY NONHARDY
ADHNOOTU AUNTHOOD
ADHNOSTU HANDOUTS
THOUSAND
ADHNOSWW DOWNWASH
ADHNRSTY HYDRANTS
ADHOOPRS HOSPODAR
ADHOOPST HOPTOADS
ADHOORRS RHODORAS
ADHOORSW ROADSHOW
ADHOPRST HARDTOPS
POTSHARD
ADHOPRSU UPHOARDS
ADHOPRSY RHAPSODY
ADHOPSST DASHPOTS
ADHORRSU DHOURRAS
ADHORRTY HYDRATOR
ADIIINRV VIRIDIAN
ADIIIQRU DAIQUIRI
ADIIKLLN KALLIDIN
ADIIKLMM MILKMAID
ADIIKLST TAILSKID
ADIIKNST ANTISKID
ADIILLMR MILLIARD
ADIILLOP LIPOIDAL
ADIILLOR ARILLOID
ADIILLST DIALLIST
ADIILLUV DILUVIAL
ADIILMSS MISDIALS
ADIILNOT DILATION
ADIILNSU INDUSIAL
ADIILNSV INVALIDS
ADIILNTW TAILWIND
ADIILNTY DAINTILY
ADIILNUV DILUVIAN
ADIILOPP DIPLOPIA
ADIILPST LAPIDIST
ADIILSST DIALISTS
ADIILSSY DIALYSIS
ADIILTVY VALIDITY
ADIIMNNS INDAMINS
ADIIMRST TRIADISM
ADIINNOT NIDATION
ADIINNOZ DIAZINON
ADIINOOT IODATION
ADIINOTU AUDITION
ADIINRST DISTRAIN
ADIINSST DISTAINS
ADIIOPSS ADIPOSIS
ADIIPRTY RAPIDITY
ADIIPSTY SAPIDITY
ADIIPTVY VAPIDITY
ADIIRSST DIARISTS
ADIIRSTT DISTRAIT
ADIJNOST ADJOINTS
ADIKLLOR ROADKILL
ADIKLNPS LANDSKIP
ADIKLNSY LADYKINS
ADIKLORS KILORADS
ADIKLOSS ODALISKS
ADIKNNST INKSTAND
ADIKNRST STINKARD
ADIKSSWY SKIDWAYS
ADILLLPY PALLIDLY
ADILLMMS MILLDAMS
ADILLMNR MANDRILL
ADILLMOU ALLODIUM
ADILLMOV VILLADOM
ADILLMSY DISMALLY
ADILLNPS LANDSLIP
ADILLOSW DISALLOW
ADILLOSY DISLOYAL
ADILLRWY WILLYARD
ADILLSTY DISTALLY
ADILMNNO MANDOLIN
ADILMNOS SALMONID
ADILMNRS MANDRILS
RIMLANDS
ADILMOPS DIPLOMAS
PLASMOID
ADILMOPT DIPLOMAT
ADILMOPY OLYMPIAD
ADILMOSY AMYLOIDS
ADILMOTY MODALITY
ADILMPRY LAMPYRID
ADILMPSS PLASMIDS
ADILMPSU PALUDISM
ADILMSSU DUALISMS
ADILMTUY MULTIDAY
ADILNNOT NONTIDAL
ADILNNOV NONVALID
ADILNNSU DISANNUL
ADILNOOR DOORNAIL
ADILNOOV VINDALOO
ADILNORS ORDINALS
ADILNORT TRINODAL
ADILNOTY NODALITY
ADILNPRS SPANDRIL
ADILNPST DISPLANT
ADILNRSU DIURNALS
ADILNRWY INWARDLY
ADILNSSU SUNDIALS
ADILNSSW WINDLASS
ADILOORT IDOLATOR
TOROIDAL
ADILOOSV OVOIDALS
ADILOPRT DIOPTRAL
TRIPODAL
ADILOPSS DISPOSAL
ADILORST DILATORS
ADILORSY SOLIDARY
ADILORTY ADROITLY
DILATORY
IDOLATRY
ADILOSST SODALIST
ADILOSTY SODALITY
ADILPRSY PYRALIDS
ADILPSST PLASTIDS
ADILPSSY DISPLAYS
ADILPSTU PLAUDITS
ADILRTTY TILTYARD
ADILRTWY TAWDRILY
ADILRWYZ WIZARDLY
ADILSSTU DUALISTS
ADIMMNOO AMMONOID
ADIMMNOS MONADISM
NOMADISM
ADIMMNSY DYNAMISM
ADIMNNOT DOMINANT
ADIMNOST SAINTDOM
ADIMNRSW MISDRAWN
ADIMNRSY MISANDRY
ADIMNSSY SYSADMIN
ADIMNSTY DYNAMIST
ADIMOPRY MYRIAPOD
ADIMOPSY SYMPODIA
ADIMORRS MIRADORS
ADIMOSST MASTOIDS
ADIMOSTT MATTOIDS
ADIMOSTY TOADYISM
ADIMPRSY PYRAMIDS
ADIMRSSW MISDRAWS
ADIMRSUU SUDARIUM
ADIMSSST DISMASTS
ADIMSSTU STADIUMS
ADINNNTU INUNDANT
ADINNOOT DONATION
ADINNOPS DIPNOANS
ADINNORS ANDIRONS
ADINNORY NONDAIRY
ADINOOPS ISOPODAN
ADINOOPT ADOPTION
ADINOORT TANDOORI
ADINOOTT DOTATION
ADINOPPS OPPIDANS
ADINOPRR RAINDROP
ADINOPRS PONIARDS
ADINOPRY PYRANOID
ADINOPST PINTADOS
SATINPOD
ADINORRY ORDINARY
ADINORSS SADIRONS
ADINORST DIATRONS
INTRADOS
ADINORSU DINOSAUR
ADINORTU DURATION
ADINOSTU SUDATION
ADINOSTX OXIDANTS
ADINOSTY DYSTONIA
ADINPSST SANDPITS
ADINPSSY SYNAPSID
ADINRSTU UNITARDS
ADINSWWY WINDWAYS
ADIOOPRT PAROTOID
ADIOOPSS APODOSIS
ADIOOSSW WOODSIAS
ADIOPPST POSTPAID
ADIOPRRS AIRDROPS
ADIOPRSS SPAROIDS
ADIOPRST PARODIST
PAROTIDS
ADIOPRTY PODIATRY
ADIOPSTY DYSTOPIA
ADIORRTT TRADITOR
ADIORSST SARODIST
ADIORSSV ADVISORS
ADIORSTU AUDITORS
ADIORSVY ADVISORY
ADIORTUY AUDITORY
ADIOSSVW DISAVOWS
ADIPRSST DISPARTS
ADIRRWYZ WIZARDRY
ADIRSSTY SATYRIDS
ADIRSSUY DYSURIAS
ADJKNRUY JUNKYARD
ADJLMORS JARLDOMS
ADJNORSU ADJOURNS
ADJORRSU ADJURORS
ADJORSTU ADJUSTOR
ADKLMRSU MUDLARKS
ADKLOORW WOODLARK
WORKLOAD
ADKMNORW MARKDOWN
ADKMOORR DARKROOM
ADKNORTU OUTDRANK
ADKOORRW ROADWORK
ADKORRWY YARDWORK
ADKORSWY DAYWORKS
WORKDAYS
ADKRSSWY SKYWARDS
ADLLMOSW WADMOLLS
ADLLNOPW PLOWLAND
ADLLNOSW LOWLANDS
ADLLOPRS POLLARDS
ADLLORSY DORSALLY
ADLLRSWY DRYWALLS
ADLMNNOO NONMODAL
ADLMNOOR MOORLAND
ADLMNORY RANDOMLY
ADLMOORS LORDOMAS
MALODORS
ADLMOPRW MOLDWARP
ADLMOPSY PSALMODY
ADLMORSU MODULARS
ADLNNORS NORLANDS
ADLNNOSW SNOWLAND
ADLNNOTU NONADULT
ADLNNSSU SUNLANDS
ADLNNTUU UNDULANT
ADLNOORS LARDOONS
ADLNOORW LOANWORD
ADLNOPRU PAULDRON
ADLNOPSU POUNDALS
ADLNOPWY DOWNPLAY
PLAYDOWN
ADLNORST TROLANDS
ADLNOSST SANDLOTS
ADLNOSTU OUTLANDS
ADLOOPRU UROPODAL
ADLOPRSU POULARDS
ADLOPRWY WORDPLAY
ADLOQSUW OLDSQUAW
ADLORRSW WARLORDS
ADLORTWY TOWARDLY
ADLPRUWY UPWARDLY
ADLRRTUY ULTRADRY
ADMMNSSU SUMMANDS
ADMNNORY MONANDRY
ADMNNOSU SOUNDMAN
ADMNOORS MADRONOS
ADMNOORW MOONWARD
ADMNOOST MASTODON
ADMNOOSW WOODSMAN
ADMNOOSZ MADZOONS
ADMNORST MORDANTS
ADMNORSW SANDWORM
SWORDMAN
ADMNOSSU OSMUNDAS
ADMOOPPP POPPADOM
ADMOORRW WARDROOM
ADMOORST DOORMATS
ADMOORSY DAYROOMS
ADMOPPPU POPPADUM
ADMORSST STARDOMS
TSARDOMS
ADMORSTW MADWORTS
ADMORSTZ TZARDOMS
ADMRSSTU DURMASTS
MUSTARDS
ADMRSTUY MUSTARDY
ADNNOOSY NOONDAYS
ADNNORTY DYNATRON
ADNOOPRS PANDOORS
ADNOOQRU QUADROON
ADNOORST DONATORS
ODORANTS
TANDOORS
TORNADOS
ADNOOSVW ADVOWSON
ADNOPRSU PANDOURS
ADNOQRSU SQUADRON
ADNORSTU ROTUNDAS
ADNORSTW SANDWORT
ADNORSTY TARDYONS
ADNORSXY SARDONYX
ADNORTUW OUTDRAWN
UNTOWARD
ADNOSSTU ASTOUNDS
ADNOSTTU OUTSTAND
STANDOUT
ADNPRSSU SANDSPUR
ADNPSSTU DUSTPANS
STANDUPS
UPSTANDS
ADNRSSUW SUNWARDS
ADOOPRRT TRAPDOOR
ADOOPRSU SAUROPOD
ADOOPSSW SAPWOODS
ADOORSWY DOORWAYS
ADOOSSSW SASSWOOD
ADOOSSTT TOSTADOS
ADOPRSSW PASSWORD
ADOPSSSU SOAPSUDS
ADORSTUW OUTDRAWS
OUTWARDS
ADORSTUY SUDATORY
ADRSSTTU STARDUST
ADSSSTUW SAWDUSTS
ADSSTUWY SAWDUSTY
AEEEEMRT EMEERATE
AEEEFRRW FREEWARE
AEEEGGNR REENGAGE
AEEEGKLS KEELAGES
AEEEGLLS LEGALESE
AEEEGLRT EGLATERE
REGELATE
RELEGATE
AEEEGLRV LEVERAGE
AEEEGLST LEGATEES
AEEEGMRT METERAGE
AEEEGNRT GENERATE
TEENAGER
AEEEGNSS AGENESES
AEEEGPRS PEERAGES
AEEEGPSS SEEPAGES
AEEEGRST EAGEREST
ETAGERES
STEERAGE
AEEEGRSW SEWERAGE
AEEEGTTV VEGETATE
AEEEHKLL KEELHALE
AEEEHLRT ETHEREAL
AEEEHMPR EPHEMERA
AEEEHRRS REHEARSE
AEEEHRRT REHEATER
AEEEHSTT AESTHETE
AEEEILNS ALIENEES
AEEEIMNX EXAMINEE
AEEEIMRT EMERITAE
AEEEIRST EATERIES
AEEEKKPS KEEPSAKE
AEEEKNRW WEAKENER
AEEELLPP APPELLEE
AEEELMNR ENAMELER
AEEELNRT LATEENER
AEEELNRV VENEREAL
AEEELNST SELENATE
AEEELPRR REPEALER
AEEELQSU SEQUELAE
AEEELRRS RELEASER
AEEELRRV REVEALER
AEEELRSS RELEASES
AEEELRST TEASELER
AEEELRTX AXLETREE
AEEELSTV ELEVATES
AEEEMMRT METAMERE
AEEEMNST EASEMENT
AEEEMPRS PERMEASE
AEEEMPRT PERMEATE
AEEENNTV VENENATE
AEEENPTT PATENTEE
AEEENRST SERENATE
AEEENRTV ENERVATE
VENERATE
AEEEPRRT REPARTEE
REPEATER
REREPEAT
AEEERRST ARRESTEE
AEEERSST ESTERASE
TESSERAE
AEEERSVW REWEAVES
AEEERTWY EYEWATER
AEEFFLLS FELAFELS
AEEFFLRT TAFFEREL
AEEFFLTT FLATFEET
AEEFFNRT AFFERENT
AEEFGILR FILAGREE
AEEFGIRR FERRIAGE
AEEFGIRT FIGEATER
AEEFGLNS FENAGLES
AEEFGLSU FUSELAGE
AEEFGRSS SERFAGES
AEEFHLLS SELFHEAL
AEEFHRST FEATHERS
AEEFHRTY FEATHERY
AEEFIIRS AERIFIES
AEEFIKLL LEAFLIKE
AEEFIKLW KALEWIFE
AEEFIKRR FREAKIER
AEEFIKRS FAKERIES
AEEFIKRW WAKERIFE
AEEFILMN FILENAME
AEEFILNR FLANERIE
AEEFILRS FILAREES
AEEFILRT FEATLIER
AEEFILST FEALTIES
FETIALES
LEAFIEST
AEEFIRRR RAREFIER
AEEFIRRS RAREFIES
AEEFIRSS FREESIAS
AEEFIRTT FETERITA
AEEFISST SAFETIES
AEEFKOPR FOREPEAK
AEEFLLNR REFALLEN
AEEFLLNV EVENFALL
AEEFLLRW FAREWELL
AEEFLLSS LEAFLESS
AEEFLLST FELLATES
LEAFLETS
AEEFLMNS ENFLAMES
AEEFLMPR PREFLAME
AEEFLMSS FAMELESS
SELFSAME
AEEFLNRU FUNEREAL
AEEFLOOV FOVEOLAE
AEEFLORV OVERLEAF
AEEFLRRR REFERRAL
AEEFLRRT FALTERER
AEEFLRSS FEARLESS
AEEFLRST REFLATES
AEEFLRSW WELFARES
AEEFMNOR FORENAME
AEEFMNRS ENFRAMES
AEEFMORS FEARSOME
AEEFMRRS REFRAMES
AEEFNRST FASTENER
FENESTRA
REFASTEN
AEEFNRTT FATTENER
AEEFNSSS SAFENESS
AEEFORRV OVERFEAR
AEEFRRST FERRATES
AEEFRSST FEASTERS
AEEFRSTU FEATURES
AEEFRSWY FREEWAYS
AEEGGINR AGREEING
AEEGGIRV AGGRIEVE
AEEGGNNR GANGRENE
AEEGGNOS GASOGENE
AEEGGNOZ GAZOGENE
AEEGGNRS ENGAGERS
AEEGGPRU PUGGAREE
AEEGGRSU REGAUGES
AEEGHIRT HERITAGE
AEEGHLOT HELOTAGE
AEEGHMOP HOMEPAGE
AEEGHMPR GRAPHEME
AEEGHNRS SHAGREEN
AEEGHNST THENAGES
AEEGHNSW WHANGEES
AEEGHORS GHERAOES
AEEGHRRT GATHERER
REGATHER
AEEGIILW WEIGELIA
AEEGIIST GAIETIES
AEEGIKLM GAMELIKE
AEEGIKLT GATELIKE
AEEGIKLU AGUELIKE
AEEGILLS GALILEES
LEGALISE
AEEGILLZ LEGALIZE
AEEGILMN LIEGEMAN
AEEGILMR GLEAMIER

AEEGILMS GELSEMIA
MILEAGES
AEEGILNR ALGERINE
AEEGILNS ENSILAGE
LINEAGES
AEEGILNT GALENITE
GELATINE
LEGATINE
AEEGILOU EULOGIAE
AEEGILPR PERIGEAL
AEEGILRS GASELIER
AEEGILST EGALITES
AEEGILSW WEIGELAS
AEEGILTV LEVIGATE
AEEGIMNT GEMINATE
AEEGIMRS REIMAGES
AEEGIMRT EMIGRATE
AEEGINNT ANTIGENE
AEEGINPR PERIGEAN
AEEGINRR REGAINER
AEEGINRS ANERGIES
GESNERIA
AEEGINRT GRATINEE
INTERAGE
AEEGINRZ RAZEEING
AEEGINSS AGENESIS
ASSIGNEE
AEEGINSU EUGENIAS
AEEGINSV ENVISAGE
AEEGINSZ AGENIZES
AEEGINTV AGENTIVE
NEGATIVE
AEEGIPPS PIPEAGES
AEEGIPQU EQUIPAGE
AEEGIRRS GREASIER
AEEGIRTT AIGRETTE
AEEGIRTV ERGATIVE
AEEGISTY GAYETIES
AEEGKLLS KLEAGLES
AEEGKNNR GENNAKER
AEEGLLNR ALLERGEN
AEEGLLPR PRELEGAL
AEEGLLRS ALLEGERS
AEEGLLSZ GAZELLES
AEEGLMNS MELANGES
AEEGLMOS MESOGLEA
AEEGLMPX MEGAPLEX
AEEGLMRS GLEAMERS
AEEGLMRT TELEGRAM
AEEGLMRY MEAGERLY
MEAGRELY
AEEGLMST MELTAGES
AEEGLNNT ENTANGLE
AEEGLNOS GASOLENE
AEEGLNOT ELONGATE
AEEGLNRR ENLARGER
AEEGLNRS ENLARGES
GENERALS
GLEANERS
AEEGLNRT REGENTAL
AEEGLNSU EUGLENAS
AEEGLNSV EVANGELS
AEEGLOOZ ZOOGLEAE
AEEGLORS AEROGELS
AEEGLRRS REGALERS
AEEGLRSS EELGRASS
GEARLESS
LARGESSE
AEEGLRSU LEAGUERS
AEEGLRSZ REGLAZES
AEEGLRTU REGULATE
AEEGLRUX EXERGUAL
AEEGLSST GATELESS
AEEGLSSV SELVAGES
AEEGLSSW WAGELESS
AEEGLSSY EYEGLASS
AEEGLSTT GALETTES
AEEGLTTU TUTELAGE
AEEGMMNR ENGRAMME
AEEGMMNS GAMESMEN
AEEGMMOS GAMESOME
AEEGMMST GEMMATES
TAGMEMES
AEEGMNSS GAMENESS
AEEGMNTT TEGMENTA
AEEGMOOT OOGAMETE
AEEGMPRS PREGAMES
AEEGMRST GAMESTER
AEEGMSSS MEGASSES
MESSAGES
AEEGMSSU MESSUAGE
AEEGNNNO ENNEAGON
AEEGNNPS PANGENES
AEEGNOPS PEONAGES
AEEGNRRV ENGRAVER
AEEGNRST ESTRANGE
GRANTEES
GREATENS
NEGATERS
REAGENTS
SERGEANT
AEEGNRSV AVENGERS
ENGRAVES
AEEGNRWY GREENWAY
AEEGNSSS SAGENESS
AEEGNSTT TENTAGES
AEEGNSTV VENTAGES
AEEGNTTV VEGETANT
AEEGORSV OVERAGES
AEEGOSTX GEOTAXES
AEEGPRRS PRESAGER
AEEGPRSS ASPERGES
PRESAGES
AEEGPRSU PUGAREES
AEEGPSST SEPTAGES
AEEGRRSS GREASERS
AEEGRRST REGRATES
AEEGRRSU REARGUES
AEEGRRSW WAGERERS
AEEGRRTT RETARGET
AEEGRSST RESTAGES
AEEGRSTT GREATEST
AEEGSSTT GESTATES
AEEGSTTZ GAZETTES
AEEHHHSS HASHEESH
AEEHHIRT HEATHIER
AEEHHLNZ HAZELHEN
AEEHHNST ENSHEATH
HEATHENS
AEEHHOOP PAHOEHOE
AEEHHRSS REHASHES
AEEHHRST HEATHERS
SHEATHER
AEEHHRTY HEATHERY
AEEHHSST SHEATHES
AEEHIKLR HARELIKE
AEEHIKRS SHIKAREE
AEEHILNP ELAPHINE
AEEHIMNT HEMATEIN
HEMATINE
AEEHIMNX HEXAMINE
AEEHIMTT HEMATITE
AEEHINRT HERNIATE
AEEHIPRS PHARISEE
AEEHIPTZ HEPATIZE
AEEHIRRT EARTHIER
HEARTIER
AEEHIRST HEARTIES
AEEHIRSV SHIVAREE
AEEHISST ESTHESIA
AEEHISTT HESITATE
AEEHISTV HEAVIEST
AEEHKLLR RAKEHELL
AEEHKLLU KEELHAUL
AEEHKMNS KHAMSEEN
AEEHKNRR HANKERER
HARKENER
AEEHKNRS HEARKENS
AEEHKPRR PHREAKER
AEEHKRST HEKTARES
AEEHLLSS SEASHELL
AEEHLMNW WHALEMEN
WHEELMAN
AEEHLMNY HYMENEAL
AEEHLMPT HELPMATE
AEEHLNOS ENHALOES
AEEHLNOT ANETHOLE
AEEHLNPT ELEPHANT
AEEHLNRT LEATHERN
AEEHLNSS HALENESS
AEEHLNTX EXHALENT
AEEHLNVY HEAVENLY
AEEHLOSU ALEHOUSE
AEEHLPRT PLEATHER
AEEHLPST HEELTAPS
AEEHLPTT TELEPATH
AEEHLRRT LATHERER
AEEHLRST HALTERES
LEATHERS
AEEHLRSV HAVERELS
AEEHLRTY LEATHERY
AEEHLSST HEATLESS
AEEHLSTT ATHLETES
AEEHLTTY ETHYLATE
AEEHMMRR HAMMERER
REHAMMER
AEEHMNPS SHEEPMAN
AEEHMNRT EARTHMEN
AEEHMNST METHANES
AEEHMNTU ATHENEUM
AEEHMNTX EXANTHEM
AEEHMPRR HAMPERER
AEEHMPSS EMPHASES
AEEHMRTY ERYTHEMA
AEEHNNTX XANTHENE
AEEHNOPR EARPHONE
AEEHNPST HAPTENES
HEPTANES
PHENATES
AEEHNRST HASTENER
HEARTENS
AEEHNRSV RESHAVEN
AEEHNRTT THREATEN
AEEHNRTU URETHANE
AEEHNRTW WATERHEN
WREATHEN
AEEHNRWY ANYWHERE
AEEHNSST ANTHESES
AEEHNSTW ENSWATHE
WHEATENS
AEEHOPRT EPHORATE
AEEHOPRV OVERHEAP
AEEHORRV OVERHEAR
AEEHORSS SEAHORSE
SEASHORE
AEEHORTV OVERHATE
OVERHEAT
AEEHOSTU TEAHOUSE
AEEHPPRS PRESHAPE
AEEHPRRS REPHRASE
RESHAPER
AEEHPRRT THREAPER
AEEHPRSS RESHAPES
AEEHPRST PREHEATS
AEEHPRUV UPHEAVER
AEEHPSUV UPHEAVES
AEEHRRSS SHEARERS
AEEHRRTU URETHRAE
AEEHRRTW WREATHER
AEEHRSSV RESHAVES
AEEHRSSW REWASHES
AEEHRSTT EARTHSET
THEATERS
THEATRES
AEEHRSTW WEATHERS
WREATHES
AEEHRTVW WHATEVER
AEEHRTXZ EXAHERTZ
AEEHSTTW SAWTEETH
AEEHSTVY HEAVYSET
AEEIINRT INERTIAE
AEEIJPRS JAPERIES
AEEIKKLL LAKELIKE
AEEIKKLP PEAKLIKE
AEEIKLLS SEALLIKE
AEEIKLMS SEAMLIKE
AEEIKLMU LEUKEMIA
AEEIKLMZ MAZELIKE
AEEIKLPT TAPELIKE
AEEIKLRW WEAKLIER
AEEIKLST LEAKIEST
AEEIKLSV VASELIKE
AEEIKLVW WAVELIKE
AEEIKMNT KETAMINE
AEEIKNRS SNEAKIER
AEEIKNRT ANKERITE
AEEIKPST PEAKIEST
AEEIKRTW TWEAKIER
AEEILLNT TENAILLE
AEEILLRT LAETRILE
AEEILLST LEALTIES
AEEILMMN MELAMINE
AEEILMMT MEALTIME
AEEILMNT MELANITE
AEEILMNZ MELANIZE
AEEILMRS MEASLIER
AEEILMRT MATERIEL
AEEILMST MEALIEST
METALISE
AEEILMTZ METALIZE
AEEILNPR PERINEAL
AEEILNPS PENALISE
SEPALINE
AEEILNPT PETALINE
TAPELINE
AEEILNPZ PENALIZE
AEEILNRR NEARLIER
AEEILNRS ALIENERS
AEEILNRT ELATERIN
ENTAILER
TREENAIL
AEEILNSV VASELINE
AEEILNSX ALEXINES
AEEILORT AEROLITE
AEEILOTT ETIOLATE
AEEILPRR PEARLIER
AEEILPRS ESPALIER
AEEILPRT PEARLITE
AEEILPST EPILATES
AEEILPSW PALEWISE
AEEILQSU EQUALISE
AEEILQUX EXEQUIAL
AEEILQUZ EQUALIZE
AEEILRRS REALISER
AEEILRRT RETAILER
AEEILRRZ REALIZER
AEEILRSS REALISES
AEEILRST ATELIERS
EARLIEST
LEARIEST
REALTIES
AEEILRSY YEARLIES
AEEILRSZ REALIZES
SLEAZIER
AEEILRTT LATERITE
LITERATE
AEEILRTV LEVIRATE
RELATIVE
AEEILRTZ LATERIZE
AEEILRVW REVIEWAL
AEEILRVZ VELARIZE
AEEILSTV ELATIVES
LEAVIEST
VEALIEST
AEEILSVW ALEWIVES
AEEILTTV LEVITATE
AEEILTUV ELUVIATE
AEEIMMNT MEANTIME
AEEIMNNS ENAMINES
AEEIMNRT ANTIMERE
AEEIMNRX EXAMINER
AEEIMNST ETAMINES
MATINEES
MISEATEN
AEEIMNSX EXAMINES
AEEIMRRS SMEARIER
AEEIMRSS SERIEMAS
AEEIMRST EMERITAS
EMIRATES
STEAMIER
AEEIMSSS MISEASES
SIAMESES
AEEIMSST SEAMIEST
AEEIMSTT ESTIMATE
MEATIEST
TEATIMES
AEEINNRS ANSERINE
AEEINNTV VENETIAN
AEEINPRS NAPERIES
AEEINPRT APERIENT
AEEINRRT RETAINER
AEEINRST ARENITES
ARSENITE
RESINATE
STEARINE
TRAINEES
AEEINRSU UNEASIER
AEEINSSS EASINESS
AEEINSST ETESIANS
TENIASES
AEEINSTT ANISETTE
TETANIES
TETANISE
AEEINSTV NAIVETES
AEEINSVW INWEAVES
AEEINTTZ TETANIZE
AEEIOOPP EPOPOEIA
AEEIPPSU EUPEPSIA
AEEIPPTT APPETITE
AEEIPRRR RARERIPE
REPAIRER
AEEIPRST PARIETES
AEEIPSST EPITASES
AEEIPSTT PEATIEST
AEEIPSTX EXPIATES
AEEIPTVX EXAPTIVE
AEEIQRSU QUEASIER
AEEIQRUZ QUEAZIER
AEEIQSTU EQUISETA
AEEIRRSS RERAISES
AEEIRRST ARTERIES
AEEIRRTW WATERIER
AEEIRSST SERIATES
AEEIRSTT ARIETTES
ITERATES
TEARIEST
TREATIES
TREATISE
AEEIRSTW SWEATIER
WASTERIE
WEARIEST
AEEIRSTY YEASTIER
AEEIRSVV AVERSIVE
AEEISTTT STEATITE
AEEISTTV ESTIVATE
AEEISTUX EUTAXIES
AEEITUVX EXUVIATE
AEEJNRST SERJEANT
AEEJRTTW WATERJET
AEEKKNOS KOKANEES
AEEKLLSS LEAKLESS
AEEKLLST SKELETAL
AEEKLMMU MAMELUKE
AEEKLMRT TELEMARK
AEEKLMRY YARMELKE
AEEKLNST KANTELES
AEEKLPSS PEAKLESS
AEEKLSSW WAKELESS
AEEKLSTY EYESTALK
AEEKMNSS KAMSEENS
AEEKMORV MAKEOVER
AEEKMOTY YOKEMATE
AEEKMRRR REMARKER
AEEKMRRS REMAKERS
AEEKMRRT MARKETER
REMARKET
AEEKMRST MEERKATS
AEEKNNNS NANKEENS
AEEKNNPS KNEEPANS
AEEKNORW REAWOKEN
AEEKNPSW NEWSPEAK
AEEKNRSS SNEAKERS
AEEKNRSW REWAKENS
WAKENERS
AEEKNSSW WEAKNESS
AEEKOOPP PEEKAPOO
AEEKORST KERATOSE
AEEKORTV OVERTAKE
TAKEOVER
AEEKORVW OVERWEAK
AEEKPRSS RESPEAKS
SPEAKERS
AEEKPRTT PARKETTE
AEEKPRTU REUPTAKE
AEEKQRSU SQUEAKER
AEEKRRST RETAKERS
STREAKER
AEEKRRSW WREAKERS
AEELLLPT PELLETAL
AEELLLTT TELLTALE
AEELLMSS MEALLESS
AEELLOTT ALLOTTEE
AEELLPTT PALLETTE
PLATELET
AEELLPTY TELEPLAY
AEELLRRT TERRELLA
AEELLRRV RAVELLER
AEELLSTT STELLATE
AEELLSWY WALLEYES
WEASELLY
AEELLTVV VALVELET
AEELMMTU MALEMUTE
AEELMNPS EMPANELS
EMPLANES
ENSAMPLE
AEELMNRT LAMENTER
AEELMNSS LAMENESS
MALENESS
MANELESS
NAMELESS
SALESMEN
AEELMNST TALESMEN
AEELMNSY AMYLENES
AEELMNTT MANTELET
AEELMOTT MATELOTE
AEELMPRS EMPALERS
RESAMPLE
AEELMPRX EXEMPLAR
AEELMPRY EMPYREAL
AEELMPSX EXAMPLES
AEELMPTT PALMETTE
TEMPLATE
AEELMSSS SEAMLESS
AEELMSST MATELESS
MEATLESS
TAMELESS
AEELMSTU EMULATES
AEELNNPS ENPLANES
AEELNNRT LANNERET
AEELNNSS LEANNESS
AEELNOPR PERONEAL
AEELNOPT ANTELOPE
AEELNORU ALEURONE
AEELNOSS ENOLASES
AEELNPPS SPALPEEN
AEELNPRR PRERENAL
AEELNPRS REPANELS
AEELNPSS PALENESS
PANELESS
AEELNQSU SQUALENE
AEELNRRS LEARNERS
RELEARNS
AEELNRRT RELEARNT
AEELNRSS REALNESS
AEELNRST ETERNALS
TELERANS
AEELNRSV ENSLAVER
AEELNRSW RENEWALS
AEELNRTV LEVANTER
RELEVANT
AEELNRTW TREELAWN
AEELNRTX EXTERNAL
AEELNRUU NEURULAE
AEELNRUV REVENUAL
AEELNSST LATENESS
AEELNSSV ENSLAVES
AEELNTUV EVENTUAL
AEELOPRS PAROLEES
AEELOPRV OVERLEAP
AEELOPSX POLEAXES
AEELOPTT TOEPLATE
AEELORST OLEASTER
AEELORSU AUREOLES
AEELORSV OVERSALE
AEELORTT TOLERATE
AEELORTV ELEVATOR
OVERLATE
AEELORVZ OVERZEAL
AEELOSTV LOVESEAT
AEELOTTT TEETOTAL
AEELPRRS PEARLERS
RELAPSER
AEELPRRT PALTERER
PREALTER
AEELPRRY PARLEYER
AEELPRSS PLEASERS
PRESALES
RELAPSES
AEELPRST PETRALES
PLEATERS
PRELATES
REPLATES
AEELPRSU PLEASURE
AEELPRSV VESPERAL
AEELPRTY PTERYLAE
AEELPRUV PREVALUE
AEELPSST TAPELESS
AEELPSTT PALETTES
AEELPSTU EPAULETS
AEELPSTZ SPAETZLE
AEELQRSU SQUEALER
AEELQSUZ QUEZALES
AEELRRST ALTERERS
REALTERS
RELATERS
AEELRRSV RAVELERS
REVERSAL
SLAVERER
AEELRRSX RELAXERS
AEELRRTU URETERAL
AEELRRTV TRAVELER
AEELRSST RESLATES
STEALERS
TEARLESS
AEELRSSV SEVERALS
AEELRSTT ALERTEST
AEELRSTU RESALUTE
AEELRSTX EXALTERS
AEELRSTY EASTERLY
AEELRSUV REVALUES
AEELRSVY AVERSELY
AEELSSST SEATLESS
AEELSSVW WAVELESS
AEELSTTY LAYETTES
AEELSTVW WAVELETS
AEEMMPSY EMPYEMAS
AEEMMRRY YAMMERER
AEEMMRST AMMETERS
METAMERS
AEEMMSST MESSMATE
AEEMNNOS ANEMONES
AEEMNNPS PENNAMES
AEEMNNRT REMANENT
AEEMNNSS MEANNESS
AEEMNOSS ANEMOSES
AEEMNOSX AXONEMES
AEEMNPRS PRENAMES
SPEARMEN
AEEMNPRT PERMEANT
AEEMNPRY EMPYREAN
AEEMNPTV PAVEMENT
AEEMNRSU USERNAME
AEEMNRSV VERSEMAN
AEEMNRSW MENSWEAR
AEEMNRTU NUMERATE

AEEMNRTV AVERMENT
AEEMNRTW WATERMEN
AEEMNRUV MANEUVER
AEEMNRVY EVERYMAN
AEEMNSSS SAMENESS
AEEMNSST TAMENESS
AEEMORTV OVERTAME
AEEMPPRR PAMPERER
AEEMPRRT TAMPERER
AEEMPRRV REVAMPER
AEEMPRST TEMPERAS
AEEMPRTT ATTEMPER
AEEMPSTU AMPUTEES
AEEMQRRU REMARQUE
AEEMQRSU MARQUEES
AEEMQTTU MAQUETTE
AEEMRRSS SMEARERS
AEEMRRST REMASTER
STREAMER
AEEMRRSU MEASURER
AEEMRRTT TETRAMER
AEEMRSST MASSETER
SEAMSTER
STEAMERS
AEEMRSSU MEASURES
REASSUME
AEEMRSTT TEAMSTER
AEEMRSTW STEMWARE
AEEMRTWY YAWMETER
AEEMSSSU MASSEUSE
AEEMSSTU MEATUSES
AEENNOST NEONATES
AEENNPST PENTANES
AEENNRRS ENSNARER
AEENNRSS ENSNARES
NEARNESS
RENNASES
AEENNRTV REVENANT
AEENNSSS SANENESS
AEENNSST NEATNESS
AEENNSTT SETENANT
AEENOPRS PERSONAE
AEENOPSU EUPNOEAS
AEENORRS REASONER
AEENORRV OVERNEAR
AEENORSS RESEASON
SEASONER
AEENORST EARSTONE
RESONATE
AEENORTV OVERNEAT
RENOVATE
AEENORVW OVENWARE
AEENOTTU OUTEATEN
AEENPPRT PETNAPER
AEENPPTT APPETENT
AEENPRUV PARVENUE
AEENPSSX EXPANSES
AEENPTTY ANTETYPE
AEENRRRW WARRENER
AEENRRSS RARENESS
AEENRRST TERRANES
AEENRRSV RAVENERS
AEENRRSW ANSWERER
AEENRRSY YEARNERS
AEENRRTT RATTENER
AEENRRTU RENATURE
AEENRRTV TAVERNER
AEENRSST ASSENTER
EARNESTS
SARSENET
AEENRSSU ANURESES
AEENRSTT ENTREATS
RATTEENS
AEENRSTU SAUTERNE
AEENRSTV VETERANS
AEENRTTV ANTEVERT
AEENRTTX EXTRANET
AEENRTTY ENTREATY
AEENRVWW NEWWAVER
AEENSSST SENSATES
AEENSTTV NAVETTES
AEENSUVW UNWEAVES
AEEOPRRT PERORATE
AEEOPRST OPERATES
PROTEASE
AEEOPRTT OPERETTA
AEEOPSTZ EPAZOTES
AEEORRSU REAROUSE
AEEORRTV OVERRATE
AEEORRVW OVERWEAR
AEEORSSV OVERSEAS
AEEORSTV OVEREATS
AEEORSVV OVERSAVE
AEEORSVW OVERAWES
AEEORSVY OVEREASY
AEEPPPRU PREPUPAE
AEEPPRRR PREPARER
AEEPPRRS PAPERERS
PREPARES
REPAPERS
AEEPPRRU PUERPERA
AEEPPRST PREPASTE
PRETAPES
AEEPPRSV PREPAVES
AEEPRRRT PARTERRE
AEEPRRSS ASPERSER
SPEARERS
AEEPRRST TAPERERS
AEEPRRSV PREAVERS
AEEPRRTT PATTERER
PRETREAT
AEEPRRTU APERTURE
AEEPRSSS ASPERSES
REPASSES
AEEPRSST TRAPESES
AEEPRSTT PEARTEST
PRETASTE
AEEPRSTZ TRAPEZES
AEEQRRUV QUAVERER
AEERRRST ARRESTER
REARREST
AEERRSST ASSERTER
REASSERT
SERRATES
TERRASES
AEERRSSU ERASURES
REASSURE
AEERRSSW SWEARERS
AEERRSTT RETREATS
TREATERS
AEERRSTU AUSTERER
TREASURE
AEERRSTV AVERTERS
TRAVERSE
AEERRSTW WATERERS
AEERRSVW WAVERERS
AEERSSSS REASSESS
AEERSSSY ESSAYERS
AEERSSTT ESTREATS
RESTATES
RETASTES
AEERSSTW SWEATERS
AEERSSTZ ERSATZES
AEERSSUU URAEUSES
AEERSTTT ATTESTER
AEERSTWW WETWARES
AEERVWYY EVERYWAY
AEESSSSS ASSESSES
AEESSTTT TESTATES
AEFFGIIL EFFIGIAL
AEFFGINR FIREFANG
AEFFGIRS GIRAFFES
AEFFGOST OFFSTAGE
AEFFGRSU GAUFFERS
SUFFRAGE
AEFFHIKY KAFFIYEH
KEFFIYAH
AEFFHILL HALFLIFE
AEFFILNY AFFINELY
AEFFILRW WAFFLIER
AEFFILUV EFFLUVIA
AEFFIMRR AFFIRMER
REAFFIRM
AEFFIMRW FARMWIFE
AEFFIPRS PIAFFERS
AEFFIRSX AFFIXERS
AEFFKORS RAKEOFFS
AEFFKOST TAKEOFFS
AEFFLNSS SNAFFLES
AEFFLNTU AFFLUENT
AEFFLRRS RAFFLERS
AEFFLRSW WAFFLERS
AEFFLSTU FEASTFUL
SUFFLATE
AEFFLSUX AFFLUXES
AEFFMRSU EARMUFFS
AEFFORST AFFOREST
AEFFOSVW WAVEOFFS
AEFFQRSU QUAFFERS
AEFFRSST RESTAFFS
STAFFERS
AEFFRTTU TARTUFFE
AEFGGGOS FOGGAGES
AEFGGILR FLAGGIER
AEFGGLRS FLAGGERS
AEFGHINR HANGFIRE
AEFGHINS SHEAFING
AEFGIIRS GASIFIER
AEFGIISS GASIFIES
AEFGIKLN FANGLIKE
AEFGIKNR FREAKING
AEFGILNR FINAGLER
AEFGILNS FINAGLES
AEFGILOS FOLIAGES
AEFGILTT LIFTGATE
AEFGIMTU FUMIGATE
AEFGINRW WAFERING
AEFGINST FEASTING
AEFGIORR FAIRGOER
AEFGIRRU ARGUFIER
AEFGIRST FRIGATES
AEFGIRSU ARGUFIES
AEFGIRTU FIGURATE
FRUITAGE
AEFGIRTW GIFTWARE
AEFGISTU FATIGUES
AEFGLLNO LONGLEAF
AEFGLLOP FLAGPOLE
AEFGLLSS FLAGLESS
AEFGLMNU FUGLEMAN
AEFGLMOP MEGAFLOP
AEFGLNOX FLEXAGON
AEFGLNRS FLANGERS
AEFGLNSS FANGLESS
AEFGLOOR FLOORAGE
AEFGLOPR LEAPFROG
AEFGLOST FLOTAGES
AEFGLOSW FLOWAGES
AEFGLPSU PAGEFULS
AEFGLRTU GRATEFUL
AEFGLSTU STAGEFUL
AEFGLTUX FLUXGATE
AEFGMNRT FRAGMENT
AEFGMORS FROMAGES
AEFGNORT FRONTAGE
AEFGNRST ENGRAFTS
AEFGOORT FOOTGEAR
AEFGOOST FOOTAGES
AEFGORRS FORAGERS
AEFGORST FAGOTERS
AEFGORTT FROTTAGE
AEFGRRST GRAFTERS
REGRAFTS
AEFHIKRS FREAKISH
AEFHIKSW WEAKFISH
AEFHILLN FELLAHIN
AEFHILLR FIREHALL
AEFHILMS FISHMEAL
AEFHILMT HALFTIME
AEFHILNS SHINLEAF
AEFHILPP HALFPIPE
AEFHILRS FLASHIER
AEFHIMSS FAMISHES
AEFHLMSU SHAMEFUL
AEFHLNOT HALFTONE
AEFHLNSS HALFNESS
AEFHLPRS PARFLESH
AEFHLRSS FLASHERS
AEFHLRTY FATHERLY
AEFHLSTU HASTEFUL
AEFHMNRS FRESHMAN
AEFHMORT FATHOMER
AEFHRSTT FARTHEST
AEFIIKLW WAIFLIKE
AEFIILMS FAMILIES
AEFIILNS FINALISE
AEFIILNT ANTILIFE
AEFIILNZ FINALIZE
AEFIILSS SALIFIES
AEFIILST FETIALIS
FILIATES
AEFIIMNS INFAMIES
AEFIIMRS RAMIFIES
AEFIINRV VINIFERA
AEFIINSZ NAZIFIES
AEFIIPRT APERITIF
AEFIIRRS FRIARIES
RARIFIES
AEFIIRRT RATIFIER
AEFIIRST RATIFIES
AEFIITVX FIXATIVE
AEFIKLMO FOAMLIKE
AEFIKLNU FAUNLIKE
AEFIKLNW FAWNLIKE
AEFIKLRY FREAKILY
AEFIKLST FLAKIEST
AEFILLNT FLATLINE
AEFILLOT FELLATIO
AEFILLRW FIREWALL
AEFILMNR INFLAMER
RIFLEMAN
AEFILMNS FLAMINES
INFLAMES
AEFILMNT FILAMENT
AEFILMST FLAMIEST
AEFILMSY MAYFLIES
AEFILNNR INFERNAL
AEFILNPS LIFESPAN
AEFILNRT INFLATER
AEFILNRU FRAULEIN
AEFILNST INFLATES
AEFILNSV FLAVINES
AEFILNTT ANTILEFT
AEFILOOR AEROFOIL
AEFILORS FORESAIL
AEFILORT FLOATIER
AEFILOST FOLIATES
AEFILPPR FLAPPIER
AEFILPRX PREFIXAL
AEFILPST FLEAPITS
AEFILRST FRAILEST
AEFILRSU FAILURES
AEFILRTT FILTRATE
AEFILRTU FAULTIER
FILATURE
AEFILRUW WEARIFUL
AEFILSST SEALIFTS
AEFILSSW SAWFLIES
AEFILSTU FISTULAE
AEFILSTV FESTIVAL
AEFILSTW FLATWISE
FLAWIEST
AEFILSTX FLAXIEST
AEFILSWY LIFEWAYS
AEFILTUU FAUTEUIL
AEFIMMRS MISFRAME
AEFIMNST MANIFEST
AEFIMORR AERIFORM
AEFIMOST FOAMIEST
AEFIMRRS FIREARMS
AEFIMRRW FIRMWARE
AEFINNST INFANTES
AEFINNSZ FANZINES
AEFINOPR PINAFORE
AEFINORS FARINOSE
AEFINOTT FETATION
AEFINPRS FIREPANS
PANFRIES
AEFINRRS REFRAINS
AEFINRRU UNFAIRER
AEFINRSS FAIRNESS
SANSERIF
AEFINRST FAINTERS
AEFINSTT FAINTEST
AEFINSTW FAWNIEST
AEFIORTV FAVORITE
AEFIPRRT FIRETRAP
AEFIQRSU AQUIFERS
AEFIRRRS FARRIERS
AEFIRRRY FARRIERY
AEFISTTT FATTIEST
AEFKLLOT FOLKTALE
AEFKLNRS FLANKERS
AEFKLRST FARTLEKS
AEFKLSST FLASKETS
AEFKNORR FORERANK
AEFKNORS FORSAKEN
AEFKNPRR PREFRANK
AEFKNRRS FRANKERS
AEFKNRST FRANKEST
AEFKORRS FORSAKER
AEFKORRW WORKFARE
AEFKORSS FORSAKES
AEFKORTU FREAKOUT
AEFLLNNS FLANNELS
AEFLLNNU UNFALLEN
AEFLLORT FELLATOR
AEFLLOST FLOATELS
AEFLLPSS FLAPLESS
AEFLLPTU PLATEFUL
AEFLLRUW AWFULLER
AEFLLRUX FLEXURAL
AEFLLSSW FLAWLESS
AEFLLSTT FLATLETS
AEFLLSTY FESTALLY
AEFLMORU FORMULAE
FUMAROLE
AEFLMORW LEAFWORM
AEFLMOSS FOAMLESS
AEFLMOTU FLAMEOUT
AEFLMSUW WAMEFULS
AEFLNNOT FONTANEL
AEFLNNOY NONLEAFY
AEFLNNTY FENTANYL
AEFLNOPR FLAPERON
AEFLNOPT PANTOFLE
AEFLNORS FARNESOL
AEFLNOSV FLAVONES
AEFLNRRU FRENULAR
AEFLNRSU FLANEURS
FUNERALS
AEFLNRTU FLAUNTER
AEFLNSST FLATNESS
AEFLNSTT FLATTENS
AEFLNSUY UNSAFELY
AEFLOORS SEAFLOOR
AEFLOORV FOVEOLAR
AEFLOOSV FOVEOLAS
AEFLOPRT TERAFLOP
AEFLOPRY FOREPLAY
AEFLOPSW PEAFOWLS
AEFLORRV FLAVORER
AEFLORSS SAFROLES
AEFLORST FLOATERS
FORESTAL
REFLOATS
AEFLORTW FLEAWORT
AEFLOSSW SEAFOWLS
AEFLOSTT FALSETTO
AEFLPPRS FLAPPERS
AEFLPPRY FLYPAPER
AEFLPRSS FELSPARS
AEFLPRSU FLAREUPS
AEFLPRSY PALFREYS
AEFLRSSU REFUSALS
AEFLRSTT FLATTERS
AEFLRSTU REFUTALS
AEFLRSZZ FRAZZLES
AEFLRTTU AFLUTTER
AEFLRTTY FLATTERY
AEFLSSTU FLATUSES
SULFATES
AEFLSTTT FLATTEST
AEFLSTTU TASTEFUL
AEFLSTUW WASTEFUL
AEFMNORS FORAMENS
AEFMNRRY FERRYMAN
AEFMNRST RAFTSMEN
AEFMNRSU FRAENUMS
AEFMORRS FOREARMS
AEFMORRT REFORMAT
AEFMORST FOREMAST
FORMATES
AEFMORVW WAVEFORM
AEFMOSUW WAMEFOUS
AEFNNSTU UNFASTEN
AEFNOPRR PROFANER
AEFNOPRS PROFANES
AEFNORRW FOREWARN
AEFNORST SEAFRONT
AEFNORSU FURANOSE
AEFNPRSU SUPERFAN
AEFNRRST TRANSFER
AEFNRRUY FUNERARY
AEFNSSST FASTNESS
AEFNSTUY UNSAFETY
AEFOORTW FOOTWEAR
AEFOPRRT FOREPART
AEFOPRST FOREPAST
AEFOPRSW FOREPAWS
AEFORRSV FAVORERS
AEFORRSW FORSWEAR
AEFORRSY FORAYERS
AEFORRUV FAVOURER
AEFORSTV OVERFAST
AEFORSTW SOFTWARE
AEFORSTY FORESTAY
AEFOSTTU OUTFEAST
AEFRRSST STRAFERS
AEFRSSTW FRETSAWS
AEFRSTTU TARTUFES
AEFRSTUW WAFTURES
AEGGGINN ENGAGING
AEGGGLSU LUGGAGES
AEGGHIRS SHAGGIER
AEGGHISS HAGGISES
AEGGHJRY JAGGHERY
AEGGHLRS HAGGLERS
AEGGHMOS HEMAGOGS
AEGGHMSU MESHUGGA
AEGGHOPY GEOPHAGY
AEGGHORU ROUGHAGE
AEGGIINV GINGIVAE
AEGGIJST JAGGIEST
AEGGILLN ALLEGING
AEGGILLR GRILLAGE
AEGGILMN GLEAMING
AEGGILNN ANGELING
GLEANING
AEGGILNR GANGLIER
LAGERING
REGALING
AEGGILNT GELATING
LEGATING
AEGGILNU LEAGUING
AEGGILNV GAVELING
AEGGILOT TALEGGIO
AEGGILRS SLAGGIER
AEGGILRW WAGGLIER
AEGGIMSU MISGAUGE
AEGGINNR ANGERING
ENRAGING
AEGGINNT AGENTING
NEGATING
AEGGINNU UNAGEING
AEGGINNV AVENGING
AEGGINOS SEAGOING
AEGGINRS GEARINGS
GREASING
SNAGGIER
AEGGINRW WAGERING
AEGGINSS SIGNAGES
AEGGINST NAGGIEST
AEGGIOPR ARPEGGIO
AEGGIOSS ISAGOGES
AEGGIQRU QUAGGIER
AEGGIRST STAGGIER
AEGGIRSU GARIGUES
AEGGISST SAGGIEST
STAGGIES
AEGGISSW SWAGGIES
AEGGLNPT EGGPLANT
AEGGLNRS GANGRELS
AEGGLORY GARGOYLE
AEGGLRRS GARGLERS
AEGGLRST STRAGGLE
AEGGLRSY GREYLAGS
AEGGMNOR GENOGRAM
AEGGMORT MORTGAGE
AEGGNORW WAGGONER
AEGGNRRS GRANGERS
AEGGNRST GANGSTER
AEGGRSST GAGSTERS
STAGGERS
AEGGRSSW SWAGGERS
AEGGRSTY STAGGERY
AEGHHMSU MESHUGAH
AEGHILLM MEGILLAH
AEGHILLS SHIGELLA
AEGHILMT MEGALITH
AEGHILNR NARGHILE
NARGILEH
AEGHILNS LEASHING
SHEALING
AEGHILNT ATHELING
AEGHILNX EXHALING
AEGHILRT LITHARGE
THIRLAGE
AEGHIMNW WEIGHMAN
AEGHIMST MEGAHITS
AEGHINNN HENNAING
AEGHINNT NAETHING
AEGHINNV HAVENING
AEGHINRS HEARINGS
HEARSING
SHEARING
AEGHINRT EARTHING
HEARTING
INGATHER
AEGHINRV HAVERING
AEGHINST GAHNITES
AEGHINSV SHEAVING
AEGHINTT GNATHITE
AEGHIOPS ESOPHAGI
AEGHIPPR EPIGRAPH
AEGHIPRT GRAPHITE
AEGHIRRS GHARRIES
AEGHLNOS HALOGENS
AEGHLNOY HYALOGEN
AEGHLOPY HYPOGEAL
AEGHLOSS GALOSHES
AEGHLRSU LAUGHERS
AEGHLRTU LAUGHTER
AEGHLRTY LETHARGY
AEGHLSTW THALWEGS
AEGHMNOS HOGMANES
AEGHMNOY HOGMENAY
AEGHMOPT APOTHEGM
AEGHMORS HOMAGERS
AEGHMORT ETHOGRAM
AEGHNNST HANGNEST
AEGHNOPT HEPTAGON
PATHOGEN
AEGHNOPY HYPOGEAN
AEGHNORV HANGOVER
OVERHANG
AEGHNOSX HEXAGONS
AEGHNSST STENGAHS
AEGHOPPR PROPHAGE
AEGHOPPY APOPHYGE
AEGHORST SHORTAGE
AEGHOSST HOSTAGES
AEGHOSSU GASHOUSE
AEGHPRTU UPGATHER
AEGHRTTU RETAUGHT
AEGIILLU AIGUILLE

AEGIILMN EMAILING
AEGIILMR REMIGIAL
AEGIILNN ALIENING
AEGIILNR GAINLIER
AEGIILRR GLAIRIER
AEGIILTT LITIGATE
AEGIILTV LIGATIVE
AEGIIMNR IMAGINER
MIGRAINE
AEGIIMNS IMAGINES
AEGIIMTT MITIGATE
AEGIINNR ARGININE
AEGIINRR GRAINIER
AEGIIRRT IRRIGATE
AEGIISTV VESTIGIA
AEGIJLNR JANGLIER
AEGIKLNS LINKAGES
SNAGLIKE
AEGIKLNT GNATLIKE
AEGIKLNW WEAKLING
AEGIKLOT GOATLIKE
AEGIKMNR REMAKING
AEGIKMRW WIGMAKER
AEGIKNNS SNEAKING
AEGIKNNW WAKENING
AEGIKNPS SPEAKING
AEGIKNRT RETAKING
AEGIKNRW REWAKING
WREAKING
AEGIKNSS SINKAGES
AEGIKNTW TWEAKING
AEGIKPRS GARPIKES
AEGIKSTW GAWKIEST
AEGILLLS ILLEGALS
AEGILLMS LEGALISM
MEGILLAS
MILLAGES
AEGILLNR ALLERGIN
AEGILLNS GALLEINS
NIGELLAS
AEGILLNU LINGULAE
AEGILLNY GENIALLY
AEGILLPR PILLAGER
AEGILLPS PILLAGES
SPILLAGE
AEGILLRU GUERILLA
AEGILLRV VILLAGER
AEGILLST LEGALIST
TILLAGES
AEGILLSV VILLAGES
AEGILLTU LIGULATE
AEGILLTY LEGALITY
AEGILMMR AGLIMMER
AEGILMNP EMPALING
AEGILMNR GERMINAL
MALIGNER
MALINGER
AEGILMNT LIGAMENT
METALING
TEGMINAL
AEGILMRS GREMIALS
AEGILMTU MULTIAGE
AEGILNNP PANELING
AEGILNNR LEARNING
AEGILNNS EANLINGS
LEANINGS
AEGILNNT GANTLINE
LATENING
AEGILNNU UNGENIAL
AEGILNNW WEANLING
AEGILNNY YEANLING
AEGILNOR GERANIOL
REGIONAL
AEGILNOS GASOLINE
AEGILNOT GELATION
LEGATION
AEGILNPR GRAPLINE
PEARLING
AEGILNPS ELAPSING
PLEASING
AEGILNPT PLEATING
AEGILNQU EQUALING
AEGILNRR GNARLIER
AEGILNRS ALIGNERS
ENGRAILS
NARGILES
REALIGNS
SIGNALER
SLANGIER
AEGILNRT ALERTING
ALTERING
INTEGRAL
RELATING
TANGLIER
TRIANGLE
AEGILNRV RAVELING
AEGILNRX RELAXING
AEGILNRY LAYERING
RELAYING
YEARLING
AEGILNSS GAINLESS
GLASSINE
LEASINGS
AEGILNST GELATINS
GENITALS
STEALING
TAGLINES
AEGILNSV LEAVINGS
SLEAVING
AEGILNSY YEALINGS
AEGILNTV VALETING
AEGILNTX EXALTING
AEGILNTZ TEAZLING
AEGILOPS SPOILAGE
AEGILOPT PILOTAGE
AEGILORS GASOLIER
GIRASOLE
SERAGLIO
AEGILOSS SOILAGES
AEGILOST LATIGOES
OTALGIES
AEGILOSU EULOGIAS
AEGILPPS SLIPPAGE
AEGILPPU PUPILAGE
AEGILRSS GLASSIER
AEGILRST GLARIEST
AEGILRSY GREASILY
AEGILRSZ GLAZIERS
AEGILRTT AGLITTER
AEGILRTU LIGATURE
AEGILRTY REGALITY
AEGILRVW LAWGIVER
AEGILRYZ GLAZIERY
AEGILSSS GLASSIES
AEGILSTZ GLAZIEST
AEGIMMST GAMMIEST
AEGIMNNO NONIMAGE
AEGIMNNR RENAMING
AEGIMNNS MEANINGS
AEGIMNRR REARMING
AEGIMNRS SMEARING
AEGIMNRT EMIGRANT
REMATING
AEGIMNRU GERANIUM
AEGIMNSS GAMINESS
AEGIMNST MANGIEST
MINTAGES
MISAGENT
STEAMING
AEGIMNSV VEGANISM
AEGIMNTU TEGUMINA
UMANGITE
AEGIMOOS OOGAMIES
AEGIMORR ARMIGERO
AEGIMPRS EPIGRAMS
PRIMAGES
AEGIMPRU UMPIRAGE
AEGIMPSS MISPAGES
AEGIMQRU QUAGMIRE
AEGIMRRS ARMIGERS
AEGIMRSS GISARMES
AEGIMRST MAGISTER
MIGRATES
RAGTIMES
STERIGMA
AEGIMSSU MISUSAGE
AEGINNNX ANNEXING
AEGINNOS ANGINOSE
AEGINNOT NEGATION
AEGINNPS SNEAPING
SPEANING
AEGINNRS AGINNERS
EARNINGS
ENGRAINS
GRANNIES
AEGINNRV RAVENING
AEGINNRY YEARNING
AEGINNST ANTIGENS
GENTIANS
AEGINNSU GUANINES
SANGUINE
AEGINORR ORANGIER
AEGINORS ORGANISE
AEGINORZ ORGANIZE
AEGINOSS AGONISES
AEGINOSZ AGONIZES
AEGINPPR PAPERING
AEGINPPS GENIPAPS
AEGINPRS SPEARING
AEGINPRT RETAPING
TAPERING
AEGINPRV REPAVING
AEGINPRY REPAYING
AEGINPSS SPAEINGS
SPINAGES
AEGINPSY GYPSEIAN
AEGINPTY EGYPTIAN
AEGINQTU EQUATING
AEGINRRS EARRINGS
GRAINERS
AEGINRRV AVERRING
AEGINRSS ASSIGNER
REASSIGN
SERINGAS
AEGINRST ANGRIEST
ASTRINGE
GANISTER
GANTRIES
GRANITES
INGRATES
RANGIEST
AEGINRSV VINEGARS
AEGINRSW RESAWING
SWEARING
AEGINRSY RESAYING
SYNERGIA
AEGINRTT GNATTIER
TREATING
AEGINRTV AVERTING
GRIEVANT
VINTAGER
AEGINRTW TWANGIER
WATERING
AEGINRTX RETAXING
AEGINRVW WAVERING
AEGINRVY VINEGARY
AEGINRWX REWAXING
AEGINRWY WEARYING
AEGINSST EASTINGS
GIANTESS
SEATINGS
AEGINSSY ESSAYING
AEGINSTT ESTATING
TANGIEST
AEGINSTU SAUTEING
UNITAGES
AEGINSTV VINTAGES
AEGINSTW SWEATING
AEGINSTY YEASTING
AEGINSTZ TZIGANES
AEGIOPRR PROGERIA
AEGIORSS ARGOSIES
AEGIORSV VIRAGOES
AEGIORTV RAVIGOTE
AEGIOSTU AGOUTIES
AEGIOSTX GEOTAXIS
AEGIPPST GAPPIEST
AEGIPRST GRAPIEST
AEGIPRTY PTERYGIA
AEGIRRSS GRASSIER
AEGIRRSU SUGARIER
AEGIRRSZ GRAZIERS
AEGIRSTV VIRGATES
AEGIRSUU AUGURIES
AEGISSST GASSIEST
AEGISSTT STAGIEST
AEGISTUZ GAUZIEST
AEGJLNOR JARGONEL
AEGJLNRS JANGLERS
AEGJLTUU JUGULATE
AEGKMRSY KERYGMAS
AEGLLNNO NONLEGAL
AEGLLNOS ALLONGES
GALLEONS
AEGLLNRS LANGRELS
AEGLLNST GELLANTS
AEGLLNSY LANGLEYS
AEGLLOOZ ZOOGLEAL
AEGLLOPR GALLOPER
AEGLLORS ALLEGROS
AEGLLORY ALLEGORY
AEGLLOSS GOALLESS
AEGLLOST TOLLAGES
AEGLLOTT TOLLGATE
AEGLLRVY GRAVELLY
AEGLLSSU GALLUSES
SEAGULLS
SULLAGES
AEGLMNNO MANGONEL
AEGLMNOY AMYLOGEN
AEGLMNRS MANGLERS
AEGLMNSS GLASSMEN
AEGLMNTU GUNMETAL
AEGLMOPS MEGALOPS
AEGLMORS GOMERALS
AEGLMOSU MOULAGES
AEGLMOTU OUTGLEAM
AEGLMOTV MEGAVOLT
AEGLMPSU PLUMAGES
AEGLNNOR NONGLARE
AEGLNNPT PLANGENT
AEGLNNSY LANGSYNE
AEGLNNTU UNTANGLE
AEGLNOPT GANTLOPE
AEGLNORY YEARLONG
AEGLNOST TANGELOS
AEGLNOSU ANGULOSE
AEGLNPRS GRAPNELS
AEGLNPSS SPANGLES
AEGLNRRW WRANGLER
AEGLNRST STRANGLE
TANGLERS
AEGLNRSU GRANULES
AEGLNRSW WANGLERS
WRANGLES
AEGLNRSY LARYNGES
AEGLNRTW TWANGLER
AEGLNSTT GANTLETS
AEGLNSTU LANGUETS
AEGLNSTW TWANGLES
AEGLNSUW GUNWALES
AEGLNTTU GAUNTLET
AEGLNTUU UNGULATE
AEGLOOOZ ZOOGLOEA
AEGLOOPU APOLOGUE
AEGLOORY AEROLOGY
AREOLOGY
AEGLOOSZ ZOOGLEAS
AEGLOPRS PERGOLAS
AEGLOPRY PLAYGOER
AEGLOPTT PLOTTAGE
AEGLORST GLOATERS
LEGATORS
AEGLORSV VORLAGES
AEGLORTU OUTGLARE
AEGLORTV TRAVELOG
AEGLORTW WATERLOG
AEGLOSTV VOLTAGES
AEGLPPRR GRAPPLER
AEGLPPRS GRAPPLES
AEGLPRSU EARPLUGS
GRAUPELS
PLAGUERS
AEGLPSSU PLUSSAGE
AEGLRRSU REGULARS
AEGLRRUV VULGARER
AEGLRSTU GESTURAL
AEGLSSTT GESTALTS
AEGLSSUV VALGUSES
AEGLSTUV VULGATES
AEGLSUUY GUAYULES
AEGMMNOR GAMMONER
AEGMMRRU RUMMAGER
AEGMMRSU RUMMAGES
AEGMNNOS AGNOMENS
AEGMNNOT MAGNETON
AEGMNORR RENOGRAM
AEGMNORV MANGROVE
VENOGRAM
AEGMNOST MAGNETOS
MEGATONS
MONTAGES
AEGMNOXY XENOGAMY
AEGMNRST GARMENTS
MARGENTS
AEGMNRTU ARGENTUM
ARGUMENT
AEGMNSTU AUGMENTS
MUTAGENS
AEGMOORS MOORAGES
AEGMOPRW GAPEWORM
AEGMOPST POSTGAME
AEGMORRW WORMGEAR
AEGMORSS GOSSAMER
AEGMPRUZ GAZUMPER
AEGMPSTU STUMPAGE
AEGNNOPT PENTAGON
AEGNNORT NEGATRON
AEGNNOST NEGATONS
TONNAGES
AEGNNPRT PREGNANT
AEGNNSTT TANGENTS
AEGNNSTU TUNNAGES
AEGNNTUU UNGUENTA
AEGNOORS OREGANOS
AEGNOPRR PARERGON
AEGNORRS GROANERS
AEGNORRY ORANGERY
AEGNORST ESTRAGON
NEGATORS
AEGNORSW WAGONERS
AEGNORTT TETRAGON
AEGNORTU OUTRANGE
AEGNOSSY NOSEGAYS
AEGNOTUY AUTOGENY
AEGNPPRU GUNPAPER
AEGNPRRS RESPRANG
AEGNPRST TREPANGS
AEGNPRSU SPEARGUN
AEGNRRST GRANTERS
REGRANTS
STRANGER
AEGNRSST STRANGES
AEGNRSSY GRAYNESS
AEGNRSTW TWANGERS
AEGNSSST GASTNESS
AEGNSSSY SYNGASES
AEGNSTTU GAUNTEST
AEGOORST ROOTAGES
AEGOPPST STOPPAGE
AEGOPRST PORTAGES
AEGOPSST GESTAPOS
POSTAGES
AEGOPSTT GATEPOST
POTTAGES
AEGORRRT GARROTER
AEGORRST GARROTES
AEGORRTT GAROTTER
GARROTTE
AEGORSST STORAGES
AEGORSTT GAROTTES
AEGORSTU OUTRAGES
AEGORSVY VOYAGERS
AEGORTTU TUTORAGE
AEGORTUU OUTARGUE
AEGORUVY VOYAGEUR
AEGOSSTW STOWAGES
AEGOSSYZ AZYGOSES
AEGOSTTV GAVOTTES
AEGOSTUZ OUTGAZES
AEGPRRSS GRASPERS
SPARGERS
AEGPRSTU UPSTAGER
AEGPSSTU UPSTAGES
AEGRRSSU SUGARERS
AEGRRSSY RYEGRASS
AEGRRSUU AUGURERS
AEGRRSUV GRAVURES
AEGRSSUV SEVRUGAS
AEGRSTTY STRATEGY
AEGRSTUU AUGUSTER
AEHHIMPY HYPHEMIA
AEHHINST INSHEATH
AEHHISVY YESHIVAH
AEHHNRSS HARSHENS
AEHHRRST THRASHER
AEHHRSST HARSHEST
THRASHES
AEHIIKLR HAIRLIKE
AEHIIKST SHIITAKE
AEHIILMO HEMIOLIA
AEHIILMT LITHEMIA
AEHIILNR HAIRLINE
AEHIIMNT THIAMINE
AEHIINTZ THIAZINE
AEHIIRRW WIREHAIR
AEHIIRST HAIRIEST
AEHIKKLW HAWKLIKE
AEHIKLLO HALOLIKE
AEHIKLMS SHEKALIM
AEHIKLNP KEPHALIN
AEHIKLRS RASHLIKE
AEHIKMNZ KHAZENIM
AEHIKSST SHAKIEST
SHITAKES
AEHILMNY HYMENIAL
AEHILMOS HEMIOLAS
AEHILMQS SHEQALIM
AEHILMRU HAULMIER
AEHILMSY LEHAYIMS
AEHILNOP APHELION
PHELONIA
AEHILNRS INHALERS
AEHILNRU INHAULER
AEHILNSY HYALINES
AEHILNTX ANTHELIX
AEHILNTZ ZENITHAL
AEHILORS AIRHOLES
SHOALIER
AEHILORT AEROLITH
AEHILOTZ THIAZOLE
AEHILPRS EARLSHIP
HARELIPS
PLASHIER
AEHILPST HAPLITES
AEHILRSS HAIRLESS
AEHILRSU HAULIERS
AEHILRSV LAVISHER
SHRIEVAL
AEHILRTY EARTHILY
HEARTILY
AEHILSST HELIASTS
SHALIEST
AEHILSSV LAVISHES
AEHILSTT LATHIEST
AEHILSTY HYALITES
AEHIMMSS SHAMMIES
AEHIMMST HAMMIEST
AEHIMMSW WHAMMIES
AEHIMNNU INHUMANE
AEHIMNRS HARMINES
AEHIMNSS SHAMISEN
AEHIMNST HEMATINS
AEHIMNSU HUMANISE
AEHIMNUZ HUMANIZE
AEHIMPRS SAMPHIRE
SERAPHIM
AEHIMPRT TERAPHIM
AEHIMPSS EMPHASIS
MISSHAPE
AEHIMPST MATESHIP
SHIPMATE
AEHIMRRS MARSHIER
AEHIMRSS MARISHES
MISHEARS
AEHIMSSS MESSIAHS
AEHIMSST ATHEISMS
AEHINNPZ PHENAZIN
AEHINNSS SHANNIES
AEHINNTX XANTHEIN
XANTHINE
AEHINORT ANTIHERO
AEHINOTT THIONATE
AEHINPPY EPIPHANY
AEHINPRS HEPARINS
SERAPHIN
AEHINPRT PERIANTH
AEHINPST THESPIAN
AEHINRRU UNHAIRER
AEHINRST HAIRNETS
INEARTHS
THERIANS
AEHINRSV ENRAVISH
VANISHER
AEHINSSS ASHINESS
HESSIANS
AEHINSST ANTHESIS
SHANTIES
SHEITANS
STHENIAS
AEHINSSV VANISHES
AEHINSSZ HAZINESS
AEHINSTT HESITANT
AEHINSTW INSWATHE
AEHIOPRS APHORISE
AEHIOPRU EUPHORIA
AEHIOPRZ APHORIZE
AEHIOPTT THIOTEPA
AEHIORST HOARIEST
AEHIORTU THIOUREA
AEHIPPRS SAPPHIRE
AEHIPPST EPITAPHS
HAPPIEST
AEHIPRSS PARISHES
SHARPIES
AEHIPRST TRIPHASE
AEHIPSTZ ZAPTIEHS
AEHIRRRS HARRIERS
AEHIRRST TRASHIER
AEHIRRSV RAVISHER
AEHIRRTW WRATHIER
AEHIRSSV RAVISHES
AEHIRSTU THESAURI
AEHIRSTW WATERISH
AEHIRSTY HYSTERIA
AEHIRSWY HAYWIRES
AEHIRTYZ YAHRZEIT
AEHISSTT ATHEISTS
HASTIEST
STAITHES
AEHISSTU HIATUSES
AEHISSTW WASHIEST
AEHISSVY YESHIVAS
AEHJNNOS JOHANNES
AEHKNNSU UNSHAKEN
AEHKNOSW HAWKNOSE
AEHKNRST THANKERS
AEHKNSSU ANKUSHES
AEHKNSWW NEWSHAWK
AEHKOOPR REAPHOOK
AEHKOSTU SHAKEOUT
AEHKPSSU SHAKEUPS
AEHKRRSS SHARKERS
AEHLLLTY LETHALLY
AEHLLMTY METHYLAL

AEHLLNRT ENTHRALL
AEHLLNTU UNLETHAL
AEHLLORW HALLOWER
AEHLLSST HALTLESS
AEHLMMNS HELMSMAN
AEHLMNOS MANHOLES
AEHLMNOT HOTELMAN
METHANOL
AEHLMNUY HUMANELY
AEHLMORS ARMHOLES
AEHLMOSU HAMULOSE
AEHLMPPT PAMPHLET
AEHLMRSS HARMLESS
AEHLMRST THERMALS
AEHLMRSU HUMERALS
AEHLNOST ANETHOLS
ETHANOLS
AEHLNPRS SHRAPNEL
AEHLNPTY ENTHALPY
AEHLNRST ENTHRALS
AEHLNSST NATHLESS
AEHLNSSU UNLASHES
AEHLNTUZ HAZELNUT
AEHLOPRT PLETHORA
AEHLOPSS HAPLOSES
AEHLOPST TAPHOLES
AEHLORST LOATHERS
RATHOLES
AEHLORSY HOARSELY
AEHLORUV OVERHAUL
AEHLOSST SHOALEST
AEHLPRSS PLASHERS
SPLASHER
AEHLPSSS SPLASHES
AEHLPSST PATHLESS
AEHLPSTU SULPHATE
AEHLRRTU URETHRAL
AEHLRSSS SLASHERS
AEHLRSST HARSLETS
SLATHERS
AEHLSSSS SASHLESS
AEHLSSTT STEALTHS
AEHLSSTW THAWLESS
AEHLSTTY STEALTHY
AEHMMRSS SHAMMERS
AEHMNNPY NYMPHEAN
AEHMNORS HORSEMAN
MENORAHS
RHAMNOSE
AEHMNOSU HOUSEMAN
AEHMNPRU PREHUMAN
AEHMNRST TRASHMEN
AEHMNSTU HUMANEST
AEHMOPRT METAPHOR
AEHMOPST APOTHEMS
AEHMORST TERAOHMS
AEHMOSTT HEMOSTAT
AEHMOSTU OUTSHAME
AEHMOSTW SOMEWHAT
AEHMOSTY HOMESTAY
AEHMRSSS SMASHERS
AEHMRSST HAMSTERS
AEHMSSSU SHAMUSES
AEHMSTTY AMETHYST
AEHMSUZZ MEZUZAHS
AEHNNOPT PANTHEON
AEHNNOTX XANTHONE
AEHNNPSU UNSHAPEN
AEHNNSUV UNSHAVEN
AEHNOPPY HYPOPNEA
AEHNOPST PHAETONS
PHONATES
STANHOPE
AEHNOPSY HYPONEAS
AEHNORSS HOARSENS
SENHORAS
AEHNOSSX HEXOSANS
AEHNPRSS SHARPENS
AEHNPRST PANTHERS
AEHNPSTY PHYTANES
AEHNRSSS RASHNESS
AEHNRSTU HAUNTERS
UNEARTHS
URETHANS
AEHNRTTU EARTHNUT
AEHNSSTW WHATNESS
AEHNSSTY SHANTEYS
AEHNSTUW UNSWATHE
AEHOPPRS PROPHASE
AEHOPRRY PYORRHEA
AEHOPRSS PHAROSES
AEHOPRST PHORATES
AEHOPSST PATHOSES
POTASHES
SPATHOSE
TEASHOPS

AEHOPSTT POSTHEAT
AEHOPSTU PHASEOUT
TAPHOUSE
AEHORRRW HARROWER
AEHORRSV OVERRASH
AEHORRSW WARHORSE
AEHORSST EARSHOTS
HOARSEST
AEHORSSW SAWHORSE
AEHORSTT RHEOSTAT
AEHORSTU OUTHEARS
AEHORSTX OXHEARTS
THORAXES
AEHOSSTU HOUSESAT
AEHPPRSW WHAPPERS
AEHPPSSU SHAPEUPS
AEHPRRSS SHARPERS
AEHPRSST SHARPEST
AEHPRSUX HARUSPEX
AEHPRSUY EUPHRASY
AEHPSTTT PHATTEST
AEHQRSSU QUASHERS
SQUASHER
AEHQSSSU SQUASHES
AEHRRSST TRASHERS
AEHRRSTU URETHRAS
AEHRRTTW THWARTER
AEHRSSSW SWASHERS
AEHRSSTT SHATTERS
AEHRSSTV HARVESTS
AEHRSSTW SWATHERS
AEHRSTUU HAUTEURS
AEHSSTUX EXHAUSTS
AEIIINTT INITIATE
AEIIIRRT RETIARII
AEIIKLLT TAILLIKE
AEIIKNRS KAISERIN
AEIIKNST KAINITES
AEIIKRTY TERIYAKI
AEIILLMR MILLIARE
RAMILLIE
AEIILLTV ILLATIVE
AEIILMNN MAINLINE
AEIILMNS ALIENISM
MILESIAN
AEIILMPR IMPERIAL
AEIILMRS RAMILIES
AEIILMTT MILITATE
AEIILNNS ANILINES
AEIILNQU AQUILINE
QUINIELA
AEIILNRR AIRLINER
AEIILNRS AIRLINES
AEIILNRT INERTIAL
AEIILNST ALIENIST
LITANIES
AEIILNSZ SALINIZE
AEIILNTZ LATINIZE
AEIILPPT TAILPIPE
AEIILPRT REPTILIA
AEIILQSU SILIQUAE
AEIILRST LISTERIA
AEIILRSV VIRELAIS
AEIILRTT LITERATI
AEIILSSS SILESIAS
AEIILSTV VITALISE
AEIILSTX LAXITIES
AEIILTVZ VITALIZE
AEIIMMRT MARITIME
AEIIMMSX MAXIMISE
AEIIMMTX MAXIMITE
AEIIMMXZ MAXIMIZE
AEIIMNNT ANTIMINE
AEIIMNRU URINEMIA
AEIIMNSZ SIMAZINE
AEIIMNTT INTIMATE
AEIIMNTU MINUTIAE
AEIIMNTV VITAMINE
AEIIMPRR IMPAIRER
AEIIMPSY EPIMYSIA
AEIIMRSS MISRAISE
AEIIMRST AIRTIMES
SERIATIM
AEIIMRSV VIREMIAS
AEIIMSTT IMITATES
AEIINNRS SIRENIAN
AEIINNRT TRIENNIA
AEIINPRT PAINTIER
AEIINPTZ PATINIZE
AEIINRSS AIRINESS
AEIINRST INERTIAS
RAINIEST
AEIINRTZ TRIAZINE

AEIINSST ISATINES
SANITIES
SANITISE
TENIASIS
AEIINSTV VANITIES
AEIINSTZ SANITIZE
AEIINSVV INVASIVE
AEIINTTT TITANITE
AEIINTTU UINTAITE
AEIIPRRS PRAIRIES
AEIIPRST PARITIES
AEIIPRTZ TRAPEZII
AEIIPRZZ PIZZERIA
AEIIPSST EPITASIS
AEIIRRST RARITIES
AEIIRRSV RIVIERAS
AEIIRRTT IRRITATE
AEIIRSST SATIRISE
AEIIRSTW WISTERIA
AEIIRSTX SEXTARII
AEIIRSTZ SATIRIZE
AEIIRSVV VIVARIES
AEIIRTVZ VIZIRATE
AEIISTTV VITIATES
AEIITTTV TITIVATE
AEIJKLZZ JAZZLIKE
AEIJLNSV JAVELINS
AEIJLNSW JAWLINES
AEIJLOPS JALOPIES
AEIJLOSU JALOUSIE
AEIJMMST JAMMIEST
AEIJMNSS JASMINES
AEIJNRTU JAUNTIER
AEIJORST JAROSITE
AEIJORVZ JAROVIZE
AEIJSTZZ JAZZIEST
AEIKKLMS MASKLIKE
AEIKKLNT TANKLIKE
AEIKKLPR PARKLIKE
AEIKKMNO KAKIEMON
AEIKKNRS SKANKIER
AEIKLLMP PALMLIKE
AEIKLLMS SELAMLIK
AEIKLLPY PLAYLIKE
AEIKLLST SALTLIKE
AEIKLMOT MOATLIKE
AEIKLMST MASTLIKE
AEIKLNOS KAOLINES
AEIKLNOV NOVALIKE
AEIKLNPS SKIPLANE
AEIKLNSS SEALSKIN
AEIKLNST LANKIEST
AEIKLNSW SWANLIKE
AEIKLNSY SNEAKILY
AEIKLNTU AUNTLIKE
AEIKLOPS SOAPLIKE
AEIKLOST KEITLOAS
AEIKLPRS SPARLIKE
AEIKLPRT TRAPLIKE
AEIKLPSW WASPLIKE
AEIKLQUY QUAYLIKE
AEIKLRST LARKIEST
STALKIER
STARLIKE
AEIKLRTW WARTLIKE
AEIKLRVY VALKYRIE
AEIKLRWY WALKYRIE
AEIKLSTT TALKIEST
AEIKMMSS MISMAKES
AEIKMNRS RAMEKINS
AEIKMNST MISTAKEN
AEIKMPRS RAMPIKES
AEIKMPSS MISSPEAK
AEIKMRST MISTAKER
AEIKMSST MISTAKES
AEIKNNST NEATNIKS
AEIKNNTU ANTINUKE
AEIKNPRS RANPIKES
AEIKNPST SNAKEPIT
AEIKNRSS SNARKIER
AEIKNRST KERATINS
AEIKNRSW SWANKIER
AEIKNRTW KNITWEAR
AEIKNSST SNAKIEST
AEIKNSSY KYANISES
AEIKNSTU UNAKITES
AEIKNSTW TWANKIES
AEIKNSTY KYANITES
AEIKNSYZ KYANIZES
AEIKOSST STOKESIA
AEIKPRRS SPARKIER
AEIKPSTW PAWKIEST
AEIKQSTU QUAKIEST
AEIKRSST ASTERISK
SARKIEST
AEIKRSTW WATERSKI

AEILLLMO MALLEOLI
AEILLLMS ALLELISM
AEILLLNY LINEALLY
AEILLMNS MANILLES
AEILLMNY MENIALLY
AEILLMSS MAILLESS
AEILLMSY MESIALLY
AEILLNNO LANOLINE
AEILLNPS SPLENIAL
AEILLNPY ALPINELY
AEILLNQU QUINELLA
AEILLNRY LINEARLY
AEILLNSS AINSELLS
SENSILLA
AEILLNVY VENIALLY
AEILLOSS LOESSIAL
AEILLOTV VOLATILE
AEILLPRS PERILLAS
AEILLPST PALLIEST
PASTILLE
AEILLQSU LALIQUES
SQUILLAE
AEILLRRS RALLIERS
AEILLRRY RAILLERY
AEILLRSS SALLIERS
AEILLRST LITERALS
TALLIERS
AEILLRSY SERIALLY
AEILLRTU TAILLEUR
AEILLRVX VEXILLAR
AEILLSSS SAILLESS
AEILLSST TAILLESS
TALLISES
AEILLSUV ALLUSIVE
AEILLSYZ SLEAZILY
AEILLTUZ LAZULITE
AEILMMNS MELANISM
AEILMMOR MEMORIAL
AEILMMOT IMMOLATE
AEILMMSS MELISMAS
AEILMMST MALMIEST
AEILMMTU MALEMIUT
AEILMNNS LINESMAN
MELANINS
AEILMNOS LAMINOSE
SEMOLINA
AEILMNPS IMPANELS
MANIPLES
AEILMNRS MARLINES
MINERALS
MISLEARN
AEILMNRT TERMINAL
TRAMLINE
AEILMNST AILMENTS
ALIMENTS
MANLIEST
MELANIST
SMALTINE
AEILMNSU ALUMINES
AEILMOOV MOVIEOLA
AEILMOPR PROEMIAL
AEILMOPS EPISOMAL
AEILMORS MORALISE
AEILMORT AMITROLE
ROLAMITE
AEILMORZ MORALIZE
AEILMOST LOAMIEST
AEILMOSV SEMIOVAL
AEILMOSW WAILSOME
AEILMPRS IMPALERS
IMPEARLS
LEMPIRAS
AEILMPRU PLUMERIA
AEILMPRV PRIMEVAL
AEILMPST PALMIEST
AEILMPTY PLAYTIME
AEILMQRU QUALMIER
AEILMRSS REALISMS
AEILMRST LAMISTER
MARLIEST
MARLITES
MISALTER
AEILMRSY MISLAYER
AEILMRTT REMITTAL
AEILMRUV VELARIUM
AEILMSSX SMILAXES
AEILMSTT MALTIEST
METALIST
SMALTITE
AEILMSTU SIMULATE
AEILMSTY STEAMILY
TALEYSIM
AEILMSUV MISVALUE
AEILMTTU MUTILATE
ULTIMATE
AEILNNOS SOLANINE

AEILNNPU PINNULAE
AEILNNRT INTERNAL
AEILNNSY INSANELY
AEILNNTY INNATELY
AEILNOPR PELORIAN
AEILNOPS OPALINES
AEILNOPT ANTIPOLE
AEILNORS AILERONS
ALIENORS
AEILNORT ORIENTAL
RELATION
AEILNORV OVERLAIN
AEILNOSS ANISOLES
AEILNOST ELATIONS
INSOLATE
TOENAILS
AEILNOSX SILOXANE
AEILNPPT PIEPLANT
AEILNPRS PRALINES
AEILNPRT INTERLAP
TRAPLINE
TRIPLANE
AEILNPSS PAINLESS
SPANIELS
AEILNPST PANELIST
PANTILES
PLAINEST
AEILNPSU SPINULAE
AEILNPSW PINWALES
AEILNPSX EXPLAINS
AEILNPTT TINPLATE
AEILNPTY PENALITY
AEILNQSU QUINELAS
AEILNQTU QUANTILE
AEILNRRS SNARLIER
AEILNRSS RAINLESS
AEILNRST ENTRAILS
LATRINES
RATLINES
RETINALS
TRENAILS
AEILNRSV RAVELINS
AEILNRSX RELAXINS
AEILNRSY INLAYERS
AEILNRTU AUNTLIER
RETINULA
TENURIAL
AEILNRTV INTERVAL
AEILNRTY INTERLAY
AEILNSST ELASTINS
NAILSETS
SALIENTS
SALTINES
AEILNSSU INULASES
AEILNSSZ LAZINESS
AEILNSTU ALUNITES
INSULATE
AEILNSTV VENTAILS
AEILNSUW LAUWINES
AEILNSUY UNEASILY
AEILNTVY NATIVELY
VENALITY
AEILNUVV UNIVALVE
AEILOORV OVARIOLE
AEILOPPR OILPAPER
AEILOPPT OPPILATE
AEILOPRS PELORIAS
POLARISE
AEILOPRT EPILATOR
PETIOLAR
AEILOPRZ POLARIZE
AEILOPST SPOLIATE
AEILORRT RETAILOR
AEILORSS SOLARISE
AEILORSV VALORISE
VARIOLES
AEILORSZ SOLARIZE
AEILORTV VIOLATER
AEILORTZ TRIAZOLE
AEILORVZ VALORIZE
AEILOSST ISOLATES
AEILOSSX OXALISES
AEILOSTT TOTALISE
AEILOSTV VIOLATES
AEILOTTZ TOTALIZE
AEILPPQU APPLIQUE
AEILPPRS APPLIERS
AEILPRRS REPRISAL
AEILPRRT PALTRIER
PRETRIAL
AEILPRST PILASTER
PLAISTER
PLAITERS
AEILPRSU SPIRULAE
AEILPRSV PREVAILS
AEILPRSW SLIPWARE

AEILPRTV LIVETRAP
AEILPRXY PYREXIAL
AEILPSSY PAISLEYS
AEILPSTT PLATIEST
AEILPSUV PLAUSIVE
AEILQRTU QUARTILE
REQUITAL
AEILQSTU LIQUATES
TEQUILAS
AEILQSUY QUEASILY
AEILQTUY EQUALITY
AEILRRST RETRIALS
TRAILERS
AEILRRSU RURALISE
AEILRRTU RURALITE
AEILRRTY LITERARY
AEILRRUZ RURALIZE
AEILRSST REALISTS
SALTIERS
SALTIRES
AEILRSSV REVISALS
AEILRSTT TERTIALS
AEILRSTU URALITES
AEILRSVV REVIVALS
AEILRSVY VIRELAYS
AEILRTTY ALTERITY
AEILRTUV VAULTIER
AEILRTUZ LAZURITE
AEILRTVV TRIVALVE
AEILRTWY WATERILY
AEILSSTT SALTIEST
SLATIEST
AEILSTVY VILAYETS
AEILSTWY SWEATILY
AEILSTYY YEASTILY
AEIMMNNT IMMANENT
AEIMMNOS SEMINOMA
AEIMMNOT AMMONITE
AEIMMNSS MISNAMES
AEIMMPST PSAMMITE
AEIMMRRS SMARMIER
AEIMMRST MARMITES
RAMMIEST
AEIMMRTU IMMATURE
AEIMMSST MISMATES
AEIMMSTT SEMIMATT
AEIMNNOT ANTINOME
NOMINATE
AEIMNNRS REINSMAN
AEIMNNRT TRAINMEN
AEIMNNST MANNITES
AEIMNOPT PTOMAINE
AEIMNORS MORAINES
ROMAINES
ROMANISE
AEIMNORW AIRWOMEN
AEIMNORZ ROMANIZE
AEIMNOSS ANEMOSIS
AEIMNOST AMNIOTES
MASONITE
MISATONE
AEIMNOSW WOMANISE
AEIMNOTZ MONAZITE
AEIMNOUX EXONUMIA
AEIMNOWZ WOMANIZE
AEIMNPSX PANMIXES
AEIMNQRU RAMEQUIN
AEIMNRRS MARINERS
AEIMNRSS SEMINARS
AEIMNRST MINARETS
RAIMENTS
AEIMNRSU ANEURISM
AEIMNRSY SEMINARY
AEIMNRTT INTERMAT
MARTINET
AEIMNRTU RUMINATE
AEIMNRTY TYRAMINE
AEIMNSSS SAMISENS
AEIMNSST MANTISES
MATINESS
AEIMNSSU ANIMUSES
AEIMNSSZ MAZINESS
AEIMOOPS IPOMOEAS
AEIMOPRS MEROPIAS
AEIMOPSX APOMIXES
AEIMORRS ARMOIRES
ARMORIES
AEIMORST AMORTISE
ATOMISER
AEIMORTT AMORETTI
AEIMORTZ AMORTIZE
ATOMIZER
AEIMOSST AMITOSES
AMOSITES
ATOMISES
AEIMOSTX TOXEMIAS

AEIMOSTZ ATOMIZES
AEIMOTTV MOTIVATE
AEIMPRRT IMPARTER
TRAMPIER
AEIMPRSS IMPRESAS
MISPARSE
AEIMPRST PRIMATES
AEIMPRSV VAMPIRES
AEIMPRSW SWAMPIER
AEIMPRTU APTERIUM
AEIMPSSS IMPASSES
AEIMPSST IMPASTES
PASTIMES
AEIMPSTV VAMPIEST
AEIMQRSU MARQUISE
AEIMRRRS MARRIERS
AEIMRSST ASTERISM
MISRATES
SMARTIES
AEIMRSSV MISAVERS
AEIMRSSY EMISSARY
AEIMRSTT MISTREAT
TERATISM
AEIMRSTU MURIATES
AEIMRSTV VITAMERS
AEIMRSTW WARTIMES
AEIMRSTX MATRIXES
AEIMRSWW SWIMWEAR
AEIMSSST MASSIEST
MISSEATS
AEIMSSTT ETATISMS
MISSTATE
AEIMSSTX MASTIXES
AEIMSSTZ MESTIZAS
AEIMTTUV MUTATIVE
AEINNOPS SAPONINE
AEINNOPV PAVONINE
AEINNORS RAISONNE
AEINNORT ANOINTER
REANOINT
AEINNOST ENATIONS
SONATINE
AEINNOTT INTONATE
AEINNOTV INNOVATE
VENATION
AEINNPRS PANNIERS
AEINNRRS INSNARER
AEINNRRT INERRANT
AEINNRSS INSNARES
AEINNRST ENTRAINS
TRANNIES
AEINNRSU ANEURINS
AEINNRTT INTRANET
AEINNSST INSANEST
STANINES
AEINNSSV VAINNESS
AEINNSSZ ZANINESS
AEINNSTT STANNITE
AEINOPPT ANTIPOPE
AEINOPRT ATROPINE
AEINOPSS SENOPIAS
AEINOPST SAPONITE
AEINOPTZ TOPAZINE
AEINOQRU AEQUORIN
AEINOQTU EQUATION
AEINORRT ANTERIOR
AEINORRW IRONWARE
AEINORSS ERASIONS
SENSORIA
AEINORST NOTARIES
SENORITA
AEINORSV AVERSION
AEINORTT TENTORIA
AEINORTZ NOTARIZE
AEINOSST ASTONIES
AEINOSSV EVASIONS
AEINOSSX SAXONIES
AEINOSXZ OXAZINES
AEINOTVX VEXATION
AEINPPPS PANPIPES
AEINPPRS SNAPPIER
AEINPPRY PAPYRINE
AEINPPSS PINESAPS
AEINPPST NAPPIEST
AEINPRRT PRETRAIN
TERRAPIN
AEINPRRU UNREPAIR
AEINPRST PAINTERS
PANTRIES
PERTAINS
PINASTER
PRISTANE
REPAINTS
AEINPRTT TRIPTANE
AEINPSST SAPIENTS
STEAPSIN
AEINPSSW WINESAPS
AEINPSTT PATIENTS
AEINPSTU PETUNIAS
SUPINATE
AEINPSTY EPINASTY
AEINPTTY ANTITYPE
AEINQRTU ANTIQUER
QUAINTER
AEINQSTU ANTIQUES
AEINQTTU EQUITANT
AEINQTUZ QUANTIZE
AEINRRST RESTRAIN
RETRAINS
STRAINER
TERRAINS
TRAINERS
AEINRRTT RETIRANT
AEINRRTV VERATRIN
AEINRRTW INTERWAR
AEINRRUW UNWARIER
AEINRSST ARTINESS
RETSINAS
STAINERS
STEARINS
AEINRSSU ANURESIS
SENARIUS
AEINRSSW WARINESS
AEINRSTT INTREATS
NITRATES
STRAITEN
TERTIANS
AEINRSTU RUINATES
TAURINES
URANITES
URINATES
AEINRSTW TINWARES
AEINRSUZ SUZERAIN
AEINRSVV VERVAINS
AEINRSZZ SNAZZIER
AEINSSST SESTINAS
AEINSSSV VINASSES
AEINSSTT ANTSIEST
INSTATES
NASTIEST
SATINETS
TITANESS
AEINSSTU SINUATES
AEINSSTX SEXTAINS
AEINSSVW WAVINESS
AEINSSWX WAXINESS
AEINSTTT NATTIEST
AEINSTTW TAWNIEST
AEINSUVV VESUVIAN
AEINTTUU AUTUNITE
AEIOOPTT PATOOTIE
AEIOPPST APPOSITE
AEIOPRRT PRIORATE
AEIOPRRW AIRPOWER
AEIOPRSV VAPORISE
AEIOPRTX EXPIATOR
AEIOPRVZ VAPORIZE
AEIOPSST SOAPIEST
AEIOPTTV OPTATIVE
AEIOQSSU SEQUOIAS
AEIORRSS ROSARIES
AEIORRST ROTARIES
AEIORRSV SAVORIER
AEIORSSV SAVORIES
AEIORSTT TOASTIER
AEIORSTU OUTRAISE
SAUTOIRE
AEIORSTV TRAVOISE
VIATORES
VOTARIES
AEIORTTV ROTATIVE
AEIOSSTZ AZOTISES
AEIOSTZZ AZOTIZES
AEIPPPST PAPPIEST
AEIPPRRS APPRISER
AEIPPRRZ APPRIZER
AEIPPRSS APPRISES
AEIPPRST PERIAPTS
AEIPPRSZ APPRIZES
AEIPPSST SAPPIEST
AEIPPSTZ ZAPPIEST
AEIPQRTU PRATIQUE
AEIPRRRS PARRIERS
SPARRIER
AEIPRRSS ASPIRERS
PRAISERS
AEIPRRST PARTIERS
AEIPRRSU UPRAISER
AEIPRRTV PRIVATER
AEIPRSST PASTRIES
PIASTERS
PIASTRES
RASPIEST
TRAIPSES
AEIPRSSU UPRAISES
AEIPRSSV PARVISES
PAVISERS
AEIPRSSX PRAXISES
AEIPRSTV PRIVATES
AEIPRSTW WIRETAPS
AEIPRSTY ASPERITY
AEIPRSVY VESPIARY
AEIPRSWW WARPWISE
AEIPRSXY PYREXIAS
AEIPSSST PASTISES
AEIPSSSV PASSIVES
PAVISSES
AEIPSSTT PASTIEST
AEIPSSTW WASPIEST
AEIPSSTY EPISTASY
AEIPSZZZ PIZAZZES
PIZZAZES
AEIPTTUV PUTATIVE
AEIQRRRU QUARRIER
AEIQRRSU QUARRIES
AEIQRRTU QUARTIER
AEIRRRST STARRIER
TARRIERS
AEIRRRSV ARRIVERS
AEIRRSST TARSIERS
AEIRRSTT STRAITER
TARRIEST
AEIRRSTW STRAWIER
AEIRRTTY TERTIARY
AEIRSSST ASSISTER
AEIRSSTT ARTISTES
ARTSIEST
STRIATES
AEIRSSTW WAISTERS
WAITRESS
WASTRIES
AEIRSTTT ATTRITES
RATTIEST
TARTIEST
TITRATES
TRISTATE
AEIRSTTW WARTIEST
AEIRSTTZ TRISTEZA
AEIRSTUZ AZURITES
AEIRSTVY VESTIARY
AEIRSWWY WIREWAYS
AEIRTTTW ATWITTER
AEISSSST SASSIEST
AEISSSTY ESSAYIST
AEISSTTT TASTIEST
AEISSTTU SITUATES
AEISSTTV STATIVES
VASTIEST
AEISSTVV SAVVIEST
AEISTTTT TATTIEST
AEJKPSTU KAJEPUTS
AEJLNSUV JUVENALS
AEJLORTV TOLARJEV
AEJLOSUY JEALOUSY
AEJLOSUZ AZULEJOS
AEKKKMRU KRUMKAKE
AEKKMNOO KAKEMONO
AEKKNRSS SKANKERS
AEKLMORS LARKSOME
AEKLMOSU LEUKOMAS
AEKLMRUW LUKEWARM
AEKLMRUY YARMULKE
AEKLNNSS LANKNESS
AEKLNOSY ANKYLOSE
AEKLNPRT PLANKTER
AEKLNRSS RANKLESS
AEKLNRSV KLAVERNS
AEKLNSST TANKLESS
AEKLOPRT LAKEPORT
AEKLOPRW ROPEWALK
AEKLORTV OVERTALK
AEKLORVW WALKOVER
AEKLOSST SKATOLES
AEKLOSVZ ZELKOVAS
AEKLPPST PEPTALKS
AEKLPRRS SPARKLER
AEKLPRSS SPARKLES
AEKLPRST SPARKLET
AEKLRSST STALKERS
AEKMMNRS MARKSMEN
AEKMNRSU UNMAKERS
UNMASKER
AEKMORTW TEAMWORK
WORKMATE
AEKMPRTU UPMARKET
AEKNNRSS RANKNESS
AEKNORRV OVERRANK
AEKNPPRS KNAPPERS
AEKNPRSS SPANKERS
AEKNPSSU UNSPEAKS
AEKNSSTW SWANKEST
AEKOORSV OVERSOAK
AEKOPRRT PARROKET
AEKOPRSS PRESOAKS
AEKOPSTU OUTSPEAK
AEKORSSS KAROSSES
AEKORSTV OVERTASK
AEKORSTW SEATWORK
AEKOSTTU OUTSKATE
OUTTAKES
STAKEOUT
TAKEOUTS
AEKPRRSS SPARKERS
AEKPSSSY PASSKEYS
AEKQRSUW SQUAWKER
AEKRRSST STARKERS
AEKRSSTT STARKEST
AEKSSSTT TSATSKES
AELLMNTY MENTALLY
TALLYMEN
AELLMORS SLALOMER
AELLMORT MARTELLO
AELLMOSS LOAMLESS
AELLMOTY TOMALLEY
AELLMRST TRAMELLS
AELLMSST SMALLEST
AELLMSWX MAXWELLS
AELLNOOT ATENOLOL
AELLNOPV VOLPLANE
AELLNOSV NOVELLAS
AELLNPRU PRUNELLA
AELLNPSS PLANLESS
AELLNPTT PLANTLET
AELLNRUY NEURALLY
UNREALLY
AELLNRVY VERNALLY
AELLNSST TALLNESS
AELLNTTY LATENTLY
AELLNTUU LUNULATE
AELLNTUY LUNATELY
AELLOOPS PALEOSOL
AELLOPPR APPELLOR
AELLOPRT PREALLOT
AELLOPRW WALLOPER
AELLOPTY ALLOTYPE
AELLORST REALLOTS
ROSTELLA
AELLORSV ALLOVERS
OVERALLS
AELLORSW SALLOWER
AELLORTT ALLOTTER
AELLORWW WALLOWER
AELLOSTY LOYALEST
AELLOSUV ALVEOLUS
AELLPRSS SPALLERS
AELLPSSY PLAYLESS
AELLPSTY PLAYLETS
AELLQRSU SQUALLER
AELLRRSU ALLURERS
AELLRRTY RETRALLY
AELLRTTY LATTERLY
AELLRTVY TREVALLY
AELLRTYY LYRATELY
AELLRWYY LAWYERLY
AELLSSST SALTLESS
AELLSTUU ULULATES
AELLSTVY VESTALLY
AELLSUVV VALVULES
AELLSUXY SEXUALLY
AELMMORW MEALWORM
AELMMOSY MYELOMAS
AELMMRSS SLAMMERS
AELMMRST TRAMMELS
AELMMSST STAMMELS
AELMMSSY MALMSEYS
AELMNNOT NONMETAL
AELMNNOU NOUMENAL
AELMNNRY MANNERLY
AELMNOPS NEOPLASM
PLEONASM
AELMNORS ALMONERS
AELMNOSU MELANOUS
AELMNOWY LAYWOMEN
AELMNOYY YEOMANLY
AELMNRSU MENSURAL
NUMERALS
AELMNSTT MANTLETS
AELMNSTY MESNALTY
AELMOORS SALEROOM
AELMOPRR PREMOLAR
PREMORAL
AELMOPRS RAMPOLES
AELMOPRT TEMPORAL
AELMOPSU AMPOULES
AELMOPSY MAYPOLES
AELMOPTT PALMETTO
AELMORSU RAMULOSE
AELMORSV REMOVALS
AELMORSY RAMOSELY
AELMORTU EMULATOR
AELMORTZ METRAZOL
AELMOSSS MOLASSES
AELMOSST MALTOSES
AELMOSSY AMYLOSES
AELMOSTT MATELOTS
AELMOSTU SOULMATE
AELMOTVZ MAZELTOV
AELMPRRT TRAMPLER
AELMPRSS SAMPLERS
AELMPRST TEMPLARS
TRAMPLES
AELMPRSY LAMPREYS
AELMPSUX AMPLEXUS
AELMRSST LAMSTERS
TRAMLESS
AELMRSTT MALTSTER
MARTLETS
AELMRSTU STAUMREL
AELMRSTY MASTERLY
AELMRTUY MATURELY
AELMSSSS MASSLESS
AELMSSST MASTLESS
AELNNOOP NAPOLEON
AELNNOOX NALOXONE
AELNNOPT PENTANOL
AELNNOQU NONEQUAL
AELNNORU NEURONAL
AELNNOSU ANNULOSE
AELNNPRS PLANNERS
AELNNRSS ENSNARLS
AELNNRST LANTERNS
AELNNRSU UNLEARNS
AELNNRTU UNLEARNT
AELNNSTU ANNULETS
AELNOOTZ ENTOZOAL
AELNOPPY POLYPNEA
AELNOPRS PERSONAL
PSORALEN
AELNOPRV OVERPLAN
AELNOPST POLENTAS
AELNOPSU APOLUNES
AELNOPTW TOWPLANE
AELNORSU ALEURONS
NEUROSAL
AELNORTT TOLERANT
AELNORTU OUTLEARN
AELNORTY ORNATELY
AELNOSSV OVALNESS
AELNOSTY ANOLYTES
AELNPPRS PREPLANS
AELNPPRT PREPLANT
AELNPPSY PLAYPENS
AELNPRST PLANTERS
REPLANTS
AELNPRSU PURSLANE
SUPERNAL
AELNPSSS SNAPLESS
SPANLESS
AELNPSSU SPANSULE
AELNPSTX EXPLANTS
AELNPTTU PATULENT
PETULANT
AELNPTTY PATENTLY
AELNQSUU UNEQUALS
AELNRRSS SNARLERS
AELNRRTY ERRANTLY
AELNRRUU NEURULAR
AELNRSST SALTERNS
AELNRSTT SLATTERN
AELNRSTU NEUTRALS
AELNRSTV VENTRALS
AELNRSUU NEURULAS
AELNRSUV UNRAVELS
AELNRSXY LARYNXES
AELNRTTW TRAWLNET
AELNSSST SALTNESS
AELNSUUX UNSEXUAL
AELNTTUX EXULTANT
AELOORRS ROSEOLAR
AELOORSS AEROSOLS
ROSEOLAS
AELOORTW WATERLOO
AELOORTZ ZOOLATER
AELOPPRS PROLAPSE
SAPROPEL
AELOPPSU PAPULOSE
AELOPPTU POPULATE
AELOPPXY APOPLEXY
AELOPQUY OPAQUELY
AELOPRRV REPROVAL
AELOPRSS REPOSALS
AELOPRST PETROSAL
POLESTAR
AELOPRSV OVERLAPS
AELOPRVY OVERPLAY
AELOPSSS SOAPLESS
AELOPSST APOSTLES
AELOPSSU ESPOUSAL
SEPALOUS
AELOPSSX EXPOSALS
AELOPSTT PALETOTS
AELOPSTU OUTLEAPS
PETALOUS
AELOPTTU OUTLEAPT
AELORRST REALTORS
RELATORS
RESTORAL
AELORSSS LASSOERS
AELORSST OLESTRAS
AELORSTT RETOTALS
AELORSTU ROSULATE
AELORSTV LEVATORS
OVERSALT
AELORSUU ROULEAUS
AELORSVY LAYOVERS
OVERLAYS
AELORTYZ ZEALOTRY
AELORUUX ROULEAUX
AELOSSTV SOLVATES
AELOSSVY SAVELOYS
AELOSTTU TOLUATES
AELOSTTW WASTELOT
AELOSTUV OVULATES
AELOSTUY AUTOLYSE
AELOTUUV OUTVALUE
AELOTUYZ AUTOLYZE
AELPPPRU PREPUPAL
AELPPPRY PREAPPLY
AELPPRSS SLAPPERS
AELPPSSU APPULSES
AELPRRRU LARRUPER
AELPRRSW SPRAWLER
AELPRRTT PRATTLER
AELPRSST PERSALTS
PLASTERS
PSALTERS
STAPLERS
AELPRSSU PERUSALS
AELPRSSY PARSLEYS
SPARSELY
AELPRSTT PARTLETS
PLATTERS
PRATTLES
SPLATTER
SPRATTLE
AELPRSTY PEYTRALS
PLASTERY
PSALTERY
AELPRSUY SUPERLAY
AELPSSSS PASSLESS
AELPSSST PASTLESS
AELPSSTT PELTASTS
AELPSSTU PULSATES
AELPSSTZ SPATZLES
AELQRRSU QUARRELS
AELQRSUY SQUARELY
AELQSTUZ QUETZALS
AELRRSSW WARSLERS
AELRRSTT RATTLERS
STARTLER
AELRRSTW TRAWLERS
WARSTLER
AELRRTVY VARLETRY
AELRSSST STARLESS
AELRSSSW WRASSLES
AELRSSTT STARLETS
STARTLES
AELRSSTU SALUTERS
AELRSSTW WARSTLES
WARTLESS
WASTRELS
WRASTLES
AELRSSUW WALRUSES
AELRSTTT TARTLETS
TATTLERS
AELRSTTU LUSTRATE
TUTELARS
AELRSTUV VAULTERS
VESTURAL
AELRSTWY TRAWLEYS
AELRSTWZ WALTZERS
AELRTTUX TEXTURAL
AELRTTUY TUTELARY

AELSSTTW WATTLESS
AELSTTTW TWATTLES
AELSTTUU USTULATE
AELSTTUY ASTUTELY
AEMMNNOY MONEYMAN
AEMMNRTU RAMENTUM
AEMMOORT ROOMMATE
AEMMORST MARMOSET
AEMMORSW WOMMERAS
AEMMPRSS SPAMMERS
AEMMRSST STAMMERS
AEMMRTUY MAUMETRY
AEMMSSTU SUMMATES
AEMMSSUW WAMMUSES
AEMNNORS MONERANS
SONARMEN
AEMNNORT ORNAMENT
AEMNNOSS MANNOSES
AEMNNOST MONTANES
AEMNNOSZ MENAZONS
AEMNNRST REMNANTS
AEMNOORT ANTEROOM
AEMNOORY AERONOMY
AEMNOOSZ MESOZOAN
AEMNOOTZ METAZOON
AEMNOPRS MANROPES
AEMNOPRW MANPOWER
AEMNORRS RANSOMER
AEMNORST MONSTERA
ONSTREAM
TONEARMS
AEMNORSU ENAMOURS
NEUROMAS
AEMNORSV OVERMANS
AEMNORTU ROUTEMAN
AEMNORTY MONETARY
AEMNORVY OVERMANY
AEMNORYY YEOMANRY
AEMNOSTU SEAMOUNT
AEMNPRSS PRESSMAN
AEMNPRSU SUPERMAN
AEMNPSTY PAYMENTS
AEMNRRSU MANURERS
SURNAMER
AEMNRRUY NUMERARY
AEMNRSST SARMENTS
SMARTENS
AEMNRSSU SURNAMES
AEMNRSSW WARMNESS
AEMNRSTU MENSTRUA
AEMNRSTV VARMENTS
AEMNRSUY ANEURYSM
AEMNSTTU NUTMEATS
AEMOORRW WAREROOM
AEMOORST TEAROOMS
AEMOORSW WOOMERAS
AEMOORTT AMORETTO
AEMOOSST MAESTOSO
OSTEOMAS
AEMOOSSV VAMOOSES
AEMOOSTT OSTOMATE
TOMATOES
AEMOOSTU AUTOSOME
AEMOOTTY TOMATOEY
AEMOPPRS PAMPEROS
AEMOPRTW TAPEWORM
AEMOQSSU SQUAMOSE
AEMORRRS ARMORERS
AEMORRRU ARMOURER
AEMORRST REARMOST
AEMORRSV OVERARMS
AEMORRSW EARWORMS
AEMORRSY ROSEMARY
AEMORRVW OVERWARM
AEMORSSS MORASSES
AEMORSST MAESTROS
AEMORSSY MAYORESS
AEMORTTU TAUTOMER
AEMOSSTT STOMATES
AEMOSSTW TWASOMES
AEMOSSWY SOMEWAYS
AEMOSTTZ MOZETTAS
AEMOTTZZ MOZZETTA
AEMPPRST PRESTAMP
AEMPRRST TRAMPERS
AEMPRRSW PREWARMS
AEMPRRSY SPERMARY
AEMPRSST RESTAMPS
STAMPERS
AEMPRSSW SWAMPERS
AEMPRSTU TEMPURAS
UPSTREAM
AEMPSSUW WAMPUSES
AEMPSTTT ATTEMPTS
AEMQRSSU MARQUESS
MASQUERS

AEMRRSST ARMRESTS
AEMRRSSW SWARMERS
AEMRRSTU MATURERS
AEMRRTUV VERATRUM
AEMRSSSU ASSUMERS
MASSEURS
AEMRSSTT MATTRESS
SMARTEST
SMATTERS
AEMRSTTU MATUREST
AEMRTUUX TRUMEAUX
AENNNPST PENNANTS
AENNOOTZ ENTOZOAN
AENNOPRX NAPROXEN
AENNOPST PENTOSAN
AENNORST RESONANT
AENNORSU UNREASON
AENNORSY ANNOYERS
AENNORTU UNORNATE
AENNORTW WANTONER
AENNORUX NEURAXON
AENNOSTU TONNEAUS
AENNOSTX NONTAXES
AENNOTUX TONNEAUX
AENNPRSS SPANNERS
AENNRRST ENTRANTS
AENNRSWY SWANNERY
AENNRTTY TENANTRY
AENOOPST TEASPOON
AENOORRT RATOONER
AENOOSTZ OZONATES
AENOPPRS PROPANES
AENOPRSS PERSONAS
RESPONSA
AENOPRST OPERANTS
PRONATES
PROTEANS
AENOPRSY PYRANOSE
AENOPRTT PATENTOR
AENOPRWY WEAPONRY
AENOPSTU AUTOPENS
AENORRRW NARROWER
AENORRSS SERRANOS
AENORRST ANTRORSE
AENORSST ASSENTOR
SANTEROS
SENATORS
STARNOSE
TREASONS
AENORSSU ANSEROUS
ARSENOUS
AENORSTU OUTEARNS
AENORSUV RAVENOUS
AENORTTV TEVATRON
AENORTTY ATTORNEY
AENORTWW TOWNWEAR
AENOSSTU SOUTANES
AENOSSUU NAUSEOUS
AENPPRSS SNAPPERS
AENPRRST PARTNERS
AENPRRSW PRAWNERS
PREWARNS
AENPRSST PASTERNS
RAPTNESS
AENPRSSW SPAWNERS
AENPRSTT PATTERNS
TRANSEPT
TRAPNEST
AENPRSUV PARVENUS
AENPSSST PASTNESS
AENPSSSY SYNAPSES
AENPSSTW STEWPANS
AENQRRTU QUARTERN
AENRRRTY ERRANTRY
AENRSSST SARSNETS
AENRSSTT TARTNESS
AENRSSTU ANESTRUS
SAUNTERS
AENRSSTV SERVANTS
VERSANTS
AENRSSUW UNSWEARS
AENRSTTU TAUNTERS
AENRSTUV VAUNTERS
AENRSTWY STERNWAY
AENRTWYY ENTRYWAY
AENSSSTV VASTNESS
AENSSTTU TAUTNESS
UNSTATES
AENSSTTX SEXTANTS
AENSSTXY SYNTAXES
AEOOPPPS PAPPOOSE
AEOOPPSS PAPOOSES
AEOOPRRT OPERATOR
AEOOPSTT POTATOES
AEOORRST SORORATE
AEOORTTT TATTOOER

AEOPPRRV APPROVER
AEOPPRSS APPOSERS
AEOPPRST TRAPPOSE
AEOPPRSV APPROVES
AEOPQRTU PAROQUET
AEOPQSTU OPAQUEST
AEOPRRRT PARROTER
AEOPRRSS ASPERSOR
AEOPRRST PRAETORS
PRORATES
AEOPRRSV VAPORERS
AEOPRRUV VAPOURER
AEOPRRWW WARPOWER
AEOPRSST ESPARTOS
PROTASES
SEAPORTS
AEOPRSSV OVERPASS
PASSOVER
AEOPRSTT PROSTATE
AEOPRSTU APTEROUS
AEOPRSTV OVERPAST
AEOPRSVY OVERPAYS
AEOPRSWY ROPEWAYS
AEOPTTUY AUTOTYPE
AEOQRSTU EQUATORS
QUAESTOR
AEOQRSUV VAQUEROS
AEOQRTTU TORQUATE
AEOQRTUZ QUATORZE
AEORRRST ARRESTOR
AEORRSST ASSERTOR
ASSORTER
ORATRESS
REASSORT
ROASTERS
AEORRSSU AROUSERS
AEORRSSV SAVORERS
SEROVARS
AEORRSTT ROSTRATE
AEORRSUV SAVOURER
AEORRTTV OVERTART
AEORRTZZ TERRAZZO
AEORRVWY OVERWARY
AEORSSSS ASSESSOR
AEORSSST OSSETRAS
AEORSSTT TOASTERS
AEORSSTU OSSATURE
AEORSSTV VOTARESS
AEORSSTX STORAXES
AEORSSUU ROUSSEAU
AEORSTTT ATTESTOR
TESTATOR
AEORSTTU OUTRATES
OUTSTARE
SEATROUT
AEORSTUV OUTRAVES
AEORSTUW OUTSWARE
OUTSWEAR
OUTWEARS
AEORSTVY OVERSTAY
AEORTUWY OUTWEARY
ROUTEWAY
AEOSTTTU OUTSTATE
AEOSTTUW OUTWASTE
AEPPPRSU PREPUPAS
AEPPRRST STRAPPER
TRAPPERS
AEPPRRSW PREWRAPS
WRAPPERS
AEPPRSSW SWAPPERS
AEPPSSTU PASTEUPS
AEPQRSTU PARQUETS
AEPRRSSY RESPRAYS
SPRAYERS
AEPRRSTU PASTURER
RAPTURES
AEPRRSTY PARTYERS
AEPRSSST SPARSEST
TRESPASS
AEPRSSTT SPATTERS
TAPSTERS
AEPRSSTU PASTURES
UPSTARES
AEPRSTTU UPSTATER
AEPRSTTY TAPESTRY
AEPRSTUX SUPERTAX
AEPRTUVY PYRUVATE
AEPSSSSU PASSUSES
AEPSSTTU UPSTATES
AEQRRSSU SQUARERS
AEQRRSTU QUARTERS
AEQRSSTU SQUAREST
AEQRSTTU QUARTETS
SQUATTER
AEQRSTUZ QUARTZES
AERRSSSU ASSURERS

AERRSSTT RESTARTS
STARTERS
AERRSSTV STARVERS
AERRSSTY STRAYERS
AERRSTUY TREASURY
AERSSSST STRASSES
AERSSTTT STRETTAS
AERSSTTU STATURES
AERSSTTW SWATTERS
AERSSTUX SURTAXES
AERSSTXY STYRAXES
AERSTTVY TRAVESTY
AERTTUXY TEXTUARY
AESSSTTU STATUSES
AESSTTTU STATUTES
AFFFFIRR RIFFRAFF
AFFFLLOS FALLOFFS
AFFGHIRT AFFRIGHT
AFFGIINP PIAFFING
AFFGIINX AFFIXING
AFFGIIRT GRAFFITI
AFFGILNR RAFFLING
AFFGILNW WAFFLING
AFFGINQU QUAFFING
AFFGINST STAFFING
AFFGIORT GRAFFITO
AFFHILLS FALLFISH
AFFHILST FLATFISH
AFFHILTU FAITHFUL
AFFIINTY AFFINITY
AFFIISTX FIXATIFS
AFFILLMM FLIMFLAM
AFFILSUX SUFFIXAL
AFFIMSST MASTIFFS
AFFINOSU AFFUSION
AFFINRSU FUNFAIRS
RUFFIANS
AFFIPSTT TIPSTAFF
AFFIRSSU SUFFARIS
AFFLLOOT FOOTFALL
AFFLOOTT FLATFOOT
AFFLOPSY PLAYOFFS
AFFLRRUU FURFURAL
AFFMOPRS OFFRAMPS
AFFNORSS SAFFRONS
AFFNORST AFFRONTS
AFFNRRUU FURFURAN
AFGGGILN FLAGGING
AFGGGINR FRAGGING
AFGGILNN FLANGING
AFGGILOP GIGAFLOP
AFGGINOR FORAGING
AFGGINOT FAGOTING
AFGGINRT GRAFTING
AFGHIINT FAITHING
AFGHILNS FLASHING
AFGHILNT FANLIGHT
AFGHILPS FLAGSHIP
AFGHINRT FARTHING
AFGHINRW WHARFING
AFGHINST SHAFTING
AFGHIOST GOATFISH
AFGHIRSY GRAYFISH
AFGHLNSU FLASHGUN
AFGHLSTU GHASTFUL
AFGHRSTU FRAUGHTS
AFGIILLN FLAILING
AFGIILNS FAILINGS
AFGIINNT FAINTING
AFGIINRS FAIRINGS
AFGIINTX FIXATING
AFGIKLNN FLANKING
AFGIKNNR FRANKING
AFGILLNT FLATLING
AFGILMMN FLAMMING
AFGILMNO FLAMINGO
AFGILNOT FLOATING
AFGILNPP FLAPPING
AFGILNRU INFRUGAL
AFGILNST FATLINGS
AFGILNTT FLATTING
AFGILNTU FAULTING
AFGIMNRS FARMINGS
FRAMINGS
AFGIMNTU FUMIGANT
AFGIMORS GASIFORM
AFGIMRST MISGRAFT
AFGINNRS SNARFING
AFGINNSU SNAFUING
AFGINORV FAVORING
AFGINORY FORAYING
AFGINPPR FRAPPING
AFGINRST INGRAFTS
STRAFING
AFGINRSY FRAYINGS
AFGINRTU FIGURANT

AFGINSST FASTINGS
AFGIORST ISOGRAFT
AFGIPRTW GIFTWRAP
AFGLLNOT FLATLONG
AFGLLRUY FRUGALLY
AFGLLSSU GLASSFUL
AFGLNNOO GONFALON
AFGNNNOO GONFANON
AFHIILSS SAILFISH
AFHIILST FISHTAIL
AFHIIMST MISFAITH
AFHIINST FAINTISH
AFHILLSY FLASHILY
AFHILOSY OAFISHLY
AFHILSTT FLATTISH
AFHIMNSU HAFNIUMS
AFHINOSS FASHIONS
AFHINSTU UNFAITHS
AFHIOSSU FASHIOUS
AFHIRSST STARFISH
AFHISSWY FISHWAYS
AFHKLNTU THANKFUL
AFHKORSY HAYFORKS
AFHKRSTU FUTHARKS
AFHLLOTU LOATHFUL
AFHLNSUY UNFLASHY
AFHLOSTY HAYLOFTS
AFHLRTUW WRATHFUL
AFHOOPTT FOOTPATH
AFHOORST HAFTOROS
AFHOORTT HAFTOROT
AFIILLLY FILIALLY
AFIILLNU UNFILIAL
AFIILMMS FAMILISM
AFIILMNS FINALISM
AFIILNRU UNIFILAR
AFIILNST FINALIST
TAILFINS
AFIILNTY FINALITY
AFIILORS AIRFOILS
AFIILRST AIRLIFTS
AFIIMNPR RIFAMPIN
AFIIMRSY FAIRYISM
AFIINNOS SAINFOIN
SINFONIA
AFIINOTX FIXATION
AFIIORRT TRIFORIA
AFIJMNOR JANIFORM
AFIKLNNR FRANKLIN
AFIKLOST FLOKATIS
AFIKMNNR FINNMARK
AFIKMNRS FINMARKS
AFIKNRST RATFINKS
AFILLLOT FLOTILLA
AFILLMUY AIMFULLY
AFILLPST PITFALLS
AFILLPSU PAILFULS
PAILSFUL
AFILLTUY FAULTILY
AFILMNOR FORMALIN
INFORMAL
AFILMNOS FOILSMAN
AFILNNNO NONFINAL
AFILNORT FLATIRON
INFLATOR
AFILNOSU FUSIONAL
AFILNPPT FLIPPANT
AFILNRTU TRAINFUL
AFILNRUY UNFAIRLY
AFILOORT FAROLITO
AFILORSW AIRFLOWS
AFILOSTX FOXTAILS
AFILRSSU FISSURAL
AFILRSTU FISTULAR
AFILSSTU FISTULAS
AFILSTTU FLAUTIST
AFIMMNOY AMMONIFY
AFIMMORR RAMIFORM
AFIMNOPR NAPIFORM
AFIMNOSU INFAMOUS
AFIMOOSS MAFIOSOS
AFIMORRU AURIFORM
AFIMORRV VARIFORM
AFIMORSV VASIFORM
AFIMRSUU FUSARIUM
AFIMSSUV FAUVISMS
AFINNOST FONTINAS
AFINNOTU FOUNTAIN
AFINNRTY INFANTRY
AFINOPSY SAPONIFY
AFINQTUY QUANTIFY
AFINRSTX TRANSFIX
AFINSSTU FUSTIANS
AFIOOPRR AIRPROOF
AFIORSTU FAITOURS
AFIRSTTY STRATIFY

AFISSTUV FAUVISTS
AFKLNOTU OUTFLANK
AFKLNSTU TANKFULS
AFKLORTW FLATWORK
AFKLOSWY FOLKWAYS
AFKMOORT FOOTMARK
AFKMORRW FARMWORK
AFKRRSTU FRAKTURS
AFLLLORY FLORALLY
AFLLLUWY LAWFULLY
AFLLMNUY MANFULLY
AFLLMORY FORMALLY
AFLLMPSU PALMFULS
AFLLNOOV FLAVONOL
AFLLNOSW SNOWFALL
AFLLNUUW UNLAWFUL
AFLLOOTW FOOTWALL
AFLLOSTU FALLOUTS
OUTFALLS
AFLLRTUY ARTFULLY
AFLMNNUU UNMANFUL
AFLMNOPR PLANFORM
AFLMOPRT PLATFORM
AFLMORSU FORMULAS
AFLMORSW WOLFRAMS
AFLMORTW FLATWORM
AFLMOSST FLOTSAMS
AFLMOSUY FAMOUSLY
AFLNORST FRONTALS
AFLNRTUU UNARTFUL
AFLNTUUV VAUNTFUL
AFLOOTTU OUTFLOAT
AFLOPSTT FLATTOPS
AFLORSUV FLAVOURS
AFLORUVY FLAVOURY
AFLPRSTY FLYTRAPS
AFLPSSTY FLYPASTS
AFLRSTUY TRAYFULS
AFMNNNUY FUNNYMAN
AFMNNORT FRONTMAN
AFMNORST FORMANTS
AFMNOSUU UNFAMOUS
AFMOOPRR PROFORMA
AFMORSSU AUSFORMS
AFMORTUY FUMATORY
AFMOSSTU SFUMATOS
AFNNOTTY NONFATTY
AFNORSTW FANWORTS
AFNOSTUW OUTFAWNS
AFOORSTZ SFORZATO
AFOOSTWY FOOTWAYS
AFOSSTTU OUTFASTS
AFOSSTUU FASTUOUS
AGGGGILN GAGGLING
AGGGHILN HAGGLING
AGGGHINS SHAGGING
AGGGILNN GANGLING
AGGGILNR GARGLING
AGGGILNS LAGGINGS
SLAGGING
AGGGILNW WAGGLING
AGGGINNS SNAGGING
AGGGINST STAGGING
AGGGINSW SWAGGING
AGGGIYZZ ZIGZAGGY
AGGHILNU LAUGHING
AGGHILST GASLIGHT
AGGHILSY SHAGGILY
AGGHIMNO HOMAGING
AGGHIMNS GINGHAMS
AGGHINNS GNASHING
HANGINGS
AGGHINNW WHANGING
AGGHINPR GRAPHING
AGGHISTT GASTIGHT
AGGHJMNO MAHJONGG
AGGHLOOT GOLGOTHA
AGGIILNN ALIGNING
AGGIILNR GLAIRING
AGGIILNT LIGATING
AGGIILNV GINGIVAL
AGGIIMNS IMAGINGS
AGGIINNR GRAINING
AGGIINNZ AGNIZING
AGGIINRT TRIAGING
AGGIINST AGISTING
AGGIJLNN JANGLING
AGGIKNSS GASKINGS
AGGILLNS GINGALLS
AGGILLNY GALLYING
AGGILMNN MANGLING
AGGILMNO GLOAMING
AGGILNNO GANGLION
AGGILNNR GNARLING
AGGILNNS ANGLINGS
SLANGING

AGGILNNT TANGLING
AGGILNNW WANGLING
AGGILNOP GALOPING
AGGILNOT GLOATING
AGGILNPU PLAGUING
AGGILNPY GAPINGLY
AGGILNRY GRAYLING
RAGINGLY
AGGILNSS GLASSING
AGGILNSZ GLAZINGS
AGGINNOR GROANING
AGGINNOT TANGOING
AGGINNOW WAGONING
AGGINNPR PRANGING
AGGINNRR GNARRING
AGGINNRT GRANTING
AGGINNST STANGING
AGGINNSW GNAWINGS
AGGINNTW TWANGING
AGGINNUZ UNGAZING
AGGINORT GAROTING
AGGINOST GIGATONS
AGGINOVY VOYAGING
AGGINOWY WAYGOING
AGGINPRS GRASPING
PARGINGS
SPARGING
AGGINPUZ UPGAZING
AGGINRSS GRASSING
AGGINRST GRATINGS
AGGINRSU SUGARING
AGGINRSZ GRAZINGS
AGGINRTY GYRATING
AGGINRUU AUGURING
AGGINSSS GASSINGS
AGGINSST STAGINGS
AGGINSWY GAYWINGS
AGGIRTUZ ZIGGURAT
AGGLLLOY LOLLYGAG
AGGLLOOY ALGOLOGY
AGGLMOOR LOGOGRAM
AGGLNOPW GANGPLOW
AGGLOORY AGROLOGY
AGGLRSTY STRAGGLY
AGGMORRS GROGRAMS
AGGMOSTY MYSTAGOG
AGGNOSSY SYNAGOGS
AGGNUWZZ ZUGZWANG
AGHHIILT HIGHTAIL
AGHHISWY HIGHWAYS
AGHHLOTU ALTHOUGH
AGHIILNN INHALING
AGHIILNS NILGHAIS
AGHIINRT AIRTHING
AGHIIRTT AIRTIGHT
AGHIJNRT NIGHTJAR
AGHIKNNS SHANKING
AGHIKNNT THANKING
AGHIKNRS SHARKING
AGHIKNSW HAWKINGS
AGHILLNO HALLOING
HOLLAING
AGHILMTY ALMIGHTY
AGHILNOO HOOLIGAN
AGHILNOR LONGHAIR
AGHILNOS SHOALING
AGHILNOT LOATHING
AGHILNPR RALPHING
AGHILNPS PLASHING
AGHILNRS RINGHALS
AGHILNSS HASSLING
LASHINGS
SLASHING
AGHILNST LATHINGS
AGHILNSU LANGUISH
NILGHAUS
SHAULING
AGHILNSW SHAWLING
WHALINGS
AGHILNSY NYLGHAIS
AGHILOST GOLIATHS
AGHILRSY GARISHLY
AGHILSUY AGUISHLY
AGHIMMNS SHAMMING
AGHIMMNW WHAMMING
AGHIMNPR PHARMING
AGHIMNSS SMASHING
AGHIMOST OGHAMIST
AGHINNOT GNATHION
AGHINNTU HAUNTING
AGHINNTY ANYTHING
AGHINORS ORANGISH
AGHINPPW WHAPPING
AGHINPRS HARPINGS
PHRASING
SHARPING

AGHINPSW PSHAWING
AGHINQSU QUASHING
AGHINRRY HARRYING
AGHINRST TRASHING
AGHINRTW THRAWING
WRATHING
AGHINSST STASHING
AGHINSSV SHAVINGS
AGHINSSW SWASHING
WASHINGS
AGHINSTW SWATHING
AGHINUZZ HUZZAING
AGHIOPRS ISOGRAPH
AGHIPRRT TRIGRAPH
AGHIRSTT STRAIGHT
AGHISSTW SIGHTSAW
AGHJMNOS MAHJONGS
AGHKOSSW GOSHAWKS
AGHLMOOR HOLOGRAM
AGHLMOOY HOLOGAMY
AGHLMPSU GALUMPHS
AGHLNOSU SHOGUNAL
AGHLNSUY NYLGHAUS
AGHLOOSS GASOHOLS
AGHLOTUU OUTLAUGH
AGHMMOOY HOMOGAMY
AGHMNPSU SPHAGNUM
AGHMOOPY OMOPHAGY
AGHMOPRY MYOGRAPH
AGHNNSTU SHANTUNG
AGHNOSTU HANGOUTS
AGHNTTUU UNTAUGHT
AGHORSTW WARTHOGS
AGIIIKMR KIRIGAMI
AGIIILNS LIAISING
AGIIINNS INSIGNIA
AGIIKNNT ANTIKING
AGIIKNRT TRAIKING
AGIILLLM MILLIGAL
AGIILLNV VIALLING
AGIILMNP IMPALING
AGIILMNS MAILINGS
MISALIGN
AGIILMNU MIAULING
AGIILNNP PLAINING
AGIILNNS SNAILING
AGIILNNU INGUINAL
AGIILNNV ANVILING
AGIILNNY INLAYING
AGIILNOP PIGNOLIA
AGIILNOR ORIGINAL
AGIILNOT INTAGLIO
LIGATION
AGIILNOX GLOXINIA
AGIILNPT PLAITING
AGIILNQU QUAILING
AGIILNRS RAILINGS
AGIILNRT RINGTAIL
TRAILING
AGIILNRV RIVALING
VIRGINAL
AGIILNSS SAILINGS
AGIILNST TAILINGS
AGIILNSU LINGUISA
AGIILNTT LITIGANT
AGIILNTV VIGILANT
AGIILORU OLIGURIA
AGIILPST PIGTAILS
AGIILTVY VAGILITY
AGIIMMSS IMAGISMS
AGIIMNNR INARMING
AGIIMNOR IGNORAMI
AGIIMNOU MIAOUING
AGIIMNOW MIAOWING
AGIIMNST GIANTISM
AGIIMORS ORIGAMIS
AGIIMSST IMAGISTS
AGIINNPT PAINTING
PATINING
AGIINNRS INGRAINS
AGIINNRT TRAINING
AGIINNRV RAVINING
AGIINNST SAINTING
STAINING
AGIINNTT TAINTING
AGIINOPT OPIATING
AGIINORT RIGATONI
AGIINPRS ASPIRING
PAIRINGS
PRAISING
AGIINPRT PIRATING
AGIINRRV ARRIVING
AGIINRSS RAISINGS
AGIINRTT ATTIRING
AGIINSTW WAISTING
WAITINGS

AGIJLLNS JINGALLS
AGIJLNPY JAPINGLY
AGIJMNOR MAJORING
AGIJNNTU JAUNTING
AGIKKNNS SKANKING
AGIKLMOR KILOGRAM
AGIKLNNP PLANKING
AGIKLNNR RANKLING
AGIKLNOP POLKAING
AGIKLNOS SKOALING
AGIKLNST STALKING
TALKINGS
AGIKLNSW WALKINGS
AGIKLNTY TAKINGLY
AGIKMNNU UNMAKING
AGIKMNRS MARKINGS
AGIKMNSS MASKINGS
AGIKNNPP KNAPPING
AGIKNNPR PRANKING
AGIKNNPS SPANKING
AGIKNNRS RANKINGS
AGIKNNSW SWANKING
AGIKNORT TROAKING
AGIKNOST GOATSKIN
AGIKNPRS PARKINGS
SPARKING
AGIKNRST KARTINGS
AGIKNSST SKATINGS
AGILLMNS MALLINGS
AGILLMNU MULLIGAN
AGILLMNY MALIGNLY
AGILLMSU GALLIUMS
AGILLNOW ALLOWING
AGILLNOY ALLOYING
AGILLNPS SPALLING
AGILLNRU ALLURING
LINGULAR
AGILLNRY RALLYING
AGILLNST STALLING
AGILLNSU LINGUALS
AGILLNSY SALLYING
SIGNALLY
SLANGILY
AGILLNTY TALLYING
AGILLOPT GALLIPOT
AGILLORS GORILLAS
AGILLOST GALLIOTS
AGILLPRY PLAYGIRL
AGILLPUY PLAGUILY
AGILLSSU LUGSAILS
AGILLSSY GLASSILY
AGILMMNS SLAMMING
AGILMNNT MANTLING
AGILMNPS PSALMING
SAMPLING
AGILMNRS MARLINGS
AGILMORS ALGORISM
AGILNNNP PLANNING
AGILNNOP PANGOLIN
AGILNNOS LOANINGS
AGILNNPT PLANTING
AGILNNRS SNARLING
AGILNNSS LINSANGS
AGILNNST SLANTING
AGILNNUY UNGAINLY
UNLAYING
AGILNOOO OOGONIAL
AGILNOOS ISOGONAL
AGILNOPR PAROLING
AGILNORT TRIGONAL
AGILNOSS GLOSSINA
LASSOING
AGILNOST ANTILOGS
SOLATING
AGILNOSV SALVOING
AGILNOTT TOTALING
AGILNOTY ANTILOGY
AGILNPPS SLAPPING
AGILNPPY APPLYING
AGILNPRS GRAPLINS
SPARLING
SPRINGAL
AGILNPSS SAPLINGS
AGILNPST PLATINGS
STAPLING
AGILNPSW LAPWINGS
AGILNPSY PALSYING
SPLAYING
AGILNPTT PLATTING
AGILNRSS RASSLING
AGILNRST STARLING
AGILNRSU SINGULAR
AGILNRSW WARSLING
AGILNRTT RATTLING
AGILNRTW TRAWLING
AGILNRVY RAVINGLY

AGILNSST LASTINGS
SALTINGS
SLATINGS
AGILNSTT SLATTING
AGILNSTU SALUTING
AGILNSUV AVULSING
AGILNSVY SAVINGLY
AGILNTTT TATTLING
AGILNTTW WATTLING
AGILNTUV VAULTING
AGILNTUX LUXATING
AGILNTWZ WALTZING
AGILNTXY TAXINGLY
AGILOOPY APIOLOGY
AGILOOXY AXIOLOGY
AGILOPST GALIPOTS
AGILORSS GIRASOLS
AGILORSW AIRGLOWS
AGILRSSY GRASSILY
AGILSYYZ SYZYGIAL
AGIMMNPS SPAMMING
AGIMMNRT TRAMMING
AGIMMOSY MISOGAMY
AGIMNNOS MASONING
AGIMNNOW WOMANING
AGIMNNRU MANURING
UNARMING
AGIMNNSW SWINGMAN
AGIMNORR ARMORING
AGIMNORS ORGANISM
AGIMNORU ORIGANUM
AGIMNORY AGRIMONY
AGIMNOST ANTISMOG
AGIMNOSV VAMOSING
AGIMNPPS MAPPINGS
AGIMNPRT TRAMPING
AGIMNPSS SPASMING
AGIMNPST STAMPING
AGIMNPSW SWAMPING
AGIMNRRY MARRYING
AGIMNRST MIGRANTS
SMARTING
AGIMNRSW SWARMING
AGIMNRTU MATURING
AGIMNSSU ASSUMING
AGIMNSTT MATTINGS
AGIMNTTU MUTATING
AGIMORRT MIGRATOR
AGIMORSS ISOGRAMS
AGIMORSU GOURAMIS
AGIMQRUY QUAGMIRY
AGIMRRST TRIGRAMS
AGINNNOY ANNOYING
AGINNNPS SPANNING
AGINNNST TANNINGS
AGINNNSW SWANNING
AGINNNUW UNWANING
AGINNOPR APRONING
AGINNOPT POIGNANT
AGINNORT IGNORANT
AGINNOSU ANGINOUS
AGINNOTT NOTATING
AGINNPPS SNAPPING
AGINNPRW PRAWNING
AGINNPSW SPAWNING
WINGSPAN
AGINNPUY UNPAYING
AGINNQTU QUANTING
AGINNRSW WARNINGS
AGINNSUY UNSAYING
AGINNTTU ATTUNING
NUTATING
TAUNTING
AGINNTUV VAUNTING
AGINOOPS POGONIAS
AGINOORT ROGATION
AGINOPPS APPOSING
AGINOPQU OPAQUING
AGINOPRV VAPORING
AGINORRS GARRISON
ROARINGS
AGINORRW ARROWING
AGINORRZ RAZORING
AGINORSS ASSIGNOR
SIGNORAS
SOARINGS
AGINORST ORGANIST
ROASTING
AGINORSU AROUSING
AGINORSV SAVORING
AGINORTT ROTATING
AGINORTV GRAVITON
AGINORTY GYRATION
AGINOSST AGONISTS
AGINOSTT TOASTING
AGINOSTU OUTGAINS

AGINPPRT TRAPPING
AGINPPRW WRAPPING
AGINPPST TAPPINGS
AGINPPSW SWAPPING
AGINPPTU PUPATING
AGINPRRS SPARRING
AGINPRRY PARRYING
AGINPRSS PINGRASS
RASPINGS
AGINPRST PARTINGS
AGINPRSY SPRAYING
AGINPRTU UPRATING
AGINPRTY PARTYING
AGINPSSS PASSINGS
AGINPSTT SPATTING
AGINPSWY YAWPINGS
AGINQRSU SQUARING
AGINRRST STARRING
AGINRRTY TARRYING
AGINRSST GASTRINS
AGINRSSU ASSURING
AGINRSSY SYRINGAS
AGINRSTT STARTING
AGINRSTV STARVING
AGINRSTW RINGTAWS
STRAWING
AGINRSTY STINGRAY
STRAYING
AGINRTYY GYNIATRY
AGINSTTT TATTINGS
AGINSTTW SWATTING
AGINSVVY SAVVYING
AGINSWWX WAXWINGS
AGIOORSZ GRAZIOSO
AGIOORTU AUTOGIRO
AGIOPPRT AGITPROP
AGIOPRUY UROPYGIA
AGIORSST ORGIASTS
AGIOSUUY OUGUIYAS
AGIRSSTU SASTRUGI
AGIRSTUZ ZASTRUGI
AGIRTTUY GRATUITY
AGJLRSUU JUGULARS
AGJNOORS JARGOONS
AGKMMORY KYMOGRAM
AGKMNOPS KAMPONGS
AGKMPRSU PUGMARKS
AGKORSSW GASWORKS
AGLLNOOS GALLOONS
AGLLNSTU GALLNUTS
NUTGALLS
AGLLOOST GALLOOTS
AGLLOPSU PLUGOLAS
AGLLPRSU SPURGALL
AGLLRUVY VULGARLY
AGLMOPYY POLYGAMY
AGLMORSU GLAMOURS
AGLNORSU LANGUORS
AGLNOSST GLASNOST
AGLNOSUU ANGULOUS
AGLNOSWY LONGWAYS
AGLNPSUY GUNPLAYS
AGLNSSSU SUNGLASS
AGLOOPST GOALPOST
AGLORSSY GLOSSARY
AGLPSSSY SPYGLASS
AGLRTTUU GUTTURAL
AGLSTUUY AUGUSTLY
AGMMNOOR MONOGRAM
NOMOGRAM
AGMMNOOY MONOGAMY
AGMMOORT TOMOGRAM
AGMMORYZ ZYMOGRAM
AGMNNOSW GOWNSMAN
AGMNOORS SONOGRAM
AGMNOORY AGRONOMY
AGMNORST ANGSTROM
AGMNORSU ORGANUMS
AGMNSSTU MUSTANGS
AGMNSSTY GYMNASTS
SYNTAGMS
AGMOOOSU OOGAMOUS
AGMOOTVY VAGOTOMY
AGMOPRRS PROGRAMS
AGNNNOOS NONAGONS
AGNNOORS ORGANONS
AGNNOQTU QUANTONG
AGNNORSU NONSUGAR
AGNNOTUW OUTGNAWN
AGNORRST GRANTORS
AGNORTUY NUGATORY
AGNOSTUW OUTGNAWS
AGNPPRSU UPSPRANG
AGNRSSTU NUTGRASS
AGOORRTY ROGATORY
AGOORTUY AUTOGYRO

AGOPPSST STOPGAPS
AGORRSTW RAGWORTS
AGORRSTY GYRATORS
AGORRTYY GYRATORY
AGORSTTY GYROSTAT
AGORSTUY GRAYOUTS
AHHIKKRS KHIRKAHS
AHHIKLSS SHASHLIK
AHHILNPT PHTHALIN
AHHILPSW WHIPLASH
AHHIMMSS MISHMASH
AHHIMNSU HAHNIUMS
AHHINSST SHANTIHS
AHHISSTT SHITTAHS
AHHKMOTW HAWKMOTH
AHHKRSTU KASHRUTH
AHHLNOPT NAPHTHOL
AHHLNPTY NAPHTHYL
AHHMPRRU HARRUMPH
AHHMPRSU HARUMPHS
AHHNORTW HAWTHORN
AHHOPRSS SHOPHARS
AHHOPSTU APHTHOUS
AHHPSTUZ HUTZPAHS
AHIIILMN MALIHINI
AHIIKRSS RIKISHAS
SHIKARIS
AHIILPTW WHIPTAIL
AHIILRTY HILARITY
AHIIMNNO HOMINIAN
AHIIMNOT HIMATION
AHIIMNST HISTAMIN
ISTHMIAN
THIAMINS
AHIIMOPX AMPHIOXI
AHIIMRST ISARITHM
AHIIMSSS SASHIMIS
AHIINOTT TITHONIA
AHIINPRS HAIRPINS
AHIINPST ANTISHIP
AHIINSSW SWAINISH
AHIINSTZ THIAZINS
AHIIOPST HOSPITIA
AHIIPRSS AIRSHIPS
AHIKLRSY RAKISHLY
AHIKLSSS SHASLIKS
AHIKMNSS KHAMSINS
AHIKMRSS KASHMIRS
AHIKNPRS PRANKISH
AHIKNPST TANKSHIP
AHIKORRW HAIRWORK
AHIKPRSS SPARKISH
AHIKRSSW RIKSHAWS
AHILLMPS PHALLISM
AHILLMSS SMALLISH
AHILLMTU THALLIUM
AHILLNRT INTHRALL
AHILLNST ANTHILLS
AHILLPST PHALLIST
AHILLSTT TALLITHS
AHILLSVY LAVISHLY
AHILMQSU QUALMISH
AHILMTUZ HALUTZIM
AHILNOPS SIPHONAL
AHILNORT HORNTAIL
AHILNRST INTHRALS
AHILOORT LOTHARIO
AHILOPSS ALPHOSIS
HAPLOSIS
AHILOPST HOSPITAL
AHILOSTZ THIAZOLS
AHILPPSS PALSHIPS
SHIPLAPS
AHILPRTU ULTRAHIP
AHILPSXY PHYLAXIS
AHILRSTY TRASHILY
AHILRTWY WRATHILY
AHIMMNSU HUMANISM
AHIMMORZ MAHZORIM
AHIMMOSS SHAMOSIM
AHIMMOSV MOSHAVIM
AHIMNOST MANIHOTS
AHIMNOSW WOMANISH
AHIMNSTU HUMANIST
AHIMNTUY HUMANITY
AHIMOOSY YAHOOISM
AHIMOPRS APHORISM
MORPHIAS
AHIMORRW HAIRWORM
AHIMPPSS SAPPHISM
AHIMPRST TRAMPISH
AHIMPSSW SWAMPISH
AHIMSSSU HASSIUMS
AHIMSSTV MITSVAHS
AHIMSTUZ AZIMUTHS
AHIMSTVZ MITZVAHS

AHINNNSY NANNYISH
AHINNOPT ANTIPHON
AHINNSTX XANTHINS
AHINOOPY HYPONOIA
AHINOSST ASTONISH
AHINOSTZ HOATZINS
AHINPPSS SNAPPISH
AHINPRST TRANSHIP
AHINPRSY SYRPHIAN
AHINPSWW WHIPSAWN
AHINQSUV VANQUISH
AHINRSVY HRYVNIAS
VARNISHY
AHIOOPPT PHOTOPIA
AHIOPRST APHORIST
AHIOPRSV VAPORISH
AHIOPSXY HYPOXIAS
AHIORSST AIRSHOTS
SHORTIAS
AHIORSSW AIRSHOWS
AHIORSTV TOVARISH
AHIORSUV HAVIOURS
AHIPPSST SAPPHIST
AHIPRSST HARPISTS
STARSHIP
AHIPRSSW WARSHIPS
AHIPRSWY WHIPRAYS
AHIPSSWW WHIPSAWS
AHIPSSWY SHIPWAYS
AHIQRSSU SQUARISH
AHIRSSTW TRISHAWS
AHISSSTU SHIATSUS
AHISSTTW WHATSITS
AHISSTUZ SHIATZUS
AHKLOPST SHOPTALK
AHKLORTW LATHWORK
AHKMOORR MARKHOOR
AHKMORRS MARKHORS
AHKNOTTU OUTTHANK
AHKRSSTU KASHRUTS
AHLLLOOP POOLHALL
AHLLNOOS SHALLOON
AHLLNOUW UNHALLOW
AHLLNRTU TURNHALL
AHLLOPSS SHALLOPS
AHLLOSST SHALLOTS
AHLLOSSW SHALLOWS
AHLLOSTU THALLOUS
AHLLOSTY TALLYHOS
AHLLPRYY PHYLLARY
AHLMMOPY LYMPHOMA
AHLMNOOR HORMONAL
AHLMOOPS OMPHALOS
AHLMOPTY POLYMATH
AHLMOSUU HAMULOUS
AHLMSTYZ SHMALTZY
AHLNNORT LANTHORN
AHLNOPRS ALPHORNS
AHLNOPST HAPLONTS
NAPHTOLS
AHLNORST ALTHORNS
AHLNRTWY THRAWNLY
AHLOOPSW WHOOPLAS
AHLOOSTW WOOLHATS
AHLORRTY HARLOTRY
AHLORTTU ULTRAHOT
AHLOSTUU OUTHAULS
AHLRTTWY THWARTLY
AHMMMOST MAMMOTHS
AHMNNNOU NONHUMAN
AHMNNSTU HUNTSMAN
MANHUNTS
AHMNOPST PHANTOMS
AHMNORRS RAMSHORN
AHMOOPPT PHOTOMAP
AHMOOPSS SHAMPOOS
AHMOORSW WASHROOM
AHMOPTYY MYOPATHY
AHMORTUW WARMOUTH
AHMPSSSU SMASHUPS
AHMPSTYY SYMPATHY
AHMQSSUU MUSQUASH
AHNOOPPY APOPHONY
AHNOOPRS HARPOONS
AHNOORRY HONORARY
AHNOPPSW PAWNSHOP
AHNOPPSY PANSOPHY
AHNOPSST SNAPSHOT
AHNORSSX SAXHORNS
AHNOSTTW WHATNOTS
AHNOSTUX XANTHOUS
AHOOSSTY SOOTHSAY
AHOOSTTW SAWTOOTH
AHOPSTTW TOWPATHS
AHOPSTUW SOUTHPAW
AHORTTUW WATTHOUR
AHOSSTUW WASHOUTS
AHRSTUWY THRUWAYS
AIIILLVX LIXIVIAL
AIIILMST MILITIAS
AIIILNST INITIALS
AIIILRVZ VIZIRIAL
AIIKKSUY SUKIYAKI
AIIKLNRR LARRIKIN
AIIKMNNN MANNIKIN
AIIKMNNS MANIKINS
AIIKMNPR MINIPARK
AIIKNNNP PANNIKIN
AIIKNNST TANKINIS
AIIKORTY YAKITORI
AIILLLUV ILLUVIAL
AIILLMRY MILLIARY
AIILLMST TALLISIM
AIILLMTT TALLITIM
AIILLNNV VANILLIN
AIILLNOP POLLINIA
AIILLNOT ILLATION
AIILLNPT ANTIPILL
AIILLNSV VILLAINS
AIILLNVY VILLAINY
AIILLPRS SPIRILLA
AIILLQSU QUILLAIS
AIILLUWW WILLIWAU
AIILLWWW WILLIWAW
AIILMMNS MINIMALS
AIILMNNS LAMININS
AIILMNPS ALPINISM
AIILMNPT PALMITIN
AIILMNTT MILITANT
AIILMNTU MINUTIAL
AIILMRST MISTRIAL
AIILMRTY LIMITARY
MILITARY
AIILMSTV VITALISM
AIILNOPV PAVILION
AIILNOSS LIAISONS
AIILNOSV VISIONAL
AIILNPST ALPINIST
ANTISLIP
PINTAILS
TAILSPIN
AIILNRSU SILURIAN
AIILNSTY SALINITY
AIILNTTY LATINITY
AIILORSV RAVIOLIS
AIILSTTV VITALIST
AIILSTTW WAITLIST
AIILTTVY VITALITY
AIIMMMST MAMMITIS
AIIMMNNY MINYANIM
AIIMMNSS ANIMISMS
AIIMMNSX MAXIMINS
AIIMNNOS INSOMNIA
AIIMNNSV MINIVANS
AIIMNPSS PIANISMS
SINAPISM
AIIMNPST IMPAINTS
MISPAINT
AIIMNPSX PANMIXIS
AIIMNRST MARTINIS
MISTRAIN
AIIMNSST ANIMISTS
AIIMNSTT TITANISM
AIIMNSTV NATIVISM
VITAMINS
AIIMNTTU TITANIUM
AIIMOPSX APOMIXIS
AIIMORTT IMITATOR
AIIMOSST AMITOSIS
AIIMPPRS PRIAPISM
AIIMPRTY IMPARITY
AIIMRSST SIMITARS
AIIMRSTU TIRAMISU
AIIMRUVV VIVARIUM
AIIMSSTT MASTITIS
AIINNOSV INVASION
AIINNQSU QUININAS
AIINNQTU QUINTAIN
AIINNSTY INSANITY
AIINOPSS SINOPIAS
AIINORTT ANTIRIOT
AIINOSTT OSTINATI
AIINPRSS ASPIRINS
AIINPSST PIANISTS
AIINRRTT IRRITANT
AIINRSTV VITRAINS
AIINRSTZ TRIAZINS
AIINSTTV NATIVIST
VISITANT
AIINTTVY NATIVITY
AIIORRST SARTORII
AIIORSTV OVARITIS
AIIORTTV VITIATOR
AIIPRRST AIRSTRIP
AIIRSSTT SATIRIST
SITARIST
AIJKKNOU KINKAJOU
AIJLLOVY JOVIALLY
AIJLNTUY JAUNTILY
AIJLOTVY JOVIALTY
AIJMORTY MAJORITY
AIJNOPPY POPINJAY
AIJNORST JANITORS
AIKKMOST KOMATIKS
AIKKOPSY KOPIYKAS
AIKKRTUZ ZIKKURAT
AIKLLSTY STALKILY
AIKLMNNS LINKSMAN
AIKLNRSY SNARKILY
AIKLNSWY SWANKILY
AIKLOSUV SOUVLAKI
AIKLOTTW KILOWATT
AIKLPRSY SPARKILY
AIKLRSTT TITLARKS
AIKLSSSY SKYSAILS
AIKMMNOO MAKIMONO
AIKMMRSS MISMARKS
AIKMRSTZ SITZMARK
AIKNNOOS NAINSOOK
AIKNNSSW SWANSKIN
AIKNORTY KARYOTIN
AIKNOSTT STOTINKA
AIKRSTUZ ZIKURATS
AILLLNOO LINALOOL
AILLLNOS LINALOLS
AILLLPSU LAPILLUS
AILLMNST STILLMAN
AILLMOST MAILLOTS
MISALLOT
AILLMOSY LOYALISM
AILLMOTY MOLALITY
AILLMPSU PALLIUMS
AILLMSSW SAWMILLS
AILLMUUV ALLUVIUM
AILLNNOS LANOLINS
AILLNOPP PAPILLON
AILLNOPV PAVILLON
AILLNORT ANTIROLL
AILLNOST STALLION
AILLNOSU ALLUSION
AILLNOUV ALLUVION
AILLNPSY SPINALLY
AILLNPTY PLIANTLY
AILLNSST INSTALLS
AILLORSY SAILORLY
AILLORSZ ZORILLAS
AILLORTT LITTORAL
TORTILLA
AILLOSTY LOYALIST
AILLPPTU PULPITAL
AILLPRSY SPIRALLY
AILLPRTY PALTRILY
AILLPSTY PLAYLIST
AILLPSUV PLUVIALS
AILLPSWY SPILLWAY
AILLQSSU SQUILLAS
AILLRSTY RALLYIST
AILLRTUY RITUALLY
AILLRTWY WILLYART
AILLSUVY VISUALLY
AILLWWYY WILLYWAW
AILMMNOO MONOMIAL
AILMMNUU ALUMINUM
AILMMOOR MAILROOM
AILMMORS MORALISM
AILMMORT IMMORTAL
AILMMRSY SMARMILY
AILMMSTU SUMMITAL
AILMNNOS NOMINALS
AILMNNOT MANNITOL
AILMNOOP PALOMINO
AILMNOOR MONORAIL
AILMNOOS MOONSAIL
AILMNOOT MOTIONAL
AILMNOPR PROLAMIN
AILMNOPS LAMPIONS
AILMNOPY PALIMONY
AILMNOSS MALISONS
AILMNOSU LAMINOUS
AILMNPSS MISPLANS
PLASMINS
AILMNPST IMPLANTS
MISPLANT
AILMNPTU PLATINUM
AILMNRUY LUMINARY
AILMNSTU SIMULANT
AILMOOSV MOVIOLAS
AILMOPRX PROXIMAL
AILMORSS ORALISMS
SOLARISM
AILMORST MORALIST
AILMORSU SOLARIUM
AILMORSY ROYALISM
AILMORTY MOLARITY
MORALITY
AILMOSTT TOTALISM
AILMOSTU SOLATIUM
AILMOSTV VOLTAISM
AILMPPSY MISAPPLY
AILMPRSU PRIMULAS
AILMPSST PALMISTS
PSALMIST
AILMPSSY MISPLAYS
AILMPSTY PTYALISM
AILMRRSU RURALISM
AILMRSST MISTRALS
AILMRSSU SIMULARS
AILMRSTU ALTRUISM
MURALIST
ULTRAISM
AILNNOOT NOTIONAL
AILNNORV NONRIVAL
NONVIRAL
AILNNOSS SOLANINS
AILNNOST ANTLIONS
AILNNOSU UNISONAL
AILNNOTU LUNATION
AILNNOTV NONVITAL
AILNNPRU PINNULAR
AILNNPTU UNPLIANT
AILNNSTU INSULANT
AILNOOPT NOPALITO
OPTIONAL
AILNOOST SOLATION
AILNOPPT OPPILANT
AILNOPRU UNIPOLAR
AILNOPRV PARVOLIN
AILNOPTV ANVILTOP
AILNOPTY PONYTAIL
AILNORST TONSILAR
AILNOSTY LANOSITY
AILNOSUV AVULSION
AILNOSVY SYNOVIAL
AILNOTTV VOLITANT
AILNOTTY TONALITY
AILNOTUX LUXATION
AILNPPSY SNAPPILY
AILNPRUV PULVINAR
AILNPSTU NUPTIALS
UNPLAITS
AILNPSTY PTYALINS
AILNPSUU NAUPLIUS
AILNQRTU TRANQUIL
AILNQSTU QUINTALS
AILNQTUY QUAINTLY
AILNRSSU INSULARS
AILNRTTU RUTILANT
AILNRUWY UNWARILY
AILNSSTU STUNSAIL
AILNSTTU LUTANIST
AILNSTUU NAUTILUS
AILOOPRT TROOPIAL
AILOORST ISOLATOR
OSTIOLAR
AILOORSW WOORALIS
AILOORTV VIOLATOR
AILOPRRV PROVIRAL
AILOPRTU TROUPIAL
AILOPRTY POLARITY
AILOPRUY POLYURIA
AILOPSST APOSTILS
TOPSAILS
AILOPSTT TALIPOTS
AILOQSTU ALIQUOTS
AILORSST ORALISTS
AILORSTY ROYALIST
SOLITARY
AILORSVY SAVORILY
AILORTTU TUTORIAL
AILORTUV OUTRIVAL
AILOSSTT ALTOISTS
AILOSSTU OUTSAILS
AILOSTTT TOTALIST
AILOTTTY TOTALITY
AILPPRUY PUPILARY
AILPQSSU PASQUILS
AILPRSSU SPIRULAS
AILPRSTU STIPULAR
AILPSSWY SLIPWAYS
AILPSTUY PLAYSUIT
AILRRSTU RURALIST
AILRRTUY RURALITY
AILRSSTU TISSULAR
AILRSSTY TRYSAILS
AILRSTTU ALTRUIST
TITULARS
ULTRAIST
AILRSTTY STRAITLY
AILRSUVV SURVIVAL
AILRTTUY TITULARY
AILSSTUW LAWSUITS
AIMMMNOU AMMONIUM
AIMMMSUX MAXIMUMS
AIMMNORT MORTMAIN
AIMMNOSW WOMANISM
AIMMNPTU TIMPANUM
AIMMNSTU MANUMITS
AIMMOSST ATOMISMS
AIMMPSST MISSTAMP
AIMMRSUU MASURIUM
AIMNNOPT POINTMAN
AIMNNOSS MANSIONS
ONANISMS
AIMNNOTU MOUNTAIN
AIMNNOTY ANTIMONY
ANTINOMY
AIMNNRTU RUMINANT
AIMNOORV OMNIVORA
AIMNOOST AMOTIONS
AIMNOOTY MYOTONIA
AIMNOPRS RAMPIONS
AIMNOPRT PROTAMIN
AIMNOPST MAINTOPS
PTOMAINS
TAMPIONS
AIMNOPTV PIVOTMAN
AIMNORTY MINATORY
AIMNOSST STASIMON
AIMNOSTU MANITOUS
TINAMOUS
AIMNOSTW WOMANIST
AIMNOTTU MUTATION
AIMNRRSU MURRAINS
AIMNRSSU URANISMS
AIMNRSTT TANTRISM
TRANSMIT
AIMNRSTU NATRIUMS
NATURISM
AIMNRSTV VARMINTS
AIMNRSUU URANIUMS
AIMNSSTU TSUNAMIS
AIMNSTTU ANTISMUT
AIMOPRSS PROSAISM
AIMOPRST ATROPISM
PASTROMI
AIMOPSST IMPASTOS
AIMOPSSY SYMPOSIA
AIMORRSU ROSARIUM
AIMORRUV VARIORUM
AIMORSST AMORISTS
AIMORSTT TRITOMAS
AIMORSTY RAMOSITY
AIMOSSTT ATOMISTS
AIMPPRUU PUPARIUM
AIMPRSST MISPARTS
AIMRSSST TSARISMS
AIMRSSTT MISSTART
AIMRSSTZ TZARISMS
AIMRSTTU STRIATUM
AIMRTTUY MATURITY
AIMSSSTT STATISMS
AINNNOST SANTONIN
AINNOOTT NOTATION
AINNOOTV NOVATION
AINNOOTZ ZONATION
AINNOPRT ANTIPORN
AINNOPSS SAPONINS
AINNOPST PINTANOS
AINNOSST ONANISTS
AINNOTTU NUTATION
AINNQSTU QUINNATS
QUINTANS
AINNRSTT INTRANTS
AINNRSTU INSURANT
AINNSSTT INSTANTS
AINNSTTY NYSTATIN
AINOOPTT POTATION
AINOORST ORATIONS
AINOORTT ROTATION
AINOOSTT OSTINATO
AINOOSTV OVATIONS
AINOPPST APPOINTS
AINOPPTU PUPATION
AINOPRST ATROPINS
AINOPSSS PASSIONS
AINOPSTU OPUNTIAS
UTOPIANS
AINOPTTU OUTPAINT
AINOPTWY WAYPOINT
AINORRTT NITRATOR
AINORRTU URINATOR
AINORSST ARSONIST
AINORSSW WARISONS
AINORSTT STRONTIA
AINORSTU RAINOUTS
AINORSTW WAITRONS
AINORTVY VANITORY
AINOSSSU SUASIONS
AINOSSTT STATIONS
AINOSSVY SYNOVIAS
AINOSTTU TITANOUS
AINPPRSS PARSNIPS
AINPRSST SPIRANTS
AINPRSTT TRIPTANS
AINPRSTU PURITANS
AINPSSSY SYNAPSIS
AINPSSTU PUISSANT
AINPSTTU PANTSUIT
AINQRSTU QUINTARS
AINQSSSU QUASSINS
AINQTTUY QUANTITY
AINRSSTT TRANSITS
AINRSTTT TITRANTS
AINRSTTU ANTIRUST
NATURIST
AINRSTTY TANISTRY
AINSSSTU SUSTAINS
AIOOORRT ORATORIO
AIOORRSW WOORARIS
AIOPRRST AIRPORTS
AIOPRRTT PORTRAIT
AIOPRSST AIRPOSTS
PROSAIST
PROTASIS
AIOPRSTT PATRIOTS
AIOPRSUV PAVIOURS
AIOPSSTT PASTITSO
AIORRRSW WARRIORS
AIORRSTT TRAITORS
AIORRSTV VARISTOR
AIORRTTT TITRATOR
AIORSSST ASSISTOR
AIORSSTU SAUTOIRS
AIORSSUV SAVIOURS
AIORSTTU TOURISTA
AIORSTTV VOTARIST
AIORSTUV VIRTUOSA
AIOSSSTY ISOSTASY
AIOSTTUW OUTWAITS
AIPRSSTU UPSTAIRS
AIPRSSTY SPARSITY
AIPYZZZZ PIZZAZZY
AIRRSTTY ARTISTRY
AIRSSSTT TSARISTS
AIRSSTTU TURISTAS
AIRSSTTZ TZARISTS
AISSSTTT STATISTS
AJKMNSTU MUNTJAKS
AJLNORSU JOURNALS
AJMNNOOR NONMAJOR
AJORRTUY JURATORY
AKKLRSSY SKYLARKS
AKKLSSWY SKYWALKS
AKKMOOST TOKOMAKS
AKKORSTW TASKWORK
AKKOSUVZ KUVASZOK
AKLMNOOW MOONWALK
AKLNNOPT PLANKTON
AKLORSTW SALTWORK
AKLOSTTU OUTTALKS
AKLOSTUW OUTWALKS
WALKOUTS
AKLPRRSU LARKSPUR
AKMNOOOT TOKONOMA
AKMOPRST POSTMARK
AKMORSST OSTMARKS
AKMQSTUU KUMQUATS
AKMRSSTU MUSKRATS
AKNOORST OSTRAKON
AKNOOUYZ YOKOZUNA
AKNORSTU OUTRANKS
AKORRSTW ARTWORKS
AKORRSWW WARWORKS
AKORSWWX WAXWORKS
AKOSSTTU OUTTASKS
ALLLOSWY SALLOWLY
ALLLPPUY PULPALLY
ALLLPRUY PLURALLY
ALLMNORY NORMALLY
ALLMNOSY ALLONYMS
ALLMNPSU PULLMANS
ALLMOPSX SMALLPOX
ALLMORTY MORTALLY
ALLMPRUU PLUMULAR
ALLMTUUY MUTUALLY
ALLNNOOY NONLOYAL

ALLNNOUY NOUNALLY
ALLNOOPS PLANOSOL
ALLOOSST LATOSOLS
ALLOOSTX AXOLOTLS
ALLOPRSY PAYROLLS
ALLOPSTY POSTALLY
ALLOPTYY ALLOTYPY
ALLORSST ALLSORTS
ALLORSWY ROLLWAYS
ALLORTUW ULTRALOW
ALLOSSWW SWALLOWS
ALLOSTWY TOLLWAYS
ALLRUUVY UVULARLY
ALMMNRUU NUMMULAR
ALMNNOOR NONMORAL
ALMNOOPS LAMPOONS
ALMNOPSS PLASMONS
ALMNORTY MATRONLY
ALMNOSSU SOLANUMS
ALMNPSSU SUNLAMPS
ALMOOPRS PROSOMAL
ALMOOPRY PLAYROOM
ALMOOPSY POLYOMAS
ALMOORTU ALUMROOT
ALMOPPST LAMPPOST
PALMTOPS
ALMOPRST MARPLOTS
ALMORSUU RAMULOUS
ALMOSTTU MULATTOS
ALMPRSTU PLASTRUM
ALMRRTYY MARTYRLY
ALMSSSUY ALYSSUMS
ALNNNOOT NONTONAL
ALNNOOPR NONPOLAR
ALNNOORS NONSOLAR
ALNNOORY NONROYAL
ALNNOPSY NONPLAYS
ALNNORRU NONRURAL
ALNNOTWY WANTONLY
ALNNRSSU UNSNARLS
ALNOOPRS POLARONS
ALNOOPST PLATOONS
ALNOOPSV VANPOOLS
ALNOOPYZ POLYZOAN
ALNOOPZZ POZZOLAN
ALNOORST ORTOLANS
ALNOPRST PLASTRON
ALNOPRTY PATRONLY
ALNOPSTU OUTPLANS
ALNOPSYY POLYNYAS
ALNORRWY NARROWLY
ALNORSVY SOVRANLY
ALNPPSTU SUPPLANT
ALNRRTUU NURTURAL
ALNRTTUY TRUANTLY
ALOOPPRS PROPOSAL
ALOOPRST POSTORAL
ALOOPRTU UPROOTAL
ALOORSUV VALOROUS
ALOORTYZ ZOOLATRY
ALOPPRYY POLYPARY
ALOPPSSU SUPPOSAL
ALOPRRSU PARLOURS
SPORULAR
ALOPRSTU POSTURAL
PULSATOR
ALOPRSTY PASTORLY
ALOPSSSU SPOUSALS
ALOPSTUU PATULOUS
ALOPSTUY OUTPLAYS
ALOQRRSU RORQUALS
ALOQRSSU SQUALORS
ALORRSUY SURROYAL
ALORSTTW SALTWORT
ALORSTWW AWLWORTS
ALORTUWY OUTLAWRY
ALOSSTTU OUTLASTS
ALOSSTXY OXYSALTS
ALPPSTUY PLATYPUS
ALPRSTUU PUSTULAR
AMMNOORT MOTORMAN
AMMNOPSS PSAMMONS
AMMNPTUY TYMPANUM
AMMOPSTU POMATUMS
AMMORRWY ARMYWORM
AMNNOOSX MONAXONS
AMNNOSTW TOWNSMAN
AMNNOSTY ANTONYMS
AMNNOTYY ANTONYMY
AMNNSSTU STANNUMS
AMNNSTTU STUNTMAN
AMNOOPPS POMPANOS
AMNOOSTT OTTOMANS
AMNOOSTZ MATZOONS
AMNOOTUY AUTONOMY
AMNOOTXY TAXONOMY
AMNOPRSW SPANWORM
AMNOPRSY PARONYMS
AMNOPSTU PANTOUMS
AMNORSST TRANSOMS
AMNORSTU ROMAUNTS
AMNORSTY STRAMONY
AMNOSSYZ ZYMOSANS
AMNOSTUY AUTONYMS
AMNOTTUY TAUTONYM
AMNRSTTU TANTRUMS
AMOOPRSS PROSOMAS
AMOOPRST TAPROOMS
AMOORRTY MORATORY
AMOORTWY MOTORWAY
AMOOSSTU ASTOMOUS
AMOOSTVY VASOTOMY
AMOOTTUY AUTOTOMY
AMOPRSXY PAROXYSM
AMOPSSTT TOPMASTS
AMOQSSUU SQUAMOUS
AMORRTUY MORTUARY
AMORSTTU OUTSMART
AMORSWWX WAXWORMS
AMPRSTYY SYMPATRY
AMRSSTTU STRATUMS
ANNNOSSY SYNANONS
ANNOOQTU NONQUOTA
ANNOORST SONORANT
ANNOPRTY NONPARTY
ANNOPSST NONPASTS
ANNOSSTU STANNOUS
ANOOPRRT PRONATOR
ANOOPRSS SOPRANOS
ANOOPRST PATROONS
ANOORSST SANTOORS
ANOORSSU ARSONOUS
ANOORSTT ARNOTTOS
RATTOONS
ANOPRRSS SPORRANS
ANOPRTTU TRAPUNTO
ANOPSSTU OUTSPANS
ANORSSTU SANTOURS
ANORSTVY SOVRANTY
ANORSUVY UNSAVORY
ANOTTUUV OUTVAUNT
ANPRSSTU UNSTRAPS
ANPRSTUU PURSUANT
ANRRTTUY TRUANTRY
AOOOPRSZ SPOROZOA
AOOOPRTZ PROTOZOA
AOOPPRSY APOSPORY
AOOPRSSU SAPOROUS
AOOPRSTT TAPROOTS
AOOPRSTW SOAPWORT
AOOPRSUV VAPOROUS
AOOPRTTY POTATORY
AOORRSTT ROTATORS
AOORRSTU OUTROARS
AOORRTTY ROTATORY
AOORSSTU OUTSOARS
AOORSSUV SAVOROUS
AOORSTUV OUTSAVOR
AOPPRRST RAPPORTS
AOPPRSST PASSPORT
AOPPRSTU TRAPPOUS
AOPRRSSW SPARROWS
AOPRRSTY PORTRAYS
AOPRSTTY PYROSTAT
AOPRSTUY OUTPRAYS
AOPTTUYY AUTOTYPY
AORRSSSU ASSURORS
AORRSTTW STARWORT
AORSSTTU STRATOUS
AORSTTTU OUTSTART
AORSUVVY VOUVRAYS
AOSSTTUY OUTSTAYS
APPRRSUU PURPURAS
APRSSTTU STARTUPS
UPSTARTS
ASVYYZZZ ZYZZYVAS
BBBCEOWY COBWEBBY
BBBDENOU UNBOBBED
BBBEGILN BLEBBING
BBBEILRU BUBBLIER
BBBEILSU BUBBLIES
BBBEINOT BOBBINET
BBBELRSU BLUBBERS
BUBBLERS
BBBELRUY BLUBBERY
BBBGILNO BLOBBING
BOBBLING
BBBGILNU BLUBBING
BUBBLING
BBBOOSXY BOBBYSOX
BBCCIKOS BIBCOCKS
BBCDEILR CRIBBLED
BBCDERSU SCRUBBED
BBCDIMOY BOMBYCID
BBCEEHOS BOBECHES
BBCEHIRU CHUBBIER
BBCEILRS SCRIBBLE
BBCEILRU CLUBBIER
BBCEIOST COBBIEST
BBCEIRRS CRIBBERS
BBCEKKOS KEBBOCKS
BBCEKKSU KEBBUCKS
BBCEKLSU BLESBUCK
BBCELORS CLOBBERS
COBBLERS
BBCELRSU CLUBBERS
BBCEMNOU BUNCOMBE
BBCERRSU SCRUBBER
BBCGIINR CRIBBING
BBCGILNO COBBLING
BBCGILNU CLUBBING
BBCHILSU CLUBBISH
BBCHILUY CHUBBILY
BBCHKOOS BOSCHBOK
BBCHKSUU BUSHBUCK
BBCILRSY SCRIBBLY
BBCIPSUU SUBPUBIC
BBCKLOSU SUBBLOCK
BBDDEEMO DEMOBBED
BBDDEEMU BEDUMBED
BBDDEERU REDUBBED
BBDDEILR DRIBBLED
BBDDENUU UNDUBBED
BBDEEGIR GIBBERED
BBDEEGIT GIBBETED
BBDEEMNU BENUMBED
BBDEERRU RUBBERED
BBDEERSU SUBBREED
BBDEFILR FRIBBLED
BBDEHORT THROBBED
BBDEILLR BELLBIRD
BBDEILQU QUIBBLED
BBDEILRR DRIBBLER
BBDEILRS DIBBLERS
DRIBBLES
BBDEILRT DRIBBLET
BBDEILRU BLUEBIRD
BBDEIMOV DIVEBOMB
BBDEINOR RIBBONED
BBDEINRU UNRIBBED
BBDEIQSU SQUIBBED
BBDELLMU DUMBBELL
BBDELOOS BEBLOODS
BBDELOSS BOBSLEDS
BBDELSTU STUBBLED
BBDERRSU DRUBBERS
BBDERSUU SUBURBED
BBDFLSUU FLUBDUBS
BBDGIILN DIBBLING
BBDGIINR DRIBBING
BBDGINRU DRUBBING
BBDGINSU DUBBINGS
BBDIIKMU DIBBUKIM
BBDIKMUY DYBBUKIM
BBDIOORS BOOBIRDS
BBDOSUYY BUSYBODY
BBEEERSU BEBEERUS
BBEEIIRR BERIBERI
BBEEILPR PEBBLIER
BBEEIMTT BIMBETTE
BBEEINRR BERBERIN
BBEEIRRS BERBERIS
BBEEISTW WEBBIEST
BBEEJLMU BEJUMBLE
BBEELLLU BLUEBELL
BBEEOPPR BEBOPPER
BBEFILRR FRIBBLER
BBEFILRS FRIBBLES
BBEFIMOR FIREBOMB
BBEFLRSU FLUBBERS
BBEGIIST GIBBSITE
BBEGILNP PEBBLING
BBEGILOR GLOBBIER
BBEGILRS GRIBBLES
BBEGILST GLIBBEST
BBEGINSW WEBBINGS
BBEGIRRU GRUBBIER
BBEGLORS GOBBLERS
BBEGRRSU GRUBBERS
BBEHINSY NEBBISHY
BBEHIOTW BOBWHITE
BBEHLORS HOBBLERS
BBEHORRT THROBBER
BBEIIMRS IMBIBERS
BBEIIRST RIBBIEST
BBEIKNOR KNOBBIER
BBEIKNRU KNUBBIER
BBEILLLU BLUEBILL
BBEILNRS NIBBLERS
BBEILNRU NUBBLIER
BBEILORS SLOBBIER
BBEILORW WOBBLIER
BBEILOST BIBELOTS
BBEILOSW WOBBLIES
BBEILQRU QUIBBLER
BBEILQSU QUIBBLES
BBEILRRU BURBLIER
RUBBLIER
BBEILRRY BILBERRY
BBEIMNOS BOMBESIN
BBEIMRSU BRUMBIES
BBEINORS SNOBBIER
BBEINOST NOBBIEST
BBEINRSU SNUBBIER
BBEINSTU NUBBIEST
BBEIORTU OUTBRIBE
BBEIRSTU STUBBIER
SUBTRIBE
BBEISTTU TUBBIEST
BBEKLOOU BLUEBOOK
BBEKLOSS BLESBOKS
BBEKNOOT BONTEBOK
BBELLOSY BELLBOYS
BBELLRUY LUBBERLY
BBELLSTU BULBLETS
BBELMOST BOMBLETS
BBELMRSU BUMBLERS
BBELNORS NOBBLERS
BBELORSS SLOBBERS
BBELORSW WOBBLERS
BBELORSY LOBBYERS
SLOBBERY
BBELOTUW BLOWTUBE
BBELRRSU BURBLERS
BBELRSSU SLUBBERS
BBELSSTU STUBBLES
BBEMOSXY BOMBYXES
BBENORSY SNOBBERY
BBENRSSU SNUBBERS
BBEORRXY BOXBERRY
BBEORSSW SWOBBERS
BBEPRSUW BREWPUBS
BBFGILNU FLUBBING
BBGGILNO GOBBLING
BBGGINRU GRUBBING
BBGHILNO HOBBLING
BBGIIIMN IMBIBING
BBGIIKLN KIBBLING
BBGIILNN NIBBLING
BBGIINNS SNIBBING
BBGIINRS RIBBINGS
BBGILLSU BILLBUGS
BBGILMNU BUMBLING
BBGILNNO NOBBLING
BBGILNOW WOBBLING
BBGILNOY LOBBYING
BBGILNRU BLURBING
BURBLING
RUBBLING
BBGILNSU SLUBBING
BBGILRUY GRUBBILY
BBGIMNOS BOMBINGS
BBGINNSU SNUBBING
BBGINOST STOBBING
BBGINOSW SWOBBING
BBGINRSU RUBBINGS
BBGINSSU SUBBINGS
BBGINSTU STUBBING
BBGLOOWY LOBBYGOW
BBHILOSS SLOBBISH
BBHINOSS SNOBBISH
BBHIOSTY HOBBYIST
BBHIRSUY RUBBISHY
BBHKOOSS BOSHBOKS
BBHRSSUU SUBSHRUB
BBIILLSU SILLIBUB
BBIILSST BIBLISTS
BBIJMOOS JIBBOOMS
BBIKLNOO BOBOLINK
BBILMOSY LOBBYISM
BBILNOSY SNOBBILY
BBILOSTY LOBBYIST
BBILOSUU BIBULOUS
BBILRSTU BLURBIST
BBILSTUY STUBBILY
BBIMMOSS MOBBISMS
BBIMNOSS SNOBBISM
BBLLOUYY BULLYBOY
BBNOORSU BOURBONS
BBNORSTU STUBBORN
BCCCIILY BICYCLIC
BCCDEILY BICYCLED
BCCEEIRR CEREBRIC
BCCEHIRU CHERUBIC
BCCEHORS BESCORCH
BCCEIIIS CICISBEI
BCCEIILO LIBECCIO
BCCEIIOS CICISBEO
BCCEILOS ECBOLICS
BCCEILOY BIOCYCLE
BCCEILRU CRUCIBLE
BCCEILRY BICYCLER
BCCEILSU CUBICLES
BCCEILSY BICYCLES
BCCEMRUU CUCUMBER
BCCHIKOY BOYCHICK
BCCIIMOR MICROBIC
BCCIISTU CUBISTIC
BCCIITUY CUBICITY
BCCIKLLO COCKBILL
BCCILMOU COLUMBIC
BCCILOOR BROCCOLI
BCCILOSU BUCOLICS
BCCINORR CORNCRIB
BCCIRTUU CUCURBIT
BCCLOOOO COCOBOLO
BCCMOOSX COXCOMBS
BCCMSSUU SUCCUMBS
BCCNOORS CORNCOBS
BCCSSUUU SUCCUBUS
BCDDEEEK BEDECKED
BCDDEENU BEDUNCED
BCDDEHIL CHILDBED
BCDDESUU SUBDUCED
BCDEEEHR BREECHED
BCDEEGLU BECUDGEL
BCDEEHLN BLENCHED
BCDEEHNR BEDRENCH
BCDEEHOU DEBOUCHE
BCDEEIKN BENEDICK
BCDEEIKR BICKERED
BCDEEILR CREDIBLE
BCDEEILS DECIBELS
BCDEEILU EDUCIBLE
BCDEEIMR BECRIMED
BCDEEINT BENEDICT
BCDEEIRS DESCRIBE
BCDEEIST BISECTED
BCDEEJOT OBJECTED
BCDEEKMO BEMOCKED
BCDEEKNO BECKONED
BCDEEKRU REEDBUCK
BCDEEKTU BUCKETED
BCDEELNU BEUNCLED
BCDEELOR CORBELED
BCDEEMOR RECOMBED
BCDEEMRU CUMBERED
BCDEENSU BEDUNCES
BCDEEORV BEDCOVER
BCDEEOTT OBTECTED
BCDEERSU BECURSED
BCDEHLOT BLOTCHED
BCDEHNRU BRUNCHED
BCDEIIOS BIOCIDES
BCDEIIRR RICEBIRD
BCDEIKRR REDBRICK
BCDEIKSS SICKBEDS
BCDEIKST BEDTICKS
BCDEILRY CREDIBLY
BCDEIMNO COMBINED
BCDEINOU ICEBOUND
BCDEIRSU SUBCIDER
BCDEKOOO CODEBOOK
BCDEKORS BEDROCKS
BCDELMRU CRUMBLED
BCDELMSU SCUMBLED
BCDELOSU BECLOUDS
BCDEMNOU UNCOMBED
BCDEMOOY COEMBODY
BCDEMORY CORYMBED
BCDENRUU UNCURBED
BCDEOORT CODEBTOR
BCDEOOWY COWBOYED
BCDEORSU OBSCURED
BCDEORSW BECROWDS
BCDEOSSU SUBCODES
BCDESSUU SUBDUCES
BCDIIMOR BROMIDIC
BCDIIPSU BICUSPID
BCDIKLLU DUCKBILL
BCDILMOY MOLYBDIC
BCDILORU COLUBRID
BCDIMOOR COMORBID
BCDIMORS SCOMBRID
BCDINOSW COWBINDS
BCDINRUU RUBICUND
BCDIORSW COWBIRDS
BCDKNOOO BOONDOCK
BCDKORSU BURDOCKS
BCDSSTUU SUBDUCTS
BCEEEFIN BENEFICE
BCEEEHIR BEECHIER
BCEEEHRS BREECHES
BCEEENRS BESCREEN
BCEEERSU BERCEUSE
BCEEFILN FENCIBLE
BCEEFKLS BEFLECKS
BCEEFLTU CLUBFEET
BCEEGIRS ICEBERGS
BCEEHKSU BUCKSHEE
BCEEHLNR BLENCHER
BCEEHLNS BLENCHES
BCEEHLOT BECLOTHE
BCEEHLRS BELCHERS
BCEEHNRS BENCHERS
BCEEHNRU UNBREECH
BCEEHNTU BEECHNUT
BCEEHOSU BOUCHEES
BCEEIILM IMBECILE
BCEEIKRR BICKERER
BCEEILNR BERNICLE
BCEEIMRS BECRIMES
BCEEINOT CENOBITE
BCEEIOSX ICEBOXES
BCEEIPSS BICEPSES
BCEEJORT REOBJECT
BCEEKNOR BECKONER
BCEEKNSU BUCKEENS
BCEEKSUY BUCKEYES
BCEELOOR BORECOLE
BCEELRTU TUBERCLE
BCEEMMOR COMEMBER
BCEEMNRU ENCUMBER
BCEEMRRU CEREBRUM
CUMBERER
BCEENORS OBSCENER
BCEERSSU BECURSES
BCEERSTU SUBERECT
BCEERSXY CYBERSEX
BCEERTVY BREVETCY
BCEFFIIR FEBRIFIC
BCEFHISU SUBCHIEF
BCEFILOR FORCIBLE
BCEGHILN BELCHING
BCEGHINN BENCHING
BCEGIINO BIOGENIC
BCEGIMNO BECOMING
BCEGKMSU GEMSBUCK
BCEGLNOO CONGLOBE
BCEHIIOT BIOETHIC
BCEHIIRT BITCHIER
BCEHILMY CHIMBLEY
BCEHIMOR BICHROME
BCEHIMRS BESMIRCH
BCEHIMRU CHERUBIM
BCEHINNO CHINBONE
BCEHINRU BUNCHIER
BCEHINSU SUBNICHE
BCEHIORS BRIOCHES
BCEHIORT BOTCHIER
BCEHIOST BIOTECHS
BCEHIRST BRITCHES
BCEHIRTY BITCHERY
BCEHLOST BLOTCHES
BCEHLRSU BLUCHERS
BCEHNOPT BENCHTOP
BCEHNRRU BRUNCHER
BCEHNRSU BRUNCHES
BCEHOORS BROOCHES
BCEHOPSU SUBEPOCH
BCEHORRU BROCHURE
BCEHORSS BORSCHES
BCEHORST BOTCHERS
BCEHORSW COWHERBS
BCEHORTY BOTCHERY
BCEHRSTU BUTCHERS
BCEHRTUY BUTCHERY
BCEIIKLN ICEBLINK
BCEIIKRR BRICKIER
BCEIILMS MISCIBLE
BCEIILNV VINCIBLE
BCEIILOP EPIBOLIC
BCEIINRS INSCRIBE
BCEIKLMO COMBLIKE
BCEIKLMS LIMBECKS
BCEIKLOO BOOKLICE
BCEIKLOR BLOCKIER
BCEIKLRS BRICKLES
BCEIKLTU BLUETICK
BCEILMRS CLIMBERS
BCEILNOS BINOCLES
BCEILNYZ BENZYLIC
BCEILORS BRICOLES
CORBEILS
BCEILOSU CIBOULES
BCEILPRU REPUBLIC

BCEIMNOR COMBINER
BCEIMNOS COMBINES
BCEIMNRU INCUMBER
BCEIMORS MICROBES
BCEIMRRU CRUMBIER
BCEINORS BICORNES
BCEINORU BOUNCIER
BCEINOVX BICONVEX
BCEINRSU BRUCINES
BCEIOOPS BIOSCOPE
BCEIORST BISECTOR
BCEIRRSS SCRIBERS
BCEIRTTY YTTERBIC
BCEJOORT OBJECTOR
BCEJSSTU SUBJECTS
BCEKLLNU BULLNECK
BCEKLNUU UNBUCKLE
BCEKLORS BLOCKERS
BCEKLRSU BUCKLERS
SUBCLERK
BCEKOORU BUCKEROO
BCEKORST BROCKETS
BCEKORSU ROEBUCKS
BCELLOSW COWBELLS
BCELLRUW WELLCURB
BCELLSSU SUBCELLS
BCELMRSU CLUMBERS
CRUMBLES
BCELMSSU SCUMBLES
BCELNOSW BECLOWNS
BCEMRRSU CRUMBERS
BCENOOOX ECONOBOX
BCENORSU BOUNCERS
BCEORRSU OBSCURER
BCEORRWY COWBERRY
BCEORSSU BESCOURS
OBSCURES
BCERSSTU BECRUSTS
BCESSSTU SUBSECTS
BCESSTUU SUBCUTES
BCFIIMOR MORBIFIC
BCFIIORT FIBROTIC
BCFILORY FORCIBLY
BCFIMORU CUBIFORM
BCFLOOTU CLUBFOOT
BCFSSSUU SUBFUSCS
BCGHIINR BIRCHING
BCGHIINT BITCHING
BCGHINNU BUNCHING
BCGHINOT BOTCHING
BCGHINPU PINCHBUG
BCGIIKNR BRICKING
BCGIIKST BIGSTICK
BCGIILMN CLIMBING
BCGIILOO BIOLOGIC
BCGIINRS SCRIBING
BCGIKLNO BLOCKING
BCGIKLNU BUCKLING
BCGILMNY CYMBLING
BCGIMNOS COMBINGS
BCGIMNRU CRUMBING
BCGINNOU BOUNCING
BUNCOING
BCGINRSU CURBINGS
BCHIILTY BITCHILY
BCHIIOPS BIOCHIPS
BCHIISSU HIBISCUS
BCHIKLOS BLOCKISH
BCHIKOSU CHIBOUKS
BCHIKOSY BOYCHIKS
BCHILNUY BUNCHILY
BCHILOTY BOTCHILY
BCHIOORY CHOIRBOY
BCHIOPRS PIBROCHS
BCHIORRT BIRROTCH
BCHIOTTU OUTBITCH
BCHKOSTU BUCKSHOT
BCHLNOUX LUNCHBOX
BCHNOORS BRONCHOS
BCHNORSU BRONCHUS
BCHORSST BORSCHTS
BCIIILMU UMBILICI
BCIIIOTT BIOTITIC
BCIIKLNS NIBLICKS
BCIILLSY SIBYLLIC
BCIILMSU BULIMICS
BCIILNVY VINCIBLY
BCIILOTY BIOLYTIC
BCIIMNOO BIONOMIC
BCIIMORU CIBORIUM
BCIINORT BORNITIC
BCIINORV VIBRONIC
BCIIOPTY BIOTYPIC
BCIIORST BISTROIC
BCIIOSTT BISCOTTI
BCIISSTU BISCUITS
BCIISTUY BISCUITY
BCIKKNSU BUCKSKIN
BCIKLOOT BOOTLICK
BCIKLOST LOBSTICK
BCIKORRW CRIBWORK
BCIKOSTT BITSTOCK
BITTOCKS
BCILLPUY PUBLICLY
BCILMOSY SYMBOLIC
BCILMOTU OUTCLIMB
BCILMPSU UPCLIMBS
BCILNOUY BOUNCILY
BCILOORS BICOLORS
BROCOLIS
BCILOORU BICOLOUR
BCIMORSU MICROBUS
BCINOSSU SUBSONIC
BCINOSTU SUBTONIC
BCINSTUU SUBTUNIC
BCIOOPSY BIOSCOPY
BCIOORST ROBOTICS
BCIOOSTT BISCOTTO
BCIOPSTU SUBOPTIC
SUBTOPIC
BCIORRSU CRIBROUS
BCISSTUU SUBCUTIS
BCJKMSUU JUMBUCKS
BCKKOOOO COOKBOOK
BCKLLOOS BOLLOCKS
BCKLLOSU BULLOCKS
BCKLLOUY BULLOCKY
BCKLNOSU SUNBLOCK
UNBLOCKS
BCKNNOOS BONNOCKS
BCKOOOPY COPYBOOK
BCKOSTTU BUTTOCKS
BCLMOORU CLUBROOM
BCLMOOSU COULOMBS
BCLMOOTU OUTCLOMB
BCLOORTU CLUBROOT
BCLOOSSU SUBCOOLS
BCLSSTUU SUBCULTS
BCMMRSUU CRUMBUMS
BCMORSUU CUMBROUS
BCMOSSTU COMBUSTS
BCNNOUUY UNBOUNCY
BCOOPSYY COPYBOYS
BCOORSSW CROSSBOW
BCOOSTTY BOYCOTTS
BCORSTTU OBSTRUCT
BCSTUUZZ BUZZCUTS
BDDDEEEM EMBEDDED
BDDDEEIM IMBEDDED
BDDDEEIR DEBRIDED
BDDEEESS SEEDBEDS
BDDEEFIR BIRDFEED
BDDEEFLU BEFUDDLE
BDDEEGGU DEBUGGED
BDDEEGIR BEGIRDED
BDDEEGTU BUDGETED
BDDEEIMM BEDIMMED
BDDEEIMO EMBODIED
BDDEEINR REBIDDEN
BDDEEINT INDEBTED
BDDEEINW BINDWEED
BDDEEIOR REBODIED
BDDEEIRR REEDBIRD
BDDEEIRS BIRDSEED
DEBRIDES
BDDEEISS BEDSIDES
BDDEEKNU DEBUNKED
BDDEELMU BEMUDDLE
BDDEENNU UNBENDED
BDDEENRU BURDENED
BDDEEORR BORDERED
BDDEEORS DESORBED
BDDEEOTT BEDOTTED
BDDEFOOR FORBODED
BDDEGINS BEDDINGS
BDDEIIMO IMBODIED
BDDEILNR BRINDLED
BDDEILOO BLOODIED
BDDEINNU UNBIDDEN
BDDEINOU UNBODIED
BDDEINRU UNDERBID
BDDEIORS DISROBED
BDDEIOWY WIDEBODY
BDDEIRRS REDBIRDS
BDDEISSU SUBSIDED
BDDELMRU DRUMBLED
BDDELOOR BLOODRED
BDDENNOU UNBONDED
BDDENOTU OBTUNDED
BDDENRUU UNDERBUD
BDDEORTU OBTRUDED
BDDGIINS BIDDINGS
BDDGINSU BUDDINGS
BDDGINUY BUDDYING
BDDGIORS BIRDDOGS
BDDGOOSY DOGSBODY
BDDHIIRY DIHYBRID
BDDINOOW WOODBIND
BDDINOSU DISBOUND
BDDINPUU PUDIBUND
BDEEEEMS BESEEMED
BDEEEGIS BESIEGED
BDEEEHST BEDSHEET
BDEEEHTU HEBETUDE
BDEEEILN BEELINED
BDEEEILV BELIEVED
BDEEEIRW DWEEBIER
BDEEELLR REBELLED
BDEEELLV BEVELLED
BDEEELMM EMBLEMED
BDEEELRS BLEEDERS
BDEEELUW BLUEWEED
BDEEEMMR MEMBERED
BDEEEMNS BEDESMEN
BDEEERRS BREEDERS
REBREEDS
BDEEERRV REVERBED
BDEEERTT BETTERED
BDEEERTV BREVETED
BDEEFFRU BUFFERED
REBUFFED
BDEEFFTU BUFFETED
BDEEFGGO BEFOGGED
BDEEFGLU BEGULFED
BDEEFILR BELFRIED
BDEEFINR BEFRIEND
BDEEFIRS DEBRIEFS
BDEEFITT BEFITTED
BDEEFLOO BEFOOLED
BDEEFLOU BEFOULED
BDEEFOOR FOREBODE
BDEEFOOW BEEFWOOD
BDEEGGIW BEWIGGED
BDEEGGRU BEGRUDGE
BUGGERED
DEBUGGER
BDEEGILN BLEEDING
BDEEGILR BEGIRDLE
BDEEGILU BEGUILED
BDEEGIMR BEGRIMED
BDEEGINR BERINGED
BREEDING
BDEEGINW BEDEWING
BEWINGED
BDEEGLNO BELONGED
BDEEGMSU BESMUDGE
BDEEGOOY BOOGEYED
BDEEGORU BEROUGED
BDEEGRSV SVEDBERG
BDEEGRTU BUDGETER
BDEEGSSU BUGSEEDS
BDEEHISW DWEEBISH
BDEEHLNO BEHOLDEN
BDEEHLOR BEHOLDER
BDEEHLOW BEHOWLED
BDEEHLSU BUSHELED
BDEEHMOR HOMEBRED
BDEEHMRY BERHYMED
BDEEHOOV BEHOOVED
BDEEHORT BOTHERED
BDEEIILL ELIDIBLE
BDEEIILN INEDIBLE
BDEEIKSS BEKISSED
BDEEILLL LIBELLED
BDEEILLR REBILLED
BDEEILLT BILLETED
BDEEILMP BEDIMPLE
BDEEILMR LIMBERED
BDEEILMS BESLIMED
BESMILED
BDEEILNR LINEBRED
RENDIBLE
BDEEILNU UNEDIBLE
BDEEILNV VENDIBLE
BDEEILOR ERODIBLE
REBOILED
BDEEILOS OBELISED
BDEEILOZ OBELIZED
BDEEILRV BEDRIVEL
BDEEILRW BEWILDER
BDEEILSV BEDEVILS
BDEEIMOR EMBODIER
BDEEIMOS EMBODIES
BDEEIMRT TIMBERED
BDEEIMST BEDTIMES
BEMISTED
BDEEINOS EBONISED
BDEEINOT OBEDIENT
BDEEINOZ EBONIZED
BDEEINRS INBREEDS
BDEEINRT INTERBED
BDEEINST BENDIEST
BDEEINSW BENDWISE
BDEEINSZ BEDIZENS
BDEEIORS REBODIES
BDEEIRRU REBURIED
BDEEIRRV RIVERBED
BDEEIRST BESTRIDE
BISTERED
BDEEIRSU DEBRUISE
BDEEIRSY BIRDSEYE
BDEEIRTT BITTERED
BDEEKMOS BESMOKED
EMBOSKED
BDEEKNRU BUNKERED
DEBUNKER
BDEEKOOR REBOOKED
BDEEKORR BROKERED
BDEELLMU UMBELLED
BDEELLOW BELLOWED
BOWELLED
BDEELLTU BULLETED
BDEELLUW BULLWEED
BDEELMNO EMBOLDEN
BDEELMOR REBELDOM
BDEELMRT TREMBLED
BDEELMRU LUMBERED
BDEELNNO ENNOBLED
BDEELNRS BLENDERS
REBLENDS
BDEELNTU UNBELTED
BDEELORU REDOUBLE
BDEELOSV BELOVEDS
BDEELSST DEBTLESS
BDEEMNOT BODEMENT
ENTOMBED
BDEEMNOW ENWOMBED
BDEEMNRU NUMBERED
BDEEMORR EMBORDER
BDEEMORW BEWORMED
BDEEMORY REEMBODY
BDEEMOSS EMBOSSED
BDEEMPRU BUMPERED
BDEEMRTU EMBRUTED
BDEENNOT BONNETED
BDEENORS DEBONERS
REDBONES
BDEENOSW BESNOWED
BDEENPRS PREBENDS
BDEENRRU BURDENER
BDEENSUV SUBVENED
BDEEOORT REBOOTED
BDEEOPRR REPROBED
BDEEORRR BORDERER
BDEEORRS RESORBED
BDEEORRV OVERBRED
BDEEORSS BEDSORES
BDEEORST BESTRODE
BDEEORSV OBSERVED
BDEEORTU OUTBREED
BDEEORTV OBVERTED
BDEEOSSS OBSESSED
BDEEOSTT BESOTTED
OBTESTED
BDEEOSTW BESTOWED
BDEEPRRU PUREBRED
BDEERRTU TRUEBRED
BDEERRWY DEWBERRY
BDEERSSU BURSEEDS
BDEERSUW BURWEEDS
BDEERTTU BUTTERED
REBUTTED
BDEFIILR BIRDLIFE
BDEFIIRR FIREBIRD
BDEFIKOR BIFORKED
BDEFILSU SUBFIELD
BDEFIMOR BIFORMED
BDEFOORS FORBODES
BDEFOORY FOREBODY
BDEGHHIR HIGHBRED
BDEGHILT BLIGHTED
BDEGHIST BEDIGHTS
BDEGIILN BIELDING
BDEGIINT BETIDING
DEBITING
BDEGILNN BLENDING
BDEGINNO DEBONING
BDEGINTU DEBUTING
BDEGLMRU GRUMBLED
BDEGLNOU BLUDGEON
BDEGLRSU BLUDGERS
BDEGNOSW BEDGOWNS
BDEGOOSY GOODBYES
BDEGORRY DOGBERRY
BDEHIKOS KIBOSHED
BDEHIOPS BISHOPED
BDEHKOSY KYBOSHED
BDEHLSUV BUSHVELD
BDEHMOOY HOMEBODY
BDEHOOOO BOOHOOED
BDEHORSU BESHROUD
BDEIIIKN BIKINIED
BDEIIKLR BIRDLIKE
BDEIIKTZ KIBITZED
BDEIILMR BIRDLIME
BDEIILNY INEDIBLY
BDEIILTY DEBILITY
BDEIIMOS IMBODIES
BDEIINNZ BENZIDIN
BDEIIOPS BIOPSIED
BDEIKNSU BUSKINED
BDEILLMU BDELLIUM
BDEILLNU UNBILLED
BDEILLNW WINDBELL
BDEILLOW BILLOWED
BDEILLOX BOLLIXED
BDEILMNO IMBOLDEN
BDEILMSU SUBLIMED
BDEILNNO BLONDINE
BDEILNOU UNBOILED
UNILOBED
BDEILNRS BLINDERS
BRINDLES
BDEILNRU UNBRIDLE
BDEILNST BLINDEST
BDEILNVY VENDIBLY
BDEILOOR BLOODIER
BDEILOOS BLOODIES
BDEILOPU UPBOILED
BDEILOQU OBLIQUED
BDEILORT TRILOBED
BDEILORV LOVEBIRD
BDEILOSS BODILESS
BDEILOSW DISBOWEL
BDEILPRU PREBUILD
BDEILQTU BEDQUILT
BDEILRRS BRIDLERS
BDEILRRY LYREBIRD
BDEILRST BRISTLED
DRIBLETS
BDEILRSU BUILDERS
REBUILDS
BDEILRTT BRITTLED
BDEILSST BILSTEDS
BDEIMNOT INTOMBED
BDEIMNSU NIMBUSED
BDEIMNUU UNIMBUED
BDEIMORS BROMIDES
BDEIMORY EMBRYOID
BDEIMORZ BROMIZED
BDEIMRTU IMBRUTED
BDEINOOS NOBODIES
BDEINOOW WOODBINE
BDEINORV OVENBIRD
BDEINOSU BEDOUINS
BDEINOTU BOUNTIED
BDEINPRS PREBINDS
BDEINRUU UNBURIED
BDEINSUX SUBINDEX
BDEINTTU UNBITTED
BDEIOORR BROODIER
BDEIORRS BROIDERS
DISROBER
BDEIORRU BOURRIDE
BDEIORRY BROIDERY
BDEIORSS DISROBES
BDEIORST DEORBITS
BDEIORSV OVERBIDS
BDEIORTU TUBEROID
BDEIOSSY DISOBEYS
BDEIOSUX SUBOXIDE
BDEIRSSU DISBURSE
SUBSIDER
BDEISSSU SUBSIDES
BDEISSTU SUBEDITS
BDEKNOOS BOOKENDS
BDELLOOR BORDELLO
DOORBELL
BDELLOOX BOLLOXED
BDELLORS BEDROLLS
BDELLOUZ BULLDOZE
BDELMOSY SYMBOLED
BDELMRSU DRUMBLES
BDELMSTU STUMBLED
BDELNNUU UNBUNDLE
BDELNOOS DOBLONES
BDELNOSS BOLDNESS
BONDLESS
BDELNOST BLONDEST
BDELNOTU UNBOLTED
BDELNOUU UNDOUBLE
BDELNRSU BLUNDERS
BUNDLERS
BDELOORS BOODLERS
BDELOORV OVERBOLD
BDELOOUW BLUEWOOD
BDELORSU BOULDERS
DOUBLERS
BDELORSW BOWLDERS
BDELORTU TROUBLED
BDELORUU DOUBLURE
BDELORUY BOULDERY
BDELOSTU DOUBLETS
BDEMNNOS BONDSMEN
BDEMNSSU DUMBNESS
BDEMOORS BEDROOMS
BOREDOMS
BDEMOOSY SOMEBODY
BDEMOOTT BOTTOMED
BDEMSSUU SUBSUMED
BDENNOTU DUBONNET
BDENNRUU UNBURDEN
UNBURNED
BDENOOTU UNBOOTED
BDENOOTW BENTWOOD
BDENOPRU PREBOUND
UNPROBED
BDENORSU BOUNDERS
REBOUNDS
SUBORNED
BDENOTTU BUTTONED
BDENRSTU SUBTREND
BDENRUUY UNDERBUY
BDENSSTU SUBTENDS
BDENSTUU UNBUSTED
BDEOORRS BROODERS
BDEOORRW BORROWED
BDEOOTUX OUTBOXED
BDEOOWWW BOWWOWED
BDEOPSST BEDPOSTS
BDEOPSTU SUBDEPOT
BDEORRSU BORDURES
SUBORDER
BDEORRTU OBTRUDER
BDEORRUW BURROWED
BDEORSSU ROSEBUDS
BDEORSTU DOUBTERS
OBTRUDES
REDOUBTS
BDEORSUV OVERDUBS
BDERSSUU SUBDUERS
BDFGNOOU FOGBOUND
BDFIIITY BIFIDITY
BDFIIORS FIBROIDS
BDFILLLO BILLFOLD
BDFILNOO BLOODFIN
BDFILSUU SUBFLUID
BDFINRUU FURIBUND
BDFIRRSU SURFBIRD
BDFLOTUU DOUBTFUL
BDFORSUY BODYSURF
BDGGIINR BRIDGING
BDGGILNU BLUDGING
BDGGLOSU GOLDBUGS
BDGHOOUY DOUGHBOY
BDGIIKNR KINGBIRD
BDGIILNN BLINDING
BDGIILNR BRIDLING
BDGIILNU BUILDING
BDGIINNS BINDINGS
BDGIINRS BIRDINGS
BDGIIOOS GOBIOIDS
BDGILNNU BUNDLING
BDGILNOO BLOODING
BOODLING
BDGILNOU DOUBLING
BDGILNOY BODINGLY
BDGILNTU BLINDGUT
BDGILOOS GLOBOIDS
BDGINNOS BONDINGS
BDGINNOU BOUNDING
BDGINOOR BROODING
BDGINORS BIRDSONG
SONGBIRD
BDGINOTU DOUBTING
BDGINSUU SUBDUING
BDGLLOSU BULLDOGS
BDGNRUUY BURGUNDY
BDGOOOSW BOGWOODS
BDHILNOS BLONDISH
BDHIMOOR RHOMBOID
BDHIMSUU SUBHUMID
BDHIORST BIRDSHOT
BDHIOSSU BUSHIDOS
BDHLOOOT HOTBLOOD
BDHOOOSY BOYHOODS

BDIIIORV VIBRIOID
BDIILMSU MISBUILD
BDIILOOS BIOSOLID
BDIILORS OILBIRDS
BDIIMNSS MISBINDS
BDIIMRUU RUBIDIUM
BDILLOOY BLOODILY
BDILMORY MORBIDLY
BDILNOOO DIOBOLON
BDILNPRU PURBLIND
BDILNSUU UNBUILDS
BDILOORY BROODILY
BDILOPRY POLYBRID
BDILOTUU OUTBUILD
BDILPSUU BUILDUPS
UPBUILDS
BDILRTUY TURBIDLY
BDIMNORU MORIBUND
BDIMNOSU MISBOUND
BDIMNSUU DUBNIUMS
BDIMOOSS DISBOSOM
BDIMOSTU MISDOUBT
BDINNOSU INBOUNDS
BDINNRUW WINDBURN
BDINOORS BRIDOONS
BDINOOSW WOODBINS
BDINORSW SNOWBIRD
BDINRSSU SUNBIRDS
BDINSSTU BUNDISTS
DUSTBINS
BDIOORSU BOUDOIRS
BDIOORTY BOTRYOID
BDIOSTUY BODYSUIT
BDIRSSTU DISTURBS
BDKNOOOR DOORKNOB
BDKOOORW WORDBOOK
BDKOORWY BODYWORK
BDKOOSTU STUDBOOK
BDLNOOOU DOUBLOON
BDLNOOUY UNBLOODY
BDLNOOWW BLOWDOWN
BDLOOOSX OXBLOODS
BDLORSUW SUBWORLD
BDMOOSSS BOSSDOMS
BDMORSUW BUDWORMS
BDNOOPTU POTBOUND
BDNOORSU BOURDONS
BDNOOSUX SOUNDBOX
BDNOOSWW DOWNBOWS
BDNOOTUU OUTBOUND
BDNORSUW RUBDOWNS
BDOOOSWX BOXWOODS
BDORUWZZ BUZZWORD
BEEEEFLN ENFEEBLE
BEEEEFRS FREEBEES
BEEEENPS PEEBEENS
BEEEENRT TEREBENE
BEEEFIRS FREEBIES
BEEEFIST BEEFIEST
BEEEFLSS BEEFLESS
BEEEFLST FEEBLEST
BEEEGIRS BESIEGER
BEEEGISS BESIEGES
BEEEGRRS BERGERES
BEEEGRTT BEGETTER
BEEEHIST BHEESTIE
BEEEHISV BEEHIVES
BEEEHNOY HONEYBEE
BEEEHNSS SHEBEENS
BEEEILLL LIBELLEE
BEEEILLS LIBELEES
BEEEILNS BEELINES
BEEEILRV BELIEVER
BEEEILSV BELIEVES
BEEEIRRZ BREEZIER
BEEEIRST BEERIEST
BEEEJLSW BEJEWELS
BEEEJLSZ JEZEBELS
BEEEJSUZ BEJEEZUS
BEEEKLLS BELLEEKS
BEEELLRV BEVELLER
BEEELMNS ENSEMBLE
BEEELMRS RESEMBLE
BEEELMZZ EMBEZZLE
BEEELPRS BLEEPERS
BEEELRST BEETLERS
BEEELRSV BEVELERS
BEEEMMRR REMEMBER
BEEEMRSS BERSEEMS
BEEENNSZ BENZENES
BEEERSTT BESETTER
BEEFFRTU BUFFETER
BEEFGINR BEFINGER
BEFRINGE
BEEFHILS FEEBLISH
BEEFIIRZ FIBERIZE
BEEFILLX FLEXIBLE
BEEFILNU UNBELIEF
BEEFILRS BELFRIES
BEEFINST BENEFITS
BEEFIRRS BRIEFERS
BEEFIRSS FRISBEES
BEEFIRST BRIEFEST
BEEFLORU BEFOULER
BEEFLORW BEFLOWER
BEEFNORR FREEBORN
BEEFOORT FREEBOOT
BEEGGNRU GREENBUG
BEEGIILL ELIGIBLE
BEEGIILX EXIGIBLE
BEEGILLR GERBILLE
BEEGILMN BEMINGLE
BEEGILNP BLEEPING
BEEGILNT BEETLING
BEEGILNV BEVELING
BEEGILOS OBLIGEES
BEEGILRU BEGUILER
BEEGILSU BEGUILES
BEEGIMRS BEGRIMES
BEEGINNR BEGINNER
BEEGINRS REBEGINS
BEEGINRZ BREEZING
BEEGINST BEIGNETS
BEEGINSU BEGUINES
BEEGINSW BEESWING
BEEGMNOS GOMBEENS
BEEGMNOY BOGEYMEN
BEEGMRSU SUBMERGE
BEEGNOOW WOBEGONE
BEEGNOTT BEGOTTEN
BEEGNRSU SUBGENRE
BEEGOOPR GEOPROBE
BEEGOPSX PEGBOXES
BEEHHMOT BEHEMOTH
BEEHIKLR HERBLIKE
BEEHIMOT BOEHMITE
BEEHIRST HERBIEST
BEEHIRSV BESHIVER
BEEHLLNT HELLBENT
BEEHLOOR BOREHOLE
BEEHLRSS HERBLESS
BEEHLRST BLETHERS
BEEHLRSU BUSHELER
BEEHMORW HOMEBREW
BEEHMRSY BERHYMES
BEEHMSTU SUBTHEME
BEEHNRRT BRETHREN
BEEHOOST BESOOTHE
BEEHOOSV BEHOOVES
BEEHRRST SHERBERT
BEEHRSST SHERBETS
BEEHRSSW BESHREWS
BEEIILNZ ZIBELINE
BEEIIORS BOISERIE
BEEIISTU UBIETIES
BEEIJLSU JUBILEES
BEEIKLNY EYEBLINK
BEEIKLTU TUBELIKE
BEEIKLWY BIWEEKLY
BEEIKSSS BEKISSES
BEEILLLR LIBELLER
BEEILLNO LOBELINE
BEEILLNT BELTLINE
BEEILLNU BLUELINE
BEEILLRS LIBELERS
BEEILLRT BILLETER
BEEILLSV BILEVELS
BEEILLTT BELITTLE
BEEILLTU TULLIBEE
BEEILMOS EMBOLIES
BEEILMPP BEPIMPLE
BEEILMPR PERIBLEM
BEEILMRR LIMBERER
BEEILMSS BESLIMES
BESMILES
BEEILNNS BLENNIES
BEEILNRS BERLINES
BEEILNRY BERYLINE
BEEILNSS SENSIBLE
BEEILNST STILBENE
TENSIBLE
BEEILNSU NEBULISE
BEEILNUZ NEBULIZE
BEEILORS EROSIBLE
BEEILOSS OBELISES
BEEILOSZ OBELIZES
BEEILRRT TERRIBLE
BEEILRSU BLUESIER
BEEILRSV VERBILES
BEEILRYZ BREEZILY
BEEIMORT BIOMETER
BEEIMRST BIMESTER
BEEIMRTT EMBITTER
BEEINNSZ BENZINES
BEEINOSS EBONISES
BEEINOST BETONIES
EBONITES
BEEINOSZ EBONIZES
BEEINRSZ ZEBRINES
BEEIORSW BOWERIES
BEEIORSZ SOBERIZE
BEEIORTV OVERBITE
BEEIQSUZ BEZIQUES
BEEIRRSU REBURIES
BEEIRRSV BREVIERS
BEEIRRTT BITTERER
BEEIRSSU SUBERISE
BEEIRSSW BREWISES
BEEIRSUZ SUBERIZE
BEEISSTW WEBSITES
BEEKMOSS BESMOKES
BEEKNOPS BESPOKEN
BEEKNOST BETOKENS
STEENBOK
BEEKRRSS BERSERKS
BEEKRRSU REBUKERS
BEELLMTU UMBELLET
BEELLORW BELLOWER
BEELLSST BELTLESS
BEELLSUV SUBLEVEL
BEELMNNO NOBLEMEN
BEELMNSU BLUESMEN
BEELMOSW EMBOWELS
BEELMRRT TREMBLER
BEELMRRU LUMBERER
BEELMRST TREMBLES
BEELMSTU BLUESTEM
BEELMUZZ BEMUZZLE
BEELNNOR ENNOBLER
BEELNNOS ENNOBLES
BEELNOSS BONELESS
NOBLESSE
BEELNOSU BLUENOSE
NEBULOSE
BEELNOSZ BENZOLES
BEELNSSU BLUENESS
BEELNTTU BETELNUT
BEELNTUY BUTYLENE
BEELOOST OBSOLETE
BEELORTT REBOTTLE
BEELORVW OVERBLEW
BEELOSTY EYEBOLTS
BEELPRSS PREBLESS
BEELRSSS BLESSERS
BEELRSSV VERBLESS
BEELRTUU TRUEBLUE
BEELSSTU TUBELESS
BEEMNRRU NUMBERER
RENUMBER
BEEMOORS BORESOME
BEEMORSS EMBOSSER
BEEMORSW EMBOWERS
BEEMOSSS EMBOSSES
BEEMRSSU SUBMERSE
BEEMRSTU EMBRUTES
BEEMRTTU UMBRETTE
BEENNOOS NONOBESE
BEENNOOT BOTONNEE
BEENOPTY TEENYBOP
BEENORRS ENROBERS
BEENORTV VERBOTEN
BEENOSST BONESETS
BEENOSTU TUBENOSE
BEENOSTY BONEYEST
BEENPRST BESPRENT
BEENRSTW BESTREWN
BEENRTTU BRUNETTE
BEENSSSU SUBSENSE
BEENSSTU SUBTEENS
BEENSSUV SUBVENES
BEEOORRV OVERBORE
BEEOORTT BEETROOT
BEEOPRRS REPROBES
BEEOPSSU BESPOUSE
BEEORRSU BOURREES
BEEORRSV OBSERVER
BEEORRTU BOURTREE
BEEORSST SOBEREST
BEEORSSU SUBEROSE
BEEORSSV OBSERVES
OBVERSES
BEEORSTU TUBEROSE
BEEORSTV OVERBETS
BEEORSTW BESTOWER
BEEORSWY EYEBROWS
BEEOSSSS OBSESSES
BEEPPRSU PREPUBES
BEEPRRSU SUPERBER
BEEPRRSV PREVERBS
BEEQSSTU BEQUESTS
BEERRTTU REBUTTER
BEERSSSU SUBSERES
BEERSSTW BESTREWS
WEBSTERS
BEERSSUV SUBSERVE
BEERSTTU BURETTES
BEERSTTY BYSTREET
BEFFISTU BUFFIEST
BEFFLRSU BLUFFERS
BEFFLSTU BLUFFEST
BEFGIILS FILIBEGS
BEFGIINR BRIEFING
BEFGILNU FUNGIBLE
BEFGIRSU FIREBUGS
BEFHILSU BLUEFISH
BEFHINOS BONEFISH
FISHBONE
BEFHIRSU BUSHFIRE
BEFILLXY FLEXIBLY
BEFILMOR FORELIMB
BEFILNOS LOBEFINS
BEFILNSU BLUEFINS
BEFILOST BOTFLIES
BEFILOSU BIOFUELS
BEFILRST FILBERTS
BEFILSSU SUBFILES
BEFINORS BONFIRES
BEFIORSS FIBROSES
BEFIRSST FIBSTERS
BEFISSTU FUBSIEST
BEFISSUX SUBFIXES
BEFLLLUY BELLYFUL
BEFLLSTY FLYBELTS
BEFLMRSU FUMBLERS
BEFLORUW FURBELOW
BEFMOOOR FOREBOOM
BEFNOORR FORBORNE
BEGGIINN BINGEING
BEGGINOY BOGEYING
BEGGIOST BOGGIEST
BEGGISTU BUGGIEST
BEGGLORS BLOGGERS
BOGGLERS
BEGHIILP PHILIBEG
BEGHIKNT BEKNIGHT
BEGHILRT BLIGHTER
BEGHINOR NEIGHBOR
BEGHINOV BEHOVING
BEGHINRT BERTHING
BRIGHTEN
BEGHIOST GOBSHITE
BEGHIRRT BRIGHTER
BEGHLNOU BUNGHOLE
BEGHNOTU BOUGHTEN
BEGHORTU REBOUGHT
BEGHOSTU BESOUGHT
BEGHOSUU BUGHOUSE
BEGHRRSU BURGHERS
BEGIILLN LIBELING
BEGIILLY ELIGIBLY
BEGIILST BILGIEST
BEGIIMNR BEMIRING
BERIMING
BEGIIMNS MISBEGIN
BEGIIMNX BEMIXING
BEGIIMNY BIGEMINY
BEGIINNS INBEINGS
BEGIINTW BITEWING
BEGIKNRU REBUKING
BEGILLLU BLUEGILL
GULLIBLE
BEGILLNS BELLINGS
BEGILLNY BELLYING
BEGILNNY BENIGNLY
BEGILNOW BOWELING
ELBOWING
BEGILNRT TREBLING
BEGILNSS BLESSING
GLIBNESS
BEGILNST BELTINGS
BEGILNSU BLUEINGS
BEGILORS OBLIGERS
BEGILRST GILBERTS
BEGILSTU BULGIEST
BEGIMNOW EMBOWING
BEGIMNRU EMBRUING
UMBERING
BEGIMNSU BEMUSING
MISBEGUN
BEGIMOST MISBEGOT
BEGINNNO NONBEING
BEGINNNU UNBENIGN
BEGINNOR ENROBING
RINGBONE
BEGINORR REBORING
BEGINORS SOBERING
BEGINORW BOWERING
BEGINRRS BRINGERS
BEGINRRY BERRYING
BEGINRSW BREWINGS
BEGINRUY REBUYING
BEGKMOSS GEMSBOKS
BEGLLORY GORBELLY
BEGLLOSU GLOBULES
BEGLMOOS BEGLOOMS
BEGLMRRU GRUMBLER
BEGLMRSU GRUMBLES
BEGLMSUU BLUEGUMS
BEGLNRSU BLUNGERS
BUNGLERS
BEGLOOST BOOTLEGS
BEGLOSUV LOVEBUGS
BEGLOTUU OUTBULGE
BEGMNOOY BOOGYMEN
BEGNOORU BOURGEON
BEGNORSU BURGEONS
BEGNORTU BURGONET
BEGNSSUU SUBGENUS
BEGORRUY BROGUERY
BEGPRSUU SUPERBUG
BEHIISST BHISTIES
BEHIISTX EXHIBITS
BEHIKLSU BUSHLIKE
BEHIKNST BETHINKS
BEHIKOSS KIBOSHES
BEHILLOS SHOEBILL
BEHILLTY BLITHELY
BEHILMRW WHIMBREL
BEHILMST THIMBLES
BEHILMTY BIMETHYL
BEHILNPY BIPHENYL
BEHILORR HORRIBLE
BEHILOSS BOLSHIES
BEHILRST BLITHERS
BEHILRTU THURIBLE
BEHILSTT BLITHEST
BEHIMNOO BONHOMIE
BEHIMOOS SEMIHOBO
BEHIMORS BIOHERMS
BEHIMOSY YOHIMBES
BEHINNOS SHINBONE
BEHINOPS HIPBONES
BEHINOSW WISHBONE
BEHIPRRT PREBIRTH
BEHIRRST REBIRTHS
BEHIRRSU BRUSHIER
BEHIRSSU HUBRISES
BEHIRSSY HYBRISES
BEHISSTU BUSHIEST
BEHKOSSY KYBOSHES
BEHLLOOT BOLTHOLE
BEHLLOOW BLOWHOLE
BEHLLOPS BELLHOPS
BEHLLSSU SUBSHELL
BEHLMRSU HUMBLERS
BEHLMSTU HUMBLEST
BEHLORST BROTHELS
BEHLRSSU BLUSHERS
BEHLSSSU BUSHLESS
BEHMOOOX HOMEOBOX
BEHMOOST BESMOOTH
BEHMOOSY HOMEBOYS
BEHMPSTU BETHUMPS
BEHNNOST BENTHONS
BEHNNOUY HONEYBUN
BEHNORST BETHORNS
BEHNRSTU BURTHENS
BEHOOOPZ ZOOPHOBE
BEHOORST THEORBOS
BEHOOSTX HOTBOXES
BEHOOSUY HOUSEBOY
BEHOPRST POTHERBS
BEHORRST BROTHERS
BEHORSSU ROSEBUSH
BEHORSTT BETROTHS
BEHOSSTU BESHOUTS
BEHRRSSU BRUSHERS
BEHRSTTU TURBETHS
BEIIIKMN MINIBIKE
BEIIKRTZ KIBITZER
BEIIKSTZ KIBITZES
BEIILLST LIBELIST
BEIILMMO IMMOBILE
BEIILMOS MOBILISE
BEIILMOZ MOBILIZE
BEIILMST LIMBIEST
BEIILNRS RINSIBLE
BEIILRSS RISIBLES
BEIILRST TRILBIES
BEIILRTT LIBRETTI
BEIILSTT STILBITE
BEIIMNNR RENMINBI
BEIIMNNU BIENNIUM
BEIIMRTT IMBITTER
BEIINORS BRIONIES
BEIINOST NIOBITES
BEIINQUU BIUNIQUE
BEIINRST BRINIEST
BEIINSST STIBINES
BEIINSTT STIBNITE
BEIIOPSS BIOPSIES
BEIIOSTT BIOTITES
BEIISSTT BITSIEST
BEIISTTT BITTIEST
BEIKKLNO KNOBLIKE
BEIKLLOT BOLTLIKE
BEIKLLOW BOWLLIKE
BEIKLMOT TOMBLIKE
BEIKLNRS BLINKERS
BEIKLOSS OBELISKS
BEIKLOTY KILOBYTE
BEIKLRUY RUBYLIKE
BEIKLSTU BULKIEST
BEIKNOST STEINBOK
BEIKNRRY INKBERRY
BEIKOORS BROOKIES
BEIKOORT BROOKITE
BEIKORST REITBOKS
BEIKOSST BOSKIEST
BEIKRSST BRISKEST
BRISKETS
BEIKRSSW BREWSKIS
BEIKRSTU BURKITES
BEILLMRY LIMBERLY
BEILLMSS LIMBLESS
BEILLNTU BULLETIN
BEILLORS BROLLIES
BEILLORV OVERBILL
BEILLOSU LIBELOUS
BEILLOSX BOLLIXES
BEILLPRS PREBILLS
BEILLSTU BULLIEST
BEILMMOS EMBOLISM
BEILMNOR BROMELIN
BEILMNOU NOBELIUM
BEILMNRU UNLIMBER
BEILMNST NIMBLEST
BEILMOOR BLOOMIER
BEILMORS EMBROILS
BEILMOSS OBELISMS
BEILMRSS BRIMLESS
BEILMRST TIMBRELS
BEILMRSU SUBLIMER
BEILMSSU LIMBUSES
SUBLIMES
BEILNNTU BUNTLINE
BEILNOPS BONSPIEL
BEILNOSU NUBILOSE
BEILNOSW BOWLINES
BEILNOVY BOVINELY
BEILNRSY BYLINERS
BEILNSSU SUBLINES
BEILNSSY SENSIBLY
BEILNSTU BUSTLINE
BEILNSTY TENSIBLY
BEILNSTZ BLINTZES
BEILOORV BOILOVER
OVERBOIL
BEILOPPW BLOWPIPE
BEILOPRS PREBOILS
BEILOPSS POSSIBLE
BEILOQRU BELIQUOR
BEILOQSU OBLIQUES
BEILORRS BROILERS
BEILORST STROBILE
BEILORSU BLOUSIER
BEILORSW BLOWSIER
BEILORTT BLOTTIER
LIBRETTO
BEILORWZ BLOWZIER
BEILOSSY BIOLYSES
BEILOSTW BLOWIEST
BEILPRTU PREBUILT
BEILRRRU BLURRIER
BEILRRTT BRITTLER
BEILRRTY TERRIBLY
BEILRSST BLISTERS
BRISTLES
BEILRSTT BRITTLES
BEILRSTU BURLIEST
SUBTILER
BEILRSTY BLISTERY
BEILRSTZ BLITZERS
BEILRSUY BRULYIES
BEILRSUZ BRULZIES
BEILRTTY BITTERLY

BEILSTTU SUBTITLE
BEIMMRRS BRIMMERS
BEIMNORS BROMINES
BEIMNRUZ BRUNIZEM
BEIMNSSU NIMBUSES
BEIMNSTU BITUMENS
BEIMOORR BROOMIER
BEIMOORS RIBOSOME
BEIMOOST BOOMIEST
BEIMORSW IMBOWERS
BEIMORSZ BROMIZES
BEIMORTY BIOMETRY
BEIMORYZ RIBOZYME
BEIMOSTV BEVOMITS
BEIMOSTW WOMBIEST
BEIMOSTY SYMBIOTE
BEIMPSTU BUMPIEST
BEIMRSTU IMBRUTES
RESUBMIT
TERBIUMS
BEIMSSTU SUBITEMS
BEINNOPS PINBONES
BEINNOSS BENISONS
BONINESS
BEINNOST BONNIEST
BEINNOSZ BENZOINS
BEINNTTU UNBITTEN
BEINOOST BONITOES
EOBIONTS
BEINORRW BROWNIER
BEINORRZ BRONZIER
BEINORST BORNITES
BEINORSW BROWNIES
BEINORSY BRYONIES
BEINOSSX BOXINESS
BEINOSTU BOUNTIES
BEINRSSU SUBERINS
BEINRSTT BITTERNS
BEINRSTU TRIBUNES
TURBINES
BEINRTTU UNBITTER
BEINSSSU BUSINESS
BEIOOPST BIOTOPES
BEIOORTZ ROBOTIZE
BEIOOSTZ BOOZIEST
BEIOPSTY BIOTYPES
BEIOQTUU BOUTIQUE
BEIORRST ORBITERS
BEIORSTY SOBRIETY
BEIORSUV BOUVIERS
BEIOSSST BOSSIEST
BEIOSSSU SOUBISES
BEIPPRSU PREPUBIS
BEIQRSTU BRIQUETS
BEIRRSSU BRUISERS
BEIRRSTU BRUITERS
BURRIEST
BEIRSSTU BUSTIERS
BEIRSTTU TRIBUTES
BEISSSTU SUBSITES
BEISSTTU BUSTIEST
BEJLMRSU JUMBLERS
BEJORTTU TURBOJET
BEKLNORY BROKENLY
BEKLOOOR BOOKLORE
BEKLOORT BROOKLET
BEKLOOST BOOKLETS
BEKLRSSU BURLESKS
BEKNNORU UNBROKEN
BEKNOOOT NOTEBOOK
BEKNORSY SKYBORNE
BEKOOORV OVERBOOK
BEKOOPRS PREBOOKS
BEKOORST BOOKREST
BEKOOTTX TEXTBOOK
BEKORSWW WEBWORKS
BEKORTUW TUBEWORK
BEKOSSXY SKYBOXES
BEKRSSTU BRUSKEST
BELLLLPU BELLPULL
BELLLMSU BLELLUMS
BELLMRUY LUMBERLY
BELLNOPS BONSPELL
BELLNORW WELLBORN
BELLNOSU BULLNOSE
BELLNOSW SNOWBELL
BELLNPSU BULLPENS
BELLOOSU LOBULOSE
BELLOOSX BOLLOXES
BELLOPTY POTBELLY
BELLORTW BELLWORT
BELLOSST BLOTLESS
BOLTLESS
BELLOSSU SOLUBLES
BELLOSWY SOWBELLY
BELMMRSU MUMBLERS
BELMNOSU NELUMBOS
BELMNOSY BENOMYLS
BELMOORS BLOOMERS
REBLOOMS
BELMOORY BLOOMERY
BELMOOST BOOMLETS
BELMOPRS PROBLEMS
BELMORST TEMBLORS
BELMORSY SOMBERLY
SOMBRELY
BELMOSST TOMBLESS
BELMPRSU PLUMBERS
REPLUMBS
BELMPRUY PLUMBERY
BELMRRSU RUMBLERS
BELMRRUY MULBERRY
BELMRSSU SLUMBERS
BELMRSTU STUMBLER
TUMBLERS
TUMBRELS
BELMRSUY SLUMBERY
BELMSSTU STUMBLES
BELNNNOO NONNOBLE
BELNOORS BORNEOLS
BELNOOSS BOONLESS
BELNOOSY BOLONEYS
BELNOSTW SNOWBELT
BELNOSUU NEBULOUS
BELNOSYZ BENZOYLS
BELNOTTU UNBOTTLE
BELNSSTU SUNBELTS
BELNSTTU BLUNTEST
BELNSTUU UNSUBTLE
BELOOPRS BLOOPERS
BELOOPRT BOLTROPE
BELOORVW OVERBLOW
BELOOSST BOOTLESS
BELOOTUV OBVOLUTE
BELORRTU TROUBLER
BELORSST BOLSTERS
LOBSTERS
BELORSSW BROWLESS
BELORSTT BLOTTERS
BOTTLERS
BELORSTU TROUBLES
BELOSSTU OUTBLESS
BELOSTUU TUBULOSE
BELOSTUY OBTUSELY
BELPRSUY SUPERBLY
BELRRSTU BLURTERS
BELRSSTU BLUSTERS
BUSTLERS
BELRSSUU SUBRULES
BELRSTUY BLUSTERY
BELRTUUU TUBULURE
BELSSTTU SUBTLEST
BELSTTUY SUBTLETY
BEMMOOSS EMBOSOMS
BEMMRRUU BEMURMUR
BEMNNSSU NUMBNESS
BEMNOORT TROMBONE
BEMNORSW EMBROWNS
BEMNORSY EMBRYONS
BEMNSSUU SUBMENUS
BEMOORRS SOMBRERO
BEMOORTT BOTTOMER
BEMORSST MOBSTERS
BEMORSWW WEBWORMS
BEMORTUW TUBEWORM
BEMOSTUX BUXOMEST
BEMSSSUU SUBSUMES
BEMSSTUW STEWBUMS
BENNNOTU UNBONNET
BENNORSW NEWBORNS
BENNSSSU SNUBNESS
BENOORRV OVERBORN
BENOORSU BURNOOSE
BENORRSU SUBORNER
BENORRSZ BRONZERS
BENORRTU TRUEBORN
BENORRUV OVERBURN
BENORSST SORBENTS
BENORSTU BURSTONE
BENORSTW BESTROWN
BROWNEST
BENORTTU BUTTONER
REBUTTON
BENOSSTU SUBTONES
BENOSSUZ SUBZONES
BENOSSWY NEWSBOYS
BENRSSTU SUBRENTS
BENRSTUY SUBENTRY
BENSSSUY BUSYNESS
BEOORRRW BORROWER
BEOORSSS OBSESSOR
SORBOSES
BEOORSST BOOSTERS
BEOORSTY BOTRYOSE
BEOOSTUX OUTBOXES
BEOPRRSV PROVERBS
BEOQSSTU BOSQUETS
BEOQSTUU BOUQUETS
BEORRRUW BURROWER
BEORRSSW BROWSERS
BEORRSTU ROBUSTER
BEORSSTW BESTROWS
BEORSSUU SUBEROUS
BEORSTUU TUBEROUS
BEORSUVY OVERBUSY
OVERBUYS
BEOSSTTU OBTUSEST
BEPRRSTU PERTURBS
BEPSSTUY SUBTYPES
BEQRRSUU BRUSQUER
BERRSSTU BURSTERS
BERSSTTU BUTTRESS
BERSSTUV SUBVERTS
BESSSSUY BYSSUSES
BESSSTTU SUBTESTS
BESSTTUX SUBTEXTS
BFFGILNU BLUFFING
BFFHORSU BRUSHOFF
BFFILOOS BOILOFFS
BFFLOOSW BLOWOFFS
BFFLOTUU OUTBLUFF
BFFNOOSU BUFFOONS
BFFNOSUX SNUFFBOX
BFGILMNU FUMBLING
BFGIOOST BIGFOOTS
BFGLLORU BULLFROG
BFHIILLS BILLFISH
BFHILOST FISHBOLT
BFHILOSW BLOWFISH
FISHBOWL
BFHIMNSU NUMBFISH
BFHLLSUU BLUSHFUL
BFIILMOS BIOFILMS
BFIINORS FIBROINS
BFIIORSS FIBROSIS
BFIKLOOP FLIPBOOK
BFILLMRU BRIMFULL
BFILLSSU BLISSFUL
BFIMORTU TUBIFORM
BFIORSTT FROSTBIT
BFKLOOSU BOOKFULS
BFLLNOWY FLYBLOWN
BFLLOSUW BOWLFULS
BFLLOSWY FLYBLOWS
BFLOORSU SUBFLOOR
BFNOORTW BOWFRONT
BFOOOSTY FOOTBOYS
BGGGIINS BIGGINGS
BGGGILNO BLOGGING
BOGGLING
BGGHIINT BIGHTING
BGGIILNO OBLIGING
BGGIILNY GIBINGLY
BGGIINNR BRINGING
BGGILNNU BLUNGING
BUNGLING
BGGILNRU BURGLING
BGGINOOY BOOGYING
BGHHHISU HIGHBUSH
BGHHINOR HIGHBORN
BGHHIORW HIGHBROW
BGHHIOSY HIGHBOYS
BGHIINRT BIRTHING
BGHILMNU HUMBLING
BGHILNSU BLUSHING
BGHILRTY BRIGHTLY
BGHIMNTU THUMBING
BGHIMOTU BIGMOUTH
BGHINORS BIGHORNS
BGHINRSU BRUSHING
BGHINRTU UNBRIGHT
BGHINSSU BUSHINGS
BGHIORSU BROGUISH
BGHIPSSU BUSHPIGS
BGHLRSUU BULGHURS
BGHMORSU HOMBURGS
BGHNOTUU UNBOUGHT
BGHOOPTU BOUGHPOT
BGHOORSU BOROUGHS
BGIIJLNY JIBINGLY
BGIIKLNN BLINKING
BGIIKNRS BRISKING
BGIILLNS BILLINGS
BGIILMNW WIMBLING
BGIILNNY BYLINING
BGIILNOR BROILING
BGIILNPP BLIPPING
BGIILNRS BIRLINGS
BRISLING
BGIILNSS BLISSING
SIBLINGS
BGIILNTY BITINGLY
BGIILNTZ BLITZING
BGIIMMNR BRIMMING
BGIIMNRU IMBRUING
BGIINORT ORBITING
BGIINRSU BRUISING
BGIINRTU BRUITING
BGIINSTT BITTINGS
BGIJLMNU JUMBLING
BGIJOSUU BIJUGOUS
BGIKLNOT KINGBOLT
BGIKNNOU BUNKOING
BGIKNOOR BROOKING
BGIKNOOS BOOKINGS
BGIKNORS BROKINGS
BGIKNSTU STINKBUG
BGILLLUY GULLIBLY
BGILLNOU GLOBULIN
BGILLNRU BULLRING
BGILLNUY BULLYING
BGILMMNU MUMBLING
BGILMNOO BLOOMING
BGILMNPU PLUMBING
BGILMNRU RUMBLING
BGILMNTU TUMBLING
BGILMORY GORBLIMY
BGILMOSU GUMBOILS
BGILMOTU GUMBOTIL
BGILNNTU BLUNTING
BGILNOOP BLOOPING
BGILNORT RINGBOLT
BGILNORY BORINGLY
BGILNOST BILTONGS
BGILNOSU BLOUSING
BGILNOSW BOWLINGS
BGILNOTT BLOTTING
BOTTLING
BGILNOWY BOWINGLY
BGILNRRU BLURRING
BGILNRTU BLURTING
BGILNSTU BUSTLING
BGILOORS OBLIGORS
BGILRSSU BUSGIRLS
BGIMNOOR BROOMING
BGIMNOOS BOSOMING
BGIMOSSY BOGYISMS
BGINNORU UNROBING
BGINNORW BROWNING
BGINNORZ BRONZING
BGINNOUW UNBOWING
BGINNOUX UNBOXING
BGINNRSU BURNINGS
BGINNSTU BUNTINGS
BGINOOST BONGOIST
BOOSTING
BGINORSW BROWSING
BGINOSWW WINGBOWS
BGINRSSU SUBRINGS
BGINRSTU BURSTING
BGINSSSU BUSSINGS
BGINSSWY SWINGBYS
BGISUWZZ BUZZWIGS
BGKLOOOS LOGBOOKS
BGKNOOOS SONGBOOK
BGLLNOOY OBLONGLY
BGLNOOSW LONGBOWS
BGLNOSUW BLOWGUNS
BGLOORYY BRYOLOGY
BGMNOOOR GOMBROON
BGMOOSTU GUMBOOTS
BGMORRUW GRUBWORM
BGOPRSUU SUBGROUP
BGORSTUU BURGOUTS
BHIIINNS INHIBINS
BHIIINST INHIBITS
BHIILMPS BLIMPISH
BHIIOPRT PROHIBIT
BHIKLLOO BILLHOOK
BHIKMNTU THUMBKIN
BHILLNOR HORNBILL
BHILLPUW BULLWHIP
BHILORRY HORRIBLY
BHILORUY BIHOURLY
BHILOSTU HOLIBUTS
BHILOSYY BOYISHLY
BHIMNORT THROMBIN
BHIMOOPR BIOMORPH
BHIMOOSS HOBOISMS
BHIMOPRS BIMORPHS
BHIMORSU BOHRIUMS
BHIMORTU BOTHRIUM
BHIMSSTU BISMUTHS
BHINORSW BROWNISH
BHIRSTTU TURBITHS
BHISSTTU BUSHTITS
BHKLORUW BUHLWORK
BHKMNOOY HYMNBOOK
BHKNOOOR HORNBOOK
BHKOOOPS BOOKSHOP
BHLLNORU BULLHORN
BHLLOSTU BULLSHOT
BHLLRSUU BULLRUSH
BHLOOOTT TOLBOOTH
BHLOSTUU OUTBLUSH
BHMNTTUU THUMBNUT
BHMORSTU THROMBUS
BHNOORTX BOXTHORN
BHNOSSUW SNOWBUSH
BHOOPSSY SHOPBOYS
BHOORTTU OUTTHROB
BHOOSSTW BOWSHOTS
BHPRSSUU BRUSHUPS
BIIKLOST KILOBITS
BIILLMOR MORBILLI
BIILLMSS MISBILLS
BIILLNOS BILLIONS
BIILLSTW TWIBILLS
BIILMOTY MOBILITY
BIILMSTU MISBUILT
SUBLIMIT
BIILNOOV OBLIVION
BIILNOTY NOBILITY
BIILNSTU SUBTILIN
BIILNSVY BIVINYLS
BIILNTUY NUBILITY
BIILORST STROBILI
BIILOSSY BIOLYSIS
BIIMMOSZ ZOMBIISM
BIIMNOSU NIOBIUMS
BIIMSSTU STIBIUMS
BIINOOTX BIOTOXIN
BIINORSV VIBRIONS
BIINOTVY BOVINITY
BIIQTUUY UBIQUITY
BIIRSSTU BURSITIS
BIJNOSSU SUBJOINS
BIKLLSSU SUBSKILL
BIKLNOST INKBLOTS
BIKLNOSY LINKBOYS
BIKMNOOS BOOMKINS
BIKMNPSU BUMPKINS
BIKOOSUU BOUSOUKI
BIKOOUUZ BOUZOUKI
BILLNOOU BOUILLON
BILLNOSU BULLIONS
BILLOSUY BLOUSILY
BILLOSWY BLOWSILY
BILLOWYZ BLOWZILY
BILLRRUY BLURRILY
BILMMPSU PLUMBISM
BILMNORS NOMBRILS
BILMOSTU BOTULISM
BILMRSTU TUMBRILS
BILNOSTU BOTULINS
BILNOSUU NUBILOUS
BILNSTUU TUBULINS
BILOOPST POTBOILS
BILOORST SORBITOL
BILOPSSY POSSIBLY
BILORSST BRISTOLS
STROBILS
BILOSSSU SUBSOILS
BILOSTUY ISOBUTYL
BILOTTUU OUTBUILT
BILSTTUY SUBTILTY
BIMMOOSS IMBOSOMS
BIMMORSS BROMISMS
BIMNNUUU UNUNBIUM
BIMNORSW IMBROWNS
BIMNOSSY SYMBIONS
BIMNOSTY SYMBIONT
BIMNRUUV VIBURNUM
BIMOORST ROBOTISM
BIMOSSSS BOSSISMS
BIMOSSTW MISTBOWS
BIMOSSTY SYMBIOTS
BIMRSSTU BRUTISMS
BIMRSSUX BRUXISMS
BINNORTW TWINBORN
BINOORST BIOTRONS
BINORSSU BOURSINS
BINRSSTU INBURSTS
BINRSTUY BUTYRINS
BINSSTUU SUBUNITS
BIOPRSTW BOWSPRIT
BIORRSTU BURRITOS
BIORRSTW RIBWORTS
BIORSSTT BISTORTS
BIORSTTY BOTRYTIS
BIORSTUY BISTOURY
BIOSTTUY OBTUSITY
BIRSSUUV SUBVIRUS
BISSSSTU SUBSISTS
BKKOOORW WORKBOOK
BKLOSTUU OUTBULKS
BKMOOORW BOOKWORM
BKNNOOOS NONBOOKS
BKNOOSTW BOWKNOTS
BKORSUWY BUSYWORK
BLLLLOOY LOBLOLLY
BLLMOORW BOLLWORM
BLLOPTUU BULLPOUT
BLLOTUUY OUTBULLY
BLMMPSUU PLUMBUMS
BLMOOOST TOMBOLOS
BLMOOOTU OUTBLOOM
BLMOOOTY LOBOTOMY
BLMOORSW LOBWORMS
BLMOOSSS BLOSSOMS
BLMOOSSY BLOSSOMY
BLMOPSUU PLUMBOUS
BLNOOSSU BLOUSONS
BLNSTUUY UNSUBTLY
BLOOPSWY PLOWBOYS
BLOORSWW LOWBROWS
BLOOSSTY SLYBOOTS
BLOOSTUW BLOWOUTS
BLOPSSTU SUBPLOTS
BLORSTUY ROBUSTLY
BLOSTUUU TUBULOUS
BLRSTUYY BUTYRYLS
BMNOOOSW MOONBOWS
BMNOOOTW BOOMTOWN
BMNOOSSU UNBOSOMS
BMOORSSU SOMBROUS
BMOORSTU MOTORBUS
BMOORTTY BOTTOMRY
BNNORTUW NUTBROWN
BNNOTTUU UNBUTTON
BNNRSSUU SUNBURNS
BNNRSTUU SUNBURNT
BNOOOSUY SONOBUOY
BNOORTUW BROWNOUT
BNOPRSTU POSTBURN
BNORSTUU BURNOUTS
OUTBURNS
BNORTTUU OUTBURNT
BNRSSTUU SUNBURST
BOOPSSTY POSTBOYS
BORSTTUU OUTBURST
BORSTUUY BUTYROUS
CCCDIILY DICYCLIC
CCCDIOOS COCCOIDS
CCCDKLOO COLDCOCK
CCCEEILT ECLECTIC
CCCEGOSY COCCYGES
CCCEILNY ENCYCLIC
CCCEOSXY COCCYXES
CCCHIORY CHICCORY
CCCIINSU SUCCINIC
CCCILLYY CYCLICLY
CCCILNOY CYCLONIC
CCCINSTU SUCCINCT
CCCIOORS SCIROCCO
CCCKOORW COCKCROW
CCCNOOST CONCOCTS
CCDDEENO CONCEDED
CCDDEEOT DECOCTED
CCDDELOU OCCLUDED
CCDDENOU CONDUCED
CCDEEENR CREDENCE
CCDEEHLN CLENCHED
CCDEEILN LICENCED
CCDEEIOP CODPIECE
CCDEEIOS ECOCIDES
CCDEEIRV CREVICED
CCDEEKOR COCKERED
RECOCKED
CCDEEKOY COCKEYED
CCDEELRY RECYCLED
CCDEENOR CONCEDER
CCDEENOS CONCEDES
CCDEESSU SUCCEEDS
CCDEHHRU CHURCHED
CCDEHILN CLINCHED
CCDEHIPU HICCUPED
CCDEHKLU CHUCKLED
CCDEHLTU CLUTCHED
CCDEHNRU CRUNCHED
CCDEHOOS SCOOCHED
CCDEHORS SCORCHED
CCDEHORT CROTCHED
CCDEHORU CROUCHED
CCDEHOST SCOTCHED

CCDEHRTU CRUTCHED
CCDEHSTU SCUTCHED
CCDEIILO CLEIDOIC
CCDEIINO COINCIDE
CCDEIIRT CRICETID
CCDEIIST DEICTICS
CCDEILYZ CYCLIZED
CCDEINOR CORNICED
CCDEINOT OCCIDENT
CCDEIOPP COPPICED
CCDEIOPU OCCUPIED
CCDEIORT CODIRECT
CCDEKNOU UNCOCKED
CCDEKOOU CUCKOOED
CCDELNOU CONCLUDE
CCDELOSU OCCLUDES
CCDELOTU OCCULTED
CCDENOOO COCOONED
CCDENORU CONDUCER
CCDENOSU CONDUCES
CCDEORRU OCCURRED
CCDEORSU SUCCORED
CCDEOSTU STUCCOED
CCDHIILS CICHLIDS
CCDHIIOR DICHROIC
CCDHIIOT DICHOTIC
CCDHINOO CONCHOID
CCDIILNU NUCLIDIC
CCDIILOS CODICILS
CCDIILSU CULICIDS
CCDIINOS SCINCOID
CCDIIORS CRICOIDS
CCDIIORT DICROTIC
CCDILOSY CYCLOIDS
CCDKLOSU CUCKOLDS
CCDKOOOW WOODCOCK
CCDNOORS CONCORDS
CCDNOSTU CONDUCTS
CCEEEILN LICENCEE
CCEEFFOT COEFFECT
CCEEHIKS CHICKEES
CCEEHILN ELENCHIC
CCEEHISV CEVICHES
CCEEHKNS SCHNECKE
CCEEHKPR PRECHECK
CCEEHKRS CHECKERS
RECHECKS
CCEEHLNR CLENCHER
CCEEHLNS CLENCHES
CCEEHRSY SCREECHY
CCEEIILS CICELIES
CCEEIIST CECITIES
CCEEILMU LEUCEMIC
CCEEILNR ENCIRCLE
LICENCER
CCEEILNS LICENCES
CCEEILNT ELENCTIC
CCEEILPY EPICYCLE
CCEEILRR RECIRCLE
CCEEILRT ELECTRIC
CCEEIMNU ECUMENIC
CCEEINOR CICERONE
CROCEINE
CCEEINOV CONCEIVE
CCEEINSS SCIENCES
CCEEIORS CICOREES
CCEEIORV COERCIVE
CCEEIRSS CERCISES
CCEEIRSV CERVICES
CRESCIVE
CREVICES
CCEEITTU EUTECTIC
CCEEKLOR COCKEREL
CCEEKNRW CREWNECK
CCEEKOSY COCKEYES
CCEELMNY CLEMENCY
CCEELNSU LUCENCES
CCEELOSS SCOLECES
CCEELRRY RECYCLER
CCEELRSY RECYCLES
CCEEMMNO COMMENCE
CCEEMMOR COMMERCE
CCEENNOS ENSCONCE
CCEENORT CONCRETE
CCEENRST CRESCENT
CCEEORRS COERCERS
CCEEORST COERECTS
CCEFFHKO CHECKOFF
CCEFIIPS SPECIFIC
CCEFINOT COINFECT
CCEFIRRU CRUCIFER
CCEFLLOU FLOCCULE
CCEFLOOS FLOCCOSE
CCEFNOST CONFECTS
CCEGHIKN CHECKING
CCEGILOO ECOLOGIC
CCEGILRY GLYCERIC
CCEGINOR COERCING
CCEGINPS SPECCING
CCEHHIIR CHICHIER
CCEHHINS CHINCHES
CCEHHRSU CHURCHES
CCEHIIMR CHIMERIC
CCEHIIMS ISCHEMIC
CCEHIINZ ZECCHINI
CCEHIKNP PINCHECK
CCEHIKNS CHICKENS
CCEHIKSU CHUCKIES
CCEHILNR CLINCHER
CCEHILNS CLINCHES
CCEHILOR CHOLERIC
CCEHILOY CHOICELY
CCEHILTY HECTICLY
CCEHINOR CORNICHE
ENCHORIC
CCEHINOS CONCHIES
CCEHINOZ ZECCHINO
CCEHINSS CHICNESS
CCEHINST TECHNICS
CCEHINSZ ZECCHINS
CCEHIORT RICOCHET
CCEHIOST CHOICEST
CCEHKLRU CHUCKLER
CCEHKLSU CHUCKLES
CCEHKMSU CHECKSUM
CCEHKORW CHECKROW
CCEHKOTU CHECKOUT
CCEHKPSU CHECKUPS
CCEHLMOR CROMLECH
CCEHLNNU UNCLENCH
CCEHLSSU SCULCHES
CCEHLSTU CLUTCHES
CULTCHES
CCEHNRRU CRUNCHER
CCEHNRSU CRUNCHES
CCEHOOSS SCOOCHES
CCEHORRS SCORCHER
CCEHORSS SCORCHES
CCEHORST CROCHETS
CROTCHES
CCEHORSU COUCHERS
CROUCHES
CCEHORTT CROTCHET
CCEHOSST SCOTCHES
CCEHRSTU CRUTCHES
SCUTCHER
CCEHRTUY CUTCHERY
CCEHSSTU SCUTCHES
CCEIIKLN NICKELIC
CCEIILNO COLICINE
CCEIILNT ENCLITIC
CCEIILNU CULICINE
CCEIILOR LICORICE
CCEIILPT ECLIPTIC
CCEIILST SCILICET
CCEIILTU LEUCITIC
CCEIINOR CICERONI
CCEIIRST ICTERICS
CCEIIRTU EUCRITIC
CCEIKKLO COCKLIKE
CCEIKLRS CLICKERS
CCEIKOST COCKIEST
CCEIKRST CRICKETS
CCEILMOO COELOMIC
CCEILMOP COMPLICE
CCEILNOR CORNICLE
CCEILNUY UNICYCLE
CCEILOSS SCOLICES
CCEILRRS CIRCLERS
CCEILRRU CURRICLE
CCEILRST CIRCLETS
CCEILRSY CRESYLIC
CCEILRTY TRICYCLE
CCEILRUU CURLICUE
CCEILSTU CUTICLES
CCEILSYZ CYCLIZES
CCEIMNOO ECONOMIC
CCEIMOPR COPREMIC
CCEIMOST COSMETIC
CCEIMRRU MERCURIC
CCEINNOV CONVINCE
CCEINOOR COERCION
CCEINOOZ CENOZOIC
CCEINOPR COPRINCE
CCEINOPT CONCEPTI
CCEINORS CONCISER
CORNICES
CROCEINS
CCEINORT CONCERTI
NECROTIC
CCEINOST CONCEITS
CCEINOTT TECTONIC
CCEINPRT PRECINCT
CCEINRTU CINCTURE
CCEINSTY SYNECTIC
CCEIOORT CROCOITE
CCEIOPPS COPPICES
CCEIOPRU OCCUPIER
CCEIOPSU OCCUPIES
CCEIOPTY ECOTYPIC
CCEIORST CORTICES
CCEIOTXY EXOCYTIC
CCEIPSST SCEPTICS
CCEIRSSU CIRCUSES
CCEKLORS CLOCKERS
CCEKNOSY COCKNEYS
CCEKOPST PETCOCKS
CCEKORRY CROCKERY
CCEKORST CROCKETS
CCEKORSU COCKSURE
CCELLOST COLLECTS
CCELMOPT COMPLECT
CCELNOSY CYCLONES
CCELOPSY CYCLOPES
CCELORTU OCCULTER
CCELOSSY CYCLOSES
CCELRUUY CURLYCUE
CCENNORS CONCERNS
CCENNOST CONCENTS
CONNECTS
CCENOORT CONCERTO
CCENOPST CONCEPTS
CCENORST CONCERTS
CCENORTY CORNETCY
CCENOSTV CONVECTS
CCENRRUY CURRENCY
CCEOOSTT COCOTTES
CCEOPRUY REOCCUPY
CCEORRST CORRECTS
CCEORRSU REOCCURS
SUCCORER
CCEORSSU CROCUSES
CCEORSTU STUCCOER
CCEOSSTU STUCCOES
CCERSTUW CREWCUTS
CCESSSUU CUSCUSES
CCFGILNO FLOCCING
CCFHKLOU CHOCKFUL
CCFIIRUX CRUCIFIX
CCFILLOU FLOCCULI
CCFILNOT CONFLICT
CCFKLOOT COCKLOFT
CCFLOOOO LOCOFOCO
CCGHHIOU HICCOUGH
CCGHIINN CINCHING
CCGHIKNO CHOCKING
CCGHIKNU CHUCKING
CCGHINOU COUCHING
CCGIIKLN CLICKING
CCGIIKNR CRICKING
CCGIILNR CIRCLING
CCGIILNU GLUCINIC
CCGIKLNO CLOCKING
COCKLING
CCGIKLNU CLUCKING
CCGIKNOR CROCKING
CCGILLOY GLYCOLIC
CCGILNOY GLYCONIC
CCGILNSY CYCLINGS
CCGILOSU GLUCOSIC
CCGINNOS SCONCING
CCGKOORS GORCOCKS
CCHHIITY ICHTHYIC
CCHHINOT CHTHONIC
CCHHLRUY CHURCHLY
CCHHNRUU UNCHURCH
CCHHOOWW CHOWCHOW
CCHIINUZ ZUCCHINI
CCHIIORT ORCHITIC
CCHIKMPU CHIPMUCK
CCHIKORY CHICKORY
CCHIKSST SCHTICKS
CCHILNNU UNCLINCH
CCHILNUY UNCHICLY
CCHINORS CHRONICS
CCHIPSSY PSYCHICS
CCHKLOSS SCHLOCKS
CCHKLOSY SCHLOCKY
CCHKMNUU NUMCHUCK
CCHKMSSU SCHMUCKS
CCHKOSTU COCKSHUT
CCHKPSUU UPCHUCKS
CCHNRSUY SCRUNCHY
CCHOORST SCROOTCH
CCIIIMSV CIVICISM
CCIIIPRT PICRITIC
CCIIKKPW PICKWICK
CCIIKNPY PICNICKY
CCIILNOS COLICINS
CCIILORT CLITORIC
CCIIMNSY CYNICISM
CCIINORZ ZIRCONIC
CCIINOTY CONICITY
CCIIRSTU CIRCUITS
CCIIRTUY CIRCUITY
CCIKKLOP PICKLOCK
CCIKKOTT TICKTOCK
CCIKLOSW COWLICKS
CCIKNOPR PRINCOCK
CCIKOPST COCKPITS
CCILLOTY CYCLITOL
CCILNOOS COLONICS
CCILNOSU COUNCILS
CCILNSUY SUCCINYL
CCILOOPS PICCOLOS
CCILORUU CURCULIO
CCILOSSY CYCLOSIS
CCILSSTY CYCLISTS
CCINOPSY SYNCOPIC
CCINOPTY PYCNOTIC
CCINORSY CRYONICS
CCINOSTV CONVICTS
CCIOOPST SCOTOPIC
CCIOORSS SIROCCOS
CCIOOTXY OXYTOCIC
CCIOPRST COSCRIPT
CCIOPSTU OCCIPUTS
CCJNNOTU CONJUNCT
CCKKLMUU MUCKLUCK
CCKMOOOR MOORCOCK
CCKOOPRT CROCKPOT
CCKOOPST STOPCOCK
CCKOPRSU COCKSPUR
CCLLOTUY OCCULTLY
CCLMOOPU COCOPLUM
CCMOOORS MOROCCOS
CCNOOPSU PUCCOONS
CCNOORSU CONCOURS
CCNOOSTU COCONUTS
CCOOSSUU COUSCOUS
CCORSSTU CROSSCUT
CCORSSUU SUCCOURS
CDDDEETU DEDUCTED
CDDEEEEX EXCEEDED
CDDEEEFN DEFENCED
CDDEEEFT DEFECTED
CDDEEEIR REDECIDE
CDDEEEIV DECEIVED
CDDEEEJT DEJECTED
CDDEEENR DECERNED
CDDEEENT DECEDENT
CDDEEEPR PRECEDED
CDDEEERS SCREEDED
CDDEEETT DETECTED
CDDEEFOR DEFORCED
CDDEEGLU CUDGELED
CDDEEHIS DEHISCED
CDDEEHIT CHEDDITE
CDDEEHNR DRENCHED
CDDEEIIM MEDICIDE
CDDEEIIS DEICIDES
CDDEEIKR DICKERED
CDDEEIKT DETICKED
CDDEEILN DECLINED
CDDEEILP PEDICLED
CDDEEINR CINDERED
CDDEEINZ DEZINCED
CDDEEIOT COEDITED
CDDEEIOV DEVOICED
CDDEEIPT DEPICTED
CDDEEIRS DECIDERS
DESCRIED
CDDEEIRT CREDITED
DIRECTED
CDDEEKNU UNDECKED
CDDEEKOR REDOCKED
CDDEEKOT DOCKETED
CDDEEKUW DUCKWEED
CDDEELPU DECUPLED
CDDEELSU SECLUDED
CDDEELUX EXCLUDED
CDDEELUY DEUCEDLY
CDDEENOS SECONDED
CDDEENSS DESCENDS
CDDEEOPR PRECODED
CDDEEORR RECORDED
CDDEEORS DECODERS
CDDEERUV DECURVED
CDDEESUW CUDWEEDS
CDDEFIIO CODIFIED
CDDEFINO CONFIDED
CDDEGIIN DECIDING
CDDEGINO DECODING
CDDEGINU DEDUCING
CDDEHIOW COWHIDED
CDDEHRSU CHUDDERS
CDDEIINT INDICTED
CDDEIISU SUICIDED
CDDEIKOS DOCKSIDE
CDDEILLO COLLIDED
CDDEILNU INCLUDED
CDDEILOR CLODDIER
CDDEILRU CUDDLIER
CDDEIMOS MISCODED
CDDEINTU INDUCTED
CDDEIORV DIVORCED
CDDEIRRU CRUDDIER
CDDEKNOU UNDOCKED
CDDELLOU COLLUDED
CDDELNOO CONDOLED
CDDELORS CODDLERS
CDDELRSU CUDDLERS
CDDENNOO CONDONED
CDDENOOR CORDONED
CDDEOORR CORRODED
CDDEOORT DOCTORED
CDDEOPRU PRODUCED
CDDGHILO GODCHILD
CDDGILNO CODDLING
CDDGILNU CUDDLING
CDDGINRU CRUDDING
CDDGINSU SCUDDING
CDDHIIRY DIHYDRIC
CDDHILOS CLODDISH
CDDIIOSS DISCOIDS
CDDIKOPS PIDDOCKS
CDDIORSS DISCORDS
CDDKORSU RUDDOCKS
CDDOOORW CORDWOOD
CDEEEERX EXCEEDER
CDEEEFFT EFFECTED
CDEEEFHL FLEECHED
CDEEEFNR REFENCED
CDEEEFNS DEFENCES
CDEEEFRT REDEFECT
REFECTED
CDEEEHLR CHEERLED
LECHERED
CDEEEHOR REECHOED
CDEEEHRS CREESHED
CDEEEHRW RECHEWED
CDEEEHSW ESCHEWED
CDEEEINV EVIDENCE
CDEEEIRV DECEIVER
RECEIVED
CDEEEISV DECEIVES
CDEEEJRT REJECTED
CDEEELLX EXCELLED
CDEEELNR CRENELED
CDEEELOS COLESEED
CDEEELST DESELECT
SELECTED
CDEEEMNT CEMENTED
CDEEEMOR COREDEEM
CDEEENNT TENDENCE
CDEEENRS SCREENED
SECERNED
CDEEENRT CENTERED
DECENTER
DECENTRE
CDEEEPRS PRECEDES
CDEEEPTX EXCEPTED
EXPECTED
CDEEERRS DECREERS
CDEEERSS RECESSED
SECEDERS
CDEEERST RESECTED
SECRETED
CDEEERTT DETECTER
CDEEERTX EXCRETED
CDEEESSX EXCESSED
CDEEESTX EXSECTED
CDEEETUX EXECUTED
CDEEFFOR COFFERED
CDEEFHLN FLENCHED
CDEEFHLT FLETCHED
CDEEFHNR FRENCHED
CDEEFIIS EDIFICES
CDEEFIIT FETICIDE
CDEEFINT INFECTED
CDEEFKLR FRECKLED
CDEEFKOR FOREDECK
CDEEFLST DEFLECTS
CDEEFNNU UNFENCED
CDEEFNOR ENFORCED
CDEEFORR DEFORCER
CDEEFORS DEFORCES
FRESCOED
CDEEFORT DEFECTOR
CDEEGIIR REGICIDE
CDEEGINO GENOCIDE
CDEEGINR RECEDING
CDEEGINS SECEDING
CDEEGIOS GEODESIC
CDEEGIOT GEODETIC
CDEEGIRZ GRECIZED
CDEEGLRU CUDGELER
CDEEHILN LICHENED
CDEEHILP CHELIPED
CDEEHILS CHISELED
CDEEHINR ENRICHED
RICHENED
CDEEHIPR CIPHERED
DECIPHER
CDEEHIPS CEPHEIDS
CDEEHIRW RICHWEED
CDEEHISS DEHISCES
CDEEHIST CHEDITES
CDEEHKST SKETCHED
CDEEHKTV KVETCHED
CDEEHLSU SCHEDULE
CDEEHNQU QUENCHED
CDEEHNRR DRENCHER
CDEEHNRS DRENCHES
CDEEHNRT TRENCHED
CDEEHNRW WRENCHED
CDEEHNUW UNCHEWED
CDEEHORS COSHERED
CDEEHORT HECTORED
TOCHERED
CDEEHPRY CYPHERED
CDEEHRTW WRETCHED
CDEEIILT ELICITED
CDEEIIMN MEDICINE
CDEEIIMP EPIDEMIC
CDEEIINT INDICTEE
CDEEIIOS DIOECIES
CDEEIIRT DIERETIC
CDEEIISV DECISIVE
CDEEIITT DIETETIC
CDEEIJNT INJECTED
CDEEIJOR REJOICED
CDEEIKLN NICKELED
CDEEIKNR NICKERED
CDEEIKNS SICKENED
CDEEIKPT PICKETED
CDEEIKRT DETICKER
CDEEIKRW WICKEDER
CDEEIKST TICKSEED
CDEEIKTT TICKETED
CDEEILNP PENCILED
CDEEILNR DECLINER
RECLINED
CDEEILNS DECLINES
LICENSED
SILENCED
CDEEILNT DENTICLE
CDEEILOR RECOILED
CDEEILPS ECLIPSED
PEDICELS
PEDICLES
CDEEILRS SCLEREID
CDEEILRT DERELICT
CDEEIMNR ENDERMIC
CDEEIMNS ENDEMICS
CDEEIMOR MEDIOCRE
CDEEIMOS COMEDIES
CDEEIMPR PREMEDIC
CDEEIMRV DECEMVIR
CDEEINNS INCENSED
CDEEINNT INCENTED
INDECENT
CDEEINOR RECOINED
CDEEINOS CODEINES
CDEEINPT INCEPTED
CDEEINRU REINDUCE
CDEEINTU INDUCTEE
CDEEINTV INVECTED
CDEEIOPR RECOPIED
CDEEIORV CODERIVE
DIVORCEE
REVOICED
CDEEIOSS DIOCESES
CDEEIOSV DEVOICES
CDEEIPRR REPRICED
CDEEIPRS PRECISED
CDEEIPRT DECREPIT
DEPICTER
PRECITED
CDEEIPRU PEDICURE
CDEEIPTZ PECTIZED
CDEEIRRS DECRIERS
DESCRIER
CDEEIRRT DIRECTER
REDIRECT
CDEEIRSS DESCRIES

CDEEIRST DESERTIC
DISCREET
DISCRETE
CDEEIRSU DECURIES
CDEEIRSV SCRIEVED
SERVICED
CDEEIRTU DEUTERIC
CDEEISUV SEDUCIVE
CDEEITUV EDUCTIVE
CDEEJKOY JOCKEYED
CDEEKLOR RELOCKED
CDEEKLPS SPECKLED
CDEEKNOR RECKONED
CDEEKOOR RECOOKED
CDEEKOPT POCKETED
CDEEKORR RECORKED
CDEEKORT ROCKETED
CDEEKORV OVERDECK
CDEEKORW ROCKWEED
CDEEKOST SOCKETED
CDEEKPRU PUCKERED
CDEEKRSU SUCKERED
CDEEKRTU TUCKERED
CDEELLOR CORDELLE
CDEELLOT COLLETED
CDEELLPU CUPELLED
CDEELMOW WELCOMED
CDEELNOS ENCLOSED
CDEELNPU PEDUNCLE
CDEELNTY DECENTLY
CDEELOOW LOCOWEED
CDEELOPU DECOUPLE
CDEELORV CLOVERED
CDEELOSS CODELESS
CDEELOST CLOSETED
CDEELPRU PRECLUDE
CDEELPSU DECUPLES
CDEELRTU LECTURED
RELUCTED
CDEELRUX EXCLUDER
CDEELSSU SECLUDES
CDEELSUX EXCLUDES
CDEEMOPR COMPERED
CDEEMOPT COEMPTED
COMPETED
CDEEMORT ECTODERM
CDEEMSTU TUMESCED
CDEENNOR RECONNED
CDEENNOS CONDENSE
CDEENNOU DENOUNCE
ENOUNCED
CDEENNOV CONVENED
CDEENNPY PENDENCY
CDEENNTY TENDENCY
CDEENORR CORNERED
CDEENORS CENSORED
ENCODERS
NECROSED
SECONDER
CDEENORU COENDURE
CDEENOSS SECONDES
CDEENOSY ECDYSONE
CDEENOTU DUECENTO
CDEENOTX COEXTEND
CDEENOVY CONVEYED
CDEENPRU PRUDENCE
CDEENRSU CENSURED
CDEENRUV VERECUND
CDEENRUW UNCREWED
CDEENSST DESCENTS
CDEENSSU CENSUSED
CDEENSTY ENCYSTED
CDEEOOPR COOPERED
CDEEOOTV DOVECOTE
CDEEOPPR COPPERED
CDEEOPRS PRECODES
PROCEEDS
CDEEOPRU RECOUPED
CDEEORRR RECORDER
RERECORD
CDEEORRS RESCORED
CDEEORST CORSETED
ESCORTED
SECTORED
CDEEORSW ESCROWED
CDEEORSY DECOYERS
CDEEORTT COTTERED
DETECTOR
CDEEORTV VECTORED
CDEEOSST CESTODES
COSSETED
CDEEPRRU PRECURED
CDEEPRST SCEPTRED
CDEERRRU RECURRED
CDEERRSU CURSEDER
REDUCERS
CDEERRUV RECURVED
CDEERSSU SEDUCERS
CDEERSUV DECURVES
CDEERTTU CURETTED
CDEERTUV CURVETED
CDEFFINO COFFINED
CDEFFISU SUFFICED
CDEFFLSU SCUFFLED
CDEFFNUU UNCUFFED
CDEFHILN FLINCHED
CDEFHILT FLITCHED
CDEFHIMO CHIEFDOM
CDEFHMOS CHEFDOMS
CDEFIIIL FILICIDE
CDEFIIIT CITIFIED
CDEFIIOR CODIFIER
CDEFIIOS CODIFIES
CDEFIIST DEFICITS
CDEFIITY CITYFIED
CDEFINNO CONFINED
CDEFINNU INFECUND
CDEFINOR CONFIDER
CDEFINOS CONFIDES
CDEFIORY RECODIFY
CDEFKORS DEFROCKS
CDEFLNOU FLOUNCED
CDEFLORY FORCEDLY
CDEFNORU FROUNCED
UNFORCED
CDEFNOSU CONFUSED
CDEFNOTU CONFUTED
CDEFOSSU FOCUSSED
CDEGHLNU GLUNCHED
CDEGHORU GROUCHED
CDEGHRTU GRUTCHED
CDEGIILP DIPLEGIC
CDEGIINX EXCIDING
CDEGIKNS DECKINGS
CDEGINNO ENCODING
CDEGINNS SCENDING
CDEGINOR RECODING
CDEGINOS CODESIGN
COGNISED
COSIGNED
CDEGINOY DECOYING
GYNECOID
CDEGINOZ COGNIZED
CDEGINRU REDUCING
CDEGINRY DECRYING
CDEGINSU SEDUCING
CDEGINSY DYSGENIC
CDEGKOSU GEODUCKS
CDEGKSUW GWEDUCKS
CDEGLNOO COLOGNED
CDEGORSU SCOURGED
SCROUGED
CDEHHNOO HONCHOED
CDEHIILO HELICOID
CDEHIILS CEILIDHS
CDEHIIMO HOMICIDE
CDEHIINO ECHINOID
CDEHIIVV CHIVVIED
CDEHILNR CHILDREN
CDEHILOR CHLORIDE
CDEHILOS CHELOIDS
CDEHILRT ELDRITCH
CDEHIMOR CHROMIDE
CDEHIMOT METHODIC
CDEHIMRS SMIRCHED
CDEHINOS HEDONICS
CDEHINST SNITCHED
CDEHIOOR CHOREOID
CDEHIOSW COWHIDES
CDEHIOTU OUTCHIDE
CDEHIOTY THEODICY
CDEHIRST DITCHERS
CDEHISTT STITCHED
CDEHISTW SWITCHED
CDEHITTW TWITCHED
CDEHKLSU SHELDUCK
CDEHKNOU UNCHOKED
CDEHLOOR COHOLDER
CDEHLOOS SCHOOLED
CDEHLORT CHORTLED
CDEHLOSU SLOUCHED
CDEHMNTU DUTCHMEN
CDEHMOOS SMOOCHED
CDEHMSTU SMUTCHED
CDEHNOOP CHENOPOD
PONCHOED
CDEHOOST COHOSTED
CDEHORSU CHORUSED
CDEHORSW CHOWDERS
COWHERDS
CDEHOSSU HOCUSSED
CDEHOSSW COWSHEDS
CDEHSSSU SCHUSSED
CDEIIILS SILICIDE
CDEIIIMT MITICIDE
CDEIIIOS IDIOCIES
CDEIIIRV VIRICIDE
CDEIIKKS SIDEKICK
CDEIIKLS DISCLIKE
SICKLIED
CDEIIKMM MIMICKED
CDEIIKST DICKIEST
CDEIILMM DILEMMIC
CDEIILMO DOMICILE
CDEIILNN INCLINED
CDEIILNO INDOCILE
CDEIILOT IDIOLECT
CDEIILPS DISCIPLE
CDEIILPU PULICIDE
CDEIILRU RIDICULE
CDEIIMOS DIOECISM
CDEIIMRT DIMETRIC
CDEIIMST MISCITED
CDEIINNT INCIDENT
CDEIINOS DECISION
CDEIINOV INVOICED
CDEIINRT INDICTER
INDIRECT
REINDICT
CDEIINTY CYTIDINE
CDEIIOPR PERIODIC
CDEIIOPS EPISODIC
CDEIIOPT EPIDOTIC
CDEIIOSU DIECIOUS
CDEIIOSV OVICIDES
CDEIIPPT PEPTIDIC
CDEIIPRR CIRRIPED
CDEIIRTU DIURETIC
CDEIIRUV VIRUCIDE
CDEIISSU SUICIDES
CDEIISTT DICTIEST
CDEIITWY CITYWIDE
CDEIJNOO COJOINED
CDEIJSST DISJECTS
CDEIKLNR CRINKLED
CDEIKLNU UNLICKED
CDEIKLOR CORDLIKE
CDEIKLPR PRICKLED
CDEIKLRT TRICKLED
CDEIKLST STICKLED
CDEIKLWY WICKEDLY
CDEIKMSU MUSICKED
CDEIKNPU UNPICKED
CDEIKOST DIESTOCK
CDEIKRRS DERRICKS
CDEIKSTU DUCKIEST
CDEILLOR COLLIDER
CDEILLOS COLLIDES
CDEILLOU LODICULE
CDEILLOY DOCILELY
CDEILLPU PELLUCID
CDEILMNO DOLMENIC
CDEILMOP COMPILED
COMPLIED
CDEILMOY MYCELOID
CDEILMPR CRIMPLED
CDEILMRU DULCIMER
CDEILNOS INCLOSED
CDEILNOU NUCLEOID
UNCOILED
UNDOCILE
CDEILNRY CYLINDER
CDEILNSU INCLUDES
NUCLIDES
UNSLICED
CDEILOPU CLUPEOID
UPCOILED
CDEILORS SCLEROID
CDEILORU CLOUDIER
CDEILORV COVERLID
CDEILOSS DISCLOSE
CDEILPPR CRIPPLED
CDEILPSU CLUPEIDS
CDEILRTY DIRECTLY
CDEILSXY DYSLEXIC
CDEILTTU CUITTLED
CDEIMMOX COMMIXED
CDEIMORT MORTICED
CDEIMOSS MISCODES
CDEIMOST DEMOTICS
DOMESTIC
CDEIMPRS SCRIMPED
CDEINNOU UNCOINED
CDEINNOV CONNIVED
CDEINOOZ ENDOZOIC
CDEINORS CONSIDER
CDEINORT CENTROID
DOCTRINE
CDEINORU DECURION
CDEINORV CODRIVEN
CDEINOTU EDUCTION
CDEINOUV UNVOICED
CDEINPRS PRESCIND
CDEINPRU UNPRICED
CDEINPSY DYSPNEIC
CDEINRRU INCURRED
CDEINRSS DISCERNS
RESCINDS
CDEINRSU INDUCERS
CDEINRTU REINDUCT
CDEINRUV INCURVED
CDEINSSX EXSCINDS
CDEINSTY SYNDETIC
CDEIOORS CORODIES
CDEIOORT COEDITOR
CDEIOPRS PERCOIDS
CDEIOPRT DEPICTOR
CDEIOPST DESPOTIC
CDEIOPTY COPYEDIT
CDEIORRT CREDITOR
DIRECTOR
CDEIORRV CODRIVER
DIVORCER
CDEIORST CORDITES
CDEIORSV CODRIVES
DISCOVER
DIVORCES
CDEIORSW CROWDIES
CDEIORTU OUTCRIED
CDEIOSST CESTOIDS
CDEIPRST PREDICTS
SCRIPTED
CDEIPRTU PICTURED
CDEIPSST DISCEPTS
CDEIPSSU CUSPIDES
CDEIRRSU SCURRIED
CDEIRSTU CRUDITES
CURDIEST
CURTSIED
CDEIRSTV VERDICTS
CDEISSST DISSECTS
CDEISSSU DISCUSES
CDEJNORU CONJURED
CDEKKLNU KNUCKLED
CDEKLMOR CLERKDOM
CDEKLNOU UNLOCKED
CDEKLOSW WEDLOCKS
CDEKLRTU TRUCKLED
CDEKNOOU UNCOOKED
CDEKNOOV CONVOKED
CDEKNORS DORNECKS
CDEKNORU UNCORKED
CDEKNSSU SUNDECKS
CDEKNTUU UNTUCKED
CDEKOPSY COPYDESK
CDELLOOP CLODPOLE
CDELLORS SCROLLED
CDELLORU COLLUDER
CDELLOSU COLLUDES
CDELLOTU CLOUDLET
CDELLTUY DULCETLY
CDELMNOO MONOCLED
CDELMNOU COLUMNED
CDELMPRU CRUMPLED
CDELNOOR CONDOLER
CDELNOOS CONDOLES
CONSOLED
CDELNOOU UNCOOLED
CDELNOSS COLDNESS
CDELNOSU UNCLOSED
CDELNOSY CONDYLES
SECONDLY
CDELNOUY UNCLOYED
CDELNRUU UNCURLED
CDELNSUY SECUNDLY
CDELOORS DECOLORS
CDELOORU COLOURED
DECOLOUR
CDELOORV OVERCOLD
CDELOOTT DOLCETTO
CDELOPTU OCTUPLED
CDELORSS CORDLESS
SCOLDERS
CDELORSU CLOSURED
CDELORSW CLOWDERS
CDELORTU CLOTURED
CDELOSTU COULDEST
CDELPRSU SCRUPLED
CDELPRUU UPCURLED
CDELPSTU SCULPTED
CDELRRSU CURDLERS
CDELRSUY CURSEDLY
CDELRTUU CULTURED
CDELRUVY CURVEDLY
CDELSSTU DUCTLESS
CDELSSUY CUSSEDLY
CDELSTTU SCUTTLED
CDELSTUU DUCTULES
CDEMMNOS COMMENDS
CDEMMNOU COMMUNED
CDEMMOOS COMMODES
CDEMMOOV COMMOVED
CDEMMOTU COMMUTED
CDEMMRSU SCRUMMED
CDEMNNOS CONDEMNS
CDEMNOOW COMEDOWN
DOWNCOME
CDEMNOPS COMPENDS
CDEMNOSU CONSUMED
CDEMNOTU DOCUMENT
CDEMNSUU SECUNDUM
CDEMOOPS COMPOSED
CDEMOPTU COMPUTED
CDEMORSU DECORUMS
CDEMOSTU COSTUMED
CDENNOOR CONDONER
CDENNOOS CONDONES
CDENNOOT CONNOTED
CDENNOST CONTENDS
CDENOORS CONDORES
CDENOORT CREODONT
CDENOOTT COTTONED
CDENOOVY CONVOYED
CDENORSU CRUNODES
CDENORSW DECROWNS
CDENORTU CORNUTED
TROUNCED
CDENOSSY ECDYSONS
CDENOSTU CONTUSED
CDENRSUU UNCURSED
CDENRTUU UNDERCUT
CDEOOPPS COPEPODS
CDEOOPRS SCROOPED
CDEOOPST POSTCODE
CDEOORRS CORRODES
CDEOORSU DECOROUS
CDEOORSV VOCODERS
CDEOOSTV DOVECOTS
CDEOPRRU PROCURED
PRODUCER
CDEOPRSU PRODUCES
CDEORRSW CROWDERS
CDEORRTU REDUCTOR
CDEORSSW SCOWDERS
CDEORSTU EDUCTORS
CDEORSUU DOUCEURS
CDEOSSTU CUSTODES
CDEPRSTY DECRYPTS
CDEPRUUV UPCURVED
CDERSTTU DESTRUCT
CDFIILSU FLUIDICS
CDFIKORS DISFROCK
CDFNNOOU CONFOUND
CDFNOOSU COFOUNDS
CDGHIILN CHILDING
CDGHIILO CHILIDOG
CDGHIINT DITCHING
CDGHILOS GLOCHIDS
CDGHINOR CHORDING
CDGHINOU DOUCHING
CDGIINNU INDUCING
CDGIINOS DISCOING
CDGIKLNU DUCKLING
CDGIKLOR GRIDLOCK
CDGILNOS CODLINGS
LINGCODS
SCOLDING
CDGILNOU CLOUDING
CDGILNRU CURDLING
CDGINORS CORDINGS
CDGINORW CROWDING
CDGINSTU DUCTINGS
CDHHIILS CHILDISH
CDHIIOOR CHORIOID
CDHIIORT HIDROTIC
TRICHOID
CDHIIOSZ SCHIZOID
CDHIISST DISTICHS
CDHILOOP CHILOPOD
CDHILORS CHLORIDS
CDHINORY HYDRONIC
CDHIOORS CHOROIDS
CDHIOORT TROCHOID
CDHIOPRW WHIPCORD
CDHIOPRY HYDROPIC
CDHIPSTY DIPTYCHS
CDHIRSTY CHYTRIDS
CDHLOOPY COPYHOLD
CDHOORRU UROCHORD
CDIIIMNS MINIDISC
CDIIIMNU INDICIUM
CDIIINSV INVISCID
CDIIIORT DIORITIC
CDIIKMNO DOMINICK
CDIIKPST DIPSTICK
CDIILMOS DOMICILS
CDIILOPP DIPLOPIC
CDIILOTY DOCILITY
CDIILSVY VISCIDLY
CDIILTUY LUCIDITY
CDIIMNOU CONIDIUM
MUCINOID
ONCIDIUM
CDIIMTUY MUCIDITY
CDIINORS CRINOIDS
CDIINORT INDICTOR
CDIINOST DICTIONS
CDIINOSV VIDICONS
CDIINPRY CYPRINID
CDIINPTU PUNDITIC
CDIINSTT DISTINCT
CDIIOOSU DIOICOUS
CDIIOPRT DIOPTRIC
DIPROTIC
TRIPODIC
CDIIORSU SCIUROID
CDIIOSSS CISSOIDS
CDIIPTUY CUPIDITY
CDIIRSSU SCIURIDS
CDIIRSTT DISTRICT
CDIJNSTU DISJUNCT
CDIKKOPR DROPKICK
CDIKNNSU NUDNICKS
CDIKNORS DORNICKS
CDIKNOSW WINDSOCK
CDIKNOTW DOWNTICK
CDIKNPSU DUCKPINS
CDILLOOS COLLOIDS
CDILLOUY CLOUDILY
CDILMSTU MIDCULTS
CDILOOPS PODSOLIC
CDILOOPZ PODZOLIC
CDILOORS DISCOLOR
CDILOORT LORDOTIC
CDILOOTY COTYLOID
CDILOSTY DICOTYLS
CDIMMOSU MODICUMS
CDIMOORT MICRODOT
CDINNQUU QUIDNUNC
CDINOOOR CORONOID
CDINOOTU NOCTUOID
CDINOPSY DYSPNOIC
CDINORSW DISCROWN
CDINORTU INDUCTOR
CDINOSTU CONDUITS
DISCOUNT
NOCTUIDS
CDINOSTY DYSTONIC
CDIOOPRS PROSODIC
CDIOORRR CORRIDOR
CDIOPRRS RIPCORDS
CDIOPRSU CUSPIDOR
CDIOSSTY CYSTOIDS
CDIOSTUV OVIDUCTS
CDJLNOUY JOCUNDLY
CDKLNOOW LOCKDOWN
CDKMORSU MUDROCKS
CDKNOORS DORNOCKS
CDKOOORW CORKWOOD
CDKORTUW DUCTWORK
CDLLLOOP CLODPOLL
CDLNOOOW COOLDOWN
CDLNOSUU UNCLOUDS
CDLNOUUY UNCLOUDY
CDLOOPSY LYCOPODS
CDLOORTY DOCTORLY
CDLOOSTU OUTSCOLD
CDMNOOPU COMPOUND
CDMNORUU CORUNDUM
CDNNOOOT CONODONT
CDNOSTUW CUTDOWNS
CDOOOPST OCTOPODS
CDOOPSST POSTDOCS
CDOORRUY CORDUROY
CDOORTUW OUTCROWD
CDOOSTUW WOODCUTS
CDOPRSTU PRODUCTS
CDORSSUW CUSSWORD
CEEEEIPY EYEPIECE
CEEEEJRT REJECTEE
CEEEELST ELECTEES
SELECTEE
CEEEFFRT EFFECTER
CEEEFHLS FLEECHES
CEEEFILR FLEECIER
CEEEFLRS FLEECERS

CEEEFNOR CONFEREE
CEEEFNRS REFENCES
CEEEGIMN EMCEEING
CEEEGINX EXIGENCE
CEEEGITX EXEGETIC
CEEEGMNR MERGENCE
CEEEGNRV VERGENCE
CEEEHIKR CHEEKIER
CEEEHIRR CHEERIER
REECHIER
CEEEHIRS CHEESIER
CEEEHLLS ECHELLES
CEEEHORS REECHOES
CEEEHPRS CHEEPERS
CEEEHPSS SPEECHES
CEEEHRRS CHEERERS
CEEEHRSS CREESHES
CEEEHRSW ESCHEWER
CEEEIJTV EJECTIVE
CEEEILNN LENIENCE
CEEEILNS LICENSEE
CEEEILRS CELERIES
CEEEILRT ERECTILE
CEEEILTV CLEVEITE
ELECTIVE
CEEEIMNN EMINENCE
CEEEIMRR REREMICE
CEEEINNT ENCEINTE
CEEEINPS EPICENES
CEEEIOPT TOEPIECE
CEEEIPRR CREEPIER
CEEEIPRS CREEPIES
CEEEIPRV PERCEIVE
CEEEIRRV RECEIVER
CEEEIRSV RECEIVES
CEEEIRSX EXERCISE
CEEEIRTV ERECTIVE
CEEEISSS ECESISES
CEEEISTV EVICTEES
CEEEJRRT REJECTER
CEEEJRST REEJECTS
CEEELLNR CRENELLE
CEEELOPR OPERCELE
CEEELOSS COLESSEE
CEEELPRT PREELECT
CEEELRRV CLEVERER
CEEELRST REELECTS
RESELECT
CEEELRTT ELECTRET
TERCELET
CEEELSST CELESTES
CEEEMNRT CEMENTER
CEREMENT
RECEMENT
CEEEMORT ECTOMERE
CEEEMRTY CEMETERY
CEEENNPT TENPENCE
CEEENNST SENTENCE
CEEENPRS PRESENCE
CEEENPRT PRETENCE
CEEENQSU SEQUENCE
CEEENRRS RESCREEN
SCREENER
CEEENRRT RECENTER
CEEENSSS ESSENCES
CEEENSST CENTESES
CEEEPRRS CREEPERS
CEEEPRRT PREERECT
CEEEPRTX EXPECTER
CEEERRST ERECTERS
REERECTS
SECRETER
CEEERRSU RESECURE
CEEERRTX EXCRETER
CEEERSSS RECESSES
CEEERSST SECRETES
SESTERCE
CEEERSSU CEREUSES
CEEERSTX EXCRETES
CEEERTUX EXECUTER
CEEESSSX EXCESSES
CEEESTUX EXECUTES
CEEFFNOS OFFENCES
CEEFFORT EFFECTOR
CEEFGILN FLEECING
CEEFHIKR KERCHIEF
CEEFHIST CHIEFEST
FETICHES
CEEFHKLU CHEEKFUL
CEEFHLNS FLENCHES
CEEFHLRT FLETCHER
CEEFHLRU CHEERFUL
CEEFHLST FLETCHES
CEEFHNRS FRENCHES
CEEFHORU FOURCHEE
CEEFHRST FETCHERS
CEEFILLY FLEECILY
CEEFILRY FIERCELY
CEEFINRT FRENETIC
INFECTER
REINFECT
CEEFIRST FIERCEST
CEEFKLRS FRECKLES
CEEFKLSS FECKLESS
CEEFLNOR FLORENCE
CEEFLNTU FECULENT
CEEFLRST REFLECTS
CEEFNNSU UNFENCES
CEEFNORR CONFRERE
ENFORCER
RECONFER
CEEFNORS ENFORCES
CEEFNORW FENCEROW
CEEFNOTU OUTFENCE
CEEFNRVY FERVENCY
CEEFOPRR PERFORCE
CEEFOPRT PERFECTO
CEEFORRS FRESCOER
CEEFORSS FRESCOES
CEEFORTW CROWFEET
CEEFPRST PERFECTS
PREFECTS
CEEGHIKN CHEEKING
CEEGHILN LEECHING
CEEGHINP CHEEPING
CEEGHINR CHEERING
CEEGHINS CHEESING
CEEGHLOW COGWHEEL
CEEGIINP EPIGENIC
CEEGIJNT EJECTING
CEEGIKLN CLEEKING
CEEGILNR CREELING
CEEGILNT ELECTING
CEEGILOT ECLOGITE
CEEGILRS CLERGIES
CEEGINOO COOEEING
CEEGINOR EROGENIC
CEEGINPR CREEPING
CEEGINRS GENERICS
CEEGINRT ERECTING
GENTRICE
CEEGINST GENETICS
CEEGINSU EUGENICS
CEEGINXY EXIGENCY
CEEGIORX EXOERGIC
CEEGIRSZ GRECIZES
CEEGLLOR COLLEGER
CEEGLLOS COLLEGES
CEEGLNST NEGLECTS
CEEGLOSU ECLOGUES
CEEGMNOY CYMOGENE
CEEGNNOO ONCOGENE
CEEGNNOR CONGENER
CEEGNORV CONVERGE
CEEGORST CORTEGES
CEEHHIRS CHESHIRE
CEEHHMNN HENCHMEN
CEEHIITZ ETHICIZE
CEEHIKLY CHEEKILY
CEEHIKMS KIMCHEES
CEEHILLN CHENILLE
CEEHILRS CHISELER
SCHLIERE
CEEHILRW CLERIHEW
CEEHILRY CHEERILY
CEEHILSV VEHICLES
CEEHILSY CHEESILY
CEEHIMRS CHIMERES
CEEHIMRT HERMETIC
CEEHIMSS CHEMISES
CEEHINOR COINHERE
CEEHINPR ENCIPHER
CEEHINPT PHENETIC
CEEHINPU EUPHENIC
CEEHINRR ENRICHER
CEEHINRS ENRICHES
CEEHINST SITHENCE
CEEHINTT ENTHETIC
CEEHIORS CHEERIOS
CEEHIOSU ICEHOUSE
CEEHIOSV COHESIVE
CEEHIPRR CIPHERER
CEEHIPRT HERPETIC
CEEHIRRS CHERRIES
CEEHIRRT CHERTIER
CEEHIRST CHESTIER
HERETICS
CEEHIRTT TETCHIER
CEEHISSV SEVICHES
CEEHISTT ESTHETIC
TECHIEST
CEEHISTW CHEWIEST
CEEHKLPR KREPLECH
CEEHKLRS HECKLERS
CEEHKNPS HENPECKS
CEEHKRST RESKETCH
SKETCHER
CEEHKRTV KVETCHER
CEEHKSST SKETCHES
CEEHKSTV KVETCHES
CEEHLMOO HEMOCOEL
CEEHLMSZ SCHMELZE
CEEHLNOO HOLOCENE
CEEHLNOS ECHELONS
CEEHLNPS PLENCHES
CEEHLNPU PENUCHLE
CEEHLNSU ELENCHUS
CEEHLORT RECLOTHE
CEEHLOSS ECHOLESS
CEEHLRSU HERCULES
CEEHLRSW WELCHERS
CEEHMNNS MENSCHEN
CEEHMNOR CHOREMEN
CEEHMNSS CHESSMEN
MENSCHES
CEEHMORT COMETHER
CEEHMOTY HEMOCYTE
CEEHMRSS SCHEMERS
SCHMEERS
CEEHNNRT ENTRENCH
CEEHNOPS PENOCHES
CEEHNORS RECHOSEN
CEEHNORT COHERENT
CEEHNORV CHEVERON
CEEHNPSU PENUCHES
CEEHNQRU QUENCHER
CEEHNQSU QUENCHES
CEEHNRRT RETRENCH
TRENCHER
CEEHNRRW WRENCHER
CEEHNRST TRENCHES
CEEHNRSW WENCHERS
WRENCHES
CEEHNSST STENCHES
CEEHNSTU CHUTNEES
CEEHOOPR POECHORE
CEEHOORS RECHOOSE
CEEHOPRS PRECHOSE
CEEHOPRY CORYPHEE
CEEHOPST SHEEPCOT
CEEHORRS COHERERS
CEEHORRT TORCHERE
CEEHORST TROCHEES
CEEHOSUV VOUCHEES
CEEHPRRS PERCHERS
CEEHQRSU CHEQUERS
CEEHRSTV CHEVRETS
CEEHRSTW WRETCHES
CEEIIKLP EPICLIKE
CEEIIMPR EPIMERIC
CEEIIMRT EREMITIC
CEEIINRT REINCITE
CEEIINST NICETIES
CEEIINVV EVINCIVE
CEEIJNOT EJECTION
CEEIJNRT REINJECT
CEEIJORR REJOICER
CEEIJORS REJOICES
CEEIJRUV VERJUICE
CEEIKKLN NECKLIKE
CEEIKKLO COKELIKE
CEEIKLMU LEUKEMIC
CEEIKLNN NECKLINE
CEEIKLPR PICKEREL
CEEIKNRS SICKENER
CEEIKNST NECKTIES
CEEIKPRS PICKEERS
CEEIKPRT PICKETER
CEEIKPST PECKIEST
CEEILLLP PELLICLE
CEEILLMS MICELLES
CEEILLNT LENTICEL
CEEILMOR COMELIER
CEEILMPS SEMPLICE
CEEILNNY LENIENCY
CEEILNOP PLIOCENE
CEEILNOS CINEOLES
CEEILNOT ELECTION
CEEILNOV VIOLENCE
CEEILNPR PENCILER
CEEILNPU PULICENE
CEEILNRR RECLINER
CEEILNRS LICENSER
RECLINES
SILENCER
CEEILNRV VERNICLE
CEEILNSS LICENSES
SILENCES
CEEILNST CENTILES
CEEILNSU LEUCINES
CEEILORR RECOILER
CEEILORS CREOLISE
CEEILORZ CREOLIZE
CEEILOSS SOLECISE
CEEILOSZ SOLECIZE
CEEILPRS ECLIPSER
PRESLICE
RESPLICE
CEEILPRY CREEPILY
CEEILPSS ECLIPSES
CEEILPSX EXCIPLES
CEEILRST RETICLES
SCLERITE
TIERCELS
TRISCELE
CEEILRSV VERSICLE
CEEILRTU RETICULE
CEEILRTY CELERITY
CEEILSSV CLEVISES
VESICLES
VICELESS
CEEILSTT TELESTIC
TESTICLE
CEEILSTU LEUCITES
CEEIMMPY EMPYEMIC
CEEIMMRS MESMERIC
CEEIMMST MEMETICS
CEEIMNNY EMINENCY
CEEIMNPS SPECIMEN
CEEIMNST CENTIMES
TENESMIC
CEEIMORT METEORIC
CEEIMRSX EXCIMERS
CEEIMSTT SMECTITE
CEEINNOP PINECONE
CEEINNOT NEOTENIC
CEEINNRT INCENTER
CEEINNSS INCENSES
NICENESS
CEEINNST NESCIENT
CEEINOPU EUPNOEIC
CEEINORT ERECTION
NEOTERIC
CEEINORV OVERNICE
CEEINORX EXOCRINE
CEEINOSS SENECIOS
CEEINOST SEICENTO
CEEINOTV EVECTION
CEEINPRT PRENTICE
TERPENIC
CEEINPST PECTINES
CEEINPSX SIXPENCE
CEEINQRU QUERCINE
CEEINRRS SINCERER
CEEINRST ENTERICS
ENTICERS
SECRETIN
CEEINRSU INSECURE
SINECURE
CEEINRTT RETICENT
CEEINRTU CEINTURE
ENURETIC
CEEINSST CENTESIS
CEEINSTY CYSTEINE
CEEIOPPR PERICOPE
CEEIOPPS EPISCOPE
CEEIOPRS RECOPIES
CEEIOPST PICOTEES
CEEIORST COTERIES
ESOTERIC
CEEIORSV REVOICES
CEEIORSX EXORCISE
CEEIORTV ORECTIVE
CEEIORTX EXOTERIC
CEEIORXZ EXORCIZE
CEEIOSST COESITES
CEEIPPRR PREPRICE
CEEIPPRS PRECIPES
CEEIPPTU EUPEPTIC
CEEIPRRS PIERCERS
PRECISER
REPRICES
CEEIPRSS PRECISES
CEEIPRST CREPIEST
RECEIPTS
CEEIPRSU EPICURES
CEEIPRUX PRECIEUX
CEEIPSTZ PECTIZES
CEEIRRST RECITERS
CEEIRRSV SERVICER
CEEIRRSW SCREWIER
CEEIRRTU URETERIC
CEEIRSSV SCRIEVES
SERVICES
CEEIRSTU CERUSITE
CUTESIER
EUCRITES
CEEIRSTV VERTICES
CEEIRSTX EXCITERS
CEEIRSVX CERVIXES
CEEISTTT TECTITES
CEEJKOTT JOCKETTE
CEEJORRT REJECTOR
CEEJORST EJECTORS
CEEKKNOS KNEESOCK
CEEKLNPU PENUCKLE
CEEKLNSS NECKLESS
CEEKLPSS SPECKLES
CEEKLRSS RECKLESS
CEEKNORR RECKONER
CEEKOPRT POCKETER
CEEKOPRX OXPECKER
CEEKORRT ROCKETER
CEEKOSSY SOCKEYES
CEEKPRRU PUCKERER
CEEKRRSW WRECKERS
CEELLLSU CELLULES
CEELLMOU MOLECULE
CEELLNOS COLLEENS
CEELLNOU NUCLEOLE
CEELLPRU CUPELLER
CEELLRRU CRUELLER
CEELLRVY CLEVERLY
CEELLSSU CLUELESS
CEELLSTY SELECTLY
CEELMOOS COELOMES
CEELMOPT COMPLETE
CEELMORW WELCOMER
CEELMOST TELECOMS
CEELMOSW WELCOMES
CEELMRTU ELECTRUM
CEELNNOP PENONCEL
CEELNNOT NONELECT
CEELNOPU OPULENCE
CEELNOPY LYCOPENE
CEELNORS ENCLOSER
ENSORCEL
CEELNORT ELECTRON
CEELNOSS ENCLOSES
CEELNPTU CENTUPLE
CEELNRST LECTERNS
CEELNRSU LUCERNES
CEELNRTU RELUCENT
CEELNRTY RECENTLY
CEELNSTU ESCULENT
CEELOOVV COEVOLVE
CEELOPRU OPERCULE
RECOUPLE
CEELORSS CORELESS
SCLEROSE
CEELORST CORSELET
ELECTORS
ELECTROS
SELECTOR
CEELORTV COVERLET
CEELOSSU COLEUSES
CEELPRST PRELECTS
CEELPRSU CUPELERS
CEELRRTU LECTURER
CEELRSSU CURELESS
RECLUSES
CEELRSSW CREWLESS
CEELRSTU CRUELEST
LECTURES
CEELRSTY SECRETLY
CEELRSUY SECURELY
CEELSTTU LETTUCES
CEEMMNTU CEMENTUM
CEEMNORW NEWCOMER
CEEMNORY CEREMONY
CEEMNOYZ COENZYME
CEEMNRSU CERUMENS
CEEMOORV OVERCOME
CEEMOPRS COMPEERS
COMPERES
CEEMOPST COMPETES
CEEMSSTU TUMESCES
CEENNOOS CONENOSE
CEENNORS ONSCREEN
CEENNORT CRETONNE
CEENNORU RENOUNCE
CEENNORV CONVENER
CEENNOST CENTONES
CEENNOSU ENOUNCES
CEENNOSV CONVENES
CEENNRST CENTNERS
CEENOOST ECOTONES
CEENOPST POTENCES
CEENOPTW TWOPENCE
CEENORRS RECENSOR
CEENORSS NECROSES
CEENORSU COENURES
CEENORSV CONSERVE
CONVERSE
CEENORSZ COZENERS
CEENORTT TRECENTO
CEENORVY CONVEYER
RECONVEY
CEENOSVX CONVEXES
CEENPPTU TUPPENCE
CEENPRSS SPENCERS
CEENPRST PERCENTS
PRECENTS
CEENQSUY SEQUENCY
CEENRRSU CENSURER
CEENRSSU CENSURES
CEENSSSU CENSUSES
CEENSSTU CUTENESS
CEEOORST CREOSOTE
CEEOPRRS PRESCORE
CEEOPRRT RECEPTOR
CEEOPRTY CEROTYPE
CEEOPSTY ECOTYPES
CEEOQTTU COQUETTE
CEEORRRS SORCERER
CEEORRSS RESCORES
CEEORRST ERECTORS
SECRETOR
CEEORRSU RECOURSE
RESOURCE
CEEORRSV COVERERS
RECOVERS
CEEORRUV OVERCURE
CEEORRVY RECOVERY
CEEORSTV COVETERS
CEEORSTX COEXERTS
CORTEXES
CEEORTTV CORVETTE
CEEORTUX EXECUTOR
CEEOSTTT OCTETTES
CEEPPRST PERCEPTS
PRECEPTS
CEEPPRSU PREPUCES
CEEPRRSU PRECURES
CEEPRSST RESPECTS
SCEPTERS
SCEPTRES
SPECTERS
SPECTRES
CEEPRSSY CYPRESES
CEEPRSTX EXCERPTS
CEERRSSU RECUSERS
SECURERS
CEERRSSW SCREWERS
CEERRSUV RECURVES
CEERSSST CRESSETS
CEERSSTU SECUREST
CEERSSTW SETSCREW
CEERSSUX EXCUSERS
CEERSTTU CURETTES
CEESSSTU CESTUSES
CEESTTUV CUVETTES
CEFFGHIN CHEFFING
CEFFHIRU CHUFFIER
CEFFHSTU CHUFFEST
CEFFIILR CLIFFIER
CEFFIORS OFFICERS
CEFFIORU COIFFEUR
COIFFURE
CEFFIRSU SUFFICER
CEFFISSU SUFFICES
CEFFLORU FORCEFUL
CEFFLRSU SCUFFLER
CEFFLSSU CUFFLESS
SCUFFLES
CEFFORSS SCOFFERS
CEFFORST COFFRETS
CEFFRSSU SCUFFERS
CEFGHINT FETCHING
CEFGIKLN FLECKING
CEFGILNT CLEFTING
CEFGINNS FENCINGS
CEFHIIMS MISCHIEF
CEFHILNR FLINCHER
CEFHILNS FLINCHES
CEFHILRS FILCHERS
CEFHILRT FLICHTER
CEFHILST FLITCHES
CEFHINSU FUCHSINE
CEFHISTT FITCHETS
CEFHISTW FITCHEWS
CEFHLSSY FLYSCHES
CEFHLSTU CHESTFUL
CEFIIIST CITIFIES
CEFIILLM MELLIFIC
CEFIILNO OLEFINIC

CEFIILST FELSITIC
CEFIILTY FELICITY
CEFIIORS ORIFICES
CEFIIRRT FERRITIC
TERRIFIC
CEFIKLOR FIRELOCK
FLOCKIER
CEFIKLRS FLICKERS
CEFIKLRY FLICKERY
CEFIKLST FICKLEST
CEFILLLO FOLLICLE
CEFILMRU MERCIFUL
CEFILNOT FLECTION
CEFILNST INFLECTS
CEFILNSU FUNICLES
CEFILOUV VOICEFUL
CEFILRSU FLUERICS
LUCIFERS
CEFIMOST COMFIEST
CEFINNOR CONFINER
CEFINNOS CONFINES
CEFINORS COINFERS
CONIFERS
FORENSIC
FORNICES
CEFINORT INFECTOR
CEFINOTT CONFETTI
CEFIOPRS FORCIPES
CEFIORTY FEROCITY
CEFIRRSU SCURFIER
CEFKLLOS ELFLOCKS
CEFKLOOR FORELOCK
CEFKLOST FETLOCKS
CEFKLPSY FLYSPECK
CEFKLRUW WRECKFUL
CEFLNOSU FLOUNCES
CEFLNRUU FURUNCLE
CEFLOPTY COPYLEFT
CEFMORSY COMFREYS
CEFNOOTT CONFETTO
CEFNORSU FROUNCES
CEFNORTU CONFUTER
CEFNOSSU CONFUSES
CEFNOSTU CONFUTES
CEFOORST SOFTCORE
CEFOPRSU PREFOCUS
CEFORRST CROFTERS
CEFORSSU FOCUSERS
CEFORSTU FRUCTOSE
CEFOSSSU FOCUSSES
CEGGHIRS CHIGGERS
CEGGHRSU CHUGGERS
CEGGILOO GEOLOGIC
CEGGILOR CLOGGIER
CEGGIORS GEORGICS
CEGGLNOY GLYCOGEN
CEGGLORS CLOGGERS
CEGHIINY HYGIENIC
CEGHIKLN HECKLING
CEGHILNT LETCHING
CEGHILNW WELCHING
CEGHILST GLITCHES
CEGHIMNS SCHEMING
CEGHINNW WENCHING
CEGHINOR COHERING
OCHERING
CEGHINPR PERCHING
CEGHINRS GRINCHES
CEGHINRT RETCHING
CEGHINRU EUCHRING
CEGHINST ETCHINGS
CEGHINVY CHEVYING
CEGHIRTU THEURGIC
CEGHLNSU GLUNCHES
CEGHMRUY CHEMURGY
CEGHNORS GROSCHEN
CEGHORSU CHOREGUS
COUGHERS
GROUCHES
CEGHRSTU GRUTCHES
CEGIILNR CLINGIER
CEGIILNS CEILINGS
CEGIILOS LOGICISE
CEGIILOZ LOGICIZE
CEGIINNT ENTICING
CEGIINNV EVINCING
CEGIINOP EPIGONIC
CEGIINOS ISOGENIC
CEGIINPR PIERCING
CEGIINPS PIECINGS
CEGIINRT RECITING
CEGIINSS GNEISSIC
CEGIINSX EXCISING
CEGIINTV EVICTING
CEGIINTX EXCITING
CEGIIOST EGOISTIC
CEGIKKLN KECKLING
CEGIKLNR CLERKING
CEGIKNNR RINGNECK
CEGIKNNS NECKINGS
CEGIKNPS SPECKING
CEGIKNRW WRECKING
CEGILMNO COMINGLE
CEGILNOO NEOLOGIC
CEGILNPU CUPELING
CEGILNRS CLINGERS
CRINGLES
CEGILNRU ULCERING
CEGILNRY GLYCERIN
CEGILNSY GLYCINES
CEGILNTU CULTIGEN
CEGIMNOS GENOMICS
CEGIMNOY MYOGENIC
CEGIMNUY GYNECIUM
CEGINNOR ENCORING
CEGINNOZ COZENING
CEGINNRT CENTRING
CEGINNST SCENTING
CEGINNSY ENSIGNCY
SYNGENIC
CEGINOOP GEOPONIC
CEGINOOR OROGENIC
CEGINOOY COOEYING
CEGINOOZ ZOOGENIC
CEGINOPY PYOGENIC
CEGINORS COREIGNS
COSIGNER
CEGINORT GERONTIC
CEGINORV COVERING
CEGINORW COWERING
CEGINORZ COGNIZER
CEGINOSS COGNISES
CEGINOST ESCOTING
CEGINOSZ COGNIZES
CEGINOTV COVETING
CEGINOXY OXYGENIC
CEGINRRS CRINGERS
CEGINRST CRESTING
CEGINRSU RECUSING
RESCUING
SECURING
CEGINRSW SCREWING
CEGINRSY SYNERGIC
CEGINRTU ERUCTING
CEGINSUX EXCUSING
CEGKLNNO LONGNECK
CEGLLOOU COLLOGUE
CEGLLORY GLYCEROL
CEGLLRYY GLYCERYL
CEGLNOOS COLOGNES
CEGLNOTY COGENTLY
CEGLOOOY OECOLOGY
CEGLOOTY CETOLOGY
CEGLOSSU GLUCOSES
CEGMNNOO COGNOMEN
CEGNNPUY PUNGENCY
CEGNOOTY GONOCYTE
CEGNORSS CONGRESS
CEGNORSU SCROUNGE
CEGNORSY CRYOGENS
CEGNORYY CRYOGENY
CEGNOSST CONGESTS
CEGNOTYY CYTOGENY
CEGNRTUY TURGENCY
CEGOORSS SCROOGES
CEGORRSU SCOURGER
CEGORSSU SCOURGES
SCROUGES
CEHHINPY HYPHENIC
CEHHIOOS HOOCHIES
CEHHIRST HITCHERS
CEHHOOSS COHOSHES
CEHHOOST HOOTCHES
CEHHOPTY HYPOTHEC
CEHHOSSU CHOUSHES
CEHIIKNR CHINKIER
CEHIILLR CHILLIER
CEHIILLS CHILLIES
CEHIILMT LITHEMIC
CEHIILNN LICHENIN
CEHIILNT LECITHIN
CEHIILOT EOLITHIC
CEHIILTY HELICITY
CEHIIMOS ISOCHEIM
ISOCHIME
CEHIIMPT MEPHITIC
CEHIIMRT HERMITIC
CEHIINST ICHNITES
CEHIIPPR CHIPPIER
CEHIIPPS CHIPPIES
CEHIIPRR CHIRPIER
CEHIIPRT PITCHIER
CEHIIRST CHRISTIE
CEHIIRSZ SCHIZIER
CEHIIRTT TRICHITE
CEHIIRTW WITCHIER
CEHIISTT CHITTIES
ETHICIST
ITCHIEST
THEISTIC
CEHIISVV CHIVVIES
CEHIKLPT KLEPHTIC
CEHIKLRS CLERKISH
CEHIKLSU SUCHLIKE
CEHIKMOS HOMESICK
CEHIKNRU CHUNKIER
CEHIKNST KITCHENS
THICKENS
CEHIKNSW CHEWINKS
CEHIKOST CHOKIEST
CEHIKRSS KIRSCHES
SHICKERS
CEHIKRST CHIRKEST
CEHIKRSW WHICKERS
CEHIKSST KITSCHES
CEHIKSTT THICKEST
THICKETS
THICKSET
CEHIKTTY THICKETY
CEHILLPR PRECHILL
CEHILLRS CHILLERS
SCHILLER
CEHILLST CHILLEST
CEHILMSY CHIMLEYS
CEHILMTY METHYLIC
CEHILNOP PHENOLIC
PINOCHLE
CEHILNOR CHLORINE
CEHILNOS CHOLINES
HELICONS
CEHILNPY PHENYLIC
CEHILNSS CHINLESS
CEHILOPT CHIPOTLE
HELICOPT
CEHILORS CEORLISH
CEHILORT CHLORITE
CLOTHIER
CEHILPTY PHYLETIC
CEHILRSV CHERVILS
CEHILSTY CHESTILY
LECYTHIS
CEHILTTY TETCHILY
CEHIMMRU CHUMMIER
CEHIMMSS CHEMISMS
CEHIMNOP PHONEMIC
CEHIMNPT PITCHMEN
CEHIMNSU MUNCHIES
CEHIMNSY CHIMNEYS
CEHIMOOT HOMEOTIC
CEHIMORR CHROMIER
CEHIMORT CHROMITE
TRICHOME
CEHIMORZ CHROMIZE
CEHIMOSS ECHOISMS
MISCHOSE
CEHIMOTW CHOWTIME
CEHIMRSS SMIRCHES
CEHIMSST CHEMISTS
CEHINNOS CHINONES
CEHINNRT INTRENCH
CEHINOOS COHESION
CEHINOPR PROCHEIN
CEHINOPS CHOPINES
CEHINOPT PHONETIC
CEHINOPU EUPHONIC
CEHINORS CHORINES
CEHINORU UNHEROIC
CEHINOSY HYOSCINE
CEHINPRS PINCHERS
PINSCHER
CEHINPRU PUNCHIER
CEHINPSU PENUCHIS
CEHINRSS RICHNESS
CEHINRST CHRISTEN
CITHERNS
CITHRENS
SNITCHER
CEHINRSW WINCHERS
CEHINRTU RUTHENIC
CEHINSST CHINTSES
SNITCHES
CEHINSTZ CHINTZES
CEHIOORS CHOOSIER
ISOCHORE
CEHIOPPR CHOPPIER
CEHIOPRU EUPHORIC
POUCHIER
CEHIOPSS HOSPICES
CEHIOPST POSTICHE
POTICHES
CEHIOPSU COPIHUES
CEHIOPTU EUPHOTIC
CEHIORRT RHETORIC
TORCHIER
CEHIORRV OVERRICH
CEHIORSS ORCHISES
CEHIORTU COUTHIER
TOUCHIER
CEHIOSTV CHEVIOTS
CEHIPPRS CHIPPERS
CEHIPRRS CHIRPERS
CEHIPRSS SPHERICS
CEHIPRST PITCHERS
CEHIQSTU QUITCHES
CEHIRSTT CHITTERS
RESTITCH
STITCHER
CEHIRSTW SWITCHER
CEHIRSTY HYSTERIC
CEHIRTTW TWITCHER
CEHIRTWY WITCHERY
CEHISSTT STITCHES
CEHISSTU CUSHIEST
CEHISSTW SWITCHES
CEHISTTW TWITCHES
CEHKKRSU CHUKKERS
CEHKLMOS HEMLOCKS
CEHKLORS SHERLOCK
CEHKNOSU SUNCHOKE
UNCHOKES
CEHKNPUY KEYPUNCH
CEHKORSS SHOCKERS
CEHKPSTU KETCHUPS
CEHKRSSU SHUCKERS
CEHKRSTU HUCKSTER
CEHLNNOU LUNCHEON
CEHLNNSU CHUNNELS
CEHLNOST CHOLENTS
CEHLNOTU UNCLOTHE
CEHLNPRU PRELUNCH
CEHLNRSU LUNCHERS
CEHLNRSY LYNCHERS
CEHLOORS RESCHOOL
CEHLORRT CHORTLER
CEHLORST CHORTLES
CEHLORSU SLOUCHER
CEHLOSSU SLOUCHES
CEHLOSTU SELCOUTH
CEHLPPSS SCHLEPPS
CEHLQSUY SQUELCHY
CEHLRRSU LURCHERS
CEHLSTUY LECYTHUS
CEHMNRSU MUNCHERS
CEHMNSSU MUCHNESS
CEHMOORS MOOCHERS
SMOOCHER
CEHMOOSS SCHMOOSE
SMOOCHES
CEHMOOSZ SCHMOOZE
CEHMOPRS CHOMPERS
CEHMORUV OVERMUCH
CEHMRSTU CHETRUMS
CEHMSSTU SMUTCHES
CEHNNOPU PUNCHEON
CEHNNOSU NONESUCH
UNCHOSEN
CEHNOOPS HENCOOPS
CEHNOORS SCHOONER
CEHNORST CHORTENS
NOTCHERS
CEHNORSV CHEVRONS
CEHNOSSZ SCHNOZES
CEHNPPRU PREPUNCH
CEHNPRSU PUNCHERS
CEHNPSST PSCHENTS
CEHNRRSU CHURNERS
CEHNRSTU CHUNTERS
CEHNSSSU SUCHNESS
CEHNSTTU CHESTNUT
CEHNSTUY CHUTNEYS
CEHOOORZ ZOOCHORE
CEHOORSS CHOOSERS
SOROCHES
CEHOORST CHEROOTS
CEHOORSU OCHEROUS
OCHREOUS
CEHOPPRS CHOPPERS
CEHOPPRY PROPHECY
CEHORSSU CHORUSES
CHOUSERS
CEHORSSZ SCHERZOS
CEHORSTU SCOUTHER
TOUCHERS
CEHORSUV VOUCHERS
CEHOSSSU HOCUSSES
CEHOSTTU COUTHEST
CEHPSSTU PUTSCHES
CEHRRSSU CRUSHERS
CEHRSSSU SCHUSSER
CEHRSTTY STRETCHY
CEHSSSSU SCHUSSES
CEIIILSV CIVILISE
CEIIILVZ CIVILIZE
CEIIINSV INCISIVE
CEIIINSZ SINICIZE
CEIIJSTU JUICIEST
CEIIKKST KICKIEST
CEIIKLMR LIMERICK
CEIIKLRS SICKLIER
CEIIKLSS SICKLIES
CEIIKMMR MIMICKER
CEIIKMST KISMETIC
CEIIKNSS ICKINESS
KINESICS
CEIIKNST KINETICS
CEIIKPRR PRICKIER
CEIIKPST PICKIEST
CEIIKQSU QUICKIES
CEIIKRRT TRICKIER
CEIIKRST STICKIER
CEIIKSST EKISTICS
STICKIES
CEIIKTTT TEKTITIC
CEIILLPT ELLIPTIC
CEIILLSS SILICLES
CEIILMNS LEMNISCI
CEIILMNT LIMNETIC
CEIILMNY MYELINIC
CEIILNNR INCLINER
CEIILNNS INCLINES
CEIILNOP PICOLINE
CEIILNOS ISOCLINE
SILICONE
CEIILNPS PENICILS
CEIILOPS POLICIES
CEIILORT ELICITOR
CEIILOTZ ZEOLITIC
CEIILPRT PERLITIC
CEIILPSS ECLIPSIS
CEIILPTX EXPLICIT
CEIILPTY PYELITIC
CEIILQRU CLIQUIER
CEIILRSY LYRICISE
CEIILRTV VERTICIL
CEIILRYZ LYRICIZE
CEIILSSS SCISSILE
CEIIMNRS CREMINIS
CEIIMNRU URINEMIC
CEIIMNST MINCIEST
CEIIMOPT EPITOMIC
CEIIMORS ISOMERIC
CEIIMOST COMITIES
SEMIOTIC
CEIIMPRR CRIMPIER
CEIIMPRS EMPIRICS
MISPRICE
CEIIMPTU PUMICITE
CEIIMRRT TRIMERIC
CEIIMRST MERISTIC
SCIMITER
TRISEMIC
CEIIMRTT TERMITIC
CEIIMSST MISCITES
CEIINNOS CONIINES
OSCININE
CEIINNOT COTININE
NICOTINE
CEIINNRS CINERINS
CEIINOPR PECORINI
CEIINORS RECISION
SORICINE
CEIINOSV INVOICES
CEIINOSX EXCISION
CEIINOTV EVICTION
CEIINPPR PRINCIPE
CEIINRSS SERICINS
CEIINRST CITRINES
CRINITES
INCITERS
CEIINRSU INCISURE
SCIURINE
CEIINRTU NEURITIC
CEIINSSU CUISINES
CEIINSTU CUTINISE
CEIINSTY SYENITIC
CEIINSTZ CITIZENS
ZINCITES
CEIINTUZ CUTINIZE
CEIIOPRT PERIOTIC
CEIIOPSW WICOPIES
CEIIOSTT OSTEITIC
CEIIPRRS CRISPIER
CEIIPRST PICRITES
PRICIEST
CEIIPSST SPICIEST
CEIIQRTU CRITIQUE
CEIIRSST ERISTICS
CEIIRSTV VERISTIC
CEIISTVV VIVISECT
CEIJNORT INJECTOR
CEIJNORU JOUNCIER
CEIJSSTU JUSTICES
CEIKKLOR CORKLIKE
ROCKLIKE
CEIKKNRS KNICKERS
CEIKLLTU CULTLIKE
CEIKLMOR CORMLIKE
CEIKLMST MICKLEST
CEIKLMSU SCUMLIKE
CEIKLNRS CLINKERS
CRINKLES
CEIKLNRU CLUNKIER
CEIKLNSS SLICKENS
CEIKLOSV LOVESICK
CEIKLOTU LEUKOTIC
CEIKLPRS PRICKLES
CEIKLPRU PLUCKIER
CEIKLRSS SLICKERS
CEIKLRST STICKLER
STRICKLE
TICKLERS
TRICKLES
CEIKLRSY SICKERLY
CEIKLSST SLICKEST
STICKLES
CEIKLSSW WICKLESS
CEIKLSTU LUCKIEST
CEIKMNOR MONICKER
CEIKMNST STICKMEN
CEIKMSTU MUCKIEST
CEIKNNOT NEKTONIC
CEIKNOTY CYTOKINE
CEIKNQSU QUICKENS
CEIKNRSS SNICKERS
CEIKNRST STRICKEN
CEIKNRSU UNSICKER
CEIKNRSY SNICKERY
CEIKNSSS SICKNESS
CEIKOPST POCKIEST
CEIKORST CORKIEST
ROCKIEST
STOCKIER
CEIKORSV OVERSICK
CEIKPRRS PRICKERS
CEIKPRST PRICKETS
CEIKPSST SKEPTICS
CEIKQSTU QUICKEST
QUICKSET
CEIKRRST TRICKERS
CEIKRRTY TRICKERY
CEIKRSST STICKERS
CEIKSSTU SUCKIEST
CEIKSTUY YUCKIEST
CEILLMOY COMELILY
CEILLNOU NUCLEOLI
CEILLOPS POLLICES
CEILLOQU COQUILLE
CEILLORS COLLIERS
CEILLORY COLLIERY
CEILLRTU TELLURIC
CEILLSST CELLISTS
CEILLSSU CULLISES
CEILMMUY MYCELIUM
CEILMNOP COMPLINE
CEILMOOP PICOMOLE
CEILMOPR COMPILER
COMPLIER
CEILMOPS COMPILES
COMPLIES
POLEMICS
CEILMOSS SOLECISM
CEILMOSU COLISEUM
CEILMPRS CRIMPLES
CEILMPRU CLUMPIER
CEILMPUU PECULIUM
CEILMRSU CLUMSIER
CEILMTUU LUTECIUM
CEILNNSU NUCLEINS
CEILNNSY SYNCLINE
CEILNOOS COLONIES
COLONISE
ECLOSION
CEILNOOZ COLONIZE
CEILNOPR REPLICON
CEILNOPS PINOCLES
CEILNOPT LEPTONIC

CEILNOPY POLYENIC
CEILNORS INCLOSER
LICENSOR
CEILNOSS INCLOSES
CEILNOST LECTIONS
TELSONIC
CEILNOSX LEXICONS
CEILNPRY PRINCELY
CEILNRUV CULVERIN
CEILNSST STENCILS
CEILNSTU CUTLINES
LINECUTS
TUNICLES
CEILOORZ COLORIZE
CEILOPPS POPSICLE
CEILOPRS POLICERS
CEILOPRT LEPROTIC
PETROLIC
CEILOPTU POULTICE
CEILOPTY EPICOTYL
LIPOCYTE
CEILORST CLOISTER
COISTREL
COSTLIER
CEILORTY CRYOLITE
CEILOSSS OSSICLES
CEILOSST SOLECIST
SOLSTICE
CEILOSSU COULISSE
CEILOTVY VELOCITY
CEILPPRR CRIPPLER
CEILPPRS CLIPPERS
CRIPPLES
CEILPRSS SPLICERS
CEILPRSU SURPLICE
CEILPSSU SPICULES
CEILRRSU SCURRILE
CEILRSTU CURLIEST
UTRICLES
CEILSTTU CUITTLES
CEIMMNNO MNEMONIC
CEIMMNOU ENCOMIUM
MECONIUM
CEIMMORT RECOMMIT
CEIMMORU COREMIUM
CEIMMOSX COMMIXES
CEIMMRRS CRIMMERS
CEIMMRRU CRUMMIER
CEIMMRSU CRUMMIES
SCUMMIER
CEIMNNOR NONCRIME
CEIMNNOY NEOMYCIN
CEIMNOOT EMOTICON
CEIMNOPT PENTOMIC
CEIMNOPY EPONYMIC
CEIMNORS INCOMERS
SERMONIC
CEIMNORT INTERCOM
CEIMNOST CENTIMOS
CEIMNRST CENTRISM
CEIMNRSU NUMERICS
CEIMNSSU MENISCUS
CEIMOOSZ MESOZOIC
CEIMOOUZ ZOOECIUM
CEIMOPRS COMPRISE
CEIMOPRX PROXEMIC
CEIMOPRZ COMPRIZE
CEIMORST MORTICES
CEIMORSX EXORCISM
CEIMOSTV VICOMTES
CEIMPRRS CRIMPERS
SCRIMPER
CEIMPRSU PUMICERS
CEIMRRTU TURMERIC
CEIMSSTY SYSTEMIC
CEINNNOT INNOCENT
CEINNORU NEURONIC
CEINNORV CONNIVER
CEINNORW COWINNER
CEINNOSV CONNIVES
CEINNOTU CONTINUE
CEINNOTV COINVENT
CEINOOPR PECORINO
CEINOOSS CONIOSES
CEINOOST COONTIES
CEINOOTZ ENTOZOIC
ENZOOTIC
CEINOPPT PEPTONIC
CEINOPRS CONSPIRE
INCORPSE
CEINOPRT ENTROPIC
INCEPTOR
CEINOPRV PROVINCE
CEINOPTU UNPOETIC
CEINORRS RESORCIN
CEINORRT TRICORNE
CEINORSS NECROSIS
CEINORST COINTERS
CORNIEST
NOTICERS
CEINORSU COINSURE
CEINORTT CONTRITE
CEINORTU NEUROTIC
UNEROTIC
CEINORTV CONTRIVE
CEINOSSS CESSIONS
COSINESS
CEINOSST SECTIONS
CEINOSSZ COZINESS
CEINOSTT STENOTIC
TONETICS
CEINOSTU COUNTIES
CEINOSTX EXCITONS
CEINOSTY CYTOSINE
CEINOSUV UNVOICES
CEINOTUX UNEXOTIC
CEINPRSS CRISPENS
PRINCESS
CEINPSST INSPECTS
CEINRRSU REINCURS
CEINRSST CISTERNS
CEINRSTT CENTRIST
CITTERNS
CEINRSUV INCURVES
CEINRTTU INTERCUT
TINCTURE
CEINSSTY CYSTEINS
CYSTINES
CEINSTTX EXTINCTS
CEIOOTUV OUTVOICE
CEIOOTXX EXOTOXIC
CEIOPPRS CROPPIES
CEIOPRRU CROUPIER
CEIOPRSU PRECIOUS
CEIOPRTU OUTPRICE
CEIOPSSU SPECIOUS
CEIORRSS CROSIERS
CEIORRSU COURIERS
CEIORRSZ CROZIERS
CEIORRTU COURTIER
CEIORRTW COWRITER
CEIORRUZ CRUZEIRO
CEIORSST CROSSTIE
CEIORSTT COTTIERS
CEIORSTU CITREOUS
OUTCRIES
CEIORSTV EVICTORS
VORTICES
CEIORSTW COWRITES
CEIORSTX EXCITORS
EXORCIST
CEIORSVY VICEROYS
CEIORTTU TOREUTIC
CEIOSSSV VISCOSES
CEIOSSTT SCOTTIES
CEIOSSTU COITUSES
CEIOSSTX COEXISTS
CEIPPSTU CUPPIEST
CEIPQSTU PICQUETS
CEIPRRSS CRISPERS
CEIPRRST RESCRIPT
SCRIPTER
CEIPRRSU SPRUCIER
CEIPRSST CRISPEST
CEIPRSTU CUPRITES
PICTURES
PIECRUST
CEIPSSST CESSPITS
CEIRRRSU CURRIERS
CEIRRRUY CURRIERY
CEIRRSSU CRUISERS
SCURRIES
CEIRRSTT CRITTERS
RESTRICT
STRICTER
CEIRRSTU CRUSTIER
RECRUITS
CEIRRSUV SCURVIER
CEIRSSSU SCISSURE
CEIRSSTT TRISECTS
CEIRSSTU CITRUSES
CURTSIES
RICTUSES
CEIRSSTV VICTRESS
CEIRSSUV CURSIVES
SCURVIES
CEIRSTUV CURVIEST
CEIRSTUY SECURITY
CEIRSUZZ SCUZZIER
CEISSSTU CISTUSES
CEJLOOSY JOCOSELY
CEJNORRU CONJURER
CEJNORSU CONJURES
CEJNRTUU JUNCTURE
CEJOPRST PROJECTS
CEKKLNRU KNUCKLER
CEKKLNSU KNUCKLES
CEKKNORS KNOCKERS
CEKLLOOV LOVELOCK
CEKLLSSU LUCKLESS
CEKLNRSU CLUNKERS
CEKLOOSS COOKLESS
CEKLOPST LOCKSTEP
CEKLORSS ROCKLESS
CEKLOSSS SOCKLESS
CEKLOSST LOCKSETS
CEKLPRSU PLUCKERS
CEKLRRTU TRUCKLER
CEKLRSSU SCULKERS
SUCKLERS
CEKLRSTU TRUCKLES
CEKLSSSU SUCKLESS
CEKMNOST STOCKMEN
CEKMNRTU TRUCKMEN
CEKNOORV CONVOKER
CEKNOOSV CONVOKES
CEKNOPST PENSTOCK
CEKNPRUU UNPUCKER
CEKNRSTU STRUCKEN
CEKNRSWY WRYNECKS
CEKOOORV OVERCOOK
CEKOOPRS PRECOOKS
CEKOOPSW COWPOKES
CEKOORRS ROCKROSE
CEKOORRW COWORKER
CEKOORRY CROOKERY
CEKOORST CROOKEST
CEKOPRST SPROCKET
CEKORRTY ROCKETRY
CEKORSST RESTOCKS
STOCKERS
CEKRRSTU RESTRUCK
TRUCKERS
CEKRSSUU RUCKUSES
CELLMOSU COLUMELS
CELLNOOS COLONELS
CELLNORS ENSCROLL
CELLNSUU NUCELLUS
CELLNTUU LUCULENT
CELLNTUY LUCENTLY
CELLRRSU CRULLERS
CELLRSSU SCULLERS
CELLRSUY SCULLERY
CELMNOOR COLORMEN
CELMNOOS MONOCLES
CELMNOUY UNCOMELY
CELMNSSU MESCLUNS
CELMOOOT LOCOMOTE
CELMOOPY COEMPLOY
CELMOSYY CYMOSELY
CELMPRSU CRUMPLES
CELMPRTU PLECTRUM
CELMPSUU SPECULUM
CELMSSSU SCUMLESS
CELNNOSU NUCLEONS
CELNOORS CONSOLER
CORONELS
CELNOOSS CONSOLES
COOLNESS
CELNOOVV CONVOLVE
CELNOPRT PLECTRON
CELNOPUU UNCOUPLE
CELNOPUY OPULENCY
CELNORWY CLOWNERY
CELNOSSU CLONUSES
COUNSELS
UNCLOSES
CELNOSTU NOCTULES
CELNOSUV CONVULSE
CELNOSVY SOLVENCY
CELNOVXY CONVEXLY
CELOOORV OVERCOOL
CELOOPRS PRECOOLS
CELOOPSS CESSPOOL
CELOORRS COLORERS
RECOLORS
CELOORRU COLOURER
CELOORSS COLESSOR
CREOSOLS
CELOORTW COLEWORT
CELOOSTU CLOSEOUT
CELOPRSS CROPLESS
CELOPRSU COUPLERS
CELOPSSU CLOSEUPS
CELOPSTU COUPLETS
OCTUPLES
CELOPSUU OPUSCULE
CELOPTTU OCTUPLET
CELOPTUX OCTUPLEX
CELORRSU CORULERS
CELORSST CORSLETS
COSTRELS
CROSSLET
CELORSSU CLOSURES
SCLEROUS
CELORSSW SCOWLERS
CELORSTU CLOTURES
CLOUTERS
COULTERS
CELORSUU ULCEROUS
CELORSUY CROUSELY
CELORTVY COVERTLY
CELOSSST COSTLESS
CELOSTTU CULOTTES
CELPRSSU SCRUPLES
CELPRSTU RESCULPT
CELPRSUY SPRUCELY
CELRSSTU CLUSTERS
CELRSSTY CLYSTERS
CELRSTTU CLUTTERS
CELRSTUU CULTURES
CELRSTUV CULVERTS
CELRSTUY CLUSTERY
CELRTTUY CLUTTERY
CELSSTTU SCUTTLES
CELSSTUU CULTUSES
CEMMNOOR COMMONER
CEMMNOOS CONSOMME
CEMMNORU COMMUNER
CEMMNOST COMMENTS
CEMMNOSU COMMUNES
CEMMOOSV COMMOVES
CEMMORTU COMMUTER
CEMMOSTU COMMUTES
CEMMRSSU SCUMMERS
CEMNNOST CONTEMNS
CEMNOOPT CONTEMPO
CEMNOOTY MONOCYTE
CEMNOPRS CORPSMEN
CEMNOPTT CONTEMPT
CEMNORSU CONSUMER
MUCRONES
CEMNOSSU CONSUMES
CEMNRSTU CENTRUMS
CEMOOPRS COMPOSER
CEMOOPSS COMPOSES
CEMOOPST COMPOTES
CEMOOPSY MYOSCOPE
CEMOORSY SYCOMORE
CEMOOSSS COSMOSES
CEMOOSTU OUTCOMES
CEMOPRSS COMPRESS
CEMOPRTU COMPUTER
CEMOPSTU COMPUTES
CEMORSTU COSTUMER
CUSTOMER
CEMOSSTU COSTUMES
CEMOSTUY COSTUMEY
CEMOTXYY MYXOCYTE
CEMPRSTU CRUMPETS
SPECTRUM
CENNOOPR CORNPONE
CENNOORV CONVENOR
CENNOOST CONNOTES
CENNORTU NOCTURNE
CENNOSST CONSENTS
CENNOSTT CONTENTS
CENNOSTV CONVENTS
CENNRSSU SCUNNERS
CENOOOTZ ECTOZOON
CENOOPSS POCOSENS
CENOORRS CORONERS
CROONERS
CENOORST CORONETS
CENOORSU CORNEOUS
CENOORSV CONVERSO
CENOORVY CONVEYOR
CENOPRSU POUNCERS
CENOPRSY NECROPSY
CENOPSSY PYCNOSES
SYNCOPES
CENOQRSU CONQUERS
CENOQSTU CONQUEST
CENORRSS SCORNERS
CENORRSW CROWNERS
RECROWNS
CENORRTU TROUNCER
CENORSSU CORNUSES
CENORSTU CONSTRUE
COUNTERS
RECOUNTS
TROUNCES
CENORSTV CONVERTS
CENORSTW CROWNETS
CENORSUU CERNUOUS
COENURUS
CENORSUV UNCOVERS
CENORSUY CYNOSURE
CENOSSTT CONTESTS
CENOSSTU CONTUSES
COUNTESS
CENOSTTX CONTEXTS
CENPRSTY ENCRYPTS
CENPRTUU PUNCTURE
CENRRSTU CURRENTS
CENRSSTU CURTNESS
ENCRUSTS
CENRSSUW UNSCREWS
CEOOOPST OTOSCOPE
CEOOPRRV OVERCROP
CEOOPRSS SCOOPERS
CEOOPSWX COWPOXES
CEOORSST SCOOTERS
CEOORSTU ECOTOURS
OUTSCORE
CEOOSTUV COVETOUS
CEOPPRRS CROPPERS
CEOPPRST PROSPECT
CEOPPRSU SUPERCOP
CEOPRRRU PROCURER
CEOPRRSU PROCURES
CEOPRSST PROSECTS
CEOPRSSU CORPUSES
CEOPRSTT PROTECTS
CEOPRSTW CROWSTEP
CEOPRSUU CUPREOUS
CEOPRSUV COVERUPS
CEOQRSTU CROQUETS
CEOQRTUY COQUETRY
CEORRSSS CROSSERS
CEORRSSU COURSERS
SCOURERS
CEORRSTU COURTERS
CEORRSTY CORSETRY
CEORSSST CROSSEST
CEORSSSU SUCROSES
CEORSSTU CRUSTOSE
SCOUTERS
CEORSTUU COUTURES
OUTCURSE
CEORSTUV CUTOVERS
OVERCUTS
CEORSTUY COURTESY
CEORTUUV OUTCURVE
CEPPRRSU CRUPPERS
CEPPRSSU SCUPPERS
CEPPRTUU UPPERCUT
CEPRSSTU SPRUCEST
CEPRSSUW SCREWUPS
CEPRSSUY CYPRUSES
CEPRSTUU CUTPURSE
CEPRSUUV UPCURVES
CEPSSSTU SUSPECTS
CERSSTTU SCUTTERS
CERSSTUY CURTSEYS
CERSSUUX EXCURSUS
CFFGHINU CHUFFING
CFFGIINO COIFFING
CFFGILNO COFFLING
CFFGINOS SCOFFING
CFFGINSU SCUFFING
CFFHINOS CHIFFONS
CFFIKKOS KICKOFFS
CFFIKLNU CUFFLINK
CFFIKOPS PICKOFFS
CFFINNOU UNCOFFIN
CFFIRTUY FRUCTIFY
CFFKKNOO KNOCKOFF
CFFKOOOS COOKOFFS
CFGHIILN FILCHING
CFGIIKLN FLICKING
CFGIKLNO FLOCKING
CFGIKNOR FROCKING
CFGINOSU FOCUSING
CFHIINOO FINOCHIO
CFHIIORR HORRIFIC
CFHIKORS ROCKFISH
CFHIKSSU SUCKFISH
CFHINSSU FUCHSINS
CFHORSTU FUTHORCS
CFIIIKNN FINICKIN
CFIIILSY SILICIFY
CFIIKNNY FINNICKY
CFIILMNU FULMINIC
CFIILNST INFLICTS
CFIILNUU FUNICULI
CFIILOPR PROLIFIC
CFIILSTU SULFITIC
CFIIMOPR PICIFORM
CFIINOPT PONTIFIC
CFIINORT FRICTION
CFIINOST FICTIONS
CFIKLORY FROLICKY
CFIKLSTU STICKFUL
CFIKOSSS FOSSICKS
CFILMOOR COLIFORM
CFILNOSU SULFONIC
CFILRSUU SULFURIC
CFIMNORS CONFIRMS
CFIMNORU CUNIFORM
UNCIFORM
CFIMOSSU MISFOCUS
CFINNOTU FUNCTION
CFIOPRUY COPURIFY
CFKLRTUU TRUCKFUL
CFKNORSU UNFROCKS
CFKOSTTU FUTTOCKS
CFLLOORU COLORFUL
CFLMRSUU FULCRUMS
CFLMRUUU FURCULUM
CFLNORSU SCORNFUL
CFLOOPSU SCOOPFUL
CFLOOPSW COWFLOPS
CFMNOORS CONFORMS
CFMOORST COMFORTS
CFNNOORT CONFRONT
CFNORSTU FUNCTORS
CFOOORTW CROWFOOT
CFRSTUUU USUFRUCT
CGGGHINU CHUGGING
CGGGILNO CLOGGING
CGGHINOU COUGHING
CGGIILNN CLINGING
CGGIINNO COIGNING
CGGIINNR CRINGING
CGGILLOY CLOGGILY
CGHHIINT HITCHING
CGHHINNU HUNCHING
CGHHINOT HOTCHING
CGHHINTU HUTCHING
CGHIIKNN CHINKING
CGHIIKNO HOICKING
CGHIIKNR CHIRKING
CGHIILLN CHILLING
CGHIILNT CHITLING
LICHTING
CGHIIMNR CHIRMING
CGHIINNN CHINNING
CGHIINNP PINCHING
CGHIINNW WINCHING
CGHIINOR CHOIRING
CGHIINPP CHIPPING
CGHIINPR CHIRPING
CGHIINPT PITCHING
CGHIINRR CHIRRING
CGHIINST ITCHINGS
CGHIINTW WITCHING
CGHIINVY CHIVYING
CGHIKNNU CHUNKING
CGHIKNOS SHOCKING
CGHIKNSU SHUCKING
CGHILMNU MULCHING
CGHILNNU LUNCHING
CGHILNNY LYNCHING
CGHILNOT CLOTHING
CGHILNRU LURCHING
CGHIMMNU CHUMMING
CGHIMNNU MUNCHING
CGHIMNOO MOOCHING
CGHIMNOP CHOMPING
CGHIMNOR CHROMING
CGHIMNOU MOUCHING
CGHIMNPU CHUMPING
CGHIMPSY SPHYGMIC
CGHINNOS CHIGNONS
CGHINNOT NOTCHING
CGHINNPU PUNCHING
CGHINNRU CHURNING
CGHINNSY SYNCHING
CGHINOOP POOCHING
CGHINOOS CHOOSING
CGHINOPP CHOPPING
CGHINOPU POUCHING
CGHINORT TORCHING
CGHINOSU CHOUSING
HOCUSING
CGHINOSW CHOWSING
CGHINOTU TOUCHING
CGHINOUV VOUCHING
CGHINPSY PSYCHING
CGHINRRU CHURRING
CGHINRSU CRUSHING
RUCHINGS
CGHINSTY SCYTHING
CGHNOOOS SOOCHONG
CGHNOOSU SOUCHONG

CGIIILNT LIGNITIC
CGIIINNS INCISING
CGIIINNT INCITING
CGIIKLNN CLINKING
NICKLING
CGIIKLNP PICKLING
CGIIKLNS LICKINGS
SICKLING
SLICKING
CGIIKLNT TICKLING
CGIIKMMS GIMMICKS
CGIIKMMY GIMMICKY
CGIIKNNS SNICKING
CGIIKNNZ ZINCKING
CGIIKNPR PRICKING
CGIIKNPS PICKINGS
CGIIKNRT TRICKING
CGIIKNRW WRICKING
CGIIKNST STICKING
TICKINGS
CGIIKNSW WICKINGS
CGIIKPST PIGSTICK
CGIILLOS ILLOGICS
CGIILNOP POLICING
CGIILNPP CLIPPING
CGIILNPS SPLICING
CGIILNQU CLIQUING
CGIILNSU SLUICING
CGIILOST LOGISTIC
CGIILRTU LITURGIC
CGIIMNNO INCOMING
CGIIMNPR CRIMPING
CGIIMNPU PUMICING
CGIIMNSU MISCUING
CGIINNOT NOTICING
CGIINNSU INCUSING
CGIINNTT TINCTING
CGIINOOS ISOGONIC
CGIINOPT PICOTING
CGIINOSV VOICINGS
CGIINPRS CRISPING
CGIINRSU CRUISING
CGIINRSV SCRIVING
CGIJNNOU JOUNCING
CGIKKNNO KNOCKING
CGIKLNNO CLONKING
CGIKLNNU CLUNKING
CGIKLNOR ROCKLING
CGIKLNPU PLUCKING
CGIKLNRU RUCKLING
CGIKLNSU SCULKING
SUCKLING
CGIKMNOS SMOCKING
CGIKNOOR CROOKING
CGIKNOOS COOKINGS
CGIKNORT TROCKING
CGIKNOST STOCKING
CGIKNPSU KINGCUPS
CGIKNRTU TRUCKING
CGILLNOY COLLYING
CGILLNSU SCULLING
CGILLNUY CULLYING
CGILMNOP CLOMPING
CGILMNPU CLUMPING
CGILMNSU MUSCLING
CGILMNSY CYMLINGS
CGILMNTU MULCTING
CGILMNUU CINGULUM
GLUCINUM
CGILMOOY MYOLOGIC
CGILNNNO NONCLING
CGILNNOS CLONINGS
CGILNNOW CLOWNING
CGILNOOR COLORING
CGILNOOY COOINGLY
CGILNOPP CLOPPING
CGILNOPU COUPLING
CGILNORU CLOURING
CGILNOSS CLOSINGS
CGILNOSW COWLINGS
SCOWLING
CGILNOTT CLOTTING
CGILNOTU CLOUTING
CGILNPSU SCULPING
CGILNRSU CURLINGS
CGILNRYY CRYINGLY
CGILNTTU CUTTLING
CGILOOOZ ZOOLOGIC
CGILOORU UROLOGIC
CGILOPRY COPYGIRL
CGILORSW COWGIRLS
CGILPSTY GLYPTICS
CGIMMNSU SCUMMING
CGIMNNOO GNOMONIC
ONCOMING
CGIMNOPT COMPTING

CGIMNOPU UPCOMING
CGIMNPRU CRUMPING
CGIMRRUY MICRURGY
CGINNNSU CUNNINGS
CGINNOOR CROONING
CGINNOPU POUNCING
CGINNORS SCORNING
CGINNORW CROWNING
CGINNOSS CONSIGNS
CGINNOTU COUNTING
CGINOOPS SCOOPING
CGINOOPT COOPTING
CGINOOST SCOOTING
CGINOOTV COGNOVIT
CGINOPPR CROPPING
CGINORSS CROSSING
CGINORSU COURSING
SCOURING
SOURCING
CGINORTU COURTING
CGINOSST GNOSTICS
CGINOSTU SCOUTING
CGINPPSU CUPPINGS
CGINPRSU SPRUCING
CGINRRUY CURRYING
CGINRSTU CRUSTING
CGINSTTU CUTTINGS
TUNGSTIC
CGKLNOSU GUNLOCKS
CGKNOSTU GUNSTOCK
CGLLOSYY GLYCOSYL
CGLMOOYY MYCOLOGY
CGLNOOOY ONCOLOGY
CGLOOOTY TOCOLOGY
CGLOOTYY CYTOLOGY
CGNORSUY SCROUNGY
CHHIIKST THICKISH
CHHIIPST PHTHISIC
CHHILRSU CHURLISH
CHHIMPSU CHUMSHIP
CHHIMRTY RHYTHMIC
CHHKOOPS HOCKSHOP
CHHNORSU RHONCHUS
CHHOOPTT HOTCHPOT
CHIIKLST TICKLISH
CHIIKRST TRICKISH
CHIILLLY CHILLILY
CHIILNNP LINCHPIN
CHIILNST CHITLINS
CHIILOPT HOPLITIC
CHIILORT TROCHILI
CHIILOST HOLISTIC
CHIILPRY CHIRPILY
CHIILPTY PITCHILY
CHIILQSU CLIQUISH
CHIIMOPT PHIMOTIC
CHIIMORZ RHIZOMIC
CHIINOPS SIPHONIC
CHIINORT ORNITHIC
CHIIORST HISTORIC
ORCHITIS
CHIIRSTT TRISTICH
CHIKLLOS HILLOCKS
CHIKLLOY HILLOCKY
CHIKLNUY CHUNKILY
CHIKMNNU MUNCHKIN
CHIKMNPU CHIPMUNK
CHIKMNTU MUTCHKIN
CHIKNOOS CHINOOKS
CHIKOPTY KYPHOTIC
CHIKOSST STOCKISH
CHILLMSU CHILLUMS
CHILLOOT OILCLOTH
CHILMMUY CHUMMILY
CHILMOSU SCHOLIUM
CHILMPSU CLUMPISH
CHILNNPY LYNCHPIN
CHILNORS CHLORINS
CHILNOSW CLOWNISH
CHILNPUY PUNCHILY
CHILOOOZ HOLOZOIC
CHILOOYZ HYLOZOIC
CHILOPPY CHOPPILY
CHILORST TROCHILS
CHILOTUY TOUCHILY
CHIMMOOR MICROMHO
CHIMMORS MICROHMS
CHIMMORU CHROMIUM
CHIMNNOO NONOHMIC
CHIMNOOR HORMONIC
CHIMNORS CHRISMON
CHIMNORW INCHWORM
CHIMNOSU INSOMUCH
CHIMNOSY CHYMOSIN
CHIMOORU MOUCHOIR
CHIMORSS CHRISOMS

CHIMOSTU MISTOUCH
CHIMSSTY CHYMISTS
CHINOOPT PHOTONIC
CHINOORS CHORIONS
ISOCHRON
CHINOORT ORTHICON
CHINOPTY HYPNOTIC
PHYTONIC
PYTHONIC
TYPHONIC
CHINORTU COTHURNI
CHINOSSU CUSHIONS
CHINOSTZ SCHIZONT
CHINOSUY CUSHIONY
CHINSTTU UNSTITCH
CHIOOPPT PHOTOPIC
CHIOOPTY OOPHYTIC
CHIOORSS ISOCHORS
CHIOORSU ICHOROUS
CHIOORSZ CHORIZOS
CHIOORTT ORTHOTIC
CHIOPRST STROPHIC
CHIOPTTU OUTPITCH
PITCHOUT
CHIPRRSU CHIRRUPS
CHIPRRSY PYRRHICS
CHIPRRUY CHIRRUPY
CHIPRTTY TRIPTYCH
CHIRRSSU SCIRRHUS
CHISSTTU CHUTISTS
CHKLOSSY SHYLOCKS
CHKMMOOS HOMMOCKS
CHKMMOSU HUMMOCKS
CHKMMOUY HUMMOCKY
CHKNOOSS SCHNOOKS
CHKNORSU CORNHUSK
CHKOOOPS COOKSHOP
CHKOPSTU TUCKSHOP
CHLMORSY CHROMYLS
CHLMPSSU SCHLUMPS
CHLMPSUY SCHLUMPY
CHLNOOOP COLOPHON
CHLOORSU CHLOROUS
CHLOPSTY SPLOTCHY
CHMNORRU CRUMHORN
CHMOORSU CHROMOUS
CHMOOSYZ SCHMOOZY
CHNNOORS CHRONONS
CHNOOPTT TOPNOTCH
CHNOORST TORCHONS
CHNOPRSU SUNPORCH
CHNOPTUU OUTPUNCH
CHNORSSY SYNCHROS
CHNORSTU COTHURNS
CHOPSTUU TOUCHUPS
CHORSTTU SHORTCUT
CIIILMPT IMPLICIT
CIIILMSU SILICIUM
CIIILNOV OLIVINIC
CIIILTVY CIVILITY
CIIIMNRS CRIMINIS
CIIINNOS INCISION
CIIINNRT CITRININ
CIIINOTY IONICITY
CIIINPPR PRINCIPI
CIIINPST INCIPITS
CIIINTVY VICINITY
CIIJRSTU JURISTIC
CIIKKLLS KILLICKS
CIIKKMSS MISKICKS
CIIKLLSY SICKLILY
CIIKLOPT POLITICK
CIIKLPST LICKSPIT
LIPSTICK
CIIKLRTY TRICKILY
CIIKLSTY STICKILY
CIIKNPPR PINPRICK
CIIKNPST NITPICKS
STICKPIN
CIIKNPTY NITPICKY
CIIKPSUW WICKIUPS
CIILLNOP POLLINIC
CIILMOPY IMPOLICY
CIILMOSS SCIOLISM
CIILMRSY LYRICISM
CIILNOPS CIPOLINS
PICOLINS
PSILOCIN
CIILNORT NITROLIC
CIILNOSS SILICONS
CIILNOST COLISTIN
CIILOOPT POLITICO
CIILOPPT POPLITIC
CIILOPST COLPITIS
POLITICS
PSILOTIC

CIILORST CLITORIS
COISTRIL
CIILOSST SCIOLIST
SOLICITS
CIILOSVV SLIVOVIC
CIILPRSY CRISPILY
CIILRSTY LYRICIST
CIILRTUU UTRICULI
CIILSTTY STYLITIC
CIIMNOOS ISONOMIC
CIIMNOSS MISCOINS
CIIMNOST MONISTIC
NOMISTIC
CIIMNOVY VIOMYCIN
CIIMORST TRISOMIC
CIIMOSST STOICISM
CIIMOSYZ ISOZYMIC
CIIMPRST SCRIMPIT
CIIMRTTU TRITICUM
CIINNNOO NONIONIC
CIINNORU UNIRONIC
CIINNOST NICOTINS
CIINNSTT INSTINCT
CIINOOPP CIOPPINO
CIINOOSS CONIOSIS
CIINOOST COITIONS
ISOTONIC
CIINOPRS PORCINIS
CIINORSS INCISORS
CIINORST CROSTINI
CIINORSY INCISORY
CIINOSSS SCISSION
CIINOSTT STICTION
CIINOTTY TONICITY
CIINPSTU SINCIPUT
CIINQSTU QUINTICS
CIIOOPST ISOTOPIC
CIIOPSTT OPTICIST
CIIOPSTY ISOTYPIC
CIIOQTUX QUIXOTIC
CIIOTTXY TOXICITY
CIIPRRTU PRURITIC
CIIPRSTU PURISTIC
CIIRSTTU TRUISTIC
CIISSTTY CYSTITIS
CIJKOSTY JOYSTICK
CIJNNOOS CONJOINS
CIJNNOOT CONJOINT
CIJNNOTU JUNCTION
CIJOOSTY JOCOSITY
CIKKLLOS KILLOCKS
CIKKOPST TOPKICKS
CIKKOSTU OUTKICKS
CIKLLORS ROLLICKS
CIKLLORY ROLLICKY
CIKLLPUY PLUCKILY
CIKLNOST LINSTOCK
CIKLOOOS OLICOOKS
CIKLOPST LOPSTICK
CIKLOSTU OUTSLICK
CIKLOSTY STOCKILY
CIKMOORS SICKROOM
CIKMOOSS MISCOOKS
CIKMORRS RIMROCKS
CIKMSSTU STICKUMS
CIKNNOOS COONSKIN
CIKNNOST NONSTICK
CIKNNOSW WINNOCKS
CIKNOPTY PYKNOTIC
CIKNOSSW COWSKINS
CIKNPSTU NUTPICKS
CIKNSSTU UNSTICKS
CIKOPSTT TIPSTOCK
CIKORTTU OUTTRICK
CIKOSSTT STOCKIST
CIKOSSTU SICKOUTS
CIKOSTTU STICKOUT
CIKPSSTU STICKUPS
CIKPSUWY WICKYUPS
CILLMSUY CLUMSILY
CILLNOOT COTILLON
CILLNORS INSCROLL
CILLNOSU CULLIONS
SCULLION
CILLOOOT OCOTILLO
CILLOORS CRIOLLOS
CILMMSUY SCUMMILY
CILMNOPS COMPLINS
CILMNOPU PULMONIC
CILMNOSS CLONISMS
CILMNOUU INOCULUM
CILMNUUV VINCULUM
CILMOORS COLORISM
MISCOLOR
CILMOOSS LOCOISMS
CILMORUX MICROLUX

CILMPSUU SPICULUM
CILMSSTU CULTISMS
CILMSTYY MYSTICLY
CILNNORY NONLYRIC
CILNOORS ORCINOLS
CILNOORU UNICOLOR
CILNOOST COLONIST
STOLONIC
CILNOOTU LOCUTION
CILNOPTU PLUTONIC
CILNORSY LYRICONS
CILNOSTU LINOCUTS
CILNOSUY COUSINLY
CILNPSSU INSCULPS
SCULPINS
CILOOPST COPILOTS
CILOOPYZ POLYZOIC
CILOORRT TRICOLOR
CILOORST COLORIST
CORTISOL
CILOORSU COULOIRS
CILOPPRY PROPYLIC
CILOPRRY PYRROLIC
CILOPRUY CROUPILY
POLYURIC
CILOPSSW COWSLIPS
CILOSSTU OCULISTS
CILOSSTY SYSTOLIC
CILOSSUU LUSCIOUS
CILPRSTU CULPRITS
CILRSTTY STRICTLY
CILRSTUY CRUSTILY
RUSTICLY
CILRSUVY SCURVILY
CILSSTTU CULTISTS
CIMMOSSS COSMISMS
CIMNNOSU NONMUSIC
CIMNOORS OMICRONS
CIMNOOTY MYOTONIC
CIMNORSS CRIMSONS
CIMNORSY CRONYISM
CIMNOSTU MISCOUNT
CIMNOSUU MUCINOUS
CIMNOSUY SYCONIUM
CIMOOOTZ ZOOTOMIC
CIMOSSST COSMISTS
CIMOSTUU MUTICOUS
CIMOSTUY MUCOSITY
CINNNOOT NONTONIC
CINNNOSU INCONNUS
CINNOOTU CONTINUO
CINNOOTX NONTOXIC
CINNORSU UNICORNS
CINNOSTU UNCTIONS
CINNOSTY SYNTONIC
CINNQUUX QUINCUNX
CINOOOPT COOPTION
CINOOOTZ ZOONOTIC
CINOOPRS SCORPION
CINOOPRT PROTONIC
CINOOPSS POCOSINS
CINOORST CROSTINO
CINOOTXY OXYTOCIN
CINOPSSY PYCNOSIS
CINOPSTY SYNOPTIC
CINORRST TRICORNS
CINORSST CISTRONS
CINORSTT STRONTIC
CINORSTU RUCTIONS
CINORSUY COUSINRY
CINORTUX COTURNIX
CINOSSST CONSISTS
CINOSSTU SUCTIONS
CINOSTUV VISCOUNT
CINRSSTU INCRUSTS
CINRSTTU INSTRUCT
CINRSTUY SCRUTINY
CIOOOPRS OOSPORIC
CIOOOTTX OTOTOXIC
CIOOPRST PORTICOS
CIOOQSTU COQUITOS
CIOPSSTY COPYISTS
CIORSSSS SCISSORS
CIORSTUU RUCTIOUS
CIPPRRUU PURPURIC
CIPSSTTY STYPTICS
CIRRSTTU CRITTURS
CJNNOOTU CONJUNTO
CJNOORRU CONJUROR
CKKNOOTU KNOCKOUT
CKKOORRW ROCKWORK
CKLLMOSU MULLOCKS
CKLLMOUY MULLOCKY
CKLLOOPS POLLOCKS
CKLNOSTU LOCKNUTS
CKLOORSW ROWLOCKS

CKLOOSTU LOCKOUTS
CKLOPSTU POTLUCKS
CKMMORUW MUCKWORM
CKNOOORS ROCKOONS
CKOOOPST COOKTOPS
CKOOOSTU COOKOUTS
OUTCOOKS
CKOOPSTT STOCKPOT
CKOORSTU OUTROCKS
CKORSTUW CUTWORKS
SCUTWORK
CKOSSSTU TUSSOCKS
CKOSSTUY TUSSOCKY
CKSSSTUU TUSSUCKS
CLLMOSSU MOLLUSCS
CLLOOPSS SCOLLOPS
CLLOOQUY COLLOQUY
CLMMNOOY COMMONLY
CLMOOOTY COLOTOMY
CLMOOPST COMPLOTS
CLMOSUUU CUMULOUS
CLNNOOOR NONCOLOR
CLNOORST CONTROLS
CLNOSSTU CONSULTS
CLOOOPRT PROTOCOL
CLOOPPSW COWPLOPS
CLOOPSTY POLYCOTS
CLOORTUY LOCUTORY
CLOOSSSU COLOSSUS
CLOOSSTY CYTOSOLS
CLOPRSTU SCULPTOR
CMMNNOOU UNCOMMON
CMNOOOST MONOCOTS
CMOOPRST COMPORTS
CMOOPSST COMPOSTS
CMORSSTU SCROTUMS
CMORSTUW CUTWORMS
CNNORSTU NOCTURNS
CNNORSUW UNCROWNS
CNOOOORT OCTOROON
CNOOOPSS POCOSONS
CNOOPPRS POPCORNS
CNOOPSSU SOUPCONS
CNOORRSW CORNROWS
CNOORRTY CRYOTRON
CNOORSST CONSORTS
CNOORSTT CONTORTS
CNOORSTU CONTOURS
CORNUTOS
CROUTONS
OUTSCORN
CNOOTTUU OUTCOUNT
CNOPSSTY POSTSYNC
CNOSTUUU UNCTUOUS
COOOPSTU OUTSCOOP
COOOPSTY OTOSCOPY
COOPPSTU POSTCOUP
COOPRRST PROCTORS
COOPRSST TOPCROSS
COOPRSTU OUTCROPS
COOPRSUU CROUPOUS
COOPRSUY UROSCOPY
COORSSTU OUTCROSS
COORSTUW OUTCROWS
COOSSTTY OTOCYSTS
COPRRSTU CORRUPTS
DDDDEEOR DODDERED
DDDEEEFN DEFENDED
DDDEEENP DEPENDED
DDDEEENR REDDENED
DDDEEERT TEDDERED
DDDEEERW REWEDDED
DDDEEFNU DEFUNDED
DDDEEFOR FODDERED
DDDEEHRS SHREDDED
DDDEEJRU JUDDERED
DDDEELRT TREDDLED
DDDEENOS SODDENED
DDDEENUW UNWEDDED
DDDEEORR DODDERER
DDDEEORS RESODDED
DDDEERTU DETRUDED
DDDEGILR GRIDDLED
DDDEIILS DIDDLIES
DDDEIINV DIVIDEND
DDDEILNW DWINDLED
DDDEILRS DIDDLERS
DDDEILSY DIDDLEYS
DDDEILTW TWIDDLED
DDDEINOR DENDROID
DDDEINRU UNDERDID
DDDEIQSU SQUIDDED
DDDENORW DROWNDED
DDDGIILN DIDDLING
DDEEEEMR REDEEMED
DDEEEENP DEEPENED

DDEEEERS RESEEDED
DDEEEERW DEERWEED
DDEEEFIR REDEFIED
DDEEEFLU DEFUELED
DDEEEFLX DEFLEXED
DDEEEFNR DEFENDER
FENDERED
DDEEEFNS DEFENSED
DDEEEFRR DEFERRED
DDEEEGMR DEGERMED
DEMERGED
DDEEEGNR DEGENDER
GENDERED
DDEEEGRT DETERGED
DDEEEHLW WHEEDLED
DDEEEHNU UNHEEDED
DDEEEILS DIESELED
DDEEEIMR REMEDIED
DDEEEINR REDENIED
DDEEEINV DEVEINED
DDEEEIRT REEDITED
DDEEEIST DEEDIEST
DDEEELPT DEPLETED
DDEEELRW REWELDED
DDEEELSS DEEDLESS
DDEEELTW TWEEDLED
DDEEEMNR REMENDED
DDEEEMNT DEMENTED
DDEEEMPR DEPERMED
DDEEENNU UNNEEDED
DDEEENPX EXPENDED
DDEEENRR RENDERED
DDEEENRT TENDERED
DDEEENSU UNSEEDED
DDEEENTX EXTENDED
DDEEENUW UNWEEDED
DDEEERRT DETERRED
DDEEERST DESERTED
DDEEERSV DESERVED
DDEEESTT DETESTED
DDEEESTV DEVESTED
DDEEESWY DYEWEEDS
DDEEFFIR DIFFERED
DDEEFFNO OFFENDED
DDEEFGGO DEFOGGED
DDEEFGIT FIDGETED
DDEEFINR FRIENDED
DDEEFLNO ENFOLDED
DDEEFLOR REFOLDED
DDEEFMOR DEFORMED
DDEEFNRU REFUNDED
UNDERFED
DDEEGHNU UNHEDGED
DDEEGILN ENGILDED
DDEEGILR REGILDED
DDEEGINR ENGIRDED
DDEEGINS DESIGNED
DDEEGIRV DIVERGED
DDEEGIST DIGESTED
DDEEGJRU REJUDGED
DDEEGLNU UNGELDED
DDEEGMMU DEGUMMED
DDEEGRRS DREDGERS
DDEEGSTU DEGUSTED
DDEEHILS SHIELDED
DDEEHINO HOIDENED
DDEEHINR HINDERED
DDEEHIRT DITHERED
DDEEHNOR DEHORNED
DDEEHNOY HOYDENED
DDEEHORT DEHORTED
DDEEHRRS SHREDDER
DDEEHRSS SHEDDERS
DDEEIINT INEDITED
DDEEIIRV REDIVIDE
DDEEILLV DEVILLED
DDEEILMN MILDENED
DDEEILMW MILDEWED
DDEEILNR REDLINED
DDEEILNT DENTILED
DDEEILRS DREIDELS
DDEEILRV DRIVELED
DDEEILRW WILDERED
DDEEILST DELISTED
DDEEIMNP IMPENDED
DDEEIMNR REMINDED
DDEEIMSS MISDEEDS
DDEEIMTT DEMITTED
DDEEINNT INDENTED
INTENDED
DDEEINNU UNDENIED
DDEEINRT DENDRITE
DDEEINRW REWINDED
DDEEINST DESTINED
DDEEINTU UNEDITED
DDEEIPPR REDIPPED

DDEEIPRR PREDRIED
DDEEIPRS PRESIDED
DDEEIPRV DEPRIVED
DDEEIPSS DEPSIDES
DESPISED
DDEEIPST DESPITED
DDEEIRRS DERIDERS
DDEEIRTV DIVERTED
DDEEISST DESISTED
DDEEISTV DIVESTED
DDEELLMO MODELLED
DDEELLOW DOWELLED
DDEELLOY YODELLED
DDEELMOR MOLDERED
REMOLDED
DDEELMPU DEPLUMED
DDEELMRS MEDDLERS
DDEELNOU LOUDENED
DDEELNUW UNWELDED
DDEELOOW DEWOOLED
DDEELOPR DEPLORED
DDEELOPX EXPLODED
DDEELOPY DEPLOYED
DDEELORS SOLDERED
DDEELOSU DELOUSED
DDEELOVV DEVOLVED
DDEELPRS PEDDLERS
DDEELPRU PRELUDED
DDEELPRY PEDDLERY
DDEELPUX DUPLEXED
DDEELRSS SLEDDERS
DDEELRST TREDDLES
DDEELRSU DELUDERS
DDEEMNNU UNMENDED
DDEEMNOR ENDODERM
DDEEMORR DORMERED
DDEEMORW DEWORMED
DDEEMRRU DEMURRED
MURDERED
DDEENNOR DONNERED
REDONNED
DDEENNTU UNDENTED
UNTENDED
DDEENOPR PONDERED
DDEENOPW PONDWEED
DDEENORS ENDORSED
DDEENORW WONDERED
DDEENRRU DURNEDER
DDEENRSU DENUDERS
SUNDERED
DDEEOPRT DEPORTED
DDEEOPRW POWDERED
DDEEOPSS SEEDPODS
DDEEORRW REWORDED
DDEEORTU DETOURED
DDEEORUV DEVOURED
DDEEORVY OVERDYED
DDEEOTUX TUXEDOED
DDEEPRRU PERDURED
DDEERRUV VERDURED
DDEERSTU DETRUDES
DDEERTUX EXTRUDED
DDEFFISU DIFFUSED
DDEFIIIN NIDIFIED
DDEFIILM MIDFIELD
DDEFIIMO MODIFIED
DDEFIIMW MIDWIFED
DDEFILNO INFOLDED
DDEFILRS FIDDLERS
DDEFLNOU UNFOLDED
DDEFLOPU UPFOLDED
DDEFNNUU UNFUNDED
DDEGGINR DREDGING
DDEGGLOY DOGGEDLY
DDEGGNOO DOGGONED
DDEGHINS SHEDDING
DDEGIINR DERIDING
DDEGIIST GIDDIEST
DDEGILMN MEDDLING
DDEGILNP PEDDLING
DDEGILNR REDDLING
DDEGILNS SLEDDING
DDEGILNU DELUDING
INDULGED
DDEGILOS DISLODGE
DDEGILRS GRIDDLES
DDEGILUV DIVULGED
DDEGIMOS DEMIGODS
DDEGINNS SNEDDING
DDEGINNU DENUDING
DDEGINRU UNGIRDED
DDEGINSW WEDDINGS
DDEGINUU UNGUIDED
DDEGIOST DODGIEST
DDEGIPRU UPGIRDED
DDEGIRRS GRIDDERS

DDEGJNUU UNJUDGED
DDEGLOPS SPLODGED
DDEGLOSS DOGSLEDS
DDEGMOOS DOGEDOMS
DDEGNORU GROUNDED
UNDERDOG
UNDERGOD
DDEGNOSS GODSENDS
DDEGNOSU DUDGEONS
DDEGOOTU OUTDODGE
DDEGRRSU DRUDGERS
DDEGRRUY DRUDGERY
DDEHILNY HIDDENLY
DDEHINOR DIHEDRON
DDEHIORS SHODDIER
DDEHIOSS SHODDIES
DDEHIRSY HYDRIDES
DDEHLRSU HUDDLERS
DDEHNOOU UNHOODED
DDEHNRSU HUNDREDS
DDEHOOOO HOODOOED
DDEHOOSW WOODSHED
DDEHORSU SHROUDED
DDEHRSSU SHUDDERS
DDEHRSUY SHUDDERY
DDEIIKLS DISLIKED
DDEIIKRS SKIDDIER
DDEIILNR DIELDRIN
DDEIILOS IDOLISED
DDEIILOZ IDOLIZED
DDEIIMSZ MIDSIZED
DDEIIMVW MIDWIVED
DDEIINRT NITRIDED
DDEIINTU UNTIDIED
DDEIIOPR PERIODID
DDEIIOPS DIOPSIDE
DIPODIES
DDEIIOST ODDITIES
DDEIIOSX DIOXIDES
OXIDISED
DDEIIOXZ OXIDIZED
DDEIIRSV DIVIDERS
DDEIIRUV REDUVIID
DDEIKNRS KINDREDS
DDEIKOOS SKIDOOED
DDEIKOSY DISYOKED
DDEIKRSS SKIDDERS
DDEIKSVY SKYDIVED
DDEILMOP IMPLODED
DDEILMRS MIDDLERS
DDEILMSU MUDSLIDE
DDEILNPS SPINDLED
SPLENDID
DDEILNRT TRINDLED
DDEILNRU UNRIDDLE
DDEILNSW DWINDLES
SWINDLED
DDEILOPS DISPLODE
LOPSIDED
DDEILOST DELTOIDS
DDEILPRS PIDDLERS
DDEILPRU PUDDLIER
DDEILRRS RIDDLERS
DDEILRST TIDDLERS
DDEILRTW TWIDDLER
DDEILRZZ DRIZZLED
DDEILSTW TWIDDLES
DDEILSTY LYDDITES
DDEILSUV DIVULSED
DDEIMMNU UNDIMMED
DDEIMNSU MUEDDINS
DDEIMORS DERMOIDS
DDEIMOSS DESMOIDS
DDEIMOSU MEDUSOID
DDEIMSTU MUDDIEST
DDEINORS INDORSED
DDEINORT TRENDOID
DDEINOSW DISENDOW
DISOWNED
DOWNSIDE
DDEINOWW WINDOWED
DDEINPSS DISPENDS
DDEINRST STRIDDEN
DDEINRTU INTRUDED
DDEINSST DISTENDS
DDEINSSW SWIDDENS
DDEIOORZ ODORIZED
DDEIOPRS DROPSIED
DDEIOPRV PROVIDED
DDEIOPSS DISPOSED
DDEIORRS DISORDER
DDEIOSTW DOWDIEST
DDEIPSTU DISPUTED
DDEIRSSU DRUIDESS
DDEIRSTU RUDDIEST
STURDIED

DDEISSTU STUDDIES
DDEKMOSU DUKEDOMS
DDELLNUU UNDULLED
DDELLOOP DOLLOPED
DDELMNOU UNMOLDED
DDELMRSU MUDDLERS
DDELNOSY SODDENLY
DDELNRTU TRUNDLED
DDELNSUY SUDDENLY
DDELOORS DOODLERS
DDELOPRS PLODDERS
DDELORST TODDLERS
DDELPRSU PUDDLERS
DDEMMSSU SMEDDUMS
DDEMNOST ODDMENTS
DDEMNOUU DUODENUM
DDEMNPUU PUDENDUM
DDEMOOTU OUTMODED
DDENNORS DENDRONS
DDENOOPS ENDOPODS
DDENOOUW UNWOODED
DDENOPSS DESPONDS
DDENORSU REDOUNDS
DDENOSTU STOUNDED
DDENOSUW SWOUNDED
DDENOTTU UNDOTTED
DDENRSTU DURNDEST
DDEOOOOV VOODOOED
DDEOORSW REDWOODS
DDEOOSWY DYEWOODS
DDEOPRRS PRODDERS
DDEOPRSW DEWDROPS
DDEPRSSU SPUDDERS
DDFGIILN FIDDLING
DDFGILNU FUDDLING
DDFIILSU DISULFID
DDFMNOUU DUMFOUND
DDGGIINY GIDDYING
DDGGINNO DINGDONG
DDGGINRU DRUDGING
DDGHIINW WHIDDING
DDGHILNU HUDDLING
DDGHINTU THUDDING
DDGHOOOS GODHOODS
DDGIIINO INDIGOID
DDGIIINV DIVIDING
DDGIIKNS SKIDDING
DDGIILMN MIDDLING
DDGIILNN DINDLING
DDGIILNP PIDDLING
DDGIILNR RIDDLING
DDGIILNW WIDDLING
DDGILMNU MUDDLING
DDGILNNO NODDLING
DDGILNOO DOODLING
DDGILNOP PLODDING
DDGILNOT TODDLING
DDGILNPU PUDDLING
DDGILNRU RUDDLING
DDGIMNUY MUDDYING
DDGINOPR PRODDING
DDGINPSU PUDDINGS
SPUDDING
DDGINSTU STUDDING
DDGOOOSW DOGWOODS
DDHILOSY SHODDILY
DDHILSUY DUDISHLY
DDHIORSY HYDROIDS
DDHIOSWY DOWDYISH
DDHLMOOO HOODMOLD
DDHLNOOW HOLDDOWN
DDIILOPS DIPLOIDS
DDIILOPY DIPLOIDY
DDIIMMUY DIDYMIUM
DDIIMRSU DRUIDISM
SIDDURIM
DDIIQTUY QUIDDITY
DDIKOOSS SKIDDOOS
DDILOOPP DIPLOPOD
DDILOOWW WILDWOOD
DDILORSY SORDIDLY
DDIMOOSS DODOISMS
DDIMOSUY DIDYMOUS
DDINNOWW DOWNWIND
DDINOOOT ODONTOID
DDINOOWW WOODWIND
DDLMORSU DOLDRUMS
DDMNOORS DROMONDS
DDNOORTW DOWNTROD
DEEEEFRR REFEREED
DEEEEGKR KEDGEREE
DEEEEHLR REHEELED
DEEEEMMS MESEEMED
DEEEEMRR REDEEMER
DEEEEMST ESTEEMED
DEEEENPR DEEPENER

DEEEENRV VENEERED
DEEEERTT TEETERED
DEEEFHLO FEEDHOLE
DEEEFHST SHEETFED
DEEEFINR REDEFINE
DEEEFIPT TEPEFIED
DEEEFIRS REDEFIES
DEEEFIRW FIREWEED
DEEEFLLR REFELLED
DEEEFLRR FERRELED
DEEEFLRT TELFERED
DEEEFLRU REFUELED
DEEEFLRX REFLEXED
DEEEFMNR FREEDMEN
DEEEFNRS ENSERFED
DEEEFNRT DEFERENT
DEEEFNSS DEFENSES
DEEEFORV OVERFEED
DEEEFRRR DEFERRER
REFERRED
DEEEFRRT FERRETED
DEEEFRST FESTERED
DEEEFRTT FETTERED
DEEEGGPR REPEGGED
DEEEGILS ELEGISED
DEEEGILZ ELEGIZED
DEEEGINS DESIGNEE
DEEEGIPR PEDIGREE
DEEEGIRR GREEDIER
DEEEGISW EDGEWISE
DEEEGLPR REPLEDGE
DEEEGLPS PLEDGEES
DEEEGLSS EDGELESS
DEEEGLSV SELVEDGE
DEEEGMRR DEMERGER
REMERGED
DEEEGMRS DEMERGES
DEEEGNNR ENGENDER
DEEEGNRV REVENGED
DEEEGRRT DETERGER
DEEEGRSS EGRESSED
DEEEGRST DETERGES
DEEEGRTT GETTERED
DEEEHLMT HELMETED
DEEEHLPW WHEEPLED
DEEEHLRW WHEEDLER
DEEEHLSS HEEDLESS
DEEEHLSW WHEEDLES
DEEEHMMR REHEMMED
DEEEHMNS ENMESHED
DEEEHMPS HEMPSEED
DEEEHMPW HEMPWEED
DEEEHPRT THREEPED
DEEEHRTT TETHERED
DEEEIKLR DEERLIKE
REEDLIKE
DEEEIKLS SEEDLIKE
DEEEIKLW WEEDLIKE
DEEEILNS SELENIDE
DEEEILRV RELIEVED
DEEEILVW WEEVILED
DEEEIMRS REMEDIES
DEEEIMST SEEDTIME
DEEEINNX ENDEXINE
DEEEINRR REINDEER
DEEEINRS NEREIDES
REDENIES
DEEEINST NEEDIEST
DEEEINTV EVENTIDE
DEEEIPRS SPEEDIER
DEEEIPTX EXPEDITE
DEEEIRRR DERRIERE
DEEEIRSS DIERESES
DEEEIRST REEDIEST
DEEEIRSZ RESEIZED
DEEEIRTW TWEEDIER
DEEEIRVW REVIEWED
DEEEISST SEEDIEST
DEEEISSV DEVISEES
DEEEISTW WEEDIEST
DEEEJLLW JEWELLED
DEEEJNRU DEJEUNER
DEEEJRRS JERREEDS
DEEEJRSY JERSEYED
DEEEKLNN KENNELED
DEEEKLNR KERNELED
DEEEKLNU UNKEELED
DEEEKNSW WEEKENDS
DEEEKOPW POKEWEED
DEEEKORV REEVOKED
DEEEKPRR REPERKED
DEEEKRST STREEKED
DEEEKRSW SKEWERED
DEEELLLV LEVELLED
DEEELLPR REPELLED
DEEELLPT PELLETED

DEEELLPX EXPELLED
DEEELLRV REVELLED
DEEELMRT REMELTED
DEEELNPU UNPEELED
DEEELNRS NEEDLERS
DEEELNRT RELENTED
DEEELNRU UNREELED
DEEELNSS LESSENED
NEEDLESS
DEEELNTT TELNETED
DEEELOPP DEPEOPLE
DEEELOPV DEVELOPE
DEEELPRT DEPLETER
PELTERED
DEEELPST DEPLETES
STEEPLED
DEEELRST STREELED
DEEELRTT LETTERED
DEEELRTW WELTERED
DEEELSSS SEEDLESS
DEEELSSV VESSELED
DEEELSSW WEEDLESS
DEEELSTW TWEEDLES
DEEELTVV VELVETED
DEEEMNRS EMENDERS
DEEEMNSS DEMESNES
SEEDSMEN
DEEEMPRT TEMPERED
DEEEMPTX EXEMPTED
DEEEMRRU MURDEREE
DEEEMRST DEEMSTER
DEEENOPR REOPENED
DEEENORS ENDORSEE
DEEENPRT REPENTED
REPETEND
DEEENPRX EXPENDER
DEEENPSS DEEPNESS
DEEENPSX EXPENSED
DEEENRRR RENDERER
DEEENRRT RERENTED
TENDERER
DEEENRRV REVEREND
DEEENRST RENESTED
RESENTED
DEEENRTT TENTERED
DEEENRTU NEUTERED
DEEENRTX EXTENDER
DEEENRUV REVENUED
UNREEVED
DEEENSSY EYEDNESS
DEEENSTT DETENTES
DEEENSUV VENDEUSE
DEEEOPRT DEPORTEE
DEEEORRZ REZEROED
DEEEORST STEREOED
DEEEORSV OVERSEED
DEEEOSTV DEVOTEES
DEEEPPPR PEPPERED
DEEEPRSS SPEEDERS
DEEEPRST PESTERED
DEEEPRTX EXPERTED
DEEEQSUZ SQUEEZED
DEEERRRT DETERRER
DEEERRRV VERDERER
DEEERRST DESERTER
DEEERRSV DESERVER
RESERVED
REVERSED
DEEERRTV REVERTED
DEEERSSV DESERVES
DEEERSTT DETESTER
RETESTED
DEEERSTV REVESTED
DEEERSTW WESTERED
DEEERSTX EXSERTED
DEEERTTV REVETTED
DEEERTTW REWETTED
DEEESTTV VEDETTES
DEEFFGLU EFFULGED
DEEFFGOR GOFFERED
DEEFFINR NIFFERED
DEEFFINS EFFENDIS
DEEFFIRS SERIFFED
DEEFFNOR FOREFEND
OFFENDER
DEEFFRSU SUFFERED
DEEFGGOR DEFOGGER
DEEFGILR FLEDGIER
DEEFGINR FINGERED
DEEFGINX FEDEXING
DEEFGIRT FIDGETER
DEEFGLNU ENGULFED
DEEFGLUW GULFWEED
DEEFGORR REFORGED
DEEFGORY FROGEYED
DEEFHLOR FREEHOLD

DEEFHLRS FELDSHER
DEEFIINT DEFINITE
DEEFIIRS DEIFIERS
EDIFIERS
FIRESIDE
DEEFIIRV VERIFIED
DEEFILLR REFILLED
DEEFILLT FILLETED
DEEFILMR REFILMED
DEEFILMS MEDFLIES
DEEFILNX INFLEXED
DEEFILPR PILFERED
PREFILED
DEEFILRS DEFILERS
FIELDERS
DEEFILRT FILTERED
DEEFIMSS MISFEEDS
DEEFIMTU TUMEFIED
DEEFINRR INFERRED
DEEFINRS DEFINERS
DEEFINRZ FRENZIED
DEEFINSS FINESSED
DEEFINST INFESTED
DEEFIORS FORESIDE
DEEFIPRR PREFIRED
DEEFIPRX PREFIXED
DEEFIRST RESIFTED
DEEFIRTT REFITTED
DEEFLLOW FELLOWED
DEEFLLRU FULLERED
DEEFLNNU FUNNELED
DEEFLNOR ENFOLDER
DEEFLNSU NEEDFULS
DEEFLNTU UNFELTED
DEEFLNUX UNFLEXED
DEEFLORW DEFLOWER
FLOWERED
REFLOWED
DEEFLOST FEEDLOTS
DEEFLOSY EYEFOLDS
DEEFLRRU FERRULED
DEEFLRUX REFLUXED
DEEFMNOT FOMENTED
DEEFMORR DEFORMER
REFORMED
DEEFMORS FREEDOMS
DEEFMPRU PERFUMED
DEEFNOOR FOREDONE
DEEFNOST SOFTENED
DEEFNRRU REFUNDER
DEEFNSST DEFTNESS
DEEFOORR REROOFED
DEEFOORS FOREDOES
DEEFORST DEFOREST
FORESTED
FOSTERED
DEEFORUY FOUREYED
DEEFPRSU PERFUSED
DEEFRSSU DEFUSERS
DEEGGHHO HEDGEHOG
DEEGGHIP HEDGEPIG
DEEGGIJR JIGGERED
REJIGGED
DEEGGINR GINGERED
RENIGGED
DEEGGIRR DREGGIER
RERIGGED
DEEGGLOR DOGGEREL
DEEGGNOR ENGORGED
DEEGGNPU UNPEGGED
DEEGGORR REGORGED
DEEGGORT GORGETED
DEEGGQSU SQUEGGED
DEEGGRRU RUGGEDER
DEEGHHOP HEDGEHOP
DEEGHILS SLEIGHED
DEEGHINR REHINGED
DEEGHIST HEDGIEST
DEEGHITW WEIGHTED
DEEGHNRU HUNGERED
DEEGHOPS SHEEPDOG
DEEGHORW HEDGEROW
DEEGHOSW HOGWEEDS
DEEGHOTT DOGTEETH
GHETTOED
DEEGIINN INDIGENE
DEEGILMP IMPLEDGE
DEEGILMT GIMLETED
DEEGILNN NEEDLING
DEEGILNO ELOIGNED
DEEGILNR ENGIRDLE
LINGERED
REEDLING
DEEGILNS SEEDLING
DEEGILNT DELETING
DEEGILNU EUGLENID
DEEGILNV DEVELING
DEEGILNW WEDELING
DEEGILRW WEREGILD
DEEGILRY GREEDILY
DEEGILST LEDGIEST
DEEGIMMR IMMERGED
DEEGIMNN EMENDING
DEEGIMRU DEMIURGE
DEEGINPS SPEEDING
DEEGINRR DERINGER
DEEGINRS DESIGNER
ENERGIDS
REDESIGN
REEDINGS
RESIGNED
DEEGINRY REDYEING
DEEGINSS EDGINESS
DEEGINST INGESTED
SIGNETED
DEEGINSX DESEXING
DEEGIPRU PREGUIDE
DEEGIPSW PIGWEEDS
DEEGIRST DIGESTER
REDIGEST
DEEGIRSV DIVERGES
DEEGISST SEDGIEST
DEEGISTW WEDGIEST
DEEGJPRU PREJUDGE
DEEGJRSU REJUDGES
DEEGKMOS GEEKDOMS
DEEGLLRU GRUELLED
DEEGLNOR GOLDENER
DEEGLNRY LEGENDRY
DEEGLOPR PLEDGEOR
DEEGLORV GROVELED
DEEGLORW GLOWERED
REGLOWED
DEEGLOSY GOLDEYES
DEEGLPRS PLEDGERS
DEEGLPST PLEDGETS
DEEGLRSW WERGELDS
DEEGMNOR MONGERED
DEEGMSUW GUMWEEDS
DEEGNNOS ENDOGENS
DEEGNNOY ENDOGENY
DEEGNOPU GEEPOUND
DEEGNORV GOVERNED
DEEGNPRU REPUGNED
DEEGNPUX EXPUNGED
DEEGNRUY UNGREEDY
DEEGNSTU NUTSEDGE
DEEGRRSU RESURGED
DEEGRSTU GESTURED
DEEGRTTU GUTTERED
DEEGSSTU GUSSETED
DEEHHNPY HYPHENED
DEEHHPRS SHEPHERD
DEEHHRST THRESHED
DEEHIKLR HERDLIKE
DEEHIKLS SHEDLIKE
DEEHIKRS SHRIEKED
DEEHIKSV KHEDIVES
DEEHILRS HIRSELED
RELISHED
SHIELDER
DEEHILSS HIDELESS
DEEHILSV DISHEVEL
DEEHIMMS IMMESHED
DEEHIMNS INMESHED
DEEHINPR EPHEDRIN
DEEHINRR HINDERER
DEEHINRS RESHINED
DEEHINTW WHITENED
DEEHIORZ HEROIZED
DEEHIPRS PERISHED
DEEHIRRT DITHERER
DEEHIRRW WHERRIED
DEEHIRST DIETHERS
DEEHIRSV SHIVERED
SHRIEVED
DEEHIRSW SHREWDIE
DEEHIRTW WITHERED
DEEHIRTY HEREDITY
DEEHKNOS KEESHOND
DEEHKNRU HUNKERED
DEEHKORS KOSHERED
DEEHLLOR HOLLERED
DEEHLLOV HOVELLED
DEEHLMNU UNHELMED
DEEHLNPU UNHELPED
DEEHLORV OVERHELD
DEEHLOST HOSTELED
DEEHLOSU HOUSELED
DEEHLOSV SHOVELED
DEEHLPPS SHLEPPED
DEEHLSTU SLEUTHED
DEEHMNRS HERDSMEN
DEEHMNSU UNMESHED
DEEHMORT MOTHERED
DEEHNOPY PHONEYED
DEEHNORR DEHORNER
DEEHNORT DETHRONE
THRENODE
DEEHNOWY HONEYDEW
DEEHNSTU ENTHUSED
DEEHOORV HOOVERED
DEEHOPRT POTHERED
DEEHORRS REDHORSE
DEEHORSU REHOUSED
DEEHORSW RESHOWED
SHOWERED
DEEHORTX EXHORTED
DEEHPRSY SYPHERED
DEEHRRSW SHREWDER
DEEHRTUW WUTHERED
DEEIIKLT TIDELIKE
DEEIILNS SIDELINE
DEEIILRV LIVERIED
DEEIILRW WIELDIER
DEEIIMRZ DIMERIZE
DEEIIMST ITEMISED
DEEIIMTZ ITEMIZED
DEEIINOZ DEIONIZE
DEEIIPRU PRIEDIEU
DEEIIRSS DIERESIS
DEEIIRST SIDERITE
DEEIIRSV DERISIVE
DEEIIRSW WEIRDIES
DEEIISSS DISSEISE
DEEIISSW SIDEWISE
DEEIISSX DEIXISES
DEEIISSZ DISSEIZE
DEEIJNNO ENJOINED
DEEIJNOR REJOINED
DEEIJRTT JITTERED
DEEIKLLR KILLDEER
DEEIKLLS KILLDEES
DEEIKLMO DOMELIKE
DEEIKLMW MILKWEED
DEEIKLNN ENKINDLE
DEEIKLNR REKINDLE
RELINKED
DEEIKLNU DUNELIKE
DEEIKLOV DOVELIKE
DEEIKLSW SILKWEED
DEEIKMSW MIDWEEKS
DEEIKNNP PINKENED
DEEIKNRS DEERSKIN
DEEIKNRT TINKERED
DEEIKNTT KITTENED
DEEIKOSV DOVEKIES
DEEIKPPR KIPPERED
DEEIKSTT DISKETTE
DEEILLMP IMPELLED
MILLEPED
DEEILLNO NIELLOED
DEEILLPR PERILLED
DEEILLRT TILLERED
DEEILLVY VEILEDLY
DEEILMNU DEMILUNE
DEEILMOS MELODIES
MELODISE
DEEILMOZ MELODIZE
DEEILNOS LESIONED
DEEILNOT DELETION
ENTOILED
DEEILNPP LIPPENED
DEEILNRR REDLINER
DEEILNRS REDLINES
DEEILNRU UNDERLIE
DEEILNSS IDLENESS
LINSEEDS
DEEILNST ENLISTED
LISTENED
TINSELED
DEEILNSV SNIVELED
DEEILNTT ENTITLED
DEEILNUV UNLEVIED
UNVEILED
DEEILOPT LEPIDOTE
PETIOLED
DEEILORT DOLERITE
LOITERED
DEEILORV EVILDOER
OVERIDLE
DEEILOSS OILSEEDS
DEEILOTT TOILETED
DEEILPPR LIPPERED
DEEILPRX DIPLEXER
DEEILPSY SPEEDILY
DEEILRRV DRIVELER
DEEILRST RELISTED
DEEILRSU LEISURED
DEEILRSV DELIVERS
DESILVER
SILVERED
SLIVERED
DEEILRSW WIELDERS
DEEILRSY YIELDERS
DEEILRTT LITTERED
RETITLED
DEEILRVY DELIVERY
DEEILSSS IDLESSES
DEEILSST TIDELESS
DEEILSUV DELUSIVE
DEEILSVW SWIVELED
DEEILTUY YULETIDE
DEEIMMNS ENDEMISM
DEEIMMOS SEMIDOME
DEEIMMRS IMMERSED
SIMMERED
DEEIMMSS MISDEEMS
DEEIMNOR DOMINEER
DEEIMNOS DEMONISE
DEEIMNOZ DEMONIZE
DEEIMNPT PEDIMENT
DEEIMNRR REMINDER
REREMIND
DEEIMNRT REMINTED
DEEIMNST SEDIMENT
DEEIMNSU SEMINUDE
DEEIMNTT MITTENED
DEEIMORS EMEROIDS
DEEIMPRR PERIDERM
DEEIMPRS DEMIREPS
EPIDERMS
IMPEDERS
PREMISED
SIMPERED
DEEIMPRX PREMIXED
DEEIMRSS DERMISES
DEEIMRST DEMERITS
DEMISTER
DIMETERS
DEEIMRTT REMITTED
DEEINNPR REPINNED
DEEINNRT INDENTER
INTENDER
INTERNED
DEEINNRV INNERVED
DEEINNST DENTINES
DESINENT
DEEINNSZ DENIZENS
DEEINNTV INVENTED
DEEINNTW ENTWINED
DEEINNUV UNENVIED
UNVEINED
DEEINORS INDORSEE
DEEINORT ORIENTED
DEEINORW IRONWEED
DEEINOSV NOSEDIVE
DEEINOTV DENOTIVE
DEEINPRS SPENDIER
DEEINPSS DISPENSE
DEEINPSW PINWEEDS
DEEINQRU ENQUIRED
DEEINQSU SEQUINED
DEEINRRT INTERRED
TRENDIER
DEEINRRV REDRIVEN
DEEINRRW REWINDER
DEEINRSS DIRENESS
DEEINRST INSERTED
NERDIEST
RESIDENT
SINTERED
TRENDIES
DEEINRSV INVERSED
DEEINRSW REWIDENS
WIDENERS
DEEINRSX INDEXERS
DEEINRTT RETINTED
DEEINRTU RETINUED
REUNITED
DEEINRTV INVERTED
DEEINRTW WINTERED
DEEINRTX DEXTRINE
DEEINSST DESTINES
DEEINSSW DEWINESS
WIDENESS
DEEINSTT DINETTES
INSETTED
DEEINSTU DETINUES
DEEINSTV INVESTED
DEEINSUZ UNSEIZED
DEEINTUV DUVETINE
DEEIOPRT PROTEIDE
DEEIOPRX PEROXIDE
DEEIOPSS EPISODES
DEEIOPST EPIDOTES
POETISED
DEEIOPSX EPOXIDES
DEEIOPTZ POETIZED
DEEIORRV OVERRIDE
DEEIORSV OVERSIDE
DEEIORSW DOWERIES
WEIRDOES
DEEIORTV OVEREDIT
DEEIORTZ EROTIZED
DEEIORVW OVERWIDE
DEEIOTVX VIDEOTEX
DEEIPPQU EQUIPPED
DEEIPPRZ ZIPPERED
DEEIPPST PEPTIDES
DEEIPPTT PIPETTED
DEEIPPTZ PEPTIZED
DEEIPRRS PREDRIES
PRESIDER
REPRISED
RESPIRED
DEEIPRRV DEPRIVER
DEEIPRRW PREWIRED
DEEIPRSS DESPISER
DISPERSE
PRESIDES
DEEIPRST PREEDITS
PRIESTED
RESPITED
DEEIPRSU DUPERIES
DEEIPRSV DEPRIVES
PREVISED
DEEIPRTT PRETTIED
DEEIPSSS DESPISES
DEEIPSST DESPITES
SIDESTEP
DEEIPSTU DEPUTIES
DEEIPTUZ DEPUTIZE
DEEIQRRU REQUIRED
DEEIQRSU ESQUIRED
DEEIQRTU REQUITED
DEEIQRUV QUIVERED
DEEIQTUU QUIETUDE
DEEIRRSS DERRISES
DESIRERS
DRESSIER
RESIDERS
DEEIRRST DESTRIER
DEEIRRSU RUDERIES
DEEIRRSV DERIVERS
REDRIVES
DEEIRRTV DIVERTER
VERDITER
DEEIRRWW WIREDREW
DEEIRSST DIESTERS
EDITRESS
RESISTED
SISTERED
DEEIRSSU DIURESES
REISSUED
RESIDUES
DEEIRSSV DEVISERS
DISSERVE
DISSEVER
DEEIRSTT TIREDEST
DEEIRSTW WEIRDEST
DEEIRTTT TITTERED
DEEIRTTV RIVETTED
DEEISSSU DISEUSES
DEEISTTV VIDETTES
DEEJKNTU JUNKETED
DEEJPRRU PERJURED
DEEKKOOY OKEYDOKE
DEEKLNST SKLENTED
DEEKLOOR RELOOKED
DEEKMNOY MONKEYED
DEEKNNNU UNKENNED
DEEKNOTW KNOTWEED
DEEKNOTY KEYNOTED
DEEKNSSW NEWSDESK
DEEKORRW REWORKED
DEEKORST RESTOKED
DEEKOSVY DOVEKEYS
DEELLMOR MODELLER
DEELLMOW MELLOWED
DEELLNOP POLLENED
DEELLNOR ENROLLED
RONDELLE
DEELLOPR REPOLLED
DEELLORR REROLLED
DEELLORW ROWELLED
WELLDOER
DEELLORY YODELLER
DEELLOTW TOWELLED
DEELLOTX EXTOLLED
DEELLOVY VOLLEYED
DEELLOWY YELLOWED
DEELLPUW UPWELLED
DEELLRSU DUELLERS
DEELLRSW DWELLERS
DEELLSSW WELDLESS
DEELLSUX DUXELLES
DEELMMOP POMMELED
DEELMMPU PUMMELED
DEELMNOO MELODEON
DEELMNTU UNMELTED
DEELMNTW WELDMENT
DEELMOOS DOLESOME
DEELMOPY EMPLOYED
DEELMORS MODELERS
MORSELED
REMODELS
DEELMOST MOLESTED
DEELMPPU PEPLUMED
DEELMPSU DEPLUMES
DEELMRUY DEMURELY
DEELNNTU TUNNELED
DEELNOOS LOOSENED
DEELNORT REDOLENT
RONDELET
DEELNORV OVERLEND
DEELNOSS LESSONED
DEELNOSU ENSOULED
DEELNPRY DEPRENYL
DEELNRTU UNDERLET
DEELNRTY TENDERLY
DEELNSSW LEWDNESS
DEELNTTU UNLETTED
DEELNWWY NEWLYWED
DEELOORT RETOOLED
DEELOPPR LOPPERED
DEELOPRR DEPLORER
DEELOPRS DEPLORES
DEELOPRW REPLOWED
DEELOPRX EXPLODER
EXPLORED
DEELOPRY DEPLOYER
REDEPLOY
DEELOPSV DEVELOPS
DEELOPSX EXPLODES
DEELORRS RESOLDER
SOLDERER
DEELORSU DELOUSER
URODELES
DEELORSV RESOLVED
DEELORSY YODELERS
DEELORTT DOTTEREL
DEELORTV REVOLTED
DEELORTW TROWELED
DEELORUV LOUVERED
DEELORVV REVOLVED
DEELORVW OVERLEWD
DEELOSSU DELOUSES
DEELOSVV DEVOLVES
DEELPRRU PRELUDER
DEELPRSU PRELUDES
REPULSED
DEELPRTU DRUPELET
DEELPRUX DUPLEXER
DEELPSUX DUPLEXES
EXPULSED
DEELPTTY PETTEDLY
DEELRSTU DELUSTER
LUSTERED
RESULTED
DEELRSTW WRESTLED
DEELRSTY RESTYLED
DEELRSUV REVULSED
DEEMMORS MESODERM
DEEMMRSU SUMMERED
DEEMNOOS ENDOSOME
MOONSEED
DEEMNOQU QUEENDOM
DEEMNORR MODERNER
DEEMNORS MODERNES
DEEMNORT ENTODERM
MENTORED
DEEMNOSS DEMONESS
DEEMNOST DEMETONS
DEEMNOSU EUDEMONS
DEEMOOPR PODOMERE
DEEMOORT ODOMETER
DEEMORRW DEWORMER
DEEMORST MODESTER
DEEMORSW WORMSEED
DEEMORSX EXODERMS
DEEMORTU UDOMETER
DEEMPPRU REPUMPED
DEEMPRST DEMPSTER
DEEMPRSU PRESUMED
DEEMPRTU PERMUTED

DEEMPSUW SUMPWEED
DEEMRRRU DEMURRER
MURDERER
DEEMRSTU DEMUREST
MUSTERED
DEEMRTTU MUTTERED
DEENNNOP PENNONED
DEENNNPU UNPENNED
DEENNOPT DEPONENT
DEENNOPU UNOPENED
DEENNORW RENOWNED
DEENNOSS DONENESS
DEENNOST ENDNOTES
SONNETED
DEENNOSY DOYENNES
DEENNPST PENDENTS
DEENNRTU UNRENTED
DEENNRUV UNNERVED
DEENNSSU NUDENESS
DEENNTTU UNTENTED
DEENOORT ENROOTED
DEENOORV OVERDONE
DEENOORW WOODENER
DEENOOSV NOSEDOVE
DEENOPRR PONDERER
DEENOPRW PREOWNED
DEENOPSS SPONDEES
DEENOPST PENTODES
DEENORRS ENDORSER
DEENORRW WONDERER
DEENORSS ENDORSES
DEENORSW ENDOWERS
REENDOWS
WORSENED
DEENORTU DEUTERON
DEENOSST STENOSED
DEENPPRS PERPENDS
DEENPRSS SPENDERS
DEENPRST PRETENDS
DEENRRSU ENDURERS
SUNDERER
DEENRRTU RETURNED
DEENRSSU RUDENESS
DEENRSTU DENTURES
SEDERUNT
UNDERSET
UNRESTED
DEENRSUU UNDERUSE
DEENRSUV UNSERVED
UNVERSED
DEENRTUV VENTURED
DEENSSSY SYNDESES
DEENSTTU UNTESTED
DEENSTUV UNVESTED
DEENTTUW UNWETTED
DEENTUVY DUVETYNE
DEEOOPPR PEREOPOD
DEEOORRV OVERDOER
OVERRODE
DEEOORSV OVERDOES
OVERDOSE
DEEOPPST ESTOPPED
DEEOPRRR PREORDER
DEEOPRRT DEPORTER
PORTERED
REPORTED
DEEOPRRU REPOURED
DEEOPRRV REPROVED
DEEOPRRW POWDERER
DEEOPRSS DEPOSERS
DEEOPRST DOPESTER
DEEOPRSY EYEDROPS
DEEOPRTT POTTERED
REPOTTED
DEEOPRTX EXPORTED
DEEOPRUZ DOUZEPER
DEEOPSSU ESPOUSED
DEEOPSTU OUTSPEED
DEEOQRTU ROQUETED
DEEORRRS ORDERERS
REORDERS
DEEORRRV VERDEROR
DEEORRST RESORTED
RESTORED
DEEORRTT RETORTED
DEEORRTU REROUTED
DEEORRUV DEVOURER
OVERRUDE
DEEORRVW OVERDREW
DEEORRVY OVERDYER
DEEORSST DOSSERET
OERSTEDS
DEEORSTT TETRODES
DEEORSTX DEXTROSE
DEEORSTY OYSTERED
STOREYED

DEEORSUV OVERUSED
DEEORSVY OVERDYES
DEEORTTT TOTTERED
DEEORTTX EXTORTED
DEEORTUV DEVOUTER
DEEOSSUX EXODUSES
DEEOSTUX TUXEDOES
DEEPPRTY PRETYPED
DEEPPSSU SPEEDUPS
DEEPRRSU PERDURES
DEEPRTTU PUTTERED
DEEPRUVY PURVEYED
DEERRSSS DRESSERS
DEERRSUV VERDURES
DEERRTTU TURRETED
DEERRTUX EXTRUDER
DEERSSST DESSERTS
STRESSED
DEERSSSU DURESSES
DEERSTTU TRUSTEED
DEERSTUV VESTURED
DEERSTUX EXTRUDES
DEERSUVY SURVEYED
DEERTTUX TEXTURED
DEFFHILW WHIFFLED
DEFFHLSU SHUFFLED
DEFFHORS SHROFFED
DEFFIINT TIFFINED
DEFFIIPS SPIFFIED
DEFFIKLS SKIFFLED
DEFFILNS SNIFFLED
DEFFILOV FIVEFOLD
DEFFIMOS FIEFDOMS
DEFFIOSS OFFSIDES
DEFFIQSU SQUIFFED
DEFFIRSU DIFFUSER
DEFFISSU DIFFUSES
DEFFISUX SUFFIXED
DEFFLNSU SNUFFLED
DEFFLOSU SOUFFLED
DEFFLRTU TRUFFLED
DEFFNORS FORFENDS
DEFFNOSS SENDOFFS
DEFFSSUU SUFFUSED
DEFFSTUY DYESTUFF
DEFGGILN FLEDGING
DEFGHILT FLIGHTED
DEFGHIRT FRIGHTED
DEFGIIIN IGNIFIED
DEFGIILN DEFILING
FIELDING
DEFGIILU UGLIFIED
DEFGIINN DEFINING
DEFGIINY DEIFYING
EDIFYING
DEFGIIST DIGESTIF
DEFGILNU INGULFED
DEFGILRU DIRGEFUL
DEFGILTY GIFTEDLY
DEFGINSU DEFUSING
DEFGINTU UNGIFTED
DEFGINUZ DEFUZING
DEFGIOOW GOODWIFE
DEFGIORS FIREDOGS
DEFGJORU FORJUDGE
DEFGNORU UNFORGED
DEFHIIMU HUMIFIED
DEFHIINS FIENDISH
FINISHED
DEFHINSU UNFISHED
DEFHIOOW WIFEHOOD
DEFHIRST REDSHIFT
DEFHLOOS SELFHOOD
DEFHOORS SERFHOOD
DEFIIILV VILIFIED
DEFIIIMN MINIFIED
DEFIIINS NIDIFIES
DEFIIINV VINIFIED
DEFIIIVV VIVIFIED
DEFIILLP FILLIPED
DEFIILLW WILDLIFE
DEFIILMR MIDLIFER
DEFIILMS MISFIELD
MISFILED
DEFIILNO DIOLEFIN
DEFIILNS INFIDELS
INFIELDS
DEFIILRW WILDFIRE
DEFIILSU FLUIDISE
DEFIILTY FIDELITY
DEFIILUZ FLUIDIZE
DEFIIMNR INFIRMED
DEFIIMOR MODIFIER
DEFIIMOS MODIFIES
DEFIIMRS MISFIRED
DEFIIMSS FIDEISMS

DEFIIMSW MIDWIFES
DEFIINOT NOTIFIED
DEFIINTU FINITUDE
DEFIINTY IDENTIFY
DEFIIOSS OSSIFIED
DEFIIPRU PURIFIED
DEFIIPSS FISSIPED
DEFIIPTY TYPIFIED
DEFIIRRT DRIFTIER
DEFIISST FIDEISTS
DEFIITTY FETIDITY
DEFILLNU UNFILLED
DEFILMNU FULMINED
UNFILMED
DEFILNNO NINEFOLD
DEFILNOR INFOLDER
DEFILNOU UNFOILED
DEFILNRS FLINDERS
DEFILNRU UNRIFLED
DEFILNRY FRIENDLY
DEFILOPR PROFILED
DEFILORU FLUORIDE
DEFILORV FRIVOLED
DEFILOTU OUTFIELD
DEFILPRU PRIDEFUL
DEFILPTU UPLIFTED
DEFILRRU FLURRIED
DEFILRVY FERVIDLY
DEFILRZZ FRIZZLED
DEFILSSU SULFIDES
DEFIMNOR INFORMED
DEFIMOPR PEDIFORM
DEFIMORY REMODIFY
DEFIMOSW WIFEDOMS
DEFIMRRU DRUMFIRE
DEFINSTU UNSIFTED
DEFINTTU UNFITTED
DEFIOORW FIREWOOD
DEFIOPRT PIEDFORT
PROFITED
DEFIORTU OUTFIRED
DEFIOTXY DETOXIFY
DEFIRRST DRIFTERS
DEFIRSSU FISSURED
SURFSIDE
DEFISSTU FEUDISTS
DEFKLORY FORKEDLY
DEFKNORU UNFORKED
DEFLLOOR FOLDEROL
DEFLLOOW FOLLOWED
DEFLMOSS SELFDOMS
DEFLNORS FONDLERS
DEFLNORU FLOUNDER
UNFOLDER
DEFLNOST TENFOLDS
DEFLNRUU UNFURLED
DEFLNTUU UNFLUTED
DEFLOORS FLOODERS
REFLOODS
DEFLOORT FORETOLD
DEFLOOSS FOODLESS
DEFLOOUW FUELWOOD
DEFLOPUW UPFLOWED
DEFLORSS FORDLESS
DEFLORST TELFORDS
DEFLRSUU DESULFUR
SULFURED
DEFMNORU UNFORMED
DEFMOOOR FOREDOOM
DEFMORSS SERFDOMS
DEFNNOSS FONDNESS
DEFNNOUW NEWFOUND
DEFNOORS FRONDOSE
DEFNOORU UNROOFED
DEFNOORV OVERFOND
DEFNORRU FRONDEUR
DEFNORSU FOUNDERS
REFOUNDS
DEFNORTU FORTUNED
DEFNORUV OVERFUND
DEFNPRSU PREFUNDS
DEFNRRUU UNDERFUR
DEFNTTUU UNTUFTED
DEFOORRW FOREWORD
DEFOOSSU DOOFUSES
DEFOOTUX OUTFOXED
DEFORRUW FURROWED
DEFORSST DEFROSTS
FROSTEDS
DEFORSTW FROWSTED
DEGGHIRS DREGGISH
DEGGHRSU SHRUGGED
DEGGIINN DEIGNING
DEGGILNP PLEDGING

DEGGILNS GELDINGS
SLEDGING
SNIGGLED
DEGGILNU DELUGING
DEGGILRW WRIGGLED
DEGGINRU UNRIGGED
DEGGIORS DISGORGE
DEGGIOST DOGGIEST
DEGGIPRS SPRIGGED
DEGGIRRU DRUGGIER
DEGGIRSU DRUGGIES
DEGGLMSU SMUGGLED
DEGGLNSU SNUGGLED
DEGGLORS DOGGRELS
DEGGLORY GORGEDLY
DEGGLRUY RUGGEDLY
DEGGNOOR DOGGONER
DEGGNOOS DOGGONES
DEGGNOSU GUDGEONS
DEGGRRSU GRUDGERS
DEGGRSTU DRUGGETS
DEGHIINS DINGHIES
DEGHIKNT KNIGHTED
DEGHILNS SHINGLED
DEGHILPT PLIGHTED
DEGHILST DELIGHTS
SLIGHTED
DEGHINNS SHENDING
DEGHINNU UNHINGED
DEGHIOPS DOGESHIP
DEGHIORU DOUGHIER
DEGHLOPU PLOUGHED
DEGHLORY HYDROGEL
DEGHLOSU SLOUGHED
DEGHMOSU GUMSHOED
DEGHNORT THRONGED
DEGHNORY HYDROGEN
DEGHOOSU DOGHOUSE
DEGIIITZ DIGITIZE
DEGIIKNS KINGSIDE
DEGIILMN DELIMING
DEGIILNS SIDELING
DEGIILNT DILIGENT
DEGIILNV DEVILING
DEGIILNW WIELDING
DEGIILNY YIELDING
DEGIILTY GELIDITY
DEGIIMNP IMPEDING
IMPINGED
DEGIIMNS DEMISING
DEGIIMSU MISGUIDE
DEGIINNR NIDERING
DEGIINNS INDIGENS
DEGIINNT ENDITING
INDIGENT
DEGIINNW WIDENING
DEGIINNX INDEXING
DEGIINNZ DIZENING
DEGIINOS INDIGOES
DEGIINRS DESIRING
RESIDING
RINGSIDE
DEGIINRV DERIVING
DEGIINRW WEIRDING
DEGIINST DINGIEST
DEGIINSV DEVISING
DEGIIRST RIDGIEST
DEGIISSU DISGUISE
DEGIJMSU MISJUDGE
DEGIKLRU KLUDGIER
DEGILLNU DUELLING
DEGILLNW DWELLING
DEGILMNO MODELING
DEGILMOS MISLODGE
DEGILMPS GLIMPSED
DEGILNOS SIDELONG
DEGILNOW DOWELING
DEGILNOY YODELING
DEGILNRU INDULGER
DEGILNSU INDULGES
DEGILNSW SWINGLED
DEGILNWY WINGEDLY
DEGILOOR GOODLIER
DEGILOOY IDEOLOGY
DEGILORV OVERGILD
DEGILOST GODLIEST
DEGILRRS GIRDLERS
DEGILRSU GUILDERS
SLUDGIER
DEGILRSW WERGILDS
DEGILRUV DIVULGER
DEGILRZZ GRIZZLED
DEGILSUV DIVULGES
DEGIMMNO MODEMING
DEGIMNNS MENDINGS

DEGIMNOS MENDIGOS
SMIDGEON
DEGIMNOT DEMOTING
DEGIMNPU IMPUGNED
DEGIMNSS SMIDGENS
DEGIMRSU SMUDGIER
DEGINNNU UNENDING
DEGINNOP DEPONING
DEGINNOT DENOTING
DEGINNOV DOVENING
DEGINNOW ENDOWING
DEGINNOZ DOZENING
DEGINNPS SPENDING
DEGINNPU UPENDING
DEGINNRT TRENDING
DEGINNRU ENDURING
DEGINNSU UNSIGNED
DEGINNTU UNTINGED
DEGINOOR RODEOING
DEGINOPS DEPOSING
DEGINORR ORDERING
DEGINORS NEGROIDS
DEGINORU GUERIDON
DEGINORV RINGDOVE
DEGINORW DOWERING
DEGINOSW WENDIGOS
WIDGEONS
DEGINOTV DEVOTING
DEGINOTX DETOXING
DEGINPRS SPRINGED
DEGINPTU DEPUTING
DEGINRRS GRINDERS
REGRINDS
DEGINRRY GRINDERY
REDRYING
DEGINRSS DRESSING
DEGINRST STRINGED
DEGINRSW REDWINGS
DEGINRSY SYNERGID
SYRINGED
DEGINSSU DINGUSES
DEGINSTU DUNGIEST
DEGINTTU DUETTING
DEGIOPRR PORRIDGE
DEGIOPRT RIDGETOP
DEGIOPSS GOSSIPED
DEGIOPST PODGIEST
DEGIORRV OVERGIRD
DEGIORST DIGESTOR
GRODIEST
STODGIER
DEGIOTUU OUTGUIDE
DEGIPSTU PUDGIEST
DEGJMNTU JUDGMENT
DEGLLNOY GOLDENLY
DEGLMNOT LODGMENT
DEGLNOOT GOLDTONE
DEGLNOUV UNGLOVED
DEGLNRTU GRUNTLED
DEGLOOPR PROLOGED
DEGLOOPY PEDOLOGY
DEGLOOUU DUOLOGUE
DEGLOPRS PLEDGORS
DEGLOPSS SPLODGES
DEGLPRSU SPLURGED
DEGMOOPR POGROMED
DEGNNOSU DUNGEONS
DEGNNOUW UNGOWNED
DEGNOOSS GOODNESS
DEGNOOST STEGODON
DEGNOPPU OPPUGNED
DEGNORRU GROUNDER
REGROUND
DEGNORSU GUERDONS
DEGNORTU TRUDGEON
DEGNPRUU UNPURGED
DEGNRSTU TRUDGENS
DEGOORSV OVERDOGS
DEGOORTT GROTTOED
DEGPRSUU UPSURGED
DEGRRSTU TRUDGERS
DEHHILTW WITHHELD
DEHHISTW WHISHTED
DEHHLSUY HUSHEDLY
DEHHOOSW WHOOSHED
DEHIIKLS DISHLIKE
DEHIILLS HILLSIDE
SIDEHILL
DEHIILSV DEVILISH
DEHIIMMS SHIMMIED
DEHIIMNS MINISHED
DEHIIMST DITHEISM
DEHIIMSW WHIMSIED
DEHIINNS SHINNIED
DEHIINNW WHINNIED
DEHIINSS SHINDIES

DEHIIPSS SHIPSIDE
DEHIIRRW WHIRRIED
DEHIIRST DISHERIT
DEHIISST DISHIEST
DEHIISTT DITHEIST
STITHIED
DEHIJMNO DEMIJOHN
DEHIKLMS MILKSHED
DEHIKLOO HOODLIKE
DEHIKMOS SHEIKDOM
DEHILLRS SHRILLED
DEHILLRT THRILLED
DEHILMOS DEMOLISH
DEHILMSS DISHELMS
DEHILMTY DIMETHYL
DEHILNOR INHOLDER
DEHILNPY DIPHENYL
DEHILOOS DHOOLIES
DEHILOPS DEPOLISH
POLISHED
DEHILOTY HOLYTIDE
DEHILPRT PHILTRED
DEHILPSU SULPHIDE
DEHILSTW WHISTLED
DEHILTTW WHITTLED
DEHIMNOS HEDONISM
MONISHED
DEHIMORS HEIRDOMS
DEHIMOST ETHMOIDS
DEHIMPRS SHRIMPED
DEHINOPS SIPHONED
SPHENOID
DEHINORS HORDEINS
DEHINOST HEDONIST
DEHINPSU PUNISHED
DEHINSUW UNWISHED
DEHIOOST DHOOTIES
HOODIEST
DEHIOPRS SPHEROID
DEHIOPRT TROPHIED
DEHIORRR HORRIDER
DEHIORSS HIDROSES
DEHIORTW WITHEROD
DEHIORTY THYREOID
DEHIOSSW SIDESHOW
DEHIOSTU HIDEOUTS
DEHIQSSU SQUISHED
DEHIRRST REDSHIRT
DEHIRRSU DHURRIES
DEHIRSTT THIRSTED
DEHIRTWW WITHDREW
DEHKLNOU ELKHOUND
DEHKNOOU UNHOOKED
DEHKNSUU UNHUSKED
DEHLLOOO HOLLOOED
DEHLLOOU HULLOOED
DEHLLOOW HOLLOWED
DEHLLOPY PHYLLODE
DEHLMOOT HOTELDOM
DEHLMORY HYDROMEL
DEHLMOSU MUDHOLES
DEHLMPSU SHLUMPED
DEHLNTUY HUNTEDLY
DEHLOOPT POTHOLED
DEHLOORV HOLDOVER
OVERHOLD
DEHLOOSS HOODLESS
DEHLOOST TOEHOLDS
TOOLSHED
DEHLOOSW WOOLSHED
DEHLOPRU UPHOLDER
DEHLOPSS SPLOSHED
DEHLORSU SHOULDER
DEHLRRSU HURDLERS
DEHLRSWY SHREWDLY
DEHLSTTU SHUTTLED
DEHMMRTU THRUMMED
DEHMNRUY UNRHYMED
DEHMOORW WHOREDOM
DEHMOOSS SMOOSHED
DEHMOOST SMOOTHED
DEHMOOSZ SHMOOZED
DEHMOPRY HYPODERM
DEHMORUU HUMOURED
DEHNOORU HONOURED
DEHNOOSW HOEDOWNS
WOODHENS
DEHNOPSY SYPHONED
DEHNORSU ENSHROUD
HOUNDERS
UNHORSED
DEHNORTY THRENODY
DEHNOSSW SNOWSHED
DEHNOSTZ DOZENTHS
DEHNOSUU UNHOUSED
DEHNRSTU THUNDERS

DEHNRSUU UNRUSHED
DEHNRTUY THUNDERY
DEHOOPRT THEROPOD
DEHOOSSW SWOOSHED
DEHOPRST POTSHERD
DEHPRSUU UPRUSHED
DEHQSSUU SQUUSHED
DEHRRSTU DRUTHERS
DEHRSTTU THRUSTED
DEIIIMST DIMITIES
DEIIINSV DIVINISE
DEIIINVZ DIVINIZE
DEIIISVV DIVISIVE
DEIIKKLS DISKLIKE
DEIIKLMS MISLIKED
DEIIKLNR KINDLIER
DEIIKLNV DEVILKIN
DEIIKLRS DISLIKER
DEIIKLSS DISLIKES
DEIIKNST DINKIEST
DEIIKSVV SKIVVIED
DEIILLMP MILLIPED
DEIILMMS SEMIMILD
DEIILMNS MIDLINES
DEIILMPR DIMPLIER
DEIILMRU DELIRIUM
DEIILMST DELIMITS
LIMITEDS
DEIILMSU SEDILIUM
DEIILMSV MIDLIVES
MISLIVED
DEIILMSW SEMIWILD
DEIILNNU INDULINE
DEIILNOS LIONISED
DEIILNOT TOLIDINE
DEIILNOZ LIONIZED
DEIILNPV VILIPEND
DEIILNTT INTITLED
DEIILNVY DIVINELY
DEIILNXY XYLIDINE
DEIILOPS PLOIDIES
DEIILORS IDOLISER
DEIILORZ IDOLIZER
DEIILOSS IDOLISES
DEIILOSZ IDOLIZES
DEIILPSS SIDESLIP
DEIILSTU UTILISED
DEIILTUV DILUTIVE
DEIILTUZ UTILIZED
DEIIMMRS DIMERISM
DEIIMMST MISTIMED
DEIIMNOS DOMINIES
DEIIMNRT DIRIMENT
DEIIMNTU MUTINIED
DEIIMPRU PERIDIUM
DEIIMRSV MISDRIVE
DEIIMSST MISEDITS
DEIIMSTT TIMIDEST
DEIIMSVW MIDWIVES
DEIINNOP PINIONED
DEIINNPP PINNIPED
DEIINNTW INTWINED
DEIINORS DERISION
IRONSIDE
RESINOID
DEIINORT RETINOID
DEIINORZ IRONIZED
DEIINOST EDITIONS
SEDITION
DEIINOSV VISIONED
DEIINOTY IDONEITY
DEIINPPW WINDPIPE
DEIINPRS INSPIRED
DEIINPRT INTREPID
DEIINPRY PYRIDINE
DEIINPSS SIDESPIN
DEIINPTU UNPITIED
DEIINQRU INQUIRED
DEIINQSU QUINSIED
DEIINRSS INSIDERS
DEIINRST DISINTER
INDITERS
NITRIDES
DEIINRSU URIDINES
DEIINRSV DIVINERS
DEIINRTU UNTIDIER
DEIINSST INSISTED
TIDINESS
DEIINSTU DISUNITE
NUDITIES
UNTIDIES
DEIINSTV DIVINEST
DEIINSTW WINDIEST
DEIINTTU INTUITED
DEIINTTY IDENTITY
DEIINTUZ UNITIZED

DEIIOPRS PRESIDIO
DEIIOPTY IDIOTYPE
DEIIORST DIORITES
DEIIORSX OXIDISER
DEIIORSZ IODIZERS
DEIIORTX TRIOXIDE
DEIIORXZ OXIDIZER
DEIIOSSX OXIDISES
DEIIOSTT OTITIDES
DEIIOSXZ OXIDIZES
DEIIPPRR DRIPPIER
DEIIPPST DIPPIEST
DEIIPRST RIPTIDES
SPIRITED
TIDERIPS
DEIIPRSZ DISPRIZE
DEIIPTTY TEPIDITY
DEIIQSTU DISQUIET
DEIIRRVV VIVERRID
DEIIRSSU DIURESIS
DEIIRSTT DIRTIEST
DEIISSTT DITSIEST
DEIISTTZ DITZIEST
DEIISTVV VIVIDEST
DEIISTZZ DIZZIEST
DEIJNNOU UNJOINED
DEIJNORS JOINDERS
DEIJORRY JOYRIDER
DEIJORSY JOYRIDES
DEIKKLNO KLONDIKE
DEIKKNNU UNKINKED
DEIKLLOR LORDLIKE
DEIKLMRU DRUMLIKE
DEIKLNNU UNLINKED
DEIKLNOW DOWNLIKE
DEIKLNPU UPLINKED
DEIKLNRS KINDLERS
DEIKLNRW WRINKLED
DEIKLNSS KINDLESS
DEIKLNTW TWINKLED
DEIKLSTU DUSTLIKE
DEIKMNOO KIMONOED
DEIKMOSY MISYOKED
DEIKNNOR DONNIKER
DEIKNNRU UNKINDER
DEIKNNSS KINDNESS
DEIKNORV OVERKIND
DEIKNOSS DOESKINS
DEIKNRRS DRINKERS
DEIKNSSU UNKISSED
DEIKORSS DROSKIES
DEIKORST DORKIEST
DEIKOSSY DISYOKES
DEIKRSVY SKYDIVER
DEIKSSTU DUSKIEST
DEIKSSVY SKYDIVES
DEILLMNU UNMILLED
DEILLNSW INDWELLS
DEILLNTU UNTILLED
DEILLNUW UNWILLED
DEILLOPW PILLOWED
DEILLORR LORDLIER
DEILLORT TROLLIED
DEILLORU LOUDLIER
DEILLOWW WILLOWED
DEILLPRR PREDRILL
DEILLRRS DRILLERS
REDRILLS
DEILLSTU DUELLIST
DEILMNSS MILDNESS
MINDLESS
DEILMOOT DOLOMITE
DEILMOPR IMPLORED
DEILMOPS IMPLODES
DEILMORU LEMUROID
MOULDIER
DEILMORV OVERMILD
DEILMOSS MIDSOLES
DEILMOST MELODIST
MODELIST
MOLDIEST
DEILMOSU EMULSOID
DEILMOTV DEMIVOLT
DEILMPPU PLUMIPED
DEILMPSU DISPLUME
IMPULSED
DEILMPTU MULTIPED
DEILMRRU DRUMLIER
DEILMRSU MISRULED
DEILMSTU MUSTELID
DEILNNOT INDOLENT
DEILNOOS EIDOLONS
SOLENOID
DEILNOST LENTOIDS

DEILNOSU DELUSION
INSOULED
UNSOILED
DEILNOTU OUTLINED
DEILNOVV INVOLVED
DEILNPRS SPINDLER
DEILNPRU UNDERLIP
DEILNPSS SPINDLES
DEILNPST SPLINTED
DEILNRSS RINDLESS
DEILNRST TENDRILS
TRINDLES
DEILNRSW SWINDLER
DEILNRTU UNDERLIT
DEILNRTY TRENDILY
DEILNSSW SWINDLES
WILDNESS
WINDLESS
DEILNSTU DILUENTS
INSULTED
UNLISTED
DEILNTTU UNTILTED
UNTITLED
DEILNTUY UNITEDLY
DEILNUWY UNWIELDY
DEILOOPS POOLSIDE
DEILOOPW WOODPILE
DEILOORR DROOLIER
DEILOPPY POLYPIDE
DEILOPRS LEPORIDS
DEILOPSS DESPOILS
DIPLOSES
DEILOPST PISTOLED
DEILOPSU EUPLOIDS
DEILOPUY EUPLOIDY
DEILOQRU LIQUORED
DEILORRW LOWRIDER
DEILORSS SOLDIERS
DEILORST STOLIDER
DEILORSY SOLDIERY
DEILORTY ELYTROID
DEILOSST SOLIDEST
DEILOSSV DISSOLVE
DEILOSTU SOLITUDE
TOLUIDES
DEILOSVW OLDWIVES
DEILOTUV OUTLIVED
DEILOTUW OUTWILED
DEILOTUY OUTYIELD
DEILPPST STIPPLED
DEILPPSU SUPPLIED
DEILPRSS DRIPLESS
DEILPSTU STIPULED
DEILPTTU UPTILTED
DEILRRSU SLURRIED
DEILRSSY DRESSILY
DEILRSTU DILUTERS
STUDLIER
DEILRSZZ DRIZZLES
DEILRTVY DEVILTRY
DEILSSTU DUELISTS
DEILSSTY STYLISED
DEILSSUV DIVULSES
DEILSTUY SEDULITY
DEILSTYZ STYLIZED
DEILSWZZ SWIZZLED
DEIMMNOO OMNIMODE
DEIMMNOS DEMONISM
DEIMMOOV MOVIEDOM
DEIMMOST IMMODEST
DEIMMOSV MISMOVED
DEIMMRST MIDTERMS
DEIMMSTU SUMMITED
DEIMNNSU MINUENDS
DEIMNOOS DOMINOES
MONODIES
DEIMNOOT DEMOTION
MOTIONED
DEIMNOOX MONOXIDE
DEIMNOPT PIEDMONT
DEIMNORT DORMIENT
DEIMNOST DEMONIST
DEIMNOTW DOWNTIME
DEIMNPRU UNPRIMED
DEIMNPSS MISSPEND
DEIMNPTU IMPUDENT
DEIMNRTU RUDIMENT
UNMITRED
DEIMNSSS MISSENDS
DEIMNSST MINDSETS
MISTENDS
DEIMNSTU MISTUNED
DEIMOORS MOIDORES
DEIMOOSS SODOMIES

DEIMOOST DOOMIEST
MOODIEST
SODOMITE
DEIMOOSZ SODOMIZE
DEIMOPRS PROMISED
DEIMOPRT IMPORTED
DEIMOPRV IMPROVED
DEIMOPST IMPOSTED
DEIMORRR MIRRORED
DEIMORRS MISORDER
DEIMORSS MISDOERS
DEIMORST MORTISED
DEIMORSU DIMEROUS
DEIMORSV MISDROVE
DEIMORUX EXORDIUM
DEIMOSST DISTOMES
MODISTES
DEIMOSTT DEMOTIST
DEIMPSTU DUMPIEST
DUMPSITE
DEIMPSTY MISTYPED
DEIMQRSU SQUIRMED
DEIMRSSU SURMISED
DEIMRSTU DIESTRUM
DEIMRSUU RESIDUUM
DEINNNOU INNUENDO
DEINNNPU UNPINNED
DEINNOOT NOONTIDE
DEINNOPT ENDPOINT
DEINNORT INDENTOR
DEINNORU UNIRONED
DEINNOWW WINNOWED
DEINNPRU UNDERPIN
DEINNRSU UNRINSED
DEINNRTU INTURNED
DEINNRUW UNWINDER
DEINNSTU DUNNITES
DEINNTUU UNUNITED
DEINNTUW UNTWINED
DEINOOPS POISONED
DEINOOPT OPTIONED
DEINOOPW PINEWOOD
DEINOOSU IDONEOUS
DEINOOSZ OZONIDES
OZONISED
DEINOOTV DEVOTION
DEINOOZZ OZONIZED
DEINOPPR PROPINED
DEINOPPW DOWNPIPE
DEINOPRS PRISONED
DEINOPRT DIPTERON
DEINOPRU INPOURED
DEINOPRY PYRENOID
DEINOPSS DOPINESS
DEINOPSU UNPOISED
DEINORRS INDORSER
DEINORSS INDORSES
SORDINES
DEINORSU DOURINES
SOURDINE
DEINORTT INTORTED
DEINORVW OVERWIND
DEINOSSV VOIDNESS
DEINOSSZ DOZINESS
DEINOSTW DOWNIEST
DEINOSWZ DOWNSIZE
DEINOTUV INDEVOUT
DEINPPRU UNRIPPED
DEINPPTU UNTIPPED
DEINPPUZ UNZIPPED
DEINPRST SPRINTED
DEINPRUZ UNPRIZED
DEINPSST STIPENDS
DEINPTTU INPUTTED
UNPITTED
DEINQSTU SQUINTED
DEINRRTU INTRUDER
DEINRSSU INSUREDS
SUNDRIES
DEINRSTT STRIDENT
TRIDENTS
DEINRSTU INTRUDES
DEINRSTX DEXTRINS
DEINSSST DISSENTS
DEINSSSY SYNDESIS
DEINSSTT DENTISTS
DEINSSUU UNISSUED
DEINSTUU UNSUITED
DEINTTUW UNWITTED
DEIOOPRR DROOPIER
DEIOORSW WOODSIER
DEIOORSZ ODORIZES
DEIOOSST OSTEOIDS
DEIOOSTW WOODIEST
DEIOPRRV PROVIDER

DEIOPRSS DISPOSER
DROPSIES
DEIOPRST DIOPTERS
DIOPTRES
PERIDOTS
PORTSIDE
PROTEIDS
RIPOSTED
TOPSIDER
DEIOPRSV DISPROVE
PROVIDES
DEIOPRSX PEROXIDS
DEIOPSSS DISPOSES
DEIOPSST DEPOSITS
TOPSIDES
DEIOPSTV POSTDIVE
DEIORRRT TORRIDER
DEIORRSS DROSSIER
DEIORRSW DROWSIER
DEIORRSY DERISORY
DEIORRTU OUTRIDER
DEIORRTW WORRITED
DEIORSSS DOSSIERS
DEIORSST STEROIDS
DEIORSSU DESIROUS
DEIORSSV DEVISORS
DEIORSTU OUTRIDES
OUTSIDER
DEIORSTW ROWDIEST
WORDIEST
DEIORSWW WIDOWERS
DEIORTTX TETROXID
DEIORTUV OUTDRIVE
DEIOSSTU OUTSIDES
DEIOSTTT DOTTIEST
DEIOSTUW WIDEOUTS
DEIOSTUZ OUTSIZED
DEIPPRRS DRIPPERS
DEIPPRST STRIPPED
DEIPRRTU IRRUPTED
DEIPRSSU SUSPIRED
DEIPRSTU DISPUTER
STUPIDER
DEIPRSTZ SPRITZED
DEIPSSTU DISPUTES
DEIPTTTU TITTUPED
DEIQRSTU SQUIRTED
DEIRRSST STRIDERS
DEIRRSTU STURDIER
DEIRSSST DISSERTS
DISTRESS
DEIRSSTU DIESTRUS
STUDIERS
STURDIES
DEIRSTTU DETRITUS
DEIRSUVV SURVIVED
DEISSSTU SUDSIEST
DEISSTTU DUSTIEST
DEISTTTU DUETTIST
DEKKSSTT TSKTSKED
DEKMNOSU UNSMOKED
DEKNNOSS NONSKEDS
DEKNORUW UNWORKED
DEKNRSTU DRUNKEST
DEKOOPRV PROVOKED
DEKOOTWW KOWTOWED
DEKOPSST DESKTOPS
DEKORSWY KEYWORDS
DEKPRSSU PREDUSKS
DELLLOOP LOLLOPED
DELLMOSY SELDOMLY
DELLNOPU UNPOLLED
DELLNORU UNROLLED
DELLNSSU DULLNESS
DELLOPRS REDPOLLS
DELLOPTU POLLUTED
DELLORRY DROLLERY
DELLORSS LORDLESS
DELLORST DROLLEST
STROLLED
DELLOSTY OLDSTYLE
DELLRSWY DRYWELLS
DELMNORY MODERNLY
DELMNOTW MELTDOWN
DELMNPUU PENDULUM
DELMOPRS PREMOLDS
DELMORSS SMOLDERS
DELMORSU MOULDERS
SMOULDER
DELMOSTY MODESTLY
DELNOOSU NODULOSE
UNLOOSED
DELNOOSZ SNOOZLED
DELNOOWY WOODENLY
DELNOPRS SPLENDOR
DELNOPUW UNPLOWED

DELNORSU ROUNDELS
UNSOLDER
DELNORTU ROUNDLET
DELNOSSU LOUDNESS
DELNOSSW DOWNLESS
DELNOSTW LETDOWNS
DELNOSUV UNSOLVED
DELNOTWY WONTEDLY
DELNPRSU PLUNDERS
DELNRRTU TRUNDLER
DELNRSTU RUNDLETS
TRUNDLES
DELOOORW WOODLORE
DELOOPPS PLEOPODS
DELOORRV OVERLORD
DELOORSS DOORLESS
LORDOSES
ODORLESS
DELOORSV OVERSOLD
DELOORUV OVERLOUD
DELOOSSW WOODLESS
DELOOTUV OUTLOVED
DELOPPST STOPPLED
DELOPPSY POLYPEDS
DELOPRST DROPLETS
DELOPSTU POSTLUDE
DELORSST OLDSTERS
DELORSSW WORDLESS
DELORSTT DOTTRELS
DELORSUY DELUSORY
DELOSSUU SEDULOUS
DELOSTTY SOTTEDLY
DELOSTUU OUTDUELS
DELOSTUW WOULDEST
DELOTUVY DEVOUTLY
DELPSTUU PUSTULED
DELRSSTU STRUDELS
DELSSSSU SUDSLESS
DELSSSTU DUSTLESS
DEMMNOSU SUMMONED
DEMMRRSU DRUMMERS
DEMMRRUU MURMURED
DEMMRSTU STRUMMED
DEMNNOSU SOUNDMEN
DEMNOOOP MONOPODE
DEMNOORU UNMOORED
DEMNOOSS ENDOSMOS
DEMNOOSW WOODSMEN
DEMNORST MORDENTS
DEMNORSW SWORDMEN
DEMNORSY SYNDROME
DEMNOSTU DEMOUNTS
MUDSTONE
DEMOOPPS POPEDOMS
DEMOOPRR PRODROME
DEMOOPRT PROMOTED
DEMOORST DOOMSTER
DEMOORSU DORMOUSE
DEMOORTY ODOMETRY
DEMOOSTU OUTMODES
DEMOOTUV OUTMOVED
DEMOPPRT PROMPTED
DEMORRUU RUMOURED
DEMORTUY UDOMETRY
DEMPRSTU DUMPSTER
DENNOOWZ DOWNZONE
DENNOSTU UNSTONED
DENNOTUW UNWONTED
DENNPRUU UNPRUNED
DENNRRUU UNDERRUN
DENNRTUU UNTURNED
DENNRTUY UNTRENDY
DENOOORT OREODONT
DENOOOTW WOODNOTE
WOODTONE
DENOOPPR PROPONED
DENOORRS ENDORSOR
DENOORTU UNROOTED
DENOORTX NEXTDOOR
DENOOSTU DUOTONES
DENOPPRS PROPENDS
DENOPRSS RESPONDS
DENOPRST PORTENDS
PROTENDS
DENOPRSU POUNDERS
DENOPRUV UNPROVED
DENOPSTU OUTSPEND
UNPOSTED
DENOPSUX EXPOUNDS
DENOPTTU UNPOTTED
DENOQTUU UNQUOTED
DENORRSU RONDURES
ROUNDERS
DENORRSW DROWNERS

DENORSSU DOURNESS
RESOUNDS
SOUNDERS
DENORSTU ROUNDEST
TONSURED
UNSORTED
DENORSTY DRYSTONE
DENORSUU UNSOURED
DENORTUW UNDERTOW
DENOSSTU SOUNDEST
DENOTUUV UNDEVOUT
DENPRSTU UPTRENDS
DENPRTUU UPTURNED
DENPSSSU SUSPENDS
DENRRTUU NURTURED
DENRSSSU SUNDRESS
DENRSTTU STRUNTED
DENRSTUU UNRUSTED
DENSSTTU STUDENTS
DENSTUVY DUVETYNS
DEOOORSW ROSEWOOD
DEOOPPRS PROPOSED
DEOOPPRT PTEROPOD
DEOOPRST DOORSTEP
TORPEDOS
DEOOPRTU UPROOTED
DEOOPWWW POWWOWED
DEOORRST REDROOTS
DEOORRSW SORROWED
DEOORRVW OVERWORD
DEOORSTU OUTDOERS
DEOORTUV OUTDROVE
DEOORTUW OUTROWED
DEOOTTUV OUTVOTED
DEOPPRRS DROPPERS
DEOPPRST STROPPED
DEOPPRSU PURPOSED
DEOPPSSU SUPPOSED
DEOPRRTU PROTRUDE
DEOPRSTU POSTURED
PROUDEST
SPROUTED
DEOPRSUU UPROUSED
DEOPSSTU UPTOSSED
DEORRTTU TORTURED
DEORSSTU OUTDRESS
DEORSSTW WORSTEDS
DEORSSTY DESTROYS
DEORSSUV OVERSUDS
DEORSTUX DEXTROUS
DEOSSSYY ODYSSEYS
DEOSSTTU TESTUDOS
DEPPSSYY DYSPEPSY
DEPRRTUU RUPTURED
DERSTTTU STRUTTED
DFFIIMRS MIDRIFFS
DFFIORSU DIFFUSOR
DFFLOORU FOURFOLD
DFFOORUW WOODRUFF
DFFOSSTU DUSTOFFS
DFGGHIOT DOGFIGHT
DFGHILOS GOLDFISH
DFGIIIRY RIGIDIFY
DFGIILRY FRIGIDLY
DFGIINNS FINDINGS
DFGIINRT DRIFTING
DFGILNNO FONDLING
DFGILNOO FLOODING
DFGINNOU FONDUING
FOUNDING
DFGINOOR FORDOING
DFGINOSU FUNGOIDS
DFHIIMUY HUMIDIFY
DFHILSSU DISHFULS
DFHIMRSU DRUMFISH
DFHINOPS FISHPOND
DFHISSTU STUDFISH
DFHLOOOT FOOTHOLD
DFHNOOUX FOXHOUND
DFIILMTU MULTIFID
DFIILOSY SOLIDIFY
DFIILTUY FLUIDITY
DFIINPRT DRIFTPIN
DFILLOOT FLOODLIT
DFILLORY FLORIDLY
DFILLOWW WILDFOWL
DFILMMOS FILMDOMS
DFILNNOU NONFLUID
DFILNOPS PINFOLDS
DFILORSU FLUORIDS
DFIMOOOR IODOFORM
DFINOSTU OUTFINDS
DFINRSUW WINDSURF
DFIOOPRS DISPROOF
DFKMMOPU DUMMKOPF
DFLMOSUW MUDFLOWS

DFLOORUU ODOURFUL
DFLOOSTU FOLDOUTS
DFLOOSTW TWOFOLDS
DFLOPRUU PROUDFUL
DFNOOPRU PROFOUND
DFNOOTUU OUTFOUND
DFOOOSTW SOFTWOOD
DGGGIINS DIGGINGS
DGGGINRU DRUGGING
GRUDGING
DGGHIINT DIGHTING
DGGIILNR GIRDLING
RIDGLING
DGGIILNS GILDINGS
DGGIINNR GRINDING
DGGIINNW WINGDING
DGGIKLNU KLUDGING
DGGILNOS GODLINGS
LODGINGS
DGGILNSU SLUDGING
DGGIMNSU SMUDGING
DGGINNOO NOODGING
DGGINOST STODGING
DGGINRTU TRUDGING
DGGIRSTU DRUGGIST
DGHIILNS HILDINGS
DGHIIMNT MIDNIGHT
DGHIINPS SPHINGID
DGHIINSS SHINDIGS
DGHIKNOO KINGHOOD
DGHILLNU DUNGHILL
DGHILNNO HONDLING
DGHILNOS HOLDINGS
DGHILNRU HURDLING
DGHILOOR GIRLHOOD
DGHINNOU HOUNDING
DGHINNUZ NUDZHING
DGHINOWY HOWDYING
DGHINSTU HINDGUTS
DGHIOPSS GODSHIPS
DGHNOTUU DOUGHNUT
DGHOOOTT DOGTOOTH
DGHORRUY ROUGHDRY
DGHORSTU DROUGHTS
DGHORTUY DROUGHTY
DGIIINNT INDITING
DGIIINNV DIVINING
DGIIINOS IODISING
DGIIINOZ IODIZING
DGIIIRTY RIGIDITY
DGIIKLNN KINDLING
DGIIKNNR DRINKING
DGIILLNR DRILLING
DGIILLNU ILLUDING
DGIILLNW WILDLING
DGIILLOU LIGULOID
DGIILMNP DIMPLING
DGIILNNP PINDLING
DGIILNNW WINDLING
DGIILNNY INDIGNLY
DGIILNSW WILDINGS
DGIILNTU DILUTING
DGIIMNOS MISDOING
DGIIMNOU GONIDIUM
DGIIMNSS SMIDGINS
DGIIMOSS SIGMOIDS
DGIIMPUY PYGIDIUM
DGIINNOP POINDING
DGIINNOR NONRIGID
DGIINNOW INDOWING
DGIINNSW WINDINGS
DGIINORR GRIDIRON
DGIINOSW WINDIGOS
DGIINOSX DIGOXINS
DGIINOTT DITTOING
DGIINOWW WIDOWING
DGIINPPR DRIPPING
DGIINPUV UPDIVING
DGIINRST STRIDING
DGIINRSV DRIVINGS
DGIINRTY DIRTYING
DGIINSSU DISUSING
DGIINVVY DIVVYING
DGIINYZZ DIZZYING
DGIKMNOS KINGDOMS
DGIKNOOW KINGWOOD
DGIKNORU DROUKING
DGILLNOR DROLLING
LORDLING
DGILLNOY DOLLYING
DGILLOOW GOODWILL
DGILMNOS MOLDINGS
DGILMNOU MOULDING
DGILMNPU DUMPLING
DGILMSUY SMUDGILY
DGILNNOO NOODLING

DGILNOOR DROOLING
DGILNORS LORDINGS
DGILNOTY DOTINGLY
DGILOSTY STODGILY
DGILRTUY TURGIDLY
DGIMMNRU DRUMMING
DGIMMNUY DUMMYING
DGIMNNOU MOUNDING
DGIMNPSU DUMPINGS
DGINNOOS SNOODING
DGINNOPU POUNDING
DGINNORU INGROUND
ROUNDING
DGINNORW DROWNING
DGINNOSU SOUNDING
UNDOINGS
DGINNOUW WOUNDING
DGINOOPR DROOPING
DGINOOTU OUTDOING
DGINOPPR DROPPING
DGINORSW DROWSING
WORDINGS
DGINPRUY UPDRYING
DGINSSTU DUSTINGS
DGINSTUY STUDYING
DGIOOPRU GROUPOID
DGIOPRRY PORRIDGY
DGIOSUYZ DIZYGOUS
DGISSSTU DISGUSTS
DGLNORSU GOLDURNS
DGLOOOSW LOGWOODS
DGLOOOXY DOXOLOGY
DGMNNOUU MUNDUNGO
DGMOOSUW GUMWOODS
DGMOPRSU GUMDROPS
DGMOPSYY GYPSYDOM
DGNNORUU UNGROUND
DGNOOORS GODROONS
DGOORSTT DOGTROTS
DGOPRRSU PRODRUGS
DGOPRSTU POSTDRUG
DHHILOTW WITHHOLD
DHHIOPPS PHOSPHID
DHIIIMNS DIMINISH
DHIIINST HISTIDIN
DHIIMNOO HOMINOID
DHIIMNOS HOMINIDS
DHIIMOST ISTHMOID
DHIIMPSS MIDSHIPS
DHIIMTUY HUMIDITY
DHIINRSU HIRUDINS
DHIIOPSX XIPHOIDS
DHIIORSS HIDROSIS
DHIIORSZ RHIZOIDS
DHIKNOOW HOODWINK
DHIKORSY HYDROSKI
DHILLNOW DOWNHILL
DHILLOPY PHYLLOID
DHILMOPY LYMPHOID
DHILMOSY MODISHLY
DHILNOPS DOLPHINS
DHILOPRS LORDSHIP
DHILOPSS SLIPSHOD
DHILORRY HORRIDLY
DHILPSSU SULPHIDS
DHILPSSY SYLPHIDS
DHIMMNOT MIDMONTH
DHIMNOST HINDMOST
DHIMNOSU UNMODISH
DHIMOPRS DIMORPHS
DHIMORSU HUMIDORS
RHODIUMS
DHINNOTW THINDOWN
DHINOOPR PHORONID
DHINOORS DISHONOR
DHINORSU ROUNDISH
DHINOTUW WHODUNIT
DHIOOOPR IODOPHOR
DHIOOPRZ RHIZOPOD
DHIOPSTY TYPHOIDS
DHIORSTY THYROIDS
THYRSOID
DHIORSWY ROWDYISH
DHIPRSSY SYRPHIDS
DHJOPRSU JODHPURS
DHKMNOOO MONKHOOD
DHLMOOSU HOODLUMS
DHLOOORT ROOTHOLD
DHLOORSY HYDROSOL
DHLOOSTU HOLDOUTS
DHLORXYY HYDROXYL
DHLOSSTU SHOULDST
DHMMRSUU HUMDRUMS
DHNOOOSS SONHOODS
DHNOOSWW SHOWDOWN
DHNOPSUW PUSHDOWN

DHNOSTUW SHUTDOWN
DHOOORTX ORTHODOX
DHOOPRST DROPSHOT
DHOPRSSU PUSHRODS
DHOPRSYY HYDROPSY
DIIILLQU ILLIQUID
DIIILTVY LIVIDITY
DIIIMOST IDIOTISM
DIIIMRSU IRIDIUMS
DIIIMTTY TIMIDITY
DIIINOSV DIVISION
DIIINTVY DIVINITY
DIIIPRST DISPIRIT
DIIIRTVY VIRIDITY
DIIJNOSS DISJOINS
DIIJNOST DISJOINT
DIIKKNSS KIDSKINS
DIILLMNW WINDMILL
DIILLMOU LIMULOID
DIILLMPY LIMPIDLY
DIILLQUY LIQUIDLY
DIILLSST DISTILLS
DIILLSTY IDYLLIST
DIILMNSS DISLIMNS
DIILMOSS IDOLISMS
DIILMSST MIDLISTS
DIILMUUV DILUVIUM
DIILNNSU INDULINS
DIILNOST TOLIDINS
DIILNOTU DILUTION
TOLUIDIN
DIILNOUV DILUVION
DIILNSXY XYLIDINS
DIILNTUY UNTIDILY
DIILOPRT TRIPLOID
DIILOPSS DIPLOSIS
DIILOQSU SOLIQUID
DIILORSU SILUROID
DIILORTU UTILIDOR
DIILOSTY SOLIDITY
DIILPPRY DRIPPILY
DIILRSSU SILURIDS
DIILSSTY IDYLISTS
DIIMMNOU DOMINIUM
DIIMNNOO DOMINION
DIIMNOPT MIDPOINT
DIIMNORS MIDIRONS
DIIMNSUU INDUSIUM
DIIMOPRS PRISMOID
DIIMPUXY PYXIDIUM
DIIMRUUV DUUMVIRI
DIIMTTUY TUMIDITY
DIINNOSU DISUNION
DIINOOPS IODOPSIN
DIINOOPU DOUPIONI
DIINOQSU QUINOIDS
DIINOSSU SINUSOID
DIINSTUY DISUNITY
DIIORSST SISTROID
DIIORSSV DIVISORS
DIIORSTX TRIOXIDS
DIIORSUV VIRUSOID
DIIPSTTY TIDYTIPS
DIJOSSTU JUDOISTS
DIKLMOOW MILKWOOD
DIKLNNOW DOWNLINK
DIKLNNUY UNKINDLY
DIKNOOSW INKWOODS
DIKNORTU OUTDRINK
DILLMNOP MILLPOND
DILLMSSU MUDSILLS
DILLOORS DOORSILL
DILLOSTY STOLIDLY
DILLPSSY PSYLLIDS
DILMNRSU DRUMLINS
DILMOOSU MODIOLUS
DILNNOOS NONSOLID
DILNOPST DIPLONTS
DILNOSXY INDOXYLS
DILNRSUY SUNDRILY
DILOOPPY POLYPOID
DILOOPRY DROOPILY
DILOORSS LORDOSIS
DILOOSUY ODIOUSLY
DILOPRTY TORPIDLY
DILORRTY TORRIDLY
DILORSTU DILUTORS
DILORSWY DROWSILY
DILPRTUY PUTRIDLY
DILPSTUY STUPIDLY
DILRSTUY STURDILY
DIMMNORY MYRMIDON
DIMMOSST MIDMOSTS
DIMNNOOS MIDNOONS
DIMNOOST MONODIST
DIMNOPSU IMPOUNDS

DIMNOSSU MISSOUND
DIMNOSTU DISMOUNT
DIMNOSTW MIDTOWNS
DIMNOSUW UNWISDOM
DIMOOPRY MYRIOPOD
DIMOOSST SODOMIST
DIMORSSW MISWORDS
DIMORSTY MIDSTORY
DIMORSWY ROWDYISM
DIMRSTUU TRIDUUMS
DIMRSUUV DUUMVIRS
DINNOPSW DOWNSPIN
DINOOORW IRONWOOD
DINOORRS INDORSOR
DINOOSTY NODOSITY
DINOPRTY DRYPOINT
DINORSWW WINDROWS
DINOSTUW OUTWINDS
DINPRTUY PUNDITRY
DINRSTUY INDUSTRY
DIOOPRTX PROTOXID
DIOORSST DISROOTS
DIOORSTT RIDOTTOS
DIOPRSST DISPORTS
DIORRSST STRIDORS
DIORSSTT DISTORTS
DIOSSTUU STUDIOUS
DIPRSSTU DISRUPTS
DIRSSTTU DISTRUST
DKLNOOOW LOOKDOWN
DKMNOOOR KOMONDOR
DKNORTUU OUTDRUNK
DKOOOPRW PORKWOOD
DKOOORWW WOODWORK
DKORSTUW STUDWORK
DLLMORRU DRUMROLL
DLLMORSU SLUMLORD
DLMNOOSW SNOWMOLD
DLNOOSUU NODULOUS
DLNOOSWW LOWDOWNS
SLOWDOWN
DLNORTUY ROTUNDLY
DLOOORRS DOLOROSO
DLOOOPSS SPODOSOL
DLOOORSU DOLOROUS
DLOOOSTW WOODLOTS
DLOOPPSY POLYPODS
DLOOPPUW PULPWOOD
DLOOPPYY POLYPODY
DLOOPSTU OUTPLODS
DLOOPSWY PLYWOODS
DMMOOORT MOTORDOM
DMMOORSU MUDROOMS
DMNOOOPS MONOPODS
DMNOOOPY MONOPODY
DMNOOSTU MOONDUST
DMNOOSTW TOWMONDS
DMOOOQSU QUOMODOS
DMOOORWW WOODWORM
WORMWOOD
DMOPPPUY PUPPYDOM
DMPPPUUY MUDPUPPY
DNNOOOWY NONWOODY
DNNOORSW NONWORDS
DNNOOTWW DOWNTOWN
DNNORRUU RUNROUND
DNNORSUU UNROUNDS
DNNORSUW RUNDOWNS
DNNORTUW DOWNTURN
TURNDOWN
DNNOSSUW SUNDOWNS
DNOOPPRU PROPOUND
DNOOPRSW SNOWDROP
DNOOPRUW DOWNPOUR
DNOOPSUY DUOPSONY
DNOORSUW WONDROUS
DNOOSTUW NUTWOODS
DNOOSUUV VOUDOUNS
DNOPRSSU SUNDROPS
DNOPRSUU ROUNDUPS
DNOPSTUW PUTDOWNS
DNORRSUU SURROUND
DOOOPPRT PROTOPOD
DOOOPRST DOORPOST
DOORSTOP
DOOORSTU OUTDOORS
DOOORSUW SOURWOOD
DOOOSTTU OUTSTOOD
DOOPRRTW DROPWORT
DOOPRSTU DROPOUTS
OUTDROPS
DOOPRSTW STOPWORD
DOORRSUU ORDUROUS
DOSTTUUY OUTSTUDY
EEEEFRRS REFEREES
EEEEFRRZ REFREEZE

EEEEGGRR GREEGREE
EEEEGMRR REEMERGE
EEEEGQSU SQUEEGEE
EEEEGSSX EXEGESES
EEEEGSTX EXEGETES
EEEEHTTY EYETEETH
EEEELLPX EXPELLEE
EEEENRRV VENEERER
EEEEPPSW PEESWEEP
EEEEPTTW PEETWEET
EEEFFFOS FEOFFEES
EEEFFLOR FOREFEEL
EEEFFLTY EFFETELY
EEEFFNRT EFFERENT
EEEFFORT FOREFEET
EEEFFOTU ETOUFFEE
EEEFFRVW FEVERFEW
EEEFGMRR GERMFREE
EEEFGRSU REFUGEES
EEEFHRSS SHEREEFS
EEEFIPST TEPEFIES
EEEFIRST REEFIEST
EEEFLRSX REFLEXES
EEEFLSST FEETLESS
EEEFLSTT FLEETEST
EEEFNORS FORESEEN
EEEFNRRT REFERENT
EEEFNRSS FREENESS
EEEFNRSV ENFEVERS
EEEFNRTT ENFETTER
EEEFNRUZ UNFREEZE
EEEFORRS FORESEER
EEEFORRV OVERFREE
EEEFORSS FORESEES
EEEFRRRR REFERRER
EEEFRRRT FERRETER
EEEFRRSZ FREEZERS
EEEFRRTT FETTERER
EEEGGILN NEGLIGEE
EEEGHINT EIGHTEEN
EEEGHMNU HEGUMENE
EEEGIKST GEEKIEST
EEEGILMN LIEGEMEN
EEEGILNV LEVEEING
EEEGILPS ESPIEGLE
EEEGILRT GLEETIER
EEEGILSS ELEGISES
EEEGILSZ ELEGIZES
EEEGINNR ENGINEER
EEEGINRR GREENIER
EEEGINRS ENERGIES
ENERGISE
GREENIES
RESEEING
EEEGINRZ ENERGIZE
EEEGIPRS PERIGEES
EEEGIRTY TIGEREYE
EEEGISSX EXEGESIS
EEEGISTV EGESTIVE
EEEGITVV VEGETIVE
EEEGKLRS KEGELERS
EEEGLMOS GLEESOME
EEEGLNRT GREENLET
EEEGMNOS MONGEESE
EEEGMNRT EMERGENT
EEEGMNRU MERENGUE
EEEGMORT GEOMETER
EEEGMRRS REMERGES
EEEGNPRS EPERGNES
EEEGNRRS REGREENS
RENEGERS
EEEGNRRV REVENGER
EEEGNRRY GREENERY
EEEGNRST GREENEST
EEEGNRSV REVENGES
EEEGNSTT GENETTES
EEEGOPRT PROTEGEE
EEEGRRST GREETERS
REGREETS
EEEGRSSS EGRESSES
EEEGRSUX EXERGUES
EEEHILRW EREWHILE
EEEHILSW WHEELIES
EEEHINRS SHEENIER
EEEHINSY EYESHINE
EEEHIRSS HERESIES
EEEHIRSX HEXEREIS
EEEHIRTZ ETHERIZE
EEEHIRWZ WHEEZIER
EEEHKLNO KNEEHOLE
EEEHLLSS HEELLESS
EEEHLMNW WHEELMEN
EEEHLMPT HELPMEET
EEEHLNSW ENWHEELS
EEEHLNTV ELEVENTH
EEEHLNTY ETHYLENE

EEEHLOPP PEEPHOLE
EEEHLOSY EYEHOLES
EEEHLPSW WHEEPLES
EEEHLRSW WHEELERS
EEEHMNNT MENTHENE
EEEHMNPS SHEEPMEN
EEEHMNSS ENMESHES
EEEHMNTV VEHEMENT
EEEHNNPT NEPENTHE
EEEHNNQU HENEQUEN
EEEHNPRS ENSPHERE
EEEHNRTV REVEHENT
EEEHNRVW WHENEVER
EEEHNSSS SNEESHES
EEEHORST SHOETREE
EEEHPRSS PHERESES
EEEHRRVW WHEREVER
EEEHRSST SHEEREST
SHEETERS
EEEHRSTT TEETHERS
EEEHRSWZ WHEEZERS
EEEHSSST ESTHESES
EEEHSSTT ESTHETES
EEEIKLRS SLEEKIER
EEEIKLRT TREELIKE
EEEIKLSW WEEKLIES
EEEIKNSS KNEESIES
EEEIKNTX EKTEXINE
EEEIKRST REEKIEST
EEEILLRV REVEILLE
EEEILMRS SEEMLIER
EEEILNPR PELERINE
EEEILNRY EYELINER
EEEILNST ENLISTEE
SELENITE
EEEILPRS SLEEPIER
EEEILRRV RELIEVER
EEEILRST LEERIEST
SLEETIER
STEELIER
EEEILRSV RELIEVES
EEEILSST STEELIES
EEEILSTV TELEVISE
EEEILTVW TELEVIEW
EEEIMNRU MEUNIERE
EEEIMNST EMETINES
EEEIMPRR PREMIERE
EEEIMPRS EMPERIES
EPIMERES
PREEMIES
EEEIMRRS MISERERE
EEEIMRST EREMITES
EEEINNNT NINETEEN
EEEINNRT INTERNEE
RETINENE
EEEINRRS SNEERIER
EEEINRSS EERINESS
ESERINES
EEEINRST ETERNISE
TEENSIER
EEEINRSV VENERIES
EEEINRSW WEENSIER
EEEINRSZ SNEEZIER
EEEINRTZ ETERNIZE
EEEINSSW SWEENIES
EEEINSTT TEENIEST
EEEINSTW TWEENIES
WEENIEST
EEEINTUX EUXENITE
EEEIPRRV REPRIEVE
EEEIPRSW SWEEPIER
EEEIPSST EPEEISTS
SEEPIEST
EEEIPSTW WEEPIEST
EEEIQSUX EXEQUIES
EEEIRRST RETIREES
EEEIRRSV REVERIES
EEEIRRTV RETRIEVE
EEEIRRVW REREVIEW
REVIEWER
EEEIRSSZ RESEIZES
EEEIRTVX EXERTIVE
EEEISSTW SWEETIES
EEEJLLRW JEWELLER
EEEJLRSW JEWELERS
EEEJNPSY JEEPNEYS
EEEKLLSS KEELLESS
EEEKLLSU UKELELES
EEEKLNRS KNEELERS
EEEKLNSS SLEEKENS
EEEKLPSW EKPWELES
EEEKLRSS SLEEKERS
EEEKLSST SLEEKEST
EEEKMNSS MEEKNESS
EEEKMORV OVERMEEK
EEEKMRSS KERMESSE
EEEKNNSS KEENNESS
EEEKNORS KEROSENE
EEEKNORV OVERKEEN
EEEKORSV REEVOKES
EEEKRRST STREEKER
EEEKRSST KEESTERS
SKEETERS
EEELLLRV LEVELLER
EEELLNOR ENROLLEE
EEELLNQU QUENELLE
EEELLPRR REPELLER
EEELLPRX EXPELLER
EEELLRRS RESELLER
EEELLRRV REVELLER
EEELLRSV LEVELERS
EEELMNST ELEMENTS
EEELMOPY EMPLOYEE
EEELMORT TELOMERE
EEELMOTT OMELETTE
EEELMRTU MULETEER
EEELNOPV ENVELOPE
EEELNRRU UNREELER
EEELNRSW NEWSREEL
EEELNRSY SERENELY
EEELNRTY TERYLENE
EEELOPPR REPEOPLE
EEELPPRS PRESLEEP
EEELPRSS PEERLESS
SLEEPERS
EEELPRST REPLETES
EEELPRSX REEXPELS
EEELPSST STEEPLES
EEELPTTY TELETYPE
EEELRRSV REVELERS
EEELRRTT LETTERER
RELETTER
EEELRSST TREELESS
EEELRSTT RESETTLE
EEELRSTV LEVERETS
EEELRSVY SEVERELY
EEELRTVV VELVERET
EEELSSTU EUSTELES
EEELTTTX TELETEXT
EEEMMORS MESOMERE
EEEMMRUZ MEZEREUM
EEEMNNTT TENEMENT
EEEMNORZ MEZEREON
EEEMNRSV VERSEMEN
EEEMNRVY EVERYMEN
EEEMNSST MEETNESS
EEEMORRV EVERMORE
EEEMPRRT RETEMPER
TEMPERER
EEEMRRTX EXTREMER
EEEMRSST SEMESTER
EEEMRSTX EXTREMES
EEENNOPR NEOPRENE
EEENNOSV VENENOSE
EEENNPST PENTENES
EEENNRUV UNEVENER
EEENNSSV EVENNESS
EEENNSTT ENTENTES
EEENORSV OVERSEEN
EEENORVW OVERWEEN
EEENORVY EVERYONE
EEENOSTY EYESTONE
EEENPPRS PREPENSE
EEENPRRS PREENERS
EEENPRRT REPENTER
EEENPRST PRETEENS
PRETENSE
TERPENES
EEENPSST STEEPENS
EEENPSSX EXPENSES
EEENRRSS SNEERERS
EEENRRST ENTERERS
REENTERS
TERREENS
TERRENES
EEENRRSW RENEWERS
EEENRRTU RETURNEE
EEENRRTV REVERENT
EEENRRUV REVENUER
EEENRSST SERENEST
EEENRSSU ENURESES
EEENRSSZ SNEEZERS
EEENRSTW TWEENERS
EEENRSTX EXTERNES
EEENRSTY YESTREEN
EEENRSUV REVENUES
UNREEVES
EEENSSTW SWEETENS
TWEENESS
EEENSSWY SWEENEYS
EEEOPRSX REEXPOSE
EEEORRSV OVERSEER
EEEORRSX XEROSERE
EEEORRSZ REZEROES
EEEORSSV OVERSEES
EEEORSSY EYESORES
EEEPPPRR PEPPERER
EEEPRRST PESTERER
EEEPRRSV PERVERSE
PRESERVE
EEEPRRTW PEWTERER
EEEPRSST STEEPERS
EEEPRSSW SWEEPERS
EEEPSSTT STEEPEST
EEEPSTTT SEPTETTE
EEEQRSTU QUEEREST
EEEQRSUZ SQUEEZER
EEEQSSUZ SQUEEZES
EEERRRSV RESERVER
REVERERS
REVERSER
EEERRRTV REVERTER
EEERRSST STEERERS
EEERRSSV RESERVES
REVERSES
EEERRSTT RESETTER
EEERSSTV SEVEREST
EEERSTTW TWEETERS
EEERSTVX VERTEXES
EEERSTWZ TWEEZERS
EEESSTTW SWEETEST
EEESTTTX SEXTETTE
EEFFFNOS ENFEOFFS
EEFFFORS FEOFFERS
EEFFGIIS EFFIGIES
EEFFGLSU EFFULGES
EEFFHIKY KEFFIYEH
EEFFINST FIFTEENS
EEFFISUV EFFUSIVE
EEFFLNTU EFFLUENT
EEFFLORT FOREFELT
EEFFLSUX EFFLUXES
EEFFMORR FREEFORM
EEFFMOTT MOFFETTE
EEFFNOSS OFFENSES
EEFFORRS OFFERERS
REOFFERS
EEFFRRSU SUFFERER
EEFGIILR FILIGREE
EEFGILNR FLEERING
EEFGILNS FEELINGS
EEFGILNT FLEETING
EEFGINNP PFENNIGE
EEFGINRR FINGERER
EEFGINRS FEIGNERS
EEFGINRV FEVERING
EEFGINRZ FREEZING
EEFGIRRU REFIGURE
EEFGLMNU FUGLEMEN
EEFGLNRY GREENFLY
EEFGLNUV VENGEFUL
EEFGLORS FORELEGS
EEFGLOSS SOLFEGES
EEFGNOOR FOREGONE
EEFGOORR FOREGOER
EEFGOORS FOREGOES
EEFGORRS REFORGES
EEFGORSY FROGEYES
EEFHILLR HELLFIRE
EEFHILRS FLESHIER
EEFHIRSV FEVERISH
EEFHIRTY ETHERIFY
EEFHISST FETISHES
EEFHISSY FISHEYES
EEFHISTT HEFTIEST
EEFHLLWY FLYWHEEL
EEFHLMNS FLEHMENS
EEFHLNSU SHEENFUL
EEFHLRSS FLESHERS
EEFHLSTY FLYSHEET
EEFHMNRS FRESHMEN
EEFHNRSS FRESHENS
EEFHORRT THEREFOR
EEFHRRSU FUEHRERS
EEFHRSST FRESHEST
FRESHETS
EEFIIKLL LIFELIKE
EEFIIKLW WIFELIKE
EEFIILLN LIFELINE
EEFIILMT LIFETIME
EEFIILRW WIFELIER
EEFIIMNN FEMININE
EEFIIMNS FEMINISE
EEFIIMNZ FEMINIZE
EEFIINRS FINERIES
EEFIIRRS REIFIERS
EEFIIRRV VERIFIER
EEFIIRST FEISTIER
FERITIES
FIERIEST
EEFIIRSV VERIFIES
EEFIKLLT FELTLIKE
EEFIKLMU FUMELIKE
EEFIKLNR FERNLIKE
EEFIKLRS SERFLIKE
EEFIKLSU FUSELIKE
EEFIKNNP PENKNIFE
EEFILLMT TELEFILM
EEFILLNY FELINELY
EEFILLRW FREEWILL
EEFILLSS LIFELESS
EEFILMNR RIFLEMEN
EEFILMTX FLEXTIME
EEFILNOS FELONIES
OLEFINES
EEFILPRR PILFERER
EEFILPRS PREFILES
EEFILRRT FILTERER
REFILTER
EEFILRSS FIRELESS
EEFILRSU FUSILEER
EEFILSST FELSITES
EEFILSSW WIFELESS
EEFILSTY EYELIFTS
EEFIMORT FORETIME
EEFIMRRS MISREFER
EEFIMSTU TUMEFIES
EEFINNSS FINENESS
EEFINNST FENNIEST
EEFINRRR INFERRER
EEFINRRS REFINERS
EEFINRRY REFINERY
EEFINRSS RIFENESS
EEFINRST FERNIEST
INFESTER
EEFINRSU REINFUSE
EEFINRSZ FRENZIES
EEFINSSS FINESSES
EEFIORRV OVERRIFE
EEFIPRRS PREFIRES
EEFIPRSX PREFIXES
EEFIRRST FERRITES
EEFIRRSU SUREFIRE
EEFIRRTT FRETTIER
EEFIRRVY REVERIFY
EEFIRSTT FRISETTE
EEFIRSTY ESTERIFY
EEFIRTTZ FRIZETTE
EEFISSSW FESSWISE
EEFISTWW WEFTWISE
EEFKNORW FOREKNEW
EEFLLNSS FELLNESS
EEFLLORT FORETELL
EEFLLRSU FUELLERS
EEFLLRXY REFLEXLY
EEFLLSSS SELFLESS
EEFLMNSU MENSEFUL
EEFLMSSU FUMELESS
EEFLNORU FLUORENE
EEFLNOST FELSTONE
EEFLNRSS FERNLESS
FLENSERS
FRESNELS
EEFLNRSU SNEERFUL
EEFLNRTU REFLUENT
EEFLNSSS SELFNESS
EEFLNSSU SENSEFUL
EEFLNTUV EVENTFUL
EEFLOOSV FOVEOLES
EEFLOOTV FOVEOLET
EEFLORRW FLOWERER
REFLOWER
EEFLORTV LEFTOVER
EEFLORTW FLOWERET
EEFLORVW OVERFLEW
EEFLORWW WEREWOLF
EEFLOSTU OUTFEELS
EEFLOSTV LOVEFEST
EEFLOSUX FLEXUOSE
EEFLRRSU FERRULES
EEFLRSST FRETLESS
EEFLRSUX FLEXURES
REFLUXES
EEFLSSSU FUSELESS
EEFMNORT FOMENTER
EEFMNRRY FERRYMEN
EEFMNRST FERMENTS
EEFMORRR REFORMER
EEFMORST FRETSOME
EEFMOSTT MOFETTES
EEFMPRRU PERFUMER
EEFMPRSU PERFUMES
EEFMSTTU FUMETTES
EEFNORRZ REFROZEN
EEFNORST RESOFTEN
SOFTENER
EEFNORTU FOURTEEN
EEFNORTW FOREWENT
EEFNOSTT OFTENEST
EEFNQRTU FREQUENT
EEFNRTTU UNFETTER
EEFOORRT ROOFTREE
EEFOPRRZ PREFROZE
EEFORRST FORESTER
FOSTERER
REFOREST
EEFORRSU FERREOUS
EEFORRSV FOREVERS
EEFORRTY FERETORY
EEFORSUV FEVEROUS
EEFOSSTT FOSSETTE
EEFOSSTU FOETUSES
EEFOSTTU FOUETTES
EEFPRSSU PERFUSES
EEFRRSSU REFUSERS
EEFRRSTT FRETTERS
EEFRRSTU REFUTERS
EEGGHLLS EGGSHELL
EEGGHMSU MESHUGGE
EEGGHSTU THUGGEES
EEGGIJRR REJIGGER
EEGGIKLN GLEEKING
EEGGILNS NEGLIGES
EEGGILNT GLEETING
EEGGILNY GINGELEY
EEGGILOR LEGGIERO
EEGGILST LEGGIEST
EEGGIMNR EMERGING
EEGGINNR GREENING
RENEGING
EEGGINRT GREETING
EEGGINST EGESTING
EEGGINSU SEGUEING
EEGGJLRU REJUGGLE
EEGGLNSS GLEGNESS
EEGGLOOR GEOLOGER
EEGGNNSS GENSENGS
EEGGNORS ENGORGES
EEGGORRS REGORGES
EEGGPRRS PREGGERS
EEGGPRSU PUGGREES
EEGHHINT HEIGHTEN
EEGHIIST EIGHTIES
EEGHILNS HEELINGS
EEGHILNW WHEELING
EEGHILRS SLEIGHER
EEGHIMNW WEIGHMEN
EEGHINNS SHEENING
EEGHINPW WHEEPING
EEGHINRS GREENISH
REHINGES
SHEERING
EEGHINST SEETHING
SHEETING
EEGHINSY HYGIENES
EEGHINTT TEETHING
EEGHINWZ WHEEZING
EEGHIOTT GOETHITE
EEGHIPRW PREWEIGH
EEGHIRSW REWEIGHS
WEIGHERS
EEGHIRTW WEIGHTER
EEGHISST SIGHTSEE
EEGHISTY EYESIGHT
EEGHKRSS SKREEGHS
EEGHLNNT LENGTHEN
EEGHMNOS HEGEMONS
EEGHMNOY HEGEMONY
EEGHMNSU HEGUMENS
EEGHMNUY HEGUMENY
EEGHNOOP GEOPHONE
EEGHNOPS PHOSGENE
EEGHNOPY HYPOGENE
EEGHNRST GREENTHS
EEGHNRSY GREYHENS
EEGHNSSU HUGENESS
EEGHOPTY GEOPHYTE
EEGHORTT TOGETHER
EEGHOSTT GHETTOES
EEGIILNR LINGERIE
EEGIILNV INVEIGLE
EEGIINRT REIGNITE
RETIEING
EEGIINTV GENITIVE
EEGIJLNW JEWELING
EEGIKLLN GLENLIKE
EEGIKLLU GLUELIKE
EEGIKLMR GERMLIKE
EEGIKLNN KNEELING
EEGIKLNS SLEEKING
EEGIKMNS SMEEKING
EEGIKNPS KEEPINGS
EEGIKNRY REKEYING
EEGIKNST STEEKING
EEGILLNV LEVELING
EEGILMOS EGLOMISE
EEGILNOR ELOIGNER
EEGILNPS PEELINGS
SLEEPING
SPEELING
EEGILNRR LINGERER
EEGILNRS REELINGS
EEGILNRT GREENLIT
EEGILNRU REGULINE
EEGILNRV LEVERING
REVELING
EEGILNST GENTILES
SLEETING
STEELING
EEGILNSV SLEEVING
EEGILNTX TELEXING
EEGILOPU EPILOGUE
EEGILOSU EULOGIES
EULOGISE
EEGILOUZ EULOGIZE
EEGILPSS SPIEGELS
EEGILQSU SQUILGEE
EEGILRSV VELIGERS
EEGILRTY LEGERITY
EEGILSST ELEGISTS
EEGIMMRS GREMMIES
IMMERGES
EEGIMMST GEMMIEST
EEGIMNNS MENINGES
EEGIMNRS REGIMENS
EEGIMNRT METERING
REGIMENT
EEGIMNRU MERINGUE
EEGIMNSS SEEMINGS
EEGIMNST MEETINGS
EEGIMRST GERMIEST
EEGINNPR PREENING
EEGINNQU QUEENING
EEGINNRS SNEERING
EEGINNRT ENTERING
EEGINNRW RENEWING
EEGINNRY ENGINERY
EEGINNSU INGENUES
UNSEEING
EEGINNSV EVENINGS
EEGINNSZ SNEEZING
EEGINOOS OOGENIES
EEGINOPS EPIGONES
EEGINORR ERIGERON
EEGINORS ERINGOES
EEGINOSS GENOISES
EEGINOST EGESTION
EEGINPRR PEREGRIN
EEGINPRS SPEERING
EEGINPRT PETERING
EEGINPRU PUREEING
EEGINPST STEEPING
EEGINPSW SWEEPING
WEEPINGS
EEGINQRU QUEERING
EEGINQUU QUEUEING
EEGINRRS RESIGNER
EEGINRRV REVERING
EEGINRSS GREISENS
EEGINRST GENTRIES
INTEGERS
REESTING
STEERING
EEGINRSU SEIGNEUR
EEGINRSV SEVERING
EEGINRSW RESEWING
SEWERING
EEGINRTU GENITURE
EEGINRTV EVERTING
EEGINRTX EXERTING
EEGINSSS GNEISSES
EEGINSSU GENIUSES
EEGINSTU EUGENIST
EEGINSTV STEEVING
EEGINSTW SWEETING
EEGINTTV VIGNETTE
EEGINTTW TWEETING
EEGINTWZ TWEEZING
EEGIOPSU EPIGEOUS
EEGIPRST PRESTIGE
EEGIRRST REGISTER
EEGIRRSV GRIEVERS
EEGIRSTT GRISETTE
TERGITES
EEGISSTV VESTIGES

EEGISTTV VEGETIST
EEGKLNOW WEEKLONG
EEGKNORS KEROGENS
EEGKNRSU GERENUKS
EEGLLRRU GRUELLER
EEGLMMSU GEMMULES
EEGLMORS GOMERELS
EEGLMOSS GLOSSEME
EEGLNNTU UNGENTLE
EEGLNOPY POLYGENE
EEGLNOSU EUGENOLS
EEGLNOSZ LOZENGES
EEGLNOTY TELEGONY
EEGLNPRU REPLUNGE
EEGLNSTT GENTLEST
EEGLOPRS GOSPELER
EEGLORRV GROVELER
EEGLORVY LEVOGYRE
EEGLRRSU GRUELERS
EEGLRSTW WERGELTS
EEGMNOST GEMSTONE
EEGMNOYZ ZYMOGENE
EEGMNSST SEGMENTS
EEGMNTTU TEGUMENT
EEGMORSU GRUESOME
EEGMORSW GREWSOME
EEGMORTY GEOMETRY
EEGMRSTU GUMTREES
EEGNNNOR NONGREEN
EEGNNORT ROENTGEN
EEGNNOSS GONENESS
EEGNNOSV EVENSONG
EEGNNOXY XENOGENY
EEGNOPTY GENOTYPE
EEGNORST ESTROGEN
EEGNORSU GENEROUS
EEGNORSY ERYNGOES
EEGNOTYZ ZYGOTENE
EEGNPRUX EXPUNGER
EEGNPSUX EXPUNGES
EEGNRSSY GREYNESS
EEGNRSUY GUERNSEY
EEGOORRV REGROOVE
EEGOPRST PROTEGES
EEGOPRSU SUPEREGO
EEGORRUV OVERURGE
EEGORRVW OVERGREW
EEGORSSS OGRESSES
EEGPPRRS PREPREGS
EEGRRSSU RESURGES
EEGRRSTU GESTURER
EEGRRSUY GRUYERES
EEGRSSSU GUESSERS
EEGRSSTU GESTURES
EEHHIPSS SHEEPISH
EEHHIRST ETHERISH
EEHHIRTW HEREWITH
EEHHLLLO HELLHOLE
EEHHNOPT ETHEPHON
EEHHNOSU HENHOUSE
EEHHRRST THRESHER
EEHHRSST THRESHES
EEHIJMNR MIJNHEER
EEHIKLLT HELLKITE
EEHIKLMO HOMELIKE
EEHIKLMP HEMPLIKE
EEHIKLMS SHEKELIM
EEHIKLOS HOSELIKE
EEHIKLRW WHELKIER
EEHIKLWY WHEYLIKE
EEHIKRRS SHRIEKER
EEHILLMS SHLEMIEL
EEHILLRS HELLERIS
SHELLIER
EEHILMNS HEMLINES
EEHILMOR HOMELIER
EEHILNOP ENOPHILE
EEHILNPW PINWHEEL
EEHILNST THEELINS
EEHILOPS PIEHOLES
EEHILORT HOTELIER
EEHILRSS HEIRLESS
RELISHES
EEHILRSV SHELVIER
EEHILSST SHELTIES
EEHILSSV HIVELESS
EEHILWYZ WHEEZILY
EEHIMMSS IMMESHES
EEHIMNRT THEREMIN
EEHIMNSS INMESHES
EEHIMOST HOMESITE
EEHIMPRT HEMIPTER
EEHIMPST HEMPIEST
EEHIMRRU RHEUMIER
EEHIMRST ERETHISM
EEHIMRTT THERMITE
EEHIMSST MESHIEST
EEHINNQU HENEQUIN
HENIQUEN
EEHINNRS ENSHRINE
EEHINNRT INHERENT
EEHINORS HEROINES
EEHINORT HEREINTO
EEHINPRS INSPHERE
EEHINPRT NEPHRITE
TREPHINE
EEHINPSX PHENIXES
EEHINRRS ERRHINES
EEHINRSS RESHINES
EEHINRTT THIRTEEN
EEHINRTW WHITENER
EEHIOPPS HOSEPIPE
EEHIORST ISOTHERE
THEORIES
THEORISE
EEHIORSZ HEROIZES
EEHIORTZ THEORIZE
EEHIOSTX ETHOXIES
EEHIPPST PSEPHITE
EEHIPPTY EPIPHYTE
EEHIPRRS SPHERIER
EEHIPRSS PERISHES
PHERESIS
EEHIPRTT TEPHRITE
EEHIPSST STEEPISH
EEHIPSTT EPITHETS
TIPSHEET
EEHIQRSU QUEERISH
EEHIRRSS SHERRIES
EEHIRRSV SHIVERER
EEHIRRSW WHERRIES
EEHIRRTW WITHERER
EEHIRRTX HERETRIX
EEHIRSST HEISTERS
EEHIRSSV SHRIEVES
EEHIRTVY THIEVERY
EEHISSST ESTHESIS
HESSITES
EEHISSTW SWEETISH
EEHISTTW THEWIEST
EEHKLOSY KEYHOLES
EEHKOOSY EYEHOOKS
EEHLLLOW WELLHOLE
EEHLLMPS PHELLEMS
EEHLLMSS HELMLESS
EEHLLOSS HOLELESS
EEHLLOST THEELOLS
EEHLLPSS HELPLESS
EEHLLRSS SHELLERS
EEHLMMNS HELMSMEN
EEHLMNOT HOTELMEN
EEHLMOSS HOMELESS
EEHLMOYZ HEMOLYZE
EEHLMRST THERMELS
EEHLNOPT PHENETOL
EEHLNOTT TELETHON
EEHLOPSS HOPELESS
EEHLOPST HEELPOST
PESTHOLE
TELESHOP
EEHLORST HOSTELER
EEHLORSV SHOVELER
EEHLOSSS SHOELESS
EEHLPRST TELPHERS
EEHLPRSU SPHERULE
EEHLPSSY PHYLESES
EEHLRSST SHELTERS
EEHLRSSV SHELVERS
EEHLRSSW WELSHERS
EEHLSSTT SHTETELS
EEHLSSTW THEWLESS
EEHMMOPR MORPHEME
EEHMMORT OHMMETER
EEHMNOPS PHONEMES
EEHMNORS HORSEMEN
EEHMNOSU HOUSEMEN
EEHMNOSW SOMEWHEN
EEHMNRSY MYNHEERS
EEHMNSSU UNMESHES
EEHMNTTU UMTEENTH
EEHMORST THEOREMS
EEHMORVW WHOMEVER
EEHMRSUX EXHUMERS
EEHNNORT ENTHRONE
EEHNOORS HONOREES
EEHNOPRU HEREUPON
EEHNOPST POTHEENS
EEHNOPTY NEOPHYTE
EEHNORSS SENHORES
EEHNORST HONESTER
EEHNORSW NOWHERES
EEHNORTU HEREUNTO
EEHNOSST ETHNOSES
EEHNPRSU UNSPHERE
EEHNRTTU UNTETHER
EEHNSSTU ENTHUSES
EEHNSSTV SEVENTHS
EEHOOPRS OOSPHERE
EEHOOPRV OVERHOPE
EEHOOPSW WHOOPEES
EEHOORSV OVERSHOE
EEHOOSST TOESHOES
EEHOOTTY EYETOOTH
EEHOPPRY HYPEROPE
EEHOPPSW PEEPSHOW
EEHOPRSU EUPHROES
EEHOPRVY OVERHYPE
EEHOPSST HEPTOSES
EEHORRSV HOVERERS
EEHORRSW RESHOWER
SHOWERER
EEHORRTX EXHORTER
EEHORSSU REHOUSES
EEHORSVW WHOSEVER
EEHOSSTY EYESHOTS
EEHRSSSU RHESUSES
EEHRSTTW WHETTERS
EEHSSTUY SHUTEYES
EEIIKKLT KITELIKE
EEIIKLLN LINELIKE
EEIIKLLR LIKELIER
EEIIKLLT TILELIKE
EEIIKLLV VEILLIKE
EEIIKLNP PINELIKE
EEIIKLNV VEINLIKE
EEIIKLPP PIPELIKE
EEIIKLRW WIRELIKE
EEIIKLSV VISELIKE
EEIIKLSW LIKEWISE
EEIILLMM MILLIEME
EEIILLMT MELILITE
EEIILLOP EOLIPILE
EEIILLRV LIVELIER
EEIILMNT ILMENITE
MELINITE
TIMELINE
EEIILMRT TIMELIER
EEIILNPP PIPELINE
EEIILNST LENITIES
EEIILNTV LENITIVE
EEIILRSV LIVERIES
EEIILRSW WISELIER
EEIILSTV LEVITIES
EEIILSTW LEWISITE
EEIIMMTT MIMETITE
EEIIMNST ENMITIES
EEIIMOST MOIETIES
EEIIMRSS MISERIES
EEIIMRTZ ITEMIZER
EEIIMSST ITEMISES
EEIIMSSV EMISSIVE
EEIIMSTZ ITEMIZES
EEIINNST EINSTEIN
NINETIES
EEIINPPR PIPERINE
EEIINPRS PINERIES
EEIINPRV VIPERINE
EEIINRRV RIVERINE
EEIINRST NITERIES
EEIINRSV VINERIES
EEIINRSW WINERIES
EEIINRTT INTERTIE
RETINITE
EEIINRTV REINVITE
EEIINSST SIENITES
EEIINSSW EISWEINS
EEIINSTT ENTITIES
EEIINSTV INVITEES
VEINIEST
EEIIOPTZ EPIZOITE
EEIIPRSX EXPIRIES
EEIIQSTU EQUITIES
EEIIRRSV RIVIERES
EEIIRRTV TIRRIVEE
EEIIRSTV VERITIES
EEIISTVW VIEWIEST
EEIJKLTU JUTELIKE
EEIJKRST JERKIEST
EEIJLNNU JULIENNE
EEIJLNRT JETLINER
EEIJLNUV JUVENILE
EEIJNNOR ENJOINER
EEIJNRRU REINJURE
EEIJSTTT JETTIEST
EEIKLMST STEMLIKE
EEIKLNOS NOSELIKE
EEIKLNOV OVENLIKE
EEIKLNRU RUNELIKE
EEIKLNSS LIKENESS
EEIKLNST NESTLIKE
EEIKLNTT TENTLIKE
EEIKLOPP POPELIKE
EEIKLOPR ROPELIKE
EEIKLOPT POETLIKE
EEIKLORS ROSELIKE
EEIKLORT LORIKEET
EEIKLPST SPIKELET
STEPLIKE
EEIKLRST TRISKELE
EEIKLSTV VESTLIKE
EEIKMPSS MISKEEPS
EEIKMRSS KERMISES
EEIKNORS KEROSINE
EEIKNORV REINVOKE
EEIKNPSY PINKEYES
EEIKNRRT TINKERER
EEIKNRST KERNITES
EEIKNSWY EYEWINKS
EEIKOQUV EQUIVOKE
EEIKORSU EUROKIES
EEIKPPRR KIPPERER
EEIKPRST PERKIEST
EEIKPSST PESKIEST
EEIKRRSS SKERRIES
EEIKRRST RESTRIKE
EEIKRSST KEISTERS
KIESTERS
EEIKRSTU KEIRETSU
EEIKSTTT TEKTITES
EEILLMPR IMPELLER
EEILLMRS SMELLIER
EEILLMSS LIMELESS
EEILLNOR LONELIER
EEILLNPS SPINELLE
EEILLNSS LINELESS
EEILLNSY SENILELY
EEILLOOP EOLOPILE
EEILLORV LOVELIER
EEILLOSV LOVELIES
EEILLPSS ELLIPSES
PILELESS
EEILLPSY SLEEPILY
EEILLPZZ PIZZELLE
EEILLSSS ISLELESS
EEILLSTT STELLITE
EEILLSTV EVILLEST
EEILLSTW WELLSITE
EEILLTVY VELLEITY
EEILLVWY WEEVILLY
EEILMNNO LIMONENE
EEILMNNS LINESMEN
EEILMNOP PEMOLINE
EEILMNRU LEMURINE
RELUMINE
EEILMNSU SELENIUM
EEILMNSY MYELINES
EEILMOPZ POLEMIZE
EEILMQTU MIQUELET
EEILMRSV VERMEILS
EEILMSST TIMELESS
EEILMSUV EMULSIVE
EEILNNOT NONELITE
EEILNNST SENTINEL
EEILNNSV ENLIVENS
EEILNOPR LEPORINE
EEILNORS ELOINERS
EEILNOSV NOVELISE
EEILNOVV LOVEVINE
EEILNOVZ NOVELIZE
EEILNPPZ ZEPPELIN
EEILNPRS PILSENER
EEILNPRU PERILUNE
EEILNPRV REPLEVIN
EEILNPST PENLITES
PLENTIES
EEILNQUY EQUINELY
EEILNRSS REINLESS
EEILNRST ENLISTER
LISTENER
REENLIST
SILENTER
EEILNRSV LIVENERS
SNIVELER
EEILNRTT NETTLIER
EEILNRTY ENTIRELY
LIENTERY
EEILNSST LITENESS
SETLINES
EEILNSSV EVILNESS
LIVENESS
VEINLESS
VILENESS
EEILNSSW WINELESS
EEILNSTT ENTITLES
EEILNSTV VEINLETS
EEILNSUV VEINULES
EEILNTUV VEINULET
EEILOPST PETIOLES
EEILORRT LOITERER
EEILORSV OVERLIES
RELIEVOS
VOLERIES
EEILORVV OVERLIVE
EEILOSTZ ZEOLITES
EEILOTTT TOILETTE
EEILOVWZ VOWELIZE
EEILPPSS PIPELESS
EEILPPSY EPILEPSY
EEILPRRS REPLIERS
EEILPRSS SPIELERS
EEILPRST EPISTLER
PELTRIES
PERLITES
REPTILES
EEILPRSU SUPERLIE
EEILPRSV PRELIVES
EEILPSSS PELISSES
EEILPSST EPISTLES
EEILPSSV PELVISES
EEILPSTY EPISTYLE
EEILQRSU RELIQUES
EEILRRSV RESILVER
REVILERS
SILVERER
SLIVERER
EEILRRTT LITTERER
EEILRSST LEISTERS
TIRELESS
EEILRSSU LEISURES
EEILRSSW WIRELESS
EEILRSTT RETITLES
EEILSSTX EXITLESS
SEXTILES
EEILSSVW VIEWLESS
EEILSSVX SILVEXES
EEILSTTX TEXTILES
EEILSTUX ULEXITES
EEIMMNRS IMMENSER
EEIMMORS MEMORIES
MEMORISE
EEIMMORZ MEMORIZE
EEIMMOST SOMETIME
EEIMMRSS IMMERSES
EEIMMRST MERISTEM
STEMMIER
EEIMMRTT TERMTIME
EEIMMSST MISMEETS
EEIMMSTU SEMIMUTE
EEIMNNOS NOMINEES
EEIMNNRS REINSMEN
EEIMNOPS SEMIOPEN
EEIMNORS EMERSION
EEIMNORV OVERMINE
VOMERINE
EEIMNOST MONETISE
SEMITONE
EEIMNOTZ MONETIZE
ZONETIME
EEIMNPRS SPERMINE
EEIMNPRU PERINEUM
EEIMNRST MISENTER
EEIMNRTU MUTINEER
EEIMNSSS MISSENSE
EEIMNSTV MISEVENT
EEIMOPRS MOPERIES
PROMISEE
REIMPOSE
EEIMOPSS EPISOMES
EEIMOPST EPISTOME
EPITOMES
EEIMORST TIRESOME
EEIMORSZ SIEROZEM
EEIMORTV OVERTIME
EEIMORTX OXIMETER
EEIMOSSS SEMIOSES
EEIMOSSW SOMEWISE
EEIMOTTT TOTEMITE
EEIMPPST PIPESTEM
EEIMPRRS PREMIERS
SIMPERER
EEIMPRSS EMPRISES
IMPRESES
PREMISES
SPIREMES
EEIMPRST EMPTIERS
EEIMPRSX PREMIXES
EEIMPRSZ EMPRIZES
EEIMPSST SEPTIMES
EEIMPSTT EMPTIEST
EEIMQRSU REQUIEMS
EEIMQSTU MESQUITE
EEIMQTUZ MEZQUITE
EEIMRRST MERRIEST
MITERERS
RIMESTER
TRIREMES
EEIMRRTT REMITTER
TRIMETER
EEIMRSST MEISTERS
MISSTEER
TRISEMES
EEIMRSTT EMITTERS
TERMITES
EEIMRSTU EMERITUS
EEIMRTTY TEMERITY
EEIMSSST MESSIEST
METISSES
EEINNNPS PENNINES
EEINNOPS PENSIONE
EEINNPTT PENITENT
EEINNRST INTENSER
INTERNES
EEINNRSU NEURINES
EEINNRSV INNERVES
NERVINES
EEINNRTT RENITENT
EEINNRTV INVENTER
REINVENT
EEINNSST TENNISES
EEINNSTT SENTIENT
EEINNSTW ENTWINES
WENNIEST
EEINNSTZ NETIZENS
EEINOOPT OPTIONEE
EEINOPPR PEPERONI
EEINOPRS ISOPRENE
PEREIONS
PIONEERS
EEINOPTY EYEPOINT
EEINORRR ORNERIER
EEINORRT ORIENTER
REORIENT
EEINORST ONERIEST
SEROTINE
EEINORSV EVERSION
EEINORTT TENORITE
EEINORTX EXERTION
EEINOSSS ENOSISES
NOESISES
EEINOSST ESSONITE
EEINOSTT NOISETTE
TEOSINTE
EEINPPSS PEPSINES
EEINPRRS PRERINSE
REPINERS
RIPENERS
EEINPRSS EREPSINS
RIPENESS
EEINPRSU PENURIES
RESUPINE
EEINPRTU PREUNITE
EEINPRTX INEXPERT
EEINQRSU ENQUIRES
SQUIREEN
EEINQSTU QUIETENS
EEINRRST INSERTER
REINSERT
REINTERS
RENTIERS
TERRINES
EEINRRSU REINSURE
EEINRRSV VERNIERS
EEINRRTU REUNITER
UNRETIRE
EEINRRTV INVERTER
EEINRRTW WINTERER
EEINRRTX INTERREX
EEINRSST SENTRIES
EEINRSSU ENURESIS
EEINRSSV INVERSES
VERSINES
EEINRSTT INSETTER
INTEREST
STERNITE
TRIENTES
EEINRSTU ESURIENT
RETINUES
REUNITES
EEINRSTV NERVIEST
REINVEST
SIRVENTE
EEINRSTX INTERSEX
EEINRSTY SERENITY
EEINRSUV UNIVERSE
EEINRSVX VERNIXES
EEINRSWW NEWSWIRE

EEINRTTY ENTIRETY
ETERNITY
EEINSSST SESTINES
EEINSSSW WISENESS
EEINSSSX SEXINESS
EEINSSTW NEWSIEST
EEINSSTX SIXTEENS
EEINSSTY SYENITES
EEINSSUX UNISEXES
EEINSTTT NETTIEST
TENTIEST
EEINSTTW TWENTIES
EEINSTTX EXISTENT
EEIOPPST EPITOPES
EEIOPRRS ROPERIES
EEIOPRRT PORTIERE
EEIOPRRV OVERRIPE
EEIOPRST POETISER
POETRIES
EEIOPRTZ POETIZER
EEIOPSST POETISES
EEIOPSTZ POETIZES
EEIORRRS ORRERIES
EEIORRSS ROSERIES
EEIORRTV OVERTIRE
EEIORRTW TOWERIER
EEIORRTX EXTERIOR
EEIORSTZ EROTIZES
EEIORSVW OVERWISE
EEIORSVZ OVERSIZE
EEIORVVW OVERVIEW
EEIPPPRR PREPPIER
EEIPPPRS PREPPIES
EEIPPPST PEPPIEST
EEIPPQRU EQUIPPER
EEIPPRRS PERSPIRE
EEIPPRRT PERIPTER
EEIPPRTY PERIPETY
EEIPPRTZ PEPTIZER
EEIPPSTT PIPETTES
EEIPPSTZ PEPTIZES
EEIPQRSU PERIQUES
REEQUIPS
EEIPRRSS PRISERES
REPRISES
RESPIRES
EEIPRRSW PREWIRES
EEIPRRSX EXPIRERS
EEIPRRTT PRETERIT
PRETTIER
EEIPRSST RESPITES
EEIPRSSV PREVISES
EEIPRSTT PRETTIES
EEIPRSTX PREEXIST
EEIPRSTY YPERITES
EEIPRSVW PREVIEWS
EEIPRTUV ERUPTIVE
EEIPSSSS SPEISSES
EEIPSSTT PESTIEST
EEIPSSTW STEPWISE
EEIPSTTT PETTIEST
EEIQRRRU REQUIRER
EEIQRRSU QUERIERS
REQUIRES
EEIQRRTU REQUITER
EEIQRRUV QUIVERER
EEIQRSSU ESQUIRES
EEIQRSTU QUIETERS
REQUITES
EEIQSTTU QUIETEST
EEIRRRST RETIRERS
TERRIERS
EEIRRRTW REWRITER
EEIRRSST RESISTER
TRESSIER
EEIRRSSU REISSUER
EEIRRSSV REVISERS
EEIRRSTV RESTRIVE
RIVETERS
EEIRRSTW REWRITES
EEIRRSVV REVIVERS
EEIRRTTT TITTERER
EEIRSSSU REISSUES
SEISURES
EEIRSSTU SURETIES
EEIRSSTV SIEVERTS
VESTRIES
EEIRSSUZ SEIZURES
EEIRSTVV VETIVERS
EEIRSTVY SEVERITY
EEIRTTVV VETIVERT
EEISSSTV VITESSES
EEISSTTT TESTIEST
EEISSTTZ ZESTIEST
EEJJLNUY JEJUNELY
EEJKNRTU JUNKETER
EEJKORST JOKESTER
EEJLPSTU PULSEJET
EEJNORSY ENJOYERS
REENJOYS
EEJORSST RESOJETS
EEJPRRRU PERJURER
EEJPRRSU PERJURES
EEJPRSTU SUPERJET
EEKKORWW WORKWEEK
EEKKRRST TREKKERS
EEKLLNRY KERNELLY
EEKLLSUU UKULELES
EEKLMRSZ KLEZMERS
EEKLNNNU UNKENNEL
EEKLNOSS KEELSONS
EEKLNOST SKELETON
EEKLOSSU LEUKOSES
EEKLOSSY YOKELESS
EEKLRSST KESTRELS
SKELTERS
EEKNOPRS RESPOKEN
EEKNORTY KEYNOTER
EEKNOSTY KEYNOTES
KEYSTONE
EEKNSSST KNESSETS
EEKNSSSW SKEWNESS
EEKNSSTU NETSUKES
EEKOOPPS PEKEPOOS
EEKOPSTU OUTKEEPS
EEKORRSV REVOKERS
EEKORSST RESTOKES
EEKRRSUZ KREUZERS
EEKRRTUZ KREUTZER
EEKRSSTY KEYSTERS
EELLLLMP PELLMELL
EELLMORS MORELLES
EELLMORW MELLOWER
EELLMPTU PLUMELET
EELLMRSS SMELLERS
EELLNNOV NONLEVEL
EELLNORR ENROLLER
REENROLL
EELLNORS RELLENOS
EELLNOUV NOUVELLE
EELLNPRU PRUNELLE
EELLNRSU SULLENER
EELLNSSS LENSLESS
EELLNSST SNELLEST
EELLNSSW WELLNESS
EELLNSTU ENTELLUS
EELLNSUV UNLEVELS
EELLOPSS POLELESS
EELLORRR REROLLER
EELLORSS ROSELLES
EELLORST SOLLERET
EELLORSV OVERSELL
EELLORTX EXTOLLER
EELLORVY VOLLEYER
EELLORWY YELLOWER
EELLOSSS SOLELESS
EELLOSSV LOVELESS
EELLOSUV LEVULOSE
EELLPRSS PRESELLS
RESPELLS
SPELLERS
EELLPRST PRETELLS
EELLPSST PELTLESS
EELLQRSU QUELLERS
EELLRSSU RULELESS
EELLSSTW SWELLEST
EELLSTVY SVELTELY
EELMMPUX EXEMPLUM
EELMNOOS LONESOME
OENOMELS
EELMNORS SOLEMNER
EELMNSUY UNSEEMLY
EELMNTUY UNMEETLY
EELMOOSV LOVESOME
EELMOPRY EMPLOYER
REEMPLOY
EELMOPSY EMPLOYES
EELMORST MOLESTER
EELMORSW EELWORMS
EELMORTV OVERMELT
EELMORTY MOTLEYER
REMOTELY
EELMOSSV MOVELESS
EELMOTVW TWELVEMO
EELMPPRU EMPURPLE
EELMPSTT TEMPLETS
EELMRRTU MURRELET
EELMRSST RESMELTS
SMELTERS
TERMLESS
EELMRSTY SMELTERY
EELMSSST STEMLESS
EELNNOSS LONENESS
EELNNRTU TUNNELER
EELNNUVY UNEVENLY
EELNOORS LOOSENER
EELNOPPU UNPEOPLE
EELNOPRT PETRONEL
EELNOPSV ENVELOPS
EELNOPSY POLYENES
EELNOPTY POLYTENE
EELNOQTU ELOQUENT
EELNORST ENTRESOL
EELNORTV OVERLENT
EELNOSSS NOSELESS
SOLENESS
EELNOSST NOTELESS
TONELESS
EELNOSSU SELENOUS
EELNOSSZ ZONELESS
EELNOSTU TOLUENES
EELNOSUV VENULOSE
EELNRSST NESTLERS
EELNRSTT NETTLERS
EELNRSUV NERVULES
EELNSSSW NEWSLESS
EELNSSTT TENTLESS
EELNSSTU TUNELESS
UNSTEELS
EELNSSTV VENTLESS
EELNSTTU LUNETTES
UNSETTLE
EELOORVV OVERLOVE
EELOPPRS PEOPLERS
EELOPPSS PEPLOSES
POPELESS
EELOPPST ESTOPPEL
EELOPPSZ ZEPPOLES
EELOPRRX EXPLORER
EELOPRSV PRESOLVE
EELOPRSX EXPLORES
EELOPRTT TELEPORT
EELOPSST POETLESS
EELOPSTU EELPOUTS
OUTSLEEP
EELORRSV RESOLVER
EELORRTV REVOLTER
EELORRTW TROWELER
EELORRUV OVERRULE
EELORRVV REVOLVER
EELORSST SOLERETS
EELORSSV RESOLVES
EELORSTU RESOLUTE
EELORSTV OVERLETS
EELORSVV EVOLVERS
REVOLVES
EELORTTU ROULETTE
EELORTUV REVOLUTE
TRUELOVE
EELOSSSU SOLEUSES
EELOSSTT TELEOSTS
EELOSSTU SETULOSE
EELOSSTV VOTELESS
EELOSTUV EVOLUTES
VELOUTES
EELPPSSU PEPLUSES
EELPPSTU SEPTUPLE
EELPQRSU PREQUELS
EELPRRSU REPULSER
EELPRSST SPELTERS
EELPRSSU REPULSES
EELPRSTY PEYTRELS
EELPRSTZ PRETZELS
EELPRTXY EXPERTLY
EELPSSTZ SPELTZES
EELPSSUX EXPULSES
PLEXUSES
EELPSTUX SEXTUPLE
EELRRSTW WRESTLER
EELRSSST RESTLESS
TRESSELS
EELRSSTT SETTLERS
STERLETS
TRESTLES
EELRSSTU STREUSEL
EELRSSTW SWELTERS
WRESTLES
EELRSSTY RESTYLES
EELRSSTZ SELTZERS
EELRSTWY WESTERLY
EELSSSTV VESTLESS
EELSSSTZ ZESTLESS
EELSSTTV SVELTEST
EELSSTTX TEXTLESS
EEMMNNOY MONEYMEN
EEMMNOST MEMENTOS
EEMMNOTV MOVEMENT
EEMMOOSS MESOSOME
EEMMRSST STEMMERS
EEMMRSTY STEMMERY
EEMMRTUX EXTREMUM
EEMNNOPR PRENOMEN
EEMNNOSV ENVENOMS
EEMNOOSS SOMEONES
EEMNOOSY MOONEYES
EEMNORSS MORENESS
EEMNORSV VENOMERS
EEMNORSY MONEYERS
EEMNORTU ROUTEMEN
EEMNPRSS PRESSMEN
EEMNPRSU SUPERMEN
EEMNPRTU ERUMPENT
EEMNRSTU MUENSTER
EEMNSSTU MUTENESS
TENESMUS
EEMNSTTV VESTMENT
EEMOOPRT PROTEOME
EEMOORRT OROMETER
EEMOORRV MOREOVER
EEMOORTT ROOMETTE
EEMOOSSX EXOSMOSE
EEMOPRRS EMPERORS
PREMORSE
EEMOPRSW EMPOWERS
EEMOQRSU MORESQUE
EEMOQTTU MOQUETTE
EEMORRSS REMORSES
EEMORRSV REMOVERS
EEMORSST SOMERSET
EEMORSTT REMOTEST
EEMOSSST MESTESOS
EEMOTTTU TEETOTUM
EEMOTTZZ MOZZETTE
EEMPPRST PREEMPTS
EEMPRRST PRETERMS
EEMPRRSU PRESUMER
SUPREMER
EEMPRSSU PRESUMES
SUPREMES
EEMPRSTT TEMPTERS
EEMPRSTU PERMUTES
EEMPSSTT TEMPESTS
EEMRRSSU RESUMERS
EEMRRSUU EREMURUS
EEMRRTTU MUTTERER
EEMSSTTU MUSETTES
EENNNOSS NONSENSE
EENNNOTV NONEVENT
EENNNPTY TENPENNY
EENNOORT ROTENONE
EENNOPSS OPENNESS
EENNOPTX EXPONENT
EENNORST ENTERONS
TENONERS
EENNORSU NEURONES
EENNRSUV UNNERVES
EENOORST OESTRONE
EENOORTV OVERTONE
EENOPPRS PROPENES
PROPENSE
EENOPPST PEPTONES
EENOPRSS RESPONSE
EENOPRTT ENTREPOT
EENOPRTU OUTPREEN
EENOPRXY PYROXENE
EENOPSST PENTOSES
POSTEENS
EENOPSTT POSTTEEN
POTTEENS
EENOPSTY NEOTYPES
EENORRTT ROTTENER
EENORSSS SORENESS
EENORSST ESTRONES
EENORSSU NEUROSES
EENORSTX EXTENSOR
EENORSVW OVERSEWN
EENOSSST STENOSES
EENOSTTT TONETTES
EENPPRST PERPENTS
EENPRSST PENSTERS
PERTNESS
PRESENTS
SERPENTS
EENPRSSU PURENESS
EENPRSTV PREVENTS
EENPRTUX UNEXPERT
EENPSSSU SUSPENSE
EENPSTTU PETUNTSE
EENPTTUZ PETUNTZE
EENQSSTU SEQUENTS
EENRRRTU RETURNER
EENRRSSU ENSURERS
EENRRSUV NERVURES
EENRRTUV VENTURER
EENRSSSU SURENESS
EENRSSTT STERNEST
EENRSSTU TRUENESS
EENRSSTW WESTERNS
EENRSSTY STYRENES
EENRSTUV VENTURES
EEOOPPRS REOPPOSE
EEOOPRST PROTEOSE
EEOOPRSX EXOSPORE
EEOORRVW OVERWORE
EEOORTVV OVERVOTE
EEOOSSST OSTEOSES
EEOPPRRR PROPERER
EEOPRRRT REPORTER
EEOPRRRV REPROVER
EEOPRRSS REPOSERS
EEOPRRST PRESTORE
EEOPRRSV REPROVES
EEOPRRSW REPOWERS
EEOPRRTT POTTERER
EEOPRRTV OVERPERT
EEOPRRTX EXPORTER
REEXPORT
EEOPRSSS ESPRESSO
EEOPRSSU ESPOUSER
REPOUSSE
EEOPRSSX EXPOSERS
EXPRESSO
EEOPRSTT PROETTES
TREETOPS
EEOPRSTV OVERSTEP
EEOPRSTY SEROTYPE
EEOPRSUX EXPOSURE
EEOPSSSU ESPOUSES
EEOPSSTW SWEETSOP
EEOPSSTY EYESPOTS
EEOPSTUW OUTSWEEP
OUTWEEPS
EEOQRTTU ROQUETTE
EEORRRST RESORTER
RESTORER
RETRORSE
EEORRRTT RETORTER
EEORRSST RESTORES
EEORRSSV REVERSOS
EEORRSTU REROUTES
EEORRSTV EVERTORS
RESTROVE
EEORRSTX EXTRORSE
EEORRSTY OYSTERER
EEORRSUV OVERSURE
EEORRTTT TOTTERER
EEORRTTX EXTORTER
EEORRTUV OVERTURE
TROUVERE
EEORSSTT ROSETTES
EEORSSTV ESTOVERS
OVERSETS
EEORSSUV OVERUSES
EEORSSVW OVERSEWS
EEORSTTU OUTSTEER
EEORSTUV OUTSERVE
EEORSTVW OVERWETS
EEORSTVX VORTEXES
EEPPRRSS PREPRESS
EEPPRSST STEPPERS
EEPPRSTY PRETYPES
EEPPSSUW UPSWEEPS
EEPRRSSS PRESSERS
EEPRRSST PRESTERS
EEPRRSSU PERUSERS
PRESSURE
EEPRRSTV PERVERTS
EEPRRSUU REPURSUE
EEPRRTTU PUTTERER
EEPRSSTT PRETESTS
EEPRSSUX SUPERSEX
EEPRSTTU UPSETTER
EEPRSTTX PRETEXTS
EEPSSTTY TYPESETS
EEQRSSTU QUESTERS
REQUESTS
EERRSSST RESTRESS
EERRSSTU TRESSURE
EERRSSTW STREWERS
WRESTERS
EERRSSVW SWERVERS
EERRSTTU REUTTERS
UTTERERS
EERRSUVY RESURVEY
EERSSSST STRESSES
EERSSSTU ESTRUSES
EERSSTTU TRUSTEES
EERSSTTY SYRETTES
EERSSTUU UTERUSES
EERSSTUV VESTURES
EERSTTUX TEXTURES
EFFFGINO FEOFFING
EFFFILRU FLUFFIER
EFFFINOS INFEOFFS
EFFFLRSU FLUFFERS
EFFFOORS FEOFFORS
EFFGINOR OFFERING
EFFGINSU EFFUSING
EFFGIRRU GRUFFIER
EFFGRSTU GRUFFEST
EFFHIILS FILEFISH
EFFHIISW FISHWIFE
EFFHIITT FIFTIETH
EFFHILRW WHIFFLER
EFFHILSW WHIFFLES
EFFHIRSS SHERIFFS
EFFHIRSW WHIFFERS
EFFHISTU HUFFIEST
EFFHISTW WHIFFETS
EFFHLLSU SHELFFUL
EFFHLRSU SHUFFLER
EFFHLSSU SHUFFLES
EFFHOOOR FOREHOOF
EFFHOORS OFFSHORE
EFFIIMST MIFFIEST
EFFIINRS SNIFFIER
EFFIINSS IFFINESS
EFFIIPRS SPIFFIER
EFFIIPSS SPIFFIES
EFFIKLLO FOLKLIFE
EFFIKLRU RUFFLIKE
EFFIKLSS SKIFFLES
EFFILNRS SNIFFLER
EFFILNSS SNIFFLES
EFFILRRS RIFFLERS
EFFILRRU RUFFLIER
EFFILRSU SIFFLEUR
EFFINOSU EFFUSION
EFFINRSS SNIFFERS
EFFINRSU SNUFFIER
EFFINSST STIFFENS
EFFIORST FORFEITS
EFFIORSX FOXFIRES
EFFIPSTU PUFFIEST
EFFIRSTU STUFFIER
EFFISSTT STIFFEST
EFFISSUX SUFFIXES
EFFLLOSS SELLOFFS
EFFLMNUU UNMUFFLE
EFFLMRSU MUFFLERS
EFFLNRSU SNUFFLER
EFFLNSSU SNUFFLES
EFFLOSSU SOUFFLES
EFFLRRSU RUFFLERS
EFFLRSTU TRUFFLES
EFFNRSSU SNUFFERS
EFFNSSTU FUNFESTS
EFFOOORT FOREFOOT
EFFOORRS OFFERORS
EFFOPRRS PROFFERS
EFFORRST TROFFERS
EFFORRUV OVERRUFF
EFFRRSUU FURFURES
EFFRSSTU RESTUFFS
STUFFERS
EFFSSSUU SUFFUSES
EFGGIINN FEIGNING
EFGGILOS SOLFEGGI
EFGGINRU REFUGING
EFGGIORR FROGGIER
EFGGIOST FOGGIEST
EFGGIRTU EGGFRUIT
EFGGISTU FUGGIEST
EFGGLORS FLOGGERS
EFGHHIIL HIGHLIFE
EFGHIILS FLEISHIG
EFGHILNS FLESHING
EFGHINRS FRESHING
EFGHINRT FRIGHTEN
EFGHIOSY FOGEYISH
EFGHIPRT PREFIGHT
EFGHIRST FIGHTERS
FREIGHTS
REFIGHTS
EFGHNOTU FOUGHTEN
EFGHORTU REFOUGHT
EFGIIINS IGNIFIES
EFGIILNR REFILING
EFGIILNT FILETING
EFGIILNU FIGULINE
EFGIILRU UGLIFIER
EFGIILSU UGLIFIES
EFGIINNR INFRINGE
REFINING
EFGIINNT FEINTING

EFGIINRR FRINGIER
REFIRING
EFGIINRU FIGURINE
EFGIINRX REFIXING
EFGIINRY REIFYING
EFGIITUV FUGITIVE
EFGIKLLU GULFLIKE
EFGIKLOR FROGLIKE
EFGILLNO LIFELONG
EFGILLNU FUELLING
EFGILLUU GUILEFUL
EFGILMOR FILMGOER
EFGILNNS FLENSING
EFGILNOR FLORIGEN
EFGILNRS FLINGERS
EFGILNRU FERULING
EFGILNRY REFLYING
EFGILNST FELTINGS
EFGILNTT FETTLING
EFGILNTW LEFTWING
EFGILPRU FIREPLUG
EFGILSST GIFTLESS
EFGILSTU GULFIEST
EFGIMNST FIGMENTS
EFGIMOSY FOGEYISM
EFGIMRUU REFUGIUM
EFGINNPS PFENNIGS
EFGINORV FORGIVEN
EFGINORW FOREWING
EFGINRRY FERRYING
REFRYING
EFGINRSU GUNFIRES
REFUSING
EFGINRTT FRETTING
EFGINRTU REFUTING
EFGINRTY GENTRIFY
EFGIOOST GOOFIEST
EFGIOPTT PETTIFOG
EFGIORRV FORGIVER
EFGIORSV FORGIVES
EFGIRRST GRIFTERS
EFGIRRSU FIGURERS
EFGLOOTY FETOLOGY
EFGLOOVX FOXGLOVE
EFGLORST FROGLETS
EFGLSSTU SLUGFEST
EFGNOSST SONGFEST
EFGNSSUU FUNGUSES
EFGOORRS FORGOERS
EFGORSTU FOREGUTS
EFHIIKLS FISHLIKE
EFHIILLT HELILIFT
EFHIILNS FISHLINE
EFHIILRT FILTHIER
EFHIILST TILEFISH
EFHIINRS FINISHER
REFINISH
EFHIINSS FINISHES
EFHIIPPS PIPEFISH
EFHIIPRS FIRESHIP
EFHIIRST SHIFTIER
EFHIISST FISHIEST
EFHIKLOO HOOFLIKE
EFHILLSY ELFISHLY
FLESHILY
EFHILOPS FISHPOLE
EFHILSSS FISHLESS
EFHILTWY WHITEFLY
EFHINNOT FENTHION
EFHINSST FISHNETS
EFHIORRT FROTHIER
EFHIORSS ROSEFISH
EFHIORSV OVERFISH
EFHIORTT FORTIETH
EFHIRRTU THURIFER
EFHIRSST SHIFTERS
EFHISSUW HUSWIFES
EFHLNORS HORNFELS
EFHLNOUY HONEYFUL
EFHLOOSS HOOFLESS
EFHLOOSX FOXHOLES
EFHLOPST FLESHPOT
EFHLOPSU HOPEFULS
EFHLORSY HORSEFLY
EFHLORVY HOVERFLY
EFHLOSUU HOUSEFUL
EFHLOSUY HOUSEFLY
EFHLRSSU FLUSHERS
EFHLSSTU FLUSHEST
EFHLSTTW TWELFTHS
EFHNOSUU FUNHOUSE
EFHOORSW FORESHOW
EFHORRST FROTHERS
EFHRRSTU FURTHERS
EFHRSTTU FURTHEST
EFIIILRV VILIFIER
EFIIILSV VILIFIES
EFIIIMNS MINIFIES
EFIIINNT INFINITE
EFIIINSV VINIFIES
EFIIIRVV VIVIFIER
EFIIISTX FIXITIES
EFIIISVV VIVIFIES
EFIIKLLM FILMLIKE
EFIIKLNT FLINKITE
EFIIKNPR FIREPINK
EFIIKRRS FRISKIER
EFIILLNT TEFILLIN
EFIILLRR FRILLIER
EFIILMRS FLIMSIER
EFIILMSS FLIMSIES
MISFILES
EFIILMST FILMIEST
EFIILNRT FLINTIER
EFIILNTY FELINITY
FINITELY
EFIILRRT FLIRTIER
EFIILRST FILISTER
EFIILRSU FUSILIER
EFIILSTY FEISTILY
EFIIMMNS FEMINISM
EFIIMNRS MISINFER
EFIIMNST FEMINIST
EFIIMNTY FEMINITY
EFIIMRRS RIMFIRES
EFIIMRSS MISFIRES
EFIINNOS SINFONIE
EFIINNST FINNIEST
EFIINORR INFERIOR
EFIINORT NOTIFIER
EFIINOST NOTIFIES
EFIINPSV FIVEPINS
EFIINPSX SPINIFEX
EFIINRRT FERRITIN
EFIINRSU UNIFIERS
EFIINRSY RESINIFY
EFIINSTT NIFTIEST
EFIINSUV INFUSIVE
EFIIORSS OSSIFIER
EFIIOSSS OSSIFIES
EFIIPRRU PURIFIER
EFIIPRST SPITFIRE
EFIIPRSU PURIFIES
EFIIPRTY TYPIFIER
EFIIPSTY TYPIFIES
EFIIRRST FIRRIEST
EFIIRRTU FRUITIER
EFIIRRZZ FRIZZIER
EFIIRSZZ FRIZZIES
EFIIRVVY REVIVIFY
EFIISTTW WIFTIEST
EFIISTZZ FIZZIEST
EFIJLORS FRIJOLES
EFIJLOST JETFOILS
EFIKKLLO FOLKLIKE
EFIKKLOR FORKLIKE
EFIKLLOT LOFTLIKE
EFIKLLOW WOLFLIKE
EFIKLMOR FOREMILK
EFIKLNSU FLUNKIES
EFIKLOOR ROOFLIKE
EFIKLOOT FOOTLIKE
EFIKLORS FOLKSIER
EFIKLORW LIFEWORK
EFIKLOST FOLKIEST
EFIKLRSU SURFLIKE
EFIKLRTU TURFLIKE
EFIKLSTU FLUKIEST
LUTEFISK
EFIKNORS FORESKIN
EFIKNRSU REFUSNIK
EFIKNSTU FUNKIEST
EFIKORRW FIREWORK
EFIKORST FORKIEST
EFIKRRSS FRISKERS
EFIKRSST FRISKETS
EFILLMSS FILMLESS
EFILLORV OVERFILL
EFILLORW LOWLIFER
EFILLOSW LOWLIFES
EFILLRRS FRILLERS
EFILLRUY IREFULLY
EFILLSTY STELLIFY
EFILLTUY FUTILELY
EFILMNOS FOILSMEN
EFILMNSU FULMINES
EFILMSST FILMSETS
LEFTISMS
EFILMSUY EMULSIFY
EFILNNTU INFLUENT
EFILNOOR ROOFLINE
EFILNORU FLUORINE
EFILNOSX FLEXIONS
EFILNRYZ FRENZILY
EFILNSUX INFLUXES
EFILNUWY UNWIFELY
EFILOOSS FLOOSIES
EFILOOSZ FLOOZIES
EFILOPPR FLOPPIER
EFILOPPS FLOPPIES
EFILOPRR PROFILER
EFILOPRS PROFILES
EFILORRV FRIVOLER
EFILORSS FLOSSIER
EFILORST TREFOILS
EFILORTU FLUORITE
EFILOSSS FLOSSIES
EFILOSTT LOFTIEST
EFILOSTU OUTFLIES
EFILPPRS FLIPPERS
EFILPPST FLIPPEST
EFILPPSU PIPEFULS
EFILPRTU UPLIFTER
EFILPSTU SPITEFUL
EFILRRST FLIRTERS
TRIFLERS
EFILRRSU FLURRIES
EFILRRZZ FRIZZLER
EFILRSST RIFTLESS
STIFLERS
EFILRSTT FLITTERS
EFILRSTW FEWTRILS
EFILRSTY FLYTIERS
EFILRSVV FLIVVERS
EFILRSZZ FRIZZLES
EFILRTTU FRUITLET
EFILSSTT LEFTISTS
EFILSSTU SULFITES
EFILSTTU FLUTIEST
EFILSTTW SWIFTLET
EFIMMRSU FERMIUMS
EFIMNORR INFORMER
REINFORM
RENIFORM
EFIMNORS ENSIFORM
FERMIONS
EFIMNRSS FIRMNESS
EFIMNSTT FITMENTS
EFIMOORR FIREROOM
EFIMORRT RETIFORM
EFIMORRW FIREWORM
EFIMORST SETIFORM
EFIMOSST SEMISOFT
EFIMOSTT OFTTIMES
EFIMPRRU FRUMPIER
EFIMRSTU FREMITUS
EFINNORS INFERNOS
EFINNPSU FINESPUN
EFINNRST FERNINST
EFINNSTU FUNNIEST
EFINOPTX PONTIFEX
EFINORRT FRONTIER
EFINORTY RENOTIFY
EFINOSSX FOXINESS
EFINOSSZ FOZINESS
EFINOSTT FISTNOTE
EFINRRRU FURRINER
EFINRSST SNIFTERS
EFINRSSU INFUSERS
EFIOOSST FOOTSIES
EFIOOSTT FOOTIEST
EFIOPRRT PROFITER
EFIOPRST FIREPOTS
PIEFORTS
POSTFIRE
EFIORRST FROSTIER
ROTIFERS
EFIORRSW FROWSIER
EFIORRTT RETROFIT
EFIORRUZ FROUZIER
EFIORRWZ FROWZIER
EFIORSTU OUTFIRES
EFIORTTU REOUTFIT
EFIPPRRY FRIPPERY
EFIPRRUY REPURIFY
EFIPRSST PRESIFTS
EFIPRSUX SUPERFIX
EFIPRTTY PRETTIFY
EFIRRRSU FURRIERS
EFIRRRUY FURRIERY
EFIRRSSU FRISEURS
EFIRRSTT FRITTERS
EFIRRSTU FRUITERS
FURRIEST
EFIRRSZZ FRIZZERS
EFIRSSSU FISSURES
EFIRSSTU SURFEITS
SURFIEST
EFIRSSTW SWIFTERS
EFIRSTTU TURFIEST
EFIRSTUX FIXTURES
EFIRSTUZ FURZIEST
EFISSSTU FUSSIEST
EFISSTTU FUSTIEST
EFISSTTW SWIFTEST
EFISTTTU TUFTIEST
EFISTUZZ FUZZIEST
EFKLLOOR FOLKLORE
EFKLMNOS MENFOLKS
EFKLMOOT FOLKMOTE
EFKLNRSU FLUNKERS
EFKLNSUY FLUNKEYS
EFKLORSS FORKLESS
EFKNOORW FOREKNOW
EFKORRTW FRETWORK
EFLLLOOW WOOLFELL
EFLLLOWY FELLOWLY
EFLLNSSU FULLNESS
EFLLNTUY FLUENTLY
EFLLOORW FOLLOWER
EFLLORUV OVERFULL
EFLLORUW WOFULLER
EFLLOSST LOFTLESS
EFLLOUWY WOEFULLY
EFLLRUUY RUEFULLY
EFLLSUUY USEFULLY
EFLMMRUY FLUMMERY
EFLMNOOU MONOFUEL
EFLMNRUU FRENULUM
EFLMORRY FORMERLY
EFLMORSS FORMLESS
EFLMOSTT LEFTMOST
EFLNORSU FLEURONS
EFLNORTT FRONTLET
EFLNORYZ FROZENLY
EFLNOSSU FOULNESS
SULFONES
EFLNOSTY STONEFLY
EFLNSSUY SYNFUELS
EFLOOPRV FLOPOVER
EFLOORRS FLOORERS
EFLOORSS ROOFLESS
EFLOORST FOOTLERS
EFLOORSZ FOOZLERS
EFLOORUV OVERFOUL
EFLOORVW OVERFLOW
EFLOOSST FOOTLESS
EFLOPPRS FLOPPERS
EFLOPRUW POWERFUL
EFLOPRUX FOURPLEX
EFLORSSS FLOSSERS
EFLORSTU FLOUTERS
EFLORSTW FELWORTS
EFLORSUY YOURSELF
EFLORSVY FLYOVERS
EFLOSUUX FLEXUOUS
EFLPRRSU PURFLERS
EFLRSSTU FLUSTERS
TURFLESS
EFLRSTTU FLUTTERS
EFLRSTUU FRUSTULE
SULFURET
EFLRTTUY FLUTTERY
EFMNNNUY FUNNYMEN
EFMNNORT FRONTMEN
EFMNORTY FROMENTY
EFMNRTUY FRUMENTY
FURMENTY
EFMOORST FOREMOST
EFMOORSU FOURSOME
EFMOPRRS PERFORMS
PREFORMS
EFMOPRST POMFRETS
EFNNOOOR FORENOON
EFNNORSU FENURONS
EFNNORUZ UNFROZEN
EFNOOOTT FOOTNOTE
EFNOORRW FOREWORN
EFNOOSST EFTSOONS
FESTOONS
EFNOPRST FORSPENT
EFNORRST REFRONTS
EFNORRSU FORERUNS
EFNORRSW FROWNERS
EFNORSTU FORTUNES
EFNOSSST SOFTNESS
EFNOTUZZ FUZZTONE
EFOOOPRT FOOTROPE
EFOOORST FOOTSORE
EFOOPRRS PROOFERS
REPROOFS
EFOOPRSS SPOOFERS
EFOOPRST FORETOPS
EFOOPRSY SPOOFERY
EFOOPRTW WETPROOF
EFOOPSTT FOOTSTEP
EFOORRSW FORSWORE
EFOORSTT FOOTREST
EFOORSTV OVERSOFT
EFOOSTUX OUTFOXES
EFORRRUW FURROWER
EFORRSST FORTRESS
EFORRSTY FORESTRY
EFORRSUV FERVOURS
EFORRTTU FROTTEUR
EGGGIILR GIGGLIER
EGGGILNS LEGGINGS
EGGGILOR GOGGLIER
EGGGILRS GIGGLERS
EGGGIORR GROGGIER
EGGGLORS GOGGLERS
EGGGORRY GROGGERY
EGGHIINN NEIGHING
EGGHIINW WEIGHING
EGGHILRS HIGGLERS
EGGHLORU ROUGHLEG
EGGHRTUY THUGGERY
EGGIIJLR JIGGLIER
EGGIIJST JIGGIEST
EGGIILLN GINGELLI
EGGIILNR NIGGLIER
EGGIILNS GINGELIS
EGGIILRW WIGGLIER
EGGIINNN ENGINING
EGGIINNR REIGNING
EGGIINNS SINGEING
EGGIINNT TINGEING
EGGIINRV GRIEVING
REGIVING
EGGIIPST PIGGIEST
EGGIIRTW TWIGGIER
EGGIISTW WIGGIEST
EGGIKLNO GONGLIKE
EGGIKLNS KEGLINGS
EGGIKNOS GINGKOES
GINKGOES
EGGILLNY GINGELLY
EGGILNNO LONGEING
EGGILNNT GENTLING
EGGILNRS NIGGLERS
SNIGGLER
EGGILNRU GRUELING
REGLUING
EGGILNRY GINGERLY
EGGILNSS SNIGGLES
EGGILNSY GLEYINGS
EGGILOOS GOOGLIES
EGGILOST LOGGIEST
EGGILQSU SQUIGGLE
EGGILRRW WRIGGLER
EGGILRSW WIGGLERS
WRIGGLES
EGGIMORS SMOGGIER
EGGIMSTU MUGGIEST
EGGINNSS GINSENGS
EGGINORR GORGERIN
ROGERING
EGGINORU ROGUEING
EGGINOUV VOGUEING
EGGINRRU GRUNGIER
EGGINRSS SERGINGS
SNIGGERS
EGGINSSU GUESSING
SNUGGIES
EGGINSTU GUESTING
EGGIOSST SOGGIEST
EGGIPRRS SPRIGGER
EGGIPRRY PRIGGERY
EGGIPRSU PUGGRIES
EGGIPSTU PUGGIEST
EGGIRRST TRIGGERS
EGGIRRSW SWIGGERS
EGGIRSTT TRIGGEST
EGGISTUV VUGGIEST
EGGJLORS JOGGLERS
EGGJLRSU JUGGLERS
EGGJLRUY JUGGLERY
EGGLMOOY GEMOLOGY
EGGLMRSU SMUGGLER
EGGLMSSU SMUGGLES
EGGLNSSU SNUGGLES
EGGLORSS SLOGGERS
EGGLORST TOGGLERS
EGGLPRSU PLUGGERS
EGGLRSSU SLUGGERS
EGGLRSTU GURGLETS
STRUGGLE
EGGMSSTU SMUGGEST
EGGNOOSY GEOGNOSY
EGGNRRSU GRUNGERS
EGGNRSUY SNUGGERY
EGGNSSTU SNUGGEST
EGGOORSU GORGEOUS
EGGOPRRS PROGGERS
EGGSSSTU SUGGESTS
EGHHHIST HEIGHTHS
EGHHIIMS SEMIHIGH
EGHHIIRS HIGHRISE
EGHHILTY EIGHTHLY
EGHHINSS HIGHNESS
EGHHIORV OVERHIGH
EGHHORUW ROUGHHEW
EGHIIKLS SIGHLIKE
EGHIILLS GHILLIES
EGHIILNR HIRELING
EGHIILNS SHIELING
EGHIIMRT MIGHTIER
EGHIINNR INHERING
EGHIINRR REHIRING
EGHIINST HEISTING
NIGHTIES
EGHIINSV INVEIGHS
EGHIINTV THIEVING
EGHIIRST RIGHTIES
TIGERISH
EGHIISTY HYGIEIST
EGHIKNRS GHERKINS
EGHIKRSS SKREIGHS
EGHILLNO HELLOING
EGHILLNS SHELLING
EGHILMNW WHELMING
EGHILMOR HOMEGIRL
EGHILMPS MEGILPHS
EGHILNOV HOVELING
EGHILNPS HELPINGS
EGHILNPT PENLIGHT
EGHILNPW WHELPING
EGHILNRS SHINGLER
EGHILNSS SHINGLES
EGHILNST LIGHTENS
EGHILNSV SHELVING
EGHILNSW WELSHING
EGHILNUW GLUHWEIN
EGHILORT REGOLITH
EGHILOSU GHOULIES
EGHILPRT PLIGHTER
EGHILRST LIGHTERS
RELIGHTS
SLIGHTER
EGHILSSS SIGHLESS
EGHILSST SLEIGHTS
EGHILSTT LIGHTEST
EGHIMNOR HOMERING
EGHIMNUX EXHUMING
EGHIMPRU GRUMPHIE
EGHINNOY HONEYING
EGHINNSS NIGHNESS
EGHINNST SENNIGHT
EGHINNSU UNHINGES
EGHINORV HOVERING
EGHINOST HISTOGEN
EGHINOSY HOSEYING
EGHINPRS SPHERING
EGHINPSS SPHINGES
EGHINRRS HERRINGS
EGHINRRU HUNGRIER
EGHINRRY HERRYING
EGHINRSU USHERING
EGHINRSW SHREWING
WHINGERS
EGHINSTT TIGHTENS
EGHINTTW WHETTING
EGHINTUW UNWEIGHT
EGHIOPSS PISHOGES
EGHIOPSU PISHOGUE
EGHIORST GHOSTIER
EGHIORSU ROUGHIES
EGHIOSTT GOTHITES
EGHIOSTU TOUGHIES
EGHIOSTV EIGHTVOS
EGHIOTUW OUTWEIGH
EGHIRRST RIGHTERS
EGHIRRUY HIERURGY
EGHIRSST RESIGHTS
SIGHTERS
EGHIRSTT RIGHTEST
EGHISSTU GUSHIEST
EGHISSTY HYGEISTS
EGHISTTT TIGHTEST
EGHKLNOU GUNKHOLE
EGHLNORS LEGHORNS
EGHLOOOR HOROLOGE
EGHLOORY RHEOLOGY
EGHLOOSS GOLOSHES
EGHLOOST THEOLOGS

EGHLOOTY ETHOLOGY
THEOLOGY
EGHLOPRU PLOUGHER
EGHLOPRY HYPERGOL
EGHMNOOY HOMOGENY
EGHMOPUY HYPOGEUM
EGHMOSSU GUMSHOES
EGHNOOSS HOGNOSES
EGHNOOTY THEOGONY
EGHNORSU ROUGHENS
EGHNORUV HUNGOVER
OVERHUNG
EGHNOSTU TOUGHENS
EGHNRSTT STRENGTH
EGHOOOSW HOOSEGOW
EGHORRSU ROUGHERS
EGHORRTW REGROWTH
EGHORSTU RESOUGHT
ROUGHEST
EGHOSTTU TOUGHEST
EGIIJLNR JINGLIER
EGIIKKLN KINGLIKE
EGIIKLNN LIKENING
EGIIKLNR KINGLIER
RINGLIKE
EGIIKLNW WINGLIKE
EGIIKLTW TWIGLIKE
EGIIKNNR REINKING
EGIIKNNS SKEINING
EGIILMMN IMMINGLE
EGIILNNO ELOINING
EGIILNNR RELINING
EGIILNNS ENISLING
ENSILING
EGIILNNT LENITING
EGIILNNU LINGUINE
EGIILNNV LIVENING
EGIILNOR LIGROINE
RELIGION
REOILING
EGIILNPR PERILING
EGIILNPS SPEILING
SPIELING
EGIILNRS RESILING
RIESLING
EGIILNRT GLINTIER
RETILING
TINGLIER
EGIILNRV LIVERING
RELIVING
REVILING
EGIILNST LIGNITES
LINGIEST
EGIILNSV VEILINGS
EGIILRRS GRISLIER
EGIILRST GIRLIEST
EGIILRTU GUILTIER
EGIILRTZ GLITZIER
EGIIMMNO MIMEOING
EGIIMNPR IMPINGER
EGIIMNPS IMPINGES
EGIIMNRS REMISING
EGIIMNRT MERITING
MITERING
RETIMING
EGIIMNRX REMIXING
EGIIMNST MINGIEST
EGIIMNSV MISGIVEN
EGIIMNTT EMITTING
EGIIMOPT IMPETIGO
EGIIMPST GIMPIEST
EGIIMRST GRIMIEST
EGIIMSSV MISGIVES
EGIINNPR REPINING
RIPENING
EGIINNRS RESINING
EGIINNST GINNIEST
EGIINNSV VEININGS
EGIINNSW SINEWING
EGIINNTU UNTIEING
EGIINNWZ WIZENING
EGIINOPR PEIGNOIR
EGIINORS SEIGNIOR
EGIINPRS SPEIRING
SPIERING
EGIINPRX EXPIRING
EGIINQTU QUIETING
EGIINRRS RERISING
EGIINRRT RETIRING
EGIINRRW REWIRING
EGIINRST IGNITERS
RESITING
STINGIER
EGIINRSV REVISING
EGIINRSW SWINGIER
EGIINRSZ RESIZING
EGIINRTU INTRIGUE
EGIINRTV RIVETING
EGIINRVV REVIVING
EGIINSSS SEISINGS
EGIINSSZ SEIZINGS
EGIINSTW WINGIEST
EGIINSTX EXISTING
EGIINSTZ ZINGIEST
EGIINSVW VIEWINGS
EGIIOPRS PIROGIES
EGIIPPRR GRIPPIER
EGIIPRST GRIPIEST
EGIIPRSW PERIWIGS
EGIIPSST PIGSTIES
EGIIRRTT GRITTIER
EGIITUXY EXIGUITY
EGIJKNOS JINGKOES
EGIJLLNY JELLYING
EGIJLNRS JINGLERS
EGIJLNRU JUNGLIER
EGIJMMNY JEMMYING
EGIJNNOS JONESING
EGIJNNOY ENJOYING
EGIJNSST JESTINGS
EGIJNTTY JETTYING
EGIKKNRT TREKKING
EGIKLLNN KNELLING
EGIKLLNV KVELLING
EGIKLNOS SONGLIKE
EGIKLNPS SKELPING
EGIKLNRS ERLKINGS
EGIKLNSS KINGLESS
EGIKLNST KINGLETS
EGIKMNRS SMERKING
EGIKNNNS KENNINGS
EGIKNNOT TOKENING
EGIKNNSY ENSKYING
EGIKNORV REVOKING
EGIKNSTU GUNKIEST
EGILLMNS SMELLING
EGILLNNO LONGLINE
EGILLNNS SNELLING
EGILLNOV LIVELONG
EGILLNPS SPELLING
EGILLNQU QUELLING
EGILLNST GILLNETS
EGILLNSW SWELLING
EGILLNTU GLUTELIN
EGILLOOR GLORIOLE
EGILLORS GIROLLES
EGILLRRS GRILLERS
EGILLRRY GRILLERY
EGILMMNS LEMMINGS
EGILMMRS GLIMMERS
EGILMNNU UNMINGLE
EGILMNOT LONGTIME
EGILMNRS GREMLINS
MINGLERS
EGILMNRU RELUMING
EGILMNST SMELTING
EGILMNSU GUMLINES
LEGUMINS
EGILMOOR GLOOMIER
OLIGOMER
EGILMORS GOMERILS
EGILMOUU EULOGIUM
EGILMPRS GLIMPSER
EGILMPRU GLUMPIER
EGILMPSS GLIMPSES
EGILNNST NESTLING
EGILNNTT NETTLING
EGILNNTU GLUTENIN
EGILNOPP PEOPLING
EGILNORS RESOLING
EGILNORW LOWERING
ROWELING
EGILNOSS LOGINESS
EGILNOSU LIGNEOUS
EGILNOSW LONGWISE
EGILNOTW TOWELING
EGILNOVV EVOLVING
EGILNPRY REPLYING
EGILNPST PESTLING
EGILNPTT PETTLING
EGILNRRY ERRINGLY
EGILNRSS SLINGERS
EGILNRST RINGLETS
STERLING
TINGLERS
EGILNRSW NEWSGIRL
EGILNRUV VELURING
EGILNSST GLISTENS
SINGLETS
SNIGLETS
EGILNSSU GLUINESS
UGLINESS
EGILNSSW SWINGLES
WINGLESS
EGILNSTT SETTLING
EGILNSTW WELTINGS
WINGLETS
EGILNSUV EVULSING
EGILNSUY GUYLINES
EGILNTUX EXULTING
EGILNVXY VEXINGLY
EGILOOOS OOLOGIES
EGILOOSU ISOLOGUE
EGILOOTY ETIOLOGY
EGILOPPR GLOPPIER
EGILORRW GROWLIER
EGILORSS GLOSSIER
EGILORTV OVERGILT
EGILOSSS GLOSSIES
EGILOSTU EULOGIST
EGILPSTU GULPIEST
EGILRRZZ GRIZZLER
EGILRSST GLISTERS
GRISTLES
EGILRSTT GLITTERS
EGILRSUV VIRGULES
EGILRSZZ GRIZZLES
EGILRTTY GLITTERY
EGILSSTW TWIGLESS
EGIMMNST STEMMING
EGIMMRST GRIMMEST
EGIMMSTU GUMMIEST
GUMMITES
EGIMNNNO MIGNONNE
EGIMNNOV VENOMING
EGIMNNSW SWINGMEN
EGIMNNUW UNMEWING
EGIMNORV REMOVING
EGIMNOST MITOGENS
EGIMNOSY MOSEYING
EGIMNPRS IMPREGNS
EGIMNPRU IMPUGNER
EGIMNPST EMPTINGS
PIGMENTS
EGIMNPTT TEMPTING
EGIMNPTY EMPTYING
EGIMNRSS GRIMNESS
EGIMNRSU RESUMING
EGIMORSS OGREISMS
EGIMORST ERGOTISM
EGIMOSST EGOTISMS
EGIMPRRU GRUMPIER
EGIMSSSU MISGUESS
EGINNNOT TENONING
EGINNOOS IONOGENS
EGINNOPS OPENINGS
EGINNORS NEGRONIS
EGINNORT NITROGEN
EGINNORV VIGNERON
EGINNORZ REZONING
EGINNOSU ENGINOUS
EGINNPSU PENGUINS
EGINNRRS GRINNERS
EGINNRRU UNERRING
EGINNRSU ENSURING
EGINNRSV NERVINGS
EGINNRTU RETUNING
TENURING
EGINNSTT NETTINGS
EGINNSUW UNSEWING
EGINNSUX UNSEXING
EGINOOSS ISOGONES
EGINOOST GOONIEST
EGINOPRS PERIGONS
REPOSING
SPONGIER
EGINOPRW POWERING
EGINOPSU EPIGONUS
EGINOPSX EXPOSING
EGINOPXY EPOXYING
EGINORRS IGNORERS
EGINORSS GORINESS
EGINORST GENITORS
EGINORSW RESOWING
EGINORSY SEIGNORY
EGINORTV REVOTING
EGINORTW TOWERING
EGINORVW WINGOVER
EGINORXX XEROXING
EGINOTUV OUTGIVEN
EGINPPPR PREPPING
EGINPPST STEPPING
EGINPRRS RESPRING
SPRINGER
EGINPRSS PRESSING
SPRINGES
EGINPRSU PERUSING
SUPERING
EGINPRTU ERUPTING
REPUTING
EGINPRTY RETYPING
EGINPRUV PREVUING
EGINPRYY PERIGYNY
EGINPSSY PIGSNEYS
EGINPSTT PETTINGS
EGINQRUY QUERYING
EGINQSTU QUESTING
EGINRRST RESTRING
STRINGER
EGINRRSW WRINGERS
EGINRRSY SERRYING
EGINRRTY RETRYING
EGINRSST STINGERS
TRIGNESS
EGINRSSV SERVINGS
EGINRSSW SWINGERS
EGINRSSY SYRINGES
EGINRSTT GITTERNS
EGINRSTW STREWING
WRESTING
EGINRSVW SWERVING
EGINRTTU UTTERING
EGINSSTT SETTINGS
EGINSSTV VESTINGS
EGINSSTW WESTINGS
EGINSTTT STETTING
EGINSTTW WETTINGS
EGIOOPST GOOPIEST
EGIOORRV GROOVIER
EGIOOSST GOOSIEST
EGIOPRSS GOSSIPER
SERPIGOS
EGIOPRSU GROUPIES
PIROGUES
EGIORRTT GROTTIER
EGIORRTU GROUTIER
EGIORRTV OVERGIRT
EGIORSST GORSIEST
STRIGOSE
EGIORSSU GRISEOUS
EGIORSTV VERTIGOS
EGIORSUV GRIEVOUS
EGIOSSTT EGOTISTS
EGIOSTTU GOUTIEST
EGIOSTUV OUTGIVES
EGIOSUUX EXIGUOUS
EGIPPRRS GRIPPERS
EGIPRSUU GUIPURES
EGIRRSST GRISTERS
EGIRRSTT GRITTERS
EGIRRSTY REGISTRY
EGIRSTTU TURGITES
EGISSTTU GUSTIEST
GUTSIEST
EGISSUWY WISEGUYS
EGISSYYZ SYZYGIES
EGISTTTU GUTTIEST
EGJLNORU JONGLEUR
EGJLNOTU JELUTONG
EGJOSSTT GJETOSTS
EGKLORSW LEGWORKS
EGLLMORW GROMWELL
EGLLOPSY GOSPELLY
EGLLPSSU PLUGLESS
EGLMMSTU GLUMMEST
EGLMNOOS LONGSOME
EGLMNOOY MENOLOGY
EGLMNORS MONGRELS
EGLMNSSU GLUMNESS
EGLMOORS LEGROOMS
EGLMOPRU PROMULGE
EGLMORSS GORMLESS
EGLMOSSS SMOGLESS
EGLNNOOR LONGERON
EGLNNOSS LONGNESS
EGLNNTUY UNGENTLY
EGLNOOOY OENOLOGY
EGLNOOPR PROLONGE
EGLNOOPY PENOLOGY
EGLNOORV OVERLONG
EGLNOOVY VENOLOGY
EGLNORSU LOUNGERS
EGLNORUU LONGUEUR
EGLNOSSS SONGLESS
EGLNOSSY LYSOGENS
EGLNOSUV UNGLOVES
EGLNOSYY LYSOGENY
EGLNPRSU PLUNGERS
EGLNRSSU RUNGLESS
EGLNRSTU GRUNTLES
EGLNRTUY URGENTLY
EGLOOPRU PROLOGUE
EGLOOPTY LOGOTYPE
EGLOORSS REGOSOLS
EGLOORSY SEROLOGY
EGLOOSXY SEXOLOGY
EGLOPSTU GLUEPOTS
EGLORRSW GROWLERS
EGLORSSS GLOSSERS
EGLORSSU ROSESLUG
EGLORSUU RUGULOSE
EGLORSUY RUGOSELY
EGLPRRSU SPLURGER
EGLPRSSU SPLURGES
EGLPRSUY GYPLURES
EGLRSTTU GUTTLERS
EGLRSUZZ GUZZLERS
EGLSSSTU GUSTLESS
EGLSSUUV VULGUSES
EGMMNOOR MONOGERM
EGMMORST GROMMETS
EGMMOSSU GUMMOSES
EGMMRSTU GRUMMEST
GRUMMETS
EGMNNOOY MONOGENY
EGMNNOSW GOWNSMEN
EGMNOOOS MONGOOSE
EGMNOOSU MUNGOOSE
EGMNOSYZ ZYMOGENS
EGMNSSSU SMUGNESS
EGMOORRS GROOMERS
REGROOMS
EGMORSTU GOURMETS
EGNNOOTY ONTOGENY
EGNNORST RONTGENS
EGNNOSTU NONGUEST
EGNNOTTU UNGOTTEN
EGNNSSSU SNUGNESS
EGNNSTTU TUNGSTEN
EGNNSTUU UNGUENTS
EGNOOOPR GONOPORE
EGNOOPRS PROGNOSE
EGNOORRV GOVERNOR
EGNOOTUX OXTONGUE
EGNOPPRU OPPUGNER
EGNOPRSS SPONGERS
EGNOPRSY PYROGENS
EGNORRST STRONGER
EGNORRSW WRONGERS
EGNORSST SONGSTER
EGNORSSU SURGEONS
EGNORSTU STURGEON
EGNORSTW WRONGEST
EGNORSUY YOUNGERS
EGNOSTUY YOUNGEST
EGNPRRSU RESPRUNG
EGNRRSTU GRUNTERS
RESTRUNG
EGOOPRRU PROROGUE
EGOORRSV GROOVERS
EGOORRVW OVERGROW
EGOORSTT GROTTOES
EGOPRRSS PROGRESS
EGOPRRSU GROUPERS
REGROUPS
EGOPSSUY GYPSEOUS
EGORRSSS GROSSERS
EGORRSSU GROUSERS
EGORRSTU GROUTERS
EGORSSST GROSSEST
EGOSSTUU OUTGUESS
EGPRSSTY GYPSTERS
EGPRSSUU UPSURGES
EHHIIPRS HEIRSHIP
EHHIISTV THIEVISH
EHHILMNT HELMINTH
EHHILOPR RHEOPHIL
EHHINOPT THIOPHEN
EHHIORTT HITHERTO
EHHIPSST PHTHISES
EHHIRSSW SHREWISH
EHHLOOST SHOTHOLE
EHHNOORS SHOEHORN
EHHOOSSW WHOOSHES
EHHOOSTU HOTHOUSE
EHHRSSSU SHUSHERS
EHHRSSTU THRUSHES
EHIIIPSX PIXIEISH
EHIIKLPW WHIPLIKE
EHIIKNST HINKIEST
EHIIKSSW WHISKIES
EHIILLST HILLIEST
EHIILMOS HOMILIES
EHIILNPS HIPLINES
EHIILPSU HUIPILES
EHIILRRW WHIRLIER
EHIILRSV LIVERISH
EHIILRSW WHIRLIES
EHIILSTT THELITIS
EHIIMMSS SHIMMIES
EHIIMNNO HOMININE
EHIIMNOS HOMINIES
EHIIMNOZ HOMINIZE
EHIIMNSS MINISHES
EHIIMPST MEPHITIS
EHIIMSST SMITHIES
EHIIMSSW WHIMSIES
EHIINNOS INHESION
EHIINNOT THIONINE
EHIINNRS INSHRINE
EHIINNRW WHINNIER
EHIINNSS SHINNIES
EHIINNSW WHINNIES
EHIINRST INHERITS
EHIINSST SHINIEST
EHIINSTW WHINIEST
EHIINSVX VIXENISH
EHIIPPRW WHIPPIER
EHIIPPST HIPPIEST
EHIIPRSV VIPERISH
EHIIPSTT PITHIEST
EHIIRRST SHIRTIER
EHIIRRSW WHIRRIES
EHIIRRTX HERITRIX
EHIIRSSW SWISHIER
EHIIRSTT THIRTIES
EHIIRWZZ WHIZZIER
EHIISSST HISSIEST
EHIISSTT STITHIES
EHIISTTW WHITIEST
WITHIEST
EHIISTTX SIXTIETH
EHIJNNOS JOHNNIES
EHIKKLOO HOOKLIKE
EHIKKLSU HUSKLIKE
EHIKKRSS SHIKKERS
EHIKLMNY HYMNLIKE
EHIKLMOT MOTHLIKE
EHIKLNOR HORNLIKE
EHIKLNOS SINKHOLE
EHIKLOOP HOOPLIKE
EHIKLOSY YOKELISH
EHIKLOTY LEKYTHOI
EHIKLRSU RUSHLIKE
EHIKLSTU HULKIEST
EHIKMNST METHINKS
EHIKNOSS HOKINESS
EHIKNPSU SHUNPIKE
EHIKNRRS SHRINKER
EHIKNRST RETHINKS
THINKERS
EHIKNSTU HUNKIEST
EHIKOOST HOOKIEST
EHIKRRSS SHIRKERS
EHIKRSSW WHISKERS
EHIKRSWY WHISKERY
EHIKSSTU HUSKIEST
EHIKSSWY WHISKEYS
EHILLLMO MOLEHILL
EHILLMOP PHILOMEL
EHILLNOS HELLIONS
EHILLOOS OILHOLES
EHILLOPY LYOPHILE
EHILLPTY PHYLLITE
EHILLRRS SHRILLER
EHILLRRT THRILLER
EHILLSST HILTLESS
EHILLSVY ELVISHLY
EHILMNOS LEMONISH
EHILMOOR HEIRLOOM
EHILMOST HELOTISM
EHILNOPS PINHOLES
EHILNOPT THOLEPIN
EHILNORU UNHOLIER
EHILNOSS HOLINESS
EHILNOST HOLSTEIN
HOTLINES
NEOLITHS
EHILNOTX XENOLITH
EHILNSTY ETHINYLS
EHILOOPZ ZOOPHILE
EHILOPRS POLISHER
REPOLISH
EHILOPRT HELIPORT
EHILOPSS POLISHES
EHILOPST HELISTOP
HOPLITES
ISOPLETH
EHILOPXY OXYPHILE
EHILORSS SLOSHIER
EHILORSU HOURLIES
EHILORTY RHYOLITE
EHILOSST HOSTILES
EHILPRST PHILTERS
PHILTRES
EHILPRSU PLUSHIER

EHILPSSS SHIPLESS
EHILPSST PITHLESS
EHILPSSY PHYLESIS
EHILPSTU SULPHITE
EHILRRSW WHIRLERS
EHILRSST SLITHERS
EHILRSSU SLUSHIER
EHILRSSV SHRIVELS
EHILRSTU LUTHIERS
EHILRSTW WHISTLER
EHILRSTY SLITHERY
EHILRTTW WHITTLER
EHILRTTY TRIETHYL
EHILSSSW WISHLESS
EHILSSTT THISTLES
EHILSSTW WHISTLES
EHILSTTW WHITTLES
EHIMMNUY HYMENIUM
EHIMMRSS SHIMMERS
EHIMMRSY SHIMMERY
EHIMNOPR MORPHINE
EHIMNORT THERMION
EHIMNOSS HOMINESS
MONISHES
EHIMNOTT MONTEITH
EHIMNPRS NEPHRISM
EHIMNPST SHIPMENT
EHIMNRRU MURRHINE
EHIMNRSU INHUMERS
RHENIUMS
EHIMNSTY THYMINES
EHIMOOST SMOOTHIE
EHIMOPSS PHIMOSES
EHIMORSS HEROISMS
EHIMORST ISOTHERM
EHIMORSZ RHIZOMES
EHIMORTU MOUTHIER
EHIMOSTT MOTHIEST
EHIMOSTW SHOWTIME
EHIMPRRS SHRIMPER
EHIMPRSU MURPHIES
EHIMPRSW WHIMPERS
EHIMPSTU HUMPIEST
EHIMPSUU EUPHUISM
EHIMRRTY HERMITRY
EHIMRSST SMITHERS
EHIMRSTT THERMITS
EHIMRSTW MISTHREW
EHIMRSTY SMITHERY
EHIMRTUU HUMITURE
EHIMSSTU MUSHIEST
EHIMSSWY WHIMSEYS
EHIMSTTY MYTHIEST
THYMIEST
EHINNORT INTHRONE
EHINNOTW NONWHITE
EHINNRST THINNERS
EHINNRSY SHINNERY
EHINNSST THINNESS
EHINNSSU SUNSHINE
EHINNSSY SHINNEYS
EHINNSTT THINNEST
EHINOPPR HORNPIPE
EHINOPST PHONIEST
EHINOPSW WINESHOP
EHINORRT THORNIER
EHINORST HORNIEST
ORNITHES
EHINORTV OVERTHIN
EHINORZZ HIZZONER
EHINOSST HISTONES
EHINOSTU OUTSHINE
EHINPPSS SHIPPENS
EHINPRSU PUNISHER
EHINPSSU PUNISHES
EHINPSSX SPHINXES
EHINRSSU INRUSHES
EHINRSTZ ZITHERNS
EHINSSUW UNWISHES
EHIOOPST ISOPHOTE
EHIOOPSW WHOOPIES
EHIOORTT TOOTHIER
EHIOOSTT HOOTIEST
EHIOPPST HOPPIEST
EHIOPPSU EOHIPPUS
EHIOPRSS ROSEHIPS
EHIOPRST TROPHIES
EHIORRST HERITORS
EHIORRTW WORTHIER
EHIORSST HOISTERS
HORSIEST
SHORTIES
EHIORSTT THEORIST
THORITES
EHIORSTW WORTHIES
EHIORTWZ HOWITZER
EHIOSSSW WHOSISES
EHIOSSTU HOUSESIT
EHIOSSTW SHOWIEST
EHIOSSTY ISOHYETS
EHIOSTVY YESHIVOT
EHIOTTUW WHITEOUT
EHIPPRSS PRESHIPS
SHIPPERS
EHIPPRSW WHIPPERS
EHIPPSTW WHIPPETS
EHIPQSUY PHYSIQUE
EHIPRSST HIPSTERS
EHIPRSSW WHISPERS
EHIPRSTU SUPERHIT
EHIPRSWY WHISPERY
EHIPSSTU PUSHIEST
EHIPSTUU EUPHUIST
EHIQSSSU SQUISHES
EHIRRRSU HURRIERS
EHIRRSSV SHRIVERS
EHIRRSTT THIRSTER
EHIRRSTV THRIVERS
EHIRRSTW WRITHERS
EHIRSSSW SWISHERS
EHIRSSTU RUSHIEST
EHIRSSTW SWITHERS
EHIRSTTW WHITTERS
EHIRSWZZ WHIZZERS
EHIRTTTW WHITTRET
EHISSUVW HUSWIVES
EHKLNOOT KNOTHOLE
EHKLOOSS HOOKLESS
EHKLOOST HOOKLETS
EHKLOOSZ KOLHOZES
EHKLOSTY LEKYTHOS
EHKLSTUY LEKYTHUS
EHKMOORW HOMEWORK
EHKMORSW MESHWORK
EHKNNRSU SHRUNKEN
EHKNOOOS HOOKNOSE
EHKNORSU UNKOSHER
EHKOPSSY KYPHOSES
EHLLMOPY PHYLLOME
EHLLNSSU UNSHELLS
EHLLNSTU NUTSHELL
EHLLOOOP LOOPHOLE
EHLLOORW HOLLOWER
EHLMNOST MENTHOLS
EHLMNSSY HYMNLESS
EHLMOORW WORMHOLE
EHLMOOST LOTHSOME
EHLMOPSY MESOPHYL
EHLMORTY MOTHERLY
EHLMOTXY METHOXYL
EHLMPSSU HUMPLESS
EHLNOPSU SULPHONE
EHLNORSS HORNLESS
EHLNOSTY HONESTLY
EHLNRSTU LUTHERNS
EHLNSSSU LUSHNESS
EHLNSTYY ETHYNYLS
EHLOOPRT PORTHOLE
EHLOOPSS HOOPLESS
EHLOOPST POSTHOLE
POTHOLES
EHLOOPTY HOLOTYPE
EHLOORVY OVERHOLY
EHLOPSSS SPLOSHES
EHLORSST HOLSTERS
HOSTLERS
EHLORSTT THROSTLE
EHLORSTW WHORTLES
EHLORSTY HOSTELRY
EHLORSUV OVERLUSH
EHLORTTT THROTTLE
EHLOSSTW THOWLESS
EHLOSTXY ETHOXYLS
EHLPSSTU PLUSHEST
EHLRSSTU HURTLESS
HUSTLERS
RUTHLESS
EHLRSTTU SHUTTLER
EHLSSTTU SHUTTLES
EHMMOOOR HOMEROOM
EHMMOOSS HOMMOSES
EHMMRRTU THRUMMER
EHMMSSUU HUMMUSES
EHMNNOTY ETHNONYM
EHMNNSTU HUNTSMEN
EHMNOOPR NEOMORPH
EHMNOORS HORMONES
MOORHENS
EHMNOOST SMOOTHEN
EHMNOOTW HOMETOWN
TOWNHOME
EHMNOOTY THEONOMY
EHMNOPSU HOMESPUN
EHMNPSTY NYMPHETS
EHMNSTTU HUTMENTS
EHMOOPRT HOMEPORT
EHMOORST RESMOOTH
SMOOTHER
EHMOORTU OUTHOMER
EHMOOSSS SMOOSHES
EHMOOSST SMOOTHES
EHMOOSSZ SHMOOZES
EHMORSST SMOTHERS
EHMORSTU MOUTHERS
EHMORSTY SMOTHERY
EHMORTUV VERMOUTH
EHMOTUZZ MEZUZOTH
EHMPRSTU THUMPERS
EHMRRSTU MURTHERS
EHMRSTUV VERMUTHS
EHMRTUYY EURYTHMY
EHMSSTUY THYMUSES
EHNNOPRS NEPHRONS
EHNNORRT NORTHERN
EHNNORTU UNTHRONE
EHNNRSSU SHUNNERS
EHNOOPTY HONEYPOT
EHNOORRS HONORERS
EHNOORRU HONOURER
EHNOORSW WHORESON
EHNOORTW HONEWORT
EHNOOSSW SNOWSHOE
EHNOOSTU OUTSHONE
EHNOPRSW PRESHOWN
EHNOPRSY HYPERONS
EHNOPSSS POSHNESS
EHNOPSSY HYPNOSES
EHNORRRS SHNORRER
EHNORRST NORTHERS
EHNORRTY ERYTHRON
EHNORSST SHORTENS
EHNORSSU ONRUSHES
UNHORSES
EHNORSTU SOUTHERN
EHNORTUV OVERHUNT
EHNOSSUU UNHOUSES
EHNOSTUU NUTHOUSE
EHNOSTUY YOUTHENS
EHNPSSXY SPHYNXES
EHNRSSTU HUNTRESS
SHUNTERS
EHOOPRST HOOPSTER
EHOOPRSW WHOOPERS
EHOOPRSX HORSEPOX
EHOOPRTY ORTHOEPY
EHOOPSTT PHOTOSET
EHOOPSTU HOUSETOP
POTHOUSE
EHOOPSTY OOPHYTES
EHOOPTYZ ZOOPHYTE
EHOORSST ORTHOSES
RESHOOTS
SHEROOTS
SHOOTERS
SOOTHERS
EHOORSTV OVERSHOT
EHOOSSSW SWOOSHES
EHOOSSTT SOOTHEST
EHOOSTUU OUTHOUSE
EHOPPRSS SHOPPERS
EHOPPRST PROPHETS
EHOPPRSW WHOPPERS
EHOPPRSY PROPHESY
EHOPRRSY ORPHREYS
EHOPRSST HOTPRESS
STROPHES
EHOPRSSW PRESHOWS
EHOPRSTU SUPERHOT
EHOPRSUV PUSHOVER
EHOPRTUY EUTROPHY
EHORRSTW THROWERS
EHORRSTY HERSTORY
EHORSSTT SHORTEST
EHORSSTU SHOUTERS
SOUTHERS
EHORTTUW OUTTHREW
EHPRSSUU UPRUSHES
EHPRSTTU TURPETHS
EHPSSTUY TYPHUSES
EHQRSSUU QURUSHES
EHQSSSUU SQUUSHES
EHRRSTTU THRUSTER
EHRSSSTY SHYSTERS
EHRSSTTU SHUTTERS
EIIILNRV INVIRILE
EIIILPPR LIRIPIPE
EIIILRVZ VIRILIZE
EIIIMMNS MINIMISE
EIIIMMNZ MINIMIZE
EIIIRSST IRITISES
EIIJNRSU INJURIES
EIIKKLLS SILKLIKE
EIIKKLLT KILTLIKE
EIIKKLNS SKINLIKE
EIIKKNST KINKIEST
EIIKLLLY LILYLIKE
EIIKLLMN LIMEKILN
EIIKLLNO LIONLIKE
EIIKLLST SLITLIKE
EIIKLMRS MISLIKER
EIIKLMSS MISLIKES
EIIKLMST MILKIEST
EIIKLNOR IRONLIKE
EIIKLNRS SLINKIER
EIIKLNRT TINKLIER
EIIKLPSS PLISKIES
EIIKLPSW WISPLIKE
EIIKLSST SILKIEST
EIIKLSTU SUITLIKE
EIIKMPRS SKIMPIER
EIIKMRRS SMIRKIER
EIIKMRST MIRKIEST
EIIKNNRS SKINNIER
EIIKNNSS INKINESS
EIIKNNST KINETINS
EIIKNNSW WINESKIN
EIIKNRST STINKIER
EIIKNSTW TWINKIES
EIIKPSST SPIKIEST
EIIKQRRU QUIRKIER
EIIKRSST RISKIEST
EIIKSSVV SKIVVIES
EIILLLVY LIVELILY
EIILLMMR MILLIREM
EIILLMMS MILLIMES
EIILLMNR MILLINER
EIILLMNS MILLINES
EIILLMNU ILLUMINE
EIILLMRS MILLIERS
EIILLNST NIELLIST
EIILLNSV VILLEINS
EIILLNTV VITELLIN
EIILLPSS ELLIPSIS
EIILLRST STILLIER
EIILLRVY VIRILELY
EIILLSST SILLIEST
EIILLSTT TILLITES
EIILLSUV ILLUSIVE
EIILMMOS MILESIMO
EIILMMOT IMMOTILE
EIILMNNT LINIMENT
EIILMNOT LIMONITE
EIILMNSS LIMINESS
EIILMOPT IMPOLITE
EIILMPPR PIMPLIER
EIILMPRS IMPERILS
LIMPSIER
EIILMPRT PRELIMIT
EIILMRSS SLIMSIER
EIILMRST LIMITERS
EIILMSSS MISSILES
EIILMSST ELITISMS
SLIMIEST
EIILMSSV MISLIVES
EIILMSTT MILTIEST
MISTITLE
EIILMSTY MYELITIS
EIILNNOT LENITION
EIILNORS LIONISER
EIILNORZ LIONIZER
EIILNOSS ELISIONS
ISOLINES
LIONISES
OILINESS
EIILNOSV OLIVINES
EIILNOSZ LIONIZES
EIILNQTU QUINTILE
EIILNRSS RESILINS
EIILNRST NITRILES
EIILNSSW WILINESS
EIILNSTT INTITLES
LINTIEST
EIILNSTY SENILITY
EIILNTTU INTITULE
EIILNTUV VITULINE
EIILOPPT POPLITEI
EIILOPRS LIRIOPES
EIILOPST PISOLITE
POLITIES
EIILORST ROILIEST
EIILORTT TROILITE
EIILOTVV VOLITIVE
EIILPPRR RIPPLIER
EIILPPRS SLIPPIER
EIILPPST LIPPIEST
EIILPRST TRIPLITE
EIILPSST PITILESS
EIILPSTY PYELITIS
EIILQSSU SILIQUES
EIILRRSW SWIRLIER
EIILRRTW TWIRLIER
EIILRSTT SLITTIER
EIILRSTU UTILISER
EIILRTUZ UTILIZER
EIILSSTT ELITISTS
SILTIEST
EIILSSTU UTILISES
EIILSTUZ UTILIZES
EIIMMNNT IMMINENT
EIIMMNSU IMMUNISE
EIIMMNUZ IMMUNIZE
EIIMMPRU IMPERIUM
EIIMMRSW SWIMMIER
EIIMMSSS SEISMISM
EIIMMSST MISTIMES
EIIMNOPT PIMIENTO
EIIMNOSS EMISSION
SIMONIES
EIIMNOSZ SIMONIZE
EIIMNOTV MONITIVE
EIIMNPRS PRIMINES
EIIMNRSS MIRINESS
RIMINESS
EIIMNRST INTERIMS
MINISTER
MISINTER
EIIMNRSV MINIVERS
EIIMNRTT INTERMIT
EIIMNRTX INTERMIX
EIIMNSTT MINTIEST
EIIMNSTU MUTINIES
EIIMOPRX MIREPOIX
EIIMOPSS MISPOISE
EIIMOPST OPTIMISE
EIIMOPSZ EPIZOISM
EIIMOPTZ OPTIMIZE
EIIMOSSS SEMIOSIS
EIIMOSSV OMISSIVE
EIIMOSUX EXIMIOUS
EIIMOTVV VOMITIVE
EIIMPRSS PISMIRES
EIIMPRSZ MISPRIZE
EIIMPSST PIETISMS
EIIMPSTW WIMPIEST
EIIMQSTU QUIETISM
EIIMRSTT METRITIS
EIIMRSTW MISWRITE
EIIMSSSS MISSISES
EIIMSSSV MISSIVES
EIIMSSTT MISTIEST
SEMITIST
EIINNNPS NINEPINS
EIINNOSS INOSINES
EIINNOSU UNIONISE
EIINNOSV ENVISION
EIINNOUZ UNIONIZE
EIINNPSS SPINNIES
EIINNQSU QUININES
EIINNRTV INVERTIN
EIINNSST TININESS
EIINNSTT TINNIEST
EIINNSTW INTWINES
EIINOPRS RIPIENOS
EIINOPRT POINTIER
EIINOPTT PETITION
EIINORRT INTERIOR
EIINORSV REVISION
EIINORSZ IONIZERS
IRONIZES
EIINOSST INOSITES
NOISIEST
EIINPPRS SNIPPIER
EIINPPSS PIPINESS
EIINPPST NIPPIEST
EIINPRRS INSPIRER
EIINPRSS INSPIRES
EIINPRST PRISTINE
EIINPSST SPINIEST
EIINPSSX PIXINESS
EIINPSTZ PINTSIZE
EIINPTUV PUNITIVE
EIINQRRU INQUIRER
EIINQRSU INQUIRES
EIINQSSU QUINSIES
EIINQSTU INQUIETS
EIINQTUY EQUINITY
INEQUITY
EIINRRTW WINTRIER
EIINRSST INSISTER
SINISTER
EIINRSSW WIRINESS
EIINRSTT NITRITES
EIINRSTU NEURITIS
EIINRSTV INVITERS
VITRINES
EIINRTUZ UNITIZER
EIINRTVY INVERITY
EIINSSSZ SIZINESS
EIINSTTT NITTIEST
EIINSTTW TWINIEST
EIINSTUZ UNITIZES
EIIOPRRS PRIORIES
EIIOPSTV POSITIVE
EIIOSSTT OSTEITIS
OTITISES
EIIOSSTZ ZOISITES
EIIPPQRU QUIPPIER
EIIPPRRT TRIPPIER
EIIPPSTT TIPPIEST
EIIPPSTZ ZIPPIEST
EIIPRRSS PRISSIER
EIIPRRST STRIPIER
EIIPRRSU SIRUPIER
EIIPRRTW TRIPWIRE
EIIPRSSS PRISSIES
EIIPRSST SPIRIEST
EIIPRSTU PURITIES
EIIPRSTV PREVISIT
PRIVIEST
EIIPSSTT PIETISTS
STIPITES
TIPSIEST
EIIPSSTW WISPIEST
EIIQSTTU QUIETIST
EIIRRSTW WRISTIER
EIIRSSTV REVISITS
VISITERS
EIIRSTTW TWISTIER
EIIRSTTZ RITZIEST
EIISSSST SISSIEST
EIISTTTW WITTIEST
EIJJNTUY JEJUNITY
EIJKNOSS JOKINESS
EIJKNSTU JUNKIEST
EIJKORRS SKIJORER
EIJLLORS JOLLIERS
EIJLLOST JOLLIEST
EIJLMTTU MULTIJET
EIJLOSTT JOLTIEST
EIJLOSTW JOWLIEST
EIJMPSTU JUMPIEST
EIJNORST JOINTERS
EIJNORTU JOINTURE
EIJNOSTT JETTISON
EIJNPRSU JUNIPERS
EIJNRRSU INJURERS
EIJNRRUY REINJURY
EIJNSTTW TWINJETS
EIJSSSUV JUSSIVES
EIKKLNOO NOOKLIKE
EIKKLNOT KNOTLIKE
EIKKLSTU TUSKLIKE
EIKKNRSS SKINKERS
EIKKNRSU SKUNKIER
EIKKOOST KOOKIEST
EIKKSTUY YUKKIEST
EIKLLMOO KILOMOLE
EIKLLMPU PLUMLIKE
EIKLLMSS MILKLESS
EIKLLNSW INKWELLS
EIKLLNUY UNLIKELY
EIKLLOOW WOOLLIKE
EIKLLORV OVERKILL
EIKLLOSU SOULLIKE
EIKLLSSS SKILLESS
EIKLLSST SKILLETS
EIKLMNNS LINKSMEN
EIKLMNOO MOONLIKE
EIKLMNOS MOLESKIN
EIKLMNRS KREMLINS
EIKLMORV OVERMILK
EIKLMORW WORMLIKE
EIKLMOSS MOSSLIKE
EIKLMPPU PUMPLIKE
EIKLNOSW SNOWLIKE
EIKLNPRS PLINKERS
SPRINKLE
EIKLNPRU PLUNKIER
EIKLNRRU KNURLIER
EIKLNRST TINKLERS
EIKLNRSW WRINKLES
EIKLNRTW TWINKLER
EIKLNSSS SKINLESS
EIKLNSST LENTISKS
EIKLNSSY SKYLINES
EIKLNSTW TWINKLES

EIKLOORT ROOTLIKE
EIKLOPSU SOUPLIKE
EIKLORTY KRYOLITE
EIKLOSSU LEUKOSIS
EIKLOSTY YOLKIEST
EIKLPSSU PUSSLIKE
EIKLRSSS RISKLESS
EIKLRSST KLISTERS
EIKLRTUZ KLUTZIER
EIKLSSTT SKITTLES
EIKLSSTU SULKIEST
EIKLSTTT KITTLEST
EIKMMRRS KRIMMERS
EIKMMRSS SKIMMERS
EIKMNNOO MONOKINE
EIKMNORS MONIKERS
EIKMNOST TOKENISM
EIKMOPSS MISSPOKE
EIKMORTW TIMEWORK
EIKMOSST SMOKIEST
EIKMOSSU KOUMISES
EIKMOSSY MISYOKES
EIKMPSSU MUSPIKES
EIKMRRSS SMIRKERS
EIKMRSTU MURKIEST
EIKMSSSU KUMISSES
EIKMSSTU MUSKIEST
EIKNNORS EINKORNS
NONSKIER
EIKNNOST INKSTONE
EIKNNPSS PINKNESS
EIKNNRSS SKINNERS
EIKNOPSS POKINESS
EIKNORST INSTROKE
EIKNORSV INVOKERS
EIKNORTT KNOTTIER
EIKNOSTW WONKIEST
EIKNPRRS PRINKERS
EIKNPRSU SPUNKIER
EIKNPRTU TURNPIKE
EIKNPSSU SPUNKIES
EIKNPSTU PUNKIEST
EIKNRSST STINKERS
EIKNRSTT KNITTERS
TRINKETS
EIKNSTUZ KUNZITES
EIKOOPRS SPOOKIER
EIKOORST ROOKIEST
EIKOPPRS PORKPIES
EIKOPRST PORKIEST
EIKORRWW WIREWORK
EIKPPRSS SKIPPERS
EIKPPSST SKIPPETS
EIKRRSST SKIRRETS
SKIRTERS
STRIKERS
EIKRSSTT SKITTERS
EIKRSTTY SKITTERY
EIKRSTWY SKYWRITE
EILLLNOY LONELILY
EILLLOVY LOVELILY
EILLMNNO MONELLIN
EILLMNOS SEMILLON
EILLMNOU LINOLEUM
EILLMNST STILLMEN
EILLMNSU MULLEINS
EILLMOPR IMPELLOR
EILLMOPS PLIMSOLE
EILLMOST MELILOTS
EILLMPSS MISSPELL
EILLMPTU MULTIPLE
EILLMSTU MULLITES
EILLMUVX VEXILLUM
EILLNOPT PLOTLINE
EILLNOTU LUTEOLIN
EILLNSST LINTLESS
EILLNSTY SILENTLY
TINSELLY
EILLNSUV LEVULINS
EILLNUVY UNLIVELY
EILLOORW WOOLLIER
EILLOOSW WOOLLIES
EILLOPSS SLIPSOLE
EILLOPTY POLITELY
EILLORST TROLLIES
EILLORSU ROUILLES
EILLORSZ ZORILLES
EILLORWW WILLOWER
EILLOSSS SOILLESS
EILLOSTW LOWLIEST
EILLOSVW LOWLIVES
EILLPRSS SPILLERS
EILLPSSS SLIPLESS
EILLQSTU QUILLETS
EILLRRST TRILLERS
EILLRSSW SWILLERS
EILLRSVY SILVERLY
EILLSSST LISTLESS
SLITLESS
EILLSSTT STILLEST
EILLSTTT LITTLEST
EILLSTUV VITELLUS
EILMMPRU PLUMMIER
EILMMRSS SLIMMERS
EILMMRSU SLUMMIER
EILMMSST SLIMMEST
EILMNOOS OINOMELS
SIMOLEON
EILMNORS MISENROL
EILMNOSU EMULSION
EILMNOTY MYLONITE
EILMNPSS LIMPNESS
PLENISMS
EILMNPSU SPLENIUM
EILMNPTU TUMPLINE
EILMNRST MINSTREL
EILMNSSS SLIMNESS
EILMNTUY MINUTELY
UNTIMELY
EILMOOPS LIPOSOME
EILMOOST TOILSOME
EILMOPRR IMPLORER
EILMOPRS IMPLORES
EILMOPST MILEPOST
POLEMIST
EILMORRS LORIMERS
EILMORSY RIMOSELY
EILMOSTT MOTLIEST
EILMOSTU OUTSMILE
EILMPRRU RUMPLIER
EILMPRUY IMPURELY
EILMPSST MISSPELT
SIMPLEST
EILMPSSU IMPULSES
EILMPSTU LUMPIEST
PLUMIEST
EILMRSSU MISRULES
EILMRSSY REMISSLY
EILMSSTU LITMUSES
EILMSSTY MISSTYLE
EILMSTUU MULTIUSE
EILMSUUV ELUVIUMS
EILMTTUU LUTETIUM
EILNNOST INSOLENT
EILNNOSV NONLIVES
EILNNOTT NONTITLE
EILNNPSU PINNULES
EILNNSTU UNSILENT
EILNNTTY INTENTLY
EILNOOST LOONIEST
OILSTONE
EILNOOSV VIOLONES
EILNOPRS PROLINES
EILNOPRT TERPINOL
EILNOPSS EPSILONS
EILNOPST POTLINES
TOPLINES
EILNOPTU UNPOLITE
EILNOPTY LINOTYPE
EILNORRS LORINERS
EILNORST RETINOLS
EILNORTT TROTLINE
EILNORTU OUTLINER
EILNORVV INVOLVER
EILNOSSU ELUSIONS
EILNOSSW LEWISSON
EILNOSTU ELUTIONS
OUTLINES
EILNOSTV NOVELIST
EILNOSTW TOWLINES
EILNOSUV EVULSION
EILNOSVV INVOLVES
EILNOTUV INVOLUTE
EILNPRSS PILSNERS
EILNPRST SPLINTER
EILNPRSU PURLINES
EILNPRUY UNRIPELY
EILNPSSS SPINLESS
EILNPSST PLENISTS
EILNPSSU SPINULES
SPLENIUS
EILNPSUY SUPINELY
EILNQUUY UNIQUELY
EILNRRUU UNRULIER
EILNRSTU INSULTER
EILNRTUV VIRULENT
EILNRTWY WINTERLY
EILNSSTT TINTLESS
EILNSSTU UTENSILS
EILNSSVY SYLVINES
EILNSTTU LUTENIST
EILNSUWY UNWISELY
EILOOPST LOOPIEST
EILOORST OESTRIOL
EILOORTV OVERTOIL
EILOOSST OSTIOLES
STOOLIES
EILOOSTW WOOLIEST
EILOOSTY OTIOSELY
EILOPPRS SLOPPIER
EILOPPST LOPPIEST
EILOPRRT PORTLIER
EILOPRSS SPOILERS
EILOPRST POITRELS
EILOPRSU PERILOUS
EILOPRSV OVERSLIP
SLIPOVER
EILOPRTT PLOTTIER
EILOPRTW PILEWORT
EILOPRYZ PYROLIZE
EILOPSSS PSILOSES
EILOPSST PISTOLES
EILOPSSV PLOSIVES
EILOPSTT PLOTTIES
POLITEST
EILOPSTX EXPLOITS
EILOPSUV PLUVIOSE
EILORRTU ULTERIOR
EILORSSS RISSOLES
EILORSST ESTRIOLS
EILORSSU SOILURES
EILORSTT TRIOLETS
EILORSTU OUTLIERS
EILORSUV RIVULOSE
EILORTTY TOILETRY
EILORTUV OUTLIVER
EILORVWY OVERWILY
EILOSSTU LOUSIEST
EILOSTTT STILETTO
EILOSTUV OUTLIVES
EILOSTUW OUTWILES
EILOTVVY VOTIVELY
EILPPPRY PREPPILY
EILPPRRS RIPPLERS
EILPPRSS SLIPPERS
EILPPRST PRESPLIT
RIPPLETS
STIPPLER
TIPPLERS
EILPPRSU SUPPLIER
EILPPRSY SLIPPERY
EILPPSST STIPPLES
EILPPSSU SUPPLIES
EILPPSSW SWIPPLES
EILPPSTU PULPIEST
EILPRSST RESPLITS
EILPRSTT SPLITTER
TRIPLETS
EILPRSTY PRIESTLY
EILPRSUU PURLIEUS
EILPRSUY PLEURISY
EILPRTTY PRETTILY
EILPSSSU PUSSLIES
EILPSSTT SPITTLES
EILPSSTU STIPULES
EILQRRSU SQUIRREL
EILQRSTU QUILTERS
EILQRSUU LIQUEURS
EILRRSSU SLURRIES
EILRRSTU SULTRIER
EILRRSTW TWIRLERS
EILRRTWY WRITERLY
EILRSSTT SLITTERS
EILRSSTU SURLIEST
EILRSSTY SISTERLY
STYLISER
EILRSSUV SURVEILS
EILRSSZZ SIZZLERS
EILRSTTU SLUTTIER
SURTITLE
EILRSTTW WRISTLET
EILRSTUV RIVULETS
EILRSTYZ STYLIZER
EILRSUUX LUXURIES
EILRSWZZ SWIZZLER
EILSSSTY STYLISES
EILSSTTU LUSTIEST
EILSSTTY STYLITES
EILSSTVY SYLVITES
EILSSTYZ STYLIZES
EILSSWZZ SWIZZLES
EIMMNNTU MUNIMENT
EIMMNORS MISNOMER
EIMMOPRU EMPORIUM
EIMMOSSV MISMOVES
EIMMOSTT TOTEMISM
EIMMPRST PRIMMEST
EIMMPRSU PREMIUMS
EIMMRRST TRIMMERS
EIMMRSST MISTERMS
EIMMRSSW SWIMMERS
EIMMRSTT TRIMMEST
EIMMRSTU RUMMIEST
EIMMSTUY YUMMIEST
EIMNNOOT NOONTIME
EIMNNOPT POINTMEN
EIMNNOST MENTIONS
EIMNNOTT OINTMENT
EIMNOOPS EMPOISON
EIMNOORS IONOMERS
MOONRISE
EIMNOORT MOTIONER
REMOTION
EIMNOORV OMNIVORE
EIMNOOST EMOTIONS
MOONIEST
EIMNOPPU PEPONIUM
EIMNOPRS PROMINES
EIMNOPRT ORPIMENT
EIMNOPSS MOPINESS
PEONISMS
EIMNOPST NEPOTISM
PIMENTOS
EIMNOPTT IMPOTENT
EIMNOPTV PIVOTMEN
EIMNORSU MONSIEUR
EIMNORSW WINSOMER
EIMNORTW TIMEWORN
EIMNORTY ENORMITY
EIMNOSST MESTINOS
MOISTENS
SENTIMOS
EIMNPRSS PRIMNESS
EIMNPSST MISSPENT
EIMNRSST MINSTERS
TRIMNESS
EIMNRSTU TERMINUS
UNMITERS
UNMITRES
EIMNRSTY MISENTRY
EIMNSSTU MISTUNES
EIMNSTTU MINUTEST
EIMNSUZZ MUEZZINS
EIMOORST MOORIEST
MOTORISE
ROOMIEST
EIMOORTZ MOTORIZE
EIMOOSST OSTOMIES
EIMOPPRR IMPROPER
EIMOPRRS PRIMEROS
PRIMROSE
PROMISER
EIMOPRRT IMPORTER
REIMPORT
EIMOPRRV IMPROVER
EIMOPRSS IMPOSERS
PROMISES
SEMIPROS
EIMOPRST IMPOSTER
EIMOPRSV IMPROVES
EIMOPRSW IMPOWERS
EIMOPRUU EUROPIUM
EIMOQSTU MISQUOTE
EIMORRSS MORRISES
EIMORRST MORTISER
STORMIER
EIMORRTT REMITTOR
EIMORRTV OVERTRIM
EIMORRWW WIREWORM
EIMORSST EROTISMS
MORTISES
TRISOMES
EIMORSSV VERISMOS
EIMORSTT OMITTERS
EIMORSTU MISROUTE
MOISTURE
EIMORSTV VOMITERS
EIMORSTW MISWROTE
WORMIEST
EIMORSTY ISOMETRY
EIMORTXY OXIMETRY
EIMOSSST MOSSIEST
EIMOSSTT MOISTEST
EIMOSSTU MOUSIEST
EIMOSSTX EXOTISMS
EIMOSSTZ MESTIZOS
EIMOSSYZ ISOZYMES
EIMOSTTT TOTEMIST
EIMOSTTU TIMEOUTS
TITMOUSE
EIMPRRST PRETRIMS
EIMPRSST IMPRESTS
EIMPRSSU PRIMUSES
EIMPRSTU IMPUREST
IMPUTERS
STUMPIER
EIMPSSST MISSTEPS
EIMPSSTU SPUMIEST
EIMPSSTY MISTYPES
EIMQRRSU SQUIRMER
EIMQSSTU MESQUITS
EIMQSTUY MYSTIQUE
EIMQSTUZ MEZQUITS
EIMRRSSU SURMISER
EIMRSSST MISTRESS
EIMRSSSU MISUSERS
SURMISES
EIMRSSTT METRISTS
EIMRSTTU SMUTTIER
EIMRSTUX MIXTURES
EIMSSSSU MISSUSES
EIMSSSTU MUSSIEST
EIMSSTTU MUSTIEST
EIMSTUZZ MUZZIEST
EINNNORT NONINERT
EINNOPPT PENPOINT
EINNOPRU PREUNION
EINNOPRY PYRONINE
EINNOPSS PENSIONS
EINNOQSU QUINONES
EINNORSS IRONNESS
EINNORST INTONERS
TERNIONS
EINNORSU REUNIONS
EINNORSV ENVIRONS
EINNORTU NEUTRINO
EINNORTV INVENTOR
EINNORWW WINNOWER
EINNOSSS NOSINESS
EINNOSST TENSIONS
EINNOSSU NONISSUE
UNSONSIE
EINNOSSV VENISONS
EINNOSTT TINSTONE
TONTINES
EINNPRSS SPINNERS
EINNPRSY SPINNERY
EINNPSSU PUNINESS
EINNPSSY SPINNEYS
EINNPSTU PUNNIEST
EINNPSXY SIXPENNY
EINNRSTU RUNNIEST
EINNRSTV VINTNERS
EINNRTTU NUTRIENT
EINNSSTT TENNISTS
EINNSSTU SUNNIEST
EINNSSWY SWINNEYS
EINNSTUW UNTWINES
EINOOPRS POISONER
SNOOPIER
SPOONIER
EINOOPSS SPOONIES
EINOOPSZ OPSONIZE
EINOORSS EROSIONS
EINOORST SNOOTIER
EINOORSW SWOONIER
EINOORSZ SNOOZIER
EINOORZZ OZONIZER
EINOOSST ISOTONES
EINOOSSZ OOZINESS
OZONISES
EINOOSTW TWOONIES
EINOOSZZ OZONIZES
EINOOTXX EXOTOXIN
EINOPPRS PROPINES
EINOPRRS PRISONER
EINOPRSS ROPINESS
EINOPRST POINTERS
PORNIEST
PROTEINS
TROPINES
EINOPRSU PRUINOSE
EINOPRSV OVERSPIN
EINOPRTU ERUPTION
EINOPSSW WINESOPS
EINOPSTT NEPOTIST
EINOPSTU POUTINES
EINOPSWX SWINEPOX
EINOQSTU QUESTION
EINOQTTU QUOTIENT
EINORRST INTRORSE
EINORRTV INVERTOR
EINORRTW INTERROW
EINORSSS ROSINESS
EINORSST OESTRINS
EINORSSU NEUROSIS
RESINOUS
EINORSSV VERSIONS
EINORSTT SNOTTIER
TENORIST
TRITONES
EINORSTU ROUTINES
SNOUTIER
EINORSTV INVESTOR
EINORSTY SEROTINY
TYROSINE
EINORSUV SOUVENIR
EINOSSSS SESSIONS
EINOSSST SONSIEST
STENOSIS
EINOSSTT STONIEST
EINOSSTW SNOWIEST
EINOSTVY VENOSITY
EINPPRRT PREPRINT
EINPPRSS SNIPPERS
EINPPSST SNIPPETS
EINPPSTY SNIPPETY
EINPRRST PRINTERS
REPRINTS
SPRINTER
EINPRRTU PRURIENT
EINPRRTY PRINTERY
EINPRSST SPINSTER
EINPRSTU UNRIPEST
EINPRTTU INPUTTER
EINPSTTY TINTYPES
EINQRSTU SQUINTER
EINQRTTU QUITRENT
EINQSSTU INQUESTS
EINQSTTU QUINTETS
EINQSTUU UNIQUEST
UNQUIETS
EINRRSSU INSURERS
EINRSSSU SUNRISES
EINRSSTT STINTERS
EINRSSXY SYRINXES
EINRSTTU RUNTIEST
EINRSTUV VENTURIS
EINSSTTU NUTSIEST
EINSSTTW ENTWISTS
TWINSETS
EINSSTUW UNWISEST
EINSTTTU NUTTIEST
EIOOPPRS PORPOISE
EIOOPPST OPPOSITE
EIOOPRSW SWOOPIER
EIOOPSST ISOTOPES
EIOOPTYZ EPIZOOTY
EIOORSTT ROOTIEST
TORTOISE
EIOOSSST OSTEOSIS
EIOOSSTT SOOTIEST
TOOTSIES
EIOOSTTZ ZOOTIEST
EIOOSTWZ WOOZIEST
EIOPPSST SOPPIEST
EIOPPTTY TIPPYTOE
EIOPQRSU PIROQUES
EIOPQSTU POSTIQUE
EIOPRRSS PRIORESS
EIOPRRST PIERROTS
SPORTIER
EIOPRRSU SUPERIOR
EIOPRRSV PREVISOR
EIOPRSSS PROSSIES
EIOPRSST PROSIEST
PROSTIES
REPOSITS
RIPOSTES
TRIPOSES
EIOPRSTT SPOTTIER
EIOPRSTU ROUPIEST
EIOPRSTV OVERTIPS
SORPTIVE
SPORTIVE
EIOPRSUV PERVIOUS
PREVIOUS
VIPEROUS
EIOPSSSU POUSSIES
EIOPSSTU SOUPIEST
EIOPSSTX EXPOSITS
EIOPSSTY ISOTYPES
EIOPSTTT POTTIEST
EIOPSTTU POUTIEST
EIOPSTUW WIPEOUTS
EIOQSTUX QUIXOTES
EIORRSSW WORRIERS
EIORRRTU ROTURIER
EIORRSST RESISTOR
ROISTERS
SORRIEST
EIORRSSV REVISORS
EIORRSTV OVERSTIR
SERVITOR

EIORRSUV REOVIRUS
EIORRSVY REVISORY
EIORRTTU TROUTIER
EIORSSTY SEROSITY
EIORSTUV VIRTUOSE
VITREOUS
EIORTTUW OUTWRITE
EIOSSTUZ OUTSIZES
EIPPQRSU QUIPPERS
EIPPRRST STRIPPER
TRIPPERS
EIPPRRSY PERSPIRY
EIPPRSTT TRIPPETS
EIPQRSTU QUIPSTER
EIPRRRSU SPURRIER
EIPRRSST STRIPERS
EIPRRSSU SPURRIES
SURPRISE
UPRISERS
EIPRRSTZ SPRITZER
EIPRRSUV UPRIVERS
EIPRRSUY SYRUPIER
EIPRRSUZ SURPRIZE
EIPRSSST PERSISTS
EIPRSSSU SUSPIRES
EIPRSSTT SPITTERS
TIPSTERS
EIPRSSTU PURSIEST
EIPRSSTZ SPRITZES
EIPRSTTU PURTIEST
PUTTIERS
EIPRSUVW PURVIEWS
EIPSSSTU PUSSIEST
EIQRRSTU SQUIRTER
EIQRSSTU QUERISTS
EIQRSTTU QUITTERS
EIQRSTUU SEQUITUR
EIQRSUZZ QUIZZERS
EIRRRSST STIRRERS
EIRRSSTV STRIVERS
EIRRSTTU TRUSTIER
EIRRSUVV SURVIVER
EIRSSTTU RUSTIEST
TRUSTIES
EIRSSTTW RETWISTS
TWISTERS
EIRSSTUV REVUISTS
STUIVERS
EIRSSUVV SURVIVES
EIRSTTTU RUTTIEST
EIRSTTTW TWITTERS
EIRTTTWY TWITTERY
EIRTTUWZ WURTZITE
EISSSSTU TUSSISES
EISSSTUW WUSSIEST
EISSTTUW WETSUITS
EJLOPSTU PULSOJET
EJLORSST JOSTLERS
EJLRSSUY JURYLESS
EJNORSUY JOURNEYS
EJNSSSTU JUSTNESS
EJOORSVY OVERJOYS
EJOPPRST PROPJETS
EJOPRSTT JETPORTS
EJORSSTU JOUSTERS
EJORSTUV OVERJUST
EKKLNPRU KERPLUNK
EKKLOOSZ KOLKOZES
EKKLRSSU SKULKERS
EKLLMSSU SKELLUMS
EKLLNORS KNOLLERS
EKLLRRSU KRULLERS
EKLNOOOR ONLOOKER
EKLNORSS SNORKELS
EKLNOSST KNOTLESS
EKLNPRSU PLUNKERS
EKLNPSSU SPELUNKS
EKLOOORV OVERLOOK
EKLOOPSW SLOWPOKE
EKLORSSW WORKLESS
EKLSSSTU TUSKLESS
EKMNOSUX MUSKOXEN
EKMOOPST SMOKEPOT
EKMOOSTU OUTSMOKE
EKMOSSUY KOUMYSES
EKMRSTUY MUSKETRY
EKNNOORT KENOTRON
EKNNOPSU UNSPOKEN
EKNOOPRW OPENWORK
EKNOORSS SNOOKERS
EKNOPSSY PYKNOSES
EKNORSTT KNOTTERS
EKNORSTW NETWORKS
EKNORSUY YOUNKERS
EKNRSTUY TURNKEYS
EKOOOPRT POKEROOT
EKOOORTV OVERTOOK
EKOOPRRV PROVOKER
EKOOPRSV PROVOKES
EKOOPRSY SPOOKERY
EKOOPSTU OUTSPOKE
EKOORRVW OVERWORK
EKOORSST STOOKERS
EKOORSTW KOTOWERS
EKOORSUU EUROKOUS
EKOORTWW KOWTOWER
EKOPRRSW PREWORKS
EKOPRSTU UPSTROKE
EKOPRSUY KOUPREYS
EKORRSST STROKERS
EKORSSTU KURTOSES
EKORSTWY SKYWROTE
EKPPSSUU SEPPUKUS
ELLLMOWY MELLOWLY
ELLLNSUY SULLENLY
ELLLOWYY YELLOWLY
ELLMNOSY SOLEMNLY
ELLMNOTY MOLTENLY
ELLMNOUW UNMELLOW
ELLMOORS MORELLOS
ELLMOSTU OUTSMELL
ELLMPSUU PLUMULES
ELLNOORV LOVELORN
ELLNOOSW WOOLLENS
ELLNOPRU PRUNELLO
ELLNOSST STOLLENS
ELLNOSVY SLOVENLY
ELLNOUVY UNLOVELY
ELLOORRV ROLLOVER
ELLOOSST TOOLLESS
ELLOOSTU TOLUOLES
ELLOPRST POLLSTER
ELLOPRTU POLLUTER
ELLOPRUV PULLOVER
ELLOPSST PLOTLESS
ELLOPSTU OUTSPELL
POLLUTES
ELLORRST STROLLER
TROLLERS
ELLORSTY TROLLEYS
ELLOSSSS LOSSLESS
ELLOSSSU SOULLESS
ELLOSSTU OUTSELLS
SELLOUTS
ELLOSTTU OUTTELLS
ELLOSTUY OUTYELLS
ELLPPSSU PULPLESS
ELLPPSUY SUPPLELY
ELLPSSUW UPSWELLS
ELMMNOTU LOMENTUM
ELMMNOTY MOMENTLY
ELMMOPSU PUMMELOS
ELMMORST TROMMELS
ELMMOSUX LUMMOXES
ELMMPSTU PLUMMEST
PLUMMETS
ELMMRSSU SLUMMERS
ELMMRSTU TUMMLERS
ELMMRSUY SUMMERLY
ELMNNOTU UNMOLTEN
ELMNOOOP MONOPOLE
ELMNOOSS MOONLESS
ELMNOOST MOONLETS
ELMNORSS NORMLESS
ELMNOSTW SNOWMELT
ELMNPPSU PLUMPENS
ELMNUUZZ UNMUZZLE
ELMOOPSY POLYSOME
ELMOORST TREMOLOS
ELMOORSY MOROSELY
ELMOOSSY LYSOSOME
ELMOPRSY POLYMERS
ELMOPSYY POLYSEMY
ELMORSTT MOTTLERS
ELMORSTU MOULTERS
ELMORUUV VERMOULU
ELMOSTTU OUTSMELT
ELMOSTUU TUMULOSE
ELMOSYYZ LYSOZYME
ELMPPRSU PLUMPERS
ELMPPSSU PUMPLESS
ELMPPSTU PLUMPEST
ELMPRSSU RUMPLESS
ELMRSTUU MULTURES
ELMRSUZZ MUZZLERS
ELNNNOOV NONNOVEL
ELNNOOSU UNLOOSEN
ELNNOPSU NONPULES
ELNNORSS LORNNESS
ELNNOSSU NOUNLESS
ELNNOSTY NONSTYLE
ELNNRSTU TRUNNELS
ELNOOPPR PROPENOL
ELNOOPST PELOTONS
ELNOOSST SOLONETS
ELNOOSSU UNLOOSES
ELNOOSSZ SNOOZLES
ELNOOSTZ SOLONETZ
ELNOPPRY PROPENYL
ELNOPRVY PROVENLY
ELNOPSTU PLEUSTON
ELNOPTTY POTENTLY
ELNOPTYY POLYTENY
ELNORSTU TURNSOLE
ELNORTTY ROTTENLY
ELNOSSST LOSTNESS
ELNOSSSW SLOWNESS
SNOWLESS
ELNOSSTV SOLVENTS
ELNOSSTW TOWNLESS
ELNOSTTW TOWNLETS
ELNOSUUV VENULOUS
ELNOSUVY VENOUSLY
ELNPRTUU PURULENT
ELNPRUUY UNPURELY
ELNPUUZZ UNPUZZLE
ELNRSUUY UNSURELY
ELNRSUZZ NUZZLERS
ELOOPPRY POLYPORE
ELOOPRSS RESPOOLS
SPOOLERS
ELOOPRTV OVERPLOT
ELOOPSSS SESSPOOL
ELOORSST ROOTLESS
ELOORSTT ROOTLETS
TOOTLERS
ELOORSUV OVERSOUL
ELOORSVW OVERSLOW
ELOOSSTU OUTSOLES
ELOOSTUV OUTLOVES
ELOOSVVX VOLVOXES
ELOPPRRY PROPERLY
ELOPPSST STOPPLES
ELOPPTYY POLYTYPE
ELOPRRSW PROWLERS
ELOPRRSY PYRROLES
ELOPRSSS PLESSORS
ELOPRSST PORTLESS
ELOPRSSU SPORULES
ELOPRSTT PLOTTERS
ELOPRSTU POULTERS
ELOPRSTY PROSTYLE
PROTYLES
ELOPRSUV OVERPLUS
ELOPRYYZ PYROLYZE
ELOPSSST SPOTLESS
ELOPSSSU SOUPLESS
ELOPSTTU OUTSLEPT
OUTSPELT
ELOPSTUY OUTYELPS
ELORSSTT SETTLORS
SLOTTERS
ELORSTUY ELYTROUS
UROSTYLE
ELOSSSTY SYSTOLES
ELOSSTUU SETULOUS
ELPPRSTU PURPLEST
ELPPRSUY RESUPPLY
ELPPSSTU SUPPLEST
ELPRSSTU SPURTLES
ELPRSTTU SPLUTTER
ELPRSUZZ PUZZLERS
ELPSSSUY PUSSLEYS
ELPSSTUU PUSTULES
ELPSTUXY SEXTUPLY
ELRRSSTU RUSTLERS
ELRRSTTU TURTLERS
ELRSSSTU RUSTLESS
ELRSTUUV VULTURES
ELSSSTUY STYLUSES
EMMMNOTU MOMENTUM
EMMNNOTU MONUMENT
EMMNOOOS MONOSOME
EMMNOORS MONOMERS
EMMNOORT MOTORMEN
EMMNOOST MOMENTOS
EMMNORSU RESUMMON
SUMMONER
EMMNOSTU OMENTUMS
EMMNOSTY METONYMS
EMMNOTTU TOMENTUM
EMMNOTYY METONYMY
EMMOOSTY MYOTOMES
EMMOPRSU SUPERMOM
EMMRRRUU MURMURER
EMMRRSTU STRUMMER
EMMRSTYY SYMMETRY
EMNNNOOU NOUMENON
EMNNNOOY NONMONEY
EMNNOOOT MONOTONE
EMNNOORT NONMETRO
EMNNOPTY NONEMPTY
EMNNOSTW TOWNSMEN
EMNNOSYY SYNONYME
EMNNSTTU STUNTMEN
EMNOOPST METOPONS
EMNOOPTY MONOTYPE
EMNOORST MESOTRON
MONTEROS
EMNOORSU ENORMOUS
EMNOORSW NEWSROOM
EMNOOSST MOONSETS
MOOTNESS
EMNOOSUV VENOMOUS
EMNOOTTY TENOTOMY
EMNOPSSU SPUMONES
EMNORRSU MOURNERS
EMNORRTY RETRONYM
EMNORSST MONSTERS
EMNORSTT TORMENTS
EMNORSTU MOUNTERS
REMOUNTS
EMNORSUU NUMEROUS
EMNOSSST STEMSONS
EMNOSUUY EUONYMUS
EMNOSUVY EVONYMUS
EMNRSSTU MUNSTERS
STERNUMS
EMOOPRRT PROMOTER
EMOOPRSS OOSPERMS
EMOOPRST PROMOTES
EMOOPRSZ ZOOSPERM
EMOORRST RESTROOM
EMOORTYZ ZOOMETRY
EMOOSSTW TWOSOMES
EMOOSSTY MYOSOTES
EMOOSSXY OXYSOMES
EMOOSTUV OUTMOVES
EMOPPRRT PROMPTER
EMOPPRUV OVERPUMP
EMOPPSTU UPTEMPOS
EMOPRSST STOMPERS
EMOPRSSU SPERMOUS
SUPREMOS
EMORSSTU OESTRUMS
STRUMOSE
EMOSSSTT MOSTESTS
EMOSSTTW WESTMOST
EMOSSTVZ ZEMSTVOS
EMOSTTTU TETOTUMS
EMPRRTUY TRUMPERY
EMPRSSTU STUMPERS
SUMPTERS
EMPRSSUU RUMPUSES
EMPRSTTU STRUMPET
TRUMPETS
ENNNOORW NONOWNER
ENNNOOVW NONWOVEN
ENNNORTY NONENTRY
ENNOOOTZ ENTOZOON
ENNOOPPT OPPONENT
ENNOORTV NONVOTER
ENNOPRSU UNPERSON
ENNOPRUV UNPROVEN
ENNOPTWY TWOPENNY
ENNORSST STERNSON
ENNORSSU NONUSERS
ENNORSSW WORNNESS
ENNORSTU NEUTRONS
ENNOSSTU NEUSTONS
SUNSTONE
ENNPPTUY TUPPENNY
ENNRSSTU STUNNERS
ENOOORSV OVERSOON
ENOOOSSZ ZOONOSES
ENOOPPRS PROPONES
ENOOPPST POSTPONE
ENOOPRSS POORNESS
SNOOPERS
ENOOPSSY SPOONEYS
ENOOPSTT POTSTONE
TOPSTONE
ENOORRVW OVERWORN
ENOORSSW SWOONERS
ENOORSSZ SNOOZERS
ENOORSTU OUTSNORE
ENOOSSTT TESTOONS
ENOOSTXY OXYTONES
ENOPRSST POSTERNS
ENOPRSTT PORTENTS
ENOPRTUW UPTOWNER
ENOPSSST STEPSONS
ENOPSSSY SYNOPSES
ENOPSTTU OUTSPENT
ENOQSTUU UNQUOTES
ENORRSST SNORTERS
ENORRSTT TORRENTS
ENORRSUV OVERRUNS
RUNOVERS
ENORRTUV OVERTURN
TURNOVER
ENORSSSU SOURNESS
ENORSSTT STENTORS
ENORSSTU TONSURES
ENORSTUY TOURNEYS
ENOSSSTT STETSONS
ENOSSSUU SENSUOUS
ENOSSTTU STOUTENS
ENPRRSSU PRESSRUN
SPURNERS
ENPRSSSY SPRYNESS
ENPRSSTU PUNSTERS
ENPRSSUU PRUNUSES
ENPRTTUY UNPRETTY
ENRRRTUU NURTURER
ENRRSTUU NURTURES
ENRSSSTU UNSTRESS
ENRSSTTU ENTRUSTS
ENRSTTUU UNTRUEST
EOOOPRSS OOSPORES
EOOOPRSZ ZOOSPORE
EOOORRST ROSEROOT
EOOPPRRS PROPOSER
EOOPPRSS OPPOSERS
PROPOSES
EOOPPRSV POPOVERS
EOOPPSST POSTPOSE
EOOPPTTY TOPOTYPE
EOOPRRST TROOPERS
EOOPRRTU UPROOTER
EOOPRSST STOOPERS
EOOPRSSW SWOOPERS
EOOPRSTV OVERTOPS
STOPOVER
EOOPRSTW TOWROPES
EOOPRTUW OUTPOWER
EOOQTTUU OUTQUOTE
EOORRRSW SORROWER
EOORRSST ROOSTERS
EOORSSTU OESTROUS
EOORSTUW OUTSWORE
EOORTTUW OUTTOWER
OUTWROTE
EOOSTTUV OUTVOTES
EOPPRRSS PROSPERS
EOPPRRST STROPPER
EOPPRRSU SUPERPRO
EOPPRRTY PROPERTY
EOPPRSST STOPPERS
EOPPRSSU PURPOSES
SUPPOSER
EOPPSSSU SUPPOSES
EOPRRSSS PRESSORS
EOPRRSST PORTRESS
PRESORTS
SPORTERS
EOPRRSTU POSTURER
RESPROUT
TROUPERS
EOPRRUVY PURVEYOR
EOPRSSTT PROTESTS
SPOTTERS
EOPRSSTU OUTPRESS
POSTURES
SPOUTERS
EOPRSSUU UPROUSES
EOPRSSUV OVERSUPS
EOPSSSTU UPTOSSES
EOPSSTTT POSTTEST
EOPSTTUW OUTSWEPT
EOQRRSTU TORQUERS
EOQRSSTU QUESTORS
EORRRTTU TORTURER
EORRSSST STRESSOR
EORRSSTT STERTORS
EORRSSTU ROUSTERS
TRESSOUR
TROUSERS
EORRSSTW TROWSERS
EORRSSTY ROYSTERS
STROYERS
EORRSTTT TROTTERS
EORRSTTU TORTURES
EORRSUVY SURVEYOR
EORRTUUV TROUVEUR
EORSSSTU TUSSORES
EORSSTTT STRETTOS
EORSSTTU OUTSERTS
TUTORESS
EORSSTTW SWOTTERS
EORSTTUY TUTOYERS
EOSSTTTU STOUTEST
EPPPRTUY PUPPETRY
EPPRRSUU PURPURES
EPPRSSSU SUPPRESS
EPPRSSUY SUPERSPY
EPRRRSSU SPURRERS
EPRRSSTU SPURTERS
EPRRSSUU PURSUERS
USURPERS
EPRRSSUY SPURREYS
EPRRSTUU RUPTURES
EPRSSTTU SPUTTERS
EPRSTTUY SPUTTERY
ERRSSSTU TRUSSERS
ERRSSTTU TRUSTERS
ERRSSTTY TRYSTERS
ERRSTTTU STRUTTER
ERSSTTTU STUTTERS
FFFGILNU FLUFFING
FFFILLUY FLUFFILY
FFFILOST LIFTOFFS
FFGGINRU GRUFFING
FFGHIINW WHIFFING
FFGHIORS FROGFISH
FFGHIRSU GRUFFISH
FFGIILNP PIFFLING
FFGIILNR RIFFLING
FFGIINNS SNIFFING
FFGIINPS SPIFFING
FFGIINRS GRIFFINS
FFGIINST STIFFING
FFGILMNU MUFFLING
FFGILNRU RUFFLING
FFGILNSU SLUFFING
FFGILRUY GRUFFILY
FFGINNSU SNUFFING
FFGINORS GRIFFONS
FFGINSTU STUFFING
FFGIORTU FOGFRUIT
FFHIINSS SNIFFISH
FFHIISST STIFFISH
FFHIISTY FIFTYISH
FFHILOOS FOOLFISH
FFHILOSW WOLFFISH
FFHILOSY OFFISHLY
FFHIRSSU SURFFISH
FFHOOOST OFFSHOOT
FFHOOSSW SHOWOFFS
FFHOSSTU SHUTOFFS
FFIILMOR FILIFORM
FFIILNSY SNIFFILY
FFIILPSY SPIFFILY
FFIKLORT FORKLIFT
FFILLLSU FULFILLS
FFILLOPP FLIPFLOP
FFILLTUY FITFULLY
FFILNSUY SNUFFILY
FFILRTUU FRUITFUL
FFILSSTU FISTFULS
FFILSTUY STUFFILY
FFIMORSU FUSIFORM
FFINOOST FINFOOTS
FFINOPRT OFFPRINT
FFINOPSS SPINOFFS
FFINOPST PONTIFFS
FFJMOPSU JUMPOFFS
FFKLORSU FORKFULS
FORKSFUL
FFLMNOOU MOUFFLON
FFNORSTU TURNOFFS
FFNSTUUY UNSTUFFY
FFOOPSST STOPOFFS
FFOORRUU FROUFROU
FGGGIINR FRIGGING
FGGGILNO FLOGGING
FGGGINOR FROGGING
FGGGINRU FRUGGING
FGGHIINT FIGHTING
FGGHIISS FISHGIGS
FGGHINTU GUNFIGHT
FGGIILNN FLINGING
FGGIINNR FRINGING
FGGIINRT GRIFTING
FGGIINRU FIGURING
FGGILNOS GOLFINGS
FGGINOOR FORGOING
FGGINORS FORGINGS
FGHIIKNS KINGFISH
FGHIILNT INFLIGHT
FGHIINSS FISHINGS
FGHIINST INFIGHTS
SHIFTING
FGHILLTU LIGHTFUL
FGHILNSU FLUSHING
LUNGFISH

FGHILRTU RIGHTFUL
FGHINOOW WHOOFING
FGHINORT FROTHING
FGHINOTU INFOUGHT
FGHIOTTU OUTFIGHT
FGHLORUU FURLOUGH
FGHNOORS FOGHORNS
FGHNOTUU UNFOUGHT
FGIIIKNN FINIKING
FGIIINNX INFIXING
FGIIKNRS FRISKING
FGIILLNR FRILLING
FGIILLNS FILLINGS
FGIILNNT FLINTING
FGIILNOO FOLIOING
FGIILNPP FLIPPING
FGIILNRS RIFLINGS
FGIILNRT FLIRTING
TRIFLING
FGIILNST STIFLING
FGIILNTT FLITTING
FGIILNZZ FIZZLING
FGIINNSU INFUSING
FGIINNUX UNFIXING
FGIINNUY UNIFYING
FGIINOST FOISTING
FGIINRTT FRITTING
FGIINRTU FRUITING
FGIINRZZ FRIZZING
FGIINSST SIFTINGS
FGIINSTT FITTINGS
FGIKLNNU FLUNKING
FGILMNPU FLUMPING
FGILMNUY FUMINGLY
FGILNNTU GUNFLINT
FGILNOOR FLOORING
FGILNOOT FOOTLING
FGILNOOZ FOOZLING
FGILNOPP FLOPPING
FGILNORU FLOURING
FGILNOSS FLOSSING
FGILNOSU FOULINGS
FGILNOSW FOWLINGS
FGILNOTU FLOUTING
FGILNPRU PURFLING
FGILNPSU UPFLINGS
FGILNSTU FLUTINGS
FGILNSTY FLYTINGS
FGIMORRU GRUIFORM
FGIMOSSY FOGYISMS
FGINNORT FRONTING
FGINNORW FROWNING
FGINOOPR PROOFING
FGINOOPS SPOOFING
FGINOORS ROOFINGS
FGINOOST FOOTINGS
FGINORST FROSTING
FGINRRSU FURRINGS
FGINRSSU SURFINGS
FGINSTTU TUFTINGS
FGIORSTW FIGWORTS
FGISSTUU FUGUISTS
FGKLNOOS FOLKSONG
FGLLMOOU GLOOMFUL
FGLLNSUU LUNGFULS
FGLNORSU FURLONGS
FGLNORUW WRONGFUL
FGLOOOST FOOTSLOG
FGNOORSU FOURGONS
FGNOORTU UNFORGOT
FHHIKOOS FISHHOOK
FHHOORST SHOFROTH
FHIIKLLS FISHKILL
FHIIKLMS MILKFISH
FHIILLTY FILTHILY
FHIILNOS LIONFISH
FHIILSTY SHIFTILY
FHIKMNOS MONKFISH
FHILLOOT FOOTHILL
FHILMPSU LUMPFISH
FHILMRTU MIRTHFUL
FHILOPST SHOPLIFT
FHILORSU FLOURISH
FHILORTY FROTHILY
FHIMNOOS MOONFISH
FHIMORSW FISHWORM
FHIMPRSU FRUMPISH
FHINSSTU UNSHIFTS
FHIORSTY FORTYISH
FHIPSSTU UPSHIFTS
FHKORSTU FUTHORKS
FHLLOSTU SLOTHFUL
FHLMORUU HUMORFUL
FHLMOTUU MOUTHFUL
FHLORTUW WORTHFUL
WROTHFUL
FHLORTUY FOURTHLY
FHLOTUUY YOUTHFUL
FHLRTTUU TRUTHFUL
FHNOSTUX FOXHUNTS
FHOOORST FORSOOTH
FHOOOSTT HOTFOOTS
FIIINNOX INFIXION
FIIINNTY INFINITY
FIIKLRSY FRISKILY
FIILLMOP PLIOFILM
FIILLMOS MILFOILS
FIILLMSY FLIMSILY
FIILLNTY FLINTILY
FIILLSSU FUSILLIS
FIILMNRY INFIRMLY
FIILMOPR PILIFORM
FIILMPSY SIMPLIFY
FIILNOST TINFOILS
FIILRTUY FRUITILY
FIILRYZZ FRIZZILY
FIILTTUY FUTILITY
FIIMOPRR PIRIFORM
FIIMOPRS PISIFORM
FIINNOSU INFUSION
FIINORTU FRUITION
FIINOSSS FISSIONS
FIKKLNOS KINFOLKS
KINSFOLK
FIKLLLSU SKILLFUL
FIKLLOSY FOLKSILY
FIKLNSSU SKINFULS
FIKLSSTU KISTFULS
LUTFISKS
FIKNOSSX FOXSKINS
FIKRSSTU TURFSKIS
FILLLUWY WILFULLY
FILLNSUY SINFULLY
SULFINYL
FILLOPPY FLOPPILY
FILLOSSY FLOSSILY
FILMNOOS MONOFILS
FILMOPRS SLIPFORM
FILMORRY LYRIFORM
FILMOSTU MOISTFUL
FILMPRUY FRUMPILY
FILNNSUU UNSINFUL
FILNORSU FLUORINS
FILNOSUX FLUXIONS
FILOOOPR OILPROOF
FILOOSTW WITLOOFS
FILORSST FLORISTS
FILORSTU FLORUITS
FILORSTY FROSTILY
FILORWYZ FROWZILY
FILRSTTU TRISTFUL
FILSSTTU FLUTISTS
FILSTTUY STULTIFY
FIMMNOOR OMNIFORM
FIMMORSS MISFORMS
FIMNORSU UNIFORMS
FIMOORRT ROTIFORM
FIMOORSS ISOFORMS
FIMOPRRY PYRIFORM
FIMORRSU URSIFORM
FIMORTUY FUMITORY
FIMRSTUU FUTURISM
FINOOPSY OPSONIFY
FINOPRST FROSTNIP
FINORSSS FRISSONS
FIORTTUY FORTUITY
FIOSTTTU TOFUTTIS
FIRSTTUU FUTURIST
FIRTTUUY FUTURITY
FJLLOUYY JOYFULLY
FJLNOUUY UNJOYFUL
FKKLOORW WORKFOLK
FKLMOOOT FOLKMOOT
FKLMOOST FOLKMOTS
FKLNOOTW TOWNFOLK
FKLNRTUU TRUNKFUL
FKLOORWW WORKFLOW
FKMOORRW FORMWORK
FKOOORTW FOOTWORK
FKRSSSUY SKYSURFS
FLLNOSUY SULFONYL
FLLOOPUW FOLLOWUP
FLLRSUUY SULFURYL
FLMNOOSU MOUFLONS
FLMNORUU MOURNFUL
FLMOOORW MOORFOWL
FLMOOOST TOMFOOLS
FLMOORSU ROOMFULS
FLNOOPSU SPOONFUL
FLNOOTUW OUTFLOWN
FLOOOSTU OUTFOOLS
FLOOPTTY TOPLOFTY
FLOOSTUW OUTFLOWS
FLOPRSTU SPORTFUL
FLRSTTUU TRUSTFUL
FMNOOOOR MOONROOF
FMOOPRST POSTFORM
FMRSSTUU FRUSTUMS
FNNOORST FRONTONS
FNOOORTW FOOTWORN
FNOOPRSU SUNPROOF
FNOORRSW FORSWORN
FNOORSSU SUNROOFS
FNOORTUW OUTFROWN
FOOOPRST ROOFTOPS
FOOOSTTU OUTFOOTS
FOORSTTX FOXTROTS
FOPSSSTU FUSSPOTS
GGGGIILN GIGGLING
GGGGILNO GOGGLING
GGGGILNU GLUGGING
GUGGLING
GGGHIILN HIGGLING
GGGHINOS SHOGGING
GGGIIJLN JIGGLING
GGGIILNN NIGGLING
GGGIILNW WIGGLING
GGGIINPR PRIGGING
GGGIINRS RIGGINGS
GGGIINRT TRIGGING
GGGIINSW SWIGGING
WIGGINGS
GGGIINTW TWIGGING
GGGIJLNO JOGGLING
GGGIJLNU JUGGLING
GGGIJNOS JOGGINGS
GGGILNOS LOGGINGS
SLOGGING
GGGILNOT TOGGLING
GGGILNPU PLUGGING
GGGILNRU GURGLING
GGGILNSU SLUGGING
GGGILORY GROGGILY
GGGIMNSU MUGGINGS
GGGINNOS NOGGINGS
SNOGGING
GGGINNSU SNUGGING
GGGINOPR PROGGING
GGHHIINT HIGHTING
GGHHISTU THUGGISH
GGHIILNT LIGHTING
GGHIINNO HONGIING
GGHIINNW WHINGING
GGHIINRT GIRTHING
RIGHTING
GGHIINST SIGHTING
GGHIIPRS PRIGGISH
GGHILSSU SLUGGISH
GGHINORU ROUGHING
GGHINOST GHOSTING
GGHINOSU SOUGHING
GGHINOTU OUGHTING
TOUGHING
GGHINOTY HOGTYING
GGHOOPRS GROGSHOP
GGIIILLN GINGILLI
GGIIILNS GINGILIS
GGIIINNT IGNITING
GGIIJLNN JINGLING
GGIILLNR GRILLING
GGIILLNY GILLYING
GGIILMNN MINGLING
GGIILNNS SINGLING
SLINGING
GGIILNNT GLINTING
TINGLING
GGIILNTZ GLITZING
GGIIMPRS PRIGGISM
GGIINNNR GRINNING
GGIINNNS GINNINGS
GGIINNOR GROINING
IGNORING
GGIINNOT INGOTING
GGIINNRW WRINGING
GGIINNST STINGING
GGIINNSW SWINGING
GGIINNTW TWINGING
GGIINNUV UNGIVING
GGIINPPR GRIPPING
GGIINPSY GIPSYING
GGIINRST RINGGITS
GGIINRTT GRITTING
GGIITTUU GUITGUIT
GGIKKNOR GROKKING
GGILLNUW GULLWING
GGILLNUY GULLYING
GGILLOOW GOLLIWOG
GGILMMNO GLOMMING
GGILMNOO GLOOMING
GGILMNOS LONGINGS
GGILNNOU LOUNGING
GGILNNPU PLUNGING
PUNGLING
GGILNNUU UNGLUING
GGILNOPP GLOPPING
GGILNORW GROWLING
GGILNORY GLORYING
GGILNOSS GLOSSING
GOSLINGS
GGILNOTU GLOUTING
GGILNRUY URGINGLY
GGILNTTU GLUTTING
GUTTLING
GGILNUZZ GUZZLING
GGILQSUY SQUIGGLY
GGIMNOOR GROOMING
GGIMNPRU GRUMPING
GGINNNSU GUNNINGS
GGINNOPR PRONGING
GGINNOPS SPONGING
GGINNORW WRONGING
GGINNOSS SINGSONG
GGINNOTU TONGUING
GGINNRTU GRUNTING
GGINOORV GROOVING
GGINOOST STOOGING
GGINOOTU OUTGOING
GGINOPRU GROUPING
GGINORSS GROSSING
GGINORSU GROUSING
GGINORTU GROUTING
GGINOSUV VOGUINGS
GGINPRSU PURGINGS
GGINPSYY GYPSYING
GGINSSUY GUSSYING
GGLLOOWY GOLLYWOG
GGLPUUY PLUGUGLY
GHHIILST LIGHTISH
GHHIINSW WHISHING
GHHILOSU GHOULISH
GHHIMNPU HUMPHING
GHHINSSU SHUSHING
GHHIOPST HIGHSPOT
HIGHTOPS
GHHIORSU ROUGHISH
GHHIOSTU TOUGHISH
GHHOORTU THOROUGH
GHHOSTTU THOUGHTS
GHIIILNS SHILINGI
GHIIJNOS JINGOISH
GHIIKNNT THINKING
GHIIKNPS KINGSHIP
GHIIKNRS SHIRKING
GHIIKNSW WHISKING
GHIILLNO HILLOING
GHIILLNS SHILLING
GHIILMST MISLIGHT
GHIILMTY MIGHTILY
GHIILNOT LITHOING
GHIILNPR HIRPLING
GHIILNRS HIRSLING
GHIILNRT THIRLING
GHIILNRW WHIRLING
GHIILOTT OILTIGHT
GHIILTTW TWILIGHT
GHIIMMNS SHIMMING
GHIIMNNU INHUMING
GHIIMRST RIGHTISM
GHIINNNS SHINNING
GHIINNNT THINNING
GHIINNNY HINNYING
GHIINNRS SHRINING
GHIINOST HOISTING
GHIINPPS SHIPPING
GHIINPPW WHIPPING
GHIINRRS SHIRRING
GHIINRRW WHIRRING
GHIINRST SHIRTING
GHIINRSV SHRIVING
GHIINRTT TRITHING
GHIINRTV THRIVING
GHIINRTW WRITHING
GHIINSSS HISSINGS
GHIINSST INSIGHTS
GHIINSSW SWISHING
GHIINSTT TITHINGS
GHIINSTW WHISTING
WHITINGS
GHIINTTW TWINIGHT
GHIINWZZ WHIZZING
GHIIORSV VIGORISH
GHIIRSTT RIGHTIST
GHIKLNTY KNIGHTLY
GHIKLSTY SKYLIGHT
GHIKNNTU THUNKING
GHIKNSSU HUSKINGS
GHIKRSTU TUGHRIKS
GHILLNOO HOLLOING
GHILLNOU HULLOING
GHILLOTW LOWLIGHT
GHILLSTY SLIGHTLY
GHILNOOS SHOOLING
GHILNOPP HOPPLING
GHILNOPS LONGSHIP
GHILNOPY HOPINGLY
GHILNOSS SLOSHING
GHILNRSU HURLINGS
GHILNRTU HURTLING
GHILNRUY HUNGRILY
GHILNSSU SLUSHING
GHILNSTU HUSTLING
SUNLIGHT
GHILOPRS SHOPGIRL
GHILORSW SHOWGIRL
GHILORSY OGRISHLY
GHILPRTY TRIGLYPH
GHILPSTU UPLIGHTS
GHIMNOPR MORPHING
GHIMNOPW WHOMPING
GHIMNORU HUMORING
GHIMNOSS MOSHINGS
GHIMNOTU MOUTHING
GHIMNPTU THUMPING
GHIMNPUW WHUMPING
GHIMNSSU SMUSHING
GHIMNSTU GUNSMITH
GHIMPRSU GRUMPISH
GHIMPSYY PYGMYISH
GHINNNSU SHUNNING
GHINNOOR HONORING
GHINNOPY PHONYING
GHINNORS HORNINGS
GHINNORT NORTHING
THORNING
THRONING
GHINNOST NOTHINGS
GHINNSTU HUNTINGS
SHUNTING
GHINOOPT PHOTOING
GHINOOPW WHOOPING
GHINOOST SHOOTING
SOOTHING
GHINOOSW WOOSHING
GHINOOTT TOOTHING
GHINOPPS HOPPINGS
SHOPPING
GHINOPPW WHOPPING
GHINORSS SHORINGS
GHINORST SHORTING
GHINORSW SHOWRING
GHINORTT TROTHING
GHINORTW INGROWTH
THROWING
WORTHING
GHINOSSU HOUSINGS
GHINOSSW SHOWINGS
GHINOSTT SHOTTING
TONIGHTS
GHINOSTU SHOUTING
SOUTHING
GHINOSUY YOUNGISH
GHINPPUW WHUPPING
GHINPSSU GUNSHIPS
GHINRRUY HURRYING
GHINRSSU RUSHINGS
GHINSSTU HUSTINGS
UNSIGHTS
GHINSTTU SHUTTING
GHIORTTU OUTRIGHT
GHIOSTTU OUTSIGHT
GHIPRSST SPRIGHTS
GHIPRSTU UPRIGHTS
GHIPRSUU GURUSHIP
GHIPSSYY GYPSYISH
GHLMOOOS HOMOLOGS
GHLMOOOY HOMOLOGY
GHLNNOOR LONGHORN
GHLNOORU HOURLONG
GHLNOOYY HOLOGYNY
GHLOOORY HOROLOGY
GHMNOOOY HOMOGONY
GHMORSSU SORGHUMS
GHMPSSUY SPHYGMUS
GHNOPRSY GRYPHONS
GHNOPYYY HYPOGYNY
GHNOSSTU GUNSHOTS
SHOTGUNS
GHNOSTUU UNSOUGHT
GHOOOSSW HOOSGOWS
GHOORTUY YOGHOURT
GHOPRTUW UPGROWTH
GHORSTUY YOGHURTS
GIIILMNT LIMITING
GIIILNNU LINGUINI
GIIILOTV VITILIGO
GIIIMMNX IMMIXING
GIIINNOS IONISING
GIIINNOT IGNITION
GIIINNOZ IONIZING
GIIINNTV INVITING
GIIINORS SIGNIORI
GIIINSTV VISITING
GIIJMMNY JIMMYING
GIIJMNOS JINGOISM
GIIJNNOS JOININGS
GIIJNNOT JOINTING
GIIJNNRU INJURING
GIIJNOST JINGOIST
JOISTING
GIIKKNNS SKINKING
GIIKLLNS KILLINGS
SKILLING
GIIKLNNP PLINKING
GIIKLNNS INKLINGS
SLINKING
GIIKLNNT TINKLING
GIIKLNNW WINKLING
GIIKLNRS SKIRLING
GIIKLNST KILTINGS
KITLINGS
GIIKLNTT KITTLING
GIIKMMNS SKIMMING
GIIKMNPS SKIMPING
GIIKMNRS SMIRKING
GIIKNNNS SKINNING
GIIKNNOV INVOKING
GIIKNNPR PRINKING
GIIKNNPS KINGPINS
PINKINGS
GIIKNNST STINKING
GIIKNNSW SWINKING
GIIKNNTT KNITTING
GIIKNORS SKIORING
GIIKNPPS SKIPPING
GIIKNPSS PIGSKINS
GIIKNQRU QUIRKING
GIIKNRRS SKIRRING
GIIKNRSS GRISKINS
GIIKNRST SKIRTING
STRIKING
GIILLMNS MILLINGS
GIILLMNU ILLUMING
GIILLNPR PRILLING
GIILLNPS SPILLING
GIILLNQU QUILLING
GIILLNRT TRILLING
GIILLNST STILLING
GIILLNSW SWILLING
GIILLNTW TWILLING
GIILLNVY LIVINGLY
GIILLNWY WILLYING
GIILLTUY GUILTILY
GIILMMNS SLIMMING
GIILMNPR RIMPLING
GIILMNPW WIMPLING
GIILMNPY IMPLYING
GIILMNSY MISLYING
GIILMNZZ MIZZLING
GIILMPRS PILGRIMS
GIILMPSU PUGILISM
GIILNNPS SPLINING
GIILNNPU UNPILING
GIILNNTW WINTLING
GIILNNUV UNLIVING
GIILNOPS PIGNOLIS
SPOILING
GIILNOPT PILOTING
GIILNORS LIGROINS
GIILNPPR RIPPLING
GIILNPPS LIPPINGS
SLIPPING
GIILNPPT TIPPLING
GIILNPPU UPPILING
GIILNPPY PIPINGLY
GIILNPRT TRIPLING
GIILNPSS SPILINGS
GIILNQSU QUISLING
GIILNQTU QUILTING
GIILNRSW SWIRLING
GIILNRTW TWIRLING
GIILNSST LISTINGS
GIILNSTT SLITTING
STILTING
GIILNSTU LINGUIST
GIILNSTW WITLINGS
GIILNSTY STINGILY

GIILNSZZ SIZZLING
GIILNTTV VITTLING
GIILNZZZ ZIZZLING
GIILPSTU PUGILIST
GIILRSST STRIGILS
GIILRTTY GRITTILY
GIIMMNPR PRIMMING
GIIMMNRT TRIMMING
GIIMMNRU IMMURING
GIIMMNSW SWIMMING
GIIMNNOP IMPONING
GIIMNNOR MINORING
GIIMNNOY IGNOMINY
GIIMNNTU MINUTING
MUTINING
GIIMNNUX UNMIXING
GIIMNOPS IMPOSING
GIIMNOTT OMITTING
GIIMNOTV MOTIVING
VOMITING
GIIMNPPR PRIMPING
GIIMNPRS PRIMINGS
GIIMNPRU UMPIRING
GIIMNPTU IMPUTING
GIIMNSSU MISUSING
GIIMNSTY STIMYING
GIIMORRS RIGORISM
GIINNNOT INTONING
GIINNNPS SPINNING
GIINNNRU INURNING
GIINNNSW WINNINGS
GIINNNTW TWINNING
GIINNOPT POINTING
GIINNOQU QUOINING
GIINNORS IRONINGS
NIGROSIN
ROSINING
GIINNORT IGNITRON
GIINNPPS SNIPPING
GIINNPRT PRINTING
GIINNRSS RINSINGS
GIINNRSU INSURING
GIINNRTU UNTIRING
GIINNSTT STINTING
TINTINGS
GIINOPST POSITING
SOPITING
GIINOPTV PIVOTING
GIINOQTU QUOITING
GIINORSS SIGNIORS
GIINORST IGNITORS
GIINORSV VISORING
GIINORSY SIGNIORY
GIINORVZ VIZORING
GIINPPQU QUIPPING
GIINPPRT TRIPPING
GIINPRSS PRISSING
GIINPRST SPIRTING
STRIPING
GIINPRSU SIRUPING
UPRISING
GIINPSTT PITTINGS
SPITTING
GIINPSTW WINGTIPS
GIINPSUZ UPSIZING
GIINQRSU SQUIRING
GIINQRTU QUIRTING
GIINQTTU QUITTING
GIINQUZZ QUIZZING
GIINRRST STIRRING
GIINRSTV STRIVING
GIINRSTW WRITINGS
GIINSSTT SITTINGS
GIINSSTU SUITINGS
TISSUING
GIINSTTW TWISTING
WITTINGS
GIINTTTW TWITTING
GIIORRST RIGORIST
GIIORSSV ISOGRIVS
GIJKLNOY JOKINGLY
GIJLLNOY JOLLYING
GIJLNOST JOSTLING
GIJLNSTU JUSTLING
GIJNOSTT JOTTINGS
GIJNOSTU JOUSTING
GIJNTTUY JUTTYING
GIKKLNSU SKULKING
GIKKNNSU SKUNKING
GIKLLNNO KNOLLING
GIKLLNSU SKULLING
GIKLNNOP PLONKING
GIKLNNPU PLUNKING
GIKLNNRU KNURLING
RUNKLING
GIKLNNUY UNKINGLY

GIKNNOOS SNOOKING
GIKNNOSW KNOWINGS
GIKNNOTT KNOTTING
GIKNNOTU KNOUTING
GIKNNOUY UNYOKING
GIKNNPSU SPUNKING
GIKNOOPS SPOOKING
GIKNOOST STOOKING
GIKNOOTW KOTOWING
GIKNOPST KINGPOST
GIKNORST STROKING
GIKNORSW WORKINGS
GILLMOOY GLOOMILY
GILLMPUY GLUMPILY
GILLNORS ROLLINGS
GILLNORT TROLLING
GILLNOSY LOSINGLY
GILLNOVY LOVINGLY
GILLNPUY PULINGLY
GILLNPYY PLYINGLY
GILLNRUY LURINGLY
GILLNSUY SULLYING
GILLOOPW POLLIWOG
GILLOSSY GLOSSILY
GILMMNSU SLUMMING
GILMNOPY MOPINGLY
GILMNOTT MOTTLING
GILMNOTU MOULTING
GILMNOUV VOLUMING
GILMNOVY MOVINGLY
GILMNPPU PLUMPING
GILMNPRU RUMPLING
GILMNPSU SLUMPING
GILMNSUY MUSINGLY
GILMNUZZ MUZZLING
GILMOOSY MISOLOGY
GILMOOXY MIXOLOGY
GILMPRUY GRUMPILY
GILNNOOS GLONOINS
SNOOLING
GILNNOTU NONGUILT
GILNNOUV UNLOVING
GILNNRSU NURSLING
GILNNSSU UNSLINGS
GILNNUZZ NUZZLING
GILNOOOY OINOLOGY
GILNOOPS SPOOLING
GILNOORT ROOTLING
GILNOOST STOOLING
TOOLINGS
GILNOOSY SINOLOGY
GILNOOTT TOOTLING
GILNOOWY WOOINGLY
GILNOPPP PLOPPING
POPPLING
GILNOPPS SLOPPING
GILNOPPT TOPPLING
GILNOPRW PROWLING
GILNOPSY POSINGLY
SPONGILY
GILNOPTT PLOTTING
GILNOPTZ PLOTZING
GILNORVY ROVINGLY
GILNOSTT SLOTTING
GILNOSTU TOUSLING
GILNOTUY OUTLYING
GILNOTUZ TOUZLING
GILNPPRU PURPLING
GILNPPSU SUPPLING
GILNPRSU PURLINGS
SLURPING
GILNPRYY PRYINGLY
GILNPUZZ PUZZLING
GILNRRSU SLURRING
GILNRSTU LUSTRING
RUSTLING
GILNRTTU TURTLING
GILNRTYY TRYINGLY
GILNSSTU TUSSLING
GILNSSTY STYLINGS
GILOOOST OOLOGIST
GILOORSS GIROSOLS
GILOORSU GLORIOUS
GILOORVY VIROLOGY
GILOOSSS ISOGLOSS
GILOOSST OLOGISTS
GILOOSTY SITOLOGY
GILOSTUY GULOSITY
GIMMMNUY MUMMYING
GIMMNSTU STUMMING
GIMMOSSU GUMMOSIS
GIMMPSYY PYGMYISM
GIMNNORS MORNINGS
GIMNNORU MOURNING
GIMNNOTU MOUNTING
GIMNNOUV UNMOVING

GIMNNSTU MUNTINGS
GIMNOOOU OOGONIUM
GIMNOOPR PROMOING
GIMNOORS MOORINGS
GIMNOORT MOTORING
GIMNOORV VROOMING
GIMNOOSS OSMOSING
GIMNOPRT TROMPING
GIMNOPST STOMPING
GIMNOPTU GUMPTION
GIMNORRU RUMORING
GIMNORRW RINGWORM
GIMNORST STORMING
GIMNORSW MISGROWN
GIMNOSST GNOMISTS
GIMNOSSU MOUSINGS
MOUSSING
GIMNOSYY MISOGYNY
GIMNPRTU TRUMPING
GIMNPSTU STUMPING
GIMNSTTU SMUTTING
GIMNSTYY STYMYING
GIMORSSW MISGROWS
GIMPSSYY GYPSYISM
GINNNOOS NOONINGS
GINNNOSU NONUSING
GINNNRSU RUNNINGS
GINNNSTU STUNNING
GINNNTUU UNTUNING
GINNOOPS SNOOPING
SPOONING
GINNOOST SNOOTING
GINNOOSW SWOONING
GINNOOSZ SNOOZING
GINNOPSS SPONGINS
GINNOPTU GUNPOINT
GINNORST SNORTING
GINNORSU GRUNIONS
GINNOSTU SNOUTING
GINNOSUW SWOUNING
GINNPRSU SPURNING
GINNRSSU NURSINGS
GINNRSTU TURNINGS
UNSTRING
GINNSTTU NUTTINGS
STUNTING
GINOOPPS OPPOSING
POGONIPS
GINOOPRS SPOORING
GINOOPRT TROOPING
GINOOPST STOOPING
GINOOPSW SWOOPING
WOOPSING
GINOORST ROOSTING
GINOPPPR PROPPING
GINOPPST STOPPING
TOPPINGS
GINOPPSW SWOPPING
GINOPRST SPORTING
GINOPRSU INGROUPS
GINOPRTU TROUPING
GINOPSST POSTINGS
SIGNPOST
GINOPSSU SPOUSING
GINOPSTT SPOTTING
GINOPSTU SPOUTING
GINOQRTU TORQUING
GINORRWY WORRYING
GINORSST RINGTOSS
GINORSTU OUTGRINS
OUTRINGS
ROUSTING
TOURINGS
GINORSTW STROWING
WORSTING
GINORSTY STORYING
STROYING
GINORTTT TROTTING
GINORTTU TUTORING
GINOSSTU OUTSINGS
GINOSTTT STOTTING
GINOSTTW SWOTTING
GINOSTUW OUTSWING
GINOTUVY OUTVYING
GINPPRSU UPSPRING
GINPRRSU SPURRING
GINPRSTU SPURTING
GINPRSUU PURSUING
USURPING
GINPRSUY SYRUPING
GINPSSUW UPSWINGS
GINPTTUY PUTTYING
GINRSSTU TRUSSING
GINRSTTU TRUSTING
GINRSTTY TRYSTING
GINRSTUU SUTURING

GIOOORSV VIGOROSO
GIOORRSU RIGOROUS
GIOORSTU GOITROUS
GIOORSUV VIGOROUS
GIOPRRSU PRURIGOS
GIOPRSSY GOSSIPRY
GIORSTUY RUGOSITY
GIOSTYYZ ZYGOSITY
GJLMNOPU LONGJUMP
GKLOOOTY TOKOLOGY
GLLLOORS LOGROLLS
GLLOOPTY POLYGLOT
GLLOOPWY POLLYWOG
GLMMSSUU SLUMGUMS
GLMNOOOS MONOLOGS
GLMNOOOT MONOGLOT
GLMNOOOY MONOLOGY
NOMOLOGY
GLMNORUW LUNGWORM
GLMNRTUU NGULTRUM
GLMOOOPY POMOLOGY
GLMOORWW GLOWWORM
GLMOOYYZ ZYMOLOGY
GLMORSUW LUGWORMS
GLNNOORS LORGNONS
GLNOOOSY NOSOLOGY
GLNOOOTY ONTOLOGY
GLNOOPRS PROLONGS
GLNOOPSY POLYGONS
GLNOOPYY POLYGONY
GLNOPRSU LONGSPUR
GLNOPYYY POLYGYNY
GLNORSTY STRONGLY
STRONGYL
GLNORTUW LUNGWORT
GLNOSSUW SUNGLOWS
GLNOSTTU GLUTTONS
GLNOTTUY GLUTTONY
GLOOOPSY POSOLOGY
GLOOOPTY TOPOLOGY
GLOOPRYY PYROLOGY
GLOOPSSY GOSSYPOL
GLOOPTYY LOGOTYPY
TYPOLOGY
GLOORSUU ORGULOUS
GLOOSTUW OUTGLOWS
GMMPSUUW MUGWUMPS
GMNNOOYY MONOGYNY
GMNOORSU GUNROOMS
GMORSTUW MUGWORTS
GNNPRSUU UNSPRUNG
GNNRSTUU UNSTRUNG
GNOOOSSS GOSSOONS
GNOORTUW OUTGROWN
GNOPRSUW GROWNUPS
GNOSTUUW OUTSWUNG
GNPPRSUU UPSPRUNG
GOOPRSST GOSPORTS
GOOPRTUU OUTGROUP
GOORSSTU OUTGROSS
GOORSTUW OUTGROWS
HHIINNST THINNISH
HHIIPSST PHTHISIS
HHILPSSY SYLPHISH
HHIMMOSS MISHMOSH
HHINOPPS PHOSPHIN
HHIORSST SHORTISH
HHOOPPRS PHOSPHOR
HHOOSSTT HOTSHOTS
HIIILMNS NIHILISM
HIIILNST NIHILIST
HIIILNTY NIHILITY
HIIINRST RHINITIS
HIIISSTV SHIVITIS
HIIKMNST MISTHINK
HIIKMRSS SKIRMISH
HIIKNPSS KINSHIPS
HIIKOPRS PIROSHKI
HIIKOPRZ PIROZHKI
HIIKQRSU QUIRKISH
HIIKSSTT SKITTISH
HIILLMMO MILLIMHO
MILLIOHM
HIILLSTT LITTLISH
HIILMOST HOMILIST
HIILMPSY IMPISHLY
HIILMSTU LITHIUMS
HIILMTUY HUMILITY
HIILOPST PISOLITH
HIILPSSY SYPHILIS
HIILRSTT TRILITHS
HIIMNSTT TINSMITH
HIIMOPSS PHIMOSIS
HIIMSSTT SHITTIMS
HIINNNSY NINNYISH
HIINNOST THIONINS

HIINPSTW TWINSHIP
HIIPPQSU QUIPPISH
HIIQRSSU SQUIRISH
HIISSSSY SISSYISH
HIISSTXY SIXTYISH
HIITTTZZ TZITZITH
HIKLNOST HOTLINKS
HIKLORTY KRYOLITH
HIKNNORS INKHORNS
HIKNNSTU UNTHINKS
HIKNOTTU OUTTHINK
HIKOOPRZ PIROZHOK
HIKOOPSS SPOOKISH
HIKOPSSY KYPHOSIS
HILLMSUY MULISHLY
HILLNOUY UNHOLILY
HILLOOST LITHOSOL
HILLOPST HILLTOPS
HILLOSWY OWLISHLY
HILLPSUY PLUSHILY
HILLSSUY SLUSHILY
HILMMOSU HOLMIUMS
HILMNOOT MONOLITH
HILMOPSY MOPISHLY
HILMOSSW WHOLISMS
HILMOTUY MOUTHILY
HILMPPSU PLUMPISH
HILMPRTU PHILTRUM
HILMSTUU THULIUMS
HILNORTY THORNILY
HILNOSTY THIONYLS
TONISHLY
HILOOPYZ ZOOPHILY
HILOOSTT OTOLITHS
HILOOTTY TOOTHILY
HILOPSXY OXYPHILS
HILORSTU UROLITHS
HILORSUU URUSHIOL
HILORTUW OUTWHIRL
HILORTWY WORTHILY
HILOSTWW WHITLOWS
HILPPRSU PURPLISH
HILPPSUY UPPISHLY
HILSSTTU SLUTTISH
HIMNOPRS MORPHINS
HIMNOSTY THYMOSIN
HIMNSSTY HYMNISTS
HIMOOPRS ISOMORPH
HIMOPRRT TRIMORPH
HIMOPRSS ORPHISMS
HIMOPRSW SHIPWORM
HIMOPRWW WHIPWORM
HIMOPSSS SOPHISMS
HIMORSST RIMSHOTS
HIMORSTU HUMORIST
THORIUMS
HIMORSTW MISTHROW
HIMOSTTV MITSVOTH
HIMOTTVZ MITZVOTH
HIMPRSTU TRIUMPHS
HIMRSTTU MISTRUTH
HINNORST TINHORNS
HINNSSUY SUNSHINY
HINOORST HORNITOS
HINOORSZ HORIZONS
HINOPPSS SHIPPONS
HINOPSSS SONSHIPS
HINOPSSY HYPNOSIS
HINOPSTW TOWNSHIP
HINORSST HORNISTS
HINORTXY THYROXIN
HINOSSTU SNOUTISH
HINPPSSU PUSHPINS
HIOOPRTT POORTITH
HIOORSST ORTHOSIS
HIOPRSSW WORSHIPS
HIOPRSUZ RHIZOPUS
HIOPSSST SOPHISTS
HIOSSTTU STOUTISH
HIOSTTUW WITHOUTS
HIPPPSUY PUPPYISH
HKKLOOSY KOLKHOSY
HKKLOOYZ KOLKHOZY
HKKOOPYY HOKYPOKY
HKKOOSSY SKYHOOKS
HKMNORRU KRUMHORN
HKMOOORW HOOKWORM
HKNNRSUU UNSHRUNK
HKOOOPST POTHOOKS
HKOOPRSW WORKSHOP
HKOORRUW WORKHOUR
HKOOSVYZ SOVKHOZY
HLLLOOWY HOLLOWLY
HLLMNOOU MONOHULL
HLMOOSTY SMOOTHLY
HLOOSTUW OUTHOWLS

HLPRSSUU SULPHURS
HLPRSUUY SULPHURY
HMMNOOSY HOMONYMS
HMMNOOYY HOMONYMY
HMMOORSU MUSHROOM
HMNOOOST MOONSHOT
HMNOORRW HORNWORM
HMNOPSYY HYPONYMS
SYMPHONY
HMNOPYYY HYPONYMY
HMOOOPRZ ZOOMORPH
HMOOORSW SHOWROOM
HMOORSUU HUMOROUS
HMOORTUU OUTHUMOR
HNNORTTU NONTRUTH
HNOOPPYY HYPOPYON
HNOOPRSW SHOPWORN
HNOOPRTU HORNPOUT
HNOOPSTY TYPHOONS
HNOORRTW HORNWORT
HNOORSTU SOUTHRON
HNOPPSTY SYNTHPOP
HNOPRTUW UPTHROWN
HNORTUWY UNWORTHY
HNOSTTUU OUTHUNTS
HNRSTTUU UNTRUTHS
HOOOSTTU OUTSHOOT
SHOOTOUT
HOOPSSTT HOTSPOTS
POTSHOTS
HOOPSSTU UPSHOOTS
HOOPSSTW POSTSHOW
HOOPSSTY TOYSHOPS
HOOQSSUY SQUOOSHY
HOORTTUW OUTTHROW
HOOSTTUU OUTSHOUT
HOPPRRYY PORPHYRY
HOPRSSTU HOTSPURS
HOPRSTUW UPTHROWS
HORRSTTU THRUSTOR
HOSSTTUU SHUTOUTS
HPRSTTUU THRUPUTS
UPTHRUST
IIIKLNPS SPILIKIN
IIIKMNNS MINIKINS
IIIKMNSS MINISKIS
IIILLMMN MINIMILL
IIILLMNP MINIPILL
IIILLMNU ILLINIUM
IIILMRSV VIRILISM
IIILMUVX LIXIVIUM
IIILRTVY VIRILITY
IIIMMPRS IMPRIMIS
IIIMNSTT INTIMIST
IIINPRST INSPIRIT
IIINQTUY INIQUITY
IIIOSTTU OUISTITI
IIJJSTUU JIUJITSU
IIJLLNOS JILLIONS
IIJMNOSS MISJOINS
IIKKLNOS KOLINSKI
IIKKNPSS KIPSKINS
IIKLLNSY SLINKILY
IIKLMNPS LIMPKINS
IIKLMPSY SKIMPILY
IIKLMRSY SMIRKILY
IIKLNOSS OILSKINS
IIKLQRUY QUIRKILY
IIKNOSTT STOTINKI
IILLLMUX MILLILUX
IILLLPTU LILLIPUT
IILLLPUV PULVILLI
IILLMNOS MILLIONS
IILLMRTU TRILLIUM
IILLMUUV ILLUVIUM
IILLNOPS PILLIONS
IILLNORT TRILLION
IILLNOSU ILLUSION
IILLNOSZ ZILLIONS
IILLNSST INSTILLS
IILLPPSY SLIPPILY
IILMMNSU LUMINISM
IILMMPSS SIMPLISM
IILMMSWY SWIMMILY
IILMNORT MIRLITON
IILMNSTU LUMINIST
IILMORST TROILISM
IILMOTTY MOTILITY
IILMPSST SIMPLIST
IILMRSSY MISSILRY
IILNNOQU QUINOLIN
IILNNOST NITINOLS
IILNNSSU INSULINS
IILNOOST INOSITOL
IILNOOTV VOLITION
IILNOPST PINITOLS

IILNORSS SIRLOINS
IILNPPSY SNIPPILY
IILNRTWY WINTRILY
IILOPRST TRIPOLIS
IILOPSSS PSILOSIS
IILOPSTY PILOSITY
IILORSTV VITRIOLS
IILOSSTV VIOLISTS
IILPRSSY PRISSILY
IILSSTTT TITLISTS
IILSTUUV UVULITIS
IILSTUVV VULVITIS
IIMMMNSU MINIMUMS
IIMMNTUY IMMUNITY
IIMMOPST OPTIMISM
IIMMOPSU OPIUMISM
IIMMSTTU MITTIMUS
IIMNNOOT MONITION
IIMNNOSU MISUNION
UNIONISM
IIMNNOTU MUNITION
IIMNOOSS OMISSION
IIMNOPRS IMPRISON
IIMNOPST MISPOINT
IIMNORTT INTROMIT
IIMNORTY MINORITY
IIMNOSSS MISSIONS
IIMNOSST SIMONIST
IIMNPRST IMPRINTS
MISPRINT
IIMNPTUY IMPUNITY
IIMNRSTY MINISTRY
IIMOPSTT OPTIMIST
IIMORSTY RIMOSITY
IIMOSSTY MYOSITIS
IIMOTTVY MOTIVITY
IIMPRTUY IMPURITY
IIMRRTUV TRIUMVIR
IIMRSTTU TRITIUMS
IIMSSSTU MISSUITS
IIMSSTUW SWIMSUIT
IINNOOPS OPINIONS
IINNOPPT PINPOINT
IINNOPTU PUNITION
IINNOSTU UNIONIST
IINNPSST TINSNIPS
IINNQSTU QUINTINS
IINNSTTU TINNITUS
IINOOPST POSITION
IINOPSSS ISOSPINS
IINORSST IRONISTS
IINORSTT INTROITS
IINOSTTU TUITIONS
IINOSTVY VINOSITY
IINRTTUY TRIUNITY
IINSSTTW INTWISTS
IIOOPSTV OVIPOSIT
IIOOSTTY OTIOSITY
IIOPRRTY PRIORITY
IIOPRSSS PISSOIRS
IIORSSTV VISITORS
IIORSTUV VIRTUOSI
IJJMSSUU JUJUISMS
IJJSSTUU JUJITSUS
JUJUISTS
IJJSTUUU JIUJUTSU

IJKLLOSY KILLJOYS
IJLNOQSU JONQUILS
IJMPSTUU JUMPSUIT
IJNNOSTU UNJOINTS
IKKLNORW LINKWORK
IKKLNOSY KOLINSKY
IKLLMORW MILLWORK
IKLLOOTV KILOVOLT
IKLLOSTU OUTKILLS
IKLMOOSS LOOKISMS
LOOKSISM
IKLMOPSS MILKSOPS
IKLMORSW SILKWORM
IKLMORTW MILKWORT
IKLMOSSY SOYMILKS
IKLNOOST KILOTONS
IKLNOOSW WOOLSKIN
IKLNOPST SLIPKNOT
IKLNOTTY KNOTTILY
IKLNPSUY SPUNKILY
IKLOOPSY SPOOKILY
IKLOOSST LOOKISTS
IKLOSSSU SOUSLIKS
IKMNNOSW MISKNOWN
IKMNOORS OMIKRONS
IKMNOSSW MISKNOWS
IKMNPPSU PUMPKINS
IKMNRSTU TRINKUMS
IKNOOPRT PINKROOT
IKNOORRW IRONWORK
IKNOPRSW PINWORKS
IKNOPSSY PYKNOSIS
IKNOPSTT STINKPOT
IKNORSTW TINWORKS
IKNPSSTU SPUTNIKS
IKORSSTU KURTOSIS
IKORSTTU OUTSKIRT
ILLLMOPS PLIMSOLL
ILLLOOPP LOLLIPOP
ILLLOOWY WOOLLILY
ILLMNOSU MULLIONS
ILLMNRSU MILLRUNS
ILLMOOST TIMOLOLS
ILLMOPSS PLIMSOLS
ILLMOSSY LISSOMLY
ILLMPSUY PSYLLIUM
ILLMPTUY MULTIPLY
ILLNOORT TORNILLO
ILLNPSUU LUPULINS
ILLOORSZ ZORILLOS
ILLOORTT ROTOTILL
ILLOPPSS SLIPSLOP
ILLOPPSY SLOPPILY
ILLOPRXY PROLIXLY
ILLOPSST POLLISTS
ILLORSUY ILLUSORY
ILLOSTUW OUTWILLS
ILLOSTXY XYLITOLS
ILLRSTUY SULTRILY
ILMMSSSU SLUMISMS
ILMNOOPU POLONIUM
ILMNOSUU LUMINOUS
ILMNOTTU MULTITON
ILMOPPSU POPULISM
ILMORSTU TURMOILS
ILMORSTY STORMILY

ILMSSTUU STIMULUS
ILMSTTUY SMUTTILY
ILNNORSU LINURONS
ILNOOPRT PLIOTRON
ILNOOPSS PLOSIONS
ILNOOPSY SNOOPILY
SPOONILY
ILNOORSS ROSINOLS
ILNOORTW TOILWORN
ILNOOSST SOLITONS
ILNOOSTU SOLUTION
ILNOOSTY SNOOTILY
ILNOOTUV VOLUTION
ILNOPRSU PURLOINS
ILNOPSSU PULSIONS
UPSILONS
ILNOPSTU UNSPOILT
ILNORSST NOSTRILS
ILNORSTY NITROSYL
ILNOSSTY TYLOSINS
ILNOSTTY SNOTTILY
ILNOSTUV VOLUTINS
ILNOSUVY VINOUSLY
ILNPSUUV PULVINUS
ILOOORSS ROSOLIOS
ILOOPPRS PROPOLIS
ILOOPSST POLOISTS
TOPSOILS
ILOOSSST SOLOISTS
ILOPPSTU POPULIST
ILOPPTUU OUTPUPIL
ILOPRSTY SPORTILY
ILOPSSTU SLIPOUTS
ILOPSTTY SPOTTILY
ILOPSUUV PLUVIOUS
ILRSTTUY TRUSTILY
ILSSSTTY STYLISTS
IMMNOORS MORONISM
IMMNOSUU MUONIUMS
IMMOPSTU OPTIMUMS
IMMRSTUY SUMMITRY
IMNNNOSU MUNNIONS
IMNNOOTT MONOTINT
IMNNOSUU NUMINOUS
IMNOOPST TOMPIONS
IMNOORRS MORRIONS
IMNOORST MONITORS
IMNOORTY MONITORY
MORONITY
IMNOPRSW PINWORMS
IMNOPSSU SPUMONIS
IMNOSTUU MUTINOUS
IMOOPRRS PROMISOR
IMOOPRST IMPOSTOR
IMOOPRSU IMPOROUS
IMOOQSTU MOSQUITO
IMOORRTT TRIMOTOR
IMOORSTT MOTORIST
IMOORSTU TIMOROUS
IMOORSTY MOROSITY
IMOORTVY VOMITORY
IMOOSSTY MYOSOTIS
IMOOSTUV VOMITOUS
IMOPPRRU PROPRIUM
IMOPRSST TROPISMS
IMOPRSTU PROTIUMS

IMOPSSST MISSTOPS
IMOPSSTU UTOPISMS
IMORSSST MISSORTS
IMORSSTU TOURISMS
IMORSTTU MISTUTOR
IMOSSSTU MISSOUTS
SUMOISTS
IMOSSTUW OUTSWIMS
IMRSSSTU SISTRUMS
IMRSSTTU MISTRUST
IMRSSTTY MISTRYST
IMRSTTUY YTTRIUMS
INNNNOOU NONUNION
INNNOOPT NONPOINT
INNNOPRT NONPRINT
INNNORTU TRUNNION
INNOOPRT TROPONIN
INNOOPRU PROUNION
INNOOPSS OPSONINS
SPONSION
INNOORST NOTORNIS
INNORTTU NOTTURNI
INNOSSTU NONSUITS
INOOOSSZ ZOONOSIS
INOOPRST PORTIONS
POSITRON
SORPTION
INOOPSTT SPITTOON
INOOPTTU OUTPOINT
INOORSST TORSIONS
INOORSSU ROSINOUS
INOORSTT TORTONIS
INOORSTY SONORITY
INOOSTTV STOTINOV
INOPPSST TOPSPINS
INOPRTTU PRINTOUT
INOPRTUY PUNITORY
INOPSSSY SYNOPSIS
INOPSSTU SPINOUTS
INOSSTUW SNOWSUIT
INPPRRUU PURPURIN
INPRRSTU SURPRINT
INPRSSTY TRYPSINS
INPRSTTU TURNSPIT
INRSSTTU INTRUSTS
INRSTTUU UNITRUST
INSSSTUU SUNSUITS
INSSTTUW UNTWISTS
IOOPRSSV PROVISOS
IOOPRSSY ISOSPORY
IOOPRSTT POSTRIOT
IOOPRSTY ISOTROPY
POROSITY
IOORRSTY SORORITY
IOORSSTT RISOTTOS
IOORSSUV VOUSSOIR
IOORSTTU TORTIOUS
IOORSTTY TOROSITY
IOORSTUV VIRTUOSO
IOORSUUX UXORIOUS
IOPPRSST RIPSTOPS
IOPRRSUV PROVIRUS
IOPRSSTT PROTISTS
IOPRSSUU SPURIOUS
IOPRSTTU OUTSTRIP
IOPRSTUY PYRITOUS

IOPRSUVX POXVIRUS
IOPSSTTU UTOPISTS
IOQRSTTU QUITTORS
IOQRSTUU TURQUOIS
IOQRTUXY QUIXOTRY
IORRSSST TSORRISS
IORRSUVV SURVIVOR
IORSSTTU TOURISTS
IORSSUUU USURIOUS
IORSTTUY TOURISTY
IORSTUUV VIRTUOUS
IPPTTTUY TITTUPPY
IPRRSSTU STIRRUPS
IPRRSTUU PRURITUS
IPRSSTUU PURSUITS
JJSSTUUU JUJUTSUS
JLNSTUUY UNJUSTLY
JLOOSUYY JOYOUSLY
JMOPSTUU OUTJUMPS
JNNOORRU NONJUROR
JNOORSSU SOJOURNS
KLLMNSUU NUMSKULL
KLLMOSSU MOLLUSKS
KLNORSTY KLYSTRON
KLOOORWW WOOLWORK
KLOOOSTU LOOKOUTS
OUTLOOKS
KLOOPRSW SLOPWORK
KLOSSTUU OUTSULKS
KMOOORRW WORKROOM
KMOORSTU MUSKROOT
KNNNOSUW UNKNOWNS
KNOOPSTT TOPKNOTS
KNOPPSTU POSTPUNK
KNOPRSTY KRYPTONS
KOOPRSTW TOPWORKS
KOORSTUW OUTWORKS
WORKOUTS
KORRSTWY TRYWORKS
LLLOOPPY LOLLYPOP
LLMOOPRS ROLLMOPS
LLOOPRST TROLLOPS
LLOOPRTY TROLLOPY
LLOOPSTU OUTPOLLS
LLOORSTU OUTROLLS
ROLLOUTS
LLOPSTUU OUTPULLS
PULLOUTS
LLOSUUVV VOLVULUS
LMNOOOPY MONOPOLY
LMOOOOPR POOLROOM
LMOOORT TOOLROOM
LMOOPRTU PULMOTOR
LMOORSWW SLOWWORM
LMOOTXYY XYLOTOMY
LMOPPRTY PROMPTLY
LMOSTUUU TUMULOUS
LMRSSTUU LUSTRUMS
LNOOPRT POLTROON
LNOOPPRY PROPYLON
LNOOPSSU UNSPOOLS
LNOOPSWW SNOWPLOW
LOOORSS OLOROSOS
LOOPPSUU POPULOUS
LOOPPSUY POLYPOUS
LOOPRSTT STOLPORT

LOOPRSUY POROUSLY
LOOPSTTU OUTPLOTS
LORSSTUU LUSTROUS
MMNOOOSY MONOSOMY
MMOORTTY TOMMYROT
MMOPSSTY SYMPTOMS
MMNOOOSS MONSOONS
MNNOOOTY MONOTONY
MNNOORSU MONURONS
MNNOPRTU NONTRUMP
MNNOSSYY SYNONYMS
MNNOSYYY SYNONYMY
MNOOOPRT MOONPORT
MNOOORTW MOONWORT
MNOOORXY OXYMORON
MNOOPRTU PRONOTUM
MNOOPSTY TOPONYMS
MNOOPTYY TOPONYMY
MNOORSSU SUNROOMS
MNOOSTTW TOWMONTS
MNORSSTU NOSTRUMS
MNORSTUU SURMOUNT
MOOORRTW MOORWORT
ROOTWORM
TOMORROW
WORMROOT
MOOPSSSU OPOSSUMS
MOORSTUU TUMOROUS
MOPRTTUU OUTTRUMP
MORRSSTU ROSTRUMS
MORSSTUU STRUMOUS
NNOOOPST PONTOONS
SPONTOON
NNOOPRSU PRONOUNS
NNOOPSSS SPONSONS
NNOOPSST NONSTOPS
NNOORSTY NONSTORY
NNOORTTU NOTTURNO
NOOORSSU SONOROUS
NOOPRSSS SPONSORS
NOORSTUW OUTSWORN
NOPSSSTU SUNSPOTS
NORSTTUU OUTTURNS
TURNOUTS
NOSTTTUU OUTSTUNT
NRSTTUUY UNTRUSTY
OOORRSTU OUTROOTS
OOPRSSSU SOURSOPS
OOPRSSTV PROVOSTS
OOPRSTTU OUTPORTS
OOPRSTUU OUTPOURS
OOPSSSTT TOSSPOTS
OOPSSTTU OUTPOSTS
OORSTTTU OUTTROTS
OORSTTUU TORTUOUS
OPPRRSTU PURPORTS
OPPRSSTU SUPPORTS
OPRSSSUU SOURPUSS
ORRSSTTU TRUSTORS
ORSSTTUU SURTOUTS
RRSSSUUU SUSURRUS

ACKNOWLEDGMENTS

Thanks are in order to many people who have contributed directly or indirectly:

To whomever invented Cross-O-Grams, produced in 1932.

To the late Alfred Butts, for devising Lexico, alias Criss-Crossword Game, alias SCRABBLE, circa 1933, 1934, or 1935 ... ish.

To Dr. Dan Matthews, for helping start New Mexico's first SCRABBLE Club, and Grace Cummins, Patty Wayne, Gertrude Savage, Laraine Chapman, Steve Needler, Carol Spitz, Frank Tarr, Susan Beard, and Nancee Mancel for carrying the torch ever since.

To Stu Goldman, who hosted the first SCRABBLE Club I attended on Memorial Day 1980 and who suggested I attend my first tournament the following weekend. Stu, your prolific contributions to *SCRABBLE News* in its early days are appreciated. You've played in more club and tournament games than anyone on Earth, and you've got the scores of every turn of every game on one sheet of paper to prove it.

To Joe Leonard, the Word List Master General, for your hand-generated alphabetical lists of words, categorized by length, of the entire dictionary, and your provision of new words that were instrumental in updating the *Official SCRABBLE® Players Dictionary* (OSPD). Your gratis 8,000+ hours of pre–Computer Age efforts are astounding, and all SCRABBLE players are indebted to you.

To Al Weissman, for your seminal articles on taking probability of tile selection into account when determining words to learn. Your Letters for Expert Game Players in the early 1980s, especially the in-depth analyses of consensus solitaire games by empaneled experts from around North America, was ahead of its time.

To Jim Lamerand, for being the first person to digitize the OSPD matching Joe Leonard's word count. This allowed all future techno-savvy word list makers to be devising programs rather than pushing a pencil while leafing through almost 700 dictionary pages.

To Dan Pratt, for your correspondence in the early 1980s on theories of selecting and learning words, and for being the quintessential example of "unflappable" at the SCRABBLE board.

To Jim Houle, former Executive Director of the National SCRABBLE Association, for publishing my articles and lists in the 1980s, for listening to and implementing the idea to make the National Championship an Open event (a subconscious ploy by which to meet my future wife), and for not dismissing dialogue on staging a first World Championship and on "infiltrating" the schools, tasks left to your successors.

To Charles Goldstein, for your inspirational playmanship and word knowledge, including your innocent little KNUR in 1980, which had me going to the OSPD and keeping me off the streets afterward with word list making.

To Jere Guin, for allowing me to get back into the streets when, in one evening in 1987, you would computer-generate a word list that took me the summer of 1982 to do by hand on the beaches of Long Island. Of course, I did acquire a much nicer suntan.

To Steve Williams, for introducing me in 1981 to SCRABBLE marathons, the idea that presumably grown men and women might play ten or more games of SCRABBLE in one day.

To the late Dr. Stan Rubinsky, for your "excellent" co-coordination of "the Wimbledon of SCRABBLE," the Annual Grand Canyon event (1981–92). We should each be half the student that you were a teacher.

To Mark Powell, for your delightful philosophical insights on SCRABBLE as a metaphor for life. I treasure the way you frame SCRABBLE's and life's challenges.

To Viraf Mehta, Brian Sugar, Phil Appleby, Allan Simmons, and Philip Nelkon, for extending a warm welcome to me in London in 1987, graciously accepting the deluxe OSPDs (the North American–only lexicon), compliments of the National SCRABBLE Association, pummeling me at my own game (using my lexicon instead of yours), then gracing us in the U.S. with the first British reps at our following year's North American Championship.

To the late Sam Orbaum, who started the world's largest attended SCRABBLE Club in Jerusalem, and the triplets Donna, Odelia, and Nomi, for making my family and me feel like royalty in Israel.

To Jim Homan and Brian Sheppard, for your able assistance on prior word list projects and for developing software programs whereby anyone with a computer can play against "an expert."

To Alan Frank for your Matchups, Nick Ballard for your Medleys, Jim Geary for your JG Newsletter, Allan Simmons for your Onwords, and others seeking to enhance the caliber of players through your newsletters.

To Sherrie Saint John, for overseeing the Crossword-Games-Pro listserv for SCRABBLE tourney players around the world, allowing the ridiculous and the sublime to emerge at lightning speed. It has been a wonderful medium through which to share not simply things SCRABBLE, including celebrating our friends' victories, but, more importantly, to support them during times of great difficulty. You have shepherded the electronic medium as a way to reach out to our SCRABBLE family members away from the board.

To Stefan Fatsis, SCRABBLE's Scribe, whose glorious bestseller *Word Freak* has infused still greater interest in our game. With formal competitive SCRABBLE having begun in the 1970s, you have captured some of the game's personalities and history at a time when the "first generation" is yielding to the "next generation" of players. Your descriptions of my earlier *Wordbooks*, I feel, made this one possible.

To Ron Tiekert and David Gibson, the 2003 SCRABBLE All Stars finalists, exemplifying gentlemanliness at and away from the board, and doing your SCRABBLE family proud as two of our reps.

To Yvonne Lieblein, for overseeing and growing the School SCRABBLE program.

To Hasbro, John Williams, and the staff at the National SCRABBLE Association, for putting together our biennial family reunion, the National SCRABBLE Championship, and otherwise promoting our favorite pastime.

To Brian Cappelletto, "my caballero amigo," for the example you set in achieving and maintaining the pinnacle of success at our game with humility and humor. Your belting out "Born to Be Wild," originally released about the time you were born, as we "got on down the highway" from UCLA to the San Jose tournament, confirmed for me you were a champion-in-the-making who would defy any geek labeling. You're cool.

To Chris Cree, for your humor, passion, and friendship, even when I invariably get both blanks ... except that time I lost fifteen games in a row to you, at which point I was the best friend you ever had. "Sure." From that first phone inquiry ("Y'all play SCRABBLE thayre?") to today, I savor the frowns we have reduced and the smiles we have shared.

To Jim Barrett, the late Margaret Bauer, the late Edith Berman, the late Jim Bodenstedt, John Chew, K.C. Conter, Martha Downey, Polly DuBois, Joe Edley, Ann Ferguson, R.A. Fontes, Mady Garner, Bernie Gottlieb, John Green, Ruth Hamilton, Matt Hopkins, Laura Klein, the late Mike Martin, Karen Merrill, Rich Moyer, Johnny Nevarez, Jim Pate, Bryan Pepper, the late Steve Pfieffer, Hildegard Powell, Larry Rand, Mary Rhoades, Bonnie Rudolph, Bill and Bobbie Sageser, Dee Segrest, Chris Sigel, Charlie Southwell, Alan Stern, Paul Terry, Mary Lou Thurman, Susi Tiekert, Siri Tillerkeratne, Barbara Van Alen, Jeff Widergren, Mike Willis, the late Mike Wise, Rick Wong, and the hundreds of other tournament coordinators and directors worldwide who are the lifeblood of our competitive sport. Without you all, SCRABBLE reverts to just a rainy day game.

Other extended SCRABBLE family members have added delight to my and my family's word gaming journeys. Just some of the many include: Steve Alexander, Judy Amiran, Maureen Apone, Chuck Armstrong, Paul Arseneau, Julie Ashe, Paul Avrin, Penny Baker, Jim and Pat Barrett, Lynne Butler, Sheree Bykofsky, Cheryl Cadieux, Holly Cappelletto, Eric Chaikin, Jim and Gloria Cilke, Jeff Commings, the late June Cosma, Lynn Cushman, Chris and Carla Cree, Dr. Al Demers, Terry Double, Chris Economos, Lou Edwards, Jack Eichenbaum, Marni Elci,

Paul Epstein, the late Bob Felt, Steve Fisher, Gregg Foster, Ann and Bob and Jessica and Libby and Andy Fullerton, Helaine Garren, Jim and Jane and Colleen Geary, June Gladney, Steve Goldberg, Mady Golob, the late Moreen Green, Roz Grossman, the late Bill Hamilton, John Hart, Lana Henson, Peggy Henson, Marlon Hill, John Holgate, Doug Honig, Dee Jackson, Carl Johnson, Robert Kahn, Dennis Kaiser, Sam Kantimathi, Jim Kramer, Mark Landsberg, Chris Lennon, Jerry Lerman, Steve Lockwood, John Luebkemann, Richie Lund, Tom Machiorletti, Rick Mastelli, Paul McCarthy, Ron "Zax" McGill, Shane Meyers, Gloria Miller, Joan Mocine, Ed Napolitano, Jim Neuberger, Ed Neugroschl, Rita Norr, Mark Nyman, Tom O'Bannon, Dr. Robert Parker, Barbara Platt, Jeff and Mary Reeves, Ann Sanfedele, Manley and Linda Sarnowsky, Gertrude and the late Irv Savage, Bob Schoenman, Les Schonbrun, Marjorie Schoneboom, Joel Sherman, Larry Sherman, Ken Shoemaker, Mike Senkiewicz, David and Shirra and Fiona Stone, the late Graeme Thomas, Joan and the late Dave Thomas, Joel Wapnick, Allan and Karen and Kassie White, Ellis Wilson, Randy Winograd, Gail Wolford, Dr. Greg and Elizabeth Wood, Geoff Wright, and so many more who have extended and continue to extend kindnesses and smiles. I am truly blessed to have crossed your paths.

To the many correspondents over the years, even the few not in correctional facilities, for your interest in my work.

To Milo Miller, for your computer wizardry, turning a huge job into a merely large one. Miniature "Milo dolls" should be attached to everyone's computers.

To Dr. Amit Chakrabarti, Assistant Professor of Computer Science at Dartmouth College, and U.S. rep at the 2003 World SCRABBLE Championship, for your incredibly speedy and efficient assistance in updating and formatting these word lists. You've been so gentle with this technoklutz. This project would not have been possible without your able efforts.

To my literary agent, Mike Baron, for believing a literary agent was not necessary, thereby putting this work in the fast track ... a mere 16-year track.

To my editor, Peter Gordon, for his unwavering support in having *SCRABBLE Wordbook* reach a wider audience. Your patience with my, uh, challenged abilities to send readable email attachments has secured your place in Patient Editor Heaven.

To Harvey Baron, Marlene Baron, the late Henry "Pop" Kammerer, Dr. Marshall Deutsch, and Reverend Judy Deutsch for putting up with, indeed indulging, me and my obsession.

To my late parents, George and Edith Baron, for teaching me to play and, more importantly, to be playful.

To Melina Baron-Deutsch for the joy your very being gives me. Never lose your curiosity, creativity, and caring, nor your zest, zeal, and zaniness.

To Pamina Deutsch for not challenging my play when I proposed to you on a SCRABBLE board. In ways none of the nearly 100,000 words in our SCRABBLE lexicon, even on a Triple-Triple Word Score, could ever adequately express, you enrich my life.

ABOUT THE AUTHOR

Sometimes referred to as "The Johnny Appleseed of SCRABBLE," for his national and international promotion of the game, MIKE BARON cut his teeth on word games growing up in New York, and developed his intractable addiction to the game after he started New Mexico's first club and attended his first tournament in 1980. Among the country's best players and winner of over 30 tournaments since then, Baron was the primary contributing author to the National SCRABBLE Association's *SCRABBLE News* in the 1980s, and has since served on the Association's Advisory Board and Rules Committee. His promotion of the game has included appearances on NBC's *Good Morning America* with Erma Bombeck and NPR's *All Things Considered* with SCRABBLE inventor Alfred Butts (with whom he was named as a charter inductee to the "Matchups" Hall of Fame). Baron was profiled in Stefan Fatsis's bestseller *Word Freak*. He describes as the best play he ever made his marriage proposal to his wife Pamina on a SCRABBLE board (see page 8), a play she found acceptable and chose not to challenge. They make their home in Corrales, New Mexico, with their daughter Melina, two cats, one dog, and a pretty nifty treehouse he built. Between tournaments and overseeing his daughter's school SCRABBLE club, "Dr. Mike," a licensed clinical psychologist, has been in private practice since 1980 and also consults with Los Alamos Public Schools.